Operations Management

TITLES OF RELATED INTEREST

ADA, *DPL Decision Programming Language for Windows*
Berk/Carey, *Data Analysis with Microsoft Excel*
Carlson, *Cases in Managerial Data Analysis*
Chisman, *Industrial Cases in Simulation Modeling*
Clauss, *Applied Management Science and Spreadsheet Modeling*
Clemen, *Making Hard Decisions,* 2nd ed.
Colley, *Case Studies in Service Operations*
Cryer/Miller, *Statistics for Business,* 2nd ed.
Davis, *Business Research for Decision Making,* 4th ed.
Dielman, *Applied Regression Analysis for Business and Economics,* 2nd ed.
Farnum, *Modern Statistical Quality Control and Improvement*
Finch/Luebbe, *Operations Management*
Gaither, *Production and Operations Management,* 7th ed.
Hildebrand/Ott, *Basic Statistical Ideas for Managers*
Kao, *Introduction to Stochastic Processes*
Keller/Warrack, *Statistics for Management and Economics,* 4th ed.
Kirkwood, *Strategic Decision Making: Multiobjective Decision Analysis with Spreadsheets*
Lapin/Whisler, *Cases in Management Science*
Lapin, *Quantitative Methods for Business Decisions,* 6th ed.
Lindo Systems, *What's Best!*
Middleton, *Data Analysis Using Microsoft Excel*
SAS Institute, *JMP IN 3 for Windows*
Sower/Motwani/Savoie, *Classic Readings in Operations Management*
Winston, *Simulation Modeling Using @RISK*
Winston, *Introduction to Mathematical Programming: Applications and Algorithms,* 2nd ed.
Winston, *Operations Research: Applications and Algorithms,* 3rd ed.

PRACTICAL MANAGEMENT SCIENCE

Spreadsheet Modeling and Applications

Wayne L. Winston

School of Business, Indiana University

S. Christian Albright

School of Business, Indiana University

With Case Studies by

Mark Broadie

Graduate School of Business, Columbia University

D U X B U R Y   P R E S S

An Imprint of Wadsworth Publishing Company

I(T)P® An International Thomson Publishing Company

Belmont, CA • Albany, NY • Bonn • Boston • Cincinnati • Detroit • Johannesburg • London • Madrid
Melbourne • Mexico City • New York • Paris • San Francisco • Singapore • Tokyo • Toronto • Washington

Editor CURT HINRICHS
Assistant Editor JULIE McDONALD
Editorial Assistant CYNTHIA MAZOW
Advertising Project Manager JOSEPH JODAR
Project Editor SANDRA CRAIG
Print Buyer KAREN HUNT
Permissions Editor PEGGY MEEHAN
Text and Cover Designer CLOYCE WALL
Cover Photo TONY STONE IMAGES
Copy Editor ERIN MILNES
Accuracy Checking LAUREL TECHNICAL SERVICES
Illustrations LAUREL TECHNICAL SERVICES
Composition SUPERSCRIPT
Prepress PURE IMAGING
Printer VON HOFFMANN PRESS

Printed in the United States of America
5 6 7 8 9 10

For more information, contact Duxbury Press at Wadsworth Publishing Company, 10 Davis Drive, Belmont, California 94002, or electronically at http://www.thomson.com/wadsworth.html

International Thomson Publishing Europe
Berkshire House 168-173
High Holborn
London, WC1V 7AA, England

International Thomson Publishing GmbH
Königswinterer Strasse 418
53227 Bonn, Germany

Thomas Nelson Australia
102 Dodds Street
South Melbourne 3205
Victoria, Australia

International Thomson Publishing Asia
221 Henderson Road
#05-10 Henderson Building
Singapore 0315

Nelson Canada
1120 Birchmount Road
Scarborough, Ontario
Canada M1K 5G4

International Thomson Publishing Japan
Hirakawacho Kyowa Building, 3F
2-2-1 Hirakawacho
Chiyoda-ku, Tokyo 102, Japan

International Thomson Editores
Campos Eliseos 385, Piso 7
Col. Polanco
11560 México D.F. México

International Thomson Publishing Southern Africa
Building 18, Constantia Park
240 Old Pretoria Road
Halfway House, 1685 South Africa

Library of Congress Cataloging-in-Publication Data

Winston, Wayne L.
Practical management science : spreadsheet modeling and applications /
Wayne L. Winston, S. Christian Albright : with case studies by Mark Broadie.
p. cm.
Includes bibliographical references and index.
ISBN 0-534-21774-5
1. Management science—Computer simulation. 2. Management science—Mathematical models
3. Electronic spreadsheets. I. Albright, S. Christian. II. Broadie, Mark Nathan. III. Title.
T57.62.W56 1997
658'.001'13—dc20 96-18223

Photo Credits

Chapter 1 Greg Pease, © Tony Stone Images; **Chapter 2** © Tony Freeman, PhotoEdit; **Chapter 3** © Kenneth Murray, Photo Researchers, Inc.; **Chapter 4** © 1984 Peter Menzel, Stock, Boston; **Chapter 5** © 1994 Don Mason, The Stock Market; **Chapter 6** © 1995 The Stock Market; **Chapter 7** © 1994 Rob Lewine, The Stock Market; **Chapter 8** © 1991 Fredrik D. Bodin, Stock, Boston; **Chapter 9** © 1983 Ira Wexler, Folio, Inc.; **Chapter 10** © Robert Brenner, PhotoEdit; **Chapter 11** © Tony Freeman, PhotoEdit; **Chapter 12** © 1988 John Riley, Folio, Inc.; **Chapter 13** © 1988 Laima Druskis, Photo Researchers, Inc.; **Chapter 14** © 1984 Don Landwehrle, The Image Bank.

Printed on acid-free recycled paper

About the Authors

WAYNE L. WINSTON

Wayne is professor of decision sciences in the School of Business at Indiana University, where he has taught since 1975. He received the S.B. degree in mathematics from MIT and his Ph.D. in operations research from Yale University. He has written three successful textbooks—*Operations Research: Applications and Algorithms, Introduction to Mathematical Programming: Applications and Algorithms,* and *Simulation Modeling Using @RISK*—all published by Duxbury Press. In addition, he has published more than 20 articles in leading journals and has won many teaching awards, including the Indiana University schoolwide MBA award four times.

Wayne enjoys swimming and basketball, and he appeared on the television series *Jeopardy!* (winning two games). He is married to the lovely and talented Vivian, and they have two children, Gregory and Jennifer.

S. CHRISTIAN ALBRIGHT

Chris received his B.S. degree in mathematics from Stanford University in 1968 and his Ph.D. in operations research from Stanford in 1972. Since then he has been teaching in the decision sciences area of the Business School at Indiana University in Bloomington. His research interests are in the area of applied probability models. Recently he also did research on a favorite topic: streakiness in baseball hitting. He has taught courses in management science, computer simulation, and statistics to all levels of business students: undergraduates, MBAs, and doctoral students. He has authored a book entitled *Statistics for Business and Economics* and a user manual for the Execustat statistical software package.

On the personal side, Chris has been married to his wife, Mary, for 25 years and has one son, Sam, who is now in his third year at Indiana University. Chris has many interests outside the academic area, including activities with his family, playing the piano (classical music), attending cultural events at the university, playing golf and tennis, running, and reading.

MARK BROADIE

The case studies appearing at the ends of chapters were created by Mark Broadie and his colleagues at the Columbia Business School. These cases are outgrowths of real-world applications, including several based on work done by Columbia Business School graduates.

Mark applies management science and operations research techniques to problems arising in managerial decision making. His current research focuses on issues of computational finance, including option pricing, portfolio management, and risk management. Mark worked for Shearson Lehman Brothers to develop pricing and hedging models for government and mortgage-backed securities. He has done extensive consulting work for various investment banks and brokerage firms and has also lectured worldwide. Mark holds a B.S. from Cornell University and a Ph.D. from Stanford University. He joined the faculty of the Graduate School of Business at Columbia University in 1983.

Mark is happily married to Nancy Morgan and they have one son, Christopher. Mark enjoys sports, especially golf (he is lucky enough to have had two holes-in-one).

To our wonderful families

Vivian

Mary

Sam

Gregory

Jennifer

Brief Contents

Contents

3 Linear Programming Formulations 71

4 Network Models 149

Preface

We believe management science has a great deal to offer students—in fact, now more than ever before—and we hope this book will help reverse negative attitudes toward quantitative methods in business. We wrote this book to provide instructors and students with a new yet highly successful approach to teaching and learning management science. We teach by example and adopt a practical spreadsheet-based approach to the modeling of a wide variety of business problems from finance, marketing, and operations. This spreadsheet approach is not brand new, but we believe we have developed the application of management science concepts more than any competing textbook. Based on our own experience with this material in the classroom, both at the undergraduate and MBA levels, we know that the impact can be enormous. Our students are thoroughly interested because they learn skills they will remember and use in their eventual jobs.

A New Paradigm

The relevance of management science for students has been discussed for several years. Many people have suggested that the way to obtain relevance is to include more examples of real-world implementations of MS. We agree, and have adapted many real applications in this book. However, upon reading about large-scale success stories such as American Airlines or Hewlett Packard, a student might argue that MS is an important discipline but that you don't really need to know MS concepts—just someone who does. We have tried to write a book that gives valuable skills and insight to common problems to the "masses," not just to large problems and the elite few.

The ability to think through complex problems and relate quantities in a spreadsheet is valuable for all business students. This skill provides real competitive advantages in finance, operations, and marketing. The essence of our approach provides skills that are fourfold:

Problem Solving

The modeling process stressed in this book forces students to think through complex problems, identify variables under a decision-maker's control, identify constraints on these decision variables, quantify the effects of uncertainty, and develop structural relationships between all important quantities. This is nothing new—it is the essence of MS—but the spreadsheet approach puts the entire procedure within the capability of virtually all business students, regardless of their mathematical background.

Interdisciplinary Approach

Students see how MS pertains to a variety of business disciplines. Traditionally, MS textbooks have emphasized problems in the operations area. We have also included many examples and problems from finance and marketing, among others. For example, we have included discussions of portfolio selection, options pricing, cash management, currency transactions, and other important finance topics that can be formulated easily as MS models and solved with spreadsheets. Our MBA students, predominantly finance and marketing, love this feature.

Insights

It is not easy to read the statement of a problem and "guess" the answer; there are usually too many relationships and constraints involved. However, it is instructive to look at a spreadsheet solution and see whether this solution looks reasonable or whether it's useful to change input parameters and see whether the effects of these changes on the solution can be anticipated. This what-if analysis, which we attempt to do with many examples in the book, provides valuable insights and helps develop mathematical intuition.

Spreadsheet Skills

Finally, students gain spreadsheet facility by working through many of our examples. Students enter our courses with a wide variety of spreadsheet skills—some have excellent skills, others have few or no skills—but all students leave our courses as very competent spreadsheet users. The particular spreadsheet package we use, Microsoft Excel, is the premier spreadsheet package in today's business world, and students who know Excel have a definite edge in the job market.

New Content and Methods

Most adopters of our approach will need to change the way they teach MS. For some instructors, the change may be great; for others it will be a natural step in a process that has already begun. In terms of content, **we have given up teaching algorithms to the mass MS audiences.** Software packages make algorithms unnecessary for all but MS/OR specialists. In this book **we have also eliminated all but a few traditional algebraic formulations in favor of spreadsheet formulations.** We agree, at least in principle, with some of our reviewers who argue that something is lost by not going through the algebra. However, we are convinced that the benefits of spreadsheet modeling outweigh any potential loss.

Our approach is to teach modeling rather than a collection of well-known models. Admittedly, many of the examples in this book fall into traditional categories, but our emphasis is different. For example, when we discuss the transportation model in Chapter 4, our intent is not to teach every detail about this type of model (and have students memorize these details). Instead, our intent is to introduce a type of model that is very flexible for modeling a variety of problems.

Regarding the teaching method itself, we have found that **the more hands-on we can make the classes, the more students enjoy them and the more they learn.** At the very least, instructors should be equipped with computer projection equipment so that they can develop spreadsheet solutions (or manipulate our files) in real time.

Although many instructors probably agree in principle that a spreadsheet approach is a good idea, they might not be aware of the difficulties this approach can entail. We do not want to ignore these difficulties, but we believe that with proper planning they can be managed. We have found that grading is the biggest challenge. Grading 50 spreadsheet files (on 50 floppy disks) can definitely take more time than grading 50 algebraic formulations on paper. Similarly, giving an exam in a computer lab, where each student must create one or more spreadsheet files on a PC, can be a real headache unless the details are carefully planned.

One way to avoid some of these problems is to employ spreadsheet "shells," where the structure of the spreadsheet is given and the students then "fill in the blanks" with appropriate formulas. We discuss these below. Another problem can be the distribution of computerized materials to the students. However, by setting up a Web page or placing files on a network, an instructor can easily distribute files, even with daily updates if desired. This way, for instance, if an example spreadsheet is nearly completed during class, the completed file can be distributed right after class—for immediate reinforcement. Various methods for dealing with these issues are discussed in the Instructor's Resource and Media Manual.

Using This Book

This book teaches by example. Students learn the subjects by working through the examples. There is not much "up front" discussion of basic content in most of the chapters; students can usually dive right into the examples. We believe this is the way students learn the modeling process best, and we believe it is most likely to hold their interest. Of course, some concepts must be discussed generally before specific examples can be given. A good illustration is Chapter 11, on queueing models, where we believe it is necessary to discuss such key concepts as the exponential distribution, Little's formula, and steady state before students can really understand queueing models.

Organization

Largely because of this example-based approach, **the book is very modular,** which allows instructors to cover only those topics and examples that are of most interest to them. For example, in the mathematical programming chapters (2 through 6), students need to read through Section 2.4 of Chapter 2, particularly Section 2.3, which explains the basic concepts of spreadsheet LP models and Excel's Solver. If instructors plan to cover nonlinear models, students should also read Section 6.2 of Chapter 6, which covers some basic concepts of nonlinear optimization. However, beyond these introductory discussions, instructors can move freely from example to example and chapter to chapter, choosing only those that interest them. This modular approach is discussed more thoroughly in the Instructor's Resource and Media Manual, which outlines several possible study plans.

Problems and Cases

The book contains a greater variety and number of problems than any competing text. These range from very straightforward to challenging. The difficulty level is indicated by the headings "Skill-Building Problems" and "Skill-Extending Problems," the latter being more challenging. There are also a number of "Modeling Problems." These are less structured than the other problems and may require students to discuss the nature of the data that would be necessary to solve a particular problem. Finally, most chapters include one or two cases (written by Mark Broadie of Columbia University). These cases, which are often challenging, should be appreciated particularly by MBA students because of the way they integrate with other business disciplines.

Accompanying Materials

The package of materials that accompanies this book is much more than a set of "ancillaries"; it is an integrated package and is essential to the successful teaching of the course.

- **Instructor's Resource and Media Manual.** Contains suggestions for teaching the course, including discussions of classroom presentation, homework assignments, team projects, and testing approaches; course syllabi; optional uses of the book for different objectives and audiences—for instance, for undergraduates or MBA students, or for a finance or marketing emphasis; plus instructions for the two $3^1/_2$ - inch disks that come with the IRMM: the Excel Solutions Disk and the Presentation Disk. Available to all adopting instructors.

- **Excel Solutions Disk.** Contains complete "live" Excel worksheet solutions for every example, problem, and case study in the book. Also contains shell, or template, worksheets for the problems that provide the structure for the worksheet solution with the numbers and formulas stripped out. Instructors may use these shells as is, strip them further, or add a few hints. We find these shells are helpful for larger classes or for undergraduates who might need extra help formulating spreadsheet models, plus they force students to enter pertinent information in particular cells and thus make grading easier. For further assistance, grading macros have been included for selected problems. These automatically check whether certain cells contain correct information. In some cases they also enter new inputs and check whether a student's formulas react correctly to the new inputs. A list of solution and shell filenames is included in the IRMM.

- **Presentation Disk.** Contains PowerPoint slides and accompanying Excel worksheets corresponding to the examples, concepts, and chapter outlines.

- **Student Excel Disk.** Included with every new copy of the book; contains Excel worksheets for all in-text examples, data sets for problems, and Excel add-ins, described below.

- **Web Page.** Provides an open communication line for instructors and students to discuss our approach to teaching MS, plus updates on software and spreadsheet information and additional information about the book (www.indiana.edu/~mgtsci).

- **Videotape.** This video introduction to the book and course highlights our approach with in-class sequences and an interview with the authors.

Software

Several options are available. One is to order the book with the following Excel add-ins, which are available at no additional cost when ordered with the book:

- **EXCEL SOLVER UPGRADE** from Frontline Systems, the developers of Excel Solver, improves the performance and robustness of your Excel 5.0 or 7.0 Solver. For more information on the Solver and Frontline Systems, go to: http://www.frontsys.com

- **TREEPLAN** by Michael Middleton is an add-in that will generate decision trees for the material in Chapter 8. This shareware version is compatible with Excel 5.0 and later.

- **MONTE CARLO/DISCRETE EVENT SIMULATION MODULES** from Sam Savage's *Insight: Business Analysis Tools for Microsoft Excel* (Duxbury, 1998), is an add-in for the Monte Carlo and queueing problems in Chapters 11 and 13.

- **RETAILER** is software for the case study in Chapter 10.

If you favor more powerful software for decision analysis and simulation, the following programs are available at extra cost from the publisher:

- **DPL** by Applied Decision Analysis is Windows-based professional software for both decision trees and influence diagrams. The student version is identical to the professional version in capability but runs slower. DPL is compatible with Excel.

- **@RISK** by Palisade Corporation is a professional add-in for Excel and Lotus for Windows for Monte Carlo simulation. Many examples in Chapter 13 use @RISK. If you want more finance examples like those in Chapter 13, order this software and the accompanying book, *Simulation Modeling Using @RISK,* by Wayne Winston. This student version is identical to the professional version in capability and contains many more financial, marketing, and operations applications.

- **WHAT'S BEST!** by Lindo Systems, an add-in for optimization, is highly recommended for Lotus 1-2-3 users. An introduction to What's Best! can be found in the appendix to Chapter 2.

Acknowledgments

This book has gone through more than its fair share of reviews, and it is a much better product because of them. The majority of the reviewers' suggestions were very good ones, and we have attempted to incorporate them. Thanks to: Mark Broadie, Columbia University; Susan Cohen, University of Illinois, Urbana/Champaign; Abe Feinberg, California State University, Northridge; Paul Fishbeck, Carnegie Mellon University; James Flynn, Cleveland State University; Gregory Frazier, University of Oregon; Robert M. Freund, Massachusetts Institute of Technology; Phil Fry, Boise State University; Daniel Fylstra, Frontline Systems, Inc.; Mark Gershon, Temple University; Anjani Jain, University of Pennsylvania; Thomas R. Jefferson, University of California, Los Angeles; L. Robin Keller, University of California, Irvine; Jerry May, University of Pittsburgh; Kevin McCardle, Duke University; Jennifer L. Meyer, University of Nebraska, Lincoln; John B. Moore, University of Waterloo; Danny Myers, Bowling Green State University; Pierre Ndilikilikesha, Duke University; Susan Palocsay, James Madison University; Steve Powell, Dartmouth College; Sam Savage, Stanford University; Carl R. Schultz, University of New Mexico; Jerry F. Shapiro, Massachusetts Institute of Technology; Stuart Smith, Purdue University; Rakesh Vohra, Ohio State University; Rick Wilson, Oklahoma State University; and Martin Young, University of Michigan.

We would also like to thank two special people at Duxbury. First, we want to thank Curt Hinrichs, our editor, for being the guiding light of this project. Throughout its development, Curt kept up incredible enthusiasm for this new approach to MS, and it rubbed off on us. In fact, his enthusiasm and vision kept us going through the tough times when we thought we'd never see the light at the end of the tunnel. Thanks to Curt, the end of the tunnel has finally arrived. If the book is a success, it will be in large part because of his efforts. Sandra Craig, our production editor, was wonderful to work with. Any MS book is bound to contain a lot of details, and one based on spreadsheets has even more details. Trying to get all of these details correct is a difficult task—to say the least!—and Sandra had the patience and the perfectionist attitude to help us "get it right."

We would also like to thank Jerry May (University of Pittsburgh) for class testing the manuscript; Daniel Fylstra (Frontline Systems) for checking the accuracy of the Microsoft Solver operations; Abe Feinberg for accuracy checking the pageproofs. And finally, thanks to over 300 faculty members involved in the Duxbury/INFORMS MS/OR teaching survey conducted in the spring of 1995. We have tried to address many of the teaching issues and problems the survey brought to our attention. Finally, we thank our students for their candid comments and suggestions on early drafts of this manuscript.

We would also enjoy hearing from you—we can be reached via e-mail.

Wayne L. Winston (winston@indiana.edu)
S. Christian Albright (albright@indiana.edu)

Bloomington, Indiana
June 1996

PRACTICAL MANAGEMENT SCIENCE

CHAPTER

1

Introduction to Modeling

What Is Management Science?

The purpose of this book is to expose you to a variety of problems that have been solved successfully with management science methods and to give you experience in modeling these problems on a spreadsheet. The subject of management science has evolved for approximately 50 years and is now a mature field within the broad category of applied mathematics. Our intent in this book is to emphasize both the applied and mathematical aspects of management science. Beginning in this chapter and continuing throughout the rest of the book, we will discuss many successful management science applications, where teams of highly trained people have implemented solutions to the problems faced by major companies and have saved these companies millions of dollars. Many airlines and oil companies, for example, could hardly operate as they do today without the support of management science. In this book we will lead you through the solution procedure of many interesting and realistic problems, and you will experience firsthand what is required to solve these problems successfully. We recognize that most of you are not highly trained in mathematics. Therefore, we will solve most of the problems using spreadsheets, which makes the quantitative analysis much more understandable and intuitive.

The key to virtually every management science application is a **mathematical model**. In simple terms, a mathematical model is a quantitative representation, or approximation, of a real problem. This representation might be phrased in terms of mathematical expressions (equations and inequalities) or as a series of interrelated cells in a spreadsheet. We prefer the latter, especially for teaching purposes, and we will concentrate primarily on spreadsheet models in this book. However, in either case the purpose of a mathematical model is to represent the essence of a problem in a concise form. This has several advantages. First, it enables an analyst to understand the problem better. In particular, it helps to define the scope of the problem, the possible solutions, and the data requirements. Second, it allows the analyst to employ a variety of the mathematical solution procedures that have been developed over the past half-century. These solution procedures are often very computer intensive, but with today's cheap and abundant computing power, they are usually feasible. Finally, the modeling process itself, if it is done correctly, often helps to "sell" the solution to the people who must work with the system that is eventually implemented.

In this chapter we will introduce the concept of a mathematical model with a simple queueing model. Then we will describe a seven-step model-building process that should be followed—in essence if not in strict conformance—in all management science applications. We will then describe three successful applications of management science. For all three of these applications, we will illustrate how the seven-step model-building process was followed. Finally, we will discuss why the study of management science is valuable, not only to large corporations, but also to students like yourselves who are about to enter the business world. ■

1.1 A Waiting Line Example

As indicated earlier, a mathematical model is a set of mathematical relationships that represent, or approximate, a real situation. Some models simply describe a situation. Such models are called **descriptive models**. Other models suggest a desirable course of action. Such models are called **prescriptive**, or **optimization**, **models**. To get us started, we discuss the following simple example of a mathematical model. It begins as a descriptive model, but we then expand it to become an optimization model.

Consider a 7–Eleven store with a single cash register. The manager of the store suspects that customers might be waiting too long in line at the checkout register and that these excessive waiting times might be hurting business. Customers who have to wait a long time might not come back, and potential customers who see a long line might not enter the store at all. Therefore, the manager wants to build a mathematical model to help understand the problem. The manager wants to build a model that reflects the current situation at the store but that will also be able to improve the current situation if possible.

A Descriptive Model

This example is a typical waiting line (or **queueing**) problem. (Such problems will be studied in detail in Chapter 11.) As mentioned earlier, the manager first wants to build a model that reflects the *current* situation at the store. Later he will alter the model to predict what might make the situation better. To describe the current situation, the manager realizes that there are two important "inputs" to the problem: (1) the arrival rate of potential customers to the store and (2) the rate at which customers can be served by the single cashier. It is intuitively clear that as the arrival rate increases and/or the service rate decreases the waiting line will tend to increase and each customer will tend to wait longer in line. In addition, it is likely that more potential customers will decide not to enter at all. It is common to refer to these latter quantities (length of waiting line, time in line per customer, fraction of customers who don't enter) as "outputs." The manager believes he has some understanding of the relationship between the inputs and the outputs, but he is not at all sure of the *exact* relationship between them.

This is where a mathematical model is useful. By making several simplifying assumptions about the nature of the arrival and service process at the store (as will be discussed in Chapter 11), we can relate the inputs to the outputs. In some cases, when the model is sufficiently simple, we can write an *equation* for an output in terms of the inputs. For example, in the simplest of all queueing models, if we let A be the arrival rate of customers per minute, S be the service rate of customers per minute, and W be the average time a typical customer waits in line (assuming all potential customers enter the store), then the following relationship can be derived:

$$W = \frac{A}{S(S - A)} \tag{1.1}$$

This relationship is intuitive in one sense. It correctly predicts that as the service rate S increases, the average waiting time W will decrease, and as the arrival rate A increases, the average waiting time W will increase. Also, if the arrival rate is just barely less than the service rate, that is, $S - A$ is positive but very small, the average waiting time will become quite large. (This model requires that the arrival rate is *less than* the service rate; otherwise, Equation 1.1 makes no sense.)

In other models there is no such "closed-form" relationship between inputs and outputs (or if there is, it is quite complex). Nevertheless, there may still be a mathematical procedure for calculating outputs from inputs, and it may be possible to implement this procedure in a spreadsheet. This is the case for the 7–Eleven problem. Again, by making certain simplifying assumptions, including the assumption that potential customers won't enter if the waiting line is sufficiently long, a spreadsheet model of the situation at the store can be developed.

Before presenting it, however, we need to discuss how the manager can obtain the inputs he will need for the spreadsheet model. There are actually three inputs: the arrival rate A, the service rate S, and the number in the store, labeled N, that will induce future customers not to enter. The first two of these can be measured with a stopwatch. For example, the manager can request an employee to measure the times between customer arrivals. Let's say the employee does this for several hours, and the average time between arrivals is observed to be 2 minutes. Then the arrival rate can be estimated as $A = 1/2 = .5$ (1 customer every 2 minutes). Similarly, the employee can record the times it takes the cashier to serve successive customers. If the average of these times (taken over many customers) is, say, 2.5 minutes, then the service rate can be estimated as $S = 1/2.5 = .4$ (1 customer every 2.5 minutes). Finally, if the manager notices that potential customers tend to take their business elsewhere when there are 5 customers in line, then he can let $N = 5$.

These input estimates can now be entered in the spreadsheet model shown in Figure 1.1. Don't worry about the details of this spreadsheet—they will be covered in Chapter 11. Just trust us that the formulas built into this spreadsheet reflect an adequate approximation of the 7–Eleven store's situation. For now, the important thing is that this spreadsheet allows the manager to enter any values for the inputs in cells B4 through B6

FIGURE 1.1 Spreadsheet Model for 7–Eleven Store with Current Inputs

	A	B	C	D
1	Spreadsheet descriptive model for 7-Eleven store example			
2				
3	Inputs			
4	Arrival rate (customers per minute)	0.5		
5	Service rate (customers per minute)	0.4		
6	Maximum customers (before others go elsewhere)	5		
7				
8	Outputs			
9	Average number in line	2.22		
10	Average time (minutes) spent in line	6.09		
11	Percentage of potential arrivals who don't enter	27.1%		

and observe the resulting outputs in cells B9 through B11. The input values in Figure 1.1 represent the store's current input values. These values indicate that on average there are slightly more than 2 customers waiting in line, an average customer waits slightly more than 6 minutes in line, and about 27% of all potential customers don't enter the store at all (due to the perception that waiting times will be long).

The information in Figure 1.1 may not be all that useful to the manager. After all, he probably already has a sense of how long waiting times are and how many customers are being lost. The power of the model is that it allows the manager to ask many what-if questions. For example, what if he could somehow speed up the cashier, say, from 2.5 minutes per customer to 1.8 minutes per customer. He might guess that since the average service time has decreased by 28%, all of the outputs should also decrease by 28%. Is this the case? Evidently not, as shown in Figure 1.2. The average line length decreases to 1.41, a 36% decrease; the average waiting time decreases to 3.22, a 47% decrease; and the percentage of customers who don't enter decreases to 12.6%, a 54% decrease. To illustrate an even more extreme change, suppose the manager could cut the service time in half, from 2.5 minutes to 1.25 minutes. The spreadsheet in Figure 1.3 shows that the average number in line decreases to .69, a 69% decrease

FIGURE 1.2 **Spreadsheet Model for Faster Service Rate**

	A	B	C	D
1	**Spreadsheet descriptive model for 7-Eleven store example**			
2				
3	**Inputs**			
4	Arrival rate (customers per minute)	0.5		
5	Service rate (customers per minute)	0.556		
6	Maximum customers (before others go elsewhere)	5		
7				
8	**Outputs**			
9	Average number in line	1.41		
10	Average time (minutes) spent in line	3.22		
11	Percentage of potential arrivals who don't enter	12.6%		

FIGURE 1.3 **Spreadsheet Model for Fastest Service Rate**

	A	B	C	D
1	**Spreadsheet descriptive model for 7-Eleven store example**			
2				
3	**Inputs**			
4	Arrival rate (customers per minute)	0.5		
5	Service rate (customers per minute)	0.8		
6	Maximum customers (before others go elsewhere)	5		
7				
8	**Outputs**			
9	Average number in line	0.69		
10	Average time (minutes) spent in line	1.42		
11	Percentage of potential arrivals who don't enter	3.8%		

from the original value; the average waiting time decreases to 1.42, a 77% decrease; and the percentage of customers who don't enter decreases to 3.8%, a whopping 86% decrease. The important lesson to be learned from the spreadsheet model is that as the manager increases the service rate, the output measures improve more than he would have expected.

In reality, the manager would attempt to validate the spreadsheet model before trusting its answers to these what-if questions. At the very least, the manager should examine the reasonableness of the assumptions. For example, one assumption is that the arrival rate remains *constant* for the time period under discussion. If the manager intends to use this model—with the *same* input parameters—during periods of time when the arrival rate varies quite a lot (such as peak lunchtime traffic followed by slack times in the early afternoon), then he is almost certainly asking for trouble. Besides determining whether the assumptions are reasonable, the manager can also check the outputs predicted by the model when the current inputs are used. For example, Figure 1.1 predicts that the average time a customer waits in line is approximately 6 minutes. At this point, the manager could ask his employee to use a stopwatch again to time customers' waiting times. If they average close to 6 minutes, then the manager can put more confidence in the model. However, if they average much more or much less than 6 minutes, then the manager probably needs to search for a new model.

An Optimization Model

As the model stands so far, it fails to reflect any *economic* information such as the cost of speeding up service, the cost of making customers wait in line, or the cost of losing customers. Given the spreadsheet model developed above, however, it is relatively straightforward to incorporate economic information and then make rational choices. To make this example simple, we will assume that the manager can do one of three things: (1) leave the system as it is, (2) hire a second person to help the first cashier process customers more quickly, or (3) lease a new model of cash register that will speed up the service process significantly. The effect of (2) is to decrease the average service time from 2.5 to 1.8 minutes. The effect of (3) is to decrease the service time from 2.5 to 1.25 minutes. What should the manager do?

He needs to examine three types of costs. The first is the cost of hiring the extra person or leasing the new cash register. We assume that these costs are known. For example, we will assume that the hourly wage for the extra person is $5 and the cost to lease a new cash register (converted to a per-hour rate) is $8 per hour. The second cost is the "cost" of making a person wait in line. Although this is not an out-of-pocket cost to the store, it does represent the cost of potential future business—a customer who has to wait a long time might not return. This cost is clearly difficult to estimate on a per-minute or per-hour basis, but we'll make a rough estimate of it as $10 per customer per hour in line.[1] Finally, there is the opportunity cost for customers who decide not to enter the store. The store loses not only their current revenue but also potential future revenue if they decide not to return. Again, this is a difficult cost to measure, but we will assume it is $20 per lost customer.

The next step in the modeling process is to combine these costs for each possible decision. Let's find the total cost per hour for decision (3), where the new cash register is leased. The lease cost is $8 per hour. From Figure 1.3 we see there are, on average, .69 customers in line at any time. Therefore, the average waiting cost per hour is $.69 \times \$10 = \$6.90$. (This is because .69 customer-hours are spent in line each hour on average.)

[1] Here we are charging only for time in the queue. An alternative model is to charge for time in the queue and for time in service.

Finally, from Figure 1.3 we see that the average number of potential arrivals per hour is 30 (= 60 × 1/2), and 3.8% of them don't enter. Therefore, the average cost per hour from lost customers is .038 × 30 × \$20 = \$22.80. The combined cost for decision (3) is \$8 + \$6.90 + \$22.80 = \$37.70 per hour.

The spreadsheet model in Figure 1.4 incorporates these calculations and similar calculations for the other two decisions. (The discrepancy between the \$37.70 above and the \$37.67 in cell D24 is due to roundoff error.) As we see from row 24, the option to lease the new cash register is the clear winner from a cost standpoint. However, if the manager wants to see how sensitive these cost figures are to the rather uncertain input costs we assessed for waiting time and lost customers, it is simple to enter new values in rows 10 and 11 and see how the "bottom lines" in row 24 change. This flexibility is the power of spreadsheets. They not only allow us to build realistic and complex models, they allow us to answer many what-if questions simply by changing input values.

FIGURE 1.4 **Spreadsheet Model with Decision Alternatives**

	A	B	C	D
1	**Spreadsheet decision model for 7-Eleven store example**			
2				
3	**Inputs**	Decision 1	Decision 2	Decision 3
4	Arrival rate (customers per minute)	0.5	0.5	0.5
5	Service rate (customers per minute)	0.4	0.556	0.8
6	Maximum customers (before others go elsewhere)	5	5	5
7				
8	Cost of extra person per hour	\$0	\$5	\$0
9	Cost of leasing new cash register per hour	\$0	\$0	\$8
10	Cost per customer per hour waiting in line	\$10	\$10	\$10
11	Cost per customer who doesn't enter the store	\$20	\$20	\$20
12				
13	**Outputs**			
14	Average number in line	2.22	1.41	0.69
15	Average time (minutes) spent in line	6.09	3.22	1.42
16	Percentage of potential arrivals who don't enter	27.1%	12.6%	3.8%
17				
18	**Cost information**			
19	Cost of extra person per hour	\$0	\$5	\$0
20	Cost of leasing new cash register per hour	\$0	\$0	\$8
21	Cost per hour of waiting time	\$22.20	\$14.08	\$6.85
22	Cost per hour of lost customers	\$162.63	\$75.61	\$22.82
23				
24	Total cost per hour	\$184.84	\$94.70	\$37.67

1.2 The Seven-Step Modeling Process

The discussion of the queueing problem in the previous section presented some of the basic principles of management science modeling. In this section we will further explain these ideas by characterizing the modeling process as a seven-step procedure.

Step 1 **Define the Problem** The management scientist first defines the organization's problem. Defining the problem includes specifying the organization's objectives and the parts of the organization that must be studied before the problem can be solved. In our simple queueing model the organization's problem was how to minimize the total costs associated with the operation of the store's cash register.

Step 2 **Observe the System and Collect Data** After defining the problem, the analyst collects data to estimate the value of parameters that affect the organization's problem. These estimates are used to develop (in Step 3) a mathematical model of the organization's problem and predict solutions (Step 4). In the 7–Eleven queueing example the manager would need to observe the arrivals and the checkout process in order to estimate A and S.

Step 3 **Formulate a Mathematical Model** In the third step the analyst develops a mathematical model of the problem. In this book we will describe many methods that can be used to model systems. Models such as Equation 1.1, where we use an equation to relate parameters such as A and S to quantities of interest such as W are called **analytic models**. The spreadsheet models from the previous section, which depended on complex equations that were not shown, are also analytic models. Many realistic applications are so complex, however, that an analytic model does not exist or is too complex to work with. For example, if the 7–Eleven store had more than one register and customers were allowed to join any line or jump from one line to another, there would be no analytic model—no equation or system of equations—that could be used to determine W from knowledge of A, S, and the number of lines. When no tractable analytic model exists, we often rely instead on a **simulation model**, which enables a computer to approximate the behavior of the actual system. We will discuss simulation models in Chapters 12 and 13.

Step 4 **Verify the Model and Use the Model for Prediction** The management scientist now tries to determine whether the mathematical model developed in the previous step is an accurate representation of reality. A first step in determining how well the model fits reality is to check whether the model is valid for the current situation. As we discussed earlier, to validate Equation 1.1 the manager might observe actual customer waiting times for several hours. As we have already seen, Equation 1.1 predicts that when $A = .5$ and $S = .4$, the average customer spends 6.09 minutes in line. Now suppose the manager observes that 120 customers spend a total of 750 minutes in line. This indicates an average of $750/120 = 6.25$ minutes in line per customer. Since 6.25 is reasonably close to 6.09, the manager's observations would appear to lend credibility to the model. In contrast, if the 120 customers had spent 1200 minutes total in line, for an average of 10 minutes per customer, this would not agree very well with the model's prediction of 6.09 minutes, and we would doubt the validity of the model.

Step 5 **Select a Suitable Alternative** Given a model and a set of alternatives, the management scientist must now choose the alternative that best meets the organization's objectives. For example, the model represented by Equation 1.1 allowed us to determine the service rate that would minimize cost. In many situations, however, the organization has more than one objective. For example, a firm considering the purchase of a microcomputer might want to buy the computer that best satisfies the following criteria: (1) it is economical, (2) it is easy to use, (3) it can run useful software, and (4) it is fast. It is likely that no single computer will be the best with respect to all four criteria. So which computer should the company purchase? This question can be answered with one of the multi-objective decision-making procedures that we will discuss in Chapter 7.

Step 6 **Present the Results of the Study to the Organization** In this step, the analyst presents the model and the recommendations from the previous step to the organization. In some situations the analyst might present several alternatives and let the organization choose the one that best meets its needs.

Step 7 **Implement and Evaluate Recommendations** If the organization has accepted the validity and usefulness of the study, the analyst then helps to implement its recommendations. The implemented system must be monitored constantly (and updated dynamically as the environment changes) to ensure that the model enables the organization to meet its objectives.

The flowchart in Figure 1.5 illustrates this seven-step process. As the arrows back to the left indicate, there is a lot of room for feedback in the process. For example, at various steps the analyst may realize that the current model is not capturing some key aspects of the real problem. In this case the analyst may need to revise the problem definition or develop a new model.

FIGURE 1.5 Flowchart for Seven-Step Process

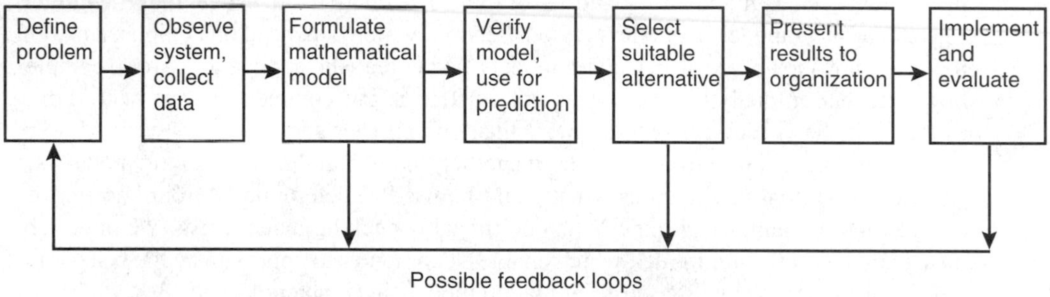

Discussion of the Seven Steps

Now that we have defined the seven steps of model building, we discuss them in more detail.

Step 1 **Problem Definition** Typically, a management science model is commissioned when an organization believes it has a problem. Perhaps the company is losing money, perhaps its market share is declining, perhaps its customers are waiting too long for service; any number of problems might be evident. The organization (which we will refer to as the client) calls in a management scientist (the analyst) to solve this problem. In such cases the problem has probably already been defined by the client, and the client hires the analyst to solve *this particular problem*. As Miser [3] and Volkema [5] point out, however, the analyst should do some investigating before accepting the client's claim that the problem is already well defined. Failure to do so could mean solving the wrong problem and wasting valuable time and energy.

For example, Miser cites the experience of an analyst who was hired by the military to investigate overly long turnaround times between fighter planes' landing and taking off again to rejoin the battle. The military (the client) was convinced that the problem was caused by inefficient ground crews; if they were sped up, turnaround times would decrease. The analyst nearly accepted this statement of the problem and was about to do classical time-and-motion studies on the ground crew to pinpoint the sources of their inefficiency. However, by snooping around he found that the problem obviously lay elsewhere. It seems that the trucks that refueled the planes were frequently late, which in turn was due to the inefficient way they were refilled from storage tanks at another location. Once this latter problem was solved—and its solution was embarrassingly simple—the turnaround times decreased to an acceptable level without any changes on the part of the ground crews. If the analyst had accepted the client's statement of the problem, the *real* problem might never have been located or solved.

The moral of this story is clear: If an analyst defines a problem incorrectly or too narrowly, the best solution to the real problem might never emerge. In his article, Volkema [5] advocates spending as much time thinking about the problem and defining it properly as modeling and solving it. This is undoubtedly good advice, especially in real-world applications where problem boundaries are often difficult to define.

Step 2 **Data Collection** This crucial step in the process is often the most tedious. All organizations keep track of various data on their operations, but these data might not be in the form the analyst requires. They also might be scattered in different places throughout the organization, in all kinds of different formats. Therefore, one of the first jobs of the analyst is to gather exactly the right data and put the data into exactly the right form required by the model. This typically requires asking questions of key people (such as the accountants) throughout the organization, studying existing organizational databases, and performing time-consuming observational studies of the organization's processes. In short, it usually entails a lot of leg work.

In this book, as in most management science textbooks, we tend to shield you from this data-collection process by supplying the appropriate data to formulate and solve a model. Although this makes the overall modeling process seem easier than it really is, it is simply not practical in most class settings to have students go out to companies and gather data. (In many cases it wouldn't even be allowed for proprietary reasons.) Nevertheless, in several exercises we will ask you to list the types of data you would need to model a given problem successfully.

Step 3 **Model Formulation** This step (along with Step 5) is where the management scientist brings his or her special skills into play. After defining the client's problem and gathering the necessary data, the analyst must formulate a mathematical model of the problem. Several properties are desirable for a good model. First, it should represent the client's real problem accurately. If it uses a linear (straight-line) function for costs when the real cost function is highly nonlinear (curved), the recommendations of the model could be very misleading. Similarly, if it ignores an important constraint such as an upper bound on capacity, its recommendations might not be possible to implement.

On the other hand, the model should be simple enough to allow a mathematical solution. Most good models capture the essence of the problem without getting bogged down in minor details. They should be *approximations* of the real world, not mirror images in every last detail. Overly complex models are often of little practical use. First, overly complex models are often too difficult to solve with the solution algorithms and computers available. Second, complex models tend to be incomprehensible to clients. As you can imagine, if a client can't understand a thing about a model, the chances are not too good that the model's recommendations will ever be implemented. Therefore, the skill in model formulation lies in being able to achieve the right balance between too simplistic and too complex.

Step 4 **Model Verification** This step is particularly important in real management science applications. A client is much more likely to accept an analyst's model if the analyst can provide some type of verification. This verification might take several forms. For example, the analyst could use the model with the company's current values of the input parameters. If the model's outputs are then in line with the outputs currently observed by the client, the analyst has at least shown that the model can duplicate the current situation. We mentioned earlier how this could be done in the 7–Eleven queueing example. That is, if the model represented by Equation 1.1 is able to predict the current average waiting time, given the current arrival rate and service rate as inputs, then it has passed the first test, and it *might* be able to predict the average waiting time for new inputs.

A second way to verify a model is to enter a number of sets of input parameters (even if they are not the company's current inputs) and see whether the outputs from the model are reasonable. One common approach is to use extreme values of the inputs to see whether the outputs behave as they should. For example, for the 7–Eleven queueing model we could enter an extremely large service rate or a service rate just barely above the arrival rate in Equation 1.1. In the first case we would expect the average waiting time to approach 0, whereas in the latter case we would expect it to become very large. You can check this expectation with Equation 1.1 to see that this is exactly what happens. Therefore, we have another piece of evidence that this model is reasonable.

What if certain inputs are entered in the model, and the model's outputs are *not* as expected? There could be two causes. First, the model could simply be a poor representation of the actual situation. In this case it is up to the analyst to refine the model until it provides reasonably accurate predictions. The second possible cause is that the model is fine but our intuition is not very good. That is, when asked what we think would happen if the inputs were set equal to certain values, we might provide totally wrong predictions. In this case the fault lies with us, not the model.

A typical example of this occurs with random sequences of zeros and ones, such as might occur with successive flips of a fair coin. Most people guess that heads and tails will alternate and that there will be very few sequences of, say, four or more heads (or tails) in a row. However, a perfectly accurate simulation model of these flips will show, contrary to what most people expect, that fairly long runs of heads or tails are not at all uncommon. In fact, one or two long runs should be expected if there are enough flips.

Actually, the fact that outcomes sometimes defy intuition is an important reason why mathematical models have been, and continue to be, important. Such models prove that people's ability to predict outcomes in complex environments is often not very good. Nevertheless, if a model's predictions are not in line with what the client expects, it may be difficult for the analyst to explain that it is the client, not the model, that is in error!

Step 5 **Selection of an Alternative** Once the problem has been defined, the data have been collected, and the model has been formulated and verified, it is time to use the model to recommend decisions or strategies. In the majority of management science models this requires the optimization of an objective function, such as maximizing profit or minimizing cost. As we mentioned earlier, it can also mean finding the alternatives that best achieve multiple objectives, as we will discuss in Chapter 7.

The optimization phase is typically the most difficult phase from a mathematical standpoint. Indeed, much of the management science literature (mostly from academics) has focused on complex solution algorithms for various classes of models. Fortunately for all of us, this research has led to a number of solution algorithms (and computer packages that incorporate these algorithms) that can now be used to solve real problems. Undoubtedly the most famous of these is the simplex algorithm that spreadsheet Solvers and other commercial software packages use on a daily basis to solve companies' linear programming problems.

Not all solution procedures find the optimal solution to a problem. Many models are too large or complex to be solved exactly. Therefore, many complex problems use heuristic methods to locate good solutions. A heuristic is a solution method that is guided by common sense, intuition, and trial and error to achieve a good, but probably not optimal, solution. Sometimes heuristics are "quick and dirty," while others are quite sophisticated. As models become larger and more complex, good heuristics are sometimes the best that can be hoped for.

For years optimization algorithms (and some heuristics) formed the basis for courses in management science. For example, all students were required to learn the inner workings of the simplex method. This focus on algorithms is now being deemphasized, and we will say very little about algorithms in this book. Many instructors (and certainly most students!) agree that this is the proper way to proceed, arguing by analogy that an automobile driver doesn't need to know how everything under the hood works in order to drive the car successfully. We buy this analogy—to a point. In contrast to most of us, race car drivers who drive cars for a living *do* need to know what's going on under the hood in order to achieve their best performance. In the same way, professional management scientists, the analysts who solve real companies' problems, must understand the algorithms that are being used to solve their models. Admittedly, most of you will not be professional management scientists, but you should appreciate that a few people out there have to understand how the computerized "black boxes" really work!

Step 6 **Presentation of the Results** Sooner or later, the analyst must communicate the model and its recommendations to the client. To appreciate this step, you must appreciate the large gap that typically exists between the technical analyst and the managers of the organization. Managers know their business but often do not understand much about mathematics and mathematical models. The burden is therefore on the analyst to present the model in terms that nonmathematical people can understand; otherwise, a perfectly good model may never see the light of day. The best strategy for successful presentation is to involve key people in the organization, including top executives, in the project *right from the beginning*. If these people have been working with the analyst, helping to supply appropriate data and helping the analyst to understand the way the organization really works, they are much more likely to accept the eventual model. Step 6, therefore, should really occur throughout the modeling process, not just toward the end.

The analyst should also try to make the model as intuitive and as user-friendly as possible. Clients appreciate menu-driven systems with plenty of graphics. They also appreciate the ability to ask what-if questions and obtain answers quickly and in a form that is easy to understand. This is one reason for favoring spreadsheets. While not all models can be developed on spreadsheets, due to size and/or complexity, we believe the spreadsheet approach we take in this book is a good choice whenever possible because most business people are comfortable with spreadsheets. Spreadsheet packages support the use of graphics, customized menus and toolbars, data tables and other tools for what-if analyses, and even macros (that can be made transparent to the users) for running complex programs.

Step 7 **Implementation of the Model** A real management science application is not complete until it has been implemented. Obviously, a successful implementation can occur only when Step 6 has been accomplished. That is, the analyst must demonstrate the model to the client, and the client must be convinced that the model adds real value and that it can be used by the people who will have to use it. For this reason, the analyst's job is not really complete until the system is up and running on a daily basis. To achieve a successful implementation, it is not just sufficient for upper management to accept the model; the people who will run it every day must be thoroughly trained in its use. At the very least, they should understand how to enter appropriate inputs, run what-if analyses, and interpret the model's output correctly. If they conclude that the model is more trouble than it's worth, they may simply refuse to use it, and the whole exercise will have been a waste of time.

It is interesting to observe how many successful management science applications take a life of their own after the initial implementation. Once an organization sees the benefits of a useful model (and of management science in general), it is likely to expand the model (or create new models) for uses beyond those originally intended. Knowing that this is often the case, the best analysts design models that can be expanded. They try to anticipate problems the organization might face besides the current problem. Also, they stay in contact with the organization after the initial implementation, just in case the organization needs their guidance in expanding the scope of the model.

This discussion of the seven-step modeling process has taken an optimistic point of view. That is, we have assumed that a successful study will employ these seven steps, in approximately this chronological order, and everything will go smoothly. It doesn't always work out this way. Numerous potential applications are never implemented even though the *technical* aspects of the models are perfectly correct. Probably the most frequent cause is a failure to communicate. The analyst builds a complex mathematical model, but the people in the organization can't understand how it works and hence are reluctant to use it. Also, company politics can be a model's downfall if the model recommends a course of action that top management simply doesn't want to follow—for whatever reasons.

Even for applications that are eventually implemented, however, the analyst may not proceed through the seven steps exactly as described above. He or she may backtrack considerably throughout the process. For example, based on a tentative definition of the problem, a model is built and demonstrated to management. Management says that the model is impressive, but it doesn't really solve the company's problem. Therefore, the analyst goes back to Step 1, redefines the problem, and builds a new model (or modifies the original model). In this way, the analyst may generate several iterations of some or all of the seven steps before the project is considered complete.

1.3

Successful Management Science Applications

In this section we discuss three successful management science applications. We will give a detailed (but nonquantitative) description of each application. We will tie our discussion of each application to the seven-step model-building process discussed in the previous section.

Citgo Petroleum

Klingman et al. [1] applied a variety of management science techniques to Citgo Petroleum. Their work saved the company an estimated $70 million per year, making this study one of the most successful applications of management science. Citgo is an oil refining and marketing company that was purchased in 1983 by Southland Corporation, the 7–Eleven convenience store giant. Southland's goal was to make Citgo as successful in the downstream petroleum business (refining and marketing) as Southland was in the convenience store industry, while supplying Southland's 7–Eleven stores with quality motor fuels. Until that time, Citgo had concentrated primarily on its oil refinery operations and had paid too little attention to the downstream market. As a result, it was losing money—a pretax loss of over $50 million in 1984. Southland called in a management science team headed by Darwin Klingman to turn things around. The results were extremely impressive, as demonstrated by Citgo's pretax profit of over $70 million in 1985.

We will focus on two aspects of the study. The first, referred to as model 1, is a mathematical model that has been used to optimize the operations of Citgo's refineries. The second, referred to as model 2 (or SDM by the authors), is a mathematical model that has been used to develop a multiweek supply, distribution, and marketing plan for the entire business. In each case we will go through the seven-step process that made this study a huge success.

Model 1: Optimizing Refinery Operations

Step 1 Klingman's team first concentrated on oil refinery operations at Citgo's Lake Charles refinery. Because of various changes that were occurring in the oil industry and because of some obvious inefficiencies the team spotted at Citgo's operations, it became apparent that

Citgo had a multifaceted problem. It was not taking advantage of available cost-saving opportunities; it wasn't making the correct mix of products; it wasn't using its resources (equipment, labor, and energy) efficiently; and its data-gathering mechanism needed updating.

Step 2 The Lake Charles, Louisiana, refinery was closely observed in an attempt to estimate key data and relationships such as

- How the cost of producing each of Citgo's products (motor fuel, number 2 fuel oil, turbine fuel, naptha, and several blended motor fuels) depends on the inputs used to produce each product;
- The amount of energy needed to produce each product (which required the installation of a new metering system);
- The yield associated with each input-output combination;
- Maintenance costs and their relationship to parts inventories and equipment breakdowns.

Obtaining accurate data required the installation of a new database management system and an integrated maintenance information system. A process-control system was also installed to accurately monitor the inputs and resources used to manufacture each product.

Step 3 Using linear programming (the main topic of the next few chapters), a large, complex model was developed to optimize refinery operations. The model determines the cost-minimizing method for mixing or blending available inputs to produce desired outputs. The model contains constraints to ensure that inputs are blended in such a way that each output is of sufficiently high quality. The model also ensures that plant capacities are not exceeded and allows for the fact that each refinery may carry an inventory of each end-product. (We will discuss blending constraints in Section 3.3 and inventory constraints in Sections 2.9 and 3.5.)

Step 4 To validate the model, inputs and outputs from the Lake Charles refinery were collected for one month. Given the actual inputs used at the refinery during the month, the actual outputs were compared to the outputs predicted by the model. After several modifications, the revised model did indeed predict outputs that were sufficiently close to the actual outputs.

Step 5 Although Citgo had been using a linear programming model prior to the study, Klingman's team replaced Citgo's linear programming software package with the most powerful package then available in order to solve the model in a more timely manner. This package was able to solve the model on a daily basis and suggest detailed strategies for running the refinery. For example, the model might recommend producing 400,000 gallons of turbine fuel by blending 300,000 gallons of crude 1 and 100,000 gallons of crude 2.

Step 6 The linear programming software package implemented in the previous step was not only more powerful, but it was also much more user-friendly. This made it possible for Klingman's team to demonstrate the model's capabilities to Citgo staff in a way they could understand and trust.

Step 7 Once the database and process control were in place, the model was used to guide day-to-day refinery operations. Citgo staff were immediately impressed with its versatility and flexibility in demonstrating how large cost-saving improvements could be made in refinery yields, labor efficiency, maintenance of equipment, and other areas. As further proof of its effects, Citgo had voluntarily participated, *before* the study, in an independent refinery evaluation with 75 other companies. Citgo's rankings on six key measures of performance varied from 38th to 58th, placing it in the middle of the third quartile. A similar evaluation in 1985, *after* implementation of the model, placed Citgo in the upper half of the second quartile of competing refineries. Such a jump, together with clear dollar cost savings of up to $50 million annually, could not help but convince management of the model's worth.

Model 2: The Supply Distribution Marketing (SDM) System

Step 1 Prior to the study, Citgo had concentrated primarily on its refinery operations. Southland wanted Citgo to become more aware of its downstream marketing operations. Specifically, Southland wanted Citgo to change its mindset from trying to produce as much volume at its refinery as possible—even if this meant losing money overall—to a profit-maximization focus. This new focus generated such questions as

- Where should crude oil be purchased?
- Where should products be sold?
- What price should Citgo charge for its products?
- How much of each product should Citgo hold in inventory?

Citgo had largely ignored these questions in the past, and it could not afford to do so in the future if it wanted to remain a viable business within Southland.

Step 2 A database was developed to keep track of sales, inventory, and trades and exchanges of all refined products. Also, regression analysis (discussed in Chapter 14) was used to develop forecasts for wholesale prices and wholesale demand for each of Citgo's products. Klingman's team realized that this was a time (in the mid-1980s) when more and more data were becoming available. The trick was to gather the correct data, put it into a usable form, and take advantage of it in appropriate mathematical models.

Step 3 The team developed a "minimum cost network flow" model (as discussed in Section 4.6) to determine an 11-week supply, marketing, and distribution strategy. This model was characterized by many algebraic equations, but it could also be portrayed graphically as a network, where goods are shipped from one location to another. This network representation had the advantage that it was more intuitive to most people. The model addressed all of the concerns discussed in Step 1.

Step 4 The forecasting modules were continuously evaluated to ensure that they provided accurate forecasts.

Step 5 Besides being more intuitive, the network nature of the model had the advantage that it was easier to solve. The solution procedure made use of special algorithms and computer software. Impossible problems became possible, and hard problems became easy. For example, a typical run of the model involving 3000 equations and 15,000 decision variables required only 30 seconds on an IBM mainframe computer. This not only enabled real-time solutions, but it allowed the model to be run repeatedly to answer what-if questions.

Step 6 Klingman's team was able to demonstrate the benefits of the integrated database management system, the forecasting models, and the optimization models to Southland and Citgo top management. The benefits included better communication and coordination between supply, distribution, marketing, and refining groups; improved data; reduced inventories; added insights into pricing policies; better forecasts; and, of course, lower costs.

Step 7 Probably the most important key to the success of the project was the support of the organization's top executives from the start. The president and CEO of Citgo, the chairman of the board of Southland, and the CEO of Southland created the management science team and were receptive to its needs and recommendations throughout the process. In addition, the project benefited from the enthusiastic and dedicated support of many operational managers during the process. Implementing the SDM required several organizational changes. A new vice president was appointed to coordinate the operation of the SDM and the linear programming refinery model. The product supply and product scheduling departments were combined to improve communication and information flow.

San Francisco Police Scheduling

In the late 1980s Taylor and Huxley [4] developed the Police Patrol Scheduling System (PPSS) for the San Francisco Police Department (SFPD). It is estimated that PPSS created an extra 170,000 productive hours per year, thereby saving the city of San Francisco $5.2 million annually. PPSS enabled SFPD to make strategic changes (such as adopting the 4/10 work schedule described below) that made officers happier and increased productivity. Response times to calls decreased by 20% after PPSS was adopted. All San Francisco precincts now use PPSS to schedule their officers. Other cities (Virginia Beach, Virginia, and Richmond, California) have also adopted PPSS. We now see how the seven-step process made this success possible.

Step 1 For years the SFPD had scheduled its officers manually to various shifts. Because of the large size of the police force (about 1900 officers), the process was very complex, and the SFPD had no idea whether the manual scheduling procedure was producing good schedules. The SFPD had three main goals: (1) to have enough officers on duty to ensure citizens' safety at all times of day, (2) to keep costs low, and (3) to keep officer morale high. This involved difficult trade-offs, and the decisions were becoming even more difficult with increased demand for police services and decreasing budgets. Beyond this, the SFPD wanted a method for evaluating two new proposals that might or might not improve efficiency. The first was a change in shift schedules from the traditional 5/8 shift (five days a week, eight hours per day) to a 4/10 shift (four days a week, ten hours per day), the latter of which was favored by the police officers. The second proposal was to convert some of the traditional two-officer cars into one-officer cars.

Believing that a computerized scheduling system was necessary, the SFPD appointed a task force from its staff to locate existing software that would solve the problem. No such software was found, so the task force hired Taylor and Huxley to develop a scheduling model.

Step 2 The SFPD already had a sophisticated computer-aided dispatch (CAD) system. CAD kept track of all calls for police help, police travel time, police response time, and other pertinent data. Because the SFPD wanted each officer to be busy on calls approximately the same percentage of his or her shift, it was relatively straightforward, using CAD, to determine the number of officers needed each hour. For example, if each officer ought to be busy about 80% of the time and CAD indicates that 30 hours worth of work is generated from 1 to 2 A.M. on a Sunday morning, then approximately 38 officers are required during this time period ($.8 \times 38 \simeq 30$ hours).

Step 3 The SFPD wanted a method to schedule officers in each precinct that would quickly (in less than one hour) produce a schedule and graphically display the schedule. The program needed to determine the staffing requirements for each hour of the week (as discussed in Step 2). For example, 38 officers might be needed between 1 and 2 A.M. Sunday morning, but only 14 officers might be needed between 4 and 5 A.M. Sunday morning. Officers needed to be scheduled to minimize the sum, over each hour of the week, of the shortages and surpluses relative to the required number of officers. For example, if 20 officers were assigned to the 12 to 8 A.M. Sunday morning shift, there would be a shortage of 18 officers ($= 38 - 20$) from 1 to 2 A.M. and a surplus of 6 officers ($= 20 - 14$) from 4 to 5 A.M. The program needed to minimize the maximum of the hourly shortages. This is because a shortage of 10 officers during a single hour is far more serious than a shortage of one officer during 10 different hours. The SFPD further wanted a model that would make it easy for precinct captains to fine-tune the optimal schedule to account for last-minute occurrences.

The analysts developed a linear programming model to solve the scheduling problem. (See Section 3.2 for a scaled-down scheduling model of this type.) The primary objective was to minimize the sum of hourly shortages and surpluses. The constraints in the PPSS model reflected the limited number of officers available and the relationship of the number of officers working each hour to the shortages and surpluses for that hour. At first, they allowed only 5/8 shifts and only three shift starting times (such as 6 A.M., 2 P.M., and 10 P.M.). Eventually, they modified the model to allow for more possibilities, including 4/10 shifts and more than three possible starting times.

The primary purpose of the PPSS model was to decide how many officers should start work at each possible shift time. For example, PPSS might recommend that 20 officers should start work at 6 A.M. Monday (working 6 A.M. to 2 P.M. Monday through Friday), 30 officers should start work at 2 P.M. Saturday (working 2 P.M. to 10 P.M. Saturday through Wednesday), and so on. The analysts also expanded the capabilities of the model so that a scheduling person could, for example, see the effect of adding an officer to any schedule, opening a new starting time or closing an old one, or increasing or decreasing the percentage of one-officer cars.

Step 4 Prior to implementing PPSS, the SFPD tested the PPSS schedules against manually created schedules. PPSS produced approximately a 50% reduction in both surpluses and shortages. The outputs from these tests convinced the SFPD that PPSS was not only working correctly, but that it could greatly improve overall efficiency.

Step 5 Given the starting times for shifts and the type of work schedule (5/8 or 4/10), PPSS was able to produce a nearly optimal schedule within a matter of minutes on a PC. More importantly, PPSS was designed so that it could be used to experiment with shift times and work rules. Specifically, PPSS was able to show that if only three shift times were allowed, a 5/8 schedule would be superior to a 4/10 schedule, whereas if five shift times were allowed, a 4/10 schedule would be superior to a 5/8 schedule. This finding was of critical importance because it enabled the SFPD to achieve two objectives at once: more efficiency in covering workloads and higher morale by instituting the 4/10 schedules favored by police officers. PPSS also enabled the SFPD to experiment with a mix of one-officer and two-officer patrol cars. This analysis convinced them to use several one-officer cars during certain times of the day.

Step 6 Since the SFPD task force worked closely with the management science team of Taylor and Huxley from the start of the project, ease of use and flexibility of the model were always priorities. The resulting model allowed users to ask all kinds of what-if questions. The answers were obtained quickly, the data displays were easy to view and understand, and many graphical views were available. In short, the PPSS was very user-friendly, and this feature enabled it to gain immediate acceptance by the SFPD.

Step 7 Certain implementation issues had to be ironed out. For example, the model recommended several one-officer patrol cars, which needed to be purchased. Management anticipated a problem convincing the city to fund these additional vehicles. However, after testing the model at one particular police station and demonstrating the effectiveness of the new scheduling system at this site, the city was persuaded to allocate an initial sum of $470,000 for additional cars.

Despite some minor problems, implementation was not difficult. The user-friendly features of the PPSS made it possible for police officers to learn the system in an average of two days. The graphical displays assisted in this training since they explained why a given schedule was good or bad. Also, the system provided an environment in which trainees could learn by challenging the system to see whether they could do better. The officers quickly learned to use the many features of the system and to trust the value of its recommendations.

GE Capital

GE Capital, a subsidiary of the General Electric Company's financial services business, provides credit card service to 50 million accounts. The average total outstanding balance exceeds $12 billion. GE Capital, led by Makuch et al. [2], developed the PAYMENT system to reduce delinquent accounts and the cost of collecting from delinquent accounts.

Step 1 At any time, GE Capital has over $1 billion in delinquent accounts. The company spends $100 million annually processing these accounts. Each day workers contact over 200,000 delinquent credit card holders with letters, taped phone messages, or live phone calls. However, there was no real scientific basis for the methods used to collect on various types of accounts. For example, GE Capital had no idea whether a two-month due account should receive a taped phone message, a live phone call, some combination of these, or no contact at all. The company's goal was to reduce delinquent accounts and the cost of processing these accounts, but it wasn't sure how to accomplish this. Therefore, GE Capital's retail financial services component, together with management scientists and statisticians from GE's corporate research and development group, studied the problem and eventually developed a model called PAYMENT. The purpose of this model was to assign the most cost-effective collection methods to delinquent accounts.

Step 2 The key data requirements for modeling delinquent accounts are **delinquency movement matrices** (DMMs). A DMM shows how the probability of the payment on a delinquent account depends on the collection action taken (no action, live phone call, taped message, or letter), the size of the unpaid balance, and the account's performance score. (The higher the performance score associated with a delinquent account, the more likely the account is to be collected.) For example, if a $250 account is two months delinquent, has a high performance score, and is contacted with a phone message, then certain events might occur with certain probabilities. The events and the probabilities listed in Table 1.1 illustrate one possibility. The key is to estimate these probabilities for each possible collection action and each account type.

Fortunately, since GE Capital had millions of delinquent accounts, there was plenty of data to estimate the DMMs accurately. To illustrate, suppose there are 1000 two-month delinquent accounts, each with balances under $300 and a high performance score. Also, suppose that each of these is contacted with a phone message. If 300 of these accounts are completely paid off by the next month, then an estimate of the probability of an account being completely paid off by next month is .30 (= 300/1000). By collecting the necessary data to estimate similar probabilities for all account types and collection actions, GE Capital finally had the basis for seeing which collection strategies were most cost effective.

TABLE 1.1 Sample DMM Entries

Event	Probability
Account completely paid off	.30
One month is paid off	.40
Nothing is paid off	.30

Step 3 After collecting the required data and expressing it in the form of DMMs, the company needed to discover which collections worked best in which situations. Specifically, they wanted to maximize the expected delinquent accounts collected during the following six months. However, they realized that this is a **dynamic** decision problem. For example, one strategy is called **creaming**. In this strategy most collection resources are concentrated on

live phone calls to the delinquent accounts classified as most likely to pay up—the best customers. This creaming strategy is attractive because it is likely to generate short-term cash flows from these customers. However, it also has two negative aspects. First, it is likely to cause a loss of goodwill among the best customers; and second, it gains nothing in the long run from the customers who are most likely to default on their payments. Therefore, the analysts developed the PAYMENT model to find the best **decision strategy**, that is, a contingency plan for each type of customer, specifying which collection strategy to use at each stage of the account's delinquency. The constraints in the PAYMENT model ensure that available resources are not overused.

Step 4 A key aspect of GE Capital's problem is uncertainty. When the PAYMENT model specifies the collection method to use for a certain type of account, it implies that the probability of collecting on this account with this collection method is relatively high. However, there is still a chance that the collection method will fail. With this high degree of uncertainty, it is difficult to convince skeptics that the model will work as advertised until it has been demonstrated in an actual environment. This is exactly what GE Capital did. It piloted the PAYMENT model on a $62 million portfolio for a single department store chain. To see the real effect of PAYMENT's recommended strategies, the pilot study used manager-recommended strategies for some accounts and PAYMENT-recommended strategies for others. (They referred to this as the "champion" versus the "challenger.") The challenger (PAYMENT) strategies were the clear winners, with an average monthly improvement of $185,000 over the champion strategies during a five-month period. In addition, because the PAYMENT strategies included more "no contact" actions (don't bother the customer this month), they led to lower collection costs and greater customer goodwill. This demonstration was very convincing. In no time, other account managers wanted to take advantage of PAYMENT.

Step 5 As described in Step 3, the output from the PAYMENT model is a contingency plan. The model uses a very complex optimization scheme, along with the DMMs from Step 2, to decide what collection strategy to use for each type of delinquent account at each stage (month) of its delinquency. At the end of each month, after the appropriate collection methods have been used and the results (actual payments) have been observed, the model then uses the status of each account to recommend the collection method for the next month. In this way, the model is used dynamically through time.

Step 6 In general, the management scientist demonstrates the model to the client in Step 6. In this application, however, the management science team members were GE's own people—they came from GE Capital and the GE corporate research and development group. Throughout the model-building process, the team of analysts strived to understand the requirements of the collection managers and staff—the end users—and tried to involve them in shaping the final system. This early and continual involvement, plus the impressive performance of PAYMENT in the pilot study, made it easy to "sell" the model to the people who would have to use it.

Step 7 After the pilot study, PAYMENT was applied to the $4.6 billion Montgomery Ward department store portfolio with 18 million accounts. Compared to the collection results from a year earlier, PAYMENT increased collections by $1.6 million per month, or over $19 million per year. (This is actually a conservative estimate of the benefit obtained from PAYMENT, because PAYMENT was first applied to the Montgomery Ward portfolio during the depths of a recession, when it is much more difficult to collect delinquent accounts.) Since then, PAYMENT has been applied to virtually all of GE Capital's accounts, with similar success. Overall, GE Capital estimates that PAYMENT has increased collections by $37 million per year and uses less resources than previous strategies. The model is now being expanded in several directions. For example, the original model assumed that collection resources (such as the amount available for live phone calls) were fixed. The model is now being expanded to treat these resource levels as decision variables in a more encompassing optimization model.

1.4 Why Study Management Science?

After reading the previous section, you may be convinced that management science is an important area and that highly trained analysts are needed to solve the large and complex problems faced by the business world. However, unless you are one of the relatively few students who intends to become a professional management scientist, you are probably wondering why you need to study management science. This is a legitimate concern. Indeed, for many years we in the field of management science education have received criticism from students and educators that management science courses were irrelevant to the majority of students who were required to take them. Looking back, it is difficult to argue with these critics. Typical management courses were centered primarily around a collection of very specific models and, worse, a collection of mind-numbing mathematical solution techniques, techniques that students were often required to implement *by hand*! (Some courses are undoubtedly still taught this way, but we hope the number is decreasing rapidly.)

There are two forces that have helped to change this tendency toward irrelevance. First, the critics have become sufficiently loud and numerous to have motivated many of us to examine our course materials and teaching methods. Certain topics have been eliminated and replaced by material that is more relevant and interesting to students. The second force is the emergence of powerful personal computers (PCs) and the accompanying easy-to-use software, especially spreadsheet software. With the availability of computers to do the number crunching, there is no need—except in very advanced courses—to go into the mathematical details of the solution techniques. We can delegate this task to machines that are far better at it than we humans are. We can now use the time formerly spent on such details to develop modeling skills that are valuable to a wide audience.

Our intent in this book is not just to cover specific models and specific approaches to these models, but to teach a more general approach to the model-building process. Furthermore, we believe the spreadsheet approach is the best way to do this and appeals to the largest audience. We have been teaching our own courses with this spreadsheet-modeling approach for several years—to a wide range of business students—and we have received very few complaints about irrelevance. Indeed, many students have said openly that this is one of the most valuable business courses they've ever taken. The following are some of the reasons for this new-found relevance.

1 The modeling approach emphasized throughout this book is an important way to think about problems in general, not just the specific problems we discuss. These problems force you to think logically. You must discover how given data can be used (or, as in some of the modeling problems, which data are necessary), you must determine the elements of the problem that you can control (the "decision variables"), and you must determine how the elements of the problem are logically related. Most students are intelligent enough to realize that these logical thinking skills will be valuable in their careers, regardless of the specific careers they enter.

2 Management science is unashamedly built around *quantitative* skills—we deal primarily with numbers and relationships between numbers. Some critics object that not everything in the real world can be reduced to numbers, but as one of our reviewers correctly pointed out, "a great deal that is of importance can." As you work

through the many models in this book, your quantitative skills will be sharpened immensely. In a business world driven increasingly by numbers, quantitative skills are an obvious asset.

3 When you enter this course, your spreadsheet abilities may not be very good. By the time this course is over, however, we can promise you that you will be a proficient spreadsheet user. We deliberately chose the spreadsheet package Excel, which is arguably the most widely used package (other than word-processing packages) in the business world today. Many of our former students have told us that the facility they gained in Excel was worth the price of the course. (Much of the analysis can also be done with Excel's two principal competitors, Lotus 1-2-3 and Quattro Pro.) We do not mean to imply that this is a course in spreadsheet fundamentals and neat tricks, although you will undoubtedly pick up a few useful tricks along the way. A great spreadsheet package—and we strongly believe that Excel is the greatest spreadsheet package written to date—gives you complete control over your problem. You can apply spreadsheets to an endless variety of problems. Spreadsheets give you the flexibility to work in a way that suits *your* style best, and spreadsheets present results (and catch errors) almost immediately. As you succeed with relatively easy problems, your confidence will build, and before long you will be able to tackle more difficult problems successfully. In short, spreadsheets enable everyone, not just technical people, to develop and use their quantitative skills.

4 Management science modeling helps you to develop your intuition, and it also indicates where intuition alone sometimes falls short. When we confront a problem, we often make an educated (or maybe not so educated) guess at the solution. If the problem is sufficiently complex, as most of the problems in this book are, this guess will frequently be wide of the mark. In this sense the study of management science can be a humbling experience: we find that our unaided intuition is often not very good. But by studying many models and examining their solutions, we can sharpen our intuition considerably. This might be called the "Aha!" effect. All of a sudden, we see why a certain solution is best. The chances are that when we originally thought about the problem, we forgot to consider an important constraint or a key relationship, and this caused the poor initial guess. Presumably, the more problems we analyze, the better we become at recognizing the critical elements of new problems. Experienced management scientists tend to have excellent intuition, that is, the ability to see through to the essence of a problem almost immediately. They aren't, however, born with this talent; it comes through the kind of analysis you will be performing as you work through this book.

1.5 Conclusion

On this chapter we introduced the field of management science and the process of mathematical model building. To provide a more concrete understanding of these concepts, we described a small hypothetical queueing system and chronicled three very successful management science applications. We also emphasized a seven-step model-building process that begins with problem definition and proceeds through final implementation. Finally, we discussed why the study of management science is a valuable experience, even if you don't intend to have a professional career in this field.

Don't worry if you didn't understand some of the terms such as *linear programming* or *regression analysis* that were used in this chapter. Although the seven-step process is not too difficult to comprehend, especially when it is discussed in the context of real applications, it typically entails some rather complex logical relationships and mathematical concepts. These ideas will be presented to you in greater detail in the rest of this book. Specifically, you will learn how to build mathematical models (usually on a spreadsheet), how to use them to answer what-if questions, and how to find optimal solutions with the help of a spreadsheet Solver. For practical reasons most of your work will take place in the classroom as you work on the examples and problems we have provided. The primary emphasis of this book, therefore, is on Steps 3 through 6, that is, model formulation, testing the model with different inputs, optimizing the model, and presenting (and interpreting) your results to a client—probably your instructor.

It is nevertheless important to keep in mind that with real problems there are crucial steps you must take before and after the procedures you'll be practicing in this book. Because real problems don't come as nicely packaged as those we will study and because the necessary data are seldom given to you on a platter, you will have to wrestle with the problem's scope and its precise data requirements when solving a problem in a real setting. (We have included several "modeling problems" at the end of each chapter. These problems are not as well structured as the "skill" problems so the burden is on you to determine an appropriate structure and decide which data are needed.) Further, because a mathematically accurate model does not necessarily result in a successful implementation, your work is not necessarily over once the numbers check out. To gain acceptance for a model, an analyst must have the right combination of technical skills *and* people skills. Try to keep this in mind as you write up your solutions to the problems in this book. Don't just hand in a mass of numbers with little or no explanation. *Sell* your solution!

REFERENCES

1 Klingman, D., N. Phillips, D. Steiger, and W. Young. "The Successful Deployment of Management Science Throughout Citgo Petroleum Corporation." *Interfaces* 17, no. 1 (1987): 4–25.

2 Makuch, W., J. Dodge, J. Ecker, D. Granfors, and G. Hahn. "Managing Consumer Credit Delinquency in the US Economy: A Multi-Billion Dollar Management Science Application." *Interfaces* 22, no. 1 (1992): 90–109.

3 Miser, H. "Avoiding the Corrupting Lie of a Poorly Stated Problem." *Interfaces* 23, no. 6 (1993): 114–19.

4 Taylor, P., and S. Huxley. "A Break from Tradition for the San Francisco Police: Patrol Officer Scheduling Using an Optimization-Based Decision Support Tool." *Interfaces* 19, no. 1 (1989): 4–24.

5 Volkema, R. "Managing the Process of Formulating the Problem." *Interfaces* 25, no. 3 (1995): 81–87.

2

CHAPTER

Introduction to Linear Programming

Management Science Success Stories

One of the many classic applications of linear programming is the "diet problem." This problem appears, often in a somewhat humorous guise, as a prototype linear programming example in almost all management science textbooks. Basically, it involves finding a group of foods—a diet—that meets all daily nutritional requirements at minimum cost. These textbook examples may or may not have any relevance to real meal planning. However, the problem is important in many real settings, as outlined by Lancaster [2] in the article "The Diet Model." A number of versions of this model have actually been used by institutions such as hospitals, nursing homes, schools, prisons, and other food-systems operations. In many of these applications, the computer-generated menus have provided a 10 to 30% cost savings, the nutritional requirements are guaranteed (in contrast to menus generated by traditional, non-MS methods), and, surprisingly, the acceptance of the menus by consumers has been very high.

This problem provides a good example of how to distinguish between good models and poor models. In the simplified diet problems in most textbooks, it is easy to develop a model that satisfies the conditions of low cost and minimal daily nutritional requirements but is so bland (or weird) that no one would eat it. The trick is to incorporate suitable "constraints" (mathematical equations or inequalities) that rule out unappetizing menus. For example, the applications cited in the article obtained more acceptable diets in one of two ways. Either they included a separation constraint (such as requiring at least three days between successive servings of mashed potatoes) or a frequency constraint (such as requiring that mashed potatoes can be served at most three times per week). By adding enough of these types of constraints, they obtained optimal menus that people were perfectly willing to eat.

A related article, "The Diet Problem" by Dantzig [1] (one of the founders of linear programming), illustrates the humorous side of the problem. When

Dantzig was developing his famous solution technique for linear programming in the late 1940s, he decided to use it to solve his *own* diet problem, one that would prescribe what he would actually eat each day. Even he was surprised by the outcome. His first solution called for various amounts of "normal" foods, plus 500 gallons of vinegar—he had forgotten a constraint! So he reformulated the problem, and his next solution called for 200 bouillon cubes per day. Still not (too) discouraged, he reformulated the problem (with an upper limit on bouillon cubes) and his resulting solution called for two pounds of bran per day. After an upper limit on bran was imposed, his next diet called for two pounds of blackstrap molasses. By this time, he started to get the point: it is possible to generate a low-cost, nutritional, and tasty diet using management science techniques, but it's not as easy as it appears! ■

2.1

Introduction

The most successful modeling tool developed by MS is **linear programming** (LP). It is used in all types of organizations, often on a daily basis, and it is used to solve an extremely wide variety of problems. These include problems in human resource scheduling, inventory management, selection of advertising media, bond trading, management of cash flows, operation of an electrical utility's hydroelectric system, routing of delivery vehicles, blending in oil refineries, hospital staffing, and many others. Because of LP's importance in MS, we single it out for special study. However, in line with the goals of this textbook, we will concentrate primarily on how to formulate problems as LP models and how to interpret output; we will not describe how the computer actually solves these problems.

2.2

A Brief History of Linear Programming

A brief history of LP is enlightening. Mathematically, every LP problem involves optimizing a linear function subject to several linear constraints, expressed as linear inequalities or equalities. For example, the objective might be profit, and the constraints might be upper limits on resource availabilities. Until World War II, mathematicians knew a great deal, at least theoretically, about systems of linear equations and inequalities. Among other things, they realized that a huge number of arithmetic operations are necessary to solve such systems and that without computing power, humans are simply not able to perform the required calculations in a reasonable amount of time. Therefore, no one seriously considered the potential uses of such systems.

During World War II, however, two things fortuitously came together. First, complex military logistics problems arose that could be modeled as LP problems (although the name linear programming did not yet exist). Second, computers were just being developed. All that was needed was a method for solving this new class of problem—a method that could take advantage of computer power. Fortunately, a young mathematician, George Dantzig, developed a method he called the **simplex method**. It involved a systematic, arithmetic-intensive search through the set of all possible solutions for the solution that optimized a given objective. It appeared to work efficiently on the problems he tried, and it was not too difficult to program on a computer.

The surprising thing is that Dantzig's method, with relatively minor modifications, is still the most important solution method for LP problems. For reasons that are not entirely understood even by mathematicians, it works quickly on problems that are orders of magnitude larger than any problems Dantzig could have imagined in the early days, and all large companies own or have access to a commercial version of the simplex computer code. Recently, an entirely different type of solution method developed by Karmarkar at Bell Labs has emerged as a competitor to the simplex method, particularly for extremely large problems, but the simplex method is still comfortably in first place.

2.3

Introduction to LP Modeling

We will not learn the simplex method. Instead, we will learn how to formulate problems as LP models. Once a problem is properly formulated, then we will see that it is fairly easy to solve it on a computer and interpret the resulting solution. Actually, there are two ways to formulate an LP problem, the traditional way and the more recent spreadsheet way. We will illustrate both methods on problems in this chapter, just for comparison. However, in later chapters we will focus exclusively on spreadsheet formulations. The first problem we will examine is often considered the prototype LP problem because various versions of it are so common. This basic problem is to select the optimal mix of products to produce in order to maximize profit. We will refer to this problem as the **product mix** problem.

A Product Mix Problem

EXAMPLE 2.1

The Monet Company produces four types of picture frames, which we label 1, 2, 3, and 4. The four types of frames differ with respect to size, shape, and materials used. Each type requires a certain amount of skilled labor, metal, and glass, as shown in Table 2.1. This table also lists the profit Monet makes from each type of frame, where the profit is the selling price minus the cost of the labor and materials. During the coming week Monet has 4000 hours of skilled labor, 6000 ounces of metal, and 10,000 ounces of glass (of the same thickness) available. Also, market constraints are such that it is impossible to sell more than 1000 type 1 frames, 2000 type 2 frames, 500 type 3 frames, and 1000 type 4 frames. The company wants to maximize its weekly profit.

TABLE 2.1 **Data for Monet Picture Frame Example**

	Skilled Labor	Metal	Glass	Profit
Frame 1	2	4	6	\$6
Frame 2	1	2	2	\$2
Frame 3	3	1	1	\$4
Frame 4	2	2	2	\$3

Solution

If we follow traditional solution method we first identify the decision variables for the problem. In this small problem they are the number of frames of types 1, 2, 3, and 4 to be produced. We label these x_1, x_2, x_3, and x_4 (although any other labels would do). Next, we write total profit and the constraints in terms of the x's. Finally, since only nonnegative amounts can be produced, we add explicit constraints to ensure that the x's are nonnegative. The resulting formulation is shown below:

$$\begin{aligned}
\text{maximize } 6x_1 + 2x_2 + 4x_3 + 3x_4 & \text{ (profit objective)} \\
\text{subject to } 2x_1 + x_2 + 3x_3 + 2x_4 \le 4000 & \text{ (labor constraint)} \\
4x_1 + 2x_2 + x_3 + 2x_4 \le 6000 & \text{ (metal constraint)} \\
6x_1 + 2x_2 + x_3 + 2x_4 \le 10{,}000 & \text{ (glass constraint)} \\
x_1 \le 1000 & \text{ (frame 1 sales constraint)} \\
x_2 \le 2000 & \text{ (frame 2 sales constraint)} \\
x_3 \le 500 & \text{ (frame 3 sales constraint)} \\
x_4 \le 1000 & \text{ (frame 4 sales constraint)} \\
x_1, x_2, x_3, x_4 \ge 0 & \text{ (nonnegativity constraints)}
\end{aligned}$$

To understand this formulation, consider the profit objective first. The profit from x_1 frames of type 1 is $6x_1$ because each frame contributes \$6 to profit. The same goes for the other three types of frames, and the total profit is the sum of the profits from the four products. Next, consider the skilled labor constraint. The right-hand side, 4000, is the number of hours available. On the left-hand side each type 1 frame uses two hours of labor, so x_1 units require $2x_1$ hours of labor. Similar statements hold for the other three products, and the total number of labor hours used is the sum over the four products. In short, according to the constraint, the number of hours used cannot exceed the number of hours available. The constraints for metal and glass are similar. Finally, the maximum sales constraints and the nonnegativity constraints simply put upper and lower limits on the quantities that can be produced.

For many years all LP problems were formulated this way. Because of this, most LP computer packages are written to accept LP problems in essentially this format. For example, in a popular package called LINDO (for the mainframe or the PC), you would type in almost exactly what you see above. Recently, however, a more intuitive method of expressing LP problems has emerged. This method takes advantage of the power and flexibility of spreadsheets. Actually, LP problems could always be *formulated* on spreadsheets, but now with the addition of add-in Solvers, spreadsheets have the capability of *solving* (that is, optimizing) LP problems as well. Specifically, Microsoft Excel, Lotus 1-2-3 for Windows, and Quattro Pro for Windows all have built-in Solvers, and there is an LP add-in called What's Best! that can be used with all three. We will refer to these generically as Solvers. All examples in this book will be illustrated with Excel's Solver. However, for Lotus users the appendix to this chapter summarizes the procedure to use with What's Best!

How are LP models expressed on a spreadsheet? If you have done any work on a spreadsheet, you are aware that there are many ways to set up a spreadsheet model, LP or otherwise. Each user has his or her own preferences for arranging the data in the various cells. The same goes for spreadsheet LPs. We will not give any exact prescriptions, but we will present enough examples to get you started. The only common elements in all spreadsheet LP models are the following.

Spreadsheet Elements

1 **Inputs.** All numerical **inputs**, that is, the data needed to form the objective and the constraints, must appear somewhere in the spreadsheet. Although it is not absolutely necessary, our convention is to enclose all inputs in a blue border with shading. We try to put most of the inputs in the upper left section of the spreadsheet. However, we

have felt free to deviate from this convention when certain inputs fit more naturally somewhere else.

2 **Changing cells.** Instead of using variable names, such as x's, there is a set of designated cells that play the role of the decision variables. The values in these cells can be changed in order to optimize the objective. In Excel these cells are called the **changing cells** or **adjustable cells**. To designate these clearly, our convention is to enclose the changing cells within a red border.

3 **Target (objective) cell.** One cell, called the **target cell** or the **objective cell**, contains the value of the objective. The Solver systematically varies the values in the changing cells in order to optimize the value in the target cell. Our convention is to enclose the target cell within a black double-line border. Our red-blue-black color scheme shows up very effectively on a color monitor. The shading (for input cells) and double-line border (for the target cell) are used for clarification on the printed page.

4 **Constraints.** Although the various spreadsheet packages differ on this point, Excel does not show the constraints directly on the spreadsheet. Instead, you specify constraints in a dialog box. For example, you might designate a set of similar constraints by

B15:D15<=B16:D16

This implies three separate constraints. The value in B15 must be less than or equal to the value in B16, the value in C15 must be less than or equal to the value in C16, and the value in D15 must be less than or equal to the value in D16.

5 **Nonnegativity.** Normally we want the decision variables, that is, the values in the changing cells, to be nonnegative. In current versions of Excel, these nonnegativity constraints must be specified explicitly. For example, to specify that the values in the range C5:C9 are nonnegative, you must include the constraint

C5:C9>=0

In general, the complete solution of a problem involves two stages. The first stage is to enter all of the inputs, trial values for the changing cells, and formulas relating these in a spreadsheet. This stage is the most crucial because it is here that all of the "ingredients" of the model are included and related appropriately. For example, the spreadsheet must include a formula that relates the objective to the changing cells, so that if the values in the changing cells vary, the objective value varies accordingly. Similarly, the spreadsheet must include expressions for the various constraints (usually their left-hand sides) that are related appropriately to the changing cells. After the spreadsheet is set up correctly, we can proceed to the second stage: invoking the Solver. At this point, we formally designate the objective cell, the changing cells, and the constraints, and we tell the Solver to find the *optimal* solution. If the first stage has been done correctly, the second stage is usually very straightforward.

The spreadsheet in Figure 2.1 illustrates the solution procedure for Monet's product mix problem. (See the file PRODMIX.XLS.) The first stage is to set up the spreadsheet, as explained in step-by-step fashion below. (We will provide the essential details. However, it is up to you to supply the cell formatting and column widths that make your spreadsheet look nice. Also, it is up to you to enter the various descriptive labels.)

Developing the Spreadsheet Model

1 **Inputs.** Enter the various inputs in the ranges B6:E8, H6:H8, B10:E10, and B17:E17.

2 **Production levels.** Enter *any* four values in cells B15:E15. These do *not* have to be the values shown in Figure 2.1. These cells are the changing cells, that is, the cells where the decision variables are placed. Any trial values can be used initially; the

FIGURE 2.1 **An Initial Solution for Monet's Product Mix Example**

	A	B	C	D	E	F	G	H
1	**Product Mix Problem with Initial (Nonoptimal) Solution**							
2								
3	**Input data**							
4			**Frame Type**					
5		1	2	3	4	Total used		Total available
6	Labor hours per frame	2	1	3	2	6000	<=	4000
7	Metal (oz.) per frame	4	2	1	2	7000	<=	6000
8	Glass (oz.) per frame	6	2	1	2	8000	<=	10000
9						**Total profit**		
10	Profit per frame	$6.00	$2.00	$4.00	$3.00	$10,700.00		
11								
12	**Production plan**							
13			**Frame Type**					
14		1	2	3	4			
15	Frames produced	500	800	400	1500			
16		<=	<=	<=	<=			
17	Maximum sales	1000	2000	500	1000			

Solver will eventually find the *optimal* values. For the sake of discussion, however, if you enter the four values shown in Figure 2.1 (which are *not* optimal), notice that they do not even satisfy the constraints. Specifically, this plan uses more labor hours and metal than are available, and it produces more type 4 frames than can be sold. However, you don't need to worry about satisfying constraints at this point; the Solver will take care of this later.

3 **Resources used.** Enter the formula

=SUMPRODUCT(B6:E6,$B$15:$E$15)

in cell F6 and copy it to the range F7:F8. These formulas calculate the units of labor, metal, and glass used by the current product mix. The SUMPRODUCT function is especially useful in LP models. Here it means to multiply each value in the range B6:E6 by the corresponding value in the range B15:E15 and then sum these products. (The purpose of the dollar signs—absolute cell addresses—in the B15:E15 range is to permit copying this formula to the range F7:F8.)

4 **Profit earned.** Enter the formula

=SUMPRODUCT(B10:E10,B15:E15)

in cell F10. This formula calculates the total profit from the current product mix.

Normally, the next step is to specify the changing cells, the objective cell, and the constraints and then instruct the solver to find the optimal solution. However, before doing this, it is often useful to try a few of your own guesses in the changing cells. This has two purposes. First, by entering different sets of values in the changing cells, you can confirm that the formulas in the other cells are calculating correct values. In other words, you can see whether you have set up your spreadsheet correctly.

The second purpose of trying a few guesses of your own is to give you more of a feel for the model. For example, it is tempting to guess that the frame types with the highest unit profits should be produced to the greatest extent possible. To try this out, begin by entering zeros in the changing cells B15:E15; that is, produce nothing, which obviously will earn no profit. Next, because frame 1 has the highest unit profit ($6) and its market constraint permits at most 1000 frames, enter 1000 in cell B15. You'll notice that none of the resources are used up completely. Therefore, you can make some type 3 frames, the type with the next highest unit profit. Since its market constraint permits at most 500 frames, enter 500 in cell D15. You'll notice that there is still some availability of each resource. This allows you to make some type 4 frames, the type with the next largest unit profit. However, you'll notice that the most you can make is 250 type 4 frames, because at that point you completely exhaust the available labor hours. The resulting solution appears in Figure 2.2; its corresponding profit is $8750.

We've now produced as much as possible of the three frame types with the three highest unit profits. Does this guarantee that this solution is the best possible product mix? Unfortunately, it does not! In fact, the solution in Figure 2.2 is *not* optimal. Even in this small model it is difficult to guess the optimal solution, even when using a relatively intelligent trial and error procedure. The problem is that a frame type with a high unit profit can use up a lot of the resources and preclude other profitable frames from being produced. So although it is instructive and sometimes enlightening to enter several sets of trial values into the changing cells, you might never hit upon the best solution. This is where the Solver enters the picture.

The Solver actually accomplishes two purposes. First, it enables you to specify the objective cell, the changing cells, and the constraints. Then it solves the model by adjusting the values in the changing cells until all of the constraints hold and the objective—here the profit—is made as large as possible. You need not be concerned with the details of the optimization procedure except to know that it uses a well-known method (the simplex method) in its calculations.

Using the Solver To invoke Excel's Solver, select the menu item Solver from the Tools menu.[1] The dialog box in Figure 2.3 appears. It has three important sections that you must fill in: the target cell, the changing cells, and the constraints. For the product mix problem, you can fill in these sections in two ways: type in cell references or point, click, and drag in the usual way. If you have named any of the ranges, you can use these range names instead of cell addresses. (If you decide to point, click, and drag, you may need to move the Solver dialog box so that it isn't in the way of the cells you want to select.)

FIGURE 2.2 **Another Possible Solution for Monet's Product Mix Example**

	A	B	C	D	E	F	G	H
1	**Product Mix Problem with Another Possible Solution**							
2								
3	**Input data**							
4			**Frame Type**					
5		1	2	3	4	Total used		Total available
6	Labor hours per frame	2	1	3	2	4000	<=	4000
7	Metal (oz.) per frame	4	2	1	2	5000	<=	6000
8	Glass (oz.) per frame	6	2	1	2	7000	<=	10000
9						**Total profit**		
10	Profit per frame	$6.00	$2.00	$4.00	$3.00	$8,750.00		
11								
12	**Production plan**							
13			**Frame Type**					
14		1	2	3	4			
15	Frames produced	1000	0	500	250			
16		<=	<=	<=	<=			
17	Maximum sales	1000	2000	500	1000			

[1] Although the Solver comes with the Excel package, it is an Excel *add-in*. If there is no Solver menu item under Tools, you will have to add it in. To do this, use the Tools/Add-Ins menu item, then Browse until you find the SOLVER.XLA file (usually under the Excel\Library\Solver directory) and select it. If you can't find the SOLVER.XLA file, it may not have been installed when Excel was installed. In that case, you'll have to go back to the Excel Setup program and install the Solver.

FIGURE 2.3 **Excel Solver Window for Monet's Product Mix Problem**

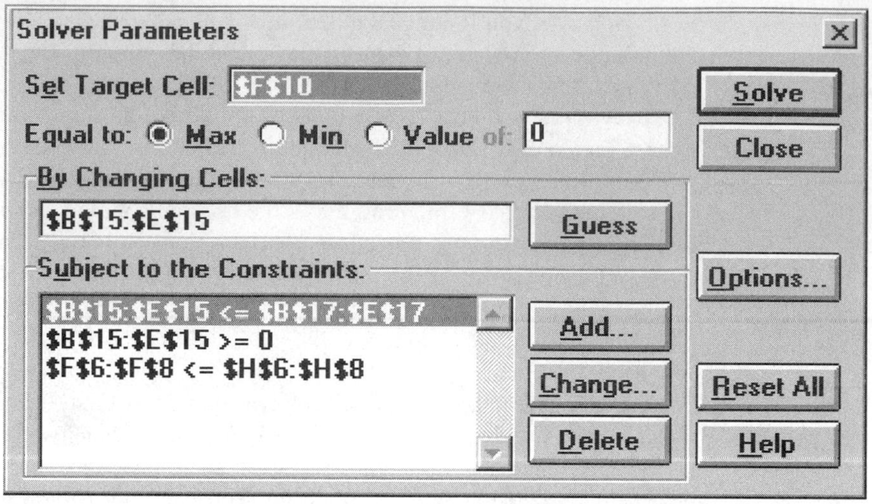

1 **Objective.** Select cell F10, total profit, as the target cell, and click on the Maximize button.[2]

2 **Changing cells.** Select the range B15:E15, the numbers of frames to produce, as the changing cells.

3 **Constraints.** Click on the Add button to add the following constraints:

F6:F8 <= H6:H8

B15:E15 <= B17:E17

B15:E15 >= 0

The first set constrains the solution to use no more of each resource than is available; the second set to produce no more of each product than can be sold; and the last set to reject all negative production quantities.[3]

Note: The <= signs in column G and row 16 are not needed in Excel. In fact, they are entered simply as *labels* in the spreadsheet and have no effect on any calculations. However, they help to identify the constraints, so we include them in all of the examples. (You are not required to do so when you formulate your own problems.) There are no such inequality signs entered for the nonnegativity constraints on the changing cells because these are always taken for granted.

4 **Linear model.** There is one other step to perform before clicking on the Solve button. The Solver uses one of several numerical methods to solve various types of problems. The problems discussed in this chapter, including the current product mix problem, are all *linear* problems. (We will discuss the properties of linear problems in the next section.) Linear problems can be solved most efficiently by the simplex method. In order to instruct Excel to use this method, click on the Options button to obtain a new dialog box. Check the Assume Linear Model box and click on OK to return to the original Solver dialog box.

[2] The Solver window includes dollar signs next to cell addresses. They will appear automatically when you point to cells or ranges, but we will omit them when we specify the entries in this window.

[3] You can enter the constraints in any order. However, the Solver will display them sorted in alphabetical order of the call addresses or names, as shown in Figure 2.3.

5 **Optimize.** Click on the Solve button.

At this point, the Solver searches through a number of possible solutions until it finds the optimal solution. (You can watch the progress on the lower left of the screen.) When the Solver is finished, it displays a message to the effect that the optimal solution has been found. You can then tell it to return the values in the changing cells to their original (probably nonoptimal) values or retain the optimal values found by the Solver. In most cases you will choose the latter. Also, at this point you can ask for any of three summary reports. We'll return to these in Section 2.6. For now, click on the OK button to keep the Solver solution. You should see the solution shown in Figure 2.4.

The optimal plan is to produce 1000 type 1 frames, 800 type 2 frames, 400 type 3 frames, and no type 4 frames. This is close to the production plan from Figure 2.2, but the current plan earns $1200 more profit. Also, it uses all of the available labor hours and metal, but only 8000 of the 10,000 ounces of glass available. Finally, in terms of maximum sales, the optimal plan could produce more of frame types 2, 3, and 4 (if there were more skilled labor and/or metal). This is typical of an LP solution. Some of the constraints are met exactly (that is, as equalities), while others contain a certain amount of *slack*. We'll say more about this property of LP solutions in Section 2.6.

Experimenting with New Inputs If you want to experiment with different inputs to this problem—the unit profits or resource availabilities, for example—you can simply change the inputs and then rerun the Solver. You'll notice that the second time you use the Solver, you don't have to respecify the target and changing cells or the constraints. Excel remembers all of these settings, and it saves them when you save the file. As a simple what-if example, consider the modified model in Figure 2.5. Here the unit profit for frame type 4 has increased from $3 to $8, and all other inputs have remained the same. By making type 4 frames more profitable, we might expect them to enter the optimal mix. This is exactly what happens. The new optimal plan discontinues production of frame types 2 and 3 and instead calls for production of 1000 units of frame type 4. This increases the total profit to $14,000.

There is one technical note you should be aware of. Because of the way numbers are stored and calculated on a computer, the optimal values in the changing cells and elsewhere may contain small roundoff errors. For example, the value that really appeared in cell E15

FIGURE 2.4 **Optimal Solution for Monet's Product Mix Example**

	A	B	C	D	E	F	G	H
1	**Product Mix Problem with Optimal Solution**							
2								
3	**Input data**							
4			**Frame Type**					
5		1	2	3	4	Total used		Total available
6	Labor hours per frame	2	1	3	2	4000	<=	4000
7	Metal (oz.) per frame	4	2	1	2	6000	<=	6000
8	Glass (oz.) per frame	6	2	1	2	8000	<=	10000
9						**Total profit**		
10	Profit per frame	$6.00	$2.00	$4.00	$3.00	$9,200.00		
11								
12	**Production plan**							
13			**Frame Type**					
14		1	2	3	4			
15	Frames produced	1000	800	400	0			
16		<=	<=	<=	<=			
17	Maximum sales	1000	2000	500	1000			

FIGURE 2.5 Solution to Product Mix Example with New Inputs

	A	B	C	D	E	F	G	H
1	Product Mix Problem with New Input							
2								
3	Input data							
4		Frame Type						
5		1	2	3	4	Total used		Total available
6	Labor hours per frame	2	1	3	2	4000	<=	4000
7	Metal (oz.) per frame	4	2	1	2	6000	<=	6000
8	Glass (oz.) per frame	6	2	1	2	8000	<=	10000
9						Total profit		
10	Profit per frame	$6.00	$2.00	$4.00	$8.00	$14,000.00		
11								
12	Production plan							
13		Frame Type						
14		1	2	3	4			
15	Frames produced	1000	0	0	1000			
16		<=	<=	<=	<=			
17	Maximum sales	1000	2000	500	1000			

(in Figure 2.4) on our PC was 8.731E-09, a very small number (.000000008731). For all practical purposes, this number can be treated as zero, as shown in Figure 2.4. ■

2.4

The Linear Assumptions

Linear programming is an important subset of a larger class of models called **mathematical programming models**.[4] All such models select the levels of various activities that can be performed, subject to a set of constraints, in order to maximize or minimize an objective such as total profit or total cost. In Monet's product mix example, the activities are the production of the four frame types, and the purpose of the model is to find the levels of these activities that maximize total profit subject to specified constraints.

In terms of this general setup—selecting the optimal levels of activities—there are three important properties that LP models possess that differentiate them from general mathematical programming models: proportionality, additivity, and divisibility. We will discuss these properties briefly in this section.

Proportionality

Proportionality means that when the level of any activity is multiplied by a constant factor, then the contribution of this activity to the objective, or to any of the constraints in which the activity is involved, is multiplied by the same factor. For example, suppose that the production of type 1 frames is cut from its optimal value of 1000 (see Figure 2.4) to 500, that is, it is multiplied by .5. Then the amounts of labor, metal, and glass consumed by type 1 frames are all cut in half, and the profit contribution from type 1 frames is also cut

[4]By the way, the word *programming* in linear programming or mathematical programming has nothing to do with computer programming. It originated with the British term *programme*, which is essentially a plan or a schedule of operations.

in half. In contrast, suppose that certain efficiencies could be gained by producing type 1 frames in larger quantities. Then, contrary to the proportionality assumption, the required amount of labor per frame might *decrease* as more type 1 frames are produced. This would represent a *nonlinear* relationship between the level of the type 1 frame activity and labor usage, and it would take us outside of the linear realm.

Additivity

The additivity property implies that the sum of the contributions from the various activities to a particular constraint equals the total contribution to that constraint. For example, if the four types of frames use, respectively, 1000, 800, 1200, and 3000 labor hours (as in Figure 2.1), then the total number of labor hours used is the *sum* of these amounts, 6000 hours. Similarly, the additivity property applies to the objective. That is, the value of the objective is the *sum* of the contributions from the various activities. The additivity property also implies that the contribution of any decision variable to the objective or to any constraint is independent of the levels of the other decision variables.

Divisibility

The divisibility property simply means that we allow both integer and noninteger levels of the activities. In the product mix example it fortunately turned out that the optimal quantities of frame types 1 through 4 were all integers. However, it is more frequent that the optimal quantities are nonintegers, such as 47.53. In LP models we allow such values. In reality, however, they might not make physical sense. For example, if product 1 is a refrigerator, it makes no sense to make 47.53 refrigerators. (There are products, such as salt measured in pounds, where 47.53 units makes sense, but refrigerators is not one of them!) If we want the levels of some activities to be integer values, then there are two possible approaches: (1) we can solve the LP model without integer constraints, and if the solution turns out to have noninteger values, we can attempt to round them to integer values or (2) we can explicitly constrain certain changing cells to contain integer values. The latter approach, however, takes us into the realm of *integer programming*, a much more difficult topic than LP. (We will study integer programming in Chapter 5.)

Whenever we model a real problem, we usually make some simplifying assumptions. This is certainly the case with LP models. The world is frequently not linear, which means that a completely realistic model will typically violate some or all of the above three properties. However, many successful applications of LP have demonstrated the usefulness of linear models, even if they are only approximations to reality. If we suspect that the violations are serious enough to invalidate a linear model, then we should use an integer or nonlinear model, as discussed in Chapters 5 and 6. However, for now we will only discuss problems that can be represented reasonably well by linear models.

In terms of Excel's Solver, if the model is linear, that is, if it satisfies the proportionality, additivity, and divisibility properties, then you should check the Assume Linear Models box mentioned earlier. (Recall that it appears under Options in the Solver window.) Then the Solver will use the simplex method to solve the problem, which is the most efficient method for a linear model.

In some cases you may think your model is linear, but when you check the Assume Linear Model box, you get a message from the Solver that "the conditions for Assume Linear Model are not satisfied." This may mean that you have a logical error in your formulation and the proportionality, additivity, or divisibility conditions are not satisfied, or that the Solver erroneously *thinks* that the linearity conditions are not satisfied due to roundoff error in its calculations. If this happens to you, and you are convinced that your formulation is correct, try *not* checking the Assume Linear Model box and see if that works. If it doesn't, consult your instructor. It's possible that the (nonsimplex) algorithm employed by the Solver when this box isn't checked simply cannot find the solution to your problem. This latter possibility unfortunately occurs now and then, as we will discuss in Chapter 6.

You can minimize the chance that roundoff error will cause the Solver to think that the linearity conditions are not satisfied by ensuring that your model is *well scaled.* In a well-scaled model, all of the large numbers are roughly the same magnitude. If your model contains some very large numbers (say 100,000 or more) and some which are very small (say .001 or less), it is *poorly scaled* for the methods used by the Solver, and roundoff error is far more likely to cause problems—not only in the Solver's test of the linearity conditions but in all of its algorithmic methods.

If you are using the version of the Excel Solver software provided with this book, you can ensure that your model is well scaled by simply checking the Use Automatic Scaling box in the Options dialog. In the standard version of Excel, however, the Use Automatic Scaling box is not effective for linear models, so you may have to rescale your model manually. To do this, redefine the units in which your changing cells, target cell, or constraints are defined. For example, in the Monet model a natural rescaling would be to

1. Define the changing cells as the number of frames of each type produced in thousands.
2. Define maximum sales limitations in thousands.
3. Define profit in thousands of dollars.
4. Define resource availability in thousands.

If you rescale according to the steps above, no number less than .4 or greater than 11 will appear in the final spreadsheet.

2.5

Graphical Solution Method

Once LP problems are formulated, they are almost always solved numerically with computer software. The amount of computation makes manual calculation prohibitive for realistically sized problems. However, it is instructive to look at a graphical solution procedure for problems with only two decision variables. Admittedly, almost no real problems have only two variables, but the graphical solution is useful for the insights it provides, even for larger problems.

EXAMPLE 2.2

To illustrate the graphical approach, we will use a slightly different scaled-down version of Monet's product mix problem. Now there are only two frame types, 1 and 2, and only two scarce resources, labor hours and metal. The problem statement is given below:

$$\max\ 2.25x_1 + 2.60x_2 \text{ (profit objective)}$$

$$\text{subject to } 2x_1 + x_2 \leq 4000 \text{ (labor constraint)}$$

$$x_1 + 2x_2 \leq 5000 \text{ (metal constraint)}$$

$$x_1, x_2 \geq 0 \text{ (nonnegativity constraints)}$$

The objective implies that each type 1 frame contributes a profit of \$2.25, whereas each type 2 frame contributes a profit of \$2.60. The first constraint is a labor hour constraint. There are 4000 hours available. Each type 1 frame requires two labor hours, and each type 2 frame requires one labor hour. Similarly, the second constraint is a metal constraint. There are 5000 ounces of metal available. Each type 1 frame requires one ounce of metal, and each type 2 frame requires two ounces of metal.

Solution

The idea is to graph the constraints on a two-dimensional graph to see which points (x_1, x_2) satisfy all of the constraints. This set of points is labeled the **feasible region**. Then we see which point in the feasible region provides the largest profit.

The graphical solution appears in Figure 2.6. To produce this graph, we first locate the lines where the constraints hold as equalities. For example, the line for labor hours is $2x_1 + x_2 = 4000$. The easiest way to graph this is to find the two points where it crosses the axes. It crosses the x_1-axis when $x_2 = 0$, that is, at $x_1 = 4000/2 = 2000$. Similarly, it crosses the x_2-axis when $x_1 = 0$, that is, at $x_2 = 4000$. Joining the points (0,4000) and (2000,0), we get the line where the labor constraint is satisfied exactly, that is, as an equality. All points below and to the left of this line are also feasible; these are the points where less than the maximum of 4000 labor hours are used. (To see this, try the point (0,0). It obviously satisfies the labor hour constraint, so it must be on the feasible side of the line. If (0,0) did not satisfy the constraint, then the feasible side would be the side not including (0,0).) We indicate the feasible side of the line by the short arrows pointing down to the left from the labor constraint line.

FIGURE 2.6 **Graphical Solution for Monet's Two-Variable Problem**

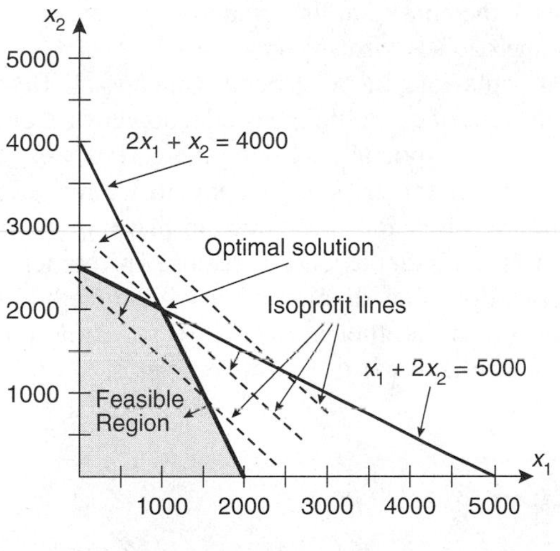

Similarly, the metal constraint line crosses the axes at the points (0,2500) and (5000,0), so we join these two points to find the line where all 5000 ounces of metal are used. Then all points below this line, indicated by the short arrows, use less than 5000 ounces of metal. Finally, the points on or below both of these lines constitute the feasible region. These are the points below the heavy lines, as indicated in Figure 2.6. (Of course, the feasible region only includes points to the right of the vertical axis and above the horizontal axis, since negative production quantities are impossible.) You can think of the feasible region as all points on or inside the figure formed by four points: (0,0), (0,2500), (2000,0), and the point where the labor hour and metal constraint lines intersect.

The next step is to bring profit into the picture. This is done by looking at "isoprofit" lines, that is, lines where total profit is a constant. Any such line can be written as

$$2.25x_1 + 2.60x_2 = P$$

where P is a constant profit level. Solving for x_2, we can put this equation in slope-intercept form:

$$x_2 = P/2.60 - (2.25/2.60)x_1$$

This shows that any isoprofit line has slope $-2.25/2.60$, and it crosses the vertical axis at the value $P/2.60$. Three of these isoprofit lines appear in Figure 2.6 as dotted lines. Clearly, as the dotted line moves up and to the right, the profit P increases. So we want to move the dotted line up and to the right until it just barely touches the feasible region. Graphically, you can see that the last feasible point it will touch is the point indicated in the figure, where the labor hour and metal constraint lines cross. (The corresponding isoprofit line is the middle dotted line.) We can then solve two equations in two unknowns to find the coordinates of this point. They are $x_1 = 1000$ and $x_2 = 2000$, with a corresponding profit of $P = \$7,450$.

Notice that if the slope of the isoprofit lines were much steeper, then the optimal point would be (2000,0). On the other hand, if the slope were much *less* steep, the optimal point would be (0,2500). These statements make intuitive sense. If the isoprofit lines are steep, this is because the unit profit from frame type 1 is large relative to the unit profit from frame type 2. If there is a large enough disparity, Monet will produce only frame type 1 and none of frame type 2. The opposite statement is true if the isoprofit lines are much less steep, inducing Monet to produce only frame type 2 and none of type 1. The crucial point, however, is that only three points can be optimal: (2000,0), (0,2500), or (1000,2000), the three "corner" points (other than (0,0)) in the feasible region.[5] The best of these depends on the relative slopes of the constraint lines and isoprofit lines in the graph.

This graphical approach is virtually never used to solve real problems, but it does provide important insights into LP in general. Namely, all LP problems have feasible regions that can be thought of as multidimensional polygons (figures with straight edges). The only points that can be optimal (except in the case of ties) are the corner points of this polygon. To see which corner point is optimal, we move an isoprofit plane as far as possible in the desired direction (the direction that improves the objective function) until it just barely intersects with the feasible region. The corner point that is touched last is then the optimal solution. The simplex method—the method Excel's Solver uses for LP problems—is really just an efficient method of searching through the thousands (or millions) of corner points that occur in realistic problems. ■

PROBLEMS

Skill-Building Problems

1 Leary Chemical manufactures three chemicals: A, B, and C. These chemicals are produced via two production processes: 1 and 2. Running process 1 for an hour costs \$4 and yields three units of A, one unit of B, and one unit of C. Running process 2 for an hour costs \$1 and yields

[5]This is not quite true. If the slope of the isoprofit lines is *exactly* the same as the slope of one of the constraint lines, then a whole line segment can be optimal. We call this the **multiple optimal solution case**—the case of ties. Even in the case of ties, however, we can still restrict the search for optimal solutions to corner points.

one unit of A and one unit of B. To meet customer demands, at least ten units of A, five units of B, and three units of C must be produced daily.

a Use a spreadsheet Solver to determine a daily production plan that minimizes the cost of meeting Leary's daily demands.

b Confirm graphically that the daily production plan from Part (a) minimizes the cost of meeting Leary's daily demands.

2 Furnco manufactures desks and chairs. Each desk uses four units of wood, and each chair uses three units of wood. A desk contributes $40 to profit, and a chair contributes $25. Marketing restrictions require that the number of chairs produced be at least twice the number of desks produced. There are 20 units of wood available.

a Use a spreadsheet Solver to maximize Furnco's profit.

b Confirm graphically that the solution in Part (a) maximizes Furnco's profit.

3 A farmer in Iowa owns 45 acres of land. She is going to plant each acre with wheat or corn. Each acre planted with wheat yields $200 profit; each with corn yields $300 profit. The labor and fertilizer used for each acre are given in Table 2.2. One hundred workers and 120 tons of fertilizer are available.

a Use a spreadsheet Solver to help the farmer maximize the profit from her land.

b Confirm graphically that the solution from Part (a) maximizes the farmer's profit from her land.

TABLE 2.2 **Data for Farmer Problem**

	Wheat	Corn
Labor	3 workers	2 workers
Fertilizer	2 tons	4 tons

Skill-Extending Problem

4 Truckco manufactures two types of trucks, types 1 and 2. Each truck must go through the painting shop and the assembly shop. If the painting shop were completely devoted to painting type 1 trucks, 800 per day could be painted, whereas if the painting shop were completely devoted to painting type 2 trucks, 700 per day could be painted. If the assembly shop were completely devoted to assembling truck 1 engines, 1500 per day could be assembled, and if the assembly shop were completely devoted to assembling truck 2 engines, 1200 per day could be assembled. Each type 1 truck contributes $300 to profit; each type 2 truck contributes $500. Use a spreadsheet Solver to maximize Truckco's profit. (*Hint*: Try a graphical procedure first. Then deduce the constraints from the graph.) ■

2.6 Solver Reports and Sensitivity Analysis

Virtually all LP software packages, including spreadsheet Solvers, provide more information than the optimal values of the decision variables and the optimal value of the objective. First, many of the constraints are inequalities, either of the $\geq$ or $\leq$ variety. A typical $\leq$ constraint is like those in Monet's product mix problem, where the amount of a resource used cannot be greater than the amount available. A typical $\geq$ constraint might be that the amount produced must be at least as great as the amount required. In either case, it is of interest to know whether, in the optimal solution, the two sides of the $\leq$ or $\geq$ inequality are equal or not. If they are equal, then the constraint is called **binding**. If they are not, the constraint is called **nonbinding**, and the difference between the two sides is called the **slack**. To understand these concepts better, we discuss two types of reports the Excel Solver produces.

Excel's Solver produces optional answer and sensitivity reports. You may request these right after the Solver has found an optimal solution. If you do request them, they are automatically inserted as new sheets in your spreadsheet file. (You may also ask for a limits report, but its information is not particularly useful.)

The answer report for Monet's (original) product mix problem from Section 2.3 is shown in Figure 2.7.[6] Among other things, it lists the final (optimal) values of the objective function and the decision variables, and for each constraint it lists its status (binding or nonbinding) and the amount of slack. This information is of most interest when it pertains to scarce resources. From Figure 2.7 we see that the labor and metal constraints are binding, but there are 2000 ounces of slack in the glass constraint. That is, only 8000 of the 10,000 available ounces are used. The next four constraints are nonnegativity constraints. The information on them is more straightforward (and less interesting). For example, because frame type 4 is not produced, its nonnegativity constraint is binding (at value 0). But because frame types 1, 2, and 3 are produced at positive levels, their slacks are simply their production quantities. Finally, the last four constraints are the maximum sales constraints. Only one of these (for frame type 1) is binding. For the other three frame types, production is *less* than the maximum sales level.

FIGURE 2.7 **Excel's Answer Report for the Product Mix Example**

Target Cell (Max)

Cell	Name	Original Value	Final Value
$F$10	Total profit	$9,200.00	$9,200.00

Adjustable Cells

Cell	Name	Original Value	Final Value
$B$15	Type 1 frames produced	1000	1000
$C$15	Type 2 frames produced	800	800
$D$15	Type 3 frames produced	400	400
$E$15	Type 4 frames produced	0	0

Constraints

Cell	Name	Cell Value	Formula	Status	Slack
$F$6	Labor hours	4000	$F$6<=$H$6	Binding	0
$F$7	Metal (oz.)	6000	$F$7<=$H$7	Binding	0
$F$8	Glass (oz.)	8000	$F$8<=$H$8	Not Binding	2000
$B$15	Type 1 frames nonnegativity	1000	$B$15>=0	Not Binding	1000
$C$15	Type 2 frames nonnegativity	800	$C$15>=0	Not Binding	800
$D$15	Type 3 frames nonnegativity	400	$D$15>=0	Not Binding	400
$E$15	Type 4 frames nonnegativity	0	$E$15>=0	Binding	0
$B$15	Maximum type 1 frames	1000	$B$15<=$B$17	Binding	0
$C$15	Maximum type 2 frames	800	$C$15<=$C$17	Not Binding	1200
$D$15	Maximum type 3 frames	400	$D$15<=$D$17	Not Binding	100
$E$15	Maximum type 4 frames	0	$E$15<=$E$17	Not Binding	1000

[6] We have changed the labels in the rows of this report (and in the sensitivity report below) to make them more meaningful. Excel tries to use the labels in appropriate cells of the spreadsheet, but these are often not very meaningful for the reports.

FIGURE 2.8 Excel's Sensitivity Report for the Product Mix Example

Changing Cells

Cell	Name	Final Value	Reduced Cost	Objective Coefficient	Allowable Increase	Allowable Decrease
$B$15	Type 1 frames produced	1000	2	6	1E+30	2
$C$15	Type 2 frames produced	800	0	2	6	0.25
$D$15	Type 3 frames produced	400	0	4	2	0.5
$E$15	Type 4 frames produced	0	-0.2	3	0.2	1E+30

Constraints

Cell	Name	Final Value	Shadow Price	Constraint R.H. Side	Allowable Increase	Allowable Decrease
$F$6	Labor hours	4000	1.2	4000	250	1000
$F$7	Metal (oz.)	6000	0.4	6000	2000	500
$F$8	Glass (oz.)	8000	0	10000	1E+30	2000

Excel also produces an optional sensitivity report, as in Figure 2.8. This is a bit more challenging to interpret. First, consider the top part of the report. There is a separate line for each decision variable (each changing cell). If a decision variable, such as the number of type 4 frames produced, is zero, then it is evidently not profitable to include this activity (producing type 4 frames) in the optimal mix. The **reduced cost** (sometimes called the **dual value**) of this activity then indicates how much *more* profitable each unit of this activity would have to be before it would be optimal to include it in the optimal mix. The unit profit for frame type 4 is now $3. According to the reduced cost, this unit profit would have to increase by $.20, that is, up to $3.20, before frames of type 4 would be worth producing. This is also reflected in the allowable increase column.

On the other hand, when an activity is already being performed at a positive level, then the allowable increase and allowable decrease indicate how much more or less profitable this activity would have to be before the current optimal solution would no longer be optimal. For example, if the unit profit for frame type 3 stays between $3.50 (= $4 – $.50) and $6 (= $4 + $2), then the current product mix will remain optimal (although the total profit will change). But if the unit profit for frame type 3 goes beyond this range, then the optimal product mix will change. Presumably, if type 3 frames become less profitable, Monet will make less of them and more of something else. Similarly, if they become more profitable, the company will make more of them and less of something else. To see how the optimal product mix changes when the unit profit for type 3 frames goes beyond its range, the best way is simply to change the input cell and rerun the Solver; it is too difficult to guess what might happen.

Notice that an allowable increase (or decrease) can be shown as 1E+30. This is a huge number that essentially means infinity. In this case the unit profit can increase (or decrease) without bound, and the optimal solution will not change. Usually there is a simple explanation for this. For example, the allowable increase for type 1 frames is infinite. This is because type 1 frames are already being produced at the maximum sales level. Because we constrain the amount produced to be less than or equal to this maximum sales level, we can't go above this limit, regardless of the profitability of the product.[7] In contrast, the allowable decrease for type 4 frames is also infinite. Here the reason is simply that if type 4 frames are currently not attractive enough to be included in the optimal product mix, they certainly wouldn't be included if we *decreased* their unit profit!

Now consider the bottom part of Figure 2.8. There is a line for every constraint (not including simple upper and lower bound constraints on the changing cells—the maximum

[7] You might argue that we should then eliminate the constraint, but that would mean changing the basic model.

sales and nonnegativity constraints). Here's the idea. Each constraint for this problem prevents Monet from using more of a scarce resource than is available. If a constraint is binding, then the company has used all the available resource, and it might consider buying more of it. The **shadow price** indicates how much an extra unit of the resource is worth in terms of increasing the total profit objective. Specifically, the shadow price is the change in the objective value per unit change in the availability of the resource; it is always measured in units of the objective per unit of the constraint.

In this problem the labor hour and metal constraints are binding, so Monet ought to be willing to pay for more of these. The shadow price for labor, \$1.20, means that each extra labor hour (on top of the 4000 already available) would add \$1.20 to total profit. Therefore, the company should be willing to pay *up to* \$1.20 for each extra labor hour. For example, if it could purchase one extra labor hour for \$1.00, say, the net increase in profit would be \$.20. It works the other way as well. If Monet lost any of the 4000 labor hours, each hour lost would mean a loss of \$1.20 profit.

However, these statements are true only up to a point. This point is why the allowable increase and decrease, 250 and 1000, are relevant. Essentially, they indicate the range in which the stated shadow price is relevant. Every extra labor hour gained, up to the first 250, is worth \$1.20 in extra profit, and every labor hour lost, up to the first 1000, means a loss of \$1.20 in profit. Beyond this range, it is difficult to tell what will happen. Actually, it can be shown that beyond the upper limit of the range, every extra hour is worth *less* than \$1.20, and beyond the lower limit of the range, every extra lost hour means a loss of *more* than \$1.20. However, the only way to find out how much less or more is to change the amount of labor available and rerun the Solver.

The explanation of the shadow price is exactly the same for any other binding constraint, such as the metal constraint. Now the shadow price per ounce of metal is 40¢, which means that an extra ounce of metal is worth an extra 40¢ in profit. Also, this value is relevant for the range 5500 (= 6000 − 500) to 8000 (= 6000 + 2000).

In contrast to binding constraints, the shadow price for any nonbinding constraint is always equal to zero. This makes economic sense. If Monet already has more ounces of glass than it is using, then it certainly isn't willing to pay for more glass. In this case the allowable increase is infinity because the shadow price remains zero no matter how many more ounces of glass are available. But the allowable decrease is 2000, exactly the same as the amount of slack for the glass constraint. This also makes sense. If the company loses more than 2000 ounces of glass, then the current solution will no longer be optimal, and the shadow price for glass will almost certainly become positive, indicating that it is now a scarce resource.

The type of information given in Figures 2.7 and 2.8 is available each time you solve an LP problem with Excel's Solver. The information in the answer report gives you a quick look at the optimal solution, and it tells you which resources are fully used and which have slack. The information in the sensitivity report allows you to answer a number of what-if questions easily—without changing the data in the original LP formulation and rerunning the Solver.

An important proviso when interpreting the sensitivity report is that we are changing *only one input at a time*. When we make the statements about the metal constraint, for example, we imply that all of the other parameters in the problem are held constant. If you want to know what happens if several inputs change simultaneously, the best way to find out is to make the changes and rerun the Solver.

You should get used to looking at these reports and interpreting the information contained in them. The information in these reports is generally used to answer questions such as the ones addressed above. For example, if some product is currently not being produced, it is worth asking how much more profitable that product would have to be before it would be included in the optimal mix. You can find this figure by looking at the product's reduced cost. Or, if the entire availability of a resource is being used, you might want to know how much it would be worth to obtain more of this resource. You can find this figure by looking at the resource's shadow price.

These sensitivity reports can sometimes be misleading. To understand why, you need to be familiar with some historical background. The traditional way of formulating LP problems, with algebraic expressions instead of spreadsheets, used two conventions. First, the objective had to be similar to

$$6x_1 + 2x_2 + 4x_3 + 3x_4$$

That is, it had to be a sum of objective coefficients multiplied by variables. Second, each constraint had to be similar to

$$2x_1 + x_2 + 3x_3 + 2x_4 < 4000$$

That is, it had to be a sum of coefficients multiplied by variables on the left-hand side and a constant on the right-hand side.

Once an LP was formulated this way, it became natural to perform sensitivity analysis on the objective coefficients (often unit profits) and the right-hand side constants (often resource availabilities). To do this, mathematicians developed methods to calculate how much an objective coefficient or right-hand side constant could change before something about the optimal solution would change. This is exactly the type of information provided in Excel's sensitivity report. However, in order for this information to be used as originally intended, the spreadsheet model must be a fairly literal translation of the types of algebraic expressions shown above.

The problem is that you are *not* forced to set up a spreadsheet formulation this way. For example, it is perfectly acceptable to enter the labor hour constraint as H6>=F6 (rather than F6<=H6). Then the right-hand side is *not* a constant but is instead an expression involving the changing cells.[8] Excel treats such a constraint internally as H6−F6>=0, and it performs sensitivity analysis on the constraint in this form—which may be confusing.

Below are some guidelines that you can use to interpret the sensitivity output from Excel for *any* type of formulation. Of course some information is naturally more useful than others, and you must decide what is most important. Also, remember that when you are not sure whether the information in a report can be used to answer a particular what-if question, you can always answer your question by changing the relevant inputs and rerunning the Solver.

Guidelines for the Sensitivity Report

1 In the changing cell section of the report, if a decision variable is currently zero, its reduced cost indicates how much more attractive (for example, lower cost or higher profit) its objective coefficient must be in order to induce us to use this variable at some positive level. (You can ignore the sign of the reduced cost, since sign conventions from Solvers are usually difficult to unravel, and instead concentrate only on its magnitude.)

2 In the changing cell section of the report, if there is an upper bound constraint on a decision variable and that variable is currently equal to its upper bound, the reduced cost indicates how much *less* attractive (for example, higher cost or lower profit) its objective coefficient must be in order to induce us to reduce the value of this variable.

3 In the constraint section of the report, the magnitude of the shadow price indicates how much the optimal objective value will improve for a maximization problem (for example, higher profit) or deteriorate for a minimization problem (for example, higher cost) if the right-hand side of that constraint increases by one unit.

[8] Some people still insist that it is "good programming practice" to enter the objective and constraints in a spreadsheet so that they follow the traditional conventions. For example, they suggest that the right-hand side of each constraint should be a constant or a formula that does not depend on the changing cells. While we agree that this is a good idea, we have found that it is sometimes not the most natural way to form the spreadsheet.

One final note: if you do *not* check the Assume Linear Models box, the sensitivity report will be in a different format and will no doubt confuse you. In these cases the Solver uses a nonsimplex algorithm to solve the problem, and the accompanying output is somewhat different. In fact, it requires concepts that we will not cover in this book.

2.7 Sensitivity Analysis with Graphs

As we mentioned earlier, the traditional sensitivity analysis indicates how the optimal solution changes if a single objective coefficient or a single right-hand side constant changes. The effects of such changes are relatively easy to see on a graph for two-variable problems.

Here we refer to the two-variable product mix problem from Section 2.5. This problem and its graphical solution in Figure 2.9 are repeated here for convenience.

$$\max 2.25x_1 + 2.60x_2$$
$$\text{subject to } 2x_1 + x_2 \leq 4000$$
$$x_1 + 2x_2 \leq 5000$$
$$x_1, x_2 \geq 0$$

The objective coefficients in this problem are 2.25 and 2.60. These yield isoprofit lines with slope $-2.25/2.60$. This implies that the slope of these isoprofit lines is *between* the slopes of the constraint lines, and the effect is that the optimal solution is where the two constraint lines cross. In this solution both types of frames are produced at a positive level.

FIGURE 2.9 Graphical Solution for Monet's Two-Variable Problem

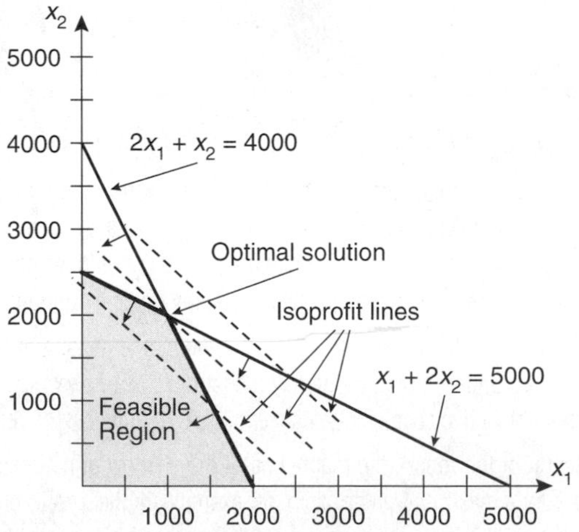

Now consider a sensitivity analysis on the objective coefficient 2.25. If this value is decreased sufficiently, the isoprofit lines become flatter than either constraint line, and the effect is that the optimal point becomes the corner point (0,2500) where only type 2 frames are produced, as shown in Figure 2.10.

FIGURE 2.10 **Graphical Solution with Low Unit Profit for Frame Type 1**

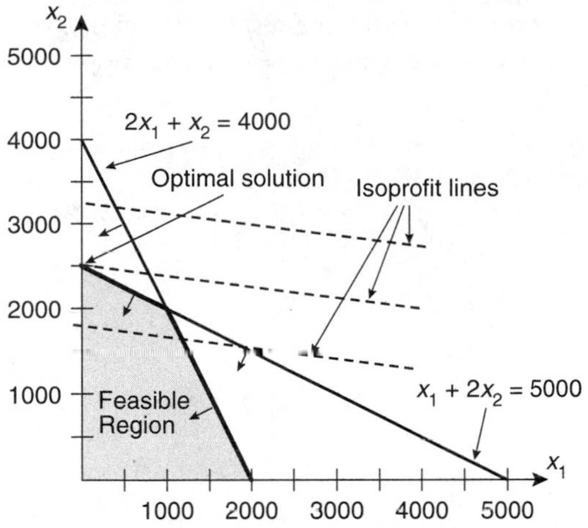

On the other hand, if this objective coefficient is increased sufficiently, the isoprofit lines become steeper than either constraint line, and the effect is that the optimal point becomes the corner point (2000,0) where only type 1 frames are produced, as shown in Figure 2.11.

FIGURE 2.11 **Graphical Solution with High Unit Profit for Frame Type 1**

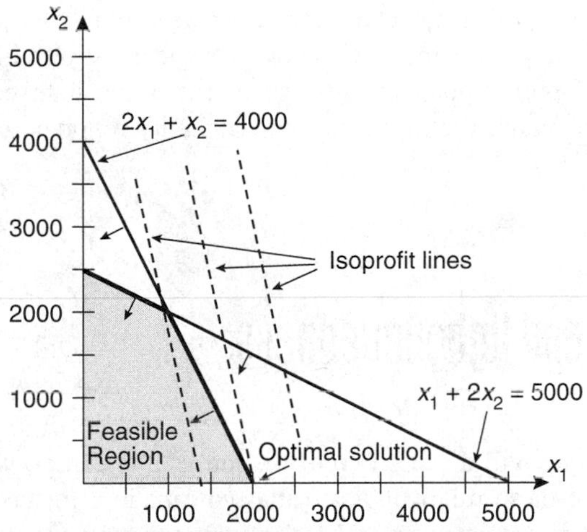

In general, if we change an objective coefficient, we change the "tilt" of the isoprofit lines. For small changes the original optimal corner point remains optimal. But for sufficiently large changes a new corner point becomes optimal. The ranges in the sensitivity reports indicate how large "sufficiently large" is.

The interpretation of right-hand side changes is somewhat different. If the right-hand side of some constraint changes, then the corresponding constraint line moves parallel to itself in one direction or the other. For example, consider the labor hour constraint with right-hand side value 4000. If we decrease this value, the constraint line will move down and to the left. For small changes the optimal solution will still be the point where the two constraint lines cross. But if the right-hand side value decreases sufficiently, the optimal point will be where this first constraint intersects with the vertical axis. For example, when the right-hand side decreases to 2000, the result is the situation shown in Figure 2.12. In this case the second constraint becomes irrelevant, and we produce only type 2 frames.

FIGURE 2.12 Graphical Solution with New Right-Hand Side

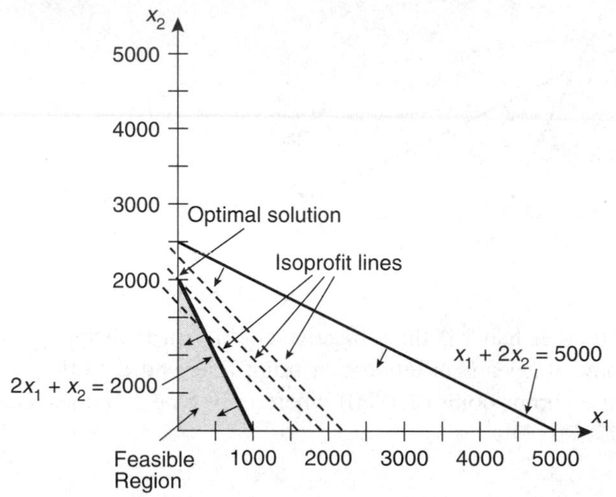

In general, when we change a right-hand side value, a constraint line moves parallel to itself in some direction. For small changes the *coordinates* of the optimal point change, but the optimal point is still at the intersection of the same constraint lines. But for sufficiently large changes the optimal point changes so that it is the intersection of a different set of constraint lines. Again, the ranges in the sensitivity report indicate exactly how large "sufficiently large" is.

2.8 Infeasibility and Unboundedness

In this section we will discuss two of the things that can go wrong when you invoke the Solver. Both of these might indicate that you made a mistake in your formulation, but because mistakes are common in LP formulations, you should be aware of the error messages you might encounter.

Infeasibility

The first problem is infeasibility. If a solution satisfies all of the constraints, we say that it is **feasible**. Among all of the feasible solutions, we are looking for the one that optimizes the objective. Now, it is possible that there are no feasible solutions to the model. There are generally two possible reasons for this: (1) there is a mistake in the formulation (an input entered wrong, such as a $\geq$ instead of a $\leq$) or (2) the problem has been so constrained that there are no solutions that satisfy all of them. In the former case a careful check of the formulation should find the error. In the latter case the modeler might simply have to change, or even eliminate, some of the constraints.

To show how an infeasible problem could occur, suppose that in Monet's product mix problem we incorrectly enter the maximum sales constraints with the wrong inequality: B15:E15>=B17:E17 instead of B15:E15<=B17:E17. Now Monet must produce *at least* as much as the maximum sales values. If the constraint is changed this way and the Solver is then used, a message appears indicating that the Solver cannot find a feasible solution. The reason is clear. There is no way, given the resource availabilities, that the company can meet these production constraints. If you are observant, you'll notice the error in the formulation, change the direction of the inequality, and proceed. However, there is no foolproof way of finding the problem when a "no feasible solution" message appears. Careful checking and rethinking are required.

Unboundedness

A second type of problem is **unboundedness**. In this case the model has been formulated in such a way that the objective is unbounded, that is, it can be made as large (or as small, for minimization problems) as you like. If this occurs, you've probably either entered a wrong input or you've forgotten some constraints. (Or you've found a way to become infinitely rich!) To see how this could occur in the product mix problem, suppose that we enter both the maximum sales constraints and the resource constraints with $\geq$ instead of $\leq$. Now there is no upper bound on how much of each product Monet can make because there is no upper bound on the amount of the resources available. Since each frame is generating a profit, the total profit is unlimited. If these changes in the formulation are made and the Solver is then used, a message appears stating that the target cell does not converge. In other words, the total profit is growing without bound.

Infeasibility and unboundedness are quite different in a practical sense. It is quite possible for a reasonable model to have no feasible solutions. For example, the people in the marketing department might impose several constraints, the people in the production department might add some more, the people in engineering might add some more, and so on. Together, they might very well constrain the problem so much that there are no feasible solutions left! The only way out is for them to change or eliminate some of their constraints. An unboundedness problem is quite different, however. There is no way a realistic model can have an unbounded solution. If your model does have an unbounded solution, then you must have made a mistake—either you made an input error or you omitted one or more constraints.

2.9 A Multiperiod Production Problem

The product mix example is a common type of LP model. However, LP models come in many forms. For variety, we will now illustrate a quite different type of problem that can also be solved with LP. (In the next two chapters we will illustrate many other examples.) The distinguishing feature of the following problem is that it relates decisions made in several time periods. This type of problem occurs when a company must make a decision now that will have ramifications in the future. The company doesn't want to focus completely on the near future to the possible detriment of its success in the long run.

EXAMPLE 2.3

The Pigskin Company produces footballs. Pigskin must decide how many footballs to produce each month. It has decided to use a six-month planning horizon. The forecasted demands for the next six months are 10,000, 15,000, 30,000, 35,000, 25,000, and 10,000. Pigskin wants to meet these demands on time, knowing that it currently has 5000 footballs in inventory and it can use a given month's production to help meet the demand for that month. During each month there is enough production capacity to produce up to 30,000 footballs, and there is enough storage capacity to store up to 10,000 footballs at the end of the month. The forecasted production costs per football for the next six months are \$12.50, \$12.55, \$12.70, \$12.80, \$12.85, and \$12.95, respectively. The holding cost per football held in inventory at the end of any month is figured at 5% of the production cost for that month. (This cost includes the cost of storage and also the cost of money tied up in inventory.) The selling price for footballs is not considered relevant to the production decision because it is assumed that all demand will be met exactly when it occurs— at whatever the selling price is. Therefore, Pigskin wants to determine the production schedule that minimizes the total production and holding costs.

Solution

In the traditional formulation, the decision variables are the production quantities for the six months, labeled P_1 through P_6. It is also convenient to let I_1 through I_6 be the corresponding end-of-month inventories. For example, I_3 is the number of footballs left over at the end of month 3. (From here on, to minimize on the number of zeros shown, we will express all quantities in 100s of footballs.) Therefore, the obvious constraints are on production and inventory storage capacities: $P_j \leq 300$ and $I_j \leq 100$ for each month j, $1 \leq j \leq 6$.

In addition to these constraints, we need "balance" constraints that relate the P's and I's. In any month the inventory from the previous month plus the current production must equal the current demand plus leftover inventory. We can represent this relation in symbols: if D_j is the forecasted demand for month j, then the balance equation for month j is

$$I_{j-1} + P_j = D_j + I_j$$

The first of these constraints, for month $j = 1$, uses the known beginning inventory, 50, for the previous inventory (the I_{j-1} term). By putting all variables (P's and I's) on the left and all known values on the right (a standard LP convention), these balance equations become

$$\begin{aligned}
P_1 - I_1 &= 100 - 50 \\
I_1 + P_2 - I_2 &= 150 \\
I_2 + P_3 - I_3 &= 300 \\
I_3 + P_4 - I_4 &= 350 \\
I_4 + P_5 - I_5 &= 250 \\
I_5 + P_6 - I_6 &= 100
\end{aligned} \tag{2.1}$$

As usual, we impose nonnegativity constraints: all P's and I's must be nonnegative. What about meeting demand on time? This requires that in each month the inventory from the preceding month plus the current production must be at least as large as the current demand. But take a look, for example, at the balance equation for month 3. By rearranging it slightly, we can write it as

$$I_3 = I_2 + P_3 - 300$$

Now, the nonnegativity constraint on I_3 implies that the right-hand side of this equation, $I_2 + P_3 - 300$, is also nonnegative. But this implies that demand in month 3 is covered—beginning inventory in month 3 plus month 3 production is at least 300. Therefore, the nonnegativity constraints on the I's *automatically* guarantee that all demands will be met on time, and no other constraints are needed. Finally, the objective is obvious. It is the sum of unit production costs multiplied by P's, plus unit holding costs multiplied by I's.

Developing the Spreadsheet Model The spreadsheet version of Pigskin's production problem appears in Figure 2.13. (See the file PRODUCE.XLS.) The main feature that distinguishes this model from the product mix model is that some of the constraints, namely, the balance equations 2.1, are built into the spreadsheet itself by means of formulas. In other words, the only changing cells are the production quantities. The ending inventories shown in row 28 are determined by the production quantities and Equations 2.1. To form the spreadsheet in Figure 2.13, you must enter the following information.

1 **Inputs.** Enter the various inputs in the ranges B5, B10:G12, B24:G24, B26:G26, and B30:G30. The zeros in B26:G26 provide lower limits for ending inventory. They are used in constraints to ensure that demands are met on time, as discussed above. Also, the range B12:G12 actually contains formulas. Cell B12 contains the formula

=.05*B11

which is then copied to the range C12:G12. The cells in row 12 indicate that the unit holding cost is 5% of the unit production cost.

FIGURE 2.13 **Nonoptimal Solution to Pigskin's Production Problem**

	A	B	C	D	E	F	G
1	**Multiperiod Production Problem with Initial (Nonoptimal) Solution**						
2							
3	**Input data**						
4							
5	Beginning inventory	50					
6							
7	Demands, unit production costs, and unit inventory holding costs:						
8				Month			
9		1	2	3	4	5	6
10	Demand	100	150	300	350	250	100
11	Production cost/unit	$12.50	$12.55	$12.70	$12.80	$12.85	$12.95
12	Holding cost/unit	$0.625	$0.628	$0.635	$0.640	$0.643	$0.648
13							
14	**Summary of costs**						
15	Total production cost	$15,915.00					
16	Total holding cost	$285.25					
17	**Total cost**	$16,200.25					
18							
19	**Production plan**						
20				Month			
21		1	2	3	4	5	6
22	Units produced	150	150	300	300	250	100
23		<=	<=	<=	<=	<=	<=
24	Production capacity	300	300	300	300	300	300
25							
26	Lower limit (no backlog)	0	0	0	0	0	0
27		<=	<=	<=	<=	<=	<=
28	Ending inventory	100	100	100	50	50	50
29		<=	<=	<=	<=	<=	<=
30	Storage capacity	100	100	100	100	100	100

2 **Production quantities.** Enter *any* six values in the cells B22:G22 as initial values for the production quantities. As usual, you can try entering values that you believe are good, maybe even optimal. This is not crucial, however, since the Solver will eventually find the best production quantities.

3 **Ending inventory in month 1.** Enter the formula

=B5+B22–B10

in cell B28. This calculates the first month ending inventory as initial inventory plus production in month 1 minus demand in month 1.

4 **Ending inventory in other months.** Enter the "typical" formula

=B28+C22–C10

for ending inventory in cell C28 and copy it to the range D28:G28. This formula calculates ending inventory in the current month as ending inventory from the previous month plus production in the current month minus demand in the current month.

5 **Total production cost.** Enter the formula

=SUMPRODUCT(B11:G11,B22:G22)

for total production cost in cell B15. This is the sum of unit production costs multiplied by production quantities.

6 **Total inventory holding cost.** Enter the formula

=SUMPRODUCT(B12:G12,B28:G28)

for total inventory holding cost in cell B16. This is the sum of unit holding costs multiplied by ending inventories.

7 **Total cost.** Enter the formula

=B15+B16

for total cost, the sum of production cost and holding cost, in cell B17.

The logic behind the constraints is now straightforward. All we have to guarantee is that the production quantities are nonnegative and do not exceed the production capacities and that the ending inventories are nonnegative and do not exceed the storage capacities. Remember that if the ending inventories are nonnegative, then all demands will automatically be met on time.

Using the Solver To use the Solver, specify the following and then Solve.

1 **Objective.** Select cell B17 (total cost) as the target cell and click on the Minimize button.

2 **Changing cells.** Select the range B22:G22 (production quantities) as the changing cells.

3 **Constraints.** Enter the constraints

B22:G22 >= 0

B22:G22 <= B24:G24

B28:G28 >= B26:G26

B28:G28 <= B30:G30

These indicate that, respectively, production must be nonnegative, production cannot exceed production capacity, ending inventory must be nonnegative, and ending inventory cannot exceed storage capacity.

The Solver window should appear as shown in Figure 2.14.

FIGURE 2.14 **Excel Solver Window for Production Problem**

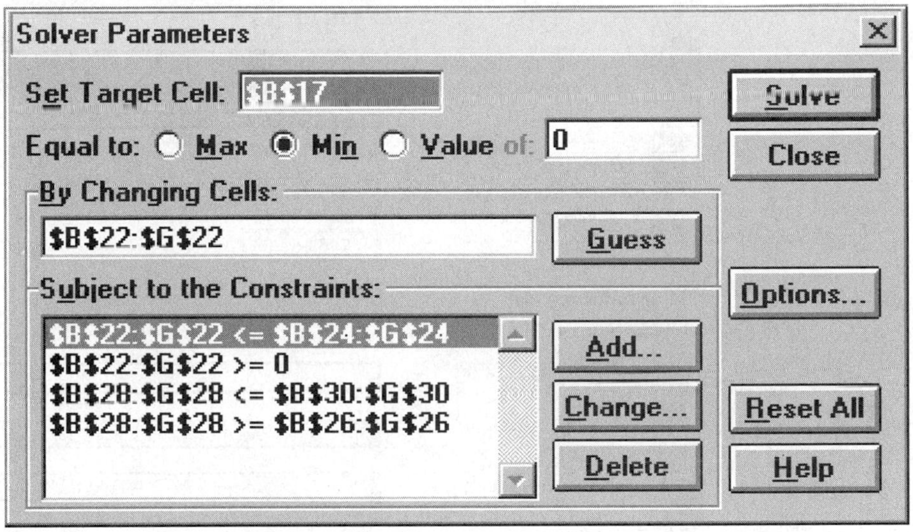

4 **Linear model, optimize.** Check the Assume Linear Model box and then Solve.

The Solver solution appears in Figure 2.15, and the accompanying answer report is shown in Figure 2.16. The solution is also represented graphically in Figure 2.17. We can interpret the solution by comparing production quantities with demands. (Also, remember that all quantities are in units of 100 footballs.) In month 1 Pigskin should produce just enough to meet month 1 demand (taking into account the initial inventory of 5000). In month 2 it should produce 5000 more footballs than month 2 demand, and then in month 3 it should produce just enough to meet month 3 demand, still carrying the extra 5000 footballs in inventory from month 2 production. In month 4 Pigskin should finally use these 5000 footballs, along with the maximum production amount, 30,000, to meet month 4 demand. Then in the last two months it should produce exactly enough to meet these months' demands. The total cost is $1,535,563, most of which is production cost. (Don't feel sorry for Pigskin, however. Remember that we ignored the selling price. The revenues from these sales should make Pigskin a handsome profit.)

Would you have guessed that this is the optimal solution? Upon some reflection, we see it makes perfect sense. Because the monthly holding costs are large relative to the differences in monthly production costs, there is little incentive to produce footballs before they are needed to take advantage of a "cheap" production month. Therefore, the Solver elects to produce, if possible, footballs in the month in which they are needed. The only exception to this rule is the 20,000 footballs produced during month 2 when only 15,000 are needed. The extra 5000 units produced during month 2 are needed, however, to meet month 4's demand of 35,000, because month 3 production capacity is used entirely to meet month 3 demand. Thus month 3 capacity is not available to meet month 4 demand, and 5000 units of month 2 capacity are used to meet month 4 demand.

FIGURE 2.15 Optimal Solution for Pigskin Production Problem

	A	B	C	D	E	F	G
1	**Multiperiod Production Problem with Optimal Solution**						
2							
3	**Input data**						
4							
5	Beginning inventory	50					
6							
7	Demands, unit production costs, and unit inventory holding costs:						
8				**Month**			
9		1	2	3	4	5	6
10	Demand	100	150	300	350	250	100
11	Production cost/unit	$12.50	$12.55	$12.70	$12.80	$12.85	$12.95
12	Holding cost/unit	$0.625	$0.628	$0.635	$0.640	$0.643	$0.648
13							
14	**Summary of costs**						
15	Total production cost	$15,292.50					
16	Total holding cost	$63.13					
17	**Total cost**	$15,355.63					
18							
19	**Production plan**						
20				**Month**			
21		1	2	3	4	5	6
22	Units produced	50	200	300	300	250	100
23		<=	<=	<=	<=	<=	<=
24	Production capacity	300	300	300	300	300	300
25							
26	Lower limit (no backlog)	0	0	0	0	0	0
27		<=	<=	<=	<=	<=	<=
28	Ending inventory	0	50	50	0	0	0
29		<=	<=	<=	<=	<=	<=
30	Storage capacity	100	100	100	100	100	100

Notice in the bottom section of the answer report in Figure 2.16 that the 24 constraints are arranged in four groups of six each: upper bounds for ending inventory, nonnegativity of ending inventory, nonnegativity of production, and upper bounds for production. In the last group there are two binding constraints, in months 3 and 4. These are the two months where production is limited by production capacities; in the other four months production is below capacity. In the second group there are four binding constraints, in months 1, 4, 5, and 6. These are the months where ending inventory is 0, that is, where demand is met exactly, with nothing to spare. In months 2 and 3 ending inventory is positive, so that demand is met with something left over.

Sensitivity Report Excel's sensitivity report for this model is shown in Figure 2.18. The top part of each report is a bit more difficult to unravel than in the Monet product mix model. For example, in the top row of the report, where does the objective coefficient 16.3175 for production in month 1 come from? The difficulty here is that we have to go back through the spreadsheet and see where the production quantity in cell B22 has an effect on the objective in cell B17. It has the obvious effect of the unit production cost 12.50 in month 1. But then this production in month 1 could be carried over to any or all of the following months as inventory, and hence it could be subject to the unit holding costs in row 12. Because each of these holding costs is, by assumption, 5% of the corresponding production cost above it, the 16.3175 figure is actually the following:

$$16.3175 = 12.50 + .05 * (12.50 + 12.55 + 12.70 + 12.80 + 12.85 + 12.85 + 12.95)$$

FIGURE 2.16 Excel Answer Report for Pigskin Production Problem

Target Cell (Min)

Cell	Name	Original Value	Final Value
$B$17	Total cost	$16,200.25	$15,355.63

Adjustable Cells

Cell	Name	Original Value	Final Value
$B$22	Units produced Month	150	50
$C$22	Units produced	150	200
$D$22	Units produced	300	300
$E$22	Units produced	300	300
$F$22	Units produced	250	250
$G$22	Units produced	100	100

Constraints

Cell	Name	Cell Value	Formula	Status	Slack
$B$28	Storage capacity month 1	0	$B$28<=$B$30	Not Binding	100
$C$28	Storage capacity month 2	50	$C$28<=$C$30	Not Binding	50
$D$28	Storage capacity month 3	50	$D$28<=$D$30	Not Binding	50
$E$28	Storage capacity month 4	0	$E$28<=$E$30	Not Binding	100
$F$28	Storage capacity month 5	0	$F$28<=$F$30	Not Binding	100
$G$28	Storage capacity month 6	0	$G$28<=$G$30	Not Binding	100
$B$28	End inv nonnegative month 1	0	$B$28>=$B$26	Binding	0
$C$28	End inv nonnegative month 2	50	$C$28>=$C$26	Not Binding	50
$D$28	End inv nonnegative month 3	50	$D$28>=$D$26	Not Binding	50
$E$28	End inv nonnegative month 4	0	$E$28>=$E$26	Binding	0
$F$28	End inv nonnegative month 5	0	$F$28>=$F$26	Binding	0
$G$28	End inv nonnegative month 6	0	$G$28>=$G$26	Binding	0
$B$22	Production nonnegative month 1	50	$B$22>=0	Not Binding	50
$C$22	Production nonnegative month 2	200	$C$22>=0	Not Binding	200
$D$22	Production nonnegative month 3	300	$D$22>=0	Not Binding	300
$E$22	Production nonnegative month 4	300	$E$22>=0	Not Binding	300
$F$22	Production nonnegative month 5	250	$F$22>=0	Not Binding	250
$G$22	Production nonnegative month 6	100	$G$22>=0	Not Binding	100
$B$22	Production capacity month 1	50	$B$22<=$B$24	Not Binding	250
$C$22	Production capacity month 2	200	$C$22<=$C$24	Not Binding	100
$D$22	Production capacity month 3	300	$D$22<=$D$24	Binding	0
$E$22	Production capacity month 4	300	$E$22<=$E$24	Binding	0
$F$22	Production capacity month 5	250	$F$22<=$F$24	Not Binding	50
$G$22	Production capacity month 6	100	$G$22<=$G$24	Not Binding	200

FIGURE 2.17 Graphical Solution to Pigskin Production Problem

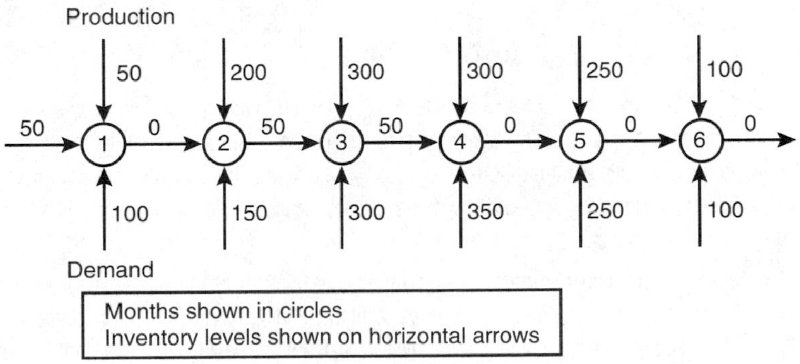

FIGURE 2.18 Sensitivity Report for Pigskin Production Problem

Changing Cells

Cell	Name	Final Value	Reduced Cost	Objective Coefficient	Allowable Increase	Allowable Decrease
$B$22	Production month 1	50	0	16.3175	1E+30	0.575
$C$22	Production month 2	200	0	15.7425	0.4775	1.6025
$D$22	Production month 3	300	-0.4775	15.265	0.4775	1E+30
$E$22	Production month 4	300	-1.0125	14.73	1.0125	1E+30
$F$22	Production month 5	250	0	14.14	1.6025	0.5425
$G$22	Production month 6	100	0	13.5975	0.5425	13.5975

Constraints

Cell	Name	Final Value	Shadow Price	Constraint R.H. Side	Allowable Increase	Allowable Decrease
$B$28	Storage capacity month 1	0	0	100	1E+30	100
$C$28	Storage capacity month 2	50	0	100	1E+30	50
$D$28	Storage capacity month 3	50	0	100	1E+30	50
$E$28	Storage capacity month 4	0	0	100	1E+30	100
$F$28	Storage capacity month 5	0	0	100	1E+30	100
$G$28	Storage capacity month 6	0	0	100	1E+30	100
$B$28	End inv nonnegative month 1	0	1	0	100	50
$C$28	End inv nonnegative month 2	50	0	0	50	1E+30
$D$28	End inv nonnegative month 3	50	0	0	50	1E+30
$E$28	End inv nonnegative month 4	0	2	0	50	50
$F$28	End inv nonnegative month 5	0	1	0	50	200
$G$28	End inv nonnegative month 6	0	14	0	100	100

Similarly, the objective coefficient for month 3, say, is the unit production cost in month 3 plus the sum of the unit holding costs in months 3 through 6.

Usually, we use a sensitivity report to see how much an input to the problem can change before the optimal solution changes. For example, we might ask how much cheaper production in month 1 would have to be before we would produce more in month 1. Unfortunately, this is very difficult to answer from the information in these reports. The allowable decrease shown in the first row of the Excel report is for the objective coefficient we calculated above, which includes not only the production cost in month 1 but other costs as well. The trouble is that it is difficult to *isolate* the effect of a particular cost because it is combined with other costs. Therefore, we won't pursue this analysis any further. However, if you want to see the effect of a change in any particular input, you can simply change the value of this input and rerun the Solver. ■

MODELING ISSUES

1 We assumed that Pigskin is using a six-month planning horizon. Why six months? In multiperiod problems such as this, the company has to make forecasts about the future, such as the level of customer demand. Therefore, the length of the planning horizon is usually the length of time for which the company can make reasonably accurate forecasts. Here, Pigskin evidently believes that it can forecast up to six months from now, so it uses a six-month planning horizon.

2 The optimal solution to Pigskin's model specifies the production level for each of the next six months. In reality, however, the company might only implement the model's recommendation for the *first* month. Then at the beginning of the second month, it will gather new forecasts for the *next* six months, that is, months 2 through 7, solve a new six-month model, and again implement the model's recommendation for the first of these months, month 2. If it continues in this manner, we say that it is following a six-month **rolling planning horizon**.

PROBLEMS

Skill-Building Problems

5 A customer requires during the next four months, respectively, 50, 65, 100, and 70 units of a commodity, and no backlogging is allowed (that is, the customer's requirements must be met on time). Production costs are $5, $8, $4, and $7 per unit during these months. The storage cost from one month to the next is $2 per unit (assessed on ending inventory). It is estimated that each unit on hand at the end of month 4 could be sold for $6. Determine how to minimize the net cost incurred in meeting the demands for the next four months.

6 A company faces the following demands during the next three weeks: week 1, 20 units; week 2, 10 units; week 3, 15 units. The unit production cost during each week is as follows: week 1, $13; week 2, $14; week 3, $15. A holding cost of $2 per unit is assessed against each week's ending inventory. At the beginning of week 1, the company has five units on hand. In reality, not all goods produced during a month can be used to meet the current month's demand. To model this fact, we assume that only one half of the goods produced during a week can be used to meet the current week's demands. Determine how to minimize the cost of meeting the demand for the next three weeks.

7 James Beerd bakes cheesecakes and Black Forest cakes. During any day he can bake at most 65 cakes. The costs per cake and the demands for cakes, which must be met on time, are listed in Table 2.3. It costs 50 cents to hold a cheesecake and 40 cents to hold a Black Forest cake in inventory for a day. Determine how to minimize the total cost of meeting the next three days' demands. ■

TABLE 2.3 **Data for Cake Problem**

	Day 1		Day 2		Day 3	
	Demand	**Cost/Cake**	**Demand**	**Cost/Cake**	**Demand**	**Cost/Cake**
Cheesecake	40	$3.00	30	$3.40	20	$3.80
Black Forest	20	$2.50	30	$2.80	10	$3.40

2.10 A Decision Support System

If your job is to develop an LP spreadsheet model to solve a problem such as Pigskin's production problem, then you will be considered the "expert" in LP. Many people who need to use such models, however, are *not* experts. They may know what the purpose of LP is and what problems it is intended to solve, but they will not know the details that we are presenting in this book. In this case it is necessary to provide these users with a **decision support system** (DSS) that can help them solve problems but will shield them from technical details.

We will not teach you in this book how to build full-scale DSSs, but we will indicate what they look like and what they can do. (We will consider only DSSs built around spreadsheets. There are many other platforms for developing DSSs that we won't consider.) Basically, they contain a spreadsheet model of a problem, such as the one in Figure 2.13. However, the users might never even see this model. Instead, they see a "front end" and a "back end." The front end allows them to select input values for their particular problem. The user interface for this front end can include several features, such as buttons, dialog boxes, toolbars, and menus—the things you are used to seeing in Windows applications. The back end then produces a report that explains the optimal policy in nontechnical terms.

We illustrate a DSS for a slight variation of the Pigskin problem in the file PIGSKIN.XLS. When you open this file, you'll see that it contains five sheets.[9] The user will see the Control sheet upon opening the file. (See Figure 2.19.) It contains two buttons, one for setting up the problem (getting the user's inputs) and one for solving the problem (running the Solver). When you press the Set Up Problem button, you will be asked for a series of inputs: the initial inventory, the number of months in the planning horizon, the forecasted demands for each month, and others. An example appears in Figure 2.20, where you must enter information about the holding costs. These input boxes should be self-explanatory, so that all you need to do is enter the values you want to try. After you have entered all of these inputs, take a look at the Formulation sheet. This sheet contains the spreadsheet model we saw earlier in Figure 2.13, but with the inputs you just entered.

FIGURE 2.19 **Control Sheet for Pigskin Application**

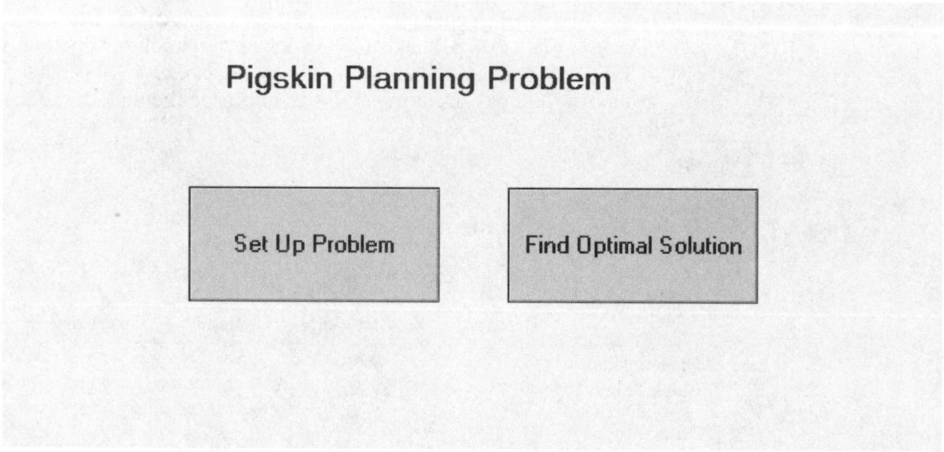

FIGURE 2.20 **Input Dialog Box for Holding Costs**

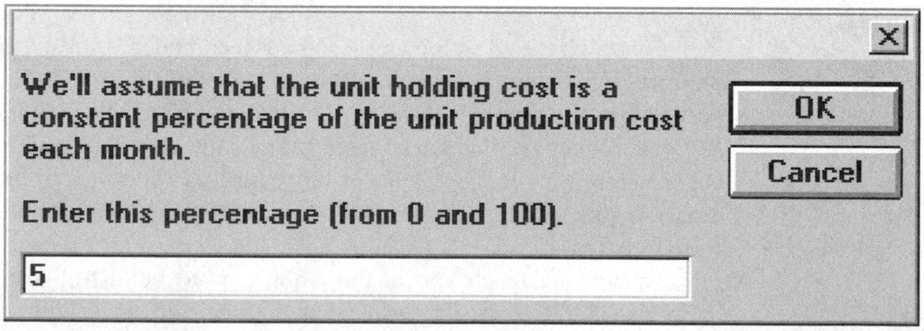

Now go back to the Control sheet and press the Find Optimal Solution button. This automatically sets up the Solver dialog box and runs the Solver. There are two cases. First,

[9] When you open this file, you may encounter an error message about a Sub or Function not defined. Since this application uses the Solver in an Excel macro, it must be able to find the SOLVER.XLA file; otherwise, you get an error. If you encounter this error message, click on OK in the error dialog box, then use the Tools/References menu item and check the SOLVER.XLA box. (You may have to "Browse" to find the SOLVER.XLA file. It is usually under the Excel\Library\Solver directory.) Once this reference is established, the application should work.

it is possible that there is no feasible solution to the problem with the inputs you entered. In this case you will see the NoSolution sheet. (See Figure 2.21.) It simply indicates that the Solver was unable to find a solution to your problem. In most cases, however, the problem will have a feasible solution. In this case you will see the Report sheet, which summarizes the optimal solution in nontechnical terms. (See Figure 2.22, which presents a solution for a four-month problem.) After studying this report, you are then allowed to push the Solve Another Problem button, which takes you back to the Control sheet so that you can solve a new problem.

FIGURE 2.21 **No Solution Sheet for Pigskin Application**

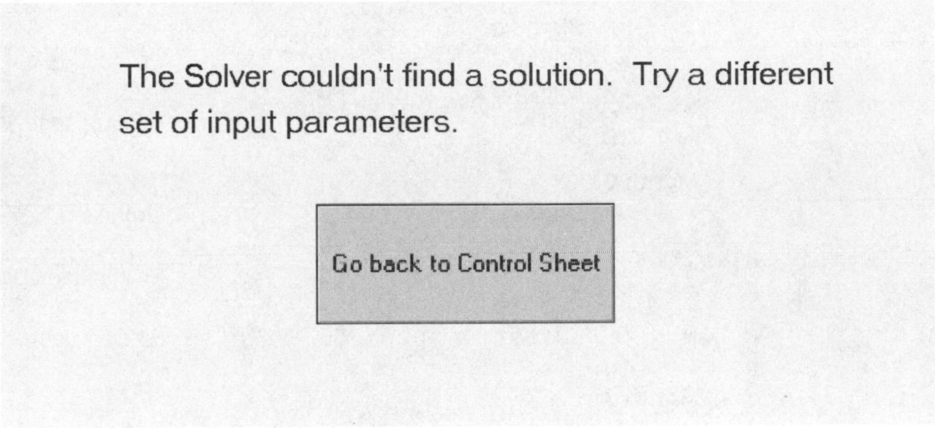

All of this is done automatically by means of the Excel macros on the Module sheet. These macros use Microsoft's Visual Basic for Applications (VBA) programming language to automate various tasks. We will not explain any of the details of this language, but you are welcome to look at the code in the Module sheet and see if you can get some sense of what it's doing. Of course, in most professional applications the Formulation and Module sheets would be hidden (and protected) from the end user. These nontechnical people have no need to know the details behind the application (and should not be given access to anything that they could inadvertently damage). They only need to enter inputs and look at reports.

2.11 Conclusion

This chapter has provided you with a good start in both LP modeling and spreadsheet modeling in general. You have learned how to formulate two simple LP models on spreadsheets, how to recognize whether a mathematical programming model satisfies the linear assumptions, how to use a spreadsheet Solver to find the optimal solution for an LP model, and how to interpret the information in the Solver's answer and sensitivity reports. In the next two chapters you will see a variety of other LP models, some considerably more complex than those discussed so far. Then in Chapters 5 and 6, you will get a chance to relax the linear assumptions and solve problems with integer variables and/or nonlinear relationships.

FIGURE 2.22 Report Sheet for Pigskins Application

Summary of optimal solution

Planning horizon (months)	4	
Total production cost	$10,839.00	
Total holding cost	$63.44	
Total cost	$10,902.44	

Solve Another Problem

Monthly schedule (scroll down to see more)

Month 1

Units		**Dollars**	
Start with	50		
Produce	50	Production cost	$625.00
Demand is	100		
End with	0	Holding cost	($0.00)

Month 2

Units		**Dollars**	
Start with	0		
Produce	200	Production cost	$2,525.00
Demand is	150		
End with	50	Holding cost	$31.57

Month 3

Units		**Dollars**	
Start with	50		
Produce	300	Production cost	$3,825.39
Demand is	300		
End with	50	Holding cost	$31.88

Month 4

Units		**Dollars**	
Start with	50		
Produce	300	Production cost	$3,863.64
Demand is	350		
End with	0	Holding cost	$0.00

REVIEW PROBLEMS

Skill-Building Problems

8 Peg and Al Fundy have a limited food budget, so Peg is trying to feed the family as cheaply as possible. However, Peg still wants to make sure her family members meet their daily nutritional requirements. Peg can buy two foods. Food 1 sells for $7 per pound, and each pound contains three units of vitamin A and one unit of vitamin C. Food 2 sells for $1 per pound, and each pound contains one unit of each vitamin. Each day, the family needs at least twelve units of vitamin A and six units of vitamin C.

a Verify that Peg should purchase twelve units of food 2 each day and thus oversatisfy the vitamin C requirement by six units.

b Al has put his foot down and demanded that Peg fulfill the family's daily nutritional requirement exactly by obtaining precisely twelve units of vitamin A and six units of vitamin C. The optimal solution to the new problem will involve ingesting less vitamin C, but it will be more expensive. Why?

9 Bloomington Brewery produces beer and ale. Beer sells for $5 per barrel, and ale sells for $2 per barrel. Producing a barrel of beer requires 5 pounds of corn and 2 pounds of hops. Producing a barrel of ale requires 2 pounds of corn and 1 pound of hops. The brewery has 60 pounds of corn and 25 pounds of hops.

a Use Excel's Solver to maximize Bloomington Brewery's revenue.

b Confirm graphically that the solution in Part (a) maximizes Bloomington Brewery's revenue.

10 A gourmet cook bakes two types of cake (chocolate and vanilla) to supplement her income. Each chocolate cake can be sold for $12, and each vanilla cake can be sold for $9. Each chocolate cake requires 20 minutes of baking time and uses 4 eggs. Each vanilla cake requires 40 minutes of baking time and uses 1 egg. The baker has 8 hours of baking time and 30 eggs.

a Use Excel's Solver to determine how the cook can maximize her profit.

b Confirm graphically that the solution in Part (a) maximizes the cook's profit.

11 For a telephone survey, a marketing research group needs to contact at least 150 wives, 120 husbands, 100 single adult males, and 110 single adult females. It costs $2 to make a daytime call and (because of higher labor costs) $5 to make an evening call. Table 2.4 lists the results that can be expected. For example, 30% of all daytime calls are answered by a wife, and 15% of all evening calls are answered by a single male. Because of a limited staff, at most half of all phone calls can be evening calls. Determine how to minimize the cost of completing the survey.

TABLE 2.4 Data for Phone Problem

Person Responding	Percentage of Daytime Calls	Percentage of Evening Calls
Wife	30	30
Husband	10	30
Single male	10	15
Single female	10	20
None	40	5

12 Woodco manufactures tables and chairs. Each table and chair must be made entirely out of oak or entirely out of pine. A total of 150 board feet of oak and 210 board feet of pine are available. A table requires either 17 board feet of oak or 30 board feet of pine, and a chair requires either 5 board feet of oak or 13 board feet of pine. Each table can be sold for $40, and each chair for $15. Determine how Woodco can maximize its revenue.

13 Alden Enterprises produces two products. Each product can be produced on one of two machines. The length of time needed to produce each product (in hours) on each machine is shown in Table 2.5. Each month, 500 hours of time are available on each machine. Each month, customers are willing to buy up to the quantities of each product at the prices given in Table 2.6. The company's goal is to maximize the revenue obtained from selling units during the next two months. Determine how it can meet this goal.

TABLE 2.5 Machine Times for Alden Problem

	Machine 1	Machine 2
Product 1	4	3
Product 2	7	4

14 There are three factories on the Momiss River: 1, 2, and 3. Each emits two types of pollutants, labeled P1 and P2, into the river. If the waste from each factory is processed, the pollution

TABLE 2.6 **Demands and Prices for Alden Problem**

	Demands		Prices	
	Month 1	**Month 2**	**Month 1**	**Month 2**
Product 1	100	190	$55	$12
Product 2	140	130	$65	$32

in the river can be reduced. It costs $15 to process a ton of factory 1 waste, and each ton processed reduces the amount of P1 by 0.10 ton and the amount of P2 by 0.45 ton. It costs $10 to process a ton of factory 2 waste, and each ton processed will reduce the amount of P1 by 0.20 ton and the amount of P2 by 0.25 ton. It costs $20 to process a ton of factory 3 waste, and each ton processed will reduce the amount of P1 by 0.40 ton and the amount of P2 by 0.30 ton. The state wants to reduce the amount of P1 in the river by at least 30 tons and the amount of P2 by at least 40 tons.

a Use Excel's Solver to determine how to minimize the cost of reducing pollution by the desired amounts.

b Do you think that the LP assumptions (proportionality, additivity, and divisibility) are reasonable for this problem?

Skill-Extending Problems

15 Money manager Boris Milkem deals with French currency (the franc) and American currency (the dollar). At 12 midnight, he can buy francs by paying 0.25 dollars per franc, and he can buy dollars by paying 3 francs per dollar. Assume that both types of transactions take place simultaneously and the only constraint is that Boris must have a nonnegative number of francs and dollars at 12:01 A.M.

a Use Excel's Solver to maximize the number of dollars Boris can obtain after all transactions are completed.

b Confirm graphically that the solution in Part (a) maximizes the number of dollars Boris has after all transactions are completed.

16 U.S. Labs manufactures mechanical heart valves from the heart valves of pigs. Different heart operations require valves of different sizes. U.S. Labs purchases pig valves from three different suppliers. The cost and size mix of the valves purchased from each supplier are given in Table 2.7. Each month, U.S. Labs places an order with each supplier. At least 500 large, 300 medium, and 300 small valves must be purchased each month. Because of limited availability of pig valves, at most 500 valves per month can be purchased from each supplier. Use Excel's Solver to determine how U.S. Labs can minimize the cost of acquiring the needed valves.

TABLE 2.7 **Data for U.S. Labs Problem**

	Cost per Valve	Percentage Small	Percentage Medium	Percentage Large
Supplier 1	$5	40	40	20
Supplier 2	$4	30	35	35
Supplier 3	$3	20	20	60

17 Sailco Corporation must determine how many sailboats to produce during each of the next four quarters. The demand during each of the next four quarters is as follows: first quarter, 40 sailboats; second quarter, 60 sailboats; third quarter, 75 sailboats; fourth quarter, 25 sailboats. Sailco must meet demands on time. At the beginning of the first quarter, Sailco has an inventory of 10 sailboats. At the beginning of each quarter, Sailco must decide how many sailboats to produce during that quarter. For simplicity, we assume that sailboats manufactured during a quarter can be used to meet demand for that quarter. During each quarter, Sailco can produce up to 40 sailboats with regular-time labor at a total cost of $400 per sailboat. By having employees work overtime during a quarter, Sailco can produce additional sailboats with overtime labor at a total cost of $450 per sailboat. At the end of each quarter (after production has occurred and the current quarter's demand has been satisfied), a holding cost of $20 per sailboat is incurred. Determine a production schedule to minimize the sum of production and inventory holding costs during the next four quarters.

18 Manufactco produces two types of products: A and B. The company has agreed to deliver the products on the schedule shown in Table 2.8. The company has two assembly lines, 1 and 2, with available production hours shown in Table 2.9. The production rate for each assembly line and product combination, in terms of hours per product, is shown in Table 2.10. For example, it takes 0.15 hour to manufacture one unit of product A on line 1, and so on. It costs $5 per hour of line time to produce any product. The inventory carrying cost per month for each product is 20¢ per unit (charged on each month's ending inventory). At present, there are 500 units of A and 750 units of B in inventory. Manufactco would like at least 1000 units of each product in inventory at the end of April. Determine the production schedule that minimizes the total cost incurred in meeting the company's demands on time.

TABLE 2.8 **Demands for Manufactco Problem**

	A	B
March 31	5000	2000
April 30	8000	4000

TABLE 2.9 **Production Hours for Manufactco Problem**

	Line 1	Line 2
March	8000	2000
April	4000	1200

TABLE 2.10 **Production Rates for Manufactco Problem**

	Line 1	Line 2
Product A	.15	.16
Product B	.12	.14

19 During the next two months General Cars must meet (on time) the following demands for trucks and cars: month 1, 400 trucks and 800 cars; month 2, 300 trucks and 300 cars. During each month at most 1000 vehicles can be produced. Each truck uses two tons of steel, and each car uses one ton of steel. During month 1, steel costs $400 per ton; during month 2, steel costs $600 per ton. At most 2500 tons of steel can be purchased each month. (Steel can be used only during the month in which it is purchased.) At the beginning of month 1, 100 trucks and 200 cars are in inventory. At the end of each month, a holding cost of $150 per vehicle is assessed. Each car gets 20 mpg, and each truck gets 10 mpg. During each month, the vehicles produced by the company must average at least 16 mpg. Determine how to meet the demand and mileage requirements at minimum total cost.

20 The Deckers Clothing Company produces shirts and pants. Each shirt requires two square yards of cloth, and each pair of pants requires three square yards of cloth. During the next two months the following demands for shirts and pants must be met (on time): month 1, 1000 shirts and 1500 pairs of pants; month 2, 1200 shirts and 1400 pairs of pants. During each month the following resources are available: month 1, 9000 square yards of cloth; month 2, 6000 square yards of cloth. (Cloth that is available during month 1 and is not used can be used during month 2.) During each month it costs $4 to make an article of clothing with regular-time labor and $8 with overtime labor. During each month a total of at most 2500 articles of clothing can be produced with regular-time labor, and an unlimited number of articles of clothing can be produced with overtime labor. At the end of each month, a holding cost of $3 per article of clothing is assessed. Determine how to meet demands for the next two months (on time) at minimum cost. Assume that at the beginning of month 1, 100 shirts and 200 pairs of pants are available.

21 Each year, Comfy Shoes faces demands (which must be met on time) for pairs of shoes as shown in Table 2.11. Workers work three consecutive quarters and then receive one quarter off. For example, a worker might work during quarters 3 and 4 of one year and quarter 1 of the next year. During a quarter in which a worker works, he or she can produce up to 500 pairs of shoes. Each worker is paid $5000 per quarter. At the end of each quarter, a holding cost of $10 per pair of shoes is assessed. Determine how to minimize the cost per year (labor plus holding) of meeting the demands for shoes. To simplify matters, assume that at the end of each year, the ending inventory is zero. (*Hint*: You may assume that a given worker will get the *same* quarter off during each year.)

TABLE 2.11 Demands for Comfy Shoes Problem

	Demand
Quarter 1	6000
Quarter 2	3000
Quarter 3	8000
Quarter 4	1000

22 A company must meet (on time) the following demands: quarter 1, 3000 units; quarter 2, 2000 units; quarter 3, 4000 units. Each quarter, up to 2700 units can be produced with regular-time labor, at a cost of $40 per unit. During each quarter, an unlimited number of units can be produced with overtime labor, at a cost of $60 per unit. Of all units produced, 20% are unsuitable and cannot be used to meet demand. Also, at the end of each quarter, 10% of all units on hand spoil and cannot be used to meet any future demands. After each quarter's demand is satisfied and spoilage is accounted for, a cost of $15 per unit is assessed against the quarter's ending inventory. Determine how to minimize the total cost of meeting the next three quarters' demands. Assume that 1000 usable units are available at the beginning of quarter 1. ■

Appendix: What's Best! for Lotus

On this book we have chosen Microsoft Excel as the preferred spreadsheet package. For many reasons, including its Solver, its statistical capabilities, and its macro language, it is today's premier spreadsheet package. However, Lotus 1-2-3, particularly the Windows version, is a worthy competitor with much of the same functionality of Excel. While we do not believe that the built-in Solver packaged with Lotus for Windows is comparable to Excel's Solver, there is an excellent Lotus add-in called What's Best! that we recommend. In this appendix we will briefly describe how to use What's Best! With this explanation Lotus users should be able to follow the mathematical programming chapters (2 through 7) with no difficulty.

Before getting into details about What's Best! it is important to understand that LP problem solving on a spreadsheet is a two-step procedure. The first step is to model the problem on the spreadsheet by entering all of the inputs and using formulas to relate various quantities. The second step is then to invoke the Solver. Here we specify the target cell, the changing cells, and the constraints and then ask the Solver to find the optimal solution. Excel and Lotus are virtually identical in the first step. The only real difference is that every formula in Excel begins with an equals sign, such as

Excel:=SUMPRODUCT(C7:C9,D7:D9)

whereas Lotus formulas begin with one of several symbols (usually @, +, or a left parenthesis), as in

Lotus:@SUMPRODUCT(C7..C9,D7..D9)

(Also, as this formula illustrates, Lotus uses two periods rather than a colon to indicate a range.) Other than these syntax differences, which we assume Lotus users are aware of, the spreadsheet LP setups in Lotus and Excel are virtually indistinguishable. In fact, we have purposely set up all of the Excel spreadsheets in the mathematical programming chapters so that they can be translated directly to Lotus spreadsheets.

The second step, however, is different. As we mentioned, Lotus for Windows also has a built-in Solver, but we do not recommend using it. A much better option for Lotus users is the third-party add-in What's Best! It must be installed separately from Lotus for Windows. Once it is installed, it appears as a WB! main menu item. You use the first three submenu items—Adjustable, Best, and Constrain—to identify the changing cells, the target cell, and the constraints. You then use the Solve submenu item to solve the problem. We now discuss each of these for Monet's product mix problem.

The layout of the spreadsheet itself is almost exactly the same as in Excel. The only difference is that the *optional* constraint indications we used in Excel, that is, the cells with <=, >=, or = labels, are replaced with special What's Best! formulas, as discussed below.[10] So the starting point for a What's Best! setup is basically the same as the starting point for Excel. The first step is then to use the WB!/Adjustable menu item to identify the changing cells (which What's Best! calls **adjustable cells**). This produces the dialog box in Figure 2.23. A convenient feature of Lotus is that you can click on the arrow next to any input box and the whole dialog box will disappear until you select the relevant range. This keeps the dialog box out of your way while you make your selection.

FIGURE 2.23 **What's Best! Adjustable Dialog Box**

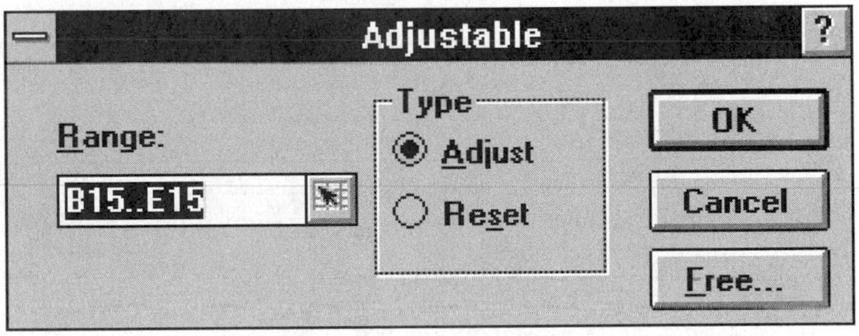

Notice the Free box. Unlike Excel's Solver, What's Best! assumes that all of the changing cells are nonnegative unless you specify otherwise. Therefore, you do *not* need to specify nonnegativity constraints explicitly. If you do have changing cells that are allowed to be negative, you specify them with the Free option. Free simply means that these values are "free" to be positive or negative.

You next set the target cell (called the **best cell** by What's Best!) with the WB!/Best menu item. The corresponding dialog box appears in Figure 2.24. You'll notice that after

[10]In fact, we used these optional labels in our Excel formulations for two reasons. First, we believe they are helpful in setting up and understanding the constraints. For example, they almost require you to put the left-hand sides and right-hand sides of constraints near each other on the spreadsheet. Second, however, these Excel labels make the Excel formulation look identical to the What's Best! formulation.

FIGURE 2.24 **What's Best! "Best" Dialog Box**

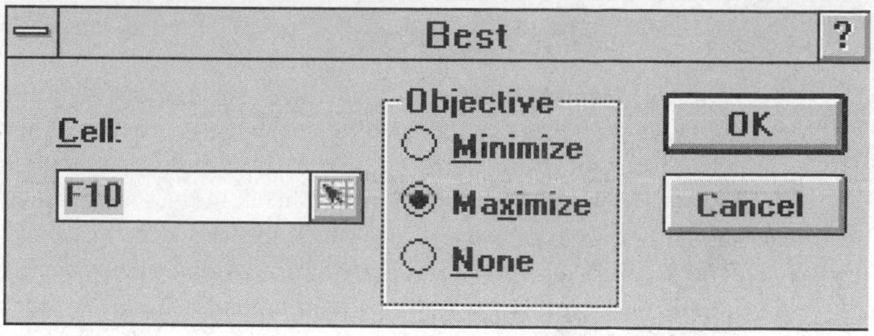

you select the target cell, this cell is automatically named WBMAX (or WBMIN for a minimization problem).

The final step before solving is to specify the constraints. When you choose the WB!/Constrain menu item, you'll see the dialog box shown in Figure 2.25. It includes boxes for the left-hand side and right-hand side ranges of the constraint, as well as the type of constraint (<=, >=, or =). You must also specify a range to store the constraints. Typically, you should select this range as the "gutter" between the left-hand side and right-hand side of the constraints. (This is where we put the <=, >=, or = labels in Excel.) What's Best! puts its own formulas in these cells just to remind it what the constraints are. For example, the formula in cell G6 is

@<<WB>>WB(F6,"<=",H6)

What's Best! enters this formula automatically in G6—you don't type it in—from the information in the constrain dialog box. You may open this dialog box as many times as you need to enter all of your constraints.

FIGURE 2.25 **What's Best! Constrain Dialog Box**

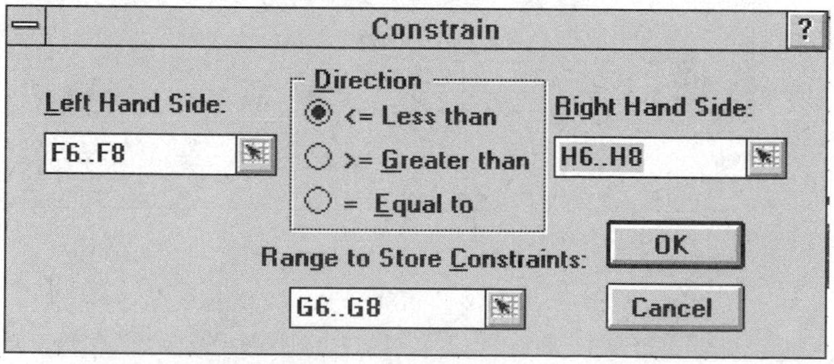

It is not necessary that the left-hand side, the information about the constraints, and the right-hand side be in nearby rows (or columns). However this is a good programming practice. In fact, we have set up all of the examples in the book this way, which has allowed us to use the same basic spreadsheets for both Excel and Lotus.

Once all of the information about the problem—the adjustable cells, the target cell, and the constraints—has been entered, you find the optimal solution with the WB!/Solve menu item. (Unlike Excel, you do *not* need to check an Assume Linear Model box. What's Best! automatically uses the simplex method whenever it recognizes that the model is linear.) When you select WB!/Solve, you see the dialog box shown in Figure 2.26. By default, What's Best! saves your current (probably nonoptimal) spreadsheet in a file WBTO, and it saves the spreadsheet with optimal values in a file WBFR. (It also saves error messages, if there are any, in a file WBERR.) Eventually, you will probably want to change these file names to more informative names.

FIGURE 2.26 **What's Best! Solve Dialog Box**

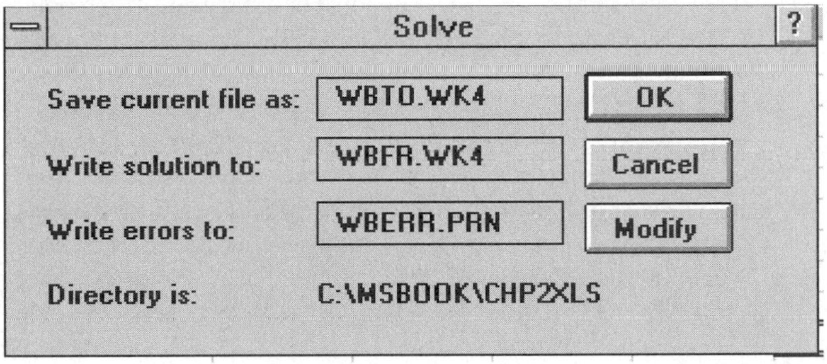

When you finally click on OK in the Solve dialog box, What's Best! appears to take you out of Lotus into never-never land. It displays a screen that shows its progress, and it shows you a blank screen for awhile. However, don't panic. You will eventually be returned to Lotus, with the optimal solution shown.

The solution to this problem appears in Figure 2.27. This is exactly the same solution that Excel's Solver produced, as we would expect. The only reason for showing it again is to point out how What's Best! indicates whether inequality constraints are binding (equality) or nonbinding. For example, the labor constraint in the labor hours row turns out to be a binding constraint—all 4000 labor hours are used. What's Best! indicates this with a "=<=" sign. However, the glass constraint in the glass row turns out to be nonbinding—not all of the 10,000 units are used. What's Best! indicates this with a "<=" sign. So if

FIGURE 2.27 **What's Best! Solution for Monet's Product Mix Example**

A	A	B	C	D	E	F	G	H
1	**Product Mix Problem with Optimal Solution**							
2								
3	**Input data**							
4			**Frame Type**					
5		1	2	3	4	Total used		Total available
6	Labor hours per frame	2	1	3	2	4000	=<=	4000
7	Metal (oz.) per frame	4	2	1	2	6000	=<=	6000
8	Glass (oz.) per frame	6	2	1	2	8000	<=	10000
9						**Total profit**		
10	Profit per frame	$6.00	$2.00	$4.00	$3.00	$9,200.00		
11								
12	**Production plan**							
13			**Frame Type**					
14		1	2	3	4			
15	Frames produced	1000	800	400	0			
16		=<=	<=	<=	<=			
17	Maximum sales	1000	2000	500	1000			

the original inequality sign is preceded by an equals sign, that constraint is an equality; otherwise, it is a strict inequality.

Besides providing indications of binding versus nonbinding constraints with the =<= symbols, What's Best! provides an optional solution report analogous to Excel's sensitivity report. To obtain it, you use the WB!/Report command and then check the Enable box under Solution. You can also specify the name of the file where this report will be placed. After you solve the problem, you can then use the WB!/Report command again to retrieve the solution report.

The solution report for the product mix problem appears in Figure 2.28. There are three areas in this report. The first just lists the value of the objective. The second area has a row for each adjustable (changing) cell. The final (optimal) values are shown, as well as dual values. (In this area dual values are analogous to Excel's reduced costs, except for a minus sign.) As we described for reduced costs, the dual value for any variable at a positive level is always zero. However, if a variable is currently zero, such as the number of type 4 frames produced, then its dual value indicates how much more profitable it would have to be before the company would begin to produce it. Since the current unit profit for type 4 frames is $3.00, this would have to increase to $3.20 before type 4 frames would be attractive.

FIGURE 2.28 What's Best! Solution Report for Monet's Product Mix Problem

OBJECTIVE CELL:

CELL ADDRESS	VALUE	INITIAL VALUE	TYPE
_A_F10	9200	9200	MAX

ADJUSTABLE CELLS:

CELL ADDRESS	VALUE	INITIAL VALUE	TYPE	DUAL VALUE	UPPER RANGE	LOWER RANGE
_A_B15	1000	1000	>	0	1000	+Inf
_A_C15	800	800	>	0	800	+Inf
_A_D15	400	400	>	0	400	+Inf
_A_E15	0	0	>	.2000001	1000	250

CONSTRAINT CELLS:

CELL ADDRESS	VALUE	TYPE	DUAL VALUE	UPPER RANGE	LOWER RANGE	FORMULA
_A_G6	0	<	1.2	250	1000	F6,<=,H6
_A_G7	0	<	.4	1999	500	F7,<=,H7
_A_G8	2000	<	0	+Inf	2000	F8,<=,H8
_A_B16	0	<	2	400	600	B15,<=,B17
_A_C16	1200	<	0	+Inf	1200	C15,<=,C17
_A_D16	100	<	0	+Inf	100	D15,<=,D17
_A_E16	1000	<	0	+Inf	1000	E15,<=,E17

The third area of the report, the constraint area, has a row for each of the constraints (not including the nonnegativity constraints). For this problem there are two groups of constraints—the availability constraints for the scarce resources and the upper bounds for the adjustable cells. The availability constraints are listed first. For each of them there is a dual value. (In this area dual values correspond to the shadow prices in the Excel report.) The dual value for a binding constraint indicates how much Monet would be willing to pay for an extra unit of that resource. For example, the dual value of 1.2 for the labor hour constraint means that the company would be willing to purchase an extra labor hour for $1.20.

The upper and lower ranges indicate where this dual value is applicable. That is, each extra labor hour, up to the first 250, is worth an extra $1.20 in profit, whereas each labor hour lost, up to the first 1000, means a loss of $1.20 in profit. Beyond these ranges, we cannot tell the value of an extra labor hour except by rerunning What's Best!

If a constraint is nonbinding, then its dual value is automatically zero. This is especially intuitive for a nonbinding resource constraint like the glass constraint. If the company currently has more of a resource than it is using, then it certainly makes no sense to pay for more of it. Hence, its dual value is zero. In fact, it will stay zero no matter how much *larger* the availability of glass might be, and it will stay zero unless the availability of glass is reduced below its current slack, that is, 2000 ounces. Therefore, the upper and lower ranges for the glass constraint are "infinity" and 2000, respectively.

Summary of Important Differences Between Excel's Solver and What's Best!

1 You do *not* have to specify nonnegativity constraints explicitly in What's Best!; in current versions of Excel, you do.

2 You *must* designate cells for special constraint formulas in What's Best! (although What's Best! enters these formulas for you when you specify the constraints in the dialog box); in Excel, such cells are not needed, but we have used them for optional labels to indicate the constraints.

3 What's Best! indicates whether constraints are binding or nonbinding in the spreadsheet itself (with such notation as =<= or <=); Excel does not do this, but you can find the same information in its answer report.

4 You do *not* have to check an Assume Linear Model box in What's Best!; in Excel, you do if you want it to use the simplex method.

5 What's Best!'s solution report refers to *dual values*; Excel's sensitivity report refers to *reduced costs* and *shadow prices*. However, these concepts are identical.

6 What's Best! does not support array formulas or functions, such as TRANSPOSE, MMULT, and VLOOKUP, which we use in several examples in this book.

7 What's Best! must be purchased separately from Lotus for Windows; Excel's Solver is part of the Excel package.

CASE STUDY

Shelby Shelving

Shelby Shelving is a small company that manufactures two types of shelves for grocery stores. Model S is the standard model, and model LX is a heavy-duty model. Shelves are manufactured in three major steps: stamping, forming, and assembly. In the stamping stage, a large machine is used to stamp, i.e., cut, standard sheets of metal into appropriate sizes. In the forming stage, another machine bends the metal into shape. Assembly involves joining the parts with a combination of soldering and riveting. Shelby's stamping and forming machines work on both models of shelves. Separate assembly departments are used for the final stage of production.

Table 2.12 shows the amount of machine time needed for each product. For example, the production of one model S shelf requires 0.25 hour on the forming machine. Both the stamping and forming machines can operate for 800 hours each month. The model S assembly department has a monthly capacity of 1900 units. The model LX assembly department has a monthly capacity of only 1400 units. Currently Shelby is producing and selling 400 units of model S and 1400 units of model LX per month.

Model S shelves are sold for $1800, and model LX shelves are sold for $2100. Shelby's operation is fairly small in the industry, and management at Shelby believes it cannot raise prices beyond these levels because of the competition. However, the marketing department feels that Shelby can sell as much as it can produce at these prices. The costs of production are summarized in Tables 2.13 and 2.14.

Management at Shelby just met to discuss next month's operating plan. Although the shelves are selling well, the overall profitability of the company was a concern. The plant's engineer suggested that the current production of model S shelves be cut back. "Model S shelves are sold for $1800 per unit, but our costs are $1839. Even though we're only selling 400 units a month, we're losing money on each one. We should decrease production of model S." The controller disagreed. He said that the problem was the model S assembly department trying to absorb a large overhead with a small production volume. "The model S units are making a contribution to overhead. Even though production doesn't cover all of the fixed costs, we'd be worse off with lower production."

Questions

What would you recommend to Shelby? How would their profitability change under your recommendation?

Note on Tables 2.13 and 2.14: The fixed overhead is distributed using activity-based costing principles. For example, at current production levels, the forming machine spends 100 hours on model S shelves and 700 hours on model LX shelves. The forming machine is used 800 hours of the month, of which 12.5% of the time is spent on model S shelves and 87.5% is spent on model LX shelves. The $95,000 of fixed overhead in the forming department is distributed as $11,875 (= 95,000 × 0.125) to model S shelves and $83,125 (= 95,000 × 0.875) to model LX shelves. The fixed overhead *per unit of output* is allocated as $29.69 (= 11,875/400) for model S and $59.38 (= 83,125/1400) for model LX. In the calculation of the standard overhead cost, the fixed and variable costs are added together. In Table 2.13, the overhead cost for the forming department allocated to a model S shelf is $149.69 (= 29.69 + 120). Similarly, the overhead cost for the forming department allocated to a model LX shelf is $229.38 (= 59.38 + 170). ■

Acknowledgment: This case was adapted from the Sherman Motor Company case. Thanks to Ram Ramakrishnan for his helpful comments.

TABLE 2.12 Machine Usage Requirements (hours per unit)

Machine	Model S	Model LX
Stamping	0.30	0.30
Forming	0.25	0.50

TABLE 2.13 Standard Costs of the Shelves

	Model S		Model LX	
Direct materials		1000		1200
Direct labor				
Stamping	35		35	
Forming	60		90	
Assembly	80		85	
Subtotal		175		210
Overhead†				
Stamping	149		159	
Forming	150		229	
Assembly	365		246	
Subtotal		664		635
Total		1839		2045

†See Table 2.14 and the note that follows.

TABLE 2.14 Overhead Budget

	Total Overhead per Month (in \$1000s)†	Fixed Overhead per Month (in \$1000s)	Variable Overhead per Unit	
			Model S	Model LX
Stamping	283	125	80	90
Forming	381	95	120	170
Model S Assembly	146	80	165	—
Model LX Assembly	344	85	—	185
Total	1154	385	365	445

†Based on current production of 400 units of model S and 1400 units of model LX.

REFERENCES

1 Dantzig, G. "The Diet Problem." *Interfaces* 20, no. 4 (1990): 43–47.

2 Lancaster, L. "The Evolution of the Diet Model in Managing Food Systems." *Interfaces* 22, no. 5 (1992): 59–68.

3

Linear Programming Formulations

CHAPTER

Management Science Success Stories

As we saw in the previous chapter, LP can be used for product mix decisions and inventory planning. This was the case at Libbey-Owens-Ford (LOF), a large plate glass company with 9000 employees and annual sales of $900 million. In the article "Integrated Production, Distribution, and Inventory Planning at Libbey-Owens-Ford," Martin, Dent, and Eckhart [16] describe the process of building and implementing a large-scale LP model of the plate glass production and distribution process at LOF. The model (named FLAGPOL for *FLA*t *G*lass *P*roducts *O*ptimization Mode*L*) deals with four manufacturing plants, over 200 separate glass products, and over 40 demand centers in a 12-month planning horizon. The development of the model took over two years to complete, but since then it has resulted in annual savings of over $2 million.

The production of plate glass is an extremely complex manufacturing process. The glass is produced in large batches, each batch producing a certain color or tint of glass. The reason the batches are large is that the time required to change from one tint to another is very long (on the order of two to four days). Therefore, production occurs in cycles of approximately ten months, and a particular tint is produced only once during a cycle. Given these long cycles, inventory planning is crucial. The production quantity of a particular tint in a cycle must be large enough to cover orders, both planned and forecasted, for a long period of time. Another complication is the cutting process. The glass is produced in long "ribbons" that can be cut to various dimensions. If the cuts are made during the production processing, yields tend to be higher than if they are made off-line, after processing. However, off-line cuts are sometimes necessary when orders arrive for nonstandard dimensions of glass.

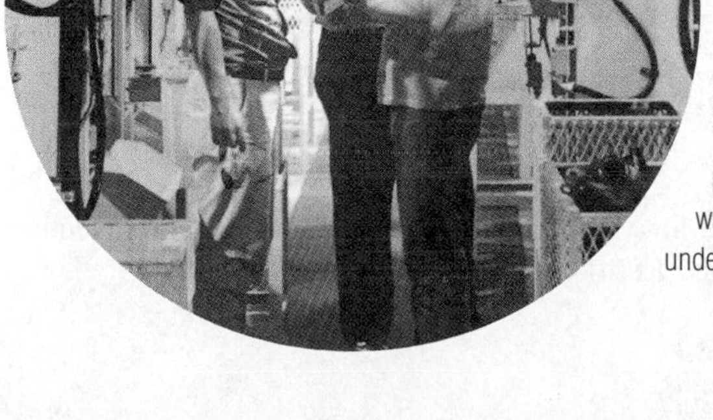

The management at LOF decided that the complexity of the entire process necessitated a formal model. Therefore, the company appointed a task force to develop an LP model of the process. Since the task force included staff members from finance, marketing, MIS, materials management, transportation, production planning, and representatives from the plants, the scope of the resulting model became very broad. The first step was to develop the database that would support the model. This was a major undertaking since data were required on market demand and sales prices, freight rates, production rates and yields, manufacturing costs, inventory levels, and interplant rail schedules. Once these data were available, the FLAGPOL model was then built, tested, and finally implemented. The implementation process itself took about nine months. During this time, several changes to the original model were required. For example, the company realized that differences in the cost accounting systems of the various plants needed to be addressed. Also, the model's reports were redesigned to make them more useful and comprehensible to the eventual users.

Now that FLAGPOL is fully implemented, it is run 10 to 20 times each month for short-run tactical plans, as well as for longer-range strategical decisions. At the tactical level, the model recommends how much of each product to produce at each plant each month, how much of each product to ship between plants each month, how much of each product to cut off-line at each plant each month, and how much inventory to hold of each product at each plant each month. At the strategic level, FLAGPOL has been used to address such issues as (1) planning the transition from a two-plant operation to a four-plant operation, (2) introducing new products or eliminating existing products from plants, (3) developing schedules for major construction and plant maintenance, and (4) analyzing possible locations and sizing for new facilities. Management at LOF now considers FLAGPOL an integrated part of the company's planning process. It helps the company to reduce costs, increase profits, and enhance overall customer service. ■

3.1 Introduction

In a survey of Fortune 500 firms, 85% of those responding said that they used linear programming. In this chapter we will discuss some of the LP models that are most often applied to real-world applications. In the chapter's examples and problems you will discover how to

- schedule bank clerks for check encoding
- optimize the operation of an oil refinery
- plan dairy production at a creamery
- schedule production of fiberglass products at Owens-Corning Fiberglass
- optimize a Wall Street firm's bond portfolio

Actually, these problems are just a sampling of the many problems we will model with LP in this chapter. There are two basic goals in this chapter. The first is to illustrate some of the many real applications that can take advantage of LP. You'll see that these applications cover a wide range; from oil production to worker scheduling to cash management. The second goal is to increase your facility in modeling LP problems on a spreadsheet. We will present a few principles that will help you model a wide variety of problems. The best way to learn, however, is to see many examples and work through numerous problems. In short, mastering the art of LP spreadsheet modeling takes hard work and practice. You'll have plenty of opportunity to do each with the material in this chapter.

3.2 Static Workforce Scheduling

Many organizations must determine how to schedule employees to provide adequate service. Here is an example of how to use LP to schedule employees.

EXAMPLE 3.1

A post office requires different numbers of full-time employees on different days of the week. The number of full-time employees required each day is given in Table 3.1. Union rules state that each full-time employee must work five consecutive days and then receive two days off. For example, an employee who works Monday to Friday must be off on Saturday and Sunday. The post office wants to meet its daily requirements using only full-time employees. Its objective is to minimize the number of full-time employees that must be hired.

TABLE 3.1 Employee Requirements for Post Office

	Minimum Employees Required
Monday	17
Tuesday	13
Wednesday	15
Thursday	19
Friday	14
Saturday	16
Sunday	11

Solution

To model the Post Office problem with a spreadsheet, we must keep track of the following:

- number of employees starting work on each day of the week
- number of employees working each day
- total number of employees

It is important to keep track of the number of employees starting work each day, because this is the only way to incorporate the fact that workers work five consecutive days. If you don't believe this, try solving the problem by just keeping track of the total number of employees and the number of employees working each day.

Developing the Spreadsheet Model The spreadsheet model for this problem appears in Figure 3.1. (See the file POSTAL.XLS.) To form this spreadsheet, proceed as follows.

1 **Daily requirements.** Enter the number of employees needed on each day of the week (from Table 3.1) in the range B9:H9.

FIGURE 3.1 Initial (Nonoptimal) Solution to Post Office Problem

	A	B	C	D	E	F	G	H	I
1	Post Office Scheduling Problem - Nonoptimal Solution								
2									
3					Starting day of 5-day shift				
4		Monday	Tuesday	Wednesday	Thursday	Friday	Saturday	Sunday	Total employees
5	Number starting	13	4	5	4	0	3	0	29
6									
7	Number working on each day	20	20	25	26	26	16	12	
8		>=	>=	>=	>=	>=	>=	>=	
9	Minimal number required each day	17	13	15	19	14	16	11	

2 **Employees beginning each day.** Enter *any* trial values for the number of employees beginning work on each day of the week in the range B5:H5.

3 **Employees on hand each day.** The important key to this solution is to realize that the numbers in row 5 do not represent the number of workers who will show up each day. As an example, the number who show up on Monday are those whose shifts start on either Monday or Thursday through Sunday. Therefore, calculate the number who show up on Monday by entering the formula

=B5+SUM(E5:H5)

in cell B7. Similarly, calculate the number who show up on Tuesday (those whose shift starts Monday, Tuesday, or Friday through Sunday) in cell C7 with the formula

=SUM(B5:C5)+SUM(F5:H5)

Continue this same logic through the rest of the range D7:H7 to calculate the number of employees who show up on each day. (Unfortunately, you can't use the copy command to do it all at once!)

4 **Total employees.** Calculate the total number of employees in cell I5 with the formula

=SUM(B5:H5)

At this point, you might want to try rearranging the numbers in row 5 to see if you can "guess" an optimal solution. It's not that easy! Each worker who starts on a given day works the next four days as well, so when you find a solution that meets the minimal requirements for the various days, you usually have many more workers available on some days than are needed.

Using the Solver Now invoke the Solver and specify the following:

1 **Objective.** Choose cell I5 (total number of employees) as the target cell to minimize.

2 **Changing cells.** Choose the range B5:H5 (number of employees beginning work each day) as the changing cells and constrain these to be nonnegative.

3 **Daily requirement constraints.** Enter the constraints B7:H7>=B9:H9. These constraints ensure that enough people are working each day.[1] After completing these steps, the Solver dialog box should appear as shown in Figure 3.2.

4 **Linear model and optimize.** Select the Assume Linear Model option and Solve to obtain the optimal solution shown in Figure 3.3.

This optimal solution requires the number of employees starting work on some days to be a fraction. Because part-time employees are not allowed, this solution is unrealistic. We will now show you how to solve the post office problem when the number of employees beginning work each day must be an integer.

Using the Solver with Integer Constraints In Excel's Solver, simply go to the Subject to the Constraints option and add the constraint B5:H5=Integer. To do this, you select "int" instead of <=, =, or >= in the Add Constraint window. When you select Assume Linear Model and then Solve, you obtain the solution in Figure 3.4.[2] This solution is represented graphically in Figure 3.5. Thus the post office needs to hire 23 full-time employees. This solution reveals an aspect of some modeling problems. Because of the

[1]Remember from the previous chapter that if you point to these ranges, they will appear in the Solver window as absolute cell addresses (that is, with $ signs). However, these $ signs are completely unnecessary, and we will not show them in the text.

[2]If you are using What's Best! for Lotus, you specify integer constraints with the WB!/Integer command. Then you choose the General option and select the range that you want to be integers (here B5..H5). What's Best! will label this range with a range name beginning with WBINT.

FIGURE 3.2 **Solver Dialog Box for Post Office Problem**

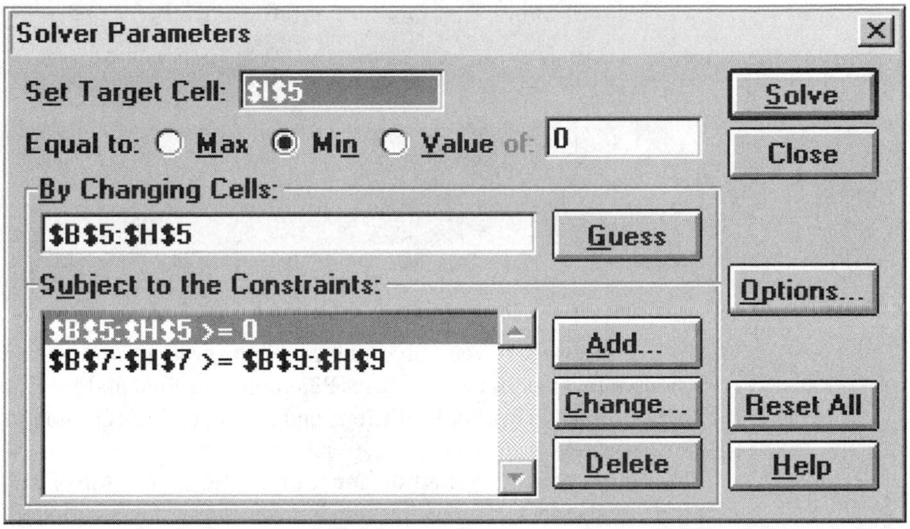

FIGURE 3.3 **Optimal (Noninteger) Solution to Post Office Problem**

	A	B	C	D	E	F	G	H	I
1	Post Office Scheduling Problem - Optimal Solution								
2									
3				Starting day of 5-day shift					
4		Monday	Tuesday	Wednesday	Thursday	Friday	Saturday	Sunday	Total employees
5	Number starting	6.33	3.33	2.00	7.33	0.00	3.33	0.00	22.33
6									
7	Number working on each day	17.00	13.00	15.00	19.00	19.00	16.00	12.67	
8		>=	>=	>=	>=	>=	>=	>=	
9	Minimal number required each day	17	13	15	19	14	16	11	

FIGURE 3.4 **Optimal Integer Solution to Post Office Problem**

	A	B	C	D	E	F	G	H	I
1	Post Office Scheduling Problem with Integer Constraints								
2									
3				Starting day of 5-day shift					
4		Monday	Tuesday	Wednesday	Thursday	Friday	Saturday	Sunday	Total employees
5	Number starting	7	4	2	8	0	2	0	23
6									
7	Number working on each day	17	13	15	21	21	16	12	
8		>=	>=	>=	>=	>=	>=	>=	
9	Minimal number required each day	17	13	15	19	14	16	11	

irregular daily requirements and two-consecutive-days-off contraint, no solution can match available workers to daily requirements. All solutions will have surplus workers some days. Sometimes the optimal solution to a modeling problem isn't the "perfect" solution you were looking for.

FIGURE 3.5 Graphical Representation of Solution to Post Office Problem

	Mon	Tues	Wed	Thurs	Fri	Sat	Sun
	7	7	7	7	7		
		4	4	4	4	4	
			2	2	2	2	2
	8			8	8	8	8
	0	0			0	0	0
	2	2	2			2	2
	0	0	0	0			0
Totals	17	13	15	21	21	16	12

By the way, if you solve this problem on your computer, you may get a different schedule that is still optimal (uses 23 employees total and meets all constraints). This is a case of **multiple optimal solutions** and is not at all uncommon in LP problems.

Creating a "Fair" Schedule for Employees The Solver solution to the post office problem shown in Figure 3.5 requires seven employees to start work on Monday, four on Tuesday, two on Wednesday, eight on Thursday, and two on Saturday. Certainly the four employees who begin work on Saturday will be unhappy, because they never get a weekend off! The Solver solution can be used to implement a "fairer" schedule that treats all employees in an equal fashion. We simply rotate the schedules of the employees over a 23-week period. To see how this is done, consider the following schedule:

- Weeks 1–7: Start on Monday
- Weeks 8–11: Start on Tuesday
- Weeks 12–13: Start on Wednesday
- Weeks 14–21: Start on Thursday
- Weeks 22–23: Start on Saturday

Employee 1 follows this schedule for a 23-week period. Employee 2 starts with week 2 of this schedule (start on Monday) and follows the schedule through week 23. For the last week of the 23-week period, employee 2 follows week 1 of the schedule (starts on Monday). We continue in this fashion to generate a 23-week schedule for each employee. For example, employee 13 will have the following schedule:

- Week 1: Start on Wednesday
- Weeks 2–9: Start on Thursday
- Weeks 10–11: Start on Saturday
- Weeks 12–18: Start on Monday
- Weeks 19–22: Start on Tuesday
- Week 23: Start on Wednesday

This method of scheduling treats each employee equally.

MODELING ISSUES

1 This example is called a **static** scheduling problem, because we assume that the post office faces the same situation each week. In reality, demands change over time, workers take vacations in the summer, and so on, so the post office does not face the same situation each week. **Dynamic** scheduling problems are discussed in Sections 3.5 and 3.6.

2 If you wanted to set up a weekly scheduling model for a supermarket or a fast-food restaurant, the number of variables could be very large and the computer might have difficulty finding an exact solution. In this situation *heuristic* methods can be used to find a good solution to the problem. See Love and Hoey [14] for an example of how this can be done.

3 Our model can easily be expanded to handle part-time employees, the use of overtime, and alternative objective functions such as maximizing the number of weekend days off received by employees. (See Problems 1, 3, and 4.)

4 How did we determine the number of workers needed each day? Perhaps the post office wants to have enough employees to ensure that 95% of all letters are sorted within an hour. To determine the number of employees that are needed to provide adequate service, the post office would need to use queueing theory, which is discussed in Chapter 11, and forecasting, which is discussed in Chapter 14. ■

EXAMPLE 3.1 CONTINUED

Sensitivity Analysis The most obvious type of sensitivity analysis involves examining how the work schedule and the total number of employees change as the number of employees required each day changes. When changing cells are required to be integers, the Solver will not produce a sensitivity report, since it would contain no useful information. Therefore, the only way to find the new optimal solution is to change the appropriate inputs and rerun the Solver.

Here is an example of what-if analysis. Suppose the number of employees needed on each day of the week increases by two, four, or six. How does this change the total number of employees needed? We simply solve the original problem three times. The first time we add two to each cell in the range B9:H9, the second time we add four, and the third time we add six. The results are shown in Table 3.2. When the requirement increases by two each day, only two extra employees are necessary (scheduled appropriately). However, when the requirement increases by four each day, *more* than four extra employees are necessary. This may surprise you at first, but there is an intuitive explanation: each extra worker works only five days of the week. ■

TABLE 3.2 **Sensitivity Results for Post Office Problem**

Increase in Daily Employee Requirement	Total Number of Employees Needed
2	25 (increase of 2 over original solution)
4	28 (increase of 5 over original solution)
6	31 (increase of 8 over original solution)

REAL-WORLD APPLICATION

Encoder Scheduling at Ohio National Bank

Krajewski, Ritzman, and McKenzie [12] used LP to schedule clerks who process checks at Ohio National Bank. Their model determined the minimum cost combination of part-time employees, full-time employees, and overtime labor needed to complete the processing of the checks received each day by the end of the workday (10 P.M.). The major input to their model was a forecast of the number of checks arriving at the bank each hour. This forecast was generated with a multiple regression (see Chapter 14). The major output of the LP was a work schedule. For example, the LP might suggest that 2 full-time employees work daily from 11 A.M. to 8 P.M., 33 part-time employees work every day from 1 P.M. to 6 P.M., and 27 part-time employees work from 6 P.M. to 10 P.M. on Monday, Tuesday, and Friday.

The LP approach to scheduling encoder clerks saved an estimated $80,000 per year in labor costs. The LP approach also resulted in faster processing of the checks. Before LP was used to schedule encoder clerks, the day's checks were rarely processed by the end of the day, whereas after LP was used, the day's checks were processed by the end of the day 98% of the time! For a simplified version of encoder scheduling see Problem 91. ■

PROBLEMS

Skill-Building Problems

1 In the post office example suppose that each full-time employee works eight hours per day. Thus, Monday's requirement of 17 workers can be viewed as a requirement of $8(17) = 136$ hours. The post office can meet its daily labor requirements by using both full-time and part-time employees. During each week a full-time employee works eight hours a day for five consecutive days, and a part-time employee works four hours a day for five consecutive days. A full-time employee costs the post office $15 per hour, whereas a part-time employee (with reduced fringe benefits) costs the post office only $10 per hour. Union requirements limit part-time labor to 25% of weekly labor requirements. Use the Solver to minimize the post office's weekly labor costs. Discuss how a change in the part-time labor limitation influences the problem's optimal solution.

2 During each four-hour period, the Smalltown police force requires the following number of on-duty police officers: eight from midnight to 4 A.M.; seven from 4 A.M. to 8 A.M.; six from 8 A.M. to noon; six from noon to 4 P.M.; five from 4 P.M. to 8 P.M.; and four from 8 P.M. to midnight. Each police officer works two consecutive four-hour shifts. Determine how to minimize the number of police officers needed to meet Smalltown's daily requirements.

Skill-Extending Problems

3 In the post office example, suppose that the post office can force employees to work one day of overtime each week. For example, an employee whose regular shift is Monday to Friday can also be required to work on Saturday. Each employee is paid $50 a day for each of the first five days worked during a week and $62 for the overtime day (if any). Determine how the post office can minimize the cost of meeting its weekly work requirements.

4 Suppose the post office has 25 full-time employees and is not allowed to hire or fire any employees. Determine a schedule that maximizes the number of weekend days off received by the employees. ■

3.3 Blending Problems

In many situations various inputs must be blended together to produce desired outputs. In many of these situations LP can find the optimal combination of outputs as well as the "mix" of inputs that are used to produce the desired outputs. Some examples of blending problems follow:

Inputs	**Outputs**
Meat, filler, water	Different types of sausage
Various types of oil	Heating oil, gasolines, aviation fuels
Carbon, iron, molybdenum	Different types of steels
Different types of pulp	Different kinds of recycled paper

The following example illustrates how to model a typical blending problem on a spreadsheet. Although this example is small relative to blending problems in real applications, we think you'll agree that it is fairly complex. If you are able to guess the optimal solution, your intuition is much better than ours!

EXAMPLE 3.2

Chandler Oil has 5000 barrels of crude oil 1 and 10,000 barrels of crude oil 2 available. Chandler sells gasoline and heating oil. These products are produced by blending together the two crude oils. Each barrel of crude oil 1 has a "quality level" of 10 and each barrel of crude oil 2 has a quality level of 5. Gasoline must have an average quality level of at least 8, while heating oil must have an average quality level of at least 6. Gasoline sells for $25 per barrel and heating oil sells for $20 per barrel. The advertising cost to sell one barrel of gasoline is $0.20 and the advertising cost to sell one barrel of heating oil is $0.10. We assume that demand for heating oil and gasoline is unlimited, so that all of Chandler's production can be sold. Chandler wants to use a spreadsheet Solver to maximize its profit.

Solution

To model Chandler's problem with a spreadsheet, we must keep track of the following:

- the number of barrels of gasoline and heating oil produced (the outputs)
- the number of barrels of each crude oil (the inputs) used to produce each output
- the quality levels of the inputs used to make the outputs
- the total profit earned

Developing the Spreadsheet Model The spreadsheet model for this problem appears in Figure 3.6. (See the file BLENDING.XLS.) To set it up, proceed as follows.

1 **Monetary and quality inputs.** Enter the unit profit contribution and advertising cost for each output in the range B4:C5. Enter the quality levels for each crude oil in the range B8:B9 and the quality standards for each output in the range B13:C13.

2 **Inputs blended into each output.** Although it may not be immediately apparent, the quantities Chandler must choose in order to specify any solution are the barrels of each input used to produce each output. Therefore, enter *any* trial values for these values in the range B17:C18. For example, the value in cell B17 is the amount of crude oil 1 used to make gasoline and the value in cell C17 is the amount of crude oil 1 used to make heating oil. The range B17:C18 will be the changing cell range.

3 **Inputs used.** Calculate the amount of crude oils 1 and 2 used by entering the formula

=SUM(B17:C17)

in cell D17 and copying it to cell D18. We will later ensure that the amount of each oil used does not exceed the amount available.

4 **Outputs sold.** Calculate the amount of gasoline and heating oil sold by entering the formula

=SUM(B17:B18)

in cell B19 and copying it to cell C19.

5 **Profits from outputs.** Compute the profit per barrel for each output in the range B29:C29. Specifically, in B29 compute the profit/barrel for gasoline with the formula

=B4–B5

and copy this formula to C29 to compute the profit per barrel for heating oil.

6 **Total profit.** In cell B31 compute total profit with the formula

=SUMPRODUCT(B29:C29,B19:C19)

FIGURE 3.6 **Initial (Nonoptimal) Solution to Chandler Blending Problem**

	A	B	C	D	E	F
1	**Chandler Blending Problem (nonoptimal solution)**					
2						
3	**Monetary inputs**	Gasoline	Heating oil			
4	Selling price/barrel	$25.00	$20.00			
5	Advertising cost/barrel	$0.20	$0.10			
6						
7	**Quality level per barrel of crudes**					
8	Crude oil 1	10				
9	Crude oil 2	5				
10						
11	**Required quality level per barrel of product**					
12		Gasoline	Heating oil			
13		8	6			
14						
15	**Blending plan (barrels of crudes in each product)**					
16		Gasoline	Heating oil	Barrels used		Barrels available
17	Crude oil 1	0	3000	3000	<=	5000
18	Crude oil 2	5000	0	5000	<=	10000
19	Barrels sold	5000	3000			
20						
21	**Constraints on quality**					
22		Gasoline	Heating oil			
23	Quality "points" obtained	25000	30000			
24		>=	>=			
25	Quality "points" required	40000	18000			
26						
27	**Profit summary**					
28		Gasoline	Heating oil			
29	Profit/barrel	$24.80	$19.90			
30						
31	**Total profit**	$183,700				

7 **Quality achieved.** Keeping track of the quality level of gasoline and heating oil is tricky. Begin by computing for each product the number of quality points (QP) in the inputs used to produce the output:

$$\text{QP in gasoline} = 10 * (\text{Oil 1 in gasoline}) + 5 * (\text{Oil 2 in gasoline})$$

$$\text{QP in heating oil} = 10 * (\text{Oil 1 in heating oil}) + 5 * (\text{Oil 2 in heating oil})$$

For the gasoline produced to have a quality level of at least 8 we must have

$$\text{QP in gasoline} \geq 8 * \text{Gasoline sold} \quad \textbf{(3.1)}$$

For the heating oil produced to have a quality level of at least 6 we must have

$$\text{QP in heating oil} \geq 6 * \text{Heating oil sold} \quad \textbf{(3.2)}$$

In preparation for generating the quality constraints corresponding to Inequalities 3.1 and 3.2, determine the QP for gasoline in cell B23 with the formula

=SUMPRODUCT(B17:B18,$B$8:$B$9)

Then copy this formula to cell C23 to generate the QP for heating oil.

8 **Quality required.** In cells B25 and C25 compute the required quality points for gasoline and heating oil. Specifically, in cell B25 determine the required quality points for gasoline with the formula

=B13*B19

Then copy this formula to cell C25 to compute the required quality points for heating oil.

Using the Solver To solve Chandler's problem with Excel's Solver, proceed as follows. (When you are finished, the Solver dialog box should appear as shown in Figure 3.7)

1 **Objective.** Maximize profit by choosing cell B31 as the target cell.
2 **Changing cells.** Select the range B17:C18 as changing cells and constrain these to be nonnegative. These cells specify the amount of each input used to produce each output.
3 **Crude oil availability constraints.** Enter the constraints D17:D18<=F17:F18. These constraints ensure that no more of any oil is used than is available.
4 **Quality constraints.** Enter the constraints B23:C23>=B25:C25. These constraints ensure that the gasoline and heating oil produced are of acceptable quality.
5 **Linear model and optimize.** Specify the Assume Linear Model option and select Solve to obtain the optimal solution shown in Figure 3.8.

The solution implies that Chandler should make 5000 barrels of gasoline with 3000 barrels of crude oil 1 and 2000 barrels of crude oil 2. It should also make 10,000 barrels of heating oil with 2000 barrels of crude oil 1 and 8000 barrels of crude oil 2. The solution is shown graphically in Figure 3.9. With this blend Chandler will earn a profit of $323,000.

As stated earlier, we believe this problem is sufficiently complex to defy intuition. Clearly, gasoline is more profitable per barrel than heating oil, but given the crude availability and the quality constraints, it turns out that Chandler should sell twice as much heating oil as gasoline. This would have been very difficult to guess ahead of time.

FIGURE 3.7 **Solver Dialog Box for Chandler Blending Problem**

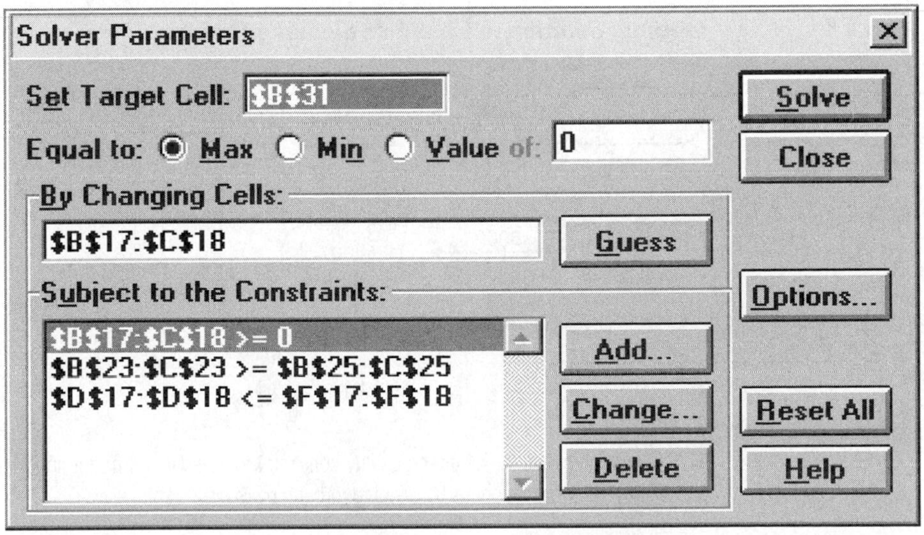

FIGURE 3.8 Optimal Solution to Chandler Blending Problem

	A	B	C	D	E	F
1	**Chandler Blending Problem (optimal solution)**					
2						
3	**Monetary inputs**	Gasoline	Heating oil			
4	Selling price/barrel	$25.00	$20.00			
5	Advertising cost/barrel	$0.20	$0.10			
6						
7	**Quality level per barrel of crudes**					
8	Crude oil 1	10				
9	Crude oil 2	5				
10						
11	**Required quality level per barrel of product**					
12		Gasoline	Heating oil			
13		8	6			
14						
15	**Blending plan (barrels of crudes in each product)**					
16		Gasoline	Heating oil	Barrels used		Barrels available
17	Crude oil 1	3000	2000	5000	<=	5000
18	Crude oil 2	2000	8000	10000	<=	10000
19	Barrels sold	5000	10000			
20						
21	**Constraints on quality**					
22		Gasoline	Heating oil			
23	Quality "points" obtained	40000	60000			
24		>=	>=			
25	Quality "points" required	40000	60000			
26						
27	**Profit summary**					
28		Gasoline	Heating oil			
29	Profit/barrel	$24.80	$19.90			
30						
31	**Total profit**	$323,000				

FIGURE 3.9 Optimal Solution to Chandler Blending Problem

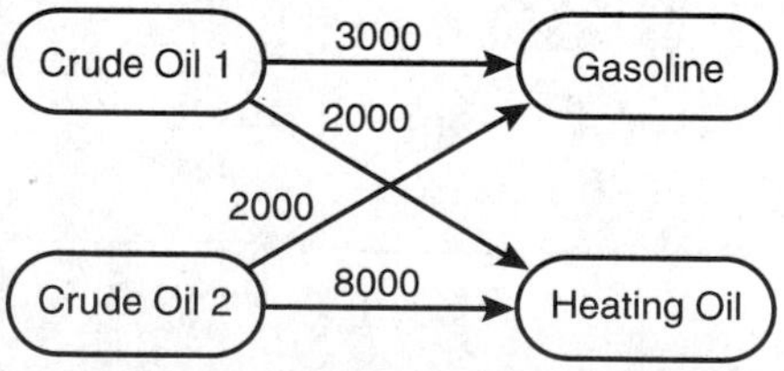

MODELING ISSUES

1 We used Inequality 3.1 as the quality constraint for gasoline. It might appear more intuitive to write this in terms of average quality points by dividing through by Gasoline sold:

$$(\text{QP in gasoline})/(\text{Gasoline sold}) \geq 8 \qquad \textbf{(3.1a)}$$

While this is logically correct, we prefer Inequality 3.1 for two reasons. First, it is conceivable that no gasoline should be sold. In this case we would be dividing by zero in Inequality 3.1a, which would certainly cause a problem for Excel. The second reason is that Inequality 3.1a is technically nonlinear, as the Solver will inform you if you check the Assume Linear Model box and attempt to solve. The lesson, therefore, is to "clear denominators" in blending problem constraints.

2 We have assumed that the quality level of a mixture is a *linear* function of the fraction of each input used in the mixture. For example, we have assumed that if gasoline is made with a fraction 3/5 of crude oil 1 and 2/5 of crude oil 2 (as in the optimal solution), then

$$\text{Quality Level for Gasoline} = (3/5) * \text{Quality Level for Oil 1} + (2/5) * \text{Quality Level for Oil 2}$$

If the quality level of the output is not a linear function of the fraction of each input used in the mixture, then we no longer have a linear programming problem; we have a *non*linear programming problem. For example, let g_i be the fraction of gasoline made with crude oil i. Suppose that

$$\text{Quality Level for Gasoline} = g_1^{.5} * \text{Quality Level for Oil 1} + g_2^{.4} * \text{Quality Level for Oil 2}$$

Then we do not have an LP problem. The reason for this is that the quality level of gasoline is not a linear function of g_1 and g_2. We will discuss nonlinear programming models in Chapter 6.

3 In reality, a company using a blending model would run the model periodically (each day, say) and set production on the basis of the current inventory of inputs and the current demand forecasts. Then the forecasts and the input levels would be updated, and the model would be run again to determine the next day's production. ■

EXAMPLE 3.2 CONTINUED

Sensitivity Analysis The shadow prices from Excel's sensitivity report appear in Figure 3.10. Representative interpretations are given below.

1 The shadow price of the constraint D17<=F17 is $29.70. This implies that if Chandler obtains an extra barrel of crude oil 1, its profit will increase by $29.70. This shadow price is valid as long as the amount of crude oil 1 available is between 2500 (= 5000 − 2500) and 15,000 (= 5000 + 10,000) barrels.

FIGURE 3.10 Sensitivity Report for Chandler Blending Problem

Changing Cells

Cell	Name	Final Value	Reduced Cost	Objective Coefficient	Allowable Increase	Allowable Decrease
$B$17	Crude oil 1 Gasoline	3000	0	24.8	58.1666667	8.16666667
$C$17	Crude oil 1 Heating oil	2000	0	19.9	8.16666667	58.1666667
$B$18	Crude oil 2 Gasoline	2000	0	24.8	87.25	6.125
$C$18	Crude oil 2 Heating oil	8000	0	19.9	6.125	14.5416667

Constraints

Cell	Name	Final Value	Shadow Price	Constraint R.H. Side	Allowable Increase	Allowable Decrease
$D$17	Crude oil 1 Barrels used	5000	29.7	5000	10000	2500
$D$18	Crude oil 2 Barrels used	10000	17.45	10000	10000	6666.66667
$B$23	Quality points obtained Gasoline	40000	-2.45	0	5000	20000
$C$23	Quality points obtained Heating oil	60000	-2.45	0	10000	6666.66667

2 The shadow price of the constraint C23<=C25 is −$2.45. This means that a unit increase in the total number of quality points needed to make heating oil will decrease Chandler's profit by $2.45. Since the company is presently producing 10,000 barrels of heating oil, this means that an increase of $1/10{,}000 = .0001$ in the per barrel gasoline quality requirement will cost Chandler $2.45.

Here is another example of what-if analysis. Suppose we want to know how a change in the price per barrel of gasoline changes Chandler's optimal product mix. We reason as follows. Since heating oil is easier to make than gasoline (in the sense that a lower quality level is acceptable), it seems unreasonable to consider a case where gasoline would sell for a lower price than heating oil. If we systematically increase the price of gasoline from $20 (the price of heating oil) and rerun the Solver several times, we find that the product mix (10,000 barrels of heating oil and 5000 barrels of gasoline) remains the same until the price of gasoline increases to approximately $59.80. When the per barrel price of gasoline exceeds this price, the optimal solution is to produce all gasoline (approximately 8333 barrels) and no heating oil. ■

REAL-WORLD APPLICATIONS

Blending at Texaco

Texaco (see Dewitt et al. [4]) uses a nonlinear programming model (OMEGA) to plan and schedule its blending applications. Their model is nonlinear because blend volatilities and octanes are nonlinear functions of the amount of each input used to produce a particular gasoline. ■

Blending in the Steel Industry

Fabian [6] describes a complex LP model that can be used to optimize the production of iron and steel. For each product produced there are several blending constraints. For example, basic pig iron must contain at most 1.5% silicon, at most .05% sulphur, between .11% and .90% phosphorus, between .4% and 2% manganese, and between 4.1% and 4.4% carbon. See Problem 57 (in the Review Problems section) for a simple example of blending in the steel industry. ■

Blending in the Oil Industry

Many oil companies use LP to optimize their refinery operations. Problem 18 contains an example (based on Magoulas and Marinos-Kouris [15]) of a blending model that can be used to maximize a refinery's profit. ■

PROBLEMS

Skill-Building Problems

5 NewAge Pharmaceuticals produces the drug NasaMist from four chemicals. Today the company must produce 1000 pounds of the drug. The three active ingredients in NasaMist are A, B, and C. By weight, at least 8% of NasaMist must consist of A, at least 4% of B, and at least 2% of C. The cost per pound of each chemical and the amount of each active ingredient in 1 pound of each chemical are given in Table 3.3. It is necessary that at least 100 pounds of chemical 2 be used. Determine the cheapest way of producing today's batch of NasaMist.

6 You have decided to enter the candy business. You are considering producing two types of candies: Slugger candy and Easy Out candy, both of which consist solely of sugar, nuts, and chocolate. At present you have in stock 10,000 ounces of sugar, 2000 ounces of nuts, and 3000 ounces of chocolate. The mixture used to make Easy Out candy must contain at least 20% nuts. The mixture used to make Slugger candy must contain at least 10% nuts and 10% chocolate.

TABLE 3.3 **Costs and Ingredients for NewAge Problem**

	Cost/Pound	A	B	C
Chemical 1	$8	.03	.02	.01
Chemical 2	$10	.06	.04	.01
Chemical 3	$11	.10	.03	.04
Chemical 4	$14	.12	.09	.04

Each ounce of Easy Out candy can be sold for 50¢, and each ounce of Slugger candy for 40¢. Determine how you can maximize your revenue from candy sales.

7 Sunblessed Juice Company sells bags of oranges and cartons of orange juice. Sunblessed grades oranges on a scale of 1 (poor) to 10 (excellent). At present Sunblessed has 100,000 pounds of grade 9 oranges and 120,000 pounds of grade 6 oranges on hand. The average quality of oranges sold in bags must be at least 7, and the average quality of the oranges used to produce orange juice must be at least 8. Each pound of oranges that is used for juice yields a revenue of $1.50 and incurs a variable cost (consisting of labor costs, variable overhead costs, inventory costs, and so on) of $1.05. Each pound of oranges sold in bags yields a revenue of $1.50 and incurs a variable cost of 70¢.

a Determine how Sunblessed can maximize its profit.

b Discuss how a change in the required average quality required for juice changes the problem's optimal solution.

8 A bank is attempting to determine where its assets should be invested during the current year. At present $500,000 is available for investment in bonds, home loans, auto loans, and personal loans. The annual rate of return on each type of investment is known to be the following: bonds, 10%; home loans, 16%; auto loans, 13%; personal loans, 20%. To ensure that the bank's portfolio is not too risky, the bank's investment manager has placed the following three restrictions on the bank's portfolio:

- The amount invested in personal loans cannot exceed the amount invested in bonds.
- The amount invested in home loans cannot exceed the amount invested in auto loans.
- No more than 25% of the total amount invested may be in personal loans.

Help the bank maximize the annual return on its investment portfolio.

9 Young MBA Erica Cudahy can invest up to $1000. She can invest her money in stocks and loans. Each dollar invested in stocks yields 10¢ profit, and each dollar invested in a loan yields 15¢ profit. At least 30% of all money invested must be in stocks, and at least $400 must be in loans. Determine how Erica can maximize the profit earned on her investments.

10 Bullco blends silicon and nitrogen to produce two types of fertilizers. Fertilizer 1 must be at least 40% nitrogen and sells for $70 per pound. Fertilizer 2 must be at least 70% silicon and sells for $40 per pound. Bullco can purchase up to 8000 pounds of nitrogen at $15 per pound and up to 10,000 pounds of silicon at $10 per pound. Assuming that all fertilizer produced can be sold, determine how Bullco can maximize its profit.

11 Eli Daisy uses chemicals 1 and 2 to produce two drugs. Drug 1 must be at least 70% chemical 1, and drug 2 must be at least 60% chemical 2. Up to 4000 ounces of drug 1 can be sold at $6 per ounce; up to 3000 ounces of drug 2 can be sold at $5 per ounce. Up to 4500 ounces of chemical 1 can be purchased at $6 per ounce, and up to 4000 ounces of chemical 2 can be purchased at $4 per ounce. Determine how to maximize Daisy's profit.

12 Hiland's TV-Radio Store must determine how many TVs and radios to keep in stock. A TV requires 10 square feet of floorspace, whereas a radio requires 4 square feet; 5000 square feet of floorspace is available. A TV sale results in an $80 profit, and a radio earns a profit of $20. The store stocks only TVs and radios. Marketing requirements dictate that at least 60% of all appliances in stock be radios. Finally, a TV ties up $200 in capital, and a radio $50. Hiland wants to have at most $60,000 worth of capital tied up at any time. Determine how to maximize Hiland's profit.

13 Linear programming models are used by many Wall Street firms to select a desirable bond portfolio. The following is a simplified version of such a model. Solodrex is considering investing in four bonds; $1 million is available for investment. The expected annual return, the worst-case annual return on each bond, and the "duration" of each bond are given in Table 3.4.

TABLE 3.4 Bond Returns and Durations for Solodrex Problem

	Expected Return	Worst Case Return	Duration
Bond 1	13%	6%	3
Bond 2	8%	8%	4
Bond 3	12%	10%	7
Bond 4	14%	9%	9

(The duration of a bond is a measure of the bond's sensitivity to interest rates.) Solodrex wants to maximize the expected return from its bond investments, subject to three constraints:

- The worst-case return of the bond portfolio must be at least 8%.
- The average duration of the portfolio must be at most 6. For example, a portfolio that invests \$600,000 in bond 1 and \$400,000 in bond 4 has an average duration of

$$[600{,}000(3) + 400{,}000(9)]/1{,}000{,}000 = 5.4$$

- Because of diversification requirements, at most 40% of the total amount invested can be invested in a single bond. Determine how Solodrex can maximize the expected return on its investment.

14 Coalco produces coal at three mines and ships it to four customers. The cost per ton of producing coal, the ash and sulfur content (per ton) of the coal, and the production capacity (in tons) for each mine are given in Table 3.5. The number of tons of coal demanded by each customer is given in Table 3.6. The cost (in dollars) of shipping a ton of coal from a mine to each customer is given in Table 3.7. The total amount of coal shipped must contain at most 6% ash and at most 3.5% sulfur. Show Coalco how to minimize the cost of meeting customer demands.

TABLE 3.5 Cost and Other Data for Coalco Problem

	Production Cost	Capacity	Ash Content	Sulfur Content
Mine 1	\$50	120	.08 ton	.05 ton
Mine 2	\$55	100	.06 ton	.04 ton
Mine 3	\$62	140	.04 ton	.03 ton

TABLE 3.6 Customer Demand for Coalco Problem

	Customer 1	Customer 2	Customer 3	Customer 4
Demand	80	70	60	40

TABLE 3.7 Shipping Costs for Coalco Problem

	Customer 1	Customer 2	Customer 3	Customer 4
Mine 1	4	6	8	12
Mine 2	9	6	7	11
Mine 3	8	12	3	5

Skill-Extending Problems

15 Sunco Oil manufactures three types of gasoline (gas 1, gas 2, and gas 3). Each type is produced by blending three types of crude oil (crude 1, crude 2, and crude 3). The sales price per barrel of gasoline and the purchase price per barrel of crude oil are given in Table 3.8. Sunco can purchase up to 5000 barrels of each type of crude oil daily. The three types of gasoline differ in their octane rating and sulfur content. The crude oil blended to form gas 1 must have an average octane rating of at least 10 and contain at most 1% sulfur. The crude oil

TABLE 3.8 Sales and Purchase Prices for Sunco Problem

	Sales Price per Barrel		Purchase Price per Barrel
Gas 1	$70	**Crude 1**	$45
Gas 2	$60	**Crude 2**	$35
Gas 3	$50	**Crude 3**	$25

blended to form gas 2 must have an average octane rating of at least 8 and contain at most 2% sulfur. The crude oil blended to form gas 3 must have an octane rating of at least 6 and contain at most 1% sulfur. The octane rating and the sulfur content of the three types of oil are given in Table 3.9. It costs $4 to transform one barrel of oil into one barrel of gasoline, and Sunco's refinery can produce up to 14,000 barrels of gasoline daily. Sunco's customers require the following amounts of each gasoline: gas 1, 3000 barrels per day; gas 2, 2000 barrels per day; gas 3, 1000 barrels per day. The company considers it an obligation to meet these demands.

TABLE 3.9 Octane Rating and Sulfur Content for Sunco Problem

	Octane Rating	Sulphur Content
Crude 1	12	0.5%
Crude 2	6	2.0%
Crude 3	8	3.0%

Sunco also has the option of advertising to stimulate demand for its products. Each dollar spent daily in advertising a particular type of gas increases the daily demand for that type of gas by 10 barrels. For example, if Sunco decides to spend $20 daily in advertising gas 2, the daily demand for gas 2 will increase by 200 barrels. Determine how Sunco can maximize its profit.

16 The risk index of an investment can be obtained by taking the absolute values of percentage changes in the value of the investment for each year and averaging them. Suppose you are trying to determine what percentage of your money you should invest in T-bills, gold, and stocks. Table 3.10 lists the annual returns (percentage changes in value) for these investments for the years 1968–88. Let the risk index of a portfolio be the weighted average of the risk indices of these investments, where the weights are the fractions of your money assigned to the investments. Suppose that the amount of each investment must be between 20% and 50% of the total invested. You would like the risk index of your portfolio to equal .15, and your goal is to maximize the expected return on your portfolio. Determine the maximum expected return on your portfolio, subject to the stated constraints. Use the average return earned by each investment during the years 1968–88 as your estimate of expected return.

TABLE 3.10 Returns for Investment Problem

	1968	1969	1970	1971	1972	1973	1974
Stocks	11	−9	4	14	19	−15	−27
Gold	11	8	−14	44	44	66	64
T-bills	5	7	7	4	4	7	8

	1975	1976	1977	1978	1979	1980	1981
Stocks	37	24	−7	7	19	33	−5
Gold	0	−22	18	31	59	99	−25
T-bills	6	5	5	7	10	11	15

	1982	1983	1984	1985	1986	1987	1988
Stocks	22	23	6	32	19	5	17
Gold	4	−11	−15	−12	16	22	−2
T-bills	11	9	10	8	6	5	6

17 The owner of Sunco (see Problem 15) does not believe that our optimal LP solution will maximize the company's daily profit. He reasons, "We have 14,000 barrels of daily refinery capacity, but your optimal solution produces only 13,500 barrels. Therefore, it cannot be maximizing profit." How would you respond?

18 (Based on Magoulas and Marinos-Kouris [15]) Oilco produces two products: regular and premium gasoline. Each product contains 0.15 gram of lead per liter. The two products are produced from six inputs: reformate, fluid catalytic cracker gasoline (FCG), isomerate (ISO), polymer (POL), MTBE, and butane (BUT). Each input has four attributes: research octane number (RON), RVP, ASTM volatility at 70 degrees Celsius, and ASTM volatility at 130 degrees Celsius. The attributes and daily availability (in liters) of each input are given in Table 3.11. The requirements for each output are given in Table 3.12. The daily demand (in thousands of liters) for each product must be met, but more can be produced if desired. The RON and ASTM requirements are minimums; the RVP requirement is a maximum. Regular gasoline sells for 29.49¢ per liter, premium gasoline for 31.43¢. Before being ready for sale, 0.15 gram per liter of lead must be removed from each product. The cost of removing 0.1 gram per liter is 8.5¢. At most 38% of each type of gasoline can consist of FCG. Show Oilco how to maximize its daily profit. ■

TABLE 3.11 **Inputs for Oilco Problem**

	Availability	RON	RVP	ASTM (70)	ASTM (130)
Reformate	15,572	98.9	7.66	−5	46
FCG	15,434	93.2	9.78	57	103
ISO	6,709	86.1	29.62	107	100
POL	1,190	97.0	14.51	7	73
MTBE	748	117.0	13.45	98	100
BUT	unlimited	98.0	166.99	130	100

TABLE 3.12 **Output Requirements for Oilco Problem**

	Demand	RON	RVP	ASTM (70)	ASTM (130)
Regular	9.8	90	21.18	10	50
Premium	30.0	96	21.18	10	50

3.4

Production Process Models

LP is often used to determine the optimal method of operating a production process. In particular, many oil refineries use LP to manage their production operations. (For example, see Garvin et al. [8].) The following example shows how spreadsheets can be used to optimize production processes.

EXAMPLE 3.3

Drugco produces three drugs, A, B, and C, and can sell these drugs in unlimited quantities at unit prices $8, $70, and $100, respectively. Producing a unit of A requires one hour of labor. Producing a unit of B requires two hours of labor and two units of A. Producing a unit of C requires three hours of labor and one unit of B. Any product A that is used to produce B cannot be sold, and any product B that is used to produce C cannot be sold. A total of 40 hours of labor are available. Drugco wants to use LP to maximize its sales revenue.

Solution

To model Drugco's operations we need to keep track of the following:

- the number of units produced of each product
- the number of units sold of each product
- the number of units of A and B used to produce other products
- the number of labor hours used
- the revenue received

Developing the Spreadsheet Model The key to setting up the spreadsheet model is as follows. Once we know how much is produced of each product, we can then compute total labor usage, quantity sold of each product, and total revenue. For example, for any product

$$\text{Amount Sold} = \text{Amount Produced} - \text{Amount Used to Produce Other Products} \quad \textbf{(3.3)}$$

We must also ensure that the amount sold of each product is nonnegative and the amount produced of each product is nonnegative. If you omit the nonnegativity requirement on the amount sold of each product, your spreadsheet solver will tell you that you can make an infinite amount of money!

The spreadsheet model for Drugco appears in Figure 3.11. (See the file DRUGCO.XLS.) To proceed, carry out the following steps:

1 **Inputs.** Enter the number of labor hours needed to produce a unit of each product in the range B5:D5 and enter the number of units of each product needed to manufacture each other product in the range B6:D8. For example, the 2 in C6 indicates that two units of A are needed to produce each unit of B. Then enter the unit selling price for each product in the range B11:D11, and enter the number of available labor hours in cell D18.

2 **Units produced.** Enter *any* trial values for the number of units produced of each product in the range B15:D15.

3 **Labor hours used.** Compute the total number of labor hours used in cell B18 with the formula

=SUMPRODUCT(B5:D5,B15:D15)

4 **Units used to make other products.** In the range B22:D24 compute the total number of units of each product that are used to produce other products. Begin by computing the amount of A used to produce B in cell C22 with the formula

=C6*C$15

and copy this formula to the range B22:D24 for the other combinations of products. Then compute the total number of units of A used to produce other products in cell E22 with the formula

=SUM(B22:D22)

and copy this to the range E23:E24 to compute the total number of units of B and C used to produce other products.

5 **Units sold.** Use Equation 3.3 to determine the number of units sold of each product. That is, enter the formulas

=B15-E22
=C15-E23

FIGURE 3.11 Initial (Nonoptimal) Solution to Drugco Production Problem

	A	B	C	D	E
1	**Drugco Production Problem (nonoptimal solution)**				
2					
3	**Inputs used (along side) to make one unit of product (along top)**				
4		Product A	Product B	Product C	
5	Labor hours	1	2	3	
6	Product A	0	2	0	
7	Product B	0	0	1	
8	Product C	0	0	0	
9					
10	**Unit selling price**	Product A	Product B	Product C	
11		$8	$70	$100	
12					
13	**Production plan (units produced)**				
14		Product A	Product B	Product C	
15		10	5	10	
16					
17	**Labor hour constraint**	Hours used		Hours available	
18		50	<=	40	
19					
20	**Units of products used (along side) to make products (along top)**				
21		Product A	Product B	Product C	Total used
22	Product A	0	10	0	10
23	Product B	0	0	10	10
24	Product C	0	0	0	0
25					
26	**Units sold**	0	-5	10	
27		>=	>=	>=	
28		0	0	0	
29					
30	**Profit**	$650			

and

=D15-E24

in cells B26, C26, and D26, respectively, to compute the units of A, B, and C sold.

6 **Total profit.** Compute Drugco's profit in cell B30 with the formula

=SUMPRODUCT(B11:D11,B26:D26)

Using the Solver To use the Excel Solver to solve the Drugco problem, proceed as follows. When you are finished, your Solver dialog box should appear as shown in Figure 3.12.

1 **Objective.** Select B30 (total profit) as the target cell to maximize.

2 **Changing cells.** Select the range B15:D15 as the changing cells. These represent the units produced of each product.

3 **Labor availability constraint.** Enter the constraint B18<=D18. This ensures that at most 40 hours of labor are used.

FIGURE 3.12 **Solver Dialog Box for Drugco Problem**

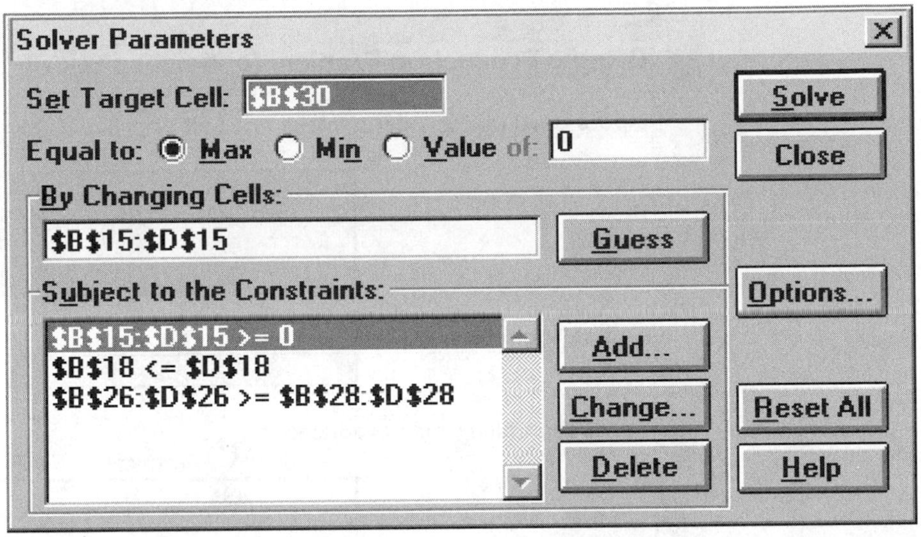

4 **Nonnegativity constraints.** Enter the constraints B15:D15>=0 to ensure that a nonnegative amount of each product is produced. Also, enter the constraints B26:D26>=B28:D28 to ensure that a nonnegative amount of each product is sold.

5 **Linear model and optimize.** Check the Assume Linear Model option and select Solve to obtain the optimal solution shown in Figure 3.13. This solution is also shown graphically in Figure 3.14. We see that Drugco obtains a profit of $700 by producing 20 units of product A, which are then used to produce 10 units of product B. All units of product B produced are sold. Even though product C earns the most money, Drugco produces none of product C. This is because of the high labor requirement for product C.

Sensitivity Analysis The shadow prices of the constraints for the Drugco example are listed in the sensitivity report in Figure 3.15. They can be interpreted as follows.

1 The shadow price of the constraint B18<=D18 is $17.50. This means that an additional hour of labor will increase profit by $17.50. This result holds for any nonnegative availability of labor.

2 The constraint B26>=0 states that the number of units of A sold must be nonnegative. The shadow price of this constraint is −$9.50. This means that if we change the constraint B26>=0 to B26>=1, the profit drops by $9.50. Thus we see that each unit of product A Drugco is forced to sell reduces the company's profit by $9.50. From the Allowable Increase for this constraint we see that this holds up to the point where Drugco is forced to sell more than 40 units of product A.

3 The constraint C26>=0 states that the number of units of product B sold must be nonnegative. The shadow price of this constraint is $0.00. This means that if we change the constraint C26>=0 to C26>=1, Drugco's profit is unchanged. This is reasonable, because the company is already selling ten units of product B. This shadow price is valid up to the point where Drugco is forced to sell more than ten units of product B.

We now consider two other sensitivity questions we might ask about the Drugco example. First, what would happen to the optimal solution if the price of product C increased

FIGURE 3.13 **Optimal Solution for Drugco Production Problem**

	A	B	C	D	E
1	**Drugco Production Problem (optimal solution)**				
2					
3	**Inputs used (along side) to make one unit of product (along top)**				
4		Product A	Product B	Product C	
5	Labor hours	1	2	3	
6	Product A	0	2	0	
7	Product B	0	0	1	
8	Product C	0	0	0	
9					
10	**Unit selling price**	Product A	Product B	Product C	
11		$8	$70	$100	
12					
13	**Production plan (units produced)**				
14		Product A	Product B	Product C	
15		20	10	0	
16					
17	**Labor hour constraint**	Hours used		Hours available	
18		40	<=	40	
19					
20	**Units of products used (along side) to make products (along top)**				
21		Product A	Product B	Product C	Total used
22	Product A	0	20	0	20
23	Product B	0	0	0	0
24	Product C	0	0	0	0
25					
26	**Units sold**	0	10	0	
27		>=	>=	>=	
28		0	0	0	
29					
30	**Profit**	$700			

FIGURE 3.14 **Optimal Solution for Drugco Problem**

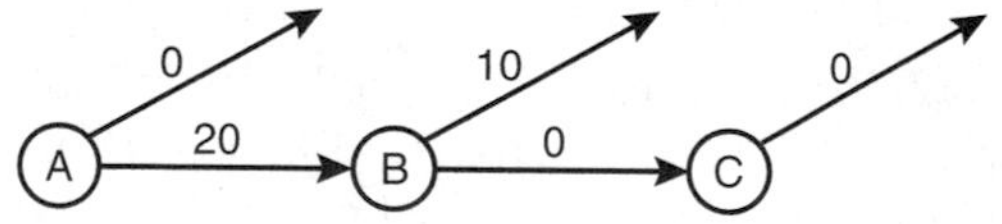

Diagonal arrows: units sold
Horizontal arrows: units used to make other products

by $30? Here, we simply change the entry in cell D11 to $130 and rerun the Solver. You can check that only product C is sold (specifically, 5.71 units of product C are sold). Second, what would happen to the optimal solution if the price of product A increased by $20? Now we change the entry in B11 to $28 and rerun the Solver. You can check that the optimal solution is to sell only product A (specifically, 40 units of product A are sold).[3] ■

[3]Note that neither of these questions can be answered, at least not easily, by appealing directly to the sensitivity report. Therefore, it is easiest to make the changes and rerun the Solver.

FIGURE 3.15 Sensitivity Report for Drugco Production Problem

Changing Cells

Cell	Name	Final Value	Reduced Cost	Objective Coefficient	Allowable Increase	Allowable Decrease
$B$15	Product A	20	0	8	19	15
$C$15	Product B	10	0	54	1E+30	30
$D$15	Product C	0	0	30	22.5	1E+30

Constraints

Cell	Name	Final Value	Shadow Price	Constraint R.H. Side	Allowable Increase	Allowable Decrease
$B$18	Hours used	40	17.5	40	1E+30	40
$B$26	Units sold Product A	0	-9.5	0	40	40
$C$26	Units sold Product B	10	0	0	10	1E+30
$D$26	Units sold Product C	0	-22.5	0	5.71428571	0

REAL-WORLD APPLICATION

Production Process Modeling for a Creamery

Sullivan and Secrest [25] developed an LP model to aid Dairyman's Cooperative Creamery Association in their production of dairy products. Each day their program took as input the amount of available raw milk and cream. As an output the LP told the creamery how much cottage cheese, sour cream, raw milk, buttermilk, and cottage cheese to produce. The problem was complicated by the relationships between the products. For example, if cottage cheese is produced then whey is produced as a by-product. Then the whey is used to produce cream, which is used in other products. The model has increased the creamery's profit by $48,000 per year. See Problem 25 for a simplified version of this model. ■

PROBLEMS

Skill-Building Problems

19 Rylon Corporation manufactures Brute and Chanelle perfumes. The raw material needed to manufacture each type of perfume can be purchased for $3 per pound. Processing one pound of raw material requires one hour of laboratory time. Each pound of processed raw material yields three ounces of Regular Brute Perfume and four ounces of Regular Chanelle Perfume. Regular Brute can be sold for $7 per ounce and Regular Chanelle for $6 per ounce. Rylon also has the option of further processing Regular Brute and Regular Chanelle to produce Luxury Brute, sold at $18 per ounce, and Luxury Chanelle, sold at $14 per ounce. Each ounce of Regular Brute processed further requires an additional three hours of laboratory time and a $4 processing cost and yields one ounce of Luxury Brute. Each ounce of Regular Chanelle processed further requires an additional two hours of laboratory time and a $4 processing cost and yields one ounce of Luxury Chanelle. Each year Rylon has 6000 hours of laboratory time available and can purchase up to 4000 pounds of raw material.

a Determine how Rylon can maximize its profit. Assume that the cost of the laboratory hours is a fixed cost (so that it can be ignored for this problem).

b Suppose that one pound of raw material can be used to produce either three ounces of Brute or four ounces of Chanelle. How does your answer to Part (a) change?

20 Sunco Oil has three different processes that can be used to manufacture various types of gasoline. Each process involves blending oils in the company's catalytic cracker. Running process 1 for an hour costs $5 and requires two barrels of crude oil 1 and three barrels of crude oil 2. The output from running process 1 for an hour is two barrels of gas 1 and one barrel of gas 2. Running process 2 for an hour costs $4 and requires one barrel of crude 1 and three barrels of crude 2. The output from running process 2 for an hour is three barrels of gas 2. Running process 3 for an hour costs $1 and requires two barrels of crude 2 and three barrels of gas 2. The output from running process 3 for an hour is two barrels of gas 3. Each week 200 barrels of crude 1, at $2 per barrel, and 300 barrels of crude 2, at $3 per barrel, can be purchased. All gas produced can be sold at the following per barrel prices: gas 1, $9; gas 2, $10; gas 3, $24. Determine how to maximize Sunco's profit (revenues less costs). Assume that only 100 hours of time on the catalytic cracker are available each week.

21 Furnco manufactures tables and chairs. A table requires 40 board feet of wood, and a chair requires 30 board feet of wood. Wood can be purchased at a cost of $1 per board foot, and 40,000 board feet of wood are available for purchase. It takes two hours of skilled labor to manufacture an unfinished table or an unfinished chair. Three more hours of skilled labor will turn an unfinished table into a finished table, and two more hours of skilled labor will turn an unfinished chair into a finished chair. A total of 6000 hours of skilled labor are available (and have already been paid for). All furniture produced can be sold at the following unit prices: an unfinished table, $70; a finished table, $140; an unfinished chair, $60; a finished chair, $110.

a Determine how to maximize Furnco's profit from manufacturing tables and chairs.

b Discuss how additional skilled labor would increase Furnco's profit.

c Discuss how a change in the price of finished chairs would change the optimal solution to the problem.

22 Chemco produces three products, 1, 2, and 3. Each pound of raw material costs $25. The raw material undergoes processing and yields three ounces of product 1 and one ounce of product 2. It costs $1 and takes two hours of labor to process each pound of raw material. Each ounce of product 1 can be used in one of three ways. First, it can be sold for $10 per ounce. Second, it can be processed into one ounce of product 2. This requires two hours of labor and costs $1. Third, it can be processed into one ounce of product 3. This requires three hours of labor and costs $2. Each ounce of product 2 can be used in one of two ways. First, it can be sold for $20 per ounce. Second, it can be processed into one ounce of product 3. This requires one hour of labor and costs $6. Product 3 is sold for $30 per ounce. The maximum numbers of ounces of products 1, 2, and 3 that can be sold are, respectively, 5000, 5000, and 3000. A maximum of 25,000 hours of labor are available. Determine how Chemco can maximize its profit.

23 A company produces three products, A, B, and C, and can sell these products in unlimited quantities at the following unit prices: A, $10; B, $56; C, $100. Producing a unit of A requires one hour of labor; a unit of B, two hours of labor plus two units of A; and a unit of C, three hours of labor plus one unit of B. Any A that is used to produce B cannot be sold. Similarly, any B that is used to produce C cannot be sold. A total of 40 hours of labor are available. Determine how to maximize the company's revenue.

Skill-Extending Problems

24 Capsule Drugs manufactures two drugs, 1 and 2. The drugs are produced by blending two chemicals, 1 and 2. By weight, drug 1 must contain at least 65% chemical 1, and drug 2 must contain at least 55% chemical 1. Drug 1 sells for $6 per ounce, and drug 2 sells for $4 per ounce. Chemicals 1 and 2 can be produced by one of two production processes. Running process 1 for an hour requires three ounces of raw material and two hours skilled labor and yields three ounces of each chemical. Running process 2 for an hour requires two ounces of raw material and three hours of skilled labor and yields three ounces of chemical 1 and one ounce of chemical 2. A total of 120 hours of skilled labor and 100 ounces of raw material are available. Determine how to maximize Capsule's sales revenues.

25 (Based on Sullivan and Secrest [25]) Lizzie's Dairy produces cream cheese and cottage cheese. Milk and cream are blended to produce these two products. Both high-fat and low-fat milk can be used to produce cream cheese and cottage cheese. High-fat milk is 60% fat; low-fat milk is 30% fat. The milk used to produce cream cheese must average at least 50% fat; for cottage cheese, at least 35% fat. At least 40% of the inputs (by weight) to cream cheese and at least 20% of the inputs (by weight) to cottage cheese must be cream.

Both cottage cheese and cream cheese are produced by putting milk and cream through the cheese machine. It costs 40¢ to process one pound of inputs into a pound of cream cheese. It costs 40¢ to produce one pound of cottage cheese, but every pound of input for cottage cheese yields 0.9 pound of cottage cheese and 0.1 pound of waste.

Cream can be produced by evaporating high-fat and low-fat milk. It costs 40¢ to evaporate one pound of high-fat milk. Each pound of high-fat milk that is evaporated yields 0.6 pound of cream. It costs 40¢ to evaporate one pound of low-fat milk. Each pound of low-fat milk that is evaporated yields 0.3 pound of cream.

Each day up to 3000 pounds of input can be sent through the cheese machine. Each day at least 1000 pounds of cottage cheese and 1000 pounds of cream cheese must be produced. Up to 1500 pounds of cream cheese and 2000 pounds of cottage cheese can be sold each day.

Cottage cheese is sold for $2.10 per pound and cream cheese for $2.50 per pound. High-fat milk is purchased for 80¢ per pound and low-fat milk for 40¢ per pound. The evaporator can process at most 2000 pounds of milk daily. Determine how to maximize Lizzie's daily profit.

26 Flexco produces six products in the following manner. Each unit of raw material purchased yields four units of product 1, two units of product 2, and one unit of product 3. Up to 1200 units of product 1 can be sold, and up to 300 units of product 2 can be sold. Demand for products 3 and 4 is unlimited. Each unit of product 1 can be sold or processed further. Each unit of product 1 that is processed yields a unit of product 4. Each unit of product 2 can be sold or processed further. Each unit of product 2 that is processed further yields 0.8 unit of product 5 and 0.3 unit of product 6.

Up to 1000 units of product 5 can be sold, and up to 800 units of product 6 can be sold. Up to 3000 units of raw material can be purchased at $6 per unit. Leftover units of products 5 and 6 must be destroyed. It costs $4 to destroy each leftover unit of product 5 and $3 to destroy each leftover unit of product 6. Ignoring raw material purchase costs, the per unit sales price and production cost for each product are shown in Table 3.13. Determine a profit-maximizing production schedule for Flexco.

TABLE 3.13 Prices and Costs for Flexco Problem

	Sales Price	Production Cost
Product 1	$7	$4
Product 2	$6	$4
Product 3	$4	$2
Product 4	$3	$1
Product 5	$20	$5
Product 6	$35	$5

27 Each week Chemco can purchase unlimited quantities of raw material at $6 per pound. Each pound of purchased raw material can be used to produce either input 1 or input 2. Each pound of raw material can yield two ounces of input 1, requiring two hours of processing time and incurring $2 in processing costs. Each pound of raw material can yield three ounces of input 2, requiring two hours of processing time and incurring $4 in processing costs.

Two production processes are available. It takes two hours to run process 1, requiring two ounces of input 1 and one ounce of input 2. It costs $1 to run process 1. Each time process 1 is run, one ounce of product A and one ounce of liquid waste are produced. Each time process 2 is run requires three hours of processing time, two ounces of input 2, and one ounce of input 1. Each process 2 run yields one ounce of product B and .8 ounce of liquid waste. Process 2 incurs $8 in costs. Chemco can dispose of liquid waste in the Port Charles River or use the waste to produce product C or product D. Government regulations limit the amount of waste Chemco is allowed to dump into the river to 1000 ounces per week.

One ounce of product C costs $4 to produce and sells for $11. One hour of processing time, two ounces of input 1, and .8 ounce of liquid waste are needed to produce an ounce of product C. One ounce of product D costs $5 to produce and sells for $7. One hour of processing time, two ounces of input 2, and 1.2 ounces of liquid waste are needed to produce an ounce of product D. At most 5000 ounces of product A and 5000 ounces of product B can be sold each week, but weekly demand for products C and D is unlimited. Product A sells for $18 per ounce and product B sells for $24 per ounce. Each week 6000 hours of processing time are available. Determine how Chemco can maximize its weekly profit.

28 Limeco owns a lime factory and sells six grades of lime (grades 1 through 6). The sales price per pound of each grade is given in Table 3.14. Lime is produced by kilns. If a kiln is run for an eight-hour shift, the amounts (in pounds) of each grade of lime given in Table 3.14 are

TABLE 3.14 Sales Prices and Other Data for Limeco Problem

	Grade					
	1	**2**	**3**	**4**	**5**	**6**
Price	$12	$14	$10	$18	$20	$25
Amount Produced	2	2	3	1	1.5	2
Maximum Demand	20	30	40	35	25	50
Disposal Cost	$3	$2	$3	$2	$4	$2

produced. It costs $150 to run a kiln for an eight-hour shift. Each day the factory believes it can sell up to the amounts (in pounds) of lime given in Table 3.14. Lime that is produced by the kiln can be reprocessed by using any one of the five processes described in Table 3.15. For example, at a cost of $1 per pound, a pound of grade 4 lime can be transformed into .5 pound of grade 5 lime and .5 pound of grade 6 lime. Any extra lime leftover at the end of each day must be disposed of, with the disposal costs (per pound) given in Table 3.14. Determine how Limeco can maximize its daily profit. (You may assume that the number of eight-hour shifts used can be fractional, or you can constrain it to be an integer.)

TABLE 3.15 Input and Output Data for Limeco Problem

Input	Cost	Output
1 lb. of Grade 1	$2	.3 lb. of Grade 3 .2 lb. of Grade 4 .3 lb. of Grade 5 .2 lb. of Grade 6
1 lb. of Grade 2	$1	1 lb. of Grade 6
1 lb. of Grade 3	$1	.8 lb. of Grade 4
1 lb. of Grade 4	$1	.5 lb. of Grade 5 .5 lb. of Grade 6
1 lb. of Grade 5	$2	.9 lb. of Grade 6

29 Abotte Products produces three products, A, B, and C. The company can sell up to 300 pounds of each product at the following prices (per pound): product A, $10; product B, $12; product C, $20. Abotte purchases raw material at $5 per pound. Each pound of raw material can be used to produce either one pound of A or one pound of B. For a cost of $3 per pound processed, product A can be converted to .6 pound of product B and .4 pound of product C. For a cost of $2 per pound processed, product B can be converted to .8 pound of product C. Determine how Abotte can maximize its profit.

30 Molecular Products produces 3 chemicals, B, C, and D. The company begins by purchasing chemical A for a cost of $6 per 100 liters. For an additional cost of $3 and the use of three hours of skilled labor, 100 liters of A can be transformed into 40 liters of C and 60 liters of B. Chemical C can either be sold or processed further. It costs $1 and one hour of skilled labor to process 100 liters of C into 60 liters of D and 40 liters of B. For each chemical the sales price per 100 liters and the maximum amount (in 100s of liters) that can be sold are given in Table 3.16. A maximum of 200 labor hours are available. Determine how Molecular can maximize its profit.

31 Bexter Labs produces three products: A, B, and C. Bexter can sell up to 30 units of product A, up to 20 units of product B, and up to 20 units of product C. Each unit of product C uses two units of A and three units of B and incurs $5 in processing costs. Products A and B are produced from either raw material 1 or raw material 2. It costs $6 to purchase and process one unit of raw material 1. Each processed unit of raw material 1 yields two units of A and three units of B. It costs $3 to purchase and process a unit of raw material 2. Each processed unit of raw material 2 yields one unit of A and two units of B. The sales prices per unit of each product are: A, $5; B, $4; C, $25. The quality levels of each product are: A, 8; B, 7; C, 6. The average quality level of the units sold must be at least 7. Determine how to maximize Bexter's profit. ■

TABLE 3.16 Prices and Demands for Molecular Problem

	B	C	D
Price	$12	$16	$26
Maximum Demand	30	60	40

3.5

Aggregate Planning Models

In this section we extend the inventory model discussed in Chapter 2 to include a situation where the number of workers available influences the possible production levels. We allow the workforce level to be modified each period through the hiring and firing of workers. We also allow demand to be backlogged, that is, demand need not be met on time. **Aggregate planning models** can accommodate workforce variability and backlogging. We will discuss several such models in this section.

EXAMPLE 3.4

During the next four months Shoeco must meet (on time) the following demands for pairs of shoes: 300 in month 1; 500 in month 2; 100 in month 3; and 100 in month 4. At the beginning of month 1, 50 pairs of shoes are on hand, and Shoeco has three workers. A worker is paid $1500 per month. Each worker can work up to 160 hours a month before he or she receives overtime. A worker may be forced to work up to 20 hours of overtime per month and is paid $25 per hour for overtime labor. It takes four hours of labor and $5 of raw material to produce a pair of shoes. At the beginning of each month workers can be hired or fired. Each hired worker costs $1600, and each fired worker costs $2000. At the end of each month, a holding cost of $30 per pair of shoes left in inventory is incurred. Production in a given month can be used to meet that month's demand. Shoeco wants to use LP to determine its optimal production schedule and labor policy.

Solution

To model Shoeco's problem we need to keep track of the following:

- the number of workers hired, fired, and available during each month
- the number of pairs of shoes produced each month with regular time and overtime labor
- the number of overtime hours used each month
- the beginning and ending inventory of shoes each month
- the monthly costs and the total cost

Developing the Spreadsheet Model The spreadsheet model appears in Figure 3.16. (See the file SHOECO.XLS.) It can be developed as follows.

1 **Inputs.** Enter the input data in the range B4:B14 and (for monthly demands) in the range B36:E36.

2 **Production, hiring and firing plan.** Enter *any* trial values for the number of pairs of shoes produced each month in the range B32:E32, the overtime hours used each

FIGURE 3.16 **Initial (Nonoptimal) Solution to Shoeco Problem**

	A	B	C	D	E	F
1	**Shoeco Aggregate Planning Problem (nonoptimal solution)**					
2						
3	**Input data**					
4	Beginning inventory of shoes	50				
5	Beginning number of workers	3				
6	Regular hours/worker/month	160				
7	Maximum overtime hours/worker/month	20				
8	Hiring cost/worker	$1,600				
9	Firing cost/worker	$2,000				
10	Regular wages/worker/month	$1,500				
11	Overtime wage rate/hour	$25				
12	Labor hours/pair of shoes	4				
13	Raw material cost/per of shoes	$5				
14	Holding cost/pair of shoes in inventory/month	$30				
15						
16	**Worker plan**					
17	Month	1	2	3	4	
18	Workers from previous month	3	3	3	3	
19	Workers hired	0	0	0	0	
20	Workers fired	0	0	0	0	
21	Workers available after hiring and firing	3	3	3	3	
22						
23	Regular-time hours available	480	480	480	480	
24	Overtime labor hours used	0	0	0	0	
25		<=	<=	<=	<=	
26	Maximum overtime labor hours available	60	60	60	60	
27						
28	Total hours for production	480	480	480	480	
29						
30	**Production plan**					
31	Month	1	2	3	4	
32	Shoes produced	200	200	200	200	
33		<=	<=	<=	<=	
34	Production capacity	120	120	120	120	
35						
36	Demand	300	500	100	100	
37	Ending inventory	-50	-350	-250	-150	
38		>=	>=	>=	>=	
39	Must be nonnegative to meet demand	0	0	0	0	
40						
41	**Summary of costs**					
42	Month	1	2	3	4	Totals
43	Hiring cost	$0	$0	$0	$0	$0
44	Firing cost	$0	$0	$0	$0	$0
45	Regular-time wages	$4,500	$4,500	$4,500	$4,500	$18,000
46	Overtime wages	$0	$0	$0	$0	$0
47	Raw material cost	$1,000	$1,000	$1,000	$1,000	$4,000
48	Holding cost	($1,500)	($10,500)	($7,500)	($4,500)	($24,000)
49	Totals	$4,000	($5,000)	($2,000)	$1,000	
50						
51	**Total cost**	($2,000)				

month in the range B24:E24, the workers hired each month in the range B19:E19, and the workers fired each month in the range B20:E20. These four ranges are the changing cells.

If we define A_t as the number of available workers in month t, after hiring or firing, and we let H_t and F_t be the number of workers hired and/or fired at the beginning of month t, then A_0 is given as 3 (the initial number of workers in cell B5), and for any month $t \geq 1$, we have the "balance" equation

$$A_t = A_{t-1} + H_t - F_t \tag{3.4}$$

This is the rationale behind the next step.

3 **Workers available each month.** In cell B18 enter the initial number of workers available with the formula

=B5

Since the number of workers available at the beginning of any other month (before hiring or firing) is equal to the number of workers from the previous month, enter the formula

=B21

in cell C18 and copy it to the range D18:E18. Then in cell B21 calculate the number of workers available in month 1 (after hiring or firing) with the formula

=B18+B19–B20

and copy this formula to the range C21:E21 for months 2 through 4. This formula is based on Equation 3.4.

4 **Overtime capacity.** Since each available worker can work up to 20 hours of overtime in a month, enter the formula

=$B$7*B21

in cell B26 and copy it to the range C26:E26 to compute the overtime hours capacity for months 2 through 4.

5 **Production capacity.** Since each worker can work 160 regular-time hours per month, calculate the regular-time hours available in month 1 in cell B23 with the formula

=$B$6*B21

and copy it to the range C23:E23 for the other months. Then calculate the total hours available for production in cell B28 with the formula

=SUM(B23:B24)

and copy it to the range C28:E28 for the other months. Finally, since it takes four hours of labor to make a pair of shoes, enter the formula

=B28/$B$12

in cell B34 and copy it to the range C34:E34.

As in Section 2.9, let I_t and P_t be, respectively, the ending inventory in month t and the number of pairs of shoes produced in month t. Also, let D_t be the demand in month t. Then, since ending inventory in month $t-1$ is the same as beginning inventory in month t, we have the following balance equation:

$$I_t = I_{t-1} + P_t - D_t \tag{3.5}$$

This leads to the following step.

6 **Ending inventory each month.** In cell B37 calculate month 1's ending inventory with the formula

=B4+B32–B36

Then in cell C37 calculate the ending inventory in month 2 with the formula

=B37+C32–C36

and copy this to the range D37:E37 for months 3 and 4.

7 **Monthly costs.** Calculate the various costs shown in rows 43 through 48 for month 1 by entering the formulas

```
=$B$8*B19
=$B$9*B20
=$B$10*B21
=$B$11*B24
=$B$13*B32
=$B$14*B37
```

in cells B43, B44, B45, B46, B47, and B48. Then copy the range B43:B48 to the range C43:E48 to calculate these costs for the other months. If you like, calculate row sums in column F (to sum the different cost categories over the four months) and column sums in row 49 (to find monthly totals).

8 **Total cost.** In cell B51 compute the total cost with the formula

```
=SUM(B43:E48)
```

Using the Solver The final Solver dialog box should appear as shown in Figure 3.17. To accomplish this, proceed as follows.

1 **Objective.** Select cell B51 as the target cell to minimize.

2 **Changing cells.** Select the ranges B19:E20 (hiring and firing), B24:E24 (overtime hours), and B32:E32 (shoe production) as changing cells. *Note:* as shown in Figure 3.17, the proper procedure for selecting multiple ranges is to select the first range, type a comma, select the second range, type a comma, and select the third range. Constrain each of these ranges to be nonnegative.

3 **Overtime constraints.** Enter the constraints B24:E24<=B26:E26. These ensure that overtime hours during each month do not exceed the allowable amount.

4 **Production capacity constraints.** Enter the constraints B32:E32<=B34:E34. These ensure that each month's production does not exceed the limit set by the number of available hours.

FIGURE 3.17 **Solver Dialog Box for Shoeco Problem**

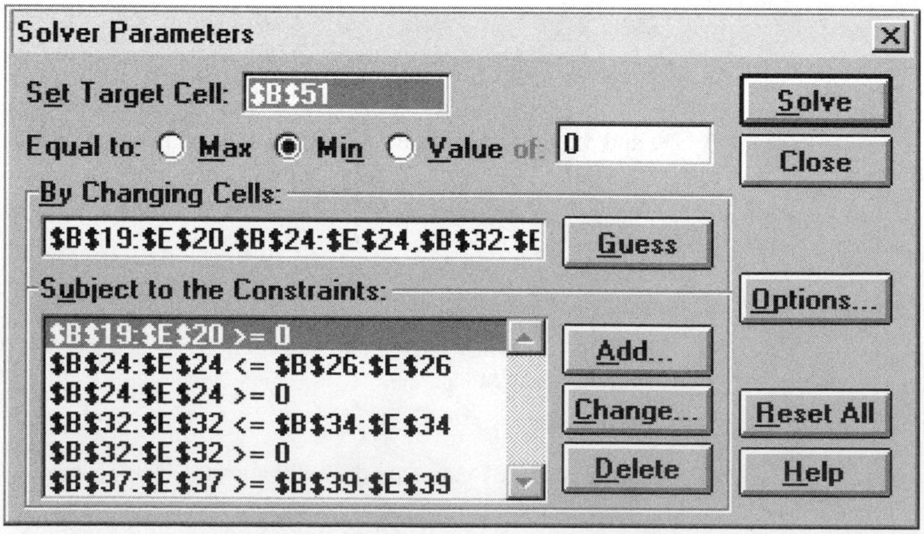

5 **Demand constraints.** Enter the constraints B37:E37>=B39:E39. These constraints ensure that each month's demand is met on time.

6 **Linear model and optimize.** Check the Assume Linear Model option and select Solve to obtain the optimal solution shown in Figure 3.18. Observe that Shoeco should hire 6.375 workers in month 1 and fire 6.875 workers in month 3. (We are assuming fractional hires and fires are allowed.) No overtime is used. Shoeco

FIGURE 3.18 **Optimal Solution to Shoeco Problem**

	A	B	C	D	E	F
1	**Shoeco Aggregate Planning Problem (optimal solution)**					
2						
3	**Input data**					
4	Beginning inventory of shoes	50				
5	Beginning number of workers	3				
6	Regular hours/worker/month	160				
7	Maximum overtime hours/worker/month	20				
8	Hiring cost/worker	$1,600				
9	Firing cost/worker	$2,000				
10	Regular wages/worker/month	$1,500				
11	Overtime wage rate/hour	$25				
12	Labor hours/pair of shoes	4				
13	Raw material cost/per of shoes	$5				
14	Holding cost/pair of shoes in inventory/month	$30				
15						
16	**Worker plan**					
17	Month	1	2	3	4	
18	Workers from previous month	3	9.375	9.375	2.5	
19	Workers hired	6.375	0	0	0	
20	Workers fired	0	0	6.875	0	
21	Workers available after hiring and firing	9.375	9.375	2.5	2.5	
22						
23	Regular-time hours available	1500	1500	400	400	
24	Overtime labor hours used	0	0	0	0	
25		<=	<=	<=	<=	
26	Maximum overtime labor hours available	187.5	187.5	50	50	
27						
28	Total hours for production	1500	1500	400	400	
29						
30	**Production plan**					
31	Month	1	2	3	4	
32	Shoes produced	375	375	100	100	
33		<=	<=	<=	<=	
34	Production capacity	375	375	100	100	
35						
36	Demand	300	500	100	100	
37	Ending inventory	125	0	0	0	
38		>=	>=	>=	>=	
39	Must be nonnegative to meet demand	0	0	0	0	
40						
41	**Summary of costs**					
42	Month	1	2	3	4	Totals
43	Hiring cost	$10,200	$0	$0	$0	$10,200
44	Firing cost	$0	$0	$13,750	$0	$13,750
45	Regular-time wages	$14,063	$14,063	$3,750	$3,750	$35,625
46	Overtime wages	$0	$0	$0	$0	$0
47	Raw material cost	$1,875	$1,875	$500	$500	$4,750
48	Holding cost	$3,750	$0	$0	$0	$3,750
49	Totals	$29,888	$15,938	$18,000	$4,250	
50						
51	**Total cost**	$68,075				

produces 375 pairs of shoes during each of the first two months and 100 pairs of shoes during each of the last two months. A total cost of $68,075 is incurred.

Using the Solver (Integer Solution) If we assume that the number of hires, fires, and shoes produced each month must be integers, Figure 3.19 gives the optimal solution. (See the file SHOECO.XLS.) This solution is represented graphically in Figures 3.20 (which

FIGURE 3.19 **Optimal Integer Solution to Shoeco Problem**

	A	B	C	D	E	F
1	**Shoeco Aggregate Planning Problem with Integer Constraints**					
2						
3	**Input data**					
4	Beginning inventory of shoes	50				
5	Beginning number of workers	3				
6	Regular hours/worker/month	160				
7	Maximum overtime hours/worker/month	20				
8	Hiring cost/worker	$1,600				
9	Firing cost/worker	$2,000				
10	Regular wages/worker/month	$1,500				
11	Overtime wage rate/hour	$25				
12	Labor hours/pair of shoes	4				
13	Raw material cost/per of shoes	$5				
14	Holding cost/pair of shoes in inventory/month	$30				
15						
16	**Worker plan**					
17	Month	1	2	3	4	
18	Workers from previous month	3	9	9	3	
19	Workers hired	6	0	0	0	
20	Workers fired	0	0	6	0	
21	Workers available after hiring and firing	9	9	3	3	
22						
23	Regular-time hours available	1440	1440	480	480	
24	Overtime labor hours used	0	120	0	0	
25		<=	<=	<=	<=	
26	Maximum overtime labor hours available	180	180	60	60	
27						
28	Total hours for production	1440	1560	480	480	
29						
30	**Production plan**					
31	Month	1	2	3	4	
32	Shoes produced	360	390	100	100	
33		<=	<=	<=	<=	
34	Production capacity	360	390	120	120	
35						
36	Demand	300	500	100	100	
37	Ending inventory	110	0	0	0	
38		>=	>=	>=	>=	
39	Must be nonnegative to meet demand	0	0	0	0	
40						
41	**Summary of costs**					
42	Month	1	2	3	4	Totals
43	Hiring cost	$9,600	$0	$0	$0	$9,600
44	Firing cost	$0	$0	$12,000	$0	$12,000
45	Regular-time wages	$13,500	$13,500	$4,500	$4,500	$36,000
46	Overtime wages	$0	$3,000	$0	$0	$3,000
47	Raw material cost	$1,800	$1,950	$500	$500	$4,750
48	Holding cost	$3,300	($0)	($0)	($0)	$3,300
49	Totals	$28,200	$18,450	$17,000	$5,000	
50						
51	**Total cost**	$68,650				

shows workers) and 3.21 (which shows production). To obtain this solution we simply designate the ranges B19:E20 and B32:E32 to be integer. Note that this results in a slight increase in total cost. Note also that overtime is now used, whereas no overtime was used in the noninteger solution.

FIGURE 3.20 **Workers in Optimal Shoeco Solution**

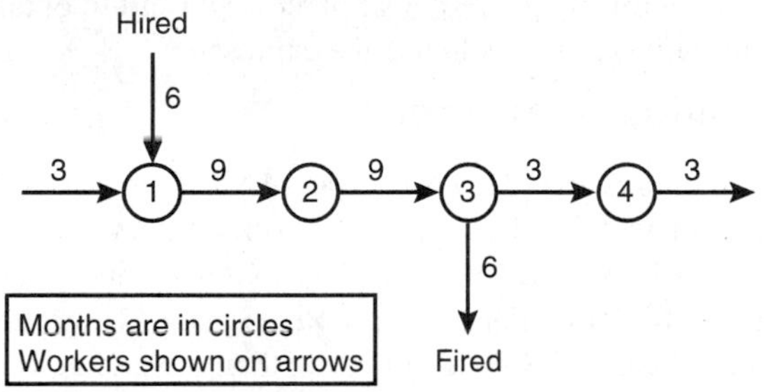

FIGURE 3.21 **Production in Optimal Shoeco Solution**

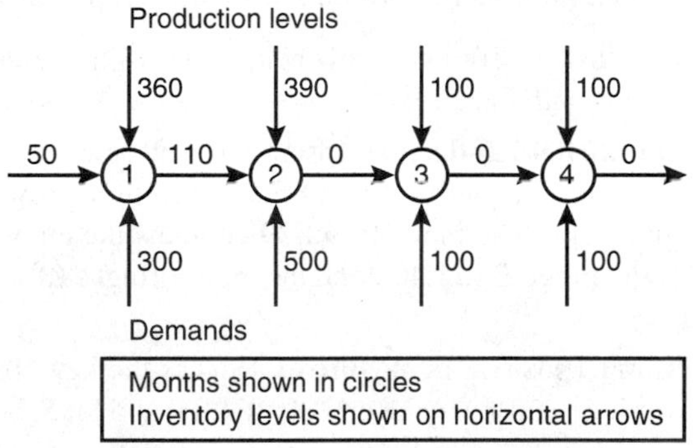

In general, we would probably not force the number of pairs of shoes produced each month to be an integer. It makes little difference whether we produce 350 or 351 pairs of shoes during a month, and forcing each month's shoe production to be an integer can greatly increase the time the computer needs to find an optimal solution. On the other hand, it is somewhat more important to ensure that the number of workers hired and fired each month is an integer, given the small numbers of workers involved.

Finally, if you want to ensure that the Solver finds the optimal solution in a problem where some or all of the changing cells must be integers, it is a good idea to go into Options (in the Solver dialog box) and set the "tolerance" to 0. Otherwise, the Solver might stop when it finds a solution that is *close* to optimal.

Model with Backlogging Allowed In many situations backlogging is allowed, that is, customer demand can be met later than it occurs. We now show how to modify the Shoeco formulation to include the option of backlogged demand. We assume that at the end of each month a cost of \$20 is incurred for each unit of demand that remains unsatisfied at the end of the month. This is easily modeled by allowing a month's ending inventory to be negative. For example, if month 1's ending inventory is −10, a shortage cost of \$200 (and no holding cost) is incurred. To ensure that Shoeco produces any shoes at all, we require that month 4's ending inventory is nonnegative. This also ensures that all demand will eventually be met by the end of the four-month horizon. We now need to modify the monthly cost computations to incorporate the costs due to shortages.

To begin, we enter the per unit monthly shortage cost in cell B15. To take shortages into account, one possibility is to replace the formula in cell B48 with

=IF(B37>=0,$B$14*B37,–$B$15*B37)

While this accurately computes the holding or shortage cost, the IF function makes the objective function nonlinear, and Excel's Solver might fail to obtain an optimal solution to the problem. Alternatively, we could use the expression

=MAX($B$14*B37,0)+MAX(0,–$B$15*B37)

instead of the IF expression. However, the MAX function is also nonlinear and can cause Excel's Solver to fail. (There is a new spreadsheet Solver called GeneHunter [9] that can handle IF, MAX, and MIN functions. GeneHunter uses **genetic algorithms** to solve optimization problems. For most problems genetic algorithms are slower than the algorithms used by the Excel Solver. However, their advantage is that they can handle *any* spreadsheet model.)

We can, however, handle shortages and maintain a linear formulation. The method is illustrated in Figure 3.22. (See the file SHOECO.XLS.) We again assume that the number of workers hired and fired each month, as well as the number of pairs of shoes produced each month, must be an integer. To develop this modified spreadsheet, proceed as follows.

1 **Enter shortage cost.** Insert a new row below row 14 and enter the shortage cost per pair of shoes per month in cell B15.

2 **Rows for amounts held and short.** Insert five new rows (which will now be rows 38 through 42) between the Demand and Ending inventory rows. The range B39:E40 will be changing cells. The range B39:E39 contains the amounts left in inventory (if any), whereas the range B40:E40 contains the shortages (if any). Enter any values in these ranges.

3 **Ending inventory (positive or negative).** Here is the key observation. Let L_t be the amount leftover in inventory at the end of month t, and let S_t be the amount short at the end of month t. Then $L_t = 0$ if $S_t \geq 0$, and $S_t = 0$ if $L_t \geq 0$. So if we allow ending inventory to be negative (meaning that there is a shortage), then for each month we have

$$I_t = L_t - S_t$$

For example, if $I_2 = 6$, then $L_2 = 6$ and $S_2 = 0$, indicating that Shoeco has six pairs of shoes leftover at the end of month 2. But if $I_2 = -3$, then $L_2 = 0$ and $S_2 = 3$, indicating that Shoeco has a shortage of three pairs of shoes at the end of month 2. To incorporate this into the spreadsheet, enter the formula

=B39–B40

in cell B41 and copy it to the range C41:E41.

4 **Monthly costs.** Insert a new row (which will be row 55) below the holding cost row. Modify the holding cost for month 1 by entering the formula

=$B$14*B39

in cell B54. Calculate the shortage cost for month 1 in cell B55 with the formula

=$B$15*B40

FIGURE 3.22 **Shoeco Model with Backlogging Allowed**

	A	B	C	D	E	F
1	**Shoeco Aggregate Planning Problem with Backlogging Allowed**					
2						
3	**Input data**					
4	Beginning inventory of shoes	50				
5	Beginning number of workers	3				
6	Regular hours/worker/month	160				
7	Maximum overtime hours/worker/month	20				
8	Hiring cost/worker	$1,600				
9	Firing cost/worker	$2,000				
10	Regular wages/worker/month	$1,500				
11	Overtime wage rate/hour	$25				
12	Labor hours/pair of shoes	4				
13	Raw material cost/per of shoes	$5				
14	Holding cost/pair of shoes in inventory/month	$30				
15	Shortage cost/pair of shoes/month	$20				
16						
17	**Worker plan**					
18	Month	1	2	3	4	
19	Workers from previous month	3	6	6	6	
20	Workers hired	3	0	0	0	
21	Workers fired	0	0	0	0	
22	Workers available after hiring and firing	6	6	6	6	
23						
24	Regular-time hours available	960	960	960	960	
25	Overtime labor hours used	0	0	0	0	
26		<=	<=	<=	<=	
27	Maximum overtime labor hours available	120	120	120	120	
28						
29	Total hours for production	960	960	960	960	
30						
31	**Production plan**					
32	Month	1	2	3	4	
33	Shoes produced	240	240	237	233	
34		<=	<=	<=	<=	
35	Production capacity	240	240	240	240	
36						
37	Demand	300	500	100	100	
38						
39	Held in inventory	0	0	0	0	
40	Shortage	10	270	133	0	
41	Net leftover	-10	-270	-133	0	
42		=	=	=	=	
43	Ending inventory	-10	-270	-133	0	
44					>=	
45	Must eventually meet demand				0	
46						
47	**Summary of costs**					
48	Month	1	2	3	4	Totals
49	Hiring cost	$4,800	$0	$0	$0	$4,800
50	Firing cost	$0	$0	$0	$0	$0
51	Regular-time wages	$9,000	$9,000	$9,000	$9,000	$36,000
52	Overtime wages	$0	$0	$0	$0	$0
53	Raw material cost	$1,200	$1,200	$1,185	$1,165	$4,750
54	Holding cost	$0	$0	$0	($0)	($0)
55	Shortage cost	$200	$5,400	$2,660	$0	$8,260
56	Totals	$15,200	$15,600	$12,845	$10,165	
57						
58	**Total cost**	$53,810				

Then copy the range B54:B55 to the range C54:E55 for the other months. Make sure the totals in row 56 and column F are updated to include the shortage costs. Also make sure the total cost in cell B58 is updated correctly. It should now be

=SUM(B49:E55)

Using the Solver for the Backlog Model The changes from the previous Solver setup are as follows.

1 **Extra changing cells.** Add the range B39:E40 as changing cells and ensure that they are nonnegative. This allows the Solver to adjust each month's amount held and amount short to be consistent with the desired ending inventory for the month.

2 **Nonnegativity constraint on ending inventory only in last month.** Change the constraints that were previously listed as B37:E37>=B39:E39. Change these constraints so that they become just E43>=E45. This allows months 1 through 3 to have negative ending inventory, whereas we keep the E43>=E45 constraint to ensure that all demand is met by the end of month 4.

3 **Logical constraints on ending inventory.** Add the constraints B41:E41=B43:E43. If you study the model closely, you'll notice that we've calculated ending inventory in two different ways (in rows 41 and 43). These constraints ensure that both ways produce the same values.

4 **Optimize.** Select Solve to obtain the optimal solution shown in Figure 3.22. Observe that Shoeco should hire workers in month 1 and never fire them. The company holds no inventory, but it incurs planned shortages during months 1 through 3. The production and inventory levels appear in Figure 3.23, where the negative values on the horizontal arrows indicate the shortages. Note that allowing shortages has greatly reduced Shoeco's total cost ($53,810 versus $68,650). This is because the cost of a shortage is small relative to the cost of hiring workers. Allowing shortages enables Shoeco to reduce the total hires from six to three and the total fires from six to zero.

FIGURE 3.23 **Production and Inventory Levels in Optimal Shoeco Solution**

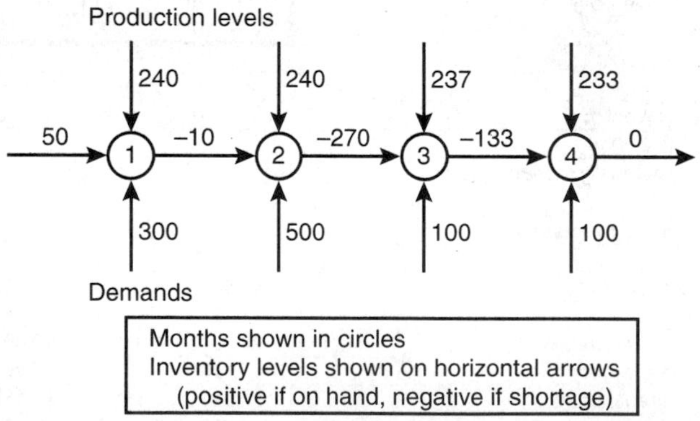

The Rolling Planning Horizon Approach In reality, an aggregate planning model is usually implemented via a rolling planning horizon. To illustrate, we assume that Shoeco works with a four-month planning horizon. To implement the Shoeco model in the rolling planning horizon context, we view the "demands" as forecasts and solve a four-month model with these forecasts. However, we implement only the month 1 production and work scheduling recommendation. Thus (assuming that the number of workers hired and fired in a month must be an integer and that shortages are allowed) Shoeco should hire 3 workers and produce 240 pairs of shoes with regular time labor in month 1. Next, we observe month 1's actual demand. Suppose that it is 280. Then Shoeco begins month 2 with 10 (= 50 + 240 − 280) pairs of shoes and 6 (= 3 + 3) workers. We would now enter 10 in cell B4 and 6 in cell B5 (referring to Figure 3.22). Then we would replace the demands in cells B37:E37 with the updated forecasts for the *next* four months. Now we would rerun the Solver and use the production levels and hiring and firing recommendations in column B as the production level and workforce policy for month 2. Just like the caissons, the planning horizon goes rolling along!

Sensitivity Analysis We now interpret the sensitivity report shadow prices, shown in Figure 3.24, for the Figure 3.18 spreadsheet (the original model, which does not require integers and does not allow shortages).

1 The constraints B24:E24<=B26:E26 all have shadow prices of 0. This indicates that an increase during any month in the number of available overtime hours will not change costs. This is reasonable, since Shoeco is currently not using any overtime.

2 The constraint B32<=B34 has a shadow price of −$67.50. This indicates that if (given the current labor force utilization) Shoeco were able to make one more pair of

FIGURE 3.24 **Sensitivity Report for Shoeco Example**

Changing Cells

Cell	Name	Final Value	Reduced Cost	Objective Coefficient	Allowable Increase	Allowable Decrease
$B$19	Workers hired	6.375	0	7600	200	3600
$C$19	Workers hired	0	1200	6100	1E+30	1200
$D$19	Workers hired	0	3600	4600	1E+30	3600
$E$19	Workers hired	0	3100	3100	1E+30	3100
$B$20	Workers fired	0	3600	-4000	1E+30	3600
$C$20	Workers fired	0	2400	-2500	1E+30	2400
$D$20	Workers fired	6.875	0	-1000	200	2400
$E$20	Workers fired	0	500	500	1E+30	500
$B$24	Overtime labor hours used	0	8.125	25	1E+30	8.125
$C$24	Overtime labor hours used	0	0.625	25	1E+30	0.625
$D$24	Overtime labor hours used	0	18.750	25	1E+30	18.750
$E$24	Overtime labor hours used	0	25	25	1E+30	25
$B$32	Shoes produced	375	0	125	5	65
$C$32	Shoes produced	375	0	95	65	5
$D$32	Shoes produced	100	0	65	102.5	55
$E$32	Shoes produced	100	0	35	55	35

Constraints

Cell	Name	Final Value	Shadow Price	Constraint R.H. Side	Allowable Increase	Allowable Decrease
$B$24	Overtime labor hours used	0	0	0	1E+30	187.5
$C$24	Overtime labor hours used	0	0	0	1E+30	187.5
$D$24	Overtime labor hours used	0	0	0	1E+30	50
$E$24	Overtime labor hours used	0	0	0	1E+30	50
$B$32	Shoes produced	375	-67.5	0	510	250
$C$32	Shoes produced	375	-97.5	0	250	750
$D$32	Shoes produced	100	-25	0	0	275
$E$32	Shoes produced	100	0	0	1E+30	0
$B$37	Ending inventory	125	0	0	125	1E+30
$C$37	Ending inventory	0	102.50	0	0	183.333
$D$37	Ending inventory	0	55	0	100	0
$E$37	Ending inventory	0	35	0	0	100

shoes in month 1, its cost would drop by \$67.50. A similar interpretation can be given to the shadow prices for the C32<=C34, D32<=D34, and E32<=E34 constraints.

3 The constraint C37>=0 has a shadow price of \$102.50. This indicates that if Shoeco were required to hold one pair of shoes in inventory at the end of month 2, its total cost would increase by \$102.50. A similar statement can be made about the constraints B37>=0, D37>=0, E37>=0.

Shoeco might ask other what-if questions that cannot be answered by the sensitivity report. First, suppose that Shoeco must maintain a "safety stock" of at least 100 pairs of shoes in inventory at the end of each month. How does the optimal solution to the problem change? To answer this, we simply change the constraints B37:E37>=0 to B37:E37>=100 and rerun the Solver. You can check that the total cost increases to \$87,325, and more workers (7.625) must be hired during month 1. Second, suppose that the cost of overtime drops during each month to \$15 per hour. How does the solution to the problem change? Now we simply change the entry in cell B11 to \$15 and rerun the Solver. You can check that the total cost decreases, fewer workers need to be hired, and overtime is now used during months 1 and 2. ■

MODELING ISSUES

1 Hiring costs include training costs as well as the cost of decreased productivity due to the fact that a new worker must learn his or her job (the "learning curve" effect).

2 Firing costs include severance costs and costs due to loss of morale.

3 Peterson and Silver [18] recommend that when demand is seasonal, the planning horizon should extend beyond the next seasonal peak.

4 Beyond a certain point, the cost of using extra hours of overtime labor increases because workers become less efficient. We haven't modeled this type of behavior because it would make the model nonlinear. ■

REAL-WORLD APPLICATION

Multiproduct Production Scheduling at Owens-Corning Fiberglass

Oliff and Burch [17] developed an aggregate planning LP that is used to schedule production of fiberglass products at Owens-Corning Fiberglass. Their model minimizes the sum of direct payroll costs, overtime costs, hiring and firing costs, and inventory holding costs. They also take into account (using integer programming, see Chapter 5) the cost (due to lost production time) incurred when a machine changes from making one product to making a different product. Their model has saved Owens-Corning over \$100,000 per year. See Problem 39 for a simplified version of this situation. ■

PROBLEMS

Skill-Building Problems

32 Mondo Motorcycles is determining its production schedule for the next four quarters. Demands for motorcycles are forecasted to be 40 in quarter 1; 70 in quarter 2; 50 in quarter 3; 20 in quarter 4. Mondo incurs four types of costs:

- It costs Mondo \$400 to manufacture each motorcycle.

- At the end of each quarter, a holding cost of $100 per motorcycle left in inventory is incurred.
- Increasing production from one quarter to the next incurs costs for training employees. It is estimated that a cost of $700 per motorcycle is incurred if production is increased from one quarter to the next.
- Decreasing production from one quarter to the next incurs costs for severance pay, decreasing morale, and so forth. It is estimated that a cost of $600 per motorcycle is incurred if production is decreased from one quarter to the next.

All demands must be met on time, and a quarter's production can be used to meet demand for the current quarter (as well as future quarters). During the quarter immediately preceding quarter 1, 50 Mondos were produced. Assume that at the beginning of quarter 1, no Mondos are in inventory.

a Determine how to minimize Mondo's total cost during the next four quarters.

b Discuss how Mondo's optimal production schedule would be affected by a change in the cost of increasing production from one quarter to the next.

c Discuss how Mondo's optimal production schedule would be affected by a change in the cost of decreasing production from one quarter to the next.

33 Referring to the previous problem, suppose that Mondo no longer must meet demands on time. For each quarter that demand for a motorcycle is not met, a shortage cost of $110 per motorcycle short is assessed. Thus, demand can now be backlogged. All demands must be met, however, by the end of quarter 4. Determine the optimal solution to this modified problem.

34 A bus company believes that it will need the following number of bus drivers during each of the next five years: 60 drivers in year 1; 70 drivers in year 2; 50 drivers in year 3; 65 drivers in year 4; 75 drivers in year 5. At the beginning of each year the bus company must decide how many drivers to hire or fire. It costs $4000 to hire a driver and $2000 to fire a driver. A driver's salary is $10,000 per year. At the beginning of year 1 the company has 50 drivers. A driver hired at the beginning of a year can be used to meet the current year's requirements and is paid full salary for the current year. Determine how to minimize the bus company's salary, hiring, and firing costs over the next five years.

35 Shoemakers of America forecasts the following demand for the next six months: 5000 pairs in month 1; 6000 pairs in month 2; 5000 pairs in month 3; 9000 pairs in month 4; 6000 pairs in month 5; 5000 pairs in month 6. It takes a shoemaker 15 minutes to produce a pair of shoes. Each shoemaker works 150 hours per month plus up to 40 hours per month of overtime. A shoemaker is paid a regular salary of $2000 per month plus $50 per hour for overtime. At the beginning of each month, Shoemakers can either hire or fire workers. It costs the company $1500 to hire a worker and $1900 to fire a worker. The monthly holding cost per pair of shoes is 3% of the cost of producing a pair of shoes with regular-time labor. The raw materials in a pair of shoes cost $10. At the beginning of month 1, Shoemakers has 13 workers. Determine how to minimize the cost of meeting (on time) the demands of the next six months.

Skill-Extending Problems

36 Clothco manufactures pants. During each of the next six months, Clothco can sell up to the numbers of pants given in Table 3.17. Demand that is not met during a month is lost (not backlogged). A pair of pants sells for $40, requires two hours of labor, and uses $10 of raw material. At the beginning of month 1 Clothco has four workers. A worker can sew pants for up to 200 hours per month and is paid $2,000 per month (regardless of how many hours he or she works). At the beginning of each month workers can be hired and/or fired. It costs $1500

TABLE 3.17 Demand for Clothco Problem

	Maximum Demand
Month 1	500
Month 2	600
Month 3	300
Month 4	400
Month 5	300
Month 6	800

to hire a worker and $1000 to fire a worker. A holding cost of $5 per pair of pants is assessed against each month's ending inventory. Determine how Clothco can maximize its profit for the next six months.

37 During the next four quarters Dorian Auto must meet (on time) the following demands for cars: 4000 in quarter 1; 2000 in quarter 2; 5000 in quarter 3; 1000 in quarter 4. At the beginning of quarter 1, there are 300 autos in stock. The company has the capacity to produce at most 3000 cars per quarter. At the beginning of each quarter, the company can change production capacity. It costs $100 to increase quarterly production capacity by one unit. For example, it would cost $10,000 to increase capacity from 3000 to 3100. It also costs $50 per quarter to maintain each unit of production capacity (even if it is unused during the current quarter). The variable cost of producing a car is $2000. A holding cost of $150 per car is assessed against each quarter's ending inventory. It is required that at the end of quarter 4, plant capacity must be at least 4000 cars. Determine how to minimize the total cost incurred during the next four quarters.

38 Carco uses robots to manufacture cars. The following demands for cars must be met (not necessarily on time, but all demands must be met by end of quarter 4): 600 in quarter 1; 800 in quarter 2; 500 in quarter 3; 400 in quarter 4. At the beginning of the year Carco has two robots. Robots can be purchased at the beginning of each quarter, but a maximum of two per quarter can be purchased. Each robot can build up to 200 cars per quarter. It costs $5000 to purchase a robot. Each quarter a robot incurs $500 in maintenance costs (even if it is not used to build any cars). Robots can also be sold at the beginning of each quarter for $3000. At the end of each quarter a holding cost of $200 per car left in inventory is incurred. If any demand is backlogged, a cost of $300 per car is incurred for each quarter the shortage lasts. At the end of quarter 4, Carco must have at least two robots. Determine how to minimize the total cost incurred in meeting demand for the next four quarters.

39 Owens-Wheat uses two production lines to produce three types of fiberglass mat. The demand requirements (in tons) for each of the next four months are shown in Table 3.18. If it were dedicated entirely to the production of one product, a line 1 machine could produce either 20 tons of type 1 mat or 30 tons of type 2 mat during a month. Similarly, a line 2 machine could produce either 25 tons of type 2 mat or 28 tons of type 3 mat. It costs $5000 per month to operate a machine on line 1 and $5500 per month to operate a machine on line 2. A cost of $2000 is incurred each time a new machine is purchased, and a cost of $1000 is incurred if a machine is retired from service. At the end of each month Owens would like to have at least 50 tons of each product in inventory. At the beginning of month 1 Owens has five line 1 machines and eight line 2 machines. Assume the per ton cost of holding either product in inventory for one month is $5.

a Determine a minimum cost production schedule for the next four months.

b There is an important aspect of this situation that cannot be modeled by linear programming. What is it? (*Hint*: If Owens makes product 1 and product 2 on line 1 during a month, is this as efficient as making just product 1 on line 1?) ■

TABLE 3.18 **Demands for Owens-Wheat Problem**

	Type 1	Type 2	Type 3
Month 1	200	300	400
Month 2	300	100	300
Month 3	200	400	200
Month 4	300	200	100

3.6 Dynamic Workforce Planning Models

We have already discussed how to adjust workforce levels in our discussion of the aggregate planning model. Here is another illustration.

EXAMPLE 3.5

CSL is a chain of computer stores. During the next five months the following number of skilled repair hours will be needed: 6000 in January; 7000 in February; 8000 in March; 9500 in April; 11,000 in May. At the beginning of January, CSL employs 50 skilled technicians. Each skilled technician can work up to 160 hours per month. To meet future demands, new technicians must be trained. It takes one month to train a new technician. During the month of training, a trainee must be supervised for 50 hours by an experienced technician. Experienced technicians are paid $2000 per month and trainees are paid $1000 per month during their month of training. Historical data indicate that 5% of CSL's skilled technicians quit each month. CSL wants to use LP to determine a training schedule that minimizes the cost of meeting the demands for the next five months.

Solution

To model CSL's situation we must keep track of the following:

- the number of workers trained each month
- the number of experienced workers on hand each month
- the number of skilled hours available to meet each month's needs
- the monthly and total costs

Developing the Spreadsheet Model The spreadsheet model for CSL's problem is shown in Figure 3.25.[4] (See the file CSL.XLS.) To develop this spreadsheet, proceed as follows.

1 **Inputs.** Enter all of the relevant data in the range D4:D9 and (for the number of repair hours required each month) in the range B19:F19.

FIGURE 3.25 **Optimal Solution to CSL Problem**

	A	B	C	D	E	F	G
1	CSL Dynamic Workforce Planning Problem						
2							
3	Data inputs						
4	January skilled technicians			50			
5	Hours/month/skilled technician			160			
6	Supervision hours/trainee/month			50			
7	Monthly pay/skilled technician			$2,000			
8	Monthly pay/trainee			$1,000			
9	Percentage quitters/month			5%			
10							
11	Planning schedule						
12	Month	1	2	3	4	5	
13	# of trainees	0	8.45	11.45	9.52	0	
14	# of skilled technicians	50	47.5	53.58	62.35	68.75	
15	# of quitters at end of month	2.5	2.38	2.68	3.12	3.44	
16							
17	Available hours for repair	8000	7177.34	8000	9500	11000	
18		>=	>=	>=	>=	>=	
19	Required hours for repair	6000	7000	8000	9500	11000	Total cost
20	Cost	$100,000	$103,453	$118,606	$134,217	$137,500	$593,777

[4]From this point on, to save space we will show only the spreadsheet with the optimal solution. Remember, however, that when you develop your model, you can enter *any* trial values in the changing cells; the Solver will find the optimal solution.

2 **Number of trainees each month.** The only decision CSL must make is the number of trainees to hire each month. This will automatically determine the number of skilled technicians needed (and available) each month. Therefore, enter *any* trial values for trainees in the range B13:F13.

3 **Skilled technicians available each month.** In cell B14 enter the formula

=D4

This corresponds to the 50 workers available at the beginning of January. Now, let S_t, Q_t, and T_t be, respectively, the number of skilled workers available in month t, the number of quitters at the end of month t, and the number of trainees in month t. Then we have the following balance equation:

$$S_t = S_{t-1} - Q_{t-1} + T_{t-1}$$

This follows because all of the trainees in month $t - 1$ are skilled by month t, and all but the quitters come back the following month. Use this relationship to compute the number of skilled technicians available during February by entering the following formula

=B14–B15+B13

in cell C14. Then copy this formula to the range D14:F14 for the other months.

4 **Quitters each month.** Since 5% of the skilled technicians quit each month, calculate the number who quit at the end of month 1 in cell B15 with the formula

=$D$9*B14

and copy this to the range C15:F15 for the quitters in the other months.

5 **Hours available for repair each month.** Let H_t be the number of hours available for repair in month t. Then the following equation relates the number of hours available for repair to the number of skilled workers and the number of trainees:

$$H_t = 160S_t - 50T_t$$

Use this relationship to compute the available repair hours for January in cell B17 with the formula

=$D$5*B14–$D$6*B13

Then copy this formula to the range C17:F17 for the other months.

6 **Payroll costs.** Compute the January payroll cost in cell B20 with the formula

=$D$8*B13+$D$7*B14

and copy it to the range C20:F20 for the other months. Then compute total cost in cell G20 with the formula

=SUM(B20:F20)

Using the Solver To use the Solver to solve CSL's problem, proceed as follows. (When you are finished, the Solver dialog box should appear as shown in Figure 3.26.)

1 **Objective.** Select cell G20 (total cost) as the target cell to minimize.

2 **Changing cells.** Select the range B13:F13 (the number of workers trained during each month) as the changing cells and constrain these to be nonnegative.

3 **Skilled technician requirement constraints.** Enter the constraints B17:F17>= B19:F19. These ensure that enough skilled technician hours are available each month to meet requirements.

FIGURE 3.26 **Solver Dialog Box for CSL Problem**

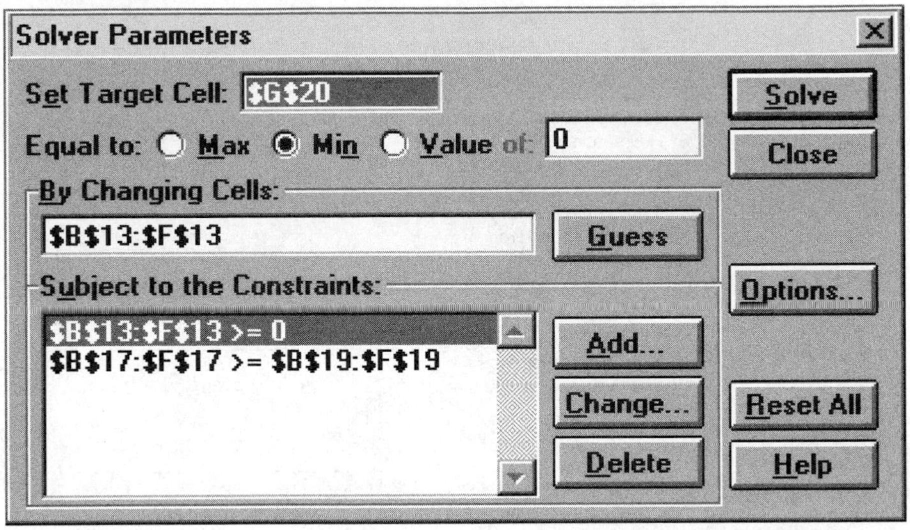

4 **Linear model and optimize.** Check the Assume Linear Model option and select Solve to obtain the optimal solution shown in Figure 3.25. We see that a minimum cost of $593,777 is obtained by the following training schedule: train 0 in January, 8.45 in February, 11.45 in March, 9.52 in April, and 0 in May. This solution is also represented graphically in Figure 3.27.

FIGURE 3.27 **Optimal Solution to CSL Problem**

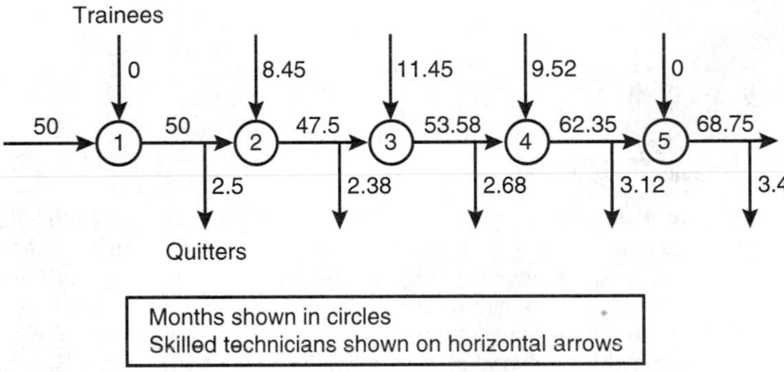

If the number of trainees during each month is required to be an integer, then we can add the constraint that the range B13:F13 be integer. The optimal integer solution is shown in Figure 3.28. Notice that the total cost has increased slightly, to $601,583. Unfortunately, there is still a problem—the number of skilled technicians during each month is still fractional. Unfortunately, there is no easy way to fix this problem.

Sensitivity Analysis A typical shadow price for the CSL problem (from the sensitivity report) is $9.88, for the constraint D17>=D19. (*Note*: From here on, to save space we will not show sensitivity reports. However, remember that they are always available after running the Solver.) This means that a unit increase in the number of repair hours needed

FIGURE 3.28 Optimal Solution to CSL Problem with Integer Constraints

	A	B	C	D	E	F	G
1	CSL Dynamic Workforce Planning Problem with Integer Constraints						
2							
3	Data inputs						
4	January skilled technicians			50			
5	Hours/month/skilled technician			160			
6	Supervision hours/trainee/month			50			
7	Monthly pay/skilled technician			$2,000			
8	Monthly pay/trainee			$1,000			
9	Percentage quitters/month			5%			
10							
11	Planning schedule						
12	Month	1	2	3	4	5	
13	# of trainees	0	9	12	10	0	
14	# of skilled technicians	50	47.5	54.13	63.42	70.25	
15	# of quitters at end of month	2.5	2.38	2.71	3.17	3.51	
16							
17	Available hours for repair	8000	7150.00	8060	9647	11239.65	
18		>=	>=	>=	>=	>=	
19	Required hours for repair	6000	7000	8000	9500	11000	Total cost
20	Cost	$100,000	$104,000	$120,250	$136,838	$140,496	$601,583

for March would increase labor costs by $9.88. After checking the allowable increase and allowable decrease for this constraint, we find that this conclusion is valid as long as the March repair hour requirement is between 6246 hours (= 8000 − 1754) and 8736 hours (= 8000 + 736).

What if CSL had to pay trainees more during their month of training? How would the optimal training schedule change? To answer this question we changed the monthly pay per trainee (in cell D8) to $1500 and then to $2000. We then reran the Solver twice and found each time that the training schedule remained unchanged. You can check whether this solution remains optimal for further increases in the monthly pay. ■

PROBLEMS

Skill-Building Problems

40 An insurance company believes that it will require the following numbers of personal computers during the next six months: January, 9; February, 5; March, 7; April, 9; May, 10; June, 5. Computers can be rented for a period of one, two, or three months at the following unit rates: one-month rate, $200; two-month rate, $350; three-month rate, $450. Determine how to minimize the cost of renting the required computers. You can assume that if a machine is rented for a period of time extending beyond June, the cost of the rental is prorated. For example, if a computer is rented for three months at the beginning of May, then a rental fee of (2/3)450 = $300 is assessed.

41 The IRS has determined that during each of the next 12 months it will need the number of supercomputers given in Table 3.19. To meet these requirements the IRS rents supercomputers for a period of one, two, or three months. It costs $100 to rent a supercomputer for one month, $180 for two months, and $250 for three months. At the beginning of month 1 the IRS has no supercomputers. Determine the rental plan that meets the requirements for the next 12 months at minimum cost. You can assume that fractional rentals are allowed. Thus, if your solution says to rent 140.6 computers for one month, you can round this up to 141 or down to 140 without much effect on the total cost.

TABLE 3.19 Computer Requirements for IRS Problem

	Computer Requirements
Month 1	800
Month 2	1000
Month 3	600
Month 4	500
Month 5	1200
Month 6	800
Month 7	800
Month 8	600
Month 9	400
Month 10	500
Month 11	800
Month 12	600

Skill-Extending Problems

42 You own a wheat warehouse with a capacity of 20,000 bushels. At the beginning of month 1 you have 6000 bushels of wheat. Each month wheat can be bought and sold at the prices per 1000 bushels shown in Table 3.20. The sequence of events during each month is as follows:

- You observe your initial stock of wheat.
- You can sell any amount of wheat up to your initial stock at the current month's selling price.
- You can buy as much wheat as you want, subject to the warehouse size limitation.

Your goal is to determine how to maximize the profit earned over the next ten months.

TABLE 3.20 Selling and Purchasing Prices for Wheat Problem

	Selling Price	Purchase Price
Month 1	$3	$8
Month 2	$6	$8
Month 3	$7	$2
Month 4	$1	$3
Month 5	$4	$4
Month 6	$5	$3
Month 7	$5	$3
Month 8	$1	$2
Month 9	$3	$5
Month 10	$2	$5

43 Suppose that in the CSL computer example it takes two months to train a technician and that during the second month of training, each trainee requires ten hours of experienced technician time. Modify the formulation in the text to account for these changes. ■

3.7 A Dynamic Financial Model

Often a company must determine the optimal level of investment and/or borrowing at different points in time. In this section we show how LP can be used to model such situations.

EXAMPLE 3.6

A small toy store, Tyco, projects the monthly cash inflows listed in Table 3.21 (in thousands of dollars) during the year 2000. A negative cash flow means that cash outflows exceed cash inflows to the business. To pay its bills Tyco will need to borrow money early in the year. The company can borrow money in two ways: (1) It can obtain a long-term one year loan and receive the total amount in January. Beginning in February 2000, 1% interest will be charged each month on this loan. The loan must be paid back by the beginning of January 2001. (2) Each month Tyco can borrow money from a short-term bank line of credit with a monthly interest rate of 1.5%. All short-term loans must be paid off by the beginning of January 2001. At the end of each month excess cash earns 0.4% interest. Tyco wants to use LP to maximize its cash position at the beginning of January 2001.

TABLE 3.21 **Cash Inflows for Tyco**

	Cash Inflow		Cash Inflow
January	−12	**July**	−7
February	−10	**August**	−2
March	−8	**September**	15
April	−10	**October**	12
May	−4	**November**	−7
June	5	**December**	45

Solution

To model Tyco's problem, we must keep track of the following:

- the amount of the long-term loan
- the amount of the short-term loan each month
- the cash balance at the end of each month
- the cash balance at the end of the problem (the beginning of January 2001)
- the interest paid each month on loans
- the interest received each month on last month's ending balance

There are three key points to consider when modeling this problem. First, Tyco can take out a short-term loan each month and close out the short-term loan at the beginning of the next month. Second, letting CB_t be the cash balance at the end of month t, note that

$$\begin{aligned} CB_t = {} & \text{Cash balance from month } t-1 \\ & + \text{Interest on cash balance from month } t-1 \\ & + \text{Loan(s) received during month } t \\ & + \text{Cash inflow in month } t \\ & - \text{Interest paid on long-term loan during month } t \\ & - \text{Interest paid on month } t-1 \text{ short-term loan} \\ & - \text{Long-term loan payback (only in January 2001)} \\ & - \text{Payback of month } t-1 \text{ short-term loan} \end{aligned} \tag{3.6}$$

Third, all bills will have been paid on time if and only if each month's ending cash balance is nonnegative.

Developing the Spreadsheet Model The spreadsheet model for Tyco's problem appears in Figure 3.29. (See the file TYCO.XLS.) To set up this spreadsheet, proceed as follows.

1 **Inputs.** Enter the relevant interest rates in the range D4:D6 and the monthly cash inflows in the range F9:F20.

2 **Loan amounts.** Enter *any* trial value in cell D9 for the long-term loan, and enter *any* trial values in the range E9:E20 for the short-term loans.

3 **Beginning cash balance each month.** Column B is used to keep track of the cash balance from the previous month. Enter a 0 in cell B9, because there was no mention of a carryover from December 1999. Then enter the formula

```
=K9
```

in cell B10. This is the entering cash balance for month 2, which equals the ending cash balance for month 1. Copy this formula to the range B11:B21 for the other months.

4 **Interest earned on cash balance each month.** Column C is used to keep track of the interest earned on the cash balance. In January 2000 no interest is earned, so enter \$0 in cell C9. During February 2000 the interest earned equals .004 times the ending January 2000 balance. So enter the formula

```
=$D$6*B10
```

in cell C10 and copy it to the range C11:C21 for the other months.

5 **Interest paid on long-term loan each month.** The range G10:G21 is used to compute the interest paid on the long-term loan each month. We assume that the interest payments on the long-term loan begin in February 2000 and end at the beginning of January 2001. For each month the interest payment on the long-term loan is the amount of the loan multiplied by the long-term interest rate. Therefore, compute the interest paid in February in cell G10 with the formula

```
=$D$4*$D$9
```

and copy this formula to the range G11:G21 for the other months.

6 **Interest paid on short-term loans each month.** The range H10:H21 is used to compute the interest payment on short-term loans each month. Note that the interest

FIGURE 3.29 **Optimal Solution to Tyco Cash Flow Problem**

	A	B	C	D	E	F	G	H	I	J	K
1	Tyco Investment/Borrowing Problem										
2											
3	**Data inputs**										
4	Interest rate on long-term loan			1.0%							
5	Interest rate on short-term loan			1.5%							
6	Interest rate earned on excess cash			0.4%							
7											
8	Month	Cash balance from previous month	Interest on cash balance	Long-term loan	Short-term loan	Cash inflow	Interest paid this month on long-term loan	Interest paid this month on short-term loan	Long-term loan payback	Short-term loan payback	Cash balance at end of month
9	Jan-00	\$0.00	\$0.00	\$32,102.28	\$0.00	(\$12,000.00)					\$20,102.28
10	Feb-00	\$20,102.28	\$80.41		\$0.00	(\$10,000.00)	\$321.02	\$0.00		\$0.00	\$9,861.67
11	Mar-00	\$9,861.67	\$39.45		\$0.00	(\$8,000.00)	\$321.02	\$0.00		\$0.00	\$1,580.09
12	Apr-00	\$1,580.09	\$6.32		\$8,734.61	(\$10,000.00)	\$321.02	\$0.00		\$0.00	\$0.00
13	May-00	\$0.00	\$0.00		\$13,186.65	(\$4,000.00)	\$321.02	\$131.02		\$8,734.61	\$0.00
14	Jun-00	\$0.00	\$0.00		\$8,705.47	\$5,000.00	\$321.02	\$197.80		\$13,186.65	\$0.00
15	Jul-00	\$0.00	\$0.00		\$16,157.08	(\$7,000.00)	\$321.02	\$130.58		\$8,705.47	(\$0.00)
16	Aug-00	(\$0.00)	(\$0.00)		\$18,720.46	(\$2,000.00)	\$321.02	\$242.36		\$16,157.08	\$0.00
17	Sep-00	\$0.00	\$0.00		\$4,322.29	\$15,000.00	\$321.02	\$280.81		\$18,720.46	\$0.00
18	Oct-00	\$0.00	\$0.00		\$0.00	\$12,000.00	\$321.02	\$64.83		\$4,322.29	\$7,291.86
19	Nov-00	\$7,291.86	\$29.17		\$0.00	(\$7,000.00)	\$321.02	\$0.00		\$0.00	(\$0.00)
20	Dec-00	(\$0.00)	(\$0.00)		\$0.00	\$45,000.00	\$321.02	\$0.00		\$0.00	\$44,678.98
21	Jan-01	\$44,678.98	\$178.72				\$321.02	\$0.00	\$32,102.28	\$0.00	\$12,434.39
22											**Final cash balance**

payment in month t is the short-term loan amount in month $t-1$ times the short-term interest rate. So in cell H10 compute the February interest payment with the formula

=$D$5*E9

and copy this formula to the range H11:H21 for the other months.

7 **Repayment of long-term loan.** In cell I21 enter the repayment of the long-term loan at the beginning of January 2001 with the formula

=D9

8 **Repayment of short-term loans.** Column J is used to compute the amount of short-term loan principal paid back each month. Note that the amount repayed in month t is simply the amount borrowed in month $t-1$. So in cell J10 compute the February 2000 short-term loan principal repayment with the formula

=E9

and copy this formula to the range J11:J21 for the other months.

9 **Ending cash balance each month.** Column K is used to compute the ending cash balance for each month. In cell K9 compute the January 2000 ending cash balance with the formula

=SUM(B9:F9)–SUM(G9:J9)

This formula operationalizes the cash balance Equation 3.6. Then copy this formula to the range K10:K21 for the other months. (*Note*: Even though the value in cell K21 is listed in the "end-of-month" column, it really represents the cash at the *beginning* of January 2001, after loans have been repaid.)

Using the Solver To solve the Tyco problem with Excel's Solver, proceed as follows. (When you are finished, the Solver dialog box should appear as shown in Figure 3.30.)

1 **Objective.** Select cell K21 (January 2001 cash position) as the target cell to maximize.

2 **Changing cells.** Select cell D9 (the long-term loan) and the range E9:E20 (the short-term loans) as the changing cells and constrain these to be nonnegative.

3 **Cash requirement constraints.** Add the constraints K9:K20>=0. These ensure that each month's cash requirements are met on time.

4 **Linear model and optimize.** Check the Assume Linear Model option and select Solve to obtain the optimal solution shown in Figure 3.29. The solution recommends a long-term loan of $32,102.28 along with short-term loans of various amounts during the six months from April to September. At the beginning of January 2001, Tyco's cash position will be $12,434.39.

Sensitivity Analysis The shadow prices for the Tyco example are difficult to interpret. We therefore limit the discussion to three what-if questions. First, how does the solution change if Tyco's excess cash earns 0.8% per month? Here we simply enter 0.8% in cell D6 and rerun the Solver. You can check that a larger long-term loan is taken out, and short-term loans are taken out in May, July, and August. Similarly, how does the solution change if the long-term loan interest rate is increased to 1.3% per month? By entering 1.3% in cell D4 and rerunning the Solver, you can check that the amount of the long-term loan is reduced, and short-term loans are taken out in the nine months from March to November. Finally, how does the solution change if the short-term interest rate is cut to 0.8% per month? By entering 0.8% in cell D5 and rerunning the Solver, you can check that no long-term loan is taken, and short-term loans are taken out in all months except for

FIGURE 3.30 Solver Dialog Box for Tyco Problem

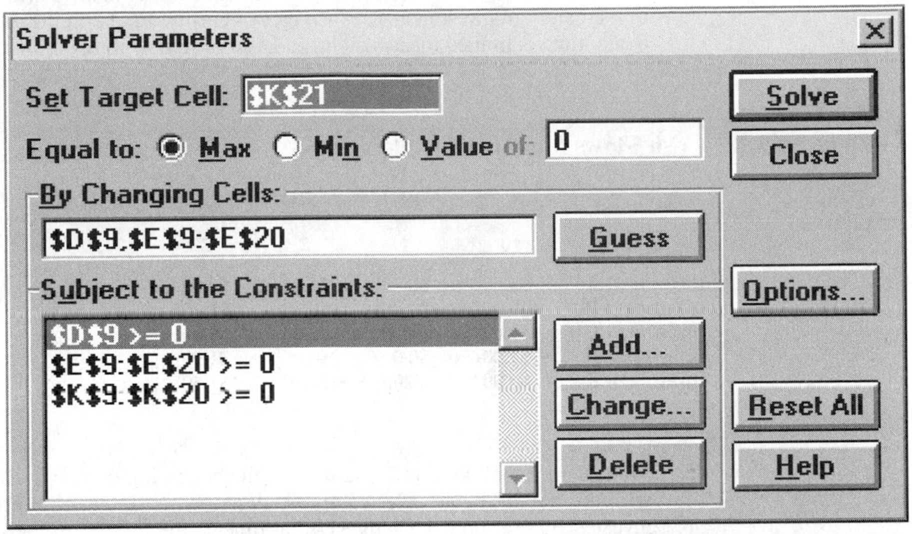

December. These examples should convince you that in reasonably complex models, it is not easy to guess the effects of changes in the input parameters! ■

MODELING ISSUES

1 In reality, we do not know future short-term interest rates and future cash needs; we must forecast them using the forecasting methods discussed in Chapter 14.

2 As in Section 3.5, Tyco's model would be implemented with a rolling planning horizon. ■

REAL-WORLD APPLICATION

Using LP to Optimize Bond Portfolios

Many Wall Street firms buy and sell bonds. Rohn [20] discusses a bond selection model that maximizes profit from bond purchases and sales subject to constraints that minimize the firm's risk exposure. The method used to model this situation is closely related to the method we used to model the Tyco problem. See Problem 47 for a simplified version of this model. ■

PROBLEMS

Skill-Building Problems

44 Finco Investment Corporation must determine an investment strategy for the firm for the next three years. At present (time 0), $100,000 is available for investment. Investments A, B, C, D, and E are available. The cash flow associated with investing $1 in each investment is given in Table 3.22. For example, $1 invested in investment B requires a $1 cash outflow at time 1 and returns 50¢ at time 2 and $1 at time 3. To ensure that the company's portfolio is diversified, Finco requires that at most $75,000 be placed in any single investment. In addition to investments A through E, Finco can earn interest at 8% per year by keeping uninvested cash in money market funds. Returns from investments can be reinvested immediately. For example, the positive cash flow received from investment C at time 1 can be reinvested immediately in investment B. Finco cannot borrow funds, so the cash available for investment at any time is limited to cash on hand. Determine how to maximize cash on hand at time 3.

TABLE 3.22 Cash Flows for Finco Problem

	Cash Flow at Time			
	0	1	2	3
Investment A	−$1.00	$0.50	$1.00	$0.00
Investment B	$0.00	−$1.00	$0.50	$1.00
Investment C	−$1.00	$1.20	$0.00	$0.00
Investment D	−$1.00	$0.00	$0.00	$1.90
Investment E	$0.00	$0.00	−$1.00	$1.50

45 Moneyco has $1000 to invest at time 1 (the beginning of year 1). The cash flows associated with the five available investments are described in Table 3.23. For example, every dollar invested in A at time 1 yields $1.40 at time 4. In addition to these investments, Moneyco can invest as much money each year as it wants in CDs. CDs pay 6% interest. The company wants to maximize its available cash at time 4. Assuming it can put no more than $500 in any investment, formulate an LP to help Moneyco achieve its goal.

TABLE 3.23 Cash Flows for Moneyco Problem

	A	B	C	D	E
Time 1	−1.00	−1.00	−1.00		
Time 2		+1.15			−1.00
Time 3			+1.28	−1.00	
Time 4	+1.40			+1.15	+1.32

46 At time 0 you have $10,000. Investments A and B are available; their cash flows are shown in Table 3.24. Assume that any money not invested in A or B earns interest at an annual rate of 8%. Determine how to maximize your cash on hand at time 3.

TABLE 3.24 Cash Flows for Investment Problem

	A	B
Time 0	−$1.00	$0.00
Time 1	$0.20	−$1.00
Time 2	$1.50	$0.00
Time 3	$0.00	$1.90

Skill-Extending Problems

47 Broker Sonya Wong is currently trying to maximize her profit in the bond market. Four bonds are available for purchase and sale at the bid and ask prices shown in Table 3.25. Sonya can buy up to 1000 units of each bond at the ask price or sell up to 1000 units of each bond at the bid price. During each of the next three years, the person who sells a bond will pay the owner of the bond the cash payments shown in Table 3.26. Sonya's goal is to maximize her revenue from selling bonds less her payment for buying bonds, subject to the constraint that after each year's payments are received, her current cash position (due only to cash payments from bonds and not purchases or sales of bonds) is nonnegative. Note that her current cash position can

depend on past coupons and that cash accumulated at the end of each year earns 11.111% annual interest. Determine how to maximize net profit from buying and selling bonds, subject to the constraints previously described. Why do you think we limit the number of units of each bond that can be bought or sold?

TABLE 3.25 Bid and Ask Prices for Bond Problem

	Bid Price	Ask Price
Bond 1	980	990
Bond 2	970	985
Bond 3	960	972
Bond 4	940	954

TABLE 3.26 Cash Payments for Bond Problem

	Bond 1	Bond 2	Bond 3	Bond 4
Year 1	100	80	70	60
Year 2	110	90	80	50
Year 3	1100	1120	1090	1110

48 Consider the Tyco example with the following modification. Each month Tyco can delay payments on some or all of the cash owed for the current month. (This is possible only for months where cash is due, indicated by negative amounts in column F of Figure 3.29.) This is called **stretching payments**. Payments can be stretched for only one month, and a 1% penalty is charged on the amount stretched. Thus, if Tyco stretches its payments on \$10,000 of the \$12,000 cash owed in January, it must pay \$10,100 (= 10000 * 1.01) in February. With this modification, determine how Tyco can maximize its cash on hand at the beginning of January 2001.

49 You are managing a company pension fund. The fund needs to make the payments shown in Table 3.27 (in thousands) on the first day of each year. You are going to finance these payments by buying bonds. Three bonds are available for purchase on January 1, 1995. The price and coupons for each bond are as follows. (All coupon payments are received on January 1 and arrive in time to meet cash demands for the date on which they arrive.)

TABLE 3.27 Payments for Pension Problem

	Payment		Payment		Payment
1995	11	**2000**	18	**2005**	25
1996	12	**2001**	20	**2006**	30
1997	14	**2002**	21	**2007**	31
1998	15	**2003**	22	**2008**	31
1999	16	**2004**	24	**2009**	31

- Bond 1 costs \$980 and yields a \$60 coupon in 1996–99 and a \$1060 payment in year 2000.
- Bond 2 costs \$970 and yields a \$65 coupon in 1996–2005 and a \$1065 payment in 2006.
- Bond 3 costs \$1050 and yields a \$75 coupon in 1996–2008 and a \$1075 payment in 2009.

On January 1, 1995, you purchase bonds and then meet your demand of \$11,000. During each year your cash on hand earns 4% interest. You must determine the bonds that should be purchased in order to minimize the January 1, 1995, investment needed to meet the 1995–2009 cash requirements. You may assume that fractional numbers of bonds can be purchased. ■

3.8

Data Envelopment Analysis (DEA)

Often we wonder if a university, hospital, restaurant, or other business is operating efficiently. The **Data Envelopment Analysis** (DEA) method can be used to answer this question. Specifically, DEA can be used by inefficient organizations to benchmark efficient and "best-practice" organizations. Quoting a paper by Sherman and Ladino [23],

> Many managers of service organizations would describe benchmarking and best-practice analysis as basic, widely accepted concepts already used in their businesses. Closer examination indicates that the traditional techniques used to identify and promulgate best practices are not very effective, largely because the operations of these service organizations are too complex to allow them to identify best practices accurately. DEA provides an objective way to identify best practices in these service organizations and has consistently generated new insights that lead to substantial productivity gains that were not otherwise identifiable.

The following example illustrates DEA.

EXAMPLE 3.7

Consider a group of three hospitals. To simplify matters, we assume that each hospital "converts" two inputs into three different outputs. The two inputs used by each hospital are

- input 1 = capital (measured by hundreds of hospital beds)
- input 2 = labor (measured by thousands of labor hours used in a month)

The outputs produced by each hospital are

- output 1 = hundreds of patient-days during month for patients under age 14
- output 2 = hundreds of patient-days during month for patients between 14 and 65
- output 3 = hundreds of patient-days for patients over 65

The inputs and outputs for these hospitals are given in Table 3.28. Which of these three hospitals is efficient in terms of using its inputs and producing outputs?

TABLE 3.28 **Input and Output for Hospital Example**

	Inputs		Outputs		
	1	**2**	**1**	**2**	**3**
Hospital 1	5	14	9	4	16
Hospital 2	8	15	5	7	10
Hospital 3	7	12	4	9	13

Solution

To determine whether a hospital is efficient, we define a price per unit of each output and a cost per unit of each input. Then the efficiency of a hospital is defined to be

$$\text{Efficiency of hospital} = \frac{\text{Value of hospital's outputs}}{\text{Value of hospital's inputs}}$$

The DEA approach uses the following four ideas to determine whether a hospital is efficient:

1 No hospital can be more than 100% efficient. Thus the efficiency of each hospital is constrained to be less than or equal to 1. To ensure that this is a linear constraint, we express it in this form:

$$\text{Value of hospital's outputs} \leq \text{Value of hospital's inputs}$$

2 When we are trying to determine whether a hospital is efficient, it simplifies matters to scale input prices so that the value of the hospital's inputs equals 1. Then the efficiency of the hospital will simply equal the value of the hospital's outputs.

3 If we are interested in evaluating the efficiency of a hospital, we attempt to choose input and output prices that maximize the hospital's efficiency. If the hospital's efficiency equals 1, then the hospital is efficient; if the hospital's efficiency is less than 1, then the hospital is inefficient.

4 We must ensure that each input cost and output price is nonnegative.

Determining Whether Hospital 1 Is Efficient Figure 3.31 contains the spreadsheet used to determine whether hospital 1 is efficient. (See the file DEA.XLS.) To develop this model, proceed as follows.

1 **Input given data.** Enter the input and output information for each hospital in the range B5:F7.

2 **Input costs.** Enter *any* trial values for the input costs in the range B10:C10.

3 **Output prices.** Enter *any* trial values for the output prices in the range D10:F10.

4 **Input costs for each hospital.** In the range B13:B15 compute the cost of the inputs produced by each hospital. Begin by entering the formula

=SUMPRODUCT(B$10:C$10,B5:C5)

in cell B13 for hospital 1. Then copy this formula to the range B14:B15 for the other hospitals.

FIGURE 3.31 **DEA for Hospital 1**

	A	B	C	D	E	F
1	DEA Hospital 1					
2						
3	Quantities used/produced					
4		Input 1	Input 2	Output 1	Output 2	Output 3
5	Hospital 1	5	14	9	4	16
6	Hospital 2	8	15	5	7	10
7	Hospital 3	7	12	4	9	13
8						
9		Input 1	Input 2	Output 1	Output 2	Output 3
10	Unit costs/prices for inputs/outputs	0	0.071	0	0	0.062
11						
12	Costs/Prices of inputs/outputs used	Input costs		Output Values		
13	Hospital 1	1	>=	1		
14	Hospital 2	1.071	>=	0.625		
15	Hospital 3	0.857	>=	0.812		
16						
17	Hospital 1 input cost	1	=	1		
18	Hospital 1 output value (maximize)	1				

5 **Output values for each hospital.** In the range D13:D15 compute the value of the outputs produced by each hospital. To begin, enter the formula

=SUMPRODUCT(D$10:F$10,D5:F5)

in cell D13 for hospital 1. Then copy this formula to the range D14:D15 for the other hospitals.

6 **Recopy input cost and output value for hospital 1.** Recopy the value of hospital 1's inputs by entering the formula

=B13

in cell B17 and enter a 1 in cell D17. Also, recopy the value of hospital 1's outputs by entering the formula

=D13

in cell B18.

Using the Solver to Determine Whether Hospital 1 Is Efficient To see whether hospital 1 is efficient, use the Solver as follows. (When you are finished, the Solver window should appear as shown in Figure 3.32.)

1 **Objective.** Select cell B18 as the target cell to maximize. Since the cost of hospital 1 inputs equals 1, this will cause the Solver to maximize the efficiency of hospital 1.

2 **Changing cells.** Choose the range B10:F10 (the input and output prices) as the changing cells and constrain these to be nonnegative.

3 **Hospital 1's input cost constraint.** Add the constraint B17=D17. This sets the value of hospital 1 inputs equal to 1.

4 **Maximum efficiency constraints.** Add the constraints B13:B15>=D13:D15. This ensures that no hospital is more than 100% efficient.

5 **Linear model and optimize.** Check the Assume Linear Model option and select Solve.

FIGURE 3.32 **Solver Dialog Box for DEA of Hospital 1**

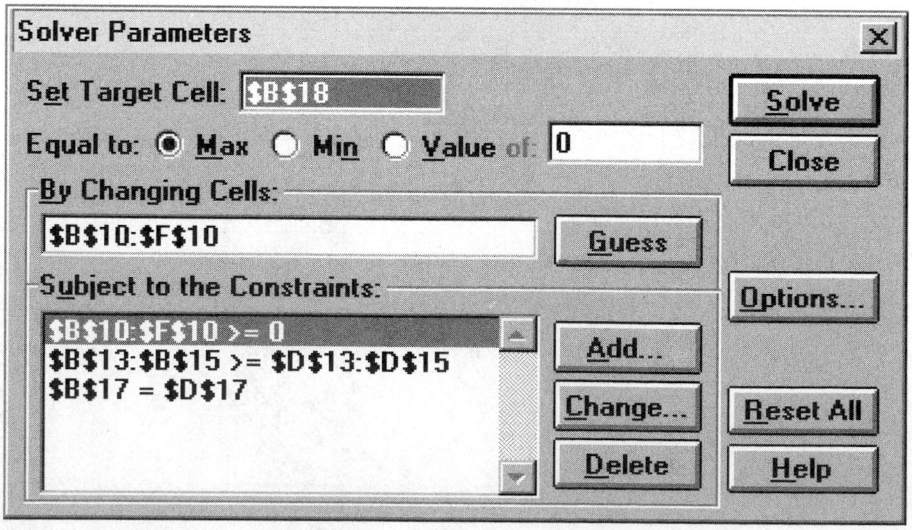

The 1 in cell B18 of Figure 3.31 means that we have been able to find a set of unit costs for the inputs and the unit values of the outputs such that the total value of hospital 1's outputs equals the total cost of its inputs. In other words, hospital 1 is efficient.

Determining Whether Hospital 2 Is Efficient To determine whether hospital 2 is efficient, we simply replace the formula in cell B17 with the value of hospital 2's inputs (from cell B14) and replace the formula in cell B18 with the value of hospital 2's outputs (from cell D14). The optimal solution appears in Figure 3.33. From the value of .773 in cell B18, we see that hospital 2 is *not* efficient.

FIGURE 3.33 **DEA for Hospital 2**

	A	B	C	D	E	F
1	DEA Hospital 2					
2						
3	Quantities used/produced					
4		Input 1	Input 2	Output 1	Output 2	Output 3
5	Hospital 1	5	14	9	4	16
6	Hospital 2	8	15	5	7	10
7	Hospital 3	7	12	4	9	13
8						
9		Input 1	Input 2	Output 1	Output 2	Output 3
10	Unit costs/prices for inputs/outputs	0	0.067	0.080	0.053	0
11						
12	Costs/Prices of inputs/outputs used	Input costs		Output Values		
13	Hospital 1	0.933	>=	0.933		
14	Hospital 2	1	>=	0.773		
15	Hospital 3	0.8	>=	0.8		
16						
17	Hospital 2 input cost	1	=	1		
18	Hospital 2 output value (maximize)	0.773				

Determining Whether Hospital 3 Is Efficient Similarly, to determine whether hospital 3 is efficient, we replace the formula in cell B17 with the value of hospital 3's inputs (from cell B15) and replace the formula in cell B18 with the value of hospital 3's outputs (from cell D15). The optimal solution appears in Figure 3.34. From the value of 1 in cell B18, we see that hospital 3 is efficient.

In summary, we have found that hospitals 1 and 3 are efficient, but hospital 2 is inefficient.

What Does It Mean to Be Inefficient? If DEA finds that a hospital is inefficient, then a "combination" of the efficient hospitals can be found that uses no more inputs than the inefficient hospital, yet produces at least as much of each output as the inefficient hospital. At least one of these inequalities will be strict. In our example it can be shown that, together, 26.2% of hospital 1 and 66.15% of hospital 3 produce the same amount of outputs 1 and 2 as hospital 2, but produce 27.9% more of output 3. Also, 26.2% of hospital 1 and 66.15% of hospital 3 together use less of each input than hospital 2. This indicates where hospital 2 is inefficient.

To demonstrate the inefficiency of hospital 2, note that

$$\text{Output 1 produced by composite hospital} = .262(9) + .6615(4)$$
$$= 5$$
$$= \text{Output 1 produced by hospital 2}$$

FIGURE 3.34 **DEA for Hospital 3**

	A	B	C	D	E	F
1	DEA Hospital 3					
2						
3	Quantities used/produced					
4		Input 1	Input 2	Output 1	Output 2	Output 3
5	Hospital 1	5	14	9	4	16
6	Hospital 2	8	15	5	7	10
7	Hospital 3	7	12	4	9	13
8						
9		Input 1	Input 2	Output 1	Output 2	Output 3
10	Unit costs/prices for inputs/outputs	0	0.083	0.1	0.067	0
11						
12	Costs/Prices of inputs/outputs used	Input costs		Output Values		
13	Hospital 1	1.167	>=	1.167		
14	Hospital 2	1.25	>=	0.967		
15	Hospital 3	1	>=	1		
16						
17	Hospital 3 input cost	1	=	1		
18	Hospital 3 output value (maximize)	1				

$$\text{Output 2 produced by composite hospital} = .262(4) + .6615(9)$$
$$= 7$$
$$= \text{Output 2 produced by hospital 2}$$
$$\text{Output 3 produced by composite hospital} = .262(16) + .6615(13)$$
$$= 12.79$$
$$> 10 = \text{Output 3 produced by hospital 2}$$
$$\text{Input 1 needed by composite hospital} = .262(5) + .6615(7)$$
$$= 5.94$$
$$< 8 = \text{Input 1 required by hospital 2}$$
$$\text{Input 2 needed by composite hospital} = .262(14) + .6615(12)$$
$$= 11.6$$
$$< 15 = \text{Input 2 required by hospital 2}$$

Thus, there exists a "combination" of hospitals 1 and 3 that produces a better combination of outputs than hospital 2 by using fewer inputs. Clearly hospital 2 has some problems!

In general, to determine the linear combination of efficient units that dominates a particular inefficient unit, we simply look at the shadow prices of the "value of unit i inputs >= value of unit i outputs" constraints (those in rows 13–15). The "weight" of any efficient unit is then the absolute value of its shadow price. In the hospital 2 spreadsheet the binding constraints in Figure 3.33 are in rows 13 and 15. The associated sensitivity report (not shown) tells us that the absolute values of the shadow prices for these binding constraints are .262 and .6615. Therefore, as we stated above, the combination of .262 times hospital 1 plus .6615 times hospital 3 is a "better" hospital than hospital 2. ■

MODELING ISSUE

Sexton, Sleeper, and Taggart [22] used DEA to evaluate the efficiency of school bus transportation for the counties of North Carolina. For each county they used two inputs: buses used and total operating expense. They used a single output: pupils transported per day. However, they noted a problem with "traditional" DEA. Consider two counties (county 1 and county 2) that use exactly the same inputs and produce the same outputs. Suppose that county 1 is very sparsely populated and county 2 is densely populated. Then it is clear that county 1 is transporting pupils more efficiently than county 2, but a DEA conducted by the method we have described will not show this. Realizing this, the authors developed a method to adjust the output of county 2 downward and the output of county 1 upward to compensate for this problem. The North Carolina Department of Education penalized the inefficient counties by reducing their budgetary appropriations. Since the time DEA was performed, most counties have greatly increased their efficiency. ■

REAL-WORLD APPLICATION

DEA in the Banking Industry

Sherman and Ladino [23] discuss the use of DEA in identifying the most and least efficient branches in a banking firm with 33 branch banks. They found efficiency ratings that varied from 37% to 100%, with 23 of the 33 branches rated below 100% and 10 below 70%. Each of the inefficient branches was compared to a reference set of "best-practice" branches—efficient branches that offered similar services as the inefficient branch. This allowed them to make specific suggestions as to how the inefficient branches could improve. For example, they showed that branch 1 should be able to provide its current level and mix of services with 4.5 fewer customer-service personnel, 1.8 fewer sales service personnel, 0.3 fewer managers, $222,928 less in operating expenses, and 1304 fewer square feet. They also indicated the added amount of service that the inefficient branches could provide, in addition to resource savings, if these branches were as efficient as the best-practice branches. For example, branch 1 could handle (per year) about 15,000 additional deposits, withdrawals, and checks cashed, 2000 added bank checks, bonds, and travelers' checks, and eight additional night deposits, while reducing the resources needed if it attained the efficiency level of the best-practice branches. ■

PROBLEMS

Skill-Building Problems

50 The Salem Board of Education wants to evaluate the efficiency of the town's four elementary schools. The three outputs of the schools are

- output 1 = average reading score
- output 2 = average mathematics score
- output 3 = average self-esteem score

The three inputs to the schools are

- input 1 = average educational level of mothers (defined by highest grade completed: 12 = high school graduate; 16 = college graduate, and so on)
- input 2 = number of parent visits to school (per child)
- input 3 = teacher to student ratio

The relevant information for the four schools is given in Table 3.29. Determine which (if any) schools are inefficient.

TABLE 3.29 Input/Output Table for School Problem

	Inputs			Outputs		
	1	2	3	1	2	3
School 1	13	4	.05	9	7	6
School 2	14	5	.05	10	8	7
School 3	11	6	.06	11	7	8
School 4	15	8	.08	9	9	9

51 Pine Valley Bank has three branches. You have been asked to evaluate the efficiency of each. The following inputs and outputs are to be used for the study:

- input 1 = labor hours used (hundreds per month)
- input 2 = space used (in hundreds of square feet)
- input 3 = supplies used per month (in dollars)
- output 1 = loan applications per month
- output 2 = deposits processed per month (in thousands)
- output 3 = checks processed per month (in thousands)

The relevant information is given in Table 3.30. Use these data to determine whether any bank branches are inefficient.

TABLE 3.30 Input/Output Table for Bank Problem

	Input			Output		
	1	2	3	1	2	3
Bank 1	15	20	50	200	15	35
Bank 2	14	23	51	220	18	45
Bank 3	16	19	51	210	17	40

52 You have been asked to evaluate the efficiency of the Port Charles Police Department. Three precincts are to be evaluated. The inputs and outputs for each precinct are as follows:

- input 1 = number of policemen
- input 2 = number of vehicles used
- output 1 = number of patrol units responding to service requests (thousands per year)
- output 2 = number of convictions obtained each year (in hundreds)

You are given the data in Table 3.31. Use this information to determine which precincts, if any, are inefficient.

53 You have been commissioned by Indiana University to evaluate the relative efficiency of four degree-granting units: Business, Education, Arts and Sciences, and Health, Physical Education, and Recreation (HPER). You are given the information in Table 3.32. Use DEA to find all inefficient units. ■

TABLE 3.31 Input/Output Table for Police Problem

	Input		Output	
	1	2	1	2
Precinct 1	200	60	6	8.0
Precinct 2	300	90	8	9.5
Precinct 3	400	120	10	11.0

TABLE 3.32 Input/Output Table for University Problem

	Faculty	Support Staff	Supply Budget (in millions)	Credit Hours (in thousands)	Research Pubs
Business	150	70	5	15.0	225
Education	60	20	3	5.4	70
Arts & Sciences	800	140	20	56.0	1300
HPER	30	15	1	2.1	40

3.9 Conclusion

On this chapter we have formulated LP spreadsheet models of many diverse situations. There is no standard procedure that can be used to attack all problems. However, there are several keys to most formulations.

1 First, determine the changing cells. For example, in blending problems it is vital to realize that the changing cells are the amount of each input used to produce each output, or, as in the post office scheduling example, it is critical to realize that the changing cells are the number of people who start work each day of the week.

2 Set up the spreadsheet so that you can easily compute what you wish to maximize or minimize (usually profit or cost). For example, in the aggregate planning model the easiest way to compute total cost is to compute the monthly cost of operation in each row.

3 Set up the spreadsheet so that the relationships between the cells in the spreadsheet and the problem constraints are readily apparent. For example, in the post office scheduling example it is convenient to compute the number of people working each day of the week near the number of people needed for each day of the week.

4 You cannot always pigeonhole an LP model into a particular box. For example, a problem might involve a combination of the ideas discussed in the inventory scheduling, blending, and production process examples of this chapter. Many of the review problems are not strictly analogous to any of the models we have discussed. However, the practice you have gained in this chapter should enable you to solve these and other complex problems.

REVIEW PROBLEMS

Skill-Building Problems

54 You now have $10,000, and the following investments are available to you during the next three years:

- Investment A: Every dollar invested now yields $0.10 a year from now and $1.30 three years from now.
- Investment B: Every dollar invested now yields $0.20 a year from now and $1.10 two years from now.
- Investment C: Every dollar invested a year from now yields $1.50 three years from now.

During each year, you can place uninvested cash in money market funds that yield 6% interest per year. However, you can invest at most $5000 in any one of A, B, or C. Determine how to maximize your cash on hand three years from now.

55 Sunco processes oil into aviation fuel and heating oil. It costs $40 to purchase each 1000 barrels of oil, which is then distilled and yields 500 barrels of aviation fuel and 500 barrels of heating oil. Output from the distillation can be sold directly or processed in the catalytic cracker. If sold after distillation without further processing, aviation fuel sells for $60 per 1000 barrels, and heating oil sells for $40 per 1000 barrels. It takes one hour to process 1000 barrels of aviation fuel in the catalytic cracker, and these 1000 barrels can be sold for $130. It takes 45 minutes to process 1000 barrels of heating oil in the cracker, and these 1000 barrels can be sold for $90. Each day at most 20,000 barrels of oil can be purchased, and eight hours of cracker time are available. Determine how to maximize Sunco's profit.

56 The following investments are available to Finco:

- Investment 1: For each dollar invested at time 0, Finco receives $0.10 at time 1 and $1.30 at time 2 (where time 0 = now, time 1 = one year from now, and so on).
- Investment 2: For each dollar invested at time 1, Finco receives $1.60 at time 2.
- Investment 3: For each dollar invested at time 2, Finco receives $1.20 at time 3.

At any time, leftover cash can be invested in T-bills, which pay 10% per year. At time 0, Finco has $10,000. At most $5000 can be invested in any one of investments 1, 2, or 3. Determine how to maximize Finco's cash on hand at time 3.

57 All steel manufactured by Steelco must meet the following requirements: between 3.2% and 3.5% carbon; between 1.8% and 2.5% silicon; between 0.9% and 1.2% nickel; tensile strength of at least 45,000 pounds per square inch (psi). Steelco manufactures steel by combining two alloys. The cost and properties of each alloy are given in Table 3.33. Assume that the tensile strength of a mixture of the two alloys can be determined by averaging the tensile strength of the alloys that are mixed together. For example, a one-ton mixture that is 40% alloy 1 and 60% alloy 2 has a tensile strength of 0.4(42000) + 0.6(50000). Determine how to minimize the cost of producing a ton of steel.

TABLE 3.33 Requirements for Steelco Problem

	Alloy 1	Alloy 2
Cost per Ton	$190	$200
Percent Silicon	2%	2.5%
Percent Nickel	1%	1.5%
Percent Carbon	3%	4.0%
Tensile Strength	42,000 psi	50,000 psi

58 Steelco manufactures two types of steel at three different steel mills. During a given month each steel mill has 200 hours of blast furnace time available. Because of differences in the furnaces at each mill, the time and cost to produce a ton of steel differs for each mill. The time and cost for each mill are shown in Table 3.34. Each month Steelco must manufacture at least 500 tons of steel 1 and 600 tons of steel 2. Formulate an LP to minimize the cost of manufacturing the desired steel.

TABLE 3.34 Times and Costs for Steelco Problem

	Steel 1		Steel 2	
	Cost	Time (minutes)	Cost	Time (minutes)
Mill 1	$10	20	$11	22
Mill 2	$12	24	$9	18
Mill 3	$14	28	$10	30

59 (Based on Heady and Egbert [11]) Walnut Orchard has two farms that grow wheat and corn. Because of differing soil conditions, there are differences in the yields and costs of growing crops on the two farms. The yields and costs are shown in Table 3.35. Each farm has 100 acres available for cultivation; 11,000 bushels of wheat and 7000 bushels of corn must be grown. Determine a planting plan that will minimize the cost of meeting these requirements. How could an extension of this model be used to allocate crop production efficiently throughout a nation?

TABLE 3.35 Yields and Costs for Walnut Orchard Problem

	Farm 1	Farm 2
Corn Yield per Acre	500 bushels	650 bushels
Cost per Acre of Corn	$100	$120
Wheat Yield per Acre	400 bushels	350 bushels
Cost per Acre of Wheat	$90	$80

60 Candy Kane Cosmetics (CKC) produces Leslie Perfume, which requires chemicals and labor. Two production processes are available. Process 1 transforms one unit of labor and two units of chemicals into three ounces of perfume. Process 2 transforms two units of labor and three units of chemicals into five ounces of perfume. It costs CKC $3 to purchase a unit of labor and $2 to purchase a unit of chemicals. Each year up to 20,000 units of labor and 35,000 units of chemicals can be purchased. In the absence of advertising, CKC believes it can sell 1000 ounces of perfume. To stimulate demand for Leslie, CKC can hire the lovely model Jenny Nelson. Jenny is paid $100 per hour. Each hour Jenny works for the company is estimated to increase the demand for Leslie Perfume by 200 ounces. Each ounce of Leslie Perfume sells for $5. Determine how CKC can maximize its profit.

61 Carco has a $150,000 advertising budget. To increase its automobile sales the firm is considering advertising in newspapers and on television. The more Carco uses a particular medium, the less effective each additional ad is. Table 3.36 shows the number of new customers reached by each ad. Each newspaper ad costs $1000 and each television ad costs $10,000. At most 30 newspaper ads and 15 television ads can be placed. How can Carco maximize the number of new customers created by advertising?

TABLE 3.36 Ad Exposures for Carco Problem

	Number of Ads	New Customers
Newspaper	1–10	900
	11–20	600
	21–30	300
Television	1–5	10000
	6–10	5000
	11–15	2000

62 Sunco Oil has refineries in Los Angeles and Chicago. The Los Angeles refinery can refine up to two million barrels of oil per year, and the Chicago refinery up to three million. Once refined, oil is shipped to two distribution points, Houston and New York City. Sunco estimates that each distribution point can sell up to five million barrels per year. Because of differences in shipping and refining costs, the profit earned (in dollars) per million barrels of oil shipped depends on where the oil was refined and on the point of distribution. This information is listed in Table 3.37. Sunco is considering expanding the capacity of each refinery. Each million barrels of annual refining capacity that is added will cost $120,000 for the Los Angeles

TABLE 3.37 Profits for Sunco Problem

	Profit per Million Barrels	
	To Houston	To New York
From Los Angeles	$20,000	$15,000
From Chicago	$18,000	$17,000

refinery and \$150,000 for the Chicago refinery. Determine how Sunco can maximize its profit (including expansion costs) over a ten-year period.

63 Feedco produces two types of cattle feed, both consisting totally of wheat and alfalfa. Feed 1 must contain at least 80% wheat, and feed 2 must contain at least 60% alfalfa. Feed 1 sells for \$1.50 per pound, and feed 2 sells for \$1.30 per pound. Feedco can purchase up to 1000 pounds of wheat at 50 cents per pound and up to 800 pounds of alfalfa at 40 cents per pound. Demand for each type of feed is unlimited. Determine how to maximize Feedco's profit.

64 Feedco (from the preceding problem) has decided to give its customer a quantity discount. (Assume that it has only one customer.) If the customer purchases over 300 pounds of feed 1, each pound over the first 300 will sell for only \$1.25 per pound. Similarly, if the customer purchases more than 300 pounds of feed 2, each pound over the first 300 will sell for \$1.00 per pound. Determine how to maximize Feedco's profit.

65 Dexter Chemical produces two compounds, A and B. These compounds are produced via two manufacturing processes. Process 1 requires two hours of labor and one pound of raw material to produce two ounces of A and one ounce of B. Process 2 requires three hours of labor and two pounds of raw material to produce three ounces of A and two ounces of B. Sixty hours of labor and 40 pounds of raw material are available. Demand for A is unlimited, but only 20 ounces of B can be sold. A sells for \$16 per ounce, and B sells for \$14 per ounce. Any B that is unsold must be disposed of at a cost of \$2 per ounce. Determine how to maximize Dexter's revenue less disposal costs.

66 Natural Furniture manufactures tables and chairs. Each table and chair must be made entirely out of oak or entirely out of pine. A total of 1500 board feet of oak and 2100 board feet of pine are available. A table requires either 17 board feet of oak or 30 board feet of pine, and a chair requires either 5 board feet of oak or 13 board feet of pine. Each table can be sold for \$40, and each chair for \$15. Determine how Natural can maximize its revenue.

Skill-Extending Problems

67 (Based on Franklin and Koenigsberg [7]) The city of Busville contains three school districts. The number of minority and nonminority students in each district is given in Table 3.38. The local court has decided that each of the town's two high schools (Cooley High and Walt Whitman High) must have approximately the same percentage of minority students (within 5%) as the entire town. The distances (in miles) between the school districts and the high schools are given in Table 3.39. Each high school must have an enrollment of 300 to 500 students. Determine an assignment of students to schools that minimizes the total distance students must travel to school.

TABLE 3.38 Student Counts for Busville Problem

	Minority Students	Nonminority Students
District 1	50	200
District 2	50	250
District 3	100	150

TABLE 3.39 Distances for Busville Problem

	Cooley High	Walt Whitman High
District 1	1	2
District 2	2	1
District 3	1	1

68 (Based on Carino and Lenoir [1]) Brady Corporation produces cabinets. Each week, Brady requires 90,000 cubic feet of processed lumber. The company can obtain lumber in two ways. First, it can purchase lumber from an outside supplier and then dry it at the Brady kiln. Second, Brady can chop down trees on its land, cut them into lumber at its sawmill, and then dry the lumber at its kiln. The company can purchase grade 1 or grade 2 lumber. Grade 1 lumber costs

\$3 per cubic foot and when dried yields 0.7 cubic feet of useful lumber. Grade 2 lumber costs \$7 per cubic foot and when dried yields 0.9 cubic feet of useful lumber. It costs the company \$3 to chop down a tree. After being cut and dried, a log yields 0.8 cubic feet of lumber. Brady incurs costs of \$4 per cubic feet of lumber it dries. It costs \$2.50 per cubic feet of logs sent through the sawmill. Each week the sawmill can process up to 35,000 cubic feet of lumber. Each week up to 40,000 cubic feet of grade 1 lumber and up to 60,000 cubic feet of grade 2 lumber can be purchased. Each week 40 hours of time are available for drying lumber. The time it takes to dry one cubic foot of lumber is as follows: grade 1, two seconds; grade 2, 0.8 second; log, 1.3 seconds. Determine how Brady can minimize the weekly cost of meeting its demand for processed lumber.

69 (Based on Cheung and Auger [3]) The Canadian Parks Commission controls two tracts of land. Tract 1 consists of 300 acres and tract 2, 100 acres. Each acre of tract 1 can be used for spruce trees, hunting, or both. Each acre of tract 2 can be used for spruce trees, camping, or both. The capital (in hundreds of dollars) and labor (in worker-days) required to maintain one acre of each tract and the profit (in thousands of dollars) per acre for each possible use of land are given in Table 3.40. Capital of \$150,000 and 200 worker-days of labor are available. How should the land be allocated to various uses to maximize profit received from the two tracts?

TABLE 3.40 Data for Canadian Parks Problem

		Capital	Labor	Profit
Tract 1	**Spruce**	3	.10	.20
	Hunting	3	.20	.04
	Both	4	.20	.05
Tract 2	**Spruce**	1	.05	.06
	Camping	30	5.00	.09
	Both	10	1.01	1.10

70 (Based on Dobson and Kalish [5]) Chandler Enterprises produces two competing products, A and B. The company wants to sell these products to two groups of customers, group 1 and group 2. The values each customer places on a unit of A and B are shown in Table 3.41. Each customer will buy either product A or product B, but not both. A customer is willing to buy product A if she believes that

$$\text{Premium of product A} \geq \text{Premium of product B}$$

and

$$\text{Premium of product A} \geq 0$$

Here, the "premium" of a product is its value minus its price. Similarly, a customer is willing to buy B if she believes

$$\text{Premium of product B} \geq \text{Premium of product A}$$

and

$$\text{Premium of product B} \geq 0$$

Group 1 has 1000 members, and group 2 has 1500 members. Chandler wants to set prices for each product to ensure that group 1 members purchase product A and group 2 members purchase product B. Determine how Chandler can maximize its revenue.

TABLE 3.41 Customers' Values for Chandler Problem

	Group 1 Customer	Group 2 Customer
Value of A	\$10	\$12
Value of B	\$8	\$15

71 Juiceco manufactures two products, premium orange juice and regular orange juice. Both products are made by combining two types of oranges, grade 6 and grade 3. The oranges in premium juice must have an average grade of at least 5; those in regular juice, at least 4. During each of the next two months, Juiceco can sell up to 1000 gallons of premium juice and up to 2000 gallons of regular juice. Premium juice sells for $1.00 per gallon, while regular juice sells for 80¢ per gallon. At the beginning of month 1 Juiceco has 3000 gallons of grade 6 oranges and 2000 gallons of grade 3 oranges. At the beginning of month 2 Juiceco can purchase additional grade 3 oranges for 40¢ per gallon and additional grade 6 oranges for 60¢ per gallon. Juice spoils at the end of the month, so Juiceco cannot make extra juice during month 1 to help meet month 2 demand. Oranges left over at the end of month 1 can be used to produce juice for month 2. At the end of month 1 a holding cost of 5¢ is assessed against each gallon of leftover grade 3 oranges, and 10¢ against each gallon of leftover grade 6 oranges. In addition to the cost of the oranges, it costs 10¢ to produce each gallon of (regular or premium) juice. Determine how Juiceco can maximize its profit during the next two months.

72 Each day Eastinghouse produces capacitors during three shifts: 8 A.M. to 4 P.M., 4 P.M. to midnight, and midnight to 8 A.M.. The hourly salary paid to the employees on each shift, the price charged for each capacitor made during each shift, and the number of defects in each capacitor produced during a given shift are shown in Table 3.42. The company can employ up to 25 workers, and each worker can be assigned to one of the three shifts. A worker produces ten capacitors during a shift, but due to machinery limitations, no more than ten workers can be assigned to any shift. Each capacitor produced can be sold, but the average number of defects per capacitor for the day's production cannot exceed three. Determine how Eastinghouse can maximize its daily profit.

TABLE 3.42 **Data for Eastinghouse Problem**

	Hourly Salary	Defects per Capacitor	Price
8 A.M. to 4 P.M.	$12	4	$18
4 P.M.to Midnight	$16	3	$22
Midnight to 8 A.M.	$20	2	$24

73 During the next three months Airco must meet (on time) the following demands for air conditioners: month 1, 300; month 2, 400; month 3, 500. Air conditioners can be produced in either New York or Los Angeles. It takes 1.5 hours of skilled labor to produce an air conditioner in Los Angeles, and two hours in New York. It costs $400 to produce an air conditioner in Los Angeles, and $350 in New York. During each month each city has 420 hours of skilled labor available. It costs $100 to hold an air conditioner in inventory for a month. At the beginning of month 1 Airco has 200 air conditioners in stock. Determine how Airco can minimize the cost of meeting air conditioner demands for the next three months.

74 During the next three months Steelco faces the following demands for steel: month 1, 100 tons; month 2, 200 tons; month 3, 50 tons. During any month a worker can produce up to 15 tons of steel. Each worker is paid $5000 per month. Workers can be hired or fired at a cost of $3000 per worker fired and $4000 per worker hired. The cost of holding a ton of steel in inventory for one month is $100. Demand can be backlogged at a cost of $70 per ton per month. For example, if one ton of month 1 demand is met during month 3, a backlogging cost of $140 is incurred. At the beginning of month 1, Steelco has eight workers. During any month, at most two workers can be hired. All demand must be met by the end of month 3. The raw material used to produce a ton of steel costs $300. Determine how to minimize Steelco's costs.

75 Gotham City National Bank is open Monday through Friday from 9 A.M. to 5 P.M. From past experience the bank knows that it needs the number of tellers shown in Table 3.43. Gotham City Bank hires two types of tellers. Full-time tellers work 9 A.M. to 5 P.M. five days a week, with one hour off each day for lunch. The bank determines when a full-time employee takes his or her lunch hour, but each teller must go between noon and 1 P.M. or between 1 P.M. and 2 P.M. Full-time employees are paid (including fringe benefits) $8 per hour, which includes payment for lunch hour. The bank can also hire part-time tellers. Each part-time teller must work exactly three consecutive hours each day. A part-time teller is paid $5 per hour and receives no fringe benefits. To maintain adequate quality of service, the bank has decided that at most five part-time tellers can be hired. Determine how to meet the bank's teller requirements at minimum cost.

TABLE 3.43 Teller Requirements for Gotham Bank Problem

Time Period	Tellers Required
9–10	4
10–11	3
11–Noon	4
Noon–1	6
1–2	5
2–3	6
3–4	8
4–5	8

76 (Based on Rothstein [21]) The Springfield City Police Department employs 30 police officers. Each officer works five days per week. The crime rate fluctuates with the day of the week, so the number of police officers required each day depends on the day of the week: Saturday, 28; Sunday, 18; Monday, 18; Tuesday, 24; Wednesday, 25; Thursday, 16; Friday, 21. The police department wants to schedule police officers to minimize the number whose days off are *not* consecutive. Determine how to accomplish this goal.

77 (Based on Charnes and Cooper [2]) Alex Cornby makes his living buying and selling corn. On January 1 he has 50 tons of corn and $1000. On the first day of each month Alex can buy corn at the following prices per ton: January, $300; February, $350; March, $400; April, $500. On the last day of each month Alex can sell corn at the following prices per ton: January, $250; February, $400; March, $350; April, $550. Alex stores his corn in a warehouse that can hold at most 100 tons of corn. He must be able to pay cash for all corn at the time of purchase. Determine how Alex can maximize his cash on hand at the end of April.

78 (Based on Robichek, Teichroew, and Jones [19]) At the beginning of month 1, Finco has $400 in cash. At the beginning of months 1, 2, 3, and 4, Finco receives certain revenues, after which it pays bills. (See Table 3.44.) Any money left over can be invested for one month at the interest rate of 0.1% per month; for two months at 0.5% per month; for three months at 1% per month; or for four months at 2% per month. Determine an investment strategy that maximizes cash on hand at the beginning of month 5.

TABLE 3.44 Data for Finco Problem

	Revenues	Bills
Month 1	$400	$600
Month 2	$800	$500
Month 3	$300	$500
Month 4	$300	$250

79 City 1 produces 500 tons of waste per day, and city 2 produces 400 tons of waste per day. Waste must be incinerated at incinerator 1 or 2, and each incinerator can process up to 500 tons of waste per day. The cost to incinerate waste is $40 per ton at incinerator 1 and $30 per ton at incinerator 2. Incineration reduces each ton of waste to 0.2 tons of debris, which must be dumped at one of two landfills. Each landfill can receive at most 200 tons of debris per day. It costs $3 per mile to transport a ton of material (either debris or waste). Distances (in miles) between locations are shown in Table 3.45. Determine how to minimize the total cost of disposing of the waste from both cities.

TABLE 3.45 Distances for Landfill Problem

	Incinerator 1	Incinerator 2
City 1	30	5
City 2	36	42
Landfill 1	5	9
Landfill 2	8	6

80 (Based on Smith [24]) Silicon Valley Corporation (Silvco) manufactures transistors. An important aspect of the manufacture of transistors is the melting of the element germanium (a major component of a transistor) in a furnace. Unfortunately, the melting process yields germanium of highly variable quality. There are two methods that can be used to melt germanium. Method 1 costs $50 per transistor, and method 2 costs $70 per transistor. The qualities of germanium obtained by methods 1 and 2 are shown in Table 3.46. Silvco can refire melted germanium in an attempt to improve its quality. It costs $25 to refire the melted germanium for one transistor. The results of the refiring process are shown in Table 3.47. For example, if grade 3 germanium is refired, half of the resulting germanium will be grade 3 and the other half will be grade 4. Silvco has sufficient furnace capacity to melt or refire germanium for at most 20,000 transistors per month. Silvco's monthly demands are for 1000 grade 4 transistors, 2000 grade 3 transistors, 3000 grade 2 transistors, and 3000 grade 1 transistors. Determine how to minimize the cost of producing the needed transistors.

TABLE 3.46 Germanium Qualities for Silvco Problem

	Yield (percent)	
	Method 1	**Method 2**
Defective	30	20
Grade 1	30	20
Grade 2	20	25
Grade 3	15	20
Grade 4	5	15

TABLE 3.47 Refiring Results for Silvco Problem

	Yield from Refiring (percent)				
	Defective	**Grade 1**	**Grade 2**	**Grade 3**	**Grade 4**
Defective	30	25	15	20	10
Grade 1	0	30	30	20	20
Grade 2	0	0	40	30	30
Grade 3	0	0	0	50	50

81 The Wild Turkey Company produces two types of turkey cutlets for sale to fast-food restaurants. Each type of cutlet consists of white meat and dark meat. Cutlet 1 sells for $4 per pound and must consist of at least 70% white meat. Cutlet 2 sells for $3 per pound and must consist of at least 60% white meat. At most 50 pounds of cutlet 1 and 30 pounds of cutlet 2 can be sold. The two types of turkey used to manufacture the cutlets are purchased from the GobbleGobble Turkey Farm. Each type 1 turkey costs $10 and yields 5 pounds of white meat and 2 pounds of dark meat. Each type 2 turkey costs $8 and yields 3 pounds of white meat and 3 pounds of dark meat. Determine how to maximize Wild Turkey's profit.

82 The production line employees at Grummins Engine work four days a week, ten hours a day. Each day of the week, the following minimum number of line employees are needed: Monday through Friday, 7 employees; Saturday and Sunday, 3 employees. Grummins employs 11 line employees. Determine how to maximize the number of consecutive days off received by these employees. For example, a worker who gets Sunday, Monday, and Wednesday off receives two consecutive days off.

83 (Based on Lanzenauer et al. [13]) To process income tax forms, the IRS first sends each form through the data preparation (DP) department, where information is coded for computer entry. Then the form is sent to data entry (DE), where it is entered into the computer. During the next three weeks, the following number of forms will arrive: week 1, 40,000; week 2, 30,000; week 3, 60,000. All employees work 40 hours per week and are paid $500 per week. Data preparation of a form requires 15 minutes, and data entry of a form requires 10 minutes. Each week an employee is assigned to either data entry or data preparation. The IRS must complete processing all forms by the end of week 5 and wants to minimize the cost of accomplishing

this goal. Assume that all workers are full-time employees and that the IRS will have the same number of employees each week. Assume all employees are capable of performing data preparation and data entry. Determine how many workers should be working and how the workers should allocate their hours during the next five weeks.

84 The mayor of Llanview is trying to determine the number of judges needed to handle the judicial caseload. The estimated number of judicial hours needed during each month of the year is given in Table 3.48.

a Suppose each judge works all 12 months and can handle up to 120 hours per month of casework. To avoid creating a backlog, all cases must be handled by the end of December. Determine how many judges Llanview needs.

b If each judge receives one month of vacation each year, how does your answer change?

TABLE 3.48 **Hours for Judicial Problem**

	Hours		Hours
January	400	**July**	200
February	300	**August**	400
March	200	**September**	300
April	600	**October**	200
May	800	**November**	100
June	300	**December**	300

85 (Based on Robichek, Teichroew, and Jones [19]) The Korvair Department Store has $100,000 in available cash. At the beginning of each of the next six months, Korvair will receive revenues and pay bills as shown in Table 3.49. It is clear that Korvair will have a short-term cash flow problem until the store receives revenues from the Christmas shopping season. To solve this problem, Korvair must borrow money. At the beginning of July, the company takes out a six-month loan. Any money borrowed for a six-month period must be paid back at the end of December along with 9% interest (early payback does not reduce the total interest of the loan). Korvair can also meet cash needs through month-to-month borrowing. Any money borrowed for a one-month period incurs an interest cost of 4% per month. Determine how Korvair can minimize the cost of paying its bills on time.

TABLE 3.49 **Revenues and Bills for Korvair Problem**

	Revenues	Bills
July	$100,000	$500,000
August	$200,000	$500,000
September	$200,000	$600,000
October	$400,000	$200,000
November	$700,000	$200,000
December	$900,000	$100,000

86 (Based on Garvin et al. [8]) Ole Oil produces three products: heating oil, gasoline, and jet fuel. The average octane levels must be at least 4.5 for heating oil, 8.5 for gas, and 7.0 for jet fuel. To produce these products Ole purchases two types of oil: crude 1 (at $12 per barrel) and crude 2 (at $10 per barrel). Each day at most 10,000 barrels of each type of oil can be purchased. Before crude can be used to produce products for sale, it must be distilled. Each day at most 15,000 barrels of oil can be distilled. It costs 10¢ to distill a barrel of oil. The result of distillation is as shown in Table 3.50. Distilled naphtha can be used only to produce gasoline or jet fuel. Distilled oil can be used to produce heating oil or it can be sent through the catalytic cracker (at a cost of 15¢ per barrel). Each day at most 5000 barrels of distilled oil can be sent through the cracker, with the results as shown in Table 3.51. Cracked oil can be used to produce gasoline and jet fuel but not heating oil. The octane level of each type of oil is as follows: naphtha, 8; distilled 1, 4; distilled 2, 5; cracked 1, 9; cracked 2, 6. All heating

TABLE 3.50 Distillation Results for Ole Oil Problem

	Yield (in barrels)		
	Naphtha	Distilled 1	Distilled 2
Crude 1	.6	.3	.1
Crude 2	.4	.2	.4

TABLE 3.51 Catalytic Cracker Results for Ole Oil Problem

	Yield (in barrels)	
	Cracked 1	Cracked 2
Distilled 1	.8	.2
Distilled 2	.7	.3

oil produced can be sold at $14 per barrel; all gasoline produced, $18 per barrel, all jet fuel produced, $16 per barrel. Marketing considerations dictate that at least 3000 barrels of each product must be produced daily. Determine how Ole can maximize its profit.

87 Mackk Engine produces diesel trucks. New government emission standards have dictated that the average pollution emissions of all trucks produced in the next three years cannot exceed 10 grams per truck. Mackk produces two types of trucks. Each type 1 truck sells for $20,000, costs $15,000 to manufacture, and emits 15 grams of pollution. Each type 2 truck sells for $17,000, costs $14,000 to manufacture, and emits 5 grams of pollution. Production capacity limits total truck production during each year to at most 320 trucks. The maximum number of each truck type that can be sold during each of the next three years is given in Table 3.52.

TABLE 3.52 Demand for Mackk Problem

	Type 1	Type 2
Year 1	100	200
Year 2	200	100
Year 3	300	150

Demand can be met from previous production or the current year's production. It costs $2000 to hold one truck (of any type) in inventory for one year. Determine how Mackk can maximize its profit during the next three years.

88 Priceler manufactures sedans and wagons. The numbers of vehicles that can be sold in each of the next three months are listed in Table 3.53. Each sedan sells for $13,000, and each wagon sells for $11,500. It costs $9000 to produce a sedan and $8500 to produce a wagon. To hold a vehicle in inventory for one month costs $250 per sedan and $200 per wagon. During each month at most 1500 vehicles can be produced. Production line restrictions dictate that during month 1, at least two-thirds of all cars produced must be sedans. At the beginning of month 1, 200 sedans and 100 wagons are available. Determine how to maximize Priceler's profit during the next three months.

TABLE 3.53 Demands for Priceler Problem

	Sedans	Wagons
Month 1	1100	600
Month 2	1500	700
Month 3	1200	500

89 Each day, workers at the Gotham City Police Department work two six-hour shifts chosen from midnight to 6 A.M., 6 A.M. to noon, noon to 6 P.M., and 6 P.M. to midnight. The following number of workers are needed during each shift: 15 from midnight to 6 A.M.; 5 from 6 A.M. to noon; 12 from noon to 6 P.M.; and 6 from 6 P.M. to midnight. Workers whose two shifts are consecutive are paid $12 per hour, whereas workers whose shifts are not consecutive are paid $18 per hour. Determine how to minimize the cost of meeting the daily workforce demands of the Gotham City Police Department.

90 During each six-hour period of the day, the Bloomington Police Department needs at least the number of police officers shown in Table 3.54. Police officers can be hired to work either 12 consecutive hours or 18 consecutive hours. Police officers are paid $4 per hour for each of the first 12 hours they work in a day and $6 per hour for each of the next 6 hours they work in a day. Determine how to minimize the cost of meeting Bloomington's daily police requirements.

TABLE 3.54 **Requirements for Bloomington Police Problem**

Time Period	Police Officers Required
Midnight to 6 A.M.	12
6 A.M. to Noon	8
Noon to 6 P.M.	6
6 P.M. to Midnight	15

91 Each hour from 10 A.M. to 7 P.M., Bank One receives checks and must process them. Its goal is to process all checks the same day they are received. The bank has 13 check processing machines, each of which can process up to 500 checks per hour. It takes one worker to operate each machine. Bank One hires both full-time and part-time workers. Full-time workers work either 10 A.M. to 6 P.M., 11 A.M. to 7 P.M., or noon to 8 P.M. and are paid $160 per day. Part-time workers work either 2 P.M. to 7 P.M. or 3 P.M. to 8 P.M. and are paid $75 per day. The numbers of checks received each hour are shown in Table 3.55. In the interest of maintaining continuity, Bank One believes that it must have at least three full-time workers under contract. Develop a work schedule that processes all checks by 8 P.M. and minimizes daily labor costs.

TABLE 3.55 **Checks Received for Bank One Problem**

	Checks Received		Checks Received
10 A.M.	5000	**3 P.M.**	3000
11 A.M.	4000	**4 P.M.**	4000
Noon	3000	**5 P.M.**	4500
1 P.M.	4000	**6 P.M.**	3500
2 P.M.	2500	**7 P.M.**	3000

92 (Based on Glassey and Gupta [10]) A paper recycling plant processes box board, tissue paper, newsprint, and book paper into pulp that can be used to produce three grades of recycled paper (grades 1, 2, and 3). The prices per ton and the pulp contents of the four inputs are shown in Table 3.56. Two methods, de-inking and asphalt dispersion, can be used to process

TABLE 3.56 **Data for Paper Problem**

	Cost	Pulp Content
Box Board	$5	15%
Tissue Paper	$6	20%
Newsprint	$8	30%
Book Paper	$10	40%

the four inputs into pulp. It costs $20 to de-ink a ton of any input. The process of de-inking removes 10% of the input's pulp, leaving 90% of the original pulp. It costs $15 to apply asphalt dispersion to a ton of material. The asphalt dispersion process removes 20% of the input's pulp. At most 3000 tons of input can be run through the asphalt dispersion process or the de-inking process. Grade 1 paper can only be produced with newsprint or book paper pulp; grade 2 paper, only with book paper, tissue paper, or box board pulp; and grade 3 paper, only with newsprint, tissue paper, or box board pulp. To meet its current demands, the company needs 500 tons of pulp for grade 1 paper, 500 tons of pulp for grade 2 paper, and 600 tons of pulp for grade 3 paper. Determine how to minimize the cost of meeting the demands for pulp.

93 At the beginning of month 1, GE Capital has 50 million accounts. Of these, 40 million are paid up (0-due), 4 million are one month overdue (1-due), 4 million are two months overdue (2-due), and 2 million are three months overdue (3-due). Once an account is more than three months overdue, it is written off as a bad debt. For each overdue account GE Capital can either phone the cardholder, send a letter, or do nothing. A letter requires an average of 0.05 hour of labor, while a phone call requires an average of 0.10 hour of labor. Each month 500,000 hours of labor are available. We assume that the average amount of a monthly payment is $30. Thus, if a 2-due account remains 2-due, it means that one month's payment ($30) has been received, and if a 2-due account becomes 0-due, it means that three months' payments ($90) have been received. By examining thousands of accounts, DMMs (Delinquency Movement Matrices), shown in Tables 3.57, 3.58, and 3.59, have been estimated. Your goal is to determine how to allocate your workforce over the next four months in order to maximize the expected collection revenue received during that time. *Note*: 0-due accounts are never contacted, which accounts for the lack of 0-due rows in Tables 3.57 and 3.58.

TABLE 3.57 DMM If Account Receives a Letter

	0-Due	1-Due	2-Due	3-Due	Bad Debt
1-Due	.60	.10	.30	.00	0.00
2-Due	.15	.15	.40	.30	0.00
3-Due	.00	.00	.20	.60	.20
Bad Debt	.00	.00	.00	.00	1.00

TABLE 3.58 DMM If Account Receives a Phone Call

	0-Due	1-Due	2-Due	3-Due	Bad Debt
1-Due	.70	.20	.10	.00	0.00
2-Due	.30	.25	.30	.15	0.00
3-Due	.00	.00	.50	.40	.10
Bad Debt	.00	.00	.00	.00	1.00

TABLE 3.59 DMM for Do Nothing Action

	0-Due	1-Due	2-Due	3-Due	Bad Dept
0-Due	.90	.10	.00	.00	0.00
1-Due	.20	.25	.55	.00	0.00
2-Due	.10	.10	.20	.60	0.00
3-Due	.00	.00	.10	.40	.50
Bad Debt	.00	.00	.00	.00	1.00

Modeling Problems

94 You have been assigned to develop a model that can be used to schedule employees at a local fast-food restaurant. Assume that computer technology has advanced to the point where very large problems can be solved on a PC at the restaurant.

a What data would you collect as inputs to your model?

b Describe in words several appropriate objective functions for your model.

c Describe in words the constraints needed for your model.

95 You have been assigned to develop a model that can be used to schedule the nurses working in a maternity ward.

a What data would you collect as inputs to your model?

b Describe in words several appropriate objective functions for your model.

c Describe in words the constraints needed for your model.

96 Keefer Paper produces recycled paper from paper purchased from local offices and universities. The company sells three grades of paper: high brightness paper, medium brightness paper, and low brightness paper. The high brightness paper must have a brightness level of at least 90, the medium brightness paper must have a brightness level of between 80 and 90, and the low brightness paper must have a brightness level no greater than 80. Discuss how Keefer might use a blending model to maximize its profit.

97 In this chapter we give you the cost of producing a product and other inputs that are used in the analysis. Do you think that it is easy for most companies to determine the cost of producing a product? What difficulties might arise?

98 Discuss how the aggregate planning model could be extended to handle a company that produces several products on several types of machines. What information would you need to model this type of problem?

99 Explain how Tyco could use a rolling planning horizon to implement its borrowing strategy.

100 A banking firm has many branch banks located throughout the state. You have been asked to determine which of these are operating inefficiently and why.

a What information would you collect and how would you use it?

b Would you have any reservations about using DEA in this situation?

101 A large CPA firm currently has 100 junior staff members and 20 partners. In the long run, say, 20 years from now, the firm would like to consist of 130 junior staff members and 20 partners. During a given year 10% of all partners and 30% of all junior staff members leave the firm. The firm can control the number of hires each year and the fraction of junior employees who are promoted to partner each year. Can you develop a personnel strategy that would meet the CPA firm's goals?

102 Bed T. Rock owns a small company that produces three grades of rocks at two quarries. Five major customers purchase the different grades of rocks. How could you use LP to help Bed T. Rock schedule his monthly production? ■

C A S E   S T U D Y

Lakefield Corporation's Oil Trading Desk

Lakefield Corporation's oil trading desk buys and sells oil products (crude oil and refined fuels), options, and futures in international markets. The trading desk is responsible for buying raw material for Lakefield's refining and blending operations and for selling final products. In addition to trading for the company's operations, the desk also takes speculative positions. In speculative trades, the desk attempts to profit from its knowledge and information about conditions in the global oil markets.

One of the traders, Lisa Davies, is responsible for transactions in the cash market (as opposed to the futures or options markets). Lisa has been trading for several years and has seen the prices of oil-related products fluctuate tremendously. Figure 3.35 shows the prices of heating oil #2 and unleaded gasoline from January 1986 through July 1992. While excessive volatility of oil prices is undesirable for most businesses, Lakefield's oil trading desk often makes substantial profits in periods of high volatility.

The prices of various oil products tend to move together over long periods of time. Since finished oil products are refined from crude oil, the prices of all finished products will tend to rise if the price of crude increases. Because finished oil products are not perfect substitutes, the prices of individual products do not move in lock step. Indeed, over short time periods, the price movements of two products can have a low correlation. For example, in late 1989 and early 1990, there was a severe cold wave in the northeastern United States. The price of heading oil rose from 60¢ per gallon to over $1 per gallon. In the same time period, the price of gasoline rose just over 10¢ per gallon.

F I G U R E 3 . 3 5   **Price of Heating Oil #2 and Unleaded Gasoline**

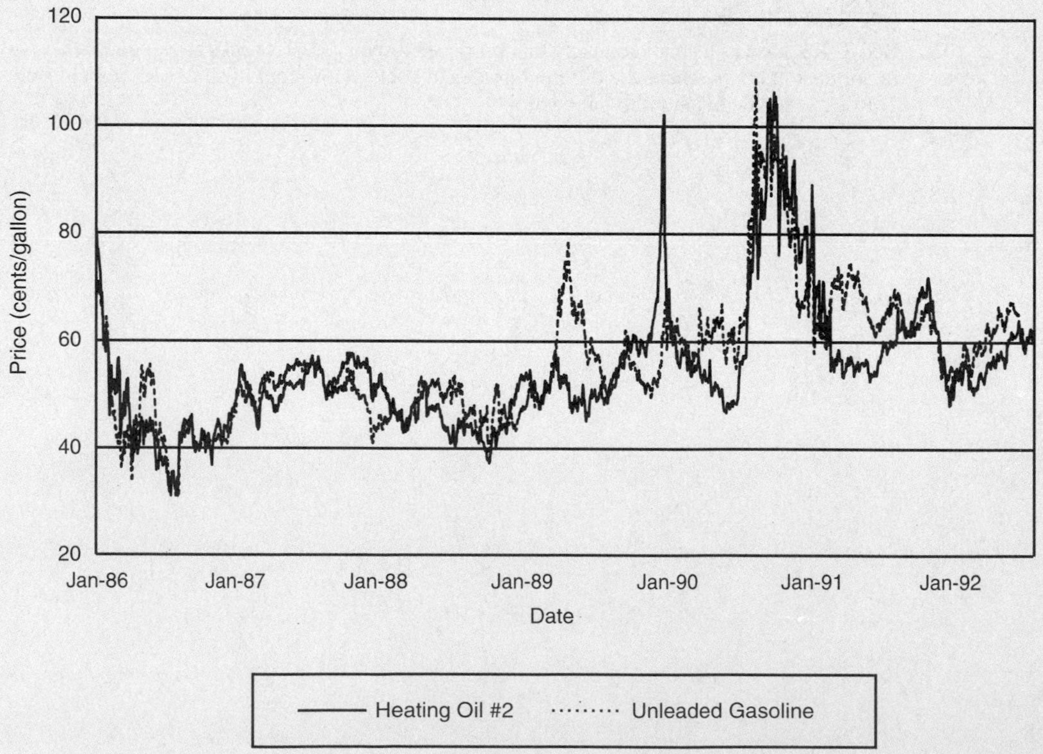

Lisa Davies feels that some mathematical analysis might be helpful to spot trading opportunities in the cash markets. The next section provides background about a few important characteristics of fuel oils. The properties of blended fuels and some implications for pricing are then discussed.

Characteristics of Hydrocarbon Fuels

The many varieties of hydrocarbon fuels include heating oil, kerosene, gasoline, and diesel oil. Each type of fuel has many characteristics, e.g., heat content, viscosity, freeze point, luminosity, volatility (speed of vaporization), and so on. The relative importance of each characteristic depends on the intended use of the fuel. For example, octane rating is one of the most important characteristics of gasoline. Octane is a measure of resistance to ignition under pressure. An engine burning low octane fuel is susceptible to "engine knock," which reduces its power output. Surprisingly, for gasoline octane rating is more important than heat content. In contrast, the most important characteristic of kerosene jet fuel is its heat content, but viscosity is also important. High viscosity fuels do not flow as smoothly through fuel lines.

For the types of fuels Lisa Davies usually trades, the most important characteristics are density, viscosity, sulphur content, and flash point, which will be described below. When trading and blending other fuels, characteristics besides these four are important to consider.

Density The density of a substance is its mass per unit volume (e.g., grams per cubic centimeter). The density of water is 1 g/cc. A related measure is American Petroleum Institute gravity (API), which is measured in degrees. API is related to density by

$$API = \frac{141.5}{D} - 131.5$$

where D is density measured in g/cc. Water has an API of 10°. Note that density and API are *inversely* related.

The specifications for kerosene jet fuel are nearly identical for all civilian airlines worldwide. Kerosene jet fuel should have an API gravity between 37° and 51°. Diesel fuel and heating oil are required to have an API not less than 30°. API is important for controlling the flow of fuel in a combustion engine. It can also be used to limit the concentration of heavy hydrocarbon compounds in the fuel.

Viscosity Viscosity refers to the resistance of a liquid to flow. A highly viscous liquid, such as ketchup or molasses, does not pour easily. Viscosity is measured by the amount of time a specified volume of liquid takes to flow through a tube of a certain diameter. It is commonly measured in units of centistokes (hundredths of stokes). Most fuel specifications place upper limits on viscosity. Less viscous fuel flows easily through lines and atomizes easily for efficient combustion. More viscous fuels must be heated initially to reduce viscosity.

Sulphur Content The content of sulphur is measured in percentage of total sulphur by weight. For example, a fuel with 2% sulphur content has 2 grams of sulphur for every 100 grams of fuel. Sulphur causes corrosion and abrasion of metal surfaces. Low sulphur content is important for maintaining the proper operation of equipment.

Flash Point The flash point of a substance is the lowest temperature at which the substance ignites when exposed to a flame. The product description of kerosene jet fuel from the American Society for Testing and Materials specifies a flash point of at least 100°F. The New York Mercantile Exchange futures contract for heating oil #2 specifies a flash point of at least 130°F. Flash-point restrictions are often prescribed for safety reasons.

Table 3.60 gives a description of some fuels and their prices on a given day. In Table 3.60 the units of viscosity are centistokes, sulphur is given in percentage by weight, and flash point is in degrees Fahrenheit. For convenience, all prices in Table 3.60 are given in dollars per barrel. In practice, the prices of heating oil, gasoline, and kerosene jet fuel are typically quoted in cents per gallon. (There are 42 gallons in a barrel.)

Blending Fuels

Since hydrocarbon fuels are made of similar compounds and have similar characteristics, there is a certain degree of substitutability among fuels. Different fuels can also be blended to form a new fuel. Next we describe how the characteristics of the individual fuels combine in the blended fuel.

Sulphur combines linearly by weight. This means, for example, that mixing equal weights of a 1% sulphur oil with a 3% sulphur oil produces a 2% sulphur oil. To a close approximation, sulphur

TABLE 3.60 Description of Available Fuels

	Fuel 1 1% Sulphur Fuel Oil	Fuel 2 3% Sulphur Fuel Oil	Fuel 3 0.7% Sulphur Fuel Oil	Fuel 4 Heating Oil	Fuel 5 1% Vacuum Gas Oil	Fuel 6 2% Vacuum Gas Oil
API	10.50	10.50	10.50	34.00	25.00	25.00
Viscosity	477.00	477.00	477.00	3.50	25.00	25.00
Sulphur	1.00	3.00	0.70	0.20	1.00	2.00
Flash Point	140.00	140.00	140.00	130.00	200.00	200.00
Price	16.08	13.25	17.33	24.10	20.83	20.10

	Fuel 7 0.5% Vacuum Gas Oil	Fuel 8 Straight Run (Low Sulphur)	Fuel 9 Straight Run (High Sulphur)	Fuel 10 Kerosene Jet Fuel	Fuel 11 Diesel Fuel	Fuel 12 Slurry
API	25.00	21.00	17.00	46.000	35.00	−4.50
Viscosity	25.00	212.00	212.00	1.500	2.50	261.00
Sulphur	0.50	0.30	2.75	0.125	0.20	2.37
Flash Point	200.00	250.00	250.00	123.000	150.00	109.00
Price	21.46	21.00	20.00	25.520	24.30	11.50

combines linearly by volume (because the densities of oils are not very different). That is, combining 0.5 barrel of 1% sulphur oil with 0.5 barrel of 3% sulphur oil gives 1 barrel of very nearly 2% sulphur oil.

In general, to say that a certain property of oil combines linearly (by volume) means the following: Suppose x_j barrels of oil j (for $j = 1, 2, \ldots, n$) are blended together to form one barrel of oil. That is, $\sum_{j=1}^{n} x_j = 1$. Also suppose that c_j is the measure of the property of oil j. Then if the property combines linearly, the measure of the property for the blended oil is a linear combination of the c_js, that is $\sum_{j=1}^{n} c_j x_j$.

API gravity does not combine linearly, but density does combine linearly. For example, consider blending 0.5 barrel of oil that has a density of 0.8 g/cc with 0.5 barrel of oil with a density of 1.2 g/cc. The resulting barrel of oil has a density of 1.0 ($= 0.8[0.5] + 1.2[0.5]$). The 0.8 g/cc density oil has an API of 45.38° and the 1.2 g/cc density oil has an API of −13.58°. If API combined linearly, the blended barrel of oil would have an API of 15.90° ($= 45.38°[0.5] - 13.58°[0.5]$). However, an API of 15.90°corresponds to a density of 0.96 g/cc, not 1.0 g/cc.[5]

Viscosity, measured in centistokes, does not combine linearly. However, chemical engineers have determined that viscosity can be transformed to another measure, called linear viscosity, which (nearly) combines linearly.[6] Similarly, flash points measured in degrees Fahrenheit do not combine linearly. But chemical engineers defined a new measure, termed linear flash point, which does combine linearly.[7] Table 3.61 summarizes the properties of the twelve fuels measured in units that combine linearly.

Implications for Pricing

Sulphur in oil is a contaminant. Therefore, oil with a low sulphur content is more valuable than oil with a higher sulphur content, all other characteristics being equal. This relationship can be seen in Table 3.60 by comparing the prices of fuels 1, 2, and 3 and fuels 5, 6, and 7. Lower density oils are generally preferred to higher density oils, because energy per unit mass is higher for low density fuels, which reduces the weight of the fuel. Lower viscosity oils are preferred because they flow more easily through fuel lines than oils with higher viscosities. High flash points are preferred for safety reasons. However, since flash point and linear flash point are inversely related, this means that lower linear flash point oils are preferred to higher linear flash point oils.

That fuels can be blended cheaply to form new fuels affects price as well. For example, fuel 2 and fuel 3 from Table 3.60 can be blended to form a fuel with the same API, viscosity, sulphur, and flash point as fuel 1. In particular, 0.1304 barrel of fuel 2 and 0.8696 barrel of fuel 3 can be blended to form 1 barrel of a new fuel, which, in terms of the four main characteristics, is identical to fuel 1. Since the cost of

[5]To convert API to density use $D = 141.5/(API + 131.5)$.

[6]Let vs represent viscosity measured in centistokes. Then linear viscosity, denoted v, is defined $v = \ln(\ln[vs + 0.08])$.

[7]Let fp denote flash point measured in degrees Fahrenheit. Then linear flash point is defined $f = 10^{42}(fp + 460)^{-14.286}$. Empirical analysis of oil blending data confirms that the measure f combines nearly linearly.

TABLE 3.61 Properties of Available Fuels Measured in Units That Combine Linearly

	Fuel 1 1% Sulphur Fuel Oil	Fuel 2 3% Sulphur Fuel Oil	Fuel 3 0.7% Sulphur Fuel Oil	Fuel 4 Heating Oil	Fuel 5 1% Vacuum Gas Oil	Fuel 6 2% Vacuum Gas Oil
Density	0.996	0.996	0.996	0.855	0.904	0.904
Linear Visc.	1.819	1.819	1.819	0.243	1.170	1.170
Sulphur	1.000	3.000	0.700	0.200	1.000	2.000
Linear Flash	204.800	204.800	204.800	260.400	52.500	52.500
Price	16.080	13.250	17.330	24.100	20.830	20.100

	Fuel 7 0.5% Vacuum Gas Oil	Fuel 8 Straight Run (Low Sulphur)	Fuel 9 Straight Run (High Sulphur)	Fuel 10 Kerosene Jet Fuel	Fuel 11 Diesel Fuel	Fuel 12 Slurry
Density	0.904	0.928	0.953	0.797	0.850	1.114
Linear Visc.	1.170	1.678	1.678	−.782	−.054	1.716
Sulphur	0.500	0.300	2.750	0.125	0.200	2.370
Linear Flash	52.500	18.500	18.500	308.800	161.700	437.000
Price	21.460	21.000	20.000	25.520	24.300	11.500

blending is quite small, prices combine nearly linearly. The cost to create the blended fuel is \$16.80 per barrel (\$16.80 = 0.1304[13.25] + 0.8696[17.33]). If the price of fuel 1 were greater than \$16.80, say \$17.10, Lisa Davies could create an arbitrage. She could buy fuels 2 and 3 in the appropriate proportions, Lakefield Corporation could blend them together, and Lisa could sell the blend at the price of fuel 1. The profit would be 30¢ per barrel minus any blending and transaction costs. However, the actual price of fuel 1 is \$16.08, so this plan does not represent an arbitrage opportunity.

The *no-arbitrage pricing principle* is simply a generalization of the previous example. No arbitrage means that the price of any fuel must be less than or equal to the cost of any blend of fuels of equal or better quality. As mentioned above, better means larger API, lower viscosity, lower sulphur content, and higher flash point. In terms of linear properties, better means lower density, lower linear viscosity, lower sulphur content, and lower linear flash point. Any number of fuels (not just two) can be blended together.

Lisa Davies would like to develop a system that automatically checks the no-arbitrage pricing condition for all of the fuels. If the condition is violated, she would like to know the appropriate amounts of the fuels to buy to create the arbitrage, the profit per barrel of the blended fuel, and the characteristics of the blended fuel.

Questions

1 Suppose that 0.3 barrel of fuel 2, 0.3 barrel of fuel 3, and 0.4 barrel of fuel 4 are blended together. What is the cost of the blended fuel? What are the (linear) properties of the blended fuel (i.e., density, linear viscosity, sulphur content, and linear flash point)?

2 Using the data from Table 3.61, check whether any of the fuels violate the no-arbitrage pricing condition. If no fuel violates the condition, which fuel's price comes the closest to the no-arbitrage upper bound? If there is a violation, give the explicit recipe.

3 What modifications would you make to the analysis to account for blending costs?

4 What would be the important issues or steps involved in creating a real system for this problem? ■

CASE STUDY

Foreign Currency Trading

Daily trading volume in the foreign exchange markets often exceeds $1 trillion. Participants trade in the spot currency markets, forward markets, and futures markets. In addition, currency options, currency swaps, and other derivative contracts are traded. For simplicity, we focus on the spot currency market only.

A spot currency transaction is simply an agreement to buy some amount of one currency using another currency.[8] For example, a British company might need to pay a Japanese supplier 150 million yen. Suppose that the spot yen/pound rate is 154.7733. Then the British company could use the spot currency market to buy 150 million yen at a cost of 969,159.41 (= 150,000,000/154.7733) British pounds. A sample of today's cross currency spot rates is given in Table 3.62.

To continue the example, suppose the company canceled the order from the supplier and wanted to convert the 150 million yen back into British pounds. From Table 3.62 the pound/yen spot rate is 0.00645. So the company could use the 150 million yen to buy 967,500 (= 150,000,000 × 0.00645) pounds. Notice that the 967,500 pounds is less than the original 969,159.41 pounds. The difference is the result of the bid-offer spread: the price to buy yen (the bid price) is greater than the price to sell yen (the offer price). The bid-offer spread represents a transactions cost to the company.

[8] A spot transaction agreed to today is *settled* (i.e., the money changes hands) two business days from today. By contrast a three-month forward transaction agreed to today is settled (approximately) three months from today.

Occasionally market prices may become "out of line" in the sense that there are arbitrage opportunities. In this context, arbitrage means that there is a set of spot currency transactions that creates positive wealth but does not require any funds to initiate, i.e., it is a "money pump." When such pure arbitrage opportunities exist, supply and demand forces will generally move prices to eliminate the opportunities. Hence, it is desirable to be able to quickly identify arbitrage opportunities when they do exist and to take advantage of them to the greatest extent possible.

Questions

1 Formulate a decision model to determine whether there are any arbitrage opportunities with the spot currency rates given in Table 3.62. Note that an arbitrage opportunity could involve several currencies. If there is an arbitrage opportunity, your model should specify the exact set of transactions to achieve it.

2 Find the cross currency rates in a recent paper—for example, in the *Wall Street Journal*. (Note that the meaning of the entries could be the opposite of Table 3.62.) Check the numbers for an arbitrage opportunity. If you find one, do you think it represents a real arbitrage opportunity? Why or why not? ■

TABLE 3.62 Cross Currency Spot Rates

		To				
		US Dollar	**Pound**	**FFranc**	**DMark**	**Yen**
	US Dollar	—	0.63900	5.37120	1.57120	98.8901
	Pound	1.56480	—	8.43040	2.45900	154.7733
From	**FFranc**	0.18560	0.11860	—	0.29210	18.4122
	DMark	0.63610	0.40630	3.42330	—	62.9400
	Yen	0.01011	0.00645	0.05431	0.01588	—

REFERENCES

1 Carino, H., and C. Lenoir. "Optimizing Wood Procurement in Cabinet Manufacturing." *Interfaces* 18, no. 2 (1988): 11–19.

2 Charnes, A., and L. Cooper. "Generalization of the Warehousing Model." *Operational Research Quarterly* 6 (1955): 131–72.

3 Cheung, H., and J. Auger. "Linear Programming and Land Use Allocation." *Socio-Economic Planning* 10 (1976): 43–45.

4 DeWitt, C., L. Lasdon, A. Waren, D. Brenner, and S. Melhem. "OMEGA: An Improved Gasoline Blending System for Texaco." *Interfaces* 19, no. 1 (1989): 85–101.

5 Dobson, G., and S. Kalish. "Positioning and Pricing a Product Line." *Marketing Science* 7 (1988): 107–26.

6 Fabian, T., "A Linear Programming Model of Integrated Iron and Steel Production." *Management Science* 4 (1958): 415–49.

7 Franklin, A., and E. Koenigsberg. "Computer School Assignments in a Large District." *Operations Research* 21 (1973): 413–26.

8 Garvin, W., W. Crandall, J. John, and R. Spellman. "Applications of Linear Programming in the Oil Industry." *Management Science* 3 (1957): 407–30.

9 GeneHunter. Ward Systems Group, Frederick, Maryland, 1995.

10 Glassey, R., and V. Gupta. "A Linear Programming Analysis of Paper Recycling." *Studies in Mathematical Programming*. Ed. H. Salkin and J. Saha. New York: North-Holland, 1978.

11 Heady, E., and A. Egbert. "Regional Planning of Efficient Agricultural Patterns." *Econometrica* 32 (1964): 374–86.

12 Krajewski, L., L. Ritzman, and P. McKenzie. "Shift Scheduling in Banking Operations: A Case Application." *Interfaces* 10, no. 2 (1980): 1–8.

13 Lanzenauer, C., E. Harbauer, B. Johnston, and D. Shuttleworth. "RRSP Flood: LP to the Rescue." *Interfaces* 17, no. 4 (1987): 27–40.

14 Love, R., and J. Hoey. "Management Science Improves Fast Food Operations." *Interfaces* 20, no. 2 (1990): 21–29.

15 Magoulas, K., and D. Marinos-Kouris. "Gasoline Blending LP." *Oil and Gas Journal* (July 1988): 44–48.

16 Martin, C., D. Dent, and J. Eckhart. "Integrated Production, Distribution, and Inventory Planning at Libbey-Owens-Ford." *Interfaces* 23, no. 3 (1993): 68–78.

17 Oliff, M., and E. Burch. "Multiproduct Production Scheduling at Owens-Corning Fiberglass." *Interfaces* 15, no. 5 (1985): 25–34.

18 Peterson, R., and E. Silver. *Decision Systems for Inventory Management And Production Planning*. 2nd ed. New York: Wiley, 1985.

19 Robichek, A., D. Teichroew, and M. Jones. "Optimal Short-Term Financing Decisions." *Management Science* 12 (1965): 1–36.

20 Rohn, E. "A New LP Approach to Bond Portfolio Management." *Journal of Financial and Quantitative Analysis* 22 (1987): 439–67.

21 Rothstein, M. "Hospital Manpower Shift Scheduling by Mathematical Programming." *Health Services Research* (1973).

22 Sexton, T., S. Sleeper, and R. Taggart. "Improving Pupil Transportation in North Carolina." *Interfaces* 24, no. 1 (1994): 87–103.

23 Sherman, H. D., and G. Ladino. "Managing Bank Productivity Using Data Envelopment Analysis (DEA)." *Interfaces* 25, no. 2 (1995): 60–80.

24 Smith, S. "Planning Transistor Production by Linear Programming." *Operations Research* 13 (1965): 132–39.

25 Sullivan, R., and S. Secrest. "A Simple Optimization DSS for Production Planning at Dairyman's Cooperative Creamery Association." *Interfaces* 15, no. 5 (1985): 46–54.

C H A P T E R

4

Network Models

Management Science Success Stories

Many of the models in this chapter can be characterized as **logistics problems**, that is, problems of finding the least expensive way to transport products from their origin to their destination. In addition, real logistics problems are often coupled with manufacturing or plant location decisions; the company must decide where to locate its manufacturing plants and what products to produce at each plant. Computer manufacturer Digital Equipment Corporation (DEC) faced such a problem, as reported by Arntzen et al. [2] in "Global Supply Chain Management at Digital Equipment Corporation." DEC faces a huge global manufacturing and distribution problem with its wide range of products (mainframe computers, minicomputers, PCs, and many types of computer parts and peripherals). It must decide where (or whether) to manufacture these products and how to get them to its customers around the world in the most economical manner.

Until the late 1980s DEC specialized primarily in mainframes and minicomputers, using a manufacturing and distribution system that had proved very successful for over 20 years. But as PCs revolutionized the industry, DEC realized that it had to change—quickly and radically—if it wanted to remain a thriving company. It had too many plants, and too much overhead, and too many groups within DEC were making decisions without central coordination. In 1989 the company began to redesign its supply and delivery network and to reengineer its manufacturing and logistics processes. A key step in these corporate changes was the development of the Global Supply Chain Model (GSCM), an extremely complex linear programming model.[1] Since that time, DEC has used GSCM to perform thousands of optimizations in scores of studies.

The typical models run with GSCM are huge. They generally contain from 2000 to 6000 constraints and from 5000 to 20,000 decision variables. (They are *not* suitable for spreadsheets!) The objective typically minimizes total cost, where total cost includes production costs, inventory holding costs, facility material handling costs, taxes, facility fixed charges, production line fixed costs, transportation costs, and duty costs.

[1] The GSCM is actually more than an LP model; it is a mixed-integer model with 0-1 (binary) variables for the plant location decisions. We will study problems with binary variables in the next chapter.

The constraints include customer demand requirements, "balance" constraints for production and inventory, limits on the weight of products through the facilities, production capacities, storage capacities, and others. Also, the models become even more complicated because of multiple products, multiple time periods (planning for four consecutive quarters, for example), and the complexities of international trade. Nevertheless, by taking advantage of the special structure of these models and the advanced software that is now available, DEC is able to solve these models routinely.

To illustrate, DEC ran a large study during 1992 to determine the optimal supply chain design for all of DEC's manufacturing. The study recommended an 18-month plan to restructure the manufacturing infrastructure completely in order to cut costs. Specifically, it recommended that the number of worldwide plants be reduced from 33 to 12, it called for the three basic customer regions (Pacific Rim, Americas, and Europe) to be served primarily by plants within their own regions, and it included a quarter-by-quarter implementation plan. This 18-month plan has since been implemented. By spring 1994 it led to a decrease of $167 million in manufacturing costs (with another $160 million expected by June 1995) and a decrease of over $200 million in logistics costs. This is quite impressive considering that the number of units manufactured and shipped increased dramatically during this same time period. ■

4.1

Introduction

Many important optimization models have a natural graphical network representation. In this chapter we will consider five specific types of these optimization models: the transportation model, the assignment model, the critical path model, the maximum flow model, and the shortest path model. All of these models are special cases of the **minimum cost network flow model** (MCNFM), which we will also discuss. Network models are among the most used management science models. There are two reasons for this. First, many companies have real problems, often extremely large problems, that can be formulated as network models. For example, Delta Airlines has recently used a type of network model to schedule its entire fleet of passenger airplanes. Second, there are specialized solution techniques that have been developed specifically for network models. Although we will not discuss the details of these solution techniques, they are extremely important because they allow us to solve large problems that could not be solved by the usual LP algorithms.

4.2

The Transportation Model

In many situations a company produces products at locations called **supply points** and ships these products to customer locations called **demand points**. Typically, each supply point has a limited amount that it can ship, and each customer must receive a required quantity of the product. Spreadsheet solvers can be used to determine the minimum-cost shipping method for satisfying customer demands.

For now we assume that the only possible shipments are those directly from a supply point to a demand point. That is, no shipments between supply points or between demand points are possible. Such a problem is called a **transportation problem**.

EXAMPLE 4.1

Powerco has three electric power plants that supply the power needs of four cities. Each power plant can supply the amounts shown in Table 4.1 (in millions of kilowatt-hours of electricity). The peak power demand (again in millions of kwh) at each city is given in Table 4.2. Finally, the cost (in dollars) of sending a million kwh from each plant to each city is given in Table 4.3. Powerco wants to find the lowest-cost method for meeting the demand of the four cities.

TABLE 4.1 **Plant Supplies in Powerco Example**

	Supply
Plant 1	35
Plant 2	50
Plant 3	40

TABLE 4.2 **City Requirements for Powerco Example**

	Demand
City 1	45
City 2	20
City 3	30
City 4	30

TABLE 4.3 **Shipping Costs for Powerco Example**

	City 1	City 2	City 3	City 4
Plant 1	8	6	10	9
Plant 2	9	12	13	7
Plant 3	14	9	16	5

Solution

To set up a spreadsheet model for Powerco's power distribution situation we need to keep track of the following:

- the power shipped (in millions of kwh) from each plant to each city
- the total power shipped out of each plant
- the total power received by each city
- the total shipping cost incurred

Developing the Spreadsheet Model The spreadsheet model is shown in Figure 4.1. (See the file POWERCO.XLS.) To develop this model, perform the following steps.

1 **Inputs.** Enter the unit shipping costs for each plant to each city in the range C6:F8.

2 **Amounts shipped.** Enter *any* trial values for the shipments from each plant to each city in the range C13:F15. These are the changing cells.

3 **Amounts shipped out of plants.** To ensure that a plant does not ship more than its available supply, we need to compute the amount shipped out of each plant. In cell G13 compute the amount shipped out of plant 1 with the formula

=SUM(C13:F13)

FIGURE 4.1 **Optimal Solution to Powerco Example**

	A	B	C	D	E	F	G	H	I
1	Powerco Transportation Problem								
2									
3	Unit shipping costs								
4				To					
5			City 1	City 2	City 3	City 4			
6		Plant 1	$8	$6	$10	$9			
7	From	Plant 2	$9	$12	$13	$7			
8		Plant 3	$14	$9	$16	$5			Total cost
9									$1,020
10	Shipments								
11				To					
12			City 1	City 2	City 3	City 4	Total shipped		Total available
13		Plant 1	0	10	25	0	35	<=	35
14	From	Plant 2	45	0	5	0	50	<=	50
15		Plant 3	0	10	0	30	40	<=	40
16		Total received	45	20	30	30			
17			>=	>=	>=	>=			
18		Total required	45	20	30	30			

Copy this formula to the range G14:G15 to compute the amounts shipped out of the other plants. Then enter the supply capacity of each plant in the range I13:I15.

4 **Amounts received by cities.** To ensure that each city receives the needed power, we keep track of the power received by each city in the range C16:F16. In cell C16 compute the power received by city 1 with the formula

=SUM(C13:C15)

Copy this formula to the range D16:F16 to compute the power received by the other cities. Then enter the power needs of each city in the range C18:F18.

5 **Total shipping cost.** Compute the total cost of shipping power from the plants to the cities in cell I9 with the formula

=SUMPRODUCT(C6:F8,C13:F15)

This formula simply sums all units' shipping costs multiplied by amounts shipped.

Using the Solver

1 **Objective.** Select cell I9 (total cost) as the objective to minimize.

2 **Changing cells.** Select the range C13:F15 as the changing cells and constrain these to be nonnegative. These cells correspond to the amounts shipped from each plant to each city.

3 **Supply constraints.** Add the constraints G13:G15<=I13:I15. These constraints (called **supply constraints**) ensure that no plant ships an amount of power exceeding its capacity.

4 **Demand constraints.** Add the constraints C16:F16>=C18:F18. These constraints (called **demand constraints**) ensure that each city receives enough power.

5 **Linear model and optimize.** Check the Assume Linear Model box and Solve.

The Solver solution is shown in Figure 4.1 and is illustrated graphically in Figure 4.2. A minimum cost of $1020 is incurred by using the shipments listed in Figure 4.1. Except for these six routes listed, no other routes are used. ■

FIGURE 4.2 Optimal Shipments for Powerco Example

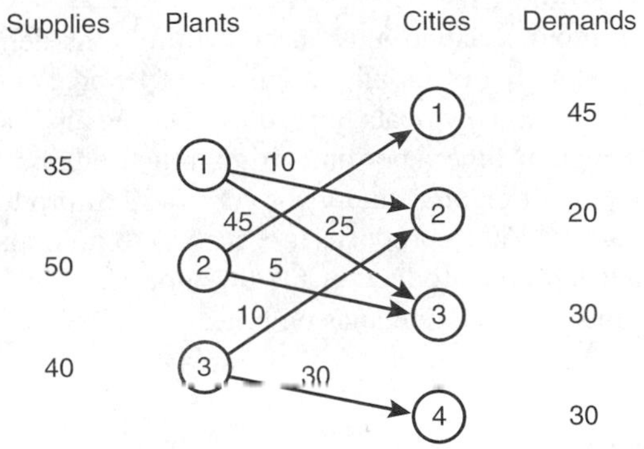

MODELING ISSUES

1 If all the supplies and demands for a transportation problem are integers, then the optimal Solver solution will automatically have integer-valued shipments.

2 Shipping costs are often nonlinear due to quantity discounts. For example, if it costs $3 per item to ship up to 100 items between cities and $2 per item for each additional item, the proportionality assumption of LP is violated and the transportation model we have developed is not valid. Shipping problems that involve quantity discounts are generally very difficult to solve.

3 Spreadsheet Solvers solve transportation problems by the simplex method. There is a simplified version of the simplex method, called the **transportation simplex method**, which is much more efficient than the ordinary simplex method for transportation problems. Large transportation problems are usually solved with the transportation simplex method or the network simplex method (briefly discussed in Section 4.6). See Winston [19] for a discussion of the transportation and network simplex methods.

4 Note that city 1 receives none of its power from the closest plant (plant 1). The reason for this is that plant 2 is a good "second option" for city 1 because it only costs $1 more per million kilowatt-hours than plant 1. On the other hand, for cities 2 and 3 plant 1 is still the best option, but the best second option (plants 3 and 2, respectively) are $3 per million kilowatt-hours more expensive than plant 1. Therefore the Solver uses all of plant 1's capacity for cities 2 and 3 and none for plant 1. ■

REAL-WORLD APPLICATION

Allocating Electric Power in Norway

The Powerco example is based on Aarvik and Randolph [1]. Their work was used to allocate electric power in Norway. They solved transportation problems having up to 75 supply and up to 92 demand points. ■

4.3 A Dynamic Inventory Model

It is possible to formulate some problems that do not involve shipping goods as transportation models. In this section we will illustrate one such example, a dynamic inventory model. (Compare this to the solution of similar inventory models in Sections 2.9 and 3.5.)

EXAMPLE 4.2

During the next four months Sailco must meet (on time) the demand for sailboats listed in Table 4.4. At the beginning of month 1, Sailco has 10 boats in inventory. Each month Sailco must determine how many boats to produce. During any month Sailco can produce up to 40 boats with regular-time labor and an unlimited number of boats with overtime labor. Boats produced with regular time labor cost $400 to produce, and boats produced with overtime labor cost $450 to produce. It costs $20 to hold a sailboat in inventory for a month. Sailco wants to find a production and inventory schedule that minimizes the cost of meeting the next four months' demands on time.

TABLE 4.4 Demand for Sailco Example

	Demand
Month 1	40
Month 2	60
Month 3	75
Month 4	25

Solution

Although this problem can be solved much like the Pigskin problem in the previous chapter, an alternative is to model it as a transportation problem. We describe the details of this procedure next.

Developing the Spreadsheet Model We set up Sailco's problem as a transportation model in Figure 4.3. (See the file SAILCO.XLS.) The following steps lead you through the spreadsheet development. They also explain how this production problem can be represented as a transportation model.

1 **Supplies.** The supply points are the initial inventory, each month's regular time production, and each month's overtime production. The demand points are the demands for each month. A shipment from a supply point to a demand point specifies how much of a given type of supply is used to meet a given month's demand. For example, shipping five units from initial inventory to month 3 demand means that five units of the initial inventory are used to meet month 3 demand. The supplies for each supply point are shown in Table 4.5. Begin by entering these supplies in the range I26:I34.

TABLE 4.5 Supplies for Sailco Example

Supply Point	Supply
Initial Inventory	10
Months 1–4 regular time	40
Months 1–4 overtime	150

Why do we use a supply of 150 for each month's overtime production? We do not know how much will be produced during a given month with overtime production. We do know, however, that an amount equal to 190 units (total demand − 10) will be produced. Even if we made all of these units during a single month, we would

FIGURE 4.3 **Optimal Solution to the Sailco Example**

	A	B	C	D	E	F	G	H	I
1	Sailco Production/Inventory Problem Solved as a Transportation Problem								
2									
3	Input data								
4	Beginning inventory			10					
5	Regular-time capacity (boats/month)			40					
6	Regular-time cost/boat			$400					
7	Overtime cost/boat			$450					
8	Holding cost/boat/month			$20					
9									
10	Unit "shipping" costs								
11				To					
12			Month 1	Month 2	Month 3	Month 4			
13		Initial inventory	$0	$20	$40	$60			
14		RT, month 1	$400	$420	$440	$460			
15		OT, month 1	$450	$470	$490	$510			
16		RT, month 2	$1,000,000	$400	$420	$440			
17	From	OT, month 2	$1,000,000	$450	$470	$490			
18		RT, month 3	$1,000,000	$1,000,000	$400	$420			
19		OT, month 3	$1,000,000	$1,000,000	$450	$470			
20		RT, month 4	$1,000,000	$1,000,000	$1,000,000	$400			
21		OT, month 4	$1,000,000	$1,000,000	$1,000,000	$450			Total cost
22									$78,450
23	Production plan								
24				To					
25			Month 1	Month 2	Month 3	Month 4	Totals		Capacity
26		Initial inventory	0	10	0	0	10	<=	10
27		RT, month 1	40	0	0	0	40	<=	40
28		OT, month 1	0	0	0	0	0	<=	150
29		RT, month 2	0	40	0	0	40	<=	40
30	From	OT, month 2	0	10	0	0	10	<=	150
31		RT, month 3	0	0	40	0	40	<=	40
32		OT, month 3	0	0	35	0	35	<=	150
33		RT, month 4	0	0	0	25	25	<=	40
34		OT, month 4	0	0	0	0	0	<=	150
35		Total received	40	60	75	25			
36			>=	>=	>=	>=			
37		Total needed	40	60	75	25			

not make more than 190 − 40 = 150 units with overtime. Therefore, we are not excluding any possible production plans by allowing at most 150 units to be produced each month with overtime. In other words, 150 is a valid upper bound on the number of units that would ever be produced with overtime in a single month.

In general, we make the capacity for each month's overtime production equal to

$$\text{Overtime production "supply"} = \text{Total demand} - \text{Beginning inventory}$$
$$- \text{Regular time boat capacity for that month}$$

2 **Demands.** The demand points correspond to each month's demand requirements. The demands for the monthly demand points are listed in Table 4.4. Enter these demands in the range C37:F37.

3 **Unit shipping costs.** Enter the "unit shipping costs" in cells C13:F21. Note that production cannot be used to meet demand from a previous month. To model this we enter a ridiculously large shipping cost, such as $1,000,000, in these cases. For example, if the cost of shipping from month 3 regular time to month 2 demand is $1,000,000, this will force the number of month 3 regular time units used to meet month 2 demand to be zero. Note that as we go across each row, the shipping costs increase by $20 per month. This is because as we move across the spreadsheet, the number of months a unit is held in inventory increases by one month per column. To illustrate the computation of the shipping costs, consider the cost of making a sailboat with month 2 regular time and using it to meet month 4 demand. In this case a boat

produced during month 2 will be held in inventory for two months and will incur a cost of

$$\$400 + 2 * (\$20) = \$440$$

4 **Amounts shipped.** In the range C26:F34 enter *any* trial values for the shipments.

5 **Amounts shipped out of supply points.** In the range G26:G34 compute the total shipped out of each supply point. To begin, compute the total amount of initial inventory used to meet demands in cell G26 with the formula

=SUM(C26:F26)

Then copy this formula to the range G27:G34 to compute the total amount shipped out of the other supply points.

6 **Amounts received by demand points.** Compute the total amount received by each demand point. Specifically, in cell C35 compute the total amount of month 1 demand that is met with the formula

=SUM(C26:C34)

Then copy this formula to the range D35:F35 to compute the total amount of demand that is met for the other months.

7 **Total production cost.** Compute the total production and holding costs in cell I22 with the formula

=SUMPRODUCT(C13:F21,C26:F34)

Using the Solver

1 **Objective.** Choose cell I22 (total production cost) as the objective to minimize.

2 **Changing cells.** Choose the range C26:F34 as the changing cells and constrain these to be nonnegative.

3 **Supply constraints.** Add the constraints G26:G34<=I26:I34. These "supply" constraints ensure that no supply point will ship more than its capacity.

4 **Demand constraints.** Add the constraints C35:F35>=C37:F37. These "demand" constraints ensure that each month's demand is met on time.

5 **Linear model and optimize.** Check the Assume Linear Model box and Solve.

The Solver solution appears in Figure 4.3. We see that Sailco can meet its demands at a minimum cost of $78,450. Month 1 demand is met with 40 units of month 1 regular time production. Month 2 demand is met with 10 units of initial inventory, 40 units of month 2 regular time, and 10 units of month 2 overtime production. Month 3 demand is met with 40 units of month 3 regular time production and 35 units of month 3 overtime production. Month 4 demand is met with 25 units of month 4 regular time production. This solution is represented graphically in Figure 4.4.

This solution makes intuitive sense. Sailco wishes to avoid expensive holding costs and overtime costs and to take advantage of relatively cheap regular-time production costs whenever possible. This is exactly what this solution allows Sailco to do. Of course, some overtime is required to meet demand. ■

MODELING ISSUE

This model can easily be extended to handle backlogged demand, lost sales, and purchasing from a subcontractor (the make or buy decision). See Problem 75 for an example. ■

FIGURE 4.4 **Graphical Representation of Solution to Sailco Example**

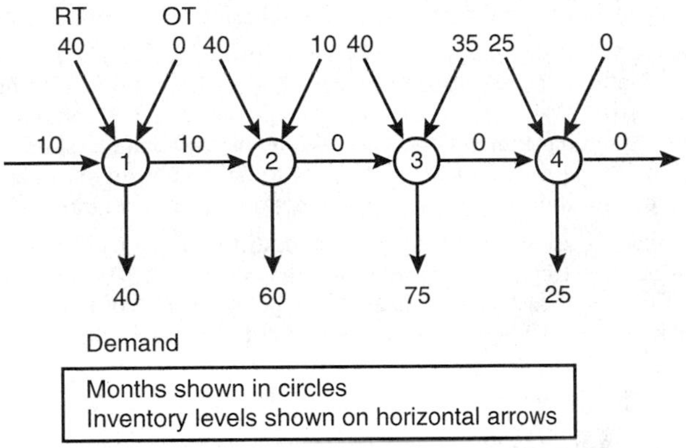

REAL-WORLD APPLICATION

Merging Data Records at the Treasury Department

The U.S. Treasury Department maintains two huge data files: the Current Population Survey and Statistics of Income. The Current Population Survey contains demographic data concerning U.S. families. A typical record in this survey might state that 1000 Jewish families with two children are headed by white males. A typical record in the Statistics of Income file might state that 10,000 families with three members make an income of $22,000 per year. To analyze the effects of changes in government policy, information from both files is needed. This necessitates merging information from the two files. Merging the files necessitates that some information will be lost. Glover and Klingman [7] devised a transportation model whose solution described how to merge the records and minimize the resulting information loss. See Problem 12 for an example. Using computing power available in 1977, they solved a transportation model with 2500 supply and 2500 demand constraints! ■

PROBLEMS

Skill-Building Problems

1 Transportco supplies goods to three customers, who each require 30 units. The company has two warehouses. In warehouse 1, 40 units are available, and in warehouse 2, 30 units are available. The costs of shipping one unit from each warehouse to each customer are shown in Table 4.6. There is a penalty for each unsatisfied customer unit of demand—with customer 1 a penalty cost of $90 is incurred; with customer 2, $80; and with customer 3, $110. Determine how to minimize the sum of shortage and shipping costs.

TABLE 4.6 **Shipping Costs for Transportco Problem**

		To		
		Customer 1	Customer 2	Customer 3
From	Warehouse 1	$15	$35	$25
	Warehouse 2	$10	$30	$40

2 Referring to the previous problem, suppose that Transportco can purchase and ship extra units to either warehouse for a total cost of $100 per unit and that all customer demand must be met. Determine how to minimize the sum of purchasing and shipping costs.

3 The Wingtip shoe company forecasts the following demands during the next six months: month 1, 200; month 2, 260; month 3, 240; month 4, 340; month 5, 190; month 6, 150. It costs $7 to produce a pair of shoes with regular-time labor (RT) and $11 with overtime labor (OT). During each month regular-time production is limited to 200 pairs of shoes, and overtime production is limited to 100 pairs. It costs $1 per month to hold a pair of shoes in inventory. Determine how Wingtip can minimize the total cost of meeting the next six months' demand on time.

4 Steelco manufactures three types of steel at different plants. The time required to manufacture one ton of steel (regardless of type) and the costs at each plant are shown in Table 4.7. Each week, 100 tons of each type of steel (1, 2, and 3) must be produced. Each plant is open 40 hours per week. Determine how to minimize the cost of meeting Steelco's weekly requirements.

TABLE 4.7 Times and Costs for Steelco Problem

	Cost			Time (minutes)
	Steel 1	Steel 2	Steel 3	
Plant 1	$60	$40	$28	20
Plant 2	$50	$30	$30	16
Plant 3	$43	$20	$20	15

5 In the previous problem suppose that the time required to produce one ton of steel depends on the type of steel as well as on the plant at which it is produced. (See Table 4.8.) Could a transportation problem still be formulated?

TABLE 4.8 Plant-dependent Times for Steelco Problem

	Time (minutes)		
	Steel 1	Steel 2	Steel 3
Plant 1	15	12	15
Plant 2	15	15	20
Plant 3	10	10	15

6 A hospital needs to purchase three gallons of a perishable medicine for use during the current month and four gallons for use during the next month. Because the medicine is perishable, it can only be used during the month of purchase. Two companies (Daisy and Laroach) sell the medicine. The medicine is in short supply. Thus, during the next two months the hospital is limited to buying at most five gallons from each company. The companies charge the prices shown in Table 4.9. Determine how to minimize the cost of purchasing the needed medicine.

TABLE 4.9 Prices for Hospital Problem

	Price/Gallon	
	Current Month	Next Month
Daisy	$800	$720
Laroach	$710	$750

7 Bankco has two check processing sites. Site 1 can process 10,000 checks per day, and site 2 can process 6000 checks per day. The bank processes three types of checks: vendor, salary, and personal. The processing cost per check depends on the site, as listed in Table 4.10. Each day 5000 checks of each type must be processed. Determine how to minimize the daily cost of processing checks.

TABLE 4.10 Processing Costs for Bankco Problem

Check Type	Site 1	Site 2
Vendor	5¢	3¢
Salary	4¢	4¢
Personal	2¢	5¢

8 The government is auctioning off oil leases at two sites: 1 and 2. At each site 100,000 acres of land are to be auctioned. Cliff Ewing, Blake Barnes, and Alexis Pickens are bidding for the oil. Government rules state that no bidder can receive more than 40% of the land being auctioned. Cliff has bid $1000 per acre for site 1 land and $2000 per acre for site 2 land. Blake has bid $900 per acre for site 1 land and $2200 per acre for site 2 land. Alexis has bid $1100 per acre for site 1 land and $1900 per acre for site 2 land. Determine how to maximize the government's revenue.

9 The Amorco Oil Company controls two oil fields. Field 1 can produce up to 40 million barrels of oil per day, and field 2 can produce up to 50 million barrels of oil per day. At field 1 it costs $3 to extract and refine a barrel of oil; at field 2 the cost is $2. Amorco sells oil to two countries: United Kingdom and Japan. The shipping costs per barrel are shown in Table 4.11. Each day the U.K. is willing to buy up to 40 million barrels (at $6 per barrel), and Japan is willing to buy up to 30 million barrels (at $6.50 per barrel). Determine how to maximize Amorco's profit.

TABLE 4.11 Shipping Costs for Amorco Oil Problem

		To	
		U.K.	**Japan**
From	**Field 1**	$1	$2
	Field 2	$2	$1

10 Touche Young has three auditors. Each can work up to 160 hours during the next month, during which time three projects must be completed. Project 1 takes 130 hours, project 2 takes 140 hours, and project 3 takes 160 hours. The amount per hour that can be billed for assigning each auditor to each project is given in Table 4.12. Determine how to maximize total billings during the next month.

TABLE 4.12 Billing Costs for Auditing Problem

	Project 1	Project 2	Project 3
Auditor 1	$120	$150	$190
Auditor 2	$140	$130	$120
Auditor 3	$160	$140	$150

Skill-Extending Problems

11 (Based on Glassey and Gupta [6]) Paperco recycles newsprint, uncoated paper, and coated paper into recycled newsprint, recycled uncoated paper, and recycled coated paper. Recycled newsprint can be produced by processing newsprint or uncoated paper. Recycled coated paper can be produced by recycling any type of paper. Recycled uncoated paper can be produced by processing uncoated paper or coated paper. The process used to produce recycled newsprint removes 20% of the input's pulp, leaving 80% of the input's pulp for recycled paper. The process used to produce recycled coated paper removes 10% of the input's pulp. The process used to produce recycled uncoated paper removes 15% of the input's pulp. The purchasing costs, processing costs, and availability of each type of paper are shown in Table 4.13. To meet demand Paperco must produce at least 250 tons of recycled newsprint pulp, at least 300 tons of recycled uncoated paper pulp, and at least 150 tons of recycled coated paper pulp. Determine how to minimize the cost of meeting Paperco's demands.

TABLE 4.13 Data for Paperco Problem

	Purchase Cost per Ton of Pulp	Processing Cost per Ton of Input	Availability (tons)
Newsprint	$10		500
Coated paper	$9		300
Uncoated paper	$8		200
NP used for RNP		$3	
NP used for RCP		$4	
UCP used for RNP		$4	
UCP used for RUP		$1	
UCP used for RCP		$6	
CP used for RUP		$5	
CP used for RCP		$3	

12 (Based on Glover and Klingman [7]) The government has many computer files that must be merged frequently. For example, consider the Survey of Current Income (SOI) and the Consumer Price Service (CPS) files, which keep track of family income and family size. The breakdown of records in each file is given in Table 4.14. SOI and CPS files contain other pieces of data, but the only variables common to the two files are income and family size. Suppose that the SOI and CPS files must be merged to create a file that will be used for an important analysis of government policy. How should the files be merged? We would like to lose as little information as possible in merging the records. For example, merging an SOI record for a family with income $25,000 and family size 2 with a CPS record for a family with income $26,000 and family size 2 results in a smaller loss of information than if an SOI record for a family with income $25,000 and family size 2 is merged with a CPS record for a family with income $29,000 and family size 3. Let the "cost" of merging an SOI record with a CPS record be

$$|I_{SOI} - I_{CPS}| + |FS_{SOI} - FS_{CPS}|$$

where I_{SOI} and I_{CPS} are the incomes from the SOI and CPS records and FS_{SOI} and FS_{CPS} are the family sizes. Determine the least expensive way to merge the SOI and CPS records.

TABLE 4.14 Data for Computer Files Problem

File	Income	Family Size	Number of Records
SOI	$20,000	4	10,000
SOI	$24,000	3	6,000
SOI	$25,000	2	8,000
CPS	$26,000	2	3,000
CPS	$27,000	1	5,000
CPS	$29,000	3	4,000
CPS	$22,000	2	12,000

13 Bloomington has two hospitals. Hospital 1 has four ambulances, and hospital 2 has two ambulances. Ambulance service is deemed adequate if there is only a 10% chance that no ambulance will be available when an ambulance call is received by a hospital. The average length of an ambulance service call is 20 minutes. Given this information, queueing theory tells us that hospital 1 can be assigned up to 4.9 calls per hour and that hospital 2 can be assigned up to 1.5 calls per hour. Bloomington has been divided into 12 districts. The average number of calls per hour emanating from each district is given in Table 4.15. This table also shows the travel time (in minutes) needed to travel from each district to each hospital. The objective is to minimize the average travel time needed to respond to a call. Determine the proper assignment of districts to hospitals. (*Hint*: Be careful about defining the supply points!) ■

TABLE 4.15 **Data for Ambulance Problem**

	Calls/Hour	Time to Hospital 1	Time to Hospital 2
District 1	0.5	5	8
District 2	0.6	6	9
District 3	0.4	7	10
District 4	0.3	5	7
District 5	0.4	6	8
District 6	0.6	7	9
District 7	0.7	9	5
District 8	0.9	10	6
District 9	1.0	11	7
District 10	0.2	7	3
District 11	0.6	8	4
District 12	0.1	9	5

4.4

The Assignment Model

Consider the following situations:

1 Five employees are available to perform four jobs. Each employee can be assigned to at most one job. What job assignment schedule minimizes the amount of time needed to complete the jobs?

2 Twenty drivers have bid on 12 school bus routes. To minimize the cost to the city of bussing the students, which drivers should be assigned to which routes?

3 Thirty men and 30 women are taking a class in management science. The instructor wants to pair them up into 30 two-person project teams with a man and a woman on each team. Which men should be paired with which women in order to maximize the total "effectiveness" (or possibly minimize the total "conflict") of the 30 teams?

In each of these situations, members of one group of objects (employees, drivers, or men) must be assigned to members of another group of objects (jobs, bus routes, or women) to minimize or maximize an objective. Such a problem is called an **assignment problem**. An assignment problem can be viewed as a special case of a transportation problem in which all supplies and demands equal 1. That is, we can think of the employee's assignment to the job as a transporting of one unit of "supply" from the employee to the job. The question is which job to match with each employee. The following example illustrates how to model an assignment problem with a spreadsheet Solver.

EXAMPLE 4.3

Four jobs need to be completed at Machinco. Five machines are available for assignment to these jobs. Each machine can be assigned to at most one job. The time required (in hours) for each machine to complete each job is shown in Table 4.16. The problem is to determine an assignment of machines to jobs that minimizes the time needed to complete the jobs.

TABLE 4.16 **Machine Times for Machinco Example**

	Job 1	Job 2	Job 3	Job 4
Machine 1	14	5	8	7
Machine 2	2	12	6	5
Machine 3	7	8	3	9
Machine 4	2	4	6	10
Machine 5	5	5	4	8

Solution

We would like to assign each machine to the job that it performs most quickly, but this is not possible. For example, this would require that machine 2 do job 1, machine 4 do job 2, machine 3 do job 3, and machine 2 do job 4. Unfortunately, this requires machine 2 to perform two jobs, which is not allowed. So this assignment problem may not be as simple as it looks!

The trick here is to solve a harder problem. Imagine that a machine can be assigned to do portions of more than one job, as long as the total "number" of jobs assigned to a machine does not exceed 1. For example, machine 1 could be assigned to do 40% of job 1, 30% of job 2, 10% of job 3, and 20% of job 4. Fortunately, the spreadsheet Solver never assigns a machine to do a "fractional" portion of a job. This means that we will get the correct answer to the original assignment problem. To model Machinco's problem we must keep track of the following:

- the fraction of each job assigned to each machine
- the fraction of each job completed
- the number of jobs completed by each machine
- the total time needed to complete the jobs

Developing the Spreadsheet Model You can now set up the spreadsheet as follows. See Figure 4.5 (and the file MACHINCO.XLS).

1 **Inputs.** Enter the time needed for each machine to complete each job in the range C6:F10.

2 **Job assignments.** Enter *any* trial values for the fraction of each job assigned to each machine in the range C15:F19.

3 **Jobs assigned to machines.** In the range G15:G19 keep track of the total number of jobs assigned to each machine. For example, in cell G15 enter the formula

=SUM(C15:F15)

This computes the total number of jobs assigned to machine 1. Copy this formula to the range G16:G19 to compute the total number of jobs assigned to the other machines.

FIGURE 4.5 Optimal Solution to Machinco Assignment Example

	A	B	C	D	E	F	G	H	I
1	Machinco Assignment of Jobs to Machines Problem								
2									
3	Times to perform jobs on various machines								
4				Job					
5			1	2	3	4			
6	Machine	1	14	5	8	7			
7		2	2	12	6	5			
8		3	7	8	3	9			
9		4	2	4	6	10			
10		5	5	5	4	8			Total time
11									15
12	Assignments								
13				Job					
14			1	2	3	4	Total jobs assigned to		Capacity
15	Machine	1	0	1	0	0	1	<=	1
16		2	0	0	0	1	1	<=	1
17		3	0	0	1	0	1	<=	1
18		4	1	0	0	0	1	<=	1
19		5	0	0	0	0	0	<=	1
20		Completed	1	1	1	1			
21			>=	>=	>=	>=			
22		Required	1	1	1	1			

4 **Jobs completed.** In the range C20:F20 compute the fraction of each job that is completed. Specifically, compute the fraction of job 1 that is completed in cell C20 with the formula

=SUM(C15:C19)

Copy this formula to the range D20:F20 to compute the fraction of the other jobs completed.

5 **Total time.** Compute the total time needed to complete the jobs in cell I11 with the formula

=SUMPRODUCT(C6:F10,C15:F19)

Using the Solver

1 **Objective.** Choose cell I11 (total time needed to complete jobs) as the objective to minimize.

2 **Changing cells.** Select the range C15:F19 as the changing cells and constrain these to be nonnegative.

3 **Machine capacity constraints.** Add the constraints G15:G19<=I15:I19. (Note that the right-hand sides stored in I15:I19 are all equal to 1.) These constraints ensure that no machine is assigned to more than one job.

4 **Job completion constraints.** Add the constraints C20:F20>=C22:F22. (The right-hand sides are again all equal to 1.) These constraints ensure that each job is completed.

5 **Linear model and optimize.** Check the Assume Linear Model box and Solve.

The optimal solution is shown in Figure 4.5. Machine 1 completes job 2, machine 2 completes job 4, machine 3 completes job 3, machine 4 completes job 1, and machine 5 is left idle. Note that three of the four jobs (1, 3, and 4) are assigned to the machine that does them most efficiently. A total of 15 hours is needed to complete all jobs.

Figure 4.6 contains a network representation of the Solver solution. The idle machine (machine 5) can be thought of as being assigned to a "dummy" job. This idea will come in handy in Section 4.6. ■

FIGURE 4.6 **Optimal Job Assignments**

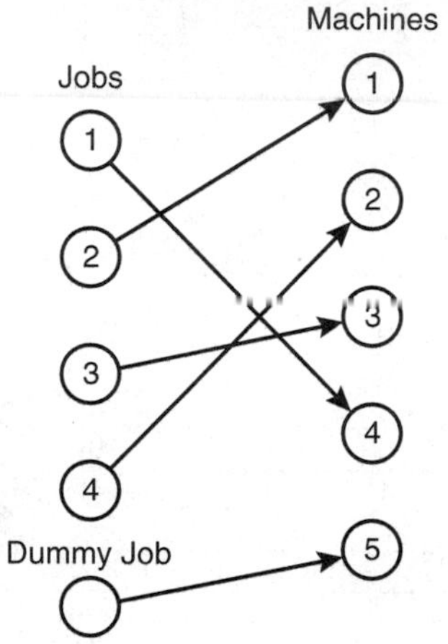

MODELING ISSUES

1 Recall from our discussion of the transportation problem that a transportation problem in which all supplies and demands are integers automatically has an optimal solution in which all changing cells are integers. Because an assignment problem is a transportation problem with all supplies and demands equal to 1, it automatically has an optimal solution in which all changing cells are nonnegative integers. But because the only way to make a group of nonnegative integers sum to 1 is to have one of the integers be 1 and the rest be 0, we know (even though the changing cells are not constrained to be integers) that the computer will assign each job to a *single* machine.

2 A spreadsheet Solver solves an assignment problem by using the simplex method. Assignment problems can be solved more efficiently with the **Hungarian method**. See Winston [19] for details. ■

REAL-WORLD APPLICATIONS

Assigning School Buses to Routes

Each year school bus drivers "bid" on the bus routes they are willing to drive. For example, driver 1 may submit a bid of $40,000 for transporting the students on route 8, and so on. After receiving all bids, the local school board must allocate the routes to the drivers. An assignment model can be used to minimize the cost of covering all routes. Our local school district (Monroe County of Indiana) actually uses such a model. See Problem 17 for more details of this procedure. ■

Saving on Airline Commuting

Consider the business commuter who must make multiple air trips between two cities such as Pittsburgh and Chicago. In today's deregulated world, the price of a round-trip ticket varies greatly. For example, if you leave on a Sunday and return on a Monday you pay much more than if you leave on a Saturday and return on a Monday. Hansen and Wendell [10] realized that a business commuter who makes many air trips between two cities can use the assignment model to save a great deal on airfare. See Problem 72 (in the Review Problems section) for details. The trick is to buy several round-trip tickets and for each trip use ticket coupons from parts of two *different* round-trip tickets. ■

Workforce Assignment in the Military

Using a version of the assignment model, Klingman and Phillips [12] assigned army personnel to jobs. Their problem involved 10,000 people and 10,000 jobs! Their actual model involved multiple objectives (see Chapter 7). Two objectives were involved: (1) maximize the number of jobs filled by a qualified person and (2) maximize the fit between people and jobs, where there is a rating given for the assignment of each person to each job. ■

PROBLEMS

Skill-Building Problems

14 Five employees are available to perform four jobs. The time it takes each person to perform each job is given in Table 4.17. Determine the assignment of employees to jobs that minimizes the total time required to perform the four jobs. (A dash indicates that a person cannot do that particular job.)

TABLE 4.17 Times for Job Assignment Problem

	Time (hours)			
	Job 1	**Job 2**	**Job 3**	**Job 4**
Person 1	22	18	30	18
Person 2	18	—	27	22
Person 3	26	20	28	28
Person 4	16	22	—	14
Person 5	21	—	25	28

15 (Based on Machol [14]) Doc Councillman is putting together a relay team for the 400-meter relay. Each swimmer must swim 100 meters of breaststroke, backstroke, butterfly, or freestyle. Doc believes that each swimmer will attain the times given in Table 4.18. To minimize the team's time for the race, which swimmer should swim which stroke?

TABLE 4.18 Times for Swimming Relay Problem

	Time (seconds)			
	Free	**Breast**	**Butterfly**	**Back**
Gary Hall	54	54	51	53
Mark Spitz	51	57	52	52
Jim Montgomery	50	53	54	56
Chet Jastremski	56	54	55	53

16 A company is taking bids on four construction jobs. Three contractors have placed bids on the jobs. Their bids (in thousands of dollars) are given in Table 4.19. (A dash indicates that the contractor did not bid on the given job.) Contractor 1 can do only one job, but contractors 2

TABLE 4.19 Bids for Contractor Problem

	Job 1	Job 2	Job 3	Job 4
Contractor 1	50	46	42	40
Contractor 2	51	48	44	—
Contractor 3	—	47	45	45

and 3 can each do up to two jobs. Determine the minimum cost assignment of contractors to jobs.

Skill-Extending Problem

17 The Chicago Board of Education is taking bids on the city's four school bus routes. Four companies have made the bids in Table 4.20.

TABLE 4.20 Bids for Bussing Problem

	Route 1	Route 2	Route 3	Route 4
Company 1	\$2500	\$3000	\$1500	—
Company 2	—	\$4000	—	\$4000
Company 3	\$3000	—	\$2000	—
Company 4	—	—	\$4000	\$5000

a Suppose each bidder can be assigned only one route. Use the assignment method to minimize Chicago's cost of running the four bus routes.

b Suppose that each company can be assigned two routes. Use the assignment method to minimize Chicago's cost of running the four bus routes. (*Hint*: Two supply points are needed for each company.) ■

4.5 The Critical Path Model (CPM)

Network models can be used as an aid in the scheduling of large, complex projects that consist of many activities. If the duration of each activity is known with certainty, the **critical path model** (CPM) can be used to determine the length of time needed to complete a project. If the durations of the activities are not known with certainty, then **Monte Carlo simulation** (see Chapters 12 and 13) can be used to estimate the probability that a project will be completed by a given deadline.

CPM has been successfully used in many applications including the following:

- scheduling construction projects such as office buildings, highways, and swimming pools
- scheduling the movement of a 400-bed hospital from Portland, Oregon, to a suburban location
- developing a countdown and "hold" procedure for space flights
- installing a new computer system
- designing and marketing a new product
- completing a corporate merger
- building a ship

To apply CPM we need a list of the activities that make up the project. The project is considered complete when all of the activities have been completed. For each activity there is a set of activities called the **predecessors** of the activity that must be completed before the activity begins. A project network is used to represent the precedence relationships between activities. In our discussion nodes (or circles) in a network represent the completion of activities and arcs joining the nodes represent the activities. This type of project network is called an **activity on arc** (AOA) network.[2]

To understand how an AOA network represents precedence relationships, suppose that activity A is a predecessor of activity B. Each node in an AOA network represents the completion of one or more activities. Thus, node 2 in Figure 4.7 represents the completion of activity A and the beginning of activity B. As another example, suppose that activities A and B must both be completed before activity C can begin. In Figure 4.8 node 3 represents the completion of activities A and B. As a final example Figure 4.9 expresses the relationship that activities B and C can begin as soon as activity A is completed.

FIGURE 4.7 **Activity A, Then B**

FIGURE 4.8 **Activities A and B, Then C**

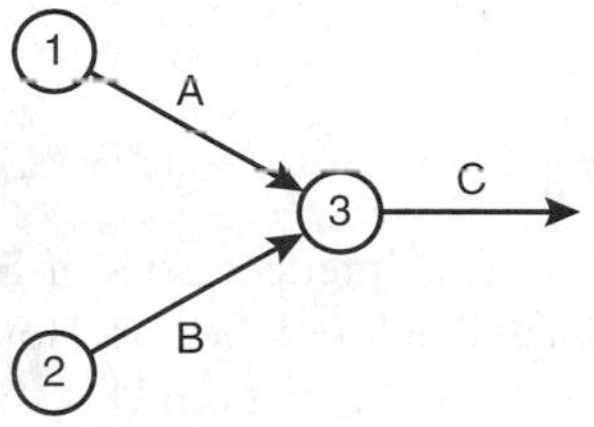

FIGURE 4.9 **Activity A, Then B and C**

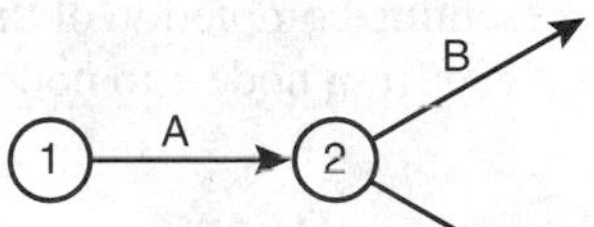

Given a list of activities and predecessors, an AOA representation of a project (called a **project network** or **project diagram**) can be constructed by using the following rules:

1 Node 1 represents the start of the project.

2 A node (called the **finish node**) is included in the network to represent the completion of the project.

[2]There is an alternative graphical representation called activity on node (AON) that is favored by some analysts. Here nodes represent activities and arcs are used to represent predecessor information.

3 The nodes are numbered so that the node representing the completion of an activity always has a larger number than the node representing the beginning of an activity. (There may be more than one numbering scheme satisfying this rule.)

The next example illustrates a project network.

EXAMPLE 4.4

Widgetco is about to introduce a new product. One unit of this product is produced by assembling subassembly 1 and subassembly 2. Before production begins on either subassembly, raw materials must be purchased and workers must be trained. Before the subassemblies can be assembled into the final product, the finished subassembly 2 must be inspected. A list of activities, their predecessors, and their durations is given in Table 4.21. Draw a project diagram for this project.

TABLE 4.21 **Data for Widgetco Example**

Activity	Predecessors	Duration (days)
A (Train Workers)	None	6
B (Purchase Raw Materials)	None	9
C (Make Subassembly 1)	A, B	8
D (Make Subassembly 2)	A, B	7
E (Inspect Subassembly 2)	D	10
F (Assemble Subassemblies)	C, E	12

Solution

Observe that although we list only C and E as predecessors of F, it is actually true that activities A, B, and D must also be completed before F begins. However, because C cannot begin until A and B are completed and E cannot begin until D is completed, it is redundant to state that A, B, and D are predecessors of F. Thus, in drawing the project network, we need only be concerned with the *immediate* predecessors of each activity.

The AOA network for this project is shown in Figure 4.10, where the number next to each activity represents the activity's duration in days. Node 1 is the beginning of the project and node 5 is the finish node, representing completion of the project. Note that two arcs, corresponding to activities A and B, lead from node 1 to node 2. This is because both

FIGURE 4.10 **Project Network for Widgetco Example**

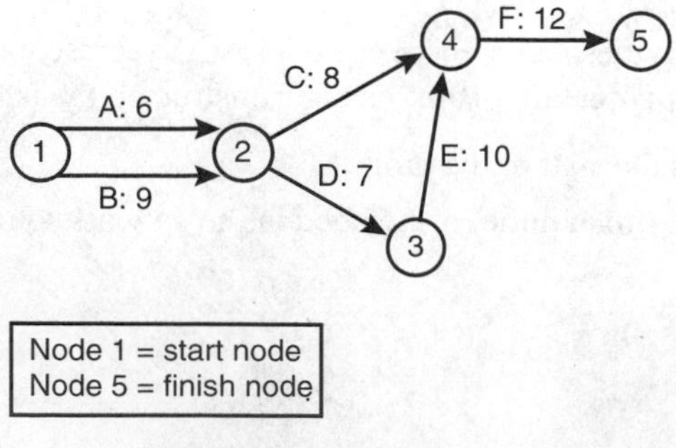

activities A and B can start at the same time, and activities C and D can start as soon as both A and B are finished.[3]

Critical Activities and the Critical Path If any increase in the duration of an activity increases the time needed to complete the project, then the activity is called a **critical activity**. A path from node 1 to the finish node that consists entirely of critical activities is called a **critical path**. Since any delay in the duration of a critical activity delays the completion of the project, it is advisable to monitor closely the completion of critical activities. Essentially, the critical activities are the "bottleneck" activities that are likely to slow up the entire project.

Using a Spreadsheet Solver to Identify Critical Activities and the Critical Path We now show how to use a spreadsheet Solver to determine the duration of the project and the critical path for the Widgetco example. See Figure 4.11 (and the file WIDGETCO.XLS).

FIGURE 4.11 **Optimal Solution to Widgetco CPM Example**

	A	B	C	D	E	F	G	H	I	J	K
1	**Widgetco Project Scheduling Problem**										
2											
3	**Start times for nodes**										
4					**Node**						
5			1	2	3	4	5			**Project time**	
6			0	9	16	26	38			38	
7											
8	**Matrix of activity/node incidences**										
9	Note: An entry is +1 if the activity's arc enters the node. It is -1 if the activity's arc leaves the node.										
10	Otherwise, the entry is 0.										
11					**Node**						
12			1	2	3	4	5			Duration	On critical path?
13	**Activity**	A	-1	1	0	0	0	9	>=	6	No
14		B	-1	1	0	0	0	9	>=	9	Yes
15		C	0	-1	0	1	0	17	>=	8	No
16		D	0	-1	1	0	0	7	>=	7	Yes
17		E	0	0	-1	1	0	10	>=	10	Yes
18		F	0	0	0	-1	1	12	>=	12	Yes

1 **Inputs.** Enter the durations of the activities in the range J13:J18.

2 **Node event times.** Designate a changing cell for each node in the project network. Each node's changing cell will equal the time at which the event corresponding to that node occurs. Without loss of generality, we assume that node 1 (the start of the project) occurs at time 0. To ensure this, enter 0 in cell C6. Then enter *any* trial values for each node's occurrence in the range D6:G6.

3 **Activity-node incidence matrix.** Let a be any activity. The arc corresponding to activity a leads from some node, say node i, to another node, say node j, where $j > i$. Let t_i and t_j be the times nodes i and j occur, and let d_a be the duration of activity a. Then

$$t_j \geq t_i + d_a \qquad \textbf{(4.1)}$$

The reasoning is that activity a can start, at the *earliest*, at time t_i, and it takes time d_a to complete activity a once it starts. Therefore, the earliest node j can occur is at time

[3]Some management scientists do not allow two arcs to connect the same two nodes, and they use extra nodes and "dummy" arcs to get around the problem. We believe this is quite confusing and is not necessary with the LP formulation we are using.

$t_i + d_a$. (The time node j occurs could be delayed even more than this if it is held up by *other* activities leading into node j.) We can rewrite Inequality 4.1 as

$$t_j - t_i \geq d_a \tag{4.2}$$

There will be exactly one such constraint for each activity.

In preparation for generating the constraints in Inequality 4.2, enter +1's, −1's, and 0's in the range C13:G18. There is a row in this range for each activity and a column for each node. A given entry is a +1 if there is an arc for an activity leading *into* a node, a −1 if there is an arc for an activity leading *out of* a node, and a 0 otherwise. For example, the arc for activity A leads out of node 1 and into node 2, so the first two entries in row 13 (cells C13 and D13) are −1 and +1; the other entries in that row are 0. We call this collection of +1's, −1's, and 0's the project network's **activity-node incidence matrix**. It essentially provides enough information to reconstruct the network shown in Figure 4.10.

4 **Duration of project.** The goal is to complete the project as quickly as possible, so we would like to minimize the duration of the project. Since the starting time of the project is 0, the duration of the project is simply the time node 5 is reached. Enter the duration of the project in cell J6 with the formula

=G6

5 **Timing of activities.** In the range H13:H18 compute the left-hand side of the constraints from Inequality 4.2. Specifically, in H13 compute the left-hand-side of 4.2 corresponding to activity A [arc (1,2)] with the formula

=SUMPRODUCT($C$6:$G$6,C13:G13)

Then copy this formula to the range H14:H18 to generate the left-hand side of 4.2 for the other activities.

Using the Solver To find the critical path and the total length of the project with the Solver, proceed as follows.

1 Choose cell J6 (project duration) as the objective to minimize.

2 Choose the range D6:G6 as the changing cells and constrain these to be nonnegative.

3 Add the constraints H13:H18>=J13:J18. These are the timing constraints from Inequality 4.2.

The optimal solution is given in Figure 4.11. It shows that the project can be completed in 38 days. Using the node times in row 6, we can better illustrate the solution with a **Gantt chart**, as shown in Figure 4.12. The dotted vertical lines indicate when the various nodes occur. Each rectangle corresponds to an activity, with length equal to the activity's duration, and time increases from left to right. Gantt charts are very useful for depicting starting and finishing times of a complex project.

Now that we have found the length of the project, there are two ways to find the critical path. First, by examining Figure 4.12, we see that there are two activities, A and C, that can "slide" a bit (as indicated by the horizontal arrows) without affecting the overall project length. For example, activity C could start at time 10 instead of 9, and it would not delay the entire project at all. The other activities, however, cannot be delayed without delaying the entire project. These activities, B, D, E, and F, are therefore the critical activities.

A second way to locate the critical activities is to examine Excel's sensitivity report. It can be shown that the shadow price for each constraint in 4.2 is either 1 or 0. From the discussion of shadow prices in Chapter 2, this means that increasing the duration of the corresponding activity by a small amount Δ will (1) increase the length of the project by

FIGURE 4.12 **Gantt Chart for Widgetco**

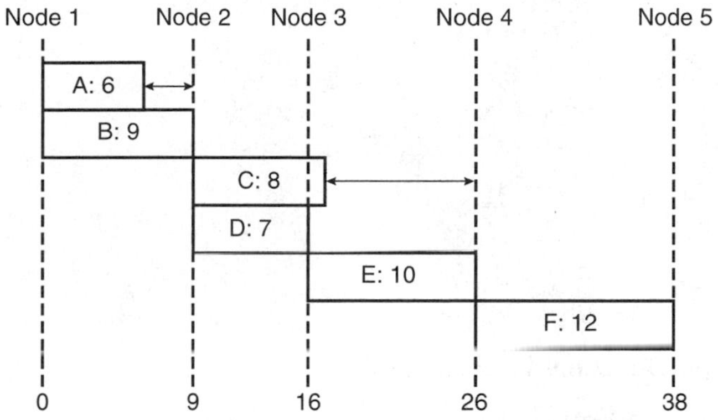

FIGURE 4.13 **Sensitivity Report for Widgetco Example**

Cell	Name	Final Value	Shadow Price	Constraint R.H. Side	Allowable Increase	Allowable Decrease
$H$13	A	9	0	6	3	1E+30
$H$14	B	9	1	9	1E+30	3
$H$15	C	17	0	8	9	1E+30
$H$16	D	7	1	7	1E+30	9
$H$17	E	10	1	10	1E+30	9
$H$18	F	12	1	12	1E+30	38

Δ if the shadow price of the constraint in 4.2 is 1 or (2) leave the duration of the project unchanged if the shadow price is 0. The relevant part of Excel's sensitivity report for this example appears in Figure 4.13. As we see, the shadow prices of 1 correspond to activities B, D, E, and F, which further confirms that these are the critical activities. If any of their durations increase, the length of the entire project will necessarily increase.

We now know, therefore, that *any activity with a shadow price of 1 is a critical activity*. Following the critical activities from the start to the finish node yields a critical path. We note that a project network can have several critical paths, but a spreadsheet Solver will identify only a *single* critical path.

MODELING ISSUES

1 A spreadsheet Solver determines critical activities with the simplex method. There are more efficient methods for determining critical activities, but they do not allow the project network to have two or more arcs joining any pair of nodes. See Winston [19] for a discussion of other methods for finding the critical path.

2 CPM assumes that the duration of each activity is known with certainty. In reality, this is usually not true. Painting a house, for example, will go slowly if the painter encounters poor weather. If the duration of activities is uncertain, then there is a probability that each activity will be on a critical path. For example, consider the project network shown in Figure 4.14. Assume that the duration of each activity is equally likely to assume one of the three values in Table 4.22. Then it can be shown (see Problem 24) that the probability of each activity being on the critical path will be those shown in Table 4.23.

FIGURE 4.14 Project with Uncertain Activity Durations

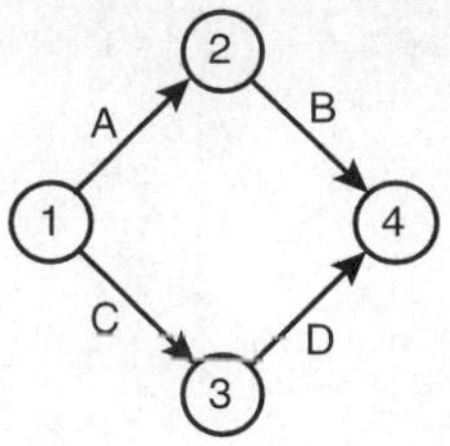

TABLE 4.22 Multiple Durations for Activities

Activity	Possible Durations
A	1, 9, 5
B	6, 14, 10
C	5, 7, 6
D	7, 9, 8

TABLE 4.23 Probabilities of Being on Critical Path

Activity	Probability Activity is Critical
A	17/27
B	17/27
C	12/27
D	12/27

This example shows that it doesn't make sense to talk about *the* critical path. Instead we should determine the probability that an activity is critical. For a more complex project, Monte Carlo simulation (see Chapters 12 and 13) can be used to determine the probability that each activity will be a critical activity. ■

Crashing the Project

In many situations the project manager is under pressure to complete the project in a time that is less than the length of the critical path. The problem of finding the minimum cost method for reducing the duration of activities in order to meet a deadline is called **crashing** a project.

EXAMPLE 4.4 CONTINUED

Assume Widgetco believes that to have any chance of being a success, the new product must be available for sale before the competitor's product hits the market. Widgetco knows that the competitor's product is scheduled to hit the market 26 days from now, so Widgetco must introduce its product within 25 days. Since the current critical path length is 38 days, Widgetco will have to expend extra resources to meet the 25-day deadline. In such a situation, linear programming can often be used to determine an allocation of resources that minimizes the cost of meeting the project deadline.

Suppose that by allocating additional resources to an activity, Widgetco can reduce the duration of any activity by up to five days. The cost per day of reducing the duration of each activity is shown in Table 4.24. We now show how to use a spreadsheet Solver to crash a project.

TABLE 4.24 Costs of Crashing Activities

	Activity					
	A	B	C	D	E	F
Cost/Day	$10	$20	$3	$30	$40	$50

Developing the Spreadsheet Model The key to crashing the project is to introduce changing cells for the number of days by which each activity's duration is reduced. Then we can write

New duration of activity = Original duration of activity

− Number of days by which duration is crashed

Now the constraints in 4.2 are replaced by

$$t_j - t_i \geq d'_a \tag{4.3}$$

where d'_a is the *new* duration for activity *a*. We also need to add a constraint to ensure that the project is completed in 25 days or less. The objective is to minimize the cost of crashing the project to 25 days.

The spreadsheet for crashing the project is shown in Figure 4.15. (See the file CRASHING.XLS.) It can be formed as follows.

1 **Inputs.** Beginning with the previous critical path worksheet (Figure 4.11), insert nine rows (which will be rows 3 through 11). Enter the costs per day of crashing in the range B5:B10 and the maximum allowable reductions in the range H5:H10. Also, move the original durations (which were in the range J13:J18 of Figure 4.11) to the range D5:D10. Finally, enter the project deadline in cell L15.

2 **Reductions in durations.** In the range F5:F10 enter *any* trial value for the reduction in the duration of each activity.

3 **New durations.** Calculate the new durations (after crashing) in the range J22:J27. Specifically, enter the formula

=D5–F5

in cell J22 and copy this formula to the range J23:J27 for the other activities.

4 **Cost of crashing.** Compute the total cost of crashing the project in cell B29 with the formula

=SUMPRODUCT(F5:F10,B5:B10)

Using the Solver

1 **Objective.** Choose cell B29 (total crashing cost) as the objective to minimize.

2 **Extra changing cells.** Choose the range F5:F10 as additional changing cells and constrain them to be nonnegative. (Remember that the cells in the range D15:G15 are already changing cells.)

FIGURE 4.15 Optimal Solution for Crashing in Widgetco Example

	A	B	C	D	E	F	G	H	I	J	K	L
1	Widgetco Project Scheduling Problem - Crashing to Meet a Deadline											
2												
3	**Data on crashing**											
4	Activity	Cost/day of reduction		Original duration		Reduction		reduction (days)				
5	A	$10		6		2	<=	5				
6	B	$20		9		5	<=	5				
7	C	$3		8		0	<=	5				
8	D	$30		7		5	<=	5				
9	E	$40		10		3	<=	5				
10	F	$50		12		0	<=	5				
11												
12	**Start times for nodes**											
13					**Node**							
14			1	2	3	4	5			Project time		Deadline
15			0	4	6	13	25			25	<=	25
16												
17	**Matrix of activity/node incidences**											
18	Note: An entry is -1 if the activity's arc leaves the node. It is +1 is the activity's arc enters the node.											
19	Otherwise, it is 0.											
20					**Node**							
21			1	2	3	4	5			Duration after crashing		
22	**Activity**	A	-1	1	0	0	0	4	>=	4		
23		B	-1	1	0	0	0	4	>=	4		
24		C	0	-1	0	1	0	9	>=	8		
25		D	0	-1	1	0	0	2	>=	2		
26		E	0	0	-1	1	0	7	>=	7		
27		F	0	0	0	-1	1	12	>=	12		
28												
29	**Total cost**	$390										

3 **Maximum reduction constraints.** Add the constraints F5:F10<=H5:H10. These ensure that we do not crash any activity by more than the allowed amount.

4 **Deadline constraint.** Add the constraint J15<=L15. This ensures that the project will be completed within 25 days.

5 **Linear model and optimize.** Check the Assume Linear Model box and Solve.

The optimal solution is shown in Figure 4.15. This solution entails reducing the duration of each activity as indicated in Table 4.25, with a total cost of $390. With the new durations of each activity, the new Gantt chart appears as shown in Figure 4.16. We see now that activity C is the only activity that can "slide." All other activities are critical. Note that although activity C is the least expensive to crash, it is not crashed at all. The reason is that in the original solution (see Figure 4.12) activity C is so far from being critical that crashing it simply doesn't help. ■

FIGURE 4.16 Gantt Chart for Widgetco After Crashing

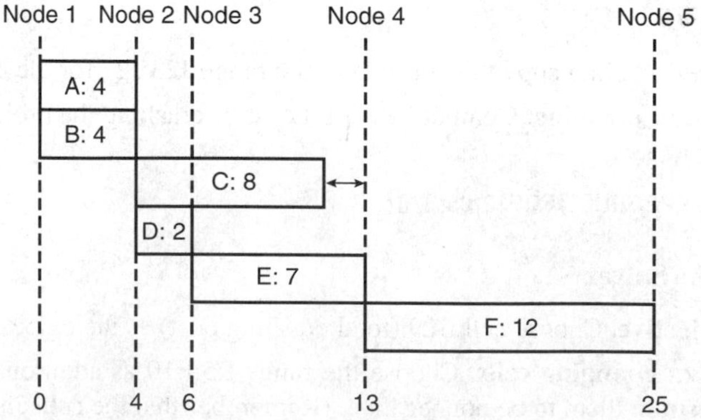

TABLE 4.25 Optimal Crash Amounts

	Activity					
	A	B	C	D	E	F
Reduction	2	5	0	5	3	0

MODELING ISSUE

Often the cost of reducing an activity's duration is not a *linear* function of the amount of time by which an activity's duration is reduced. In such cases crashing the project leads to a nonlinear model ■

PROBLEMS

Skill-Building Problems

18 A company has a project that consists of 11 activities, as illustrated in Figure 4.17. Nodes 1 and 9 are the start and finish nodes. The numbers on the arcs represent the activity durations (in days). Use LP to find the critical path and the minimum number of days to complete this project.

FIGURE 4.17 Project Network for 11-Activity Problem

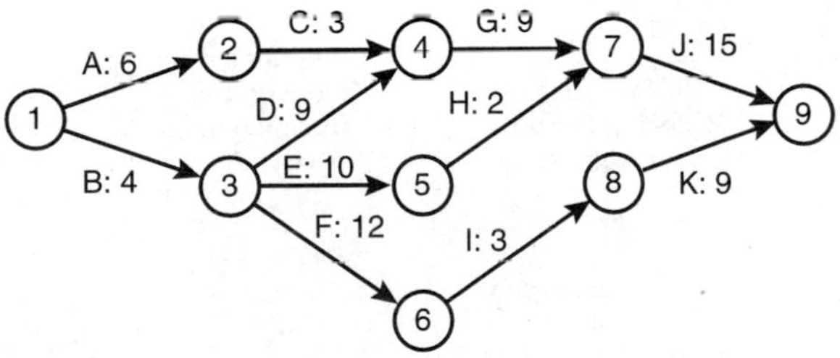

19 The promoters of a rock concert in Indianapolis must perform the tasks shown in Table 4.26 before the concert can be held. (All durations are in days.)

TABLE 4.26 Rock Concert Activities

	Description	Predecessors	Duration
Activity A	Find Site	—	3.0
Activity B	Find Engineers	A	2.0
Activity C	Hire Opening Act	A	6.0
Activity D	Set Radio and TV Ads	C	2.0
Activity E	Set Up Ticket Agents	A	3.0
Activity F	Prepare Electronics	B	3.0
Activity G	Print Advertising	C	5.0
Activity H	Set Up Transportation	C	1.0
Activity I	Rehearsals	F, H	1.5
Activity J	Last-Minute Details	I	2.0

a Draw the project network.

b Use LP to find the critical path and the minimum number of days needed to prepare for the concert.

20 Consider the (simplified) list of activities and predecessors that are involved in building a house, as listed in Table 4.27.

TABLE 4.27 House-Building Activities

	Description	Predecessors	Duration (days)
Activity A	Build Foundation	—	5
Activity B	Build Walls and Ceilings	A	8
Activity C	Build Roof	B	10
Activity D	Do Electrical Wiring	B	5
Activity E	Put In Windows	B	4
Activity F	Put On Siding	E	6
Activity G	Paint House	C, F	3

a Draw a project network and use LP to find the critical path and the minimum number of days needed to build the house.

b Suppose that by hiring additional workers, the duration of each activity can be reduced. The costs per day of reducing the duration of the activities are given in Table 4.28. Use LP to find the strategy that minimizes the cost of completing the project within 20 days.

TABLE 4.28 Reducing House-Building Activity Times

Activity	Cost per Day of Reducing Duration of Activity	Maximum Possible Reduction in Duration of Activity (days)
Foundation	\$30	2
Walls and ceiling	\$15	3
Roof	\$20	1
Electrical wiring	\$40	2
Windows	\$20	2
Siding	\$30	3
Paint	\$40	1

21 Horizon Cable is about to expand its cable TV offerings in Smalltown by adding MTV and other exciting stations. The activities in Table 4.29 must be completed before the service expansion can be completed. Draw the project network and use LP to find the critical path and the minimum number of weeks needed to complete the project.

TABLE 4.29 Cable Company Activities

	Description	Predecessors	Duration (weeks)
Activity A	Choose stations	—	2
Activity B	Get town council to approve expansion	A	4
Activity C	Order converters	B	3
Activity D	Install new dish	B	2
Activity E	Install converters	C, D	10
Activity F	Change billing system	B	4

22 A company is planning to manufacture a product that consists of three parts (A, B, and C). The company anticipates that it will take five weeks to design the three parts and determine the way in which these parts must be assembled to make the final product. Then the company estimates that it will take four weeks to make part A, five weeks to make part B, and three weeks to make part C. The company must test part A after it is completed, and this takes two weeks. The assembly line process will then proceed as follows: assemble parts A and B (two weeks) and then attach part C (one week). Then the final product must undergo one week of testing.

a Draw the project network.

b Use LP to find the critical path and the minimum amount of time needed to complete the project.

23 When an accounting firm audits a corporation, the first phase of the audit involves obtaining "knowledge of the business." This phase of the audit requires the activities listed in Table 4.30.

a Draw the project network and use LP to determine the critical path and the minimum number of days needed to complete the first phase of the audit.

TABLE 4.30 **Audit Activities**

	Description	Predecessors	Duration (days)
Activity A	Determine terms of engagement	—	3
Activity B	Appraisal of auditability risk and materiality	A	6
Activity C	Identification of types of transactions and possible errors	A	14
Activity D	Systems description	C	8
Activity E	Verification of systems description	D	4
Activity F	Evaluation of internal controls	B, E	8
Activity G	Design of audit approach	F	9

b Assume that the first phase must be completed within 30 days. The duration of each activity can be reduced by incurring the costs shown in Table 4.31. Use LP to find the strategy that minimizes the cost of meeting this deadline.

TABLE 4.31 **Reducing Audit Activity Times**

	Cost per Day of Reducing Duration of Activity	Maximum Possible Reduction in Duration of Activity (days)
Activity A	$100	3
Activity B	$80	4
Activity C	$60	5
Activity D	$70	2
Activity E	$30	4
Activity F	$20	4
Activity G	$50	4

Skill-Extending Problem

24 Consider the project described by Table 4.22 (Mutiple Durations for Activities). Assume that each activity's duration is equally likely to be any of the durations listed in the table. Verify that the probabilities in Table 4.23 are correct. For example, verify that activity A has probability 17/27 of being critical. ■

4.6 The Minimum Cost Network Flow Model

The transportation model, the assignment model, and the critical path model (as well as maximum flow and shortest path models, discussed in Sections 4.7 and 4.8) are all special cases of the **minimum cost network flow model** (MCNFM). In a general sense this class of problems entails sending "goods" along the arcs of a network at a minimal cost when there are possibly capacity restrictions on some or all of the arcs.

To motivate the MCNFM, consider a food processing company that ships products from plants to warehouses. Customers are supplied from warehouses. This is *not* a transportation problem because shipments do not occur directly from the supply points (plants) to the demand points (customers). To model general distribution problems, we need a model that allows shipments into and out of every point.

Figure 4.18 provides an example of this situation. (This figure is the basis for the following example.) The plants (points 1, 2, and 3) can ship to the warehouses (points 4 and 5) or directly to the customers (points 6 and 7). The warehouses can ship only to the customers (points 6 and 7).

FIGURE 4.18 **Typical Network for Minimum Cost Network Flow Model**

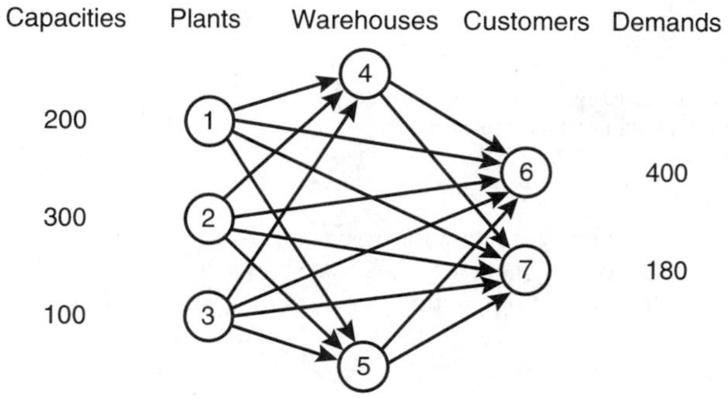

The network flow model of this situation requires the following elements:

1. There must be a changing cell that represents the possible flow through each arc in the network.
2. Each arc must have a **unit shipping cost** (or unit shipping profit), which is the cost (or profit) received per unit shipped along the arc.
3. Each arc in the network must have a lower bound (usually 0) and an upper bound (often infinity) on the flow through the arc. These upper bounds are called **arc capacities**.
4. Each node in the network must have a **net supply**. For each node i in the network, the flows through the arcs must satisfy the following **flow constraint**:

$$\text{Flow out of node } i - \text{Flow into node } i = \text{Net supply at node } i \quad \textbf{(4.4)}$$

Any node with a positive net supply is called a **supply point**; it is a net shipper of goods. Any node with a negative net supply is called a **demand point**; it is a net receiver of goods. A node with a net supply of zero is called a **transshipment point**; goods neither originate nor end up there.

To formulate a problem as a MCNFM, it is necessary that the sum of all the net supplies in the network equal zero. If this is not the case, we simply add a dummy node with a net supply equal to the negative of the sum of the net supplies for all other nodes:

$$\text{Net supply for dummy node} = -(\text{Sum of net supplies for all other nodes})$$

There are two cases where a dummy node is necessary: when the net supply for the dummy node is *negative* and when it is *positive*. The first case is when there is more capacity than demand; the second is when demand exceeds capacity. In the first case, no shipments *out of* the dummy node are allowed. To model this, we make the arc capacity for any shipment out of the dummy node equal to 0, and we insert an arc from each "real" node to the dummy node. The unit shipping cost for each of these arcs equals 0, and the capacity of each of these arcs equals the *negative* of the net supply of the dummy node.

As an example, consider Figure 4.18, where the three plants have capacities of 200, 300, and 100 units, and the two customers have demands of 400 and 180 units. Then the net supplies for nodes 1, 2, and 3 are 200, 300, and 100, the net supplies for nodes 4 and 5 are 0, and the net supplies for nodes 6 and 7 are −400 and −180. Since the sum of these is 20, the net supply for the dummy node is −20. There would then be an arc from each of nodes 1–7 to the dummy node. These would each have unit shipping cost 0 and capacity 20. A "shipment" from node 1, say, to the dummy node would correspond to unused capacity at the first plant.

In the second case, where the net supply of the dummy node is positive, no shipments *into* the dummy node are allowed. To model this, we make the arc capacity for any shipment into the dummy node equal to 0, and we insert an arc from the dummy node to each "real" node. The unit shipping cost for each of these arcs equals 0, and the capacity of each of these arcs equals the net supply of the dummy node.

As an example, consider changing Figure 4.18 slightly so that the second customer's demand increases to 250. Then nodes 1, 2, and 3 have net supplies of 200, 300, and 100, nodes 4 and 5 have net supplies of 0, and nodes 6 and 7 have net supplies of −400 and −250. Since the sum of these is −50, the net supply for the dummy node is 50. There would then be an arc from the dummy node to each of nodes 1–7. These arcs would each have unit shipping cost 0 and capacity 50. A "shipment" from the dummy node to node 6, say, would correspond to unsatisfied demand for the first customer.

We are now ready to set up and solve a network flow problem. The changing cells will represent the flows through the arcs in the network. The constraints will consist of arc capacity constraints and the conservation of flow described in Equation 4.4.

EXAMPLE 4.5

Foodco produces food at three plants (nodes 1, 2, and 3). Food can be shipped directly to customers (nodes 6 and 7) or it can first be shipped to warehouses (nodes 4 and 5) and then to the customers. (See Figure 4.18.) The cost of producing food at each plant is the same, so Foodco is concerned with minimizing the total shipping cost incurred in meeting customer demands. The production capacity of each plant (in tons per year) and the demand of each customer are listed in Tables 4.32 and 4.33. The cost of shipping a ton of food (in thousands of dollars) between each pair of points is given in Table 4.34, where a dash indicates that Foodco cannot ship from a node to itself. At most 200 tons of food can be shipped between any two nodes. Foodco wants to determine a minimum cost shipping schedule.

Solution

We do not know exactly how much food will be shipped out of nodes 1 through 3, so we set the net supply for each of these nodes equal to the plant's capacity. Thus nodes 1 through

TABLE 4.32 Capacities at Plants for Foodco Example

	Capacity
Plant 1 (Node 1)	200
Plant 2 (Node 2)	300
Plant 3 (Node 3)	100

TABLE 4.33 Customer Demands for Foodco Example

	Demand
Customer 1 (Node 6)	400
Customer 2 (Node 7)	180

TABLE 4.34 Shipping Costs for Foodco Example

		To Node						
		1	**2**	**3**	**4**	**5**	**6**	**7**
	1	—	5	3.0	2.0	1.0	2	4
	2	9.0	—	9.0	1.0	1.0	8	9
	3	0.4	8	—	1.0	0.5	10	8
From Node	**4**	1.0	1	0.5	—	1.2	5	1
	5	2.0	1	0.6	0.8	—	2	7
	6	2.0	9	1.0	0.6	0.7	—	3
	7	7.0	3	6.0	1.0	0.3	7	—

3 are supply points with net supplies 200, 300, and 100, respectively. Any amount shipped into a warehouse must eventually leave the warehouse, so nodes 4 and 5 are transshipment points with net supplies equal to zero. Finally, nodes 6 and 7 are customers, so their net supplies are (by convention) the negatives of their demands, −400 and −180.

Since the sum of the net supplies over all nodes is 200 + 300 + 100 − 400 − 180 = 20, we need to add a dummy demand node (node 8) with net supply −20. In essence, node 8 will "receive" the 20 units of unused capacity from one or more of the plants; in reality, of course, these 20 units are not physically shipped.

Developing the Spreadsheet Model To set up the spreadsheet model, proceed as follows. (See Figure 4.19 and the file FOODCO.XLS. Also, refer to the graph in Figure 4.18.)

1. **Unit shipping costs.** Enter the unit shipping costs (in thousands of dollars) in the range C6:J13. Note that the cost of shipping along any node leading to or from the dummy node is zero. (*Note*: In the FOODCO.XLS file, we gave this range the name "Costs." We also used range names for the arc capacities and the flows. This was done purely for ease of reference.)
2. **Arc capacities.** Enter the arc capacities in the range C35:J42. Note that the zero entries in the range C42:J42 prohibit shipments out of the dummy node. Also note that zero arc capacities are used to rule out shipments from any node to itself.
3. **Amounts shipped.** Enter any trial values for the shipments between points in the range C18:J25.
4. **Flows out of nodes.** In preparation for creating the conservation of flow constraints for each node, we need to compute the flow out of and the flow into each node. In the range K18:K25 compute the flow out of each node. For example, to compute the flow out of node 1, we add all the flows out of node 1. To do this, enter the formula

   =SUM(C18:J18)

FIGURE 4.19 Optimal Solution to Foodco Example

	A	B	C	D	E	F	G	H	I	J	K
1	**Foodco Minimum Cost Network Flow Problem**										
2											
3	**Unit shipping costs**										
4							To				
5			Plant 1	Plant 2	Plant 3	Warehouse 1	Warehouse 2	Customer 1	Customer 2	Dummy	
6	**From**	Plant 1	$0.00	$5.00	$3.00	$2.00	$1.00	$2.00	$4.00	$0.00	
7		Plant 2	$9.00	$0.00	$9.00	$1.00	$1.00	$8.00	$9.00	$0.00	
8		Plant 3	$0.40	$8.00	$0.00	$1.00	$0.50	$10.00	$8.00	$0.00	
9		Warehouse 1	$1.00	$1.00	$0.50	$0.00	$1.20	$5.00	$1.00	$0.00	
10		Warehouse 2	$2.00	$1.00	$0.60	$0.80	$0.00	$2.00	$7.00	$0.00	
11		Customer 1	$2.00	$9.00	$1.00	$0.60	$0.70	$0.00	$3.00	$0.00	
12		Customer 2	$7.00	$3.00	$6.00	$1.00	$0.30	$7.00	$0.00	$0.00	
13		Dummy	$0.00	$0.00	$0.00	$0.00	$0.00	$0.00	$0.00	$0.00	
14											**Total cost**
15	**Shipments**										$1,310.00
16							To				
17			Plant 1	Plant 2	Plant 3	Warehouse 1	Warehouse 2	Customer 1	Customer 2	Dummy	Total outflow
18	**From**	Plant 1	0	0	0	0	0	200	0	0	200
19		Plant 2	0	0	0	180	100	0	0	20	300
20		Plant 3	0	0	0	0	100	0	0	0	100
21		Warehouse 1	0	0	0	0	0	0	180	0	180
22		Warehouse 2	0	0	0	0	0	200	0	0	200
23		Customer 1	0	0	0	0	0	0	0	0	0
24		Customer 2	0	0	0	0	0	0	0	0	0
25		Dummy	0	0	0	0	0	0	0	0	0
26		Total inflow	0	0	0	180	200	400	180	20	
27		Total outflow	200	300	100	180	200	0	0	0	
28		Net outflow	200	300	100	0	0	-400	-180	-20	
29			=	=	=	=	=	=	=	=	
30		Given net outflow	200	300	100	0	0	-400	-180	-20	
31											
32	**Arc capacities**										
33							To				
34			Plant 1	Plant 2	Plant 3	Warehouse 1	Warehouse 2	Customer 1	Customer 2	Dummy	
35	**From**	Plant 1	0	200	200	200	200	200	200	20	
36		Plant 2	200	0	200	200	200	200	200	20	
37		Plant 3	200	200	0	200	200	200	200	20	
38		Warehouse 1	200	200	200	0	200	200	200	20	
39		Warehouse 2	200	200	200	200	0	200	200	20	
40		Customer 1	200	200	200	200	200	0	200	20	
41		Customer 2	200	200	200	200	200	200	0	20	
42		Dummy	0	0	0	0	0	0	0	0	

in cell K18. Then copy this formula to the range K19:K25 to compute the flow out of the other nodes.

5 **Flows into nodes.** Compute the flow into each node in the range C26:J26. First, compute the total flow into node 1 by adding the flow into node 1 from all other nodes. To do this, enter the formula

=SUM(C18:C25)

in cell C26. Then copy this formula to the range D26:J26 to compute the flow into the other nodes.

6 **Transpose flows out of nodes.** It is convenient to "copy" the flows out of the nodes to the *horizontal* range C27:J27. To do this, enter the flow out of node 1 in cell C27 with the formula

=K18

Then continue in this fashion to "copy" the flow out of nodes 2 through 8 to the range D27:J27. *Note*: An easy way to "copy" or transpose in one step in Excel is to highlight the range C27:J27 and then enter in cell C27 the *array* formula[4]

=TRANSPOSE(K18:K25)

To enter this formula you must press *Control, Shift, and then Enter*, not just Enter. You will notice that the numbers in the *vertical* range K18:K25 have been transposed to the *horizontal* range C27:J27. (We will use the transposing command in other

[4]Array formulas and functions such as TRANSPOSE cannot be used with the What's Best! add-in for Lotus 1-2-3. You will have to copy the values by hand from K18:K25 to C27:J27.

examples in the chapter. Its purpose is to allow us to calculate the net outflows in the next step easily.)

7 **Net outflows.** Now prepare for the creation of the flow constraints by computing the actual net outflow for each node in the range C28:J28. Begin by entering the formula

=C27–C26

in cell C28. Then copy this formula to the range D28:J28 to compute the flow out of the other nodes.

8 **Net supplies (inputs).** Enter the net supply for each node in the range C30:J30. (These are labeled "Given net outflow" in the spreadsheet.)

9 **Total shipping cost.** In cell K15 compute the total shipping cost (in hundreds of dollars) with the formula

=SUMPRODUCT(C6:J13,C18:J25)

Note that you can take advantage of the range names we have included in the FOODCO.XLS file to write this as

=SUMPRODUCT(Costs,Flows)

Using the Solver

1 **Objective.** Choose cell K15 (total shipping cost) as the objective to minimize.

2 **Changing cells.** Choose the range C18:J25 (the possible shipments) as the changing cells and constrain these to be nonnegative.

3 **Flow balance constraints.** Add the constraints C28:J28=C30:J30. These ensure that Equation 4.4 is satisfied for each node.

4 **Arc capacity constraints.** Add the constraints C18:J25<=C35:J42. These ensure that the flow through each arc does not exceed the arc's capacity.

5 **Linear model and optimize.** Check the Assume Linear Model box and Solve.

The optimal solution is shown in Figure 4.19. We find that Foodco's customer demand can be satisfied for a shipping cost of $1,310,000. Plant 1 ships 200 tons to customer 1 (node 6). Plant 2 produces 280 units. It sends 180 of these units to warehouse 1 (node 4) and 100 units to warehouse 2 (node 5). Plant 3 ships 100 units to node 5 (warehouse 2). Warehouse 1 (node 4) ships its 180 units to customer 2 (node 7). Warehouse 2 (node 5) ships its 200 units to customer 1 (node 6). The optimal shipping plan is displayed in Figure 4.20. The 20 units shipped from plant 2 to the dummy (not shown in the figure) indicate that plant 2 has 20 units of unused capacity. ■

FIGURE 4.20 **Optimal Shipments for Foodco Example**

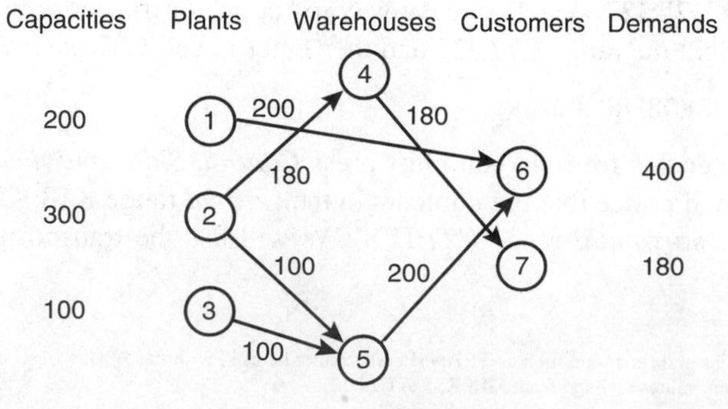

MODELING ISSUES

1 Spreadsheet Solvers use the simplex method to solve network flow models. For network flow models the simplex method can be simplified dramatically. The simplified version of the simplex method, called the **network simplex method**, is much more efficient than the ordinary simplex method. Specialized computer codes have been written to implement the network simplex method, and all large network flow problems are solved by using the network simplex method. See Winston [19] for a discussion of this method.

2 If the net supplies for each node and all arc capacities are integers, then the network flow problem will always have an optimal solution for which the flow in every arc is an integer. ■

REAL-WORLD APPLICATION

Production Distribution and Inventory at Agrico

Agrico Chemical Company is a large producer of chemical fertilizers. Glover et al. [8] developed a network flow model to help Agrico answer questions such as

- How many units of each fertilizer should be produced each month?
- How should products be shipped to distribution centers and customers?

The key to the Agrico model was to create a **dynamic network**. For each location in a dynamic network, there are nodes representing the location at different points in time. For example, there might be a node for plant 1 at times 1, 2, and 3. A "flow" from the plant 1–time 1 node to the plant 1–time 2 node, for example, corresponds to holding inventory. See Problems 67 and 69 (in the Review Problems section) for examples of dynamic network modeling. The Agrico model saves the company an estimated $8 million a year in holding, production, and distribution costs. See Problem 76 for a further discussion of the Agrico situation.

A similar model developed by Klingman et al. [13] helped Citgo Petroleum to optimize its refinery and distribution operations. This model saves Citgo over $16 million annually. (This model was also discussed in Chapter 1.) ■

PROBLEMS

Skill-Building Problems

25 Widgetco manufactures widgets at two factories, one in Memphis and one in Denver. The Memphis factory can produce up to 150 widgets per day, and the Denver factory can produce up to 200 widgets per day. Widgets are shipped by air to customers in Los Angeles and Boston. The customers in each city require 130 widgets per day. Because of the deregulation of air fares, Widgetco believes that it might be cheaper to first fly some widgets to New York or Chicago and then fly them to their final destinations. The costs of flying a widget are shown in Table 4.35. Determine how to minimize the total cost of shipping the required widgets to the customers.

26 General Ford produces cars at L.A. and Detroit and has a warehouse in Atlanta. The company supplies cars to customers in Houston and Tampa. The costs of shipping a car between various points are listed in Table 4.36, where a dash means that a shipment is not allowed. L.A. can produce up to 1100 cars, and Detroit can produce up to 2900 cars. Houston must receive 2400 cars, and Tampa must receive 1500 cars.

a Determine how to minimize the cost of meeting demands at Houston and Tampa.

b Modify the answer to Part (a) if shipments between L.A. and Detroit are not allowed.

c Modify the answer to Part (a) if shipments between Houston and Tampa are allowed at a cost of $5 per car.

TABLE 4.35 Shipping Costs for Widgetco Problem

		To					
		Memphis	Denver	N.Y.	Chicago	L.A.	Boston
From	Memphis	—	—	$8	$13	$25	$28
	Denver	—	—	$15	$12	$26	$25
	N.Y.	—	—	—	$6	$16	$17
	Chicago	—	—	$6	—	$14	$16
	L.A.	—	—	—	—	—	—
	Boston	—	—	—	—	—	—

TABLE 4.36 Shipping Costs for General Ford Problem

		To				
		L.A.	Detroit	Atlanta	Houston	Tampa
From	L.A.	—	$140	$100	$90	$225
	Detroit	$145	—	$111	$110	$119
	Atlanta	$105	$115	—	$113	$78
	Houston	$89	$109	$121	—	—
	Tampa	$210	$117	$82	—	—

27 Sunco Oil produces oil at two wells. Well 1 can produce up to 150,000 barrels per day, and well 2 can produce up to 200,000 barrels per day. It is possible to ship oil directly from the wells to Sunco's customers in Los Angeles and New York. Alternatively, Sunco could transport oil to the ports of Mobile and Galveston and then ship it by tanker to New York or Los Angeles. Los Angeles requires 160,000 barrels per day, and New York requires 140,000 barrels per day. The costs of shipping 1000 barrels between various locations are shown in Table 4.37, where a dash indicates shipments that are not allowed. Determine how to minimize the transport costs in meeting the oil demands of Los Angeles and New York.

TABLE 4.37 Shipping Costs for Sunco Problem

		To					
		Well 1	Well 2	Mobile	Galveston	N.Y.	L.A.
From	Well 1	—	—	$10	$13	$25	$28
	Well 2	—	—	$15	$12	$26	$25
	Mobile	—	—	—	$6	$16	$17
	Galveston	—	—	$6	—	$14	$16
	N.Y.	—	—	—	—	—	$15
	L.A.	—	—	—	—	$15	—

28 In the previous problem assume that before being shipped to Los Angeles or New York, all oil produced at the wells must be refined at either Galveston or Mobile. To refine 1000 barrels of oil costs $12 at Mobile and $10 at Galveston. Assuming that both Mobile and Galveston have infinite refinery capacity, determine how to minimize the daily cost of transporting and refining the oil requirements of Los Angeles and New York.

29 Rework the previous problem under the assumption that Galveston has a refinery capacity of 150,000 barrels per day and Mobile has a refinery capacity of 180,000 barrels per day.

30 Nash Auto has two plants, two warehouses, and three customers. The locations of these are as follows: the plants are in Detroit and Atlanta, the warehouses are in Denver and New York, and the customers are in Los Angeles, Chicago, and Philadelphia. Cars are produced at plants, then shipped to warehouses, and finally shipped to customers. Detroit can produce 150 cars per week, and Atlanta can produce 100 cars per week. Los Angeles requires 80 cars per week,

Chicago requires 70, and Philadelphia requires 60. It costs $10,000 to produce a car at each plant. The costs of shipping a car between various cities are listed in Table 4.38. Assume that during a week, at most 50 cars can be shipped from a warehouse to any particular city. Determine how to meet Nash's weekly demands at minimum cost.

TABLE 4.38 Shipping Costs for Nash Auto Problem

		To				
		Denver	N.Y.	L.A.	Chicago	Philadelphia
From	Detroit	$1253	$637	—	—	—
	Atlanta	$1398	$841			—
	Denver	—	—	$1059	$996	$1691
	N.Y.	—	—	$2786	$802	$100

31 Each hour an average of 900 cars enter the network in Figure 4.21 at node 1 and seek to travel to node 6. The number above each arc in this figure is the maximum number of cars that can pass by any point on the arc during a one-hour period. The times it takes a car to traverse the various arcs are shown in Table 4.39. Determine how to minimize the total time required for all cars to travel from node 1 to node 6.

FIGURE 4.21 Network Representation of Traffic Problem

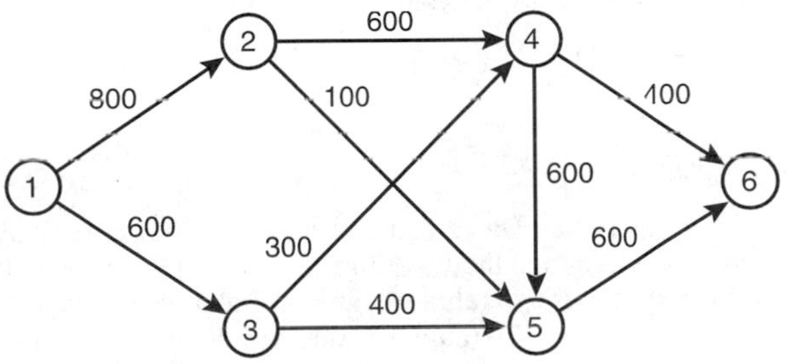

TABLE 4.39 Travel Times for Traffic Problem

Arc	Time (minutes)
(1,2)	10
(1,3)	50
(2,5)	70
(2,4)	30
(5,6)	30
(4,5)	30
(4,6)	60
(3,5)	60
(3,4)	10

32 Fordco produces cars in Detroit and Dallas. The Detroit plant can produce up to 6500 cars, and the Dallas plant can produce up to 6000 cars. Producing a car costs $2000 in Detroit and $1800 in Dallas. Cars must be shipped to three cities. City 1 must receive 5000 cars, city 2 must receive 4000 cars, and city 3 must receive 3000 cars. The costs of shipping a car from each plant to each city are given in Table 4.40. At most 2700 cars can be sent from a given plant to a given city. Determine how to minimize the cost of meeting all demands.

TABLE 4.40 Shipping Costs for Fordco Problem

		To		
		City 1	City 2	City 3
From	Detroit	$800	$600	$300
	Dallas	$500	$200	$200

33 Each year Data Corporal produces up to 400 computers in Boston and up to 300 computers in Raleigh. Los Angeles customers must receive 400 computers, and 300 computers must be supplied to Austin customers. Producing a computer costs $800 in Boston and $900 in Raleigh. Computers are transported by plane and can be sent through Chicago. The costs of sending a computer between pairs of cities are shown in Table 4.41.

a Determine how to minimize the total (production plus distribution) cost of meeting Data Corporal's annual demand.

b How would you modify the model in Part (a) if at most 200 units could be shipped through Chicago?

TABLE 4.41 Shipping Costs for Data Corporal Problem

		To		
		Chicago	Austin	Los Angeles
From	Boston	$80	$220	$280
	Raleigh	$100	$140	$170
	Chicago	—	$40	$50

Skill-Extending Problems

34 Oilco has oil fields in San Diego and Los Angeles. The San Diego field can produce up to 500,000 barrels per day, and the Los Angeles field can produce up to 400,000 barrels per day. Oil is sent from the fields to a refinery, either in Dallas or in Houston. (Assume that each refinery has unlimited capacity.) To refine 100,000 barrels costs $700 at Dallas and $900 at Houston. Refined oil is shipped to customers in Chicago and New York. Chicago customers require 400,000 barrels per day, and New York customers require 300,000 barrels per day. The costs of shipping 100,000 barrels of oil (refined or unrefined) between cities are shown in Table 4.42.

a Determine how to minimize the total cost of meeting all demands.

b If each refinery had a capacity of 380,000 barrels per day, how would you modify the model in Part (a)?

TABLE 4.42 Shipping Costs for Oilco Problem

		To			
		Dallas	Houston	New York	Chicago
From	Los Angeles	$300	$110	—	—
	San Diego	$420	$100	—	—
	Dallas	—	—	$450	$550
	Houston	—	—	$470	$530

35 (Based on Glover et al. [9]) Braneast Airlines must determine how many airplanes should serve the Boston–New York air corridor and which flights to fly. Braneast can fly any of the daily flights shown in Table 4.43. The fixed cost of operating an airplane is $800 per day. Determine how to maximize Braneast's daily profit. (*Hint*: Each node in the network

TABLE 4.43 Flight Data for Braneast Problem

Leaves		Arrives		Flight	Flight
City	Time	City	Time	Revenue	Variable Cost
N.Y.	9 A.M.	Boston	11 A.M.	$800	$400
N.Y.	11 A.M.	Boston	1 P.M.	$900	$450
N.Y.	2 P.M.	Boston	4 P.M.	$1050	$500
N.Y.	4 P.M.	Boston	6 P.M.	$1200	$450
Boston	10 A.M.	N.Y.	Noon	$900	$420
Boston	Noon	N.Y.	2 P.M.	$1100	$620
Boston	2 P.M.	N.Y.	4 P.M.	$1300	$600
Boston	5 P.M.	N.Y.	7 P.M.	$1200	$580

represents a city and a time. In addition to arcs representing flights, you must allow for the possibility that an airplane will stay on the ground for an hour or more. You must also ensure that the model includes the fixed cost of operating a plane. To include this cost, the following arcs can be included in the network: from Boston 7 P.M. to Boston 10 A.M. and from New York 7 P.M. to New York 9 A.M.)

36 At present there are 500 long-distance calls that must be routed from New York to Los Angeles and 400 calls that must be routed from Philadelphia to L.A. On route to L.A. from Philly or New York, calls are sent through Indianapolis or Cleveland, then through Dallas or Denver, and finally to L.A. The number of calls that can be routed between any pair of cities is shown in Table 4.44. The phone company wants to know how many of the $500 + 400 = 900$ calls originating in New York and Philadelphia can be routed to L.A. Set this up as a MCNFM, that is, specify the nodes, arcs, shipping costs, and arc capacities. (*Hint*: You will need a dummy supply (DS) and dummy demand point (DD) to set this up. DS will have a net supply of 900 and DD will have a net supply of -900. Shipments are allowed on the arcs DS-LA and DS-DD. Shipments are also allowed on the arcs NY-DD and PHIL-DD.) ■

TABLE 4.44 Data for Phone Call Problem

Cities	Maximum calls
N.Y.-Indy	300
N.Y.-Clev.	200
Phil.-Indy	250
Phil.-Clev.	250
Indy-Denver	180
Indy-Dallas	220
Clev.-Denver	160
Clev.-Dallas	260
Denver-L.A.	500
Dallas-L.A.	400

4.7 The Maximum Flow Model

Many situations can be modeled by a network in which each arc has a capacity that limits the quantity of a product that can be shipped through that arc. In these situations it is often desired to transport the maximum amount of flow from a starting point (called the **source**) to a terminal point (called the **sink**). Such problems represent a special case of the network flow model known as the **maximum flow model**. The following is an example of the maximum flow model.

EXAMPLE 4.6

Sunco Oil wants to ship the maximum amount of oil (per hour) via pipeline from a source (an Alaskan well) to a sink (a California refinery), as depicted in Figure 4.22. On its way from the source to the sink, the oil must pass through some or all of the three stations: 1, 2, and 3. The various arcs represent pipelines of different diameters. The maximum number of barrels of oil (millions of barrels per hour) that can be pumped through each arc is shown in Figure 4.22. Sunco wants to determine the maximum number of barrels per hour that can be sent from the source to the sink. (In this figure, the source and sink are abbreviated as *so* and *si*.)

FIGURE 4.22 **Network for Sunco Maximum Flow Example**

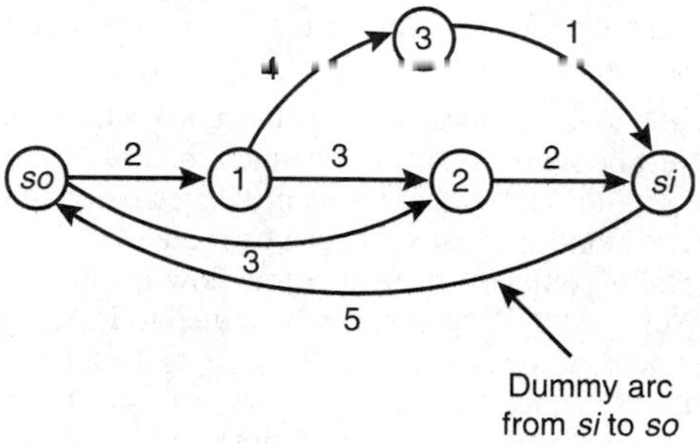

Solution

To represent a maximum flow problem as a network flow model, we add a dummy arc flowing from the sink to the source. We set the net outflow for each node in the network equal to zero. Then we use Equation 4.4 of Section 4.6 to ensure that the flow through the dummy arc will equal the flow into the sink. Therefore, we need only maximize the flow through the dummy arc, that is, the arc from the sink to the source. Since we do not know what the flow through the dummy arc will be, we make the capacity of the dummy arc equal to the sum of the arc capacities leading out of the source. In this case the total flow out of the source cannot exceed $2 + 3 = 5$, so we make the capacity of the dummy arc equal to 5.

Developing the Spreadsheet Model In setting up a spreadsheet for the maximum flow model, we must keep track of the arc capacities, the flow through each arc, and the net outflow for each node (which should be zero). The spreadsheet solution appears in Figure 4.23. (See the file SUNCO.XLS.) To develop it, proceed as follows.

1 **Arc capacities.** Enter the arc capacities in the range C20:G24. Observe that the arc capacity of 5 for the dummy arc from the sink to the source is entered in cell C24. For arcs that do not exist, enter an arc capacity of zero.

2 **Net supplies.** Enter the net supply (zero) for each node in the range C15:G15.

3 **Flows.** Enter *any* trial values of the flow through each arc in the network in the range C6:G10.

4 **Outflows from nodes.** Compute the outflow from each node in the range H6:H10. Specifically, compute the outflow from the source in cell H6 with the formula

```
=SUM(C6:G6)
```

FIGURE 4.23 Optimal Solution for Sunco Example

	A	B	C	D	E	F	G	H	I	J
1	**Sunco Oil Maximum Flow Problem**									
2										
3	**Flows**									
4					**To**					
5			Source	Node 1	Node 2	Node 3	Sink	Total Outflow		**Total flow**
6	**From**	Source	0	1	2	0	0	3		3
7		Node 1	0	0	0	1	0	1		
8		Node 2	0	0	0	0	2	2		
9		Node 3	0	0	0	0	1	1		
10		Sink	3	0	0	0	0	3		
11		Total inflow	3	1	2	1	3			
12		Total outflow	3	1	2	1	3			
13		Net outflow	0	0	0	0	0			
14			=	=	=	=	=			
15		Given net outflow	0	0	0	0	0			
16										
17	**Arc capacities**									
18					**To**					
19			Source	Node 1	Node 2	Node 3	Sink			
20	**From**	Source	0	2	3	0	0			
21		Node 1	0	0	3	4	0			
22		Node 2	0	0	0	0	2			
23		Node 3	0	0	0	0	1			
24		Sink	5	0	0	0	0			

Then copy this formula to the range H7:H10 to compute the outflow from the other nodes.

5 **Inflows to nodes.** Compute the inflow to each node in the range C11:G11. Specifically, compute the inflow to the source in cell C11 with the formula

=SUM(C6:C10)

Then copy this formula to the range D11:G11 to compute the inflow for the other nodes.

6 **Transpose outflows from nodes.** To compute the net outflow for each node, "copy" the outflow from each node to the range C12:G12. For example, transpose the outflow from node 1 to cell C12 with the formula

=H6

Remember that with Excel, an easy way to do this for all nodes at once is to highlight the range C12:G12 and enter in cell C12 the *array* formula

=TRANSPOSE(H6:H10)

(Don't forget to press Control, Shift, and then Enter instead of just Enter!)

7 **Net outflows from nodes.** In the range C13:G13 compute the net outflow from each node. Specifically, compute the net outflow from the source in cell C13 with the formula

=C12–C11

Then copy this formula to the range D13:G13 to compute the net outflow for the other nodes.

8 **Total flow from source to sink.** In cell J6 compute the total flow from the source to the sink, which equals the flow through the arc from the sink to the source, with the formula

=C10

(Equivalently, we could use cell H6 in this formula since the flow out of the source must equal the flow into the source.)

Using the Solver

1 **Objective.** Choose cell J6 as the objective to maximize. This maximizes the flow through the artificial arc. As previously explained, this maximizes the flow from the source to the sink.

2 **Changing cells.** Select the range C6:G10 as the changing cells and constrain these to be nonnegative.

3 **Flow balance constraints.** Add the constraints C13:G13=C15:G15. These are the conservation of flow equations.

4 **Arc capacity constraints.** Add the constraints C6:G10<=C20:G24. These are the arc capacity constraints.

5 **Linear model and optimize.** Check the Assume Linear Model box and Solve.

The optimal solution appears in Figure 4.23 and is shown graphically in Figure 4.24. (The numbers in this figure represent flows, not arc capacities. Also, we don't show the arc from the sink to the source since it doesn't represent a real flow.) We see that a maximum of three million barrels per hour can be transported from the source to the sink. The solution is fairly obvious for such a small problem. The arc capacities of the arcs leading into the sink limit the total flow to 3, and it is easy to find a feasible solution with total flow 3. But in large networks the solution is usually far from obvious. ■

FIGURE 4.24 **Optimal Flows for Sunco Example**

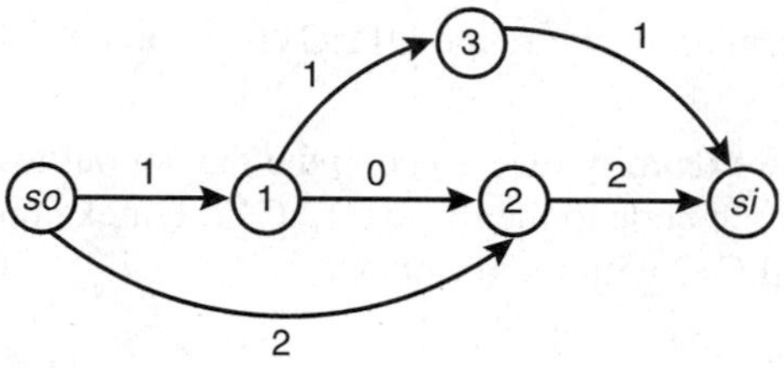

REAL-WORLD APPLICATION

Determining Manufacturing Throughput with the Maximum Flow Model

Maxwell and Wilson [15] used the maximum flow model to determine the maximum number of parts per minute that a manufacturing system could produce. See Problem 80 for an example of this type of application. ■

PROBLEMS

Skill-Building Problems

37 Fly-by-Night Airlines must determine how many connecting flights daily can be arranged between Juneau, Alaska, and Dallas, Texas. Connecting flights must stop in Seattle and then stop in Los Angeles or Denver. Because of limited landing space, Fly-by-Night is limited to making the number of daily flights between pairs of cities shown in Table 4.45. Determine how to maximize the number of connecting flights daily from Juneau to Dallas.

TABLE 4.45 **Data for Fly-by-Night Problem**

	Maximum daily flights
Juneau-Seattle	3
Seattle-L.A.	2
Seattle-Denver	3
L.A.-Dallas	1
Denver-Dallas	2

38 Flying Lion Airlines needs to ship 20 tons of freight from New York to Los Angeles by tomorrow night. The number of tons that can be shipped on each of Flying Lion's flights is listed in Table 4.46. Can 20 tons of freight make it by tomorrow?

TABLE 4.46 **Freight Capacities for Flying Lion Problem**

	Capacity (in tons)
N.Y.-Pittsburgh	10
N.Y.-Indy	11
N.Y.-Chicago	3
N.Y.-Dallas	3
Pittsburgh-Indy	2
Pittsburgh-Minneapolis	8
Indy-Chicago	10
Indy-L.A.	2
Chicago-Minneapolis	4
Chicago-L.A.	8
Minneapolis-L.A.	7
Dallas-L.A.	13

39 Excron Oil Company has a pipeline distribution network as shown in Figure 4.25. Each node corresponds to a storage tank, and the numbers represent flow capacities. Note that flow is allowed in both directions between some, but not all, of the tanks.

a Determine the maximum flow that can be sent from tank 1 to tank 8.

b If Excron doubles the capacity of all arcs leading out of tank 1 and all arcs leading into tank 8, will the maximum flow from tank 1 to tank 8 double?

FIGURE 4.25 **Pipeline Distribution for Excron Problem**

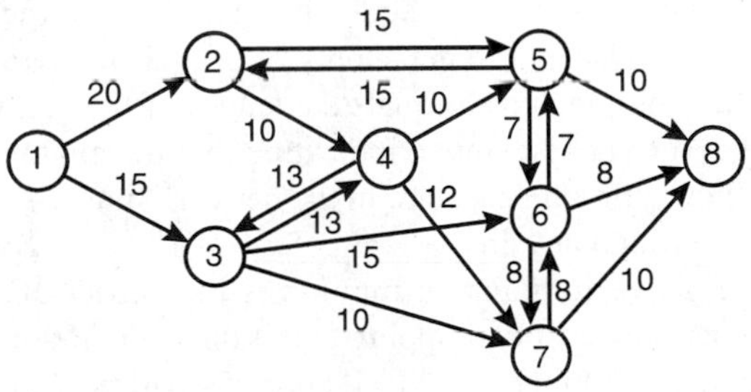

Skill-Extending Problems

40 Seven types of packages are to be delivered by five trucks. There are three packages of each type, and the capacities of the five trucks are 6, 4, 5, 4, and 3 packages, respectively. Determine whether the packages can be loaded so that no truck carries two packages of the same type.

41 Four workers are available to perform jobs 1, 2, 3, and 4. Unfortunately, three workers can do only certain jobs: worker 1, only job 1; worker 2, only jobs 1 and 2; worker 3, only job 2; worker 4, any job. Determine whether all jobs can be assigned to a suitable worker.

42 The Hatfields, Montagues, McCoys, and Capulets are going on their annual family picnic. Four cars are available to transport the families to the picnic. The cars can carry the following number of people: car 1, four; car 2, three; car 3, three; and car 4, four. There are four people in each family, and no car can carry more than two people from any one family. Determine the maximum number of people that can be transported to the picnic.

43 Suppose the number of cars per hour given in Table 4.47 can travel between any two of the cities 1, 2, 3, and 4. Determine how many cars can be sent from city 1 at noon to city 4 at 3 P.M. (*Hint*: Have portions of the network represent noon–1 P.M., 1 P.M.–2 P.M., and 2 P.M.–3 P.M.)

TABLE 4.47 **Data for Car Travel Problem**

		To			
		1	2	3	4
From	1	—	200	150	250
	2	200	—	220	230
	3	150	220	—	180
	4	250	230	180	—

44 During the next four months a construction firm must complete three projects. Project 1 must be completed within three months and requires eight months of labor. Project 2 must be completed within four months and requires 10 months of labor. Project 3 must be completed at the end of two months and requires 12 months of labor. Each month, eight workers are available. During a given month, no more than six workers can work on a single job. Determine whether all three projects can be completed on time. (*Hint*: If the maximum flow in the network is 30, all projects can be completed on time.) ■

4.8

The Shortest Path Model

In many applications it is important to find the shortest path between two points in a network. This is a special case of the MCNFM. Suppose that we want to find the shortest path between node i and node j in a network. To find this shortest path we create a MCNFM in which the net supply for node i is equal to 1 and the net supply for node j is equal to -1. All other nodes have a net supply of 0. If there is an arc joining nodes i and j in the network, the "shipping cost" equals the length of the arc. Otherwise, the shipping cost for arc (i, j) is a very large number, indicating that travel along this nonexistent arc is not allowed. The "flow" through each arc in the network must be nonnegative, but there is no limit on the flow through any arc.

Essentially, the above formulation minimizes the "cost" of shipping one unit from node i to node j, where the cost of shipping a unit through an arc equals the length of the arc. In the optimal solution to the MCNFM, all flows will be 1 or 0. Each arc with a flow of 1 will be a part of a shortest path from node i to node j.

Although shortest path problems often involve traveling through a network (such as driving from Los Angeles to New York), this is not always the case. For example, when should you trade your car in for a new car? As a car gets older, the maintenance cost per year increases and it may become worthwhile to buy a new car. If your goal is to minimize the average annual cost of owning a car (we will ignore discounting), then it is possible to set up a shortest path representation of this problem. Actually, the method we discuss can be used in any situation where equipment replacement is an issue. We note, of course, that many people trade in a car very often because they like the "feel" of a new car; we are just looking at the financial aspects of the problem. The following is an example of how the equipment replacement problem can be modeled as a shortest path problem.

EXAMPLE 4.7

Jane Driver has just purchased (at time 1) a new car for \$12,000. The cost of maintaining a car during a year depends on the age of the car at the beginning of the year, as given in Table 4.48. To avoid the high maintenance costs associated with an older car, Jane can trade in a car and purchase a new car. The prices she receives on a trade-in are also given in Table 4.48. To simplify the computations, we assume that at any time it costs Jane \$12,000 to purchase a new car. Jane's goal is to minimize the net costs (purchasing costs plus maintenance costs minus money received in trade-ins) incurred during the next five years. We will formulate this as a shortest path problem.

TABLE 4.48 Maintenance Costs and Trade-in Values

Age of Car (years)	Annual Maintenance Cost	Trade-in Price
0	\$2000	N/A
1	\$4000	\$7000
2	\$5000	\$6000
3	\$9000	\$2000
4	\$12000	\$1000
5	N/A	\$0

Solution

The network for this model has six nodes (1, 2, 3, 4, 5, and 6). (See Figure 4.26.) Node i represents the beginning of year i. For $i < j$, an arc (i, j) corresponds to the purchase of a new car at the beginning of year i and keeping it until the beginning of year j. The length of arc (i, j), labeled c_{ij}, is the total net cost incurred by owning and operating a car from

FIGURE 4.26 Network Representation of Car Replacement Problem

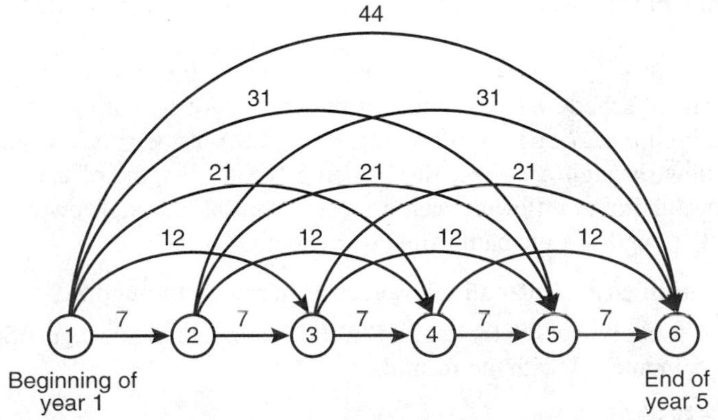

the beginning of year i to the beginning of year j if a new car is purchased at the beginning of year i and this car is traded in at the beginning of year j. Thus,

$$c_{ij} = \text{Maintenance cost during years } i,\ i+1, \ldots\ j-1$$
$$+ \text{ Cost of purchasing a car at beginning of year } i$$
$$- \text{ Trade-in value received at beginning of year } j$$

Applying this formula to the given information yields (all costs are in thousands of dollars) the following:

$$c_{12} = 2 + 12 - 7 = 7$$
$$c_{13} = 2 + 4 + 12 - 6 = 12$$
$$c_{14} = 2 + 4 + 5 + 12 - 2 = 21$$
$$c_{15} = 2 + 4 + 5 + 9 + 12 - 1 = 31$$
$$c_{16} = 2 + 4 + 5 + 9 + 12 + 12 - 0 = 44$$
$$c_{23} = 2 + 12 - 7 = 7$$
$$c_{24} = 2 + 4 + 12 - 6 = 12$$
$$c_{25} = 2 + 4 + 5 + 12 - 2 = 21$$
$$c_{26} = 2 + 4 + 5 + 9 + 12 - 1 = 31$$
$$c_{34} = 2 + 12 - 7 = 7$$
$$c_{35} = 2 + 4 + 12 - 6 = 12$$
$$c_{36} = 2 + 4 + 5 + 12 - 2 = 21$$
$$c_{45} = 2 + 12 - 7 = 7$$
$$c_{46} = 2 + 4 + 12 - 6 = 12$$
$$c_{56} = 2 + 12 - 7 = 7$$

We now see that the length of any path from node 1 to node 6 in Figure 4.26 is the net cost incurred during the next five years corresponding to a particular trade-in strategy. For example, suppose Jane trades in her car at the beginning of year 3 and next trades in her car at the end of year 5 (the beginning of year 6). This strategy corresponds to the path 1-3-6 in Figure 4.26. The length of this path ($c_{13} + c_{36}$) is the total net cost incurred during the next five years if Jane trades in her car at the beginning of year 3 and at the beginning of year 6. Thus, the length of the *shortest* path from node 1 to node 6 in Figure 4.26 is the minimum net cost that can be incurred in operating a car during the next five years.

Developing the Spreadsheet Model We now use a spreadsheet model to find the replacement schedule that minimizes the net cost of operating a car for the next five years. (See Figure 4.27 and the file REPLACE.XLS.) In the spreadsheet we must keep track of the flow through each arc, the shipping "cost" (length) of each arc, the *actual* outflow, inflow, and net outflow at each node, the *required* net outflow at each node, and the total "cost" (length) of the path from node 1 to node 6.

1 **Input costs.** Enter all relevant costs in rows 4 through 8.

2 **Costs on arcs.** In the range D13:H18 compute the costs c_{ij}. Specifically, in cell D13 compute c_{12} with the formula

=$B$4+B$7–C$8

FIGURE 4.27 Optimal Solution for Car Replacement Example

	A	B	C	D	E	F	G	H	I
1	**Car Replacement Problem Solved as a Shortest Path Problem**								
2									
3	**Data inputs**								
4	Cost of new car	$12,000							
5									
6	Age of car	0	1	2	3	4	5		
7	Annual maintenance cost	$2,000	$4,000	$5,000	$9,000	$12,000	N/A		
8	Trade-in price	N/A	$7,000	$6,000	$2,000	$1,000	$0		
9									
10	**Unit costs on arcs**								
11			**Hold till beginning of year**						
12			1	2	3	4	5	6	
13	**Buy at beginning of year**	1	$1,000,000	$7,000	$12,000	$21,000	$31,000	$44,000	
14		2	$1,000,000	$1,000,000	$7,000	$12,000	$21,000	$31,000	
15		3	$1,000,000	$1,000,000	$1,000,000	$7,000	$12,000	$21,000	
16		4	$1,000,000	$1,000,000	$1,000,000	$1,000,000	$7,000	$12,000	
17		5	$1,000,000	$1,000,000	$1,000,000	$1,000,000	$1,000,000	$7,000	
18		6	$1,000,000	$1,000,000	$1,000,000	$1,000,000	$1,000,000	$1,000,000	
19									
20	**Buying/trade-in schedule**						**Total cost**	$31,000	
21			**Hold till beginning of year**						
22			1	2	3	4	5	6	Total outflow
23	**Buy at beginning of year**	1	0	0	1	0	0	0	1
24		2	0	0	0	0	0	0	0
25		3	0	0	0	0	1	0	1
26		4	0	0	0	0	0	0	0
27		5	0	0	0	0	0	1	1
28		6	0	0	0	0	0	0	0
29		Total inflow	0	0	1	0	1	1	
30		Total outflow	1	0	1	0	1	0	
31		Net outflow	1	0	0	0	0	-1	
32			=	=	=	=	=	=	
33		Required net outflow	1	0	0	0	0	-1	

In cell E13 compute c_{13} with the formula

=D13+C$7+(C$8–D$8)

Copy the formula in E13 to the range F13:H13 to compute the other c_{1j}'s, that is, the costs of arcs out of node 1. Next, in cell E14 compute c_{23} from the fact that $c_{23} = c_{12}$ with the formula

=D13

Copy this formula in cell E14 to the ranges F14:H14, F15:H15, G16:H16, and to H17 to generate all of the other c_{ij}'s.

3 **Costs on arcs that don't exist.** Enter a large cost (such as $1,000,000) for each (i, j) combination that does not have an arc in Figure 4.26.

4 **Amounts "shipped."** Enter *any* trial values for the amounts "shipped" through the arcs in the range C23:H28.

5 **Outflows from nodes.** Compute the outflow from each node in the range I23:I28. Specifically, compute the outflow from node 1 in cell I23 with the formula

=SUM(C23:H23)

Copy this formula to the range I24:I28 to compute the outflows from the other nodes.

6 **Inflows to nodes.** Compute the inflow to each node in the range C29:H29. Specifically, compute the inflow to node 1 in cell C29 with the formula

=SUM(C23:C28)

Copy this formula to the range D29:H29 to compute the inflows for the other nodes.

7 **Transpose node outflows.** To compute the net outflow for each node, "copy" the outflow from each node to the range C30:H30. For example, put the outflow from

node 1 in cell C30 with the formula

=I23

As in previous examples, an easy way to put all of the outflows in the range C30:H30 is to highlight the range C30:H30 and enter in cell C30 the *array* formula

=TRANSPOSE(I23:I28)

(Don't forget to press Control, Shift, and then Enter instead of just Enter!)

8 **Net outflows.** In the range C31:H31 compute the actual net outflow from each node. Specifically, compute the actual net outflow from node 1 in cell C31 with the formula

=C30–C29

Then copy this formula to the range D31:H31 to compute the actual net outflow for each node.

9 **Required net outflows.** Enter the required net outflow for each node in the range C33:H33. Recall that the starting node of the path (node 1) must have a net outflow of +1 and the ending node of the path (node 6) must have a net outflow of −1. All other nodes must have a net outflow of 0.

10 **Total cost.** To compute the total "cost" of the flow through the network, enter in cell H20 the formula

=SUMPRODUCT(C13:H18,C23:H28)

Using the Solver

1 **Objective.** Choose cell H20 as the objective to minimize. This minimizes the cost of shipping one unit from node 1 to node 6.

2 **Changing cells.** Select the range C23:H28 as the changing cells and constrain these to be nonnegative.

3 **Flow balance constraints.** Add the constraints C31:H31=C33:H33. These are the conservation of flow equations.

4 **Linear Model and Optimize.** Check the Assume Linear Model box and Solve.

The optimal solution appears in Figure 4.27. By following the 1's in the range C23:H28, we see that the shortest path from node 1 to node 6 is 1-3-5-6. The corresponding network solution appears in Figure 4.28. The "length" of the shortest path from node 1 to node 6 is the sum of the relevant arc lengths: $\$31,000 = \$12,000 + \$12,000 + \$7000$. This means that the minimum cost incurred in operating a car for the next 5 years is $31,000. (You can check that 1-2-4-6 and 1-3-4-6 are also shortest paths from node 1 to node 6.) ■

FIGURE 4.28 **Network Representation of Optimal Solution for Car Replacement Example**

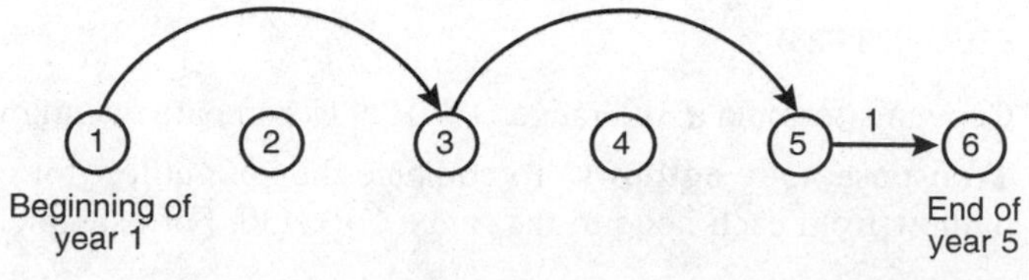

REAL-WORLD APPLICATION

Replacing Vehicles at Phillips Petroleum Company

Waddell [18] used the shortest path method to help Phillips Petroleum Company schedule replacement of individual highway tractors, cars, and trucks. The model allowed for the possibility of leasing vehicles, as well as purchasing them. Replacement of vehicles was allowed at three-month intervals. The goal was to find a vehicle replacement policy that would minimize discounted costs over a planning horizon of 20 years. The following costs were included in the model:

- maintenance and operating costs such as fuel, oil, salaries of repair personnel, and so on
- leasing cost for leased vehicles
- purchase cost for purchased vehicles
- state license fees and road taxes
- cost of purchasing vehicle
- savings due to investment tax credits and investment depreciation

When the model was applied to cars and trucks, vehicles were grouped according to their age, odometer mileage, and function. It is estimated that the equipment replacement model saves Phillips $90,000 annually when applied to tractors alone. ■

PROBLEMS

Skill-Building Problems

45 Suppose it costs $10,000 to purchase a new car. The annual operating cost and resale value of a used car is shown in Table 4.49. Assuming that you have a new car at present, determine a replacement policy that minimizes your net costs of owning and operating a car for the next six years.

TABLE 4.49 **Data for Car Resale Problem**

Age of Car (years)	Resale Value	Operating Cost
1	$7000	$300
2	$6000	$500
3	$4000	$800
4	$3000	$1200
5	$2000	$1600
6	$1000	$2200

46 It costs $40 to buy a telephone from the department store. Assume that I can keep a telephone for at most five years and that the estimated maintenance cost each year of operation is as follows: year 1, $20; year 2, $30; year 3, $40; year 4, $60; year 5, $70. I have just purchased a new telephone. Assuming that a telephone has no salvage value, determine how to minimize the total cost of purchasing and operating a telephone for the next six years.

47 At the beginning of year 1, a new machine must be purchased. The cost of maintaining a machine, depending on its age, is given in Table 4.50. The cost of purchasing a machine at the beginning of each year is given in Table 4.51. There is no trade-in value when a machine is replaced. Your goal is to minimize the total (purchase plus maintenance) cost of having a machine for five years. Determine the years in which a new machine should be purchased.

TABLE 4.50 Maintenance Costs for Machine Problem

Age at Beginning of Year	Maintenance Cost for Next Year
0	$38,000
1	$50,000
2	$97,000
3	$182,000
4	$304,000

TABLE 4.51 Purchase Costs for Machine Problem

	Purchase Cost
Year 1	$170,000
Year 2	$190,000
Year 3	$210,000
Year 4	$250,000
Year 5	$300,000

Skill-Extending Problems

48 (Based on Ravindran [17]) A library must build shelving to shelve 200 4-inch high books, 100 8-inch high books, and 80 12-inch high books. Each book is 0.5 inch thick. The library has several ways to store the books. For example, an 8-inch high shelf can be built to store all books of height less than or equal to 8 inches, and a 12-inch high shelf can be built for the 12-inch books. Alternatively, a 12-inch high shelf can be built to store all books. The library believes it costs $2300 to build a shelf and that a cost of $5 per square inch is incurred for book storage. (Assume that the area required to store a book is given by the height of the storage area times the book's thickness.) Determine how to shelve the books at minimum cost. (*Hint*: Create nodes 0, 4, 8, and 12, and make the cost associated with the arc joining nodes i and j equal to the total cost of shelving all books of height $> i$ and $\leq j$ on a single shelf.)

49 A company sells seven types of boxes, ranging in volume from 17 to 33 cubic feet. The demand and size of each box are given in Table 4.52. The variable cost (in dollars) of producing each box is equal to the volume of the box. A fixed cost of $1000 is incurred to produce any of a particular box. If the company desires, demand for a box can be satisfied by a box of a larger size. Determine how to minimize the cost of meeting the demand for boxes. ■

TABLE 4.52 Data for Box Problem

	Box						
	1	**2**	**3**	**4**	**5**	**6**	**7**
Size	33	30	26	24	19	18	17
Demand	400	300	500	700	200	400	200

4.9

Conclusion

In this chapter we have discussed a number of management science problems that can be formulated as network problems. Often these problems are of a logistics nature—shipping goods from one set of locations to another. However, we have also seen that problems that do not involve shipping or traveling along a physical network can sometimes be formulated as network problems. Examples include the dynamic inventory problem in Section 4.3 and the car replacement problem in Section 4.8.

There are two advantages to formulating a problem as a network model. First, streamlined versions of the simplex method exist for various forms of network models. These enable companies to solve extremely large problems that might not be solvable with ordinary LP solution algorithms. Second, network models' graphical representations often make it easier to visualize a problem. Once a problem can be visualized graphically, then it may be simpler to formulate (on a spreadsheet or otherwise) and ultimately solve.

REVIEW PROBLEMS

Skill-Building Problems

50 Televco produces TV picture tubes at three plants. Plant 1 can produce up to 50 tubes per week; plant 2, up to 100 tubes per week; and plant 3, up to 50 tubes per week. Tubes are shipped to three customers. The profit earned per tube depends on the site where the tube was produced and on the customer who purchases the tube, as listed in Table 4.53. Customer 1 is willing to purchase up to 80 tubes per week; customer 2, up to 90; and customer 3, up to 100. Find a shipping and production plan that will maximize Televco's profit.

TABLE 4.53 **Profits for TV Problem**

		To		
		Customer 1	**Customer 2**	**Customer 3**
	Plant 1	\$75	\$60	\$69
From	**Plant 2**	\$79	\$73	\$68
	Plant 3	\$85	\$76	\$70

51 Five workers are available to perform four jobs. The time it takes each worker to perform each job is given in Table 4.54. Determine how to assign workers to jobs so as to minimize the total time required to perform the four jobs.

TABLE 4.54 **Times for Job Assignment Problem**

	Job 1	**Job 2**	**Job 3**	**Job 4**
Worker 1	10	15	10	15
Worker 2	12	8	20	16
Worker 3	12	9	12	18
Worker 4	6	12	15	18
Worker 5	16	12	8	12

52 A company must meet the following demands for a product: January, 30 units; February, 30 units; March, 20 units. Demand can be backlogged at a cost of \$5 per unit per month. All demand must be met by the end of March. Thus, if one unit of January demand is met during March, a backlogging cost of 5(2) = \$10 is incurred. Monthly production capacity and unit production cost during each month are given in Table 4.55. A holding cost of \$20 per unit is assessed on the inventory at the end of each month. Determine how to minimize the total cost (including backlogging, holding, and production costs) of meeting demand.

TABLE 4.55 Data for Production Problem

	Production Capacity	Unit Production Cost
January	35	\$400
February	30	\$420
March	35	\$410

53 Appletree Cleaning has five maids. To complete cleaning my house, they must vacuum, clean the kitchen, clean the bathroom, and do general straightening up. The time (in minutes) it takes each maid to do each job is shown in Table 4.56. Each maid is assigned one job. Determine assignments that minimize the total number of maid-hours needed to clean my house.

TABLE 4.56 Cleaning Times for Appletree Problem

	Vacuum	Clean Kitchen	Clean Bathroom	Straighten Up
Maid 1	60	50	20	10
Maid 2	90	80	70	30
Maid 3	80	50	90	40
Maid 4	70	70	80	30
Maid 5	50	50	60	40

54 (Based on Evans [5]) Currently, State University can store 200 files on hard disk, 100 files in computer memory, and 300 files on tape. Users want to store 300 word-processing files, 100 packaged-program files, and 100 data files. Each month a typical word-processing file is accessed eight times; a typical packaged-program file, four times; and a typical data file, two times. When a file is accessed, the time it takes for the file to be retrieved depends on the type of file and on the storage medium. (See Table 4.57.) The goal is to minimize the total time per month that users spend accessing their files. Determine where files should be stored.

TABLE 4.57 Retrieval Times for Computer Problem

	Word Processing	Packaged Program	Data
Hard Disk	5	4	4
Memory	2	1	1
Tape	10	8	6

55 The Gotham City Police have just received three calls for police. At present, five cars are available. The distance (in city blocks) of each car from each call is given in Table 4.58. Gotham City wants to minimize the total distance cars must travel to respond to the three police calls. Determine which cars should respond to which call.

TABLE 4.58 Distances for Gotham City Problem

	Call 1	Call 2	Call 3
Car 1	10	11	18
Car 2	6	7	7
Car 3	7	8	5
Car 4	5	6	4
Car 5	9	4	7

56 There are three school districts in the town of Busville. The numbers of black and white students in each district are shown in Table 4.59. The Supreme Court requires the schools in Busville to be racially balanced. Thus, each school must have exactly 300 students, and each school must have the same number of black students. The distances between districts are also shown in Table 4.59. Determine how to minimize the total distance that students must be bussed while still satisfying the Supreme Court's requirements. Assume that a student who remains in his or her own district will not be bussed.

TABLE 4.59 Data for Busville Problem

	Students		Distance to	
	Whites	Blacks	District 2	District 3
District 1	210	120	3 miles	5 miles
District 2	210	30	—	4 miles
District 3	180	150	4 miles	—

57 Delko is considering hiring people for four types of jobs. The company would like to hire the number of people in Table 4.60 for each type of job. Delko can hire four types of people. Each type is qualified to perform two types of jobs, as shown in Table 4.61. A total of 20 type 1, 30 type 2, 40 type 3, and 20 type 4 people have applied for jobs. Determine how Delko can maximize the number of employees assigned to suitable jobs, assuming that each person can be assigned to at most one job. (*Hint*: Set this up as a transportation model where the "supplies" are the applicants.)

TABLE 4.60 Number of People Required for Delko Problem

	Job			
	1	2	3	4
Number of People	30	30	40	20

TABLE 4.61 Jobs Qualified for in Delko Problem

	Person Type			
	1	2	3	4
Jobs Qualified for	1,2	2,3	3,4	1,4

58 A truck must travel from New York to Los Angeles. As shown in Figure 4.29, a variety of routes are available. The number associated with each arc is the number of gallons of fuel required by the truck to traverse the arc. Determine the route from New York to Los Angeles that uses the minimum amount of gas.

59 Telephone calls from New York to Los Angeles are transported as follows. The call is sent first to either Chicago or Memphis, then routed through either Denver or Dallas, and finally sent to Los Angeles. The number of phone lines joining each pair of cities is shown in Table 4.62. Determine the maximum number of calls that can be sent from New York to Los Angeles at any given time.

60 Before a new product can be introduced at Jiffyco, the activities shown in Table 4.63 must be completed (all times are in weeks).

a Draw the project network and use LP to determine a critical path and the minimum number of weeks required before the new product can be introduced.

b The duration of each activity can be reduced by up to two weeks at the following cost per week: A, \$80; B, \$60; C, \$30; D, \$60; E, \$40; F, \$30; G, \$20. Determine how to minimize

FIGURE 4.29 Network for Truck Problem

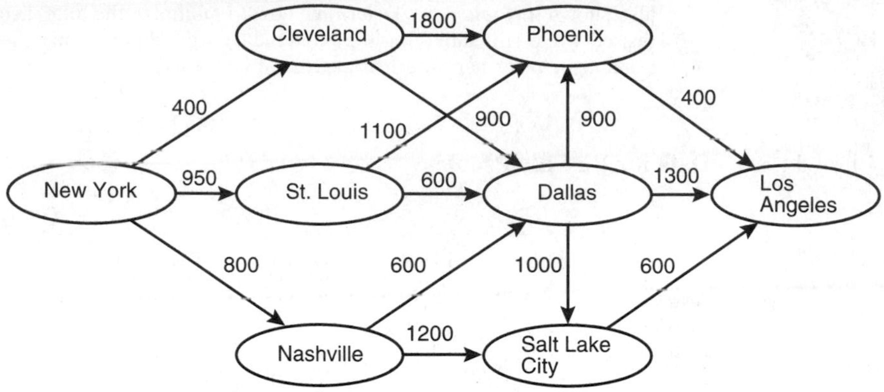

TABLE 4.62 Data for Telephone Problem

	Number of Telephone Lines
N.Y.-Chicago	500
N.Y.-Memphis	400
Chicago-Denver	300
Chicago-Dallas	250
Memphis-Denver	200
Memphis-Dallas	150
Denver-L.A.	400
Dallas-L.A.	350

TABLE 4.63 Data for Jiffyco Problem

	Description	Predecessors	Duration (weeks)
Activity A	Design product	—	6
Activity B	Survey the market	—	5
Activity C	Place orders for raw material	A	3
Activity D	Receive raw materials	C	2
Activity E	Build prototype of product	A,D	3
Activity F	Develop ad campaign	B	4
Activity G	Set up plant for mass production	E	4
Activity H	Deliver product to stores	G,F	2

the cost of getting the product into the stores by Christmas. (It is now 12 weeks until Christmas.)

61 During each of the next two months you can produce up to 50 units per month of a product at a cost of $12 per unit during month 1 and $15 per unit during month 2. The customer is willing to buy up to 60 units per month during each of the next two months. The customer will pay $20 per unit during month 1 and $16 per unit during month 2. It costs $1 per unit to hold a unit in inventory for a month. Determine how to maximize profit.

Skill-Extending Problems

62 (Based on Jacobs [11]) The Carter Caterer Company must have the following number of clean napkins available at the beginning of each of the next four days: day 1, 1500; day 2, 1200; day 3, 1800; day 4, 600. After being used, a napkin can be cleaned by one of two methods: fast service or slow service. Fast service costs 10 cents per napkin, and a napkin cleaned via fast service is available for use the day after it is last used. Slow service costs 6 cents per napkin, and these napkins can be reused two days after they are last used. New napkins can be purchased for a cost of 20 cents per napkin. Determine how to minimize the cost of meeting the demand for napkins during the next four days.

63 Braneast Airlines must staff the daily flights between New York and Chicago shown in Table 4.64. Each of Braneast's crews lives in either New York or Chicago. Each day a crew must fly one New York–Chicago and one Chicago–New York flight with at least one hour of downtime between flights. Braneast wants to schedule the crews to minimize the total downtime. Of course, some assignments are not possible. Find the flight assignments that minimize the total downtime. (*Hint*: The trick is to set this up as an assignment model. Select a changing cell for each possible pairing of a Chicago–New York flight with a New York–Chicago flight. How many crews should be based in each city? Assume that at the end of the day, each crew must be in its home city.)

TABLE 4.64 Flight Data for Braneast Problem

Flight	Leave Chicago	Arrive N.Y.	Flight	Leave N.Y.	Arrive Chicago
1	6 A.M.	10 A.M.	1	7 A.M.	9 A.M.
2	9 A.M.	1 P.M.	2	8 A.M.	10 A.M.
3	Noon	4 P.M.	3	10 A.M.	Noon
4	3 P.M.	7 P.M.	4	Noon	2 P.M.
5	5 P.M.	9 P.M.	5	2 P.M.	4 P.M.
6	7 P.M.	11 P.M.	6	4 P.M.	6 P.M.
7	8 P.M.	Midnight	7	7 P.M.	8 P.M.

64 Kellwood, a company that produces a single product, has three plants and four customers. The three plants will produce 3000, 5000, and 5000 units, respectively, during the next time period. Kellwood has made a commitment to sell 4000 units to customer 1, 3000 units to customer 2, and at least 3000 units to customer 3. Both customers 3 and 4 also want to buy as many of the remaining units as possible. The profit associated with shipping a unit from each plant to each customer is given in Table 4.65. Determine how to maximize Kellwood's profit.

TABLE 4.65 Profits for Kellwood Problem

		To			
		Customer 1	Customer 2	Customer 3	Customer 4
	Plant 1	$65	$63	$62	$64
From	Plant 2	$68	$67	$66	$62
	Plant 3	$63	$60	$59	$60

65 Sonico can produce up to 35 units per month. The demands of its primary customers must be met on time each month. If it wishes, Sonico can also sell units to secondary customers each month. A holding cost of $10 per unit is assessed against each month's ending inventory. The relevant data are shown in Table 4.66. Determine how Sonico can maximize its profit during the next three months.

TABLE 4.66 Data for Sonico Problem

	Production Cost/Unit	Primary Demand	Available for Secondary Demand	Sales Price/Unit
Month 1	$130	20	15	$160
Month 2	$120	15	20	$150
Month 3	$130	25	15	$170

66 During the next three months Shoemakers must meet (on time) the following demands for shoes: month 1, 1000 pairs; month 2, 1500 pairs; month 3, 1800 pairs. It takes one hour of labor to produce a pair of shoes. During each of the next three months, the following number of regular-time labor hours are available: month 1, 1000 hours; month 2, 1200 hours; month 3, 1200 hours. Each month the company can require workers to put in up to 400 hours of overtime. Workers are only paid for the hours they work, and a worker receives $4 per hour for regular-time work and $6 per hour for overtime work. At the end of each month, a holding cost of $1.50 per pair of shoes is incurred.

a Use a MCNFM to minimize the total cost incurred in meeting the demands of the next three months.

b How would you modify your answer if demand could be backlogged at a cost of $20 per pair per month? (*Note*: All demand must still be met by the end of month 3.)

67 Excelco produces a product at two plants: 1 and 2. The unit production cost and production capacity during each period are given in Table 4.67. The product is instantaneously shipped to the company's only customer according to the unit shipping costs given in Table 4.68. If a unit is produced and shipped during period 1, it can still be used to meet a period 2 demand, but a holding cost of $13 per unit in inventory is assessed. At the end of period 1, at most 600 units can be held in inventory. Demands are as follows: 900 in period 1, 1100 in period 2. Determine how to minimize the cost of meeting all demands on time.

TABLE 4.67 Production Costs and Capacities for Excelco Problem

	Unit Production Cost	Capacity
Plant 1 (Period 1)	$33	700
Plant 1 (Period 2)	$43	400
Plant 2 (Period 1)	$30	900
Plant 2 (Period 2)	$41	900

TABLE 4.68 Shipping Costs for Excelco Problem

	Period 1	Period 2
Plant 1 to Customer	$51	$60
Plant 2 to Customer	$42	$71

68 (Based on Mulvey [16]) State University has three professors who each teach four courses per year. Each year, four sections of marketing, finance, and production must be offered. At least one section of each class must be offered during each semester (fall and spring). Each professor's time preference and preference for teaching various courses are given in Table 4.69. The total satisfaction a professor earns teaching a class is the sum of the semester satisfaction and the course satisfaction. Thus, professor 1 derives a satisfaction of $3 + 6 = 9$ from teaching marketing during the fall semester. Use a MCNFM to assign professors to courses so as to maximize the total satisfaction of the three professors.

TABLE 4.69 Preferences for University Problem

	Professor 1	Professor 2	Professor 3
Fall Preference	3	5	4
Spring Preference	4	3	4
Marketing	6	4	5
Finance	5	6	4
Production	4	5	6

69 (Based on Brown, Geoffrion, and Bradley [3]) During the next two months Machineco must meet (on time) the demands for three types of products, shown in Table 4.70. Two machines are available to produce these products. Machine 1 can only produce products 1 and 2, and machine 2 can only produce products 2 and 3. Each machine can be used for up to 40 hours per month. Table 4.71 shows the time required to produce one unit of each product (independent of the type of machine), the cost of producing one unit of each product on each type of machine, and the cost of holding one unit of each product in inventory for one month. Determine how Machineco can minimize the total cost of meeting all demands on time.

TABLE 4.70 **Demands for Machineco Problem**

	Product 1	Product 2	Product 3
Month 1	50 units	70 units	80 units
Month 2	60 units	90 units	120 units

TABLE 4.71 **Other Data for Machineco Problem**

	Production Time (minutes)	Production Cost		Holding Cost
		Machine 1	Machine 2	
Product 1	30	$40	—	$15
Product 2	20	$45	$60	$10
Product 3	15	—	$55	$5

70 I have put four valuable paintings up for sale. Four customers are bidding for the paintings. Customer 1 is willing to buy two paintings, but each other customer is willing to purchase at most one painting. The prices that each customer is willing to pay are given in Table 4.72. Determine how to maximize the total revenue received from the sale of the paintings.

TABLE 4.72 **Bids for Painting Problem**

	Painting 1	Painting 2	Painting 3	Painting 4
Customer 1	$8000	$11,000	—	—
Customer 2	$9000	$13,000	$12,000	$7000
Customer 3	$9000	—	$11,000	—
Customer 4	—	—	$12,000	$9000

71 Powerhouse produces capacitors at three locations: Los Angeles, Chicago, and New York. Capacitors are shipped from these locations to public utilities in five regions of the country: northeast (NE), northwest (NW), midwest (MW), southeast (SE), and southwest (SW). The cost of producing and shipping a capacitor from each plant to each region of the country is given in Table 4.73. Each plant has an annual production capacity of 100,000 capacitors. Each year, each region of the country must receive the following number of capacitors: NE, 55,000; NW, 50,000; MW, 60,000; SE, 60,000; SW, 45,000. Powerhouse believes that shipping costs are too high, and it is therefore considering building one or two more production plants. Possible sites are Atlanta and Houston. The costs of producing a capacitor and shipping it to each region of the country are given in Table 4.74. It costs $3 million (in current dollars) to build a new plant, and operating each plant incurs a fixed cost (in addition to variable shipping and production costs) of $50,000 per year. A plant at Atlanta or Houston will have the capacity to produce 100,000 capacitors per year. Assume that future demand patterns and production costs will remain unchanged. If costs are discounted at a rate of 11.11% per year, how can Powerhouse minimize the present value of all costs associated with meeting current and future demands?

TABLE 4.73 Costs at Current Locations for Powerhouse Problem

		To				
		NE	NW	MW	SE	SW
From	L.A.	$27.86	$4.00	$20.54	$21.52	$13.87
	Chicago	$8.02	$20.54	$2.00	$6.74	$10.67
	N.Y.	$2.00	$27.86	$8.02	$8.41	$15.20

TABLE 4.74 Costs at New Locations for Powerhouse Problem

		To				
		NE	NW	MW	SE	SW
From	Atlanta	$8.41	$21.52	$6.74	$3.00	$7.89
	Houston	$15.20	$13.87	$10.67	$7.89	$3.00

72 (Based on Hansen and Wendell [10]) During the month of July, Pittsburgh resident Bill Fly must make four round-trip flights between Pittsburgh and Chicago. The dates of the trips are shown in Table 4.75. Bill must purchase four round-trip tickets. Without a discounted fare a round-trip ticket between Pittsburgh and Chicago costs $500. If Bill's stay in a city includes a weekend, he gets a 20% discount on the round-trip fare. If his stay in a city is at least 21 days, he receives a 35% discount, and if his stay is more than 10 days, he receives a 30% discount. However, at most one discount can be applied toward the purchase of any ticket. Determine how to minimize the total cost of purchasing the four round-trip tickets. (*Hint*: It might be beneficial to pair one half of one round-trip ticket number with half of another round-trip ticket.)

TABLE 4.75 Flights for Bill Fly Problem

Leave Pittsburgh	Leave Chicago
Monday, July 1	Friday, July 5
Tuesday, July 9	Thursday, July 11
Monday, July 15	Friday, July 19
Wednesday, July 24	Thursday, July 25

73 Three professors must be assigned to teach six sections of finance. Each professor must teach two sections of finance, and each has ranked the six time periods during which finance is taught, as shown in Table 4.76. A ranking of 10 means that the professor wants to teach at that time, and a ranking of 1 means that he or she does not want to teach at that time. Determine an assignment of professors to sections that will maximize the total satisfaction of the professors.

TABLE 4.76 Preferences for Teaching Problem

	9 A.M.	10 A.M.	11 A.M.	1 P.M.	2 P.M.	3 P.M.
Professor 1	8	7	6	5	7	6
Professor 2	9	9	8	8	4	4
Professor 3	7	6	5	6	9	5

74 (Based on Denardo, Rothblum, and Swersey [4]) Three fires have just broken out in New York. Fires 1 and 2 each require two fire engines, and fire 3 requires three fire engines. The "cost" of responding to each fire depends on the time at which the fire engines arrive. Let t_{ij} be the time in minutes when the jth engine arrives at fire i (if it is dispatched to that location). Then the cost of responding to each fire is as follows: fire 1, $6t_{11} + 4t_{12}$; fire 2, $7t_{21} + 3t_{22}$; fire 3,

$9t_{31} + 8t_{32} + 5t_{33}$. There are three fire companies that can respond to the three fires. Company 1 has three engines available, and companies 2 and 3 each have two engines available. The time (in minutes) it takes an engine to travel from each company to each fire is shown in Table 4.77.

a Determine how to minimize the cost associated with assigning the fire engines. (*Hint*: Seven demand points are necessary.)

b Would the formulation in Part (a) still be valid if the cost of fire 1 were $4t_{11} + 6t_{12}$?

TABLE 4.77 Travel Times for Fire Problem

	Fire 1	Fire 2	Fire 3
Company 1	6	7	9
Company 2	5	8	11
Company 3	6	9	10

Modeling Problems

75 Solve the Sailco example (Example 4.2) for each of the following modifications. (Solve each part independently.)

a Suppose that demand can be backlogged at a cost of \$30 per sailboat per month. (*Hint*: Now it is permissible to "ship" from, say, month 2 production to month 1 demand.)

b If demand for a sailboat is not met on time, the sale is lost and an opportunity cost of \$450 is incurred.

c Sailboats can be held in inventory for a maximum of two months.

d At a cost of \$440 per sailboat, Sailco can purchase up to ten sailboats per month from a subcontractor.

76 A company produces several products at several different plants. The products are then shipped to two warehouses for storage and are finally shipped to one of many customers. How would you use a MCNFM to help the company reduce its production and distribution costs? Pay particular attention to discussing the data you would need to implement a MCNFM.

77 You want to start a campus business to match compatible male and female students for dating. How would you use the models in this chapter to help you run your business?

78 A company sells lengths of wood varying from 1 to 12 feet in length. It might not be desirable to stock lengths of each type of wood sold. For example, demand for an 8-foot board might be met by cutting a 9-foot board. Develop a network model to determine which lengths of wood should be stocked, given a typical demand pattern for various lengths.

79 You have been assigned to ensure that each high school in the Indianapolis area is racially balanced. Explain how you would use a network model to help attain this goal.

80 A drug must go through three stages of production before production is complete. Stage 1 must be completed at machine 1. Stage 2 can be completed at either machine 2 or machine 3. Stage 3 can be completed at either machine 4 or machine 5. Each stage of the production process results in a batch size of a certain number of units being processed in a given time period. For example, machine 2 may be able to process 300 units in a two-hour time period. Show how a maximum flow model could be used to determine the maximum number of finished units of the drug that could be produced during an eight-hour period.

81 Consider a building that must be evacuated if a disaster occurs. How could you use a maximum flow model to determine the maximum number of people who could be evacuated in a 30-minute period?

82 Show how a maximum flow model with several sources and sinks could be converted into a maximum flow model with a single source and sink.

83 You own a plot large enough for a single tree. At various times you cut down the tree to obtain some wood to sell. As soon as the tree is cut down, you can plant another tree. Develop a shortest (or longest) path model that would help you determine how to maximize your revenue from selling wood during the next 100 years. Would this model still be applicable if your plot contained *many* trees? ■

CASE STUDY

Optimized Motor Carrier Selection at Westvaco

A typical paper mill might produce 1200 tons of paper per day to fill orders from 250 customers. One hundred truckload shipments per day would not be unusual for a mill served by 20 motor carriers. The carriers will generally accept shipments to any destination that they serve, subject to daily volume commitments and equipment availability. Each carrier has a different and somewhat complex rate structure. Given a pool of orders that must be shipped on a given day, the mill's problem is to assign truckloads to carriers in order to minimize its total shipping cost.

Westvaco Company Overview

Each year Westvaco sells over $2 billion worth of manufactured paper, paperboard, and specialty chemicals. Production occurs at five domestic paper mills and four chemical plants. In addition, Westvaco has many converting locations, which manufacture liquid packaging, envelopes, folding cartons, and corrugated boxes. Some of Westvaco's products include

- Fine papers, often used in printing applications (magazines and annual reports)
- Bleached paperboard, used in packaging (milk and juice cartons, freezer to oven entrees, and so forth)
- Kraft paper, used for corrugated boxes and decorative laminates (such as Formica)
- Chemicals, including activated carbon printing ink resins

Transportation Function

The *corporate transportation function* has a dual role at Westvaco. It supports the operating locations by negotiating freight rates and service commitments with rail, truck, and ocean carriers. In addition, it serves as an internal consulting group for reviewing operations in the field and making recommendations on streamlining tasks, making organizational changes to support changing customer requirements, and supporting the implementation of new technology.

Local traffic departments are responsible for day-to-day operations of mills and plants, including carrier assignments, dispatching, and switching lists for the railroads.

Production Overview

The production cycle is summarized in Figure 4.30.

Orders The majority of paper orders are for rolls, where customers request a specific grade and size of paper (diameter and width), amount (pounds, or linear or square feet), and delivery date. The orders typically range in width from 8 to 70 inches. With greater emphasis on just-in-time production by Westvaco's customers, delivery dates are sometimes specified in half-hour time windows. Orders that arrive before or after the time window are not accepted.

Scheduling Once orders are received, they are scheduled on paper machines up to 200 inches wide. The paper business is heavily capital intensive: new machines can cost over $400 million each. Machines usually run 24 hours a day and scheduling is done to minimize waste while meeting shipping date requirements. After production of a "parent" roll, the orders are cut on a rewinder into the exact order size.

Load Planning Each morning a load planner must review the previous day's production to divide large orders and consolidate less-than-truckload (LTL) orders into truckload quantities. Special attention is necessary to ensure that delivery requirements are met for orders that are consolidated. Orders typically weigh between 1000 and 150,000 pounds. A truck can generally pull a trailer with 46,000 to 48,000 pounds of paper. Depending on the construction of the trailer, this is the maximum weight limit that can be loaded while remaining under federal weight limits. Some care must also be taken to remain within axle weight limits. The goal of the load planner is to maximize the weight on a trailer while determining a route that minimizes the total number of miles traveled per day, with no truck making more than four stops (three stops plus the final destination).

Distribution This case focuses on the distribution problem shown in the bold box in Figure 4.30. After loads are planned, they are turned over to a transportation planner to assign carriers to loads. The planner has a contract for each carrier that gives the rates to each destination served (state or zip code range). The rates include a mileage charge, a stop-off charge, and a minimum charge per truckload. The transportation planner also has a list of the trailers available for each carrier. The planner will select a carrier for a given shipment based on the knowledge of the best carriers for a given traffic lane, subject to availability. Some carriers have minimum daily volume commitments that must be met.

After the carrier is selected for a given load, the planner updates the information in the mill's mainframe computer and displays this information in the shipping area. The selected carrier's trailer is spotted and brought to the loading dock and loading commences. The shipment information is then phoned or faxed to the carrier.

A Sample Distribution Problem

Table 4.78 contains a scaled-down version of a typical distribution problem faced by a transportation planner at Westvaco's paper mill in Wickliffe, Kentucky. The load planner has determined that 32 truckloads are needed to distribute last night's production. In the shipping area there are 33 drivers from 6 carriers waiting for their trucks to be loaded. One truck will not be needed today. The carrier PSST has 4 trucks in the shipping area, and Westvaco has a contractual obligation to use all 4 of these trucks today. (In practice, it would not be unusual for a transportation planner to assign 25 truckloads to 20 carriers in a single day.)

The mileage numbers in Table 4.78 represent the total number of miles for the trip from Wickliffe to the final destination, including any intermediate stops. The total charge is calculated as follows. Suppose that the Roseville, Minnesota, trip is assigned to carrier IRST. The cost to Westvaco would be $600(1.13) + 3(75) = \$903$. (If the cost calculated this way was less than IRST's minimum truckload charge of \$400, the cost to Westvaco would be \$400.) Stop-off charges only apply to intermediate stops and not the final destination. Four truckloads are needed to go to Atlanta, Georgia. These truckloads can be assigned to a single carrier, or they can be split among several carriers. If carrier MRST is assigned one of these truckloads, the cost is $612(0.87) = \$532$.

Question

For the distribution data shown in Table 4.78, what is the least cost assignment of truckloads to carriers that meets the necessary requirements? What is the cost of this distribution plan?

FIGURE 4.30 Production Cycle Overview

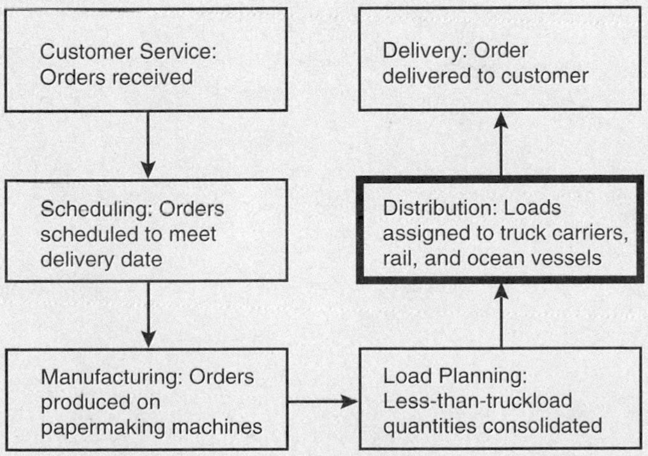

TABLE 4.78 Current Distribution Data for Westvaco Case Study

					Carrier					
Destination	**State**	**Trips**	**Stops**	**Miles**	**ABCT**	**IRST**	**LAST**	**MRST**	**NEST**	**PSST**
Atlanta	GA	4	0	612	*	0.88	1.15	0.87	0.95	1.05
Everett	MA	1	3	612	*	1.18	1.27	1.39	1.35	1.28
Ephrata	PA	3	0	190	*	3.42	1.73	1.71	1.82	2.00
Riverview	MI	5	0	383	0.79	1.01	1.25	0.96	0.95	1.11
Carson	CA	1	2	3063	*	0.80	0.87	*	1.00	*
Chamblee	GA	1	0	429	*	1.23	1.61	1.22	1.33	1.47
Roseville	MN	1	3	600	1.24	1.13	1.89	1.32	1.41	1.41
Hanover	PA	1	0	136	*	4.78	2.23	2.39	2.26	2.57
Sparks	NV	2	0	2439	*	1.45	*	1.20	*	*
Parsippany	NJ	1	1	355	*	1.62	1.36	1.39	1.03	1.76
Effingham	IL	5	0	570	0.87	0.87	1.25	0.87	0.90	1.31
Kearny	NJ	7	0	324	*	2.01	1.54	1.53	1.28	1.95
	Minimum Charge per Truckload				350	400	350	300	350	300
	Stop-off Charge				50	75	50	35	50	50
	Available Pulls				4	8	7	7	3	4
	Commitment				1	7	6	0	0	4

Note: Asterisks (*) indicate carrier does not travel to the destination; rates in dollars/mile.

Epilogue

Carrier selection at Westvaco was done manually (with pencil and paper!) by transportation planners in the past. A side-by-side test of a spreadsheet linear programming solution versus manual selection indicated daily savings in the range of 3% to 6%, and so the project was approved. With annual trucking costs of about $15 million, the total savings with the new approach have been very significant. In addition to this benefit, there have been a number of serendipitous side-effects. The optimization technique removes the guesswork from carrier selection, especially on weekends, where revolving coverage added significant variability to the carrier selection process. The technique adds accountability to the transportation planner's position and, tied to a reason code for changing the carrier, offers a clear answer to management questions regarding carrier selection. Finally, the time savings have also been significant. The carrier assignment portion of the transportation planner's job can be done much faster than before. ■

Acknowledgment: This case was co-authored with Dave Rimple, who identified and implemented this project at Westvaco.

REFERENCES

1 Aarvik, O., and P. Randolph. "The Application of Linear Programming to the Determination of Transmission Line Fees in an Electrical Power Network. *Interfaces* 6 (1975): 17–31.

2 Arntzen, B., G. Brown, T. Harrison, and L. Trafton. "Global Supply Chain Management at Digital Equipment Corporation." *Interfaces* 25, no. 1 (1995): 69–93.

3 Brown, G., A. Geoffrion, and G. Bradley. "Production and Sales Planning with Limited Shared Tooling at the Key Operation." *Management Science* 27 (1981): 247–59.

4 Denardo, E., U. Rothblum, and A. Swersey. "Transportation Problem in Which Costs Depend on Order of Arrival." *Management Science* 34 (1988): 774–84.

5 Evans, J. "The Factored Transportation Problem." *Management Science* 30 (1984): 1021–24.

6 Glassey, R., and V. Gupta. "A Linear Programming Analysis of Paper Recycling." *Studies in Mathematical Programming*. Ed. H. Salkin and J. Saha. New York: North-Holland, 1978.

7 Glover, F., and D. Klingman. "Network Applications in Industry and Government." *AIIE Transactions* 9 (1977): 363–76.

8 Glover, F., G. Jones, D. Karney, D. Klingman, and J. Mote. "An Integrated Production, Distribution, and Inventory System." *Interfaces* 9, no. 5 (1979): 21–35.

9 Glover, F., et al. "The Passenger-Mix Problem in the Scheduled Airlines." *Interfaces* 12 (1982): 873–80.

10 Hansen, P., and R. Wendell. "A Note on Airline Commuting." *Interfaces* 11, no. 12 (1982): 85–87.

11 Jacobs, W. "The Caterer Problem." *Naval Logistics Research Quarterly* 1 (1954): 154–65.

12 Klingman, D., and N. Phillips. "Topological and Computations Aspects of Preemptive Multicriteria Military Personnel Assignment Problems." *Management Science* 30, no. 11 (1984): 1362–75.

13 Klingman, D., N. Phillips, D. Steiger, and W. Young. "The Successful Deployment of Management Science throughout Citgo Petroleum Corporation." *Interfaces* 17, no. 1 (1987): 4–25.

14 Machol, R. "An Application of the Assignment Problem." *Operations Research* 18 (1970): 745–46.

15 Maxwell, W., and R. Wilson. "Dynamic Network Flow Modelling of Fixed Path Material Handling Systems." *AIIE Transactions* 13, no. 1 (1981): 12–21.

16 Mulvey, M. "Strategies in Modeling: A Personnel Example." *Interfaces* 9, no. 3 (1982): 66–75.

17 Ravindran, A. "On Compact Book Storage in Libraries." *Opsearch* 8 (1971): 245–52.

18 Waddell, R. "A Model for Equipment Replacement Decisions and Policies." *Interfaces* 13, no. 4 (1983): 1–8.

19 Winston, W. L. *Operations Research: Applications and Algorithms*. 3rd ed. Belmont, California: Duxbury Press, 1994.

5

C H A P T E R

Integer Programming Models

Management Science Success Stories

As we discussed in Chapter 3, many management sciences applications deal with workforce scheduling. These problems can be extremely complex and frequently require an integer programming approach to handle a variety of constraints. As an example, Dijkstra et al. [6] report the use of integer programming in their article "Planning the Size and Organization of KLM's Aircraft Maintenance Personnel." KLM Royal Dutch Airlines, the major Dutch carrier since 1919, owns (as of 1993) about 90 aircraft of eight different types. To guarantee safety, KLM carries out high quality aircraft maintenance, both on its own aircraft and on aircraft belonging to about 30 other carriers, according to fairly strict schedules. Maintenance standards require KLM engineers to perform routine maintenance between flights and major inspections after a certain number of flight hours. The company employs about 400 maintenance engineers, many of whom are highly skilled for their demanding jobs. Each of these highly skilled engineers is licensed to work on at most two types of aircraft (B737s and B747s, for example) and at most one particular skill (mechanical, electrical, or radio operations). For this reason the engineers operate in nearly identical teams of about 20 engineers each, so that each team has the capabilities required to service all aircraft.

The workload varies considerably across days of the week and within a given day. In order to respond to this workload in a timely manner, it is important for KLM to determine the composition of its maintenance teams and to schedule these teams optimally. KLM realized that its workforce scheduling problem was too complex for "manual" analysis and therefore employed a management science team.

The team built a decision support system (DSS) to help KLM solve its maintenance scheduling problem. The DSS includes a database module, an analysis module, and a graphical user interface. In simple terms, the database module gathers all of the necessary data about flight timetables, required maintenance, required skill levels, and other necessary information. It then feeds these data into the analysis module, which uses integer programming to either (1) minimize the size of the maintenance teams subject to meeting a specified service level or (2) maximize the service level subject to the composition of existing teams. Because both of these problems result in large and difficult integer programming models, good approximations have been developed to yield near-optimal results. The graphical user interface then allows the users to see the results of the analysis and ask a number of what-if questions.

The managers at KLM have been quite satisfied with the DSS. They consider it a valuable tool for analyzing both strategic and tactical problems, and they have advocated expanding its use into other departments of KLM such as the helicopter department. ■

5.1 Introduction

In this chapter we see how many complex problems can be modeled using 0-1 variables and other variables that are forced to assume integer values. A **0-1 variable** is simply a variable that must equal 0 or 1. Usually a 0-1 variable corresponds to an activity that is or is not undertaken. If the 0-1 variable corresponding to the activity equals 0, then the activity is not undertaken; if it equals 1, the activity is undertaken. A 0-1 variable is often called a **binary variable**.

Optimization models in which some or all of the variables must be integers are known as **integer programming** (IP) models. We first saw an integer programming model in our discussion of scheduling postal workers in Example 3.1 of Chapter 3. In this chapter we illustrate many of the "tricks of the trade" that are needed to formulate IP models of complex situations. You should be aware that a spreadsheet Solver typically has a much harder time solving an IP problem than an LP problem! In fact, in some cases a spreadsheet Solver is unable to solve an IP problem, even if the IP problem has an optimal solution. The reason is simply that these problems are inherently difficult to solve, no matter what software package is used. However, as we will see in this chapter, our ability to model complex problems increases tremendously when we are able to use integer programming.

5.2 Capital Budgeting Models

We introduce our study of IP models with the following capital budgeting example. This example illustrates perfectly the "go–no go" nature of many IP models.

EXAMPLE 5.1

Stockco is considering four investments. The cash required for each investment as well as the NPV the investment adds to the firm are given in Table 5.1. The cash available for investment is $14,000. Stockco wants to find the investment policy that maximizes its

TABLE 5.1 **Data for Stockco Capital Budgeting Example**

	Cash Required	NPV Added
Investment 1	$5,000	$16,000
Investment 2	$7,000	$22,000
Investment 3	$4,000	$12,000
Investment 4	$3,000	$8,000

NPV. The crucial assumption here is that if Stockco wishes to take part in any of these investments, it must go "all the way." It can't, for example, go halfway in investment 1, investing \$2500 and realizing an NPV of \$8000. (If partial investments were allowed, we wouldn't need IP; we could use LP.)

Solution

The solution of this problem is quite straightforward. Stockco must keep track of

- the investments chosen
- the total cash required for the chosen investments
- the total NPV from the chosen investments

Developing the Spreadsheet Model To keep track of which investments are chosen, we use a 0-1 variable for each investment. If a particular investment is undertaken, the 0-1 variable for this investment will equal 1; if it is not undertaken, the 0-1 variable will equal 0. To form the spreadsheet model, proceed as follows. (See Figure 5.1 and the file STOCKCO.XLS.)

1 **Inputs.** Enter the NPV for each investment in the range B7:E7, the cost required by each investment in the range B9:E9, and the amount of available cash in cell H9.

2 **0-1 values for investments.** Enter *any* trial 0-1 values for the investments in cells B5:E5.[1]

3 **NPV contributions.** In cell B11 compute the NPV contributed by the investments with the formula

=SUMPRODUCT(B5:E5,B7:E7)

Observe that this formula "picks up" the NPV *only* for those investments whose 0-1 variables equal 1.

4 **Cash invested.** In cell F9 compute the cash invested with the formula

=SUMPRODUCT(B5:E5,B9:E9)

Again, this picks up only the costs of the investments whose 0-1 variables equal 1.

FIGURE 5.1 **Optimal Solution for Stockco Capital Budgeting Example**

	A	B	C	D	E	F	G	H
1	**Stockco Capital Budgeting Problem**							
2								
3			Investment					
4		1	2	3	4			
5	Investment level	0	1	1	1			
6								
7	NPV	\$16,000	\$22,000	\$12,000	\$8,000			
8						Total cost		Budget
9	Investment cost	\$5,000	\$7,000	\$4,000	\$3,000	\$14,000	<=	\$14,000
10								
11	Total NPV	\$42,000						

[1]Even fractional values such as 0.5 can be entered in these cells. The Solver constraints will eventually force them to be 0 or 1.

Using the Solver

1 **Objective.** Choose cell B11 as the objective to maximize.

2 **Changing cells.** Choose the range B5:E5 as the changing cells. These cells correspond to the 0-1 variables that indicate whether an investment is chosen or not.

3 **0-1 constraints.** Constrain the changing cells to be 0 or 1. To do this in current versions of Excel, you proceed as follows. First, constrain the changing cells to be nonnegative as usual. Next, constrain them to be less than or equal to 1. Finally, constrain them to be "integer." (Notice in the Solver dialog box that when you add a constraint, "int" is a fourth option, after "<=," ">=," and "=.") Thus, you actually need three sets of constraints to constrain the changing cells to 0 or 1. If a variable is nonnegative, less than or equal to 1, and an integer, it must be 0 or 1![2]

4 **Investment constraint.** Add the constraint F9<=H9. This ensures that we do not invest more than the available cash.

5 **Linear model and optimize.** Check the Assume Linear Model box and Solve.

The completed Solver window should appear as shown in Figure 5.2. The optimal solution is shown in Figure 5.1. This indicates that a maximum NPV of $42,000 can be obtained by selecting investments 2, 3, and 4.

FIGURE 5.2 **Solver Window for Stockco Capital Budgeting Example**

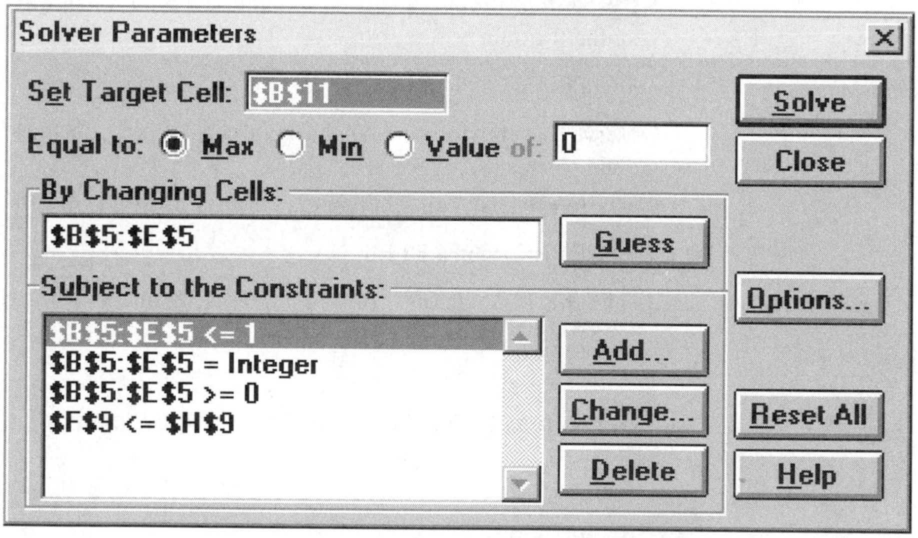

If we rank Stockco's investments on the basis of NPV per dollar invested, then investment 1 yields $3.20 per dollar invested, investment 2 yields $3.14, investment 3 yields $3.00, and investment 4 yields $2.67. Therefore, investment 1 can be thought of as the "best" investment, but our optimal solution does not use investment 1 at all! To understand why this is the case, observe that any investment combination that uses investment 1 cannot use more than $12,000. This means that choosing investment 1 forces Stockco to forego investing $2000 of its total $14,000. On the other hand, the *optimal* investment

[2] If you're using What's Best! with Lotus, the specification of 0-1 variables is easier. From the WB! menu, choose the command Integer and then the command Binary. Now select the range B5..E5. This tells What's Best! to force the values in cells B5..E5 to equal 0 or 1.

combination allows Stockco to invest $14,000. This enables Stockco to achieve a higher NPV than it could with any combination that includes investment 1. ■

MODELING ISSUES

1 The following modifications of the Stockco example can be handled easily:

- Suppose that at most two projects can be selected. In this case we add a constraint that the sum of the 0-1 variables for the four investments is less than or equal to 2, that is, SUM(B5:E5)<=2. This constraint will be satisfied if 0, 1, or 2 investments are chosen, and it will be violated if 3 or 4 investments are chosen.
- Suppose that if investment 2 is selected, then investment 1 must also be selected. In this case we add a constraint saying that the 0-1 variable for investment 2 is less than or equal to the 0-1 variable for investment 1, that is, B5>=C5. This constraint rules out the one possibility that is not allowed, namely, where investment 2 is selected but investment 1 is not.
- Suppose that either investment 1 or investment 3 (or both) *must* be selected. In this case we add a constraint that the sum of the 0-1 variables for investments 1 and 3 must be greater than or equal to 1, that is, B5+D5>=1. This rules out the possibility that both of these 0-1 variables is 0, that is, neither investment is selected.

2 If Stockco could choose a fractional amount of an investment, then we could maximize its NPV by deleting the integer constraint. The optimal solution to the resulting LP model would have a total NPV of $44,000. All of investments 1 and 2 and half of investment 3 would be chosen. Notice that there is no way to round off the solution to the LP that yields the optimal IP solution! Often solving an IP *without* the integer constraints yields a solution that bears no resemblance to the optimal IP solution.

3 Any IP involving 0-1 variables with only one constraint is called a **knapsack problem**. Think of the problem faced by a hiker going on an overnight hike. For example, imagine that the hiker's knapsack can hold only 14 pounds, and he must choose which of four available items to take on the hike. The benefit derived from each item is analogous to the NPV of each project and the "weight" of each item is analogous to the cash required by each investment. The single constraint is analogous to the budget constraint, that is, only 14 pounds can fit in the knapsack. In a knapsack problem the goal is to get the most value in the knapsack without overloading it.

4 It can be proved (see Morton [13]) that if the "weight" of the knapsack is sufficiently large, then the best item (in terms of NPV per dollar invested) *will* be used in the optimal solution. ■

REAL-WORLD APPLICATIONS

Integer Programming at Monsanto

Monsanto (see Boykin [3]) used an IP model to determine the settings of its chemical reactors that minimized the annual cost of meeting customer demands. The model is credited with saving Monsanto between $1 and $3 million annually. The model contained a 0-1 variable for each possible setting of each reactor. See Problem 55 (in the Review Problems section) for a scaled-down version of the Monsanto IP model. ■

Integer Programming in the Steel Industry

Fagersta AB, a Swedish steel company, used an integer programming model (see Westerberg, Bjorklund and Hultman [21]) to determine how to combine steel ingots, scrap steel, and alloys to produce different kinds of steel. The model contained a 0-1 variable for each ingot that was available for purchase. The model is credited with reducing Fagersta AB's production costs by 6%. See Problem 54 (in the Review Problems section) for an example of the use of IP in the steel industry. ■

The Solver Tolerance Option

If you click on Options in the Excel Solver dialog box, you will see Tolerance option. Excel's default tolerance is .05. To explain the Tolerance option, we must first define the **LP relaxation** of an IP problem, which is the same model as the IP model, except that all integer constraints are ignored. In particular, cells that are originally constrained to be 0 or 1 are allowed, under the LP relaxation, to have any fractional values between 0 and 1. For the Stockco example, it is easy to show that the optimal solution to the LP relaxation has an optimal objective value of $44,000, using changing cell values 1, 1, 0.5, and 0.[3,4]

The implication is that if you set the tolerance to 0, the Solver will (in theory) run until it finds the *optimal* integer solution. So why don't we always use a tolerance setting of 0? The problem is that for many IP models, it might take the Solver days (or even years!) to find the optimal solution. On the other hand, finding a solution that is *close* to the optimal solution might not be so difficult. Thus, if the Solver fails to find an optimal solution to an IP problem, you might be able to find a *near optimal* solution by increasing the tolerance setting.

PROBLEMS

Skill-Building Problems

1 Suppose that in the Stockco example each investment requires $2000 during year 2 and only $5000 is available for investment during year 2.

a Assuming that available money uninvested at the end of year 1 cannot be used during year 2, what combination of investments maximizes NPV?

b Suppose that any uninvested money at the end of year 1 is available for investment in year 2. How does your answer to Part (a) change?

2 Coach Night is trying to choose the starting lineup for the basketball team. The team consists of seven players who have been rated on a scale of 1 (poor) to 3 (excellent) according to their ball-handling, shooting, rebounding, and defensive abilities. The positions that each player is allowed to play and the players' abilities are listed in Table 5.2. The five-player starting lineup must satisfy the following restrictions:

- At least four members must be able to play guard, at least two members must be able to play forward, and at least one member must be able to play center.
- The average ball-handling, shooting, and rebounding level of the starting lineup must each be at least 1.8.
- Either player 2 or player 3 must start.

Given these constraints, Coach Night wants to maximize the total defensive ability of the starting team. Determine his starting team.

3 To graduate from Basketweavers University with a major in operations research (OR), a student must complete at least two math courses, at least two OR courses, and at least two computer courses. Some courses can be used to fulfill more than one requirement: Calculus can fulfill the math requirement; Operations Research can fulfill the math and OR requirements; Data Structures can fulfill the computer and math requirements; Business Statistics can fulfill the math and OR requirements; Computer Simulation can fulfill the OR and computer requirements; Introduction to Computer Programming can fulfill the computer requirement; and Forecasting

[3]This optimal objective value serves as an initial "best bound" on the optimal integer solution: Satisfying the integer constraints, in addition to the other constraints in the LP problem, can only yield an objective value which is the same or worse.

[4]A tolerance setting of 0.5 means that the Solver will stop as soon as it finds a feasible (integer) solution to the IP model that is within 5% of the "best bound." Initially, the optimal objective value of the LP relaxation serves as the best bound. As the Solver proceeds to find trial solutions satisfying the integer constraints, it eliminates various alternative solutions and updates the best bound to be the best objective value of the remaining possibilities. Thus, when the Solver stops, it is guaranteed to have an integer solution that is within at least 5% of the "true" integer optimal solution.

TABLE 5.2 **Data for Basketball Problem**

	Position	Ball-Handling	Shooting	Rebounding	Defense
Player 1	G	3	3	1	3
Player 2	C	2	1	3	2
Player 3	G/F	2	3	2	2
Player 4	F/C	1	3	3	1
Player 5	G/F	1	3	1	2
Player 6	F/C	3	1	2	3
Player 7	G/F	3	2	2	1

can fulfill the OR and math requirements. Some courses are prerequisites for others: Calculus is a prerequisite for Business Statistics, Introduction to Computer Programming is a prerequisite for Computer Simulation and for Data Structures; and Business Statistics is a prerequisite for Forecasting. Determine how to minimize the number of courses needed to satisfy the major requirements. (*Hint*: Since Calculus is a prerequisite for Business Statistics, for example, you will need a constraint that ensures that the changing cell for Calculus is greater than or equal to the changing cell for Business Statistics.)

4 (Based on Bean, Noon, and Salton [2]) Boris Milkem's firm owns six assets. The expected sales price (in millions of dollars) for each asset is given in Table 5.3. For example, if asset 1 is sold in year 2, the firm receives $20 million. To maintain a regular cash flow, Milkem must sell at least $20 million of assets during year 1, at least $30 million worth during year 2, and at least $35 million worth during year 3. Determine how Milkem can maximize his total revenue from assets sold during the next three years. In implementing this model, how might the idea of a rolling planning horizon be used?

TABLE 5.3 **Sale Prices for Milkem Problem**

	Sold in		
	Year 1	**Year 2**	**Year 3**
Asset 1	15	20	24
Asset 2	16	18	21
Asset 3	22	30	36
Asset 4	10	20	30
Asset 5	17	19	22
Asset 6	19	25	29

5 The Cubs are trying to determine which of the following free agent pitchers should be signed: Rick Sutcliffe (RS), Bruce Sutter (BS), Dennis Eckersley (DE), Steve Trout (ST), or Tim Stoddard (TS). The cost of signing each pitcher and the predicted number of victories each pitcher will add to the Cubs are shown in Table 5.4. Subject to the following restrictions, the Cubs want to sign the pitchers who will add the most victories to the team.

- At most $12 million can be spent.
- At most two right-handed pitchers can be signed.
- The Cubs cannot sign both BS and RS.

Determine who the Cubs should sign.

TABLE 5.4 **Data for Baseball Problem**

Pitcher	Cost of Signing Pitcher (millions)	Victories Added to Cubs
RS (righty)	$6	6
BS (righty)	$4	5
DE (righty)	$3	3
ST (lefty)	$2	3
TS (righty)	$2	2

6 NASA must determine how many of three types of objects to bring on board the space shuttle. The weight and benefit of each of the items are given in Table 5.5. If the space shuttle can carry up to 26 pounds of items 1 through 3, which items should be taken on the space shuttle?

TABLE 5.5 **Data for NASA Problem**

	Benefit	Weight (pounds)
Item 1	10	3
Item 2	15	4
Item 3	17	5

7 I am moving from New Jersey to Indiana and have rented a truck that can haul up to 1100 cubic feet of furniture. The volume and value of each item I am considering moving on the truck are given in Table 5.6. Which items should I bring to Indiana?

TABLE 5.6 **Data for Moving Problem**

	Value	Volume (cubic feet)
Bedroom set	\$60	800
Dining room set	\$48	600
Stereo	\$14	300
Sofa	\$31	400
TV set	\$10	200

8 Four projects are available for investment. The projects require the cash flows and yield the net present values (in millions) shown in Table 5.7. If \$6 million is available for investment at time 0, find the investment plan that maximizes NPV.

TABLE 5.7 **Data for Project Selection Problem**

	Cash Outflow at Time 0	NPV
Project 1	\$3	\$5
Project 2	\$5	\$8
Project 3	\$2	\$3
Project 4	\$4	\$7

9 Consider the following puzzle. You are to select four three-letter "words" from the following list:

DBA DEG ADI FFD GHI BCD FDF BAI

For each word you earn a score equal to the position of the word's third letter in the alphabet. For example, DBA earns a score of 1, DEG earns a score of 7, and so on. Your goal is to choose the four words that maximize your total score, subject to the following constraint. The sum of the positions in the alphabet for the first letters of the four words chosen must be at least as large as the sum of the positions in the alphabet for the second letters of the words chosen. Use a spreadsheet Solver to solve this problem.

10 You are given a group of possible investment projects for your company's capital. For each project you are given the NPV the project would add to the firm, as well as the cash outflow required by each project during each year. Given the information in Table 5.8, determine the investments that maximize the firm's NPV. The firm has 30 million dollars available during each of the next five years. All numbers are in millions of dollars.

TABLE 5.8 Data for Capital Budgeting Problem

	NPV	Year 1	Year 2	Year 3	Year 4	Year 5
Project 1	20	1	3	4	1	1
Project 2	25	3	4	2	1	2
Project 3	30	4	4	3	2	1
Project 4	35	6	5	3	2	3
Project 5	40	5	1	2	3	8
Project 6	42	4	5	2	5	5
Project 7	31	2	3	1	4	6
Project 8	33	0	0	3	6	7
Project 9	35	1	1	4	8	3
Project 10	37	3	2	4	1	6
Project 11	38	9	2	4	1	1
Project 12	39	8	7	1	1	1

Skill-Extending Problems

11 Thailand inducts naval draftees at three drafting centers. Then the draftees must be sent to one of three naval bases for training. The cost of transporting a draftee from a drafting center to a base is given in Table 5.9. Each year 1000 men are inducted at center 1; 600 at center 2; and 700 at center 3. Base 1 can train 1000 men a year; base 2, 800 men; and base 3, 700 men. After the inductees are trained, they are sent to Thailand's main naval base. They may be transported on either a small ship or a large ship. Seven small and five large ships are available. It costs \$5000 plus \$2 per mile to use a small ship. A small ship can transport up to 200 men to the main base and can visit up to two bases on its way to the main base. It costs \$10,000 plus \$3 per mile to use a large ship. A large ship can visit up to three bases on its way to the main base and can transport up to 500 men. The possible "tours" for each type of ship are given in Table 5.10. (In this table, B stands for the main base.) Assume that draftees are assigned to training bases using the transportation method. Now determine how to minimize the total cost incurred in sending the men from the training bases to the main base.

TABLE 5.9 Transport Costs for Draftee Problem

		To		
		Base 1	**Base 2**	**Base 3**
	Center 1	\$200	\$200	\$300
From	**Center 2**	\$300	\$400	\$220
	Center 3	\$300	\$400	\$250

TABLE 5.10 Travel Data for Draftee Problem

	Locations Visited	Miles Traveled
Tour 1	B-1-B	370
Tour 2	B-1-2-B	515
Tour 3	B-2-3-B	665
Tour 4	B-2-B	460
Tour 5	B-3-B	600
Tour 6	B-1-3-B	640
Tour 7	B-1-2-3-B	720

12 You have been assigned to arrange the songs on the cassette version of Madonna's latest album. A cassette tape has two sides (1 and 2). The songs on each side of the cassette must total between 14 and 16 minutes in length. The length and type of each song are given in Table 5.11. The assignment of songs to the tape must satisfy the following conditions:

- Each side must have exactly two ballads.

TABLE 5.11 Data for Madonna Problem

	Type	Length (minutes)
Song 1	Ballad	4
Song 2	Hit	5
Song 3	Ballad	3
Song 4	Hit	2
Song 5	Ballad	4
Song 6	Hit	3
Song 7	Filler	5
Song 8	Ballad and Hit	4

- Side 1 must have at least three hit songs.
- Either song 5 or song 6 must be on side 1.

Determine whether there is an arrangement of songs satisfying these restrictions. (*Hint*: You need not have an objective function when using a spreadsheet Solver. In the Solver dialog box, just leave the Target Cell box empty.)

13 Cousin Bruzie of radio station WABC schedules radio commercials in 60-second blocks. This hour, the station has sold commercial time for commercials of 15, 16, 20, 25, 30, 35, 40, and 50 seconds. Determine the minimum number of 60-second blocks of commercials that must be scheduled to fit in all the current hour's commercials. (*Hint*: Certainly no more than eight blocks of time are needed.)

14 (Based on Brown et al. [4]) A Sunco oil delivery truck contains five compartments, holding up to 2700, 2800, 1100, 1800, and 3400 gallons of fuel, respectively. The company must deliver three types of fuel (super, regular, and unleaded) to a customer. The demands, penalty per gallon short, and the maximum allowed shortage are given in Table 5.12. Each compartment of the truck can carry only one type of gasoline. Determine how to load the truck in a way that minimizes shortage costs.

TABLE 5.12 Data for Sunco Problem

Type of Gasoline	Demand	Cost per Gallon Short	Maximum Shortage Allowed
Super	2900	$10	500
Regular	4000	$8	500
Unleaded	4900	$6	500

15 (Based on Bean et al. [1]) Simon's Mall has 10,000 square feet of space to rent and wants to determine the types of stores that should occupy the mall. The minimum number and maximum number of each type of store (along with the square footage of each type) are given in Table 5.13. The annual profit made by each type of store depends on how many stores of that type are in the mall. This dependence is given in Table 5.14 (where all profits are in units of $10,000). Thus, if there are two department stores in the mall, each department store will earn $210,000 profit per year. Each store pays 5% of its annual profit as rent to Simon's. Determine how Simon can maximize its rental income from the mall.

TABLE 5.13 Store Data for Simon Mall Problem

Store Type	Square Footage	Minimum	Maximum
Jewelry	500	1	3
Shoe	600	1	3
Department	1500	1	3
Book	700	0	3
Clothing	900	1	3

TABLE 5.14 Profits for Simon Mall Problem

Type of Store	Number of This Type in Mall 1	2	3
Jewelry	9	8	7
Shoe	10	9	5
Department	27	21	20
Book	16	9	7
Clothing	17	13	10

16 WSP Publishing sells textbooks to college students. WSP has two sales reps available to assign to the A–G state area. The number of college students (in thousands) in each state is given in Figure 5.3. Each sales rep must be assigned to two adjacent states. For example, a sales rep could be assigned to A and B, but not A and D. WSP's goal is to maximize the number of total students in the states assigned to the sales reps. Determine where the sales reps should be assigned.

FIGURE 5.3 Map for WSP Problem

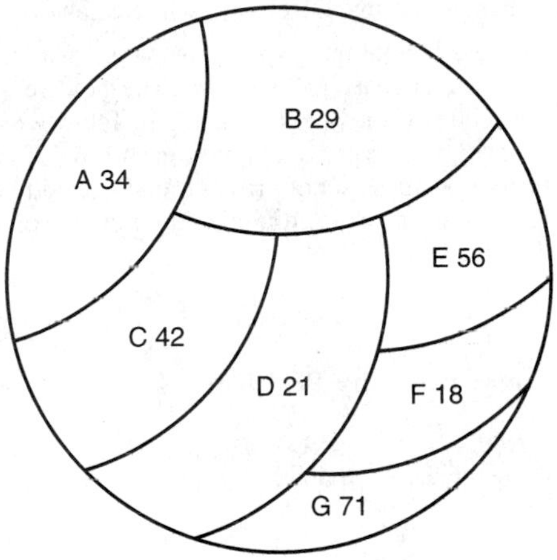

17 A power plant has three boilers. If a given boiler is operated, it can be used to produce a quantity of steam (in tons) between the minimum and maximum given in Table 5.15. The cost of producing a ton of steam on each boiler is also given. Steam from the boilers is used to produce power on three turbines. If operated, each turbine can process an amount of steam (in tons) between the minimum and maximum given in Table 5.16. The cost of processing a ton of steam and the power produced by each turbine is also given. Determine how to minimize the cost of producing 8000 kwh of power.

TABLE 5.15 Boiler Data for Power Plant Problem

	Minimum Steam	Maximum Steam	Cost/Ton
Boiler Number 1	500	1000	$10
Boiler Number 2	300	900	$8
Boiler Number 3	400	800	$6

18 (Based on Salkin and Lin [16]) An Ohio company, Clevcinn, consists of three subsidiaries. Each has the respective average payroll, unemployment reserve fund, and estimated payroll given in Table 5.17. (All figures are in millions of dollars.) Any employer in the state of Ohio

TABLE 5.16 **Turbine Data for Power Plant Problem**

	Minimum Steam	Maximum Steam	Kwh per Ton of Steam	Processing Cost
Turbine 1	300	600	4	$2
Turbine 2	500	800	5	$3
Turbine 3	600	900	6	$4

TABLE 5.17 **Data for Clevcinn Problem**

	Average Payroll	Reserve	Estimated Payroll
Subsidary 1	300	400	350
Subsidary 2	600	510	400
Subsidary 3	800	600	500

whose reserve to average payroll ratio is less than 1 must pay 20% of its estimated payroll in unemployment insurance premiums. Otherwise, if the ratio is at least 1, the employer pays 10%. Clevcinn can aggregate its subsidiaries and label them as separate employers. For example, if subsidiaries 2 and 3 are aggregated, they must pay 20% of their combined payroll in unemployment insurance premiums. Determine which subsidiaries should be aggregated.

19 Indiana University's Business School has two rooms that seat 50 students, one room that seats 100 students, and one room that seats 150 students. Classes are held five hours a day. At present, the four types of requests for rooms are listed in Table 5.18. The business school must decide how many requests of each type to assign to each type of room. Suppose that classes that cannot be assigned to a business school room are assigned to another campus building. Determine how to assign classes so as to minimize the number of hours students spend each week outside the business building. ■

TABLE 5.18 **Room Requests for Indiana University Problem**

	Size Room Requested	Hours Requested	Number of Requests
Type 1	50 seats	2, 3, 4	3
Type 2	150 seats	1, 2, 3	1
Type 3	100 seats	5	1
Type 4	50 seats	1, 2	2

5.3 The Fixed-Charge Model

In many situations a fixed cost is incurred if an activity is undertaken at *any* positive level. This cost is independent of the level of the activity and is known as a **fixed charge**. Here are three examples of fixed charges:

1. Construction of a warehouse incurs a fixed cost that is the same whether the warehouse is used at a low or a high level.
2. A cash withdrawal from a bank incurs a fixed cost, independent of the size of the withdrawal, due to the time spent at the bank.
3. A machine that is used to produce several products must be set up for the production of each product. No matter how many units the company produces of a product, it incurs the same fixed cost (lost production due to the setup time) for producing the product.

In these examples a fixed cost is incurred if an activity is undertaken at any positive level, whereas zero fixed cost is incurred if the activity is not undertaken at all. Although it might not be obvious, this feature makes the problem inherently *non*linear, which means that a straightforward application of LP is not possible. However, we will illustrate how a clever use of 0-1 variables can result in a *linear* model. In the next three sections we consider three interesting examples of the fixed charge model.

EXAMPLE 5.2

Gandy Cloth Company is capable of manufacturing three types of clothing: shirts, shorts, and pants. The manufacture of each type of clothing requires that Gandy have the appropriate type of machinery available. The machinery needed to manufacture each type of clothing must be rented at the following rates: shirt machinery, $200 per week; shorts machinery, $150 per week; pants machinery, $100 per week. The manufacture of each type of clothing requires the amounts of cloth and labor given in Table 5.19. This table also shows the variable unit cost and selling price for each type of clothing. There are 150 hours and 160 square yards of cloth available. Gandy wants to find a solution that maximizes its weekly profit.

TABLE 5.19 **Data for Gandy Example**

	Labor Hours	Cloth (sq. yds.)	Sales Price	Variable Cost
Shirts	3	4	$12	$6
Shorts	2	3	$8	$4
Pants	6	4	$15	$8

Solution

We first note that the cost, $f(x)$, of producing x shirts during a week is 0 if $x = 0$, but it is $200 + 6x$ if $x > 0$. This cost structure violates the proportionality assumption (discussed in Chapter 2), which is needed for a linear model. If proportionality were satisfied, then the cost of making, say, 10 shirts would be double the cost of making 5 shirts. However, because of the fixed cost, the total cost of making 5 shirts is 230, and the cost of making 10 shirts is only 260. Therefore, the proportionality assumption is violated.

To model the Gandy problem, we need to keep track of the following:

- the number of shirts, shorts, and pants produced
- a 0-1 variable for each type of clothing indicating whether any of that type of clothing is produced
- the total profit, which equals revenue from sales minus the cost of renting machines minus the variable cost of producing clothing
- the resource usage of labor and cloth

We must also ensure that if any shirts are produced, for example, then the 0-1 variable for shirts equals 1. (Similar statements apply to shorts and pants.)

Developing the Spreadsheet Model The spreadsheet model can now be formulated as follows. (See Figure 5.4 and the file GANDY.XLS.)

1 **Inputs.** Enter the given inputs in the ranges B6:D7, B10:D12, and D23:D24.

FIGURE 5.4 Spreadsheet for Gandy Clothing Example

	A	B	C	D
1	**Gandy Fixed Charge Clothing Problem**			
2				
3	**Input data**			
4			**Product**	
5		Shirts	Shorts	Pants
6	Labor hours/unit	3	2	6
7	Cloth (sq. yd.)/unit	4	3	4
8	Maximum production	40	53.33	25
9				
10	Selling price/unit	$12	$8	$15
11	Variable cost/unit	$6	$4	$8
12	Fixed charge for equipment	$200	$150	$100
13				
14	**Production plan**			
15		Shirts	Shorts	Pants
16	Produce any? (1 if yes, 0 if no)	0	0	1
17				
18	Units produced	0	0	25
19		<=	<=	<=
20	Logical upper bound	0	0	25
21				
22	**Constraints on resources**	Used		Available
23	Labor hours	150	<=	150
24	Cloth	100	<=	160
25				
26	**Summary of costs**			
27	Revenue	$375		
28	Variable cost	$200		
29	Fixed charge for equipment	$100		
30				
31	**Profit**	$75		

2 **0-1 values for shirts, shorts, and pants.** Enter *any* trial values for the 0-1 variables for shirts, shorts, and pants in the range B16:D16. For example, if you enter a 1 in cell C16, you are implying that some shorts are produced.

3 **Shirts, shorts, and pants produced.** Enter *any* trial values for the number of shirts, shorts, and pants that are produced in the range B18:D18.

4 **Total revenue.** In cell B27 compute total sales revenue with the formula

=SUMPRODUCT($B$18:$D$18,B10:D10)

5 **Total variable cost.** In cell B28 compute total variable cost by copying the formula for revenue in cell B27 to cell B28.

6 **Total fixed cost.** In cell B29 compute total fixed cost with the formula

=SUMPRODUCT(B16:D16,B12:D12)

Note that this formula picks up the fixed costs only for those products with 0-1 variables equal to 1.

7 **Total profit.** In cell B31 compute total profit with the formula

=B27–SUM(B28:B29)

8 **Labor and cloth used.** Calculate the total amount of labor hours used by entering the formula

=SUMPRODUCT($B$18:$D$18,B6:D6)

in cell B23. Then copy this to cell B24 to calculate the amount of cloth used.

9 **Upper limits on production quantities.** Now we come to the tricky part of the formulation. We need to ensure that the following constraints hold:

- If any shirts are produced, the 0-1 shirts variable equals 1.
- If any shorts are produced, the 0-1 shorts variable equals 1.
- If any pants are produced, the 0-1 pants variable equals 1.

Together these ensure that the model "picks up" the cost of renting a machine if Gandy produces any positive amount of the product. We could easily implement these constraints with IF statements. For example, to implement the shirts constraint, we could enter the following formula in cell B16:

=IF(B18>0,1,0)

Unfortunately, spreadsheet Solvers often obtain incorrect answers when IF statements are used. Beware of using a spreadsheet Solver when your spreadsheet contains IF statements![5] We instead model the fixed charge constraints as follows:

$$\text{Shirts produced} \leq (\text{Maximum number of shirts that can be produced}) * (\text{0-1 variable for shirts}) \tag{5.1}$$

with similar inequalities for shorts and pants.

Here is the logic behind Inequality 5.1. If the 0-1 variable for shirts is 0, then the right-hand side of the inequality is 0, which means that the left-hand side must be 0—no shirts can be produced. That is, if the 0-1 variable for shirts is 0, so that no fixed cost for shirts is picked up, then Inequality 5.1 does not allow Gandy to "cheat" and produce a positive number of shirts. On the other hand, if the 0-1 variable for shirts is 1, then the inequality is certainly true (and is essentially redundant); it simply says that the number of shirts produced must be no greater than the *maximum* number that can be produced. Inequality 5.1 rules out the one case we want it to rule out, namely, that Gandy could produce shirts but avoid the fixed cost. However, it will allow the 0-1 variable to be 1 (thus picking up the fixed cost) even if Gandy plans to produce no shirts. Fortunately, this is not a problem; when the Solver minimizes total cost, it will never obtain such a solution because the total cost could be lowered by setting the 0-1 variable equal to 0 instead of 1.

To implement Inequality 5.1, we need an upper limit on the number of shirts that can be produced. However, observe that the number of shirts that can be produced is limited by the smaller of

$$\frac{\text{Available labor hours}}{\text{Labor hours per shirt}}$$

[5] We note that the GeneHunter solver mentioned in Chapter 3 is capable of handling IF statements in a spreadsheet.

and

$$\frac{\text{Available square yards of cloth}}{\text{Square yards of cloth per shirt}}$$

Therefore, the smaller of these can be used as the maximum needed in Inequality 5.1. So in cell B8 compute an upper limit on the number of shirts that can be produced with the formula

=MIN($D$23/B6,$D$24/B7)

Copy this formula to the range C8:D8 to compute upper limits on the numbers of shorts and pants that can be produced. For example, we see that at most

$$\min\{(150/3), (160/4)\} = 40$$

shirts can be produced.[6]

10 **Logical upper limits.** Now model the fixed-charge constraints in the range B18:D20. The left-hand sides are already in the range B18:D18. Generate the right-hand sides of the fixed charge constraints in the range B20:D20. Specifically, in cell B20 compute the right-hand-side of Inequality 5.1 by entering the formula

=B8*B16

Then copy this formula to the range C20:D20 to generate the right-hand-sides for shorts and pants.

Using the Solver

1 **Objective.** Choose cell B31 (total profit) as the objective to maximize.

2 **Changing cells.** Choose the ranges B18:D18 (units produced of each product) and B16:D16 (0-1 fixed charge variable for each product) as the changing cells.

3 **Nonnegative integer constraints on production quantities.** Constrain the range B18:D18 to be nonnegative and integers. This ensures that an integer number of each product is produced.[7]

4 **0-1 constraints.** Constrain the range B16:D16 to be 0-1. This ensures that the fixed charge variables will be 0 or 1.

5 **Resource availability constraints.** Add the constraint B23:B24<=D23:D24. This ensures that we do not use more labor and cloth than are available.

6 **Logical fixed charge constraints.** Add the constraint B18:D18<=B20:D20. This ensures that if we make any quantity of a product, the fixed charge variable for that product will equal 1. As discussed above, these constraints do not place unnecessary restrictions on the amount that can be produced of a given product.

7 **Linear model and optimize.** Check the Assume Linear Model box and Solve.

The optimal solution is shown in Figure 5.4. We see that Gandy should produce 25 pairs of pants but no shirts or shorts. The total profit is $75. Note that the fixed-charge 0-1 variables for shirts and shorts are both 0, which forces production of these products to be zero. However, the fixed-charge for pants, the product that is produced, is 1, which ensures that the fixed charge of producing pants is included in the total cost.

[6] Why not set the maximum number of shirts that can be produced equal to a huge number like 1,000,000? The reason is that spreadsheet Solvers work most efficiently when the maximum is as "tight" (that is, as low) as possible.

[7] In What's Best!, choose the command WB!/Integer followed by General. This makes the variables integers but not necessarily 0-1.

It may be helpful to think of this solution as occurring in two stages. In the first stage the Solver determines which products to produce, in this case pants only. Then in the second stage the Solver specifies how many pairs of pants to produce. Since each pair of pants is profitable (once the fixed cost has been paid), Gandy makes as many pairs of pants as possible, which is 25 because of the labor constraint. Of course, these two stages are interrelated, and the Solver considers them both in its solution process. ■

REAL-WORLD APPLICATIONS

Locating Distribution Centers

When Dow Consumer Products (a manufacturer of food-care products) acquired the Texize home-care product lines of Morton Thiokol in 1985 to form DowBrands, Inc., the distribution channels of the two organizations remained, for the most part, separate. Each had its own district and regional distribution centers for storing and then shipping products to the customer regions. This led to possible inefficiencies in a business where keeping logistics costs low can be the key to survival. Robinson, Gao, and Muggenborg [15], acting as consultants for DowBrands, modeled the problem as a fixed-cost network problem—which distribution centers to keep open and which routes to use to satisfy which customers with which products. The study was highly successful and convinced DowBrands to close a significant number of distribution centers in order to reduce costs. ■

Locating Out-of-State Audit Offices

To increase the collection of state taxes from companies doing business in Texas, the state auditors must often travel out of state. To reduce the cost associated with these trips, the state of Texas decided to locate auditors at several locations throughout the country. Fitzsimmons and Allen [10] used a fixed charge model to help the state of Texas locate out-of-state audit offices. See Problem 57 (in the Review Problems section) for a scaled-down version of this model. ■

Using Integer Programming to Immunize a Bond Portfolio

In order to minimize the interest-rate risk associated with an organization's assets and liabilities, it is important to match the *duration* of an organization's financial assets with the duration of its liabilities. This process is called **immunization**. In Problem 35 (based on Strong [19]), we indicate how an IP model can be used to minimize the transactions costs associated with immunizing holdings against interest-rate risk.

PROBLEMS

Skill-Building Problems

20 Because of excessive pollution on the Momiss River, the state of Momiss is going to build some pollution control stations. Three sites (1, 2, and 3) are under consideration. Momiss is interested in controlling the pollution levels of two pollutants (1 and 2). The state legislature requires that at least 80,000 tons of pollutant 1 and at least 50,000 tons of pollutant 2 be removed from the river. The relevant data for this problem are shown in Table 5.20. (The last two columns indicate the number of tons of pollutants removed per ton treated.) Determine how to minimize the cost of meeting the state legislature's goals.

21 A manufacturer can sell product 1 at a profit of \$2 per unit and product 2 at a profit of \$5 per unit. Three units of raw material are needed to manufacture one unit of product 1, and six units of raw material are need to manufacture one unit of product 2. A total of 120 units of raw material are available. If any of product 1 is produced, a setup cost of \$10 is incurred, and if

TABLE 5.20 Data for Momiss Pollution Problem

	Cost of Building Station	Cost of Treating One Ton of Water	Amount Removed (tons) Pollutant 1	Pollutant 2
Site 1	$100,000	$20	0.40	0.30
Site 2	$60,000	$30	0.25	0.20
Site 3	$40,000	$40	0.20	0.25

any of product 2 is produced, a setup cost of $20 is incurred. Determine how to maximize the manufacturer's profit.

22 A company is considering opening warehouses in four cities: New York, Los Angeles, Chicago, and Atlanta. Each warehouse can ship 100 units per week. The weekly fixed cost of keeping each warehouse open is $400 for New York, $500 for Los Angeles, $300 for Chicago, and $150 for Atlanta. Region 1 of the country requires 80 units per week, region 2 requires 70 units per week, and region 3 requires 40 units per week. The costs (including production and shipping costs) of sending one unit from a plant to a region are shown in Table 5.21. The company wants to meet weekly demands at minimum cost, subject to the preceding information and the following restrictions:

- If the New York warehouse is opened, then the Los Angeles warehouse must be opened.
- At most two warehouses can be opened.
- Either the Atlanta or the Los Angeles warehouse must be opened.

TABLE 5.21 Costs for Warehouse Shipping Problem

		To Region 1	Region 2	Region 3
From	**New York**	$20	$40	$50
	Los Angeles	$48	$15	$26
	Chicago	$26	$35	$18
	Atlanta	$24	$50	$35

23 Glueco produces three types of glue on two different production lines. Each line can be utilized by up to seven workers at a time. Workers are paid $500 per week on production line 1 and $900 per week on production line 2. For a week of production it costs $1000 to set up production line 1 and $2000 to set up production line 2. During a week on a production line each worker produces the number of units of glue shown in Table 5.22. Each week at least 120 units of glue 1, at least 150 units of glue 2, and at least 200 units of glue 3 must be produced. Determine how to minimize the total cost of meeting weekly demands.

TABLE 5.22 Production Data for Glueco Problem

	Glue 1	Glue 2	Glue 3
Line 1	20	30	40
Line 2	50	35	45

24 Fruit Computer produces two types of computers: Pear computers and Apricot computers. The relevant data are given in Table 5.23. The equipment cost is a fixed cost; it is incurred if any of this type of computer is produced. A total of 3000 chips and 1200 hours of labor are available. Determine how Fruit can maximize its profit.

25 Consider the Pigskin example (Example 2.3) from Chapter 2. Find Pigskin's optimal production policy if, in addition to the given production and holding costs, there is a fixed cost

TABLE 5.23 Data for Fruit Computer Problem

	Labor (hours)	Number of Chips	Equipment Cost	Selling Price
Pear	1	2	$5000	$400
Apricot	2	5	$7000	$900

of $1000 during any month in which there is positive production. Assume now that maximum storage capacity is 200 footballs.

26 A product can be produced on four different machines. Each machine has a fixed setup cost, variable production cost per unit processed, and a production capacity, given in Table 5.24. A total of 2000 units of the product must be produced. Determine how to minimize the total cost.

TABLE 5.24 Data for Machine Setup Problem

	Fixed Cost	Variable Cost	Capacity
Machine 1	$1000	$20	900
Machine 2	$920	$24	1000
Machine 3	$800	$16	1200
Machine 4	$700	$28	1600

27 Bookco Publishers is considering publishing five textbooks. The maximum number of copies of each textbook that can be sold, the variable cost of producing each textbook, the sales price of each textbook, and the fixed cost of a production run for each book are given in Table 5.25. For example, producing 2000 copies of book 1 brings in a revenue of $(2000)(50) = \$100,000$ but costs $80,000 + 25(2000) = \$130,000$. Determine how Bookco can maximize its profit if it can produce at most 10,000 books.

TABLE 5.25 Data for Bookco Problem

	Maximum Demand	Fixed Cost	Variable Cost	Sales Price
Book 1	5000	$80,000	$25	$50
Book 2	4000	$50,000	$20	$40
Book 3	3000	$60,000	$15	$38
Book 4	4000	$30,000	$18	$32
Book 5	3000	$40,000	$22	$40

28 Comquat owns four production plants at which personal computers are produced. Comquat can sell up to 20,000 computers per year at a price of $3500 per computer. For each plant, the production capacity, the production cost per computer, and the fixed cost of operating a plant for a year are given in Table 5.26. Determine how Comquat can maximize its yearly profit from computer production.

29 In the Sailco example (Example 4.2) suppose that a fixed cost of $20,000 is incurred during each quarter that production takes place. Determine how Sailco can minimize the total cost of meeting the demands for the four quarters.

TABLE 5.26 Data for Comquat Computer Problem

	Production Capacity	Plant Fixed Cost	Cost per Computer
Plant 1	10,000	$9 million	$1000
Plant 2	8,000	$5 million	$1700
Plant 3	9,000	$3 million	$2300
Plant 4	6,000	$1 million	$2900

30 Eastinghouse sells air conditioners. The annual demand for air conditioners in each region of the country is as follows: East, 100,000; South, 150,000; Midwest, 110,000; West, 90,000. Eastinghouse is considering building its air conditioners in four different cities: New York, Atlanta, Chicago, and Los Angeles. The cost of producing an air conditioner in a city and shipping it to a region of the country is given in Table 5.27. Any factory can produce up to 150,000 air conditioners per year. The annual fixed cost of operating a factory in each city is given in Table 5.28. At least 50,000 units of the Midwest demand for air conditioners must come from New York and at least 50,000 units of the Midwest demand must come from Atlanta. Determine how Eastinghouse can minimize the annual cost of meeting demand for air conditioners.

TABLE 5.27 Production and Shipping Costs for Eastinghouse Problem

	East	South	Midwest	West
New York	$206	$225	$230	$290
Atlanta	$225	$206	$221	$270
Chicago	$230	$221	$208	$262
Los Angeles	$290	$270	$262	$215

TABLE 5.28 Fixed Costs for Eastinghouse Problem

	Annual Fixed Cost
New York	$6.0 million
Atlanta	$5.5 million
Chicago	$5.8 million
Los Angeles	$6.2 million

31 During the next five periods the demands in Table 5.29 must be met on time. At the beginning of period 1, the inventory level is 0. Each period that production occurs a setup cost of $250 and a per unit production cost of $2 are incurred. At the end of each period a per unit holding cost of $1 is incurred. Determine the cost-minimizing production schedule.

TABLE 5.29 Demands for Production-Inventory Problem

	Demand
Period 1	220
Period 2	280
Period 3	360
Period 4	140
Period 5	270

Skill-Extending Problems

32 (Based on Efroymson and Ray [8]). Breadco Bakeries is a new bakery chain that sells bread to customers throughout the state of Indiana. Breadco is considering building bakeries in three locations: Evansville, Indianapolis, and South Bend. Each bakery can bake up to 900,000 loaves of bread each year. The cost of building a bakery at each site is $5 million in Evansville, $4 million in Indianapolis, and $4.5 million in South Bend. To simplify the problem, we assume that Breadco has only three customers. Their demands each year are 700,000 loaves (customer 1); 400,000 loaves (customer 2); and 300,000 loaves (customer 3). The total cost of baking and shipping a load of bread to a customer is given in Table 5.30. Assume that future shipping and production costs are discounted at a rate of 11.11% per year. Assume that once built, a bakery lasts forever. How would you minimize Breadco's total cost of meeting demand, present and future? (*Note*: Although your model is actually linear, the Excel Solver may report that "the conditions for Assume Linear Model are not satisfied" if you do not scale

TABLE 5.30 Costs for Breadco Problem

		To		
		Customer 1	Customer 2	Customer 3
From	Evansville	16¢	34¢	26¢
	Indianapolis	40¢	30¢	35¢
	South Bend	45¢	45¢	23¢

your changing cells and costs in "natural" units, as discussed in Chapter 2. For example, costs can be expressed in units of $1 million or $100,000, and annual shipments can be expressed in units of 100,000 loaves.)

33 A company sells seven types of boxes, ranging in volume from 17 to 33 cubic feet. The demand and size of each box are given in Table 5.31. The variable cost (in dollars) of producing each box is equal to the box's volume. A fixed cost of $1000 is incurred to produce any quantity of a particular box. If the company desires, demand for a box can be satisfied by a box of a larger size. Determine how to minimize the cost of meeting the demand for boxes.

TABLE 5.31 Data for Box Problem

	Box						
	1	2	3	4	5	6	7
Size	33	30	26	24	19	18	17
Demand	400	300	500	700	200	400	200

34 A large drug company must determine how many sales representatives to assign to each of four sales districts. The cost of having n representatives in a district is $88,000 + 80,000n$ dollars per year. If a sales rep is based in a given district, the time it takes to complete a call on a doctor is that given in Table 5.32, where times are in hours. Each sales rep can work up to 160 hours per month. Each month a certain number of calls, given in Table 5.33, must be made in each district. A fractional number of representatives in a district is not permissible. Determine how many representatives should be assigned to each district.

TABLE 5.32 Times for Calls in Drug Rep Problem

	Actual Sales Call District			
Rep's Base District	1	2	3	4
1	1	4	5	7
2	4	1	3	5
3	5	3	1	2
4	7	5	2	1

TABLE 5.33 Required Calls for Drug Rep Problem

	Number of Calls
District 1	50
District 2	80
District 3	100
District 4	60

35 (Based on Strong [19]) In this problem you will use integer programming and the concept of bond duration to show how Wall Street firms can select an optimal bond portfolio. The duration of a bond (or any stream of payments) is defined as follows: Let $C(t)$ be the payment of the bond at time t ($t = 1, 2, \ldots, n$). Let r be the market interest rate. If the time-weighted average of the bond's payments is given by

$$\sum_{t=1}^{n} tC(t)/(1+r)^t$$

and the market price P of the bond is given by

$$P = \sum_{t=1}^{n} C(t)/(1+r)^t$$

then the duration D of the bond is given by

$$D = (1/P)\sum_{t=1}^{n} tC(t)/(1+r)^t$$

The duration of a bond measures the "average" time (in years) at which a randomly chosen \$1 of NPV is received. Suppose an insurance company needs to make payments of \$20,000 every 6 months for the next 10 years. If the market rate of interest is 10% per year, this stream of payments has an NPV of \$251,780 and a duration of 4.47 years. If we want to minimize the sensitivity of the bond portfolio to interest-rate risk (that is, *immunize* the bond portfolio) and still meet our payment obligations, then it has been shown that we should invest \$251,780 at the beginning of year 1 in a bond portfolio having a duration equal to the duration of the payment stream.

Suppose that the only cost of owning a bond portfolio is the transaction cost associated with the cost of purchasing the bonds. Let's suppose that six bonds are available. The payment streams for these six bonds are given in Table 5.34. The transaction cost of purchasing any units of bond i equals \$500 plus \$5 per bond purchased. Thus, purchasing one unit of bond 1 costs \$505 and purchasing ten units of bond 1 costs \$550. Assume that a fractional number of bond i unit purchases is permissible, but in the interest of diversification, at most 100 units of any bond can be purchased. Treasury bonds can also be purchased (with no transaction cost). A treasury bond costs \$980 and has a duration of .25 year (90 days). After computing the price and duration for each bond, determine the immunized bond portfolio that incurs the smallest total transaction cost. You may assume that the duration of a portfolio is a weighted average of the durations of the bonds included in the portfolio, where the weight associated with each bond is equal to the money invested in that bond.

TABLE 5.34 Payment Streams for Bond Problem

	Bond 1	Bond 2	Bond 3	Bond 4	Bond 5	Bond 6
Year 1	50	100	130	20	100	120
Year 2	60	90	130	20	100	100
Year 3	70	80	130	20	100	80
Year 4	80	70	130	20	100	140
Year 5	90	60	130	20	100	100
Year 6	100	50	130	80	100	90
Year 7	110	40	130	40	100	110
Year 8	120	30	130	150	100	130
Year 9	130	20	130	200	100	180
Year 10	1010	1040	1130	1200	1100	950

36 (Based on Calloway, Cummins, and Freeland [5]) To satisfy telecommunication needs for the next 20 years, Telstar Corporation estimates that the number of circuits required between the United States and Germany, France, Switzerland, and the United Kingdom will be as given in Table 5.35. Two types of circuits can be created: cable and satellite. Two types of cable circuits (TA7 and TA8) are available. The fixed cost of building each type of cable and the circuit capacity of each type are given in Table 5.36. TA7 and TA8 cable go underseas from the United States to the English Channel. Thus, it costs an additional amount to extend these circuits to other European countries. The annual variable cost per circuit is given in Table 5.37. To create and use a satellite circuit, Telstar must launch a satellite, and each country using the satellite must have an earth station (or stations) to receive the signal. It costs $3 billion to launch a satellite. Each launched satellite can handle up to 140,000 circuits. All earth stations have a maximum capacity of 190 circuits and cost $6000 per year to operate. Determine how to supply the needed circuits and minimize total cost incurred during the next 20 years.

TABLE 5.35 Required Circuits for Telstar Problem

	Required Circuits
France	20,000
Germany	60,000
Switzerland	16,000
United Kingdom	60,000

TABLE 5.36 Building Costs and Capacities for Telstar Problem

	Fixed Building Cost	Capacity
Cable TA7	$1.6 billion	8,500
Cable TA8	$2.3 billion	37,800

TABLE 5.37 Variable Costs for Telstar Problem

	Variable Cost per Circuit
France	$0
Germany	$310
Switzerland	$290
United Kingdom	$0

37 On Monday morning you have $3000 in cash on hand. For the following seven days the following cash requirements must be met: Monday, $5000; Tuesday, $6000; Wednesday, $9000; Thursday, $2000; Friday, $7000; Saturday, $2000; Sunday, $3000. At the beginning of each day you must decide how much money (if any) to withdraw from the bank. It costs $10 to make a withdrawal of any size. You believe that the opportunity cost of having $1 of cash on hand for a year is $0.20. Assume that opportunity costs are incurred on each day's ending balance. Determine how much money you should withdraw from the bank during each of the next seven days. ■

5.4 The Lockbox Problem

Companies (such as banks and credit card companies) that receive payments by mail must determine how many payment centers they should have for customers to mail payments to. Having too few payment centers results in a large amount of customer receipts being in the mail at any given time. This causes the company to lose a great deal of interest on its receipts. Having too many payment centers, however, results in large fixed costs. The problem of determining the number and location of payment centers that minimize the sum of fixed operating costs and lost interest costs is called a **lockbox problem**. The following is an example of a lockbox problem.

EXAMPLE 5.3

JC Nickles receives credit card payments from four regions of the country (West, Midwest, East, and South). The average daily amount of payments mailed from each region is as follows: West, $70,000; Midwest, $50,000; East, $60,000; South, $40,000. Nickles must decide where customers should mail their payments. An annual interest of 20% can be earned on revenues. Nickles is considering setting up payment centers (lockboxes) in four cities: Los Angeles, Chicago, New York, and Atlanta. The average number of days that elapse between the time a check is mailed and the check is credited to the Nickles account is given in Table 5.38. The annual cost of running a lockbox is $50,000. Each region must send all its money to a single city, and there is no limit on the amount of money a lockbox can handle. Nickles wants to determine the lockbox configuration that minimizes the sum of lost interest and lockbox costs.

TABLE 5.38 **Times for Nickles Lockbox Example**

	L.A.	Chicago	N.Y.	Atlanta
West	2	6	8	8
Midwest	6	2	5	5
East	8	5	2	5
South	8	5	5	2

Solution

To solve this problem, we must keep track of the following:

- the location of the lockboxes
- the city to which each region sends its money
- the annual lost interest cost if a particular region sends its money to a particular city
- the total annual lost interest cost
- the total annual fixed cost

We must also ensure (1) that each region sends its money somewhere and (2) that each lockbox that is used is paid for.

Developing the Spreadsheet Model The spreadsheet can be developed with the following steps. (See Figure 5.5 and the file NICKLES.XLS.)

1 **Inputs.** Enter the given data in the ranges C6:F9, C13:C14, and C17:C20.

2 **0-1 values for lockbox locations.** We will use 0-1 variables to keep track of the cities where lockboxes are located. Enter *any* trial 0-1 values in the range C33:F33. For example, a 1 in cell D33 means that there is a lockbox in Chicago, while a 0 in cell F33 means that there is no lockbox in Atlanta.

3 **0-1 values for cities where regions send their money.** In the range C38:F41 enter *any* 0-1 trial values to keep track of the city to which each region sends its money. For example, a 1 in cell D38 means that the West sends its money to Chicago, while a 0 in cell E41 means that the South does not send its money to New York.

4 **Number of cities each region sends money to.** Compute the number of cities to which each region sends its money in the range G38:G41. Specifically, to compute the number of cities to which the West sends its money, enter the formula

=SUM(C38:F38)

FIGURE 5.5 Spreadsheet for Nickles Lockbox Example

	A	B	C	D	E	F	G	H	I	J
1	**Nickles Lockbox Problem**									
2										
3	**Days in transit**									
4				Lockbox location						
5			Los Angeles	Chicago	New York	Atlanta				
6	Origin of	West	2	6	8	8				
7	checks	Midwest	6	2	5	5				
8		East	8	5	2	5				
9		South	8	5	5	2				
10										
11	**Financial data**									
12										
13	Annual interest rate		20%							
14	Cost per lockbox		$50,000							
15										
16	Payments per day									
17		West	$70,000							
18		Midwest	$50,000							
19		East	$60,000							
20		South	$40,000							
21										
22	**Annual lost interest for origin/location pair**									
23				Lockbox location						
24			Los Angeles	Chicago	New York	Atlanta				
25	Origin of	West	$28,000	$84,000	$112,000	$112,000				
26	checks	Midwest	$60,000	$20,000	$50,000	$50,000				
27		East	$96,000	$60,000	$24,000	$60,000				
28		South	$64,000	$40,000	$40,000	$16,000				
29										
30	**Assignments and lockbox decisions**									
31	Locations of lockboxes (1 if located there, 0 if not)									
32			Los Angeles	Chicago	New York	Atlanta				
33			1	0	1	0				
34										
35	Assignments (1 if origin and lockbox location are paired, 0 if not)									
36				To lockbox location						
37			Los Angeles	Chicago	New York	Atlanta	Sent?		Required	
38	Send	West	1	0	0	0	1	=	1	
39	from	Midwest	0	0	1	0	1	=	1	
40		East	0	0	1	0	1	=	1	
41		South	0	0	1	0	1	=	1	
42										
43	**Logical lockbox constraints**									
44			1	0	0	0				
45			0	0	1	0	←		Duplication of range C38:F41	
46			0	0	1	0				
47			0	0	1	0				
48					<=					
49			1	0	1	0				
50			1	0	1	0			4 duplications of range C33:F33	
51			1	0	1	0	←			
52			1	0	1	0				
53										
54	**Cost summary**									
55	Lost interest	$142,000								
56	Lockbox cost	$100,000								
57	**Total cost**	$242,000								

in cell G38. Then copy this formula to the range G39:G41 to compute the number of cities to which the other regions send their money.

5 **Total fixed cost.** Compute the annual fixed cost in cell B56 with the formula

=C14*SUM(C33:F33)

6 **Lost interest for each region-city combination.** To determine how much interest Nickles loses annually, we must determine how much revenue is lost if payments are sent from a particular region to a particular city. For example, how much in annual interest is lost if customers from the West send their money to N.Y.? On a given day, eight days worth, or $560, 000 (= 8[70,000]), of West payments would be in the mail and not earning interest. Since Nickles can earn 20% annually, each year West funds will result in $112,000 (= .20[560,000]) in lost interest. Compute the annual lost

interest costs for each region-city combination in the range C25:F28. Specifically, in cell C25 compute the annual lost interest cost for sending money from the West to L.A. with the formula

```
=$C$13*C6*$C17
```

Then copy this formula to the range C25:F28 to compute the annual lost interest cost for every other region-city combination.

7 **Total lost interest.** Compute the total annual lost interest cost in cell B55 with the formula

```
=SUMPRODUCT(C25:F28,C38:F41)
```

Using 0-1 variables for the assignment of regions to cities ensures that this formula picks up only the lost interest costs that are due to *actual* assignments of regions to cities.

8 **Total cost.** In cell B57 compute the total annual cost (the sum of annual fixed lockbox costs and annual lost interest costs) with the formula

```
=SUM(B55:B56)
```

9 **Copy 0-1 variables.** Next we ensure that if a lockbox is used, Nickles pays for it. To do this, we add constraints of the following form for each possible combination of a region and city:

$$\text{Assignment variable for region } i\text{, city } j \leq \text{Fixed charge variable for city } j \tag{5.2}$$

This constraint ensures that if region i sends its money to city j, then the fixed charge variable for city j must equal 1, and Nickles pays for a lockbox at city j. If no region is assigned to city j, then the Solver can make the fixed charge variable for city j equal to 0 or 1. However, because setting a fixed charge variable to 0 is cheaper, this will be done if possible. We insert the 16 constraints of type 5.2 in the range C44:F52 by duplicating the range C38:F41 (the left-hand sides of 5.2) in the range C44:F47. To do this, enter the formula

```
=C38
```

in cell C44. Then copy this formula to the range C44:F47. Similarly, to put the right-hand sides of Inequality 5.2 in the range C49:F52, enter the formula

```
=C$33
```

into cell C49, and copy this formula to the range C49:F52. Essentially, this puts four copies of the lockbox fixed charge variables in rows 49–52.

Using the Solver

1 **Objective.** Choose cell B57 (total annual cost) as the objective to minimize.

2 **Changing cells.** Choose the ranges C38:F41 (corresponding to region-city assignments) and C33:F33 (fixed charge variables for lockboxes) as the changing cells.

3 **0-1 constraints.** Constrain the ranges C38:F41 and C33:F33 to be 0-1 variables.

4 **Assignment constraints.** Add the constraints G38:G41=1 (or, equivalently, G38:G41=I38:I41 since 1's are entered in the range I38:I41) to ensure that each region is assigned to exactly one city.

5 **Logical fixed charge constraints.** Add the constraints C44:F47<=C49:F52. These operationalize the logical constraints in Inequality 5.2.

6 **Linear model and optimize.** Check the Assume Linear Model box and Solve.

The optimal solution appears in Figure 5.5. We see that Nickles needs lockboxes in L.A. and N.Y. The West sends its money to L.A., and all other regions send their money to N.Y. An annual cost of $242,000 is incurred. Note that row 33 (and its four duplicates in rows 49–52) have 1's corresponding to L.A. and N.Y. These 1's pick up the fixed costs of locating lockboxes in L.A. and N.Y., and they allow the four regions to send their money to these two cities. The 1's in rows 38–41 (and in their duplicates in rows 44–47) indicate where the regions send their money. The logical fixed charge constraints ensure that these rows can have 1's only in the columns where row 33 has 1's. That is, a region can send its money to a city only if a lockbox is located in that city. ■

MODELING ISSUE

The **cash disbursement model** involves dispersing sites around the country to extend the time between the mailing of a check and the time the check clears. Shanker and Zoltners [18] use a model similar to the lockbox model to solve this problem. See Problem 42 for an example of this model. ■

PROBLEMS

Skill-Building Problems

38 Ford has four automobile plants. Each is capable of producing the Taurus, Lincoln, or Escort, but it can only produce one of these cars. The fixed cost of operating each plant for a year and the variable cost of producing a car of each type at each plant are given in Table 5.39. Ford faces the following restrictions:

- Each plant can produce only one type of car.
- The total production of each type of car must be at a single plant. For example, if any Tauruses are made at plant 1, then all Tauruses must be made there.

Each year Ford must produce 5 million of each type of car. Determine how to minimize the annual cost of producing these cars.

TABLE 5.39 **Fixed and Variable Costs for Ford Problem**

		Variable Cost		
	Fixed Cost	**Taurus**	**Lincoln**	**Escort**
Plant 1	$70 billion	$12,000	$16,000	$9,000
Plant 2	$60 billion	$15,000	$18,000	$11,000
Plant 3	$40 billion	$17,000	$19,000	$12,000
Plant 4	$20 billion	$19,000	$22,000	$14,000

39 At a machine tool plant five jobs must be completed each day. The time it takes to do each job depends on the machine used to do the job. If a machine is used at all, there is a setup time required. The relevant times (in minutes) are given in Table 5.40. Determine how to minimize the sum of the setup and machine operation times needed to complete all jobs.

40 How would the Nickles lockbox formulation change if each city could handle at most $120,000 per day in payments?

TABLE 5.40 Times for Machine Tool Problem

	Job 1	Job 2	Job 3	Job 4	Job 5	Setup Time
Machine 1	42	70	93	X	X	30
Machine 2	X	85	45	X	X	40
Machine 3	58	X	X	37	X	50
Machine 4	58	X	55	X	38	60
Machine 5	X	60	X	54	X	20

Skill-Extending Problems

41 A 3×3 magic square is an arrangement of the digits 1 through 9 for which all three rows, three columns, and both diagonals of the square add up to the same number. For example,

1	4	9
2	6	5
3	7	8

is not a magic square. Use a spreadsheet solver to find a 3x3 magic square. (*Hint*: You will have $9 * 9 = 81$ variables that you can put in a range consisting of 9 rows and 9 columns. The variable in row i and column j will equal 1 if digit i is assigned to position j in the square and will equal 0 otherwise.)

42 (Based on Shanker and Zoltners [18]) Speaker's Clearinghouse must disburse sweepstakes checks to winners in four different regions of the country: Southeast (SE), Northeast (NE), Far West (FW), and Midwest (MW). The average daily amounts of the checks written to winners in each region of the country are as follows: SE, \$40,000; NE, \$60,000; FW, \$30,000; MW, \$50,000. Speaker's must issue the checks the day they find that a customer has won. They can delay winners from quickly cashing their checks by giving a winner a check drawn on an out-of-the-way bank (this will cause the check to clear slowly). Four bank sites are under consideration: Frostbite Falls, Montana (FF), Redville, South Carolina (R), Painted Forest, Arizona (PF), and Beanville, Maine (B). The annual cost of maintaining an account at each bank is as follows: FF, \$50,000; R, \$40,000; PF, \$30,000; B, \$20,000. Each bank has a requirement that the average daily amount of checks written cannot exceed \$90,000. The average number of days it takes a check to clear is given in Table 5.41. Assuming that money invested by Speaker's earns 15% per year, where should the company have bank accounts, and from which bank should a given customer's check be written?

TABLE 5.41 Data for Clearinghouse Problem

	FF	R	PF	B
SE	7	2	6	5
NE	8	4	5	3
FW	4	8	2	11
MW	5	4	7	5

43 You have nine circles. Three are red, three are green, and three are orange. You want to assign these circles to a 3×3 chessboard so that each row, column, and diagonal has one circle of each color. Use the Solver to accomplish this goal. ■

5.5 The Warehouse Location Problem

Consider a company that must produce its goods at plants and store its goods at warehouses before shipping these goods to customers. Suppose that there is a fixed cost associated with the operation of each plant and warehouse. If the company is allowed to determine which warehouses and plants are opened, then we have an IP problem called a **fixed charge plant and warehouse location problem**. By solving such a problem, companies such as Hunt's Foods have saved millions of dollars in production and distribution costs. See Geoffrion and Graves [11] for a documented application of a fixed charge plant and warehouse location model that saved Hunt-Wesson over $1 million annually.

The following is an example of a fixed charge plant and warehouse location problem.

EXAMPLE 5.4

Huntco produces tomato sauce at five different plants. The capacity (in tons) of each plant is given in Table 5.42. The tomato sauce is stored at one of three warehouses. The per ton cost of producing tomato sauce at each plant and shipping it to each warehouse is given in Table 5.43. Huntco has four customers. The cost of shipping a ton of sauce from each warehouse to each customer is given in Table 5.44. Each customer must receive the amount (in tons) of sauce given in Table 5.45. The annual fixed cost of operating each plant and warehouse is listed in Table 5.46. Huntco's goal is to minimize the annual cost of meeting customer demands. The company wants to determine which plants and warehouses to open, as well as the optimal shipping plan.

TABLE 5.42 **Capacities for Huntco Example**

	Plant				
	1	2	3	4	5
Tons	300	200	300	200	400

TABLE 5.43 **Production and Shipping Costs for Huntco Example**

		To		
		Warehouse 1	Warehouse 2	Warehouse 3
From	Plant 1	$800	$1000	$1200
	Plant 2	$700	$500	$700
	Plant 3	$800	$600	$500
	Plant 4	$500	$600	$700
	Plant 5	$700	$600	$500

TABLE 5.44 **Shipping Costs to Customers for Huntco Example**

		To			
		Customer 1	Customer 2	Customer 3	Customer 4
From	Warehouse 1	$40	$80	$90	$50
	Warehouse 2	$70	$40	$60	$80
	Warehouse 3	$80	$30	$50	$60

TABLE 5.45 **Customer Requirements for Huntco Example**

	Customer			
	1	2	3	4
Requirement	200	300	150	250

TABLE 5.46 **Fixed Costs for Huntco Example**

	Fixed Annual Cost
Plant 1	$35,000
Plant 2	$45,000
Plant 3	$40,000
Plant 4	$42,000
Plant 5	$40,000
Warehouse 1	$40,000
Warehouse 2	$20,000
Warehouse 3	$60,000

Solution

To model Huntco's situation we need to keep track of the following:

- the shipments from plants to warehouses
- the shipments from warehouses to customers
- the fixed costs of operating plants and warehouses
- the shipping and production costs from plants to warehouses
- the shipping costs from warehouses to customers
- the total amount shipped out of each plant

We must also ensure that (1) Huntco pays the fixed costs for all plants and warehouses that are used, (2) the amount shipped into each warehouse equals the amount received by each warehouse, and (3) each customer receives the specified demand.

Developing the Spreadsheet Model The completed spreadsheet appears in Figure 5.6. (See the file HUNTCO.XLS.) It can be formed as follows.

1 **Inputs.** Enter the given data. Specifically, enter the plant-to-warehouse units costs in the range C6:E10, the fixed costs in the ranges G6:G10 and H15:H17, the warehouse-to-customer unit costs in C15:F17, the plant capacities in J22:J26, and the customer requirements in C39:F39.

2 **Shipments.** Enter *any* trial values for the shipments from each plant to each warehouse in the range C22:E26 and *any* trial values for the shipment from each warehouse to each customer in the range C34:F36.

3 **0-1 fixed-charge values.** In the range I22:I26 enter *any* trial 0-1 values of the fixed charge variable for each plant. The fixed charge variable for a plant equals 1 if the plant is used and 0 if the plant is not used. Similarly, in the range J34:J36 enter *any* trial 0-1 values of the fixed charge variables for each warehouse. The fixed charge variable for a warehouse equals 1 if the warehouse is used and 0 if the warehouse is not used.

4 **Amount shipped out of each plant.** In the range F22:F26 compute the total amount shipped out of each plant. Specifically, in cell F22 compute the amount shipped out of plant 1 with the formula

=SUM(C22:E22)

FIGURE 5.6 **Optimal Solution for Huntco Example**

	A	B	C	D	E	F	G	H	I	J	K
1	**Huntco Plant/Warehouse Location Problem**										
2											
3	**Plant to warehouse unit production, shipping costs, plant fixed costs**										
4				**Warehouse**							
5			1	2	3		Fixed cost				
6		1	$800	$1,000	$1,200		$35,000				
7		2	$700	$500	$700		$45,000				
8	**Plant**	3	$800	$600	$500		$40,000				
9		4	$500	$600	$700		$42,000				
10		5	$700	$600	$500		$40,000				
11											
12	**Warehouse to customer unit shipping costs, warehouse fixed costs**										
13				**Customer**							
14			1	2	3	4		Fixed cost			
15		1	$40	[illegible]	[illegible]	$50		$40,000			
16	**Warehouse**	2	$70	$40	$60	$80		$20,000			
17		3	$80	$30	$50	$60		$60,000			
18											
19	**Plant to warehouse shipments (tons)**										
20				**Warehouse**							
21			1	2	3	Shipped		Logical upper bound	Use plant?	Capacity	
22		1	0	0	0	0	<=	0	0	300	
23		2	0	200	0	200	<=	200	1	200	
24	**Plant**	3	0	0	300	300	<=	300	1	300	
25		4	0	0	0	0	<=	0	0	200	
26		5	0	0	400	400	<=	400	1	400	
27		Received	0	200	700						
28			=	=	=						
29		Shipped	0	200	700						
30											
31	**Warehouse to customer shipments (tons)**										
32				**Customer**							
33			1	2	3	4	Shipped		Logical upper bound	Use warehouse?	Total demand
34		1	0	0	0	0	0	<=	0	0	900
35	**Warehouse**	2	200	0	0	0	200	<=	900	1	900
36		3	0	300	150	250	700	<=	900	1	900
37		Received	200	300	150	250					
38			>=	>=	>=	>=					
39		Required	200	300	150	250					
40											
41	**Summary of costs**										
42	Plant to warehouse costs			$450,000							
43	Warehouse to customer costs			$45,500							
44	Plant fixed costs			$125,000							
45	Warehouse fixed costs			$80,000							
46	**Total cost**			$700,500							

Then copy this formula to the range F23:F26 to compute the amounts shipped out of the other plants.

5 **Upper limit on amount shipped out of each plant.** For each plant i we need a constraint of the form

$$\text{Total shipped out of plant } i \leq \text{ Plant } i \text{ capacity} \qquad \textbf{(5.3)}$$
$$*\text{Fixed charge variable for plant } i$$

This inequality ensures that if Huntco uses plant i, then this plant's fixed charge variable will equal 1 and the company will pay the plant i operating cost. In this case Inequality 5.3 simply states that the total shipped out of plant i is less than or equal to the plant's capacity. We generate the right-hand sides of 5.3 in the range H22:H26. Specifically, to generate the right-hand side of 5.3 for plant 1, enter the formula

=I22*J22

in cell H22. Then copy this formula to the range H23:H26 to generate the right-hand sides for the other plants. Of course, if plant i is not used, the Solver is free to make the plant i fixed charge variable 0, and no fixed cost for plant i will be incurred. Then Inequality 5.3 will be trivially satisfied ($0 \leq 0$).

6 **Upper limit on amount shipped out of each warehouse.** Similarly, for warehouse i we need a constraint of the form

$$\text{Total shipped out of warehouse } i \leq \text{Total demand} * \text{Fixed charge variable for warehouse } i \quad \textbf{(5.4)}$$

This formula ensures that if Huntco uses warehouse i, then this warehouse's fixed charge variable will equal 1 and Huntco will pay the warehouse i operating cost. In preparation for entering the inequalities of the form 5.4, we will enter the total demand in the range K34:K36. (This will help to construct the right-hand sides of these inequalities.) First, compute the total demand in cell K34 with the formula

=SUM(C$39:F$39)

Then copy this formula to the range K35:K36 to create two "copies" of the total demand. Next, construct the right-hand side of the warehouse 1 constraint 5.4 by entering the formula

=J34*K34

in cell I34. Then copy this formula to the range I35:I36 to compute the right-hand sides of Inequality 5.4 for warehouses 2 and 3.

7 **Amount shipped out of each warehouse.** As in the MCNFM (discussed in Section 4.6), we need the following constraint for each warehouse:

$$\text{Total shipments into warehouse } i = \text{Total shipments out of warehouse } i \quad \textbf{(5.5)}$$

To model Equation 5.5 we begin by computing the amount shipped out of each warehouse in the range G34:G36. In cell G34 compute the total shipped out of warehouse 1 with the formula

=SUM(C34:F34)

Copy this formula to the range G35:G36 to compute the total amounts shipped out of the other warehouses. Then recopy the shipments out of each warehouse to the range C29:E29. (We do this because the two ranges we want to make equal, C27:E27 and G34:G36, are not the same shape—one is a row and the other is a column. So we copy the contents of G34:G36 to a row.) The easiest way to recopy is to use the Excel Transpose command. Simply highlight the range C29:E29 and type the *array* formula

=TRANSPOSE(G34:G36)

Don't forget to hit Control Shift and Enter to enter this array formula.

8 **Amount received by each warehouse.** Similarly, compute the amount received by each warehouse in the range C27:E27. In cell C27 compute the amount received by warehouse 1 with the formula

=SUM(C22:C26)

Then copy this formula to the range D27:E27 to compute the totals received by the other warehouses.

9 **Amount received by each customer.** In the range C37:F37 compute the total amount received by each customer. Specifically, compute the amount received by customer 1 in cell C37 with the formula

=SUM(C34:C36)

Then copy this formula to the range D37:F37 to compute the total amount received by each customer.

10 **Shipping costs.** Compute the total cost of shipping from plants to warehouses in cell D42 with the formula

=SUMPRODUCT(C6:E10,C22:E26)

Compute the total cost of shipping items from the warehouses to the customers in cell D43 with the formula

=SUMPRODUCT(C15:F17,C34:F36)

11 **Fixed costs.** Compute the annual fixed costs for operating plants in cell D44 with the formula

=SUMPRODUCT(G6:G10,I22:I26)

Compute the annual fixed cost for operating warehouses in cell D45 with the formula

=SUMPRODUCT(H15:H17,J34:J36)

12 **Total cost.** Finally, compute the total annual cost in cell D46 with the formula

=SUM(D42:D45)

Using the Solver

1 **Objective.** Choose cell D46 (total annual cost) as the objective to minimize.

2 **Changing cells.** Choose the following as changing cells: C22:E26 (shipments from plants to warehouses); C34:F36 (shipments from warehouses to customers); I22:I26 (fixed charge variables for operating plants); J34:J36 (fixed charge variables for operating warehouses). Constrain C22:E26 and C34:F36 to be nonnegative.

3 **0-1 constraints.** Constrain the ranges I22:I26 and J34:J36 to be 0-1 variables. This ensures that all fixed charge variables will equal 0 or 1.

4 **Logical plant constraints.** Add the constraints F22:F26<=H22:H26. These constraints operationalize Inequality 5.3.

5 **Logical warehouse constraints.** Add the constraints G34:G36<=I34:I36. These operationalize Inequality 5.4.

6 **Warehouse balance constraints.** Add the constraints C27:E27=C29:E29. These operationalize Equation 5.5.

7 **Demand constraints.** Add the constraints C37:F37>=C39:F39. These ensure that each customer receives the required amount.

8 **Linear model and optimize.** Check the Assume Linear Model box and Solve.

The optimal solution appears in Figure 5.6.[8] Plants 2, 3,and 5 are used, and warehouses 2 and 3 are used. A total annual cost of $700,500 is incurred by making the following shipments: 200 tons from plant 2 to warehouse 2; 300 tons from plant 3 to warehouse 3; 400 tons from plant 5 to warehouse 3; 200 tons from warehouse 2 to customer 1; 300 tons from warehouse 3 to customer 2; 150 tons from warehouse 3 to customer 3; 250 tons from warehouse 3 to customer 4. A graphical representation of this solution appears in Figure 5.7.

[8] To solve this rather difficult problem, you will need to use the version of the Solver software included with this book (or perhaps a newer version of Excel), and be sure to check the Use Automatic Scaling box as well as the Assume Linear Model box. In current versions of Excel, you are likely to experience the problems with scaling described in Chapter 2—including the message "the conditions for Assume Linear Model are not satisfied," even though the model is linear, and the message "Solver could not find a feasible solution," even though such a solution exists.

FIGURE 5.7 Plants, Warehouses Used, and Optimal Shipments for Huntco Example

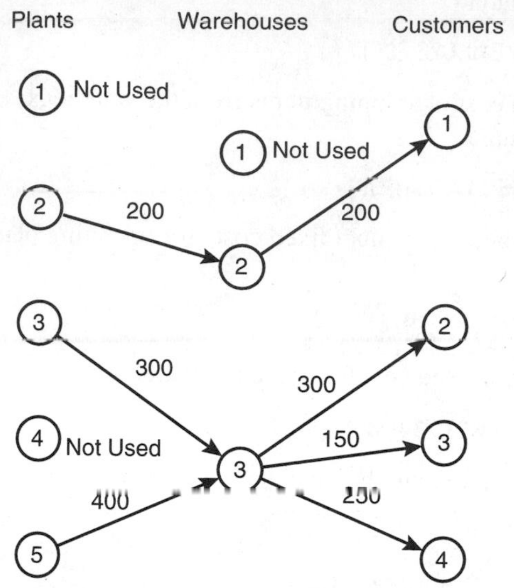

At this point, you might want to review the inputs for this problem and see whether the optimal solution appears reasonable from an economic point of view. For example, although plant 1 has a relatively small fixed cost, it has relatively large unit shipping costs. This is evidently the reason for not using plant 1. However, the situation is not so obvious for plant 4 or warehouse 1. We think you'll agree that on logistics problems such as this—and this isn't even a large problem—more than intuition is necessary! ■

PROBLEMS

Skill-Building Problems

44 Heinsco produces tomato sauce at five different plants. The plant capacities (in tons) are listed in Table 5.47. The tomato sauce is stored at one of three warehouses. The cost per ton of producing tomato sauce at each plant and shipping it to each warehouse is given in Table 5.48. Heinsco has four customers. The cost of shipping a ton of sauce from each warehouse to each customer is given in Table 5.49. Each customer must be delivered the amount (in tons) of sauce given in Table 5.50. There is a fixed annual cost of operating each plant and warehouse, given in Table 5.51. Determine the minimum cost method for meeting customer demands.

TABLE 5.47 Capacities for Heinsco Problem

	Plant				
	1	2	3	4	5
Capacity	500	200	300	400	400

45 Suppose in the previous problem that each customer's demand must be met from a *single* warehouse. Solve the previous problem with this restriction. ■

TABLE 5.48 **Production and Shipping Costs for Heinsco Problem**

		To		
		Warehouse 1	Warehouse 2	Warehouse 3
From	Plant 1	$600	$700	$500
	Plant 2	$700	$500	$700
	Plant 3	$800	$400	$900
	Plant 4	$500	$600	$700
	Plant 5	$700	$600	$500

TABLE 5.49 **Shipping Costs to Customers for Heinsco Problem**

		To			
		Customer 1	Customer 2	Customer 3	Customer 4
From	Warehouse 1	$60	$80	$40	$70
	Warehouse 2	$70	$40	$60	$80
	Warehouse 3	$50	$50	$50	$50

TABLE 5.50 **Customer Requirements for Heinsco Problem**

	Customer			
	1	2	3	4
Requirement	400	300	250	350

TABLE 5.51 **Fixed Costs for Heinsco Problem**

	Fixed Annual Cost
Plant 1	$25,000
Plant 2	$35,000
Plant 3	$40,000
Plant 4	$50,000
Plant 5	$40,000
Warehouse 1	$30,000
Warehouse 2	$40,000
Warehouse 3	$30,000

5.6 Set Covering Problems

In a set covering problem each member of a given set (set 1) must be "covered" by an acceptable member of another set (set 2). The objective in a set covering problem is to minimize the number of elements in set 2 that are needed to cover all the elements in set 1. For example, set 1 might consist of the cities in a given county and set 2 might consist of the cities in which a fire engine is located. A member of set 2 "covers" a member of set 1 if the fire engine is located within ten minutes of a city. The goal is to minimize the number of fire engines needed to cover all cities. Set covering problems have been applied to areas as diverse as airline crew scheduling, truck dispatching, political resdistricting, and capital investment. The following is an example of a set covering problem.

EXAMPLE 5.5

Western Airlines has decided that it needs to have three hubs in the United States. Western runs flights between the following cities: Atlanta, Boston, Chicago, Denver, Houston, Los Angeles, New Orleans, New York, Pittsburgh, Salt Lake City, San Francisco, and Seattle. Western needs to have a hub within 1000 miles of each of these cities. The company wants to determine the smallest number of hubs needed to meet this requirement. Table 5.52 lists which cities cover (that is, are within 1000 miles of) other cities.

TABLE 5.52 **Data for Western Set Covering Example**

	Cities Within 1000 Miles
Atlanta (AT)	AT, CH, HO, NO, NY, PI
Boston (BO)	BO, NY, PI
Chicago (CH)	AT, CH, NY, NO, PI
Denver (DE)	DE, SL
Houston (HO)	AT, HO, NO
Los Angeles (LA)	LA, SL, SF
New Orleans (NO)	AT, CH, HO, NO
New York (NY)	AT, BO, CH, NY, PI
Pittsburgh (PI)	AT, BO, CH, NY, PI
Salt Lake City (SL)	DE, LA, SL, SF, SE
San Francisco (SF)	LA, SL, SF, SE
Seattle (SE)	SL, SF, SE

Solution

The model must keep track of the following:

- the set of cities that cover other cities (For example, San Francisco covers Los Angeles, Salt Lake City, San Francisco, and Seattle.)
- the cities that are selected as hubs (We will use a 0-1 variable for each city to indicate whether a city is selected as a hub. If a city's 0-1 variable equals 1, the city is selected as a hub; if the city's 0-1 variable equals 0, the city is not selected as a hub.)
- the total number of cities chosen to be hubs
- whether or not each city is covered by a hub

Developing the Spreadsheet Model The spreadsheet for Western can now be developed as follows. (See Figure 5.8 and the file WESTERN.XLS.)

1 **Inputs.** Enter the information from Table 5.52 about which cities cover which other cities in the range B5:M16. A 1 in a cell indicates that the column city covers the row city, while a 0 indicates that the column city does not cover the row city. For example, the three 1's in row 6 indicate that Boston, New York, and Pittsburgh are the only cities within 1000 miles of Boston. Also, enter 1's in the range P5:P16 to indicate that we need at least one hub within 1000 miles of each city.

2 **0-1 values for hub locations.** Enter *any* trial values of 0's or 1's in the range B18:M18 to keep track of which cities are used as hubs.

3 **Number of hubs.** In cell N18 compute the total number of hubs used with the formula

=SUM(B18:M18)

FIGURE 5.8 Optimal Solution to Western Set Covering Example

	A	B	C	D	E	F	G	H	I	J	K	L	M	N	O	P
1	Western Airlines Set Covering Problem															
2																
3							Potential hub									
4	Cities covered	AT	BO	CH	DE	HO	LA	NO	NY	PI	SL	SF	SE	# covered by		Required
5	AT	1	0	1	0	1	0	1	1	1	0	0	0	2	>=	1
6	BO	0	1	0	0	0	0	0	1	1	0	0	0	1	>=	1
7	CH	1	0	1	0	0	0	1	1	1	0	0	0	1	>=	1
8	DE	0	0	0	1	0	0	0	0	0	1	0	0	1	>=	1
9	HO	1	0	0	0	1	0	1	0	0	0	0	0	1	>=	1
10	LA	0	0	0	0	0	1	0	0	0	1	1	0	1	>=	1
11	NO	1	0	1	0	1	0	1	0	0	0	0	0	1	>=	1
12	NY	1	1	1	0	0	0	0	1	1	0	0	0	1	>=	1
13	PI	1	1	1	0	0	0	0	1	1	0	0	0	1	>=	1
14	SL	0	0	0	1	0	1	0	0	0	1	1	1	1	>=	1
15	SF	0	0	0	0	0	1	0	0	0	1	1	1	1	>=	1
16	SE	0	0	0	0	0	0	0	0	0	1	1	1	1	>=	1
17														Total hubs		
18	Used as hub?	0	0	0	0	1	0	0	1	0	1	0	0	3		

4 **Cities covered by hubs.** We now determine whether each city is covered by a hub. Compute the total number of hubs within 1000 miles of Atlanta in cell N5 with the formula

=SUMPRODUCT(B5:M5,$B$18:$M$18)

Then copy this formula to the range N6:N16 to compute the number of hubs covering each other city.

Using the Solver

1 **Objective.** Choose cell N18 (total number of hubs) as the objective to minimize.

2 **Changing cells.** Choose the range B18:M18 as the changing cells.

3 **0-1 constraints.** Constrain the range B18:M18 to be 0-1 variables.

4 **City coverage constraints.** Add the constraints N5:N16>=P5:P16. These ensure that each city will be covered by at least one hub.

5 **Linear model and optimize.** Check the Assume Linear Model box and Solve.

The optimal solution to Western's problem appears in Figure 5.8. A graphical representation appears in Figure 5.9, where the double ovals indicate hub locations and the large circles indicate ranges covered by the hubs. (These large circles aren't drawn to scale. In reality, they should be circles of radius 1000 miles centered at the hubs.) Three hubs—in Houston, New York, and Salt Lake City—are needed. Would you have guessed this? The Houston hub covers Houston, Atlanta, and New Orleans. The New York hub covers Atlanta, Pittsburgh, Boston, New York, and Chicago. The Salt Lake City hub covers Denver, Los Angeles, Salt Lake City, San Francisco, and Seattle. Note that Atlanta is the only city covered by two of these hubs; it can be serviced by either New York or Houston. ■

REAL-WORLD APPLICATIONS

Station Staffing at Pan Am

Like many other airlines, Pan Am used management science to determine optimal staffing levels for its support staff (for ticket counters, baggage loading and unloading, mechanical maintenance, and so on). Schindler and Semmel [17] describe how Pan Am used a set covering model to determine flexible shifts of full-time and part-time personnel in the United States, Latin and South America, and Europe. The model allowed the company to reduce its deployment of staff (by up to 11% in work-hour requirements) and suggested how existing staff could be used more efficiently. ■

FIGURE 5.9 Graphical Representation of Western Set Covering Solution

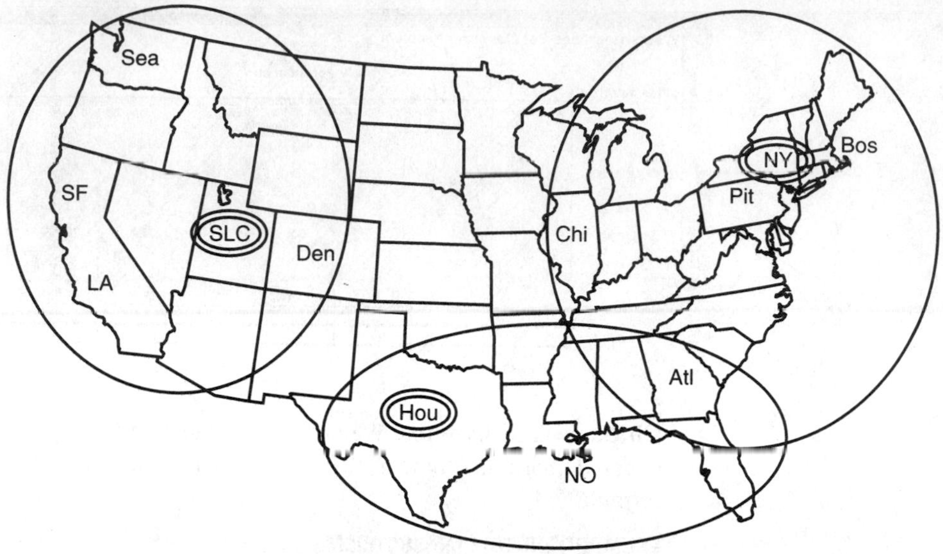

Locating Ambulances in Austin, Texas

Eaton et al. [7] used a set covering model to determine where emergency medical vehicles should be located in Austin, Texas. They determined the location of emergency medical facilities and vehicles that maximized (with a limited budget) the number of people receiving adequate emergency service. See Problem 48 for a scaled-down version of this model. The Eaton model is estimated to have saved Austin, Texas, over $10 million. ■

PROBLEMS

Skill-Building Problems

46 (Based on Walker [20]) The Smalltown Fire Department currently has seven conventional ladder companies and seven alarm boxes. The two closest ladder companies to each alarm box are listed in Table 5.53. The town council wants to maximize the number of conventional ladder companies that can be replaced with tower ladder companies. Unfortunately, political considerations dictate that a conventional company can be replaced only if, after replacement, at least one of the two closest companies to each alarm box is still a conventional company. Determine how to maximize the number of conventional companies that can be replaced by tower companies.

TABLE 5.53 Data for Fire Department Problem

	Two Closest Ladder Companies
Alarm Box 1	2, 3
Alarm Box 2	3, 4
Alarm Box 3	1, 5
Alarm Box 4	2, 6
Alarm Box 5	3, 6
Alarm Box 6	4, 7
Alarm Box 7	5, 7

47 At Blair General Hospital six types of surgical operations are performed. The types of operations each surgeon is qualified to perform (indicated by an X) are listed in Table 5.54. Suppose that surgeons 1 and 2 dislike each other and cannot be on duty at the same time. Determine the minimum number of surgeons required so that the hospital can perform all types of surgery.

TABLE 5.54 Data for Hospital Problem

	Operation Number					
	1	**2**	**3**	**4**	**5**	**6**
Surgeon 1	X	X		X		
Surgeon 2			X		X	X
Surgeon 3			X		X	
Surgeon 4	X					
Surgeon 5		X				
Surgeon 6				X	X	

Skill-Extending Problem

48 (Based on Eaton et al. [7]) Gotham City has been divided into eight districts. The time (in minutes) it takes an ambulance to travel from one district to another is shown in Table 5.55. The population of each district (in thousands) is as follows: district 1, 40; district 2, 30; district 3, 35; district 4, 20; district 5, 15; district 6, 50; district 7, 45; district 8, 60. Suppose Gotham City has n ambulance locations. Determine the locations of ambulances that maximize the number of people who live within two minutes of an ambulance. Do this separately for $n = 1$; $n = 2$; $n = 3$; $n = 4$. ■

TABLE 5.55 Travel Distances for Gotham City Problem

		To							
		1	**2**	**3**	**4**	**5**	**6**	**7**	**8**
	1	0	3	4	6	8	9	8	10
	2	3	0	5	4	8	6	12	9
	3	4	5	0	2	2	3	5	7
From	**4**	6	4	2	0	3	2	5	4
	5	8	8	2	3	0	2	2	4
	6	9	6	3	2	2	0	3	2
	7	8	12	5	5	2	3	0	2
	8	10	9	7	4	4	2	2	0

5.7 Either-Or Constraints

Consider a company that makes x units of a product, where x is a decision variable. It is possible that the company has only two options, due to economy-of-scale considerations. Either it produces no more than 100 units of the product, or it produces at least 1000 units of the product. This is a typical example of a problem with **either-or constraints**. The company's solution must satisfy either

$$x \leq 100$$

or

$$x \geq 1000$$

To generalize this situation, suppose we are given two functions f and g of the decision variables and we want to ensure that *at least one* of the following inequalities holds:

$$f \leq 0 \tag{5.6}$$

or

$$g \leq 0 \tag{5.7}$$

(We can always use less-than-or-equal-to constraints by multiplying through by -1 if necessary.) To ensure that at least one of these holds, we construct the following two constraints, where y is a 0-1 variable:

$$f \leq M_1 * y \tag{5.8}$$

$$g \leq M_2 * (1 - y) \tag{5.9}$$

In Inequality 5.8, M_1 is chosen large enough to ensure that $f \leq M_1$ always holds, while in Inequality 5.9, M_2 is chosen large enough to ensure that $g \leq M_2$ always holds. We now argue that if both 5.8 and 5.9 are satisfied, either 5.6 or 5.7 must be satisfied. Either $y = 0$ or $y = 1$. If $y = 0$, then 5.8 and 5.9 become $f \leq 0$ and $g \leq M_2$. Thus if $y = 0$, then 5.6 (and possibly 5.7) must be satisfied. Similarly, if $y = 1$, then 5.8 and 5.9 become $f \leq M_1$ and $g \leq 0$. Thus if $y = 1$, then 5.7 (and possibly 5.6) must be satisfied. Therefore, whether $y = 0$ or $y = 1$, 5.8 and 5.9 together ensure that at least one of (and possibly both) 5.6 and 5.7 is satisfied. The strategy, then, when faced with either-or constraints of the form 5.6 and 5.7 is to form constraints of the form 5.8 and 5.9 (by introducing a 0-1 variable) and require that both of these hold.

Here is an example of either-or constraints in action.

EXAMPLE 5.6

Dorian Auto is considering manufacturing three types of autos: compact, midsize, and large. The resources required and the profits yielded by each type of car are shown in Table 5.56. At present, 6000 tons of steel and 60,000 hours of labor are available. If any cars of a given type are produced, production of that type of car will be economically feasible only if at least 1000 cars of that type are produced. Dorian wants to find a production schedule that maximizes its profit.

TABLE 5.56 Data for Dorian Car Example

	Compact	Midsize	Large
Steel Required	1.5 tons	3 tons	5 tons
Labor Required	30 hours	25 hours	40 hours
Profit	$2000	$3000	$4000

Solution

The model for this example must keep track of the following:

- the number of each car type produced
- the labor hours and steel used
- the profit earned

Also, we must ensure that Dorian produces either 0 or at least 1000 cars of each type.

Developing the Spreadsheet Model The example can be modeled with the following steps. (See Figure 5.10 and the file DORIAN.XLS.)

1 **Inputs.** Begin by entering the input data. In the range B6:D8 enter the steel and hour requirements per car and the minimum production level for each type of car. In the range D20:D21 enter the amount available of each resource. In the range B11:D11 enter the unit profit for each type of car.

2 **Number of cars produced.** Enter *any* trial values for the number of cars of each type produced in the range B16:D16.

3 **Steel and labor used.** In cell B20 compute the tons of steel used with the formula

```
=SUMPRODUCT($B$16:$D$16,B6:D6)
```

Copy this formula to cell B21 to compute the labor hours used.

FIGURE 5.10 **Optimal Solution for Dorian Car Example**

	A	B	C	D	E
1	**Dorian Auto Production Problem with Either-Or Constraints**				
2					
3	**Data inputs**				
4			**Type of car**		
5		Compact	Midsize	Large	
6	Steel (tons)/unit	1.5	3	5	
7	Labor hours/unit	30	25	40	
8	Minimum production (if any)	1000	1000	1000	
9	Maximum production	2000	2000	1200	
10					
11	Profit/unit	$2,000	$3,000	$4,000	
12					
13	**Production plan**				
14			**Type of car**		
15		Compact	Midsize	Large	
16	Units produced	0	2000	0	
17	Produce at least minimum?	0	1	0	
18					
19	**Constraints on resources**	Used		Available	
20	Steel	6000	<=	6000	
21	Labor hours	50000	<=	60000	
22					
23					
24	**Logical constraints**				
25	First set	0	2000	0	
26		<=	<=	<=	
27		0	2000	0	
28					
29	Second set	1000	-1000	1000	
30		<=	<=	<=	
31		1000	0	1000	
32					
33	**Profit**	$6,000,000			

4 **Profit.** In cell B33 compute the profit earned with the formula

=SUMPRODUCT(B11:D11,B16:D16)

5 **Upper limits on cars produced.** We need to ensure that one of the following constraints holds:

$$\text{Compact cars produced} = 0 \tag{5.10}$$

or

$$\text{Compact cars produced} \geq \text{Minimum production level for compacts} \tag{5.11}$$

(Similar constraints hold for midsize cars and large cars.) Define the functions f and g by

$$f = \text{Compact cars produced}$$

and

$$g = \text{Minimum production level for compacts} - \text{Compact cars produced}$$

Then we can operationalize 5.10 and 5.11 by including the following two constraints:

$$\text{Compact cars produced} \leq (\text{Maximum compact production}) * y_c \tag{5.12}$$

and

$$\text{Minimum production level for compacts} - \text{Compacts produced} \leq (\text{Minimum production level for compacts}) * (1 - y_c) \tag{5.13}$$

Here y_c (c for compact) is the 0-1 variable that operationalizes the either-or constraint. Notice that the left-hand side of 5.12 is f and the left-hand side of 5.13 is g, so that these constraints are exactly like those in our general discussion of either-or constraints.

Before generating constraints 5.12 and 5.13 (and similar constraints for midsize cars and large cars), we must find the maximum production level (really an upper bound for production) for each type of car. One way to do so is as follows. Note that the number of compacts that can be produced cannot exceed (1) the available amount of steel divided by the amount of steel required per compact or (2) the available amount of labor divided by the amount of labor required per compact. In other words, the number of compacts produced cannot exceed the *smaller* of (1) and (2). So in cell B9 compute this upper bound on the number of compact cars that can be produced with the formula

=MIN($D$20/B6,$D$21/B7)

Then copy this formula to the range C9:D9 to compute similar upper bounds for midsize and large cars.

6 **0-1 values for car production.** Enter *any* trial values for the 0-1 variables for the either-or constraints in the range B17:D17. (For example, the value in cell B17 corresponds to y_c for compacts.) The 0-1 variable for any type of car will equal 1 if and only if that type of car is produced at a positive level.

7 **Ingredients for Inequality 5.12.** Enter the left-hand side of the constraint 5.12 in cell B25 with the formula

=B16

Copy this formula to the range C25:D25 to compute similar left-hand sides for midsize and large cars. Then enter the right-hand side of the constraint 5.12 in cell B27 with the formula

=B9*B17

and copy it to the range C27:D27 for midsize and large cars.

8 **Ingredients for Inequality 5.13.** Proceeding as in the previous step, enter the left-hand side of 5.13 in cell B29 with the formula

=B8–B16

and copy it to the range C29:D29. Then enter the right-hand side of 5.13 in cell B31 with the formula

=B8*(1–B17)

and copy it to the range C31:D31.

Using the Solver

1 **Objective.** Choose cell B33 (total profit) as the objective to maximize.

2 **Changing cells.** Choose the ranges B16:D17 (production levels and 0-1 variables for either-or constraints) as the changing cells.

3 **0-1 constraints.** Constrain the range B17:D17 to be 0-1 variables.

4 **Nonnegative integer constraints on cars produced.** Constrain the range B16:D16 to be general (not necessarily 0-1) nonnegative integer variables.

5 **Resource availability constraints.** Add the constraints B20:B21<=D20:D21. These ensure that Dorian does not exceed its resource limitations.

6 **Logical constraints in Inequality 5.12.** Add the constraints B25:D25<=B27:D27. These operationalize Inequality 5.12 (and similar inequalities for midsize and large cars).

7 **Logical constraints in Inequality 5.13.** Add the constraints B29:D29<=B31:D31. These operationalize Inequality 5.13 (and similar inequalities for midsize and large cars).

8 **Linear model and optimize.** Check the Assume Linear Model box and Solve.

The optimal solution is shown in Figure 5.10. It implies that Dorian should make 2000 midsize cars and no large or compact cars. The profit from this strategy is $6 million.

This is possibly the trickiest formulation we have seen so far, so we'll go over the logic once more, with reference to Figure 5.10. First, each maximum production level in row 9 represents the most Dorian could make of a type of car if *all* of its labor and steel resources were used for that single type of car. The first group of logical constraints, in rows 25–27, refers to these maximum limits on production. If the 0-1 variable for a car type in row 17 is 0, then the constraint in rows 25–27 simply states that this type of car won't be produced at all. But if the 0-1 variable is 1, then the constraint limits production by the maximum limit on production, which is essentially a redundant constraint.

Now consider the second group of logical constraints, in rows 29–31. If the 0-1 variable in row 17 for a car type is 0, then the constraint in rows 29–31 is essentially redundant. For example, for compact cars it is B8–B16<=B8*(1–0), which is equivalent to B16>=0, a nonnegativity constraint on production. However, if the 0-1 variable in row 17 is 1, then the constraint in rows 29–31 is equivalent to requiring the minimum level of production specified in row 8. For example, for midsize cars it is C8–C16<=C8*(1–1), or C16>=C8.

In short, whichever value a 0-1 variable has, it forces an appropriate constraint and a redundant constraint on that type of car. The optimal solution reflects this. The 0-1 variables for compact and large cars are 0, forcing zero production of these types. However, the 0-1 variable for midsize cars is 1, requiring production to be at least 1000. Actually, a production level of 2000 midsize cars turns out to be optimal. Once Dorian decides to produce only midsize cars, it might as well make as many as its labor hours and steel allow. ■

PROBLEMS

Skill-Building Problems

49 State University must purchase 1100 computers from three vendors. Vendor 1 charges $500 per computer plus a total delivery charge of $5000. Vendor 2 charges $350 per computer plus a total delivery charge of $4000. Vendor 3 charges $250 per computer plus a total delivery charge of $6000. Vendor 1 will sell the university at most 500 computers, vendor 2, at most 900, and vendor 3, at most 400. The minimum order from a vendor is 200 computers. Determine how to minimize the cost of purchasing the needed computers.

50 Eastinghouse ships 12,000 capacitors per month to its customers. The capacitors can be produced at three different plants. The production capacity, fixed monthly cost of operation, and variable cost of producing a capacitor at each plant are given in Table 5.57. The fixed cost for a plant is incurred only if the plant is used to make any capacitors. If a plant is used at all, at least 3000 capacitors per month must be produced at the plant. Determine how to minimize the company's monthly costs of meeting its customers' demands. ■

TABLE 5.57 **Data for Eastinghouse Problem**

	Fixed Cost	Variable Cost	Production Capacity
Plant 1	$80,000	$20	6000
Plant 2	$40,000	$25	7000
Plant 3	$30,000	$30	6000

5.8 Conclusion

Three important points emerge from this chapter. First, a wide variety of important problems can be modeled as IP problems. These can generally be identified as problems where at least some of the "activities" (such as producing at a particular plant, locating a lockbox at a particular city, making a particular investment, and so on) must either be done or not done; there is no in between. Regular LP cannot be used for these problems; they must be modeled as IP problems.

The second point is that many important IP models are not simply LP models with integer constraints on the variables, such as a constraint that the number of refrigerators produced must be an integer. There are certainly IP examples of this type, where fractional values of the decision variables make no physical sense, but they can generally be solved by solving the associated LP problem and then rounding the solution to integer values. While there is no guarantee that the rounded solution will be optimal, it is often close to optimal. In contrast, the problems discussed in this chapter introduce 0-1 decision variables that specify whether an activity is done or not. Using these 0-1 variables, the problem can then be modeled with linear constraints. However, if the resulting model is solved as an LP problem, *without* the integer constraints on the 0-1 variables, it is generally very difficult to round the fractional values of the 0-1 variables appropriately. Therefore, problems with 0-1 variables require a different solution approach than LP problems.

Third, the solution approach required for IP problems, especially those with 0-1 variables, is inherently more difficult than the simplex method for LP problems. The relatively small examples in this chapter may have given the impression that a spreadsheet Solver can handle IP models just as easily as it handles LP models, but this is definitely not the case. If you continue to solve IP problems with a spreadsheet Solver, you will eventually run into a problem that the Solver is simply unable to solve, at least not in a reasonable amount of time. In fact, even with the most sophisticated IP computer codes on the most powerful computers, there are IP problems—from real applications—that continue to defy solution.

REVIEW PROBLEMS

Skill-Building Problems

51 (Based on Ellis and Corn [9]) The Transylvania Olympic Gymnastics Team consists of six people. Transylvania must choose three people to enter both the balance beam and floor exercises. They must also enter a total of four people in each event. The score that each individual gymnast can attain in each event is shown in Table 5.58. Determine how to maximize the total score attained by the Transylvania gymnasts.

TABLE 5.58 **Data for Gymnastics Problem**

	Balance Beam	Floor Exercise
Gymnast 1	8.8	7.9
Gymnast 2	9.4	8.3
Gymnast 3	9.2	8.5
Gymnast 4	7.5	8.7
Gymnast 5	8.7	8.1
Gymnast 6	9.1	8.6

52 (Based on Liggett [12]) A court decision has stated that the enrollment of each high school in Metropolis must be at least 20% black. The numbers of black and white high school students in each of the city's five school districts are shown in Table 5.59. The distance (in miles) that a student in each district must travel to each high school is shown in Table 5.60. School board policy requires that all students in a given district must attend the same school. Assuming that each school must have an enrollment of at least 150 students, determine how to minimize the total distance that Metropolis students must travel to high school.

53 Esperantia has coins with the following monetary values: 1¢, 5¢, 10¢, 20¢, 25¢, and 50¢. You work at the Two-Twelve Convenience Store and must give a customer 91¢ in change. Determine how to minimize the number of coins needed to give the correct change.

TABLE 5.59 **Students in Districts for School Problem**

	Whites	Blacks
District 1	80	30
District 2	70	5
District 3	90	10
District 4	50	40
District 5	60	30

TABLE 5.60 Distances for School Problem

	High School 1	High School 2
District 1	1.0	2.0
District 2	0.5	1.7
District 3	0.8	0.8
District 4	1.3	0.4
District 5	1.5	0.6

54 (Based on Westerberg, Bjorklund, and Hultman [21]) Newcor's steel mill has received an order for 25 tons of steel. The steel must be 5% carbon and 5% molybdenum by weight. The steel is manufactured by combining three types of metal: steel ingots, scrap steel, and alloys. Four individual steel ingots are available. At most, one of each can be purchased. The weight (in tons), cost per ton, and the carbon and molybdenum content of each ingot are given in Table 5.61. Three types of alloys can be purchased. The cost per ton and chemical makeup of each alloy are given in Table 5.62. Steel scrap can be purchased at a cost of $100 per ton. Steel scrap contains 3% carbon and 9% molybdenum. Determine how Newcor can minimize the cost of filling its order.

TABLE 5.61 Ingot Data for Newcor Problem

	Weight	Cost per Ton	Carbon %	Molybdenum %
Ingot 1	5	$350	5	3
Ingot 2	3	$330	4	3
Ingot 3	4	$310	5	4
Ingot 4	6	$280	3	4

TABLE 5.62 Alloy Data for Newcor Problem

	Cost per Ton	Carbon %	Molybdenum %
Alloy 1	$500	8	6
Alloy 2	$450	7	7
Alloy 3	$400	6	8

55 (Based on Boykin [3]) Monsanto annually produces 359 million pounds of the chemical maleic anhydride. A total of four reactors are available to produce maleic anhydride. Each reactor can be run on one of three settings. The cost (in thousands of dollars) and pounds produced (in millions) annually for each reactor and each setting are given in Table 5.63. A reactor can only be run on one setting for the entire year. Determine how Monsanto can minimize the cost of meeting its annual demand for maleic anhydride.

TABLE 5.63 Data for Monsanto Problem

	Setting	Cost	Pounds
Reactor 1	1	50	80
	2	80	140
	3	100	170
Reactor 2	1	65	100
	2	90	140
	3	120	215
Reactor 3	1	70	112
	2	90	153
	3	110	195
Reactor 4	1	40	65
	2	60	105
	3	70	130

56 (Based on Zangwill [22]) Hallco runs a day shift and a night shift. Regardless of the number of units produced, the only production cost during a shift is a setup cost. It costs $8000 to run the day shift and $4500 to run the night shift. Demand for the next two days is as follows: day 1, 2000; night 1, 3000; day 2, 2000; night 2, 3000. It costs $1 per unit to hold a unit in inventory for a shift.

a Determine a production schedule that minimizes the sum of setup and inventory costs. All demand must be met on time. (*Note*: All shifts do not have to be run.)

b After listening to a seminar on the virtues of the Japanese theory of production, Hallco has cut its day shift setup cost to $1000 per shift and its night shift setup cost to $3500 per shift. Now determine a production schedule that minimizes the sum of setup and inventory costs. All demand must be met on time. Show that the decrease in setup costs has actually raised the average inventory level.

57 (Based on Fitzsimmons and Allen [10]) The State of Texas frequently audits companies doing business in Texas. Since these companies often have headquarters located outside the state, auditors must be sent to out-of-state locations. Each year, auditors must make 500 trips to cities in the Northeast, 400 trips to cities in the Midwest, 300 trips to cities in the West, and 400 trips to cities in the South. Texas is considering basing auditors in Chicago, New York, Atlanta, and Los Angeles. The annual cost of basing auditors in any city is $100,000. The cost of sending an auditor from any of these cities to a given region of the country is given in Table 5.64. Determine how to minimize the annual cost of conducting out-of-state audits.

TABLE 5.64 **Costs for Auditing Problem**

	Northeast	Midwest	West	South
New York	$1100	$1400	$1900	$1400
Chicago	$1200	$1000	$1500	$1200
Los Angeles	$1900	$1700	$1100	$1400
Atlanta	$1300	$1300	$1500	$1050

Skill-Extending Problems

58 Arthur Ross, Inc., must complete many corporate tax returns during the period February 15 to April 15. This year the company must begin and complete the five jobs shown in Table 5.65 during this eight-week period. Arthur Ross employs four full-time accountants who normally work 40 hours per week. If necessary, however, they can work up to 20 hours of overtime per week for which they are paid $100 per hour. Determine how Arthur Ross can minimize the overtime cost incurred in completing all jobs by April 15.

TABLE 5.65 **Data for Ross Accounting Problem**

	Duration (weeks)	Accountant Hours per Week
Job 1	3	120
Job 2	4	160
Job 3	3	80
Job 4	2	80
Job 5	4	100

59 (Based on Muckstadt and Wilson [14]) PSI believes it will need the amounts of generating capacity (in millions of kwh) shown in Table 5.66 during the next five years. The company has a choice of building (and then operating) power plants with the capacities (in millions of kwh) and costs (in millions of dollars) shown in Table 5.67. Determine how to minimize the total cost of meeting PSI's generating capacity requirements for the next five years.

TABLE 5.66 Generating Capacities for PSI Problem

	Generating Capacity
Year 1	80
Year 2	100
Year 3	120
Year 4	140
Year 5	160

TABLE 5.67 Plant Data for PSI Problem

	Generating Capacity	Construction Cost	Annual Operating Cost
Plant 1	70	\$20	\$1.5
Plant 2	50	\$16	\$0.8
Plant 3	60	\$18	\$1.3
Plant 4	40	\$14	\$0.6

60 Houseco Developers is considering erecting three office buildings. The time (in years) required to complete each of them and the number of workers required to be on the job at all times are shown in Table 5.68. Once a building is completed, it brings in the following amount of rent per year: building 1, \$50,000; building 2, \$30,000; building 3, \$40,000. Houseco faces the following constraints:

- During each year 60 workers are available.
- At most one building can be started during any year.
- Building 2 must be completed by the end of year 4.

Determine the maximum total rent that can be earned by Houseco by the end of year 4.

TABLE 5.68 Data for Houseco Problem

	Project Duration	Workers Required
Building 1	2	30
Building 2	2	20
Building 3	3	20

61 Four trucks are available to deliver milk to five grocery stores. The capacity and daily operating cost of each truck are shown in Table 5.69. The demand of each grocery store can be supplied by only one truck, but a truck can deliver to more than one grocery. The daily demands of each grocery are as follows: grocery 1, 100 gallons; grocery 2, 200 gallons; grocery 3, 300 gallons; grocery 4, 500 gallons; grocery 5, 800 gallons. Determine how to minimize the daily cost of meeting the demands of the four groceries.

62 A county is going to build two hospitals. There are nine cities in which the hospitals can be built. The number of hospital visits per year made by people in each city and the x-y coordinates of each city are listed in Table 5.70. The county's goal is to minimize the total distance that patients must travel to hospitals. Where should it locate the hospitals? (*Hint*: You will need to determine the distance between each pair of cities. An easy way to do this is with lookup tables.)

Modeling Problems

63 We have assumed that there is a fixed annual cost of running a lockbox operation that does not depend on the size of the operation. Can you improve on this assumption?

64 (This problem and the next three refer to the Huntco example in Section 5.5.) Huntco Foods produces hundreds of products. Modeling the shipment of each of these products would result in an IP that no computer could solve exactly. How might you deal with this problem?

TABLE 5.69 Data for Milk Delivery Problem

	Capacity (gallons)	Daily Operating Cost
Truck 1	400	$45
Truck 2	500	$50
Truck 3	600	$55
Truck 4	1100	$60

TABLE 5.70 Data for Hospital Problem

	x	y	Hospital Visits per Year
City 1	0	0	3000
City 2	10	3	4000
City 3	12	15	5000
City 4	14	13	6000
City 5	16	9	4000
City 6	18	6	3000
City 7	8	12	2000
City 8	6	10	4000
City 9	4	8	1200

65 Huntco Foods has thousands of customers. Modeling the shipment to each customer would result in an IP that no computer could solve exactly. How might you deal with this problem?

66 Why do you think that Huntco insisted on each customer being serviced from a single distribution center?

67 Describe how you might estimate the fixed annual cost and variable shipping costs needed for the Huntco model. How would quantity discounts for large shipments influence your model?

68 Suppose that you want to divide a state containing 12 cities into five congressional districts. How might you use IP to assign cities to districts?

69 (Based on Geoffrion and Graves [11]) Huntco Foods produces tomato sauce at three plants. The plants are located in Los Angeles, New York, and St. Louis. The annual production capacity (in millions of pounds) of each plant is shown in Table 5.71. The variable cost of producing a pound of tomato sauce at any plant is 30¢ per pound.

TABLE 5.71 Production Capacities for Huntco Problem

Plant	Production Capacity
New York	9
Los Angeles	7
St. Louis	8

Tomato sauce can be stored at one of five potential warehouse sites. The potential warehouse sites are located in Philadelphia, Chicago, Atlanta, Indianapolis, and Kansas City. For it to be economical to use a warehouse, between 4.8 million and 10 million pounds of tomato sauce per year must be shipped through the warehouse. If a warehouse site is not used, it incurs no cost. To get some idea of the annual cost of operating a warehouse, Huntco has tabulated in the file HUNTDAT.XLS the annual cost of operating warehouses and the total amount of sauce shipped through the warehouse during a given year.

Huntco ships tomato sauce to six distributors. For administrative reasons, each distributor must receive all its sauce from a single warehouse. Each distributor receives two shipments per month of tomato sauce, and the annual amount of tomato sauce required by each distributor is shown in Table 5.72. You may assume that monthly demand for tomato sauce at each site is relatively constant.

TABLE 5.72 Annual Requirements for Huntco Problem

	Location	Annual Requirements (millions of pounds)
Distributor 1	Boston	2.0
Distributor 2	Memphis	2.5
Distributor 3	Detroit	4.0
Distributor 4	Denver	2.0
Distributor 5	Dallas	3.5
Distributor 6	San Francisco	5.0

The cost per pound of shipping tomato sauce depends on the distance the sauce is shipped. In order to relate the cost of shipping to the distance shipped, you may use the data in file HUNTDAT.XLS, which lists for the various shipments the weight of the shipment, the distance shipped, and the cost of the shipment.

The distance between each plant and potential warehouse site is shown in Table 5.73, and the distance between each warehouse and each distributor is shown in Table 5.74. (All distances are in miles.)

Determine how Huntco can minimize the annual total cost of getting tomato sauce from the plants to the customers.

TABLE 5.73 Distances Between Plants and Warehouses

	Philadelphia	Chicago	Atlanta	Indianapolis	Kansas City
New York	100	802	841	713	1189
Los Angeles	2706	2054	2182	2073	1589
St. Louis	868	289	541	235	257

TABLE 5.74 Distances Between Warehouses and Distributors

	Boston	Memphis	Detroit	Denver	Dallas	San Francisco
Philadelphia	296	1000	576	1691	1452	2866
Chicago	963	530	266	996	917	2142
Atlanta	1037	371	699	1398	795	2496
Indianapolis	906	435	278	1058	865	2256
Kansas City	1391	451	743	600	489	1835

70 The Wanderers Insurance Company has hired you to determine the number of sales divisions into which the country should be divided. Each division will need a president, vice president, and a divisional staff. The time needed to call on a client will depend on the distance of the salesperson from the client. Discuss how you would determine the optimal number of sales divisions and the allocation of the company's salesforce to the various divisions.

71 Ten different types of brownies are sold. You are thinking of developing a new brownie for sale. Brownies are rated on the basis of five qualities: price, chocolateness, chewiness, sweetness, and ease of preparation. You want to group the ten brownies on the market into three clusters. Each cluster should contain brownies that are relatively similar.

a Why would this be useful to you?

b How would you do it?

72 Telco, a national telemarketing firm, usually picks a number of sites around the country from which to make its calls. As a service, AD&D's telecommunication marketing department wants to help Telco choose the number and location of its sites. How can integer programming be used to approach this problem? ■

CASE STUDY

Giant Motor Company I

Preface

This problem deals with strategic planning issues for a large company. The main issue is planning the company's production capacity for the coming year. At issue is the overall level of capacity and the type of capacity—for example, the degree of *flexibility* in the manufacturing system. The main tool used to aid the company's planning process in GMC I is a mixed integer programming (MIP) model. A *mixed* integer program has both integer and continuous variables. A continuation of this problem, GMC II (at the end of Chapter 8), deals with capacity planning in a multiperiod, multiscenario framework. In GMC II the MIP model is extended to handle the multiperiod stochastic nature of the problem.

Problem Statement

The Giant Motor Company (GMC) produces three lines of cars for the domestic (U.S.) market: Lyras, Libras, and Hydras. The Lyra is a relatively inexpensive subcompact car that appeals mainly to first-time car owners and to households using it as a second car for commuting. The Libra is a sporty compact car that is sleeker, faster, and roomier than the Lyra. Without any options, the Libra costs slightly more than the Lyra; additional options increase the price further. The Hydra is the luxury car of the GMC line. It is significantly more expensive than the Lyra and Libra, and it has the highest profit margin of the three cars.

Retooling Options for Capacity Expansion

Currently GMC has three manufacturing plants in the U.S. Each plant is dedicated to producing a single line of cars. In its planning for the coming year, GMC is considering the retooling of its Lyra and/or Libra plants. Retooling either plant would represent a major expense for the company. The retooled plants would have significantly increased production capacities. Although having greater *fixed* costs, the retooled plants would be more efficient and have lower *marginal* production costs—that is, higher *marginal* profit contributions. In addition, the retooled plants would be *flexible*—they would have the capability of producing more than one line of cars.

The characteristics of the current plants and the retooled plants is given in Table 5.75. The retooled Lyra and Libra plants are prefaced by the word *new*. The fixed costs and capacities in Table 5.75 are given on an annual basis. A dash in the profit margin section indicates that the plant cannot manufacture that line of car. For example, the new Lyra plant would be capable of producing both Lyras and Libras but not Hydras. The new Libra plant would be capable of producing any of the three lines of cars. Note, however, that the new Libra plant has a slightly lower profit margin for producing Hydras than the Hydra plant. The flexible new Libra plant is capable of producing the luxury Hydra model but is not quite as efficient as the current Hydra plant that is dedicated to Hydra production.

The fixed costs are annual costs that are incurred by GMC independent of the number of cars that are produced by the plant. For the current plant configurations, the fixed costs include property taxes, insurance, payments on the loan that was taken out to construct the plant, and so on. If a plant is retooled, the fixed costs will include the previous fixed costs plus the additional cost of the renovation. The additional renovation cost will be an annual cost representing the cost of the renovation amortized over a long period.

Demand for GMC Cars

Short-term demand forecasts have been very reliable in the past and are expected to be reliable in the future. Longer-term forecasts are not so accurate; this complication will be considered in GMC II. The demand for GMC cars for the coming year is given in Table 5.76.

TABLE 5.75 Plant Characteristics

	Lyra	Libra	Hydra	New Lyra	New Libra
Capacity (in 1000s)	1000	800	900	1600	1800
Fixed Cost (in $millions)	2000	2000	2600	3400	3700
			Profit Margin by Car Line (in $1000s)		
Lyra	2	—	—	2.5	2.3
Libra	—	3	—	3.0	3.5
Hydra	—	—	5	—	4.8

TABLE 5.76 Demand for GMC Cars

	Demand (in 1000s)
Lyra	1400
Libra	1100
Hydra	800

A quick comparison of plant capacities and demands in Tables 5.75 and 5.76 indicates that GMC is faced with insufficient capacity. Partially offsetting the lack of capacity is the phenomenon of **demand diversion**. If a potential car buyer walks into a GMC dealer showroom wanting to buy a Lyra but the dealer is out of stock, frequently the salesperson can convince the customer to purchase the better Libra car, which is in stock. Unsatisfied demand for the Lyra is said to be *diverted* to the Libra. Only rarely in this situation can the salesperson convince the customer to switch to the luxury Hydra model.

From past experience GMC estimates that 30% of unsatisfied demand for Lyras is diverted to demand for Libras and 5% to demand for Hydras. Similarly, 10% of unsatisfied demand for Libras is diverted to demand for Hydras. For example, if the demand for Lyras is 1,400,000 cars, then the unsatisfied demand will be 400,000 if no capacity is added. Out of this unsatisfied demand, 120,000 ($= 400{,}000 \times .3$) will materialize as demand for Libras, and 20,000 ($= 400{,}000 \times .05$) will materialize as demand for Hydras. Similarly, if the demand for Libras is 1,220,000 cars (1,100,000 original demand plus 120,000 demand diverted from Lyras), then the unsatisfied demand for Lyras would be 420,000 if no capacity is added. Out of this unsatisfied demand, 42,000 ($= 420{,}000 \times .1$) will materialize as demand for Hydras. All other unsatisfied demand is lost to competitors. The pattern of demand diversion is summarized in Table 5.77.

Question

GMC wants to decide whether or not to retool the Lyra and Libra plants. In addition, GMC wants to determine its production plan at each plant in the coming year. Based on the previous data, formulate a mixed integer programming model for solving GMC's production planning–capacity expansion problem for the coming year. ■

Acknowledgment: The idea for GMC I and II came from Eppen, Martin, and Schrage. "A Scenario Approach to Capacity Planning." *Operations Research* 37, no. 4 (July–August 1989): 517–27.

TABLE 5.77 Demand Diversion Matrix

	Lyra	Libra	Hydra
Lyra	NA	0.3	.05
Libra	0	NA	.10
Hydra	0	0.0	NA

REFERENCES

1 Bean, J., C. Noon, S. Ryan, and G. Salton. "Selecting Tenants in a Shopping Mall." *Interfaces* 18, no. 2 (1988): 1–10.

2 Bean, J., C. Noon, and G. Salton. "Asset Divestiture at Homart Development Company." *Interfaces* 17, no. 1 (1987): 48–65.

3 Boykin, R. "Optimizing Chemical Production at Monsanto." *Interfaces* 15, no. 1 (1985): 88–95.

4 Brown, G., et al. "Real-Time Wide Area Dispatch of Mobil Tank Trucks." *Interfaces* 17, no. 1 (1987): 107–20.

5 Calloway, R., M. Cummins, and J. Freeland. "Solving Spreadsheet-Based Integer Programming Models: An Example from International Telecommunications." *Decision Sciences* 21 (1990): 808–24.

6 Dijkstra, M., L. Kroon, M. Salomon, J. van Nunen, and L. Wassenhove. "Planning the Size and Organization of KLM's Aircraft Maintenance Personnel." *Interfaces* 24, no. 6 (1994): 47–65.

7 Eaton, D., et al. "Determining Emergency Medical Service Vehicle Deployment in Austin, Texas." *Interfaces* 15, no. 1 (1985): 96–108.

8 Efroymson, M., and T. Ray. "A Brand-Bound Algorithm for Plant Location." *Operations Research* 14 (1966): 361–68.

9 Ellis, P., and R. Corn. "Using Bivalent Integer Programming to Select Teams for Intercollegiate Women's Gymnastics Competition." *Interfaces* 14, no. 3 (1984): 41–46.

10 Fitzsimmons, J., and L. Allen. "A Warehouse Location Model Helps Texas Comptroller Select Out-of-State Audit Offices." *Interfaces* 13, no. 5 (1983): 40–46.

11 Geoffrion, A., and G. Graves. "Better Distribution Planning with Computer Models." *Harvard Business Review* (July–August 1976).

12 Liggett, R. "The Application of an Implicit Enumeration Algorithm to the School Desegregation Problem." *Management Science* 20 (1973): 159–68.

13 Morton, T. "Planning Horizons for Dynamic Programming." *Operations Research* 27 (1979): 730–43.

14 Muckstadt, J., and R. Wilson. "An Application of Mixed Integer Programming Duality to Scheduling Thermal Generating Systems." *IEEE Transactions on Power Apparatus and Systems* (1968): 1968–78.

15 Robinson, P., L. Gao, and S. Muggenborg. "Designing an Integrated Distribution System at DowBrands, Inc." *Interfaces* 23, no. 3 (1993): 107–17.

16 Salkin, H., and C. Lin. "Aggregation of Subsidiary Firms for Minimal Unemployment Compensation Payments via Integer Programming." *Management Science* 25 (1979): 405–8.

17 Schindler, S., and T. Semmel. "Station Staffing at Pan American World Airways." *Interfaces* 23, no. 3 (1993): 91–106.

18 Shanker, R., and A. Zoltners. "The Corporate Payments Problem." *Journal of Bank Research* (1972): 47–53.

19 Strong, R. "LP Solves Problem: Eases Duration Matching Process." *Pension and Investment Age* 17, no. 26 (1989): 21.

20 Walker, W. "Using the Set Covering Problem to Assign Fire Companies to Firehouses." *Operations Research* 22 (1974): 275–77.

21 Westerberg, C., B. Bjorklund, and E. Hultman. "An Application of Mixed Integer Programming in a Swedish Steel Mill." *Interfaces* 7, no. 2 (1977): 39–43.

22 Zangwill, W. "The Limits of Japanese Production Theory." *Interfaces* 22, no. 5 (1992): 14–25.

CHAPTER

6

Nonlinear Programming Models

Management Science Success Stories

Since the 1950s oil companies have been among the most dedicated users of management science methods, particularly mathematical programming models. They often run optimization models on a daily basis and consider them absolutely indispensable to their operations. DeWitt et al. [4] describe one company's experiences in the article "OMEGA: An Improved Gasoline Blending System for Texaco." Texaco began using computerized blending models in many of its refineries in the 1960s. By the early 1980s, however, the company realized that these models were not being used routinely by all of its refineries, partly because the optimization routines themselves did not always work correctly. Therefore, a fresh analysis began and culminated in OMEGA, a decision support system that combines data acquisition with nonlinear optimization and presents the blending technicians at Texaco's refineries with graphical descriptions of the results. Texaco estimates (somewhat conservatively) that OMEGA has increased profits up to 30%, which translates to more than $30 million annually.

Generally, Texaco develops aggregated plans at a fairly broad level for medium-range decisions. For example, it creates a monthly operating plan for the entire downstream operation of a regional subdivision of the company. At this broad level of planning, the company makes enough simplifying assumptions to permit the use of linear programming for the blending portion of the model. However, for the short-term day-to-day scheduling of blending at the refineries, linear programming is unable to capture the complex chemical relationships between inputs and outputs. Therefore a nonlinear model is required.

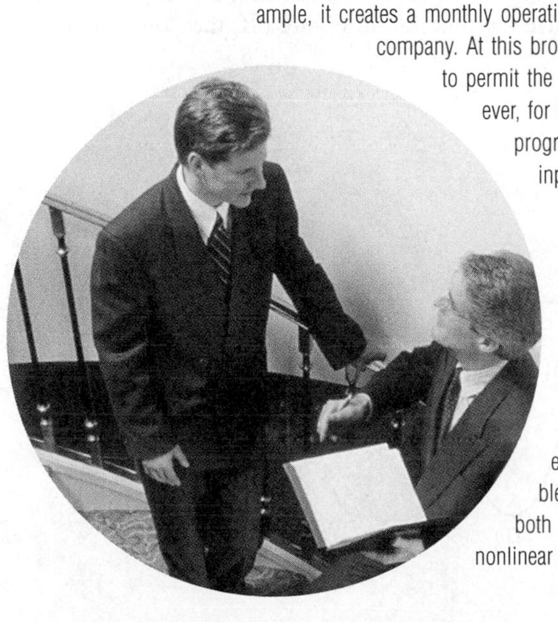

The cause of the complexity of the problem is that Texaco uses various grades of crude oil, refines them into intermediate stocks with particular chemical properties, and finally blends these stocks into required blends of gasoline (such as the regular unleaded and super unleaded we buy at the gas station). Sometimes as many as 15 stocks are used to blend up to eight blends. The qualities of the blends are determined by the qualities of the stocks. Typical stock qualities include percentage of sulfur, octane indices, percentage of aromatics, lead content, and others. There are a number of equations that translate these stock qualities into blend qualities. Of particular importance are blend volatilities and octanes, both of which are related to input stock qualities by *nonlinear* equations. These nonlinear equations require Texaco to employ nonlinear programming. The resulting nonlinear models must take into account constraints on the availabilities of the stocks, the technical requirements on the various blends (such as the maximum percentage of lead allowed), and market considerations. The nonlinear optimizer within OMEGA has been able to perform the optimization quickly and accurately, with the performance results noted earlier.

An interesting aspect of the DeWitt article is its discussion of Texaco's experience with nonlinear optimizers. Until OMEGA, Texaco used a nonlinear optimization package that gave rather inconsistent results. Not only was it very slow, but it sometimes failed to provide *any* feasible solution to the problem, and it sometimes stopped at *different* solutions, depending on which initial solution was used. (Based on your experience with Excel's Solver in previous chapters, imagine how you would feel if you and your classmates all used the same spreadsheet model but all got different answers because of different initial trial values. You wouldn't have much faith in the Solver!) This was simply the state of the art at the time—nonlinear optimizers were far from perfect. Fortunately, advances have been made, and the nonlinear optimizer currently used by OMEGA does not seem to suffer from these early problems. ■

6.1 Introduction

In many complex optimization problems the objective function and/or the constraints are not linear functions of the decision variables. Such an optimization problem is called a **nonlinear programming problem** (NLP). In this chapter we will discuss how to use a spreadsheet Solver to find optimal solutions to NLPs. We will discuss many interesting applications, including the important portfolio optimization model.

6.2 Basic Ideas of Nonlinear Optimization

When we solve an LP problem with a spreadsheet Solver, we can guarantee that the solution obtained by the computer is an optimal solution. When we solve an NLP problem, however, it is very possible that the spreadsheet Solver will obtain the wrong answer. For example, if we use a Solver to maximize the function in Figure 6.1, the Solver may have

FIGURE 6.1 **Function with Local Maxima and Minima**

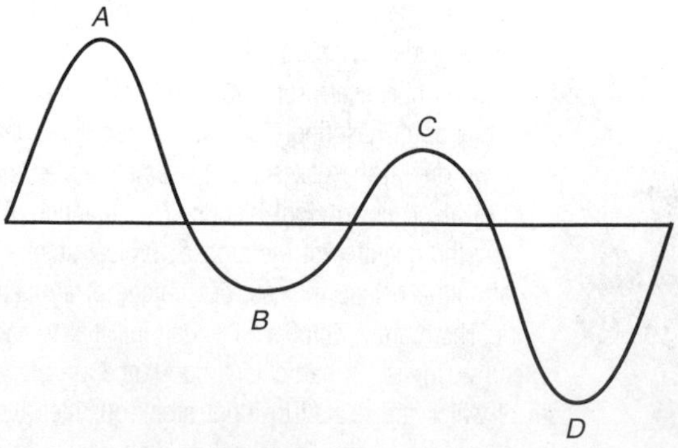

difficulty. For the function graphed in this figure, points A and C are called **local maxima** because the function is larger at A and C than at nearby points. However, only point A actually maximizes the function; it is called the **global maximum**. The problem is that a spreadsheet Solver might get "stuck" near point C, concluding that C maximizes the function, and not find point A. Similarly, points B and D are **local minima** because the function has a lower value at B and D than at nearby points. However, only point D is a **global minimum**. If you ask a spreadsheet Solver to minimize this function, it might conclude—incorrectly—that point B is optimal.

Convex and Concave Functions

Fortunately, there are certain types of NLPs that a spreadsheet Solver will solve correctly. To describe these NLPs, we need to define **convex** and **concave** functions. A function of one variable is *convex* in a region if its slope (rate of change) in that region is always nondecreasing. Equivalently, a function of one variable is convex if a line drawn connecting two points on the function never lies below the function.[1] See Figures 6.2 and 6.3 for two examples of convex functions. In Figure 6.2 the function first decreases and then increases, but the slope is always increasing, first becoming less and less negative and then becoming more and more positive. In contrast, the function in Figure 6.3 is always decreasing, but again the slope is constantly increasing—it is becoming less and less negative.

The following are examples of convex functions:

$$y = cx^a, \text{ where } a \geq 1, c \geq 0, \text{ and } x \geq 0$$

$$y = ce^x, \text{ where } c \geq 0$$

Similarly, a function of one variable is *concave* in a region if its slope is always nonincreasing. Equivalently, a function of one variable is concave if a line drawn connecting two points on the function never lies above the function. See Figures 6.4 and 6.5 for examples of concave functions. The first has a global maximum and the second is increasing, but the slopes of both are constantly decreasing.

FIGURE 6.2 **A Convex Function with a Global Minimum**

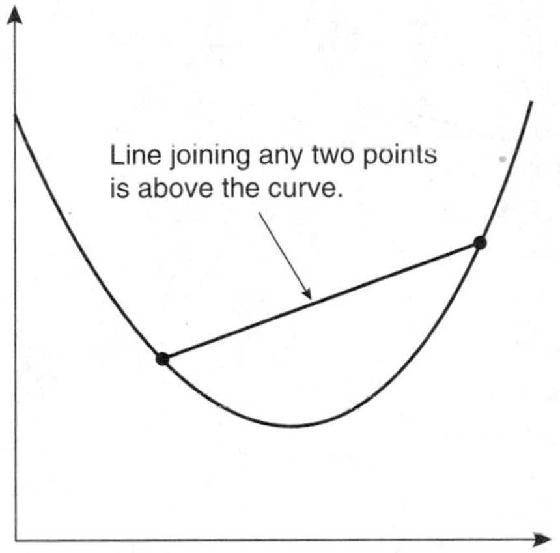

[1]For functions of several variables, the precise definition of convexity is more difficult to state. However, the geometric idea of convexity we give here will suffice for this book.

FIGURE 6.3 **A Decreasing Convex Function**

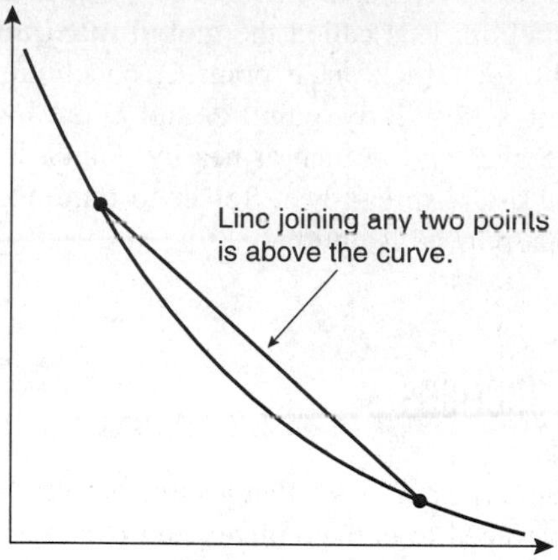

FIGURE 6.4 **A Concave Function with a Global Maximum**

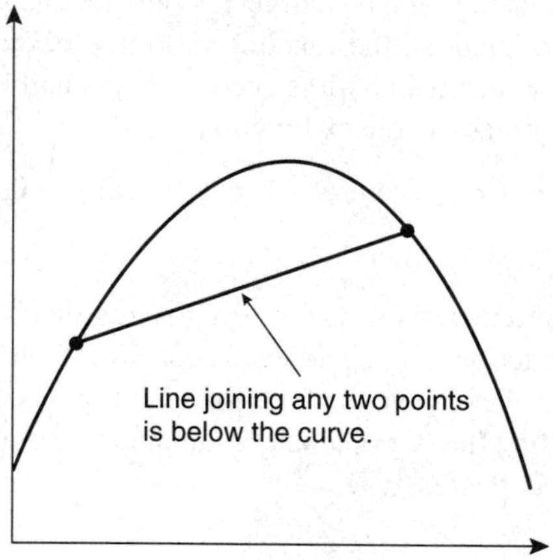

FIGURE 6.5 **An Increasing Concave Function**

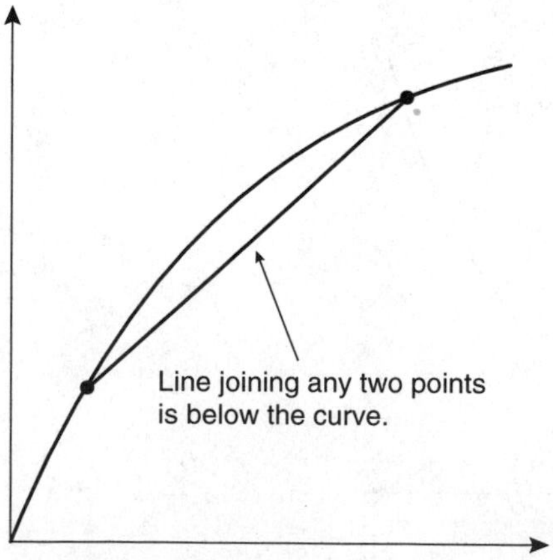

The following are examples of concave functions:

$$y = c \ln x, \quad \text{where } c \geq 0 \text{ and } x > 0$$

$$y = cx^a, \quad \text{where } 0 < a \leq 1,\ c \geq 0, \text{ and } x \geq 0$$

A linear function ($y = ax + b$) is both convex and concave. This is because the slope of a linear function is a constant.

Another, possibly more intuitive way to think about convex and concave functions is as follows. Imagine that you are walking up a hill. If you're on a stretch where the hill keeps getting steeper every step you take, you're on the convex part of the hill. If it keeps getting less steep, then you're on the concave part of the hill. Alternatively, if you are walking down a hill and it is getting less steep with every step you take, you're on the convex part of the hill; if it's getting more steep, you're on the concave part. In either case (walking uphill or downhill), if the steepness is not changing, you're on the linear part of the hill, which means it is both convex and concave.

It can be shown that the sum of convex functions is convex and the sum of concave functions is concave. Also, if you multiply any convex function by a positive constant, the result is still convex, and if you multiply any concave function by a positive constant, the result is still concave. However, if you multiply a convex function by a negative constant, the result is concave, and if you multiply a concave function by a negative constant, the result is convex.

Problems That Solvers Always Solve Correctly

As Figure 6.2 suggests, a Solver will perform well for a minimization problem if the objective function is convex. This is because convex functions can't have any local minima that aren't global minima. Similarly, Figure 6.4 suggests that a Solver will perform well for a maximization problem if the objective function is concave. These statements can be generalized to the situation where there are many decision variables (x's) and constraints. In fact, the following conditions imply that a Solver is guaranteed to find the global minimum or global maximum if it exists. (There are actually more general conditions than these, but the conditions stated here will suffice.)[2]

- **Conditions for Maximization Problems** A Solver is guaranteed to find the global maximum (if it exists) if

  1. the objective function is concave or the logarithm of the objective function is concave
  2. the constraints are linear

- **Conditions for Minimization Problems** A Solver is guaranteed to find the global minimum (if it exists) if

  1. the objective function is convex
  2. the constraints are linear

Therefore, if the constraints are linear, we need only check for the appropriate concavity or convexity of the objective function to assure that the Solver will find the optimal solution (as opposed to a local but nonglobal optimum).

[2]The following discussion assumes that your spreadsheet contains no IF, MAX, MIN, or ABS statements that depend on changing cells. The current generation of spreadsheet Solvers are not equipped to deal with these functions, and errors often occur if they are present.

When the Assumptions Do Not Hold There are many problems for which the above conditions do not hold or cannot be verified. Since we are then not sure whether the Solver's solution is the correct solution, the best strategy is to try several possible starting values for the changing cells, use the Solver with each of these, and take the best solution the Solver finds.

For example, consider the following NLP:

$$\max\ (x-1)(x-2)(x-3)(x-4)(x-5) \qquad \textbf{(6.1)}$$

$$\text{subject to } x \geq 1 \text{ and } x \leq 5$$

This is the function shown in Figure 6.1, where the graph extends from $x = 1$ to $x = 5$. Obviously, this function equals 0 when x equals 1, 2, 3, 4, or 5. (Just substitute any of these values for x in the function.) From the graph we see that the global maximum is between $x = 1$ and $x = 2$, but that there is a local maximum between $x = 3$ and $x = 4$. The spreadsheet in Figure 6.6 shows the results of using the Solver to solve this problem. In columns A and B we show what happened when the starting value in the changing cell was $x = 1.5$. The Solver eventually found $x = 1.355567$ with a corresponding objective value of 3.631432. (The objective in cell B11 is the product of the five numbers above it, and the constraints are B5<=5 and B5>=1.) However, given the identical setup in columns D and E, but with a starting value of $x = 3.5$, the Solver found the local maximum $x = 3.543912$ and its corresponding objective value of 1.418697. Clearly this second solution is not the correct solution to the problem in Equation 6.1, but the Solver found it because of an "unlucky" starting value of x.

FIGURE 6.6 **Function with Local and Global Maxima**

	A	B	C	D	E
1	**Function with Local and Global Maxima**				
2					
3	The function is: y = (x-1)(x-2)(x-3)(x-4)(x-5)				
4					
5	x	1.355567		x	3.54391
6	x-1	0.355567		x-1	2.54391
7	x-2	-0.64443		x-2	1.54391
8	x-3	-1.64443		x-3	0.54391
9	x-4	-2.64443		x-4	-0.45609
10	x-5	-3.64443		x-5	-1.45609
11	Product	3.631432		Product	1.4187

In general, if you try several starting combinations for the changing cells and the Solver obtains the same optimal solution in all cases, you can be fairly confident—but still not absolutely sure—that you have found the optimal solution to the NLP. On the other hand, if you try different starting values for the changing cells and obtain several different solutions, then the best you can do is keep the "best" solution you have found. That is, you should keep the solution with the lowest objective value (for a minimization problem) or the highest objective value (for a maximization problem).

6.3

Managerial Economics Applications

Many problems that are discussed in managerial economics are nonlinear but can be solved with a spreadsheet Solver. We illustrate two important examples in this section: output maximization and peak-load pricing.

Output Maximization

Here is an example of output maximization when the function relating inputs to a single output has a special form. This function is usually called the **Cobb-Douglas production function**.

EXAMPLE 6.1

Redhound Bus Lines currently owns 700 buses and employs 2200 workers. The company can purchase new buses for $25,000 per bus or sell its current buses for a salvage value of $8000 per bus. The yearly maintenance cost per bus is $1000. Redhound can also hire or fire workers. The hiring and firing costs per worker are $1000 and $800. The annual wage per worker is $30,000. The fuel cost per thousand gallons is $1100. Redhound must have at least three workers per bus, and each bus can consume at most 10,000 gallons of fuel. (This is figured on a maximum of 100,000 miles traveled at 10 miles per gallon.) The number of vehicle miles, measured in thousands, is a function of the number of buses owned, the number of workers employed, and the fuel consumed (in thousands of gallons). This function is estimated to be

$$\text{Vehicle Miles} = 10.8 * \text{Buses}^{.06} * \text{Workers}^{.32} * \text{Fuel}^{.56} \qquad \textbf{(6.2)}$$

The company would like to stay within its budget of $80 million per year and maximize the number of vehicle miles driven.

Solution

To solve this problem we must keep track of the following:

- the number of buses purchased and sold
- the number of workers hired and fired
- the amount of fuel used per bus
- the total net cost
- the number of vehicle miles driven

Developing the Spreadsheet Model The spreadsheet model is shown in Figure 6.7. (See the file BUS.XLS.) It can be formed with the following steps.

1. **Inputs.** Enter the various inputs in the ranges B10:E10, B12:B14, B18:D18, B21:D21, B23, F28, and D44.
2. **Decision variables.** Redhound must decide how many buses to buy or sell, how many workers to hire or fire, and how many thousands of gallons of fuel to consume per bus. Enter *any* trial values for these quantities in the range B26:F26.

FIGURE 6.7 **Optimal Solution to Redhound Bus Example**

	A	B	C	D	E	F
1	**Output Maximization with the Cobb-Douglas Production Function**					
2						
3	The output is measured in 1000s of vehicle miles for a bus line. We assume that output is of the form:					
4	Vehicle miles = a(Number of buses)^b(Number of workers)^c(Fuel)^d					
5						
6	Note: Fuel is measured in 1000s of gallons					
7						
8	**Parameters of production function, other inputs**					
9		a	b	c	d	
10		10.8	0.06	0.32	0.56	
11						
12	Buses already owned	700				
13	Workers already employed	2200				
14	Minimum workers per bus	3				
15						
16	**Unit costs**					
17	Buses	Purchase cost	Salvage value	Maintenance		
18		$25,000	$8,000	$1,000		
19						
20	Workers	Hiring cost	Firing cost	Annual wage		
21		$1,000	$800	$30,000		
22						
23	Fuel	$1,100				
24						
25	**Decision variables**	Buses purchased	Buses sold	Workers hired	Workers fired	Fuel per bus
26		66.92	0	100.77	0	10.000
27						<=
28					Max per bus	10
29	**Inputs to production function**					
30		Buses	Workers	Fuel		
31		766.92	2300.77	7669.23		
32			>=			
33		Required workers	2300.77			
34						
35	**Monetary information**					
36	Buses	Purchase cost	Salvage value	Maintenance		
37		$1,673,077	$0	$766,923		
38						
39	Workers	Hiring cost	Firing cost	Wages		
40		$100,769	$0	$69,023,077		
41						
42	Fuel	$8,436,154				
43				Budget		
44	Total cost	$80,000,000	<=	$80,000,000		
45						
46	**Vehicle miles**	28692.56				

3 **Inputs to production function.** The inputs to the function in Equation 6.2 are the number of buses owned, the number of workers employed, and the amount of fuel used. Calculate these quantities in the cells B31, C31, and D31 with the formulas

=B12+B26–C26
=B13+D26–E26

and

=B31*F26

4 **Workers required.** Calculate the minimal number of workers required in cell C33 with the formula

=B14*B31

5 **Cost information for buses.** Calculate the purchase cost and salvage value for buses by entering the formula

=B18*B26

in cell B37 and copying it to cell C37. Then calculate the annual maintenance cost in cell D37 with the formula

=D18*B31

6 **Cost information for workers.** Calculate the hiring and firing costs for workers by entering the formula

=B21*D26

in cell B40 and copying it to cell C40. Then calculate the annual wages in cell D40 with the formula

=D21*C31

7 **Fuel cost.** Calculate the fuel cost in cell B42 with the formula

=B23*D31

8 **Total cost.** Calculate the total (net) cost in cell B44 with the formula

=SUM(B37,D37,B40:D40,B42)–C37

(Note how several ranges can be included in the SUM function provided they are separated by commas.)

9 **Vehicle miles.** Use Equation 6.2 to calculate the total vehicle miles (in thousands) in cell B46 with the formula

=B10*B31^C10*C31^D10*D31^E10

Using the Solver

1 **Objective.** Choose cell B46 (vehicle miles) as the objective to maximize.

2 **Changing cells.** Choose the range B26:F26 as the changing cells and constrain these cells to be nonnegative.

3 **Fuel constraint.** Add the constraint F26<=F28. This ensures that no bus will use more than 10,000 gallons of fuel per year.

4 **Worker constraint.** Add the constraint C31>=C33. This ensures that there will be at least three workers per bus.

5 **Budget constraint.** Add the constraint B44<=D44. This ensures that spending will stay within the budget.

6 **Optimize.** Make sure that the Assume Linear Model box is *not* checked and click on Solve. (We will not continue to remind you throughout this chapter, but Excel users should always make sure that the Assume Linear Model box is unchecked for nonlinear problems. Otherwise, an error message will appear when the Solver begins its work.)

The Solver solution appears in Figure 6.7. It indicates that Redhound should purchase about 67 buses, hire about 101 workers, and consume the maximum amount of fuel per bus. The $80 million budget is used up entirely, and the estimated number of vehicle miles driven is about 28.7 million.

Is the Solver Solution Optimal? The objective function in Equation 6.2 is a positive constant multiplied by the product of variables raised to positive powers. It can be shown that the logarithm of this type of function is concave. Since the constraints are all linear, the conditions for a maximization problem are satisfied. Therefore, we know for certain that the Solver's solution is optimal. ■

MODELING ISSUES

1 In general, a function of the form $y = ax_1^b x_2^c x_3^d$, where y is the output, the x's are inputs, and a, b, c, and d are positive constants, is called a Cobb-Douglas production function. (Of course, there can be more or fewer than three inputs.) Economists refer to this as a **constant elasticity relationship**, where the constants b, c, and d are the constant elasticities of inputs 1, 2, and 3. Each elasticity measures the percentage change in the output for a 1% increase in the input. For example, in the Redhound problem the elasticity of fuel is .56. This means that if the amount of fuel used increases by 1% (and the number of buses and workers remains constant), the number of vehicle miles increases by .56%.

2 The elasticities used in the Redhound example, .06 for buses, .32 for workers, and .56 for fuel, were estimated from actual data on several bus lines (from National Mass Transportation Statistics, U.S. Department of Transportation, 1983). ■

Peak-Load Pricing

In many situations there is peak-load and off-peak-load demand for a product. In such a situation it is optimal for a producer to charge a larger price for peak-load service than for off-peak service. Here is a typical example.

EXAMPLE 6.2

Florida Power and Light faces demands during both peak-load and off-peak-load times. FPL must determine the price per kilowatt hour (kwh) to charge during both peak and off-peak periods. The daily demand for power during each period (in kwh) is related to price as follows:

$$D_p = 60 - .5P_p + .1P_o \qquad \textbf{(6.3)}$$

$$D_o = 40 - P_o + .1P_p \qquad \textbf{(6.4)}$$

Here, D_p and P_p are demand and price during peak times, whereas D_o and P_o are demand and price during off-peak times. Note that because of the signs of the coefficients, an increase in the peak-load price decreases the demand for power during the peak period but increases the demand for power during the off-peak period. Similarly, an increase in the price for the off-peak period decreases the demand for the off-peak period but increases the demand for the peak period. In economic terms, this implies that peak-load power and off-peak power are **substitutes** for one another. It costs FPL $10 per day to maintain a kwh of capacity. The company wants to determine a pricing strategy and capacity level that maximize its daily profit.

Solution

Due to the relationships between the demand and price variables, it is not at all obvious what FPL should do. The pricing decisions determine demand, and larger demand requires larger capacity, which costs money. In addition, revenue is price multiplied by demand, so it is not clear whether price should be low or high in order to increase revenue.

To solve this problem, we must keep track of the following:

- the peak and off-peak price
- the peak and off-peak demand
- the peak and off-peak revenue
- the capacity (in kwh)
- the cost of capacity
- the total profit

Developing the Spreadsheet Model The spreadsheet model is shown in Figure 6.8. (See the file PEAKLOAD.XLS.) It can be formed as follows.

1 **Inputs.** Enter the constants and coefficients of peak price and off-peak price (from Equations 6.3 and 6.4) in the range B7:D8 and enter the cost per kwh of capacity in cell B10.

2 **Prices and capacity level.** Enter *any* trial prices (per kwh) for peak and off-peak power in cells B14 and C14. Also, enter *any* trial value for the capacity level in

FIGURE 6.8 **Optimal Solution for Peak-Load Example**

	A	B	C	D
1	Florida Power and Light Peak-Load Pricing Problem			
2				
3	**Input data**			
4				
5	Coefficients of demand functions			
6		Constant	Peak price	Off-peak price
7	Peak-load demand	60	-0.5	0.1
8	Off-peak demand	40	0.1	-1
9				
10	Cost of capacity/kwh	$10		
11				
12	**Pricing, capacity decisions**			
13		Peak price	Off-peak price	Capacity
14		$70.31	$26.53	27.50
15				
16	**Demands**			
17		Demand		Capacity
18	Peak-load	27.50	<=	27.50
19	Off-peak	20.50	<=	27.50
20				
21	**Summary of revenues, costs**			
22	Cost of capacity	$275.00		
23	Revenue	$2,477.30		
24	**Profit**	$2,202.30		

cell D14. These are the three values FPL has control over, so they become the changing cells.

3 **Demands.** In cell B18 compute the peak-load demand with the formula

=B7+SUMPRODUCT($B$14:$C$14,C7:D7)

Then copy this formula to cell B19 to compute the off-peak demand. These formulas operationalize Equations 6.3 and 6.4.

4 **Revenue.** In cell B23 compute the daily revenue with the formula

=B18*B14+B19*C14

5 **Cost of capacity.** In cell B22 compute the daily cost of operating this level of capacity with the formula

=B10*D14

6 **Profit.** In cell B24 compute the daily profit (revenue minus cost) with the formula

=B23–B22

7 **Copy capacity level.** "Copy" the capacity level to cell D18 with the formula

=$D$14

and copy it to cell D19. (This step isn't absolutely necessary, but it makes it easier to specify capacity constraints.)

Using the Solver

1 **Objective.** Choose cell B24 (total daily profit) as the objective to maximize.

2 **Changing cells.** Choose the range B14:D14 as the changing cells and constrain these to be nonnegative.

3 **Capacity constraints.** Add the constraints B18:B19<=D18:D19. These ensure that capacity is sufficient to meet both peak and off-peak demand.

4 **Optimize.** Click on Solve.

The Solver solution appears in Figure 6.8. It shows that FPL should charge $70.31 per kwh during the peak-load period and $26.53 during the off-peak-load period. These prices generate demands of 27.5 (peak) and 20.5 (off-peak), so that a capacity of 27.5 kwh is needed. The cost of this capacity is $275. When this is subtracted from the revenue of $2477.30, the daily profit becomes $2202.30.

To gain some insight into this solution, let's see what happens if FPL changes the peak-load price slightly from its optimal value of $70.31. If FPL decreases the price to $70, say, you can check that the peak-load demand increases to 27.65 and the off-peak demand decreases to 20.47. The net effect is that revenue increases slightly to $2478.78. However, the peak-load demand is now greater than capacity, so FPL must increase its capacity from 27.50 to 27.65. This costs an extra $1.50, which more than offsets the increase in revenue. A similar chain of effects occurs if FPL increases the peak price to $71. Now peak-load demand decreases, off-peak demand increases, and total revenue decreases. Although FPL can get by with lower capacity, the net effect is slightly less profit.

Is the Solver Solution Optimal? All of the constraints in this example are linear, so they certainly meet the assumptions for a maximization problem. Also, it can be shown that the objective (daily profit) is a concave function of peak price, off-peak price, and capacity level (although this is not obvious). Algebraically, this objective function is called

quadratic, meaning that it is a sum of squared terms (such as P_p^2) and cross-product terms (such as P_pP_o). Not all quadratic functions are concave, but there is a test to check whether a given quadratic function is concave. We will not cover the details of this test, but we assure you that the quadratic function for this example passes the test. Therefore, the assumptions for a maximization problem are satisfied, and the Solver's solution is guaranteed to be optimal. ■

PROBLEMS

Skill-Building Problems

1 Widgetco produces widgets at plants 1 and 2. It costs $20x^{1/2}$ dollars to produce x units at plant 1 and $40x^{1/3}$ dollars to produce x units at plant 2. Each plant can produce up to 70 units. Each unit produced can be sold for $10. At most 120 widgets can be sold. Determine how Widgetco can maximize its profit.

2 If a monopolist produces q units, she can charge $100 - 4q$ dollars per unit. The fixed cost of production is $50 and the variable cost is $2 per unit.

a How can the monopolist maximize her profit?

b If the monopolist must pay a sales tax of $2 per unit, will she increase or decrease production (relative to the situation with no sales tax)?

3 It costs a company $12 to purchase an hour of labor and $15 to purchase an hour of capital. If L hours of labor and K units of capital are available, then $L^{2/3}K^{1/3}$ machines can be produced. If the company has $10,000 to purchase labor and capital, what is the maximum number of machines it can produce?

4 In the previous problem what is the minimum cost method of producing 100 machines? (Ignore the $10,000 budget constraint.)

5 A total of 160 hours of labor are available each week at $15 per hour. Additional labor can be purchased at $25 per hour. Capital can be purchased in unlimited quantities at a cost of $45 per unit. If K units of capital and L units of labor are available during a week, then $L^{1/2}K^{1/3}$ machines can be produced. Each machine sells for $270. How can the firm maximize its weekly profit?

6 A monopolist can purchase up to 17.25 ounces of a chemical for $10 per ounce. At a cost of $3 per ounce, the chemical can be processed into an ounce of product 1, or at a cost of $5 per ounce, the chemical can be processed into an ounce of product 2. If x_1 ounces of product 1 are produced, it sells for a price of $30 - x_1$ dollars per ounce. If x_2 ounces of product 2 are produced, it sells for a price of $50 - 2x_2$ dollars per ounce. Determine how the monopolist can maximize profit.

7 The cost per day of running a hospital is $200{,}000 + .002x^2$ dollars, where x is the number of patients served per day. What number of patients served per day minimizes the cost per patient of running the hospital?

8 A company can sell all it produces of a given output for $2 per unit. The output is produced by combining two inputs, 1 and 2. If q_1 units of input 1 and q_2 units of input 2 are used, the company can produce $q_1^{1/3} + q_2^{2/3}$ units of the output. If it costs $1 to purchase a unit of input 1 and $1.50 to purchase a unit of input 2, how can the company maximize its profit?

9 There are two firms producing widgets. It costs the first firm q_1^2 dollars to produce q_1 widgets and the second firm $0.5q_2^2$ dollars to produce q_2 widgets. If a total of q widgets are produced, consumers will pay $200 - q$ dollars for each widget. If the two manufacturers want to collude in an attempt to maximize the sum of their profits, how many widgets should each company produce? The model for this sort of problem is called a **collusive duopoly model**.

10 A company manufactures two products. If it charges price p_i for product i, it can sell q_i units of product i, where $q_1 = 60 - 3p_1 + p_2$ and $q_2 = 80 - 2p_2 + p_1$. It costs $25 to produce a unit of product 1 and $72 to produce a unit of product 2. How many units of each product should the company produce, and what prices should it charge, to maximize its profit?

11 (Based on Littlechild [10]) A power company faces demands during both peak and off-peak times. If a price of p_1 dollars per kilowatt hour is charged during the peak time, customers will demand $60 - 0.5p_1$ kwh of power. If a price of p_2 dollars is charged during the off-peak time, customers will demand $40 - p_2$ kwh. The power company must have sufficient capacity to meet demand during both the peak and off-peak times. It costs $10 per day to maintain each kilowatt-hour of capacity. Determine how the power company can maximize its daily revenues less operating costs.

Skill-Extending Problems

12 Each morning during rush hour 10,000 people want to travel from New Jersey to New York City. If a person takes the commuter train, the trip lasts 40 minutes. If x thousand people per morning drive to New York, it takes $20 + 5x$ minutes to make the trip. This problem illustrates a basic fact of life: If people make their decisions individually, they will cause more congestion than need actually occur!

a Show that if people make their decisions individually, an average of 4000 people will travel by road from New Jersey to New York. Here you should assume that people will divide up between the trains and roads in a way that makes the average travel time by road equal to the travel time by train. When this "equilibrium" occurs, nobody has an incentive to switch from the road to the train or vice versa.

b Show that the average travel time per person is minimized if 2000 people travel by road.

13 (Based on Grossman and Hart [6]) A salesperson for Fuller Brush has three options: quit, put forth a low effort level, or put forth a high effort level. Suppose for simplicity that each salesperson will sell either $0, $5000, or $50,000 worth of brushes. The probability of each sales amount depends on the effort level as described in Table 6.1. If a salesperson is paid w dollars, he or she earns a "benefit" of $w^{1/2}$ units. In addition, low effort costs the salesperson 0 benefit units, while high effort costs 50 benefit units. If a salesperson were to quit Fuller and work elsewhere, he or she could earn a benefit of 20 units. Fuller wants all salespeople to put forth a high effort level. The question is how to minimize the cost of encouraging them to do so. The company cannot observe the level of effort put forth by a salesperson, but it can observe the size of his or her sales. Thus, the wage paid to the salesperson is completely determined by the size of the sale. This means that Fuller must determine w_0, the wage paid for sales of $0; w_{5000}, the wage paid for sales of $5000; and $w_{50,000}$, the wage paid for sales of $50,000. These wages must be set so that the salespeople value the expected benefit from high effort more than quitting and more than low effort. Determine how to minimize the expected cost of ensuring that all salespeople put forth high effort. (This problem is an example of **agency theory**.) ■

TABLE 6.1 Probabilities for Sales Effort Problem

Size of Sale	Low Effort	High Effort
$0	.6	.3
$5,000	.3	.2
$50,000	.1	.5

6.4 Salesforce Allocation

How should a business allocate its salesforce? Many companies have applied NLP to answer this question. For example, Syntex Labs (see Lodish et al. [11]) increased the profitability of the company by over $1 million per year by using NLP to allocate its salesforce among the company's seven main drugs. Here is a simplified sales force allocation model.

EXAMPLE 6.3

Drugco sells four drugs. It costs Drugco $50,000 per year per salesperson. The annual revenue generated from drug i ($i = 1, 2, 3,$ or 4) is a function of the number of salespeople assigned to the drug. This dependence is shown in Table 6.2, where x_i is the number of salespeople assigned to drug i (revenue is shown in thousands of dollars). In order to maximize profit (revenue from sales less salesperson costs), how many salespeople should be assigned to each drug?

TABLE 6.2 **Revenue Functions for Drugco Example**

	Revenue
Drug 1	$200x_1^{.5}$
Drug 2	$150x_2^{.75}$
Drug 3	$180x_3^{.6}$
Drug 4	$300x_4^{.3}$

Solution

One might intuit that as more salespeople are assigned to any particular drug, the marginal effect on revenue decreases. That is, each additional salesperson generates less revenue than the previous salesperson. This is due to the fact that all exponents in Table 6.2 are less than 1. Therefore, it is not at all obvious how many salespeople Drugco should assign to each drug.

To build a spreadsheet model for Drugco, we need to keep track of the following:

- the number of salespeople assigned to each drug
- the sales revenue from each drug
- the total profit (revenue from sales less salesperson costs)

Developing the Spreadsheet Model To build a spreadsheet model, proceed as follows. (See Figure 6.9 and the file DRUGCO1.XLS.)

1 **Inputs.** Observe that the revenue (in thousands of dollars) for each drug equals a constant times the number of salespeople assigned to the drug raised to a power. Enter these constants and powers in the range B9:E10. Also, enter the cost per salesperson in cell C12.

2 **Number of salespeople assigned to each drug.** Enter *any* trial values for the number of salespeople assigned to each drug in the range B17:E17.

3 **Revenue from each drug.** In the range B18:E18 compute the revenue earned by each drug. Specifically, in B18 compute the revenue earned by drug 1 with the formula

```
=1000*B9*B17^B10
```

Then copy this formula to the range C18:E18 for the other drugs.

4 **Total number of salespeople and total revenue.** Compute the total number of salespeople in cell F17 with the formula

```
=SUM(B17:E17)
```

Copy this to cell F18 to calculate the total revenue.

FIGURE 6.9 Optimal Solution to Drugco Salesforce Example

	A	B	C	D	E	F	G	H
1	**Drugco Salesforce Problem**							
2								
3	**Input data**							
4								
5	Coefficients of revenue functions							
6	Note: Revenue for any drug is a constant times the number of salespeople raised to a power							
7			**Drug**					
8		1	2	3	4			
9	Constant	200	150	180	300			
10	Power	0.5	0.75	0.6	0.3			
11								
12	Cost/salesperson		$50,000					
13								
14	**Salesforce allocations**							
15			**Drug**					
16		1	2	3	4	Totals		
17	# assigned	4.000	25.629	6.857	2.316	38.802		**Profit**
18	Revenue	$400,000	$1,708,592	$571,117	$[illegible],044	$[illegible]		$1,125,876

5 **Total profit.** Compute the profit (revenue minus cost of salespeople) in cell H18 with the formula

=F18-C12*F17

Using the Solver

1 **Objective.** Choose cell H18 (profit) as the objective to maximize.

2 **Changing cells.** Choose the range B17:E17 as the changing cells and constrain these cells to be nonnegative. There are no other constraints.

3 **Optimize.** Click on Solve.

The Solver solution appears in Figure 6.9. We see that Drugco can earn a profit of $1,125,876 by assigning the following number of salespeople to each drug: drug 1, 4.00; drug 2, 25.63; drug 3, 6.86; drug 4, 2.32.

Is the Solver Solution Optimal? Since the only constraints for Drugco are the nonnegativity constraints, we know the Solver will find the optimal solution to the problem if the objective function is concave. Recall that for $x \geq 0$, the function cx^a is concave for $0 < a \leq 1$ and $c \geq 0$. Therefore, the revenue from each drug is a concave function of the number of salespeople assigned to the drug. Also, the total cost of the salespeople assigned to each region is a linear (hence concave) function of the number of people assigned to the region. Since the sum of concave functions is concave, we know that the profit is a concave function. Thus we know that the Solver solution is indeed optimal.

Using the Solver (Integer Solution) It might be impractical to have a fractional number of salespeople. In this case we need to constrain the changing cells to be integers. With these integer constraints, we find that a maximum profit of $1,124,996 can be earned with the following assignments: drug 1, 4; drug 2, 26; drug 3, 7; drug 4, 2. (See Figure 6.10 and the file DRUGCO2.XLS.) Note that the optimal integer solution is the noninteger solution rounded off to the nearest integers. This is not always the case. Also, note that the "sacrifice" in profit by requiring integers is very slight—less than $1000.

This optimal solution, which assigns by far the most salespeople to drug 2, might surprise you. After all, drug 2 has the smallest coefficient in Table 6.2. However, it has the

FIGURE 6.10 **Optimal Integer Solution to Drugco Salesforce Example**

	A	B	C	D	E	F	G	H
1	Drugco Salesforce Problem with Integer Constraints							
2								
3	Input data							
4								
5	Coefficients of revenue functions							
6	Note: Revenue for any drug is a constant times the number of salespeople raised to a power							
7			Drug					
8		1	2	3	4			
9	Constant	200	150	180	300			
10	Power	0.5	0.75	0.6	0.3			
11								
12	Cost/salesperson		$50,000					
13								
14	Salesforce allocations							
15			Drug					
16		1	2	3	4	Totals		
17	# assigned	4	26	7	2	39		Profit
18	Revenue	$400,000	$1,727,115	$578,537	$369,343	$3,074,996		$1,124,996

largest exponent. This means that the decreasing marginal revenue effect is less important for drug 2 than any other drug—extra salespeople assigned to drug 2 continue to generate significant revenue. ■

Using NLP to Estimate the Sales Response Function

The following example illustrates how NLP can be used to estimate the sales response function. It indicates how functions such as those in Table 6.2 of the Drugco example might be estimated from real data.

EXAMPLE 6.4

Syntex Labs needs to determine the optimal allocation of its salesforce to sell the seven drugs it produces. Lodish et al. [11] used NLP to model Syntex Labs's problem.

Solution

Before their analysis could be performed, Lodish and colleagues had to estimate the sales from each drug as a function of the amount of sales effort assigned to the drug. In order to estimate this response function, the authors asked Syntex management the following four questions for each drug.

1. What would the sales of the drug be if no sales effort were assigned to the drug?
2. What would sales of the drug be if half the current effort were assigned to the drug?
3. What would sales of the drug be if 50% more than the current effort were assigned to the drug?
4. What would sales of the drug be if Syntex used a saturation level (a very large amount) of sales effort for the drug?

The answers to these questions for each drug were relative to the current salesforce allocation generating a sales level of "100." Using the answers to these questions, the authors fit the following response curve for each drug:

$$\text{Sales of drug } i \text{ when } x \text{ calls are made for drug } i = a + \frac{(b-a)x^c}{d+x^c} \qquad \textbf{(6.5)}$$

For each drug, the four parameters a, b, c, and d were estimated using the answers to questions 1–4.

This estimation process can easily be implemented with a spreadsheet Solver. For example, for the drug Naprosyn, Syntex management felt that

- having no sales allocation to Naprosyn would decrease sales to 47% of the current level;
- cutting the salesforce allocation to Naprosyn by 50% would reduce sales to 68% of the current level;
- raising sales allocation by 50% would increase sales by 26% over the current level;
- a saturation level of sales effort would result in a 52% increase in Naprosyn sales.

Suppose that 350,000 sales calls per year are currently made on behalf of Naprosyn. To fit Equation 6.5 we need to find values of a, b, c, and d that "best fit" the data in Table 6.3, where we assume that saturation effort is ten times the current effort level (x is in units of 1000 calls).

TABLE 6.3 Values for Sales Response Function

Number of Calls x	Sales
0	47
175	68
350	100
525	126
3500	152

We use a spreadsheet approach to find a, b, c, and d. The objective we will use is "squared-error" minimization, that is, we will choose a, b, c, and d to minimize the sum of squared errors between the observed and predicted values of sales levels.

Developing the Spreadsheet Model The following steps are required to build a spreadsheet model. (See Figure 6.11 and the file SYNTEX.XLS.)

1 **Inputs.** Enter the subjective estimates of sales given by Syntex management in the range A5:B9.

2 **Parameter values.** Enter *any* trial values for a, b, c, and d in the range A13:D13. A close look at Equation 6.5 shows that a should equal sales when $x = 0$ and b should be close to sales when $x = 3500$. Therefore, it is a good idea to enter these (47 and 152) as trial values for a and b.

3 **Predicted sales values.** In cell C5 determine the predicted value of sales when there are zero sales calls with the formula

=$A$13+((B$13–A$13)*A5^$C$13)/($D$13+A5^$C$13)

This is simply Equation 6.5 evaluated at $x = 0$. Then copy this formula to the range C6:C9 to generate the predictions for the other sales calls values.

FIGURE 6.11 Estimates of Parameters for Syntex Example

	A	B	C	D
1	Estimating the Sales Response Function at Syntex Labs			
2				
3	Estimates from management			
4	Sales calls (1000s)	Sales level	Sales estimate (model)	Squared error
5	0	47	47.480	0.230
6	175	68	66.746	1.572
7	350	100	102.068	4.276
8	525	126	124.325	2.805
9	3500	152	152.381	0.145
10			Sum of squared errors	9.028
11	Model parameters			
12	a	b	c	d
13	47.480	152.914	2.264	534164.139

4 **Squared prediction errors.** In the range D5:D9 construct a set of squared errors, where

Error = Estimate by Syntex – Prediction from Equation 6.5

Specifically, in cell D5 compute the squared error when there are zero sales calls with the formula

```
=(B5–C5)^2
```

Then copy this formula to the range D6:D9 for the other sales calls values.

5 **Sum of squared errors.** Compute the sum of the squared errors in cell D10 with the formula

```
=SUM(D5:D9)
```

Using the Solver

1 **Objective.** Choose cell D10 as the objective to minimize. This will minimize the sum of the squared prediction errors.

2 **Changing cells.** Choose cells A13:D13 as the changing cells.

3 **Nonnegativity constraints on two parameters.** Since a equals sales when $x = 0$ and b equals sales when x is large, both a and b must be nonnegative. On the other hand, c and d can be negative. Therefore, constrain a and b (cells A13 and B13) to be nonnegative.

4 **Optimize.** Click on Solve.

The optimal solution is shown in Figure 6.11. The parameters that minimize the sum of squared errors are $a = 47.480$, $b = 152.914$, $c = 2.264$, and $d = 534{,}164.139$.

Once the response curve for each drug was fit, the authors determined the revenue per unit sold of each drug and then proceeded to find the allocation of salespersons that maximized profit, much as we did in the Drugco example. Due to the work of Lodish and colleagues, the Syntex salesforce was increased by over 200 people. Syntex earned a better than 100% return from this increase in the salesforce. ■

PROBLEMS

Skill-Building Problems

14 Q&H Company advertises during soap operas and football games. Each soap opera ad costs \$50,000, and each football game ad costs \$100,000. If S soap opera ads are purchased, they will be seen by $5S^{1/2}$ million men and $20S^{1/2}$ million women. If F football ads are purchased, they will be seen by $17F^{1/2}$ million men and $7F^{1/2}$ million women. The company wants at least 40 million men and at least 60 million women to see its ads.

a Determine how to minimize Q&H's cost of reaching the required number of viewers.

b How does this model violate the proportionality and additivity assumptions of LP?

c Suppose that the number of women (in millions) reached by F football ads and S soap opera ads is $7F^{1/2} + 20S^{1/2} - 0.2(FS)^{1/2}$. Why might this be a more realistic representation of the number of women viewers seeing Q&H's ads?

15 Beerco has \$100,000 to spend on advertising in four markets. The sales revenue (in thousands of dollars) that can be created in each market by spending x_i thousand dollars in market i is given in Table 6.4. To maximize its sales revenue, how much money should Beerco spend in each market?

TABLE 6.4 **Sales Revenue Functions for Beerco Problem**

	Sales Revenue
Market 1	$10x_1^{.4}$
Market 2	$8x_2^{.5}$
Market 3	$12x_3^{.3}$
Market 4	$6x_4^{.6}$

16 It costs a company \$6 per unit to produce a product. If the company charges price p dollars per unit and spends a dollars on advertising, it can sell $10{,}000p^{-2}a^{1/6}$ units of the product. Find the price and advertising level that maximizes the company's profit.

17 A beer company has divided Bloomington into two territories. If the company spends x_1 dollars on promotion in territory 1, it can sell $60x_1^{1/2}$ cases of beer there, and if it spends x_2 dollars on promotion in territory 2, it can sell $40x_2^{1/2}$ cases of beer there. Each case of beer sold in territory 1 sells for \$10 and incurs \$5 in shipping and production costs. Each case of beer sold in territory 2 sells for \$9 and incurs \$4 in shipping and production costs. A total of \$5000 is available for promotion.

a How can the beer company maximize its profit?

b If an extra dollar could be spent on promotion, by approximately how much would the company's profit increase? By how much would its revenue increase?

18 A firm is planning to spend \$10,000 on advertising. It costs \$3000 per minute to advertise on television and \$1000 per minute to advertise on radio. If the firm buys x minutes of television advertising and y minutes of radio advertising, its revenue in thousands of dollars is given by $-2x^2 - y^2 + xy + 8x + 3y$. How can the firm maximize its revenue?

19 Proctor and Ramble has given you \$12 million to spend on advertising Huggys diapers during the next 12 months. At the beginning of January, Huggys has a 30% market share. During any month 10% of the people who purchase Huggys defect to Brand X, and a fraction $.2a^{1/2}$ of customers who usually buy Brand X switch to Huggys, where a is the amount spent on advertising in millions of dollars. For example, if you spend \$4 million during a month, 40% of Brand X's customers switch to Huggys. Your goal is to maximize Proctor and Ramble's average market share during the next 12 months, where the average is computed from each month's ending share. Determine an appropriate advertising policy. (*Hint*: Make sure you enter a nonzero trial value for each month's advertising expense or the Solver may give you an error message.) ■

6.5

Facility Location Models

Suppose you need to find a location for a facility such as a warehouse, a tool crib in a factory, or a fire station. Your goal is to locate the facility so as to minimize the total distance that must be traveled to provide required services. Facility location problems such as these can usually be set up as NLP models. Here is a typical example.

EXAMPLE 6.5

The Wareco company wants to locate a warehouse from which it will ship products to four customers. The location (in the x-y plane) of the four customers and the number of shipments per year needed by each customer are given in Table 6.5. (All locations are in miles, relative to the point $x = 0$ and $y = 0$.) A single warehouse must be used to service all of the customers. Wareco wants to find the location of the warehouse that minimizes the total distance traveled from the warehouse to the customers.

TABLE 6.5 **Data for Wareco Example**

	x	y	Shipments per Year
Customer 1	5	10	200
Customer 2	10	5	150
Customer 3	0	12	200
Customer 4	12	0	300

Solution

For the spreadsheet model we need to keep track of the following:

- the x and y coordinates of the warehouse and each customer
- the distance between the warehouse and each customer
- the total annual distance traveled from the warehouse to customers

Developing the Spreadsheet Model To develop the spreadsheet model, use the following steps. (See Figure 6.12 and the file WARECO.XLS.)

1 **Inputs.** Enter the given customer data in the ranges B5:C8 and E5:E8.

2 **Coordinates of warehouse.** Enter *any* trial values in cells B12 and C12 for the x- and y-coordinates of the warehouse.

3 **Distance from warehouse to each customer.** In the range B16:B19 compute the distance from the proposed warehouse location to each customer. Recall that the (straight-line) distance between the two points (a, b) and (c, d) is

$$\sqrt{(c - a)^2 + (d - b)^2}$$

Therefore in cell B16 compute the distance from the warehouse to customer 1 with the formula

=SQRT((B5–$B$12)^2+(C5-$C$12)^2)

Then copy this formula to the range B17:B19 for the other customers.

FIGURE 6.12 **Optimal Solution to Wareco Example**

	A	B	C	D	E
1	**Wareco facility location problem**				
2					
3	**Current customer data**				
4		X-coordinate	Y-coordinate		Annual shipments
5	Customer 1	5	10		200
6	Customer 2	10	5		150
7	Customer 3	0	12		200
8	Customer 4	12	0		300
9					
10	**Warehouse location**				
11		X-coordinate	Y-coordinate		
12		9.314	5.029		
13					
14	**Customer distances from warehouse**				
15		Distance			
16	Customer 1	6.582			
17	Customer 2	0.686			
18	Customer 3	11.634			
19	Customer 4	5.701			
20					
21	**Annual distance traveled**	5456.540			

4 **Total distance traveled annually.** The total annual distance traveled from the warehouse to meet the demands of all customers is

$$\sum_{i=1}^{4} n_i d_i$$

where n_i is the number of trips per year for customer i and d_i is the distance from the warehouse to customer i. Therefore compute the total annual distance traveled from the customers to the warehouse in cell B21 with the formula

=SUMPRODUCT(B16:B19,E5:E8)

Using the Solver

1 **Objective.** Choose cell B21 (total annual distance) as the objective to minimize.

2 **Changing cells.** Choose the range B12:C12 as the changing cells. Do not constrain these to be nonnegative; it is perfectly possible for the x or y coordinate of the warehouse to be negative.

3 **Optimize.** Click on Solve.

The Solver solution appears in Figure 6.12 and is represented graphically in Figure 6.13. The warehouse should be located at $x = 9.31$ and $y = 5.03$. Each year a total of 5456.54 miles will be traveled annually from the warehouse to the customers. This solution represents a compromise. On the one hand, Wareco would like to position the facility near customer 4 because the largest number of trips are made to customer 4. However, since customer 4 is fairly far from the other customers, the warehouse is located in a more central position.

Is the Solver Solution Optimal? The Wareco problem has no constraints. An NLP with no constraints is called an **unconstrained NLP**. Therefore, we know that the Solver

FIGURE 6.13 Graph of Solution to Wareco Example

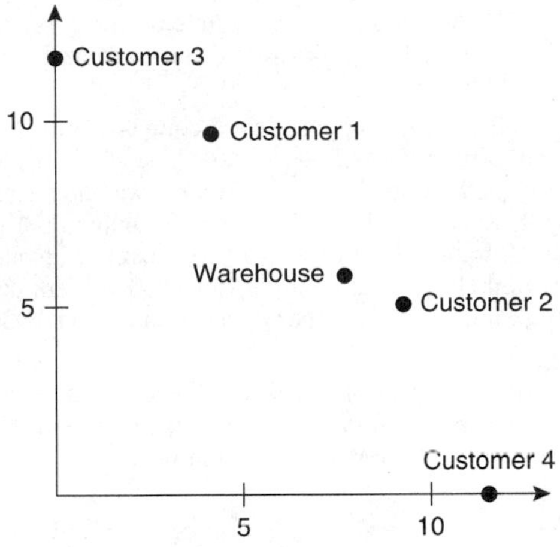

will find an optimal solution if the objective function is a convex function of the x- and y-coordinates of the warehouse. It can be shown (with some difficulty) that the annual distance traveled is indeed a convex function of the coordinates of the warehouse. Therefore, we know that the Solver solution is optimal. ■

MODELING ISSUE

The straight-line distance function we used in the Wareco example is relevant if the company is shipping by air. However, if it is shipping by road, we must take into account that most roads are built in a north-south or east-west direction. Then the relevant distance between points (a, b) and (c, d) is $|a-c|+|b-d|$, and this objective should be used in place of the square root objective. (See Problem 24.)

If our objective was to minimize the total distance traveled to meet customer demand, then it can be shown (see Problem 23) that the warehouse should be located at the "center of gravity" of all customer demands. For example, if one customer was located at $(2, 3)$ and another at $(4, 5)$, then the warehouse would need to be located at the "average" of these coordinates: $(3, 4)$. ■

REAL-WORLD APPLICATION

Facility Location at Coastal Construction

Love and Yerex [12] used a facility location model similar to Wareco's to help Coastal Construction Company of Portsmouth, Virginia, locate two new production facilities. See Problem 24 for a scaled-down version of this type of application. ■

PROBLEMS

Skill-Building Problems

20 The area of a triangle with sides of length a, b, and c is

$$\sqrt{s(s-a)(s-b)(s-c)}$$

where s is half the perimeter of the triangle. Suppose that we have 600 feet of fence and we want to fence a triangular-shaped area. Determine how to maximize the fenced area.

21 Three cities are located at the vertices of an equilateral triangle. An airport is to be built at a location that minimizes the total (straight-line) distance from the airport to the three cities. Determine where to build the airport.

22 (Based on Kolesar and Blum [9]) Suppose that a company must service customers lying in an area of A square miles with n warehouses. Kolesar and Blum showed that by locating the warehouse(s) properly, the average distance between a warehouse and a customer is $(A/n)^{1/2}$. Assume that it costs the company $60,000 per year to maintain a warehouse and $400,000 to build a warehouse. Also, assume that a $400,000 cost is equivalent to incurring a cost of $40,000 per year indefinitely. The company fills 160,000 orders per year, and the shipping cost per order is $1 per mile. If the company serves an area of 100 square miles, how many warehouses should it have?

23 A company has five factories. The x- and y-coordinates of the location of each factory are given in Table 6.6. The company wants to locate a warehouse at a point that minimizes the sum of the squared distances of the plants from the warehouse. Where should the warehouse be located?

TABLE 6.6 **Locations for Factory Problem**

	x	y
Factory 1	6	−5
Factory 2	8	4
Factory 3	5	2
Factory 4	−5	4
Factory 5	−3	2

24 (Based on Love and Yerex [12]) Steelco's main plant currently has a steel manufacturing area and shipping area located as shown in Figure 6.14 (where distances are in hundreds of feet). The company must determine where to locate a casting facility and an assembly and storage facility to minimize the daily cost of moving material through the plant. The number of trips made each day and the cost per 100 feet of each trip are as shown in Table 6.7.

a Assuming that all travel is in an east-west or north-south direction, determine where the casting and assembly/storage plants should be located in order to minimize daily

FIGURE 6.14 **Existing Locations for Steelco Problem**

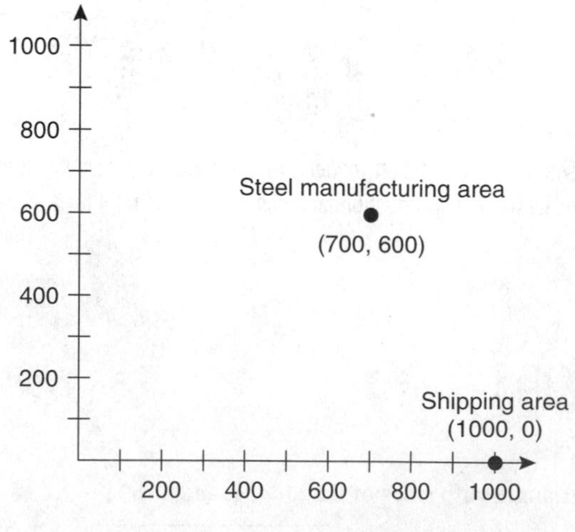

transportation costs. (*Hint*: Use changing cells for the amount by which each area is east, west, north, and south of each facility.)

b Assuming that all travel is in a straight line, determine where the casting and assembly/storage plants should be located.

TABLE 6.7 **Data for Steelco Problem**

	Daily Trips	Cost/100 Feet
From Casting to Assembly & Storage	40	10¢
From Steel manufacturing to Casting	8	10¢
From Steel manufacturing to Assembly & Storage	8	10¢
From Shipping to Assembly & Storage	2	20¢

25 Monroe County is trying to determine where to place the county fire station. The locations of the county's four major towns are as follows. Town 1 is at the point (10, 20); town 2 is at (60, 20); town 3 is at (40, 30); and town 4 is at (80, 60). (See Figure 6.15.) Town 1 averages 20 fires per year; town 2, 30 fires; town 3, 40 fires; and town 4, 25 fires. The county wants to build the fire station in a location that minimizes the average distance that a fire engine must travel to respond to a fire. Since most roads run in either an east-west or a north-south direction, we assume that the fire engine must do the same. For example, if the fire station is located at (30,40) and a fire occurs at town 4, the fire engine has to travel $|80 - 30| + |60 - 40| = 70$ miles to the fire. Determine where the fire station should be located. ■

FIGURE 6.15 **Existing Locations for Fire Station Problem**

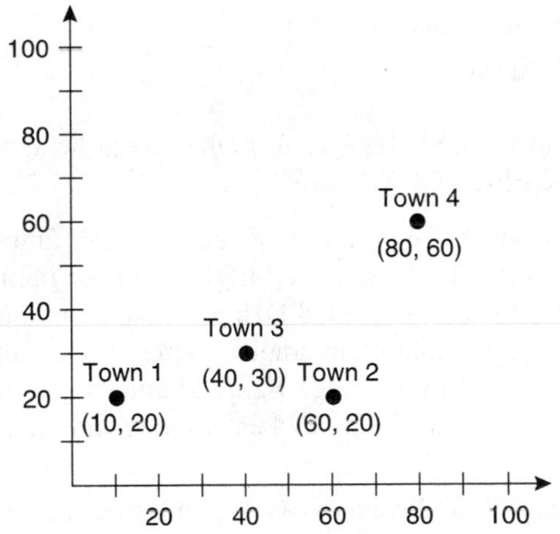

6.6

Improving Product Quality

To successfully compete in today's world, it is necessary to produce high quality products. In many situations the solution to an NLP model can help improve product quality or minimize the cost of producing a product of a desired quality. Here is an example of such a situation.

EXAMPLE 6.6

(Based on Nicholson [16]) Firerock produces rubber used for tires by combining three ingredients: rubber, oil, and carbon black. The cost of rubber is 4¢ per pound, the cost of oil is 1¢ per pound, and the cost of carbon black is 7¢ per pound. The rubber used in automobile tires must have a hardness between 25 and 35, an elasticity of at least 16, and a tensile strength of at least 12. To manufacture a set of four automobile tires, 100 pounds of product is needed. The material used to make a set of four tires must contain between 25 and 60 pounds of rubber and at least 50 pounds of carbon black. Let R, O, and C be, respectively, the number of pounds of rubber, oil, and carbon black used in the production of a set of four tires. Then statistical analysis has shown that the tensile strength, elasticity, and hardness of a 100-pound mixture of rubber, oil, and carbon black are as follows:

$$\text{Tensile strength} = 12.5 - .10O - .001O^2$$

$$\text{Elasticity} = 17 + .35R - .04O - .002R^2$$

$$\text{Hardness} = 34 + .10R + .06O - .3C + .001RO + .005O^2 + .001C^2$$

Firerock wants to find the minimal cost mixture that produces an acceptable set of automobile tires.

Solution

A spreadsheet model for Firerock must include

- the amount of each input in the 100-pound mix
- the tensile strength, elasticity, and hardness of the mixture
- the total weight of the mixture
- the total cost of the mixture

Developing the Spreadsheet Model To form the spreadsheet, proceed as follows. (See Figure 6.16 and the file FIREROCK.XLS.)

1 **Inputs.** Enter the costs of the inputs in the range B6:D6. Enter the required weight of the mixture in cell G16. In the range B14:D14 enter the minimum amount allowed of each ingredient. In the range B18:D18 enter the maximum allowed of each ingredient. (If no explicit minimum amount is prescribed, enter 0; if no maximum is prescribed, enter 100.) In the range B22:B24 enter the minimum allowable level for each objective. In the range F22:F24 enter the maximum allowable level for each objective.

2 **Amount of rubber, oil, and carbon black in mixture.** Enter *any* trial values for the amount of rubber, oil, and carbon black in the mixture in the range B16:D16.

3 **Total weight of mixture.** In cell E16 compute the total weight of the mixture with the formula

=SUM(B16:D16)

4 **Total cost of mixture.** Compute the total cost of the mixture in cell B26 with the formula

=SUMPRODUCT(B16:D16,B6:D6)

5 **Qualities of mixture.** In cell D22 compute the tensile strength of the mixture with the formula

=12.5–.10*C16–.001*C16ˆ2

FIGURE 6.16 Optimal Solution for Firerock Tire Example

	A	B	C	D	E	F	G	H	I	J
1	**Firerock Tire Composition Problem**									
2										
3	**Input data**									
4	Cost per pound of inputs									
5		Rubber	Oil	Carbon black						
6		$0.04	$0.01	$0.07						
7										
8	Tensile strength function:		12.5-.10*Oil-.001*Oil^2							
9	Elasticity function:		17+.35*Rubber-.04*Oil-.002*Rubber^2							
10	Hardness function:		34+.10*Rubber+.06*Oil-.3*CarbonBlack+.001*Rubber*Oil+.005*Oil^2+.001*CarbonBlack^2							
11										
12	**Tire composition**									
13		Rubber	Oil	Carbon black						
14	Minimum	25	0	50						
15		<=	<=	<=	Total		Required			
16	Pounds used	45.23	4.77	50.00	100	=	100			
17		<=	<=	<=						
18	Maximum	60	100	100						
19										
20	**Constraints on qualities of products**									
21		Minimum		Actual		Maximum				
22	Tensile strength	12	<=	12.00		None				
23	Elasticity	16	<=	28.55		None				
24	Hardness	25	<=	26.64	<=	35				
25										
26	**Total cost**	$5.36								

Similarly, in cells D23 and D24 compute the elasticity and hardness of the mixture with the formulas

=17+.35*B16–.04*C16–.002*B16^2

and

=34+.10*B16+.06*C16–.3*D16+.001*B16*C16+.005*C16^2+.001*D16^2

Using the Solver

1. **Objective.** Choose the cell B26 (total cost) as the objective to minimize.
2. **Changing cells.** Choose the range B16:D16 as the changing cells.
3. **Weight constraint.** Add the constraint E16=G16. This ensures that the mixture has the proper weight.
4. **Minimum constraints on ingredients of mixture.** Add the constraints B14:D14<=B16:D16. These ensure that the amount of each ingredient in the mixture is no less than the minimum allowed value. (They also take care of nonnegativity of the changing cells.)
5. **Maximum constraints on ingredients of mixture.** Add the constraints B16:D16<=B18:D18. These ensure that the amount of each ingredient in the mixture does not exceed the maximum allowed value.
6. **Minimum constraints on qualities.** Add the constraints B22:B24<=D22:D24. These ensure that the tensile strength, elasticity, and hardness of the mixture are no less than the minimum values.
7. **Maximum constraint on hardness.** Add the constraint D24<=F24. This ensures that the hardness of the mixture does not exceed the maximum value. (There is no such constraint on tensile strength or elasticity.)
8. **Optimize.** Click on Solve.

The Solver solution is shown in Figure 6.16. The minimum cost of producing an acceptable 100-pound mixture is \$5.36. Firerock should combine 45.23 pounds of rubber, 4.77 pounds of oil, and 50 pounds of carbon black. Note that of all the minimum and maximum constraints, the only two that are binding are the minimun constraints on carbon black and tensile strength. If the minimum level (50) on carbon black could be lowered (say, to 45), the minimum cost of a 100-pound mixture would decrease. Similarly, if the minimum tensile strength could be lowered, the cost would also decrease.

Is the Solver Solution Optimal? While the Firerock objective function is linear, it is difficult to determine whether the left-hand side of the constraints involving tensile strength, hardness, and elasticity are convex or concave. This makes it difficult to determine whether the assumptions for a minimization problem are satisfied. We tried many different combinations of rubber, oil, and carbon black as initial solutions for the Solver and never found a mixture with a cost smaller than \$5.36. This leads us to believe that the Solver found the optimal solution to the Firerock problem. ■

REAL-WORLD APPLICATION

Manufacturing for Quality

Montgomery and Del Castillo [13] discuss how NLP can be used to ensure that a manufacturer produces a product of minimum variability that attains a desired quality level. NLP can also be used to help a manufacturer maximize product quality subject to a desired level of variability. ■

PROBLEMS

Skill-Building Problems

26 The yield Y of a chemical process depends on the length of time T (in minutes) that the process is run and the temperature C (in degrees centigrade) at which the process is operated. This dependence is described by the equation

$$Y = 87 - 1.4T' + .4C' - 2.2T'^2 - 3.2C'^2 - 4.9T'C'$$

where $T' = (T - 90)/10$ and $C' = (C - 150)/5$. Also, T must be between 60 and 120 minutes, and C must be between 100 and 200 degrees. Determine how to maximize the yield of the process.

27 Suppose that the seal strength Y of a plastic storage bag is a function of the sealing temperature T and the percentage P of an additive used to make the plastic. The relationship between T, P, and Y is as follows:

$$Y = -20 + .8T + 1.4P - .0025T^2 - .375P^2 + .025TP$$

The temperature T is measured in degrees Fahrenheit and must be between 100 and 200; P must be between 20% and 40%. What values of T and P maximize seal strength?

28 (Based on Myers [15]) Eli Daisy wants to maximize blank absorbance B of the drug gentamicin, where B is a function of reagent volume R and antibody volume A as follows:

$$B = 62 + .22R + .18A + .06RA - .02R^2$$
$$-.06A^2 - .16R^2A - .22RA^2$$

Reagent volume must be between 1 and 4; antibody volume must be between 2 and 5. Determine the values of R and A that maximize B. ■

6.7

Estimating the Beta of a Stock

Often we are interested in predicting the value of one variable (the **dependent variable**) from another variable (the **independent variable**). For example, the **return** on an investment over a time period is the percentage change in its value over the time period. In finance it is important to be able to predict the return on a stock from the return on the market, that is, on a market index such as the S&P 500 index. It is often hypothesized that

$$r_s = \alpha + \beta r_m + \varepsilon \qquad \textbf{(6.6)}$$

where r_s is the return on a stock during a time period, r_m is the return on the market during the same time period, ε is a random "error" term, and α and β are constants that must be estimated. The true value of β in Equation 6.6 (which we will never know, but can only estimate) is called the **beta** of the stock.

From Equation 6.6 we find that an increase in the market return of 1% will increase the return on the stock by β% (on average). Thus β is a measure of the responsiveness of a stock's return to changes in the market return. The return on stocks with large positive or negative β's are highly sensitive to the business cycle.

Sharpe's **capital asset pricing model** (CAPM) implies that stocks with large beta values are riskier and therefore must yield higher returns than those with small beta values. This implies that if you can estimate beta values more accurately than people on Wall Street, then you can better identify overvalued and undervalued stocks and make a lot of money!

How do people usually estimate the beta of a stock? Most often, they run a linear regression with the dependent variable being the return (usually monthly) on the stock and the independent variable being the return (usually monthly) on the stock market.[3] To run a regression with Excel, we can use the Regression option from the Tools/Data Analysis menu items.

In this section we will focus on four methods that (in conjunction with a spreadsheet Solver) can be used to estimate α and β in Equation 6.6. This requires a set of observations, where an observation gives both the market return and the return on the stock during a particular time period. Let a and b denote potential estimates of the unknown parameters α and β. Then for time period i we generate a prediction of the return on the stock with the equation

$$\widehat{r}_{si} = a + br_{mi} \qquad \textbf{(6.7)}$$

Here, $\widehat{r}_{si}$ is the predicted stock return for period i, and r_{mi} is the actual market return for period i. The *error* for period i, labeled e_i, is defined as

$$e_i = r_{si} - \widehat{r}_{si} \qquad \textbf{(6.8)}$$

That is, the error is the actual return of the stock minus the predicted return. If our predictions were perfect, then all of the errors in Equation 6.8 would equal 0. However, this is generally impossible, so we will instead try to choose the estimates a and b in order to make the errors close to 0. We now discuss four criteria for choosing these estimates.

Criterion 1: Sum of Squared Errors (Least Squares) Here we try to minimize the sum of the squared errors over all observations. The sum of the squared errors is a convex

[3]See Chapter 14 for a more general discussion of regression.

function of the estimates a and b, so the spreadsheet Solver is guaranteed to find the (unique) estimates of α and β that minimize the sum of squared errors. The main problem with the least squares criterion is that outliers (points for which the error in Equation 6.8 is especially large) exert a disproportionate influence on the estimates of α and β.

Criterion 2: Weighted Sum of Squared Errors Criterion 1 gives equal weight to older and more recent observations. It stands to reason that more recent observations might have more to say about the beta of a stock than older observations. To incorporate this idea, we can give a smaller weight to the squared errors for older observations. While this method usually leads to more accurate predictions of the future than least squares, the least squares method has many desirable statistical properties weighted least squares estimates do not possess.

Criterion 3: Least Absolute Deviations (LAD) Instead of minimizing the sum of the squared errors, we can minimize the sum of the absolute errors for all observations. This is often called the **least absolute deviations** (LAD) approach. This method has the advantage of not being greatly affected by outliers. Unfortunately, little is known about the statistical properties of LAD estimators. Another drawback to LAD is that there may be more than one combination of a and b that minimize LAD. However, LAD estimates have the advantage that they can be obtained with *linear* programming.

Criterion 4: Minimax Here we try to minimize the absolute value of the *maximum* estimation error over all observations. This method may be appropriate for a highly risk-averse decision maker. (See Chapter 8.) This "minimax" criteria can also be implemented using LP.

Implementing the Estimation Procedures We now describe how to use a spreadsheet Solver to obtain estimates of α and β for the four criteria above.

EXAMPLE 6.7

High Fidelity is considering including Dow Chemical stock in its new mutual fund. HiFi has asked us to determine the α and β for Dow stock. We will consider the four criteria above and will examine the annual returns on Dow stock and annual returns on a market index during the years 1956–80 to obtain estimates of α and β for Dow stock.

Solution

Developing the Spreadsheet Model for Least Squares In Figure 6.17 we obtain least squares estimates of α and β using the following steps. (See the file BETA1.XLS.) The given data on stock and market returns have already been entered in the range A10:C34. (In general, you would obtain such data from a financial database.) For example, during 1960 Dow Chemical lost 21.84% of its value and the market dropped 1.56%.

1 **Estimates of alpha and beta.** Enter *any* trial estimates of α and β in the range A6:B6.

2 **Predictions.** In the range D10:D34 create the predictions given by Equation 6.7 for the annual return on Dow Chemical. To begin, predict the 1956 return in cell D10 with the formula

=\$A\$6+\$B\$6*C10

Then copy this formula to the range D11:D34 for the other years.

FIGURE 6.17 **Least Squares Estimates of Alpha and Beta**

	A	B	C	D	E	F
1	**Estimating the Beta for Dow Chemical**					
2	**Sum of Squared Errors Criterion**					
3						
4	**Parameters of prediction model**					
5	Alpha	Beta				
6	0.0238	0.6099				
7						
8	**Historical returns**					
9	Year	DowChem	Market	Prediction	Error	Squared Error
10	1956	15.03%	6.92%	6.60%	8.43%	0.00710
11	1957	-17.95%	-14.31%	-6.35%	-11.60%	0.01347
12	1958	47.50%	59.68%	38.78%	8.72%	0.00760
13	1959	33.52%	15.41%	11.78%	21.74%	0.04726
14	1960	-21.84%	-1.56%	1.43%	-23.27%	0.05415
15	1961	0.28%	29.45%	20.34%	-20.06%	0.04025
16	1962	-21.84%	-12.75%	-5.39%	-16.45%	0.02705
17	1963	29.83%	18.69%	13.78%	16.05%	0.02576
18	1964	13.62%	18.13%	13.44%	0.18%	0.00000
19	1965	5.31%	28.61%	19.83%	-14.52%	0.02109
20	1966	-17.52%	-7.06%	-1.92%	-15.60%	0.02432
21	1967	45.26%	50.38%	33.11%	12.15%	0.01477
22	1968	-7.78%	30.55%	21.01%	-28.79%	0.08288
23	1969	-8.75%	-20.30%	-10.00%	1.25%	0.00016
24	1970	11.42%	-2.90%	0.61%	10.81%	0.01168
25	1971	64.94%	19.47%	14.26%	50.68%	0.25688
26	1972	31.19%	8.45%	7.54%	23.65%	0.05595
27	1973	15.32%	-29.31%	-15.49%	30.81%	0.09495
28	1974	-2.32%	-26.53%	-13.80%	11.48%	0.01318
29	1975	69.55%	61.90%	40.13%	29.42%	0.08653
30	1976	-3.39%	45.49%	30.13%	-33.52%	0.11233
31	1977	-36.06%	9.50%	8.18%	-44.24%	0.19568
32	1978	-2.14%	14.02%	10.93%	-13.07%	0.01709
33	1979	35.82%	35.31%	23.92%	11.90%	0.01417
34	1980	5.13%	30.99%	21.28%	-16.15%	0.02609
35				**Sum of squared errors**		1.25039

3 **Prediction errors.** In the range E10:E34 use Equation 6.8 to compute the errors for each of the annual predictions. Specifically, compute the error for the 1956 prediction in cell E10 with the formula

=B10–D10

and copy it to the range E11:E34 for the other years.

4 **Squared errors.** Compute the squared error for 1956 in cell F10 with the formula

=E10^2

and copy it to the range F11:F34 to compute the squared errors for the other years.

5 **Sum of squared errors.** Compute the sum of the squared errors in cell F35 with the formula

=SUM(F10:F34)

Using the Solver to Find Least Squares Estimates

1 **Objective.** Choose cell F35 as the objective to minimize.

2 **Changing cells.** Choose the range A6:B6 as the changing cells. Nonnegativity constraints are *not* required.

3 **Optimize.** Click on Solve.

The Solver solution to this unconstrained model appears in Figure 6.17. The least squares estimates are $a = .024$ and $b = .610$. The prediction for the return on Dow Chemical during any year is then given by

$$\text{Predicted return} = .024 + .610 * \text{Market return}$$

The fact that the estimated value of β is less than 1 implies that Dow Chemical (for the period observed) was not a very volatile (risky) stock. Specifically, if the market rose or fell by 1%, the Dow Chemical stock tended to change by about 0.6% (in the same direction as the market).

Developing the Spreadsheet Model for Weighted Least Squares We now modify the spreadsheet in Figure 6.17 to give more weight to more recent observations. The resulting spreadsheet apprears in Figure 6.18. (See the file BETA2.XLS.) When calculating the sum of squared errors, we now give an error from n years before 1980 a weight of $(.95)^n$. Thus the 1980 error receives a weight of 1, the 1979 error a weight of .95, the 1978 error a weight of $.95^2$, and so on. To see how much this weighting function "discounts" remote values, note that the 1956 error receives a weight of only $.95^{24} = .08$. (Any other function that gives more weight to recent observations could be used, but this exponential weighting function is quite popular.)

The necessary modifications to the previous (least squares) spreadsheet are as follows.

1 **Weighting constant.** Insert two rows after row 3. In cell C4 enter the weighting constant .95.

2 **Weighted sum of squared prediction errors.** To give less weight to older observations, replace the previous formulas in column F. Specifically, enter the formula

```
=$C$4^(1980–A12)*E12^2
```

in cell F12 and copy it to the range F13:F36.

Using the Solver to Find Weighted Least Squares Estimates We now can invoke the spreadsheet Solver *exactly* as we did in the least squares case. From Figure 6.18 we see that the weighted least squares estimates are $a = .029$ and $b = .559$. Note that the least squares and weighted least squares estimates are very similar. In particular, the estimate of β is still close to .6. The weighted least squares predictions for annual return on Dow Chemical are obtained from

$$\text{Predicted return} = .029 + .559 * \text{Market return}$$

Developing the Spreadsheet Model for LAD In Figure 6.19 we illustrate the LAD approach, which minimizes the sum of the absolute errors in order to estimate α and β. (See the file BETA3.XLS.) A straightforward approach would be to change the squared errors in column F of Figure 6.17 to absolute errors (with Excel's ABS function) and then minimize the average of these absolute errors. However, for technical reasons, this approach is not guaranteed to lead to the correct solution. Therefore, we present a somewhat different approach, which leads to a linear model. Because the model is linear, the Solver is guaranteed to find the optimal solution. The following steps explain how to modify the original (least squares) spreadsheet in Figure 6.17 appropriately.

FIGURE 6.18 **Weighted Least Squares Estimates of Alpha and Beta**

	A	B	C	D	E	F
1	Estimating the Beta for Dow Chemical					
2	Weighted Least Squares Criterion					
3						
4	Weighting constant		0.95			
5						
6	Parameters of prediction model					
7	Alpha	Beta				
8	0.0288	0.5589				
9						
10	Historical returns					
11	Year	DowChem	Market	Prediction	Error	Weighted Squared Error
12	1956	15.03%	6.92%	6.75%	8.28%	0.00200
13	1957	-17.95%	-14.31%	-5.12%	-12.83%	0.00506
14	1958	47.50%	59.68%	36.24%	11.26%	0.00410
15	1959	33.52%	15.41%	11.50%	22.02%	0.01652
16	1960	-21.84%	-1.56%	2.01%	-23.85%	0.02039
17	1961	0.28%	29.45%	19.34%	-19.06%	0.01371
18	1962	-21.84%	-12.75%	-4.24%	-17.60%	0.01230
19	1963	29.83%	18.69%	13.33%	16.50%	0.01139
20	1964	13.62%	18.13%	13.02%	0.60%	0.00002
21	1965	5.31%	28.61%	18.87%	-13.56%	0.00852
22	1966	-17.52%	-7.06%	-1.06%	-16.46%	0.01321
23	1967	45.26%	50.38%	31.04%	14.22%	0.01038
24	1968	-7.78%	30.55%	19.96%	-27.73%	0.04156
25	1969	-8.75%	-20.30%	-8.46%	-0.29%	0.00000
26	1970	11.42%	-2.90%	1.26%	10.16%	0.00618
27	1971	64.94%	19.47%	13.76%	51.18%	0.16506
28	1972	31.19%	8.45%	7.61%	23.58%	0.03690
29	1973	15.32%	-29.31%	-13.50%	28.82%	0.05800
30	1974	-2.32%	-26.53%	-11.95%	9.63%	0.00681
31	1975	69.55%	61.90%	37.48%	32.07%	0.07959
32	1976	-3.39%	45.49%	28.31%	-31.70%	0.08183
33	1977	-36.06%	9.50%	8.19%	-44.25%	0.16789
34	1978	-2.14%	14.02%	10.72%	-12.86%	0.01492
35	1979	35.82%	35.31%	22.62%	13.20%	0.01656
36	1980	5.13%	30.99%	20.20%	-15.07%	0.02272
37			Sum of weighted squared errors			0.81563

1 **Trial values of overpredictions and underpredictions.** Insert four blank columns (E–H) to the right of column D of the least squares spreadsheet. Then enter *any* trial values for the overpredictions and underpredictions in the range E10:F34.

Columns E and F (labeled Overpredict and Underpredict, respectively) contain the amount by which we overpredict or underpredict each year's return on Dow Chemical. The key to understanding this procedure is to realize that at least one of the values in columns E and F (in each row) will be zero in the Solver's solution. That is, we will either overpredict or underpredict in a given year, but not both. This means that the sum of the absolute prediction errors is just the sum of the total overprediction errors plus the total underprediction errors.

2 **Prediction errors.** Enter the formula

=E10–F10

FIGURE 6.19 LAD Estimates of Alpha and Beta

	A	B	C	D	E	F	G	H	I
1	Estimating the Beta for Dow Chemical								
2	Least Absolute Deviation Criterion								
3									
4	Parameters of prediction model								
5	Alpha	Beta							
6	0.0553	0.7033							
7									
8	Historical returns								
9	Year	DowChem	Market	Prediction	OverPredict	UnderPredict	Over-Under		Error
10	1956	15.03%	6.92%	10.39%	4.64%	0.00%	4.64%	=	4.64%
11	1957	-17.95%	-14.31%	-4.54%	0.00%	13.41%	-13.41%	=	-13.41%
12	1958	47.50%	59.68%	47.50%	0.00%	0.00%	0.00%	=	0.00%
13	1959	33.52%	15.41%	16.36%	17.16%	0.00%	17.16%	=	17.16%
14	1960	-21.84%	-1.56%	4.43%	0.00%	26.27%	-26.27%	=	-26.27%
15	1961	0.28%	29.45%	26.24%	0.00%	25.96%	-25.96%	=	-25.96%
16	1962	-21.84%	-12.75%	-3.44%	0.00%	18.40%	-18.40%	=	-18.40%
17	1963	29.83%	18.69%	18.67%	11.16%	0.00%	11.16%	=	11.16%
18	1964	13.62%	18.13%	18.28%	0.00%	4.66%	-4.66%	=	-4.66%
19	1965	5.31%	28.61%	[illegible]	0.00%	20.34%	-20.34%	=	-20.34%
20	1966	-17.52%	-7.06%	0.56%	0.00%	18.08%	-18.08%	=	-18.08%
21	1967	45.26%	50.38%	40.96%	4.30%	0.00%	4.30%	=	4.30%
22	1968	-7.78%	30.55%	27.01%	0.00%	34.79%	-34.79%	=	-34.79%
23	1969	-8.75%	-20.30%	-8.75%	0.00%	0.00%	0.00%	=	0.00%
24	1970	11.42%	-2.90%	3.49%	7.93%	0.00%	7.93%	=	7.93%
25	1971	64.94%	19.47%	19.22%	45.72%	0.00%	45.72%	=	45.72%
26	1972	31.19%	8.45%	11.47%	19.72%	0.00%	19.72%	=	19.72%
27	1973	15.32%	-29.31%	-15.09%	30.41%	0.00%	30.41%	=	30.41%
28	1974	-2.32%	-26.53%	-13.13%	10.81%	0.00%	10.81%	=	10.81%
29	1975	69.55%	61.90%	49.06%	20.49%	0.00%	20.49%	=	20.49%
30	1976	-3.39%	45.49%	37.52%	0.00%	40.91%	-40.91%	=	-40.91%
31	1977	-36.06%	9.50%	12.21%	0.00%	48.27%	-48.27%	=	-48.27%
32	1978	-2.14%	14.02%	15.39%	0.00%	17.53%	-17.53%	=	-17.53%
33	1979	35.82%	35.31%	30.36%	5.46%	0.00%	5.46%	=	5.46%
34	1980	5.13%	30.99%	27.32%	0.00%	22.19%	-22.19%	=	-22.19%
35				Totals	177.79%	290.81%			
36									
37				Average of Absolute Errors		18.74%			

in cell G10 and copy this formula to the range G11:G34 for the other years. For example, if E10 and F10 contain the values 1 and 0, say, then we overpredicted in this year, and the difference of +1 is the prediction error. But if the values in E10 and F10 are 0 and 1, then we underpredicted in this year, and the difference of −1 is the prediction error. Whether we overpredict or underpredict the difference in column G is the prediction error.

Note that the actual prediction errors (from Equation 6.8) are in column I. Unless the trial values for overprediction and underprediction in columns E and F are perfect, the resulting prediction errors in column G will be different from those in column I. The idea is that we are calculating the prediction errors in two different ways: from Equation 6.8 and as overpredictions minus underpredictions. The only way to make these two equal is to *constrain* them to be equal, which we will do when we use the Solver.

3 **Total overpredictions and underpredictions.** In cell E35 compute the total of the overpredictions with the formula

=SUM(E10:E34)

Copy this formula to cell F35 to compute the total of the underpredictions.

4 **Average absolute error.** In cell F37 compute the average of the absolute errors with the formula

=(E35+F35)/25

where the denominator is the number of observations.

Using the Solver to Find the LAD Estimates We modify the Solver settings from the original least squares spreadsheet as follows.

1 **Objective.** Choose cell F37 as the objective to minimize.

2 **Extra changing cells.** Add the range E10:F34 (overpredictions and underpredictions) as extra changing cells and constrain them to be nonnegative.

3 **Consistency constraints on overpredictions and underpredictions.** Add the constraints G10:G34=I10:I34. As discussed above, these ensure that the prediction errors implied by the overpredictions and underpredictions in columns E and F are consistent with the actual errors derived from Equation 6.8.

4 **Linear model and optimize.** Check the Assume Linear Model box (since all of the constraints are linear) and Solve.

The Solver solution appears in Figure 6.19. We see that the LAD estimates are $a =$ .055 and $b = .703$. With this criterion, the predicted return on Dow Chemical is given by

$$\text{Predicted return} = .055 + .703 * \text{Market return}$$

Note that this estimate of β is slightly larger than with the least squares approaches, but it is still less than 1. Also, note that for each observation, either the amount of overprediction or underprediction is 0. We claimed the Solver solution would have this property.

Developing the Spreadsheet Model for Minimax Since the minimax method is also concerned with *absolute* prediction errors, it is simplest to develop its spreadsheet by modifying the LAD spreadsheet. The modifications appear in Figure 6.20. (See the file BETA4.XLS.) The following steps are required.

1 **Trial value of maximum absolute error.** Enter *any* trial value in cell D36 for the maximum absolute error. Then "copy" this value to cell D38 by entering the formula

```
=D36
```

in cell D38. (The reason for placing this value in two cells is that cell D38 will eventually be the objective cell, and the Solver requires a *formula* to be in the objective cell.)

Observe that the maximum absolute error is just the largest number in the range E10:F34 of the LAD spreadsheet (Figure 6.19). We could use Excel's MAX function to capture this maximum error, but as we have stated before, the Solver performs unpredictably when the MAX function is used. Therefore, we resort to a more indirect method.

2 **Copy the maximum absolute error.** Insert two columns (F and G) to the right of column E in the LAD spreadsheet. (We use column F only to indicate constraints.) We want "copies" of the value in cell D36 in the entire range G10:G34, so enter the formula

```
=$D$36
```

in cell G10 and copy it to the range G11:G34. Similarly, insert two columns (I and J) to the right of column H. (We use column I only to indicate constraints.) Again, "copy" the trial value of the maximum error to column J by entering the formula

```
=$D$36
```

in cell J10 and copying it to the range J11:J34.

FIGURE 6.20 Minimax Estimates of Alpha and Beta

	A	B	C	D	E	F	G	H	I	J	K	L	M
1	Estimating the Beta for Dow Chemical												
2	Minimax Criterion												
3													
4	Parameters of prediction model												
5	Alpha	Beta											
6	0.0129	0.9078											
7													
8	Historical returns												
9	Year	DowChem	Market	Prediction	OverPredict		Maximum	UnderPredict		Maximum	Over-Under		Error
10	1956	15.03%	6.92%	7.57%	7.46%	<=	45.97%	0.00%	<=	45.97%	7.46%	=	7.46%
11	1957	-17.95%	-14.31%	-11.70%	0.00%	<=	45.97%	6.25%	<=	45.97%	-6.25%	=	-6.25%
12	1958	47.50%	59.68%	55.47%	0.00%	<=	45.97%	7.97%	<=	45.97%	-7.97%	=	-7.97%
13	1959	33.52%	15.41%	15.28%	18.24%	<=	45.97%	0.00%	<=	45.97%	18.24%	=	18.24%
14	1960	-21.84%	-1.56%	-0.12%	0.00%	<=	45.97%	21.72%	<=	45.97%	-21.72%	=	-21.72%
15	1961	0.28%	29.45%	28.02%	0.00%	<=	45.97%	27.74%	<=	45.97%	-27.74%	=	-27.74%
16	1962	-21.84%	-12.75%	-10.28%	0.00%	<=	45.97%	11.56%	<=	45.97%	-11.56%	=	-11.56%
17	1963	29.83%	18.69%	18.26%	11.57%	<=	45.97%	0.00%	<=	45.97%	11.57%	=	11.57%
18	1964	13.62%	18.13%	17.75%	0.00%	<=	45.97%	4.13%	<=	45.97%	-4.13%	=	-4.13%
19	1965	5.31%	28.61%	27.26%	0.00%	<=	45.97%	21.95%	<=	45.97%	-21.95%	=	-21.95%
20	1966	-17.52%	-7.06%	-5.12%	0.00%	<=	45.97%	12.40%	<=	45.97%	-12.40%	=	-12.40%
21	1967	45.26%	50.38%	47.02%	0.00%	<=	45.97%	1.76%	<=	45.97%	-1.76%	=	-1.76%
22	1968	-7.78%	30.55%	29.02%	0.00%	<=	45.97%	36.80%	<=	45.97%	-36.80%	=	-36.80%
23	1969	-8.75%	-20.30%	-17.14%	8.39%	<=	45.97%	0.00%	<=	45.97%	8.39%	=	8.39%
24	1970	11.42%	-2.90%	-1.34%	12.76%	<=	45.97%	0.00%	<=	45.97%	12.76%	=	12.76%
25	1971	64.94%	19.47%	18.97%	45.97%	<=	45.97%	0.00%	<=	45.97%	45.97%	=	45.97%
26	1972	31.19%	8.45%	8.96%	22.23%	<=	45.97%	0.00%	<=	45.97%	22.23%	=	22.23%
27	1973	15.32%	-29.31%	-25.32%	40.64%	<=	45.97%	0.00%	<=	45.97%	40.64%	=	40.64%
28	1974	-2.32%	-26.53%	-22.79%	20.47%	<=	45.97%	0.00%	<=	45.97%	20.47%	=	20.47%
29	1975	69.55%	61.90%	57.48%	12.07%	<=	45.97%	0.00%	<=	45.97%	12.07%	=	12.07%
30	1976	-3.39%	45.49%	42.58%	0.00%	<=	45.97%	45.97%	<=	45.97%	-45.97%	=	-45.97%
31	1977	-36.06%	9.50%	9.91%	0.00%	<=	45.97%	45.97%	<=	45.97%	-45.97%	=	-45.97%
32	1978	-2.14%	14.02%	14.02%	0.00%	<=	45.97%	16.16%	<=	45.97%	-16.16%	=	-16.16%
33	1979	35.82%	35.31%	33.34%	2.48%	<=	45.97%	0.00%	<=	45.97%	2.48%	=	2.48%
34	1980	5.13%	30.99%	29.42%	0.00%	<=	45.97%	24.29%	<=	45.97%	-24.29%	=	-24.29%
35													
36	Trial value for maximum error			45.97%									
37													
38	Maximum absolute error			45.97%									

Using the Solver to Find the Minimax Estimates We modify the LAD Solver settings as follows. (These are all *additions* to the previous Solver settings. Therefore, the Assume Linear Model box should still be checked.)

1 **Objective.** Choose cell D38 as the objective to minimize. Combined with the next step, this will minimize the largest of the absolute errors.

2 **Constraints on individual absolute errors.** Add the constraints E10:E34<=G10:G34 and H10:H34<=J10:J34. These ensure that the maximum absolute error will be at least as large as each of the absolute errors. That is, the value in cell D36 (or D38) will be at least as large as each of the overpredictions and underpredictions.

3 **Optimize.** Click on Solve.

The Solver solution appears in Figure 6.20. We see that the minimax estimates are $a = .013$ and $b = .908$. With this criterion the predicted return on Dow Chemical is given by

$$\text{Predicted return} = .013 + .908 * \text{Market return}$$

Note that the estimate of β is now .908, a bit larger than the estimates from any of the other methods but still less than 1. Also, note that the maximum absolute error in Figure 6.20, .4597, is smaller than the maximum absolute error in any of the other spreadsheets. ■

PROBLEMS

Skill-Building Problems

29 Given the information in Table 6.8, use the four criteria discussed in this section to estimate the β (and α) for GM.

TABLE 6.8 Returns for GM Problem

	Return on GM Stock	Return on S&P 500
1961	12%	21%
1962	2%	−3%
1963	38%	15%
1964	26%	20%
1965	18%	12%
1966	−10%	0%
1967	0%	10%
1968	9%	10%
1969	−2%	2%
1970	−1%	−15%

30 Widco has observed the daily production and daily variable production cost of widgets produced at its New York City plant. The data in Table 6.9 have been collected. Widco believes that daily production and daily variable costs are related as follows. For some numbers α and β,

$$\text{Daily variable cost} = \alpha + \beta * \text{Daily production} + \text{Error term}$$

Use the four methods of this section to estimate α and β. ■

TABLE 6.9 Data for Widco Problem

	Production	Variable Cost
Day 1	4000	\$9,000
Day 2	6000	\$12,000
Day 3	7000	\$14,000
Day 4	1000	\$5,000
Day 5	3000	\$8,000

6.8 Rating Sports Teams

Sports fans always wonder which team is best in a given sport. Was Florida State, Notre Dame, or Nebraska number 1 during the 1993 NCAA football season? A spreadsheet Solver can be used to rate sports teams. We examine one method for rating sports teams in the following example.

EXAMPLE 6.8

We wish to determine the rating of NFL teams for the 1991 season.

Solution

We examined the results of 127 NFL games from the 1991 season and entered the data into a spreadsheet, shown in Figure 6.21 (see the file NFL.XLS). (Some of these results are hidden in Figure 6.21 for reasons of space.) The teams are indexed 1–28. For example, team 1 is Miami, team 2 is Buffalo, and so on. The first game entered (row 37) was team 1 (Miami) versus team 2 (Buffalo) at Buffalo. The margin of victory for the home team is given in column C. Thus, Buffalo won the game in row 37 by 4 points. A negative score in

FIGURE 6.21 Ratings of NFL Teams

	A	B	C	D	E	F
1	**Rating NFL teams**					
2					**Ordered rankings (best first)**	
3	**Team name**	**ID number**	**Rating**		**Team name**	**Rating**
4	Miami Dolphins	1	-5.9689		Washington Redskins	17.0311
5	Buffalo Bills	2	0.1248		Houston Oilers	14.0854
6	Dallas Cowboys	3	4.8942		New Orleans Saints	9.5119
7	Cleveland Browns	4	-1.0092		Kansas City Chiefs	6.8991
8	Atlanta Falcons	5	1.0180		San Francisco 49ers	6.1276
9	Kansas City Chiefs	6	6.8991		Seattle Seahawks	5.2495
10	New England Patriots	7	-7.0868		Dallas Cowboys	4.8942
11	Indianapolis Colts	8	-14.5852		Denver Broncos	3.6381
12	Philadelphia Eagles	9	2.0648		Minnesota Vikings	2.1752
13	Green Bay Packers	10	-3.2568		Philadelphia Eagles	2.0648
14	Cincinnati Bengals	11	-6.6860		Atlanta Falcons	1.0180
15	Denver Broncos	12	3.6381		Chicago Bears	0.7074
16	Phoenix Cardinals	13	-5.3258		Buffalo Bills	0.1248
17	Los Angeles Rams	14	-3.0181		Los Angeles Raiders	-0.0996
18	Minnesota Vikings	15	2.1752		New York Jets	-0.2724
19	Chicago Bears	16	0.7074		Cleveland Browns	-1.0092
20	Detroit Lions	17	-7.0382		New York Giants	-1.4143
21	Washington Redskins	18	17.0311		Los Angeles Rams	-3.0181
22	Tampa Bay Buccaneers	19	-10.4712		San Diego Chargers	-3.2360
23	New York Jets	20	-0.2724		Green Bay Packers	-3.2568
24	Seattle Seahawks	21	5.2495		Pittsburgh Steelers	-3.9163
25	New Orleans Saints	22	9.5119		Phoenix Cardinals	-5.3258
26	San Diego Chargers	23	-3.2360		Miami Dolphins	-5.9689
27	Pittsburgh Steelers	24	-3.9163		Cincinnati Bengals	-6.6860
28	Los Angeles Raiders	25	-0.0996		Detroit Lions	-7.0382
29	Houston Oilers	26	14.0854		New England Patriots	-7.0868
30	San Francisco 49ers	27	6.1276		Tampa Bay Buccaneers	-10.4712
31	New York Giants	28	-1.4143		Indianapolis Colts	-14.5852
32						
33	Home team advantage	3	Actual average		Desired average	
34			0.0	=	0	
35	Results of games					
36	Visitor	Home team	Home team score minus visitor score	Predicted difference	Squared error	
37	1	2	4	9.0937	25.9453	
38	3	4	-12	-2.9034	82.7480	
39	5	6	11	8.8812	4.4895	
159	1	8	-4	-5.6164	2.6127	
160	13	3	20	13.2200	45.9688	
161	4	12	2	7.6473	31.8917	
162	19	15	15	15.6464	0.4178	
163	28	10	23	1.1575	477.0947	
164				Sum of squared errors	14347.1678	

column C means that the home team lost. Our goal is to determine a set of ratings for the 28 NFL teams that most accurately predicts the outcomes of the games listed.

Suppose that team i plays at home against team j. Then our prediction for the outcome of the game is that team i will win by

$$\text{Predicted margin} = \text{Team } i \text{ rating} + 3 - \text{Team } j \text{ rating}$$

The "+3" is due to the fact that NFL home teams outscore their opponents by an average of three points per game. (In other words, the average home-team advantage is three points. This value appears in cell B33.) We define the error in predicting a game to be

$$\text{Error} = \text{Actual victory margin for home team}$$
$$- \text{Predicted victory margin for home team}$$

We wish to determine ratings that minimize the sum of squared prediction errors. To "normalize" the ratings, we will require that the average of the 28 ratings equals 0. Thus a team with a rating of 0 is an "average" team.

Developing the Spreadsheet Model The spreadsheet in Figure 6.21 is formed as follows.

1 **Predictions.** To generate the predictions, enter the formula

=$B$33+VLOOKUP(B37,$B$4:$C$31,2)–VLOOKUP(A37,$B$4:$C$31,2)

in cell D37. The first VLOOKUP term "looks up" the rating of the home team. More precisely, this term tells Excel to proceed as follows:

a Find the number in column 1 of the "lookup table range" $B$4:$C$31 that matches the number in cell B37. This is the "2" in cell B5 since the home team for the first game is Buffalo.

b Then find the number in the second column of the lookup table range—second because 2 is the last argument of the VLOOKUP function—that is in the same row as the "2" found in the previous step. This is Buffalo's rating.[4]

Similarly, the second VLOOKUP term looks up the visiting team's rating. Now copy the formula in cell D37 to the range D38:D163 to compute the predictions for all other games.

2 **Squared prediction errors.** In column E compute the squared error of the prediction for each game: enter the formula

=(C37–D37)^2

in cell E37 and copy it to the range E38:E163. Then in cell E164 compute the sum of squared errors with the formula

=SUM(E37:E163)

3 **Average rating.** Compute the average rating of all 28 teams in cell C34 with the formula

=AVERAGE(C4:C31)

Also, enter the desired average rating (0) in cell E34.

Using the Solver

1 **Objective.** Choose cell E164 (sum of squared errors) as the objective to minimize.

2 **Changing cells.** Choose the range C4:C31 as the changing cells. These do *not* need to be nonnegative; the ratings can be positive or negative.

3 **Average rating constraint.** Add the constraint C34=E34. This constraint forces the average rating to be 0.

4 **Optimize.** Click on Solve.

The ratings found by the Solver are shown in Figure 6.21. We have sorted the ratings of the teams from best to worst in the range F4:F31. We see that Washington and Houston were the two best teams and the Colts were the worst team (no surprise to us Indiana fans!). If Washington had hosted the Colts that year, they would have been favored by $17.03 + 3 - (-14.59) = 34.62$ points!

Is the Solver Solution Optimal? It turns out that the squared error for each game is a convex function of the ratings of the teams playing in the game. Since the total squared error is the sum of the individual squared errors, it follows that the total squared error is a convex function of all the team ratings. The only constraint is linear, so we know that the Solver has found the best ratings. ■

[4] For Lotus users, the last argument in the VLOOKUP table is always one less than the similar argument in Excel. Lotus refers to it as the "offset." However, the bad news is that What's Best! does not support the VLOOKUP command—Lotus does but What's Best! doesn't. So to rate teams in Lotus, you must manually type in the code numbers of the teams in each game.

MODELING ISSUES

1 We can improve the future predictive accuracy by giving more weight to more recent games. To do this, we multiply the squared error for a game k weeks ago by a factor such as $(0.95)^k$. As an example of how this "discounts" the importance of past games, this weighting gives a game from five weeks ago about 77% of the weight given to this week's game.

2 We can also use a Solver to find the set of ratings that minimize the average absolute deviation of the predictions.

3 You can make the home field edge an additional changing cell (instead of a given input cell) and have the Solver determine the value of this cell that minimizes the prediction errors. For example, in college basketball the home field edge is about five points, while in pro basketball it is about three points.

4 The average absolute error for the games in Figure 6.21 was 8.12 points per game. If we used our ratings to forecast the next week of NFL games, we would probably see an average absolute error exceeding 8.12 points. This is because most forecasting methods fail to perform as well on data they have not yet seen as they perform on the data used to generate the forecasts. This phenomenon is called **overfitting**. ■

PROBLEMS

Skill-Building Problems

31 In the Bloomington Girls Club Basketball League, the following games have been played: team A beat team B by 7 points, team C beat team A by 8 points, team B beat team C by 6 points, and team B beat team C by 9 points. Let A, B, and C represent "ratings" for the teams in the sense that if, say, team A plays team B, we predict that team A will win by $A - B$ points (or lose by $A - B$ points if $A - B$ is negative). (We assume that there is no home-court advantage.) Determine values of A, B, and C that best fit (in the least-squares sense) these results. To obtain a unique set of ratings, add the constraint that $A + B + C = 0$. This ensures that an "average" team will have a rating of 0.

32 The file BIG94.XLS contains the scores of the 1994 Big Ten Basketball season. Develop ratings for the 11 teams. Use a home team advantage of 5 points. Which was the best team? The worst team? If you are an Indiana fan, try it again after deleting Indiana's huge loss to Minnesota. See how much this "outlier" affects the results. ■

6.9

Finding Implied Stock Volatilities

Some problems that do not have an objective to minimize or maximize can still be modeled and solved using a spreadsheet Solver. To illustrate, we show how a spreadsheet Solver can be used in conjunction with the Black-Scholes option pricing formula to estimate the volatility (standard deviation) of the annual return on a stock.

What Is an Option?

A **European option** on a stock gives the owner of the option the right to buy (if the option is a *call* option) or sell (if the option is a *put* option) one share of a stock for a particular price on a particular date. The price at which the option holder can buy or sell a stock is called the **exercise price**. The date on which the option must be "exercised" is called the **expiration date**.

For example, suppose that a stock is currently selling for $50 and you purchase a call option with an exercise price of $50 and a three-month expiration date. What cash flows do you obtain from this option? Let S_T denote the price of the stock at the expiration date. Then your cash flow from this option, ignoring the cost of buying the option, is 0 if $S_T \leq 50$, or $S_T - 50$ if $S_T > 50$. In the first case we say that you're "out of the money," whereas in the second case you're "in the money."

The reasoning behind these expressions is that if the price of the stock three months from now exceeds $50, you can buy one share of the stock for $50 and sell it on the open market for its current price; the difference is your profit. However, if the price of the stock at the expiration date is less than $50, then you cannot make any money by exercising your option, so you simply let the option expire and do nothing. In short,

$$\text{Cash flow from call option} = \max(0, S_T - 50) \qquad \textbf{(6.9)}$$

Pricing a Call Option

Since option trading is a multibillion dollar business, it is natural to ask how a "fair" price for a given option is determined. Black and Scholes [1] were the first to derive a formula for pricing options. Their work revolutionized investments and corporate finance. The work of Black and Scholes shows that the call option price for a European option is a function of the current price of the stock, the exercise price of the option, the duration (time until expiration) of the option, the risk-free interest rate, and the standard deviation of the annual return of the stock. If we label these five quantities *SP*, *EP*, *DUR*, *IR*, and *VOL* (for volatility), then the Black-Scholes formula can be developed as follows. First, define the quantities d_1 and d_2 as

$$d_1 = \frac{\ln(\frac{SP}{EP}) + (IR + VOL^2/2) * DUR}{VOL * \sqrt{DUR}}$$

and

$$d_2 = d_1 - VOL * \sqrt{DUR}$$

Then the Black-Scholes option price is given by

$$\text{Black-Scholes option price} = SP * N(d_1) - EP * e^{-DUR*IR} * N(d_2)$$

where $N(d_i)$ represents the cumulative normal distribution function evaluated at d_i, that is, $N(d_i)$ is the probability that a standard normal random variable (mean 0, standard deviation 1) is less than or equal to d_i ($i = 1$ or 2).

In reality, the first four inputs (*SP*, *EP*, *DUR*, and *IR*) are usually known, but the fifth, *VOL*, is not. The volatility of a stock can be estimated as the standard deviation of the stock's return based on past data. However, a better prediction of the *future* volatility of a stock can be found by a "back-door" approach. After observing the first four inputs and today's *actual* option price, we ask what standard deviation (volatility) would make the price from Black-Scholes equal to today's actual price. The answer to this question is called the stock's **implied volatility**. That is, the implied volatility is the volatility of the stock implied by today's quoted option price. We can find this implied volatility fairly easily on a spreadsheet, as we demonstrate in the following example.

EXAMPLE 6.9

My broker wants to determine the implied volatility of RocoCo stock. The current stock price is \$50, the exercise price is \$50, the option expires in three months (.25 year), the annual risk-free interest rate is 8%, and today's quoted price of the option is \$3.97.

Solution

Although there is no objective to maximize or minimize, we can use a spreadsheet Solver to model and solve this problem. The spreadsheet model is formed as follows. (See Figure 6.22 and the file OPTION.XLS.)

Developing the Spreadsheet Model

1 **Inputs.** Enter the above inputs in the range B5:B8 and cell B13.

2 **Volatility.** Enter *any* trial value for volatility of the stock in cell B10.

3 **Quantities for Black-Scholes formula.** Calculate the quantities d_1 and d_2 in cells B16 and B17 with the formulas

=(LN(B5/B6)+(B8+B10^2/2)*B7)/(B10*SQRT(B7))

and

=B16–B10*SQRT(B7)

4 **Values from normal distribution.** Calculate the normal distribution, evaluated at d_1, in cell E16 with the formula

=NORMSDIST(B16)

Then copy this formula to cell E17 to do the same for d_2. Note that the built-in NORMSDIST function is designed precisely to calculate standard normal cumulative probabilities.

5 **Option price.** Calculate the Black-Scholes option price in cell D13 with the formula

=B5*E16–B6*EXP(–B7*B8)*E17

Using the Solver

1 **No objective.** Clear the Target cell box; there is no objective to minimize or maximize.

2 **Changing cell.** Choose cell B10 as the only changing cell and constrain it to be nonnegative.

3 **Prediction constraint.** Add the constraint B13=D13.

4 **"Optimize."** Click on Solve.

The above settings tell the Solver to find a nonnegative value in cell B10 (the implied volatility) that makes the Black-Scholes formula (in cell D13) yield the actual option price (\$3.97). From Figure 6.22 we see that implied volatility of the option equals 35%.

The Goal Seek Tool It may appear strange to use the Solver, an optimization tool, when there is no objective to maximize or minimize. It turns out that this is perfectly acceptable—the above procedure works—but there is another Excel tool that also does the job. This is the Goal Seek tool, found under the Tools menu. It can be used any time you want to force a single output cell to equal a specified value when there is a single changing cell that affects this output cell. For the current example, instead of using the Solver, try using Goal Seek. When you see the Goal Seek dialog box, enter D13 in the *Set cell* box,

FIGURE 6.22 **Solution to Option Pricing Example**

	A	B	C	D	E	F
1	**Black-Scholes Option Pricing Problem**					
2	**Using the Option Price to Find the Implied Volatility**					
3						
4	**Input data**					
5	Stock price	$50				
6	Exercise price	$50				
7	Duration	0.25				
8	Interest rate	8%				
9						
10	Implied volatility (stdev)	35.01%				
11						
12	Option price	Actual		Predicted		
13		$3.97	=	$3.97		
14						
15	Other quantities for option price					
16	d1	0.20178		N(d1)	0.57996	
17	d2	0.02674		N(d2)	0.51067	

3.97 in the *To value* box, and B10 in the *By changing cell* box. You should obtain the same implied volatility of 35%. ■

MODELING ISSUES

1 The same basic spreadsheet can also be used to find the price of an option if the volatility is known. Then the known volatility should be entered in cell B10 and the Black-Scholes price is calculated automatically in cell D13. (Cell B13 can be left blank, and there is no need for the Solver or Goal Seek at all.)

2 An option is often called a **derivative** because it derives its value from another quantity (the price of the stock on which the option is written). ■

PROBLEMS

Skill-Building Problems

33 A stock is currently selling for $36. A call option with a duration of three months on this stock has an exercise price of $40. Currently the option is selling for $2.26 and the risk-free rate is 5%. What is the implied volatility of the stock?

34 A stock is currently selling for $50. A call option with a duration of 199 days on this stock has an exercise price of $49. Currently the option is selling for $5.85 and the risk-free rate is 7%. What is the implied volatility of the stock?

35 The **yield** of a bond is the interest rate that makes the present value of its payments equal to the price of the bond. Suppose a bond sells for $980 and yields the following payments:

One year from now: $100

Two years from now: $90

Three years from now: $110

Four years from now: $1100

Use the Goal Seek tool in Excel to find the yield of the bond. ■

6.10

Portfolio Optimization

Given a set of investments, how do we find the portfolio that has the minimum variance and yields an acceptable expected return? This question was answered by Harry Markowitz in the 1950s. For his work on this and other investment topics, he received the Nobel Prize in economics in 1991. The ideas discussed in this section are the basis for most methods of **asset allocation** used by Wall Street firms. **Asset allocation models** are used, for example, to determine the percentage of assets to invest in stocks, gold, and Treasury bills. To begin we need to review some important formulas involving the mean and variance of sums of random variables.

Sums of Random Variables: Mean and Variance

Let S_i be the (random) return earned during a year on a dollar invested in investment i. Thus if $S_i = .10$, a dollar invested at the beginning of the year grows to \$1.10 at the end of the year, whereas if $S_i = -.20$, a dollar invested at the beginning of the year decreases in value to \$0.80. We assume that n investments are available. Let x_i be the fraction of our money invested in investment i. We assume that $x_1 + x_2 + \cdots + x_n = 1$, so that all of our money is invested. To rule out shorting a stock, that is, selling shares we don't own, we assume that $x_i \geq 0$. Then the annual return on our investments is given by the random variable R, where

$$R = x_1 S_1 + x_2 S_2 + \cdots + x_n S_n$$

Let μ_i be the expected value of S_i, let σ_i^2 be the variance of S_i (so that σ_i is the standard deviation of S_i), and let ρ_{ij} be the correlation between S_i and S_j. To do any work with investments, you must understand how to use the following formulas, which relate the data for the individual investments to the expected return and the variance of return for a *portfolio* of investments.

$$\text{Expected value of } R = x_1\mu_1 + x_2\mu_2 + \cdots + x_n\mu_n \quad \textbf{(6.10)}$$

$$\text{Variance of } R = x_1^2\sigma_1^2 + x_2^2\sigma_2^2 + \cdots + x_n^2\sigma_n^2 + \sum_{i \neq j} x_i x_j \rho_{ij}\sigma_i\sigma_j \quad \textbf{(6.11)}$$

Since we never actually know the true expected values (μ_i's), variances (σ_i^2's), and correlations (ρ_{ij}'s), we must estimate them. If historical data are used, we proceed as follows.

1 Estimate μ_i by $\overline{X}_i$, the sample average of returns on investment i over several previous years. You can use the Excel AVERAGE function to obtain $\overline{X}_i$.

2 Estimate σ_i^2 by s_i^2, the sample variance of returns on investment i over several previous years. You can use the Excel VAR function to obtain s_i^2.

3 Estimate σ_i by s_i, the sample standard deviation of returns on investment i. You can obtain s_i with the Excel STDEV function. (Alternatively, of course, you can obtain s_i as the square root of s_i^2.)

4 Estimate ρ_{ij} by r_{ij}, the sample correlation between past returns on investments i and j. You can find all of the r_{ij}'s by using Excel's Correlation option from the Tools/Data Analysis menu item. The input range should consist of n columns of historical returns.

We now estimate the mean and variance of the return on a portfolio by replacing each parameter in Equations 6.10 and 6.11 with its sample estimate. This yields

$$\text{Estimated expected value of } R = x_1\overline{X}_1 + x_2\overline{X}_2 + \cdots + x_n\overline{X}_n \quad \textbf{(6.12)}$$

and

$$\text{Estimated variance of } R = x_1^2 s_1^2 + x_2^2 s_2^2 + \cdots + x_n^2 s_n^2 + \sum_{i \neq j} x_i x_j r_{ij} s_i s_j \quad \textbf{(6.13)}$$

In keeping with common practice, we express the annual return on investments as decimals. Thus a return of .10 on a stock means that the stock has increased in value by 10%.

Most investors have two objectives in forming portfolios: to obtain a large expected return and to obtain a small variance (in order to minimize risk). The most common way of handling this two-objective problem is to specify a minimal expected return that we require and then minimize the variance subject to this expected return requirement. The following example shows how we can use a spreadsheet Solver to do this.

EXAMPLE 6.10

Stockco can invest in three stocks. From past data, the means and standard deviations of annual returns have been estimated as shown in Table 6.10 (where we express percentages as decimals). The correlation between the annual returns on the stocks are listed in Table 6.11. Stockco wants to find a minimum variance portfolio that yields an expected annual return of at least .12.

TABLE 6.10 **Estimated Means and Standard Deviations for Stockco Example**

	Mean	Standard Deviation
Stock 1	.14	.20
Stock 2	.11	.15
Stock 3	.10	.08

TABLE 6.11 **Estimated Correlations for Stockco Example**

Combination	Correlation
Stocks 1 and 2	.6
Stocks 1 and 3	.4
Stocks 2 and 3	.7

Solution

To model Stockco's problem, we must keep track of the following:

- the fraction of money invested in each stock
- the total fraction of Stockco's money invested
- the expected annual return of the portfolio
- the variance of the annual portfolio return

Developing the Spreadsheet Model The individual steps are now listed. (See Figure 6.23 and the file PORTFOL1.XLS.)

FIGURE 6.23 Optimal Portfolio for Stockco Example

	A	B	C	D	E	F	G
1	**Stockco Portfolio Problem**						
2							
3	**Stock input data**						
4		Stock 1	Stock 2	Stock 3			
5	Mean return	0.14	0.11	0.1			
6	StDev of return	0.2	0.15	0.08			
7							
8	Correlations						
9		Stock 1	Stock 2	Stock 3			
10	Stock 1	1	0.6	0.4			
11	Stock 2	0.6	1	0.7			
12	Stock 3	0.4	0.7	1			
13							
14	**Investment decision**						
15		Stock 1	Stock 2	Stock 3	Total		Required
16	Fractions to invest	0.5	0	0.5	1	=	1
17							
18	Expected portfolio return						
19		Actual		Required			
20		0.12	>=	0.12			
21							
22	Standard deviations times fractions invested						
23		Stock 1	Stock 2	Stock 3			
24		0.1	0	0.04			
25							
26	Portfolio variance	0.0148					
27							
28	Portfolio stdev	0.1217					

1 **Inputs.** Enter the data from Tables 6.10 and 6.11 in the ranges B5:D6 and B10:D12. (Note that the correlation between any stock's return and itself is 1.)

2 **Fractions invested.** Enter *any* trial values in the range B16:D16 for the fractions of Stockco's money placed in the three investments.

3 **Total fraction invested.** Calculate the total fraction of money invested in cell E16 with the formula

=SUM(B16:D16)

Then enter a 1 in cell G16 to indicate that 100% of the money will be invested in the available investments.

4 **Expected annual return.** Use Equation 6.12 to compute the expected annual return. Specifically, enter the formula

=SUMPRODUCT(B16:D16,B5:D5)

in cell B20. Then enter the required annual mean return (.12) in cell D20.

5 **Variance of portfolio return.** In preparation for computing the variance of the portfolio return, compute for each stock the quantity

(Standard deviation of return on stock i) $*$ (Fraction of money invested in stock i)

Specifically, enter the formula

=B6*B16

in cell B24 for stock 1 and copy this formula to the range C24:D24 for the other two stocks. Now, using the entries in cells B24:D24, compute the estimated variance of the portfolio's annual return in cell B26 (from Equation 6.13) with the formula

```
=SUMPRODUCT(B24:D24,B24:D24)+2*B24*C24*C10
+2*B24*D24*D10+2*C24*D24*D11
```

The term SUMPRODUCT(B24:D24,B24:D24) corresponds to the first n variance terms in Equation 6.13, while the remaining terms correspond to the summation expression in Equation 6.13.

Using the Solver

1 **Objective.** Select cell B26 (portfolio variance) as the objective to minimize.

2 **Changing cells.** Choose the range B16:D16 as the changing cells and constrain these to be nonnegative.

3 **Constraint on expected return.** Add the constraint B20>=D20. This ensures that the portfolio will have an expected return of at least .12.

4 **Investment constraint.** Add the constraint E16=G16. This ensures that all of Stockco's money is invested.

5 **Optimize.** Click on Solve.

The Solver solution is shown in Figure 6.23. This portfolio has a variance of .0148 (or a standard deviation of $\sqrt{.0148} = .1217$). Stockco's optimal portfolio places half of the money in stock 1 and half in stock 3.

Is the Solver Solution Optimal? It can be shown that the variance of a portfolio is a convex function of the fractions invested in the various stocks. All of the constraints are linear. Therefore, the assumptions for a minimization problem are satisfied, and we are assured that the Solver will find the minimum variance portfolio. ■

MODELING ISSUES

1 What does it mean to say that the standard deviation of the annual return on the portfolio is .1217? If portfolio returns are normally distributed (which is usually a reasonable assumption), then during the year there is (1) a 68% chance that the portfolio return is between −.0017 (=.12−.1217) and .2417 (=.12+.1217), (2) a 95% chance that the portfolio return is between −.1234 (=.12−.2434) and .3634 (=.12+.2434), and (3) a 99.7% chance that the portfolio return is between −.2451 (=.12−.3651) and .4851 (=.12+.3651).

2 If Stockco is allowed to short a stock, we simply allow the fraction invested in that stock to be negative. That is, we simply eliminate the nonnegativity constraints on the changing cells.

3 An alternative objective might be to minimize the probability that the portfolio loses money. (See Problem 39.) ■

Matrix Multiplication and Portfolio Optimization (Optional)

The formula for the estimated variance of Stockco's portfolio was very tedious to enter in the spreadsheet. If we had ten investments, typing this variance formula would take forever. Using **matrix multiplication**, however, it is easy to express the variance of a portfolio. Before describing how this is done, we briefly review the mechanics of matrix multiplication.

A **matrix** is a rectangular array of numbers. We say a matrix is an $i \times j$ matrix if it consists of i rows and j columns. For example,

$$\begin{bmatrix} 1 & 2 & 3 \\ 4 & 5 & 6 \end{bmatrix}$$

is a 2×3 matrix, and

$$\begin{bmatrix} 1 & 2 & 3 & 4 \end{bmatrix}$$

is a 1×4 matrix. If the matrix has only a single row, it is sometimes called a **row vector**. Similarly, if it has only a single column, it is sometimes called a **column vector**.

If matrix A has the same number of columns as matrix B has rows, then we can construct the matrix product of A and B, which is denoted AB. The ij'th entry in AB is obtained by summing the products of the elements in row i of A with the corresponding elements in column j of B. If A is an $i \times r$ matrix and B is an $r \times j$ matrix, then AB is an $i \times j$ matrix.

For example, if

$$A = \begin{bmatrix} 1 & 2 & 3 \\ 2 & 4 & 5 \end{bmatrix}$$

and

$$B = \begin{bmatrix} 1 & 2 \\ 3 & 4 \\ 5 & 6 \end{bmatrix}$$

then AB is the following 2×2 matrix:

$$AB = \begin{bmatrix} 1(1)+2(3)+3(5) & 1(2)+2(4)+3(6) \\ 2(1)+4(3)+5(5) & 2(2)+4(4)+5(6) \end{bmatrix} = \begin{bmatrix} 22 & 28 \\ 39 & 50 \end{bmatrix}$$

The Excel MMULT function performs matrix multiplication in a single step.[5] The spreadsheet in Figure 6.24 shows how to multiply the above matrices A and B. (See the file

FIGURE 6.24 **Matrix Multiplication with Excel**

	A	B	C	D	E	F	G
1	**Matrix Multiplication with Excel**						
2							
3	Matrix A						
4		1	2	3			
5		2	4	5			
6							
7	Matrix B						
8		1	2				
9		3	4				
10		5	6				
11							
12	Matrix A times B, with formula =MMULT(B4:D5,B8:C10)						
13	Select range with 2 rows, 2 columns, enter formula, press Ctrl-Shift-Enter.						
14							
15		22	28				
16		39	50				

[5] Although you can use MMULT with Excel's Solver, the What's Best! add-in does not support this function.

MATRIX.XLS.) Matrix A is in the range B4:D5 and matrix B is in the range B8:C10. We know that the product AB will be a 2×2 matrix. To use MMULT to find AB, we highlight a blank 2×2 range in the spreadsheet, say B15:C16. Now type the *array* formula

=MMULT(B4:D5,B8:C10)

and press Control, Shift, and Enter (all at the same time). When you do so, the product matrix AB appears in the range B15:C16.

We can now explain how to use matrix multiplication to compute the variance of a portfolio. Suppose that n investments are available. Let x_i be the fraction of money invested in investment i; let s_i be the sample standard deviation of return on investment i; and let C be the $n \times n$ matrix whose ij'th entry is r_{ij}, the sample correlation between the returns on investments i and j.

It is not hard to show (see Problem 38) that the estimated portfolio variance, computed from Equation 6.13, can be written as

$$\text{Portfolio variance} = \begin{bmatrix} x_1s_1 & x_2s_2 & \cdots & x_ns_n \end{bmatrix} C \begin{bmatrix} x_1s_1 & x_2s_2 & \cdots & x_ns_n \end{bmatrix}^T \qquad \textbf{(6.14)}$$

Here $\begin{bmatrix} x_1s_1 & x_2s_2 & \cdots & x_ns_n \end{bmatrix}^T$ is the $n \times 1$ matrix (or column vector)

$$\begin{bmatrix} x_1s_1 \\ x_2s_2 \\ \vdots \\ x_ns_n \end{bmatrix}$$

Referring to the Stockco spreadsheet in Figure 6.23, if we use the MMULT function to compute the estimated variance of the return on Stockco's portfolio, there is no change except in the portfolio variance cell B26. Note that we have already computed the row vector

$$\begin{bmatrix} x_1s_1 & x_2s_2 & \cdots & x_ns_n \end{bmatrix}$$

in the range B24:D24. Also, the matrix C of correlations is already in the range B10:D12. So to compute the estimated portfolio variance, we enter the array formula

=MMULT(B24:D24,MMULT(B10:D12,TRANSPOSE(B24:D24)))

in cell B26. (See the file PORTFOL2.XLS.) Note that TRANSPOSE(B24:D24) creates the column vector

$$\begin{bmatrix} x_1s_1 & x_2s_2 & \cdots & x_ns_n \end{bmatrix}^T$$

Therefore, the inner MMULT finds the product

$$C\begin{bmatrix} x_1s_1 & x_2s_2 & \cdots & x_ns_n \end{bmatrix}^T$$

Then the outer MMULT multiplies this product on the left by the row vector

$$\begin{bmatrix} x_1s_1 & x_2s_2 & \cdots & x_ns_n \end{bmatrix}$$

to obtain the variance.

We could now use the Solver with the same settings as before to find the variance-minimizing portfolio that yields an expected return of at least 12%. Again, the main benefit from calculating the portfolio variance with the MMULT function is that it generalizes easily to *any* number of stocks, whereas the "brute force" formula used earlier becomes too tedious for a large number of stocks.

Note that in Equation 6.14 we first multiply a $1 \times n$ matrix by an $n \times n$ matrix. This yields a $1 \times n$ matrix, which is then multiplied by an $n \times 1$ matrix. The final result is a 1×1 matrix—a number.

PROBLEMS

Skill-Building Problems

36 The annual returns on three different types of assets (T-bonds, stocks, and gold) during the years 1968–88 are listed in Table 6.12. (See the file INV68.XLS.) For example, $1 invested in T-bonds at the beginning of 1978 grew to $1.07 by the end of 1978. You have $1000 to invest in these three investments. Your goal is to minimize the variance of the annual dollar return of your portfolio subject to the constraint that the expected return on the portfolio for a one-year period is at least .10.

TABLE 6.12 **Data for Security Problem**

	Stocks	Gold	T-Bonds		Stocks	Gold	T-Bonds
1968	.11	.11	.05	**1979**	.19	.59	.10
1969	−.09	.08	.07	**1980**	.33	.99	.11
1970	.04	.11	.07	**1981**	−.05	−.25	.15
1971	.14	.14	.04	**1982**	.22	.04	.11
1972	.19	.44	.04	**1983**	.23	−.11	.09
1973	−.15	.66	.07	**1984**	.06	−.15	.10
1974	−.27	.64	.08	**1985**	.32	−.12	.08
1975	.37	.00	.06	**1986**	.19	.16	.06
1976	.24	−.22	.05	**1987**	.05	.22	.05
1977	−.07	.18	.05	**1988**	.17	−.02	.06
1978	.07	.31	.07				

a Determine how much money you should invest in each investment.

b Find an interval such that you are 95% sure that the change in the value of your assets during the next year will be within this interval (assuming normally distributed returns).

c Find an interval such that you are 95% sure that the percentage annual return on your portfolio will be within this interval (assuming normally distributed returns).

37 Consider three investments. You are given the following means, standard deviations, and correlations for the annual return on these three investments. The means are .12, .15, and .20. The standard deviations are .20, .30, and .40. The correlation between stocks 1 and 2 is .65, between stocks 1 and 3 is .75, and between stocks 2 and 3 is .41. You have $10,000 to invest and can invest no more than half of your money in any single stock. Determine the minimum variance portfolio that yields an expected annual return of at least .14.

Skill-Extending Problems

38 Using the notation from this section, show algebraically that the portfolio variance in Equation 6.13 can be written in matrix form as the product

$$[\, x_1 s_1 \;\; x_2 s_2 \;\; \cdots \;\; x_n s_n \,]\, C\, [\, x_1 s_1 \;\; x_2 s_2 \;\; \cdots \;\; x_n s_n \,]^T$$

39 Reconsider the Stockco portfolio example (Example 6.10). Suppose that your goal is to find (among all portfolios that invest all of your money in stocks 1, 2, and 3) the portfolio that minimizes the probability that you will lose money during the next year. Use the Excel Solver to solve this problem. (*Hint*: You will need to assume that the returns on any portfolio follow a normal distribution. Then the Excel function NORMSDIST(x) will return the area under a standard normal curve to the left of a given number x. For example, NORMSDIST(1) returns .84, and NORMSDIST(−1) returns .16.)

40 The file STOCK83.XLS contains the percentage return on the market for the years 1984–91 as well as the closing stock price for Ford, Lilly, Kellogg, Merck, and Hewlett-Packard for the same years. Use the approach outlined in Example 6.10 to determine the minimum variance portfolio (of the stocks listed) that yields an expected return of at least .22. ■

6.11

Portfolio Optimization: The Scenario Approach

Historical estimates of the means, standard deviations, and correlations needed for portfolio optimization may be poor predictors of the future. An alternative approach to portfolio optimization is the **scenario approach**.[6] In the scenario approach we identify a few scenarios (less than ten, say) that might occur during the next year. For each scenario we estimate the return on each investment. Then we estimate the expected return on the portfolio with the formula

$$\text{Expected portfolio return} = ER = \sum_i r_i p_i \tag{6.15}$$

and the variance of the portfolio with the formula

$$\text{Variance of portfolio return} = \sum_i (r_i - ER)^2 p_i \tag{6.16}$$

Here r_i is the portfolio return under scenario i, ER is the expected portfolio return, p_i is the probability that scenario i will occur, and each summation is over all possible scenarios. Then we use the Solver as before to find the minimum variance portfolio that yields an acceptable expected return. Here is an example of the scenario approach.

EXAMPLE 6.11

During the next year the Security Analysis Company (SAC) has identified seven equally likely scenarios. For each of three stocks the annual return earned under each scenario is given in Table 6.13. SAC wants to find the minimum variance portfolio that yields an expected annual return of at least .13.

Solution

To model SAC's scenario example we need to keep track of the following:

- the fraction of the portfolio invested in each stock
- the fraction of the money invested
- the return of the portfolio under each scenario
- the expected annual return of the portfolio
- the variance of the annual return on the portfolio

TABLE 6.13 **Returns for the SAC Example**

	Stock 1	Stock 2	Stock 3
Scenario 1	−.071	.144	.169
Scenario 2	.056	.107	−.035
Scenario 3	.038	.321	.133
Scenario 4	.089	.305	.732
Scenario 5	.090	.195	.021
Scenario 6	.083	.390	.131
Scenario 7	.035	−.072	.006

[6]This section is based on Schrage [17].

Developing the Spreadsheet Model The problem can be modeled as follows. (See Figure 6.25 and the file SCENARIO.XLS.)

1 **Inputs.** Enter the data from Table 6.13 in the range B6:E12. This includes the probabilities of the various scenarios, which are all 1/7.

2 **Fractions invested.** Enter *any* trial values in the range B16:D16 for the fractions invested in the various stocks.

3 **Total fraction invested.** In cell E16 compute the fraction of money invested with the formula

=SUM(B16:D16)

Then enter a 1 in cell G16 to denote that SAC intends to invest all of its money.

4 **Return for each portfolio.** In cell B19 compute the return for the portfolio under scenario 1 with the formula

=SUMPRODUCT($B$16:$D$16,B6:D6)

Copy this formula to the range B20:B25 for the other scenarios.

5 **Expected annual return.** In cell B28 compute the expected annual return of the portfolio (using Equation 6.15) with the formula

=SUMPRODUCT(E6:E12,B19:B25)

This formula weights the portfolio return under each scenario by the probability that the scenario occurs.

6 **Squared differences.** In the range C19:C25 compute the squared difference between each scenario's return and the expected portfolio return. To begin, enter the formula

=(B19–$B$28)^2

in cell C19 for the first scenario. Then copy this formula to the range C20:C25 for the other scenarios.

7 **Portfolio variance.** In cell B30 use Equation 6.16 to compute the portfolio variance with the formula

=SUMPRODUCT(C19:C25,E6:E12)

Using the Solver

1 **Objective.** Choose cell B30 (portfolio variance) as the objective to minimize.

2 **Changing cells.** Choose the range B16:D16 as the changing cells and constrain these to be nonnegative.

3 **Investment constraint.** Add the constraint E16=G16. This ensures that all of the money is invested.

4 **Constraint on expected return.** Add the constraint B28>=D28. This ensures that the expected annual return on the portfolio will be at least .13.

5 **Optimize.** Click on Solve.

The Solver solution is shown in Figure 6.25. We see that SAC obtains a minimum portfolio variance of .008285. This corresponds to a standard deviation of .091. SAC's optimal portfolio is to invest 44.5% of its money in stock 1, 53.8% in stock 2, and 1.7% in stock 3.

FIGURE 6.25 Scenario Approach Solution to SAC Example

	A	B	C	D	E	F	G
1	**Scenario Model of Portfolio Selection**						
2							
3	**Scenario input data**						
4			**Returns**				
5	Scenario	Stock 1	Stock 2	Stock 3	Probability		
6	1	-0.071	0.144	0.169	0.143		
7	2	0.056	0.107	-0.035	0.143		
8	3	0.038	0.321	0.133	0.143		
9	4	0.089	0.305	0.732	0.143		
10	5	0.09	0.195	0.021	0.143		
11	6	0.083	0.39	0.131	0.143		
12	7	0.035	-0.072	0.006	0.143		
13							
14	**Investment decision**						
15		Stock 1	Stock 2	Stock 3	Total		Required
16	Fractions to invest	0.445	0.538	0.017	1	=	1
17							
18	Scenario	Portfolio return	Squared deviation				
19	1	0.049	0.0065953				
20	2	0.082	0.0023168				
21	3	0.192	0.0038279				
22	4	0.216	0.0074423				
23	5	0.145	0.0002339				
24	6	0.249	0.0141539				
25	7	-0.023	0.0234267				
26							
27	Overall expected return	Actual		Required			
28		0.13	>=	0.13			
29							
30	Overall return variance	0.008285					
31							
32	Overall return stdev	0.0910					

Is the Solver Solution Optimal? It can be shown that the variance of a portfolio is a convex function of the fractions invested in the various stocks. All of the constraints are linear. Therefore, the assumptions for a minimization problem are satisfied, and we know that the Solver solution is indeed optimal. ■

MODELING ISSUES

1 If we assume that portfolio returns are normally distributed, then (1) we are 68% sure that the annual return on the portfolio is between .039 (=.13−.091) and .221 (=.13+.091), (2) we are 95% sure that it is between −.052 (=.13−.182) and .312 (=.13+.182), and (3) we are 99.7% sure that it is between −.143 (=.13−.273) and .403 (=.13+.273).

2 In portfolio problems, minimizing **downside risk** of return might be a more reasonable objective than minimizing portfolio variance. Given a target return rate, the downside risk of a portfolio is the expected amount by which the return on the portfolio falls short of the target return. For example, suppose there are three equally likely scenarios, the target return is .13, and the portfolio returns under scenarios 1, 2, and 3 are .12, .14, and .11. Then we can determine the expected downside risk with this equation:

Downside risk=(1/3)(.01)+(1/3)(0)+(1/3)(.02)=.01 ■

REAL-WORLD APPLICATIONS

Using the Scenario Approach at GM

Eppen, Martin, and Schrage [5] used the scenario approach to help General Motors analyze its plant capacities. In their integer programming model, GM was able to adjust the capacity of plants and the types of products each plant could make. For example, plant 1 could be changed from a plant with a production capacity of 500,000 compacts per year into a plant with a production capacity of 200,000 compacts and 250,000 large cars per year. GM management identified five possible scenarios for each year (high inflation, recession, and so on) and forecasted demand for each product for each scenario. Given the choice of plant configurations at the beginning of each year, the model computed the profit for each scenario. Then the integer programming model computed the capacities and configurations for each plant that minimized the downside risk associated with the company's profit for the next five years. The model was instrumental in convincing top GM management that the company had a great deal of excess capacity. (See Problem 44 for an example of this type of model.) ■

Asset and Liability Management at Pacific Financial

Mulvey [14] describes how he used a scenario approach at Pacific Financial Asset Management Company to allocate financial assets. The problem was to balance the risk and rewards of investment decisions in concert with the movements of the projected liabilities. Mulvey's approach extended the asset-only Markowitz model described in this section and the previous section to handle liabilities. The objective of the integrative asset-liability system was to preserve the firm's wealth as measured by assets minus the present value of its liabilities. Although this approach requires greater information, Mulvey claims that "its recommendations are more closely tailored to the investor's circumstances." ■

PROBLEMS

Skill-Building Problems

41 Assume there are four equally likely states of the world possible next year. The annual returns on gold, stocks, and T-bills for these scenarios are shown in Table 6.14. Determine the minimum-variance portfolio that has an expected return of at least .08.

TABLE 6.14 **Data for Four-Scenario Problem**

	Gold	Stocks	T-bills
Scenario 1	.20	.03	.12
Scenario 2	.12	.05	.10
Scenario 3	.06	.10	.08
Scenario 4	.01	.15	.06

42 There are five possible scenarios for the economy next year. The probability of each scenario, as well as the annual percentage return on stocks, bonds, and gold, are listed in Table 6.15.

TABLE 6.15 **Data for Five-Scenario Problem**

	Probability	Stocks	Bonds	Gold
Depression	.05	−.05	.01	.30
Recession	.20	.00	.02	.16
Zero Growth	.30	.10	.06	.10
Moderate Growth	.20	.15	.08	.04
High Growth	.25	.20	.04	−.02

a Find the minimum variance portfolio that yields an expected return of at least .09.

b Find the portfolio that yields an expected return of at least .09 and minimizes the downside risk.

Skill-Extending Problems

43 If interest rates rise, GM will make less profit because fewer consumers will purchase cars. In this problem we will explore how the scenario approach to portfolio optimization could be used to aid GM in modifying its risk profile. Suppose that during the next year GM believes that five different interest rate scenarios can occur. The annual profit from GM's operations (in billions) and the probability of each scenario are listed in Table 6.16.

TABLE 6.16 Interest Rate Scenarios for GM Problem

Interest Rate	Probability	Profit
5%	.10	$6
7%	.30	$4
8%	.35	$2
10%	.15	$1
11%	.10	$0

To hedge against decreases in profits caused by increased interest rates, GM can pursue the following three derivative strategies:

Strategy 1. Go long (or short) on T-bill futures contracts. Each futures contract costs $1000. For each interest rate, the percentage profit associated with a long position is listed in Table 6.17. (For a short position, take the negatives of the profits listed.)

TABLE 6.17 Profits from T-bill Futures

Interest Rate	Percent Profit on Long Futures Position
5%	24%
7%	1%
8%	−8%
10%	−24%
11%	−34%

Strategy 2. Purchase put option 1 (on a long-term bond) at a cost of $1 per option. For each interest rate the percentage profit associated with put option 1 is that shown in Table 6.18.

TABLE 6.18 Profits from Put Option 1

Interest Rate	Percent Profit on Put Option 1
5%	−100%
7%	−100%
8%	−100%
10%	200%
11%	400%

Strategy 3. Purchase put option 2 (on a long-term bond) at a cost of $5 per option. For each interest rate the percentage profit associated with put option 2 is that shown in Table 6.19.

TABLE 6.19 Profits for Put Option 2

Interest Rate	Percent Profit on Put Option 2
5%	−100%
7%	−100%
8%	12%
10%	48%
11%	92%

a Compute the mean and variance of GM's annual profit from operations.

b GM wants to minimize the variance of its annual profit, subject to the constraint that its expected annual profit is at least \$2.65 billion. Determine how GM can use the three derivatives to achieve this goal. (*Note*: You should scale profits to be in billions of dollars and purchases of the three derivatives to be in millions of units. Otherwise, the Solver might have difficulty obtaining the correct solution.)

c Given a target, the **downside variance** of a random variable is the expected value of the square of the amount by which the target is unsatisfied on the low side. For example, suppose the target for a random variable is 2, and the value of the random variable is 0 or 3 with probability .5 each. Then the downside variance is

$$\text{Downside variance} = .5(2)^2 + .5(0)^2 = 2$$

Determine how GM can use the three derivatives to minimize the downside variance associated with a target of \$3.2 billion annual profit, subject to the constraint that GM's expected annual profit is at least \$2.65 billion.

44 You have been assigned to adjust the capacity of GM's three automobile production plants. The company believes that one of three demand scenarios (high, medium, or low) will persist indefinitely. Information about these three scenarios is listed in Table 6.20. For each of GM's three plants there are three options: keep the current configuration, expand the plant, or close the plant. If a plant's configuration is changed, a changeover cost is incurred. There is an annual fixed cost of operating each plant in any configuration. The variable cost of producing a car at a plant also depends on the plant's configuration. The information about plant changes is listed in Table 6.21. Suppose that GM's goal is to maximize its expected discounted profit over an infinite horizon. Assume that a stream of annual profits can be converted to a discounted profit by multiplying the annual profit by 10. Determine a plant configuration and production schedule for each scenario that will achieve GM's goal. ■

TABLE 6.20 Demand Scenarios for GM Problem

	Annual Demand	Price per Car	Probability
High Demand	3.0 million	\$15,000	.25
Medium Demand	2.4 million	\$13,000	.60
Low Demand	1.6 million	\$12,000	.15

TABLE 6.21 Plant Change Data for GM Problem

	Changeover Cost (\$ billions)	Fixed Cost (\$ billions)	Variable Cost per Car	Annual Capacity (millions)
Plant 1 Expanded	3.0	1.5	\$6000	1.0
Plant 1 Current	0.0	1.0	\$8000	0.6
Plant 1 Closed	1.0	0.0	—	0.0
Plant 2 Expanded	4.0	1.8	\$5000	1.2
Plant 2 Current	0.0	0.8	\$7500	0.8
Plant 2 Closed	1.5	0.0	—	0.0
Plant 3 Expanded	3.0	2.0	\$4000	1.3
Plant 3 Current	0.0	1.5	\$6000	0.7
Plant 3 Closed	1.2	0.0	—	0.0

6.12

Portfolio Optimization with Transaction Costs

In reality, there is a charge for buying or selling stocks. How can we incorporate these **transaction costs** into the portfolio optimization model? To illustrate, reconsider the Stockco portfolio optimization example (Example 6.10) in Section 6.10.

EXAMPLE 6.12

Suppose that for every \$1 traded in stock 1 or 2, Stockco must pay \$0.01, and for every dollar traded in stock 3 it must pay \$.005. Suppose the company begins with 10% of its money invested in stock 1, 40% in stock 2, and 50% in stock 3. Stockco's goal is to obtain a portfolio of minimum variance that yields an expected annual return of at least .12.[7]

Suppose (without loss of generality) that Stockco initially has \$1.00 invested total in these three stocks. Then initially it has 10¢ invested in stock 1, 40¢ in stock 2, and 50¢ in stock 3. It must now decide how to adjust its holdings in stocks 1 through 3. If, for example, it increases its holdings in stock 1 to 30¢, there is a transaction cost of $.01(20) = .2$¢. The transactions are governed by the following balance equation:

$$\text{Final amount invested} + \text{Transaction costs} = \text{Initial amount invested} = \$1.00 \tag{6.17}$$

Stockco's goal is to minimize the variance of the annual expected return on the final portfolio, subject to Equation 6.17 and the constraint that the expected value of its stocks a year from now must be at least \$1.12.

Before discussing the details of the spreadsheet model, we note that this problem is more difficult to model than the problem without transaction costs. The main reason it is more difficult is that if \$1 is currently invested and the company then makes some changes in its investments, the amount it will have invested after the changes is somewhat *less* than \$1. This is due to the transaction costs. Strictly speaking, then, when the company requires the expected value of its stocks a year from now to be at least \$1.12, it is requiring a return of slightly *greater* than .12. Do you see why?

Solution

To develop the transactions cost model, we need to keep track of the following:

- the amount of stock that is bought and sold
- the final amount of money invested in each stock
- the total amount invested in the portfolio (after transactions) plus the fraction of the total wealth spent on transaction costs
- the expected return on the final portfolio
- the variance of the annual return on the final portfolio

Developing the Spreadsheet Model We now proceed as follows. (See Figure 6.26 and the file TRANSACT.XLS.)

[7] This section is also based on Schrage [17].

1 **Inputs.** Enter the given data in the ranges B5:D6, B10:D12, B16:D16, B20:D20, and D31.

2 **Amounts transacted.** Enter *any* trial values in the range B21:D22 for the amount (in terms of the whole portfolio) bought and sold of each stock. For example, the values .55 and 0 in cells B21 and B22 mean that Stockco increases its holding of stock 1 to .10 + .55 = .65 (65¢). Similarly, the values 0 and .50 in cells D21 and D22 mean that Stockco reduces its holding in stock 3 to .50 − .50 = 0.

3 **Final holdings.** In the range B24:D24 compute the final holding of each stock. Specifically, enter the formula

=B20+B21–B22

in cell B24 for stock 1. Then copy this formula to the range C24:D24 for the other two stocks. Also, enter lower bounds (zeroes) for these final holdings in the range B26:D26.

4 **Expected value of holdings a year from now.** Calculate the amount to which $1 of each stock is expected to increase in one year in the range B28:D28. Specifically, enter the formula

=B5+1

in cell B28 for stock 1 and copy it to the range C28:D28 for the other two stocks. Then in cell B31 compute the expected value of holdings one year from now with the formula

=SUMPRODUCT(B28:D28,B24:D24)

5 **Transactions costs for each stock.** In the range B23:D23 compute the transactions costs incurred. The transactions cost for stock *i* equals the total dollar amount of stock *i* traded multiplied by the transaction cost rate for stock *i*. Therefore, in cell B23 compute the transaction cost for stock 1 with the formula

=B16*SUM(B21:B22)

Then copy this formula to the range C23:D23 for the other two stocks.

6 **Total transactions costs.** In cell E23 compute the total transactions costs with the formula

=SUM(B23:D23)

7 **Total amount invested.** In cell E24 compute the total amount invested in stocks (after transactions have occurred) with the formula

=SUM(B24:D24)

8 **Sum of transactions costs and amount invested.** Recall from Equation 6.17 that we must keep track of the final amount invested in stocks plus total transactions costs. Compute this quantity in cell E25 with the formula

=SUM(E23:E24)

Then enter the required amount ($1) in cell G25.

9 **Portfolio variance.** In the range B35:D35 compute the amount invested in each stock (in the final portfolio) multiplied by the standard deviation of annual return of the stock. Specifically, enter the formula

=B24*B6

in cell B35 for stock 1 and copy it to the range C35:D35 for the other two stocks.

FIGURE 6.26 Portfolio Model with Transaction Costs

	A	B	C	D	E	F	G
1	**Stockco Portfolio Problem**						
2							
3	**Stock input data**						
4		Stock 1	Stock 2	Stock 3			
5	Mean return	0.14	0.11	0.1			
6	StDev of return	0.2	0.15	0.08			
7							
8	Correlations						
9		Stock 1	Stock 2	Stock 3			
10	Stock 1	1	0.6	0.4			
11	Stock 2	0.6	1	0.7			
12	Stock 3	0.4	0.7	1			
13							
14	Transactions costs ($ per $ bought or sold)						
15		Stock 1	Stock 2	Stock 3			
16		0.01	0.01	0.005			
17							
18	**Investment decision**						
19		Stock 1	Stock 2	Stock 3			
20	Fractions owned now	0.1	0.4	0.5			
21	Amount bought	0.553992	0	0			
22	Amount sold	0	0.062658	0.5	Totals		
23	Transactions costs	0.00554	0.000627	0.0025	0.008667		
24	Final fractions owned	0.653992	0.337342	0	0.991334		Required
25		>=	>=	>=	1	=	1
26	Minimum owned	0	0	0			
27							
28	Expected returns plus	1.14	1.11	1.1			
29	Expected cash one year from now						
30		Actual		Required			
31		1.12	>=	1.12			
32							
33	Standard deviations times fractions invested						
34		Stock 1	Stock 2	Stock 3			
35		0.130798	0.050601	0			
36							
37	Portfolio variance	0.027611					
38							
39	Portfolio stdev	0.1662					

Then compute the portfolio variance in cell B37 with the formula

=SUMPRODUCT(B35:D35,B35:D35)+2*B35*C35*C10
+2*B35*D35*D10+2*C35*D35*D11

(You could also use the MMULT formula we discussed earlier.)

Using the Solver

1. **Objective.** Choose cell B37 (portfolio variance) as the objective to minimize.
2. **Changing cells.** Choose cells B21:D22 (buys and sells) as the changing cells and constrain these to be nonnegative.
3. **Balance constraint.** Add the constraint E25=G25. This ensures that Equation 6.17 is satisfied.

4 **Nonnegativity constraints on final amounts invested.** Add the constraints B24:D24>=B26:D26. These ensure that Stockco does not end with a negative amount invested in any stock.

5 **Constraint on expected return.** Add the constraint B31>=D31. This ensures that the expected value of the portfolio one year from now will be at least $1.12.

6 **Optimize.** Click on Solve.

The Solver solution appears in Figure 6.26. Stockco should increase its holdings of stock 1 to 65.4¢, decrease its holdings of stock 2 to 33.7¢, and eliminate its holdings of stock 3. The variance of the annual return on the final portfolio is .0276, and the standard deviation is .166.

Is the Solver Solution Optimal? As before, the variance of the final portfolio is a convex function of the decision variables, and all constraints are linear. Therefore, the Solver solution is guaranteed to be optimal. ■

MODELING ISSUE

This analysis was performed for a typical dollar of investment. For an initial amount of *many* dollars, we simply treat each dollar the same way, as prescribed by the Solver solution. This is shown graphically in Figure 6.27 for a total investment amount of $10,000. Notice that the final value of the holdings is slightly less than $10,000. The difference (aside from roundoff) is the transactions cost. ■

PROBLEM

Skill-Building Problem

45 (Refer to Problem 36 for data.) Suppose that at present you have $10,000 invested, with 30% of your investment in stocks, 50% in T-bonds, and 20% in gold. Assume that transactions incur costs. Every $100 of stocks traded costs you $1, every $100 of your gold portfolio traded costs you $2, and every $100 of your T-bonds portfolio traded costs you $5. Find the minimum variance portfolio that yields an expected holdings one year from now of at least $11,000. ■

FIGURE 6.27 **Optimal Solution with $10,000 Total Investment**

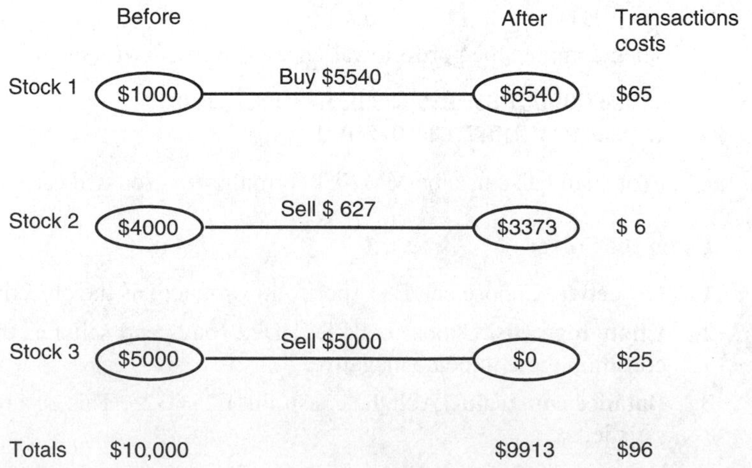

6.13

Conclusion

Although a large number of real-world problems can be approximated well by linear models, there are also many problems that are inherently nonlinear. We have analyzed a number of these in this chapter, including the important class of portfolio selection models where the risk (measured by portfolio variance) is a nonlinear function of the decision variables. We have purposely neglected much of the mathematics behind nonlinear optimization because of its technical difficulty. However, it is important to realize that nonlinear models present many more hazards for spreadsheet Solvers than linear models. Unless we can verify that the assumptions for a minimization or maximization problem are satisfied—and this can be very difficult to do—there is no guarantee that a Solver will converge to the optimal solution (or even converge at all). The examples in this chapter were purposely kept small and "nice" so that the Solver could handle them and produce optimal solutions. Larger and more complex nonlinear models are not always so accommodating and frequently require solution methods beyond the scope of this book.

REVIEW PROBLEMS

Skill-Building Problems

46 Refer back to the Widgetco project scheduling example (Example 4.4) and let A be the number of days the duration of A is reduced, B be the number of days the duration of B is reduced, and so on. The costs of crashing the various activities are shown in Table 6.22. Each activity can be "crashed" to a duration of 0 days, if desired. Determine how to minimize the cost of finishing the project in 25 days or less.

TABLE 6.22 **Costs in Activity Crashing Problem**

	Cost to Crash
Activity A	$5A^2$
Activity B	$20B^2$
Activity C	$2C^2$
Activity D	$20D^2$
Activity E	$10E^2$
Activity F	$15F^2$

47 Suppose that a cylindrical soda can must have a volume of 26 cubic inches. If the soda company wants to minimize the surface area of the soda can, what should the ratio of the height to the radius of the can be? (*Hint*: The volume of a right circular cylinder is $\pi r^2 h$, and the surface area of a right circular cylinder is $2\pi r^2 + 2\pi rh$, where r is the radius and h is the height. Also, the value of π can be obtained in Excel with the function PI().)

48 I have \$1000 to invest in three stocks. Let S_i be the random variable representing the annual return on \$1 invested in stock i. For example, if $S_i = 0.12$, then \$1 invested in stock i at the beginning of a year is worth \$1.12 at the end of the year. The means are: $E(S_1) = 0.14$, $E(S_2) = 0.11$, $E(S_3) = 0.10$. The variances are: $Var\ S_1 = 0.20$, $Var\ S_2 = 0.08$, $Var\ S_3 = 0.18$. The correlations are: $r_{12} = .8$, $r_{13} = .7$, and $r_{23} = .9$. Determine the minimum variance portfolio that attains an expected annual return of at least .12.

49 Fruit Computer Company produces Pear and Apricot computers. If the company charges price p_1 for Pear computers and p_2 for Apricot computers, it can sell q_1 Pear and q_2 Apricot computers, where $q_1 = 4000 - 10p_1 + p_2$ and $q_2 = 2000 - 9p_2 + 0.8p_1$. Manufacturing a Pear computer requires two hours of labor and three computer chips. An Apricot computer

uses three hours of labor and one computer chip. At present, 5000 hours of labor and 4500 chips are available.

a Determine how to maximize Fruit's revenue.

b What is the most that Fruit would be willing to pay for another hour of labor?

c What is the most that Fruit would be willing to pay for another computer chip?

50 Oilco must determine how many barrels of oil to extract during each of the next two years. If Oilco extracts x_1 million barrels during year 1, each barrel can be sold for $30 - x_1$ dollars. If Oilco extracts x_2 million barrels during year 2, each barrel can be sold for $35 - x_2$ dollars. The cost of extracting x_1 million barrels during year 1 is x_1^2 million dollars, and the cost of extracting x_2 million barrels during year 2 is $2x_2^2$ million dollars. A total of 20 million barrels of oil are available, and at most $250 million can be spent on extraction. Determine how Oilco can maximize its profit (revenues less costs) for the next two years.

51 Five of a store's major customers are located as shown in Figure 6.28. Determine where the store should be located to minimize the sum of the squares of the (straight-line) distances that the customers will have to travel to the store.

FIGURE 6.28 **Customers for Store Location Problem**

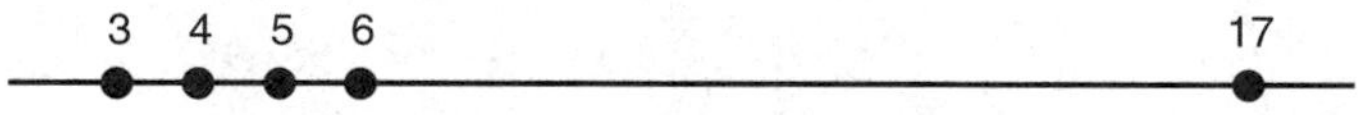

52 A company uses a raw material to produce two types of products. When processed, each unit of raw material yields two units of product 1 and one unit of product 2. If x_1 units of product 1 are produced, each unit can be sold for $49 - x_1$ dollars, and if x_2 units of product 2 are produced, each unit can be sold for $30 - 2x_2$ dollars. It costs $5 to purchase and process each unit of raw material. Determine how the company can maximize its profit.

53 If a company charges price p dollars per unit for a product and spends a dollars on advertising, it can sell $10{,}000 + 5a^{1/2} - 100p$ units of the product. If the product costs $10 per unit to produce, how can the company maximize its profit?

54 With L labor hours and M machine hours, a company can produce $L^{1/3}M^{2/3}$ computer disk drives. Each disk drive sells for $150. If labor can be purchased at $50 per hour and machine hours can be purchased at $100 per hour, determine how the company can maximize its profit.

55 Suppose that we are hiring a weather forecaster to predict the probability that next summer will be rainy or sunny. The following suggests a method that can be used to ensure that the forecaster is accurate. Suppose that the actual probability of next summer being rainy is .6. (For simplicity, we assume that the summer can only be rainy or sunny.) If the forecaster announces a probability p that the summer will be rainy, he receives a payment of $1 - (1 - p)^2$ if the summer is rainy and a payment of $1 - p^2$ if the summer is sunny. Show that the forecaster will maximize his expected profit by announcing that the probability of a rainy summer is .6.

56 Consider the points (0,0), (1,1), and (2,3). Determine the circle of smallest radius enclosing these three points. (*Note*: To "determine" a circle, you must specify its center and its radius.)

57 The cost of producing x units of a product during a month is $x^{1/2}$ dollars. Show that the minimum-cost method of producing 40 units during the next two months is to produce all 40 units during a single month.

58 A company uses raw material to produce two products. For $15 dollars, a unit of raw material can be purchased and processed into four units of product 1 and two units of product 2. If x_1 units of product 1 are produced, they can be sold at $25 - x_1$ dollars per unit. If x_2 units of product 2 are produced, they can be sold at $14 - x_2$ dollars per unit. (Negative prices are not permitted.) The company can choose the number of units of raw material that are purchased and processed. How can the company maximize its profit?

Skill-Extending Problem

59 Reconsider the Chandler Oil blending problem (Example 3.2) with the following modification. Suppose that Chandler can add a chemical called Superquality (SQ) to improve the quality level of gasoline and heating oil. If it adds an amount x of SQ to each barrel of gasoline, the quality level improves by $x^{1/2}$ over what it would have been. If the company adds an amount x of SQ to each barrel of heating oil, its quality level improves by $.6x^{.6}$ over what it would have been. The amount of SQ added to heating oil cannot exceed (by weight) 5% of the oils used to make heating oil. Similarly, the amount of SQ added to gasoline cannot exceed (by weight) 5% of the oils used to make gasoline. SQ can be purchased at a cost of $20 per barrel. Determine how Chandler Oil can maximize its profit.

Modeling Problems

60 For the product mix example (Example 2.1), discuss where you think the assumptions of a linear model are most likely to break down. How might an NLP formulation look in this situation?

61 For the Chandler Oil blending example (Example 3.2), discuss where you think the assumptions of a linear model are most likely to break down. How might an NLP formulation look in this situation?

62 For the Shoeco aggregate planning example (Example 3.4), is it likely that the cost per worker of changing the size of the workforce during a month would be constant (as we assumed)? How could an NLP formulation account for a situation in which the cost per worker of changing the size of the workforce is not constant?

63 (Problems 63 and 64 refer to sports ratings [Section 6.8].) If you were going to give more recent games more weight, how might you determine whether the weight given to a game from k weeks ago should be, say, $(.95)^k$ or $(.9)^k$?

64 If you were going to use the approach from Section 6.8 to forecast future sports contests, what problems might you encounter early in the season? How might you resolve these problems?

65 Kellpost Cereal Company sells four products: (1) Special L (a low-calorie, high-nutrition cereal); (2) Corn Bran (another low-calorie, high-nutrition cereal); (3) Admiral Smacks (a sugary cereal pitched at the children's market); and (4) Honey Pops (another sweet cereal pitched at the children's market). Kellpost has sufficient production capacity to produce a total of 10,000 boxes of cereal per month. For each of the last 16 months, Kellpost has kept track of the price and sales of each product. (These data are listed in the file CEREAL.XLS.) Market executives believe that Special L and Corn Bran may be substitutes for each other, as may be Admiral Smacks and Honey Pops. For example, this means that an increase in the price of Special L may raise the sales of Corn Bran. The variable cost of bringing a box of each cereal to market is as follows: Special L, $2.00; Corn Bran, $2.20; Admiral Smacks, $2.30; Honey Pops, $2.40.

a Use the given information to determine the price for each cereal that will enable Kellpost to maximize profits.

b Now suppose that Kellpost can increase its monthly production capacity. The cost (per year) of doing this is $20,000 per thousand boxes of added monthly capacity. Can you determine an optimal capacity level?

66 UE is going to invest $400 million dollars to acquire companies in the auto and/or electronics industry. How would you apply portfolio optimization to determine which companies should be purchased?

67 Your family owns a large farm that can grow wheat, corn, cotton, alfalfa, barley, pears, and apples. Each product requires a certain amount of labor each month and a certain number of hours of machine time. You have just studied portfolio optimization and want to help your family run its farm. What would you do?

68 A power company is trying to determine how much generating capacity to add for the next ten years. If more capacity must be added later, the per unit cost of adding capacity will drastically increase. Demand for the next ten years is, of course, uncertain. How would you structure this problem to determine the amount of capacity that should be added today?

69 Your company is about to market a new golf club. You have convened a focus group of 100 golfers and asked them to compare your club to the clubs produced by your competitors. You have found, for exmple, that 30 customers in the focus group would purchase your club if you charged $20, 28 customers would purchase your club if you charged $25, and so on. How would you use this information to determine the price at which your club should be sold? ■

CASE STUDY

GMS Stock Hedging

Kate Torelli, a security analyst for LionFund, has identified a gold mining stock (ticker symbol GMS) as a particularly attractive investment. Torelli believes that the company has invested wisely in new mining equipment. Furthermore, the company has recently purchased mining rights on land that has high potential for successful gold extraction. Torelli notes that gold has underperformed the stock market in the last decade and believes that the time is ripe for a large increase in gold prices. In addition, she reasons that conditions in the global monetary system make it likely that investors may once again turn to gold as a safe haven in which to park assets. Finally, supply and demand conditions have improved to the point where there could be significant upward pressure on gold prices.

GMS is a highly leveraged company, so it is quite a risky investment by itself. Torelli is mindful of a passage from the annual report of a competitor, Baupost, which has an extraordinarily successful investment record: "Baupost has managed a decade of consistently profitable results despite, and perhaps in some respect due to, consistent emphasis on the avoidance of downside risk. We have frequently carried both high cash balances and costly market hedges.... Our results are particularly satisfying when considered in the light of this sustained risk aversion." She would therefore like to *hedge* the stock purchase—that is, reduce the risk of an investment in GMS stock.

Currently GMS is trading at $100 per share. Torelli has constructed seven scenarios for the price of GMS stock one month from now. These scenarios and corresponding probabilities are shown in Table 6.23.

In order to hedge an investment in GMS stock, Torelli can invest in other securities whose prices tend to move in the direction opposite to that of GMS stock. In particular, she is considering over-the-counter put options on GMS stock as potential hedging instruments. The value of a put option increases as the price of the underlying stock decreases.[8] For example, consider a put option with a strike price of $100 and a time to expiration of one month. This means that the owner of the put has the right to sell GMS stock at $100 per share one month in the future. Suppose that the price of GMS falls to $80 at that time. Then the holder of the put option can exercise the option and receive $20 (= 100 – 80). If the price of GMS falls to $70, the option would be worth $30 (= 100 – 70). However, if the price of GMS rises to $100 or more, the option expires worthless.

Torelli called an options trader at a large investment bank for quotes. The prices for three (European-style) put options are shown in Table 6.24. Torelli wishes to invest $10 million in GMS stock and put options.

Questions

1 Based on Torelli's scenarios, what is the expected return of GMS stock? What is the standard deviation of the return of GMS stock?

2 After a cursory examination of the put option prices, Torelli suspects that a good strategy is to buy one put option A for each share of GMS stock purchased. What are the mean and standard deviation of return for this strategy?

3 Assuming that Torelli's goal is to minimize the standard deviation of the portfolio return, what is the optimal portfolio that invests all $10 million? (For simplicity, assume that fractional numbers of stock shares and put options can be purchased. Assume that the amounts invested in each security must be nonnegative. However, the number of options purchased need *not* equal the number of shares of stock purchased.) What are the expected return and standard deviation of return of this portfolio? How many shares of GMS stock and how many of each put option does this portfolio correspond to?

4 Suppose that short selling is permitted—that is, the nonnegativity restrictions on the portfolio weights are removed. Now what portfolio minimizes the standard deviation of return?

[8] For a brief introduction to options see, for example, Cox and Rubinstein [3], pp. 1–8, or Jarrow and Turnbull [8], pp. 14–18.

Hint: A good way to attack this problem is to create a table of security returns, as indicated in Table 6.25. Only a few of the table entries are shown. To correctly compute the standard deviation of portfolio return, you will need to incorporate the scenario probabilities. If r_i is the portfolio return in scenario i, and p_i is the probability of scenario i, then the standard deviation of portfolio return is

$$\sqrt{\sum_{i=1}^{7} p_i(r_i - \mu)^2}$$

where $\mu = \sum_{i=1}^{7} p_i r_i$ is the expected portfolio return. ■

TABLE 6.23 Scenarios and Probabilities for GMS Stock in One Month

	Scenario 1	Scenario 2	Scenario 3	Scenario 4	Scenario 5	Scenario 6	Scenario 7
Probability	0.05	0.10	0.20	0.30	0.20	0.10	0.05
GMS Stock Price	150	130	110	100	90	80	70

TABLE 6.24 Put Option Prices (Today) for GMS Case Study

	Put Option A	Put Option B	Put Option C
Strike Price	90	100	110
Option Price	\$2.20	\$6.40	\$12.50

TABLE 6.25 Table of Security Returns

	GMS Stock	Put Option A	Put Option B	Put Option C
Scenario 1			−100%	
2	30%			
⋮				
7				220%

CASE STUDY

Durham Asset Management

Durham Asset Management (DAM) is a small firm with 50 employees that manages the pension funds of small to medium-sized companies. Durham was founded in 1975 and has grown considerably throughout the years. Initially, DAM managed the pension funds of three small companies whose asset values totaled $30 million. By 1991 DAM's funds under management were valued at $2 billion.

James Franklin is a senior vice president at DAM, in charge of managing the equity portion of one of its largest pension funds. Franklin meets on a quarterly basis with company officials who supervise his decisions and oversee his performance. His work is measured on several levels, including both subjective and objective criteria. The subjective criteria include estimates of the quality of research reports. The objective criteria include the actual performance of Franklin's portfolio relative to a customized index of companies in DAM's investment universe. Franklin attempts to "beat" the index not by trying to time market moves, but by investing more heavily in those companies he expects to outperform the customized index and less heavily in those companies he expects to underperform the index.

Franklin has several research analysts who are charged with following the performance of several companies within specific industries. The research analysts prepare reports that analyze the past performance of the companies and prepare projections of future performance. The projections include assessments of the "most likely" or average performance anticipated over the next month.

Franklin analyzes their findings and often asks for additional information or suggests modifications to the analyses. After a period of careful review, the final forecasts for the next month are assembled and summarized. Each month the analysts' forecasts are compared to the actual results. Annual bonuses for the analysts are based in part on the comparison of these numbers.

It is now late December 1991, and the projections for January 1992 are indicated in Table 6.26. The projections have been made for 15 U.S. companies divided into five industry groups. The five industry groups are metals, retail, computer, automotive, and aviation.

Franklin would like to use the portfolio optimization approach to see what portfolios it would

TABLE 6.26 Projections for January 1992 for DAM Case Study

Company	Forecasted Mean Return
Aluminum Co. of America (ALCOA)	0.6%
Reynolds Metals	0.9%
Alcan Aluminum, Ltd.	0.8%
Walmart Store, Inc.	1.5%
Sears, Roebuck & Co.	0.8%
K-Mart Corporation	1.3%
International Business Machines (IBM)	0.4%
Digital Equipment Corporation (DEC)	1.1%
Hewlett Packard Co. (HP)	0.7%
General Motors Corp. (GM)	1.2%
Ford Motor Co. (FORD)	0.9%
Chrysler Corp.	1.3%
Boeing Co.	0.3%
McDonnell Douglas Corp.	0.2%
United Technologies Corp.	0.7%

recommend. He has data containing end-of-month prices for the last two years for each of the companies. The data is contained in the spreadsheet DAM.XLS. Also included in the spreadsheet is information about dividends and stock splits. Using this data James constructs a history of 24 monthly returns for each of the 15 companies.

The past data provides useful information about the volatility (standard deviation) of stock returns. It also gives useful information about the degree of association (correlation) of returns between pairs of stocks. However, average returns from the past do not tend to be good predictors of future average returns. Rather than using the raw historical data directly, Franklin creates 24 future return scenarios by adjusting the 24 historical returns. The adjustments are made so that the means of the future scenario returns are consistent with the forecasts from Table 6.26. The adjustments are also made so that the volatilities and correlations of the future scenario returns are the same as in the historical data.

The exact procedure that Franklin uses for developing future scenario returns is described next. Let r_{ij}^0 denote the historical return of security j in month i (for $j = 1, \ldots, 15$ and $i = 1, \ldots, 24$). Suppose that the average historical return of security j is μ_j^0. For security j, denote the forecasted mean return in Table 6.26 by μ_j. (For example, $\mu_1 - 0.6\%$ and $\mu_2 = 0.9\%$, where the index 1 refers to ALCOA and 2 refers to Reynolds Metals.) Franklin creates the future scenario return r_{ij} for security j in scenario i using the following equation:

$$r_{ij} = r_{ij}^0 + \mu_j - \mu_j^0 \tag{6.18}$$

Franklin assumes that any of the scenarios defined by Equation 6.18 can occur with equal probability. DAM's policy is never to invest more than 30% of the funds in any one industry group. Franklin measures the risk of a portfolio by its standard deviation of return. He then solves a portfolio optimization model for various minimum levels of mean return to see which portfolios are recommended. After analyzing the trade-off between risk and return, Franklin makes a judgment as to which portfolio to hold for the coming month.

Questions

1. Use the information in the spreadsheet DAM.XLS to create a history of 24 monthly returns for the 15 companies. Compute the historical average return of each stock. In particular, what was the historical return of ALCOA from 12/29/89 to 1/31/90? What was the historical return of Boeing from 5/31/90 to 6/29/90? Explain how you account for dividends and stock splits in computing monthly returns.
2. Develop 24 future scenario returns using Equation 6.18. What is the explanation underlying it? In particular, what is the return of ALCOA if scenario 1 occurs? What is the return of Reynolds Metals if scenario 3 occurs?
3. Compute and graph the mean-standard deviation efficient frontier. Compute at least six points on the efficient frontier (including the minimum standard deviation and maximum expected return points). Create a table of results showing the following for each of your points on the efficient frontier: (1) the optimal portfolio weights, (2) mean portfolio return, and (3) standard deviation. (Briefly explain the equations and optimization model used in the spreadsheet.) ■

Acknowledgment: Thanks to Ziv Katalan and Aliza Schachter for assistance in developing this case.

REFERENCES

1 Black, F., and M. Scholes. "The Pricing of Options and Corporate Liabilities." *Journal of Political Economy* 81 (1973): 637–54.

2 Cournot, A. *Mathematical Principles of the Theory of Wealth*. New York: Macmillan, 1897.

3 Cox, J., and M. Rubinstein. *Options Markets*. Englewood Cliffs, NJ: Prentice Hall, 1985.

4 DeWitt, C., L. Lasdon, A. Waren, D. Brenner, and S. Melhem. "OMEGA: An Improved Gasoline Blending System for Texaco." *Interfaces* 19, no. 1 (1989): 85–101.

5 Eppen, G., K. Martin, and L. Schrage. "A Scenario Approach to Capacity Planning." *Operations Research* 37, no. 4 (1989): 517–27.

6 Grossman, S., and O. Hart. "An Analysis of the Principal Agent Problem." *Econometrica* 51 (1983): 7–45.

7 Hull, J. *Options, Futures, and Other Derivative Securities*. 2nd edition. Englewood Cliffs, NJ: Prentice Hall, 1993.

8 Jarrow and Turnbull. *Derivative Securities*. Cincinnati: South-Western College Publishing, 1996.

9 Kolesar, P., and E. Blum. "Square Root Laws for Fire Engine Response Distances." *Management Science* 19 (1973): 1368–78.

10 Littlechild, S. "Marginal Pricing with Joint Costs." *Economic Journal* 80 (1970): 323–34.

11 Lodish, L., et al. "Salesforce Sizing and Deployment Using a Decision Calculus Model at Syntex Laboratories." *Interfaces* 18, no. 1 (1986): 5–20.

12 Love, R., and L. Yerex. "An Application of a Facilities Location Model in the Prestressed Concrete Industry." *Interfaces* 6, no. 4 (1976): 45–49.

13 Montgomery, D., and E. Del Castillo. "A Nonlinear Programming Response to the Dual Response Problem." *Journal of Quality Technology* 25, no. 3 (1993): 199–204.

14 Mulvey, J. "An Asset-Liability Investment System." *Interfaces* 24, no. 3 (1994): 22–33.

15 Myers, R. *Classical and Modern Regression with Applications*. Belmont, CA: Duxbury Press, 1990.

16 Nicholson, T. *Optimization in Industry: Volume 2 Applications*. Chicago: Aldine-Atherton, 1971.

17 Schrage, L., *WHAT'S BEST! Release 2.0*. Belmont, CA: Duxbury Press, 1996.

C H A P T E R

7

Multiple-Objective Decision Making

Management Science Success Stories

The government is a prime candidate for performing decision making that involves multiple (conflicting) objectives. Most governmental decisions have political ramifications, with each constituency benefiting along some dimensions but losing along others. A real example of such governmental decision making is discussed by Chrisman et al. [1] in their paper "A Multiobjective Linear Programming Methodology for Public Sector Tax Planning." During the 1980s the city of Peoria, Illinois, experienced a deterioration of its industrial base. As a result, its population and property values declined, which meant a decrease in property taxes. Because Peoria had always relied heavily on property taxes, it became more difficult for it to generate sufficient revenue for existing public services.

In response, the city funded a management science study to determine new ways to generate revenue that would be politically acceptable. Several forms of sales tax were suggested, such as a sales tax on everything but food, drugs, and durable goods, a sales tax on food and drugs, a sales tax on durable goods, and a sales tax on gasoline. Politically, the city had several objectives. It certainly needed to maintain its current level of tax revenue, but it also wanted to put less tax burden on low income families, it wanted to reduce the property tax rate, and it wanted to keep businesses from moving out of Peoria. This suggested a multiple-objective linear programming (MOLP) approach. Specifically, the study identified four objectives: (1) reduce the property tax rate, (2) minimize the tax burden on low income households, (3) minimize the flight of businesses and shoppers to the suburbs to escape higher sales taxes, and (4) minimize the gasoline tax rate.

Using these four objectives, the model then formulated a number of constraints, including (1) maintain the current level of tax revenues (at least), (2) ensure that the property tax rate does not increase, (3) ensure that the general sales tax rate excluding food, drugs, and durable goods is between 1%

and 3%, and others. (Actually, as the city manager studied the model's output and saw results he didn't agree with, he suggested more constraints in order to produce different types of solutions. Remember that this took place in a *political* context!) The decision variables were the various tax rates, including the property tax rate and the proposed sales tax rates.

Unlike examples in previous chapters where there was a single objective, an MOLP model produces *many* solutions. The solutions worth examining are called **efficient solutions**, in the sense that any change in an efficient solution that makes one objective better automatically makes another objective worse. This means that the set of efficient solutions is the only set decision makers need to choose from, and they can make the choice by using their own preference function. This is indeed what happened in the Peoria study. After the city manager studied the set of efficient solutions, he was finally able to select a solution that he deemed best—it satisfied the constraints, it did well across the various objectives, and it was politically acceptable. Because of the political context, it might be hard to argue that the accepted solution was really "optimal," but the MOLP approach did what it was supposed to do. It allowed the city to make a decision based on rational criteria, it illustrated the trade-offs between the objectives associated with planning the tax structure, and it decreased the property tax rate from 2.76% to 1.64% while maintaining the level of tax revenue. (See Problem 40 of the Review Problems section for an illustration of this problem.) ■

7.1 Introduction

In many of your classes, you have probably discussed how to make good decisions. Usually, you assume that the correct decision optimizes a *single* objective, such as profit maximization or cost minimization. In most situations you encounter in business and life, however, there are more than one relevant objective. For example, when you graduate you will (we hope) receive several job offers. Which should you accept? Before deciding which job offer to accept, you might consider how each job "scores" on several objectives, such as salary, interest in work, quality of life in the city you will live in, and nearness to family. In this situation it is difficult to combine your four objectives into a single objective. Similarly, in determining an optimal investment portfolio, you want to maximize expected return but you also want to minimize risk. How do you reconcile these conflicting objectives? In this chapter we will discuss three tools, *goal programming*, *trade-off curves*, and the *Analytic Hierarchy Process* (*AHP*), that decision makers can use to solve multiple-objective problems. Fortunately, all three of these tools can be implemented fairly easily on a spreadsheet.

7.2 Goal Programming

In many situations a company wants to achieve several objectives. Given limited resources, it may prove impossible to meet all objectives simultaneously. If the company can prioritize its objectives, then **goal programming** can often be used to choose good decisions. The following media selection problem is typical of the situations in which goal programming is useful.

EXAMPLE 7.1

The Leon Burnit Ad Agency is trying to determine a TV advertising schedule for Priceler Auto Company. Priceler has three goals (listed here in descending order of importance). Priceler wants its ads to be seen by

- Goal 1: at least 40 million high-income men (HIM)
- Goal 2: at least 35 million high-income women (HIW)
- Goal 3: at least 60 million low-income people (LIP)

Burnit can purchase two types of ads: ads shown on football games and ads shown during soap operas. At most $600,000 can be spent on ads. The advertising costs and potential audiences (in millions of viewers) of a one-minute ad of each type are shown in Table 7.1. The company wants to find the advertising plan that best meets its goals.

TABLE 7.1 **Data for Advertising Example**

Ad Type	HIM	LIP	HIW	Cost
Football	7	10	5	$100,000
Soap opera	3	5	4	$60,000

Solution

First, we build a spreadsheet model and see whether all of the goals can be met simultaneously. In the spreadsheet we must keep track of the following:

- the number of football and soap opera ads placed
- the cost of the ads
- the number of exposures to each group (HIM, HIW, and LIP)
- the deviation from the exposure goal of each group

Developing the Spreadsheet Model The spreadsheet model can be formed as follows. (See Figure 7.1 and the file BURNIT.XLS.)

1 **Inputs.** In the range B5:C7 enter the number of exposures (in millions) to each group generated by each type of ad. In the range B9:C9 enter the cost of each type of ad. In the range D20:D22 enter the exposure goal for each group (in millions) and in cell D16 enter the budget limitation.

2 **Numbers of ads.** Enter trial values for the number of football and soap opera ads in the range B13:C13.

3 **Exposures obtained.** In the range B20:B22 compute the number of people (in millions) in each group that the ads reach. Specifically, compute the number of HIM exposures in cell B20 with the formula

=SUMPRODUCT($B$13:$C$13,B5:C5)

Copy this formula to the range B21:B22 to generate the exposures to HIW and LIP.

4 **Total cost.** Calculate the total amount spent on ads in cell B16 with the formula

=SUMPRODUCT(B9:C9,B13:C13)

We are now ready to see whether it is possible to reach the desired number of people in each group simultaneously.

FIGURE 7.1 Infeasible Solution to Burnit Advertising Example

	A	B	C	D
1	**Advertising Problem Where Not All Goals Can Be Met**			
2				
3	**Exposures (in millions) to various groups per unit of advertising**			
4		Football ad	Soap opera ad	
5	High-income men	7	3	
6	High-income women	5	4	
7	Low-income people	10	5	
8				
9	Cost/unit	$100,000	$60,000	
10				
11	**Advertising plan**			
12		Football ad	Soap opera ad	
13	Number purchased	5	1.67	
14				
15	**Cost constraint**	Total cost		Budget
16		$600,000	<=	$600,000
17				
18	**Achievement of goals**			
19		Total exposures		Goal
20	High-income men	40	>=	40
21	High-income women	31.67	>=	35
22	Low-income people	58.33	>=	60

Can All of the Exposure Goals Be Met?

1 **Objective.** There is no explicit objective to minimize or maximize, so make the Set Target Cell box empty. (We are simply trying to find *any* feasible solution to the constraints.)

2 **Changing cells.** Choose the range B13:C13 as the changing cells and constrain these to be nonnegative.

3 **Exposure constraints.** Add the constraints B20:B22>=D20:D22. This constrains the total exposures to meet or exceed the exposure goals.

4 **Budget constraint.** Add the constraint B16<=D16. This ensures that the budget limit will not be exceeded.

5 **Linear model and "optimize."** Check the Assume Linear Model box and Solve.

The solution we found using the Solver appears in Figure 7.1. However, we also obtained a message stating that no feasible solution exists. You may obtain a different solution, but you should receive the same "no feasible solution" message. This means that there is no way to meet the exposure goals for each group simultaneously and stay within the budget.

When there is no solution that meets all goals simultaneously (and satisfies other constraints such as a budget constraint), we can use a **preemptive goal programming** approach. This method entails the following steps.

Steps for Implementing Preemptive Goal Programming

1 Try to come as close as possible to meeting the highest priority (HIM) goal.

2 Try to come as close as possible to meeting the second highest priority goal (HIW) *but ensure that the highest priority goal is not compromised.*

3 Try to come as close as possible to meeting the third highest priority goal (LIP), *but ensure that no higher priority goal is compromised.*

EXAMPLE 7.1 CONTINUED

For example, if we meet the HIM goal in Step 1, then in Step 2 we try to achieve the HIW goal, but add a constraint to ensure that the HIM goal remains satisfied. However, if we come within two units, say, of meeting the HIM goal in Step 1, then in Step 2 we add a constraint to ensure that the deviation from the HIM goal remains at value 2. Then in Step 3 we minimize the deviation from the LIP goal, but add constraints to ensure that the deviations from the two higher priority goals attained in Steps 1 and 2 are not compromised. In general, of course, the number of steps is equal to the total number of goals.

To implement preemptive goal programming for the Leon Burnit example, we need to compute the deviation from each goal. We could compute the deviation from the HIM goal with the formula

=MAX(D20–B20,0)

or the formula

=IF(D20–B20>=0,D20–B20,0)

Either of these formulas ensures that if we reach fewer than 40 million HIM, a deviation of (40 minus the number of HIM) is recorded, whereas if we reach at least 40 million HIM, a deviation of 0 is recorded. Copying either formula would then compute the deviation from the LIP and HIW goals. The problem with both of these formulas is that the IF or MAX functions create a nonlinear objective function and nonlinear constraints. In many cases these nonlinearities will cause a spreadsheet Solver to obtain an incorrect solution to the goal programming model.

Fortunately, there is a way to obtain a *linear* formulation of the goal programming model. To do so, we modify the spreadsheet in Figure 7.1 as follows.

1 **Amounts under or over goals.** Move the goals from the range D20:D22 to the range G20:G22. In the range C20:C22 enter *any* trial values for the amount by which we are under each of the three goals. Similarly, in the range D20:D22 enter *any* trial values of the amount by which we are over each of the three goals. The range C20:D22 will be additional changing cells.

2 **Logical expressions for goals.** In the range E20:E22 we will compute the quantity

$$\text{Amount of goal achieved} + \text{Amount under goal} - \text{Amount over goal} \qquad \textbf{(7.1)}$$

for each goal. To do this, enter the formula

=B20+C20–D20

in cell E20 and copy this formula to the range E21:E22 to compute Quantity 7.1 for the other goals. Later we will add constraints to ensure that for each goal, the desired value for the goal equals Quantity 7.1. By making the range C20:D22 changing cells and setting the range E20:E22 equal to the range G20:G22, we ensure that the computer accurately records, for each choice of advertising media, the deviation from each goal. Note that we keep track of the amounts under *and* the amounts over each goal because either might be nonzero. However, because Burnit wants the number of exposures to be *at least as large* as the goals, we will only try to minimize the amounts *under* the goals.

3 **Copy amounts under goals.** "Copy" the amounts under the goals to the range B25:B27 by entering the formula

=C20

in cell B25 and copying this formula to the range B26:B27. These will be used as objectives to minimize.

We are now ready to implement preemptive goal programming. For step 1, we try to minimize the amount under the highest priority (HIM) goal. (See Figure 7.2 and the file BURNIT.XLS.)

Implementing Step 1 Modify the Solver settings from the previous spreadsheet as follows.

1 **Objective.** Choose cell B25 (amount under the HIM goal) as the objective to be minimized.

2 **Extra changing cells.** Choose the range C20:D22 as extra changing cells and constrain these to be nonnegative.

3 **Logical constraints on the goal levels.** Add the constraints E20:E22=G20:G22. As explained above, this ensures that the range C20:D22 contains the amount by which we fail to meet each goal.

4 **Budget constraint.** Remember that the budget constraint was already incorporated before.

5 **Optimize.** Click on Solve.

FIGURE 7.2 **Preemptive Goal Programming Step 1 for Burnit Example**

	A	B	C	D	E	F	G
1	**Advertising Problem with Goal Programming - Step 1**						
2							
3	**Exposures (in millions) to various groups per unit of advertising**						
4		Football ad	Soap opera ad				
5	High-income men	7	3				
6	High-income women	5	4				
7	Low-income people	10	5				
8							
9	Cost/unit	$100,000	$60,000				
10							
11	**Advertising plan**						
12		Football ad	Soap opera ad				
13	Number purchased	5	1.67				
14							
15	**Cost constraint**	Total cost		Budget			
16		$600,000	<=	$600,000			
17							
18	**Achievement of goals**						
19		Total exposures	Amt under goal	Amt over goal	Sum		Goal
20	High-income men	40	0	0	40	=	40
21	High-income women	31.67	3.333	0	35	=	35
22	Low-income people	58.33	1.667	0	60	=	60
23							
24							
25	**Deviation from goal 1**	0					
26	Deviation from goal 2	3.333					
27	Deviation from goal 3	1.667					

The Solver solution to Step 1 appears in Figure 7.2. This solution meets the HIM goal (see cell B25), but fails to meet the HIW and LIP goals (see cells B26 and B27). You should not be surprised that goals 2 and 3 are not met in this solution. The model in Figure 7.2 contains absolutely no incentive to achieve these goals; it focuses entirely on goal 1 and only records the deviations from the other goals.

Implementing Step 2 We now try to minimize the amount under the second highest priority goal (HIW), keeping the amount under the highest priority goal (HIM) at value 0. (See Figure 7.3 and the file BURNIT.XLS.) The only modification to the previous spreadsheet is that in cell D25 we enter a 0, indicating that we will add a constraint to ensure that the Step 1 amount under the HIM goal will still be achieved at the conclusion of Step 2. Then we modify the Solver settings as follows.

1 **Objective.** Choose cell B26 (amount under the HIW goal) as the objective to minimize.

2 **Constraint on goal 1.** Add the constraint B25=D25. This ensures that the HIM goal will still be met.

FIGURE 7.3 **Preemptive Goal Programming Step 2 for Burnit Example**

	A	B	C	D	E	F	G
1	**Advertising Problem with Goal Programming - Step 2**						
2							
3	**Exposures (in millions) to various groups per unit of advertising**						
4		Football ad	Soap opera ad				
5	High-income men	7	3				
6	High-income women	5	4				
7	Low-income people	10	5				
8							
9	Cost/unit	$100,000	$60,000				
10							
11	**Advertising plan**						
12		Football ad	Soap opera ad				
13	Number purchased	5	1.67				
14							
15	**Cost constraint**	Total cost		Budget			
16		$600,000	<=	$600,000			
17							
18	**Achievement of goals**						
19		Total exposures	Amt under goal	Amt over goal	Sum		Goal
20	High-income men	40	0	0	40	=	40
21	High-income women	31.67	3.333	0	36	=	36
22	Low-income people	58.33	1.667	0	60	=	60
23							
24		Current level		Previous level			
25	**Deviation from goal 1**	0	=	0			
26	Deviation from goal 2	3.333					
27	Deviation from goal 3	1.667					

The Solver solution to Step 2 is shown in Figure 7.3. We see that the HIM goal is still met (see cell B25), and we come within 3.333 units of meeting the HIW goal. In cell B27 we see that we fail to meet the LIP goal by 1.67 units. The bad news is that this solution is no better than the solution from Step 1. In fact, it is identical. This doesn't always occur in goal programming, but it occurred in this example. As you might guess, Step 3 won't do any better, but we will show it in order to complete the procedure.

Implementing Step 3 In Step 3 we try to minimize the amount under the lowest priority goal (LIP) subject to the constraints that the HIM deviation remains at value 0 and the LIP deviation remains at value 3.333. (See Figure 7.4 and the file BURNIT.XLS.) We enter the Step 2 amount under the HIW goal (3.333) in cell D26. Then we add a constraint to ensure that in Step 3 we still come within 3.333 units of the HIW goal. The previous Solver settings are modified as follows.

FIGURE 7.4 **Preemptive Goal Programming Step 3 for Burnit Example**

	A	B	C	D	E	F	G
1	**Advertising Problem with Goal Programming - Step 3**						
2							
3	**Exposures (in millions) to various groups per unit of advertising**						
4		Football ad	Soap opera ad				
5	High-income men	7	3				
6	High-income women	5	4				
7	Low-income people	10	5				
8							
9	Cost/unit	$100,000	$60,000				
10							
11	**Advertising plan**						
12		Football ad	Soap opera ad				
13	Number purchased	5	1.67				
14							
15	**Cost constraint**	Total cost		Budget			
16		$600,000	<=	$600,000			
17							
18	**Achievement of goals**						
19		Total exposures	Amt under goal	Amt over goal	Sum		Goal
20	High-income men	40	0	0	40	=	40
21	High-income women	31.67	3.333	0	35	=	35
22	Low-income people	58.33	1.667	0	60	=	60
23							
24		Current level		Previous level			
25	**Deviation from goal 1**	0	=	0			
26	Deviation from goal 2	3.333	=	3.333			
27	Deviation from goal 3	1.667					

1 **Objective.** Choose cell B27 (deviation from the LIP goal) as the objective to minimize.

2 **Constraint on Goal 2.** Add the constraint B26=D26. This ensures that we will not compromise the HIW goal when we minimize the deviation from the LIP goal.

The Solver solution to Step 3 appears in Figure 7.4. As we indicated, there is again no improvement over the Step 1 solution. Preemptive goal programming suggests that Burnit should use 5 football ads and 1.667 soap opera ads. The HIM goal will be met, and Burnit will come within 3.333 units ($3\frac{1}{3}$ million viewers) of meeting the HIW goal and within 1.667 units ($1\frac{2}{3}$ million viewers) of meeting the LIP goal. This is the closest it can come to meeting all of its goals, given the priorities it has set.

How Does a Change in Priorities Affect the Solution? With three goals, there are six possible orderings of the three goals. The preemptive goal programming solutions corresponding to each possible ordering of the three goals are listed in Table 7.2. The second row corresponds to the ordering we used in the example. Obviously, the solution can change if the priorities of the goals change. (Problem 1 asks you to verify the details.) ■

TABLE 7.2 **Solutions for Different Priority Orderings**

Priority			Ad Type		Deviation from		
Highest	Middle	Lowest	Football	Soap Opera	HIM	LIP	HIW
HIM	LIP	HIW	6	0	0	0	5
HIM	HIW	LIP	5	5/3	0	5/3	10/3
LIP	HIM	HIW	6	0	0	0	5
LIP	HIW	HIM	6	0	0	0	5
HIW	HIM	LIP	3	5	4	5	0
HIW	LIP	HIM	3	5	4	5	0

MODELING ISSUE

The goal programming method we have discussed works fine if some or all of the changing cells must be integers. If there are any nonlinearities, however, then the Solver might not find an optimal solution. ■

REAL-WORLD APPLICATIONS

Goal programming has been applied to many situations where multiple objectives are present. Here are some examples.

- Optimally blending sausage. The conflicting objectives are cost, protein content, and fat content. See Problem 6 and Steuer [8].
- Admitting students to a college. The conflicting objectives involve class size, diversity, in-state versus out-of-state mix, and academic quality of the class. See Problem 9 and Lee and Moore [4].
- Assigning different types of employees (partners, junior associates, and so on) to different jobs at a CPA firm. The conflicting objectives are monthly billings and the number of workers of each type that the company can hire. See Problem 7 and Welling [12].
- Determining the projects that a manufacturing firm should implement. The conflicting objectives include return on investment, cost, technological risk, and productivity improvement.
- Determining the type of recreation facilities that a city should build. The conflicting objectives include limitations on land use and maintenance cost, as well as desired usage of each facility. See Problem 12 and Taylor and Keown [9].
- Determining the optimal product mix. The conflicting objectives include profit, maintaining a desired cash balance, and maintaining a desired value of the firm's current ratio. See Problem 41 (of the Review Problems section) and Sartoris and Spruill [7].
- Determining the optimal set of ingot molds to use for steel production. Bethlehem Steel did this. Their primary goal was to minimize the number of molds used for steel production. Their secondary goal was to minimize the weight of the steel that needed to be produced to fill the company's orders. See Vasko, Wolfe, and Stott [10]. ■

PROBLEMS

Skill-Building Problems

1 For each set of priorities of goals, solve the Leon Burnit problem and verify that the values in Table 7.2 are correct.

2 Gotham City must determine how to allocate ambulances during the next year. It costs $5000 per year to run an ambulance. Each ambulance must be assigned to one of two districts. Let x_i be the number of ambulances assigned to district i, $i = 1, 2$. The average time (in minutes) it takes for an ambulance to respond to a call from district 1 is $40 - 3x_1$; for district 2 the time is $50 - 4x_2$. Gotham City has three goals (listed in order of priority):

- Goal 1: At most $100,000 per year should be spent on ambulance service.
- Goal 2: Average response time in district 1 should be at most five minutes.
- Goal 3: Average response time in district 2 should be at most five minutes.

a Use preemptive goal programming to determine how many ambulances to assign to each district.

b How would your answer change if goal 2 had the highest priority, then goal 3, and then goal 1?

3 Fruit Computer Company is ready to make its annual purchase of computer chips. Fruit can purchase chips (in lots of 100) from three suppliers. Each chip's quality is rated as excellent, good, or mediocre. During the coming year Fruit needs 5000 excellent chips, 3000 good chips, and 1000 mediocre chips. The characteristics of the chips purchased from each supplier are shown in Table 7.3. Each year, Fruit has budgeted $28,000 to spend on chips. If Fruit does not obtain enough chips of a given quality, it can special-order additional chips at $10 per excellent chip, $6 per good chip, and $4 per mediocre chip. Fruit assesses a penalty of $1 for each dollar it goes over the annual budget (in payments to suppliers). Determine how Fruit can minimize the penalty associated with meeting the annual chip requirements. Also use preemptive goal programming to determine a purchasing strategy. Let the budget constraint have the highest priority, followed in order by the restrictions on excellent, good, and mediocre chips.

TABLE 7.3 Data for Fruit Computer Problem

	Number of Chips per Lot of 100			
	Excellent	**Good**	**Mediocre**	**Price per 100**
Supplier 1	60	20	20	$400
Supplier 2	50	35	15	$300
Supplier 3	40	20	40	$250

4 Hiland Appliance must determine how many color TVs and VCRs to stock. It costs Hiland $300 to purchase a color TV and $200 to purchase a VCR. A color TV requires three square yards of storage space, and a VCR requires one square yard. The sale of a color TV earns Hiland a profit of $150, and each VCR sale earns a profit of $100. Hiland has set the following goals (listed in order of importance):

- Goal 1: A maximum of $20,000 can be spent on purchasing color TVs and VCRs.
- Goal 2: Highland should earn at least $11,000 profit from the sale of color TVs and VCRs.
- Goal 3: Color TVs and VCRs should not use up more than 200 square yards of storage space.

Use a preemptive goal programming model to determine how many color TVs and VCRs Hiland should order. How would the preemptive goal formulation be modified if Hiland's second goal were to have a profit of *exactly* $11,000?

5 Stockco produces two products. Relevant information for each product is shown in Table 7.4. Stockco has a goal of $48 in profits and incurs a $1 penalty for each dollar it falls short of this goal. A total of 32 hours of labor are available. A $2 penalty is incurred for each hour of overtime (labor over 32 hours) used, and a $1 penalty is incurred for each hour of available labor that is unused. Marketing considerations require that at least seven units of product 1 be produced and at least ten units of product 2 be produced. For each unit (of either product) by which production falls short of demand, a penalty of $5 is assessed.

TABLE 7.4 Data for Stockco Problem

	Product 1	Product 2
Labor Hours Required	4	2
Contribution to Profit	\$4	\$2

a Determine how to minimize the total penalty incurred by Stockco.

b Suppose the company sets (in order of importance) the following goals:

- Goal 1: Avoid underutilization of labor.
- Goal 2: Meet demand for product 1.
- Goal 3: Meet demand for product 2.
- Goal 4: Do not use any overtime.

Use preemptive goal programming to determine an optimal production schedule.

6 (Based on Steuer [8]) Deancorp produces sausage by blending beef head, pork chuck, mutton, and water. The cost per pound, fat per pound, and protein per pound for these ingredients are listed in Table 7.5. Deancorp needs to produce 100 pounds of sausage and has set the following goals, listed in order of priority:

- Goal 1: Sausage should consist of at least 15% protein.
- Goal 2: Sausage should consist of at most 8% fat.
- Goal 3: Cost per pound of sausage should not exceed 8¢.

Use preemptive goal programming model to determine the composition of sausage.

TABLE 7.5 Data for Deancorp Sausage Problem

	Beef Head	Pork Chuck	Mutton	Water
Fat (per lb.)	.05	.24	.11	0
Protein (per lb.)	.20	.26	.08	0
Cost (in cents)	12	9	8	0

7 (Based on Welling [12]) The Touche Young accounting firm must complete three jobs during the next month. Job 1 will require 500 hours of work, job 2 will require 300 hours, and job 3 will require 100 hours. At present the firm consists of five partners, five senior employees, and five junior employees, each of whom can work up to 40 hours per month. The dollar amount (per hour) that the company can bill depends on the type of accountant assigned to each job, as shown in Table 7.6. (The "X" indicates that a junior employee does not have enough experience to work on job 1.) All jobs must be completed. Touche Young has also set the following goals, listed in order of priority:

- Goal 1: Monthly billings should exceed \$74,000.
- Goal 2: At most one partner should be hired.
- Goal 3: At most three senior employees should be hired.
- Goal 4: At most one junior employee should be hired.

Use preemptive goal programming to help Touche solve its problem.

TABLE 7.6 Data for Touche Accounting Problem

	Job 1	Job 2	Job 3
Partner	160	120	110
Senior Employee	120	90	70
Junior Employee	X	50	40

8 There are four teachers in the Faber College Business School. Each semester, 200 students take each of the following courses: Marketing, Finance, Production, and Statistics. The "effectiveness" of each teacher in teaching each course is given in Table 7.7. Each teacher can teach a total of 200 students during the semester. The dean has set a goal of obtaining an average teaching effectiveness level of at least 6 in each course. Deviations from this goal in any course are considered equally important. Determine the semester's teaching assignments.

TABLE 7.7 Data for Teaching Problem

	Marketing	Finance	Production	Statistics
Teacher 1	7	5	8	2
Teacher 2	7	8	9	4
Teacher 3	3	5	7	9
Teacher 4	5	5	6	7

Skill-Extending Problems

9 (Based on Lee and Moore [4]) Faber College is admitting students for the class of 2001. Data on its applicants are shown in Table 7.8. It has set four goals for this class, listed in order of priority:

- Goal 1: The entering class should include at least 5000 students.
- Goal 2: The entering class should have an average SAT score of at least 640.
- Goal 3: The entering class should consist of at least 25% out-of-state students.
- Goal 4: At least 2000 members of the entering class should not be business majors.

Use preemptive goal programming to determine how many applicants of each type to admit. Assume that all applicants who are admitted will decide to attend Faber.

TABLE 7.8 Data on Faber's Applicants

	SAT Score	Business Majors	Non-Business Majors
In-state	700	1500	400
In-state	600	1300	700
In-state	500	500	500
Out-of-state	700	350	50
Out-of-state	600	400	400
Out-of-state	500	400	600

10 During the next four quarters Wivco faces the following demands for globots: quarter 1, 13; quarter 2, 14; quarter 3, 12; quarter 4, 15. Globots can be produced by regular-time labor or by overtime labor. Production capacity (number of globots) and production costs during the next four quarters are shown in Table 7.9. Wivco has set the following goals in order of importance:

- Goal 1: Each quarter's demand should be met on time.
- Goal 2: Inventory at the end of each quarter should not exceed three units.
- Goal 3: Total production cost should be no greater than $250.

Use a preemptive goal programming model to determine Wivco's production schedule for the next four quarters. Assume that at the beginning of the first quarter, one globot is in inventory.

TABLE 7.9 Data for Wivco Production Problem

	Regular Time		Overtime	
	Capacity	Cost per Unit	Capacity	Cost per Unit
Quarter 1	9	\$4	5	\$6
Quarter 2	10	\$4	5	\$7
Quarter 3	11	\$5	5	\$8
Quarter 4	12	\$6	5	\$9

11 Lucy's Music Store at present employs five full-time employees and three part-time employees. The normal workload is 40 hours per week for full-time employees and 20 hours per week for part-time employees. Each full-time employee is paid \$6 per hour for work up to 40 hours per week and can sell five recordings per hour. A full-time employee who works overtime is paid \$10 per hour. Each part-time employee is paid \$3 per hour and can sell three recordings per hour. It costs Lucy \$6 to buy a recording, and each recording sells for \$9. Lucy has weekly fixed expenses of \$500. She has established the following weekly goals, listed in order of priority:

- Goal 1: Sell at least 1600 recordings per week.
- Goal 2: Earn a profit of at least \$2200 per week.
- Goal 3: Full-time employees should work at most 100 hours of overtime.
- Goal 4: To promote a sense of job security, the number of hours by which each full-time employee fails to work 40 hours should be minimized.

Use a preemptive goal programming model to determine how many hours per week each employee should work.

12 (Based on Taylor and Keown [9]) Gotham City is trying to determine the type and location of recreational facilities to build during the next decade. Four types of facilities are under consideration: golf courses, swimming pools, gymnasiums, and tennis courts. Six sites are under consideration. If a golf course is built it must be built at either site 1 or site 6. Other facilities can be built at sites 2–5. The amounts of available land (in thousands of square feet) at sites 2–5 are given in Table 7.10. The cost of building each facility (in thousands of dollars), the annual maintenance cost (in thousands of dollars) for each facility, and the land (in thousands of square feet) required for each facility are given in Table 7.11. The number of user days (in thousands) for each type of facility, shown in Table 7.12, depends on where it is built.

a Consider the following set of priorities:

- Priority 1: The amount of land used at each site should be no greater than the amount of land available.
- Priority 2: Construction costs should not exceed \$1.2 million.
- Priority 3: User days should exceed 200,000.
- Priority 4: Annual maintenance costs should not exceed \$200,000.

For this set of priorities, use preemptive goal programming to determine the type and location of recreation facilities in Gotham City.

b Consider the following set of priorities:

- Priority 1: The amount of land used at each site should be no greater than the amount of land available.
- Priority 2: User days should exceed 200,000.
- Priority 3: Construction costs should not exceed \$1.2 million.
- Priority 4: Annual maintenance costs should not exceed \$200,000.

For this set of priorities, use preemptive goal programming to determine the type and location of recreation facilities in Gotham City.

TABLE 7.10 Available Land for Gotham Problem

	Site			
	2	3	4	5
Available Land	70	80	95	120

TABLE 7.11 Costs and Land Requirements for Gotham Problem

	Construction Cost	Maintenance Cost	Land Required
Golf	$340	$80	Not relevant
Swimming	$300	$36	29
Gymnasium	$840	$50	38
Tennis Courts	$85	$17	45

TABLE 7.12 User Days for Gotham Problem

	Site					
	1	2	3	4	5	6
Golf	31	X	X	X	X	27
Swimming	X	25	21	32	32	X
Gymnasium	X	37	29	28	38	X
Tennis Courts	X	20	23	22	20	X

13 A small aerospace company is considering eight projects:

- Project 1: Develop an automated test facility.
- Project 2: Bar code all company inventory and machinery.
- Project 3: Introduce a CAD/CAM system.
- Project 4: Buy a new lathe and deburring system.
- Project 5: Institute an FMS (Flexible Manufacturing System).
- Project 6: Install a LAN (Local Area Network).
- Project 7: Develop an AIS (Artificial Intelligence Simulation).
- Project 8: Set up a TQM (Total Quality Management) program.

Each project has been rated on five attributes: return on investment (ROI), cost, productivity improvement, workforce requirements, and degree of technological risk. These ratings are given in Table 7.13. The company has set the following five goals (listed in order of priority):

- Goal 1: Achieve a return on investment of at least $3250.
- Goal 2: Limit cost to $1300.
- Goal 3: Achieve a productivity improvement of at least 6.
- Goal 4: Limit workforce use to 108.
- Goal 5: Limit technological risk to a total of 4.

Use preemptive goal programming to determine which projects should be undertaken.

14 A new president has just been elected and has set the following economic goals (listed from highest to lowest priority):

- Goal 1: Balance the budget (this means revenues are at least as large as costs).
- Goal 2: Cut spending by at most $150 billion.
- Goal 3: Raise at most $550 billion in taxes from the upper class.
- Goal 4: Raise at most $350 billion in taxes from the lower class.

TABLE 7.13 Ratings for Aerospace Problem

	Project							
	1	2	3	4	5	6	7	8
Return on Investment (ROI)	$2070	$456	$670	$350	$495	$380	$1500	$480
Cost	$900	$240	$335	$700	$410	$190	$500	$160
Productivity Improvement	3	2	2	0	1	0	3	2
Workforce Requirements	18	18	27	36	42	6	48	24
Degree of Technological Risk	3	2	4	1	1	0	2	3

Currently the government spends $1 trillion per year. Revenue can be raised in two ways: through a gas tax and through an income tax. You must determine: G, the per gallon tax rate (in cents); T_1, the tax rate charged on the first $30,000 of income; T_2, the tax rate charged on any income earned over $30,000; and C, the cut in spending (in billions). If the government chooses G, T_1, and T_2, then we assume that the revenue given in Table 7.14 (in billions of dollars) is raised. Of course, the tax rate on income over $30,000 must be at least as large as the tax rate on the first $30,000 of income. Use preemptive goal programming to help the president meet his goals.

TABLE 7.14 Data for Government Economy Problem

	Low Income	High Income
Gas Tax	G	$0.5 * G$
Tax on Income Up to $30,000	$20 * T_1$	$5 * T_1$
Tax on Income Over $30,000	0	$15 * T_2$

15 The HAL computer must determine which of eight research and development (R&D) projects to undertake. For each project four quantities are of interest: (1) the net present value (NPV, in millions of dollars) of the project; (2) the annual growth rate in sales generated by the project; (3) the probability that the project will succeed; and (4) the cost (in millions of dollars) of the project. The relevant information is given in Table 7.15. HAL has set the following four goals:

- Goal 1: The total NPV of all chosen projects should be at least $200 million.
- Goal 2: The average probability of success for all projects chosen should be at least .75.
- Goal 3: The average growth rate of all projects chosen should be at least 15%.
- Goal 4: The total cost of all chosen projects should be at most $1 billion.

For the following sets of priorities, use preemptive (integer) goal programming to determine the projects that should be selected.

a Goal 2, Goal 4, Goal 1,Goal 3.

b Goal 1, Goal 3, Goal 4, Goal 2.

TABLE 7.15 Data for R&D Problem

	NPV (millions)	Annual Growth Rate	Probability of Success	Cost (millions)
Project 1	$40	20%	.75	$220
Project 2	$30	16%	.70	$140
Project 3	$60	12%	.75	$280
Project 4	$45	8%	.90	$240
Project 5	$55	18%	.65	$300
Project 6	$40	18%	.60	$200
Project 7	$40	18%	.60	$200
Project 8	$90	19%	.65	$440

16 (Based on Klingman and Phillips [3]) The Marines need to fill three types of jobs in two cities (Los Angeles and Chicago). The numbers of jobs of each type that must be filled in each city are shown in Table 7.16. The Marines available to fill these jobs have been classified into six groups according to the types of jobs each person is capable of doing, the type of job each person prefers, and the city in which each person prefers to live. The data for each of these six groups are shown in Table 7.17. The Marines have the following three goals, listed from highest priority to lowest priority.

- Ensure that all jobs are filled by qualified workers.
- Ensure that at least 8000 employees are assigned to the jobs they prefer.
- Ensure that at least 8000 employees are assigned to their preferred cities.

Determine how the Marines should assign their workers. (*Note*: You may allow fractional assignments of workers.)

17 (Based on Vasko, Wolfe, and Stott [10]) Bethlehem Steel can fill orders using five different types of steel molds. Up to three different molds of each type can be purchased. Each individual mold can be used to fill up to 100 orders per year. Six different types of orders must be filled during the coming year. The waste (in tons) incurred if a type of mold is used to fill an order is shown in Table 7.18 (where an "x" indicates that a type of mold cannot be used to fill an order). The number of each order type that must be filled during the coming year is shown in Table 7.19. Bethlehem Steel has the following two goals, listed in order of priority.

- Since molds are very expensive, Bethlehem wants to use at most five molds.
- Bethlehem wants to have at most 600 tons of total waste.

Use preemptive goal programming to determine how Bethlehem should fill the coming year's orders. ■

TABLE 7.16 Marine Jobs to Be Filled

	Job Type	Jobs to Fill
Los Angeles	1	1000
Los Angeles	2	2000
Los Angeles	3	1500
Chicago	1	2000
Chicago	2	1000
Chicago	3	1000

TABLE 7.17 Group Data for Marine Problem

	Number of People	Jobs They Can Do	Preferred Job	Preferred City
Group 1	1500	1, 2	1	Los Angeles
Group 2	1500	2, 3	2	Los Angeles
Group 3	1500	1, 3	1	Chicago
Group 4	1500	1, 3	3	Chicago
Group 5	1500	2, 3	3	Los Angeles
Group 6	1500	3	3	Chicago

TABLE 7.18 Waste in Bethlehem Problem

	Order Type					
	1	2	3	4	5	6
Mold 1	1	2	3	4	5	6
Mold 2	x	1	2	3	4	5
Mold 3	x	x	1	2	3	4
Mold 4	x	x	x	1	2	3
Mold 5	x	x	x	x	1	2

TABLE 7.19 Number of Orders for Bethlehem Problem

	Number of Orders
Order 1	80
Order 2	60
Order 3	40
Order 4	100
Order 5	120
Order 6	140

7.3 Pareto Optimality and Trade-off Curves

On a multiple objective problem with no uncertainty, we often search for Pareto optimal solutions. We will assume that the decision maker has exactly two objectives and that the set of feasible points under consideration must satisfy a prescribed set of constraints.

Definition 7.1

A solution (call it *A*) to a multiple objective problem is called **Pareto optimal** if no other feasible solution is at least as good as *A* with respect to every objective and strictly better than *A* with respect to at least one objective. ■

If we define a **dominated solution** as follows, then we can rephrase the definition of Pareto optimality.

Definition 7.2

A feasible solution *B* *dominates* a feasible solution *A* to a multiple objective problem if *B* is at least as good as *A* with respect to every objective and is strictly better than *A* with respect to at least one objective. ■

From this definition it follows that the Pareto optimal solutions are the set of all undominated feasible solutions.

If we graph the "score" of all Pareto optimal solutions in the x–y plane with the x-axis score being the score on objective 1 and the y-axis score being the score on objective 2, the graph is called a **trade-off curve**. It is also called the **efficient frontier**.

To illustrate, suppose that the set of feasible solutions for a multiple objective problem is the shaded region bounded by the curve *AB* and the first quadrant in Figure 7.5. If we want to maximize both objectives 1 and 2, then the curve *AB* is the set of Pareto optimal points.

For another illustration, suppose the set of feasible solutions for a multiple objective problem is all shaded points in the first quadrant bounded from below by the curve *AB* in Figure 7.6. If our goal is to maximize objective 1 and minimize objective 2, then the curve *AB* is the set of Pareto optimal points.

To find a trade-off curve, proceed according to the following steps.

Steps for Finding a Trade-off Curve

1 Choose an objective, say objective 1, and determine its best attainable value v_1. For the solution attaining v_1, find the value of objective 2 (call it v_2). Then (v_1, v_2) is a point on the trade-off curve.

FIGURE 7.5 **Trade-off Curve for Maximizing Two Objectives**

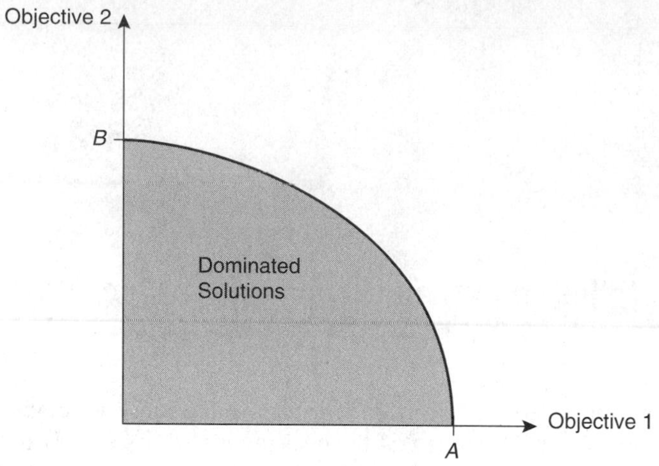

FIGURE 7.6 **Trade-off Curve for Maximizing Objective 1, Minimizing Objective 2**

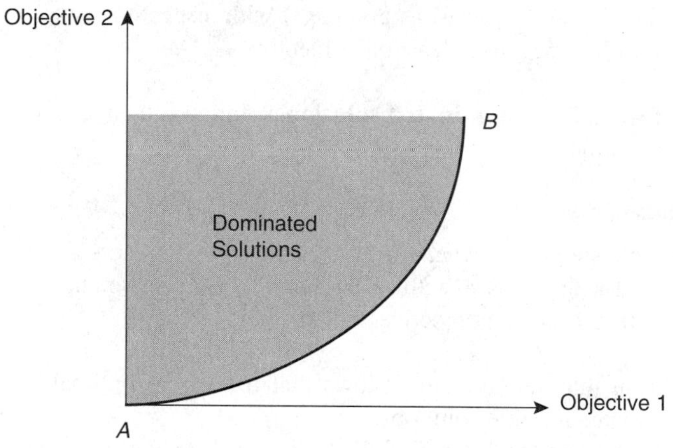

2 For values v of objective 2 that are better than v_2, solve the optimization problem in Step 1 with the additional constraint that the value of objective 2 is at least as good as v. Varying v (over values of v preferred to v_2) yields other points on the trade-off curve.

3 In Step 1 we obtained one "endpoint" of the trade-off curve. If we determine the best value of objective 2 that can be attained, we obtain the other endpoint of the trade-off curve. ■

We will illustrate the concept of Pareto optimality (and how to determine Pareto optimal solutions) with the following example.

EXAMPLE 7.2

Chemco plans to produce three products. The profit per unit, the labor and raw material used per unit produced, and the pollution emitted per unit produced are given in Table 7.20. Currently 1300 labor hours and 1000 units of raw material are available. Chemco's two

TABLE 7.20 **Data for Chemco Example**

	Product 1	Product 2	Product 3
Profit	$10	$9	$8
Labor	4 hrs	3 hrs	2 hrs
Raw Material	3 units	2 units	2 units
Pollution	10 units	6 units	3 units

objectives are to maximize profit and minimize pollution produced. Chemco wants to graph the trade-off curve for this problem.

Solution

To find this trade-off curve, we will solve a number of LP problems where profit is maximized for various levels of pollution. The first LP problem will not constrain pollution at all. Succeeding problems will constrain pollution to lower and lower levels.

Developing the Spreadsheet Model To set up a spreadsheet model to analyze the trade-off between pollution and profit, proceed as follows. (See Figure 7.7 and the file CHEMCO.XLS.)

1 **Inputs.** Enter the labor and raw material used (per unit) by each product in the range B5:D6, the unit profit contribution for each product in the range B10:D10, the pollution created by one unit of each product in the range B8:D8, and the amount of available labor and raw material in the range D19:D20.

FIGURE 7.7 **First Optimal Point for Chemco Example**

	A	B	C	D
1	Chemco Profit/Pollution Problem			
2				
3	Input data			
4		Product 1	Product 2	Product 3
5	Labor hours/unit	4	3	2
6	Raw material/unit	3	2	2
7				
8	Pollution/unit	10	6	3
9				
10	Profit/unit	$10	$9	$8
11				
12	Production plan			
13			Product	
14		1	2	3
15	Units produced	0	300	200
16				
17	Constraints on resources			
18		Used		Available
19	Labor hours	1300	<=	1300
20	Raw material	1000	<=	1000
21				
22	Total pollution	2400		
23				
24	Profit	$4,300		

2 **Units produced.** Enter *any* trial values for the units produced of each product in the range B15:D15.

3 **Labor and raw material used.** Compute the total labor used in cell B19 with the formula

=SUMPRODUCT($B$15:$D$15,B5:D5)

and copy this formula to cell B20 to compute the total raw material used.

4 **Pollution created.** Copy the formula in cell B19 to cell B22 to compute the total pollution created.

5 **Total profit.** Copy the formula in cell B19 to cell B24 to compute total profit.

To find the first point on the profit-pollution trade-off curve, we must find the profit maximizing production plan.

Finding the First Point on the Trade-off Curve

1 **Objective.** Choose cell B24 (profit) as the objective to maximize.

2 **Changing cells.** Choose the range B15:D15 as the changing cells and constrain these to be nonnegative. These correspond to the quantity produced of each product.

3 **Resource availability constraints.** Add the constraints B19:B20<=D19:D20. These constraints ensure that production does not use more labor and raw material than are available.

4 **Linear model and optimize.** Check the Assume Linear Model box and Solve.

The Solver solution appears in Figure 7.7. A maximum profit of $4300 can be obtained by producing 0 units of product 1, 300 units of product 2, and 200 units of product 3. This combination yields 2400 units of pollution (see cell B22). Assuming that we plot profit on the x-axis and pollution on the y-axis, this yields the point (4300,2400) on the trade-off curve.

Finding Other Points on the Trade-off Curve To obtain other points on the profit-pollution trade-off curve, we follow Step 2 of the general procedure. (See Figure 7.8 and the file CHEMCO.XLS.) We choose a pollution level "better" (that is, lower) than 2400, say 2100, and add a constraint to indicate that the pollution produced must be less than or equal to 2100. To do this, first insert two rows (22 and 23) for appropriate labels. Then enter 2100 in cell D24 and add the constraint B24<=D24. By using the Solver, we find that the pollution level produced is 2100 and a profit of $4200 is obtained. This yields the point (4200,2100) on the trade-off curve.

Then by successively changing the number in cell D24 and invoking the Solver, we obtain other points on the trade-off curve. For example, if we change the "allowable" pollution level in cell D24 to 1800 and invoke the Solver, the resulting profit is $4100, and the corresponding point on the trade-off curve is (4100,1800). In a similar fashion we find the points on the trade-off curve given in the range A30:B38 of Figure 7.8. Using the spreadsheet's graphical capabilities (specifically, Option 2 for an X-Y chart), we obtain the profit-pollution trade-off curve in Figure 7.9. Observe that for a profit less than or equal to $4000, an extra dollar of profit increases pollution by 0.375 units. For a profit greater than $4000, however, an extra dollar of profit increases pollution by 3 units. Thus, squeezing out high profits requires great increases in pollution. ■

FIGURE 7.8 **Finding Other Points on the Trade-off Curve**

	A	B	C	D	E	F	G
1	Chemco Profit/Pollution Problem						
2							
3	**Input data**						
4		Product 1	Product 2	Product 3			
5	Labor hours/unit	4	3	2			
6	Raw material/unit	3	2	2			
7							
8	Pollution/unit	10	6	3			
9							
10	Profit/unit	$10	$9	$8			
11							
12	**Production plan**						
13			**Product**				
14		1	2	3			
15	Units produced	0	200	300			
16							
17	**Constraints on resources**						
18		Used		Available			
19	Labor hours	1200	<=	1300			
20	Raw material	1000	<=	1000			
21							
22	**Constraint on total pollution (to obtain new point on trade-off curve)**						
23		Pollution		Upper bound			
24		2100	<=	2100			
25							
26	**Profit**	$4,200					
27							
28	**Same procedure as above was used to find other points on trade-off curve:**						
29	Profit	Pollution					
30	$0	0					
31	$800	300					
32	$1,600	600					
33	$2,400	900					
34	$3,200	1200					
35	$4,000	1500					
36	$4,100	1800					
37	$4,200	2100					
38	$4,300	2400					

Trade-off Curves for Nonlinear Models

Trade-off curves are not confined to linear models. Here is an example of a trade-off curve in a case where the objective is a nonlinear function of the changing cells.

EXAMPLE 7.3

Proctor and Ramble places ads on football games and soap operas. If F one-minute ads are placed on football games and S one-minute ads are placed on soap operas, then the number of men and women (in millions) who view the ads and the cost of the ads (in thousands of dollars) are the values given in Table 7.21. (The square roots in this table indicate the decreasing marginal effectiveness of each succeeding ad.) P&R has a $1 million advertising

FIGURE 7.9 Trade-off Curve for Chemco

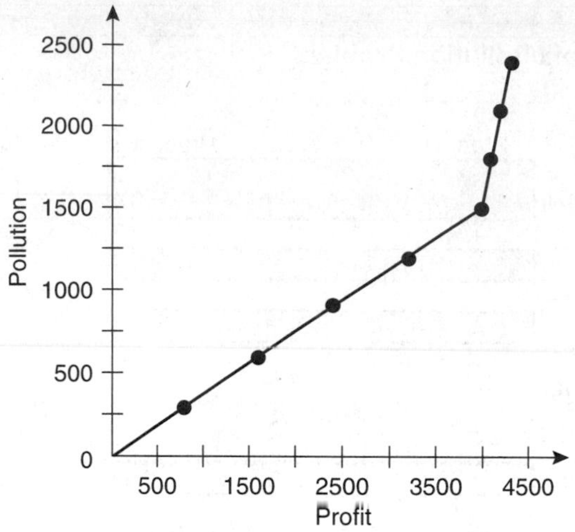

TABLE 7.21 Data for P&R Example

Ad Type	Men Reached	Women Reached	Cost per Ad
Football	$20 * \sqrt{F}$	$4 * \sqrt{F}$	100
Soap Opera	$4 * \sqrt{S}$	$15 * \sqrt{S}$	60

budget; its two objectives are to maximize the number of men and the number of women who see its ads. The company wants to construct a trade-off curve for this situation.

Solution

As in the previous example we need to solve a sequence of problems, now NLP problems. The first will maximize the number of men reached. Each successive problem will maximize this same objective but will impose larger and larger requirements on the number of women reached.

Developing the Spreadsheet Model P&R's spreadsheet model can be formed as follows. (See Figure 7.10 and the file PROCTOR.XLS.)

1 **Inputs.** Enter the costs per ad in the range B8:C8 and the budget in cell C16.

2 **Numbers of ads.** Enter *any* trial values for the number of football and soap opera ads in cells B12 and C12.

3 **Numbers watching ads.** In cell B5 compute the number of men (in millions) watching football ads with the formula

=20*SQRT(B12)

Similarly, in cells B6, C5, and C6 compute the number of women watching football ads, the number of men watching soap opera ads, and the number of women watching soap opera ads (all in millions) with the formulas

=4*SQRT(B12)
=4*SQRT(C12)

FIGURE 7.10 First Optimal Solution for P&R Example

	A	B	C
1	**Proctor & Ramble Advertising Problem**		
2			
3	**Input data (exposures are in millions)**		
4		Football ads	Soap opera ads
5	Men reached/ad	61.24	4.08
6	Women reached/ad	12.25	15.31
7			
8	Cost/ad ($1,000s)	100	60
9			
10	**Advertising strategy**		
11		Football ads	Soap opera ads
12	Number of ads	9.37	1.04
13			
14	**Budget constraint**		
15	Total cost		Budget
16	1000	<=	1000
17			
18	**Women reached**	27.56	
19			
20	**Men reached**	65.32	

and

=15*SQRT(C12)

4 **Total men and women reached.** In cell B20 compute the total number of men reached (in millions) with the formula

=SUM(B5:C5)

Similarly, compute the total number of women reached (in millions) in cell B18 with the formula

=SUM(B6:C6)

5 **Amount spent on ads.** In cell A16 compute the amount (in thousands of dollars) spent on ads with the formula

=SUMPRODUCT(B8:C8,B12:C12)

To find a first point on the trade-off curve, we maximize the number of men that can see P&R's ads, subject to the budget constraint.

Finding the First Point on the Trade-off Curve

1 **Objective.** Choose cell B20 (the number of men reached) as the objective to maximize.

2 **Changing cells.** Choose the range B12:C12 as the changing cells and constrain these cells to be nonnegative. These correspond to the number of football and soap opera ads purchased.

3 **Budget constraint.** Add the constraint A16<=C16. This constraint ensures that the budget is not exceeded.

4 **Optimize.** Make sure the Assume Linear Model box is not checked and Solve.

The Solver solution appears in Figure 7.10. We see that the maximum number of men that P&R's ads can reach is 65.32 million. To reach this many men, P&R needs 9.37

football and 1.04 soap opera ads. From cell B18 we see that this combination reaches 27.56 million women. Essentially, this solution sacrifices exposures to women by placing more ads that are effective with men. If we put the number of women reached on the x-axis, we obtain the point (27.56,65.32) on the trade-off curve.

Finding Other Points on the Trade-off Curve To obtain other points on the trade-off curve, we choose a number of women reached greater than 27.56 (say 30) and add a constraint to indicate that the number of women reached is no less than 30. To do this, insert two rows (18 and 19) for labels. Then enter the value 30 in cell D20, and add the constraint B20<=D20. (See Figure 7.11 and the file PROCTOR.XLS.) By using the Solver, we find that 30 million women and 65.26 million men are reached. This yields the point (30,65.26) on the trade-off curve.

Then by successively changing the number in cell D20 (to 35, 40, 45, 50, 55, 60, and so on) and invoking the Solver repeatedly, we obtain other points on the trade-off curve. For example, if the number of women reached in cell D20 is 35, the Solver indicates an optimal solution reaching 35 million women and 64.7 million men. In a similar fashion we find the points on the trade-off curve given in the range A26:B34 of Figure 7.11. Finally, if

FIGURE 7.11 **Finding Other Points on the Trade-off Curve**

	A	B	C	D	E
1	**Proctor & Ramble Advertising Problem**				
2					
3	**Input data (exposures are in millions)**				
4		Football ads	Soap opera ads		
5	Men reached/ad	60.48	4.77		
6	Women reached/ad	12.10	17.90		
7					
8	Cost/ad ($1,000s)	100	60		
9					
10	**Advertising strategy**				
11		Football ads	Soap opera ads		
12	Number of ads	9.15	1.42		
13					
14	**Budget constraint**				
15		Total cost		Budget	
16		1000	<=	1000	
17					
18	**Constraint on women reached (to obtain a new point on trade-off curve)**				
19		Number reached		Minimum	
20		30.00	>=	30	
21					
22	**Men reached**	65.26			
23					
24	**Same procedure as above used to find other points on trade-off curve:**				
25	Women reached	Men reached			
26	27.56	65.32			
27	30	65.26			
28	35	64.7			
29	40	63.48			
30	45	61.43			
31	50	58.23			
32	55	53.22			
33	60	44.13			
34	62.5	30.59			

we simply maximize the number of women reached, subject to the budget constraint, we obtain another point, (62.5,30.59), on the trade-off curve.

If we graph these points, we obtain the trade-off curve shown in Figure 7.12. Observe that as we move to the right the slope becomes more negative. This means that as the number of women reached by the ads increases, the "cost" (in terms of the loss of male viewers) increases at an increasing rate. ■

FIGURE 7.12 **Trade-off Curve for P&R Example**

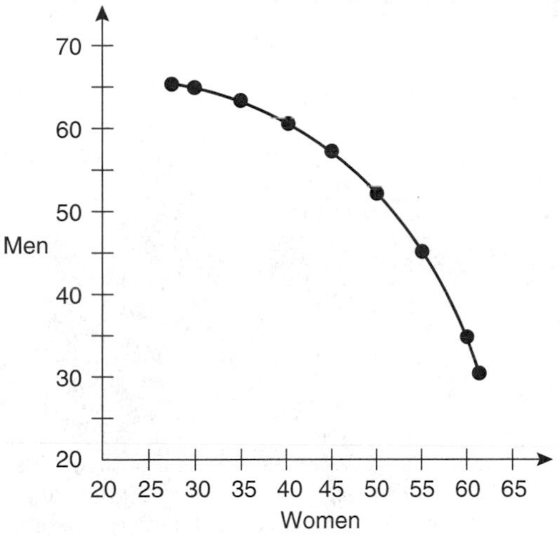

MODELING ISSUE

In a situation where there are more than two objectives, the obvious generalization is to construct trade-off curves between *pairs* of objectives. ■

PROBLEMS

Skill-Building Problems

18 Widgetco produces two types of widgets. Each widget is made of steel and aluminum and is assembled with skilled labor. The resources used and the per-unit profit contribution (ignoring cost of overtime labor purchased) for each type of widget are given in Table 7.22. At present, 200 pounds of steel, 300 pounds of aluminum, and 300 hours of labor are available. Extra overtime labor can be purchased for $10 per hour. Construct a trade-off curve between the objectives of maximizing profit and minimizing overtime labor.

TABLE 7.22 **Data for Widgetco Problem**

	Type 1	Type 2
Steel	6 lbs	12 lbs
Aluminum	8 lbs	20 lbs
Skilled Labor	11 hrs	24 hrs
Profit Contribution	$500	$1100

19 Plantco produces three products. Three workers work for Plantco, and the company must determine which product(s) each worker should produce. The number of units each worker would produce if he or she spent the whole day producing each type of product is given in Table 7.23. The company is also interested in maximizing the happiness of its workers. The amount of happiness "earned" by a worker who spends the entire day producing a given product is given in Table 7.24. Construct a trade-off curve between the objectives of maximizing total units produced daily and total worker happiness.

TABLE 7.23 **Worker Productivity for Plantco Problem**

	Product 1	Product 2	Product 3
Worker 1	20	12	10
Worker 2	12	15	9
Worker 3	6	5	10

TABLE 7.24 **Happiness Values for Plantco Problem**

	Product 1	Product 2	Product 3
Worker 1	6	8	10
Worker 2	6	5	9
Worker 3	9	10	8

20 If a company spends a on advertising (measured in thousands of dollars) and charges a price of p dollars per unit, then it can sell $1000 - 100p + 20a^{1/2}$ units of the product. The cost per unit of producing the product is \$6. Construct a trade-off curve between the objectives of maximizing profit and maximizing the number of units sold.

21 GMCO produces three types of cars: compact, medium, and large. The variable cost per car and production capacity (per year) for each type of car are given in Table 7.25. The annual demand for each type of car depends on the prices of the three types of cars, given in Table 7.26. In this latter table, P_C is the price charged for a compact car (in thousands of dollars). The variables P_M and P_L are defined similarly for medium and large cars. Suppose that each compact gets 30 mpg, each medium car gets 25 mpg, and each large car gets 18 mpg. GMCO wants to keep the planet pollution free, so in addition to maximizing profit, it wants to maximize the average miles per gallon attained by the cars it sells. Construct a trade-off curve between these two objectives.

TABLE 7.25 **Variable Costs and Production Capacities for GMCO Problem**

	Cost	Production Capacity
Compact	\$10,000	2000
Medium	\$14,000	1500
Large	\$18,000	1000

TABLE 7.26 **Demand Functions for GMCO Problem**

	Demand
Compact	$2500 - 100P_C + 3P_M$
Medium	$1800 - 30P_M + 2P_C + P_L$
Large	$1300 - 20P_L + P_M$

22 In Section 4.5 of Chapter 4, we discussed crashing the length of the Widgetco project. For this example construct a trade-off curve between the cost of crashing the project and duration of the project.

23 Referring to the Stockco example from Chapter 6 (see Example 6.10), construct a trade-off curve between the chosen portfolio's expected return and variance. In finance terminology this trade-off curve is usually called the **efficient frontier**. ■

7.4

The Analytic Hierarchy Process

When multiple objectives are important to a decision maker, it is often difficult to choose between alternatives. For example, if you are choosing a job, one job might offer the highest starting salary but rate poorly on other objectives such as quality of life in the city where the job is located and the nearness of the job to your family. Another job offer might rate highly on these latter objectives but have a relatively low starting salary. In this case it might be difficult for you to choose between job offers. Thomas Saaty's **Analytic Hierarchy Process (AHP)** provides a powerful tool that can be used to make decisions in situations where multiple objectives are present. We present an example to illustrate such a case.[1] (*Note*: We will use matrix notation and matrix multiplication in this section. You may need to review the discussion of matrices in Section 6.10.)

EXAMPLE 7.4

Jane is about to graduate from college and is trying to determine which job to accept. She plans to choose between the offers by determining how well each job offer meets the following four objectives:

- Objective 1: High starting salary
- Objective 2: Quality of life in city where job is located
- Objective 3: Interest of work
- Objective 4: Nearness of job to family

Solution

To illustrate how AHP works, suppose that Jane is facing three job offers and must determine which offer to accept. In this example there are four objectives, as listed above. For each objective, AHP generates a weight (by a method to be described shortly). By convention, the weights are always chosen so that they sum to 1. Suppose that Jane's weights are $w_1 = .5115$, $w_2 = .0986$, $w_3 = .2433$, and $w_4 = .1466$. These weights indicate that a high starting salary is the most important objective, followed by interest of work, nearness to family, and quality of life.

Next suppose that Jane determines (again by a method that will be described shortly) how well each job "scores on" each objective. For example, suppose these scores are those listed in Table 7.27. We see from this table that job 1 best meets the objective of a high starting salary, but scores worst on all other objectives. Note that the scores of the jobs on

[1] The leading software package for implementing AHP is Expert Choice, developed by Expert Choice Inc.

TABLE 7.27 Job Scores on Objectives in AHP Example

	Salary	Quality of Life	Interest of Work	Nearness to Family
Job 1	.5714	.1593	.0882	.0824
Job 2	.2857	.2519	.6687	.3151
Job 3	.1429	.5889	.2431	.6025

each objective are "normalized" so that for each objective, the sum of the scores of the jobs on that objective is 1.

Given the weights for the objectives and the scores shown in Table 7.27, Jane can now determine which job offer to accept. Specifically, for each job we calculate an overall score that is a weighted sum of the scores for that job, using the w's as weights. For example, the overall score for job 1 weights the scores in the first row of Table 7.27:

$$\begin{aligned}\text{Job 1 score} &= .5115(.5714) + .0986(.1593) + .2433(.0882) + .1466(.0824)\\ &= .3415\end{aligned}$$

Similarly, the overall scores for jobs 2 and 3 are obtained by weighting the scores in the second and third rows of Table 7.27:

$$\begin{aligned}\text{Job 2 score} &= .5115(.2857) + .0986(.2519) + .2433(.6687) + .1466(.3151)\\ &= .3799\end{aligned}$$

$$\begin{aligned}\text{Job 3 score} &= .5115(.1429) + .0986(.5889) + .2433(.2431) + .1466(.6025)\\ &= .2786\end{aligned}$$

Because the overall score for job 2 is the largest, AHP suggests that Jane should accept this job.

Pairwise Comparison Matrices To obtain the weights, we begin by forming a matrix A, known as the pairwise comparison matrix. The entry in row i and column j of A, labeled a_{ij}, indicates how much more (or less) important objective i is than objective j. "Importance" is measured on an integer-valued 1–9 scale with each number having the interpretation shown in Table 7.28. The phrases in this table, such as "strongly more important than," are suggestive only. They simply indicate discrete points on a continuous scale that can be used to compare the relative importance of any two objectives.

For example, if $a_{13} = 3$, then objective 1 is slightly more important than objective 3. If $a_{ij} = 4$, a value not in the table, then objective i is somewhere between slightly and strongly more important than objective j. If objective i is *less* important than objective j, we use the reciprocal of the appropriate index. For example, if objective i is slightly less important than objective j, then $a_{ij} = 1/3$. Finally, for all objectives i, we use the convention that $a_{ii} = 1$.

For consistency, it is necessary to set $a_{ji} = 1/a_{ij}$. For example, if $a_{13} = 3$, then it is necessary to have $a_{31} = 1/3$. This states the obvious fact that if objective 1 is slightly

TABLE 7.28 Interpretation of Values in Pairwise Comparison Matrix

Value of a_{ij}	Interpretation
1	Objectives i and j are equally important.
3	Objective i is slightly more important than j.
5	Objective i is strongly more important than j.
7	Objective i is very strongly more important than j.
9	Objective i is absolutely more important than j.

more important than objective 3, then objective 3 is slightly less important than job 1. It is usually easier to determine all a_{ij}'s that are greater than 1 and then use the relationship $a_{ji} = 1/a_{ij}$ to determine the remaining entries in the pairwise comparison matrix.

To illustrate, suppose that Jane has identified the following pairwise comparison matrix for her four objectives:

$$A = \begin{bmatrix} 1 & 5 & 2 & 4 \\ 1/5 & 1 & 1/2 & 1/2 \\ 1/2 & 2 & 1 & 2 \\ 1/4 & 2 & 1/2 & 1 \end{bmatrix}$$

The rows and columns of A each correspond to Jane's four objectives: salary, quality of life, interest of work, and nearness to family. Considering the first row, for example, she believes that salary is more important, in various degrees, than quality of life, interest of work, and nearness to family.

The entries in this matrix have built-in pairwise consistency since we require $a_{ij} = 1/a_{ji}$ for each i and j. However, they may not be consistent when three (or more) alternatives are considered simultaneously. For example, Jane claims that salary is strongly more important than quality of life ($a_{12} = 5$) and that salary is very slightly more important than interesting work ($a_{13} = 2$). But she also says that interesting work is very slightly more important than quality of life ($a_{32} = 2$). The question is whether these raatings are all consistent with one another. They are not, at least not exactly. It can be shown that some of Jane's pairwise comparisons are slightly inconsistent. When a person is asked to make this many pairwise comparisons, slight inconsistencies are common and fortunately do not cause serious difficulties. An index that can be used to measure the consistency of Jane's preferences will be discussed later in this section.

Determining the Weights Although the ideas behind AHP are fairly intuitive, the mathematical reasoning required to derive the weights for the objectives is quite advanced. Therefore, we simply describe how it is done.

Starting with the pairwise comparison matrix A, we find the weights for Jane's four objectives using the following two steps.

1 For each of the columns of A, divide each entry in the column by the sum of the entries in the column. This yields a new matrix (call it A_{norm}, for "normalized") in which the sum of the entries in each column is 1.

For Jane's pairwise comparison matrix, this step yields

$$A_{\text{norm}} = \begin{bmatrix} .5128 & .5000 & .5000 & .5333 \\ .1026 & .1000 & .1250 & .0667 \\ .2564 & .2000 & .2500 & .2667 \\ .1282 & .2000 & .1250 & .1333 \end{bmatrix}$$

2 Estimate w_i, the weight for objective i, as the average of the entries in row i of A_{norm}.

For Jane's matrix this yields

$$w_1 = \frac{.5128 + .5000 + .5000 + .5333}{4} = .5115$$

$$w_2 = \frac{.1026 + .1000 + .1250 + .0667}{4} = .0986$$

$$w_3 = \frac{.2564 + .2000 + .2500 + .2667}{4} = .2433$$

$$w_4 = \frac{.1282 + .2000 + .1250 + .1333}{4} = .1466$$

Intuitively, why does w_1 approximate the weight for objective 1 (salary)? Here is the reasoning. The proportion of weight that salary is given in pairwise comparisons of each objective to salary is .5128. Similarly, .50 represents the proportion of total weight that salary is given in pairwise comparisons of each objective to quality of life. Therefore, we see that each of the four numbers averaged to obtain w_1 represents a measure of the total weight attached to salary. Averaging these numbers should give a good estimate of the proportion of the total weight given to salary.

Determining the Score of Each Decision Alternative on Each Objective Now that we have determined the weights, we need to determine how well each job scores on each objective. To determine these scores, we use the same scale described in Table 7.28 to construct a pairwise comparison matrix for each objective. Consider the salary objective, for example. Suppose that Jane assesses the following pairwise comparison matrix. We denote this matrix as A_1 since it reflects her comparisons of the three jobs with respect to the first objective, salary.

$$A_1 = \begin{bmatrix} 1 & 2 & 4 \\ 1/2 & 1 & 2 \\ 1/4 & 1/2 & 1 \end{bmatrix}$$

The rows and columns of this matrix correspond to the three jobs. For example, the first row means that Jane believes job 1 is superior to job 2 (and even more superior to job 3) in terms of salary. To find the relative scores of the three jobs on salary, we now apply the *same* two-step procedure as above to the salary pairwise comparison matrix A_1. That is, we first divide each column entry by the column sum to obtain

$$A_{1,\text{norm}} = \begin{bmatrix} .5714 & .5714 & 5714 \\ .2857 & .2857 & .2857 \\ .1429 & .1429 & .1429 \end{bmatrix}$$

Then we average the numbers in each row to obtain the vector of scores for the three jobs on salary, denoted by S_1:

$$S_1 = \begin{bmatrix} .5714 \\ .2857 \\ .1429 \end{bmatrix}$$

That is, the scores for jobs 1, 2, and 3 on salary are .5714, .2857, and .1429. In terms of salary, job 1 is clearly the favorite.

Next, we repeat these calculations for Jane's other objectives. Each of these objectives requires a pairwise comparison matrix, which we will denote as A_2, A_3, and A_4. Suppose that Jane's pairwise comparison matrix for quality of life is

$$A_2 = \begin{bmatrix} 1 & 1/2 & 1/3 \\ 2 & 1 & 1/3 \\ 3 & 3 & 1 \end{bmatrix}$$

Then the corresponding normalized matrix is

$$A_{2,\text{norm}} = \begin{bmatrix} .1667 & .1111 & .2000 \\ .3333 & .2222 & .2000 \\ .5000 & .6667 & .6000 \end{bmatrix}$$

and by averaging, we obtain

$$S_2 = \begin{bmatrix} .1593 \\ .2519 \\ .5889 \end{bmatrix}$$

Here, job 3 is the clear favorite. However, this might not have much impact since Jane puts relatively little weight on quality of life.

For interest of work, suppose the pairwise comparison matrix is

$$A_3 = \begin{bmatrix} 1 & 1/7 & 1/3 \\ 7 & 1 & 3 \\ 3 & 1/3 & 1 \end{bmatrix}$$

Then the same types of calculations show that the scores for jobs 1, 2, and 3 on interest of work are

$$S_3 = \begin{bmatrix} .0882 \\ .6687 \\ .2431 \end{bmatrix}$$

Finally, suppose the pairwise comparison matrix for nearness to family is

$$A_4 = \begin{bmatrix} 1 & 1/4 & 1/7 \\ 4 & 1 & 1/2 \\ 7 & 2 & 1 \end{bmatrix}$$

In this case the scores for jobs 1, 2, and 3 on nearness to family are

$$S_4 = \begin{bmatrix} .0824 \\ .3151 \\ .6025 \end{bmatrix}$$

Determining the Best Alternative Let's summarize what we've determined so far. Jane first assesses a pairwise comparison matrix A that measures the relative importance of each of her objectives to one another. From this matrix we obtain a vector of weights w that summarizes the relative importance of the objectives. Next, Jane assesses a pairwise comparison matrix A_i for each objective i. This matrix measures how well each job compares to other jobs with regard to this objective. For each matrix A_i we obtain a vector of scores S_i that summarizes how the jobs compare in terms of achieving objective i.

The final step is to combine the scores in the S_i vectors with the weights in the w vector. Actually, we have already done this. Note that the columns of Table 7.27 are all the same as the S_i vectors we just obtained. If we form a matrix S of these score vectors and multiply this matrix by w, we obtain a vector of overall scores for each job, as shown below:

$$S_w = \begin{bmatrix} .5714 & .1593 & .0882 & .0824 \\ .2857 & .2519 & .6687 & .3151 \\ .1429 & .5889 & .2431 & .6025 \end{bmatrix} * \begin{bmatrix} .5115 \\ .0986 \\ .2433 \\ .1466 \end{bmatrix} = \begin{bmatrix} .3415 \\ .3799 \\ .2786 \end{bmatrix}$$

These are the same overall scores that we obtained earlier. As before, the largest of these overall scores is for job 2, so AHP suggests that Jane should accept this job. Job 1 follows closely behind, with job 3 a distant third.

Checking for Consistency As mentioned earlier, any pairwise comparison matrix can suffer from inconsistencies. We now describe a procedure to check for inconsistencies. We illustrate this on the A matrix and its associated vector of weights w. However, the same procedure can be used on any of the A_i matrices and their associated "weights" vector S_i.

1 Compute Aw. For the example, we obtain

$$Aw = \begin{bmatrix} 1 & 5 & 2 & 4 \\ 1/5 & 1 & 1/2 & 1/2 \\ 1/2 & 2 & 1 & 2 \\ 1/4 & 2 & 1/2 & 1 \end{bmatrix} * \begin{bmatrix} .5115 \\ .0986 \\ .2433 \\ .1466 \end{bmatrix} = \begin{bmatrix} 2.0774 \\ 0.3958 \\ 0.9894 \\ 0.5933 \end{bmatrix}$$

2 Find the ratio of each element of Aw to the corresponding weight in w and average these ratios. For the example, this calculation is

$$\frac{\frac{2.0774}{.5115} + \frac{.3958}{.0986} + \frac{.9894}{.2433} + \frac{.5933}{.1466}}{4} = 4.0477$$

3 Compute the consistency index (labeled CI) as

$$CI = \frac{(\text{Step 2 result}) - n}{n - 1}$$

where n is the number of objectives. For the example this is $CI = \frac{4.0477-4}{4-1} = .0159$

4 Compare CI to the random index (labeled RI) in Table 7.29 for the appropriate value of n.

For a perfectly consistent decision maker, each ratio in Step 2 equals n. This implies that a perfectly consistent decision maker has $CI = 0$. The values of RI in Table 7.29 give the average value of CI if the entries in A were chosen at random (subject to the constraints that a_{ii}'s must equal 1, and $a_{ij} = 1/a_{ji}$). If the ratio of CI to RI is sufficiently small, then the decision maker's comparisons are probably consistent enough to be useful. Saaty suggests that if $CI/RI < .10$, then the degree of consistency is satisfactory, whereas if $CI/RI > .10$, serious inconsistencies exist and AHP may not yield meaningful results. In Jane's example, $CI/RI = .0159/.90 = .0177$, which is much less than .10. Therefore, Jane's pairwise comparison matrix A does not exhibit any serious inconsistencies. (You can check that the same is true of her other pairwise comparison matrices A_1 through A_4.)

TABLE 7.29 **Random Indices for Consistency Check for AHP Example**

n	2	3	4	5	6	7	8	9	10
RI	0	.58	.90	1.12	1.24	1.32	1.41	1.45	1.51

AHP on a Spreadsheet We now show how to implement AHP on a spreadsheet. (See Figure 7.13 and the file AHP.XLS.)

1 **Inputs.** Enter the pairwise comparison matrices in the ranges B5:E8, B12:D14, B18:D20, B24:D26, and B30:D32. (Note that you can enter fractions such as 1/7 in cell C24, and have them appear as fractions, by formatting the cells with the Fraction option.)

2 **Normalized matrix.** Compute the normalized matrix for the first pairwise comparison matrix in the range G5:J8. This can be done quickly as follows. Starting with the cursor in cell G5, drag the cursor so that the range G5:J8 is highlighted. Then type the formula

```
=B5/SUM(B$5:B$8)
```

and press Control-Enter (both keys at once). You've just learned a quicker way than copying and pasting!

3 **Weights of objectives.** In the range L5:L8 compute the weights for each objective. We'll again do this the quick way. Starting with the cursor in cell L5, highlight the range L5:L8. Then type the formula

```
=AVERAGE(G5:J5)
```

and press Control-Enter.

FIGURE 7.13 **Spreadsheet Implementation of AHP**

	A	B	C	D	E	F	G	H	I	J	K	L
1	Job Selection Using Analytical Hierarchy Process											
2												
3	**Pairwise comparisons among objectives**						**Normalized matrix**					**Weights**
4		Salary	Life quality	Work interest	Near family							
5	Salary	1	5	2	4		0.5128	0.5000	0.5000	0.5333		0.5115
6	Life quality	1/5	1	1/2	1/2		0.1026	0.1000	0.1250	0.0667		0.0986
7	Work interest	1/2	2	1	2		0.2564	0.2000	0.2500	0.2667		0.2433
8	Near family	1/4	2	1/2	1		0.1282	0.2000	0.1250	0.1333		0.1466
9												
10	**Pairwise comparisons among jobs on salary**						**Normalized matrix**					**Scores**
11		Job 1	Job 2	Job 3								
12	Job 1	1	2	4			0.5714	0.5714	0.5714			0.5714
13	Job 2	1/2	1	2			0.2857	0.2857	0.2857			0.2857
14	Job 3	1/4	1/2	1			0.1429	0.1429	0.1429			0.1429
15												
16	**Pairwise comparisons among jobs on quality of life**						**Normalized matrix**					**Scores**
17		Job 1	Job 2	Job 3								
18	Job 1	1	1/2	1/3			0.1667	0.1111	0.2000			0.1593
19	Job 2	2	1	1/3			0.3333	0.2222	0.2000			0.2519
20	Job 3	3	3	1			0.5000	0.6667	0.6000			0.5889
21												
22	**Pairwise comparisons among jobs on interest of work**						**Normalized matrix**					**Scores**
23		Job 1	Job 2	Job 3								
24	Job 1	1	1/7	1/3			0.0909	0.0968	0.0769			0.0882
25	Job 2	7	1	3			0.6364	0.6774	0.6923			0.6687
26	Job 3	3	1/3	1			0.2727	0.2258	0.2308			0.2431
27												
28	**Pairwise comparisons among jobs on nearness to family**						**Normalized matrix**					**Scores**
29		Job 1	Job 2	Job 3								
30	Job 1	1	1/4	1/7			0.0833	0.0769	0.0870			0.0824
31	Job 2	4	1	1/2			0.3333	0.3077	0.3043			0.3151
32	Job 3	7	2	1			0.5833	0.6154	0.6007			0.6025
33												
34	**Determining best job**											
35	Matrix of scores						Overall scores					
36		Salary	Life quality	Work interest	Near family							
37	Job 1	0.5714	0.159	0.088	0.082		0.3415		job 2 has the			
38	Job 2	0.2857	0.252	0.669	0.315		0.3799	←	highest score			
39	Job 3	0.1429	0.589	0.243	0.602		0.2786					

4 **Scores for jobs on various objectives.** Repeat the same calculations in Steps 2 and 3 for the other pairwise comparison matrices to obtain the normalized matrices in columns G through I and scores vectors in column L.

5 **Overall job scores.** In the range B37:E39 form a matrix of job scores on the various objectives. To get the score vector in the range L12:L14 into the range B37:B39, for example, highlight the range B37:B39, type the formula

=L12

and press Control-Enter. Do likewise for the other three scores vectors in column L. Then to obtain the overall job scores (from the formula *Sw*), highlight the range G37:G39, type the formula

=MMULT(B37:E39,L5:L8)

and press Control-Shift-Enter. (Remember that Control-Shift-Enter is used to enter a matrix function. In contrast, Control-Enter is equivalent to copying a formula to a highlighted range.)

Again we see that job 2 is the preferred of the three jobs.

Computing the Consistency Index We now show how to compute the consistency index *CI* for each of the pairwise comparison matrices. (See Figure 7.14, which is also in the file AHP.XLS. Note that we have hidden columns G through K in order to save space. These contain the normalized matrices from Step 2, above.) The following steps are relevant for the first pairwise comparison matrix. The others are done in analogous fashion.

FIGURE 7.14 Computing the Consistency Index for AHP Example

	A	B	C	D	E	F	L	M	N	O	P
1	**Consistency of Pairwise Comparison Matrices**										
2											
3	**Pairwise comparisons among objectives**						**Weights**	**Product**	**Ratios**		
4		Salary	Life quality	Work interest	Near family						
5	Salary	1	5	2	4		0.5115	2.0774	4.0611		
6	Life quality	1/5	1	1/2	1/2		0.0986	0.3958	4.0161		
7	Work interest	1/2	2	1	2		0.2433	0.9894	4.0672		
8	Near family	1/4	2	1/2	1		0.1466	0.5933	4.0459		
9								CI	0.0159	CI/RI	0.0176
10	**Pairwise comparisons among jobs on salary**						**Scores**				
11		Job 1	Job 2	Job 3							
12	Job 1	1	2	4			0.5714	1.7143	3		
13	Job 2	1/2	1	2			0.2857	0.8571	3		
14	Job 3	1/4	1/2	1			0.1429	0.4286	3		
15								CI	0	CI/RI	0.0000
16	**Pairwise comparisons among jobs on quality of life**						**Scores**				
17		Job 1	Job 2	Job 3							
18	Job 1	1	1/2	1/3			0.1593	0.4815	3.0233		
19	Job 2	2	1	1/3			0.2519	0.7667	3.0441		
20	Job 3	3	3	1			0.5889	1.8222	3.0943		
21								CI	0.0270	CI/RI	0.0465
22	**Pairwise comparisons among jobs on interest of work**						**Scores**				
23		Job 1	Job 2	Job 3							
24	Job 1	1	1/7	1/3			0.0882	0.2648	3.0018		
25	Job 2	7	1	3			0.6687	2.0154	3.0139		
26	Job 3	3	1/3	1			0.2431	0.7306	3.0054		
27								CI	0.0035	CI/RI	0.0061
28	**Pairwise comparisons among jobs on nearness to family**						**Scores**				
29		Job 1	Job 2	Job 3							
30	Job 1	1	1/4	1/7			0.0824	0.2473	3.0005		
31	Job 2	4	1	1/2			0.3151	0.9460	3.0019		
32	Job 3	7	2	1			0.6025	1.8096	3.0035		
33								CI	0.0010	CI/RI	0.0017

1 **Product of comparison matrix and vector of weights (or scores).** Compute the product of the first pairwise comparison matrix and the weights vector in the range M5:M8 by highlighting this range, typing

=MMULT(B5:E8,L5:L8)

and pressing Control-Shift-Enter.

2 **Ratios.** In cell N5 calculate the ratio of the two cells to its left with the formula

=M5/L5

and copy this to the range N6:N8.

3 **Consistency index.** Calculate the consistency index *CI* in cell N9 with the formula

=(AVERAGE(N5:N8)–4)/3

Then in cell P9 calculate the ratio of *CI* to *RI* (for $n = 4$) with the formula

=N9/.90

(The .90 comes from Table 7.29. For the other four pairwise comparison matrices in Figure 7.14, we use $n = 3$ and $RI = .58$.)

As Figure 7.14 illustrates, all of the pairwise comparison matrices are quite consistent; the CI/RI ratio for each is quite a bit less than .10. ■

MODELING ISSUE

In Jane's job selection example, suppose that quality of life depends on two "subobjectives": recreational and educational facilities. Then we need a pairwise comparison matrix to calculate the proportion of the quality of life score that is determined by recreational facilities and the proportion that is determined by educational facilities. Next, we need to determine how each job scores (separately) on recreational facilities and educational facilities. Then we can again determine a "quality of life score" for each job and proceed with AHP as before. Using this idea, AHP can handle a hierarchy of objectives and subobjectives. (See Problem 30.) ■

REAL-WORLD APPLICATIONS

Automated Manufacturing Decisions Using AHP

Weber [11] reports the successful use of AHP in deciding which of several technologies to purchase for automated manufacturing. As he discusses, these decisions can have several types of impacts: quantitative financial (such as purchase cost), quantitative nonfinancial (such as throughput, cycle time, and scrap, which are difficult to translate directly into dollars), and qualitative (such as product quality and manufacturing flexibility, which are also difficult to translate into dollars). When the decision maker is trying to rate the different technologies along nonmonetary criteria, then he or she should use the method discussed in this section. (For example, how much more do you prefer technology 1 to technology 2 in the area of product quality?) However, he advises that when quantitative financial data are available (for example, technology 1 costs twice as much as technology 2), then this "objective" information should be used in the AHP preference matrices. Weber developed a software package called AutoMan to implement the AHP method. This software has been purchased by over 800 decision makers since its first release in 1989. ■

Other Applications of AHP

We close by noting that AHP has been used by decision makers in many areas, including accounting, finance, marketing, energy resource planning, microcomputer selection, sociology, architecture, and political science. See Zahedi [13], Golden, Wasil, and Harker [2], and Saaty [6] for a discussion of applications of AHP. ■

PROBLEMS

Skill-Building Problems

24 Each professor's annual salary increase is determined by his performance in three areas: teaching, research, and service to the university. The administration has assessed the pairwise comparison matrix for these objectives as shown in Table 7.30. The administration has compared two professors with regards to their teaching, research, and service over the past year. The pairwise comparison matrices are shown in Table 7.31.

a Which professor should receive a bigger raise?

b Does AHP indicate how large a raise each professor should be given?

c Check the pairwise comparison matrix for consistency.

TABLE 7.30 **Pairwise Comparisons of Objectives in Salary Problem**

	Teaching	Research	Service
Teaching	1	1/3	5
Research	3	1	7
Service	1/5	1/7	1

TABLE 7.31 Pairwise Comparisons of Professors in Salary Problem

Teaching	Professor 1	Professor 2
Professor 1	1	4
Professor 2	1/4	1

Research	Professor 1	Professor 2
Professor 1	1	1/3
Professor 2	3	1

Service	Professor 1	Professor 2
Professor 1	1	6
Professor 2	1/6	1

25 Your company is about to purchase a new personal computer. Three objectives are important in determining which computer you should purchase: cost, user-friendliness, and software availability. The pairwise comparison matrix for these objectives is shown in Table 7.32. Three computers are being considered for purchase. The performance of each computer with regard to each objective is indicated by the pairwise comparison matrices in Table 7.33.

a Which computer should you purchase?

b Check the pairwise comparison matrices for consistency.

TABLE 7.32 Pairwise Comparisons of Objectives in Computer Problem

	Cost	User-friendliness	Software Availability
Cost	1	1/4	1/5
User-friendliness	4	1	1/2
Software Availability	5	2	1

TABLE 7.33 Pairwise Comparisons of Computers in Computer Problem

Cost	Computer 1	Computer 2	Computer 3
Computer 1	1	3	5
Computer 2	1/3	1	2
Computer 3	1/5	1/2	1

User-friendliness	Computer 1	Computer 2	Computer 3
Computer 1	1	1/3	1/2
Computer 2	3	1	5
Computer 3	2	1/5	1

Software Availability	Computer 1	Computer 2	Computer 3
Computer 1	1	1/2	1/7
Computer 2	2	1	1/5
Computer 3	7	5	1

26 You are ready to select your mate for life and have determined that physical attractiveness, intelligence, and personality are key factors in selecting a satisfactory mate. Your pairwise comparison matrix for these objectives is shown in Table 7.34. Three people (Chris, Jamie, and Pat) are begging to be your mate. (This problem attempts to be gender-neutral!) Your view of these people's attractiveness, intelligence, and personality is given in the pairwise comparison matrices in Table 7.35.

a Who should you choose as your lifetime mate?

b Evaluate all pairwise comparison matrices for consistency.

TABLE 7.34 Pairwise Comparisons of Objectives in Mating Problem

	Attractiveness	Intelligence	Personality
Attractiveness	1	3	5
Intelligence	1/3	1	3
Personality	1/5	1/3	1

TABLE 7.35 Pairwise Comparisons of People in Mating Problem

Attractiveness	Chris	Jamie	Pat
Chris	1	5	3
Jamie	1/5	1	1/2
Pat	1/3	2	1

Intelligence	Chris	Jamie	Pat
Chris	1	1/6	1/4
Jamie	6	1	2
Pat	4	1/2	1

Personality	Chris	Jamie	Pat
Chris	1	4	1/4
Jamie	1/4	1	1/9
Pat	4	9	1

27 In determining where to invest your money, two objectives, expected rate of return and degree of risk, are considered to be equally important. Two investments (1 and 2) have the pairwise comparison matrices shown in Table 7.36.

a How would you rank these investments?

b Now suppose another investment (investment 3) is available. The pairwise comparison matrices for these investments are shown in Table 7.37. (Observe that the entries in the comparison matrices for investments 1 and 2 have not changed.) How would you now rank the investments? Contrast your ranking of investments 1 and 2 with your answer from Part (a).

TABLE 7.36 Pairwise Comparisons in Investment Problem

Expected Return	Investment 1	Investment 2
Investment 1	1	1/2
Investment 2	2	1

Degree of Risk	Investment 1	Investment 2
Investment 1	1	3
Investment 2	1/3	1

TABLE 7.37 Expanded Pairwise Comparisons in Investment Problem

Expected Return	Investment 1	Investment 2	Investment 3
Investment 1	1	1/2	4
Investment 2	2	1	8
Investment 3	1/4	1/8	1

Degree of Risk	Investment 1	Investment 2	Investment 3
Investment 1	1	3	1/2
Investment 2	1/3	1	1/6
Investment 3	2	6	1

28 You are trying to determine which MBA program to attend. You have been accepted at two schools: Indiana and Northwestern. You have chosen three attributes to use in helping you make your decision: cost, starting salary for graduates, and ambience of school (can we party there?). Your pairwise comparison matrix for these attributes is shown in Table 7.38. For each attribute the pairwise comparison matrix for Indiana and Northwestern is shown in Table 7.39. Which MBA program should you attend?

TABLE 7.38 Pairwise Comparisons of Attributes in School Problem

	Cost	Salary	Ambience
Cost	1	1/4	2
Salary	4	1	7
Ambience	1/2	1/7	1

TABLE 7.39 Pairwise Comparisons of Indiana and Northwestern

Cost	Indiana	Northwestern
Indiana	1	6
Northwestern	1/6	1

Salary	Indiana	Northwestern
Indiana	1	1/6
Northwestern	6	1

Ambience	Indiana	Northwestern
Indiana	1	4
Northwestern	1/4	1

29 You are trying to determine which of two secretarial candidates (John or Sharon) to hire. The three objectives that are important to your decision are personality, typing ability, and intelligence. You have assessed the pairwise comparison matrix for the three objectives in Table 7.40. The score of each employee on each objective is shown in Table 7.41. If you follow the AHP method, which employee should you hire?

TABLE 7.40 Pairwise Comparison of Objectives in Secretary Problem

	Personality	Typing Ability	Intelligence
Personality	1	1/4	1/3
Typing Ability	4	1	1/2
Intelligence	3	2	1

TABLE 7.41 Candidate Scores in Secretary Problem

	Personality	Typing Ability	Intelligence
John	.4	.6	.2
Sharon	.6	.4	.8

Skill-Extending Problems

30 A consumer is trying to determine which type of frozen dinner to eat. She considers three attributes to be important: taste, nutritional value, and price. Nutritional value is considered to be determined by cholesterol and sodium level. Three types of dinners are under consideration. The pairwise comparison matrix for the three attributes is shown in Table 7.42. Between the three frozen dinners the pairwise comparison matrix for each attribute is shown in Table 7.43. To determine how each dinner rates on nutrition, you will need the pairwise comparison matrix for cholesterol and sodium in Table 7.44. Which frozen dinner would the consumer prefer? (*Hint*: The nutrition score for a dinner equals the score of the dinner on sodium multiplied by the weight for sodium plus the score for the dinner on cholesterol multiplied by the weight for cholesterol.)

TABLE 7.42 Pairwise Comparisons of Attributes for Food Problem

	Taste	Nutrition	Price
Taste	1	3	1/2
Nutrition	1/3	1	1/5
Price	2	5	1

TABLE 7.43 Pairwise Comparisons of Dinners in Food Problem

Taste	Dinner 1	Dinner 2	Dinner 3
Dinner 1	1	5	3
Dinner 2	1/5	1	1/2
Dinner 3	1/3	2	1

Sodium	Dinner 1	Dinner 2	Dinner 3
Dinner 1	1	1/7	1/3
Dinner 2	7	1	2
Dinner 3	3	1/2	1

Cholesterol	Dinner 1	Dinner 2	Dinner 3
Dinner 1	1	1/8	1/4
Dinner 2	8	1	2
Dinner 3	4	1/2	1

Price	Dinner 1	Dinner 2	Dinner 3
Dinner 1	1	4	1/2
Dinner 2	1/4	1	1/6
Dinner 3	2	6	1

TABLE 7.44 Pairwise Comparison of Sodium and Cholesterol in Food Problem

	Cholesterol	Sodium
Cholesterol	1	5
Sodium	1/5	1

31 (Based on Lin, Mock, and Wright [5]) You have been hired by Arthur Ross to determine which of the following accounts receivable methods should be used in an audit of the Keating Five and Dime Store: analytic review (method 1), confirmations (method 2), or test of subsequent collections (method 3). The three criteria used to distinguish between the methods are reliability, cost, and validity. The pairwise comparison matrix for the three criteria is shown in Table 7.45. The pairwise comparison matrices of the three accounting methods for the three criteria are shown in Table 7.46. Use AHP to determine which auditing procedure should be used. Also check the first pairwise comparison matrix for consistency. ■

TABLE 7.45 Pairwise Comparisons of Criteria in Accounting Problem

	Reliability	Cost	Validity
Reliability	1	5	7
Cost	1/5	1	2
Validity	1/7	1/2	1

TABLE 7.46 Pairwise Comparisons of Methods in Accounting Problem

Reliability	Method 1	Method 2	Method 3
Method 1	1	1/6	1/2
Method 2	6	1	4
Method 3	2	1/4	1

Cost	Method 1	Method 2	Method 3
Method 1	1	5	3
Method 2	1/5	1	1/2
Method 3	1/3	2	1

Validity	Method 1	Method 2	Method 3
Method 1	1	3	2
Method 2	1/3	1	1/2
Method 3	1/2	2	1

7.5 Conclusion

Whenever we face a problem with multiple competing objectives, as is the case in many real-world problems, we are forced to make trade-offs between these objectives. This is usually a very difficult task, and not all management scientists agree on the best way to proceed. When the objectives are very different in nature, no method can disguise the inherent complexity of comparing "apples to oranges." Although one method, finding Pareto optimal solutions and drawing the resulting trade-off curve, locates solutions that are not dominated by any others, we still face the problem of choosing one of the (many) Pareto optimal solutions to implement. The other two methods we have discussed in this chapter, goal programming and AHP, make trade-offs and ultimately locate an "optimal" solution. These methods are not without their critics, but when they are used carefully, they have the potential to help solve some difficult and important real-world problems.

REVIEW PROBLEMS

Skill-Building Problems

32 The Pine Valley Board of Education must hire teachers for the coming school year. The types of teachers and the salaries that must be paid are given in Table 7.47. For example, 20 teachers who are qualified to teach history and science have applied for jobs, and each of these teachers must be paid an annual salary of $21,000. Each teacher who is hired teaches the two subjects he or she is qualified to teach. Pine Valley needs to hire 35 teachers qualified to teach history, 30 teachers qualified to teach science, 40 teachers qualified to teach math, and 32 teachers qualified to teach English. The board has $1.4 million to spend on teachers' salaries. A penalty cost of $1 is incurred for each dollar the board goes over budget. For each teacher by which Pine Valley's goals are unmet, the following costs are incurred (because of the lower quality of education): science, $30,000; math, $28,000; history, $26,000; and English, $24,000. Determine how the board can minimize its total cost due to unmet goals.

TABLE 7.47 **Data for Pine Valley Problem**

Teacher Can Teach	Number Applying	Annual Salary
History and science	20	$21,000
History and math	15	$22,000
English and science	12	$23,000
English and math	14	$24,000
English and history	13	$25,000
Science and math	12	$26,000

33 Stockco fills orders for three products for a local warehouse. Stockco must determine how many of each product should be ordered at the beginning of the current month. This month, 400 units of product 1, 500 units of product 2, and 300 units of product 3 will be demanded. The cost and space taken up by one unit of each product are shown in Table 7.48. If Stockco runs out of stock before the end of the month, the stockout costs shown in Table 7.48 are incurred. Stockco has $17,000 to spend on ordering products and has 3700 square feet of warehouse space. A $1 penalty is assessed for each dollar spent over the budget limit, and a $10 cost is assessed for every square foot of warehouse space needed.

TABLE 7.48 **Data for Stockco Problem**

	Space (sq ft)	Cost	Stockout Cost
Product 1	6	$20	$16
Product 2	5	$18	$10
Product 3	4	$16	$8

a Determine Stockco's optimal ordering policy.

b Suppose that Stockco has set the following goals, listed in order of priority:

- Goal 1: Spend at most $17,000.
- Goal 2: Use at most 3700 square feet of warehouse space.
- Goal 3: Meet demand for product 1.
- Goal 4: Meet demand for product 2.
- Goal 5: Meet demand for product 3.

Develop a preemptive goal programming model for Stockco.

34 BeatTrop Foods is trying to choose one of three companies to merge with. In making this decision seven factors are important:

- Factor 1: Contribution to profitability
- Factor 2: Growth potential
- Factor 3: Labor environment
- Factor 4: R&D ability of company
- Factor 5: Organizational fit
- Factor 6: Relative size
- Factor 7: Industry commonality

The pairwise comparison matrix for these factors is as follows:

$$\begin{bmatrix} 1 & 3 & 7 & 5 & 1 & 7 & 1 \\ 1/3 & 1 & 9 & 1 & 1 & 5 & 1 \\ 1/7 & 1/9 & 1 & 1/7 & 1/5 & 1/2 & 1/4 \\ 1/5 & 1 & 7 & 1 & 1/4 & 7 & 1/3 \\ 1 & 1 & 5 & 4 & 1 & 5 & 3 \\ 1/7 & 1/5 & 2 & 1/7 & 1/5 & 1 & 1/6 \\ 1 & 1 & 4 & 3 & 1/3 & 6 & 1 \end{bmatrix}$$

The three contenders for merger have the following pairwise comparison matrices for each factor:

$$\text{Factor 1: } \begin{bmatrix} 1 & 9 & 3 \\ 1/9 & 1 & 1/5 \\ 1/3 & 5 & 1 \end{bmatrix}$$

$$\text{Factor 2: } \begin{bmatrix} 1 & 7 & 4 \\ 1/7 & 1 & 1/3 \\ 1/4 & 3 & 1 \end{bmatrix}$$

$$\text{Factor 3: } \begin{bmatrix} 1 & 1/5 & 1/3 \\ 5 & 1 & 2 \\ 3 & 1/2 & 1 \end{bmatrix}$$

$$\text{Factor 4: } \begin{bmatrix} 1 & 6 & 3 \\ 1/6 & 1 & 1/2 \\ 1/3 & 2 & 1 \end{bmatrix}$$

$$\text{Factor 5: } \begin{bmatrix} 1 & 1/9 & 1/5 \\ 9 & 1 & 4 \\ 5 & 1/4 & 1 \end{bmatrix}$$

$$\text{Factor 6: } \begin{bmatrix} 1 & 1/7 & 1/4 \\ 7 & 1 & 3 \\ 4 & 1/3 & 1 \end{bmatrix}$$

$$\text{Factor 7: } \begin{bmatrix} 1 & 1/7 & 1/3 \\ 7 & 1 & 3 \\ 3 & 1/3 & 1 \end{bmatrix}$$

Use AHP to determine the company that BeatTrop should merge with.

35 Productco produces three products. Each product requires labor, lumber, and paint. The resource requirements, unit price, and variable cost (exclusive of raw materials) for each product are given in Table 7.49. At present, 900 labor hours, 1550 gallons of paint, and 1600 board feet of lumber are available. Additional labor can be purchased at \$6 per hour. Additional paint can be purchased at \$2 per gallon. Additional lumber can be purchased at \$3 per board foot. For the following two sets of priorities, use preemptive goal programming to determine an optimal production schedule. For set 1:

- Priority 1: Obtain profit of at least $10,500.
- Priority 2: Purchase no additional labor.
- Priority 3: Purchase no additional paint.
- Priority 4: Purchase no additional lumber.

For set 2:

- Priority 1: Purchase no additional labor.
- Priority 2: Obtain profit of at least $10,500.
- Priority 3: Purchase no additional paint.
- Priority 4: Purchase no additional lumber.

TABLE 7.49 Data for Productco Problem

	Labor	Lumber	Paint	Price	Variable Cost
Product 1	1.5	2	3	$26	$10
Product 2	3.0	3	2	$28	$6
Product 3	2.0	4	2	$31	$7

Skill-Extending Problems

36 Jobs at Indiana University are rated on three factors:

- Factor 1: Complexity of duties
- Factor 2: Education required
- Factor 3: Mental and/or visual demands

For each job at IU, the requirement for each factor has been rated on a scale of 1–4, with a 4 in factor 1 representing high complexity of duty, a 4 in factor 2 representing high educational requirement, and a 4 in factor 3 representing high mental and/or visual demands. IU wants to determine a formula for grading each job. To do this, it will assign a point value to the score for each factor that a job requires. For example, suppose that level 2 of factor 1 yields a point total of 10, level 3 of factor 2 yields a point total of 20, and level 3 of factor 3 yields a point total of 30. Then a job with these requirements has a point total of $10 + 20 + 30 = 60$. A job's hourly salary equals half its point total. IU has two goals (listed in order of priority) in setting up the points given to each level of each job factor.

- Goal 1: When increasing the level of a factor by 1, the points should increase by at least 10. For example, level 2 of factor 1 should earn at least 10 more points than level 1 of factor 1. Goal 1 is to minimize the sum of deviations from this requirement.
- Goal 2: For the benchmark jobs referred to in Table 7.50, the actual point total for each job should come as close as possible to the point total listed in the table. Goal 2 is to minimize the sum of the absolute deviations of the point totals from the desired scores.

Use preemptive goal programming to find appropriate point totals. What salary should a job with skill levels of 3 for each factor be paid?

TABLE 7.50 Data for IU Benchmark Jobs

	Factor 1 Level	Factor 2 Level	Factor 3 Level	Desired Score
Job 1	4	4	4	105
Job 2	3	3	2	93
Job 3	2	2	2	75
Job 4	1	1	2	68

37 A hospital outpatient clinic performs four types of operations. The profit per operation, as well as the minutes of X-ray time and laboratory time used, are given in Table 7.51. The clinic has 500 private rooms and 500 intensive care rooms. Type 1 and type 2 operations require a patient to stay in an intensive care room for one day, while type 3 and type 4 operations require a patient to stay in a private room for one day. Each day the hospital is required to perform at least 100 operations of each type. The hospital has set the following goals (listed in order of priority):

- Goal 1: Earn a daily profit of at least $100,000.
- Goal 2: Use at most 50 hours daily of X-ray time.
- Goal 3: Use at most 40 hours daily of laboratory time.

Use preemptive goal programming to determine the types of operations that should be performed.

TABLE 7.51 Data for Hospital Problem

	Type of Operation			
	1	**2**	**3**	**4**
Profit	$200	$150	$100	$80
X-ray Time (minutes)	6	5	4	3
Lab Time (minutes)	5	4	3	2

38 You are trying to determine which city to live in. New York and Chicago are under consideration. Four objectives will determine your decision: housing cost, cultural opportunities, quality of schools and universities, and crime level. The weight for each objective is in Table 7.52. For each objective (except for quality of schools and universities), New York and Chicago scores are given in Table 7.53. Suppose that the score for each city on the quality of schools and universities depends on two things: a score on public school quality and a score on university quality. The pairwise comparison matrix for public school and university quality is shown in Table 7.54. To see how each city scores on public school quality and university quality, use the pairwise comparison matrices in Table 7.55. You should be able to derive a score for each city on the quality of schools and universities objective. Then use AHP to determine where you should live.

TABLE 7.52 Weights for Objectives in City Problem

Objective	Weight
Housing cost	.50
Culture	.10
Education	.20
Crime	.20

TABLE 7.53 Scores for Cities in City Problem

	New York	Chicago
Housing Cost	.30	.70
Culture	.70	.30
Crime	.40	.60

TABLE 7.54 Pairwise Comparison of Education Objectives in City Problem

	Public School Quality	University Quality
Public School Quality	1	4
University Quality	1/4	1

TABLE 7.55 Pairwise Comparison of Cities for Education in City Problem

Public School Quality	New York	Chicago
New York	1	4
Chicago	1/4	1

University Quality	New York	Chicago
New York	1	1/3
Chicago	3	1

39 At Lummins Engine Corporation, production employees work ten hours per day, four days per week. Each day of the week, at least the following number of employees must be working: Monday–Friday, seven employees; Saturday and Sunday, three employees. Lummins has set the following goals, listed in order of priority:

- Goal 1: Meet employee requirements with 11 workers.
- Goal 2: The average number of weekend days off per employee should be at least 1.5 days.
- Goal 3: The average number of consecutive days off an employee gets during the week should exceed 2.8 days.

Use preemptive goal programming to determine how to schedule Lummins employees.

40 You are the mayor of Gotham City and you must determine a tax policy for the city. Five types of taxes are used to raise money:

- Property taxes. Let p be the property tax rate.
- A sales tax on all items except food, drugs, and durable goods. Let s be the sales tax rate.
- A sales tax on durable goods. Let d be the durable goods sales tax rate.
- A gasoline sales tax. Let g be the gasoline sales tax rate.
- A sales tax on food and drugs. Let f be the sales tax on food and drugs.

The city consists of three groups of people: low income (LI), middle income (MI), and high income (HI). The amount of revenue (in millions of dollars) raised from each group by setting a particular tax at a 1% level is given in Table 7.56. For example, a 3% tax on durable good sales will raise 360 million dollars from low income people. Your tax policy must satisfy the following restrictions:

- Restriction 1: The tax burden on MI people cannot exceed \$2.8 billion.
- Restriction 2: The tax burden on HI people cannot exceed \$2.4 billion.
- Restriction 3: The total revenue raised must exceed the current level of \$6.5 billion.
- Restriction 4: s must be between 1% and 3%.

Given these restrictions, the city council has set the following three goals (listed in order of priority):

- Goal 1: Limit the tax burden on LI people to \$2 billion.
- Goal 2: Keep the property tax rate under 3%.

TABLE 7.56 Data for Gotham City Tax Problem

	p	s	d	g	f
LI	900	300	120	30	90
MI	1200	400	100	20	60
HI	1000	250	60	10	40

- Goal 3: If their tax burden becomes too high, 20% of the LI people, 20% of the MI people, and 40% of the HI people may consider moving to the suburbs. Suppose that this will happen if their total tax burden exceeds \$1.5 billion. To discourage this exodus, goal 3 is to keep the total tax burden on these people below \$1.5 billion.

Use preemptive goal programming to determine an optimal tax policy.

41 (Based on Sartoris and Spruill [7]) Wivco produces two products, which it sells on both a cash and credit basis. Revenues from credit sales will not have been received but are included in determining profit earned during the current six-month period. Sales during the next six months can be made either from units produced during the next six months or from beginning inventory. Relevant information about products 1 and 2 is as follows. During the next six months, at most 150 units of product 1 can be sold on a cash basis, and at most 100 units of product 1 can be sold on a credit basis. It costs \$35 to produce each unit of product 1, and each sells for \$40. A credit sale of a unit of product 1 yields 50¢ less profit than a cash sale (because of delays in receiving payment). Two hours of production time are needed to produce each unit of product 1. At the beginning of the six-month period, 60 units of product 1 are in inventory.

During the next six months, at most 175 units of product 2 can be sold on a cash basis, and at most 250 units of product 2 can be sold on a credit basis. It costs \$45 to produce each unit of product 2, and each sells for \$52.50. A credit sale of a unit of product 2 yields \$1.00 less profit than a cash sale. Four hours of production time are needed to produce each unit of product 2. At the beginning of the six-month period, 30 units of product 2 are in inventory.

During the next six months, Wivco has 1000 hours for production available. At the end of the next six months, Wivco incurs a 10% holding cost on the value of ending inventory (measured relative to production cost). An opportunity cost of 5% is also assessed against any cash on hand at the end of the six-month period.

a Formulate and solve an LP that yields Wivco's maximum profit during the next six months. What is Wivco's ending inventory position? Assuming an initial cash balance of \$0, what is Wivco's ending cash balance?

b Since an ending inventory and cash position of \$0 is undesirable (for ongoing operations), Wivco is considering other options. At the beginning of the six-month period, Wivco can obtain a loan (secured by ending inventory) that incurs an interest cost equal to 5% of the value of the loan. The maximum value of the loan is 75% of the value of the ending inventory. The loan will be repaid one year from now. Wivco has the following goals (listed in order of priority):

- Goal 1: Make the ending cash balance of Wivco come as close as possible to \$75.
- Goal 2: Make profit come as close as possible to the profit level obtained in Part (a).
- Goal 3: At any time, Wivco's current ratio is defined to be

$$\text{Current ratio} = \frac{\text{Wivco's assets}}{\text{Wivco's liabilities}}$$

Assuming initially that current liabilities equal \$150, six months from now Wivco's current ratio will equal

$$\text{Current ratio} = \frac{\text{CB} + \text{AR} + \text{EI}}{150 + \text{Size of loan}}$$

where CB is the ending cash balance, AR is the value of accounts receivable, and EI is the value of the ending inventory. Six months from now, Wivco wants the current ratio to be as close as possible to 2.

Use preemptive goal programming to determine Wivco's production and financial strategy.

Modeling Problems

42 How might you use preemptive goal programming to help Congress balance the budget?

43 A company is considering buying up to five other businesses. Given knowledge of the company's view of the trade-off between risk and return, how could trade-off curves be used to determine the companies that should be purchased?

44 How would you use AHP to determine the greatest sports record of all time? (Many believe it is Joe Dimaggio's 56-game hitting streak.)

45 You are planning to renovate a hospital. How would you use AHP to help determine what improvements to include in the renovation?

46 You are planning to overhaul a hospital computer system. How would you use AHP to determine the type of computer system to install?

47 You have been commissioned to assign 100 remedial education teachers to the 10 schools in the St. Louis School System. What are some objectives you might consider in assigning the teachers to schools?

48 You have been hired as a consultant to help design a new airport in northern Indiana that will supplant O'Hare as Chicago's major airport. Discuss the objectives you consider important in designing and locating the airport.

49 In the Indiana MBA program we need to divide a class of 60 students into ten six-person teams. In the interest of diversity we have the following goals (listed in descending order of importance):

- at least one woman per team
- at least one member of a minority per team
- at least one student with a financial or accounting background per team
- at least one engineer per team

Explain how you could use the material in this chapter to develop a model to assign students to teams. ■

CASE STUDY

Play Time Toy Company

Play Time Toy faces a highly seasonal pattern of sales. In the past, Play Time has used a *seasonal* production schedule, where the amount produced each month matches the sales for that month. Under this production plan, inventory is maintained at a constant level. The production manager, Thomas Lindop, is proposing a switch to a *level*, or constant, production schedule. This schedule would result in significant savings in production costs but would have higher storage and handling costs, fluctuating levels of inventories, and would also have implications for financing. Jonathan King, president of Play Time Toy, has been reviewing pro forma income statements, cash budgets, and balance sheets for the coming year under the two production scenarios. Table 7.57 shows the pro forma analysis under seasonal production, and Table 7.58 shows the pro forma analysis under level production.

Greg Cole, chief financial officer of Play Time, prepared the two tables. He explained that the pro forma analyses in Tables 7.57 and 7.58 take fully into account the 11% interest payments on the unsecured loan from Bay Trust Company and the 3% interest received from its cash account. An interest charge of 11%/12 on the balance of the loan at the end of a month must be paid the next month. Similarly, an interest payment of 3%/12 on the cash balance at the end of a month is received in the next month.

The inventory available at the end of December 1990 is $530,000 (measured in terms of cost to produce). Mr. Cole assumed that this inventory represents a sales value of $813,300 (= $530,000/0.651667).

The inventory and overtime costs in Tables 7.57 and 7.58 are based on the cost information developed by Mr. Lindop. This information is summarized in Table 7.59.

Mr. Cole further explained how the cost information was used in the pro forma analyses. For example, in Table 7.57, the production in August is $1,458,000. The overtime cost in August is therefore calculated to be $61,000 (= 0.15 × (1,458,000 – 1,049,000)). Play Time uses LIFO (last-in, first-out) accounting, so overtime costs are always charged in the month that they occur.[2] The annual overtime cost for the seasonal production plan is $435,000. In Table 7.58, under level production, finished goods worth $5,164,000 are in inventory at the end of July. The inventory cost for the month is $20,000 (= 0.07/12 × (5,164,000 – 1,663,000)). The annual inventory cost for the level production plan is $100,000.

Mr. Lindop felt that a minimum of $813,300 of inventory (measured in terms of sales value, or $530,000 measured in terms of cost to produce) must be kept on hand at the end of each month. This inventory level represents a reasonable safety stock, required since orders do not occur uniformly during a month.

Mr. King was impressed at the possible increase in profit from $237,000 under the seasonal production plan to $373,000 under level production. While studying the pro forma projections, it occurred to Mr. King that some combination of the two production plans might be even better. He asked Mr. Lindop to try to find a production plan with a higher profit than the seasonal and level plans.

Mr. Lindop proceeded to develop a spreadsheet-based linear programming model to maximize annual net profit.

[2]This assumes that overtime production is used only to satisfy current demand and not to build up inventory.

TABLE 7.57 Seasonal Production

Annual net profit **237** **Play Time Toy Company**

	Actual Dec 1990	Jan	Feb	Mar	Apr	May	June	July	Aug	Sept	Oct	Nov	Dec	Total
		Projected for 1991												
Production (sales value)	850	108	126	145	125	125	125	145	1,458	1,655	1,925	2,057	1,006	9000
Inventory (sales value)	813	813	813	813	813	813	813	813	813	813	813	813	813	

INCOME STATEMENT	Jan	Feb	Mar	Apr	May	June	July	Aug	Sept	Oct	Nov	Dec	Total
Net sales	108	126	145	125	125	125	145	1,458	1,655	1,925	2,057	1,006	9,000
Cost of goods sold													
Materials & regular wages	70	82	94	81	81	81	94	950	1,079	1,254	1,340	656	5,865
Overtime wages	0	0	0	0	0	0	0	61	91	131	151	0	435
Gross profit	38	44	51	44	44	44	51	447	486	539	565	350	2,700
Operating expenses	188	188	188	188	188	188	188	188	188	188	188	183	2,256
Inventory cost	0	0	0	0	0	0	0	0	0	0	0	0	0
Profit before int & taxes	(150)	(144)	(137)	(144)	(144)	(144)	(137)	259	298	351	377	162	444
Net interest payments	10	2	1	1	2	2	2	3	7	18	19	19	86
Profit before taxes	(160)	(146)	(138)	(146)	(146)	(147)	(140)	256	290	333	359	144	358
Taxes	(55)	(50)	(47)	(50)	(50)	(50)	(48)	87	99	113	122	49	122
Net profit	(106)	(97)	(91)	(96)	(97)	(97)	(92)	169	192	220	237	95	237

BALANCE SHEET	Actual Dec 1990	Jan	Feb	Mar	Apr	May	June	July	Aug	Sept	Oct	Nov	Dec
		Projected for 1991											
Cash	175	782	1,365	1,116	934	803	604	450	175	175	175	175	175
Accts receivable	2,628	958	234	271	270	250	250	270	1,603	3,113	3,580	3,982	3,063
Inventory	530	530	530	530	530	530	530	530	530	530	530	530	530
Net P/E	1,070	1,070	1,070	1,070	1,070	1,070	1,070	1,070	1,070	1,070	1,070	1,070	1,070
Total Assets	4,403	3,340	3,199	2,987	2,804	2,653	2,454	2,320	3,378	4,388	5,355	5,757	4,838
Accts payable	255	32	38	44	38	33	38	44	437	497	578	617	302
Notes payable	680	0	0	0	0	0	0	0	408	1,500	1,653	1,656	966
Accrued taxes	80	25	(24)	(151)	(232)	(282)	(363)	(411)	(324)	(256)	(143)	(21)	(4)
Long term debt	450	450	450	450	450	450	425	425	425	425	425	425	400
Equity	2,938	2,832	2,736	2,644	2,548	2,452	2,355	2,263	2,431	2,523	2,843	3,080	3,175
Total liab & equity	4,403	3,340	3,199	2,987	2,804	2,658	2,454	2,320	3,378	4,388	5,355	5,757	4,838

TABLE 7.58 Level Production

Annual net profit **373** **Play Time Toy Company**

	Actual Dec 1990	Projected for 1991												
		Jan	Feb	Mar	Apr	May	June	July	Aug	Sept	Oct	Nov	Dec	Total
Production (sales value)	850	750	750	750	750	750	750	750	750	750	750	750	750	9000
Inventory (sales value)	813	1455	2079	2684	3309	3934	4559	5164	4456	3551	2376	1069	813	

INCOME STATEMENT	Jan	Feb	Mar	Apr	May	June	July	Aug	Sept	Oct	Nov	Dec	Total
Net sales	108	126	145	125	125	125	145	1,4[illegible]8	1,655	1,925	2,057	1,006	9,000
Cost of goods sold													
Materials & regular wages	70	82	94	81	81	81	94	9[illegible]0	1,079	1,254	1,340	656	5,865
Overtime wages	0	0	0	0	0	0	0	0	0	0	0	0	0
Gross profit	38	44	51	44	44	44	51	5[illegible]8	576	671	717	350	3,135
Operating expenses	188	188	188	188	188	188	188	188	188	188	188	188	2,256
Inventory cost	0	2	6	10	13	17	20	[illegible]6	11	4	0	0	100
Profit before int & taxes	(150)	(147)	(143)	(154)	(158)	(161)	(158)	3[illegible]4	377	478	529	162	779
Net interest payments	10	3	2	5	10	15	21	[illegible]6	32	37	31	22	214
Profit before taxes	(160)	(149)	(146)	(159)	(168)	(177)	(179)	2[illegible]7	346	441	498	141	565
Taxes	(55)	(51)	(50)	(54)	(57)	(60)	(61)	[illegible]4	118	150	169	48	192
Net profit	(106)	(99)	(96)	(105)	(111)	(117)	(118)	1[illegible]3	228	291	329	93	373

BALANCE SHEET	Actual Dec 1990	Projected for 1991 Jan	Feb	Mar	Apr	May	June	July	Aug	Sept	Oct	Nov	Dec
Cash	175	556	724	175	175	175	175	175	175	175	175	175	175
Accts receivable	2,628	958	234	271	270	250	250	270	1,6[illegible]3	3,113	3,580	3,982	3,063
Inventory	530	948	1,355	1,749	2,157	2,564	2,971	3,365	2,9[illegible]4	2,314	1,549	697	530
Net P/E	1,070	1,070	1,070	1,070	1,070	1,070	1,070	1,070	1,070	1,070	1,070	1,070	1,070
Total Assets	4,403	3,533	3,383	3,265	3,672	4,059	4,466	4,880	5,7[illegible]2	6,672	6,374	5,924	4,838
Accts payable	255	225	225	225	225	225	225	225	225	225	225	225	225
Notes payable	680	0	0	108	704	1,259	1,900	2,493	3,0[illegible]7	3,693	2,953	2,005	836
Accrued taxes	80	25	(25)	(155)	(240)	(297)	(389)	(450)	(3[illegible]5)	(269)	(119)	50	66
Long term debt	450	450	450	450	450	450	425	425	425	425	425	425	400
Equity	2,938	2,832	2,734	2,637	2,533	2,422	2,305	2,187	2,3[illegible]0	2,599	2,890	3,218	3,311
Total liab & equity	4,403	3,533	3,383	3,265	3,672	4,059	4,466	4,880	5,7[illegible]2	6,672	6,374	5,924	4,838

TABLE 7.59 Play Time Cost Information

- **Gross margin.** The cost of goods sold (excluding overtime costs) is 65.1667% of sales under any production schedule. Materials costs are 30% of sales. All other nonmaterials costs, including regular wages but excluding overtime wages, are 35.1667% of sales.
- **Overtime cost.** Running at capacity but without using any overtime, the plant can produce $1,049,000 of monthly sales. Units produced in excess of this capacity in a month incur an additional overtime cost of 15% of sales. (The monthly production capacity of the plant running on full overtime is $2,400,000 of sales. Since November has the maximum level of projected sales at $2,057,000, the capacity on full overtime should never pose a problem.)
- **Inventory cost.** The plant has a limited capacity to store finished goods. It can store $1,663,000 worth of sales at the plant. Additional units must be moved and stored in rented warehouse space. The cost of storage, handling, and insurance of finished goods over this capacity is 7% of the sales value of the goods per year, or 7%/12 per month.

Questions

Note: Mr. Lindop's model is contained in the spreadsheet file PLAYTIME.XLS. The spreadsheet is ready to be optimized, but it has not been optimized yet.

1 Run the optimization model in the spreadsheet PLAYTIME.XLS. What is the optimal production plan? What is the optimal annual net profit? How does this optimal production plan compare to the seasonal and level production plans?

2 Suppose that Play Time's bankers will not extend any credit over $1.9 million—in other words, the loan balance in any month cannot exceed $1.9 million. Modify the spreadsheet to take into account this restriction. What is the optimal production plan in this case? What is the optimal annual net profit?

3 Annual profit is a measure of reward for Play Time Toy. The maximum loan balance is a measure of risk for the bank. Construct a trade-off curve between optimal annual profit and the maximum loan balance. ■

REFERENCES

1 Chrisman, J., T. Fry, G. Reeves, H. Lewis, and R. Weinstein. "A Multiobjective Linear Programming Methodology for Public Sector Tax Planning." *Interfaces* 19, no. 5 (1989): 13–30.

2 Golden, B., E. Wasil, and P. Harker. *The Analytic Hierarchy Process*. New York: Springer-Verlag, 1989.

3 Klingman, D., and N. Phillips. "Topological and Computational Aspects of Preemptive Multicriteria Assignment Problems." *Management Science* 30, no. 11 (1984): 1362–75.

4 Lee, S., and L. Moore. "Optimizing University Admissions Planning." *Decision Sciences* 5 (1974): 405–14.

5 Lin, W., T. Mock, and A. Wright. "The Use of AHP as an Aid in Planning the Nature and Extent of Audit Procedures." *Auditing: A Journal of Practice and Theory* 4, no. 1 (1984): 89–99.

6 Saaty, T. *The Analytic Hierarchy Process*. New York: McGraw-Hill, 1988.

7 Sartoris, W., and M. Spruill. "Goal Programming and Working Capital Management." *Financial Management* 3 (1974): 67–74.

8 Steuer, R. "Sausage Blending Using Multiple Objective Programming." *Management Science* 30 (1984): 1376–84.

9 Taylor, B., and A. Keown. "Planning Urban Recreational Facilities with Goal Programming." *Journal of Operational Research Society* 29, no. 8 (1984): 751–58.

10 Vasko, F., J. Wolfe, and K. Stott. "Optimal Selection of Ingot Sizes via Set Covering." *Operations Research* 35 no. 3 (1955): 346–53.

11 Weber, S. "A Modified Analytic Hierarchy Process for Automated Manufacturing Decisions." *Interfaces* 23, no. 4 (1993): 75–84.

12 Welling, P. "A Goal Programming Model for Human Resource Allocation in a CPA Firm." *Accounting, Organizations and Society* 2 (1977): 307–16.

13 Zahedi, F. "The Analytic Hierarchy Process—A Survey of the Method and Its Applications." *Interfaces* 16, no. 4 (1986): 96–108.

CHAPTER

8

Decision Making Under Uncertainty

Management Science Success Stories

Formal decision analysis in the face of uncertainty frequently occurs at the most strategic levels of a company's planning process and typically involves teams of high-level managers from all areas of the company. This is certainly the case with Du Pont, as reported by two internal decision analysis experts, Krumm and Rolle [10], in their article "Management and Application of Decision and Risk Analysis in Du Pont." Du Pont's formal use of decision analysis began in the 1960s, but because of a lack of computing power and distrust of the method by senior-level management, it never really got a foothold. However, by the mid-1980s things had changed considerably. The company was involved in a faster-moving, more uncertain environment, more people throughout the company were empowered to make decisions, and these decisions had to be made more quickly. In addition, the computing power had arrived to make large-scale quantitative analysis feasible. Since that time, Du Pont has embraced formal decision-making analysis in all of its businesses, and the trend is almost certain to continue.

The article describes a typical example of decision analysis within the company. One of Du Pont's businesses, Business Z (so-called for reasons of confidentiality), was stagnating. It was not set up to respond quickly to changing customer demands, and its financial position was declining due to lower prices and market share. A decision board and a project team were empowered to turn things around. The project team developed a detailed timetable to accomplish three basic steps: frame the problem, assess uncertainties and perform the analysis, and implement the recommended decision. The first step involved setting up a "strategy table" to list the possible strategies and the factors that would affect or be affected by them. The three basic strategies were (1) a base-case strategy (continue operating as is), (2) a product differentiation strategy (develop new products), and (3) a cost leadership strategy (shut down the plant and streamline the product line).

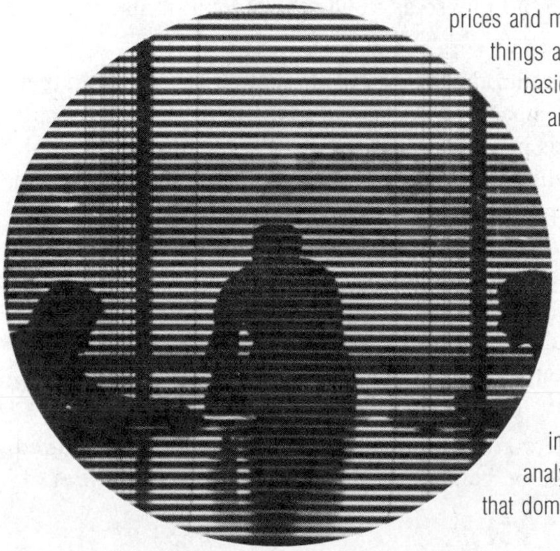

In the second step the team asked a variety of experts throughout the company for their assessments of the likelihood of key uncertain events. In the analysis step they then used all of the information gained to determine the strategy with the largest expected net present value. Two important aspects of this analysis step were the extensive use of sensitivity analysis (many what-if questions) and the emergence of new "hybrid" strategies that dominated the strategies that had been considered to that point. In particular, the team finally decided on a product differentiation strategy that also decreased costs by shutting down some facilities in each plant.

By the time of the third step, implementation, the decision board needed little convincing. Since all of the key people had been given the opportunity to provide input to the process, everyone was convinced that the right strategy had been selected. All that was left was to put the plan in motion and monitor its results. The results were impressive. Business Z made a complete turnaround, and its net present value increased by close to $200 million. Besides this tangible benefit, there were definite intangible benefits from the overall process. As Du Pont's vice president for finance said, "The D&RA [decision and risk analysis] process improved communication within the business team as well as between the team and corporate management, resulting in rapid approval and execution. As a decision maker, I highly value such a clear and logical approach to making choices under uncertainty and will continue to use D&RA whenever possible." ■

8.1 Introduction

This chapter marks a departure from the type of analysis we have done so far. Until now, we have assumed that all of the data that are needed to evaluate strategies and choose optimal strategies are known with certainty. Unfortunately this is not always the case. For example, when a company periodically orders a product from a supplier in order to meet customer demand, this demand is not known with certainty but can only be forecasted. If the forecasts are low, causing the company to order too little, lost demand (and lost rcvcnuc) will occur. On the other hand, if the forecasts are high, causing the company to order too much, excess inventory will occur, and this also results in higher costs.

Many other examples of decision making under uncertainty exist in the business world. Here are several examples.

1 Companies routinely place bids for contracts such as government contracts to complete a certain project within a set time frame. Often these are sealed bids, where each of several companies presents a bid in a sealed envelope for completing the project, then the envelopes are opened, and the low bidder is awarded the bid amount to complete the project. Any particular company in the bidding competition must deal with the possible uncertainty of the *actual* cost of completing the project (should it win the bid), as well as the uncertainty involved in what the other companies will bid. Essentially, each company wants to bid low so as to win the bid, but it also wants to bid high in order to make a profit.

2 Whenever a company contemplates introducing a new product into the market, there are a number of uncertainties that impact the decision, the most important probably being the customers' reaction to this product. If it turns out that the product generates high demand, then the company will make a large profit. But if demand is low (and, after all, the vast majority of new products do poorly), then the company might not even recoup its development costs. Since the level of customer demand is critical, the company might try to gauge this level by first test marketing the product in a small region of the country. Then if this test market is a big success, the company can be somewhat more optimistic that a full-scale national marketing of the product will also be successful. But if the test market is a failure, the company can cut its losses by abandoning the product.

3 Should athletes be required to undergo drug testing? And if drug testing is required, should an athlete who tests positive be banned from the sport? Several sources of

uncertainty, as well as several "costs," are relevant here. The uncertainties involve the fraction of the total athlete population who use drugs and the reliability of the tests. The costs include the obvious cost of the tests, but also the less obvious "cost" of invading an athlete's privacy and the "cost" of declaring an athlete a drug-user when in fact he or she isn't (because of a faulty test).

4 A recent *Interfaces* article describes an application of formal decision analysis by Oglethorpe Power Corporation (OPC), a Georgia-based electricity supplier. (See Borison [2].) The basic decision OPC faced was whether to build a new transmission line to supply large amounts of electricity to parts of Florida and, if they decided to build it, how to finance this project. OPC had to deal with several sources of uncertainty: the cost of building new facilities, the demand for power in Florida, and various market conditions, such as the spot price of electricity.

5 Another *Interfaces* article describes the decision analysis performed by the U.S. Postal Service regarding the purchase of automation equipment. (See Ulvila [12].) One of the investment decisions was which type of OCR (optical character recognition) equipment the postal service should purchase (or convert) for reading single- and/or multiple-line addresses on packages. An important factor in this decision was the use by businesses of the "zip+4" (nine-digit zip codes). Zip+4 usage had been recommended for some time but was used only sporadically. The postal service was uncertain about the future level of business zip+4 usage. If businesses would be using the nine-digit codes heavily in the future, then a certain type of (expensive) OCR equipment would be most economical. If business use of zip+4 did not increase, then purchasing this equipment would be a waste of money. The decision was an extremely important one, given the expense of the proposed equipment and the fact that the postal service would have to live with whatever equipment it purchased for a number of years.

6 Utility companies must make many decisions that have significant environmental and economic consequences. (A good discussion of such consequences appears in an *Interfaces* article by Balson, Welsh, and Wilson [1].) For these companies it is not necessarily enough to conform to federal or state environmental regulations. Recent court decisions have found companies liable—for huge settlements—when accidents occurred, even though the companies followed all existing regulations. Therefore, when utility companies decide, say, whether to replace equipment or mitigate the effects of environmental pollution, they must take into account the possible environmental consequences (injuries to people, for example) as well as economic consequences (lawsuits, for example). An aspect of these situations that makes decision analysis particularly difficult is that the "disasters" that might occur are often extremely improbable; hence, their likelihoods are very difficult to assess accurately.

In this chapter we will provide a formal framework for analyzing problems that include uncertainties. We will discuss the most frequently used criteria for choosing among alternative actions, how probabilities are used in the decision-making process, how decisions made at an early stage are dependent upon decisions made at a later stage, how a decision maker can quantify the value of information, and how attitudes toward risk can affect the analysis. Throughout, we will employ a graphical tool called a decision tree to aid the analysis. A decision tree enables the decision maker to view all important aspects of the problem at once: the decision alternatives, the uncertain outcomes and their probabilities, the economic consequences, and the chronological order of events. Also, we will take advantage of TreePlan, an Excel add-in that allows us to build decision trees on Excel spreadsheets.

8.2

Elements of a Decision Analysis

Although decision making under uncertainty exists in a wide variety of contexts, all problems have three elements in common. These three elements are (1) the set of decisions (or strategies) available to the decision maker, (2) the set of outcomes that are possible and the probabilities of these outcomes, and (3) a **value model** that prescribes results, usually monetary values, for the various combinations of decisions and outcomes. Once these elements are known, the decision maker can then find an "optimal" decision, depending on the optimality criterion chosen. The following example illustrates these concepts.

EXAMPLE 8.1

Precision Incorporated, a company that specializes in scientific instruments, has been invited to make a bid on a government contract. The contract calls for a specific number of these instruments to be delivered during the coming year. The bids must be sealed (so that no company knows what the others are bidding), and the low bid wins the contract. Precision estimates that it will cost \$5000 to prepare a bid and \$95,000 to supply the instruments if it wins the contract. On the basis of past contracts of this type, Precision believes that the possible low bids from the competition, if there is any competition, and the associated probabilities are those shown in Table 8.1. In addition, Precision believes there is a 30% chance that there will be no competing bids.

TABLE 8.1 Data for Bidding Example

Low Bid	Probability
Less than \$115,000	.2
Between \$115,000 and \$120,000	.4
Between \$120,000 and \$125,000	.3
Greater than \$125,000	.1

Solution

Let's discuss the three elements of Precision's problem. First, Precision has two basic strategies: submit a bid or do not submit a bid. If Precision submits a bid, then it must decide how much to bid. Based on Precision's cost to prepare the bid and its cost to supply the instruments, there is obviously no point in bidding less than \$100,000—Precision wouldn't make a profit even if it won the bid. Although any bid amount over \$100,000 might be considered, the data in Table 8.1 might lead Precision to limit its choices to \$115,000, \$120,000, and \$125,000.[1]

The next element of the problem involves the uncertain outcomes and their probabilities. We have assumed that Precision knows exactly how much it will cost to prepare a bid and how much it will cost to supply the instruments if it wins the bid. (In reality, these are probably estimates of the actual costs.) Therefore, the only source of uncertainty is the behavior of the competitors—will they bid, and if so, how much? From Precision's

[1]The problem with a bid such as \$117,000 is that the data in Table 8.1 make it impossible to calculate the probability of Precision winning the contract if it bids this amount. Other than this, however, there is nothing that obviously rules out such an "in-between" bid.

standpoint, this is difficult information to obtain. The behavior of the competitors depends on (1) how many competitors are likely to bid and (2) how the competitors assess *their* costs of supplying the instruments. However, we will assume that Precision has been involved in similar bidding contests many times in the past and can, therefore, predict competitor behavior from past competitor behavior. The result of such prediction is the assessed probability distribution shown in Table 8.1 and the 30% estimate of the probability of no competing bids.

The last element of the problem is the value model that transforms decisions and outcomes into monetary values for Precision. This value model is straightforward for Precision's problem, but it can become quite complex in realistic applications, especially when the time value of money is involved and some quantities (such as environmental pollution) are difficult to quantify. If Precision decides right now not to bid, then its monetary value is \$0—no gain, no loss. If it makes a bid and is underbid by a competitor, then it loses \$5000, the cost of preparing the bid. If it bids B dollars and wins the contract, then it makes a profit of B – \$100,000, that is, B dollars for winning the bid less \$5000 for preparing the bid less \$95,000 for supplying the instruments. For example, if it bids \$115,000 and the lowest competing bid, if any, is greater than \$115,000, then Precision makes a profit of \$15,000.

It is often convenient to list the monetary outcomes in a **payoff table**, as shown in Table 8.2. For each possible decision and each possible outcome, the payoff table lists the monetary value to Precision, where a positive value represents a profit and a negative value represents a loss. At the bottom of the table, we also list the probabilities of the various outcomes. For example, the probability that the competitors' low bid is less than \$115,000 is 0.7 (the probability of at least one competing bid) multiplied by 0.2 (the probability that the lowest competing bid is less than \$115,000, given that there is at least one competing bid).

It is sometimes possible to simplify payoff tables in order to better understand the essence of the problem. In the present example, if Precision bids, then the only necessary information about the competitors' bid is whether it is lower or higher than Precision's bid. That is, Precision only cares whether it wins the contract or not. Therefore, an alternative way of presenting the payoff table is shown in Table 8.3.

The third and fourth columns of this table indicate the payoffs to Precision, depending on whether it wins or loses the bid. The right-most column shows the probability that Precision wins the bid for each possible decision. For example, if Precision bids \$120,000,

TABLE 8.2 Payoff Table for Precision Bidding Example

		Competitors' Low Bid (\$1000s)				
		No Bid	<115	>115, <120	>120, <125	>125
Precision's Bid (\$1000s)	No Bid	0	0	0	0	0
	115	15	−5	15	15	15
	120	20	−5	−5	20	20
	125	25	−5	−5	−5	25
Probability		.3	.7(.2)	.7(.4)	.7(.3)	.7(.1)

TABLE 8.3 Alternative Payoff Table for Precision Bidding Example

		Monetary value		
		Precision Wins	Precision Loses	Probability That Precision Wins
Precision's Bid (\$1000s)	No bid	NA	0	0.00
	115	15	−5	0.86
	120	20	−5	0.58
	125	25	−5	0.37

then it wins the bid if there are no competing bids (probability .3) or if there are competing bids but the lowest of these is greater than $120,000 (probability .7(.3 + .1)). In this case the total probability that Precision wins the bid is .3 + .28 = .58.

Risk Profiles From Table 8.3 we obtain the **risk profiles** for each of Precision's alternatives. For any alternative, the risk profile simply lists all possible monetary values and their corresponding probabilities. For example, if Precision bids $120,000, there are two monetary values possible, a profit of $20,000 or a loss of $5000, and their probabilities are .58 and .42, respectively. On the other hand, if Precision decides not to bid, there is a sure monetary value of $0—no profit, no loss.

Risk profiles can perhaps be understood more easily by using graphs. An alternative's risk profile is simply a bar chart, with bars located at each possible monetary value with heights proportional to the probabilities. The risk profiles for Precision's four alternatives appear in Figures 8.1 through 8.4.

FIGURE 8.1 **Risk Profile for No Bid Alternative**

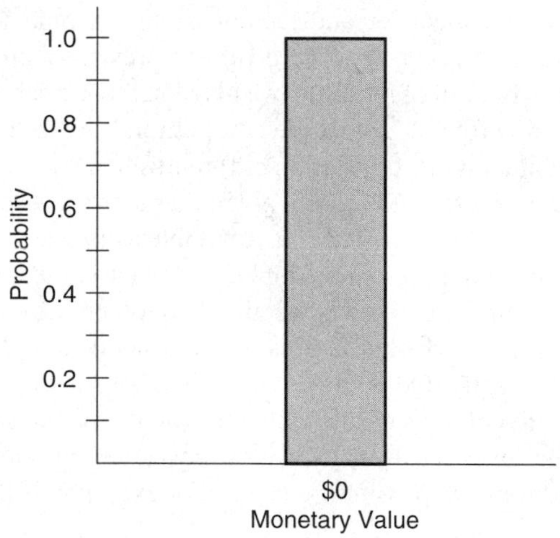

FIGURE 8.2 **Risk Profile for $115,000 Bid**

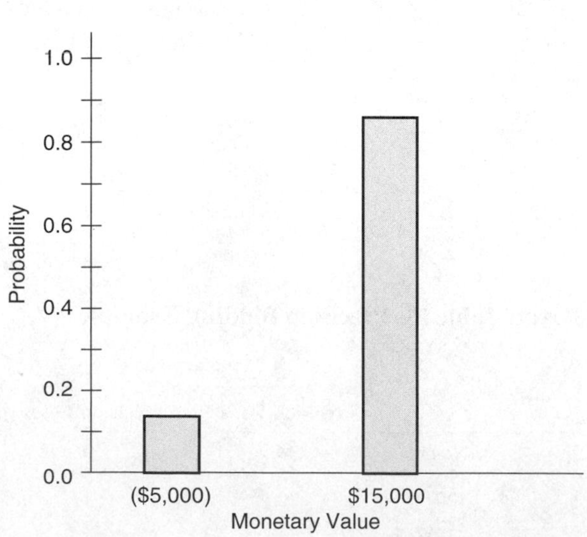

FIGURE 8.3 **Risk Profile for $120,000 Bid**

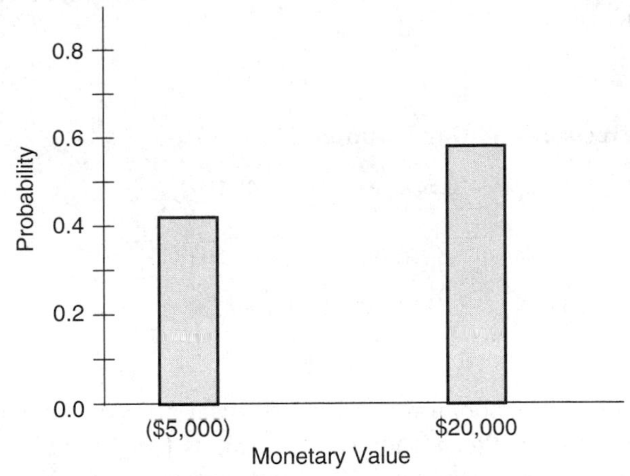

FIGURE 8.4 **Risk Profile for $125,000 Bid**

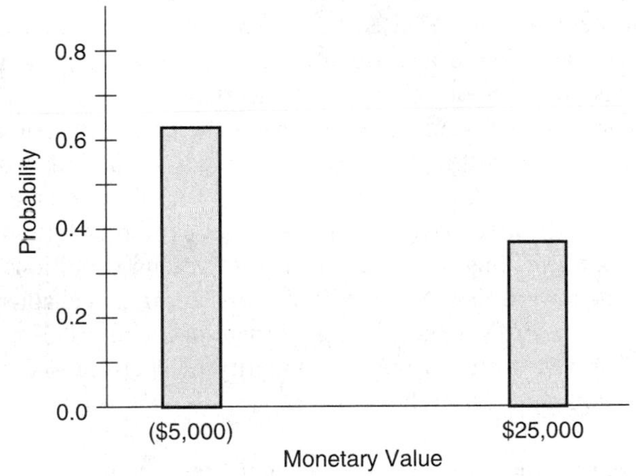

Expected Monetary Value (EMV) From the risk profiles in Figures 8.1 through 8.4, it is not at all obvious which decision Precision should make. For example, the no bid decision is certainly safe, but it is certain to make zero profit. If Precision decides to bid, the probability that it will lose $5000 is smallest with the $115,000 bid, but this bid has the smallest potential profit. Of course, if Precision knew what the competitors were going to do, its decision would be easy. However, that uncertainty is the defining aspect of the problems in this chapter. The decision must be made *before* the uncertainty is removed.

The most popular way to make the choice is to calculate the **expected monetary value** (*EMV*) of each alternative and then choose the alternative with the largest EMV. The EMV is simply a weighted average of the possible monetary values, weighted by their probabilities. Formally, if v_i is the monetary value corresponding to outcome i, and p_i is its probability, then EMV is defined as

$$\text{EMV} = \sum v_i p_i$$

The EMVs for Precision's problem are listed in Table 8.4. They indicate that if Precision wants to use the EMV criterion for making its decision, it should bid $115,000, as this yields the largest EMV.

TABLE 8.4 EMVs for Precision Bidding Example

Alternative	EMV Calculation	EMV
No bid	0(1)	$0
Bid $115,000	15,000(.86) + (−5000)(.14)	$12,200
Bid $120,000	20,000(.58) + (−5000)(.42)	$9,500
Bid $125,000	25,000(.37) + (−5000)(.63)	$6,100

It is extremely important to understand what an EMV implies and what it doesn't imply. For example, if Precision bids $115,000, its EMV is $12,200. However, Precision will certainly *not* earn a profit of $12,200. It will earn $15,000 or it will lose $5000. So what does the EMV of $12,200 really mean? It means that if Precision could enter many "gambles" like this, where on each gamble it would win $15,000 with probability .86 or lose $5000 with probability .14, then *on average* it would win $12,200 per gamble. In other words, the EMV can be interpreted as a long-term average.

It might seem peculiar, then, to base a one-time decision on EMV, which represents a long-term average. There are two ways to explain this apparent paradox. First, most companies make frequent decisions under uncertainty. Although each decision might have its unique characteristics, it makes sense that if the company is going to make many such decisions, it should be willing to "play the averages," as it does when it uses EMV as the decision criterion. Second, even if this is the only such decision the company is *ever* going to make, decision theorists have proven that under certain conditions, maximizing EMV is a rational basis for making this decision. These "certain conditions" relate to the decision maker's attitude toward risk. As we will discuss later in this chapter, if the decision maker is risk averse, then EMV is not the appropriate decision criterion to use. However, this criterion has proved useful in the vast majority of decision-making applications, so we will use it throughout most of this chapter.

Using a Decision Tree By now, we have gone through most of the steps of solving Precision's problem. We have listed the decision alternatives, the probabilities of the uncertain outcomes, and the profits or losses from all combinations of decisions and outcomes. We have then calculated the EMV for each alternative and have chosen the alternative with the largest EMV. All of this can be done efficiently using a graphical tool called a **decision tree**. The decision tree that corresponds to Precision's problem appears in Figure 8.5 (where all monetary values are in thousand of dollars).

To understand Figure 8.5, you need to know the following conventions that have been established for decision trees.

Decision Tree Conventions

1 Decision trees are composed of **nodes** (circles and squares) and **branches** (straight lines).

2 The nodes represent points in time. A **decision node** (a square) is a time when the decision maker makes a decision. A **probability node** (a circle) is a time when the result of an uncertain event becomes known.

3 Time proceeds from left to right. This means that any sequence of branches leading into a node (from the left) have already occurred. Any branches leading out of a node (to the right) have not yet occurred.

FIGURE 8.5 Decision Tree for Precision Bidding Example

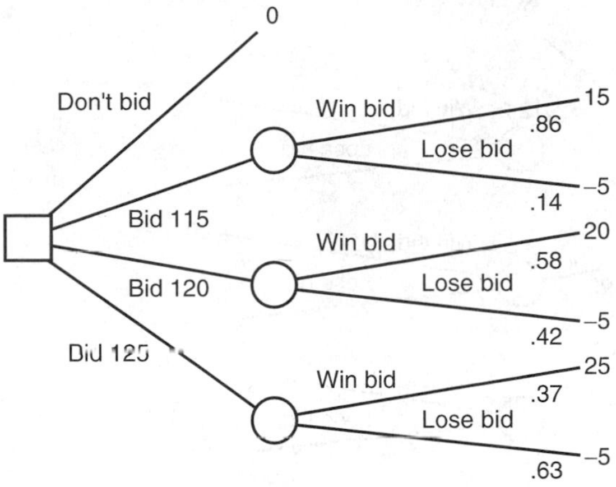

Note: All monetary values are in thousands of dollars.

4 Branches leading out of a decision node represent the possible decisions; the decision maker can choose the preferred branch. Branches leading out of probability nodes represent the possible outcomes of uncertain events; the decision maker has no control over which of these will occur.

5 Probabilities are listed on probability branches. These probabilities are "conditional" on the events that have already been observed. Also, the probabilities on branches leading out of any particular probability node must sum to 1.

6 Monetary values are shown at the tips of the right-most branches. These monetary values depend on the decisions and outcomes to the left of them. ■

EXAMPLE 8.1 CONTINUED

The decision tree in Figure 8.5 illustrates these conventions for a **single-stage decision problem**, the simplest type of decision problem. In a single-stage problem a decision maker is faced with an immediate decision. Once this decision is made, the decision maker waits for the resulting outcome to occur. Based on this outcome and the decision that is chosen, a payoff or cost results. Therefore, in all single-stage decision problems there is a single decision node at the left. Emanating from this node are as many branches as there are possible decisions. Each of these may be followed by a probability node, and these are followed by the resulting monetary values. If there is no uncertainty following a particular decision, such as the "no bid" decision in Figure 8.5, then no probability node follows this branch.

Once a decision tree is drawn and labeled with probabilities and monetary values, it can be solved easily. The solution for the decision tree in Figure 8.5 is shown in Figure 8.6. Among other things, it shows that the decision to bid $115,000 is optimal, with a corresponding EMV of $12,200. This is consistent with what we saw earlier.

The solution procedure used to develop Figure 8.6 is called **folding back** on the tree. Starting at the right of the tree and working back to the left, the procedure consists of two types of calculations.

FIGURE 8.6 Folding Back for Precision Bidding Example

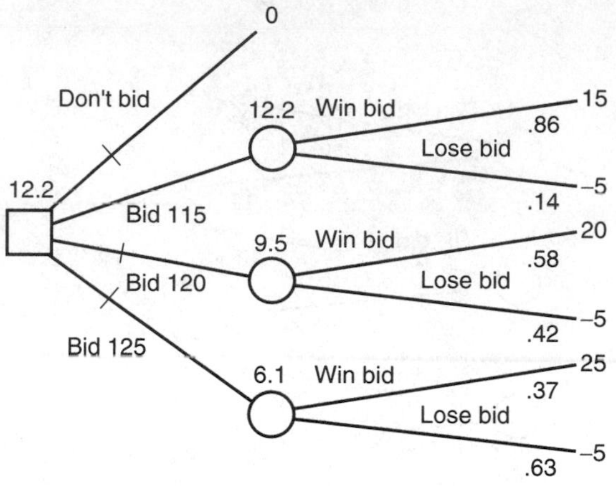

Note: All monetary values are in thousands of dollars.

Folding Back Procedure

1. At each probability node, calculate the EMV (sum of monetary values times probabilities), and write it above the node.
2. At each decision node, find the maximum of the EMVs and write it above the node. It is also customary to put a mark on all decision branches except the optimal one (the one with the largest EMV) to indicate that these alternatives will *not* be chosen.

TreePlan, an Excel Add-In For all of the problems we have discussed in previous chapters, Excel has provided a very natural means for both formulating and solving the associated models. Decision trees present a challenge for Excel, however. We must somehow take advantage of Excel's calculating capabilities (to calculate EMVs, for example) and also its graphical capabilities to depict the decision tree. Fortunately, we are able to use a third-party Excel add-in called TreePlan developed by Michael Middleton to set up and solve decision trees in Excel.[2] Although the process can be somewhat tedious and slow (for large problems on slow PCs), it has one great advantage: it can be used to perform sensitivity analysis. That is, once we develop the decision tree and enter all of the numerical inputs (monetary values and probabilities), it is easy to vary inputs and see how the EMVs and the optimal decision change.

The first thing you must do to use TreePlan is to "add it in." We suggest that you copy the add-in file TREEPLAN.XLA to the Excel\Library directory of your hard drive (unless your school or instructor has already done this for you). Then in Excel, use the Tools/Add-Ins menu item, Browse to find this .XLA file, and click on OK. Once TreePlan has been added in, it can be invoked from the Tools menu or by pressing Ctrl-t.

TreePlan is quite easy to use—at least its most basic items are—but it can be confusing at first. We'll lead you through the steps for the Precision example.

1. **Inputs.** Enter the inputs shown in columns A and B of Figure 8.7 for the Precision's problem.

[2]There are a number of other software packages (not spreadsheet based) designed to solve decision problems with uncertainty. One of the most popular of these is DPL.

FIGURE 8.7 **Inputs and Initial Tree**

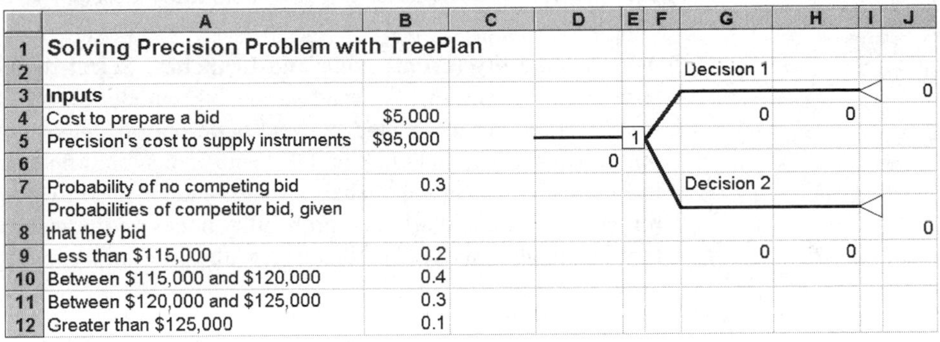

2 **New tree.** With the cursor in cell D1, select Tools/TreePlan and click on New Tree. The tree in Figure 8.7 should appear. As in the general decision tree conventions, TreePlan uses squares for decision nodes and circles for probability nodes (it calls them **event nodes**). It also uses triangles as **terminal nodes**, that is, the right-hand tips of the branches. So for this starting tree, there is a single decision node, with two decision branches, each followed by terminal nodes. Obviously, we need to expand the tree.

3 **More decision branches.** Select the cell (currently E5) that contains the decision node, then invoke TreePlan and select the Add Branch option. This adds a third decision branch. Repeat the procedure to add a fourth branch. Your decision tree should now look like the one shown in Figure 8.8. Then change the Decision 1

FIGURE 8.8 **Tree with Four Decision Branches**

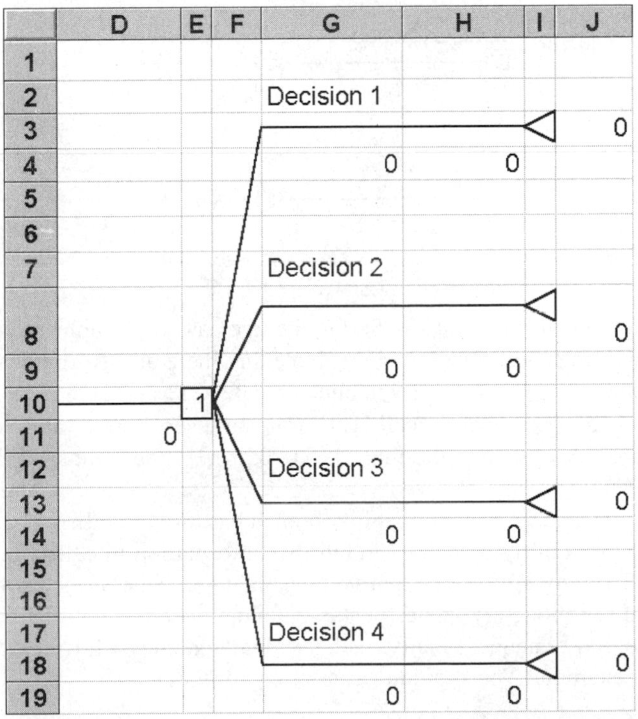

through Decision 4 labels in cells G2 through G17 to No bid, Bid $115,000, Bid $120,000, and Bid $125,000. These are simply descriptive labels for the possible alternatives.

4 **Add probability (event) node and branches.** Select the cell with the second terminal node (cell I8). We want a probability node to start there. To do this, invoke TreePlan, select the Change to event node option, make sure the Two Branches option is checked, and click on OK. Your tree should now look like the one shown in Figure 8.9. Change the labels Event 5 and Event 6 to Win bid and Lose bid. At this point, you could also add probability nodes and branches to the third and fourth terminal nodes, but we'll do that later with TreePlan's copying capabilities.

FIGURE 8.9 **Tree with a Probability Node and Branches Added**

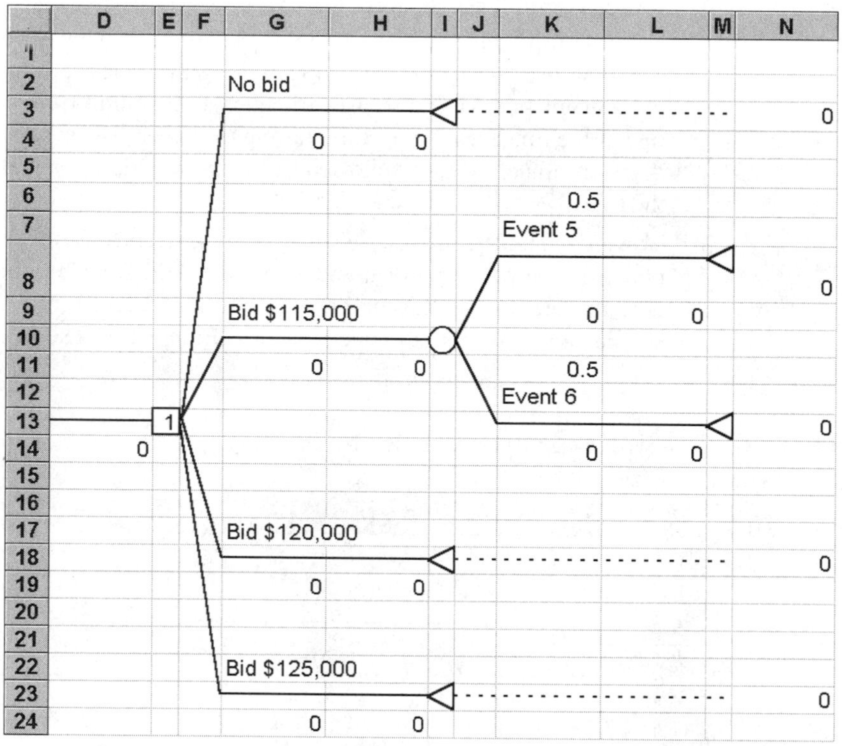

5 **Numerical information.** So far, the tree has only graphical information—a skeleton. Now we'll add some numbers. Note that there are two numbers under each decision branch. For example, if you click on cells G11 and H11, you'll see a *value* (0) in cell G11, but a *formula* in cell H11. You can insert a new value, namely, the immediate payoff or cost from bidding $115,000, in G11, but you shouldn't change the formula in H11.

Similarly, each probability branch has three numbers next to it. For example, the top probability branch (Win bid) has information in cells K6, K9, and L9. Cells K6 and K9 contain values that you can change, namely, the probability of this branch and the monetary value for this outcome, whereas cell L9 has a formula that you shouldn't change. Finally, each terminal node has a formula cell to its right, cell N8, for example. You shouldn't change any of these.

To see how these work, enter the value 0 in cell G11 (no immediate monetary value from bidding $115,000), replace the .5 value in cell K6 with the formula

=$B$7+(1–$B$7)*SUM($B$10:$B$12)

and replace the .5 value in cell K11 with the formula

=1–K6

Finally, replace the zeros in cells K9 and K14 with the formulas

=115000–$B$4–$B$5

and

=–$B$4

Your spreadsheet should now look like the one shown in Figure 8.10. The formulas you have entered have transferred the appropriate inputs into the correct cells in the tree. (You could have entered numbers such as .86 directly, but it is always better to refer to the input cells by formulas.) But notice what TreePlan has done automatically—it has folded back the tree for you! For example, it has calculated the EMV from bidding $115,000 in cell H11, $12,200. This is the purpose of TreePlan's built-in formulas, the formulas you should never change.

6 **Add other probability branches.** We need probability nodes and branches very similar to the ones we just built for the "bid $120,000" and "bid $125,000" branches. The easiest way to do this is to take advantage of TreePlan's copy and paste capabilities. Select the probability node in cell I10, invoke TreePlan, and select Copy Subtree. Then select the terminal node in cell I18, invoke TreePlan, select Paste

FIGURE 8.10 **Tree with Numerical Information**

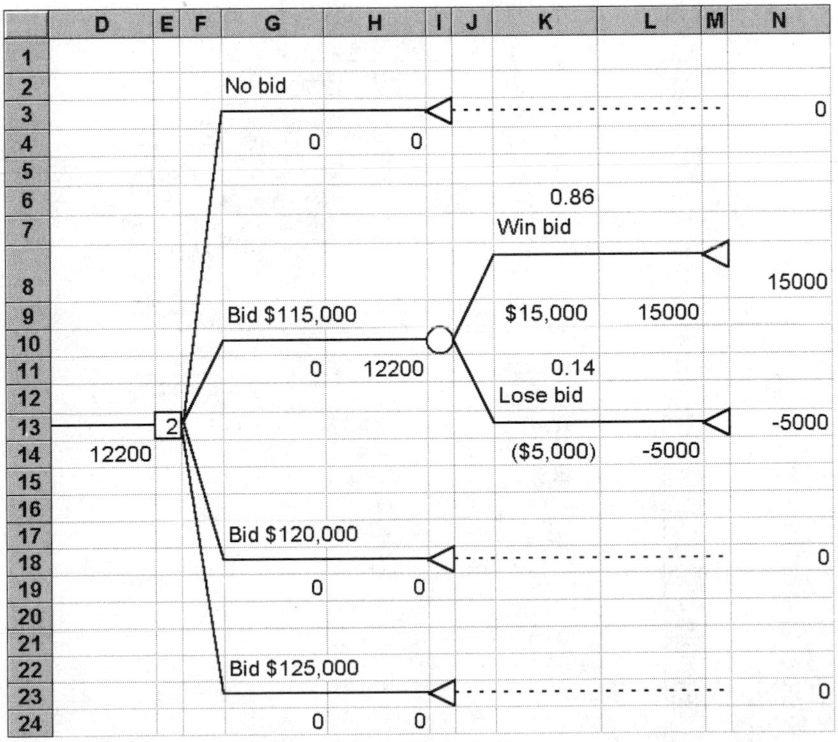

Subtree, and click on OK twice. Then repeat the procedure (you'll have to copy again) for the other terminal node (which is now in cell I28).

The formulas next to the probability branches you just built (probabilities and monetary values) are almost correct—that's why we used absolute references earlier—but you will need to fix them up slightly. In cells K16 and K26, change the $B$10 reference to $B$11 and $B$12, respectively. Then in cells K19 and K29, change the 115,000 to 120,000 and 125,000, respectively.

You're finished! The completed tree should appear as shown in Figure 8.11. (See the Tree1 sheet in the PRECISN.XLS file.) It is virtually identical to the tree we did by hand in Figure 8.6. The EMVs for the four alternatives appear in cells H4, H11, H21, and H31. The maximum of these appears in cell D17. Also, note the 2 in the decision node in cell E16. This signifies that the second of the four alternatives (from top to bottom) is the one with the largest EMV.

An Equivalent Tree There are often equivalent (correct) ways to build a decision tree in TreePlan. Recall that the values under the decision branches (now in cells G4, G11,

FIGURE 8.11 **Completed Tree for Precision Example**

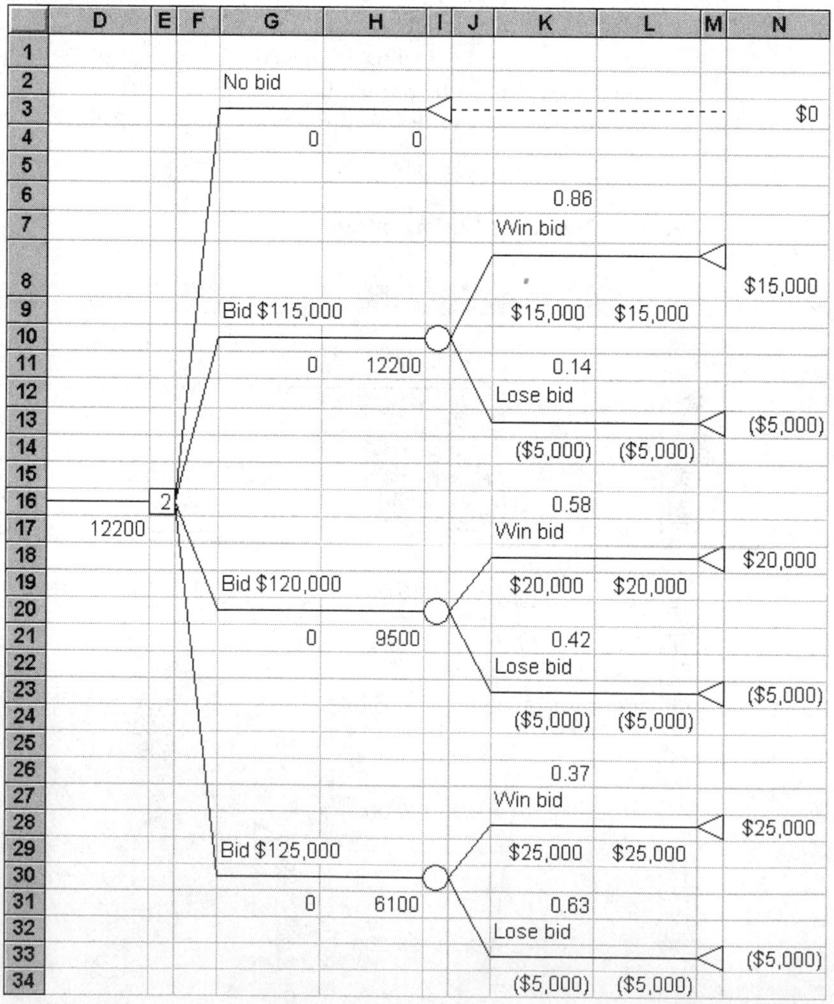

G21, and G31) represent immediate payoffs or costs from making these decisions. In the Precision example, if Precision bids at all it incurs a sure $5000 cost to prepare the bid, regardless of what happens later on. Therefore, you could enter these values in cells G11, G21, and G31. (Actually, you would enter the formula

=–$B$4

in cell G11 and copy it to G21 and G31.) However, if you enter this cost in these cells, you must remove it from the cells to the right—otherwise, you would be double counting. Therefore, you should remove the reference to cell B4 in the formulas in cells K9, K19, and K29. You should also remove it in cells K14, K24, and K34. For these cells you can simply enter the value 0.

The modified tree should appear as shown in Figure 8.12. (See the Tree2 sheet in the PRECISN.XLS file.) This tree is completely equivalent to the one in Figure 8.11. The only difference is in the timing of the monetary values. Now the $5000 bid cost occurs as soon as the decision to bid is made, and the eventual profit, if any, is realized when we learn

FIGURE 8.12 **Modified Tree for Precision Example**

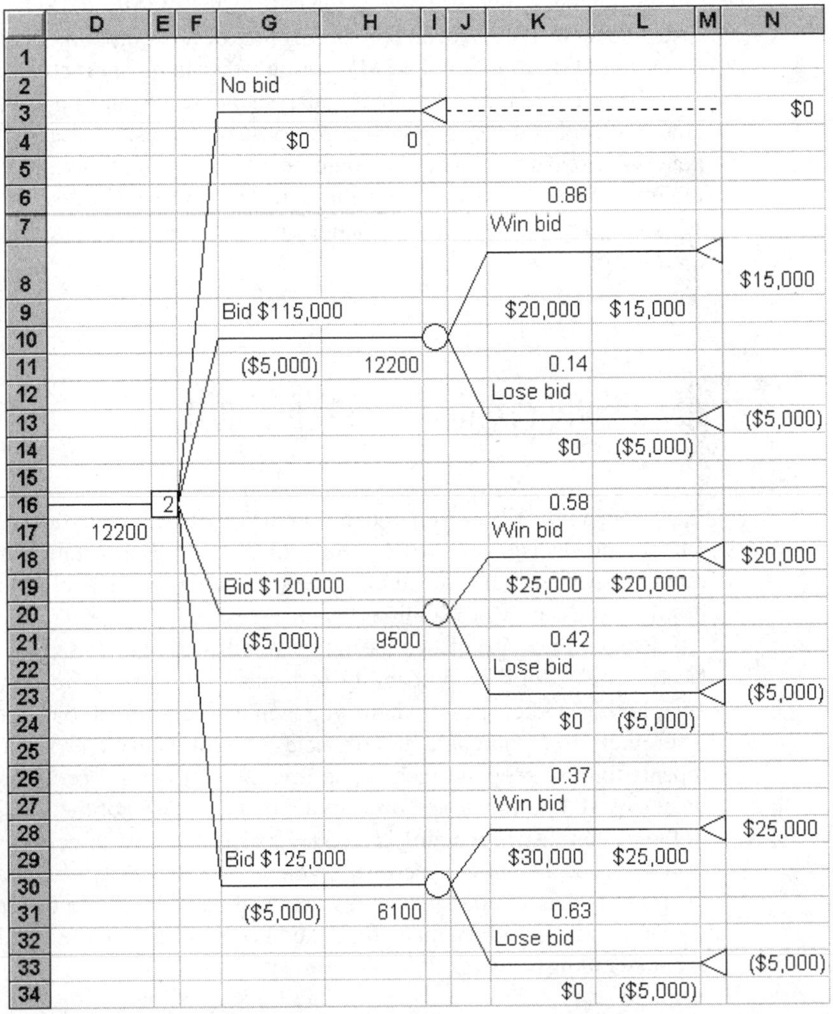

whether Precision wins the bid. In some sense, this is a more natural way to model the problem. But as far as the decision tree is concerned, it really doesn't matter.

Sensitivity Analysis TreePlan can be a bit slow and tedious. It also takes up a lot of room on a spreadsheet, so that you will probably want to use the Zoom feature of Excel at a level of 75% or even lower. However, once you go to all this trouble, it is nice to know that you can easily perform a sensitivity analysis on any or all of the input parameters of the problem. For example, you might want to see how sensitive the optimal decision is to Precision's cost to prepare the bid, its cost to supply the instruments, and/or the probability of no competing bids. In real applications quantities such as these are often educated guesses at best, so it is extremely important to check whether the optimal decision remains optimal for changes in the inputs.

To perform sensitivity analysis in the Precision example, all you need to do is enter new values for the inputs in column B. Since all of the formulas in the tree are tied to these input cells, the entire tree will recompute automatically. For example, you can check that if the cost to prepare a bid increases to $10,000, the largest EMV becomes $7200, but the $115,000 bid is still the best alternative. In fact, for a variety of "moderate" changes to the cost of the bid, the cost of supplying the instruments, and the probability of no competing bids, the $115,000 bid remains the best alternative. However, this isn't necessarily true for "large" changes. For example, if the cost of the bid is $10,000, the cost of supplying the instruments is $105,000, and the probability of no competing bids is 0, the best alternative is not to bid. In this case the EMVs of the other three alternatives are all negative.

We reiterate that a sensitivity analysis is always an important aspect in real decision analysis applications. If you had to construct decision trees by hand—with paper and pencil—a sensitivity analysis would be virtually out of the question. You would have to recompute everything each time through. Therefore, one of the most valuable features of a software package such as TreePlan is that it enables you to perform sensitivity analyses in a matter of seconds. ■

8.3 Assessing Probabilities (Optional)

We began the discussion of decision making under uncertainty by listing three basic elements: the decision alternatives, the probabilities of uncertain outcomes, and the resulting monetary values. The second of these is probably the most elusive. In this section we will briefly discuss how probabilities can be assessed.[3]

Probabilities are of two basic types: **subjective** or based on **historical frequencies**. Most people think of probability in terms of historical frequencies. Suppose that you are playing a dice game where you win if the sum of two dice is 7 or 11, and you lose otherwise. You could approximate the probability of winning by throwing two dice repeatedly and keeping track of the fraction of time a 7 or 11 appears. If you throw the dice, say, 10,000 times, and observe a 7 or 11 on 2450 of these throws, then your estimate of the probability of winning is .245 (= 2450/10,000). Of course, this is only an estimate. If you repeat the entire experiment, you will undoubtedly obtain a different estimate. But the point is that it is possible, at least conceptually, to obtain the probability of winning by repeating an experiment many times and keeping track of the fraction of time the specified event (winning) occurs.

[3]Readers who do not feel they need a review of probability assessment may wish to skip this section.

Not all probabilities can be estimated in this way. Many situations are "one-time" occurrences that cannot be repeated at all, let alone indefinitely. A common situation is sporting events. Suppose that the Atlanta Falcons and the Seattle Seahawks are about to play in the upcoming Super Bowl. (Well, we can dream!) You are thinking about placing a bet on Atlanta, so you want to assess the probability that Atlanta will win. This is much different than throwing dice, because there are no historical data to rely on. You must use whatever information you have, such as the seasonal records for the two teams, how they appear to match up, whether they have any significant injuries, and so on, and then *subjectively* assess Atlanta's probability of winning. It is important to realize that another sports fan might look at the same information available to you and assess a very different probability for the same event. What's more, neither of you is wrong. This is why we call such probabilities subjective—different people can come to different conclusions.

Although there are not necessarily right or wrong subjective probabilities, there are systematic methods for assessing them. When a company is about to make an important decision, it frequently hires a decision analysis expert to help analyze the problem. In this case the company executives know the details of their problem best, but the expert can help them model the problem. This is particularly true of the probability assessments. We will use the Precision example as an illustration, where the probability in question is p, the probability that there will be no competing bids.

There are three common methods the expert might use to obtain a "reasonable" value of p from Precision (the client). The first is very straightforward. The expert can simply ask, "How likely do you believe it is that there will be no competing bids?" Surprisingly, however, this direct approach does not always yield the most useful results. The client might not feel comfortable about answering such a direct question and might not put a lot of confidence in the answer. Therefore, the other two methods are roundabout ways to help the client think more carefully about the problem.

The first of these methods presents the client with a bet that the client can take either side of. The outcome of this bet will depend on the value of p. The trick is to adjust the bet until the client is indifferent as to which side of the bet to take. To be specific, suppose that the expert presents the following two bets to Precision:

$$\text{Bet 1:} \begin{cases} \text{win } x \text{ dollars if there are no competing bids} \\ \text{lose } y \text{ dollars if there is at least one competing bid} \end{cases}$$

$$\text{Bet 2:} \begin{cases} \text{lose } x \text{ dollars if there are no competing bids} \\ \text{win } y \text{ dollars if there is at least one competing bid} \end{cases}$$

Note that these bets and the monetary values involved (x and y) are *not* necessarily related to Precision's real decision problem discussed earlier. They are simply hypothetical bets that are used to help the client assess the value of p. Also, note that bet 2 is the "flip side" of bet 1.

If the client chooses bet 1, the EMV is

$$\text{EMV from bet 1} = xp - y(1-p)$$

Similarly, if the client chooses bet 2, the EMV is

$$\text{EMV from bet 2} = -xp + y(1-p)$$

Now suppose that x and y are eventually chosen such that the client is *indifferent* between the two bets, that is, the client is equally comfortable with bets 1 and 2. This means that their EMVs must be equal. Setting $xp - y(1-p)$ equal to $-xp + y(1-p)$ and solving for p gives

$$p = \frac{y}{x+y}$$

The role of the expert is to "zero in" on the values of x and y such that the client is indifferent between the two bets. For example, if $x = \$10{,}000$ and $y = \$500$, Precision will almost surely prefer bet 1. The client would rather take a chance of winning \$10,000 and possibly losing \$500 than the other way around. At the other extreme, if $x = \$500$ and $y = \$10{,}000$, Precision will almost surely prefer bet 2. But what about $x = \$1000$ and $y = \$700$? In this case Precision can either take a bet where it wins \$1000 or loses \$700 or a bet where it wins \$700 or loses \$1000. On the surface, bet 1 may appear to be the obvious choice, but it depends on the probability p. As we see in Figure 8.13, if Precision believes the value of p is approximately .41, then it will have a hard time choosing between these two bets. (Compare the EMVs of \$3 and −\$3.) To put it the other way around, if Precision believes these two bets are equally preferable, then its subjective estimate of p must be close to .41 (more precisely, $p = 700/(1000 + 700) = .412$).

FIGURE 8.13 One Method of Assessing Probabilities

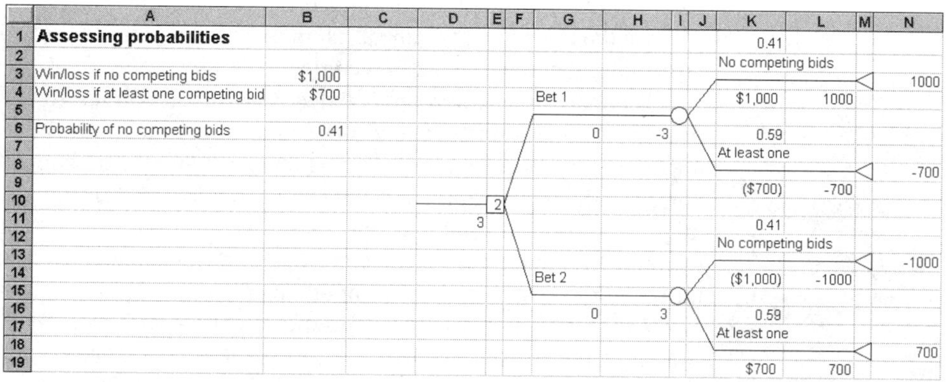

To summarize, with this method the expert will vary the monetary values x and y until the client is indifferent between bets 1 and 2. Then it will conclude that the client's assessment of p is $y/(x + y)$.

The second method for assessing probability is similar to the first. Again the expert presents the client with two bets, described as follows:

$$\text{Bet 1:} \begin{cases} \text{win \$1000 dollars if there are no competing bids} \\ \text{lose \$500 dollars if there is at least one competing bid} \end{cases}$$

(The monetary values are arbitrary. We have selected \$1000 and \$500 as simple round numbers.) The second bet contains the same monetary values but is based on some probabilistic mechanism that the client can easily understand. One possibility is the "probability wheel," shown in Figure 8.14, where the fraction of the wheel that is red, f_{red}, can easily be adjusted.

$$\text{Bet 2:} \begin{cases} \text{win \$1000 dollars if the spinner lands on red} \\ \text{lose \$500 dollars if the spinner lands on blue} \end{cases}$$

The trick is again to find the point where Precision is indifferent between the two bets. Now, however, the expert adjusts the value of f_{red}, that is, the portion of the wheel that is red. When Precision is indifferent between the two bets, then it must believe that p equals the final setting of f_{red}. Otherwise the EMVs of the two bets would not be equal.

FIGURE 8.14 Probability Wheel

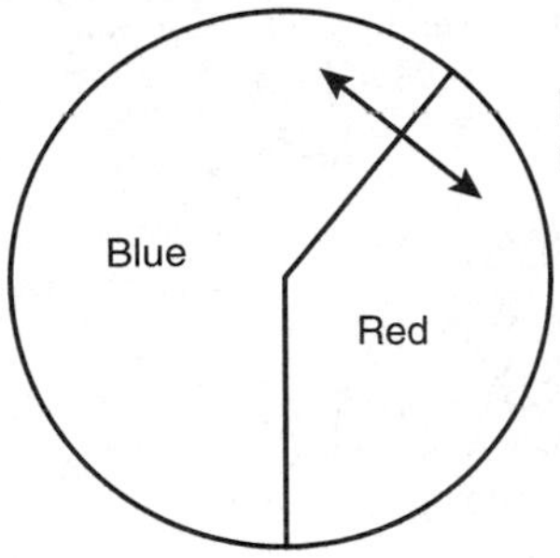

Assessing subjective probabilities—or helping a client assess probabilities—is not easy. For most people, probability is not an intuitive concept, and unwanted personal biases and inconsistencies can complicate the assessment process. The final assessment inevitably contains a certain amount of imprecision. This is one of the reasons why a sensitivity analysis is so crucial. If the client assesses a key probability to be .4, say, but believes this probability could easily be as low as .35 or as high as .45, it is comforting to know whether this amount of "error" really makes a difference. If a sensitivity analysis confirms that the best alternative for .4 is also best for .35 or .45, then the probability assessment is evidently as accurate as it needs to be.

One last comment about probability assessment is that many probabilities in real applications are combinations of subjective estimates and estimates from historical frequencies. This happens when the situation in question is unique in some aspects, so that subjective assessments are required, but is similar in other ways to situations that have occurred in the past. This might well be the case in Precision's problem. The company has probably bid on similar contracts in the past, so it probably has some record of what its competitors have done. It should certainly take this historical data into account, but it should also think subjectively about any unique aspects of this bidding situation that distinguish it from situations in the past.

PROBLEMS

Skill-Building Problems

1 You are playing a casino game where two dice are thrown and the outcome depends on the sum of the two faces showing. This sum can be any number from 2 to 12; the probabilities of the possible outcomes appear in Table 8.5. Suppose that you lose \$10 if the sum is 2, you win \$$w$ if the sum is 7 or 11, and you lose \$1 otherwise. From an EMV standpoint, how large must w be to make this game attractive to you?

TABLE 8.5 Outcome Probabilities for Betting Problem

Sum	2	3	4	5	6	7	8	9	10	11	12
Probability	1/36	2/36	3/36	4/36	5/36	6/36	5/36	4/36	3/36	2/36	1/36

2 Pizza King and Noble Greek are the two main pizza restaurants in town. Pizza King is trying to decide whether to undertake a small, medium, or large advertising campaign. The costs of these campaigns are, respectively, \$5000, \$10,000, and \$20,000. Pizza King knows that Noble Greek will also undertake a small, a medium, or a large advertising campaign. The changes in revenue for Pizza King depend on the actions chosen by each restaurant, as shown (in thousands of dollars) in Table 8.6. Determine the payoff table for Pizza King, where each element in this table lists the change in profit for Pizza King.

TABLE 8.6 Revenues for Pizza King Problem

		Noble Greek's Decision		
		Small	**Medium**	**Large**
Pizza King's Decision	**Small**	\$10	\$1	−\$5
	Medium	\$16	\$2	−\$6
	Large	\$30	\$18	\$3

3 Suppose in the previous problem that Pizza King assesses the probabilities of Noble Greek's actions to be Pr(small) = .5, Pr(medium) = .4, and Pr(large) = .1. For each of Pizza King's possible decisions, find the EMV of the company's change in profit.

4 Referring to the two previous problems, suppose that each dollar in extra revenue entails a 30¢ increase in operating costs—more pepperonis, more cheese, more help in the kitchen, and so forth. Rework the previous two problems with this assumption.

5 Build on the previous three problems in the following way. Suppose that the advertising costs, revenues, and operating costs are monthly figures that will continue throughout the next 12 months. Now determine the payoff table, where each element is a net present value over the next 12 months of the change in Pizza King's profit. Use an annual interest rate of 12%.

6 Sodaco is considering producing a new product: Chocovan soda. Sodaco estimates that the annual demand for Chocovan, D (in thousands of cases), has the following probability distribution: $\Pr(D = 30) = .30$, $\Pr(D = 50) = .40$, $\Pr(D = 80) = .30$. Each case of Chocovan sells for \$5 and incurs a variable cost of \$3. It costs \$800,000 to build a plant to produce Chocovan. Assume that if \$1 is received every year (forever), this is equivalent to receiving \$10 at the present time. If Sodaco decides to build the plant and produce Chocovan, find the expected net present value of its profit.

7 Many decision problems have the following simple structure. A decision maker has two possible decisions, 1 and 2. If decision 1 is made, a *sure* cost of c is incurred. If decision 2 is made, there are two possible outcomes, with costs c_1 and c_2 and probabilities p and $1 - p$. We assume that $c_1 < c < c_2$. The idea is that decision 1, the riskless decision, has a "moderate" cost, whereas decision 2, the risky decision, has a "low" cost c_1 or a "high" cost c_2.

a Find the decision maker's cost table, that is, the cost for each possible decision and each possible outcome.

b Calculate the expected cost from the risky decision.

c List as many scenarios as you can think of that have this structure. (Here's an example to get you started. Think of insurance, where you pay a sure premium in order to avoid a large possible loss.)

Skill-Extending Problem

8 Suppose that Pizza King and Noble Greek stop advertising but must determine the price they will charge for each pizza sold. Pizza King believes that Noble Greek's price will be \$6, \$8, or \$10 with probabilities .25, .50, and .25. If Pizza King charges price p_1 and Noble Greek charges price p_2, then Pizza King estimates that it will sell $1000 + 250(p_2 - p_1)$ pizzas during the next month. It costs Pizza King \$4 to make a pizza. Pizza King is considering charging \$5, \$6, \$7, \$8, or \$9 per pizza. For each of these possible choices, find the expected value of Pizza King's profit during the next month. ■

8.4

Decision Analysis Examples

All applications of decision making under uncertainty follow the procedures discussed so far. We first identify the possible decision alternatives, assess relevant probabilities, and calculate monetary values. Then we use a decision tree analysis to identify the alternative with the largest EMV and follow this up with a thorough sensitivity analysis. If it is feasible, we also examine the risk profiles for the various alternatives. This is particularly useful if criteria other than straight EMV maximization are considered, as we will discuss in Section 8.6. In this section we will illustrate the process with several examples. The first of these is another single-stage example, where the decision maker makes one decision and then learns which of several uncertain outcomes occurs. Later in this section we will also examine multistage examples, where two or more sequential decisions must be made.

A Purchasing Example

EXAMPLE 8.2

A chain of supermarkets requires 24,000 fluorescent light bulbs for its stores. There are two suppliers of these bulbs. Supplier A offers them at \$4.00 per bulb and will replace any defectives with guaranteed good ones for \$4.00 each. Supplier B offers them at \$4.15 per bulb and guarantees to replace defectives for \$1.00 each. The probability distributions of the percentage of defective bulbs from the two suppliers, listed in Table 8.7, have been estimated from historical data. For example, the probability is 0.4 that 5%, or 1200, of the 24,000 bulbs will be defective if they are purchased from supplier A. The supermarket plans to sell these bulbs for \$4.40 apiece and charge nothing for replacement of defectives. Which supplier should be chosen in order to maximize the supermarket's EMV?

TABLE 8.7 **Distributions of Percentage Defective for Purchasing Example**

	Probability of % Defective if Supplied by	
Percentage Defective	**Supplier A**	**Supplier B**
3%	0.10	0.05
4%	0.20	0.10
5%	0.40	0.60
6%	0.30	0.25

Solution

There are two alternatives in this problem: buy bulbs from A or buy bulbs from B. The necessary probabilities are listed in Table 8.7. We note that these probabilities are based primarily on historical frequencies, that is, previous experience with these suppliers. Also, they are clearly an approximation of reality, in that the *actual* percentage of bulbs that could fail is not restricted to 3%, 4%, 5%, and 6%. However, it is normal to limit the possible number of outcomes for computational ease, as we have done here.

The relevant monetary values in this example are the eventual profits for the supermarket, depending on the supplier chosen and the percentage of defective bulbs. For example, if supplier A is chosen and 4% (or 960) of the 24,000 bulbs are defective, then the supermarket's profit is

$$24000(4.40) - 24000(4.00) - 960(4.00) = \$5760$$

Alternatively, if they are purchased from B and 4% are defective, then the profit is

$$24000(4.40) - 24000(4.15) - 960(1.00) = \$5040$$

Continuing in this way, we find the profits for each combination of supplier and percentage defective in Table 8.8.

TABLE 8.8 Payoff Table for Purchasing Example

	Profit if Supplied by	
Percentage Defective	**Supplier A**	**Supplier B**
3%	\$6720	\$5280
4%	\$5760	\$5040
5%	\$4800	\$4800
6%	\$3840	\$4560

Using the probabilities in Table 8.7 and the profits in Table 8.8, we can form the risk profiles for the two alternatives. These appear in Figures 8.15 and 8.16.

FIGURE 8.15 Risk Profile for Choosing Supplier A

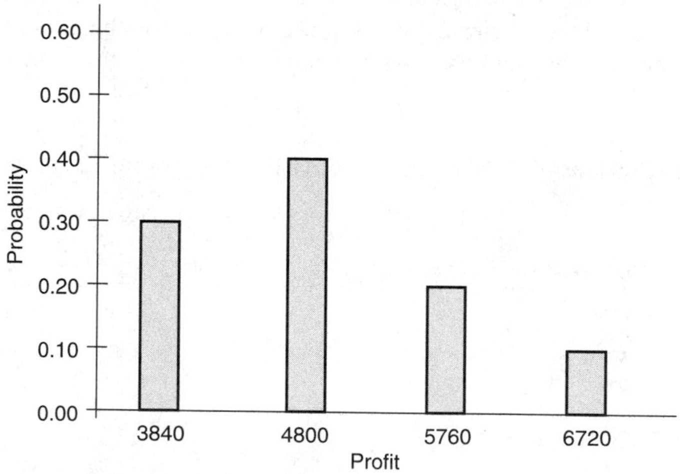

As we see, the choice is not entirely clear. The best outcome for supplier A is better and has higher probability than for supplier B, but the worst outcome for supplier A is worse and has higher probability than for supplier B. Therefore, we now turn to the decision tree analysis.

Using TreePlan To develop a decision tree with TreePlan, it is first convenient to enter the inputs for the problem and use appropriate Excel formulas to calculate the profits in

FIGURE 8.16 Risk Profile for Choosing Supplier B

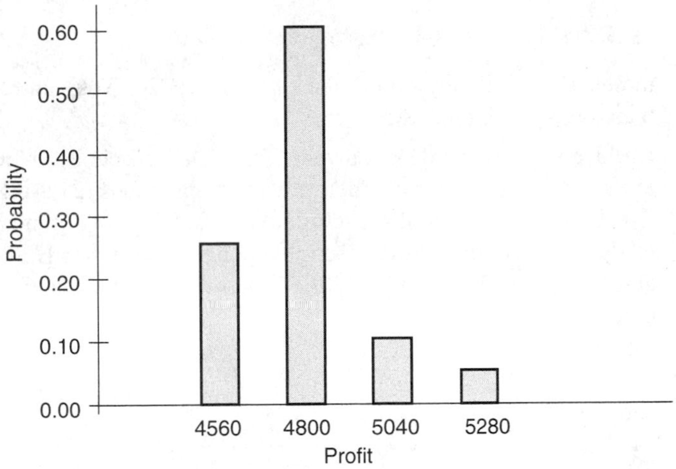

Table 8.8. Then we can refer to them in the decision tree. The steps are as follows. (See Figure 8.17 and the file BULB.XLS.)

1 **Inputs.** Enter the inputs in rows 3–17, columns A–C.

2 **Profit table.** The profits from each alternative and each outcome can be developed

FIGURE 8.17 Inputs and Profit Table for Purchasing Example

	A	B	C
1	Light bulb example		
2			
3	Number of bulbs	24000	
4			
5	Probabilities for percent defective		
6	Percent	Supplier A	Supplier B
7	3%	0.10	0.05
8	4%	0.20	0.10
9	5%	0.40	0.60
10	6%	0.30	0.25
11			
12	Monetary information		
13		Supplier A	Supplier B
14	Cost per bulb	$4.00	$4.15
15	Cost of replacing	$4.00	$1.00
16			
17	Selling price per bulb	$4.40	
18			
19	Table of profits		
20	Percent defective	Supplier A	Supplier B
21	3%	$6,720	$5,280
22	4%	$5,760	$5,040
23	5%	$4,800	$4,800
24	6%	$3,840	$4,560

from a single formula if absolute/relative addresses are used properly. To do so, enter the formula

=$B$3*($B$17–B$14–$A21*B$15)

in cell B21 and copy this to the range B21:C24. You can check that these profits match those in Table 8.8.

3 **Build tree.** Select cell E1, invoke TreePlan, and choose New Tree. This new tree already has the correct number of decision branches (2). Add a probability node with four branches to each of the terminal nodes. (Copying branches isn't very efficient in this problem.) Change the descriptive labels in columns H and L appropriately. Then enter formulas for the probabilities and monetary values in column L. For example, enter the formulas

=B7

and

–D21

in cells L1 and L4. After you enter these, everything else should recalculate automatically. Your final tree should appear as in Figure 8.18.

As we see from the decision tree, the decision is more clear-cut than it appeared. The EMV for supplier A is $4896, whereas the EMV for supplier B is only $4788. Supplier A is the best choice. Is this because of supplier B's higher cost of bulbs or because supplier A has a "better" probability distribution of defectives? This is where sensitivity analysis enters the picture. If we change supplier B's cost per bulb (in cell C14) to $4.10—just a nickel decrease—the EMV for supplier B increases to $5988, and of course, the EMV for supplier A doesn't change. So now supplier B is preferred! On the other hand, if supplier B keeps its cost at $4.15 but its probabilities change to .1, .2, .4, and .3, the same as for supplier A, the EMV for supplier B increases to $4824. This is slightly below the $4896 EMV for supplier A, but it is obviously closer than before.

Therefore, we see from this sensitivity analysis that although supplier A is the best choice with the original problem parameters, it doesn't take much to turn the tables. ■

A Medical Insurance Example

The following example illustrates a decision problem most of us face on an annual basis, although most of us probably don't go to the trouble of analyzing it formally.

EXAMPLE 8.3

Each year employees at State University are asked to decide on one of three health care plans. The terms of these are as follows:[4]

Plan 1: The monthly cost is $24. There is a $500 deductible. The participant pays all expenses until payments for the year equal $500. After that, 90% of remaining expenses are paid by the insurer.

Plan 2: This is the same as plan 1, except that the monthly cost is $1 and the deductible amount is $1000.

[4]We assume that these terms apply only to the employee, that is, these are not family plans.

FIGURE 8.18 Decision Tree for Purchasing Example

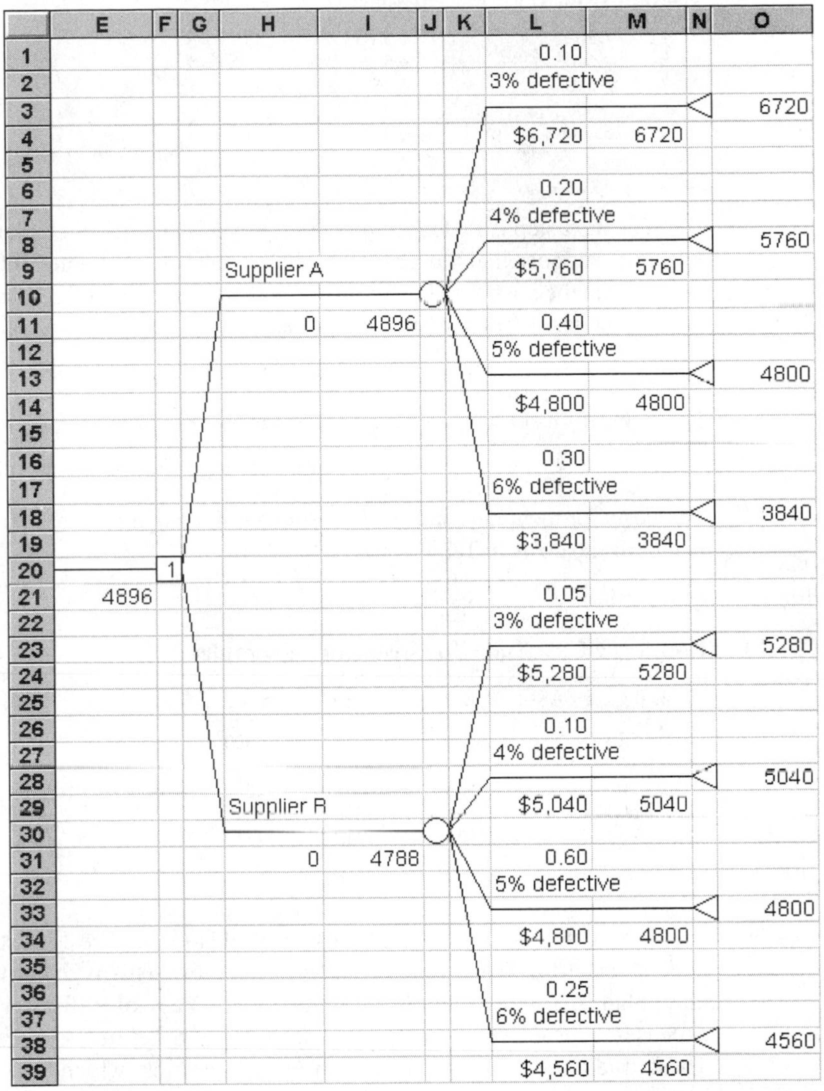

Plan 3: The monthly cost is $20. There is no deductible. The employee pays 30% of all medical expenses. The rest is paid by the insurer.

Which of these three plans should an employee choose?

Solution

Clearly, the solution will vary from one employee to another, depending on the assessed probability distribution of medical expenses. To illustrate, however, we will consider an employee who assesses the distribution of yearly medical expenses shown in Table 8.9. These expenses include hospital visits, surgery, office visits, and prescriptions, all of which are covered under the terms of the plans. As in the light bulb purchasing example, this distribution is only an approximation of the real distribution, which would contain a continuum of expenses. However, it is probably adequate for making a decision between the three plans.

TABLE 8.9 **Distribution of Medical Expenses for Insurance Example**

Total Medical Expense	Probability
$200	0.30
$600	0.50
$1000	0.15
$5000	0.03
$15,000	0.02

The next step is to determine the employee's cost for each plan and each outcome. For example, suppose that the employee chooses plan 1 and incurs $600 in expenses. Then the total cost is the cost of the insurance plus the full amount of the first $500 in expenses plus 10% of the last $100 in expenses, that is,

$$24(12) + 500 + .1(100) = \$798$$

However, if this employee's medical expenses are only $200, then the cost is

$$24(12) + 200 = \$488$$

The costs for the other plans and other outcomes can be calculated in a similar manner. We list all of the costs in Table 8.10.

TABLE 8.10 **Employee Cost Table for Insurance Example**

Medical Expense	Plan 1	Plan 2	Plan 3
$200	$488	$212	$300
$600	$798	$612	$420
$1000	$838	$1012	$540
$5000	$1238	$1412	$1740
$15,000	$2238	$2412	$4740

The choice is certainly not clear from this table. The lowest-premium plan, plan 2, looks good if the year's medical expenses are low. This is also true for the no-deductible plan, plan 3, although its cost is quite large in case of a disaster. For moderate medical expenses, plan 1 is obviously inferior, but it is the best for guarding against a disaster. These trade-offs could be illustrated by risk profiles, which you might want to develop. Instead, we turn directly to the decision tree.

Using TreePlan

1 **Inputs.** Enter the inputs for the three plans and the probabilities from Table 8.9 in the top left portion of the spreadsheet (down to row 15). (See Figure 8.19 and the file MEDICAL.XLS.)

2 **Cost table.** For later use in the decision tree, calculate the costs to the employee in the range B19:D23. To do this, enter the formula

=12*B$5+IF($A19<=B$6,$A19,B$6+B$7*($A19–B$6))

in cell B19 and copy this to the range B19:D23. The first term in this sum is the insurance premium. Then the IF function says that if the medical expense is less than the deductible, the employee pays it all. Otherwise, the employee pays the deductible amount plus a percentage of the remainder.

3 **Decision tree.** Select cell F1 and use TreePlan to start a new tree. Add one decision branch. Then add a probability node with five branches to the top terminal

FIGURE 8.19 **Inputs and Cost Table for Medical Insurance Example**

	A	B	C	D
1	**Medical insurance example**			
2				
3	Information about plans			
4		Plan 1	Plan 2	Plan 3
5	Monthly cost	$24	$1	$20
6	Deductible	$500	$1,000	$0
7	Percent paid after deductible	10%	10%	30%
8				
9	Probability distribution of medical expenses for the year			
10	Expense	Probability		
11	$200	0.30		
12	$600	0.50		
13	$1,000	0.15		
14	$5,000	0.03		
15	$15,000	0.02		
16				
17	Employee cost table			
18	Expense	Plan 1	Plan 2	Plan 3
19	$200	$488	$212	$300
20	$600	$798	$612	$420
21	$1,000	$838	$1,012	$540
22	$5,000	$1,238	$1,412	$1,740
23	$15,000	$2,238	$2,412	$4,740

node. Change the descriptive labels on all branches. Then enter formulas for the probabilities. Enter them as absolute references, so that the entire subtree can be copied to the other two terminal nodes. For example, enter the formula

=$B$11

in cell M1. Now select the probability node (cell K13) and use TreePlan's options to copy this subtree to the other two terminal nodes attached to the decision branches. Finally, enter the costs in all relevant cells in column M. For example, enter the formula

=B19

in cell M4.

4 **Minimize costs.** If you quit here, you would mistakenly choose the *worst* of the three plans. This is because TreePlan maximizes EMV by default, and in this problem you want to *minimize* the EMV of the costs. However, this is simple to change. Invoke TreePlan, click on the Options button, and check the Minimize costs option.

The final tree is quite large. We show only the probability node for Plan 3, which turns out to be the best plan, in Figure 8.20. Its EMV—an expected *cost*—is $528. The EMVs for plans 1 and 2 are $753 and $612. Evidently, this employee's chances of large medical expenses where plan 3 is at its worst are not so large that they outweigh plan 3's no-deductible benefit. However, you might want to experiment with various inputs, either the properties of the plans or the employee's medical expense distribution, to see whether plan 3 continues to be the preferred plan. For example, if the probabilities in Table 8.9 change to .30, .40, .15, .10, .05, so that large expenses are much more probable, the EMVs for the three plans become \$827, \$722, and \$750. Now plan 2 is preferred, although the difference in EMV between plans 2 and 3 is quite small.

FIGURE 8.20 Probability Node and Branches for Plan 3

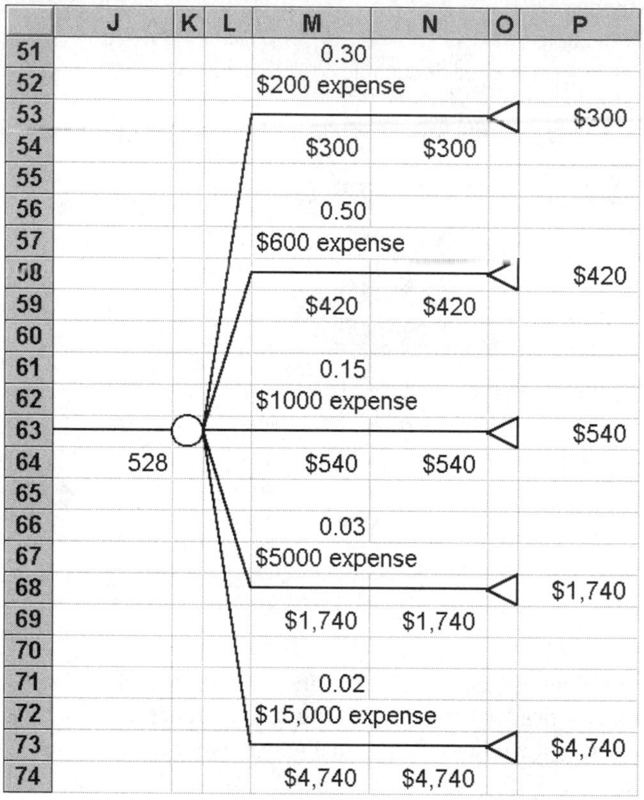

We can use this insurance example to illustrate one *non*monetary aspect of decision problems that is difficult to incorporate into a decision tree. At the university where we teach, there is another insurance plan in addition to the types in the example. Its premiums are low, and there are *no* copayments—the insurer pays all medical expenses. This plan is clearly the cheapest of all plans offered, but it is not chosen by many employees. Why? The plan is through an HMO, where all employees must go to a specified set of physicians; otherwise, the plan doesn't pay their expenses. Evidently, many employees believe that the "cost" of having to go to physicians they wouldn't choose otherwise outweighs the dollar savings from the plan. ■

A Marketing Example

So far, all of the examples have required a single decision. We now examine problems where the decision maker must make at least two decisions that are separated in time, such as when a company must decide whether to buy information that will help it make a second decision. The following example illustrates this type of problem.

EXAMPLE 8.4

The Acme Company is trying to decide whether to market a new product. As in many new-product situations, there is considerable uncertainty about whether the new product will eventually "catch on." Acme believes that it might be prudent to introduce the product in a regional test market before introducing it nationally. Therefore, the company's first decision is whether to conduct the test market. Acme estimates that the net cost of the test market is $50,000. If it decides to conduct the test market, it must then wait for the results of the test market. Based on these results, it can then decide whether to market the product nationally. On the other hand, if the original decision is *not* to run a test market, then the final decision—whether to market the product nationally—can be made without further delay. Acme figures that a successful product (in the national market) is worth $1,200,000, whereas a failure will cost the company $500,000. The company wants to use a decision tree approach to find the best strategy.

Solution

We begin by discussing the three basic elements of this decision problem: the possible strategies, the possible outcomes and their probabilities, and the value model. The possible strategies are clear. Acme must first decide whether to conduct a test market. Then it must decide whether to introduce the product nationally. It is important to realize that if Acme decides to conduct a test market, it can then take advantage of the results of the test market when making the national market decision. Therefore, its final strategy might be a **contingency plan**, where it conducts the test market, then introduces the product nationally if it receives positive test market results and abandons the product if it receives negative test market results. The optimal strategies from many multistage decision problems involve similar types of contingency plans.

Regarding the uncertain outcomes and their probabilities, we will simplify the problem to some extent by assuming that the results of the test market (if there is a test market) are either "success" or "failure." Similarly, if the product is marketed nationally, we will assume that the only possible outcomes are "success" and "failure." If Acme were able to distinguish finer degrees of outcomes, such as "huge success," "moderate success," and so on, these could be used instead. They would not change the basic structure of the analysis; they would only add to the amount of data needed and the size of the decision tree—and possibly to the realism of the model. However, as we have discussed in previous examples, it is not at all unusual in real decision analyses to sacrifice some degree of detail in order to simplify the analysis.

The probabilities of these outcomes undoubtedly reflect a blend of expert judgment and historical experience with similar products. We will assume that Acme has assessed that the probability of a successful product in the national market, without any test market information, is .5—success and failure are equally likely. However, if a test market is conducted and it is successful, then Acme believes the probability of success in the national market increases to .7, whereas if the test market is unsuccessful, the probability of success in the national market decreases to .2. Finally, Acme has assessed that the probability of a successful test market is .6.

Finally, from the problem statement we see that Acme has estimated three monetary values: $50,000 as the cost of the test market, $1,200,000 as the profit (not counting the test market cost, if any) from a successful national market, and $500,000 as the cost (again, not counting the test market cost) from an unsuccessful national market. All of these figures include any relevant marketing costs, operating costs, administrative costs, and so on, as well as eventual revenues. If the planning horizon is long (several years), the time value of money has presumably also been taken into account, so that the payoffs and costs then represent net present values. Clearly, accountants and other relevant people in the organization are required to obtain all of the necessary monetary information.

The monetary values required in the decision tree are then straightforward. For example, if Acme conducts a test market, then decides to market nationally, and the product is successful in the national market, the net profit is \$1,200,000 – \$50,000 = \$1,150,000. Or if Acme conducts a test market, then decides not to market nationally, there is a loss of \$50,000.

Using TreePlan Although most of the details of the decision tree will be done automatically by TreePlan, it is important to understand the basic structure of the tree. This basic structure appears, without numbers, in Figure 8.21. (The numbers inside the nodes of this tree are for identification purposes only.) The key to understanding this tree is to remember that time goes from left to right. Nodes and branches to the right of other nodes and branches occur *after* these other nodes and branches. Acme first decides whether to conduct a test market (node 1). If it decides not to conduct a test market, then it immediately decides whether to market nationally (node 7). If it does so, then it waits for the eventual success or failure of the product (node 8). If it abandons the product, the problem is over. On the other hand, if Acme runs a test market, it must then wait for the results of the test market (node 2). After these results are available, it must then decide whether to market nationally (nodes 3 and 4) and, if it markets nationally, wait for the eventual national market results (nodes 5 and 6).

Note that there are three identical-looking decision nodes (nodes 3, 4, and 7) in Figure 8.21 where Acme must decide whether to market nationally. However, these are not really identical because of the information available when each is made. At node 7, no test market information is available. At node 3, information that the product was successful in the test market is available, and at node 4 information that the product was unsuccessful in the test market is available. The result is that the probabilities on the probability branches following these three decision nodes differ. Specifically, they are shown in Figure 8.22. The probability of a national success, given no test market, is .5. But it increases to .7 following a successful test market, and it decreases to .2 following an unsuccessful test market. Figure 8.22 also shows the probabilities of the test market results and the eventual profits (or losses, if negative) at the tips of the branches.

FIGURE 8.21 **Structure of Decision Tree for Acme Example**

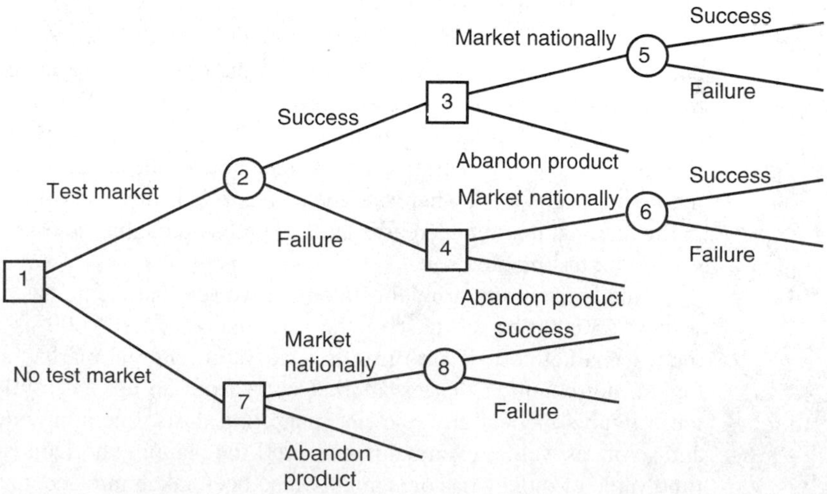

FIGURE 8.22 Decision Tree for Acme Example

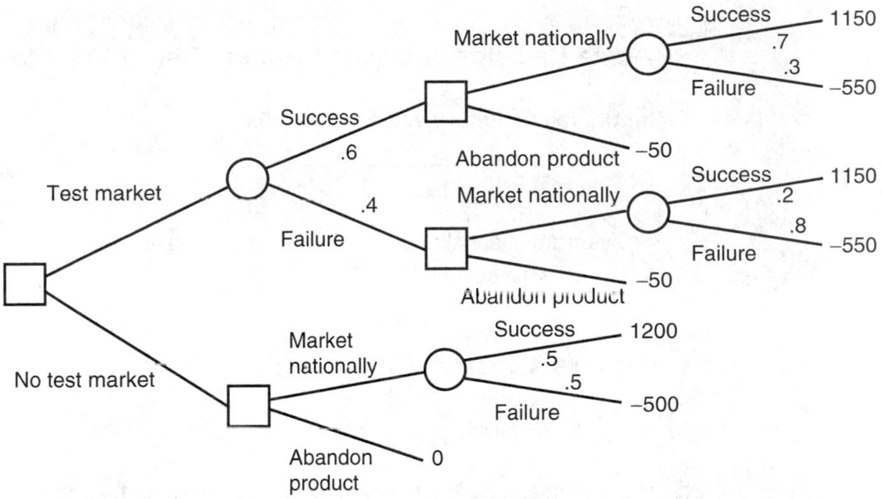

Note: All monetary values are in thousands of dollars.

Once you understand the structure of the decision tree, it is straightforward to build it with TreePlan. As usual, we enter the inputs and calculate important monetary values first and then refer to these in building the tree. The inputs and monetary values appear in Figure 8.23. The tree itself appears in Figure 8.24, where all monetary values are in thousands of dollars. (See the file ACME.XLS.)

To help you build this rather involved tree, we found it useful to build the subtree starting with the decision node in cell M39 and enter its descriptive labels and monetary values. For example, the formula in cell S34 is

=B8

Then we copied this subtree to obtain the subtrees starting in cells Q9 and Q24. Finally, we entered formulas for all remaining quantities, relating them to the inputs in Figure 8.23. For example, the formulas in cells K17 and W1 are

=-B5

and

=B20

Note that the cost of the test market is entered on the branch where it occurs in time (cell K17). Some analysts prefer to enter 0 in this cell and instead subtract the test market cost from the monetary values in later branches (cells S14, W4, W9, S29, W19, and W24). These approaches are entirely equivalent, and the one you choose is largely a matter of taste. Just make certain that you don't subtract the test market cost in *both* places; this would be double-counting.

Interpreting the Solution The interpretation of this tree is fairly straightforward if you realize that each value just below and to the left of each node is an EMV. For example, the 364 in cell H28 is the EMV for the entire decision problem. It means that Acme's best EMV is $364,000. As another example, the 640 in cell P10 means that if Acme ever gets to that point—the test market has been conducted and it has been successful—the EMV

FIGURE 8.23 Inputs for Acme Example

	A	B	C	D	E	F
1	**Acme Decision Analysis Problem Using TreePlan**					
2						
3	**Inputs (all monetary values in $1000s)**					
4						
5	Cost of test market	50				
6						
7	Profits from national market if marketed nationally					
8	If success	1200				
9	If failure	-500				
10						
11	Probabilities of test market outcomes					
12	Success	0.6				
13	Failure	0.4				
14						
15	Probabilities of national market outcomes, given no test market					
16	Success	0.5				
17	Failure	0.5				
18						
19	Probabilities of national market outcomes, given successful test market					
20	Success	0.7				
21	Failure	0.3				
22						
23	Probabilities of national market outcomes, given failure in test market					
24	Success	0.2				
25	Failure	0.8				

for ACME is $640,000. You should check that each of these EMVs has been calculated by the folding-back procedure we discussed earlier, starting from the right and working back toward the left—take EMVs at probability nodes and maximums at decision nodes.

Each decision node has a number in it, indicating which of the decision branches is favored if that decision node is ever reached. (Recall that the numbering goes from top branch to bottom branch.) Therefore, we can read the optimal contingency plan as follows. Because of the 1 in cell I27, Acme's first decision should be to conduct a test market. Then because of the 1 in cell Q9 and the 2 in cell Q24, it should market nationally if the test market is a success and abandon the product if the test market is a failure. Its EMV under this strategy is $364,000. Note that there is also a 1 in cell M39. This indicates that *if* Acme decided not to conduct a test market, for whatever reason, then its best decision would be to market nationally right away. Of course, this is essentially irrelevant if Acme conducts the test market, as the decision tree suggests.

Sensitivity Analysis There are three input sources that might be varied in this example: the cost of the test market, the payoff or loss from the national marketing of the product, and the probabilities. We will consider only the first two for now. It turns out that the probabilities are related to one another, as we will see when we discuss Bayes' rule, so it is not appropriate to vary them "randomly." We can, however, change the payoff of $1,200,000 or the loss of $500,000 and see if it affects Acme's optimal strategy. For example, if the payoff from a successful national market increases to slightly more than $1,375,000, then the best strategy is to market nationally right away, without a test market.

FIGURE 8.24 Completed Decision Tree for Acme Example

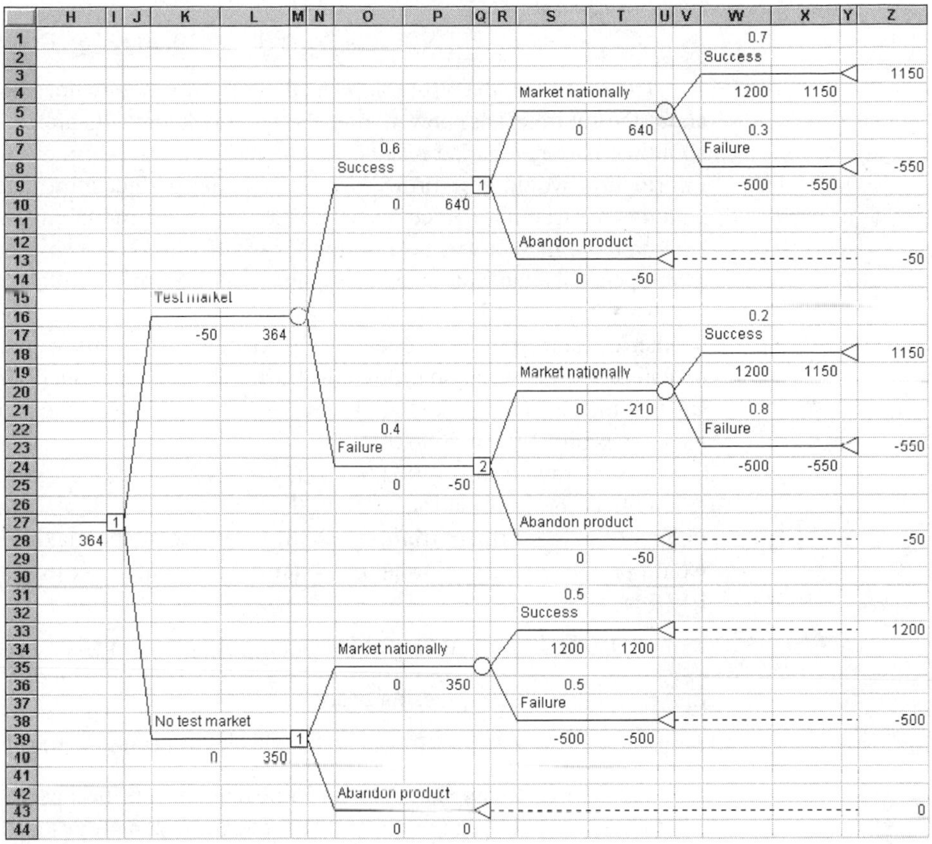

Similarly, if the loss from an unsuccessful national market is slightly less than \$460,000, the best strategy is again to market nationally right away.

The effect of the test market cost is easier to gauge. Currently, the EMV from not test marketing is \$350,000, which is \$14,000 less than the EMV from test marketing. Therefore, since the test market cost is a sure thing—no uncertainty is involved—if it increases by more than \$14,000 and everything else stays constant, the test market will no longer be worth its cost, and marketing nationally right away will be optimal. Of course, if the test market cost decreases, the decision to test market will be much more attractive, and the overall EMV for Acme will decrease by the amount of the decrease in the test market cost.

Value of Information Continuing the thought in the previous paragraph, the role of the test market is to provide information in the form of more accurate probabilities of national market results. Information usually costs something, as it does in Acme's problem. Currently, the cost of the test market is \$50,000, which is evidently not too much to pay since Acme's best strategy is to conduct the test market. However, we might ask how much this test market is worth. This is easy to answer. From the previous paragraph, we saw that if the test market cost increased by more than \$14,000, the test market would no longer be worth its cost. Therefore, the *most* Acme should pay for the test market is \$64,000. This value is called the **expected value of sample information**, or EVSI. In general, we can write the following expression for EVSI:

$$\text{EVSI} = \text{EMV with } \textit{free} \text{ information} - \text{EMV without information}$$

In Acme's problem, the EMV with free information must be \$414,000 since its EMV less the \$50,000 test market cost is \$364,000. Therefore,

$$\text{EVSI} = \$414{,}000 - \$350{,}000 = \$64{,}000$$

The reason for the term *sample* is that the information does not remove all uncertainty about the future. That is, even after the test market results are in, there is still uncertainty about the national market results. We might go one step further and ask how much *perfect* information would be worth. You can imagine perfect information as an envelope that contains the true final outcome. That is, either "the national market will be successful" or "the national market will be a failure" is written inside the envelope. Admittedly, no such envelope exists, but if it were, how much would Acme be willing to pay for it?

This is answered by the simple decision tree in Figure 8.25. Now the probability node on the left corresponds to opening the envelope. Once the contents of the envelope are revealed, Acme's decision is obvious. It should market nationally if the envelope's contents say that the national market will be successful and abandon the product otherwise. Folding back gives an EMV of \$600,000.

Now compare this \$600,000 with the EMV in the bottom part of Figure 8.24 that results from no information, \$350,000. The difference, \$250,000, is called the **expected value of perfect information**, or EVPI. It represents the maximum amount the company would pay for perfect information about the final outcome. In general, the expression for EVPI is

$$\text{EVPI} = \text{EMV with } \textit{free} \text{ perfect information} - \text{EMV with no information}$$

In Acme's case this expression becomes

$$\text{EVPI} = \$600{,}000 - \$350{,}000 = \$250{,}000$$

The EVPI may appear to be an irrelevant concept because perfect information is almost never available—at any price. However, it is sometimes useful because it represents an *upper bound* on the EVSI for any potential sample information. That is, no sample information is ever worth more than the EVPI. For example, if Acme is contemplating an expensive test market with an anticipated cost of more than \$250,000, then there is really no point in pursuing it any further. The information gained from this test market, no matter how reliable it is, cannot possibly justify its cost because its cost is greater than the EVPI. ■

FIGURE 8.25 Decision Tree with Perfect Information

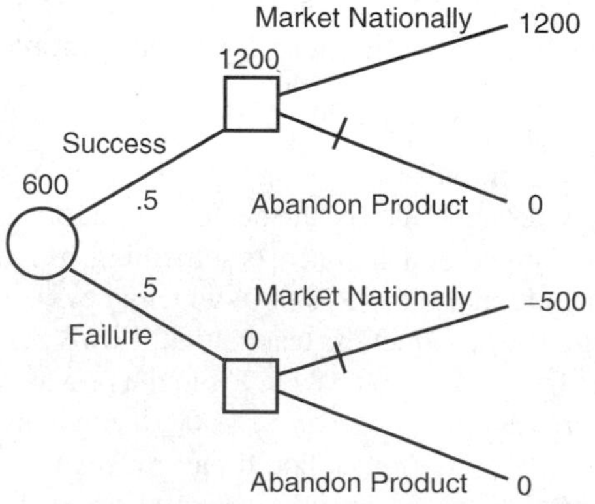

Note: All monetary values are in thousands of dollars.

An Investment Example

EXAMPLE 8.5

The Westhouser Paper Company in the state of Washington currently has an option to purchase a piece of land with good timber forest on it. It is now May 1, and the current price of the land is $2,200,000. Westhouser does not actually need the timber from this land until the beginning of July, but its management people fear that another company might buy the land between now and the beginning of July. They assess that there is 1 chance out of 20 that a competitor will buy the land during May. If this does not occur, then they assess that there is 1 chance out of 10 that the competitor will buy the land during June. If Westhouser does not take advantage of its current option, it can attempt to buy the land at the beginning of June or the beginning of July, providing that it is still available.

Westhouser's incentive for delaying the purchase is that its financial experts believe that the price of the land might fall significantly in one or both of the next two months. The possible price decreases and their probabilities are shown in Tables 8.11 and 8.12. Table 8.11 shows the probabilities of the possible price decreases during May. Table 8.12 shows the *conditional* probabilities of the possible price decreases in June, *given* the price decrease in May. For example, if the price decrease in May is $60,000, then the possible price decreases in June are $0, $30,000, and $60,000 with respective probabilities .6, .2, and .2.

TABLE 8.11 **Distribution of Price Decrease in May**

Price Decrease	Probability
$0	0.5
$60,000	0.3
$120,000	0.2

TABLE 8.12 **Distribution of Price Decrease in June**

Price Decrease in May					
$0		$60,000		$120,000	
June Decrease	Probability	June Decrease	Probability	June Decrease	Probability
$0	0.3	$0	0.6	$0	0.7
$60,000	0.6	$30,000	0.2	$20,000	0.2
$120,000	0.1	$60,000	0.2	$40,000	0.1

If Westhouser purchases the land, it believes that it can gross $3 million. (This does not count the cost of purchasing the land.) But if it does not purchase the land, it believes that it can make $650,000 from alternative investments. What should the company do?

Solution

This example illustrates how decision trees can get very "bushy" very quickly. The structure of the tree is shown in Figure 8.26. At the beginning of each month (May, June, and July), Westhouser decides whether to buy the land, assuming it is available. Then (in May and June) uncertainty is resolved concerning the competitor's action and the price decrease of the land. Note that as soon as Westhouser or the competitor buys the land,

FIGURE 8.26 **Structure of Tree for Westhouser Example**

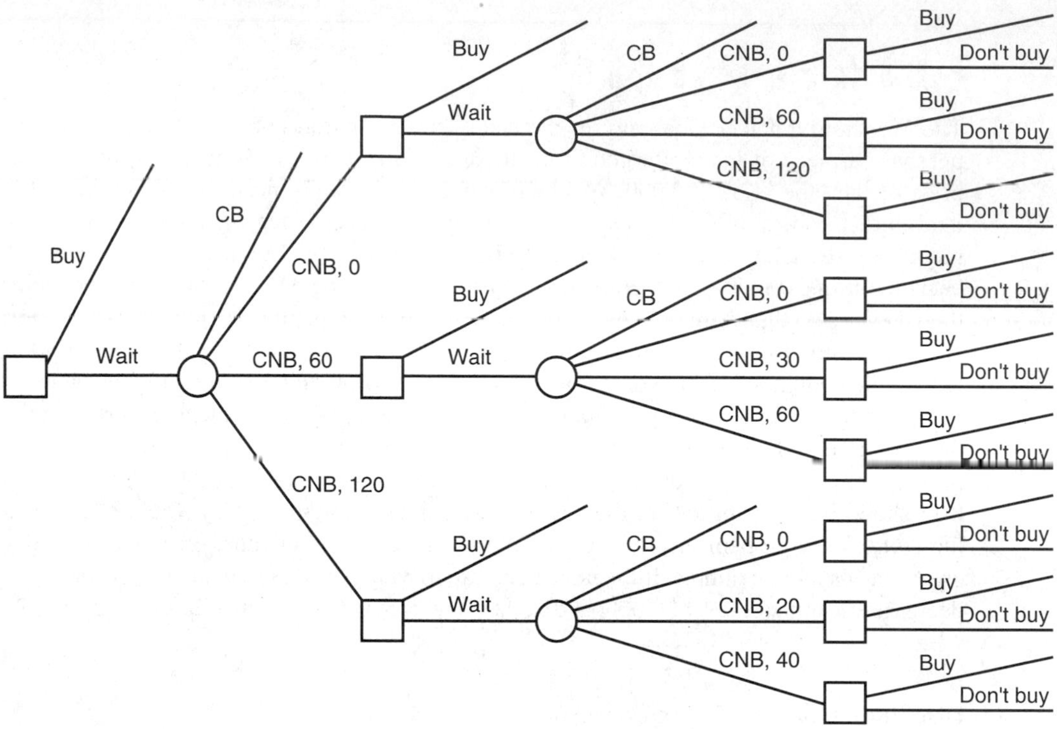

the problem is over—no branches follow. Also note how we have saved room by putting two uncertain outcomes on the same probability branch. Specifically, we have abbreviated the events where the competitor buys or does not buy the land as CB and CNB, and we have designated a price decrease by the amount of this decrease (in thousands of dollars). Then notation such as "CNB, 60" means that the competitor does not buy the land *and* the price decreases by \$60,000. (An alternative would be to have separate probability nodes and branches for the competitor's action and the price decreases, but this isn't necessary and only makes the tree bigger.) The probability of this joint event is the product of the individual probabilities.[5] For example, the probability of CNB, 60 in May is

$$\Pr(\text{CNB,60 in May}) = \Pr(\text{CNB in May})\,\Pr(\text{60 in May}) = (.95)(.3) = .285$$

Using TreePlan It is admittedly *very* tedious to build the tree for this problem with TreePlan. You can take a look at it in the file LAND.XLS, but the tree itself takes up too much room to show it here. Instead, we show a "hand" drawing of the completed tree (without labels, to keep the clutter to a minimum) in Figure 8.27. This figure shows the probabilities on the probability branches, the monetary values at the tips of all the branches, the EMVs on all nodes (from the folding back procedure), and marks on all decision branches that are not optimal. As this figure shows, Westhouser's optimal EMV is \$845,795. The optimal strategy is interesting. Westhouser should delay purchasing in May. Then if the land is still available in June, it should observe the new price. If the June price is the same as the May price, it should delay again and buy the land in July if it is

[5]We can multiply because of the implicit assumption that the competitor's action and the price decrease are probabilistically independent. This could easily be changed to increase the realism, but it makes sense if the price change doesn't take effect until after the competitor's action.

FIGURE 8.27 Completed Tree for Westhouser Example

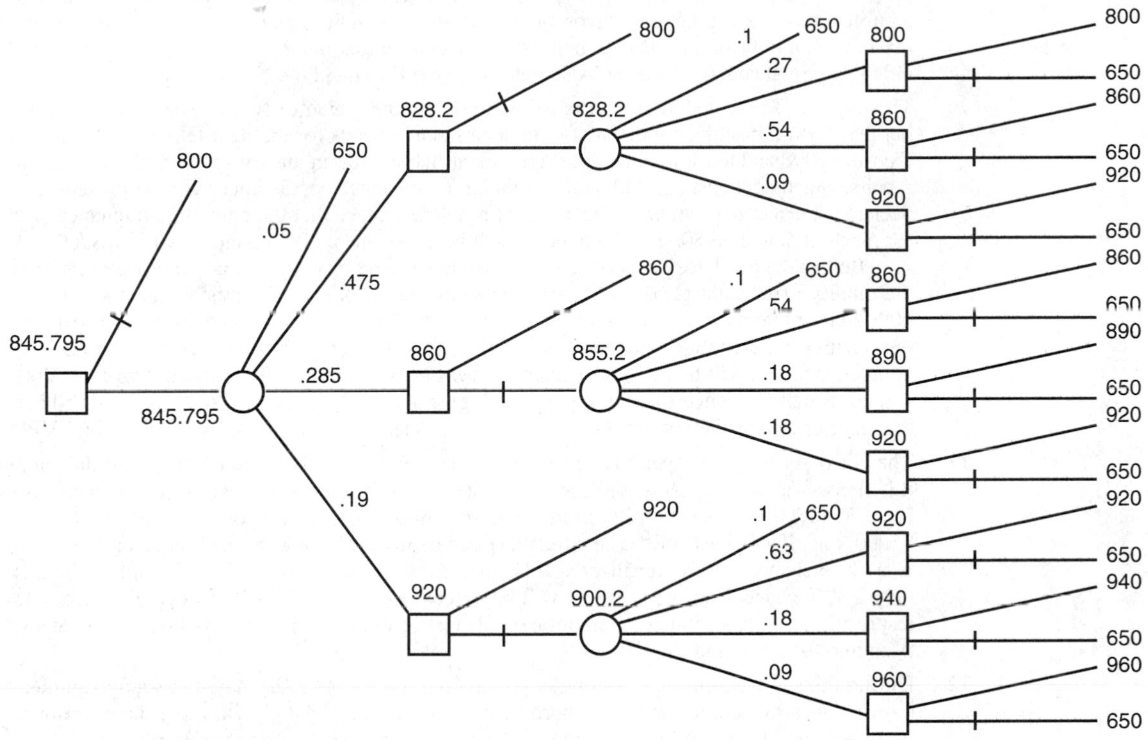

still available. Otherwise, if the June price is lower than the May price, it should buy the land in June.

If you try to build this decision tree with TreePlan (or even look at the one we built in the LAND.XLS file), you'll quickly see why a spreadsheet is not the best tool for solving large decision problems. They quickly go beyond the dimensions of the screen, and it is difficult to get a grasp of the entire tree. There are other decision analysis (nonspreadsheet) software packages available for solving larger problems, but we will not discuss them here.

Despite TreePlan's bulkiness in a problem such as Westhouser's, it does have one very good feature—its usefulness for sensitivity analysis. For example, after we build the tree in the LAND.XLS file, which has all probabilities and monetary values linked to input cells, it is easy to see what happens if Westhouser's payoff from other investments increases from \$650,000 to \$700,000. The new optimal EMV increases to \$850,727, and the optimal strategy changes only slightly. Now, if Westhouser observes either no change or a \$60,000 decrease in the land price in May, it should wait in June and buy in July. But as before, if the price decrease in May is \$120,000, it should buy the land in June. We found all of this new information just by changing the value in one input cell of the spreadsheet! ■

PROBLEMS

Skill-Building Problems

9 Oilco must determine whether or not to drill for oil in the South China Sea. It costs \$100,000 to drill, and if oil is found it is estimated that its value will be \$600,000. At present, Oilco believes there is a 45% chance that the field contains oil. Before drilling, Oilco can hire (for

$10,000) a geologist to obtain more information about the likelihood that the field will contain oil. There is a 50% chance that the geologist will issue a favorable report and a 50% chance of an unfavorable report. Given a favorable report, there is an 80% chance that the field contains oil. Given an unfavorable report, there is a 10% chance that the field contains oil. Determine Oilco's optimal course of action. Also determine the EVSI and the EVPI.

10 The decision sciences department is trying to determine which of two copying machines to purchase. Both machines will satisfy the department's needs for the next ten years. Machine 1 costs $2000 and has a maintenance agreement, which, for an annual fee of $150, covers all repairs. Machine 2 costs $3000, and its annual maintenance cost is uncertain. At present, the decision sciences department believes there is a 40% chance that the annual maintenance cost for machine 2 will be $0, a 40% chance it will be $100, and a 20% chance it will be $200.

Before the purchase decision is made, the department can have a trained repairer evaluate the quality of machine 2. If the repairer believes that machine 2 is satisfactory, there is a 60% chance that its annual maintenance cost will be $0 and a 40% chance it will be $100. If the repairer believes that machine 2 is unsatisfactory, there is a 20% chance that the annual maintenance cost will be $0, a 40% chance it will be $100, and a 40% chance it will be $200. If there is a 50% chance that the repairer will give a satisfactory report, what is the EVSI? If the repairer charges $40, what should the decision sciences department do? What is the EVPI?

11 The Nitro Fertilizer Company is developing a new fertilizer. If Nitro markets the product and it is successful, the company will earn a $50,000 profit; if it is unsuccessful, the company will lose $35,000. In the past, similar products have been successful 60% of the time. At a cost of $5000, the effectiveness of the new fertilizer can be tested. If the test result is favorable, there is an 80% chance that the fertilizer will be successful. If the test result is unfavorable, there is only a 30% chance that the fertilizer will be successful. There is a 60% chance of a favorable test result and a 40% chance of an unfavorable test result. Determine Nitro's optimal strategy. Also find the EVSI and the EVPI.

12 During the summer, Olympic swimmer Adam Johnson swims every day. On sunny summer days he goes to an outdoor pool, where he may swim for no charge. On rainy days he must go to a domed pool. At the beginning of the summer, he has the option of purchasing a $15 season pass to the domed pool, which allows him use for the entire summer. If he doesn't buy the season pass, he must pay $1 each time he goes there. Past meteorological records indicate that there is a 60% chance that the summer will be sunny (in which case there is an average of 6 rainy days during the summer) and a 40% chance the summer will be rainy (an average of 30 rainy days during the summer).

Before the summer begins, Adam has the option of purchasing a long-range weather forecast for $1. The forecast predicts a sunny summer 80% of the time and a rainy summer 20% of the time. If the forecast predicts a sunny summer, there is a 70% chance that the summer will actually be sunny. If the forecast predicts a rainy summer, there is an 80% chance that the summer will actually be rainy. Assuming that Adam's goal is to minimize his total expected cost for the summer, what should he do? Also find the EVSI and the EVPI.

13 Pete is considering placing a bet on the NCAA playoff game between Indiana and Purdue. Without any further information, he believes that each team has an equal chance to win. If he wins the bet, he will win $10,000; if he loses, he will lose $11,000. Before betting, he may pay Bobby $1,000 for his inside prediction on the game. Bobby will predict that Indiana will win 60% of the time, and 40% of the time, Bobby will predict that Purdue will win. When Bobby says that IU will win, IU has a 70% chance of winning, and when Bobby says that Purdue will win, IU has only a 20% chance of winning. Determine how Pete can maximize his total expected profit. What is the EVSI? What is the EVPI?

14 Erica is going to fly to London on August 5, 1994, and return home on August 20, 1994. It is now July 1, 1994. On July 1, 1994, she may buy a one-way ticket (for $350) or a round-trip ticket (for $660). She may also wait until August 1, 1994, to buy a ticket. On August 1, 1994, a one-way ticket will cost $370, and a round-trip ticket will cost $730. It is possible that between July 1 and August 1, her sister (who works for the airline) will be able to obtain a free one-way ticket for Erica. The probability that her sister will obtain the free ticket is .30. If Erica has bought a round-trip ticket on July 1 and her sister has obtained a free ticket, she may return "half" of her round-trip to the airline. In this case, her total cost will be $330 plus a $50 penalty. Use a decision tree approach to determine how to minimize Erica's expected cost of obtaining round-trip transportation to London.

15 I am a contestant on the TV show *Remote Jeopardy*, which works as follows. I am first asked a question in the category British Videos. If I answer correctly, I earn $100. I believe that I have an 80% chance of answering such a question correctly. If I answer incorrectly, the game is over, and I win nothing. If I answer correctly, I may leave with $100 or go on and answer a question in the category British TV Shows. If I answer this question correctly, I earn another $300, but if I answer incorrectly, I lose all previous earnings and am sent home. My chance of answering this question correctly is .60. If I answer the British TV Shows question correctly, I may leave with my earnings or go on and answer a question in the category Statistics. If I answer this question correctly, I earn another $500, but if I answer it incorrectly, I lose all previous earnings and am sent home. My chance of answering this question correctly is .40. Draw a decision tree that can be used to maximize my expected earnings. What are my expected earnings?

16 A candy company knows that it will need ten tons of sugar six months from now. The company has two basic options. It can buy the sugar at the going price when it needs it, six months from now, or it can buy a futures contract today. This contract guarantees delivery of the sugar in six months but at today's price. There are two futures contracts available, a five-ton contract and a ten-ton contract. This gives the company three options: (1) buy a single ten-ton contract, (2) buy a single five-ton futures contract and buy the other five tons in six months, or (3) buy all ten tons in six months.

The price of sugar bought now for delivery in six months is 8.51¢ per pound. The transaction cost for a five-ton futures contract is $65; for a ten-ton contract it is $110. (This explains why the company does not need to consider two five-ton contracts; the transaction cost would be larger than for a single ten-ton contract.) Finally, the company assumes that the possible prices of sugar six months from now (in cents per pound) are 7.8, 8.3, 8.7, 9.1, and 9.6, with corresponding probabilities .04, .28, .38, .18, and .12. Which decision minimizes the company's expected cost of obtaining the required sugar?

17 A drugstore that provides film-developing services is trying to decide on its pricing policy for 24-print rolls of color film. It will choose one of the following options (and then use it for all customers): (1) charge a flat $5.25 per roll, or (2) charge 24¢ for each print the customer decides to accept. From past data, a typical customer will refuse either 0, 1, 2, 3, or 4 prints with corresponding probabilities .60, .15, .10, .08, and .07. Use a decision tree to find the pricing policy that maximizes the store's EMV. If the store's cost of developing a 24-print roll is C dollars, is the answer to the problem dependent on the value of C?

Skill-Extending Problems

In many decision tree problems, the decision maker's goal is to maximize the probability of a favorable event occurring. To incorporate this goal into a decision tree, we simply assign a reward of 1 to any terminal branch that results in the favorable event occurring and a reward of 0 to any terminal branch that results in the favorable event not occurring. Then maximizing the expected reward is the same as maximizing the probability that the favorable event occurs. Use this idea to solve the next two problems.

18 The American chess master Jonathan Meller is playing the Soviet expert Yuri Gasparov in a two-game exhibition match. Each win earns a player one point, and each draw earns a half point. The player who has the most points after two games wins the match. If the players are tied after two games, they play until one wins a game; then the first player to win a game wins the match. During each game, Meller has two possible strategies: to play a daring strategy or to play a conservative strategy. His probabilities of winning, losing, and drawing when he follows each strategy are shown in Table 8.13. To maximize his probability of winning the match, what should the American do?

TABLE 8.13 Probabilities for Chess Problem

Strategy	Win	Loss	Draw
Daring	0.45	0.55	0.00
Conservative	0.00	0.10	0.90

19 Yvonne Delaney is playing Chris Becker a single point for the women's world tennis championship. She has won the coin toss and elected to serve. If she tries a hard serve, her probability of getting the serve into play is .60. Given that the hard serve is in play, she has a .60 chance of winning the point. If she tries a soft serve, her probability of getting the serve in play is .90, but if the soft serve is in play, her probability of winning the point is only .50. To maximize her probability of winning the point, what should Yvonne do?

20 In trying to decide how to design a space vehicle, NASA needs to know whether to provide zero, one, or two backup systems for an important part of the vehicle. The first backup system (if provided) comes into use only if the original system fails. The second backup (if provided) comes into use only if the original system and the first backup both fail. The engineers claim that each system, independently of the others, has a .01 probability of failing if called into use. Each backup system costs $70,000 to produce and install. Once in flight, the mission will fail only if the original system and all backups fail. The cost of a mission failure (in addition to production costs) is assessed at $8 million. How many backups should be provided in order to minimize the total expected cost?

21 Ms. Foyt has just bought a new $15,000 car. Being an average driver, she believes that her chances of having an accident in the next year are 1 out of 20. If she does have an accident, she assesses that the possible damage amounts are $100, $500, $2000, and $15,000 with (conditional) probabilities .6, .2, .1, and .1. (These probabilities are conditional on having an accident.) How much should Ms. Foyt be willing to pay for a $150-deductible collision insurance policy? (With this type of insurance, she pays the first $150 if she causes an accident, and the insurance company pays the rest.)

22 In the previous problem, suppose that a $250-deductible insurance policy is also available. How much less would Ms. Foyt be willing to pay for this than for the $150-deductible insurance policy? Intuitively, why is a $150-deductible insurance policy not worth $100 more than a $250-deductible insurance policy?

23 A patient enters the hospital with severe abdominal pains. Based on past experience, Dr. Craig believes there is a 28% chance that the patient has appendicitis and a 72% chance that the patient has nonspecific abdominal pains. Dr. Craig may operate on the patient now or wait 12 hours to gain a more accurate diagnosis. In 12 hours, Dr. Craig will surely know whether the patient has appendicitis. The problem is that in the meantime, the patient's appendix may perforate (if he has appendicitis), thereby making the operation much more dangerous. Again based on past experience, Dr. Craig believes that if she waits 12 hours, there is a 6% chance that the patient will end up with a perforated appendix, a 22% chance the patient will end up with "normal" appendicitis, and a 72% chance that the patient will end up with nonspecific abdominal pain. From past experience, Dr. Craig assesses the following probabilities that the patient will die. If she operates on a patient with appendicitis, this probability is .0009; if she operates on a patient with nonspecific abdominal pain, it is .0004; if she operates on a perforated appendix, it is .0064; and if she does not operate on a patient with nonspecific abdominal pain, it is 0. Assume that Dr. Craig's goal is to maximize the probability that the patient will survive. Use a decision tree to help Dr. Craig make the right decision. ■

8.5 Bayes' Rule

Until now we have taken the probabilities on the probability branches as given. The only restriction is that the probabilities emanating from any probability node must sum to 1. When uncertain events are probabilistically dependent, however, there are certain "consistency" conditions that must be met. As an example, we look again at Acme's marketing problem (Example 8.4). Three types of probabilities are given:

Type 1: Probabilities of national market outcomes without any test market

Type 2: Probabilities of test market outcomes

Type 3: Probabilities of national market outcomes given the possible test market outcomes

As we mentioned briefly when we discussed sensitivity analysis for Acme's problem, these probabilities are related. In fact, the relationship between these probabilities is Acme's real incentive for spending money on the test market information. By obtaining this information, it is able to "update" the probabilities of national market success or failure on the basis of the test market results it observes. Specifically, it uses a result called **Bayes' rule** to update these probabilities.

We'll show how Bayes' rule works for Acme's problem and then discuss it in general. For Acme's problem, let S_N and F_N denote success and failure in the national market, and let S_T and F_T denote success and failure in the test market. We used the following probabilities (of types 1, 2, and 3) for the decision tree:

$$\Pr(S_N) = 1 - \Pr(F_N) = .5 \tag{8.1}$$

$$\Pr(S_T) = 1 - \Pr(F_T) = .6 \tag{8.2}$$

and

$$\Pr(S_N|S_T) = 1 - \Pr(F_N|S_T) = .7$$

$$\Pr(S_N|F_T) = 1 - \Pr(F_N|F_T) = .2 \tag{8.3}$$

(Recall in general that a probability such as $\Pr(A|B)$ is a *conditional* probability and should be read as "the probability of A given B." Therefore, the probability $\Pr(S_N|S_T)$, for example, is the probability of national market success, given that the test market was successful.)

It is common to refer to the probabilities in 8.1, 8.2, and 8.3 by name. The probabilities in 8.1 are called **prior probabilities**. They are the probabilities of national market outcomes prior to any test market information. In contrast, the probabilities in 8.3 are called **posterior probabilities**. They are the probabilities of national market outcomes *after* (or posterior to) the test market results. Finally, the probabilities in 8.2 are the **information probabilities**. They are the probabilities of the different information (test market) outcomes. Recall from the Acme example that these three sets of probabilities are exactly the probabilities we needed in the decision tree. (See Figure 8.22, for example.)

Sometimes, however, the probabilities in 8.2 and 8.3 are *not* the probabilities that are most easily assessed. Let's consider what historical information Acme might use to assess various probabilities. First, the company might have observed that approximately half of similar products marketed nationally in the past were successes. This would lead directly to the probability assessment in 8.1—the prior probabilities. Next, it might have observed that of all those products that were eventually national successes and were first test marketed, 84% had successful test markets. This would lead to the probability assessment

$$\Pr(S_T|S_N) = 1 - \Pr(F_T|S_N) = .84 \tag{8.4}$$

Finally, it might have observed that of all those products that were eventually national failures and were first test marketed, only 36% had successful test markets. This would lead to the probability assessment

$$\Pr(S_T|F_N) = 1 - \Pr(F_T|F_N) = .36 \tag{8.5}$$

The probabilities in 8.4 and 8.5 are often called **likelihoods**, or more specifically, likelihoods of sample information (test market outcomes) given the eventual national market results. As we see, these likelihoods might be easy to assess from historical data. Unfortunately, they are "backward" from the probabilities needed in the decision tree. Contrast, for example, $\Pr(S_T|F_N)$ with $\Pr(F_N|S_T)$. The first is a likelihood assessed from historical data; the second is a posterior probability needed in the decision tree.

Bayes' rule transforms prior probabilities and likelihoods into posterior probabilities. As a by-product it also gives us the information probabilities (of test market results). For Acme's problem Bayes' rule can be stated as follows. Let B be either of the national market outcomes (S_N or F_N), let $\overline{B}$ be the opposite of B (for example, $\overline{B} = S_N$ if $B = F_N$), and let A be either of the test market outcomes (S_T or F_T). Then Bayes' rule is

$$\Pr(B|A) = \frac{\Pr(A|B)\Pr(B)}{\Pr(A|B)\Pr(B) + \Pr(A|\overline{B})\Pr(\overline{B})} \tag{8.6}$$

For example, if $B = S_N$, $\overline{B} = F_N$, and $A = S_T$ (so that a successful test market has been observed), then using the assessed probabilities in 8.1, 8.4, and 8.5 in the right-hand side of Bayes' rule, we obtain

$$\Pr(S_N|S_T) = \frac{\Pr(S_T|S_N)\Pr(S_N)}{\Pr(S_T|S_N)\Pr(S_N) + \Pr(S_T|F_N)\Pr(F_N)}$$

$$= \frac{.84(.5)}{.84(.5) + .36(.5)} = \frac{.42}{.60} = .7 \tag{8.7}$$

which implies that $\Pr(F_N|S_T) = 1 - .7 = .3$.

Similarly, if $B = S_N$, $\overline{B} = F_N$, and $A = F_T$ (so that an unsuccessful test market has been observed), then

$$\Pr(S_N|F_T) = \frac{\Pr(F_T|S_N)\Pr(S_N)}{\Pr(F_T|S_N)\Pr(S_N) + \Pr(F_T|F_N)\Pr(F_N)}$$

$$= \frac{.16(.5)}{.16(.5) + .64(.5)} = \frac{.08}{.40} = .2 \tag{8.8}$$

This implies that $\Pr(F_N|F_T) = 1 - .2 = .8$. You can check Figure 8.22 to see that these are exactly the posterior probabilities that were used in the decision tree.

Finally, the denominators in Equations 8.7 and 8.8 give useful by-products that are also needed in the decision tree. Specifically, the denominator of 8.7 is the probability of a successful test market:

$$\Pr(S_T) = .6$$

Similarly, the denominator of 8.8 is the probability of an unsuccessful test market:

$$\Pr(F_T) = .4$$

Again, you can check that these probabilities were used in the decision tree in Figure 8.22.

Bayes' rule is a formal mechanism for updating probabilities as new information becomes available. However, it is also intuitive. For example, Acme started by thinking that national market success and national market failure are equally likely, each with probability .5. If the company receives the information that a test market was successful, then the probability of a national market success ought to increase. Equation 8.7 confirms this—the probability of a national market success increases from .5 to .7. If Acme receives the information that the test market was a failure, then the probability of a national market success ought to decrease. Again, Equation 8.8 confirms this—the probability of a national market success decreases from .5 to .2.

Bayes' Rule in a Spreadsheet

The above formulas make Bayes' rule look more complex than it really is. We can use these formulas to implement Bayes' rule in Excel, which will probably help to simplify the rule. We show the calculations in Figure 8.28. (See the File BAYES.XLS.) Here, SN and FN are the same as S_N and F_N, and ST and FT are the same as S_T and F_T. To produce this spreadsheet, we use the following steps.

FIGURE 8.28 **Bayes' Rule in Excel**

	A	B	C	D	E	F
1	**Illustration of Bayes' rule using Acme example**					
2						
3	Prior probabilities					
4		SN	FN			
5		0.5	0.5			
6						
7	Likelihoods					
8		SN	FN			
9	ST	0.84	0.36			
10	FT	0.16	0.64			
11						
12	Joint probabilities (multiply priors by likelihoods)					
13		SN	FN		Information probabilities (sum)	
14	ST	0.42	0.18		0.6	
15	FT	0.08	0.32		0.4	
16						
17	Posteriors (divide by information probabilities)					
18		SN	FN			
19	ST	0.7	0.3			
20	FT	0.2	0.8			

1 **Inputs.** Enter the prior probabilities in the range B5:C5 and enter the likelihoods in the range B9:C10. Make sure you get them in the right order. To check, make sure that the priors add to 1 and the sum of the likelihoods in each column is 1.

2 **Joint probabilities.** As an intermediate step, multiply each likelihood by the prior in its column and put the results in the range B14:C15. Specifically, enter the formula

=B$5*B9

in cell B14 and copy it to the range B14:C15. These products have meaning in their own right. For example, the probability in cell B14 is the probability of the "joint" event that the test market is a success *and* the national market is a success.

3 **Information probabilities.** Sum the joint probabilities in each row and put the results in the range E14:E15. For example, the probability in cell E14 is the probability that the test market is a success. To check, make sure the information probabilities add to 1.

4 **Posterior probabilities.** Divide each joint probability by the information probability in its row to obtain the posterior probabilities in the range B19:C20. Specifically, enter the formula

=B14/$E14

in cell B19 and copy it to the range B19:C20. To check, make sure the posterior probabilities in each *row* add to 1.

This spreadsheet procedure can be used regardless of the size of the problem, that is, regardless of the number of national market outcomes or the number of test market outcomes. For example, Figure 8.29 demonstrates the same procedure where the national market and the test market each have "moderate success" and "moderate failure"

FIGURE 8.29 **Bayes' Rule with More Than Two Outcomes**

	A	B	C	D	E	F	G
1	**Bayes' rule with more outcomes**						
2							
3	Prior probabilities						
4		SN	MSN	MFN	FN		
5		0.20	0.30	0.40	0.10	1	
6							
7	Likelihoods						
8		SN	MSN	MFN	FN		
9	ST	0.64	0.34	0.12	0.10		
10	MST	0.20	0.40	0.35	0.26		
11	MFT	0.10	0.16	0.29	0.30		
12	FT	0.06	0.10	0.24	0.34		
13		1	1	1	1		
14	Joint probabilities (multiply priors by likelihoods)						
15		SN	MSN	MFN	FN		Information probabilities (sum)
16	ST	0.128	0.102	0.048	0.010		0.288
17	MST	0.040	0.120	0.140	0.026		0.326
18	MFT	0.020	0.048	0.116	0.030		0.214
19	FT	0.012	0.030	0.096	0.034		0.172
20							1
21	Posteriors (divide by information probabilities)						
22		SN	MSN	MFN	FN		
23	ST	0.444	0.354	0.167	0.035	1	
24	MST	0.123	0.368	0.429	0.080	1	
25	MFT	0.093	0.224	0.542	0.140	1	
26	FT	0.070	0.174	0.558	0.198	1	

categories, designated by MSN, MFN, MST, and MFT, in addition to the original success and failure categories. (This spreadsheet is also in the BAYES.XLS file.) The main difficulty here is that Acme has to assess more prior probabilities and likelihoods. However, once they are assessed, the computational procedure to implement Bayes' rule is exactly as before. Note that we have included several row and column sums in this spreadsheet, just to remind you which probabilities ought to sum to 1.

A Drug-Testing Example

The following problem concerning drug testing of athletes is another example of Bayes' rule that shows even more clearly how prior probabilities are combined with sample information to obtain posterior probabilities. (See Feinstein [5] for a real application of this example.)

EXAMPLE 8.6

If an athlete is tested for a certain type of drug usage (steroids, say), then the test will come out either positive or negative. However, these tests are never perfect. Some athletes who are drug free test positive, and some who are drug users test negative. (The former are called false positives; the latter are called false negatives.) The question then is what we can conclude from a positive or negative test result.

Solution

Let D and $\overline{D}$ denote that the athlete is or is not a drug user, and let $T+$ and $T-$ indicate a positive or negative test result. We will first identify the priors, the posteriors, and the likelihoods for this example. The prior probabilities reflect the chances that a randomly chosen athlete uses drugs. For example, if 5% of the total athlete population are drug users, then the priors are $\Pr(D) = .05$ and $\Pr(\overline{D}) = .95$.

The likelihoods reflect the "reliability" of the test. For example, let's suppose that the test produces 8% false negatives and 3% false positives. In words, 8% of athletes who use drugs test negative, and 3% of athletes who do not use drugs test positive. Then two of the likelihoods are $\Pr(T-|D) = .08$ and $\Pr(T+|\overline{D}) = .03$. These are error probabilities. They imply the other two likelihoods, the probabilities of correct test results: $\Pr(T+|D) = .92$ and $\Pr(T-|\overline{D}) = .97$.

Given these priors and likelihoods, we want posteriors such as $\Pr(D|T+)$, the probability that an athlete who tested positive is a drug user, or $\Pr(\overline{D}|T-)$, the probability that an athlete who tested negative is drug free. These are calculated in Figure 8.30, using exactly the same procedure as in the Acme example. (See the file DRUGS.XLS.)

FIGURE 8.30 **Bayes' Rule for Drug-Testing Example**

	A	B	C	D	E
1	**Bayes' rule for drug-testing example**				
2					
3	Prior probabilities				
4		Drug user	Drug free		
5		0.05	0.95		
6					
7	Likelihoods				
8		Drug user	Drug free		
9	Tests positive	0.92	0.03		
10	Tests negative	0.08	0.97		
11					
12	Joint probabilities (multiply priors by likelihoods)				
13		Drug user	Drug free		Information probabilities (sum)
14	Tests positive	0.046	0.029		0.075
15	Tests negative	0.004	0.922		0.926
16					
17	Posteriors (divide by information probabilities)				
18		Drug user	Drug free		
19	Tests positive	0.617	0.383		
20	Tests negative	0.004	0.996		

Notice that a negative test result leaves little doubt that the athlete is drug free. The posterior probability that the athlete is drug free, given a negative test result, is .996. However, there is still a lot of doubt about an athlete who tests positive. The posterior probability that the athlete uses drugs, given a positive test result, is only .617. This asymmetry occurs because of the prior probabilities. We are fairly certain that a randomly selected athlete is drug free because only 5% of the athletes use drugs. It takes a lot of evidence to convince us otherwise. This initial bias, plus the fact that the test produces a few false positives, means that athletes with positive test results still have a decent chance (probability .383) of being drug free. Is this a valid argument for not requiring drug testing of athletes? We explore this question in the following continuation of the drug-testing example. It all depends on the "costs." (It might also depend on whether there is a second type of test that could help confirm the findings of the first test. However, we won't consider such a test.) ■

EXAMPLE 8.7

The administrators at State University are trying to decide whether to institute mandatory drug testing for the athletes. They have the same information about priors and likelihoods as above, but now they want to use a decision tree approach to see whether benefits outweigh the costs.[6]

Solution

We have already discussed the uncertain outcomes and their probabilities. Now we need to discuss the decision alternatives and the monetary values—the other two elements of a decision analysis. We will assume that there are only two alternatives: perform drug testing on all athletes or don't perform any drug testing. In the former case, we assume that if an athlete tests positive, this athlete is barred from sports.

The "monetary" values are more difficult to assess. They include

- the benefit B from correctly identifying a drug user and barring him or her from sports
- the cost C_1 of the test itself for a single athlete (materials and labor)
- the cost C_2 of falsely accusing a non-user (and barring him or her from sports)
- the cost C_3 of not identifying a drug user (either by not testing at all or by obtaining a false negative)
- the cost C_4 of violating a non-user's privacy by performing the test

It is clear that only C_1 is a direct monetary cost that is easy to measure. However, the other "costs" and the benefit B are real, and they must be compared on some scale in order for the administrators to make a rational decision. We will do so by comparing everything to the cost C_1, to which we will assign value 1. (This does not mean that the cost of testing an athlete is necessarily $1; it just means that we will express all other costs as multiples of C_1.) Clearly, there is a lot of subjectivity involved in making these comparisons, so sensitivity analysis on the final decision tree is a must.

Before developing this decision tree, it is useful to form a benefit-cost table for both alternatives and all possible outcomes. Because we will eventually maximize expected net *benefit*, all benefits in this table have a positive sign and all costs have a negative sign. These net benefits appear in Table 8.14. The first two columns are relevant if no tests are performed; the last four are relevant when testing is performed. For example, if a positive test is obtained for a non-user, there are three costs: the cost of the test (C_1), the cost of falsely accusing the athlete (C_2), and the cost of violating the non-user's privacy (C_4). The other entries are obtained similarly.

[6] Again, see Feinstein [5] for an enlightening discussion of this drug-testing problem at a particular university.

TABLE 8.14 Net Benefit for Drug-Testing Example

Don't Test		Perform Test			
D	$\overline{D}$	D and $T+$	$\overline{D}$ and $T+$	D and $T-$	$\overline{D}$ and $T-$
$-C_3$	0	$B - C_1$	$-(C_1 + C_2 + C_4)$	$-(C_1 + C_3)$	$-(C_1 + C_4)$

Using TreePlan The solution with TreePlan is now fairly straightforward. We first enter all of the benefits and costs in an input section. These, together with the Bayes' rule calculations from before, appear in Figure 8.31. (See the file DRUGS.XLS.) Then we use TreePlan to build the tree in the usual way and enter the links to the values and probabilities in Figure 8.31. The completed tree appears in Figure 8.32.

FIGURE 8.31 Inputs for Drug-Testing Example Decision Tree

	A	B	C	D	E
1	Drug testing decision analysis				
2					
3	Benefits/costs (per athlete)				
4	Identifying drug user (B)	25			
5	Cost of test (C1)	1			
6	Barring non-user (C2)	50			
7	Not identifying user (C3)	20			
8	Violation of privacy (C4)	2			
9					
10	Prior probabilities				
11		Drug user	Drug free		
12		0.05	0.95		
13					
14	Likelihoods				
15		Drug user	Drug free		
16	Tests positive	0.92	0.03		
17	Tests negative	0.08	0.97		
18					
19	Joint probabilities (multiply priors by likelihoods)				
20		Drug user	Drug free		Information probabilities (sum)
21	Tests positive	0.046	0.029		0.075
22	Tests negative	0.004	0.922		0.926
23					
24	Posteriors (divide by information probabilities)				
25		Drug user	Drug free		
26	Tests positive	0.617	0.383		
27	Tests negative	0.004	0.996		

Before we interpret this solution, there are a couple of things you should note. First, look at the timing (from left to right). If drug testing is performed, the result of the drug test is observed first (a probability node). Each test result leads to an action (bar from sports or don't), and then the eventual benefit or cost depends on whether the athlete uses drugs (again a probability node). (You might argue that the university never knows for

FIGURE 8.32 Decision Tree for Drug-Testing Example

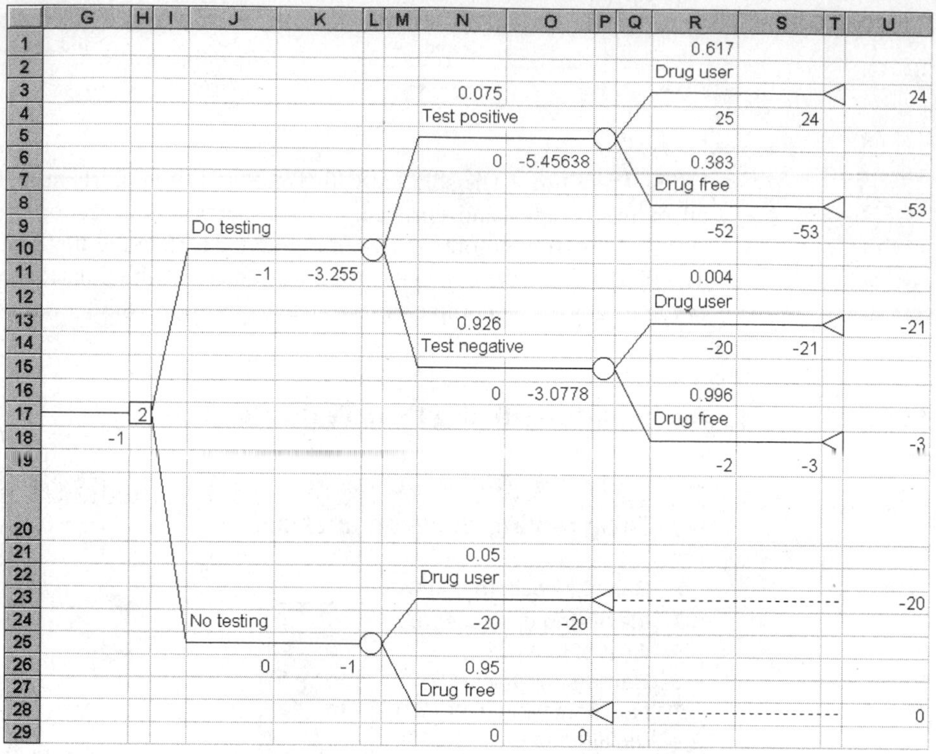

certain whether the athlete uses drugs, but we must include this information in the tree in order to get the benefits and costs correct.) If no drug testing is performed, then there is no intermediate test result node or branches. Second, note that we entered the cost of testing where it occurs in time—in cell J11. We could have left this cell equal to 0 and included the testing cost in cells R4, R9, R14, and R19. It doesn't matter which way you do it—just don't include this cost in *both* places.

Now to the interpretation. First, we discuss the benefits and costs shown in Figure 8.31. These were chosen fairly arbitrarily, but with some hope of reflecting reality. They say that the largest cost is falsely accusing (and barring) a non-user. This is 50 times as large as the cost of the test. The benefit of identifying a drug user is only half this large, and the cost of not identifying a user is 40% as large as barring a non-user. The violation of privacy of a non-user is only twice as large as the cost of the test. Based on these values, the decision tree implies that drug testing should *not* be performed. The EMVs for testing and for not testing are both negative, indicating that the costs outweigh the benefits for each, but the EMV for not testing is slightly less negative.[7]

What would it take to change this decision? We'll start with the assumption, probably accepted by most people in our society, that the cost of falsely accusing a non-user (C_2) ought to be the largest of the benefits or costs in the range B4:B8. In fact, because of possible legal costs, you might argue that C_2 should be *more* than 50 times the cost of the test. But if you increase C_2, the scales are tipped even farther in the direction of not testing. On the other hand, if the benefit B from identifying a user or the cost C_3 for not identifying a user increase, then testing might be the preferred alternative. We tried this, keeping C_2 constant at 50. When B and C_3 both had value 45, no testing was still the

[7] The university in the Feinstein study [5] came to the same conclusion.

winner, but when they both increased to 50—the same magnitude as C_2—then testing won out by a small margin. However, it would be difficult to argue that B and C_3 should be of the same magnitude as C_2.

Other than the benefits and costs, the only other thing we might vary is the accuracy of the test, measured by the error probabilities in cells B17 and C16. Presumably, if the test makes fewer false positives and false negatives, testing might be a more attractive alternative. We tried this, keeping the benefits and costs the same as those shown in Figure 8.31 but changing the error probabilities. Even when each error probability was decreased to .01, however, the no-testing alternative was still the winner—by a fairly wide margin.

In summary, based on a number of reasonable assumptions and parameter settings, this example has shown that it is difficult to make a case for mandatory drug testing. ■

PROBLEMS

Skill-Building Problems

24 Consider a population of 1000 people, 400 of whom are college graduates. It is known that 150 of the college graduates earn at least \$30,000 per year, and 100 of the non–college graduates make at least \$30,000 per year.

- **a** What is the probability that a randomly chosen person makes at least \$30,000 per year?
- **b** If a randomly chosen person is observed to make at least \$30,000 per year, what is the probability that this person is a college graduate?
- **c** If a randomly chosen person is observed to make less than \$30,000 per year, what is the probability that this person is not a college graduate?

25 Most baseball teams win much more regularly when they play at their home field. One particular team wins 58% of its home games and only 45% of its away games. Half of its games are at home and half are away. If we hear that this team has just won a game but we are not told where the game was played, what is the probability that it was played at the team's home field?

26 In a state with mandatory yearly automobile inspections, it is estimated that 15% of all cars have problems that need to be corrected. Unfortunately, the inspections fail to catch these problems, when they are present, 10% of the time. Consider a car that is inspected and nothing is found to be wrong. What is the probability that there is indeed something wrong that the inspection has failed to catch? (Assume that if there is really nothing wrong, the inspection will not find anything wrong.)

27 A financial analyst has just received information that could affect the price of a particular stock in the next few days. He is 75% certain that the information is correct. If it is correct, he assesses that the price of the stock will fall in the next few days with probability .8, and that it will rise or remain unchanged with probability .2. If the information is incorrect, he believes that the two possibilities just described are equally likely.

- **a** If the price of the stock falls in the next few days, what is the probability that the information was correct?
- **b** If the price of the stock does not fall, what is the probability that the information was correct?

28 A customer has approached a bank for a \$50,000 one-year loan at a 12% interest rate. If the bank does not approve the loan, the \$50,000 will be invested in bonds that earn a 6% annual return. Without further information, the bank believes that there is a 4% chance that the customer will totally default on the loan. If the customer totally defaults, the bank loses \$50,000. At a cost of \$500, the bank can thoroughly investigate the customer's credit record and supply a favorable or unfavorable recommendation. Past experience indicates that

$$\text{Pr(Favorable recommendation}|\text{customer doesn't default)} = 77/96$$

$$\text{Pr(Favorable recommendation}|\text{customer defaults)} = 1/4$$

How can the bank maximize its expected profits? Also find the EVSI and the EVPI.

29 A nuclear power company is deciding whether or not to build a nuclear power plant at Diablo Canyon or at Roy Rogers City. The cost of building the power plant is \$10 million at Diablo and \$20 million at Roy Rogers City. If the company builds at Diablo, however, and an earthquake occurs at Diablo during the next five years, construction will be terminated and the company will lose \$10 million (and will still have to build a power plant at Roy Rogers City). Without further expert information the company believes there is a 20% chance that an earthquake will occur at Diablo during the next five years. For \$1 million, a geologist can be hired to analyze the fault structure at Diablo Canyon. She will either predict that an earthquake will occur or that an earthquake will not occur. The geologist's past record indicates that she will predict an earthquake on 95% of the occasions for which an earthquake will occur and no earthquake on 90% of the occasions for which an earthquake will not occur. Should the power company hire the geologist? Also find the EVSI and the EVPI.

30 Farmer Jones must determine whether to plant corn or wheat. If he plants corn and the weather is warm, he earns \$8000; if he plants corn and the weather is cold, he earns \$5000. If he plants wheat and the weather is warm, he earns \$7000; if he plants wheat and the weather is cold, he earns \$6500. In the past, 40% of all years have been cold and 60% have been warm. Before planting, Jones can pay \$600 for an expert weather forecast. If the year is actually cold, there is a 90% chance that the forecaster will predict a cold year. If the year is actually warm, there is an 80% chance that the forecaster will predict a warm year. How can Jones maximize his expected profits? Also find the EVSI and the EVPI.

31 The NBS television network earns an average of \$400,000 from a hit show and loses an average of \$100,000 on a flop. Of all shows reviewed by the network, 25% turn out to be hits and 75% turn out to be flops. For \$40,000, a market research firm will have an audience view a pilot of a prospective show and give its view about whether the show will be a hit or a flop. If a show is actually going to be a hit, there is a 90% chance that the market research firm will predict the show to be a hit. If the show is actually going to be a flop, there is an 80% chance that the market research firm will predict the show to be a flop. Determine how the network can maximize its expected profits. Also find the EVSI and the EVPI.

32 We are thinking of filming the life of Dennis Robman. We know that if the film is a flop, we will lose \$4 million, and if the film is a success, we will earn \$15 million. Beforehand, we believe that there is a 10% chance that the Dennis Robman story will be a hit. Before filming, we have the option of paying the noted movie critic Paulene Keel \$1 million for her view of the film. In the past, Keel has predicted 60% of all actual hits to be hits and 90% of all actual flops to be flops. We want to maximize our expected profits. Use a decision tree to determine our best strategy. What is the EVSI? What is the EVPI?

Skill-Extending Problems

33 Ms. Stevens wishes to buy a tractor lawn mower from the Rider company. The company buys these mowers for \$5000 and is currently selling them for \$5200. Because \$5200 is more cash than Ms. Stevens has, she asks if she can pay on an installment plan. Under this plan she pays a \$200 down payment and the other \$5000 over the next 15 months. The company needs to decide whether to let her do this, because it has recently been having problems with people defaulting on installment loans. The company's experience shows that 10% of its customers default, and on these it can expect to recover only 20% of the loan value.

Before making a decision on Ms. Stevens's request, Rider can buy information about her credit rating. This information will show that she is in the high risk (HR), medium risk (MR), or low risk (LR) category. Also, the credit-rating service claims the following conditional probabilities (obtained from historical frequencies). Here D stands for default, and ND stands for no default.

$$\Pr(\text{HR}|\text{D}) = .65,\ \Pr(\text{MR}|\text{D}) = .30,\ \Pr(\text{LR}|\text{D}) = .05$$

$$\Pr(\text{HR}|\text{ND}) = .20,\ \Pr(\text{MR}|\text{ND}) = .25,\ \Pr(\text{LR}|\text{ND}) = .55$$

For example, 65% of people who eventually default are rated in the high-risk category. The rating service charges R dollars for its information.

a If $R = \$50$, what is Rider's best strategy. (The strategy must specify whether to obtain the rating's services and whether to give Ms. Stevens the loan.)

b For what values of R should Rider purchase the rating's services?

34 A company is considering whether to market a new product. For simplicity, assume that if the product is marketed, there are only two possible outcomes, success (S) or failure (F). The company assesses that the probabilities of these two outcomes are p and $1 - p$. If the product is marketed and it is a failure, the company will suffer a loss of \$300,000. If the product is marketed and it is a success, the company will gain \$500,000. There is no cost (or gain) from not marketing the product. The company is also considering whether to take a survey, the results of which can be classified as favorable, neutral, or unfavorable. The conditional probabilities for the results of the survey, conditional on whether the product would eventually be a success or a failure, are

$$\text{Pr(Favorable|S)} = .6, \ \text{Pr(Neutral|S)} = .3, \ \text{Pr(Unfavorable|S)} = .1$$

$$\text{Pr(Favorable|F)} = .1, \ \text{Pr(Neutral|F)} = .2, \ \text{Pr(Unfavorable|F)} = .7$$

(These probabilities have been estimated from the successes and failures of previous products.) The survey costs C dollars.

a Make up some specific data on past products that could lead to these conditional probabilities.

b What is the *largest* amount the company should pay for perfect information if $p = .4$; if $p = .5$?

c If $p = .4$, find the EVSI. What is the expected net gain from the survey (over no survey) if $C = \$10,000$ and $p = .4$?

35 The government is attempting to determine whether immigrants should be tested for a contagious disease. Let's assume that the decision will be made on a financial basis. Assume that each immigrant who is allowed into the country and has the disease costs the United States \$100,000, and each immigrant who enters and does not have the disease will contribute \$10,000 to the national economy. Assume that 10% of all potential immigrants have the disease. The government can admit all immigrants, admit no immigrants, or test immigrants for the disease before determining whether they should be admitted. It costs \$100 to test a person for the disease; the test result is either positive or negative. A person who does not have the disease always tests negative. However, 20% of all people who *do* have the disease test negative. The government's goal is to maximize (per potential immigrant) expected benefits minus expected costs. Use a decision tree to aid in this undertaking. Also determine the EVSI and the EVPI. ■

8.6

Incorporating Attitudes Toward Risk

Rational decision makers are sometimes willing to violate the EMV maximization criterion when large amounts of money are at stake. These decision makers are willing to sacrifice some EMV in order to reduce risk. Are you ever willing to do so personally? Consider the following scenarios.

1 You have a chance to enter a lottery where you will win \$100,000 with probability .10 or win nothing with probability .90. Alternatively, you can receive \$5000 for certain. How many of you (truthfully) would take the certain \$5000, even though the EMV of the lottery is \$10,000? Or change the \$100,000 to \$1,000,000 and the \$5000 to \$50,000 and ask yourself whether you'd prefer the sure \$50,000!

2 You can either buy collision insurance on your expensive new car or not buy it, where the insurance costs a certain premium and carries some deductible provision. If you decide to pay the premium, then you are essentially paying a certain amount in order to avoid a gamble—the possibility of wrecking your car and not having it insured. You can be sure that the premium is greater than the expected cost of damage; otherwise, the insurance company would not stay in business. Therefore, from an

EMV standpoint you should not purchase the insurance. But how many of you drive without this type of insurance?

These examples, the second of which is certainly realistic, illustrate situations where rational people do not behave as EMV maximizers. Then how do they act? This question has been studied extensively by many researchers, both mathematically and behaviorally. Although the answer is still not agreed upon universally, most researchers believe that if certain basic behavioral assumptions hold, people are **expected utility** maximizers, that is, they choose the alternative with the largest expected utility. Although we will not go deeply into the subject of expected utility maximization, the discussion in this section will give you some idea of what it is all about.

Utility Functions

We begin by discussing an individual's **utility function**. This is a mathematical function that transforms monetary values—payoffs and costs—into **utility values**. Essentially, an individual's utility function specifies the individual's preferences for various monetary payoffs and costs and in doing so, automatically encodes the individual's attitudes toward risk. Most individuals are **risk averse**, which means intuitively that they are willing to sacrifice some EMV in order to avoid risky gambles. In terms of the utility function, this means that every extra dollar of payoff is worth slightly less utility to the individual than the previous dollar, and every extra dollar of cost is considered slightly more costly (in terms of utility) than the previous dollar. The resulting utility functions are shaped as shown in Figure 8.33. Mathematically, these functions are said to be **increasing** and **concave**. The increasing part means that they go uphill—everyone prefers more money to less money. The concave part means that they increase at a decreasing rate. This is the risk-averse behavior.

There are two problems involved in implementing utility maximization in a real decision analysis. The first is obtaining an individual's (or company's) utility function; this will be discussed below. The second is using the resulting utility function to find the best decision. This second step is actually quite straightforward. You simply substitute utility values for monetary values in the decision tree and then fold back as usual. That is, you calculate expected utilities at probability branches and take maximums (of expected utilities)

FIGURE 8.33 Utility Function for a Risk-Averse Decision Maker

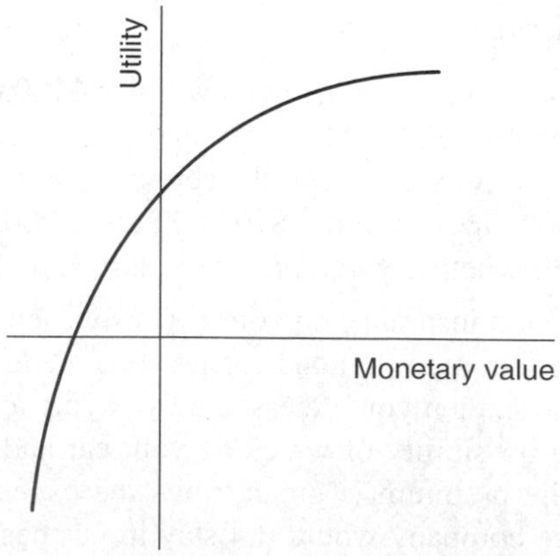

at decision branches. (We will look at a numerical example later in this section.) So the real work involves finding an individual's (or company's) utility function in the first place.

Assessing a Utility Function

We will outline a method that can be used to estimate a person's utility function. There are two things you must understand about this method. First, it asks the person to make a series of trade-offs. Because each of us has different attitudes toward risk, we will not all make the trade-offs in the same way. Therefore, each of us will obtain our own unique utility function. Second, even a particular person's utility function is not unique. If $U(x)$ represents a person's utility function, then it turns out that $aU(x) + b$ also describes that person's utility function, for any constants a and b with $a > 0$.

We actually take advantage of this non-uniqueness in assessing the utility function by specifying two points on the utility function. Specifically, we will begin by asking the person for two monetary values that represent the worst possible loss and the best possible gain imaginable. Let's say these values are $-A$ and B. Then we arbitrarily assign utility values 0 and 1 to these two monetary values, that is, $U(-A) = 0$ and $U(B) = 1$. You should not worry about the absolute magnitudes, 0 and 1, we've assigned—we could assign any other values, such as 14 and 320. The important thing is to use these as "anchors" and then obtain other utility values in terms of these anchors.

The procedure then is as follows. Given any two utility values that are known, say, $U(x)$ and $U(y)$, where x and y are monetary values, we present the person with a choice between the following two options:

1 a certain payoff of z

2 a payoff of either x or y, depending on the flip of a fair coin

Then we ask the person to select the monetary value z in option 1 so that he or she is *indifferent* between the two options. If the person is indifferent, then the expected utilities from the two options must be equal. We will call the resulting value of z the **indifference value**. This leads to the equation for $U(z)$:

$$U(z) = .5U(x) + .5U(y) \tag{8.9}$$

In words, we have generated a new utility value from two known utility values. This process continues until we have enough utility values to approximate a utility curve. (Note that if any of x, y, and z are negative, then "payoff" really means "cost.") We'll illustrate this procedure with an example.

EXAMPLE 8.8

John Jacobs owns his own business. Because he is about to make an important decision where large losses or large gains are at stake, he wants to use the expected utility criterion to make his decision. He knows that he must first assess his own utility function, so he hires a decision analysis expert, Susan Schilling, to help him out. How might the session between John and Susan proceed?

Solution

Susan first asks John for the largest loss and largest gain he can imagine. He answers with the values \$200,000 and \$300,000, so she assigns utility values $U(-200000) = 0$ and

$U(300000) = 1$ as anchors for the utility function. Now she presents John with the choice between two options:

1 a payoff of z (really a loss if z is negative)

2 a loss of \$200,000 or a payoff of \$300,000, depending on the flip of a fair coin

Susan reminds John that the EMV of option 2 is \$50,000 (halfway between −\$200,000 and \$300,000). He realizes this, but because he is quite risk averse, he would far rather have \$50,000 for certain than take the gamble in option 2. Therefore, the indifference value of z must be less than \$50,000. Susan then poses several values of z to John. Would he rather have \$10,000 for sure or take option 2? He'd rather take the \$10,000. Would he rather *pay* \$5000 for sure or take the gamble in option 2? (This would be like an insurance premium.) He answers that in this case he'd rather take option 2. By this time, they know that the indifference value of z must be less than \$10,000 and greater than −\$5000. With a few more questions of this type, John finally decides on $z = \$5000$ as his indifference value. He is indifferent between \$5000 for sure and the gamble in option 2. We can substitute these values into Equation 8.9:

$$U(5000) = .5U(-200000) + .5U(300000) = .5(0) + .5(1) = .5$$

Note that John is giving up \$45,000 in EMV because of his risk averseness. The EMV of the gamble in option 2 is \$50,000, and he is willing to accept a *sure* \$5000 in its place.

The process would then continue. For example, since she now knows $U(5000)$ and $U(300000)$, Susan could ask John to choose between these options:

1 a payoff of z

2 a payoff of \$5000 or a payoff of \$300,000, depending on the flip of a fair coin

If John decides that his indifference value is now $z = \$130,000$, then with Equation 8.9 we know that

$$U(130000) = .5U(5000) + .5U(300000) = .5(.5) + .5(1) = .75$$

Note that John is now giving up \$22,500 in EMV, since the EMV of the gamble in option 2 is \$152,500. By continuing in this manner, Susan can help John to assess enough utility values to approximate a continuous utility curve. ■

As this example illustrates, utility assessment is not easy. Even in the best of circumstances, when a trained consultant attempts to assess the utility function of a single person, the process requires the person to make a series of choices between hypothetical alternatives involving uncertain outcomes. Unless the person has some training in probability, these choices can be difficult to understand, let alone make, and it is unlikely that the person will answer consistently as the questioning proceeds. The process is even more difficult when a company's utility function is being assessed. Because the executives involved typically have different attitudes toward risk, it is difficult to have these people reach a consensus on a common utility function.

Exponential Utility

For these reasons there are classes of "ready-made" utility functions that have been developed. One important class is called **exponential utility** and has been used in many financial investment analyses. An exponential utility function has only one adjustable numerical parameter, and there are relatively straightforward ways to discover the most appropriate value of this parameter for a particular individual or company. So the advantage of using an exponential utility function is that it is relatively easy to assess. The drawback is that exponential utility functions do not capture all types of attitudes toward risk. Nevertheless, their ease of use has made them popular.

An exponential utility function has the following form:

$$U(x) = 1 - e^{-x/R} \tag{8.10}$$

Here x is a monetary value (a payoff if positive, a cost if negative), $U(x)$ is the utility of this value, and $R > 0$ is an adjustable parameter called the **risk tolerance**. Basically, the risk tolerance measures how much risk the decision maker will tolerate. The larger the value of R, the less risk averse the decision maker is. That is, a person with a large value of R is more willing to take risks than a person with a small value of R.

To assess a person's (or company's) exponential utility function, we need only assess the value of R. There are a couple of tips for doing this. First, it has been shown that the risk tolerance is approximately equal to that dollar amount R such that the decision maker is indifferent between the following two options:

1 no payoff at all

2 a payoff of R dollars or a loss of $R/2$ dollars, depending on the flip of a fair coin

For example, if you are indifferent between a bet where you win \$1000 or lose \$500, with probability .5 each, and not betting at all, then your R is approximately \$1000. From this criterion it certainly makes intuitive sense that a wealthier person (or company) ought to have a larger value of R. This has been found in practice.

A second tip for finding R is based on empirical evidence found by Ronald Howard, a prominent decision analyst. Through his consulting experience with several large companies, he discovered tentative relationships between risk tolerance and several financial variables—net sales, net income, and equity. (See [8].) Specifically, he found that R was approximately 6.4% of net sales, 124% of net income, and 15.7% of equity for the companies he studied. For example, according to this prescription, a company with net sales of \$30 million should have a risk tolerance of approximately \$1.92 million. Howard admits that these percentages are only guidelines. However, they do indicate that larger and more profitable companies tend to have larger values of R, which means that they are more willing to take risks.

We illustrate the use of the expected utility criterion, and exponential utility in particular, with the following example.

EXAMPLE 8.9

Venture Limited is a company with net sales of \$30 million. The company currently must decide whether to enter a risky venture or do nothing. The possible outcomes of the risky venture are a \$1 million loss, a \$0.5 million gain, and a \$3 million gain. The probabilities of these outcomes are .35, .60, and .05. Should the company enter this risky venture?

Solution

We will assume that Venture has an exponential utility function. Also, based on Howard's guidelines, we will assume that Venture's risk tolerance is 6.4% of its net sales, or \$1.92 million (we'll do a sensitivity analysis on this parameter later). We can substitute into the exponential utility formula 8.10 to find the expected utility from each alternative. First, the gain from doing nothing is \$0, and its (expected) utility is

$$\text{EU(Doing nothing)} = U(0) = 1 - e^{-0/1.92} = 1 - 1 = 0$$

Next, the utility for any outcome from the risky venture is found by plugging into the exponential utility function. For example, the utility of the \$1 million loss is

$$U(-1) = 1 - e^{-(-1)/1.92} = 1 - e^{.5208} = 1 - 1.683 = -.683$$

Similarly, the utility of the \$0.5 million gain is

$$U(.5) = 1 - e^{-.5/1.92} = 1 - e^{-.2604} = 1 - .771 = .229$$

and the utility of the \$3 million gain is

$$U(3) = 1 - e^{-3/1.92} = 1 - e^{-1.5625} = 1 - .210 = .790$$

Therefore, the expected utility of the risky venture is a weighted average of these utility values, weighted by their probabilities:

$$\text{EU(Risky venture)} = (-.683)(.35) + .229(.60) + .790(.05) = -.062$$

Because this is less than zero, the expected utility from doing nothing, the expected utility criterion specifies that the company should *not* enter the risky venture.

For the sake of comparison, however, note that the EMV from the risky venture is positive:

$$\text{EMV(Risky venture)} = (-1)(.35) + .5(.60) + 3(.05) = \$0.1 \text{ million}$$

So from an EMV standpoint, the company *should* enter the risky venture. The reason it doesn't take this action is its aversion to risk.

Using TreePlan The TreePlan add-in uses the EMV criterion by default, but it can also be used for exponential utility functions and the expected utility criterion. The solution for Venture's decision problem appears in Figure 8.34. (See the file VENTURE.XLS.) To form this spreadsheet, enter the inputs in columns A and B and use TreePlan in the usual way to construct the decision tree, just as though you were going to use EMV. After you have linked the appropriate cells in the decision tree to the input cells, you must do two things to incorporate exponential utility. First, you *must* name cell B5 (the cell that contains the risk tolerance) RiskTolerance. TreePlan uses this range name, so it must be

FIGURE 8.34 **Decision Tree for Risky Venture Example**

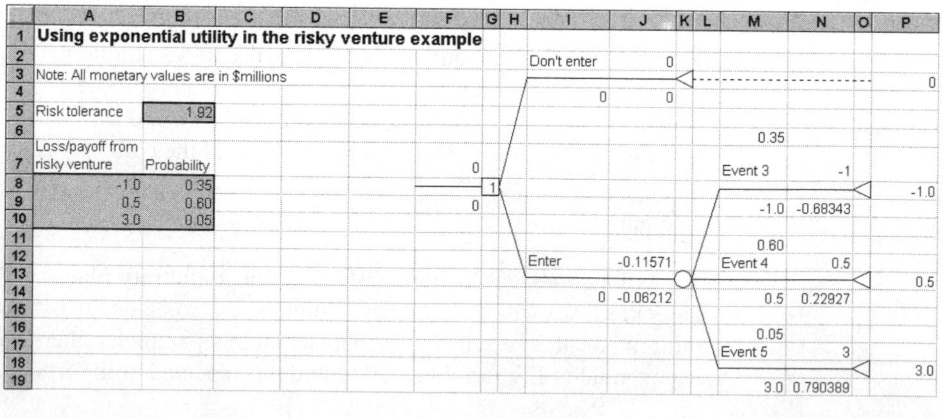

able to locate it. Then invoke TreePlan, click on the Options button, and select the Use Exponential Utility Function option. The tree shown in Figure 8.34 should result.

Now the cells just to the left and below the nodes are expected utilities, not EMVs. For example, the value -0.06212 in cell J14 is the expected utility from entering the risky venture, the same as we calculated above. Since it is less than 0, the utility from doing nothing, the decision node in cell G8 indicates that the company should not enter the risky venture.

What if the company were less risk averse, that is, it had a larger risk tolerance? Would it then enter the risky venture? This is easy to check in TreePlan. We gradually increased the risk tolerance from its current value until the decision node in cell G8 contained a 2 rather than a 1. This occurred somewhere between $R = 4$ and $R = 4.5$. Since the company's risk tolerance is evidently far below these levels, it can be fairly confident that the best decision is to avoid the risky venture.

Certainty Equivalents Now suppose that the company has only two options. It can either enter the risky venture or pay some amount x to avoid the gamble altogether. (You can think of x as a type of insurance premium.) We want to find the dollar amount x such that the company is indifferent between these two options. If it enters the risky venture, its expected utility is $-.062$, calculated above. If it pays x dollars to avoid the gamble altogether, its (expected) utility is

$$\text{EU(Avoiding gamble)} = U(-x) = 1 - e^{-(-x)/1.92} = 1 - e^{x/1.92}$$

To find the indifference value x, we set $1 - e^{x/1.92}$ equal to $-.062$, or $e^{x/1.92} = 1.062$, and solve for x. Taking natural logs of both sides and multiplying by 1.92, we obtain

$$x = 1.92 \ln(1.062) \simeq \$0.115 \text{ million}$$

This value is called the **certainty equivalent** of the risky venture. The company is indifferent between entering the risky venture and paying \$115,000 to avoid it. Although the EMV of the risky venture is a positive \$100,000, the company acts as if it is equivalent to a \$115,000 loss!

Now look at the decision tree in Figure 8.34 again. We already saw how the value in cell J14 is the expected utility from entering the venture. The number above it, in cell J12, is $-x$, where x is the certainty equivalent we just calculated. So TreePlan automatically calculates the expected utilities and the certainty equivalents.

Is Expected Utility Maximization Used? This discussion indicates that utility maximization is a fairly involved task. The bottom line, then, is whether the difficulty is worth the trouble. Theoretically, expected utility maximization might be interesting to researchers, but is it really used? The answer appears to be not very often. For example, one recent article on the practice of decision making (see Kirkwood [9]) quotes Ronald Howard, a prominent academician and consultant in the field, as having found risk aversion to be of practical concern in only 5 to 10% percent of business decision analyses. This same article quotes the president of a Fortune 500 company as saying, "Most of the decisions we analyze are for a few million dollars. It is adequate to use expected value (EMV) for these."

With these comments in mind, it is clear that knowledge of expected utility maximization is an important requirement for anyone intending to specialize in the field. In some of the greatest success stories expected utility maximization was indeed implemented. For nonspecialists, however, a passing knowledge of the concepts is sufficient. ■

REAL-WORLD APPLICATION

Maximizing Utility at Fannie Mae

Holmer [7] reports the use by Fannie Mae (the Federal National Mortgage Association) of expected utility to optimize its portfolio composition of assets and liabilities. (Refer to Chapter 6 for more discussion on portfolio maximization.) Fannie Mae supports a highly leveraged portfolio of home mortgage assets. Its asset-liability management strategy employs a combination of security cash-flow simulation methods and options-based pricing methods to estimate the return distribution (the inputs we required in Chapter 6) for each asset and liability considered in the portfolio optimization. The use of expected utility rather than EMV as the decision criterion allows Fannie Mae to incorporate degrees of risk aversion into the optimization procedure. ■

PROBLEMS

Skill-Building Problems

Note: For problems with utility functions other than exponential utility, you can still use Treeplan. However, instead of entering monetary values on branches, you should enter formulas that yield utility values. Then Treeplan will calculate expected utilities and find the maximum of these over all decisions.

36 Suppose a decision maker's utility function for wealth is $U(x) = \ln x$ (the natural logarithm of x).

a Is this decision maker risk averse?

b The decision maker now has \$20,000 and has two possible decisions. For decision 1, he loses \$1000 for certain. For decision 2, he loses \$0 with probability .9 and loses \$10,000 with probability .1. Which decision maximizes the expected utility of his final wealth?

37 A decision maker has a utility function for monetary gains x given by $U(x) = (x + 10000)^{1/2}$.

a Show that this decision maker is indifferent between doing nothing (no loss, no gain) and entering a risky situation where she gains \$80,000 with probability 1/3 and loses \$10,000 with probability 2/3.

b If there is a 10% chance that a painting valued at \$10,000 will be stolen during the next year, what is the most (per year) that the decision maker would be willing to pay for insurance covering the loss of the painting?

38 A decision maker is going to invest \$1000 for a period of six months. Two potential investments are available: T-bills and gold. If he invests the \$1000 in T-bills, the decision maker is certain to end the six-month period with \$1296 (a gain of \$296). If he invests in gold, there is a .75 probability that he will end the six-month period with \$400 and a .25 probability that he will end with \$10,000. His utility function of ending with x dollars is $U(x) = x^{1/2}$. Should he invest in gold or T-bills?

39 In the previous problem allow the decision maker to invest a proportion y of his \$1000 in T-bills and the rest in gold. In this case his gain or loss from either investment is reduced proportionally. For example, if he invests half of his money in gold, he will either lose \$300 or gain \$4500—half of the values from investing all of his money in gold. Using the same square utility function as before, find the investor's best value of y. Is it 0 or 1 (invest all in gold or all in T-bills), or is it somewhere in between? (*Hint*: Use a data table.)

40 An investor has \$5000 in assets and can choose between investments 1 and 2. If she invests in investment 1 there is a .8 probability that she will increase her assets by \$295,000 and a .2 probability that she will increase her assets by \$95,000. If she invests in investment 2 she has a fifty-fifty chance of increasing her assets by \$595,000 or \$5000. The investor has an exponential utility function for final assets that has a risk tolerance parameter equal to \$300,000. Which investment will she prefer?

41 My current income is \$80,000. I believe that I owe \$16,000 in taxes. For \$500, I can hire a CPA to review my tax return. There is a 20% chance that he will save me \$6000 in taxes and a probability of .8 that he won't save me anything. My utility function for disposable income x is $U(x) = x^{1/2}$. Here, disposable income is current income minus taxes minus payment to the CPA. Should I hire the CPA?

42 Edwina, a commodities broker, has acquired an option to buy 1000 ounces of gold from South Africa at \$50 per ounce. If she takes the option and if Congress relaxes import quotas, she can sell the gold for \$80 per ounce. If she takes the option and Congress does not relax the import quotas, however, the company will lose \$10 per ounce. Edwina believes that there is a 50% chance that the government will relax the quota. She also has the option of waiting until Congress decides whether to relax the import quota. If she adopts this strategy, however, there is a 70% chance that some other broker will have already taken the option.

a If Edwina is risk neutral, what should she do?

b If Edwina's utility function for a change x in her asset position is given by $U(x) = (10000 + x)^{1/2}$, what should she do?

43 Revisit the examples from Sections 8.2 and 8.4 that used the EMV criterion. Now, using TreePlan, solve them with the expected utility criterion and exponential utility. Experiment with different values of R, the risk tolerance, to see whether you get different optimal decisions than with EMV.

Skill-Extending Problem

44 Suppose that an investor's utility function for wealth x is $U(x) = x^{1/2}$. The investor has \$10,000 at present and has a chance to play a game where he either gains \$1025 or loses \$199, with probability 1/2 each.

a This game is obviously a good one from the investor's point of view, but he must pay B dollars to play it. Find the value B such that he would be indifferent between paying B (and playing the game) and not playing.

b Now suppose that the investor owns the right to play the game but he can sell this right to another investor for S dollars. What value S should he charge so that he is indifferent between selling (and giving up his right to play) or not selling (and playing)?

c Answer Part (b) under the assumption that the investor begins with only \$1000. ■

8.7 Conclusion

On this chapter we have discussed methods that can be used in decision-making problems in which future uncertainty is a key element. Perhaps the most important skill you can gain from this chapter is the ability to approach systematically problems that include uncertainty. This systematic approach requires the decision maker to list all possible decisions or strategies, list all possible future outcomes, assess the probabilities of these outcomes (possibly with the aid of Bayes' rule), calculate all necessary monetary values, and finally use the appropriate decision criterion to obtain the best decision. If large dollar amounts are at stake, it might also be necessary to perform a formal utility analysis, where the decision maker's feelings toward risk are assessed. Once the basic analysis has been completed, using "best guesses" for the various parameters of the problem, it is then possible—and usually mandatory—to conduct a sensitivity analysis in order to see whether the best decision continues to be best within a range of problem parameters.

REVIEW PROBLEMS

Skill-Building Problems

45 We have \$1000 to invest. All the money must be placed in one of three investments: gold, stock, or money market certificates. Each dollar placed in money market certificates earns a 10% annual return for certain. Each dollar invested in stock earns a return of 0%, 10%, or 20% depending on three possible states of the economy. Similarly, each dollar invested in gold earns a return of 60%, −70%, or 40%, depending on the same three states of the economy. (In the second case the investor's \$1000 would decrease to \$300.) Assume that each state of the economy is equally likely. If the investor must put all of her money in a single investment, which investment maximizes the EMV of her wealth a year from now?

46 In the previous problem suppose that the utility function for the investor's wealth x a year from now is given by $U(x) = \ln x$. Determine which investment she should choose. Again, assume she must put all of her money into a single investment.

47 Jay Boyville Corporation is being sued by Lark Dent. Lark can settle out of court and win \$40,000, or go to court. If Lark goes to court, there is a 30% chance that he will win the case. If he wins, a small and a large settlement are equally likely. A small settlement nets \$50,000, and a large settlement nets \$300,000.

a If Lark is risk neutral, what should he do? What should Lark do if his utility function for an increase x in his cash position is given by $U(x) = x^{1/2}$?

b For \$10,000, Lark can hire a consultant who will predict who will win the trial. The consultant is correct 90% of the time. Should he hire the consultant? (Assume that Lark is risk neutral.) What is the EVSI?

c If Lark is risk neutral, what is the EVPI?

48 Rolla Megabux has \$1 million to invest in stocks or bonds. The percentage yield on each investment during the coming year depends on whether the economy has a good or a bad year. If the economy has a good year, the return on stocks is 22% and the return on bonds is 16%. If the economy has a bad year, these returns drop to 10% and 14%. It is equally likely that the economy will have a good or a bad year.

a If Rolla is risk neutral, how should she invest her money?

b For \$15,000, Rolla can hire a consulting firm to forecast the state of the economy. The consulting firm's forecasts have the following properties:

$$\Pr(\text{Good forecast}|\text{Economy good}) = .8$$
$$\Pr(\text{Good forecast}|\text{Economy bad}) = .2$$

Should Rollo hire the consulting firm? What are the EVSI and the EVPI?

Skill-Extending Problems

49 (Based on Balson, Welsh, and Wilson [1]) An electric utility company is trying to decide whether to replace its PCB transformer in a generating station with a new and safer transformer. To evaluate this decision the utility needs information about the likelihood of an incident, such as a fire, the cost of such an incident, and the cost of replacing the unit. Suppose that the total cost of replacement as a present value is \$75,000. If the transformer is replaced, there is virtually no chance of a fire. However, if the current transformer is retained, the probability of a fire is assessed to be .0025. If a fire occurs, then the cleanup cost could be high (\$80 million) or low (\$20 million). The probability of a high cleanup cost, given that a fire occurs, is assessed at .2.

a If the company uses EMV as its decision criterion, should it replace the transformer?

b Perform a sensitivity analysis on the key parameters of the problem that are difficult to assess, namely, the probability of a fire, the probability of a high cleanup cost, and the high and low cleanup costs. Does the optimal decision from Part (a) remain optimal for a "wide" range of these parameters?

c Do you believe EMV is the correct criterion to use in this type of problem involving environmental accidents?

50 (Based on Engemann and Miller [3]) A large bank is considering whether to install an emergency generator in its operations facility. The cost of the generator, expressed as an annualized cost, is \$800,000. With this generator, nothing "bad" can happen. However, without the generator there could be a power outage. The bank assesses that the probability of a power outage is .1. If there is a power outage, the bank's losses could be "large" or "small." The bank assesses that the probability of a large loss, given a power outage, is .05. In terms of annualized earnings, a large loss amounts to \$80 million, and a small loss amounts to \$1 million.

a If the bank uses EMV as its criterion, should it purchase the generator?

b Suppose that the bank uses the expected utility criterion, with an exponential utility function. Experiment with the risk-tolerance parameter to see when the best decision switches from "don't purchase generator" to "purchase generator."

c In a decision environment like this one, do you believe expected utility is a more appropriate criterion than EMV?

51 (Based on Mellichamp, Miller, and Kwon [11]) Construction equipment managers typically have many large pools of engines, transmissions, and other equipment units to maintain. One approach to this maintenance is to use oil analysis, where the oil from any of these is subjected periodically to an inspection. These inspections can sometimes signal an impending failure (for example, too much iron in the oil), and preventive maintenance is then performed (at a relatively low cost), eliminating the risk of failure (failure would result in a relatively high cost). However, oil analysis costs money, and it is not perfect. That is, it can indicate that a unit is defective when in fact it is not about to fail, and it can indicate that a unit is nondefective when in fact it is about to fail. As a possible substitute for oil analysis, the company could simply change the oil periodically, thereby reducing the probability of a failure.

Suppose the company has four alternatives: (1) do nothing, (2) use oil analysis only, (3) replace oil only, or (4) replace oil and do oil analysis. For option (1) the probability of a failure is p_1, and the cost of a failure is C_1. For option (2), the probability of a failure remains at p_1. If the unit is about to fail, the oil analysis will indicate this with probability $1 - \alpha$; if the unit is not about to fail, the oil analysis will indicate this with probability $1 - \beta$. (Therefore, α and β are the error probabilities of the oil analysis.) The oil analysis itself costs C_2, and if it indicates that a failure is about to occur, the oil will be changed, at cost C_3, and preventive maintenance will be performed. The cost of maintenance to restore a unit that is about to fail is C_4, whereas the cost of maintenance for a unit that is not about to fail is C_5. The only difference between options (3) and (4) is that the probability of a failure decreases to p_2 after changing the oil. The values of these parameters for a particular class of units (engines in light trucks, say) appear in Table 8.15.

TABLE 8.15 Parameters for Oil Analysis Problem

Parameter	Value
p_1	0.10
p_2	0.04
α	0.30
β	0.20
C_1	\$1200.00
C_2	\$20.00
C_3	\$14.80
C_4	\$500.00
C_5	\$250.00

a For these parameters, develop a decision tree to find the company's best decision and the corresponding expected cost.

b If the company has 500 units, what should it do? What is the expected cost for the entire fleet?

c Suppose that the company has different types of units. For example, the cost of an oil change might be higher for some, or the cost of a failure might be higher or lower. Run a sensitivity analysis on any of the parameters you believe might be "key" parameters and see whether the optimal decision changes in ways you would anticipate.

Modeling Problems

52 (Based on Hess [6]) A company that is heavily involved in R&D projects believes it might have the potential to develop a very lucrative commercial product that would (if successful) reduce pulp mill water pollution. At the current stage, however, everything is quite uncertain, and the company is trying to decide whether to go ahead with its R&D or abandon the product. The following are the primary risks:

- Would market tests confirm that there is a significant market for the product?
- Could the company develop a new process for making this product, that is, is it technically feasible?
- Even if there is a significant market and the process is technically feasible, would the company's board sanction the new plant capital necessary to produce the product on a commercial scale?
- Assuming the answers to the above questions are all yes and the plant is built, would the venture turn out to be successful?

We assume that each of these questions has a yes or no answer. The probabilities of yes answers are shown in Table 8.16. The plus-or-minus value indicates the company's uncertainty about the true probabilities.

TABLE 8.16 Probabilities for Water Pollution Problem

Event	Probability
Significant market	0.6 ± 0.15
Technically feasible	0.6 ± 0.15
Board sanctions plant expenditures	0.8 ± 0.2
Commercial success	0.8 ± 0.2

The primary economic factors are the following:

- the research expenses to identify a new production process for the product
- the marketing development cost to determine whether there is a significant market
- the process development costs, including presanction engineering
- the commercial development costs, both before and after the board's sanction
- the venture value (net present value) if successful

The estimates of these values are shown in Table 8.17. Again, the plus-or-minuses indicate the company's considerable uncertainty about the values. All dollar values are in millions of dollars.

TABLE 8.17 Monetary Estimates for Water Pollution Problem

Expense or Gain	Net Present Value
Research expense	\$0.8 ± 25%
Market development expense	\$0.2 ± 25%
Process development expense (presanction)	\$3.0 ± 25%
Commercial development expense (presanction)	\$0.5 ± 25%
Commercial development expense (postsanction)	\$1.0 ± 25%
Value if successful	\$25.0 ± 50%

The timing of events is as follows:

- Decide whether to abandon product now. (This is really the only nontrivial decision the company will make.) If not, then

- Spend on research and marketing development. If marketing development indicates an insignificant market for the product *or* research indicates that the process is technically infeasible, cut expenses and quit. Otherwise,
- Spend on process and commercial development. If company board then declines to sanction money for plant, cut expenses and quit. Otherwise,
- Spend on further commercial development. By this time, the company has made all of its decisions. If the venture turns out to be a commercial success, then it gains the venture value for a success (less expenses so far). Otherwise, the company has lost the money spent so far, but that is all.

Analyze the company's problem. Obviously, with the high degree of uncertainty, sensitivity analysis is the key. Note that there are many uncertainties about the input parameters in Tables 8.16 and 8.17. In fact, there are way too many to allow you to try every combination. Therefore, just try a few combinations that you believe might be the most important.

53 Many drug companies use decision trees to evaluate new drugs during the development process. Fewer than 10% of all compunds under development eventually make it to market. Discuss the probabilities and payoffs that would have to be estimated in order to use decision trees to evaluate prospective drugs. ■

CASE STUDY

Giant Motor Company II

This case is a continuation of GMC I (from Chapter 5). Management at GMC is generally pleased with the modeling effort that has been done for capacity planning in the coming year. However, some managers have asked about the effect demand forecasts for the second year out could have on the recommended strategy.

While demand forecasts for the coming year are considered to be quite reliable, forecasts two or more years in the future have been less accurate. Accordingly, analysts at GMC formulate several demand scenarios in the future, and assign probabilities to each scenario. The situation for the coming two years is summarized in Table 8.18.

Three demand scenarios are possible in the second year. Scenario A corresponds to a robust economic expansion and increasing market share for GMC cars. Scenario B represents little change from the first year, although there is a relative shift away from the smaller Lyra to the larger Libra and Hydra models. Scenario C represents an economic recession and decreased demand for all car lines. In scenario C, the decrease in demand for Libras and Hydras is larger than for the economical Lyras. Analysts give scenario A a slightly higher probability of occurring than scenarios B or C.

Management at GMC wants to consider all possible configurations of capacity in the next two years. As before, the Lyra and/or Libra plants can be retooled, *but retooling can be done in either the first or second year.* Because of the enormous costs of changing a plant configuration, a plant that is retooled in the first year cannot be returned to its original configuration in the second year. The costs and characteristics of the original and retooled plants are the same in either year. For convenience, these are repeated in Table 8.19.

In addition to selecting the plant configurations for each year, GMC needs to determine the production plan at each plant in each year. The sequence of events and decisions is as follows. At the beginning of a year, GMC must decide on the plant configurations. Demand occurs during the year, and based on the observed demand, GMC plans its production accordingly. For example, in the second year, GMC must decide on its plant configurations *before* the demand scenario is revealed, but can determine its production plan *after* the demand scenario is revealed. This sequence of events is consistent with the relative time periods involved. Reconfiguring a plant is a major undertaking that must be planned in advance, so this decision must be made before the demand scenario is revealed. Production during a year can be altered to best meet the demand as it develops during the year. For modeling purposes, the production decision can be made after the demand scenario is revealed. Also, no inventory is carried from one year to the next.

The demand diversion matrix is assumed to be constant for both years. For convenience, it is repeated in Table 8.20.

Questions

1 GMC wants to decide whether to retool the Lyra and Libra plants in each of the coming two years. In addition, GMC wants to determine its production plan at each plant for each year. Based on the previous data, formulate a mixed integer programming model for solving GMC's production planning–capacity expansion problem for the coming two years. Assume that GMC's objective is to maximize total average profit for the two years. For simplicity, assume that no discounting of profits is done for the second year.

2 In the past, GMC had solved problems separately for each scenario. The three optimal solutions were compared and then a final decision was made. What are the three optimal solutions corresponding to each scenario? (For example, assuming that scenario A occurs with probability one, what is the optimal solution? Then repeat for scenarios B and C.) How do the three separate optimal solutions compare to the overall optimal solution found before? ■

Acknowledgment: The idea for GMC I and II came from Eppen, Martin, and Schrage [4], pp. 517–27.

TABLE 8.18 Demand Forecasts and Probabilities for GMC Case Study

Model	First Year	Second Year: Scenario A	Scenario B	Scenario C
Lyra	1,400	1,700	1,300	1,300
Libra	1,100	1,500	1,200	800
Hydra	800	1,100	850	600
Probability	1	0.4	0.3	0.3

TABLE 8.19 Plant Characteristics for GMC Case Study

	Lyra	Libra	Hydra	New Lyra	New Libra
Capacity (in 1000s)	1,000	800	900	1,600	1,800
Fixed Cost (in $millions)	2,000	2,000	2,600	3,400	3,700
	Profit Margin by Car Line (in 1000s)				
Lyra	2	–	–	2.5	2.3
Libra	–	3	–	3	3.5
Hydra	–	–	5	–	4.8

TABLE 8.20 Demand Diversion Matrix for GMC Case Study

	Lyra	Libra	Hydra
Lyra	–	0.3	0.05
Libra	0	–	0.10
Hydra	0	0.0	–

REFERENCES

1 Balson, W., J. Welsh, and D. Wilson. "Using Decision Analysis and Risk Analysis to Manage Utility Environmental Risk." *Interfaces* 22, no. 6 (1992): 126–39.

2 Borison, A. "Oglethorpe Power Corporation Decides about Investing in a Major Transmission System." *Interfaces* 25, no. 2 (1995): 25–36.

3 Engemann, K., and H. Miller. "Operations Risk Management at a Major Bank." *Interfaces* 22, no. 6 (1992): 140–49.

4 Eppen, Martin, and Schrage. "A Scenario Approach to Capacity Planning." *Operations Research* 37, no. 4 (1989): 517–27.

5 Feinstein, C. "Deciding Whether to Test Student Athletes for Drug Use." *Interfaces* 20, no. 3 (1990): 80–87.

6 Hess, S. "Swinging on the Branch of a Tree: Project Selection Applications." *Interfaces* 23, no. 6 (1993): 5–12.

7 Holmer, M. "The Asset-Liability Management Strategy System at Fannie Mae." *Interfaces* 24, no. 3 (1994): 3–21.

8 Howard, R. "Heathens, Heretics, and Cults: The Religious Spectrum of Decision Aiding." *Interfaces* 22, no. 6 (1992): 15–27.

9 Kirkwood, C. "An Overview of Methods for Applied Decision Analysis" *Interfaces* 22, no. 6 (1992): 28–39.

10 Krumm, F., and C. Rolle. "Management and Application of Decision and Risk Analysis in Du Pont." *Interfaces* 22, no. 6 (1992): 84–93.

11 Mellichamp, J., D. Miller, and O. Kwon. "The Southern Company Uses a Probability Model for Cost Justification of Oil Sample Analysis." *Interfaces* 23, no. 3 (1993): 118–24.

12 Ulvila, J. "Postal Automation (ZIP+4) Technology: A Decision Analysis." *Interfaces* 17, no. 2 (1987): 1–12.

COMPAQ
PLUS

9

CHAPTER

Deterministic Inventory Models

Management Science Success Stories

All inventory models have the common characteristic that they attempt to find the right balance between having enough inventory on hand in order to meet customer demand but not so much as to incur excess costs. However, there are many variations of the basic inventory model. One of these is described by Lee, Billington, and Carter [3] in their article "Hewlett-Packard Gains Control of Inventory and Service through Design for Localization." The article discusses HP's Deskjet-Plus Printer Division and its problem of manufacturing and distributing these printers. The printers are manufactured in Vancouver and are then shipped by sea to three distribution centers (DCs), one in North America, one in the Far East, and one in Europe. These DCs then supply the printers to the customers in their regions. The problem is to determine the quantity and location for printer inventory. In particular, should the printers be stored in Vancouver or at the DCs?

This problem is complicated by a "localization" issue. Different regions require slightly different specifications on their printers. For example, the type of power supply module (with the correct voltage and plugs) and the appropriate manual vary from region to region. In the past, HP had "localized" the printers at the manufacturing plant in Vancouver. It bundled the various packages together in the factory—some for Asian markets, some for European markets, and so on—and then sent the appropriate bundles to the DCs as demand forecasts dictated. However, this policy was not terribly effective from a cost or a customer service standpoint. The policy forced HP to carry too much inventory at its factory, and (largely because of the long shipping times) it didn't allow HP to respond quickly enough to changes in forecasts of demands.

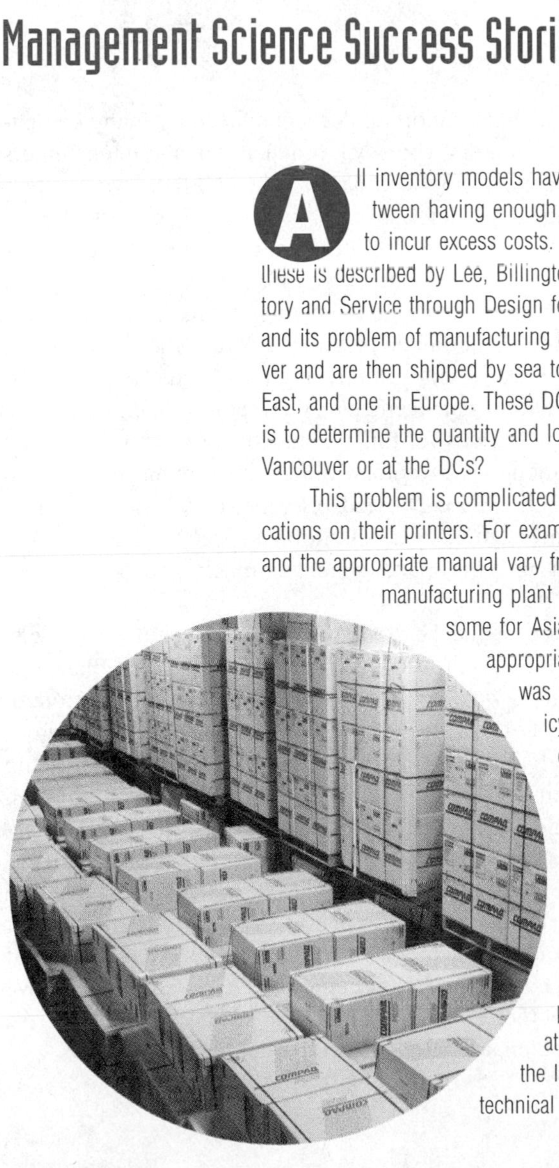

The company decided to try a "DC-localization" policy instead, at least for its Far East and European DCs. Under this policy the Vancouver factory shipped only the "generic" printers to the DCs and allowed the DCs to carry the bulk of the printer inventory. These DCs also carried an ample supply of localization materials, such as appropriate power supply modules and manuals. An important key in being able to implement this policy was that the printers had to be redesigned slightly so that the staff at the DCs could simply attach the localization materials to the printers at the last minute. (Without these design changes, the DCs would have lacked the technical skills to assemble the parts!) The rationale for this DC-localization policy was fairly obvious. The DCs could carry just enough printer inventory to meet customer demand on time and could react quickly to changes in the demand forecasts. The Vancouver plant wouldn't have to carry a wide range of inventory just to be able to respond to every possible contingency. In addition, there were other less obvious benefits. For example, the unbundled printers were less bulky and hence less costly to transport.

Although this change in policy sounded good, HP developed a mathematical inventory model (of the type we'll discuss in this chapter and the next chapter) to verify that it would save costs. The model predicted that a smaller *total* printer inventory would be carried under the new policy, although there would be more inventory in localization materials at the DCs. Nevertheless, since the value of a printer is much greater than the value of a power supply module or a manual, the total dollar value of inventory would be reduced by about 18%—a very significant figure considering the millions of dollars involved. In addition, the models were run with a *fixed* level of customer service. In other words, HP could satisfy its customers just as well with 18% less money tied up in inventory. (Alternatively, this implied that HP could *increase* the level of customer service by carrying the same amount of inventory as before.) The company not only went ahead with this new policy, but it adapted it to other new products in Vancouver and other parts of Hewlett-Packard. ■

9.1

Introduction

Inventory management is one of the most important decisions faced by many companies. These companies include not only retailers who stock products for sale to customers like yourself, but also companies who supply other companies. They all face two competing pressures. The first is the pressure to have enough inventory on hand. The most obvious reason for this is that they do not want to run out of products that customers demand. Another prominent reason, however, is the cost of ordering (which we will discuss throughout this chapter). If there is a fixed cost incurred each time the company orders from its supplier, and this cost does not depend on the number of units ordered, then there is an incentive for the company to place large orders, thus minimizing its annual ordering costs.

The second pressure related to inventory management is the pressure to carry as little inventory as possible. The most obvious reasons for this are the cost of storing items and the interest costs involved in tying up money in inventory. If the company has to pay cash for items that end up sitting on the shelf for long periods of time, it is losing potential interest on this money (that could be invested elsewhere). Storage space is often an issue as well. Some companies simply don't have the space to store as much inventory as they might like.

These two competing pressures are at the heart of virtually all inventory models. Companies want to order enough, but they don't want to order too much. The balance is, typically, not easy to find, so we need models to help us find the best ordering (or production) policy. These models are the subject of this chapter and the next chapter. An inventory problem can usually be broken up into two parts: (1) *how much* to order on each ordering opportunity and (2) *when* to order. In this chapter we will deal primarily with the former. When we assume that customer demand is known, the resulting models are called **deterministic** models. If customer demand is known, then once the order amount has been determined, it is fairly easy to specify when the orders should be placed. In the next chapter we will assume a more realistic situation, where only the probability distribution of customer demand is known—we do not know exactly how much will be demanded in any period of time. In this case the decision on when to place orders becomes much more important. We want to place them early enough so that the chance of running out before the orders arrive is fairly small. These more difficult problems require **probabilistic** inventory models.

9.2

Categories of Inventory Models

The number of types of inventory models, both deterministic and probabilistic, that have been analyzed is extremely large. We will discuss only the most basic of these models, which have been used extensively in real applications. Before beginning our study of these models, it will be useful to discuss several important issues and introduce some terminology.

Deterministic Versus Probabilistic Models

An important factor in inventory modeling is the choice between deterministic and probabilistic models (which we have already touched upon). In deterministic models we assume that all inputs to the problem, particularly customer demand, are known when the decisions are being made. In reality, a company must always forecast future demands with some type of forecasting model. The outputs of this forecasting model might include a mean demand and a standard deviation of demand. In deterministic models, on the other hand, we use only the mean and discard any information about the uncertainty, such as the standard deviation. This makes the resulting models simpler, but usually less realistic. Probabilistic models use this information about uncertainty explicitly. They are typically more difficult to analyze, but they are likely to produce better decisions, especially when the level of uncertainty is high.

External Versus Internal Demand

A second factor in inventory modeling is whether demand for the product is generated *externally* or *internally*. **External demand**, often referred to as **independent demand**, occurs when the company that sells the product cannot directly control the extent or the timing of customer demand. For example, a retailer who orders products from a supplier and then waits to see how many customers will request these products is operating in a situation of external demand. Ordering decisions are influenced by but do not influence customer demand.

In contrast, **internal demand**, often called **dependent demand**, occurs in most assembly and manufacturing processes. Consider, for example, a company that manufactures refrigerators. There is external demand for the finished product, but there is internal demand for the parts that go into the finished product. That is, once the company forecasts how many refrigerators its customers will require in the next month, say, it must determine an appropriate production schedule to produce these. This production schedule will necessitate having inventories of the refrigerator's component parts and subassemblies on hand at the right time. In short, the production schedule determines, in large part, the inventory required for all of the individual parts and subassemblies. The coordination of all of these—ensuring that everything is on hand when it is needed—is a complex problem that we will not discuss in this book. We will consider only external demand.

Ordering Versus Production

A third factor in inventory modeling is whether the company orders the products from a supplier or produces them internally. If the products are ordered, then there is typically an order **lead time**, the time elapsed from when the order is placed until it arrives. In ordering models there is also usually a fixed cost (also called a **setup** or **ordering cost**) each time an order is placed, where this cost is independent of the order amount. In contrast, if products are produced internally, then it takes time to produce a batch of items. This time is determined by a production rate, such as ten units per hour, and also possibly by a setup time, the fixed time necessary to set up any machinery in order to produce a specific type of product. As in the ordering models, there may also be a setup cost each time a batch is produced that is independent of the batch size.

Continuous Versus Periodic Review

Another factor in inventory modeling is whether the inventory is reviewed continuously or periodically. In a **continuous review** model the inventory is monitored continually and orders can be placed at any time. Typically, there is a **reorder point**—a specific inventory level—such that when the inventory on hand reaches this reorder point, an order is placed immediately. This could happen Wednesday afternoon, Friday morning, or any other time. In contrast, in **periodic review** models there is some standard time, such as every Monday morning, when the inventory is reviewed and an ordering decision is made. Except possibly for emergency orders, these are the only times when orders are placed. Continuous review models can certainly be implemented, given today's computerized access to inventory levels in real time, and these models may result in lower annual costs than periodic review models. However, when a company stocks many products (hundreds or even thousands), it may be more convenient to order these only on, say, Monday mornings.

In this chapter we will consider only continuous review models. However, versions of periodic review models have already been discussed in earlier chapters, where we modeled them with linear programming. See Examples 2.3, 3.4, and 4.2.

Single-Product Versus Multiple-Product Models

A final factor in inventory modeling concerns the number of products involved. Models that consider only a single product are conceptually and mathematically simpler, so we will initially analyze single-product models. However, most companies have many different products that must be analyzed simultaneously. If the company orders these items from a supplier, then it may be wise to synchronize the orders in some way in order to minimize ordering costs. We will look at one such model of synchronization in Section 9.8.

9.3 Costs Involved in Inventory Models

We now discuss the costs involved in inventory modeling.

Ordering (or Setup) Cost

We have already mentioned the ordering cost (also referred to as the setup cost). This is the fixed cost incurred every time an order is placed or a batch is produced. Its key property is that it is independent of the amount ordered or produced. This ordering cost includes the cost of paperwork and billing each time an order is placed and could include other costs as well, such as paying a truck driver to deliver the order to the company's warehouse. If the product is produced rather than ordered, this cost might include the cost to set up equipment and/or the cost of worker idle time while the equipment is being set up.

Unit Purchasing (or Production) Cost

The **unit purchasing** or **production cost** is the additional cost for each additional unit purchased or produced. For example, to order 100 units the company might have to pay a setup cost of $500 plus $3 per unit, for a total of $800. Here, $3 is the unit purchasing cost. If the company produces the product, then the unit production cost might include the cost of raw materials and the labor cost for each unit produced. Sometimes the unit purchasing cost is not constant, but changes according to some quantity discount schedule. We will consider a quantity discount model in Section 9.5.

Holding (Carrying) Cost

The **holding** or **carrying cost** is the cost that motivates the company to keep less inventory on hand. This cost generally has two components, the **financial holding cost** and the **nonfinancial holding cost**. The nonfinancial holding cost is usually called the **storage cost**. It includes any cost, such as renting warehouse space, that involves the physical storage of the product. The financial holding cost has to do with the time value of money. It is the opportunity cost of having money tied up in inventory when that money could instead be earning interest in other investments. Actually, there may be other holding costs, such as spoilage, insurance, and overhead, that vary according to the amount and type of inventory on hand.

Shortage (Penalty) Cost

We also need to measure the cost of running out of inventory. This cost, called a **shortage** or **penalty cost**, is often the most difficult cost to measure. For one thing, it depends on how the company handles shortages. At one extreme, there are **lost sales** models, where any demands that occur when inventory is zero are simply lost. These customers take their business elsewhere. At the other extreme, there are **complete backlogging** models, where demands that occur when inventory is zero are satisfied as soon as a new order arrives.[1] Both of these models—or any in between, the **partial backlogging** models—have negative effects for the company. There is lost business, loss of goodwill, and possibly emergency shipments with higher costs. The problem, however, is that it can be difficult to put a dollar value on the "cost" of running out of inventory. Although

[1] We also say the excess demand is **backordered**. Both terms, backlog and backorder, mean that these orders are kept on the books and are satisfied when additional shipments arrive.

we will look at models that assume specific shortage costs, an alternative is to specify a **service level**, such as meeting at least 95% of the demand on time.

Revenue

Finally, there is the **selling price** of the product and the resulting revenue to the company. In many situations the revenue is a fixed amount that is not affected by any ordering decisions. This occurs when the selling price is constant and the company intends to satisfy all demand eventually. In such cases we can add the total revenue to the relevant costs, but it will not affect any decisions. On the other hand, there are times, such as in the lost sales case mentioned earlier, when the selling price affects the ordering decision. Here the shortage cost is a function of how much revenue is lost by not having enough inventory on hand, and this clearly depends on the selling price. We will see an example of this in the next chapter when we examine the "newsvendor" model.

9.4 The Basic EOQ Model

We now examine a class of models called **economic order quantity** (EOQ) models. These are the most basic of all the inventory models. Developed originally in 1915 by F. W. Harris of Westinghouse Corporation, they are also among the earliest management science models. Despite their simplicity, they have been applied by numerous companies, and they continue to play a prominent role in inventory management. We begin by studying a very basic EOQ model in some detail. Then we will examine interesting variations of this basic model. All of these variations are categorized by the following assumptions.

Assumptions of EOQ Models

1. There is a constant, known demand rate, usually expressed in units per year (annual demand).
2. The models use continuous review.
3. There is a constant, known lead time for delivery. ■

The constant demand rate means, for example, that if the yearly demand is 52,000 units, then each week's demand is approximately 1000 units; there are no peaks or valleys during the year. Continuous review means that the company can place an order at any time, not just at the beginning of the week, say. Finally, the known lead time means that if the company places an order on Monday and the lead time is three days, then the order will arrive with certainty on Thursday. We now analyze the basic EOQ model in the context of the following example.

EXAMPLE 9.1

Machey's Department Store sells 1200 cameras per year, and the demand pattern throughout the year is very steady. The store orders its cameras from a regional warehouse, and it usually takes a week for the cameras to arrive once an order has been placed. Each time an order is placed, an ordering cost of $35 is incurred. The store pays $100 for each camera and sells them for $130 apiece. There is no physical storage cost, but the store's cost of capital is estimated at 10% per year, that is, it can earn 10% on any excess cash it invests. The store wants to determine how often it should order cameras, when it should place orders, and how many cameras it should order in each order.

Solution

In developing the solution to Machey's problem, we will introduce some ideas and notation that will be useful throughout this chapter. First, we make an important observation. Because the demand for cameras is assumed to be steady throughout the year—its rate could be expressed as 1200 per year, 100 per month, 1200/52 per week, and so on—there is really only one decision Machey's must make, namely, the order quantity of each order. We label this order quantity Q. Once Q is determined, the number of orders per year can be calculated easily. For example, if $Q = 50$, then since yearly demand is 1200, there must be 24 ($= 1200/50$) orders per year, and the time between orders will be 1/24 of a year (once every half-month). In general, if D is the yearly demand, then we have

$$\text{Number of orders per year} = D/Q \tag{9.1}$$

$$\text{Time between orders} = Q/D \tag{9.2}$$

where time is measured as a fraction of a year.

It is also straightforward to determine the timing of orders. Since the ordering lead time is known to be one week, Machey's should place an order when there is exactly one week's worth of demand left in inventory. This way, the order will arrive just as inventory is depleted—the best possible state of affairs. In general, if L is the length of the lead time, expressed as a fraction of a year, and D is the annual demand, then an order should be placed when the inventory level reaches the value LD.[2] In Machey's case this is 1200/52, or approximately 23 cameras.

This timing is best illustrated graphically, as in Figure 9.1. Here we see how the inventory level follows a "saw-tooth" pattern. It decreases at rate D until it reaches level LD. At this point an order for Q units is triggered, and this order arrives exactly L time units later, just as the inventory reaches zero. The order arrival takes the inventory level back up to Q, at which time the process repeats itself. We call the time between orders an **order cycle**; its length is Q/D.

The problem now is to find an ordering quantity Q that maximizes Machey's annual profit. We will examine each component of the annual profit. First, each time Machey's places an order, it incurs a fixed ordering cost, labeled K, where $K = \$35$. Since there are D/Q orders placed per year, the annual ordering cost is

$$\text{Annual ordering cost} = KD/Q \tag{9.3}$$

In the example this is $35(1200)/Q = 42{,}000/Q$.

On top of this, Machey's pays a variable cost, labeled c, for each camera purchased. Here, $c = \$100$. Since the annual demand is $D = 1200$, and all demand must be met, the annual variable cost is

$$\text{Annual variable cost} = cD \tag{9.4}$$

[2]Unfortunately, this analysis is not quite correct when Q is smaller than the demand during the lead time. We will discuss this case later on.

FIGURE 9.1 Graph of Inventory Level for Basic EOQ Example

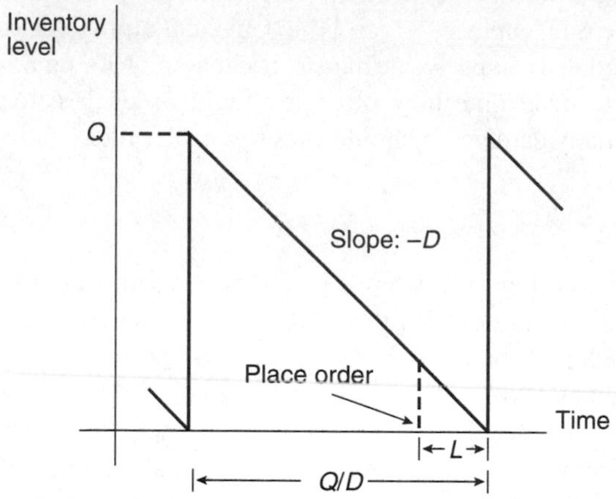

or \$120,000. Note that this cost does *not* depend on Q. Similarly, since the company's revenue from each camera, labeled r, is $r = \$140$, its annual revenue is

$$\text{Annual revenue} = rD \tag{9.5}$$

or \$156,000. This is also unaffected by the order quantity Q.

Now we consider the annual holding cost. There is no cost for physically storing the cameras, but Machey's loses money from potential investments by having excess cash tied up in inventory. If we let i be Machey's annual cost of capital, where $i = 0.10$ (that is, 10%), then it can be shown from a net present value argument that the relevant annual holding cost is i multiplied by the average monetary value of inventory, where this average is over the entire year. Since the inventory during a cycle decreases linearly from Q to 0, the average level of the inventory at a typical point in time is $(Q + 0)/2 = Q/2$, which implies that the average monetary value of inventory is

$$\text{Average monetary value of inventory} = cQ/2$$

Therefore, the annual holding cost from money tied up in inventory, sometimes called the **financial holding cost**, is

$$\text{Annual financial holding cost} = icQ/2$$

In the example this is $(.1)(100)Q/2 = 5Q$.

In general, the annual holding cost also includes a storage cost (which is zero in Machey's case). If there is a storage cost of s dollars per unit held in storage per year, then the annual storage cost is $sQ/2$, as the average inventory is $Q/2$. Therefore, the entire annual holding cost is

$$\text{Annual holding cost} = (s + ic)Q/2 \tag{9.6}$$

We can now develop a spreadsheet to optimize Machey's annual profit.

Developing the Spreadsheet Model The spreadsheet solution appears in Figure 9.2. (See the file EOQ1.XLS.) It can be formed as follows.

1 **Inputs.** Enter the inputs in the range B5:B11. Note that the lead time in cell B11 is entered as a formula (=1/52) in order to express it as a fraction of a year. Also, note that we have entered a storage cost (even though it is zero) in cell B6. This way, the same basic spreadsheet can be used in cases where the storage cost is nonzero.

FIGURE 9.2 **Spreadsheet for Basic EOQ Example**

	A	B
1	**Basic Economic Order Quantity Example**	
2		
3	**Inputs**	
4		
5	Setup cost (K)	$35
6	Storage cost per unit per year (s)	$0
7	Annual interest rate (i)	10%
8	Unit purchasing cost (c)	$100
9	Selling price per unit (r)	$130
10	Annual demand (D)	1200
11	Lead time in years (L)	0.0192
12		
13	**Analysis using the Solver**	
14		
15	Order quantity Q	91.65
16	Time between orders	0.076
17	Orders per year	13.09
18		
19	Costs affected by order quantity	
20	Annual setup cost	$458.25
21	Annual holding cost	$458.26
22	Total affected cost	$916.52
23		
24	Costs/revenues unaffected by order quantity	
25	Annual purchasing cost	$120,000.00
26	Annual revenue	$156,000.00
27		
28	Total annual profit	$35,083.48
29		
30	**Reorder point**	23

2 **Order quantity.** Enter *any* order quantity in cell B15.

3 **Order cycles.** Calculate the length of the order cycle and the number of cycles per year in the cells B16 and B17 with the formulas

=B15/B10

and

=1/B16

These follow directly from Equations 9.1 and 9.2.

4 **Costs affected by the order quantity.** Calculate the annual ordering cost (from Equation 9.3), the annual holding cost (from Equation 9.6), and their sum in the range B20:B22 with the formulas

=B5*B17

=(B6+B7*B8)*B15/2

and

=SUM(B20:B21)

5 **Cost or revenue unaffected by order quantity.** Enter the annual purchasing cost and the annual revenue (from Equations 9.4 and 9.5) in cells B25 and B26 with the formulas

=B8*B10

and

=B9*B10

These are not really relevant in terms of finding the optimal order quantity, but we include them in order to find Machey's annual profit.

6 **Profit.** Calculate the annual profit in cell B28 with the formula

=B26–B25–B22

7 **Reorder point.** Recall that the reorder point is the inventory level (number of cameras in stock) that triggers an order. Calculate it in cell B30 with the formula

=MOD(B11*B10,B15)

This takes a bit of explaining. Normally, as we discussed earlier, the reorder point is *LD* (cell B11 times cell B10), the amount of demand during a lead time. In this example, $LD = (1/52)1200 \simeq 23$. However, suppose that the order quantity turned out to be $Q = 15$. Then the inventory level would never *reach* 23 (see Figure 9.1), so that 23 certainly could not be the appropriate reorder point. In this case Machey's should order when the inventory level is 8 and one order of size 15 is already on the way. Or if Q turned out to be 10, Machey's should order when the inventory level is 3 and *two* orders of size 10 are already on the way. In general, to account for the situation where Q is less than *LD*, we should divide *LD* by Q and use the *remainder* as the reorder point. For example, 23 divided by 15 gives a remainder of 8, and 23 divided by 10 gives a remainder of 3. This is exactly what the MOD function in the above formula does—it gives the remainder when *LD* is divided by Q.

Using the Solver

1 **Objective.** Select cell B22 as the objective to minimize. (We could also maximize the profit in cell B28 since the only difference between these is a constant that is independent of the order quantity.)

2 **Changing cell.** Select cell B15 as the only changing cell, and constrain it to be nonnegative. (You can also constrain it to be an integer if you like, although we have not done so.)

3 **Optimize.** Click on Solve. (Do *not* check the Assume Linear Model box. The objective is not a linear function of the order quantity Q.)

As we see from Figure 9.2, the optimal order quantity is $Q = 91.65$, the associated annual cost that is affected by the order quantity is \$916.52, and the annual profit is \$35,083.48.[3] Note that the annual setup cost and the annual holding cost are equal. It turns out that this is always the case. Also, because the order quantity Q is larger than the demand during a lead time (23), the reorder point is simply $LD = 23$. Therefore, Machey's should place an order for about 92 cameras every time its inventory falls to 23 cameras. This will require about 13 orders per year.

[3] It can be shown the objective is a convex function, so that the Solver solution is really optimal.

The Square Root EOQ Formula To solve Machey's problem, we have used the Solver in the usual way. However, it is possible to give a *formula* for the optimal order quantity under fairly general conditions. As in Machey's example, the model should have the following elements:

1 There is a single product that the company orders from a supplier.

2 The yearly customer demand for this product is D units.

3 The cost of ordering Q units is $K + cQ$, where K is the setup cost and c is the unit purchasing cost.

4 The holding cost per unit in inventory per year is $s + ic$, where s is the storage cost per unit per year and i is the annual interest rate (sometimes called the **cost of capital**). For notational convenience, we will let $h = s + ic$, that is, h will be the combined holding cost per unit per year. The important thing is that the annual holding cost should be of the form $hQ/2$, that is, linear in Q.[4]

5 The selling price is r per unit.

6 No shortages are allowed.

7 The lead time is L (measured as a fraction of a year).

8 The objective is to maximize the total annual profit. (As in the example, this is equivalent to minimizing the costs affected by the order quantity—the sum of annual setup and holding costs.)

With these assumptions, it can be shown (by using calculus) that the optimal order quantity is given by the following formula. This formula is referred to as the **square root** or **EOQ formula**, and we refer to the optimal order quantity Q as the **EOQ**.

$$Q = \sqrt{\frac{2KD}{h}} \tag{9.7}$$

As we will see, this EOQ formula gives the same optimal value of Q as the Solver. However, it provides additional useful information. Namely, it shows explicitly how the optimal order quantity varies with K, D, and h. For example, if the demand rate D doubles, the optimal order quantity Q increases by about 40% (because $\sqrt{2} = 1.414$). Or if the ordering cost K is cut in half, the optimal order quantity decreases by about 40%.

The optimal order quantity Q in Equation 9.7 achieves the best balance between annual setup costs and annual holding costs. This balance is illustrated in Figure 9.3. The annual setup cost is decreasing in Q; as the order quantity increases, there are fewer orders per year and therefore fewer setup costs. In contrast, as the order quantity increases, the annual holding cost increases (linearly in Q). The sum of these functions is minimized at the EOQ, which just happens to be where the annual setup and holding cost curves intersect.[5]

To verify that the EOQ formula produces the same order quantity as the Solver for Machey's example, we simply substitute Machey's input values, $K = 35$, $D = 1200$, and $h = s + ic = 0 + .10(100) = 10$, into Equation 9.7:

$$Q = \sqrt{\frac{2(35)(1200)}{10}} = 91.65$$

[4]Frequently the unit holding cost h is expressed as a percentage of the unit purchase cost c. For example, if we are told that the unit purchase cost is \$10 and the unit holding cost is 15% of the purchase cost, then we would use $h = \$1.50$ in the EOQ model.

[5]We observed this latter fact in Machey's example, and it can be proved mathematically. However, you should not conclude that the sum of an increasing curve and a decreasing curve always has its minimum where the two curves intersect; this is usually *not* the case.

FIGURE 9.3 Optimal Order Quantity for Basic EOQ Example

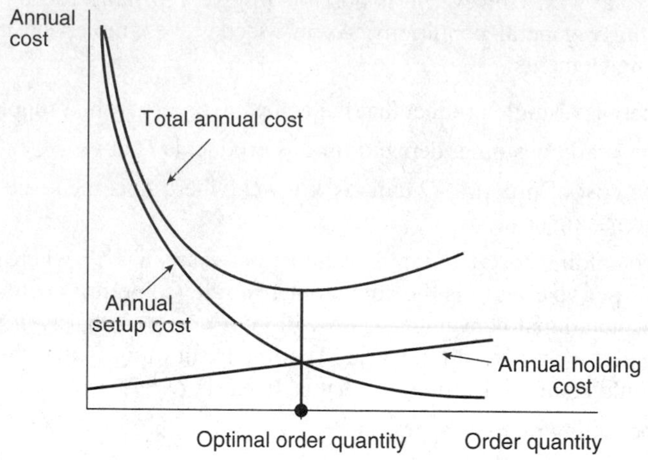

Therefore, we could have avoided the Solver altogether by entering the formula

=SQRT(2*B5*B10/(B6+B7*B8))

in cell B15 of Figure 9.2. (See the file EOQ1A.XLS, which uses this formula rather than the Solver.)

A further advantage to using this formula instead of the Solver is that it is then easy to see how sensitive the total annual setup and holding cost is to the order quantity Q. To do this, we calculate a data table in the range A35:B49 that shows the total annual setup plus holding costs as a function of the optimal order quantity Q. To produce this table, which is shown in Figure 9.4, enter a set of possible values for Q in column A, enter the formula

=B22

in cell B35 to keep track of the sum of setup and holding costs, and select the range A35:B49 as the data table range. Then use the Data/Table menu item with cell B15 as the column input cell. Finally, create a line graph using the data in columns A and B to show the total annual cost as a function of Q. As we see from the graph, the total annual cost is fairly flat in the neighborhood of the optimal value of Q. This is useful information for the

FIGURE 9.4 Data Table for Basic EOQ Example

Table of total annual costs (affected by order quantity) as a function of Q

Q	Total affected cost
	$916.52
60	$1,000.00
65	$971.15
70	$950.00
75	$935.00
80	$925.00
85	$919.12
90	$916.67
95	$917.11
100	$920.00
105	$925.00
110	$931.82
115	$940.22
120	$950.00
125	$961.00

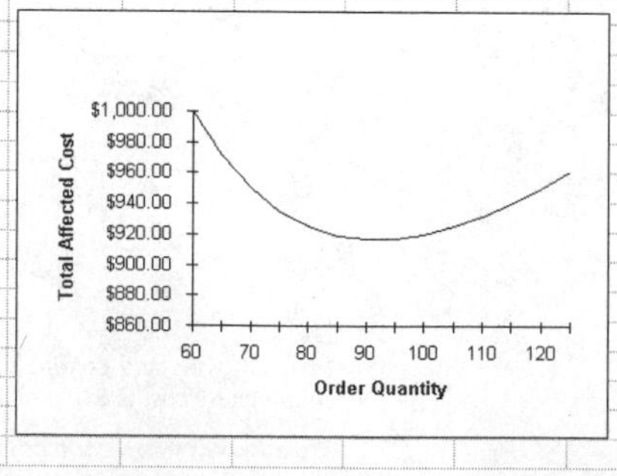

manager, since it means that slight deviations from the optimal Q will have minor effects on total cost.

It is also possible to generate other data tables and corresponding graphs. For example, Figure 9.5 contains another data table and an associated graph, this time of the optimal Q (from Equation 9.7) for various values of the setup cost K. The corresponding graph shows that the optimal Q increases at a decreasing rate as K increases (and all of the other inputs stay constant). Of course, the reason for this behavior is the square root in the EOQ formula.

FIGURE 9.5 **Data Table for Sensitivity of Q to Ordering Cost K**

	A	B
51	Table of optimal Q versus ordering cost K	
52		
53	K	Optimal Q
54		91.65
55	5	34.64
56	10	48.99
57	15	60.00
58	20	69.28
59	25	77.46
60	30	84.85
61	35	91.65
62	40	97.98
63	45	103.92
64	50	109.54
65	55	114.89
66	60	120.00
67	65	124.90
68	70	129.61
69	75	134.16
70	80	138.56
71	85	142.83

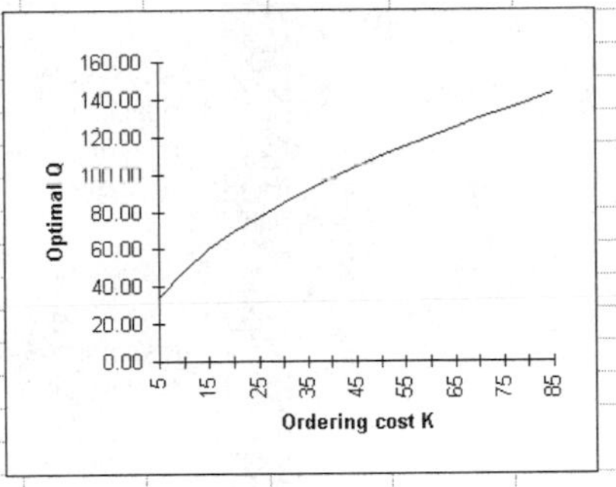

A Variation of the Model It is important to understand when the assumptions behind the basic EOQ formula apply and when they don't. Suppose that a company has the option to rent a warehouse at cost S per year, and this warehouse has room for as many as C units (C for capacity). Then the annual storage cost is *not* a function of Q; it is a flat S per year. In particular, the annual storage cost does not have the form $sQ/2$ as assumed by the basic EOQ model.

There are two ways to proceed on such variations of the basic model. We could try to salvage as much of the EOQ solution as possible. A better approach is to go directly to the Solver solution and not bother with a square root formula. Both methods are possible for this particular problem. The EOQ solution, using $h = ic$ instead of $h = s + ic$, is $Q = \sqrt{2KD/ic}$, which is optimal if this Q is no greater than C. But if it is greater than C, then the best feasible solution is to order C units.

The spreadsheet model shown in Figure 9.6 uses the Solver to confirm this. (See the file EOQ2.XLS.) It uses the same parameters as in Machey's example, with the addition that $S = \$1000$ and $C = 80$. Because the EOQ formula prescribes $Q = 91.65$ (see Figure 9.2), which is greater than capacity, the best solution for this problem is $Q = 80$. Notice that we now separate the holding cost into two parts in cells B22 and B26, the financial holding cost and the warehouse rental charge. Only the first is affected by the choice of Q, so we can use the Solver to minimize the quantity in cell B23 and essentially ignore the fixed rental charge. Again, the only changing cell is B16, and the constraints are now B16>=0 and B16<=B7. As we predicted, the optimal order quantity is $Q = 80$. The company would like to order more, for reasons of cost, but capacity doesn't allow it.

FIGURE 9.6 **EOQ Model with Flat Storage Cost**

	A	B	C
1	**Variation of EOQ Model with Flat Storage Cost**		
2			
3	**Inputs**		
4			
5	Setup cost (K)	$35	
6	Warehouse rental charge per year (S)	$1,000	
7	Warehouse capacity (C)	80	
8	Annual interest rate (i)	10%	
9	Unit purchasing cost (c)	$100	
10	Selling price per unit (r)	$130	
11	Annual demand (D)	1200	
12	Lead time in years (L)	0.0192	
13			
14	**Analysis using the Solver**		
15			
16	Order quantity Q	80	
17	Time between orders	0.0667	
18	Orders per year	15.00	
19			
20	Costs affected by order quantity		
21	Annual setup cost	$525.00	
22	Annual financial holding cost	$400.00	
23	Total affected cost	$925.00	
24			
25	Costs/revenue unaffected by order quantity		
26	Annual storage cost	$1,000.00	
27	Annual purchasing cost	$120,000.00	
28	Annual revenue	$156,000.00	
29			
30	Total annual profit	$34,075.00	
31			
32	**Reorder point**	23	

The point here is that not all problems fit the framework of the basic EOQ model exactly. By extending the mathematical analysis or using a spreadsheet Solver, we can often handle these EOQ variations without too much difficulty. In the next section we will look at a special variation of the EOQ model where quantity discounts are available. ■

PROBLEMS

Skill-Building Problems

1 Each month, a gas station sells 4000 gallons of gasoline. Each time the parent company refills the station's tanks, it charges the station $50 plus 70¢ per gallon. The annual cost of holding a gallon of gasoline is 30¢.

a How large should the station's orders be?

b How many orders per year will the station place?

c How long will it be between orders?

d Would the EOQ assumptions be satisfied in this situation? Why or why not?

e If the lead time is two weeks, what is the reorder point? If the lead time is ten weeks, what is the reorder point?

2 A bakery that orders cartons of bread mix has used an EOQ model to determine that an order quantity of 90 cartons per order is economically optimal. The bakery needs 150 cartons per

month to meet demand. It takes L days for the bakery's supplier to deliver an order. When should the bakery place its orders when $L = 2$, when $L = 5$, and when $L = 10$? (Assume that the bakery and its supplier both work seven-day weeks and that there are 30 days per month.)

3 Consider the basic EOQ model. We want to know the sensitivity of (1) the optimal order quantity, (2) the sum of the annual order cost and the annual holding cost (not including the annual purchase cost cD), and (3) the time between orders to various parameters of the problem.

a How do (1), (2), and (3) change if the setup cost K decreases by 10%?

b How do (1), (2), and (3) change if the annual demand doubles?

c How do (1), (2), and (3) change if the cost of capital increases by 10%. (For this part, assume that the storage cost s is zero.)

d How do (1), (2), and (3) change if the changes in Parts (a), (b), and (c) all occur simultaneously?

4 (Based on Baumol [1]) Money in your savings account earns interest at a 10% annual rate. Each time you go to the bank, you waste 15 minutes in line, and your time is worth \$10 per hour. During each year you need to withdraw \$10,000 to pay your bills.

a How often should you go to the bank?

b Each time you go to the bank, how much money should you withdraw?

c If your need for cash increases, will you go to the bank more often or less often?

d If the interest rate increases, will you go to the bank more often or less often?

e If the bank adds more tellers, will you go to the bank more often or less often?

5 The efficiency of an inventory system is often measured by the **turnover ratio**. The turnover ratio (TR) is defined by

$$TR = \frac{\text{Cost of goods sold per year}}{\text{Average value of on-hand inventory}}$$

a Does a high turnover ratio indicate an efficient inventory system?

b If the EOQ model is being used, determine TR in terms of K, D, h, and Q.

c Suppose that D increases. Show that TR will also increase. Does this make intuitive sense?

Skill-Extending Problems

6 (Based on Ignall and Kolesar [2]) Father Dominic's Pizza Parlor receives 30 calls per hour for delivery of pizza. It costs Father Dominic's \$10 to send out a truck to deliver pizzas. It is estimated that each minute a customer spends waiting for a pizza costs the pizza parlor 20¢ in lost future business.

a How often should Father Dominic's send out a truck?

b What would the answer be if a truck could only carry five pizzas?

7 Suppose that instead of ordering the amount Q specified by the EOQ formula, we use the order quantity $0.8Q$. Show that the sum of the annual ordering cost and the annual holding cost increases by 2.5%.

8 In terms of K, D, and h, what is the average length of time that an item spends in inventory before being used to meet demand? Explain how this result can be used to characterize a fast- or slow-moving item.

9 A drug store sells 30 bottles of antibiotics per week. Each time it orders antibiotics, there is a fixed ordering cost of \$10 and a cost of \$10 per bottle. Assume that the store's cost of capital is 10% and there is no storage cost, and suppose that antibiotics spoil and cannot be sold if they spend more than one week in inventory. When the drug store places an order, how many bottles of antibiotics should it order?

10 During each year, CSL Computer Company needs to train 27 service representatives. No matter how many students are trained, it costs \$12,000 to run a training program. Since service reps earn a monthly salary of \$1500, CSL does not want to train them before they are needed. Each training session takes one month.

a State the assumptions needed for the EOQ model to be applicable.

b How many service representatives should be in each training group?

c How many training programs should CSL undertake each year?

d How many trained service reps will be available when each training program begins? ■

9.5

EOQ Models with Quantity Discounts

One of the incentives for ordering large quantities in real applications is the availability of quantity discounts. In the basic EOQ model we assume that the unit purchasing cost is a constant c, regardless of the number of units purchased. We now examine two types of quantity discounts where the marginal purchasing cost decreases as the company orders more. The most intuitive type of quantity discount is illustrated in Figure 9.7. The slope at any point on this curve is the marginal cost of that unit. Because the slopes decrease as quantity increases, the marginal cost decreases—the quantity discount effect. This curve has natural price breaks, q_1 and q_2, where the unit cost of the first $q_1 - 1$ units is c_1, the unit cost of units q_1 through $q_2 - 1$ is c_2 (less than c_1), and the cost of units q_2 and up is c_3 (less than c_2). For example, it might cost \$10 per unit for the first 99 units, \$9.75 per unit for units 100 through 199, and \$9.50 per unit for all units after the first 199. Then we would have $q_1 = 100$, $q_2 = 200$, $c_1 = \$10$, $c_2 = \$9.75$, and $c_3 = \$9.50$.

Surprisingly, however, most real-world quantity discounts are not of this type. They are of the type illustrated in Figure 9.8. Here again there are price breaks at q_1 and q_2, but the total cost curve has *discontinuities* at these price breaks. Specifically, if fewer than q_1 units are purchased, the cost of each unit is c_1. If the quantity ordered is at least q_1 but less than q_2, then *each* unit costs c_2. Finally, if at least q_2 units are ordered, the cost of *each* unit is c_3. This type of quantity discount has the interesting property that it can be cheaper to purchase more than less. For example, if $c_1 = \$26$, $c_2 = \$25$, and $q_1 = 100$, then it costs \$2,522 to purchase 97 units ($= 97 \times \$26$), but only \$2,500 to purchase 100 units ($= 100 \times \$25$). So would any company purchase 97 units when it could have the extra three units essentially for free (with a few extra dollars thrown in)? The answer is probably not unless the storage cost makes the extra three units unattractive.

We now examine the EOQ model when either of these quantity discounts is in effect. The following example is typical.

FIGURE 9.7 **Continuous Discount Purchasing Cost Function**

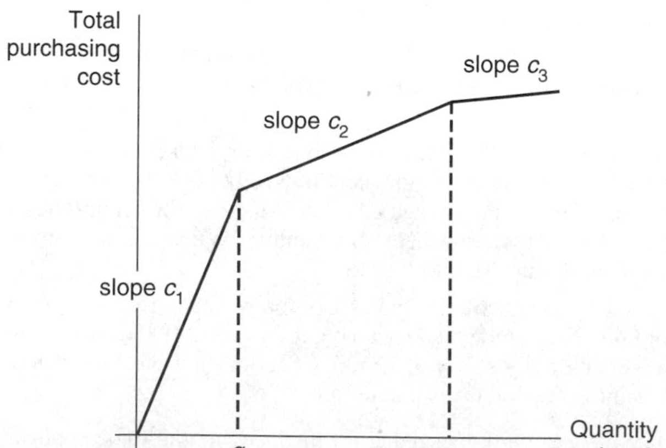

FIGURE 9.8 **Discontinuous Discount Purchasing Cost Function**

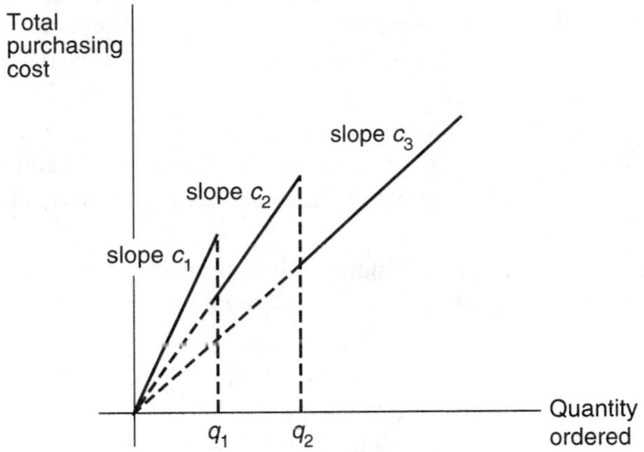

EXAMPLE 9.2

The accounting firm of AJ Taylor buys boxes of floppy disks (ten disks to a box) from a large mail-order distributor. The firm uses approximately 5000 boxes per year at a fairly constant rate. The distributor offers a quantity discount of the type illustrated in Figure 9.8. If fewer than 500 boxes are ordered, the cost per box is \$10. If at least 500 but fewer than 800 boxes are ordered, the cost per box is \$9.50. If at least 800 boxes are ordered, the cost per box is \$9.25. The fixed cost of placing an order is \$25. The company's cost of capital is 12% per year, and there is no storage cost. The firm wants to find the optimal order quantity and the corresponding total annual cost.

Solution

In general, let $c(Q)$ be the cost of purchasing Q units. As in the basic EOQ model, if D is the annual demand, then there are D/Q orders placed per year, so the sum of annual setup cost and purchasing cost is

$$\text{Annual setup and purchasing cost} = [K + c(Q)]D/Q$$

The annual holding cost is i times the average monetary value of the inventory on hand. Since the inventory fluctuates between 0 and Q, which have monetary values 0 and $c(Q)$, we have

$$\text{Annual holding cost} = i[c(Q) + 0]/2 = ic(Q)/2$$

(When $c(Q) = cQ$, this reduces to the expression from the basic EOQ model.) Then the total annual cost is the sum of these:

$$\text{Total annual cost} = [K + c(Q)]D/Q + ic(Q)/2$$

There are two ways to find the value of Q that minimizes this total cost function: a mathematical approach and a spreadsheet approach. Although a mathematical approach is possible, it is fairly difficult. Therefore, we illustrate the spreadsheet approach. For either of the types of quantity discounts illustrated in Figures 9.7 and 9.8, it is not difficult to generate values of $c(Q)$ with appropriate IF functions and thus obtain a single spreadsheet formula for $c(Q)$. But from this point on we must be careful. There are certain types of nonlinear functions that spreadsheet Solvers do not handle well, and functions incorporating IF functions are among these. (We made this same point in Chapter 6.) Sometimes the Solver works, but sometimes it gives the wrong answer (or doesn't converge to any solution).

Fortunately, there is a simple and safe way out. Suppose that there are exactly two price breaks (as shown in Figures 9.7 and 9.8), which lead to three possible regions: below q_1, between q_1 and q_2, and above q_2. We break the spreadsheet into three parts, corresponding to these three regions, and use the Solver three separate times, each with a different constraint on Q. Then we take the minimum of the three optimal total costs and the corresponding Q. We illustrate this approach for AJ Taylor's problem.

Developing the Spreadsheet Model The spreadsheet solution appears in Figure 9.9. (See the file EOQ3.XLS.) There are three separate sections, depending on where the order quantity falls in relation to the price breaks. Because all of these sections are treated similarly, we'll concentrate only on the middle section, where the order quantity must satisfy $500 \leq Q \leq 799$. (Of course, all three sections depend on the same inputs in cells B6 through B14.) To form the middle part of Figure 9.9, use the following steps.

1 **Inputs.** Enter the inputs, including the price breaks, in the range B6:B14.

2 **Order quantity.** Enter *any* trial order quantity in cell B28. Although it could be set initially at any value, it is natural to enter a value within the price break region, that is, a value from 500 to 799.

3 **Formulas for order cycle and annual costs.** Enter the following formulas in the middle section of the spreadsheet. Except for the purchasing cost in B32, these are analogous to the formulas in Example 9.1 (see Figure 9.2), so we just briefly indicate the Excel formulas. In cells B29 through B34 enter the formulas

```
=B9/B28
=B12*B28
=B6*B29
=B30*B29
=B7*B28/2+B8*B30/2
```

and

```
=SUM(B31:B33)
```

The key formula for the quantity discounting aspect of the problem is in cell B30. It says that for this region, the purchasing cost per order is the relevant unit cost, \$9.50, times the *total* number of units ordered. Then the annual purchasing cost (cell B32) is the cost per order times the number of orders per year, and the financial holding cost (cell B33) is the interest rate times half the purchase cost per order.

Using the Solver

1 **Objective.** Select cell B34 as the objective to minimize.

2 **Changing cell.** Select cell B28 as the only changing cell.

3 **Constraints.** Add the constraints B28>=500 and B28<=799. (You may also add the constraint that B28 is an integer.)

4 **Optimize.** Click on Solve.

As we see from Figure 9.9, the Solver solution is $Q = 500$, with a corresponding total annual cost of \$48,035.00. This implies that if we *force* the order quantity to be within the price breaks 500 and 799, then the best order quantity in this region is 500.

The first and third analysis sections of the spreadsheet are completely analogous. (For each section, we have to reset the Solver settings.) In the first section the changing

FIGURE 9.9 Solution to Discontinuous Quantity Discount Example

	A	B
1	**Quantity Discount Version of EOQ Model**	
2	Quantity discount is of type: discontinuous purchase cost function	
3		
4	**Inputs**	
5		
6	Setup cost (K)	$25
7	Storage cost per unit per year (s)	$0
8	Annual interest rate (i)	12%
9	Annual demand (D)	5000
10	Unit purchasing cost below first price break (c1)	$10
11	First price break (q1)	500
12	Unit purchasing cost between first and second price breaks (c2)	$9.50
13	Second price break (q2)	800
14	Unit purchasing cost above second price break (c3)	$9.25
15		
16	**Analysis when Q is below first price break**	
17		
18	Order quantity Q	456
19	Orders per year	11.0
20	Purchasing cost per order	$4,560.00
21	Annual setup cost	$274.12
22	Annual purchasing cost	$50,000.00
23	Annual holding cost	$273.60
24	Total annual cost	$50,547.72
25		
26	**Analysis when Q is between first price break and second price break**	
27		
28	Order quantity Q	500
29	Orders per year	10.0
30	Purchasing cost per order	$4,750.00
31	Annual setup cost	$250.00
32	Annual purchasing cost	$47,500.00
33	Annual holding cost	$285.00
34	Total annual cost	$48,035.00
35		
36	**Analysis when Q is above second price break**	
37		
38	Order quantity Q	800
39	Orders per year	6.3
40	Purchasing cost per order	$7,400.00
41	Annual setup cost	$156.25
42	Annual purchasing cost	$46,250.00
43	Annual holding cost	$444.00
44	Total annual cost	$46,850.25
45		
46	Optimal Q (overall)	800
47	Minimum total cost	$46,850.25

cell is B18, the constraints are B18>=0, B18<=499, and B18 is an integer, and the cell to minimize is B24. In the third section the changing cell is B38, the constraints are B38>=800 and B38 is an integer, and the cell to minimize is B44. After running the Solver on each of these, we see that the best order quantity under 500 is 456, whereas the best order quantity at least 800 is 800. The corresponding total costs are $50,547.72 and $46,850.25.

We summarize the three sections of Figure 9.9 in cells B46 and B47. The formula in B47 is

=MIN(B24,B34,B44)

and the formula in B46 is

=IF(B47=B24,B18,IF(B47=B34,B28,B38)

The formula in B47 simply selects the smallest of the three "optimal" costs, whereas the formula in B46 records the corresponding order quantity. The bottom line is that AJ Taylor should order 800 units at a total annual cost of $46,850.25.

This spreadsheet solution is not necessarily as elegant as the mathematical solution found in many textbooks, but it has two advantages. First, it is relatively easy to understand. Second, and more importantly, it carries over to other types of quantity discounts where mathematical derivations may be quite difficult. For example, suppose that the supplier of floppy disks in this example gives discounts like those shown in Figure 9.7. Then if AJ Taylor purchases 900 boxes, for example, the total purchasing cost is $10 × 499 for the first 500 boxes, $9.50 × 300 for the next 300 boxes, and $9.25 × 101 for the last 101 boxes, for a total of $8774.25. (The price would have been $9.25 × 900 = $8325 with the discontinuous quantity discount in the example.)

Virtually the same spreadsheet as that shown in Figure 9.9 solves this new problem. The solution appears in Figure 9.10. (See the file EOQ4.XLS.) The only difference between this spreadsheet and the one in Figure 9.9 is in the purchasing cost per order in cells B20, B30, and B40. For example, the formula in cell B30 is now

=B10*(B11–1)+B12*(B28–B11+1)

because the first 499 units cost $10 apiece and any units after the first 500 (up to 799 total) cost $9.50 apiece. As we see, the solution changes fairly dramatically. The optimal order quantity is now 2067 units, and the total annual cost, $48,571.33, is almost $2000 higher than before.

The only drawback to this Solver approach for quantity discount problems is that if we want to see how sensitive the optimal order quantity and the total annual cost are to any of the problem parameters, such as K or i, we must rerun the Solver several times, once for each section of the spreadsheet. (This procedure can be steamlined, however. Excel allows you to save Solver settings in case you need to solve several related problems on the same sheet. You can then load any of these settings quickly, without having to respecify them each time. We refer to an Excel manual for details.) ■

PROBLEMS

Skill-Building Problems

11 A consulting firm is trying to determine how to minimize the annual costs associated with purchasing computer paper. Each time an order is placed an ordering cost of $20 is incurred. The price per box of computer paper depends on Q, the number of boxes ordered, as shown in Table 9.1. The annual holding cost is 20% of the dollar value of inventory. During each month, the consulting firm uses 80 boxes of computer paper. Determine the optimal order quantity and the number of orders placed each year.

FIGURE 9.10 Solution to Continuous Quantity Discount Example

	A	B
1	**Quantity Discount Version of EOQ Model**	
2	Quantity discount is of type: continuous purchase cost function	
3		
4	**Inputs**	
5		
6	Setup cost (K)	$25
7	Storage cost per unit per year (s)	$0
8	Annual interest rate (i)	12%
9	Annual demand (D)	5000
10	Unit purchasing cost below first price break (c_1)	$10
11	First price break (q_1)	500
12	Unit purchasing cost between first and second price breaks (c	$9.50
13	Second price break (q_2)	800
14	Unit purchasing cost above second price break (c_3)	$9.25
15		
16	**Analysis when Q is below first price break**	
17		
18	Order quantity Q	456
19	Orders per year	11.0
20	Purchasing cost per order	$4,560.00
21	Annual setup cost	$274.12
22	Annual purchasing cost	$50,000.00
23	Annual holding cost	$273.60
24	Total annual cost	$50,547.72
25		
26	**Analysis when Q is between first price break and second price break**	
27		
28	Order quantity Q	799
29	Orders per year	6.3
30	Purchasing cost per order	$7,840.00
31	Annual setup cost	$156.45
32	Annual purchasing cost	$49,061.33
33	Annual holding cost	$470.40
34	Total annual cost	$49,688.17
35		
36	**Analysis when Q is above second price break**	
37		
38	Order quantity Q	2067
39	Orders per year	2.4
40	Purchasing cost per order	$19,569.00
41	Annual setup cost	$60.47
42	Annual purchasing cost	$47,336.72
43	Annual holding cost	$1,174.14
44	Total annual cost	$48,571.33
45		
46	Optimal Q (overall)	2067
47	Minimum total cost	$48,571.33

TABLE 9.1 Data for Computer Paper Problem

Number of Boxes Ordered	Price per Box
$Q < 300$	$10.00
$300 \le Q < 500$	$9.80
$Q \ge 500$	$9.70

12 Each year Shopalot Stores sells 10,000 cases of soda. The company is trying to determine how many cases should be ordered each time. It costs \$5 to process each order, and the cost of carrying a case of soda in inventory for one year is 20% of the purchase price. The soda supplier offers Shopalot the schedule of quantity discounts shown in Table 9.2, where Q is the number of cases ordered per order. Each time an order is placed, how many cases of soda should the company order?

TABLE 9.2 **Data for Shopalot Problem**

Number of Cases Ordered	Price per Case
$Q < 200$	\$4.40
$200 \le Q < 400$	\$4.20
$Q \ge 400$	\$4.00

13 The Gilette Company buys a product using the price schedule given in Table 9.3. The company estimates the unit holding cost at 10% of the purchase price and the ordering cost at \$10 per order. Gilette's annual demand is 460 units.

a Determine how often the company should order.

b Determine the optimal order quantity.

c At what price should the company order?

TABLE 9.3 **Data for Gilette Problem**

Order Quantity	Price per Unit
0–99 units	\$20.00
100–199	\$19.50
200–499	\$19.00
500 or more	\$18.75

Skill-Extending Problems

14 A hospital orders its thermometers from a hospital supply firm. The cost per thermometer depends on the order quantity Q, as shown in Table 9.4. The annual holding cost is 25% of the purchasing cost. Let EOQ_{80} be the EOQ if the cost per thermometer is 80¢, and let EOQ_{79} be the EOQ if the cost per thermometer is 79¢.

a Explain why EOQ_{79} will be larger than EOQ_{80}.

b Explain why the optimal order quantity must be either EOQ_{79}, EOQ_{80}, or 100.

c If $EOQ_{80} > 100$, explain why the optimal order quantity must be EOQ_{79}.

d If $EOQ_{80} < 100$ and $EOQ_{79} < 100$, explain why the optimal order quantity must be either EOQ_{80} or 100.

e If $EOQ_{80} < 100$ and $EOQ_{79} > 100$, explain why the optimal order quantity must be EOQ_{79}.

TABLE 9.4 **Data for Hospital Problem**

Order Quantity	Price per Thermometer
$Q < 100$	80¢
$Q \ge 100$	79¢

15 In the previous problem suppose that the cost per order is \$1 and the monthly demand is 50 thermometers. What is the optimal order quantity? What would be the smallest discount the supplier could offer that would still be accepted by the hospital? ■

9.6

EOQ Model with Shortages Allowed

In the basic EOQ model we assume that the company decides, as a matter of policy, not to allow any shortages. Because the demand rate and the lead time are known, the ordering can be done so that an order arrives just as the inventory reaches zero. That is, it is possible to prevent shortages from occurring. However, it may be in the company's best interests to allow a few shortages if the "penalty" for a shortage is not too large. As discussed in the introduction to this chapter, this opens up a wide range of possible models.

First, are shortages backlogged or are these demands simply lost? And what about the penalty cost for a shortage? Does the penalty relate only to the number of units short per year or also to the amount of time shortages last? After all, a customer might be twice as unhappy if he has to wait two days instead of one day for his demand to be satisfied. Whichever type of shortage cost we assume, the practical difficulty is then assessing a specific dollar value for this cost. For example, what is the cost of having a customer wait at all? What is the cost of having a customer wait three days?

We will illustrate only the complete backlog case where the penalty cost is charged per unit short per amount of time short. In this case the annual penalty cost is a constant p multiplied by the product of the average number of units backlogged and the average amount of time a customer has to wait for a backlogged unit. The constant p is the penalty cost charged for each customer who has to wait one unit of time for a backlogged item. Mathematical models are available for this particular shortage model and for any of the others described above. However, these mathematical models are fairly difficult. We will instead use a spreadsheet approach that adapts easily to other versions of the shortage model. The following example illustrates this approach.

EXAMPLE 9.3

GMB is a mail-order distributor of audio CDs that sells approximately 50,000 CDs per year. Each CD is packaged in a jewel case that GMB buys from a supplier. The fixed cost of placing an order for jewel cases is \$100. GMB pays 50¢ for each jewel case, and its cost of capital is 10%. The cost of storing a jewel case for one year is 50¢. GMB believes it can afford to run out of jewel cases from time to time, reasoning that this will simply make the time between customer orders and customer deliveries a bit longer. It knows that there is some cost of doing this—impatient customers might take their business elsewhere—but it is not sure what dollar amount p to attach to this cost. It decides to use a trial value of $p = \$52$, reasoning that this value implies a \$1 penalty for each extra week a customer has to wait because of a backlogged jewel case. GMB wants to develop a spreadsheet model to find the optimal order quantity, the optimal amount to backlog, and the optimal annual cost, and it also wants to see how sensitive these quantities are to the shortage cost parameter p.

Solution

As before, the first step of the solution is to develop the components of the total annual cost. The key is, again, a saw-toothed graph, shown in Figure 9.11. Now there are two

FIGURE 9.11 EOQ Model with Shortages Allowed

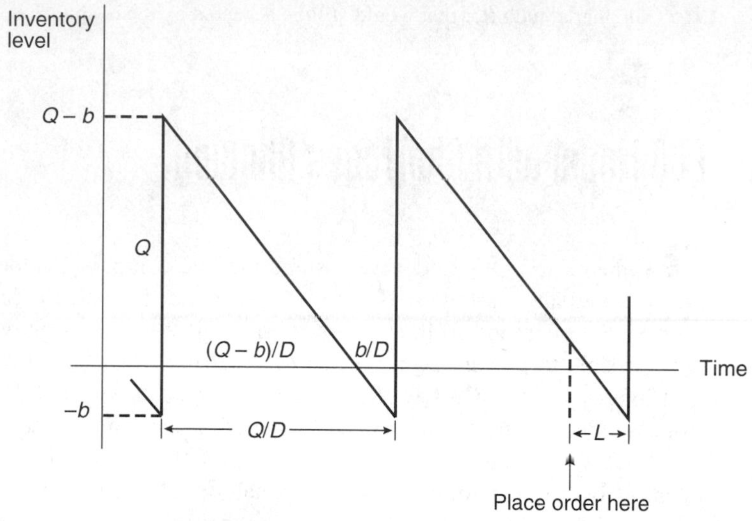

decision variables: Q, the order quantity, and b, the maximum amount backlogged. Each cycle has length Q/D, the time to deplete Q units at demand rate D. But now a cycle has two parts. During time $(Q - b)/D$ (the time required to deplete the first $Q - b$ units), there is positive inventory and demands are being met on time. During the last section of each cycle, of length b/D, the inventory is negative, which means that shortages exist. The order for Q units is placed so that it arrives precisely when the inventory level reaches $-b$. When this order arrives, b units are used immediately to satisfy backlogged demand and the other $Q - b$ units go into on-hand inventory. Therefore, at the beginning of any cycle, there are $Q - b$ units in inventory. Note that if there is an order lead time of L, then the order is placed when the inventory level is DL units above its lowest point, $-b$. This is exactly analogous to the basic EOQ model, since DL is the amount of demand during the lead time. (As before, this must be modified slightly if $DL > Q$.)

The total cost function, a function of both Q and b, is now fairly straightforward. The annual setup cost is KD/Q, the same as before, because there are D/Q orders per year. The annual purchase cost is cD because all demand is eventually satisfied. (In this section we assume a constant marginal purchasing cost; no quantity discounts are available.) The annual financial holding cost is, as usual, the interest rate times half of the purchase cost of an order, $icQ/2$.

To find the annual storage cost, refer to Figure 9.11. The storage cost per cycle is the unit storage cost s multiplied by the average inventory when inventory is positive $([Q - b]/2)$ multiplied by the amount of time during a cycle when inventory is positive $([Q - b]/D)$. To obtain the annual storage cost, we multiply the cost per cycle by the number of cycles per year (D/Q) to obtain

$$\text{Annual storage cost} = s[(Q - b)/2][(Q - b)/D](D/Q) = s(Q - b)^2/(2Q) \qquad \textbf{(9.8)}$$

Again referring to Figure 9.11, the average shortage cost per cycle is p multiplied by the average amount short when the inventory level is negative $(b/2)$ multiplied by the amount of time during a cycle when inventory is negative (b/D). Multiplying the shortage cost per cycle by the number of cycles per year (D/Q) gives

$$\text{Annual shortage cost} = p(b/2)(b/D)(D/Q) = pb^2/(2Q) \qquad \textbf{(9.9)}$$

We can now develop the spreadsheet model for GMB.

Developing the Spreadsheet Model The spreadsheet solution to GMB's problem appears in Figure 9.12. (See the file EOQ5.XLS.) The following steps can be used to develop the spreadsheet.

1 **Inputs.** Enter the inputs in the range B5:B10.

2 **Order quantity and maximum backlog.** Enter *any* values for the order quantity and the maximum backlog allowed in cells B14 and B15.

3 **Order cycle.** Calculate the time between orders and the number of orders per year in cells B16 and B17 with the same formulas as before.

4 **Costs.** Calculate the annual costs that are affected by the decision variables in cells B20:B24 and then the purchasing cost and the total annual cost in cells B26 and B27. The only new formulas here are the storage cost and shortage costs in cells B22 and B23. Using Equations 9.8 and 9.9, calculate these with the formulas

=B6*(B14–B15)^2/(2*B14)

and

=B9*B15^2/(2*B14)

The other formulas are analogous to previous EOQ spreadsheets.

FIGURE 9.12 **EOQ Model with Shortages Allowed**

	A	B
1	**Basic EOQ Model with Shortages Allowed**	
2		
3	**Inputs**	
4		
5	Setup cost (K)	$100
6	Storage cost per unit per year (s)	$0.50
7	Annual interest rate (i)	10%
8	Unit purchasing cost (c)	$0.50
9	Shortage cost per unit per year (p)	$52
10	Annual demand (D)	50000
11		
12	**Analysis using the Solver**	
13		
14	Order quantity Q	4283
15	Maximum backlog b	41
16	Time between orders	0.086
17	Orders per year	11.7
18		
19	Costs affected by decision variables	
20	Annual setup cost	$1,167.41
21	Annual financial holding cost	$107.08
22	Annual storage cost	$1,050.35
23	Annual shortage cost	$10.20
24	Total affected cost	$2,335.03
25		
26	Annual purchasing cost	$25,000.00
27	Total annual cost	$27,335.03

Using the Solver

1 **Objective.** Select cell B24 (total affected cost) as the objective to minimize. (Cell B27 could be used instead with the same result.)

2 **Changing cells.** Choose the range B14:B15 as the changing cells, and constrain them to be nonnegative. (You can also constrain them to be integers if you like.)

3 **Optimize.** Click on Solve.

As we see in Figure 9.12, the optimal solution calls for GMB to place orders for 4283 jewel cases and let shortages occur until the backlog is 41. The total annual cost is approximately $27,300, of which $25,000 is the unavoidable annual purchase cost.

Since GMB is somewhat uncertain about the shortage cost p to use, we then ran the Solver several additional times, each time using a different value of p in cell B9, and transferred the optimal values of Q, b, and total annual cost (without the $25,000 purchasing cost) to a sensitivity table shown in Figure 9.13.[6] The entries in this table show that Q, b, and the total annual cost are quite insensitive to p, except possibly that b becomes fairly large when p is very small. (This makes sense. Why should GMB worry about making customers wait if it believes that the penalty for waiting is very low?) This information should make GMB more comfortable, knowing that its estimate of p is not that crucial. ■

FIGURE 9.13 **Sensitivity of Ordering Policy to Penalty Cost**

	A	B	C	D
29	Sensitivity of Q, b, and total affected cost to p			
30				
31	p	Q	b	TotCost
32	$10	4359	208	$2,293.88
33	$30	4296	70	$2,327.67
34	$50	4283	42	$2,334.63
35	$70	4278	30	$2,337.64
36	$90	4275	24	$2,339.31
37	$110	4273	19	$2,340.38

PROBLEMS

Skill-Building Problems

16 The manager of a hardware store decides to use the model from this section to determine her ordering policy for tape measures. Using economic considerations, she determines that she should use an order quantity of $Q = 30$ and have a maximum shortage of $b = 3$. The lead time for her supplier to deliver an order is L working days, where there are six working days in a week. (Essentially, you can ignore Sundays.) The weekly demand is for 20 tape measures. What reorder point should the manager use if $L = 3$; if $L = 5$; if $L = 10$? (*Hint*: Now the manager should plan her orders so that the inventory level when an order arrives is $-b$.)

[6]This table was *not* formed by using the Data/Table command. Unfortunately, this command cannot be used when each entry is an output from a separate run of the Solver.

17 A Mercedes dealer must pay $20,000 for each car purchased. The annual holding cost is estimated to be 25% of the dollar value of inventory. The dealer sells an average of 500 cars per year. He is willing to backlog some demand but estimates that if he is short one car for one year he will lose $20,000 worth of future profits. Each time the dealer places an order for cars, the ordering cost is $10,000. Determine the Mercedes dealer's optimal ordering policy. What is the maximum shortage that will occur? Assume it costs $5000 to store a car for a year (this is in addition to the holding cost above).

Skill-Extending Problems

18 Suppose that instead of measuring shortage in terms of cost per shortage per year, a cost of P dollars is incurred for each unit the firm is short. This cost does not depend on the length of time before the backlogged demand is satisfied. Determine a new expression for the annual shortage cost as a function of Q and b, and solve GMB's problem with this way of costing shortages for reasonable values of P. (What values of P do you think are reasonable?)

19 The penalty cost p used in the backlog model might be very difficult to estimate. Instead, a company might use a service level constraint, such as, "95% of all demand must be met from on-hand inventory." Solve the Mercedes problem (Problem 17) with this constraint instead of the $20,000 penalty cost. Now the problem is to minimize the total annual ordering and holding costs subject to meeting the service level constraint. ■

9.7 Reducing the Setup Cost

There has been a lot of talk in the past few years about striving for zero inventory. The argument is that the less inventory a company carries, the more efficiently it is operating its business. (See the article by Zangwill [6] for a discussion of the merits of keeping inventory low.) The question is whether this argument can be justified from an economic point of view, at least in the context of the economic order quantity models we have been discussing. We have seen that the main factor driving up inventory levels in these models is the fixed setup cost K. If K is large, it is economical to order in larger quantities, which means that the average inventory level is large. So if this is true, what incentive is there for a company to strive for zero inventory?

One possible answer to this question is to reconsider whether the setup cost is really fixed. Is a company automatically stuck with some value of K, or is it possible to reduce this value of K and thereby justify smaller order quantities and smaller inventory levels? This is an interesting modeling question: how can we mathematically model the cost of reducing K?

One researcher, Evan Porteus, has proposed a model where a company can make a one-time investment to reduce the value of K. (See Porteus [4].) Specifically, if the company's initial setup cost is K_0, he assumes that by investing $f(K)$ dollars, it can reduce the setup cost from K_0 down to K (where $K < K_0$). Having a smaller value of K will certainly imply a lower total annual cost, but this reduction must be weighed against the one-time investment to reduce the setup cost. Also, the optimal *amount* of setup cost reduction must be found. That is, K becomes a decision variable along with the order quantity Q in the basic EOQ model. (To keep the model reasonably simple, we will not allow quantity discounts or shortages in this section.)

There are two modeling problems here. The first is to choose a reasonable form for the function $f(K)$. The second is to find a way to turn a one-time investment cost, $f(K)$, into an equivalent *annual* cost, so that the cost of reducing the setup cost is comparable to the annual operating costs we have been discussing. For the first problem Porteus assumes that the investment required to reduce the setup cost from K_0 to K is of the form

$$f(K) = a_0 + a_1 \ln(K), 0 < K \le K_0$$

for some constants a_0 and a_1. This form is not as strange as it might look. It implies that each 10% decrease in K costs a fixed dollar amount. (The 10% figure is chosen for convenience; the same argument can be used for any other percentage.) In fact, it can be shown that the cost of reducing K by 10% is $a_1 \ln(.9) = -.1054a_1$ dollars, regardless of whether the reduction is from \$300 to \$270, \$30 to \$27, \$3 to \$2.70, or any other 10% change. This constant cost per 10% decrease is a reasonable property for $f(K)$ to have.

We can now fully specify the $f(K)$ function, that is, find a_0 and a_1, if we are given two inputs: the initial setup cost K_0 and the cost of a 10% reduction in K. To illustrate, suppose that the initial setup cost is $K_0 = \$500$ and it takes a one-time investment of \$1000 to reduce this by 10%. Then we set $-.1054a_1 = 1000$ to obtain $a_1 = -9491$. Also, because it costs zero dollars to stay at level K_0, we have $f(K_0) = 0$, which implies that

$$0 = a_0 + a_1 \ln(K_0) = a_0 - 9491 \ln(500) = a_0 - 58984$$

or

$$a_0 = 58984$$

Now we tackle the second problem. The investment cost $f(K)$ is a one-time investment. However, it is equivalent to an annual investment in perpetuity of $if(K)$ dollars, where i is again the annual interest rate. This follows from a net present value argument that we will not present here. In words, if the company were to pay $if(K)$ dollars at the beginning of each year forever, this would be equivalent in net present value terms to a one-time payment of $f(K)$ dollars. Putting all of this together, the total annual cost to the company is $if(K)$ plus the annual operating cost from any of our previous models. In addition to any previous decision variables such as Q, we now need to choose K, subject to the constraint $K \le K_0$. The procedure is illustrated in the following example.

EXAMPLE 9.4

The CompServe Company stocks expensive laser printers. The annual demand for this product is 300 units. The cost from CompServe's supplier is \$1000 per printer, the cost of capital is 10%, and the storage cost per printer per year is \$30. CompServe currently incurs a setup cost of \$800 per order, but it believes that by streamlining its ordering and delivery operations, it can reduce this value and thereby achieve smaller inventory levels. Specifically, it assumes that each 10% reduction in setup cost requires a \$1500 investment. However, preliminary analysis shows that it is physically impossible to reduce the setup cost below \$50, regardless of the amount invested. Should the company invest in setup cost reductions, and if so, how will this affect its ordering policy?

Solution

We must first find the parameters a_0 and a_1 of the investment cost function $f(K)$ by using the information on the original setup cost, \$800, and the cost per 10% setup cost reduction, \$1500. Then we can express all annual costs in terms of the decision variables K and Q and use the Solver to optimize. The details are explained below.

Developing the Spreadsheet Model The spreadsheet solution shown in Figure 9.14 is very similar to the solution for the basic EOQ model. (See the file EOQ6.XLS.) It can be formed as follows.

FIGURE 9.14 **Solution to Setup Cost Reduction Example**

	A	B	C
1	**Basic EOQ Model When the Setup Cost Can Be Reduced**		
2			
3	**Inputs**		
4			
5	Initial setup cost (K_0)	\$800	
6	Minimal setup cost achievable (K_{min})	\$50	
7	Storage cost per unit per year (s)	\$30	
8	Annual interest rate (i)	10%	
9	Unit purchasing cost (c)	\$1,000	
10	Annual demand (D)	300	
11	Cost of 10% reduction in setup cost	\$1,500	
12			
13	**Parameters of setup cost reduction function**		
14	a_0	95168	
15	a_1	-14237	
16			
17	**Analysis using the Solver**		
18			
19	Setup cost K after reduction	\$104.48	
20	Order quantity Q	22	
21	Time between orders	0.073	
22	Orders per year	13.64	
23			
24	Costs affected by decision variables		
25	One-time investment to reduce setup cost	\$28,980	
26	Equivalent annual cost to reduce setup cost	\$2,898	
27	Annual setup cost	\$1,425	
28	Annual holding cost	\$1,430	
29	Total affected cost	\$5,753	
30			
31	Annual purchasing cost	\$300,000	
32	Total annual cost	\$305,753	

1 **Inputs.** Enter the inputs in cells B5 through B11.

2 **Parameters of setup cost reduction function.** Calculate the parameters a_0 and a_1 of the setup cost reduction function in cells B14 and B15 using the procedure outlined above. Specifically, calculate a_1 in cell B15 with the formula

=B11/LN(.9)

Then calculate a_0 in cell B14 with the formula

=-B15*LN(B5)

3 **Setup cost (after reduction) and order quantity.** In the analysis section enter *any* trial values for K and Q in cells B19 and B20. Notice that this value of K refers to the setup cost after the setup cost reduction, that is, it is the setup cost the company will be using.

4 **Order cycle.** As in previous models, calculate the time between orders and the number of orders per year in cells B21 and B22.

5 **Cost of reducing setup cost.** Enter the one-time investment in setup cost reduction in cell B25 with the formula

=B14+B15*LN(B19)

Then enter the equivalent annual cost in cell B26 with the formula

```
=B8*B25
```

6 **Other costs.** Calculate the other costs in cells B27:B29 and B31:B32 exactly as in previous EOQ models. Note that the total affected cost in cell B29 is the sum of the three costs above it, that is, you should *not* include the cost in cell B25 in this sum.

Using the Solver

1 **Objective.** Select cell B29 as the objective to minimize. (As usual, cell B32 could be used instead.)

2 **Changing cells.** Choose cells B19 and B20 as the changing cells. Constrain cell B20 to be nonnegative (and integer, if you like).

3 **Constraints.** Add the constraints B19>=B6 and B19<=B5. These simply force the eventual setup cost to be between the initial setup cost and the minimal value achievable.

4 **Optimize.** Click on Solve.

As Figure 9.14 indicates, CompServe should first invest $28,980 to reduce the setup cost from $800 to $104.48. Then its optimal order quantity is 22 printers, and the total affected cost, including the investment in setup cost reduction, is $5753.

Has setup cost reduction worked? If this example is solved with the basic EOQ model, using the original $800 as the setup cost, you can check that the optimal order quantity is 61 units and the total affected cost is approximately $7900. When setup cost reduction is allowed, the company reduces its setup cost from $800 to slightly over $100, and the ordering quantity drops sharply to 22 units. Instead of ordering about five times a year (300/61), it now orders almost 14 times a year (300/22). Also, the total affected cost drops by over $2000. Since the company's initial investment of almost $29,000 is equivalent to about $2900 per year (as shown in cell B26), the saving in annual ordering and holding costs is about $4900. In addition, there may be other intangible benefits from holding less inventory, as Zangwill [6] and many other authors have noted. ■

PROBLEMS

Skill-Building Problems

20 Reconsider Example 9.1 from Section 9.4. Each time Machey's orders cameras, it incurs a $35 ordering cost. Assume that Machey's could make an investment to decrease this ordering cost. Suppose that any 10% decrease costs a fixed amount C dollars. Using $i = .10$ and a spreadsheet Solver, experiment with different values of C to see how Machey's optimal order quantity is affected. Assume the minimum possible ordering cost is $10.

21 The particular logarithmic function proposed by Porteus is just one possibility for the cost of a setup reduction. Suppose instead that in the previous problem Machey's has only three possibilities. It can either leave the setup cost as it is, it can spend C_1 dollars to reduce the setup cost to $25, or it can spend C_2 dollars to reduce it to $15. Analyze these possibilities for various values of C_1 and C_2 on a spreadsheet to see which is optimal in terms of total annual cost. ■

9.8

Synchronizing Orders for Several Products

Until now, we have assumed that the company orders only a single product. If it orders several products, it could calculate the EOQ for each product and order them according to separate schedules. However, there might be economies, particularly reduced setup costs, from synchronizing the orders so that several products are ordered simultaneously. This should be particularly attractive for products that come from the same supplier. Then, for example, the same truck might be able to deliver orders for several products, thereby reducing the setup cost involved with the delivery. We will develop a model in this section that takes advantage of synchronization, and we will compare it to the "individual EOQs" policy that involves no synchronization and treats the separate products independently. Although this model can be developed for any number of products, we will keep things relatively simple by assuming that there are only *two* products. We illustrate the approach in the following example.

EXAMPLE 9.5

Sleepease, a retailer of bedding supplies, orders king-size and queen-size mattresses from a regional supplier. There is a fairly constant demand for each of these products. The annual demand for the queens is 2200; for the kings it is 250. The unit purchasing costs for queen-size and king-size mattresses are \$100 and \$120, and the company's cost to store either of these for one year is \$15. Sleepease's ordering cost is based primarily on the fixed cost of delivering a batch of mattresses. This ordering cost is \$500 if either queens or kings are ordered separately, but the ordering cost is only \$650 if both are ordered together. The retailer's cost of capital is 13%. Sleepease wants to know whether synchronizing orders is better than not synchronizing them, and if so, what the best synchronized ordering policy is.

Solution

The only real cost benefit from synchronization is reduced setup costs. Let $K_1 = \$500$ be the setup cost for ordering queens when this is the only product ordered. Define $K_2 = \$500$ similarly for kings. When both of the products are ordered simultaneously, we denote the setup cost for the order by $K_{12} = \$650$. The important point is that K_{12} is considerably less than $K_1 + K_2$. This reflects the economy of scale achieved when both products are ordered together rather than individually. All other parameters (s, c, i, and D) are defined as before, except that each product has its own values of s, c, and D.

To model this problem, consider the graph shown in Figure 9.15, which depicts a synchronization policy. Let t_1 and t_2, respectively, be the time between orders of queens and kings, and let T be the cycle time, defined as the larger of t_1 and t_2. (In the graph, $t_2 > t_1$, so $T = t_2$.) Also, let n_1 and n_2, respectively, be the number of times queens and kings are ordered during a cycle. (In the graph, $n_1 = 3$ and $n_2 = 1$.) Then under a synchronization model, n_1 and n_2 are both positive integers, and at least one of them equals 1. (Actually, they could both be 1, in which case queens and kings are always ordered together.)

FIGURE 9.15 EOQ with Synchronization

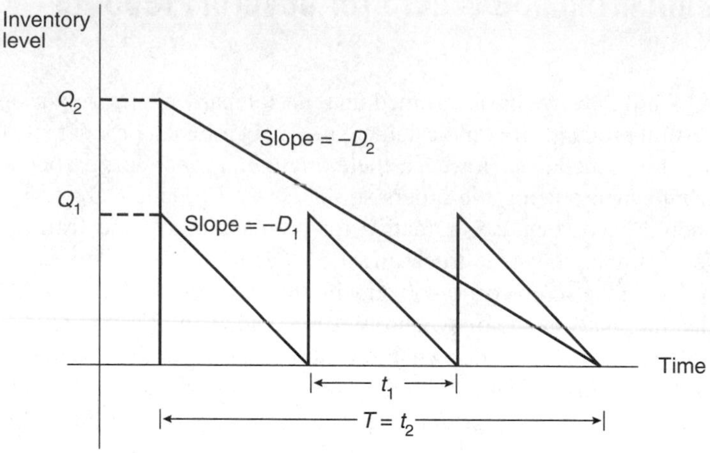

For the optimization model it is convenient to let T, n_1, and n_2 be the decision variables, that is, the changing cells in the spreadsheet. We can easily recover the order quantities Q_1 and Q_2 from these values as follows. First, we know that t_1, the time between orders of queens, is T/n_1, and similarly, $t_2 = T/n_2$. Then given t_1 and t_2, the order quantities Q_1 and Q_2 must be given by $Q_1 = D_1 t_1$ and $Q_2 = D_2 t_2$ (because we want each Q to decrease to zero in time t at rate D).

To develop the total annual cost, the purchasing and holding costs are exactly as before (for each product). Therefore, we concentrate on the setup cost. During a cycle, both products are ordered together exactly once, for a setup cost of K_{12}. Then product j (for $j = 1$ or $j = 2$) is ordered $n_j - 1$ times by itself, for a setup cost of $K_j(n_j - 1)$. (For at least one of the two products, this latter term is 0. For example, it is 0 for product 2 in Figure 9.15.) The number of cycles per year is $1/T$, so the total annual setup cost is

$$\text{Annual setup cost} = [K_{12} + (n_1 - 1)K_1 + (n_2 - 1)K_2]/T \qquad \textbf{(9.10)}$$

We are now ready to develop the spreadsheet model.

Developing the Spreadsheet Model The spreadsheet model appears in Figure 9.16. (See the file EOQ7.XLS.) The top part of the spreadsheet shows the analysis for the synchronized ordering policy. It can be formed as follows.

1 **Inputs.** Enter the inputs in rows 3, 4, 7, and 8. Note that (as usual) the combined holding costs in the range E7:E8 are storage costs plus the interest rate multiplied by the purchasing costs.

2 **Orders per cycle and cycle time.** Enter *any* trial values in the range B13:B14 and cell B16 for the number of orders of queens and kings per cycle and the cycle time (measured as a fraction of a year).

3 **Timing of orders.** Calculate the times between orders (t_1 and t_2) and the numbers of orders per year in the range C13:D14. Specifically, enter the formulas

=$B$16/B13

and

=1/C13

in cells C13 and D13 and then copy them to cells C14 and D14.

FIGURE 9.16 **Solution to Synchronized Ordering Policy Example**

	A	B	C	D	E	F
1	**Synchronized Ordering of Two Products**					
2						
3	Interest rate	13%				
4	Joint setup cost	$650				
5						
6	Product	Setup cost (individual)	Storage cost	Purchasing cost	Combined holding cost	Annual demand
7	Queens	$500	$15	$100	$28	2200
8	Kings	$500	$15	$120	$31	250
9						
10	**Optimal synchronized policy**					
11						
12	Product	Number of orders per cycle	Time between orders	Orders per year	Order quantity	
13	Queens	2	0.122	8.2	269	
14	Kings	1	0.245	4.1	61	
15						
16	Cycle time (years)	0.245				
17						
18	Costs affected by ordering policy					
19	Annual setup cost	$4,702				
20	Annual holding cost	$4,702				
21	Total affected cost	$9,404				
22						
23	Annual purchasing cost	$250,000				
24	Total annual cost	$259,404				
25						
26	**Optimal policy with no synchronization (using individual EOQs)**					
27						
28	Product	EOQ	Time between orders	Orders per year	Annual setup costs	Annual holding costs
29	Queens	280	0.127	7.8	$3,924	$3,924
30	Kings	90	0.362	2.8	$1,383	$1,383
31					$5,307	$5,307
32	Annual purchasing cost	$250,000				
33	Total annual cost	$260,614				

4 **Order quantities.** Calculate the order quantity for queens in cell E13 with the formula

=F7*C13

and copy this to cell E14 for the kings. Again, this expresses the order quantity as the annual demand multiplied by the time between orders.

5 **Annual setup cost.** Calculate the annual setup cost in cell B19 with the formula

=(B4+(B13–1)*B7+(B14–1)*B8)/B16

This follows directly from the expression in Equation 9.10.

6 **Other costs.** Calculate the other costs in cells B20, B21, B23, and B24 exactly as in previous EOQ models, except that now the holding and purchasing costs must be summed over the two products, queens and kings.

We can now use the Solver to find the optimal synchronized policy.

Using the Solver

1 **Objective.** Select cell B21 as the objective to minimize.

2 **Changing cells.** Choose B13:B14 and B16 as the changing cells.

3 **Constraints.** Constrain cell B16 to be nonnegative, add the constraint B13:B14>=1, and constrain cells B13:B14 to be integers. These latter two ensure that Sleepease will order each product a positive integer number of times per cycle.

4 **Optimize.** Click on Solve.

We see that there are about four cycles every year. Queens are ordered twice every cycle, and kings are ordered only once. The total affected cost (setup plus holding) from this synchronized ordering policy is $9404.

The bottom part of the spreadsheet in Figure 9.16 shows the unsynchronized policy from using individual EOQs for comparison. (The order quantity for each product is found from the basic EOQ square root formula.) Now queens and kings are both ordered slightly less frequently than before, but because the orders aren't synchronized, there are more ordering times per year. By comparing setup and holding costs, we see that this unsynchronized policy is about 11% higher than the best synchronized policy ($10,614 versus $9404). In addition, there might be an important noneconomic advantage of synchronizing orders: the ordering process is simply easier to manage.

Could you have guessed that queens would be ordered more frequently than kings? The reason is that the number of orders per year (for either product) is D/Q. Because the optimal Q from the EOQ formula, as a function of D, increases in proportion to the square root of D, the optimal number of orders per year is proportional to the square root of D. (This is because $D/\sqrt{D} = \sqrt{D}$.) Now, kings and queens have very similar setup costs K (if ordered separately) and holding costs h. Therefore, their relative ordering frequencies are determined by their demand rates, and queens have a much larger demand rate. Thus it makes sense to order queens more frequently. (The analysis wouldn't be this straightforward if kings and queens had different values for all three parameters K, D, and h.) ■

More Than Two Products

Virtually the same spreadsheet could be used for more than two products, provided that we make a simplifying assumption. This assumption is that a setup cost reduction is available only when the company places an order for all of the products simultaneously. Unfortunately, it is probably more realistic to assume that there is a setup cost reduction when *any* subset of products is ordered simultaneously. To illustrate, suppose that there are four products, product 1 is ordered once per cycle, products 2 and 3 are ordered twice per cycle, and product 4 is ordered four times per cycle. (See Figure 9.17.) When all four products are ordered together at the beginning of a cycle, there is definitely a setup cost reduction, but there is probably also some setup cost reduction when products 2, 3, and 4 are ordered together in the middle of a cycle. If we allow this possibility, however, and then try to optimize over all possible synchronizations, the problem becomes difficult to

FIGURE 9.17 **Another Way to Synchronize**

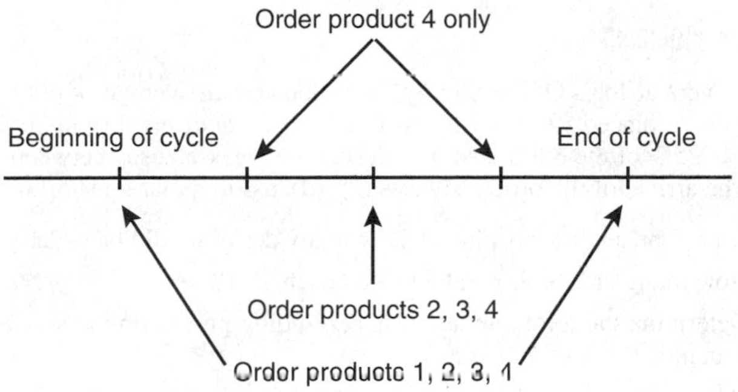

model on a spreadsheet. Therefore, we will not pursue this multiple-product model any further here.

PROBLEMS

Skill-Building Problems

22 Chicago Nope Hospital needs to order drugs that are used to treat heart attack victims. Annually 500 units of drug 1 and 800 units of drug 2 are used. The unit purchasing cost for drug 1 is $150 per unit, and the unit cost of purchasing drug 2 is $300. It costs $20 to store a unit of each drug for a year. When only drug 1 is ordered, an order for drug 1 costs $400. When only drug 2 is ordered, an order for drug 2 costs $600. If both drugs are ordered at the same time, the cost of placing an order is $800. Chicago Nope's annual cost of capital is 18%. Determine a cost-minimizing ordering policy.

23 Software EG orders two kinds of software from TeleHard Software. Annually they sell 800 units of product 1 and 400 units of product 2. The unit purchasing cost is $30 per unit of product 1 and $25 per unit of product 2. It costs $5 to store a unit of either product for a year. The cost of placing an order for either product separately or both products together is $100. Software EG's annual cost of capital is 14%. Determine a cost-minimizing ordering policy. ■

9.9 Conclusion

We have examined a variety of inventory/ordering models in this chapter. The general theme is the balance companies try to find between two competing costs. If they order frequent small quantities, they have little extra inventory on hand but they incur large setup costs. In contrast, if they order infrequent large quantities, then they have small setup costs, but they have large inventories on hand and incur large holding costs. The basic EOQ model and its many variations we have discussed here are able to find the right balance. These models are relatively straightforward, although the multiproduct models introduce significant complications. The main reason we were able to handle such complex problems in a reasonably simple way is that we have assumed that customer demand is *known*. In the next chapter we will relax this simplifying (and often unrealistic) assumption and assume that future demand is random with a known probability distribution. This complicates the analysis immensely, but we will still be able to obtain useful results.

REVIEW PROBLEMS

Skill-Building Problems

24 Customers at Joe's Office Supply Store demand an average of 6000 desks per year. Each time an order is placed, an ordering cost of $300 is incurred. The annual holding cost for a single desk is 25% of the $200 cost of a desk. One week elapses between the placement of an order and the arrival of the order. In Parts (a)–(d), assume that no shortages are allowed.

a Each time an order is placed, how many desks should be ordered?

b How many orders should be placed each year?

c Determine the total annual costs (excluding purchasing costs) of meeting the customers' demands for desks.

d Determine the reorder point. If the lead time is five weeks, what is the reorder point? (One year equals 52 weeks.)

e How do the answers to Parts (a) and (b) change if shortages are allowed and a cost of $80 is incurred if Joe's is short one desk for one year?

25 A camera store sells an average of 100 cameras per month. The cost of holding a camera in inventory for a year is 30% of the price the camera shop pays for the camera. It costs $120 each time the camera store places an order with its supplier. The price charged per camera depends on the number of cameras ordered (see Table 9.5). Each time the camera store places an order, how many cameras should it order?

TABLE 9.5 **Data for Camera Problem**

No. of Cameras Ordered	Price per Camera
1–10	$10.00
11–40	$9.00
41–100	$7.00
More than 100	$5.50

Skill-Extending Problems

26 A newspaper has 500,000 subscribers who pay $4 per month for the paper. It costs the company $200,000 to bill all its customers. Assume that the company can earn interest at a rate of 20% per year on all revenues. Determine how often the newspaper should bill its customers. (*Hint*: Consider unpaid subscriptions as the inventoried good.)

27 Consider a firm that knows that the price of the product it is ordering is going to increase permanently by X dollars. It wants to know how much of the product it should order before the price increase goes into effect. Here is one approach to this problem. Suppose the firm places one order for Q units before the price increase goes into effect.

a What extra holding cost is incurred by ordering Q units now?

b How much in purchasing costs is saved by ordering Q units now?

c What value of Q maximizes purchasing cost savings less extra holding costs?

d Suppose that the annual demand is 1000 units, the holding cost per unit per year is $7.50, and the price of the item is going to increase by $10. How large an order should the firm place before the price increase goes into effect?

28 (Based on Riccio et al. [5]) The borough of Staten Island has two sanitation districts. In district 1 street litter piles up at an average rate of 2000 tons per week, and in district 2, at an average rate of 1000 tons per week. Each district has 500 miles of streets. Staten Island has ten sanitation crews and each crew can clean 50 miles per week of streets. To minimize the average level of the total amount of street litter in the two districts, how often should each district be cleaned? Assume that litter in a district grows at a constant rate until it is picked up, and assume that pickup is instantaneous. (*Hint*: Let p_i equal the average number of times that each district is cleaned per week. Then $p_1 + p_2 = 1$.)

29 A company inventories two items. The relevant data for each item are shown in Table 9.6. Determine the optimal inventory policy if no shortages are allowed and if the average investment in inventory is not allowed to exceed $700. If this constraint could be relaxed by $1, by how much would the company's annual costs decrease? (*Hint*: Use the Solver.)

TABLE 9.6 **Data for Two-Item Inventory Problem**

	Item 1	Item 2
Annual Demand	6000	4000
Per-Unit Cost	$4.00	$3.50
Annual Holding Cost	30% per year	25% per year
Price per Order	$35	$20

Modeling Problem

30 An *exchange curve* can be used to display the trade-offs between the average investment in inventory and the annual ordering cost. To illustrate the usefulness of a trade-off curve, suppose that a company must order two products with the attributes shown in Table 9.7.

TABLE 9.7 **Data for Exchange Curve Problem**

	Order Cost	Annual Demand	Unit Purchase Cost
Product 1	$50	10,000	$200.00
Product 2	$80	20,000	$2.50

a Draw a curve that displays annual order cost on the horizontal axis and average inventory investment on the vertical axis.

b Currently the firm is ordering each product ten times per year. Demonstrate that this is an unsatisfactory ordering policy.

c Suppose management limits the company's average inventory investment to $10,000. Use the exchange curve to determine the best ordering policy. ■

CASE STUDY

Subway Token Hoarding

Riders of the subway system in the city of Metropolis must pay for the ride by purchasing a token. The same token can also be used to ride the buses in Metropolis. A single token is good for a trip to any destination served by the system. (Tokens are also used by millions of commuters for bridge, tunnel, and highway tolls in many areas of the country.)

Late in 1996 Metropolis transit officials announced that they were seeking a fare increase from \$1.50 to \$2.00. Later negotiations with politicians in the state capital reduced the requested increase to \$1.75. It usually takes a few weeks between the announcement of a fare increase and the time that the increase goes into effect. Knowing that an increase will occur gives users of mass transit an opportunity to mitigate the effect of the increase by hoarding tokens—that is, by purchasing a large supply of tokens before the fare increase goes into effect.

There is a clear motivation for hoarding tokens—namely, the purchase of tokens before a fare increase offers a savings over purchasing the same tokens at a higher price after the change in fare. Why wouldn't riders wish to purchase a very large supply of tokens? The reason is the inventory cost that arises because of the time value of money.[7] The larger the supply that is hoarded, the longer the time until the tokens are used. Purchasing the supply of tokens represents an immediate cost, but the benefit is only realized over a longer period of time. Thus, there is a trade-off between the immediate cost and the prolonged benefit. The optimal number of tokens to hoard balances these two effects to maximize the present value of the net benefit of the hoarding strategy.

Suppose that the current price of subway tokens is $p_1 = \$1.50$ and the fare is due to rise to $p_2 = \$1.75$. Suppose that you use the subway to commute twice per day, five days per week, 50 weeks per year. Also, suppose that you can purchase (or *hoard*) any number of tokens before the price increase takes effect. The hoarded tokens will be used by you during your normal usage of the mass transit system. After your hoard runs out, you will start purchasing tokens each day at the higher price. Suppose that your cost of capital is 15% per year. This means that you can borrow money to purchase your token supply, but the interest cost on the borrowed money is 15% per year.[8]

Questions

1. What is the optimal number of tokens to hoard?
2. What is the present value of the savings over not hoarding at all?
3. Suppose that the optimal quantity to hoard is Q^*. What is the present value of the savings if you decide to hoard only $0.8Q^*$? ■

[7] We are assuming that the hoarded tokens will be used by the hoarder for rides on the mass transit system, not for the immediate sale to other riders. In fact, such sales are illegal in Metropolis.

[8] Using 250 commuting days per year, you can assume that the daily interest cost is 0.05592% ($= 1.15^{(1/250)} - 1$).

REFERENCES

1 Baumol, W. "The Transactions Demand for Cash: An Inventory Theoretic Approach." *Quarterly Journal of Economics* 16 (1952): 545–56.

2 Ignall, E., and P. Kolesar. "Operating Characteristics of a Simple Shuttle under Local Dispatching Rules." *Operations Research* 20 (1972): 1077–88.

3 Lee, H., C. Billington, and B. Carter. "Hewlett-Packard Gains Control of Inventory and Service through Design for Localization." Interfaces 23, no. 4 (1993): 1–11.

4 Porteus, E. "Investing in Reduced Setups in the EOQ Model." *Management Science* 31, no. 8 (1985): 998–1010.

5 Riccio, L., J. Miller, and A. Little. "Polishing the Big Apple." *Interfaces* 16, no. 1 (1986): 83–88.

6 Zangwill, W. "The Limits of Japanese Production Theory." *Interfaces* 22, no. 5 (1992): 14–25.

CHAPTER

10

Probabilistic Inventory Models

Management Science Success Stories

When we think of inventory, we usually think of items stored on shelves, hung on racks, or parked in new car lots. However, American Airlines manages a different type of inventory: the seat reservations on its planes. As described by Smith et al. [4] in their article "Yield Management at American Airlines," American has used management science methods to great advantage, starting in the 1960s and continuing to today. There are two primary problems it has attacked: the overbooking problem and the discount allocation problem. The company estimates that its analysis of these problems has generated a gain of $1.4 billion over the past three years, and it expects an annual revenue of over $500 million to continue into the future.

The overbooking problem is a classic one. The airline knows that if it has, say, 150 seats on a plane and it sells only 150 tickets, a significant number of these ticketholders will either cancel or fail to show up, causing the airline to lose revenue. Therefore, American and all other airlines have overbooked for years, selling more tickets than there are seats and hoping that the number of passengers who show up will be close to the number of seats. Of course, if you have ever been "bumped" from a flight, you know that there is a cost to the airline. They have to book you a seat on another flight, they may give you a free ticket for a future flight, and they may even give you free lodging and/or meals while you are waiting. So the airline must find a balance between not enough overbooking and too much overbooking. A simple model of overbooking is not difficult to solve, but on the scale at which American Airlines operates, the problem is very complex and requires data that are difficult to collect (or estimate). For example, the airline needs to know the probability distribution of passenger cancellations and no-shows. However, this distribution continually changes as flight time draws nearer, so that any good overbooking policy must take into account the time until the flight and the latest data from the flight reservation database.

The overbooking problem is a special case of a problem we will discuss in this chapter. American's discount allocation is unlike any problem we will discuss, but it is extremely important to American's overall inventory management system. The problem is one of allocating an optimal (or near-optimal) number of tickets of various classes in order to maximize revenue. You are probably aware that there are many different fares offered for a given flight, but you may not be aware that the airline makes only a certain number of tickets of each fare available. For example, suppose that there are only two fares: discount and full-price. The airline uses the discount fares to attract customers, so that seats that would otherwise be empty generate at least some revenue. But the airline also realizes that there are business travelers who need to take a certain flight and are willing to pay the full price. Therefore, it makes sense to cut off the supply of the discount tickets at some point and force the business travelers to pay full price. American Airlines has made an exact science of this practice, and as the numbers quoted earlier show, it has paid off handsomely. ■

10.1 Introduction

We continue the analysis of inventory models in this chapter, but we now assume that demand for the company's product is not known with certainty. Instead, only the *probability distribution* of demand is known. This tends to make the models more realistic, because demand is usually not known in real applications, and it makes the analysis more difficult mathematically. Therefore, we will examine only a few of the simpler models in this chapter, namely, the one-period "newsvendor" model and the widely used continuous review (R, Q) model. Many other probabilistic models have been investigated by specialists in this area, but they are beyond the level of this book.

As in the previous chapter, there are two possible problems in probabilistic inventory models—having too much inventory and not having enough. When demand is known, a good balance between the two can be found relatively easily by arranging for the inventory level to reach zero just as a new order arrives. However, when demand is probabilistic, this may not be possible. Typically, a company places an order when its inventory level gets sufficiently low, hoping that when the order arrives (after a certain lead time), the inventory level will be close to zero. However, the company realizes that because the demand during lead time is random, its inventory might be depleted before the order arrives.

Therefore, there is a natural incentive to order a bit earlier, that is, when the inventory level is not too low, so that when the order arrives, there is a good chance that there will still be some inventory in stock. This remaining inventory is called **safety stock**. It provides a cushion in case the demand during lead time is greater than expected. Of course, excess safety stock—playing it more conservatively than necessary—implies larger inventory levels than needed and excess inventory holding costs. The purpose of the models in this chapter is to find a good balance.

In the previous chapter we discussed the difficulty of measuring the cost of running out of inventory. This cost becomes even more crucial when demand is random because, unless the company keeps excessive amounts of inventory on hand, there is always the possibility of running out. In the first model in this chapter, the newsvendor model, we will see that the penalty for running out is simple—potential revenue is lost from sales that could have been made if inventory had been on hand. In the (R, Q) model discussed next, however, we will assume that demands that occur when no inventory is on hand are backlogged. That is, these demands are not lost; the company eventually obtains revenue from these customers when the next order arrives. So we have to look elsewhere for the "cost" of running out. It may be loss of goodwill, emergency shipments, or other factors. Because this cost is typically difficult to measure in dollar terms, many companies instead specify a service level, such as promising to meet 98% of all customer demands on time. This service level constraint may ultimately have the same effect on decisions as assuming, say, a $3 cost for each unit that is backlogged, but it is usually easier for managers to understand.

Mathematically, there are two difficulties we face with probabilistic inventory models. The first difficulty is deriving an expression for the total cost from any particular ordering policy. In contrast to the models in the previous chapter, we must now take the probability distribution of demand into account. When demand is random, the total annual cost is also random, and it has a probability distribution. In Chapters 12 and 13 we will learn how to use computer simulation to generate this probability distribution and estimate its important summary measures, such as its mean and standard deviation. In this chapter, however, we will use probability arguments to derive expressions for the total expected annual cost as a function of the decision variables. This is a very difficult problem for all but a few probabilistic inventory models. This explains why the models in this chapter are somewhat limited. (It also explains why many analysts prefer simulation for probabilistic inventory models—the mathematics is simpler, and more complex problems can be analyzed.)

Even if we can find an expression for the expected annual cost, we are still faced with a second difficulty, namely, optimizing this cost with respect to the decision variables. In a few cases this optimization can be performed with differential calculus—by setting the first derivative(s) equal to zero and solving for the decision variable(s). However, this approach presumes quite a lot of calculus background on the part of the user. For the models in this chapter we will instead rely on the spreadsheet Solver to perform the optimization. Therefore, our main emphasis is on deriving cost functions for the Solver to optimize.

10.2 The Newsvendor Model

The essence of probabilistic inventory models is that a company places an order at a certain time for a certain quantity and then waits to see whether this is enough to satisfy the eventual customer demand. This is exactly what happens in the following example, a version of the "newsvendor" model. In a newsvendor model a company has one chance to order a product that will be sold for one period of time. This period could be a day, a month, a year, or any other length of time. At the end of this period, the product is essentially out of date and can no longer be sold, except possibly at a reduced price. A rather trivial example of this problem concerns a boy selling newspapers on the street corner, where he must decide how many newspapers to stock on a given day—hence, the term *newsvendor model*.

EXAMPLE 10.1

H. H. Craig, a retailer of kitchen appliances is about to place its last order for a certain model of dishwasher. This model will be phased out in a few months and will be replaced by a new model. The company buys these dishwashers from its supplier for $400 apiece and sells them for $550. However, after the new model comes out, the company plans to lower its price on any leftover dishwashers to $350, just to clear them out. It assumes that all leftovers will be purchased at this reduced price. But demand is limited for these dishwashers (at the $550 price). The company assumes that this demand, D, has the discrete distribution given in Table 10.1. For example, the probability that exactly ten customers will request dishwashers at the $550 price is 0.2. Finally, the company assumes that a $50 loss will result from each customer who requests one of these dishwashers when there are none left in stock. This cost captures the loss of goodwill from not satisfying customer demand. The company wants to know the consequences of different order amounts on expected profit.

TABLE 10.1 Probability Distribution of Demand for Dishwasher Example

k	$\Pr(k)$
6	0.02
7	0.05
8	0.10
9	0.15
10	0.20
11	0.15
12	0.15
13	0.10
14	0.05
15	0.03

Solution

Our first task is to develop a method for calculating the expected profit for a given order quantity. Then we can use the Solver to find the *optimal* order quantity. Let Q be the number of dishwashers ordered, a decision variable, and let D be the number of customers who order dishwashers, so that D follows the probability distribution in Table 10.1. If Q is greater than D, then all potential demand can be satisfied, and some dishwashers will be left over. If Q is less than D, then some customer demand will go unsatisfied. Of course, if Q is exactly equal to D, everything turns out perfectly, but the probability of this occurring is usually small. The company's problem is exactly like the ones we discussed in Chapter 8 on decision making under uncertainty. That is, it has to choose Q now, although the demand D will not be known until later.

There are several monetary values in the model. Each unit costs the company $c =$ \$400 to purchase, and the company sells each unit for $r_1 =$ \$550. After several months, when the new model comes out, any leftover dishwashers will be sold at the sale price of $r_2 =$ \$350. Finally, the "goodwill cost" per unit of unsatisfied demand is $p =$ \$50.

We can express Craig's profit as follows. Let $P(Q, D)$ denote the profit for given values of Q and D. Then there are two cases: $Q \geq D$ and $Q < D$. If $Q \geq D$, then Q units are ordered, D units are sold, and $Q - D$ units are left over. However, if $Q < D$, then Q units are ordered, only Q units are sold, and $D - Q$ units of customer demand cannot be satisfied. Therefore, we can express the profit thus:

$$P(Q, D) = \begin{cases} -cQ + r_1 D + r_2(Q - D) = -(c - r_2)Q + (r_1 - r_2)D & \text{if } Q \geq D \\ -cQ + r_1 Q - p(D - Q) = (r_1 - c + p)Q - pD & \text{if } Q < D \end{cases} \quad \textbf{(10.1)}$$

Now comes the hard part. Because D is random, so is the profit function $P(Q, D)$. We want to take the expected value of $P(Q, D)$ with respect to the probability distribution of D. This expected profit is the objective we will attempt to maximize.

Let $\Pr(k)$ be the probability D that equals k. Table 10.1 lists these probabilities for various values of k. Also, let $F(k)$ be the probability that demand D is less than or equal to k. For example, from Table 10.1, $F(8)$ is given by

$$F(8) = \Pr(D \leq 8) = \Pr(6) + \Pr(7) + \Pr(8) = .02 + .05 + .10 = .17$$

Then it can be shown that the expected profit for a given value of Q, labeled $EP(Q)$, is given by the following expression:

$$EP(Q) = (r_1 - c + p)Q - pE(D) + (r_1 - r_2 + p)\left[\left(\sum_{k \leq Q} k \Pr(k)\right) - QF(Q)\right] \quad \textbf{(10.2)}$$

Although this expression is quite complex, we will now see how it can be incorporated into a spreadsheet model.

Developing the Spreadsheet Model The spreadsheet in Figure 10.1 can be used to solve Craig's problem. (See the file NEWSBOY1.XLS.) It can be formed as follows.

1 **Inputs.** Enter the given inputs in the ranges B5:B8 and B12:K13 (the latter from Table 10.1).

2 **Order quantity.** Enter *any* trial value for the order quantity Q in cell B20.

3 **Cumulative probabilities.** Calculate the cumulative probabilities $F(k)$ in row 14. Specifically, calculate $F(6)$ in cell B14 with the formula

=B13

Then calculate $F(7)$ in cell C14 with the formula

=B14+C13

and copy this to the range D14:K14 to calculate the other $F(k)$ values. For example, the probability that demand is less than or equal to 12 (cell H14) is the probability that demand is less than or equal to 11 (cell G14) plus the probability that demand is exactly 12 (cell H13).

4 **Other probability terms.** Calculate the terms $k\,\Pr(k)$ in row 15 and the cumulative sums of these products in row 16. Specifically, enter the formula

=B12*B13

in cell B15 and copy this formula to the range C15:K15. Then copy the range B14:K14 to the range B16:K16 (since row 16 is related to row 15 in exactly the same way row 14 is to row 13).

5 **Mean demand.** Calculate the mean demand in cell B18 with the formula

=SUMPRODUCT(B12:K12,B13:K13)

FIGURE 10.1 **Spreadsheet Solution to Dishwasher Example**

	A	B	C	D	E	F	G	H	I	J	K
1	**H.H. Craig Dishwasher Example**										
2											
3	**Inputs**										
4											
5	Regular selling price (r_1)	$550									
6	Cost from supplier (c)	$400									
7	Sale price (r_2)	$350									
8	Loss of goodwill cost (p)	$50									
9											
10	Probability distribution of demand										
11											
12	k	6	7	8	9	10	11	12	13	14	15
13	P(k)	0.02	0.05	0.1	0.15	0.2	0.15	0.15	0.1	0.05	0.03
14	F(k)	0.02	0.07	0.17	0.32	0.52	0.67	0.82	0.92	0.97	1
15	kP(k)	0.12	0.35	0.8	1.35	2	1.65	1.8	1.3	0.7	0.45
16	Sum of kP(k)	0.12	0.47	1.27	2.62	4.62	6.27	8.07	9.37	10.07	10.52
17											
18	Mean demand	10.52									
19											
20	Order quantity (Q)	12									
21											
22	**Calculation of expected profit**										
23											
24	First term	$2,400		(r_1-c+p)Q							
25	Second term	($526)		-pE(D)							
26	Third term	($443)		(r_1-r_2+p) times [sum of kP(k) for k<=Q minus QF(Q)]							
27											
28	Expected profit	$1,431									

6 **Terms for expected profit.** Calculate the three terms for the expression in equation 10.2 in cells B24 through B26. In cell B24 enter

```
=(B5–B6+B8)*B20
```

In cell B25 enter

```
=–B8*B18
```

For the third term in Equation 10.2, it is convenient to first name the range B12:K16 as "LTable." Then in cell B26 use the horizontal lookup function with the formula

```
=(B5–B7+B8)*HLOOKUP(B20,LTable,5)–B20*HLOOKUP(B20,LTable,3)
```

This formula uses the LTable range. Specifically, since $Q = 12$ in cell B20, it finds the term $\sum_{k \le Q} kP(k)$ under the value 12 (column H) in the fifth row of the table, and it finds the value $F(Q)$ under the value 12 in the third row of the lookup table. By entering the formula in this way, if the value of Q in cell B20 changes, the formula will automatically refer to the appropriate column of the lookup table.

7 **Expected profit.** Calculate the expected profit in cell B28 with the formula

```
=SUM(B24:B26)
```

Using the Solver

1 **Objective.** Select cell B28 (expected profit) as the cell to maximize.

2 **Changing cells.** Specify cell B20 (order quantity) as the only changing cell and constrain it to be a nonnegative integer. There are no other constraints.

3 **Optimize.** Click on Solve. (Do *not* check the Assume Linear Model box; this is a nonlinear model.)

The Solver solution appears in Figure 10.1. We see that the maximum expected profit of \$1431 results from ordering 12 dishwashers.

It is important to realize that there is an entire probability distribution of profit for any value of Q. Depending on the random value of demand, this profit could be smaller than expected or larger than expected. However, we are focusing only on the mean, or expected value, of this profit distribution. As we see from Figure 10.1, this mean is maximized by ordering 12 dishwashers. The entire probability distribution of profit, that is, the spread of possible profits around the mean, is best analyzed with computer simulation—the topic of Chapters 12 and 13.

Since cell B28 gives the expected profit for *any* order quantity, it is a good idea to build a data table for the expected profit as a function of the order quantity Q. Then we can see how sensitive the expected profit is to Q. Such a data table and a corresponding line graph appear in Figure 10.2. (The formula =B28 is used in cell B33, and cell B20 is the column input cell for the data table.) As we see, the graph is quite flat in the range from $Q = 11$ to $Q = 15$. This means Craig should not worry about ordering slightly more or less than 12 dishwashers—it will have little effect on the expected profit.

In addition, Craig might want to consider other consequences, besides expected profit, in making the ordering decision. For example, if it orders 12 dishwashers, the number of units of lost demand will be 0, 1, 2, or 3 with probabilities .82, .10, .05, and .03. (To see this, note that there will be 1 unit of lost demand if total demand is 13, and the probability of this is .10. Similar arguments apply for the other probabilities.) On the other hand, if the company orders 13 dishwashers, the number of units of lost demand will be 0, 1, or 2 with probabilities .92, .05, and .03. Since the expected profits from ordering 12 or 13 are so similar, the company might go with 13 because it has smaller probability of unsatisfied demand. ■

FIGURE 10.2 Sensitivity of Expected Profit to Order Quantity

Data table for expected profit as a function of Q

Q	E(Q)
	\$1,431
6	\$674
7	\$869
8	\$1,052
9	\$1,209
10	\$1,329
11	\$1,399
12	\$1,432
13	\$1,427
14	\$1,397
15	\$1,354

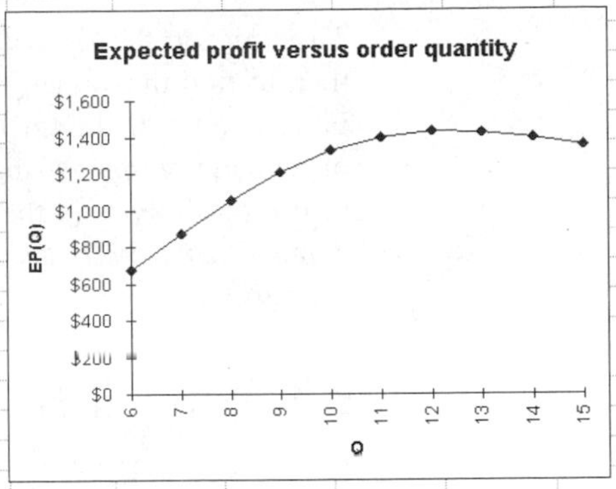

Generalizing the Newsvendor Model

The spreadsheet shown in Figure 10.1 can be used with minor modifications to find the optimal order quantity and associated expected profit for any *discrete* probability distribution for demand. However, it turns out that we can do a bit more. First, notice that Equation 10.1 for the profit can be written as

$$P(Q, D) = \begin{cases} -(c - r_2)Q + \text{Terms not involving } Q & \text{if } Q \geq D \\ (r_1 - c + p)Q + \text{Terms not involving } Q & \text{if } Q < D \end{cases}$$

The coefficient $(c - r_2)$ in the first expression, which is always positive in any realistic application, can be considered the unit cost of overstocking.[1] If $Q \geq D$ and we increase Q to $Q + 1$, then profit decreases by $c - r_2$ dollars. Similarly, the coefficient $(r_1 - c + p)$ in the second expression, which is always positive, can be considered the unit cost of understocking. That is, if $Q < D$ and we reduce Q to $Q - 1$, the profit decreases by $r_1 - c + p$ dollars. To remind us of the meaning of these coefficients, we let $c_{over} = c - r_2$ and $c_{under} = r_1 - c + p$.

Now, it can be shown that for any discrete distribution, the order quantity that maximizes expected profit is the smallest integer Q that satisfies the following:

$$F(Q) \geq \frac{c_{under}}{c_{over} + c_{under}} \qquad \textbf{(10.3)}$$

For the dishwasher example the ratio on the right of Inequality 10.3 is

$$\frac{c_{under}}{c_{over} + c_{under}} = \frac{550 - 400 + 50}{(400 - 350) + (550 - 400 + 50)} = .8$$

From row 14 of Figure 10.1, we see that $F(11) < .8$ and $F(12) > .8$. Therefore, $Q = 12$ is the smallest integer that satisfies Inequality 10.3. This confirms what we found from the Solver, namely, that $Q = 12$ is the optimal order quantity. However, given the optimality condition 10.3, we don't really need the Solver.

This optimality condition holds for continuous demand distributions as well. However, because $F(Q)$ is a *continuous* function of Q in this case, the inequality holds as an equality,

[1] If $c - r_2$ were negative, that is, the reduced sale price were *greater* than the company's cost of purchasing, the company could make an unlimited profit by purchasing huge quantities and selling them at the reduced sale price.

that is, the optimal Q satisfies

$$F(Q) = \frac{c_{under}}{c_{over} + c_{under}} \tag{10.4}$$

The ratio on the right is always a fraction between 0 and 1, such as .8. The problem is then to find the value Q with this fraction to the left of it under the demand distribution. For example, if the fraction is .8, we need the value Q such that there is an 80% chance of demand being less than or equal to Q. This will be the optimal Q, and we won't need to use the Solver. In the next example we illustrate how this can be accomplished when demand is *normally* distributed.

EXAMPLE 10.2

We revisit the H. H. Craig dishwasher example (Example 10.1), but now we assume that the dishwashers are being ordered for an entire chain of retailers. The dollar figures from before still apply, but now the total demand is much larger, and we assume its probability distribution is normal with mean 1500 and standard deviation σ. That is, the demand distribution is bell-shaped, it is centered at 1500, and its spread is determined by the value of σ. (See Figure 10.3. This figure compares two such distributions, one with a large σ and one with a small σ.) The company wants to find the optimal order quantity Q for various values of σ in order to test its sensitivity to the variability of the demand distribution.

Solution

The solution is straightforward. Given the parameters of the problem, we must calculate c_{under} and c_{over} and then find the value of Q that satisfies Equation 10.4 when F corresponds to a normal distribution. The procedure, explained in detail below, may appear much easier than the procedure required to form the spreadsheet in Figure 10.1. However, we are sacrificing something, namely, the ability to calculate the expected profit for any value of Q. Although Equation 10.4 is a result of maximizing expected profit, the expression for expected profit is quite complex and will not be given here. (We discuss this further at the end of the example.)

FIGURE 10.3 **Two Normal Curves**

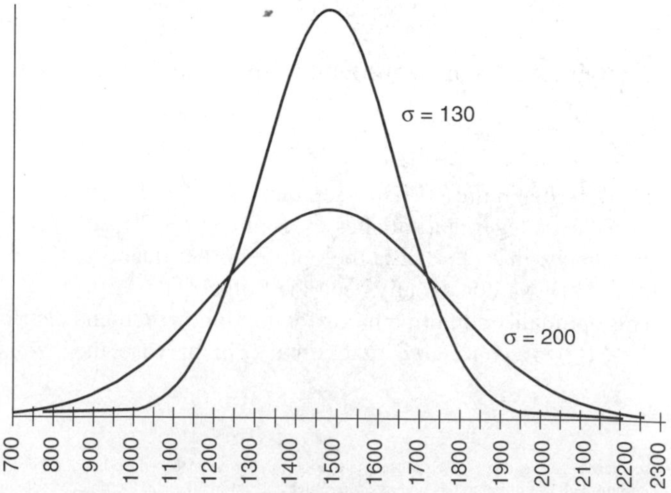

Developing the Spreadsheet Solution Fortunately, Excel has a built-in function that solves this problem easily. The relevant function has the form NORMINV(*probability, mean,stdev*). That is, you must specify the mean and standard deviation as the second and third arguments of this function, as well as a probability for the first argument. The function then returns the value with the specified probability to the left of it—exactly what we want in order to solve Equation 10.4. (See Figure 10.4.) The spreadsheet solution is shown in Figure 10.5. (See the file NEWSBOY2.XLS.) It can be formed with the following steps.

1 **Inputs.** Enter the inputs in cells B5:B8 and B14.

2 **Understocking and overstocking costs.** Calculate the understocking cost c_{under} and overstocking cost c_{over} in cells B10 and B11 with the formulas

=B5–B6+B8

and

=B6–B7

Then calculate the ratio $c_{under}/(c_{over} + c_{under})$ in cell B12 with the formula

=B10/(B10+B11)

3 **Standard deviations of demand.** Enter the range of standard deviations shown in cells A19 through A26. (Here we allow the standard deviation to increase from 50 to 400 in increments of 50, but any other reasonable values could be used.)

4 **Optimal order quantities.** To find the corresponding optimal values of Q, enter the formula

=NORMINV($B$12,$B$14,A19)

in cell B19 and copy it to the range B20:B26. Then use the values in A19:B26 to create a line graph showing the optimal Q as a function of the standard deviation σ.

Notice in Step 4 of the solution procedure that we are appealing to Equation 10.4 to obtain the optimal order quantities; we are *not* using the Solver.

As we stated earlier, the expression for the expected profit is quite complex. However, it can be calculated on a spreadsheet, and then the Solver can be used to optimize it. This has been done on the second sheet of the NEWSBOY2.XLS file, as shown in Figure 10.6. We will not pursue the details (specifically, the complex formula in cell B16), but as Figure 10.6 shows, when the standard deviation of demand is 150, for example, the optimal order quantity is the same as before, 1626. In addition, we see that the expected profit is $214,501.

FIGURE 10.4 **NORMINV Function**

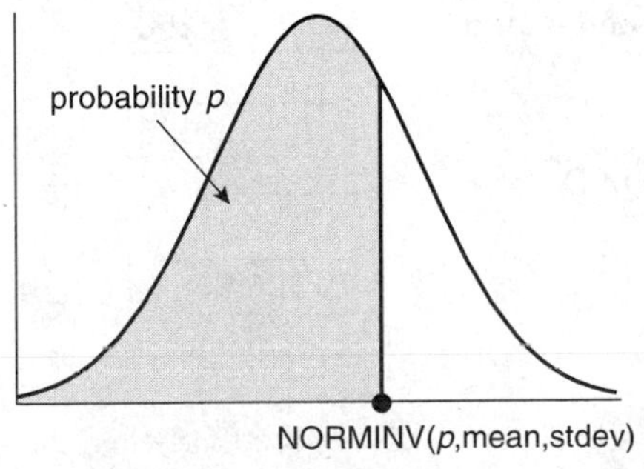

FIGURE 10.5 Solution to Dishwasher Example with Normally Distributed Demand

	A	B	C	D	E	F	G	H
1	**H.H. Craig Dishwasher Example with Normally Distributed Demand**							
2								
3	**Inputs**							
4								
5	Regular selling price (r_1)	$550						
6	Cost from supplier (c)	$400						
7	Sale price (r_2)	$350						
8	Loss of goodwill cost (p)	$50						
9								
10	Understocking cost (c_{under})	$200						
11	Overstocking cost (c_{over})	$50						
12	Ratio ($c_{under}/(c_{over}+c_{under})$)	0.8						
13								
14	Mean demand	1500						
15								
16	**Optimal Q as a function of standard deviation of demand (using Equation 10.4)**							
17								
18	Standard deviation of demand (σ)	Optimal Q						
19	50	1542						
20	100	1584						
21	150	1626						
22	200	1668						
23	250	1710						
24	300	1752						
25	350	1795						
26	400	1837						
27								
28								
29								
30								
31								
32								

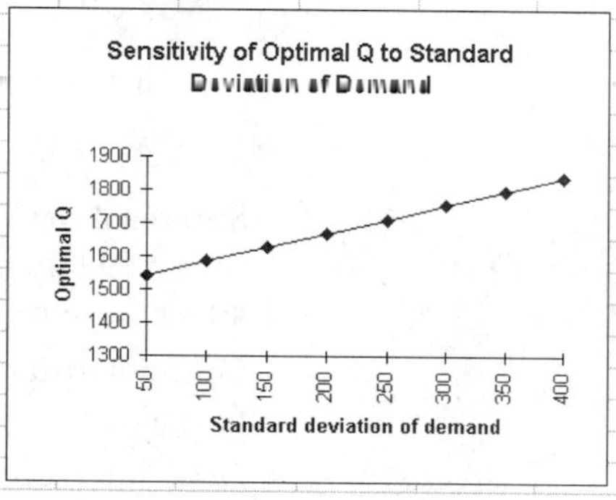

FIGURE 10.6 Solver Solution to Dishwasher Example

	A	B	C
1	**Using the Solver to Optimize Expected Cost**		
2			
3	**Inputs**		
4			
5	Regular selling price (r_1)	$550	
6	Cost from supplier (c)	$400	
7	Sale price (r_2)	$350	
8	Loss of goodwill cost (p)	$50	
9			
10	Mean demand	1500	
11	Standard deviation of demand	150	
12			
13	Order quantity Q	1626	
14	Standardized value of Q	0.842	
15			
16	Total expected cost	$214,501	

From the graph shown in Figure 10.5, we see that when there is more uncertainty in the demand distribution, that is, when σ increases, the optimal order quantity Q increases in a linear manner. However, this increase is not very rapid. For example, if the standard deviation increases by 700% from 50 to 400, the optimal value of Q increases only from 1542 to 1837, which is approximately a 19% increase. Finally, notice that the cost of overstocking, \$50, is small in comparison to the cost of understocking, \$200. Therefore, the company always orders *more* than the mean demand, sometimes considerably more. ■

Airline Overbooking

We conclude our discussion of newsvendor models with an example that is not a traditional inventory model but can be formulated as a newsvendor model nevertheless. (You should recognize it as a scaled-down version of American Airlines's problem described in the introduction to this chapter.) The key to the solution is determining the unit costs of understocking and overstocking.

EXAMPLE 10.3

The ticket price for a flight from New York to Indianapolis is \$200. Each plane can hold up to 100 passengers. Usually, some of the passengers who have purchased tickets for a flight fail to show up. We call these the no-shows. To protect against no-shows, the airline tries to sell more than 100 tickets for each flight. Federal law states that any ticketed customer who is unable to board the plane is entitled to a "bonus" compensation, say, \$100—in addition to being reimbursed for the \$200 ticket. Past data indicate that the number of no-shows for each New York–Indianapolis flight is approximately normally distributed with mean 20 and standard deviation 5. To maximize expected revenues less compensation costs, the airline company wants to determine the optimal number of tickets to issue. (We assume that any passenger who purchases a ticket for \$200 but decides not to use it also receives a full \$200 refund.)

Solution

We let Q, the decision variable, be the number of tickets sold by the airline in excess of 100, and we let D be the number of no-shows. (We'll assume that the airline can sell as many tickets as it wants.) For example, if $Q = 5$, the airline sells $Q + 100 = 105$ tickets. Then $(Q + 100) - D$ is the number of ticketed customers who actually show up for the flight. There are two cases: (1) $Q < D$ (more no-shows than extra tickets), and (2) $Q \geq D$ (more extra tickets than no-shows). If $Q < D$, then all customers who show up are able to board the plane, and the revenue for the airline is $200[(Q + 100) - D]$. (Note that the D no-shows pay \$200 for their tickets but are reimbursed when they don't show up.) If $Q \geq D$, then 100 passengers board the plane, paying $\$200 \times 100 = \$20,000$, and $Q - D$ customers are turned away. These latter customers not only receive their \$200 back but are compensated \$100 apiece, for a cost of $100(Q - D)$ to the airline. In summary, the profit for the airline, $P(Q, D)$, is given by

$$P(Q, D) = \begin{cases} -100Q + 100D + 20000 & \text{if } Q \geq D \\ 200Q - 200D + 20000 & \text{if } Q < D \end{cases}$$

This is exactly the same form as the profit function for the newsvendor problem, where $c_{over} = 100$, the negative of the coefficient of Q in the top expression, and $c_{under} = 200$, the coefficient of Q in the bottom expression. (This makes intuitive sense. When Q is too low, the airline loses \$200 in potential revenue for every extra seat not filled. When Q is too high, the airline loses \$100 in extra compensation for every extra passenger who is bumped from the plane.) Therefore, the spreadsheet in Figure 10.7 (see the file OVERBOOK.XLS) obtains the optimal number of extra tickets to sell. The formulas in cells B12, B14, and B16 are

=B9/(B9+B10)
=NORMINV(B12,B6,B7)

and

=B3+B14

As we see, the airline should sell 122 or 123 tickets for the 100-seat flight. A graphic explanation for the formula in cell B14 appears in Figure 10.8.

This solution derives the optimal value of Q from Equation 10.4; it does not rely on the Solver to maximize expected profit. As in Example 10.2 (see Figure 10.6), a complex expression for the expected profit could be optimized, and it would lead to the same value of Q, but we will not present that approach here. ■

FIGURE 10.7 **Spreadsheet for Airline Overbooking Example**

	A	B
1	**Airline Overbooking Example**	
2		
3	Number of seats on plane	100
4		
5	Distribution of number of no-shows	
6	Mean	20
7	StDev	5
8		
9	Ticket cost (understocking cost)	$200
10	Compensation for being bumped (overstocking cost)	$100
11		
12	Critical ratio	0.67
13		
14	Number of tickets to issue in excess of capacity	22.15
15		
16	Total number of tickets to issue	122.15

FIGURE 10.8 **Finding Appropriate Value of Q**

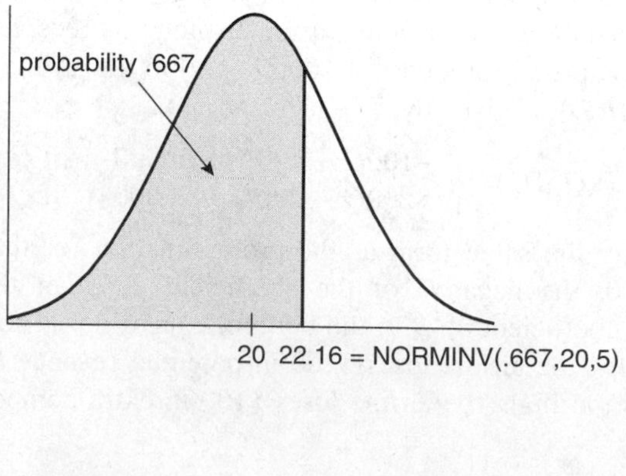

PROBLEMS

Skill-Building Problems

1 Each day, a newsvendor must determine how many *New York Herald Wonderfuls* to order. She pays 25¢ for each paper and sells each for 50¢. Any leftover papers are a total loss. From past experience, she believes that the number of papers she can sell each day is governed by the probability distribution shown in Table 10.2. How many papers should she order each day?

TABLE 10.2 Demand Distribution for Newspaper Problem

No. of Papers Demanded	Probability
50	.30
70	.15
90	.25
110	.10
130	.20

2 Joe is selling Christmas trees to pay his college tuition. He purchases trees for \$10 each and sells them for \$25 each. The number of trees he can sell is normally distributed with a mean of 200 and standard deviation of 60. How many trees should Joe purchase? (Leftover trees are worthless.)

3 A hot dog vendor at Yankee Stadium sells hot dogs for \$1.50 each. She buys them for \$1.20 each. All the hot dogs she fails to sell at Yankee Stadium during the afternoon can be sold that evening at Shea Stadium for \$1 each. The daily demand for hot dogs at Yankee Stadium is normally distributed with a mean of 400 and a standard deviation of 100.

a If the vendor buys hot dogs once a day, how many should she buy?

b If she buys 520 hot dogs, what is the probability that she will meet all of the day's demand for hot dogs at Yankee Stadium?

4 A department store is trying to decide how many of JP Desksquirt II printers to order. Since JP is about to come out with a new model in a few months, the store will only order a limited number of model IIs. The cost per printer is \$200, and each printer is sold for \$230. If any model IIs are still in stock when the next model comes out, they will be sold for \$150 apiece. If a customer wants a model II and there are none left, the store will special order the printer at an extra cost (to the store) of \$25. These printers are not in great demand. The store estimates that the number of model IIs that will be demanded during the next few months (before the next model comes out) is equally likely to be any value from 10 to 20, inclusive.

a Identify the parameters c, r_1, r_2, and p for this problem.

b Assume that the store orders $Q = 17$ model IIs. Use Equation 10.2 and a spreadsheet to find the components of expected profit. That is, calculate separately the parts in Equation 10.2.

c Find the value of Q that maximizes the store's expected profit from the model II printers.

5 In the previous problem perform the following sensitivity analyses. (Do each part separately.)

a Find the optimal Q and the corresponding optimal expected profit for each selling price from \$220 to \$250 in increments of \$5.

b Repeat Part (a) for each reduced sale price from \$130 to \$170 in increments of \$10.

c Repeat Part (a) for each special-order extra cost from \$10 to \$40 in increments of \$5.

d Now suppose that the demand is equally likely to be any value from 10 to M. Repeat Part (a) for each M from 16 to 32 in increments of 4.

6 In August 1996, a car dealer is trying to determine how many 1997 models to order. Each car costs the dealer \$10,000. The demand for the dealer's 1997 models has the probability distribution shown in Table 10.3. Each car sells for \$15,000. If the demand for 1997 cars exceeds the number of cars ordered in August, the dealer must reorder at a cost of \$12,000

TABLE 10.3 Demand Distribution for New Car Problem

No. of Cars Demanded	Probability
20	.30
25	.15
30	.15
35	.20
40	.20

per car. If the demand for 1997 cars falls short, the dealer can dispose of excess cars in an end-of-model-year sale for \$9000 per car. How many 1997 models should he order in August?

Skill-Extending Problems

7 In the basic newsvendor problem suppose that each leftover item (when $Q > D$) can either be sold at a reduced price of r_3 or must be hauled away at cost c_1 (because no one would buy it at the reduced sale price). We model this by assuming that each leftover item will be purchased at price r_3 with probability p_1, independently of the others, and must be hauled away with probability $1 - p_1$. How could you use the basic newsvendor model in this case? In particular, what is the relevant value of r_2?

8 Continuing the previous problem, assume that the Overhead Garage Door Company is trying to decide how many of a particular door to stock. The selling price per door is \$450, and the cost per door to Overhead is \$400. If extra doors are left over when next year's model is available, the company will sell these leftovers at \$350 each. Overhead figures it will be able to sell a given leftover door at this price with probability .7. However, with probability .3 there will be no demand for a given leftover, and the company will have to dispose of the door at a cost of \$50. The loss of goodwill for not having a door when it is demanded is estimated to be \$45.

a If the demand for these doors is normally distributed with mean 130 and standard deviation 40, how many should the company stock in order to maximize its profit?

b The loss of goodwill cost and the probability that a given leftover will be sold at the reduced price are difficult to estimate. Therefore, perform a sensitivity analysis (using a two-way data table) to find the optimal order quantity when the goodwill cost varies from \$25 to \$70 in increments of \$5 and the probability of selling a leftover varies from .5 to .9 in increments of .1.

9 Referring to the previous problem, suppose that Overhead places its order in March, expecting shipment in June. However, in April its marketing research shows that it may not have ordered enough. In March it believed demand would be normally distributed with mean 130 and standard deviation 40, as given above. However, by April, having observed an increase in home construction, it believes eventual demand for this type of door will be normally distributed with mean 150 and standard deviation 45. An order for the previous optimal order quantity, labeled Q_1, has already been placed, but the supplier is willing to change this to the new optimal order quantity, labeled Q_2, at a fixed cost of C. (This cost is for the extra paperwork and so forth.) Find the value of Q_2. Then find the largest value of C such that it would be worth it to Overhead to change its order quantity to Q_2 in April. (*Hint*: Use the formula for expected profit in cell B16 of the "Using Solver" sheet in the NEWSBOY2.XLS file.)

10 In the basic newsvendor model we argued that $c - r_2$ should always be positive. The reasoning is that if, for example, it cost \$50 to purchase an item and the reduced sale price were \$60, so that $c - r_2 = 50 - 60 = -\$10$, then the company could make an unlimited amount of money by ordering an infinite amount and selling leftovers at the (attractive) reduced sale price. From a realistic point of view, what would happen if in fact $c = \$50$ and $r_2 = \$60$? How might you model a realistic version of this problem so that the optimal order quantity is *not* infinite?

11 Every four years, Blockbuster Publishers revises its textbooks. It has been three years since the best-selling book *The Joy of Excel* has been revised. At present, 2000 copies of the book are in stock, and Blockbuster must determine how many copies of the book to print for the next year. The sales department believes that sales during the next year are governed by the distribution in Table 10.4. Each copy of *Joy* sold during the next year brings the publisher a revenue of \$35.Any copies left at the end of the next year cannot be sold at full price but can

TABLE 10.4 Distribution for Blockbuster Problem

Copies Demanded	Probability
5000	.30
6000	.20
7000	.40
8000	.10

be sold for \$5 to Bonds Ennoble and Gitano's bookstores. The cost of a printing of the book is \$50,000 plus \$15 per book printed. How many copies of *Joy* should be printed? Would the answer change if 4000 copies were currently in stock?

12 Some universities allow an employee to put an amount Q into an account at the beginning of each year, to be used for child-care expenses. The amount Q is not subject to federal income tax. Assume that all other income is taxed by the federal government at a 30% rate. If child-care expenses for the year (call them D) are less than Q, the employee in effect loses $Q - D$ dollars in before-tax income. If child-care expenses exceed Q, the employee must pay the excess out of his or her own pocket but may credit 25% of that as a savings on his or her state income tax.

Suppose Professor Sharon Donaldson believes that there is an equal chance that her child-care expenses for the coming year will be \$3000, \$4000, \$5000, \$6000, or \$7000. At the beginning of the year, how much money should she place in the child-care account? Assume that her annual salary is \$50,000 and that her objective is to maximize her expected disposable income.

13 Motorama TV estimates the annual demand for its TVs is (and will be in the future) normally distributed with a mean of 6000 and standard deviation of 2000. Motorama must determine its optimal production capacity. The cost of building enough production capacity to make 1000 sets per year is \$1 million (equivalent in present value terms to a cost of \$100,000 per year forever). Exclusive of the cost of building capacity, each set sold contributes \$250 to profit. How much production capacity should Motorama have?

14 L. L. Pea is a well-known mail order company. During the Christmas rush (from November 1 to December 15), the number of orders that L. L. Pea must fill each day (five days per week) is normally distributed with a mean of 2000 and a standard deviation of 500. L. L. Pea must determine how many employees to schedule during the Christmas rush. Each employee works five days a week, eight hours a day, can process 50 orders per day, and is paid \$10 per hour. If the full-time work force cannot handle the day's orders during regular hours, some employees will have to work overtime. Each employee is paid \$15 per hour for overtime work. For example, if 300 orders are received in a day and there are four employees, then $300 - 4(50) = 100$ orders must be processed by employees who are working overtime. Since each employee can fill $50/8 = 6.25$ orders per hour, L. L. Pea would need to pay workers $100/6.25 = 16$ hours of overtime for that day. To minimize its expected labor costs, how many full-time employees should L. L. Pea employ during the Christmas rush? ■

10.3 Analysis of (R, Q) Policies

Many products that companies order are not like a newspaper, which is ordered only once and is then phased out. The ordering of these products requires a model more like the EOQ model from the previous chapter. Demand for the product occurs continually, at a fairly constant rate, and the company must place an order for the product when its inventory reaches a sufficiently low level. In these situations many companies use a **reorder point, reorder quantity policy**, called an (R, Q) policy. This is a continuous review policy that is determined by two numbers, R and Q. The reorder point R is the "trigger" point. When the company's inventory level reaches R, this automatically triggers the placement of an order. The order quantity Q specifies how much to order each time an order is placed.

When we studied EOQ policies in the previous chapter, we were actually talking about (R, Q) policies. However, we didn't place much emphasis on the reorder point R. This was because the demand rate was a *known* quantity, D per year. That is, for a given lead time L, we knew that if an order was placed when the inventory level was LD, the inventory level would exactly reach zero when the order arrived. So we determined very easily that the reorder point R should equal LD.[2] This argument also showed that the company could avoid any possibility of shortages unless (as in Section 9.6) it *planned* to have a few shortages.

In this section we keep the same EOQ model, but with one important difference. Now the demand during any period of time is random and only its probability distribution is known. Most importantly, the **demand during lead time** is not known for certain. This demand is defined as the number of items demanded between the time when the order is placed and when it arrives. So if the company orders when the inventory level drops to R, for any chosen value of R, it is uncertain about the inventory level L time units later when the order arrives. There might still be some units in stock, or there might be a shortage.

This discussion implies that when the company chooses R, it must take into account the effects of running out of inventory. If it believes shortages are very expensive or undesirable, it should choose a relatively large value of R. This leads to a relatively large value of **safety stock**, the expected amount of inventory left over—the cushion—by the time the next order arrives. On the other hand, if shortages are not considered too expensive or undesirable, the company can afford to use a lower value of R, with a smaller resulting level of safety stock. In this section we will show how to determine an appropriate balance between leftovers and shortages.

We also must determine the appropriate order quantity Q. As we will see, the choices of R and Q can be made almost independently. The choice of R depends largely on how we measure shortage costs (or customer service), whereas the choice of Q depends mostly on the same cost factors we considered in the EOQ model. That is, the company wants to order enough to avoid a lot of setup costs but as little as possible to avoid excessive holding costs. In particular, the same EOQ square root formula for Q (with the annual demand replaced by the *expected* annual demand) is nearly optimal. Therefore, most of the work in this section centers around finding the optimal reorder point R. We will discuss methods for doing this in the context of the following example.

EXAMPLE 10.4

In Example 9.1 we considered the Machey's department store that sells, on average, 1200 cameras per year. The store pays a setup cost of \$35 per order, and the holding cost is \$10 per camera per year. It takes one week for an order to arrive once it is placed. In that example the optimal order quantity Q was found from the EOQ formula to be 92 cameras. Now we assume that the annual demand is normally distributed with mean 1200 and standard deviation 70. Machey's wants to know when to order and how many cameras to order at each ordering opportunity.

Solution

Suppose the company places an order for Q cameras every time its inventory level reaches R. Our goal is to find "good" values of Q and R. There are two aspects of this model that are critical to its solution: (1) the demand during lead time and (2) the "cost" of running out of inventory.

[2] Actually, as we pointed out in the previous chapter, this is not quite correct if the lead time demand LD is greater than the order quantity Q. However, the important point is that the company can plan the timing of its order so that the order arrives just as inventory reaches zero.

Demand During Lead Time and Safety Stock The most critical probabilistic quantity in the (R, Q) model is the amount of demand during an order lead time. To illustrate, suppose that Machey's uses $R = 30$ as the reorder point. This means that an order is placed as soon as the inventory level drops to 30 cameras. This order will arrive one week later. If the demand during this lead time is 25 cameras, say, then no shortage will occur, and there will be 5 cameras on hand when the order arrives. However, if the demand during this period is 35 cameras, then there will be a shortage of 5 cameras by the time the order arrives. Therefore, the demand during lead time, in conjunction with the choice of R, determines the extent of shortages. Before we can continue, we need to find the probability distribution of this quantity.

Let D be the annual demand, and let D_L be the demand during an order lead time. From the statement of the problem, D is normally distributed with mean $E(D) = 1200$ and standard deviation $\sigma = 70$, but what about D_L? By making appropriate probability assumptions, it can be shown that D_L is also normally distributed, and its mean and standard deviation are $E(D_L) = LE(D)$ and $\sigma_L = \sqrt{L}\sigma$. Since the lead time is one week $(L = 1/52)$, Machey's expected demand during lead time is $E(D_L) = 1200/52 \simeq 23$ cameras, and the standard deviation of demand during lead time is $\sigma_L = \sqrt{1/52} \times 70 \simeq 9.7$ cameras.

Given these values, you might think that Machey's should set its reorder point R equal to 23, the mean demand during lead time. But then there would be a fifty-fifty chance of stocking out before the order arrives (because the probability is 1/2 that a normal random variable is greater than its mean). What if it instead sets R equal to one standard deviation above the mean, that is, $R = 23 + 9.7 \simeq 33$? Then the probability of a stockout is $P(D_L > 33)$. This can be found from normal probability tables (by finding $P(Z > 1)$, where Z is normal with mean 0 and standard deviation 1) or, alternatively, with the NORMDIST function in Excel. The syntax for this function is NORMDIST(*value,mean,stdev*,1). It returns the probability of a normal random variable with mean *mean* and standard deviation *stdev* being to the left of *value*. Therefore, we find $P(D_L > 33)$, the probability of a stockout, with the formula

=1–NORMDIST(33,23,9.7,1)

which has approximate value .15. (See Figure 10.9.)

In general, suppose that Machey's decides to set R equal to k standard deviations above the mean, where k is an appropriate multiplier that must be determined. That is, it uses the reorder level

$$R = E(D_L) + k\sigma_L = E(D_L) + \text{Safety stock} \tag{10.5}$$

In effect, the multiplier k becomes the decision variable. Usually k is positive. The term $k\sigma_L$ then becomes the safety stock. To summarize the reasoning, Machey's expects an amount

FIGURE 10.9 **Probability of a Stockout for Camera Example**

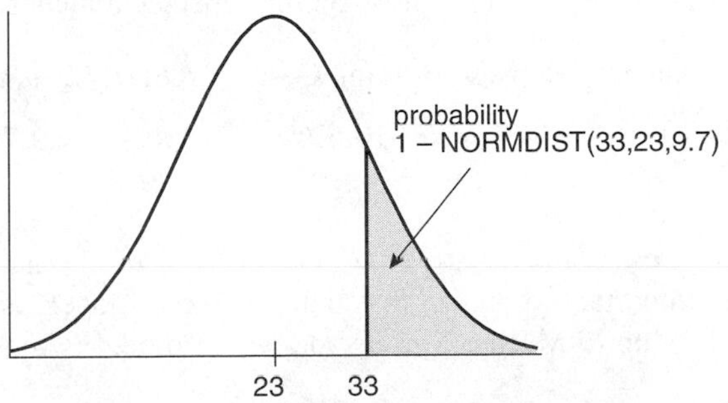

$E(D_L)$ to be demanded during the one-week lead time. However, because shortages are undesirable, it orders when the inventory level is $k\sigma_L$ above $E(D_L)$. Therefore, it expects the inventory level to be $k\sigma_L$, a positive value, when the order arrives. This value is its cushion against larger than expected demand—hence the term *safety stock*. But although the company plans for this safety stock to exist, there is no guarantee that it will exist. As we saw in the previous probability calculation (with $k = 1$), there is about a 15% chance that the safety stock of ten units will be depleted before the order arrives and a stockout will occur. We will see shortly how to choose k and the order quantity Q in an intelligent manner.

Finding the Expected Costs We now develop an expression for Machey's expected total annual cost as a function of the order quantity Q and k, the parameter that determines the amount of safety stock (and the reorder point). Actually, because there are several ways Machey's could value the "cost" of having shortages, we will develop several expressions for the total expected annual cost. In the following discussion we will refer to an **order cycle**. Such a cycle begins each time an order arrives and ends just before the next order arrives. (See Figure 10.10.)

FIGURE 10.10 **Order Cycle**

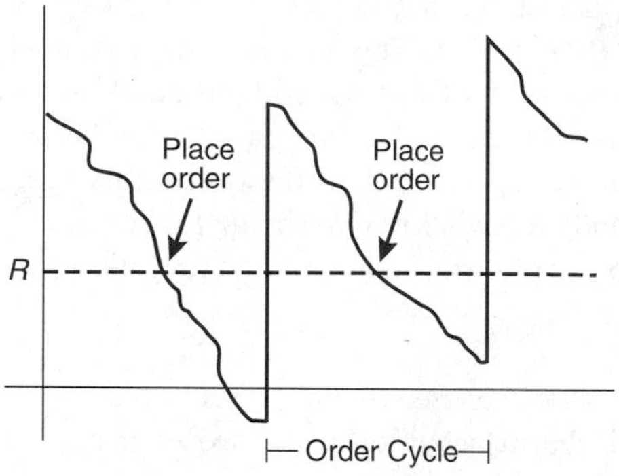

We first consider the annual setup and holding costs. If an order quantity Q is used, then it takes an expected amount of time $Q/E(D)$ to deplete this inventory. Therefore, there are an expected $E(D)/Q$ order cycles per year, and the expected annual setup cost is $KE(D)/Q$. For the holding cost, consider any order cycle. The lowest inventory level during a cycle is expected to be $k\sigma_L$, the safety stock. The highest inventory level then occurs when the order arrives and the expected inventory jumps up to $Q + k\sigma_L$. Therefore, the expected average inventory level during a typical cycle is $[k\sigma_L + (Q + k\sigma_L)]/2$, and we multiply this by h to obtain the expected annual holding cost. Simplifying the algebra slightly, we obtain the following expression for expected annual setup and holding costs:

$$\text{Expected Annual Setup and Holding Costs} = KE(D)/Q + hQ/2 + hk\sigma_L \qquad \textbf{(10.6)}$$

where (for Machey's) $K = \$35$, $h = \$10$, $E(D) = 1200$, $\sigma_L = 9.7$, and Q and k need to be determined.

Four Ways to "Cost" Shortages Now we look at four alternative models of "costing" shortages. It is important to realize that none of these models is clearly superior to any of the others. It is up to Machey's to decide which model is most in line with its goals.

Model 1 assumes that there is a shortage cost of p_1 dollars during each cycle in which a shortage occurs. This cost is independent of the *amount* of the shortage; it depends only on whether there is a shortage. Model 2 assumes that there is a shortage cost of p_2 per unit short. In this model a cycle with a total shortage of five units is five times as costly as a cycle with a shortage of only one unit (whereas these would have the *same* cost under model 1). For example, if Machey's uses model 1 with $p_1 = \$100$, and there is a stockout on two of its order cycles during the year, then its annual shortage cost is \$200. In contrast, suppose it uses model 2 with $p_2 = \$5$. If the *average* number of shortages during each of its order cycles per year is 2 and there are 13 order cycles during the year, then its annual shortage cost is \$130.

Models 3 and 4 get around the difficult problem of assessing *dollar* shortage costs by instead specifying *service levels*. Model 3 specifies a service level s_1 (a number between 0 and 1) and requires that the expected fraction of all order cycles with no shortages must be s_1. Model 4 specifies a service level s_2 (again a number between 0 and 1) and requires that the fraction of demand that can be met from on-hand inventory must be s_2. For example, if Machey's uses model 3 with $s_1 = .95$, then it will choose its ordering policy so that there is a stockout during only 5% of all order cycles. However, if it uses model 4 with $s_2 = .98$, then it will choose its ordering policy so that 98% of all customer demand can be met from on-hand inventory.

Before we can solve Machey's problem on a spreadsheet, we must develop formulas for the shortage costs (or service levels) for these four shortage-costing models.

Expected Shortage Cost for Model 1 In model 1 there is a shortage cost of p_1 during any order cycle only if the demand during lead time, D_L, is greater than the reorder point R. Therefore, the expected shortage cost per order cycle is p_1 multiplied by the probability that D_L is greater than R, $P(D_L > R)$. Because $R = E(D_L) + k\sigma_L$, we can standardize the normally distributed random variable D_L in the usual way to obtain

$$P(D_L > R) = P\left(\frac{D - E(D_L)}{\sigma_L} > k\right) = P(Z > k)$$

where Z is a standard normal random variable. Therefore, since the expected number of order cycles per year is $E(D)/Q$, the total expected annual cost in model 1 is

$$\text{Model 1 expected annual shortage cost} = p_1 P(Z > k)E(D)/Q \qquad \textbf{(10.7)}$$

Developing the Spreadsheet for Model 1 Here we will assume that Machey's decides to use model 1 to cost its shortages, using $p_1 = \$100$ as the cost for each cycle that experiences a shortage. Then the relevant spreadsheet is shown in Figure 10.11. (See the file CAMERA1.XLS.)

1 **Inputs.** Enter the inputs in cells B5 through B9 and B12. (Notice that the lead time in cell B9 is entered in units of years, that is, 1/52.)

2 **Demand during lead time.** In cells B10 and B11 calculate the mean and standard deviation of demand during lead time with the formulas

=B7*B9

and

=B8*SQRT(B9)

3 **Order quantity and factor for reorder level.** Enter *any* trial values for Q and k in cells B16 and B17.

FIGURE 10.11 Spreadsheet Solution for Model 1

	A	B	C	D	E	F	G	H
1	Optimal (R,Q) inventory policy for model 1							
2								
3	Inputs							
4								
5	K	$35		Setup cost per order				
6	h	$10		Holding cost per unit per year				
7	E(D)	1200		Expected annual demand				
8	StDev(D)	70		StDev of annual demand				
9	L	0.0192		Lead time in years				
10	E(D_L)	23.077		Expected demand during lead time				
11	StDev(D_L)	9.707		StDev of demand during lead time				
12	p_1	$100		Shortage cost incurred each cycle with a shortage				
13								
14	Optimal solution using Solver to choose Q and k							
15								
16	Q	96.2		Changing cells				
17	k	1.81		for Solver				
18	k*σ_L	17.6		Safety stock				
19	P(Z>k)	0.04		Probability of a shortage during an ordering cycle				
20	R	40.6		Reorder point				
21								
22	Annual setup cost	$437						
23	Annual holding cost	$656						
24	Annual shortage cost	$44						
25	Total annual cost	$1,137						

4 **Safety stock, probability of shortage, and reorder level.** Enter the following formulas for the safety stock $k\sigma_L$, the probability $P(Z > k)$ of a shortage, and the reorder level R (from Equation 10.5) in cells B18, B19, and B20:

=B17*B11
=1–NORMSDIST(B17)

and

=B10+B18

Here we have used the NORMSDIST function (with the S in the middle), which requires only one argument and is relevant for the *standard* normal distribution, to find the probability of a shortage during an order cycle.

5 **Expected annual costs.** Using Equations 10.6 and 10.7, calculate the expected annual setup cost, the expected annual holding cost, the expected annual shortage cost, and the total expected annual cost in cells B22 through B25 with the formulas

=B5*B7/B16
=B6*(B18+B16/2)
=B12*B19*B7/B16

and

=SUM(B22:B24)

Using the Solver for Model 1

1 **Objective.** Select cell B25 as the cell to minimize.

2 **Changing cells.** Select cells B16 and B17 as the changing cells and constrain them to be nonnegative. (*Note*: The order quantity obviously must be nonnegative, but why do we make k nonnegative? Actually, this is not logically necessary. Machey's could allow k to be negative, which would imply a *negative* safety stock. However, this is unusual and can cause a problem with the way we've set up the spreadsheet. Therefore, we constrain k to be nonnegative.)

3 **Optimize.** Click on Solve.

As we see from Figure 10.11, Machey's should order approximately 96 cameras each time it orders, and it should place an order each time its inventory level reaches 41 cameras. (Here, we've rounded up the spreadsheet solution.) Note how this solution works. The expected demand during the lead time of one week is approximately 23 cameras (cell B10), and the corresponding standard deviation is almost 10 cameras (cell B11). Machey's should let the inventory drop until it is $k = 1.81$ standard deviations above the mean, that is, until it drops to about $R = 41$ cameras. Then it should place an order for $Q = 96$ cameras. With this policy, there is about one chance in 25 of a stockout during the lead time, so that the shortage cost of \$100 will be incurred in about one out of every 25 order cycles.

Expected Shortage Cost for Model 2 In model 2 Machey's assesses a shortage cost of p_2 per unit short during any order cycle. Therefore, to evaluate the expected annual shortage cost, we must find the expected number of shortages per order cycle. Let B be the number of units short during a typical order cycle. Then the expected shortage cost during this cycle is $p_2E(B)$, and the expected annual shortage cost is the expected shortage cost per cycle multiplied by the expected number of cycles per year, $E(D)/Q$. This leads to the following expected total annual cost:

$$\text{Model 2 expected annual shortage cost} = p_2E(B)E(D)/Q \qquad \textbf{(10.8)}$$

The problem is to find an expression for $E(B)$. It can be shown that this expected value is related to a well-known quantity called the **normal loss function**. Fortunately, it can be calculated fairly easily with Excel spreadsheet functions. The formula for $E(B)$ is

$$E(B) = \sigma_L\left(\frac{1}{\sqrt{2\pi}}e^{-k^2/2} - kP(Z > k)\right) \qquad \textbf{(10.9)}$$

You might recognize the first term inside parentheses as the standard normal *density* function evaluated at k. We now show how to implement model 2 for the camera example.

Developing the Spreadsheet for Model 2 Now we will assume that Machey's decides to use model 2, with $p_2 = \$10$ as the cost per camera that cannot be supplied to a customer from existing inventory. The spreadsheet solution appears in Figure 10.12. (See the file CAMERA2.XLS.)

We will not repeat all of the instructions that we gave for the spreadsheet shown in Figure 10.11 because the present spreadsheet is almost exactly the same. The only differences are in cells B12, B19, and B24. Now the input in cell B12 is p_2, the \$10 cost per camera backordered. In cell B19 we use Equation 10.9 to calculate the expected number of backorders per order cycle, $E(B)$, with the formula

=B11*(NORMDIST(B17,0,1,0)–B17*(1–NORMSDIST(B17)))

Finally, from Equation 10.8 the expected annual shortage cost in cell B24 is

=B12*B19*B7/B16

The quantity in B19 is now the expected number of backorders per cycle rather than the probability of a backorder in a typical cycle.

FIGURE 10.12 Spreadsheet Solution for Model 2

	A	B	C	D	E	F
1	**Optimal (R,Q) inventory policy for model 2**					
2						
3	**Inputs**					
4						
5	K	$35		Setup cost per order		
6	h	$10		Holding cost per unit per year		
7	E(D)	1200		Expected annual demand		
8	StDev(D)	70		StDev of annual demand		
9	L	0.0192		Lead time in years		
10	$E(D_L)$	23.077		Expected demand during lead time		
11	$StDev(D_L)$	9.707		StDev of demand during lead time		
12	p_2	$10		Shortage cost per unit short		
13						
14	**Optimal solution using Solver to choose Q and k**					
15						
16	Q	96.2		Changing cells		
17	k	1.40		for Solver		
18	$k^*\sigma_L$	13.6		Safety stock		
19	E(B)	0.35		Expected shortage per cycle		
20	R	36.7		Reorder point		
21						
22	Annual setup cost	$437				
23	Annual holding cost	$617				
24	Annual shortage cost	$44				
25	Total annual cost	$1,098				

Note that the formula in cell B19 uses two related functions, NORMDIST and NORMSDIST. The first of these takes four arguments: a value, the mean, the standard deviation, and a 0 or 1. When the fourth argument is 1 (the usual case), the function returns a cumulative (left-hand tail) probability, but when this argument is 0, it returns the value of the density function. Here it is used, with a fourth argument equal to 0, to evaluate the standard normal density at value k (in cell B17). The second function, the NORMSDIST function, takes only one argument, a value. It returns the probability to the *left* of this value under the standard normal curve. To obtain the probability to the *right* of the value k, we subtract the NORMSDIST probability from 1. (See Figure 10.13.)

The interpretation of the Solver solution in Figure 10.12 is that Machey's waits until the inventory level reaches approximately 37 cameras and then places an order for 96 cameras. The actual number of backorders during the order lead time is a discrete random variable with possible values of 0, 1, 2, and so on. However, the *expected* number of backorders, a weighted average of these possible values, is $E(B) = .35$, so that the expected shortage cost during any order cycle is $p_2E(B) = \$3.50$. Multiplying this by the expected number of cycles per year (1200/96.2) gives the expected annual shortage cost of approximately $44.

Service Levels for Models 3 and 4 The final two models use service level constraints instead of dollar shortage costs. Model 3 specifies a fraction s_1 of order cycles that should not experience stockouts, whereas model 4 specifies a fraction s_2 of demands that must be

FIGURE 10.13 **NORMSDIST and NORMDIST Functions**

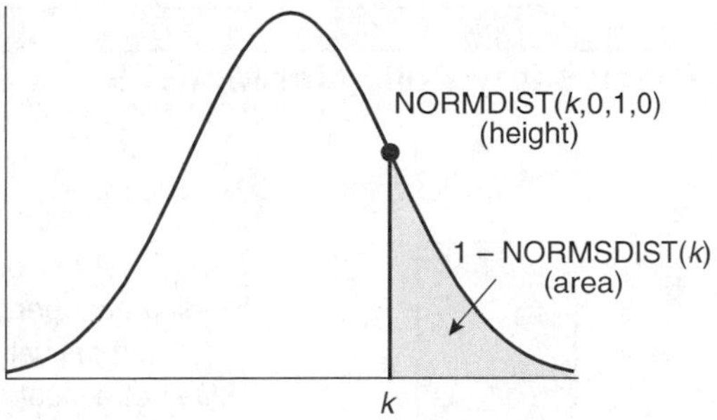

met on time. The fundamental difference between these models and models 1 and 2 is that there is now no explicit shortage *cost*. Instead, Machey's minimizes the expected setup and holding costs, subject to meeting a service level constraint.

To model the service level constraints, we need an expression for the fraction of cycles that have no stockouts (model 3) and the fraction of demand met on time (model 4). The fraction of cycles that have no stockouts is the probability that a typical cycle has no stockout. We already saw in model 1 that the probability of having a stockout in a cycle is $P(Z > k)$, so the probability of no stockout is $P(Z \leq k)$. Therefore, the model 3 service level constraint is as follows:

$$s_1 = P(Z \leq k) \tag{10.10}$$

For model 4 note that Q items are ordered each cycle, and the expected shortage each cycle is $E(B)$ (which we evaluated for model 2). Therefore, the expected fraction of demand met on time is $1 - E(B)/Q$, and the model 4 service level constraint becomes the following:

$$s_2 = 1 - E(B)/Q \tag{10.11}$$

Developing the Spreadsheets for Models 3 and 4 The solutions for models 3 and 4 appear in Figures 10.14 and 10.15. (See the files CAMERA3.XLS and CAMERA4.XLS.) The first assumes that Machey's specifies its service level to be no stockouts on 95% ($s_1 = .95$) of its order cycles. The second assumes a service level where 98% ($s_2 = .98$) of its demands for cameras are satisfied with existing inventory.

Since these spreadsheets are very similar to those in Figures 10.11 and 10.12, we explain only the differences, which occur in cells B19 and B20. Specifically, the formulas in cells B19 and B20 for the fraction of cycles with no shortages and the fraction of demand met on time follow directly from Equations 10.10 and 10.11:

=NORMSDIST(B17)

and

=1–(B11*(NORMDIST(B17,0,1,0)–B17*(1–B19)))/B16

(This latter formula uses Equation 10.9, developed for model 2, for $E(B)$.) Actually, the quantity in B19 isn't really needed in model 4, and the quantity in cell B20 isn't really needed in model 3, but we calculate both of them in order to compare the two models.

Note that there is no annual shortage *cost* in these models. The total annual cost is simply the sum of the setup and holding costs. We use the Solver to minimize this total annual cost, subject to the service level constraint B19=B12 (for model 3) or B20=B12 (for model 4).

FIGURE 10.14 Spreadsheet Solution for Model 3

	A	B	C	D	E	F
1	**Optimal (R,Q) Inventory Policy for Model 3**					
2						
3	**Inputs**					
4						
5	K	$35		Setup cost per order		
6	h	$10		Holding cost per unit per year		
7	E(D)	1200		Expected annual demand		
8	StDev(D)	70		StDev of annual demand		
9	L	0.0192		Lead time in years		
10	$E(D_L)$	23.077		Expected demand during lead time		
11	$StDev(D_L)$	9.707		StDev of demand during lead time		
12	s_1	0.95		Fraction of cycles with no shortages		
13						
14	**Optimal solution using Solver to choose Q and k**					
15						
16	Q	91.7		Changing cells		
17	k	1.64		for Solver		
18	$k^*\sigma_L$	16.0		Safety stock		
19	P(Z<=k)	0.95		Fraction of cycles with no shortages		
20	1-E(B)/Q	0.998		Fraction of all demand met on time		
21	R	39.0		Reorder point		
22						
23	Annual setup cost	$458				
24	Annual holding cost	$618				
25	Total annual cost	$1,076				

As we stated earlier, in model 3 it was not really necessary to calculate the fraction of demand met on time (cell B20), and in model 4 it was not really necessary to calculate the fraction of cycles with no stockouts (cell B19). However, we calculated them for comparison purposes. The optimal policy for model 3 shows that when Machey's prescribes no stockouts on 95% of its order cycles, it will automatically meet 99.8% of its demands on time (see cell B20 of Figure 10.14). In comparison, if Machey's uses model 4 with a service level constraint that 98% of its demands be met on time, then an automatic consequence is that only 69% of its order cycles will have no stockouts (see cell B19 of Figure 10.15). Therefore, we see that model 3, with a 95% service level constraint, is more stringent than model 4, with a 98% service level constraint. This more stringent service level constraint results in a larger total expected annual cost ($1076 versus $966). As we see, the service level constraint in model 4 allows Machey's to order larger quantities less frequently ($Q = 98.1$ versus $Q = 91.7$) and to order when the inventory has fallen to a lower level ($R = 27.8$ versus $R = 39.0$). This causes smaller setup and holding costs.

Shortage Cost Versus Service Level Models Service level constraints may be more meaningful to a manager than trying to estimate an ambiguous shortage cost. However, you should realize that any service level constraint *implies* an associated shortage cost. For example, in Figure 10.11 we saw that when the shortage cost is $p_1 = \$100$, the optimal k turns out to be slightly greater than 1.8, with an associated probability $P(Z > k) = .04$ of stocking out in any order cycle. But it works the other way around. If we had used

FIGURE 10.15 **Spreadsheet Solution for Model 4**

	A	B	C	D	E	F
1	**Optimal (R,Q) Inventory Policy for Model 4**					
2						
3	**Inputs**					
4						
5	K	$35		Setup cost per order		
6	h	$10		Holding cost per unit per year		
7	E(D)	1200		Expected annual demand		
8	StDev(D)	70		StDev of annual demand		
9	L	0.0192		Lead time in years		
10	$E(D_L)$	23.077		Expected demand during lead time		
11	$StDev(D_L)$	9.707		StDev of demand during lead time		
12	s_2	0.98		Fraction of demand met on time		
13						
14	**Optimal solution using Solver to choose Q and k**					
15						
16	Q	98.1		Changing cells		
17	k	0.49		for Solver		
18	$k^*\sigma_L$	4.7		Safety stock		
19	P(Z<=k)	0.69		Fraction of cycles with no shortages		
20	1-E(B)/Q	0.980		Fraction of all demand met on time		
21	R	27.8		Reorder point		
22						
23	Annual setup cost	$428				
24	Annual holding cost	$538				
25	Total annual cost	$966				

model 3 with $s_1 = .96$, then we would have obtained the same solution as the one derived in model 1. That is, model 3 with a service level of 96% is equivalent to model 1 with a shortage cost of $100.

Similarly, suppose that Machey's prescribes a model 3 service level of $s_1 = .98$. That is, it wants to have shortages on only 2% of its order cycles. The company wants to know what model 1 shortage cost p_1 is equivalent to this service level. One way to proceed is to run the Solver repeatedly in Figure 10.11, with different values of p_1, until the probability of a shortage during a cycle (one minus the probability in cell B19) is approximately .98. We know that $p_1 = \$100$ is too small because it yields a service level of only 96%. So we try slightly larger values of p_1 and keep running the Solver for Figure 10.11. The results are shown in Table 10.5. As we see, a service level of $s_1 = .98$ is equivalent to a shortage cost of $p_1 = \$160$.

TABLE 10.5 **Equivalent Shortage Costs and Service Levels for Camera Example**

p_1	Service Level
$120	2.8%
$130	2.6%
$140	2.3%
$150	2.2%
$160	2.0%

As one final comparison, suppose that Machey's wants to know what model 2 shortage cost p_2 is equivalent to a model 4 service level of $s_2 = .99$. Now we can use the Solver repeatedly in Figure 10.12, with different values of p_2, until the expected percentage of demands met on time is approximately 99%. Note that Figure 10.12 reports only $E(B)$, the expected number of backorders during an order cycle, whereas we saw that the expected fraction of demands met on time is $1 - E(B)/Q$. Therefore, we insert a row in the spreadsheet to monitor the quantity $1 - E(B)/Q$. Table 10.6 shows the results. We see that the original value of $p_2 = \$10$ gives too high a service level, namely, 99.6%. By lowering p_2 to about $4.50, we eventually achieve the desired service level of 99%.

TABLE 10.6 **Equivalent Shortage Costs and Service Levels for Camera Example**

p_2	Service Level
$10	99.6%
$8	99.5%
$6	99.3%
$4.50	99.0%

The point of these comparisons is that if a company attempts to avoid the difficult problem of specifying a shortage cost by instead specifying a service level, there is still an *implied* shortage cost.

The Case of Random Lead Time Throughout this section, we have assumed that the lead time for orders is a known quantity. It is not difficult to modify the analysis for the case where the lead time L is random. This is important, because it is not at all uncommon in real applications for ordering lead times to be uncertain; suppliers may not be able to deliver according to a precise schedule.

When L is random, we need to know $E(L)$ and $Var(L)$, the expected lead time and the variance of the lead time distribution. If these are known, then the expected demand during lead time becomes

$$E(D_L) = E(L)E(D)$$

and the standard deviation of demand during lead time becomes

$$\sigma_L = \sqrt{E(L)\sigma^2 + E(D)^2 Var(L)}$$

For example, suppose as before that $E(D) = 1200$ and $\sigma = 70$. However, instead of L being fixed at $1/52$, it is uncertain with mean $E(L) = 1/52$ and $Var(L) = (1/104)^2$, so that the standard deviation of the lead time is half a week ($1/104$). Then $E(D_L)$ is still 23.077 units ($= 1200/52$), but the standard deviation of demand during lead time is

$$\sigma_L = \sqrt{(1/52)70^2 + 1200^2(1/104)^2} \simeq 15$$

This is considerably larger than $\sigma_L = 9.7$ when L was known with certainty. Intuitively we can see that the extra amount of uncertainty about the length of the lead time adds to the uncertainty about the amount of demand during the lead time.

Given these formulas for $E(D_L)$ and σ_L, the analysis we use to find the optimal (R, Q) will be the same as the one we used in the nonrandom lead time case. ■

PROBLEMS

Skill-Building Problems

15 Suppose that the annual demand for Soni CD players at an appliance store is normally distributed with mean 150 and standard deviation 45. When the store orders these CD players from its supplier, it takes an amount of time L for the order to arrive, where L is measured as a fraction of a year. In each of the following, find the mean $E(D_L)$ and the standard deviation σ_L of the demand during lead time.

a Assume that L is known to be $3/52$, that is, three weeks.

b Assume that L is uncertain, with mean $3/52$ and standard deviation $1/52$.

16 In the previous problem assume that it costs $300 to place an order. The holding cost per CD player held in inventory per year is $15. The cost each time a customer orders a CD player that is not in stock is estimated at $40. (All demand is backlogged.)

a Find the optimal ordering policy for Parts (a) and (b) of the previous problem (when lead time is known for certain and when it is not).

b How much more is the expected annual holding cost when L is random than when it is known with certainty? Why is this cost greater in the random case?

17 How do your answers to Part (a) of the previous problem change if, instead of incurring a $40 penalty cost for each shortage, the store has a service level requirement of meeting 95% of all customer demands on time? In each case (L known with certainty and L random) what model 2 penalty cost p_2 is this service level requirement equivalent to?

18 Again refer to the Soni CD problem (Problem 15), and use the ordering and holding costs from Problem 16. Now, however, assume that the store's service level requirement obligates it to meet customer demand on 95% of all order cycles. What (R, Q) policy should it use? Then find the model 1 penalty cost p_1 that gives an equivalent (R, Q) policy. Answer these questions for the case where L is known with certainty and where it is random.

19 A hospital orders its blood from a regional blood bank. Each year, the hospital uses an average of 1040 pints of type O blood. Each order placed with the regional blood bank incurs a cost of $20. The lead time for each order is five days. It costs the hospital $20 to hold one pint of blood in inventory for a year. The per-pint stockout cost is estimated to be $50. This cost is incurred for each pint backlogged. Annual demand for type O blood is normally distributed with standard deviation 43.26 pints.

a Determine the optimal order quantity, reorder point, and safety stock level. Assume that 365 days equal one year and that all demand is backlogged.

b What model 4 service level requirement is equivalent to this $50 stockout cost?

20 Furnco sells secretarial chairs. Annual demand is normally distributed with mean 1040 chairs and standard deviation 130 chairs. Furnco orders its chairs from its flagship store. It costs $100 to place an order, and the lead time is two weeks. Furnco estimates that each order cycle in which there is a stockout causes a loss of $250 in future goodwill. Furnco pays $60 for each chair and sells it for $100. The annual cost of holding a chair in inventory is 30% of its purchase cost.

a Assuming that all demand is backlogged, what are the reorder point and the safety stock level?

b What model 3 service level is this $250 stockout cost equivalent to?

c Is the $100 selling price relevant information for solving this problem? Why or why not?

21 A firm experiences demand with a mean of 100 units per day. Lead time demand is normally distributed with a mean of 1000 units and a standard deviation of 200 units. It costs $6 to hold one unit for one year. If the firm wants to meet 90% of all demand on time, what will be the annual cost of holding safety stock? (Assume that each order costs $50.)

Skill-Extending Problem

22 Explain the following statement: Faster-moving items require larger safety stocks than slower-moving items. (*Hint*: If $Q/E(D)$ is large, does this imply that an item is fast moving or slow moving?) ■

10.4 Conclusion

We have considered two important classes of models in this chapter. The first is usually called the newsvendor problem, where a company has one chance to order a product that will soon have little or no value. We saw that the key to this problem is determining the unit costs of understocking and overstocking. Once these costs are known, the determination of the optimal order quantity is relatively straightforward and depends only on the form of the probability distribution of demand. The second class of model we examined is a continuous review ordering model, where a company must determine when to order and how much to order at each ordering opportunity. We saw that these two decisions can be made practically independently. The decision on how much to order can be made in essentially the same way as in the EOQ model from the previous chapter. In contrast, the reorder point decision is more difficult and depends on the probability distribution of demand during lead time as well as the type of shortage cost or service level chosen by the company.

The models in this chapter, while relatively complex mathematically, are among the simplest of all probabilistic inventory models. Realistic models can quickly become much more complex, requiring tools well beyond the level of this book (and the abilities of most managers). However, there is another solution method that can be used for complex models, namely, computer simulation. Although computer simulation has its drawbacks, it allows us to analyze much more difficult (and often realistic) models fairly easily. We will revisit some inventory models when we study the topic of simulation in Chapters 12 and 13.

REVIEW PROBLEMS

Skill-Building Problems

23 The Chocochip Cookie Store bakes its cookies every morning before opening. It costs the store 30¢ to bake each cookie, and each cookie is sold for 65¢. At the end of the day, leftover cookies may be sold to a thrift bakery for 15¢ per cookie.

a If the daily demand for cookies is described by the discrete distribution shown in Table 10.7, how many dozen cookies should be baked before the store opens?

b If the daily demand (in dozens) for cookies is instead normal with mean 100 and standard deviation 35, how many dozen cookies should be baked?

c Suppose that the daily demand (in dozens) for cookies has the *exponential* density function with mean 100:

$$f(d) = \frac{e^{-d/100}}{100} \qquad (d \geq 0)$$

How many dozen cookies should be baked? (*Hint*: The cumulative demand distribution in this case is $F(d) = 1 - e^{-d/100}$; this is the probability that demand is less than or equal to d.)

24 The power at Ice Station Lion is supplied via solar cells. Once a year, a plane flies in and sells solar cells to the ice station at a price of $20 per cell. Because of uncertainty about future

TABLE 10.7 **Distribution for Cookie Problem**

Demand (dozens)	Probability
20	.30
30	.20
40	.20
50	.15
60	.15

power needs, the ice station can only guess the number of cells that will be required during the coming year (see probability distribution shown in Table 10.8). If the ice station runs out of solar cells, a special order must be placed at a cost of $30 per cell. (*Hint*: Find the distribution of total cost, and then the expected total cost, for any order quantity. Then use a data table to find the best order quantity.)

TABLE 10.8 **Distribution of Cells for Ice Station Problem**

Number of Cells	Probability
50	.20
60	.15
70	.30
80	.10
90	.15
100	.10

25 (Based on Bruno [3]) The daily demand for substitute teachers in the Los Angeles teaching system follows the distribution given in Table 10.9. Los Angeles wants to know how many teachers to keep in its substitute teacher pool. Whether or not the substitute teacher is needed, it costs $50 per day to keep a substitute teacher in the pool. If not enough substitute teachers are available on a given day, regular teachers are used to cover classes at a cost of $84 (extra) per regular teacher. How many teachers should Los Angeles have in its substitute teacher pool? (See the hint in the previous problem.)

TABLE 10.9 **Distribution for L.A. Teacher Problem**

Number Needed	Probability
200	.03
275	.03
350	.03
400	.05
450	.40
500	.30
550	.06
600	.07
650	.03

26 Condo Construction Company is going to First National Bank for a loan. At the present time, the bank is willing to lend Condo up to $1 million, with an interest cost of 10%. Condo believes that the amount of borrowed funds needed during the current year is normally distributed with a mean of $700,000 and a standard deviation of $200,000. If Condo needs to borrow more money during the year, the company will have to go to Louie the Loan Shark. The cost per dollar borrowed from Louie is 25¢. To minimize expected interest costs for the year, how much money should Condo borrow from the bank?

27 If c_{under} is fixed, will an increase in c_{over} increase or decrease the optimal order quantity? If c_{over} is fixed, will an increase in c_{under} increase or decrease the optimal order quantity?

28 In the airline overbooking example (Example 10.3), form a data table that finds the optimal *Q* as a function of the extra bonus paid to each bumped ticketholder. This bonus was \$100. In the data table let it vary from \$50 to \$300 in increments of \$50.

29 An optometrist orders eyeglass frames at a cost of \$40 per frame and sells each frame for \$70. The annual holding cost is 20% of the optometrist's cost of purchasing a frame. Each time frames are ordered, a cost of \$200 is incurred. Because of lost goodwill, a cost of \$50 is incurred each time a customer wants a frame that is not in stock. Frames are delivered one week after an order is placed. The annual demand for frames is normally distributed with mean 1000 and standard deviation 250.

a Assuming all shortages are backlogged, determine the order quantity and reorder point.

b What order quantity and reorder point should be used to meet 95% of all orders from stock?

c What order quantity and reorder point should be used to have shortages occur during an average of two order cycles per year?

30 We are given the following information about a product: (1) the cost of placing an order is \$100, (2) the cost per item is \$5, (3) the sales price per item is \$8, (4) the annual holding cost per item is 40% of the cost of the item, (5) the annual demand is 5000 units, and (6) the lead time demand is normally distributed with mean 30 and standard deviation 10.

a If the reorder point that minimizes expected annual cost is 50, what is the implied shortage cost per unit short? (Assume all shortages are backlogged.)

b What order quantity and reorder point should be used to satisfy 99% of all demand on time?

31 We are given the following information for a product: (1) the ordering cost is \$50, (2) the annual demand is normally distributed with mean 960 and standard deviation 60, (3) the holding cost per item per year is \$6, (4) the shortage cost per unit short is \$80, and (5) the lead time is random with mean four weeks and standard deviation one week.

a Determine the order quantity and the reorder point under the assumption that all demands are backordered.

b For the policy in Part (a), find the implied service levels. That is, find the fraction of all order cycles where all demand is met and the fraction of all customer demands that are met from existing stock.

32 A hospital must order the drug Porapill from Daisy Drug Company. It costs \$500 to place an order. Annual demand for the drug is normally distributed with mean 10,000 and standard deviation 3000, and it costs \$5 to hold one unit in inventory for one year. (A unit is a standard container for the drug.) Orders arrive one month after being placed. Assume that all shortages are backlogged.

a What (R, Q) policy should the company use if it wants to meet 95% of all customer demand from existing inventory?

b Suppose the company could pay *C* dollars per year to decrease its lead time per order from one month to half a month. What is the most it would be willing to pay to do this (and still have a 95% service level)?

33 Chicago's Treadway Tires Dealer must order tires from its national warehouse. It costs \$10,000 to place an order. Annual tire sales are normally distributed with mean 20,000 and standard deviation 5000. It costs \$10 per year to hold a tire in inventory, and the lead time for delivery of an order is normally distributed with mean three weeks and standard deviation one week. Assume that all shortages are backlogged.

a Find the (R, Q) policy the company should use to meet a service level where 96% of all order cycles experience no stockouts.

b Assume that the company could pay *C* dollars per year to decrease the variability in lead times to essentially zero. That is, the lead time would then be a certain three weeks. What is the most it would be willing to pay (and still meet the service level in Part (a))?

Skill-Extending Problems

34 A business believes that its needs for cash during the next month are those described by the probability distribution shown in Table 10.10. At the beginning of the month, \$10,000 is available to the business, and the business manager must determine how much of the money to place in an account bearing 24% annual interest. If any money must be withdrawn before the end of the month, all interest on the withdrawn money is forfeited, and a penalty equal to 2% of the withdrawn money must be paid. How much money should be placed in the 24% annual interest account?

TABLE 10.10 Distribution for Cash Management Problem

Cash Needs	Probability
\$4000	.30
\$5000	.20
\$6000	.10
\$7000	.30
\$8000	.10

35 A fur dealer buys fur coats for \$100 each and sells them for \$200 each. He believes that the demand for coats is normally distributed with mean 100 and standard deviation 10. Any coat not sold can be sold to a discount house for \$100, but the fur dealer believes he must charge himself a cost of 10¢ per dollar invested in a fur coat that is sold at discount.

a How many coats should the dealer order?

b If the price at which the dealer sold his coats increased (assuming demand is unchanged), would he buy more or fewer coats?

36 A company currently has two warehouses. Each warehouse services half the company's demand, and the annual demand serviced by each warehouse is normally distributed with mean 10,000 and standard deviation 1000. The lead time for meeting demand is $1/10$ year. The company wants to meet 95% of all demand on time. Assume that each warehouse uses the EOQ formula to determine its order quantity and that this leads to $Q = 2000$ for each warehouse.

a How much safety stock must be held at each warehouse?

b Show that if the company had only one warehouse, it would hold less safety stock than it does when it has two warehouses.

c A young MBA argues, "By having one central warehouse, I can reduce the total amount of safety stock needed to meet 95% of all customer demands on time. Therefore, we can save money by having only one central warehouse instead of several branch warehouses." How might this argument be rebutted?

Modeling Problems

37 A trucking firm must decide at the beginning of the year on the size of its trucking fleet. If on a given day the firm does not have enough trucks, the firm will have to rent trucks from Hertz. Discuss how you would determine the optimal size of the trucking fleet?

38 A computer manufacturer produces computers for 40 different stores. In order to monitor its inventory policies the manufacturer needs to estimate the mean and standard deviation of its weekly demand. Do you have any ideas about how to do this?

39 An **exchange curve** is a helpful way to visualize trade-offs between inventory investments and shortages. To illustrate the idea, suppose that expected lead time demand is 200 units, standard deviation of lead time demand is 50 units, expected annual demand is 100,000 units, cost per order is \$12.50, annual holding cost is \$10 per unit, and per-unit purchase cost is \$100.

a Construct a curve that plots the average inventory investment on the horizontal axis and the number of stockouts per year on the vertical axis.

b Construct a curve that plots the average inventory investment on the horizontal axis and the percentage of annual demand that is unfilled on the vertical axis.

c How can these curves be used to illustrate the trade-offs between inventory investment and customer service?

40 (Based on Brout [2]) Planner's Peanuts sells 100 products. The company has been disappointed with the high level of inventory it keeps of each product and its low service level (percentage of demand met on time). Describe how you would help Planner's improve its performance on both these objectives. Pay close attention to the data you would need to collect and how the data would be used.

41 Austin [1] conducted an extensive inventory analysis for the U.S. Air Force. He found that for over 250,000 items the annual holding cost was assumed to equal 32% of the item's purchase price. He also found that when an order was placed for most items, a fixed cost of over $200 was incurred. The Air Force held one month of safety stock for each item. Given this limited information, discuss how you could improve the Air Force's inventory policies. ■

CASE STUDY

Retail Pricing Using Retailer

Retailer is an exercise designed to simulate the pricing decisions faced by the management of a large chain of retail clothing stores. The simulation focuses on two important aspects of the pricing decision: *timing* and *magnitude* of price reductions. The retailer must decide when to take a price cut, if at all. If a price cut is taken, the magnitude of the cut must also be determined. These decisions are interrelated and further complicated because price reductions cannot be rescinded.

To place this problem in perspective, we give an overview of the fashion retail industry. Then we present a description of the production and distribution process, followed by a brief discussion of the technology and issues involved in pricing and markdowns. The implication of a markdown strategy for overall corporate earnings is illustrated for a specific company.

To help you develop a good pricing strategy for playing Retailer, historical data is provided in the spreadsheet RETAIL.XLS. Specific instructions and suggestions for preparing to play Retailer are described in the final section.

The Fashion Retail Industry

The fashion retail industry is highly fragmented. Companies range in size from small boutiques operated as sole proprietorships to multinational specialty retailers such as Benetton, The Limited, and Gap Inc. Other important outlets include national department store chains, such as Macy's and Nordstrom's in the U.S., Marks and Spencer in Europe, and the rapidly growing mail order segment (Spiegel, J. Crew, etc.).

While many retailers only serve as intermediaries between producers and consumers, there is an increasing trend in the industry toward *private label* merchandise, which is manufactured exclusively for a particular retailer. Because it is exclusive, private label merchandise gives a store greater pricing power. It also helps differentiate a store's merchandise mix. Specialty retailers (Benetton, The Limited, etc.) have always manufactured (or subcontracted the manufacture of) their own exclusive designs. Recently, department stores such as Macy's are following this pattern by introducing their own private label lines.

While there is a tremendous variety in the range of merchandise sold by fashion retailers, from an operations standpoint the merchandise can be broken down into two main categories:

- **Staple Items.** Also known as *basic goods*, these are items that consumers purchase regularly and that do not become obsolete quickly. Socks, underwear, T-shirts, and core denim garments like five-pocket jeans are considered staples. Also included in this category are "classic" garments, such as black gabardine skirts, khaki pants, white button-down Oxford shirts, and other items that are relatively immune to shifting fashion trends. Staple items are characterized by relatively stable and predictable demand.
- **Fashion Items.** These are items with a strong fashion component that quickly become obsolete or outdated. Fashion items are targeted for specific seasons (fall, spring, cruise, holiday, etc.) and in many cases are marketed over a series of "mini-seasons" lasting as short as eight weeks. These items are used to enliven the presentation within a store and are frequently featured in its window display. In many ways, they also define the "style" of a store and help position the store relative to its competitors.

A range of garment types are found in the fashion category. Demand for fashion items is highly unpredictable and erratic; an item can be a hit and sell out in a matter of weeks, or consumers might utterly reject the style, resulting in only a fraction of the total stock selling during its targeted season.

Of course, a store's merchandise portfolio can be broken down in many different ways. For example, some stores categorize merchandise by fabric type (knits vs. wovens) or department (sportswear, accessories, etc.). However, the staple-fashion classification turns out to be most useful in understanding the relationship between production, distribution, and pricing.

Production and Distribution

Garment production involves four major stages. First, and perhaps most important, is the design of the garments themselves. This is a highly creative process that, in most cases, begins one year in advance of the target season. Basic silhouettes, colors, and fabrics are chosen at this stage. Designs of individual garments or *styles* are often based on a particular theme (for example, the "Victorian look" or the "Western look") to form an entire *line* of clothes. The line projects a unified image and also helps ensure that garments coordinate well with each other.

Once designs are finalized, production quantities are determined. These quantities are based on very rough forecasts of the likely sales of individual styles. Given the vagaries of fashion trends and the long lead times involved, these forecasts are typically highly inaccurate.

Materials are then procured for production. Fabric is ordered from textile mills. Mills range in size from large national firms such as Burlington, Cone Mills, and Galey and Lord, to small specialty mills that produce silks and woolens. The lead time for fabric procurement can range from one to two weeks for standard in-stock fabrics to several months for special-order fabrics (for example, fabrics with custom colors or weaves). Buttons, zippers, and other accessories must also be ordered at this stage.

While materials are being ordered, production time is arranged either at a firm's own facilities or through subcontractors. Firms that specialize in particular fabric types, such as Italy's Benetton, with its core line of natural fiber knitwear, or Levi Strauss and Co., with its signature denim jeans, are more likely to own their own facilities; those without strong materials orientation often use subcontractors.

Subcontractors provide two key advantages to retailers: (1) flexible production capacity and (2) production expertise in particular fabric types. Both can be significant advantages when faced with fast moving fashion trends. For example, Ireland is well regarded as a source for high quality woolen knits, while Hong Kong is the preferred source for silk garments, since it is close to the sources of raw materials and has the machinery and skilled labor necessary to work with this delicate fiber. Denim and gabardine are relatively easy fabrics with which to work and garments made from these fabrics can be produced in a variety of locations, for example Indonesia, Puerto Rico, or the U.S. As a result, it is not uncommon for a retailer to have production contracts in dozens of countries in any given season. Lead times can range from under four weeks for an in-house domestic shop producing a simple garment to several months for an overseas contractor who requires advance production agreements.

Finally, once garments are cut and assembled, they are shipped to distribution centers and then from distribution centers to individual stores. The distribution process can be quick (1–2 weeks) for a domestic supplier, but in the case of overseas suppliers it may take 4–6 weeks if garments are transported in container ships. Overall, the total lead time for production is typically 6–12 weeks for a domestic contractor producing from standard fabric stock, 3–4 months for an overseas contractor using stock fabrics, and more than six months for an overseas contractor using a special-order fabric.

For staple items, periodic production runs can be scheduled to ensure a steady flow of merchandise from production facilities to stores. The management of this process is carried out using many of the traditional tools of inventory control. Indeed, the primary concern with staple items is reducing lead time and costs for reordering. This is accomplished through better communication via Electronic Data Interchange (EDI)[3] and better materials handling technology.[4] Fashion items, however, are usually produced in a *single production run* because the fabrics and patterns change significantly from one season to the next and the lead times involved in production are usually too long to permit restocking within a tight 8–15 week sales season.

Pricing, Markdowns, and Leftovers

With perfect forecasts, merchandise is available in the exact quantities demanded by consumers and a store sells out its entire stock at full price. In practice, this is rarely the case. More often, a store may find itself short of stock on hit items, while selling only a fraction of its initial stock if a style proves unpopular. Items that remain unsold at the end of the selling season are typically sold in factory outlets (if available) or sold to discounters ("jobbers"). In the latter case,

[3]EDI refers to a collection of technologies for computer-to-computer transmission of standard trading documents such as purchase orders and invoices. The technology is based on the ANSI X.12 standard, a detailed set of standards for protocols and message formats.

[4]The term *quick response* is often used in the industry to refer to lead-time reduction techniques.

labels are often removed to prevent devaluation of the company's or designer's image.

Without the option to restock fashion items during a sales season, merchandise managers are left with few alternatives to match supply and demand for individual styles. One option is to transfer merchandise from stores where sales are weak to those where sales are strong. The second option is to change the price, usually by marking down styles that are not selling. The main decisions in taking a markdown are its timing and magnitude. For most retailers, the process of making markdown decisions is more of an art than a science. It is based mainly on the judgment of experienced merchandise managers.

POS Data and Markdown Control

A major technological trend in the retail industry is the development of point-of-sale (POS) technology. Essentially, a POS system links computerized cash registers (which are often equipped with laser scanners for automated reading of bar-coded tags) and scanners at distribution centers with a central computer in a retailer's home office. Local computers (usually PC based) in the individual retail locations and distribution centers collect data on sales and inventories and are polled periodically by the central computer to update the status of each style in a store's line. Through a POS system, senior managers have a real-time view of the sales activities throughout their entire distribution chain.

Currently, most POS data is used only to identify ("flag") particular styles that are not performing up to expectations. For example, many retailers use an index of weekly sell-through percentage, defined as the ratio of a given week's sales to the in-store inventory at the start of that week. Each week items are sorted by sell-through percentages. These lists are used by merchandise managers to make markdown decisions. To date, however, very little analysis of POS data is performed beyond this simple exception reporting.

Financial Implications

To understand the financial impact of a markdown policy it is useful to examine a specific company's earnings. Gap Inc. provides a good example. Gap Inc. has several subsidiaries: Gap Stores, Gap Kids, and Banana Republic. Each sells casual clothes and denim.

In the *New York Times* article shown in Figure 10.16, a sharp earnings increase for Gap Inc. is partially attributed to its markdown strategy.[5] Financial information for Gap Inc. is shown in Figures 10.17–10.19. They show that in 1992, Gap had almost $3 billion in sales, producing a net income of approximately $210 million. With 144 million shares of stock outstanding in 1992, this represented earnings per share of $1.47.

Suppose that Gap could increase revenues 2% by changing its markdown strategy. This would represent a $59 million increase in sales. Since the cost of goods sold is not affected by the pricing strategy, pretax income would also increase by $59 million. This represents a 17% increase in pretax income and thus provides a 17% increase in net income and earnings per share. Likewise, a 2% decrease in revenue would decrease net income by 17%. *Relatively small changes in revenue can have a substantial impact on a company's bottom line.*

Preparation for Retailer

In the retailer simulation exercise, the player plays the role of upper management at a large chain of retail stores. The stores start with an initial stock of 2000 units of a fashion item initially priced at $60. *There are high hopes that the item will fly off the shelves, but only some items do.* The length of the selling season is 15 weeks. Production and distribution costs for the item have been paid, so that cost is sunk. *The goal is to maximize the revenue* from the 2000 units during the selling season plus any salvage value. Management has decided to allow four price levels: full price ($60), 10% off ($54), 20% off ($48), or 40% off ($36). By observing sales for the current item (and historical data from roughly similar fashion items), in any given week management can leave the price the same or cut the price. Once the price is cut company policy does *not* allow the price to be raised. If the price has been cut to 40% off, further markdowns are not possible in later weeks.

[5] The article does not contain enough information to determine whether Gap Inc.'s markdown strategy changed or whether items were simply selling faster so that fewer markdowns were required.

FIGURE 10.16 Article in the *New York Times*, November 12, 1993

Gap's 3d-Quarter Earnings Climbed 27.3%

By ANDREA ADELSON

Gap Inc. said yesterday that its third-quarter income rose 27.3 percent because of leaner inventories, fewer markdowns and the addition of fashion merchandise for women.

The results were a record for the San Francisco-based company and exceeded expectations of some industry analysts. Gap shares rose $3.125, to $39.50, on the New York Stock Exchange.

The Gap's results also marked a turnaround following four consecutive quarters where the company's earnings have declined compared with the previous year's periods. The specialty retailer that made jeans and T-shirts a fashion statement has struggled over the last 12 months as once-rapid sales growth has slowed and profit margins have eroded.

"This was a welcome change," said Robert F. Buchanan, a retail analyst for Alex Brown. He noted, however, that the period a year ago, when the company's earnings had declined 14 percent and the yearlong slide began, "was easy to beat."

In this year's third quarter, sales increased 9 percent from the period a year earlier. However, sales at stores open at least one year, which analysts say is a better measure of sales strength, declined 1 percent. The company has 1,385 stores currently, a 7 percent increase over the 1992 period.

Inventories Cut by 15%

The company overcame sluggish sales volume by cutting inventories 15 percent and adding more fashionable merchandise for women, such as long knit skirts and ribbed vests, alongside its standard stock of jeans and sweatshirts.

"It's very current, younger, not quite as preppy-basic as a year ago," said Alice Ruth, a retail analyst for Montgomery Securities. She said sales of the new merchandise had been brisk with little left over to be marked down. Price markdowns hurt profits in earlier periods.

With fewer clearance items and lower inventory, which meant the company had lower interest expense to finance the cost of goods, the company's gross profit margins rose in the quarter by 2.5 percentage points, to 37.8 percent, compared with a 4.5 percent decline in the period a year ago, the analysts said.

"This strategy should continue into the fourth quarter," said Thomas H. Tashjian, a retail analyst with First Manhattan. Holiday shoppers "will be hard pressed to find fleece or denim" at a Gap store, he predicted.

FIGURE 10.17 Gap Inc.: Estimated Sales and Income by Division

	1989	1990	1991	1992	1993E
SALES ($ millions)					
Gap Stores	$1,307	$1,554	$1,944	$2,185	$2,335
Gap Kids	$70	$140	$264	$375	$500
Banana Republic	$210	$240	$310	$400	$480
Total Sales	$1,587	$1,934	$2,518	$2,960	$3,315
% Change		21.9%	30.2%	17.6%	12.0%
OPERATING INCOME					
Gap Stores	$174	$223	$315	$278	$301
% of Sales	13.3%	14.4%	16.2%	12.7%	12.9%
Gap Kids	$6	$12	$29	$34	$45
% of Sales	8.6%	8.6%	11.0%	9.1%	9.0%
Banana Republic	($5)	$5	$31	$32	$43
% of Sales	−2.4%	2.1%	10.0%	8.0%	9.0%
Total Op. Income	$175	$240	$375	$344	$389
% of Sales	11.0%	12.4%	14.9%	11.6%	11.7%
CONTRIBUTION TO SALES					
Gap Stores	82.4%	80.4%	77.2%	73.8%	70.4%
Gap Kids	4.4%	7.2%	10.5%	12.7%	15.1%
Banana Republic	13.2%	12.4%	12.3%	13.5%	14.5%
CONTRIBUTION TO PROFITS					
Gap Stores	99.4%	92.9%	84.0%	80.8%	77.4%
Gap Kids	3.4%	5.0%	7.7%	9.9%	11.6%
Banana Republic	−2.9%	2.1%	8.3%	9.3%	11.1%

FIGURE 10.18 Gap Inc.: Operating Statement Information

	1989	1990	1991	1992	1993E
Net Sales ($ millions)	$1,587.0	$1,934.0	$2,518.0	$2,960.0	$3,315.2
Cost of Goods Sold	1,046.2	1,241.2	1,568.0	1,955.6	2,182.3
S, G & A	364.1	454.2	575.7	661.3	743.8
Interest Expense	2.8	1.4	3.5	3.8	6.0
Pretax Income	162.7	237.1	370.8	339.8	383.0
Taxes	65.1	92.4	140.9	129.1	145.5
Net Income	97.6	144.7	229.9	210.7	237.5
EPS	$0.69	$1.02	$1.62	$1.47	$1.65
Shares Out (millions)	141.0	141.6	142.0	143.7	144.2
Sales % Change	26.8%	21.9%	30.3%	17.7%	16.0%
Comp Stores	15.0	14.0	13.0	5.0	5.0
% OF SALES					
Cost of Goods Sold	65.9	64.2	62.3	66.1%	65.8%
S, G & A	22.9	23.5	22.9	22.3	22.4
Interest Expense	0.2	0.1	0.1	0.1	0.2
Pretax Income	10.3	12.3	14.7	11.5	11.6
Tax Rate	40.0	39.0	38.0	38.0	38.0

Source: Company reports & C. J. Lawrence estimates.

FIGURE 10.19 Gap Inc.: Estimated Store Profile

	1989	1990	1991	1992	1993E
TOTAL					
Number of Stores	960	1,092	1,216	1,307	1,416
Average Store Size	4,226	4,361	4,637	4,980	5,390
Beginning Year Square Feet	3,843	4,067	4,762	5,638	6,509
Year-End Square Feet	4,057	4,762	5,638	6,509	7,632
% Change	5.6%	17.4%	18.4%	15.4%	17.3%
Average Square Feet	3,950	4,415	5,200	6,074	7,071
% Change	5.8%	11.8%	17.8%	16.8%	16.4%
Total Sales ($ million)	$1,587	$1,934	$2,518	$2,960	$3,315
% Change	27.9%	21.9%	30.2%	17.6%	12.0%
Sales/Average Square Foot	$402	$438	$484	$487	$469
% Change	20.9%	9.0%	10.5%	0.6%	−3.8%
Operating Income	$175	$240	$375	$344	$389
Operating Margin	11.0%	12.4%	14.9%	11.6%	11.7%
Comparable Store Sales	15.0%	14.0%	13.0%	5.0%	3.0%

Source: Company reports & C. J. Lawrence estimates.

In the first week the price is set at $60. Thus, there are 14 weeks remaining for price cut decisions. All unsold inventory at the end of 15 weeks is sold for a salvage value of $25 per unit.

In order to make more informed markdown decisions, historical data for 15 different items is available in the spreadsheet RETAIL.XLS. These are all fashion items, and some turned out to be very popular items while some did not sell so well.[6] Although the items are different, their responsiveness to price cuts are quite similar. The historical data in RETAIL.XLS has been "deseasonalized." That is, the data has been normalized to remove the predictable effects of seasons and holidays on sales figures. These effects are also removed from the Retailer simulation

[6] In other words, weekly demand for each item (at a given price) is sampled from a distribution with a mean that is different for each item. This "true mean" is unknown at the beginning of each selling season but can be estimated with greater accuracy as additional weeks of sales are observed.

exercise.[7] Nevertheless, the unpredictable component of sales is quite significant. Even at the same price, sales can vary considerably from week to week because of weather, competitors, and a host of other factors. The historical data in RETAIL.XLS has also been normalized, so that the initial prices of all items are scaled to $60 and the initial quantities are scaled to 2000 units.

Before playing Retailer, you should carefully analyze the historical data and try to develop a sensible markdown strategy. You should work out any desired formulas in advance, so that necessary calculations can be done simply and quickly. In analyzing the historical data, you might want to attempt to answer the following questions:

- What is the average effect on sales of each size price cut? For example, for a price cut from $60 to $54, what is the average increase in weekly sales?
- How variable are sales from one item to the next?

In developing a strategy, you might want to consider the following:

- If demand was not variable, what would be the optimal price cut strategy? For example, suppose the demand at a price of $60 was a constant 80 items per week. Using your estimated demand sensitivities, to what level would you cut the price and when would you cut the price?
- How might your strategy be altered to account for uncertainty in demand?
- How would your strategy have performed on the historical data? ■

[7] In statistical terms, sales from one week to the next are independent. Sales are also identically distributed if the price is not changed.

Acknowledgment: This case was coauthored with Garrett van Ryzin.

REFERENCES

1 Austin, L. "Project EOQ: A Success Story in Implementing Academic Research." *Interfaces* 7, no. 4 (1977): 1–14

2 Brout, D. "Scientific Management of Inventory on a Hand-Held Calculator. *Interfaces* 11, no. 6 (1981): 57–69.

3 Bruno, J. "The Use of Monte-Carlo Techniques for Determining the Size of Substitute Teacher Pools." *Socio-Economic Planning Science* 4 (1970): 415–28.

4 Smith, B., J. Leimkuhler, and R. Darrow. "Yield Management at American Airlines." *Interfaces* 22, no. 1 (1992): 8–31.

C H A P T E R

11

Queueing Models

Management Science Success Stories

Long waiting lines in service organizations can be bad for business, and the money spent to reduce these lines is often money well spent. This is the conclusion of two studies reported in *Interfaces*, one relating to the mail order company L. L. Bean and the other to Lourdes Hospital in New York State. Each study employed a queueing model to determine the staffing levels necessary to reduce congestion to an acceptable level.

The article "Staffing a Centralized Appointment Scheduling Department in Lourdes Hospital," by Agnihothri and Taylor [1], describes how Lourdes Hospital decided to use a centralized system to schedule by phone appointments for outpatients and inpatients and ambulatory services requested by physicians, their staff, hospital personnel, and patients. The decision to centralize certainly made sense. Instead of having doctors and patients call many different departments for appointments and information, the system allowed them to call a well-trained and centrally located staff. However, a disadvantage quickly became obvious: the staff were not able to handle the large numbers of calls, particularly at peak periods during the day. Their goal of being able to answer 90% of all arriving calls was not being met, and all parties involved–doctors, patients, and staff–were frustrated with long waits and busy signals.

The authors collected data on the rates of incoming calls and the times required to "service" these calls. They found, among other things, that the pattern of calls was approximately the same each day of the week but the rate of calls differed during various times of the day. Therefore, they solved several queueing models, each for a different time of day, in order to determine staffing levels that would eliminate much of the congestion and many of the complaints. The study proved to be a big success. As the authors state, "Prior to the study, three to four formal complaints were made each week about the busy phone lines. They fell to less than one per week immediately after the staffing changes, and since July 1988, complaints have been very infrequent and can usually be attributed to a known factor, such as an unexpected absence of a staff member."

The L. L. Bean study reported in the article "Establishing Telephone-Agent Staffing Levels through Economic Optimization," by Andrews and Parsons [2], is similar to the hospital study in that L. L. Bean also experienced high levels of telephone congestion. Too many customers calling to order merchandise either got a busy signal or had to wait a long time on line for an operator. The company had not ignored the problem in the past. In fact, it set a goal of having no more than 15% of the calls wait more than 20 seconds before reaching an operator, and it attempted to meet this goal with its rule-of-14: employ enough operators so that each handles about 14 calls per hour.

The problem was that there was little scientific basis for this rule-of-14; it was essentially an intuitive guideline. Worse yet, there was no guarantee that the company's goal of answering 85% of the calls within 20 seconds was a good one from an *economic* point of view. Before the study, L. L. Bean had never really analyzed the relevant costs, particularly the cost of lost business from fed-up customers who took their business elsewhere. After all, it was difficult to track customers who got busy signals or hung up after waiting a few minutes. Would they call L. L. Bean again or not? This study gathered data on lost business due to impatient customers, analyzed these data statistically, and then used a queueing model to determine the number of operators to employ (at various times of the day) in order to maximize expected profit. The authors report that for the first year it was used (1988) their new system resulted in an annualized profit gain of over $200,000. ■

11.1 Introduction

A basic fact of life is that we all spend a great deal of time waiting in queues. This occurs when we wait in line at a bank, at the supermarket, at a fast-food restaurant, at a stoplight, and many other situations. Of course, people are not the only entities that wait in queues. For example, at a television repair shop, all of the televisions other than the one(s) being repaired are essentially waiting in line to be repaired. Or when people submit computer jobs to a mainframe computer via remote terminals, these jobs typically wait in a queue (according to some priority system) until the computer has time to run them.

In terms of the mathematical analysis of queues, it doesn't really matter whether the entities waiting are people or televisions or computer jobs. The same type of analysis is appropriate for all of these. The purpose of such an analysis is generally twofold. First, we want to examine an existing system in order to quantify its operating characteristics. For example, a fast-food restaurant currently employs 12 people in various jobs; we might be interested in determining the amount of time a typical customer must wait in line or how many customers are typically waiting in line at a given time. The second purpose of queueing analysis is to learn how to make a system better. We might find, for example, that the fast-food restaurant would be better off economically employing only 10 workers and deploying them in a different manner.

The first objective, analyzing the characteristics of a particular system, is quite difficult from a mathematical point of view. Usually, several simplifying assumptions must be made; otherwise, the mathematical model is too complex to solve. For example, a commonly observed queueing situation is the one at a typical supermarket, where customers join one of several lines (probably the shortest), possibly switch lines if they see that another is moving faster, and eventually get served by one of the checkout people. However, as common as this is—and as simple as it is to describe—it is *very* difficult to analyze mathematically. Therefore, we will only be able to analyze the simplest of queueing models in this chapter. Usually, when management scientists need to analyze more complex systems, they resort to computer simulation, a method quite different than the approach we use in this chapter.

The second objective, queueing optimization, is also difficult but for a different reason. Of course, in order to find the *best* system, we need to be able to analyze each of several competing systems, which we have already said is difficult. But beyond this, we must make difficult choices. For example, if the fast-food restaurant is trying to decide how many employees to hire for various times of day, it must analyze the trade-off between more employees (better service) and fewer employees (less wages). The cost of extra employees is simple to gauge—the marginal cost of one more employee is simply the wage rate. However, it is difficult to estimate the "cost" of making a customer wait an extra two minutes in line. In some sense it costs the restaurant nothing, at least not in terms of immediate out-of-pocket costs. But it might have long-range implications—fewer customers will bring their business to this restaurant if they have to wait a long time in line. Thus, there is definitely an incentive for the restaurant manager to consider service as well as employee wages. In order to find the optimal number of employees, the restaurant must estimate the dollar cost of having a customer wait in line for some amount of time, such as a minute. Only by estimating this cost can it make an economic choice between the cost of waiting and the cost of more efficient service.

The examples in this chapter will highlight these two objectives. First, we will learn how to calculate important characteristics, such as expected waiting times, of specific systems. Then we will illustrate how a balance can be found in order to obtain economically optimal systems.

11.2

Elements of Queueing Models

On this section we will list some of the features of queueing systems that distinguish one system from another. Almost all queueing systems are alike in that customers enter a system, possibly wait in one or more queues, are served, and then depart.[1] This general description of a queueing system—customers entering, waiting in line, and being served—hardly suggests the variety of queueing systems that exist. We now discuss some of the key features and their variations.

Characteristics of Arrivals

First, we must specify the arrival process. This includes the timing of arrivals as well as the types of arrivals. Regarding timing, it is most common to specify the **interarrival times**, the times between successive customer arrivals. It is possible that these interarrival times are known, that is, they are nonrandom. For example, at some doctors' offices, arrivals are scheduled fairly precisely. However, it is much more common that interarrival times are random and that only their probability distribution is known. In this case we must specify this probability distribution.

Regarding the types of arrivals, there are at least two issues. First, do customers arrive one at a time or in batches (carloads, for example)? The simplest system to analyze is when customers arrive one at a time, as we will assume in all of the models in this chapter. Second, are all customers essentially alike, or can they be separated into priority classes? At a computer center, for example, certain jobs might receive higher priority and run first, while the lower priority jobs go to the back of the line and run only after midnight.

[1]From here on, we will refer to the entities requesting service as "customers," whether or not they are actually people. Also, we will refer to "servers" performing service on these customers, regardless of the type of work being performed and whether the servers are people or machines.

Service Discipline

When customers enter the system, they might have to wait in line until a server becomes available. In this case we must specify the **service discipline**. The service discipline is the rule that states which customer, from all who are waiting, goes into service next. The most common service discipline is **first-come-first-served** (FCFS). Here customers are served in the order in which they arrive. All of the models we will discuss will use the FCFS discipline. However, other service disciplines are possible, including **service-in-random-order** (SRO), **last-come-first-served** (LCFS), and various priority disciplines (if there are customer classes with different priorities). For example, a type of priority discipline used in some manufacturing settings is called the **shortest-processing-time** (SPT) discipline. In this case the jobs that are waiting to be processed are ranked according to their eventual processing (service) times—which are assumed to be known—and the job with the shortest processing time is processed next.

A related issue is whether (or how long) customers will wait in line. A customer might arrive at the system, see that too many customers are waiting in line, and decide not to enter the system after all. This is called **balking**. Actually, the choice might be made by the customer or the system. In the latter case the system might set a limit (possibly based on waiting room size) such that if the number of customers in the system is at the limit, no newly arriving customers are allowed to enter the system until a customer finishes service. Most of our examples will have this feature. Another type of behavior is called **reneging**. This is when a customer already in line becomes impatient and leaves the system before being served.

One final aspect of the waiting process is whether there is a *single* line or *multiple* lines. For example, most banks now have a single line. An arriving customer joins the end of the line. When any teller finishes service, the customer at the head of the line then goes to that teller. In contrast, most supermarkets have multiple lines. When a customer goes to a checkout counter, often she must choose which of several lines to enter. Presumably, she will choose the shortest line, but she may use other criteria in her decision. Once she joins a line (inevitably the slowest moving one!), she might decide to **jockey**, that is, move to another line that seems to be moving faster.

Service Characteristics

Now we discuss the service itself. In the simplest systems each customer is served by exactly one server, even though there may be multiple servers. For example, when you enter a bank, you are eventually served by a single teller, even though several tellers are working. Also, the service time is typically random, with constant service times as a special case. When service times are random, we need to specify the probability distribution of a typical service time. This probability distribution can be the same for all customers and servers, or it can depend on the server and/or the customer type.

In a situation like the typical bank, where customers join a single line and are then served by the first available teller, we say the servers (tellers) are in **parallel**. (See Figure 11.1.) A different type of service process is found in many manufacturing settings. For example, various types of parts (which are considered the customers) might enter a system with several types of machines (which are considered the servers). Each part type then follows a certain machine routing, such as machine 1, then machine 4, and then machine 2. Each machine has its own service time distribution, and a typical part might have to wait

FIGURE 11.1 Queueing System with Servers in Parallel

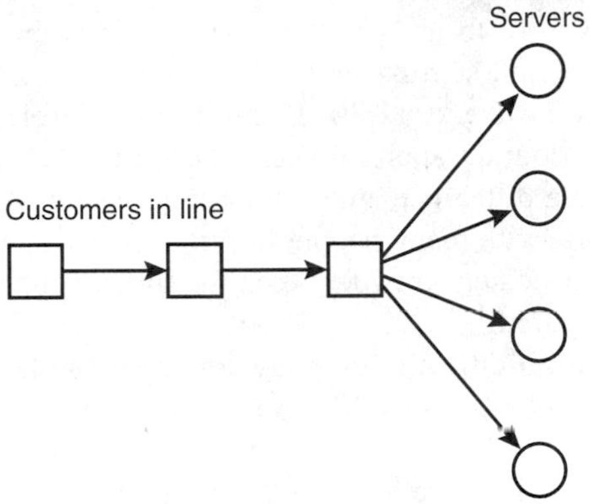

in line behind each machine on its routing. This type of system is called a **queueing network**. The simplest type of queueing network is called a **series system**, where all parts go through the machines in numerical order: first machine 1, then machine 2, then machine 3, and so on. (See Figure 11.2.) We will examine only parallel systems in this chapter. Queueing networks are extremely important, but they are, unfortunately, quite difficult to analyze.

FIGURE 11.2 Queueing System with Servers in Series

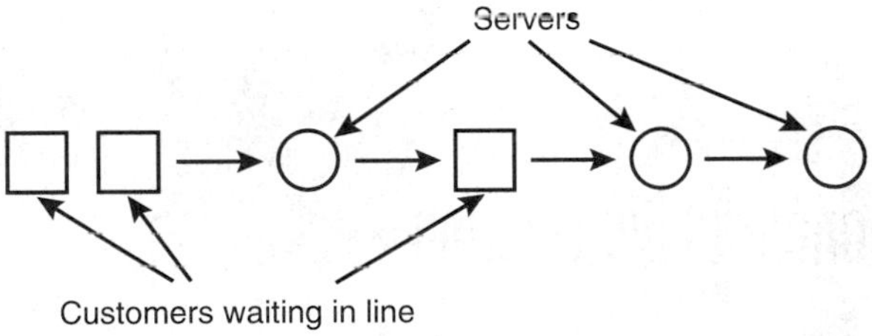

11.3 Short-Run Versus Steady-State Behavior

If you run a fast-food restaurant, you are probably interested in studying the queueing patterns during your peak lunch-time period. During this time the customer arrival rate increases sharply, and you might employ more workers to meet the increased customer load. In this case you might guess your primary interest is in short-run behavior (as opposed to long-run behavior). Unfortunately, short-run behavior is the most difficult to analyze. But how do we draw the line between the short run and the long run? Basically, the answer depends on how long the effects of **initial conditions** last. In the restaurant example the initial conditions are determined by the number of customers already in line at the beginning of the lunch period, say, 11:30. Let's say the restaurant manager is interested in the average number of customers waiting in line over the two-hour peak period. The question then is whether this average is strongly affected by the number of customers in line at 11:30. That is, do the effects of the initial conditions get "washed out" in a period as long as two hours, or do they persist?

Ultimately, the only way to answer this question is with empirical evidence. We might compare a lunch period starting with no people in line at 11:30 with one where many people are already in line at 11:30. If the average levels of congestion over the entire two-hour lunch period are approximately the same, then the initial conditions at 11:30 evidently make little difference, and a long-run analysis is permitted. However, if the lunch period that starts with many people in line is never quite able to overcome this initial load, that is, it tends to stay crowded, then the initial conditions are important, and a short-run analysis is required.

Due to the mathematical difficulty of analyzing short-run behavior, we will deal exclusively with long-run results—results that apply when the time period is long enough to allow the effects of initial conditions to wash out. This type of analysis is usually called **steady-state analysis** and will be the focus of this chapter.

One requirement for any steady-state analysis is that the parameters of the system remain constant for the entire time period. In particular, the arrival rate must remain constant. In the restaurant example, if the objective is to study a two hour peak lunch time period where the arrival rate is significantly larger than normal, and if we decide to employ steady-state analysis, we must be aware that the results of this two-hour analysis do *not* apply to the rest of the day, when the arrival rate is much lower. If the parameters of the system change from one time period to another, then separate steady-state analyses are required for each time period.

Another requirement for steady-state analysis is that the system must be **stable**. Basically, this means that the servers must serve fast enough to keep up with arrivals; otherwise, the queue could theoretically grow without limit. For example, in a single-server system where all arriving customers join the system, the requirement for system stability is simply that the arrival rate must be less than the service rate.

11.4 The Exponential Distribution

Queueing systems generally contain uncertainty. For example, the times between customer arrivals (interarrival times) and the customer service times are generally considered random variables. The most common probability distribution used to model these uncertain quantities is the **exponential distribution**. As we will illustrate in this chapter, many queueing models can be analyzed in a fairly straightforward manner, even on a spreadsheet, if we assume exponentially distributed interarrival times and service times. This exponential assumption buys us a lot, in terms of simplified analysis, but it is quite strong. Therefore, it is important that you understand the exponential distribution and its ramifications for queueing applications.

The random variable X has an exponential distribution with parameter λ (with $\lambda > 0$) if the density of X has the form $f(x) = \lambda e^{-\lambda x}$ for $x > 0$. This exact form is not as important as the shape of the graph it implies, as shown in Figure 11.3.[2] Because the density decreases continually from left to right, its mode (the most likely value) is at 0. That is, X is more likely to be near 0 than any other value. Or another way to state this is that if we collect many observations from an exponential distribution and draw a histogram (frequency

[2] You might want to compare this density to the more familiar bell-shaped, symmetric normal curve. In contrast to the normal distribution, the exponential is very un–bell-shaped, with a heavy skew to the right.

FIGURE 11.3 **Exponential Density Function (with Mean 1)**

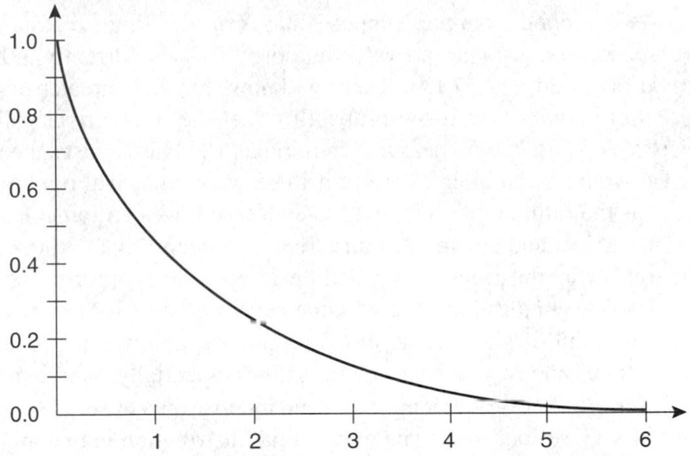

diagram) of the observed values, then we should expect it to resemble the smooth curve in Figure 11.3, with the tallest bars to the left. The mean (or expected value) and standard deviation are easy to remember. They are both equal to the reciprocal of the parameter λ. For example, an exponential distribution with parameter $\lambda = 0.1$ has mean (and standard deviation) equal to 10.

In this chapter the random variable X will always be expressed in some time unit, such as minutes. For example, X might be the number of minutes it takes to serve a customer. Now, suppose that the mean service time is three minutes. Then $1/\lambda = 3$, so that $\lambda = 1/3$. Therefore, we see that λ can be interpreted as a rate, in this case one customer every three minutes (on average). Of course, the value of λ depends on the unit of time. If we switched from minutes to hours, say, λ would change from 1/3 (one every three minutes) to $60(1/3) = 20$ (20 every hour). The corresponding mean would then be $1/\lambda = 1/20$ of an hour.

The Memoryless Property

The property that makes the exponential distribution so useful in queueing models (and in other management science models) is called the **memoryless property**. It can be stated as follows. Let x and h be any positive numbers that represent amounts of time. Then if X is exponentially distributed, the following equation holds:

$$\Pr(X > x + h | X > x) = \Pr(X > h)$$

The probability on the left is a conditional probability, the probability that X is greater than $x + h$, *given* that it is greater than x. The memoryless property states that this conditional probability is the same as the (unconditional) probability that X is greater than h. We now interpret this important property in several contexts.

First, suppose that X is the time, measured in hours, until failure of some item such as a lightbulb. Now consider two lightbulbs with the same exponential time to failure. The only difference is that the first lightbulb has already survived x hours, whereas the second lightbulb is brand new. We want the probabilities that lightbulbs 1 and 2 will survive at least h additional hours. The memoryless property says that these probabilities are the *same* for the two lightbulbs! That is, the lightbulb that has been in use for x hours has the same chance of surviving at least h more hours as the brand new lightbulb. For this reason, the memoryless property is sometimes called the "no-wear-out" property.

As a second example, suppose that X is the time, measured in minutes, between two successive customer arrivals. Suppose that it is currently 3:00 P.M. and the previous arrival occurred at 2:57 P.M. Then we know that X is greater than three minutes. Given this information, what is the probability that the *next* arrival will occur after 3:05 P.M.? (Here $x = 3$ and $h = 5$, measured in minutes.) This is same as the probability that the next arrival would occur after 3:05 P.M. if there were an arrival right now, at 3:00 P.M. That is, as far as the future (after 3:00 P.M.) is concerned, we can forget how long it has been since the last arrival and assume that an arrival just occurred, at 3:00 P.M. This example clearly illustrates why the property is called the *memoryless* property.

These examples illustrate why the exponential distribution is attractive from a mathematical point of view. If we observe a process at any time, all exponential times (interarrival times and service times, for example) essentially "start over" probabilistically—we don't have to know how long it's been since various events (the last arrival or the beginning of service) occurred. The exponential distribution is the only continuous probability distribution with this property.

However, is the exponential distribution, with this strong memoryless property, valid for use in real applications? In the lightbulb example you might dismiss the exponential assumption immediately on the grounds that lightbulbs *do* wear out—a bulb that has been in continuous use for 100 hours is *not* as good as a brand new one. However, the ultimate test is whether sample data fit an exponential curve. We illustrate how you might check the suitability of an exponential distribution in the following example.

EXAMPLE 11.1

A bank manager would like to use a queueing model to analyze the congestion at the bank's automatic teller machines (ATMs). A simple model of this system requires that the interarrival times (times between customer arrivals to the machines) and service times (times customers spend with the machines) are exponentially distributed. During a period of time when business was fairly steady, several employees used stopwatches to gather data on interarrival times and service times. These are shown in Figure 11.4. The bank manager wants to know, based on these data, whether it is reasonable to assume exponentially distributed interarrival times and service times. In each case he also wants to know the appropriate value of λ.

Solution

To see whether these times are consistent with the exponential distribution, we plot histograms of the interarrival times and the service times. (See the file EXPONFIT.XLS.) This can be done in Excel with the Tools/Data Analysis menu item, using the Histogram option. (This option asks for a "bin range," which defines the categories for the histogram. We entered the values 15, 30, 45, 60, 75, and 90 in the range A41:A46 and referred to this as the bin range.) The histograms appear in Figures 11.5 and 11.6. The histogram of the interarrival times appears to be quite consistent with the exponential density curve shown in Figure 11.3. Its highest bar is at the left, and the remaining bars fall off gradually from left to right. On the other hand, the histogram of the service times is somewhat at odds with the exponential density. Its highest bar is *not* the one farthest to the left but instead corresponds to the category from 15 to 30 seconds. Considering the way automatic teller

FIGURE 11.4 Interarrival and Service Times for ATM Example

	A	B	C	D	E	F	G
1	**Interarrival times and service times at a bank**						
2							
3	Interarrival times (seconds)				Service times (seconds)		
4	8	5	12		11	10	15
5	33	13	16		20	27	63
6	9	5	7		16	13	33
7	11	26	9		8	18	18
8	5	33	10		12	20	47
9	24	23	29		17	16	19
10	4	84	45		41	33	16
11	46	1	27		7	36	18
12	25	17	29		19	15	14
13	10	4	21		43	21	32
14	31	50	64		21	17	46
15	30	17	14		10	7	27
16	16	11	19		26	50	16
17	88	11	16		7	19	15
18	2	21	25		23	27	23
19	4	30	19		18	14	10
20	4	13	35		7	7	21
21	94	37	18		16	15	17
22	24	2	40		20	12	12
23	56	2	2		18	17	17
24	154	13	82		19	11	6
25	41	16	43		18	33	34
26	28	14	30		14	16	11
27	11	12	15		40	48	9
28	20	7	15		16	28	44
29	28	19	3		46	13	11
30	31	58	14		21	14	16
31	11	21	17		8	28	30
32	36	3	17		23	18	24
33	38	8	3		30	57	31
34	84	10	42		62	19	59
35	16	10	112		26	16	22
36	7	46	17		27	7	40
37	3	38	5		17	22	11
38							
39	Average interarrival time		25.3		Average service time		22.3

machines operate, this is not surprising. There is some minimum time required to process *any* customer, regardless of the task, so that the most likely times are *not* close to zero. Therefore, the exponential assumption for interarrival times is reasonable, but for service times it is questionable.

In either case, if the manager decides to accept the exponential assumption, the parameter λ is the rate of arrivals (or services) and is estimated by the average of the observed times. For interarrival times, this estimate of λ is the reciprocal of the average in cell C39, $1/25.3 = 0.0395$, that is, 1 arrival every 25.3 seconds. For service times, the estimated λ is the reciprocal of the average in cell G39, $1/22.3 = 0.0448$, that is, 1 service every 22.3 seconds. ■

FIGURE 11.5 Histogram of Interarrival Times for ATM Example

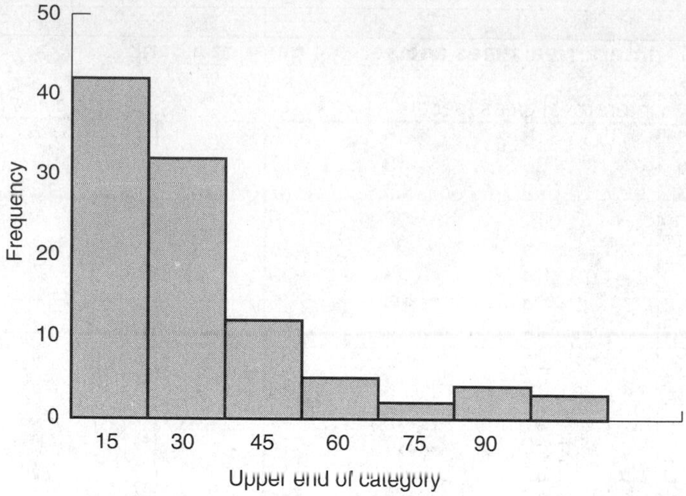

FIGURE 11.6 Histogram of Service Times for ATM Example

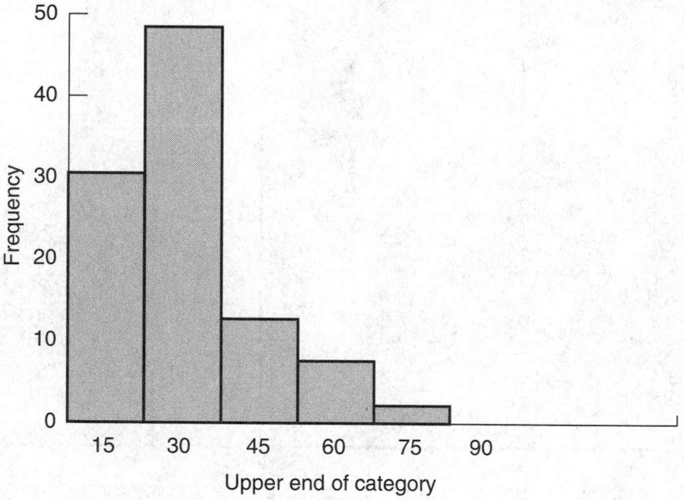

The Poisson Process Model

When the times between arrivals are exponentially distributed, you sometimes hear that "arrivals occur according to a Poisson process." It turns out that there is a close relationship between the exponential distribution, which measures *times* between events such as arrivals, and the **Poisson distribution**, which counts the *number* of events in a certain length of time. The details of this relationship are slightly beyond the level of this book, so we will not explore the topic any further here. However, if you hear, say, that customers arrive at a bank according to a Poisson process with rate one every three minutes, this means that the interarrival times are exponentially distributed with parameter $\lambda = 1/3$ (in units of customers per minute).

PROBLEMS

Skill-Building Problems

1 An extremely important concept in queueing models is the difference between rates and times. If λ represents a rate (customers per hour, say), then argue why $1/\lambda$ is a time and vice versa.

2 Explain the basic relationship between the exponential distribution and a Poisson process. Also, explain how the exponential distribution and the Poisson distribution are fundamentally different. (*Hint*: What type of data does each describe?)

3 It is possible to generate on a spreadsheet random numbers that have an exponential distribution with a given mean. For example, to generate 200 such numbers from an exponential distribution with $\lambda = 1/3$, enter the formula =–3*LN(RAND()) in cell A1 and copy it to the range A2:A200. Then (for technical reasons that we will discuss in the next chapter) select the A1:A200 range, choose the Edit/Copy command, and choose the Edit/Paste Special command with the Values option. (This "freezes" the random numbers, so that they don't change each time the spreadsheet recalculates.) Explore the properties of these numbers as follows.

a In cell A201, find the average of the 200 numbers with the AVERAGE function. What theoretical value should this average be close to?

b In cell A202, find the standard deviation of the 200 numbers with the STDEV function. What theoretical value should this standard deviation be close to?

c To see how these numbers are distributed, first enter the values 1 through 18 in cells C1 through C18. Then use the Tools/Data Analysis menu item with the Histogram option. In the resulting dialog box, enter A1:A200 as the input range and C1:C18 as the bin range (which defines categories for the data) and make sure to check the Chart output box. You should see a histogram where the height of each bar indicates the frequency of that category. For example, the first category contains observations between 0 and 1, the second contains observations between 1 and 2, and so on. Because these data are exponentially distributed, the bars should go downhill, like the curve in Figure 11.3.

d Suppose that you collected the data in column A by timing arrivals at a store. The value in cell A1 is the time (in minutes) until the first arrival, the value in cell A2 is the time between the first and second arrivals, the value in cell A3 is the time between the second and third arrivals, and so on. How might you convince yourself that the interarrival times for this store are indeed exponentially distributed? What would be your best guess for the arrival rate (customers per minute)? ■

11.5 Important Queueing Relationships

Unlike most of the models we have analyzed in previous chapters, the calculations required in queueing models are neither simple nor obvious. For example, there is no obvious way to use the inputs to a typical queueing model—the average arrival rate, the average service time, and the number of servers, say—in order to evaluate outputs such as the average time in queue per customer or the average line length. Fortunately, there are several very useful and general relationships that hold for a wide variety of queueing models. We briefly discuss them here so that we can put them to use in all of the queueing models in succeeding sections.

There are two general types of outputs we typically calculate from a queueing model: **time averages** and **customer averages**. A typical time average is the expected length of the queue, denoted L_q. If you were going to estimate this quantity, you might observe the system at many time points, record the number of customers in the queue at each time point, and then average these numbers. In other words, you would average some measure of the system over *time*. Other time averages are L, the expected number of customers in the system, L_s, the expected number of customers in service, Pr(all idle), the probability that all the servers are idle, and Pr(all busy), the probability that all servers are busy. (To estimate a probability such as Pr(all busy), you would observe the system at many time points, record a 1 each time all servers were busy and a 0 each time at least one was idle, and then average these 0's and 1's.)

In contrast, a typical customer average is the expected time a customer waits in the queue, labeled W_q. To estimate this quantity, you would observe many customers, record the time in queue for each customer, and then average these times over the number of customers observed. Now you are averaging over *customers*. Other customer averages include W, the expected time spent in the system (waiting in line or being served), and W_s, the expected time spent in service.

Little's Formula

There is a famous formula that relates time averages and customer averages in steady state. This formula was first discovered by Little, and it is still called Little's formula. The formula is easy to state (but not always easy to apply!). Consider any queueing system or any subsystem of a queueing system. Let $\bar{\lambda}$ be the average rate at which customers enter this system, let L be the expected number of customers in the system, and let W be the expected time a typical customer spends in the system. (If we are considering only a subsystem of the entire system, then $\bar{\lambda}$, L, and W are defined in terms of the subsystem only.) Then Little's formula can be expressed as

$$L = \bar{\lambda}W$$

It can also be stated in terms of L_q and W_q or in terms of L_s and W_s. That is, two alternative versions of Little's formula are $L_q = \bar{\lambda}W_q$ and $L_s = \bar{\lambda}W_s$.

The reasoning behind Little's formula is as follows. Consider a long period of time of length t. Since we assume steady-state behavior, the expected number of customers in the system at any time during this period is L. Therefore, the expected number of customer-minutes spent in the system during this period is Lt. On the other hand, the expected number of customers who enter the system during this period is $\bar{\lambda}t$ (rate multiplied by time), and each of these customers spends, on average, W minutes in the system. Therefore, the number of customer-minutes spent in the system by these customers is $\bar{\lambda}tW$. Equating Lt and $\bar{\lambda}tW$ produces Little's formula (since t cancels out).

Typically, we use analytical methods to find one of the L's, such as L or L_q. Then we appeal to Little's formula to find the corresponding W. For example, suppose that the arrival rate to a single-server queueing system is 30 customers per hour. Also, suppose that we can use one of the methods discussed later in this chapter to calculate that the expected number of customers in the system is 2.5. Then we know that $\bar{\lambda} = 30$ and $L = 2.5$, and Little's formula can be used to show that a typical customer waits an expected time

$$W = L/\bar{\lambda} = 2.5/30 = .0833 \text{ hour} = 5 \text{ minutes}$$

in the system. If, in addition, we know that the average number of customers in the queue is 1.8, then Little's formula implies that a typical customer's expected time in the queue is

$$W_q = L_q/\bar{\lambda} = 1.8/30 = .06 \text{ hour} = 3.6 \text{ minutes}$$

Other Relationships

There are also two other formulas that we can use to relate these quantities. First, $L = L_q + L_s$, since all customers are either in service or in the queue. In the above example this implies that $L_s = 2.5 - 1.8 = 0.7$. (For a single-server system this means that exactly one customer is in service 70% of the time and no customers are in service 30% of the time.)

Second, if we let $1/\mu$ denote the mean service time, then $W_s = 1/\mu$ and $W = W_q + 1/\mu$. The latter formula follows because the time spent in the system is the time spent in the queue plus the time spent in service. In the above example it implies that the expected time a typical customer spends in service is $5 - 3.6 = 1.4$ minutes.

Two final important queueing measures are **server utilization** and **throughput**. The server utilization, denoted by U, is defined as the long-run fraction of time a server is busy. In a multiple-server system, where there are identical servers in parallel, server utilization is often defined as

$$U = L_s/s$$

That is, it is the expected number of busy servers divided by the number of servers. For example, if $s = 3$ and $L_s = 2.55$, then $U = 0.85$. In this case the expected number of busy servers is 2.55, and each of the three servers is busy about 85% of the time in the long run.

The throughput of the system, denoted by T, is defined as the rate at which customers finish service and depart from the system. It is useful to think of customers entering the "front door" and departing from the "back door." Then if you are stationed at the back door, the throughput is the rate you will see. However, assuming that the system is stable, an observer stationed at the front door ought to see the *same* rate of arrivals as you see of departures. For example, if customers enter at rate 45 per hour, they must leave at rate 45 per hour. Each of these is then equal to the throughput, which enables us to calculate the throughput in two equivalent ways. These are listed below, where μ is the service rate for each server. (The logic behind the second formula is that, on average, there are L_s servers busy, and each busy server is completing services—and sending customers out the back door—at rate μ.)

$$T = \bar{\lambda} \text{ (Throughput from front door approach)}$$

$$T = L_s\mu \text{ (Throughput from back door approach)}$$

PROBLEMS

Skill-Building Problems

4 Assume that parts arrive to a machining center at a rate of 60 parts per hour. The machining center is capable of processing 75 parts per hour, that is, the mean time to machine a part is 0.8 minute. If you are watching these parts *exiting* the machine center, what exit rate do you observe—60 or 75 per hour? Explain.

5 Little's formula applies to an entire queueing system or to a subsystem of a larger system. For example, consider a single-server system composed of two "subsystems." The first subsystem is the waiting line, and the second is the service area, where service actually takes place. Let $\bar{\lambda}$ be the rate that customers enter the system and assume that $\bar{\lambda} = 60$ per hour.

a If the expected number of customers waiting in line is 2.5, what does Little's formula applied to the first subsystem tell us?

b Let μ be the service rate of the server (in customers per hour). Assuming that $\bar{\lambda} < \mu$ (so that the server can serve customers faster than they arrive), argue why the rate into the second subsystem must be $\bar{\lambda}$. Then, letting $\mu = 80$ per hour, what does Little's formula applied to the second subsystem tell us about the expected number of customers in service?

6 Consider a bank where potential customers arrive at rate 60 customers per hour. However, because of limited space, 1 out of every 4 arriving customers finds the bank full and leaves immediately (without entering the bank). Suppose that the average number of customers waiting in line in the bank is 3.5. How long will a typical *entering* customer have to wait in line? (*Hint*: In Little's formula, $\bar{\lambda}$ refers only to customers who join the system.)

7 Consider a fast-food restaurant where customers enter at rate 75 per hour. There are three servers. Customers wait in a single line and go, in first-come-first-serve fashion, to the first of the three servers who is available. Each server can serve one customer every two minutes on average. What is the system throughput (assuming that the service rates are fast enough to keep up with arrivals)? On average, how many of the servers are busy? ■

11.6

The Basic Single-Server Model

We are now equipped to analyze several common queueing models. In this section we will begin by discussing the most basic single-server model, usually labeled the $M/M/1$ model. This shorthand notation, developed by Kendall, implies three things. The first M implies that the distribution of interarrival times is exponential.[3] The second M implies that the distribution of service times is also exponential. Finally, the 1 implies that there is a single server. It is customary to let λ be the arrival rate and μ be the service rate. In other words, $1/\lambda$ is the mean time between arrivals and $1/\mu$ is the mean service time per customer. The model in this section is sometimes called the "classical" $M/M/1$ queueing model, which means that all customers who arrive join the system and stay until they are eventually served. An example of this type follows.

EXAMPLE 11.2

The Smalltown postal branch employs a single clerk. Customers arrive at this postal branch according to a Poisson process at rate 30 customers per hour, and the average service time is exponentially distributed with mean 1.5 minutes. All arriving customers enter the branch, regardless of how many are already waiting in line. The manager of the postal branch would ultimately like to decide whether to improve the system (the topic of the next example). In order to do this, the manager first needs to develop a queueing model that describes the steady-state characteristics of the current system.

Solution

To begin, we must choose a common unit of time and then express the arrival and service rates (λ and μ) in terms of this unit. We could measure time in seconds, minutes, hours, or any other convenient unit, as long as we are consistent. Here we will choose minutes. Then, since one customer arrives every two minutes, $\lambda = 1/2$. Also, since the mean service *time* is 1.5 minutes, the service *rate* is its reciprocal, that is, $\mu = 1/1.5$. Next, it is useful to introduce the parameter ρ (the Greek letter rho) which is called the **traffic intensity**. For the $M/M/1$ model, $\rho = \lambda/\mu$, the arrival rate divided by the service rate. Then to ensure that the system is stable, we require that $\rho < 1$, so that the arrival rate is less than the service rate.

In general, the mathematical derivation of the results for the $M/M/1$ model is quite complex. Therefore, we will simply list the results and show how they can be implemented in a spreadsheet.

Let p_n be the steady-state probability that there are exactly n customers in the system (waiting in line or being served) at any point in time. This probability can be interpreted

[3]The M actually stands for "Markov," a technical term that is synonymous with the exponential distribution for continuous random variables.

as the long-run *fraction* of time when there are n customers in the system. For example, p_0 is the long-run fraction of time when zero customers are in the system, p_1 is the long-run fraction of time when one customer is in the system, and so on. These steady-state probabilities can be found from the following equation:

$$p_n = (1-\rho)\rho^n, n \geq 0 \tag{11.1}$$

Other system measures can also be calculated easily, as listed below:

$$L = \frac{\rho}{1-\rho} = \frac{\lambda}{\mu-\lambda} \tag{11.2}$$

$$L_q = \frac{\rho^2}{1-\rho} = \frac{\lambda^2}{\mu(\mu-\lambda)} \tag{11.3}$$

$$W = L/\lambda, W_q = L_q/\lambda \tag{11.4}$$

$$\Pr(\text{time in queue} > t) = \rho e^{-\mu(1-\rho)t}, t > 0 \tag{11.5}$$

Notice in particular how the Equations in 11.4 are a direct result of Little's formula. Here, the $\bar{\lambda}$ from Little's formula is λ, the arrival rate. Equation 11.5 is also useful. For any value of t, it indicates the probability that a typical customer will have to spend more than t time units in the queue. All of these quantities can be calculated easily in a spreadsheet, as we now illustrate for the Smalltown postal branch example.

Developing the Spreadsheet Model The solution is shown in Figure 11.7. (See the file MM1.XLS.) Actually, this file is structured as a "template" so that any $M/M/1$ problem can be solved with it by changing the inputs in the range B4:B6. It is formed as follows.

1 **Inputs.** Enter the label "minute" (without the quotes) in cell B4. Then since arrivals occur at rate 1 every 2 minutes, enter 0.5 in cell B5. Finally, the service rate μ is the reciprocal of the mean service time (1.5 minutes). Since $1/1.5 = .66666\ldots$, you get a more exact value for this input if you enter the *formula*

=1/1.5

in cell B6.

FIGURE 11.7 **Spreadsheet Solution to the *M/M/1* Queue Example**

	A	B	C	D	E	F	G	H	I
1	M/M/1 Queue - A "Template"								
2									
3	Inputs								
4	Unit of time	minute							
5	Arrival rate	0.50	customers/minute						
6	Service rate	0.667	customers/minute						
7									
8	Outputs								
9	Direct outputs from inputs				Distribution of number in system			Distribution of time in queue	
10	Mean time between arrivals	2.000	minutes		n (customers)	P(n in system)		t (in minutes)	P(wait > t)
11	Mean time per service	1.500	minutes		4	0.079		2.000	0.537
12	Traffic intensity	0.750							
13									
14	Summary measures								
15	Expected number in system	3.000	customers						
16	Expected number in queue	2.250	customers						
17	Expected time in system	6.000	minutes						
18	Expected time in queue	4.500	minutes						
19	Percentage who don't wait in queue	25.0%							

2 **Mean times and traffic intensity.** The mean time between arrivals and the mean service time are the reciprocals of the corresponding rates, so enter the formula

```
=1/B5
```

in cell B10 and copy it to cell B11. Then calculate the traffic intensity ρ in cell B12 with the formula

```
=B5/B6
```

3 **Summary outputs.** The entries in cells B15 through B19 are the summary measures L, L_q, W, W_q, and p_0. (Since p_0 is the fraction of time the server is idle, it can also be interpreted as the fraction of entering customers who don't have to wait in line.) The formulas for these follow directly from Equations 11.1 through 11.4. Specifically, enter the formulas

```
=B12/(1-B12)
=B12^2/(1-B12)
=B15/B5
=B16/B5
```

and

```
=1-B12
```

in cells B15 through B19. Note that Equation 11.1 reduces to $p_0 = 1 - \rho$ for $n = 0$.

4 **Probability of number in system.** Columns E and F are set up so that you can enter any number of customers in cell E11, and the steady-state probability of this number of customers in the system is calculated in cell F11. To do this, enter the formula

```
=(1-$B$12)*$B$12^E11
```

in cell F11. This is the formula for p_n in Equation 11.1. The absolute references in this formula allow you to enter other values of n in column E (below cell E11) and get the corresponding probabilities simply by copying F11 down.

5 **Probability of waiting times.** Similarly, columns H and I are set up so that you can enter any time in cell H11, and the probability that a typical customer must wait in line *at least* this much time is calculated in cell I11. Here we use Equation 11.5, so enter the formula

```
=$B$12*EXP(-$B$6*(1-$B$12)*H11)
```

in cell I11. Note that the built-in Excel function EXP is used to calculate the term $e^{-\mu(1-\rho)t}$ in Equation 11.5. (Again, the absolute references allow you to enter other times in column H and get the corresponding probabilities by copying I11 down.)

From Figure 11.7 we see, for example, that when the traffic intensity is 0.75, the expected number of customers in the queue is 2.25 and the expected time a typical customer spends in the queue is 4.5 minutes. However, 25% of all customers spend no time in the queue, while 53.7% spend more than two minutes in the queue. Also, just for illustration, we see that exactly four customers are in the system 7.9% of the time.

The spreadsheet in the MM1.XLS file not only enables us to solve the Smalltown postal branch example, but it is relevant for *any* $M/M/1$ model. We encourage you to experiment with the MM1.XLS file by entering different inputs in cells B4 through B6 (and possibly different values in cells E11 and H11). Just make certain that λ (in cell B5) is less than μ (in cell B6). Otherwise, the outputs will not be meaningful.

We now extend this example to include costs. That is, we consider an *optimization* example. ■

EXAMPLE 11.3

Suppose that the manager of the Smalltown postal branch in the previous example has an opportunity to purchase new equipment that would reduce the expected time to serve a customer by 15%, that is, from 1.5 minutes to 1.275 minutes. The purpose, of course, is to reduce the length of the waiting line and the time customers spend in the system. Should the manager purchase the new equipment?

Solution

This is a typical example of queueing optimization that involves difficult trade-offs. Let's consider the costs and benefits of purchasing the new equipment. Smalltown's only out-of-pocket cost, other than possible training costs that we'll ignore, is the cost of the new equipment. This is a one-time cost. On the benefit side, it is important to realize that the branch observes no direct monetary benefits from the new equipment. However, there is the *indirect* benefit of less time spent in the system per customer.

Specifically, let μ_{new} and μ_{old} be the new and old service rates, so that $1/\mu_{new} = 1.275$ and $\mu_{new} = 1/1.275$. By using the MM1.XLS file from the previous example with this new value of μ in cell B6, we find that the expected time spent in the "new" system, labeled W_{new}, is

$$W_{new} = 3.517 \text{ minutes}$$

In contrast, from Figure 11.7, $W_{old} = 6$ minutes for the "old" system. Therefore, a typical customer would spend an average of 2.483 minutes *less* in the new system. Since 30 customers enter the system per hour (on average), this translates to a savings of $30(2.483) = 74.49$ minutes of customer time per hour.

Let c_w be the "cost" of having a customer spend one minute in the system. (The w in c_w is for *waiting*.) Then the hourly cost saved with the new equipment is $74.49c_w$. Now there are two problems. The first is assessing a reasonable value for c_w. As we stated above, this is not an out-of-pocket cost to the postal branch. Rather, it is the goodwill loss that occurs when customers get upset by having to wait. The numerical value of this cost is certainly not obvious. The second problem is that the cost of the equipment is a *one-time* cost, whereas the cost of waiting is an hourly cost that continues indefinitely. To make these costs comparable, we need to amortize the cost of the equipment over a long time horizon.

To be specific, suppose that the cost of purchasing the equipment is equivalent to a weekly payment of \$500. Assuming five working days per week and eight hours of working time per day, this translates to a cost of $500/(5 \times 8) = \$12.50$ per working hour. Now we compare this to the hourly benefit in decreased waiting time, $74.49c_w$, of having the new equipment, and we recommend purchasing the equipment only if the benefit is greater than the cost, that is,

$$74.49c_w > 12.50$$

This is equivalent to $c_w > \$0.168$. In words, if customer time in the system is valued at more than about 17¢ per minute (or about \$10 per hour), then the cost of the new equipment is justified.

This example illustrates the cost trade-offs that must be examined in queueing applications. The difficulty is estimating the value of a customer's time spent in line. If customers are asked how valuable their time is, they will obviously place a high value on it—they have better things to do. But it is usually the manager of the queueing system, in this case the postal branch manager, who does the evaluation, and this manager might or might not place a very high value on customers' time, depending on how important the image of "timely service" is to the organization. If it is important enough (such as $c_w > \$0.168$ in the example), then money will be spent to upgrade the system; otherwise, customers will be forced to wait as they always have! ■

PROBLEMS

Skill-Building Problems

8 The MM1.XLS template file is now set up so that you can enter any integer in cell E11 and the corresponding probability of that many in the system appears in cell F11. Change this setup so that columns E and F specify the distribution of the number in the *queue* rather than the system. That is, set it up so that if you enter an integer in cell E11, the formula in cell F11 gives the probability of that many customers in the queue.

9 The MM1.XLS template file is now set up so that when you enter any time value in cell H11, the formula in cell I11 gives the probability that the wait in queue will be greater than this amount of time. Suppose that you would like the information to go the other direction. That is, you would like to specify a probability, such as .05, in cell I11 and obtain the corresponding time in cell H11. Try doing this as follows with Excel's Goal Seek tool. Use the Tools/Goal Seek menu items to get to a dialog box. Then in this dialog box, enter I11 as the set cell, enter the desired probability such as .05 in the By Value box, and enter H11 as the changing cell. Use this procedure to answer the following. In an $M/M/1$ queue where customers are entering at rate 50 per hour and the mean service time is 1 minute, find the number of minutes t such that there is a 5% chance of having to wait in the queue more than t minutes.

10 Expand the MM1.XLS file so that the steady-state probability distribution of the number in the system is shown in tabular form and graphically. That is, enter values 0, 1, and so on (up to some upper limit you can choose) in the range from cell E11 down and copy the formula in cell F11 down accordingly. Then create a column chart using the data in columns E and F.

11 The Decision Sciences Department is trying to determine whether to rent a slow or a fast copier. The department believes that an employee's time is worth \$15 per hour. The slow copier rents for \$4 per hour, and it takes an employee an average of ten minutes to complete copying. The fast copier rents for \$15 per hour, and it takes an employee an average of six minutes to complete copying. An average of four employees per hour need to use the copying machine. (Assume the copying times and interarrival times to the copying machine are exponentially distributed.) Which machine should the department rent in order to minimize expected total cost per hour?

12 For an $M/M/1$ queueing system, suppose that λ and μ are both doubled.

a How is L changed?

b How is W changed?

c How is the steady-state probability distribution changed?

13 A fast-food restaurant has one drive-through window. An average of 40 customers per hour arrive at the window. It takes an average of one minute to serve a customer. Assume that interarrival and service times are exponentially distributed.

a On the average, how many customers are waiting in line?

b On the average, how long does a customer spend at the restaurant (from time of arrival to time service is completed)?

c What fraction of the time are more than three cars in line? (Here, the line includes the car, if any, being serviced.)

Skill-Extending Problems

14 Consider an airport where taxis and customers arrive (exponential interarrival times) with respective rates of one and two per minute. No matter how many other taxis are present, a taxi will wait. If an arriving customer does not find a taxi, the customer immediately leaves.

a Model this system as an $M/M/1$ queue. (*Hint*: Think of the taxis as the customers.)

b Find the average number of taxis that are waiting for a customer.

c Suppose all customers who use a taxi pay a \$2 fare. During a typical hour, how much revenue will the taxis receive?

15 A bank is trying to determine which of two machines to rent for check processing. Machine 1 rents for \$10,000 per year and processes 1000 checks per hour. Machine 2 rents for \$15,000 per year and processes 1600 checks per hour. Assume that machines work 8 hours a day, 5 days a week, 50 weeks a year. The bank must process an average of 800 checks per hour, and the average check processed is for \$100. Assume an annual interest rate of 20%. Then determine the cost to the bank (in lost interest) for each hour that a check spends waiting for and undergoing processing. Assuming that interarrival times and service times are exponentially distributed, which machine should the bank rent?

16 A worker at the State Unemployment Office is responsible for processing a company's forms when it opens for business. The worker can process an average of 4 forms per week. In 1992 an average of 1.8 companies per week submitted forms for processing, and the worker had a backlog of .45 week. In 1993 an average of 3.9 companies per week submitted forms for processing, and the worker had a 5-week backlog. The poor worker was fired but later sued to get her job back. The court said that since the amount of work submitted to the worker had approximately doubled, the worker's backlog should also have doubled. Since her backlog increased by more than a factor of 10, she must have been slacking off, so the state was justified in firing her. Use queueing theory to defend the worker. (This is based on an actual case!)

17 For the $M/M/1$ queueing model show that the following results hold:

a $W = (L + 1)W_s$

b $W_q = LW_s$

c Interpret the results in Parts (a) and (b). ■

11.7 A Multiple-Server Model

Many service facilities such as banks and postal branches employ multiple servers. Usually, these servers work in parallel, so that each customer goes to exactly one server for service and then exits. In this section we will analyze the simplest version of this multiple-server parallel system, labeled the $M/M/s$ model. Again, the first M means that interarrival times are exponentially distributed. The second M means that the service times for *each* server are exponentially distributed. (We also assume that each server is identical to the others, in the sense that each has the same mean service time.) Finally, the s in $M/M/s$ denotes the number of servers. (Of course, if $s = 1$, then the $M/M/s$ and $M/M/1$ models are identical.)

If you think about the multiple-server facilities you typically enter, such as banks, post offices, and supermarkets, you recognize that there are two types of waiting line setups. The first, usually seen at supermarkets, is where each server has a separate line. Each customer must decide which line to join (and then either stay in that line or switch later on). The second, seen at most banks and post offices, is where there is a *single* waiting line, from which customers are served in FCFS (first-come-first-serve) fashion. We will examine only this second type in this section since the first is much more difficult to analyze.

There are three inputs to this system: the arrival rate λ, the service rate (per server) μ, and the number of servers s. In order to ensure that the system is stable, we must also assume that the traffic intensity, now given by $\rho = \lambda/(s\mu)$, is less than 1. That is, we require that the arrival rate λ is less than the *maximum* service rate $s\mu$ (which is achieved when all s servers are busy). If the traffic intensity were not less than 1, the length of the queue would eventually increase without bound.

The following example illustrates that while the $M/M/s$ model is more complex than the $M/M/1$ model, it can still be analyzed on a spreadsheet.

EXAMPLE 11.4

CountyBank has several branch locations. At one of these locations, customers arrive at a Poisson rate of 150 per hour. The branch employs six tellers. Each teller takes, on average, two minutes to serve a customer, and service times are exponentially distributed. Also, all tellers perform all tasks, so that customers can go to any of the six tellers. Customers who arrive and find all six servers busy join a single queue and are then served in FCFS fashion. The manager of this CountyBank branch eventually wants to decide whether to add one or more extra tellers (the topic of the next example). Therefore, as a first step, the manager wants to develop a queueing model of the current system.

Solution

As in the $M/M/1$ model, we must first present several equations that relate outputs to inputs. Let p_n be the steady-state probability that there are n customers in the system. (This includes those in line and those in service.) In order to find the various summary measures such as L and W, we first need to find p_0, the probability that no customers are in the system, and Pr(all busy), the probability that all s tellers are busy. Note that an entering customer waits in line only if all s servers are busy. Therefore, Pr(all busy) can also be interpreted as the fraction of arriving customers who must wait in line.

Since Pr(all busy) turns out to depend on p_0, the key is finding p_0. It is given by a complex formula that we won't list here. In terms of p_0, the other relevant quantities then follow:

$$p_n = \begin{cases} \frac{(s\rho)^n p_0}{n!} & \text{if } 1 \leq n \leq s \\ \frac{(s\rho)^n p_0}{s!s^{n-s}} & \text{if } n \geq s+1 \end{cases} \tag{11.6}$$

$$\Pr(\text{all busy}) = \frac{(s\rho)^s p_0}{s!(1-\rho)} \tag{11.7}$$

$$L_q = \frac{\Pr(\text{all busy})\rho}{1-\rho} \tag{11.8}$$

$$L = L_q + \lambda/\mu \tag{11.9}$$

$$W = L/\lambda, \; W_q = L_q/\lambda \tag{11.10}$$

$$\Pr(\text{wait in queue} > t) = \Pr(\text{all busy})e^{-s\mu(1-\rho)t}, \; t > 0 \tag{11.11}$$

Although these formulas are somewhat intimidating, they are quite easy to incorporate into a spreadsheet, as we now explain.

Developing the Spreadsheet Model The solution to CountyBank's problem appears in Figure 11.8. (See the file MMS.XLS.) Actually, it presents a spreadsheet template much like the one for the $M/M/1$ model; all you need to do to obtain all of the relevant outputs is enter the inputs and press a button. When you press the button, you actually run an Excel macro that calculates p_0 for you; then all of the other outputs recalculate automatically. Here are the steps for forming this template.

1 **Inputs.** The first thing to do is choose a unit of time. In this example we will use an hour as the unit of time, so enter the label "hour" (without the quotes) in cell B4. Then enter the arrival rate, the service rate per server, and the number of servers in cells B5 through B7.

FIGURE 11.8 Spreadsheet Solution to $M/M/s$ Queue Example

	A	B	C	D	E	F	G	H	I
1	**M/M/s Queue - A "Template"**				**Directions:**				
2					1. Enter the inputs in cells B4 through B7.				
3	**Inputs**				2. Push the "Calculate P0" button to calculate				
4	Unit of time	hour			p0 (and all of the other outputs)				
5	Arrival rate	150	customers/hour						
6	Service rate per server	30	customers/hour		Calculate P0				
7	Number of servers	6							
8									
9	**Outputs**								
10	**Direct outputs from inputs**				**Distribution of number in system**			**Distribution of time in queue**	
11	Mean time between arrivals	0.007	hours		n (customers)	P(n in system)		t (in hours)	P(wait > t)
12	Mean time per service	0.033	hours		3	0.0940		0.020	0.322
13	Traffic intensity	0.833							
14									
15	**Summary measures**								
16	P(system empty)	0.005							
17	Percentage who wait in queue	58.8%							
18	Expected number in system	7.938	customers						
19	Expected number in queue	2.938	customers						
20	Expected time in system	0.053	hours						
21	Expected time in queue	0.020	hours						
22	Percentage who don't wait in queue	41.2%							

2 **Mean times and traffic intensity.** Enter the formulas

```
=1/B5
=1/B6
```

and

```
=B5/(B6*B7)
```

in cells B11 through B13 in order to calculate the mean time between arrivals, the mean service time (per server), and the traffic intensity.

3 **Button (macro) for p_0.** Notice the "button" near cell E6 of the MMS.XLS file. When you click on this button, you run an Excel macro (a computer program) that calculates p_0. (Actually, you can look at this program; its instructions are in the sheet labeled "Module1" of the MMS.XLS file.) The macro even performs a check for you. If your inputs produce an unallowed value of ρ (greater than or equal to 1), you will be asked to change them. After you click on this button, take a look at the contents of cell B16. It does *not* contain a formula; it contains the value of p_0 that is calculated by the macro. So if you change the inputs in cells B5 through B7, you must click again on the button.

4 **Summary outputs.** From here on, the other output cells contain the formulas from Equations 11.6 through 11.11. First, in cell B17 enter the formula (from Equation 11.7) for Pr(all busy):

```
=(B7*B13)^B7*B16/(FACT(B7)*(1–B13))
```

Here, FACT is a built-in Excel function for calculating factorials. Then enter the following formulas in cells B18 through B22 for the quantities L, L_q, W, W_q, and the fraction of customers who do *not* have to wait in line, that is, 1 − Pr(all busy):

```
=B19+B5/B6
=B17*B13/(1-B13)
=B18/B5
=B19/B5
```

and

```
=1-B17
```

5 **Probability of number in system.** For any number of customers entered in cell E12, the formula in cell F12 finds the steady-state probability of this many customers in the system. This is the formula from Equation 11.6:

=IF(E12<=B$7,(B$7*B$13)^E12*B$16/FACT(E12),
(B$7*B$13)^E12*B$16/(FACT(B$7)*B$7^(E12–B$7)))

If you want to perform several of these calculations, just enter several values in column E and copy this formula down column F.[4]

6 **Probability of waiting time.** For any time entered in cell H12, the formula in cell I12 calculates the probability that a typical customer must wait in line more than this amount of time. This is the formula from Equation 11.11:

=B$17*EXP(–B$7*B$6*(1–B$13)*H12)

Note that the built-in Excel function EXP is used to evaluate the term $e^{-s\mu(1-\rho)t}$ in Equation 11.11. (Again, multiple calculations of this type can be obtained by entering a series of times in column H and copying the formula in cell I12 down column I.)

From Figure 11.8 we see that when there are 6 tellers and the traffic intensity is 0.833, the expected number of customers in the system is 7.94 and the expected time a typical customer spends in the system is 0.053 hour (about 3.2 minutes). Also, about 41% of all arriving customers can go immediately into service, whereas about 32% of all customers must wait more than 0.02 hour (1.2 minutes). Finally, we can find the server utilization (the fraction of time each teller is busy) from $U = L_s/s$. (This calculation doesn't appear in the spreadsheet.) First, we find L_s, the number of busy tellers, from

$$L_s = L - L_q = 7.938 - 2.938 = 5$$

because all customers in the system who are not in the queue must be in service. Then the server utilization is

$$U = L_s/s = 5/6 = 83.3\%$$

If this number doesn't ring a bell, it should—it is the traffic intensity. The traffic intensity is always the fraction of time each teller is busy! ■

We now continue this bank example to look at trade-offs involving the number of tellers in the system.

EXAMPLE 11.5

The manager of the CountyBank branch office would like to know the economic trade-offs involved for hiring one or two extra tellers.

Solution

As in the Smalltown postal branch example, there is a cost and a benefit of adding a teller. The cost is simple—it is the wage rate paid to the extra teller. The benefit is that customers wait less time in the bank. In this example, adding an extra teller will make both W and W_q decrease by the same amount because W is the sum of W_q and the expected service time per customer, and the latter does not change with extra tellers. That is, extra tellers only

[4]Note that since we would only copy this formula (or the formula in the next step) down a column, it suffices to have only the row references absolute.

decrease the expected time in line, not the time in service. (The expected time in service would change only if we made each teller *faster*, rather than adding tellers.) To see how W_q changes, try entering 7 and then 8 for the number of tellers in cell B7 of Figure 11.8 and recalculate (click on the button). You should observe that the value of W_q changes from 0.0196 hour (with six tellers) to 0.0054 hour (with seven tellers) to 0.0019 hour (with eight tellers). Because the arrival rate is 150 customers per hour, these waiting times translate to 2.94, 0.81, and 0.285 customer-hours spent waiting in line each hour.

Now suppose that c_r is the wage rate per hour and c_w is the cost per customer-hour spent in line. Then the net benefit of going from six to seven tellers is $-c_r + (2.94 - 0.81)c_w$, or $-c_r + 2.13c_w$ dollars per hour, and the net benefit of going from seven to eight tellers is $-c_r + (0.81 - 0.285)c_w$, or $-c_r + 0.525c_w$ dollars per hour. The CountyBank manager's most difficult task is to assess a value of c_w. A somewhat indirect way of approaching this is to see when the net benefit of an extra teller is positive.

Suppose that the wage rate is $c_r = \$8$ per hour. Then the net benefit of going from six to seven tellers is positive if $-8 + 2.13c_w > 0$, that is, if $c_w > 8/2.13 = 3.75$. This means that if the customer cost of waiting is valued at more than \$3.75 per hour, a seventh teller should be hired. In the same way, an eighth teller should be hired if $c_w > 8/.525$, or \$15.24 per hour of waiting. It's probably safe to say that a seventh teller should be hired but not an eighth—the bank probably values its customers' time at more than \$3.75 per hour but less than \$15.25 per hour (although you could debate this).

As an alternative approach, the bank might specify a service level (instead of a waiting cost c_w) such that very few customers wait in line more than five minutes, say. By entering .08333 hour (that is, five minutes) in cell H12 of the MMS.XLS file, you can check that when there are six tellers, about 4.8% of the arriving customers wait in line more than five minutes. If this 4.8% figure is too high for the bank manager, then it might be worth adding a seventh teller. It is easy to check that the percentage who wait more than five minutes decreases to 0.2% when there are seven tellers. Therefore, adding the seventh teller will certainly achieve the desired service level goal—providing that the bank is willing to pay the extra wages. ■

A Comparison of Models

Here is a question many of you have probably pondered as you've waited in line. Would you rather go to a system with one fast server or a system with several slow servers? In the latter case, we'll assume that only one waiting line forms, so that you can't get unlucky by joining the "wrong" line. The solution to the question is fairly straightforward, now that we know how to solve $M/M/1$ and $M/M/s$ models. In the following example we'll make the comparison numerically. To make a fair comparison, we'll assume that (1) the arrival rate is the same for both systems and (2) the service rate μ_f for the single fast server is equal to s times μ_s, where μ_s is the service rate for *each* of the s slow servers.

EXAMPLE 11.6

Which system has the best steady-state characteristics such as L, W, L_q, and W_q: a single-server system where the single server can serve 30 customers per hour, or a five-server system where each of the servers can serve 6 customers per hour? For each system we will assume that customers arrive according to a Poisson process at rate 25 per hour.

Solution

First, note that the two models are comparable in the sense that $\mu_f = s\mu_s$ because $\mu_f = 30$, $s = 5$, and $\mu_s = 6$. Equivalently, the traffic intensity ρ is the same for each, namely, $\rho = 5/6$. The spreadsheets in Figures 11.9 and 11.10 answer our question. (They were formed from the MM1.XLS and MMS.XLS files simply by changing the inputs.) As you see, the comparison is not entirely clear-cut. The $M/M/1$ system has a smaller L but a larger L_q. Similarly, it has a smaller W but a larger W_q. Finally, the $M/M/1$ system is worse in the sense that it has a smaller percentage of customers who experience no waiting in line (16.7% versus 38.0%) and a larger percentage who must wait in line at least 0.25 hour (23.9% versus 17.8%). The bottom line is that if you hate to *wait* in line, you should prefer the system with multiple slow servers. However, once it's your turn to be served, you will clearly prefer the system with the single fast server. In this latter system you'll spend less *total* time in the system, but more of it will be spent waiting in line. Take your choice!

The Effect of the Traffic Intensity We have mentioned that in order for an $M/M/1$ or $M/M/s$ system to be stable, the traffic intensity must be less than 1. In words, the system must be able to service the customers faster than they arrive; otherwise, the queue

FIGURE 11.9 **Single Fast Server System**

	A	B	C	D	E	F	G	H	I
1	**M/M/1 Queue - A "Template"**								
2									
3	**Inputs**								
4	Unit of time	hour							
5	Arrival rate	25	customers/hour						
6	Service rate	30	customers/hour						
7									
8	**Outputs**								
9	**Direct outputs from inputs**				**Distribution of number in system**			**Distribution of time in queue**	
10	Mean time between arrivals	0.040	hours		n (customers)	P(n in system)		t (in hours)	P(wait > t)
11	Mean time per service	0.033	hours		4	0.080		0.250	0.239
12	Traffic intensity	0.833							
13									
14	**Summary measures**								
15	Expected number in system	5.000	customers						
16	Expected number in queue	4.167	customers						
17	Expected time in system	0.200	hours						
18	Expected time in queue	0.167	hours						
19	Percentage who don't wait in queue	16.7%							

FIGURE 11.10 **System with Multiple Slow Servers**

	A	B	C	D	E	F	G	H	I
1	**M/M/s Queue - A "Template"**				**Directions:**				
2					1. Enter the inputs in cells B4 through B7.				
3	**Inputs**				2. Push the "Calculate P0" button to calculate				
4	Unit of time	hour			P_0 (and all of the other outputs)				
5	Arrival rate	25	customers/hour						
6	Service rate per server	6	customers/hour		Calculate P0				
7	Number of servers	5							
8									
9	**Outputs**								
10	**Direct outputs from inputs**				**Distribution of number in system**			**Distribution of time in queue**	
11	Mean time between arrivals	0.040	hours		n (customers)	P(n in system)		t (in hours)	P(wait > t)
12	Mean time per service	0.167	hours		3	0.1191		0.250	0.178
13	Traffic intensity	0.833							
14									
15	**Summary measures**								
16	P(system empty)	0.010							
17	Percentage who wait in queue	62.0%							
18	Expected number in system	7.267	customers						
19	Expected number in queue	3.101	customers						
20	Expected time in system	0.291	hours						
21	Expected time in queue	0.124	hours						
22	Percentage who don't wait in queue	38.0%							

length will eventually grow without limit. It is interesting to see, however, what happens to a system when the traffic intensity gets closer and closer to 1 but stays less than 1. As the following continuation of the CountyBank example will show, the effects can be disastrous. ■

EXAMPLE 11.7

Over a period of time, the CountyBank branch office from previous examples has been experiencing a steady increase in the customer arrival rate. This rate has increased from the previous value of 150 customers per hour to 160, then to 170, and is still increasing. During this time, the number of tellers has remained constant at six, and their mean service times have remained constant at two minutes per customer. The bank manager has seen an obvious increase in bank congestion. Is this reinforced by the $M/M/s$ model? What will happen if the arrival rate continues to increase?

Solution

Since the traffic intensity is $\rho = \lambda/(s\mu)$ and $s\mu$ has stayed constant at value $6(30) = 180$, ρ has climbed from $150/180 = .833$ to $160/180 = .889$ to $170/180 = .944$—and is still climbing. We know that λ must stay below 180 or the system will become unstable, but what about values of λ slightly below 180? We recalculated the spreadsheet in Figure 11.8 for several values of λ and obtained the results in Table 11.1. (W and W_q are expressed in minutes.) Although each column of this table represents a stable system, the congestion is becoming unbearable. When $\lambda = 178$, the line length is over 80 customers, and a typical customer must wait about a half hour in line. Things are twice as bad when $\lambda = 179$.

The conclusion should be clear to the bank manager. Something must be done to alleviate the congestion—probably extra tellers—and the bank will no doubt take such measures if it wants to stay in business. However, the point of the example is that systems moving toward the borderline of stability can become extremely congested. As the results in the table indicate, there is a huge difference between a system with a traffic intensity of .9 and one with a traffic intensity of .99! ■

TABLE 11.1 **Effects of Increasing Arrival Rate**

	Customer Arrival Rate (λ)					
	150	**160**	**170**	**175**	**178**	**179**
ρ	0.833	0.889	0.944	0.972	0.989	0.994
L	7.94	11.04	20.14	38.18	92.21	182.22
L_q	2.94	5.71	14.47	32.35	86.28	176.25
W	3.18	4.14	7.11	13.09	31.08	61.08
W_q	1.18	2.14	5.11	11.09	29.08	59.08

PROBLEMS

Skill-Building Problems

18 Suppose that you observe a sequence of interarrival times, such as 1.2, 3.7, 4.2, 0.5, 8.2, 3.1, 1.7, 4.2, 0.7, 0.3, and 2.0. For example, 4.2 is the time between the arrivals of customers 2 and 3. If you average these, what parameter of the $M/M/s$ model are you estimating? Use these numbers to estimate the arrival rate λ. If instead these numbers were observed service times, what would their average be an estimate of, and what would the corresponding estimate of μ be?

19 In the $M/M/s$ model, where μ is the service rate per server, explain why $\lambda < \mu$ is *not* the appropriate condition for steady state but $\lambda < s\mu$ is.

20 Expand the MMS.XLS file so that the steady-state probability distribution of the number in the system is shown in tabular form and graphically. That is, enter values 0, 1, and so on (up to some upper limit you can choose) in the range from cell E12 down and copy the formula in cell F12 down accordingly. Then create a column chart using the data in columns E and F.

21 Each airline passenger and his or her luggage must be checked to determine whether he or she is carrying weapons onto the airplane. Suppose that at Gotham City Airport, an average of 10 passengers per minute arrive, where interarrival times are exponentially distributed. To check passengers for weapons, the airport must have a checkpoint consisting of a metal detector and baggage X-ray machine. Whenever a checkpoint is in operation, two employees are required. These two employees work simultaneously to check a *single* passenger. A checkpoint can check an average of 12 passengers per minute, where the time to check a passenger is also exponentially distributed. Under the assumption that the airport has only one checkpoint, answer the following questions.

a Why is an $M/M/1$, not an $M/M/2$, model relevant here?

b What is the probability that a passenger will have to wait before being checked for weapons?

c On the average, how many passengers are waiting in line to enter the checkpoint?

d On the average, how long will a passenger spend at the checkpoint (including waiting time in line)?

22 A supermarket is trying to decide how many cash registers to keep open. Suppose an average of 18 customers arrive each hour, and the average checkout time for a customer is four minutes. Interarrival times and service times are exponentially distributed, and the system can be modeled as an $M/M/s$ system. (In contrast to the situation at most supermarkets, we'll assume all customers wait in a single line.) It costs $20 per hour to operate a cash register, and a cost of 25¢ is assessed for each minute the customer spends in the cash register area (in line or being served). How many registers should the store open in order to minimize the expected hourly cost?

23 A small bank is trying to determine how many tellers to employ. The total cost of employing a teller is $100 per day, and a teller can serve an average of 60 customers per day. An average of 50 customers per day arrive at the bank, and both service times and interarrival times are exponentially distributed. If the delay cost per customer-day is $100, how many tellers should the bank hire?

24 In this problem, all interarrival and service times are exponentially distributed.

a At present, the finance department and the marketing department each have their own typists. Each typist can type 25 letters per day. Finance requires that an average of 20 letters per day be typed, and marketing requires that an average of 15 letters per day be typed. For each department, determine the average length of time that elapses between a request for a letter and completion of the letter.

b Suppose that the two typists are grouped into a typing pool; that is, each typist is now available to type letters for either department. For this arrangement, calculate the average length of time between a request for a letter and completion of the letter.

c Comment on the results of Parts (a) and (b).

d Under the pooled arrangement, what is the probability that more than 1/5 of a day will elapse between a request for a letter and start of the letter?

25 MacBurger's is attempting to determine how many servers (or lines) to have available during the breakfast shift. During each hour, an average of 100 customers arrive at the restaurant. Each line or server can handle an average of 50 customers per hour. A server costs $5 per hour, and the cost of a customer waiting in line for one hour is $20. Assuming that an $M/M/s$

model is applicable, determine the number of lines that minimizes the sum of hourly delay and service costs.

26 An average of 100 customers arrive each hour at the Gotham City Bank. The average service time for each customer is one minute. Service times and interarrival times are exponentially distributed. The manager wants to ensure that no more than 1% of all customers will have to wait in line for more than five minutes. If the bank follows the policy of having all customers join a single line, how many tellers must the bank hire?

Skill-Extending Problems

27 In the $M/M/s$ model with $\lambda < s\mu$, we know that the throughput T is $\bar{\lambda}$ (from the front door approach) or $L_s\mu$ (from the back door approach). Verify that these are indeed equal as follows.

a Argue that $\bar{\lambda}$ equals λ.

b Find an expression for L_s and use it to show that $L_s\mu = \lambda$. (*Hint*: The expected number of customers in the system is the expected number waiting in line plus the expected number in service.)

c The service rate μ measures the number of customers each server can serve per unit time. Why then isn't the throughput equal to $s\mu$? For example, if $\mu = 75$ per hour and there are two servers, why isn't the throughput 150 customers per hour?

28 Referring to Problem 21, suppose the airline wants to determine how many checkpoints to operate to minimize operating costs and delay costs over a ten-year period. Assume that the cost of delaying a passenger for one hour is $10 and that the airport is open every day for 16 hours per day. It costs $1 million to purchase, staff, and maintain a metal detector and baggage X-ray machine for a ten-year period. Finally, assume that each passenger is equally likely to enter a given checkpoint, so that the "effective" arrival rate to any checkpoint is the total arrival rate divided by the number of checkpoints. (Assume that each checkpoint has its own waiting line.)

29 The manager of a bank wants to use an $M/M/s$ queueing model to weigh the costs of extra tellers against the cost of having customers wait in line. The arrival rate is 60 customers per hour, and the average service time is four minutes. The cost of each teller is easy to gauge: it is the $8.50 per hour wage rate. However, because it is difficult to estimate the cost per minute of waiting time the bank manager decides to hire the minimum number of tellers so that a typical customer has probability .05 of waiting more than five minutes in line.

a How many tellers will the manager use, given this criterion?

b By deciding on this many tellers as "optimal," the manager is *implicitly* using some value (or some range of values) for the cost per minute of waiting time. That is, a certain cost (or cost range) would lead to the same number of tellers as suggested in Part (a). What is this implied cost (or cost range)?

30 An average of 100 customers per hour arrive at Gotham City Bank. It takes a teller an average of two minutes to serve a customer. Interarrival and service times are exponentially distributed. The bank currently has four tellers working. The bank manager wants to compare the following two systems with regard to the average number of customers present in the bank and the probability that a customer will spend more than eight minutes in line.

System 1 Each teller has his or her own line (and no moving between lines is permitted). Arriving customers are equally likely to choose any teller.

System 2 All customers wait in a single line for the first available teller.

If you were the bank manager, which system would you prefer?

31 Consider the following two queuing systems.

System 1 An $M/M/1$ system with arrival rate λ and service rate 3μ

System 2 An $M/M/3$ system with arrival rate λ and each server working at rate μ

Which system will have the smaller W and L? ■

11.8

Variations of the Basic Models

In this section we consider two variations of the basic $M/M/1$ and $M/M/s$ models. In the first of these, the number of customers allowed to enter the queueing system is limited. The usual reason for this is a waiting room of limited capacity. When the customers waiting for service fill the waiting room, potential arrivals to the system are forced to take their business elsewhere. In the second variation we assume that the total number of customers in the entire population is fairly small. These customers cycle between being in the system and being out of the system. When they are in the system, they are either waiting for service or are in service. When they are out of the system, they are potential arrivals to the system. This means that the arrival rate to the system constantly changes depending on how many customers are potential arrivals.

A Limited Waiting Room Model

We first consider a variation of the bank example from the previous section.

EXAMPLE 11.8

In the CountyBank example from the previous section, we assumed that all customers could enter the bank, regardless of how crowded it was. Now the bank manager wants to analyze the effect of restricting the waiting room size. The assumption is that if the waiting room is full and another customer arrives, this new arrival will go to another branch.

Solution

Let N denote the maximum number of customers who are allowed in the bank at any time. Since there are $s = 6$ tellers and a single customer can be in service with each teller, the maximum number of customers who can be waiting is $N - s = N - 6$. Therefore, in addition to the inputs λ, μ, and s, we have an additional input N. We will see how the summary measures of the bank's performance depends on N.

The solution procedure is very similar to the "classical" $M/M/s$ system in the previous section (with no waiting line limitation). We need a formula for p_0, the fraction of time the bank is empty. All other quantities such as L and W will be based on p_0. Since the required formulas are quite complex and shed little light on the solution of the problem, we simply present a spreadsheet template that you can use to analyze this and other limited waiting room models.

The spreadsheet solution appears in Figure 11.11. (See the file MMSN.XLS.) It has an input section (B4:B8), in which you enter the time unit, the arrival and service rates, the number of servers, and the maximum number of customers allowed in the system. Then you press the Do Calculations button. This runs a macro that produces the values in columns E and F, and these values lead directly to the summary measures in the range B12:B17.

We will not go through all of the details of this spreadsheet since the macro does the work for you. However, there are a few key points you should be aware of.

1 Column E contains the possible numbers of customers in the system (n). (These assume $N = 10$, the input value in cell B8.) Column F contains the steady-state

FIGURE 11.11 Solution to CountyBank Example with a Limited Waiting Room

	A	B	C	D	E	F
1	**M/M/s Queue with Finite Waiting Room**				**Directions**	
2					1. Enter the inputs in cells B4 through B8.	
3	**Inputs**				2. Press the "Do Calculations" button.	
4	Unit of time	hour				
5	Arrival rate	150	customers/hour			
6	Service rate	30	customers/hour		Do Calculations	
7	Number of servers	6				
8	Maximum customers in system	10	customers			
9						
10	**Outputs**				**Steady-state probabilities**	
11	**Summary measures**				n	p_n
12	Expected number in system	5.446	customers		0	0.0059
13	Expected number in queue	0.755	customers		1	0.0295
14	Expected time in system	0.039	hours		2	0.0738
15	Expected time in queue	0.005	hours		3	0.1231
16	Entering rate	140.727	customers/hour		4	0.1538
17	Percentage who don't wait in queue	54.0%			5	0.1538
18					6	0.1282
19					7	0.1068
20					8	0.0890
21					9	0.0742
22					10	0.0618

probabilities p_n. For example, $p_3 = .1231$, which means that there are exactly three customers in the bank about 12% of the time.

2 The summary measures L, L_q, W, and W_q are calculated in the range B12:B15. The expected line length L is a weighted average of the numbers in column E, weighted by the probabilities in column F. The other measures then follow from Little's formula. The bank manager's interest is in how these measures (and the other summary measures in column B) are affected by the limited waiting room size. Table 11.2 shows this effect for $N = 7$, $N = 10$, and $N = 15$, that is, waiting room sizes of 1, 4, and 9. (In each case we entered a new value of N in cell B8 and clicked on the Do Calculations button.) For comparison, the results from Figure 11.8 are also shown in this table. This corresponds to a waiting room of unlimited size. As we see, all of these measures *increase* as the waiting room size increases. The primary reason is that as the waiting room size increases, more of the potential customers are allowed to enter the bank, so that the congestion in the bank increases.

TABLE 11.2 Queue Lengths and Waiting Times for Waiting Room Sizes

	Maximum Number in System (N)			
	7	**10**	**15**	**Unlimited**
L	4.449	5.446	6.568	7.938
L_q	0.138	0.755	1.673	2.938
W	0.034	0.039	0.045	0.053
W_q	0.001	0.005	0.011	0.020

3 The rate of arrivals who are allowed to enter appears in cell B16. Because a customer is allowed to enter only when the bank is not full, this rate is the *potential* arrival rate $\lambda = 150$ (from cell B5) multiplied by the fraction of time the bank is not full. This latter fraction is one minus the last p_n value in column F. For example, from Figure 11.11, when $N = 10$, the system is full 6.18% of the time (see cell F22), so 6.18% of potential arrivals are lost, and the entering rate is only

$$150(1 - .0618) = 140.7 \text{ customers per hour}$$

Table 11.3 shows how the fraction lost and the entering rate depend on the waiting room size. Obviously, as the waiting room size decreases, fewer potential arrivals are able to enter the bank. So the good news for the bank with a small waiting room is that there is typically less congestion; the bad news is that more potential customers take their business elsewhere.

4 Finally, the percentage of entering customers who don't have to wait in line appears in cell B17. It is the sum of the values p_0 through p_5 in column F, since an arriving customer experiences no waiting only if fewer than $s = 6$ customers are already in the bank. Table 11.4 shows how this percentage changes as a function of the waiting room size. From this table it is clear that a larger percentage of customers experience no waiting as the waiting room size decreases. But remember that this percentage is in terms of the number who are allowed to enter. Therefore, with a small waiting room size, a relatively small percentage of customers are allowed to enter, but for those who do enter, most don't have to wait in line.

We have seen in general that things are "better" for entering customers in a small waiting room model than in a large (or unlimited) waiting room model. The only catch is that some customers are now turned away, which could certainly represent a cost to the system. We explore this in the following continuation of the bank example. ■

TABLE 11.3 Percentage Lost and Entering Rate for Waiting Room Sizes

	Maximum Number in System (N)			
	7	**10**	**15**	**Unlimited**
Percentage Lost	13.78%	6.18%	2.10%	0%
Entering Rate	129.3	140.7	146.9	150

TABLE 11.4 Percentage Who Don't Wait for Waiting Room Sizes

	Maximum Number in System (N)			
	7	**10**	**15**	**Unlimited**
Percentage Who Don't Wait	69.7%	54.0%	45.6%	41.2%

EXAMPLE 11.9

Continuing the previous example, the CountyBank manager wants to explore the economic implications of providing more space for customers to wait. Assume that the bank will continue to employ six tellers.

Solution

There are potentially three costs that should be considered: c_w, the cost per hour of making a customer wait in line; c_l, the cost of losing a potential customer because the waiting room is full; and c_e, the cost of expanding the waiting room by one space. Although this latter cost is probably a one-time cost, we'll assume that it has been amortized appropriately so that it represents an hourly cost. We will also assume that there is currently room for four customers to wait ($N = 10$), as in the solution shown in Figure 11.11. Now the bank manager is trying to decide whether to expand the waiting room by one space (from four customers to five).

By changing the value in cell B8 of Figure 11.11 from 10 to 11 and clicking on the Do Calculations button, we see that the entering rate increases from 140.727 to 142.651, so that the expected number of customers lost per hour decreases from 150 – 140.727 = 9.273 to 150 – 142.651 = 7.349. Also (by increasing the number of decimal places shown), we see that the expected time in queue (W_q) increases from 0.00536 hour to 0.00675 hour. Since the former wait is experienced by 140.727 customers per hour and the latter by 142.651 customers per hour, the overall change in expected cost per hour is

$$\begin{aligned}\text{Cost change} &= c_e + c_l(7.349 - 9.273) + c_w[142.651(.00675) - 140.727(.00536)] \\ &= c_e - 1.924c_l + 0.2086c_w\end{aligned}$$

The first term is the cost of providing the extra space. The second term is the decrease in cost of lost customers (per hour). The third term is the increase in cost for more waiting in line.

Obviously, the extra space should be added only if this cost change is negative. To see whether this is the case, the bank manager must assess values for c_w, c_l, and c_e. Here we will assume that the cost per customer-hour of waiting in line is \$5 ($c_w = 5$) and the cost of losing a customer is \$8 ($c_l = 8$). Then the extra space should be added only if

$$c_e < 1.924(8) - 0.2086(5) = 14.35$$

In words, if the capital expense of expanding by one space is less than \$14.35 per hour, then the bank should expand. In fact, it should then consider expanding by two (or more) spaces instead of just one.

The cost trade-offs in this problem are difficult to compare, but the analysis indicates which cost data the bank manager must estimate in order to make a sensible decision. By the way, we are implicitly assuming that each extra additional space costs the bank the same amount. This is probably not the case; each extra space probably costs less to "install" than the previous space. However, this nonlinear expansion cost could be handled with a very similar analysis. ■

A Finite Source Model

Until now, we have implicitly assumed that the arrival rate to the system is unaffected by the number of customers currently in the system. At many service systems, such as banks or supermarkets, this is perfectly reasonable because the potential arrival population is very large. Specifically, the arrival rate doesn't tend to decrease just because a lot of customers are already in the bank or the supermarket. However, some systems have a fairly small number of potential customers. If most of these are in the system (being served or awaiting service), then the arrival rate is relatively small, simply because there aren't many customers left to enter. Think of a specialty store where only ten customers ever enter. If all ten of them are currently in the store, the potential arrival rate is 0! The following example illustrates an important example of the finite source model. It is generally called the **machine repair model**.

EXAMPLE 11.10

The Reem Paper Company runs a factory with 25 identical machines. These machines work full-time except when they are broken. Broken machines are repaired by any of

Reem's six dedicated repairmen. After a machine is repaired, it works for a random amount of time before breaking again, where this time is exponentially distributed with mean one hour. The time it takes for a repairman to repair a broken machine is also exponentially distributed, with mean 12 minutes. It takes one repairman to fix a machine, so that as many as six machines can be in the process of repair at any time. If more than six are broken, the excess machines wait in a single queue for repair. The factory manager wants to find the steady-state distribution of the number of machines broken and various summary measures such as the probability that all machines are working.

Solution

This problem is somewhat different from previous queueing models, where the customers were always people. Now the "customers" are machines, and the "servers" are the repairmen. It may be helpful to think of the factory as separated into two sections. The working machines are in section 1, and the broken machines are in section 2. (See Figure 11.12.) In section 2 broken parts are either waiting in line for repair or are being repaired. When a machine breaks down, it goes from section 1 to section 2. When a machine is repaired, it goes from section 2 to section 1. If we let n be the number of broken machines, so that $25 - n$ are working, then the arrival rate from section 1 to section 2 varies with n. (In Figure 11.12, $n = 8$.) In particular, if we let λ be the breakdown rate per working machine, then the *system* breakdown rate when n are already broken is $(25 - n)\lambda$, since each of the $25 - n$ working machines breaks down at rate λ. This varying arrival rate to the queueing part of the system distinguishes the current model from previous models.

As in the limited waiting room model, there are complex formulas for calculating the steady-state characteristics of this machine repair model. However, we will again omit these and discuss only the outputs in a spreadsheet model.

The relevant spreadsheet appears in Figure 11.13. (See the file REPAIR.XLS.) This spreadsheet is very similar to the one in Figure 11.11 for the limited waiting room model. It is again driven by a push-button macro, so that all you need to do is enter the inputs in the range B4:B8 and then click on the Do Calculations button. In this case the inputs are the time unit, the breakdown rate per machine, the repair rate per repairman, the number of repairmen, and the number of machines.

FIGURE 11.12 **Two Sections of Reem Factory**

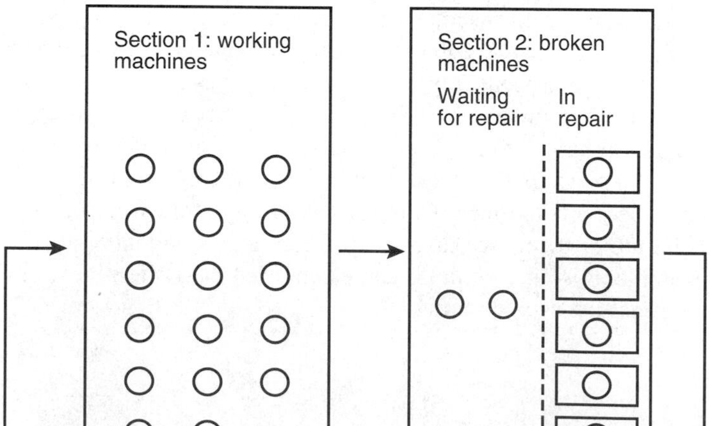

FIGURE 11.13 Spreadsheet Solution to Machine Repair Example

	A	B	C	D	E	F	G	H	I
1	**Finite Source Model (Machine Repair Model)**				**Directions**				
2					1. Enter the inputs in cells B4 through B8.				
3	**Inputs**				2. Press the "Do Calculations" button.				
4	Unit of time	hour							
5	Breakdown rate per machine	1	times/hour						
6	Repair rate	5	repairs/hour		**Do Calculations**				
7	Number of repairmen	6							
8	Number of machines	25							
9									
10	**Outputs**				**Steady-state probabilities**				
11	**Summary measures**				n	p_n			
12	Expected number broken	4.454	machines		0	0.0099			
13	Expected number waiting for repair	0.345	machines		1	0.0493			
14	Average breakdown rate	20.546	machines/hour		2	0.1184			
15	Expected time in repair shop	0.217	hours		3	0.1815			
16	Expected time waiting for repairman	0.017	hours		4	0.1997			
17	Percentage of time all machines working	1.0%			5	0.1677			
18					6	0.1118			
19					7	0.0708			
20					8	0.0425			
21					9	0.0241			
22					10	0.0128			
23					11	0.0064			
24					12	0.0030			
25					13	0.0013			
26					14	0.0005			
27					15	0.0002			
28					16	0.0001			
29					17	0.0000			
30					18	0.0000			
31					19	0.0000			
32					20	0.0000			
33					21	0.0000			
34					22	0.0000			
35					23	0.0000			
36					24	0.0000			
37					25	0.0000			

We make the following comments about the output in Figure 11.13.

1. The values in columns E and F show the steady-state distribution of the number of machines broken. Specifically, for each value of n in column E, the value in column F is the fraction of time when n machines are broken. For example, exactly 1 out of 25 is broken 4.93% of the time.

2. The values in cells B12 and B13 correspond to L and L_q. They now represent the expected number of broken machines total and the number of broken machines awaiting repair, respectively. Similarly, the values in cells B15 and B16 correspond to W and W_q. They now represent the total time per machine in the repair shop and in the repair queue, respectively. As always, Little's formula relates each L to the corresponding W, but now the "$\bar{\lambda}$" in Little's formula represents the *average* breakdown rate, which is calculated in cell B14. Note that the system breakdown rate varies from 0 per hour (when all 25 machines are already broken) to 25 per hour (when none are broken). Using the steady-state probabilities in column F, we find that the average breakdown rate for the system, a weighted average of all possibilities, is 20.546 per hour.

3. The fraction of time that all 25 machines are working, listed in cell B17, is the same as the fraction of time zero machines are broken. Therefore, it is always the first entry in the p_n column, that is, the entry in cell F12. In this example all 25 machines are working only about 1% of the time.

4. It is interesting to vary λ, the breakdown rate per machine in cell B5 and see how the summary output measures change. We did this for $\lambda = .6$, $\lambda = .8$, $\lambda = 1$, $\lambda = 1.2$, and $\lambda = 1.4$. In each case we kept all of the other inputs constant and calculated the

revised outputs by clicking on the Do Calculations button. The results are listed in Table 11.5. Obviously, as machines break down at a faster rate, more machines tend to be in the repair shop, either being repaired or awaiting repair. This creates more congestion in the repair shop, which means that each broken machine tends to spend more time there on each visit. Also, the fraction of time all 25 machines are working decreases dramatically.

By referring to Figure 11.13, the Reem factory manager sees that the percentage of time when all 25 machines are working is only 1%. She also sees that 4.454 machines are broken on average, and a broken machine must typically spend 0.217 hour in the repair shop before being fixed. Since these machines are critical for the successful operations of the factory, these statistics aren't very good. Therefore, the manager is thinking about hiring more repairmen to improve matters. We explore this in the next example. ■

TABLE 11.5 Summary Measures for Different Breakdown Rates

	Breakdown Rate per Machine (λ)				
	0.6	**0.8**	**1.0**	**1.2**	**1.4**
Expected Number Broken	2.703	3.551	4.454	5.463	6.600
Expected Number Waiting for Repair	0.027	0.119	0.345	0.775	1.449
Average Breakdown Rate	13.378	17.159	20.546	23.444	25.759
Expected Time in Repair Shop	0.202	0.207	0.217	0.223	0.256
Expected Time Waiting for Repair	0.002	0.007	0.017	0.033	0.056
Percentage of Time All Machines Working	5.9%	2.4%	1.0%	0.4%	0.2%

EXAMPLE 11.11

Suppose that Reem can hire extra repairmen at a wage rate of $15 per hour. Should it hire one or more repairmen?

Solution

As usual, there is a trade-off. The cost per hour of hiring an extra repairman is known to be $15 per hour. The manager must trade this off against the cost per hour, labeled c_w, of having a machine in the repair shop. Actually, it is probably a bit easier for Reem to estimate this c_w cost than in previous examples because it now represents a *direct* cost to the company, namely, the cost of the lost output a broken machine could be producing.

Let's see how the expected costs change if we add a seventh repairman. By entering a 7 in cell B7 of Figure 11.13 and recalculating, the expected time in the repair shop (cell B15) decreases from 0.217 hour to 0.205 hour. Also, the average breakdown rate (cell B14) increases from 20.546 per hour to 20.742 per hour.[5] Therefore, the hourly change in cost by hiring the seventh repairman is

$$\text{Cost change} = 15 + c_w[20.742(.205) - 20.546(.217)]$$
$$= 15 - .206c_w$$

This change is negative only if $c_w > 15/.206 = \$72.82$. So the wages of the seventh repairman are justified only if the cost in lost production per broken machine per hour is

[5]Counterintuitive results can occur in finite-source models. By adding a repairman, which ought to make the system "better," the average breakdown rate actually *increases*. The reason is that the machines are repaired faster, making more of them candidates for breakdowns!

greater than \$72.82. If this is the case, then the Reem manager could use a similar analysis to see whether even more repairmen are justified. ■

PROBLEMS

Skill-Building Problems

32 A service facility consists of one server who can serve an average of two customers per hour (service times are exponential). An average of three customers per hour arrive at the facility (interarrival times are assumed to be exponential). The system capacity is three customers—two waiting and one being served.

a On the average, how many potential customers enter the system each hour?

b What is the probability that the server is busy at a typical point in time?

33 An average of 40 cars per hour (interarrival times are exponentially distributed) are tempted to use the drive-through window at the Hot Dog King Restaurant. If a total of more than four cars are in line (including the car at the window), a car will not enter the line. It takes an average of four minutes (exponentially distributed) to serve a car.

a What is the average number of cars waiting for the drive-through window (not including the car at the window)?

b On the average, how many cars will be served per hour?

c I have just joined the line at the drive-through window. On the average, how long will it be before I receive my food?

34 A laundromat has five washing machines. A typical machine breaks down once every five days. A repairer can repair a machine in an average of 2.5 days. Currently, three repairers are on duty. The owner of the laundromat has the option of replacing them with a superworker, who can repair a machine in an average of 5/6 of a day. The salary of the superworker equals the pay of the three regular employees. Breakdown and service times are exponential. Should the laundromat replace the three repairers with the superworker?

35 The machine repair model may often be used to approximate the behavior of a computer's CPU (central processing unit). Suppose that 20 terminals (assumed to always be busy) feed the CPU. After the CPU responds to a user, he or she takes an average of 80 seconds before sending another request to the CPU (this is called the "think time"). The CPU takes an average of 2 seconds to respond to any request. On the average, how long will a user have to wait before the CPU acts on his or her request? How will your answer change if there are 30 terminals? 40 terminals? Of course, you must make appropriate assumptions about the exponential distribution to answer this question.

Skill-Extending Problems

36 Two one-barber shops sit side by side in Dunkirk Square. Each can hold a maximum of four people, and any potential customer who finds a shop full will not wait for a haircut. Barber 1 charges \$11 per haircut and takes an average of 15 minutes to complete a haircut. Barber 2 charges \$7 per haircut and takes an average of 10 minutes to complete a haircut. An average of 10 potential customers per hour arrive at each barber shop. Of course, a potential customer becomes an actual customer only if he or she finds that the shop is not full. Assuming that interarrival times and haircut times are exponential, which barber will earn more money?

37 A small mail-order firm Sea's Beginning has one phone line. An average of 60 people per hour call in orders, and it takes an average of one minute to handle a call. Time between calls and time to handle calls are exponentially distributed. If the phone line is busy, Sea's Beginning can put up to $c - 1$ people on hold. If $c - 1$ people are on hold, a caller gets a busy signal and calls a competitor (Air's End). Sea's Beginning wants only 1% of all callers to get a busy signal. How many people should they be able to put on hold, that is, what is the required value of c?

38 Bectol, Inc., is building a dam. A total of 10 million cubic feet of dirt is needed to construct the dam. A bulldozer is used to collect dirt for the dam. Then the dirt is moved via dumpers to the dam site. Only one bulldozer is available, and it rents for \$100 per hour. Bectol can rent, at \$40 per hour, as many dumpers as desired. Each dumper can hold 1000 cubic feet of dirt. It takes an average of 12 minutes for the bulldozer to load a dumper with dirt, and each dumper an average of five minutes to deliver the dirt to the dam and return to the bulldozer. Making appropriate assumptions about the exponential distribution, determine how Bectol can minimize the total expected cost of moving the dirt needed to build the dam. (*Hint*: There is a machine repair problem here somewhere!) ■

11.9 The Erlang Loss Model

All of the results so far have been made possible because of exponential distribution and its memoryless property. If we drop the exponential assumption, the mathematical derivations become much more difficult, and "nice" results are few and far between. In this section we will discuss one of the better-known results for nonexponential systems. Actually, we continue to assume a Poisson arrival process, that is, exponentially distributed interarrival times, but we relax the exponential service time requirement. This is important because many real-world service time distributions are definitely *not* exponential.

The model in this section is called the **Erlang loss model**. The reason for the term *loss* is that there is no waiting room at all, so that customers who arrive when all servers are busy are lost to the system. This model is illustrated in the following example.

EXAMPLE 11.12

Suppose that a fire department receives an average of 24 requests for fire engines each hour. Each request causes a fire engine to be unavailable for an average of 20 minutes. To have at most a 1% chance of being unable to respond to a request, how many fire engines should the fire department have?

Solution

To model this as a queueing problem, we identify the requests for fire engines as customers and the fire engines as servers. Then the key aspect of the problem is that there is no queueing for service. If a request occurs when at least one fire engine is available, an available fire engine serves this request. However, if no fire engine is available, then this request is not serviced at all. Therefore, this problem is essentially like the $M/M/s$ model with a waiting room size of zero, where s is the number of fire engines (a value to be determined). The only difference is that we are not assuming exponentially distributed service times. All we are told is that the mean service time is 20 minutes. Since there is probably some minimum time that all service times must exceed, the exponential assumption probably does not apply, so it is more realistic to assume nonexponentially distributed service times.

The main focus of this type of system is Pr(lost), the long-run fraction of requests that are lost. Once this fraction has been determined, we can find other key quantities from Little's formula. Specifically, the $\bar{\lambda}$ in Little's formula is the arrival rate of requests, $\lambda = 24$ per hour, multiplied by $1 - \text{Pr(lost)}$, the fraction of requests that can be serviced. The expected time W that a typical request takes to be serviced is given as 20 minutes. From these data the expected number of requests in the system, L, can be found from $L = \bar{\lambda}W$. The quantities L_q and W_q are both 0 since no queueing ever takes place.

Since the calculation of the fraction Pr(lost) is fairly complex, we again supply a push-button macro to accomplish it. The relevant spreadsheet appears in Figure 11.14. (See the file ERLANG.XLS.) We make several comments about this spreadsheet model.

1 The service rate is entered as an input as usual. For this example it is 3 per hour since each service request requires 20 minutes. However, unlike previous queueing models, there is no claim that the service time distribution be exponential; we only need to know the *mean* service time.

2 The push-button macro calculates the fraction of requests that are lost, expressed as a percentage in cell B12. Then the entering arrival rate, the expected number of requests being serviced, and the expected time a request takes to be serviced can be calculated easily in the range B13:B15 with the formulas

=B5*(1–B12)
=B13*B15

and

=1/B6

3 To ensure that the fire department achieves its goal of meeting all but 1% of the entering requests, we need to vary the number of fire engines in cell B7 until the percentage of lost requests in cell B12 is no more than 1%. We did this by trial and error; the results are shown in Table 11.6. As these results show, the required number of fire engines is 15. Using this value, which appears in Figure 11.14, the arrival rate of requests that can be serviced is 23.782 per hour, and the expected number of requests that are being serviced at any time is 7.927. ■

FIGURE 11.14 Spreadsheet Solution to Fire Engine Example

	A	B	C	D	E	F	G	H
1	Erlang Loss Model for Fire Engine Example				Directions			
2					1. Enter the inputs in cells B4 through B7.			
3	Inputs				2. Press the "Do Calculations" button.			
4	Unit of time	hour						
5	Arrival rate	24	customers/hour					
6	Service rate	3	customers/hour		Do Calculations			
7	Number of fire engines	15						
8								
9								
10	Outputs							
11	Summary measures							
12	Percentage of requests lost	0.9%						
13	Entering arrival rate	23.782	customers/hour					
14	Expected number in system	7.927	customers					
15	Expected time in system	0.333	hours					

TABLE 11.6 Outputs for Fire Engine Example

Number of Fire Engines	Percentage of Requests Lost
12	5.1%
13	3.1%
14	1.7%
15	0.9%
16	0.5%

PROBLEMS

Skill-Building Problems

39 A telephone-order sales company must determine how many telephone operators are needed to staff the phones during the nine-to-five shift. It is estimated that an average of 480 calls are received during this time period and that the average call lasts for six minutes. If the company wants to have at most one chance in 100 of a caller receiving a busy signal, how many operators should be hired for the nine-to-five shift? What assumption does the answer require?

40 At the peak usage time, an average of 200 people per hour attempt to log on to the Jade Vax, a minicomputer. The average length of time someone spends on the Vax is 20 minutes. Computing administrators want to ensure that during peak usage only 1% of all users receive an "All ports busy" message. How many ports should the Jade Vax have?

41 US Airlines receives an average of 500 calls per hour from customers who want to make a reservation (time between calls follows an exponential distribution). It takes an average of three minutes to handle each call. Each customer who buys a ticket contributes $100 to US Airlines profit. It costs $15 per hour to staff a telephone line. Any customer who receives a busy signal will purchase a ticket on another airline. How many telephone lines should US Airlines have?

Skill-Extending Problems

42 On the average, 26 patrons per year come to the I.U. library to borrow the book *I Ching*. (Assume that interarrival times are exponential.) Borrowers who find the book unavailable leave and never return. A borrower keeps a copy of *I Ching* for an average of four weeks.

a If the library has only one copy, what is the expected number of borrowers who will come to borrow *I Ching* each year and find that the book is not available?

b Suppose that each person who comes to borrow *I Ching* and is unable to is considered to cost the library $1 in goodwill. A copy of *I Ching* lasts two years and costs $11. A thief has just stolen the library's only copy. To minimize the sum of purchasing and goodwill costs over the next two years, how many copies of *I Ching* should the library purchase?

43 A company's warehouse can store up to four units of a good. Each month, an average of ten orders for the good are received. The times between the receipt of successive orders are exponentially distributed. When an item is used to fill an order, a replacement item is immediately ordered, and it takes an average of one month for a replacement item to arrive. If no items are on hand when an order is received, the order is lost. What fraction of all orders will be lost due to shortages? (*Hint*: Let the storage space for each item be a server and think about what it means for a server to be busy. Then come up with an appropriate definition of "service" time.) ■

11.10 Conclusion

We have presented several of the most widely used queueing models in this chapter. Except for the Erlang loss model in Section 11.9, all of these queueing models are exponential models, where all interarrival times and service times are exponentially distributed. This allows us to use relatively simple methods to analyze these systems, although even in these cases we hid many of the mathematical details with the push-button macros.

As queueing models become more realistic, which usually means more complex, they are often too difficult to solve using the methods in this chapter. Often the only practical alternative is computer simulation, the topic of the next two chapters. Indeed, several simulation software packages have been written explicitly to deal with complex queueing systems. The details of such queueing simulation packages are beyond the scope of this book; we will discuss them only briefly in the next chapter. However, we do want you to be aware that it is possible to analyze almost any queueing system, either by the methods employed in this chapter or by computer simulation.

REVIEW PROBLEMS

Skill-Building Problems

44 At the Franklin Post Office, patrons wait in a single line for the first open window. An average of 100 patrons per hour enter the post office, and each window can serve an average of 45 patrons per hour. The post office estimates a cost of 10¢ for each minute a patron waits in line and believes that it costs $20 per hour to keep a window open. Interarrival times and service times are exponential.

a To minimize the total expected hourly cost, how many windows should be open?

b If the post office's goal is to ensure that at most 5% of all patrons will spend more than five minutes in line, how many windows should be open?

45 The manager of a large group of employees must decide if she needs another photocopying machine. The cost of a machine is $40 per eight-hour day whether or not the machine is in use. An average of four people per hour need to use the copying machine. Each person uses the copier for an average of ten minutes. Interarrival times and copying times are exponentially distributed. Employees are paid $8 per hour, and we assume that a waiting cost is incurred when a worker is waiting in line or is using the copying machine. How many copying machines should be rented?

46 The Newcoat Painting Company has for some time been experiencing high demand for its automobile repainting service. Since it has had to turn away business, management is concerned that the limited space available to store cars awaiting painting has cost them in lost revenue. A small vacant lot next to the painting facility has recently been made available for rental on a long-term basis at a cost of $10 per day. Management believes that each lost customer costs $20 in profit. Current demand is estimated to be 21 cars per day with exponential interarrival times (including those turned away), and the facility can service at an exponential rate of 24 cars per day. Cars are processed on a FCFS basis. Waiting space is now limited to 9 cars but can be increased to 20 cars with the lease of the vacant lot. Newcoat wants to determine whether the vacant lot should be leased. Management also wants to know the expected daily lost profit due to turning away customers if the lot is leased. Only one car can be painted at a time.

47 An average of 90 patrons per hour arrive at a hotel lobby (interarrival times are exponential) waiting to check in. At present there are five clerks, and patrons wait in a single line for the first available clerk. The average time for a clerk to service a patron is three minutes (exponentially distributed). Clerks earn $10 per hour, and the hotel assesses a waiting time cost of $20 for each hour that a patron waits in line.

a Compute the expected cost per hour of the current system.

b The hotel is considering replacing one clerk with an Automatic Clerk Machine (ACM). Management estimates that 20% of all patrons will use an ACM. An ACM takes an average of one minute to service a patron. It costs $48 per day (one day equals eight hours) to operate an ACM. Should the hotel install the ACM? Assume that all customers who are willing to use the ACM wait in a separate queue.

48 An average of 50 customers per hour arrive at a small post office. Interarrival times are exponentially distributed. Each window can serve an average of 25 customers per hour. Service times are exponentially distributed. It costs $25 per hour to open a window and the post office values the time a customer spends waiting in line at $15 per customer-hour. To minimize expected hourly costs, how many postal windows should be opened?

49 An average of 300 customers per hour arrive at a huge branch of Bank 2. It takes an average of two minutes to serve each customer. It costs $10 per hour to keep a teller window open, and the bank estimates that it will lose $50 in future profits for each hour that a customer waits in line. How many teller windows should Bank 2 open?

50 Ships arrive at a port facility at an average rate of 2 ships every 3 days. On the average, it takes a single crew 1 day to unload a ship. Assume that interarrival and service times are exponential. The shipping company owns the port facility as well as the ships using that facility. The company estimates that it costs $1000 per day for each day that a ship spends in port. The crew servicing the ships consists of 100 workers, who are each paid an average of $30 per day. A consultant has recommended that the shipping company hire an additional 40 workers and split the employees into two equal-sized crews of 70 each. This would give each crew an average unloading or loading time of 1.5 days. Which crew arrangement would you recommend to the company?

51 An average of 40 jobs per day arrive at a factory. The time between arrivals of jobs is exponentially distributed. The factory can process an average of 42 jobs per day, and the time to process a job is exponentially distributed.

a On the average, how long does it take before a job is completed (measured from the time the job arrives at the factory)?

b What fraction of the time is the factory idle?

c What is the probability that work on a job will begin within two days of its arrival at the factory?

52 A printing shop receives an average of one order per day. The average length of time required to complete an order is half a day. At any given time, the print shop can work on at most one job. Interarrival times and service times are exponentially distributed.

a On the average, how many jobs are present in the print shop?

b On the average, how long will a person who places an order have to wait until it is finished?

c What is the probability that an order will begin work within two days of its arrival?

Skill-Extending Problem

53 The mail order firm of L. L. Pea receives an average of 200 calls per hour (times between calls are exponentially distributed). It takes an L. L. Pea operator an average of three minutes to handle a call. If a caller gets a busy signal, L. L. Pea assumes that he or she will call a competing mail-order company, and L. L. Pea will lose an average of $30 in profit. The cost of keeping a phone line open is $9 per hour. How many operators should L. L. Pea have on duty?

Modeling Problems

54 Bloomington Hospital knows that insurance companies are going to reduce the average length of stay of many types of patients. How can queueing theory be used to determine how changes in insurance policies will influence the hospital?

55 Recently excessive delays have been noted on New York City's 911 system. Discuss how you would use queueing theory to improve the performance of the 911 system.

56 Suppose that annually an average of λ library patrons want to borrow a book. A patron borrows the book for an average of $1/\mu$ years. Suppose we observe that the book is actually borrowed an average of R times per year. Expain how we can estimate λ, which is an unobservable quantity. (*Hint*: Let U be the expected number of times per year a patron wants to borrow the book and the book is out. Note that $\lambda = R + U$.)

57 (Based on Quinn, Andrews, and Parsons [4]) Winter Riggers handles approximately $400 million in telephone orders per year. Winter Riggers' system works as follows. Callers are connected to an agent if one is available. Otherwise, they are put on hold (if a "trunk" or line is available). At any time a customer can hang up and leave the system. Winter Riggers would like to efficiently manage the telephone system (lines and agents) used to process these orders. Of course, orders are very seasonal and depend on the time of day.

a What decisions must Winter Riggers make?

b What would be an appropriate objective function for Winter Riggers to minimize (or maximize)? What difficulties do you see in specifying the objective function?

c What data would Winter Riggers need to keep track of to improve its efficiency?

58 Zerox has 16 service centers throughout the U.S. Zerox is trying to determine how many technicians should be assigned to each service center. How would you approach this problem?

59 (Based on Kolesar et al. [3]) Metropolis PD Precinct 88 needs to determine the minimum number of police cars required to meet its needs for the next 24 hours. An average call for service requires 30 minutes. The number of calls the police department expects to receive during each hour is shown in Table 11.7. The Metropolis PD standard of service is that there should be a 90% chance that a car is available to respond to a call.

a Suppose that patrol officer teams assigned to a car work an eight-hour shift beginning at either 12 A.M., 8 A.M., or 4 P.M. Officers get an hour off for a meal. This hour can be anytime between the second and fifth hour of their shift. How many officer teams are needed to meet daily demand?

b Suppose that patrol officer teams assigned to a car begin their eight-hour shift at 12 A.M., 8 A.M., 12 P.M., 4 P.M., and 8 P.M. An hour off for meals may be taken anytime during a shift. How many teams are now needed to meet daily demand? ■

TABLE 11.7 **Calls for Metropolis PD Problem**

	Number of Calls		Number of Calls
12 A.M.–1 A.M.	9.8	12 P.M.–1 P.M.	4.3
1 A.M.–2 A.M.	9.6	1 P.M.–2 P.M.	5.0
2 A.M.–3 A.M.	8.7	2 P.M.–3 P.M.	5.9
3 A.M.–4 A.M.	7.6	3 P.M.–4 P.M.	6.6
4 A.M.–5 A.M.	6.7	4 P.M.–5 P.M.	7.8
5 A.M.–6 A.M.	5.3	5 P.M.–6 P.M.	8.6
6 A.M.–7 A.M.	4.1	6 P.M.–7 P.M.	9.4
7 A.M.–8 A.M.	3.2	7 P.M.–8 P.M.	9.8
8 A.M.–9 A.M.	2.5	8 P.M.–9 P.M.	10.2
9 A.M.–10 A.M.	2.5	9 P.M.–10 P.M.	10.4
10 A.M.–11 A.M.	2.9	10 P.M.–11 P.M.	10.2
11 A.M.–12 P.M.	3.8	11 P.M.–12 A.M.	10.0

CASE STUDY

The Catalog Company Problem

The Catalog Company is a mail and phone order company that sells generic brands of houseware items and clothing. Approximately 95% of customer orders are received by phone; the remaining 5% are received in the mail. Phone orders are accepted at Catalog Company's toll-free 800 number, 800-SAVE-NOW. The number is available nine hours per day (8 A.M. to 5 P.M.), five days a week.

Sarah Walters, a recent graduate of Columbia Business School, has just been hired by Catalog to improve its operations. Sarah would like to impress her boss, Ben Gleason, the president of Catalog Company, with some ideas that would quickly improve the company's bottom line. After spending a week learning about Catalog's operations, Sarah feels that a substantial impact can be made by a closer evaluation of the phone order system.

Currently, Catalog employs one full-time operator to take orders over the phone. Sarah wonders whether additional operators should be hired to take phone orders. Ben feels that Sarah's time might be better spent studying the catalog mailing lists. Ben reasons that the mailing lists are where customers are generated, and improving the list will bring in more revenue. And besides, Ben says, "Catalog's phone operator, Betty Wrangle, seems to be doing nothing more than half of the time that I walk by. Hiring more operators to do nothing will just waste more money." While Sarah knows the mailing lists are important, she thinks that a study of the mailing lists will take far more time than a quick evaluation of the phone order system.

Forging ahead, Sarah found out the following information about the phone order system. The phone operator, Betty Wrangle, is paid $9 per hour in wages and benefits. The average cost to Catalog for a completed 800 number call is $1.50. With only one phone line, any incoming calls that arrive when Betty is on the phone to another customer get a busy signal. The cost of the phone line is $40 per month. The phone company can immediately add up to four additional phone lines using the same 800 number, each at a cost of $40 per month per line. Catalog's phone system is such that it cannot be upgraded in the near future to allow incoming calls to be placed on hold. The average profit on an order (not including the cost of the operator or phone call) is 40% of the amount of the order. For example, an order of $100 brings a profit of $40 to Catalog.

Sarah decided that additional information needed to be collected about the frequency of incoming calls, the length of the calls, and so on. After talking to the phone company, Sarah found out that she could borrow equipment for one day that could detect when a call was coming in, even when Betty was on the phone. The caller would still get a busy signal and be lost, but Sarah would know that a call had been attempted. Sarah collected almost nine hours of data the next day. The data that Sarah collected are presented in Table 11.8. Sarah believes that most of the callers that receive a busy signal take their business elsewhere and are totally lost to Catalog. Sarah does not feel that extending the hours of operation of the 800 number

TABLE 11.8 Call Data for Catalog Case Study

Call Number	Arrival Time (hours)	Busy Signal? (1=busy, 0=not)	Call Length (hours)	Order Size (dollars)
1	0.0359	0	0.0544	65.21
2	0.1564	0	0.0503	62.47
3	0.3066	0	0.0191	62.46
4	0.3609	0	0.0109	38.11
5	0.3610	1	N/A	N/A
6	0.3689	1	N/A	N/A
7	0.4094	0	0.0877	54.02
⋮	⋮	⋮	⋮	⋮
80	8.4890	0	0.0310	10.00

would be beneficial because the hours of operation are printed prominently in all of the catalogs.

The first call arrives 0.036 hours into the day. It takes Betty 0.054 hours to process the call and record the order for $65.21 worth of merchandise. Callers 5 and 6 get a busy signal when they call, because Betty was still processing caller 4. Because calls 5 and 6 were lost, no call length information was available and no orders were placed. Data collection was stopped at call number 80.

Questions

Use the complete information in the spreadsheet CATALOG.XLS to answer the following questions.

1 Approximately what fraction of the time is Betty idle? Is Ben's estimate correct?

2 Approximately how many calls are lost in an average hour due to a busy signal?

3 Use the data to estimate the average arrival rate of all attempted calls to Catalog. Give an approximate 90% confidence interval for the estimate. Plot a frequency histogram of interarrival times. Does the distribution of interarrival times appear to be exponential?

4 Use the data to estimate the average service rate of all completed calls. Give an approximate 90% confidence interval for the estimate. Plot a frequency histogram of service times. Does the service time distribution appear to be exponential? Give an approximate 90% confidence interval for the average revenue per call.

5 Would you recommend that Catalog acquire additional phone lines and operators? If so, how many? If not, why not? Justify your answer in enough detail so that Ben Gleason would be convinced of your recommendation. ■

REFERENCES

1 Agnihothri, R., and P. Taylor. "Staffing a Centralized Appointment Scheduling Department in Lourdes Hospital." *Interfaces* 21, no. 5 (1991): 1–15.

2 Andrews, B., and H. Parsons. "Establishing Telephone-Agent Staffing Levels through Economic Optimization." *Interfaces* 23, no. 2 (1993): 14–20.

3 Kolesar, P., T. Crabill, K. Rider, and W. Walker. "A Queueing Linear Programming Approach to Scheduling Police Patrol Cars." *Operations Research* 23 (1974): 1045–62.

4 Quinn, P., B. Andrews, and H. Parsons. "Allocating Telecommunications Resources at L. L. Bean, Inc." *Interfaces* 21, no. 1 (1991): 75–91.

SIMILAR PURCHASE PROGRAMS SINCE
THE COMPANY SAID IT WAS ABOUT
SHARES OUTSTANDING.

C H A P T E R

12

Simulation

Management Science Success Stories

Simulation is a versatile tool that allows companies to ask many what-if questions about changes in their systems without actually changing the systems themselves. As reported in the article "AT&T's Call Processing Simulator (CAPS) Operational Design for Inbound Call Centers" by Brigandi et al. [2], AT&T has used a simulation model called CAPS to help its corporate customers design and operate their call centers. These call centers are the locations into which customers phone, usually using 800 numbers, for customer service, telephone shopping, and other services. The system that is used to handle these calls—the way calls are routed to agents, the number of lines open, the prerecorded messages given to customers, the way customer queues are handled, and so on—can be extremely complex and difficult to understand, let alone optimize. Therefore, AT&T developed the CAPS simulation tool to simulate a variety of operating policies for its corporate customers. AT&T reports that it has used this tool to regain more than $1 billion from a customer base of approximately 2000 corporate customers per year. The CAPS tool has improved the customers' call center operations dramatically and has helped sell these customers on further AT&T services.

As an example, a major airline's reservation system was supported by 19 separate call centers located near domestic and international airports. In 1992, the airline decided to consolidate its reservations centers. AT&T helped the airline by running a series of CAPS studies to determine the characteristics of efficient, load-balanced call centers that would accomplish the airline's goals. The airline was particularly interested in reducing its 10% blocked-call rate while using its resources more efficiently. The result of the CAPS studies was a $25 million savings in the airline's reservations call-center operations costs and an ability to handle approximately 3000 more reservation sales calls per day. At the same time, AT&T strengthened its position as the 800-number service communications carrier of choice with the airline. Its annual billed network services for the airline increased by 5% on a base of $49 million. ■

12.1

Introduction

In the previous chapters of this book we have analyzed many models. Most of these models enabled us to determine the optimal course of action for a decision maker. In many situations where uncertainty is present, however, it is difficult or even impossible to build a tractable mathematical model that will yield useful information to a decision maker. For example, the queueing models we discussed in Chapter 11 are often used to model a situation where people wait in line. For a bank where all customers wait in a single line for the first available teller, the $M/M/s$ model might adequately describe the situation. If so, then this model can be used to predict customer waiting times and evaluate how adding additional tellers would reduce customer waiting times. At present, however, no queueing models can adequately model a supermarket with express lanes where customers can move freely between lines. Simulation is used in such situations where no tractable mathematical model exists.

In most situations a simulation model is a computer model that imitates a real-life situation. The meaning of the word *imitates* will become clear as we work through the examples in this chapter. Often the simulation model can provide a decision maker with important information. For the supermarket illustration, a simulation model might help answer questions such as the following:

- If an additional express lane is added, how much will the average waiting time of a customer decrease?
- Currently baggers help people load their groceries into their cars. How much will the average waiting time of a customer change if the store eliminates this practice?
- How does the number of checkout counters needed to provide adequate service vary during the day? (This information is a great aid in scheduling employees.)

A simulation can be used to determine how sensitive a system is to changes in operating conditions. For example, if the store experiences a 20% increase in business, what will happen to the average time customers must wait for service? A simulation model can also help a company determine an "optimal" operating policy. For example, the supermarket could use simulation to determine the relationship between the number of open registers and the expected time a customer waits in line. Then this relationship, along with the cost of opening a register, could be used to determine the optimal number of registers corresponding to a range of possible arrival rates.

A great benefit of computer simulation is that it enables us to answer these types of what-if questions *without* actually changing (or building) a physical system. For example, the supermarket might want to experiment with the number of open registers to reduce customer waiting times. Of course, the only way it can physically experiment with more registers than it currently owns is to purchase more equipment. Then if it determines that this equipment is not a good investment—customer waiting times don't decrease appreciably—the company is stuck with expensive equipment it doesn't need. Computer simulation is a much less expensive alternative. It provides the company with an electronic replica of what would happen *if* the new equipment were purchased. Then, if the simulation indicates that the new equipment is worth the cost, the company can be confident that purchasing it is the right decision. Otherwise, it can abandon the idea of the new equipment *before* the equipment has been purchased.

As you will learn in this chapter, modeling simulations on a spreadsheet is quite similar to the other modeling applications in this book. We begin with input quantities and then relate these with various spreadsheet formulas to produce outputs of interest. The main difference is that simulation uses *random* numbers to drive the whole process. These are generated with a special function (the RAND function in Excel) that returns a different random number each time it is entered. Each time the spreadsheet recalculates, all of the random numbers change. This gives us the ability to model the logical process once and then use the recalculation feature repeatedly in order to generate many different scenarios. By collecting the data from these scenarios, we see which outputs are most likely and what the best-case and worst-case scenarios are. However, the modeling *process* is basically the same as before.

In this chapter we will illustrate spreadsheet models that can be developed with the basic Excel package. However, because simulation is becoming such an important tool for analyzing real problems, add-ins to Excel are being developed to streamline the process of developing simulation models. In the next chapter we will focus on one of the most popular simulation add-ins, called @RISK. This add-in not only augments the simulation capabilities of Excel but also enables users to develop models more quickly and easily. If your class has access to @RISK, we recommend that you read through Section 12.5 of this chapter and then skip to Chapter 13. If you do not have access to @RISK, you will nevertheless see through the examples in this chapter that Excel by itself—without any add-ins—is a very powerful simulation tool.

12.2 Actual Applications of Simulation

There are many published applications of simulation. These cover a wide variety of topics, as we will discuss briefly in this section.

Burger King developed a simulation model for its restaurants (see Swart and Donno [8]). This model was used to justify business decisions such as the following:

- Should a restaurant open a second drive-through window?
- How much would customer waiting time increase if a new sandwich were added to the menu?

Many companies (Cummins Engine, Merck, Proctor and Gamble, Kodak, and United Airlines, to name a few) have used simulation to determine which of several possible investment projects they should choose. This is often referred to as **risk analysis** (see Hertz [4]).

As an example, consider a situation where a company must choose a single investment. If the future cash flows for each investment project are known with certainty, then most companies advocate choosing the investment with the largest net present value (NPV). However, if future cash flows are not known with certainty, then it is not clear how to choose between competing projects. Using simulation, we can obtain a frequency distribution (or histogram) for the NPV of a project. Then we can answer such questions as these:

- Which project is the riskiest?
- What is the probability that an investment will yield at least a 20% return?
- What is the probability that the NPV of an investment will be less than −\$1 billion, that is, a loss of more than \$1 billion?

When several investments are compared using simulation, it may become apparent that some are riskier than others. Therefore, contrary to what many finance textbooks advise, the investment with the largest *expected* NPV may not be the best investment; it may be too risky! In Section 12.10 we will develop a simulation model for a single investment opportunity in order to gauge its potential for large profits as well as large losses.

To illustrate the use of simulation in corporate finance, we refer to the article "A New Tool to Help Managers" (Norton [7]). This article describes a simulation model (referred to as a **Monte Carlo model**) that was used by Merck, the world's largest drug company, to determine whether Merck should pay $6.6 billion to acquire Medco, a mail-order drug company. The model contained inputs concerning the following:

- possible scenarios for the future of the U.S. healthcare system, such as a single-payer system, universal coverage, and so forth
- possible future changes in the mix of generic and brand-name drugs
- probability distributions of profit margins for each product
- assumptions about competitors' reactions to a merger with Medco

The Merck model contained thousands of equations. A simulation was performed to see how the merger would perform under various possible scenarios. As Merck's CFO, Judy Lewent, says, "Monte Carlo techniques are a very, very powerful tool to get a more intelligent look at a range of outcomes. It's almost never useful in this kind of environment to build a single bullet forecast." Merck's model indicated that the merger with Medco would benefit Merck no matter what type of health insurance plan (if any) the federal government enacts.

Other applications of simulation include the following:

1. Companies must constantly make inventory-ordering decisions in the face of unknown demand. In special cases analytic (nonsimulation) models, such as those discussed in Chapter 10, can be used to help make decisions. However, when the problems become more complex, simulation may be the only feasible solution method. We revisit the newsvendor model from Section 10.2, but we now use simulation to study the effects of uncertainty.
2. Firms must often bid against competitors in order to win a contract. If a firm's bid is too low, it will probably win the contract, but it will make very little profit on the contract. On the other hand, if the firm bids too high, it will probably not win the contract at all. The firm must decide how much to bid, although the competitors' bids are uncertain. In Section 12.6 we will develop a simulation model that can help a firm choose the bid amount that maximizes its expected profit.
3. One of the most important challenges manufacturing firms face is achieving a high level of quality in their products. They must meet the increasingly tight specifications set by their customers. Perhaps the most visible advocate of quality, Edwards Deming, stated that many companies spend too much time "tampering" with their manufacturing processes instead of making the fundamental changes that are required to achieve lasting quality. In Section 12.7 we will build a simulation model of Deming's famous funnel experiment. It clearly shows how tampering with a stable process can have a disastrous effect on quality.
4. Large corporate projects can frequently be divided into smaller activities. (A prime example is the Apollo space mission.) To create the project's schedule the company must estimate the length of time required to finish the project. It might also wish to expedite activities most critical to finishing the project in order to speed up the schedule. We discussed a version of this problem in Chapter 4 where all of the activity times were assumed to be known with certainty. It is much more realistic to assume that these times can only be estimated with probability distributions. In this case simulation is required. We will examine this topic in Section 12.8.
5. Investors face a bewildering array of securities to choose from. Some of these, such as stocks and bonds, are reasonably straightforward (although still risky).

Others, particularly derivatives (such as futures and stock options), can be extremely complex. Simulation is the perfect tool for analyzing these investment instruments. In Section 12.9 we will illustrate a fairly simple case of an investor trading in the stock market. Although the model is not difficult to construct, it clearly shows how tricky (and risky) it can be to trade in the market.

12.3 Random Numbers

All spreadsheet packages are capable of generating random numbers between 0 and 1. These are the "building blocks" of all computer simulations. In the next three sections we will show how random numbers can be generated and then used to model the uncertainty inherent in many business situations.

In Excel, you generate a random number between 0 and 1 by entering the formula

=RAND()

in any cell. (The pair of parentheses to the right of RAND indicates that this is an Excel function with no arguments. These parentheses must be included.) In addition to being between 0 and 1, the numbers created by this command have two properties that make them behave like random numbers:

1. Each time the RAND function is used, any number between 0 and 1 has the same chance of occurring. This means, for example, that approximately 10% of the numbers generated by the RAND function will be between 0.0 and 0.1; 10% of the numbers will be between 0.65 and 0.75; 60% of the numbers will be between 0.20 and 0.80; and so on. Property 1 is often expressed by saying that the random numbers are **uniformly distributed** on the interval from 0 to 1.
2. Different random numbers generated by the computer are probabilistically independent. This implies, for instance, that if we generate a random number in cell A5 and know its value, this tells us nothing about the values of any other random numbers generated in the spreadsheet. Therefore, if one call of the RAND function yields a large random number (say, 0.98) in cell A5, then there is still a 50% chance that a number generated by RAND in cell A6 (or any other cell) will yield a value less than 0.50.

To illustrate the RAND function, we generated 500 random numbers by entering the formula

=RAND()

in cell A4 and copying it to the range A4:J53. Figure 12.1 displays the output. (See the file RANDNUM.XLS.) When you try this on your PC, you'll undoubtedly obtain different random numbers. This will happen throughout this chapter and is a characteristic of simulation. No two answers are ever exactly alike! Now try the following. Press the "recalculate" (F9) key. All of the random numbers will change. In fact, each time you press the F9 key or do anything to your spreadsheet to effect a recalculation, all of the cells containing the RAND function will change.

A frequency graph (histogram) of the 500 random numbers for our illustration is shown in Figure 12.2. Since we will be constructing similar histograms fairly often in this chapter, we will explain the procedure in some detail. (Note that if you try this on your PC, the shape of your histogram will not be identical to the one shown in Figure 12.2. Again, this is because yours will be based on different random numbers.)

FIGURE 12.1 Five Hundred Random Numbers

	A	B	C	D	E	F	G	H	I	J
1	**A table of 500 random numbers found with RAND() function**									
2	Note: These are formatted to show only 4 decimal places.									
3										
4	0.1571	0.7018	0.9296	0.8013	0.8775	0.2321	0.1337	0.4223	0.1416	0.8176
5	0.2099	0.6175	0.9196	0.1203	0.7330	0.2631	0.5256	0.9364	0.2200	0.7289
6	0.7188	0.0381	0.1189	0.3727	0.1636	0.5521	0.3845	0.9131	0.8030	0.4733
7	0.4488	0.7761	0.1667	0.5321	0.0950	0.0996	0.6187	0.0807	0.4411	0.6374
8	0.3274	0.9849	0.4958	0.5034	0.2904	0.3174	0.8729	0.6704	0.4535	0.8783
9	0.1857	0.3499	0.6503	0.5366	0.8769	0.2914	0.3049	0.5008	0.8242	0.1426
10	0.3950	0.0142	0.4984	0.7464	0.0375	0.6225	0.9145	0.3736	0.6551	0.9883
11	0.2875	0.6598	0.7592	0.5123	0.4959	0.4861	0.1349	0.6656	0.5262	0.3229
12	0.2924	0.7027	0.2816	0.0519	0.1139	0.2678	0.2556	0.9344	0.5322	0.9048
13	0.3048	0.6417	0.1822	0.3859	0.2213	0.1088	0.0474	0.2807	0.5308	0.5069
14	0.7333	0.1098	0.8169	0.5106	0.3986	0.6909	0.4632	0.7650	0.3213	0.6740
15	0.6419	0.3035	0.8029	0.5182	0.5782	0.4879	0.1593	0.3410	0.8554	0.9808
16	0.8863	0.6596	0.8478	0.5853	0.5388	0.3522	0.2427	0.1544	0.4961	0.4653
17	0.7300	0.6896	0.9112	0.2035	0.0162	0.8784	0.3193	0.4189	0.9220	0.8418
18	0.8259	0.0687	0.5259	0.8397	0.7289	0.9136	0.5454	0.0330	0.1245	0.4482
19	0.8173	0.4892	0.9399	0.4732	0.2426	0.2978	0.6404	0.9153	0.0127	0.5772
20	0.3911	0.2729	0.3018	0.9836	0.1011	0.6198	0.6771	0.3908	0.7824	0.9570
21	0.9761	0.1571	0.2685	0.5161	0.4405	0.4781	0.8746	0.3590	0.5022	0.1222
22	0.5073	0.7823	0.7298	0.2741	0.2509	0.6086	0.3160	0.1992	0.2707	0.7144
23	0.4815	0.5350	0.2633	0.0479	0.2994	0.7318	0.4452	0.7058	0.2995	0.8528
24	0.0802	0.2935	0.8556	0.8600	0.0405	0.9710	0.0774	0.0101	0.8701	0.8768
25	0.9873	0.4573	0.2545	0.1641	0.8009	0.9954	0.1681	0.0047	0.2782	0.8003
26	0.8882	0.1852	0.8230	0.9003	0.5310	0.5441	0.4131	0.4304	0.7772	0.8509
27	0.1755	0.9868	0.8844	0.8214	0.0816	0.3070	0.3985	0.9120	0.9844	0.0591
28	0.3792	0.5076	0.8573	0.3202	0.8940	0.8634	0.5059	0.3717	0.2356	0.9549
29	0.2696	0.5124	0.7092	0.6612	0.0321	0.6320	0.4680	0.7358	0.7200	0.8059
30	0.3967	0.9598	0.2661	0.4018	0.5260	0.9838	0.0840	0.2157	0.9051	0.3244
31	0.2397	0.5464	0.0623	0.7350	0.9958	0.3304	0.8519	0.9651	0.5136	0.7671
32	0.1059	0.6141	0.9479	0.9455	0.6723	0.6314	0.3561	0.4432	0.6249	0.9695
33	0.4802	0.4731	0.0785	0.2146	0.3616	0.8521	0.1187	0.8615	0.1236	0.0416
34	0.8030	0.9464	0.5835	0.3993	0.2593	0.0160	0.4777	0.4100	0.4960	0.6078
35	0.9590	0.2750	0.0413	0.9135	0.2544	0.6015	0.7557	0.2179	0.3668	0.5415
36	0.0474	0.0289	0.0937	0.2986	0.7364	0.2762	0.3746	0.7959	0.9796	0.6080
37	0.4602	0.8486	0.9310	0.2123	0.9305	0.0604	0.5127	0.0875	0.2330	0.8739
38	0.9188	0.5205	0.6819	0.9683	0.9750	0.8679	0.8820	0.7899	0.6110	0.1645
39	0.7488	0.1928	0.9000	0.9373	0.0512	0.1176	0.8773	0.2793	0.3080	0.4411
40	0.0806	0.5348	0.5693	0.3841	0.2949	0.3727	0.5477	0.1074	0.8011	0.7974
41	0.8202	0.2919	0.4224	0.5251	0.1192	0.4047	0.4243	0.7156	0.7220	0.7240
42	0.7165	0.4522	0.0021	0.4148	0.4537	0.0334	0.7813	0.8120	0.5252	0.7812
43	0.7986	0.9013	0.3610	0.8434	0.3528	0.4132	0.5251	0.8419	0.5936	0.4303
44	0.1928	0.7455	0.3903	0.6851	0.1992	0.1405	0.6031	0.3937	0.1930	0.2842
45	0.1090	0.8415	0.1694	0.4441	0.5369	0.5177	0.2014	0.0089	0.6599	0.2734
46	0.6355	0.9975	0.7155	0.3668	0.4809	0.0569	0.6830	0.1158	0.9449	0.8476
47	0.7552	0.9082	0.2980	0.8130	0.2740	0.6759	0.2817	0.7671	0.9115	0.4248
48	0.2666	0.9570	0.2365	0.0945	0.9553	0.8040	0.3593	0.4586	0.9660	0.2965
49	0.5492	0.8722	0.3391	0.8210	0.1583	0.6737	0.2224	0.6890	0.5926	0.1015
50	0.2417	0.9629	0.3951	0.7452	0.9830	0.2003	0.5491	0.0491	0.1535	0.0687
51	0.6330	0.7350	0.0997	0.9012	0.3852	0.7213	0.6602	0.8335	0.2720	0.0439
52	0.8278	0.3685	0.8210	0.1179	0.1465	0.7809	0.5550	0.9325	0.9444	0.3111
53	0.9665	0.0842	0.4802	0.6854	0.7480	0.4311	0.3202	0.3542	0.0926	0.7256

Forming Frequency Tables and Histograms

First, you may be aware that there is a Histogram option with the Tools/Data Analysis menu item. Although this provides a one-step method for generating a histogram, it has a serious drawback for this chapter, namely, it does not retain a link to the data from which it is formed. That is, if we use this method to form a histogram of the 500 numbers in Figure 12.1, and then we change these numbers by pressing the F9 recalculate key, the histogram will *not* change. The following method does not have this drawback; it retains the link to the data.

FIGURE 12.2 Histogram of the 500 Random Numbers

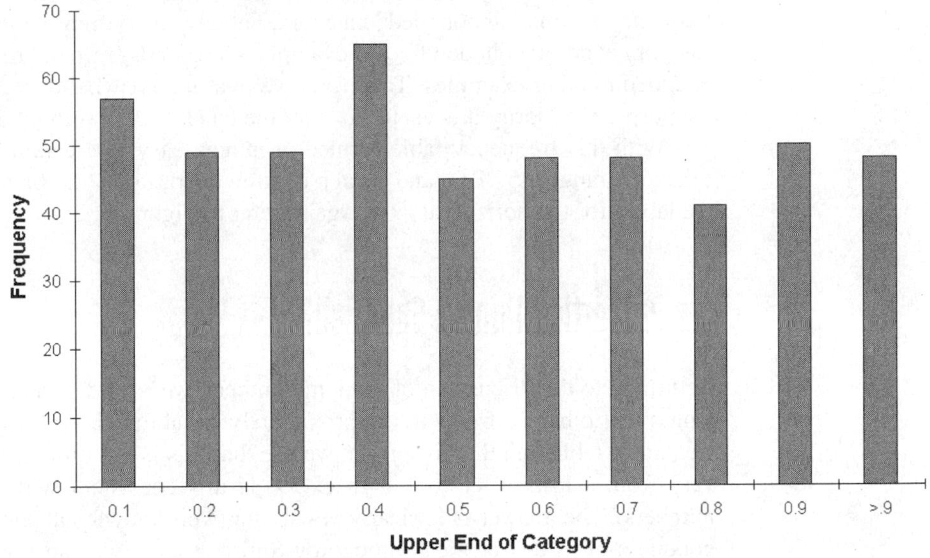

In some unused section of the spreadsheet, we first form a frequency table of the data. The frequency table for our example appears in Figure 12.3. Suppose we want to know how many of the 500 observations are between 0 and 0.1, how many are between 0.1 and 0.2, and so on up to the interval 0.9 to 1.0.

1 **Define categories.** Enter the upper limit of all of the categories *except the last category* in the range A57:A65. That is, enter 0.1 through 0.9 in these cells. (Leave cell A66 blank for now.)

2 **Calculate frequencies.** Select the range B57:B66, type the *array* formula

=FREQUENCY(A4:J53,A57:A65)

and press Ctrl-Shift-Enter. (Press all three keys at once.) This counts the numbers of observations—the frequencies—in each of the categories.

Notice that the FREQUENCY function has two arguments. The first is the range where the data are. The second is the range that defines the category boundaries. In gen-

FIGURE 12.3 Frequency Table of the 500 Random Numbers

	A	B	C
55	Distribution of random numbers		
56	Value	Frequency	
57	0.1	45	
58	0.2	45	
59	0.3	58	
60	0.4	51	
61	0.5	48	
62	0.6	48	
63	0.7	41	
64	0.8	47	
65	0.9	58	
66	>.9	59	

eral, the range where you put the frequencies (B57:B66) is one cell longer than the range that defines the category boundaries (A57:A65). The extra cell (B66) then contains the frequency for the "unbounded" category, namely, everything above 0.9. Admittedly, this category is not unbounded for our example—it extends from 0.9 to 1.0—but it is often unbounded in other examples. Therefore, we treat it somewhat differently. Nevertheless, for the purpose of clarity it is useful to enter the label ">.9" (without the quotes) in cell A66.

With this frequency table formed, it is now easy to create a histogram. You simply select the range A57:B66 and form a column chart, using the first column (column A) as the labels for the horizontal axis. Again, refer to Figure 12.2.

Are Properties 1 and 2 Satisfied?

Returning to the discussion of random numbers, we would expect each of the intervals of length 0.1 to have a frequency approximately equal to $0.1 \times 500 = 50$. By looking at the frequency table and the histogram, we see that this is not quite the case. The frequencies vary from a low of 41 to a high of 59. Is this consistent with Property 1 of random numbers? The answer is basically yes. Using well-known statistical tests (the chi-square goodness-of-fit test or the Kolmogorov-Smirnov test), we can formally test whether this sample of 500 random numbers is consistent with Property 1, that is, whether this sample has equal frequencies across categories. Due to inherent randomness, we will almost never get exactly the same frequencies in all categories, but the formal tests indicate that the apparent discrepancies in Figure 12.2 can be attributed to chance.

To check whether these random numbers are consistent with Property 2, we determined the fraction of time a "small" random number was immediately followed by a "large" random number. Here we define "small" as less than 0.5 and "large" as greater than 0.5. A straightforward count shows that 51% of the small random numbers were immediately followed by a large random number, which appears to be consistent with the independence property. Actually, this is not enough to *verify* the independence property. It could be that 90% of the time, two *consecutive* small random numbers are followed by a large random number. This would violate the independence property. Suffice it to say, it is difficult to verify that a spreadsheet's method for generating random numbers satisfies the independence property, so from here on we will assume that this property is satisfied.

Freezing Random Numbers

As you will see through this chapter, the automatic recalculation of random numbers can be useful sometimes and annoying other times. There are situations where you may want the random numbers to stay fixed, that is, you want to "freeze" them at their current values. The following method will do this.

1 **Select range.** Select the range that you want to freeze, such as A4:J53 in Figure 12.1.

2 **Copy.** Use the Copy command to copy this range.

3 **Paste Special with Values option.** With the range still selected, select Paste Special from the Edit menu, choose the Values option, and click on OK. This procedure pastes a copy of the range onto itself, except that the entries are now *numbers*, not *formulas*. Therefore, whenever you recalculate, these numbers will not change.

If you open the RANDNUM.XLS file, you'll notice that there are two "live" sheets, one for the random numbers and one for the histogram, and two frozen sheets. If you press F9, the live sheets change, whereas the frozen sheets don't.

As mentioned earlier, you may at times wish to freeze random numbers. We will tell you when to do so. By the way, this use of the Copy and Paste Special/Values commands is useful anytime you want to replace a formula (RAND or otherwise) with the value generated by the formula.

PROBLEMS

Skill-Building Problems

1 Use the RAND function and the Copy command to generate a set of 100 random numbers.

a What fraction of the random numbers are smaller than 0.5?

b What fraction of the time is a random number less than 0.5 followed by a random number greater than 0.5?

c What fraction of the random numbers are larger than 0.8?

d Freeze these random numbers. However, instead of pasting them over the original random numbers, paste them onto a new range. Then press the F9 recalculate key. The original random numbers should change, but the pasted copy should remain the same.

2 We all hate to bring change to a store. By using random numbers, we can eliminate the need for change and give the store and the customer a fair deal.

a Suppose that you buy something for 20¢. How could you use random numbers (built into the cash register system) to decide whether you should pay $1.00 or nothing? This would eliminate the need for change!

b If you bought something for $9.60, how would you use random numbers to eliminate the need for change?

c In the long run, why is this method fair to both the store and the customers? Would you personally (as a customer) be willing to abide by such a system? ■

12.4 Introduction to Spreadsheet Simulation

On this section we show how spreadsheets can be used to perform simulations in which the uncertainty occurs through one or more *discrete* random variables. For our purposes, a random variable is discrete if it has only a finite number of possible values. To illustrate, we show how to simulate a simple newsvendor problem on a spreadsheet. Such a problem, which was analyzed by other methods in Chapter 10, occurs when a company (such as a newsvendor) must make a one-time purchase of a product (such as a newspaper) to meet customer demands for a certain period of time. A "newsvendor" problem is any problem analogous to that faced by people ordering daily newspapers. If they order too few newspapers, they will lose potential profit by not having enough to satisfy their customers, but if they order too many, they will have worthless newspapers left over at the end of the day. The following example illustrates this basic problem in a slightly different context.

EXAMPLE 12.1

In August, Walton Bookstore must decide how many of next year's nature calendars to order. Each calendar costs the bookstore $7.50 and is sold for $10. After February 1 all unsold calendars are returned to the publisher for a refund of $2.50 per calendar. Walton believes that the number of calendars it can sell by February 1 follows the probability distribution shown in Table 12.1. Walton wants to maximize the expected profit from calendar sales. Specifically, the company wants to use simulation to determine the number of calendars to order in August.

TABLE 12.1 **Probability Distribution of Demand for Walton Example**

Calendars Demanded	Probability
100	0.30
150	0.20
200	0.30
250	0.15
300	0.05

Solution

For a *fixed* order quantity, we will show how Excel can be used to simulate 50 replications (or any other number of replications). Each replication is an independent replay of Walton's problem. To illustrate, suppose we want to estimate the expected profit if 200 calendars are ordered. Figure 12.4 illustrates the results obtained by simulating 50 independent replications for an order quantity of 200 calendars. (See the file WALTON1.XLS.) Here's an explanation of how we created Figure 12.4. (*Note*: To fit this spreadsheet on a single page, we've "hidden" rows 17 through 54 with the Format/Rows/Hide command.)

1 **Inputs.** Enter the cost data in the range B4:B6, the probability distribution of demand in the range D5:F9, and the proposed order quantity, 200, in cell B9. Pay particular attention to the way we entered the probability distribution. Columns D and F contain the individual probabilities and demand values from Table 12.1. It is also convenient (see Step 3 for the reasoning) to have the cumulative probabilities in column E. To obtain these, first enter the value 0 in cell E5. Then enter the formula

=D5+E5

in cell E6 and copy it to the range E7:E9 to generate the cumulative probabilities.

2 **Generate random numbers.** Enter a random number in cell B13 with the formula

=RAND()

and copy this to the range B14:B62. Finally, freeze the random numbers in the B13:B62 range as described earlier, that is, with the Copy and Paste Special/Values commands. (*Important note*: From here on, the numbers in your spreadsheet will probably differ from those shown here. They differ because your RAND functions will generate *different* random numbers than the ones we generated.)

3 **Generate demands.** The key to the simulation is the generation of the customer demands in the range C13:C62 from the random numbers in column B and the probability distribution of demand. Here's how it works. We divide the interval from 0 to 1 into five segments: from 0.0 to 0.3 (length 0.3), from 0.3 to 0.5 (length 0.2), from 0.5 to 0.8 (length 0.3), from 0.8 to 0.95 (length 0.15), and from 0.95 to 1.0 (length 0.05). These lengths are the probabilities of the various demands. Then we assign a demand to each random number depending on which interval the random number falls in. For example, the random number in cell A13, 0.5279, falls in the third interval, so we assign the third possible demand value, 200, to this replication.

There are two ways to implement this procedure. The first is to use a nested IF statement in cell C13 (and copy it down column C). However, this is quite complex

FIGURE 12.4 Simulation for Walton Example

	A	B	C	D	E	F	G	H
1	**Simulation of Walton's bookstore**							
2								
3	**Cost data**			**Demand distribution**				
4	Unit cost	$7.50		Probability	Cum Prob	Demand		
5	Unit price	$10.00		0.30	0.00	100		
6	Unit refund	$2.50		0.20	0.30	150		
7				0.30	0.50	200		
8	**Decision variable**			0.15	0.80	250		
9	Order quantity	200		0.05	0.95	300		
10								
11	**Simulation**							
12	Replication	Random number	Demand	Revenue	Cost	Refund	Profit	
13	1	0.5279	200	$2,000.00	$1,500.00	$0.00	$500.00	
14	2	0.9117	250	$2,000.00	$1,500.00	$0.00	$500.00	
15	3	0.5765	200	$2,000.00	$1,500.00	$0.00	$500.00	
16	4	0.0251	100	$1,000.00	$1,500.00	$250.00	($250.00)	
55	43	0.6565	200	$2,000.00	$1,500.00	$0.00	$500.00	
56	44	0.3903	150	$1,500.00	$1,500.00	$125.00	$125.00	
57	45	0.1965	100	$1,000.00	$1,500.00	$250.00	($250.00)	
58	46	0.3585	150	$1,500.00	$1,500.00	$125.00	$125.00	
59	47	0.0231	100	$1,000.00	$1,500.00	$250.00	($250.00)	
60	48	0.7556	200	$2,000.00	$1,500.00	$0.00	$500.00	
61	49	0.4388	150	$1,500.00	$1,500.00	$125.00	$125.00	
62	50	0.8324	250	$2,000.00	$1,500.00	$0.00	$500.00	
63						AvgProfit	$222.50	
64						StDevProfit	$328.58	
65						MinProfit	($250.00)	
66						MaxProfit	$500.00	
67								
68						95% confidence interval for mean profit		
69						Lower limit	$131.42	
70						Upper limit	$313.58	

even for a demand distribution with only five values; it becomes unmanageable for a demand distribution with many possible values. A simpler way is to use the VLOOKUP function. To do this, we create a "lookup table" in the range E5:F9. This table has the cumulative probabilities in column E and the possible demand values in column F. In fact, we entered the cumulative probabilities in column E specifically so that the VLOOKUP command could be used. To generate the simulated demands, first give the range E5:F9 the name Lookup. (Use the Insert/Name/Define command or enter the name directly in the left-hand side of the formula bar.) Then enter the formula

=VLOOKUP(B13,Lookup,2)

in cell C13 and copy it to the range C14:C62. For each random number in column B, this function compares the random number to the values in E5:E9 and returns the appropriate demand from F5:F9.[1]

This step is the key to the simulation, so make sure you understand exactly what it entails. The rest is "bookkeeping," as we illustrate in the following steps.

4 **Revenue.** Once the demand is known, the number of calendars sold is the smaller of the demand and the order quantity. For example, if 150 calendars are demanded, 150 will be sold. But if 250 are demanded, only 200 can be sold (since Walton orders only 200). Therefore, to calculate the revenue for the first replication in cell D13, enter the formula

=$B$5*MIN(C13,$B$9)

[1]You might be wondering what happens if a random number in column A falls exactly on one of the "breakpoints" in E5:E9. Fortunately, we don't have to worry about this because the chance of it happening is virtually 0.

5 **Ordering cost.** The cost of ordering the calendars does not depend on the demand; it is the unit cost multiplied by the number ordered. Calculate this cost in cell E13 with the formula

=$B$4*$B$9

6 **Refund.** If the order quantity is greater than the demand, there is a refund of $2.50 for each calendar left over; otherwise, there is no refund. Therefore, enter the total refund for the first replication in cell F13 with the formula

=$B$6*MAX($B$9–C13,0)

For example, if demand is 150, then 50 calendars are left over, and this MAX is 50, the larger of 50 and 0. However, if demand is 250, then no calendars are left over, and this MAX is 0, the larger of −50 and 0. (This calculation could also be accomplished with a slightly more complex IF function.)

7 **Profit.** Calculate the profit for the first replication in cell G13 with the formula

=D13–E13+F13

8 **Copy to other rows.** Do the same bookkeeping for the other 49 replications by copying the range D13:G13 to the range D14:G62.

9 **Summary measures.** Each profit value in column G corresponds to one randomly generated demand. We usually want to see how these vary from one replication to another. First, calculate the average and standard deviation of the 50 profits in cells G63 and G64 with the formulas

=AVERAGE(G13:G62)

and

=STDEV(G13:G62)

Then calculate the smallest and largest of the 50 profits in cells G65 and G66 with the formulas

=MIN(G13:G62)

and

=MAX(G13:G62)

10 **Confidence interval for expected profit.** Finally, calculate an approximate 95% confidence interval for the expected profit in cells G69 and G70 with the formulas

=G63–NORMSINV(.975)*G64/SQRT(50)

and

=G63+NORMSINV(.975)*G64/SQRT(50)

Here, NORMSINV(.975), which equals 1.96, is the standard normal value that cuts off probability 0.025 in each tail of the standard normal distribution. (See the next subsection for a discussion of confidence intervals.)

At this point it's a good idea to stand back and see what we've accomplished. First, in the body of the simulation, rows 13 through 62, we randomly generated 50 possible demands and the corresponding profits. Notice that because there are only five possible demand values (100, 150, 200, 250, and 300), there are only five possible profit values: −$250, $125, $500, $500, and $500. Also, notice that for our order quantity, 200, the profit is $500 regardless of whether demand is 200, 250, or 300. A look at the profit values in these rows (including the hidden rows) indicates that there were 14 trials with profit equal to −\$250 (demand 100), 9 trials with profit equal to \$125 (demand 150), and 27 trials with profit equal to \$500 (demand 200, 250, or 300). The average of these 50 profits is \$222.50, and their standard deviation is \$328.58. (Again, remember that your answers will probably differ from these because your random numbers will differ from those shown in Figure 12.4.)

Typically we want a computer simulation to yield one or more output variables, such as profit, for our analysis. These output variables depend on random inputs, such as demand. Our goal is to estimate probability distributions of the outputs. In the Walton simulation we estimate the probability distribution of profit to be:

$$\Pr(\text{Profit} = -\$250) = 14/50$$

$$\Pr(\text{Profit} = \$125) = 9/50$$

$$\Pr(\text{Profit} = \$500) = 27/50$$

We also estimate the mean of this distribution to be \$222.50 and its standard deviation to be \$328.58.

It is important to realize that if the entire simulation were run again with different random numbers (such as the ones you might have generated on your PC), the answers would be slightly different. This is the reason for the confidence interval in cells G69 and G70. This interval expresses our uncertainty about the mean of the profit distribution. Our best guess for this mean is the average of the 50 profits we happened to observe. However, because the corresponding confidence interval is very wide, from \$131.42 to \$313.58, we are not at all sure of the *true* mean of the profit distribution. If we ran this simulation again with different random numbers, the average profit might be quite different than the average profit we observed, \$222.50.

Some Notes About Confidence Intervals

It is common in computer simulations to estimate the mean of some distribution by the average of the simulated observations, just as we estimated the mean of the profit distribution by the average of 50 profits. The usual practice is then to accompany this estimate with a **confidence interval**, which indicates the accuracy of the estimate. You should recall from statistics that in order to obtain a confidence interval for the mean, you start with the estimated mean and then add and subtract a multiple of the *standard error* of the estimated mean. If we denote the estimated mean (that is, the average) by $\overline{X}$, we have

$$\text{Confidence interval for the mean} = \overline{X} \pm (\text{Multiple} \times \text{Standard Error of } \overline{X})$$

The standard error of $\overline{X}$ is the standard deviation of the observations divided by the square root of n, the number of observations:

$$\text{Standard error of } \overline{X} = \frac{\text{Standard deviation of observations}}{\sqrt{n}} = \frac{s}{\sqrt{n}}$$

Here, s is the symbol for the standard deviation of the observations. We obtain it with the STDEV function in Excel.

The "multiple" in the confidence interval formula depends on the confidence level and the number of observations. If the confidence level is 95%, for example, then the multiple is usually very close to 2, so a good guideline is to go out two standard errors on either side of the average to obtain an approximate 95% confidence interval for the mean:

$$\overline{X} \pm 2\frac{s}{\sqrt{n}}$$

To be more precise, if n is reasonably large (which is almost always the case in simulations), the Central Limit Theorem from statistics implies that the correct multiple is the number from the standard normal distribution that cuts off probability .025 in each tail. We found this number, 1.96, by using the NORMSINV function in the Walton example. Of course, since 1.96 is very close to 2, it would be acceptable for all practical purposes to use 2 instead of 1.96 when forming the confidence interval.

Analysts often plan a simulation so that the confidence interval for the mean of some important output will be sufficiently narrow. The reasoning is that narrow confidence intervals imply more precision about the estimated mean of the output variable. If the confidence level is fixed at some value such as 95%, then the only way to narrow the confidence interval is to simulate more trials. Assuming that the confidence level is 95%, the following value of n is required to ensure that the resulting confidence interval will have length equal to some prespecified value L.

$$n = \frac{16 \times (\text{Estimated Stdev})^2}{L^2}$$

To use this formula, we must have an estimate of the standard deviation of the output variable.

For example, in the Walton simulation we saw that with $n = 50$, the resulting 95% confidence interval for the mean profit had length \$313.58 − \$131.42 = \$182.16. Suppose that we want to reduce this length to \$50, that is, we want $L =$ \$50. We are not sure what the exact standard deviation of the profit distribution is, but an estimate from the simulation is \$328.58. Therefore, to obtain (approximately) the required L, we need to simulate n trials, where

$$n = \frac{16 \times 328.58^2}{50^2} = 690.97$$

(The usual practice is to round this up to 691.) The claim, then, is that if we rerun the simulation with 691 trials rather than 50 trials, the length of the 95% confidence interval for the mean profit should be close to \$50.

Finding the Best Order Quantity

We are not yet finished with the Walton example.

EXAMPLE 12.1 CONTINUED

So far, we have run the simulation for only a single order quantity, 200. Walton's ultimate goal is to find the *best* order quantity, that is, the order quantity that maximizes the mean profit.

Solution

We can do this with a data table. Specifically, we can use a data table to rerun the simulation (using the *same* 50 random demands) for other order quantities. We show this data table in Figure 12.5. (This is still part of the WALTON1.XLS file.) To form this table, enter the trial order quantities shown in the range A76:A84, enter the formula

=G63

in cell B75 and select the data table range, A75:B84. Then use the Data/Table command,

FIGURE 12.5 **Data Table for Walton Example**

	A	B	C	D	E
72	Data table for average profit as a function of the order quantity				
73					
74	Order quantity	AvgProfit			
75		$222.50			
76	100	$250.00			
77	125	$260.00			
78	150	$270.00			
79	175	$246.25			
80	200	$222.50			
81	225	$146.25			
82	250	$70.00			
83	275	($47.50)			
84	300	($165.00)			

FIGURE 12.6 **Average Profit Versus Order Quantity for Walton Example**

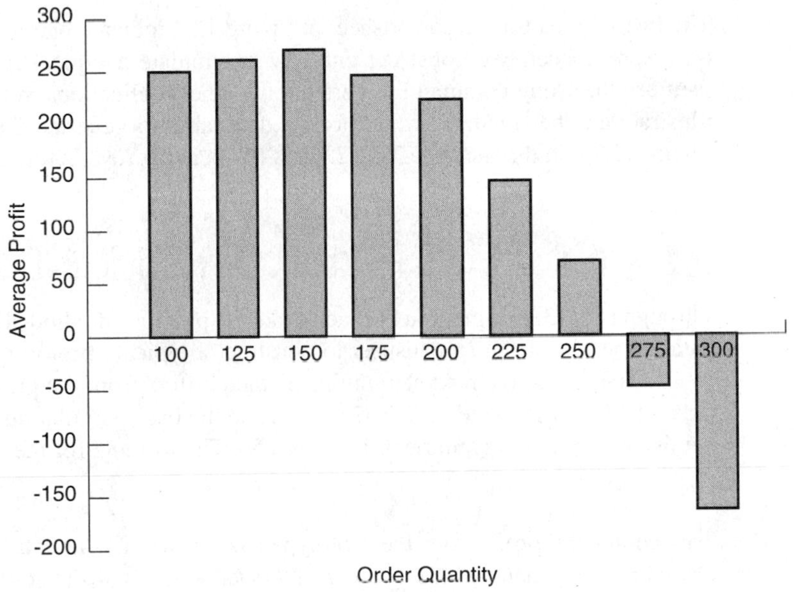

specifying that the single (column) input cell is B9 (see Figure 12.4). Finally, construct a bar chart of the average profits in the data table (see Figure 12.6).

Notice that an order quantity of 150 appears to maximize the average profit. Its average profit of $270 is slightly higher than the average profits from nearby order quantities and much higher than the profit gained from an order of 225 or more calendars. However, again keep in mind that this is a simulation, so that all of these average profits depend on the particular random numbers generated. If we reran the simulation with different random numbers, it is conceivable that some other order quantity could be best.

Before concluding this subsection, we make one other observation. In the Walton simulation we suggested that you freeze the random numbers in column B. If you neglect this step, then every time you press the F9 key, a new set of simulated answers (including those in the data table) will appear. Depending on the speed of your computer, this recalculation can take a long time, even for this relatively small simulation. For larger simulations the recalculation time can be quite large, which is one of the primary reasons you might want to freeze your random numbers right away.[2] However, the drawback is that once the random numbers are frozen, you are stuck with that particular set of random numbers. In most of the rest of this chapter, we will *not* freeze the random numbers. This way we will be able to generate many different scenarios simply by pressing the F9 key.

There is another advantage to freezing the random numbers in this example. When we build the data to compare order quantities, each order quantity experiences the *same* 50 demands. To see the effect of this, look at the "Walton1—Live" sheet and the accompanying live bar chart in the WALTON1.XLS file. Here we did not freeze the random numbers. Therefore, in the data table, each order quantity experiences different demands. As you can see by viewing the bar chart and pressing F9, the "best" order quantity changes considerably from one set of random demands to another. This would not occur, at least not to this extent, if all order quantities experienced the same demands.

Using a Data Table to Repeat Simulations

The instructions for the spreadsheet in Figure 12.4 indicate one way to build a simulation on a spreadsheet. We construct one row to simulate a typical replication (row 13) and then use the Copy command to perform the other replications in the simulation. We now illustrate another method, which uses a data table to generate the replications. Refer to Figure 12.7 and the file WALTON2.XLS. (Notice that rows 25 through 60 are hidden.)

EXAMPLE 12.1 CONTINUED

Through row 13, this method is exactly like the previous method. That is, we use the given data at the top of the spreadsheet to construct a typical "prototype" of the simulation in row 13. However, the next step in this method differs from the previous method: we form a data table in the range A17:B67 to replicate the basic simulation 50 times. In column A we list the replication numbers, 1 through 50. The formula for the data table in cell B17 is

=F13

This copies the profit from the prototype row for use in the data table. Then we use the Data/Table command with *any blank cell* (such as C18) as the column input cell. (No row input cell is necessary.) This tricks Excel into repeating the row 13 calculations 50 times, each time with a new random number. Each time the profit is reported. (If you wanted to see other simulated quantities, such as the revenue, for each replication, you could add extra output columns to the data table.)

To understand why this procedure works, you need to understand how a data table is formed. When you form a data table, Excel takes each value in the left-hand column of the data table (here column A), substitutes it into the cell you designate as the column input cell, recalculates the spreadsheet, and returns the "bottom line" value (or values) you've

[2] Here is a useful Excel tip for speeding up recalculation. Use the Tools/Option command, click on the Calculation tab, click on the Automatic Except Tables option, and click on OK. Now when you enter anything new into your spreadsheet, everything will recalculate in the normal way *except* data tables. Data tables will not recalculate until you intentionally press the F9 key. As you'll see after working through examples in this chapter, data tables can require lots of computing time, so this feature can come in very handy.

FIGURE 12.7 Simulation with a Data Table for Walton Example

	A	B	C	D	E	F
1	Simulation of Walton's bookstore					
2						
3	Cost data			Demand distribution		
4	Unit cost	$7.50		Probability	CumProb	Demand
5	Unit price	$10.00		0.30	0.00	100
6	Unit refund	$2.50		0.20	0.30	150
7				0.30	0.50	200
8	Decision variable			0.15	0.80	250
9	Order quantity	200		0.05	0.95	300
10						
11	Simulation					
12	Random number	Demand	Revenue	Cost	Refund	Profit
13	0.2713	100	$1,000.00	$1,500.00	$250.00	($250.00)
14						
15	Data table for replications, each shows profit from that replication					
16	Replication	Profit				
17		($250.00)				
18	1	$500.00				
19	2	($250.00)				
20	3	$500.00				
21	4	$125.00				
22	5	($250.00)				
23	6	$500.00				
24	7	$500.00				
61	44	($250.00)				
62	45	$500.00				
63	46	$500.00				
64	47	$125.00				
65	48	($250.00)				
66	49	($250.00)				
67	50	($250.00)				
68	Average	$215.00				
69	StDev	$343.53				
70	Minimum	($250.00)				
71	Maximum	$500.00				
72						
73	95% confidence interval for mean profit					
74	Lower limit	$119.78				
75	Upper limit	$310.22				

requested in the top row of the data table (such as average profit). It may seem silly to substitute each replication number from column A into a blank cell such as cell C18, but this method causes the sample simulation in row 13 to be recalculated with *new* random numbers, which is exactly what we want.

Of course, this means that you should *not* freeze the random number in cell A13 before forming the data table. The whole point of the data table is to use a different random number for each trial, and this will occur only if the random number from the typical trial in row 13 is left unfrozen. (The only reason for including a frozen sheet in the WALTON2.XLS file is that we needed a stable version in order to create Figure 12.7.)

We can carry this method one step further to see how the profit depends on the order quantity. Here we use a *two-way* data table with the replication number along the side and possible order quantities along the top. See Figure 12.8 and the file WALTON3.XLS. Now the data table range is A17:F67, and the driving formula, entered in cell A17, is again

=F13

The *column* input cell should again be any blank cell, but the *row* input cell should be B9 (the order quantity). Each cell in the body of the data table shows a simulated profit for a particular trial and a particular order quantity, and each is based on a *different* random number. (This is somewhat different than the data table in Figure 12.5, where we used the *same* random numbers for the various order quantities.)

By averaging the numbers in each column of the data table (see row 68), we again see that 150 appears to be the best order quantity. It is also helpful to construct a bar chart of these averages, as shown in Figure 12.9. To see whether 150 is always the best order quantity, try pressing the F9 key. (Again, we assume you haven't frozen any random numbers in the spreadsheet.) The entire data table, and hence the averages in row 68 and the corresponding graph, should all change. Keep pressing the F9 key to see whether an order quantity of 150 continues to be the winner!

By now you should appreciate the usefulness of data tables in spreadsheet simulations. They allow you to take a "prototype" simulation and replicate its key results as often as you like. This method makes summary statistics (over the entire group of replications) and corresponding charts easy to obtain. Admittedly, data tables can be a bit confusing at first,

FIGURE 12.8 **Average Profit Versus Order Quantity Using a Data Table for Walton Example**

	A	B	C	D	E	F
1	**Simulation of Walton's bookstore**					
2						
3	**Cost data**			**Demand distribution**		
4	Unit cost	$7.50		Probability	CumProb	Demand
5	Unit price	$10.00		0.30	0.00	100
6	Unit refund	$2.50		0.20	0.30	150
7				0.30	0.50	200
8	**Decision variable**			0.15	0.80	250
9	Order quantity	200		0.05	0.95	300
10						
11	**Simulation**					
12	Random number	Demand	Revenue	Cost	Refund	Profit
13	0.5830	200	$2,000.00	$1,500.00	$0.00	$500.00
14						
15	**Data table showing profit for replications with various order quantities**					
16	Replication			Order quantity		
17	$500.00	100	150	200	250	300
18	1	$250.00	$375.00	$500.00	($500.00)	$0.00
19	2	$250.00	$375.00	($250.00)	($125.00)	($375.00)
20	3	$250.00	$0.00	($250.00)	$250.00	$0.00
21	4	$250.00	$375.00	$500.00	$250.00	($750.00)
22	5	$250.00	$375.00	$500.00	$250.00	($750.00)
23	6	$250.00	$375.00	($250.00)	($500.00)	$0.00
24	7	$250.00	$375.00	$500.00	($125.00)	($750.00)
61	44	$250.00	$375.00	$500.00	$625.00	$0.00
62	45	$250.00	$375.00	$500.00	$625.00	($750.00)
63	46	$250.00	$375.00	($250.00)	$250.00	($750.00)
64	47	$250.00	$0.00	($250.00)	$250.00	$0.00
65	48	$250.00	$0.00	$500.00	($500.00)	($375.00)
66	49	$250.00	$375.00	$125.00	$625.00	($375.00)
67	50	$250.00	$375.00	$500.00	$625.00	$750.00
68	Averages	$250.00	$255.00	$200.00	$62.50	($345.00)

FIGURE 12.9 **Average Profit Versus Order Quantity**

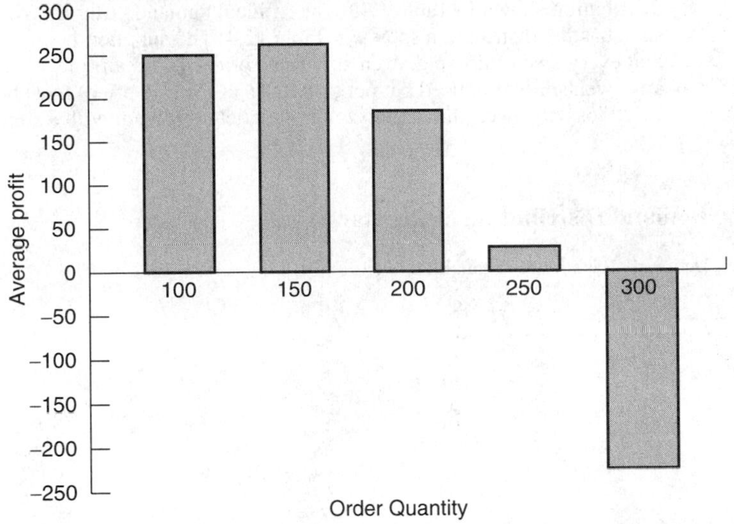

but they become second nature after a few uses. In the rest of this chapter, you will have plenty of opportunities to increase your data table skills! ■

PROBLEMS

Skill-Building Problems

3 Explain why an order quantity other than one of the possible demands cannot maximize the expected profit. (*Hint*: Consider an order of 190 calendars. If this maximizes expected profit, then it must yield a higher expected profit than an order of 150 or 100. But then an order of 200 calendars must also yield a larger expected profit than 190 calendars. Why?)

4 In August 1997, a car dealer is trying to determine how many 1998 cars to order. Each car ordered in August 1997 costs $10,000. The demand for the dealer's 1998 models has the probability distribution shown in Table 12.2. Each car sells for $15,000. If demand for 1998 cars exceeds the number of cars ordered in August, the dealer must reorder at a cost of $12,000 per car. Excess cars can be disposed of at $9000 per car. Use simulation to determine how many cars to order in August. For your optimal order quantity, find a 95% confidence interval for the expected profit.

5 In the Walton Bookstore example, suppose that Walton receives no money for the first 50 excess calendars returned but receives $2.50 for every calendar after the first 50 returned. Does this change the optimal order quantity?

6 A sweatshirt supplier is trying to decide how many sweatshirts to print for the upcoming NCAA basketball championships. The final four teams have emerged from the quarterfinal round, and there is now a week left until the semifinals, which are then followed in a couple of days by the finals. Each sweatshirt costs $10 to produce and sells for $25. However, in three weeks any

TABLE 12.2 **Demand Distribution for Car Problem**

Cars Demanded	Probability
20	0.30
25	0.15
30	0.15
35	0.20
40	0.20

leftover sweatshirts will be put on sale for half price, $12.50. The supplier assumes that the demand for his sweatshirts during the next three weeks (when interest is at its highest) has the distribution shown in Table 12.3. The residual demand, after the sweatshirts have been put on sale, has the distribution shown in Table 12.4. The supplier, being a profit maximizer, realizes that every sweatshirt sold, even at the sale price, yields a profit. However, he also realizes that any sweatshirts produced but not sold (even at the sale price) must be thrown away, resulting in a $10 loss per sweatshirt. Analyze the supplier's problem with a simulation spreadsheet. ■

TABLE 12.3 **Demand Distribution at Regular Price**

Demand (1000s)	Probability
7	.05
8	.10
9	.25
10	.30
11	.20
12	.10

TABLE 12.4 **Demand Distribution at Reduced Price**

Demand (1000s)	Probability
2	.20
3	.30
4	.20
5	.15
6	.10
7	.05

12.5 Generating Other Distributions

We have seen that the RAND function is capable of generating numbers that are uniformly distributed between 0 and 1. In words, a value generated by this function is *equally likely* to be anywhere within the 0 to 1 interval. However, in many situations we want the random numbers to have a probability distribution other than this uniform distribution. For example, it might be more realistic to have a bell-shaped distribution (like the one shown in Figure 12.10) or a skewed distribution (like the one shown in Figure 12.11). Is this possible within Excel?

If the desired distribution is discrete, with a finite (usually small) number of possible values with known probabilities, then we can use the RAND function along with a VLOOKUP function to generate the random numbers. In fact, this is exactly what we did in the Walton Bookstore example to generate demands. This method allows us to generate random numbers from any discrete distribution—symmetric, skewed, bimodal, or whatever—simply by setting up the lookup table correctly. However, it is often convenient to use *continuous* distributions in a simulation. For example, we assumed in the Walton example that the possible demands are 100, 150, 200, 250, and 300. It is more realistic to assume that the possible demands form a continuum, say, from 0 to some large value such as 500.[3]

[3]Strictly speaking, the set of possible values would not be a continuum since only integer values are allowed for a product such as calendars, but we can easily handle this by rounding fractional demands to integers.

FIGURE 12.10 **Bell-shaped Distribution**

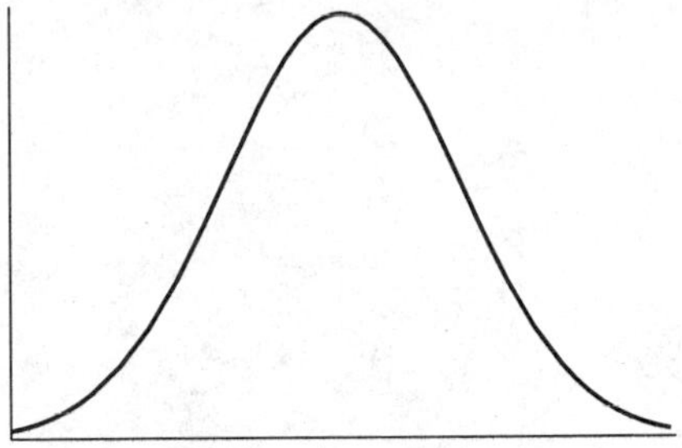

FIGURE 12.11 **Skewed Distribution**

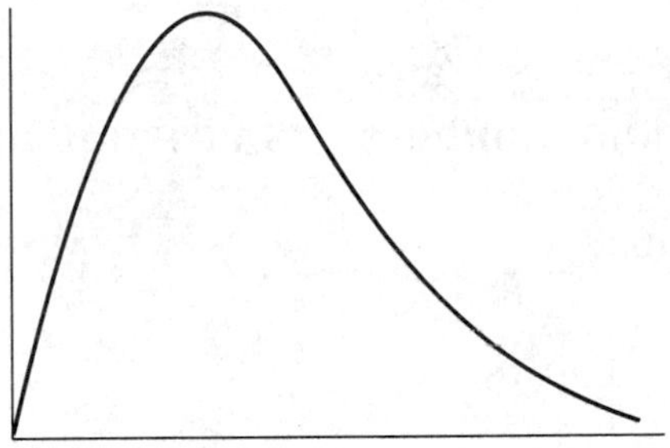

The question, then, is how to use the RAND command—the only random number command built into in Excel—to generate continuous distributions commonly used in applications. The answer is that there are a number of ways to *transform* uniform random numbers into random numbers from other distributions. We list four of these below, with the Excel function that is necessary to generate a *single* random number from one of these distributions.

1 Uniform between a and b. This is similar to the uniform on 0,1 distribution except that the random numbers are now equally likely to be anywhere between two specified numbers a and b. The Excel command is

=$a + (b - a)$***RAND()**

where you substitute the known values for a and b.

2 Normal with mean μ and standard deviation σ. The Excel function is

=NORMINV(RAND(),μ,σ)

where you substitute the known values for μ and σ.

3 Exponential with mean m. This is the distribution used most commonly in queueing models, as discussed in Chapter 11. The Excel function is

=$-m$***LN(RAND())**

where you substitute the known value for m. Here, LN is the natural logarithm function. (Note the minus sign. This is necessary because the log of a number between 0 and 1 is negative.)

4 Triangular with parameters a, c, and b. This distribution appears in Figure 12.12, where a and b are the lower and upper limits and c is the most likely value. This

FIGURE 12.12 **Triangular Distribution**

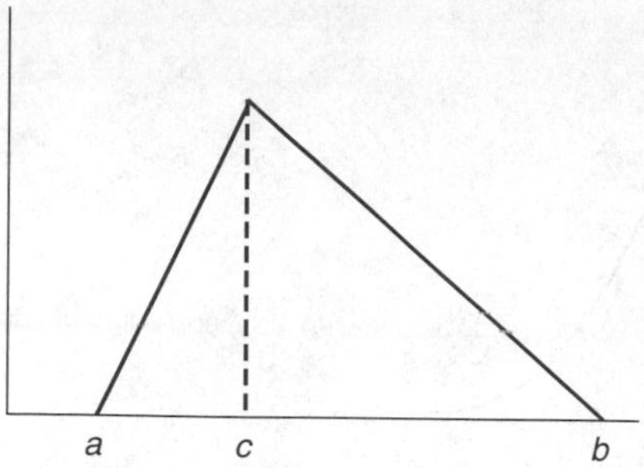

FIGURE 12.13 **Spreadsheet for Generating Triangular Random Numbers**

	A	B	C	D	E
1	**Generating random numbers from triangular distribution**				
2					
3	**Parameters of distribution**				
4	Minimum value (a)	10			
5	Most likely value (c)	12			
6	Maximum value (b)	20			
7					
8	"Standardized" c	0.2			
9					
10	Uniform on 0,1	Triangular			
11	0.033605042	10.81981756			
12	0.790430942	15.90542741			
13	0.33301895	12.69531082			
14	0.594147408	14.30191195			
15	0.830504309	16.31765628			
16	0.938053068	17.77384758			
17	0.637585452	14.61546995			
18	0.725835074	15.31671119			
19	0.203595816	12.01799933			
20	0.743609843	15.47106938			
21	0.246566774	12.23632445			

distribution is often used for times to complete an activity. Then *a* is the minimum time, *b* is the maximum time, and *c* is the most likely time.

The method for generating a random number from this distribution is slightly more complex, so we illustrate it with the spreadsheet shown in Figure 12.13. (See the file TRIGEN.XLS.) After entering values for *a*, *b*, and *c* in the B4:B6 range, we first "standardize" the value of *c* in cell B8 with the formula

=(B5–B4)/(B6–B4)

Then in cell A11 enter the =RAND() function and use this uniform 0,1 random number to generate the triangular random number in cell B11 with the formula

=$B$4+($B$6–$B$4)*IF(A11<=$B$8,SQRT(A11*$B$8), 1–SQRT((1–$B$8)*(1–A11)))

By copying cells A11 and B11 down, we can generate many such random numbers.

There are Excel add-ins that have special functions for generating random numbers from these and other distributions. For example, @RISK, the add-in discussed in the next chapter, has a function RISKTRIANG(a,c,b) for generating a triangular distributed random number. This is obviously much easier than the complex method given above—but you have to have the add-in!

PROBLEM

Skill-Building Problem

7 Six months before its annual convention, the American Medical Association must determine how many rooms to reserve. At this time the AMA can reserve rooms at a cost of $50 per room. The AMA believes the number of doctors attending the convention will be normally distributed with a mean of 5000 and a standard deviation of 1000. If the number of people attending the convention exceeds the number of rooms reserved, extra rooms must be reserved at a cost of $80 per room.

a Use simulation to determine the number of rooms that should be reserved to minimize the expected cost to the AMA.

b Rework Part (a) for the case where the number attending has a triangular distribution with minimum value 2000, maximum value 7000, and most likely value 5000. ■

12.6

Simulation and Bidding

In situations where a company must bid against competitors, simulation can often be used to determine the company's optimal bid. Usually the company does not know what its competitors will bid, but it may have an idea about the *range* of the bids its competitors will choose. In this section we will show how to use simulation to determine a bid that maximizes the company's expected profit.

EXAMPLE 12.2

The Rogers Construction Company is trying to decide whether to make a bid on a construction project. Rogers believes it will cost the company $10,000 to complete the project (if it wins the contract), and it will cost $350 to prepare a bid. Four potential competitors are going to bid against Rogers. The lowest bid will win the contract (and the winner will then be given the winning bid amount to complete the project). Based on past history Rogers believes that each competitor's bid has a triangular distribution with low and high extremes 10,000a and 10,000b and most likely value 10,000c. That is, each competitor's bid is at least a times Rogers's cost, is no more than b times Rogers's cost, and is most likely to be c times Rogers's cost. For this particular example, we will assume that $a = 1$, $b = 3$, and $c = 1.3$. These four competitors' bids are also assumed to be independent of one another. If Rogers decides to prepare a bid, then it has decided that its bid amount will be a multiple of $500 in the range from $10,500 to $15,000. The company wants to use simulation to determine which strategy to use in order to maximize its expected profit.

Solution

The solution to Rogers's problem is shown in Figure 12.14. (See the file BIDDING.XLS.) To create this spreadsheet solution, proceed as follows.

1 **Inputs.** Enter the cost to prepare the bid and the cost to complete the project in cells C3 and C4. Also, enter the parameters for the triangular distribution of competitors' bids in the range B9:B11. Here we have assumed that the competitors' bids will be between \$10,000 ($a = 1$) and \$30,000 ($b = 3$), with most likely value \$13,000 ($c = 1.3$).

2 **Triangular random numbers.** To find the competitors' bids, we need four triangularly distributed random numbers with parameters a, b, and c. Use the method described in the previous section to generate these numbers. Specifically, calculate the standardized c in cell D10 with the formula

=(B10–B9)/(B11–B9)

Then enter uniform 0,1 numbers in cells B14 through E14. Then enter the formula

=$B$9+($B$11–$B$9)*IF(B14<=$D$10,SQRT(B14*$D$10),
1–SQRT((1–$D$10)^(1–B14)))

in cell B15 and copy it to the range C15:E15.

3 **Competitor bids.** Generate bid amounts for the four competitors by entering the formula

=B15*$C$4

FIGURE 12.14 **Spreadsheet for Bidding Example**

	A	B	C	D	E
1	**Bidding Problem**				
2					
3	Company's cost to prepare a bid		$350		
4	Company's cost to complete project		$10,000		
5					
6	Competitors' bids - assumed to be triangularly distributed between a times company's cost				
7	and b times company's cost, with most likely value c times company's cost				
8					
9	a	1			
10	c	1.3	Standardized c	0.150	
11	b	3			
12					
13	**Simulation**				
14	Uniform 0,1 numbers	0.155416395	0.555744907	0.182062624	0.248354022
15	Triangular random numbers	1.305425051	1.770989294	1.332370821	1.401376741
16					
17	Competitors' bids	1	2	3	4
18		$13,054	$17,710	$13,324	$14,014
19					
20	Outcomes for company				
21	Company's bid	Wins bid?	Company's profit		
22	No bid		$0		
23	$10,500	1	$150		
24	$11,000	1	$650		
25	$11,500	1	$1,150		
26	$12,000	1	$1,650		
27	$12,500	1	$2,150		
28	$13,000	1	$2,650		
29	$13,500	0	($350)		
30	$14,000	0	($350)		
31	$14,500	0	($350)		
32	$15,000	0	($350)		

in cell B18 and copying it across to the rest of row 18. Notice in Figure 12.14 that competitor 1 has the low bid of the four competitors ($13,054). This is the bid that Rogers will have to beat in order to win the contract. Of course, for other random numbers the bids in row 18 will change.

4 **Possible decisions.** Enter the possible decisions for Rogers in the range A22:A32. This includes the no bid decision.

5 **Does Rogers win the bid?** For each bid Rogers could make, check whether Rogers will win the contract by entering the formula

=IF(A23<MIN($B$18:$E$18),1,0)

in cell B23 and copying this to the range B24:B32. A "1" in column B signifies that Rogers wins the contract; a "0" signifies that a competitor wins it.

6 **Profits.** Enter $0 in cell C22, since the no bid decision results in no costs and no revenues. For every other decision the profit depends on whether Rogers wins or loses the bid. Therefore in cell C23 enter the formula

=IF(B23=1,A23–$C$4,0)–$C$3

and copy it to the range C24:C32. Notice that the cost of preparing the bid is outside the IF function since Rogers pays this amount regardless of whether it wins the bid.

The numbers in the range C22:C32 of Figure 12.14 indicate that Rogers would be best—in this particular scenario—to bid $13,000 and make a profit of $2650. In general, if Rogers *knew* the bids of its competitors, it would naturally bid the highest amount that was still less than its competitors bids. Unfortunately, Rogers doesn't have this information when it makes its decision. So how does it decide on its "optimal" bid?

A sensible approach is to replicate the simulation many times, keep track of the profit from each possible decision on each replication, average these profits for each possible decision, and choose the decision with the highest average. This is easy to do with a data table, as we've illustrated in Figure 12.15. To create this data table, enter replication numbers (1 through 100) in the range A38:A137, enter the possible decisions (as labels) in the range B36:L36, and enter the formulas from the range C22:C32 in the range B37:L37.

Here is an easy way to enter these labels and formulas. First, select the range B36:L36 and type the *array* formula

=TRANSPOSE(A22:A32)

Enter this in the selected range by pressing Ctrl-Shift-Enter (press all three keys at once). The TRANSPOSE command simply reorients the information from A22:A32 horizontally.

FIGURE 12.15 **Data Table for Bidding Example**

	A	B	C	D	E	F	G	H	I	J	K	L
35	Data table showing profits from various bids											
36	Replication	No bid	$10,500	$11,000	$11,500	$12,000	$12,500	$13,000	$13,500	$14,000	$14,500	$15,000
37		$0	$150	$650	$1,150	$1,650	$2,150	$2,650	($350)	($350)	($350)	($350)
38	1	$0	$150	$650	$1,150	$1,650	$2,150	$2,650	$3,150	$3,650	$4,150	($350)
39	2	$0	$150	$650	$1,150	$1,650	($350)	($350)	($350)	($350)	($350)	($350)
40	3	$0	$150	$650	$1,150	$1,650	$2,150	$2,650	$3,150	($350)	($350)	($350)
41	4	$0	$150	$650	$1,150	$1,650	$2,150	$2,650	$3,150	($350)	($350)	($350)
42	5	$0	$150	$650	$1,150	$1,650	$2,150	$2,650	$3,150	$3,650	($350)	($350)
43	6	$0	$150	$650	$1,150	$1,650	$2,150	$2,650	$3,150	$3,650	$4,150	$4,650
134	97	$0	$150	$650	$1,150	$1,650	$2,150	$2,650	$3,150	$3,650	($350)	($350)
135	98	$0	$150	$650	$1,150	$1,650	$2,150	$2,650	$3,150	$3,650	($350)	($350)
136	99	$0	$150	$650	$1,150	$1,650	$2,150	($350)	($350)	($350)	($350)	($350)
137	100	$0	$150	$650	$1,150	$1,650	$2,150	($350)	($350)	($350)	($350)	($350)
138												
139	Averages	$0	$145	$580	$955	$1,230	$1,325	$1,240	$1,260	$1,090	$1,000	$700
140	Standard deviations	$0	$50	$256	$507	$819	$1,181	$1,505	$1,753	$1,930	$2,073	$2,047

Similarly, select the range B37:L37, type the array formula

=TRANSPOSE(C22:C32)

and press Ctrl-Shift-Enter. Finally, to form the data table, select the range A37:L137 and use the Data/Table command with any blank cell as the column input cell. (There is no row input cell.)

Once the data table has been formed, the average and standard deviation of the 100 numbers in each column of the data table can be calculated in rows 139 and 140 with the AVERAGE and STDEV functions. Also, bar charts of these averages and standard deviations can be created, as shown in Figures 12.16 and 12.17. As we see from Figure 12.16, a bid amount of $12,500 achieves the largest average profit from these 100 simulations. However, we also see from Figure 12.17 that there is more risk (larger standard deviation) associated with larger bids. Because of this risk, Rogers might want to settle for a smaller bid amount such as $12,000.

FIGURE 12.16 **Average Profits for Bidding Example**

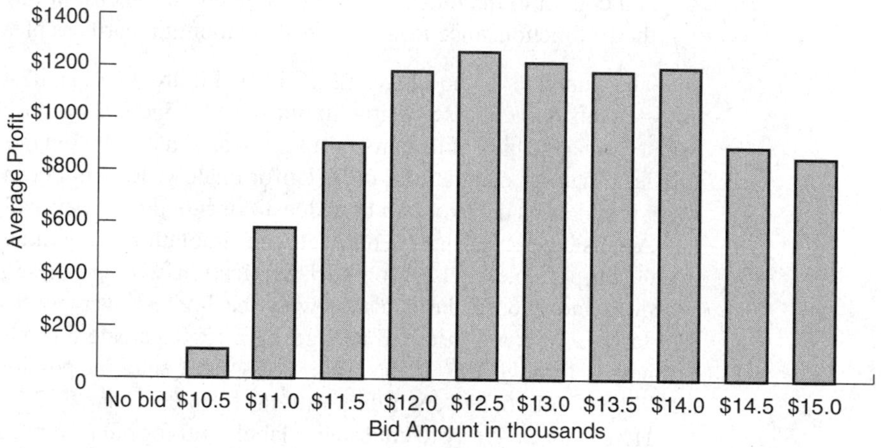

FIGURE 12.17 **Standard Deviations for Bidding Example**

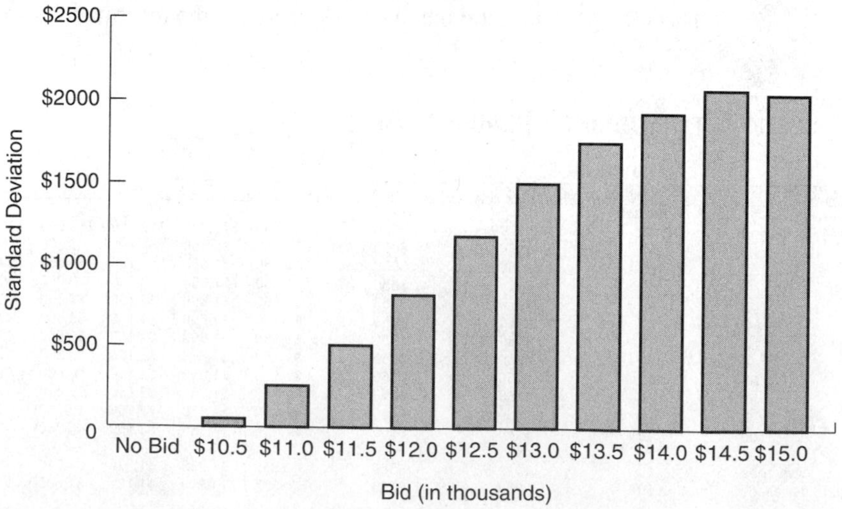

You should be aware that the numbers in Figure 12.14 and the associated graphs are not necessarily the *definitive* answer to Rogers's problem. These numbers are all based on the random numbers that happened to be generated for these 100 replications. To see how things can change, press the F9 key with the BIDDING.XLS file open and look at the "live" sheets. After a few seconds, all of the numbers, as well as the corresponding graphs, will change. It is very possible that some bid amount other than $12,500 will now correspond to the largest average profit. The only way to ensure that a simulation spreadsheet represents *the* definitive solution to a problem is to make many replications. Unfortunately, the required number of replications varies from problem to problem, so it is difficult to provide clear guidelines in general. All we can suggest is: *the more, the better*! ■

PROBLEMS

Skill-Building Problems

8 If the number of competitors in the Rogers bidding example were to double, how would the optimal bid change?

9 Again referring to the Rogers bidding example, if the average bid for each competitor stayed the same, but their bids exhibited less variability, would the optimal bid increase or decrease? To study this question assume that each competitor's bid follows each of the following distributions:

a Uniform between 12 and 24.

b Uniform between 13 and 16. ■

12.7 Deming's Funnel Experiment

Edwards Deming was an American statistician whose views on quality management revolutionized the way companies do business across the world. Deming has been given much of the credit for Japan's spectacular post–World War II economic recovery. He traveled around the U.S. giving a famous four-day seminar on quality management. After attending his seminar, many U.S. companies (including Xerox, GM, and Ford) reorganized their businesses to reflect Deming's management philosophy as embraced in his famous 14 points. For example, GM's Saturn plant is run almost completely in accordance with Deming's 14 points. We strongly recommend that you read Deming's book *Out of the Crisis* [3]. It's terrific!

An important component of Deming's seminar was his famous funnel experiment. The funnel experiment is designed to show how businesses often greatly overadjust stable processes. To illustrate the idea, suppose that you are in the business of drilling a tiny hole in the exact center of a square piece of wood. In the past the holes you have drilled were, on average, in the center of the wood, and the x- and y-coordinates had a standard deviation of 0.1 inch. Also, the drilling process has been *stable*. That is, the holes average being in the center of the square, and the deviations from the center of the square (measured in both the x- and y-coordinates) follow a normal distribution with mean 0 and standard deviation 0.1 inch. This means, for example, that for 68% of the holes the x-coordinate is within 0.1 inch of the center, for 95% of the holes the x-coordinate is within 0.2 inch of the center, and for 99.7% of the holes the x-coordinate is within 0.3 inch of the center. This describes the *inherent* variability in the drilling process. Without changing the hole-drilling process, you must live with this amount of variation.

Now suppose that you drill a hole and its x- and y-coordinates are $x = 0.1$ and $y = 0$ (where the center of the square has coordinates [0, 0]). A natural reaction is to reduce (if possible) the x-setting of the drill by 0.1 to correct for the fact that the x-coordinate was too high. Then if the next hole has coordinates $x = -0.2$ and $y = 0.1$, you might try to increase the x-coordinate by 0.2 and decrease the y-coordinate by 0.1. Deming's funnel experiment shows that this method of continually readjusting a stable process—he called it "tampering"—will actually *increase* the variability of the coordinates of the position where the hole is drilled. That is, tampering will generally make the process worse!

To illustrate the effects of tampering, Deming placed a funnel above a target on the floor and dropped small balls through the funnel in an attempt to hit the target. As he demonstrated, many balls did *not* hit the target. His goal, therefore, was to make the balls fall as close to the target as possible. Deming proposed four rules for adjusting the positioning of the funnel.

Rules for Funnel Experiment

1 Never move the funnel.

2 After each ball is dropped, move the funnel—*relative to its previous position*—to compensate for any error. To illustrate, suppose the target has coordinates $(0, 0)$ and the funnel begins directly over the target. If the ball lands at $(.5, .1)$ on the first drop, we compensate by repositioning the funnel at $(0 - .5, 0 - .1) = (-.5, -1)$. If the second drop has coordinates $(1, -2)$, we now reposition the funnel at $(-.5 - 1, -.1 - (-2)) = (-1.5, 1.9)$.

3 Move the funnel—*relative to its original position at* $(0, 0)$—to compensate for any error. If the ball lands at $(.5, .1)$ on the first drop, we compensate by repositioning the funnel at $(0 - .5, 0 - .1) = (-.5, -1)$. If the second drop has coordinates $(1, -2)$, we now reposition the funnel at $(0 - 1, 0 - (-2)) = (-1, 2)$.

4 Always reposition the funnel directly over the last drop. Thus if the first ball lands at $(.5, 1)$, we position the funnel at $(.5, 1)$. If the second drop has coordinates $(1, 2)$, we position the funnel at $(1, 2)$. This rule might be followed, for example, by an automobile manufacturer's painting department. With each new batch of paint, they attempt to match the color of the previous batch (whether or not the previous color was "correct"). ■

Does it appear to you (intuitively) that any of these latter three rules ought to outperform rule 1, the "leave it alone" rule? Is so, read on—you might surprised.

To see how these rules work, we make the following assumptions. We assume that the x-coordinate on each drop is normally distributed with a mean equal to the x-coordinate of the funnel position and a standard deviation of 1. A similar statement holds for the y-coordinate. Also, we assume that the x- and y-coordinates are selected independently of one another. These assumptions describe the inherent variability in the process of dropping the balls.

We now develop four spreadsheets to simulate the four rules. In each spreadsheet we simulate 50 consecutive drops of the ball and then use the Data/Table command to find the distance from the target of the 50th ball for 100 replications of the 50-drop experiment. A good rule should have a small average distance, and the standard deviation of the distances (across the 100 replications) should also be small.

Simulating Rule 1

Figure 12.18 shows the results of simulating 50 drops with rule 1. (See the file FUNNEL1 .XLS.) The details for forming this spreadsheet are explained below. (Fewer details will be given for the other three rules since the overall plan of the spreadsheets is very similar.)

1 **Inputs.** Enter the drop numbers (1 through 50) in column A. Then, since this rule starts with the funnel positioned over the target at (0, 0) and always leaves it there, enter 0's in the range B6:C55.

FIGURE 12.18 Simulation of Funnel Experiment Using Rule 1

	A	B	C	D	E	F
1	**Deming's funnel experiment: Rule 1**					
2						
3	Never move the funnel!					
4		Funnel positioned at:		Drop lands at:		
5	Drop #	x-coord	y-coord	x-coord	y-coord	
6	1	0	0	-2.09	0.45	
7	2	0	0	1.57	-0.71	
8	3	0	0	1.22	-2.70	
9	4	0	0	-0.69	-1.31	
10	5	0	0	1.10	0.65	
11	6	0	0	-0.25	-0.36	
12	7	0	0	-0.80	-0.42	
52	47	0	0	0.89	0.05	
53	48	0	0	-1.01	-0.33	
54	49	0	0	0.68	1.03	
55	50	0	0	-0.05	0.42	
56						
57	**Data table for replicating distance from center of 50th drop**					
58	Replication	Distance		Value	Frequency	
59		0.42		0	0	
60	1	3.31		0.5	11	
61	2	1.68		1	25	
62	3	2.31		1.5	26	
63	4	1.10		2	22	
64	5	1.08		2.5	11	
65	6	1.45		3	3	
66	7	0.54		>3	2	
67	8	1.36				
68	9	2.74				
156	97	1.81				
157	98	1.08				
158	99	1.25				
159	100	1.53				
160	Average	1.31				
161	StDev	0.70				
162	Maximum	3.31				

2 **Generate random coordinates.** The x-coordinate for any drop is, in general, the x-coordinate of the funnel position (in column B) plus a normally distributed random "error." The same is true for the y-coordinate. Therefore, in cell D6 generate the x-coordinate of the first drop with the formula

=B6+NORMINV(RAND(),0,1)

Then copy this to the range D6:E55.

3 **Data table for simulation.** Now use a data table to replicate the distance of the 50th drop from the target 100 times. To do this, enter the replication numbers (1 through 100) in the range A60:A159, enter the formula

=SQRT(D55^2+E55^2)

in cell B59 (remember that the straight-line distance between points is the square root of the sum of squares), select the range A59:B159, and use the Data/Table command with any blank cell as the column input cell.

4 **Summary statistics.** Finally, use the AVERAGE, STDEV, and MAX functions to find the average, standard deviation, and largest of the values in the range B60:B159, and use the FREQUENCY function to count the number of distances in various categories.

To appreciate what this simulation tells us, several graphs are useful. First, a scattergram of the x- and y-coordinates of the 50 drops (using the data in the range D6:E55) appears in Figure 12.19. However, since the *time sequence* of the drops is not apparent from this graph, it is also useful to graph the time sequences of the x- and y-coordinates (individually) of the 50 drops, as shown in Figure 12.20. (This graph uses a line chart with the data from the combined ranges A6:A55 and D6:E55.) Finally, to see how the distances from the target of the 50th drop vary over the 100 replications, we form a histogram from the frequency table found in the range D59:E66. This histogram is shown in Figure 12.21. These three graphs indicate that when the funnel is never moved, the drops tend to occur randomly around the target, with no apparent time series patterns, and most drops are no more than three units from the target.

FIGURE 12.19 **Scatterplot of 50 Drops Using Rule 1**

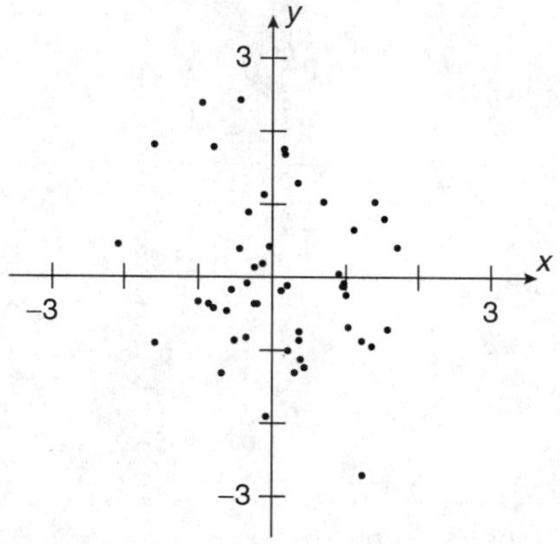

FIGURE 12.20 **Time Series Graph of Coordinate Positions Using Rule 1**

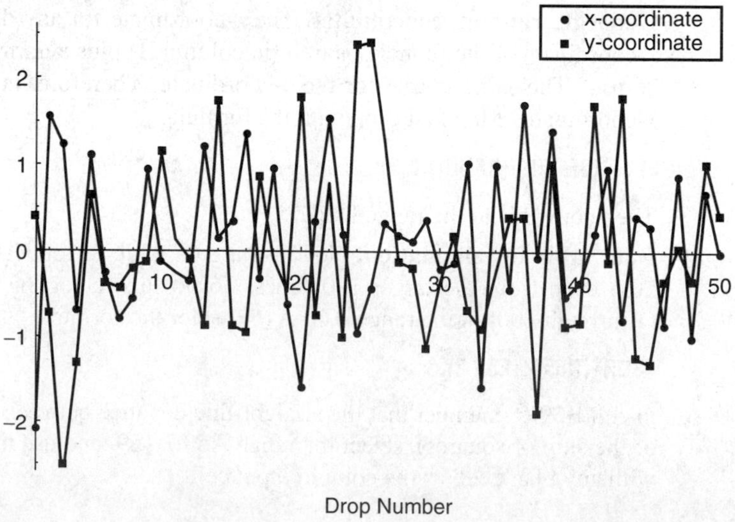

FIGURE 12.21 **Histogram of Distances on 50th Drop Using Rule 1**

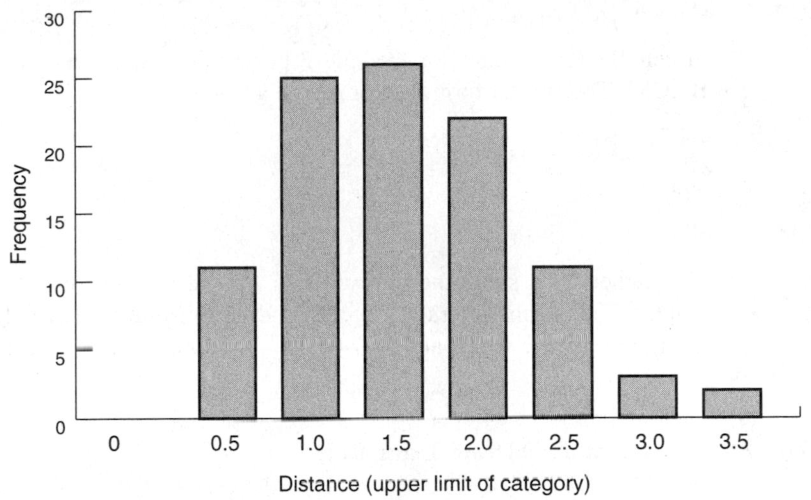

Before continuing, we mention that all of the live graphs in the file FUNNEL1.XLS are linked to the numbers in Figure 12.18. Therefore, by pressing the F9 key, all of the random numbers, and hence all of the graphs, will change. (This change will take a few seconds because of all the recalculations.) You can check (by pressing F9 several times) that the patterns continue to be very much like those shown in Figures 12.19, 12.20, and 12.21 for rule 1. However, this is not the case with the other rules, particularly rules 3 and 4, as you will see.

Simulating Rules 2, 3, and 4

The difference between rule 2 and rule 1 is that we now move the funnel. Specifically, we check how far from the target the previous drop was and then compensate for this error, relative to the previous funnel position, in the new positioning of the funnel. Let's say the funnel position for the previous drop had x-coordinate Pos_{prev} and that the x-coordinate of the previous drop was $Drop_{prev}$. Then the funnel position for the next drop has x-coordinate Pos_{new} given by

$$Pos_{new} = Pos_{prev} - Drop_{prev} \qquad \textbf{(Rule 2 Positioning Equation)}$$

The same equation also governs the y-coordinate.

There are similar positioning equations for rules 3 and 4. For rule 3 the compensation is always relative to the *original* funnel position (that is, over the target), so it is given by

$$Pos_{new} = 0 - Drop_{prev} = -Drop_{prev} \qquad \textbf{(Rule 3 Positioning Equation)}$$

In contrast, rule 4 always places the funnel over the previous drop, so its positioning equation is

$$Pos_{new} = Drop_{prev} \qquad \textbf{(Rule 4 Positioning Equation)}$$

Using these positioning equations, it is easy to modify the spreadsheet in Figure 12.18 to account for the different rules. (See the files FUNNEL2.XLS, FUNNEL3.XLS, and FUNNEL4.XLS.) The only changes that need to be made are in the range B7:C55, where we record the positioning of the funnel. For example, for rule 2 we enter the formula

=B6–D6

in cell B7 (to account for the rule 2 positioning equation) and copy this to the range B7:C55. The similar formulas for rules 3 and 4 are

=–D6

and

=D6

Rather than show the spreadsheets for these rules, we show their accompanying graphs. The graphs for rule 2 corresponding to Figures 12.19, 12.20, and 12.21 appear in Figures 12.22, 12.23, and 12.24. The only noticeable difference between these graphs

FIGURE 12.22 **Scatterplot of 50 Drops Using Rule 2**

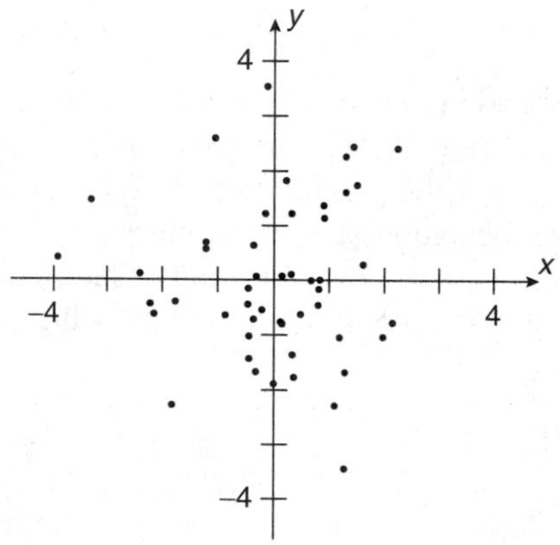

FIGURE 12.23 **Time Series Graph of Coordinate Positions Using Rule 2**

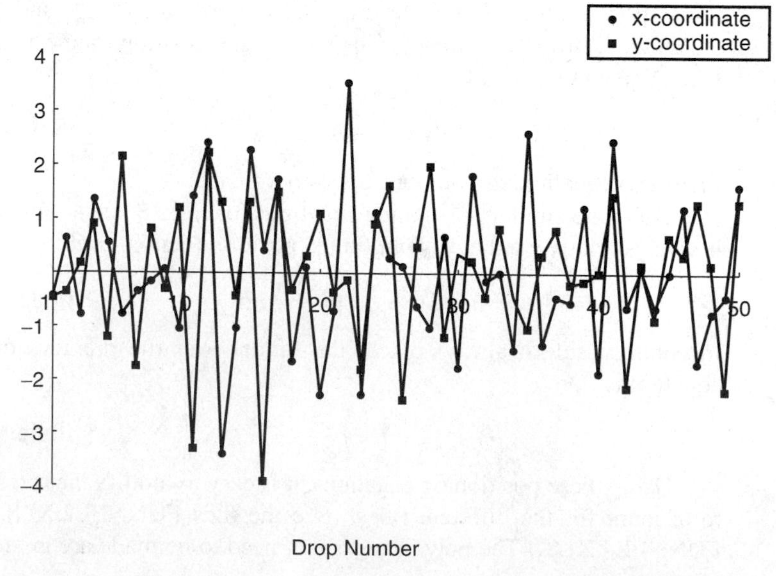

FIGURE 12.24 Histogram of Distances on 50th Drop Using Rule 2

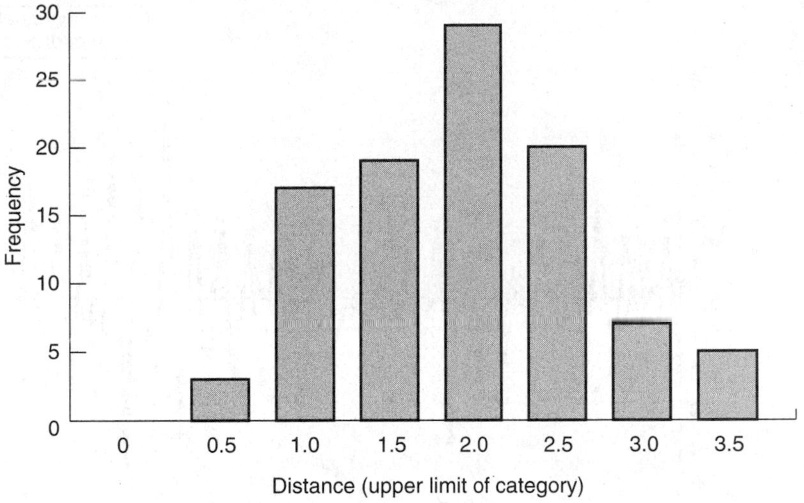

and the graphs for rule 1 is that the rule 2 histogram in Figure 12.24 is shifted slightly further to the right and is slightly more spread out. That is, the distances (for drop 50) tend to be slightly larger and vary slightly more than those for rule 1. So rule 2 is somewhat worse than rule 1. (Actually, it's a bit worse than it might look. Mathematically, it can be shown that the variance for rule 2 is *twice* as large as for rule 1.)

In contrast, rule 3 can have disastrous behavior, as illustrated in Figures 12.25, 12.26, and 12.27. If the drops start to get off track, then we make a big adjustment in the opposite direction, so that the next drop also tends to be off track, but on the opposite side of the target. This oscillating behavior is apparent in Figure 12.26. The effect is that by drop 50, the ball is likely to be way off in some direction, as is evident from Figure 12.27. (Notice that the scale on the horizontal axis of Figure 12.27 is much different than in the corresponding figures for rules 1 and 2.) If you open the FUNNEL3.XLS file, try pressing the F9 key several times and look at the graphs. You'll be surprised at the different types of behavior that are possible.

FIGURE 12.25 Scatterplot of 50 Drops Using Rule 3

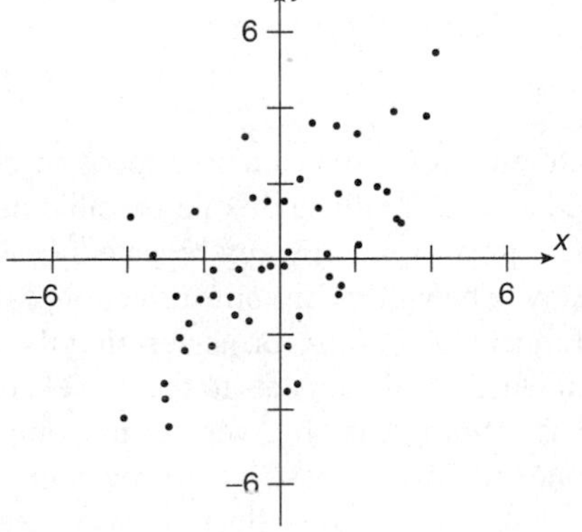

FIGURE 12.26 **Time Series Graph of Coordinate Positions Using Rule 3**

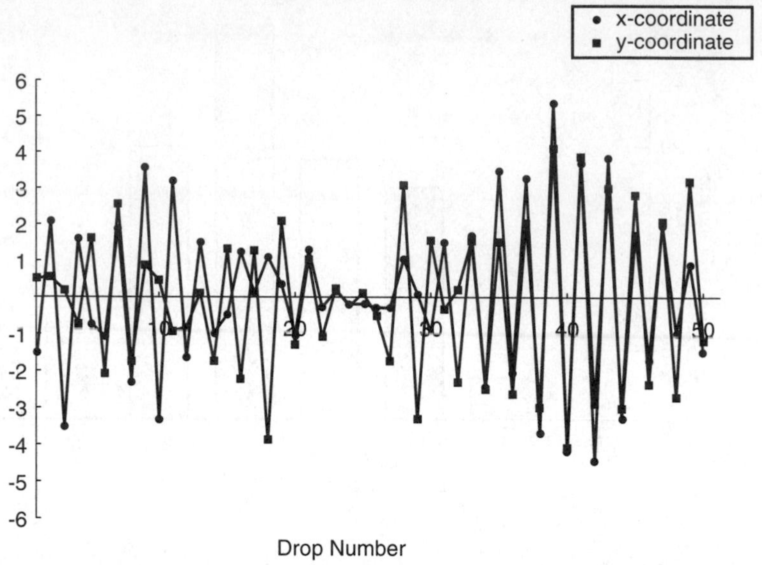

FIGURE 12.27 **Histogram of Distances on 50th Drop Using Rule 3**

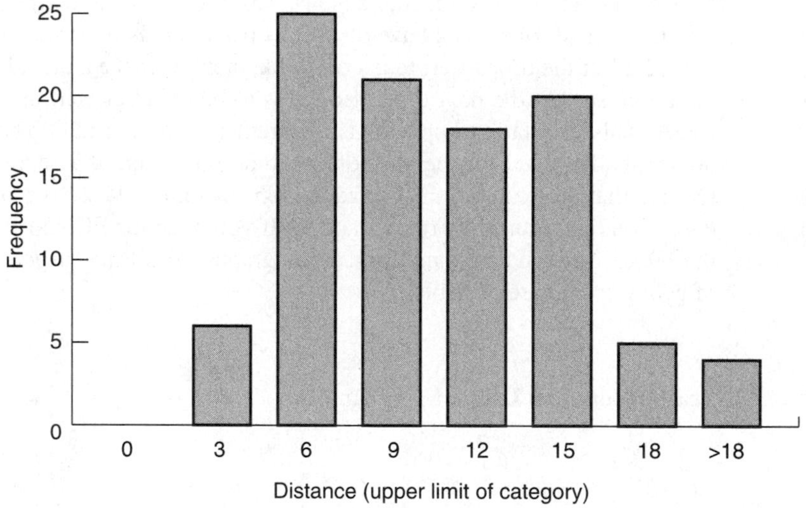

Rule 4 is just as bad, although the behavior now tends to be a constant drifting in some direction. Figures 12.28 and 12.29 illustrate one possible behavior, although others are possible (as can be seen by pressing the F9 key repeatedly). The bottom line is again that by drop 50, the ball is likely to be way off in some direction, as Figure 12.30 illustrates.

Without running these funnel simulations (or performing the experiment physically), you could argue forever about whether adjustments to the funnel are beneficial. The answer is simply not obvious. (And as Deming has observed, many companies apparently do not understand that the "let it alone" rule works best, since they continually adjust the settings of their processes.) However, these simulations illustrate very clearly that when a process is stable, nothing good can be gained by tampering with it. The only way to really improve performance is to redesign the entire process.

FIGURE 12.28 **Scatterplot of 50 Drops Using Rule 4**

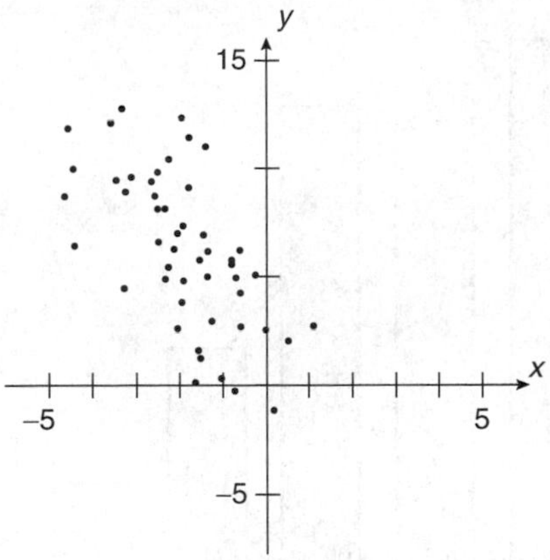

FIGURE 12.29 **Time Series Graph of Coordinate Positions Using Rule 4**

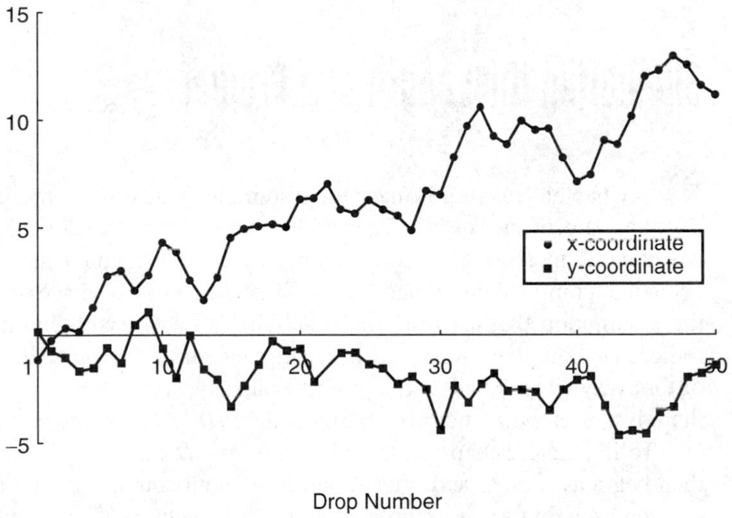

PROBLEMS

Skill-Building Problems

10 Simulate 400 trials of the 50th drop for rule 3. Then evaluate the average and standard deviation of the x-coordinate for the 50th drop.

11 Simulate 400 trials of the 50th drop for rule 4. Then evaluate the average and standard deviation of the x-coordinate for the 50th drop.

12 A car company paints all its cars yellow. In the company vault is a sample of the original yellow used to paint this year's cars. Suppose that each time a new batch of yellow paint is mixed up, the company matches the new batch to the most recent batch (not the original). Which of the four funnel rules does this illustrate?

13 Suppose that missile tests indicate that on average, a missile misses the target by 50 feet. Suppose a missile is fired, and it lands 80 feet east of the target. Then the army adjusts the control mechanism on the missile to a setting 80 feet west of the current setting. Which rule is being followed here? ■

FIGURE 12.30 **Histogram of Distances on 50th Drop Using Rule 4**

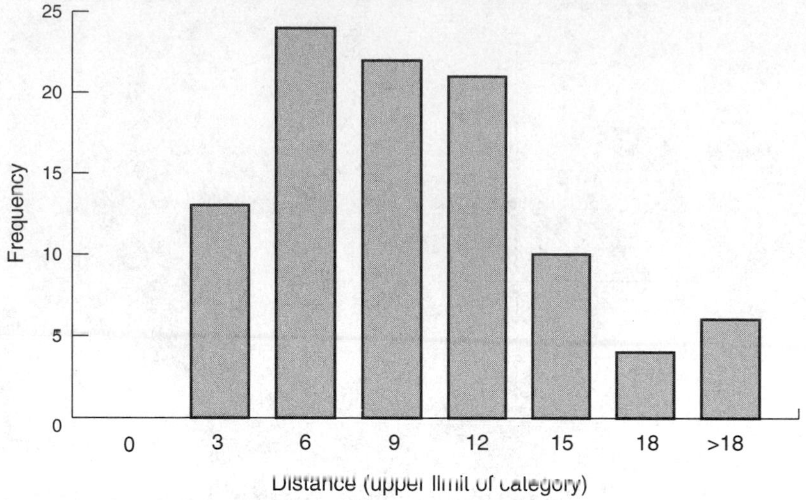

12.8

Simulating the Length of a Project

In Chapter 4 we used linear programming to determine the length of time needed to complete a project. We also learned how to identify critical activities, where an activity is critical if increasing its activity time by a small amount increases the length of time needed to complete the project by the same amount. Our discussion in Chapter 4 required the assumption that the time of an activity is known with certainty. In reality, the time required to complete an activity is usually uncertain. Of course, this implies that the length of time needed to complete the project is also uncertain. It also implies that for any activity there is a *probability* (not necessarily equal to 0 or 1) that the activity is critical.

To illustrate, suppose that activities *A* and *B* can begin immediately. Activity *C* can then begin as soon as activities *A* and *B* are both completed, and the project is completed as soon as activity *C* is completed. Obviously, activity *C* is on the critical path, but what about *A* and *B*? Let's say that the *expected* activity times of *A* and *B* are 10 and 12. If we use these expected times and ignore any uncertainty about the actual times, that is, if we proceed as we did in Chapter 4, then activity *B* is definitely a critical activity. However, suppose there is some positive probability that *A* can have duration 12 and *B* can have duration 11. Under this scenario, *A* is a critical activity. In other words, we can't say in advance which of the activities, *A* or *B*, will be critical. However, by using simulation we can see how *likely* it is that each of these activities is critical. Of course, we can also see how long the entire project is likely to take. We illustrate with the following example.

EXAMPLE 12.3

Tom Lingley, an independent contractor, has agreed to build a new room on an existing house. He plans to begin work on Monday morning, June 1. The main question is when will he complete his work, given that he works only on weekdays. The owner of the house is particularly hopeful that the room will be ready by Saturday, June 27, that is, in 20 or fewer working days. Lingley has told the owner that he is "pretty sure" this deadline can

TABLE 12.5 Activities for Room Construction Example

	Description	Immediate Predecessors
Activity A	Prepare foundation	None
Activity B	Put up frame	A
Activity C	Order custom windows	None
Activity D	Erect outside walls	B
Activity E	Do electrical wiring	D
Activity F	Do plumbing	D
Activity G	Put in duct work	D
Activity H	Hang dry wall	E, F, G
Activity I	Install windows	B, C
Activity J	Paint and clean up	H

be met. The work proceeds in stages, labeled *A* through *J*, as summarized in Table 12.5. Three of these activities, *E*, *F*, and *G*, will be done by separate independent subcontractors. Lingley would like to use computer simulation to see (1) how long the project is likely to take, (2) how likely it is that the project will be completed by the deadline, and (3) which activities are likely to be critical.

Solution

From Table 12.5 we see that Tom can begin immediately on Monday to prepare the foundation and order the windows. When the foundation has been prepared, he can put up the frame. When the frame has been put up, he can erect the outside walls. When the outside walls are up, he can call in the three subcontractors to install the electrical wiring, the plumbing, and the duct work for the heating. When all of these subcontractors have finished their work, Tom can hang the dry wall and then paint. Also, he can install the windows as soon as the windows arrive, assuming that the frame has been finished by that time. When there are no explicit precedence relationships, work on various stages can occur concurrently. For example, it is possible for the electrical subcontractor, the plumbing subcontractor, and the heating subcontractor to work simultaneously. In fact, it is possible that they could all be working at the same time that Tom is installing windows. The room is completed when all of the activities have been completed.

A diagram of the project that shows the precedence relationships appears in Figure 12.31.[4] Each of the circles corresponds to one of the activities. If one of the activities is an immediate predecessor of another activity, an arrow is drawn from the predecessor to

FIGURE 12.31 Diagram for Room Construction Example

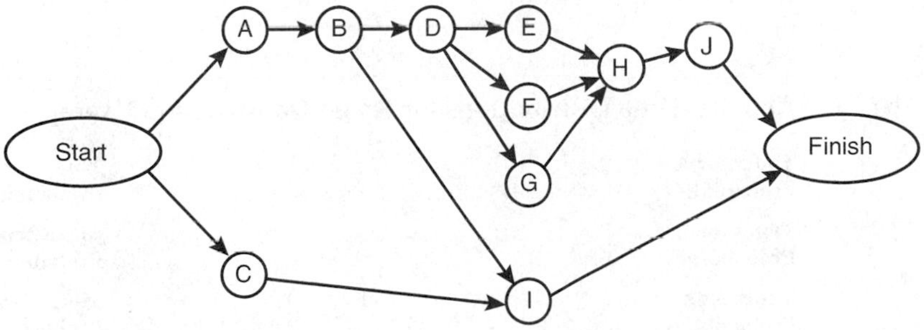

[4]We've gone from the "activity-on-arc" convention used in Chapter 4 to the "activity-on-node" convention in Figure 12.31. In this example we believe the latter convention produces a graph that is easier to understand.

its successor. For example, there are arrows from D to E, F, and G. For convenience, there are two extra circles, a "start" and a "finish," that denote the beginning and completion of the project. Arrows lead from the "start" to activities A and C, indicating that these activities can begin immediately. Also, there are arrows from activities I and J to the "finish," indicating that when these two activities are both completed, the entire project has been completed.

Each activity has a corresponding time. For example, the time for activity E is the time (measured in days) necessary to complete the electrical wiring once it has been started. All of these times can be uncertain, as they would be in most real projects. The time to complete the foundation could be delayed because of rain, the time to receive the custom window order could be delayed because the windows are temporarily out of stock, and the subcontractor times could be delayed because the subcontractors are busy on other jobs. We assume that the activities have the discrete probability distributions shown in Table 12.6. For example, the time to complete the electrical work, once the electrical subcontractor has been called, is either 2, 3, 4, or 5 days with corresponding probabilities .2, .3, .3, and .2. We also assume that these random times are probabilistically independent of one another. Notice that all of these times are measured in *working* days. So, for example, if the electrical contractor begins work on Friday morning and it takes him three days to complete his work, he will finish at the end of the following Tuesday.

For any *specific* values of the activity times, it can be shown that the length of the project is the length of the longest path from the "start" to the "finish." There are five possible paths:

$$Start \rightarrow A \rightarrow B \rightarrow D \rightarrow E \rightarrow H \rightarrow J \rightarrow Finish \text{ (Path 1)}$$

$$Start \rightarrow A \rightarrow B \rightarrow D \rightarrow F \rightarrow H \rightarrow J \rightarrow Finish \text{ (Path 2)}$$

$$Start \rightarrow A \rightarrow B \rightarrow D \rightarrow G \rightarrow H \rightarrow J \rightarrow Finish \text{ (Path 3)}$$

$$Start \rightarrow A \rightarrow B \rightarrow I \rightarrow Finish \text{ (Path 4)}$$

$$Start \rightarrow C \rightarrow I \rightarrow Finish \text{ (Path 5)}$$

You can check that when each of the activities has its minimum possible time, the longest path is path 3 with length 13 days; when each of the activities has its maximum possible time, the longest path is path 1 with length 24 days. Therefore, the project will certainly take at least 13 days to complete but no more than 24 days.

Of course, there are numerous combinations of values for the various activity times, and these combinations are not equally likely. Therefore, the whole purpose of simulation is to repeatedly generate random activity times for the activities, calculate the five path lengths, and declare the maximum of these path lengths the length of the project. The spreadsheet that accomplishes this is shown in Figure 12.32. (See the file PROJECT.XLS.) It can be formed as follows.

TABLE 12.6 Activity Time Distributions for Room Construction Example

Times for A	2	3	4	5			**Times for F**	2	3	4
Probabilities	0.3	0.4	0.2	0.1			**Probabilities**	0.2	0.6	0.2
Times for B	2	3	4				**Times for G**	3	4	
Probabilities	0.1	0.5	0.4				**Probabilities**	0.2	0.8	
Times for C	5	7	9	10	15	18	**Times for H**	2	3	
Probabilities	0.1	0.15	0.25	0.2	0.2	0.1	**Probabilities**	0.7	0.3	
Times for D	2	3	4				**Times for I**	1	2	
Probabilities	0.3	0.5	0.2				**Probabilities**	0.5	0.5	
Times for E	2	3	4	5			**Times for J**	2	3	
Probabilities	0.2	0.3	0.3	0.2			**Probabilities**	0.5	0.5	

FIGURE 12.32 Spreadsheet for Room Construction Example

	A	B	C	D	E	F	G	H	I	J	K	L	M	N
1	**Simulation of Room Construction Project**													
2														
3	Deadline	20	days											
4														
5	**Probability distributions of activity times (cumulative probabilities shown)**													
6														
7	Activity A			Activity B			Activity C			Activity D			Activity E	
8	Cum Prob	Time		Cum Prob	Time		Cum Prob	Time		Cum Prob	Time		Cum Prob	Time
9	0	2		0	2		0	5		0	2		0	2
10	0.3	3		0.1	3		0.1	7		0.3	3		0.2	3
11	0.7	4		0.6	4		0.25	9		0.8	4		0.5	4
12	0.9	5					0.5	10					0.8	5
13							0.7	15						
14							0.9	18						
15														
16	Activity F			Activity G			Activity H			Activity I			Activity J	
17	Cum Prob	Time		Cum Prob	Time		Cum Prob	Time		Cum Prob	Time		Probability	Time
18	0	2		0	3		0	2		0	1		0	2
19	0.2	3		0.2	4		0.7	3		0.5	2		0.5	3
20	0.8	4												
21														
22	**Simulation**													
23	Activity information				Path information									
24	Activity	Time	On critical path?		Path	Length	Critical path?							
25	A	4	1		1	21	1							
26	B	3	1		2	19	0							
27	C	18	0		3	20	0							
28	D	4	1		4	9	0							
29	E	5	1		5	20	0							
30	F	3	0											
31	G	4	0		Critical path length									
32	H	2	1			21								
33	I	2	0		Meet deadline?									
34	J	3	1			0								

1 **Inputs.** Enter the deadline (20 days) in cell B3. Also, enter the labels and probability distributions of the activity times as shown in rows 7 through 20. As in the Walton Bookstore example, we enter the *cumulative* probabilities so that we can use the VLOOKUP function to generate random activity times later on. With this in mind, it is useful to name the various ranges Lookup*X*, where *X* is the activity. For example, give the range A9:B12 the name LookupA, give the range D9:E11 the name LookupB, and so on.

2 **Generate activity times.** To generate one replication of the simulation, generate possible activity times in the range B25:B34. For example, enter the formula

=VLOOKUP(RAND(),LookupA,2)

in cell B25. This formula actually does two things. First, it generates a random number for the first argument of the VLOOKUP function. Then it compares this random number with the lookup table called LookupA to generate a single activity time for activity A. Enter similar formulas in the range B26:B34 for the other activities by referring to their lookup tables.

3 **Path lengths.** Calculate the path lengths in the range F25:F29 by summing the activity times for the activities on each path. For example, the length of path 1 is the sum of the activity times for *A*, *B*, *D*, *E*, *H*, and *J*, so in cell F25 enter the formula

=B25+B26+B28+B29+B32+B34

Enter similar formulas for the other four paths by referring to Figure 12.31.

4 **Critical path.** Calculate the critical path length in cell F32 as the maximum of the path lengths with the formula

=MAX(F25:F29)

5 **Is the deadline met?** Check whether the deadline is met in cell F34 with the formula

=IF(F32<=B3,1,0)

This records a "1" if the deadline is met and a "0" otherwise.

6 **Which paths are critical?** To see which *paths* are critical, check whether a given path length is equal to the maximum path length. To do this, enter the formula

=IF(F25=$F$32,1,0)

in cell G25 and copy it to the range G26:G29. A "1" in a cell in this range signifies that the corresponding path is critical.

7 **Which activities are critical?** Use the information in the range G25:G29 to check which of the *activities* are critical. For example, activity *A* is on paths 1, 2, 3, and 4 (from Figure 12.31), so if any of these paths is critical, activity *A* is critical. Therefore, in cell C25 enter the formula

=IF(OR(G25=1,G26=1,G27=1,G28=1),1,0)

This "OR" condition says that if *any* of the entries in G25, G26, G27, and G28 is 1, then we record a "1" in cell C25 to signify that activity *A* is on a critical path. Use the same logic (and refer to Figure 12.31) to enter similar formulas for the other activities in cells C26 through C34.

8 **Data table to replication simulation.** Now form a data table in the range A39:M139 to replicate the simulation 100 times. (See Figure 12.33.) To do this, enter the formula

=F32

in cell B39 to keep track of the total project time, enter

=F34

in cell C39 to keep track of whether the deadline is met, and (after selecting the range D39:M39) type the *array* formula

=TRANSPOSE(C25:C34)

and press Ctrl-Shift-Enter to keep track of which activities are critical. As usual, to complete the table, select the entire table range A39:M139 and use the Data/Table command with any blank cell as the column input cell.

9 **Summary statistics.** Find the averages of the numbers in the various columns of the data table by entering the formula

=AVERAGE(B40:B139)

in cell B140 and copying it to the rest of row 140.

The average in cell B140 shows that the average total project time for these 100 replications is 18.50 days. (You will be asked to find a 95% confidence interval for the mean total project time in Problem 14.) The average in cell C140 shows that the deadline was met on 92 of the 100 replications. It is also useful to create a histogram of the 100 total project times that were generated. Such a histogram appears in Figure 12.34. It shows that for these particular 100 replications, the most likely total project time is 18 days. However, there is also quite a bit of variation. In fact, one of the replications had a total project time of 14 days, whereas another had a total project time of 22 days.

If Tom wants to speed up the project, where should he put his effort? This depends on which activities are critical most often. This information appears in the range D140:M140.

FIGURE 12.33 Data Table for Room Construction Example

	A	B	C	D	E	F	G	H	I	J	K	L	M
36	Data table to replicate simulation												
37				On critical path?									
38	Replication	Total time	Meet deadline?	A	B	C	D	E	F	G	H	I	J
39		21	0	1	1	0	1	1	0	0	1	0	1
40	1	19	1	1	1	0	1	1	0	0	1	0	1
41	2	19	1	0	0	1	0	0	0	0	0	1	0
42	3	19	1	0	0	1	0	0	0	0	0	1	0
136	97	20	1	0	0	1	0	0	0	0	0	1	0
137	98	16	1	1	1	0	1	0	0	1	1	0	1
138	99	19	1	1	1	0	1	1	0	0	1	0	1
139	100	18	1	1	1	0	1	1	0	0	1	0	1
140	Averages	18.50	92%	85%	85%	18%	85%	48%	19%	53%	85%	18%	85%
141													
142	Probability distribution of time to complete project												
143	Time	Frequency	Probability										
144	13	0	0										
145	14	1	0.01										
146	15	1	0.01										
147	16	6	0.06										
148	17	17	0.17										
149	18	25	0.25										
150	19	23	0.23										
151	20	19	0.19										
152	21	7	0.07										
153	22	1	0.01										
154	23	0	0										
155	24	0	0										
156		0											

FIGURE 12.34 Histogram of Total Project Time

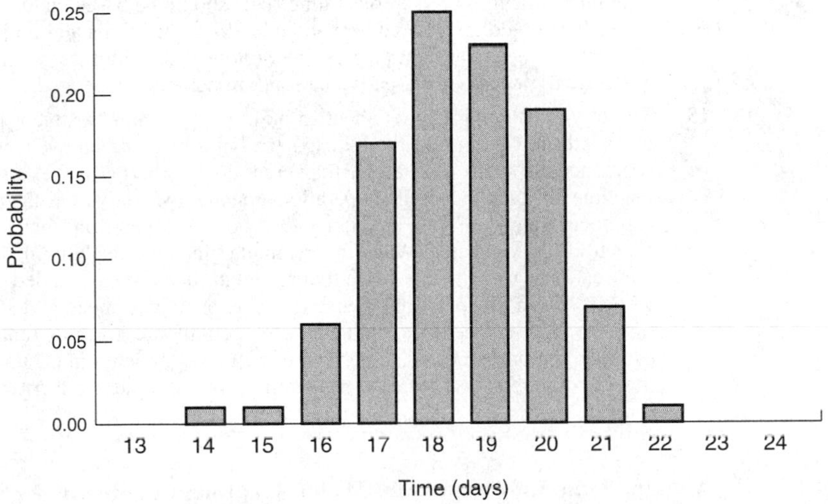

For example, activity A is critical in 85 of the 100 replications. These percentages are graphed in Figure 12.35. We see that activities A, B, D, H, and J are critical most often. These are where Tom should devote his efforts if he wants to complete the project sooner. However, this extra effort still *might* not help; there were times when these activities were *not* on the critical path. Unlike the nonprobabilistic example in Chapter 4, we cannot say for certain which activities will be critical. The simulation only tells us which activities are most *likely* to be critical. ■

FIGURE 12.35 **Probabilities of Activities Being Critical**

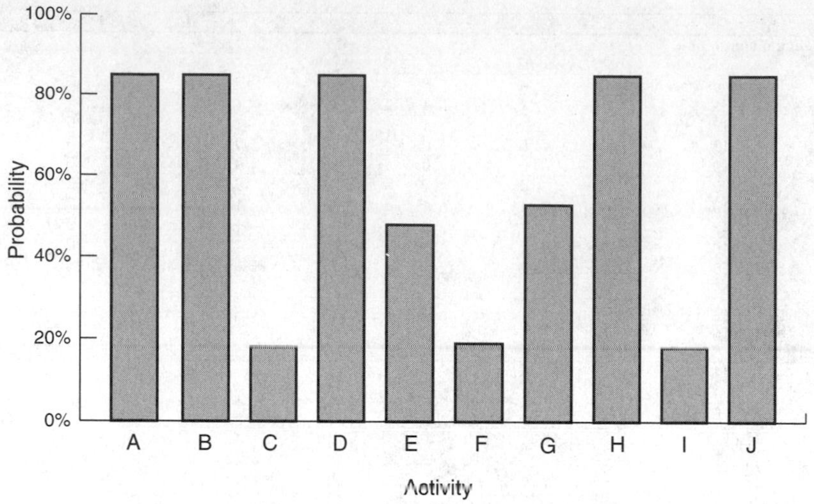

PROBLEMS

Skill-Building Problems

14 For the simulation shown in Figure 12.32, use the PROJECT.XLS file to find a 95% confidence interval for the mean total project time. This should be based on the 100 simulated total project times. Then redo the data table to include 200 replications and find the new 95% confidence interval for the mean total project time. (*Note*: Don't look for a unique answer; everyone's answer will depend on the particular random numbers generated.)

15 The city of Bloomington is about to build a new water treatment plant. Once the plant is designed (D) we can select the site (S), the building contractor (C), and the operating personnel (P). Once the site is selected we may erect the building (B). We can order the water treatment machine (W) and prepare the operations manual (M) only after the contractor is selected. We can begin training (T) the operators when both the operations manual and operating personnel selection are completed. When the treatment plant and the building are finished, we can install the treatment machine (I). Once the treatment machine is installed and operators are trained, we can obtain an operating license (L). The estimated mean and standard deviation of the time (in months) needed to complete each activity are given in Table 12.7. Use simulation to estimate the probability that the project will be completed in (a) under 50 days and (b) more than 55 days. Also estimate the probability that B, I, and T are critical activities.

TABLE 12.7 **Activity Time Information for Water Treatment Problem**

	Mean	Standard Deviation
Activity D	6	1.5
Activity S	2	0.3
Activity C	4	1.0
Activity P	3	1.0
Activity B	24	0.6
Activity W	14	4.0
Activity M	3	0.4
Activity T	4	1.0
Activity I	6	1.0
Activity L	3	6.0

16 In order to complete an addition to the Business Building, the activities in Table 12.8 need to be completed (all times are in months). The project is completed once Room 111 has been destroyed and the main structure has been built.

a Estimate the probability that it will take at least three years to complete the addition.

b For each activity, estimate the probability that it will be a critical activity.

TABLE 12.8 **Information on Activities for Business Building Problem**

	Predecessors	Mean Time	Standard Deviation
Activity A: Hire Workers	—	4	0.6
Activity B: Dig Big Hole	A	9	2.5
Activity C: Pour Foundation	B	5	1.0
Activity D: Destroy Room	A	7	2.0
Activity E: Build Main Structure	C	10	1.5

17 In order to build Indiana University's new law building, the activities in Table 12.9 must be completed (all times are in months).

a Estimate the probability that the project will take less than 30 months to complete.

b Estimate the probability that the project will take more than 3 years to complete.

c For each of the activities A, B, C, and G, estimate the probability that it is a critical activity. ■

TABLE 12.9 **Information on Activities for Law Building Problem**

	Predecessors	Mean Time	Standard Deviation
Activity A: Obtain Funding	—	6	0.6
Activity B: Design Building	A	8	1.3
Activity C: Prepare Site	A	2	0.2
Activity D: Lay Foundation	B, C	2	0.3
Activity E: Erect Walls and Roof	D	3	1.0
Activity F: Finish Exterior	E	3	0.6
Activity G: Finish Interior	D	7	1.5
Activity H: Landscape Grounds	F, G	5	1.2

12.9

Investing in the Stock Market

There are numerous strategies for investing in the stock market. These vary from the very simple to the very complex. Perhaps the only thing they have in common is that the serious investors who devise these strategies believe they can be used to "beat the market." Is this possible? In this section we will build a spreadsheet model to simulate a particular investment strategy and keep track of how well it does over time. You can then modify the spreadsheet to incorporate your own strategy and see how successful it is. Although we believe the model developed here is a very interesting one, we do not claim it will help you beat the market. In fact, the principal insight you gain from this model may be that inherent randomness can ruin just about any strategy!

We will confine the model to an investor trading a single stock over a period of time. At the beginning of any day, the investor checks how the price of the stock has changed from the previous day and then decides how many shares (if any) to buy or sell at the new price. There are two key ingredients to this model. The first is the random aspect, namely, how the price of the stock changes from one day to the next. (We will only consider trading done at the *beginning* of the day, that is, we won't get into the details of how the stock price changes throughout a given day.) This random behavior can take many forms, and many researchers and traders have spent considerable effort trying to understand the underlying probabilistic mechanism that drives stock price changes. We will consider a fairly simple type of behavior.

The other key element is the trading strategy. Each day the investor must decide whether to buy or sell (or do nothing). Also, if a buy or sell decision is made, the investor must decide how *much* to buy or sell. In reality, these decisions can be based on everything the investor has observed up to the current time: how the price has moved recently, how many shares are currently owned, and maybe even a random element (I feel lucky today). We will develop only a fairly simple "buy low, sell high" strategy, but you are welcome to incorporate your own strategies.

EXAMPLE 12.4

Mary Higgins is a freelance writer with enough spare time on her hands to play the stock market fairly seriously. Each morning she observes the change in stock price of a particular stock and decides whether to buy or sell, and if so, how many shares to buy or sell. We will assume that on day 1, she has $100,000 cash to invest and that she spends part of this to buy her first 500 shares of the stock. From that point on, she follows a fairly simple "buy low, sell high" strategy. Specifically, if the price has increased three days in a row, she sells 25% of her shares of the stock. If the price has increased two days in a row (but not three), she sells 10% of her shares. In the other direction, if the price has decreased three days in a row, she buys 25% more shares, whereas if the price has decreased only two days in a row, she buys 10% more shares. She wants to simulate how this strategy will do over a period of 75 trading days.

Solution

Although Mary can specify her strategy, she cannot determine how the price of the stock will change. She probably doesn't even know the probability distribution of stock price changes, so we will supply one for her. (In reality, this is the most difficult aspect of the problem to model.) We will build a type of trend into the stock price changes. First, we will allow the price to increase or decrease by $1 or $2, or not change at all, each trading day. Then we will assume that decreases are more likely to be followed by decreases, increases are more likely to be followed by increases, and a symmetric distribution follows a "no change." That is, there are three possible probability distributions for the current change in price, and these depend on whether the *previous* change was a decrease, an increase, or no change. These distributions appear in Table 12.10. For example, if the price decreases by

TABLE 12.10 Price Change Distributions for Investment Example

	Probabilities Following		
Price Change	**Decrease**	**Increase**	**No Change**
−$2	0.20	0.10	0.15
−$1	0.25	0.15	0.20
$0	0.30	0.30	0.30
+$1	0.15	0.25	0.20
+$2	0.10	0.20	0.15

$1 from Tuesday to Wednesday, the Decrease column of the table shows the probabilities of the various price changes from Wednesday to Thursday.

We should point out that these probabilities would be very difficult to obtain in a realistic situation. In fact, many investors might argue whether a stable set of probabilities such as these even exist. However, without some specific probability distribution(s), we cannot run the simulation at all. Therefore, we have chosen the probabilistic structure in Table 12.10 as a "reasonable" starting point.

The rest is now a matter of bookkeeping, as we explain below. The relevant spreadsheet appears in Figure 12.36. (See the file INVEST.XLS.)

1 **Inputs.** Enter Mary's initial cash ($100,000) in cell B3. Also, enter the probability distributions from Table 12.10 in rows 8 through 12. As in previous examples, it is convenient to enter *cumulative* probabilities so that we can use the VLOOKUP function to generate price changes. To simplify VLOOKUP formulas, name the probability distribution ranges Lookup1, Lookup2, and Lookup3. For example,

FIGURE 12.36 **Investment Simulation**

Investment example

Initial cash: $100,000

Probability distributions (lookup tables)

Lookup table following decrease		Lookup table following increase		Lookup table following no change	
Cum prob	Change	Cum prob	Change	Cum prob	Change
0.00	-2	0.00	-2	0.00	-2
0.20	-1	0.10	-1	0.15	-1
0.45	0	0.25	0	0.35	0
0.75	1	0.55	1	0.65	1
0.90	2	0.80	2	0.85	2

Day	Previous share price	Change in share price	Current share price	Previous shares owned	Shares sold	Shares purchased	Current shares owned	Previous cash	Change in cash	Current cash	Current worth of shares	Cumulative gain/loss	Random number
1	$50	($2)	$48	0	0	500	500	$100,000	($24,000)	$76,000	$24,000	$0	0.1148373
2	$48	($2)	$46	500	0	50	550	$76,000	($2,300)	$73,700	$25,300	($1,000)	0.028227
3	$46	($1)	$45	550	0	138	688	$73,700	($6,210)	$67,490	$30,960	($1,550)	0.4284472
4	$45	$2	$47	688	0	0	688	$67,490	$0	$67,490	$32,336	($174)	0.9911291
5	$47	($2)	$45	688	0	0	688	$67,490	$0	$67,490	$30,960	($1,550)	0.0902571
6	$45	$0	$45	688	0	0	688	$67,490	$0	$67,490	$30,960	($1,550)	0.6266208
7	$45	($1)	$44	688	0	0	688	$67,490	$0	$67,490	$30,272	($2,238)	0.2538854
8	$44	$0	$44	688	0	0	688	$67,490	$0	$67,490	$30,272	($2,238)	0.6194214
70	$45	($2)	$43	801	0	0	801	$64,794	$0	$64,794	$34,443	($763)	0.1486562
71	$43	($2)	$41	801	0	80	881	$64,794	($3,280)	$61,514	$36,121	($2,365)	0.163828
72	$41	($2)	$39	881	0	220	1101	$61,514	($8,580)	$52,934	$42,939	($4,127)	0.1661718
73	$39	($2)	$37	1101	0	275	1376	$52,934	($10,175)	$42,759	$50,912	($6,329)	0.1847205
74	$37	($1)	$36	1376	0	344	1720	$42,759	($12,384)	$30,375	$61,920	($7,705)	0.3508895
75	$36	($1)	$35	1720	0	430	2150	$30,375	($15,050)	$15,325	$75,250	($9,425)	0.2973186

Data table to replicate gain/loss over 75 days

Replication	Gain/loss		Positive?
	($9,425)		
1	$10,007		1
2	$5,256		1
3	$1,232		1
4	($32,799)		0
5	$846		1
6	$7,399		1
7	$3,353		1
8	($22,278)		0
9	$5,719		1
10	$10,353		1
97	$3,815		1
98	$5,023		1
99	($8,360)		0
100	$7,202		1
Average	$785	% positive	76%
StDev	$8,055		
Minimum	($32,799)		
Maximum	$14,766		

Frequency table

Value	Frequency
($10,000)	8
($7,500)	4
($5,000)	1
($2,500)	0
$0	11
$2,500	27
$5,000	26
$7,500	16
$10,000	2
	5

Lookup1 is the name of the range A8:B12 that is relevant when the previous price change was a decrease.

2 **Day numbers.** Each row from row 15 to row 89 corresponds to the beginning of a particular trading day. The data in these rows comprise a *single* replication of the simulation. Begin by entering the values 1 through 75 in the range A15:A89.

3 **Uniform 0,1 random numbers.** Enter random numbers in column N by entering the formula

```
=RAND()
```

in cell N15 and copying it to the range N16:N89. Each random number will be used to drive that day's stock price change.

4 **Share prices.** The data in columns B, C, and D concern share prices. Enter $50 as the original share price in cell B15. We will assume that the previous change in price (one we can't see) was no change, so generate the current change in price in cell C15 with the formula

```
=VLOOKUP(N15,Lookup3,2)
```

Then calculate the new share price in cell D15 with the formula

```
=B15+C15
```

and copy it to the range D16:D89.

5 **Price changes.** Since the previous share price on day 2 is the current share price from day 1, enter the formula

```
=D15
```

in cell B16 and copy it to the range B17:B89. Then generate the change in share price for day 2 in cell C16 with the formula

```
=IF(C15<0,VLOOKUP(N16,Lookup1,2),
IF(C15>0,VLOOKUP(N16,Lookup2,2),
VLOOKUP(N16,Lookup3,2)))
```

and copy it to the range C17:C89. This formula (a nested IF) is not as complex as it looks. It simply says to look at the previous price change (in cell C15). If this price change is negative, we use the Lookup1 table to generate the next price change. If the previous price change is positive we use the Lookup2 table, and if it is zero we use the Lookup3 table.

6 **Shares owned and traded.** In columns E through H we keep track of the number of the shares owned and traded. Since Mary begins by buying her first 500 shares on day 1, enter the values 0, 0, 500, and 500 in the range E15:H15. Then enter the formulas

```
=H15
```

and

```
=E16–F16+G16
```

in cells E16 and H16 and copy these down their respective columns. The former formula shows the carryover from one day to the next; the latter represents the trading activity.

7 **Selling activity.** Columns F and G reflect Mary's trading strategy. We will explain the selling first; the buying is exactly the same except the greater than sign (>) is replaced by a less than sign (<). Recall that Mary first checks whether there have been three

price increases in a row. On day 2, however, there are only two price changes to check. So enter the formula

```
=IF(AND(C16>0,C15>0),ROUND(.1*E16,0),0)
```

in cell F16. (The ROUND function, with second argument 0, means to round the quantity .1*E16 to the nearest integer. This is because Mary can't sell *part* of a share of stock.) Then in cell F17 enter the typical formula

```
=IF(AND(C17>0,C16>0,C15>0),ROUND(.25*E17,0),
IF(AND(C17>0,C16>0),ROUND(.1*E17,0),0))
```

and copy it to the range F18:F89. Again, this nested IF isn't as complicated as it appears. Mary first checks if the three most recent price changes were positive. If so, she sells 25% of her shares. Otherwise, she checks whether the *two* most recent price changes were positive, in which case she sells 10% of her shares. Otherwise, she sells no shares.

8 **Buying activity.** As explained in the previous step, fill in column G (for buying shares) in the same way you filled column F, but replace each > with <.

9 **Initial wealth.** Since Mary keeps changing shares into cash and vice versa, we keep track of whether she is "winning" or "losing" by evaluating her total worth—her cash plus the value of her stock—each day and comparing it to her original cash of $100,000. We do this in columns I through M. Begin by entering her initial wealth in cell I15 with the formula

```
=B3
```

10 **Cash inflow and outflow.** Calculate the amount of cash spent to purchase shares or the amount earned by selling shares in cell J15 with the formula

```
=D15*(F15–G15)
```

and copy it down column J. Notice that either the value in cell F15 or the value in G15 (or both) will be 0, since Mary won't sell *and* buy on the same day. So this formula accurately reflects cash inflow or outflow.

11 **Current cash, worth, and cumulative gain or loss.** In columns K, L, and M we keep track of Mary's current cash, the current worth of her shares of stock, and her cumulative gain or loss relative to her original $100,000. Therefore, enter the formulas

```
=I15+J15
=D15*H15
```

and

```
=K15+L15–$B$3
```

in cells K15, L15, and M15 and copy these down the respective columns. Also, since her previous cash on any day is her current cash from the day before, enter the formula

```
=K15
```

in cell I16 and copy it down column I.

12 **Data table to replicate simulation.** Use a data table to replicate the entire 75-day scenario 100 times in the range A93:B193, where each replication finds the cumulative gain or loss after 75 days. To do this, enter the formula

```
=M89
```

in cell B93 and use the Data/Table command with any blank cell as the column input cell.

13 **Summary statistics.** Use the AVERAGE, STDEV, MIN, and MAX functions in the range B194:B197 to calculate these statistics for the 100 replicated gains and losses. Also, for each replication check whether she ends up ahead or behind. Specifically, enter the formula

=IF(B94>0,1,0)

in cell D94 and copy it to the range D95:D193. Then use the AVERAGE function in cell D194 to calculate the fraction of replications she ends up ahead.

For the particular 75-day scenario shown in the middle of Figure 12.36, Mary ends up with a net loss of $9425, that is, with a cash equivalent of $90,575. (It represents a loss because she started with $100,000.) However, a look at the replications at the bottom of the spreadsheet shows that her luck is sometimes very good and sometimes *very* bad. Her best 75-day period earned her $14,766 and her worst gave her a $32,799 loss.

In reality, this underestimates how bad things can get. By repeatedly pressing F9 to produce new sets of 100 simulations, we found that Mary sometimes loses more than $100,000. How is it possible that she could lose this much when she started with only $100,000? A close look at the formulas in column G shows that Mary is able to purchase more shares than her cash allows. So we are essentially allowing her to borrow money to purchase shares. Figure 12.37 shows a time series chart of gains and losses for such a disastrous replication. Basically, what happens is that the price of the stock goes down consistently. Mary keeps buying shares, hoping that the price will eventually go back up, but it doesn't!

For the 100 replications shown in Figure 12.36, Mary gains on average $785 (cell B194), and she realizes a gain on 76 of the 100 replications (cell D194). However, the large standard deviation in cell B195 suggests a skewness in the distribution of the 75-day gains and losses. We can see this more clearly with a histogram of these gains and losses, as shown in Figure 12.38. The large spikes in the middle (representing gains between $0 and $5000) indicate the most likely outcomes. However, the relatively large spike on the left (representing losses of more than $10,000) shows that large losses are certainly possible—and they certainly distort the average!

FIGURE 12.37 A Disastrous Scenario for Investment Example

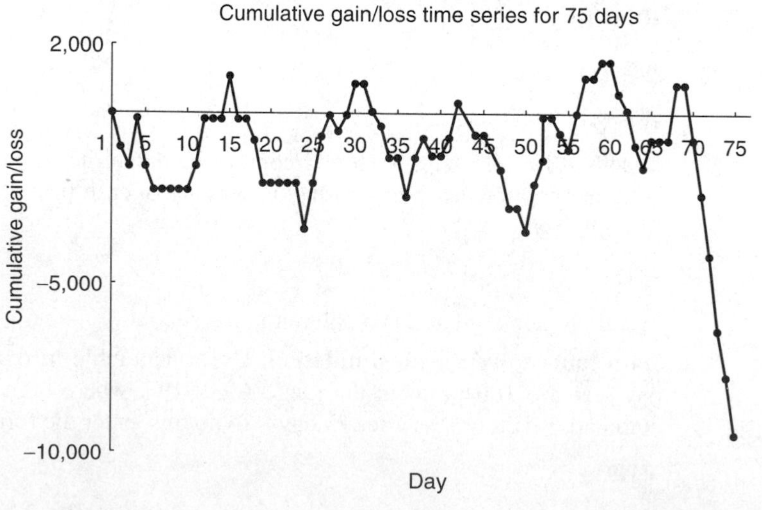

FIGURE 12.38 Histogram of 75-Day Gains and Losses for Investment Example

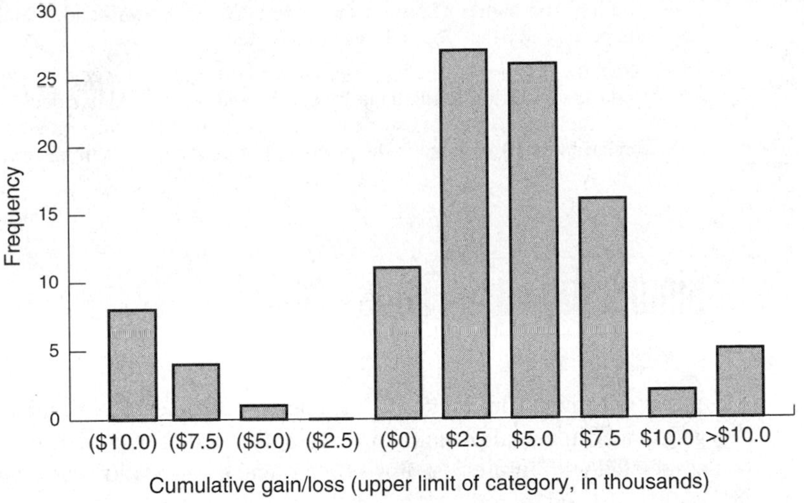

Is Mary's investment strategy a good one? Most people would probably say no. On the plus side, it earns her a modest 75-day profit about 76% of the time. However, it has a lot of downside risk, a quality investors uniformly dislike. In the problems you are asked to see whether you can devise a strategy that has a higher average gain *and* less downside risk. Unfortunately, without getting into very complex mathematical models, the only way to search for better strategies is by trial and error! ■

PROBLEMS

Skill-Building Problems

18 (Based on Kelly [5]) You currently have \$100. Each week you can invest any amount of money you currently have in a risky investment. With probability .4 the amount you invest is tripled (e.g., if you invest \$100, you increase your asset position by \$300), and with probability .6 the amount you invest is lost. Consider the following investment strategies:

- **a** Each week invest 10% of your money.
- **b** Each week invest 30% of your money.
- **c** Each week invest 50% of your money.

Simulate 100 weeks of each strategy 50 times. Which strategy appears to be best? In general, if you can multiply your investment by M with probability p and lose your investment with probability q, you should invest a fraction $\frac{p(M-1)-q}{M-1}$ of your money each week. This strategy maximizes (for a favorable game) the expected growth rate of your fortune and is known as the **Kelly Criterion**.

19 (Based on Marcus [6]) The Balboa mutual fund has beaten the Standard and Poor's 500 during 11 of the last 13 years. People use this as an argument that you can "beat the market." Here's another way to look at it that shows that Balboa's beating the market 11 out of 13 times is not unusual. Consider 50 mutual funds, each of which has a 50% chance of beating the market during a given year. Use simulation to estimate the probability that over a 13-year period the "best" of the 50 mutual funds will beat the market for at least 11 out of 13 years. This probability turns out to exceed 40%, which means that the best mutual fund's beating the market 11 out of 13 years is not an unusual occurrence!

20 You now have \$3. You will toss a fair coin four times. Before each toss you can bet any amount of your money (including none) on the outcome of the toss. If heads comes up you win the amount you bet. If tails comes up you lose the amount you bet. Your goal is to reach \$6. It turns out that you can maximize your chance of reaching \$6 by betting either the money you have on hand or \$6 minus the money you have on hand, whichever is smaller. Estimate the probability that you will reach your goal.

21 Amanda is presently a 25-year-old hard-working employee of Enright Enterprises. Her goal is to have \$1 million in the bank by age 55 and retire. She has decided to invest \$5000 per year in a stock index fund. Historically, the mean annual return on stocks is 13% with a standard deviation of 10%. What is the probability that Amanda will be able to retire on time? ■

12.10 Simulating Cash Flows

As mentioned in Section 12.2, many companies use simulation in their capital budgeting and financial planning processes. Simulation can be used to model the uncertainty associated with future cash flows. In particular, simulation can be used to answer questions such as the following:

- What is the mean and variance of a project's net present value (NPV)?
- What is the probability that a project will have a negative NPV?
- What are the mean and variance of a company's profit during the next fiscal year?
- What is the probability that a company will have to borrow more than \$2 million during the next year?

The following example illustrates how simulation can be used to evaluate an investment opportunity.

EXAMPLE 12.5

The General Ford (GF) Auto Corporation is trying to determine the profitability of a new type of compact car it is in the process of developing. The car is assumed to generate sales for the next ten years. In order to determine whether development of the car should continue, information has been gathered through focus groups with the marketing and engineering departments. In particular, GF has analyzed the fixed cost of developing the car, the variable cost of producing each car, the sales price per car, the demand during each of the next ten years, the production policy, and the interest rate used for discounting future cash flows. Based on this analysis, GF has decided to use the following inputs in a simulation model.

The fixed cost of developing the car is not known with certainty. GF models this uncertainty with a normal distribution, mean \$2.2 billion and standard deviation \$0.3 billion. The entire fixed cost is assumed to occur at the beginning of year 1.

The variable production cost in year 1 is also modeled with a normal distribution, mean \$7200, standard deviation \$250. Each year after year 1, the variable production cost is the previous year's variable production cost multiplied by an inflation factor. Each year this inflation factor is assumed to be normally distributed with mean 1.05 (a 5% increase) and standard deviation .02. All production costs are assumed to occur at the ends of the respective years.

The sales price in year 1 is already set at \$11,000. After year 1, the sales price will increase by the same inflation factor that drives production costs. Specifically, the sales price will be the previous year's sales price multiplied by the inflation factor. Like production costs, revenues from sales are assumed to occur at the ends of the respective years.

The demand for cars in year 1 is assumed to be normally distributed with mean 100,000 and standard deviation 10,000. After year 1, the demand in a given year is assumed to be normally distributed with mean equal to the *actual* demand in the previous year and standard deviation 10,000. For example, if the observed demand in year 3 is 105,000, then the demand distribution in year 4 is assumed to be normal with mean 105,000 and standard deviation 10,000. An implication of this assumption is that demands in successive years are *not* probabilistically independent. If the demand in one year is large, for example, the mean demand for the next year is large, so that the actual demand for the next year will tend to be large.

In any particular year the company plans to base its production policy on the probability distribution of demand for that year—*before* the actual demand for that year is observed. In particular, if the expected demand in year t is ED_t and the standard deviation of demand is σ_t, then GF's policy is to produce $ED_t + k\sigma_t$ cars, where k is a decision variable that GF will have to select. For example, if it chooses $k = 1$, then its production quantity in any year will be one standard deviation above the expected demand. From the properties of the normal distribution, this implies that the chances are approximately five out of six of meeting all demand for the year. (This is because a normal random variable has approximate probability 5/6 of being no more than one standard deviation above the mean.) If demand in any year is greater than production, the excess demand is lost. However, if production in any year is greater than demand, GF will sell the excess cars at an end-of-year discount of 30%.

GF plans to use a 10% interest rate to discount future cash flows. This means, for example, that a cash flow of \$1 at the beginning of year 1 is equivalent to a cash flow of \$1.10 at the end of year 1.

Given these assumptions, GF wants to develop a simulation spreadsheet that will evaluate its NPV over the ten-year time horizon.

Solution

The simulation spreadsheet for GF appears in Figure 12.39. (See the file NEWCAR.XLS.) It can be formed as follows.

1 **Inputs.** Enter the various inputs through row 27. As usual, it is a good practice to enter all of the input values in cells so that they can be referenced in formulas later on. Notice that we have used a value of 1 for the decision variable k in cell G24. This can easily be changed to see the effects of other ordering policies.

2 **Variable cost inflation factors.** Rows 32 through 46 contain a single ten-year simulation. The approach is to enter appropriate formulas in columns B and C for years 1 and 2, then copy the year 2 formulas to the columns for the other years, and finally calculate the values in rows 40, 43, 44, and 46. Begin by entering the variable production cost inflation factor relating year 2 to year 1 in cell C32 with the formula

=NORMINV(RAND(),$B$19,$B$20)

and copy this across to the rest of row 32.

3 **Production quantities.** The production quantity in year 1 is based on the expected demand and the standard deviation of demand in year 1, so enter the formula

=G7+G24*G8

in cell B33. For other years, the expected demand is the previous year's actual demand, which is used to calculate the production quantity. Therefore, for year 2 enter the formula

=B34+$G$24*$G$13

FIGURE 12.39 Simulation for New Car Example

	A	B	C	D	E	F	G	H	I	J	K	L
1	**Simulation of costs/sales for a new model of car**											
2												
3	**Probability distributions used, other inputs**											
4												
5	**Fixed costs (assumed to occur at the beginning of year 1)**					**Demand for cars in year 1**						
6	Normal distribution ($billions)					Normal distribution (1000's of cars)						
7	Mean	2.2				Mean	100					
8	StDev	0.3				StDev	10					
9												
10						**Demand for cars in year t (t>1)**						
11	**Variable production cost per car in year 1**					Normal distribution of error term (1000's of cars)						
12	Normal distribution ($1000s)					Mean	demand from previous year					
13	Mean	7.2				StDev	10					
14	StDev	0.25										
15						**Discount rate (used to find NPV) in all years**						
16							9%					
17	**Variable production cost inflation factor in succeeding years**											
18	Normal distribution					**Production policy**						
19	Mean	1.05				Production each year is the mean demand plus a multiple of the stdev of						
20	StDev	0.02				demand (for that year). If demand is greater than supply, the excess demand is lost.						
21						If the supply is greater than the demand, the excess are sold at a discount.						
22	**Sales price in year 1 (all sales are assumed to occur at the end of the year)**											
23	No uncertainty ($1000s)					Multiple (k) of stdev used for setting production quantity						
24		11					1					
25												
26	**Sales price inflation factor for succeeding years**					**Year-end percentage discount for leftover cars at the end of the year**						
27	Same as variable production cost inflation factor						30%					
28												
29	**Simulation**											
30												
31	Year	1	2	3	4	5	6	7	8	9	10	
32	Inflation factor	N/A	1.039	1.083	1.059	1.055	1.049	1.078	1.051	1.043	1.061	
33	Production (1000s)	110.00	89.81	106.05	109.46	124.44	135.28	114.98	105.92	92.88	91.37	
34	Demand (1000s)	79.81	96.05	99.46	114.44	125.28	104.98	95.92	82.88	81.37	79.45	
35	VarProd cost ($1000s)	7.30	7.58	8.22	8.70	9.18	9.63	10.38	10.91	11.39	12.08	
36	Sales price ($1000s)	11.00	11.43	12.38	13.11	13.83	14.51	15.65	16.45	17.16	18.21	
37	Production cost ($millions	803	681	871	952	1142	1303	1194	1156	1057	1104	
38	Revenue ($millions)	1110	1027	1289	1435	1721	1831	1709	1628	1534	1599	
39												
40	Fixed cost ($1000s)	$2,823,707										
41												
42	NPV's ($1000s)											
43	Production costs	$6,362,541										
44	Revenue	$9,238,880										
45												
46	Total NPV ($1000s)	$52,632										

in cell C33 and copy it across to the rest of row 33.

4 **Demands.** Generate the demand in year 1 in cell B34 with the formula

=NORMINV(RAND(),G7,G8)

As in the previous step, the expected demand in year 2 is the actual demand from year 1, so generate the demand for year 2 in cell C34 with the formula

=NORMINV(RAND(),B34,$G$13)

Then copy this to the rest of row 34 to generate demands for the other years.

5 **Variable production costs.** Generate the variable production cost for year 1 in cell B35 with the formula

=NORMINV(RAND(),B13,B14)

Then use the inflation factor in row 32 to generate the variable production cost for year 2 in cell C35 with the formula

=B35*C32

and copy this across to the rest of row 35.

6 **Sales prices.** Enter the (nonrandom) sales price for year 1 in cell B36 with the formula

=B24

Then generate the sales price for year 2 in cell C36 with the formula

=B36*C32

and copy this across to the rest of row 36.

7 **Production costs.** The production cost for any year is the production quantity multiplied by the variable production cost, so enter the formula

=B33*B35

in cell B37 and copy it to the rest of row 37. (Notice that because the production quantity is in thousands of cars and variable production cost is in thousands of dollars, the resulting product will automatically be in millions of dollars.)

8 **Revenues.** The revenue in any year is calculated in one of two possible ways. If demand is greater than the production quantity, then revenue is the sales price multiplied by the production quantity. Otherwise, if demand is less than the production quantity, then revenue is the sales price multiplied by the demand, plus the discounted sales price multiplied by the number of cars left over. So calculate the revenue for year 1 in cell B38 with the formula

=IF(B33<B34,B36*B33,B36*(B34+(1–$G$27)*(B33–B34)))

and copy it to the rest of row 38.

9 **Fixed cost.** Generate the fixed cost of developing the car (in thousands of dollars) in cell B40 with the formula

=NORMINV(RAND(),B7,B8)*1000000

10 **NPVs.** Calculate the NPV of all production costs (in thousands of dollars) in cell B43 with the formula

=NPV($G$16,B37:K37)*1000

Then copy this to cell B44 to calculate the NPV of all revenues (in thousands of dollars). Notice that the NPV function takes two arguments: the interest rate used for discounting, and a stream of cash flows beginning with the flow at the end of year 1.

11 **Total NPV.** Finally, calculate the total NPV in cell B46 with the formula

=B44–B40–B43

Because the fixed costs occur at the *beginning* of year 1, they are not discounted when calculating total NPV.

As in other simulations we have considered, the calculations to this point show only one possible scenario for the ten-year horizon. As we see from cell B46 of Figure 12.39, the future of this car looks good—the NPV represents a $52 million gain. However, this might be due to a lucky set of random numbers. To check this, we form a data table in the range A50:B150 in order to replicate the ten-year simulation 100 times, each time recording the total NPV. This can be done by entering the formula

=B46

in cell B50 and using the Data/Table command with any blank cell as the column input cell. Some of the results appear in Figure 12.40, including the average, standard deviation, minimum, and maximum of the 100 total NPVs. The average and standard deviation are

FIGURE 12.40 Data Table for New Car Simulation

	A	B	C	D	E	F
48	**Data table to replicate the simulation 100 times**				**Frequency Table**	
49	Replication	Total NPV		Value ($1000s)	Value ($billions)	Frequency
50		$52,632		($1,000,000)	-1	0
51	1	$406,202		($500,000)	-0.5	1
52	2	$269,824		$0	0	7
53	3	$1,321,790		$500,000	0.5	26
54	4	$1,054,873		$1,000,000	1	35
55	5	$9,974		$1,500,000	1.5	23
56	6	$111,560		$2,000,000	2	7
57	7	$1,115,318			>2	1
58	8	$1,411,550				
59	9	$405,058				
148	98	$855,381				
149	99	$1,381,527				
150	100	$92,742				
151	Average	$744,868		95% confidence interval for total NPV		
152	StDev	$536,592		Lower limit	$637,549	
153	Minimum	($604,894)		Upper limit	$852,186	
154	Maximum	$2,486,890				

also used to form a 95% confidence interval for the mean total NPV. To calculate this confidence interval, enter the formulas

=B151–2*B152/SQRT(100)

and

=B151+2*B152/SQRT(100)

in cells E152 and E153.

Now an entirely different picture emerges. On average, the company can expect to make an average of approximately $745 million, and in the best case it made almost $2.5 billion. Also, the confidence interval shows that GF can be quite sure that its *expected* NPV is over $637 million. On the other hand, the standard deviation is quite high, meaning that there is a chance the company will lose a lot of money. In fact, the worst case out of 100 resulted in a loss of over $600 million. This information is summarized in the frequency table in Figure 12.40 and the accompanying histogram in Figure 12.41. In particular, we see that in $0 + 1 + 7 = 8$ of the 100 simulations, the company lost money (1 time losing in excess of $500 million), whereas its most likely scenario—in 35 out of 100 cases—was a gain of somewhere between $500 and $1000 million.

This example illustrates the value of simulation, but it points out two potential misuses of simulation. First, it can be very misleading to make only a *single* replication. This single result could easily be overly optimistic or pessimistic. Second, even if many replications are made, it can be very misleading to report only the *average* of the outputs. For example, if GF looks only at the average of the 100 total NPVs, it might form an overly optimistic view of this car's future. If it instead looks at the entire distribution of total NPV, as shown in Figure 12.41, it will see the potential for large losses and might decide *not* to continue development of the car after all. ■

PROBLEMS

Skill-Building Problems

22 Recall from the GF example that the company's ordering policy is determined by the factor k, the number of standard deviations above the mean for the production quantity. Rerun the

FIGURE 12.41 Histogram of NPV for New Car Simulation

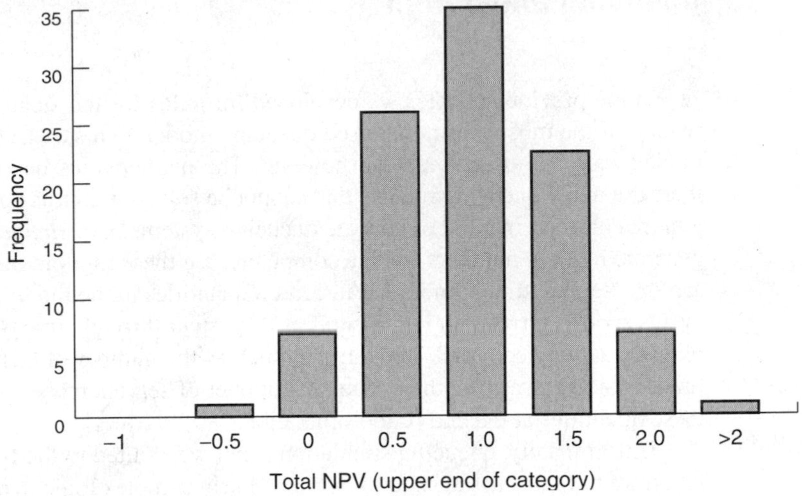

simulation using several different values of k. Is the total NPV very sensitive to this parameter? Which value of k would you recommend that GF use?

23 Dord Motors is considering whether to introduce a new model called the Racer. The profitability of the Racer will depend on the following factors:

a Fixed cost of developing the Racer: Fixed cost is equally likely to be \$3 or \$5 billion.

b Sales: Assume that year 1 sales will be normally distributed with mean 200,000 and standard deviation 50,000. Then assume that year 2 sales are normally distributed with mean equal to year 1 sales and standard deviation 50,000 and that year 3 sales are normally distributed with mean equal to year 2 sales and standard deviation 50,000.

c Price: Assume year 1 price is \$13,000. Then the year 2 price will be

$$1.05 * (\text{year 1 price} + \$30 * \%\ \text{diff1})$$

where % diff1 is the percentage by which actual year 1 sales differ from expected year 1 sales. The 1.05 factor accounts for inflation. For example, if the year 1 sales figure is 180,000, which is 10% below the expected year 1 sales, then the year 2 price will be

$$1.05 * [13,000 + 30 * (-10)] = \$13,335$$

Similarly, the year 3 price will be

$$1.05 * (\text{year 2 price} + \$30 * \%\ \text{diff2})$$

where % diff2 is the percentage by which actual year 2 sales differ from expected year 2 sales.

d Variable cost per car: Variable cost is equally likely to be \$5000, \$6000, \$7000, or \$8000 during year 1 and is assumed to increase by 5% each year.

Your goal is to estimate the NPV of the new car during its first three years. Assume cash flows are discounted at 10%, that is, \$1 received now is equivalent to \$1.10 received a year from now. Simulate 400 trials and estimate the mean and standard deviation of the NPV for the first three years of sales. Also determine a 95% confidence interval for the mean NPV of the Racer during its first three years of operation. ■

12.11

Queueing Simulation

On the previous chapter we developed formulas for the steady-state characteristics of several of the most commonly used queueing models. This *analytic* approach to queueing models can take us only so far, however. The mathematics becomes very involved, and there are many queueing models that cannot be solved with this approach at all. Therefore, a more common method to analyze queueing systems is to *simulate* them. In this case we generate random numbers (with a computer), use these random numbers as times between arrivals, service times, and other uncertain quantities in the model, and then "play out" the events such as arrivals and departures as they occur through time. As these events are being played out, we keep track of quantities such as the number of customers in the queue, the times customers wait in the queue, the number of servers busy, and so on, and then report these quantities at the end of the simulation.

Unfortunately, queueing simulation is not well suited to the type of spreadsheet simulation we have discussed so far. It requires fairly complex logic in order to keep track of the timing of events and this logic is handled much better through a programming language than by simply entering formulas into a spreadsheet.

However, in order to provide a glimpse of what queueing simulation is all about, we have taken advantage of Excel's built-in programming (macro) language, Visual Basic for Applications, to develop a queueing simulation that you can run. This is in the QUEUESIM.XLS file. When you open this file, you see a Report sheet. (See Figure 12.42.) This sheet shows the inputs for the queueing model—the same inputs we discussed in Chapter 11—and the outputs from the simulation. There are also three buttons, one for entering new inputs, one for running the simulation, and one for creating a graph of selected outputs. (See Figure 12.43.) All random times generated in this simulation application are exponentially distributed. Therefore, by changing the inputs, you can simulate most of the models we discussed in Chapter 11, including the $M/M/1$ and $M/M/s$ models with or without a finite waiting room.

When you click on any of the buttons on the Report sheet, macros on the Module1 sheet are activated. (You can look at the computer code in this module sheet, but we won't attempt to explain it here.) In particular, when you click on the button to run the simulation, a new set of random numbers is generated, events are played out again, and statistical information is stored in the output section of the Report sheet. For example, if you choose to run the simulation for 480 minutes, the statistics listed in the output section show what happens for one simulated eight-hour period.

It is important to understand the difference between the results in the previous chapter and simulation results. The earlier results are theoretical long-run averages obtained from mathematical formulas. For given inputs, they never change. In contrast, simulation results are only "snapshots" of a system during a particular period of time, and they depend on the particular random numbers generated for that period of time. Therefore, each time you run the simulation, even with the same inputs, the results will change.

It is interesting to compare the theoretical steady-state results with simulation results. For example, when we studied the $M/M/s$ model with a finite waiting room in Section 11.8, we used the following inputs:

- arrival rate = 150 per hour
- service rate per server = 30 per hour
- number of servers = 6
- maximum number of customers allowed in the system = 10

FIGURE 12.42 **Inputs and Outputs for Queueing Simulation**

Multiple Server Queueing Simulation

Change inputs

Run simulation

Create Chart

Inputs

Time unit	minute	
Customer arrival rate	2.5	
Mean time between arrivals	0.4	minutes
Service rate per server	0.5	
Mean time for each service	2.0	minutes
Number of servers	6	
Maximum allowed in system	10	
Simulation run length (minutes)	480	minutes

Simulation Outputs

(Page down for more output)

Average time in queue per customer	0.31	minutes
Maximum time a customer was in queue	3.69	minutes
Average number of customers in queue	0.70	
Maximum number in queue	4	
Fraction of time each server is busy	74.3%	
Number of customers processed	1101	
Number of customers turned away	74	
Fraction of customers turned away	6.3%	

Probability distribution of number in queue

Number in queue	% of time
0	70.62%
1	9.24%
2	6.62%
3	7.08%
4	6.65%

FIGURE 12.43 **Graph Generated by Queueing Simulation**

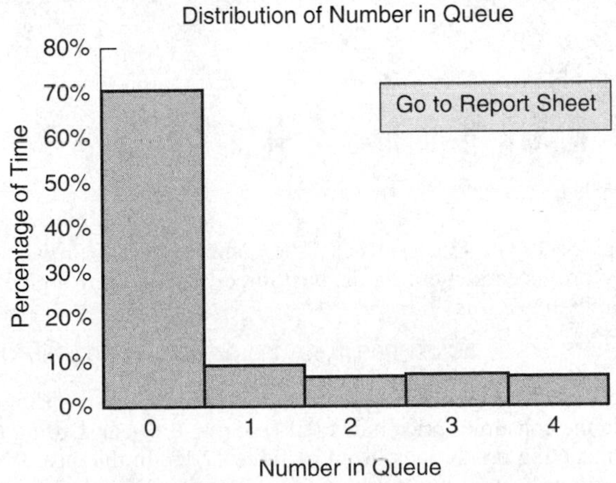

Table 12.11 shows several of the steady-state results that we obtained earlier for this model, as well as results from five replications of the simulation with the same inputs. Each simulation was run for 480 minutes of simulated time, that is, one eight-hour day. As we see, the simulated results are close to the theoretical results, but each simulated day is slightly different from every other one.

We will not pursue queueing simulation any further in this book because it requires computer programming skills or a special-purpose simulation package (such as SIMSCRIPT) that automates much of the programming and allows users to develop simulation models fairly easily. Both of these are beyond the scope of this book.

TABLE 12.11 Steady-State Versus Simulated Queueing Results

	Steady-State	Run 1	Run 2	Run 3	Run 4	Run 5
Average Number in Queue	.76	.62	.64	.80	.88	.70
Average Time in Queue (minutes)	.32	.26	.28	.34	.39	.31
Percentage of Customers Lost	6.2%	4.1%	4.5%	7.2%	7.5%	6.3%

12.12 Conclusion

Computer simulation is one of the most versatile of all management science tools, and its popularity is growing constantly. We have seen in this chapter how the single RAND function in Excel allows us to simulate a wide variety of problems. However, this represents only a small fraction of what simulation can accomplish. In the next chapter we will revisit spreadsheet simulation, but we will take advantage of a powerful add-in package, @RISK, that facilitates simulation, particularly statistics gathering and presentation of results. This add-in, along with the functionality of Excel itself, allows individuals with virtually no programming skills to perform complex and realistic simulations. Even this, however, is only the tip of the iceberg in terms of what simulation can accomplish. As we discussed briefly in Section 12.11, there are many special-purpose simulation packages that can simulate complex queueing systems and a variety of other processes, and these packages are being using increasingly often in the business world. The material in this chapter has given you a good start in simulation, but be aware that there is a whole lot more out there!

REVIEW PROBLEMS

Skill-Building Problem

24 Truckco produces the Goatco truck. The company wants to gain information about the discounted profits earned during the next three years. During a given year the total number of trucks sold in the U.S. is

$$500,000 + 50,000 * GNP - 40,000 * INF$$

where *GNP* is the percentage increase in GNP during the year and *INF* is the percentage increase in the consumer price index (CPI) during the year. During the next three years Value Line has made the predictions listed in Table 12.12. In the past, 95% of Value Line's *GNP* predictions have been accurate within 6%, and 95% of Value Line's *INF* predictions have been accurate within 5%. We assume that the actual *GNP* and *INF* values are normally distributed each year.

TABLE 12.12 **Predictions for Truckco Problem**

	Year		
	1	2	3
GNP	3%	5%	4%
INF	4%	7%	3%

At the beginning of each year a number of competitors may enter the trucking business. At the beginning of any year, the probability distribution of the number of competitors that will enter the trucking business is that given in Table 12.13. Before competitors join the industry at the beginning of year 1 there are two competitors. During a year that begins with *c* competitors (after competitors have entered the business, but before any have left), Goatco will have a market share given by $.5 * (.9)^c$. At the end of each year there is a 20% chance that each competitor will leave the industry.

TABLE 12.13 **Distribution of Number of New Competitors for Truckco Problem**

Number of New Competitors	Probability
0	0.50
1	0.30
2	0.10
3	0.10

The sales price of the truck and production cost per truck are given in Table 12.14. Simulate 500 replications of Truckco's profit for the next three years. Estimate the mean and variance of the discounted three-year profits, using a discount rate of 10%. You can use Excel's NPV function here. Do the same if there is a 50% chance during each year that each competitor will leave the industry.

TABLE 12.14 **Prices and Costs for Truckco Problem**

	Year 1	Year 2	Year 3
Sales Price	$15,000	$16,000	$17,000
Variable Cost	$12,000	$13,000	$14,000

Skill-Extending Problems

25 (Based on Altman [1]) The Weaver Company, a textile firm, wants to simulate its cash budget for the year 1999. We make the following assumptions. (All cash amounts are in thousands of dollars except where noted for the long-term loan.)

- Each month the monthly "base" sales follow a normal distribution with a mean of $70,000 and a standard deviation of $15,000. Then the *actual* sales in any month is the monthly base sales multiplied by a seasonal index for the month. The seasonal indexes are listed in Table 12.15.
- Cash sales for a month are 10% of monthly sales.
- Monthly collections for January and February are each $50,000. For other months, monthly collections are 90% of sales from two months ago.
- Monthly total cash receipts equal cash sales plus monthly collections.
- Together, labor and material costs are a certain fraction (called the cost factor) of monthly sales. This cost factor (the same for each month of the year) is normally distributed with mean 0.7 and standard deviation 0.03.

TABLE 12.15 **Seasonal Indexes for Weaver Problem**

	Index		Index
Jan	0.85	Jul	1.03
Feb	0.87	Aug	1.06
Mar	0.90	Sep	1.06
Apr	0.91	Oct	1.10
May	0.94	Nov	1.12
Jun	1.02	Dec	1.13

- Monthly cash disbursements include the following:
  - Monthly labor costs equal the cost factor multiplied by 20% of monthly sales.
  - Monthly material costs are $33,000 for January. In any other month they equal the cost factor multiplied by 80% of the previous month's sales.
  - Monthly operating expenses are 19% of monthly base sales.
  - The quarterly interest payment in January is $2780. In April, July, and October, it is composed of the interest on the average loan balance for last three months, paid at the short-term rate of interest for three months, plus three months of interest on the $96 million dollar long-term loan, paid at 8.5% annually. The short-term interest rate for the year is normal with mean 14% and standard deviation 1%.
  - Taxes are paid in January, April, July, and September. Each payment is $4000.
  - Dividends of $2000 are paid in February, May, August, and November.
  - Capital Expenditures are $4500 in March, $4600 in June, $4800 in September, and $4900 in December.
- At the beginning of January, there is a cash balance of −$7015. The desired ending cash balance for a given month (after adjusting the loan balance) is 18.8% of monthly sales.
- Cash evolves as follows:
  - Beginning cash for month t equals the desired ending cash for month $t-1$.
  - End of month cash for month t equals the beginning cash for month t plus the net cash flow for month t.
  - For all but January, the ending loan balance for month t equals the ending loan balance for month $t-1$ plus the desired cash for month t minus the end-of-month cash for month t.
  - For January, the ending loan balance equals the ending January desired cash balance minus the January end-of-month cash.

Simulate Weaver's yearly cash budget 500 times. Find the mean and standard deviation of the firm's total net cash flow for 1999 as well as the mean and standard deviation of the firm's monthly average loan balance for 1999. What is the probability that the firm's 1999 net cash flow will be negative? What is the probability that the firm's ending loan balance will be negative? Note that the monthly net cash flow equals the monthly cash receipts minus the monthly cash disbursements.

26 You are considering a ten-year investment project. At present, the expected cash flow each year is $1000. Suppose, however, that each year's cash flow is normally distributed with mean equal to *last* year's actual cash flow and standard deviation $100. For example, suppose that year 1 cash flow is $1200. Then year 2 cash flow is normal with mean $1200 and standard deviation $100. Also, at the end of year 1, your best guess is that each later year's expected cash flow will be $1200.

a Estimate the mean and variance of the NPV of this project. Assume that cash flows are discounted at a rate of 10% per year.

b Now assume that the project has an abandonment option. At the end of each year you can abandon the project for the value given in Table 12.16. For instance, suppose that year 1 cash flow is $400. Then at the end of year 1, you expect cash flow for each remaining year to be $400. This has an NPV of less than $6200, so you should abandon the project and collect $6200 at the end of year 1. Estimate the mean and variance of the project with the abandonment option. How much would you pay for the abandonment option? (*Hints*: One

TABLE 12.16 **Abandonment Values for Investment Problem**

	Value		Value
Year 1	$6200	**Year 6**	$3300
Year 2	$5700	**Year 7**	$2570
Year 3	$5180	**Year 8**	$1780
Year 4	$4580	**Year 9**	$920
Year 5	$3980	**Year 10**	$0

idea you need to incorporate is that you can abandon a project at most once. Thus in year 5, for example, you abandon only if the sum of future expected NPV's is less than the year 5 abandonment value and the project has not yet been abandoned. Another idea you need to incorporate is that once you abandon the project, the actual cash flows for future years will be 0. You can't abandon more than once, and actual future cash flows after abandonment should disappear.)

27 Computco sells personal computers. The demand for their computers during a month follows a normal distribution, with a mean of 400 and standard deviation of 100. Each time an order is placed, a cost of $600 per order and $1500 per computer is incurred. Computers are sold for $2800, and if Computco does not have a computer in stock, the customer will buy a computer from a competitor. At the end of each month a holding cost of $10 per computer is incurred. Orders are placed at the end of each month, and arrive at the beginning of the next month. Four ordering policies are under consideration:

- Policy 1: Place an order for 900 computers whenever the end-of-month inventory is 50 or less.
- Policy 2: Place an order for 600 computers whenever the end-of-month inventory is 200 or less.
- Policy 3: Place an order for 1000 computers whenever end-of-month inventory is 400 or less.
- Policy 4: Place an order for 1200 computers whenever end-of-month inventory is 500 or less.

Using 500 iterations, determine which ordering policy maximizes expected profit for two years. To get a more accurate idea of expected profit, you can credit Computco with a salvage value of $1500 for each computer left at the end of the last month. Assume that 400 computers are in inventory at the beginning of the first month.

Modeling Problems

28 Big Hit Video needs to determine how many copies of a new video to purchase. Assume that the company's goal is to purchase a number of copies that will maximize its expected profit from the video during the next year. Describe how you would use simulation to solve this problem. To simplify matters assume that each time a tape is rented, it is rented for one day.

29 It is surprising (but true) that if 23 people are in the same room, there is a more than 50% chance that at least two people will have the same birthday. In this problem you will estimate the chance that if 30 people are in the same room, two of them have the same birthday. You should proceed as follows.

a Generate the "birthdays" of 30 different people. Ignoring the possibility of a leap year, each person has a 1/365 chance of having a given birthday (call the days of the year 1, 2, . . . , 365). You should use a formula involving the INT and RAND functions to generate birthdays.

b Once you have generated 30 people's birthdays, how can you tell if at least two people have the same birthday? The key here is to use Excel's RANK function. (You can learn how to use this function with the Insert/Function menu item or the Function Wizard.) This function will give the rank of a number relative to a given group of numbers. In the case of a tie, two numbers will be given the same rank. For example, if the set of numbers is 4, 3, 2, 5, the RANK function will output 2, 3, 4, 1. If the set of numbers is 4, 3, 2, 4, the RANK function will output 1, 3, 4, 1.

c After using the RANK function, you should be able to determine if at least two of your 30 people have the same birthday.

30 United Electric sells refrigerators for \$400 with a one-year warranty. The warranty works as follows. If any part of the refrigerator fails during the first year after purchase, UE replaces the refrigerator for an average cost of \$100. As soon as a replacement is made, another one-year warranty period begins for the customer. If a refrigerator fails outside the warranty period, we assume that the customer immediately purchases another UE refrigerator. Suppose that the amount of time a refrigerator lasts follows a normal distribution with a mean of 1.8 years and a standard deviation of .3 year.

a Estimate the average profit per year UE earns from a customer.

b How could the approach of this problem be used to determine the optimal warranty period?

31 Many people who are involved in a small auto accident do not file a claim because they are afraid their premiums will be raised. Suppose that City Farm Insurance has three rates. If you file a claim you are moved to the next higher rate. How would you use simulation to determine whether a particular claim should be filed?

32 You are playing Pete Sampras in tennis, and you have a 42% chance of winning each point.

a Use simulation to estimate the probability you will win a particular game. Note that the first player to score at least 4 points and have at least two more points than his or her opponent wins the game.

b Use simulation to determine your probability of winning a set. (*Note*: Assume that the first player to win six games wins the set if he or she is at least two games ahead; otherwise, the first player to win seven games wins the set.)

c Use simulation to determine your probability of winning a match. (*Note*: Assume that the first player to win three sets wins the match.)

33 A building contains 1000 light bulbs. Each bulb lasts at most five months. The company maintaining the building is trying to decide whether it is worthwhile to practice a *group replacement* policy. Under a group replacement policy all bulbs are replaced every T months (where T is to be determined). Also, bulbs are replaced when they burn out. Assume that it costs 2.5¢ to replace each bulb during a group replacement and 10¢ to replace each burned-out bulb if it is replaced individually. How would you use simulation to determine whether a group replacement policy is worthwhile?

34 Two companies, company A and company B, share practically all of the market share for a product with a large national market. (Coca Cola and Pepsi represent an example.) They compete vigorously with tactics such as advertising blitzes and coupons for reduced prices. Of course, they also try to outguess what the other is going to do. For this problem, we'll take the point of view of company A, which must decide what marketing strategies to take each week. These might be proactive or reactive. A proactive tactic might be to offer 20%-off coupons during a week, regardless of what company B is doing (or has been doing). A reactive tactic might be to offer 20%-off coupons during a week after company B does so. We'll assume that company A can only react to company B's actions the following week. For example, if company B does something in week 20, company A won't learn about this until week 20, so it won't be able to react until week 21 (or later).

Each week the total market share is divided up by companies A and B. For example, their shares might be 45% and 55%. Using these values for illustration, some of A's 45% might move to B the next week, and some of B's 55% might move to A the next week. The sizes of these movements are random, but they will depend on actions A and B take during the week. (They might even depend on actions taken in previous weeks. Consider the possible delayed effect of advertising, for example.) You can assume that the net change in company A's market share is normally distributed with mean and standard deviation that depend on current (and possibly previous) actions. You can make this dependence as simple or complex as you like.

The revenues and costs are as follows:

- Each percentage point in market share is worth a certain amount per week in net profit. This is composed of revenue (per percentage point) minus costs (per percentage point).
- An advertising blitz costs a certain amount per week. (For simplicity, we'll assume that each company advertises regularly at some "normal" level. The cost of this is included in the cost per week mentioned above. However, an advertising "blitz" represents something special, and it might be expensive!)
- Instead of, or in addition to, an advertising blitz, either company can issue coupons (at essentially no cost) for a certain percentage off the regular selling price. Then the revenue per percentage point of market share decreases by this coupon percentage.

Remember that we are taking company A's point of view. It can decide each week whether to conduct an advertising blitz, issue coupons, do both, or do neither. These decisions can be based on company B's actions in previous weeks, or company A can ignore company B's decisions. In any case, company B's actions can be generated randomly. To simplify the problem, assume that four fixed probabilities determine company B's actions each week: the probabilities of (1) an advertising blitz, (2) issuing coupons, (3) doing both, or (4) doing neither. (In reality, these probabilities shouldn't be fixed. They ought to depend on the previous actions of both companies, but this would make the simulation model extremely complex.)

Your job is to develop a strategy for company A that produces a large average weekly profit over the next two years, that is, 104 weeks. You can assume any beginning market shares for the two companies at the beginning of week 1. ■

CASE STUDY

Ski Jacket Production

Egress, Inc. is a small company that designs, produces, and sells ski jackets and other coats. The creative design team has labored for weeks over their new design for the coming winter season. It is now time to decide how many ski jackets to produce in this production run. Because of the lead times involved, no other production runs will be possible during the season.

Predicting ski jacket sales months in advance of the selling season can be quite tricky. Egress has been in operation for only three years, and their ski jacket designs were quite successful in two of those years. Based on realized sales from the last three years, current economic conditions, and professional judgment, twelve Egress employees have independently estimated demand for their new design for the upcoming season. Their estimates are:

14,000	16,000
13,000	8,000
14,000	5,000
14,000	11,000
15,500	8,000
10,500	15,000

To assist in the decision on the number of units for the production run, management has gathered the following data:

Variable production cost per unit (C):	\$80
Selling price per unit (S):	\$100
Salvage value per unit (V):	\$30
Fixed production cost (F):	\$100,000

Note that S is the price Egress charges retailers. Any ski jackets that do not sell during the season can be sold by Egress to discounters for V per jacket. F is the fixed cost of plant and equipment. This cost is incurred irrespective of the size of the production run.

Questions

1 Egress management believes that a normal distribution is a reasonable model for the unknown demand in the coming year. What mean (μ) and standard deviation (σ) parameters should Egress use for their demand distribution?

2 Use a spreadsheet to simulate 400 possible outcomes for demand in the coming year. Use the random number seed 5862. Based on these scenarios, what is the expected profit if Egress produces $Q = 7800$ ski jackets? What is the expected profit if Egress produces $Q = 12{,}000$ ski jackets? What is the standard deviation of profit in these two cases?

3 Based on the same 400 scenarios, how many ski jackets should Egress produce to maximize expected profit? Call this quantity Q^*.

4 Should $Q^* = \mu$ or not? Explain.

5 Create a frequency histogram of profit at the production level Q^*. Create a frequency histogram of profit at the production level $Q = \mu$. What is the probability of a loss greater than \$100,000 in each case? ■

CASE STUDY

The College Fund Investment Decision

Your next door neighbor, Scott Jansen, has a twelve-year-old daughter and he wants to pay the tuition for her first year of college six years from now. The tuition for the first year will be $17,500. Scott has gone through his budget and finds that he can invest $200 per month for the next six years. Scott has opened accounts at two mutual funds. The first fund follows an investment strategy designed to match the return of the S&P 500. The second fund invests in short-term Treasury bills. Both funds have very low fees.

Scott has decided to follow a strategy in which he contributes a fixed fraction of the $200 to each fund. An adviser from the first fund suggested that each month he invest 80% of the $200 in the S&P 500 fund and the other 20% in the T-bill fund. The adviser explained that the S&P 500 has averaged much larger returns than the T-bill fund. Even though stock returns are risky investments in the short run, the risk would be fairly minimal over the longer six-year period. An adviser from the second fund recommended just the opposite: invest 20% in the S&P 500 fund and 80% in T-bills, he said. Treasury bills are backed by the U.S. government. If you follow this allocation, he said, your average return will be lower, but at least you will have enough to reach your $17,500 target in six years.

Not knowing which adviser to believe, Scott has come to you for help.

Questions

1 The spreadsheet COLLEGE.XLS contains 261 monthly returns of the S&P 500 and Treasury bills from January 1970 through September 1991. Suppose that in each of the next 72 months (six years), it is equally likely that any of the historical returns will occur.

Set up a spreadsheet to simulate the two suggested investment strategies over the six-year period. Plot the value of each strategy over time for one simulation trial. What was the total value of each strategy after six years? Did either of the strategies reach the target?

2 Simulate 200 trials of the two strategies over the six-year period. Create a histogram of the final fund values. Based on your simulation results, which of the two strategies would you recommend? Why?

3 Suppose that Scott needs to have $19,500 to pay for the first year's tuition. Based on the same simulation results, which of the two strategies would you recommend now? Why?

4 What other real-world factors might be important to consider in designing the simulation and making a recommendation? ■

CASE STUDY

Ebony Bath Soap

Management of Ebony, a leading manufacturer of bath soap, is trying to control its inventory costs. The weekly cost of holding one unit of soap in inventory is \$30 (one unit is 1000 cases of soap). The marketing department estimates that weekly demand averages 120 units, with a standard deviation of 15 units, and is reasonably well modeled by a normal distribution. If demand exceeds the amount of soap on hand, those sales are *lost*—that is, there is no backlogging of demand. The production department can produce at one of three levels: 110, 120, or 130 units per week. The cost of changing production from one week to the next is \$3000.

Management would like to evaluate the following production policy. If the current inventory is less than $l = 30$ units, then produce 130 units in the next week. If the current inventory is greater than $u = 80$ units, then produce 110 units in the next week. Otherwise, continue at the previous week's production level.

Ebony currently has 60 units of inventory on hand. Last week's production level was 120.

Questions

1 Create a spreadsheet to simulate 52 weeks of operation at Ebony. Graph the inventory of soap over time. What is the total cost (inventory cost plus production change cost) for the 52 weeks?

2 Use a simulation of 200 trials to estimate the average 52-week cost with values of u ranging from 30 to 80 in increments of 10. Keep $l = 30$ for every trial.

3 Calculate the sample mean and standard deviation of the 52-week cost under each policy. Using those results, construct 90% confidence intervals for the average 52-week cost for each value of u. Graph the average 52-week cost versus u. What is the best value of u for $l = 30$?

4 What other production policies might be useful to investigate? ■

CASE STUDY

Bond Investment Strategy

An investor is considering the purchase of zero-coupon U.S. Treasury bonds. A 30-year zero-coupon bond yielding 8% can be purchased today for \$9.94. At the end of 30 years the owner of the bond will receive \$100. The yield of the bond is related to its price by the following equation:

$$P = \frac{100}{(1+y)^t} \qquad \textbf{(12.1)}$$

where P is the price of the bond, y is the yield of the bond, and t is the maturity of the bond measured in years. Evaluating Equation 12.1 for $t = 30$ and $y = 0.08$ gives $P = 9.94$.

The investor is planning to purchase a bond today and sell it one year from now. The investor is interested in evaluating the *return* on the investment in the bond. Suppose, for example, that the yield of the bond one year from now is 8.5%. Then the price of the bond one year later will be \$9.39 ($= 100/(1+0.085)^{29}$). The time remaining to maturity is $t = 29$, since one year has passed. The return for the year is −5.54% ($= (9.39 - 9.94)/9.94$).

In addition to the 30-year-maturity zero-coupon bond, the investor is considering the purchase of zero-coupon bonds with maturities of 2, 5, 10, or 20 years. All of the bonds are currently yielding 8.0%. (Bond investors describe this as a *flat yield curve*.) The investor cannot predict the future yields of the bonds with certainty. However, the investor believes that the yield of each bond one year from now can be modeled by a normal distribution with a mean of 8% and a standard deviation of 1%.

Questions

1 Suppose that the yields of the five zero-coupon bonds are all 8.5% one year from today. What are the returns of each bond over the period?

2 Using a simulation of 500 trials with a random number seed of 2814, estimate the expected return of each bond over the year. Estimate the standard deviations of the returns. Construct 90% confidence intervals for the expected returns.

3 Comment on the following statement: "The expected yield of the 30-year bond one year from today is 8%. At that yield, its price would be \$10.73. The return for the year would be 8% (= (10.73 − 9.94)/9.94). Hence, the average return for the bond should be 8% as well. A simulation isn't really necessary. Any difference between 8% and the answer in Question 2 must be due to simulation error." ■

REFERENCES

1 Altman, E. *Handbook of Corporate Finance*. New York: Wiley, 1986.

2 Brigandi, A., D. Dargon, M. Sheehan, and T. Spencer. "AT&T's Call Processing Simulator (CAPS) Operational Design for Inbound Call Centers." *Interfaces* 24, no. 1 (1994): 6–28.

3 Deming, E. *Out of the Crisis*. Cambridge, MA: MIT Center for Advanced Engineering Study, 1986.

4 Hertz, D. "Risk Analysis in Capital Investment." *Harvard Business Review* 42 (Jan.–Feb. 1964): 96–108.

5 Kelly, J. "A New Interpretation of Information Rate." *Bell System Technical Journal* 35 (1956): 917–26.

6 Marcus, A. "The Magellan Fund and Market Efficiency." *Journal of Portfolio Management* (Fall 1990): 85–88.

7 Norton, R. "A New Tool to Help Managers." *Fortune* (May 30, 1994): 135–40.

8 Swart, W., and L. Donno. "Simulation Modeling Improves Operations, Planning and Productivity of Fast-Food Restaurants." *Interfaces* 11, no. 6 (1981): 35–47.

CULLINANE ALSO SAID THE COMPANY S GOAL
TO HAVE $50 MILLION IN RE

CHAPTER

13

Simulation with Add-Ins

Management Science Success Stories

One of the key benefits of simulation methodology is that it allows a company to see how important outputs respond to various scenarios. Each scenario, which is determined by certain inputs and operating policies, can be simulated, and statistics can be collected. By running enough scenarios, the company obtains useful information about which inputs and policies tend to produce the best outputs. This methodology was used in the 1980s by the United States Postal Service (USPS), as described in the article "Management Science in Automating Postal Operations: Facility and Equipment Planning in the United States Postal Service" by Cebry, DeSilva, and DiLisio [4]. At the time, the USPS was faced with increasing competitive pressure from a variety of competitors, including other advertising media, alternative retail and delivery companies, and electronic mail. Automation technology was identified as the only way to handle an increase in mail volume, to maintain cost competitiveness, and provide adequate service.

The process of getting mail from the sender to the receiver is an extremely complex one. Mail enters the process as a mixed product—many types of mail addressed in various ways to many geographical regions—and it must be sorted in several stages before it can eventually reach the proper destination. The USPS recognized the need for automated equipment to speed up this process and to save on labor costs. In fact, by the early 1980s it had purchased OCR (optical character recognition) machines that could identify the destination (at least on some mail) and attach a bar code corresponding to the ZIP code to the mail. It had also purchased bar code sensing machines that could read these bar codes and automatically help sort the mail. Part of the cost effectiveness of these new machines relied on heavy use by businesses of the new nine-digit ZIP codes. Unfortunately, businesses were somewhat slow to use the nine-digit codes.

At about this time, the USPS realized that it needed to use management science methods in order to utilize its existing automation equipment most effectively and to plan appropriately for the future. It hired a consulting company, Kenan Systems Corporation, to help compare automation alternatives. The result was META, a simulation model that quantifies the impacts of changes in mail processing and delivery operations. The META model is very complex, but it can be described briefly as follows. Mail of various types and of various volumes enters the system and progresses through a number of "inks." Each of the links is one step in the overall sorting process that gets the mail from its origin to its final destination. The META model takes as its inputs various mail streams (types of mail with similar characteristics) and routes these streams through the links of the sorting process according to user-specified rules. For example, a rule might specify which mail streams receive highest priority on certain automation equipment at each link. Each set of mail streams and each set of rules corresponds to a single scenario in the simulation model. Given a typical scenario, the model simulates the throughput of the system, the number of errors made, the amount of labor required, and the total cost. These outputs are then compared to identify the best policies for the USPS to implement.

The META model, first developed in 1985, has proved to be extremely useful and versatile. Using this simulation tool, the USPS formulated a corporate automation plan (CAP), which was first released in 1989. By the time CAP was to be fully implemented in 1995, the postal service expected it to save 100,000 work years annually, which translates to over $4 billion. Just as important, by using the model as part of an ongoing planning process, the USPS ensured that it would implement future technologies in a timely and cost-effective manner. ■

13.1 Introduction

As spreadsheets have grown in popularity, the functionality of the basic spreadsheet packages such as Excel and Lotus 1-2-3 has increased immensely. At the same time, third-party add-ins have been developed to add even more functionality to the basic packages. Some of these, most notably the Solver for Excel, have been included in the packages themselves. Others have been developed as freeware (users can use them for free) or shareware (users are morally obligated to pay the developers a nominal fee for their use). We took advantage of one of these freeware package, Treeplan, in Chapter 8.[1] Other add-ins are full commerical packages that must be bought separately—at varying prices.

In this chapter we will look at simulation add-ins for Excel, and we will concentrate on one of the most popular of these, @RISK, which has been developed by Palisade Corporation. Given what we covered in Chapter 12, you may ask why we need an add-in to perform simulations on a spreadsheet. There are two reasons. First, an add-in provides more functionality—we can do more things—than the basic Excel package. We will discuss these extra features shortly. Second, an add-in allows us to perform simulations much more easily than is possible with Excel alone. For example, we usually needed to create data tables in Chapter 12 in order to replicate a simulation. Then we had to calculate summary statistics, such as averages, standard deviations, and confidence intervals, with built-in Excel functions. If we wanted graphs to enhance the analysis, we had to create them. In short, we had to perform a number of time-consuming steps for each simulation. Simulation add-ins such as @RISK relieve us of much of this work by performing the typical steps of a simulation automatically.

Although we will concentrate primarily on @RISK in this chapter, we emphasize that it is not the only available simulation add-in for Excel. A worthy competitor is Crystal Ball, developed by Decisioneering. Crystal Ball has most of the same functionality as @RISK. In addition, because of the relative ease of developing "home-grown" applications in Excel with Excel's built-in macro language Visual Basic for Applications, individuals are developing their own simulation add-ins for Excel. We have included one of these, written by Sam Savage, which we will discuss briefly in this chapter. Admittedly, Savage's add-in does not have the power or polish of a commercial add-in, but it is very inexpensive

[1] Treeplan falls into the shareware category, but it has been provided free with this book.

(with this book), it is quite easy to use, and it adds considerably to Excel's simulation capabilities.

We have written this chapter for schools that own a license for @RISK. If you have access to @RISK, we believe you will get more out of simulation than if you rely exclusively on Excel's built-in capabilities. Nevertheless, you should read Sections 12.1 through 12.4 of the previous chapter to learn the basic concepts of simulation; we will not repeat that material here. Instead, we will begin immediately with simulation examples using @RISK.

Before beginning these examples, we briefly mention the increased functionality you can expect from @RISK. There are three features of @RISK that add to Excel's functionality:

1. @RISK contains a number of new functions that make it easier to generate observations from the most important probability distributions. From Chapter 12, recall that the only built-in Excel function for generating random observations is the RAND function. Beyond that, we had to resort to various tricks to generate observations from, say, a normal or a triangular distribution. But with @RISK, you can generate an observation from a normal distribution with, say, mean 100 and standard deviation 10 with the @RISK formula

   =RISKNORMAL(100,10)

   Similarly, you can generate an observation from a triangular distribution with, say, minimum value 10, most likely value 30, and maximum value 100 with the @RISK formula

   RISKTRIANG(10,30,100)

   Functions for a variety of other distributions are also available.
2. You may specify any cell or range of cells in your simulation as **output cells**. When you run the simulation, @RISK will automatically keep statistics (averages and standard deviations, for example) on the values generated in these output cells across the replications. It will also create graphs such as histograms for the values in the output cells.
3. @RISK has a special function, the RISKSIMTABLE function, that allows you to run the same simulation several times, using a different value of some key input each time. For example, suppose that we would like to simulate an inventory ordering policy (such as that in the Walton Bookstore example in Chapter 12). Our ultimate purpose is to compare simulation outputs across a number of possible order quantities such as 1100, 1150, 1200, and 1250. If we use the formula

   =RISKSIMTABLE({1100,1150,1200,1250})

   the entire simulation will be performed for each of these order quantities separately. Then we can compare their outputs when attempting to choose the "best" order quantity.

13.2 Simulating an Income Statement

We begin with a relatively simple income statement example with a number of random inputs. Most business spreadsheets have an "input section" where important input values are entered. The rest of the spreadsheet then references these values and eventually produces key outputs. The value of listing the inputs separately and then referencing them is that if you want to see how the outputs vary for different input values, you need only modify a few cells. The next step is usually a sensitivity analysis. Here you change the inputs systematically and watch how the outputs change. As we have seen, data tables are especially useful for sensitivity analysis. The primary reason for performing a sensitivity analysis is that we are not always certain of the "true" values of the inputs, and therefore we do not want the entire analysis to rest on a *single* set of input values.

This is where @RISK enters the picture. Instead of entering a single number in an input cell, you enter a *probability distribution* in any input cell in which there is uncertainty. For example, if an annual interest rate is an input and you are not certain of its eventual value, then instead of entering a fixed value such as 10%, you might enter a normal distribution with mean 10% and standard deviation 1% to reflect your uncertainty. @RISK allows you to enter probability distributions in any number of cells, and it gives you a wide assortment of probability distributions to choose from. For example, one input cell might have the normal distribution just described, another might have a uniform distribution between 50 and 100, and another might have an exponential distribution with mean 5.

An important difference between a "regular" spreadsheet and one in @RISK, then, is that some of the cells in @RISK have probability distributions instead of single values. Once these probability distributions and other parts of the spreadsheet (formulas, values, and labels) have been entered, you run the simulation. Specifically, for each of several replications (@RISK calls them **iterations**), the program simulates a random value from *each* cell that contains a probability distribution, and then it calculates the rest of the spreadsheet using these simulated values in the usual manner. The number of iterations is user-controlled; it can be 50, 100, 10,000, or any desired number. As the iterations progress, the spreadsheet continually changes as it calculates outputs from the changing inputs.

The most attractive aspect of @RISK is that it automatically keeps track of all the desired outputs. For example, if the profit for a three-year period is in cell H43, then the program keeps track of all the numbers that appear in cell H43 (one for each iteration). Once the program is finished executing, these profits can be seen graphically or in tabular form. This allows you to see how low the profit might be (a worst-case scenario), how high it might be (a best-case scenario), the average profit, the standard deviation of profits, a histogram of profits, and other measures. Obviously, such information is much more useful to a manager than a single profit value based on a single set of input values (that might be wrong!). We illustrate the basic capability of @RISK in the following example.

EXAMPLE 13.1

The ABC Company wants to develop a monthly income statement for the coming year. However, ABC recognizes that many of the inputs necessary to form this income statement are at best educated guesses. Therefore, it wants to use @RISK to indicate how sensitive important bottom line figures, such as yearly net income after taxes, are to the inputs. The following assumptions are made (where all monetary values are in thousands of dollars).

- January sales are normally distributed with mean 2225 and standard deviation 150.
- The cost of goods in January is uniformly distributed between 870 and 910.
- The marketing cost in January is triangularly distributed with minimum value 90, most likely value 93, and maximum value 96.
- The administrative cost in January is triangularly distributed with minimum value 75, most likely value 78, and maximum value 81.

- The miscellaneous cost in January is triangularly distributed with minimum value 23, most likely value 24, and maximum value 25.
- The tax rate is known to be 33% (no uncertainty).
- The monthly percentage changes in sales and all costs are independent of each other and are all normally distributed with mean 1.5% and standard deviation 1.0%.

These probability distributions reflect ABC's uncertainty about the inputs. Certainly other distributions could have been chosen, but ABC believes that these particular distributions represent the uncertainty in the best way possible.

Solution

The spreadsheet in Figure 13.1 shows ABC's projected income statement for the next 12 months. (See the file ABC.XLS.) The inputs shown at the top of the spreadsheet include projected sales and costs for January, the company's tax rate, and projected monthly percentage changes in sales and costs. (As usual, they are enclosed in borders and shaded to emphasize that they are input cells.) For example, the January percentage change in sales (in cell B13) is the percentage change from January to February. The rest of the spreadsheet (in the Income Statement section) is relatively straightforward. The cells in this section use standard Excel formulas that reference the input cells. For example, the formulas in cells B21 and C21 are

=B5

and

=B21*B13

This latter formula is then copied across row 21 to generate sales for each month. You should check the other formulas in the Income Statement section to make sure you understand the logic, but since our main interest is seeing how *simulation* works, we will concentrate on this aspect.

FIGURE 13.1 **@RISK Spreadsheet for ABC Example**

	A	B	C	D	E	F	G	H	I	J	K	L	M	N
1	**Income Statement for ABC Company Using @RISK**													
2														
3	**Inputs (dollar figures in $1000's)**													
4														
5	Sales in January	$2,225												
6	Cost of goods in January	$890												
7	Marketing in January	$93												
8	Administrative in January	$78												
9	Miscellaneous in January	$24												
10	Tax rate	33%												
11														
12	Monthly % changes in	Jan	Feb	Mar	Apr	May	Jun	Jul	Aug	Sep	Oct	Nov		
13	Sales	1.5%	1.5%	1.5%	1.5%	1.5%	1.5%	1.5%	1.5%	1.5%	1.5%	1.5%		
14	Cost of goods	1.5%	1.5%	1.5%	1.5%	1.5%	1.5%	1.5%	1.5%	1.5%	1.5%	1.5%		
15	Marketing	1.5%	1.5%	1.5%	1.5%	1.5%	1.5%	1.5%	1.5%	1.5%	1.5%	1.5%		
16	Administrative	1.5%	1.5%	1.5%	1.5%	1.5%	1.5%	1.5%	1.5%	1.5%	1.5%	1.5%		
17	Miscellaneous	1.5%	1.5%	1.5%	1.5%	1.5%	1.5%	1.5%	1.5%	1.5%	1.5%	1.5%		
18														
19	**Income Statement**													
20		Jan	Feb	Mar	Apr	May	Jun	Jul	Aug	Sep	Oct	Nov	Dec	Totals
21	Sales	$2,225	$2,258	$2,292	$2,327	$2,362	$2,397	$2,433	$2,469	$2,506	$2,544	$2,582	$2,621	$29,017
22	Cost of goods sold	$890	$903	$917	$931	$945	$959	$973	$988	$1,003	$1,018	$1,033	$1,048	$11,607
23														
24	Gross margin	$1,335	$1,355	$1,375	$1,396	$1,417	$1,438	$1,460	$1,482	$1,504	$1,526	$1,549	$1,573	$17,410
25														
26	Marketing expense	$93	$94	$96	$97	$99	$100	$102	$103	$105	$106	$108	$110	$1,213
27	Administrative expense	$78	$79	$80	$82	$83	$84	$85	$87	$88	$89	$91	$92	$1,017
28	Miscellaneous expense	$24	$24	$25	$25	$25	$26	$26	$27	$27	$27	$28	$28	$313
29														
30	Total expenses	$195	$198	$201	$204	$207	$210	$213	$216	$220	$223	$226	$230	$2,543
31														
32	Net income before taxes	$1,140	$1,157	$1,174	$1,192	$1,210	$1,228	$1,247	$1,265	$1,284	$1,303	$1,323	$1,343	$14,867
33	Taxes	$376	$382	$388	$393	$399	$405	$411	$418	$424	$430	$437	$443	$4,906
34														
35	Net income after taxes	$764	$775	$787	$799	$811	$823	$835	$848	$860	$873	$886	$900	$9,961
36	Cum net income	$764	$1,539	$2,326	$3,125	$3,935	$4,758	$5,593	$6,441	$7,301	$8,175	$9,061	$9,961	

Developing the Spreadsheet Model The main difference between this spreadsheet and the usual type is that probability distributions have been entered in several of the input cells. We enter a particular probability distribution in a cell by using one of @RISK's several functions in that cell. Specifically, we will use the RISKNORMAL, RISKUNIFORM, and RISKTRIANG functions in this example.

1 **January sales.** Enter the distribution of January sales in cell B5 with the formula

   =RISKNORMAL(2225,150)

2 **January cost of goods.** Enter the distribution of the cost of goods in January in cell B6 with the formula

   =RISKUNIFORM(870,910)

3 **January marketing cost.** Enter the distribution of the marketing cost in January in cell B7 with the formula

   =RISKTRIANG(90,93,96)

4 **January administrative cost.** Enter the distribution of the administrative cost in January in cell B8 with the formula

   =RISKTRIANG(75,78,81)

5 **January miscellaneous costs.** Enter the distribution of the miscellaneous costs in January in cell B9 with the formula

   =RISKTRIANG(23,24,25)

6 **Tax rate.** Since there is no uncertainty in the tax rate, enter the *value* 33%—not a formula—in cell B10.

7 **Monthly percentage changes.** To generate the monthly percentage changes, enter the formula

   =RISKNORMAL(.015,.01)

   in cell B13 and copy it to the range B13:L17. Although all cells in this range have the same probability distribution, their individual values will be generated independently on each iteration of the simulation. Therefore, these percentage increases will all be different.

Notice that *numbers* appear in the spreadsheet in the input cells. The @RISK program indeed keeps track of the formulas entered, but it shows the *means* of these distributions in the input cells, and then it shows the outputs that are based on these means. Therefore, the outputs shown in the spreadsheet reflect one set of input values—the means. However, when @RISK executes, it simulates many different values for the inputs and calculates the corresponding outputs for each set of input values.

Using @RISK Once you have entered the inputs and the formulas relating these to outputs (specifically, the straightforward formulas in the Income Statement section for this example), you must invoke @RISK, much as you invoked the Solver to solve LP problems. This requires the following steps. First, however, note that when you open @RISK, there is a new toolbar. The buttons on this toolbar are used to perform the various @RISK functions. (See Figure 13.2.)

1 **Specify output cell(s).** Specify an output cell or a range of output cells. For this example we specify the "bottom line" output cell N35 (yearly net income after taxes) and the output range B36:M36 (the monthly cumulative net incomes after taxes). As the simulation progresses, @RISK automatically keeps track of the values in these

FIGURE 13.2 **@RISK Toolbar**

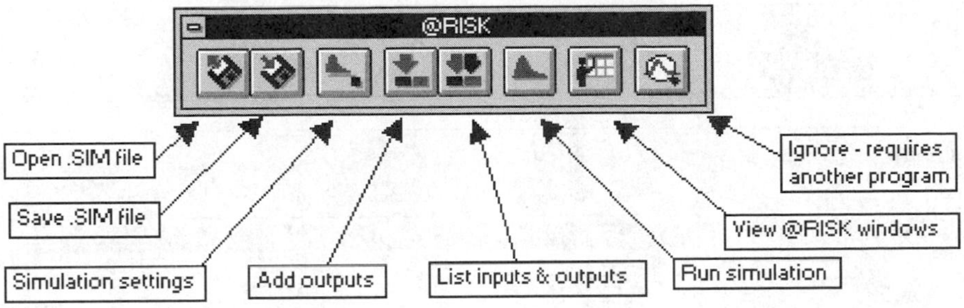

output ranges. To add these cells as output cells, select cell N35 and click on the Add Outputs button (fourth from the left) on the @RISK toolbar. Then select the range B36:M36 and again click on this button.

2 **Specify simulation settings.** We will replicate this simulation 100 times. Therefore, click on the Simulation Settings button (third from the left) and enter 100 in the # Iterations box. (There are many other settings you can make at this stage, but we will accept all of the defaults for now.)

3 **Run the simulation.** To run the simulation, click on the Run button (third from the right). As the simulation is being run, you can watch the progress in an @RISK window.

Once the 100 iterations are complete, you see an @RISK screen with a new menu bar, an expanded toolbar, and two windows of summary statistics. From this screen you can see the results of the simulation in both tabular and graphical form. The following results (among others) are available.

- The upper window (the Results window) shows summary statistics for each of the output cells and (by scrolling down) each of the input cells that contain random distributions. (See Figure 13.3.) For example, we see that the mean value of net income after taxes (averaged over the 100 replications) is \$9968.87. The minimum value is \$6129.14, and the maximum value is \$13,458.29.
- The bottom window (the Summary Statistics window) shows more detailed statistics. To see more of these, click anywhere in this window and click on the maximize button. (See Figure 13.4.) For example, the standard deviation of net income after taxes is \$1370.94. Similarly, the 5%, 50%, and 95% percentiles are \$7758.89, \$9971.32, and \$12,192.68. (This last value doesn't appear in Figure 13.4 but it is part of the output.) The 50% value is the median; it means that half of the simulated net income values are below it and half are above it. The 5% value means that 5% of the net incomes are below it. Similarly, the 95% value means that 95% of the net incomes are below it. These percentiles are often useful for gauging the worst and best cases that are likely to occur.
- To see a histogram of net income after taxes, make sure the Results window is showing and the net income cell is highlighted. Then click on the Graph button on the toolbar. You should see a histogram like the one shown in Figure 13.5. It clearly indicates a bell-shaped distribution around the mean.
- When you select an output range, such as B36:M36, that tracks a variable (cumulative net income after taxes) over time, it is useful to produce a summary chart that shows the time series behavior. To do this, highlight cell B36 in the Results window and click on the Summary button in the toolbar. A graph like the one shown in Figure 13.6

FIGURE 13.3 Summary Measures for ABC Example

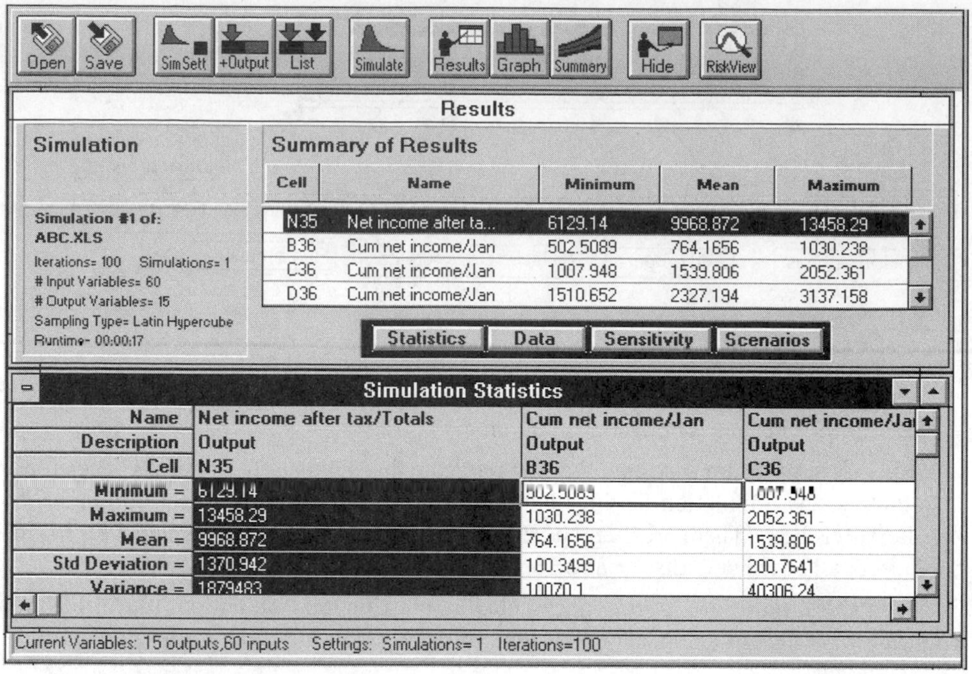

FIGURE 13.4 Detailed Statistics for ABC Example

Name	Net income after tax/Totals	Cum net income/Jan	Cum net income/Jan
Description	Output	Output	Output
Cell	N35	B36	C36
Minimum =	6129.14	502.5089	1007.948
Maximum =	13458.29	1030.238	2052.361
Mean =	9968.872	764.1656	1539.806
Std Deviation =	1370.942	100.3499	200.7641
Variance =	1879483	10070.1	40306.24
Skewness =	1.035614E-02	3.635984E-02	5.458812E-02
Kurtosis =	2.885141	2.879421	2.857365
Errors Calculated =	0	0	0
Mode =	9976.944	805.9532	1504.044
5% Perc =	7758.894	594.0823	1212.019
10% Perc =	8214.271	627.8293	1281.412
15% Perc =	8590.624	656.9828	1330.904
20% Perc =	8670.746	681.0133	1364.195
25% Perc =	8913.107	692.4655	1386.392
30% Perc =	9258.149	717.0162	1438.271
35% Perc =	9439.582	724.3917	1464.479
40% Perc =	9645.725	736.5051	1480.973
45% Perc =	9887.15	750.7533	1505.98
50% Perc =	9971.322	761.3498	1527.049
55% Perc =	10061.87	769.4075	1558.493
60% Perc =	10207.62	794.1608	1592.116
65% Perc =	10410.76	803.8126	1620.035
70% Perc =	10495.13	814.7319	1637.566

should appear. In this graph time moves from left to right. The middle line in the graph joins the means for each month. The first band around this line extends to one standard deviation on either side of the mean. The outer bands extend to the 5% and

FIGURE 13.5 **Histogram for ABC Example**

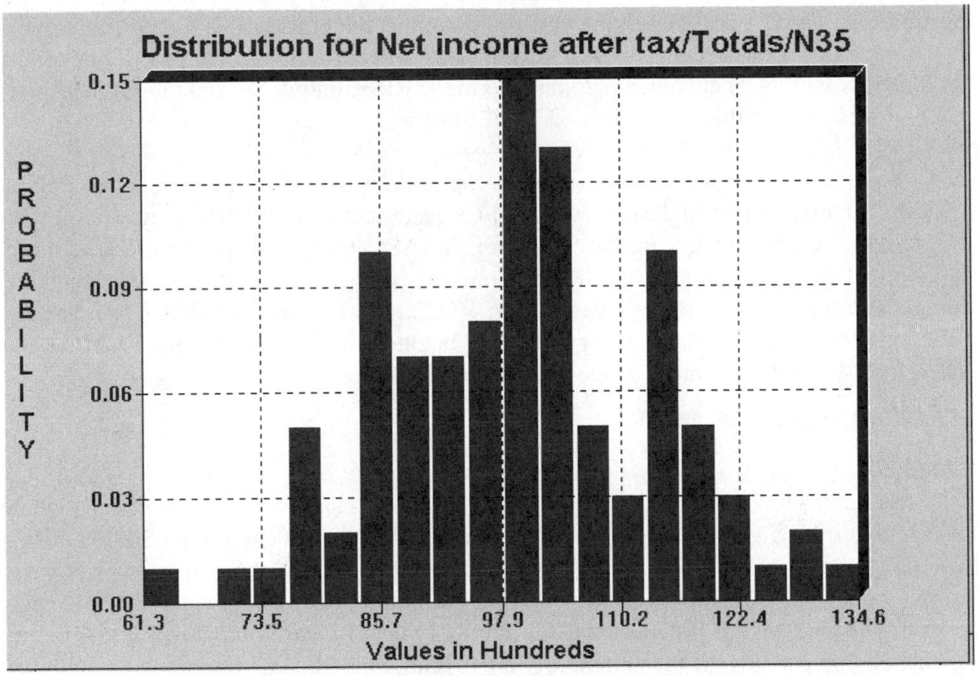

FIGURE 13.6 **Summary Chart for ABC Example**

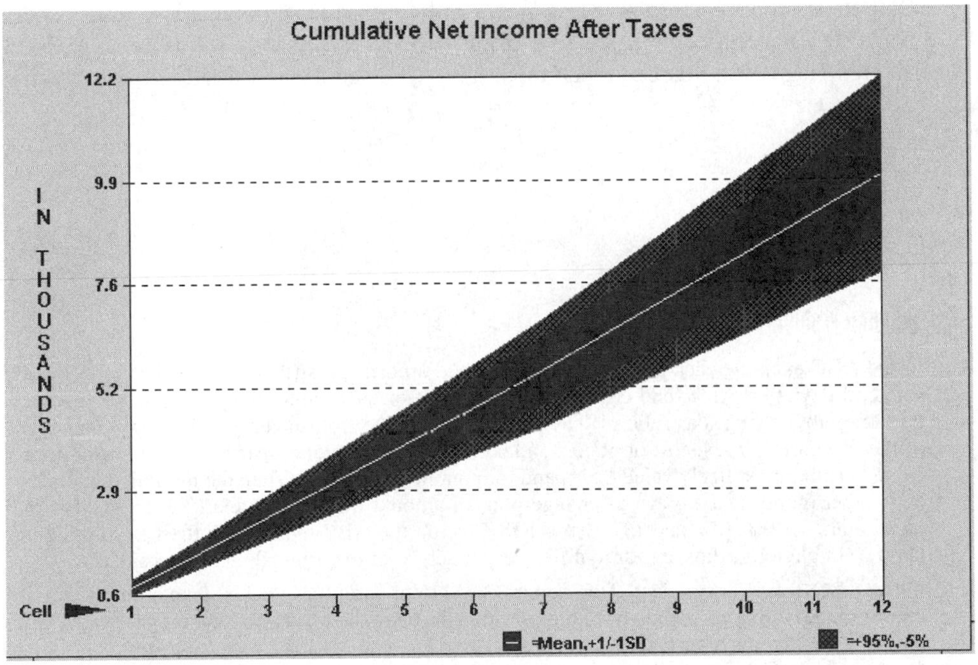

95% percentiles. The graph clearly indicates the upward movement in cumulative net income, and it also shows how the uncertainty increases as more months are included in the cumulative value.

There are two ways to proceed at this stage. First, you can save the output from the simulation in a .SIM file (a file format readable by @RISK) by clicking on the Save button. Second, you can cut portions of the @RISK output to the clipboard and then paste them into your Excel spreadsheet. To return to your spreadsheet from @RISK, you need to click on the Hide button. Then you can go back to the @RISK output by clicking on the Show button (second from the right) on the @RISK toolbar.

A Comparison with the Savage Add-In You can produce much of this same output with the simulation add-in developed by Sam Savage that is included with this book. We will briefly describe its use in the context of the ABC example. The spreadsheet setup is identical to the setup for @RISK with one exception. All of the @RISK functions for generating random numbers begin with RISK, as in RISKNORMAL. The Savage functions are mostly the same except that they begin with GEN_, as in GEN_NORMAL. Therefore, to generate January sales, we enter the formula

=GEN_NORMAL(2225,150)

in cell B5.

Instead of a toolbar, Savage's add-in adds a new menu item, Simulate, to Excel's menu bar. To enter the simulation settings and run the simulation, you choose the Simulate/Run Simulation menu item. This brings up a settings window in which you can specify the output cells (individual cells, not ranges) and the number of replications (which Savage calls trials). The outputs produced include summary data for each output cell, a histogram for which you can choose the number of "bins" (bars in the histogram), and a cumulative frequency graph that shows the percentage of values below any given level. You can also form a "convergence" graph that shows how the average output over the first n replications varies with n. This is useful for checking whether your average over, say, 100 replications is stable or whether you need more replications in order to obtain a stable average.

Outputs for the ABC example are shown in Figures 13.7 through 13.10. One aspect of Savage's outputs, in contrast to those from @RISK, is that they are all regular Excel sheets. This means that you can touch them up as you see fit (as we did in the following figures). ■

PROBLEMS

Skill-Building Problems

1 In the ABC example each percentage increase had a normal distribution with mean 1.5% and standard deviation 1.0%, and each was independent of each other. Suppose that we model these monthly changes as follows. The percentage change from January to February (for each of the categories, sales, cost of goods, and so on) has a triangular distribution with minimum value −1.0%, most likely value 1.5%, and maximum value 3.0%. Then the monthly change for each other month is the previous change plus an amount that is triangularly distributed with parameters −1.0%, 0%, and 1%. Use @RISK to run the ABC model with these assumptions. Do the simulation results appear to differ very much from the original model's results?

2 In the ABC example we selected the range B36:M36 of cumulative net income after taxes as an output range. Using the inputs from the previous problem, select instead the range B35:M35 of monthly net income after taxes as an output range and use @RISK to create a summary chart for this range. Discuss its characteristics and how it differs from the chart of cumulative net income after taxes (see Figure 13.6). ■

FIGURE 13.7 Summary Statistics from Savage Add-In

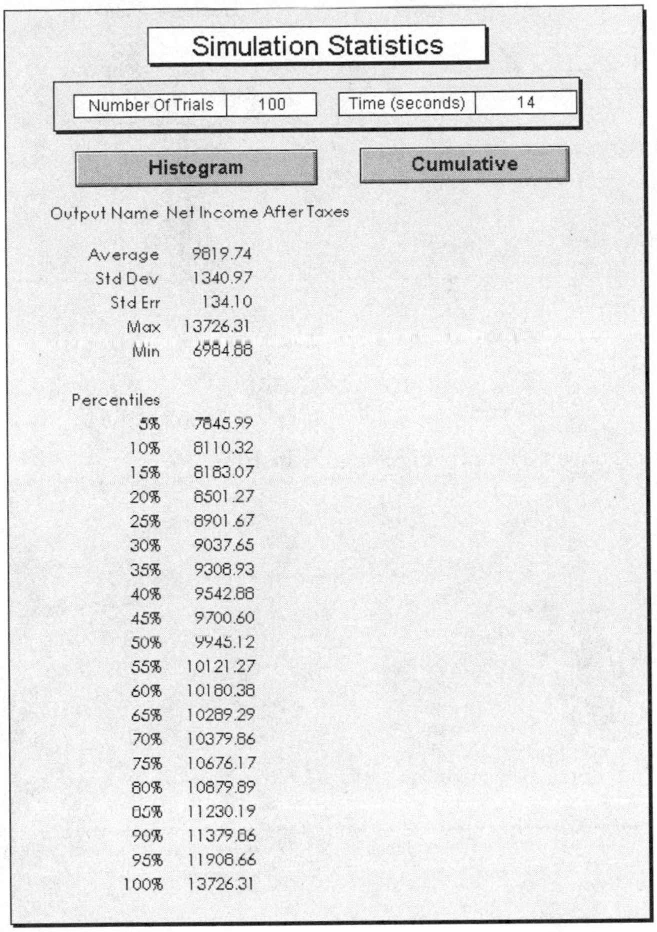

Average	9819.74
Std Dev	1340.97
Std Err	134.10
Max	13726.31
Min	6984.88
Percentiles	
5%	7845.99
10%	8110.32
15%	8183.07
20%	8501.27
25%	8901.67
30%	9037.65
35%	9308.93
40%	9542.88
45%	9700.60
50%	9945.12
55%	10121.27
60%	10180.38
65%	10289.29
70%	10379.86
75%	10676.17
80%	10879.89
85%	11230.19
90%	11379.86
95%	11908.66
100%	13726.31

FIGURE 13.8 Histogram from Savage Add-In

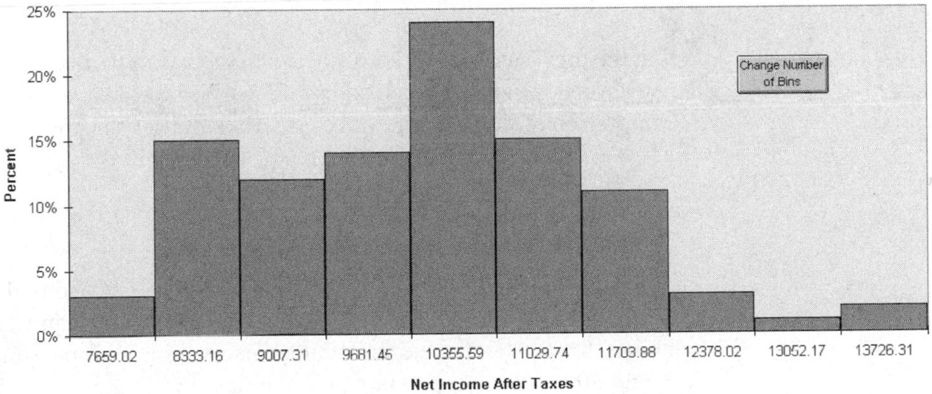

FIGURE 13.9 **Cumulative Frequency Chart from Savage Add-In**

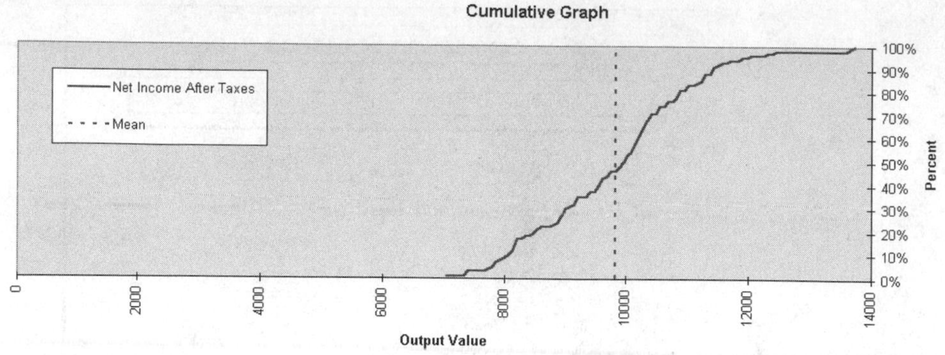

FIGURE 13.10 **Convergence Graph from Savage Add-In**

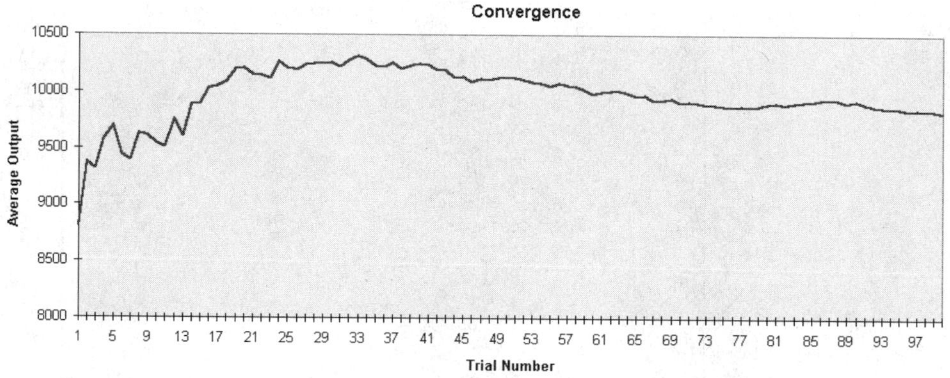

13.3

The Newsvendor Model with @RISK

On the previous chapter we illustrated Excel's simulation capabilities with a version of the newsvendor model. (See Example 12.1.) We now analyze this example using @RISK. A comparison of the two approaches clearly indicates the power and ease of @RISK.

EXAMPLE 13.2

Recall that Walton Bookstore buys calendars for \$7.50, sells them at the regular price of \$10, and gets a refund of \$2.50 for all calendars that can't be sold. The demand for calendars follows a discrete probability distribution with possible values 100, 150, 200, 250, and 300 and corresponding probabilities .30, .20, .30, .15, and .05. Walton wants to use @RISK to simulate the profits from calendars for five different order quantities: 100, 150, 200, 250, and 300.

Solution

We will take advantage of two @RISK functions to form the spreadsheet model. To simulate a demand, we will use the RISKDISCRETE function. This function generates a discrete random number from a distribution with any set of possible values and corresponding probabilities. To run the simulation several times, each with a different order quantity, we will use the RISKSIMTABLE function.

Developing the Spreadsheet Model The spreadsheet model is short and simple. (See Figure 13.11 and the file WALTONR1.XLS.) The following steps are required.

1 **Inputs.** Enter the monetary inputs in the range B4:B6, the inputs for the demand distribution in the range D4:E8, and the possible order quantities in the range G4:G8.

2 **Possible order quantities.** Indicate that the simulation should be run five times, once with each order quantity, by entering the formula

=RISKSIMTABLE(G4:G8)

in cell B9.[2] (Only the first possible demand, 100, shows in this cell, but all possible demands will eventually be used.)

3 **Simulated demand.** Generate a typical random demand by entering the formula

=RISKDISCRETE(D4:D8,E4:E8)

in cell B13. Note that this function requires two arguments (in this order): the range of possible demand values and the range of their probabilities. Also, note that the value showing in cell B13 will depend on the simulation settings (see below).

4 **Other simulated quantities.** Use the regular Excel functions to calculate the other simulated quantities (which are all determined by the order quantity and the demand) in the range C13:F13. Specifically, enter the formulas

=B5*MIN(B9,B13)
=B4*B9
=B6*MAX(B9–B13,0)

and

=C13+E13–D13

FIGURE 13.11 **@RISK Spreadsheet for Walton Example**

	A	B	C	D	E	F	G	H	I
1	Simulation of Walton's Bookstore using @RISK								
2				Demand distribution					
3	Cost data			Demand	Probability		Possible order quantities		
4	Unit cost	$7.50		100	0.30		100		
5	Unit price	$10.00		150	0.20		150		
6	Unit refund	$2.50		200	0.30		200		
7				250	0.15		250		
8	Decision variable			300	0.05		300		
9	Order quantity	100							
10									
11	Simulated quantities								
12		Demand	Revenue	Cost	Refund	Profit			
13		150	$1,000.00	$750.00	$0.00	$250.00			

[2] @RISK expects a list of values as the argument for the RISKSIMTABLE function. This list can either be in a range, as it is here, or it can be spelled out explicitly, as in =RISKSIMTABLE({100,150,200,250,300}). Note the required curly brackets.

in cells C13, D13, E13, and F13. The values showing in these cells are based on the values showing in cells B9 and B13. However, they will all change as the simulation runs.

Using @RISK Now that the spreadsheet is set up, you can use the @RISK toolbar buttons (see Figure 13.2) to run the simulation. Proceed as follows.

1 **Specify output cell(s).** The only output we will track in this simulation is profit. Therefore, select cell F13 and click on the Add Ouputs button (fourth from the left) to add profit as an output. (Always remember to select the cell or range of cells before clicking on this button because it will add whatever cell is currently selected. However, if you mistakenly add an output, you can click on the List button (fifth from the left), select the mistaken output, and click on delete.)

2 **Specify simulation settings.** Click on the Simulation Setting button (third from the left). The only crucial settings are the number of iterations, which you should set to 100, and the number of simulations, which you should set to 5. These will make @RISK run 100 iterations of the simulation for each of the five possible order quantities. The other settings are optional, but you might want to experiment.

   For example, there are three possible Standard Recalc settings: Expected Value, Monte Carlo, and True EV. If the Monte Carlo option is chosen, all random quantities will change—and the changes will show on your spreadsheet—every time you press Excel's Recalc (F9) button. On the other hand, if the Expected Value option is chosen, all random quantities will be replaced by their expected values or, in the case of discrete distributions, the possible value closest to the expected value. In this latter case, if the True EV option is chosen, the exact expected value will be shown. Be aware, however, that these settings only affect what you see on the spreadsheet; they don't affect the way the simulation is run. From now on, all spreadsheets shown in this chapter use the Monte Carlo—it allows us to see more interesting numbers on the screen!

   Another setting you might want to change is the Collect Distributions option. If this box is checked, @RISK will collect statistics on every cell that contains a probability distribution. If there are many of these cells, the amount of memory required could become huge. Therefore, for large problems you might want to uncheck this box.

   Finally, if you check the Update Display box, you will see each iteration of the simulation. This is possibly instructive for beginners, but it slows down the simulation considerably. We don't recommend using it. Similarly, you might want to uncheck the Monitor Convergence button. This will also speed up the simulation.

3 **Run the simulation.** Click on the Simulate button (third from the right). This runs the simulation. You can monitor the progress on the lower left-hand corner of your screen.

Once the simulation is completed, you can examine the outputs in graphical or tabular form. Here are a few things to be aware of.

- Sometimes there is no variation in an output variable. This occurs in the Walton example when the order quantity is 100—the profit is $250 in each iteration. (Do you see why?) Whenever this occurs, @RISK will not let you produce a histogram of the output.
- This example ran five separate simulations, one for each order quantity. You can look at the outputs from these one at a time or all at once. To do so, maximize the Results window. You'll see a couple of buttons in the bottom left-hand corner that allow you to merge the simulations or list them by simulation number. (These two buttons don't quite show unless the Results window is maximized.) See Figure 13.12, which shows

FIGURE 13.12 **Summary Statistics for Walton Example**

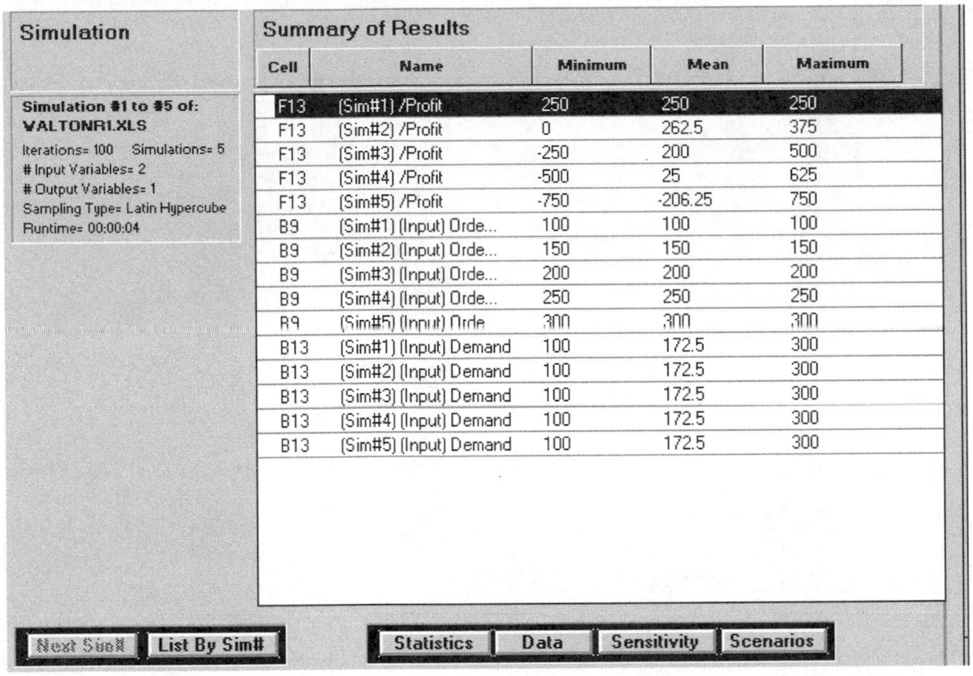

Cell	Name	Minimum	Mean	Maximum
F13	(Sim#1) /Profit	250	250	250
F13	(Sim#2) /Profit	0	262.5	375
F13	(Sim#3) /Profit	-250	200	500
F13	(Sim#4) /Profit	-500	25	625
F13	(Sim#5) /Profit	-750	-206.25	750
B9	(Sim#1) (Input) Orde...	100	100	100
B9	(Sim#2) (Input) Orde...	150	150	150
B9	(Sim#3) (Input) Orde...	200	200	200
B9	(Sim#4) (Input) Orde...	250	250	250
B9	(Sim#5) (Input) Orde...	300	300	300
B13	(Sim#1) (Input) Demand	100	172.5	300
B13	(Sim#2) (Input) Demand	100	172.5	300
B13	(Sim#3) (Input) Demand	100	172.5	300
B13	(Sim#4) (Input) Demand	100	172.5	300
B13	(Sim#5) (Input) Demand	100	172.5	300

the merged summary statistics. This shows, for example, that an order quantity of 150 (simulation #2) produced the largest mean profit. Larger order quantities produced larger best-case profits, but they also produced lower means and lower worst-case profits (actually, losses).

- Two other buttons, Statistics and Data, on the Results window toggle between detailed statistics on outputs and the simulated data. That is, by clicking on Data, you can see the outputs from *each* of the 100 iterations. (See Figure 13.13.) In contrast, the Statistics window shows summary statistics only. (See Figure 13.14.) For example, when the order quantity is 150 (simulation #2), the mean profit is \$262.50, the standard deviation is \$171.85, the 5% percentile is \$0, and the median (50% percentile) and the 95% percentile (not shown) are both \$375. However, these figures are a bit misleading. With this discrete demand distribution and an order quantity of 150, there are only two possible profits, \$0 and \$375. By looking at the 30% and 35% percentile lines, we see that somewhere between 30 and 35 of the iterations produced \$0 profit. (The exact number is 30 since $.30 * (0) + .70 * (375) =$ \$262.50, the mean profit from the simulation.)
- By selecting any output cell in the Results window (other than those with no variation) and clicking on the Graph button, you can see a histogram of the simulated results. However, when there is no *range* of output cells but instead only single output cells (as in this example), graphs from the Summary button, like those shown in Figure 13.6, are not available.
- If you feel more comfortable viewing data or graphs back in an Excel spreadsheet, you can always copy and paste. For example, you could copy the information from the Statistics window into the original Walton spreadsheet. Remember that to go from the @Risk screen back to your spreadsheet, click on the Hide button.

FIGURE 13.13 Simulated Data for Walton Example

Name	/Profit	/Profit	/Profit	/Profit
Description	Output (Sim#1)	Output (Sim#2)	Output (Sim#3)	Output (Sim#4)
Iteration# / Cell	F13	F13	F13	F13
1	250	0	-250	-500
2	250	375	500	250
3	250	375	125	-125
4	250	375	500	250
5	250	375	500	625
6	250	375	500	250
7	250	375	500	250
8	250	375	500	250
9	250	375	500	250
10	250	375	500	250
11	250	375	500	250
12	250	375	500	250
13	250	375	500	250
14	250	0	-250	-500
15	250	375	500	250
16	250	375	125	-125
17	250	375	125	-125
18	250	375	500	250
19	250	375	500	625
20	250	375	500	250
21	250	0	-250	-500
22	250	0	-250	-500
23	250	375	500	625

FIGURE 13.14 Detailed Statistics for Walton Example

Name	/Profit	/Profit	/Profit	/Profit	/Profit
Description	Output (Sim#1)	Output (Sim#2)	Output (Sim#3)	Output (Sim#4)	Output (Sim#5)
Cell	F13	F13	F13	F13	F13
Minimum =	250	0	-250	-500	-750
Maximum =	250	375	500	625	750
Mean =	250	262.5	200	25	-206.25
Std Deviation =	0	171.8466	326.9174	417.5823	451.1703
Variance =	0	29531.25	106875	174375	203554.7
Skewness =	0	-.8728716	-.3984589	3.476232E-02	.2898334
Kurtosis =	0	1.761905	1.432133	1.630593	2.072172
Errors Calculated =	0	0	0	0	0
Mode =	250	375	500	-500	-750
5% Perc =	250	0	-250	-500	-750
10% Perc =	250	0	-250	-500	-750
15% Perc =	250	0	-250	-500	-750
20% Perc =	250	0	-250	-500	-750
25% Perc =	250	0	-250	-500	-750
30% Perc =	250	0	-250	-500	-750
35% Perc =	250	375	125	-125	-375
40% Perc =	250	375	125	-125	-375
45% Perc =	250	375	125	-125	-375
50% Perc =	250	375	125	-125	-375
55% Perc =	250	375	500	250	0
60% Perc =	250	375	500	250	0
65% Perc =	250	375	500	250	0
70% Perc =	250	375	500	250	0

Walton Example with Normally Distributed Demand In the Walton example we made the rather unrealistic assumptions that demand must be one of the five values 100, 150, 200, 250, or 300. It is much more realistic to assume a continuous demand distribution, where a continuum of demand values are possible. Here we will assume that demand is normally distributed. The spreadsheet itself is almost unchanged. (See Figure 13.15 and the file WALTONR2.XLS.) All we need to do is replace the previous demand distribution inputs with the mean and standard deviation of the normal distribution. These appear in cells E5 and E6. (We chose 175 and 60 as the mean and standard deviation because these are very close to the mean and standard deviation of the discrete distribution that was used earlier.) Then replace the formula for a typical demand in cell B13 with the formula

=RISKNORMAL(E5,E6)

This is all it takes to generate a normally distributed variable. We use @RISK's RISKNORMAL function with two arguments for the mean and standard deviation of the distribution.[3]

We then run the simulation exactly as before. Now there is a continuum of profits that can be generated for any given order quantity, which makes the output a bit more interesting. Figure 13.16 shows the basic summary statistics for the five simulations. As before, an order quantity of 150 produces the largest mean profit, whereas larger order

FIGURE 13.15 **Spreadsheet for Walton Example with Normally Distributed Demand**

	A	B	C	D	E	F	G	H	I
1	**Simulation of Walton's Bookstore using @RISK**								
2									
3	**Cost data**			**Demand distribution**			**Possible order quantities**		
4	Unit cost	$7.50		**Normal with:**			100		
5	Unit price	$10.00		Mean	175		150		
6	Unit refund	$2.50		St Dev	60		200		
7							250		
8	**Decision variable**						300		
9	Order quantity	100							
10									
11	**Simulated quantities**								
12		Demand	Revenue	Cost	Refund	Profit			
13		187.63	$1,000.00	$750.00	$0.00	$250.00			

FIGURE 13.16 **Basic Summary Statistics for Walton Example**

Simulation

Simulation #1 to #5 of: VALTONR2.XLS

Iterations= 100 Simulations= 5
# Input Variables= 2
# Output Variables= 1
Sampling Type= Latin Hypercube
Runtime= 00:00:04

Summary of Results

Cell	Name	Minimum	Mean	Maximum
F13	(Sim#1) /Profit	-362.3653	226.9017	250
F13	(Sim#2) /Profit	-612.3652	273.5834	375
F13	(Sim#3) /Profit	-862.3652	211.3775	500
F13	(Sim#4) /Profit	-1112.365	39.95216	625
F13	(Sim#5) /Profit	-1362.365	-190.6423	750
B9	(Sim#1) (Input) Orde...	100	100	100
B9	(Sim#2) (Input) Orde...	150	150	150
B9	(Sim#3) (Input) Orde...	200	200	200
B9	(Sim#4) (Input) Orde...	250	250	250
B9	(Sim#5) (Input) Orde...	300	300	300
B13	(Sim#1) (Input) Demand	18.3513	174.7617	318.063
B13	(Sim#2) (Input) Demand	18.3513	174.7617	318.063
B13	(Sim#3) (Input) Demand	18.3513	174.7617	318.063
B13	(Sim#4) (Input) Demand	18.3513	174.7617	318.063
B13	(Sim#5) (Input) Demand	18.3513	174.7617	318.063

[3]There is a slight probability that a normally distributed demand could be negative, which wouldn't make any sense. Therefore, you might instead use the RISKTNORMAL function, where *T* stands for truncated. This function takes four arguments: the mean, the standard deviation, a lower limit, and an upper limit. No values below the lower limit or above the upper limit are allowed.

quantities have more upside and downside potential—profits could be large, but they could also be negative. This is confirmed by a sample of the more detailed summary statistics shown in Figure 13.17. They show, for example, that the 5% and 95% percentiles are spread further apart as the order quantity increases.

Histograms for the example are quite enlightening. You might think that with normally distributed demand, that is, a bell-shaped curve, the distribution of profits ought to be bell-shaped as well. This is far from true. Figures 13.18 and 13.19 show histograms of the profits for order quantities of 200 and 250, respectively. The histogram for an order quantity of 200 is totally skewed to the left, whereas the histogram for an order quantity of 250 is somewhat bell-shaped in the middle but has a large spike at the right. Histograms such as these are of tremendous value in analyzing simulation data. The numbers tell part of the story, if properly analyzed. For example, the fact that the mean profit is much larger than the median for an order quantity of 200 suggests the skewness to the left. However, a graph indicates the true distribution much more clearly.

We finish this example by examining some other features of @RISK that are useful for analyzing simulation output.

FIGURE 13.17 Percentiles for Walton Example

Name	/Profit	/Profit	/Profit	/Profit	/Profit
Description	Output (Sim#1)	Output (Sim#2)	Output (Sim#3)	Output (Sim#4)	Output (Sim#5)
Cell	F13	F13	F13	F13	F13
5% Perc =	33.97586	-216.0241	-466.0241	-716.0242	-966.0242
10% Perc =	213.4472	-36.55279	-286.5528	-536.5528	-786.5528
15% Perc =	250	86.47086	-163.5291	-413.5291	-663.5291
20% Perc =	250	180.7694	-69.23061	-319.2306	-569.2306
25% Perc =	250	252.1829	2.182881	-247.8171	-497.8171
30% Perc =	250	313.8221	63.82212	-186.1779	-436.1779
35% Perc =	250	375	137.8821	-112.1179	-362.1179
40% Perc =	250	375	190.6826	-59.31737	-309.3174
45% Perc =	250	375	253.1363	3.136315	-246.8637
50% Perc =	250	375	307.6284	57.6284	-192.3716
55% Perc =	250	375	379.8268	129.8268	-136.6359
60% Perc =	250	375	416.1596	166.1596	-83.84037
65% Perc =	250	375	484.6513	234.6513	-15.34869
70% Perc =	250	375	500	297.3905	47.39053
75% Perc =	250	375	500	354.4746	104.4746
80% Perc =	250	375	500	440.9597	190.9597
85% Perc =	250	375	500	514.3869	264.3869
90% Perc =	250	375	500	625	386.5727
95% Perc =	250	375	500	625	516.7124

Using the Graph Type Command Once you obtain a histogram of a selected output, you can modify the graph in a number of ways. To do so, click with the right mouse button on an open histogram. This brings up a dialog box of graph options. Under the Type options, try selecting the Cumulative Ascending option. The resulting graph (for profit and an order quantity of 200) is shown in Figure 13.20. For any particular profit value (read on the horizontal axis), the height of the bar is the proportion of simulated profits less than or equal to this value. For example, the next-to-last bar on the right indicates that about 60% of the simulated profits are less than or equal to $430. This can be confirmed by looking at the percentiles shown in Figure 13.17. If you instead choose the Cumulative Descending option, the height of any bar above any profit value is the proportion of simulated profits greater than this value. There are other graph options you might want to explore, such as changing the scale of the horizontal axis or the title of the graph.

FIGURE 13.18 **Histogram for an Order Quantity of 200**

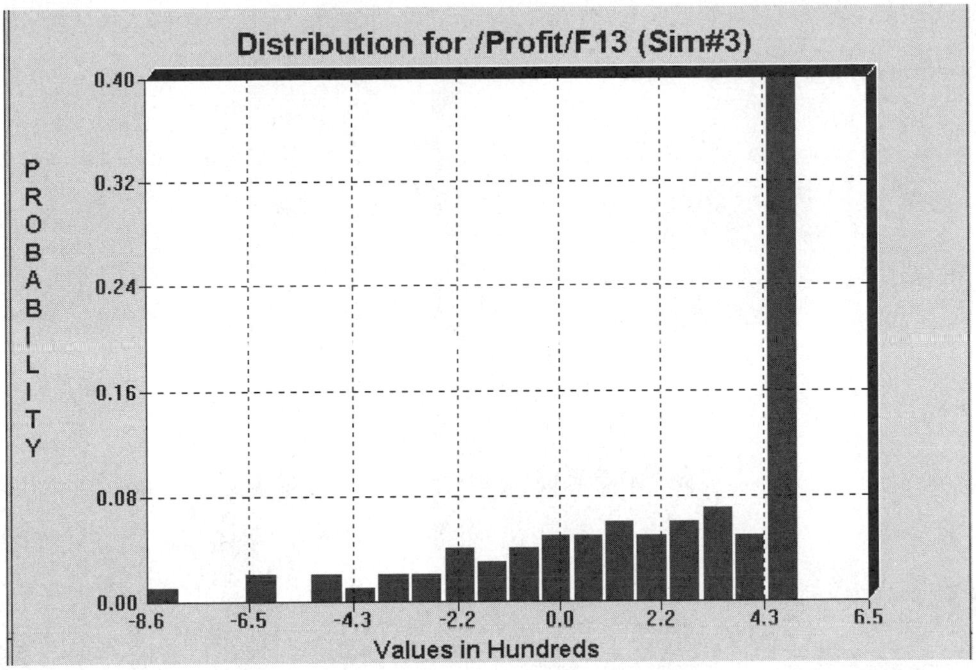

FIGURE 13.19 **Histogram for an Order Quantity of 250**

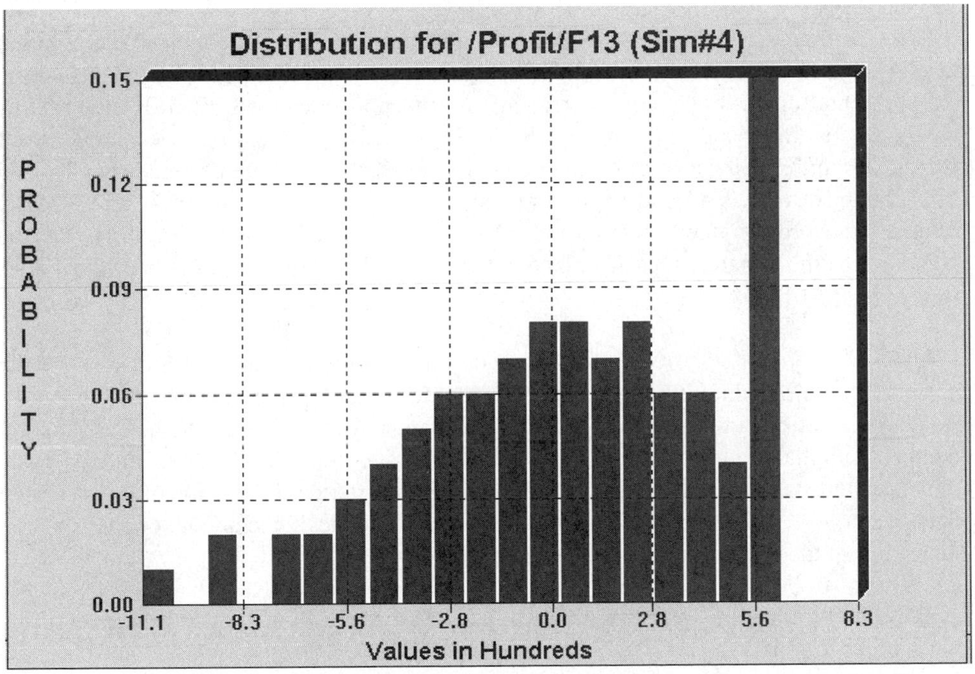

Target Values in the Statistics Output There is a section of the Simulation Statistics window in which you can select target values. This works in two directions. If you enter a dollar value for profit, @RISK will determine the percentage of simulated profits that

FIGURE 13.20 **Cumulative Ascending Graph for Walton Example**

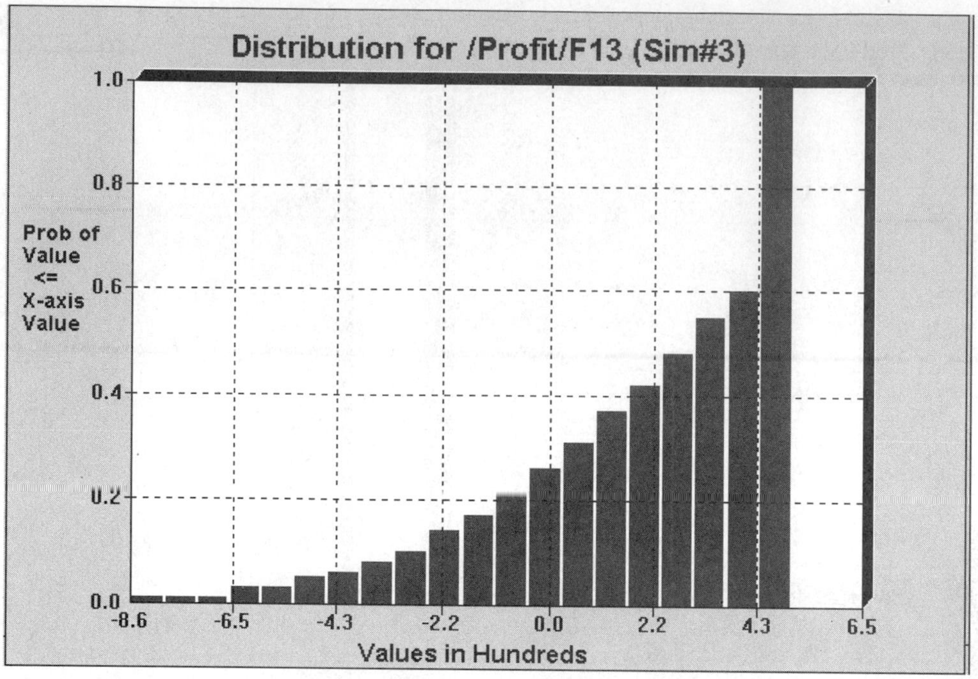

were less than or equal to this value. Conversely, if you enter a percentage, @RISK will determine the corresponding percentile, that is, the dollar value such that the given percentage of profits were below this value.

To do this, scroll down the Simulation Statistics window until you see the target headings. (See Figure 13.21, which shows results for an order quantity of 200.) For any target #, enter either a value or a percentage in the appropriate cell. @RISK then returns the corresponding value in the other cell. For example, in Figure 13.21 we entered profit values 200 and 300 for targets #1 and #2, and @RISK returned the percentages 40% and 48%. Then for targets #3 and #4, we entered the percentages 5% and 95%, and @RISK returned the profit values -466.02 and 500. Of course, these latter percentiles can be compared with the percentiles given in the upper part of the Simulation Statistics window. (See Figure 13.17.)

Which Normal Distribution? We conclude this section with a brief discussion of the normal input distribution for demand. In the Walton example we used a mean of 175 and a standard deviation of 60. How would Walton determine these values? If there are historical demand data that are relevant to the current demand situation, then Walton could estimate the mean and standard deviation by using the mean and standard deviation of the historical data. Otherwise, if there are no historical data or the historical data are out of date, Walton must choose the mean and standard deviation subjectively.

To do so, Walton should first determine the number such that it believes demand is equally likely to be above or below this number. Because of the symmetric nature of the normal curve, this value is a good estimate of the mean. Then it should determine two numbers, equidistant from the mean, such that it believes demand is 95% certain to be between these two numbers. For example, let's assume that it estimates the mean to be 175 and these two numbers to be 55 and 295. Then, because there is about a 95% chance that a normally distributed variable will be within two standard deviations of the mean, a good

FIGURE 13.21 **Target Values in @RISK**

Simulation Statistics			
Name	/Profit	Order quantity	Demand
Description	Output	Simtable(G4:G8)	Normal(E5,E6)
Cell	F13	B9	B13
Target #1 (Value)=	200		
Target #1 (Perc%)=	40%		
Target #2 (Value)=	300		
Target #2 (Perc%)=	48%		
Target #3 (Value)=	-466.024139404297		
Target #3 (Perc%)=	5%		
Target #4 (Value)=	500		
Target #4 (Perc%)=	95%		

estimate of the standard deviation is half the distance from either of these two numbers to the mean, that is, $120/2 = 60$. ■

PROBLEMS

Skill-Building Problems

3 In Problem 12.4 suppose that the demand for cars is normally distributed with mean 100 and standard deviation 15. Use @RISK to determine the "best" order quantity, that is, the one that has the largest mean profit. Using the statistics and/or graphs from @RISK, discuss whether this order quantity would or would not be considered best by the car dealer. (The point is that a decision maker can use more than just *mean* profit in making a decision.)

4 Use @RISK to analyze the sweatshirt situation in Problem 12.6. Do this for the discrete distributions given in the problem. Then do it for normal distributions. For the normal case assume that the regular demand is normally distributed with mean 9800 and standard deviation 1300 and that the demand at the reduced price is normally distributed with mean 4800 and standard deviation 1300.

Skill-Extending Problem

5 Although the normal distribution is a reasonable input distribution in many situations, it does have two potential drawbacks: (1) it allows negative values, even though they may be extremely improbable, and (2) it is a symmetric distribution. Many situations are modeled better with a distribution that allows only positive values and is skewed to the right. Two of these are the gamma and lognormal distributions, and @RISK allows you to generate observations from each of these distributions. The @RISK function for the gamma distribution is RISKGAMMA, and it takes two arguments, as in

=RISKGAMMA(3,10)

The first argument, which must be positive, determines the shape. The smaller it is, the more skewed the distribution is to the right; the larger it is, the more symmetric the distribution is. The second argument determines the scale in the sense that the product of it and the first argument equals the mean of the distribution. (The mean above is 30.) Also, the product of the second argument and the square root of the first argument is the standard deviation of the distribution. (Above, it is $\sqrt{3} * 10 = 17.32$.) The @RISK function for the lognormal distribution is RISKLOGNORM. It has two arguments, as in

RISKLOGNORM(40,10)

These arguments are the mean and standard deviation of the distribution.

Rework Example 13.2 when the demand has (a) a gamma distribution with parameters 2 and 85, (b) a gamma distribution with parameters 5 and 35, and (c) a lognormal distribution with mean 170 and standard deviation 60. Do the simulated outputs have any different qualitative properties with these skewed distributions than with the normal distribution used in the example? ■

13.4

Financial Planning Simulations

Many companies use simulation in their capital budgeting and financial planning processes. Simulation can be used to model the uncertainty associated with future cash flows and to answer questions such as the following:

- What is the estimated mean and variance of a project's net present value (NPV)?
- What is the estimated probability that a project will have a negative NPV?
- What are the estimated mean and variance of a company's profit during the next fiscal year?
- What is the estimated probability that a company will have to borrow more than $2 million during the next year?

The following example illustrates how simulation can be used to compare investment opportunities. (It generalizes Example 12.5.)

EXAMPLE 13.3

General Ford (GF) Auto Corporation is trying to determine what type of compact car to develop. Two models (model 1 and model 2) are under consideration. Each model is assumed to generate sales for ten years. In order to determine which model to build, GF has gathered information about the following quantities through focus groups with the marketing and engineering departments.

- **Fixed cost of developing car.** This cost is assumed to be normally distributed for each model. The mean and standard deviation for model 1 are $2.5 billion and $0.4 billion; for model 2 they are $2.3 billion and $0.5 billion. The fixed cost is incurred at the beginning of year 1, before any sales are recorded.
- **Variable production cost.** This cost, which includes all variable production costs required to build a single car, is assumed to be normally distributed for each model during year 1. For model 1 the mean and standard deviation are $8000 and $400; for model 2 they are $7800 and $600. Each year after year 1 the variable production cost is the previous year's variable production cost multiplied by an inflation factor. Each year this inflation factor is assumed to be normally distributed with mean 1.05 (a 5% increase) and standard deviation .015. All production costs are assumed to occur at the ends of the respective years.
- **Sales price.** The sales price in year 1 is already set at $12,000 for model 1 and $11,800 for model 2. After year 1 the sales price will increase by the same inflation factor that drives production costs. Like production costs, revenues from sales are assumed to occur at the ends of the respective years.
- **Demand.** The demand for either model in year 1 is assumed to be normally distributed with mean 100,000. The standard deviation for model 1 is 7500; for

model 2 it is 10,000. After year 1 the demand in a given year is assumed to be normally distributed with mean equal to the *actual* demand in the previous year and standard deviation 7500 for model 1 or 10,000 for model 2. For example, if the observed demand in year 3 is 105,000, then the demand distribution in year 4 has mean 105,000. An implication of this assumption is that demands in successive years are not probabilistically independent. If the demand in one year is large, for example, the mean demand for the next year is also large, so that the actual demand for the next year will tend to be large.

- **Production.** In any particular year GF plans to base its production policy on the probability distribution of demand for that year—*before* the actual demand for that year is observed. In particular, if the expected demand in year t is ED_t and the standard deviation of demand is σ_t, then GF's policy is to produce $ED_t + k\sigma_t$ cars, where k is a decision variable that GF will have to select. For example, if it chooses $k = 1$, then its production quantity in any year will be one standard deviation above the expected demand. From the properties of the normal distribution, this implies that the chances are approximately five out of six of meeting all demand for the year. (This is because a normal random variable has approximate probability 5/6 of being no more than one standard deviation above the mean.) If demand in any year is greater than production, the excess demand is lost. However, if production in any year is greater than demand, GF will sell the excess cars at an end-of-year discount of 30%.
- **Interest rate.** GF plans to use a 10% interest rate to discount future cash flows. This means, for example, that a cash flow of $1 at the beginning of year 1 is equivalent to a cash flow of $1.10 at the end of year 1.

Given these assumptions, GF wants to develop a simulation spreadsheet that will evaluate its NPV for each model over the ten-year time horizon and suggest which model to build.

Solution

The simulation spreadsheet for model 1 appears in Figure 13.22. (See the file GFAUTO.XLS.)

1 **Inputs.** Enter the various inputs through row 24. As usual, it is a good practice to enter all of the input values in cells so that they can be referenced in formulas later on. Notice that we have used a value of 1 for the decision variable k in cell H21. This can easily be changed to see the effects of other ordering policies. (In fact, this might be a good place to use the RISKSIMTABLE function.)

2 **Variable cost inflation factors.** Rows 28 through 43 contain a single ten-year simulation. The approach is to enter appropriate formulas in columns B and C for years 1 and 2, then copy the year 2 formulas to the columns for the other years, and finally calculate the values in rows 37, 40, 41, and 43. Begin by entering the variable production cost inflation factor relating year 2 to year 1 in cell C28 with the formula

=RISKNORMAL($B$17,$B$18)

and copy this across to the rest of row 28.

3 **Production quantities.** The production quantity in year 1 is based on the expected demand and the standard deviation of demand in year 1, so enter the formula

=H7+H21*H8

in cell B29. For other years the expected demand is the previous year's actual demand,

FIGURE 13.22 Spreadsheet for Model 1 of GF Auto Example

	A	B	C	D	E	F	G	H	I	J	K	L	M	N
1	GF Simulation with @RISK for model 1													
2														
3	Input section													
4														
5	Fixed costs (assumed to occur at beginning of year 1)						Demand in year 1							
6	Normal distribution ($ billions)						Normal distribution (1000s of cars)							
7	Mean	2.5					Mean	100						
8	St Dev	0.4					St Dev	7.5						
9														
10	Variable production cost per car in year 1						Demand in other years							
11	Normal distribution ($1000s)						Normal distribution (1000s of cars)							
12	Mean	8					Mean	demand from previous year						
13	St Dev	0.4					St Dev	7.5						
14														
15	Inflation factor						Production policy							
16	Normal distribution						Production each year is the mean demand plus a multiple of the st dev of							
17	Mean	1.05					demand (for that year). If demand is greater than supply, the excess demand is lost.							
18	St Dev	0.015					If the supply is greater than demand, the excess are sold at a discount.							
19														
20	Sales price in year 1						Multiple (k) of st dev used for setting production quantity							
21	No uncertainty ($1000s)	12						1						
22														
23	Interest rate	10%					Year-end discount for leftover cars at the end of the year							
24								30%						
25														
26	Simulation section													
27	Year	1	2	3	4	5	6	7	8	9	10			
28	Inflation factor	N/A	1.05	1.04	1.08	1.04	1.08	1.04	1.07	1.09	1.08			
29	Production (1000s)	107.5	96.75	98.73	109.91	118.82	124.38	123.06	114.06	120.53	118.48			
30	Demand (1000s)	89.25	91.23	102.41	111.32	116.88	115.56	106.56	113.03	110.98	114.43			
31	Var prod cost ($1000s)	7.95	8.37	8.73	9.39	9.77	10.54	10.96	11.77	12.82	13.83			
32	Sales price ($1000s)	12	12.64	13.18	14.18	14.75	15.90	16.53	17.76	19.35	20.87			
33														
34	Production cost ($ millions)	854.84	810.15	862.28	1032.57	1161.12	1310.53	1348.34	1342.50	1545.78	1638.29			
35	Sales revenue ($ millions)	1224.28	1201.65	1301.22	1558.21	1743.59	1935.62	1952.87	2020.43	2277.19	2446.92			
36														
37	Fixed cost ($ millions)	2662.622												
38														
39	NPV ($ millions)													
40	Production costs	6865.888												
41	Revenue	10177.052												
42														
43	Total NPV ($ millions)	648.542												

and this is used to calculate the production quantity. Therefore, for year 2 enter the formula

=B30+$H$21*$H$13

in cell C29 and copy it across to the rest of row 29.

4 **Demands.** Generate the demand in year 1 in cell B30 with the formula

=RISKNORMAL(H7,H8)

As in the previous step, the expected demand in year 2 is the actual demand from year 1, so generate the demand for year 2 in cell C30 with the formula

=RISKNORMAL(B30,$H$13)

Then copy this to the rest of row 30 to generate demands for the other years.

5 **Variable production costs.** Generate the variable production cost for year 1 in cell B31 with the formula

=RISKNORMAL(B12,B13)

Then use the inflation factor in row 28 to generate the variable production cost for year 2 in cell C31 with the formula

=B31*C28

and copy this across to the rest of row 31.

6 **Sales prices.** Enter the (nonrandom) sales price for year 1 in cell B32 with the formula

=B21

Then generate the sales price for year 2 in cell C32 with the formula

```
=B32*C28
```

and copy this across to the rest of row 32.

7 **Production costs.** The production cost for any year is the production quantity multiplied by the variable production cost, so enter the formula

```
=B29*B31
```

in cell B34 and copy it to the rest of row 34. (Notice that because the production quantity is in thousands of cars and variable production cost is in thousands of dollars, the resulting product will automatically be in millions of dollars.)

8 **Revenues.** The revenue in any year is calculated in one of two possible ways. If demand is greater than the production quantity, then revenue is the sales price multiplied by the production quantity. Otherwise, if demand is less than the production quantity, then revenue is the sales price multiplied by the demand, plus the discounted sales price multiplied by the number of cars left over. Therefore, calculate the revenue for year 1 in cell B35 with the formula

```
=IF(B29<B30,B32*B29,B32*(B30+(1–$H$24)*(B29–B30)))
```

and copy it to the rest of row 35.

9 **Fixed cost.** Generate the fixed cost of developing the car (in millions of dollars) in cell B37 with the formula

```
=RISKNORMAL(B7,B8)*1000
```

10 **NPVs.** Calculate the NPV of all production costs (in millions of dollars) in cell B40 with the formula

```
=NPV($B$23,B34:K34)
```

Then copy this to cell B41 to calculate the NPV of all revenues. Notice that the NPV function takes two arguments: the interest rate used for discounting and a stream of cash flows beginning with the flow at the end of year 1.

11 **Total NPV.** Finally, calculate the total NPV in cell B43 with the formula

```
=B41–B37–B40
```

Because the fixed costs occur at the *beginning* of year 1, they are not discounted when calculating total NPV.

To form the analogous spreadsheet for model 2, you can copy this sheet to a new sheet (in the same workbook file) and change the inputs. Here is an easy way to do this. With your finger on the Ctrl key, drag the sheet tab of the model 1 sheet to the right. This will create a copy of the original sheet. Then it is a good idea to name these two sheets Model 1 and Model 2. (Double-click on the sheet tab to obtain a dialog box for naming a sheet.) Finally, change the necessary inputs in the model 2 sheet.

Using @RISK A single simulation can be used to simulate the quantities for each car model.[4] To track the total NPV for each model, select cell B43 from each sheet (separately) as an output cell.[5] The simulated results from 200 iterations definitely favor model 2. The summary of results and simulation statistics shown in Figure 13.23 show that (1) model 2

[4]From here on, we will not give step-by-step instructions for using @RISK. Remember that it is basically a three-step process: (1) identify the output cell(s), (2) specify the simulation settings, and (3) run the simulation.

[5]This simulation ran successfully. However, we have had occasional problems with @RISK when using output cells from different sheets, and Palisades Corporation has acknowledged a possible bug in the program that can cause problems in this situation.

FIGURE 13.23 Summary Statistics for GF Auto Example

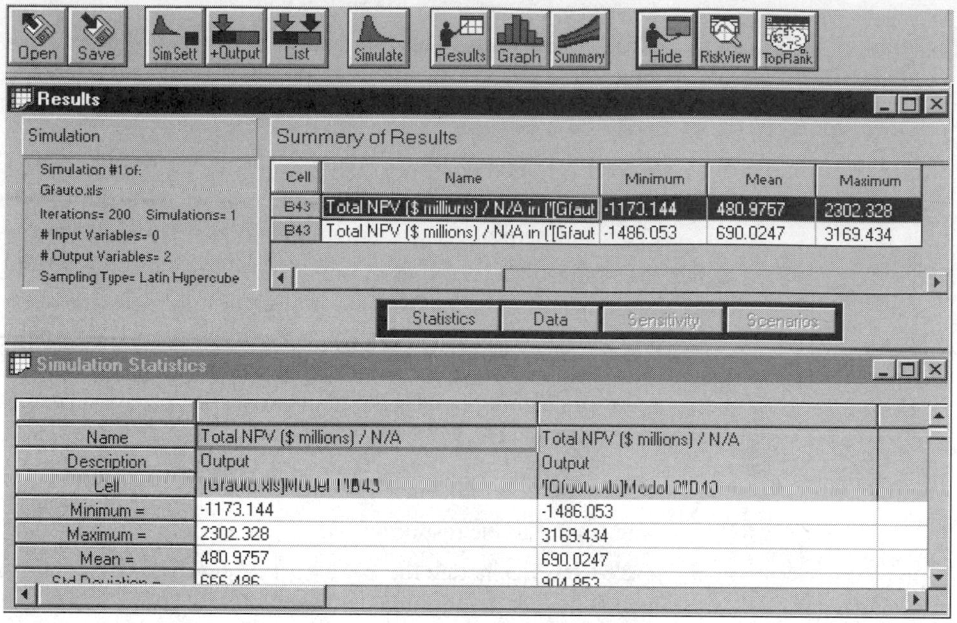

has a much larger mean NPV than model 1 ($690 million versus $480 million), (2) both models have approximately the same worst-case outcome (a loss of over $1 billion), (3) model 2 has a much better best-case outcome ($3.1 billion versus $2.3 billion), and (4) model 2 has a slightly larger standard deviation of NPVs than model 1 ($.9 billion versus $.66 billion). Usually, a larger standard deviation is not an attractive property, but in this case, since the two models have approximately the same worst-case outcomes, a larger standard deviation is encouraging. It means that model 2 has more upside potential.

The target values shown in Figure 13.24 illustrate model 2's dominance in a slightly different way. Here we entered target values of 0, 1000, 2000, and −1000 for each model. (A value of 1000, for example, corresponds to $1 billion.) The percentages show how many simulated NPVs are below each target value. Looking at the 0 and −1000 targets, we see that model 1 has a larger chance of a loss (28% versus 23%), although model 2 has a slightly larger chance of a really large loss (2.7% versus 1.3%). However, looking at the 1000 and 2000 targets, we see that model 2 has larger chances of significant gains. For example, model 2 has about an 8% chance of gaining over $2 billion, whereas model 1 has only about a 1% chance of doing this.

Finally, histograms for the two models appear in Figure 13.25. (For comparison, it is important to make the scales on the axes the same for each model. This is possible with @RISK's graphical options. You access these by right-clicking on a graph.) The two graphs don't appear to be too different. However, a close look reveals that model 1 has more chances for moderate losses, whereas model 2 has more chances for large gains. ■

MODELING ISSUES

1 When we enter two sets of @RISK functions on separate sheets, as we did in this example, @RISK uses different random numbers for the two car models when it runs the simulation. This could give the edge to one model

FIGURE 13.24 Target Values for GF Auto Example

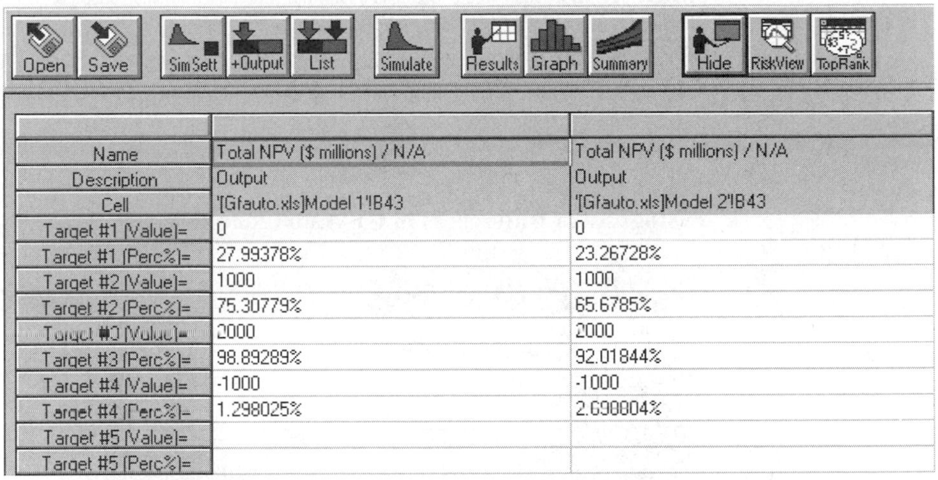

Name	Total NPV ($ millions) / N/A	Total NPV ($ millions) / N/A
Description	Output	Output
Cell	'[Gfauto.xls]Model 1'!B43	'[Gfauto.xls]Model 2'!B43
Target #1 (Value)=	0	0
Target #1 (Perc%)=	27.99378%	23.26728%
Target #2 (Value)=	1000	1000
Target #2 (Perc%)=	75.30779%	65.6785%
Target #3 (Value)=	2000	2000
Target #3 (Perc%)=	98.89289%	92.01844%
Target #4 (Value)=	-1000	-1000
Target #4 (Perc%)=	1.298025%	2.698004%
Target #5 (Value)=		
Target #5 (Perc%)=		

FIGURE 13.25 Histograms for GF Auto Example

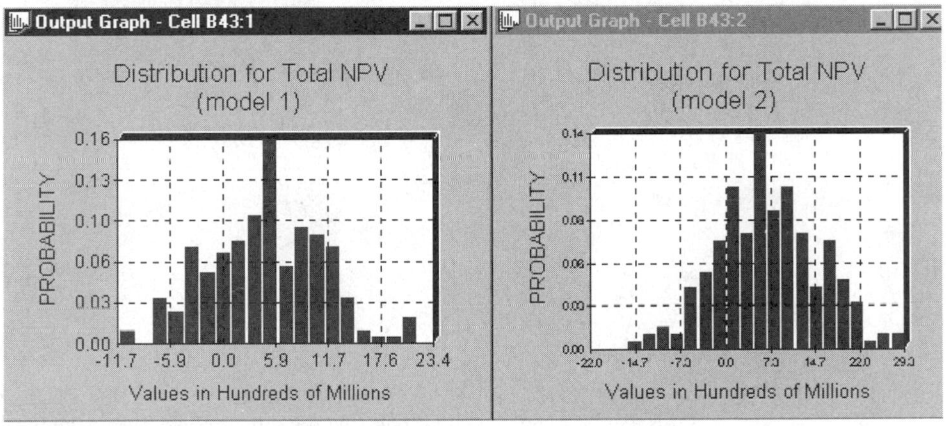

just by chance. That is, one model could obtain a larger mean NPV just because of a relatively lucky set of random numbers. This is one reason we used a larger number of iterations, 200, than before. The larger number of iterations should cancel out the effect of a few lucky or unlucky random numbers.

In general, when we are performing a comparison between several strategies (two different models, five different ordering policies, and so on), it is best if we can use the same random numbers for each strategy. For example, if we had set up a single spreadsheet for both models and then used the same stream of inflation factors for both models' production and sales prices, this would have subjected both models to more identical conditions. Hence, it would have led to a fairer comparison. Sometimes this synchronization of random numbers is easy to accomplish; other times it is awkward or difficult. In any case, we can partially overcome any chance factor due to different streams of random numbers by running more iterations of the simulation.

2 To compare NPVs for models 1 and 2, we used the NPVs in cell B43 of the respective sheets as the output cells. Another approach would be to calculate the *difference* between these two NPVs in some cell and use the difference as the output cell. Then we could analyze the statistics or the graph of differences to see whether one model is generally favored over the other. A histogram of such differences (NPV for model 2 minus NPV for model 1) appears in Figure 13.26. Although many bars indicate a negative difference (model 1 beats model 2), many more indicate a positive difference. ■

FIGURE 13.26 **Histogram of Differences in GF Auto Example**

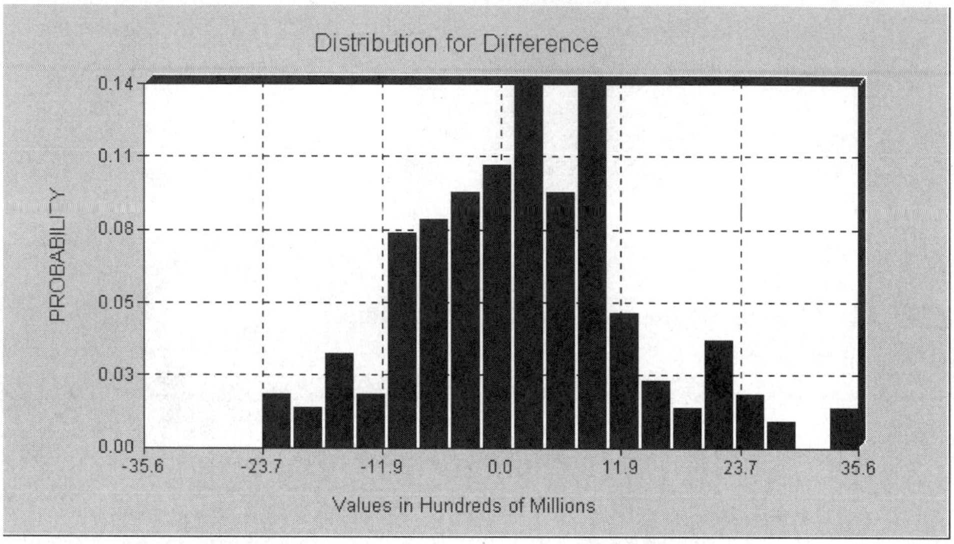

PROBLEMS

Skill-Building Problems

6 Use @RISK to solve Problem 12.23, but now assume that the fixed cost of developing the Racer is triangularly distributed with minimum, most likely, and maximum values \$3, \$4, and \$5 billion. Also, assume that the variable cost per car in year 1 is triangularly distributed with minimum, most likely, and maximum values \$5000, \$7000, and \$8000.

7 Use @RISK to solve Problem 12.24.

Skill-Extending Problems

8 Use @RISK to solve Problem 12.26.

9 Toys For U is developing a new Madonna doll. The company has made the following assumptions:

- It is equally likely that the doll will sell for two, four, six, eight, or ten years.
- At the beginning of year 1, the potential market for the doll is one million. The potential market grows by an average of 5% per year. Toys For U is 95% sure that the growth in the potential market during any year will be between 3% and 7%. It uses a normal distribution to model this.

- The company believes its share of the potential market during year 1 will be at worst 20%, most likely 40%, and at best 50%. It uses a triangular distribution to model this.
- The variable cost of producing a doll during year 1 is equally likely to be \$4 or \$6.
- Each year the sales price and variable cost of producing the doll will increase by 5%.
- The fixed cost of developing the doll (which is incurred right away, at time 0) is equally likely to be \$4, \$8, or \$12 million.
- Right now there is one competitor in the market. During each year that begins with four or fewer competitors, there is a 20% chance that a new competitor will enter the market.
- To determine year t sales (for $t > 1$) we proceed as follows. Suppose that at the end of year $t - 1$, x competitors are present. Then we assume that during year t, a fraction $.9 - .1 * x$ of the company's loyal customers (last year's purchasers) will buy a doll during the next year, and a fraction $.2 - .04 * x$ of people currently in the market who did not purchase a doll last year will purchase a doll from the company this year. We can now generate a prediction for year t sales. Of course, this prediction will not be exactly correct. We assume that it is sure to be accurate within 15%, however. (There are different ways to model this. You may choose any method that is reasonable.)
- Cash flows are discounted at 10% per year.

a Use @RISK to estimate the expected NPV of this project. Also, find a 95% confidence interval for this expected value.

b Use the percentiles in @RISK's output to find an interval such that you are 95% certain that the company's *actual* NPV will be within this interval.

c Explain the difference between the two intervals in Parts (a) and (b). ■

13.5

A Component Redundancy Simulation

To extend the useful lifetimes of various devices, redundancy is often built in. For example, in space modules, there is massive redundancy. If the primary unit fails, a backup takes over. If the backup fails, there might be a second backup to take over, and so on. In this section we will simulate the time to failure of one such system. In doing so, we will discuss the effect on simulation results of different input probability distributions. Although it is tempting to use one of the well-known distributions, particularly the normal distribution, for most simulations, you should be aware that there are quite a few candidate distributions available and that the simulated results can depend significantly on which candidate you choose. We will compare four available distributions in the following example.

EXAMPLE 13.4

The FailSafe Company operates machines, each of which depends on an important module to perform successfully. This module, in turn, relies on a specific component. If this component fails, the module fails and the machine fails. In order to extend the time until component failure, redundancy is built in at the component level. Specifically, ten identical components are placed in parallel in the module. This means that the machine lasts as long as any of the ten components are still working. In mathematical terms, if T_i is the time at which component i fails, then the time at which the machine fails is the maximum of T_1 through T_{10}. Each T_i is random with mean 100 hours and standard deviation 20 hours. FailSafe wants to use simulation to find the distribution of the time until machine failure.

Solution

The solution is straightforward. For a single replication we need to generate ten T_i's and calculate their maximum; this is the time at which the machine fails. The key question is what distribution we should use to generate the T_i's. We know that it has mean 100 and standard deviation 20, but what is its shape? Should it be symmetric and bell-shaped, or should it be skewed in one direction or the other? We will test four possible distributions: normal, lognormal, gamma, and Weibull. The normal, of course, is the symmetric bell-shaped distribution. The other three are less well known, but they are frequently used to model times to failure. They all have the attractive property that they use positive random variables only (times to failure can't be negative!). Also, all three are skewed to the right (the long tail is on the right side of the curve), a property that histograms of failure times usually possess.

Developing the Spreadsheet Model The spreadsheet module for FailSafe's simulation appears in Figure 13.27. (See the file REDUND.XLS.) It can be formed as follows.

1 **Inputs.** Enter the inputs in rows 4 through 9. The values in cells D4 and D5 are not used explicitly in the simulation, but they indicate that there is a single module that consists of ten identical components in parallel, as explained above. The inputs for each distribution, entered in rows 8 and 9, require some explanation. Each distribution "family," such as the normal family, requires two arguments to identify the particular input distribution. For the normal and lognormal distributions these arguments are the mean and standard deviation themselves.

For the gamma and Weibull distributions the arguments are indirectly related to the means and standard deviations. For these two distributions the arguments are labeled α and β (which must be positive values). They determine the shape and location of the distribution, respectively. For the gamma distribution it can be shown that the mean and standard deviation are $\alpha\beta$ and $\sqrt{\alpha}\beta$. Therefore, the values required to obtain a mean of 100 and a standard deviation of 20 are $\alpha = 25$ and $\beta = 4$.

FIGURE 13.27 Simulation Model for Component Redundancy Example

	A	B	C	D	E	F	G	H	I	J	K
1	**Component Redundancy Example**										
2											
3	**Input section**										
4	Number of modules in series			1							
5	Number of components in each module			10							
6											
7	Normal distribution			Lognormal distribution			Gamma distribution			Weibull distribution	
8	Mean	100		Mean	100		Alpha	25		Alpha	5.797
9	StDev	20		StDev	20		Beta	4		Beta	107.991
10							Mean	100		Mean	100
11							StDev	20		StDev	20
12											
13	**Simulated component lifetimes (for each distribution)**										
14	Normal			Lognormal			Gamma			Weibull	
15	Component	Time		Component	Time		Component	Time		Component	Time
16	1	107.715		1	93.560		1	147.285		1	63.133
17	2	73.316		2	94.144		2	102.113		2	104.966
18	3	118.345		3	85.492		3	83.055		3	113.932
19	4	112.545		4	137.958		4	91.989		4	101.353
20	5	117.085		5	90.328		5	75.900		5	86.100
21	6	110.930		6	103.321		6	90.212		6	71.871
22	7	87.636		7	123.033		7	111.281		7	136.569
23	8	105.886		8	84.571		8	101.301		8	56.234
24	9	85.014		9	110.681		9	96.337		9	36.658
25	10	85.893		10	82.840		10	129.347		10	110.062
26											
27	Length of time machine lasts										
28	Normal	118.345		Lognormal	137.958		Gamma	147.285		Weibull	136.569

For the Weibull distribution the relationship between α and β and the mean and standard deviation is much more complex. Therefore, we simply state that the values $\alpha = 5.797$ and $\beta = 107.991$ (obtained through special tables) are required to obtain a mean of 100 and a standard deviation of 20.

2 **Simulated component times.** To generate a single time to component failure for the various distributions, enter the formulas

=RISKNORMAL($B$8,$B$9)
=RISKLOGNORM($E$8,$E$9)
=RISKGAMMA($H$8,$H$9)

and

=RISKWEIBULL($K$8,$K$9)

in cells B16, E16, H16, and K16. Then copy these down their respective columns to generate component failure times for the other components.

3 **Simulated machine times.** To generate the time at which the machine fails for each distribution, enter the formula

=MAX(B16:B25)

in cell B28 and copy it to the cells E28, H28, and K28.

Using @RISK To keep track of the machine failure times for each distribution, select cells B28, E28, H28, and K28 as the output cells. Then run a single simulation for 1000 iterations. The summary results shown in Figure 13.28 indicate that the mean time until machine failure is fairly consistent across the four distributions. In particular, the redundancy increases the mean time until failure from 100 hours (if there were only a single component) to approximately 130 hours. However, the minimum and maximum times (over the 1000 iterations) differ fairly widely across the four distributions. For example, the lognormal produces the worst and the best times, whereas the Weibull's best time is much lower than the best times for the other distributions.

FIGURE 13.28 Summary Statistics for Component Redundancy Example

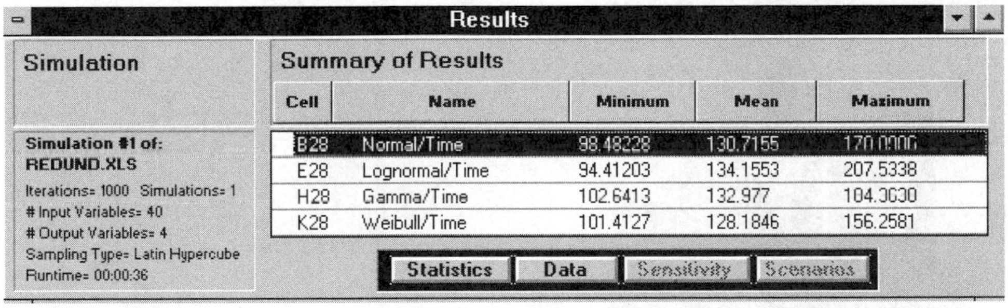

This behavior is further confirmed by the target information, as shown in Figure 13.29. For each of the four distributions we entered five percentages (1%, 5%, 50%, 95%, and 99%) to see how the distribution of machine time failure behaves in the middle and at the extremes. The lower and 50% percentiles (medians) are similar across the four distributions. However, the upper percentiles differ widely. For example, we predict that 1% of the machine times for the Weibull distribution will be greater than 150 hours; for the lognormal distribution the comparable value is 177 hours.

FIGURE 13.29 **Target Values for Component Redundancy Example**

Simulation Statistics				
Name	Normal/Time	Lognormal/Time	Gamma/Time	Weibull/Time
Description	Output	Output	Output	Output
Cell	B28	E28	H28	K28
Target #1 (Value)=	105.327430725098	106.53687286377	105.843490600586	106.861526489258
Target #1 (Perc%)=	1%	1%	1%	1%
Target #2 (Value)=	111.607879638672	111.134788513184	111.027389526367	113.185577392578
Target #2 (Perc%)=	5%	5%	5%	5%
Target #3 (Value)=	129.985580444336	132.10871887207	131.612060546875	127.876487731934
Target #3 (Perc%)=	50%	50%	50%	50%
Target #4 (Value)=	151.450271606445	162.412536621094	158.551147460938	143.628265380859
Target #4 (Perc%)=	95%	95%	95%	95%
Target #5 (Value)=	161.448684692383	177.130996704102	173.253936767578	150.056884765625
Target #5 (Perc%)=	99%	99%	99%	99%

Finally, the histograms of times until machine failure appear in Figures 13.30 through 13.33. Although these are not dramatically different, we see more skewness (longer tails to the right) in the lognormal and gamma cases and more symmetry around the mean in the normal and Weibull cases. Also, the Weibull has a significantly shorter tail on the right than any of the others. In real terms, if FailSafe's component times until failure are really Weibull distributed (as has been observed in many similar applications), then there is less potential for really long machine lifetimes than if they had one of the other distributions. ■

FIGURE 13.30 **Histogram for Normal Distribution Values**

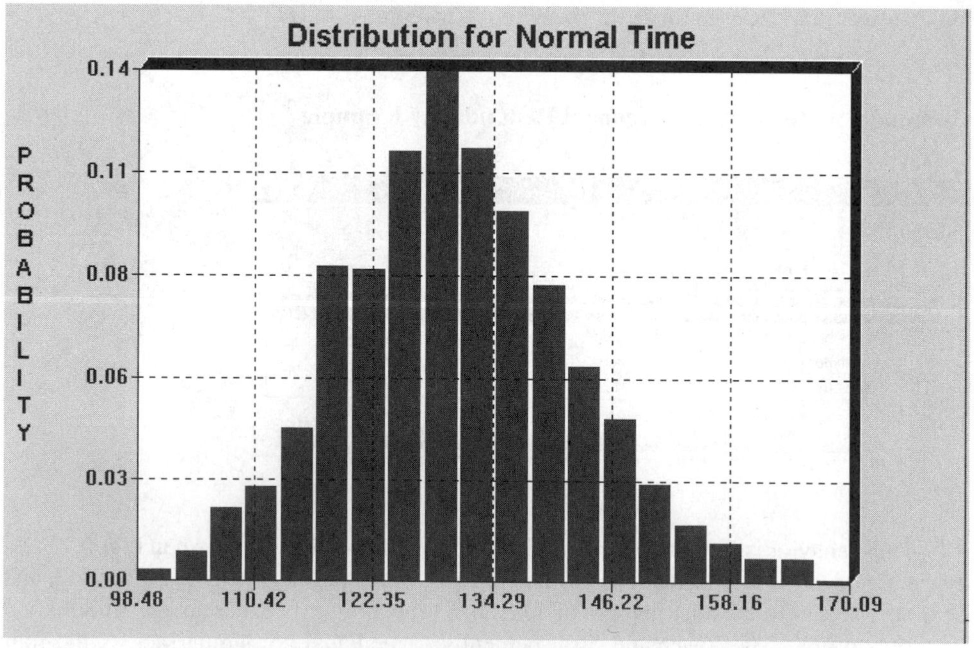

FIGURE 13.31 **Histogram for Lognormal Distribution Values**

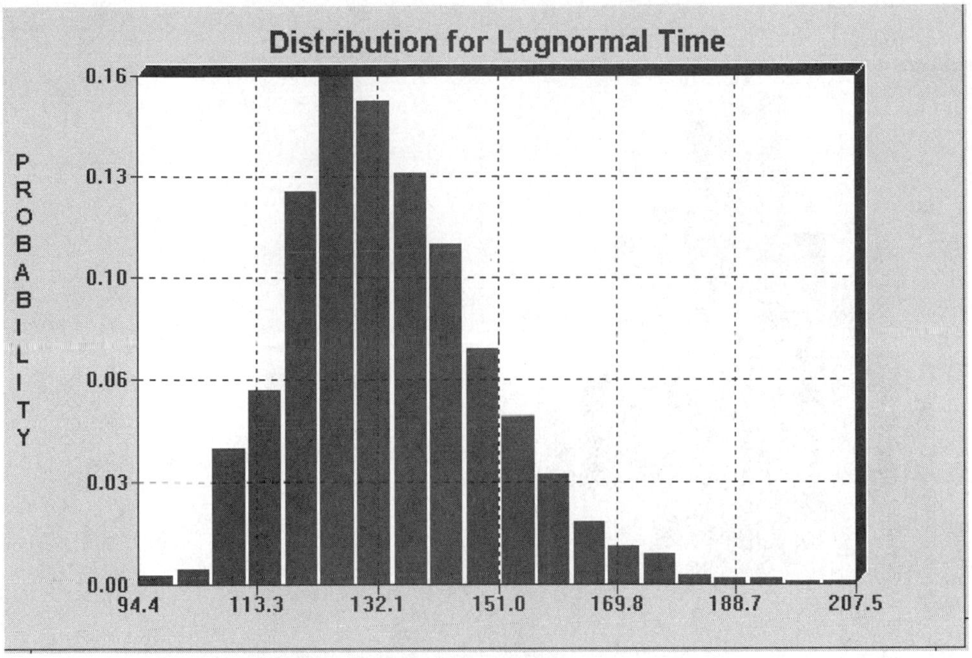

FIGURE 13.32 **Histogram for Gamma Distribution Values**

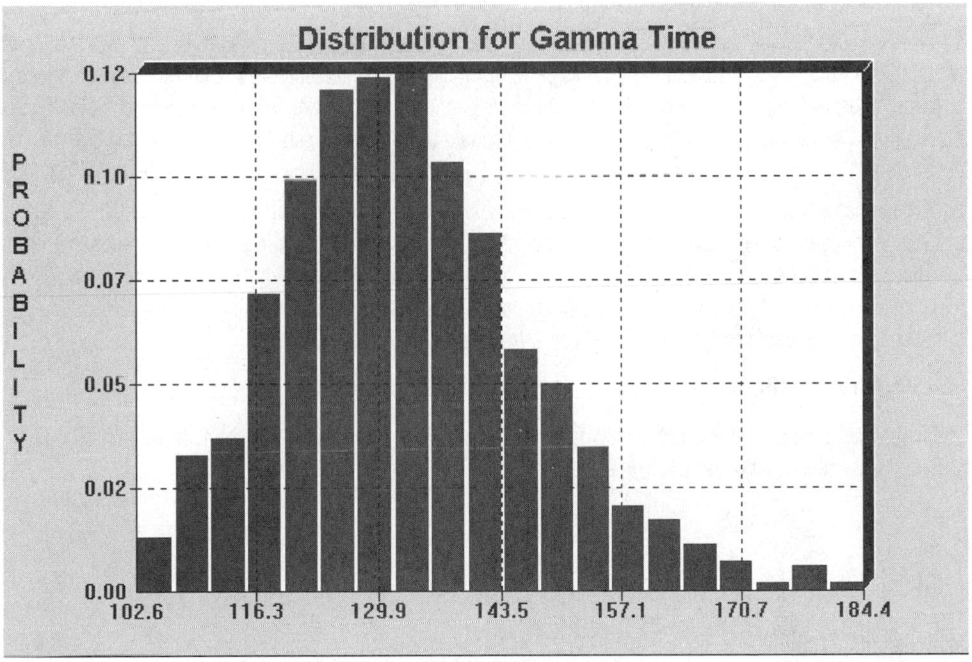

FIGURE 13.33 Histogram for Weibull Distribution Values

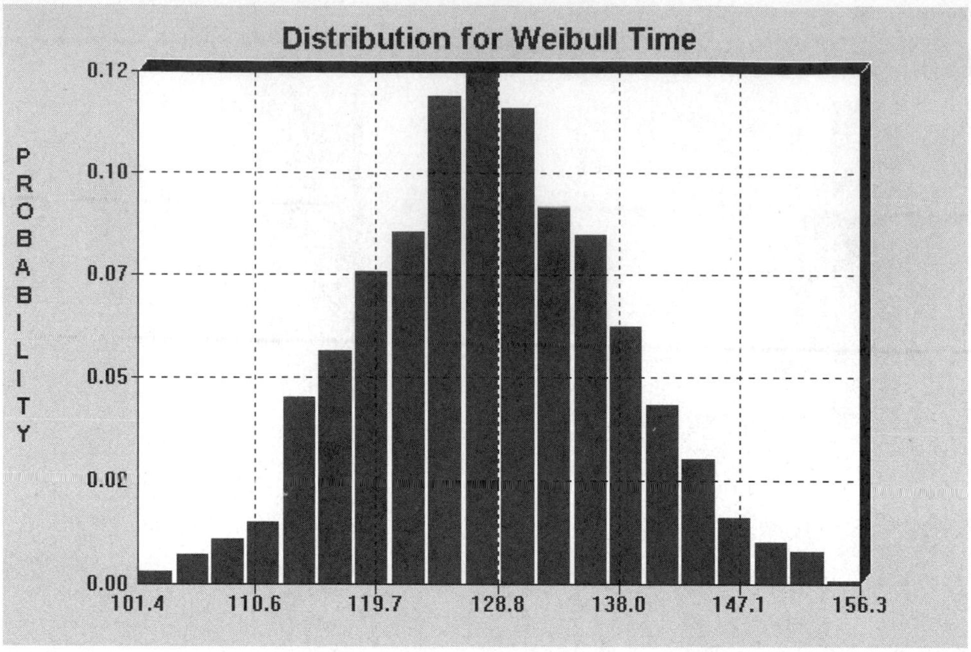

MODELING ISSUES

1 How would FailSafe know which of these distributions to use? There are several software packages available for fitting distributions to historical data, in this case, historical times until component failures. These packages suggest the best-fitting family, such as the Weibull or the gamma family, as well as the best parameters for these distributions. These packages are very easy to use and should be considered seriously by anyone doing extensive simulations. One such package, BestFit, is distributed by Palisades, the same company that distributes @RISK.

2 It is relatively straightforward to extend this simulation model to more complex forms of redundancy. For example, suppose that the machine consists of two identical modules connected in series. This means that the machine works until either of the two modules fails. However, suppose that each of the modules consists of five identical components in parallel. Then we could use the spreadsheet model shown in Figure 13.27 except that the formulas in row 28 would be modified. For example, the formula in cell B28 would be

=MIN(MAX(B16:B20),MAX(B21:B25))

The first MAX is the time at which module 1 fails; the second MAX is the time at which module 2 fails. The MIN function finds the smaller of these two times, which is the time until machine failure. ■

PROBLEMS

Skill-Building Problems

10 In Example 13.4 we simulated the time until failure of the machine. Suppose that the machine has a mission to carry out and to accomplish this mission it must survive at least 125 hours. The component times are assumed to be gamma distributed with $\alpha = 25$ and $\beta = 4$, as in the example. The company wants to know how many components to include in parallel so that there is a 95% probability that the machine will fulfill its mission. Use @RISK to determine the number of components to include.

11 Consider a device that requires two batteries to function. If either of these batteries dies, the device won't work. Currently there are two brand new batteries in the device, and there are three extra brand new batteries. Each battery, once it is placed in the device, lasts a random amount of time that is lognormally distributed with mean 20 hours and standard deviation 5 hours. When any of the batteries in the device dies, it is immediately replaced by an extra (if an extra is still available). Use @RISK to simulate the time the device can last with the batteries currently available.

Skill-Extending Problems

12 The machine in Example 13.4 is a purely parallel system: the machine works as long as *any* of the components work. Suppose instead that the machine is in a series-parallel arrangement. To understand this, think of the machine as being a series of modules. If any of these modules fails, the machine fails. To make the machine last longer, each module can consist of a parallel arrangement of identical components, as in the example. This means that a given module lasts as long as any one of its components lasts, but as soon as a single module fails, the machine fails. In general, suppose that there are m modules in series and that module i consists of n_i components in parallel. The components in module i are identical in that they have a common lognormal distribution with mean and standard deviation μ_i and standard deviation σ_i. However, these parameters can depend on i, that is, they can vary from one module to another. Use @RISK to simulate the time to machine failure when $m = 3$, $n_1 = 5$, $n_2 = 8$, and $n_3 = 3$. Use the parameters $\mu_1 = 100$, $\mu_2 = 90$, $\mu_3 = 120$, $\sigma_1 = 20$, $\sigma_2 = 25$, and $\sigma_3 = 30$. As part of your simulation, find the fraction of the iterations in which machine failure is caused by failure of module 1; by failure of module 2; by failure of module 3.

13 Referring to the previous problem, suppose your job is to build as reliable a machine as possible with a given budget. You again have $m = 3$ modules, and you already own exactly one component for each module. For c_i dollars apiece you can purchase as many extra components for module i as you like, but you have only C dollars to spend. Run several simulations, using the same distributions as in the previous problem, to see how you should best spend your money. Assume that $c_1 = \$100$, $c_2 = \$80$, $c_3 = \$140$, and $C = \$500$.

14 Rework the previous problem, but instead of basing your decision on the time until machine failure (which you want to maximize), base it on the probability that the machine will last at least 125 hours. That is, for any configuration of components your only interest is in the fraction of iterations in which the machine lasts at least 125 hours. Will you allocate your budget in the same way with this objective? ■

13.6

Simulating the Game of Craps

Most games of chance are great candidates for simulation since they are, by their very nature, driven by randomness. In this section we will examine one such game that is extremely popular in the gambling casinos, the game of craps. In its most basic form the game of craps is played as follows. A player rolls two dice and calculates the sum of the two sides turned up. If this sum is 7 or 11, the player wins right away. If this sum is 2, 3, or 12, the player loses right away. However, if this sum is any other number (4, 5, 6, 8, 9, or 10), that number becomes the player's "point." Then the dice are thrown repeatedly until the sum is the original point or 7. In case the point occurs before a 7, the player wins. But if a 7 occurs before the point, the player loses. The following example uses simulation to determine the properties of this game.

EXAMPLE 13.5

Joe Gamble loves to play craps at the casinos. He suspects that his chances of winning are less than 50-50, but he figures that he can at least play for quite awhile before losing all of his cash. Assuming that he starts with $50 and each bet is worth $5, he wants to know whether he can play 100 games without going broke.

Solution

We will solve this problem in two parts. First, we will simulate a single game. By running this simulation for many iterations, we will find the probability that Joe wins a single game. If his intuition is correct (and surely it must be, or the casino could not stay in business), this probability will be less than .5. As a byproduct, we will also see how many tosses of the dice are needed to determine the outcome of a single game. Then we will run a second simulation, using the probability from the first simulation, to determine whether Joe can play 100 games without going broke.

Developing the First Spreadsheet Model The first spreadsheet model is for a single game, which we will iterate repeatedly. (See Figure 13.34 and the file CRAPS1.XLS.) There is a subtle problem here: we don't know how many tosses of the dice are necessary to determine the outcome of a single game. Theoretically, the game could continue forever, with the player waiting for his or her point or a 7. However, it is very unlikely that more than, say, 30 tosses will be necessary in a single game. (This can be shown by a relatively straightforward probability argument, but we won't present it here.) Therefore, we will simulate 30 tosses and use only those that are necessary to determine the outcome of a single game. The steps required to simulate a single game are as follows.

1 **Simulate tosses.** Simulate the results of 30 tosses in the range B9:D38 by entering the formula

=RISKDUNIFORM({1,2,3,4,5,6})

in cells B9 and C9 and the formula

=SUM(B9:C9)

in cell D9. Then copy these to the range B10:D38. The @RISK function RISKDUNIFORM takes a single argument, a list of numbers, and randomly selects one of the numbers from this list, where each number has equal probability (in this case 1/6). DUNIFORM stands for discrete uniform.

2 **First toss outcome.** In the range G9:I9 determine the outcome (win, lose, or continue) of the first toss with the formulas

=IF(OR(D9=7,D9=11),1,0)
=IF(OR(D9=2,D9=3,D9=12),1,0)

and

=IF(AND(G9=0,H9=0),"Yes","No")

in cells G9, H9, and I9. Note that we use the OR condition to check whether Joe wins right away (in which case a 1 is recorded in cell G9). Similarly, the OR condition in cell H9 checks whether he loses right away. In cell I9, we use the AND condition to check whether both cells G9 and H9 are 0, in which case the game continues. Otherwise, the game is over.

3 **Outcomes of other tosses.** Assuming the game continues beyond toss 1, Joe's point is the value in cell D9. So we are waiting for a toss to have the value in cell D9 or 7, whichever occurs first. To operationalize this logic, enter the formulas

=IF(I9="Yes",IF(D10=$D$9,1,0),"NA")
=IF(I9="Yes",IF(D10=7,1,0),"NA")

FIGURE 13.34 **Simulation Model of a Single Game of Craps**

	A	B	C	D	E	F	G	H	I
1	**Craps Simulation**								
2									
3	**Summary of results**								
4	Win? (1 if yes, 0 if no)	0							
5	Number of tosses	3							
6									
7	**Simulated tosses**					**Results**			
8		Die 1	Die 2	Sum			Win on this toss?	Lose on this toss?	Continue?
9	Toss 1	2	2	4		Toss 1	0	0	Yes
10	Toss 2	1	2	3		Toss 2	0	0	Yes
11	Toss 3	5	2	7		Toss 3	0	1	No
12	Toss 4	6	6	12		Toss 4	NA	NA	No
13	Toss 5	5	2	7		Toss 5	NA	NA	No
14	Toss 6	3	4	7		Toss 6	NA	NA	No
15	Toss 7	4	4	8		Toss 7	NA	NA	No
16	Toss 8	3	6	9		Toss 8	NA	NA	No
17	Toss 9	5	1	6		Toss 9	NA	NA	No
18	Toss 10	6	1	7		Toss 10	NA	NA	No
19	Toss 11	1	6	7		Toss 11	NA	NA	No
20	Toss 12	3	4	7		Toss 12	NA	NA	No
21	Toss 13	1	4	5		Toss 13	NA	NA	No
22	Toss 14	3	5	8		Toss 14	NA	NA	No
23	Toss 15	2	3	5		Toss 15	NA	NA	No
24	Toss 16	4	3	7		Toss 16	NA	NA	No
25	Toss 17	1	3	4		Toss 17	NA	NA	No
26	Toss 18	1	5	6		Toss 18	NA	NA	No
27	Toss 19	4	3	7		Toss 19	NA	NA	No
28	Toss 20	3	5	8		Toss 20	NA	NA	No
29	Toss 21	5	3	8		Toss 21	NA	NA	No
30	Toss 22	1	1	2		Toss 22	NA	NA	No
31	Toss 23	3	2	5		Toss 23	NA	NA	No
32	Toss 24	6	2	8		Toss 24	NA	NA	No
33	Toss 25	5	3	8		Toss 25	NA	NA	No
34	Toss 26	2	4	6		Toss 26	NA	NA	No
35	Toss 27	5	5	10		Toss 27	NA	NA	No
36	Toss 28	4	5	9		Toss 28	NA	NA	No
37	Toss 29	6	1	7		Toss 29	NA	NA	No
38	Toss 30	2	6	8		Toss 30	NA	NA	No

and

=IF(AND(I9="Yes",G10=0,H10=0),"Yes","No")

in cells G10, H10, and I10. Then copy these to the range G11:I38. The nested IF in cell G10 should be read as follows. Check whether the game is still continuing (I9="Yes"). If so, Joe wins on this toss only if the current toss is his point (D10=$D$9). If not, that is, if the game is already over, the result of this toss is not applicable. The formula in cell H10 is similar. The formula in cell I10 states that for the game to continue, the game must have continued to this point and the game must not have been decided by this toss.

4 **Game outcomes.** We keep track of two aspects of the game: whether Joe wins or loses and how many tosses are required. To find these, enter the formulas

=SUM(G9:G38)

and

=COUNT(G9:G38)

in cells B4 and B5. Note that Joe wins only if some entry in column G is 1. Therefore, if the sum in cell B4 is 1, he wins; if it is 0, he loses. The COUNT function in cell B5 counts the number of cells with *numerical* entries. This will correctly record the number of tosses required to determine the outcome of the game since we record a "NA" in each cell after the game is over.

Using @RISK Specify cells B4 and B5 as the output cells. Then run a single simulation for 1000 iterations. The results are summarized in Figure 13.35. The average of the 0's

FIGURE 13.35 **Summary Statistics for Craps Game Example**

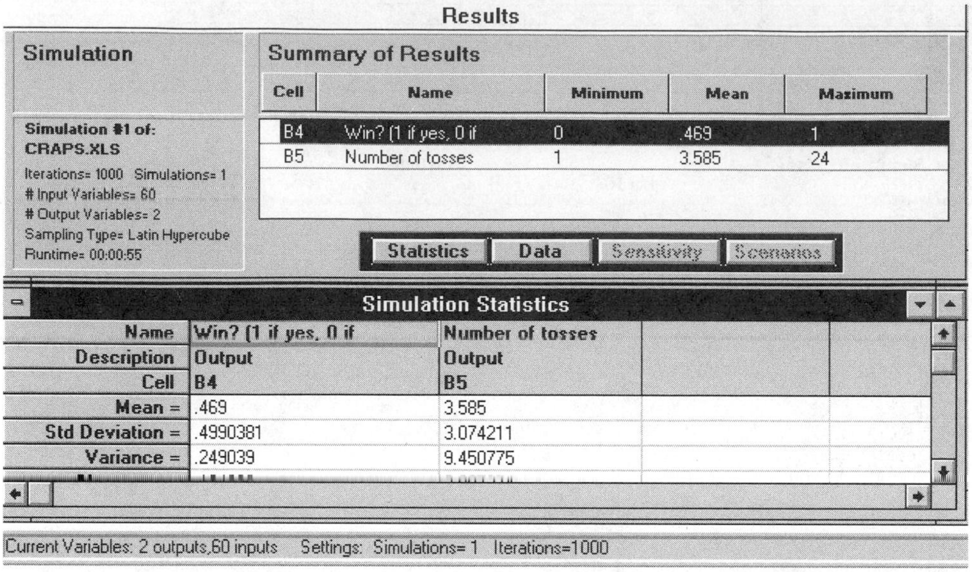

and 1's in cell B4 is .469. This means that Joe won 469 times out of 1000. Is this his true probability of winning a single game? We are not exactly sure because there is always the chance that he got lucky or unlucky in these 1000 games. However, an approximate 95% confidence interval for an unknown proportion p (here the probability of winning a single game) is of the form

$$\widehat{p} \pm 2\sqrt{\widehat{p}(1-\widehat{p})/n}$$

where $\widehat{p}$ is the sample proportion (here .469) and n is the number of observations (here 1000). Therefore, this confidence interval for the true probability of winning is

$$.469 \pm \sqrt{.469(1-.469)/1000}$$

This interval extends from .437 to .501. Now you can see why we used so many iterations. In fact, we would need even more to shrink the confidence interval appreciably. It can be shown that the exact probability of winning (from probability arguments, not simulation) is .493. Therefore, Joe was a bit unlucky in this particular simulation, but his intuition that the chances of winning are less than 50-50 is indeed correct.

Figure 13.35 also indicates that the average number of tosses required to determine the game's outcome was 3.585. However, the histogram of the number of tosses (one value for each of the 1000 games) shows that the average is quite misleading. (See Figure 13.36.) This histogram shows that about 47% of the games were determined on the first toss, but several required a large number of tosses. In fact, one game required 24 tosses! With a highly skewed distribution such as this, the histogram is much more informative than summary statistics such as the mean or the standard deviation.

Developing the Second Spreadsheet Model The purpose of the second simulation is to see whether Joe can play 100 games before going broke. In case he does go broke, we will keep track of the number of games he was able to play. The following steps are required. (See Figure 13.37 and the file CRAPS2.XLS.)

1 **Inputs.** Enter the inputs in the range B4:B7. Note that we have used the theoretical probability, .493, of winning on a particular game, not the simulated value from the previous simulation.

FIGURE 13.36 **Histogram of Number of Tosses in Craps Example**

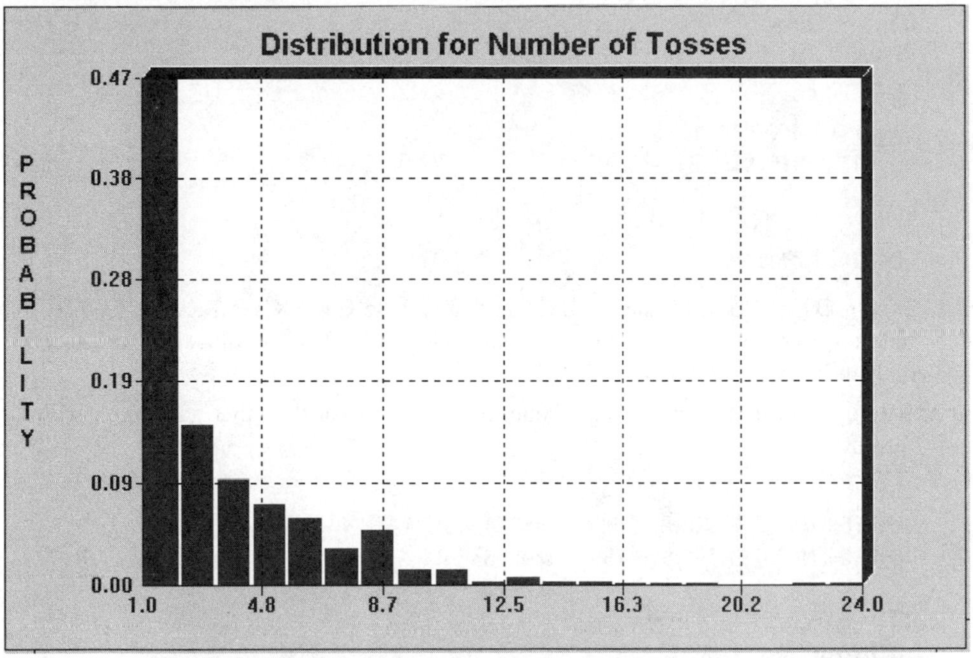

FIGURE 13.37 **Spreadsheet Model for Craps Betting Example**

	A	B	C	D	E
1	**Simulating craps to see whether Joe goes broke**				
2					
3	**Input section**				
4	Probability of winning	0.493			
5	Initial wealth	$50			
6	Bet on each game	$5			
7	Maximum games	100			
8					
9	**Summary of simulated results**				
10	Went broke?	0			
11	Number of plays	100			
12					
13	**Simulation of games**				
14	Game	Wealth before	Won?	Wealth after	Broke yet?
15	1	$50	0	$45	No
16	2	$45	0	$40	No
17	3	$40	0	$35	No
18	4	$35	1	$40	No
19	5	$40	0	$35	No
20	6	$35	0	$30	No
21	7	$30	1	$35	No
111	97	$70	1	$75	No
112	98	$75	0	$70	No
113	99	$70	0	$65	No
114	100	$65	0	$60	No

2 **First simulated game.** The results of the simulated games appear in the range B15:E114. (Some of these rows have been hidden in Figure 13.37.) Although Joe might go broke before playing all 100 games, we simulate all 100 just in case. For the first simulated game enter the formulas

=B5
=IF(RISKUNIFORM(0,1)<$B$4,1,0)
=IF(C15=1,B15+$B$6,B15–$B$6)

and

=IF(D15=0,"Yes","No")

in cells B15, C15, D15, and E15. (Note that we use @RISK's RISKUNIFORM(0,1) function to determine the outcome of a single game. This is equivalent to Excel's built-in RAND() function.)

3 **Other simulated games.** To generate the outcomes for the other games, enter the formulas

=D15
=IF(E15="No",IF(RISKUNIFORM(0,1)<$B$4,1,0),"NA")
=IF(E15="No",IF(C16=1,B16+$B$6,B16–$B$6),0)

and

=IF(D16=0,"Yes","No")

in cells B16, C16, D16, and E16. Then copy these to the range B17:E114. The formula in C16 first checks whether Joe is broke yet. If he is, it records "NA" in cell C16. Otherwise, it uses the RISKUNIFORM function to see whether he wins or loses this game. Similar logic applies to the formula in cell D16. Therefore, whenever Joe goes broke, there will be a sequence of NAs in column C.

4 **Summary results.** Joe goes broke eventually only if his final wealth in cell D114 is 0. Also, the number of games he plays is the number of *numerical* values (as opposed to NAs) in column C. Therefore, enter the formulas

=IF(D114=0,1,0)

and

=COUNT(C15:C114)

in cells B10 and B11. The first of these records a 1 if Joe eventually goes broke and a 0 otherwise. The second calculates the number of games he is able to play.

Using @RISK The settings for using @RISK are the same as in the previous craps simulation except that the output cells are now B10 and B11. The results appear numerically in Figure 13.38 and graphically in Figure 13.39. For example, Joe went broke in 571 of the 1000 simulations. Proceeding as we did earlier, this implies a 95% confidence interval from .540 to .602 for the probability that Joe will go broke.

We also see that the average number of plays was about 69, and there was at least one interation where Joe went broke in ten plays—he lost ten times in a row! However, the histogram is more revealing. It shows that Joe is still playing after 100 games about 43% of the time. When he goes broke, however, this is most likely to occur somewhere around game 50. ■

FIGURE 13.38 Summary Statistics for Betting in Craps Example

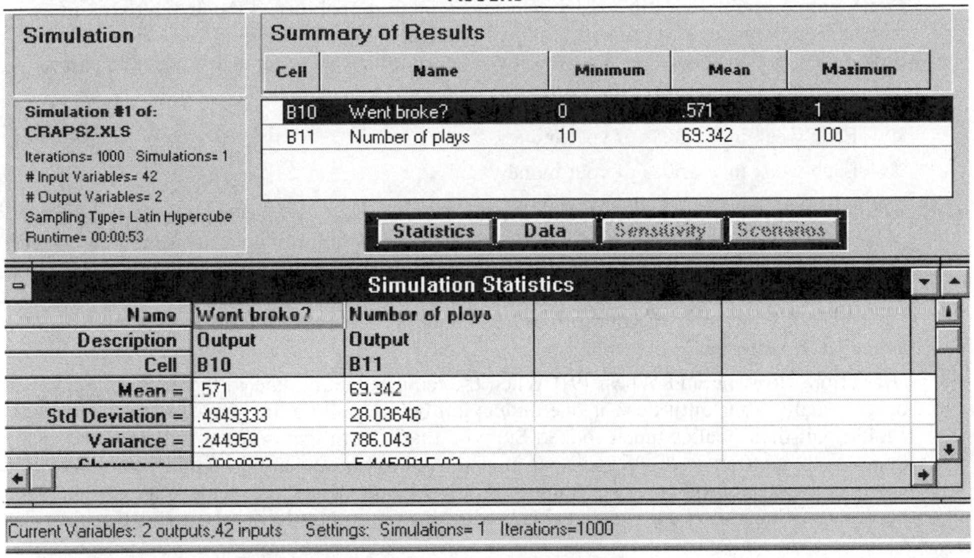

FIGURE 13.39 Histogram of Number of Games in Craps Example

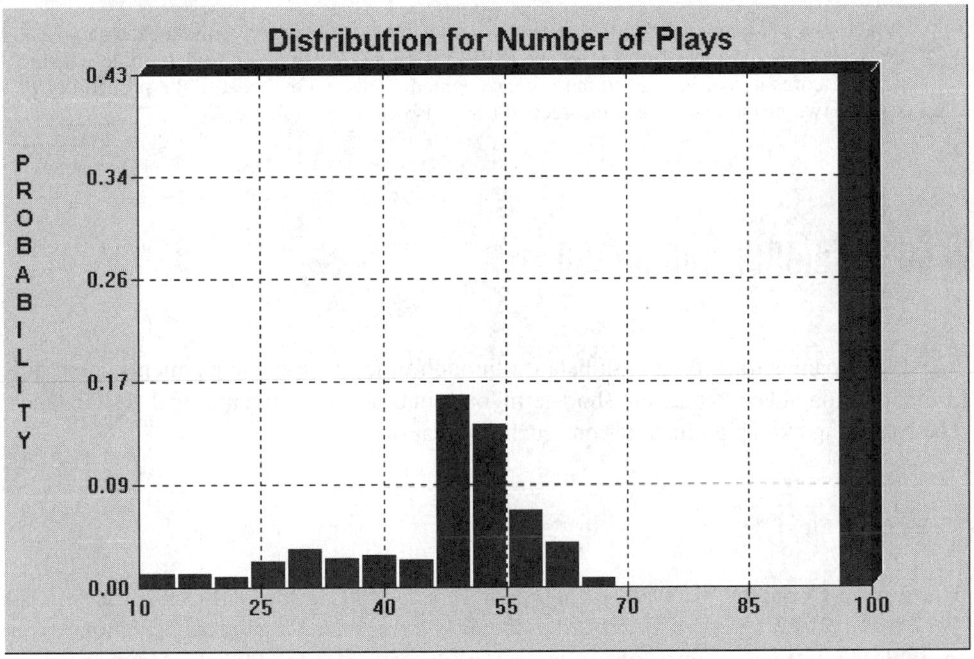

PROBLEMS

Skill-Building Problems

15 The game of Chuck-a Luck is played as follows: You pick a number between 1 and 6 and toss three dice. If your number does not appear, you lose \$1. If your number appears x times, you win \$$x$. On the average, how much money will you win or lose on each play of the game?

Skill-Extending Problems

16 (Based on Kelly [8]) You currently have \$1000. Each week you can invest any amount of money you currently have in a risky investment. With probability .4 the amount you invest is tripled. For example, if you invest \$500, you increase your wealth by \$1500. However, with probability .6, the amount you invest is lost. Consider the following investment strategies:

- Each week invest 10% of your money.
- Each week invest 30% of your money.
- Each week invest 50% of your money.

Simulate 100 weeks of each strategy for 100 iterations. Which strategy appears to be best? (*Note*: In general, it has been shown that if you can multiply your investment by a factor of M with probability p and lose your investment with probability $q = 1 - p$, then you should invest a fraction $(p(M-1) - q)/(M-1)$ of your money each week. This strategy maximizes the expected growth rate of your fortune, assuming the game is favorable to you, and is known as the **Kelly criterion**.)

17 (Based on Morrison and Wheat [9]) When the team is behind late in the game, a hockey coach usually waits until there is one minute left before pulling the goalie. Actually coaches should pull their goalies much sooner. Suppose that if both teams are at full strength, each team scores an average of .05 goals per minute. Also suppose that if you pull your goalie you score an average of .08 goals per minute while your opponent scores an average of .12 goals per minute. Suppose you are one goal behind with five minutes left in the game. Consider the following two strategies:

Strategy 1: Pull your goalie if you are behind at any point in the last five minutes of the game; put him back in if you tie the score or go ahead.

Strategy 2: Pull your goalie if you are behind at any point in the last minute of the game; put him back in if you tie the score or go ahead.

Which strategy maximizes your chance of winning or tying the game? Simulate the game using ten-second increments of time. Use the @RISKBINOMIAL function to determine whether a team scores a goal in a given ten-second segment. This is OK because the probability of scoring two or more goals in a ten-second period is near 0. ■

13.7 A Cash Balance Simulation

All companies track their cash balance through time. As specific payments come due, companies may need to take out short-term loans in order to keep a minimal cash balance. The following example illustrates one such application.

EXAMPLE 13.6

The Entson Company believes that its monthly sales during the period from November 1997 to July 1998 are normally distributed with the means and standard deviations given in Table 13.1. Each month Entson incurs fixed costs of \$250,000. In March taxes of \$150,000 and in June taxes of \$50,000 must be paid. Dividends of \$50,000 must also be paid in June. Entson estimates that its receipts in a given month are a weighted sum of sales from the current month, the previous month, and two months ago with weights .2, .6, and .2. In symbols, if R_t and S_t represent receipts and sales in month t, then

$$R_t = .2 * S_{t-2} + .6 * S_{t-1} + .2 * S_t$$

The materials and labor needed to produce a month's sales must be purchased one month in advance, and the cost of these averages to 80% of the product's sales. For example, if sales

TABLE 13.1 Monthly Sales (in Thousands of Dollars) for Entson

	Nov	Dec	Jan	Feb	Mar	Apr	May	Jun	Jul
Mean	1500	1600	1800	1500	1900	2600	2400	1900	1300
St Dev	70	75	80	80	100	125	120	90	70

in February are \$1,500,000, then the February materials and labor costs are \$1,200,000, but these must be paid in January.

At the beginning of January 1998 Entson has \$250,000 in cash. The company would like to ensure that each month's ending cash balance never dips below \$250,000. This means that Entson might have to take out short-term (one-month) loans. For example, if the ending cash balance at the end of March is \$200,000, Entson will take out a loan for \$50,000, which it will then pay back (with interest) one month later. The interest rate on a short-term loan is 1% per month. At the beginning of each month, Entson earns interest of 0.5% on its cash balance. The company would like to use simulation to estimate the maximum loan it will need to take out to meet its desired minimum cash balance. It would also like to see how sensitive the results are to the sales data, shown in Table 13.1. In particular, considering the data in this table as a "base case," it would like to run a simulation in which the means are 20% below the values in the table and another simulation in which the means are 20% above those in the table.

Solution

There is a considerable amount of bookkeeping in this simulation, so it is a good idea to list the events in chronological order that occur each month.

- Entson observes its beginning cash balance.
- Entson receives interest on its beginning cash balance.
- Receipts arrive and expenses are paid (including payback of the previous month's loan, if any, with interest).
- If necessary, Entson takes out a short-term loan.
- The final cash balance is observed, which becomes next month's beginning cash balance.

Developing the Spreadsheet Model The completed spreadsheet appears in Figure 13.40. (See the file CASHBUD.XLS.) It requires the following steps.

1 **Inputs.** Enter the inputs through row 25. Note that we are only going to simulate loans for the period from January to June. However, we need sales figures in November and December to generate receipts for January and February. Also, we need July sales to generate the material and labor costs paid in June.

2 **Scenarios.** Enter the formula

=RISKSIMTABLE({.8,1,1.2})

in cell B27. This allows us to run three simulations simultaneously. The middle value, 1, corresponds to the base case. The other two values, .8 and 1.2, correspond to the scenarios in which mean sales are 20% below or 20% above the base case.

3 **Actual sales.** Generate the sales in row 31 by entering the formula

=RISKNORMAL(\$B\$27*B6,B7)

in cell B31 and copying it to the range C31:J31.

FIGURE 13.40 Spreadsheet for Entson Cash Balance Example

	A	B	C	D	E	F	G	H	I	J
1	**Entson Cash Balance Simulation**									
2										
3	**Input section (all values are in thousands of dollars)**									
4	Monthly sales (normal distributions)									
5		Nov	Dec	Jan	Feb	Mar	Apr	May	Jun	Jul
6	Mean	1500	1600	1800	1500	1900	2600	2400	1900	1300
7	St Dev	70	75	80	80	100	125	120	90	70
8										
9	Monthly fixed cost			250	250	250	250	250	250	
10										
11	Tax, dividend expenses			0	0	150	0	0	100	
12										
13	Receipts in any month are of form: A*(sales from 2 months ago)+B*(previous month's sales)+C*(current month's sales), where:									
14		A	B	C						
15		20%	60%	20%						
16										
17	Cost of materials and labor for next month, spent this month, is a percentage of product's sales from next month, where the percentage is:									
18		80%								
19										
20	Initial cash in Jan	250								
21	Min cash balance	250								
22										
23	Monthly interest rates									
24	Loan interest rate	1%								
25	Interest rate on cash	0.50%								
26										
27	Base level of sales	80%								
28										
29	**Simulation section**									
30		Nov	Dec	Jan	Feb	Mar	Apr	May	Jun	Jul
31	Actual sales	1200.00	1280.00	1440.00	1200.00	1520.00	2080.00	1920.00	1520.00	1040.00
32										
33	Beginning cash balance			250.00	337.25	250.00	250.00	250.00	250.00	
34	Interest on cash balance			1.25	1.69	1.25	1.25	1.25	1.25	
35	Receipts			1296.00	1360.00	1312.00	1568.00	1936.00	1872.00	
36	Fixed costs			250.00	250.00	250.00	250.00	250.00	250.00	
37	Tax, dividend expenses			0.00	0.00	150.00	0.00	0.00	100.00	
38	Material, labor expenses			960.00	1216.00	1664.00	1536.00	1216.00	832.00	
39	Close out previous loan			0.00	0.00	17.23	775.66	1002.34	536.40	
40	Cash balance before loan			337.25	232.94	-517.98	-742.41	-281.09	404.85	
41	Loan amount (if any)			0.00	17.06	767.98	992.41	531.09	0.00	
42	Final cash balance			337.25	250.00	250.00	250.00	250.00	404.85	
43										
44	Maximum loan	992.41								

4 **Beginning cash balance.** For January 1998 enter the cash balance with the formula

=B20

in cell D33. Then for the other months enter the formula

=D42

in cell E33 and copy it across row 33.

5 **Incomes.** Entson's incomes (interest on cash balance and receipts) are calculated in rows 34 and 35. To calculate these, enter the formulas

=D33*$B$25

and

=SUMPRODUCT($B$15:$D$15,B31:D31)

in cells D34 and D35 and copy them across rows 34 and 35. The latter formula simply multiplies the fixed weights in row 15 by the relevant sales and adds these products to obtain receipts.

6 **Expenses.** Entson's expenses (fixed costs, taxes and dividends, material and labor costs, and payback of the previous month's loan) are calculated in rows 36 through 39. Calculate these by entering the formulas

=D9
=D11
=$B$18*E31

and

=C41*(1+$B$24)

in cells D36, D37, D38, and D39 and copying these across rows 36 through 39. (For the loan payback, we are assuming that no loan payback is necessary in January.)

7 **Cash balance before loan.** Calculate the cash balance before the loan (if any) by entering the formula

=SUM(D33:D35)–SUM(D36:D39)

in cell D40 and copying it across row 40.

8 **Amount of loan.** If the value in row 40 is below the minimum cash balance ($250,000), Entson must borrow enough to bring the cash balance up to this minimum. Otherwise, no loan is necessary. Therefore, enter the formula

=MAX($B$21–D40,0)

in cell D41 and copy it across row 41.

9 **Final cash balance.** Calculate the final cash balance by entering the formula

=SUM(D40:D41)

in cell D42 and copying it across row 42.

10 **Maximum loan.** Calculate the maximum loan from January to June in cell B44 with the formula

=MAX(D41:I41)

Using @RISK To use @RISK, specify cells B44 and the range D41:I41 as output cells. The latter allows us to see how the loan amounts vary over time. For the settings use 500 iterations and 3 as the number of simulations (one for the base case and one for each of the other two scenarios). The results appear numerically in Figures 13.41 and 13.42. The data

FIGURE 13.41 **Summary Statistics for Cash Balance Example**

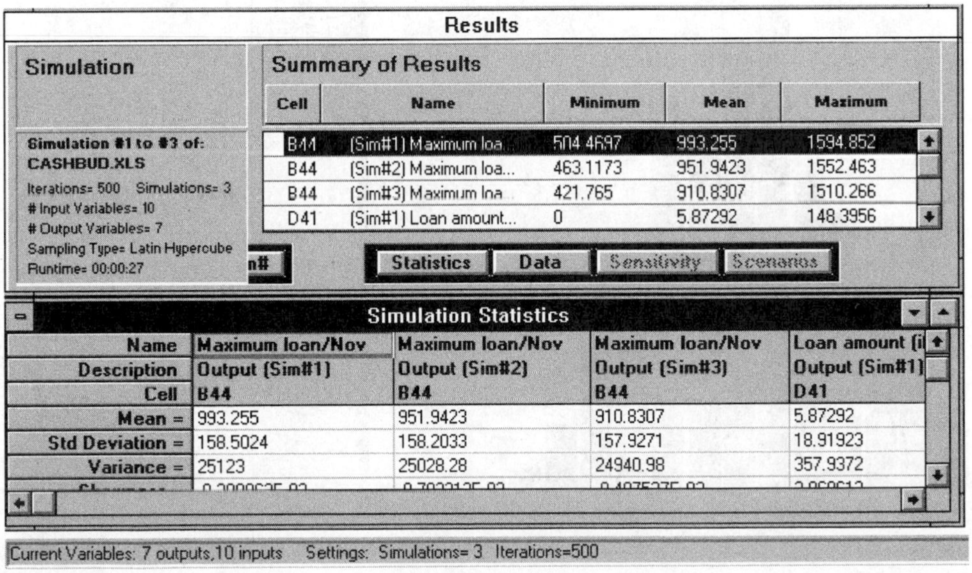

FIGURE 13.42 **Target Percentiles for Cash Balance Example**

Simulation Statistics				
Name	Maximum loan/Nov	Maximum loan/Nov	Maximum loan/Nov	Loan amount (i
Description	Output (Sim#1)	Output (Sim#2)	Output (Sim#3)	Output (Sim#1)
Cell	B44	B44	B44	D41
Target #1 (Value)=	727.7939453125	685.427429199219	649.301513671875	
Target #1 (Perc%)=	5%	5%	5%	
Target #2 (Value)=	995.586181640625	953.625732421875	912.765075683594	
Target #2 (Perc%)=	50%	50%	50%	
Target #3 (Value)=	1248.07568359375	1206.115234375	1164.15478515625	
Target #3 (Perc%)=	95%	95%	95%	

Current Variables: 7 outputs,10 inputs Settings: Simulations= 3 Iterations=500

in Figure 13.41 indicate that for the base case (simulation #2) the maximum loan varied considerably, from a low of $463,117 to a high of $1,552,463. The average was $951,942. The data in Figure 13.42 complements these figures by providing the medians and 5% and 95% percentiles of the maximum loan distribution for each of the scenarios. As you might expect, as sales increase (from the 20%-below scenario to the base case to the 20%-above scenario), the maximum loan tends to decrease. This is due to the increasing receipts that dominate the increasing material and labor costs.

Figures 13.43 and 13.44 illustrate the simulation results graphically. The histogram in Figure 13.43 supports the numerical data in Figure 13.41. The time series graph (using the Summary graph on the D41:I41 output cell range) shows the sequence of loan amount from January to June. Evidently, the extra tax payment in March typically results in large loans in both March and April. ■

FIGURE 13.43 **Histogram of Maximum Loan in Cash Balance Example**

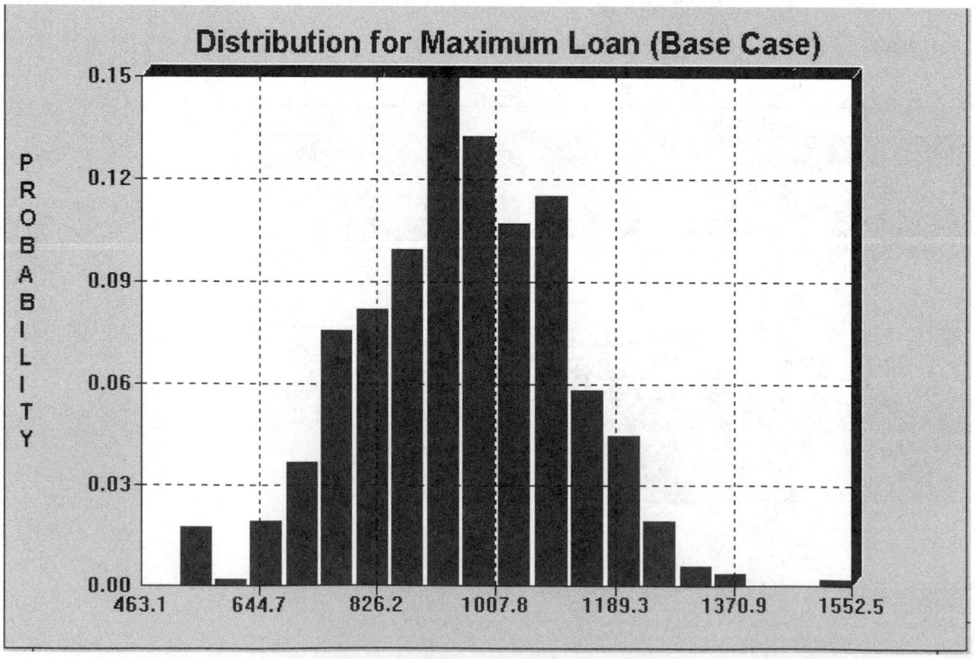

FIGURE 13.44 **Time Series of Loan Amounts in Cash Balance Example**

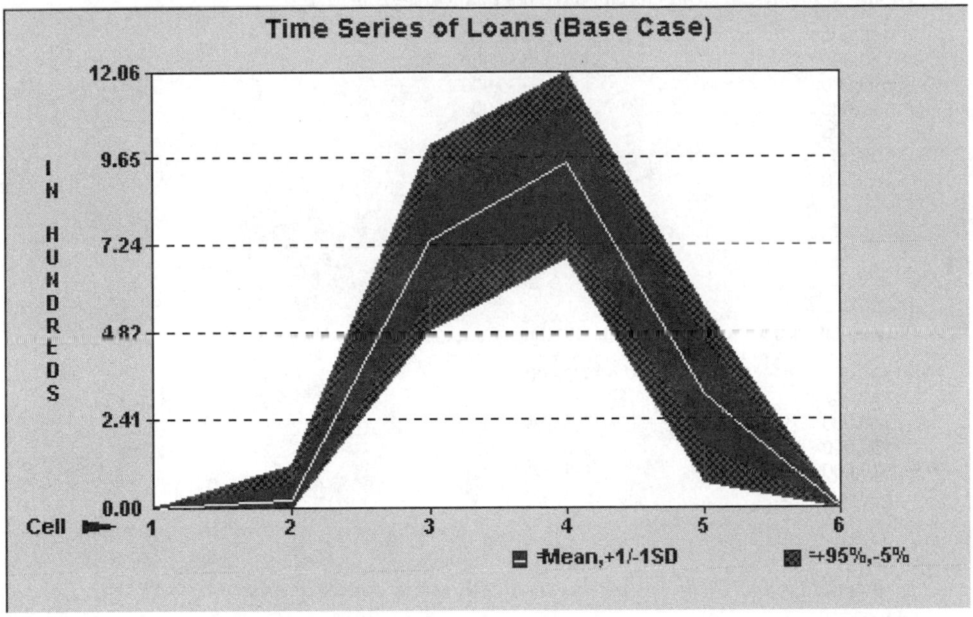

PROBLEMS

Skill-Building Problem

18 You have been asked to simulate the cash inflows to a toy company for the next year. Monthly sales are independent random variables. Mean sales for the months January–March and October–December are \$80,000, and mean sales for the months April–September are \$120,000. The standard deviation for each month's sales is 20% of the month's mean sales. We model the method used to collect monthly sales as follows:

- During each month a certain fraction of new sales will be collected. All new sales not collected become one month overdue.
- During each month a certain fraction of one-month overdue sales is collected. The remainder becomes two months overdue.
- During each month a certain fraction of two-month overdue sales is collected.
- The remainder are written off as bad debts. You are given the information in Tables 13.2–13.4 from some past months.

Using this information you should be able to build a simulation model that generates the total cash inflow for each month. Develop a simple forecasting model and build into the simulation somewhere the error of your forecasting model. Assuming that during January there are \$120,000 of one-month-old sales outstanding and \$140,000 of two-month-old sales

TABLE 13.2

New Sales	New Sales Paid During Month
\$40,000	\$25,000
\$50,000	\$32,000
\$60,000	\$35,000
\$20,000	\$10,000
\$30,000	\$21,000
\$45,000	\$29,000

TABLE 13.3

One-Month-Old Sales	One-Month-Old Sales Paid Off During Month
$50,000	$26,000
$60,000	$33,000
$80,000	$36,000
$20,000	$ 8,000
$25,000	$14,000
$30,000	$17,000
$40,000	$22,000

TABLE 13.4

Two-Month-Old Sales	Two-Month-Old Sales Collected
$30,000	$23,000
$40,000	$30,000
$50,000	$43,000
$60,000	$50,000
$70,000	$58,000
$40,000	$34,000

outstanding, you are 95% sure that total cash inflow for the year will be between ______ and ______.

Skill-Extending Problems

19 Use @RISK to solve Problem 12.25.

20 (Based on Benninga [2]) You are the chief financial officer (CFO) for Carco, a small car rental company. You are trying to get some idea of what Carco's financial and income statements will look like during the current year (year 0) and the next five years. The following relationships hold:

- Current assets for each year are a "current assets factor" multiplied by the year's sales, where the current assets factors for different years are independent normal random variables with mean 0.15 and standard deviation 0.02.
- Each year, fixed assets at cost equals depreciation plus net fixed assets.
- Accumulated depreciation in year 0 equals $330. For year t ($t \geq 1$), the depreciation equals the accumulated depreciation in year $t - 1$ plus 10% of the fixed assets at cost for year $t - 1$.
- Net fixed assets for year t equals a "net fixed assets factor" multiplied by year t sales, where the net fixed assets factors for different years are independent normal random variables with mean 0.77 and standard deviation 0.04.
- Total assets each year equals net fixed assets plus current assets.
- Current liabilities each year equals a "current liabilities factor" multiplied by the year's sales, where the current liabilities factor for different years are independent normal random variables with mean 0.08 and standard deviation 0.01.
- Long-term debt for year 0 is $280.
- For $t \geq 1$, the long-term debt for year t is the year t debt-equity ratio multiplied by the sum of year t retained earnings and the year t stock. Carco wants to have the following debt-equity ratios in years 1 through 5: 0.48, 0.46, 0.44, 0.42, and 0.40.
- Stock in year 0 is $450. For $t \geq 1$, year t stock equals the sum of year $t - 1$ stock and year t new stock.
- Year 0 retained earnings equals $110. For $t \geq 1$, year t retained earnings is the sum of year $t - 1$ retained earnings and year t retention.
- Each year, total liabilities is the sum of current liabilities, long-term debt, stock, and retained earnings.

- The amount of new stock issued each year must be enough to make total assets equal to total liabilities.
- The interest rate on current debt is 10.5%, and the interest rate on new debt is 9.5%. During each of the next five years, 20% of the current \$280 in long-term debt must be paid off. Then the *total* amount of new debt during year t is the year t long-term debt minus the amount of initial debt still remaining.
- The new debt for year t equals the *total* new debt for year t minus the *total* new debt for year $t - 1$.
- Year 0 sales equals \$1000, and for $t \geq 1$, year t sales equals a "sales factor" multiplied by year $t - 1$ sales, where the sales factors for different years are independent normal random variables with mean 1.1 and standard deviation 0.05. (This does *not* mean that sales during successive years are independent!)
- Year t expense equals an "expense factor" multiplied by year t sales, where the expense factors for different years are independent normal random variables, with mean 0.80 and standard deviation 0.06.
- To calculate yearly interest payments, remember that interest is 10.5% on old debt and 9.5% on new debt.
- Depreciation for year 0 is \$0, and for $t \geq 1$, year t depreciation is 10% of the year $t - 1$ fixed assets at cost.
- The before-tax profit each year is the sales minus the sum of expenses, interest payments, and depreciation.
- The tax rate is 47%.
- Dividends each year are 70% of after-tax profits.
- Retention each year is 30% of after-tax profits.

Set up a spreadsheet to model the current year (year 0) and next five years of Carco's financial future. Now simulate the firm's future 500 times. Use your output to answer the following questions.

a There is only a 5% chance that total new debt will exceed what value?

b On the average, total interest payments for the next five years will equal what value?

c What is the probability of profit being negative during year 5?

Note: Your spreadsheet is allowed to contain circular references. There are many of these. For example, stock purchased each year depends on long-term debt, and long-term debt depends on stock. To resolve the circular references use the Tools/Options menu item, click on the Calculations tab, check the Iterations box, and enter 20 as the Maximum Number of Iterations. This ensures that the spreadsheet will recalculate itself 20 times, which in turn ensures that the values in the spreadsheet will converge to the correct values.

21 Estimates of mean monthly sales for the months October 1997–March 1999 are as shown in Table 13.5. Your goal is to model Toyco's 1997 cash budget given the following assumptions:

- At the beginning of each month Toyco wants to have a cash balance of at least \$20,000, and it will borrow sufficient funds to achieve this goal.
- All sales are for credit; 70% of all payments are collected in the first month after sale, 20% in the second month after sale, and 10% are collected in the third month after sale.
- Inventory at the beginning of each month should equal forecasted sales for the next three months.
- Merchandise purchased for sale incurs a cost equal to 75% of sales. On purchases made each month, 70% is paid in the first month after purchase and 30% is paid in the second month after purchase.
- Selling and administrative expenses incurred during a month equal $\$8500 + .09 * (\text{Sales})$. These expenses are paid at a rate of 70% during the current month and 30% in the month following.

If money must be borrowed, it is borrowed month-to-month at an interest rate of 0.7%. Borrowing takes place in multiples of \$1000. To model this situation use the CEILING function. For example, CEILING(2500, 1000) = 3000. Note that you will need an IF statement because CEILING(−500, 1000) is not defined.

TABLE 13.5

	1997	1998	1999
January		$70,000	$130,000
February		$80,000	$130,000
March		$80,000	$140,000
April		$90,000	
May		$100,000	
June		$100,000	
July		$90,000	
August		$100,000	
September		$110,000	
October	$40,000	$120,000	
November	$50,000	$120,000	
December	$60,000	$130,000	

In February 1999 capital expenditures of $20,000 are incurred. In July and October capital expenditures of $30,000 are incurred.

Existing fixed assets are depreciated at $100 per month. Additional capital expenses are depreciated on a straight-line basis at a rate of 1% per month, beginning in the month after the capital expense is incurred.

The sales for each month have a standard deviation of 15,000 about the forecasted sales.

a Use your model to predict average profit for 1995. How high is profit likely to go? How low?

b To be sure of having enough money to borrow, how big a line of credit would you need for 1997?

c Suppose you could ensure that all accounts receivable could be collected in the month after sale and that beginning inventory for each month could be trimmed to 80% of the next three months' forecasted sales. How would this new scenario change your answers to (a) and (b)? ■

13.8

Simulating Stock Prices and Options

In this section we illustrate how you can use @RISK to simulate stock prices. Then we show how you can analyze derivative securities such as call options with @RISK.

Modeling the Price of a Stock

An enormous amount of research has been devoted to discovering the way stock prices change. Although there is not complete agreement on the best model of stock price changes, one popular model states that price changes follow a lognormal distribution. Essentially, this means that the logarithm of a stock's price at any time is a normally distributed random variable. To be more specific, the stock price p_t at any time t in the future is related to the current price p_0 by the formula

$$p_t = p_0 * \exp[(\mu - .5 * \sigma^2) * t + \sigma * Z * \sqrt{t}] \qquad \textbf{(13.1)}$$

Here, μ is the mean percentage growth rate of the stock, σ is the standard deviation of the growth rate, and Z is a normal random variable with mean 0 and standard deviation 1. Both μ and σ are expressed as decimals, such as $\mu = .06$ for a 6% mean growth rate, and all quantities are measured with respect to a common unit of time, such as a year.

The spreadsheet in Figure 13.45 illustrates how to estimate the parameters μ and σ in Equation 13.1 from monthly returns. (See the file STOCKRET.XLS.) We first enter the observed closing prices of the stock in column B. The corresponding monthly returns (percentage changes) are calculated in column C. For example, the formula in cell C6 is

=(B6–B5)/B5

The return of $-.012$ corresponds to a decrease of 1.2%. We then add 1 to each return in column C to obtain column D, and we take the natural logarithms of the numbers in column D to obtain column E. For example, the formula in cell E6 is

=LN(D6)

The average of the numbers in column E, obtained in cell E19 with the AVERAGE function, represents the monthly growth rate labeled μ_{month}. Similarly, the standard deviation calculated in cell E20 represents the standard deviation of the monthly growth rate, labeled σ_{month}. (It can be calculated with the STDEV or the STDEVP function with slightly different results; we used the latter.) To obtain the mean yearly growth rate μ_{year} in cell E22, multiply μ_{month} by 12. To obtain the standard deviation of the yearly growth rate, σ_{year}, in cell E23, multiply σ_{month} by $\sqrt{12}$. Thus, our estimate of the mean yearly growth rate of the stock price is 7.33%. The standard deviation of the growth rate is 9.99%.

Now that we know how analysts find the mean and standard deviation of a stock's growth rate, we use Equation 13.1 and simulation to value certain derivative securities.[6]

FIGURE 13.45 **Estimating Mean and Standard Deviation of Stock Returns**

	A	B	C	D	E	F	G
1	Estimating Mean and Standard Deviation of Stock Returns						
2							
3	Historical data						
4	Month	Closing	Return	1+Return	Ln(1+Return)		
5	0	$25.00					
6	1	$24.70	-0.01200	0.98800	-0.01207		
7	2	$23.70	-0.04049	0.95951	-0.04133		
8	3	$22.90	-0.03376	0.96624	-0.03434		
9	4	$22.81	-0.00393	0.99607	-0.00394		
10	5	$22.89	0.00351	1.00351	0.00350		
11	6	$22.56	-0.01442	0.98558	-0.01452		
12	7	$23.94	0.06117	1.06117	0.05937		
13	8	$24.37	0.01796	1.01796	0.01780		
14	9	$24.99	0.02544	1.02544	0.02512		
15	10	$26.09	0.04402	1.04402	0.04308		
16	11	$26.14	0.00192	1.00192	0.00191		
17	12	$26.90	0.02907	1.02907	0.02866		
18							
19	Monthly values			Mean	0.61%		
20				StDev	2.88%		
21							
22	Annual values			Mean	7.33%		
23				StDev	9.99%		

[6]Derivative securities get their name because their value is derived from the value of an underlying security such as a stock. There are a wide variety of derivative securities available in the market; we will discuss only some of the simplest ones.

Valuing a European Call Option

A **European option** on a stock gives the owner of the option the right to buy (if the option is a **call** option) or sell (if the option is a **put** option) one share of a stock on a particular date for a particular price. The price at which an option holder can buy or sell the stock is called the **exercise price** of the option. The date by which the option must be used (or "exercised") is called the **expiration date**.

For example, suppose that a stock is currently selling for \$50 and you purchase a call option with an exercise price of \$56 and a three-month expiration date. What will you earn from this option? If T represents the expiration date and p_T represents the price of the stock at time T, you will earn \$0 if $p_T \leq 56$, and you will earn $(p_T - 56)$ dollars if $p_T > 56$. Here is the reasoning. If $p_T \leq 56$, you have the option, if you want to use it, of buying a share of stock for *less* than it is worth. This would be a dumb thing to do, so you would let your option expire—without ever using it. In this case, we say that you're "out of the money." On the other hand, if $p_T > 56$, you could buy a share at the option price of \$56, sell it for the current price of p_T, and thereby make a profit of $p_T - 56$ dollars. In this case we say that you're "in the money."

We've left one thing out, however. You must pay for the option in the first place. The question is, what is a fair price for such an option? Since option trading is a multibillion-dollar business, this is an important question! As discussed briefly in Chapter 6, Black and Scholes [3] were the first to derive a formula for pricing options. In 1979 Cox, Ross, and Rubenstein [5] derived a different but equivalent method for pricing options. We will use their model below. It states that *the price of an option must be the expected discounted value of the cash flows from an option on a stock having the same standard deviation as the stock on which the option is written and growing at the risk-free rate of interest*. Here, discounting is done continuously at the risk-free rate. One surprising implication of this result is that the price of the option does *not* depend on the growth rate of the stock itself, only on the risk-free rate and the standard deviation of the growth rate of the stock.

In the following example we will use @RISK to estimate the price of a European option.

EXAMPLE 13.7

A share of AnTech stock currently sells for \$42. A European call option with an expiration date of six months and an exercise price of \$40 is available. The stock has an annual standard deviation of 20% ($\sigma_{year} = .20$). The stock price has tended to increase at a rate of 15% per year ($\mu_{year} = .15$). The risk-free rate is 10% per year. What is a fair price for this option?

Solution

According to the result of Cox et al., we need to know the mean of the cash flow from this option, discounted to time 0, assuming that the stock price increases at the risk-free rate. Therefore, we will simulate many six-month periods, each time finding the discounted cash flow of the option. The average of these discounted cash flows represents an estimate of the true mean, that is, it estimates the fair price of the option.

Developing the Spreadsheet Model The spreadsheet model is quite simple, as shown in Figure 13.46. (See the file ANTECH1.XLS.) It can be formed as follows.

FIGURE 13.46 **Spreadsheet Model for AnTech Call Option Example**

	A	B
1	AnTech Call Option Example	
2		
3	Input section	
4	Current stock price	$42
5	Exercise price	$40
6	Mean annual return	15%
7	StDev of annual return	20%
8	Risk-free rate	10%
9	Option duration (years)	0.5
10		
11	Simulation section	
12	Stock price in 6 months (growing at risk-free rate)	$45.677
13	Option cash flow at termination	$5.677
14	Discounted value of option	$5.400

1 **Inputs.** Enter the inputs in the range B4:B9. Note that the expiration date is expressed in years. Also, note that we enter the mean growth rate of the stock in cell B6. However, for reasons discussed above, this value is not used in the model.

2 **Simulated stock price at expiration date.** Using Equation 13.1 with μ equal to the risk-free rate, simulate the stock price in six months by entering the formula

=B4*EXP((B8–.5*B7^2)*B9+B7*RISKNORMAL(0,1)*SQRT(B9))

in cell B12.

3 **Cash flow from option.** Calculate the cash flow from the option by entering the formula

=MAX(B12–B5,0)

in cell B13. This simply says that if the value in cell B12 is greater than the value in cell B5, we make the difference; otherwise, we make nothing.

4 **Discount the cash flow.** Discount the cash flow in cell B14 with the formula

=EXP(–B8*B9)*B13

This represents the net present value of the cash flow (if any) realized at the expiration date.

Using @RISK To run @RISK we choose cell B14 as the only output cell, set the number of iterations to 1000, and set the number of simulations to 1. The most important outputs are shown in Figure 13.47. Recall that we are interested in the theoretical mean of the discounted value in cell B14. An estimate of this mean is the average of the 1000 simulated values, namely 4.7597. How accurate is this estimate? We can find an approximate 95% confidence for the true mean by adding and subtracting twice the standard error of the mean, where the standard error is the reported standard deviation (4.9645) divided by the square root of the number of iterations. The resulting confidence interval extends approximately from 4.45 to 5.07. Actually, the simulated average is very close to the true price of the option, $4.76, as calculated by financial analysts.

Simulating a Portfolio of the Stock and an Option on the Stock We now extend this option example. Suppose the investor buys one share of AnTech stock at the current price and an option on this stock, as described in the example, for $4.76. We will use simulation

FIGURE 13.47 **Summary Statistics for Valuing Call Option Example**

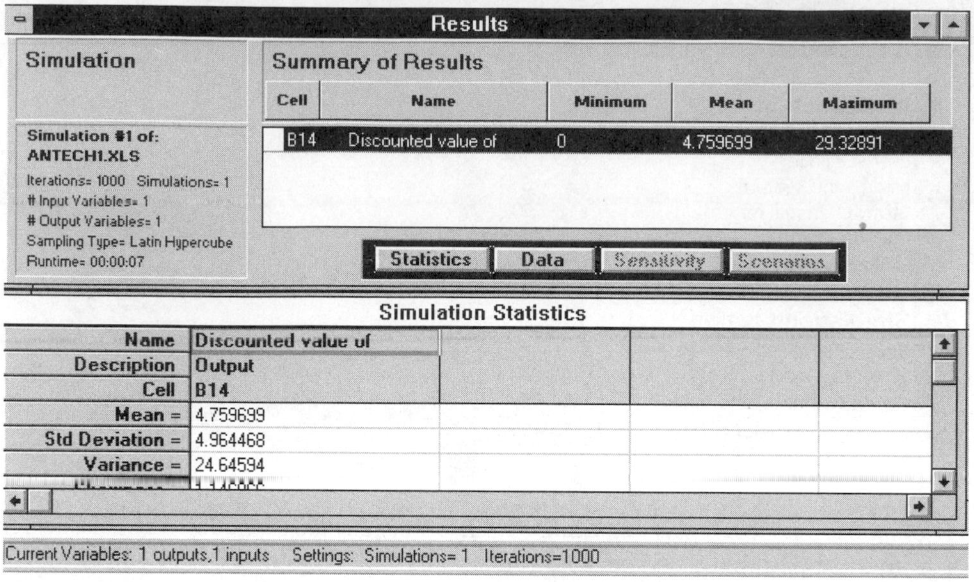

to find the return on the investor's portfolio as of the expiration date. The spreadsheet model appears in Figure 13.48. (See the file ANTECH2.XLS.) Through row 13, it is similar to the spreadsheet in Figure 13.46, so we will describe only the differences.

1 **Simulate stock price at expiration.** In cell B12 we now simulate the stock price when it grows at its own growth rate, not the risk-free rate. (The risk-free rate was used only to price the option according to the rule of Cox et al. Now we want to simulate the stock's *actual* price in six months.) Therefore, change the formula in B12 to

=B4*EXP((B6–.5*B7^2)*B9+B7*RISKNORMAL(0,1)*SQRT(B9))

FIGURE 13.48 **Spreadsheet Model for AnTech Portfolio Example**

	A	B
1	**AnTech Portfolio Example**	
2		
3	**Input section**	
4	Current stock price	$42
5	Exercise price	$40
6	Mean annual return	15%
7	StDev of annual return	20%
8	Risk-free rate	10%
9	Option duration (years)	0.5
10		
11	**Simulation section**	
12	Stock price in 6 months (growing at stock's rate)	$45.038
13	Option cash flow at termination	$5.038
14		
15	Ending value of portfolio	$50.076
16	Initial cost	$46.76
17	Return from portfolio	7.091%

2 **Return from portfolio.** The formula in cell B13 is the same as before. However, we don't need the discounted value in cell B14 any longer. Instead, we need the ending value of the portfolio, the cost of the portfolio, and the portfolio's return in the range B15:B17. These can be calculated by entering the formulas

=SUM(B12:B13)
=B4+4.76

and

=(B15–B16)/B16

in cells B15, B16, and B17. The value in cell B17 represents the percentage by which our initial investment has increased.

Using @RISK We again ran 1000 iterations with @RISK, keeping track of the single output cell B17. The outputs are summarized numerically in Figure 13.49 and graphically in Figure 13.50. These show the considerable variability possible in the portfolio's return. Although the average return was .094 (a 9.4% gain), the simulated returns varied from a worst case 40% loss to a best case 117% gain. Derivative securities are notorious for their variability; this output illustrates why. The best that can be said is that in Figure 13.50, there appears to be more potential for large gains than for large losses. ■

FIGURE 13.49 **Summary Statistics for Portfolio Example**

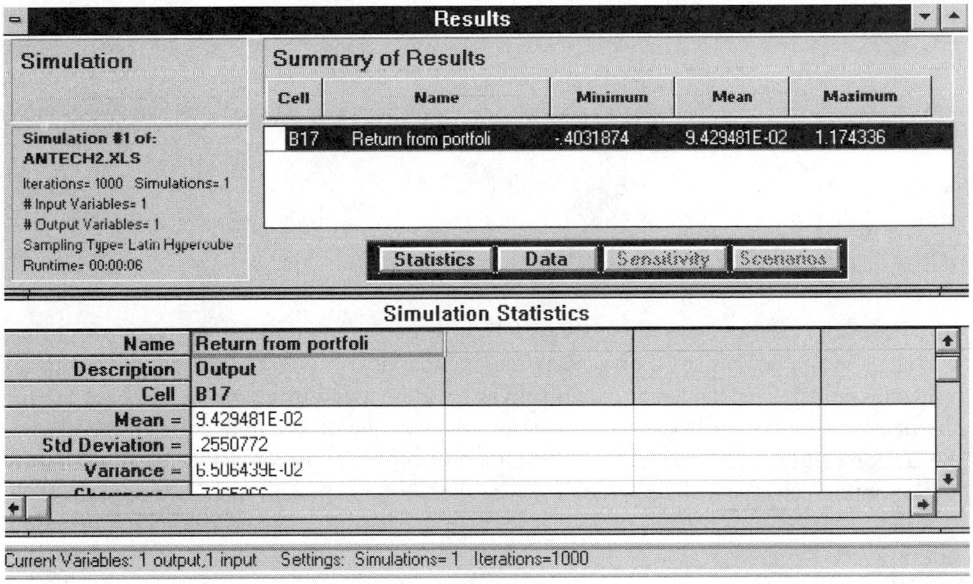

MODELING ISSUE

If you have any intuition for financial portfolios, you may have noticed that this investor is "putting all her eggs in one basket." If the stock price increases, she gains by owning the share of stock and she also gains from holding the option (since she is more likely to be in the money). However, if the price of the stock decreases, she loses money on her share of stock and her option is worthless. A safer strategy is to **hedge** the bets. She can purchase one share of the stock and purchase a *put* option on the stock. Recall that a put option allows her to *sell* a share of stock for

FIGURE 13.50 **Histogram for Portfolio Example**

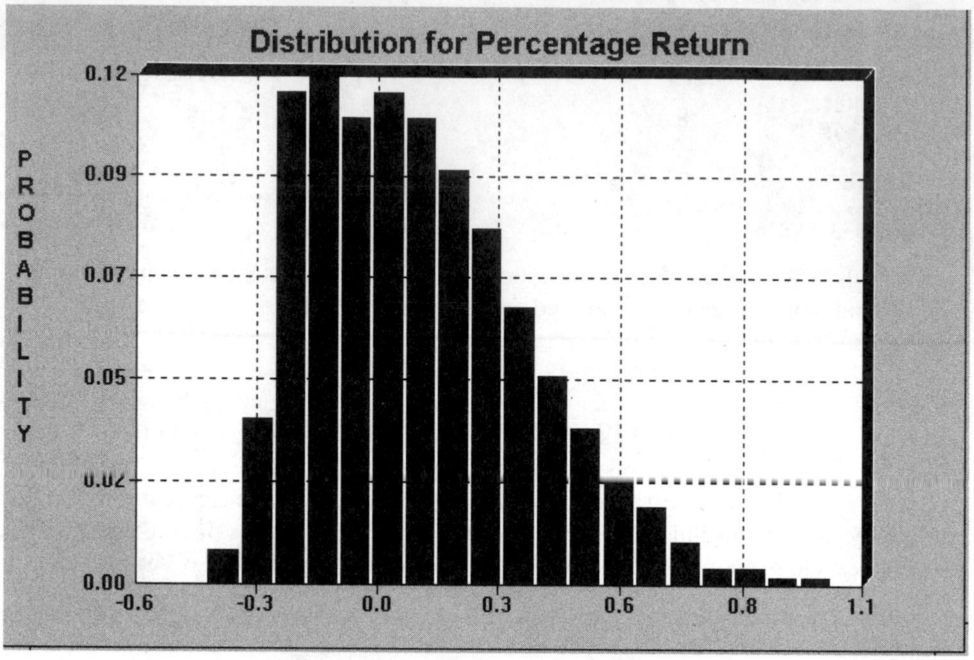

the exercise price at the expiration date. With a put option, the investor hopes the stock price will decrease because she can then sell a share at the exercise price and immediately buy it back at the decreased stock price, thus earning a profit. Therefore, a portfolio consisting of a share of stock and a put option on the stock covers the investor in both directions. It has less upside potential, but it decreases the downside risk. ■

Valuing a More Exotic Call Option

The European call option is rather simple. There are a variety of other derivative securities currently available. In fact, their variety and complexity are what make them attractive—and dangerous!—for the unsuspecting investor. Here we will examine one variation of the basic call option. It is called an **Asian** option. Its payoff depends, not on the price at expiration of the underlying stock, but on the *average* price of the stock over the lifetime of the option. That is, if the exercise price of the option is p_e and the average price of the stock over the lifetime of the option is p_{avg}, then the payoff at the expiration date from the option is the larger of $p_{avg} - p_e$ and 0.

To price an Asian option (or any number of other exotic options), we again need to find the expected discounted value of the payoff from the option, assuming that the stock grows at the risk-free rate. The following example illustrates how to approximate this expected value with simulation.

EXAMPLE 13.8

Consider a stock currently priced at \$100 per share. Its mean annual return is 15% and the standard deviation of its annual return is 30%. What is the value of an Asian option that expires in 52 weeks (one year) with an exercise price of $110? Assume that the risk-free rate is 9%.

Solution

To value this option we will base p_{avg} on the averages of the weekly (simulated) stock prices, assuming that the stock price grows at the risk-free rate. This requires us to generate weekly stock prices from Equation 13.1. The key is to interpret p_0 and p_t correctly in Equation 13.1. To generate any week's price from the previous week's price, we must identify p_0 with the previous week's price and p_t with the current week's price.

Developing the Spreadsheet Model The spreadsheet model appears in Figure 13.51. (See the file ASIAN.XLS.) It can be formed as follows.

1 **Inputs.** Enter the inputs in the range B4:B9. (As in the valuation of the European call option, we enter the mean growth rate of the stock in cell B6 even though it won't be used in the simulation.)

2 **Weekly prices.** Enter the initial price (week 0) in cell E5 with the formula

=B4

Then to generate each weekly price from the previous one, enter the formula

=E5*EXP(($B$8–.5*$B$7^2)*(1/52)+$B$7*RISKNORMAL(0,1)*SQRT(1/52))

in cell E6 and copy it to the range E7:E57. Note that the unit of time is always one week (1/52 of a year).

3 **Discounted value of option.** Enter the formulas

=AVERAGE(E5:E57)
=MAX(B12–B5,0)

FIGURE 13.51 **Spreadsheet Model for Asian Call Option Example**

	A	B	C	D	E	F	G
1	Asian Call Option Example						
2							
3	Input section			Weekly prices (growing at risk-free rate)			
4	Current stock price	$100		Week	Simulated price		
5	Exercise price	$110		0	$100.00		
6	Mean annual return	15%		1	$95.85		
7	StDev of annual return	30%		2	$94.23		
8	Risk-free rate	9%		3	$95.78		
9	Option duration (years)	1		4	$100.17		
10				5	$105.18		
11	Simulation section			6	$104.21		
12	Average of weekly prices	$115.474		7	$104.85		
13	Option cash flow at termination	$5.474		8	$102.94		
14	Discounted value of option	$5.003		9	$106.84		
15				10	$111.33		
16				11	$111.14		
51				46	$139.55		
52				47	$130.84		
53				48	$134.26		
54				49	$125.66		
55				50	$130.32		
56				51	$135.70		
57				52	$139.26		

and

=EXP(−B8*B9)*B13

in cells B12, B13, and B14. These are exactly like in the European call option example, except that the payoff in cell B13 is based on the average in cell B12, not on the ending price of the stock.

Using @RISK Using cell B14 as the single output cell, we obtained the summary results in Figure 13.52. It indicates that a good estimate of the value of the option is $4.78, the average value in cell B14 over the 1000 iterations. By going out two standard errors on either side of this estimate, we see that the interval from $4.18 to $5.38 is an approximate 95% confidence interval for the true mean of the distribution, that is, for the value at which the option should be priced. (The actual price of this particular option turns out to be $4.68.) ■

FIGURE 13.52 **Summary Statistics for Asian Option Example**

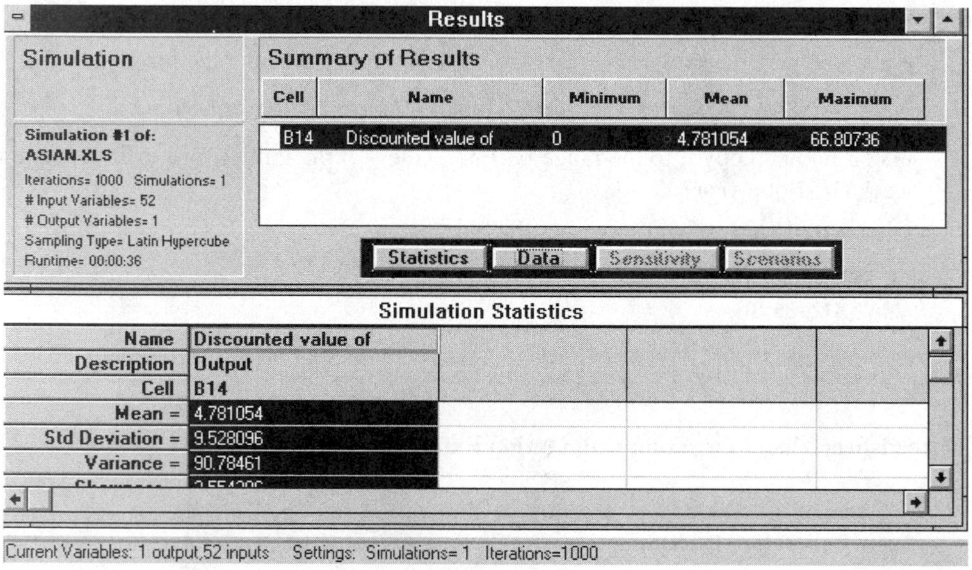

PROBLEMS

Skill-Building Problems

22 A stock currently sells for $100. The risk-free rate is 12% per year, and the stock's $\sigma = 20\%$. By considering exercise prices of $90, $100, and $110, show how the value of a call option depends on the option's exercise price. Assume the duration of the option is one year.

23 The current price of HAL computer stock is $280. Its closing price during each of the next twelve months is given in Table 13.6. Use these data to estimate the annual mean and standard deviation of the return on HAL stock.

Skill-Extending Problems

24 If you own a stock, buying a put option on the stock will greatly reduce your risk. This is the idea behind **portfolio insurance**. To illustrate, consider a stock (Trumpco) that currently sells for $56 and has $\sigma = 30\%$. Assume the risk-free rate is 8% and you estimate $\mu = 12\%$.

TABLE 13.6

	Closing Price
Month 1	$290.00
Month 2	$300.00
Month 3	$282.00
Month 4	$286.50
Month 5	$291.40
Month 6	$308.00
Month 7	$298.32
Month 8	$304.50
Month 9	$308.23
Month 10	$310.40
Month 11	$308.21
Month 12	$309.34

a You own one share of Trumpco. Use simulation to estimate the probability distribution of the percentage return earned on this stock during a one-year period.

b Now suppose you also buy a put option (for $2.38) on Trumpco. The option has an exercise price of $50 and a one-year expiration date. Use simulation to estimate the probability distribution of the percentage return on your portfolio over a one-year period. Can you see why this strategy is called a portfolio insurance strategy?

c Use simulation to show that the put option should, indeed, sell for $2.38.

25 For the data in the previous problem, the following is an example of a **butterfly spread**: Sell two calls with an exercise price of $50; buy one call with an exercise price of $40 and one call with an exercise price of $60. Simulate the cash flows from this portfolio.

26 Cryco stock currently sells for $69. The annual growth rate of the stock is 15%, and the stock's annual volatility (σ) is 35%. The risk-free rate is currently 5%. You have bought a six-month European put option on this stock with an exercise price of $70.

a Use @RISK to value this option.

b Use @RISK to analyze the distribution of percentage returns (for a six-month horizon) for the following portfolios:

Portfolio 1: Own one share of Cryco.
Portfolio 2: Own one share of Cryco and buy the put described in Part (a).

Which portfolio has the largest expected return? Explain why portfolio 2 is known as portfolio insurance.

27 A **knockout call option** loses all value at the instant the price of the stock drops below a given "knockout level." Determine a fair price for a knockout call option in the following situation:

Current Stock Price: $20.	Knockout Price: $19.50.
Exercise Price: $21.	Annual Volatility: 40%.
Risk-free Rate: 10%.	Mean Growth Rate of Stock: 12%.

Duration of Option: 1 month = 21 days; assume 250 days = 1 year. ■

13.9 Simulating Correlated Values

Until now, all of the random numbers we have generated with @RISK functions have been probabilistically independent. This means, for example, that if one value is much larger than its mean, the next value is completely unaffected. It is no more likely to be abnormally large or small than if the first value had been average or less than average. Sometimes we don't want to maintain this independence. Instead, we want the random numbers to be correlated in some way. If they are positively correlated, then large numbers tend to go with large numbers, and small with small. If they are negatively correlated, large tend to go with small and small with large. As an example, we might expect daily stock price changes for two companies in the same industry to be positively correlated. If Exxon's price increases, we might expect Amoco's price to increase as well. @RISK allows us to build in this correlated behavior with the RISKCORRMAT function, as illustrated in the following example.[7]

EXAMPLE 13.9

There are currently two brands of brownies on the market. The Bisquake Company plans to enter the brownie market with one of two new brands. Each of the existing brands and potential new brands is characterized by three attributes: sweetness (measured on a 1 to 10 scale), chewiness (measured on a 1 to 10 scale), and price per box. These attributes are listed in Table 13.7. Each customer is assumed to choose one of these brands over the others on the basis of a weighted combination of the three attributes. That is, each customer is assumed to calculate a score for each brand as

$$\text{Score} = w_s * \text{Sweetness} + w_c * \text{Chewiness} + w_p * \text{Price}$$

where the w's are weights. (We would expect w_s and w_c to be positive, since most customers prefer more of these attributes to less, but we would expect w_p to be negative since customers prefer lower prices.) The customer then purchases the brand with the largest score.

TABLE 13.7 Attributes of Brands in Brownie Example

	Sweetness	Chewiness	Price
Existing Brand 1	8	6	$3.00
Existing Brand 2	10	7	$3.80
Potential New Brand 1	8	6	$2.00
Potential New Brand 2	10	9	$4.50

Each customer's weights are different, depending on how important sweetness, chewiness, and price are to the customer. However, we might expect these weights to be correlated. For example, we might expect the sweetness and chewiness weights to be positively correlated. If a customer attaches a lot of importance to sweetness, he might also attach a lot of weight to chewiness. We will assume the population of customers have normally distributed weights with the means and standard deviations shown in Table 13.8. We will also assume that the correlations between these weights are those given in Table 13.9. Note that the correlation between a variable and itself is always 1. The other correlations, which

TABLE 13.8 Means and Standard Deviations of Weights for Brownie Example

	Mean	Standard Deviation
Sweetness	5.0	1.0
Chewiness	4.0	0.6
Price	−9.0	2.0

[7] This example is based on the work of Hauser and Gaskin [6].

TABLE 13.9 Correlations Between Weights in Brownie Example

	Sweetness	Chewiness	Price
Sweetness	1.00	0.80	0.70
Chewiness	0.80	1.00	0.65
Price	0.70	0.65	1.00

are all positive, imply that if a customer puts a large weight on one attribute, he will tend to put a large weight on the other two attributes.

Bisquake wants to use simulation in order to choose the new brand (from the two possibilities) that is likely to obtain the largest market share.

Solution

A single iteration of the simulation will simulate the behavior of a single customer. That is, it will generate this customer's weights, find the customer's scores for each of the brands, and see whether the customer prefers new brand 1 or new brand 2 to the existing brands. By performing many iterations, we can simulate the behavior of many customers and approximate the fraction of the entire customer population who would prefer either of the new brands to the existing brands.

Developing the Spreadsheet Model The relevant spreadsheet appears in Figure 13.53. (See the file BROWNIE.XLS.) It can be formed as follows.

1 **Inputs.** Enter the inputs from Tables 13.7 through 13.9 in the ranges B6:D7, B11:D13, and B17:D20.

2 **Simulated weights.** @RISK's method of generating correlated random numbers is not entirely intuitive, but it is quite easy once you see how it works. We want the weights in the range B23:D23 to be normally distributed with the means and standard deviations in the range B6:D7, but we also want them to be correlated. To accomplish this, generate the first weight (for sweetness) in cell B23 with the formula

=RISKCORRMAT(B11:D13,1)+RISKNORMAL(B6,B7)

This is not really addition. It simply instructs @RISK to generate a normal random number but to correlate it with other potential random numbers, using the correlations in the first column of the correlation range B11:D13. Similarly, enter the formulas

=RISKCORRMAT(B11:D13,2)+RISKNORMAL(C6,C7)

and

=RISKCORRMAT(B11:D13,3)+RISKNORMAL(D6,D7)

in cells C23 and D23 in order to generate weights for chewiness and price.

3 **Scores for brands.** Calculate this customer's scores for the four brands in the range B26:B29 by entering the formula

=SUMPRODUCT($B$23:$D$23,B17:D17)

in cell B26 and copying it to the range B27:B29. This formula weights the attributes of each brand with the customer's weights.

4 **Is either new brand chosen?** Either of the new brands will be chosen if its score is larger than the largest score of the existing brands. Therefore, enter the formula

=IF(B28>MAX($B$26:$B$27),1,0)

FIGURE 13.53 Spreadsheet Model for Brownie Marketing Example

	A	B	C	D	E
1	**New Product Decision with Correlated Preferences**				
2					
3	**Input section**				
4	Distribution of customers' weights for attributes (normal distribution)				
5		Sweetness	Chewiness	Price	
6	Mean	5	4	-9	
7	StDev	1	0.6	2	
8					
9	Correlations between customers' weights for attributes				
10		Sweetness	Chewiness	Price	
11	Sweetness	1	0.8	0.7	
12	Chewiness	0.8	1	0.65	
13	Price	0.7	0.65	1	
14					
15	Attributes of existing brands and possible new brands				
16		Sweetness	Chewiness	Price	
17	Existing brand 1	8	6	$3.00	
18	Existing brand 2	10	7	$3.80	
19	New brand 1	8	6	$2.00	
20	New brand 2	10	9	$4.50	
21					
22	**Simulation section**				
23	Generated weights	5.30	3.91	-8.67	
24					
25	Scores for brands				
26	Existing brand 1	39.79			
27	Existing brand 2	47.36			
28	New brand 1	48.47			
29	New brand 2	49.10			
30					
31	Will either new brand be chosen? (1 if yes, 0 if no)				
32	New brand 1	1			
33	New brand 2	1			

in cell B32 to check whether new brand 1 is preferred to the existing brands. Then copy it to cell B33 to do the same for new brand 2.

Using @RISK We set up @RISK in the usual way, choosing cells B32 and B33 as the output cells and setting the number of iterations to 1000 and the number of simulations to 1. The results, shown in Figure 13.54, indicate that 657 of the 1000 simulated customers prefer new brand 1 to the existing brands, whereas 760 prefer new brand 2 to the existing brands. Perhaps this is not *conclusive* evidence that Bisquake should market its brand 2 rather than brand 1 (since brand 2's dominance could possibly be attributed to chance), but it is fairly persuasive.

How do these results depend on the correlation structure we assumed in Table 13.9? To see, we changed the positive .80 and .65 correlations to negative values (−.80 and −.65) and reran the simulation. In this case, a large weight on sweetness tends to be accompanied by a small weight on chewiness and vice versa. Similarly, a large weight on chewiness tends to be accompanied by a small weight on price and vice versa. The new simulated results appear in Figure 13.55. New brand 2 is even more dominant in this case; there is even less doubt that it is the brand Bisquake should market. ■

FIGURE 13.54 **Summary Statistics for Brownie Example with Positive Correlation**

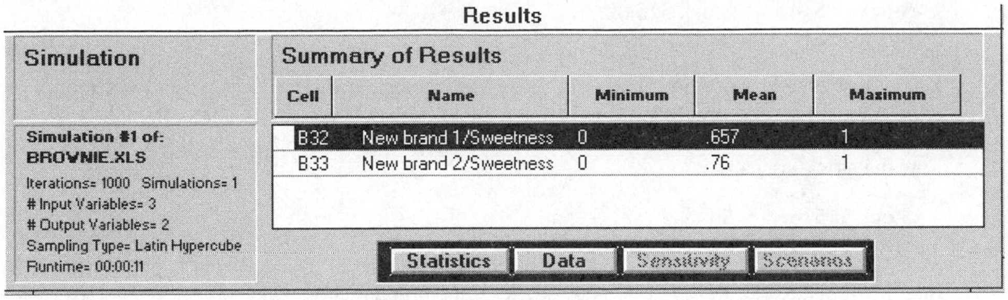

FIGURE 13.55 **Summary Statistics for Brownie Example with Negative Correlations**

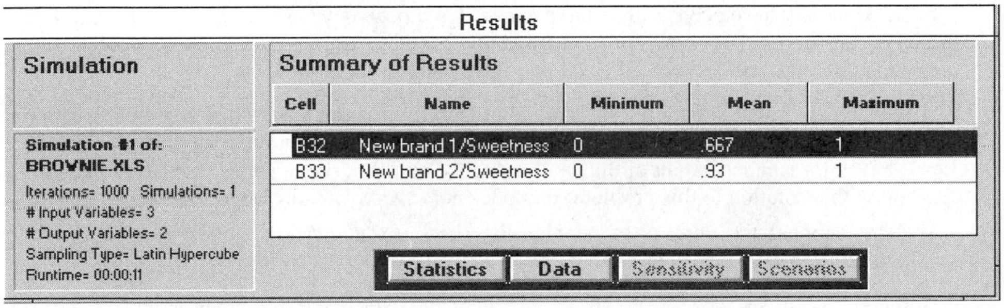

PROBLEMS

Skill-Building Problems

28 Suppose you have invested 25% of your portfolio in four different stocks. The mean and standard deviation of the annual return on each stock are as shown in Table 13.10. The correlation between the annual returns on the four stocks is as shown in Table 13.11.

a What is the probability that your portfolio's annual return will exceed 20%?

b What is the probability that your portfolio will lose money during the course of a year?

TABLE 13.10

	Mean	Standard Deviation
Stock 1	15%	20%
Stock 2	10%	12%
Stock 3	25%	40%
Stock 4	16%	20%

TABLE 13.11

	Stock 1	Stock 2	Stock 3	Stock 4
Stock 1	1.00	.80	.70	.60
Stock 2	.80	1.00	.75	.55
Stock 3	.70	.75	1.00	.65
Stock 4	.60	.55	.65	1.00

29 Suppose that the current price of each stock in the previous problem is as follows:

Stock 1: $14	Stock 3: $18
Stock 2: $16	Stock 4: $20

I have just bought an option involving these four stocks. If the price of stock 1 six months from now is $17 or more, the option enables me to buy, if I desire, one share of each stock for $20 six months from now. Otherwise the option is worthless. For example, if six months from now the stock prices are

Stock 1: $18	Stock 3: $21
Stock 2: $19	Stock 4: $22

then I would exercise my option to buy stocks 3 and 4 and receive $(21 - 20) + (22 - 20) = \$3$ in cash flow. How much is this option worth if the risk-free rate is 8%?

Skill-Extending Problems

30 The B-School at State U currently has three parking lots each containing 155 spaces. Two hundred faculty have been assigned to each lot. On a peak day, an average of 70% of all Lot 1 parking sticker holders show up, an average of 72% of all Lot 2 parking sticker holders show up, and an average of 74% of all Lot 3 parking sticker holders show up.

a Given the current situation, estimate the probability that on a peak day at least one faculty member with a sticker will be unable to find a spot. Assume that the number who show up at each lot is independent of the number who show up at the other two lots. Can you come up with a solution to this problem (that does not involve creating more parking spaces!)?

b Now suppose the number of people who show up at the three lots are correlated (correlation .9). Does your solution work as well? Why or why not?

31 Bottleco produces six-packs of soda cans. Each can is supposed to contain at least 12 oz. of soda. If the total weight in a six-pack is under 72 oz., Bottleco is fined $100 and receives no sales revenue for the six-pack. Each six-pack sells for $3.00. It costs Bottleco $0.02 per ounce of soda put in the cans. Bottleco can control the mean fill rate of its soda-filling machines. The amount put in each can by a machine is normally distributed with a standard deviation of .10 oz.

a Assume that the weight of each can in a six-pack has a .8 correlation with the weight of the other cans in the six-pack. What mean fill quantity (within .05 oz.) maximizes expected profit per six-pack?

b If the weights of the cans in the six-pack are independent, what mean fill quantity (within .05 oz.) will maximize expected profit per six-pack?

c Can you explain the difference in the answers to Parts (a) and (b)? ■

13.10 A Market Share Simulation

We conclude this chapter with a rather complex model of market share behavior. The model is based on the type of competition faced by two dominant brands in an industry, such as Coca Cola and Pepsi. These companies continually attempt to steal market share from one another. However, there are also smaller companies that enter and exit the market. They might be able to steal market share from the giants or vice versa. The following example illustrates one possible model of such behavior. Even though it is reasonably complex, it could be made much more complex by including marketing initiatives (advertising and price cuts, for example) by any of the competitors.

EXAMPLE 13.10

Sweetness and IceT are the two dominant companies in the bottled iced tea market. They each currently possess 49% of the total iced tea market, with three smaller companies splitting the remaining 2%. At the beginning of any year, a random number of new small companies enter the iced tea market. The actual number of new entries is assumed to be Poisson distributed with mean 1.[8] After the new entries enter the market, there is a random shift in market share among all competitors. Essentially, all competitors lose a random percentage of their market share to other competitors. We will assume that each of these percentages is triangularly distributed with the parameters given in Table 13.12. For example, the percentage of Sweetness's market share lost to IceT has a triangular distribution with minumum value 1%, most likely value 5%, and maximum value 10%. Similarly, the percentage of market share Sweetness will lose to *each* of the small companies has parameters 0.5%, 1%, and 3%. Therefore, the more small companies there are in the market, the more of its market share Sweetness will tend to lose to them.

At the end of each year, each of the small companies has a 50% chance of exiting the iced tea market. Each small company that exits will lose its market share to Sweetness or IceT. The percentage of this market share that goes to Sweetness is triangularly distributed with parameters 40%, 50%, and 60%; the rest goes to IceT.

The dominant companies, Sweetness and IceT, want to use simulation to see how their market share is likely to change over the next ten years.

TABLE 13.12 Parameters of Lost Market Share Percentages

	Minimum	Most Likely	Maximum
From Sweetness			
To IceT	1.0%	5%	10%
To Each Small Company	0.5%	1%	3%
From IceT			
To Sweetness	1.0%	5%	10%
To Each Small Company	0.5%	1%	3%
From Small Companies			
To Sweetness	5.0%	10%	15%
To IceT	5.0%	10%	15%

Solution

The spreadsheet model is somewhat tedious to develop, but the ideas are straightforward. At the beginning of any year, we observe the market shares of Sweetness, IceT, and the small companies (combined). Next, we simulate the number of new entrants. Then we simulate the shifts in market share during the year. Next, we simulate the number of small companies that exit at the end of the year, and we simulate their market shares that go to Sweetness or IceT. Finally, we tally the total market share at the end of the year for all competitors.

Developing the Spreadsheet Model The completed spreadsheet model appears in Figures 13.56 and 13.57. We use two figures, one for the inputs and one for the simulation results, because of the size of the spreadsheet. (See the file ICETEA.XLS.) It can be formed with the following steps.

[8] The Poisson distribution is a frequently used discrete distribution, particularly for the number of "events" that occur during some time period. This distribution is completely characterized by a single parameter, its mean. Its variance is equal to the mean. Its possible values are all nonnegative integers.

FIGURE 13.56 Inputs for Iced Tea Example

	A	B	C	D	E
1	**Iced tea market share simulation**				
2					
3	**Input section**				
4					
5	**Current market shares of dominant companies**				
6	Sweetness	49.00%			
7	IceT	49.00%			
8					
9	**Current data on small companies**				
10	Number	3			
11	Combined market share	2.00%			
12					
13	**Probability any small company will exit industry in any year**				
14		0.5			
15					
16	**Mean number of new entries in any year (Poisson distributed)**				
17		1			
18					
19	**Percentage of market share of each exiter that goes to Sweetness -**				
20	**the rest go to IceT (triangularly distributed)**				
21		Minimum	Most likely	Maximum	
22		40.00%	50.00%	60.00%	
23					
24	**Percentage of companies' market shares lost to each other and to small companies**				
25		Minimum	Most likely	Maximum	
26	Sweetness				
27	to IceT	1.00%	5.00%	10.00%	
28	to each small company	0.50%	1.00%	3.00%	
29	IceT				
30	to Sweetness	1.00%	5.00%	10.00%	
31	to each small company	0.50%	1.00%	3.00%	
32	Small companies				
33	to Sweetness	5.00%	10.00%	15.00%	
34	to IceT	5.00%	10.00%	15.00%	

1 **Inputs.** Enter the inputs shown in Figure 13.56.

2 **Beginning market shares.** For year 1 the beginning market shares are inputs. For example, find the beginning market share for Sweetness in cell B39 with the formula

=B6

For every other year, the beginning market shares are the ending market shares from the previous year. For example, find the beginning market share for Sweetness in year 2 by entering the formula

=B70

in cell C39. Then copy this to the range C39:K41 for all competitors over the remaining years.

3 **Entries to the market.** In year 1 find the number of small companies before entries, the number of new entries, and the number of small companies after entries by entering the formulas

=B10
=RISKPOISSON($B$17)

FIGURE 13.57 Spreadsheet Simulation for Iced Tea Example

	A	B	C	D	E	F	G	H	I	J	K
36	**Simulation section**										
37		Year 1	Year 2	Year 3	Year 4	Year 5	Year 6	Year 7	Year 8	Year 9	Year 10
38	**Beginning market shares**										
39	Sweetness	49.00%	48.13%	48.78%	48.78%	48.78%	48.78%	48.78%	48.78%	48.78%	48.78%
40	IceT	49.00%	48.13%	48.78%	48.78%	48.78%	48.78%	48.78%	48.78%	48.78%	48.78%
41	Small companies (combined)	2.00%	3.74%	2.44%	2.44%	2.44%	2.44%	2.44%	2.44%	2.44%	2.44%
42											
43	**Small companies before and after new entries**										
44	Number of smalls before entries	3	2	1	1	1	1	1	1	1	1
45	Number entering at beginning	1	1	1	1	1	1	1	1	1	1
46	Total number of smalls	4	3	2	2	2	2	2	2	2	2
47											
48	**Market shares lost during year**										
49	Sweetness										
50	to IceT	2.61%	2.57%	2.60%	2.60%	2.60%	2.60%	2.60%	2.60%	2.60%	2.60%
51	to smalls (combined)	2.94%	2.17%	1.46%	1.46%	1.46%	1.46%	1.46%	1.46%	1.46%	1.46%
52	IceT										
53	to Sweetness	2.61%	2.57%	2.60%	2.60%	2.60%	2.60%	2.60%	2.60%	2.60%	2.60%
54	to smalls (combined)	2.94%	2.17%	1.46%	1.46%	1.46%	1.46%	1.46%	1.46%	1.46%	1.46%
55	Small companies										
56	to Sweetness	0.20%	0.37%	0.24%	0.24%	0.24%	0.24%	0.24%	0.24%	0.24%	0.24%
57	to IceT	0.20%	0.37%	0.24%	0.24%	0.24%	0.24%	0.24%	0.24%	0.24%	0.24%
58											
59	**Information on exiters**										
60	Market share of smalls before exits	7.48%	7.32%	4.88%	4.88%	4.88%	4.88%	4.88%	4.88%	4.88%	4.88%
61	Number of smalls exiting at end	2	2	1	1	1	1	1	1	1	1
62	Number of smalls remaining	2	1	1	1	1	1	1	1	1	1
63	Combined market share of exiters	3.74%	4.88%	2.44%	2.44%	2.44%	2.44%	2.44%	2.44%	2.44%	2.44%
64											
65	**Market shares gained from exiters**										
66	to Sweetness	1.87%	2.44%	1.22%	1.22%	1.22%	1.22%	1.22%	1.22%	1.22%	1.22%
67	to IceT	1.87%	2.44%	1.22%	1.22%	1.22%	1.22%	1.22%	1.22%	1.22%	1.22%
68											
69	**Market shares at end**										
70	Sweetness	48.13%	48.78%	48.78%	48.78%	48.78%	48.78%	48.78%	48.78%	48.78%	48.78%
71	IceT	48.13%	48.78%	48.78%	48.78%	48.78%	48.78%	48.78%	48.78%	48.78%	48.78%
72	Small companies (combined)	3.74%	2.44%	2.44%	2.44%	2.44%	2.44%	2.44%	2.44%	2.44%	2.44%

and

=SUM(B44:B45)

in cells B44, B45, and B46. Note that the RISKPOISSON function, which takes a single argument, generates the number of new entries in a single year. For year 2 the number of small companies before entries is the remaining number from year 1. Therefore, enter the formula

=B62

in cell C44. Then copy the formulas in cells C44, B45, and B46 across these rows.

4 **Market shares lost during the year.** Generate the percentage of its market share Sweetness loses to IceT and to the small companies (combined) in year 1 by entering the formulas

=B39*RISKTRIANG($B$27,$C$27,$D$27)

and

=B39*RISKTRIANG($B$28,$C$28,$D$28)*B46

in cells B50 and B51 and then copy these across rows 50 and 51. Note that the latter of these multiplies the random percentage of market share lost by the number of small companies currently in the market. Next, enter similar formulas in rows 53, 54, 56, and 57 for market share lost by IceT and the small companies. For example, the formula in cell B57 is

=B41*RISKTRIANG($B$34,$C$34,$D$34)

5 **Exiters.** Rows 60 through 63 contains information about small companies before and after exiting. To calculate this information, enter the formulas

```
=SUM(B41,B51,B54)–SUM(B56:B57)
=IF(B46>0,RISKBINOMIAL(B46,$B$14),0)
=B46–B61
```

and

```
=IF(B46>0,(B61/B46)*B60,0)
```

in cells B60, B61, B62, B63. Then copy these across rows 60 through 63. The formula in B60 simply tallies the market shares lost and gained for the small companies before exiting takes place. The formula in cell B61 uses the RISKBINOMIAL function to generate the number of small companies that exit. This function takes two arguments: the number of small companies and the probability that any company exits. Since it is not defined if the number of small companies is 0, we need the IF function. Finally, the formula in B63 finds the amount of market share possessed by the exiting companies under the assumption that all small companies have an equal market share. Again, it uses an IF function to take care of the case where there are no remaining small companies—never divide by 0!

6 **Market share gained by exiters.** The assumption of the model is that the market share of the exiters in row 63 is split randomly between Sweetness and IceT. To generate the split, enter the formula

```
=B63*RISKTRIANG($B$22,$C$22,$D$22)
```

and

```
=B63–B66
```

in cells B66 and B67. Then copy these across rows 66 and 67.

7 **Year-end market shares.** Calculate the year-end market shares of Sweetness, IceT, and the small companies (combined) by entering the formulas

```
=SUM(B39,B53,B56,B66)–SUM(B50:B51)
=SUM(B40,B50,B57,B67)–SUM(B53:B54)
```

and

```
=B60–B63
```

in cells B70, B71, and B72. Then copy these across rows 70 through 72. If you like, you can check that the year-end market shares sum to 100% for each year, as they should.

Using @RISK There are a number of interesting outputs you can request for this simulation. We included the final market shares after ten years (cells K70, K71, and K72) as output cells. We also included the ranges B70:K70 and B71:K71 as output cells so that we could track the time series behavior of the two dominant companies' market shares. Selected outputs are shown numerically and graphically in Figures 13.58 through 13.62. Figure 13.58 indicates that the final market shares of the two dominant companies in year 10 averaged close to 49%—exactly where they began—but varied considerably, from a low of 38.9% for IceT to a high of 57.0% for Sweetness. Of course, Sweetness and IceT are modeled in exactly the same way in our simulation, so any differences between their outputs can be attributed entirely to chance. The small companies' combined market share averaged to about 2.4% at the end of year 10, but it also varied considerably from a low of 0% (no small companies in the market) to a high of 13.8%.

FIGURE 13.58 **Summary Statistics for Iced Tea Example**

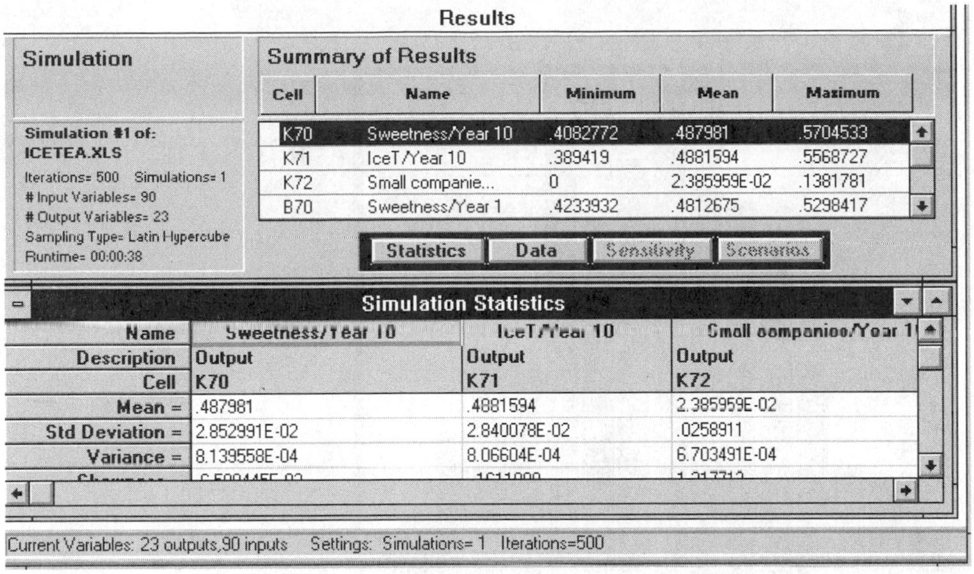

FIGURE 13.59 **Histogram for Sweetness's Ending Year 10 Market Share**

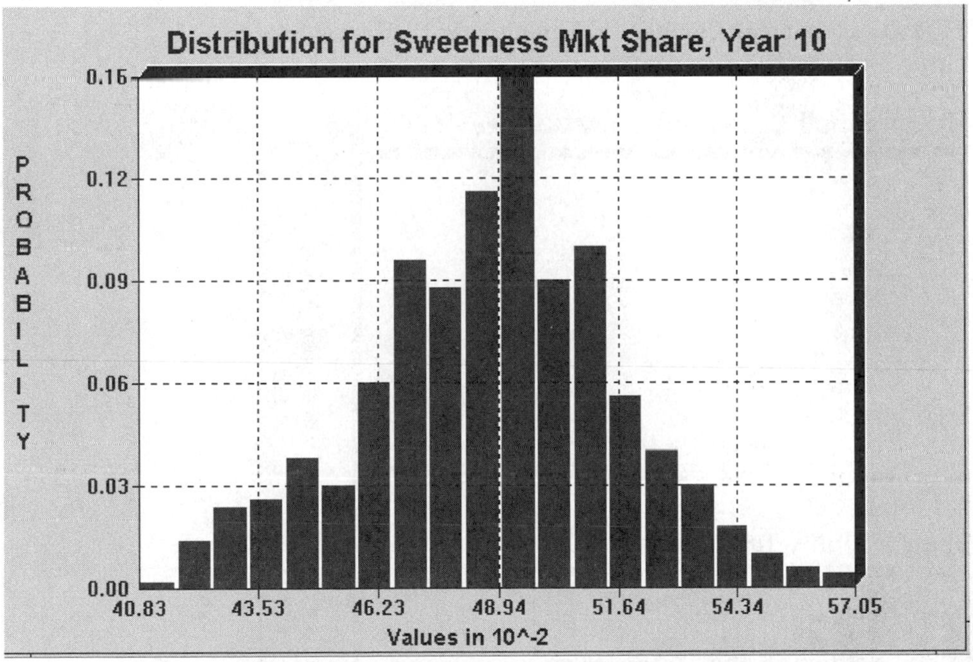

The histograms for the year 10 ending market share of the dominant companies, shown in Figures 13.59 and 13.60, represent behavior we might expect. Namely, they are reasonably bell-shaped around their means. The histogram for small companies shown in Figure 13.61, however, is quite different. We see that there were no small companies left in the market in about 37% of the iterations. When there were small companies remaining, their combined market share was skewed to the right.

FIGURE 13.60 Histogram for IceT's Ending Year 10 Market Share

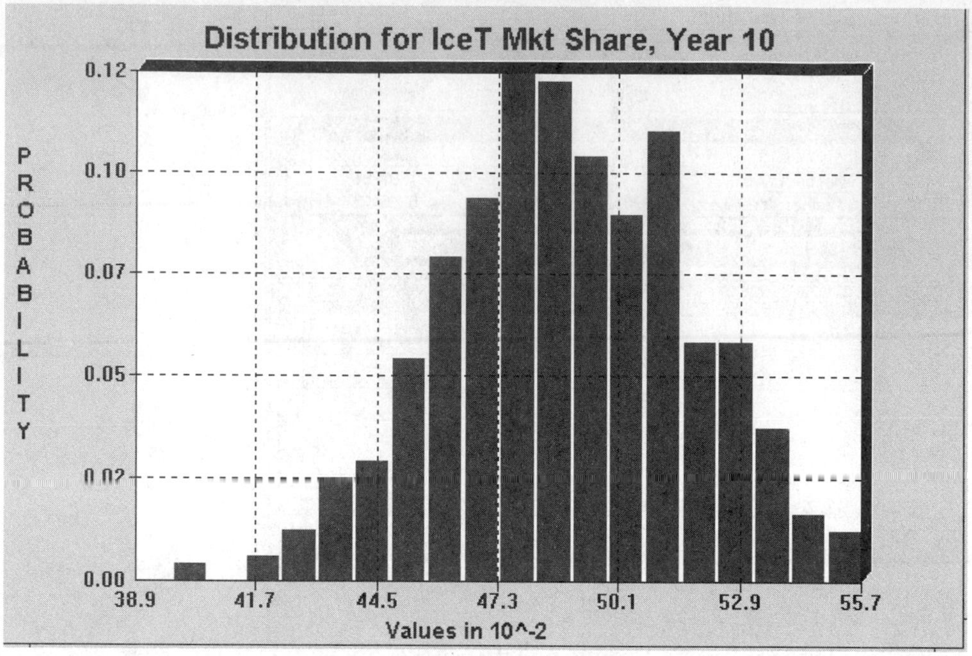

FIGURE 13.61 Histogram for Small Companies' Ending Year 10 Market Share

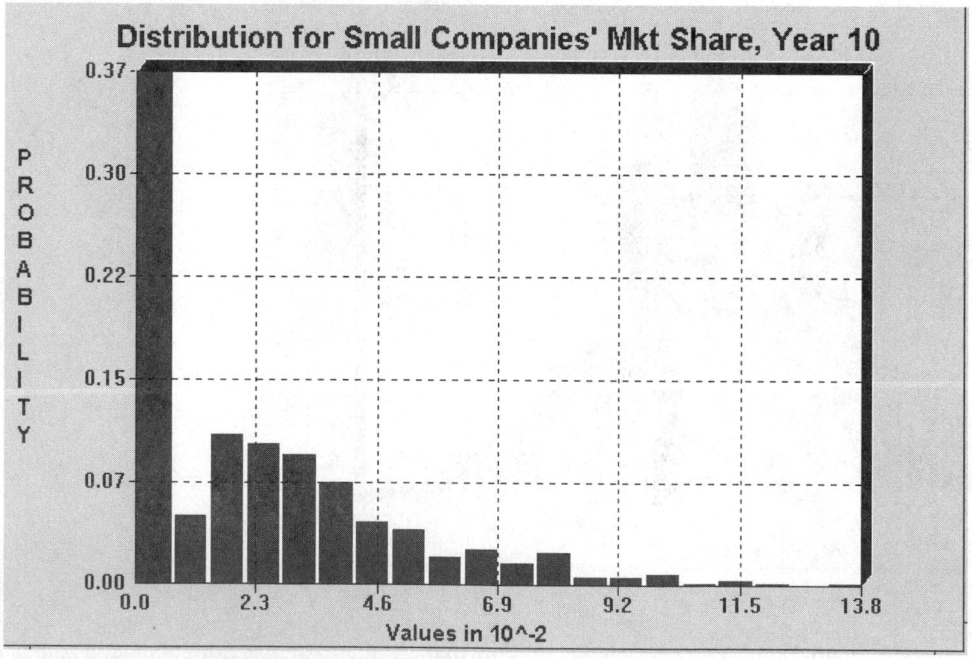

Finally, Figure 13.62 shows time series behavior of Sweetness's ending market share over the ten-year period. (This was produced by using the Summary graph option for cell B70—which is part of the output range B70:K70.) As we see, there is a slight upward trend on average, probably at the expense of the small companies.

FIGURE 13.62 Time Series of Sweetness's Ending Market Share

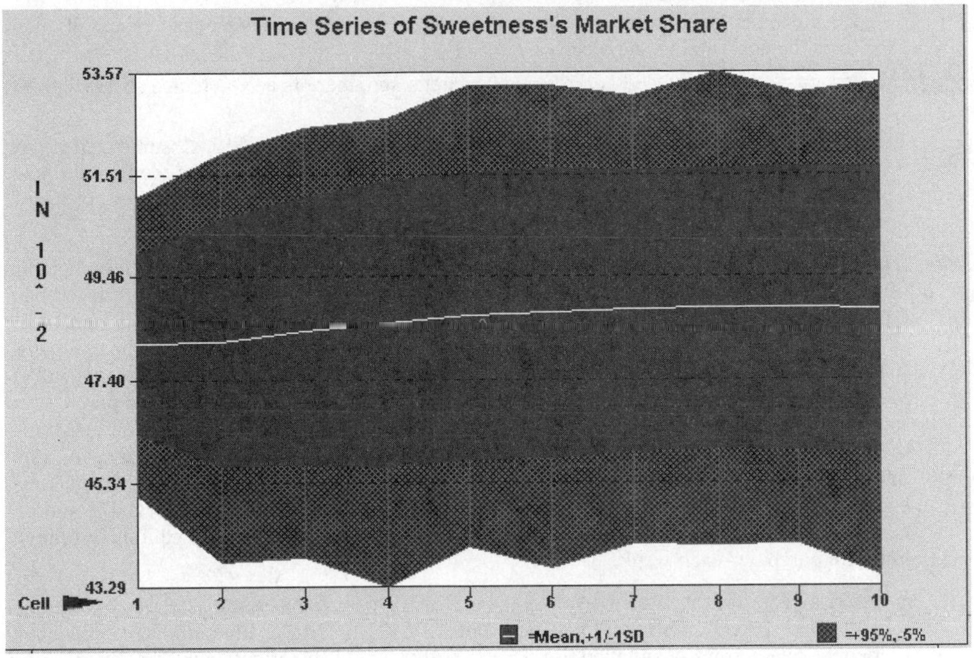

As we stated earlier, we could add marketing initiatives such as advertising or price cuts to this simulation model in order to reflect real-world behavior. The resulting output should be of enormous benefit to the companies involved. ■

PROBLEMS

Skill-Building Problems

32 Suppose that Coke and Pepsi are fighting for the cola market. Each week each person in the market buys one case of Coke or Pepsi. If the person's last purchase was Coke, there is a .90 probability that this person's next purchase will be Coke; otherwise, it will be Pepsi. (We are considering only two brands in the market.) Similarly, if the person's last purchase was Pepsi, there is a .80 probability that this person's next purchase will be Pepsi; otherwise, it will be Coke. Currently half of all people purchase Coke, and the other half purchase Pepsi. Simulate one year of sales in the cola market and estimate each company's average weekly market share. Do this by assuming that the total market size is fixed at 100 customers. (*Hint*: Use @RISK's RISKBINOMIAL function.)

33 Seas Beginning sells clothing by mail order. An important question is when to strike a customer from their mailing list. At present, they strike a customer from their mailing list if a customer fails to order from six consecutive catalogs. They want to know if striking a customer from their list after a customer fails to order from four consecutive catalogs will result in a higher profit per customer. The following data are available:

If a customer placed an order the last time she received a catalog, then there is a 20% chance she will order from the next catalog.

If a customer last placed an order one catalog ago, there is a 16% chance she will order from the next catalog she receives.

If a customer last placed an order two catalogs ago, there is a 12% chance she will order from the next catalog she receives.

If a customer last placed an order three catalogs ago, there is an 8% chance she will order from the next catalog she receives.

If a customer last placed an order four catalogs ago, there is a 4% chance she will order from the next catalog she receives.

If a customer last placed an order five catalogs ago, there is a 2% chance she will order from the next catalog she receives.

It costs $1 to send a catalog, and the average profit per order is $15. Assume a customer has just placed an order. In order to maximize expected profit per customer, would Seas Beginning make more money canceling such a customer after six non-orders or four non-orders?

34 (Based on Babich [1]) Suppose that each week every family in the United States buys a gallon of orange juice from Company A, B, or C. Let p_I = probability that a gallon produced by company I is of unsatisfactory quality. If the last gallon of juice purchased by a family is satisfactory, then the next week they will purchase a gallon of juice from the same company. If the last gallon of juice purchased by a family is not satisfactory, then the family will purchase a gallon from a competitor. Consider a week in which A families have purchased Juice A, B families have purchased Juice B, and C families have purchased Juice C. Assume that families that switch brands during a period are allocated to the remaining brands in a manner that is proportional to the current market shares of the other brands. Thus if a customer switches from Brand A there is a chance $B/(B + C)$ that he will switch to Brand B and a chance $C/(B + C)$ that he will switch to Brand C. Suppose that 1,000,000 gallons of orange juice are purchased each week.

a After a year, what will be the market share for each firm? Assume $p_A = .10$, $p_B = .15$, and $p_C = .20$. (*Hint*: You will need to use the RISKBINOMIAL function to see how many people switch from A and then use the RISKBINOMIAL function again to see how many switch from A to B and from A to C.)

b Suppose a 1% increase in market share is worth $10,000 per week to Firm A. Also suppose that currently $p_A = .10$, $p_B = .15$, and $p_C = .20$. Firm A believes that for a cost of $1 million per year they can cut the percentage of unsatisfactory juice cartons in half. Is this worthwhile?

Skill-Extending Problems

35 (Based on Hoppensteadt and Peskin [7]) The following model (the Reed-Frost model) is often used to model the spread of an infectious disease. Suppose that at the beginning of period 1 the population consists of 5 diseased people (called infectives) and 95 healthy people (called susceptibles). During any period, there is a .05 chance that a given infective person will encounter a particular susceptible. If an infective encounters a susceptible, there is a .5 chance that the susceptible will contract the disease. An infective lives an average of 10 periods with the disease. To model this, we assume that there is a .10 probability that an infective dies during a period. Use @RISK to model the evolution of the population over 100 periods. Use your results to answer the following questions:

a What is the probability that the population will die out?

b What is the probability that the disease will die out?

c On the average, what percentage of the population becomes infected by the end of period 100?

d Suppose that people use infection "protection" during encounters. The use of protection reduces from .50 to .10 the chance that a susceptible will contract the disease during a single encounter with an infective. Now answer questions (a)–(c) under the assumption that everyone uses protection. (*Hint*: During any period there is a probability $(.05) * .50 = .025$ that an infective will infect a particular susceptible. Thus the probability that a particular susceptible is not infected during a period is $(1 - .025)^I$, where I = number of infectives present at end of the previous period.)

36 You are unemployed and 21 years old and searching for a job. Until you accept a job offer the following situation occurs. At the beginning of each year you receive a job offer. The annual salary associated with the job offer is equally likely to be any number between $20,000 and $100,000. You must immediately choose whether to accept the job offer. If you accept an offer with salary $x, you receive $x per year for the rest of your life (we assume you die at age 70), including the current year. Assume that cash flows are discounted so that a cash flow received one year from now has an NPV of .9. You have adopted the following policy: you will accept the first job offer that exceeds w dollars. Within $10,000, what value of w maximizes the expected NPV of earnings you will receive the rest of your life? ■

13.11

Conclusion

Simulation has traditionally not received the attention it deserves in management science courses. The reason for this has primarily been the lack of easy-to-use simulation software. Now with Excel's built-in simulation capabilities, plus powerful and affordable add-ins such as @RISK and Crystal Ball, simulation is achieving its rightful emphasis. The world is full of uncertainty, which is what makes simulation so valuable. Simulation models provide important insights that are simply missing in models that do not incorporate uncertainty. In addition, simulation models are relatively easy to understand and (with suitable add-ins) easy to develop. Therefore, we suspect that simulation models will soon be the primary emphasis of most management science courses—if they aren't already!

REVIEW PROBLEMS

Skill-Building Problems

37 Use @RISK to analyze the AMA's situation in Problem 12.7.

38 A ticket from Indianapolis to Orlando on Deleast Airlines sells for $150. The plane can hold 100 people. It costs Deleast $8000 to fly an empty plane. Each person on the plane incurs variable costs of $30 (for food and fuel). If the flight is overbooked, anyone who cannot get a seat receives $300 in compensation. On average, 95% of all people who have a reservation show up for the flight. To maximize expected profit, how many reservations for the flight should Deleast book? (*Hint*: The @RISK function RISKBINOMIAL can be used to simulate the number who show up. It takes two arguments: the number of reservations booked and the probability that any ticketed person shows up.)

39 In the machine redundancy example (see Example 13.4) we assumed that all components in parallel have *independent* times to failure. This might not be realistic. For example, the reason for component failures might be stress from an external force that operates on all components simultaneously. This would induce positive correlation between the component failures times: if one fails early, others are likely to fail early as well. Assume that the times until component failure are lognormally distributed with mean 100 hours and standard deviation 20 hours, as in the example. However, suppose the correlation between any two component failure times is .5. Simulate the time until machine failure when there are n components in parallel. Do this for $n = 3$ through $n = 10$. (You can do this with a single simulation if you set up the spreadsheet correctly.) How do the simulated machine times with correlated component failure times compare to those with uncorrelated times?

40 Suppose you buy an electronic device that you operate continuously. The device costs you $100 and carries a one-year warranty. The warranty states that if the device fails during its first year of use, you get a new device for no cost, and this new device carries exactly the same warranty. However, if it fails after the first year of use, the warranty is of no value. You need this device for the next six years. Therefore, any time the device fails outside its warranty period, you must pay $100 for another device of the same kind. (We'll assume the price doesn't increase during the six-year period.) The time until failure for a device is gamma distributed with parameters $\alpha = 2$ and $\beta = .5$. (This implies a mean of one year.) Use @RISK to simulate the six-year period. Include as outputs (1) your total cost, (2) the number of failures during the warranty period, and (3) the number of devices owned during the six-year period.

41 Rework the previous problem for a case in which the one-year warranty requires you to pay for the new device even if failure occurs during the warranty period. Specifically, if the device fails at time t, measured relative to the time it went into use, you must pay t times $100 for a new device. For example, if the device goes into use at the beginning of April and fails nine months later, at the beginning of January, you must pay \$75. The reasoning is that you got 3/4 of the warranty period for use, so you should pay that fraction of the total cost for the next device. As before, however, if the device fails outside the warranty period, you must pay the full \$100 cost for a new device.

42 A TSB (Tax Saver Benefit plan) allows you to put money into an account at the beginning of the calendar year that may be used for medical expenses. This amount is not subject to federal tax (hence the phrase TSB). As you pay medical expenses during the year, you are reimbursed by the administrator of the TSB until the TSB account is exhausted. From that point on, you must pay your medical expenses out of your own pocket. On the other hand, if you put more money into your TSB than the medical expenses you incur, this extra money is lost to you. Your annual salary is \$50,000 and your federal income tax rate is 30%.

a Assume that your medical expenses in a year are normally distributed with mean \$2000 and standard deviation \$500. Build an @RISK model in which the output is the amount of money left to you after paying taxes, putting money in a TSB, and paying any extra medical expenses. Experiment with the amount of money put in the TSB, using a RISKSIMTABLE function.

b Rework Part (a), but this time assume a gamma distribution for your annual medical expenses. Use $\alpha = 16$ and $\beta = 125$ as the two parameters of this distribution. These imply the same mean and standard deviation as in Part (a), but the distribution of medical expenses is now skewed to the right, which is probably more realistic. Using simulation, see whether you should now put more or less money in a TSB than in the symmetric case in Part (a).

43 At the beginning of each week a machine is in one of four conditions: 1 = excellent; 2 = good; 3 = average; 4 = bad. The weekly revenue earned by a machine in state 1, 2, 3, or 4 is \$100, \$90, \$50, or \$10, respectively. After observing the condition of the machine at the beginning of the week, the company has the option, for a cost of \$200, of instantaneously replacing the machine with an excellent machine. The quality of the machine deteriorates over time, as shown in Table 13.13. Four maintenance policies are under consideration:

- Policy 1: Never replace a machine.
- Policy 2: Immediately replace a bad machine.
- Policy 3: Immediately replace a bad or average machine.
- Policy 4: Immediately replace a bad, average, or good machine.

TABLE 13.13 Description of Machine Deterioration

Present Machine State	Probability That Machine Begins Next Week As			
	Excellent	Good	Average	Bad
Excellent	.7	.3		
Good		.7	.3	
Average			.6	.4
Bad				1.0 (until replaced)

Simulate each of these policies for 50 weeks (using 250 iterations each) in an attempt to determine the policy that maximizes expected weekly profit. Assume that the machine at the beginning of week 1 is excellent.

44 Solve Problem 12.19 using @RISK.

45 You have made it to the final round of "Let's Make a Deal." You know that there is \$1 million behind either door 1, door 2, or door 3. It is equally likely that the prize is behind any of the three doors. The two doors without a prize have nothing behind them. You randomly choose door 2. Before you see whether the prize is behind door 2, Monty chooses to open a door which has no prize behind it. For the sake of definiteness, suppose that before door 2 is opened Monty reveals that there is no prize behind door 3. You now have the opportunity to switch and choose door 1. Should you switch?

Use a spreadsheet to simulate this situation 400 times. For each "trial" use an @RISK function to generate the door behind which the prize sits. Then use another @RISK function to generate the door that Monty will open. Assume that Monty plays as follows: Monty knows where the prize is and will open an empty door, but he cannot open door 2. If the prize is really behind door 2, Monty is equally likely to open door 1 or door 3. If the prize is really behind door 1, Monty must open door 3. If the prize is really behind door 3, Monty must open door 1.

46 Consider a drill press containing three drill bits. The current policy (called **individual replacement**) is to replace a drill bit when it fails. The firm is considering changing to a **block replacement** policy in which all three drill bits are replaced whenever a single drill bit fails. Each time the drill press is shut down the cost is $100. A drill bit costs $50, and the variable cost of replacing a drill bit is $10. Assume that the time to replace a drill bit is negligible. Assume that the time until failure for a drill bit follows an exponential distribution with a mean of 100 hours. This can be modeled in @RISK with the formula

=RISKEXPON(100)

Determine which replacement policy (block or individual replacement) should be implemented.

47 Freezco sells refrigerators. Any refrigerator that fails before it is three years old must be replaced. Of all refrigerators 3% fail during their first year of operation; 5% of all one-year-old refrigerators fail during their second year of operation; and 7% of all two-year-old refrigerators fail during their third year of operation.

a Estimate the fraction of all refrigerators that will have to be replaced.

b It costs $500 to replace a refrigerator, and Freezco sells 10,000 refrigerators per year. If the warranty period were reduced to two years, how much per year in replacement costs would be saved?

48 Lowland Appliance replenishes its stock of color TVs three times a year. Each order takes 1/9 of a year to arrive. Annual demand for the color TVs follows a normal distribution with a mean of 990 and a standard deviation of 40. Assume that the cost of holding a TV in inventory for a year is $100. Assume that we begin with 500 TVs in inventory, the cost of a shortage is $150, and the cost of placing an order is $500.

a Suppose that whenever inventory is reviewed and our inventory level is x, we order $480 - x$ TVs. Estimate the average annual cost of such a policy. Such a policy is called an **order-up** policy.

b Estimate average annual cost for order-up policies when we order up to 200, 400, 600, and 800 TVs.

Skill-Extending Problems

49 In the Walton Bookstore example (see Example 13.2), we assumed that there is only a single product. Suppose instead that there are two competing products sold by a company. Sales of either product tend to take away sales from the other product. That is, the demands for the two products are negatively correlated. The company first places an order for each product. Then during a period of time, there is demand D_1 for product 1 and demand D_2 for product 2. Each demand is normally distributed with means 1000 and 1200 and standard deviations 250 and 350. However, the correlation between D_1 and D_2 is ρ, where ρ is a negative number between -1 and 0. The unit cost of each product is $7.50, the unit price for each product is $10, and the unit refund for any unit of either product not sold is $2.50. The company must decide how many units of each product to order. Use @RISK to help the company by experimenting with different order quantities. Try this for $\rho = -.3$, $\rho = -.5$, and $\rho = -.7$. What recommendation can you give about the "best" order quantities as the demands become more highly correlated (in a negative direction).

50 Work the previous problem when the demands are *positively* correlated, as they might be with products like peanut butter and jelly. Now use $\rho = .3$, $\rho = .5$, and $\rho = .7$ in your simulations.

51 Simulation can be used to illustrate a number of results from statistics that are difficult to understand with nonsimulation arguments. One is the famous Central Limit Theorem, which says that if you sample enough values from *any* population distribution and then average these values, the resulting average will be approximately normally distributed. Illustrate that this is the case by using @RISK with the following population distributions (run a separate simulation for each): (a) discrete with possible values 1 and 2 and probabilities .2 and .8;

(b) exponential with mean 1 (use the RISKEXPON function with the single argument 1); (c) triangular with minimum, most likely, and maximum values equal to 1, 9, and 10. (Note that each of these distributions is very *non*normal.) Run each simulation with 10 values in each average, and run 1000 iterations in order to simulate 1000 averages. Create a histogram of the averages to see that it is indeed bell-shaped. Then repeat, using 30 values in each average. Are the histograms based on 10 qualitatively different than those based on 30?

52 In statistics we often use observed data to test a hypothesis about a population or populations. The basic method is that we use the observed data to calculate a test statistic (a single number). If the magnitude of this test statistic is sufficiently large, we reject the "null" hypothesis in favor of the "research" hypothesis. As an example, consider a researcher who believes teenage girls sleep longer than teenage boys on average. She collects observations on $n = 40$ randomly selected girls and $n = 40$ randomly selected boys. (We'll assume that each observation is the average sleep time over several nights for a given person.) The averages are $\overline{X}_1 = 7.9$ hours for the girls and $\overline{X}_2 = 7.6$ hours for the boys. The standard deviation of the 40 girl observations is $s_1 = .5$ hour; for the boys it is $s_2 = .7$ hour. The researcher, consulting her statistics textbook, then calculates the test statistic

$$\frac{\overline{X}_1 - \overline{X}_2}{\sqrt{s_1^2/40 + s_2^2/40}} = \frac{7.9 - 7.6}{\sqrt{.25/40 + .49/40}} = 2.206$$

Based on the fact that 2.206 is "large," she claims that her research hypothesis is confirmed: girls *do* sleep longer than boys.

You are skeptical of this claim, so you check it out by running a simulation. In your simulation you assume that girls and boys have the *same* mean and standard deviation of sleep times in the entire population, say, 7.7 and .6. You also assume that the distribution of sleep times is normal. Then you repeatedly simulate 40 girl and 40 boy observations from this distribution and calculate the above test statistic. The question is whether the observed test statistic, 2.206 is "extreme." If it is larger than most or all of the test statistics you simulate, then the researcher is justified in her claim; otherwise, this large a statistic could have happened just by chance, even if the girls and boys have identical population means. Use @RISK to see which is the case.

53 Chemcon has taken over the production of Wozac from a rival drug company. Chemcon must build a plant to produce Wozac by the beginning of 1997. Once the plant is built, the plant's capacity cannot be changed. Each unit sold brings in \$10 in revenue. The fixed cost (in dollars) of producing a plant that can produce x units per year of the drug is given by

$$\text{Fixed cost} = 5{,}000{,}000 + 10x$$

This cost is assumed to be incurred at the end of 1997. We assume that all cost and sales cash flows are incurred at the end of each year. If a plant of capacity x is built, the variable cost of producing a unit of Wozac is given by

$$\text{Variable cost per unit} = 6 - .1 * (x - 1{,}000{,}000)/100{,}000$$

For example, a plant capacity of 1,100,000 units has a variable cost of \$5.90. Each year a plant operating cost of \$1 per unit of capacity is also incurred.

Based on a forecasting sales model from the previous ten years, Chemcon forecasts that demand in year t, D_t, is related to the demand in the previous year, D_{t-1}, by the equation

$$D_t = 67{,}430 + .985 * D_{t-1} + e_t$$

where e_t is a random term that is normally distributed with mean 0 and standard deviation 29,320. The demand in 1996 was 1,011,000 units. If demand for a year exceeds production capacity, all sales in excess of plant capacity are assumed lost. Chemcon wants to determine a capacity level that will maximize expected discounted profits (using an interest rate of 10%) for the time period 1997–2006.

54 The Tinkan Company produces one-pound cans for the Canadian salmon industry. Each year the salmon spawn during a 24-hour period and must be canned immediately. Tinkan has the following agreement with the salmon industry. The company can deliver as many cans as it chooses. Then the salmon are caught. For each can by which Tinkan falls short of the salmon industry's needs, the company pays the industry a \$2 penalty. Cans cost Tinkan \$1 to produce and are purchased for \$2 per can. If any cans are left over, they are returned to Tinkan and the company reimburses the industry \$2 for each extra can. These extra cans are put in storage for next year. Each year a can is held in storage, a carrying cost equal to 20% of the can's production cost is incurred. It is well known that the number of salmon harvested during a year is strongly related to the number of salmon harvested the previous year. In fact, using past data, Tinkan estimates that the harvest size in year t, H_t (measured in the number of cans required), is related to the harvest size in the previous year, H_{t-1}, by the equation

$$H_t = H_{t-1} * e_t$$

where e_t is normally distributed with mean 1.02 and standard deviation .10.

Tinkan plans to use the following type of production strategy. For some value of x, it will produce enough cans at the beginning of year t to bring its inventory up to $x + \widehat{H}_t$, where $\widehat{H}_t$ is the predicted harvest size in year t. Then it will deliver these cans to the salmon industry. For example, if it uses $x = 100{,}000$, the predicted harvest size is 500,000 cans, and 80,000 cans are already in inventory, then Tinkan will produce and deliver 520,000 cans. Given that the harvest size for the previous year was 550,000 cans, use simulation to help Tinkan develop a production strategy that will maximize its expected profit over the next 20 years.

55 Use @RISK to solve Problem 12.28.

56 A highly perishable drug spoils after three days. A hospital estimates that they are equally likely to need between 1 and 9 units of the drug daily. Each time an order for the drug is placed, a fixed cost of $200 is incurred as well as a purchase cost of $50 per unit. Orders are placed at the end of each day and arrive at the beginning of the following day. It costs no money to hold the drug in inventory, but a cost of $100 is incurred each time the hospital needs a unit of the drug and does not have any available. The following three policies are under consideration:

Policy 1: If we end the day with fewer than 5 units, order enough to bring next day's beginning inventory up to 10 units.

Policy 2: If we end the day with fewer than 3 units, order enough to bring next day's beginning inventory up to 7 units.

Policy 3: If we end the day with fewer than 8 units, order enough to bring next day's beginning inventory up to 15 units.

Compare these policies with regard to expected daily costs, expected number of units short per day, and expected number of units spoiling each day. Assume that we begin day 1 with 5 units of the drug on hand. (*Hint*: You will need to keep track of the age distribution of the units on hand at the beginning of each week. Assume that the hospital uses a FIFO (first in, first out) inventory policy. The trick is to get formulas that relate the age of each unit of the drug you have at the beginning of the day to the age of each unit you have at the end of the day.) ■

REFERENCES

1 Babich, P. "Customer Satisfaction: How Good Is Good Enough?" *Quality Progress* 25 (Dec. 1992): 65–68.

2 Benninga, S. *Numerical Methods in Finance*. Cambridge, MA: MIT Press, 1989.

3 Black, F., and M. Scholes. "The Pricing of Options and Corporate Liabilities." *Journal of Political Economy* 81 (1973): 637–54.

4 Cebry, M., A. DeSilva, and F. DiLisio. "Management Science in Automating Postal Operations: Facility and Equipment Planning in the United States Postal Service." *Interfaces* 22, no. 1 (1992): 110–30.

5 Cox, J., S. Ross, and M. Rubenstein. "Option Pricing: A Simplified Approach." *Journal of Financial Economics* 7 (1979): 229–63.

6 Hauser, J., and S. Gaskin. "Application of the Defender Consumer Model." *Marketing Science* 3, no. 4 (1984): 327–51.

7 Hoppensteadt, F., and C. Peskin. *Mathematics in Medicine and the Life Sciences*. New York: Springer-Verlag, 1992.

8 Kelly, J. "A New Interpretation of Information Rate." *Bell System Technical Journal* 35 (1956): 917–26.

9 Morrison, D., and R. Wheat. "Pulling the Goalie Revisited." *Interfaces* 16, no. 6 (1984): 28–34.

CHAPTER

14

Forecasting Models

Management Science Success Stories

Unlike the previous topics we have discussed in this book, forecasting is not as likely to get credit as the key methodology in successful management science applications. This credit often goes to linear programming, decision analysis, simulation, or other methodologies we have studied. However, forecasting is a necessary ingredient in many applications. In fact, most if not all of the successful applications we have described in previous chapters used forecasting as a crucial step in the data gathering process. We list several of these here.

1 The Citgo study described in Chapter 1 developed a supply distribution and marketing system for its downstream marketing operations. It used regression analysis to forecast wholesale prices and wholesale demand for each of Citgo's products.

2 The objective of the San Francisco Police Department study described in Chapter 1 was to schedule officers appropriately. In order to do so, it first had to forecast the demand for police officers by time of day and day of week.

3 The HP Deskjet-Plus Printer study discussed in Chapter 9 focused on keeping the appropriate amount of inventory at the appropriate locations in order to satisfy customer demand quickly and at minimal cost. A necessary first step in achieving this goal was to obtain accurate forecasts of customer demand for printers.

4 In Chapter 10 we described the attempts by American Airlines to achieve an overbooking policy that would keep airplane occupancies high and costs low. In order to do so, American had to develop forecasts of its customer demand for flights and the frequency (and timing) of cancellations.

5 The objective of L. L. Bean in the study described in Chapter 11 was to find an economically optimal method of staffing its telephones. As in the San Francisco police study, this required L. L. Bean to obtain accurate forecasts of its mail order calls by time of day, day of week, and time of year.

As these and many other successful management science applications reveal, forecasting does not usually receive "top billing" as the methodology that saved the companies millions, but it is frequently one of the first steps in the solution process. Recall that the second step in the seven-step modeling process discussed in Chapter 1 is data gathering. Forecasting is often the method required to gather these data. ■

14.1

Introduction

On previous chapters we have often substituted numbers into problems without considering where the numbers came from. For example, in the Monet linear programming example (Example 2.1), we assumed that the unit profit from a type 1 frame was \$6, which is the selling price minus the variable cost of labor and materials. In reality, we would have to estimate this variable cost. This can be done using the method of simple linear regression, explained in Section 14.7.

In Chapters 9 and 10 we used inventory theory to determine production quantities and reorder points. To use the models in these chapters, we need to be able to forecast the demand for a product. In Sections 14.3–14.6, we discuss extrapolation and smoothing methods that can be used to forecast future demand for a product.

Chapter 11 on queueing models is another example of where we can use forecasting. Suppose that we want to determine how the number of tellers at a bank should vary with the day of the week and the time of day. To tackle this problem, we need to determine how the rate at which customers enter the bank depends on the time of day and the day of the week. For example, if we know that over half the bank's customers arrive during the lunch hour (noon to 1 P.M.), that would have a significant effect on the optimal staffing policy. Forecasting methods can be used to obtain these arrival rates.

In this chapter we will discuss two important types of forecasting methods: **extrapolation methods** and **causal methods**. In Sections 14.3–14.6, we discuss extrapolation methods, which are used to forecast future values of a time series from past values of the series. For example, if a company needs to forecast future sales of one of its products, it can use one of several extrapolation methods to base future sales forecasts on past sales. When we use an extrapolation forecasting method, we assume that past patterns and trends in sales will continue in future months. Thus, past data on sales—and no other information—are used to generate forecasts for sales during future months. Extrapolation methods (unlike the causal forecasting methods described in Sections 14.7–14.9) don't take into account what "caused" past data; they simply assume that past trends and patterns will continue in the future.

In contrast, causal forecasting methods attempt to forecast future values of a time series variable (called the **dependent variable**) by using past data to estimate the relationship between the dependent variable and one or more **independent variables**. For example, a company might try to forecast future monthly sales of its product by using past data to determine how sales are related to independent variables such as price, advertising, and the month of the year.

14.2

Time Series Notation

We begin our explanation by developing some time series ideas and notation that are common to all extrapolation methods. Let $y_1, y_2, \ldots, y_t, \ldots$ be observed values of a time series, where y_t is the value of the time series observed during period t. We define $f_{t,h}$ to be the forecast for period t made after observing y_{t-h}. This is called the **h-period-ahead forecast** because, standing in period $t - h$, it forecasts h periods into the future. A special case is the one-period-ahead forecast, $f_{t,1}$. For example, if t corresponds to June 1997, then $f_{t,1}$ is the forecast of June 1997 made in May 1997. Since one-period-ahead forecasts are so common, we abbreviate $f_{t,1}$ by the simpler notation f_t, so that f_t is the forecast of y_t made in period $t - 1$.

Clearly, the accuracy of a forecasting method must be judged by the **forecast errors** it makes. Consider a sequence of one-period-ahead forecasts. That is, for many consecutive time periods t, right after observing y_{t-1}, we make a forecast f_t of y_t, the value of the series one period from now. Eventually (one period later), we will observe the actual y_t. Then the difference between what we observe in period t and what we forecasted for period t, $y_t - f_t$, is called the forecast error and is denoted by e_t. For example, if the forecast of June sales (made in May) is 55, and June sales eventually turns out to be 58, then the forecast error for June is $58 - 55 = 3$. Our forecast was off by 3 units on the low side. By tracking these forecast errors over many months, we get a sense of the accuracy of the forecasting method.

One particular measure is often used to gauge forecasting accuracy. It is the **mean absolute deviation**, or MAD. It is simply the average of the absolute forecast errors. If T is the number of one-step-ahead forecasts we make, then MAD is given by the formula

$$MAD = \frac{\sum |e_t|}{T}$$

To illustrate these ideas, consider the monthly sales data shown in Table 14.1. The observations begin in December 1996, which corresponds to period $t = 0$. Then for months $t = 1$ to $t = 12$, corresponding to the 12 months of 1997, we observe the values in the y_t column and we make the forecasts listed in the f_t column. (These forecasts have been chosen fairly randomly; in later sections we will present methods for obtaining them.) Each forecast is made in the previous month and is based only on what has been observed to that point. For example, the forecast f_5 is the forecast for May 1997. It is made in April and is based only on the observations through April. Finally, the differences between the values in the y_t and f_t columns are the forecast errors and are listed in the e_t column. Their magnitudes are listed in the $|e_t|$ column. The average of these 12 absolute errors is

$$MAD = (100 + 300 + \cdots + 100 + 100)/12 = 1400/12 = 116.67$$

This is a measure of the average forecast error.

TABLE 14.1 **Forecasts and Forecast Errors**

	t	y_t	f_t	e_t	$\|e_t\|$
Dec 96	0	800	—	—	—
Jan 97	1	700	800	−100	100
Feb 97	2	600	900	−300	300
Mar 97	3	800	900	−100	100
Apr 97	4	1000	1100	−100	100
May 97	5	1400	1300	100	100
Jun 97	6	1500	1500	0	0
Jul 97	7	1700	1600	100	100
Aug 97	8	1600	1500	100	100
Sep 97	9	1300	1400	−100	100
Oct 97	10	900	1100	200	200
Nov 97	11	700	800	−100	100
Dec 97	12	600	500	100	100

14.3

Moving-Average Method

As we discussed in the introduction to this chapter, extrapolation methods use only past values of the time series variable to forecast future values. Several extrapolation methods are frequently used, including moving-average methods and exponential smoothing methods. In this section we will discuss the moving-average method. For all of these extrapolation methods, we will use the data in the following example.

EXAMPLE 14.1

Lowland Appliance Company sells TVs, compact disc players (CDs), and air conditioners (ACs). Its monthly sales of TVs, CDs, and ACs for the past 24 months, January 1995 through December 1996, are listed in Table 14.2. Lowland wants to find suitable forecasting methods for forecasting sales of these products for the next few months.

Solution

For the moving-average method the one-period-ahead forecast is given by

$$f_t = \text{Average of the last } N \text{ observations}$$
$$= \text{Average of } y_{t-1}, y_{t-1}, y_{t-2}, \ldots, y_{t-N}$$

where N is a given parameter called the **span**. To illustrate the method, we will choose $N = 3$ and forecast TV sales for the first six months of data given in Table 14.2. The results are given in Table 14.3. For months 1–3, we have not yet observed three months of data, so (for $N = 3$) we cannot develop a moving-average forecast of sales for these months. For month 4 the moving-average forecast, based on the average of the first three observations, is

$$f_4 = \frac{30 + 32 + 30}{3} = 30.67$$

Similarly, the forecasts for month 5 and 6 are

$$f_5 = \frac{32 + 30 + 39}{3} = 33.67$$

TABLE 14.2 **Data for Lowland Example**

	TV Sales	CD Sales	AC Sales		TV Sales	CD Sales	AC Sales
Month 1	30	40	13	**Month 13**	38	79	36
Month 2	32	47	7	**Month 14**	30	82	21
Month 3	30	50	23	**Month 15**	35	80	47
Month 4	39	49	32	**Month 16**	30	85	81
Month 5	33	56	58	**Month 17**	34	94	112
Month 6	34	53	60	**Month 18**	40	89	139
Month 7	34	55	90	**Month 19**	36	96	230
Month 8	38	63	93	**Month 20**	32	100	201
Month 9	36	68	63	**Month 21**	40	100	122
Month 10	39	65	39	**Month 22**	36	105	84
Month 11	30	72	37	**Month 23**	40	108	74
Month 12	36	69	29	**Month 24**	34	110	62

TABLE 14.3 Moving-Average Forecasts for TV Sets for Lowland Example

	Actual Sales	Forecasted Sales
Month 1	30	—
Month 2	32	—
Month 3	30	—
Month 4	39	30.67
Month 5	33	33.67
Month 6	34	34.00

and

$$f_6 = \frac{30 + 39 + 33}{3} = 34$$

Note that from one period to the next, the moving-average forecast "moves" by replacing the oldest observation in the average by the most recent observation.

Choice of the Span The moving-average forecasting method is determined entirely by the span N, the number of periods used to compute each moving average. It is reasonable to choose N on the basis of the MAD, the mean absolute forecasting error. That is, we find the value of N that makes the MAD as small as possible.

When $N = 3$, we see from Table 14.3 that $e_4 = 39 - 30.67 = 8.33$, $e_5 = 33 - 33.67 = -0.67$, and $e_6 = 34 - 34 = 0$. The MAD is the average of the absolute values of these errors. So when $N = 3$, we have

$$\text{MAD} = \frac{|e_4| + |e_5| + |e_6|}{3} = \frac{8.33 + 0.67 + 0}{3} = 3$$

This means that on average, our forecasts for TV sales are off by 3 TVs per month.

If we apply the moving-average technique to all 24 months of TV sales from Table 14.2, we find the values of the MAD shown in Table 14.4. Based on these results, a three- or four-period moving average appears to yield the best forecasts for TV sales.

Moving Averages on a Spreadsheet It is simple to implement the moving-average method in Excel. The AVERAGE function can be used to generate the moving averages, and then the ABS (absolute value) function can be used to generate the MAD. We illustrate the procedure with the TV data for Lowland. (See the file LOWLAND.XLS.)

1 **Data.** The original data are listed in columns A–D. For convenience, copy the TV sales data in B3:B26 to the range F3:F26, as shown in Figure 14.1.

2 **Forecasts (moving averages).** Enter the first moving average in cell G6 with the formula

=AVERAGE(F3:F5)

This is the average of the sales in the first three months, so it is a forecast of sales in month 4. Therefore, we place it next to sales in month 4. Copy this formula to the range G7:G27. Note that the value in cell G27 is a forecast for month 25, the first month for which we have *not* yet observed sales.

TABLE 14.4 MADs for Moving-Average Forecasts for Lowland Example

N	MAD
2	3.21
3	2.78
4	2.79
5	2.99
6	3.27

FIGURE 14.1 Moving-Average Forecasts (N=3) for TV Sales for Lowland Example

	F	G	H	I
1	Moving Average Calculations for TV Sales			
2	TV Sales	MovAvg	Error	AbsError
3	30			
4	32			
5	30			
6	39	30.67	8.33	8.33
7	33	33.67	-0.67	0.67
8	34	34.00	0.00	0.00
9	34	35.33	-1.33	1.33
10	38	33.67	4.33	4.33
11	36	35.33	0.67	0.67
12	39	36.00	3.00	3.00
13	30	37.67	-7.67	7.67
14	36	35.00	1.00	1.00
15	38	35.00	3.00	3.00
16	30	34.67	-4.67	4.67
17	35	34.67	0.33	0.33
18	30	34.33	-4.33	4.33
19	34	31.67	2.33	2.33
20	40	33.00	7.00	7.00
21	36	34.67	1.33	1.33
22	32	36.67	-4.67	4.67
23	40	36.00	4.00	4.00
24	36	36.00	0.00	0.00
25	40	36.00	4.00	4.00
26	34	38.67	-4.67	4.67
27		36.67	MAD	3.21

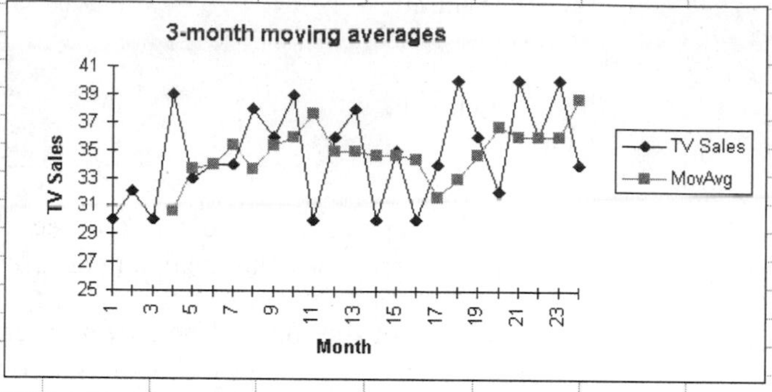

3 **Forecast errors.** Calculate the forecast error in month 4 in cell H6 with the formula

=F6–G6

and then calculate the absolute error in cell I6 with the formula

=ABS(H6)

Then copy these formulas in H6:I6 to the range H7:I26.

4 **MAD.** Calculate the MAD in cell I27 with the formula

=AVERAGE(I6:I26)

5 **Graph.** To see how the actual sales compare to the moving-average forecasts, create a line graph (using the data in columns A , F, and G, and rows 3 through 26). This graph illustrates the averaging, or "smoothing," effect of the forecasts. The forecast series is typically a much smoother series than the original series, although this depends on the span N. (The larger the value of N, the more smoothing tends to occur.)

The steps shown above are typical for forecasting methods in spreadsheets. We start with a time series variable in some column, then use a forecasting method to construct a series of forecasts in an adjacent column. Then we can calculate the differences by subtracting the forecasts from the actual observations, take their absolute values in order to form the MAD, and finally chart the forecasts against the actual observations.

Excel has several Data Analysis tools that can speed up the process. We will look at several of them in this chapter. To illustrate the moving-averages tool, go through the five-step process just described, but in Step 2 use the Tools/Data Analysis menu item. Choose the Moving Average option, which brings up the dialog window shown in Figure 14.2. Fill it out as shown to obtain column G and the graph shown in Figure 14.1 (with some minor variation). (You'll still have to add the errors and absolute errors in columns H and I exactly as in Steps 3 and 4.)

FIGURE 14.2 **Dialog Box for Moving-Average Method**

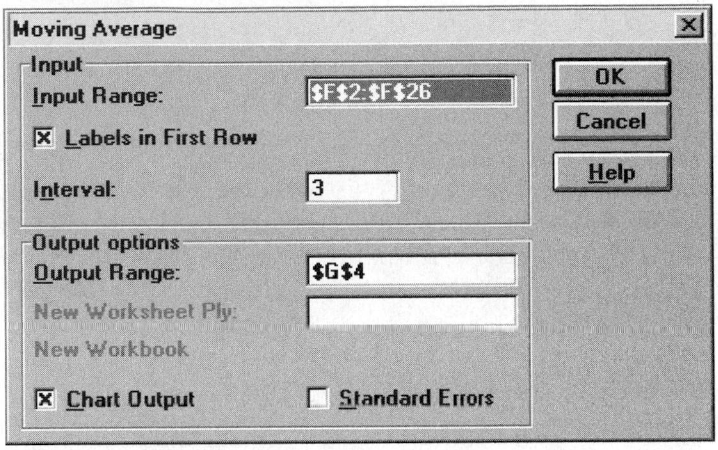

Once you've created the spreadsheet for a particular span N, it is fairly straightforward to modify your work for a different span N. For example, to use $N = 6$, delete the formulas in the range G6:I8 (since the first moving average will now be for month 7 in row 9), change the average in cell G9 to refer to the range F3:F8 (the first six months), and copy this new formula to the range G10:G27. Everything else, including the graph, should change accordingly, as shown in Figure 14.3. ■

FIGURE 14.3 **Moving-Average Forecasts (N=6) for TV Sales for Lowland Example**

	F	G	H	I	J	K	L	M	N	O	P
1	Moving Average Calculations for TV Sales										
2	TV Sales	MovAvg	Error	AbsError							
3	30										
4	32										
5	30										
6	39										
7	33										
8	34										
9	34	33.00	1.00	1.00							
10	38	33.67	4.33	4.33							
11	36	34.67	1.33	1.33							
12	39	35.67	3.33	3.33							
13	30	35.67	-5.67	5.67							
14	36	35.17	0.83	0.83							
15	38	35.50	2.50	2.50							
16	30	36.17	-6.17	6.17							
17	35	34.83	0.17	0.17							
18	30	34.67	-4.67	4.67							
19	34	33.17	0.83	0.83							
20	40	33.83	6.17	6.17							
21	36	34.50	1.50	1.50							
22	32	34.17	-2.17	2.17							
23	40	34.50	5.50	5.50							
24	36	35.33	0.67	0.67							
25	40	36.33	3.67	3.67							
26	34	37.33	-3.33	3.33							
27		36.33	MAD	2.99							

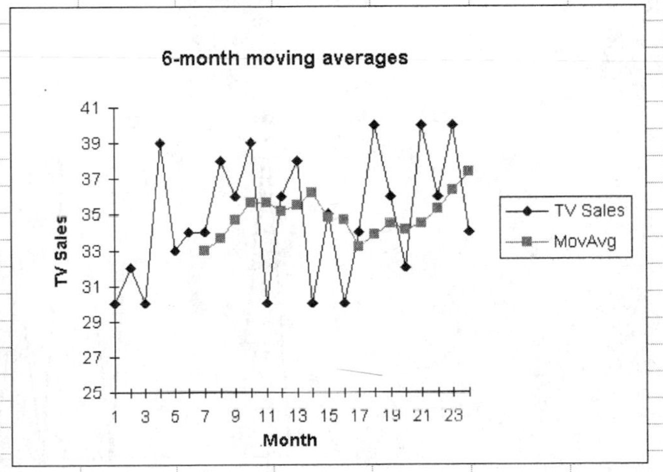

MODELING ISSUES

1 For any forecasting model in which forecast errors are normally distributed, we can use the MAD to estimate s_e, the standard deviation of the forecast errors. The approximate relationship between the MAD and s_e is given by

$$s_e \simeq 1.25 * \text{MAD} \tag{14.1}$$

Assuming that errors are normally distributed, we know that approximately 68% of the forecasts should be within s_e of the actual value and approximately 95% of the forecasts should be within $2s_e$ of the actual value. For our TV sales forecasts, we find that $s_e \simeq 1.25(3.21) = 4.01$ (based on $N = 3$). So we would expect about 14 $(= 0.68 * 21)$ of our 21 forecasts to be off by at most 4.01 TVs and about 20 $(= 0.95 * 21)$ of our 21 forecasts to be off by at most $2(4.01) = 8.02$ TVs. According to the spreadsheet (see column I of Figure 14.1), 13 of our forecasts for TV sales are accurate within 4.01, and 20 are accurate with 8.02. In general, either the MAD or s_e can be used—almost interchangeably—to measure forecasting accuracy.

2 Moving-average forecasts perform well for a time series that fluctuates about a constant "base level." From Figure 14.4, it appears that monthly TV sales fluctuate about a base level of 35. More formally, moving-average forecasts work well if we can represent the series of observations by

$$y_t = b + \varepsilon_t \tag{14.2}$$

where b is the base level for the series and ε_t is the random fluctuation in period t about the base level.

From Figures 14.5 and 14.6, we see that sales of CDs and ACs are *not* well described by Equation 14.2. Figure 14.5 exhibits an upward **trend** in CD sales, so that CD sales do not fluctuate about a base level. Figure 14.6 exhibits **seasonality** in AC sales. That is, the peaks and valleys of the series repeat at regular 12-month intervals. Figure 14.6 also shows that AC sales exhibit an upward trend. In situations where trend and/or seasonality are present, the moving-average method usually yields poor forecasts.

3 In addition to trend and seasonality, a time series may exhibit **cyclic** behavior. For example, auto sales often follow the business cycle of the national economy. Cyclic behavior is much more irregular than a seasonal pattern and is often hard to detect. ■

FIGURE 14.4 **Time Series Graph of TV Sales for Lowland Example**

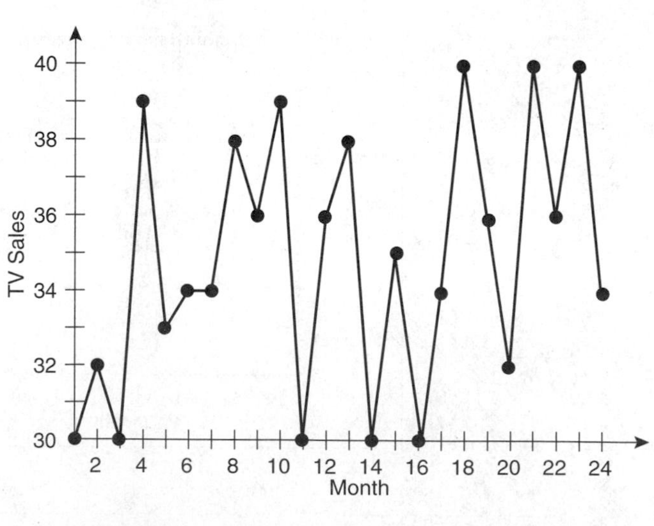

FIGURE 14.5 **Time Series Graph of CD Sales for Lowland Example**

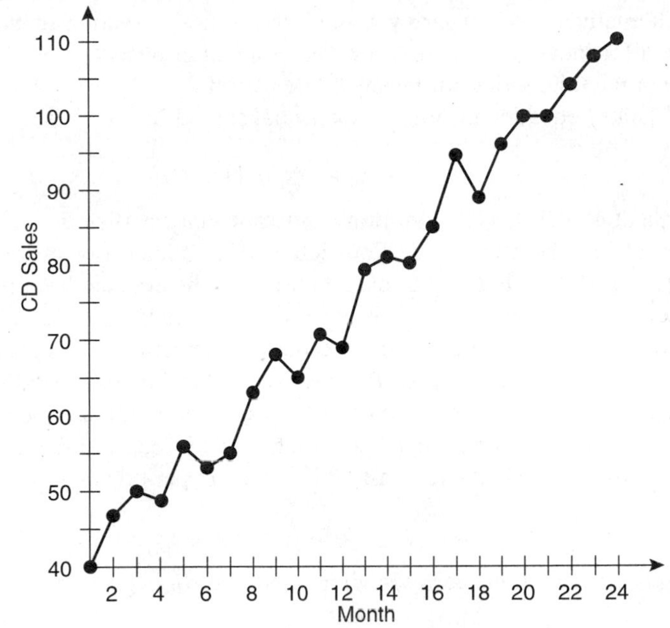

FIGURE 14.6 **Time Series Graph of AC Sales for Lowland Example**

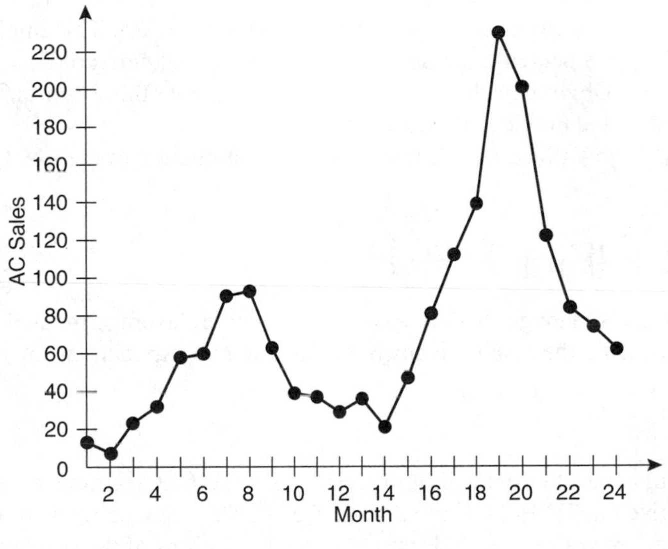

14.4 Simple Exponential Smoothing

If a time series fluctuates about a base level, **simple exponential smoothing** can be used to obtain good forecasts for future values of the series. To describe simple exponential smoothing, let L_t be the "smoothed average" of a time series after observing y_t. You can think of this smoothed average as your best guess of the level of the series after observing y_t. Alternatively, it is where you think the next observation of the series would be if it weren't for inevitable randomness. Therefore, after observing y_t, L_t is the forecast for the value of the time series during any future period.

The key equation in simple exponential smoothing is

$$L_t = \alpha y_t + (1 - \alpha)L_{t-1} \tag{14.3}$$

In Equation 14.3, α is a **smoothing constant** that satisfies $0 < \alpha < 1$. After y_t has been observed in period t, we use Equation 14.3 to update our estimate of the level of the process, from L_{t-1} to L_t. The equation says that the updated level is a weighted average of the new observation and the previous estimate of the level.

To initialize the forecasting procedure, we must have a value for L_0 (before observing y_1). Usually, we let L_0 be the observed value for the period immediately preceding period 1, although various implementations of the method choose L_0 in different ways. Then as soon as L_t is calculated, it is used as the forecast of the next period and all future periods. In particular, the forecast f_t of y_t made in period $t - 1$ is

$$f_t = L_{t-1} \tag{14.4}$$

Using this forecast, the corresponding forecast error is given by

$$e_t = y_t - f_t = y_t - L_{t-1} \tag{14.5}$$

To understand Equation 14.3 better, we use 14.5 to rewrite 14.3 as

$$L_t = L_{t-1} + \alpha(y_t - L_{t-1}) = L_{t-1} + \alpha e_t$$

That is, the new forecast L_t (for period $t + 1$ and beyond) is equal to the previous forecast (L_{t-1}) plus a fraction of the period t forecast error (e_t). This implies that if we "overpredict" y_t, we decrease the next forecast, and if we "underpredict" y_t, we increase the next forecast. Obviously, the larger the value of the smoothing constant α, the more we adjust, based on the previous forecast error.

We now illustrate the method with a continuation of the Lowland sales example.

EXAMPLE 14.2

Lowland's manager has already used the moving-average method to analyze the TV sales data. Would the results be any different if simple exponential smoothing were used?

Solution

We illustrate the method with $\alpha = 0.1$ for the first six months of TV sales. The results are given in Table 14.5. We assume that 32 TVs were sold last month, so we initialize the procedure with $L_0 = 32$. Here are some illustrations of the computations:

$$L_1 = 0.1y_1 + 0.9L_0 = 0.1(30) + 0.9(32) = 31.8$$

$$f_1 = L_0 = 32$$

$$e_1 = y_1 - f_1 = 30 - 32 = -2$$

$$f_2 = L_1 = 31.8$$

$$e_2 = y_2 - f_2 = 32 - 31.8 = 0.2$$

$$L_2 = 0.1y_2 + 0.9L_1 = 0.1(32) + 0.9(31.8) = 31.82$$

TABLE 14.5 **Simple Exponential Smoothing for TV Sales for Lowland Example ($\alpha = 0.1$)**

t	y_t	f_t	L_t	e_t
0	32	—	32.00	—
1	30	32.00	31.80	−2.00
2	32	31.80	31.82	0.20
3	30	31.82	31.64	−1.82
4	39	31.64	32.37	7.36
5	33	32.37	32.44	0.63
6	34	32.44	32.60	1.56

For months 1–6, the MAD of these forecasts is

$$\text{MAD} = \frac{|-2| + |0.2| + |-1.82| + |7.36| + |0.63| + |1.56|}{6} = 2.26$$

Simple Exponential Smoothing on a Spreadsheet The basic Equation 14.3 for simple exponential smoothing makes it easy to implement this method on a spreadsheet. We illustrate the method, again using Lowland TV sales and the spreadsheet file LOWLAND.XLS.

1 **Initialization.** Starting from the original LOWLAND.XLS file, copy the TV sales data in the range B2:B26 to the range F2:F26. To make room for the starting value L_0, insert a blank row below row 2. This will be the "month 0" row. (See Figure 14.7.)

2 **Smoothing constant.** Enter a value for the smoothing constant α such as 0.10 in cell K3.

3 **Smoothed levels.** Enter the value 32 (the assumed month 0 sales value) in cell G3. Then to implement the basic exponential smoothing equation, Equation 14.3, enter the formula

```
=$K$3*F4+(1–$K$3)*G3
```

in cell G4 and copy it to the range G5:G27.

4 **Forecasts.** The forecasts are just the smoothed levels "shifted" by one month. So enter the formula

```
=G3
```

in cell H4 and copy it to the range H5:H28. Notice that cell H28 contains the forecast for a "future" month, month 25.

5 **Forecast errors.** Calculate the forecast errors (actual minus forecast) in column I and the absolute errors and the MAD in column J in the usual way.

6 **Graph.** Create a line graph of the actual observations against the forecasts (using columns A, F, and H). Note that for a relatively small smoothing constant ($\alpha = 0.10$), the forecast series is much smoother than the actual TV sales series. This is the typical effect of using a small smoothing constant—it reacts very little to the random ups and downs of the series.

7 **Effect of smoothing constant.** To see the effect of different smoothing constants, you can either enter different values into cell K3 or you can build a data table for MAD versus α, as shown in Figure 14.8. To create this table, enter a list of α values in column A, enter the formula

```
=J28
```

in cell B46, and select the range A46:B56. Then use the Data/Table menu item with column input cell K3. It shows that a smoothing constant in the range 0.20

FIGURE 14.7 **Simple Exponential Smoothing for TV Sales for Lowland Example**

	A	B	C	D	E	F	G	H	I	J	K
1	Data for Lowland Appliance Company					Simple Exponential Smoothing Method for TV Sales					
2	Month	TV Sales	CD Sales	AC Sales		TV Sales	Smoothed Level (L_t)	Forecast	Error	AbsError	Alpha
3							32.00				0.10
4	1	30	40	13		30	31.80	32.00	-2.00	2.00	
5	2	32	47	7		32	31.82	31.80	0.20	0.20	
6	3	30	50	23		30	31.64	31.82	-1.82	1.82	
7	4	39	49	32		39	32.37	31.64	7.36	7.36	
8	5	33	56	58		33	32.44	32.37	0.63	0.63	
9	6	34	53	60		34	32.59	32.44	1.56	1.56	
10	7	34	55	90		34	32.73	32.59	1.41	1.41	
11	8	38	63	93		38	33.26	32.73	5.27	5.27	
12	9	36	68	63		36	33.53	33.26	2.74	2.74	
13	10	39	65	39		39	34.08	33.53	5.47	5.47	
14	11	30	72	37		30	33.67	34.08	-4.08	4.08	
15	12	36	69	29		36	33.91	33.67	2.33	2.33	
16	13	38	79	36		38	34.32	33.91	4.09	4.09	
17	14	30	82	71		30	33.88	34.32	-4.32	4.32	
18	15	35	80	47		35	34.00	33.88	1.12	1.12	
19	16	30	85	81		30	33.60	34.00	-4.00	4.00	
20	17	34	94	112		34	33.64	33.60	0.40	0.40	
21	18	40	89	139		40	34.27	33.64	6.36	6.36	
22	19	36	96	230		36	34.45	34.27	1.73	1.73	
23	20	32	100	201		32	34.20	34.45	-2.45	2.45	
24	21	40	100	122		40	34.78	34.20	5.80	5.80	
25	22	36	105	84		36	34.90	34.78	1.22	1.22	
26	23	40	108	74		40	35.41	34.90	5.10	5.10	
27	24	34	110	62		34	35.27	35.41	-1.41	1.41	
28								35.27	**MAD**	3.04	

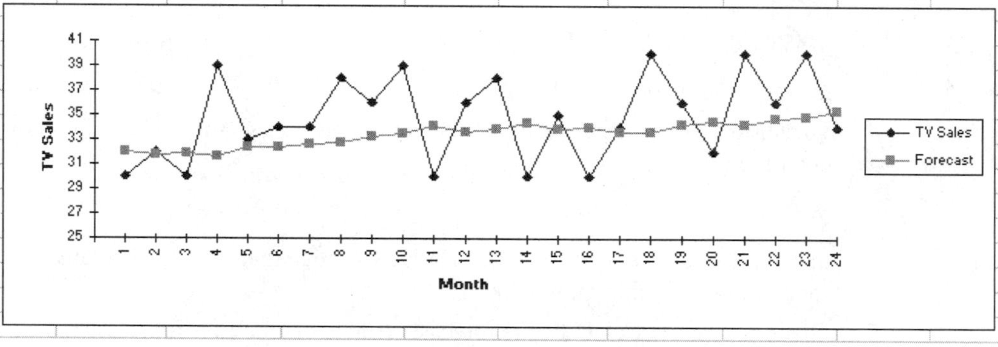

to 0.30 produces the lowest value of the MAD. Also, these values of the MAD are very comparable to the best values of the MAD from the moving-average method. Evidently, both methods work equally well for the Lowland TV sales data.

Excel also has a Exponential Smoothing tool under its Tools/Data Analysis menu item. It essentially calculates the smoothed levels in column G for a given "damping factor" $(1 - \alpha)$. However, it uses a slightly different method for getting started, that is, choosing L_0, so its forecasts will be slightly different. You can experiment with this tool, but we believe it offers no significant advantage over the step-by-step method described above. Besides, this Exponential Smoothing tool applies only to *simple* exponential smoothing, not to Holt's method or Winter's method, the subjects of the next two sections. ■

FIGURE 14.8 Effect of Smoothing Constant on MAD for Lowland Example

	A	B	C
44	Data Table for MAD versus Alpha		
45	Alpha	MAD	
46		3.04	
47	0.05	3.20	
48	0.10	3.04	
49	0.15	2.94	
50	0.20	2.89	
51	0.25	2.88	
52	0.30	2.90	
53	0.35	2.94	
54	0.40	2.98	
55	0.45	3.05	
56	0.50	3.14	

MODELING ISSUES

1 Since $\alpha < 1$, exponential smoothing "smooths out" variations in a time series by not giving total weight to the last observation. Actually, if $\alpha = 2/(N+1)$, it can be shown that simple exponential smoothing (with smoothing parameter α) and an N-period moving-average forecast will yield similar forecasts. For example, $\alpha = 0.33$ is roughly equivalent to a five-period moving average.

2 In practice, α is usually chosen to be 0.10, 0.30, or 0.50. If the value of α that minimizes the MAD exceeds 0.5, then trend, seasonality, or cyclical variation is probably present, and simple exponential smoothing is not a recommended forecasting method. In such cases, better forecasts can probably be obtained with Holt's method (exponential smoothing with trend, discussed in Section 14.5), Winter's method (exponential smoothing with trend and seasonality, discussed in Section 14.6), or some other nonexponential smoothing forecasting method.

3 Even if a time series does not fluctuate about a constant base level, simple exponential smoothing might still provide good forecasts. If $y_t = m_t + \varepsilon_t$ and $m_t = m_{t-1} + \delta_t$, where ε_t and δ_t are independent error terms each having mean 0, then simple exponential smoothing will provide good forecasts. This implies that if the mean demand (m_t) for a product is randomly shifting over time, simple exponential smoothing will still provide good forecasts of product demand.

4 To understand the term *exponential* in exponential smoothing, consider Equation 14.3 for $t-1$:

$$L_{t-1} = \alpha y_{t-1} + (1-\alpha)L_{t-2} \tag{14.6}$$

Substituting Equation 14.6 into 14.3 yields

$$\begin{aligned} L_t &= \alpha y_t + (1-\alpha)[\alpha y_{t-1} + (1-\alpha)L_{t-2}] \\ &= \alpha y_t + \alpha(1-\alpha)y_{t-1} + (1-\alpha)^2 L_{t-2} \end{aligned} \tag{14.7}$$

Similarly, using Equation 14.3 with $t-2$ we get

$$L_{t-2} = \alpha y_{t-2} + (1-\alpha)L_{t-3} \tag{14.8}$$

Substituting Equation 14.8 into 14.7 yields

$$L_t = \alpha y_t + \alpha(1-\alpha)y_{t-1} + \alpha(1-\alpha)^2 y_{t-2} + \alpha(1-\alpha)^3 L_{t-3}$$

Repeating this process yields

$$L_t = \alpha y_t + \alpha(1-\alpha)y_{t-1} + \alpha(1-\alpha)^2 y_{t-2} + \cdots + \alpha(1-\alpha)^k y_{t-k} + \cdots \tag{14.9}$$

Since $\alpha + \alpha(1-\alpha) + \alpha(1-\alpha)^2 + \cdots = 1$, Equation 14.9 shows that if we go back an "infinite" number of periods, the current smoothed average is a weighted average of all past observations. The weight given to the observation from k periods in the past declines exponentially (by a factor of $1 - \alpha$). The larger the value of α , the more weight is given to the most recent observations. For example, for $\alpha = 0.2$, the three most recent observations have 49% of the weight (20%, 16%, and 13%), whereas for $\alpha = 0.5$, the three most recent observations have 88% of the weight (50%, 25%, and 13%). ■

14.5

Holt's Method for Trend

If we believe that a time series exhibits a linear trend (and no seasonality), **Holt's method** often yields good forecasts. After observing y_t in period t, Holt's method yields an estimate of the level L_t and the per-period trend T_t of the series. For example, suppose that $L_{20} = 20$ and $T_{20} = 2$. This means that after observing y_{20}, we believe that the level of the series is 20 and that the level is increasing by two units per period. Thus, five periods from now, we estimate that the level of the series will equal 30.

After observing y_t, Equations 14.10 and 14.11 are used to update the level and trend estimates. Now, α and β are both smoothing constants, each between 0 and 1.

$$L_t = \alpha y_t + (1-\alpha)(L_{t-1} + T_{t-1}) \quad \textbf{(14.10)}$$

$$T_t = \beta(L_t - L_{t-1}) + (1-\beta)T_{t-1} \quad \textbf{(14.11)}$$

To express these equations in words, L_t is a weighted average of the following two quantities:

- y_t, the current observation
- $L_{t-1} + T_{t-1}$, an estimate of the period t level based on previous data

Similarly, T_t is a weighted average of the following two quantities:

- $L_t - L_{t-1}$, the change in the level from period $t-1$ to period t
- T_{t-1}, the previous estimate of the trend

The forecast f_t made of y_t in period $t-1$ is simply the level in period $t-1$ plus the trend in period $t-1$:[1]

$$f_t = L_{t-1} + T_{t-1} \quad \textbf{(14.12)}$$

To initialize Holt's method, we need an initial estimate L_0 of the level and an initial estimate T_0 of the trend. We might set T_0 equal to the average monthly increase in the time series during the previous year, and we might set L_0 equal to last month's observation, although various implementations of Holt's method select L_0 and T_0 in different ways.

We now illustrate Holt's method with the Lowland sales data.

[1] This can be generalized to k-period-ahead forecasts. To forecast k periods from now, add the most current value of level to k times the most recent value of trend.

EXAMPLE 14.3

We have already seen that the Lowland TV sales data is essentially without trend. However, the CD sales data is clearly trending upward. (See Figure 14.5.) The manager wants to use Holt's method to forecast CD sales.

Solution

To get started, we will assume that CD sales during each of the previous 12 months are given by 4, 6, 8, 10, 14, 18, 20, 22, 24, 28, 31, and 34. Then the average of the *changes* for these months is

$$\frac{(6-4)+(8-6)+(10-8)+\cdots+(34-31)}{11}=\frac{34-4}{11}=2.73$$

We might then use $L_0 = 34$ and $T_0 = 2.73$ to get Holt's method started.

By applying Holt's method to the first six months of CD sales, using $\alpha = 0.3$ and $\beta = 0.1$ for illustration, we obtain the results shown in Table 14.6. Here are some examples of the calculations:

$$f_1 = L_0 + T_0 = 34 + 2.73 = 36.73$$

$$e_1 = y_1 - f_1 = 40 - 36.73 = 3.27$$

$$L_1 = 0.3y_1 + 0.7(L_0 + T_0) = 0.3(40) + 0.7(34 + 2.73) = 37.71$$

$$T_1 = 0.1(L_1 - L_0) + 0.9T_0 = 0.1(37.71 - 34) + 0.9(2.73) = 2.83$$

$$f_2 = L_1 + T_1 = 37.71 + 2.83 = 40.54$$

$$e_2 = y_2 - f_2 = 47 - 40.54 = 6.46$$

For the first six months of CD sales, we find that

$$\text{MAD} = \frac{3.27 + 6.46 + 4.5 + 1.01 + 3.17 + 4.00}{6} = 3.74$$

Continuing these calculations, it turns out that the MAD for the entire 24-month period is 2.85.

TABLE 14.6 Holt's Method for CD Sales for Lowland Example

t	y_t	L_t	T_t	f_t	e_t
0	34	34.00	2.73	—	—
1	40	37.71	2.83	36.73	3.27
2	47	42.48	3.02	40.54	6.46
3	50	46.85	3.16	45.50	4.50
4	49	49.70	3.13	50.01	−1.01
5	56	53.78	3.22	52.83	3.17
6	53	55.80	3.10	57.00	−4.00

Holt's Method on a Spreadsheet It is only slightly more difficult to implement Holt's method on a spreadsheet than it is to implement simple exponential smoothing. As indicated in Table 14.6, we need a column for the smoothed levels L_t, a column for the smoothed trends T_t, and the usual columns for the forecasts and errors. We explain the procedure for the Lowland CD Sales series below.

1 **Initialization.** Starting from the original LOWLAND.XLS file, copy the CD sales data in the range C2:C26 to the range F2:F26. To make room for the starting values L_0 and T_0, insert a blank row below row 2. This will be the "month 0" row. Enter the starting values 34 and 2.73 for L_0 and T_0 in cells G3 and H3. See Figure 14.9.

2 **Smoothing constants.** Enter values for α and β, such as 0.30 and 0.10, in cells L3 and L5.

3 **Levels.** To implement Equation 14.10, enter the formula

```
=$L$3*F4+(1-$L$3)*(G3+H3)
```

in cell G4 and copy it to the range G5:G27.

4 **Trends.** To implement Equation 14.11, enter the formula

```
=$L$5*(G4-G3)+(1-$L$5)*H3
```

in cell H4 and copy it to the range H5:H27.

5 **Forecasts.** Enter the forecast for month 1 in cell I4 with the formula

```
=G3+H3
```

and copy it to the range I5:I28. Notice that the forecast in cell I28 is the forecast of month 25 made in month 24. To make a forecast of month 26 in month 24, enter the formula

```
=G27+2*H27
```

FIGURE 14.9 Holt's Method for CD Sales for Lowland Example

	F	G	H	I	J	K	L
1	Holt's Exponential Smoothing Method for CD Sales						
2	CD Sales	Smoothed Level (L_t)	Smoothed Trend (T_t)	Forecast	Error	AbsError	Alpha
3		34.00	2.73				0.30
4	40	37.71	2.83	36.73	3.27	3.27	Beta
5	47	42.48	3.02	40.54	6.46	6.46	0.10
6	50	46.85	3.16	45.50	4.50	4.50	
7	49	49.70	3.13	50.01	-1.01	1.01	
8	56	53.78	3.22	52.83	3.17	3.17	
9	53	55.80	3.10	57.00	-4.00	4.00	
10	55	57.73	2.98	58.90	-3.90	3.90	
11	63	61.40	3.05	60.72	2.28	2.28	
12	68	65.52	3.16	64.46	3.54	3.54	
13	65	67.57	3.05	68.68	-3.68	3.68	
14	72	71.04	3.09	70.62	1.38	1.38	
15	69	72.59	2.94	74.13	-5.13	5.13	
16	79	76.57	3.04	75.53	3.47	3.47	
17	82	80.33	3.11	79.61	2.39	2.39	
18	80	82.41	3.01	83.44	-3.44	3.44	
19	85	85.29	3.00	85.42	-0.42	0.42	
20	94	90.00	3.17	88.29	5.71	5.71	
21	89	91.92	3.04	93.17	-4.17	4.17	
22	96	95.27	3.07	94.96	1.04	1.04	
23	100	98.84	3.12	98.35	1.65	1.65	
24	100	101.38	3.06	101.97	-1.97	1.97	
25	105	104.61	3.08	104.44	0.56	0.56	
26	108	107.78	3.09	107.69	0.31	0.31	
27	110	110.61	3.06	110.87	-0.87	0.87	
28				113.68	MAD	2.85	
29				116.74			

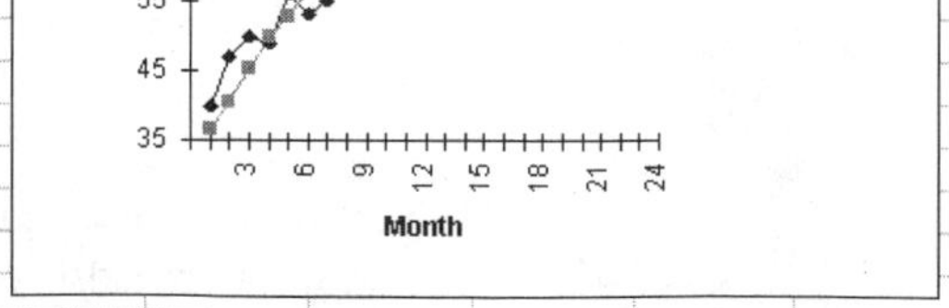

in cell I29. We could make forecasts for months 27, 28, and so on in a similar way, by adding larger multiples of the latest trend estimate (which is in cell H27).

6 **Forecast errors.** Calculate the errors, the absolute errors, and the MAD in columns J and K in the usual way.

7 **Graph.** Create a line graph of the forecasts against the actual CD sales (using columns A, F, and I). It shows that Holt's method (with these particular smoothing constants) picks up the trend quite well.

8 **Effect of smoothing constants.** To see how sensitive the MAD is to α and β, create a two-way data table in the range A49:K59. (See Figure 14.10.) To do this, enter a list of α values in column A, a list of β values in row 49, and enter the formula

=K28

in cell A49. Then use the Data/Table menu item with L5 as the Row input cell and L3 as the column input cell. This data table indicates that the best values of α and β are around .10 and .35, respectively. More importantly, however, the table shows that the value of the MAD is quite insensitive to the exact values of α and β for a fairly large range. ■

FIGURE 14.10 **Data Table for MAD Versus α and β for Lowland Example**

	A	B	C	D	E	F	G	H	I	J	K
48	Data Table for MAD versus Alpha (along side) and Beta (along top)										
49	2.85	0.05	0.10	0.15	0.20	0.25	0.30	0.35	0.40	0.45	0.50
50	0.05	4.10	3.50	3.13	2.97	2.90	2.92	2.94	2.97	2.98	2.98
51	0.10	3.07	2.86	2.80	2.80	2.78	2.74	2.70	2.70	2.73	2.75
52	0.15	2.88	2.79	2.75	2.72	2.71	2.71	2.72	2.73	2.75	2.77
53	0.20	2.82	2.77	2.74	2.73	2.75	2.76	2.78	2.79	2.81	2.84
54	0.25	2.81	2.79	2.79	2.80	2.82	2.84	2.85	2.88	2.90	2.93
55	0.30	2.86	2.85	2.86	2.87	2.89	2.91	2.93	2.95	2.97	2.99
56	0.35	2.91	2.90	2.92	2.94	2.96	2.98	3.01	3.03	3.06	3.09
57	0.40	2.95	2.96	2.98	3.00	3.03	3.05	3.08	3.11	3.14	3.17
58	0.45	3.01	3.02	3.04	3.06	3.09	3.12	3.15	3.18	3.21	3.24
59	0.50	3.07	3.07	3.10	3.13	3.16	3.19	3.22	3.25	3.28	3.31

MODELING ISSUES

1 If the values of α and β that minimize the MAD are not both less than 0.5, then seasonality or cyclical behavior is probably present, and another forecasting method should be used.

2 Holt's method tends to provide good forecasts for a series with a linear trend. Such a series can be modeled as $y_t = a + bt + \varepsilon_t$, where

$a =$ Base level at beginning of period 0

$b =$ Per-period trend

$\varepsilon_t =$ Error term for period t

3 A multiplicative version of Holt's method (see Problem 14) can be used to generate good forecasts for a series of the form $y_t = ab^t\varepsilon_t$. Here, the value of b represents the *percentage* growth in the level of the series during each period. For example, $b = 1.1$ implies that the level of the series increases by 10% per period. In this model, ε_t is a random error factor with a mean of 1. ■

14.6

Winter's Method for Seasonality

The appropriately named Winter's method is used to forecast time series when seasonality and possibly trend are present. As we saw in Figure 14.6, for example, Lowland AC sales exhibit an upward trend and seasonality, so Winter's method is a logical candidate for forecasting these sales.

To describe Winter's method, we require two quantities. First, we need c, the number of periods in the length of the seasonal pattern ($c = 4$ for quarterly data and $c = 12$ for monthly data). Second, for each period t, we need s_t, an estimate of the **seasonal factor** for month t, obtained after observing y_t. To illustrate a seasonal factor, suppose that month 7 is July and $s_7 = 2$. Then July AC sales tend to be twice as large as sales during an average month (all other things being equal). Similarly, if month 12 is December and $s_{12} = 0.4$, then December AC sales tend to be 40% as large as sales during an average month.

An important concept with seasonal data is **deseasonalizing**, that is, removing the seasonality. Again, assume that the seasonal factor for July in month 7 is $s_7 = 2$ and the seasonal factor for December in month 12 is $s_{12} = 0.4$. Also, assume the observations in months 7 and 12 are $y_7 = 200$ and $y_{12} = 45$. Then we find the deseasonalized values by dividing the observations by their seasonal factors. The deseasonalized value for July is $y_7/s_7 = 200/2 = 100$, whereas the deseasonalized value for December is $y_{12}/s_{12} = 45/0.4 = 112.5$. This makes intuitive sense. July observations tend to be twice as large as "typical" observations, so to put them on the same scale as typical observations, we divide them by 2. Similarly, we divide December observations by a number less than 1 to make them as large as typical observations.

In what follows, L_t and T_t have the same meaning as they did in Holt's method. Each period, L_t, T_t, and s_t are updated (in that order) by using Equations 14.13–14.15. We now have three smoothing constants, α, β, and γ, each of which is between 0 and 1.

$$L_t = \alpha \frac{y_t}{s_{t-c}} + (1-\alpha)(L_{t-1} + T_{t-1}) \quad \textbf{(14.13)}$$

$$T_t = \beta(L_t - L_{t-1}) + (1-\beta)T_{t-1} \quad \textbf{(14.14)}$$

$$s_t = \gamma \frac{y_t}{L_t} + (1-\gamma)s_{t-c} \quad \textbf{(14.15)}$$

Equation 14.13 updates the estimate of the series level by taking a weighted average of the following two quantities:

- $L_{t-1} + T_{t-1}$, the estimate of the current level (before observing y_t)
- y_t/s_{t-c}, the current observation after deseasonalizing by the most recent seasonal factor for that month (the one from a year ago)

Equation 14.14 is identical to the T_t Equation 14.11 used to update trend in Holt's method. Finally, Equation 14.15 updates the estimate of month t's seasonal factor by taking a weighted average of the following two quantities:

- s_{t-c}, the most recent estimate of month t's seasonal factor
- y_t/L_t, an estimate of month t's seasonal factor, obtained from the current month's observation. (*Note*: L_t is essentially a deseasonalized value. Therefore, dividing y_t by L_t yields an estimate of a seasonal factor.)

The forecast f_t of y_t made in period $t-1$ is

$$f_t = (L_{t-1} + T_{t-1})s_{t-c}$$

That is, to forecast the value of y_t, we multiply the estimate of the month t level, $L_{t-1} + T_{t-1}$, by the most recent estimate of month t's seasonal factor, s_{t-c}. For example, if month t corresponds to May 1997, we would use the seasonal factor from May 1996 (since no new seasonal factor for May 1997 is available in April 1997, when the forecast is being made).[2]

We now illustrate how Winter's method can be used to forecast Lowland AC sales.

EXAMPLE 14.4

Since Lowland AC sales exhibit obvious seasonality—low in the cold months, high in the hot months—the manager wants to use Winter's method to forecast AC sales.

Solution

To obtain good forecasts with Winter's method, we must obtain good initial estimates of the level, the trend, and all seasonal factors. Here we'll illustrate the procedure when the data are monthly and month 1 corresponds to January. Let

$$L_0 = \text{Estimate of base level at beginning of month 1}$$

$$T_0 = \text{Estimate of trend at beginning of month 1}$$

$$s_{-11} = \text{Estimate of January seasonal factor at beginning of month 1}$$

$$s_{-10} = \text{Estimate of February seasonal factor at beginning of month 1}$$

$$\vdots$$

$$s_0 = \text{Estimate of December seasonal factor at beginning of month 1}$$

Note that the subscripts -11 through 0 correspond to the 12 months prior to month 1.

A variety of methods are available to estimate these initial parameters. We choose a simple method that requires two years of previous data. For ease of notation, assume that these previous two years were 1995 and 1996, and suppose that monthly sales for 1995 and 1996 were

1995: 4, 3, 10, 14, 25, 26, 38, 40, 28, 17, 16, 13

1996: 9, 6, 18, 27, 48, 50, 75, 77, 52, 33, 31, 24

Total sales during 1995 = 234

Total sales during 1996 = 450

Then we estimate T_0 by

$$T_0 = \frac{(\text{Avg sales during 1996}) - (\text{Avg sales during 1995})}{12}$$

or

$$T_0 = \frac{\frac{450}{12} - \frac{234}{12}}{12} = 1.5$$

To estimate L_0, we first determine the average monthly demand during 1996, that is, $450/12 = 37.5$. This estimates the sales level at the middle of 1996 (month "6.5" of 1996). To bring this estimate to the end of month 12 of 1995, we add $(12 - 6.5)T_0 = 5.5T_0$ to the monthly average. Thus, our estimate of L_0 is $L_0 = 37.5 + 5.5(1.5) = 45.75$.

[2] Again, k-period-ahead forecasts can be made. We add the most recent level to k times the most recent trend. Then we multiply this sum by the relevant seasonal factor for the month being forecasted.

To estimate the seasonal factor for a given month (say, s_{-11} for January), we estimate the January seasonal factors for 1995 and 1996 and average them. In 1995, the average monthly demand was $234/12 = 19.5$, and in January of 1996, four air conditioners were sold. Therefore,

$$\text{1995 estimate of January seasonality} = \frac{4}{19.5} = 0.205$$

Similarly,

$$\text{1996 estimate of January seasonality} = \frac{9}{37.5} = 0.240$$

Therefore, the estimate of s_{-11} is

$$s_{-11} = \frac{0.205 + 0.24}{2} = 0.22$$

In a similar fashion, s_{-10} through s_0 are found to be 0.16 (February), 0.50 (March), 0.72 (April), 1.28 (May), 1.33 (June), 1.97 (July), 2.05 (August), 1.41 (September), 0.88 (October), 0.82 (November), and 0.65 (December). As a check, initial seasonal factor estimates should average to 1.

With these initial values, we now illustrate some of the calculations in Equations 14.13–14.15. Specifically, for month 1 we illustrate the computations by computing L_1, T_1, and s_1 using $\alpha = .5$, $\beta = .4$, and $\gamma = .6$.

$$L_1 = 0.5\left(\frac{y_1}{s_{-11}}\right) + 0.5(L_0 + T_0) = 0.5\left(\frac{13}{0.22}\right) + 0.5(45.75 + 1.5) = 53.17$$

$$T_1 = 0.4(L_1 - L_0) + 0.6T_0 = 0.4(53.17 - 45.75) + 0.6(1.5) = 3.87$$

$$s_1 = 0.6\left(\frac{y_1}{L_1}\right) + 0.4s_{-11} = .6\left(\frac{13}{53.17}\right) + .4(.22) = .23$$

Given these values, the forecast for month 2 is

$$f_2 = (L_1 + T_1)s_{-10} = (53.17 + 3.87)(.16) = 9.13$$

Then when February's AC sales figure is observed to be 7, the forecast error is

$$e_2 = y_2 - f_2 = 7 - 9.13 = -2.13$$

Similar calculations lead to the values given in Table 14.7.

Since these calculations are at best tedious, a spreadsheet model is obviously preferred, as we discuss next.

TABLE 14.7 Winter's Method for AC Sales for Lowland Example

t	y_t	L_t	T_t	s_t	f_t	e_t
	⋮			⋮		
0	24	45.75	1.50	0.65	—	—
1	13	53.17	3.87	0.23	10.40	2.60
2	7	50.39	1.21	0.15	9.13	−2.13
3	23	48.80	0.09	0.48	25.80	−2.80
4	32	46.67	−0.80	0.70	35.20	−3.20
5	58	45.59	−0.91	1.28	58.71	−0.71
6	60	44.90	−0.82	1.33	59.42	0.58
7	90	44.88	−0.50	1.99	86.82	3.18
8	93	44.87	−0.30	2.06	90.97	2.03
9	63	44.62	−0.28	1.41	62.84	0.16
10	39	44.33	−0.29	0.88	39.02	−0.02
11	37	44.58	−0.07	0.83	36.12	0.88
12	29	44.56	−0.05	0.65	28.93	0.07

Winter's Method on a Spreadsheet The spreadsheet implementation of Winter's method is much like Holt's method, except that we need an extra column for the seasonal factors. Also, we need a whole year's worth of extra rows at the top to hold the initial seasonal factors, s_{-11} through s_0. The following steps outline the procedure for Lowland's AC sales.

1 **Initialization.** Starting from the original LOWLAND.XLS file, copy the AC sales values in the range D2:D26 to the range F2:F26. To make room for the starting values L_0, T_0, and the initial seasonal factors, insert 12 blank rows below row 2. These rows will refer to months "−11" through "0." Then enter the values for L_0, T_0, and s_{-11} through s_0 in cells G14, H14, and the range I3:I14. (See Figure 14.11.)

2 **Smoothing constants.** Enter values of the smoothing constants α, β, and γ, such as 0.30, 0.40, and 0.60, in cells M15, M17, and M19. (The smoothing constants shown in Figure 14.11 are "optimal," as we will explain shortly.)

3 **Levels.** To implement Equation 14.13, enter the formula

=$M$15*F15/I3+(1−$M$15)*(G14+H14)

in cell G15 and copy it to the range G16:G38.

FIGURE 14.11 **Winter's Method for AC Sales for Lowland Example**

	F	G	H	I	J	K	L	M
1	Winter's Exponential Smoothing Method for AC Sales							
2	AC Sales	Smoothed Level (L_t)	Smoothed Trend (T_t)	Smoothed Seasonal Factors (s_t)	Forecast	Error	AbsError	
3				0.22				
4				0.16				
5				0.50				
6				0.72				
7				1.28				
8				1.33				
9				1.97				
10				2.05				
11				1.41				
12				0.88				
13				0.82				
14		45.75	1.50	0.65				Alpha
15	13	54.94	1.99	0.22	10.40	2.61	2.61	0.65
16	7	48.37	1.45	0.16	9.11	-2.11	2.11	Beta
17	23	47.34	1.29	0.50	24.91	-1.91	1.91	0.06
18	32	45.91	1.12	0.72	35.01	-3.01	3.01	Gamma
19	58	45.91	1.05	1.28	60.20	-2.20	2.20	0.00
20	60	45.76	0.97	1.33	62.46	-2.46	2.46	
21	90	46.05	0.93	1.97	92.06	-2.06	2.06	
22	93	45.93	0.86	2.05	96.31	-3.31	3.31	
23	63	45.42	0.77	1.41	65.98	-2.98	2.98	
24	39	44.98	0.70	0.88	40.65	-1.65	1.65	
25	37	45.32	0.67	0.82	37.45	-0.45	0.45	
26	29	45.10	0.62	0.65	29.89	-0.89	0.89	
27	36	122.28	5.47	0.22	10.06	25.94	25.94	
28	21	130.02	5.61	0.16	20.44	0.56	0.56	
29	47	108.60	3.90	0.50	67.81	-20.81	20.81	
30	81	112.50	3.90	0.72	81.00	0.00	0.00	
31	112	97.64	2.71	1.28	148.99	-36.99	36.99	
32	139	103.05	2.88	1.33	133.46	5.54	5.54	
33	230	112.96	3.33	1.97	208.69	21.31	21.31	
34	201	104.44	2.58	2.05	238.38	-37.38	37.38	
35	122	93.71	1.73	1.41	150.90	-28.90	28.90	
36	84	95.45	1.73	0.88	83.99	0.01	0.01	
37	74	92.68	1.45	0.82	79.69	-5.69	5.69	
38	62	94.94	1.50	0.65	61.18	0.82	0.82	
39					21.22	MAD	8.73	
40					15.67			

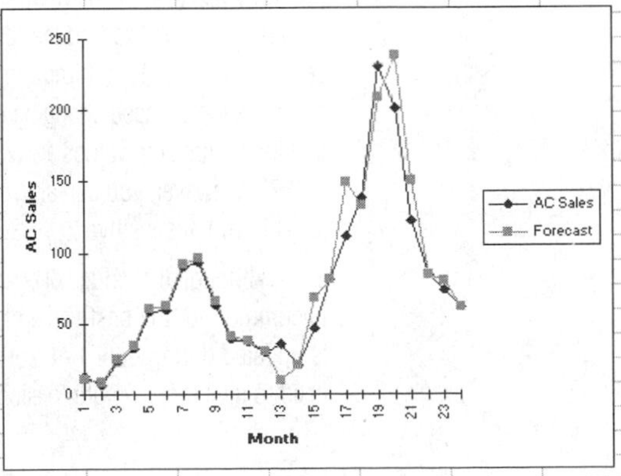

4 **Trends.** To implement Equation 14.14, enter the formula

=$M$17*(G15–G14)*(1–$M$17)*H14

in cell H15 and copy it to the range H16:H38.

5 **Seasonal factors.** To implement Equation 14.15, enter the formula

=$M$19*F15/G15+(1–$M$19)*I3

in cell I15 and copy it to the rangc I16:I38.

6 **Forecasts.** The one-month ahead forecasts can now be calculated in column J. In cell J15, enter the formula

=(G14+H14)*I3

and copy it to the range J16:J39. Note that the forecast in cell J39 is for month 25, made in month 24. We can also find a forecast for month 26, made in month 24, by entering the formula

=(G38+2*H38)*I28

in cell J40. These forecasts are really composed of two parts. The part inside parentheses is the forecast of the deseasonalized value: the level plus a multiple of the trend. Then this deseasonalized forecast is multiplied by the appropriate seasonal factor to "reseasonalize" the forecast.

7 **Forecast errors.** Calculate the errors, the absolute errors, and the MAD in the usual way in columns K and L.

8 **Graph.** Use columns A, F, and J (along with the labels in row 2) to draw a line graph of the forecasts against the actual AC sales. Although the agreement is far from perfect, the seasonality is captured quite well. The agreement between predicted and actual sales is least good during months 15 and 17. During these months the forecasts are much too high. Perhaps new salespeople were hired during these two months, causing sales to be lower than anticipated. ■

MODELING ISSUES

1 We did not use a data table in Figure 14.11 to show the sensitivity of the MAD to the smoothing constants, primarily because there are now three smoothing constants. However, for the sake of variety, we can use the Solver (in a new context!) to find the "best" smoothing constants. All we need to do is invoke the Solver with the following settings. The cell to minimize is L39 (MAD), the changing cells are M15, M17, and M19, and the only constraints are that each of these changing cells must be greater than or equal to 0 and less than or equal to 1. You can check that the minimizing values are $\alpha = 0.65$, $\beta = 0.06$, and $\gamma = 0.00$, with a corresponding value of the MAD equal to 8.73. However, you can also check that when α and β are close to these values (0.65 and 0.06), the value of the MAD is very insensitive to γ. So we would suggest using a positive value of γ, such as 0.30.

2 Although the values of α and β that minimize the MAD should not exceed 0.5 (as in the Holt method), it is not uncommon for the best value of γ to exceed 0.5. This is because for monthly data, each monthly seasonal factor is updated during only $1/12$ of all periods. Since the seasonal factors are updated so infrequently, we sometimes need to give more weight to each observation, so that $\gamma > 0.5$ is not out of the question. ■

PROBLEMS

Skill-Building Problems

1 Suppose that simple exponential smoothing (with $\alpha = 0.2$) is used to forecast monthly beer sales at Gordon's liquor store. After observing April's demand, the predicted demand for May is 4000 cans of beer.

a At the beginning of May, what is the prediction for July's beer sales?

b Actual demand during May and June is as follows: May, 4500 cans of beer; June, 3500 cans of beer. After observing June's demand, what is the forecast for July's demand?

c The demand during May and June averages out to $(4500 + 3500)/2 = 4000$ cans per month. This is the same as the forecast for monthly sales before we observed the May and June data. Yet after observing the May and June demands for beer, our forecast for July demand has decreased from what it was at the end of April. Why?

2 Now suppose that we are forecasting quarterly sales for soda at Gordon's liquor store using Winter's method. We are given the following information:

$$\text{Seasonal factors: fall} = 0.8,\ \text{spring} = 1.2,\ \text{winter} = 0.7,\ \text{summer} = 1.3$$

$$\text{Current level estimate} = 400 \text{ cases per quarter}$$

$$\text{Current trend estimate} = 40 \text{ cases per quarter}$$

$$\alpha = 0.2,\ \beta = 0.3,\ \gamma = 0.5$$

Summer quarter sales = 650 cases.

a Use this information to update the estimates of level, trend, and seasonality.

b After observing the summer demand, forecast demand for the fall quarter and the winter quarter.

3 Suppose that we use Winter's method and monthly data to forecast the GDP. (All numbers are in billions of dollars.) At the end of January 1997, $L_t = 600$ and $T_t = 5$. We are given the following seasonalities: January, 0.80; February, 0.85; December, 1.2. During February 1997, the GDP is 630. At the end of February, what is the forecast for the December 1997 GDP? Use $\alpha = \beta = \gamma = 0.5$.

4 Hiland Appliance wants to use Holt's method to forecast its monthly VCR sales. At the end of October 1997, $L_t = 200$ and $T_t = 10$. During November 1997, 230 VCRs are sold. At the end of November, MAD = 25. Hiland is 95% sure that VCR sales for December 1997 will be between ______ and ______. Use $\alpha = \beta = 0.5$. (Fill in the blanks by referring to the approximate relationship between the MAD and the standard deviation of the forecast errors.)

5 Hick's Drugs is using simple exponential smoothing to predict monthly electric shaver sales. At the end of October 1997, Hick's forecast for December 1997 sales was 40. In November 50 shavers were sold, and during December 45 shavers were sold. At the end of December 1997, what is Hick's forecast for the total number of shavers that will be sold during March and April of 1998? Use $\alpha = 0.50$.

6 Bloomington Ford is using simple exponential smoothing to predict monthly auto sales. The company believes that sales do not exhibit trend or seasonality, so simple exponential smoothing has yielded satisfactory forecasts in the past. Each March, however, Bloomington Ford has observed that sales tend to exceed the simple exponential smoothing forecast (made in February) by 200. Suppose that at the end of February 1997, $L_t = 600$. During March 1997, 900 cars are sold.

a Using $\alpha = 0.3$, determine (at the end of March 1997) a forecast for April 1997 car sales.

b Assume that at the end of March, MAD = 60. Bloomington Ford can be 95% sure that April sales will be between ______ and ______.

7 The University Credit Union is open Monday through Saturday. Winter's method is being used (with $\alpha = \beta = \gamma = 0.5$) to predict the number of customers entering the bank each day. After incorporating the arrivals of 16 October 1996, $L_t = 200$, $T_t = 1$, and the "seasonalities" are as follows: Monday, 0.90; Tuesday, 0.70; Wednesday, 0.80; Thursday, 1.1; Friday, 1.2; Saturday, 1.3. For example, this means that on a typical Monday, the number of customers is 90% of the number of customers entering the bank on an average day. On Tuesday, 17 October 1996,

182 customers enter the bank. At the close of business on 17 October 1996, make a forecast for the number of customers who will enter the bank on 25 October 1996.

8 TOD Chevy is using Holt's method to forecast weekly car sales. Currently, the level is estimated to be 50 cars per week, and the trend is estimated to be 6 cars per week. During the current week, 30 cars are sold. After observing the current week's sales, forecast the number of cars three weeks from now. Use $\alpha = \beta = 0.3$.

9 Last National Bank is using Winter's method (with $\alpha = 0.2$, $\beta = 0.1$, and $\gamma = 0.5$) to forecast the number of customers served each day. The bank is open Monday through Friday. At present, the following "seasonalities" have been estimated: Monday, 0.80; Tuesday, 0.90; Wednesday, 0.95; Thursday, 1.10; Friday, 1.25. A seasonality of 0.80 for Monday means that on a Monday, the number of customers served by the bank tends to be 80% of average. Currently, the level is estimated to be 20 customers, and the trend is estimated to equal 1 customer. After observing that 30 customers are served by the bank on Monday, forecast the number of customers who will be served by the bank on Wednesday.

10 We have been assigned to forecast the number of aircraft engines ordered each month by Commins Engine Company. At the end of February, the forecast is that 100 engines will be ordered during April. During March, 120 engines are ordered.

a Using $\alpha = 0.3$, determine a forecast (at the end of March) for the number of orders placed during April. Answer the same question for May. Use simple exponential smoothing.

b Suppose at the end of March, MAD = 16. At the end of March, Commins can be 68% sure that April orders will be between ______ and ______.

11 Suppose that Winter's method is used to forecast quarterly U.S. retail sales (in billions of dollars). At the end of the first quarter of 1997, $L_t = 300$, $T_t = 30$, and the seasonal indexes are as follows: quarter 1, 0.90; quarter 2, 0.95; quarter 3, 0.95; quarter 4, 1.20. During the second quarter of 1997, retail sales are $360 billion. Assume $\alpha = 0.2$, $\beta = 0.4$, and $\gamma = 0.5$.

a At the end of the second quarter of 1997, develop a forecast for retail sales during the fourth quarter of 1997.

b At the end of the second quarter of 1997, develop a forecast for the second quarter of 1998.

12 Simple exponential smoothing with $\alpha = 0.3$ is being used to forecast sales of radios at Lowland Appliance. Forecasts are made on a monthly basis. After observing August radio sales, the forecast for September is 100 radios.

a During September, 120 radios are sold. After observing September sales, what is the forecast for October radio sales? For November radio sales?

b It turns out that June sales were recorded as 10 radios. Actually, however, 100 radios were sold in June. After correcting for this error, develop a forecast for October radio sales.

Skill-Extending Problems

13 In our discussion of Winter's method, a monthly seasonality of 0.80 for January, say, means that during January, AC sales are expected to be 80% of the sales during an average month. An alternative approach to modeling seasonality (called an **additive model**) is to let the seasonality factor for each month represent how far above average AC sales will be during the current month. For instance, if $s_{Jan} = -50$, then AC sales during January are expected to be 50 less than AC sales during an average month. (This is 50 ACs, not 50%.) If $s_{July} = 90$, then AC sales during July are expected to be 90 more than AC sales during an average month. Let

s_t = Seasonality for month t after observing month t demand

L_t = Estimate of level after observing month t demand

T_t = Estimate of trend after observing month t demand

Then the Winter's method equations given in the text should be modified as follows:

$$L_t = \alpha * (I) + (1 - \alpha) * (L_{t-1} + T_{t-1})$$

$$T_t = \beta * (L_t - L_{t-1}) + (1 - \beta) * T_{t-1}$$

$$s_t = \gamma * (II) + (1 - \gamma) * s_{t-12}$$

a Determine (I) and (II).

b Suppose that month 13 is January, $L_{12} = 30$, $T_{12} = -3$, $s_1 = -50$, and $s_2 = -20$. Let $\alpha = \gamma = \beta = 0.5$. Suppose 12 ACs are sold during month 13. At the end of month 13, what is the prediction for AC sales during month 14?

14 Holt's method assumes an additive trend. For example, a trend of 5 means that the level will increase by 5 units per period. Suppose there is actually a **multiplicative trend**. Thus, if the current estimate of the level is 50 and the current estimate of the trend is 1.2, we would predict demand to increase by 20% per period. So we would forecast the next period's demand to be 50(1.2) and forecast the demand two periods in the future to be $50(1.2)^2$. If we want to use a multiplicative trend in Holt's method, we should use the following equations:

$$L_t = \alpha * y_t + (1 - \alpha) * (I)$$
$$T_t = \beta * (II) + (1 - \beta) * T_{t-1}$$

a Determine (*I*) and (*II*).

b Suppose we are working with monthly data and month 12 is December, month 13 January, and so on. Also suppose that $L_{12} = 100$ and $T_{12} = 1.2$. Suppose $y_{13} = 200$. At the end of month 13, what is the prediction for y_{15}? Assume $\alpha = \beta = 0.5$.

15 Winter's method assumes a multiplicative seasonality but an additive trend. For example, a trend of 5 means that the level will increase by 5 units per period. Suppose that there is actually a *multiplicative* trend. Then (ignoring seasonality) if the current estimate of the level is 50 and the current estimate of the trend is 1.2, we would predict demand to increase by 20% per period. Ignoring seasonality, we would thus forecast the next period's demand to be 50(1.2) and forecast the demand two periods in the future to be $50(1.2)^2$. If we want to use a multiplicative trend in Winter's method, we should use the following equations:

$$L_t = \alpha * \frac{y_t}{s_{t-c}} + (1 - \alpha) * (I)$$
$$T_t = \beta * (II) + (1 - \beta) * T_{t-1}$$
$$s_t = \gamma * \frac{y_t}{L_t} + (1 - \gamma) * s_{t-12}$$

a Determine (*I*) and (*II*).

b Suppose that we are working with monthly data and month 12 is December, month 13 January, and so on. Also suppose that $L_{12} = 100$, $T_{12} = 1.2$, $s_1 = 0.90$, $s_2 = 0.70$, and $s_3 = 0.95$. Suppose $y_{13} = 200$. At the end of month 13, what is the prediction for y_{15}? Assume $\alpha = \beta = \gamma = 0.5$.

16 A version of simple exponential smoothing can be used to predict the outcome of sporting events. To illustrate, consider pro football. We first assume that all games are played on a neutral field. Before each day of play, we assume that each team has a rating. For example, if the rating for the Bears is +10 and the rating for the Bengals is +6, we would predict the Bears to beat the Bengals by 10 − 6 = 4 points. Suppose that the Bears play the Bengals and win by 20 points. For this game, we "underpredicted" the Bears's performance by 20 − 4 = 16 points. The best α for pro football is $\alpha = 0.10$. After the game, we therefore increase the Bears's rating by 16(0.1) = 1.6 and decrease the Bengals's rating by 1.6 points. In a rematch, the Bears would be favored by (10 + 1.6) − (6 − 1.6) = 7.2 points.

a How does this approach relate to the equation $L_t = L_{t-1} + \alpha e_t$?

b Suppose that the home field advantage in pro football is 3 points; that is, home teams tend to outscore visiting teams by an average of 3 points a game. How could the home field advantage be incorporated into this system?

c How could we determine the best α for pro football?

d How might we determine ratings for each team at the beginning of the season?

e Suppose we tried to apply the above method to predict pro football (16-game schedule), college football (11-game schedule), college basketball (30-game schedule), and pro basketball (82-game schedule). Which sport would have the smallest optimal α? Which sport would have the largest optimal α?

f Why would this approach probably yield poor forecasts for major league baseball? ■

14.7

Simple Linear Regression

Often, we try to predict the value of one variable (the dependent variable) from the value of another variable (the independent variable). Here are several examples:

Dependent variable	*Predicted from*	Independent variable
Sales of product		Price of product
Automobile sales		Interest rate
Total production cost		Units produced
Return of a company's stock		Return on a market index

If the dependent variable and the independent variable are related linearly, simple linear regression can be used to estimate this relationship. In Section 14.8, we will discuss how to estimate nonlinear relationships.

To illustrate simple linear regression, consider the Giapetto Company, which manufactures toy trains. The company wants to determine the cost of producing a train. To estimate this cost, we observe for ten weeks the number of trains produced and the cost of producing these trains. The data are given in Table 14.8.

TABLE 14.8 **Data for Giapetto Example**

	Trains Produced	**Cost**
Week 1	10	\$257.40
Week 2	20	\$601.60
Week 3	30	\$782.00
Week 4	40	\$765.40
Week 5	45	\$895.50
Week 6	50	\$1133.00
Week 7	60	\$1152.80
Week 8	55	\$1132.70
Week 9	70	\$1459.20
Week 10	40	\$970.10

The data from Table 14.8 are plotted in Figure 14.12.[3] Observe that there appears to be a strong linear relationship between x_t, the number of trains produced during week t, and y_t, the cost of producing trains made during week t. The line plotted in Figure 14.12 appears, in a way to be made precise later, to come close to capturing the linear relationship between units produced and production cost. We will soon see how this line was chosen.

To begin, we model the linear relationship between x_t and y_t with the following equation:

$$y_t = \beta_0 + \beta_1 x_t + \varepsilon_t$$

Here ε_t is an *error term.* It represents the fact that during a week when x_t trains are produced, the production cost does not always equal $\beta_0 + \beta_1 x_t$. If $\varepsilon_t > 0$, the cost of

[3]Such a **scatterplot** is always a good place to start the analysis. You can obtain this in Excel by using the ChartWizard and specifying an X-Y chart. Keep in mind, however, that regardless of how you specify the range of the data, the leftmost column will *always* be on the horizontal axis. (Similarly, if your data are in rows, not columns, the topmost row will always be on the horizontal axis.)

FIGURE 14.12 **Scatterplot of Cost Versus Trains Produced for Giapetto Example**

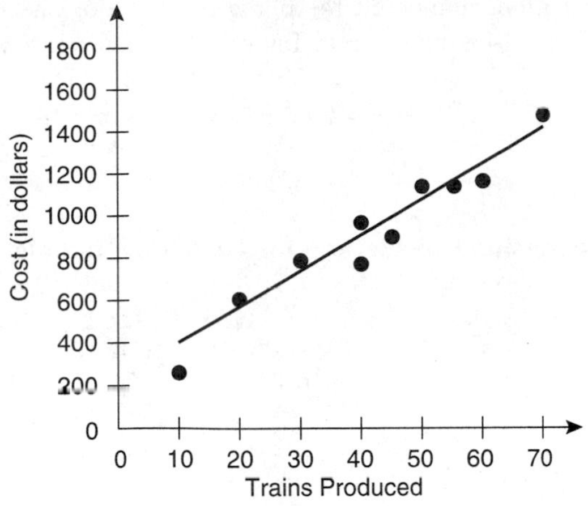

producing x_t trains during week t exceeds $\beta_0 + \beta_1 x_t$, whereas if $\varepsilon_t < 0$, the cost of producing x_t trains during week t is less than $\beta_0 + \beta_1 x_t$. However, we expect ε_t to average out to 0, so that the expected cost during a week in which x_t trains are produced is $\beta_0 + \beta_1 x_t$.

The true values of β_0 and β_1 are unknown. Suppose that we estimate β_0 by b_0 and β_1 by b_1. Then our forecast for y_t, denoted by $\hat{y}_t$, is given by

$$\hat{y}_t = b_0 + b_1 x_t$$

Suppose we have data points of the form $(x_1, y_1), (x_2, y_2), \ldots, (x_T, y_T)$. We select values of b_0 and b_1 that make the predictions $\hat{y}_t = b_0 + b_1 x_t$ close to the observed values y_t. To formalize this idea, define e_t as the error for week t, that is, the actual value minus the predicted value:

$$e_t = y_t - \hat{y}_t = y_t - (b_0 + b_1 x_t)$$

In regression terminology, this error is called a **residual**. Then we choose b_0 and b_1 to minimize the sum of the squared residuals:

$$\text{minimize} \sum e_t^2 = \sum (y_t - b_0 - b_1 x_t)^2$$

The values b_0 and b_1 minimizing the sum of squared residuals are called the **ordinary least squares** (OLS) estimates of β_0 and β_1. It can be shown that the OLS estimates are

$$b_1 = \frac{\sum (x_t - \bar{x})(y_t - \bar{y})}{\sum (x_t - \bar{x})^2} \qquad b_0 = \bar{y} - b_1 \bar{x} \qquad \textbf{(14.16)}$$

Here $\bar{x}$ is the average value of all x_t's and $\bar{y}$ is the average value of all y_t's. We call $\hat{y}_t = b_0 + b_1 x_t$ the **least squares regression line**. Usually, the least squares line is determined by computer. Lotus, Excel, Minitab, and many other popular packages provide b_0 and b_1. We illustrate how to determine the least squares line using Excel with the Giapetto train data.

EXAMPLE 14.5

Using the data in Table 14.8, find the OLS estimates b_0 and b_1. Then find the forecasts of sales from the regression line.

Solution

Referring to the equations numbered 14.16, the computations needed to determine b_0 and b_1 for the data in Table 14.8 are given in Table 14.9, where we have used

$$\bar{x} = \frac{\sum x_t}{10} = 42 \qquad \bar{y} = \frac{\sum y_t}{10} = 914.97$$

TABLE 14.9 Worksheet for Regression Calculations for Giapetto Example

	x_t	y_t	$x_t - \bar{x}$	$y_t - \bar{y}$	$(x_t - \bar{x})(y_t - \bar{y})$	$(x_t - \bar{x})^2$
Week 1	10	257.4	−32	−657.57	21042.24	1024
Week 2	20	601.6	−22	−313.37	6894.14	484
Week 3	30	782.0	−12	−132.97	1595.64	144
Week 4	40	765.4	−2	−149.57	299.14	4
Week 5	45	895.5	3	−19.47	−58.41	9
Week 6	50	1133.0	8	218.03	1744.24	64
Week 7	60	1152.8	18	237.83	4280.94	324
Week 8	55	1132.7	13	217.73	2830.49	169
Week 9	70	1459.2	28	544.23	15238.44	784
Week 10	40	970.1	−2	55.13	−110.26	4

From Table 14.9, we find that $\sum(x_t - \bar{x})(y_t - \bar{y}) = 53756.6$ and $\sum(x_t - \bar{x})^2 = 3010$. From the equations numbered 14.16, we now find that

$$b_1 = \frac{53756.6}{3010} = 17.86 \qquad b_0 = 914.97 - (17.86)42 = 164.88$$

The least squares line is $\hat{y} = 164.88 + 17.86x$. In words, we estimate that each extra train incurs a variable cost of $b_1 = \$17.86$.

Using a Spreadsheet Approach Fortunately, we can avoid these tedious calculations by using Excel's regression capabilities. The necessary information is shown in Figure 14.13. (See the file GIAPETTO.XLS.) It can be formed with the following steps.

1 **Name ranges.** Although this is not absolutely necessary, it is convenient to name the range B4:B13 Trains and the range C4:C13 Costs. The Costs range includes the dependent variable and the Trains range includes the independent variable.

2 **Intercept and slope.** We determine b_0 and b_1, called the intercept and the slope, by using the Excel INTERCEPT and SLOPE functions. Enter the formulas

=INTERCEPT(Costs,Trains)

and

=SLOPE(Costs,Trains)

in cells B15 and B16. As before, these lead to the regression line $\hat{y} = 164.88 + 17.86x$.

3 **Predictions.** The predicted costs can be found by entering the x values into the regression line. An easy way to do this is to use Excel's TREND function. To do this, enter the formula

=TREND(Costs,Trains,B4)

in cell D4 and copy it to the range D5:D13. Alternatively, you could use the regression line directly by entering the formula

=$B$15+$B$16*B4

FIGURE 14.13 **Regression Output for Giapetto Example**

	A	B	C	D
1	Giapetto Train Example			
2				
3	Week	Trains	Cost	Predictions
4	1	10	$257.40	$343.47
5	2	20	$601.60	$522.06
6	3	30	$782.00	$700.66
7	4	40	$765.40	$879.25
8	5	45	$895.50	$968.55
9	6	50	$1,133.00	$1,057.84
10	7	60	$1,152.80	$1,236.44
11	8	55	$1,132.70	$1,147.14
12	9	70	$1,459.20	$1,415.03
13	10	40	$970.10	$879.25
14				
15	INTERCEPT	164.88		
16	SLOPE	17.86		
17	RSQ	94.0%		
18	STEYX	87.82		
19	CORREL	0.969		

in cell D4, which you would then copy to the range D5:D13. For example, the predicted cost in week 10, when 40 trains are produced, is \$879.25. Since the actual cost is \$970.10, the forecast error is

$$e_{10} = 970.10 - 879.25 = \$90.85$$

4 **Other quantities.** We will shortly discuss three other measures commonly obtained in regression analysis: the R-square value, the standard error of estimate, and the correlation. Calculate these in cells B17, B18, and B19 with the formulas

=RSQ(Costs,Trains)
=STEYX(Costs,Trains)

and

=CORREL(Costs,Trains)

5 **Finishing the scatterplot.** Create the scatterplot shown in Figure 14.12 on a new sheet (as we have done in the GIAPETTO.XLS file). To do this, select the Insert/Chart/On New Sheet menu item, and then follow the ChartWizard steps. After creating the chart, click on any of the points on the scatterplot. Then select the Insert/Trendline menu item and choose the Linear box. This will insert the regression line, as shown in Figure 14.12. (As long as you're inserting, you can also click on the Options tab and check to display the regression equation and/or the R-square value on the chart.)

Every least squares line has two properties:

1 It passes through the point $(\bar{x}, \bar{y})$. Thus, during a week in which Giapetto produced $\bar{x} = 42$ trains, we would predict that these trains would cost $\bar{y} = \$914.97$ to produce.

2 The sum of the residuals ($\sum e_i$) equals 0. The least squares line "splits" the data points in the sense that the sum of the vertical distances from points above the least squares line to the least squares line equals the sum of the vertical distances from points below the least squares line to the least squares line.

Goodness of Fit How do we determine how well the least squares line fits our data points? To answer this question, we need to discuss three components of variation: sum of squares total, SST, sum of squares error, SSE, and sum of squares regression, SSR. The sum of squares total is given by $SST = \sum(y_t - \bar{y})^2$. This sum of squares measures the total variation of the y_t's about the mean $\bar{y}$. The sum of squares error is given by $SSE = \sum(y_t - \hat{y}_t)^2 = \sum e_t^2$. If the least squares line passes through all the data points, then $SSE = 0$. Thus, a small SSE indicates that the least squares line fits the data well. The sum of squares regression is defined as $SSR = \sum(\hat{y}_t - \bar{y})^2$. It can be shown that

$$SST = SSR + SSE \tag{14.17}$$

For a good fit, SSE will be small; Equation 14.17 shows that SSR will be large for a good fit. More formally, we define the **coefficient of determination** R^2 as

$$R^2 = \frac{SSR}{SST} = \text{Fraction of variation in } y \text{ explained by } x$$

We found this value for the Giapetto data with the RSQ function. From cell B17 of Figure 14.13, we see that $R^2 = .940$. Expressed in words, the *number* of trains produced explains 94.0% of the variation in the *costs* of those trains. This is a relatively large R^2 value, although we would expect it to be large in this type of example where production cost is largely determined by production level. All other factors combined can explain at most 6% of the variation in weekly cost, so we are quite sure that the linear relationship between x and y is strong.

A measure of the linear association between x and y is the **correlation coefficient** r_{xy}. A correlation near +1 indicates a strong positive linear relationship between x and y; a correlation near −1 indicates a strong negative linear relationship between x and y; and a correlation near 0 indicates a weak linear relationship between x and y. The correlation between x and y can be obtained by using Excel's CORREL function, as we did in cell B19 of Figure 14.13. For the Giapetto data, we see that the correlation between number of trains produced and the costs of these trains is quite large, 0.969.

It can be shown that if $b_1 \geq 0$, then r_{xy} equals $+\sqrt{R^2}$, whereas if $b_1 < 0$, then r_{xy} equals $-\sqrt{R^2}$. Thus, in the Giapetto example, $r_{xy} = \sqrt{0.94} = 0.97$. Both R^2 and its square root r_{xy} indicate a strong linear relationship between x and y.

Forecasting Accuracy A measure of the accuracy of predictions derived from regression is the **standard error of estimate**, labeled s_e. If we let T be the number of observations, s_e is given by

$$s_e = \sqrt{\frac{SSE}{T-2}}$$

The standard error of estimate can be found with the Excel function STEYX, as shown in cell B18 of Figure 14.13. Referring to that cell, we see that $s_e = 87.82$.

It is usually true that approximately 68% of the values of the y_t's will be within s_e of the predicted $\hat{y}_t$ values, and 95% of the values of the y_t's will be within $2s_e$ of the predicted $\hat{y}_t$ values. In the Giapetto example, we expect that 68% of our cost estimates will be within \$87.82 of the observed costs and 95% will be within \$175.64 of the observed costs. In reality, the actual cost is within s_e of the predicted cost for 80% (8 of 10) of the data points, and the actual cost is within $2s_e$ of the predicted cost for 100% (all 10) of the data points.

Any observation for which y_t is not within $2s_e$ of $\hat{y}_t$ is sometimes called an **outlier**.[4] Outliers represent unusual data points and should be carefully examined. Of course, if an

[4]This characterization of outliers is not used by everyone. Some analysts classify an observation as an outlier only if the difference between y_t and $\hat{y}_t$ is at least $3s_e$. Other analysts use even more complex definitions of outliers (in the context of regression).

outlier is the result of a data entry error, it should be corrected. If an outlier is in some way uncharacteristic of the remaining data points, it might be better to omit the outlier and reestimate the least squares line. Since all the errors in the Giapetto example are less than $2s_e$ in absolute value, there are no outliers. ■

Assumptions of the Simple Linear Regression Model

So far, we have used regression only to fit a line to a set of points and measure the goodness of the fit. Often we want to go a step further and use regression for statistical inference. In this case we consider the observed data as a *sample* from a larger population. We want to use the sample data to infer the properties of the population. Specifically, in a time series context, the sample includes historical observations, and we want to infer (or forecast) future behavior. If the statistical analysis is to rest on solid ground, the following assumptions must hold.

Assumption 1 The variance of the error term should not depend on the value of the independent variable x. This assumption is called **homoscedasticity**. If the variance of the error term depends on x, then we say that **heteroscedasticity** is present. To see whether the homoscedasticity assumption is satisfied, we plot the errors on the vertical axis and the value of x on the horizontal axis. Alternatively, we can plot the y's on the vertical axis and the x's on the horizontal axis. Figure 14.14 illustrates a situation where the homoscedasticity assumption is satisfied; the figure indicates no tendency for the variance of the points to depend on x. In Figure 14.15, however, the points vary more around the regression line (not shown) as x increases. This is an example of heteroscedasticity. Using $\ln(y)$ (the natural logarithm of y) or $\sqrt{y}$ instead of y as the dependent variable will often eliminate heteroscedasticity.

Assumption 2 The errors are normally distributed. This assumption is not as critical as the other assumptions, so we will not discuss it further.

Assumption 3 The errors should be independent. This assumption is often violated when data are collected (as in the Giapetto example) over time. Independence of the errors

FIGURE 14.14 **Example of Equal Error Variance (Homoscedasticity)**

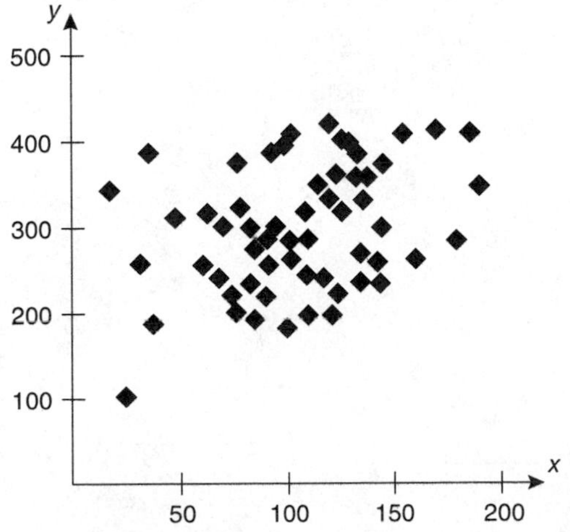

FIGURE 14.15 **Example of Nonconstant Error Variance (Heteroscedasticity)**

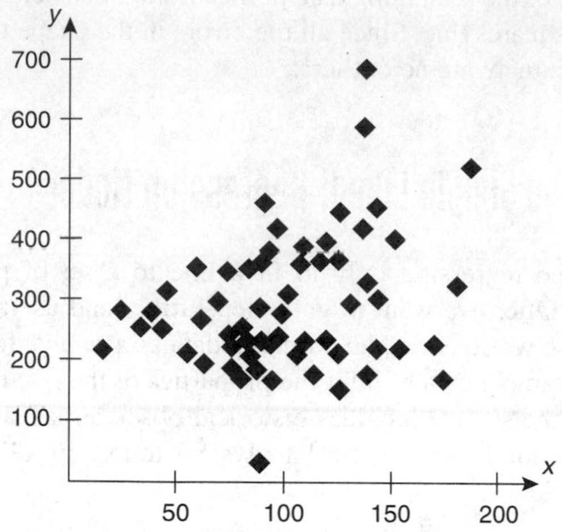

implies that knowing the value of one error tells us nothing about the value of the next error (or any other error). The validity of this assumption can be checked by plotting the errors in time-series sequence. In the example shown in Figure 14.16, we see that the errors have the following signs: $++++++------$. This sequence of errors exhibits an obvious pattern: a positive error (corresponding to underprediction of the actual value of y) is usually followed by another positive error, and a negative error (corresponding to overprediction of the actual value of y) is usually followed by another negative error. This pattern indicates that successive errors are not independent; it is referred to as **positive autocorrelation**. Positive autocorrelation indicates that successive errors have a positive linear relationship and are not independent.

If the sequence of errors in time sequence resembles that shown in Figure 14.17, we have **negative autocorrelation**. Here, the sequence of errors is $+-+-+-+-+-+-$. This indicates that a positive error tends to be followed by a negative error, and vice versa. This indicates that successive errors have a negative linear relationship and are not independent.

FIGURE 14.16 **Example of Positive Autocorrelation**

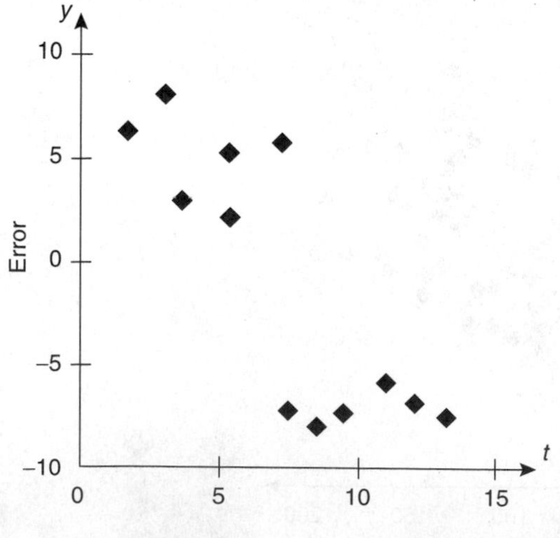

FIGURE 14.17 **Example of Negative Autocorrelation**

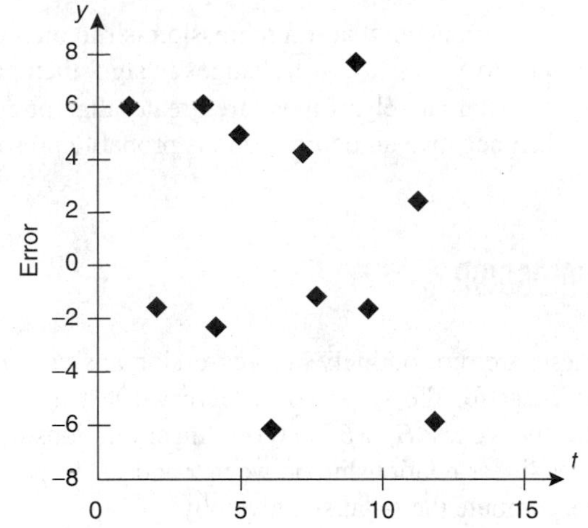

In the example shown in Figure 14.18, the sequence of errors is: $++-++++---++$. Here, no obvious pattern is present, and the independence assumption appears to be satisfied. Observe that the errors average to 0, so we expect about half of the errors to be positive and half to be negative. Thus, if there is no pattern in the errors, we expect the errors to change sign about half the time.

In general, we can check for autocorrelation—somewhat informally—as follows.[5]

1 If the errors change sign very rarely (much less than half the time), they probably violate the independence assumption, and positive autocorrelation is probably present.

2 If the errors change sign very often (much more than half the time), they probably violate the independence assumption, and negative autocorrelation is probably present.

FIGURE 14.18 **Example of No Autocorrelation**

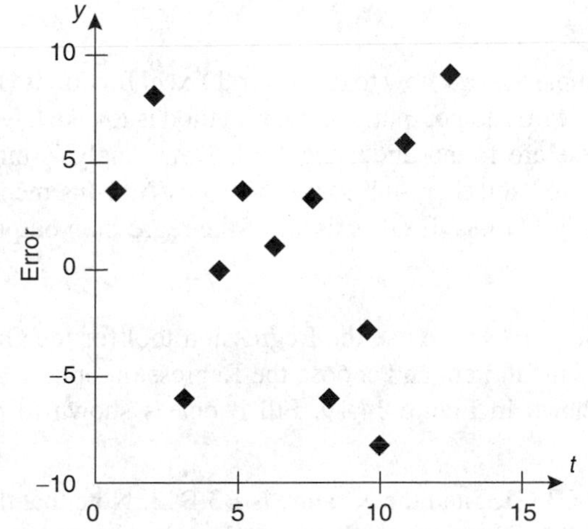

[5]There are more formal tests for autocorrelation, but we won't present them here.

3 If the errors change sign about half the time, they probably satisfy the independence assumption.

4 More formally, it can be shown that if a regression is run on n observations and there are less than or equal to $\frac{n-1}{2} - \sqrt{n-1}$ changes in sign, then positive autocorrelation is probably present. Alternatively, if there are greater than or equal to $\frac{n-1}{2} + \sqrt{n-1}$ changes in sign, then negative autocorrelation is probably present.

Inferences in Regression

Several hypothesis tests are run routinely in a regression analysis. Perhaps the most common of these is the t-test for the slope term. Here we test the significance of a linear relationship. Specifically, we test $H_0 : \beta_1 = 0$ (no linear relationship between x and y) versus $H_a : \beta_1 \neq 0$ (some linear relationship between x and y). To perform this test at a level of significance α, we compute the t-statistic given by

$$t = \frac{b_1}{\text{StErr}(b_1)}$$

Here, StErr(b_1) measures the uncertainty in our estimate of β_1; it can always be found on a computer printout. We reject H_0 if $|t|$ is sufficiently large compared to the value in a "t table."

Computer packages typically perform this table lookup for us by reporting the p-value of the test. Essentially, the p-value indicates how unlikely it would be to see a sample as unlikely as the one we observed *if* the null hypothesis H_0 were true. If this p-value is small, say, less than .05, then we can reject H_0 and conclude that β_1 is *not* 0, that is, there *is* some relationship between x and y. We illustrate this with the Giapetto data.

EXAMPLE 14.6

Given the Giapetto data in Table 14.8, can we infer that there is a statistically significant linear relationship between the number of trains produced and the weekly costs?

Solution

In the previous example we saw how to use several Excel functions (INTERCEPT, SLOPE, and so on) to obtain regression output. Another method is to take advantage of Excel's Data Analysis tools. These are found under the Tools/Data Analysis menu. (If you can't find them, you will have to "add them in" using the Tools/Add-Ins menu item.) Regression is one of the Data Analysis tools. It gives us all of the regression outputs we've discussed so far, plus some.

Using the Regression Tool To use the Regression tool for the Giapetto data, select the Tools/Data Analysis menu item and choose the Regression option. This produces a dialog box like the one shown in Figure 14.19. Fill it out as shown to produce the following outputs:

1 The Y range is C3:C13, and the X range is B3:B13. Note that these include the labels in cells C3 and B3. Therefore, we have checked the Labels box.

2 The output range, where the regression output will be placed, will start in cell E3 of the current sheet. (If you like, you can put it on a new sheet or even in a different workbook.)

FIGURE 14.19 Dialog Box for Regression Analysis for Giapetto Example

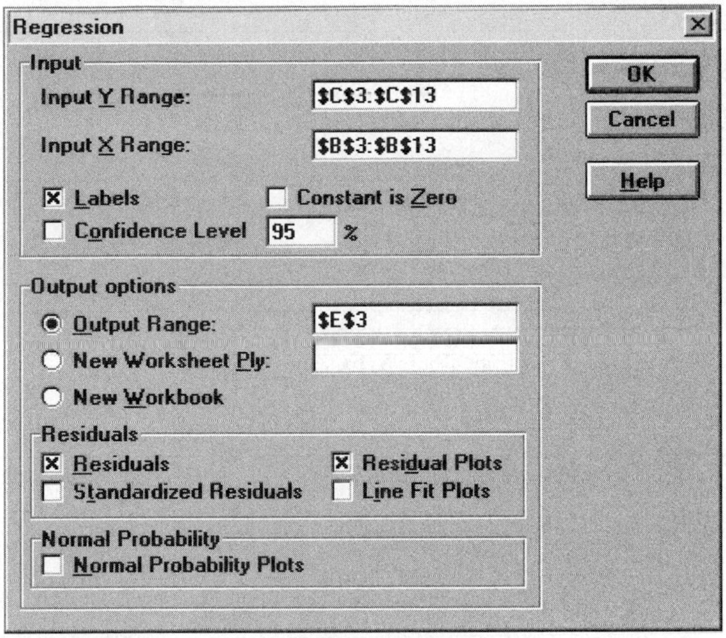

3 We have checked the Residuals and Residual Plots boxes. Checking the Residuals box gives us a list of the predicted costs and the residuals (prediction errors). Checking the Residual Plots box gives us a graph of the residuals versus the independent variable (trains produced). This allows us to check the assumptions of the linear regression model.

The output appears in Figure 14.20. (It is part of the GIAPETTO.XLS file.) We don't need to cover every piece of output in this figure. However, the following are particularly important.

1 The values of r_{xy}, R^2, and s_e appear in cells F6, F7, and F9.

2 The values of SSR, SSE, and SST (which we briefly mentioned earlier) appear in cells G14, G15, and G16. They are used to separate total variation of the dependent variable into explained and unexplained parts. Recall that $R^2 = SSR/SST$. These sums of squares are also used in a so-called ANOVA (analysis of variance) table to test the overall strength of the linear relationship. Essentially, if the "Significance F" value in cell J14 is small, say, less than .05, then there is clear evidence of a linear relationship between y and x. (We will say more about this F-test when we discuss multiple regression. For simple regression, it is equivalent to the t-test for b_1.)

3 The coefficients b_0 and b_1 appear in cells F19 and F20. Next to them are their standard errors. These are used to obtain the t-values in column H. For example, the t-value for the slope term is

$$t = 17.86/1.60 = 11.16$$

The p-value for the test of whether the true β_1 could be 0 is right next to it in cell I20. Since this p-value is extremely small, there is no doubt that the true slope β_1 is *not* 0.

4 Columns J and K contain 95% confidence intervals for the true values of β_0 and β_1. For example, we are 95% confident that the true value of β_1 is between 14.17 and 21.55. (The reason for duplicate information in columns L and M is that

FIGURE 14.20 **Regression Output from Data Analysis Tool for Giapetto Example**

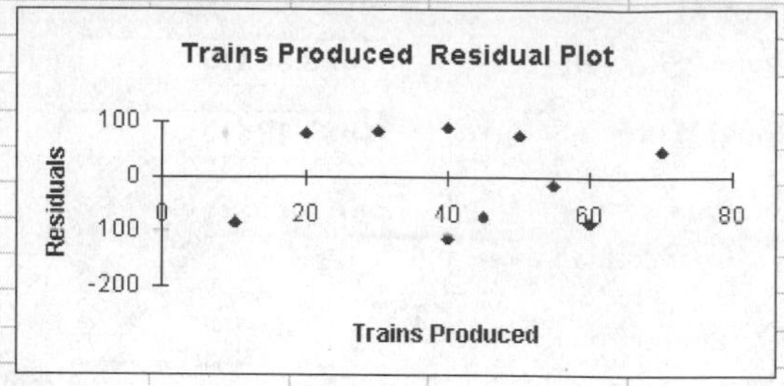

No indication of heteroscedasticity.

5 sign changes out of 9 in residuals indicates little autocorrelation.

	E	F	G	H	I	J	K	L	M
1									
2									
3	SUMMARY OUTPUT								
4									
5	*Regression Statistics*								
6	Multiple R	0.969334265							
7	R Square	0.939608917							
8	Adjusted R Square	0.932060032							
9	Standard Error	87.82464323							
10	Observations	10							
11									
12	ANOVA								
13		*df*	*SS*	*MS*	*F*	*Significance F*			
14	Regression	1	960057.1573	960057.2	124.4699	3.72837E-06			
15	Residual	8	61705.34367	7713.168					
16	Total	9	1021762.501						
17									
18		*Coefficients*	*Standard Error*	*t Stat*	*P-value*	*Lower 95%*	*Upper 95%*	*Lower 95.000%*	*Upper 95.000%*
19	Intercept	164.877907	72.7433294	2.266571	0.053174	[illegible]	[illegible]	[illegible]	[illegible]
20	Trains Produced	17.85933555	1.600785517	11.15661	3.73E-06	14.16791514	21.550756	14.16791514	21.55075596
21									
22									
23									
24	RESIDUAL OUTPUT								
25									
26	*Observation*	*Predicted Cost*	*Residuals*						
27	1	343.4712625	-86.07126246						
28	2	522.0646179	79.53538206						
29	3	700.6579734	81.34202658						
30	4	879.2513289	-113.8513289						
31	5	968.5480066	-73.04800664						
32	6	1057.844684	75.15531561						
33	7	1236.43804	-83.63803987						
34	8	1147.141362	-14.44136213						
35	9	1415.031395	44.16860465						
36	10	879.2513289	90.8486711						

the Regression tool automatically produces 95% confidence intervals (the ones in columns J and K). You are allowed to request another confidence level, such as 90% or 99%, in the dialog box. Since 95% is entered in the dialog box in Figure 14.19, we obtain two sets of 95% intervals in the output.)

5 The predicted costs and residuals appear in the range F27:G36. If you count the number of sign changes as you scan the residuals, you'll find five sign changes (out of a possible nine). This indicates that autocorrelation is probably not a problem.

6 The graph of the residuals versus the number of trains produced is also shown. The residuals appear to "swarm" randomly, as we would like. In particular, there is no indication of heteroscedasticity. ■

14.8 Fitting Nonlinear Relationships

Often a plot of points of the form (x_t, y_t) indicates that y is a *non*linear function of x. For example, if the plot of (x_t, y_t) looks like any of parts (*a*) – (*i*) of Figure 14.21, a nonlinear relationship between x and y is indicated.

The following procedure can be used to estimate a nonlinear relationship:

1 Plot a scatterplot of the points and find which graph in Figure 14.21 appears to fit the data best. For illustrative purposes, suppose the data look like graph (*c*). The second

FIGURE 14.21 Graphs of Linearizable Functions

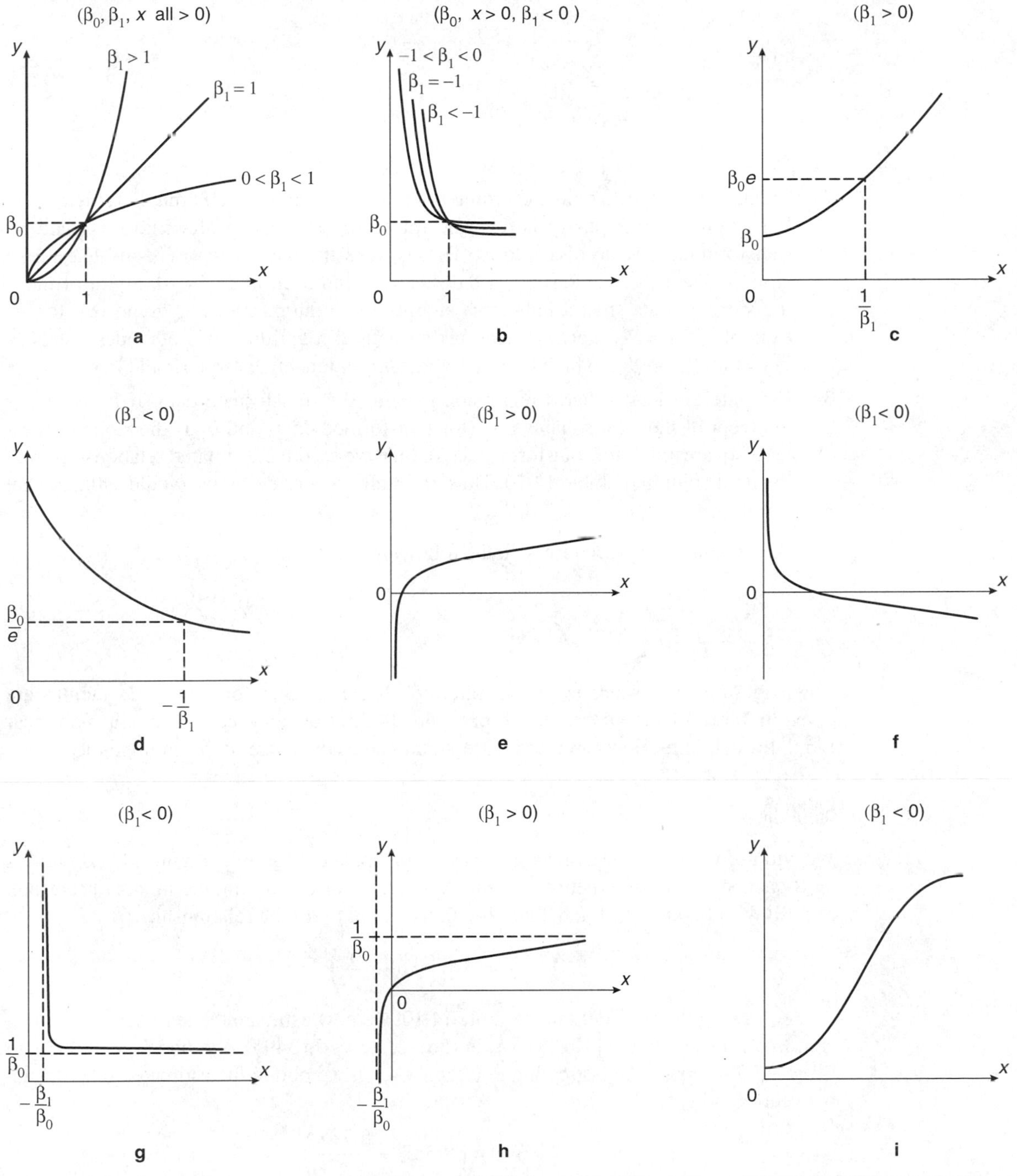

Reprinted by permission from C. Daniel and F. Wood, *Fitting Functions to Data*. Copyright 1980, John Wiley and Sons.

column of Table 14.10 gives the functional relationship between x and y. For graph (c), this indicates the relationship $y = \beta_0 \exp(\beta_1 x)$.

TABLE 14.10 **How to Fit Nonlinear Relationships**

Graph Type	Appropriate Functional Relationship	Transform (x, y) into	Estimate of Functional Relationship
(a) or (b)	$y = \beta_0 x^{\beta_1}$	$(\ln x, \ln y)$	$\hat{y} = \exp(b_0)x^{b_1}$
(c) or (d)	$y = \beta_0 \exp(\beta_1 x)$	$(x, \ln y)$	$\hat{y} = \exp(b_0 + b_1 x)$
(e) or (f)	$y = \beta_0 + \beta_1 \ln x$	$(\ln x, y)$	$\hat{y} = b_0 + b_1 \ln x$
(g) or (h)	$y = \frac{x}{\beta_0 x + \beta_1}$	$(\frac{1}{x}, \frac{1}{y})$	$\hat{y} = \frac{x}{b_0 x + b_1}$
(i)	$y = \exp(\beta_0 + \frac{\beta_1}{x})$	$(\frac{1}{x}, \ln y)$	$\hat{y} = \exp(b_0 + \frac{b_1}{x})$

2 Transform each data point according to the rules in the third column of Table 14.10. For example, if graph (c) is relevant, transform each value of y into $\ln(y)$ and transform each value of x into x. (That is, take the natural log of y and leave x alone.) Given the relationship in the second column of Table 14.10, a plot of the transformed data should indicate a straight-line relationship. For graph (c), for example, if $y = \beta_0 \exp(\beta_1 x)$, then taking natural logarithms of both sides yields $\ln y = \ln(\beta_0) + \beta_1 x$, which indicates a linear relationship between x and $\ln y$.

3 Estimate the least squares regression line for the transformed data. If b_0 is the intercept of the least squares line (for transformed data) and b_1 is the slope of the least squares line (for transformed data), then we read the estimated relationship from the final column of Table 14.10. Thus, if graph (c) is relevant, we would estimate that $\hat{y} = \exp(b_0 + b_1 x)$.

We illustrate the procedure with the following example.

EXAMPLE 14.7

Lowland Appliance wants to predict future VCR sales. Sales for the last 24 months are given in Table 14.11 and are plotted in Figure 14.22. Lowland sees an obvious nonlinear trend through time. How can it use regression to take advantage of this nonlinearity?

Solution

We will use x, the number of the month, as the independent variable. Figure 14.22 indicates an S-shaped relationship between x and y, where y is sales during the month. Therefore, according to Figure 14.21 and Table 14.10, we ought to try the relationship

$$y = \exp\left(\beta_0 + \frac{\beta_1}{x}\right)$$

Following the third column of Table 14.10, we now estimate the least squares regression line for the points $(\frac{1}{1}, \ln 23)$, $(\frac{1}{2}, \ln 156)$, ..., $(\frac{1}{24}, \ln 3495)$. We find $b_0 = 8.387$ and $b_1 = -5.788$. From the last column of Table 14.10, we obtain the estimated relationship between x and y:

$$\hat{y} = \exp\left(8.387 - \frac{5.788}{x}\right)$$

TABLE 14.11 Data for VCR Sales for Lowland Example

	VCR Sales		VCR Sales
Month 1	23	**Month 13**	3136
Month 2	156	**Month 14**	3241
Month 3	330	**Month 15**	3149
Month 4	482	**Month 16**	3524
Month 5	1209	**Month 17**	3542
Month 6	1756	**Month 18**	3312
Month 7	2000	**Month 19**	3547
Month 8	2512	**Month 20**	3376
Month 9	2366	**Month 21**	3375
Month 10	2942	**Month 22**	3403
Month 11	2872	**Month 23**	3697
Month 12	2937	**Month 24**	3495

FIGURE 14.22 Time Series Graph of VCR Sales for Lowland Example

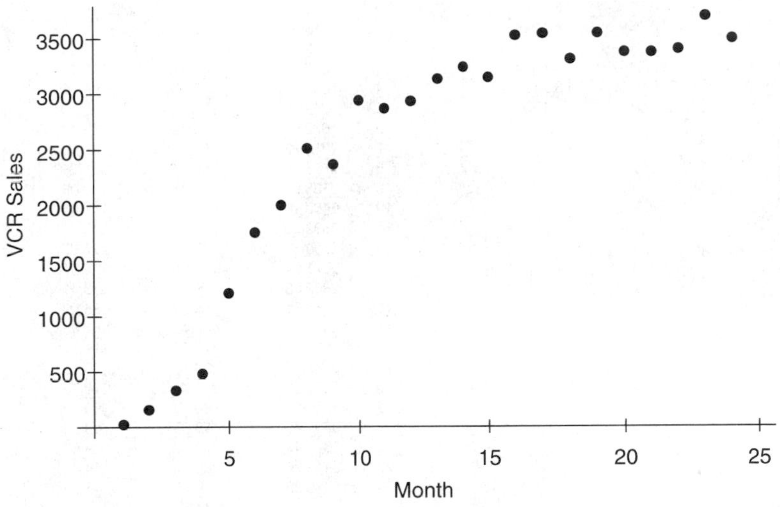

Using a Spreadsheet Estimating a nonlinear relationship can be accomplished very easily with Excel. We use the Regression tool from Tools/Data Analysis exactly as before, but now we must first transform the *x*'s and/or *y*'s. This part is fairly straightforward. You must keep in mind (when the *y*'s are transformed), however, that summary statistics such as R^2, s_e, and the predictions and residuals are in terms of the transformed *y*'s, not the original *y*'s. Therefore, the last column of Table 14.10 should be used in order to obtain valid statistics for the predictions of the original (untransformed) *y*'s. The output for the Lowland VCR data appears in Figure 14.23. (See the file VCR.XLS.) The procedure is as follows.

1 **Transform data.** First, calculate the transformed values of the *x*'s and *y*'s as suggested earlier (reciprocals of *x*'s, logs of *y*'s) in columns D and E. To do this, enter the formulas

=1/A4

and

=LN(B4)

in cells D4 and E4 and copy these to the range D5:E27.

FIGURE 14.23 Regression Output for Lowland Example

	A	B	C	D	E	F	G	H	I	J	K	L
1	**VCR Sales**			**Transformed data**								
2												
3	**Month**	**Sales**		**1/Month**	**Ln(Sales)**	SUMMARY OUTPUT						
4	1	23		1.000	3.1355							
5	2	156		0.500	5.0499	*Regression Statistics*						
6	3	330		0.333	5.7991	Multiple R	0.97610183					
7	4	482		0.250	6.1779	R Square	0.95277479					
8	5	1209		0.200	7.0975	Adjusted R Square	0.95062819					
9	6	1756		0.167	7.4708	Standard Error	0.27610817					
10	7	2000		0.143	7.6009	Observations	24					
11	8	2512		0.125	7.8288							
12	9	2366		0.111	7.7690	ANOVA						
13	10	2942		0.100	7.9868		*df*	*SS*	*MS*	*F*	*Significance F*	
14	11	2872		0.091	7.9628	Regression	1	33.83744596	33.83744596	443.8529	4.48043E-16	
15	12	2937		0.083	7.9851	Residual	22	1.677185886	0.076235722			
16	13	3136		0.077	8.0507	Total	23	35.51463185				
17	14	3241		0.071	8.0836							
18	15	3149		0.067	8.0548		*Coefficients*	*Standard Error*	*t Stat*	*P-value*	*Lower 95%*	*Upper 95%*
19	16	3524		0.063	8.1674	Intercept	8.38678863	0.071026755	118.0792881	2.5E-32	8.239487998	8.534089262
20	17	3542		0.059	8.1724	1/Month	-5.7879961	0.274731657	-21.06781657	4.48E-16	-6.35775534	-5.218236951
21	18	3312		0.056	8.1053							
22	19	3547		0.053	8.1739	Observation	Predicted	Residual	Absolute Error			
23	20	3376		0.050	8.1244	1	13.45	9.55	9.55			
24	21	3375		0.048	8.1242	2	242.93	-86.93	86.93			
25	22	3403		0.045	8.1324	3	637.44	-307.44	307.44			
26	23	3697		0.043	8.2153	4	1032.55	-550.55	550.55			
27	24	3495		0.042	8.1591	5	1379.10	-170.10	170.10			
28						6	1672.58	83.42	83.42			
29						7	1919.72	80.28	80.28			
30						8	2128.75	383.25	383.25			
31						9	2306.94	59.06	59.06			
32						10	2460.18	481.82	481.82			
33						11	2593.09	278.91	278.91			
34						12	2709.33	227.67	227.67			
35						13	2811.74	324.26	324.26			
36						14	2902.59	338.41	338.41			
37						15	2983.71	165.29	165.29			
38						16	3056.54	467.46	467.46			
39						17	3122.28	419.72	419.72			
40						18	3181.90	130.10	130.10			
41						19	3236.21	310.79	310.79			
42						20	3285.88	90.12	90.12			
43						21	3331.47	43.53	43.53			
44						22	3373.47	29.53	29.53			
45						23	3412.28	284.72	284.72			
46						24	3448.25	46.75	46.75			
47								**MAD**	223.74			
48								**Approx StErr**	279.67			

2 **Scatterplot of transformed data.** Form an X-Y graph of the transformed values, just to confirm that the transformations have indeed straightened out the points. This is apparent from Figure 14.24. There is still a hint of a slightly nonlinear shape, but a linear fit should do quite well.

3 **Regression tool.** Use the Tools/Data Analysis menu item and choose the Regression option. Fill in the dialog window as shown in Figure 14.25. Do not check the boxes for residuals, because these would produce residuals for the logs of VCR sales, not sales themselves.

4 **Forecasting untransformed values.** Fill out the range F23:I46, which corresponds to the predicted values of actual (not transformed) VCR sales and the associated residuals and their absolute values. Specifically, enter the values 1 through 24 in column F. In cell G23 enter the formula

=EXP($G$19+$G$20/F23)

and copy this to the range G24:G46. (The EXP function is the "anti-log" function.) This uses the coefficients in cells G19 and G20. Then enter the formulas

=B4–G23

FIGURE 14.24 **Scatterplot of Transformed Values**

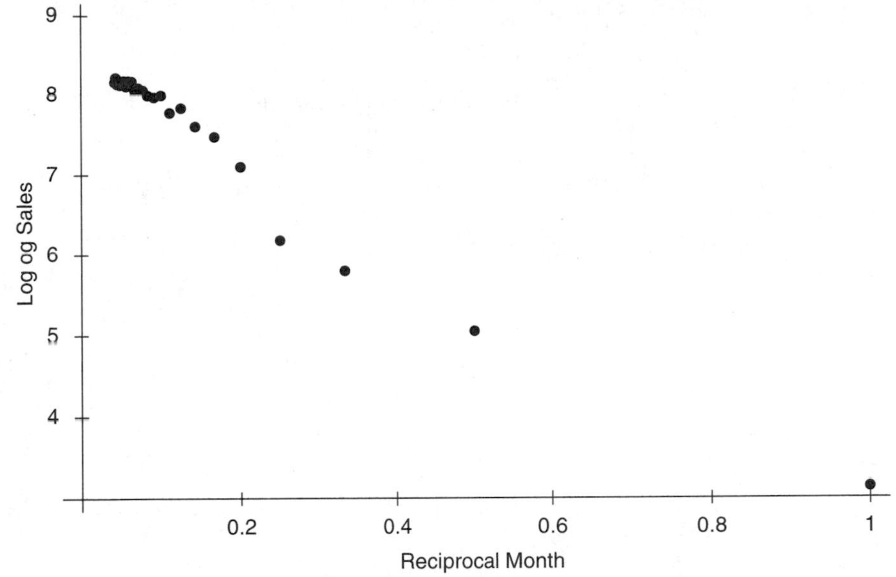

FIGURE 14.25 **Dialog Box for Regression Analysis for Lowland Example**

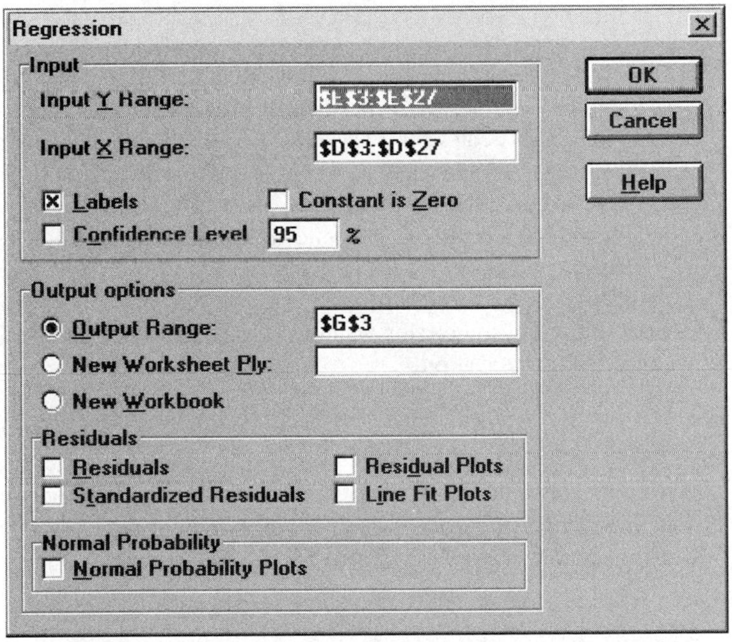

and

=ABS(H23)

in cells H23 and I23 and copy these to the range H24:I46. Finally, enter the formulas

=AVERAGE(I23:I46)

and

=1.25*I47

in cells I47 and I48.

The interpretation of the output in Figure 14.23 is as follows. The coefficients in cells G19 and G20 are the estimates of β_0 and β_1 in the nonlinear relationship

$$y = \exp(\beta_0 + \frac{\beta_1}{x})$$

Specifically, the prediction equation for $\ln y$ is

$$\ln \hat{y} = 8.387 - \frac{5.788}{x}$$

However, we are more interested in the prediction of y, not $\ln y$. Therefore, we use the last column of Table 14.10 to obtain the prediction equation

$$\hat{y} = \exp(8.387 - \frac{5.788}{x})$$

This equation is used to obtain the predictions of Lowland VCR sales in the range G23:G46. ■

14.9 Multiple Regression

In many situations more than one independent variable is useful in predicting the value of a dependent variable. We then use **multiple regression**. For example, if we are trying to predict the monthly sales for a national fast-food chicken chain, we might consider using the independent variables national income, price of chicken, dollars spent on advertising during the current month, and dollars spent on advertising during the previous month.

Suppose that we use k independent variables to predict the dependent variable y and we have n observations of the form $(y_t, x_{1t}, x_{2t}, \ldots, x_{kt})$. Here x_{it} is the value of ith independent variable for time period t, and y_t is the value of the dependent variable for time period t. In multiple regression we model the relationship between y and the k independent variables with the equation

$$y_t = \beta_0 + \beta_1 x_{1t} + \beta_2 x_{2t} + \cdots + \beta_k x_{kt} + \varepsilon_t$$

As before, ε_t is an error term with mean 0. It reflects the fact that the actual value of y_t does not usually equal $\beta_0 + \beta_1 x_{1t} + \beta_2 x_{2t} + \cdots + \beta_k x_{kt}$. The coefficient β_i can be thought of as the change in y if the value of the ith independent variable increases by 1 and all other independent variables are held constant.

Estimating the Regression Coefficients

Suppose we estimate β_i $(i = 0, 1, 2, \ldots, k)$ by b_i. Then our prediction for y_t is given by

$$\hat{y}_t = b_0 + b_1 x_{1t} + b_2 x_{2t} + \cdots + b_k x_{kt}$$

As we did in Section 14.7, we define $e_t = y_t - \hat{y}_t$ and choose $b_0, b_1, \ldots, b_k$ to minimize the sum of squared residuals, $\Sigma\, e_t^2$. Usually, these least squares estimates of $\beta_0, \beta_1, \ldots, \beta_k$

are obtained from a computer package such as Excel, SPSS, or Minitab. We call

$$\hat{y}_t = b_0 + b_1 x_{1t} + b_2 x_{2t} + \cdots + b_k x_{kt}$$

the **least squares regression equation**.

The mechanics of doing a multiple regression analysis in Excel is virtually the same as doing a simple regression analysis. The main difference is in the interpretation of the output. We illustrate this in the following example.

EXAMPLE 14.8

The Heavyhaul Truck Company wants to predict the yearly maintenance expense y for a truck using independent variables x_1 and x_2, where x_1 is the number of miles driven during the year and x_2 is the age of the truck (in years) at the beginning of the year. The company has gathered the information given in Table 14.12. Each observation corresponds to a particular truck.[6] Heavyhaul wants to use these data to see whether there is a linear relationship between maintenance cost and the independent variables miles driven and age.

TABLE 14.12 **Data for Truck Example**

y	x_1	x_2
\$908.56	10500	10
\$751.12	9700	7
\$793.55	9200	8
\$619.61	8300	9
\$380.11	6500	5
\$368.72	4500	2
\$235.32	3500	2
\$174.93	2200	3
\$256.30	1800	2

Solution

We again use Excel's Regression tool to produce the output shown in Figure 14.26. (See the file TRUCK.XLS.) The only difference is that we now have to specify the range B3:C12—two adjacent columns—as the X range. (Excel requires that the independent variables be in adjacent columns; therefore you may have to move the data around before initiating a regression analysis.) The interpretation of this output is as follows.

1 **Regression coefficients.** The estimated regression equation is

$$\hat{y} = 12.45 + .0650x_1 + 15.12x_2 \qquad \textbf{(14.18)}$$

These coefficients appear in the range B30:B32. This equation can be used to predict the maintenance cost for other trucks. For example, the predicted maintenance cost for a five-year-old truck that is driven 10,000 miles during a year is

$$\hat{y} = 12.45 + .0650(10{,}000) + 15.12(5) = \$738.05$$

[6] We have deviated from our pattern of using **time series** data sets in this chapter. The data in Table 14.12 are **cross-sectional** data, meaning that they represent a cross-section of trucks observed at the same time. However, multiple regression pertains equally well to cross-sectional data, as we illustrate in this example. In terms of forecasting, the analysis in this example might be used to forecast the total maintenance cost for the company's entire fleet of trucks in the coming year.

FIGURE 14.26 **Regression Output for Truck Example**

	A	B	C	D	E	F	G
1	**Truck Data**						
2							
3	Expense	Miles	Age				
4	$908.56	10500	10				
5	$751.12	9700	7				
6	$793.55	9200	8				
7	$619.61	8300	9				
8	$380.11	6500	5				
9	$368.72	4500	2				
10	$235.32	3500	2				
11	$174.93	2200	3				
12	$256.30	1800	2				
13							
14	SUMMARY OUTPUT						
15							
16	*Regression Statistics*						
17	Multiple R	0.96436517					
18	R Square	0.93000019					
19	Adjusted R Square	0.90666692					
20	Standard Error	83.4685517					
21	Observations	9					
22							
23	ANOVA						
24		*df*	*SS*	*MS*	*F*	*Significance F*	
25	Regression	2	555370.953	277685.5	39.85726	0.000342997	
26	Residual	6	41801.99469	6966.999			
27	Total	8	597172.9477				
28							
29		*Coefficients*	*Standard Error*	*t Stat*	*P-value*	*Lower 95%*	*Upper 95%*
30	Intercept	12.451351	61.91875576	0.201092	0.847271	-139.058497	163.9612
31	Miles	0.06495426	0.022927153	2.833071	0.029837	0.008853497	0.121055
32	Age	15.1192885	23.70048789	0.637932	0.547077	-42.8737586	73.112336

From Equation 14.18, we conclude that when the age of the truck is held constant, driving an extra thousand miles during a year increases annual maintenance costs by $65 and that an increase of one year in the age of the truck, holding miles driven constant, increases annual maintenance costs by $b_2 = \$15.12$.

2 **R-square.** The value of R^2 (in cell B18) can still be interpreted as the percentage of variation in y explained by the independent variables. For the truck data, we see that 93% of the variation of maintenance costs can be explained by knowing the miles driven and the age of the truck.

3 **Standard error of estimate.** The standard error of estimate s_e, found in cell B20, indicates the magnitude of the prediction errors. Specifically, we expect approximately 68% of the $\hat{y}$'s to be within $83.47 of the corresponding y's and approximately 95% of the $\hat{y}$'s to be within $166.94 ($2s_e$) of the y's.

4 **Inferences about regression coefficients.** For each regression coefficient β_i, we can test the null hypothesis H_0 that it is 0. The idea is that if H_0 is true, then the corresponding x variable does not have an effect on y when the other independent variables are included in the regression equation. In this case, we might decide to exclude this variable from the equation for y. However, if H_0 is rejected, then this independent variable does have an effect on y and should be included in the equation for y. To test these hypotheses, Excel calculates

$$t = \frac{b_i}{\text{StErr}(b_i)}$$

for each i, where StErr(b_i) measures the amount of uncertainty present in the estimate of β_i. The relevant StErr(b_i) and t-values appear in rows 31–32 and columns C and D. (In general, we are not interested in testing whether the intercept term is 0.) If the p-value (in column E) corresponding to each t-value is small, say, less than .05, then we can reject H_0 for that coefficient and conclude that this variable is significantly related to y. We see from the output that Miles (x_1) has a significant coefficient (low p-value), whereas the coefficient of Age (x_2) is not significant (large p-value). Therefore, it might be a good idea to reestimate the regression equation including only x_1.

5 **ANOVA Table.** Whereas the t-values for the individual coefficients are used to test whether individual variables have a significant effect on y (given the other variables in the equation), the ANOVA table is used to test whether all independent variables, taken as a whole, have a significant effect on y. The key value is the Significance F in cell F25. If it is sufficiently small, say, less than .05, then we can conclude that the independent variables, taken as a whole, help to explain the dependent variable. This is certainly the case in the Truck data, where the value in cell F25 is extremely small. ■

Multicollinearity

A problem that we often encounter when there are multiple independent variables is called **multicollinearity**. Essentially this means that several independent variables provide overlapping information about the dependent variable, and it usually occurs when two or more independent variables are highly correlated with one another. This is definitely the case in the Heavyhaul Truck example, where the miles driven and the age are positively correlated (high with high, low with low).

The problem that multicollinearity creates is that it is difficult to separate the individual effects on y of the correlated independent variables. You can check (by means of scatterplots or correlations) that the maintenance cost is highly correlated with miles driven and with age. However, regression analysis is unable to separate the individual effects of miles driven and age. As a result, one of these two, namely age, ends up with a large standard error (cell C32) and a small t-value (cell D32). This leads us to believe that age is not important for predicting maintenance cost. This is not quite true. The correct interpretation is that once the miles driven variable is included in the regression, the age variable has very little *extra* to add.

Usually, we want to include variables in the regression if they have significant t-values, that is, low p-values. However, because of multicollinearity, we now see that there can be two reasons for a large p-value (and hence exclusion from the regression): (1) the variable is not at all related to y or (2) the variable is related to y, but its influence on y has already been captured by one or more other independent variables in the regression.

To illustrate the effect of excluding variables from a regression, we consider the following time series data on sales at a restaurant.

EXAMPLE 14.9

The Bloomington Happy Chicken Restaurant has recorded sales data for the past 20 years. It has also recorded data on other potentially relevant variables. The entire data set appears in Figure 14.27. (See the file CHICKEN.XLS.) The variables are defined thus:

POP = Population within ten miles of Happy Chicken Restaurant

AD = Thousands of dollars spent on advertising during the current year

LAGAD = Thousands of dollars spent on advertising during the previous year

SALES = Sales in thousands of dollars

Happy Chicken wants to analyze these data with regression in order to see whether it is possible to make accurate forecasts of future sales.

Solution

We attempt to estimate the model

$$\text{SALES} = \beta_0 + \beta_1\text{YEAR} + \beta_2\text{POP} + \beta_3\text{AD} + \beta_4\text{LAGAD} + \varepsilon$$

We are using YEAR as an independent variable in the hopes of picking up a possible upward trend in sales. LAGAD is used as an independent variable because we believe that last year's advertising might affect this year's sales. (To obtain the LAGAD column in the spreadsheet, we copied the AD column from the range C4:C21 to D5:D22. Note that we cannot use the first year of data since LAGAD is undefined. However, we assume that AD for year 1 is 30 [see cell D4].) By using the Regression tool under Tools/Data Analysis, we obtain the output shown in Figure 14.28. In particular, this output implies the following estimated regression equation:

$$\text{SALES} = 10951.51 + 169.51 * \text{YEAR} - 0.059 * \text{POP}$$
$$+ 122.38 * \text{AD} + 276.93 * \text{LAGAD} \quad \textbf{(14.19)}$$

The t-values for YEAR, POP, AD, and LAGAD are 1.91, −0.70, 13.84, and 28.92. Their corresponding p-values are .076, .498, .000, and .000. Based on a significance level of .05, we would conclude that AD and LAGAD are significant. However, YEAR is also significant if we use a significance level of .10. Therefore, YEAR, AD, and LAGAD appear to have significant effects on sales (at the .10 significance level).

FIGURE 14.27 **Sales Data for Restaurant Example**

	A	B	C	D	E
1	Happy Chicken Regression Example				
2					
3	Year	Pop	Ad	LagAd	Sales
4	2	102558	20	30	15713
5	3	101792	15	20	12937
6	4	104347	25	15	12872
7	5	106180	30	25	16227
8	6	106562	15	30	15388
9	7	105209	25	15	13180
10	8	109185	35	25	17199
11	9	109976	40	35	20674
12	10	110659	20	40	20350
13	11	111844	25	20	14444
14	12	111576	35	25	17530
15	13	113784	5	35	16711
16	14	112482	12	5	9715
17	15	116487	16	12	12248
18	16	117316	21	16	13856
19	17	117830	22	21	15285
20	18	118148	24	22	15620
21	19	118481	26	24	17158
22	20	121069	28	26	17800

FIGURE 14.28 Regression Output with All Four Independent Variables for Restaurant Example

	G	H	I	J	K	L	M
3	SUMMARY OUTPUT						
4							
5	*Regression Statistics*						
6	Multiple R	0.99483337					
7	R Square	0.98969343					
8	Adjusted R Square	0.98674869					
9	Standard Error	314.272971					
10	Observations	19					
11							
12	ANOVA						
13		*df*	*SS*	*MS*	*F*	*Significance F*	
14	Regression	4	132778719.6	33194680	336.0891	9.7939E-14	
15	Residual	14	1382745.006	98767.5			
16	Total	18	134161464.6				
17							
18		*Coefficients*	*Standard Error*	*t Stat*	*P-value*	*Lower 95%*	*Upper 95%*
19	Intercept	10951.5091	8340.633981	1.313031	0.210288	-6937.387578	28840.4057
20	Year	169.510378	88.5466088	1.914363	0.076237	-20.4033787	359.424135
21	Pop	-0.05882686	0.084522751	-0.69599	0.497828	-0.24011029	0.12245657
22	Ad	122.376085	8.845232364	13.83526	1.48E-09	103.4049314	141.347238
23	LagAd	276.927198	9.576831814	28.91637	6.93E-14	256.3869179	297.467477

If we exclude the insignificant variable POP from the equation, we obtain the output shown in Figure 14.29, and the estimated regression equation becomes

$$\text{SALES} = 5150.94 + 108.58 * \text{YEAR}$$
$$+121.59 * \text{AD} + 274.30 * \text{LAGAD}$$

(To obtain this equation we first deleted the POP column, column B, so that YEAR, AD, and LAGAD are in adjacent columns.)

The t-values for YEAR, AD, and LAGAD are now 8.29, 14.10, and 31.72—all highly significant. The significance of these independent variables is confirmed by the fact that

FIGURE 14.29 Regression Output with POP Variable Excluded for Restaurant Example

	F	G	H	I	J	K	L
3	SUMMARY OUTPUT						
4							
5	*Regression Statistics*						
6	Multiple R	0.99465412					
7	R Square	0.98933682					
8	Adjusted R Square	0.98720418					
9	Standard Error	308.824435					
10	Observations	19					
11							
12	ANOVA						
13		*df*	*SS*	*MS*	*F*	*Significance F*	
14	Regression	3	132730876.7	44243626	463.9032	5.22251E-15	
15	Residual	15	1430587.976	95372.53			
16	Total	18	134161464.6				
17							
18		*Coefficients*	*Standard Error*	*t Stat*	*P-value*	*Lower 95%*	*Upper 95%*
19	Intercept	5150.93405	319.4120942	16.1263	6.96E-11	4470.12287	5831.74523
20	Year	108.58484	13.09470367	8.292272	5.52E-07	80.67412265	136.495557
21	Ad	121.59372	8.621406454	14.1037	4.62E-10	103.2176157	139.969824
22	LagAd	274.29791	8.647665335	31.7193	3.65E-15	255.8658366	292.729984

each variable has a p-value smaller than .001. Also, we see that $R^2 = 0.99$ and $s_e = 309$. Therefore, the fit is quite good. From the value of s_e, Happy Chicken is 95% certain that its forecast of next year's sales will be within $618,000 (about $2s_e$, expressed in dollars) of actual sales.

Multicollinearity in the Restaurant Example In certain circumstances, multicollinearity can cause an estimated regression coefficient to have the "wrong" sign. This occurred in the Happy Chicken example. We began with both YEAR and POP as independent variables. As POP and YEAR both increase over time, we would expect a strong positive linear relationship to exist between them—this is the source of the multicollinearity. Indeed, the correlation between YEAR and POP is 0.98. (This correlation appears in Figure 14.30. We obtained this entire set of correlations by selecting the Tools/Data Analysis menu item and choosing the Correlation option.)

FIGURE 14.30 **Correlations in the Restaurant Example**

	A	B	C	D	E
26		*Year*	*Pop*	*Ad*	*LagAd*
27	Year	1			
28	Pop	0.986149	1		
29	Ad	-0.02885	0.00141	1	
30	LagAd	-0.15555	-0.08592	0.16216	1

To see that the estimates of the coefficients of POP and YEAR are unreliable, note that in Equation 14.19, the coefficient of POP is negative, indicating that an increase in the number of customers near Happy Chicken decreases sales. This anomaly—and it *is* an anomaly, as the correlation between SALES and POP is positive—is due to multicollinearity. The strong linear relationship between YEAR and POP makes it difficult for the regression method to estimate the coefficients of YEAR and POP accurately. After we drop POP from the estimated equation, however, the multicollinearity problem disappears because there is no strong linear relationship among the remaining independent variables.

By the way, if an *exact* linear relationship exists between two or more independent variables, there are an infinite number of combinations of the regression coefficients that will minimize the sum of the squared errors, and most computer packages will print an error message. For example, if x_1 is the U.S. consumer expenditure during a year, x_2 is the U.S. investment during a year, x_3 is the U.S. government expenditure during a year, and x_4 is the U.S. national income during a year, it is well known that $x_4 = x_1 + x_2 + x_3$. In this case, we cannot use all four of these variables as independent variables in some regression equation. At least one must be excluded from the equation. ■

MODELING ISSUE

How can we choose between several regression equations that have different sets of independent variables? We usually want to choose the equation with the lowest value of s_e, since that will yield the most accurate forecasts. We also want the t-values for all variables in the equation to be significant (p-values less than, say, .10 or .05). These two objectives may conflict, in which case it is difficult to determine the "best" equation. ■

14.10

Categorical Independent Variables

Often, a nonquantitative or qualitative independent variable can influence the dependent variable. Some examples are as follows:

Dependent Variable	*influenced by* Categorical Independent Variable
Salary of employee	Gender of employee
Consumer expenditures during year	Whether it is a wartime or peacetime year
Customers entering bank on a given day	Day of the week
Air conditioner sales during a month	Month of the year

In each of these situations, the independent variable does not have a numerical value, but it can be classified into one of c categories. To illustrate, for monthly air conditioner sales, $c = 12$, and for the consumer expenditure example, $c = 2$.

Let the possible values of the categorical variable be "labeled" $1, 2, \ldots, c$. To model the effect of a categorical variable on a dependent variable, we define $c - 1$ **dummy variables** as follows:

$$x_1 = \begin{cases} 1 & \text{if observation takes on value 1 of categorical variable} \\ 0 & \text{otherwise} \end{cases}$$

$$x_2 = \begin{cases} 1 & \text{if observation takes on value 2 of categorical variable} \\ 0 & \text{otherwise} \end{cases}$$

$$\vdots$$

$$x_{c-1} = \begin{cases} 1 & \text{if observation takes on value } c-1 \text{ of categorical variable} \\ 0 & \text{otherwise} \end{cases}$$

We now include $x_1, x_2, \ldots, x_{c-1}$ (along with any other relevant independent variables) in the estimated regression equation.

The following example illustrates the use of dummy variables.

EXAMPLE 14.10

The University Credit Union is trying to forecast the number of customers who enter its branch each day. The manager believes that the number of customers is influenced by the day of the week (the credit union is open Monday through Friday) and by whether the day is a payday for university employees. Figure 14.31 shows data for 18 randomly chosen days, where day 1 is the present, day 6 is a week from now, and so on. (See the file CREDUN.XLS.) The objective is to develop a regression equation that can be used to forecast daily arrivals.

Solution

In this situation, there are two categorical variables of interest: the day of the week ($c = 5$) and whether or not a day is a payday ($c = 2$). For the day of the week, we give Monday through Friday the labels 1 through 5. Then we let

$$x_1 = \begin{cases} 1 & \text{if day is a Monday} \\ 0 & \text{otherwise} \end{cases}$$

$$x_2 = \begin{cases} 1 & \text{if day is a Tuesday} \\ 0 & \text{otherwise} \end{cases}$$

$$x_3 = \begin{cases} 1 & \text{if day is a Wednesday} \\ 0 & \text{otherwise} \end{cases}$$

$$x_4 = \begin{cases} 1 & \text{if day is a Thursday} \\ 0 & \text{otherwise} \end{cases}$$

(We purposely do not define a dummy variable for Friday. Recall that when there are c categories, only $c - 1$ dummy variables are required.) Similarly, to keep track of whether a day is a payday, we define a single dummy variable x_5 as

$$x_5 = \begin{cases} 1 & \text{if day is a payday} \\ 0 & \text{otherwise} \end{cases}$$

FIGURE 14.31 **Data for Credit Union Example**

	A	B	C
1	Credit Union data		
2			
3	Day	Payday?	Customers
4	Mon	No	515
5	Tues	No	360
6	Wed	Yes	548
7	Wed	No	386
8	Thurs	No	440
9	Mon	Yes	687
10	Wed	No	350
11	Tues	No	430
12	Thurs	No	370
13	Fri	No	496
14	Fri	No	506
15	Mon	No	509
16	Thurs	Yes	508
17	Thurs	No	396
18	Mon	No	600
19	Wed	No	266
20	Tues	No	360
21	Fri	Yes	521
22	Tues	No	398

To account for a possible trend in the number of customers, we include t, the number of the day, as an independent variable. To illustrate how this information would be coded on the computer, we "code" the last two observations:

t	x_1	x_2	x_3	x_4	x_5	Customers
130	0	0	0	0	1	521
152	0	1	0	0	0	398

Developing the Spreadsheet Model Once we have the data entered properly, we run the regression as usual, with the Regression option from Tools/Data Analysis. A big part of the problem, therefore, is creating the dummy variables needed for the regression. We proceed as follows.

1 **Input data.** Enter the day of the week in column A, whether or not the day was a payday in column B, the number of customers in column C, and the day number (today is day 1, next Monday is day 6, and so on) in column D. (See Figure 14.32.)

2 **Dummy variables.** Create dummy variables by entering IF formulas in columns E through I. For example, enter the formula

=IF(A4="Mon",1,0)

in cell E4 and copy it down column E. Do the same for Tuesday, Wednesday, and Thursday dummy variables in columns F, G, and H. Finally, enter the formula

=IF(B4="Yes",1,0)

in cell I4 and copy it down column I. This creates the dummy variables for paydays.

3 **Run regression.** Note that the independent variables are now in adjacent columns, D through I, whereas the dependent variable is in column C. This makes it straightforward to use the Regression tool. Its output is shown in Figure 14.33. The coefficients in the range O19:O25 imply the following estimated regression equation:

$$\hat{y} = 496.1 - 0.36t + 71.1x_1 - 78.5x_2 - 122.5x_3 - 74.8x_4 + 127.1x_5$$

4 **Locate insignificant variables.** From column R of Figure 14.33, we see that the only variable with an insignificant coefficient is the day number. This might lead us to exclude this variable and rerun the regression.

5 **Rerun regression.** Since the day number is an insignificant variable, we rerun the analysis without it. (Now the X range includes columns E through I only.) The new regression output (not shown) yields the following regression equation:

$$\hat{y} = 466.2 + 80.4x_1 - 79.2x_2 - 109.8x_3 - 68.8x_4 + 124.3x_5 \quad \textbf{(14.20)}$$

All p-values are smaller than .10, therefore all independent variables are significant at the .10 significance level, and this equation appears satisfactory. We also see that

FIGURE 14.32 **Data and Dummy Variables for Credit Union Example**

	A	B	C	D	E	F	G	H	I
3	Day	Payday?	Customers	T	D1	D2	D3	D4	P
4	Mon	No	515	1	1	0	0	0	0
5	Tues	No	360	12	0	1	0	0	0
6	Wed	Yes	548	18	0	0	1	0	1
7	Wed	No	386	23	0	0	1	0	0
8	Thurs	No	440	24	0	0	0	1	0
9	Mon	Yes	687	46	1	0	0	0	1
10	Wed	No	350	48	0	0	1	0	0
11	Tues	No	430	52	0	1	0	0	0
12	Thurs	No	370	54	0	0	0	1	0
13	Fri	No	496	55	0	0	0	0	0
14	Fri	No	506	70	0	0	0	0	0
15	Mon	No	509	81	1	0	0	0	0
16	Thurs	Yes	508	89	0	0	0	1	1
17	Thurs	No	396	104	0	0	0	1	0
18	Mon	No	600	106	1	0	0	0	0
19	Wed	No	266	108	0	0	1	0	0
20	Tues	No	360	122	0	1	0	0	0
21	Fri	Yes	521	130	0	0	0	0	1
22	Tues	No	398	152	0	1	0	0	0

FIGURE 14.33 **Regression Output for Credit Union Example**

	N	O	P	Q	R	S	T
3	SUMMARY OUTPUT						
4							
5	*Regression Statistics*						
6	Multiple R	0.919743152					
7	R Square	0.845927465					
8	Adjusted R Square	0.768891198					
9	Standard Error	48.84517416					
10	Observations	19					
11							
12	ANOVA						
13		*df*	*SS*	*MS*	*F*	*Significance F*	
14	Regression	6	157192.7349	26198.8	10.9809	0.00028229	
15	Residual	12	28630.21247	2385.85			
16	Total	18	185822.9474				
17							
18		*Coefficients*	*Standard Error*	*t Stat*	*P-value*	*Lower 95%*	*Upper 95%*
19	Intercept	496.0856516	37.66028923	13.1726	1.7E-08	414.0309317	578.14037
20	T	-0.362217611	0.279852189	-1.2943	0.21991	-0.97196314	0.2475279
21	D1	71.07694463	38.07609893	1.86671	0.08656	-11.8837468	154.03764
22	D2	-78.47826352	38.5093761	-2.0379	0.06423	-162.3829848	5.4264578
23	D3	-122.5235683	38.6517004	-3.1699	0.00807	-206.7383876	-38.308749
24	D4	-74.82254247	37.66997099	-1.9863	0.07033	-156.8983572	7.2532722
25	P	127.1085359	28.68216773	4.43162	0.00082	64.61546188	189.60161

$R^2 = 0.85$ and $s_e = 48.8$. Thus, on 95% of all days, our prediction for the number of customers entering the credit union should be accurate within $2(48.8) = 97.6$ customers.

Interpretation of Coefficients of Dummy Variables How do we interpret the coefficients of dummy variables? To illustrate, consider paydays versus nonpaydays. On a payday, $x_5 = 1$. By substituting $x_5 = 1$ into Equation 14.20, we predict that

$$466.2 + 80.4x_1 - 79.2x_2 - 109.8x_3 - 68.8x_4 + 124.3$$

customers will enter the credit union. On a day that is not a payday, $x_5 = 0$. By substituting $x_5 = 0$ into Equation 14.20, we obtain the same prediction, except that the last term, +124.3, is missing. This shows the effect of the coefficient of the payday dummy variable. Expressed in words, paydays tend to have 124.3 more customers that nonpaydays, everything else being equal.

To see how the day of the week influences credit union traffic, we note that Equation 14.20 yields a different prediction for each day of the week. For Monday, $x_1 = 1, x_2 = x_3 = x_4 = 0$, and we obtain

$$\hat{y} = 466.2 + 80.4 + 124.3x_5 = 546.6 + 124.3x_5$$

For Tuesday, $x_2 = 1, x_1 = x_3 = x_4 = 0$, and we obtain

$$\hat{y} = 466.2 - 79.2 + 124.3x_5 = 387 + 124.3x_5$$

For Wednesday, $x_3 = 1, x_2 = x_1 = x_4 = 0$, and we obtain

$$\hat{y} = 466.2 - 109.8 + 124.3x_5 = 356.4 + 124.3x_5$$

For Thursday, $x_4 = 1, x_1 = x_3 = x_2 = 0$, and we obtain

$$\hat{y} = 466.2 - 68.8 + 124.3x_5 = 397.4 + 124.3x_5$$

Finally, for Friday, $x_1 = x_2 = x_3 = x_4 = 0$, and we obtain

$$\hat{y} = 466.2 + 124.3x_5$$

Thus, we find that (all other things being equal) credit union traffic is heaviest on Mondays, next heaviest on Fridays, third heaviest on Thursdays, fourth heaviest on Tuesdays, and lightest on Wednesdays. The coefficient of each day of the week represents how many more customers we would expect on that day than on a Friday (the day with no dummy).

In summary, we would interpret our dummy variables as follows. A payday increases the number of customers entering the bank by 124.3. On Mondays, we expect 80.4 more people than on Fridays. On Tuesdays, we expect 79.2 fewer people than on Fridays. On Wednesdays, we expect 109.8 fewer people than on Fridays. On Thursdays, we expect 68.8 fewer people than on Fridays.

Using the TREND Function to Make Forecasts We already used the TREND function in simple linear regression to make forecasts. Essentially, it saves us having to plug x-values directly into the regression equation. This is even more handy in multiple regression, where there are more x's to plug in. To illustrate, suppose we want to make forecasts for the following two future days: (1) day 320, which is a Friday and not a payday, and (2) day 324, which is a Thursday and a payday. (Here we will utilize the original regression equation, with the day number included.) To proceed, use the following steps, building from the spreadsheet shown in Figure 14.33.

1 Code these two days in rows 24 and 25. (See Figure 14.34.)
2 Select (highlight) the range J24:J25, which is where you want to put the predictions. Then type the formula

=TREND(C4:C22,D4:I22,D24:I25)

and enter it as an *array* formula by pressing Ctrl-Shift-Enter. The first argument (C4:C22) is the range where the y-values used to develop the regression equation are located. The second argument (D4:I22) is the range where the x-values used to develop the regression are located. The final range (D24:I25) is the range where the x-values for the new days are located.

As we see, the regression predicts that about 380 customers will enter on day 320, and about 304 will enter on day 324. ■

FIGURE 14.34 **Predictions for Two New Days for Credit Union Example**

	D	E	F	G	H	I	J
23							Predictions
24	320	0	0	0	0	0	380.17602
25	324	0	0	0	1	0	303.9046

14.11

Multiplicative Models

Often, we believe that the relationship between the dependent variable and the independent variables is of the following form:

$$y = \beta_0 x_1^{\beta_1} x_2^{\beta_2} \cdots x_k^{\beta_k} \tag{14.21}$$

The implication of this equation—and the primary reason it is used—is that a 1% increase in x_i leads to an expected increase in y of approximately β_i percent. Thus β_i can be interpreted as a measure of the elasticity of y with respect to x_i. The model itself is called a multiplicative model because the independent variables are multiplied (rather than added) to obtain y. To estimate such a relationship, we take natural logarithms of both sides of 14.21. This gives

$$\ln y = \ln \beta_0 + \beta_1(\ln x_1) + \beta_2(\ln x_2) + \cdots + \beta_k(\ln x_k)$$

Then to estimate 14.21, we run a multiple regression with $\ln y$ as the dependent variable and $\ln x_1, \ln x_2, \ldots, \ln x_k$ as the independent variables. The estimate of the coefficient of $\ln x_i$ from the regression output will be our estimate of β_i. (The antilog of the intercept term will be our estimate of β_0, although this is usually of less interest.)

We illustrate a multiplicative model in the following example.

EXAMPLE 14.11

The All County insurance company wants to determine how its annual operating costs depend on the number of home insurance and car insurance policies that have been written. Figure 14.35 gives relevant information for ten branches of the insurance company. (See the file INSURE.XLS.) The company believes a multiplicative model might be appropriate because operating costs might increase by a constant percentage as the number of either type of policy increases by a given percentage. How should the company proceed?

Solution

We attempt to fit the model $y = \beta_0 x_1^{\beta_1} x_2^{\beta_2}$, where y is the annual operating cost, x_1 is the number of home insurance policies, and x_2 is the number of car insurance policies. Because this is a multiplicative model, we need to take logs before running the regression. This can all be done easily in a spreadsheet as follows.

Developing the Spreadsheet Model

1 **Create logs.** Create the logs of the variables in columns F through H. For example, enter the formula

=LN(B4)

in cell F4. Then copy this formula to the range F4:H13 to create the other logs.

2 **Run regression.** Use the Regression tool in the usual way with G4:H13 as the X Range and F4:F13 as the Y Range. The least squares estimates obtained are

$$\text{Constant term estimate} = 5.339$$

$$\text{Estimate for } \beta_1 = 0.583$$

$$\text{Estimate for } \beta_2 = 0.409$$

Thus our estimate of β_0 is $e^{5.339} = 208.3$ (the anti-log of 5.339), and the estimated equation for annual operating cost is

$$\hat{y} = 208.3 x_1^{0.583} x_2^{0.409} \quad \textbf{(14.22)}$$

This regression yields $R^2 = 0.998$, indicating a very good fit.

3 **Predictions.** The standard error of estimate from the regression output is very misleading because it pertains to log dollars, not dollars. To find a meaningful

FIGURE 14.35 **Data for Insurance Example**

	A	B	C	D
3	Branch	Annual operating cost (y)	# of home insurance policies (x1)	# of car insurance policies (x2)
4	1	$124,000	400	1200
5	2	$71,000	350	360
6	3	$136,000	600	800
7	4	$219,000	800	1800
8	5	$230,000	900	1600
9	6	$75,000	200	1000
10	7	$56,000	120	900
11	8	$110,000	340	1100
12	9	$120,000	490	900
13	10	$144,000	700	800

standard error of estimate, first calculate the predicted values from Equation 14.22. (See Figure 14.36.) Specifically, enter the formula

=EXP($B$31)*C4^$B$32*D4^$B$33

in cell J4 and copy this down column J. (This assumes that the regression coefficients are in cells B31, B32, and B33, as they are in the INSURE.XLS file.)

4 **Prediction Errors.** Calculate the absolute prediction errors in column K, that is, the absolute values of the differences between the values in columns B and J. Then calculate the MAD in cell K16 with the formula

=AVERAGE(K4:K13)

FIGURE 14.36 **Predictions and Prediction Errors for Insurance Example**

	J	K	L	M	N
3	Predicted Cost	Absolute Error			
4	124337	336.644			
5	70310.6	689.439			
6	133432	2568.37			
7	219825	824.969			
8	224380	5620.43			
9	77044.5	2044.5			
10	54790.8	1209.19			
11	109145	854.815			
12	124422	4422.36			
13	145977	1977.32			
14			95% of all predictions		
15	Est StErr	2568.51	accurate within $5137.		
16	MAD	2054.8			

and calculate the approximate value of s_e in cell K15 with the formula

```
=1.25*K16
```

This approximate standard error is about $2570; therefore the company knows that 95% of its predictions will be accurate within $5140. ■

PROBLEMS

Skill-Building Problems

17 The annual return on General Motors stock and the return on the Standard and Poor's market index for the years 1961–1970, are given in the file BETA.XLS.

a Let y be the return on General Motors stock during a year and x be the return on Standard and Poor's index during a year. Financial theory suggests that $y = \beta_0 + \beta_1 x + \varepsilon$, where β_1 is called the beta for General Motors stock. Give an interpretation for the beta of a stock (in this case, General Motors) and use the data in the BETA.XLS file to estimate the beta for General Motors.

b Does the Standard and Poor's index appear to have a significant effect on the return on General Motors stock?

c What percentage of the variation in the return on General Motors Stock is explained by variation in the Standard and Poor's index?

d What percentage of the variation in the return on General Motors stock is unexplained by variation in Standard and Poor's index?

e During a year in which the Standard and Poor's index increased by 15%, what would we predict for the return on General Motors stock?

18 We are trying to determine the number of labor hours required to produce a unit of a product. We are given the information in the file LEARN.XLS. For example, the second unit produced required 517 labor hours, and the 600th unit produced required 34 labor hours.

a Try to determine a relationship between the number of units already produced and the labor hours needed to produce the next unit. Why is this relationship called the *learning curve*?

b How many labor hours would be needed to produce the 800th unit?

c We are 95% sure that the prediction in Part (b) is accurate within ______ hours.

19 Quarterly sales for a department store over a six-year period are given in the file SALES.XLS.

a Use multiple regression to develop a model that can be used to predict future quarterly sales. (*Hint*: Use dummy variables and an independent variable for the quarter number—quarter 1–quarter 24.)

b Letting y_t be the sales during quarter number t, discuss how to fit the following model to the data in the SALES.XLS file.

$$y_t = \beta_0 \beta_1^t \beta_2^{x_1} \beta_3^{x_2} \beta_4^{x_3}$$

Here $x_1 = 1$ if t is a first quarter, $x_2 = 1$ if t is a second quarter, and $x_3 = 1$ if t is a third quarter. (*Hint*: Take logarithms of both sides.)

c Interpret the answer to Part (b).

d Which model appears to yield better predictions for sales, the one in Part (a) or the one in Part (b)?

20 Confederate Express Service is attempting to determine how its shipping costs for a month depend on the number of units shipped during a month. The number of units shipped and total shipping cost for the last 15 months are given in the file SHIP.XLS.

a Determine a relationship between units shipped and monthly shipping cost.

b Plot the errors for the predictions in order of time sequence. Is there any unusual pattern?

c We have been told that there was a trucking strike during months 11–15, and we believe that this may have influenced shipping costs. How could the answer to Part (a) be modified to account for the effects of the strike? After accounting for the effects of the strike, does the unusual pattern in Part (b) disappear?

21 Consider the regression equation for the All County insurance example. If the number of car insurance policies increased by 1%, by what percentage would we predict that total costs would increase?

22 In the Credit Union example, suppose that we had used five (instead of four) dummy variables to represent the days of the week. What problem would have arisen? Try working through the example in this way and see what kind of output you obtain with Excel's regression tool. ■

14.12 Conclusion

Forecasting is a topic that usually fails to receive the bright lights. However, it is an essential first step in many of the models we have discussed throughout this book. Forecasting is often needed to obtain at least some of the input data for these models. In this chapter we have discussed the two main quantitative classes of forecasting methods. The first, extrapolation methods, uses the historical values of a time series variable—and nothing else—to forecast future values. The most frequently used extrapolation methods are the moving-average method and the various exponential smoothing methods.

The second class of forecasting methods is regression analysis. This method is much more general than the extrapolation methods. It uses any number of independent variables to explain a dependent variable. Regression analysis can use time series variables or cross-sectional variables. We have tried to give a broad picture of the kinds of situations where regression can be used. However, we have really only scratched the surface of this topic. If you plan to perform regression analysis as part of your job, you will need to explore the method much more thoroughly than we have done here.

REVIEW PROBLEMS

Skill-Building Problems

23 The file PORK.XLS contains data on pork sales. Price is in dollars per hundred pounds sold, quantity sold is in billions of pounds, per-capita income is in dollars, U.S. population is in millions, and GNP is in billions of dollars.

- **a** Use the data in this file to develop a regression equation that could be used to predict the quantity of pork sold during future periods. Is autocorrelation, heteroscedasticity, or multicollinearity a problem?
- **b** Suppose that during each of the next two quarters, price is \$45, U.S. population is 240, GNP is 2620, and per-capita income is \$10,000. Predict the quantity of pork sold during each of the next two quarters.
- **c** We expect our prediction of pork sales to be accurate within what value 68% of the time?
- **d** Use Winter's method to develop a forecast for pork sales during the next two quarters. (Use the first two years to initialize.)

24 The file MOTEL.XLS contains data on a motel chain's revenue and advertising.

- **a** Use the data in this file and multiple regression to make predictions of the motel chain's revenues during the next four quarters. Assume that advertising during each of the next four quarters is \$50,000. (*Hint*: Try using advertising, lagged by one period, as an independent variable.)

b Use Holt's method to make forecasts for the motel chain's revenues during the next four quarters.

c Use simple exponential smoothing to make predictions for the motel chain's revenues during the next four quarters.

d Use Winter's method to determine predictions for the motel chain's revenues during the next four quarters.

e Which forecasts would you expect to be the most reliable?

25 The file HOUSE.XLS contains data on monthly U.S. housing sales (in thousands of houses) for 1967–72.

a Use the years 1967–68 to initialize the parameters for Winter's method. Then find values of α, β, and γ that yield a MAD (for 1969–72) as small as possible.

b We would expect 68% of our forecasts to be accurate within ______ and 95% of our forecasts to be accurate within ______.

c Check whether the data are consistent with the answer to Part (b).

d Although we have not discussed autocorrelation for smoothing methods, good forecasts derived from smoothing methods should exhibit no autocorrelation. Do the forecast errors for this problem exhibit autocorrelation?

e It has been stated that if only trend and seasonality are important factors, then α should be at most 0.5. Explain why this problem required $\alpha > 0.5$.

f At the end of December 1972, what is the forecast for housing sales during the first three months of 1973?

26 Carboco puts metal coatings on jet propeller blades. The harder the coating, the higher the quality of the coating. The coating is shot onto the blade using pressurized gas contained in an F-gun. Carboco can control the temperature and gas pressure in the F-gun and can also control the room humidity. To see how gas pressure, temperature, and humidity influence hardness, Carboco engineers have run a regression for which the dependent variable is

$$\text{HARD} = \text{Hardness of a coating}$$

and the independent variables are

$$\begin{aligned}\text{HUMID} &= \text{Room humidity}\\ \text{TEMP} &= 1 \text{ if temperature level is high}\\ &= 0 \text{ if temperature level is low}\\ \text{PRESS} &= 1 \text{ if gas pressure is high}\\ &= 0 \text{ if gas pressure is low}\\ \text{T*P} &= \text{Product of TEMP and PRESS}\end{aligned}$$

We assume that temperature and gas pressure have only two possible levels, low and high. The relevant data are given in the file TEMP.XLS.

a Ignoring considerations of heteroscedasticity, multicollinearity, and autocorrelation, which equation should be used to predict hardness? Explain.

b What combination of gas pressure and temperature setting will maximize hardness?

c Explain how changing temperature from a low level to a high level affects hardness. Be specific!

27 We have been asked to determine how the total weekly production cost for Widgetco depends on the number of widgets produced during the week. The following model has been proposed:

$$y = \beta_0 + \beta_1 x + \beta_2 x^2 + \beta_3 x^3 + \varepsilon$$

where x is the number of widgets produced during the week and y is the total production cost for the week. For 15 weeks of data, we found that $SSR = 215475$ and $SST = 229228$. For this model, we obtain the following estimated regression equation:

$$\hat{y} = -29.7 + 19.8x - 0.39x^2 + 0.005x^3$$

The t-values for the coefficients of x, x^2, and x^3 are 0.78, 0.62, and 1.25.

a Test $H_0 : \beta_i = 0$ against $H_a : \beta_i \neq 0$ for $i = 1, 2, 3$, each at the .10 significance level.

b Determine R^2 for this model. How can the high R^2 value be reconciled with the answer to Part (a)?

28 Let y_t be the sales during month t (in thousands of dollars) for a photography studio, and let p_t be the price charged for portraits during month t. The data are in the file PHOTO.XLS. Use regression to fit the following model to the data in this file:

$$y_t = \beta_0 + \beta_1 y_{t-1} + \beta_2 p_t + \varepsilon_t$$

This equation indicates that last month's sales and the current month's price are independent variables.

a If the price of a portrait during month 21 is \$10, what would we predict for sales in month 21?

b Does there appear to be a problem with autocorrelation, heteroscedasticity, or multi collinearity?

29 The U.S. GNP during the years 1975–1984 is given in the file GNP.XLS. The data are in billions of dollars.

a Plot t, the number of years after 1974, against GNP and use the plot to describe how to fit a curve that could be used to predict GNP during future years.

b When the regression on transformed data is done, we find that $b_0 = 6.86$ and $b_1 = 0.105$. What is the prediction for 1985 GNP?

Skill-Extending Problems

30 (Based on Myers, Khuri, and Carter [1]) We want to determine how speed (x_1), pressure (x_2), and distance (x_3) affect the ability (y) of a printing machine to apply colored ink package labels. For 27 combinations of x_1, x_2, and x_3, we have observed three values of y. The data are in the file PRINT.XLS.

a For each combination of settings, determine the average of the y responses and the standard deviation of the y responses.

b Use a regression equation with independent variables $x_1, x_2, x_3, x_1^2, x_2^2, x_3^2, x_1x_2, x_1x_3$, and x_2x_3 to predict the average of the y responses.

c Use a regression equation with independent variables $x_1, x_2, x_3, x_1^2, x_2^2, x_3^2, x_1x_2, x_1x_3$, and x_2x_3 to predict the standard deviation of the y responses.

d Actually, the values of x_1, x_2, and x_3 are "coded" as shown in Table 14.13. Your goal is to achieve a mean response of 500 and minimize the standard deviation of the response. Determine values of speed, pressure, and distance that will achieve this goal.

31 Suppose that the return on asset i can be estimated as $\mu_i + \beta_i r_m + \varepsilon_i$, where r_m is the return on the market. Assume that the ε_i's are independent and that the standard deviation of ε_i can be estimated by the "standard error of estimate" from the regression equation with the market return as the independent variable and the return on asset i as the dependent variable. How can you express the variance of the portfolio without knowing the correlation between each pair of investments explicitly? (*Hint*: The variance of the market will enter into the equation.) Use the estimated regression equation to estimate the mean return on asset i as a function of the market return. Refer to the file SHARPE.XLS. Use NLP (as in Section 6.10) to determine the

TABLE 14.13 Codes for Printing Problem

	Code		
	−1	0	+1
Speed	40	60	80
Pressure	80	120	160
Distance	60	110	160

minimum variance portfolio that yields an expected return of at least 22%. Why do you think this method (using regression) is useful when many potential investments are available?

Modeling Problems

32 The file EAST.XLS lists the number of customers entering the Indiana University Credit Union Eastland Plaza Branch for each day of the year. It also lists other information such as the day of the week, whether the day was a staff or faculty payday, and whether the day was the day before or after a holiday. Use this data set to develop an equation that could be used to predict the number of customers entering the Eastland Plaza Branch. Carefully interpret the coefficients in your equation and discuss whether heteroscedasticity, autocorrelation, and/or multicollinearity appear to be problems.

33 Researchers who needed to forecast annual U.S. demand for newsprint found an R^2 of .93 with a multiple linear regression involving only two independent variables. Can you guess what those two independent variables were?

34 The file AUTO.XLS gives quarterly auto sales, GNP, interest rates and unemployment rates.

a With all but the most recent two years of data, use regression to forecast auto sales. Carefully interpret the coefficients in your final equation.

b Use all but the most recent two years of data to develop an exponential smoothing model to forecast future auto sales.

c To *validate* your model, determine which model does the best job of forecasting for the most recent two years of data. It is usually recommended to hold back some of your data to validate any forecast model. This helps avoid "overfitting."

35 We have mentioned the relationship that s_e is approximately 1.25 times the MAD. Assuming that errors are normally distributed, explain how you could use simulation to validate this relationship.

36 Standard Motors would like to reduce the warranty expenses incurred in servicing truck engines. If you were going to use regression to achieve this noble goal, what type of data would you collect? How could simulation be used to solve this problem?

37 Referring to Problem 32, your goal is to determine how many tellers the Eastland Plaza Branch must have each hour in order to ensure that 95% of all customers wait at most three minutes in line.

a Carefully describe the data you must collect to answer this question.

b If you were given the relevant data, describe how you would use queueing theory to answer this question.

38 New York City has hired you to determine how to staff the Sanitation Department. Each month New York must determine how many sanitation workers to hire (or fire) and how many hours of overtime to use. Discuss how you would set up a model to help New York minimize the annual cost of collecting the city's trash. ■

REFERENCE

1 Myers, R., A. Khuri, and W. Carter. "Response Surface Methodology: 1966–1988." *Technometrics* 3 (1989): 137–57.

Index

Why Do You Need This New Edition?

If you're wondering why you should buy this new edition of *Development Through the Lifespan*, here are 10 good reasons!

1. **Updated!** Meticulously researched material, including more than 2,000 new reference citations as well as the latest in research findings, is conveyed in a clear, story-like fashion that humanizes the complex development process.

2. **New!** "Take a Moment...," an active-learning feature built into the text narrative, asks students to "take a moment" to think about an important point, integrate information on human development, or engage in an exercise or an application to clarify a challenging concept. Take a Moment... actively engages students in learning and inspires critical thinking.

3. **New** and **updated** thematic boxes—"Social Issues," "Cultural Influences," Biology and Environment," and "A Lifespan Vista"—cover a wide range of areas within human development.

4. In-text highlighting of key terms and definitions permits students to review important terms and concepts in context, thereby promoting deeper and more thorough learning. An end-of-chapter term list with page references is also included for convenient and focused student review.

5. "Ask Yourself" critical-thinking questions have been thoroughly revised and expanded into a unique pedagogical feature that promotes four approaches to connecting with the subject matter. The questions encourage students to **Review** information they have just read, **Apply** it to new situations, **Connect** it to other age periods and domains of development, and **Reflect** on how theory and research are personally relevant in their own lives.

6. Chapter summaries, organized by major section headings, highlight important terms and remind students of key points in the text discussion. Review questions are also included in the summaries to encourage active study.

7. "Applying What We Know" tables provide practical real-life applications based on the results of theory and research. Professor Berk speaks directly to students, offering real-world advice on the importance of caring for oneself and others throughout the lifespan. The tables also speak to students as parents and to those pursuing child- and family-related careers or areas of study, such as teaching, health care, counseling, or social work.

8. Stories and vignettes about real people open each chapter and continue through the text to illustrate developmental principles and teach through engaging narrative. This book "teaches while it tells a story."

9. **New** and **updated** photos, figures, and tables effectively illustrate major points and enhance student interest and understanding.

10. "Milestones" tables appear at the end of each age division of the text. These tables summarize major physical, cognitive, language, emotional, and social attainments, providing a convenient aid for reviewing the chronology of lifespan development.

Allyn & Bacon
is an imprint of
PEARSON

FIFTH EDITION

Development Through the Lifespan

Laura E. Berk
Illinois State University

Allyn & Bacon
Boston • Columbus • Indianapolis • New York • San Francisco • Upper Saddle River
Amsterdam • Cape Town • Dubai • London • Madrid • Milan • Munich • Paris • Montreal • Toronto
Delhi • Mexico City • Sao Paulo • Sydney • Hong Kong • Seoul • Singapore • Taipei • Tokyo

Dedication

In loving memory of my parents,
Sofie Lentschner Eisenberg and Philip Vernon Eisenberg

Editor in Chief: Jessica Mosher
Acquisitions Editor: Michelle Limoges
Managing Editor: Tom Pauken
Supplements Editor: Sara Harris
Development Editors: Judy Ashkenaz, Pam Barter, Lisa McLellan, Susan Messer
Editorial Assistants: Paige Clunie, Claire Christensen
Senior Marketing Manager: Wendy Albert
Senior Production Administrator: Donna Simons
Manufacturing Buyer: JoAnne Sweeney
Cover Administrator: Kristina Mose-Libon
Interior Designer: Carol Somberg
Photo Researcher: Sarah Evertson—ImageQuest
Electronic Composition: TexTech, Inc.
Copyeditor: Margaret Pinette
References Editor: William Heckman
Proofreader: Beyond Words Proofreading

Library of Congress Cataloging-in-Publication Data
Berk, Laura E.
Development through the lifespan / Laura E. Berk. — 5th ed.
p. cm.
ISBN-13: 978-0-205-68793-0
ISBN-10: 0-205-68793-8
1. Developmental psychology—Textbooks. I. Title
BF713.B465 2010
155—dc22
2009037324

10 9 8 7 6 5 4 3 2 1 CIN 13 12 11 10 09

Milestones Photo Credits
(credit sequence keyed to top-to-bottom placement of photos):
Page 212: column 1: © Ariel Skelly/Getty Images/Blend Images; column 2: © Marcus Mok/Getty Images/Asia Images; column 3: © Myrleen Ferguson Cate/PhotoEdit. **Page 213:** column 1: © Ellen B. Senisi; column 2: © Geri Engberg/The Image Works; column 3: © Laura Dwight/CORBIS.

Page 286: column 1: Don Smetzer/PhotoEdit; column 2: © John-Francis Bourke/zefa/CORBIS; column 3: © Bill Aron/PhotoEdit. **Page 287:** column 1 top: © Retna/Index Stock; column 1 bottom: Peter Hvizdak/The Image Works; column 2: © David Madison/Getty Images/Digital Vision; column 3 top: Ellen B. Senisi/The Image Works; column 3 bottom: Brand X Pictures/Jupiter Images.

Page 358: column 1 top: © Dennis MacDonald/PhotoEdit; column 1 bottom: © David Young-Wolff/PhotoEdit; column 3 top: Nancy R. Cohen/Getty Images/Digital Vision; column 3 bottom: © David Young-Wolff/Getty Images/Photographer's Choice. **Page 359:** column 1: © CP Photo/Paul Chiasson; column 2 top: Toronto Star/First Light; column 2 bottom: © David Young-Wolff/PhotoEdit; column 3 top: © Gideon Mendel/Corbis; column 3 bottom: Thomas Downs/Lonely Planet Images.

Page 428: column 1: © Catherine Wessel/Corbis; column 2: © Kayte M. Deioma/PhotoEdit; column 3 top: Rudy von Briel/PhotoEdit; column 3 bottom: © Steve Skjold/Alamy. **Page 429:** column 1: © Leland Bobbé/Corbis; column 2 top: © Journal Courier/Clayton Stalter/The Image Works; column 2 bottom: Don Smelzer/Getty Images/Stone; column 3: Ariel Skelley/Corbis.

Page 498: column 1: © Jacksonville Journal/Clayton Stalter/The Image Works; column 2 top: © Bob Daemmrich/The Image Works; column 2 bottom: © Zefa RF/Alamy; column 3 top: © moodboard/Alamy; column 3 bottom: © David Young Wolff/PhotoEdit. **Page 499:** column 1: © Jim Craigmyle/Corbis; column 2 top: © David Young-Wolff/Getty Images/Photographer's Choice; column 2 bottom: Jose Luis Pelaez, Inc./Blend Images/Getty Images; column 3 top: © Ariel Skelley/Getty Images/Blend Images; column 3 bottom: Jim Craigmyle/Corbis.

Page 560: column 1 top: © Jon Feingersh/Getty Images/Blend Images; column 1 bottom: © Golden Pixels LLC/Alamy; column 2: © Image Source/photolibrary; column 3 top: © Paul A. Souders/CORBIS; column 3 bottom: © Elyse Lewin/Getty Images/Photographer's Choice. **Page 561:** column 1 top: © Blend images RF/photolibrary; column 1 bottom: © Lee Snider/The Image Works; column 2 top: © Blend Images RF/photolibrary; column 2 bottom: © Jonathan Nourok/PhotoEdit; column 3 top: © Design Pics Inc/photolibrary; column 3 middle: © Creatas/photolibrary; column 3 bottom: © David Young-Wolff/PhotoEdit.

Page 636: column 1 top: © Choups/Alamy; column 1 bottom: © Corbis; column 2 top: © Johnny Crawford/The Image Works; column 2 bottom: AP Images/Greg Baker; column 3 top: © Jon Feingersh/Getty Images/Blend Images; column 3 bottom: © Dennis MacDonald/Alamy. **Page 637:** column 1 top: © Studio Zanello/Ken Chernus Photography/Getty Images; column 1 bottom: © Hill Street Studios/Getty Images/blend images; column 2 top: Jacobs Stock Photography/Getty Images/Digital Vision; column 2 bottom: © John Birdsall/The Image Works; column 3 top: Damon Higgins/Palm Beach Post/ZUMA Press; column 3 bottom: © Mike Kemp/Getty Images.

Allyn & Bacon
is an imprint of
PEARSON

www.pearsonhighered.com

ISBN-10: 0-205-68793-8
ISBN-13: 978-0-205-68793-0

About the Author

Laura E. Berk is a distinguished professor of psychology at Illinois State University, where she has taught human development to both undergraduate and graduate students for more than three decades. She received her bachelor's degree in psychology from the University of California, Berkeley, and her master's and doctoral degrees in child development and educational psychology from the University of Chicago. She has been a visiting scholar at Cornell University, UCLA, Stanford University, and the University of South Australia.

Berk has published widely on the effects of school environments on children's development, the development of private speech, and most recently the role of make-believe play in development. Her research has been funded by the U.S. Office of Education and the National Institute of Child Health and Human Development. It has appeared in many prominent journals, including *Child Development, Developmental Psychology, Merrill-Palmer Quarterly, Journal of Abnormal Child Psychology, Development and Psychopathology,* and *Early Childhood Research Quarterly.* Her empirical studies have attracted the attention of the general public, leading to contributions to *Psychology Today* and *Scientific American.* She has also been featured on National Public Radio's *Morning Edition* and in *Parents Magazine, Wondertime,* and *Reader's Digest.*

Berk has served as a research editor for *Young Children* and a consulting editor for *Early Childhood Research Quarterly.* Currently, she is an associate editor for the *Journal of Cognitive Education and Psychology.* She is a frequent contributor to edited volumes on early childhood development, having recently authored chapters on the importance of parenting, on make-believe play and self-regulation, and on the kindergarten child. She has also written the chapter on development for *The Many Faces of Psychological Research in the Twenty-First Century* (Society for the Teaching of Psychology); the article on social development for *The Child: An Encyclopedic Companion*; the article on Vygotsky for the *Encyclopedia of Cognitive Science*; and the chapter on storytelling as a teaching strategy for *Voices of Experience: Memorable Talks from the National Institute on the Teaching of Psychology* (Association for Psychological Science).

Berk's books include *Private Speech: From Social Interaction to Self-Regulation; Scaffolding Children's Learning: Vygotsky and Early Childhood Education; Landscapes of Development: An Anthology of Readings;* and *A Mandate for Playful Learning in Preschool: Presenting the Evidence.* In addition to *Development Through the Lifespan,* she is author of the best-selling texts *Child Development* and *Infants, Children, and Adolescents,* published by Allyn and Bacon. Her book for parents and teachers is *Awakening Children's Minds: How Parents and Teachers Can Make a Difference.*

Berk is active in work for children's causes. In addition to service in her home community, she is a member of the national board of directors and chair of the central region advisory board of Jumpstart, a nonprofit organization that provides one-to-one literacy intervention to thousands of low-income preschoolers across the United States, using college and university students as interveners. Berk is a fellow of the American Psychological Association, Division 7: Developmental Psychology.

Features at a Glance

A LIFESPAN VISTA

SOCIAL ISSUES

CULTURAL INFLUENCES

BIOLOGY AND ENVIRONMENT

APPLYING WHAT WE KNOW

Contents

CHAPTER 14
Emotional and Social Development in Early Adulthood 462

PART VIII
Middle Adulthood

CHAPTER 15
Physical and Cognitive Development in Middle Adulthood 500

CHAPTER 16

Emotional and Social Development in Middle Adulthood 530

PART IX

Late Adulthood

CHAPTER 17

Physical and Cognitive Development in Late Adulthood 562

CHAPTER 18
Emotional and Social Development in Late Adulthood 602

PART X
The End of Life

CHAPTER 19
Death, Dying, and Bereavement 638

A Personal Note to Students

My more than 30 years of teaching child development have brought me in contact with thousands of students like you—students with diverse college majors, future goals, interests, and needs. Some are affiliated with my own field, psychology, but many come from other related fields—education, sociology, anthropology, family studies, social service, nursing, and biology, to name just a few. Each semester, my students' aspirations have proved to be as varied as their fields of study. Many look toward careers in applied work—counseling, caregiving, nursing, social work, school psychology, and program administration. Some plan to teach, and a few want to do research. Most hope someday to become parents, whereas others are already parents who come with a desire to better understand and rear their children. And almost all arrive with a deep curiosity about how they themselves developed from tiny infants into the complex human beings they are today.

My goal in preparing this fifth edition of *Development Through the Lifespan* is to provide a textbook that meets the instructional goals of your course as well as your personal interests and needs. To achieve these objectives, I have grounded this book in a carefully selected body of classic and current theory and research. In addition, the text highlights the lifespan perspective on development and the interacting contributions of biology and environment to the developing person. It also illustrates commonalities and differences among ethnic groups and cultures, and discusses the broader social contexts in which we develop. I have provided a unique pedagogical program that will assist you in mastering information, integrating various aspects of development, critically examining controversial issues, applying what you have learned, and relating the information to your own life.

I hope that learning about human development will be as rewarding for you as I have found it over the years. I would like to know what you think about both the field of human development and this book. I welcome your comments; please feel free to send them to me at Department of Psychology, Box 4620, Illinois State University, Normal, IL 61790, or care of the publisher, who will forward them to me.

—*Laura E. Berk*

Preface for Instructors

My decision to write *Development Through the Lifespan* was inspired by a wealth of professional and personal experiences. First and foremost were the interests and concerns of hundreds of students of human development with whom I have worked in over three decades of college teaching. Each semester, their insights and questions have revealed how an understanding of any single period of development is enriched by an appreciation of the entire lifespan. Second, as I moved through adult development myself, I began to think more intensely about factors that have shaped and reshaped my own life course—family, friends, mentors, co-workers, community, and larger society. My career well-established, my marriage having stood the test of time, and my children launched into their adult lives, I felt that a deeper grasp of these multiple, interacting influences would help me better appreciate where I had been and where I would be going in the years ahead. I was also convinced that such knowledge could contribute to my becoming a better teacher, scholar, family member, and citizen. And because teaching has been so central and gratifying to my work life, I wanted to bring to others a personally meaningful understanding of lifespan development.

The years since *Development Through the Lifespan* first appeared have been a period of considerable expansion and change in theory and research. This fifth edition represents these rapidly transforming aspects of the field, with a wealth of new content and teaching tools:

- *Diverse pathways of change are highlighted.* Investigators have reached broad consensus that variations in biological makeup and everyday tasks lead to wide individual differences in paths of change and resulting competencies. This edition pays more attention to variability in development and to recent theories—including ecological, sociocultural, and dynamic systems—that attempt to explain it. Multicultural and cross-cultural findings, including international comparisons, are enhanced throughout the text. Biology and Environment and Cultural Influences boxes also accentuate the theme of diversity in development.

- *The lifespan perspective is emphasized.* As in previous editions, the lifespan perspective—development as lifelong, multidimensional, multidirectional, plastic, and embedded in multiple contexts—continues to serve as a unifying approach to understanding human change and is woven thoroughly into the text. In addition, special Lifespan Vista boxes discuss lifespan-perspective assumptions and consider development across a wide age span.

- *The complex bidirectional relationship between biology and environment is given greater attention.* Accumulating evidence on development of the brain, motor skills, cognitive and language competencies, temperament and personality, and developmental problems underscores the way biological factors emerge in, are modified by, and share power with experience. Interconnections between biology and environment are integral to the lifespan perspective and are revisited throughout the text narrative and in the Biology and Environment boxes with new and updated topics.

- *Inclusion of interdisciplinary research is expanded.* The move toward viewing thoughts, feelings, and behavior as an integrated whole, affected by a wide array of influences in biology, social context, and culture, has motivated developmental researchers to strengthen their ties with other fields of psychology and with other disciplines. Topics and findings included in this edition increasingly reflect the contributions of educational psychology, social psychology, health psychology, clinical psychology, neuropsychology, biology, pediatrics, geriatrics, sociology, anthropology, social welfare, and other fields.

- *The links among theory, research, and applications are strengthened.* As researchers intensify their efforts to generate findings relevant to real-life situations, I have placed even greater weight on social policy issues and sound theory- and research-based applications. Further applications are provided in the Applying What We Know tables, which give students concrete ways of building bridges between their learning and the real world.

- *The role of active student learning is made more explicit.* A new ***TAKE A MOMENT...*** feature, built into the chapter narrative, asks students to think deeply and critically or to engage in an exercise or application as they read. Ask Yourself questions at the end of each major section have been thoroughly revised to promote four approaches to engaging actively with the subject matter—*Review, Apply, Connect,* and *Reflect.* This feature assists students in thinking about what they have learned from multiple vantage points. In addition, highlighting of key terms within the text narrative reinforces student learning in context.

Text Philosophy

The basic approach of this book has been shaped by my own professional and personal history as a teacher, researcher, and parent. It consists of seven philosophical ingredients that I regard as essential for students to emerge from a course with a thorough understanding of lifespan development. Each theme is woven into every chapter:

1. **An understanding of the diverse array of theories in the field and the strengths and shortcomings of each.** The first chapter begins by emphasizing that only knowledge of multiple theories can do justice to the richness of human

development. As I take up each age period and domain of development, I present a variety of theoretical perspectives, indicate how each highlights previously overlooked aspects of development, and discuss research that evaluates it. Consideration of contrasting theories also serves as the context for an evenhanded analysis of many controversial issues.

2. **A grasp of the lifespan perspective as an integrative approach to development.** I introduce the lifespan perspective as an organizing framework in the first chapter and refer to and illustrate its assumptions throughout the text, in an effort to help students construct an overall vision of development from conception to death.

3. **Knowledge of both the sequence of human development and the processes that underlie it.** Students are provided with a discussion of the organized sequence of development along with processes of change. An understanding of process—how complex combinations of biological and environmental events produce development—has been the focus of most recent research. Accordingly, the text reflects this emphasis. But new information about the timetable of change has also emerged. In many ways, the very young and the old have proved to be far more competent than they were believed to be in the past. In addition, many milestones of adult development, such as finishing formal education, entering a career, getting married, having children, and retiring, have become less predictable. Current evidence on the sequence and timing of development, along with its implications for process, is presented for all periods of the lifespan.

4. **An appreciation of the impact of context and culture on human development.** A wealth of research indicates that people live in rich physical and social contexts that affect all domains of development. Throughout the book, students travel to distant parts of the world as I review a growing body of cross-cultural evidence. The text narrative also discusses many findings on socioeconomically and ethnically diverse people within the United States. Furthermore, the impact of historical time period and cohort membership receives continuous attention. In this vein, gender issues—the distinctive but continually evolving experiences, roles, and life paths of males and females—are granted substantial emphasis. Besides highlighting the effects of immediate settings, such as family, neighborhood, and school, I make a concerted effort to underscore the influence of larger social structures—societal values, laws, and government programs—on lifelong well-being.

5. **An understanding of the joint contributions of biology and environment to development.** The field recognizes more powerfully than ever before the joint roles of hereditary/constitutional and environmental factors—that these contributions to development combine in complex ways and cannot be separated in a simple manner. Numerous examples of how biological dispositions can be maintained as well as transformed by social contexts are presented throughout the book.

6. **A sense of the interdependency of all domains of development—physical, cognitive, emotional, and social.** Every chapter emphasizes an integrated approach to human development. I show how physical, cognitive, emotional, and social development are interwoven. Within the text narrative, and in a special series of Ask Yourself questions at the end of major sections, students are referred to other sections of the book to deepen their grasp of relationships among various aspects of change.

7. **An appreciation of the interrelatedness of theory, research, and applications.** Throughout this book, I emphasize that theories of human development and the research stimulated by them provide the foundation for sound, effective practices with children, adolescents, and adults. The link among theory, research, and applications is reinforced by an organizational format in which theory and research are presented first, followed by practical implications. In addition, a current focus in the field—harnessing knowledge of human development to shape social policies that support human needs throughout the lifespan—is reflected in every chapter. The text addresses the current condition of children, adolescents, and adults in the United States and elsewhere in the world and shows how theory and research have combined with public interest to spark successful interventions. Many important applied topics are considered, such as family planning, infant mortality, maternal employment and child care, teenage pregnancy and parenthood, domestic violence, exercise and adult health, lifelong learning, grandparents rearing grandchildren, caring for elders with dementia, adjustment to retirement, and palliative care for the dying.

Text Organization

I have chosen a chronological organization for *Development Through the Lifespan.* The book begins with an introductory chapter that describes the scientific history of the field, influential theories, and research strategies. It is followed by two chapters on the foundations of development. Chapter 2 combines an overview of biological and environmental contexts into a single integrated discussion of these multifaceted influences on development. Chapter 3 is devoted to prenatal development, birth, and the newborn baby. With this foundation, students are ready to look closely at seven major age periods: infancy and toddlerhood (Chapters 4, 5, and 6), early childhood (Chapters 7 and 8), middle childhood (Chapters 9 and 10), adolescence (Chapters 11 and 12), early adulthood (Chapters 13 and 14), middle adulthood (Chapters 15 and 16), and late adulthood (Chapters 17 and 18). Topical chapters within each chronological division cover physical development, cognitive development, and emotional and social development. The book concludes with a chapter on death, dying, and bereavement (Chapter 19).

The chronological approach assists students in thoroughly understanding each age period. It also eases the task of integrating the various domains of development because each is discussed in close proximity. At the same time, a chronologically organized book requires that theories covering several age periods be presented piecemeal. This creates a challenge for students, who must link the various parts together. To assist with this task, I frequently remind students of important earlier achievements before discussing new developments, referring back to related sections with page references. Also, chapters or sections devoted to the same topic (for example, cognitive development) are similarly organized, making it easier for students to draw connections across age periods and construct an overall view of developmental change.

New Coverage in the Fifth Edition

Lifespan development is a fascinating and ever-changing field of study, with constantly emerging new discoveries and refinements in existing knowledge. The fifth edition represents this burgeoning contemporary literature, with over 2,000 new citations. Cutting-edge topics throughout the text underscore the book's major themes. Here is a sampling:

CHAPTER 1: New extension of Sofie's story • New Lifespan Vista box on the baby-boom generation, illustrating history-graded influences (cohort effects) on the life course • Developmental cognitive neuroscience as a new area of investigation • New examples of research using systematic observation, structured interviews, ethnography, correlational research, and field experiments

CHAPTER 2: New evidence on the changing proportion of male to female births • Updated Social Issues box on the pros and cons of reproductive technologies • Updated section on development of adopted children • Enhanced attention to the impact of poverty on development • Updated research on neighborhood influences on physical and mental health of children and adults • Updated section on public policies and human development, including current statistics on the condition of children, families, and the aged in the United States compared with other Western nations • Updated Lifespan Vista box on worldwide education of girls and its transforming impact on current and future generations • New examples of environmental influences on gene expression

CHAPTER 3: Updated research on fetal sensory and behavioral capacities • Updated consideration of a wide range of teratogens • Inclusion of the new designation for harmful effects of prenatal alcohol exposure—fetal alcohol spectrum disorder—and its associated three diagnoses: fetal alcohol syndrome (FAS), partial fetal alcohol syndrome (PFAS), and alcohol-related neurodevelopmental disorder (ARND) • New evidence on the long-term consequences of emotional stress during pregnancy • New findings on older maternal age and prenatal and birth complications • Updated discussion of preterm and low-birth-weight infants, including long-term developmental outcomes in very-low-birth-weight babies • Expanded Social Issues box on health care and other policies for parents and newborn babies, including cross-national infant mortality rates and the importance of generous parental leave

CHAPTER 4: Updated introduction to major methods of assessing brain functioning, including NIROT • New research on children adopted from Romanian orphanages, bearing on the question of whether infancy is a sensitive period of development • Updated Cultural Influences box on cultural variation in infant sleeping arrangements • Updated section on breastfeeding • Expanded and updated section on newborn imitation, including the role of mirror neurons in the human capacity for imitation and other social abilities • New dynamic systems research on development of walking and reaching • Updated evidence on how environmental supports contribute to development of motor skills • New findings on development of infant speech perception, including infants' statistical learning capacity • New Biology and Environment box on "tuning in" to familiar speech, faces, and music during the second half of the first year, suggesting a sensitive period for culture-specific learning • Expanded and updated section on intermodal perception, including its contributions to all aspects of psychological development

CHAPTER 5: New research on deferred imitation in toddlerhood • New evidence on young infants' understanding of object permanence, including brain-wave findings • New research on development of categorization in toddlerhood, including the animate–inanimate distinction • Updated evidence on memory development in infancy, including salience of novel actions over object features to young babies • Updated findings on quality of child care in the United States, with consequences for cognitive and language development • Expanded discussion of the interactionist perspective on language development • New evidence on the relationship between language comprehension and production in toddlers, with implications for early language progress

CHAPTER 6: Revised and updated Biology and Environment box on parental depression and child development, with expanded treatment of the impact of paternal depression • New research on parenting and early development of emotional self-regulation • Expanded treatment of infants' developing understanding of others' emotions • New research on the self-regulatory dimension of temperament—effortful control—and consequences for children's cognitive and social competence • New findings on attachment difficulties of children adopted from deprived institutions, including neurophysiological evidence • New research on the joint contributions of infant characteristics and parental sensitivity to attachment security • Expanded section on fathers' involvement with infants, including cultural variations • Enhanced discussion of the influence of attachment quality on later development, including emergence of internal working models in the second year • Updated Social Issues box on the influence of child-care quality and long child-care hours on attachment and later development, including cross-cultural evidence • Updated section on development of self-recognition and self-awareness in the first two years, with new research on cultural variations • New evidence on joint contributions of temperament and parenting to toddlers' developing capacity to delay gratification

CHAPTER 7: Updated consideration of advances in brain development in early childhood, with emphasis on the hippocampus • New Biology and Environment box on low-level lead exposure and children's development • Updated statistics and research on childhood immunizations • New findings on the contribution of child temperament, parenting practices, and societal conditions to unintentional injury in early childhood • Updated research on development of attention, highlighting gains in inhibition • New research on Tools of the Mind, a preschool program inspired by Vygotsky's theory • Enhanced discussion of the development of autobiographical memory, including the influence of the parent–child relationship • New evidence on cognitive attainments and social experiences that contribute to mastery of false belief • Updated Biology and Environment box on "mindblindness" and autism • New findings on gains in academic and social skills associated with Montessori preschool education • Updated discussion of educational media, including effects of television and computers on cognitive and academic learning • Expanded and updated research on the diverse strategies preschoolers use to figure out word meanings

CHAPTER 8: New evidence on the contribution of attachment to parent–child narratives about emotions and, thus, to emotional understanding • Updated consideration of emotional self-regulation in early childhood, including the influence of temperament • Enhanced Cultural Influences box on ethnic differences in the consequences of physical punishment • New evidence on the importance of social skills and friendships in fostering children's successful transition to school • Updated discussion of violent media and development of aggression • Updated discussion of gender schema theory, noting individual differences among children in gender-schematic processing • New findings on the harmful impact of parental psychological control on children's adjustment • Expanded consideration of ethnic variations in child-rearing beliefs and practices • Updated consideration of consequences of child maltreatment, including new evidence on central nervous system damage • Research on Healthy Families America, an early intervention program aimed at reducing child maltreatment

CHAPTER 9: Revised and updated section on overweight and obesity, including rapid increase in developing nations • Updated statistics on physical activity and fitness among U.S. school-age children • New Social Issues box on physical, cognitive, and social benefits of school recess • Revised and updated Biology and Environment box on children with attention-deficit hyperactivity disorder • Expanded treatment of cultural influences on mathematical development, with special attention to Asian nations • Updated Lifespan Vista box on emotional intelligence • Enhanced discussion of dynamic assessment, with implications for ethnic minority children's mental test performance • Updated Social Issues box on high-stakes testing • Updated research on bilingual development • New research on inclusive classrooms and children with learning difficulties

CHAPTER 10: Enhanced attention to cultural variations in self-concept, with special attention to Asian versus U.S. comparisons • New research on the impact of gender-stereotyped expectations on school-age children's self-esteem • Updated research on parenting practices and children's achievement-related attributions, including the influence of cultural values on likelihood of developing learned helplessness • Updated research on cultural variations in children's moral judgments of truthfulness and lying • Updated evidence on school-age children's grasp of individual rights • Expanded section on development of racial and ethnic prejudice and strategies for reducing children's prejudices • Updated findings on development of gender identity in middle childhood, with implications for emotional adjustment • Consideration of the contemporary debate over how best to help children who feel gender atypical • Enhanced attention to parenting of school-age children, including the consequences of paternal involvement for children's development • Expanded attention to the role of fathers in children's development, with special attention to blended families and dual-career families •

Updated Lifespan Vista box on impact of ethnic and political violence on children • New evidence on the impact of self-care and after-school programs on school-age children's adjustment • New evidence on children's eyewitness testimony, including factors that contribute to children's suggestibility

CHAPTER 11: Updated findings on adolescent physical activity and sports participation, including gender differences and consequences for development • Updated research on adolescent brain development • New evidence on contributions of early family experiences to timing of puberty • New findings on implications of pubertal timing for psychological adjustment in adolescence and adulthood, including ethnic variations • Updated evidence on factors that contribute to anorexia nervosa and treatment outcomes • Discussion of the Internet as a hazardous "sex educator" • New evidence on the long-term consequences of adolescent parenthood and on prevention and intervention strategies • New Lifespan Vista box on intergenerational continuity in adolescent parenthood • New findings on the influence of schooling on development of propositional thought • Expanded and updated research on adolescent decision making • Updated consideration of factors contributing to sex differences in verbal, mathematical, and spatial abilities • New research on the impact of school transitions on adolescent adjustment • New research on ethnic variations in peer support for school achievement • New findings on consequences of part-time work for adolescent adjustment

CHAPTER 12: New research on identity statuses, cognitive styles, and adjustment • Updated Cultural Influences box on identity development among ethnic minority youths • New research on situational influences on care-based moral reasoning • Expanded evaluation of Kohlberg's stages, including issues raised by a pragmatic approach to moral development • Enhanced consideration of factors that promote moral self-relevance, including a compassionate and just school climate • Updated section on parenting and adolescent autonomy • Inclusion of the impact of acculturative stress on adjustment of ethnic minority teenagers • New findings on Internet friendships and adjustment • Updated section on dating • New findings on adolescent suicide, including high suicide rates among Native-American youths • Evaluations of zero tolerance policies in schools, including their failure to reduce youth misconduct

CHAPTER 13: Updated discussion of theories of biological aging • New Biology and Environment box on telomere length as a marker of the impact of life circumstances on biological aging • Updated evidence on causes and consequences of overweight and obesity in adulthood • New findings on the contribution of physical activity to psychological well-being and cognitive functioning • Updated discussion of SES variations in adult health • New evidence on substance abuse in early adulthood • Consideration of continued development of the cerebral cortex in early adulthood, including experience-dependent brain growth • Updated findings on factors that foster development of epistemic cognition • New evidence on factors influencing vocational choice, with special attention to the role of parents and teachers

CHAPTER 14: Expanded section on emerging adulthood, including new evidence on identity development, cultural influences, and cultural variations • New Cultural Influences box addressing the controversy over whether emerging adulthood really is a distinct period of development • Enhanced consideration of cultural influences on the experience of love • Updated Social Issues box on partner abuse • New findings on young adult friendships • Updated research on factors contributing to relationship satisfaction among heterosexual and gay and lesbian couples • New findings on factors influencing successful transition to parenthood • Updated evidence on life satisfaction of never-married single people and childless couples • New findings on cohabitation and durability of relationships • New evidence on career development and workplace challenges faced by women and ethnic minority young adults

CHAPTER 15: Updated evidence on risks of hormone therapy to reduce physical discomforts of menopause, including efficacy of alternatives • New findings on women's psychological reactions to menopause • Updated consideration of lifestyle changes that can reduce cancer incidence and deaths • New findings on prevalence of osteoporosis, including ethnic variations • New evidence on social dominance as an unhealthy feature of the Type A behavior pattern • Updated discussion of the contribution of processing speed to diverse cognitive changes in older adults • Updated consideration of memory changes during midlife • New research on returning students, with special attention to factors influencing women's adjustment • Revised and updated Biology and Environment box on anti-aging effects of dietary calorie restriction, including physiological processes that mediate its impact on longevity

CHAPTER 16: Inclusion of the Midlife Development in the United States (MIDUS) survey findings on emotional and social development • Expanded discussion of the midlife experience of the baby-boom generation • Enhanced attention to factors contributing to generativity, including the role of fatherhood for men • New research on "turning points" at midlife • Updated Biology and Environment box on contributions to midlife psychological well-being • New findings on gender identity, including androgyny among middle-aged baby boomers • Expanded discussion of factors contributing to involved grandparenting and satisfaction with the grandparent role • Updated Lifespan Vista box on grandparents rearing grandchildren—the "skipped generation" family • New research on middle-aged adults' relationships with their aging parents, including cultural variations • Updated findings on caring for aging parents, including gender differences • New evidence on midlife sibling relationships, highlighting warmer ties between brothers of the baby-boom than the previous generation • New evidence on challenges faced by women in advancing to high-level managerial positions in the workplace

CHAPTER 17: Inclusion of international comparisons in healthy life expectancy • New research on brain development, including neurological changes that enable elders to compensate for declines in central nervous system functioning • Updated findings on risk and protective factors associated with various aspects of physical aging • Updated section on assistive technologies • Expanded and updated discussion of stereotypes of aging and their impact on elders • New Cultural Influences box on cultural variations in sense of uselessness in late life, with implications for health and mortality • New evidence on the impact of nutrition and exercise on health status in late adulthood • New survey findings on sexual activity in late adulthood • Updated evidence on genetic and environmental contributions to arthritis • New evidence on genetic and environmental risks for Alzheimer's, and on protective factors • Updated Social Issues box on interventions for caregivers of elders with dementia • Expanded consideration of benefits of assisted living • Enhanced attention to elders' use of selective optimization with compensation in adapting to cognitive changes • Updated research on everyday problem solving in late adulthood • New findings on the impact of cognitive training on older adults' long-term health and mental functioning

CHAPTER 18: New Lifespan Vista box on the Third Age as a new phase of late adulthood spanning the years 65 to 79—a time of new goal setting and high life satisfaction • New research on late-life personality development, with emphasis on elders' resilience • Updated findings on the interrelationship between physical and mental health in late adulthood • Expanded consideration of the role of social support in elders' psychological well-being • Enhanced discussion of the importance of aging in place, with special attention to high-quality assisted living and THE GREEN HOUSE® nursing home model • Expanded attention to cultural variations in elders' social networks, including implications for psychological well-being • New evidence on elders' relationships with adult children • Updated research on elder abuse • Enhanced discussion of variations in the retirement process • New evidence on elders' contribution to society through volunteering • Discussion of factors that contribute to optimal aging

CHAPTER 19: New evidence on factors affecting death anxiety, including religiosity and gender • New section on the experience of dying in nursing homes • Updated statistics on prevalence of hospice in the United States, along with information on its affordability • Updated cross-national evidence on religiosity and attitudes toward voluntary active euthanasia • Updated Social Issues box on voluntary active euthanasia • Revised and updated discussion of assisted suicide, including cautions advised by the Academy of Hospice and Palliative Medicine and attitudes of U.S. doctors • New research supporting the dual-process model of coping with loss • Updated evidence on the course of bereavement after death of a spouse • Attention to the controversy over whether grief counseling is beneficial for most bereaved people or only those experiencing profound difficulty

Pedagogical Features

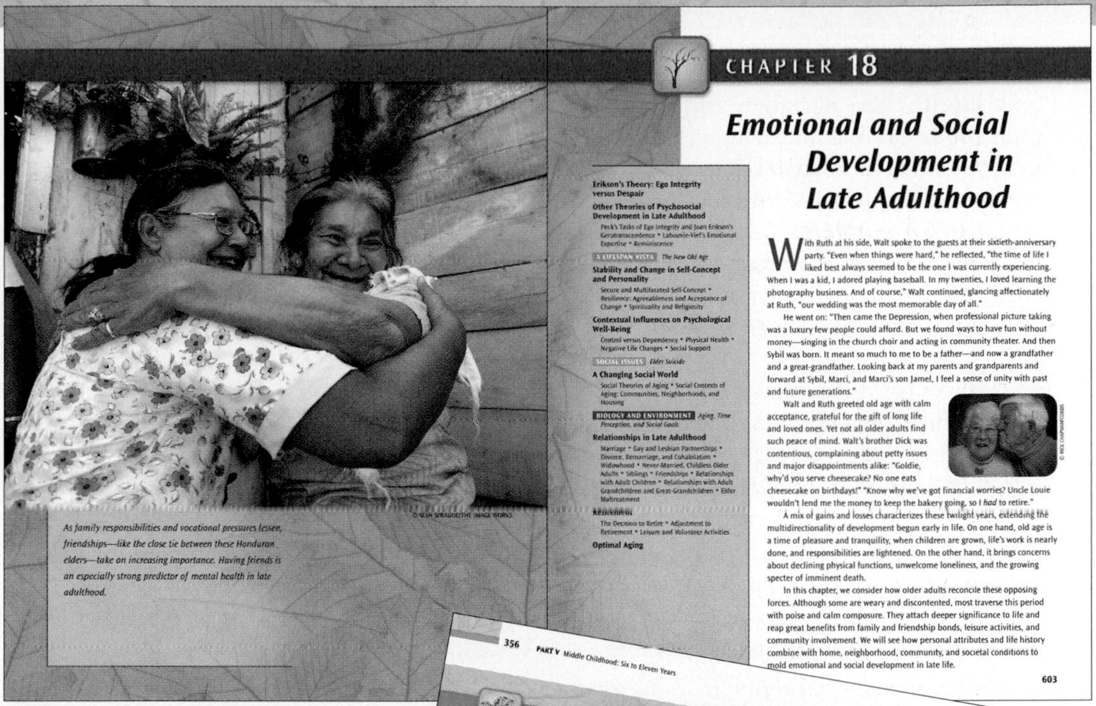

Maintaining a highly accessible writing style—one that is lucid and engaging without being simplistic—continues to be one of my major goals. I frequently converse with students, encouraging them to relate what they read to their own lives. In doing so, I hope to make the study of human development involving and pleasurable.

Stories and Vignettes About Real People. To help students construct a clear image of development and to enliven the text narrative, each chronological age period is unified by case examples woven throughout that set of chapters. For example, the middle childhood section highlights the experiences and concerns of 10-year-old Joey; 8-year-old Lizzie; their divorced parents, Rena and Drake; and their classmates. In the chapters on late adulthood, students get to know Walt and Ruth, a vibrant retired couple, along with Walt's older brother Dick and his wife Goldie and Ruth's sister Ida, a victim of Alzheimer's disease. Besides a set of main characters who bring unity to each age period, many additional vignettes offer vivid examples of development and diversity among children, adolescents, and adults.

Chapter Introductions and End-of-Chapter Summaries. To provide a helpful preview, I include an outline and overview of chapter content in each chapter introduction. Concise end-of-chapter summaries, organized according to the major divisions of each chapter and highlighting important terms, remind students of key points in the text discussion. Review questions are included in the summaries to encourage active study.

Ask Yourself Questions. Active engagement with the subject matter is also supported by four types of questions at the end of major sections, which prompt students to think about human development in diverse ways: ***Review*** questions help students recall and comprehend information they have just read; ***Apply*** questions encourage the application of knowledge to controversial issues and problems faced by children, adolescents, adults, and professionals who work with them; ***Connect*** questions help students build an image of the whole person by integrating what they have learned across age periods and domains of development; ***Reflect*** questions help make the study of human development personally meaningful by asking students to reflect on their own development and life experiences. Each question is answered on the text's MyDevelopmentLab website.

Take a Moment... This new active-learning feature, built into the text narrative, asks students to "take a moment" to think about an important point, integrate information on human development, or engage in an exercise or an application to clarify a challenging concept. ***TAKE A MOMENT...*** highlights and reinforces the text's strength in conversing with and actively engaging the student in learning and in inspiring critical thinking.

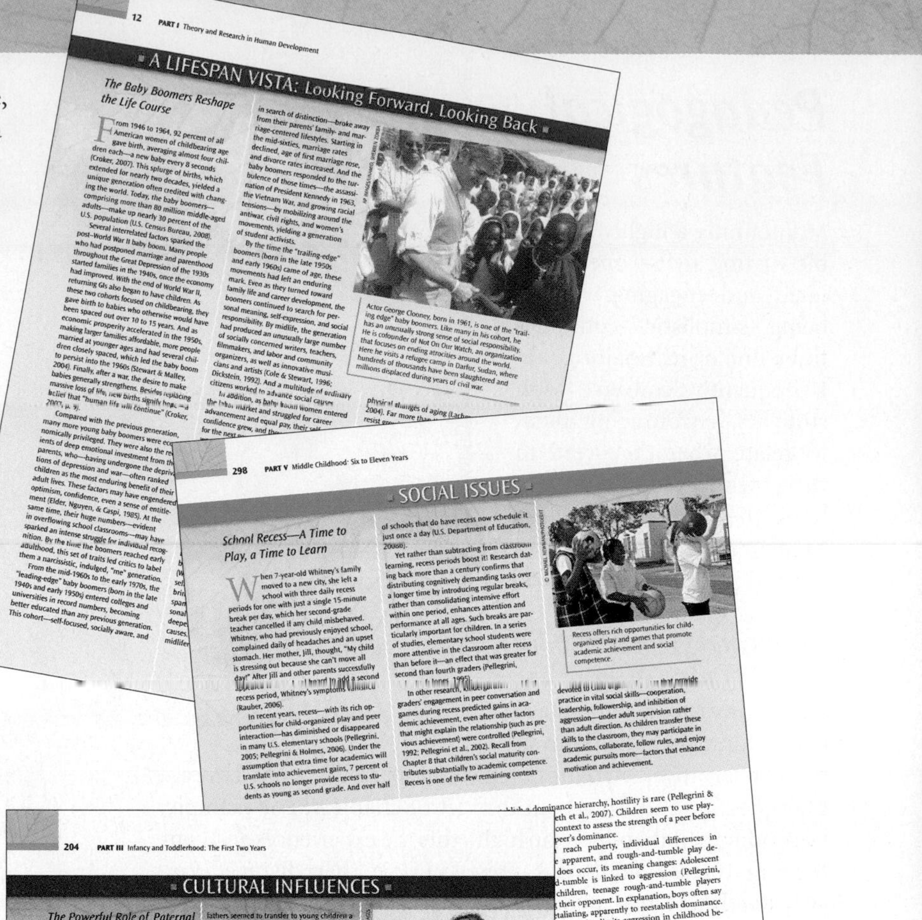

Four types of thematic boxes accentuate the philosophical themes of this book:

***A Lifespan Vista* boxes** are devoted to topics that have long-term implications for development or involve intergenerational issues. Examples include *The Baby Boomers Reshape the Life Course; The Prenatal Environment and Health in Later Life; Like Parent, Like Child: Intergenerational Continuity in Adolescent Parenthood; Childhood Attachment Patterns and Adult Romantic Relationships;* and *The New Old Age.*

***Social Issues* boxes** discuss the impact of social conditions on children, adolescents, and adults and emphasize the need for sensitive social policies to ensure their well-being—for example, *School Recess—A Time to Play, a Time to Learn; High-Stakes Testing; Masculinity at Work: Men Who Choose Nontraditional Careers; Women in "Fast-Track" Careers Who Opt to Stay Home;* and *Interventions for Caregivers of Elders with Dementia.*

***Cultural Influences* boxes** have been expanded and updated to deepen attention to culture threaded throughout the text. They highlight both cross-cultural and multicultural variations in human development—for example, *Immigrant Youths: Amazing Adaptation; Cultural Variation in Infant Sleeping Arrangements; The Powerful Role of Paternal Warmth in Development; Children in Village and Tribal Cultures Observe and Participate in Adult Work; Is Emerging Adulthood Really a Distinct Period of Development?;* and *Cultural Variations in Sense of Usefulness in Late Life.*

***Biology and Environment* boxes** highlight the growing attention to the complex, bidirectional relationship between biology and environment during development. Examples include *"Tuning In" to Familiar Speech, Faces, and Music: A Sensitive Period for Culture-Specific Learning; Bullies and Their Victims; Telomere Length: A New Marker of the Impact of Life Circumstances on Biological Aging; Anti-Aging Effects of Dietary Calorie Restriction;* and *What Factors Promote Psychological Well-Being in Midlife?*

Applying What We Know Tables. This feature provides easily accessible research-based applications on many issues, speaking directly to students pursuing child-, adult-, or family-related areas of study or careers, such as teaching, health care, counseling, or social work. They include *Signs of Developmentally Appropriate Infant and Toddler Child Care; Supporting Early Language Learning; Using Positive Discipline; Helping Children Adjust to Their Parents' Divorce; Communicating with Adolescents About Sexual Issues; Resources That Foster Resilience in Emerging Adulthood; Relieving the Stress of Caring for an Aging Parent;* and *Fostering Adaptation to Widowhood in Late Adulthood.*

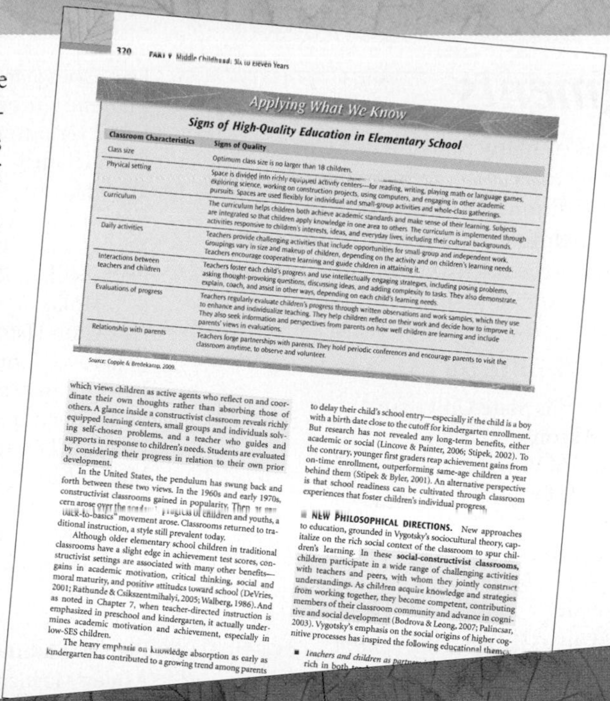

320 PART V Middle Childhood: Six to Eleven Years

Applying What We Know

Signs of High-Quality Education in Elementary School

Classroom Characteristics	Signs of Quality
Class size	Optimum class size is no larger than 18 children.
Physical setting	Space is divided into richly equipped activity centers—for reading, writing, playing math or language games, exploring science, working on construction projects, using computers, and engaging in other academic pursuits. Spaces are used flexibly for individual and small-group activities and whole-class gatherings.
Curriculum	The curriculum helps children both achieve academic standards and make sense of their learning. Subjects are integrated so that children apply knowledge in one area to others. The curriculum is implemented through activities responsive to children's interests, ideas, and everyday lives, including their cultural backgrounds.
Daily activities	Teachers provide challenging activities that include opportunities for small-group and independent work. Groupings vary in size and makeup of children, depending on the activity and on children's learning needs. Teachers encourage cooperative learning and guide children in attaining it.
Interactions between teachers and children	Teachers foster each child's progress and use intellectually engaging strategies, including posing problems, asking thought-provoking questions, discussing ideas, and adding complexity to tasks. They also demonstrate, explain, coach, and assist in other ways, depending on each child's learning needs.
Evaluations of progress	Teachers regularly evaluate children's progress through written observations and work samples, which they use to enhance and individualize teaching. They help children reflect on their work and decide how to improve it. They also seek information and perspectives from parents on how well children are learning and include parents' views in evaluations.
Relationship with parents	Teachers forge partnerships with parents. They hold periodic conferences and encourage parents to visit the classroom anytime, to observe and volunteer.

Source: Copple & Bredekamp, 2009.

Milestones Tables. A Milestones table appears at the end of each age division of the text. These tables summarize major physical, cognitive, language, emotional, and social attainments, providing a convenient aid for reviewing the chronology of lifespan development.

Enhanced Art and Photo Program. A revised art style presents concepts and research findings with clarity and attractiveness, thereby aiding student understanding and retention. Each photo has been carefully selected to portray human development and to represent the diversity of people in the United States and around the world.

In-Text Key Terms with Definitions, End-of-Chapter Term List, and End-of-Book Glossary. Mastery of terms that make up the central vocabulary of the field is promoted through in-text highlighting of key terms and definitions, which encourages students to review the terminology of the field in greater depth by rereading related information. Key terms also appear in an end-of-chapter page-referenced term list and an end-of-book page-referenced glossary.

Acknowledgments

The dedicated contributions of many individuals helped make this book a reality and contributed to refinements and improvements in this fourth edition. An impressive cast of reviewers provided many helpful suggestions, constructive criticisms, and enthusiasm for the organization and content of the text. I am grateful to each one of them.

Reviewers for the Fifth Edition

Cheryl Anagnopoulos, Black Hills State University
Toni Bisconti, University of Akron
Tracie Blumentritt, University of Wisconsin—La Crosse
Lou de la Cruz, Sheridan Institute
Karen Fingerman, Purdue University
Beth Fauth, Utah State University
Bert Hayslip, University of North Texas
Bob Heller, Athabasca University
Dale Lund, California State University, San Bernardino
David Mitchell, Kennesaw State University
Julie Patrick, West Virginia University
Aurora Sherman, Oregon State University
Carey Sherman, University of Michigan
David Shwalb, Southeastern Louisiana University
Jacqui Smith, University of Michigan
Bruce Thompson, University of Southern Maine
Laura Thompson, New Mexico State University
Paul Wink, Wellesley College

Reviewers for Previous Editions

Gerald Adams, University of Guelph
Jackie Adamson, South Dakota School of Mines and Technology
Paul C. Amrhein, University of New Mexico
Cheryl Anagnopoulos, Black Hills State University
Doreen Arcus, University of Massachusetts, Lowell
René L. Babcock, Central Michigan University
Sherry Beaumont, University of Northern British Columbia
W. Keith Berg, University of Florida
James A. Bird, Weber State University
Joyce Bishop, Golden West College
Kimberly Blair, University of Pittsburgh
Tracie L. Blumentritt, University of Wisconsin—La Crosse
Ed Brady, Belleville Area College
Michele Y. Breault, Truman State University
Dilek Buchholz, Weber State University
Lanthan Camblin, University of Cincinnati
Judith W. Cameron, Ohio State University
Joan B. Cannon, University of Massachusetts, Lowell
Michael Caruso, University of Toledo
Susan L. Churchill, University of Nebraska—Lincoln
Gary Creasey, Illinois State University
Rhoda Cummings, University of Nevada—Reno
Rita M. Curl, Minot State University
Carol Lynn Davis, University of Maine
Byron Egeland, University of Minnesota
Karen Fingerman, Purdue University
Maria P. Fracasso, Towson University
Elizabeth E. Garner, University of North Florida
Clifford Gray, Pueblo Community College
Laurie Gottlieb, McGill University
Dan Grangaard, Austin Community College
Marlene Groomes, Miami Dade College
Laura Gruntmeir, Redlands Community College
Laura Hanish, Arizona State University
Traci Haynes, Columbus State Community College
Vernon Haynes, Youngstown State University
Karl Hennig, St. Francis Xavier University
Paula Hillman, University of Wisconsin—Whitewater
Deb Hollister, Valencia Community College
Hui-Chin Hsu, University of Georgia
Lera Joyce Johnson, Centenary College of Louisiana
Janet Kalinowski, Ithaca College
Kevin Keating, Broward Community College
Wendy Kliewer, Virginia Commonwealth University
Marita Kloseck, University of Western Ontario
Karen Kopera-Frye, University of Nevada, Reno
Valerie Kuhlmeier, Queens University
Deanna Kuhn, Teachers College, Columbia University
Rebecca A. López, California State University—Long Beach
Dale Lund, University of Utah
Pamela Manners, Troy State University
Ashley Maynard, University of Hawaii
Kate McLean, University of Toronto at Mississauga
Robert B. McLaren, California State University, Fullerton
Randy Mergler, California State University
Karla K. Miley, Black Hawk College
Carol Miller, Anne Arundel Community College
Teri Miller, Milwaukee Area Technical College
Steve Mitchell, Somerset Community College
Gary T. Montgomery, University of Texas, Pan American
Feleccia Moore-Davis, Houston Community College
Ulrich Mueller, University of Victoria
Karen Nelson, Austin College
Bob Newby, Tarleton State University
Jill Norvilitis, Buffalo State College
Patricia O'Brien, University of Illinois at Chicago
Nancy Ogden, Mount Royal College
Peter Oliver, University of Hartford
Verna C. Pangman, University of Manitoba
Robert Pasnak, George Mason University
Ellen Pastorino, Gainesville College
Marion Perlmutter, University of Michigan
Warren H. Phillips, Iowa State University
Leslee K. Polina, Southeast Missouri State University
Dana Plude, University of Maryland
Dolores Pushkar, Concordia University
Leon Rappaport, Kansas State University
Pamela Roberts, California State University, Long Beach
Stephanie J. Rowley, University of North Carolina
Elmer Ruhnke, Manatee Community College
Randall Russac, University of North Florida
Marie Saracino, Stephen F. Austin State University
Edythe H. Schwartz, California State University—Sacramento
Bonnie Seegmiller, City University of New York, Hunter College
Richard Selby, Southeast Missouri State University
David Shwalb, Southeastern Louisiana University
Paul S. Silverman, University of Montana
Judi Smetana, University of Rochester
Glenda Smith, North Harris College
Jeanne Spaulding, Houston Community College
Thomas Spencer, San Francisco State University
Bruce Stam, Chemeketa Community College

JoNell Strough, West Virginia University
Vince Sullivan, Pensacola Junior College
Laura Thompson, New Mexico State University
Mojisola Tiamiyu, University of Toledo
Ruth Tincoff, Harvard University
Joe Tinnin, Richland College
Catya von Károlyi, University of Wisconsin—Eau Claire
L. Monique Ward, University of Michigan
Rob Weisskirch, California State University, Fullerton
Nancy White, Youngstown State University
Ursula M. White, El Paso Community College
Carol L. Wilkinson, Whatcom Community College
Lois J. Willoughby, Miami-Dade Community College
Deborah R. Winters, New Mexico State University

An outstanding editorial staff in my home community contributed greatly to the entire project. Sara Harris, Supplements Editor, coordinated the preparation of the teaching ancillaries and wrote major sections of the Instructor's Resource Manual, bringing to these tasks great depth of knowledge, impressive writing skill, enthusiasm, and imagination. Claire Christensen, Editorial Assistant, spent countless hours searching, gathering, and organizing scholarly literature; writing portions of the Study Guide; designing highly creative MyDevelopmentLab simulations; and contributing to the Explorations in Lifespan Development video segments and video guide. With Claire's departure for doctoral study, Amelia Benner capably assisted with completion of these tasks.

I have been fortunate to work with a highly effective editorial team at Pearson Education. It has been a great pleasure to work once again with Tom Pauken, Managing Editor, who oversaw the preparation of the third edition of *Development Through the Lifespan* and who returned to edit this fifth edition. His careful review of manuscript, keen organizational skills, responsive day-to-day communication, insightful suggestions, astute problem solving, interest in the subject matter, and thoughtfulness have greatly enhanced the quality of the text and made its preparation especially enjoyable and rewarding. Judy Ashkenaz and Pam Barter, Development Editors, carefully reviewed and commented on each chapter, helping to ensure that every thought and concept would be clearly expressed and well-developed. My appreciation, also, to Jessica Mosher, Editor in Chief of Psychology, for reorganizing the management of my projects to enable the focused work that is vital for precise, inspired writing and timely manuscript preparation.

The supplements package benefited from the talents and diligence of several other individuals. Kimberly Michaud prepared a superb Test Bank, and Heather Heinrich authored the excellent MyDevelopmentLab assessments. Diana Murphy designed and wrote a highly attractive PowerPoint presentation, and Judy Ashkenaz authored the informative biographies of major figures in the field and Careers in Lifespan Development, which appear in MyDevelopmentLab. Maria Henneberry and Phil Vandiver of Contemporary Visuals in Bloomington, IL, prepared an extraordinarily artistic and inspiring set of new video segments covering diverse topics in lifespan development.

Donna Simons, Senior Production Administrator, coordinated the complex production tasks that resulted in an exquisitely beautiful fifth edition. I am grateful for her keen aesthetic sense, attention to detail, flexibility, efficiency, and thoughtfulness. I thank Sarah Evertson for obtaining the exceptional photographs that so aptly illustrate the text narrative. I am also grateful for Susan Messer's fine contributions to the photo specifications and captions. Margaret Pinette, Bill Heckman, and Beyond Words Proofreading provided outstanding copyediting and proofreading.

Wendy Albert, Executive Marketing Manager, prepared the beautiful print ads and informative e-mails to the field about *Development Through the Lifespan*, Fifth Edition. She has also ensured that accurate and clear information reached Pearson Education's sales force and that the needs of prospective and current adopters were met.

A final word of gratitude goes to my family, whose love, patience, and understanding have enabled me to be wife, mother, teacher, researcher, and text author at the same time. My sons, David and Peter, grew up with my texts, passing from childhood to adolescence and then to adulthood as successive editions were written. David has a special connection with the books' subject matter as an elementary school teacher, and Peter is now an experienced attorney and recently married to his vivacious, talented, and caring Melissa. All three continue to enrich my understanding through reflections on events and progress in their own lives. My husband, Ken, willingly made room for yet another time-consuming endeavor in our life together and communicated his belief in its importance in a great many unspoken, caring ways.

—*Laura E. Berk*

Supplementary Materials

Instructor Supplements

A variety of teaching tools are available to assist instructors in organizing lectures, planning demonstrations and examinations, and ensuring student comprehension.

- **MyDevelopmentLab.** This interactive and instructive multimedia resource can be used as a supplement to a classroom course or to completely administer an online course. Prepared in collaboration with Laura Berk, MyDevelopmentLab includes a variety of assessments that enable continuous evaluation of students' learning. Extensive video footage, multimedia simulations, biographies of major figures in the field, and interactive activities that are unique to *Development Through the Lifespan* are also included. A new MyDevelopmentLab feature, "Careers in Lifespan Development," explains how studying human development is essential for a wide range of career paths. The power of MyDevelopmentLab lies in its design as an all-inclusive teaching and learning tool. For a sampling of its rich content, contact your Pearson representative.

- **Instructor's Resource Manual (IRM).** This thoroughly revised IRM can be used by first-time or experienced instructors to enrich classroom experiences. Each chapter includes a Chapter-at-a-Glance grid, Brief Chapter Summary, Learning Objectives, detailed Lecture Outline, Lecture Enhancements, Learning Activities, Ask Yourself questions with answers, Suggested Readings, a list of transparencies, PowerPoint Presentation, and Media Materials list.

- **Test Bank.** The Test Bank contains over 2,000 multiple-choice questions, each of which is page-referenced to chapter content and classified by type (factual, applied, or conceptual). Each chapter also includes a selection of essay questions and sample answers.

- **Computerized Test Bank.** This computerized version of the Test Bank, in easy-to-use MyTest format, lets you prepare tests for printing as well as for network and online testing. It has full editing capability. Test items are also available in CourseCompass, Blackboard, and WebCT formats.

- **PowerPoint Presentation.** The PowerPoint presentation contains illustrations and outlines of key topics for each chapter from the text, presented in a clear and visually attractive format.

- **"Explorations in Lifespan Development" DVD and Guide.** This new DVD is over three hours in length and contains more than 50 four- to ten-minute narrated segments, designed for effective classroom use, that illustrate the many theories, concepts, and milestones of human development. New additions include Reproductive Technology, High-Quality Child Care, International Adoption, Civic Engagement in Early Adulthood, Transition to Parenthood, Caring for an Elder with Alzheimer's Disease, Late-Life Creativity, and Hospice. "Explorations in Lifespan Development" DVD and DVD Guide are available to instructors who adopt the text and to students as a free supplement when packaged with the text. The DVD Guide helps students use the DVD in conjunction with the textbook, deepening their understanding and applying what they have learned to everyday life.

- **Transparencies.** Two hundred full-color transparencies taken from the text and other sources are referenced in the IRM for the most appropriate use in your classroom presentations.

Student Supplements

Beyond the study aids found in the textbook, Pearson offers a number of supplements for students:

- **MyDevelopmentLab.** This interactive and instructive multimedia resource is an all-inclusive learning tool. Prepared in collaboration with Laura Berk, MyDevelopmentLab engages students and reinforces learning through controlled assessments, extensive video footage, multimedia simulations, biographies of major figures in the field, and interactive activities that are unique to *Development Through the Lifespan.* In addition, "Careers in Lifespan Development" explains how knowledge of human development is essential for a wide range of career paths. Easy to use, MyDevelopmentLab meets the individual learning needs of every student. For a sampling of its rich content, visit *www.mydevelopmentlab.com.*

- **Study Guide with Practice Tests.** This helpful study guide offers Chapter Summaries, Learning Objectives, Study Questions organized according to major headings in the text, Suggested Readings, Crossword Puzzles for mastering important terms, and two multiple-choice Practice Tests per chapter.

- **Milestones Study Cards.** Adapted from the popular Milestones tables featured in the text, these colorfully illustrated study cards outline key developmental attainments. Easy to use, they assist students in integrating the various domains of development and constructing a vision of the whole developing person.

Legend for Photos Accompanying Sofie's Story Sofie's story is told in Chapters 1 and 19, from her birth to her death. The photos that appear at the beginning of Chapter 1 follow her through her lifespan and include family members of two succeeding generations.

Page 2

1. Sophie, age 18, high school graduation in 1926.
2. Sofie as a baby, with her mother in 1908.
3. Sofie, age 6, with her brother, age 8, in 1914.
4. Sofie's German passport.
5. Sofie, age 60, and daughter Laura on Laura's wedding day in 1968.
6. Sofie and Phil in 1968, less than two years before Sofie died.
7. Sofie's grandsons, David and Peter, ages 5 and 2, children of Laura and Ken.
8. Laura, Ken, and sons Peter and David, ages 10 and 13, on the occasion of David's Bar Mitzvah in 1985.
9. Ken and sons David and Peter as young adults, in 2005.
10. Peter and Melissa on their wedding day in 2007.

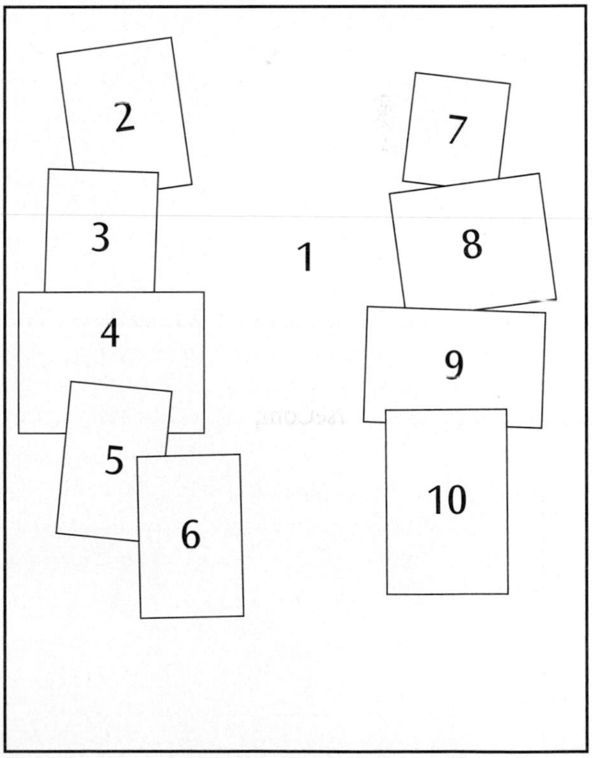

Page 3

Sofie, age 61, and her first grandchild, Ellen, October 1969, less than three months before Sofie died.

Page 4

Sofie and Phil in their midthirties, during World War II, when they became engaged.

Development Through the Lifespan

This photo essay chronicles the life course and family legacy of Sofie Lentschner. It begins in 1908 with Sofie's infancy and concludes in 2007, 37 years after Sofie's death, with the marriage of her young adult grandson, Peter, to Melissa. For a description of each photo, see the legend on page xxvii.

PHOTOS COURTESY OF LAURA E. BERK

CHAPTER 1

History, Theory, and Research Strategies

Sofie Lentschner was born in 1908, the second child of Jewish parents who made their home in Leipzig, Germany, a city of thriving commerce and cultural vitality. Her father was a successful businessman and community leader, her mother a socialite well-known for her charm, beauty, and hospitality. As a baby, Sofie displayed the determination and persistence that would be sustained throughout her life. She sat for long periods inspecting small objects with her eyes and hands. The single event that consistently broke her gaze was the sound of the piano in the parlor. As soon as Sofie could crawl, she steadfastly pulled herself up to finger its keys and marveled at the tinkling sounds.

By the time Sofie entered elementary school, she was an introspective child, often ill at ease at the festive parties that girls of her family's social standing were expected to attend. She immersed herself in her schoolwork, especially in mastering foreign languages—a regular part of German elementary and secondary education. Twice a week, she took piano lessons from the finest teacher in Leipzig. By the time Sofie graduated from high school, she spoke English and French fluently and had become an accomplished pianist. Whereas most German girls of her time married by age 20, Sofie postponed serious courtship in favor of entering the university. Her parents began to wonder whether their intense, studious daughter would ever settle into family life.

COURTESY OF LAURA E. BERK

Sofie wanted marriage as well as education, but her plans were thwarted by the political turbulence of her times. When Hitler rose to power in the early 1930s, Sofie's father, fearing for the safety of his wife and children, moved the family to Belgium. Conditions for Jews in Europe quickly worsened. The Nazis plundered Sofie's family home and confiscated her father's business. By the end of the 1930s, Sofie had lost contact with all but a handful of her aunts, uncles, cousins, and childhood friends, many of whom (she later learned) were herded into cattle cars and transported to Nazi death camps at Auschwitz and Chelmno, Poland. In 1939, as anti-Jewish laws and atrocities intensified, Sofie's family fled to the United States.

As Sofie turned 30, her parents, convinced that she would never marry and would need a career for financial security, agreed to support her return to school. Sofie earned two master's degrees, one in music and the other in librarianship. Then, on a blind date, she met Philip, a U.S. army officer. Philip's calm, gentle nature complemented Sofie's intensity and worldliness. Within six months they married. During the next four years, two daughters and a son were born. Soon Sofie's father became ill, his health shattered by the strain of

COURTESY OF LAURA E. BERK

uprooting his family and losing his home and business. After months of being bedridden, he died of heart failure.

When World War II ended, Philip left the army and opened a small men's clothing store. Sofie divided her time between caring for the children and helping Philip in the store. Now in her forties, she was a devoted mother, but few women her age were still rearing young children. As Philip struggled with the business, he spent longer hours at work, and Sofie often felt lonely. She rarely touched the piano, which brought back painful memories of youthful life plans shattered by war. Sofie's sense of isolation and lack of fulfillment frequently left her short-tempered. Late at night, she and Philip could be heard arguing.

As Sofie's children grew older, she returned to school again, this time to earn a teaching credential. Finally, at age 50, she launched a career. For the next decade, she taught German and French to high school students and English to newly arrived immigrants. Besides easing her family's financial difficulties, she felt a gratifying sense of accomplishment and creativity. These years were among the most energetic and satisfying of Sofie's life. She had an unending enthusiasm for teaching—for transmitting her facility with language, her firsthand knowledge of the consequences of hatred and oppression, and her practical understanding of how to adapt to life in a new land. She watched her children, whose young lives were free of the trauma of war, adopt many of her values and commitments and begin their marital and vocational lives at the expected time.

Sofie approached age 60 with an optimistic outlook. Released from the financial burden of paying for their children's college education, she and Philip looked forward to greater leisure. Their affection and respect for each other deepened. Once again, Sofie began to play the piano. But this period of contentment was short-lived.

One morning, Sofie awoke and felt a hard lump under her arm. Several days later, her doctor diagnosed cancer. Sofie's spirited disposition and capacity to adapt to radical life changes helped her meet the illness head on. She defined it as an enemy to be fought and overcome. As a result, she lived five more years. Despite the exhaustion of chemotherapy, Sofie maintained a full schedule of teaching duties and continued to visit and run errands for her elderly mother. But as she weakened physically, she no longer had the stamina to meet her classes. Gradually, she gave in to the ravaging illness. Bedridden for the last few weeks, she slipped quietly into death with Philip at her side. The funeral chapel overflowed with hundreds of Sofie's students. She had granted each a memorable image of a woman of courage and caring.

One of Sofie's three children, Laura, is the author of this book. Married a year before Sofie died, Laura and her husband, Ken, often think of Sofie's message, spoken privately to them on the eve of their wedding day: "I learned from my own life and marriage that you must build a life together but also a life apart. You must grant each other the time, space, and support to forge your own identities, your own ways of expressing yourselves and giving to others. The most important ingredient of your relationship must be respect."

Laura and Ken settled in a small midwestern city, near Illinois State University, where they have served on the faculty for many years—Laura in the Department of Psychology, Ken in the Department of Mathematics. They have two sons, David and Peter, to whom Laura has related many stories about Sofie's life and who carry her legacy forward. David shares his grandmother's penchant for teaching; he is a second-grade teacher. Peter, a lawyer, shares his grandmother's love of music, and his wife Melissa—much like Sofie—is both a talented linguist and a musician. When Peter asked Melissa to marry him, he placed a family heirloom on her finger—an engagement ring that had belonged to Sofie's aunt, who perished in a Nazi death camp. In the box that held the ring, Melissa found a written copy of the story of Sofie and her family.

Sofie also had a lifelong impact on many of her students. Recently, a professor of human development wrote to Laura:

> I have been meaning to contact you for a while. I teach a class in lifespan development. When I opened the textbook and saw the pictures of your mother, I was very

surprised. From 1962 to 1966, I took high school German classes from your mother. . . . I remember her as a very tough teacher who both held her students accountable and cared about each and every one of us. That she was an incredible teacher did not really sink in until I went to Germany during my [college] years and was able to both understand German and speak it.

Sofie's story raises a wealth of fascinating issues about human life histories:

- What determines the features that Sofie shares with others and those that make her unique—in physical characteristics, mental capacities, interests, and behaviors?
- What led Sofie to retain the same persistent, determined disposition throughout her life but to change in other essential ways?
- How do historical and cultural conditions—for Sofie, the persecution that destroyed her childhood home, caused the death of family members and friends, and led her family to flee to the United States—affect well-being throughout life?
- How does the timing of events—for example, Sofie's early exposure to foreign languages and her delayed entry into marriage, parenthood, and career—affect development?
- What factors—both personal and environmental—led Sofie to die sooner than expected?

These are central questions addressed by **developmental science**, a field of study devoted to understanding constancy and change throughout the lifespan (Lerner, 2006). Great diversity characterizes the interests and concerns of investigators who study development. But all share a single goal: to identify those factors that influence consistencies and transformations in people from conception to death.

A Scientific, Applied, and Interdisciplinary Field

The questions just listed are not merely of scientific interest. Each has *applied,* or practical, importance as well. In fact, scientific curiosity is just one factor that led the study of development to become the exciting field it is today. Research about development has also been stimulated by social pressures to improve people's lives. For example, the beginning of public education in the early twentieth century led to a demand for knowledge about what and how to teach children of different ages. The interest of the medical profession in improving people's health required an understanding of physical development, nutrition, and disease. The social service profession's desire to treat emotional problems and to help people adjust to major life events, such as divorce, job loss, war, natural disasters, or the death of loved ones, required information about personality and social development. And parents have continually sought expert advice about child-rearing practices and experiences that would promote their children's well-being.

Our large storehouse of information about development is *interdisciplinary*. It has grown through the combined efforts of people from many fields of study. Because of the need for solutions to everyday problems at all ages, researchers from psychology, sociology, anthropology, biology, and neuroscience have joined forces in research with professionals from education, family studies, medicine, public health, and social service, to name just a few. Together, they have created the field as it exists today—a body of knowledge that is not just scientifically important but also relevant and useful.

Basic Issues

Developmental science is a relatively recent endeavor. Studies of children did not begin until the late nineteenth and early twentieth centuries. Investigations into adult development, aging, and change over the life course emerged only in the 1960s and 1970s (Elder & Shanahan, 2006). But speculations about how people grow and change have existed for centuries. As they combined with research, they inspired the construction of *theories* of development. A **theory** is an orderly, integrated set of statements that describes, explains, and predicts behavior. For example, a good theory of infant–caregiver attachment would (1) *describe* the behaviors of babies of 6 to 8 months of age as they seek the affection and comfort of a familiar adult, (2) *explain* how and why infants develop this strong desire to bond with a caregiver, and (3) *predict* the consequences of this emotional bond for future relationships.

Theories are vital tools for two reasons. First, they provide organizing frameworks for our observations of people. In other words, they *guide and give meaning* to what we see. Second, theories that are verified by research provide a sound basis for practical action. Once a theory helps us *understand* development, we are in a much better position to know *how to improve* the welfare and treatment of children and adults.

As we will see, theories are influenced by the cultural values and belief systems of their times. But theories differ in one important way from mere opinion or belief: A theory's continued existence depends on *scientific verification*. Every theory must be tested using a fair set of research procedures agreed on by the scientific community, and the findings must endure, or be replicated, over time.

Within the field of developmental science, many theories exist, offering very different ideas about what people are like and how they change. The study of development provides no ultimate truth because investigators do not always agree on the meaning of what they see. Also, humans are complex beings; they change physically, mentally, emotionally, and socially. No single theory has explained all these aspects. But the existence of many theories helps advance knowledge as researchers continually try to support, contradict, and integrate these different points of view.

This chapter introduces you to major theories of human development and research strategies used to test them. In later chapters, we will return to each theory in greater detail and will also introduce other important but less grand theories. Although there are many theories, we can easily organize them by looking at the stand they take on three basic issues: (1) Is the course of development continuous or discontinuous? (2) Does one course of development characterize all people, or are there many possible courses? (3) Are genetic or environmental factors more important in influencing development? Let's look closely at each of these issues.

Continuous or Discontinuous Development?

How can we best describe the differences in capacities among infants, children, adolescents, and adults? As Figure 1.1 illustrates, major theories recognize two possibilities.

One view holds that infants and preschoolers respond to the world in much the same way as adults do. The difference between the immature and mature being is simply one of *amount or complexity*. For example, when Sofie was a baby, her perception of a piano melody, memory for past events, and ability to categorize objects may have been much like our own. Perhaps her only limitation was that she could not perform these skills with as much information and precision as we can. If this is so, then changes in her thinking must be **continuous**—a process of gradually augmenting the same types of skills that were there to begin with.

According to a second view, infants and children have *unique ways of thinking, feeling and behaving,* ones quite different from adults. If so, then development is **discontinuous**—a process in which new ways of understanding and responding to the world emerge at specific times. From this perspective, Sofie could not yet perceive, remember, and categorize experiences as a mature person can. Rather, she moved through a series of developmental steps, each of which has unique features, until she reached the highest level of functioning.

Theories that accept the discontinuous perspective regard development as taking place in **stages**—*qualitative* changes in thinking, feeling, and behaving that characterize specific periods of development. In stage theories, development is like climbing a staircase, with each step corresponding to a more mature, reorganized way of functioning. The stage concept also assumes that people undergo periods of rapid transformation as they step up from one stage to the next. In other words, change is fairly sudden rather than gradual and ongoing.

Does development actually occur in a neat, orderly sequence of stages? This ambitious assumption has faced significant challenges. Later in this chapter, we will review some influential stage theories.

One Course of Development or Many?

Stage theorists assume that people everywhere follow the same sequence of development. Yet the field of human development is becoming increasingly aware that children and adults live in distinct **contexts**—unique combinations of personal and environmental circumstances that can result in different paths of change. For example, a shy individual who fears social encounters

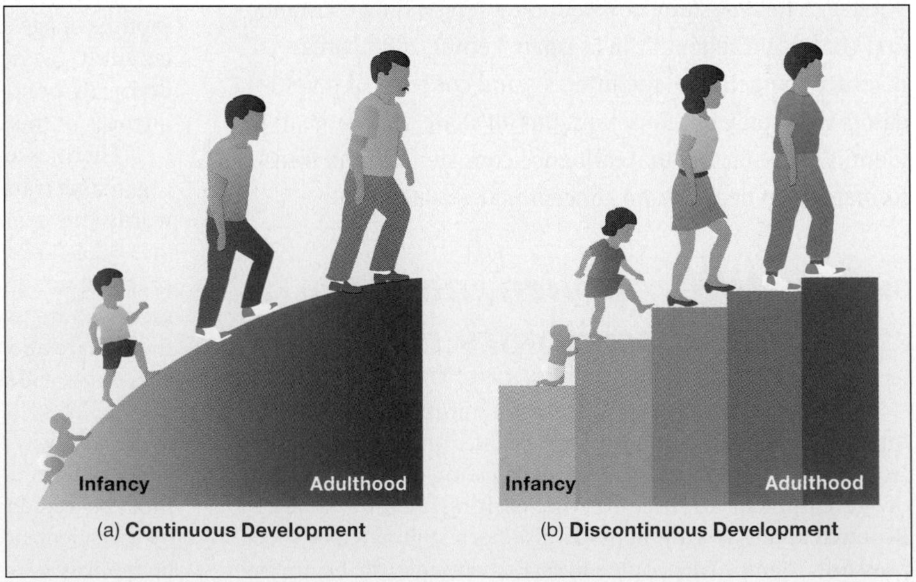

■ **FIGURE 1.1** ■ **Is development continuous or discontinuous?** (a) Some theorists believe that development is a smooth, continuous process. Individuals gradually add more of the same types of skills. (b) Other theorists think that development takes place in discontinuous stages. People change rapidly as they step up to a new level and then change very little for a while. With each new step, the person interprets and responds to the world in a qualitatively different way.

develops in very different contexts from those of an outgoing agemate who readily seeks out other people (Kagan & Fox, 2006). Children and adults in non-Western village societies have experiences in their families and communities that differ sharply from those of people in large Western cities. These different circumstances foster different intellectual capacities, social skills, and feelings about the self and others (Shweder et al., 2006).

As you will see, contemporary theorists regard the contexts that shape development as many-layered and complex. On the personal side, they include heredity and biological makeup. On the environmental side, they include both immediate settings—home, school, and neighborhood—and circumstances more remote from people's everyday lives: community resources, societal values, and historical time period. Finally, researchers today are more conscious than ever before of cultural diversity in development.

Relative Influence of Nature and Nurture?

In addition to describing the course of human development, each theory takes a stand on a major question about its underlying causes: Are genetic or environmental factors more important? This is the age-old **nature–nurture controversy.** By *nature,* we mean inborn biological givens—the hereditary information we receive from our parents at the moment of conception. By *nurture,* we mean the complex forces of the physical and social world that influence our biological makeup and psychological experiences before and after birth.

Although all theories grant at least some role to both nature and nurture, they vary in emphasis. Consider the following questions: Is the developing person's ability to think in more complex ways largely the result of an inborn timetable of growth, or is it primarily influenced by stimulation from parents and teachers? Do children acquire language rapidly because they are genetically predisposed to do so or because parents teach them from an early age? And what accounts for the vast individual differences among people—in height, weight, physical coordination, intelligence, personality, and social skills? Is nature or nurture more responsible?

A theory's position on the roles of nature and nurture affects how it explains individual differences. Theorists who emphasize *stability*—that individuals who are high or low in a characteristic (such as verbal ability, anxiety, or sociability) will remain so at later ages—typically stress the importance of *heredity.* If they regard environment as important, they usually point to *early experiences* as establishing a lifelong pattern of behavior. Powerful negative events in the first few years, they argue, cannot be fully overcome by later, more positive ones (Bowlby, 1980; Johnson, 2000; Sroufe, 2005). Other theorists, taking a more optimistic view, emphasize *plasticity*—that *change* is possible and even likely if new experiences support it (Greenspan & Shanker, 2004; Lester, Masten, & McEwen, 2006).

Since the 1960s, researchers have moved from focusing only on child development to investigating development over the entire life course. These hikers, all in their seventies, continue to change physically, mentally, and socially. They convey the health, vitality, and life satisfaction of many contemporary older adults.

Throughout this book, you will see that investigators disagree, often sharply, on the question of *stability versus plasticity.* Their answers often vary across *domains,* or aspects, of development. Think back to Sofie's story, and you will see that her linguistic ability and persistent approach to challenges were stable over the lifespan. In contrast, her psychological well-being and life satisfaction fluctuated considerably.

The Lifespan Perspective: A Balanced Point of View

So far, we have discussed basic issues of human development in terms of extremes—solutions favoring one side or the other. But as we trace the unfolding of the field, you will see that the positions of many theorists have softened. Today, some theorists believe that both continuous and discontinuous changes occur. Many acknowledge that development has both universal features and features unique to each individual and his or her contexts. And a growing number regard heredity and environment as inseparably interwoven, each affecting the potential of the other to modify the child's traits and capacities (Cole, 2006; Gottlieb, Wahlsten, & Lickliter, 2006; Huttenlocher, 2002; Lerner, 2006; Rutter, 2007).

These balanced visions owe much to the expansion of research from a nearly exclusive focus on the first two decades of life to include development during adulthood. In the first half of the twentieth century, it was widely assumed that development stopped at adolescence. Infancy and childhood were viewed as periods of rapid transformation, adulthood as a plateau, and aging as a period of decline. The changing character of the North American population awakened researchers to the idea that gains in functioning are lifelong.

Because of improvements in nutrition, sanitation, and medical knowledge, the *average life expectancy* (the number of years an individual born in a particular year can expect to live) gained more in the twentieth century than in the preceding five thousand years. In 1900, life expectancy was just under age 50; today, it is 78.1 years in the United States and even higher in most other industrialized nations, including neighboring Canada. Life expectancy continues to increase; in the United States, it is predicted to reach 84 years in 2050. Consequently, there are more older adults—a worldwide trend that is especially striking in developed countries. People age 65 and older accounted for about 4 percent of the U.S. population in 1900, 7 percent in 1950, and 13 percent in 2007 (Heron et al., 2008; U.S. Census Bureau, 2008a).

Older adults are not only more numerous but also healthier and more active. Challenging the earlier stereotype of the withering person, they have contributed to a profound shift in our view of human change and the factors that underlie it. Increasingly, researchers are envisioning *development as a dynamic system*—a perpetually ongoing process, extending from conception to death, that is molded by a complex network of biological, psychological, and social influences (Lerner, Theokas, & Bobek, 2005). A leading dynamic systems approach is the **lifespan perspective.** Four assumptions make up this broader view: that development is (1) lifelong, (2) multidimensional and multidirectional, (3) highly plastic, and (4) affected by multiple, interacting forces (Baltes, Lindenberger, & Staudinger, 2006; Smith & Baltes, 1999; Staudinger & Lindenberger, 2003).

Development Is Lifelong

According to the lifespan perspective, no single age period is supreme in its impact on the life course. Rather, events occurring during each major period, summarized in Table 1.1, can have equally powerful effects on future change. Within each period, change occurs in three broad domains: *physical, cognitive,* and *emotional/social,* which we separate for convenience

TABLE 1.1 ■ ***Major Periods of Human Development***

PERIOD	APPROXIMATE AGE RANGE	BRIEF DESCRIPTION
Prenatal	Conception to birth	The one-celled organism transforms into a human baby with remarkable capacities to adjust to life outside the womb.
Infancy and toddlerhood	Birth–2 years	Dramatic changes in the body and brain support the emergence of a wide array of motor, perceptual, and intellectual capacities and first intimate ties to others.
Early childhood	2–6 years	During the "play years," motor skills are refined, thought and language expand at an astounding pace, a sense of morality is evident, and children establish ties with peers.
Middle childhood	6–11 years	The school years are marked by improved athletic abilities; more logical thought processes; mastery of basic literacy skills; advances in self-understanding, morality, and friendship; and the beginnings of peer-group membership.
Adolescence	11–18 years	Puberty leads to an adult-sized body and sexual maturity. Thought becomes abstract and idealistic and school achievement more serious. Adolescents begin to establish autonomy from the family and to define personal values and goals.
Early adulthood	18–40 years	Most young people leave home, complete their education, and begin full-time work. Major concerns are developing a career, forming an intimate partnership, and marrying, rearing children, or establishing other lifestyles.
Middle adulthood	40–65 years	Many people are at the height of their careers and attain leadership positions. They must also help their children begin independent lives and their parents adapt to aging. They become more aware of their own mortality.
Late adulthood	65 years–death	People adjust to retirement, to decreased physical strength and health, and often to the death of a spouse. They reflect on the meaning of their lives.

© J.P. WILSON/ICON SMI/CORBIS © RONNIE KAUFMAN/CORBIS © TIM GRAHAM/ALAMY

Physical Development
Changes in body size, proportions, appearance, functioning of body systems, perceptual and motor capacities, and physical health.

Cognitive Development
Changes in intellectual abilities, including attention, memory, academic and everyday knowledge, problem solving, imagination, creativity, and language.

Emotional and Social Development
Changes in emotional communication, self-understanding, knowledge about other people, interpersonal skills, friendships, intimate relationships, and moral reasoning and behavior.

■ **FIGURE 1.2** ■ **Major domains of development.**
The three domains are not really distinct. Rather, they overlap and interact.

of discussion (see Figure 1.2 for a description of each). Yet, as you already know from reading the first part of this chapter, these domains are not really distinct; they overlap and interact.

Every age period has its own agenda, its unique demands and opportunities that yield some similarities in development across many individuals. Nevertheless, throughout life, the challenges people face and the adjustments they make are highly diverse in timing and pattern, as the remaining assumptions make clear.

Development Is Multidimensional and Multidirectional

Think back to Sofie's life and how she continually faced new demands and opportunities. From a lifespan perspective, the challenges and adjustments of development are *multidimensional*—affected by an intricate blend of biological, psychological, and social forces.

Lifespan development is also *multidirectional,* in at least two ways. First, development is not limited to improved performance. Rather, at every period, it is a joint expression of growth and decline. When Sofie directed her energies toward mastering languages and music as a school-age child, she gave up refining other skills to their full potential. Later, when she chose to become a teacher, she let go of other career options. Although gains are especially evident early in life, and losses during the final years, people of all ages can improve current skills and develop new ones, including skills that compensate for reduced functioning (Freund & Baltes, 2000). Most older adults, for example, devise compensatory techniques for dealing with their increasing memory failures. They may rely more on external aids, such as calendars and lists, or generate new internal strategies, such as visualizing exactly where they will be and what they will be doing when they must keep an appointment or take medication (Chazottes, 2004).

Second, besides being multidirectional over time, change is multidirectional within each domain of development. Although some qualities of Sofie's cognitive functioning (such as memory) probably declined in her mature years, her knowledge of both English and French undoubtedly grew throughout her life. And she also developed new forms of thinking. For example, Sofie's wealth of experience and ability to cope with diverse problems led her to become expert in practical matters—a quality of reasoning called *wisdom.* Recall Sofie's wise advice to

BIOLOGY AND ENVIRONMENT

Resilience

John and his best friend, Gary, grew up in a rundown, crime-ridden, inner-city neighborhood. By age 10, each had experienced years of family conflict followed by parental divorce. Reared from then on in mother-headed households, John and Gary rarely saw their fathers. Both dropped out of high school and were in and out of trouble with the police.

Then John's and Gary's paths diverged. By age 30, John had fathered two children with women he never married, had spent time in prison, was unemployed, and drank alcohol heavily. In contrast, Gary had returned to finish high school, had studied auto mechanics at a community college, and had become manager of a gas station and repair shop. Married with two children, he had saved his earnings and bought a home. He was happy, healthy, and well-adapted to life.

A wealth of evidence shows that environmental risks—poverty, negative family interactions and parental divorce, job loss, mental illness, and drug abuse—predispose children to future problems (Masten & Gewirtz, 2006; Sameroff, 2006). Why did Gary "beat the odds" and come through unscathed?

New evidence on **resilience**—the ability to adapt effectively in the face of threats to development—is receiving increased attention as investigators look for ways to protect young people from the damaging effects of stressful life conditions (Masten & Powell, 2003). This interest has been inspired by several long-term studies on the relationship of life stressors in childhood to competence and adjustment in adolescence and adulthood (Fergusson & Horwood, 2003; Garmezy, 1993; Masten et al., 1995; Werner & Smith, 2001). In each study, some individuals were shielded from negative outcomes, whereas others had lasting problems. Four broad factors offered protection from the damaging effects of stressful life events.

© TOM STEWART/CORBIS

This boy's special relationship with his grandmother promotes resilience. By providing social support, she helps him cope with stress and solve problems constructively.

Personal Characteristics

A child's biologically endowed characteristics can reduce exposure to risk or lead to experiences that compensate for early stressful events. High intelligence and socially valued talents (in music or athletics, for example) increase the chances that a child will have rewarding experiences in school and in the community that offset the impact of a stressful home life. Temperament is particularly powerful. Children who have easygoing, sociable dispositions and who can readily inhibit negative emotions and impulses tend

Laura and Ken on the eve of their wedding day. We will consider the development of wisdom in Chapter 17. Notice in these examples how the lifespan perspective includes both continuous and discontinuous change.

Development Is Plastic

Lifespan researchers emphasize that development is plastic at all ages. Consider Sofie's social reserve in childhood and her decision to study rather than marry as a young adult. As new opportunities arose, Sofie moved easily into marriage and childbearing in her thirties. And although parenthood and financial difficulties posed challenges to Sofie's and Philip's happiness, their relationship gradually became richer and more fulfilling. In Chapter 17, we will see that intellectual performance also remains flexible with advancing age. Elderly people respond to special training with substantial (but not unlimited) gains in a wide variety of mental abilities (Nyberg, 2005; Willis et al., 2006).

Evidence on plasticity reveals that aging is not an eventual "shipwreck," as has often been assumed. Instead, the metaphor of a "butterfly"—of metamorphosis and continued potential—provides a far more accurate picture of lifespan change (Lemme, 2006). Still, development gradually becomes less plastic, as both capacity and opportunity for change are reduced. And plasticity varies greatly across individuals. Some children and adults experience more diverse life circumstances. Also, as the Biology and Environment box above indicates, some adapt more easily than others to changing conditions.

Development Is Influenced by Multiple, Interacting Forces

According to the lifespan perspective, pathways of change are highly diverse because *development is influenced by multiple forces:* biological, historical, social, and cultural. Although these

to have an optimistic outlook on life and a special capacity to adapt to change—qualities that elicit positive responses from others. In contrast, emotionally reactive and irritable children often tax the patience of people around them (Mathiesen & Prior, 2006; Werner, 2005; Wong et al., 2006). For example, both John and Gary moved several times during their childhoods. Each time, John became anxious and angry. Gary looked forward to making new friends and exploring a new neighborhood.

A Warm Parental Relationship

A close relationship with at least one parent who provides warmth, appropriately high expectations, monitoring of the child's activities, and an organized home environment fosters resilience (Masten & Shaffer, 2006). But this factor (as well as the next one) is not independent of children's personal characteristics. Children who are relaxed, socially responsive, and able to deal with change are easier to rear and more likely to enjoy positive relationships with parents and other people. At the same time, some children may develop more attractive dispositions as a result of parental warmth and attention (Conger & Conger, 2002; Gulotta, 2008).

Social Support Outside the Immediate Family

The most consistent asset of resilient children is a strong bond to a competent, caring adult. For children who do not have a close bond with either parent, a grandparent, aunt, uncle, or teacher who forms a special relationship with the child can promote resilience (Masten & Reed, 2002). Gary received support in adolescence from his grandfather, who listened to Gary's concerns and helped him solve problems. In addition, Gary's grandfather had a stable marriage and work life and handled stressors skillfully. Consequently, he served as a model of effective coping.

Associations with rule-abiding peers who value school achievement are also linked to resilience. But children who have positive relationships with adults are far more likely to establish these supportive peer ties.

Community Resources and Opportunities

Community supports—good schools, convenient and affordable health care and social services, libraries, and recreation centers—foster both parents' and children's well-being. In addition, opportunities to participate in community life help older children and adolescents overcome adversity. Extracurricular activities at school, religious youth groups, scouting, and other organizations teach important social skills, such as cooperation, leadership, and contributing to others' welfare. As participants acquire these competencies, they gain in self-reliance, self-esteem, and community commitment (Benson et al., 2006). As a college student, Gary volunteered for Habitat for Humanity, joining a team building affordable housing in low-income neighborhoods. Community involvement offered Gary opportunities to form meaningful relationships, which further strengthened his resilience.

Research on resilience highlights the complex connections between heredity and environment. Armed with positive characteristics, which stem from innate endowment, favorable rearing experiences, or both, children and adolescents take action to reduce stressful situations.

But when many risks pile up, they are increasingly difficult to overcome (Luthar, 2006). To inoculate children against the negative effects of risk, interventions must not only reduce risks but also enhance children's protective relationships at home, in school, and in the community. This means attending to both the person and the environment—strengthening the individual's capacities while also reducing hazardous experiences.

wide-ranging influences can be organized into three categories, they work together, combining in unique ways to fashion each life course.

■ **AGE-GRADED INFLUENCES.** Events that are strongly related to age and therefore fairly predictable in when they occur and how long they last are called **age-graded influences.** For example, most individuals walk shortly after their first birthday, acquire their native language during the preschool years, reach puberty around age 12 to 14, and (for women) experience menopause in their late forties or early fifties. These milestones are influenced by biology, but social customs—such as starting school around age 6, getting a driver's license at age 16, and entering college around age 18—can create age-graded influences as well. Age-graded influences are especially prevalent in childhood and adolescence, when biological changes are rapid and cultures impose many age-related experiences to ensure that young people acquire the skills they need to participate in their society.

© DANIEL RODRIGUEZ/ISTOCKPHOTO

For this 16-year-old, getting a driver's license is a major life transition, offering new privileges and responsibilities. In industrialized nations, starting to drive independently is an age-graded influence—one that occurs at about the same age for most young people.

A LIFESPAN VISTA: Looking Forward, Looking Back

The Baby Boomers Reshape the Life Course

From 1946 to 1964, 92 percent of all American women of childbearing age gave birth, averaging almost four children each—a new baby every 8 seconds (Croker, 2007). This splurge of births, which extended for nearly two decades, yielded a unique generation often credited with changing the world. Today, the baby boomers—comprising more than 80 million middle-aged adults—make up nearly 30 percent of the U.S. population (U.S. Census Bureau, 2008a).

Several interrelated factors sparked the post–World War II baby boom. Many people who had postponed marriage and parenthood throughout the Great Depression of the 1930s started families in the 1940s, once the economy had improved. With the end of World War II, returning GIs also began to have children. As these two cohorts focused on childbearing, they gave birth to babies who otherwise would have been spaced out over 10 to 15 years. And as economic prosperity accelerated in the 1950s, making larger families affordable, more people married at younger ages and had several children closely spaced, which led the baby boom to persist into the 1960s (Stewart & Malley, 2004). Finally, after a war, the desire to make babies generally strengthens. Besides replacing massive loss of life, new births signify hope—a belief that "human life will continue" (Croker, 2007, p. 9).

Compared with the previous generation, many more young baby boomers were economically privileged. They were also the recipients of deep emotional investment from their parents, who—having undergone the deprivations of depression and war—often ranked children as the most enduring benefit of their adult lives. These factors may have engendered optimism, confidence, even a sense of entitlement (Elder, Nguyen, & Caspi, 1985). At the same time, their huge numbers—evident in overflowing school classrooms—may have sparked an intense struggle for individual recognition. By the time the boomers reached early adulthood, this set of traits led critics to label them a narcissistic, indulged, "me" generation.

From the mid-1960s to the early 1970s, the "leading-edge" baby boomers (born in the late 1940s and early 1950s) entered colleges and universities in record numbers, becoming better educated than any previous generation. This cohort—self-focused, socially aware, and in search of distinction—broke away from their parents' family- and marriage-centered lifestyles. Starting in the mid-sixties, marriage rates declined, age of first marriage rose, and divorce rates increased. And the baby boomers responded to the turbulence of those times—the assassination of President Kennedy in 1963, the Vietnam War, and growing racial tensions—by mobilizing around the antiwar, civil rights, and women's movements, yielding a generation of student activists.

AP IMAGES/UNAMID, SHERREN ZORBA

Actor George Clooney, born in 1961, is one of the "trailing edge" baby boomers. Like many in his cohort, he has an unusually strong sense of social responsibility. He is cofounder of Not On Our Watch, an organization that focuses on ending atrocities around the world. Here he visits a refugee camp in Darfur, Sudan, where hundreds of thousands have been slaughtered and millions displaced during years of civil war.

By the time the "trailing-edge" boomers (born in the late 1950s and early 1960s) came of age, these movements had left an enduring mark. Even as they turned toward family life and career development, the boomers continued to search for personal meaning, self-expression, and social responsibility. By midlife, the generation had produced an unusually large number of socially concerned writers, teachers, filmmakers, and labor and community organizers, as well as innovative musicians and artists (Cole & Stewart, 1996; Dickstein, 1992). And a multitude of ordinary citizens worked to advance social causes.

In addition, as baby-boom women entered the labor market and struggled for career advancement and equal pay, their self-confidence grew, and they paved the way for the next generation: On average, younger women attained this same level of self-confidence at a much earlier age (Stewart & Ostrove, 1998; Twenge, 1997, 2001). And as baby-boom activists pressed for gender and racial equality, they influenced national policy. The 1960s saw laws passed that banned discrimination in employment practices, in racial access to public accommodations, and in sale or rental of housing. By the 1970s, progress in civil rights served as the springboard for the gay and lesbian rights movement.

Today, the baby boomers are larger, healthier, better educated, and financially better off than any previous midlife cohort (Whitbourne & Willis, 2006). Their sense of self-empowerment and innovativeness is bringing new vitality to this period of the lifespan, including efforts to increase the personal meaningfulness of their careers and to deepen their lifelong engagement with social causes. Yet another concern of baby-boom midlifers is an intense desire to control the physical changes of aging (Lachman & Firth, 2004). Far more than their predecessors, they resist growing old, as indicated by their interest in a wide array of anti-aging products and procedures—from cosmetics to Botox to plastic surgery—that are now a multi-billion-dollar U.S. industry. Nevertheless, it is important to note that the baby boomers—though advantaged as a generation—are diverse in health status and sense of control over their lives, with those higher in education and income considerably better off.

What lies ahead as this gigantic population bulge approaches late adulthood? Most analysts focus on societal burdens, such as rising social security and health-care costs. At the same time, as the boomers continue to build on the foundation laid in middle age, they could become "our only increasing natural resource" (Freedman, 1999). After retirement, they will have more time to care about others—and more relevant experience and years left to do so—than any previous generation. Policies and programs aimed at recruiting older adults into volunteer and service roles may be one of the most effective ways to "channel good will into good deeds," combat social ills, and enhance development during all periods of life.

■ **HISTORY-GRADED INFLUENCES.** Development is also profoundly affected by forces unique to a particular historical era. Examples include epidemics, wars, and periods of economic prosperity or depression; technological advances, such as the introduction of television, computers, and the Internet; and changes in cultural values, such as attitudes toward women and ethnic minorities. These **history-graded influences** explain why people born around the same time—called a *cohort*—tend to be alike in ways that set them apart from people born at other times.

Consider the *baby boomers,* a term used to describe people born between 1946 and 1964, the post–World War II period during which birth rates soared in most Western nations. The population increase was especially sharp in the United States: By 1960, the prewar birth rate had nearly doubled, yielding the largest population increase in the nation's history. The sheer size of the baby-boom generation made it a powerful social force from the time its members became young adults; today, the baby boomers are redefining our view of middle age (see the Lifespan Vista box on page 12).

■ **NONNORMATIVE INFLUENCES.** Age-graded and history-graded influences are *normative*—meaning typical, or average—because each affects large numbers of people in a similar way. **Nonnormative influences** are events that are irregular: They happen to just one person or a few people and do not follow a predictable timetable. Consequently, they enhance the multidirectionality of development. Nonnormative influences that had a major impact on the direction of Sofie's life were piano lessons in childhood with an inspiring teacher; a blind date with Philip; delayed marriage, parenthood, and career entry; and a battle with cancer. Because they occur haphazardly, nonnormative events are difficult for researchers to capture and study. Yet, as each of us can attest from our own experiences, they can affect us in powerful ways.

Lifespan investigators point out that nonnormative influences have become more powerful and age-graded influences less so in contemporary adult development. Compared with Sofie's era, much greater diversity exists today in the ages at which people finish their education, enter careers, get married, have children, and retire. Indeed, Sofie's "off-time" accomplishments would have been less unusual had she been born a generation or two later! Age remains a powerful organizer of everyday experiences, and age-related expectations have certainly not disappeared. But age markers have blurred, and they vary across ethnic groups and cultures. The increasing role of nonnormative events in the life course adds to the fluid nature of lifespan development.

Notice that instead of a single line of development, the lifespan perspective emphasizes many potential pathways and outcomes—an image more like fibers extending in diverse directions, which may undergo both continuous and stagewise transformations (see Figure 1.3). Now let's turn to the scientific foundations of the field as a prelude to major theories that address various aspects of change.

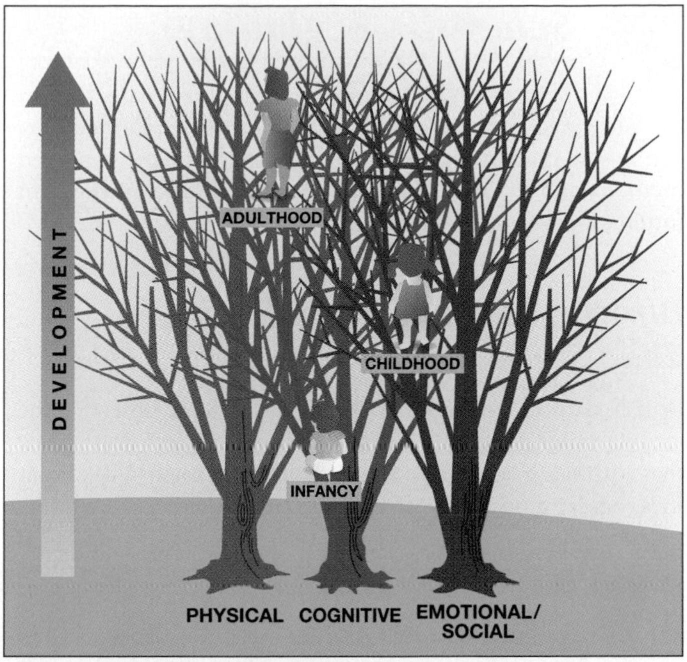

■ **FIGURE 1.3** ■ **The lifespan view of development.** Rather than envisioning a single line of stagewise or continuous change (see Figure 1.1 on page 6), lifespan theorists conceive of development as more like tree branches extending in diverse directions. Many potential pathways are possible, depending on the contexts that influence the individual's life course. Each branch in this treelike image represents a possible skill within one of the major domains of development. The crossing of the branches signifies that the domains—physical, cognitive, emotional, and social—are interrelated.

ASK YOURSELF

» REVIEW
Distinguish among age-graded, history-graded, and nonnormative influences on lifespan development. Cite an example of each in Sofie's story at the beginning of this chapter.

» APPLY
Anna, a high school counselor, has devised a program that integrates classroom learning with vocational training to help adolescents at risk for school dropout stay in school and transition smoothly to work life. What is Anna's position on *stability versus plasticity* in development? Explain.

» CONNECT
What stand does the lifespan perspective take on the issue of *one course of development or many?* How about the relative influence of *nature and nurture?* Explain.

» REFLECT
Describe an aspect of your development that differs from a parent's or a grandparent's when he or she was your age. Using influences highlighted by the lifespan perspective, explain this difference in development.

Scientific Beginnings

Scientific study of human development dates back to the late nineteenth and early twentieth centuries. Early observations of human change were soon followed by improved methods and theories. Each advance contributed to the firm foundation on which the field rests today.

Darwin: Forefather of Scientific Child Study

British naturalist Charles Darwin (1809–1882) observed the infinite variation among plant and animal species. He also saw that within a species, no two individuals are exactly alike. From these observations, he constructed his famous *theory of evolution.*

© LISA F. YOUNG/ALAMY

Darwin's theory of evolution emphasizes the adaptive value of physical characteristics and behavior. Affection and care in families are adaptive throughout the lifespan, promoting survival and psychological well-being. Here, a son helps his father adjust to using a walker.

The theory emphasized two related principles: *natural selection* and *survival of the fittest.* Darwin explained that certain species survive in particular environments because they have characteristics that fit with, or are adapted to, their surroundings. Other species die off because they are less well-suited to their environments. Individuals within a species who best meet the environment's survival requirements live long enough to reproduce and pass their more beneficial characteristics to future generations. Darwin's (1859/1936) emphasis on the adaptive value of physical characteristics and behavior found its way into important developmental theories.

During his explorations, Darwin discovered that early prenatal growth is strikingly similar in many species. Other scientists concluded from Darwin's observations that the development of the human child follows the same general plan as the evolution of the human species. Although this belief eventually proved inaccurate, efforts to chart parallels between child growth and human evolution prompted researchers to make careful observations of all aspects of children's behavior. Out of these first attempts to document an idea about development, scientific child study was born.

The Normative Period

G. Stanley Hall (1844–1924), one of the most influential American psychologists of the early twentieth century, is generally regarded as the founder of the child study movement (Cairns & Cairns, 2006). He also foreshadowed lifespan research by writing one of the few books of his time on aging. Inspired by Darwin's work, Hall and his well-known student Arnold Gesell (1880–1961) devised theories based on evolutionary ideas. They regarded development as a *maturational process*—a genetically determined series of events that unfold automatically, much like a flower (Gesell, 1933; Hall, 1904).

Hall and Gesell are remembered less for their one-sided theories than for their intensive efforts to describe all aspects of development. This launched the **normative approach,** in which measures of behavior are taken on large numbers of individuals, and age-related averages are computed to represent typical development. Using this procedure, Hall constructed elaborate questionnaires asking children of different ages almost everything they could tell about themselves—interests, fears, imaginary playmates, dreams, friendships, everyday knowledge, and more. Similarly, through careful observations and parent interviews, Gesell collected detailed normative information on the motor achievements, social behaviors, and personality characteristics of infants and children.

Gesell was also among the first to make knowledge about child development meaningful to parents by informing them of what to expect at each age. If the timetable of development is the product of millions of years of evolution, as Gesell believed, then children are naturally knowledgeable about their needs. His child-rearing advice recommended sensitivity to children's cues (Thelen & Adolph, 1992). Along with Benjamin Spock's *Baby and Child Care,* Gesell's books became a central part of a rapidly expanding child development literature for parents.

The Mental Testing Movement

While Hall and Gesell were developing their theories and methods in the United States, French psychologist Alfred Binet (1857–1911) was also taking a normative approach to child development, but for a different reason. In the early 1900s, Binet and his colleague Theodore Simon were asked by Paris school officials to find a way to identify children with learning problems who needed to be placed in special classes. To address these practical educational concerns, Binet and Simon constructed the first successful intelligence test.

In 1916, at Stanford University, Binet's test was adapted for use with English-speaking children. Since then, the English version has been known as the *Stanford-Binet Intelligence Scale.* Besides providing a score that could successfully predict school achievement, the Binet test sparked tremendous interest in individual differences in development. Comparisons of the scores of people who vary in gender, ethnicity, birth order, family background, and other characteristics became a major focus of research. And intelligence tests moved quickly to the forefront of the nature–nurture controversy.

Mid-Twentieth-Century Theories

In the mid-twentieth century, the study of human development expanded into a legitimate discipline. As it attracted increasing interest, a variety of theories emerged, each of which continues to have followers today. In these theories, the European concern with the individual's inner thoughts and feelings contrasts sharply with the North American academic focus on scientific precision and concrete, observable behavior.

The Psychoanalytic Perspective

In the 1930s and 1940s, as more people sought help from professionals to deal with emotional difficulties, a new question had to be addressed: How and why do people become the way they are? To treat psychological problems, psychiatrists and social workers turned to an emerging approach to personality development that emphasized each individual's unique life history.

According to the **psychoanalytic perspective,** people move through a series of stages in which they confront conflicts between biological drives and social expectations. How these conflicts are resolved determines the person's ability to learn, to get along with others, and to cope with anxiety. Among the many individuals who contributed to the psychoanalytic perspective, two were especially influential: Sigmund Freud, founder of the psychoanalytic movement, and Erik Erikson.

FREUD'S THEORY. Freud (1856–1939), a Viennese physician, sought a cure for emotionally troubled adults by having them talk freely about painful events of their childhoods. On the basis of these recollections, he examined the unconscious motivations of his patients and constructed his **psychosexual theory,** which emphasizes that how parents manage their child's sexual and aggressive drives in the first few years is crucial for healthy personality development.

In Freud's theory, three parts of the personality—id, ego, and superego—become integrated during five stages, summarized in Table 1.2 on page 16. The *id,* the largest portion of the mind, is the source of basic biological needs and desires. The *ego,* the conscious, rational part of personality, emerges in early infancy to redirect the id's impulses so they are discharged in acceptable ways. For example, aided by the ego, the hungry baby stops crying when he sees his mother preparing to feed him. And the more competent preschooler gets a snack from the kitchen on her own.

Between 3 and 6 years of age, the *superego,* or conscience, develops through interactions with parents, who insist that children conform to the values of society. Now the ego faces the increasingly complex task of reconciling the demands of the id, the external world, and conscience (Freud, 1923/1974). For example, when the ego is tempted to gratify an id impulse by hitting a playmate to get an attractive toy, the superego may warn that such behavior is wrong. The ego must decide which of the two forces (id or superego) will win this inner struggle, or it must work out a compromise, such as asking for a turn with the toy. According to Freud, the relations established among the id, ego, and superego during the preschool years determine the individual's basic personality.

Freud (1938/1973) believed that during childhood sexual impulses shift their focus from the oral to the anal to the genital regions of the body. In each stage, parents walk a fine line between permitting too much or too little gratification of their child's basic needs. If parents strike an appropriate balance, then children grow into well-adjusted adults with the capacity for mature sexuality and investment in family life.

Freud's theory was the first to stress the influence of the early parent–child relationship on development. But his perspective was eventually criticized. First, it overemphasized the influence of sexual feelings in development. Second, because it was based on the problems of sexually repressed, well-to-do adults in nineteenth-century Viennese society, it did not apply in other cultures. Finally, Freud had not studied children directly.

ERIKSON'S THEORY. Several of Freud's followers took what was useful from his theory and improved on his vision. The most important of these neo-Freudians is Erik Erikson (1902–1994), who expanded the picture of development at each stage. In his **psychosocial theory,** Erikson emphasized that in addition to mediating between id impulses and superego demands, the ego makes a positive contribution to development, acquiring attitudes and skills at each stage that make the individual an active, contributing member of society. A

TABLE 1.2 Freud's Psychosexual Stages

PSYCHOSEXUAL STAGE	PERIOD OF DEVELOPMENT	DESCRIPTION
Oral	Birth–1 year	The new ego directs the baby's sucking activities toward breast or bottle. If oral needs are not met appropriately, the individual may develop such habits as thumb sucking, fingernail biting, and pencil chewing in childhood and overeating and smoking in later life.
Anal	1–3 years	Toddlers and preschoolers enjoy holding and releasing urine and feces. Toilet training becomes a major issue between parent and child. If parents insist that children be trained before they are ready, or if they make too few demands, conflicts about anal control may appear in the form of extreme orderliness and cleanliness or messiness and disorder.
Phallic	3–6 years	As preschoolers take pleasure in genital stimulation, Freud's Oedipus conflict for boys and Electra conflict for girls arise: Children feel a sexual desire for the other-sex parent. To avoid punishment, they give up this desire and adopt the same-sex parent's characteristics and values. As a result, the superego is formed, and children feel guilty each time they violate its standards.
Latency	6–11 years	Sexual instincts die down, and the superego develops further. The child acquires new social values from adults and same-sex peers outside the family.
Genital	Adolescence	With puberty, the sexual impulses of the phallic stage reappear. If development has been successful during earlier stages, it leads to marriage, mature sexuality, and the birth and rearing of children. This stage extends through adulthood.

basic psychological conflict, which is resolved along a continuum from positive to negative, determines healthy or maladaptive outcomes at each stage. As Table 1.3 shows, Erikson's first five stages parallel Freud's stages, but Erikson added three adult stages.

Unlike Freud, Erikson pointed out that normal development must be understood in relation to each culture's life situation. For example, in the 1940s, he observed that Yurok Indians of the northwest coast of the United States deprived babies of breastfeeding for the first 10 days after birth and instead fed them a thin soup. At age 6 months, infants were abruptly weaned—if necessary, by having the mother leave for a few days. From our cultural vantage point, this deliberate deprivation seems cruel. But Erikson explained that because the Yurok depended on salmon, which fill the river just once a year, the development of considerable self-restraint was essential for survival. In this way, he showed that child rearing can be understood only in relation to the competencies valued and needed by an individual's society.

Children of the Lacandon Mayan people of southern Mexico look on as their father makes souvenir arrows similar to those of their ancestors. The Lacandon—descendants of hunter-gatherers and subsistence farmers who lived in isolation for hundreds of years—teach their children many ancient skills and traditions, including tool making and agricultural techniques. As Erikson recognized, these child-rearing practices can be understood only in relation to the Lacandon's distinct culture.

CONTRIBUTIONS AND LIMITATIONS OF THE PSYCHOANALYTIC PERSPECTIVE. A special strength of the psychoanalytic perspective is its emphasis on the individual's unique life history as worthy of study and understanding. Consistent with this view, psychoanalytic theorists accept the *clinical,* or *case study, method,* which synthesizes information from a variety of sources into a detailed picture of the personality of a single person. (We will discuss the clinical method further at the end of this chapter.) Psychoanalytic theory has also inspired a wealth of research on many aspects of emotional and social

■ TABLE 1.3 ■ ***Erikson's Psychosocial Stages, with Corresponding Psychosexual Stages Indicated***

PSYCHOSOCIAL STAGE	PERIOD OF DEVELOPMENT	DESCRIPTION
Basic trust versus mistrust (Oral)	Birth–1 year	From warm, responsive care, infants gain a sense of trust, or confidence, that the world is good. Mistrust occurs when infants have to wait too long for comfort and are handled harshly.
Autonomy versus shame and doubt (Anal)	1–3 years	Using new mental and motor skills, children want to choose and decide for themselves. Parents can foster autonomy by permitting reasonable free choice and not forcing or shaming the child.
Initiative versus guilt (Phallic)	3–6 years	Through make-believe play, children explore the kind of person they can become. Initiative—a sense of ambition and responsibility—develops when parents support their child's new sense of purpose. When parents demand too much self-control, they induce excessive guilt.
Industry versus inferiority (Latency)	6–11 years	At school, children develop the capacity to work and cooperate with others. Inferiority develops when negative experiences at home, at school, or with peers lead to feelings of incompetence.
Identity versus role confusion (Genital)	Adolescence	The adolescent tries to answer the questions, Who am I, and what is my place in society? By exploring values and vocational goals, the young person forms a personal identity. The negative outcome is confusion about future adult roles.
Intimacy versus isolation	Early adulthood	Young people work on establishing intimate ties to others. Because of earlier disappointments, some individuals cannot form close relationships and remain isolated.
Generativity versus stagnation	Middle adulthood	Middle-aged adults contribute to the next generation through child rearing, caring for other people, or productive work. The person who fails in these ways feels an absence of meaningful accomplishment.
Integrity versus despair	Late adulthood	Elders reflect on the kind of person they have been. Integrity results from feeling that life was worth living as it happened. Those who are dissatisfied with their lives fear death.

Erik Erikson

development, including infant–caregiver attachment, aggression, sibling relationships, child-rearing practices, morality, gender roles, and adolescent identity.

Despite its extensive contributions, the psychoanalytic perspective is no longer in the mainstream of human development research. Psychoanalytic theorists may have become isolated from the rest of the field because they were so strongly committed to the clinical approach that they failed to consider other methods. In addition, many psychoanalytic ideas, such as psychosexual stages and ego functioning, are so vague that they are difficult or impossible to test empirically (Crain, 2005; Thomas, 2005).

Nevertheless, Erikson's broad outline of lifespan change captures the essence of personality development during each major period of the life course, so we will return to it in later chapters. We will also encounter perspectives inspired by Erikson's theory that clarify the attainments of early, middle, and late adulthood and that are within the tradition of stage models of psychosocial development (Levinson, 1978, 1996; McAdams, 2001, 2008; Vaillant, 1977, 2002).

Behaviorism and Social Learning Theory

As the psychoanalytic perspective gained in prominence, the study of development was also influenced by a very different perspective. According to **behaviorism,** directly observable events—stimuli and responses—are the appropriate focus of study. North American behaviorism began in the early twentieth century with the work of psychologist John Watson (1878–1958), who, rejecting the psychoanalytic concern with the unseen workings of the mind, set out to create an objective science of psychology.

■ **TRADITIONAL BEHAVIORISM.** Watson was inspired by Russian physiologist Ivan Pavlov's studies of animal learning. Pavlov knew that dogs release saliva as an innate reflex when they are given food. But he noticed that his dogs were salivating before they tasted any food—when they saw the trainer who usually fed them. The dogs, Pavlov reasoned, must have learned to associate a neutral stimulus (the trainer) with another stimulus (food) that produces a reflexive response (salivation). Because of this association, the neutral stimulus alone could bring about a response resembling the reflex. Eager to test this idea, Pavlov successfully taught dogs to salivate at the sound of a bell by pairing it with the presentation of food. He had discovered *classical conditioning.*

Watson wanted to find out if classical conditioning could be applied to children's behavior. In a historic experiment, he taught Albert, an 11-month-old infant, to fear a neutral stimulus—a soft white rat—by presenting it several times with a sharp, loud sound, which naturally scared the baby. Little Albert, who at first had reached out eagerly to touch the furry rat, began to cry and turn his head away when he caught sight of it (Watson & Raynor, 1920). In fact, Albert's fear was so intense that researchers eventually challenged the ethics of studies like this one. Watson concluded that environment is the supreme force in development and that adults can mold children's behavior by carefully controlling stimulus–response associations. He viewed development as a continuous process, consisting of a gradual increase with age in the number and strength of these associations.

Another form of behaviorism was American psychologist B. F. Skinner's (1904–1990) *operant conditioning theory.* According to Skinner, the frequency of a behavior can be increased by following it with a wide variety of *reinforcers,* such as food, praise, or a friendly smile. It can also be decreased through *punishment,* such as disapproval or withdrawal of privileges. As a result of Skinner's work, operant conditioning became a broadly applied learning principle. We will consider these conditioning techniques further in Chapter 4.

SOCIAL LEARNING THEORY. Psychologists wondered whether behaviorism might offer a more direct and effective explanation of the development of social behavior than the less precise concepts of psychoanalytic theory. This sparked approaches that built on the principles of conditioning, offering expanded views of how children and adults acquire new responses.

Several kinds of **social learning theory** emerged. The most influential, devised by American psychologist Albert Bandura (1925–), emphasizes *modeling,* also known as *imitation* or *observational learning,* as a powerful source of development. The baby who claps her hands after her mother does so, the child who angrily hits a playmate in the same way that he has been punished at home, and the teenager who wears the same clothes and hairstyle as her friends at school are all displaying observational learning. In his early work, Bandura found that diverse factors affect children's motivation to imitate: their own history of reinforcement or punishment for the behavior, the promise of future reinforcement or punishment, and even vicarious reinforcement or punishment (observing the model being reinforced or punished).

Bandura's work continues to influence much research on social development. But today, his theory stresses the importance of *cognition,* or thinking. In fact, the most recent revision of Bandura's (1992, 2001) theory places such strong emphasis on how we think about ourselves and other people that he calls it a *social-cognitive* rather than a social learning approach.

In Bandura's revised view, children gradually become more selective in what they imitate. From watching others engage in self-praise and self-blame and through feedback about the worth of their own actions, children develop *personal standards* for behavior and *a sense of self-efficacy*—the belief that their own abilities and characteristics will help them succeed. These cognitions guide responses in particular situations (Bandura, 1999, 2001). For example, imagine a parent who often remarks, "I'm glad I kept working on that task, even though it was hard," who explains the value of persistence, and who encourages it by saying, "I know you can do a good job on that homework!" Soon the child starts to view herself as hard-working and high-achieving and selects people with these characteristics as models. In this way, as individuals acquire attitudes, values, and convictions about themselves, they control their own learning and behavior.

CONTRIBUTIONS AND LIMITATIONS OF BEHAVIORISM AND SOCIAL LEARNING THEORY. Behaviorism and social learning theory have been helpful in treating a wide range of adjustment problems. **Behavior modification** consists of procedures that combine conditioning and modeling to eliminate undesirable behaviors and increase desirable responses. It has been used to relieve a wide range of difficulties in children and

Social learning theory recognizes that children acquire many skills through modeling. By observing and imitating her mother, this Vietnamese preschooler learns to use chopsticks.

adults, ranging from poor time management and unwanted habits to serious problems, such as language delays, persistent aggression, and extreme fears (Conyers et al., 2004; Martin & Pear, 2007).

Nevertheless, many theorists believe that behaviorism and social learning theory offer too narrow a view of important environmental influences, which extend beyond immediate reinforcement, punishment, and modeled behaviors to people's rich physical and social worlds. Behaviorism and social learning theory have also been criticized for underestimating people's contributions to their own development. Bandura, with his emphasis on cognition, is unique among theorists whose work grew out of the behaviorist tradition in granting children and adults an active role in their own learning.

© BOB DAEMMRICH/THE IMAGE WORKS

In Piaget's operational stage, school-age children think in an organized, logical fashion about concrete objects. This 6-year-old girl and 7-year-old boy understand that the amount of milk remains the same after being poured into a differently shaped container, even though its appearance changes.

Piaget's Cognitive-Developmental Theory

If one individual has influenced research on child development more than any other, it is Swiss cognitive theorist Jean Piaget (1896–1980). North American investigators had been aware of Piaget's work since 1930. But they did not grant it much attention until the 1960s, mainly because Piaget's ideas were at odds with behaviorism, which dominated North American psychology in the mid-twentieth century (Cairns & Cairns, 2006). Piaget did not believe that children's learning depends on reinforcers, such as rewards from adults. According to his **cognitive-developmental theory,** children actively construct knowledge as they manipulate and explore their world.

■ **PIAGET'S STAGES.** Piaget's view of development was greatly influenced by his early training in biology. Central to his theory is the biological concept of *adaptation* (Piaget, 1971). Just as structures of the body are adapted to fit with the environment, so structures of the mind develop to better fit with, or represent, the external world. In infancy and early childhood, Piaget claimed, children's understanding is different from adults'. For example, he believed that young babies do not realize that an object hidden from view—a favorite toy or even the mother—continues to exist. He also concluded that preschoolers' thinking is full of faulty logic. For example, children younger than age 7 commonly say that the amount of a liquid changes when it is poured into a different-shaped container. According to Piaget, children eventually revise these incorrect ideas in their ongoing efforts to achieve an *equilibrium,* or balance, between internal structures and information they encounter in their everyday worlds.

In Piaget's theory, as the brain develops and children's experiences expand, they move through four broad stages, each characterized by qualitatively distinct ways of thinking. Table 1.4 on page 20 provides a brief description of Piaget's stages. Cognitive development begins in the *sensorimotor stage* with the baby's use of the senses and movements to explore the world. These action patterns evolve into the symbolic but illogical thinking of the preschooler in the *preoperational stage.* Then cognition is transformed into the more organized, logical reasoning of the school-age child in the *concrete operational stage.* Finally, in the *formal operational stage,* thought becomes the abstract, systematic reasoning system of the adolescent and adult.

Piaget devised special methods for investigating how children think. Early in his career, he carefully observed his three infant children and presented them with everyday problems, such as an attractive object that could be grasped, mouthed, kicked, or searched for. From their responses, Piaget derived his ideas about cognitive changes during the first two years. To study childhood and adolescent thought, Piaget adapted the clinical method of psychoanalysis, conducting open-ended *clinical interviews* in which a child's initial response to a task served as the basis for Piaget's next question. We will look more closely at this technique when we discuss research methods later in this chapter.

■ **CONTRIBUTIONS AND LIMITATIONS OF PIAGET'S THEORY.** Piaget convinced the field that children are active learners whose minds consist of rich structures of knowledge. Besides investigating children's understanding of the physical world, Piaget explored their reasoning about the social world. His stages have sparked a wealth of research on children's conceptions of themselves, other people, and human relationships. In practical terms, Piaget's theory encouraged the development of educational philosophies and programs that emphasize discovery learning and direct contact with the environment.

■ TABLE 1.4 ■ *Piaget's Stages of Cognitive Development*

STAGE	PERIOD OF DEVELOPMENT	DESCRIPTION
Sensorimotor	Birth–2 years	Infants "think" by acting on the world with their eyes, ears, hands, and mouth. As a result, they invent ways of solving sensorimotor problems, such as pulling a lever to hear the sound of a music box, finding hidden toys, and putting objects into and taking them out of containers.
Preoperational	2–7 years	Preschool children use symbols to represent their earlier sensorimotor discoveries. Development of language and make-believe play takes place. However, thinking lacks the logic of the two remaining stages.
Concrete operational	7–11 years	Children's reasoning becomes logical. School-age children understand that a certain amount of lemonade or play dough remains the same even after its appearance changes. They also organize objects into hierarchies of classes and subclasses. However, children think in a logical, organized fashion only when dealing with concrete information they can perceive directly.
Formal operational	11 years on	The capacity for abstract, systematic thinking enables adolescents, when faced with a problem, to start with a hypothesis, deduce testable inferences, and isolate and combine variables to see which inferences are confirmed. Adolescents can also evaluate the logic of verbal statements without referring to real-world circumstances.

Jean Piaget

Despite Piaget's overwhelming contributions, his theory has been challenged. Research indicates that Piaget underestimated the competencies of infants and preschoolers. When young children are given tasks scaled down in difficulty and relevant to their everyday experiences, their understanding appears closer to that of the older child and adult than Piaget assumed. Furthermore, many studies show that children's performance on Piagetian problems can be improved with training—findings that call into question Piaget's assumption that discovery learning rather than adult teaching is the best way to foster development (Klahr & Nigam, 2004; Siegler & Svetina, 2006). Critics also point out that Piaget's stagewise account pays insufficient attention to social and cultural influences on development. Finally, some lifespan theorists disagree with Piaget's conclusion that no major cognitive changes occur after adolescence. Several have proposed important transformations in adulthood (Labouvie-Vief, 1985; Moshman, 2005; Perry, 1981, 1970/1998).

Today, the field of developmental science is divided over its loyalty to Piaget's ideas (Desrochers, 2008). Those who continue to find merit in Piaget's stages often accept a modified view—one in which changes in thinking take place more gradually than Piaget believed (Case, 1998; Demetriou et al., 2002; Fischer & Bidell, 2006; Halford & Andrews, 2006). Among those who disagree with Piaget's stage sequence, some have embraced an approach that emphasizes continuous gains in children's cognition: information processing. And still others have been drawn to theories that focus on the role of children's social and cultural contexts. We take up these approaches in the next section.

ASK YOURSELF

» REVIEW
What aspect of behaviorism made it attractive to critics of the psychoanalytic perspective? How did Piaget's theory respond to a major limitation of behaviorism?

» APPLY
A 4-year-old becomes frightened of the dark and refuses to go to sleep at night. How would a psychoanalyst and a behaviorist differ in their views of how this problem developed?

» CONNECT
Although social learning theory focuses on social development and Piaget's theory on cognitive development, each has enhanced our understanding of other domains. Mention an additional domain addressed by each theory.

» REFLECT
Find out whether your parents read any child-rearing advice books when you were growing up. What questions most concerned them? Do you think the concerns of today's parents differ from those of your parents' generation? Explain.

Recent Theoretical Perspectives

New ways of understanding the developing person are constantly emerging—questioning, building on, and enhancing the discoveries of earlier theories. Today, a burst of fresh approaches and research emphases is broadening our understanding of lifespan development.

Information Processing

In the 1970s and 1980s, researchers turned to the field of cognitive psychology for ways to understand the development of thinking. The design of digital computers that use mathematically specified steps to solve problems suggested to psychologists that the human mind might also be viewed as a symbol-manipulating system through which information flows—a perspective called **information processing** (Klahr & MacWhinney, 1998; Munakata, 2006). From the time information is presented to the senses at *input* until it emerges as a behavioral response at *output,* information is actively coded, transformed, and organized.

■ **CONCERN WITH RIGOR AND PRECISION.** Information-processing researchers often use flowcharts to map the precise steps individuals use to solve problems and complete tasks, much like the plans devised by programmers to get computers to perform a series of "mental operations" (Siegler & Alibali, 2005). To see the usefulness of this approach, let's look at an example.

In a study of problem solving, a researcher provided a pile of blocks varying in size, shape, and weight and asked school-age children to build a bridge across a "river" (painted on a floor mat) that was too wide for any single block to span (Thornton, 1999). Figure 1.4 shows one solution: Two plank-like blocks span the water, each held in place by the counterweight of heavy blocks on the bridge's towers. Whereas older children easily built successful bridges, only one 5-year-old did. Careful tracking of her efforts revealed that she repeatedly tried unsuccessful strategies, such as pushing two planks together and pressing down on their ends to hold them in place. But eventually, her experimentation triggered the idea of using the blocks as counterweights. Her mistaken procedures helped her understand why the counterweight approach worked.

Many information-processing models exist. Some, like the one just considered, track children's mastery of one or a few tasks. Others describe the human cognitive system as a whole (Atkinson & Shiffrin, 1968; Lockhart & Craik, 1990). These general models are used as guides for asking questions about broad changes in thinking: Does a child's ability to solve problems become more organized and "planful" with age? Why is information processing slower among older than younger adults? Are declines in memory during old age evident on all types of tasks or only some?

Like Piaget's cognitive-developmental theory, the information-processing approach regards people as actively making sense of their own thinking (Halford, 2005; Munakata, 2006). But unlike Piaget's theory, it does not divide development into stages. Rather, the thought processes studied—perception, attention, memory, planning strategies, categorization of information, and comprehension of written and spoken prose—are regarded as similar at all ages but present to a lesser or greater extent. Therefore, the view of development is one of continuous change.

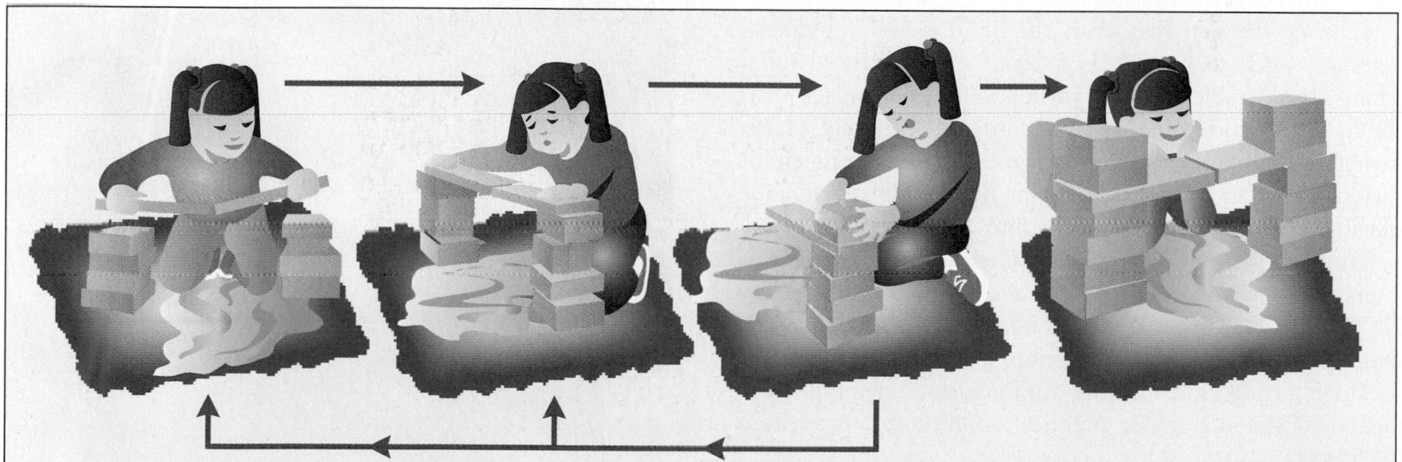

■ **FIGURE 1.4** ■ **Information-processing flowchart showing the steps that a 5-year-old used to solve a bridge-building problem.** Her task was to use blocks varying in size, shape, and weight, some of which were planklike, to construct a bridge across a "river" (painted on a floor mat) too wide for any single block to span. The child discovered how to counterweight and balance the bridge. The arrows reveal that, even after building a successful counterweight, she returned to earlier, unsuccessful strategies, which seemed to help her understand why the counterweight approach worked. (Adapted from Thornton, 1999.)

A great strength of the information-processing approach is its commitment to rigorous research methods. Because it has provided precise accounts of how children and adults tackle many cognitive tasks, its findings have important implications for education (Blumenfeld, Marx, & Harris, 2006). But information processing has fallen short in some respects. It has been better at analyzing thinking into its components than at putting them back together into a comprehensive theory. And it virtually ignores aspects of cognition that are not linear and logical, such as imagination and creativity (Birney et al., 2005).

■ **DEVELOPMENTAL COGNITIVE NEUROSCIENCE.** Over the past two decades, as information-processing research has expanded, a new area of investigation has arisen, called **developmental cognitive neuroscience.** It brings together researchers from psychology, biology, neuroscience, and medicine to study the relationship between changes in the brain and the developing person's cognitive processing and behavior patterns.

Improved methods for analyzing brain activity while children and adults perform various tasks have greatly enhanced knowledge of relationships between brain functioning, cognitive capacities, and behavior (Johnson, 2005; Westermann et al., 2007). Armed with these brain-imaging techniques (which we will consider in Chapter 4), neuroscientists are tackling questions like these: How do specific experiences at various ages influence the growth and organization of the young child's brain? What transformations in the brain make it harder for adolescents and adults than for children to acquire a second language? What neurological changes are related to declines in speed of thinking, memory, and other aspects of cognitive processing in old age?

During the first five years, the brain is highly plastic—especially open to growth as a result of experience. But it retains considerable plasticity throughout life. Neuroscientists are making rapid progress in identifying the types of experiences that support or undermine brain development at various ages. They are also clarifying the brain bases of many learning and behavior disorders, and they are contributing to effective interventions by examining the impact of various intervention techniques on both brain functioning and behavior (Munakata, Casey, & Diamond, 2004). Although much remains to be discovered, developmental cognitive neuroscience is already transforming our understanding of development and yielding major practical applications throughout the lifespan.

An advantage of having many theories is that they encourage researchers to attend to previously neglected dimensions of people's lives. The final three perspectives we will discuss focus on *contexts* for development. The first of these views emphasizes that development of many capacities is influenced by our long evolutionary history.

Ethology and Evolutionary Developmental Psychology

Ethology is concerned with the adaptive, or survival, value of behavior and its evolutionary history. Its roots can be traced to the work of Darwin. Two European zoologists, Konrad Lorenz and Niko Tinbergen, laid its modern foundations. Watching diverse animal species in their natural habitats, Lorenz and Tinbergen observed behavior patterns that promote survival. The best known of these is *imprinting,* the early following behavior of certain baby birds, such as geese, that ensures that the young will stay close to the mother and be fed and protected from danger. Imprinting takes place during an early, restricted period of development. If the mother goose is absent during this time but an object resembling her in important features is present, young goslings may imprint on it instead (Lorenz, 1952).

Observations of imprinting led to a major concept in human development: the *critical period.* It refers to a limited time span during which the individual is biologically prepared to acquire certain adaptive behaviors but needs the support of an appropriately stimulating environment. Many researchers have investigated whether complex cognitive and social behaviors must be learned during certain time periods. For example, if children are deprived of adequate food or physical and social stimulation during their early years, will their intelligence be impaired? If language is not mastered in early childhood, is the capacity to acquire it reduced?

© AP/WIDE WORLD PHOTOS

Ethology focuses on the adaptive, or survival, value of behavior and on similarities between human behavior and that of other species, especially our primate relatives. Observing this mother cuddling her 8-day-old infant helps us understand the human–infant caregiver relationship.

In later chapters, we will see that the term *sensitive period* applies better to human development than the strict notion of a critical period (Bornstein, 1989). A **sensitive period** is a time that is optimal for certain capacities to emerge and in which the individual is especially responsive to environmental influences. However, its boundaries are less well-defined than those of a critical period. Development can occur later, but it is harder to induce.

Inspired by observations of imprinting, British psychoanalyst John Bowlby (1969) applied ethological theory to the understanding of the human infant–caregiver relationship. He argued that infant smiling, babbling, grasping, and crying are built-in social signals that encourage the caregiver to approach, care for, and interact with the baby. By keeping the parent near, these behaviors help ensure that the infant will be fed, protected from danger, and provided with stimulation and affection necessary for healthy growth. The development of attachment in humans is a lengthy process that leads the baby to form a deep affectionate tie with the caregiver (Thompson, 2006). Bowlby believed that this bond has lifelong consequences for human relationships. In later chapters, we will consider research that evaluates this assumption.

Observations by ethologists have shown that many aspects of social behavior, including emotional expressions, aggression, cooperation, and social play, resemble those of our primate relatives. Recently, researchers have extended this effort in a new area of research called **evolutionary developmental psychology.** It seeks to understand the adaptive value of specieswide cognitive, emotional, and social competencies as those competencies change with age (Geary, 2006b). Evolutionary developmental psychologists ask questions like these: What role does the newborn's visual preference for facelike stimuli play in survival? Does it support older infants' capacity to distinguish familiar caregivers from unfamiliar people? Why do children play in gender-segregated groups? What do they learn from such play that might lead to adult gender-typed behaviors, such as male dominance and female investment in caregiving?

As these examples suggest, evolutionary psychologists are not just concerned with the genetic and biological roots of development. They recognize that humans' large brain and extended childhood resulted from the need to master an increasingly complex environment, so they are also interested in learning (Bjorklund & Blasi, 2005). And they realize that today's lifestyles differ so radically from those of our evolutionary ancestors that certain evolved behaviors (such as life-threatening risk taking in adolescents and male-to-male violence) are no longer adaptive (Blasi & Bjorklund, 2003). By clarifying the origins and development of such behaviors, evolutionary developmental psychology may help spark effective interventions.

In sum, evolutionary psychologists want to understand the entire *person–environment system.* The next contextual perspective we will discuss, Vygotsky's sociocultural theory, serves as an excellent complement to ethology because it highlights social and cultural contexts for development.

Vygotsky's Sociocultural Theory

The field of human development has recently seen a dramatic increase in studies addressing the cultural context of people's lives. Investigations that make comparisons across cultures, and between ethnic groups within cultures, provide insight into whether developmental pathways apply to all people or are limited to particular environmental conditions (Cole, 2005). As a result, cross-cultural and multicultural research helps us untangle the contributions of biological and environmental factors to the timing, order of appearance, and diversity of children's and adults' behaviors.

Today, much research is examining the relationship of *culturally specific beliefs and practices* to development. The contributions of Russian psychologist Lev Vygotsky (1896–1934) have played a major role in this trend. Vygotsky's (1934/1987) perspective, called **sociocultural theory,** focuses on how *culture*—the values, beliefs, customs, and skills of a social group—is transmitted to the next generation. According to Vygotsky, *social interaction*—in particular, cooperative dialogues with more knowledgeable members of society—is necessary for children to acquire the ways of thinking and behaving that make up a community's culture (Rowe & Wertsch, 2002).

© PAUL CHESLEY/GETTY IMAGES/STONE

With her mother's guidance, this Navajo child learns to use a vertical weaving loom. According to Vygotsky's sociocultural theory, social interaction between children and more knowledgeable members of their culture leads to ways of thinking and behaving essential for success in that culture.

Vygotsky believed that as adults and more expert peers help children master culturally meaningful activities, the communication between them becomes part of children's thinking. As children internalize the essential features of these dialogues, they can use the language within them to guide their own thought and actions and to acquire new skills (Berk & Harris, 2003; Winsler, Fernyhough, & Montero, 2009). The young child instructing herself while working a puzzle or preparing a table for dinner has begun to produce the same kind of guiding comments that an adult previously used to help her master important tasks.

Vygotsky's theory has been especially influential in the study of cognitive development. Vygotsky agreed with Piaget that children are active, constructive beings. But whereas Piaget emphasized children's independent efforts to make sense of their world, Vygotsky viewed cognitive development as a *socially mediated process,* in which children depend on assistance from adults and more-expert peers as they tackle new challenges.

In Vygotsky's theory, children undergo certain stagewise changes. For example, when they acquire language, their ability to participate in dialogues with others is greatly enhanced, and mastery of culturally valued competencies surges forward. When children enter school, they spend much time discussing language, literacy, and other academic concepts—experiences that encourage them to reflect on their own thinking (Bodrova & Leong, 2007; Kozulin, 2003). As a result, they gain dramatically in reasoning and problem solving.

Although most research inspired by Vygotsky's theory focuses on children, his ideas apply to people of any age. A central theme is that cultures select tasks for their members, and social interaction surrounding those tasks leads to competencies essential for success in a particular culture. For example, in industrialized nations, teachers help people learn to read, drive a car, or use a computer. Among the Zinacanteco Indians of southern Mexico, adult experts guide young girls as they master complicated weaving techniques (Greenfield, 2004; Greenfield, Maynard, & Childs, 2000). In Brazil and other developing nations, child candy sellers with little or no schooling develop sophisticated mathematical abilities as the result of buying candy from wholesalers, pricing it in collaboration with adults and experienced peers, and bargaining with customers on city streets (Saxe, 1988).

Research stimulated by Vygotsky's theory reveals that people in every culture develop unique strengths. But Vygotsky's emphasis on culture and social experience led him to neglect the biological side of development. Although he recognized the importance of heredity and brain growth, he said little about their role in cognitive change. Furthermore, Vygotsky's focus on social transmission of knowledge meant that, compared with other theorists, he placed less emphasis on children's capacity to shape their own development. Followers of Vygotsky grant the individual and society more balanced, mutually influential roles (Karpov, 2005; Rogoff, 2003).

Ecological Systems Theory

Urie Bronfenbrenner (1917–2005) is responsible for an approach that has moved to the forefront of the field because it offers the most differentiated and complete account of contextual influences on development. **Ecological systems theory** views the person as developing within a complex *system* of relationships affected by multiple levels of the surrounding environment. Because the child's biologically influenced dispositions join with environmental forces to mold development, Bronfenbrenner recently characterized his perspective as a *bioecological model* (Bronfenbrenner, 2005; Bronfenbrenner & Morris, 2006).

Bronfenbrenner envisioned the environment as a series of nested structures, including but also extending beyond the home, school, neighborhood, and workplace settings in which people spend their everyday lives (see Figure 1.5). Each layer of the environment is viewed as having a powerful impact on development.

THE MICROSYSTEM. The innermost level of the environment, the **microsystem,** consists of activities and interaction patterns in the person's immediate surroundings. Bronfenbrenner emphasized that to understand development at this level, we must keep in mind that all relationships are *bidirectional.* For example, adults affect children's behavior, but children's biologically and socially influenced characteristics—their physical attributes, personalities, and capacities—also affect adults' behavior. A friendly, attentive child is likely to evoke positive, patient reactions from parents, whereas an irritable or distractible child is more likely to receive impatience, restriction, and punishment. When these reciprocal interactions occur often over time, they have an enduring impact on development (Collins et al., 2000; Crockenberg & Leerkes, 2003).

© ELLEN B. SENISI

In ecological systems theory, development occurs within a complex system of relationships affected by multiple levels of the environment. This father says good-bye to his daughter at the start of the school day. The girl's experiences at school (microsystem) and the father's experiences at work (exosystem) affect the father–daughter relationship.

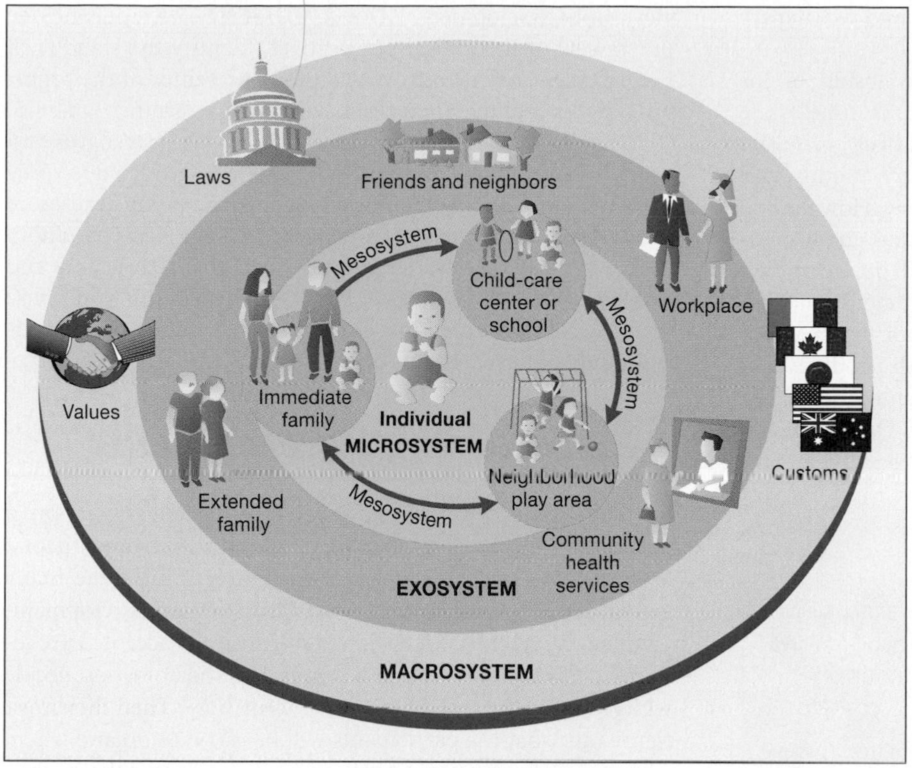

■ **FIGURE 1.5** ■ **Structure of the environment in ecological systems theory.** The *microsystem* concerns relations between the developing person and the immediate environment; the *mesosystem,* connections among immediate settings; the *exosystem,* social settings that affect but do not contain the developing person; and the *macrosystem,* the values, laws, customs, and resources of the culture that affect activities and interactions at all inner layers. The *chronosystem* (not pictured) is not a specific context. Instead, it refers to the dynamic, ever-changing nature of the person's environment.

Third parties—other individuals in the microsystem—also affect the quality of any two-person relationship. If they are supportive, interaction is enhanced. For example, when parents encourage each other in their child-rearing roles, each engages in more effective parenting. In contrast, marital conflict is associated with inconsistent discipline and hostile reactions toward children. In response, children often react with fear and anxiety or with anger and aggression, and both parent and child well-being suffers (Caldera & Lindsey, 2006; Davies & Lindsay, 2004).

■ **THE MESOSYSTEM.** The second level of Bronfenbrenner's model, the **mesosystem,** encompasses connections between microsystems. For example, a child's academic progress depends not just on activities that take place in classrooms but also on parent involvement in school life and on the extent to which academic learning is carried over into the home (Gershoff & Aber, 2006). Among adults, how well a person functions as spouse and parent at home is affected by relationships in the workplace, and vice versa (Gottfried, Gottfried, & Bathurst, 2002).

THE EXOSYSTEM. The **exosystem** consists of social settings that do not contain the developing person but nevertheless affect experiences in immediate settings. These can be formal organizations, such as the board of directors in the individual's workplace, religious institution, or community health and welfare services. Flexible work schedules, paid maternity and paternity leave, and sick leave for parents whose children are ill are examples of ways that work settings can help parents rear children and, indirectly, enhance the development of both adult and child. Exosystem supports can also be informal. Children are affected by their parents' social networks—friends and extended-family members who provide advice, companionship, and even financial assistance. Research confirms the negative impact of a breakdown in exosystem activities. Families who are socially isolated, with few personal or community-based ties, show increased rates of conflict and child abuse (Coulton et al., 2007).

■ **THE MACROSYSTEM.** The outermost level of Bronfenbrenner's model, the **macrosystem,** consists of cultural values, laws, customs, and resources. The priority that the macrosystem gives to the needs of children and adults affects the support they receive at inner levels of the environment. For example, in countries that require generous workplace benefits for employed parents and set high standards for the quality of child care, children are more likely to have favorable experiences in their immediate settings. And when the government provides a generous pension plan for retirees, it supports the well-being of the elderly.

■ **A DYNAMIC, EVER-CHANGING SYSTEM.** According to Bronfenbrenner, the environment is not a static force that affects people in a uniform way. Instead, it is ever-changing. Whenever individuals add or let go of roles or settings in their lives, the breadth of their microsystems changes. These shifts in contexts—or *ecological transitions,* as Bronfenbrenner called them—are often important turning points in development. Starting school, entering the workforce, marrying, becoming a parent, getting divorced, moving, and retiring are examples.

Bronfenbrenner called the temporal dimension of his model the **chronosystem** (the prefix *chrono* means "time"). Life changes can be imposed externally or, alternatively, can arise from within the person, since individuals select, modify, and create many of their own settings and experiences. How they do so depends on their age; their physical, intellectual, and personality characteristics; and their environmental opportunities. Therefore, in ecological systems theory, development is neither controlled by environmental circumstances nor driven solely by inner dispositions. Rather, people are both products and producers of their environments: The person and the environment form a network of interdependent effects. Our discussion of resilience on page 10 illustrates this idea. We will see many more examples in later chapters.

ASK YOURSELF

» REVIEW
Explain how each recent theoretical perspective regards children and adults as active contributors to their own development.

» APPLY
Mario wants to find out precisely how children of different ages recall stories. Anna is interested in how adult–child communication in different cultures influences children's storytelling. Which theoretical perspective has Mario probably chosen? How about Anna? Explain.

» CONNECT
Is ecological systems theory compatible with assumptions of the lifespan perspective—that development is lifelong, multidirectional, highly plastic, and influenced by multiple, interacting forces? Explain.

» REFLECT
To illustrate the chronosystem in ecological systems theory, select an important event from your childhood, such as a move to a new neighborhood, a class with an inspiring teacher, or parental divorce. How did the event affect you? How might its impact have differed had you been five years younger? How about five years older?

Comparing and Evaluating Theories

In the preceding sections, we reviewed major theoretical perspectives in human development research. They differ in many respects. First, they focus on different domains of development. Some, such as the psychoanalytic perspective and ethology, emphasize emotional and social development. Others, such as Piaget's cognitive-developmental theory, information processing, and Vygotsky's sociocultural theory, stress changes in thinking. The remaining approaches—behaviorism, social learning theory, evolutionary developmental psychology, ecological systems theory, and the lifespan perspective—discuss many aspects of human functioning. Second, every theory contains a point of view about development. ***TAKE A MOMENT...*** As we conclude our review of theoretical perspectives, identify the stand each theory takes on the controversial issues presented at the beginning of this chapter. Then check your analysis against Table 1.5.

Finally, we have seen that every theory has strengths and limitations. Perhaps you found that you were attracted to some theories, but you have doubts about others. As you read more about development in later chapters, you may find it useful to keep a notebook in which you test your theoretical likes and dislikes against the evidence. Don't be surprised if you revise your ideas many times, just as theorists have done since scientific study of development began.

Studying Development

In every science, research is usually based on a *hypothesis*—a prediction about behavior drawn from a theory. Theories and hypotheses, however, merely initiate the many activities that result in sound evidence on human development. Conducting research according to scientifically accepted procedures involves many steps and choices. Investigators must decide which participants, and how many, to include. Then they must figure out what the participants will be asked to do and when, where, and how many times each will be seen. Finally, they must examine and draw conclusions from their data.

In the following sections, we look at research strategies commonly used to study human development. We begin with *methods of gathering information*—the specific activities of participants, such as taking tests, answering questionnaires, responding to interviews, or being observed. Then we turn to *research designs*—overall plans for research studies that permit the best possible test of the investigator's hypothesis. Finally, we discuss ethical issues involved in doing research with human participants.

Why learn about research strategies? Why not leave these matters to research specialists and concentrate, instead, on what is known about the developing person and how this knowledge can be applied? There are two reasons. First, each of us must be a wise and critical consumer of knowledge. Knowing the strengths and limitations of various research strategies is important in separating dependable information from misleading results. Second, individuals who work directly with children or adults may be in a unique position to build bridges between research and practice by conducting studies, either on their own or in partnership with experienced investigators. Community agencies such as schools, mental health facilities, and parks and recreation programs sometimes collaborate with researchers in designing, implementing, and evaluating interventions aimed at enhancing development (Lerner, Fisher, & Weinberg, 2000). To broaden these efforts, a basic understanding of the research process is essential.

Common Research Methods

How does a researcher choose a basic approach to gathering information? Common methods include systematic observation, self reports (such as questionnaires and interviews), clinical or case

■ TABLE 1.5 ■ *Stances of Major Theories on Basic Issues in Human Development*

THEORY	CONTINUOUS OR DISCONTINUOUS DEVELOPMENT?	ONE COURSE OF DEVELOPMENT OR MANY?	RELATIVE INFLUENCE OF NATURE AND NURTURE?
Psychoanalytic perspective	*Discontinuous:* Psychosexual and psychosocial development takes place in stages.	*One course:* Stages are assumed to be universal.	*Both nature and nurture:* Innate impulses are channeled and controlled through child-rearing experiences. *Early experiences* set the course of later development.
Behaviorism and social learning theory	*Continuous:* Development involves an increase in learned behaviors.	*Many possible courses:* Behaviors reinforced and modeled may vary from person to person.	*Emphasis on nurture:* Development is the result of conditioning and modeling. *Both early and later experiences* are important.
Piaget's cognitive-developmental theory	*Discontinuous:* Cognitive development takes place in stages.	*One course:* Stages are assumed to be universal.	*Both nature and nurture:* Development occurs as the brain grows and children exercise their innate drive to discover reality in a generally stimulating environment. *Both early and later experiences* are important.
Information processing	*Continuous:* Children and adults change gradually in perception, attention, memory, and problem-solving skills.	*One course:* Changes studied characterize most or all children and adults.	*Both nature and nurture:* Children and adults are active, sense-making beings who modify their thinking as the brain grows and they confront new environmental demands. *Both early and later experiences* are important.
Ethology and evolutionary developmental psychology	*Both continuous and discontinuous:* Children and adults gradually develop a wider range of adaptive behaviors. Sensitive periods occur in which qualitatively distinct capacities emerge fairly suddenly.	*One course:* Adaptive behaviors and sensitive periods apply to all members of a species.	*Both nature and nurture:* Evolution and heredity influence behavior, and learning lends greater flexibility and adaptiveness to it. In sensitive periods, *early experiences* set the course of later development.
Vygotsky's sociocultural theory	*Both continuous and discontinuous:* Language development and schooling lead to stagewise changes. Dialogues with more expert members of society also lead to continuous changes that vary from culture to culture.	*Many possible courses:* Socially mediated changes in thought and behavior vary from culture to culture.	*Both nature and nurture:* Heredity, brain growth, and dialogues with more expert members of society jointly contribute to development. *Both early and later experiences* are important.
Ecological systems theory	*Not specified.*	*Many possible courses:* Biological dispositions join with environmental forces at multiple levels to mold development in unique ways.	*Both nature and nurture:* The individual's characteristics and the reactions of others affect each other in a bidirectional fashion. *Both early and later experiences* are important.
Lifespan perspective	***Both continuous and discontinuous:* Continuous gains and declines and discontinuous, stagewise emergence of new skills occur.**	***Many possible courses:* Development is influenced by multiple, interacting biological, psychological, and social forces, many of which vary from person to person, leading to diverse pathways of change.**	***Both nature and nurture:* Development is multidimensional, affected by an intricate blend of hereditary and environmental factors. Emphasizes plasticity at all ages. *Both early and later experiences* are important.**

studies of a single individual, and ethnographies of the life circumstances of a specific group of people. Table 1.6 on page 28 summarizes the strengths and limitations of each of these methods.

■ **SYSTEMATIC OBSERVATION.** Observations of the behavior of children and adults can be made in different ways. One approach is to go into the field, or natural environment, and record the behavior of interest—a method called **naturalistic observation.**

A study of preschoolers' responses to their peers' distress provides a good example (Farver & Branstetter, 1994). Observing 3- and 4-year-olds in child-care centers, the researchers recorded each instance of crying and the reactions of nearby children—whether they ignored, watched, commented on the child's

■ TABLE 1.6 ■ *Strengths and Limitations of Common Research Methods*

METHOD	DESCRIPTION	STRENGTHS	LIMITATIONS
SYSTEMATIC OBSERVATION			
Naturalistic observation	Observation of behavior in natural contexts	Reflects participants' everyday lives.	Cannot control conditions under which participants are observed.
Structured observation	Observation of behavior in a laboratory, where conditions are the same for all participants	Grants each participant an equal opportunity to display the behavior of interest.	May not yield observations typical of participants' behavior in everyday life.
SELF-REPORTS			
Clinical interview	Flexible interviewing procedure in which the investigator obtains a complete account of the participant's thoughts	Comes as close as possible to the way participants think in everyday life. Great breadth and depth of information can be obtained in a short time.	May not result in accurate reporting of information. Flexible procedure makes comparing individuals' responses difficult.
Structured interview, questionnaires, and tests	Self-report instruments in which each participant is asked the same questions in the same way	Permits comparisons of participants' responses and efficient data collection. Researchers can specify answer alternatives that participants might not think of in an open-ended interview.	Does not yield the same depth of information as a clinical interview. Responses are still subject to inaccurate reporting.
CLINICAL, OR CASE STUDY, METHOD			
	A full picture of one individual's psychological functioning, obtained by combining interviews, observations, and test scores	Provides rich, descriptive insights into factors that affect development.	May be biased by researchers' theoretical preferences. Findings cannot be applied to individuals other than the participant.
ETHNOGRAPHY			
	Participant observation of a culture or distinct social group; by making extensive field notes, the researcher tries to capture the culture's unique values and social processes	Provides a more complete description than can be derived from a single observational visit, interview, or questionnaire.	May be biased by researchers' values and theoretical preferences. Findings cannot be applied to individuals and settings other than the ones studied.

unhappiness, scolded or teased, or shared, helped, or expressed sympathy. Caregiver behaviors—explaining why a child was crying, mediating conflict, or offering comfort—were noted to see if adult sensitivity was related to children's caring responses. A strong relationship emerged. The great strength of naturalistic observation is that investigators can see directly the everyday behaviors they hope to explain.

Naturalistic observation also has a major limitation: Not all individuals have the same opportunity to display a particular behavior in everyday life. In the study just described, some children might have witnessed a child crying more often than others or been exposed to more cues for positive social responses from caregivers. For these reasons, they might have displayed more compassion.

Researchers commonly deal with this difficulty by making **structured observations,** in which the investigator sets up a laboratory situation that evokes the behavior of interest so that every participant has an equal opportunity to display the response. In one study, 2-year-olds' emotional reactions to harm that they thought they had caused were observed by asking them to take care of a rag doll that had been modified so its leg would fall off when the child picked it up. To make the child feel at fault, once the leg detached, an adult "talked for" the doll by saying, "Ow!" Researchers recorded children's facial expressions of sadness and concern for the injured doll, efforts to help the doll, and body tension—responses that indicated remorse and a desire to make amends for the mishap. In addition, mothers were asked to engage in brief conversations about emotions

© BOB DAEMMRICH/THE IMAGE WORKS

In naturalistic observation, the researcher goes into the field and records the behavior of interest. Here, the researcher observes children at a summer camp. She may be focusing on their playmate choices, cooperation, helpfulness, or conflicts.

with their children (Garner, 2003). Toddlers whose mothers more often explained the causes and consequences of emotion were more likely to express concern for the injured doll.

The procedures used to collect systematic observations vary, depending on the research problem posed. Occasionally investigators choose to record the entire stream of behavior—everything said and done over a certain time period. In one study, researchers wanted to find out whether maternal sensitivity in infancy and early childhood contributes to readiness for formal schooling at age 6 (Hirsh-Pasek & Burchinal, 2006). Between age 6 months and 4½ years, the investigators periodically videotaped mother–child 15-minute play sessions. Then they rated each session for maternal positive emotion, support, stimulating play, and respect for the child's autonomy—ingredients of sensitivity that did predict better language and academic progress when the children reached kindergarten.

Researchers have devised ingenious ways of observing difficult-to-capture behaviors. For example, to record instances of bullying, a group of investigators set up video cameras overlooking a classroom and a playground and had fourth to sixth graders wear small, remote microphones and pocket-sized transmitters (Craig, Pepler, & Atlas, 2000). Results revealed that bullying occurred often—at rates of 2.4 episodes per hour in the classroom and 4.5 episodes per hour on the playground. Yet only 15 to 18 percent of the time did teachers take steps to stop the harassment.

Systematic observation provides invaluable information on how children and adults actually behave, but it tells us little about the reasoning behind their responses. For that information, researchers must turn to self-report techniques.

■ **SELF-REPORTS.** Self-reports ask research participants to provide information on their perceptions, thoughts, abilities, feelings, attitudes, beliefs, and past experiences. They range from relatively unstructured interviews to highly structured interviews, questionnaires, and tests.

In a **clinical interview,** researchers use a flexible, conversational style to probe for the participant's point of view. In the following example, Piaget questioned a 5-year-old child about his understanding of dreams:

> *Where does the dream come from?*—I think you sleep so well that you dream.—*Does it come from us or from outside?*—From outside.—*When you are in bed and you dream, where is the dream?*—In my bed, under the blanket. I don't really know. If it was in my stomach, the bones would be in the way and I shouldn't see it.—*Is the dream there when you sleep?*—Yes, it is in the bed beside me. (Piaget, 1926/1930, pp. 97–98)

Although a researcher conducting clinical interviews with more than one participant would typically ask the same first question to establish a common task, individualized prompts are used to provide a fuller picture of each person's reasoning (Ginsburg, 1997).

The clinical interview has two major strengths. First, it permits people to display their thoughts in terms that are as close as possible to the way they think in everyday life. Second, the clinical interview can provide a large amount of information in a fairly brief period. For example, in an hour-long session, we can obtain a wide range of information on child rearing from a parent or on life circumstances from an elder—much more than we could capture by observing for the same amount of time.

A major limitation of the clinical interview has to do with the accuracy with which people report their thoughts, feelings, and experiences. Some participants, wishing to please the interviewer, may make up answers that do not represent their actual thinking. When asked about past events, some may have trouble recalling exactly what happened. And because the clinical interview depends on verbal ability and expressiveness, it may underestimate the capacities of individuals who have difficulty putting their thoughts into words.

The clinical interview has also been criticized because of its flexibility. When questions are phrased differently for each participant, responses may reflect the manner of interviewing rather than real differences in the way people think about a topic. **Structured interviews** (including tests and questionnaires), in which each participant is asked the same set of questions in the same way, eliminate this problem. These instruments are also much more efficient. Answers are briefer, and researchers can obtain written responses from an entire group simultaneously. Also, by listing answer alternatives, researchers can specify the activities and behaviors of interest—ones that participants might not think of in an open-ended clinical interview. For example, when parents were asked what they considered "the most important thing for children to prepare them for life," 62 percent checked "to think for themselves" when this choice appeared on a list. Yet only 5 percent thought of it during a clinical interview (Schwarz, 1999).

Nevertheless, structured interviews do not yield the same depth of information as a clinical interview. And they can still be affected by the problem of inaccurate reporting.

THE CLINICAL, OR CASE STUDY, METHOD. An outgrowth of psychoanalytic theory, the **clinical, or case study, method** brings together a wide range of information on one person, including interviews, observations, and sometimes test scores. The aim is to obtain as complete a picture as possible of that individual's psychological functioning and the experiences that led up to it.

The clinical method is well-suited to studying the development of certain types of individuals who are few in number but vary widely in characteristics. For example, the method has been used to find out what contributes to the accomplishments of *prodigies*—extremely gifted children who attain adult competence in a field before age 10 (Moran & Gardner, 2006). Consider Adam, a boy who read, wrote, and composed musical pieces before he was out of diapers. By age 4, Adam was deeply involved in mastering human symbol systems—French, German, Russian, Sanskrit, Greek, the computer programming language BASIC, ancient hieroglyphs, music, and mathematics. Adam's parents provided a home rich in stimulation and reared him with affection, firmness, and humor. They searched for schools in which he could both develop his abilities and form rewarding social relationships. He graduated from college at age 18 and continued to pursue musical composition (Goldsmith, 2000). Would Adam have realized his abilities without the chance combination of his special gift and nurturing, committed parents? Probably not, researchers concluded (Feldman, 2004).

The clinical method yields richly detailed case narratives that offer valuable insights into the many factors influencing development. Nevertheless, like all other methods, it has drawbacks. Because information often is collected unsystematically and subjectively, researchers' theoretical preferences may bias their observations and interpretations. In addition, investigators cannot assume that their conclusions apply, or generalize, to anyone other than the person studied (Stanovich, 2007). Even when patterns emerge across several cases, it is wise to confirm these with other research strategies.

© SPENCER GRANT/PHOTOEDIT

Using the clinical, or case study, method, this researcher combines interviews with the mother and observations and testing of the child to construct an in-depth picture of one child's psychological functioning.

METHODS FOR STUDYING CULTURE. To study the impact of culture, researchers adjust the methods just considered or tap procedures specially devised for cross-cultural and multicultural research (Triandis, 2007). Which approach investigators choose depends on their research goals.

Sometimes researchers are interested in characteristics that are believed to be universal but that vary in degree from one society to the next: Are parents warmer or more directive in some cultures than others? How strong are gender stereotypes in different nations? In each instance, several cultural groups will be compared, and all participants must be questioned or observed in the same way. Therefore, researchers draw on the self-report and observational procedures we have already considered, adapting them through translation so they can be understood in each cultural context. For example, to study cultural variation in parenting practices, the same questionnaire, asking for ratings on such items as "I often hug and kiss my child" or "I scold my child when his/her behavior does not meet my expectations," is given to all participants (Wu et al., 2002).

At other times, researchers want to uncover the *cultural meanings* of children's and adults' behaviors by becoming as familiar as possible with their way of life. To achieve this goal, investigators rely on a method borrowed from the field of anthropology—**ethnography.** Like the clinical method, ethnographic research is a descriptive, qualitative technique. But instead of aiming to understand a single individual, it is directed toward understanding a culture or a distinct social group through *participant observation.* Typically, the researcher spends months, and sometimes years, in the cultural community, participating in its daily life. Extensive field notes are gathered, consisting of a mix of observations, self-reports from members of the culture, and careful interpretations by the investigator (Miller, Hengst, & Wang, 2003; Shweder et al., 2006). Later, these notes are put together into a description of the community that tries to capture its unique values and social processes.

The ethnographic method assumes that entering into close contact with a social group will allow researchers to understand the beliefs and behaviors of its members in a way that is not possible with an observational visit, interview, or questionnaire. Some ethnographies take in many aspects of experience, as one team of researchers did in describing what it is like to grow up in a small American town. Others focus on one or a few settings and issues—for example, barriers to effective

This Western ethnographer spent months living among the Efe people of the Republic of Congo. Here he observes young children sharing food. The Efe value and encourage cooperation and generosity at an early age.

parent–school communication in a Mexican-American community or African-Caribbean adults' reactions to a diagnosis of high blood pressure, signaling elevated risk for heart disease (Higginbottom, 2006; Peshkin, 1997; Valdés, 1998). Notice how such ethnographic evidence is vital in designing effective educational and health interventions. Increasingly, researchers are supplementing traditional self-report and observational methods with ethnography when they suspect that unique meanings underlie cultural differences, as the Cultural Influences box on page 32 reveals.

Ethnographers strive to minimize their own influence on the culture they are studying by becoming part of it. Nevertheless, as with clinical studies, investigators' cultural values and theoretical commitments sometimes lead them to observe selectively or misinterpret what they see. In addition, the findings of ethnographic studies cannot be assumed to generalize beyond the people and settings in which the research was conducted.

ASK YOURSELF

» REVIEW
Why might a researcher choose structured observation over naturalistic observation? How about the reverse? What might lead the researcher to opt for clinical interviewing over systematic observation?

» APPLY
A researcher wants to study the thoughts and feelings of parents on active duty in the military and those of their school-age and adolescent children. Which method should she use? Explain.

» CONNECT
What strengths and limitations do the clinical (or case study) method and ethnography have in common?

» REFLECT
Reread the description of nonnormative influences on page 13, and cite an example from your own life. Which method would be best suited to studying the impact of such a nonnormative event on development?

General Research Designs

In deciding on a research design, investigators choose a way of setting up a study that permits them to test their hypotheses with the greatest certainty possible. Two main types of designs are used in all research on human behavior: *correlational* and *experimental*.

■ **CORRELATIONAL DESIGN.** In a **correlational design,** researchers gather information on individuals, generally in natural life circumstances, without altering their experiences. Then they look at relationships between participants' characteristics and their behavior or development. Suppose we want to answer such questions as, Do parents' styles of interacting with children have any bearing on children's intelligence? Does the arrival of a baby influence a couple's marital satisfaction? Does the death of a spouse in old age affect the surviving partner's physical health and psychological well-being? In these and many other instances, the conditions of interest are difficult or impossible to arrange and control and must be studied as they currently exist.

Correlational studies have one major limitation: We cannot infer cause and effect. For example, if we were to find that parental interaction is related to children's intelligence, we would not know whether parents' behavior actually *causes* intellectual differences among children. In fact, the opposite is possible: The behaviors of highly intelligent children may be so attractive that they cause parents to interact more favorably. Or a third variable that we did not even consider, such as the amount of noise and distraction in the home, may cause changes in both parental interaction and children's intelligence.

CULTURAL INFLUENCES

Immigrant Youths: Amazing Adaptation

Over the past several decades, a rising tide of immigrants has come to North America, fleeing war and persecution in their homelands or seeking better life chances. Today, one-fifth of the U.S. youth population have foreign-born parents; nearly one-third of these youths are foreign-born themselves, mostly from Asia and Latin America (Suarez-Orozco, Todorova, & Qin, 2006).

How well are immigrant youths adapting to their new country? To find out, researchers use multiple research methods, including academic testing, questionnaires assessing psychological adjustment, and in-depth ethnographies.

Academic Achievement and Adjustment

Although educators and laypeople often assume that the transition to a new country has a negative impact on psychological well-being, evidence reveals that children of immigrant parents adapt amazingly well. Students who are first-generation (foreign-born) and second-generation (American-born, with immigrant parents) often achieve in school as well as or better than students of native-born parents (Fuligni, 2004; Saucier et al., 2002). Findings on psychological adjustment are similar. Compared with their agemates, adolescents from immigrant families are less likely to commit delinquent and violent acts, to use drugs and alcohol, or to have early sex. They are also less likely to be obese or to have missed school because of illness. And they feel as positively about themselves as young people with native-born parents. These successes do not depend on having extensive time to adjust to a new way of life. Recently arrived high school students do as well in school and report just as favorable self-esteem as those who came at younger ages (Fuligni, 1998; Saucier et al., 2002).

These outcomes are strongest for Chinese, Filipino, Japanese, Korean, and East Indian youths, less dramatic for other ethnicities (Fuligni, 2001; Louie, 2001, Portes & Rumbaut, 2005). And a minority of young people—especially of certain ethnicities, including Cambodians and Laotians—deviate from these favorable patterns, showing high rates of school failure and dropout, delinquency, teenage parenthood, and drug use (Zhou & Xiong, 2005). Variations in parental economic resources and education contribute to these trends. Still, many first- and second-generation youths from ethnic groups that face considerable financial hardship (such as Mexican and Vietnamese) are successful (Fuligni & Yoshikawa, 2003). Factors other than income are responsible—notably, family values and strong ethnic-community ties.

© JEFF GREENBERG/ALAMY

In Miami, Florida, Asian-American girls participate in the Hong Kong Dragon Boat Race Festival. Cultural values that foster allegiance to family and community promote high achievement and protect many immigrant youths from involvement in risky behaviors.

Family and Community Influences

Ethnographies reveal that immigrant parents view education as the surest way to improve life chances (Goldenberg et al., 2001; Louie, 2001). Aware of the challenges their children face, they typically emphasize trying hard. They remind their children that, because educational opportunities were not available in their native countries, they themselves are often limited to menial jobs.

Adolescents from immigrant families internalize their parents' valuing of education, endorsing it more strongly than agemates with native-born parents (Asakawa, 2001; Fuligni, 2004). Because minority ethnicities usually stress allegiance to family and community over individual goals, first- and second-generation young people feel a strong sense of obligation to their parents. They view school success as both their own and their parents' success and as an important way of repaying their parents for the hardships they have endured (Bacallao & Smokowski, 2007; Fuligni, Yip, & Tseng, 2002). Both family relationships and school achievement protect these youths from delinquency, early pregnancy and drug use, and other risky behaviors (see the Biology and Environment box on resilience on page 10).

Immigrant parents of successful youths typically develop close ties to an ethnic community, which exerts additional control through a high consensus on values and constant monitoring of young people's activities. The following comments capture the power of these family and community forces:

> *Elizabeth, age 16, from Vietnam, straight-A student, like her two older sisters:* "My parents know pretty much all the kids in the neighborhood. . . . Everybody here knows everybody else. It's hard to get away with much." (Zhou & Bankston, 1998, pp. 93, 130)

> *Juan, teenager from Mexico:* A really big part of the Hispanic population [is] being close to family, and the family being a priority all the time. I hate people who say, "Why do you want to go to a party where your family's at? Don't you want to get away from them?" You know, I don't really get tired of them. I've always been really close to them. That connection to my parents, that trust that you can talk to them, that makes me Mexican. (Bacallao & Smokowski, 2007, p. 62)

The experiences of well-adjusted immigrant youths are not problem-free. Chinese adolescents who had arrived in the United States within the previous year described their adjustment as very difficult because they were not proficient in English and, as a result, found many everyday tasks challenging and felt socially isolated (Yeh et al., 2008). Young immigrants also encounter racial and ethnic prejudices and experience tensions between family values and the new culture—challenges we will take up in Chapter 12. In the long term, however, family and community cohesion, supervision, and high expectations promote favorable outcomes.

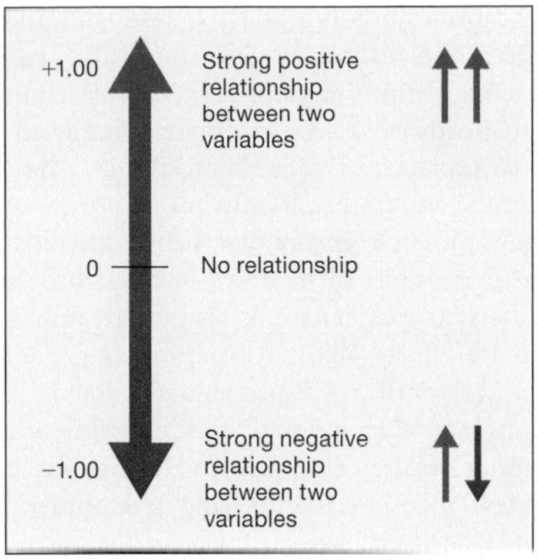

■ FIGURE 1.6 ■ The meaning of correlation coefficients. The magnitude of the number indicates the *strength* of the relationship. The sign of the number (+ or −) indicates the *direction* of the relationship.

In correlational studies and in other types of research designs, investigators often examine relationships by using a **correlation coefficient**—a number that describes how two measures, or variables, are associated with each other. We will encounter the correlation coefficient in discussing research findings throughout this book, so let's look at what it is and how it is interpreted. A correlation coefficient can range in value from +1.00 to −1.00. The *magnitude, or size, of the number* shows the *strength of the relationship.* A zero correlation indicates no relationship; the closer the value is to +1.00 or −1.00, the stronger the relationship (see Figure 1.6). For instance, a correlation of −.78 is high, −.52 is moderate, and −.18 is low. Note, however, that correlations of +.52 and −.52 are equally strong. The *sign of the number* (+ or −) refers to the *direction of the relationship.* A positive sign (+) means that as one variable *increases,* the other also *increases.* A negative sign (−) indicates that as one variable *increases,* the other *decreases.*

Let's look at some examples of how a correlation coefficient works. One researcher reported a +.55 correlation between a measure of maternal language stimulation and the size of children's vocabularies at 2 years of age (Hoff, 2003). This is a moderate correlation, which indicates that mothers who spoke more to their toddlers had children who were more advanced in language development. In two other studies, maternal sensitivity was modestly associated with children's cooperativeness in consistent ways. First, maternal warmth and encouragement during play correlated positively with 2-year-olds' willingness to comply with their mother's directive to clean up toys, at +.34 (Feldman & Klein, 2003). Second, the extent to which mothers spoke harshly, interrupted, and controlled their 4-year-olds' play correlated negatively with children's compliance, at −.31 for boys and −.42 for girls (Smith et al., 2004).

All these investigations found correlations between parenting and young children's behavior. ***TAKE A MOMENT...*** Are you tempted to conclude that the maternal behaviors influenced children's responses? Although the researchers in these studies suspected this was so, they could not be sure of cause and effect. Can you think of other possible explanations? Finding a relationship in a correlational study does suggest that tracking down its cause—using a more powerful experimental strategy, if possible—would be worthwhile.

■ **EXPERIMENTAL DESIGN.** An **experimental design** permits inferences about cause and effect because researchers use an evenhanded procedure to assign people to two or more treatment conditions. In an experiment, the events and behaviors of interest are divided into two types, independent and dependent variables. The **independent variable** is the one the investigator expects to cause changes in another variable. The **dependent variable** is the one the investigator expects to be influenced by the independent variable. Cause-and-effect relationships can be detected because the researcher directly *controls* or *manipulates* changes in the independent variable by exposing participants to the treatment conditions. Then the researcher compares their performance on measures of the dependent variable.

In one *laboratory experiment,* investigators explored the impact of adults' angry interactions on children's adjustment (El-Sheikh, Cummings, & Reiter, 1996). They hypothesized that the

Does the death of a spouse in old age affect the surviving partner's physical health and psychological well-being? A correlational design can be used to answer this question, but it does not permit researchers to determine the precise cause of their findings.

way angry encounters end (independent variable) affects children's emotional reactions (dependent variable). Four- and 5-year-olds were brought to a laboratory one at a time, accompanied by their mothers. One group was exposed to an *unresolved-anger treatment,* in which two adult actors entered the room and argued but did not work out their disagreements. The other group witnessed a *resolved-anger treatment,* in which the adults ended their disputes by apologizing and compromising. When witnessing a follow-up adult conflict, children in the resolved-anger treatment showed less distress, as measured by fewer anxious facial expressions, less freezing in place, and less seeking of closeness to their mothers. The experiment revealed that anger resolution can reduce the stressful impact of adult conflict on children.

In experimental studies, investigators must take special precautions to control for participants' characteristics that could reduce the accuracy of their findings. For example, in the study just described, if a greater number of children from homes high in parental conflict ended up in the unresolved-anger treatment, we could not tell what produced the results—the independent variable or the children's backgrounds. To protect against this problem, researchers engage in **random assignment** of participants to treatment conditions. By using an unbiased procedure, such as drawing numbers out of a hat or flipping a coin, investigators increase the chances that participants' characteristics will be equally distributed across treatment groups.

■ **MODIFIED EXPERIMENTAL DESIGNS: FIELD AND NATURAL EXPERIMENTS.** Most experiments are conducted in laboratories, where researchers can achieve the maximum possible control over treatment conditions. But, as we have already indicated, findings obtained in laboratories may not always apply to everyday situations. In *field experiments,* investigators capitalize on opportunities to assign participants randomly to treatment conditions in natural settings. In the experiment just described, we can conclude that the emotional climate established by adults affects children's behavior in the laboratory. But does it also do so in daily life?

Another study helps answer this question. Ethnically diverse, poverty-stricken families with a 2-year-old child were scheduled for a home visit, during which researchers assessed family functioning and child problem behaviors by asking parents to respond to questionnaires and videotaping parent–child interaction. Then the families were randomly assigned to either an intervention condition, called the Family Check-Up, or a no-intervention control group. The intervention consisted of three home-based sessions in which a consultant gave parents feedback about their child-rearing practices and their child's adjustment, explored parents' willingness to improve, identified community services appropriate to each family's needs, and offered follow-up sessions on parenting practices and other concerns (Dishion et al., 2008). Findings showed that families assigned to the Family Check-Up (but not controls) gained in positive parenting, which predicted a reduction in child problem behaviors—outcomes still evident a year later, when participating children were reassessed at age 3. Highly problematic children benefited most from this brief, early intervention.

Often researchers cannot randomly assign participants and manipulate conditions in the real world. Sometimes they can compromise by conducting *natural, or quasi-, experiments,* comparing treatments that already exist, such as different family environments, schools, workplaces, or retirement villages. These studies differ from correlational research only in that groups of participants are carefully chosen to ensure that their characteristics are as much alike as possible. In this way, investigators do their best to rule out alternative explanations for their treatment effects. But, despite these efforts, natural experiments cannot achieve the precision and rigor of true experimental research.

To help you compare correlational and experimental designs, Table 1.7 summarizes their strengths and limitations. It also includes an overview of designs for studying development, to which we turn next.

Designs for Studying Development

Scientists interested in human development require information about the way research participants change over time. To answer questions about development, they must extend correlational and experimental approaches to include measurements at different ages. Longitudinal and cross-sectional designs are special *developmental* research strategies. In each, age comparisons form the basis of the research plan.

■ **THE LONGITUDINAL DESIGN.** In a **longitudinal design,** participants are studied repeatedly, and changes are noted as they get older. The time spanned may be relatively short (a few months to several years) or very long (a decade or even a lifetime). The longitudinal approach has two major strengths. First, because it tracks the performance of each person over time, researchers can identify common patterns as well as individual differences in development. Second, longitudinal studies permit investigators to examine relationships between early and later events and behaviors. Let's illustrate these ideas.

A group of researchers wondered whether children who display extreme personality styles—either angry and explosive or shy and withdrawn—retain the same dispositions when they become adults. In addition, the researchers wanted to know what kinds of experiences promote stability or change in personality and what consequences explosiveness and shyness have for long-term adjustment. To answer these questions, the researchers delved into the archives of the Guidance Study, a well-known longitudinal investigation initiated in 1928 at the University of California, Berkeley, and continued for several decades (Caspi, Elder, & Bem, 1987, 1988).

Results revealed that the two personality styles were moderately stable. Between ages 8 and 30, a good number of individuals remained the same, whereas others changed substantially. When stability did occur, it appeared to be due to a "snowballing effect," in which children evoked responses from adults and peers that acted to maintain their dispositions. Explosive youngsters were likely to be treated with anger, whereas shy children were apt to be ignored. As a result, the two types of children came to view their social worlds differently.

TABLE 1.7 *Strengths and Limitations of Research Designs*

DESIGN	DESCRIPTION	STRENGTHS	LIMITATIONS
GENERAL			
Correlational	The investigator obtains information on participants without altering their experiences.	Permits study of relationships between variables.	Does not permit inferences about cause-and-effect relationships.
Experimental	Through random assignment of participants to treatment conditions, the investigator manipulates an independent variable and examines its effect on a dependent variable. Can be conducted in the laboratory or the natural environment.	Permits inferences about cause-and-effect relationships.	When conducted in the laboratory, findings may not generalize to the real world. In *field experiments,* control over the treatment is usually weaker than in the laboratory. In *natural,* or *quasi-, experiments,* lack of random assignment substantially reduces the precision of research.
DEVELOPMENTAL			
Longitudinal	The investigator studies the same group of participants repeatedly at different ages.	Permits study of common patterns and individual differences in development and relationships between early and later events and behaviors.	Age-related changes may be distorted because of participant dropout, practice effects, and cohort effects.
Cross-sectional	The investigator studies groups of participants differing in age at the same point in time.	More efficient than the longitudinal design. Not plagued by such problems as participant dropout and practice effects.	Does not permit study of individual developmental trends. Age differences may be distorted because of cohort effects.
Sequential	The investigator conducts several similar cross-sectional or longitudinal studies (called sequences) at varying times.	When the design includes longitudinal sequences, permits both longitudinal and cross-sectional comparisons. Also reveals cohort effects. Permits tracking of age-related changes more efficiently than the longitudinal design.	May have the same problems as longitudinal and cross-sectional strategies, but the design itself helps identify difficulties.

Explosive children regarded others as hostile; shy children regarded them as unfriendly (Caspi & Roberts, 2001). Together, these factors led explosive children to sustain or increase their unruliness and shy children to continue to withdraw.

Persistence of extreme personality styles affected many areas of adult adjustment. For men, the results of early explosiveness were most apparent in their work lives, in the form of conflicts with supervisors, frequent job changes, and unemployment. Since few women in this sample of an earlier generation worked after marriage, their family lives were most affected. Explosive girls grew up to be hotheaded wives and mothers who were especially prone to divorce. Sex differences in the long-term consequences of shyness were even greater. Men who had been withdrawn in childhood were delayed in marrying, becoming fathers, and developing stable careers. However, because a withdrawn, unassertive style was socially acceptable for females in the mid-twentieth century, women who had shy personalities showed no special adjustment problems.

PROBLEMS IN CONDUCTING LONGITUDINAL RESEARCH. Despite their strengths, longitudinal investigations pose a number of problems. For example, participants may move away or drop out of the research for other reasons. This biases the sample so that it no longer represents the population to whom researchers would like to generalize their findings. Also, from repeated study, people may become more aware of their own thoughts, feelings, and actions and revise them in ways that have little to do with age-related change. In addition, they may become "test-wise." Their performance may improve as a result of *practice effects*—better test-taking skills and increased familiarity with the test—not because of factors commonly associated with development.

The most widely discussed threat to longitudinal findings is **cohort effects** (see page 13): Individuals born in the same time period are influenced by a particular set of historical and cultural conditions. Results based on one cohort may not apply to people developing at other times. For example, unlike the findings on female shyness described in the preceding section, which were gathered in the 1950s, today's shy young women tend to be poorly adjusted—a difference that may be due to changes in gender roles in Western societies. Shy adults, whether male or female, feel more anxious, depressed, and

Cohort effects are particular historical and cultural conditions that affect individuals born in the same time period. Young people who witnessed this victory celebration—Barack and Michelle Obama and their two daughters standing before a jubilant crowd in Chicago's Grant Park the night of the 2008 presidential election—came away with a new sense of what is possible for members of America's ethnic minorities.

lonely and may do less well in educational and career attainment than their agemates (Caspi, 2000; Caspi et al., 2003; Mounts et al., 2006). Similarly, a longitudinal study of lifespan development would probably result in quite different findings if it were carried out in the first decade of the twenty-first century, around the time of World War II, or during the Great Depression of the 1930s.

Cohort effects don't just operate broadly on an entire generation. They also occur when specific experiences influence some groups of individuals but not others in the same generation. For example, children who witnessed the terrorist attacks of September 11, 2001 (either because they were near Ground Zero or because they saw injury and death on TV), or who lost a parent in the disaster were far more likely than other children to display persistent emotional problems, including intense fear, anxiety, and depression (Pfeffer et al., 2007; Saylor et al., 2003). A study of one New York City sample suggested that as many as one-fourth of the city's children were affected (Hoven et al., 2005).

■ **THE CROSS-SECTIONAL DESIGN.** The length of time it takes for many behaviors to change, even in limited longitudinal studies, has led researchers to turn toward a more convenient strategy for studying development. In the **cross-sectional design,** groups of people differing in age are studied at the same point in time. The cross-sectional design is an efficient strategy for describing age-related trends. And because participants are measured only once, researchers need not be concerned about such difficulties as participant dropout or practice effects.

A study in which students in grades 3, 6, 9, and 12 filled out a questionnaire about their sibling relationships provides a good illustration (Buhrmester & Furman, 1990). Findings revealed that sibling interaction was characterized by greater equality and less power assertion with age. Also, feelings of sibling companionship declined in adolescence. The researchers thought that several factors contributed to these age differences. As later-born children become more competent and independent, they no longer need, and are probably less willing to accept, direction from older siblings. And as adolescents move from psychological dependence on the family to greater involvement with peers, they may have less time and emotional need to invest in siblings. As you will see in Chapter 12, subsequent research has confirmed these intriguing ideas about the development of sibling relationships.

■ **PROBLEMS IN CONDUCTING CROSS-SECTIONAL RESEARCH.** Despite its convenience, cross-sectional research does not provide evidence about development at the level at which it actually occurs: the individual. For example, in the cross-sectional study of sibling relationships just discussed, comparisons are limited to age-group averages. We cannot tell if important individual differences exist. Indeed, longitudinal findings reveal that adolescents vary considerably in the changing quality of their sibling relationships. Although many become more distant, others become more supportive and intimate, still others more rivalrous and antagonistic (Branje et al., 2004; Kim et al., 2006; Whiteman & Loken, 2006).

Cross-sectional studies—especially those that cover a wide age span—have another problem. Like longitudinal research, they can be threatened by cohort effects. For example, comparisons of 10-year-old cohorts, 20-year-old cohorts, and 30-year-old cohorts—groups born and reared in different years—may not really represent age-related changes. Instead, they may reflect unique experiences associated with the historical period in which the age groups were growing up.

■ **IMPROVING DEVELOPMENTAL DESIGNS.** Researchers have devised ways of building on the strengths and minimizing the weaknesses of longitudinal and cross-sectional approaches. Several modified developmental designs have resulted.

Sequential Designs. To overcome some of the limitations of traditional developmental designs, investigators sometimes use **sequential designs,** in which they conduct several similar cross-sectional or longitudinal studies (called *sequences*) at varying times. As the illustration in Figure 1.7 reveals, some sequential designs combine longitudinal and cross-sectional strategies, an approach that has two advantages:

- We can find out whether cohort effects are operating by comparing participants of the same age who were born in different years. In the example in Figure 1.7, we can

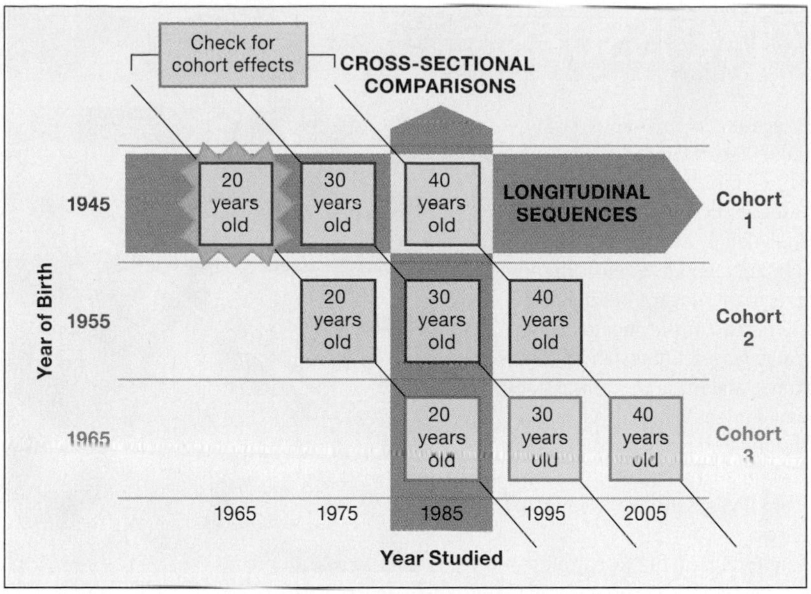

■ **FIGURE 1.7** ■ **Example of a sequential design.** Three cohorts, born in 1945 (blue), 1955 (pink), and 1965 (green), are followed longitudinally from 20 to 40 years of age. The design permits the researcher to check for cohort effects by comparing people of the same age who were born in different years. In a study that used this design, the 20-year-olds in Cohort 1 differed substantially from the 20-year-olds in Cohorts 2 and 3, indicating powerful history-graded influences. This design also permits longitudinal and cross-sectional comparisons. Similar findings lend additional confidence in the results.

compare the three longitudinal samples at ages 20, 30, and 40. If they do not differ, we can rule out cohort effects.

- We can make longitudinal and cross-sectional comparisons. If outcomes are similar in both, then we can be especially confident about our findings.

In a study that used the design in Figure 1.7, researchers wanted to find out whether adult personality development progresses as Erikson's psychosocial theory predicts (Whitbourne et al., 1992). Questionnaires measuring Erikson's stages were given to three cohorts of 20-year-olds, each born a decade apart. The cohorts were reassessed at ten-year intervals. Consistent with Erikson's theory, longitudinal and cross-sectional gains in identity and intimacy occurred between ages 20 and 30—a trend unaffected by historical time period. But a powerful cohort effect emerged for consolidation of the sense of industry: At age 20, Cohort 1 scored substantially below Cohorts 2 and 3. Look at Figure 1.7 again and notice that members of Cohort 1 reached age 20 in the mid-1960s. As college students, they were part of an era of political protest that reflected disenchantment with the work ethic. Once out of college, they caught up with the other cohorts in industry, perhaps as a result of experiencing the pressures of the work world. Followed up in 2001 at age 54, Cohort 1 showed a decline in focus on identity issues and a gain in ego integrity over middle adulthood—trends expected to continue as they reach their sixties and seventies (Sneed, Whitbourne, & Culang, 2006). Future tracking of Cohorts 2 and 3 will reveal whether they, too, follow this Erikson-predicted psychosocial path.

By uncovering cohort effects, sequential designs help explain diversity in development. Yet to date only a small number of sequential studies have been conducted.

Combining Experimental and Developmental Designs. Perhaps you noticed that all the examples of longitudinal and cross-sectional research we have considered permit only correlational, not causal, inferences. Yet causal information is desirable, both for testing theories and for finding ways to enhance development. Sometimes researchers can explore the causal link between experiences and development by experimentally manipulating the experiences. If, as a result, development improves, then we have strong evidence for a causal association. Today, research that combines an experimental strategy with either a longitudinal or a cross-sectional approach is increasingly common. For an example, refer to the Social Issues box on page 38.

ASK YOURSELF

>> REVIEW

Explain how cohort effects can affect the findings of both longitudinal and cross-sectional studies. How do sequential designs reveal cohort effects?

>> APPLY

A researcher compares older adults with chronic heart disease to those with no major health problems and finds that the first group scores lower on mental tests. Can the researcher conclude that heart disease causes a decline in intellectual functioning in late adulthood? Explain.

>> CONNECT

Review the study of the Family Check-Up, described on page 34. Explain how it combines an experimental with a developmental design. What are the independent and dependent variables? Is its developmental approach longitudinal or cross-sectional?

>> REFLECT

Suppose a researcher asks you to enroll your baby in a ten-year longitudinal study. What factors would lead you to agree and stay involved? Do your answers shed light on why longitudinal studies often have biased samples?

SOCIAL ISSUES

Can Musical Experiences Enhance Intelligence?

In a 1993 experiment, researchers reported that college students who listened to a Mozart sonata for a few minutes just before taking a test of spatial reasoning abilities did better on the test than students who took the test after listening to relaxation instructions or sitting in silence (Rauscher, Shaw, & Ky, 1993). Strains of Mozart, the investigators concluded, seem to induce changes in the brain that "warm up" neural connections, thereby improving thinking. But the gain in performance, widely publicized as the "Mozart effect," lasted only 15 minutes and proved difficult to replicate. Rather than involving a real change in ability, Mozart seemed to improve arousal and mood, yielding better concentration on the test (Schellenberg et al., 2007).

Despite mounting evidence that the Mozart effect was uncertain at best, the media and politicians were enthralled with the idea that a brief exposure of the brain to classical music in infancy, when neural connections are forming rapidly, might yield lifelong intellectual benefits. Soon, the states of Georgia, Tennessee, and South Dakota began providing free classical music CDs for every newborn baby leaving the hospital. Yet no studies of the Mozart effect have ever been conducted on infants! And an experiment with school-age children failed to demonstrate any intellectual gains as a result of simply listening to music (McKelvie & Low, 2002).

Research suggests that to produce lasting gains in mental test scores, interventions must be long-lasting and involve children's active participation. Consequently, Glenn Schellenberg (2004) wondered, Can music lessons enhance intelligence? Children who take music lessons must practice regularly, engage in extended focused attention, read music, memorize lengthy musical passages, understand diverse musical structures, and master technical skills. These experiences might foster cognitive processing, particularly during childhood, when regions of the brain are taking on specialized functions and are highly sensitive to environmental influences.

Schellenberg recruited 132 6-year-olds—children just old enough for formal lessons. First, the children took an intelligence test and were rated on social maturity, permitting the researchers to see whether music lessons would affect one aspect of development but not others. Next, the children were randomly assigned to one of four experimental conditions. Two were music groups; one received piano lessons and the other voice lessons. The third group took drama lessons—a condition that shed light on whether intellectual gains were unique to musical experiences. The fourth group—a no-lessons control—was offered music lessons the following year. All music and drama instruction took place at the prestigious Royal Conservatory of Music in Toronto, where experienced teachers taught the children in small groups. After 36 weeks of lessons, a longitudinal follow-up was conducted: The children's intelligence and social maturity were assessed again.

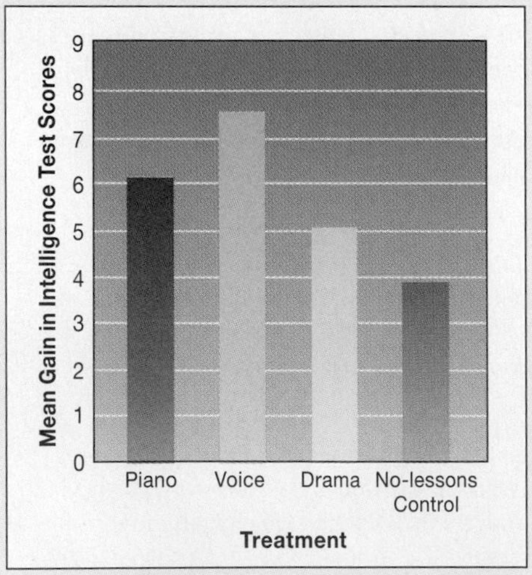

■ **FIGURE 1.8** ■ **Music lessons promote gains in intelligence.** In a study that combined experimental and longitudinal research strategies, children's mental test performance was tracked longitudinally, before and after they experienced one of four conditions: (1) piano lessons, (2) voice lessons, (3) drama lessons, or (4) no lessons. Children in the two groups receiving music lessons showed greater gains in intelligence test performance. (Adapted from Schellenberg, 2004.)

© DANITA DELIMONT/ALAMY

When children take music lessons over many weeks, they gain in mental test performance compared to children who take drama lessons or who receive no lessons at all. To make music, children must engage in diverse intellectual skills: reading musical notation, memorizing lengthy passages, analyzing musical structures, and mastering technical skills.

All four groups showed gains in mental test performance, probably because the participants had just entered grade school, which usually leads to an increase in intelligence test scores. But the two music groups consistently gained more than the control groups (see Figure 1.8). Their advantage, though just a few points, extended across many mental abilities, including verbal and spatial skills and speed of thinking. At the same time, only the drama group improved in social maturity.

In sum, active, sustained musical experiences can lead to small increases in intelligence among 6-year-olds that do not arise from comparable drama lessons. But other enrichment activities with similar properties, such as reading, science, math, and chess programs, may confer similar benefits. All demand that children invest far more time and effort than they would in listening to a Mozart sonata. Nevertheless—despite absence of evidence to support these claims—music companies persist in selling CDs entitled *Tune Your Brain with Mozart, Music for Accelerating Learning,* and *Mozart for Newborns: A Bright Beginning.*

Ethics in Lifespan Research

Research into human behavior creates ethical issues because, unfortunately, the quest for scientific knowledge can sometimes exploit people. For this reason, special guidelines for research have been developed by the federal government, by funding agencies, and by research-oriented associations, such as the American Psychological Association (2002) and the Society for Research in Child Development (2007). Table 1.8 presents a summary of basic research rights drawn from these guidelines. ***TAKE A MOMENT...*** After examining them, read about the following research situations, each of which poses a serious ethical dilemma. What precautions do you think should be taken in each instance?

- In a study of moral development, an investigator wants to assess children's ability to resist temptation by videotaping their behavior without their knowledge. She promises 7-year-olds a prize for solving difficult puzzles but tells them not to look at a classmate's correct solutions, which are deliberately placed at the back of the room. Informing children ahead of time that cheating is being studied or that their behavior is being monitored will destroy the purpose of the study.
- A researcher wants to study the impact of mild daily exercise on the physical and mental health of elderly patients in nursing homes. He consults each resident's doctor to make sure that the exercise routine will not be harmful. But when he seeks the residents' consent, he finds that many do not comprehend the purpose of the research. And some appear to agree simply to relieve feelings of isolation and loneliness.

As these examples indicate, when children or the aged take part in research, the ethical concerns are especially complex. Immaturity makes it difficult or impossible for children to evaluate for themselves what participation in research will mean. And because mental impairment rises with very advanced age, some older adults cannot make voluntary and informed choices. The life circumstances of others make them unusually vulnerable to pressure for participation (Kim et al., 2004; Society for Research in Child Development, 2007).

Virtually every organization that has devised ethical principles for research has concluded that conflicts arising in research situations often do not have simple right-or-wrong answers. The ultimate responsibility for the ethical integrity of research lies with the investigator. But researchers are advised—and often required—to seek advice from others. Committees for this purpose exist in colleges, universities, and other institutions. These *institutional review boards (IRBs)* weigh the costs of the research to participants in terms of inconvenience and possible psychological or physical injury against the study's value for advancing knowledge and improving conditions of life. If there are any risks to participants' safety and welfare that the

TABLE 1.8 ■ ***Rights of Research Participants***

RESEARCH RIGHT	DESCRIPTION
Protection from harm	Participants have the right to be protected from physical or psychological harm in research. If in doubt about the harmful effects of research, investigators should seek the opinion of others. When harm seems possible, investigators should find other means for obtaining the desired information or abandon the research.
Informed consent	All participants, including children and the elderly, have the right to have explained to them, in language appropriate to their level of understanding, all aspects of the research that may affect their willingness to participate. When children are participants, informed consent of parents as well as of others who act on the child's behalf (such as school officials) should be obtained, preferably in writing. Older adults who are cognitively impaired should be asked to appoint a surrogate decision maker. If they cannot do so, then someone should be named by an institutional review board (IRB) after careful consultation with relatives and professionals who know the person well. All participants have the right to discontinue participation in the research at any time.
Privacy	Participants have the right to concealment of their identity on all information collected in the course of research. They also have this right with respect to written reports and any informal discussions about the research.
Knowledge of results	Participants have the right to be informed of the results of research in language that is appropriate to their level of understanding.
Beneficial treatments	If experimental treatments believed to be beneficial are under investigation, participants in control groups have the right to alternative beneficial treatments if they are available.

Sources: American Psychological Association, 2002; Society for Research in Child Development, 2007.

Older adults should not be arbitrarily excluded from research. Most require only the typical informed-consent procedures, and their participation brings both personal and scientific benefits. For elders who are cognitively impaired—like this man with Alzheimer's disease—informed consent may not be possible without the assistance of a surrogate decision maker.

research does not justify, then preference is always given to the participants' interests.

The ethical principle of *informed consent* requires special interpretation when participants cannot fully appreciate the research goals and activities. Parental consent is meant to protect the safety of children, whose ability to decide is not yet mature. But as soon as children are old enough to appreciate the purpose of the research, and certainly by age 7, their own informed consent should be obtained in addition to parental consent. Around this age, changes in children's thinking permit them to better understand simple scientific principles and the needs of others. Researchers should respect and enhance these new capacities by giving school-age children a full explanation of research activities in language they can understand (Fisher, 1993). Extra care must be taken when telling children that the information they provide will be kept confidential and that they can end their participation at any time. Even adolescents may not understand, and sometimes do not believe, these promises (Bruzzese & Fisher, 2003; Ondrusek et al., 1998).

Most older adults require no more than the usual informed-consent procedures. Yet many investigators set upper age limits in studies relevant to the elderly, thereby excluding the oldest adults (Bayer & Tadd, 2000). The elderly should not be stereotyped as incompetent to decide about their own participation or to engage in research activities. Nevertheless, extra measures must be taken to protect those who are cognitively impaired or who reside in settings for the chronically ill. As noted, some individuals may agree to participate simply to engage in rewarding social interaction. Yet participation should not be automatically withheld, since it can result in personal as well as scientific benefits. In these instances, potential participants should be asked to appoint a surrogate decision maker. If they cannot do so, then someone should be named by an IRB, after careful consultation with relatives and professionals who know the person well. As an added precaution, if the elderly person is incapable of consenting and the risks of the research are more than minimal, then the study should not be done unless it is likely to directly benefit the participant (Kim et al., 2004).

Finally, all ethical guidelines advise that special precautions be taken in the use of deception and concealment, as occurs when researchers observe people from behind one-way mirrors, give them false feedback about their performance, or do not tell them the truth about the real purpose of the research. When these kinds of procedures are used, *debriefing*, in which the investigator provides a full account and justification of the activities, occurs after the research session is over. But young children often lack the cognitive skills to understand the reasons for deceptive procedures, and despite explanations, even older children may leave the research situation with their belief in the honesty of adults undermined. Ethical standards permit deception if investigators satisfy IRBs that a study's potential benefits to society are great enough to justify infringing on participants' right to informed consent and risking other harm (Fisher, 2005). Nevertheless, because deception may have serious emotional consequences for some youngsters, many experts in research ethics believe that investigators should use it with children only if the risk of harm is minimal.

ASK YOURSELF

» REVIEW
What special steps must investigators take in conducting studies of children and the aged to ensure protection from harm and informed consent?

» APPLY
As a researcher gathered observations of the activities of several elderly adults with cognitive impairments in a nursing home, one resident said, "Stop watching me!" How should the researcher respond, and why?

» CONNECT
In the experiment on music lessons and intelligence reported in the Social Issues box on page 38, why was it ethically important for the researchers to offer music lessons to the no-lessons control group during the year after completion of the study?

» REFLECT
What ethical safeguards do you regard as vital in conducting research that requires deception of children?

Summary

A Scientific, Applied, and Interdisciplinary Field

What is developmental science, and what factors stimulated expansion of the field?

» **Developmental science** is an interdisciplinary field devoted to understanding human constancy and change throughout the lifespan. Research on human development has been stimulated by both scientific curiosity and social pressures to improve people's lives.

Basic Issues

Identify three basic issues on which theories of human development take a stand.

» Each **theory** of human development takes a stand on three basic issues: (1) Is development a **continuous** process, or does it proceed in a series of **discontinuous stages?** (2) Does one general course of development characterize all individuals, or do many possible courses exist, depending on the distinct **contexts** in which children and adults live? (3) Is development determined primarily by genetic or environmental factors, and are individual differences stable or open to change?

The Lifespan Perspective: A Balanced Point of View

Describe the lifespan perspective on development.

» The **lifespan perspective** is a balanced view that envisions development as a dynamic system. It is based on assumptions that development is lifelong, multidimensional (affected by biological, psychological, and social forces), multidirectional (an expression of both growth and decline), and plastic (open to change through new experiences).

© TIM GRAHAM/ALAMY

» According to the lifespan perspective, the life course is influenced by multiple, interacting forces, which can be organized into three categories: (1) **age-graded influences,** which are predictable in timing and duration; (2) **history-graded influences,** unique to a particular historical era; and (3) **nonnormative influences,** which are unique to one or a few individuals.

Scientific Beginnings

Describe the major early influences on the scientific study of development.

» Darwin's theory of evolution influenced important developmental theories and inspired scientific child study. In the early twentieth century, Hall and Gesell introduced the **normative approach,** which produced a large body of descriptive facts about development.

© LISA F. YOUNG/ALAMY

» Binet and Simon constructed the first successful intelligence test, which sparked interest in individual differences in development and led to a heated **controversy over nature versus nurture.**

Mid-Twentieth-Century Theories

What theories influenced human development research in the mid-twentieth century?

» In the 1930s and 1940s, psychiatrists and social workers turned to the **psychoanalytic perspective** for help in treating people's emotional problems. In Freud's **psychosexual theory,** the individual moves through five stages, during which three portions of the personality—id, ego, and superego—become integrated. Erikson's **psychosocial theory** expands Freud's theory by emphasizing the development of culturally relevant attitudes and skills and the lifespan nature of development.

» As the psychoanalytic perspective gained in prominence, **behaviorism** and **social learning theory** emerged, emphasizing the study of directly observable events—stimuli and responses—and the principles of conditioning and modeling. These approaches led to practical procedures of behavior modification to eliminate undesirable behaviors and increase desirable responses.

© MARGOT GRANITSAS/THE IMAGE WORKS

» In contrast to behaviorism, Piaget's **cognitive-developmental theory** emphasizes children's active role in constructing knowledge as they manipulate and explore their world. According to Piaget, children move through four stages, from the baby's sensorimotor action patterns to the adolescent's capacity for abstract, systematic thinking. Although some of Piaget's conclusions have been challenged, his work has stimulated a wealth of research on children's thinking and encouraged educational programs that emphasize discovery learning.

Recent Theoretical Perspectives

Describe recent theoretical perspectives on human development.

» **Information processing** views the mind as a symbol-manipulating system through which information flows, much like a computer, and sees development as a process of continuous change. Because this approach provides precise accounts of how children and adults tackle cognitive tasks, its findings have important implications for education.

» Researchers in **developmental cognitive neuroscience** study the relationship between changes in the brain and the development of cognitive processing and behavior patterns. They are making rapid progress in identifying the types of experiences that support or undermine brain development at various ages.

» Three contemporary perspectives emphasize contexts of development. **Ethology,** which stresses the adaptive value and evolutionary history of behavior, inspired the **sensitive period** concept. In **evolutionary developmental psychology,** which extends this emphasis, researchers seek to understand the adaptiveness of specieswide competencies as they change with age.

» Vygotsky's **sociocultural theory,** which focuses on how culture is transmitted from one generation to the next through social interaction, views cognitive development as a socially mediated process. Through cooperative dialogues with more expert members of society, children come to use language to guide their own thought and actions and acquire culturally relevant knowledge and skills.

© PAUL CHESLEY/GETTY IMAGES/STONE

» **Ecological systems theory** views the individual as developing within a complex system of relationships affected by multiple, nested layers of the surrounding environment—**microsystem, mesosystem, exosystem,** and **macrosystem.** The **chronosystem** represents the dynamic, ever-changing nature of individuals and their experiences.

Comparing and Evaluating Theories

Identify the stand taken by each major theory on the three basic issues of human development.

» Theories vary in their focus on different domains of development and in their stand on three basic issues: whether development is continuous or discontinuous, whether there is one course of development or many, and whether nature or nurture is more influential. (For a full summary, see Table 1.5 on page 27.)

Studying Development

Describe methods commonly used in research on human development.

» **Naturalistic observations,** gathered in everyday environments, permit researchers to see directly the everyday behaviors they hope to explain. In contrast, **structured observations,** which take place in laboratories, give every participant an equal opportunity to display the behavior of interest.

» Self-report methods include the **clinical interview,** a flexible, open-ended method that permits participants to express their thoughts in ways similar to their thinking in everyday life. **Structured interviews** (including tests and questionnaires) are more efficient, permitting researchers to ask about activities and behaviors that participants may not think of mentioning in an open-ended interview. Investigators use the **clinical, or case study, method** to gain an in-depth understanding of a single individual.

» Researchers have adapted observational and self-report methods to permit direct comparisons of cultures. To uncover the cultural meanings of children's and adults' behaviors, they rely on **ethnography,** engaging in participant observation.

© ED TRONICK/ANTHRO-PHOTO

Distinguish between correlational and experimental research designs, noting the strengths and limitations of each.

» The **correlational design** examines relationships between variables as they occur, without altering people's experiences. The **correlation coefficient** is often used to measure the association between variables. Correlational studies do not permit inferences about cause and effect, but they are useful when it is difficult or impossible to control the variables of interest.

» An **experimental design** permits cause-and-effect inferences. Researchers manipulate an **independent variable** by exposing participants to two or more treatment conditions. Then they determine the effect of this variable on a **dependent variable. Random assignment** to treatment conditions reduces the chances that participant characteristics will affect the accuracy of experimental findings.

» Experiments conducted in laboratories permit a high degree of control, but findings may not apply to everyday life. Field and natural, or quasi-, experiments compare treatments in natural environments. These approaches, however, are less rigorous than laboratory experiments.

Describe designs for studying development, noting the strengths and limitations of each.

» The **longitudinal design,** in which participants are studied repeatedly over time, permits researchers to identify common patterns and individual differences in development and to examine relationships between early and later events and behaviors. Longitudinal research poses several problems, including participant dropout that biases the sample, practice effects, and **cohort effects**—difficulty generalizing to people developing in other historical times.

» In the **cross-sectional design,** groups of people differing in age are studied at the same point in time. This is an efficient way to study age-related trends, but it is limited to comparisons of age-group averages. Cross-sectional studies, especially those that cover a wide age span, are also vulnerable to cohort effects.

» Investigators have devised modified developmental designs that combine aspects of longitudinal and cross-sectional approaches. In **sequential designs,** researchers conduct several similar cross-sectional or longitudinal studies, or sequences, at varying times. This permits them to test for cohort effects and to compare longitudinal and cross-sectional findings.

» When researchers combine experimental and developmental designs, they can examine causal influences on development.

Ethics in Lifespan Research

What special ethical concerns arise in research on human development?

» Research creates ethical issues because the quest for scientific knowledge has the potential to exploit people. The ethical principle of informed consent requires special safeguards for children and for elderly people who are cognitively impaired or who live in settings for the care of the chronically ill. The use of deception in research with children is especially risky because it may undermine their basic faith in the trustworthiness of adults.

Important Terms and Concepts

age-graded influences (p. 11)
behavior modification (p. 18)
behaviorism (p. 17)
chronosystem (p. 26)
clinical interview (p. 29)
clinical, or case study, method (p. 30)
cognitive-developmental theory (p. 19)
cohort effects (p. 35)
contexts (p. 6)
continuous development (p. 6)
correlation coefficient (p. 33)
correlational design (p. 31)
cross-sectional design (p. 36)
dependent variable (p. 33)
developmental cognitive neuroscience (p. 22)
developmental science (p. 5)
discontinuous development (p. 6)
ecological systems theory (p. 24)
ethnography (p. 30)
ethology (p. 22)
evolutionary developmental psychology (p. 23)
exosystem (p. 25)
experimental design (p. 33)
history-graded influences (p. 13)
independent variable (p. 33)
information processing (p. 21)
lifespan perspective (p. 8)
longitudinal design (p. 34)
macrosystem (p. 25)
mesosystem (p. 25)
microsystem (p. 24)
naturalistic observation (p. 27)
nature–nurture controversy (p. 7)
nonnormative influences (p. 13)
normative approach (p. 14)
psychoanalytic perspective (p. 15)
psychosexual theory (p. 15)
psychosocial theory (p. 15)
random assignment (p. 34)
resilience (p. 10)
sensitive period (p. 23)
sequential designs (p. 36)
social learning theory (p. 18)
sociocultural theory (p. 23)
stage (p. 6)
structured interview (p. 29)
structured observation (p. 20)
theory (p. 5)

© RYAN MCVAY/GETTY IMAGES/DIGITAL VISION

A complex blend of genetic and environmental influences leads members of this three-generation family of Mexico to be both alike and different in physical characteristics and behavior.

CHAPTER 2

Biological and Environmental Foundations

"It's a girl!" announces the doctor, holding up the squalling little creature as her parents gaze with amazement at their miraculous creation.

"A girl! We've named her Sarah!" exclaims the proud father to eager relatives waiting for news of their new family member.

As we join these parents in thinking about how this wondrous being came into existence and imagining her future, we are struck by many questions. How could this baby, equipped with everything necessary for life outside the womb, have developed from the union of two tiny cells? What ensures that Sarah will, in due time, roll over, walk, talk, make friends, learn, imagine, and create—just like other typical children born before her? Why is she a girl and not a boy, dark-haired rather than blond, calm and cuddly instead of wiry and energetic? What difference will it make that Sarah is given a name and place in one family, community, nation, and culture rather than another?

© ARIEL SKELLEY/BLEND IMAGES/JL PITERIMAGES

To answer these questions, this chapter takes a close look at the foundations of development: heredity and environment. Because nature has prepared us for survival, all humans have features in common. Yet each of us is also unique. ***TAKE A MOMENT...*** Think about several of your friends, and jot down the most obvious physical and behavioral similarities between them and their parents. Did you find that one person shows combined features of both parents, another resembles just one parent, whereas a third is not like either parent? These directly observable characteristics are called **phenotypes.** They depend in part on the individual's **genotype**—the complex blend of genetic information that determines our species and influences all our unique characteristics. Yet phenotypes are also affected by each person's lifelong history of experiences.

We begin our discussion at the moment of conception, an event that establishes the hereditary makeup of the new individual. First we review basic genetic principles that help explain similarities and differences among us in appearance and behavior. Then we turn to aspects of the environment that play powerful roles throughout the lifespan. Finally, we consider the question of how nature and nurture *work together* to shape the course of development.

Genetic Foundations

Each of us is made up of trillions of units called *cells.* Within every cell (except red blood cells) is a control center, or *nucleus,* containing rodlike structures called **chromosomes,** which store and transmit genetic information. Human chromosomes come in 23 matching pairs (an exception is the XY pair in males, which we will discuss shortly). Each member of a pair corresponds to the other in size, shape, and genetic functions, with one chromosome inherited from the mother and the other from the father (see Figure 2.1).

The Genetic Code

Chromosomes are made up of a chemical substance called **deoxyribonucleic acid,** or **DNA.** As Figure 2.2 shows, DNA is a long, double-stranded molecule that looks like a twisted ladder. Each rung of the ladder consists of a specific pair of chemical substances called *bases,* joined together between the two sides. It is this sequence of bases that provides genetic instructions. A **gene** is a segment of DNA along the length of the chromosome. Genes can be of different lengths—perhaps 100 to several thousand ladder rungs long. An estimated 20,000 to 25,000 genes lie along the human chromosomes (International Human Genome Sequencing Consortium, 2004).

We share some of our genetic makeup with even the simplest organisms, such as bacteria and molds, and most of it with other mammals, especially primates. Between 98 and 99 percent of chimpanzee and human DNA is identical. This means that only a small portion of our heredity is responsible for the traits that make us human, from our upright gait to our extraordinary language and cognitive capacities. And the genetic variation from one human to the next is even less! Individuals around the world are about 99.1 percent genetically identical (Gibbons, 1998; Gibbons et al., 2004). But it takes a change in only a single base pair to influence human traits and capacities. And such tiny changes can combine in unique ways across multiple genes, thereby amplifying variability within the human species (National Center for Biotechnology Information, 2004).

A unique feature of DNA is that it can duplicate itself through a process called **mitosis.** This special ability permits the one-celled fertilized ovum to develop into a complex human being composed of a great many cells. Refer again to Figure 2.2, and you will see that during mitosis, the chromosomes copy themselves. As a result, each new body cell contains the same number of chromosomes and the identical genetic information.

Genes accomplish their task by sending instructions for making a rich assortment of proteins to the *cytoplasm,* the area surrounding the cell nucleus. Proteins, which trigger chemical reactions throughout the body, are the biological foundation on which our characteristics are built. How do humans, with far fewer genes than scientists once thought (only twice as many as the worm or fly), manage to develop into such complex beings? The answer lies in the proteins our genes make, which break up and reassemble in staggering variety—about 10 to 20 million altogether. Simpler species have far fewer proteins. Furthermore, the communication system between the cell nucleus and cytoplasm, which fine-tunes gene activity, is more intricate in humans than in simpler organisms. Within the cell, a wide range of environmental factors modify gene expression (Lashley, 2007). So even at this microscopic level, biological events are the result of *both* genetic and nongenetic forces.

The Sex Cells

New individuals are created when two special cells called **gametes,** or sex cells—the sperm and ovum—combine. A gamete contains only 23 chromosomes, half as many as a regular body cell. Gametes are formed through a cell division

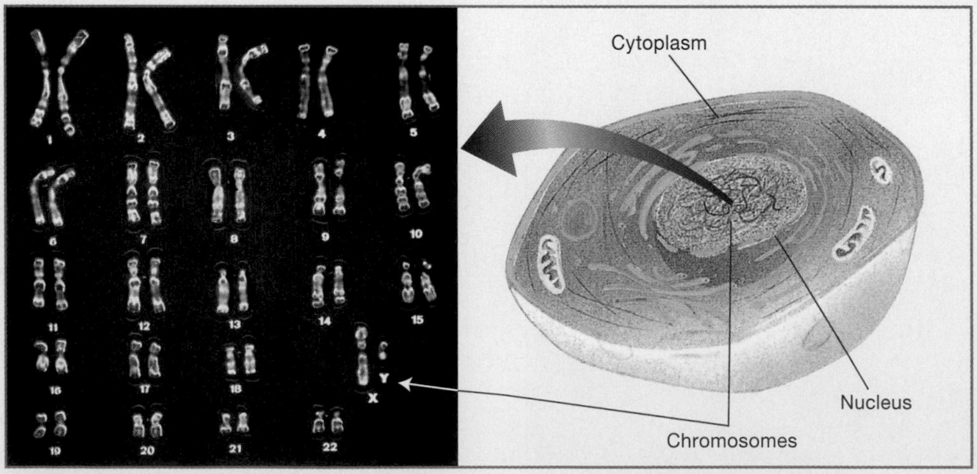

■ **FIGURE 2.1** ■ **A karyotype, or photograph, of human chromosomes.** The 46 chromosomes shown on the left were isolated from a human cell, stained, greatly magnified, and arranged in pairs according to decreasing size of the upper "arm" of each chromosome. The twenty-third pair, XY, reveals that the cell donor is a male. In a female, this pair would be XX. (Photo © CNRI/Science Photo Library/Photo Researchers, Inc.)

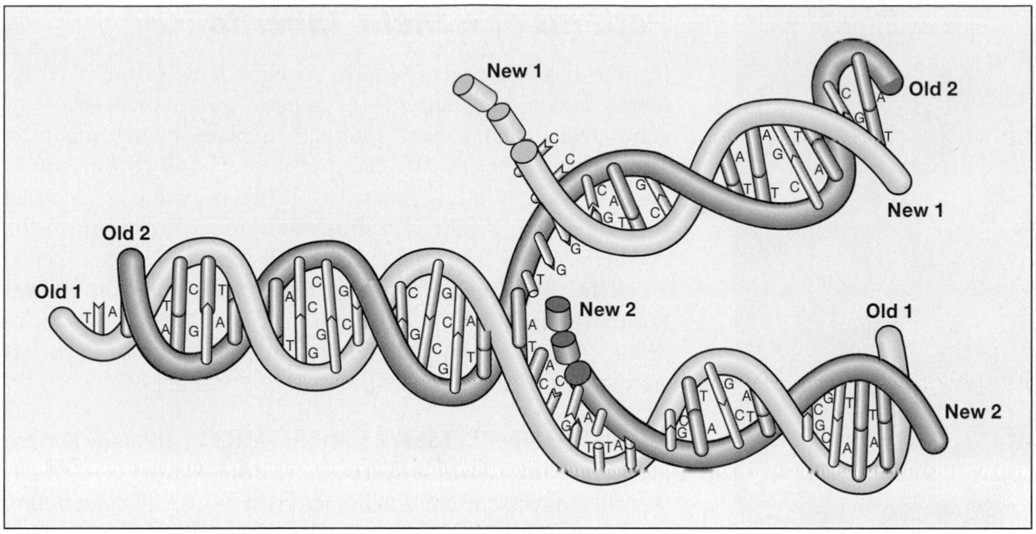

■ **FIGURE 2.2** ■ **DNA's ladder-like structure.** This figure shows that the pairings of bases across the rungs of the ladder are very specific: Adenine (A) always appears with thymine (T), and cytosine (C) always appears with guanine (G). Here, the DNA ladder duplicates by splitting down the middle of its ladder rungs. Each free base picks up a new complementary partner from the area surrounding the cell nucleus.

process called **meiosis,** which halves the number of chromosomes normally present in body cells. When sperm and ovum unite at conception, the resulting cell, called a **zygote,** will again have 46 chromosomes. Meiosis ensures that a constant quantity of genetic material is transmitted from one generation to the next.

In meiosis, the chromosomes pair up and exchange segments, so that genes from one are replaced by genes from another. Then chance determines which member of each pair will gather with others and end up in the same gamete. These events make the likelihood extremely low—about 1 in 700 trillion—that nontwin siblings will be genetically identical (Gould & Keeton, 1996). The genetic variability produced by meiosis is adaptive: It increases the chances that at least some members of a species will cope with ever-changing environments and will survive.

In the male, four sperm are produced when meiosis is complete. Also, the cells from which sperm arise are produced continuously throughout life. For this reason, a healthy man can father a child at any age after sexual maturity. In the female, meiosis results in just one ovum. In addition, the female is born with all her ova already present in her ovaries, and she can bear children for only three to four decades. Still, there are plenty of female sex cells. About 1 to 2 million are present at birth, 40,000 remain at adolescence, and approximately 350 to 450 will mature during a woman's childbearing years (Moore & Persaud, 2008).

Boy or Girl?

Return to Figure 2.1 and note that 22 of the 23 pairs of chromosomes are matching pairs, called **autosomes.** The twenty-third pair consists of **sex chromosomes.** In females, this pair is called XX; in males, it is called XY. The X is a relatively large chromosome, whereas the Y is short and carries little genetic material. When gametes form in males, the X and Y chromosomes separate into different sperm cells. The gametes that form in females all carry an X chromosome. Therefore, the sex of the new organism is determined by whether an X-bearing or a Y-bearing sperm fertilizes the ovum.

Multiple Offspring

Ruth and Peter, a couple I know well, tried for several years to have a child, without success. When Ruth reached age 33, her doctor prescribed a fertility drug, and twins—Jeannie and Jason—were born. Jeannie and Jason are **fraternal,** or **dizygotic, twins,** the most common type of multiple birth, resulting from the release and fertilization of two ova. Genetically, they are no more alike than ordinary siblings. Table 2.1 summarizes genetic

■ **TABLE 2.1** ■ ***Maternal Factors Linked to Fraternal Twinning***

FACTOR	DESCRIPTION
Ethnicity	Occurs in 4 per 1,000 births among Asians, 8 per 1,000 births among whites, 12 to 16 per 1,000 births among blacks[a]
Family history of twinning	Occurs more often among women whose mothers and sisters gave birth to fraternal twins
Age	Rises with maternal age, peaking between 35 and 39 years, and then rapidly falls
Nutrition	Occurs less often among women with poor diets; occurs more often among women who are tall and overweight or of normal weight as opposed to slight body build
Number of births	Is more likely with each additional birth
Fertility drugs and in vitro fertilization	Is more likely with fertility hormones and in vitro fertilization (see page 54), which also increase the chances of bearing triplets, quadruplets, or quintuplets

[a]Worldwide rates, not including multiple births resulting from use of fertility drugs.

Sources: Hall, 2003; Hoekstra et al., 2008; Lashley, 2007.

© RACHEL EPSTEIN/PHOTOEDIT

These identical, or monozygotic, twins were created when a duplicating zygote separated into two clusters of cells, and two individuals with the same genetic makeup developed. Identical twins look alike and tend to resemble each other in a variety of psychological characteristics.

and environmental factors that increase the chances of giving birth to fraternal twins. Older maternal age, fertility drugs, and in vitro fertilization (to be discussed shortly) are major causes of the dramatic rise in fraternal twinning and other multiple births in industrialized nations over the past several decades (Machin, 2005; Russell et al., 2003). Currently, fraternal twins account for 1 in about every 60 births in the United States (U.S. Department of Health and Human Services, 2008b).

Twins can be created in another way. Sometimes a zygote that has started to duplicate separates into two clusters of cells that develop into two individuals. These are called **identical,** or **monozygotic, twins** because they have the same genetic makeup. The frequency of identical twins is the same around the world—about 1 in every 330 births (Hall, 2003). Animal research has uncovered a variety of environmental influences that prompt this type of twinning, including temperature changes, variation in oxygen levels, and late fertilization of the ovum. In a minority of cases, the identical twinning runs in families, suggesting a genetic influence (Lashley, 2007).

During their early years, children of single births often are healthier and develop more rapidly than twins. Jeannie and Jason, like most twins, were born early—three weeks before Ruth's due date. And, like other premature infants—as you will see in Chapter 3—they required special care after birth. When the twins came home from the hospital, Ruth and Peter had to divide time between them. Perhaps because neither baby received as much attention as the average single infant, Jeannie and Jason walked and talked several months later than most other children their age, although both caught up by middle childhood (Lytton & Gallagher, 2002). Parental energies are further strained after the birth of triplets, whose early development is slower than that of twins (Feldman, Eidelman, & Rotenberg, 2004).

Patterns of Genetic Inheritance

Jeannie has her parents' dark, straight hair; Jason is curly-haired and blond. Patterns of genetic inheritance—the way genes from each parent interact—explain these outcomes. Recall that, except for the XY pair in males, all chromosomes come in corresponding pairs. Two forms of each gene occur at the same place on the chromosomes, one inherited from the mother and one from the father. Each form of a gene is called an **allele.** If the alleles from both parents are alike, the child is **homozygous** and will display the inherited trait. If the alleles differ, then the child is **heterozygous,** and relationships between the alleles determine the trait that will appear.

DOMINANT–RECESSIVE INHERITANCE. In many heterozygous pairings, **dominant–recessive inheritance** occurs: Only one allele affects the child's characteristics. It is called *dominant;* the second allele, which has no effect, is called *recessive.* Hair color is an example. The allele for dark hair is dominant (we can represent it with a capital *D*), whereas the one for blond hair is recessive (symbolized by a lowercase *b*). A child who inherits a homozygous pair of dominant alleles *(DD)* and a child who inherits a heterozygous pair *(Db)* will both be dark-haired, even though their genotypes differ. Blond hair (like Jason's) can result only from having two recessive alleles *(bb).* Still, heterozygous individuals with just one recessive allele *(Db)* can pass that trait to their children. Therefore, they are called **carriers** of the trait.

Some human characteristics that follow the rules of dominant–recessive inheritance are listed in Tables 2.2 and 2.3.

TABLE 2.2 *Examples of Dominant and Recessive Characteristics*

DOMINANT	RECESSIVE
Dark hair	Blond hair
Normal hair	Pattern baldness
Curly hair	Straight hair
Nonred hair	Red hair
Facial dimples	No dimples
Normal hearing	Some forms of deafness
Normal vision	Nearsightedness
Farsightedness	Normal vision
Normal vision	Congenital eye cataracts
Normally pigmented skin	Albinism
Double-jointedness	Normal joints
Type A blood	Type O blood
Type B blood	Type O blood
Rh-positive blood	Rh-negative blood

Note: Many normal characteristics that were previously thought to result from dominant–recessive inheritance, such as eye color, are now regarded as due to multiple genes. For the characteristics listed here, most experts agree that the simple dominant–recessive relationship holds.

Source: McKusick, 2007.

TABLE 2.3 *Examples of Dominant and Recessive Diseases*

DISEASE	DESCRIPTION	MODE OF INHERITANCE	INCIDENCE	TREATMENT
AUTOSOMAL DISEASES				
Cooley's anemia	Pale appearance, retarded physical growth, and lethargic behavior begin in infancy.	Recessive	1 in 500 births to parents of Mediterranean descent	Frequent blood transfusion; death from complications usually occurs by adolescence.
Cystic fibrosis	Lungs, liver, and pancreas secrete large amounts of thick mucus, leading to breathing and digestive difficulties.	Recessive	1 in 2,000 to 2,500 Caucasian births; 1 in 16,000 births to North Americans of African descent	Bronchial drainage, prompt treatment of respiratory infection, dietary management. Advances in medical care allow survival with good life quality into adulthood.
Phenylketonuria (PKU)	Inability to metabolize the amino acid phenylalanine, contained in many proteins, causes severe central nervous system damage in the first year of life.	Recessive	1 in 8,000 births	Placing the child on a special diet results in average intelligence and normal lifespan. Subtle deficits in memory, planning, decision making, and problem solving are often present.
Sickle cell anemia	Abnormal sickling of red blood cells causes oxygen deprivation, pain, swelling, and tissue damage. Anemia and susceptibility to infections, especially pneumonia, occur.	Recessive	1 in 400 to 600 births to North Americans of African descent	Blood transfusions, painkillers, prompt treatment of infection. No known cure; 50 percent die by age 55.
Tay-Sachs disease	Central nervous system degeneration, with onset at about 6 months, leads to poor muscle tone, blindness, deafness, and convulsions.	Recessive	1 in 3,600 births to Jews of European descent and to French Canadians	None. Death occurs by 3 to 4 years of age.
Huntington disease	Central nervous system degeneration leads to muscular coordination difficulties, mental deterioration, and personality changes. Symptoms usually do not appear until age 35 or later.	Dominant	1 in 18,000 to 25,000 births to North Americans	None. Death occurs 10 to 20 years after symptom onset.
Marfan syndrome	Tall, slender build; thin, elongated arms and legs; and heart defects and eye abnormalities, especially of the lens. Excessive lengthening of the body results in a variety of skeletal defects.	Dominant	1 in 5,000 to 10,000 births	Correction of heart and eye defects is sometimes possible. Death from heart failure in young adulthood is common.
X-LINKED DISEASES				
Duchenne muscular dystrophy	Degenerative muscle disease. Abnormal gait, loss of ability to walk between ages 7 and 13 years.	Recessive	1 in 3,000 to 5,000 male births	None. Death from respiratory infection or weakening of the heart muscle usually occurs in adolescence.
Hemophilia	Blood fails to clot normally. Can lead to severe internal bleeding and tissue damage.	Recessive	1 in 4,000 to 7,000 male births	Blood transfusions. Safety precautions may prevent injury.
Diabetes insipidus	Insufficient production of the hormone vasopressin, resulting in excessive thirst and urination. Dehydration can cause central nervous system damage.	Recessive	1 in 2,500 male births	Hormone replacement.

Note: For recessive disorders listed, carrier status can be detected in prospective parents through a blood test or genetic analyses. For all disorders listed, prenatal diagnosis is available (see page 56).

Sources: Kliegman et al., 2000; Lashley, 2007; McKusick, 2007.

As you can see, many disabilities and diseases are the product of recessive alleles. One of the most frequently occurring recessive disorders is *phenylketonuria,* or *PKU,* which affects the way the body breaks down proteins contained in many foods. Infants born with two recessive alleles lack an enzyme that converts one of the basic amino acids that make up proteins (phenylalanine) into a byproduct essential for body functioning (tyrosine). Without this enzyme, phenylalanine quickly builds to toxic levels that damage the central nervous system. By 1 year, infants with PKU are permanently mentally retarded.

Despite its potentially damaging effects, PKU provides an excellent illustration of the fact that inheriting unfavorable genes does not always lead to an untreatable condition. All U.S. states require that each newborn be given a blood test for PKU. If the disease is found, doctors place the baby on a diet low in phenylalanine. Children who receive this treatment nevertheless take slightly longer to process information and show mild deficits in certain cognitive skills, such as memory, planning, decision making, and problem solving, because even small amounts of phenylalanine interfere with brain functioning (Anderson et al., 2007; Channon, Mockler, & Lee, 2005; Christ et al., 2006). But as long as dietary treatment begins early and continues, children with PKU usually attain an average level of intelligence and have a normal lifespan.

In dominant–recessive inheritance, if we know the genetic makeup of the parents, we can predict the percentage of children in a family who are likely to display or carry a trait. Figure 2.3 illustrates this for PKU. Notice that for a child to inherit the condition, each parent must have a recessive allele.

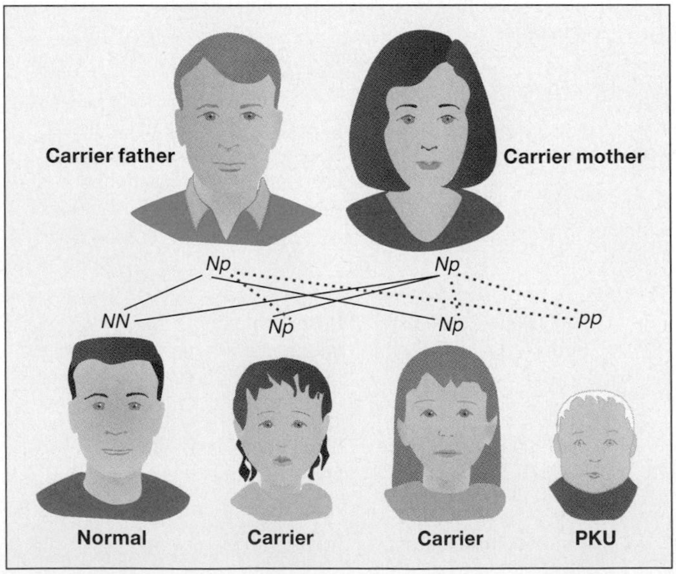

■ **FIGURE 2.3** ■ **Dominant–recessive mode of inheritance, as illustrated by PKU.** When both parents are heterozygous carriers of the recessive gene *(p),* we can predict that 25 percent of their offspring are likely to be normal *(NN),* 50 percent are likely to be carriers *(Np),* and 25 percent are likely to inherit the disorder *(pp).* Notice that the PKU-affected child, in contrast to his siblings, has light hair. The recessive gene for PKU affects more than one trait. It also leads to fair coloring.

Only rarely are serious diseases due to dominant alleles. Think about why this is so. Children who inherit the dominant allele always develop the disorder. They seldom live long enough to reproduce, so the harmful dominant allele is eliminated from the family's heredity in a single generation. Some dominant disorders, however, do persist. One is *Huntington disease,* a condition in which the central nervous system degenerates. Why has this disorder endured? Its symptoms usually do not appear until age 35 or later, after the person has passed on the dominant gene to his or her children.

■ **INCOMPLETE DOMINANCE.** In some heterozygous circumstances, the dominant–recessive relationship does not hold completely. Instead, we see **incomplete dominance,** a pattern of inheritance in which both alleles are expressed, resulting in a combined trait, or one that is intermediate between the two.

The *sickle cell trait,* a heterozygous condition present in many black Africans, provides an example. *Sickle cell anemia* (see Table 2.3) occurs in full form when a child inherits two recessive genes. They cause the usually round red blood cells to become sickle (crescent-moon) shaped, especially under low-oxygen conditions. The sickled cells clog the blood vessels and block the flow of blood, causing intense pain, swelling, and tissue damage. Despite medical advances that today allow 85 percent of affected children to survive to adulthood, North Americans with sickle cell anemia have an average life expectancy of only 55 years (Driscoll, 2007). Heterozygous individuals are protected from the disease under most circumstances. However, when they experience oxygen deprivation—for example, at high altitudes or after intense physical exercise—the single recessive allele asserts itself, and a temporary, mild form of the illness occurs.

The sickle cell allele is common among black Africans for a special reason. Carriers of it are more resistant to malaria than are individuals with two alleles for normal red blood cells. In Africa, where malaria is common, these carriers survived and reproduced more frequently than others, leading the gene to be maintained in the black population. But in regions where the risk of malaria is low, the frequency of the gene is declining. For example, only 8 percent of African Americans are carriers, compared with 20 percent of black Africans (Goldbloom, 2004).

■ **X-LINKED INHERITANCE.** Males and females have an equal chance of inheriting recessive disorders carried on the autosomes, such as PKU and sickle cell anemia. But when a harmful allele is carried on the X chromosome, **X-linked inheritance** applies. Males are more likely to be affected because their sex chromosomes do not match. In females, any recessive allele on one X chromosome has a good chance of being suppressed by a dominant allele on the other X. But the Y chromosome is only about one-third as long and therefore lacks many corresponding genes to override those on the X. A well-known example is *hemophilia,* a disorder in which the blood fails to clot normally. Figure 2.4 shows its greater likelihood of inheritance by male children whose mothers carry the abnormal allele.

Besides X-linked disorders, many sex differences reveal the male to be at a disadvantage. Rates of miscarriage, infant

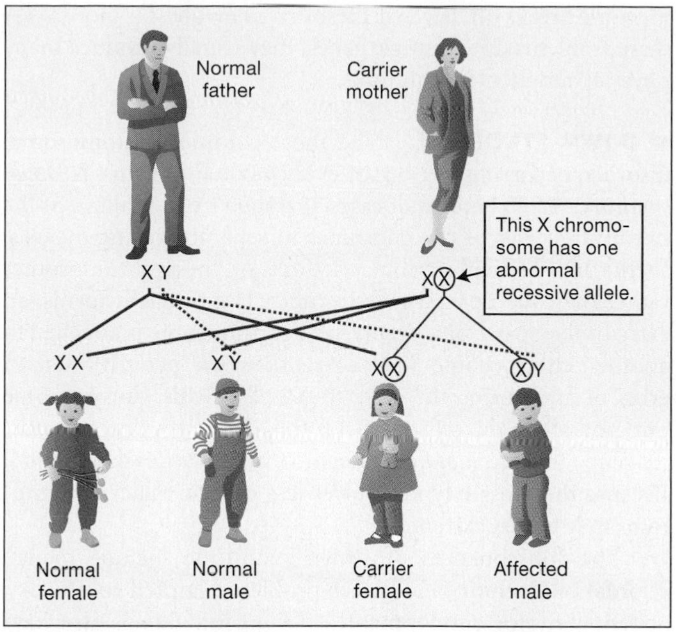

■ **FIGURE 2.4** ■ **X-linked inheritance.** In the example shown here, the allele on the father's X chromosome is normal. The mother has one normal and one abnormal recessive allele on her X chromosomes. By looking at the possible combinations of the parents' alleles, we can predict that 50 percent of these parents' male children are likely to have the disorder and 50 percent of their female children are likely to be carriers of it.

and childhood deaths, birth defects, learning disabilities, behavior disorders, and mental retardation all are higher for boys (Butler & Meaney, 2005). It is possible that these sex differences can be traced to the genetic code. The female, with two X chromosomes, benefits from a greater variety of genes. Nature, however, seems to have adjusted for the male's disadvantage. Worldwide, about 106 boys are born for every 100 girls, and judging from miscarriage and abortion statistics, an even greater number of males are conceived (United Nations, 2006b).

Nevertheless, in recent decades the proportion of male births has declined in many industrialized countries, including the United States, Canada, and European nations (Jongbloet et al., 2001). Some researchers attribute the trend to a rise in stressful living conditions, which heighten spontaneous abortions, especially of male fetuses. In a test of this hypothesis, male-to-female birth ratios in East Germany were examined between 1946 and 1999. The ratio was lowest in 1991, the year that the country's economy collapsed (Catalano, 2003). Similarly, in a California study spanning the decade of the 1990s, the percentage of male fetal deaths increased in months in which unemployment (a major stressor) also rose above its typical level (Catalano et al., 2005).

■ **GENOMIC IMPRINTING.** More than 1,000 human characteristics follow the rules of dominant–recessive and incomplete-dominance inheritance (McKusick, 2007). In these cases, whichever parent contributes a gene to the new individual, the gene responds in the same way. Geneticists, however, have identified exceptions. In **genomic imprinting,** alleles are *imprinted,* or chemically *marked,* so that one pair member (either the mother's or the father's) is activated, regardless of its makeup. The imprint is often temporary; it may be erased in the next generation, and it may not occur in all individuals (Everman & Cassidy, 2000).

Imprinting helps us understand certain puzzling genetic patterns. For example, children are more likely to develop diabetes if their father, rather than their mother, suffers from it. And people with asthma or hay fever tend to have mothers, not fathers, with the illness. Imprinting is involved in several childhood cancers and in *Prader-Willi syndrome,* a disorder with symptoms of mental retardation and severe obesity (Benarroch et al., 2007). It may also explain why Huntington disease, when inherited from the father, tends to emerge earlier and progress more rapidly (Navarrete, Martinez, & Salamanca, 1994).

Genomic imprinting can also operate on the sex chromosomes, as *fragile X syndrome*—the most common inherited cause of mental retardation—reveals. In this disorder, which affects about 1 in 2,000 males and 1 in 4,000 females, an abnormal repetition of a sequence of DNA bases occurs on the X chromosome, damaging a particular gene. Fragile X has been linked to 2 to 3 percent of cases of *autism,* a serious disorder usually diagnosed in early childhood that involves impaired social interaction, delayed or absent language and communication, and repetitive motor behavior (Goodlin-Jones et al., 2004). Research reveals that the defective gene at the fragile site is expressed only when it is passed from mother to child (Reiss & Dant, 2003).

■ **MUTATION.** Although less than 3 percent of pregnancies result in the birth of a baby with a hereditary abnormality, these children account for about 20 percent of infant deaths and contribute substantially to lifelong impaired physical and mental functioning (U.S. Department of Health and Human Services, 2008b). How are harmful genes created in the first place? The answer is **mutation,** a sudden change in a segment of DNA. A mutation may affect only one or two genes, or it may involve many genes, as in the chromosomal disorders we will discuss shortly. Some mutations occur spontaneously, simply by chance. Others are caused by hazardous environmental agents.

Although nonionizing forms of radiation—electromagnetic waves and microwaves—have no demonstrated impact on DNA, ionizing (high-energy) radiation is an established cause of mutation. Women who receive repeated doses before conception are more likely to miscarry or to give birth to children with hereditary defects. The incidence of genetic abnormalities, such as physical malformations and childhood cancer, is also higher in children whose fathers are exposed to radiation in their occupation. However, infrequent and mild exposure to radiation does not cause genetic damage (Jacquet, 2004). Rather, high doses over a long period impair DNA.

The examples just given illustrate *germline mutation,* which takes place in the cells that give rise to gametes. When the affected individual mates, the defective DNA is passed on to the next generation. In a second type, called *somatic mutation,* normal body cells mutate, an event that can occur at any time of life. The DNA defect appears in every cell derived from the affected body cell, eventually becoming widespread enough to cause disease or disability. Many cancers, including lung, colon, and prostate, originate this way. Other diseases, such as epilepsy and heart disease, are also believed to be due to somatic mutation (Gottlieb, Beitel, & Trifiro, 2001; Steinlein, 2004).

It is easy to see how disorders that run in families can result from germline mutation. But somatic mutation may be involved in these disorders as well. Some people may harbor a genetic susceptibility that causes certain body cells to mutate easily in the presence of triggering events (Weiss, 2005). This helps explain why some individuals develop serious illnesses as a result of smoking, exposure to pollutants, or psychological stress, while others do not.

Somatic mutation shows that each of us does not have a single, permanent genotype. Rather, the genetic makeup of each cell can change over time. Somatic mutation increases with age, raising the possibility that it contributes to the age-related rise in disease and to the aging process itself (Salvioli et al., 2008).

Finally, although virtually all mutations that have been studied are harmful, some spontaneous ones (such as the sickle cell allele in malaria-ridden regions of the world) are necessary and desirable. By increasing genetic variation, they help individuals adapt to unexpected environmental challenges. Scientists, however, seldom go looking for mutations that underlie favorable traits, such as an exceptional talent or an especially sturdy immune system. They are far more concerned with identifying and eliminating unfavorable genes that threaten health and survival.

■ **POLYGENIC INHERITANCE.** So far, we have discussed patterns of inheritance in which people either do or do not display a trait. These cut-and-dried individual differences are much easier to trace to their genetic origins than are characteristics that vary on a continuum among people, such as height, weight, intelligence, and personality. These traits are due to **polygenic inheritance,** in which many genes influence the characteristic in question. Polygenic inheritance is complex, and much about it is still unknown. In the final section of this chapter, we will discuss how researchers infer the influence of heredity on human attributes when they do not know the precise patterns of inheritance.

Chromosomal Abnormalities

Besides harmful recessive alleles, abnormalities of the chromosomes are a major cause of serious developmental problems. Most chromosomal defects result from mistakes occurring during meiosis, when the ovum and sperm are formed. A chromosome pair does not separate properly, or part of a chromosome breaks off. Because these errors involve far more DNA than problems due to single genes, they usually produce many physical and mental symptoms.

■ **DOWN SYNDROME.** The most common chromosomal disorder, occurring in 1 out of every 1,000 live births, is *Down syndrome.* In 95 percent of cases, it results from a failure of the twenty-first pair of chromosomes to separate during meiosis, so the new individual inherits three of these chromosomes rather than the normal two. In other, less frequent forms, an extra broken piece of a twenty-first chromosome is attached to another chromosome (called *translocation* pattern). Or an error occurs during the early stages of mitosis, causing some but not all body cells to have the defective chromosomal makeup (called *mosaic* pattern) (Saitta & Zackai, 2005). Because the mosaic type involves less genetic material, symptoms may be less extreme.

The consequences of Down syndrome include mental retardation, memory and speech problems, limited vocabulary, and slow motor development. Affected individuals also have distinct physical features—a short, stocky build, a flattened

© LAURA DWIGHT PHOTOGRAPHY

The boy on the right has facial features typical of children with Down syndrome. Despite his impaired intellectual development, he is doing well because he is growing up in a stimulating home where he is loved and accepted by family members, including his older brother.

face, a protruding tongue, almond-shaped eyes, and (in 50 percent of cases) an unusual crease running across the palm of the hand. In addition, infants with Down syndrome are often born with eye cataracts, hearing loss, and heart and intestinal defects. Because of medical advances, fewer individuals with Down syndrome die early than was the case in the past. Many survive into their fifties and a few into their sixties to eighties (Roizen & Patterson, 2003).

Infants with Down syndrome smile less readily, show poor eye-to-eye contact, have weak muscle tone, and explore objects less persistently (Slonims & McConachie, 2006). But when parents encourage them to engage with their surroundings, Down syndrome children develop more favorably. They also benefit from infant and preschool intervention programs, although emotional, social, and motor skills improve more than intellectual performance (Carr, 2002). Clearly, environmental factors affect how well children with Down syndrome fare.

The risk of bearing a Down syndrome baby rises dramatically with maternal age, from 1 in 1,900 births at age 20, to 1 in 300 at age 35, to 1 in 30 at age 45 (Halliday et al., 1995; Meyers et al., 1997). Why is this so? Geneticists believe that the ova, present in the woman's body since her own prenatal period, weaken over time. As a result, chromosomes do not separate properly as they complete the process of meiosis at conception. But in about 5 to 10 percent of cases, the extra genetic material originates with the father. The reasons for this mutation are unknown. Some studies suggest a role for advanced paternal age, while others show no age effects (Dzurova & Pikhart, 2005; Fisch et al., 2003; Sherman et al., 2005).

■ ABNORMALITIES OF THE SEX CHROMOSOMES. Disorders of the autosomes other than Down syndrome usually disrupt development so severely that miscarriage occurs. When such babies are born, they rarely survive beyond early childhood. In contrast, abnormalities of the sex chromosomes usually lead to fewer problems. In fact, sex chromosome disorders often are not recognized until adolescence when, in some deviations, puberty is delayed. The most common problems involve the presence of an extra chromosome (either X or Y) or the absence of one X in females.

A variety of myths about individuals with sex chromosome disorders have been discredited by research. For example, males with *XYY syndrome* are not necessarily more aggressive and antisocial than XY males. And most children with sex chromosome disorders do not suffer from mental retardation. Rather, their intellectual problems usually are very specific. Verbal difficulties—for example, with reading and vocabulary—are common among girls with *triple X syndrome* and boys with *Klinefelter syndrome,* both of whom inherit an extra X chromosome. In contrast, girls with *Turner syndrome,* who are missing an X, have trouble with spatial relationships—for example, drawing pictures, telling right from left, following travel directions, and noticing changes in facial expressions (Kesler, 2007; Lawrence et al., 2003; Simpson et al., 2003). Brain-imaging research confirms that adding to or subtracting from the usual number of X chromosomes alters the development of certain brain structures, yielding particular intellectual deficits (Cutter et al., 2006; Itti et al., 2006).

ASK YOURSELF

» REVIEW
Explain the genetic origins of PKU and Down syndrome. Cite evidence that both heredity and environment contribute to the development of individuals with these disorders.

» REVIEW
Using your knowledge of X-linked inheritance, explain why males are more vulnerable than females to miscarriage, infant death, genetic disorders, and other problems.

» APPLY
Gilbert's genetic makeup is homozygous for dark hair. Jan's is homozygous for blond hair. What color is Gilbert's hair? How about Jan's? What proportion of their children are likely to be dark-haired? Explain.

» CONNECT
Referring to ecological systems theory (Chapter 1, pages 24–26), explain why parents of children with genetic disorders often experience increased stress. What factors, within and beyond the family, can help these parents support their children's development?

Reproductive Choices

Two years after they married, Ted and Marianne gave birth to their first child. Kendra appeared to be a healthy infant, but by 4 months her growth slowed, and she was diagnosed as having Tay-Sachs disease (see Table 2.3 on page 49). When Kendra died at 2 years of age, Ted and Marianne were devastated. Although they did not want to bring another infant into the world who would endure such suffering, they badly wanted to have a child. They began to avoid family gatherings, where little nieces and nephews were constant reminders of the void in their lives.

In the past, many couples with genetic disorders in their families chose not to bear a child at all rather than risk the birth of an abnormal baby. Today, genetic counseling and prenatal diagnosis help people make informed decisions about conceiving, carrying a pregnancy to term, or adopting a child.

Genetic Counseling

Genetic counseling is a communication process designed to help couples understand genetic principles, genetic testing, and prevention of genetic disorders; assess their chances of giving birth to a baby with a hereditary disorder; and choose the best course of action in view of risks and family goals (Resta et al., 2006). Individuals likely to seek counseling are

SOCIAL ISSUES

The Pros and Cons of Reproductive Technologies

Some couples decide not to risk pregnancy because of a history of genetic disease. Many others—in fact, one-sixth of all couples who try to conceive—discover that they are infertile. And some never-married adults and gay and lesbian partners want to bear children. Today, increasing numbers of individuals are turning to alternative methods of conception—technologies that, although they fulfill the wish for parenthood, have become the subject of heated debate.

Donor Insemination and In Vitro Fertilization

For several decades, *donor insemination*—injection of sperm from an anonymous man into a woman—has been used to overcome male reproductive difficulties. In recent years, it has also permitted women without a male partner to become pregnant. Donor insemination is 70 to 80 percent successful, resulting in about 40,000 deliveries and 52,000 newborn babies in the United States each year (Wright et al., 2008).

In vitro fertilization is another reproductive technology that has become increasingly common. Since the first "test tube" baby was born in England in 1978, 1 percent of all children in developed countries—about 40,000 babies in the United States—have been conceived through this technique annually (Jackson, Gibson, & Wu, 2004). With in vitro fertilization, a woman is given hormones that stimulate the ripening of several ova. These are removed surgically and placed in a dish of nutrients, to which sperm are added. Once an ovum is fertilized and begins to duplicate into several cells, it is injected into the mother's uterus.

By mixing and matching gametes, pregnancies can be brought about when either or both partners have a reproductive problem. Usually, in vitro fertilization is used to treat women whose fallopian tubes are permanently damaged. But a recently developed technique permits a single sperm to be injected directly into an ovum, thereby overcoming most male fertility problems. And a "sex sorter" method helps ensure that couples who carry X-linked diseases (which usually affect males) have a daughter. Fertilized ova and sperm can even be frozen and stored in embryo banks for use at some future time, thereby guaranteeing healthy zygotes should age or illness lead to fertility problems.

The overall success rate of in vitro fertilization is about 35 percent. However, success declines steadily with age, from 40 percent in women younger than age 35 to 7 percent in women age 43 and older (Wright et al., 2008).

Children conceived through these methods may be genetically unrelated to one or both of their parents (if donor gametes are used). In addition, most parents who have used in vitro fertilization do not tell their children about their origins, even though health professionals usually encourage them to do so. Does lack of genetic ties or secrecy surrounding these techniques interfere with parent–child relationships? Perhaps because of a strong desire for parenthood, caregiving tends to be somewhat warmer for young children conceived through donor insemination or in vitro fertilization. And in vitro infants are as securely attached to their parents, and in vitro children and adolescents as well-adjusted, as their counterparts who were naturally conceived (Golombok & MacCallum, 2003; Golombok et al., 2004; Punamaki, 2006).

Although donor insemination and in vitro fertilization have many benefits, serious questions have arisen about their use. Most U.S. states have few legal guidelines for these procedures. As a result, donors are not always screened for genetic or sexually transmitted diseases. Furthermore, in many countries (including the United States and Canada), doctors are not required to keep records of donor characteristics (Richards, 2004). Canada does retain a file on donor identities, permitting contact only in cases of serious disease, where knowledge of the child's genetic background might have medical value (Bioethics Consultative Committee, 2003). Another concern is that the in vitro "sex sorter" method will lead to parental sex selection, thereby eroding the moral value that children of both sexes are equally precious.

Finally, about 50 percent of in vitro procedures result in multiple births. Most are twins, but 9 percent are triplets and higher-order multiples. Consequently, among in vitro babies, the rate of low birth weight is nearly three times as high as in the general population (Wright et al., 2008). Risk of major birth defects also doubles because of many factors, including drugs used to induce ripening of ova and delays in fertilizing the ova outside the womb (Machin, 2005). In sum, in vitro fertilization poses greater risks than natural conception to infant survival and healthy development.

Surrogate Motherhood

An even more controversial form of medically assisted conception is *surrogate motherhood.* Typically in this procedure, sperm from a man whose wife is infertile are used to inseminate a woman, called a surrogate, who is paid a fee for her childbearing services. In return, the surrogate agrees to turn the baby over to the man (who is the natural father). The child is then adopted by his wife.

Although most of these arrangements proceed smoothly, those that end up in court highlight serious risks for all concerned. In one case, both parties rejected the infant with severe disabilities who resulted from the pregnancy. In several others, the surrogate mother wanted to keep the baby, or the couple changed their mind during the pregnancy. These children came into the world in the midst of conflict that threatened to last for years.

Because surrogacy favors the wealthy as contractors for infants and the less economically advantaged as surrogates, it may promote

those who have had difficulties bearing children—for example, repeated miscarriages—or who know that genetic problems exist in their families. In addition, women who delay childbearing past age 35 are candidates for genetic counseling. After this time, the overall rate of chromosomal abnormalities rises sharply, from 1 in every 190 to as many as 1 in every 20 pregnancies at age 43 (Wille et al., 2004). But because younger mothers give birth in far greater numbers than older mothers, they bear the majority of babies with genetic defects. Therefore, some experts argue that maternal needs, not age, should determine referral for genetic counseling (Berkowitz, Roberts, & Minkoff, 2006).

If a family history of mental retardation, physical defects, or inherited diseases exists, the genetic counselor interviews the

exploitation of financially needy women. In addition, most surrogates already have children of their own who may be deeply affected by the pregnancy. Knowledge that their mother would give away a baby for profit may cause these youngsters to worry about the security of their own family circumstances.

New Reproductive Frontiers

Reproductive technologies are evolving faster than societies can weigh the ethics of these procedures. Doctors have used donor ova from younger women in combination with in vitro fertilization to help postmenopausal women become pregnant. Most recipients are in their forties, but several women in their fifties and sixties have given birth. These cases raise questions about bringing children into the world whose parents may not live to see them reach adulthood. Based on U.S. life expectancy data, 1 in 3 mothers and 1 in 2 fathers having a baby at age 55 will die before their child enters college (U.S. Census Bureau, 2009b).

Currently, experts are debating other reproductive options. At donor banks, customers can select ova or sperm on the basis of physical characteristics and even IQ. And scientists are devising ways to alter the DNA of human ova, sperm, and embryos to protect against hereditary disorders—techniques that could be used to engineer other desired characteristics. Many worry that these practices are a dangerous step toward selective breeding through "designer babies"—controlling offspring characteristics by manipulating genetic makeup.

Furthermore, scientists have successfully cloned (made multiple copies of) fertilized ova in sheep, cattle, and monkeys, and they are working on effective ways to do so in humans. By providing extra ova for injection, cloning might improve the success rate of in vitro fertilization. But it also opens the possibility of mass-producing genetically identical people. Therefore, it is widely condemned.

Fertility drugs and in vitro fertilization often lead to multiple fetuses. Although these sextuplets are healthy, reproductive technologies can pose grave ethical dilemmas. When two or more fetuses fill the womb, pregnancy complications may be so severe that doctors recommend aborting one or more to save the others.

Although reproductive technologies permit many barren couples to rear healthy newborn babies, laws are needed to regulate such practices. In Australia, New Zealand, Sweden, and Switzerland, individuals conceived with donated gametes have a right to information about their genetic origins (Frith, 2001). Pressure from those working in the field of assisted reproduction may soon lead to similar policies in the United States. Australia, Canada, and the Netherlands prohibit any genetic alteration of human gametes, with other nations following suit (Isasi, Nguyen, & Knoppers, 2006). But some scientists argue that this total ban is too restrictive because it interferes with serving therapeutic needs.

In the case of surrogate motherhood, the ethical problems are so complex that 18 U.S. states have sharply restricted the practice. Australia, Canada, and many European nations have banned it, arguing that the status of a baby should not be a matter of commercial arrangement and that a part of the body should not be rented or sold (Chen, 2003; McGee, 1997). Denmark, France, and Great Britain have prohibited in vitro fertilization for women past menopause (Bioethics Consultative Committee, 2003). At present, nothing is known about the psychological consequences of being a product of these procedures. Research on how such children grow up, including later-appearing medical conditions and knowledge and feelings about their origins, is important for weighing the pros and cons of these techniques.

couple and prepares a *pedigree,* a picture of the family tree in which affected relatives are identified. The pedigree is used to estimate the likelihood that parents will have an abnormal child, using the genetic principles discussed earlier in this chapter. For many disorders, blood tests or genetic analyses can reveal whether the parent is a carrier of the harmful gene. Carrier detection is possible for all of the recessive disorders listed in Table 2.3 on page 49, as well as others, and for fragile X syndrome.

When all the relevant information is in, the genetic counselor helps people consider appropriate options. These include taking a chance and conceiving, choosing from among a variety of reproductive technologies (see the Social Issues box above), or adopting a child.

Prenatal Diagnosis and Fetal Medicine

If couples who might bear an abnormal child decide to conceive, several **prenatal diagnostic methods**—medical procedures that permit detection of problems before birth—are available (see Table 2.4). Women of advanced maternal age are prime candidates for *amniocentesis* or *chorionic villus sampling* (see Figure 2.5). Except for *maternal blood analysis,* however, prenatal diagnosis should not be used routinely because other methods pose some risk of injury to the developing organism.

Prenatal diagnosis has led to advances in fetal medicine. For example, by inserting a needle into the uterus, doctors can administer drugs to the fetus. Surgery has been performed to repair such problems as heart, lung, and diaphragm malformations, urinary tract obstructions, and neural defects (Kunisaki & Jennings, 2008). Fetuses with blood disorders have been given blood transfusions. And those with immune deficiencies have received bone marrow transplants that succeeded in creating a normally functioning immune system (Williams, 2006).

These techniques frequently result in complications, the most common being premature labor and miscarriage (Flake, 2003). Yet parents may be willing to try almost any option, even one with only a slim chance of success. Currently, the medical profession is struggling with how to help parents make informed decisions about fetal surgery.

Advances in *genetic engineering* also offer hope for correcting hereditary defects. As part of the Human Genome Project—an ambitious international research program aimed at deciphering the chemical makeup of human genetic material (genome)—researchers have mapped the sequence of all human DNA base pairs. Using that information, they are "annotating" the genome—identifying all its genes and their functions, including their protein products and what they do. A major goal is to understand the estimated 4,000 human disorders, those due to single genes and those resulting from a complex interplay of multiple genes and environmental factors.

Already, thousands of genes have been identified, including those involved in hundreds of diseases, such as cystic fibrosis; Duchenne muscular dystrophy; Huntington disease; Marfan

■ TABLE 2.4 ■ *Prenatal Diagnostic Methods*

METHOD	DESCRIPTION
Amniocentesis	The most widely used technique. A hollow needle is inserted through the abdominal wall to obtain a sample of fluid in the uterus. Cells are examined for genetic defects. Can be performed by the 14th week after conception; 1 to 2 more weeks are required for test results. Small risk of miscarriage.
Chorionic villus sampling	A procedure that can be used if results are desired or needed very early in pregnancy. A thin tube is inserted into the uterus through the vagina, or a hollow needle is inserted through the abdominal wall. A small plug of tissue is removed from the end of one or more chorionic villi, the hairlike projections on the membrane surrounding the developing organism. Cells are examined for genetic defects. Can be performed at 9 weeks after conception; results are available within 24 hours. Entails a slightly greater risk of miscarriage than amniocentesis. Also associated with a small risk of limb deformities, which increases the earlier the procedure is performed.
Fetoscopy	A small tube with a light source at one end is inserted into the uterus to inspect the fetus for defects of the limbs and face. Also allows a sample of fetal blood to be obtained, permitting diagnosis of such disorders as hemophilia and sickle cell anemia, as well as neural defects (see below). Usually performed between 15 and 18 weeks after conception but can be done as early as 5 weeks. Entails some risk of miscarriage.
Ultrasound	High-frequency sound waves are beamed at the uterus; their reflection is translated into a picture on a video screen that reveals the size, shape, and placement of the fetus. By itself, permits assessment of fetal age, detection of multiple pregnancies, and identification of gross physical defects. Also used to guide amniocentesis, chorionic villus sampling, and fetoscopy. When used five or more times, may increase the chances of low birth weight.
Maternal blood analysis	By the second month of pregnancy, some of the developing organism's cells enter the maternal bloodstream. An elevated level of alpha-fetoprotein may indicate kidney disease, abnormal closure of the esophagus, or neural tube defects, such as anencephaly (absence of most of the brain) and spina bifida (bulging of the spinal cord from the spinal column). Isolated cells can be examined for genetic defects.
Preimplantation genetic diagnosis	After in vitro fertilization and duplication of the zygote into a cluster of about 8 to 10 cells, 1 or 2 cells are removed and examined for hereditary defects. Only if that sample is free of detectable genetic disorders is the fertilized ovum implanted in the woman's uterus.

Sources: Bianchi, 2005; Kumar & O'Brien, 2004; Moore & Persaud, 2008; Sermon, Van Steirteghem, & Liebaers, 2004.

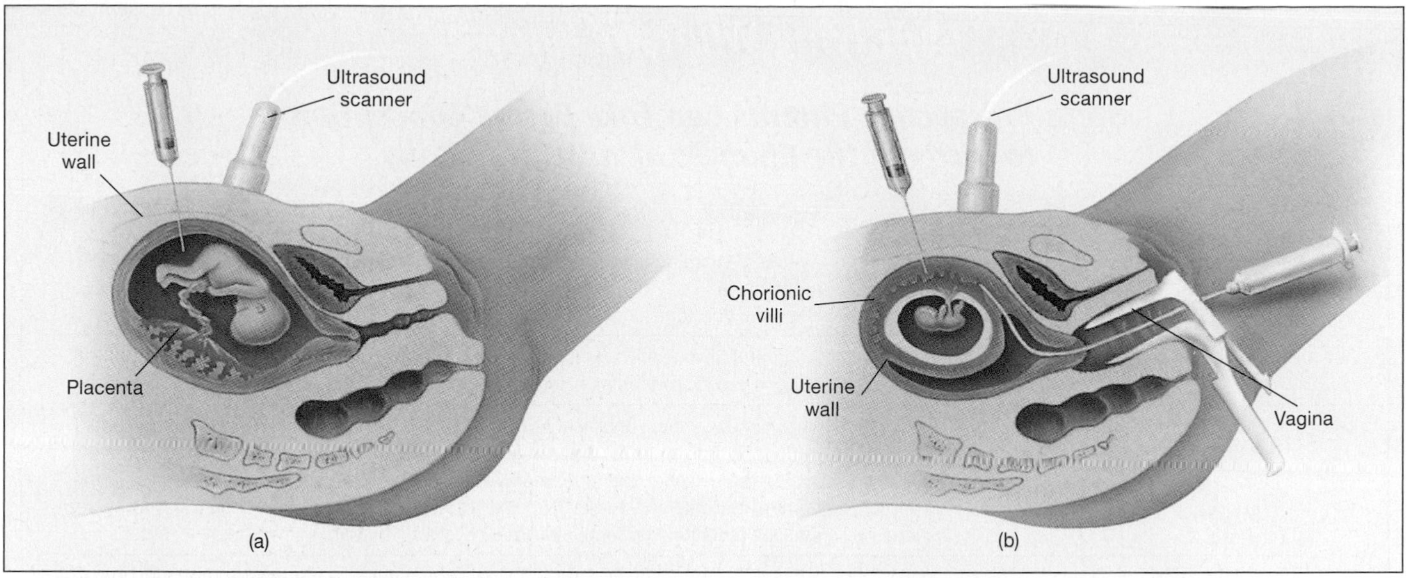

■ **FIGURE 2.5** ■ **Amniocentesis and chorionic villus sampling.** Today, hundreds of defects and diseases can be detected before birth using these two procedures. (a) In amniocentesis, a hollow needle is inserted through the abdominal wall into the uterus during the fourteenth week after conception, or later. Fluid is withdrawn, and fetal cells are cultured, a process that takes one to two weeks. (b) Chorionic villus sampling can be performed much earlier in pregnancy, at nine weeks after conception, and results are available within 24 hours. Two approaches to obtaining a sample of chorionic villus are shown: inserting a thin tube through the vagina into the uterus and inserting a needle through the abdominal wall. In both amniocentesis and chorionic villus sampling, an ultrasound scanner is used for guidance. (Adapted from *Before We Are Born, 7th ed.* by K. L. Moore and T. V. N. Persaud, p. 69. Copyright © 2008, reprinted with permission from Elsevier, Inc.)

syndrome; heart, digestive, blood, eye, and nervous system abnormalities; and many forms of cancer (National Institutes of Health, 2008). As a result, new treatments are being explored, such as *gene therapy*—correcting genetic abnormalities by delivering DNA carrying a functional gene to the cells. In recent experiments, gene therapy relieved symptoms in hemophilia patients and in patients with severe immune system dysfunction. A few, however, experienced serious side effects (Anson & Fletcher, 2007). In another approach, called *proteomics*, scientists modify gene-specified proteins involved in biological aging and disease (Bradshaw & Burlingame, 2005).

Genetic treatments seem some distance in the future for most single-gene defects, however, and even farther off for diseases involving multiple genes that combine in complex ways with one another and the environment. Applying What We Know on page 58 summarizes steps that prospective parents can take before conception to protect the genetic health of their child.

Adoption

Adults who are infertile, who are likely to pass along a genetic disorder, or who are older and single but want a family are turning to adoption in increasing numbers. Those who have children by birth, too, sometimes choose to expand their families through adoption. Adoption agencies try to ensure a good fit by seeking parents of the same ethnic and religious background as the child and, where possible, trying to choose parents who are the same age as typical biological parents. Because the availability of

This mother sings while delivering medication through a nebulizer to her 2-year-old daughter, who has cystic fibrosis. The girl also wears a vest for a twice-daily treatment that pounds her chest to clear her lungs of thick mucus. In the future, such children may benefit from the discovery of gene-based treatments for hereditary disorders.

Applying What We Know

Steps Prospective Parents Can Take Before Conception to Increase the Chances of a Healthy Baby

Recommendation	Explanation
Arrange for a physical exam.	A physical exam before conception permits detection of diseases and other medical problems that might reduce fertility, be difficult to treat after the onset of pregnancy, or affect the developing organism.
Consider your genetic makeup.	Find out if anyone in your family has had a child with a genetic disease or disability. If so, seek genetic counseling before conception.
Reduce or eliminate toxins under your control.	Since the developing organism is highly sensitive to damaging environmental agents during the early weeks of pregnancy (see Chapter 3), couples trying to conceive should avoid drugs, alcohol, cigarette smoke, radiation, pollution, chemical substances in the home and workplace, and infectious diseases. Furthermore, they should stay away from ionizing radiation and some industrial chemicals that are known to cause mutations.
Ensure proper nutrition.	A doctor-recommended vitamin–mineral supplement, begun before conception, helps prevent many prenatal problems. It should include folic acid, which reduces the chances of neural tube defects, prematurity, and low birth weight (see Chapter 3, page 93).
Consult your doctor after 12 months of unsuccessful efforts at conception.	Long periods of infertility may be due to undiagnosed spontaneous abortions, which can be caused by genetic defects in either partner. If a physical exam reveals a healthy reproductive system, seek genetic counseling.

healthy babies has declined (fewer young unwed mothers give up their babies than in the past), more people in North America and Western Europe are adopting from other countries or accepting children who are past infancy or who have known developmental problems (Schweiger & O'Brien, 2005).

Adopted children and adolescents—whether or not they are born in their adoptive parents' country—have more learning and emotional difficulties than other children, a difference that increases with the child's age at time of adoption (Brodzinsky & Pinderhughes, 2002; Nickman et al., 2005; van IJzendoorn, Juffer, & Poelhuis, 2005). There are many possible reasons for adoptees' more problematic childhoods. The biological mother may have been unable to care for the child because of problems believed to be partly genetic, such as alcoholism or severe depression, and may have passed this tendency to her offspring. Or perhaps she experienced stress, poor diet, or inadequate medical care during pregnancy—factors that can affect the child (as we will see in Chapter 3). Furthermore, children adopted after infancy often have a preadoptive history of conflict-ridden family relationships, lack of parental affection, neglect and abuse, or deprived institutional rearing. Finally, adoptive parents and children, who are genetically unrelated, are less alike in intelligence and personality than are biological relatives—differences that may threaten family harmony.

Despite these risks, most adopted children fare well, and those with preexisting problems usually make rapid progress (Bimmel et al., 2003; Johnson, 2002). In a study of internationally adopted children in the Netherlands, sensitive maternal care and secure attachment in infancy predicted cognitive and social competence at age 7 (Stams, Juffer, & van IJzendoorn, 2002).

Overall, international adoptees fare much better in development than birth siblings or institutionalized agemates who stay behind. By middle childhood, those who were adopted in infancy have mental test scores resembling those of their nonbiological siblings and school classmates, although they tend to achieve less well in school, to have more learning problems that require special treatment, and to be slightly delayed in language skills (van IJzendoorn, Juffer, & Poelhuis, 2005). Children adopted at older ages develop feelings of trust and affection for their adoptive parents as they come to feel loved and supported in their new families (Veríssimo & Salvaterra, 2006). As we will see in Chapter 4, however, later-adopted children are more likely than their agemates to have persistent cognitive, emotional, and social problems.

By adolescence, adoptees' lives are often complicated by unresolved curiosity about their roots. Some have difficulty accepting the possibility that they may never know their birth parents. Others worry about what they would do if their birth parents suddenly reappeared. Nevertheless, the decision to search for birth parents is usually postponed until early adulthood, when marriage and childbirth may trigger it. Despite concerns about their origins, most adoptees appear well-adjusted as adults. And as long as their parents took steps to help them learn about their heritage in childhood, young people adopted into a different ethnic group or culture generally develop identities that are healthy blends of their birth and rearing backgrounds (Nickman et al., 2005; Thomas & Tessler, 2007).

As we conclude our discussion of reproductive choices, perhaps you are wondering how things turned out for Ted and Marianne. Through genetic counseling, Marianne discovered a history of Tay-Sachs disease on her mother's side of the family. Ted had a distant cousin who died of the disorder. The genetic counselor explained that the chances of giving birth to another affected baby were 1 in 4. Ted and Marianne took the risk. Their son Douglas is now 12 years old. Although Douglas is a carrier of the recessive allele, he is a normal, healthy boy. In a few years, Ted and Marianne will tell Douglas about his genetic history and explain the importance of seeking genetic counseling before he has children of his own.

ASK YOURSELF

» REVIEW
Why is genetic counseling called a *communication process?* Who should seek it?

» APPLY
Imagine that you must counsel a couple considering in vitro fertilization using the wife's ova and sperm from an anonymous man to overcome the husband's infertility. What medical and ethical risks would you raise?

» CONNECT
How does research on adoption reveal resilience? Which factor related to resilience (see Chapter 1, pages 10–11) is central in positive outcomes for adoptees?

» REFLECT
Imagine that you are a woman who is a carrier of fragile X syndrome but who wants to have children. Would you become pregnant, adopt, use a surrogate mother, or give up your desire for parenthood? If you became pregnant, would you seek prenatal diagnosis? Explain your decisions.

Environmental Contexts for Development

Just as complex as genetic inheritance is the surrounding environment—a many-layered set of influences that combine to help or hinder physical and psychological well-being. ***TAKE A MOMENT...*** Think back to your childhood, and jot down a brief description of events and people that you believe significantly influenced your development. Next, do the same for your adult life. Do the items on your list resemble those of my students, who mostly mention experiences that involve their families? This emphasis is not surprising, since the family is the first and longest-lasting context for development. Other influences that make the top ten are friends, neighbors, school, workplace, and community and religious organizations.

Return to Bronfenbrenner's ecological systems theory, discussed in Chapter 1. It emphasizes that environments extending beyond the *microsystem*—the immediate settings just mentioned—powerfully affect development. Indeed, my students rarely mention one important context. Its impact is so pervasive that we seldom stop to think about it in our daily lives. This is the *macrosystem,* or broad social climate of society—its values and programs that support and protect human development. All people need help with the demands of each period of the lifespan—through affordable housing and health care, safe neighborhoods, good schools, well-equipped recreational facilities, and high-quality child care and other services that permit them to meet both work and family responsibilities. And some people, because of poverty or special tragedies, need considerably more help than others.

In the following sections, we take up these contexts for development. Because they affect every age and aspect of change, we will return to them in later chapters. For now, our discussion emphasizes that environments, as well as heredity, can enhance or create risks for development.

The Family

In power and breadth of influence, no other context equals the family. The family creates bonds among people that are unique. Attachments to parents and siblings usually last a lifetime and serve as models for relationships in the wider world of neighborhood, school, and community. Within the family, children learn the language, skills, and social and moral values of their culture. And at all ages, people turn to family members for information, assistance, and pleasurable interaction. Warm, gratifying family ties predict physical and psychological health throughout development. In contrast, isolation or alienation from the family is often associated with developmental problems (Deković & Buist, 2005; Parke & Buriel, 2006).

Contemporary researchers view the family as a *social system,* or network of interdependent relationships (Bronfenbrenner & Morris, 2006; Lerner et al., 2002). Recall from ecological systems theory that *bidirectional influences* exist in which the behaviors of each family member affect those of others. Indeed, the very term *system* implies that the responses of family members are related. These system influences operate both directly and indirectly.

■ DIRECT INFLUENCES. The next time you have a chance to observe family members interacting, watch carefully. You are likely to see that kind, patient communication evokes cooperative, harmonious responses, whereas harshness and impatience engender angry, resistive behavior. Each of these reactions, in turn, forges a new link in the interactive chain. In the first instance, a positive message tends to follow; in the second, a negative or avoidant one is likely.

These observations fit with a wealth of research on the family system. Many studies show that when parents' requests are firm but made with warmth and affection, children tend to

© ATEF HASSAN/REUTERS/CORBIS

An Iraqi family shares a morning meal before a dawn-to-dusk fast during the Muslim holy month of Ramadan. The family is a complex system of interdependent relationships in which each person's behavior influences the behavior of others, both directly and indirectly.

cooperate. And when children willingly comply, their parents are likely to be warm and gentle in the future. In contrast, children whose parents discipline with harshness and impatience are likely to refuse and rebel. And because children's misbehavior is stressful for parents, they may increase their use of punishment, leading to more unruliness by the child (Stormshak et al., 2000; Whiteside-Mansell et al., 2003). This principle also applies to other two-person family relationships—siblings, marital partners, parent and adult child. In each case, the behavior of one family member helps sustain a form of interaction in the other that either promotes or undermines psychological well-being.

■ **INDIRECT INFLUENCES.** The impact of family relationships on development becomes even more complicated when we consider that interaction between any two members is affected by others present in the setting. Bronfenbrenner calls these indirect influences the effect of *third parties.*

Third parties can serve as supports for or barriers to development. For example, parents who have a warm, considerate marital relationship praise and stimulate their children more. In contrast, parents whose marriage is tense and hostile tend to be less responsive to their children's needs and more likely to criticize, express anger, and punish (Cox, Paley, & Harter, 2001; McHale et al., 2002). Children chronically exposed to angry, unresolved parental conflict have serious emotional problems (Harold et al., 2004). These include both *internalizing difficulties* (especially among girls), such as feeling worried and afraid and trying to repair their parents' relationship, and *externalizing difficulties* (especially among boys), including verbal and physical aggression (Davies & Lindsay, 2004). These child problems can further disrupt parents' marital relationship.

Yet even when third parties strain family ties, other members may help restore effective interaction. Grandparents, for example, can promote children's development both directly, by responding warmly to the child, and indirectly, by providing parents with child-rearing advice, models of child-rearing skill, and even financial assistance. Of course, as with any indirect influence, grandparents can sometimes be harmful. When quarrelsome relations exist between grandparents and parents, parent–child communication may suffer.

■ **ADAPTING TO CHANGE.** Think back to the *chronosystem* in Bronfenbrenner's theory (see page 26 in Chapter 1). The interplay of forces within the family is dynamic and ever-changing. Important events, such as the birth of a baby, a change of jobs, or the addition to the household of an elderly parent in declining health, create challenges that modify existing relationships. The way such events affect family interaction depends on the support other family members provide and on the developmental status of each participant. For example, the arrival of a new baby prompts very different reactions in a toddler than in a school-age child. And caring for an ill elderly parent is more stressful for a middle-aged adult still rearing young children than for an adult of the same age who has no child-rearing responsibilities.

Historical time period also contributes to a dynamic family system. In recent decades, a declining birth rate, a high divorce rate, and expansion of women's roles have led to a smaller family size. This, combined with a longer lifespan, means that more generations are alive, with fewer members in the youngest ones, leading to a "top-heavy" family structure. Young people today are more likely to have older relatives than at any time in history—a circumstance that can be enriching as well as a source of tension. In sum, as this complex intergenerational system moves through time, relationships are constantly revised as members adjust to their own and others' development as well as to external pressures.

Despite these variations, some general patterns in family functioning do exist. In the United States and other Western nations, one important source of these consistencies is socioeconomic status.

Socioeconomic Status and Family Functioning

People in industrialized nations are stratified on the basis of what they do at work and how much they earn for doing it—factors that determine their social position and economic well-being. Researchers assess a family's standing on this continuum through an index called **socioeconomic status (SES),** which combines three related, but not completely overlapping, variables: (1) years of education and (2) the prestige of one's job and the skill it requires, both of which measure social status; and (3) income, which measures economic status. As SES rises and falls, people face changing circumstances that profoundly affect family functioning.

SES affects the timing and duration of phases of the family life cycle. People who work in skilled and semiskilled manual occupations (for example, construction workers, truck drivers, and custodians) tend to marry and have children earlier as well as give birth to more children than people in professional and technical occupations. The two groups also differ in values and expectations. For example, when asked about personal qualities they desire for their children, lower-SES parents tend to emphasize external characteristics, such as obedience, politeness, neatness, and cleanliness. In contrast, higher-SES parents emphasize psychological traits, such as curiosity, happiness, self-direction, and cognitive and social maturity (Duncan & Magnuson, 2003; Hoff, Laursen, & Tardif, 2002; Tudge et al., 2000).

These differences are reflected in family interaction. Parents higher in SES talk to, read to, and otherwise stimulate their infants and preschoolers more. When their children are older, higher-SES parents use more warmth, explanations, and verbal praise. Commands ("You do that because I told you to"), criticism, and physical punishment all occur more often in low-SES households (Bradley & Corwyn, 2003).

Education contributes substantially to these variations in child rearing. Higher-SES parents' interest in providing verbal stimulation and nurturing inner traits is supported by years of schooling, during which they learned to think about abstract, subjective ideas. In diverse cultures around the world, as the Lifespan Vista box on page 62 makes clear, education of women in particular fosters patterns of thinking that greatly improve quality of life, for both parents and children.

Because of limited education and low social status, many lower-SES parents feel a sense of powerlessness and lack of influence in their relationships beyond the home. At work, for example, they must obey rules of others in positions of power and authority. When they get home, their parent–child interaction seems to duplicate these experiences—but now they are in authority. Higher levels of stress combined with a stronger belief in the value of physical punishment contribute to low-SES parents' greater use of coercive discipline (Conger & Donnellan, 2007; Pinderhughes et al., 2000). Higher-SES parents, in contrast, typically have more control over their own lives. At work, they are used to making independent decisions and convincing others of their point of view. At home, they teach these skills to their children (Greenberger, O'Neil, & Nagel, 1994).

Affluence

Despite advanced education and great material wealth, affluent parents—those in highly prestigious occupations with six-figure annual incomes—too often fail to engage in family interaction and parenting that promote favorable development. In several studies, researchers tracked the adjustment of youths growing up in wealthy suburbs (Luthar & Latendresse, 2005a). By seventh grade, many showed serious problems that worsened in high school. Their school grades were poor, and they were more likely to engage in alcohol and drug use and to report high levels of anxiety and depression than low-SES youths (Luthar & Becker, 2002). Furthermore, among affluent (but not low-SES) teenagers, substance use was correlated with anxiety and depression, suggesting that wealthy youths took drugs to self-medicate—a practice that predicts persistent abuse (Luthar & Sexton, 2004).

Why are so many affluent youths troubled? Compared to their better-adjusted counterparts, poorly adjusted affluent young people report less emotional closeness and supervision from their parents, who lead professionally and socially demanding lives. As a group, wealthy parents are nearly as physically and emotionally unavailable to their youngsters as parents coping with serious financial strain. At the same time, these parents often make excessive demands for achievement (Luthar & Becker, 2002). Adolescents whose parents value their accomplishments more than their character are more likely to have academic and emotional problems.

For both affluent and low-SES youths, a simple routine—eating dinner with parents—is associated with a reduction in adjustment difficulties, even after many other aspects of parenting are controlled (see Figure 2.6) (Luthar & Latendresse, 2005b). Interventions that make wealthy parents aware of the high costs of a competitive, overscheduled lifestyle and minimal family time are badly needed.

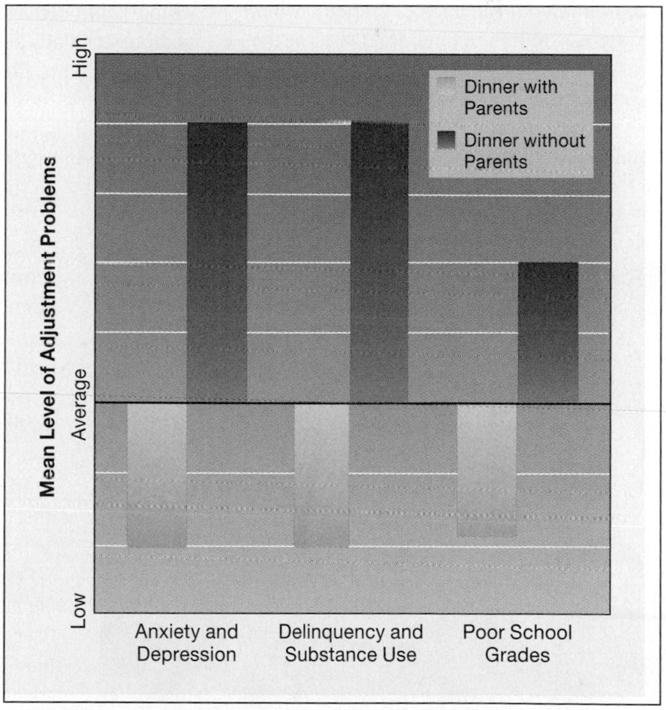

■ **FIGURE 2.6** ■ **Relationship of regularly eating dinner with parents to affluent youths' adjustment problems.** Compared with sixth graders who often ate dinner with their parents, those who rarely did so were far more likely to display anxiety and depression, delinquency and substance use, and poor school grades, even after many other aspects of parenting were controlled. In this study, frequent family mealtimes also protected low-SES youths from delinquency and substance use and from classroom learning problems. (Adapted from Luthar & Latendresse, 2005b.)

A LIFESPAN VISTA: Looking Forward, Looking Back

Worldwide Education of Girls: Transforming Current and Future Generations

When a new school opened in the Egyptian village of Beni Shara'an, some villagers complained that the school would deprive them of their children's help in the wheat fields and small businesses. Ahmen, an illiterate shopkeeper, heard an elderly merchant, who had donated space for the school, say, "I have come to believe that a girl's education is even more important than a boy's." Immediately, Ahmen enrolled his 8-year-old daughter Rawia (Bellamy, 2004, p. 19). Until that day, Rawia had divided her days between backbreaking farming and confinement to her home.

Before long, Rawia's advancing language, literacy, and reasoning skills transformed her family's quality of life. "My store accounts were in a mess, but soon Rawia started straightening out the books," Ahmen recalled. She also began helping her older sister learn to read and write and explaining to her family the instructions on prescription medicines and the news on television. In addition, Rawia began to envision a better life for herself.

AP IMAGES/JOHN McCONNICO

For these girls huddling in an open-air class in a village in Pakistan, attending school will dramatically improve their life opportunities and their nation's welfare. In both developed and developing nations, educating girls leads to gains in family income and relationships that carry over to improved health, education, and economic well-being in the next generation.

"When I grow up," she told her father, "I want to be a doctor. Or maybe a teacher."

Over the past century, the percentage of children in the developing world who go to school has increased from a small minority of boys to a majority of all children in most regions. Still, some 73 million children, most of them poverty-stricken girls, do not start elementary school, and more than 200 million, again mostly girls, do not go to secondary school (UNICEF, 2006).

Although schooling is vital for all children, educating girls has an especially powerful impact on the welfare of families, societies, and future generations. The diverse benefits of girls' schooling largely accrue in two ways: (1) through enhanced verbal skills—reading, writing, and oral communication; and (2) through empowerment—a growing desire to improve their life conditions. In studies carried out on three continents, in three cultures, and in three community settings—rural Nepal, a small Mexican town, and a large city in Zambia—the more education women obtained, the better their language and literacy skills and the higher their aspirations for a better life. Their knowledge and attitudes, in turn, dramatically influenced family health, relationships, and parenting (LeVine, LeVine, & Schnell, 2001).

Family Health

Education gives people the communicative skills and confidence to seek health services and to benefit from public health information. As a result, years of schooling strongly predicts women's preventive health behavior: prenatal visits, child immunizations, healthy diet, and sanitary practices (LeVine et al., 2004; Peña, Wall, & Person, 2000). In addition, because educated women have more life opportunities, they are more likely to take advantage of family planning services, delay marriage and childbearing, and have more widely spaced and fewer children (Stromquist, 2007). All these practices are linked to increased maternal and child survival and family health.

Family Relationships and Parenting

In developed and developing nations alike, the empowerment that springs from education is associated with more equitable husband–wife relationships and a reduction in harsh disciplining of children (LeVine et al., 1991; LeVine, LeVine, & Schnell, 2001). Also, educated mothers engage in more verbal stimulation and teaching of literacy skills to their children, which fosters success in school, higher educational attainment, reduced crime rates, and economic gains in the next generation. Regions of the world that have invested more in girls' education, such as southeast Asia and Latin America, tend to have higher levels of economic development (King & Mason, 2001).

Donor nations and international organizations are increasingly coming to the same conclusion: The education of girls is the most effective means of combating the most profound, global threats to human development: poverty, maternal and child mortality, and disease (Bellamy, 2004; Herz, 2004). As a result, the United Nations is encouraging all developing nations to make education a high priority and to take special steps to enable girls to go to school.

Rawia got the chance to go to school because of an Egyptian national initiative, which led to the establishment of several thousand one-classroom schools in rural areas with the poorest record in educating girls. Because of cultural beliefs about gender roles or reluctance to give up a daughter's work at home, parents sometimes resist. But the largest barrier is that many countries continue to charge parents a fee for each child enrolled in school, often amounting to nearly one-third of the income of poverty-stricken families. Under these conditions, parents—if they send any children—tend to send only sons.

In 2003, Kenya eliminated fees for primary school. Immediately, enrollments of both boys and girls surged—by more than 30 percent. Uganda followed suit, increasing its primary school enrollment by 70 percent (Alter, 2008; RESULTS, 2006). When governments abolish enrollment fees, provide information about the benefits of education for girls, and create employment possibilities for women, the overwhelming majority of parents—including the very poor—choose to send their daughters to school, and some make great sacrifices to do so.

Poverty

When families slip into poverty, development is seriously threatened. Consider the case of Zinnia Mae, who grew up in a close-knit black community located in a small southeastern American city (Heath, 1990). As unemployment struck in the 1980s and citizens moved away, 16-year-old Zinnia Mae caught a ride to Atlanta. Two years later, she was the mother of a daughter and twin boys, and she had moved into a high-rise in public housing.

Zinnia Mae worried constantly about scraping together enough money to put food on the table, finding baby-sitters so she could go to the laundry or grocery, freeing herself from a cycle of rising debt, and finding the twins' father, who had stopped sending money. Her most frequent words were "I'm so tired." The children had only one set meal—breakfast; otherwise, they ate whenever they were hungry or bored. Their play space was limited to the living room sofa and a mattress on the floor. Toys consisted of scraps of a blanket, spoons and food cartons, a small rubber ball, a few plastic cars, and a roller skate abandoned in the building. At the researcher's request, Zinnia Mae agreed to tape record her interactions with her children. Cut off from family and community ties and overwhelmed by financial strain and feelings of helplessness, she found herself unable to join in activities with her children. In 500 hours of tape, she started a conversation with them only 18 times.

Although poverty rates in the United States declined slightly in the 1990s, in recent years they have risen. Today, about 13 percent—nearly 40 million Americans—are affected. Those hit hardest are parents under age 25 with young children and elderly people who live alone. Poverty is also magnified among ethnic minorities and women. For example, 19 percent of U.S. children are poor, a rate that climbs to 30 percent for Hispanic children, 32 percent for Native-American children, and 34 percent for African-American children. For single mothers with preschool children and elderly women on their own, the poverty rate is close to 50 percent (DeNavas-Walt, Proctor, & Smith, 2009).

Joblessness, a high divorce rate, a lower remarriage rate among women than men, widowhood, and (as we will see later) inadequate government programs to meet family needs are responsible for these disheartening statistics. The poverty rate is higher among children than any other age group. And of all Western nations, the United States has the highest percentage of extremely poor children. Nearly 8 percent of U.S. children live in deep poverty (at less than half the poverty threshold, the income level judged necessary for a minimum living standard). In contrast, in Denmark, Finland, Norway, and Sweden, child poverty rates have remained at 5 percent or less for two decades, and deep child poverty is rare (UNICEF, 2005). The earlier poverty begins, the deeper it is, and the longer it lasts, the more devastating are its effects. Children of poverty are more likely than other children to suffer from lifelong poor physical health, persistent deficits in cognitive development and academic achievement, high school dropout, mental illness, and antisocial behavior (Aber, Jones, & Raver, 2007; Dearing, McCartney, & Taylor, 2006; Ryan, Fauth, & Brooks-Gunn, 2006).

The constant stressors that accompany poverty gradually weaken the family system. Poor families have many daily hassles—bills to pay, the car breaking down, loss of welfare and unemployment payments, something stolen from the house, to name just a few. When daily crises arise, family members become depressed, irritable, and distracted, and hostile interactions increase (Conger & Donnellan, 2007; Evans, 2006). Negative outcomes are especially severe in single-parent families and families that must live in poor housing and dangerous neighborhoods—conditions that make everyday existence even more difficult, while reducing social supports that help people cope with economic hardship (Leventhal & Brooks-Gunn, 2003).

Besides poverty, another problem—one that has become more common in the past 30 years—has reduced the life chances of many children and adults. On any given night, approximately 350,000 people in the United States have no place to live. The majority are adults on their own, many of whom suffer from serious mental illness. But 23 percent of the homeless are families with children (National Coalition for the Homeless, 2008). The rise in homelessness is mostly due to two factors: a decline in the availability of government-supported, low-cost housing and the release of large numbers of mentally ill people from institutions, without an increase in community treatment programs to help them adjust to ordinary life and get better.

Most homeless families consist of women with children under age 5. Besides health problems (which affect the majority of homeless people), many homeless children suffer from developmental delays and chronic emotional stress due to their harsh, insecure daily lives (Bratt, 2002; Pardeck, 2005). An estimated 25 to 30 percent who are old enough do not attend school. Those who do enroll achieve less well than other poverty-stricken children because of poor attendance and health and emotional difficulties (Shinn et al., 2008).

Beyond the Family: Neighborhoods, Towns, and Cities

As the concepts of *mesosystem* and *exosystem* in ecological systems theory make clear, connections between family and community are vital for psychological well-being. From our discussion of poverty, perhaps you can see why: In poverty-stricken urban areas, community life is usually disrupted. Families move often, parks and playgrounds are in disarray, and community centers providing organized leisure time activities do not exist. In such neighborhoods, family violence, child abuse and neglect, children's problem behavior, youth antisocial activity, and adult criminal behavior are especially high

A boy hugs his mother as they wait to board a bus that will take them away from Galveston, Texas, following Hurricane Ike, which in 2008 left a massive path of destruction on the island. For low-income families, dislocation caused by a natural disaster is especially likely to result in long-term homelessness, poverty, and emotional stress.

(Brody et al., 2003; Kohen et al., 2002). In contrast, strong family ties to the surrounding social context—as indicated by frequent contact with friends and relatives and regular church, synagogue, or mosque attendance—reduce family stress and enhance adjustment (Boardman, 2004; Leventhal & Brooks-Gunn, 2003).

NEIGHBORHOODS. Let's look closely at the functions of communities in the lives of children and adults by beginning with the neighborhood. What were your childhood experiences like in the yards, streets, and parks surrounding your home? How did you spend your time, whom did you get to know, and how important were these moments to you?

Neighborhoods offer resources and social ties that play an important part in children's development. In several studies, low-SES families were randomly assigned vouchers to move out of public housing into neighborhoods varying widely in affluence. Compared with their peers who remained in poverty-stricken areas, children and youths who moved into low-poverty neighborhoods showed substantially better physical and mental health and school achievement (Goering, 2003; Leventhal & Brooks-Gunn, 2003).

Neighborhood resources have a greater impact on economically disadvantaged than well-to-do young people. Higher-SES families are less dependent on their immediate surroundings for social support, education, and leisure pursuits. They can afford to reach beyond the streets near their homes, transporting their children to lessons and entertainment and, if necessary, to better-quality schools in distant parts of the community. In low-income neighborhoods, in-school and after-school programs that substitute for lack of resources by providing enrichment activities are associated with improved academic performance and a reduction in emotional and behavior problems in middle childhood (Peters, Petrunka, & Arnold, 2003; Vandell & Posner, 1999). Neighborhood organizations and informal social activities predict favorable development in adolescence, including increased self-confidence, school achievement, and educational aspirations (Barnes et al., 2007; Gonzales et al., 1996).

The Better Beginnings, Better Futures Project of Ontario, Canada, is a government-sponsored set of pilot programs aimed at preventing the dire consequences of neighborhood poverty, including child and adolescent internalizing and externalizing difficulties, antisocial activity, school failure, and high school dropout (Gershoff & Aber, 2006). The most successful of these efforts, using a local elementary school as its base, provided children with in-class and summer enrichment activities. Project staff also visited each child's parents regularly, informed them about community resources, and encouraged their involvement in the child's school and neighborhood life (Peters, 2005; Peters, Petrunka, & Arnold, 2003). An evaluation after four years revealed gains in neighborhood satisfaction, family functioning, effective parenting, and children's reading skills, along with a reduction in emotional and behavior problems.

As these outcomes suggest, neighborhoods also affect adults' well-being. An employed parent who can rely on a neighbor to assist her school-age child in her absence and who lives in an area safe for walking to and from school gains the peace of mind essential for productive work. In low-SES areas with high resident stability and social cohesion, where neighbors collaborate in keeping the environment clean and watching out for vandalism and other crimes, adults report less stress, which in turn predicts substantially better physical health (Boardman, 2004; Feldman & Steptoe, 2004).

During late adulthood, neighborhoods become increasingly important because people spend more time in their homes. Despite the availability of planned housing for elders, about 90 percent remain in regular housing, usually in the same neighborhood where they lived during their working lives (U.S. Census Bureau, 2009b). Proximity to relatives and friends is a significant factor in the decision to move or stay put late in life. In the absence of nearby family members, the elderly mention neighbors and nearby friends as resources they rely on most for physical and social support (Hooyman & Kiyak, 2008).

TOWNS AND CITIES. Neighborhoods are embedded in towns and cities, which also mold children's and adults' daily lives. In rural areas and small towns, children and youths are more likely to be given important work tasks—caring for live-

AP IMAGES/MUSCATINE JOURNAL, CONNIE STREET

At a block party in an inner-city neighborhood, children participate in a doughnut-eating contest while their parents look on with amusement. According to the social systems perspective, ties to the community are essential for families to function at their best.

stock, operating the snowplow, or playing in the town band. They usually perform these tasks alongside adults, who instill in them a strong sense of responsibility and teach them practical and social skills needed to sustain their community. Compared with large urban areas, small towns also offer stronger connections between settings that influence children's lives. For example, because most citizens know each other and schools serve as centers of community life, contact between teachers and parents occurs often—an important factor in promoting children's academic achievement (Hill & Taylor, 2004).

Adults in small towns participate in more civic groups, such as school board or volunteer fire brigade. And they are more likely to occupy positions of leadership because a greater proportion of residents are needed to meet community needs (Elder & Conger, 2000). In late adulthood, people residing in small towns and suburbs have neighbors who are more willing to provide assistance. As a result, they form a greater number of warm relationships with nonrelatives. As one 99-year-old resident of a small Midwestern community, living alone and leading an active life, commented, "I don't think I could get along if I didn't have good neighbors." The family next door helps him with grocery shopping, checks each night to make sure his basement light is off (the signal that he is out of the shower and into bed), and looks out in the morning to see that his garage door is raised (the signal that he is up and OK) (Fergus, 1995).

Of course, small-town residents cannot visit museums, go to professional baseball games, or attend orchestra concerts on a regular basis. The variety of settings is not as great as in a large city. In small towns, however, active involvement in the community is likely to be greater throughout the lifespan. Also, public places in small towns are relatively safe and secure. Responsible adults are present in almost all settings to keep an eye on children. And the elderly feel safer—a strong contributor to how satisfied they are with their place of residence (Parmelee & Lawton, 1990; Shields et al., 2002). These conditions are hard to match in today's urban environments.

The Cultural Context

Our discussion in Chapter 1 emphasized that human development can be fully understood only when viewed in its larger cultural context. In the following sections, we expand on this theme by taking up the role of the *macrosystem* in development. First, we discuss ways that cultural values and practices affect environmental contexts for development. Second, we consider how healthy development depends on laws and government programs that shield people from harm and foster their well-being.

■ **CULTURAL VALUES AND PRACTICES.** Cultures shape family interaction and community settings beyond the home—in short, all aspects of daily life. Many of us remain blind to aspects of our own cultural heritage until we see them in relation to the practices of others.

TAKE A MOMENT... Consider the question, Who should be responsible for rearing young children? How would you answer it? Here are some typical responses from my students: "If parents decide to have a baby, then they should be ready to care for it." "Most people are not happy about others intruding into family life." These statements reflect a widely held opinion in the United States—that the care and rearing of children, and paying for that care, are the duty of parents, and only parents. This view has a long history—one in which independence, self-reliance, and the privacy of family life emerged as central American values (Halfon & McLearn, 2002). It is one reason, among others, that the public has been slow to endorse government-supported benefits for all families, such as high-quality child care and paid employment leave for meeting family needs. And it has also contributed to the large number of U.S. families who remain poor, even though family members are gainfully employed (Gruendel & Aber, 2007; Pohl, 2002; UNICEF, 2005).

CULTURAL INFLUENCES

The African-American Extended Family

The African-American extended family can be traced to the African heritage of most black Americans. In many African societies, newly married couples do not start their own households. Instead, they live with a large extended family, which assists its members with all aspects of daily life. This tradition of maintaining a broad network of kin ties traveled to North America during the period of slavery. Since then, it has served as a protective shield against the destructive impact of poverty and racial prejudice on African-American family life. Today, more black than white adults have relatives other than their own children living in the same household. African-American parents also live closer to kin, often establish family-like relationships with friends and neighbors, see more relatives during the week, and perceive relatives as more important figures in their lives (Boyd-Franklin, 2006; Kane, 2000).

By providing emotional support and sharing essential resources, the African-American extended family helps reduce the stress of poverty and single parenthood. Extended-family members often help with child rearing, and adolescent mothers living in extended families are more likely to complete high school and get a job and less likely to be on welfare than mothers living on their own—factors that in turn benefit children's well-being (Gordon, Chase-Lansdale, & Brooks-Gunn, 2004; Trent & Harlan, 1994).

For single mothers who were very young at the time of their child's birth, extended-family living continues to be associated with more positive mother–child interaction during the preschool years. Otherwise, establishing an independent household with the help of nearby relatives is related to improved child rearing. Perhaps this arrangement permits the more mature teenage mother who has developed effective parenting skills to implement them (Chase-Lansdale, Brooks-Gunn, & Zamsky, 1994). In families rearing adolescents, kinship support increases the likelihood of effective parenting, which is related to adolescents' self-reliance, emotional well-being, and reduced antisocial behavior (Hamilton, 2005; Simons et al., 2006).

Finally, the extended family plays an important role in transmitting African-American culture. Compared with nuclear-family households (which include only parents and their children), extended-family arrangements place more emphasis on cooperation and on moral and religious values. And older black adults, such as grandparents and great-grandparents, regard educating children about their African heritage as especially important (Mosely-Howard & Evans, 2000; Taylor, 2000). Family reunions—sometimes held in grandparents' and great-grandparents' hometowns in the South—are especially common among African Americans, giving young people a strong sense of their roots (Boyd-Franklin, 2006). These influences strengthen family bonds, protect children's development, and increase the chances that the extended-family lifestyle will carry over to the next generation.

A grandmother shares a photo album chronicling family history with her son and grandchildren. Strong bonds with extended-family members have helped protect many African-American children against the destructive impact of poverty and racial prejudice.

Although the culture as a whole may value independence and privacy, not all citizens share the same values. Some belong to **subcultures**—groups of people with beliefs and customs that differ from those of the larger culture. Many ethnic minority groups in the United States have cooperative family structures, which help protect their members from the harmful effects of poverty. As the Cultural Influences box above indicates, the African-American tradition of **extended family households,** in which three or more generations live together, is a vital feature of black family life that has enabled its members to survive, despite a long history of prejudice and economic deprivation. Within the extended family, grandparents play meaningful roles in guiding younger generations; adults who face employment, marital, or child-rearing difficulties receive assistance and emotional support; and caregiving is enhanced for children and the elderly. Active, involved extended families also characterize other minorities, such as Asian, Native-American, and Hispanic subcultures (Becker et al., 2003; Harwood et al., 2002).

Our discussion so far reflects a broad dimension on which cultures and subcultures differ: the extent to which *collectivism* versus *individualism* is emphasized. In **collectivist societies,** people define themselves as part of a group and stress group goals over individual goals. In **individualistic societies,** people think of themselves as separate entities and are largely concerned with their own personal needs (Triandis, 1995, 2005). As these definitions suggest, the two cultural patterns are associated with two distinct views of the self. Collectivist societies value an *interdependent self,* which stresses social harmony, obligations and responsibility to others, and collaborative endeavors. In contrast, individualistic societies value an *independent self,* which emphasizes personal exploration, discovery, and achievement and individual choice in relationships. Both interdependence and independence are part of the makeup of every person and occur in varying mixtures (Greenfield et al., 2003; Tamis-LeMonda et al., 2008). But societies vary greatly in the extent to which they emphasize each alternative and—as later chapters will reveal—instill it in their young.

Although individualism tends to increase as cultures become more complex, cross-national differences remain. The United States is strongly individualistic, whereas most Western European countries lean toward collectivism. As we will see next, collectivist versus individualistic values have a powerful impact on a nation's approach to protecting the well-being of its children, families, and aging citizens.

■ **PUBLIC POLICIES AND LIFESPAN DEVELOPMENT.** When widespread social problems arise, such as poverty, homelessness, hunger, and disease, nations attempt to solve them through **public policies**—laws and government programs designed to improve current conditions. For example, when poverty increases and families become homeless, a country might decide to build more low-cost housing, raise the minimum wage, and increase welfare benefits. When reports indicate that many children are not achieving well in school, federal and state or provincial governments might grant more tax money to school districts, strengthen teacher preparation, and make sure that help reaches children who need it most. And when senior citizens have difficulty making ends meet because of inflation, a nation might increase its social security benefits.

Nevertheless, U.S. public policies safeguarding children and youths have lagged behind policies for the elderly. And compared with other industrialized nations, both sets of policies have been especially slow to emerge in the United States.

Policies for Children, Youths, and Families. We have already seen that although many U.S. children fare well, a large number grow up in environments that threaten their development. As Table 2.5 reveals, the United States does not rank well on any key measure of children's health and well-being.

The problems of children and youths extend beyond the indicators in the table. The United States is the only industrialized nation in the world without a universal, publicly funded health-care system. Hence, approximately 10 percent of U.S. children—most of them in low-income families—

■ **TABLE 2.5** ■ ***How Does the United States Compare to Other Nations on Indicators of Children's Health and Well-Being?***

INDICATOR	U.S. RANK[a]	SOME COUNTRIES THE UNITED STATES TRAILS
Childhood poverty (among 25 industrialized nations considered)	25th	Canada, Czech Republic, Germany, Norway, Sweden, Poland, Spain[b]
Infant deaths in the first year of life (worldwide)	26th	Canada, Hong Kong, Ireland, Singapore, Spain
Teenage birth rate (among 28 industrialized nations considered)	28th	Australia, Canada, Czech Republic, Denmark, Hungary, Iceland, Poland, Slovak Republic
Public expenditures on education as percentage of gross domestic product[b] (among 22 industrialized nations considered)	12th	Belgium, France, Iceland, New Zealand, Portugal, Spain, Sweden
Public expenditures on early childhood education and child care as a percentage of gross domestic product[c] (among 14 industrialized nations considered)	9th	Austria, Germany, Italy, Netherlands, France, Sweden
Public expenditures on health as a percentage of gross domestic product (among 22 industrialized nations considered)	16th	Austria, Australia, Canada, France, Hungary, Iceland, Switzerland, New Zealand

[a]1 = highest, or best, rank.

[b]U.S. childhood poverty and, especially, deep poverty rates greatly exceed poverty in these nations. For example, the poverty rate is 12 percent in Canada, 6 percent in the Czech Republic, 4 percent in Norway, and 2.5 percent in Sweden. Deep poverty affects just 2.5 percent of children in Canada, and a fraction of 1 percent in the other countries just listed.

[c]Gross domestic product is the value of all goods and services produced by a nation during a specified time period. It provides an overall measure of a nation's wealth.

Sources: Canada Campaign 2000, 2007; OECD, 2006, 2008a; UNICEF, 2005; U.S. Census Bureau, 2009b; U.S. Department of Education, 2009.

have no health insurance (DeNavas-Walt, Proctor, & Smith, 2009). Furthermore, the United States has been slow to move toward national standards and funding for child care: Affordable care is in short supply, and much of it is substandard in quality (Lamb & Ahnert, 2006; Muenchow & Marsland, 2007). In families affected by divorce, weak enforcement of child support payments heightens poverty in mother-headed households. By the time they finish high school, many American non-college-bound young people lack the vocational preparation they need to contribute fully to society. And by ages 18 to 20, about 11 percent of U.S. adolescents have not yet earned a high school diploma (U.S. Department of Education, 2009).

Why have attempts to help children and youths been difficult to realize in the United States? A complex set of political and economic forces is involved. Cultural values of self-reliance and privacy have made government hesitant to become involved in family matters. Furthermore, good social programs are expensive, and they must compete for a fair share of a country's economic resources. Children can easily remain unrecognized in this process because they cannot vote or speak out to protect their own interests, as adult citizens do (Ripple & Zigler, 2003). Instead, they must rely on the goodwill of others to become an important government priority.

Policies for the Elderly. Until well into the twentieth century, the United States had few policies in place to protect its aging population. For example, Social Security benefits, which address the income needs of retired citizens who contributed to society through prior employment, were not awarded until the late 1930s. Yet most Western nations had social security systems in place a decade or more earlier (Karger & Stoesz, 2008). In the 1960s, U.S. federal spending on programs for the elderly expanded rapidly. Medicare, a national health insurance program for older people that pays partial health-care costs, was initiated. But it mainly covers acute care services and requires participants to pay part of those costs, too. This leaves about half of elderly health spending to be covered by supplemental private insurance, government health insurance for the poor, or out-of-pocket payments (U.S. Department of Health and Human Services, 2008j).

Social Security and Medicare consume 96 percent of the U.S. federal budget for the elderly; only 4 percent is devoted to other programs. Consequently, U.S. programs for the aged have been criticized for neglecting social services (Hooyman & Kiyak, 2008). To meet this need, a national network for planning, coordinating, and delivering assistance to the aged has been established. Approximately 660 Area Agencies on Aging operate at regional and local levels, assessing community needs and offering communal and home-delivered meals, self-care education, elder abuse prevention, and a wide range of other social services. But limited funding means that the Area Agencies help far too few people in need.

As noted earlier, many senior citizens—especially women, ethnic minorities, and those living alone—remain in dire economic straits. Those who had interrupted employment histories, held jobs without benefits, or suffered lifelong poverty are not eligible for Social Security. Although all Americans age 65 and older are guaranteed a minimum income, the guaranteed amount is below the poverty line—the amount judged necessary for bare subsistence by the federal government. Furthermore, Social Security benefits are rarely adequate as a sole source of retirement income; they must be supplemented through other pensions and family savings. But a substantial percentage of U.S. aging citizens do not have access to these resources. Therefore, they are more likely than other age groups to be among the "near poor" (Greenberg, 2007).

Nevertheless, the U.S. aging population is financially much better off now than in the past. Today, the elderly are a large, powerful, well-organized constituency, far more likely than children

Overall, senior citizens in the United States are better off economically than are children. But many older adults—especially ethnic minorities, women, and those living alone—are poverty-stricken.

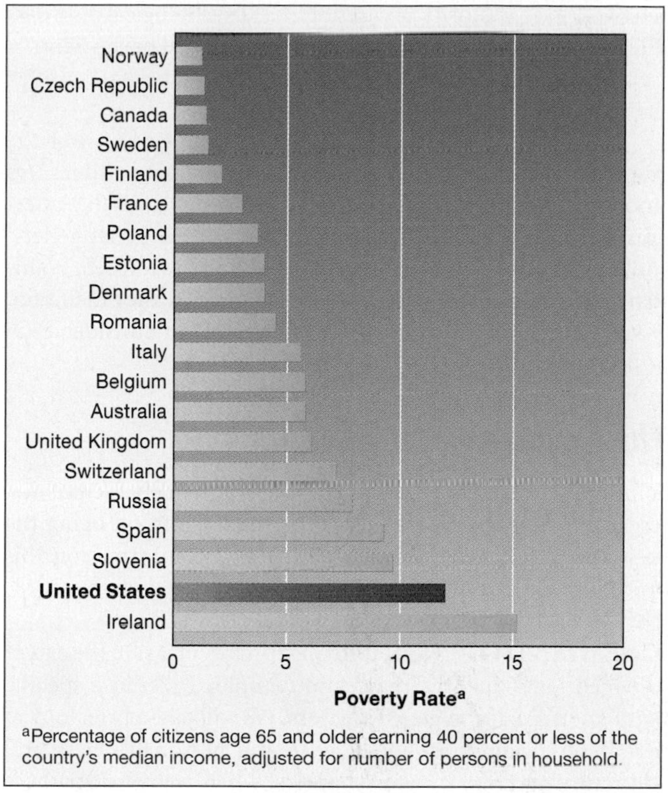

■ **FIGURE 2.7** ■ **Percentage of elderly living in poverty in twenty industrialized nations.** Among the countries listed, the United States has the highest rate of elderly living in poverty. Public expenditures on social security and other income guarantees for senior citizens are far greater in the highly ranked nations than in the United States. (Adapted from Luxembourg Income Study, 2008.)

or low-income families to attract the support of politicians. As a result, the number of aging poor has declined from 1 out of 3 people in 1960 to 1 out of 10 in the early twenty-first century (U.S. Census Bureau, 2009b). And senior citizens are healthier and more independent than ever before. Still, as Figure 2.7 shows, the elderly in the United States are less well off than those in many other Western nations, which provide more generous, government-funded income supplements to older adults.

■ **LOOKING TOWARD THE FUTURE.** Despite the worrisome state of many children, families, and aging citizens, efforts are being made to improve their condition. Throughout this book, we will discuss many successful programs that could be expanded. Also, growing awareness of the gap between what we know and what we do to better people's lives has led experts in human development to join with concerned citizens as advocates for more effective policies. As a result, several influential interest groups devoted to the well-being of children or the elderly have emerged.

In the United States, the Children's Defense Fund (CDF)—a private, nonprofit organization founded by Marian Wright Edelman in 1973—engages in research, public education, legal action, drafting of legislation, congressional testimony, and community organizing. Among its publications is its *Annual Report,* which provides a comprehensive analysis of children's condition, government-sponsored programs that serve children and families, and CDF initiatives aimed at improving those programs. To learn more about the Children's Defense Fund, visit its website at *www.childrensdefense.org.*

Nearly half of Americans over age 50, both retired and employed, are members of AARP (originally known as the American Association of Retired Persons). Founded by Ethel Percy Andrus in 1958, AARP has a large and energetic lobbying staff that works for increased government benefits of all kinds for the aged. Each year, it releases the *AARP Public Policy Agenda,* which forms the basis for advocacy activities in diverse areas, including income, health care, social services, housing, and personal and legal rights. Among AARP's programs is an effort to mobilize elderly voters, an initiative that keeps lawmakers highly sensitive to policy proposals affecting older Americans. A description of AARP and its activities can be found at *www.aarp.org.*

Besides strong advocacy, public policies that enhance human development depend on policy-relevant research that documents needs and evaluates programs to spark improvements. Today, more researchers are collaborating with community and government agencies to enhance the social relevance of their investigations. They are also doing a better job of disseminating their findings to the public in easily understandable, compelling ways, through television documentaries, newspaper

Policy-relevant research helps child advocates make the case for expanding programs like this summer day camp for Boston inner-city children. Schools coordinate with community centers to combine academic and athletic activities. Here, children participate in a science experiment, followed by gym time. They spend the summer exercising both their minds and their bodies.

stories, magazine articles, websites, and direct reports to government officials. As a result, they are helping to create a sense of immediacy about the condition of children, families, and the aged that is necessary to spur a society into action.

ASK YOURSELF

» REVIEW
Links between family and community foster development throughout the lifespan. Cite several examples from our discussion that support this idea.

» APPLY
Check your local newspaper or one or two national news magazines to see how often articles on the condition of children, families, and the aged appear. Why is it important for researchers to communicate with the general public about the well-being of these sectors of the population?

» CONNECT
How does poverty affect the family system, placing all aspects of development at risk?

» REFLECT
Review the discussion of cultural values and practices on pages 65–67. Under what circumstances do you believe government should become involved in family life?

Understanding the Relationship Between Heredity and Environment

So far in this chapter, we have discussed a wide variety of genetic and environmental influences, each of which has the power to alter the course of development. Yet people who are born into the same family (and who therefore share genes and environments) are often quite different in characteristics. We also know that some individuals are affected more than others by their homes, neighborhoods, and communities. In some cases, a child who is given many advantages nevertheless does poorly, while another, though exposed to unfavorable rearing conditions, does well. How do scientists explain the impact of heredity and environment when they seem to work in so many different ways?

All contemporary researchers agree that both heredity and environment are involved in every aspect of development. But for polygenic traits (those due to many genes), such as intelligence and personality, scientists are a long way from knowing the precise hereditary influences involved. Although they are making progress in identifying the multiple variations in DNA sequences associated with complex traits, so far these genetic markers explain only a small amount of variation in human behavior, and a minority of cases of most psychological disorders (Plomin, 2005; Plomin et al., 2003). For the most part, scientists are still limited to investigating the impact of genes on complex characteristics indirectly.

Some believe that it is useful and possible to answer the question of *how much each factor contributes* to differences among people. A growing consensus, however, regards that question as unanswerable. These investigators believe that genetic and environmental influences are inseparable (Gottlieb, Wahlsten, & Lickliter, 2006). The important question, they maintain, is *how nature and nurture work together.* Let's consider each position in turn.

The Question, "How Much?"

To infer the role of heredity in complex human characteristics, researchers use special methods, the most common being the *heritability estimate.* Let's look closely at the information this procedure yields, along with its limitations.

■ **HERITABILITY.** **Heritability estimates** measure the extent to which individual differences in complex traits in a specific population are due to genetic factors. We will take a brief look at heritability findings on intelligence and personality here and will return to them in later chapters, when we consider these topics in greater detail. Heritability estimates are obtained from **kinship studies,** which compare the characteristics of family members. The most common type of kinship study compares identical twins, who share all their genes, with fraternal twins, who, on average, share only half. If people who are genetically more alike are also more similar in intelligence and personality, then the researcher assumes that heredity plays an important role.

Kinship studies of intelligence provide some of the most controversial findings in the field of human development. Some experts claim a strong genetic influence, whereas others believe that heredity is barely involved. Currently, most kinship findings support a moderate role for heredity. When many twin studies are examined, correlations between the scores of identical twins are consistently higher than those of fraternal twins. In a summary of more than 10,000 twin pairs, the correlation for intelligence was .86 for identical twins and .60 for fraternal twins (Plomin & Spinath, 2004).

Researchers use a complex statistical procedure to compare these correlations, arriving at a heritability estimate ranging from 0 to 1.00. The value for intelligence is about .50 for child and adolescent twin samples in Western industrialized nations. This suggests that differences in genetic makeup explain half the variation in intelligence. However, heritability increases in adulthood, with some estimates as high as .80. As we will see later, one explanation is that, compared to children, adults exert greater personal control over their intellectual experiences—for example, how much time they spend reading or solving challenging problems (McClearn et al., 1997; McGue & Christensen,

2002). Adopted children's mental test scores are more strongly related to their biological parents' scores than to those of their adoptive parents, offering further support for the role of heredity (Petrill & Deater-Deckard, 2004).

Heritability research also reveals that genetic factors are important in personality. For frequently studied traits, such as sociability, anxiety, agreeableness, and activity level, heritability estimates obtained on child, adolescent, and young adult twin samples are moderate, in the .40s and .50s (Bouchard, 2004; Caspi & Shiner, 2006; Rothbart & Bates, 2006). Unlike intelligence, however, heritability of personality does not increase over the lifespan (Heiman et al., 2003; Loehlin et al., 2005).

Twin studies of schizophrenia—a psychological disorder involving delusions and hallucinations, difficulty distinguishing fantasy from reality, and irrational and inappropriate behaviors—consistently yield high heritabilities, around .80. The role of heredity in antisocial behavior and major depression, though still apparent, is less strong, with heritabilities in the .30s and .40s (Bouchard, 2004). Again, adoption studies support these results. Biological relatives of schizophrenic and depressed adoptees are more likely than adoptive relatives to share the same disorder (Plomin et al., 2001; Ridenour, 2000; Tienari et al., 2003).

LIMITATIONS OF HERITABILITY. Serious questions have been raised about the accuracy of heritability estimates, which depends on the extent to which the twin pairs studied reflect genetic and environmental variation in the population. Within a population in which all people have very similar home, school, and community experiences, individual differences in intelligence and personality would be largely genetic, and heritability estimates would be close to 1.00. Conversely, the more environments vary, the more likely they are to account for individual differences, yielding lower heritability estimates. In twin studies, most of the twin pairs are reared together under highly similar conditions. Even when separated twins are available for study, social service agencies have often placed them in advantaged homes that are alike in many ways (Rutter et al., 2001). Because the environments of most twin pairs are less diverse than those of the general population, heritability estimates are likely to exaggerate the role of heredity.

Heritability estimates are controversial measures because they can easily be misapplied. For example, high heritabilities have been used to suggest that ethnic differences in intelligence, such as the poorer performance of black children compared to white children, have a genetic basis (Jensen, 1969, 1998, 2001; Rushton & Jensen, 2005, 2006). Yet this line of reasoning is widely regarded as incorrect. Heritabilities computed on mostly white twin samples do not tell us what is responsible for test score differences between ethnic groups. We have already seen that large economic and cultural differences are involved. In Chapter 9, we will discuss research indicating that when black children are adopted into economically advantaged homes at an early age, their scores are well above average and substantially higher than those of children growing up in impoverished families.

Perhaps the most serious criticism of heritability estimates has to do with their limited usefulness. Though interesting, these statistics give us no precise information on how intelligence and personality develop or how children might respond to environments designed to help them develop as far as possible (Rutter, 2002; Wachs, 1999). Indeed, the heritability of children's intelligence increases as parental education and income increase—that is, as children grow up in conditions that allow them to make the most of their genetic endowment. In disadvantaged environments, children are prevented from realizing their potential. Consequently, enhancing their experiences through interventions—such as increasing parent education and income and providing high-quality preschool or child care—has a greater impact on development (Bronfenbrenner & Morris, 2006; Turkheimer et al., 2003).

Adriana and Tamara, identical twins born in Mexico, were separated at birth and adopted into different homes in the New York City area. They were unaware of each other until a mutual acquaintance noted resemblances between them. At age 20, when they decided to meet, they discovered many similarities: Both like the same clothing styles, were B students, and love to dance. The study of identical twins reared apart reveals that heredity contributes to many personality characteristics. But not all separated twins match up as well as this pair, and generalizing from twin evidence to the broader population is controversial.

According to one group of experts, heritability estimates have too many problems to yield any firm conclusions about the relative strength of nature and nurture (Collins et al., 2000). Although these statistics confirm that heredity contributes to complex traits, they do not tell us how environment can modify genetic influences.

The Question, "How?"

Today, most researchers view development as the result of a dynamic interplay between heredity and environment. How do nature and nurture work together? Several concepts shed light on this question.

■ REACTION RANGE. The first of these ideas is **range of reaction,** each person's unique, genetically determined response to the environment (Gottesman, 1963). Let's explore this idea in Figure 2.8. Reaction range can apply to any characteristic; here it is illustrated for intelligence. Notice that when environments vary from extremely unstimulating to highly enriched, Ben's intelligence increases steadily, Linda's rises sharply and then falls off, and Ron's begins to increase only after the environment becomes modestly stimulating.

Reaction range highlights two important points. First, it shows that because each of us has a unique genetic makeup, we respond differently to the same environment. Notice in Figure 2.8 how a poor environment results in similarly low scores for all three individuals. But when the environment provides an intermediate level of stimulation, Linda is by far the best-performing child. And in a highly enriched environment, Ben does best, followed by Ron, both of whom now outperform Linda.

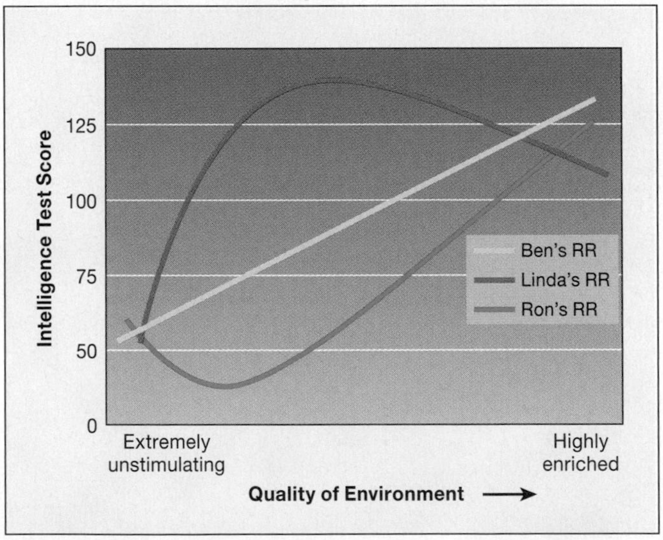

■ FIGURE 2.8 ■ Intellectual ranges of reaction (RR) for three children in environments that vary from extremely unstimulating to highly enriched. Each child, because of his or her genetic makeup, responds differently to changes in quality of the environment. Ben's intelligence test score increases steadily, Linda's rises sharply and then falls off, and Ron's begins to increase only after the environment becomes modestly stimulating. (Adapted from Wahlsten, 1994.)

Second, sometimes different genetic–environmental combinations can make two people look the same! For example, if Linda is reared in a minimally stimulating environment, her score will be about 100—average for people in general. Ben and Ron can also obtain this score, but to do so, they must grow up in a fairly enriched home. In sum, range of reaction reveals that unique blends of heredity and environment lead to both similarities and differences in behavior (Gottlieb, Wahlsten, & Lickliter, 2006).

■ CANALIZATION. Another way of understanding how heredity and environment combine comes from the concept of **canalization**—the tendency of heredity to restrict the development of some characteristics to just one or a few outcomes. A behavior that is strongly canalized develops similarly in a wide range of environments; only strong environmental forces can change it (Waddington, 1957). For example, infant perceptual and motor development seems to be strongly canalized because all normal human babies eventually roll over, reach for objects, sit up, crawl, and walk. It takes extreme conditions to modify these behaviors or cause them not to appear. In contrast, intelligence and personality are less strongly canalized; they vary much more with changes in the environment.

When we look at behaviors constrained by heredity, we can see that canalization is highly adaptive. Through it, nature ensures that children will develop certain species-typical skills under many rearing conditions, thereby promoting survival.

■ GENETIC–ENVIRONMENTAL CORRELATION. A major problem in trying to separate heredity and environment is that they are often correlated (Plomin et al., 2001; Scarr & McCartney, 1983). According to the concept of **genetic–environmental correlation,** our genes influence the environments to which we are exposed. The way this happens changes with age.

Passive and Evocative Correlation. At younger ages, two types of genetic–environmental correlation are common. The first is called *passive* correlation because the child has no control over it. Early on, parents provide environments influenced by their own heredity. For example, parents who are good athletes emphasize outdoor activities and enroll their children in swimming and gymnastics. Besides being exposed to an "athletic environment," the children may have inherited their parents' athletic ability. As a result, they are likely to become good athletes for both genetic and environmental reasons.

The second type of genetic–environmental correlation is *evocative.* Children evoke responses that are influenced by the child's heredity, and these responses strengthen the child's original style. For example, an active, friendly baby is likely to receive more social stimulation than a passive, quiet infant. And a cooperative, attentive child probably receives more patient and sensitive interactions from parents than an inattentive, distractible child. In support of this idea, the less genetically alike siblings are, the more their parents treat them differently, in both warmth and negativity. Thus, parents' treatment of identical twins is highly similar, whereas their treatment of fraternal twins and nontwin biological siblings is only moderately so. And little resemblance exists in parents' warm and negative interactions with unrelated stepsiblings (see Figure 2.9) (Reiss, 2003).

Active Correlation. At older ages, *active* genetic–environmental correlation becomes common. As children extend their experiences beyond the immediate family and are given the freedom to make more choices, they actively seek environments that fit with their genetic tendencies. The well-coordinated, muscular child spends more time at after-school sports, the musically talented youngster joins the school orchestra and practices his violin, and the intellectually curious child is a familiar patron at her local library.

This tendency to actively choose environments that complement our heredity is called **niche-picking** (Scarr & McCartney, 1983). Infants and young children cannot do much niche-picking because adults select environments for them. In contrast, older children, adolescents, and adults are increasingly in charge of their environments.

The niche-picking idea explains why pairs of identical twins reared apart during childhood and later reunited may find, to their surprise, that they have similar hobbies, food preferences, and vocations—a trend that is especially marked when twins' environmental opportunities are similar (Plomin, 1994). Niche-picking also helps us understand why identical twins become somewhat more alike, and fraternal twins and adopted siblings less alike, in intelligence with age (Bouchard, 2004; Loehlin, Horn, & Willerman, 1997). And niche-picking sheds light on why identical twins, compared to fraternal twins and other adults, select more similar spouses and best friends—in height, weight, personality, political attitudes, and other characteristics (Rushton & Bons, 2005).

The influence of heredity and environment is not constant but changes over time. With age, genetic factors may become more important in influencing the environments we experience and choose for ourselves.

This mother shares her love of running with her daughter. In addition, her child may have inherited her mother's athletic ability. When heredity and environment are correlated, they jointly foster the same capacities, and the influence of one cannot be separated from the influence of the other.

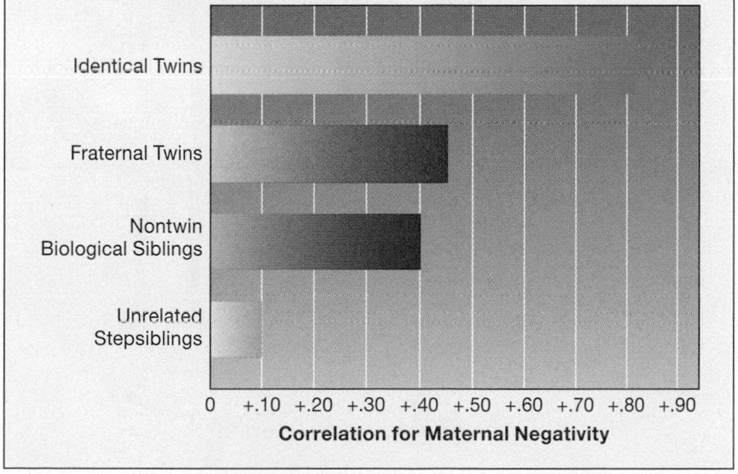

■ **FIGURE 2.9** ■ **Similarity in mothers' interactions for pairs of siblings differing in genetic relatedness.** The correlations shown are for maternal negativity. The pattern illustrates evocative genetic–environmental correlation. Identical twins evoke similar maternal treatment because of their identical heredity. As genetic resemblance between siblings declines, the strength of the correlation drops. Mothers vary their interactions as they respond to each child's unique genetic makeup. (Adapted from Reiss, 2003.)

■ **ENVIRONMENTAL INFLUENCES ON GENE EXPRESSION.** Notice how, in the concepts just considered, heredity is granted priority. In range of reaction, it *determines* individual responsiveness to varying environments. In canalization, it *restricts* the development of certain behaviors. Similarly, some theorists regard genetic–environmental correlation as entirely driven by genetics (Harris, 1998; Rowe, 1994). They believe that children's genetic makeup causes them to receive, evoke, or seek experiences that actualize their inborn tendencies.

Others argue that heredity does not dictate children's experiences or development in a rigid way. In one study, boys with a genetic tendency toward antisocial behavior (based on the presence of a gene on the X chromosome known to predispose both animals and humans to aggression) were no more aggressive than boys without this gene, *unless* they also had a history of severe child abuse (Caspi et al., 2002). Boys with and without the gene did not differ in their experience of abuse, indicating that the "aggressive genotype" did not increase exposure to abuse. And in a large Finnish adoption study, children of schizophrenic mothers reared by healthy adoptive parents showed little mental illness—no more than a control group with healthy biological and adoptive parents. In contrast, schizophrenia and other psychological impairments piled up in adoptees whose biological and adoptive parents were both disturbed (Tienari et al., 2003; Tienari, Wahlberg, & Wynne, 2006).

Furthermore, parents and other caring adults can provide children with experiences that modify the expression of heredity, yielding favorable outcomes. For example, in a study that tracked the development of 5-year-old identical twins, pair members tended to resemble each other in level of aggression. And the more aggression they displayed, the more maternal anger and criticism they received (a genetic–environmental correlation). Nevertheless, some mothers treated their twins differently. When followed up at age 7, twins who had been targets of more maternal negativity engaged in even more antisocial behavior. In contrast, their better-treated, genetically identical counterparts showed a reduction in disruptive acts (Caspi et al., 2004). Good parenting protected them from a spiraling, antisocial course of development.

Other research confirms that parents' unequal treatment of siblings is not just the straightforward result of children's heredity but is affected by aspects of family life. In single-parent families, low-income families, and families with unhappy marriages, siblings receive more differential treatment from parents (Jenkins, Rasbash, & O'Connor, 2003). Perhaps parents who are under stress concentrate their limited energies on one child.

Accumulating evidence reveals that the relationship between heredity and environment is not a one-way street, from genes to environment to behavior. Rather, like other system influences considered in this and the previous chapter, it is *bidirectional:* Genes affect people's behavior and experiences, but their experiences and behavior also affect gene expression (Gottlieb, 2000, 2003; Rutter, 2006; Ryff & Singer, 2005).

Researchers call this view of the relationship between heredity and environment the *epigenetic framework* (Gottlieb, 1998, 2007). It is depicted in Figure 2.10. **Epigenesis** means development resulting from ongoing, bidirectional exchanges between heredity and all levels of the environment. To

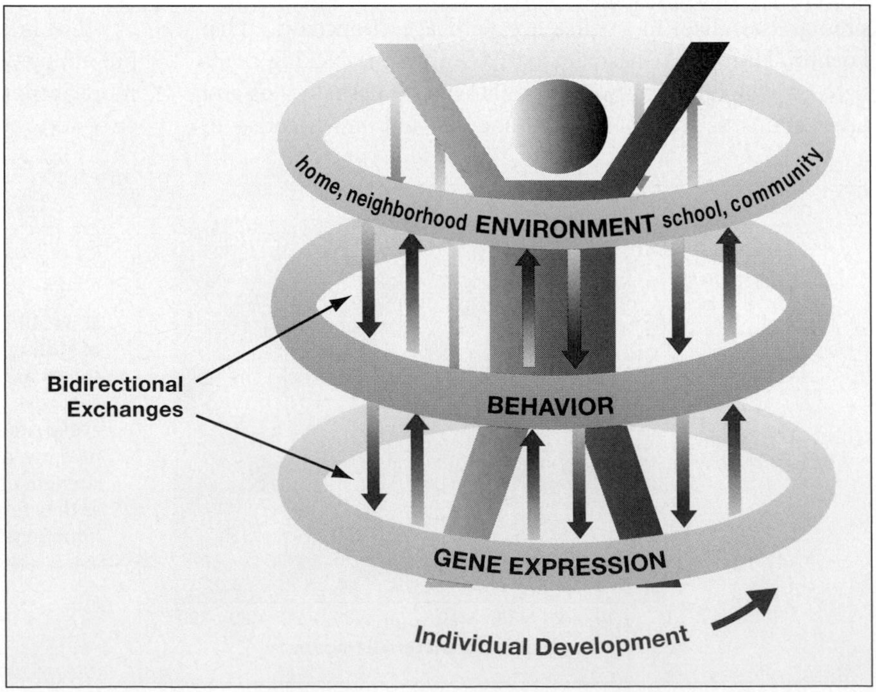

■ **FIGURE 2.10** ■ **The epigenetic framework.** Development takes place through ongoing, bidirectional exchanges between heredity and all levels of the environment. Genes affect behavior and experiences. Experiences and behavior also affect gene expression. (Adapted from Gottlieb, 2007.)

illustrate, providing a baby with a healthy diet increases brain growth, leading to new connections between nerve cells, which transform gene expression. This opens the door to new gene–environment exchanges—for example, advanced exploration of objects and interaction with caregivers, which further enhance brain growth and gene expression. These ongoing, bidirectional influences foster cognitive and social development. In contrast, harmful environments can dampen gene expression, at times so profoundly that later experiences can do little to change characteristics (such as intelligence and personality) that were flexible to begin with.

A major reason that researchers are interested in the nature–nurture issue is that they want to improve environments so that people can develop as far as possible. The concept of epigenesis reminds us that development is best understood as a series of complex exchanges between nature and nurture. Although people cannot be changed in any way we might desire, environments can modify genetic influences. The success of any attempt to improve development depends on the characteristics we want to change, the genetic makeup of the individual, and the type and timing of our intervention.

ASK YOURSELF

>> REVIEW
What is epigenesis, and how does it differ from range of reaction and genetic–environmental correlation? Provide an example of epigenesis.

>> APPLY
Bianca's parents are accomplished musicians. At age 4, Bianca began taking piano lessons. By age 10, she was accompanying the school choir. At age 14, she asked if she could attend a special music high school. Explain how genetic–environmental correlation promoted Bianca's talent.

>> CONNECT
Explain how each of the following concepts supports the conclusion that genetic influences on human characteristics are not constant but change over time: somatic mutation (page 52), niche-picking (page 73), and epigenesis (page 74).

>> REFLECT
What aspects of your own development—for example, interests, hobbies, college major, or vocational choice—are probably due to niche-picking? Explain.

Summary

Genetic Foundations

What are genes, and how are they transmitted from one generation to the next?

>> Each individual's **phenotype,** or directly observable characteristics, is a product of both **genotype** and environment. **Chromosomes,** rodlike structures within the cell nucleus, contain our hereditary endowment. Along their length are **genes,** segments of **DNA** that send instructions for making a rich assortment of proteins to the cell's cytoplasm—a process that makes us distinctly human and influences our development and characteristics. We share most of our genetic makeup with other mammals, especially primates.

>> **Gametes,** or sex cells, result from a process of cell division called **meiosis,** in which each individual receives a unique set of genes from each parent. Once sperm and ovum unite, the resulting **zygote** starts to develop into a complex human being through cell duplication, or **mitosis.**

>> If the fertilizing sperm carries an X chromosome, the child will be a girl; if it contains a Y chromosome, a boy. **Fraternal,** or **dizygotic, twins** result when two ova are released from the mother's ovaries and each is fertilized. **Identical,** or **monozygotic, twins** develop when a zygote divides in two during the early stages of cell duplication.

© RACHEL EPSTEIN/PHOTOEDIT

Describe various patterns of genetic inheritance.

>> Traits controlled by single genes follow **dominant–recessive** and **incomplete dominance** patterns of inheritance. **Homozygous** individuals have two identical **alleles,** or forms of a gene. **Heterozygous** individuals, with one dominant and one recessive allele, are **carriers** of the recessive trait.

>> **X-linked inheritance** applies when recessive disorders are carried on the X chromosome and, therefore, are more likely to affect males. In **genomic imprinting,** one parent's gene is activated, regardless of its makeup.

>> Unfavorable genes arise from **mutation,** which can occur spontaneously or be caused by hazardous environmental agents. Germline mutation affects the cells that give rise to gametes; somatic mutation can occur in body cells at any time of life.

>> **Polygenic inheritance** of human traits, such as intelligence and personality, is influenced by many genes. For such characteristics, scientists must study the influence of heredity indirectly.

Describe major chromosomal abnormalities, and explain how they occur.

>> Most chromosomal abnormalities are due to errors in meiosis. The most common, Down syndrome, results in physical defects and mental retardation. Disorders of the **sex chromosomes** are generally milder than defects of the **autosomes.** Specific intellectual problems occur in children who

have either more or fewer X chromosomes than usual, as in triple X, Klinefelter, and Turner syndromes.

© LAURA DWIGHT PHOTOGRAPHY

Reproductive Choices

What procedures can assist prospective parents in having healthy children?

» **Genetic counseling** helps couples at risk for giving birth to children with genetic abnormalities decide whether or not to conceive. **Prenatal diagnostic methods** permit early detection of genetic problems.

» Reproductive technologies such as donor insemination, in vitro fertilization, surrogate motherhood, and postmenopausal-assisted childbirth permit many individuals to become parents who otherwise would not, but they raise serious legal and ethical concerns.

» Many parents who cannot conceive or who are at high risk of transmitting a genetic disorder decide to adopt. Although adopted children have more learning and emotional problems than children in general, most fare well in the long run. Warm, sensitive parenting predicts favorable development.

Environmental Contexts for Development

Describe the social systems perspective on family functioning, along with aspects of the environment that support family well-being and development.

» Human development takes place within a complex, many-layered environment. The first and foremost context for development is the family, a dynamic system characterized by bidirectional influences, in which each family member's behaviors affect those of others. Both direct and indirect influences operate within the family system, which must continually adjust to new events and changes in its members.

» **Socioeconomic status (SES)** profoundly affects family functioning. Higher-SES families tend to be smaller, to emphasize psychological traits, and to engage in warm, verbally stimulating interaction with children. Lower-SES families often stress external characteristics and use more commands, criticism, and physical punishment. Many affluent parents are physically and emotionally unavailable, thereby impairing their children's adjustment. Poverty and homelessness can seriously undermine development.

AP IMAGES/LM OTERO

» Connections between family and community are vital for psychological well-being. Stable, socially cohesive neighborhoods in which residents have access to enrichment activities and social support promote favorable development in both children and adults. Compared with urban environments, small towns foster greater community involvement, warm ties among nonrelatives, and a sense of safety among the elderly.

» The values and practices of cultures and **subcultures** affect all aspects of daily life. **Extended-family households,** which are common among ethnic minorities, help protect family members from negative effects of poverty and other stressful life conditions.

© RICHARD LORD/THE IMAGE WORKS

» In our complex world, favorable development depends on **public policies.** Factors promoting effective social programs include cultural values emphasizing **collectivism** over **individualism,** a nation's economic resources, and the presence of organizations and individuals that work to improve quality of life. U.S. policies safeguarding children and their families are less well developed than those safeguarding the elderly, which also lag behind those of other Western nations.

Understanding the Relationship Between Heredity and Environment

Explain the various ways heredity and environment may combine to influence complex traits.

» Researchers use **kinship studies** to compute **heritability estimates,** which show that genetic factors influence such traits as intelligence and personality. However, the accuracy and usefulness of heritability estimates have been challenged.

© MYRLEEN FERGUSON CATE/PHOTOEDIT

» According to the concepts of **range of reaction** and **canalization,** heredity influences each individual's unique response to varying environments. **Genetic–environmental correlation** and **niche-picking** describe how genes affect the environments to which people are exposed. **Epigenesis** reminds us that development is best understood as a series of complex exchanges between nature and nurture that change over the lifespan.

Important Terms and Concepts

allele (p. 48)
autosomes (p. 47)
canalization (p. 72)
carrier (p. 48)
chromosomes (p. 46)
collectivist societies (p. 66)
deoxyribonucleic acid (DNA) (p. 46)
dominant–recessive inheritance (p. 48)
epigenesis (p. 74)
extended-family household (p. 66)
fraternal, or dizygotic, twins (p. 47)
gametes (p. 46)
gene (p. 46)
genetic counseling (p. 53)
genetic–environmental correlation (p. 72)
genomic imprinting (p. 51)
genotype (p. 45)
heritability estimate (p. 70)
heterozygous (p. 48)
homozygous (p. 48)
identical, or monozygotic, twins (p. 48)
incomplete dominance (p. 50)
individualistic societies (p. 66)
kinship studies (p. 70)
meiosis (p. 47)
mitosis (p. 46)
mutation (p. 51)
niche-picking (p. 73)
phenotype (p. 45)
polygenic inheritance (p. 52)
prenatal diagnostic methods (p. 56)
public policies (p. 67)
range of reaction (p. 72)
sex chromosomes (p. 47)
socioeconomic status (SES) (p. 60)
subculture (p. 66)
X-linked inheritance (p. 50)
zygote (p. 47)

© BLEND IMAGES/ALAMY

As these parents share an intimate moment with their children, they convey a sense of delight in their growing family and help their older daughter welcome the new baby.

CHAPTER 3

Prenatal Development, Birth, and the Newborn Baby

When I met Yolanda and Jay one fall in my child development class, Yolanda was just two months pregnant. After months of wondering if the time in their lives was right, they had decided to have a baby. Both were full of questions: "How does the baby grow before birth?" "When is each organ formed?" "Has its heart begun to beat?" "Can it hear, feel, or sense our presence?"

Most of all, Yolanda and Jay wanted to do everything possible to make sure their baby would be born healthy. At first, they believed that the uterus completely shielded the developing organism from any dangers in the environment. All babies born with problems, they thought, had unfavorable genes. After browsing through several pregnancy books, Yolanda and Jay realized they were wrong. Yolanda started to wonder about her diet and whether she should keep up her daily aerobics routine. And she asked me whether an aspirin for a headache, a glass of wine at dinner, or a few cups of coffee during study hours might be harmful.

In this chapter, we answer Yolanda and Jay's questions, along with a great many more that scientists have asked about the events before birth. First, we trace prenatal development, paying special attention to environmental supports for healthy growth, as well as damaging influences that threaten the child's health and survival. Next, we turn to the events of childbirth. Today, women in industrialized nations have many choices about where and how they give birth, and hospitals go to great lengths to make the arrival of a new baby a rewarding, family-centered event.

Yolanda and Jay's son Joshua reaped the benefits of his parents' careful attention to his needs during pregnancy. He was strong, alert, and healthy at birth. Sometimes, however, the birth process does not go smoothly. We will consider the pros and cons of medical interventions, such as pain-relieving drugs and surgical deliveries, designed to ease a difficult birth and protect the health of mother and baby. Our discussion also addresses the development of infants born underweight or too early, before the prenatal period is complete. We conclude with a close look at the remarkable capacities of newborns.

Prenatal Development

The sperm and ovum that unite to form the new individual are uniquely suited for the task of reproduction. The ovum is a tiny sphere, measuring $\frac{1}{175}$ inch in diameter—barely visible to the naked eye as a dot the size of the period at the end of this sentence. But in its microscopic world, it is a giant—the largest cell in the human body. The ovum's size makes it a perfect target for the much smaller sperm, which measure only $\frac{1}{500}$ inch.

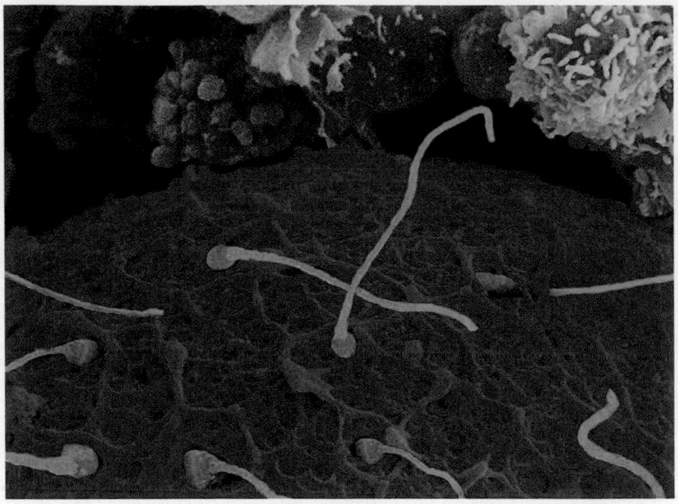

© JACK BURNS/ACE/PHOTOTAKE

In this photo taken with the aid of a powerful microscope, sperm have completed their journey up the female reproductive tract and are beginning to penetrate the surface of the enormous-looking ovum, the largest cell in the human body. When one sperm successfully fertilizes the ovum, the resulting zygote begins to duplicate.

Conception

About once every 28 days, in the middle of a woman's menstrual cycle, an ovum bursts from one of her *ovaries,* two walnut-sized organs located deep inside her abdomen, and is drawn into one of two *fallopian tubes*—long, thin structures that lead to the hollow, soft-lined uterus (see Figure 3.1). While the ovum is traveling, the spot on the ovary from which it was released, now called the *corpus luteum,* secretes hormones that prepare the lining of the uterus to receive a fertilized ovum. If pregnancy does not occur, the corpus luteum shrinks, and the lining of the uterus is discarded two weeks later with menstruation.

The male produces sperm in vast numbers—an average of 300 million a day—in the *testes,* two glands located in the *scrotum,* sacs that lie just behind the penis. In the final process of maturation, each sperm develops a tail that permits it to swim long distances upstream in the female reproductive tract, through the *cervix* (opening of the uterus) and into the fallopian tube, where fertilization usually takes place. The journey is difficult, and many sperm die. Only 300 to 500 reach the ovum, if one happens to be present. Sperm live for up to six days and can lie in wait for the ovum, which survives for only one day after being released into the fallopian tube. However, most

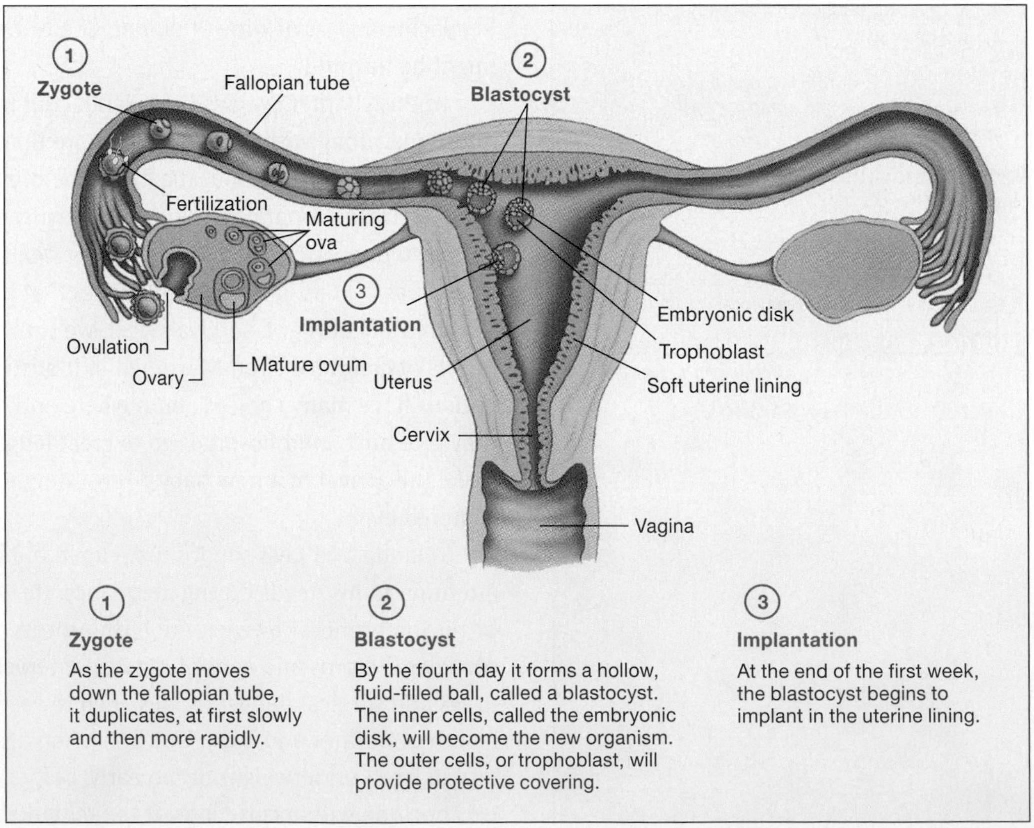

■ FIGURE 3.1 ■ Female reproductive organs, showing fertilization, early cell duplication, and implantation. (From *Before We Are Born, 6th ed.* by K. L. Moore and T. V. N. Persaud, p. 87. Copyright © 2003, reprinted with permission from Elsevier, Inc.)

■ **TABLE 3.1** ■ ***Milestones of Prenatal Development***

TRIMESTER	PERIOD	WEEKS	LENGTH AND WEIGHT	MAJOR EVENTS
First	Zygote 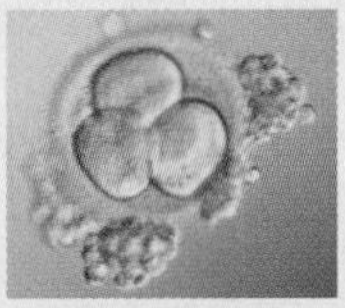	1		The one-celled zygote multiplies and forms a blastocyst.
		2		The blastocyst burrows into the uterine lining. Structures that feed and protect the developing organism begin to form—*amnion, chorion, yolk sac, placenta,* and *umbilical cord.*
	Embryo 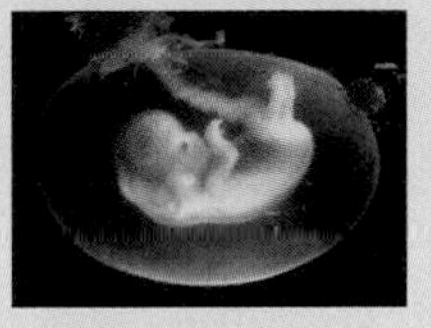	3–4	¼ inch (6 mm)	A primitive brain and spinal cord appear. Heart, muscles, ribs, backbone, and digestive tract begin to develop.
		5–8	1 inch (2.5 cm); ⅐ ounce (4 g)	Many external body structures (face, arms, legs, toes, fingers) and internal organs form. The sense of touch begins to develop, and the embryo can move.
	Fetus 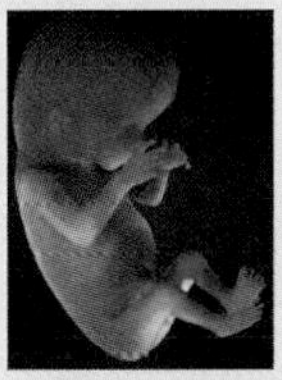	9–12	3 inches (7.6 cm); less than 1 ounce (28 g)	Rapid increase in size begins. Nervous system, organs, and muscles become organized and connected, and new behavioral capacities (kicking, thumb sucking, mouth opening, and rehearsal of breathing) appear. External genitals are well-formed, and the fetus's sex is evident.
Second	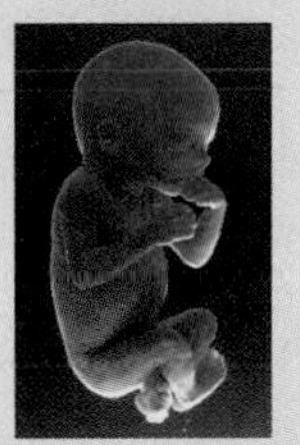	13–24	12 inches (30 cm); 1.8 pounds (820 g)	The fetus continues to enlarge rapidly. In the middle of this period, fetal movements can be felt by the mother. Vernix and lanugo keep the fetus's skin from chapping in the amniotic fluid. Most of the brain's neurons are present by 24 weeks. Eyes are sensitive to light, and the fetus reacts to sound.
Third	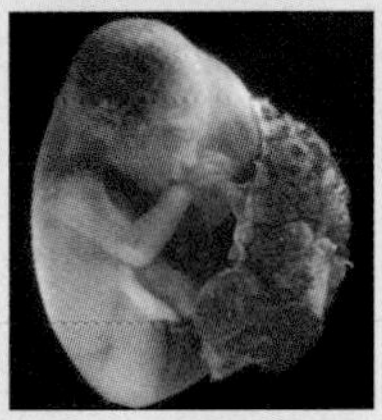	25–38	20 inches (50 cm); 7.5 pounds (3,400 g)	The fetus has a chance of survival if born during this time. Size increases. Lungs mature. Rapid brain development causes sensory and behavioral capacities to expand. In the middle of this period, a layer of fat is added under the skin. Antibodies are transmitted from mother to fetus to protect against disease. Most fetuses rotate into an upside-down position in preparation for birth.

Source: Moore & Persaud, 2008.
Photos (from top to bottom): © Claude Cortier/Photo Researchers, Inc.; © G. Moscoso/Photo Researchers, Inc.; © John Watney/Photo Researchers, Inc.; © James Stevenson/Photo Researchers, Inc.; © Lennart Nilsson, *A Child Is Born*/Bonniers.

conceptions result from intercourse occurring during a three-day period—on the day of ovulation or during the two days preceding it (Wilcox, Weinberg, & Baird, 1995).

With conception, the story of prenatal development begins to unfold. The vast changes that take place during the 38 weeks of pregnancy are usually divided into three phases: (1) the period of the zygote, (2) the period of the embryo, and (3) the period of the fetus. As we look at what happens in each, you may find it useful to refer to Table 3.1, which summarizes milestones of prenatal development.

Period of the Zygote

The period of the zygote lasts about two weeks, from fertilization until the tiny mass of cells drifts down and out of the fallopian tube and attaches itself to the wall of the uterus. The zygote's first cell duplication is long and drawn out; it is not complete until about 30 hours after conception. Gradually, new cells are added at a faster rate. By the fourth day, 60 to 70 cells exist that form a hollow, fluid-filled ball called a *blastocyst* (refer again to Figure 3.1). The cells on the inside, called the embryonic disk,

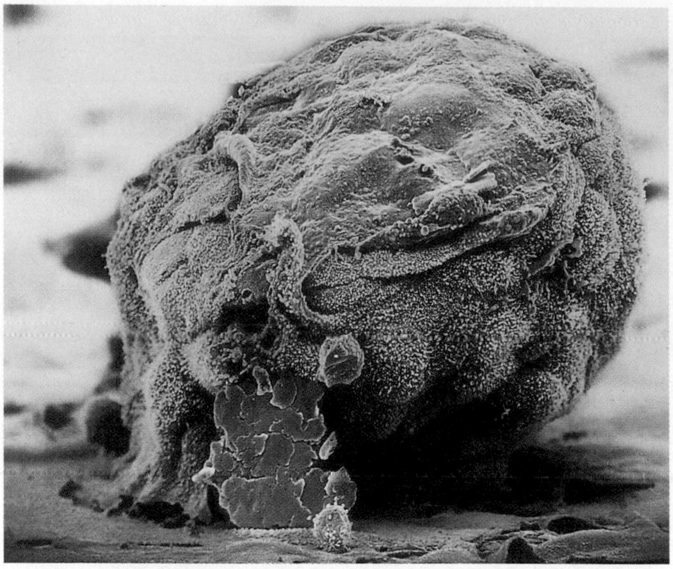

Period of the zygote: seventh to ninth day. The fertilized ovum duplicates rapidly, forming a hollow ball of cells, or blastocyst, by the fourth day after fertilization. Here the blastocyst, magnified thousands of times, burrows into the uterine lining between the seventh and ninth day.

will become the new organism; the outer ring of cells, termed the *trophoblast,* will become the structures that provide protective covering and nourishment.

■ **IMPLANTATION.** Between the seventh and ninth days, **implantation** occurs: The blastocyst burrows deep into the uterine lining. Surrounded by the woman's nourishing blood, it starts to grow in earnest. At first, the trophoblast (protective outer layer) multiplies fastest. It forms a membrane, called the **amnion,** that encloses the developing organism in *amniotic fluid,* which helps keep the temperature of the prenatal world constant and provides a cushion against any jolts caused by the woman's movements. A *yolk sac* emerges that produces blood cells until the liver, spleen, and bone marrow are mature enough to take over this function (Moore & Persaud, 2008).

The events of these first two weeks are delicate and uncertain. As many as 30 percent of zygotes do not survive this period. In some, the sperm and ovum do not join properly. In others, cell duplication never begins. By preventing implantation in these cases, nature eliminates most prenatal abnormalities (Sadler, 2006).

■ **THE PLACENTA AND UMBILICAL CORD.** By the end of the second week, cells of the trophoblast form another protective membrane—the **chorion,** which surrounds the amnion. From the chorion, tiny hairlike *villi,* or blood vessels, emerge.[1] As these villi burrow into the uterine wall, the placenta starts to develop. By bringing the embryo's and mother's blood close together, the **placenta** permits food and oxygen to reach the organism and waste products to be carried away. A membrane forms that allows these substances to be exchanged but prevents the mother's and embryo's blood from mixing directly.

The placenta is connected to the developing organism by the **umbilical cord,** which first appears as a tiny stalk and eventually grows to a length of one to three feet. The umbilical cord contains one large vein that delivers blood loaded with nutrients and two arteries that remove waste products. The force of blood flowing through the cord keeps it firm, so it seldom tangles while the embryo, like a space-walking astronaut, floats freely in its fluid-filled chamber (Moore & Persaud, 2008).

By the end of the period of the zygote, the developing organism has found food and shelter. These dramatic beginnings take place before most mothers know they are pregnant.

Period of the Embryo

The period of the **embryo** lasts from implantation through the eighth week of pregnancy. During these brief six weeks, the most rapid prenatal changes take place as the groundwork is laid for all body structures and internal organs.

■ **LAST HALF OF THE FIRST MONTH.** In the first week of this period, the embryonic disk forms three layers of cells: (1) the *ectoderm,* which will become the nervous system and skin; (2) the *mesoderm,* from which will develop the muscles, skeleton, circulatory system, and other internal organs; and (3) the *endoderm,* which will become the digestive system, lungs,

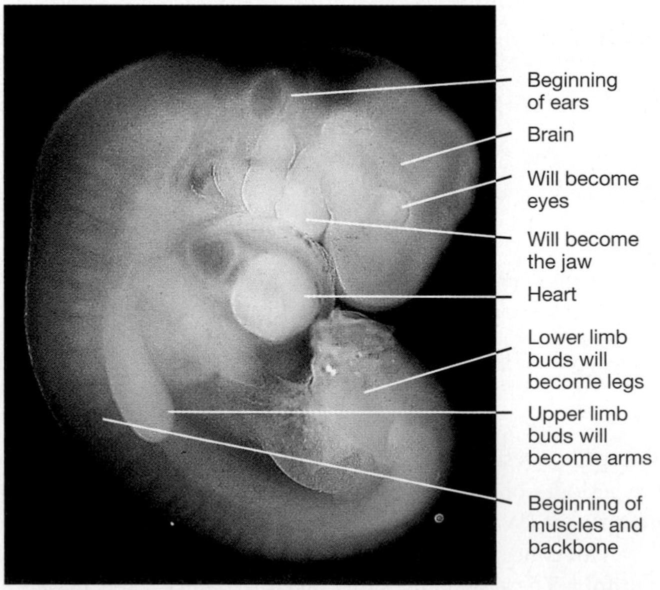

Period of the embryo: fourth week. This 4-week-old embryo is only ¼-inch long, but many body structures have already begun to form. The primitive tail will disappear by the end of the embryonic period.

[1]Recall from Table 2.4 on page 56 that *chorionic villus sampling* is the prenatal diagnostic method that can be performed earliest, at nine weeks after conception.

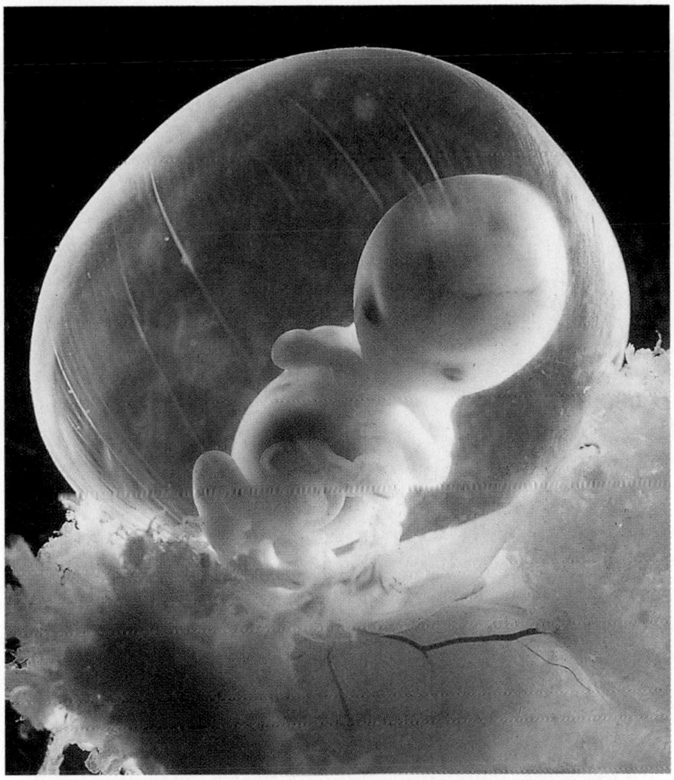

Period of the embryo: seventh week. The embryo's posture is more upright. Body structures—eyes, nose, arms, legs, and internal organs—are more distinct. An embryo of this age responds to touch. It can also move, although at less than one inch long and one ounce in weight, it is still too tiny to be felt by the mother.

urinary tract, and glands. These three layers give rise to all parts of the body.

At first, the nervous system develops fastest. The ectoderm folds over to form the **neural tube,** which will become the spinal cord and brain. At 3½ weeks, production of *neurons* (nerve cells that store and transmit information) begins deep inside the neural tube at an astounding pace—more than 250,000 per minute. Once formed, neurons travel along tiny threads to their permanent locations, where they will form the major parts of the brain (Nelson, Thomas, & de Haan, 2006).

While the nervous system is developing, the heart begins to pump blood, and the muscles, backbone, ribs, and digestive tract appear. At the end of the first month, the curled embryo—only ¼ inch long—consists of millions of organized groups of cells with specific functions.

■ **THE SECOND MONTH.** In the second month, growth continues rapidly. The eyes, ears, nose, jaw, and neck form. Tiny buds become arms, legs, fingers, and toes. Internal organs are more distinct: The intestines grow, the heart develops separate chambers, and the liver and spleen take over production of blood cells so that the yolk sac is no longer needed. Changing body proportions cause the embryo's posture to become more upright. Now 1 inch long and ⅐ ounce in weight, the embryo can sense its world. It responds to touch, particularly in the mouth area and on the soles of the feet. And it can move, although its tiny flutters are still too light to be felt by the mother (Moore & Persaud, 2008).

Period of the Fetus

The period of the **fetus,** from the ninth week to the end of pregnancy, is the longest prenatal period. During this "growth and finishing" phase, the organism increases rapidly in size.

■ **THE THIRD MONTH.** In the third month, the organs, muscles, and nervous system start to become organized and connected. When the brain signals, the fetus kicks, bends its arms, forms a fist, curls its toes, opens its mouth, and even sucks its thumb. The tiny lungs begin to expand and contract in an early rehearsal of breathing movements. By the twelfth week, the external genitals are well-formed, and the sex of the fetus can be detected with ultrasound (Sadler, 2006). Other finishing touches appear, such as fingernails, toenails, tooth buds, and eyelids that open and close. The heartbeat can now be heard through a stethoscope.

Prenatal development is sometimes divided into **trimesters,** or three equal time periods. At the end of the third month, the *first trimester* is complete.

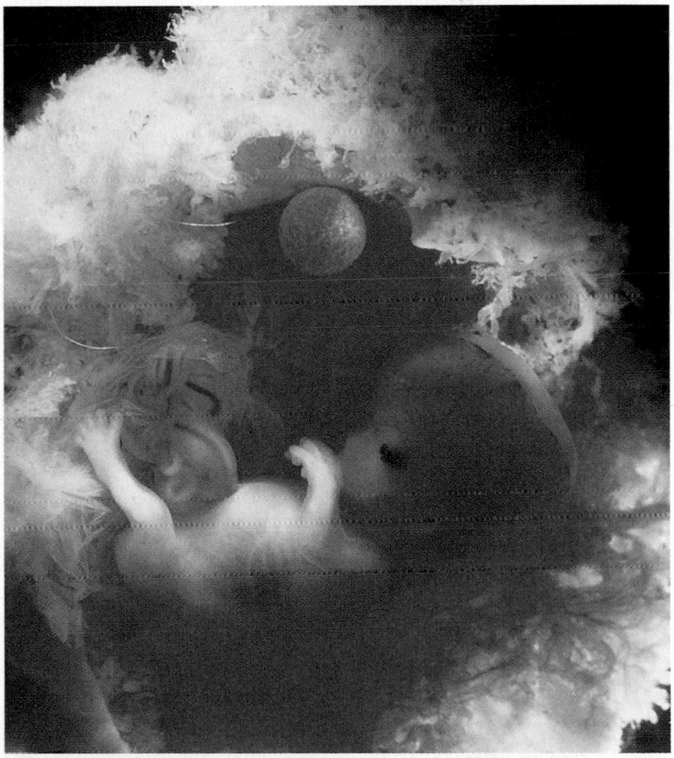

Period of the fetus: eleventh week. The organism grows rapidly. At 11 weeks, the brain and muscles are better connected. The fetus can kick, bend its arms, open and close its hands and mouth, and suck its thumb. Notice the yolk sac, which shrinks as pregnancy advances. The internal organs have taken over its function of producing blood cells.

■ **THE SECOND TRIMESTER.** By the middle of the second trimester, between 17 and 20 weeks, the new being has grown large enough that the mother can feel its movements. A white, cheeselike substance called **vernix** protects its skin from chapping during the long months spent bathing in the amniotic fluid. White, downy hair called **lanugo** also appears over the entire body, helping the vernix stick to the skin.

At the end of the second trimester, many organs are well-developed. And most of the brain's billions of neurons are in place; few will be produced after this time. However, *glial cells,* which support and feed the neurons, continue to increase at a rapid rate throughout pregnancy, as well as after birth. Consequently, brain weight increases tenfold from the twentieth week until birth (Roelfsema et al., 2004).

Brain growth means new behavioral capacities. The 20-week-old fetus can be stimulated as well as irritated by sounds. And if a doctor looks inside the uterus using fetoscopy (see Table 2.4 on page 56), fetuses try to shield their eyes from the light with their hands, indicating that sight has begun to emerge (Moore & Persaud, 2008). Still, a fetus born at this time cannot survive. Its lungs are immature, and the brain cannot yet control breathing and body temperature.

■ **THE THIRD TRIMESTER.** During the final trimester, a fetus born early has a chance for survival. The point at which the fetus can first survive, called the **age of viability,** occurs sometime between 22 and 26 weeks (Moore & Persaud, 2008). A baby born between the seventh and eighth month, however, usually needs oxygen assistance to breathe. Although the brain's respiratory center is now mature, tiny air sacs in the lungs are not yet ready to inflate and exchange carbon dioxide for oxygen.

The brain continues to make great strides. The *cerebral cortex,* the seat of human intelligence, enlarges. As neurological organization improves, the fetus spends more time awake. At 20 weeks, fetal heart rate reveals no periods of alertness. But by 28 weeks, fetuses are awake about 11 percent of the time, a figure that rises to 16 percent just before birth (DiPietro et al., 1996). Between 30 and 34 weeks, fetuses show rhythmic alternations between sleep and wakefulness that gradually increase in organization (Rivkees, 2003). Around this time, synchrony between fetal heart rate and motor activity peaks: A rise in heart rate is usually followed within five seconds by a burst of motor activity (DiPietro et al., 2006). These are clear signs that coordinated neural networks are beginning to form in the brain.

The fetus also takes on the beginnings of a personality. Fetal activity is linked to infant temperament. In one study, more active fetuses during the third trimester became 1-year-olds who could better handle frustration and 2-year-olds who were less

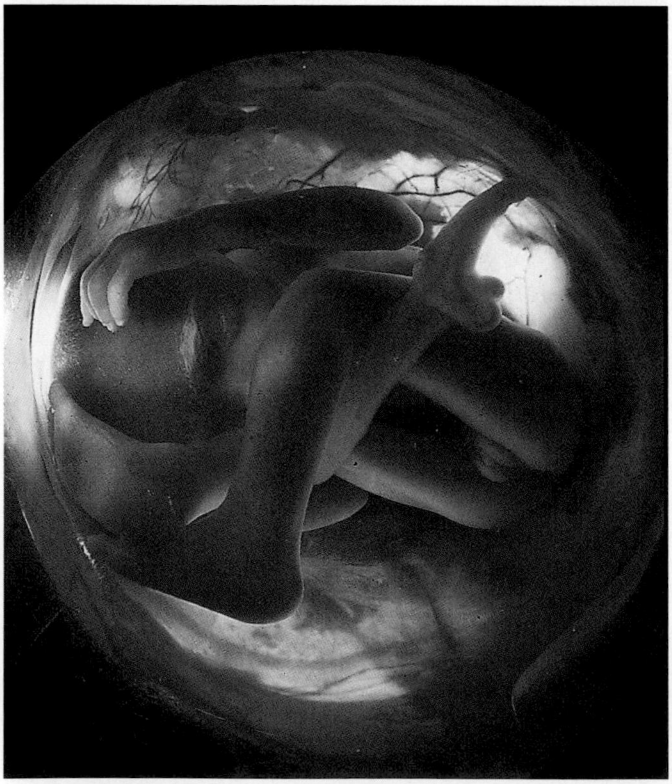

Period of the fetus: twenty-second week. This fetus is almost a foot long and weighs slightly more than one pound. Its movements can be felt easily by the mother and by other family members who place a hand on her abdomen. The fetus has reached the age of viability. If born, it has a slim chance of surviving.

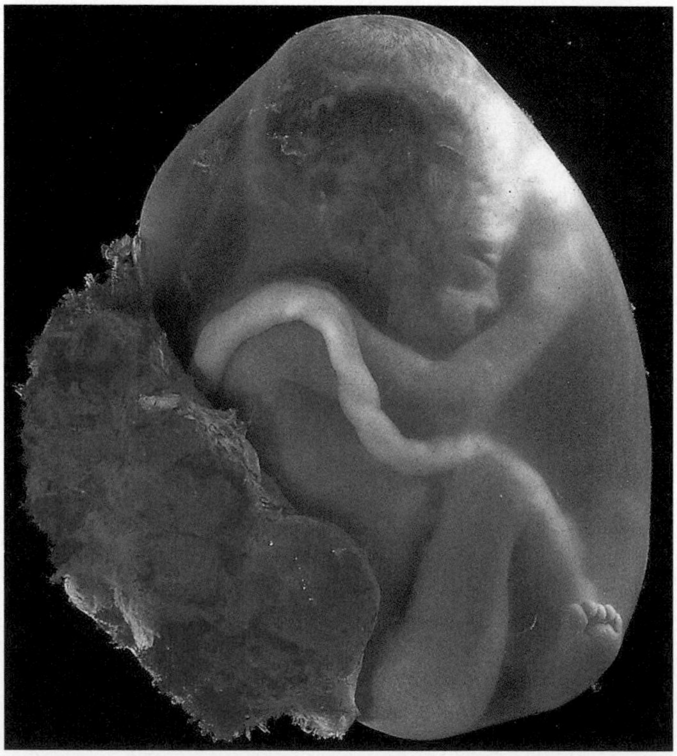

Period of the fetus: thirty-sixth week. This fetus fills the uterus. To support its need for nourishment, the umbilical cord and placenta have grown large. Notice the vernix (cheeselike substance) on the skin, which protects it from chapping. The fetus has accumulated a layer of fat to assist with temperature regulation after birth. In two more weeks, it will be full-term.

fearful, in that they more readily interacted with toys and with an unfamiliar adult in a laboratory (DiPietro et al., 2002). Perhaps fetal activity is an indicator of healthy neurological development, which fosters adaptability in childhood. The relationships just described, however, are only modest. As you will see in Chapter 6, sensitive caregiving can modify the temperaments of children who have difficulty adapting to new experiences.

The third trimester brings greater responsiveness to stimulation. As we will see later when we discuss newborn capacities, fetuses acquire taste and odor preferences from bathing in and swallowing amniotic fluid. Between 23 and 30 weeks, connections form between the cerebral cortex and brain regions involved in pain sensitivity. By this time, painkillers should be used in any surgical procedures performed on a fetus (Lee et al., 2005). Around 28 weeks, fetuses blink their eyes in reaction to nearby sounds (Kisilevsky & Low, 1998; Saffran, Werker, & Werner, 2006).

Within the next six weeks, fetuses distinguish the tone and rhythm of different voices and sounds. They show systematic heart rate changes to a male versus a female speaker, to the mother's voice versus a stranger's, and to a simple familiar melody versus an unfamiliar melody (Granier-Deferre et al., 2003; Huotilainen et al., 2005; Kisilevsky et al., 2003; Lecanuet et al., 1993). And in one clever study, mothers read aloud Dr. Seuss's lively book *The Cat in the Hat* for the last six weeks of pregnancy. After birth, their infants learned to turn on recordings of the mother's voice by sucking on nipples. They sucked hardest to hear *The Cat in the Hat*—the sound they had come to know while still in the womb (DeCasper & Spence, 1986).

In the final three months, the fetus gains more than 5 pounds and grows 7 inches. In the eighth month, a layer of fat is added to assist with temperature regulation. The fetus also receives antibodies from the mother's blood that protect against illnesses, since the newborn's own immune system will not work well until several months after birth. In the last weeks, most fetuses assume an upside-down position, partly because of the shape of the uterus and also because the head is heavier than the feet. Growth slows, and birth is about to take place.

ASK YOURSELF

» REVIEW
Why is the period of the embryo regarded as the most dramatic prenatal period? Why is the fetal period called the "growth and finishing" phase?

» APPLY
Amy, two months pregnant, wonders how the embryo is being fed and what parts of the body have formed. "I don't look pregnant yet, so does that mean not much development has occurred?" she asks. How would you respond to Amy?

» CONNECT
How is brain development related to fetal capacities and behavior?

Prenatal Environmental Influences

Although the prenatal environment is far more constant than the world outside the womb, many factors can affect the embryo and fetus. Yolanda and Jay learned that parents—and society as a whole—can do a great deal to create a safe environment for development before birth.

Teratogens

The term **teratogen** refers to any environmental agent that causes damage during the prenatal period. Scientists chose this label (from the Greek word *teras,* meaning "malformation" or "monstrosity") because they first learned about harmful prenatal influences from cases in which babies had been profoundly damaged. Yet the harm done by teratogens is not always simple and straightforward. It depends on the following factors:

- *Dose.* As we discuss particular teratogens, you will see that larger doses over longer time periods usually have more negative effects.
- *Heredity.* The genetic makeup of the mother and the developing organism plays an important role. Some individuals are better able than others to withstand harmful environments.
- *Other negative influences.* The presence of several negative factors at once, such as additional teratogens, poor nutrition, and lack of medical care, can worsen the impact of a harmful agent.
- *Age.* The effects of teratogens vary with the age of the organism at time of exposure. To understand this last idea, think of the *sensitive period* concept introduced in Chapter 1. A sensitive period is a limited time span in which a part of the body or a behavior is biologically prepared to develop rapidly. During that time, it is especially sensitive to its surroundings. If the environment is harmful, then damage occurs, and recovery is difficult and sometimes impossible.

Figure 3.2 on page 86 summarizes prenatal sensitive periods. In the *period of the zygote,* before implantation, teratogens rarely have any impact. If they do, the tiny mass of cells is usually so damaged that it dies. The *embryonic period* is the time when serious defects are most likely to occur because the foundations for all body parts are being laid down. During the *fetal period,* teratogenic damage is usually minor. However, organs such as the brain, ears, eyes, teeth, and genitals can still be strongly affected.

The effects of teratogens go beyond immediate physical damage. Some health effects are subtle and delayed. As the Lifespan Vista box on pages 88–89 illustrates, they may not show up for decades. Furthermore, psychological consequences may occur indirectly, as a result of physical damage. For example, a defect resulting from drugs the mother took during pregnancy can affect others' reactions to the child as well as the child's ability to

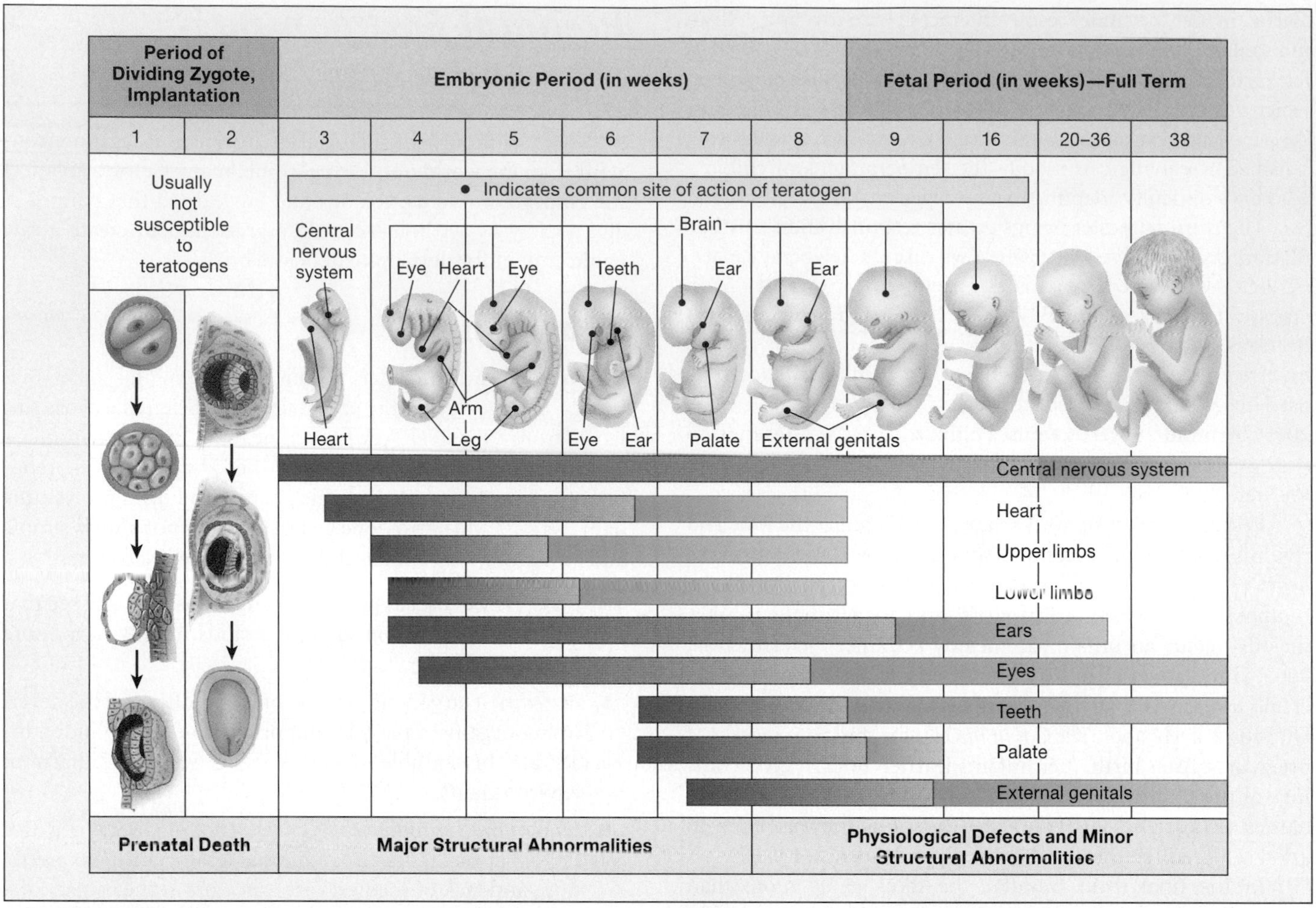

■ **FIGURE 3.2** ■ **Sensitive periods in prenatal development.** Each organ or structure has a sensitive period, during which its development may be disturbed. Blue horizontal bars indicate highly sensitive periods. Green horizontal bars indicate periods that are somewhat less sensitive to teratogens, although damage can occur. (Adapted from *Before We Are Born, 7th ed.,* by K. L. Moore and T. V. N. Persaud, p. 313. Copyright © 2008, reprinted with permission from Elsevier, Inc.)

explore the environment. Over time, parent–child interaction, peer relations, and cognitive, emotional, and social development may suffer. Furthermore, prenatally exposed children may be less resilient in the face of environmental risks, such as single parenthood, parental emotional disturbance, or maladaptive parenting (Yumoto, Jacobson, & Jacobson, 2008). As a result, their long-term adjustment may be compromised.

Notice how an important idea about development that we discussed in earlier chapters is at work here: *bidirectional influences* between child and environment. Now let's look at what scientists have discovered about a variety of teratogens.

■ **PRESCRIPTION AND NONPRESCRIPTION DRUGS.** In the early 1960s, the world learned a tragic lesson about drugs and prenatal development. At that time, a sedative called *thalidomide* was widely available in Canada, Europe, and South America. When taken by mothers four to six weeks after conception, thalidomide produced gross deformities of the embryo's arms and legs and, less frequently, damage to the ears, heart, kidneys, and genitals. About 7,000 infants worldwide were affected (Moore & Persaud, 2008). As children exposed to thalidomide grew older, many scored below average in intelligence. Perhaps the drug damaged the central nervous system directly. Or perhaps the child-rearing conditions of these severely deformed youngsters impaired their intellectual development.

Another medication, a synthetic hormone called *diethylstilbestrol (DES),* was widely prescribed between 1945 and 1970 to prevent miscarriages. As daughters of these mothers reached adolescence and young adulthood, they showed unusually high rates of cancer of the vagina, malformations of the uterus, and infertility. When they tried to have children, their pregnancies more often resulted in prematurity, low birth weight, and miscarriage than those of non-DES-exposed women. Young men showed an increased risk of genital abnormalities and cancer of the testes (Hammes & Laitman, 2003; Palmer et al., 2001).

Currently, the most widely used potent teratogen is a vitamin A derivative called *Accutane,* used to treat severe acne (also known by the generic name *isotretinoin*). Hundreds of thousands of women of childbearing age in industrialized nations take it. Exposure during the first trimester results in eye, ear, skull, brain, heart, and immune system abnormalities (Honein, Paulozzi, & Erickson, 2001). Accutane's packaging warns users to avoid pregnancy by using two methods of birth control, but many women do not heed this advice (Garcia-Bournissen et al., 2008).

Indeed, any drug with a molecule small enough to penetrate the placental barrier can enter the embryonic or fetal bloodstream. Yet many pregnant women continue to take over-the-counter medications without consulting their doctors. Aspirin is one of the most common. Several studies suggest that regular aspirin use is linked to low birth weight, infant death around the time of birth, poorer motor development, and lower intelligence scores in early childhood, although other research fails to confirm these findings (Barr et al., 1990; Kozer et al., 2003; Streissguth et al., 1987). Coffee, tea, cola, and cocoa contain another frequently consumed drug, caffeine. As amounts exceed 100 milligrams per day (equivalent to one cup of coffee), low birth weight and miscarriage increase (CARE Study Group, 2008; Weng, Odouli, & Li, 2008). And antidepressant medication taken during the third trimester is linked to increased risk of birth complications, including respiratory distress (Oberlander et al., 2006).

Because children's lives are involved, we must take findings like these seriously. At the same time, we cannot be sure that these frequently used drugs actually cause the problems just mentioned. Often mothers take more than one drug. If the embryo or fetus is injured, it is hard to tell which drug might be responsible or whether other factors correlated with drug taking are at fault. Until we have more information, the safest course of action is the one Yolanda took: Avoid these drugs entirely. Unfortunately, many women do not know that they are pregnant during the early weeks of the embryonic period, when exposure to teratogens can be of greatest threat.

■ **ILLEGAL DRUGS.** The use of highly addictive mood-altering drugs, such as cocaine and heroin, has become more widespread, especially in poverty-stricken inner cities, where these drugs provide a temporary escape from a daily life of hopelessness. Nearly 4 percent of U.S. pregnant women take these substances (U.S. Department of Health and Human Services, 2007e).

Babies born to users of cocaine, heroin, or methadone (a less addictive drug used to wean people away from heroin) are at risk for a wide variety of problems, including prematurity, low birth weight, physical defects, breathing difficulties, and death around the time of birth (Behnke et al., 2001; Schuetze & Eiden, 2006; Walker, Rosenberg, & Balaban-Gil, 1999). In addition, these infants are born drug-addicted. They are often feverish and irritable and have trouble sleeping, and their cries are abnormally shrill and piercing—a common symptom among stressed newborns (Bauer et al., 2005). When mothers with many problems of their own must care for these babies, who are difficult to calm down, cuddle, and feed, behavior problems are likely to persist.

Throughout the first year, heroin- and methadone-exposed infants are less attentive to the environment than nonexposed babies, and their motor development is slow. After infancy, some children get better, while others remain jittery and inattentive. The kind of parenting they receive may explain why problems persist for some but not for others (Cosden, Peerson, & Elliott, 1997).

Evidence on cocaine suggests that some prenatally exposed babies develop lasting difficulties. Cocaine constricts the blood vessels, causing oxygen delivered to the developing organism to fall for 15 minutes following a high dose. It also can alter the production and functioning of neurons and the chemical balance in the fetus's brain. These effects may contribute to any array of cocaine-associated physical defects, including eye, bone, genital, urinary tract, kidney, and heart deformities; brain hemorrhages and seizures; and severe growth retardation (Covington et al., 2002; Feng, 2005; Mayes, 1999). Some studies report perceptual, motor, attention, memory, language, and impulse-control problems that persist into the preschool years (Dennis et al., 2006; Lester et al., 2003; Linares et al., 2006; Noland et al., 2005; Singer et al., 2004).

But other investigations reveal no major negative effects of prenatal cocaine exposure (Behnke et al., 2006; Frank et al., 2005; Hurt et al., 2005). These contradictory findings indicate how difficult it is to isolate the precise damage caused by illegal drugs. Cocaine users often take several drugs, display other high-risk behaviors, suffer from poverty and other stresses, and engage in insensitive caregiving—factors that worsen outcomes for children (Jones, 2006). But researchers have yet to determine exactly what accounts for findings of cocaine-related damage in some studies but not in others.

Another illegal drug, marijuana, is used more widely than heroin and cocaine. Studies examining its relationship to low birth weight and prematurity reveal mixed findings (Fried, 1993). Several researchers have linked prenatal marijuana

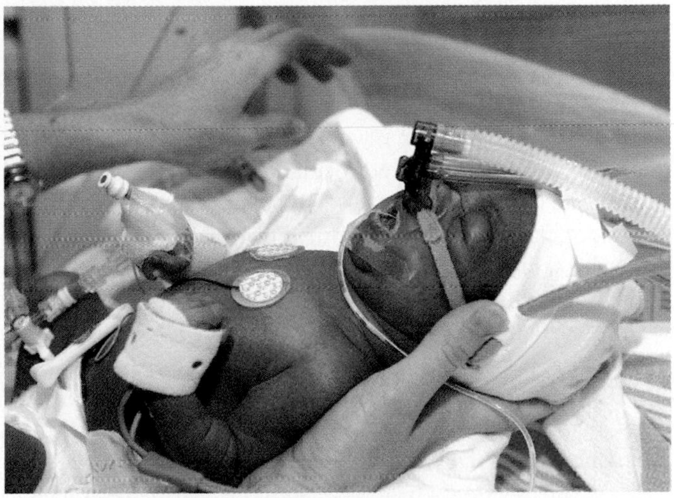

This 3-day-old infant, who was born many weeks before his due date and is underweight, breathes with the aid of a respirator. Prematurity and low birth weight can result from a variety of environmental influences during pregnancy, including maternal drug use and cigarette smoking.

A LIFESPAN VISTA: Looking Forward, Looking Back

The Prenatal Environment and Health in Later Life

When Michael entered the world 55 years ago, six weeks premature and weighing only 4 pounds, the doctor delivering him wasn't sure he would make it. Michael not only survived but enjoyed good health until his mid-forties when, during a routine medical checkup, he was diagnosed with high blood pressure and type 2 diabetes. Michael had no apparent risk factors for these conditions: He wasn't overweight, didn't smoke, and didn't eat high-fat foods. Nor did the illnesses run in his family. Could the roots of Michael's health problems date back to his prenatal development?

Increasing evidence suggests that prenatal environmental factors—ones that are not toxic (as are tobacco or alcohol) but rather fairly subtle, such as the flow of nutrients and hormones across the placenta—can affect an individual's health decades later.

Low Birth Weight and Heart Disease, Stroke, and Diabetes

Carefully controlled animal experiments reveal that a poorly nourished, underweight fetus experiences changes in body structure and function that greatly increase the risk of cardiovascular disease in adulthood (Franco et al., 2002). To explore this relationship in humans, researchers tapped public records, gathering information on the birth weights of 15,000 British men and women and the occurrence of disease in middle adulthood. Those weighing less than 5 pounds at birth had a 50 percent greater chance of dying of heart disease and stroke, even after SES and a variety of other health risks were controlled. The connection between birth weight and cardiovascular disease was strongest for people whose weight-to-length ratio at birth was very low—a sign of prenatal growth stunting (Godfrey & Barker, 2000; Martyn, Barker, & Osmond, 1996).

In other large-scale studies, a consistent link between low birth weight and heart disease, stroke, and diabetes in middle adulthood has emerged—for both sexes and in diverse countries, including Finland, India, Jamaica, and the United States (Barker, 2002; Fowden, Giussani, & Forhead, 2005; Roseboom, de Rooij, & Painter, 2006). Smallness itself does not cause later health problems; rather, researchers believe, complex factors associated with it are involved.

Some speculate that a poorly nourished fetus diverts large amounts of blood to the brain, causing organs in the abdomen such as the liver and kidney (involved in controlling cholesterol and blood pressure) to be undersized (Hales & Ozanne, 2003). The result is heightened later risk of heart disease and

Prenatal environmental factors—even subtle ones such as the flow of nutrients and hormones across the placenta—can affect an individual's health in later life. This newborn girl's high birth weight places her at increased risk for breast cancer in adulthood.

exposure to smaller head size (a measure of brain growth); to sleep, attention, and memory difficulties in childhood; and to poorer problem-solving performance in adolescence (Dahl et al., 1995; Goldschmidt et al., 2004; Gray et al., 2005; Huizink & Mulder, 2006). As with cocaine, however, lasting effects are not well-established. Overall, the effects of illegal drugs are far less consistent than the impact of two legal substances to which we now turn: tobacco and alcohol.

■ **TOBACCO.** Although smoking has declined in Western nations, an estimated 17 percent of U.S. women smoke during their pregnancies (U.S. Department of Health and Human Services, 2007e). The best-known effect of smoking during the prenatal period is low birth weight. But the likelihood of other serious consequences, such as miscarriage, prematurity, impaired heart rate and breathing during sleep, infant death, and asthma and cancer later in childhood, is also increased (Franco et al., 2000; Jaakkola & Gissler, 2004). The more cigarettes a mother smokes, the greater the chances that her baby will be affected. If a pregnant woman stops smoking at any time, even during the last trimester, she reduces the likelihood that her infant will be born underweight and suffer from future problems (Klesges et al., 2001).

Even when a baby of a smoking mother appears to be born in good physical condition, slight behavioral abnormalities may threaten the child's development. Newborns of smoking mothers are less attentive to sounds, display more muscle tension, are more excitable when touched and visually stimulated, and more often have colic (persistent crying)—findings that suggest subtle negative effects on brain development (Law et al., 2003; Sondergaard et al., 2002). Some studies report that prenatally exposed children and adolescents have shorter attention spans, poorer memories, lower mental test scores, and more behavior problems (Fried, Watkinson, & Gray, 2003; Huizink & Mulder, 2006; Nigg & Breslau, 2007; Thapar et al.,

stroke. In the case of diabetes, inadequate prenatal nutrition may permanently impair functioning of the pancreas, leading blood sugar (glucose) to rise beyond control as the person ages (Wu et al., 2004). Yet another hypothesis, supported by both animal and human research, is that the malfunctioning placentas of some expectant mothers permit high levels of stress hormones to reach the fetus, which retard fetal growth, increase fetal blood pressure, and promote excess blood glucose, predisposing the developing person to later disease (Stocker, Arch, & Cawthorne, 2005).

Finally, prenatally growth-stunted babies often gain excessive weight in childhood, once they have access to plentiful food. This excess weight usually persists, greatly magnifying the risk of diabetes (Hyppönen, Power, & Smith, 2003).

High Birth Weight and Cancer

The other prenatal growth extreme—high birth weight—is linked to breast cancer, the most common malignancy in adult women (Ahlgren et al., 2004; Vatten et al., 2002). In one sample of more than 2,000 British women, high birth weight—especially above 8.8 pounds—was associated with a greatly increased incidence of breast cancer, even after other cancer risks were controlled (see Figure 3.3) (dos Santos Silva et al., 2004). Researchers suspect that the culprit is excessive estrogen in the overweight expectant mother, which promotes large fetal size and alters the makeup of beginning breast tissue so that it may respond to estrogen in adulthood by becoming malignant.

High birth weight is also associated with increases in digestive and lymphatic cancers in both men and women (McCormack et al., 2005). As yet, the reasons are unclear.

Prevention

The relationships between prenatal development and later-life illnesses emerging in research do not mean that the illnesses are inevitable. Rather, prenatal environmental conditions *influence* adult health, and the steps people take to protect their health can prevent prenatal risks from becoming reality. Researchers advise individuals who were low-weight at birth to get regular medical checkups and to be attentive to diet, weight, fitness, and stress—controllable factors that contribute to heart disease and type 2 diabetes. And high-birth-weight women should be conscientious about breast self-exams and mammograms, which permit early detection—and, in many cases, cure—of breast cancer.

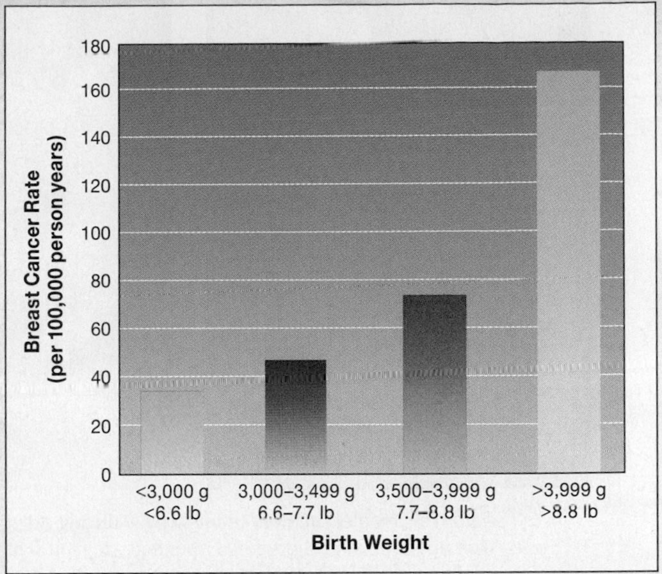

■ **FIGURE 3.3** ■ **Relationship of birth weight to breast cancer risk in adulthood.** In a study of over 2,000 British births with follow-ups in adulthood, birth weight predicted breast cancer incidence after many other prenatal and postnatal health risks were controlled. The breast cancer risk was especially high for women whose birth weights were greater than 3,999 grams, or 8.8 pounds. (Adapted from dos Santos Silva et al., 2004.)

2003). However, other factors closely associated with smoking, such as lower maternal education and income levels, may contribute to these outcomes (Huijbregts et al., 2006).

Exactly how can smoking harm the fetus? Nicotine, the addictive substance in tobacco, constricts blood vessels, lessens blood flow to the uterus, and causes the placenta to grow abnormally. This reduces the transfer of nutrients, so the fetus gains weight poorly. Also, nicotine raises the concentration of carbon monoxide in the bloodstreams of both mother and fetus. Carbon monoxide displaces oxygen from red blood cells, damaging the central nervous system and slowing body growth in the fetuses of laboratory animals (Friedman, 1996). Similar effects may occur in humans.

From one-third to one-half of nonsmoking pregnant women are "passive smokers" because their husbands, relatives, or co-workers use cigarettes. Passive smoking is also related to low birth weight, infant death, childhood respiratory illnesses, and possible long-term impairments in attention and learning (Hanke, Sobala, & Kalinka, 2004; Makin, Fried, & Watkinson, 1991; Pattenden et al., 2006). Clearly, expectant mothers should avoid smoke-filled environments.

■ **ALCOHOL.** In his moving book *The Broken Cord,* Michael Dorris (1989), a Dartmouth College anthropology professor, described what it was like to rear his adopted son Abel (called Adam in the book), whose biological mother drank heavily throughout pregnancy and died of alcohol poisoning shortly after his birth. A Sioux Indian, Abel was born with **fetal alcohol spectrum disorder (FASD),** a term encompassing a range of physical, mental, and behavioral outcomes caused by prenatal alcohol exposure. Children with FASD are given one of three diagnoses, which vary in severity:

1. **Fetal alcohol syndrome (FAS),** distinguished by (a) slow physical growth, (b) a pattern of three facial abnormalities (short eyelid openings, a thin upper lip, a smooth or flattened philtrum, or indentation running from the bottom

Left photo: This toddler's mother drank heavily during pregnancy. Her widely spaced eyes, thin upper lip, and short eyelid openings are typical of fetal alcohol syndrome (FAS). *Right photo:* This 11-year-old girl also has the facial abnormalities of FAS and shows the slow physical growth that accompanies the disorder.

of the nose to the center of the upper lip), and (c) brain injury, evident in a small head and impairment in at least three areas of functioning—for example, memory, language and communication, attention span and activity level (overactivity), planning and reasoning, motor coordination, or social skills. Other defects—of the eyes, ears, nose, throat, heart, genitals, urinary tract, or immune system—may also be present. Abel was diagnosed as having FAS. As is typical for this disorder, his mother drank heavily throughout pregnancy.

2. **Partial fetal alcohol syndrome (p-FAS),** characterized by (a) two of the three facial abnormalities just mentioned and (b) brain injury, again evident in at least three areas of impaired functioning. Mothers of children with p-FAS generally drank alcohol in smaller quantities, and children's defects vary with the timing and length of alcohol exposure. Furthermore, recent evidence suggests that paternal alcohol use around the time of conception may induce genetic alterations, thereby contributing to symptoms (Abel, 2004).
3. **Alcohol-related neurodevelopmental disorder (ARND),** in which at least three areas of mental functioning are impaired, despite typical physical growth and absence of facial abnormalities. Again, prenatal alcohol exposure, though confirmed, is less pervasive than in FAS (Chudley et al., 2005; Loock et al., 2005).

Even when provided with enriched diets, FAS babies fail to catch up in physical size during infancy and childhood. Mental impairment associated with all three FASD diagnoses is also permanent: In his teens and twenties, Abel had trouble concentrating and keeping a routine job, and he suffered from poor judgment. For example, he would buy something and not wait for change or wander off in the middle of a task. He died in 1991, at age 23, after being hit by a car.

The more alcohol a woman consumes during pregnancy, the poorer the child's motor coordination, speed of information processing, reasoning, and intelligence and achievement test scores during the preschool and school years (Burden, Jacobson, & Jacobson, 2005; Korkman, Kettunen, & Autti-Raemoe, 2003; Mattson, Calarco, & Lang, 2006). In adolescence and early adulthood, FASD is associated with persisting attention and motor-coordination deficits, poor school performance, trouble with the law, inappropriate sexual behavior, alcohol and drug abuse, and lasting mental health problems (Barr et al., 2006; Connor et al., 2006; Howell et al., 2006; Streissguth et al., 2004).

How does alcohol produce its devastating effects? First, it interferes with production and migration of neurons in the primitive neural tube. Brain-imaging research reveals reduced brain size, damage to many brain structures, and abnormalities in brain functioning, including the electrical and chemical activity involved in transferring messages from one part of the brain to another (Riley, McGee, & Sowell, 2004; Spadoni et al., 2007). Second, the body uses large quantities of oxygen to metabolize alcohol. A pregnant woman's heavy drinking draws away oxygen that the developing organism needs for cell growth.

About 25 percent of U.S. mothers report drinking at some time during their pregnancies. As with heroin and cocaine, alcohol abuse is higher in poverty-stricken women. On some Native-American reservations, the incidence of FAS is as high as 10 to 20 percent (Szlemko, Wood, & Thurman, 2006; U.S. Department of Health and Human Services, 2007e). Unfortunately, when affected girls later become pregnant, the poor judgment caused by the syndrome often prevents them from understanding why they themselves should avoid alcohol. Thus, the tragic cycle is likely to be repeated in the next generation.

How much alcohol is safe during pregnancy? Even mild drinking, less than one drink per day, is associated with reduced head size and body growth among children followed into adolescence (Jacobson et al., 2004; Martinez-Frias et al., 2004). Recall that other factors—both genetic and environmental—can make some fetuses more vulnerable to teratogens. Therefore, no amount of alcohol is safe. Couples planning a pregnancy and expectant mothers should avoid alcohol entirely.

■ **RADIATION.** Defects due to ionizing radiation were tragically apparent in children born to pregnant women who survived the bombing of Hiroshima and Nagasaki during World War II. Similar abnormalities surfaced in the nine months following the 1986 Chernobyl, Ukraine, nuclear power plant accident. After each disaster, the incidence of miscarriage and babies born with underdeveloped brains, physical deformities, and slow physical growth rose dramatically (Hoffmann, 2001; Schull, 2003).

This child's deformities are linked to radiation exposure during the Chernobyl nuclear power plant disaster of 1986. Her mother was just a few weeks pregnant at that time. She is also at risk for low intelligence and language and emotional disorders.

Even when a radiation-exposed baby seems normal, problems may appear later. For example, even low-level radiation, resulting from industrial leakage or medical X-rays, can increase the risk of childhood cancer (Fattibene et al., 1999). In middle childhood, prenatally exposed Chernobyl children had abnormal brain-wave activity, lower intelligence test scores, and rates of language and emotional disorders two to three times greater than those of nonexposed Russian children. Furthermore, the more tension parents reported, due to forced evacuation from their homes and worries about living in irradiated areas, the poorer their children's emotional functioning (Loganovskaja & Loganovsky, 1999; Loganovsky et al., 2008). Stressful rearing conditions seemed to combine with the damaging effects of prenatal radiation to impair children's development.

■ ENVIRONMENTAL POLLUTION. In industrialized nations, an astounding number of potentially dangerous chemicals are released into the environment. More than 75,000 are in common use in the United States, and many new pollutants are introduced each year. When 10 newborns were randomly selected from U.S. hospitals for analysis of umbilical cord blood, researchers uncovered a startling array of industrial contaminants—287 in all! They concluded that many babies are "born polluted" by chemicals that not only impair prenatal development but increase the chances of life-threatening diseases and health problems later on (Houlihan et al., 2005).

In the 1950s, an industrial plant released waste containing high levels of *mercury* into a bay providing seafood and water for the town of Minamata, Japan. Many children born at the time displayed physical deformities, mental retardation, abnormal speech, difficulty in chewing and swallowing, and uncoordinated movements. High levels of prenatal mercury exposure disrupt production and migration of neurons, causing widespread brain damage (Clarkson, Magos, & Myers, 2003; Hubbs-Tait et al., 2005). Pregnant women are wise to avoid eating long-lived predatory fish, such as swordfish, albacore tuna, and shark, which are heavily contaminated with mercury.

For many years, *polychlorinated biphenyls (PCBs)* were used to insulate electrical equipment until research showed that, like mercury, they entered waterways and the food supply. In Taiwan, prenatal exposure to high levels of PCBs in rice oil resulted in low birth weight, discolored skin, deformities of the gums and nails, brain-wave abnormalities, and delayed cognitive development (Chen & Hsu, 1994; Chen et al., 1994). Steady, low-level PCB exposure is also harmful. Women who frequently ate PCB-contaminated fish, compared with those who ate little or no fish, had infants with lower birth weights, smaller heads, persisting attention and memory difficulties, and lower intelligence test scores in childhood (Jacobson & Jacobson, 2003; Stewart et al., 2000; Walkowiak et al., 2001).

Another teratogen, *lead,* is present in paint flaking off the walls of old buildings and in certain materials used in industrial occupations. High levels of prenatal lead exposure are related to prematurity, low birth weight, brain damage, and a wide variety of physical defects. Even low levels may be dangerous. In some studies, affected babies showed slightly poorer mental and motor development (Bellinger, 2005). In one investigation, unfavorable effects—in the form of increased delinquent and antisocial behaviors—were evident in adolescence (Dietrich et al., 2001).

Finally, prenatal exposure to dioxins—toxic compounds resulting from incineration—is linked to brain, immune system, and thyroid damage in babies and to an increased incidence of breast and uterine cancers in women, perhaps through altering hormone levels (ten Tusscher & Koppe, 2004). Furthermore, even tiny amounts of dioxin in the paternal bloodstream cause a dramatic change in sex ratio of offspring: Affected men father nearly twice as many girls as boys (Ishihara et al., 2007; Mocarelli et al., 2000). Dioxin seems to impair the fertility of Y-bearing sperm prior to conception.

■ INFECTIOUS DISEASE. During her first prenatal visit. Yolanda's doctor asked her if she and Jay had already had measles, mumps, chickenpox, and several other illnesses. Although most infectious diseases seem to have no impact, a few—as Table 3.2 on page 92 illustrates—can cause extensive damage.

Viruses. In the mid-1960s, a worldwide epidemic of *rubella* (three-day, or German, measles) led to the birth of more than 20,000 North American babies with serious defects. Consistent with the sensitive-period concept, the greatest damage occurs when rubella strikes during the embryonic period. More than 50 percent of infants whose mothers become ill during that time show eye cataracts; deafness; heart, genital, urinary, and intestinal abnormalities; and mental retardation (Eberhart-Phillips, Frederick, & Baron, 1993). Infection during the fetal period is

■ TABLE 3.2 ■ *Effects of Some Infectious Diseases During Pregnancy*

DISEASE	MISCARRIAGE	PHYSICAL MALFORMATIONS	MENTAL RETARDATION	LOW BIRTH WEIGHT AND PREMATURITY
VIRAL				
Acquired immune deficiency syndrome (AIDS)	0	?	+	?
Chickenpox	0	+	+	+
Cytomegalovirus	+	+	+	+
Herpes simplex 2 (genital herpes)	+	+	+	+
Mumps	+	?	0	0
Rubella (German measles)	+	+	+	+
BACTERIAL				
Chlamydia	+	?	0	+
Syphilis	+	+	+	?
Tuberculosis	+	?	+	+
PARASITIC				
Malaria	+	0	0	+
Toxoplasmosis	+	+	+	+

+ = established finding, 0 = no present evidence, ? = possible effect that is not clearly established.

Sources: Jones, Lopez, & Wilson, 2003; Kliegman et al., 2008; Mardh, 2002; O'Rahilly & Müller, 2001.

less harmful, but low birth weight, hearing loss, and bone defects may still occur. And the brain abnormalities resulting from prenatal rubella increase the risk of severe mental illness in adulthood (Brown, 2006). Routine vaccination in infancy and childhood has made new rubella outbreaks unlikely in industrialized nations (Hyde et al., 2006). But an estimated 100,000 cases of prenatal infection continue to occur worldwide, primarily in developing countries in Africa and Asia with weak or absent immunization programs (Robinson et al., 2006).

The *human immunodeficiency virus (HIV),* which can lead to *acquired immune deficiency syndrome (AIDS),* a disease that destroys the immune system, has infected increasing numbers of women over the past two decades. In developing countries, where 95 percent of new infections occur, more than half affect women. In South Africa, for example, one-fourth of all pregnant women are HIV-positive (Kasmauski & Jaret, 2003; Quinn & Overbaugh, 2005). HIV-infected expectant mothers pass the deadly virus to the developing organism 20 to 30 percent of the time.

AIDS progresses rapidly in infants. By 6 months, weight loss, diarrhea, and repeated respiratory illnesses are common. The virus also causes brain damage. Most prenatal AIDS babies survive for only five to eight months after the appearance of these symptoms (O'Rahilly & Müller, 2001). The antiviral drug zidovudine (ZDV) reduces prenatal AIDS transmission by as much as 95 percent, with no harmful consequences of drug treatment for children (Culnane et al., 1999). ZDV has led to a dramatic decline in prenatally acquired AIDS in Western nations, but it is not widely available in impoverished regions of the world (United Nations, 2006a).

As Table 3.2 reveals, the developing organism is especially sensitive to the family of herpes viruses, for which no vaccine or treatment exists. Among these, *cytomegalovirus* (the most frequent prenatal infection, transmitted through respiratory or sexual contact) and *herpes simplex 2* (which is sexually transmitted) are especially dangerous. In both, the virus invades the mother's genital tract, infecting babies either during pregnancy or at birth.

Bacterial and Parasitic Diseases. Table 3.2 also includes several bacterial and parasitic diseases. Among the most common is *toxoplasmosis,* caused by a parasite found in many animals. Pregnant women may become infected from eating raw or undercooked meat or from contact with the feces of infected cats. About 40 percent of women who have the disease transmit

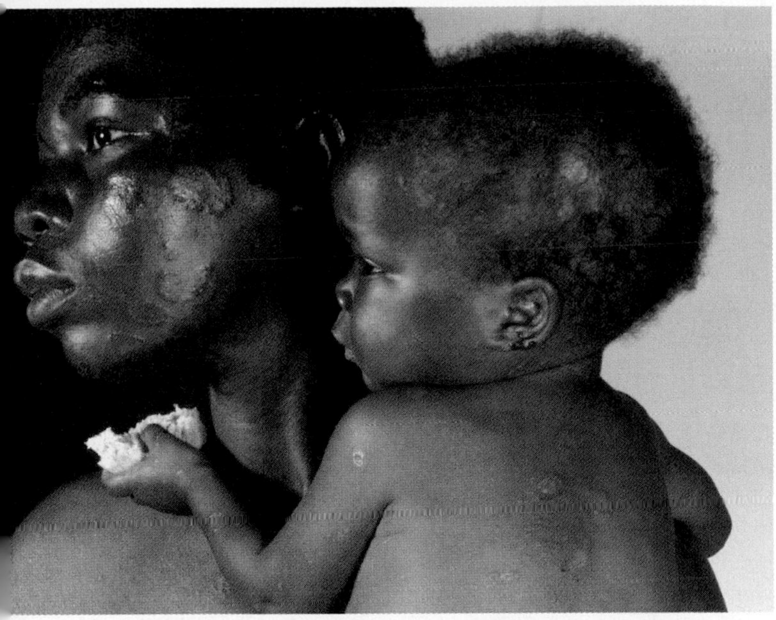

This South African mother and infant, who are suffering from AIDS, both have extensive ringworm skin rashes. Their weakened immune systems make normally harmless infections life threatening. Because AIDS progresses rapidly in infants, the baby may live only a few months.

it to the developing organism. If it strikes during the first trimester, it is likely to cause eye and brain damage. Later infection is linked to mild visual and cognitive impairments (Jones, Lopez, & Wilson, 2003). Expectant mothers can avoid toxoplasmosis by making sure that the meat they eat is well-cooked, having pet cats checked for the disease, and turning over the care of litter boxes to other family members.

Other Maternal Factors

Besides avoiding teratogens, expectant parents can support the development of the embryo and fetus in other ways. In healthy, physically fit women, regular moderate exercise, such as walking, swimming, biking, or an aerobic workout, is related to increased birth weight (Leiferman & Evenson, 2003). However, frequent, vigorous, extended exercise, especially late in pregnancy, results in lower birth weight than in healthy, nonexercising controls (Clapp et al., 2002; Pivarnik, 1998). (Pregnant women with health problems, such as circulatory difficulties or previous miscarriages, should consult their doctors about a physical fitness routine.)

In the following sections, we examine other maternal factors—nutrition, emotional stress, blood type, age, and previous births.

■ **NUTRITION.** During the prenatal period, when children are growing more rapidly than at any other time, they depend totally on the mother for nutrients. A healthy diet that results in a weight gain of 25 to 30 pounds (10 to 13.5 kilograms) helps ensure the health of mother and baby.

Consequences of Prenatal Malnutrition. Prenatal malnutrition can cause serious damage to the central nervous system. The poorer the mother's diet, the greater the loss in brain weight, especially if malnutrition occurred during the last trimester. During that time, the brain is increasing rapidly in size, and a maternal diet high in all the basic nutrients is necessary for it to reach its full potential (Morgane et al., 1993). An inadequate diet during pregnancy can also distort the structure of other organs, including the liver, kidney, and pancreas, resulting in lifelong health problems (refer again to the Lifespan Vista box on pages 88–89).

Because poor nutrition suppresses development of the immune system, prenatally malnourished babies frequently catch respiratory illnesses (Chandra, 1991). In addition, they are often irritable and unresponsive to stimulation. In poverty-stricken families, these effects quickly combine with a stressful home life. With age, low intelligence and serious learning problems become more apparent (Pollitt, 1996).

Prevention and Treatment. Many studies show that providing pregnant women with adequate food has a substantial impact on the health of their newborn babies. Yet the growth demands of the prenatal period require more than just increased quantity of food. Vitamin–mineral enrichment is also crucial. For example, taking a folic acid supplement around the time of conception greatly reduces by more than 70 percent abnormalities of the neural tube, such as *anencephaly* and *spina bifida* (see Table 2.4 on page 56). In addition, adequate folic acid intake during the last 10 weeks of pregnancy cuts in half the risk of premature delivery and low birth weight (MCR Vitamin Study Research Group, 1991; Scholl, Heidiger, & Belsky, 1996). Because of these findings, U.S. government guidelines recommend that all women of childbearing age consume 0.4 milligrams of folic acid per day. For women who have previously had a pregnancy affected by neural tube defect, the recommended amount is 4 to 5 milligrams (dosage must be carefully monitored, as excessive intake can be harmful) (American Academy of Pediatrics, 2006). Currently, bread, flour, rice, pasta, and other grain products are being fortified with folic acid.

When poor nutrition persists throughout pregnancy, infants usually require more than dietary improvement. Successful interventions must also break the cycle of apathetic mother–baby interactions. Some do so by teaching parents how to interact effectively with their infants, while others focus on stimulating infants to promote active engagement with their physical and social surroundings (Grantham-McGregor et al., 1994; Grantham-McGregor, Schofield, & Powell, 1987).

Although prenatal malnutrition is highest in poverty-stricken regions of the world, it is not limited to developing countries. The U.S. Special Supplemental Food Program for Women, Infants, and Children (WIC), which provides food packages to low-income pregnant women, reaches about 90 percent of those who qualify because of their extremely low incomes (U.S. Department of Agriculture, 2008). But many U.S. women who need nutrition intervention are not eligible for WIC.

EMOTIONAL STRESS. When women experience severe emotional stress during pregnancy, their babies are at risk for a wide variety of difficulties. Intense anxiety is associated with higher rates of miscarriage, prematurity, low birth weight, infant respiratory and digestive illnesses, sleep disturbances, and irritability during the first three years (Field et al., 2007; Mulder et al., 2002; Wadhwa, Sandman, & Garite, 2001). It is also related to several commonly occurring physical defects, such as cleft lip and palate, heart deformities, and pyloric stenosis (tightening of the infant's stomach outlet, which often must be treated surgically) (Carmichael & Shaw, 2000).

How can maternal stress affect the fetus? ***TAKE A MOMENT...*** To understand this process, list the changes you sensed in your own body the last time you were under stress. When we experience fear and anxiety, stimulant hormones released into our bloodstream cause us to be "poised for action." Large amounts of blood are sent to parts of the body involved in the defensive response—the brain, the heart, and the muscles in the arms, legs, and trunk. Blood flow to other organs, including the uterus, is reduced. As a result, the fetus is deprived of a full supply of oxygen and nutrients.

Stress hormones also cross the placenta, causing a dramatic rise in fetal heart rate (Monk et al., 2000, 2004). They also may permanently alter fetal neurological functioning, thereby heightening stress reactivity in later life (Monk et al., 2003). In one study, researchers identified mothers who had been directly exposed to the September 11, 2001, World Trade Center collapse during their pregnancies. At age 9 months, their babies were tested for saliva concentrations of *cortisol,* a hormone involved in regulating the stress response. Infants whose mothers had reacted to the disaster with severe anxiety had abnormally low cortisol levels, a symptom of reduced physiological capacity to manage stress (Yehuda et al., 2005). Consistent with this finding, maternal emotional stress during pregnancy predicts anxiety, short attention span, anger, aggression, and overactivity among preschool and school-age children, above and beyond the impact of other risks, such as maternal smoking during pregnancy, low birth weight, postnatal maternal anxiety, and low SES (de Weerth & Buitelaar, 2005; Gutteling et al., 2006; Van den Bergh, 2004).

But stress-related prenatal complications are greatly reduced when mothers have partners, other family members, and friends who offer social support (Federenko & Wadhwa, 2004). The link between social support and positive pregnancy outcomes is particularly strong for low-income women, who often lead highly stressful daily lives (Hoffman & Hatch, 1996).

RH FACTOR INCOMPATIBILITY. When the inherited blood types of mother and fetus differ, serious problems sometimes result. The most common cause of these difficulties is **Rh factor incompatibility.** When the mother is Rh-negative (lacks the Rh blood protein) and the father is Rh-positive (has the protein), the baby may inherit the father's Rh-positive blood type. If even a little of a fetus's Rh-positive blood crosses the placenta into the Rh-negative mother's bloodstream, she begins to form antibodies to the foreign Rh protein. If these enter the fetus's system, they destroy red blood cells, reducing the oxygen supply to organs and tissues. Mental retardation, miscarriage, heart damage, and infant death can occur.

It takes time for the mother to produce Rh antibodies, so firstborn children are rarely affected. The danger increases with each additional pregnancy. Fortunately, Rh incompatibility can be prevented in most cases. After the birth of each Rh-positive baby, Rh-negative mothers are routinely given a vaccine to prevent the buildup of antibodies.

MATERNAL AGE. In Chapter 2, we noted that women who delay childbearing until their thirties or forties face increased risk of infertility, miscarriage, and babies born with chromosomal defects. Are other pregnancy complications more common for older mothers? Research consistently indicates that healthy women in their thirties have about the same rates of prenatal and birth complications as those in their twenties (Bianco et al., 1996; Dildy et al., 1996; Prysak, Lorenz, & Kisly, 1995). Thereafter, as Figure 3.4 reveals, complication rates increase, with a sharp rise among women age 50 to 55—an age at which because of menopause (end of menstruation) and aging reproductive organs, few women can conceive naturally (Salihu et al., 2003).

In the case of teenage mothers, does physical immaturity cause prenatal complications? As we will see in Chapter 11,

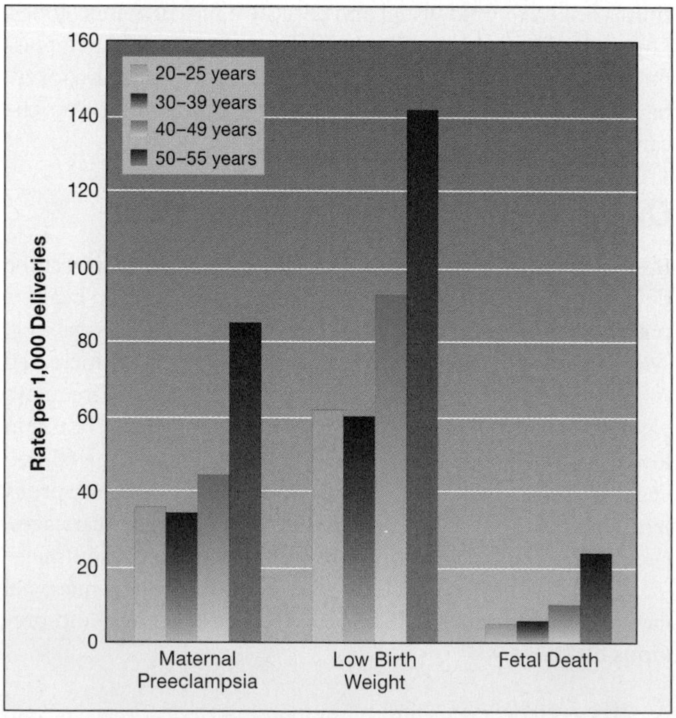

FIGURE 3.4 **Relationship of maternal age to prenatal and birth complications.** Complications increase after age 40, with a sharp rise between 50 and 55 years. See page 95 for a description of preeclampsia. (Adapted from Salihu et al., 2003.)

nature tries to ensure that once a girl can conceive, she is physically ready to carry and give birth to a baby. Infants born to teenagers have a higher rate of problems, but not directly because of maternal age. Most pregnant teenagers come from low-income backgrounds, where stress, poor nutrition, and health problems are common. Also, many are afraid to seek medical care or, in the United States, do not have access to care because they lack health insurance (U.S. Department of Health and Human Services, 2008g).

The Importance of Prenatal Health Care

Yolanda had her first prenatal appointment three weeks after missing her menstrual period. After that, she visited the doctor's office once a month until she was seven months pregnant, then twice during the eighth month. As birth grew near, Yolanda's appointments increased to once a week. The doctor kept track of her general health, her weight gain, and the capacity of her uterus and cervix to support the fetus. The fetus's growth was also carefully monitored.

Yolanda's pregnancy, like most others, was free of complications. But unexpected difficulties can arise, especially if mothers have health problems. For example, women with diabetes need careful monitoring. Extra sugar in the diabetic mother's bloodstream causes the fetus to grow larger than average, making pregnancy and birth problems more common. Another complication, experienced by 5 to 10 percent of pregnant women, is *preeclampsia* (sometimes called *toxemia*), in which blood pressure increases sharply and the face, hands, and feet swell in the last half of pregnancy. If untreated, preeclampsia can cause convulsions in the mother and fetal death. Usually, hospitalization, bed rest, and drugs can lower blood pressure to a safe level (Vidaeff, Carroll, & Ramin, 2005). If not, the baby must be delivered at once.

Unfortunately, 16 percent of pregnant women in the United States wait until after the first trimester to seek prenatal care, and 4 percent receive none at all. Most are adolescents, unmarried, or members of poverty-stricken ethnic minorities. Their infants are three times as likely to be born underweight and five times as likely to die as are babies of mothers who receive early medical attention (Child Trends, 2007). Although the poorest of these mothers are eligible for government-sponsored health services, many low-income women do not qualify. As we will see when we take up birth complications, in nations where affordable medical care is universally available, such as Australia, Canada, Japan, and European countries, late-care pregnancies and maternal and infant health problems are greatly reduced.

Besides financial hardship, some mothers have other reasons for not seeking early prenatal care. These include *situational barriers* (difficulty finding a doctor, getting an appointment, and arranging transportation) and *personal barriers* (psychological stress, the demands of taking care of other young children, ambivalence about the pregnancy, and family crises). Many also engage in high-risk behaviors, such as smoking and drug abuse (Daniels, Noe, & Mayberry, 2006; Maupin et al., 2004). These women, who had little or no prenatal care, were among those who needed it most!

Clearly, public education about the importance of early and sustained prenatal care for all pregnant women is badly needed. Refer to Applying What We Know on page 96, which lists "do's and don'ts" for a healthy pregnancy, based on our discussion of the prenatal environment.

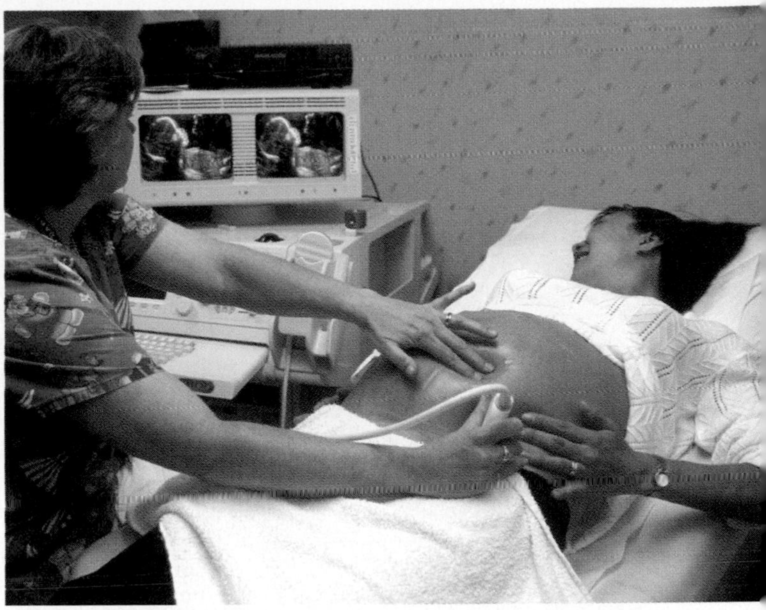

During a routine prenatal visit, a doctor uses ultrasound to evaluate the development of this expectant mother's 5-month-old fetus. All pregnant women should receive regular prenatal care to protect their own health as well as the health of their babies.

ASK YOURSELF

» REVIEW
Why is it difficult to determine the prenatal effects of many environmental agents, such as drugs and pollution?

» APPLY
Nora, pregnant for the first time, believes that a few cigarettes and a glass of wine a day won't be harmful. Provide Nora with research-based reasons for not smoking or drinking.

» CONNECT
How do teratogens illustrate the notion of epigenesis, presented in Chapter 2, that environments can affect gene expression (see page 74 to review)?

» REFLECT
If you had to choose five environmental influences to publicize in a campaign aimed at promoting healthy prenatal development, which ones would you choose, and why?

Applying What We Know

Do's and Don'ts for a Healthy Pregnancy

Do	Don't
Do make sure that you have been vaccinated against infectious diseases that are dangerous to the embryo and fetus, such as rubella, before you get pregnant. Most vaccinations are not safe during pregnancy.	Don't take any drugs without consulting your doctor.
Do see a doctor as soon as you suspect that you are pregnant, and continue to get regular medical checkups throughout pregnancy.	Don't smoke. If you are a smoker, cut down or, better yet, quit. Avoid secondhand smoke. If other members of your family are smokers, ask them to quit or to smoke outside.
Do eat a well-balanced diet and take vitamin–mineral supplements, as prescribed by your doctor, both prior to and during pregnancy. Gain 25 to 30 pounds gradually.	Don't drink alcohol from the time you decide to get pregnant.
Do obtain literature from your doctor, library, or bookstore about prenatal development. Ask your doctor about anything that concerns you.	Don't engage in activities that might expose your embryo or fetus to environmental hazards, such as radiation or pollutants.
Do keep physically fit through mild exercise. If possible, join an exercise class for expectant mothers.	Don't engage in activities that might expose your embryo or fetus to harmful infectious diseases, such as toxoplasmosis.
Do avoid emotional stress. If you are a single expectant mother, find a relative or friend on whom you can count for emotional support.	Don't choose pregnancy as a time to go on a diet.
Do get plenty of rest. An overtired mother is at risk for complications.	Don't gain too much weight during pregnancy. A very large weight gain is associated with complications.
Do enroll in a prenatal and childbirth education class with your partner or other companion. When you know what to expect, the nine months before birth can be one of the most joyful times of life.	

Childbirth

Although Yolanda and Jay completed my course three months before their baby was born, both agreed to return the following spring to share their experiences with my next class. Two-week-old Joshua came along as well. Yolanda and Jay's story revealed that the birth of a baby is one of the most dramatic and emotional events in human experience. Jay was present throughout Yolanda's labor and delivery. Yolanda explained:

> By morning, we knew I was in labor. It was Thursday, so we went in for my usual weekly appointment. The doctor said, yes, the baby was on the way, but it would be a while. He told us to go home and relax and come to the hospital in three or four hours. We checked in at three in the afternoon; Joshua arrived at two o'clock the next morning. When, finally, I was ready to deliver, it went quickly; a half hour or so and some good hard pushes, and there he was! His face was red and puffy, and his head was misshapen, but I thought, "Our son! I can't believe he's really here."

Jay was also elated by Joshua's birth. "I wanted to support Yolanda and to experience as much as I could. It was awesome, indescribable," he said, holding Joshua over his shoulder and patting and kissing him gently. In the following sections, we explore the experience of childbirth, from both the parents' and the baby's point of view.

The Stages of Childbirth

It is not surprising that childbirth is often referred to as labor. It is the hardest physical work a woman may ever do. A complex series of hormonal changes between mother and fetus initiates the process, which naturally divides into three stages (see Figure 3.5):

1. *Dilation and effacement of the cervix.* This is the longest stage of labor, lasting an average of 12 to 14 hours with a first birth and 4 to 6 hours with later births. Contractions of the uterus gradually become more frequent and powerful, causing the cervix, or uterine opening, to widen and thin to nothing, forming a clear channel from the uterus into the birth canal, or vagina.
2. *Delivery of the baby.* This stage is much shorter, lasting about 50 minutes for a first birth and 20 minutes with later births. Strong contractions of the uterus continue, but the mother also feels a natural urge to squeeze and push with her abdominal muscles. As she does so with each contraction, she forces the baby down and out.
3. *Delivery of the placenta.* Labor comes to an end with a few final contractions and pushes. These cause the placenta to separate from the wall of the uterus and be delivered in about 5 to 10 minutes.

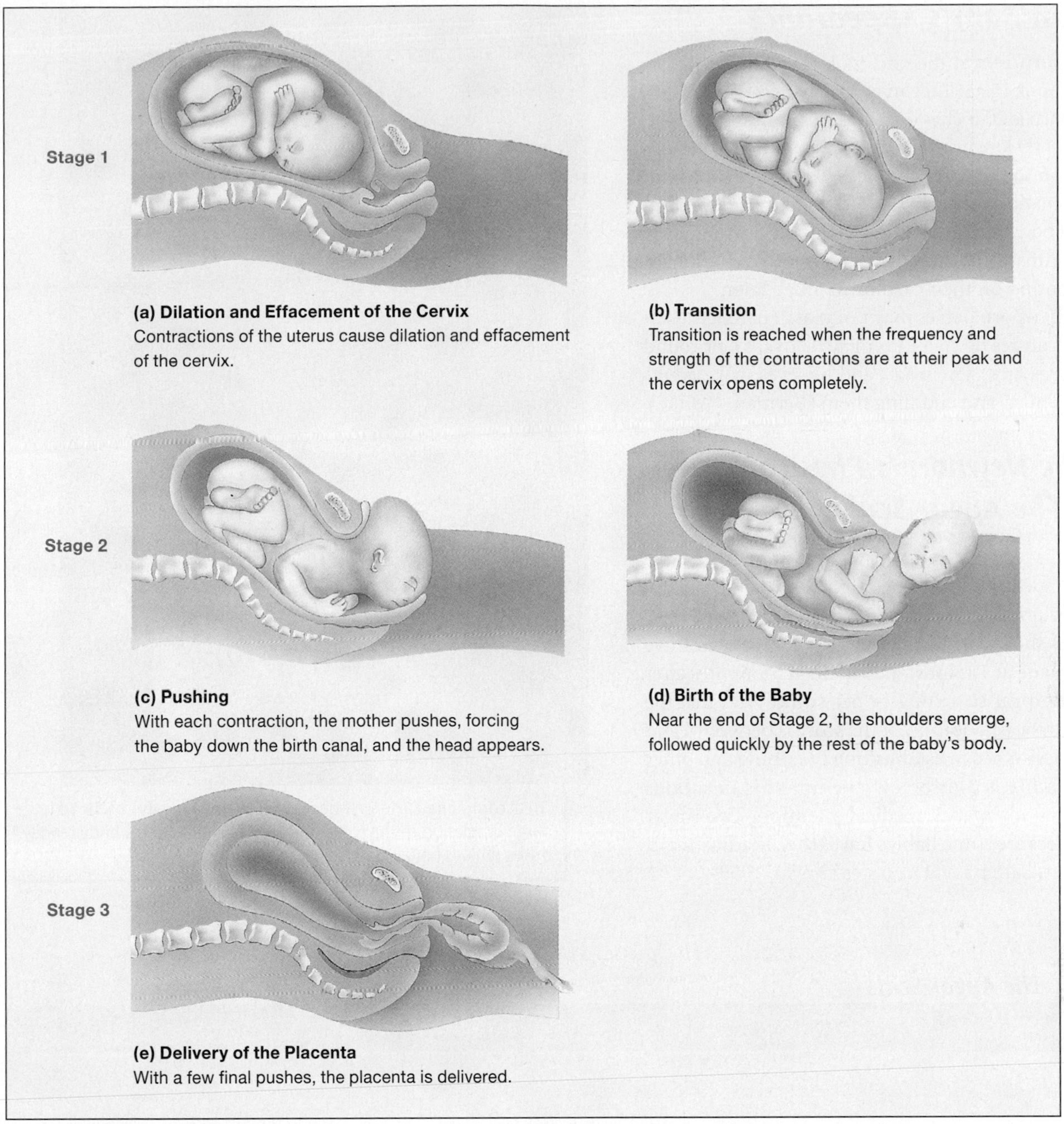

■ **FIGURE 3.5** ■ The three stages of labor.

The Baby's Adaptation to Labor and Delivery

At first glance, labor and delivery seem like a dangerous ordeal for the baby. The strong contractions exposed Joshua's head to a great deal of pressure, and they squeezed the placenta and the umbilical cord repeatedly. Each time, Joshua's supply of oxygen was temporarily reduced.

Fortunately, healthy babies are well-equipped to withstand these traumas. The force of the contractions causes the infant to produce high levels of stress hormones. But in contrast to high maternal stress levels during pregnancy, which can endanger the baby, the infant's production of stress hormones during childbirth is adaptive. It helps the baby withstand oxygen deprivation by sending a rich supply of blood to the brain and heart (Gluckman, Sizonenko, & Bassett, 1999). In addition, stress hormones prepare the baby to breathe by causing the lungs to absorb any remaining fluid and by expanding the bronchial tubes (passages leading to the lungs). Finally, stress hormones arouse the infant into alertness. Joshua was born wide awake, ready to interact with the surrounding world (Lagercrantz & Slotkin, 1986).

The Newborn Baby's Appearance

Parents are often surprised at the odd-looking newborn—a far cry from the storybook image they may have had in their minds. The average newborn is 20 inches long and 7½ pounds in weight; boys tend to be slightly longer and heavier than girls. The head is large in comparison to the trunk and legs, which are short and bowed. This combination of a large head (with its well-developed brain) and a small body means that human infants learn quickly in the first few months of life. But, unlike most other mammals, they cannot get around on their own until much later.

Even though newborn babies may not match parents' idealized image, some features do make them attractive. Their round faces, chubby cheeks, large foreheads, and big eyes make adults feel like picking them up and cuddling them (Berman, 1980).

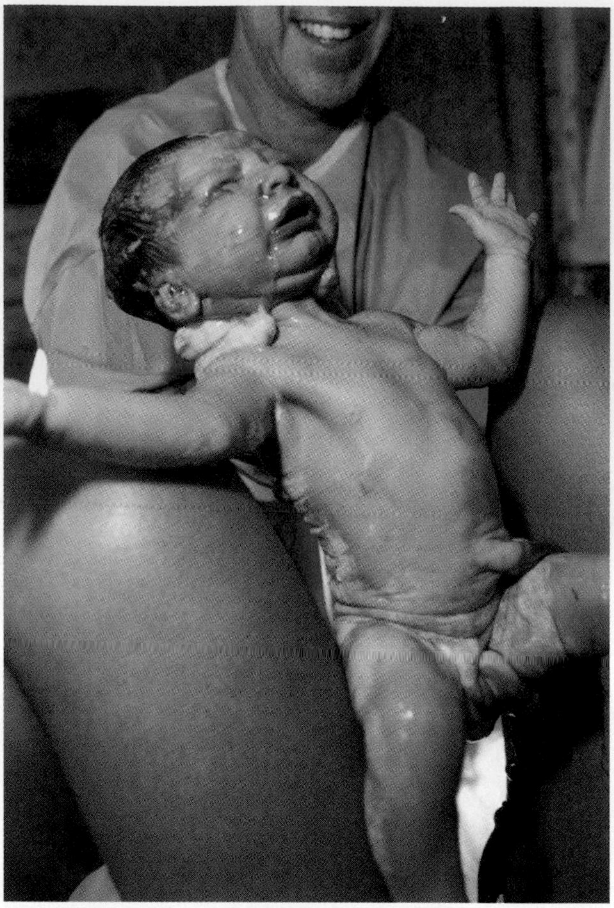

To accommodate the well-developed brain, a newborn's head is large in relation to the trunk and legs. This newborn's body readily turns pink as he takes his first few breaths.

Assessing the Newborn's Physical Condition: The Apgar Scale

Infants who have difficulty making the transition to life outside the uterus require special help at once. To assess the newborn's physical condition quickly, doctors and nurses use the **Apgar Scale.** As Table 3.3 shows, a rating of 0, 1, or 2 on each of five characteristics is made at 1 minute and again at 5 minutes after birth. A combined Apgar score of 7 or better indicates that the infant is in good physical condition. If the score is between 4 and 6, the baby needs assistance in establishing breathing and other vital signs. If the score is 3 or below, the infant is in serious danger and requires emergency medical attention. Two Apgar ratings are given because some babies have trouble adjusting at first but do quite well after a few minutes (Apgar, 1953).

■ **TABLE 3.3** ■ ***The Apgar Scale***

	RATING		
Sign[a]	***0***	***1***	***2***
Heart rate	No heartbeat	Under 100 beats per minute	100 to 140 beats per minute
Respiratory effort	No breathing for 60 seconds	Irregular, shallow breathing	Strong breathing and crying
Reflex irritability (sneezing, coughing, and grimacing)	No response	Weak reflexive response	Strong reflexive response
Muscle tone	Completely limp	Weak movements of arms and legs	Strong movements of arms and legs
Color[b]	Blue body, arms, and legs	Body pink with blue arms and legs	Body, arms, and legs completely pink

[a]To remember these signs, you may find it helpful to use a technique in which the original labels are reordered and renamed as follows: color = **A**ppearance, heart rate = **P**ulse, reflex irritability = **G**rimace, muscle tone = **A**ctivity, and respiratory effort = **R**espiration. Together, the first letters of the new labels spell **Apgar.**

[b]The skin tone of nonwhite babies makes it difficult to apply the "pink" color criterion. However, newborns of all races can be rated for pinkish glow resulting from the flow of oxygen through body tissues.

Source: Apgar, 1953.

Approaches to Childbirth

Childbirth practices, like other aspects of family life, are molded by the society of which mother and baby are a part. In many village and tribal cultures, expectant mothers are well-acquainted with the childbirth process. For example, the Jarara of South America and the Pukapukans of the Pacific Islands treat birth as a vital part of daily life. The Jarara mother gives birth in full view of the entire community, including small children. The Pukapukan girl is so familiar with the events of labor and delivery that she frequently can be seen playing at it. Using a coconut to represent the baby, she stuffs it inside her dress, imitates the mother's pushing, and lets the nut fall at the proper moment. In most nonindustrialized cultures, women are assisted during the birth process. Among the Mayans of the Yucatán, the mother leans against a woman called the "head helper," who supports her weight and breathes with her during each contraction (Jordan, 1993; Mead & Newton, 1967).

In Western nations, childbirth has changed dramatically over the centuries. Before the late 1800s, birth usually took place at home and was a family-centered event. The industrial revolution brought greater crowding to cities, along with new health problems. As a result, childbirth moved from home to the hospital, where the health of mothers and babies could be protected. Once doctors assumed responsibility for childbirth, women's knowledge of it declined, and relatives and friends no longer participated (Borst, 1995).

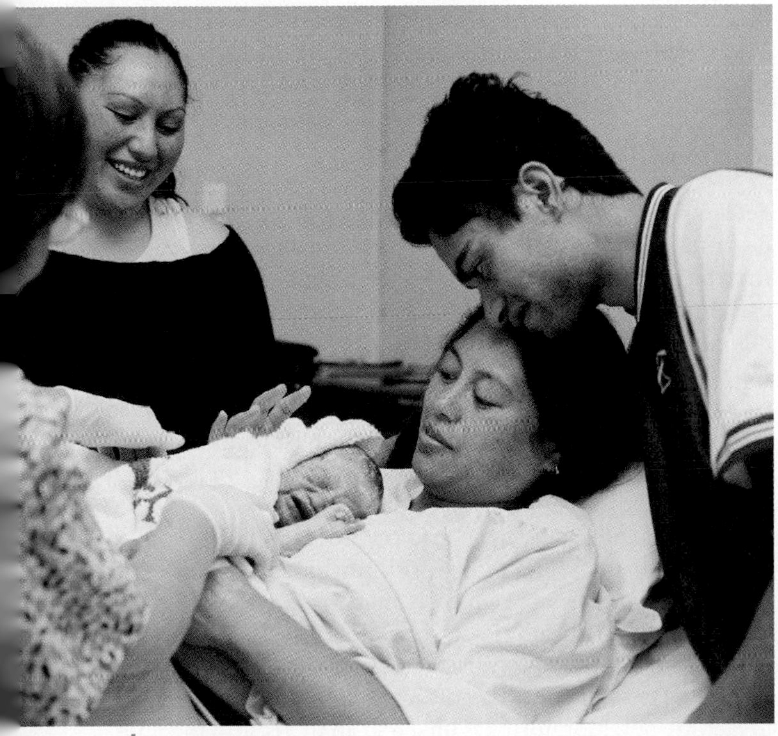

© JESSIE CASSON/CORBIS

In a hospital birthing center in New Zealand, the father and a close family friend coached and supported this Maori mother during labor and delivery. New Zealand places no limitations on the number of people parents can invite to attend a birth.

By the 1950s and 1960s, women had begun to question the medical procedures that had come to be used routinely during labor and delivery. Many felt that use of strong drugs and delivery instruments had robbed them of a precious experience and were often neither necessary nor safe for the baby. Gradually, a natural childbirth movement arose in Europe and spread to North America. Its purpose was to make hospital birth as comfortable and rewarding for mothers as possible. Today, most hospitals offer birth centers that are family-centered and homelike. *Freestanding birth centers,* which permit greater maternal control over labor and delivery, including choice of delivery positions, presence of family members and friends, and early contact between parents and baby, also exist. And a small number of North American women reject institutional birth entirely and choose to have their babies at home.

Natural, or Prepared, Childbirth

Yolanda and Jay chose **natural,** or **prepared, childbirth**—a group of techniques aimed at reducing pain and medical intervention and making childbirth as rewarding an experience as possible. Although many natural childbirth programs exist, most draw on methods developed by Grantly Dick-Read (1959) in England and Fernand Lamaze (1958) in France. These physicians recognized that cultural attitudes had taught women to fear the birth experience. An anxious, frightened woman in labor tenses muscles, turning the mild pain that sometimes accompanies strong contractions into intense pain.

In a typical natural childbirth program, the expectant mother and a companion (a partner, relative, or friend) participate in three activities:

- *Classes.* Yolanda and Jay attended a series of classes in which they learned about the anatomy and physiology of labor and delivery. Knowledge about the birth process reduces a mother's fear.
- *Relaxation and breathing techniques.* During each class, Yolanda was taught relaxation and breathing exercises aimed at counteracting the pain of uterine contractions.
- *Labor coach.* Jay learned how to help Yolanda during childbirth by reminding her to relax and breathe, massaging her back, supporting her body, and offering encouragement and affection.

Social support is important to the success of natural childbirth techniques. In Guatemalan and American hospitals that routinely isolated patients during childbirth, some mothers were randomly assigned a companion who stayed with them throughout labor and delivery, talking to them, holding their hands, and rubbing their backs to promote relaxation. These mothers had fewer birth complications and shorter labors than women with no companionship. Guatemalan mothers who received support also interacted more positively with their babies after delivery, talking, smiling, and gently stroking (Kennell et al., 1991; Sosa et al., 1980). Other studies indicate that mothers who are supported during labor and delivery less often have cesarean (surgical) deliveries, and their babies' Apgar scores are higher (Sauls, 2002). Social support also makes Western hospital-birth customs more acceptable to women from parts of the world where assistance from family and community members is the norm (Granot et al., 1996).

Home Delivery

Home birth has always been popular in certain industrialized nations, such as England, the Netherlands, and Sweden. The number of North American women choosing to have their babies at home increased during the 1970s and 1980s but remains small, at about 1 percent (Studelska, 2006). Although some home births are attended by doctors, many more are handled by certified *nurse–midwives,* who have degrees in nursing and additional training in childbirth management.

The joys and perils of home delivery are well-illustrated by the story I heard from Don, who was painting my house as I worked on this book. "Our first child was delivered in the hospital," he said. "Even though I was present, Kathy and I found the atmosphere to be rigid and insensitive. We wanted a warmer, more personal birth environment." With the coaching of a nurse–midwife, Don delivered their second child, Cindy, at their farmhouse, three miles out of town. Three years later, when Kathy went into labor with Marnie, a heavy snowstorm prevented the midwife from reaching the house on time, and Don delivered the baby alone. The birth was difficult. Marnie failed to breathe for several minutes; with great effort, Don revived her. The frightening memory of Marnie's limp, blue body convinced Don and Kathy to return to the hospital to have their last child. By then, hospital practices had changed, and the event was a rewarding one for both parents.

Don and Kathy's experience raises the question: Is it just as safe to give birth at home as in a hospital? For healthy women who are assisted by a well-trained doctor or midwife, it seems so because complications rarely occur (Fullerton, Navarro, & Young, 2007; Johnson & Daviss, 2005). However, if attendants are not carefully trained and prepared to handle emergencies, the rate of infant death is high (Mehlmadrona & Madrona, 1997). When mothers are at risk for any kind of complication, the appropriate place for labor and delivery is the hospital, where life-saving treatment is available.

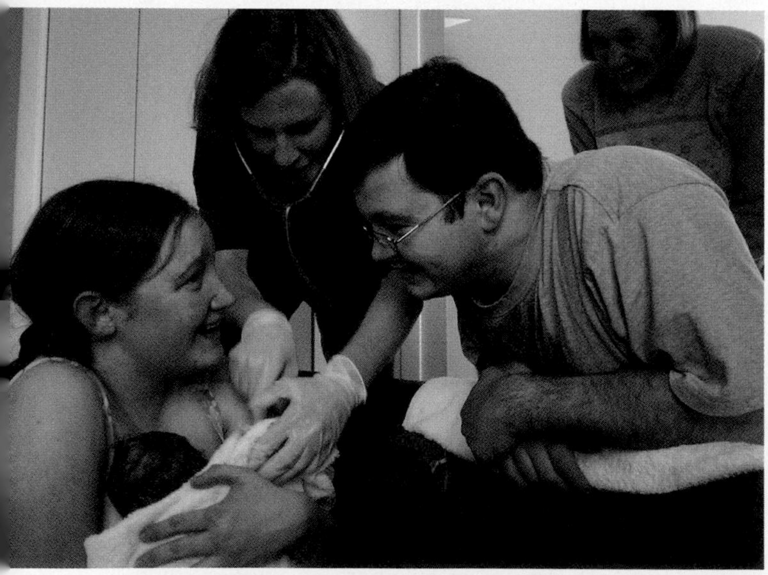

This midwife checks the baby's heartbeat minutes after he was born at home. As long as a woman is healthy and has a well-trained doctor or midwife, home birth is as safe as hospital birth.

Medical Interventions

Four-year-old Melinda walks with a halting, lumbering gait and has difficulty keeping her balance. She has *cerebral palsy,* a general term for a variety of impairments in muscle coordination caused by brain damage before, during, or just after birth. For about 10 percent of these children, including Melinda, brain damage was caused by **anoxia,** or inadequate oxygen supply, during labor and delivery (Anslow, 1998; Bracci, Perrone, & Buonocore, 2006). Her mother got pregnant accidentally, was frightened and alone, and arrived at the hospital at the last minute. Melinda was in **breech position,** turned so that the buttocks or feet would be delivered first, and the umbilical cord was wrapped around her neck. Had her mother come to the hospital earlier, doctors could have monitored Melinda's condition and delivered her surgically as soon as squeezing of the umbilical cord led to distress, thereby reducing the damage or preventing it entirely.

In cases like Melinda's, medical interventions are clearly justified. But in others, they can interfere with delivery and even pose new risks. In the following sections, we examine some commonly used medical procedures during childbirth.

Fetal Monitoring

Fetal monitors are electronic instruments that track the baby's heart rate during labor. An abnormal heartbeat may indicate that the baby is in distress due to anoxia and needs to be delivered immediately. Continuous fetal monitoring, which is required in most U.S. hospitals, is used in over 80 percent of American births (Natale & Dodman, 2003). The most popular type of monitor is strapped across the mother's abdomen throughout labor. A second, more accurate method involves threading a recording device through the cervix and placing it directly under the baby's scalp.

Fetal monitoring is a safe medical procedure that has saved the lives of many babies in high-risk situations. But in healthy pregnancies, it does not reduce the already low rates of infant brain damage and death (Priddy, 2004). Furthermore, most infants have some heartbeat irregularities during labor, so critics worry that fetal monitors identify many babies as in danger who, in fact, are not. Monitoring is linked to an increase in the number of cesarean (surgical) deliveries, which we will discuss shortly (Thacker & Stroup, 2003). In addition, some women complain that the devices are uncomfortable, prevent them from moving easily, and interfere with the normal course of labor.

Still, fetal monitors will probably continue to be used routinely in the United States, even though they are not necessary in most cases. Doctors fear that they will be sued for malpractice if an infant dies or is born with problems and they cannot show that they did everything possible to protect the baby.

Labor and Delivery Medication

Some form of medication is used in more than 80 percent of U.S. births (Althaus & Wax, 2005). *Analgesics,* drugs used to relieve pain, may be given in mild doses during labor to help a mother relax. *Anesthetics* are a stronger type of painkiller that blocks sensation. Currently, the most common approach to controlling pain during labor is *epidural analgesia,* in which a regional pain-relieving drug is delivered continuously through a catheter into a small space in the lower spine. Unlike older spinal block procedures, which numb the entire lower half of the body, epidural analgesia limits pain reduction to the pelvic region. Because the mother retains the capacity to feel the pressure of the contractions and to move her trunk and legs, she is able to push during the second stage of labor.

Although pain-relieving drugs help women cope with childbirth and enable doctors to perform essential medical interventions, they also can cause problems. Epidural analgesia, for example, weakens uterine contractions. As a result, labor is prolonged, and the chances of cesarean (surgical) delivery increase (Klein, 2006). And because drugs rapidly cross the placenta, exposed newborns tend to have lower Apgar scores, to be sleepy and withdrawn, to suck poorly during feedings, and to be irritable when awake (Caton et al., 2002; Eltzschig, Lieberman, & Camann, 2003; Emory, Schlackman, & Fiano, 1996).

Do heavy doses of childbirth medication have a lasting impact on physical and mental development? Some researchers have claimed so (Brackbill, McManus, & Woodward, 1985), but their findings have been challenged (Riordan et al., 2000). Use of medication may be related to other risk factors that could account for long-term consequences in some studies. Nevertheless, the negative impact of these drugs on the newborn's adjustment supports the current trend to limit their use.

Cesarean Delivery

A **cesarean delivery** is a surgical birth; the doctor makes an incision in the mother's abdomen and lifts the baby out of the uterus. Forty years ago, cesarean delivery was rare. Since then, cesarean rates have climbed internationally, reaching 16 percent in Finland, 20 percent in New Zealand, 22 percent in Australia, 26 percent in Canada, and 30 percent in the United States (Betrán et al., 2007; Society of Obstetricians and Gynaecologists, 2008; U.S. Department of Health and Human Services, 2008g).

Cesareans have always been warranted by medical emergencies, such as Rh incompatibility, premature separation of the placenta from the uterus, or serious maternal illness or infection (for example, the herpes simplex 2 virus, which can infect the baby during a vaginal delivery). Cesareans are also justified in breech births, in which the baby risks head injury or anoxia (as in Melinda's case). But the infant's exact position makes a difference: Certain breech babies fare just as well with a normal delivery as with a cesarean (Giuliani et al., 2002). Sometimes the doctor can gently turn the baby into a head-down position during the early part of labor.

Until recently, many women who have had a cesarean have been offered the option of a vaginal birth in subsequent pregnancies. But new evidence indicates that compared with repeated cesareans, a natural labor after a cesarean is associated with slightly increased rates of rupture of the uterus and infant death (Gerten et al., 2005). As a result, the rule, "Once a cesarean, always a cesarean," is making a comeback.

Repeated cesareans, however, do not explain the worldwide rise in cesarean deliveries. Instead, medical control over childbirth is largely responsible. Because many needless cesareans are performed, pregnant women should ask questions about the procedure before choosing a doctor. Although the operation itself is safe, mother and baby require more time for recovery. Anesthetic may have crossed the placenta, making cesarean newborns sleepy and unresponsive and at increased risk for breathing difficulties (McDonagh, Osterweil, & Guise, 2005).

ASK YOURSELF

REVIEW
Describe the features and benefits of natural childbirth. What aspect contributes greatly to favorable outcomes, and why?

APPLY
On seeing her newborn baby for the first time, Caroline exclaimed, "Why is she so out of proportion?" What observations prompted Caroline to ask this question? Explain why her baby's appearance is adaptive.

CONNECT
How might use of epidural analgesia negatively affect the parent–newborn relationship? Does your answer illustrate bidirectional influences between parent and child, emphasized in ecological systems theory? Explain.

REFLECT
If you were an expectant parent, would you choose home birth? Why or why not?

Preterm and Low-Birth-Weight Infants

Babies born three weeks or more before the end of a full 38-week pregnancy or who weigh less than 5½ pounds (2,500 grams) have for many years been referred to as "premature." A wealth of research indicates that premature babies are at risk for many problems. Birth weight is the best available predictor of infant survival and healthy development. Many newborns who weigh less than 3½ pounds (1,500 grams) experience difficulties that are not overcome, an effect that becomes stronger as length of pregnancy and birth weight decrease (see Figure 3.6) (Dombrowski, Noonan, & Martin, 2007; Bolisetty et al., 2006). Frequent illness, inattention, overactivity, sensory impairments, poor motor coordination, language delays, low intelligence test scores, deficits in school learning, and emotional and behavior problems are some of the difficulties that persist through childhood and adolescence and into adulthood (Bayless, 2007; Grunau, Whitfield, & Fay, 2004; Hultman et al., 2007; Lefebvre, Mazurier, & Tessier, 2005).

About 1 in 13 American infants is born underweight. Although the problem can strike unexpectedly, it is highest among poverty-stricken women (U.S. Department of Health and Human Services, 2007b). These mothers, as noted earlier, are more likely to be undernourished and to be exposed to other harmful environmental influences. In addition, they often do not receive adequate prenatal care.

Recall from Chapter 2 that prematurity is also common among twins, who are usually born about three weeks early. Because space inside the uterus is restricted, twins gain less weight than singletons after the twentieth week of pregnancy.

Preterm versus Small-for-Date Infants

Although low-birth-weight infants face many obstacles to healthy development, most go on to lead normal lives; about half of those born at 23 to 24 weeks gestation and weighing only a couple of pounds at birth have no disability (refer again to Figure 3.6). To better understand why some babies do better than others, researchers divide them into two groups. **Preterm** infants are those born several weeks or more before their due date. Although they are small, their weight may still be appropriate, based on time spent in the uterus. **Small-for-date** babies are below their expected weight considering length of the pregnancy. Some small-for-date infants are actually full-term. Others are preterm infants who are especially underweight.

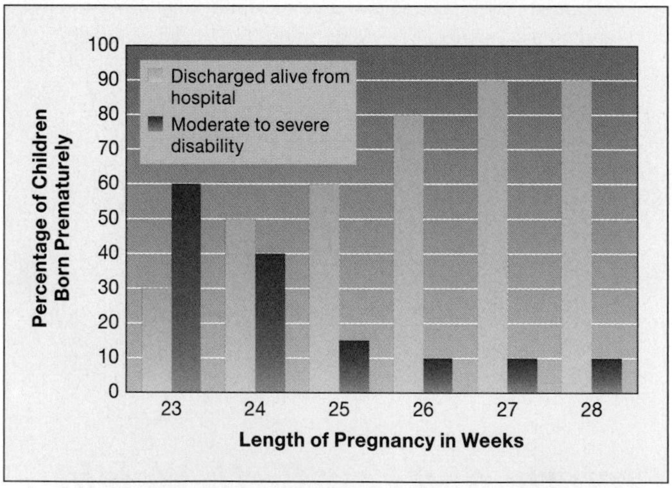

■ **FIGURE 3.6** ■ **Rates of infant survival and child disabilities by length of pregnancy.** In a follow-up of more than 2,300 babies born between 23 and 28 weeks gestation, percentage of infants who survived decreased and percentage who displayed moderate to severe disabilities (assessed during the preschool years) increased with reduced length of pregnancy. Severe disabilities included cerebral palsy (unlikely to ever walk), severely delayed mental development, deafness, and blindness. Moderate disabilities included cerebral palsy (able to walk with assistance), moderately delayed mental development, and hearing impairments partially correctable with a hearing aid. (Adapted from Bolisetty et al., 2006.)

Of the two types of babies, small-for-date infants usually have more serious problems. During the first year, they are more likely to die, catch infections, and show evidence of brain damage. By middle childhood, they have lower intelligence test scores, are less attentive, achieve less well in school, and are socially immature (Hediger et al., 2002; O'Keefe et al., 2003). Small-for-date infants probably experienced inadequate nutrition before birth. Perhaps their mothers did not eat properly, the placenta did not function normally, or the babies themselves had defects that prevented them from growing as they should. Recall that an abnormally functioning placenta is associated with ready transfer of stress hormones from mother to fetus. Consequently, small-for-date infants are especially likely to suffer from prenatal neurological impairments that permanently weaken their capacity to manage stress (Wust et al., 2005).

Even among preterm newborns whose weight is appropriate for length of pregnancy, just seven more days—from 34 to 35 weeks—greatly reduces rates of illness, costly medical procedures, and lengthy hospital stays (Gladstone & Katz, 2004). And despite being low-risk for disabilities, a substantial number of 34-week preterms are below average in physical growth and mildly to moderately delayed in cognitive development in early and middle childhood (de Haan et al., 2000; Pietz et al., 2004). Yet doctors often induce births several weeks preterm, under the misconception that these babies are developmentally "mature."

Consequences for Caregiving

Imagine a scrawny, thin-skinned infant whose body is only a little larger than the size of your hand. You try to play with the baby by stroking and talking softly, but he is sleepy and unresponsive. When you feed him, he sucks poorly. During the short, unpredictable periods in which he is awake, he is usually irritable.

The appearance and behavior of preterm babies can lead parents to be less sensitive in caring for them. Compared with full-term infants, preterm babies—especially those who are very ill at birth—are less often held close, touched, and talked to gently. At times, their mothers resort to interfering pokes and verbal commands in an effort to obtain a higher level of response from the baby (Barratt, Roach, & Leavitt, 1996; Feldman, 2007). This may explain why preterm babies as a group are at risk for child abuse. When they are born to isolated, poverty-stricken mothers who cannot provide good nutrition, health care, and parenting, the likelihood of unfavorable outcomes increases. In contrast, parents with stable life circumstances and social supports usually can overcome the stresses of caring for a preterm infant. In these cases, even sick preterm babies have a good chance of catching up in development by middle childhood (Ment et al., 2003).

These findings suggest that how well preterm infants develop has a great deal to do with the parent–child relationship. Consequently, interventions directed at supporting both sides of this tie are more likely to help these infants recover.

Interventions for Preterm Infants

A preterm baby is cared for in a special Plexiglas-enclosed bed called an *isolette.* Temperature is carefully controlled because these babies cannot yet regulate their own body temperature effectively. To help protect the baby from infection, air is filtered before it enters the isolette. Infants born more than six weeks early commonly have a disorder called *respiratory distress syndrome* (otherwise known as *hyaline membrane disease*). Their tiny lungs are so poorly developed that the air sacs collapse, causing serious breathing difficulties. When a preterm infant breathes with the aid of a respirator, is fed through a stomach tube, and receives medication through an intravenous needle, the isolette can be very isolating indeed! Physical needs that otherwise would lead to close contact and other human stimulation are met mechanically.

SPECIAL INFANT STIMULATION. At one time, doctors believed that stimulating such fragile babies could be harmful. Now we know that in proper doses, certain kinds of stimulation can help preterm infants develop. In some intensive care nurseries, preterm babies can be seen rocking in suspended hammocks or lying on waterbeds designed to replace the gentle motion they would have received while still in the mother's uterus. Other forms of stimulation have also been used—an attractive mobile or a tape recording of a heartbeat, soft music, or the mother's voice. These experiences promote faster weight gain, more predictable sleep patterns, and greater alertness (Arnon et al., 2006; Marshall-Baker, Lickliter, & Cooper, 1998; Standley, 1998).

Touch is an especially important form of stimulation. In baby animals, touching the skin releases certain brain chemicals that support physical growth—effects believed to occur in humans as well. When preterm infants were massaged several times each day in the hospital, they gained weight faster and, at the end of the first year, were advanced in mental and motor development over preterm babies not given this stimulation (Field, 2001; Field, Hernandez-Reif, & Freedman, 2004).

In developing countries where hospitalization is not always possible, skin-to-skin "kangaroo care" is the most readily available intervention for promoting the survival and recovery of preterm babies. It involves placing the infant in a vertical position between the mother's breasts or next to the father's chest (under the parent's clothing) so the parent's body functions as a human incubator. Kangaroo care offers fathers a unique opportunity to increase their involvement in caring for the preterm newborn. Because of its many physical and psychological benefits, the technique is used often in Western nations as a supplement to hospital intensive care.

Kangaroo skin-to-skin contact fosters improved oxygenation of the baby's body, temperature regulation, sleep, feeding, and infant survival (Feldman & Eidelman, 2003). In addition, the kangaroo position provides the baby with gentle stimulation of all sensory modalities: hearing (through the parent's voice), smell (through proximity of the parent's body), touch

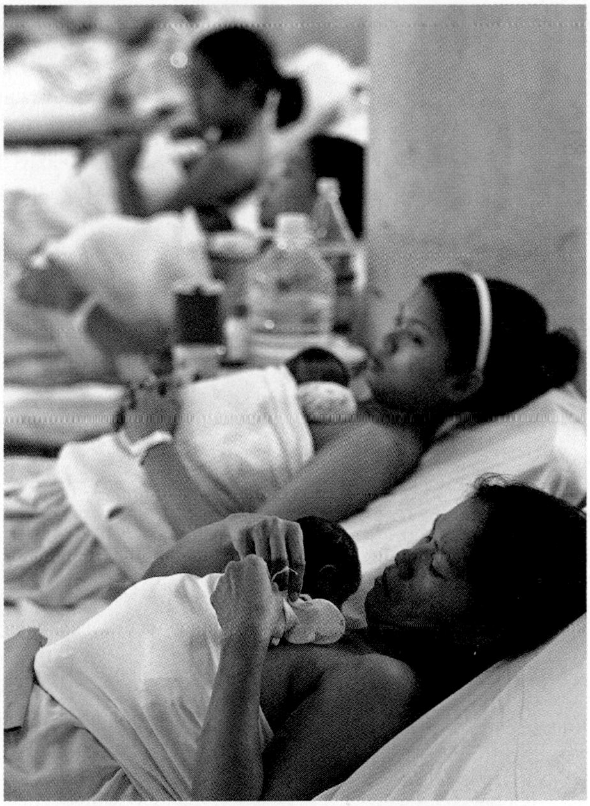

New mothers in a hospital ward in the Philippines practice skin-to-skin "kangaroo care," which is widely used in developing countries to promote the survival and recovery of preterm babies. Because of its many physical and psychological benefits, kangaroo care has spread to western nations, where it supplements hospital intensive care.

(through skin-to-skin contact), and visual (through the upright position). Mothers and fathers practicing kangaroo care feel more confident about caring for their fragile babies and interact more sensitively and affectionately with them (Dodd, 2005; Feldman et al., 2002, 2003).

Together, these factors may explain why preterm babies given many hours of kangaroo care in their early weeks, compared to those given little or no such care, score higher on measures of mental and motor development during the first year (Charpak, Ruiz-Peláez, & Figueroa, 2005; Tessier et al., 2003). Because of its diverse benefits, more than 80 percent of North American nurseries now offer kangaroo care to preterm newborns (Field et al., 2006).

TRAINING PARENTS IN INFANT CAREGIVING SKILLS. Interventions that support parents of preterm infants generally teach them about the infant's characteristics and promote caregiving skills. For parents with adequate economic and personal resources to care for a preterm infant, just a few sessions of coaching in recognizing and responding to the baby's needs are linked to steady gains in mental test performance that, after several years, resemble those of full-term children (Achenbach et al., 1990).

When preterm infants live in stressed, low-income households, long-term, intensive intervention is required to reduce

SOCIAL ISSUES

A Cross-National Perspective on Health Care and Other Policies for Parents and Newborn Babies

Infant mortality—the number of deaths in the first year of life per 1,000 live births—is an index used around the world to assess the overall health of a nation's children. The United States has the most up-to-date health care technology in the world, but it has made less progress in reducing infant deaths than many other countries. Over the past three decades, it has slipped in the international rankings, from seventh in the 1950s to twenty-sixth in 2008. Members of America's poor ethnic minorities are at greatest risk. African-American and Native-American babies are twice as likely as white infants to die in the first year of life (U.S. Census Bureau, 2009a, 2009b).

Neonatal mortality, the rate of death within the first month of life, accounts for 67 percent of the U.S. infant death rate. Two factors are largely responsible for neonatal mortality. The first is serious physical defects, most of which cannot be prevented. The percentage of babies born with physical defects is about the same in all ethnic and income groups. The second leading cause of neonatal mortality is low birth weight, which is largely preventable. African-American and Native-American babies are more than twice as likely as white infants to be born early and underweight (U.S. Census Bureau, 2009b).

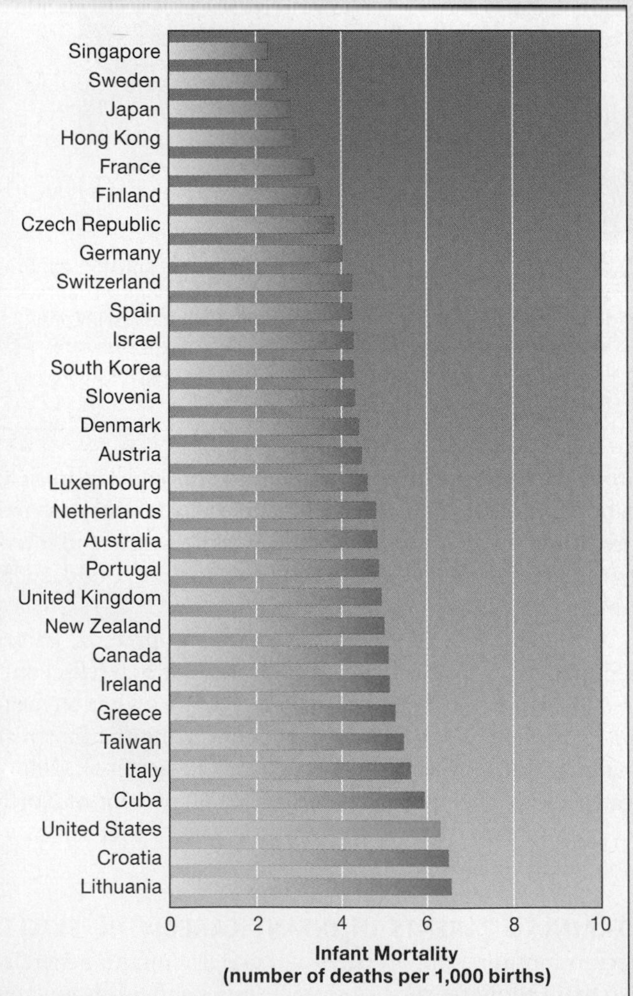

■ **FIGURE 3.7** ■ **Infant mortality in thirty-two nations.** Despite its advanced health care technology, the United States ranks poorly. It is twenty-eighth in the world, with a death rate of 6.6 infants per 1,000 births. (Adapted from U.S. Census Bureau, 2009a.)

Widespread poverty and weak health care programs for mothers and young children are largely responsible for these trends. Each country in Figure 3.7 that outranks the United States in infant survival provides all its citizens with government-sponsored health care benefits. And each takes extra steps to make sure that pregnant mothers and babies have access to good nutrition, high-quality medical care, and social and economic supports that promote effective parenting.

For example, all Western European nations guarantee women a certain number of prenatal visits at very low or no cost. After a baby is born, a health professional routinely visits the home to provide counseling about infant care and to arrange continuing medical services. Home assistance is especially extensive in the Netherlands. For a token fee, each mother is granted a specially trained maternity helper, who assists with infant care, shopping, housekeeping, meal preparation, and the care of other children during the days after delivery (Bradley & Bray, 1996; Zwart, 2007).

Paid, job-protected employment leave is another vital societal intervention for new parents. Canadian mothers are eligible for 15 weeks' maternity leave at 55 percent of prior earnings (up to a maximum of $113 per week), and Canadian mothers or fathers can take an additional year of parental leave at the same rate in certain cases—for example, when a child is ill following birth or adoption. Paid leave is widely available in other industrialized nations as well. Sweden has the most generous parental leave program in the world. Mothers can begin maternity leave 60 days prior to expected delivery, extending it to six weeks after birth; fathers are granted two weeks of birth leave. In addition, each parent can take full leave until the child reaches age 18 months at 80 percent of prior earnings, followed by an additional three months at a modest flat rate. Each parent is also entitled to another 18 months of unpaid leave. Even less-developed nations provide parental leave benefits. For example, in the People's Republic of China, a new mother is granted three months' leave at regular pay. Furthermore, many countries supplement basic paid leave. In Germany, for example, after a fully paid three-month leave, a parent may take two more years at a flat rate and a third year at no pay (OECD, 2006; Waldfogel, 2001).

Yet in the United States, the federal government mandates *only 12 weeks of unpaid leave* for employees in businesses with at least 50 workers. Most women, however, work in smaller businesses, and even those who work in large enough companies may be unable to afford to take unpaid leave (Hewlett, 2003). And because of financial pressures, many new mothers who are eligible for unpaid work leave take far less than 12 weeks, while new fathers tend to take little or none at all (OECD, 2006). In 2002, California became the first state to guarantee a mother or father paid leave—up to six weeks at half salary, regardless of the size of the company.

Nevertheless, six weeks of childbirth leave (the norm in the United States) is not enough. When a family is stressed by a baby's arrival, leaves of six weeks or less are linked to increased maternal anxiety, depression, marital dissatisfaction, sense of role overload (conflict between work and family responsibilities), and negative interactions with the baby. A longer leave (12 weeks or more) predicts favorable maternal mental health, supportive marital interaction, and sensitive caregiving (Feldman, Sussman, & Zigler, 2004; Hyde et al., 2001). Single women and their babies are most hurt by the absence of a generous national paid-leave policy. These mothers, who are usually the sole source of support for their families, can least afford to take time from their jobs.

In countries with low infant mortality rates, expectant parents need not wonder how they will get health care and other resources to support their baby's development. The powerful impact of universal, high-quality health care, generous parental leave, and other social services on maternal and infant well-being provides strong justification for these policies.

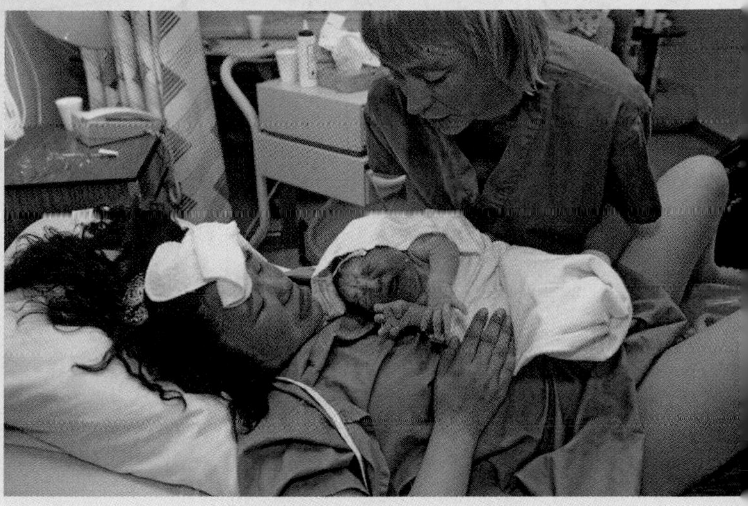

© JOANNA B. PINNEO/AURORA

This Inuit mother, from Baffin Island in northernmost Canada, experienced pregnancy complications and had to be flown 190 miles to deliver her son. Limited access to health care and social services in remote areas compromises the future of many Inuit newborns.

developmental problems. In the Infant Health and Development Program, preterm babies born into poverty received a comprehensive intervention that combined medical follow-up, weekly parent training sessions, and enrollment in cognitively stimulating child care from 1 through 3 years of age. More than four times as many intervention children as controls (39 versus 9 percent) were within normal range in intelligence, psychological adjustment, and physical growth (Bradley et al., 1994). In addition, mothers in the intervention group were more affectionate and more often encouraged play and cognitive mastery in their children—one reason their 3-year-olds may have been developing so favorably (McCarton, 1998).

At ages 5 and 8, children who had attended the child-care program regularly—for more than 350 days over the three-year period—continued to show better intellectual functioning. The more they attended, the higher they scored, with greater gains among those whose birth weights were higher—between 4½ and 5½ pounds (2,001 to 2,500 grams). In contrast, children who attended only sporadically gained little or even lost ground (Hill, Brooks-Gunn, & Waldfogel, 2003). These findings confirm that babies who are both preterm and economically disadvantaged require *intensive* intervention. And special strategies, such as extra adult–child interaction, may be necessary to achieve lasting changes in children with the lowest birth weights.

■ VERY LOW BIRTH WEIGHT, ENVIRONMENTAL ADVANTAGES, AND LONG-TERM OUTCOMES. Although very-low-birth-weight babies often have lasting problems, in a Canadian study, participants who had weighed between 1 and 2.2 pounds (500 to 1,000 grams) at birth were doing well as young adults (Saigal et al., 2006). At 22 to 25 years of age, they resembled normal-birth-weight individuals in educational attainment, rates of marriage and parenthood, and (for those who had no neurological or sensory impairments) employment status. Researchers believe that home, school, and societal advantages combine to explain these excellent outcomes (Hack & Klein, 2006). Most participants were reared in two-parent middle-SES homes, attended good schools where they received special services, and benefited from Canada's government-sponsored, universal health care system.

But even the best environments cannot "fix" the serious biological risks associated with being born severely underweight. An even better course of action would be to prevent this serious threat to infant survival and development. The high rate of underweight babies in the United States—one of the worst in the industrialized world—could be greatly reduced by improving the health and social conditions described in the Social Issues box above.

Birth Complications, Parenting, and Resilience

In the preceding sections, we considered a variety of birth complications. Now let's try to put the evidence together. Can any general principles help us understand how infants who survive a traumatic birth are likely to develop? A landmark study carried out in Hawaii provides answers to this question.

In 1955, Emmy Werner and Ruth Smith began to follow nearly 700 infants on the island of Kauai who had experienced mild, moderate, or severe birth complications. Each was matched, on the basis of SES and ethnicity, with a healthy newborn (Werner & Smith, 1982). Findings revealed that the likelihood of long-term difficulties increased if birth trauma was severe. But among mildly to moderately stressed children, those growing up in stable families did almost as well on measures of intelligence and psychological adjustment as those with no birth problems. Children exposed to poverty, family disorganization, and mentally ill parents often developed serious learning difficulties, behavior problems, and emotional disturbance.

The Kauai study tells us that as long as birth injuries are not overwhelming, a supportive home environment can restore children's growth. But the most intriguing cases in this study were the handful of exceptions. A few children with both fairly serious birth complications and troubled family environments grew into competent adults who fared as well as controls in career attainment and psychological adjustment. Werner and Smith found that these children relied on factors outside the family and within themselves to overcome stress. Some had attractive personalities that drew positive responses from relatives, neighbors, and peers. In other instances, a grandparent, aunt, uncle, or babysitter provided the needed emotional support (Werner, 1989, 2001; Werner & Smith, 1992).

Do these outcomes remind you of the characteristics of resilient children, discussed in Chapter 1? The Kauai study and other similar investigations reveal that the impact of early biological risks often wanes as children's personal characteristics and social experiences contribute increasingly to their functioning (Laucht, Esser, & Schmidt, 1997; Resnick et al., 1999). In sum, when the overall balance of life events tips toward the favorable side, children with serious birth problems can develop successfully.

ASK YOURSELF

» REVIEW
Sensitive care can help preterm infants recover, but they are less likely than full-term newborns to receive such care. Explain why.

» APPLY
Cecilia and Adena each gave birth to a 3-pound baby seven weeks preterm. Cecilia is single and on welfare. Adena and her husband are happily married and earn a good income. Plan an intervention for helping each baby develop.

» CONNECT
List factors discussed in this chapter that increase the chances that an infant will be born underweight. How many of these factors could be prevented by better health care for expectant mothers?

» REFLECT
Many people question the use of extraordinary medical measures to save extremely low-birth-weight babies because of their high risk of developing serious physical, cognitive, and emotional problems. Do you agree or disagree? Explain.

The Newborn Baby's Capacities

Newborn infants have a remarkable set of capacities that are crucial for survival and for evoking attention and care from parents. In relating to the physical world and building their first social relationships, babies are active from the very start.

Newborn Reflexes

A **reflex** is an inborn, automatic response to a particular form of stimulation. Reflexes are the newborn baby's most obvious organized patterns of behavior. As Jay placed Joshua on a table in my classroom, we saw several. When Jay bumped the side of the table, Joshua reacted by flinging his arms wide and bringing them back toward his body. As Yolanda stroked Joshua's cheek, he turned his head in her direction. When she put her finger in Joshua's palm, he grabbed on tightly. ***TAKE A MOMENT...*** Look at Table 3.4 and see if you can name the newborn reflexes that Joshua displayed.

Some reflexes have survival value. The rooting reflex helps a breastfed baby find the mother's nipple. Babies display it only when hungry and touched by another person, not when they touch themselves (Rochat & Hespos, 1997). And if newborns could not suck, our species would be unlikely to survive for a single generation! At birth, babies adjust their sucking pressure to how easily milk flows from the nipple (Craig & Lee, 1999).

A few reflexes form the basis for complex motor skills that will develop later. The stepping reflex looks like a primitive walking response. Unlike other reflexes, it appears in a wide range of situations—with the newborn's body in a sideways or upside-down orientation, with feet touching walls or ceilings, and even with legs dangling in the air (Adolph & Berger, 2006). One reason that babies frequently engage in the alternating leg

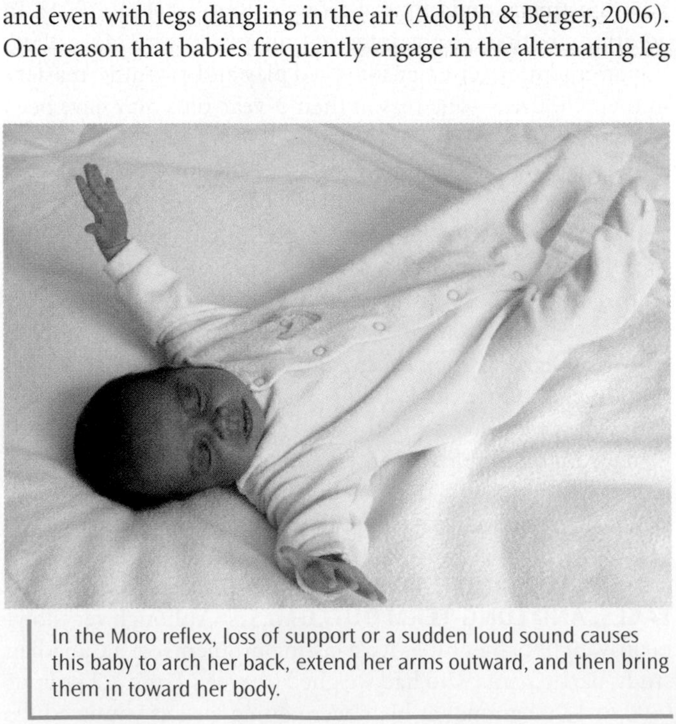

In the Moro reflex, loss of support or a sudden loud sound causes this baby to arch her back, extend her arms outward, and then bring them in toward her body.

■ TABLE 3.4 ■ *Some Newborn Reflexes*

REFLEX	STIMULATION	RESPONSE	AGE OF DISAPPEARANCE	FUNCTION
Eye blink	Shine bright light at eyes or clap hand near head.	Infant quickly closes eyelids.	Permanent	Protects infant from strong stimulation
Rooting	Stroke cheek near corner of mouth.	Head turns toward source of stimulation.	3 weeks (becomes voluntary turning at this time)	Helps infant find the nipple
Sucking	Place finger in infant's mouth.	Infant sucks finger rhythmically.	Replaced by voluntary sucking after 4 months	Permits feeding
Moro	Hold infant horizontally on back and let head drop slightly, or produce a sudden loud sound against surface supporting infant.	Infant makes an "embracing" motion by arching back, extending legs, throwing arms outward, and then bringing arms in toward the body.	6 months	In human evolutionary past, may have helped infant cling to mother
Palmar grasp	Place finger in infant's hand and press against palm.	Infant spontaneously grasps finger.	3–4 months	Prepares infant for voluntary grasping
Tonic neck	Turn baby's head to one side while lying awake on back.	Infant lies in a "fencing position." One arm is extended in front of eyes on side to which head is turned, other arm is flexed.	4 months	May prepare infant for voluntary reaching
Stepping	Hold infant under arms and permit bare feet to touch a flat surface.	Infant lifts one foot after another in stepping response.	2 months in infants who gain weight quickly; sustained in lighter infants.	Prepares infant for voluntary walking
Babinski	Stroke sole of foot from toe toward heel.	Toes fan out and curl as foot twists in.	8–12 months	Unknown

Sources: Knobloch & Pasamanick, 1974; Prechtl & Beintema, 1965; Thelen, Fisher, & Ridley-Johnson, 1984.

movements of stepping is their ease compared with other movement patterns: Repetitive movement of just one leg or of both legs at once requires more effort.

In infants who gain weight quickly in the weeks after birth, the stepping reflex drops out because thigh and calf muscles are not strong enough to lift the baby's chubby legs. But if the lower part of the infant's body is dipped in water, the reflex reappears because the buoyancy of the water lightens the load on the baby's muscles (Thelen, Fisher, & Ridley-Johnson, 1984). When stepping is exercised regularly, babies make more reflexive stepping movements and are likely to walk several weeks earlier than if stepping is not practiced (Zelazo et al., 1993). However, there is no special need for infants to practice the stepping reflex because all normal babies walk in due time.

Some reflexes help parents and infants establish gratifying interaction. A baby who searches for and successfully finds the nipple, sucks easily during feedings, and grasps when the hand is touched encourages parents to respond lovingly and feel competent as caregivers. Reflexes can also help caregivers comfort the baby because they permit infants to control distress and amount of stimulation. For example, on short trips with Joshua to the grocery store, Yolanda brought along a pacifier. If he became fussy, sucking helped quiet him until she could feed, change, or hold him.

© LAURA DWIGHT PHOTOGRAPHY

The palmar grasp reflex is so strong during the first week after birth that many infants can use it to support their entire weight.

Look at Table 3.4 again, and you will see that most newborn reflexes disappear during the first six months. Researchers believe that this is due to a gradual increase in voluntary control over behavior as the cerebral cortex develops. Pediatricians test reflexes carefully because reflexes can reveal the health of the baby's nervous system. Weak or absent reflexes, overly rigid or exaggerated reflexes, and reflexes that persist beyond the point in development when they should normally disappear can signal brain damage (Schott & Rossor, 2003; Zafeiriou, 2000).

Newborn States

Throughout the day and night, newborn infants move in and out of five **states of arousal,** or degrees of sleep and wakefulness, described in Table 3.5. During the first month, these states alternate frequently. The most fleeting is quiet alertness, which usually moves quickly toward fussing and crying. Much to the relief of their fatigued parents, newborns spend the greatest amount of time asleep—about 16 to 18 hours a day. Although newborns sleep more at night than during the day, their sleep–wake cycles are affected more by fullness–hunger than by darkness–light (Davis, Parker, & Montgomery, 2004; Goodlin-Jones, Burnham, & Anders, 2000).

However, striking individual differences in daily rhythms exist that affect parents' attitudes toward and interaction with the baby. A few newborns sleep for long periods, increasing the energy their well-rested parents have for sensitive, responsive care. Other babies cry a great deal, and their parents must exert great effort to soothe them. If these parents do not succeed, they may feel anxious, less competent, and less positively toward their infant. Babies who spend more time alert probably receive more social stimulation and opportunities to explore and, therefore, may have a slight advantage in mental development (Gertner et al., 2002; Sadeh et al., 2007; Smart & Hiscock, 2007).

Of the states listed in Table 3.5, the two extremes—sleep and crying—have been of greatest interest to researchers. Each tells us something about normal and abnormal early development.

■ **SLEEP.** Observing Joshua as he slept, Yolanda and Jay wondered why his eyelids and body twitched and his rate of breathing varied. Sleep is made up of at least two states. During irregular, or **rapid-eye-movement (REM), sleep,** brain-wave activity is remarkably similar to that of the waking state. The eyes dart beneath the lids; heart rate, blood pressure, and breathing are uneven; and slight body movements occur. In contrast, during regular, or **non-rapid-eye-movement (NREM), sleep,** the body is almost motionless, and heart rate, breathing, and brain-wave activity are slow and even.

Like children and adults, newborns alternate between REM and NREM sleep. However, they spend far more time in the REM state than they ever will again. REM sleep accounts for 50 percent of a newborn baby's sleep time. By 3 to 5 years, it has declined to an adultlike level of 20 percent (Louis et al., 1997).

Why do young infants spend so much time in REM sleep? In older children and adults, the REM state is associated with dreaming. Babies probably do not dream, at least not in the same way we do. But researchers believe that the stimulation of REM sleep is vital for growth of the central nervous system. Young infants seem to have a special need for this stimulation because they spend little time in an alert state, when they can get input from the environment. In support of this idea, the percentage of REM sleep is especially great in the fetus and in preterm babies, who are even less able than full-term newborns to take advantage of external stimulation (de Weerd & van den Bossche, 2003; DiPietro et al., 1996).

■ **TABLE 3.5** ■ ***Infant States of Arousal***

STATE	DESCRIPTION	DAILY DURATION IN NEWBORN
Regular sleep	The infant is at full rest and shows little or no body activity. The eyelids are closed, no eye movements occur, the face is relaxed, and breathing is slow and regular.	8–9 hours
Irregular sleep	Gentle limb movements, occasional stirring, and facial grimacing occur. Although the eyelids are closed, occasional rapid eye movements can be seen beneath them. Breathing is irregular.	8–9 hours
Drowsiness	The infant is either falling asleep or waking up. Body is less active than in irregular sleep but more active than in regular sleep. The eyes open and close; when open, they have a glazed look. Breathing is even but somewhat faster than in regular sleep.	Varies
Quiet alertness	The infant's body is relatively inactive, with eyes open and attentive. Breathing is even.	2–3 hours
Waking activity and crying	The infant shows frequent bursts of uncoordinated body activity. Breathing is very irregular. Face may be relaxed or tense and wrinkled. Crying may occur.	1–4 hours

Source: Wolff, 1966.

Because the normal sleep behavior of a newborn baby is organized and patterned, observations of sleep states can help identify central nervous system abnormalities. In infants who are brain-damaged or who have experienced birth trauma, disturbed REM–NREM sleep cycles are often present. Babies with poor sleep organization are likely to be behaviorally disorganized and, therefore, to have difficulty learning and evoking caregiver interactions that enhance their development. In the preschool years, they show delayed motor, cognitive, and language development (de Weerd & van den Bossche, 2003; Feldman, 2006; Holditch-Davis, Belyea, & Edwards, 2005). And the brain-functioning problems that underlie newborn sleep irregularities may culminate in sudden infant death syndrome, a major cause of infant mortality (see the Biology and Environment box on page 110.

CRYING. Crying is the first way that babies communicate, letting parents know they need food, comfort, or stimulation. During the weeks after birth, all infants have some fussy periods when they are difficult to console. But most of the time, the nature of the cry, combined with the experiences leading up to it, helps guide parents toward its cause. The baby's cry is a complex stimulus that varies in intensity, from a whimper to a message of all-out distress (Gustafson, Wood, & Green, 2000). As early as the first few weeks, individual infants can be identified by the unique vocal "signature" of their cry, which helps parents locate their baby from a distance (Gustafson, Green, & Cleland, 1994).

Young infants usually cry because of physical needs, most commonly hunger, but babies may also cry in response to temperature change when undressed, a sudden noise, or a painful stimulus. Newborns (as well as older babies) often cry at the sound of another crying baby (Dondi, Simion, & Caltran, 1999). Some researchers believe that this response reflects an inborn capacity to react to the suffering of others. Furthermore, crying typically increases during the early weeks, peaks at about six weeks, and then declines. Because this trend appears in many cultures with vastly different infant care practices, researchers believe that normal readjustments of the central nervous system underlie it (Barr, 2001).

TAKE A MOMENT... The next time you hear an infant cry, notice your own reaction. The sound stimulates strong feelings of arousal and discomfort in just about anyone (Murray, 1985). This powerful response is probably innately programmed in humans to make sure that babies receive the care and protection they need to survive.

Soothing Crying Infants. Although parents do not always interpret their baby's cry correctly, their accuracy improves with experience (Thompson & Leger, 1999). Fortunately, there are many ways to soothe a crying baby when feeding and diaper changing do not work (see Applying What We Know on page 111). The technique that Western parents usually try first, lifting the baby to the shoulder and rocking or walking, is the most effective. Another common soothing method is swaddling—wrapping the baby snugly in a blanket. The

To soothe his crying infant, this father holds his baby upright against his gently moving body. Besides encouraging infants to stop crying, this technique causes them to become quietly alert.

Quechua, who live in the cold, high-altitude desert regions of Peru, dress young babies in layers of clothing and blankets that cover the head and body. The result—a warm pouch placed on the mother's back that moves rhythmically as she walks—reduces crying and promotes sleep. It also allows the baby to conserve energy for early growth in the harsh Peruvian highlands (Tronick, Thomas, & Daltabuit, 1994).

In many tribal and village societies and non-Western developed nations, infants spend most of the day and night in close physical contact with their caregivers. Among the !Kung of the desert regions of Botswana, Africa, mothers sling their young babies on their hips, so infants can see their surroundings and nurse at will. Japanese mothers and babies also spend much time in close body contact (Small, 1998). Infants in these cultures show shorter bouts of crying than their North American counterparts (Barr, 2001).

But not all research indicates that rapid parental responsiveness reduces infant crying (van IJzendoorn & Hubbard, 2000). Parents must make reasoned choices about what to do on the basis of culturally accepted practices, the suspected reason for the cry, and the context in which it occurs—for example, in the privacy of their own home or while having dinner at a restaurant. Fortunately, with age, crying declines. Virtually all researchers agree that parents can lessen older babies' need to cry by encouraging more mature ways of expressing their desires, such as gestures and vocalizations.

Abnormal Crying. Like reflexes and sleep patterns, the infant's cry offers a clue to central nervous system distress. The cries of brain-damaged babies and those who have experienced prenatal and birth complications are often shrill, piercing, and shorter in duration than those of healthy infants (Boukydis & Lester, 1998; Green, Irwin, & Gustafson, 2000). Even newborns

BIOLOGY AND ENVIRONMENT

The Mysterious Tragedy of Sudden Infant Death Syndrome

Millie awoke with a start one morning and looked at the clock. It was 7:30, and Sasha had missed both her night waking and her early morning feeding. Wondering if she was all right, Millie and her husband Stuart tiptoed into the room. Sasha lay still, curled up under her blanket. She had died silently during her sleep.

Sasha was a victim of **sudden infant death syndrome (SIDS),** the unexpected death, usually during the night, of an infant under 1 year of age that remains unexplained after thorough investigation. In industrialized nations, SIDS is the leading cause of infant mortality between 1 and 12 months, accounting for about 20 percent of these deaths in the United States (Mathews & McDorman, 2008).

Although the precise cause of SIDS is not known, its victims usually show physical problems from the beginning. Early medical records of SIDS babies reveal higher rates of prematurity and low birth weight, poor Apgar scores, and limp muscle tone. Abnormal heart rate and respiration and disturbances in sleep–wake activity and in REM–NREM cycles while asleep are also involved (Cornwell & Feigenbaum, 2006; Kato et al., 2003). At the time of death, many SIDS babies have a mild respiratory infection (Samuels, 2003). This seems to increase the chances of respiratory failure in an already vulnerable baby.

One hypothesis about the cause of SIDS is that impaired brain functioning prevents these infants from learning how to respond when their survival is threatened—for example, when respiration is suddenly interrupted. Between 2 and 4 months, when SIDS is most likely to occur, reflexes decline and are replaced by voluntary, learned responses. Respiratory and muscular weaknesses may stop SIDS babies from acquiring behaviors that replace defensive reflexes (Lipsitt, 2003). As a result, when breathing difficulties occur during sleep, infants do not wake up, shift their position, or cry out for help. Instead, they simply give in to oxygen deprivation and death. In support of this interpretation, autopsies reveal that SIDS babies, more often than other infants, show abnormalities in brain centers controlling breathing (Paterson et al., 2006).

In an effort to reduce the occurrence of SIDS, researchers are studying environmental factors related to it. Maternal cigarette smoking, both during and after pregnancy, as well as smoking by other caregivers, strongly predicts the disorder. Babies exposed to cigarette smoke have more respiratory infections, arouse less easily from sleep, and are twice as likely as nonexposed infants to die of SIDS (Anderson, Johnson, & Batal, 2005; Shah, Sullivan, & Carter, 2006). Prenatal abuse of drugs that depress central nervous system functioning (opiates and barbiturates) increases the risk of SIDS as much as fifteenfold (Hunt & Hauck, 2006). SIDS babies are also more likely to sleep on their stomachs than on their backs and often are wrapped very warmly in clothing and blankets (Hauck et al., 2003).

Researchers suspect that nicotine, depressant drugs, excessive body warmth, and respiratory infection all lead to physiological stress, which disrupts the normal sleep pattern. When sleep-deprived infants experience a sleep "rebound," they sleep more deeply, which results in loss of muscle tone in the airway passages. In at-risk babies, the airway may collapse, and the infant may fail to arouse sufficiently to reestablish breathing (Simpson, 2001). In other cases, healthy babies sleeping face down on soft bedding may die from continually breathing their own exhaled breath.

Quitting smoking, changing an infant's sleeping position, and removing a few bedclothes can reduce the incidence of SIDS. For example, if women refrained from smoking while pregnant, an estimated 30 percent of SIDS cases would be prevented. Public education campaigns that encourage parents to put their infants down on their backs have cut the incidence of SIDS in half in many Western nations (Byard & Krous, 2003). Another protective measure is pacifier use: Sleeping babies who suck arouse more easily in response to breathing and heart-rate irregularities (Li et al., 2006). Nevertheless, compared with white infants, SIDS rates are two to six times as high in poverty-stricken minority groups, where parental stress, substance abuse, reduced access to health care, and lack of knowledge about safe sleep practices are widespread (Pickett, Luo, & Lauderdale, 2005).

When SIDS does occur, surviving family members require a great deal of help to overcome a sudden and unexpected death. As Millie commented six months after Sasha's death, "It's the worst crisis we've ever been through. What's helped us most are the comforting words of others who've experienced the same tragedy."

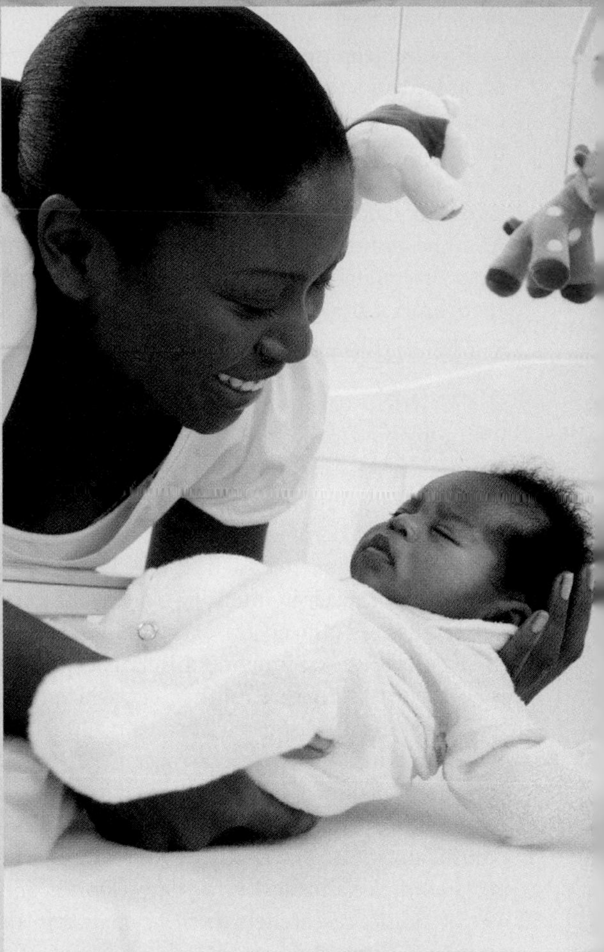

Public education campaigns encouraging parents to put their infants down on their backs to sleep have helped reduce the incidence of SIDS by half in many Western nations.

Applying What We Know

Soothing a Crying Baby

Method	Explanation
Lift the baby to the shoulder and rock or walk.	This combination of physical contact, upright posture, and motion is an effective soothing technique, causing young infants to become quietly alert.
Swaddle the baby.	Restricting movement and increasing warmth often soothe a young infant.
Offer a pacifier.	Sucking helps babies control their own level of arousal.
Talk softly or play rhythmic sounds.	Continuous, monotonous, rhythmic sounds (such as a clock ticking, a fan whirring, or peaceful music) are more effective than intermittent sounds.
Take the baby for a short car ride or a walk in a baby carriage; swing the baby in a cradle.	Gentle, rhythmic motion of any kind helps lull the baby to sleep.
Massage the baby's body.	Stroking the baby's torso and limbs with continuous, gentle motions relaxes the baby's muscles.
Combine several of the methods just listed.	Stimulating several of the baby's senses at once is often more effective than stimulating only one.
If these methods do not work, let the baby cry for a short period.	Occasionally, a baby responds well to just being put down and, after a few minutes, will fall asleep.

Sources: Evanoo, 2007; Campos, 1989; Lester, 1985; Reisman, 1987.

These Quechua women, who live in the cold, high-altitude desert regions of Peru, dress their young babies in layers of clothing and blankets that cover the head and body. In addition to reducing crying and promoting sleep, swaddling helps babies conserve energy for early growth in the harsh Peruvian highlands.

with a fairly common problem—*colic,* or persistent crying—tend to have high-pitched, harsh-sounding cries (Zeskind & Barr, 1997). Although the cause of colic is unknown, certain newborns, who react especially strongly to unpleasant stimuli, are susceptible. Because their crying is intense, they have more difficulty calming down than other babies. Colic generally subsides between 3 and 6 months (Barr et al., 2005; St James-Roberts et al., 2003).

Most parents try to respond to a crying baby with extra care and attention, but sometimes the cry is so unpleasant and the infant so difficult to soothe that parents become frustrated, resentful, and angry. Preterm and ill babies are more likely to be abused by highly stressed parents, who frequently mention a high-pitched, grating cry as one factor that caused them to lose control and harm the baby (St James-Roberts, 2007; Zeskind & Lester, 2001). We will discuss a host of additional influences on child abuse in Chapter 8.

Sensory Capacities

On his visit to my class, Joshua looked wide-eyed at my bright pink blouse and turned to the sound of his mother's voice. During feedings, he lets Yolanda know through his sucking rhythm that he prefers the taste of breast milk to a bottle of plain water. Clearly, Joshua has some well-developed sensory capacities. In the following sections, we explore the newborn's responsiveness to touch, taste, smell, sound, and visual stimulation.

■ **TOUCH.** In our discussion of preterm infants, we saw that touch helps stimulate early physical growth. As we will see in Chapter 6, it is vital for emotional development as well. Therefore, it is not surprising that sensitivity to touch is well-developed at birth. The reflexes listed in Table 3.4 reveal that the newborn baby responds to touch, especially around the mouth, on the palms, and on the soles of the feet. During the prenatal period, these areas, along with the genitals, are the first to become sensitive to touch (Humphrey, 1978; Streri, 2005).

At birth, infants are highly sensitive to pain. If male newborns are circumcised, anesthetic is sometimes not used because of the risk of giving drugs to a very young infant. Babies often respond with a high-pitched, stressful cry and a dramatic rise in heart rate, blood pressure, palm sweating, pupil dilation, and muscle tension (Lehr et al., 2007; Warnock & Sandrin, 2004). Brain-imaging research suggests that because of central nervous system immaturity, preterm and male babies feel the pain of a medical injection especially intensely (Bartocci et al., 2006).

Recent research establishing the safety of certain local anesthetics for newborns promises to ease the pain of these procedures. Offering a nipple that delivers a sugar solution is also helpful; it quickly reduces crying and discomfort in young babies, preterm and full-term alike. And combining the sweet liquid with gentle holding by the parent lessens pain even more. Research on infant mammals indicates that physical touch releases *endorphins*—painkilling chemicals in the brain (Axelin, Salanterä, & Lehtonen, 2006; Gormally et al., 2001). Allowing a baby to endure severe pain overwhelms the nervous system with stress hormones, which can disrupt the child's developing capacity to handle common, everyday stressors. The result is heightened pain sensitivity, sleep disturbances, feeding problems, and difficulty calming down when upset (Mitchell & Boss, 2002).

■ **TASTE AND SMELL.** Facial expressions reveal that newborns can distinguish several basic tastes. Like adults, they relax their facial muscles in response to sweetness, purse their lips when the taste is sour, and show a distinct archlike mouth opening when it is bitter (Steiner, 1979; Steiner et al., 2001). These reactions are important for survival: The food that best supports the infant's early growth is the sweet-tasting milk of the mother's breast. Not until 4 months do babies prefer a salty taste to plain water, a change that may prepare them to accept solid foods (Mennella & Beauchamp, 1998).

Nevertheless, newborns can readily learn to like a taste that at first evoked either a neutral or a negative response. For example, babies allergic to cow's-milk formula who are given a soy or other vegetable-based substitute (typically very strong and bitter-tasting) soon prefer it to regular formula. A taste previously disliked can come to be preferred when it is paired with relief of hunger (Harris, 1997).

As with taste, certain odor preferences are present at birth. For example, the smell of bananas or chocolate causes a relaxed, pleasant facial expression, whereas the odor of rotten eggs makes the infant frown (Steiner, 1979). During pregnancy, the amniotic fluid is rich in tastes and smells that vary with the mother's diet—early experiences that influence newborns' preferences. In a study carried out in the Alsatian region of France, where anise is frequently used to flavor foods, researchers tested newborns for their reaction to the anise odor (Schaal, Marlier, & Soussignan, 2000). The mothers of some babies had regularly consumed anise during the last two weeks of pregnancy; the other mothers had never consumed it. When presented with the anise odor on the day of birth, the babies of non-anise-consuming mothers were far more likely to turn away with a negative facial expression (see Figure 3.8). These different reactions were still apparent four days later, even though all mothers had refrained from consuming anise during this time.

In many mammals, the sense of smell plays an important role in feeding and in protecting the young from predators by helping mothers and babies identify each other. Although smell is less well-developed in humans, traces of its survival value remain.

Immediately after birth, babies placed face down between their mother's breasts spontaneously latch on to a nipple and begin sucking within an hour. If one breast is washed to remove its natural scent, most newborns grasp the unwashed breast, indicating that they are guided by smell (Varendi & Porter, 2001). At 4 days of age, breastfed babies prefer the smell of their

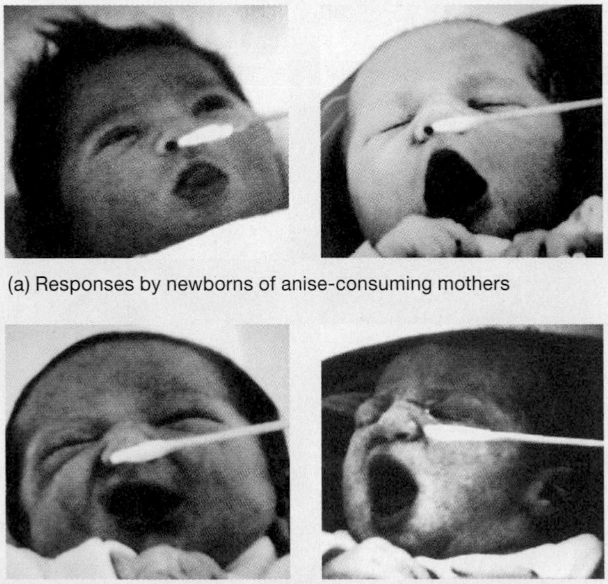

(a) Responses by newborns of anise-consuming mothers

(b) Responses by newborns of non-anise-consuming mothers

■ **FIGURE 3.8** ■ **Examples of facial expressions of newborns exposed to the odor of anise whose mothers' diets differed in anise-flavored foods during late pregnancy.** (a) Babies of anise-consuming mothers spent more time turning toward the odor and sucking, licking, and chewing. (b) Babies of non-anise-consuming mothers more often turned away with a negative facial expression. (From B. Schaal, L. Marlier, & R. Soussignan, 2000, "Human Foetuses Learn Odours from Their Pregnant Mother's Diet," *Chemical Senses, 25,* p. 731. Reprinted by permission of Benoist Schaal.)

own mother's breast to that of an unfamiliar lactating mother (Cernoch & Porter, 1985). And both breast- and bottle-fed 3- to 4-day-olds orient more and display more mouthing to the smell of unfamiliar human milk than to formula milk, indicating that (even without prior exposure) the odor of human milk is more attractive to newborns (Marlier & Schaal, 2005). Newborns' dual attraction to the odor of their mother and to that of breast milk helps them locate an appropriate food source and, in the process, begin to distinguish their caregiver from other people.

■ **HEARING.** Newborn infants can hear a wide variety of sounds, and their sensitivity improves greatly over the first few months (Saffran, Werker, & Werner, 2006; Tharpe & Ashmead, 2001). At birth, infants prefer complex sounds, such as noises and voices, to pure tones. And babies only a few days old can tell the difference between a few sound patterns—a series of tones arranged in ascending versus descending order, utterances with two versus three syllables, the stress patterns of words, such as *ma*-ma versus ma-*ma,* and happy-sounding speech as opposed to speech with negative or neutral emotional qualities (Mastropieri & Turkewitz, 1999; Sansavini, Bertoncini, & Giovanelli, 1997; Trehub, 2001).

Young infants listen longer to human speech than structurally similar nonspeech sounds (Vouloumanos & Werker, 2004). And they can detect the sounds of any human language. Newborns make fine-grained distinctions among many speech sounds. For example, when given a nipple that turns on a recording of the "*ba*" sound, babies suck vigorously and then slow down as the novelty wears off. When the sound switches to "*ga*," sucking picks up, indicating that infants detect this subtle difference. Using this method, researchers have found only a few speech sounds that newborns cannot discriminate (Aldridge, Stillman, & Bower, 2001; Jusczyk & Luce, 2002). These capacities reveal that the baby is marvelously prepared for the awesome task of acquiring language.

TAKE A MOMENT... The next time you talk to a young baby, listen carefully to yourself. You will probably speak in ways that highlight important parts of the speech stream—use a slow, high-pitched, expressive voice with a rising tone at the ends of phrases and sentences and a pause before continuing. Adults probably communicate this way because they notice that infants are more attentive when they do so. Indeed, newborns prefer speech with these characteristics (Saffran, Werker, & Werner, 2006). They will also suck more on a nipple to hear a recording of their mother's voice than that of an unfamiliar woman and to hear their native language as opposed to a foreign language (Moon, Cooper, & Fifer, 1993; Spence & DeCasper, 1987). These preferences may have developed from hearing the muffled sounds of the mother's voice before birth.

■ **VISION.** Vision is the least-developed of the newborn baby's senses. Visual structures in both the eye and the brain are not yet fully formed. For example, cells in the *retina,* a membrane lining the inside of the eye that captures light and transforms it into messages that are sent to the brain, are not as mature or densely packed as they will be in several months. The optic nerve that relays these messages, and the visual centers in the brain that receive them, will not be adultlike for several years. And the muscles of the *lens,* which permit us to adjust our visual focus to varying distances, are weak (Kellman & Arterberry, 2006).

As a result, newborns cannot focus their eyes well, and **visual acuity,** or fineness of discrimination, is limited. At birth, infants perceive objects at a distance of 20 feet about as clearly as adults do at 600 feet (Slater, 2001). In addition, unlike adults (who see nearby objects most clearly), newborn babies see unclearly across a wide range of distances (Banks, 1980; Hainline, 1998). As a result, images such as the parent's face, even from close up, look quite blurred.

Although newborns cannot see well, they actively explore their environment by scanning it for interesting sights and tracking moving objects. However, their eye movements are slow and inaccurate (von Hofsten & Rosander, 1998). Joshua's captivation with my pink blouse reveals that he is attracted to bright objects. Although newborns prefer to look at colored rather than gray stimuli, they are not yet good at discriminating colors. It will take about four months for color vision to become adultlike (Adams & Courage, 1998; Kellman & Arterberry, 2006).

Neonatal Behavioral Assessment

A variety of instruments permit doctors, nurses, and researchers to assess the behavior of newborn babies. The most widely used, T. Berry Brazelton's **Neonatal Behavioral Assessment Scale (NBAS),** evaluates the newborn's reflexes, muscle tone, state changes, responsiveness to physical and social stimuli, and other reactions (Brazelton & Nugent, 1995). A recently developed instrument consisting of similar items, the Neonatal Intensive Care Unit Network Neurobehavioral Scale (NNNS), is specially designed for use with newborns at risk for developmental problems because of low birth weight, preterm delivery, prenatal substance exposure, or other conditions (Lester & Tronick, 2004). Scores are used to understand each infant's capacity to initiate caregiver support, to adjust his or her behavior to avoid being overwhelmed by stimulation, and to recommend appropriate interventions.

The NBAS has been given to many infants around the world. As a result, researchers have learned about individual and cultural differences in newborn behavior and how child-rearing practices can maintain or change a baby's reactions. For example, NBAS scores of Asian and Native-American babies reveal that they are less irritable than Caucasian infants. Mothers in these cultures often encourage their babies' calm dispositions through holding and nursing at the first signs of discomfort (Muret-Wagstaff & Moore, 1989; Small, 1998). In contrast, close mother–infant contact throughout the day quickly changes the poor NBAS scores of undernourished newborns in Zambia, Africa. When reassessed at 1 week of age, a once unresponsive newborn appears alert and contented (Brazelton, Koslowski, & Tronick, 1976).

TAKE A MOMENT... Using these examples, can you explain why a single neonatal assessment score is not a good predictor of later development? Because newborn behavior and parenting styles combine to shape development, *changes in scores* over the first week or two of life (rather than a single score) provide the best estimate of the baby's ability to recover from the stress of birth. NBAS "recovery curves" predict intelligence and absence of emotional and behavior problems with moderate success well into the preschool years (Brazelton, Nugent, & Lester, 1987; Ohgi et al., 2003a, 2003b).

In some hospitals, health professionals use the NBAS or the NNNS to help parents get to know their newborns through discussion or demonstration of the capacities these instruments assess. Parents of both preterm and full-term newborns who participate in these programs interact more confidently and effectively with their babies (Browne & Talmi, 2005; Bruschweiler-Stern, 2004). Although lasting effects on development have not been demonstrated, NBAS-based interventions are useful in helping the parent–infant relationship get off to a good start.

Similar to women in the Zambian culture, this mother of the El Molo people of northern Kenya carries her baby all day, providing close physical contact, a rich variety of stimulation, and ready feeding.

ASK YOURSELF

» REVIEW
What functions does REM sleep serve in young infants? Can sleep tell us anything about the health of the newborn's central nervous system? Explain.

» APPLY
After a difficult delivery, Jackie observes her 2-day-old daughter Kelly being given the NBAS. Kelly scores poorly on many items. Jackie wonders if this means Kelly will not develop normally. How would you respond to Jackie's concern?

» CONNECT
How do the diverse capacities of newborn babies contribute to their first social relationships? Provide as many examples as you can.

» REFLECT
Are newborns more competent than you thought they were before you read this chapter? Which of their capacities most surprised you?

Adjusting to the New Family Unit

Because effective parental care is crucial for infant survival and optimal development, nature helps prepare expectant mothers and fathers for their new role. Toward the end of pregnancy, mothers begin producing the hormone oxytocin, which stimulates uterine contractions; causes the breasts to "let down" milk; induces a calm, relaxed mood; and promotes responsiveness to the baby (Russell, Douglas, & Ingram, 2001). And in several studies, first-time fathers enrolled in prenatal classes showed hormonal changes around the time of birth that were compatible with those of mothers—specifically, slight increases in *prolactin* (a hormone that stimulates milk production in females) and *estrogens* (sex hormones produced in larger quantities in females) and a drop in *androgens* (sex hormones produced in larger quantities in males). In animal and human research, these changes are associated with positive emotional reactions to infants and with paternal caregiving (Storey et al., 2000; Wynne-Edwards, 2001).

Although birth-related hormones can facilitate caregiving, their release and effects may depend on experiences, such as a positive couple relationship and paternal close contact with the pregnant mother. Furthermore, humans can parent effectively without experiencing birth-related hormonal changes, as successful adoption reveals. And as we have seen, a great many factors—from family functioning to social policies—are involved in good infant care.

Indeed, the early weeks after the baby's arrival are full of profound challenges. The mother needs to recuperate from childbirth. If she is breastfeeding, energies must be devoted to working out this intimate relationship. The father needs to support the mother in her recovery and become a part of this new threesome. At times, he may feel ambivalent about the baby, who constantly demands and gets the mother's attention. And as we will see in Chapter 6, siblings—especially those who are young and firstborn—understandably feel displaced. They sometimes react with jealousy and anger.

While all this is going on, the tiny infant is assertive about his urgent physical needs, demanding to be fed, changed, and comforted at odd times of the day and night. The family schedule becomes irregular and uncertain. Yolanda spoke candidly about the changes she and Jay experienced:

> When we brought Joshua home, we had to deal with the realities of our new responsibility. Joshua seemed so small and helpless, and we worried about whether we would be able to take proper care of him. It took us 20 minutes to change the first diaper! I rarely feel rested because I'm up two to four times every night, and I spend a good part of my waking hours trying to anticipate Joshua's rhythms and needs. If Jay weren't so willing to help by holding and walking Joshua, I think I'd find it much harder.

How long does this time of adjustment to parenthood last? In Chapter 14, we will see that when marital relationships are positive, social support is available, and families have sufficient income, the stress caused by the birth of a baby remains manageable. Nevertheless, as one pair of counselors who have worked with many new parents pointed out, "As long as children are dependent on their parents, those parents find themselves preoccupied with thoughts of their children. This does not keep them from enjoying other aspects of their lives, but it does mean that they never return to being quite the same people they were before they became parents" (Colman & Colman, 1991, p. 198).

Summary

Prenatal Development

List the three phases of prenatal development, and describe the major milestones of each.

» The first prenatal phase, the period of the zygote, lasts about two weeks, from fertilization until **implantation** of the blastocyst in the uterine lining. During this time, structures that will support prenatal growth begin to form, including the **placenta** and the **umbilical cord.**

» The period of the **embryo** lasts from two to eight weeks, during which the foundations for all body structures are laid down. In the first week of this period, the **neural tube** forms, and the nervous system starts to develop. Other organs follow and grow rapidly. At the end of this phase, the embryo responds to touch and can move.

» The period of the **fetus,** lasting until the end of pregnancy, involves a dramatic increase in body size and the completion of physical structures. At the end of the second **trimester,** most of the brain's neurons are in place. At the beginning of the third trimester, between 22 and 26 weeks, the fetus reaches the **age of viability.** The brain continues to develop rapidly, and new sensory and behavioral capacities emerge. The lungs gradually mature, the fetus fills the uterus, and birth is near.

Prenatal Environmental Influences

What are teratogens, and what factors influence their impact?

» **Teratogens** are environmental agents that cause damage during the prenatal period. Their impact varies with the amount and length of exposure, the genetic makeup of mother and fetus, the presence or absence of other harmful agents, and the age of the organism at time of exposure. The developing organism is especially vulnerable during the embryonic period.

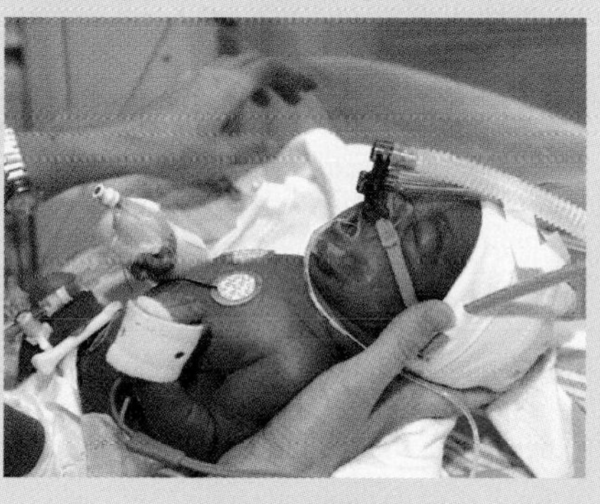

© CHET GORDON/THE IMAGE WORKS

List agents that are known or suspected teratogens, and discuss evidence supporting the harmful impact of each.

» Currently, the most widely used potent teratogen is Accutane, a drug used to treat acne. The prenatal impact of many other commonly used medications, such as aspirin and caffeine, is hard to separate from other factors correlated with drug taking. Babies whose mothers used heroin, methadone, or cocaine during pregnancy are at risk for a wide variety of problems, including prematurity, low birth weight, physical defects, and breathing difficulties around the time of birth.

» Infants of parents who use tobacco are often born underweight and may have attention, learning, and behavior problems in childhood. Maternal alcohol consumption can lead to **fetal alcohol spectrum disorder (FASD). Fetal alcohol syndrome (FAS)** involves slow physical growth, facial abnormalities, and impairment in mental functioning. Milder forms—**partial fetal alcohol syndrome (p-FAS)** and **alcohol-related neurodevelopmental disorder (ARND)**—affect children whose mothers consumed smaller quantities of alcohol.

- Prenatal exposure to high levels of radiation, mercury, lead, dioxins, and PCBs leads to physical malformations and severe brain damage. Low-level exposure has also been linked to diverse impairments, including lower intelligence test scores and, in the case of radiation, language and emotional disorders.
- Among infectious diseases, rubella (German measles) causes a wide variety of abnormalities. Babies with prenatally transmitted HIV rapidly develop AIDS, leading to brain damage and early death. Cytomegalovirus, herpes simplex 2, and toxoplasmosis can also be devastating to the fetus.

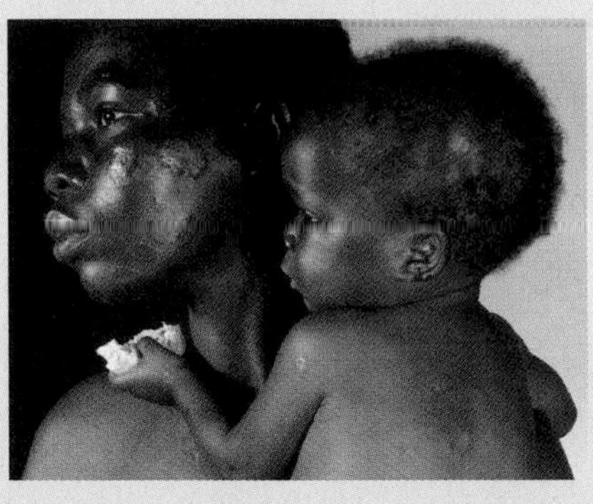

© DR. M. A. ANSARY/PHOTO RESEARCHERS, INC.

Describe the impact of other maternal factors on prenatal development.

- Regular moderate exercise during pregnancy is related to increased birth weight, but very frequent, vigorous exercise can result in lower birth weight. When the mother's diet is inadequate, low birth weight and damage to the brain and other organs are major concerns.
- Severe emotional stress is linked to many pregnancy complications, although its impact can be reduced by providing the mother with emotional support. **Rh factor incompatibility**—an Rh-negative mother carrying an Rh-positive fetus—can lead to oxygen deprivation, brain and heart damage, and infant death.
- Aside from the risk of chromosomal abnormalities in older women, maternal age through the thirties is not a major cause of prenatal problems. Poor health and environmental risks associated with poverty are the strongest predictors of pregnancy complications.

Why is early and regular health care vital during the prenatal period?

- Unexpected difficulties, such as preeclampsia, can arise, especially when mothers have health problems to begin with. Prenatal health care is especially critical for women unlikely to seek it—in particular, those who are young, single, and poor.

Childbirth

Describe the three stages of childbirth, the baby's adaptation to labor and delivery, and the newborn baby's appearance.

- In the first stage of childbirth, contractions widen and thin the cervix. In the second stage, the mother feels an urge to push the baby through the birth canal. In the final stage, the placenta is delivered. During labor, infants produce high levels of stress hormones, which help them withstand oxygen deprivation, clear the lungs for breathing, and arouse them into alertness at birth.
- Newborn babies have large heads, small bodies, and facial features that make adults feel like cuddling them. The **Apgar Scale** assesses the baby's physical condition at birth.

Approaches to Childbirth

Describe natural childbirth and home delivery, noting any benefits and concerns associated with each.

- **Natural,** or **prepared, childbirth** involves classes in which prospective parents learn about labor and delivery, relaxation and breathing techniques to counteract pain, and coaching during childbirth. The method helps reduce use of medication. Social support, a vital part of natural childbirth, is linked to fewer birth complications and shorter labors. Home birth is safe for healthy mothers who are assisted by a well-trained doctor or midwife, but mothers at risk for any kind of complication are safer giving birth in a hospital.

© NNS/BIRMINGHAM NEWS/LANDOV

Medical Interventions

List common medical interventions during childbirth, circumstances that justify their use, and any dangers associated with each.

- When pregnancy and birth complications make **anoxia** likely, **fetal monitors** help save the lives of many babies. However, when used routinely, they may identify infants as in danger who, in fact, are not.
- Medication to relieve pain is necessary in complicated deliveries. When given in large doses, it may prolong labor and produce a depressed state in the newborn that affects the early mother–infant relationship.
- **Cesarean deliveries** are justified in cases of medical emergency and serious maternal illness and sometimes when babies are in **breech position.** Many unnecessary cesareans are performed, especially in the United States.

Preterm and Low-Birth-Weight Infants

Describe risks associated with preterm birth and low birth weight, along with effective interventions.

- Low birth weight, a major cause of neonatal and **infant mortality** and wide-ranging developmental problems, is most common in infants born to poverty-stricken women. Compared with **preterm infants,** whose weight is appropriate for time spent in the uterus, **small-for-date infants** usually have longer-lasting difficulties.

© REUTERS/CHERYL RAVELO/LANDOV

- Some interventions provide special stimulation in the intensive care nursery. Others teach parents how to care for and interact with their babies. Preterm infants in stressed, low-income households need long-term, intensive intervention.

Birth Complications, Parenting, and Resilience

What factors predict positive outcomes in infants who survive a traumatic birth?

- When infants experience birth trauma, a supportive home environment can help restore their growth. Even infants with fairly serious birth complications can recover with the help of favorable experiences with parents, relatives, neighbors, and peers.

The Newborn Baby's Capacities

Describe the newborn baby's reflexes and states of arousal, including sleep characteristics and ways to soothe a crying baby.

» Infants begin life with remarkable skills for relating to their physical and social worlds. **Reflexes** are the newborn baby's most obvious organized patterns of behavior. Some have survival value, others provide the foundation for voluntary motor skills, and still others contribute to early social relationships.

» Although newborns move in and out of five different **states of arousal,** they spend most of their time asleep. Sleep consists of at least two states, **rapid-eye-movement (REM) sleep** and **non-rapid-eye-movement (NREM) sleep.** Newborns spend more time in REM sleep than they will at any later age. This state provides stimulation essential for central nervous system development.

» A crying baby stimulates strong feelings of discomfort in nearby adults. The intensity of the cry and the experiences that led up to it help parents identify what is wrong. Once feeding and diaper changing have been tried, the most effective soothing technique is lifting the baby to the shoulder and rocking and walking.

Describe the newborn baby's sensory capacities.

» The senses of touch, taste, smell, and sound are well-developed at birth. Newborns are sensitive to pain, prefer sweet tastes and smells, and orient toward the odor of their own mother's lactating breast. Already they can distinguish a few sound patterns as well as almost all speech sounds. They are especially responsive to high-pitched, expressive voices, their own mother's voice, and speech in their native tongue.

» Vision is the least mature of the newborn's senses. At birth, focusing ability and **visual acuity** are limited. In exploring the visual field, newborn babies are attracted to bright objects but have difficulty discriminating colors.

Why is neonatal behavioral assessment useful?

» The most widely used instrument for assessing the behavior of the newborn infant is Brazelton's **Neonatal Behavioral Assessment Scale (NBAS).** The NBAS has helped researchers understand individual and cultural differences in newborn behavior. Sometimes it is used to teach parents about their newborn's capacities.

Adjusting to the New Family Unit

Describe typical changes in the family after the birth of a new baby.

» The new baby's arrival is exciting but stressful, as the mother recuperates from childbirth and the family schedule becomes irregular and uncertain. When parents are sensitive to each other's needs, adjustment problems are usually temporary, and the transition to parenthood goes well.

Important Terms and Concepts

age of viability (p. 84)
alcohol-related neurodevelopmental disorder (ARND) (p. 90)
amnion (p. 82)
anoxia (p. 100)
Apgar Scale (p. 98)
breech position (p. 100)
cesarean delivery (p. 101)
chorion (p. 82)
embryo (p. 82)
fetal alcohol spectrum disorder (FASD) (p. 89)
fetal alcohol syndrome (FAS) (p. 89)
fetal monitors (p. 100)
fetus (p. 83)
implantation (p. 82)
infant mortality (p. 104)
lanugo (p. 84)
natural, or prepared, childbirth (p. 99)
Neonatal Behavioral Assessment Scale (NBAS) (p. 113)
neural tube (p. 83)
non-rapid-eye-movement (NREM) sleep (p. 108)
partial fetal alcohol syndrome (p-FAS) (p. 90)
placenta (p. 82)
preterm infants (p. 102)
rapid-eye-movement (REM) sleep (p. 108)
reflex (p. 106)
Rh factor incompatibility (p. 94)
small-for-date infants (p. 102)
states of arousal (p. 108)
sudden infant death syndrome (SIDS) (p. 110)
teratogen (p. 85)
trimesters (p. 83)
umbilical cord (p. 82)
vernix (p. 84)
visual acuity (p. 113)

© SARAH MONTE/GETTY IMAGES/WESTEND61

Babies acquire new motor skills by building on previously acquired capacities. Eager to explore his world, this baby has just about mastered the art of crawling. Once he can fully move on his own, he will make dramatic strides in understanding his surroundings.

CHAPTER 4

Physical Development in Infancy and Toddlerhood

On a brilliant June morning, 16-month-old Caitlin emerged from her front door, ready for the short drive to the child-care home where she spent her weekdays while her mother, Carolyn, and her father, David, worked. Clutching a teddy bear in one hand and her mother's arm with the other, Caitlin descended the steps. "One! Two! Threeee!" Carolyn counted as she helped Caitlin down. "How much she's changed," Carolyn thought to herself, looking at the child who, not long ago, had been a newborn. With her first steps, Caitlin had passed from *infancy* to *toddlerhood*—a period spanning the second year of life. At first, Caitlin did, indeed, "toddle" awkwardly, rocking from side to side and frequently tipping over. But her face reflected the thrill of conquering a new skill.

As they walked toward the car, Carolyn and Caitlin spotted 3-year-old Eli and his father, Kevin, in the neighboring yard. Eli dashed toward them, waving a bright yellow envelope. Carolyn bent down to open the envelope and took out a card. It read, "Announcing the arrival of Grace Ann. Born: Cambodia. Age: 16 months." Carolyn turned to Kevin and Eli. "That's wonderful news! When can we see her?"

COURTESY OF LAURA E. BERK

"Let's wait a few days," Kevin suggested. "Monica's taken Grace to the doctor this morning. She's underweight and malnourished." Kevin described Monica's first night with Grace in a hotel room in Phnom Penh. Grace lay on the bed, withdrawn and fearful. Eventually she fell asleep, clutching crackers in both hands.

Carolyn felt Caitlin's impatient tug at her sleeve. Off they drove to child care, where Vanessa had just dropped off her 18-month-old son, Timmy. Within moments, Caitlin and Timmy were in the sandbox, shoveling sand into plastic cups and buckets with the help of their caregiver, Ginette.

A few weeks later, Grace joined Caitlin and Timmy at Ginette's child-care home. Although still tiny and unable to crawl or walk, she had grown taller and heavier, and her sad, vacant gaze had given way to an alert expression, a ready smile, and an enthusiastic desire to imitate and explore. When Caitlin headed for the sandbox, Grace stretched out her arms, asking Ginette to carry her there, too. Soon Grace was pulling herself up at every opportunity. Finally, at age 18 months, she walked!

This chapter traces physical growth during the first two years—one of the most remarkable and busiest times of development. We will see how rapid changes in the infant's body and brain support learning, motor skills, and perceptual capacities. Caitlin, Grace, and Timmy will join us along the way to illustrate individual differences and environmental influences on physical development.

Body Growth

TAKE A MOMENT... The next time you're walking in your neighborhood or at the mall, observe the contrast between the capabilities of infants and those of toddlers. One reason for the vast changes in what children can do over the first two years is that their bodies change enormously—faster than at any other time after birth.

Changes in Body Size and Muscle–Fat Makeup

By the end of the first year, a typical infant's height is about 32 inches—more than 50 percent greater than at birth. By 2 years, it is nearly 75 percent greater (36 inches). Similarly, by 5 months of age, birth weight has doubled, to about 15 pounds. At 1 year it has tripled, to 22 pounds, and at 2 years it has quadrupled, to about 30 pounds.

Figure 4.1 illustrates this dramatic increase in body size. But rather than making steady gains, infants and toddlers grow in little spurts. In one study, children who were followed over the first 21 months of life went for periods of 7 to 63 days with

■ **FIGURE 4.1** ■ **Body growth during the first two years.** These photos depict the dramatic changes in body size and proportions during infancy and toddlerhood in two individuals—a boy, Chris, and a girl, Mai. In the first year, the head is quite large in proportion to the rest of the body, and height and weight gain are especially rapid. During the second year, the lower portion of the body catches up. Notice, also, how both children added "baby fat" in the early months of life and then slimmed down, a trend that continues into middle childhood.

no growth, then added as much as half an inch in a 24-hour period! Almost always, parents described their babies as irritable and very hungry on the day before the spurt (Lampl, 1993; Lampl, Veldhuis, & Johnson, 1992).

One of the most obvious changes in infants' appearance is their transformation into round, plump babies by the middle of the first year. This early rise in "baby fat," which peaks at about 9 months, helps the small infant maintain a constant body temperature. In the second year, most toddlers slim down, a trend that continues into middle childhood (Fomon & Nelson, 2002). In contrast, muscle tissue increases very slowly during infancy and will not reach a peak until adolescence. Babies are not very muscular; their strength and physical coordination are limited.

Individual and Group Differences

As with all aspects of development, children vary in body size and muscle–fat makeup. In infancy, girls are slightly shorter and lighter than boys, with a higher ratio of fat to muscle. These small sex differences persist throughout early and middle childhood and are greatly magnified at adolescence. Ethnic differences in body size are apparent as well. Grace was below the *growth norms* (height and weight averages for children her age). Early malnutrition contributed, but even after substantial catch-up Grace—as is typical for Asian children—remained below North American norms. In contrast, Timmy is slightly above average, as African-American children tend to be (Bogin, 2001).

Children of the same age also differ in *rate* of physical growth; some progress more rapidly than others. Current body size does not tell us how quickly a child's physical growth is moving along. For example, although Timmy is larger and heavier than either Caitlin or Grace, he is not physically more mature. In a moment, you will see why.

The best way of estimating a child's physical maturity is to use *skeletal age,* a measure of bone development. It is determined by X-raying the long bones of the body to see the extent to which soft, pliable cartilage has hardened into bone, a gradual process that is completed in adolescence. When skeletal ages are examined, African-American children tend to be slightly ahead of Caucasian children at all ages, and girls are considerably ahead of boys. At birth, the sexes differ by about 4 to 6 weeks, a gap that widens over infancy and childhood and explains why girls reach their full body size several years before boys (Tanner, Healy, & Cameron, 2001). Girls' greater physical maturity may contribute to their greater resistance to harmful environmental influences. As noted in Chapter 2, girls experience fewer developmental problems than boys and have lower infant and childhood mortality rates.

Changes in Body Proportions

As the child's overall size increases, different parts of the body grow at different rates. Two growth patterns describe these changes. The first is the **cephalocaudal trend**—from the Latin for "head to tail." During the prenatal period, the head develops more rapidly than the lower part of the body. At birth, the head takes up one-fourth of total body length, the legs only one-third. Notice how, in Figure 4.1, the lower portion of the body catches up. By age 2, the head accounts for only one-fifth and the legs for nearly one-half of body length.

In the second pattern, the **proximodistal trend,** growth proceeds, literally, from "near to far"—from the center of the body outward. In the prenatal period, the head, chest, and trunk grow first, then the arms and legs, and finally the hands and feet. During infancy and childhood, the arms and legs continue to grow somewhat ahead of the hands and feet.

Brain Development

At birth, the brain is nearer to its adult size than any other physical structure, and it continues to develop at an astounding pace throughout infancy and toddlerhood. We can best understand brain growth by looking at it from two vantage points: (1) the microscopic level of individual brain cells and (2) the larger level of the cerebral cortex, which is responsible for the highly developed intelligence of our species.

Development of Neurons

The human brain has 100 to 200 billion **neurons,** or nerve cells that store and transmit information, many of which have thousands of direct connections with other neurons. Unlike other body cells, neurons are not tightly packed together. Between them are **synapses**—tiny gaps where fibers from different neurons come close together but do not touch (see Figure 4.2).

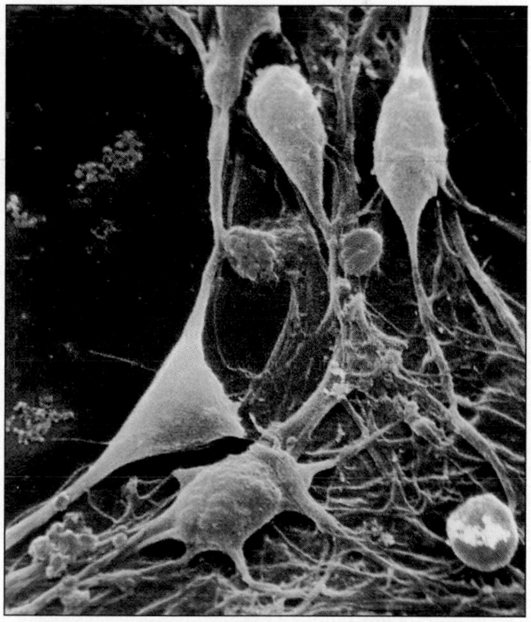

■ **FIGURE 4.2** ■ **Neurons and their connective fibers.** This photograph of several neurons, taken with the aid of a powerful microscope, shows the elaborate synaptic connections that form with neighboring cells.

Neurons send messages to one another by releasing chemicals called **neurotransmitters,** which cross the synapse.

The basic story of brain growth concerns how neurons develop and form this elaborate communication system. Figure 4.3 summarizes the major milestones of brain development. In the prenatal period, neurons are produced in the embryo's primitive neural tube. From there, they migrate to form the major parts of the brain (see page 83 in Chapter 3). Once neurons are in place, they differentiate, establishing their unique functions by extending their fibers to form synaptic connections with neighboring cells. During the first two years, neural fibers and synapses increase at an astounding pace (Huttenlocher, 2002; Moore & Persaud, 2008). Because developing neurons require space for these connective structures, a surprising aspect of brain growth is that as synapses form, many surrounding neurons die—20 to 80 percent, depending on the brain region (de Haan & Johnson, 2003; Stiles, 2001a). Fortunately, during the prenatal period, the neural tube produces far more neurons than the brain will ever need.

As neurons form connections, *stimulation* becomes vital to their survival. Neurons that are stimulated by input from the surrounding environment continue to establish synapses, forming increasingly elaborate systems of communication that support more complex abilities. At first, stimulation results in massive overabundance of synapses, many of which serve identical functions, thereby ensuring that the child will acquire the motor, cognitive, and social skills that our species needs to survive. Neurons that are seldom stimulated soon lose their synapses, in a process called **synaptic pruning** that returns neurons not needed at the moment to an uncommitted state so they can support future development. In all, about 40 percent of synapses are pruned during childhood and adolescence to reach the adult level (Webb, Monk, & Nelson, 2001). For this process to advance, appropriate stimulation of the child's brain is vital during periods in which the formation of synapses is at its peak (Nelson, Thomas, & de Haan, 2006).

If few neurons are produced after the prenatal period, what causes the dramatic increase in brain size during the first two years? About half the brain's volume consists of **glial cells,** which are responsible for **myelination,** the coating of neural fibers with an insulating fatty sheath (called *myelin*) that improves the efficiency of message transfer. Glial cells multiply dramatically from the end of pregnancy through the second year of life, a process that slows through middle childhood and accelerates again in adolescence. Gains in neural fibers and myelination are responsible for the extraordinary gain in overall size of the brain—from nearly 30 percent of its adult weight at birth to 70 percent by age 2 (Johnson, 2005; Thatcher et al., 1996).

Brain development can be compared to molding a "living sculpture." After neurons and synapses are overproduced, cell death and synaptic pruning sculpt away excess building material to form the mature brain—a process jointly influenced by genetically programmed events and the child's experiences. The resulting sculpture is a set of interconnected regions, each with specific functions—much like countries on a globe that communicate with one another (Johnston et al., 2001). This "geography" of the brain permits researchers to study its developing organization and the activity of its regions using *neurophysiological* techniques.

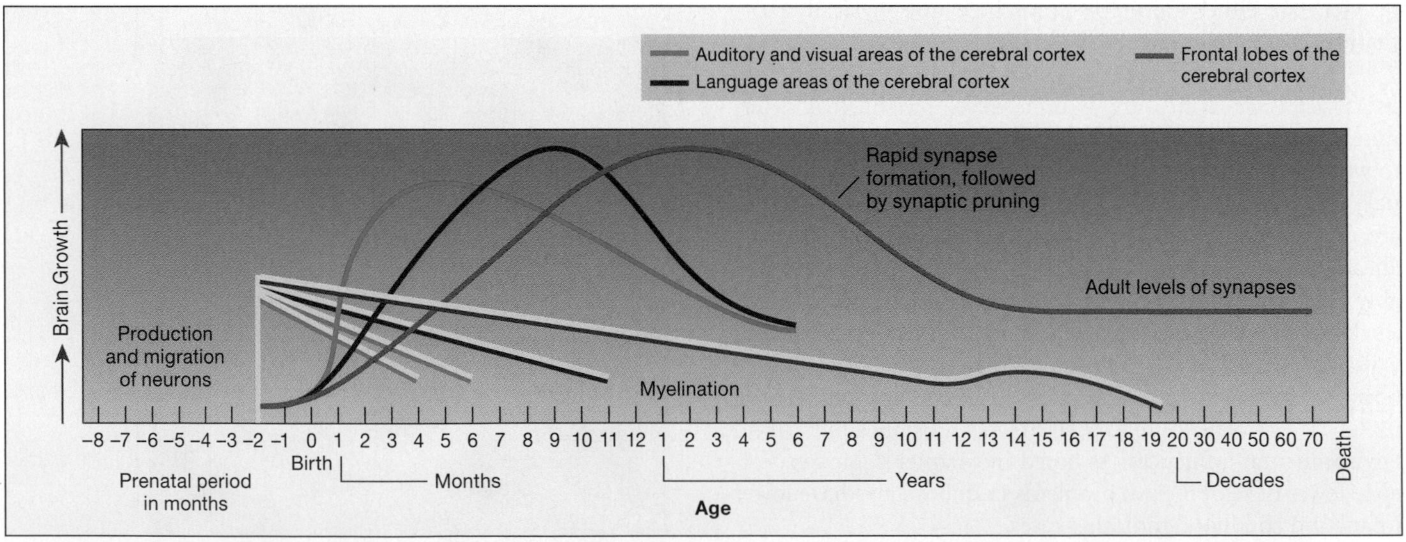

■ **FIGURE 4.3** ■ **Major milestones of brain development.** Formation of synapses is rapid during the first two years, especially in the auditory, visual, and language areas of the cerebral cortex. The frontal lobes undergo more extended synaptic growth. In each area, overproduction of synapses is followed by synaptic pruning. The frontal lobes are among the last regions to attain adult levels of synaptic connections—in mid- to late adolescence. Myelination occurs at a dramatic pace during the first two years and then at a slower pace through childhood and adolescence. The multiple yellow lines indicate that the timing of myelination varies among different brain areas. For example, neural fibers continue to myelinate over a longer period in the language areas, and especially in the frontal lobes, than in the visual and auditory areas. (Adapted from Thompson & Nelson, 2001.)

■ TABLE 4.1 ■ *Methods for Measuring Brain Functioning*

METHOD	DESCRIPTION
Electroencephalogram (EEG)	Electrodes, usually embedded in a head cap, are attached to the scalp with conductive gel to record electrical brain-wave activity in the brain's outer layers—the cerebral cortex.
Event-related potentials (ERPs)	Using the EEG, the frequency and amplitude of brain waves in response to particular stimuli (such as a picture, music, or speech) are recorded in the cerebral cortex. Enables identification of general regions of stimulus-induced activity.
Functional magnetic resonance imaging (fMRI)	While the person lies inside a tunnel-shaped apparatus that creates a magnetic field, a scanner magnetically detects increased blood flow and oxygen metabolism in areas of the brain as the individual processes particular stimuli. The result is a computerized moving picture of activity anywhere in the brain (not just its outer layers).
Positron emission tomography (PET)	After injection or inhalation of a radioactive substance, the person lies inside an apparatus with a scanner that emits fine streams of X-rays, which detect increased blood flow and oxygen metabolism in areas of the brain as the person processes particular stimuli. As with fMRI, the result is a computerized image of activity anywhere in the brain.
Near-Infrared Optical Topography (NIROT)	Using thin, flexible optical fibers attached to the scalp through a head cap, infrared (invisible) light is beamed at the brain; its absorption by areas of the cerebral cortex varies with changes in blood flow and oxygen metabolism as the individual processes particular stimuli. The result is a computerized moving picture of active areas in the cerebral cortex. Unlike fMRI and PET, NIROT is appropriate for infants and young children, who can move within limited range during testing.

Neurophysiological Methods

Table 4.1 above describes major measures of brain functioning. The first two methods detect changes in *electrical activity* in the cerebral cortex. Researchers can use an EEG to examine *brain-wave patterns* for stability and organization—signs of mature cortical functioning. As the person processes a stimulus, ERPs detect the general location of brain-wave activity in the cerebral cortex—a method often used to study preverbal infants' responsiveness to various stimuli and the impact of experience on specialization of cortical regions (DeBoer, Scott, & Nelson, 2007).

Neuroimaging techniques, which yield detailed, three-dimensional computerized pictures of the entire brain and its active areas, provide the most precise information about which brain regions are specialized for certain capacities. The most promising of these methods is fMRI. Unlike PET, fMRI does not depend on X-ray photography, which requires injection of a radioactive substance. Rather, when an individual is exposed to a stimulus, fMRI detects changes in blood flow and oxygen metabolism magnetically, yielding a colorful, moving picture of parts of the brain used to process information or perform an activity (see Figure 4.4a, b, and c).

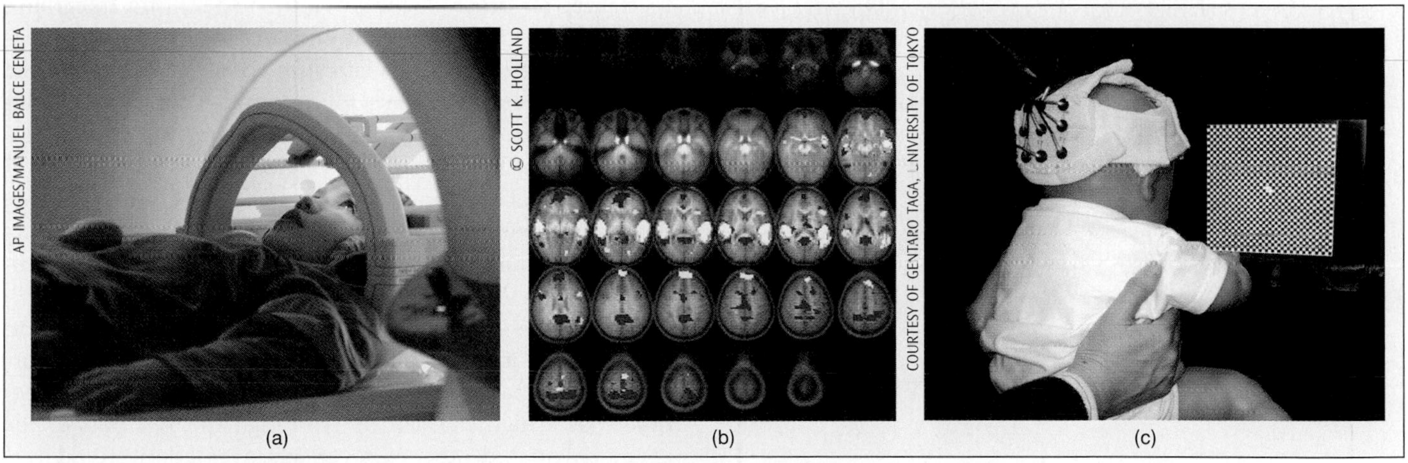

■ **FIGURE 4.4** ■ **Functional magnetic resonance imaging (fMRI) and NIROT.** (a) This 6-year-old is part of a study that uses fMRI to find out how his brain processes light and motion. (b) The fMRI image shows which areas of the child's brain are active while he views changing visual stimuli. (c) Here, NIROT is used to investigate a 2-month-old's response to a visual stimulus. During testing, the baby can move freely within a limited range. (Photo (c) from G. Taga, K. Asakawa, A. Maki, Y. Konishi, & H. Koisumi, 2003, "Brain Imaging in Awake infants by Near-Infrared Optical Topography," *Proceedings of the National Academy of Sciences, 100,* p. 10723. Reprinted by permission.)

Because PET and fMRI require the participant to lie as motionless as possible in an enclosed space filled with the noise of the surrounding machine for an extended time, they are not suitable for infants and young children (Nelson, Thomas, & de Haan, 2006). A neuroimaging technique that works well in infancy and early childhood is NIROT (refer again to Table 4.1). Because the apparatus consists only of optical fibers attached to the scalp using a head cap, a baby can sit on the parent's lap and move during testing—as Figure 4.4c illustrates (Meek, 2002; Taga et al., 2003). Unlike PET and fMRI, which map activity changes throughout the brain, NIROT is limited to examining the functioning of the cerebral cortex.

Development of the Cerebral Cortex

The **cerebral cortex** surrounds the rest of the brain, resembling half of a shelled walnut. It is the largest, most complex brain structure—accounting for 85 percent of the brain's weight and containing the greatest number of neurons and synapses. Because it is also the last brain structure to stop growing, it is sensitive to environmental influences for a much longer period than any other part of the brain.

■ **REGIONS OF THE CORTEX.** Figure 4.5 shows specific functions of regions of the cerebral cortex, such as receiving information from the senses, instructing the body to move, and thinking. The order in which cortical regions develop corresponds to the order in which various capacities emerge in the infant and growing child. For example, a burst of synaptic growth occurs in the auditory and visual cortexes and in areas responsible for body movement over the first year—a period of dramatic gains in auditory and visual perception and mastery of motor skills (Johnson, 2005). Language areas are especially active from late infancy through the preschool years, when language development flourishes (Pujol et al., 2006; Thompson, 2000).

The cortical regions with the most extended period of development are the *frontal lobes,* which are responsible for thought—in particular, consciousness, inhibition of impulses, integration of information, and use of memory, reasoning, planning, and problem-solving strategies. From age 2 months on, the frontal lobes function more effectively. But they undergo especially rapid myelination and formation and pruning of synapses during the preschool and school years, followed by another period of accelerated growth in adolescence, when the frontal lobes reach an adult level of synapses (Nelson, 2002; Nelson, Thomas, & de Haan, 2006; Sowell et al., 2002).

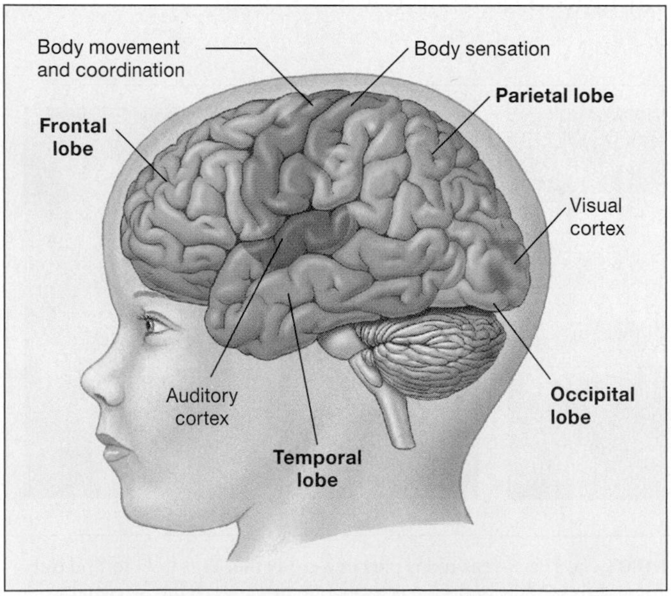

■ **FIGURE 4.5 ■ The left side of the human brain, showing the cerebral cortex.** The cortex is divided into different lobes, each containing a variety of regions with specific functions. Some major regions are labeled here.

■ **LATERALIZATION AND PLASTICITY OF THE CORTEX.** The cerebral cortex has two *hemispheres,* or sides, that differ in their functions. Some tasks are done mostly by the left hemisphere, others by the right. For example, each hemisphere receives sensory information from the side of the body opposite to it and controls only that side.* For most of us, the left hemisphere is largely responsible for verbal abilities (such as spoken and written language) and positive emotion (such as joy). The right hemisphere handles spatial abilities (judging distances, reading maps, and recognizing geometric shapes) and negative emotion (such as distress) (Banish & Heller, 1998; Nelson & Bosquet, 2000). In left-handed people, this pattern may be reversed—or, more commonly, the cerebral cortex may be less clearly specialized than in right-handers.

Why does this specialization of the two hemispheres, called **lateralization,** occur? Studies using fMRI reveal that the left hemisphere is better at processing information in a sequential, analytic (piece-by-piece) way, a good approach for dealing with communicative information—both verbal (language) and emotional (a joyful smile). In contrast, the right hemisphere is specialized for processing information in a holistic, integrative manner, ideal for making sense of spatial information and regulating negative emotion. A lateralized brain may have evolved because it enabled humans to cope more successfully with changing environmental demands (Rogers, 2000). It permits a wider array of functions to be carried out effectively than if both sides processed information in the same way. However, the popular notion of a "right-brained" or "left-brained" person is an oversimplification. The two hemispheres communicate and work together, doing so more effectively with age.

Researchers study the timing of brain lateralization to learn more about **brain plasticity.** A highly *plastic* cerebral cortex, in which many areas are not yet committed to specific functions, has a high capacity for learning. And if a part of the cortex is damaged, other parts can take over tasks it would have

*The eyes are an exception. Messages from the right half of each retina go to the right hemisphere; messages from the left half of each retina go to the left hemisphere. Thus, visual information from *both* eyes is received by *both* hemispheres.

handled. But once the hemispheres lateralize, damage to a specific region means that the abilities it controls cannot be recovered as fully or as easily as earlier.

At birth, the hemispheres have already begun to specialize. Most newborns show greater ERP brain-wave activity in the left hemisphere while listening to speech sounds or displaying a positive state of arousal. In contrast, the right hemisphere reacts more strongly to nonspeech sounds and to stimuli (such as a sour-tasting fluid) that evoke a negative reaction (Davidson, 1994; Fox & Davidson, 1986).

Nevertheless, research on brain-damaged children and adults offers dramatic evidence for substantial plasticity in the young brain, summarized in the Lifespan Vista box on page 126. Furthermore, early experience greatly influences the organization of the cerebral cortex. For example, deaf adults who, as infants and children, learned sign language (a spatial skill) depend more than hearing individuals on the right hemisphere for language processing (Neville & Bavelier, 2002). And toddlers who are advanced in language development show greater left-hemispheric specialization for language than their more slowly developing agemates (Luna et al., 2001; Mills et al., 2005). Apparently, the very process of acquiring language and other skills promotes lateralization.

In sum, the brain is more plastic during the first few years than it will ever be again. An overabundance of synaptic connections supports brain plasticity and, therefore, young children's ability to learn, which is fundamental to their survival. And although the cortex is programmed from the start for hemispheric specialization, experience greatly influences the rate and success of its advancing organization.

Sensitive Periods in Brain Development

Animal studies confirm that early, extreme sensory deprivation results in permanent brain damage and loss of functions—findings that verify the existence of sensitive periods in brain development. For example, early, varied visual experiences must occur for the brain's visual centers to develop normally. If a 1-month-old kitten is deprived of light for just three or four days, these areas of the brain degenerate. If the kitten is kept in the dark during the fourth week of life and beyond, the damage is severe and permanent (Crair, Gillespie, & Stryker, 1998). And the general quality of the early environment affects overall brain growth. When animals reared from birth in physically and socially stimulating surroundings are compared with those reared in isolation, the brains of the stimulated animals show much denser synaptic connections (Greenough & Black, 1992).

HUMAN EVIDENCE: VICTIMS OF DEPRIVED EARLY ENVIRONMENTS. For ethical reasons, we cannot deliberately deprive some infants of normal rearing experiences and observe the impact on their brains and competencies. Instead, we must turn to natural experiments, in which children were victims of deprived early environments that were later rectified. Such studies have revealed some parallels with the animal evidence just described.

For example, when babies are born with cataracts in both eyes, those who have corrective surgery within four to six months show rapid improvement in vision, except for subtle aspects of face perception, which require early visual input to the right hemisphere to develop (Le Grand et al., 2001, 2003). But the longer cataract surgery is postponed beyond infancy, the less complete the recovery in visual skills. And if surgery is delayed until adulthood, vision is severely and permanently impaired (Maurer et al., 1999).

Studies of infants placed in orphanages who were later exposed to family rearing confirm the importance of a generally stimulating environment for psychological development. In one investigation, researchers followed the progress of a large sample of children transferred between birth and 3½ years from extremely deprived Romanian orphanages to adoptive families in Great Britain (Beckett et al., 2006; O'Connor et al., 2000; Rutter et al., 1998, 2004). On arrival, most were impaired in all domains of development. By the preschool years, catch-up in physical size was dramatic. Cognitive catch-up, assessed at ages 6 and 11, was impressive for children adopted before 6 months, who attained average mental test scores and performed

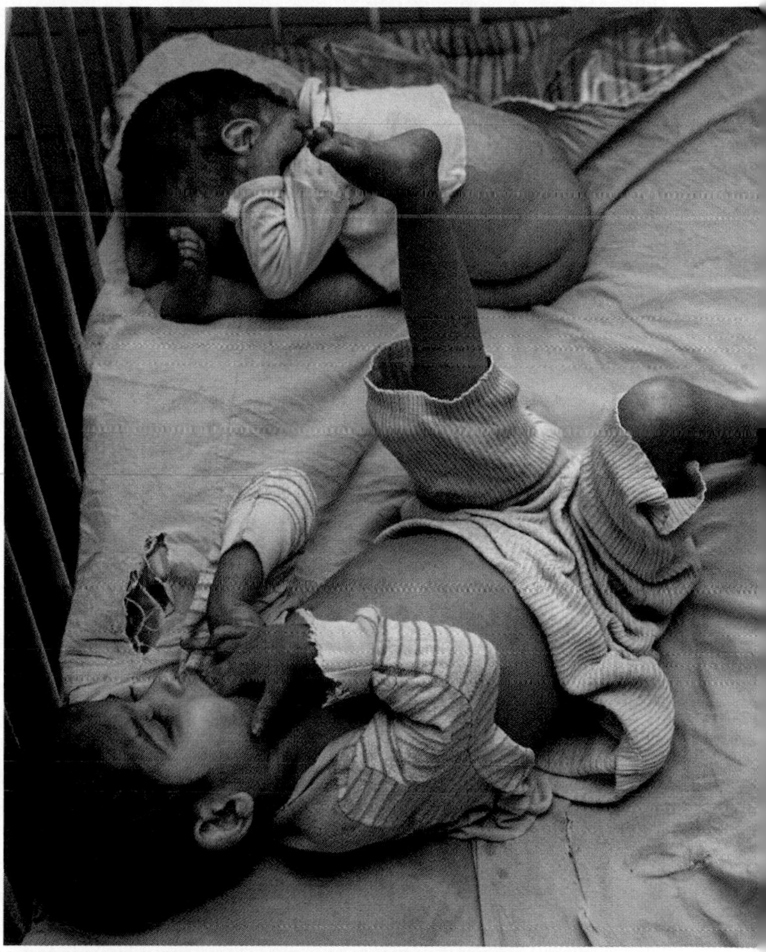

These children, in an orphanage in Romania, receive very little adult contact or stimulation. The longer they remain in this barren environment, the more they will withdraw and wither, displaying profound impairments in all domains of development.

A LIFESPAN VISTA: Looking Forward, Looking Back

Brain Plasticity: Insights from Research on Brain-Damaged Children and Adults

In the first few years of life, the brain is highly plastic. It can reorganize areas committed to specific functions in ways that the mature brain cannot. Consistently, adults who suffered brain injuries in infancy and early childhood show fewer cognitive impairments than adults with later-occurring injuries (Holland, 2004; Huttenlocher, 2002). Nevertheless, the young brain is not totally plastic. When it is injured, its functioning is compromised. The extent of plasticity depends on several factors, including age at time of injury, site of damage, and skill area. Furthermore, plasticity is not restricted to childhood. Some reorganization after injury also occurs in the mature brain.

Brain Plasticity in Infancy and Early Childhood

In a large study of children with injuries to the cerebral cortex that occurred before birth or in the first six months of life, language and spatial skills were assessed repeatedly into adolescence (Akshoomoff et al., 2002; Stiles, 2001a; Stiles et al., 2005). All the children had experienced early brain seizures or hemorrhages. Brain-imaging techniques—fMRI and PET—revealed the precise site of damage.

Regardless of whether injury occurred in the left or right cerebral hemisphere, the children showed delays in language development that persisted until about 3½ years of age. That damage to either hemisphere affected early language competence indicates that at first, language functioning is broadly distributed in the brain. But by age 5, the children caught up in vocabulary and grammatical skills. Undamaged areas—in either the left or the right hemisphere—had taken over these language functions.

Compared with language, spatial skills were more impaired after early brain injury. When preschool through adolescent-age youngsters were asked to copy designs, those with early right-hemispheric damage had trouble with holistic processing—accurately representing the overall shape. In contrast, those with left-hemispheric damage captured the basic shape but omitted fine-grained details. Nevertheless, the children's drawings improved with age—gains that did not occur in brain-injured adults (Akshoomoff et al., 2002; Stiles et al., 2003).

Clearly, recovery after early brain injury is greater for language than for spatial skills. Why is this so? Researchers speculate that spatial processing is the older of the two capacities in our evolutionary history and, therefore, more lateralized at birth (Stiles, 2001b; Stiles et al., 2002). But early brain injury has far less impact than later injury on *both* language and spatial skills. In sum, the young brain is remarkably plastic.

The Price of High Plasticity in the Young Brain

Despite impressive recovery of language and (to a lesser extent) spatial skills, children with early brain injuries show deficits in many complex mental abilities during the school years. Their progress in reading and math is slow, and in telling stories, they produce simpler narratives than agemates without early brain injuries (although many catch up in narrative skills by early adolescence) (Reilly, Bates, & Marchman, 1998; Reilly et al., 2004). Furthermore, the more brain tissue destroyed in infancy or early childhood, the poorer children score on intelligence tests (Anderson et al., 2006).

High brain plasticity, researchers explain, comes at a price. When healthy brain regions take over the functions of damaged areas, a "crowding effect" occurs: Multiple tasks must be done by a smaller-than-usual volume of brain tissue. Consequently, the brain processes information less quickly and accurately than it would if it were intact. Complex mental abilities of all kinds suffer into middle childhood, and often longer, because performing them well requires considerable space in the cerebral cortex (Huttenlocher, 2002).

Brain Plasticity in Adulthood

Brain plasticity is not restricted to early childhood. Though far more limited, reorganization in the brain can occur later, even in adulthood. For example, adult stroke victims often display considerable recovery, especially in response to stimulation of language and motor skills. Brain-imaging techniques reveal that structures adjacent to the permanently damaged area or in the opposite cerebral hemisphere reorganize to support the impaired ability (Bach-y-Rita, 2001; Hallett, 2000).

In infancy and childhood, the goal of brain growth is to form neural connections that ensure mastery of essential skills. Plasticity is greatest while the brain is forming many new synapses; it declines during synaptic pruning (Kolb & Gibb, 2001). At older ages, specialized brain structures are in place, but after injury they can still reorganize to some degree. The adult brain can produce a small number of new neurons. And when an individual practices relevant tasks, the brain strengthens existing synapses and generates new ones (Nelson, Thomas, & de Haan, 2006). Plasticity seems to be a basic property of the nervous system. Researchers hope to discover how experience and brain plasticity work together throughout life so they can help people of all ages—with and without brain injuries—develop at their best.

This preschooler, who experienced brain damage in infancy, has been spared massive impairments because of high plasticity of the brain. Here, a teacher guides his hand in drawing shapes to strengthen spatial skills, which remain more impaired than language after early brain injury.

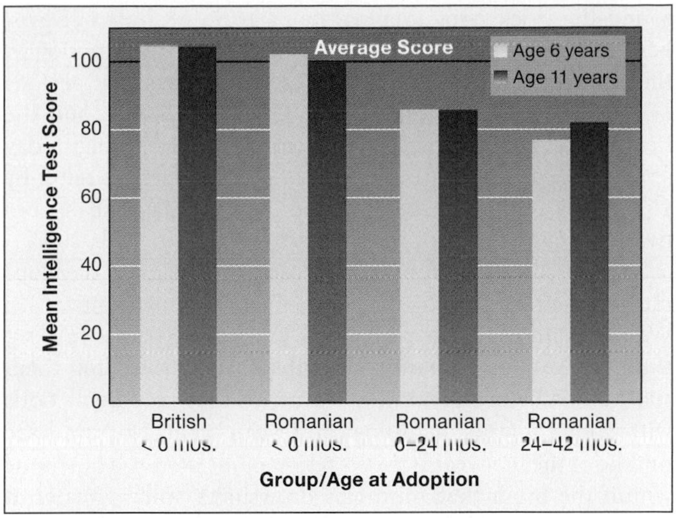

■ **FIGURE 4.6** ■ **Relationship of age at adoption to mental test scores at ages 6 and 11 among British and Romanian adoptees.** Children transferred from Romanian orphanages to British adoptive homes in the first six months of life attained average scores and fared as well as British early-adopted children, suggesting that they had fully recovered from extreme early deprivation. Romanian children adopted after 6 months of age performed well below average. And although those adopted after age 2 improved between ages 6 and 11, they continued to show serious intellectual deficits. (Adapted from Beckett et al., 2006.)

as well as a comparison group of early-adopted British-born children. But Romanian children who had been institutionalized for more than the first six months showed serious intellectual deficits (see Figure 4.6). Although they improved in test scores during middle childhood, perhaps as a result of time spent in their adopted homes and special services at school, they remained substantially below average. And most displayed at least three serious mental health problems, such as inattention, overactivity, and unruly behavior, that are seldom seen in children adopted before 6 months of age (Kreppner et al., 2007).

Additional evidence shows that the chronic stress of early, deprived orphanage rearing disrupts the brain's capacity to manage stress, with long-term physical and psychological consequences. In another investigation, researchers followed the development of children who had spent their first 8 months or more in Romanian institutions and were then adopted into Canadian homes (Gunnar et al., 2001; Gunnar & Cheatham, 2003). Compared with agemates adopted shortly after birth, these children showed extreme stress reactivity, as indicated by high concentrations of the stress hormone *cortisol* in their saliva—a physiological response linked to persistent illness, retarded physical growth, and learning and behavior problems, including deficits in attention and control of anger and other impulses. The longer the children spent in orphanage care, the higher their cortisol levels—even $6\frac{1}{2}$ years after adoption.

In other investigations, orphanage children displayed abnormally low cortisol—a blunted physiological stress response that may be the central nervous system's adaptation to earlier, frequent cortisol elevations (Carlson & Earls, 1997; Gunnar & Vasquez, 2001). Extremely low cortisol interferes with release of growth hormone (GH) and, thus, can stunt children's physical growth.

■ **APPROPRIATE STIMULATION.** Unlike the orphanage children just described, Grace, whom Monica and Kevin had adopted in Cambodia at 16 months of age, showed favorable progress. Two years earlier, they had adopted Grace's older brother, Eli. When Eli was 2 years old, Monica and Kevin sent a letter and a photo of Eli to his biological mother, describing a bright, happy child. The next day, the Cambodian mother tearfully asked an adoption agency to send her baby daughter to join Eli and his American family.

Although Grace's early environment was very depleted, her biological mother's loving care—holding tenderly, speaking softly, and breastfeeding—may have prevented irreversible damage to her brain. Besides offering gentle, appropriate stimulation, sensitive adult care helps normalize cortisol production in both typically developing and emotionally traumatized infants and young children (Gunnar & Quevedo, 2007; Tarullo & Gunnar, 2006). Good parenting seems to help protect the young brain from the potentially damaging effects of both excessive and inadequate stress-hormone exposure.

In addition to impoverished environments, ones that overwhelm children with expectations beyond their current capacities interfere with the brain's potential. In recent years, expensive early learning centers have sprung up, in which infants are trained with letter and number flash cards and slightly older toddlers are given a full curriculum of reading, math, science, art, music, gym, and more. There is no evidence that these programs yield smarter, better "superbabies" (Hirsh-Pasek & Golinkoff, 2003). To the contrary, trying to prime infants with stimulation for which they are not ready can cause them to withdraw, thereby threatening their interest in learning and creating conditions much like stimulus deprivation!

How, then, can we characterize appropriate stimulation during the early years? To answer this question, researchers distinguish between two types of brain development. The first, **experience-expectant brain growth,** refers to the young brain's rapidly developing organization, which depends on ordinary experiences—opportunities to see and touch objects, to hear language and other sounds, and to move about and explore the environment. As a result of millions of years of evolution, the brains of all infants, toddlers, and young children expect to encounter these experiences and, if they do, grow normally. The second type of brain development, **experience-dependent brain growth,** consists of additional growth and refinement of established brain structures as a result of specific learning experiences that occur throughout our lives, varying widely across individuals and cultures (Greenough & Black, 1992). Reading and writing, playing computer games, weaving an intricate rug, and practicing the violin are examples. The brain of a violinist differs in certain ways from the brain of a poet because each has

Experience-expectant brain growth takes place naturally, through ordinary, stimulating experiences. This toddler, focused on shoveling pebbles into her bucket at the beach, enjoys the type of activity that is best for promoting brain development in the early years.

exercised different brain regions for a long time (Thompson & Nelson, 2001).

Experience-expectant brain growth occurs early and naturally, as caregivers offer babies and preschoolers age-appropriate play materials and engage them in enjoyable daily routines—a shared meal, a game of peekaboo, a bath before bed, or a picture book to talk about. The resulting growth provides the foundation for later-occurring experience-dependent development (Huttenlocher, 2002; Shonkoff & Phillips, 2001). No evidence exists for a sensitive period in the first few years of life for mastering skills that depend on extensive training, such as reading, musical performance, or gymnastics (Bruer, 1999). To the contrary, rushing early learning harms the brain by overwhelming its neural circuits, thereby reducing the brain's sensitivity to the everyday experiences it needs for a healthy start in life.

Changing States of Arousal

Rapid brain growth means that the organization of sleep and wakefulness changes substantially between birth and age 2, and fussiness and crying also decline. The newborn baby takes round-the-clock naps totaling about 16 to 18 hours (Davis, Parker & Montgomery, 2004). Total sleep time declines slowly; the average 2-year-old still needs 12 to 13 hours. But periods of sleep and wakefulness become fewer and longer, and the sleep–wake pattern increasingly conforms to a night–day schedule. Most 6- to 9-month-olds take two daytime naps; by 18 months, children generally need only one nap. Finally, between ages 3 and 5, napping subsides (Iglowstein et al., 2003).

These changing arousal patterns are due to brain development, but they are also affected by the social environment. In Western nations, many parents try to get their babies to sleep through the night around 4 months of age by feeding them solid foods before bedtime—a practice that may be at odds with young infants' neurological development. Not until the middle of the first year is the secretion of *melatonin,* a hormone within the brain that promotes drowsiness, much greater at night than during the day (Sadeh, 1997). Babies of this age whose caregivers take them on regular early-afternoon outings, exposing them to more bright sunlight, sleep better at night (Harrison, 2004).

As the Cultural Influences box on the following page reveals, isolating infants to promote sleep is rare elsewhere in the world. When babies sleep with their parents, their average sleep period remains constant at three hours from 1 to 8 months of age. Only at the end of the first year, as REM sleep (the state that usually prompts waking) declines, do infants move in the direction of an adultlike sleep–waking schedule (Ficca et al., 1999).

Even after infants sleep through the night, they continue to wake occasionally. In studies carried out in Australia, Great Britain, and Israel, night wakings increased between 1½ and 2 years and then declined (Scher, Epstein, & Tirosh, 2004; Scher et al., 1995). As Chapter 6 will reveal, the challenges of toddlerhood—ability to range farther from the familiar caregiver and clearer awareness of the self as separate from others—often prompt anxiety, evident in disturbed sleep and clinginess. When parents offer comfort, these behaviors subside.

ASK YOURSELF

» REVIEW
How do overproduction of synapses and synaptic pruning support infants' and children's ability to learn?

» APPLY
Which infant enrichment program would you choose: one that emphasizes gentle talking and touching and social games, or one that includes reading and number drills and classical music lessons? Explain.

» CONNECT
Explain how inappropriate stimulation—either too little or too much—can impair cognitive and emotional development in the early years.

» REFLECT
What is your attitude toward parent–infant cosleeping? Is it influenced by your cultural background? Explain.

CULTURAL INFLUENCES

Cultural Variation in Infant Sleeping Arrangements

While awaiting the birth of a new baby, North American parents typically furnish a room as the infant's sleeping quarters. For decades, child-rearing advice from experts has strongly encouraged the nighttime separation of baby from parent. For example, the most recent edition of Benjamin Spock's *Baby and Child Care* recommends that infants be moved into their own room by 3 months of age, explaining, "By 6 months, a child who regularly sleeps in her parents' room may become dependent on this arrangement" (Spock & Needlman, 2004, p. 60).

Yet parent–infant "cosleeping" is the norm for approximately 90 percent of the world's population, in cultures as diverse as the Japanese, the rural Guatemalan Maya, the Inuit of northwestern Canada, and the !Kung of Botswana. Japanese and Korean children usually lie next to their mothers in infancy and early childhood, and many continue to sleep with a parent or other family member until adolescence (Takahashi, 1990; Yang & Hahn, 2002). Among the Maya, mother–infant cosleeping is interrupted only by the birth of a new baby, when the older child is moved next to the father or to another bed in the same room (Morelli et al., 1992). Cosleeping is also common in some American subcultures. African-American children frequently fall asleep with their parents, remaining with them for part or all of the night (Brenner et al., 2003; Buswell & Spatz, 2007). Appalachian children of eastern Kentucky typically sleep with their parents for the first two years (Abbott, 1992).

Cultural values—specifically, collectivism versus individualism (see Chapter 2)—strongly influence infant sleeping arrangements. In one study, researchers interviewed Guatemalan Mayan mothers and American middle-SES mothers about their sleeping practices. Mayan mothers stressed a collectivist perspective, explaining that cosleeping helps build a close parent–child bond, which children need to learn the ways of people around them. In contrast, American mothers took an individualistic perspective, mentioning the importance of instilling early independence, preventing bad habits, and protecting their own privacy (Morelli et al., 1992).

Over the past 15 years, cosleeping has increased dramatically in Western nations, perhaps because more mothers are breastfeeding. Today, the rate of bedsharing among U.S. mothers of young babies may be as high as 50 percent (Buswell & Spatz, 2007; Willinger et al., 2003). Research suggests that cosleeping evolved to protect infants' survival and health. During the night, cosleeping babies breastfeed three times as long as infants who sleep alone. Because infants arouse to nurse more often when sleeping next to their mothers, some researchers believe that cosleeping may actually help safeguard babies at risk for sudden infant death syndrome (SIDS) (see page 110 in Chapter 3). SIDS is rare in Asian cultures where cosleeping is widespread, including Cambodia, China, Japan, Korea, Thailand, and Vietnam (McKenna, 2002; McKenna & McDade, 2005). And contrary to popular belief, cosleeping does not reduce mothers' total sleep time, although they experience more brief awakenings, which permits them to check on their baby (Mao et al., 2004).

Infant sleeping practices affect other aspects of family life. For example, Mayan babies doze off in the midst of ongoing family activities and are carried to bed by their mothers. In contrast, for many North American parents, bedtime involves an elaborate ritual that takes a good part of the evening. Perhaps bedtime struggles, so common in Western homes but rare elsewhere in the world, are related to the stress young children feel when they are required to fall asleep without assistance (Latz, Wolf, & Lozoff, 1999).

Critics warn that cosleeping children will develop emotional problems, especially excessive dependency. Yet a longitudinal study following children from birth through age 18 showed that young people who had bedshared in the early years were no different from others in any aspect of adjustment (Okami, Weisner, & Olmstead, 2002). Another concern is that infants might become trapped under the parent's body or in soft covers and suffocate. Parents who are obese or who use alcohol, tobacco, or illegal drugs do pose a serious risk to their sleeping babies, as does the use of quilts and comforters or an overly soft mattress (Willinger et al., 2003).

But with appropriate precautions, parents and infants can cosleep safely (McKenna & Volpe, 2007). In cultures where cosleeping is widespread, parents and infants usually sleep with light covering on hard surfaces, such as firm mattresses, floor mats, and wooden planks, or infants sleep in a cradle or hammock next to the parents' bed (McKenna, 2001, 2002). And when sharing the same bed, infants typically lie on their back or side facing the mother—positions that promote frequent, easy communication between parent and baby and arousal if breathing is threatened.

Finally, breastfeeding mothers usually assume a distinctive sleeping posture: They face the infant, with knees drawn up under the baby's feet and arm above the baby's head. Besides facilitating feeding, the position prevents the infant from sliding down under covers or up under pillows (Ball, 2006). Because this posture is also seen in female great apes while sharing sleeping nests with their infants, researchers believe it may have evolved to enhance infant safety.

This Cambodian father and child sleep together—a practice common in their culture and around the globe. The family sleeps on hard wooden surfaces, which protect cosleeping children from entrapment in soft bedding.

Influences on Early Physical Growth

Physical growth, like other aspects of development, results from the continuous and complex interplay between genetic and environmental factors. Heredity, nutrition, and emotional well-being all affect early physical growth.

Heredity

Because identical twins are much more alike in body size than fraternal twins, we know that heredity is important in physical growth (Estourgie-van Burk et al., 2006). When diet and health are adequate, height and rate of physical growth are largely determined by heredity. In fact, as long as negative environmental influences such as poor nutrition and illness are not severe, children and adolescents typically show *catch-up growth*—a return to a genetically influenced growth path once conditions improve. Still, the brain, the heart, the digestive system, and many other internal organs may be permanently compromised (Hales & Ozanne, 2003). (Recall the consequences of inadequate prenatal nutrition for long-term health, discussed on page 93 in Chapter 3.)

Genetic makeup also affects body weight: The weights of adopted children correlate more strongly with those of their biological than of their adoptive parents (Sørensen, Holst, & Stunkard, 1998). At the same time, environment—in particular, nutrition—plays an especially important role.

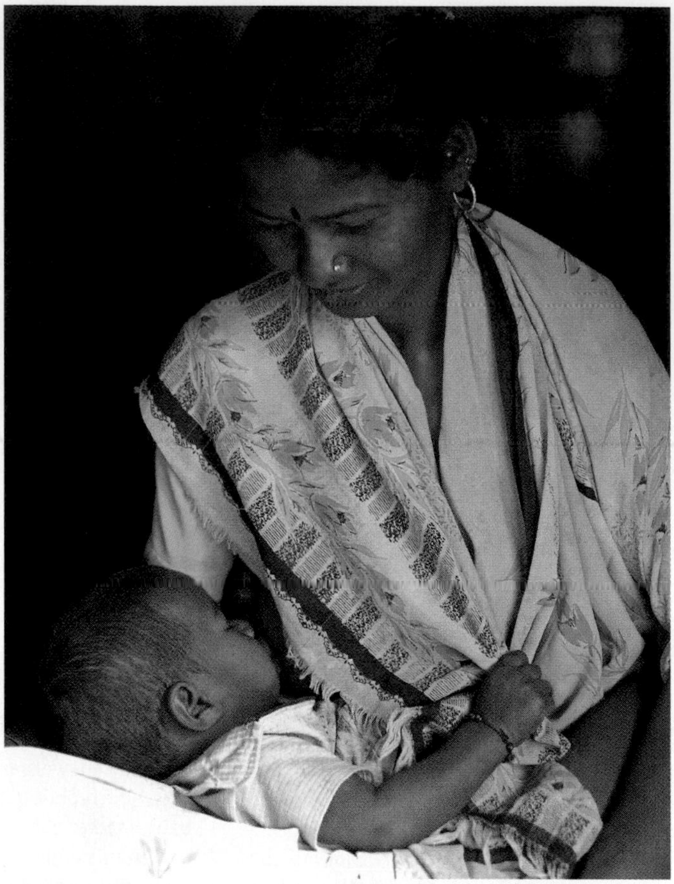

Breastfeeding is especially important in developing countries, where infants are at risk for malnutrition and early death due to widespread poverty. This baby from a village in India is likely to grow normally during the first year because his mother decided to breastfeed.

Nutrition

Nutrition is especially crucial for development in the first two years because the baby's brain and body are growing so rapidly. Pound for pound, an infant's energy needs are twice those of an adult. Twenty-five percent of infants' total caloric intake is devoted to growth, and babies need extra calories to keep rapidly developing organs functioning properly (Trahms & Pipes, 1997).

BREASTFEEDING VERSUS BOTTLE-FEEDING. Babies need not only enough food but the right kind of food. In early infancy, breastfeeding is ideally suited to their needs, and bottled formulas try to imitate it. Applying What We Know on the following page summarizes major nutritional and health advantages of breastfeeding.

Because of these benefits, breastfed babies in poverty-stricken regions are much less likely to be malnourished and 6 to 14 times more likely to survive the first year of life. The World Health Organization recommends breastfeeding until age 2 years, with solid foods added at 6 months—practices that, if widely followed, would save the lives of more than a million infants annually (World Health Organization, 2008b). Even breastfeeding for just a few weeks offers some protection against respiratory and intestinal infections, which are devastating to young children in developing countries. Also, because a nursing mother is less likely to get pregnant, breastfeeding helps increase spacing between siblings, a major factor in reducing infant and childhood deaths in nations with widespread poverty (Bellamy, 2005). (Note, however, that breastfeeding is not a reliable method of birth control.)

Yet many mothers in the developing world do not know about the benefits of breastfeeding. In Africa, the Middle East, and Latin America, most babies get some breastfeeding, but fewer than 40 percent are exclusively breastfed for the first six months (Lauer et al., 2004). In place of breast milk, mothers give their babies commercial formula or low-grade nutrients, such as rice water or highly diluted cow or goat milk. Contamination of these foods as a result of poor sanitation is common and often leads to illness and infant death. The United Nations has encouraged all hospitals and maternity units in developing countries to promote breastfeeding as long as mothers do not have viral or bacterial infections (such as HIV or tuberculosis) that can be transmitted to the baby. Today, most developing countries have banned the practice of giving free or subsidized formula to new mothers.

Partly as a result of the natural childbirth movement, breastfeeding has become more common in industrialized nations, especially among well-educated women. Today, 74 percent of

Applying What We Know

Reasons to Breastfeed

Nutritional and Health Advantages	Explanation
Provides the correct balance of fat and protein	Compared with the milk of other mammals, human milk is higher in fat and lower in protein. This balance, as well as the unique proteins and fats contained in human milk, is ideal for a rapidly myelinating nervous system.
Ensures nutritional completeness	A mother who breastfeeds need not add other foods to her infant's diet until the baby is 6 months old. The milks of all mammals are low in iron, but the iron contained in breast milk is much more easily absorbed by the baby's system. Consequently, bottle-fed infants need iron-fortified formula.
Helps ensure healthy physical growth	In the first few months, breastfed infants add weight and length slightly faster than bottle-fed infants, who catch up by the end of the first year. One-year-old breastfed babies are leaner (have a higher percentage of muscle to fat), a growth pattern that may help prevent later overweight and obesity.
Protects against many diseases	Breastfeeding transfers antibodies and other infection-fighting agents from mother to child and enhances functioning of the immune system. As a result, compared with bottle-fed infants, breastfed babies have far fewer allergic reactions and respiratory and intestinal illnesses. Breast milk also has anti-inflammatory effects, which ease the severity of illness symptoms. U.S. infant mortality rates are reduced by 21 percent in breastfed infants.
Protects against faulty jaw development and tooth decay	Sucking the mother's nipple instead of an artificial nipple helps avoid malocclusion, a condition in which the upper and lower jaws do not meet properly. It also protects against tooth decay due to sweet liquid remaining in the mouths of infants who fall asleep while sucking on a bottle.
Ensures digestibility	Because breastfed babies have a different kind of bacteria growing in their intestines than do bottle-fed infants, they rarely suffer from constipation or other gastrointestinal problems.
Smoothes the transition to solid foods	Breastfed infants accept new solid foods more easily than bottle-fed infants, perhaps because of their greater experience with a variety of flavors, which pass from the maternal diet into the mother's milk.

Sources: American Academy of Pediatrics, 2005a; Buescher, 2001; Fulhan, Collier, & Duggan, 2003; Kramer et al., 2002, 2003; Weyermann, Rothenbacher, & Brenner, 2006.

American mothers breastfeed, but nearly two-thirds of them stop after a few months (U.S. Department of Health and Human Services, 2008c). Not surprisingly, mothers who return to work sooner wean their babies from the breast earlier (Kimbro, 2006). But mothers who cannot be with their infants all the time can still combine breast- and bottle-feeding. The U.S. Department of Health and Human Services advises exclusive breastfeeding for the first 6 months and inclusion of breast milk in the baby's diet until at least 1 year.

Women who do not breastfeed sometimes worry that they are depriving their baby of an experience essential for healthy psychological development. Yet breastfed and bottle-fed children in industrialized nations do not differ in emotional adjustment (Fergusson & Woodward, 1999). Some studies report a slight advantage in intelligence test performance for children and adolescents who were breastfed, after controlling for many factors. Most, however, find no cognitive benefits (Der, Batty, & Deary, 2006).

■ ARE CHUBBY BABIES AT RISK FOR LATER OVERWEIGHT AND OBESITY? From early infancy, Timmy was an enthusiastic eater who nursed vigorously and gained weight quickly. By 5 months, he began reaching for food on his parents' plates. Vanessa wondered: Was she overfeeding Timmy and increasing his chances of being permanently overweight?

Most chubby babies thin out during toddlerhood and early childhood, as weight gain slows and they become more active. Infants and toddlers can eat nutritious foods freely without risk of becoming overweight. But recent evidence does indicate a strengthening relationship between rapid weight gain in infancy and later obesity (Botton et al., 2008; Chomtho et al., 2008). The trend may be due to the rise in overweight and obesity among adults, who promote unhealthy eating habits in their young children. Interviews with more than 3,000 U.S. parents of 4- to 24-month-olds revealed that many routinely served them french fries, pizza, candy, sugary fruit drinks, and soda. On average, infants consumed 20 percent and toddlers 30 percent more calories than they needed. At the same time, one-third ate no fruits or vegetables (Briefel et al., 2004).

How can concerned parents prevent their infants from becoming overweight children and adults? One way is to breastfeed for the first 6 months, which is associated with slower early weight gain (Kalies et al., 2005; Sloan et al., 2008). Another is to avoid giving them foods loaded with sugar, salt, and saturated fats. Once toddlers learn to walk, climb, and run, parents can also provide plenty of opportunities for energetic play. Finally, because research shows a correlation between excessive television viewing and overweight in older children, parents should limit the time very young children spend in front of the TV.

Malnutrition

Osita is an Ethiopian 2-year-old whose mother has never had to worry about his gaining too much weight. When she weaned him at 1 year, there was little for him to eat besides starchy rice-flour cakes. Soon his belly enlarged, his feet swelled, his hair fell out, and a rash appeared on his skin. His bright-eyed curiosity vanished, and he became irritable and listless.

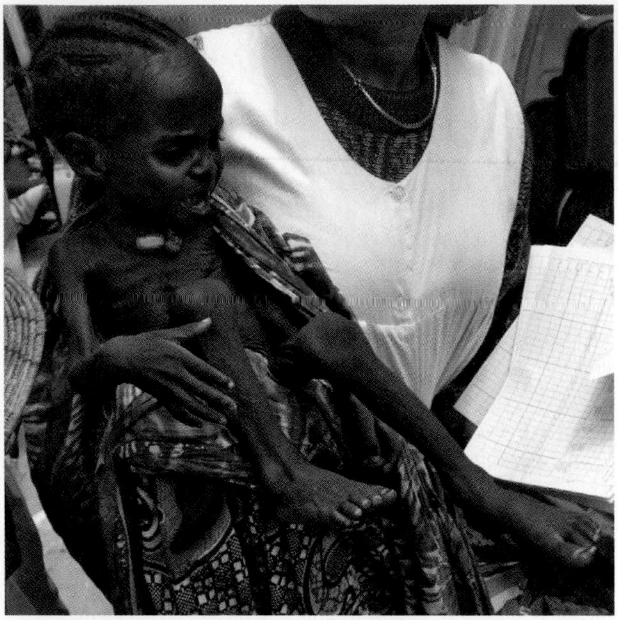
© DOMINIQUE DERDA/FRANCE 2/CORBIS

© BARRY LEWIS/ALAMY

Top photo: This baby of Niger, Africa, has marasmus, a wasted condition caused by a diet low in all essential nutrients. *Bottom photo:* The swollen abdomen of this toddler, who lives in a Rwandan refugee camp, is a symptom of kwashiorkor, which results from a diet very low in protein. If they survive, these children are likely to suffer stunted growth, damage to vital organs, and lasting intellectual and emotional impairments.

In developing countries and war-torn areas where food resources are limited, malnutrition is widespread. Recent evidence indicates that about one-third of the world's children suffer from malnutrition before age 5 (Bellamy, 2005; Pronczuk & Surdu, 2008). The 9 percent who are severely affected suffer from two dietary diseases.

Marasmus is a wasted condition of the body caused by a diet low in all essential nutrients. It usually appears in the first year of life when a baby's mother is too malnourished to produce enough breast milk and bottle-feeding is also inadequate. Her starving baby becomes painfully thin and is in danger of dying.

Osita has **kwashiorkor,** caused by an unbalanced diet very low in protein. The disease usually strikes after weaning, between 1 and 3 years of age. It is common in regions where children get just enough calories from starchy foods, but little protein. The child's body responds by breaking down its own protein reserves, which causes the swelling and other symptoms that Osita experienced.

Children who survive these extreme forms of malnutrition grow to be smaller in all body dimensions and suffer from lasting damage to the brain, heart, liver, or other organs (Müller & Krawinkel, 2005). When their diets do improve, they tend to gain excessive weight (Branca & Ferrari, 2002; Martins et al., 2004). A malnourished body protects itself by establishing a low basal metabolism rate, which may endure after nutrition improves. Also, malnutrition may disrupt appetite control centers in the brain, causing the child to overeat when food becomes plentiful.

Learning and behavior are also seriously affected. In one long-term study of marasmic children, an improved diet led to some catch-up growth in height, but not in head size (Stoch et al., 1982). The malnutrition probably interfered with growth of neural fibers and myelination, causing a permanent loss in brain weight. And animal evidence reveals that a deficient diet alters the production of neurotransmitters in the brain—an effect that can disrupt all aspects of development (Haller, 2005). These children score low on intelligence tests, show poor fine-motor coordination, and have difficulty paying attention (Galler et al., 1990; Liu et al., 2003). They also display a more intense stress response to fear-arousing situations, perhaps caused by the constant, gnawing pain of hunger (Fernald & Grantham-McGregor, 1998).

Inadequate nutrition is not confined to developing countries. Because government-supported supplementary food programs do not reach all families in need, an estimated 17 percent of U.S. children suffer from *food insecurity*—uncertain access to enough food for a healthy, active life. Food insecurity is especially high among single-parent families (33 percent) and low-income ethnic minority families—for example, Hispanics and African Americans (26 and 29 percent) (U.S. Census Bureau, 2008b). Although few of these children have marasmus or kwashiorkor, their physical growth and ability to learn are still affected.

Emotional Well-Being

We may not think of affection and stimulation as necessary for healthy physical growth, but they are just as vital as food.

Nonorganic failure to thrive, a growth disorder resulting from lack of parental love, is usually present by 18 months of age. Infants who have it show all the signs of marasmus—their bodies look wasted, and they are withdrawn and apathetic. But no organic (or biological) cause for the baby's failure to grow can be found (Black, 2005). The baby is offered enough food and has no serious illness.

Lana, an observant nurse at a public health clinic, became concerned about 8-month-old Melanie, who was 3 pounds lighter than she had been at her last checkup. Her mother claimed to feed her often. Lana noted that Melanie kept her eyes on nearby adults, anxiously watching their every move, and rarely smiled at her mother (Steward, 2001). During feeding, diaper changing, and play, Melanie's mother sometimes acted cold and distant, at other times impatient and hostile (Hagekull, Bohlin, & Rydell, 1997). Melanie tried to protect herself by tracking her mother's whereabouts and, when she approached, avoiding her gaze.

Often an unhappy marriage and parental psychological disturbance contribute to these serious caregiving problems (Drotar, Pallotta, & Eckerle, 1994; Duniz et al., 1996). Sometimes the baby is irritable and displays abnormal feeding behaviors, such as poor sucking or vomiting—circumstances that stress the parent–child relationship further (Linscheid, Budd, & Rasnake, 2005).

In Melanie's case, her alcoholic father was out of work, and her parents argued constantly. Melanie's mother had little energy to meet Melanie's psychological needs. When treated early, by helping parents or placing the baby in a caring foster home, failure-to-thrive infants show quick catch-up growth. But if the disorder is not corrected in infancy, most of these children remain small and show lasting cognitive and emotional difficulties (Drewett, Corbett, & Wright, 2006; Dykman et al., 2001).

ASK YOURSELF

» REVIEW
Explain why breastfeeding can have lifelong consequences for the development of babies born in poverty-stricken regions of the world.

» APPLY
Ten-month-old Shaun is below average in height and painfully thin. He has one of two serious growth disorders. Name them, and indicate what clues you would look for to tell which one Shaun has.

» CONNECT
How are bidirectional influences between parent and child involved in the impact of malnutrition on psychological development? After her adoption, how did those influences change for Grace?

» REFLECT
Imagine that you are the parent of a newborn baby. Describe feeding practices you would use, and ones you would avoid, to prevent overweight and obesity.

Learning Capacities

Learning refers to changes in behavior as the result of experience. Babies come into the world with built-in learning capacities that permit them to profit from experience immediately. Infants are capable of two basic forms of learning, which were introduced in Chapter 1: classical and operant conditioning. They also learn through their natural preference for novel stimulation. Finally, shortly after birth, babies learn by observing others; they can imitate the facial expressions and gestures of adults.

Classical Conditioning

Newborn reflexes, discussed in Chapter 3, make **classical conditioning** possible in the young infant. In this form of learning, a neutral stimulus is paired with a stimulus that leads to a reflexive response. Once the baby's nervous system makes the connection between the two stimuli, the neutral stimulus produces the behavior by itself. Classical conditioning helps infants recognize which events usually occur together in the everyday world, so they can anticipate what is about to happen next. As a result, the environment becomes more orderly and predictable. Let's take a closer look at the steps of classical conditioning.

As Carolyn settled down in the rocking chair to nurse Caitlin, she often stroked her baby's forehead. Soon Carolyn noticed that each time she did this, Caitlin made sucking movements. Caitlin had been classically conditioned. Here is how it happened (see Figure 4.7 on page 134):

1. Before learning takes place, an **unconditioned stimulus (UCS)** must consistently produce a reflexive, or **unconditioned, response (UCR).** In Caitlin's case, sweet breast milk (UCS) resulted in sucking (UCR).
2. To produce learning, a *neutral stimulus* that does not lead to the reflex is presented just before, or at about the same time as, the UCS. Carolyn stroked Caitlin's forehead as each nursing period began. The stroking (neutral stimulus) was paired with the taste of milk (UCS).
3. If learning has occurred, the neutral stimulus by itself produces a response similar to the reflexive response. The neutral stimulus is then called a **conditioned stimulus (CS),** and the response it elicits is called a **conditioned response (CR).** We know that Caitlin has been classically conditioned because stroking her forehead outside the feeding situation (CS) results in sucking (CR).

If the CS is presented alone enough times, without being paired with the UCS, the CR will no longer occur, an outcome called *extinction*. In other words, if Carolyn repeatedly strokes Caitlin's forehead without feeding her, Caitlin will gradually stop sucking in response to stroking.

Young infants can be classically conditioned most easily when the association between two stimuli has survival value. Learning which stimuli regularly accompany feeding improves the infant's ability to get food and survive (Blass, Ganchrow, & Steiner, 1984). In contrast, some responses, such as fear, are very

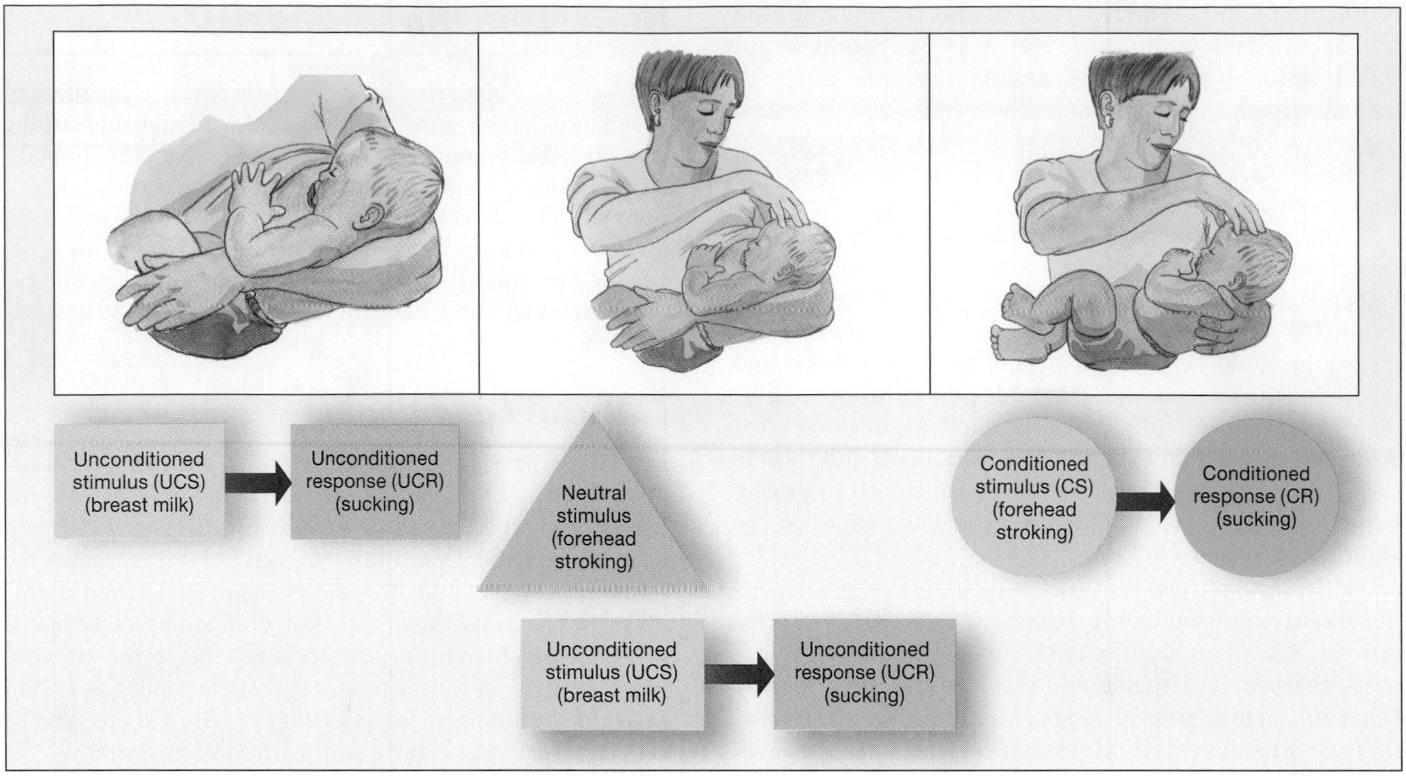

■ **FIGURE 4.7** ■ **The steps of classical conditioning.** This example shows how Caitlin's mother classically conditioned her to make sucking movements by stroking her forehead at the beginning of feedings.

difficult to classically condition in young babies. Until infants have the motor skills to escape unpleasant events, they have no biological need to form these associations. After age 6 months, however, fear is easy to condition. In Chapter 6, we will discuss the development of fear and other emotional reactions.

Operant Conditioning

In classical conditioning, babies build expectations about stimulus events in the environment, but their behavior does not influence the stimuli that occur. In **operant conditioning,** infants act, or *operate,* on the environment, and stimuli that follow their behavior change the probability that the behavior will occur again. A stimulus that increases the occurrence of a response is called a **reinforcer.** For example, sweet liquid *reinforces* the sucking response in newborns. Removing a desirable stimulus or presenting an unpleasant one to decrease the occurrence of a response is called **punishment.** A sour-tasting fluid *punishes* newborns' sucking response, causing them to purse their lips and stop sucking entirely.

Many stimuli besides food can serve as reinforcers of infant behavior. For example, newborns will suck faster on a nipple when their rate of sucking produces interesting sights and sounds, including visual designs, music, or human voices (Floccia, Christophe, & Bertoncini, 1997). As these findings suggest, operant conditioning is a powerful tool for finding out what stimuli babies can perceive and which ones they prefer.

As infants get older, operant conditioning includes a wider range of responses and stimuli. For example, researchers have hung mobiles over the cribs of 2- to 6-month-olds. When the baby's foot is attached to the mobile with a long cord, the infant can, by kicking, make the mobile turn. Under these conditions, it takes only a few minutes for infants to start kicking vigorously (Rovee-Collier, 1999; Rovee-Collier & Barr, 2001). As you will see in Chapter 5, operant conditioning with mobiles is frequently used to study infants' memory and their ability to group similar stimuli into categories. Once babies learn the response, researchers see how long and under what conditions they retain it when exposed again to the original mobile or to mobiles with varying features.

Operant conditioning also plays a vital role in the formation of social relationships. As the baby gazes into the adult's eyes, the adult looks and smiles back, and then the infant looks and smiles again. The behavior of each partner reinforces the other, so that both continue their pleasurable interaction. In Chapter 6, we will see that this contingent responsiveness contributes to the development of infant–caregiver attachment.

Habituation

At birth, the human brain is set up to be attracted to novelty. Infants tend to respond more strongly to a new element that has entered their environment, an inclination that ensures that they will continually add to their knowledge base. **Habituation** refers to a gradual reduction in the strength of a response due to repetitive stimulation. Looking, heart rate, and respiration rate may all decline, indicating a loss of interest. Once this has occurred, a new stimulus—a change in the environment—causes responsiveness to return to a high level, an increase called **recovery.** For example, when you walk through a familiar space, you notice things that are new and different—a recently hung picture on the wall or a piece of furniture that has been moved. Habituation and recovery promote efficient learning by focusing our attention on those aspects of the environment we know least about.

Researchers investigating infants' understanding of the world rely on habituation and recovery more than any other learning capacity. For example, a baby who first *habituates* to a visual pattern (a photo of a baby) and then *recovers* to a new one (a photo of a bald man) appears to remember the first stimulus and perceive the second one as new and different from it. This method of studying infant perception and cognition, illustrated in Figure 4.8, can be used with newborns, including preterm infants. It has even been used to study the fetus's sensitivity to external stimuli in the third trimester of pregnancy—for example, by measuring changes in fetal heart rate when various repeated sounds are presented (Doherty & Hepper, 2000).

Recovery to a new stimulus, or *novelty preference,* assesses infants' *recent memory*. ***TAKE A MOMENT...*** Think about what happens when you return to a place you have not seen for a long time. Instead of attending to novelty, you are likely to focus on aspects that are familiar: "I recognize that. I've been here before!" Similarly, with passage of time, infants *shift from a novelty preference to a familiarity preference.* That is, they recover to the familiar stimulus rather than to a novel stimulus (see Figure 4.8) (Bahrick & Pickens, 1995; Courage & Howe, 1998). By focusing on that shift, researchers can also use habituation to assess *remote memory,* or memory for stimuli to which infants were exposed weeks or months earlier.

As Chapter 5 will reveal, habituation research has greatly enriched our understanding of how long babies remember a wide range of stimuli. And by varying stimulus features, researchers can use habituation and recovery to study babies' ability to categorize stimuli as well.

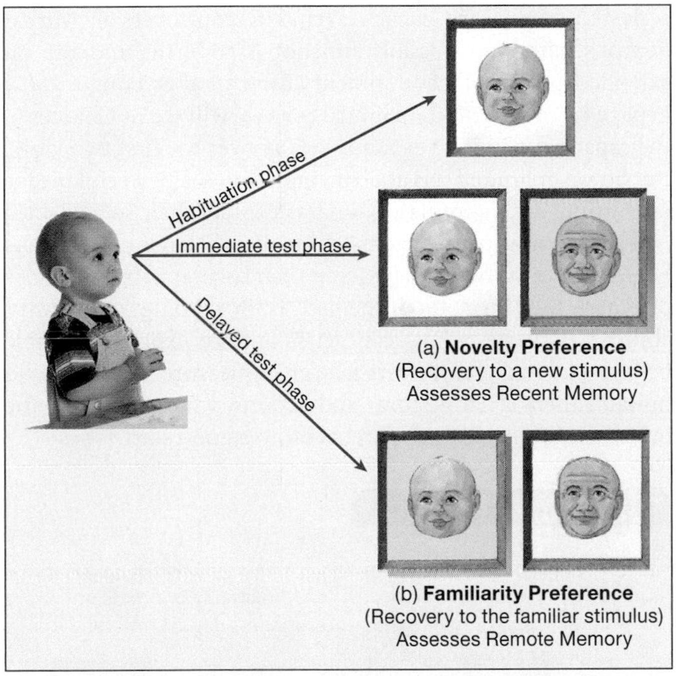

■ **FIGURE 4.8** ■ **Using habituation to study infant memory and knowledge.** In the habituation phase, infants view a photo of a baby until their looking declines. In the test phase, infants are again shown the baby photo, but this time it appears alongside a photo of a bald-headed man. (a) When the test phase occurs soon after the habituation phase (within minutes, hours, or days, depending on the age of the infants), participants who remember the baby face and distinguish it from the man's face show a *novelty preference;* they recover to (spend more time looking at) the new stimulus. (b) When the test phase is delayed for weeks or months, infants who continue to remember the baby face shift to a *familiarity preference;* they recover to the familiar baby face rather than to the novel man's face.

Imitation

Newborn babies come into the world with a primitive ability to learn through **imitation**—by copying the behavior of another person. For example, Figure 4.9 on page 136 shows a human newborn imitating two adult facial expressions (Meltzoff & Moore, 1977). The newborn's capacity to imitate extends to certain gestures, such as head movements, and has been demonstrated in many ethnic groups and cultures (Meltzoff & Kuhl, 1994; Nagy et al., 2005). As the figure reveals, even newborn chimpanzees, our closest evolutionary ancestors, imitate some facial expressions (Myowa-Yamakoshi et al., 2004).

Although newborns' capacity to imitate is widely accepted, a few studies have failed to reproduce the human findings (see, for example, Anisfeld et al., 2001). And because newborn mouth and tongue movements occur with increased frequency to almost any arousing change in stimulation (such as lively music or flashing lights), some researchers argue that certain newborn "imitative" responses are actually mouthing—a common early exploratory response to interesting stimuli (Jones, 2006). Furthermore, imitation is harder to induce in babies 2 to 3 months old than just after birth. Therefore, skeptics believe that the newborn imitative response is little more than an automatic response that declines with age, much like a reflex (Heyes, 2005).

Others claim that newborns imitate a variety of facial expressions and head movements with effort and determination, even after short delays—when the adult is no longer demonstrating the behavior (Hayne, 2002; Meltzoff & Moore, 1999). Furthermore, these investigators argue that imitation—unlike reflexes—does not decline. Human babies several months old often do not imitate an adult's behavior right away because they first try to play familiar social games—mutual gazing, cooing, smiling, and waving their arms. But when an adult models a gesture repeatedly, older human infants soon get down to business and imitate (Meltzoff & Moore, 1994). Similarly, imitation

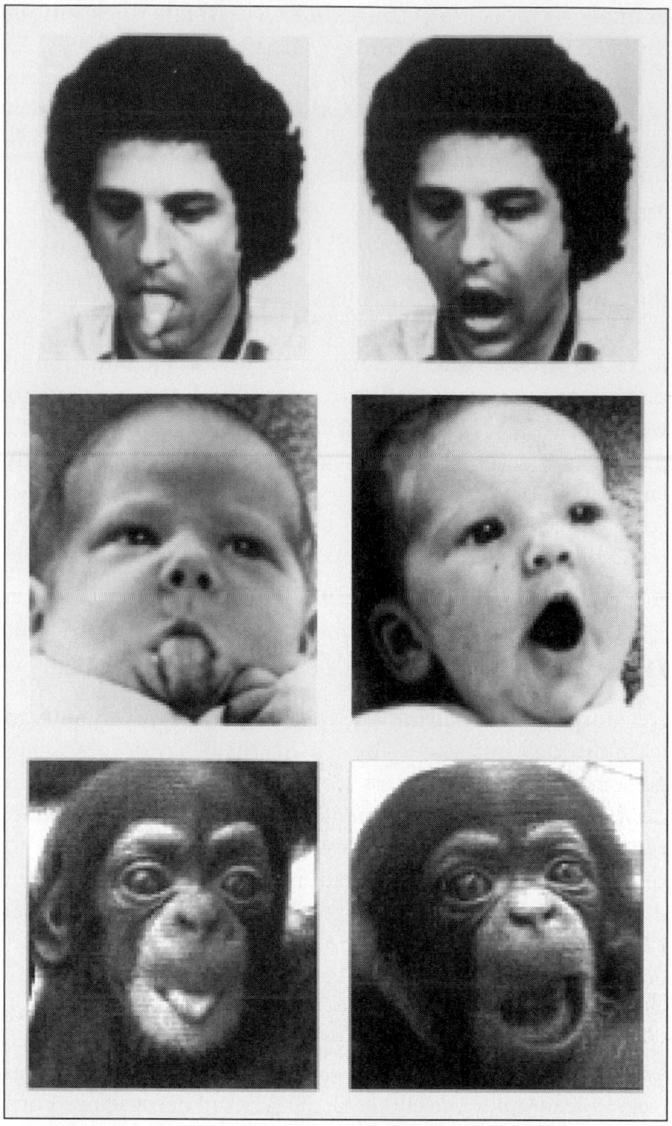

■ **FIGURE 4.9** ■ **Imitation by human and chimpanzee newborns.** The human infants in the middle row imitating (left) tongue protrusion and (right) mouth opening are 2 to 3 weeks old. The chimpanzee imitating both facial expressions is 2 weeks old. (From A. N. Meltzoff & M. K. Moore, 1977, "Imitation of Facial and Manual Gestures by Human Neonates," *Science, 198,* p.75; and M. Myowa-Yamakoshi et al., 2004, "Imitation in Neonatal Chimpanzees (Pan Troglodytes)," *Developmental Science, 7,* p. 440. Copyright © 1977 by AAAS, copyright 2004 by Blackwell Publishing. Reprinted by permission.)

declines in baby chimps around 9 weeks of age, when mother–baby mutual gazing and other face-to-face exchanges increase.

According to Andrew Meltzoff, newborns imitate much as older children and adults do—by actively trying to match body movements they *see* with ones they *feel* themselves make (Meltzoff, 2007). Later we will encounter evidence that young infants are remarkably adept at coordinating information across sensory systems.

Indeed, scientists have identified specialized cells in motor areas of the cerebral cortex in primates—called **mirror neurons**—that underlie these capacities (Rizzolatti & Craighero, 2004). Mirror neurons fire identically when a primate hears or sees an action and when it carries out that action on its own. Human adults have especially elaborate systems of mirror neurons, which enable us to observe another's behavior (such as smiling or throwing a ball) while simulating the behavior in our own brain. Mirror neurons are believed to be the biological basis of a variety of interrelated, complex social abilities, including imitation, empathic sharing of emotions, and understanding others' intentions (Iocaboni et al., 2005; Schulte-Ruther et al., 2007).

Brain-imaging findings support a functioning mirror-neuron system as early as 6 months of age. Using NIROT, researchers found that the same motor areas of the cerebral cortex were activated in 6-month-olds and in adults when they observed a model engage in a behavior that could be imitated (tapping a box to make a toy pop out) as when they themselves engaged in a motor action (Shimada & Hiraki, 2006). In contrast, when infants and adults observed an object that appeared to move on its own, without human intervention (a ball hanging from the ceiling on a string, swinging like a pendulum), motor areas were not activated.

Still, Meltzoff and Moore's view of newborn imitation as a flexible, voluntary capacity remains controversial. Mirror neurons, although possibly functional at birth, undergo an extended period of development (Bertenthal & Longo, 2007; Lepage & Théoret, 2007). Similarly, as we will see in Chapter 5, the capacity to imitate expands greatly over the first two years. But however limited it is at birth, imitation is a powerful means of learning. Using imitation, infants explore their social world and get to know people by matching their behavioral states. As babies notice similarities between their own actions and those of others, they learn about themselves. By tapping into infants' ability to imitate, adults can get infants to express desirable behaviors. Finally, caregivers take great pleasure in a baby who imitates their facial gestures and actions, which helps get the infant's relationship with parents off to a good start.

ASK YOURSELF

» REVIEW
Provide an example of classical conditioning, of operant conditioning, and of habituation/recovery in young infants. Why is each type of learning useful?

» APPLY
Nine-month-old Byron has a toy with large, colored push buttons on it. Each time he pushes a button, he hears a nursery tune. Which learning capacity is the toy's manufacturer taking advantage of? What can Byron's play with the toy reveal about his perception of sound patterns?

» CONNECT
Infants with nonorganic failure to thrive rarely smile at friendly adults but, instead, anxiously keep track of nearby people. Using the learning capacities discussed in the preceding sections, explain these reactions.

Motor Development

Carolyn, Monica, and Vanessa each kept a baby book, filled with proud notations about when their children first held up their heads, reached for objects, sat by themselves, and walked alone. Parents are understandably excited about these new motor skills, which allow babies to master their bodies and the environment in a new way. For example, sitting upright gives infants a new perspective on the world. Reaching permits babies to find out about objects by acting on them. And when infants can move on their own, their opportunities for exploration multiply.

Babies' motor achievements have a powerful effect on their social relationships. When Caitlin crawled at 7½ months, Carolyn and David began to restrict her movements by saying no and expressing mild impatience. When she walked three days after her first birthday, the first "testing of wills" occurred (Biringen et al., 1995). Despite her mother's warnings, she sometimes pulled items from shelves that were off limits. "I said, 'Don't do that!'" Carolyn would say firmly, taking Caitlin's hand and redirecting her attention.

At the same time, newly walking babies more actively attend to and initiate social interaction (Clearfield, Obsborn, & Mullen, 2008). Caitlin frequently toddled over to her parents to express a greeting, give a hug, or initiate a gleeful game of hide-and-seek. Soon after, she held out a book, then turned pages while she and her parent named the pictures. Carolyn and David, in turn, increased their expressions of affection and playful activities. Caitlin's delight as she worked on new motor skills triggered pleasurable reactions in others, which encouraged her efforts further (Mayes & Zigler, 1992). Motor, social, cognitive, and language competencies developed together and supported one another.

The Sequence of Motor Development

Gross-motor development refers to control over actions that help infants get around in the environment, such as crawling, standing, and walking. *Fine-motor development* has to do with smaller movements, such as reaching and grasping. Table 4.2 shows the average age at which North American infants and toddlers achieve a variety of gross- and fine-motor skills. It also presents the age ranges during which most babies accomplish each skill, indicating large individual differences in *rate* of motor progress. Also, a baby who is a late reacher will not necessarily be a late crawler or walker. We would be concerned about a child's development only if many motor skills were seriously delayed.

Table 4.2 reveals both organization and direction in infants' motor achievements. A *cephalocaudal trend* is evident: Motor

TABLE 4.2 ■ ***Gross- and Fine-Motor Development in the First Two Years***

MOTOR SKILL	AVERAGE AGE ACHIEVED	AGE RANGE IN WHICH 90 PERCENT OF INFANTS ACHIEVE THE SKILL
When held upright, holds head erect and steady	6 weeks	3 weeks–4 months
When prone, lifts self by arms	2 months	3 weeks–4 months
Rolls from side to back	2 months	3 weeks–5 months
Grasps cube	3 months, 3 weeks	2–7 months
Rolls from back to side	4½ months	2–7 months
Sits alone	7 months	5–9 months
Crawls	7 months	5–11 months
Pulls to stand	8 months	5–12 months
Plays pat-a-cake	9 months, 3 weeks	7–15 months
Stands alone	11 months	9–16 months
Walks alone	11 months, 3 weeks	9–17 months
Builds tower of two cubes	11 months, 3 weeks	10–19 months
Scribbles vigorously	14 months	10–21 months
Walks up stairs with help	16 months	12–23 months
Jumps in place	23 months, 2 weeks	17–30 months
Walks on tiptoe	25 months	16–30 months

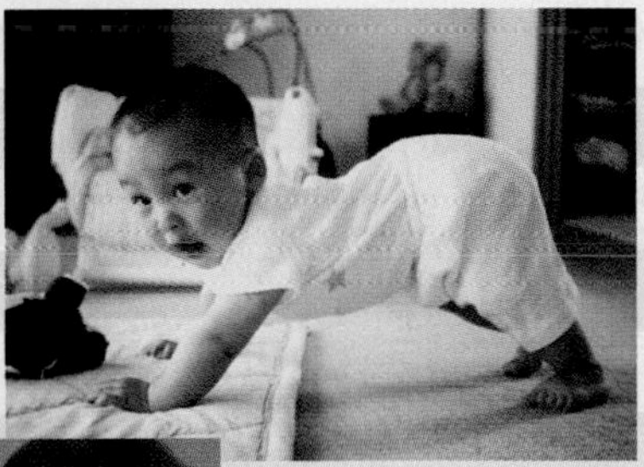
© OOTE BOE/ALAMY

© LAURA DWIGHT/CORBIS

© LAURA DWIGHT/COREIS

Note: These milestones represent overall age trends. Individual differences exist in the precise age at which each milestone is attained.
Sources: Bayley, 1969, 1993, 2005.

control of the head comes before control of the arms and trunk, which precedes control of the legs. You can also see a *proximodistal trend:* Head, trunk, and arm control precedes coordination of the hands and fingers. The similarities between physical and motor development suggest a genetic contribution to motor progress. But as we will see, some motor milestones deviate sharply from these trends.

We must be careful not to think of motor skills as unrelated accomplishments that follow a fixed maturational timetable. Rather, each skill is a product of earlier motor attainments and a contributor to new ones. And children acquire motor skills in highly individual ways. For example, before her adoption, Grace spent most of her days lying in a hammock. Because she was rarely placed on her tummy and on firm surfaces that enabled her to move on her own, she did not try to crawl. As a result, she pulled to a stand and walked before she crawled! Many influences—both internal and external to the child—join together to support the vast transformations in motor competencies of the first two years.

Motor Skills as Dynamic Systems

According to **dynamic systems theory of motor development,** mastery of motor skills involves acquiring increasingly complex *systems of action.* When motor skills work as a *system,* separate abilities blend together, each cooperating with others to produce more effective ways of exploring and controlling the environment. For example, control of the head and upper chest combine into sitting with support. Kicking, rocking on all fours, and reaching combine to become crawling. And standing, stepping, and improved upright postural control unite into walking (Thelen, 1989).

Each new skill is a joint product of four factors: (1) central nervous system development, (2) the body's movement capacities, (3) the goals the child has in mind, and (4) environmental supports for the skill. Change in any element makes the system less stable, and the child starts to explore and select new, more effective motor patterns.

The broader physical environment also profoundly influences motor skills. Infants with stairs in their home learn to crawl up stairs at an earlier age and also more readily master a back-descent strategy—the safest but also the most challenging position because the baby must turn around at the top, give up visual guidance of her goal, and crawl backward (Berger, Theuring, & Adolph, 2007). And if children were reared on the moon, with its reduced gravity, they would prefer jumping to walking or running!

When a skill is first acquired, infants must refine it. For example, in trying to crawl, Caitlin often collapsed on her tummy and moved backward. Soon she figured out how to propel herself forward by alternately pulling with her arms and pushing with her feet. By experimenting, she perfected the crawling motion (Vereijkin & Adolph, 1999). As babies attempt a new skill, related, previously mastered skills often become less secure. As the novice walker experiments with balancing the body vertically over two small moving feet, balance during sitting may become temporarily less stable (Adolph & Berger, 2006; Chen et al., 2007). In learning to walk, toddlers practice six or more hours a day, traveling the length of 29 football fields! Gradually their small, unsteady steps change to a longer stride, their feet move closer together, their toes point to the front, and their legs become symmetrically coordinated (Adolph, Vereijken, & Shrout, 2003). As movements are repeated thousands of times, they promote new connections in the brain that govern motor patterns.

Dynamic systems theory shows us why motor development cannot be genetically determined. Because it is motivated by exploration and the desire to master new tasks, heredity can map it out only at a general level (Hopkins & Butterworth, 1997; Thelen & Smith, 1998). Rather than being *hardwired* into the nervous system, behaviors are *softly assembled,* allowing for different paths to the same motor skill (Adolph & Berger, 2006; Thelen & Smith, 2006).

■ **DYNAMIC MOTOR SYSTEMS IN ACTION.** To find out how babies acquire motor capacities, some studies have tracked their first attempts at a skill until it became smooth and effortless. In one investigation, researchers held sounding toys alternately in front of infants' hands and feet, from the time they showed interest until they engaged in well-coordinated reaching and grasping (Galloway & Thelen, 2004). As Figure 4.10 shows, the infants, violating the cephalocaudal trend, first reached for the toys with their feet—as early as 8 weeks of age, at least a month before reaching with their hands!

Why did babies reach "feet first"? Because the hip joint constrains the legs to move less freely than the shoulder constrains the arms, infants could more easily control their leg movements. When they first tried reaching with their hands,

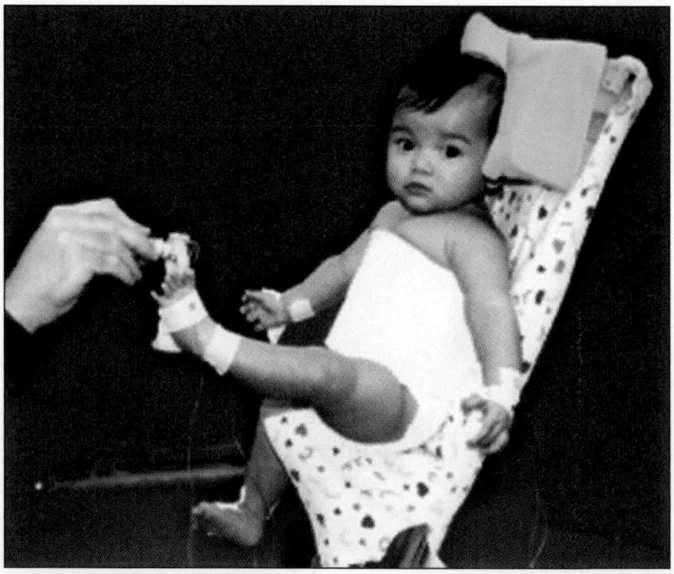

■ **FIGURE 4.10** ■ **Reaching "feet first."** When sounding toys were held in front of babies' hands and feet, they reached with their feet as early as 8 weeks of age, a month or more before they reached with their hands—a clear violation of the cephalocaudal pattern. This 2½-month-old skillfully explores an object with her foot.

The West Indians of Jamaica use a formal handling routine with their babies, believing that exercise helps infants grow up strong, healthy, and physically attractive. This mother "walks" her baby up her body—an exercise that contributes to earlier mastery of independent walking.

their arms actually moved *away* from the object! Consequently, hand reaching required far more practice than foot reaching. As these findings confirm, rather than following a strict cephalocaudal pattern, the order in which motor skills develop depends on the anatomy of the body part being used, the surrounding environment, and the baby's efforts.

CULTURAL VARIATIONS IN MOTOR DEVELOPMENT. Cross-cultural research further illustrates how early movement opportunities and a stimulating environment contribute to motor development. Half a century ago, Wayne Dennis (1960) observed infants in Iranian orphanages who were deprived of the tantalizing surroundings that induce infants to acquire motor skills. These babies spent their days lying on their backs in cribs, without toys to play with. As a result, most did not move on their own until after 2 years of age. When they finally did move, the constant experience of lying on their backs led them to scoot in a sitting position rather than crawl on their hands and knees. Because babies who scoot come up against furniture with their feet, not their hands, they are far less likely to pull themselves to a standing position in preparation for walking. Indeed, by 3 to 4 years of age, only 15 percent of the Iranian orphans were walking alone.

Cultural variations in infant-rearing practices affect motor development. ***TAKE A MOMENT...*** Take a quick survey of several parents you know: Should sitting, crawling, and walking be deliberately encouraged? Answers vary widely from culture to culture. Japanese mothers and mothers from rural India, for example, believe such efforts are unnecessary (Seymour, 1999). Among the Zinacanteco Indians of Southern Mexico, rapid motor progress is actively discouraged. Babies who walk before they know enough to keep away from cooking fires and weaving looms are viewed as dangerous to themselves and disruptive to others (Greenfield, 1992).

In contrast, among the Kipsigis of Kenya and the West Indians of Jamaica, babies hold their heads up, sit alone, and walk considerably earlier than North American infants. Kipsigi parents deliberately teach these motor skills. In the first few months, babies are seated in holes dug in the ground, with rolled blankets used to keep them upright. Walking is promoted by frequently bouncing babies on their feet (Hopkins & Westra, 1988; Super, 1981). And as parents in these cultures support babies in upright postures and rarely put them down on the floor, their infants usually skip crawling—a motor skill regarded as crucial in Western nations!

By decreasing exposure to "tummy time," the current Western practice of having babies sleep on their backs to protect them from SIDS (see page 110 in Chapter 3) delays gross motor milestones of rolling, sitting, and crawling (Majnemer & Barr, 2005; Scrutton, 2005). Regularly exposing infants to the tummy-lying position during waking hours prevents these delays.

Fine-Motor Development: Reaching and Grasping

Of all motor skills, reaching may play the greatest role in infant cognitive development because it opens up a whole new way of exploring the environment. By grasping things, turning them over, and seeing what happens when they are released, infants learn a great deal about the sights, sounds, and feel of objects.

Reaching and grasping, like many other motor skills, start out as gross, diffuse activity and move toward mastery of fine movements. Figure 4.11 on page 140 illustrates some milestones of reaching over the first nine months. Newborns make poorly coordinated swipes or swings, called *prereaching*, toward an object in front of them, but because of poor arm and hand control, they rarely contact the object. Like newborn reflexes, prereaching drops out around 7 weeks of age. Yet these early behaviors suggest that babies are biologically prepared to coordinate hand with eye in the act of exploring (Rosander & von Hofsten, 2002; von Hofsten, 2004).

At about 3 to 4 months, as infants develop the necessary eye, head, and shoulder control, reaching reappears as purposeful, forward arm movements in the presence of a nearby toy and gradually improves in accuracy (Bhat, Heathcock, & Galloway, 2005; Spencer et al., 2000). By 5 to 6 months, infants reach for an object in a room that has been darkened during the reach by switching off the lights—a skill that improves over the next few months (Clifton et al., 1994; McCarty & Ashmead, 1999). Early on, vision is freed from the basic act of reaching so it can focus on more complex adjustments. By 7 months, the arms become more independent; infants can reach for objects by extending just one arm, rather than both (Fagard & Pezé, 1997). During

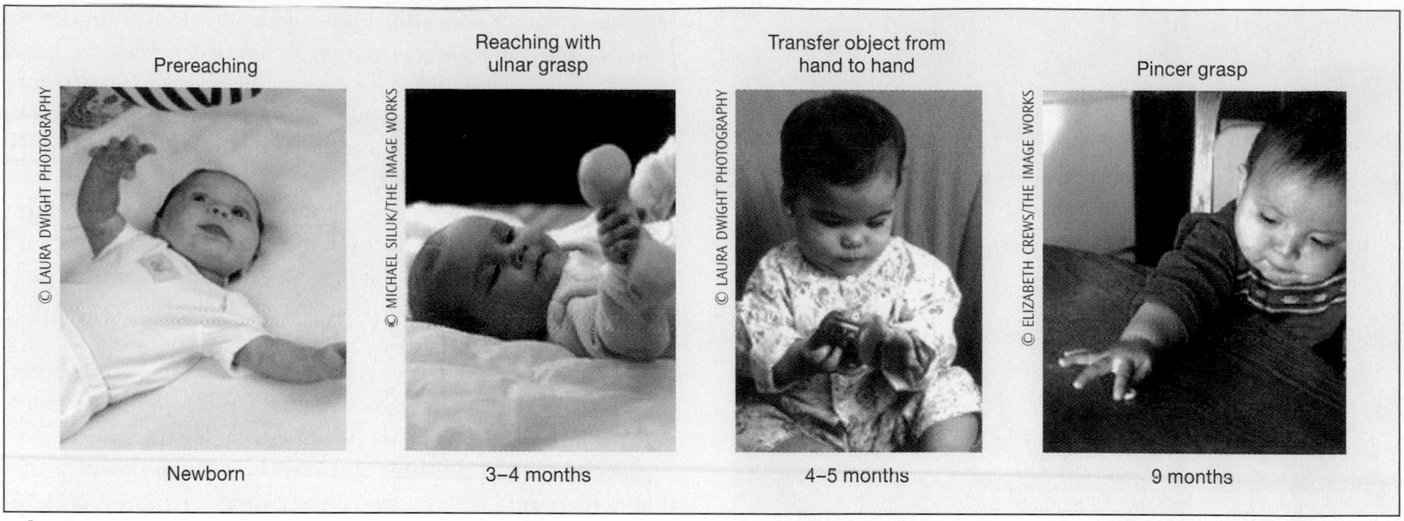

■ **FIGURE 4.11** ■ **Some milestones of reaching.** The average age at which each skill is attained is given. (Ages from Bayley, 1969; Rochat, 1989.)

the next few months, infants become better at reaching for moving objects—ones that spin, change direction, or move closer or farther away (Wentworth, Benson, & Haith, 2000).

Once infants can reach, they modify their grasp. The newborn's grasp reflex is replaced by the *ulnar grasp,* a clumsy motion in which the fingers close against the palm. Still, even 3-month-olds adjust their grasp to the size and shape of an object—a capacity that improves over the first year as infants orient the hand more precisely (Newman, Atkinson, & Braddick, 2001; Witherington, 2005). Around 4 to 5 months, when infants begin to sit up, they coordinate both hands in exploring objects. They can hold an object in one hand while the other scans it with the fingertips, and they frequently transfer objects from hand to hand (Rochat & Goubet, 1995). By the end of the first year, infants use the thumb and index finger opposably in a well-coordinated *pincer grasp.* Then the ability to manipulate objects greatly expands. The 1-year-old can pick up raisins and blades of grass, turn knobs, and open and close small boxes.

Between 8 and 11 months, reaching and grasping are well-practiced, so that attention is released from the motor skill to events that occur before and after attaining the object. For example, 10-month-olds easily adjust their reach to anticipate their next action. They reach for a ball faster when they intend to throw it than when they intend to drop it carefully through an opening (Claxton, Keen, & McCarty, 2003). Around this time, too, infants begin to solve simple problems that involve reaching, such as searching for and finding hidden toys.

Finally, the capacity to reach for and manipulate an object increases infants' attention to the way an adult reaches for and plays with that particular object (Hauf, Aschersleben, & Prinz, 2007). Perhaps with the aid of mirror neurons, babies match their own active experience of reaching to their perception of others' actions. As a result, they broaden their understanding of others' behaviors and—as they watch what others do—of the range of actions that can be performed on various objects.

ASK YOURSELF

» REVIEW
Cite evidence that motor development is a joint product of biological, psychological, and environmental factors.

» APPLY
List everyday experiences that support mastery of reaching, grasping, sitting, and crawling. Why should caregivers place young infants in a variety of waking-time body positions?

» CONNECT
Provide several examples of how motor development influences infants' social experiences. How do social experiences, in turn, influence motor development?

» REFLECT
Do you favor early, systematic training of infants in motor skills such as crawling, walking, and stair climbing? Why or why not?

Perceptual Development

In Chapter 3, you learned that the senses of touch, taste, smell, and hearing—but not vision—are remarkably well-developed at birth. Now let's turn to a related question: How does perception change over the first year? Our discussion will address hearing and vision, the focus of almost all research. Recall that in Chapter 3, we used the word *sensation* to talk about these capacities. It suggests a fairly passive process—what the baby's receptors detect when exposed to stimulation. Now we use the word *perception,* which is active: When we perceive, we organize and interpret what we see.

As we review the perceptual achievements of infancy, you may find it hard to tell where perception leaves off and thinking begins. The research we are about to discuss provides an excellent bridge to the topic of Chapter 5—cognitive development during the first two years.

Hearing

On Timmy's first birthday, Vanessa bought several CDs of nursery songs, and she turned one on each afternoon at naptime. Soon Timmy let her know his favorite tune. If she put on "Twinkle, Twinkle," he stood up in his crib and whimpered until she replaced it with "Jack and Jill." Timmy's behavior illustrates the greatest change in hearing over the first year of life: Babies organize sounds into increasingly complex patterns.

Between 4 and 7 months, infants display a sense of musical phrasing: They prefer Mozart minuets with pauses between phrases to those with awkward breaks (Krumhansl & Jusczyk, 1990). Around 6 to 7 months, they can distinguish musical tunes on the basis of variations in rhythmic patterns, including beat structure (duple or triple) and accent structure (emphasis on the first note of every beat unit or at other positions) (Hannon & Johnson, 2004). And by the end of the first year, infants recognize the same melody when it is played in different keys (Trehub, 2001). As we will see next, 6- to 12-month-olds make comparable discriminations in human speech. They readily detect sound regularities that will facilitate later language learning.

■ **SPEECH PERCEPTION.** Recall from Chapter 3 that newborns can distinguish nearly all sounds in human languages and that they prefer listening to human speech over nonspeech sounds, and to their native tongue rather than a foreign language. As they listen to people talking, they learn to focus on meaningful sound variations. ERP brain-wave recordings reveal that around 5 months, babies become sensitive to syllable stress patterns in their own language (Weber et al., 2004). Between 6 and 8 months, they start to "screen out" sounds not used in their native tongue (Anderson, Morgan, & White, 2003; Polka & Werker, 1994). As the Biology and Environment box on page 142 explains, this increased responsiveness to native-language sounds is part of a general "tuning" process in the second half of the first year—a possible sensitive period in which infants acquire a range of perceptual skills for picking up socially important information.

Soon after, infants focus on larger speech segments that are critical to figuring out meaning. They recognize familiar words in spoken passages and listen longer to speech with clear clause and phrase boundaries (Jusczyk & Hohne, 1997; Soderstrom et al., 2003). Around 7 to 9 months, infants extend this sensitivity to speech structure to individual words. They begin to divide the speech stream into wordlike units (Jusczyk, 2002; Saffran, Werker, & Werner, 2006).

■ **ANALYZING THE SPEECH STREAM.** How do infants make such rapid progress in perceiving the structure of language? Research shows that they have an impressive **statistical learning capacity.** By analyzing the speech stream for patterns—repeatedly occurring sequences of sounds—they acquire a stock of speech structures for which they will later learn meanings, long before they start to talk around age 12 months.

For example, when presented with controlled sequences of nonsense syllables, babies listen for statistical regularities: They locate words by distinguishing syllables that often occur together (indicating they belong to the same word) from syllables that seldom occur together (indicating a word boundary). Consider the English word sequence *pretty#baby.* After listening to the speech stream for just one minute, babies can discriminate a word-internal syllable pair *(pretty)* from a word-external syllable pair *(ty#ba).* They prefer to listen to new speech that preserves the word-internal pattern (Saffran, Aslin, & Newport, 1996; Saffran & Thiessen, 2003).

Once infants locate words, they focus on the words and, around 7 to 8 months, identify regular syllable-stress patterns—for example, in English and Dutch, that the onset of a strong syllable (*hap*-py, *rab*-bit) often signals a new word (Swingley, 2005; Saffran & Thiessen, 2007). By 10 months, babies can detect words that start with weak syllables, such as "sur*prise*" (Jusczyk, 2001).

Clearly, babies have a powerful ability to extract patterns from complex, continuous speech. Some researchers believe that infants are innately equipped with a general statistical learning capacity for detecting structure in the environment, which they also apply to visual stimulation (Kirkham, Slemmer, & Johnson, 2002). Indeed, because communication is often multisensory (simultaneously verbal, visual, and tactile), infants receive much support from other senses in analyzing speech. Perhaps you have observed parents name objects while demonstrating—for example, saying "doll" while moving a doll and, sometimes, having the doll touch the infant. In doing so, caregivers greatly increase the chances that babies will remember the association between the word and the object (Gogate & Bahrick, 2001).

Vision

For exploring the environment, humans depend on vision more than any other sense. Although at first a baby's visual world is fragmented, it undergoes extraordinary changes during the first 7 to 8 months of life.

Visual development is supported by rapid maturation of the eye and visual centers in the cerebral cortex. Recall from Chapter 3 that the newborn baby focuses and perceives color poorly. Around 2 months, infants can focus on objects about as well as adults can, and their color vision is adultlike by 4 months (Kellman & Arterberry, 2006). *Visual acuity* (fineness of discrimination) improves steadily throughout the first year, reaching a near-adult level of about 20/20 by 6 months (Slater, 2001).

BIOLOGY AND ENVIRONMENT

"Tuning In" to Familiar Speech, Faces, and Music: A Sensitive Period for Culture-Specific Learning

To share experiences with members of their family and community, babies must become skilled at making perceptual discriminations that are meaningful in their culture. As we have seen, at first babies are sensitive to virtually all speech sounds, but around 6 months, they narrow their focus, limiting the distinctions they make to the language they hear and will soon learn.

The ability to perceive faces shows a similar path of development. After habituating to one member of each pair of faces in Figure 4.12, 6-month-olds were shown the familiar and the novel face side-by-side. For both pairs, they recovered to (looked longer at) the novel face, indicating that they could discriminate individual faces of both humans and monkeys equally well (Pascalis, de Haan, & Nelson, 2002). But at 9 months, infants no longer showed a novelty preference when viewing the monkey pair. Like adults, they could distinguish only the human faces.

This developmental trend appears again in musical rhythm perception. Western adults are accustomed to the even-beat pattern of Western music—repetition of the same rhythmic structure in every measure of a tune—and easily notice rhythmic changes that disrupt this familiar beat. But present them with music that does not follow this typical Western rhythmic form—Baltic folk tunes, for example—and they fail to pick up on rhythmic-pattern deviations. Six-month-olds, however, can detect such disruptions in both Western and non-Western melodies. But by 12 months, after added exposure to Western music, babies are no longer aware of deviations in foreign musical rhythms, although their sensitivity to Western rhythmic structure remains unchanged (Hannon & Trehub, 2005b).

Several weeks of regular interaction with a foreign-language speaker and of daily opportunities to listen to non-Western music fully restore 12-month-olds' sensitivity to wide-ranging speech sounds and music rhythms (Hannon & Trehub, 2005a; Kuhl, Tsao, & Liu, 2003). Adults given similar extensive experiences, by contrast, show little improvement in perceptual sensitivity.

Taken together, these findings suggest a heightened capacity—or sensitive period—in the second half of the first year, when babies are biologically prepared to "zero in" on socially meaningful perceptual distinctions. Notice how, between 6 and 12 months, learning is especially rapid across several domains (speech, faces, and music) and is easily modified by experience. This suggests a broad neurological change—perhaps a special time of brain development in which babies analyze everyday stimulation of all kinds similarly, in ways that prepare them to participate in their cultural community.

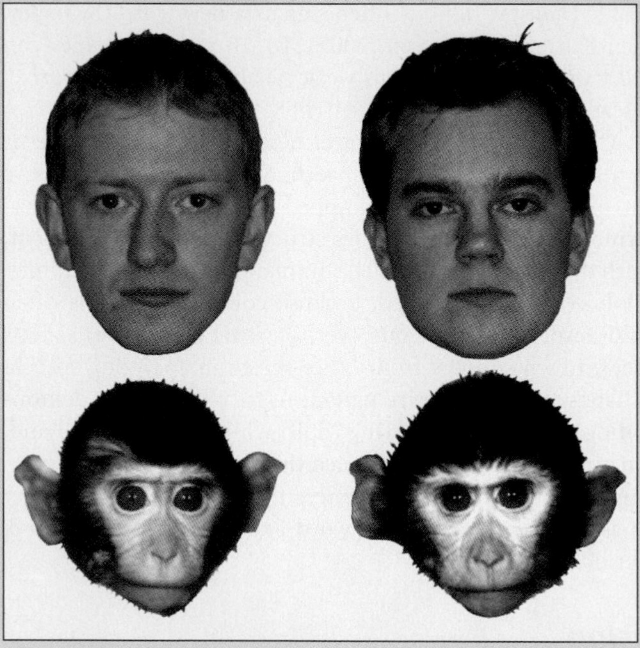

FIGURE 4.12 Discrimination of human and monkey faces. Which of these pairs is easiest for you to tell apart? After habituating to one of the photos in each pair, infants were shown the familiar and the novel face side-by-side. For both pairs, 6-month-olds recovered to (looked longer at) the novel face, indicating that they could discriminate human and monkey faces equally well. By 12 months, babies lost their ability to distinguish the monkey faces. Like adults, they showed a novelty preference only to human stimuli. (From O. Pascalis et al., 2002, "Is Face Processing Species-Specific During the First Year of Life?" *Science, 296,* p. 1322. Reprinted with permission from AAAS.)

Scanning the environment and tracking moving objects improve over the first half-year as infants better control their eye movements and build an organized perceptual world (Johnson, Slemmer, & Amso, 2004; von Hofsten & Rosander, 1998).

As babies explore their visual field, they figure out the characteristics of objects and how they are arranged in space. To understand how they do so, let's examine the development of two aspects of vision: depth and pattern perception.

DEPTH PERCEPTION. *Depth perception* is the ability to judge the distance of objects from one another and from ourselves. It is important for understanding the layout of the environment and for guiding motor activity.

Figure 4.13 shows the *visual cliff,* designed by Eleanor Gibson and Richard Walk (1960) and used in the earliest studies of depth perception. It consists of a Plexiglas-covered table with a platform at the center, a "shallow" side with a checkerboard pattern just under the glass, and a "deep" side with a checkerboard several feet below the glass. The researchers found that crawling babies readily crossed the shallow side, but most reacted with fear to the deep side. They concluded that around the time infants crawl, most distinguish deep and shallow surfaces and avoid drop-offs.

© MARK RICHARDS/PHOTOEDIT

■ **FIGURE 4.13** ■ **The visual cliff.** Plexiglas covers the deep and shallow sides. By refusing to cross the deep side and showing a preference for the shallow side, this infant demonstrates the ability to perceive depth.

Visual cliff findings show that crawling and avoidance of drop-offs are linked but not how they are related or when depth perception first appears. Recent research has looked at babies' ability to detect specific depth cues, using methods that do not require that they crawl.

Motion is the first depth cue to which infants are sensitive. Babies 3 to 4 weeks old blink their eyes defensively when an object moves toward their face as if it is going to hit (Nánez & Yonas, 1994). *Binocular depth cues* arise because our two eyes have slightly different views of the visual field. The brain blends these two images, resulting in perception of depth. Research in which two overlapping images are projected before the baby, who wears special goggles to ensure that each eye receives one image, reveals that sensitivity to binocular cues emerges between 2 and 3 months and improves rapidly over the first year (Birch, 1993; Brown & Miracle, 2003). Finally, around 6 to 7 months, babies become sensitive to *pictorial* depth cues, the ones artists use to make a painting look three-dimensional. Examples include receding lines that create the illusion of perspective, changes in texture (nearby textures are more detailed than faraway ones), overlapping objects (an object partially hidden by another object is perceived to be more distant), and shadows cast on surfaces (indicating a separation in space between the object and the surface) (Sen, Yonas, & Knill, 2001; Yonas, Elieff, & Arterberry, 2002; Yonas & Granrud, 2006).

Why does perception of depth cues emerge in the order just described? Researchers speculate that motor development is involved. For example, control of the head during the early weeks of life may help babies notice motion and binocular cues. Around the middle of the first year, the ability to turn, poke, and feel the surface of objects may promote perception of pictorial cues (Bushnell & Boudreau, 1993). And as we will see next, one aspect of motor progress—independent movement—plays a vital role in refinement of depth perception.

■ **INDEPENDENT MOVEMENT AND DEPTH PERCEPTION.** At 6 months, Timmy started crawling. "He's fearless!" exclaimed Vanessa. "If I put him down in the middle of our bed, he crawls right over the edge. The same thing's happened by the stairs." Will Timmy become more wary of the side of the bed and the staircase as he becomes a more experienced crawler? Research suggests that he will. Infants with more crawling experience (regardless of when they start to crawl) are far more likely to refuse to cross the deep side of the visual cliff (Campos et al., 2000).

From extensive everyday experience, babies gradually figure out how to use depth cues to detect the danger of falling. But because the loss of body control that leads to falling differs greatly for each body position, babies must undergo this learning separately for each posture. In one study, 9-month-olds who were experienced sitters but novice crawlers were placed

© MURRAY PRODUCTIONS/ALAMY

Infants must learn to use depth cues to avoid falling in each new position—sitting, crawling, walking—and in various situations. As this baby carefully navigates a set of stone steps, she uses vision to make postural adjustments, and her understanding of depth expands.

on the edge of a shallow drop-off that could be widened (Adolph, 2000, 2002). While in the familiar sitting position, infants avoided leaning out for an attractive toy at distances likely to result in falling. But in the unfamiliar crawling posture, they headed over the edge, even when the distance was extremely wide! And newly walking babies, while avoiding sharp drop-offs, careen down slopes and over uneven surfaces without making the necessary postural adjustments, so they fall frequently (Joh & Adolph, 2006; Witherington et al., 2005). As infants discover how to avoid falling in different postures and situations, their understanding of depth expands.

Crawling experience promotes other aspects of three-dimensional understanding. For example, seasoned crawlers are better than their inexperienced agemates at remembering object locations and finding hidden objects (Bai & Bertenthal, 1992; Campos et al., 2000). Why does crawling make such a difference? ***TAKE A MOMENT...*** Compare your own experience of the environment when you are driven from one place to another as opposed to walking or driving yourself. When you move on your own, you are much more aware of landmarks and routes of travel, and you take more careful note of what things look like from different points of view. The same is true for infants. In fact, crawling promotes a new level of brain organization, as indicated by more organized EEG brain-wave activity in the cerebral cortex (Bell & Fox, 1996). Perhaps it strengthens certain neural connections, especially those involved in vision and understanding of space.

■ **PATTERN PERCEPTION.** Even newborns prefer to look at patterned rather than plain stimuli—for example, a drawing of the human face or one with scrambled facial features rather than a black-and-white oval (Fantz, 1961). As they get older, infants prefer more complex patterns. For example, 3-week-old infants look longest at black-and-white checkerboards with a few large squares, whereas 8- and 14-week-olds prefer those with many squares (Brennan, Ames, & Moore, 1966).

A general principle, called **contrast sensitivity,** explains early pattern preferences (Banks & Ginsburg, 1985). *Contrast* refers to the difference in the amount of light between adjacent regions in a pattern. If babies *are sensitive to* (can detect) the contrast in two or more patterns, they prefer the one with more contrast. To understand this idea, look at the checkerboards in the top row of Figure 4.14. To us, the one with many small squares has more contrasting elements. Now look at the bottom row, which shows how these checkerboards appear to infants in the first few weeks of life. Because of their poor vision, very young babies cannot resolve the small features in more complex patterns, so they prefer to look at the large, bold checkerboard. Around 2 months, when detection of fine-grained detail has improved, infants become sensitive to the contrast in complex patterns and spend more time looking at them. Contrast sensitivity continues to increase during infancy and childhood (Gwiazda & Birch, 2001).

In the early weeks of life, infants respond to the separate parts of a pattern. They stare at single, high-contrast features and have difficulty shifting their gaze away toward other interesting stimuli (Hunnius & Geuze, 2004a, 2004b). In exploring drawings of human faces, for example, 1-month-olds often limited themselves to the edges of the stimulus and focus on the hairline or chin. At 2 to 3 months, when contrast sensitivity improves and infants can better control their scanning, they thoroughly explore a pattern's internal features, pausing briefly to look at each part (Bronson, 1994).

But babies' inspection of a stimulus varies with pattern characteristics. When exposed to dynamic stimuli, such as the mother's nodding, smiling face, even 6-week-olds fixate more on internal features (the mouth and eyes) than on edges. Nevertheless, thorough scanning of a dynamic stimulus emerges later—after 4 months of age (Hunnius & Geuze, 2004b). And when presented with more complex stimuli, such as a still frame or a video clip from the TV program *Sesame Street,* babies increase their inspection time over the second half-year as they try to make sense of the image (Courage, Reynolds, & Richards, 2006). Exploring complex patterns, especially those with moving stimuli, is more demanding than exploring simple, static patterns—a difference we must keep in mind as we examine research on pattern perception, which is based largely on static stimuli.

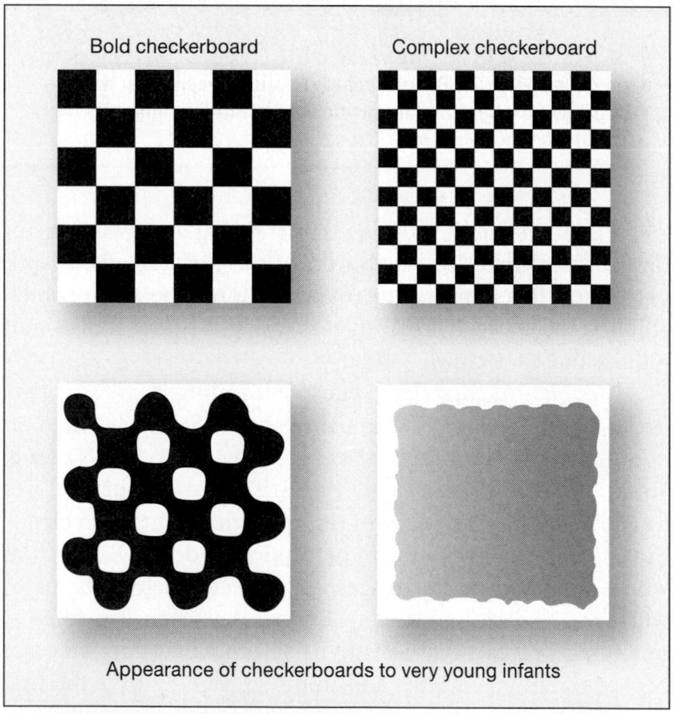

■ **FIGURE 4.14** ■ **The way two checkerboards differing in complexity look to infants in the first few weeks of life.** Because of their poor vision, very young infants cannot resolve the fine detail in the *complex checkerboard.* It appears blurred, like a gray field. The large, *bold checkerboard* appears to have more contrast, so babies prefer to look at it. (Adapted from M. S. Banks & P. Salapatek, 1983, "Infant Visual Perception," in M. M. Haith & J. J. Campos (Eds.), *Handbook of Child Psychology: Vol. 2. Infancy and Developmental Psychobiology [4th ed.],* New York: John Wiley & Sons, p. 504. Reprinted with permission from John Wiley & Sons, Inc.)

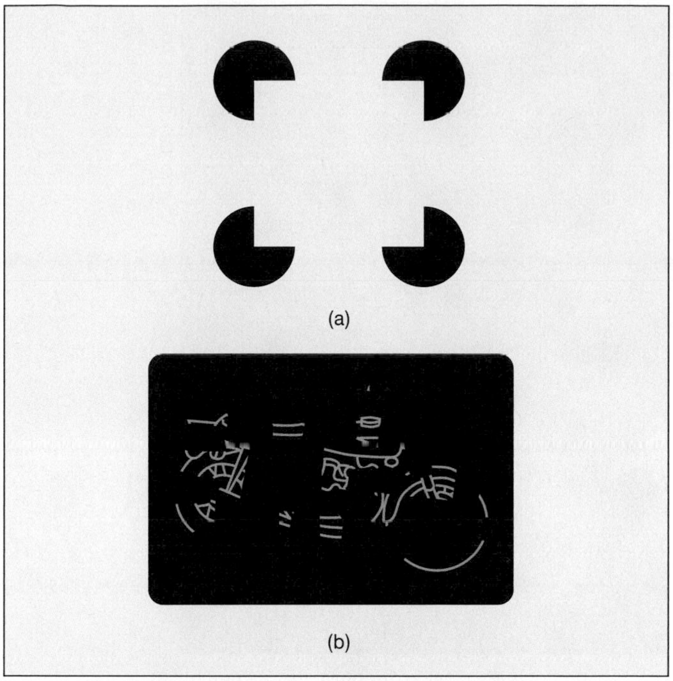

■ **FIGURE 4.15** ■ **Subjective boundaries in visual patterns.** (a) Do you perceive a square in the middle of the top figure? By 4 months of age, infants do, too. (b) What does the image on the bottom, missing two-thirds of its outline, look like to you? By 12 months, infants detect the image of a motorcycle. After habituating to the incomplete motorcycle image, they were shown an intact motorcycle figure paired with a novel form. Twelve-month-olds recovered to (looked longer at) the novel figure, indicating that they recognized the motorcycle pattern on the basis of very little visual information. (Adapted from Ghim, 1990; Rose, Jankowski, & Senior, 1997.)

Once babies can take in all aspects of a pattern, they integrate the parts into a unified whole. Around 4 months, they are so good at detecting pattern organization that they even perceive subjective boundaries that are not really present. For example, they perceive a square in the center of Figure 4.15a, just as you do (Ghim, 1990). Older infants carry this responsiveness to subjective form further, applying it to complex, moving stimuli. For example, 9-month-olds look much longer at an organized series of moving lights that resembles a human being walking than at upside-down or scrambled versions (Bertenthal, 1993). At 12 months, infants can detect familiar objects represented by incomplete drawings, even when as much as two-thirds of the drawing is missing (see Figure 4.15b) (Rose, Jankowski, & Senior, 1997). As these findings reveal, infants' increasing knowledge of objects and actions supports pattern perception.

■ **FACE PERCEPTION.** Infants' tendency to search for structure in a patterned stimulus also applies to face perception. Newborns prefer to look at photos and simplified drawings with features arranged naturally (upright) rather than unnaturally (upside-down or sideways) (see Figure 4.16a) (Cassia, Turati, & Simion, 2004; Mondloch et al., 1999). They also track a facial pattern moving across their visual field farther than they track other stimuli (Johnson, 1999). And although their ability to distinguish real faces on the basis of inner features is limited, shortly after birth babies prefer photos of faces with eyes open and a direct gaze (Farroni et al., 2002). Yet another amazing capacity is their tendency to look longer at faces judged by adults as attractive—a preference that may be the origin of the widespread social bias favoring physically attractive people (Slater et al., 2000).

Some researchers claim that these behaviors reflect a built-in capacity to orient toward members of one's own species, just as many newborn animals do (Johnson, 2001; Slater & Quinn, 2001). Others assert that newborns prefer any stimulus in which the most salient elements are arranged horizontally in the upper part of a pattern—like the "eyes" in Figure 4.16b (Turati, 2004). Possibly, however, a bias favoring the facial pattern promotes

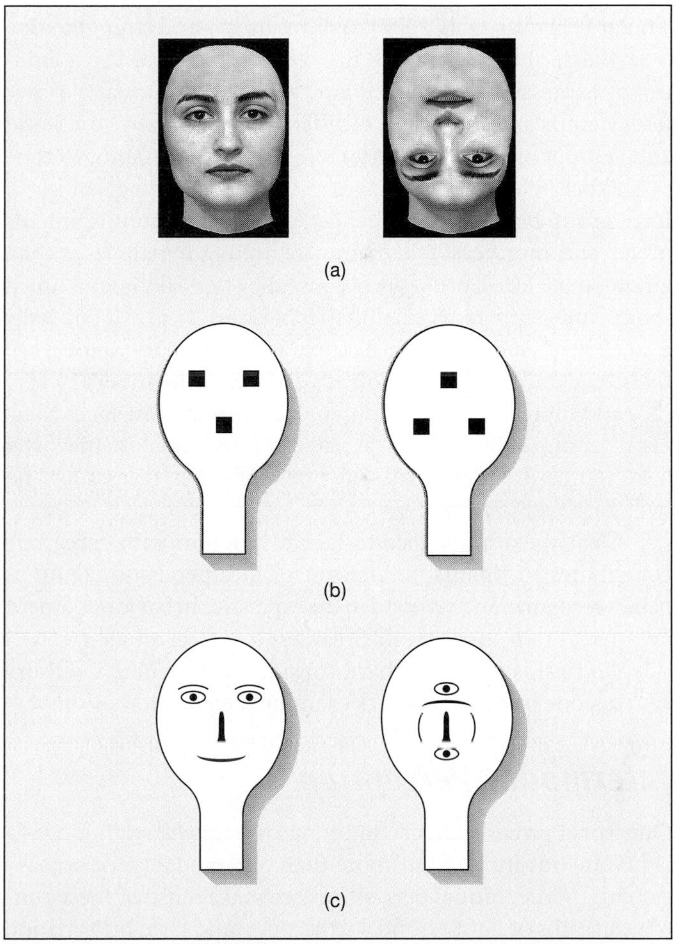

■ **FIGURE 4.16** ■ **Early face perception.** Newborns prefer to look at the upright photo of a face (a) and the simple pattern resembling a face (b) over the upside-down versions. (c) When the complex drawing of a face on the left and the equally complex, scrambled version on the right are moved across newborns' visual field, they follow the face longer. But if the two stimuli are stationary, infants show no preference for the face until around 2 months of age. (From Cassia, Turati, & Simion, 2004; Johnson, 1999; Mondloch et al., 1999.)

such preferences. Still other researchers argue that newborns are exposed to faces more often than to other stimuli—early experiences that could quickly "wire" the brain to detect faces and prefer attractive ones (Nelson, 2001).

Although newborns respond to a general facelike structure, they cannot discriminate a complex facial pattern from other, equally complex patterns (see Figure 4.16c). But from repeated exposures to their mother's face, they quickly learn to prefer her face to that of an unfamiliar woman, although they are sensitive only to its broad outlines. Around 2 months, when they can combine pattern elements into an organized whole, babies prefer a complex drawing of the human face to other equally complex stimulus arrangements (Dannemiller & Stephens, 1988). They also prefer their mother's detailed facial features to those of another woman (Bartrip, Morton, & de Schonen, 2001).

Around 3 months, infants make fine distinctions among the features of different faces—for example, between photographs of two strangers, even when the faces are moderately similar (Farroni et al., 2007). At 5 months—and strengthening over the second half of the first year—infants perceive emotional expressions as meaningful wholes. They treat positive faces (happy and surprised) as different from negative ones (sad and fearful) (Bornstein & Arterberry, 2003; Ludemann, 1991).

Experience influences face processing, leading babies to form group biases at a tender age. As early as 3 months, infants prefer and more easily discriminate among female faces than among male faces, probably because they typically spend much more time with female adults (Bar-Haim et al., 2006; Kelly et al., 2007). And 3-month-olds exposed mostly to members of their own race prefer to look at the faces of members of that race and more easily detect differences among those faces (Bar-Haim et al., 2006; Kelly et al., 2007). In contrast, babies who have frequent contact with members of other races show no own-race face preference.

Clearly, extensive face-to-face interaction with caregivers contributes to infants' refinement of face perception. And as babies recognize and respond to the expressive behavior of others, face perception supports their earliest social relationships.

Up to this point, we have considered the infant's sensory systems one by one. Now let's examine their coordination.

Intermodal Perception

Our world provides rich, continuous *intermodal stimulation*—simultaneous input from more than one modality, or sensory system. In **intermodal perception,** we make sense of these running streams of light, sound, tactile, odor, and taste information by perceiving them as unified wholes. We know, for example, that an object's shape is the same whether we see it or touch it; that breaking a glass causes a sharp, crashing sound; and that the patter of footsteps signals the approach of a person.

Recall that newborns turn in the general direction of a sound and reach for objects in a primitive way. These behaviors suggest that infants expect sight, sound, and touch to go together. Research reveals that babies perceive input from different sensory systems in a unified way by detecting *amodal sensory properties*—information that overlaps two or more sensory systems, such as rate, rhythm, duration, intensity, temporal synchrony (for vision and hearing), and texture and shape (for vision and touch). Consider the sight and sound of a bouncing ball or the face and voice of a speaking person. In each event, visual and auditory information occur simultaneously and with the same rate, rhythm, duration, and intensity.

Within the first half-year, infants master a remarkable range of intermodal relationships. This 3-month-old, assisted by her mother, quickly picks up associations between the sights, sounds, and feel of toys.

Even newborns are impressive perceivers of amodal properties. After touching an object (such as a cylinder) placed in their palms, they recognize it visually, distinguishing it from a different-shaped object (Sann & Streri, 2007). And they require just one exposure to learn the association between the sight and sound of a toy, such as a rhythmically jangling rattle (Morrongiello, Fenwick, & Chance, 1998).

Within the first half-year, infants master a remarkable range of intermodal relationships. For example, 3- and 4-month-olds can relate a child's or adult's moving lips to the corresponding sounds in speech. They can also link the age of a voice (child versus adult) and its emotional tone (happy or angry) with the appropriate face of a person (Bahrick, Netto, & Hernandez-Reif, 1998; Walker-Andrews, 1997). Between 4 and 6 months, infants can perceive and remember the unique face–voice pairings of unfamiliar adults (Bahrick, Hernandez-Reif, & Flom, 2005). By 8 months, they can match voices and faces on the basis of gender (Patterson & Werker, 2002).

How does intermodal perception develop so quickly? Young infants seem biologically primed to focus on amodal information. Their detection of amodal relations—for example, the common tempo and rhythm in sights and sounds—precedes and seems to provide the basis for detecting more specific intermodal matches, such as the relation between a particular person's face and the sound of her voice or between an object and its verbal label (Bahrick, Hernandez-Reif, & Flom, 2005).

Intermodal sensitivity is crucial for perceptual development. In the first few months, when much stimulation is unfamiliar and confusing, it enables babies to notice meaningful correlations between sensory inputs and rapidly make sense of their surroundings (Bahrick, Lickliter, & Flom, 2004). And as the examples just reviewed suggest, intermodal perception also facilitates social and language processing. Recall, also, the evidence presented in our discussion of hearing—that in their earliest efforts to make sense of language, infants profit from temporal synchrony between a speech sound and the motion of an object (page 141).

Finally, early parent–infant interaction presents the baby with a rich context—consisting of many concurrent sights, sounds, touches, and smells—for expanding intermodal knowledge (Lickliter & Bahrick, 2000). Intermodal perception is a fundamental ability that fosters all aspects of psychological development.

Understanding Perceptual Development

Now that we have reviewed the development of infant perceptual capacities, how can we put together this diverse array of amazing achievements? Widely accepted answers come from the work of Eleanor and James Gibson. According to the Gibsons' **differentiation theory,** infants actively search for *invariant features* of the environment—those that remain stable—in a constantly changing perceptual world. In pattern perception, for example, young babies—confronted with a confusing mass of stimulation—search for features that stand out and also orient toward faces. Soon they explore internal features, noticing *stable relationships* among them. As a result, they detect patterns, such as complex designs and faces. The development of intermodal perception also reflects this principle. Babies seek out invariant relationships—first, amodal properties, such as common rate and rhythm in a voice and face, and later, more detailed associations, such as unique voice–face matches.

The Gibsons described their theory as *differentiation* (where "differentiate" means "analyze" or "break down") because over time, the baby detects finer and finer invariant features among stimuli. In addition to pattern perception and intermodal perception, differentiation applies to depth perception. Recall how sensitivity to motion and binocular cues precedes detection of fine-grained pictorial features. So one way of understanding perceptual development is to think of it as a built-in tendency to search for order and consistency—a capacity that becomes increasingly fine-tuned with age (Gibson, 1970; Gibson, 1979).

Infants constantly look for ways in which the environment *affords possibilities for action* (Gibson, 2000, 2003). By exploring their surroundings, they figure out which things can be grasped, squeezed, bounced, or stroked and when a surface is safe to cross or presents a risk of falling (Adolph & Eppler, 1998, 1999). And from handling objects, they become more aware of a variety of observable object properties (Perone et al., 2008). As a result, they differentiate the world in new ways and act more competently.

To illustrate, recall how infants' changing capabilities for independent movement affect their perception. When babies crawl, and again when they walk, they gradually realize that a sloping surface *affords the possibility of falling* (see Figure 4.17). With added weeks of practicing each skill, they hesitate to crawl or walk down a risky incline. Experience in trying to keep their balance on various surfaces seems to make crawlers and walkers more aware of the consequences of their movements. Crawlers come to detect when surface slant places so much body weight on their arms that they will fall forward, and walkers come to sense when an incline shifts body weight so their legs and feet can no longer hold them upright (Adolph &

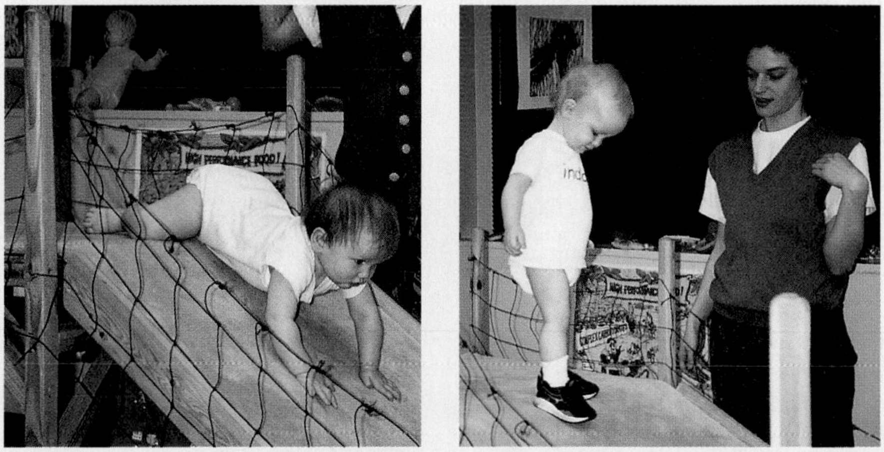

■ **FIGURE 4.17** ■ **Acting on the environment plays a major role in perceptual differentiation.** Crawling and walking change the way babies perceive a sloping surface. The newly crawling infant on the left plunges headlong down the slope. He has not yet learned that it affords the possibility of falling. The toddler on the right, who has been walking for more than a month, approaches the slope cautiously. Experience in trying to remain upright but frequently tumbling over has made him more aware of the consequences of his movements. He perceives the incline differently than he did at a younger age. (Courtesy of Karen Adolph, New York University.)

Berger, 2006). Each skill leads infants to perceive surfaces in new ways that guide their movements. ***TAKE A MOMENT...*** Can you think of other links between motor milestones and perceptual development described in this chapter?

As we conclude our discussion of infant perception, it is only fair to note that some researchers believe that babies do more than make sense of experience by searching for invariant features and action possibilities: They also *impose meaning on* what they perceive, constructing categories of objects and events in the surrounding environment. We have seen the glimmerings of this *cognitive* point of view in this chapter. For example, older babies *interpret* a familiar face as a source of pleasure and affection and a pattern of blinking lights as a moving human being. This cognitive perspective also has merit in understanding the achievements of infancy. In fact, many researchers combine these two positions, regarding infant development as proceeding from a perceptual to a cognitive emphasis over the first year of life.

ASK YOURSELF

» REVIEW
Using examples, explain why intermodal perception is vital for infants' developing understanding of their physical and social worlds.

» APPLY
After several weeks of crawling, Ben learned to avoid going headfirst down a steep incline. Now he has started to walk. Can his parents trust him not to try walking down the steep surface? Explain.

» CONNECT
According to differentiation theory, perceptual development reflects infants' active search for invariant features. Provide examples from research on hearing, pattern perception, and intermodal perception.

Summary

Body Growth

Describe major changes in body growth over the first 2 years.

» Changes in height and weight are rapid during the first 2 years. In the first 9 months, body fat is laid down quickly, while muscle development is slow and gradual. Skeletal age is the best way to estimate a child's physical maturity, which tends to vary by ethnic group and sex. Body proportions change as growth follows **cephalocaudal** and **proximodistal trends.**

Brain Development

Describe brain development during infancy and toddlerhood, including appropriate stimulation to support the brain's potential.

» Early in development, the brain grows faster than any other organ of the body. Once **neurons,** or nerve cells, are in place, they rapidly form **synapses.** To communicate, neurons release **neurotransmitters,** which cross synapses. As synapses form, to make room for new synaptic connections, many surrounding neurons die. Neurons that are seldom stimulated lose their synapses in a process called **synaptic pruning. Glial cells,** responsible for **myelination,** multiply rapidly into the second year, contributing to large gains in brain weight.

» The **cerebral cortex** is the largest, most complex brain structure and the last to stop growing. The hemispheres of the cerebral cortex specialize, a process called **lateralization.** In the first few years of life, there is high **brain plasticity,** with many areas not yet committed to specific functions.

» Both heredity and early experience contribute to brain organization. Stimulation of the brain is essential during sensitive periods in brain development—periods in which the brain is growing most rapidly. Appropriate early stimulation promotes **experience-expectant brain growth,** which depends on ordinary experiences. No evidence exists for a sensitive period in the first few years for **experience-dependent brain growth,** which relies on specific learning experiences. In fact, environments that overwhelm children with inappropriately advanced expectations can undermine the brain's potential.

© ERIN HOGAN/GETTY IMAGES/PHOTODISC

How does the organization of sleep and wakefulness change over the first two years?

» Infants' changing arousal patterns are primarily affected by brain growth, but the social environment also plays a role. Periods of sleep and wakefulness become fewer but longer, increasingly conforming to a night–day schedule. Parents in Western nations try to get their babies to sleep through the night much earlier than parents throughout most of the world, who are more likely to sleep with their babies.

Influences on Early Physical Growth

Cite evidence that heredity, nutrition, and affection and stimulation contribute to early physical growth.

» Twin and adoption studies reveal the contribution of heredity to body size and rate of physical growth.

» Breast milk is ideally suited to infants' growth needs. Breastfeeding protects against disease and prevents malnutrition and infant death in poverty-stricken areas of the world.

» Most infants and toddlers can eat nutritious foods freely, without risk of becoming overweight. However, the relationship between rapid weight gain in infancy and later obesity is strengthening. Breastfeeding, limiting sugary and fatty foods, and encouraging energetic play are ways parents can help children maintain desirable weight.

» **Marasmus** and **kwashiorkor** are dietary diseases caused by malnutrition that affect many children in developing countries and, if prolonged, can permanently stunt body growth and brain development. **Nonorganic failure to thrive,** which occurs in infants who are adequately nourished but lack affection and stimulation, illustrates the importance of these factors in normal physical growth.

Learning Capacities

Describe infant learning capacities, the conditions under which they occur, and the unique value of each.

» **Classical conditioning** is based on the infant's ability to associate events that usually occur together in the everyday world. Infants can be classically conditioned most easily when the pairing of an **unconditioned stimulus (UCS)** and a **conditioned stimulus (CS)** has survival value—for example, learning which stimuli regularly accompany feeding.

» In **operant conditioning,** infants act on their environment and their behavior is followed by either **reinforcers,** which increase the occurrence of a preceding behavior, or **punishment,** which either removes a desirable stimulus or presents an unpleasant one to decrease the occurrence of a response. In young infants, interesting sights and sounds and pleasurable caregiver interaction serve as effective reinforcers.

» **Habituation** and **recovery** reveal that at birth, babies are attracted to novelty. Novelty preference (recovery to a novel stimulus) assesses recent memory, whereas familiarity preference (recovery to the familiar stimulus) assesses remote memory.

» Newborns have a primitive ability to imitate adults' facial expressions and gestures. **Imitation** contributes to the parent–infant bond and is a powerful means of learning, though whether it is a voluntary capacity in newborns remains controversial.

Motor Development

Describe the general course of motor development during the first 2 years, along with factors that influence it.

» Motor development follows the cephalocaudal and proximodistal trends, though some milestones deviate sharply from these patterns. According to the **dynamic systems theory of motor development,** children acquire new motor skills by combining existing skills into increasingly complex systems of action. Each new skill is a joint product of central nervous system development, movement possibilities of the body, the child's goals, and environmental supports for the skill. Cultural values and child-rearing customs also contribute to the emergence and refinement of early motor skills.

© DON DESPAIN/WWW.REKINDLEPHOTO.COM/ALAMY

» During the first year, infants perfect reaching and grasping. Reaching gradually becomes more accurate and flexible, and the clumsy ulnar grasp is transformed into a refined pincer grasp.

Perceptual Development

What changes in hearing, depth and pattern perception, and intermodal perception take place during infancy?

» Infants organize sounds into increasingly complex patterns and, in the middle of the first year, become more sensitive to the sounds of their own language. They have an impressive **statistical learning capacity,** which enables them to detect regular sound patterns for which they will later learn meanings.

» Rapid maturation of the eye and visual centers in the brain supports the development of focusing, color discrimination, and visual acuity during the first half-year. The ability to scan the environment and track moving objects also improves.

» Research on depth perception reveals that responsiveness to motion cues develops first, followed by sensitivity to binocular and then to pictorial cues. Experience in crawling enhances depth perception and other aspects of three-dimensional understanding, but babies must learn to avoid drop-offs for each body position.

» **Contrast sensitivity** accounts for early pattern preferences. At first, babies stare at single, high-contrast features and often focus on the edges of a pattern. At 2 to 3 months, they explore a pattern's internal features and start to detect pattern organization. Over time, they discriminate increasingly complex, meaningful patterns.

» Newborns prefer to look at and track simple, facelike stimuli. However, researchers disagree on whether they have an innate tendency to orient toward human faces. Around 2 months, they recognize and prefer their mother's facial features, and at 3 months, they distinguish the features of different faces. In the second half-year, they perceive emotional expressions as meaningful wholes.

» From the start, infants are capable of **intermodal perception**—combining information across sensory modalities. Detection of amodal relations (such as common tempo or rhythm) precedes and may provide a basis for detecting other intermodal matches.

© LAURA DWIGHT PHOTOGRAPHY

Explain differentiation theory of perceptual development.

» According to **differentiation theory,** perceptual development is a matter of detecting invariant features in a constantly changing perceptual world. Acting on the world plays a major role in perceptual differentiation. According to a more cognitive view, at an early age, infants impose meaning on what they perceive. Many researchers combine these two ideas.

Important Terms and Concepts

brain plasticity (p. 124)
cephalocaudal trend (p. 121)
cerebral cortex (p. 124)
classical conditioning (p. 133)
conditioned response (CR) (p. 133)
conditioned stimulus (CS) (p. 133)
contrast sensitivity (p. 144)
differentiation theory (p. 147)
dynamic systems theory of motor development (p. 138)
experience-dependent brain growth (p. 127)
experience-expectant brain growth (p. 127)
glial cells (p. 122)
habituation (p. 134)
imitation (p. 135)
intermodal perception (p. 146)
kwashiorkor (p. 132)
lateralization (p. 124)
marasmus (p. 132)
mirror neurons (p. 136)
myelination (p. 122)
neurons (p. 121)
neurotransmitters (p. 122)
nonorganic failure to thrive (p. 133)
operant conditioning (p. 134)
proximodistal trend (p. 121)
punishment (p. 134)
recovery (p. 135)
reinforcer (p. 134)
statistical learning capacity (p. 141)
synapses (p. 121)
synaptic pruning (p. 122)
unconditioned response (UCR) (p. 133)
unconditioned stimulus (UCS) (p. 133)

© KEN SEET/CORBIS

This grandmother shares her grandchild's curiosity and delight in discovery. With the sensitive support of caring adults, infants' and toddlers' cognition and language develop rapidly.

CHAPTER 5

Cognitive Development in Infancy and Toddlerhood

When Caitlin, Grace, and Timmy gathered at Ginette's child-care home, the playroom was alive with activity. The three spirited explorers, each nearly 18 months old, were bent on discovery. Grace dropped shapes through holes in a plastic box that Ginette held and adjusted so the harder ones would fall smoothly into place. Once a few shapes were inside, Grace grabbed the box and shook it, squealing with delight as the lid fell open and the shapes scattered around her. The clatter attracted Timmy, who picked up a shape, carried it to the railing at the top of the basement steps, and dropped it overboard, then followed with a teddy bear, a ball, his shoe, and a spoon. Meanwhile, Caitlin pulled open a drawer, unloaded a set of wooden bowls, stacked them in a pile, knocked it over, and then banged two bowls together.

As the toddlers experimented, I could see the beginnings of spoken language—a whole new way of influencing the world. "All gone baw!" Caitlin exclaimed as Timmy tossed the bright red ball down the basement steps. "Bye-bye," Grace chimed in, waving as the ball disappeared from sight. Later that day, Grace revealed that she could use words and gestures to pretend. "Night-night," she said, putting her head down and closing her eyes, ever so pleased that in make-believe, she could decide for herself when and where to go to bed.

© MAYA BARNES JOHANSEN/THE IMAGE WORKS

Over the first two years, the small, reflexive newborn baby becomes a self-assertive, purposeful being who solves simple problems and starts to master the most amazing human ability: language. Parents wonder, How does all this happen so quickly? This question has also captivated researchers, yielding a wealth of findings along with vigorous debate over how to explain the astonishing pace of infant and toddler cognition.

In this chapter, we take up three perspectives on early cognitive development: Piaget's *cognitive-developmental theory, information processing,* and Vygotsky's *sociocultural theory.* We also consider the usefulness of tests that measure infants' and toddlers' intellectual progress. Finally, we look at the beginnings of language. We will see how toddlers' first words build on early cognitive achievements and how, very soon, new words and expressions greatly increase the speed and flexibility of their thinking. Throughout development, cognition and language mutually support each other.

Piaget's Cognitive-Developmental Theory

Swiss theorist Jean Piaget inspired a vision of children as busy, motivated explorers whose thinking develops as they act directly on the environment. Influenced by his background in biology, Piaget believed that the child's mind forms and modifies psychological structures so they achieve a better fit with external reality. Recall from Chapter 1 that in Piaget's theory, children move through four stages between infancy and adolescence. During these stages, all aspects of cognition develop in an integrated fashion, changing in a similar way at about the same time.

Piaget's first stage, the **sensorimotor stage,** spans the first two years of life. Piaget believed that infants and toddlers "think" with their eyes, ears, hands, and other sensorimotor equipment. They cannot yet carry out many activities inside their heads. But by the end of toddlerhood, children can solve practical, everyday problems and represent their experiences in speech, gesture, and play. To appreciate Piaget's view of how these vast changes take place, let's consider some important concepts.

Piaget's Ideas About Cognitive Change

According to Piaget, specific psychological structures—organized ways of making sense of experience called **schemes**—change with age. First schemes are sensorimotor action patterns. For example, at 6 months, Timmy dropped objects in a fairly rigid way, simply letting go of a rattle or teething ring and watching with interest. By 18 months, his "dropping scheme" had become deliberate and creative. In tossing objects down the basement stairs, he threw some in the air, bounced others off walls, released some gently and others forcefully. Soon, instead of just acting on objects, he will show evidence of thinking before he acts. For Piaget, this change marks the transition from sensorimotor to preoperational thought.

In Piaget's theory, two processes, *adaptation* and *organization,* account for changes in schemes.

© LAURA DWIGHT PHOTOGRAPHY

In Piaget's theory, first schemes are motor action patterns. As this 11-month-old repeatedly experiments with her "dropping scheme," her dropping behavior will become more deliberate and varied.

■ **ADAPTATION.** ***TAKE A MOMENT...*** The next time you have a chance, notice how infants and toddlers tirelessly repeat actions that lead to interesting effects. **Adaptation** involves building schemes through direct interaction with the environment. It consists of two complementary activities, *assimilation* and *accommodation.* During **assimilation,** we use our current schemes to interpret the external world. For example, when Timmy dropped objects, he was assimilating them to his sensorimotor "dropping scheme." In **accommodation,** we create new schemes or adjust old ones after noticing that our current ways of thinking do not capture the environment completely. When Timmy dropped objects in different ways, he modified his dropping scheme to take account of the varied properties of objects.

According to Piaget, the balance between assimilation and accommodation varies over time. When children are not changing much, they assimilate more than they accommodate. Piaget called this a state of cognitive *equilibrium,* implying a steady, comfortable condition. During rapid cognitive change, however, children are in a state of *disequilibrium,* or cognitive discomfort. Realizing that new information does not match their current schemes, they shift from assimilation toward accommodation. After modifying their schemes, they move back toward assimilation, exercising their newly changed structures until they are ready to be modified again.

Each time this back-and-forth movement between equilibrium and disequilibrium occurs, more effective schemes are produced. Because the times of greatest accommodation are the earliest ones, the sensorimotor stage is Piaget's most complex period of development.

■ **ORGANIZATION.** Schemes also change through **organization,** a process that takes place internally, apart from direct contact with the environment. Once children form new schemes, they rearrange them, linking them with other schemes to create a strongly interconnected cognitive system. For example, eventually Timmy will relate "dropping" to "throwing" and to his developing understanding of "nearness" and "farness." According to Piaget, schemes truly reach equilibrium when they become part of a broad network of structures that can be jointly applied to the surrounding world (Piaget, 1936/1952).

In the following sections, we will first describe infant development as Piaget saw it, noting research that supports his observations. Then we will consider evidence demonstrating that, in some ways, babies' cognitive competence is more advanced than Piaget believed.

The Sensorimotor Stage

The difference between the newborn baby and the 2-year-old child is so vast that Piaget divided the sensorimotor stage into six substages, summarized in Table 5.1. Piaget based this sequence on a very small sample: his own three children. He observed his son and two daughters carefully and also presented them with everyday problems (such as hidden objects) that helped reveal their understanding of the world.

According to Piaget, at birth infants know so little about the world that they cannot purposefully explore it. The **circular reaction** provides a special means of adapting their first schemes. It involves stumbling onto a new experience caused by the baby's own motor activity. The reaction is "circular" because, as the infant tries to repeat the event again and again, a sensorimotor response that first occurred by chance becomes strengthened into a new scheme. Consider Caitlin, who at age 2 months accidentally made a smacking noise after a feeding. Finding the sound intriguing, she tried to repeat it until she became quite expert at smacking her lips.

The circular reaction initially centers on the infant's own body but later turns outward, toward manipulation of objects. In the second year, it becomes experimental and creative, aimed at producing novel outcomes. Infants' difficulty inhibiting new and interesting behaviors may underlie the circular reaction. This immaturity in inhibition seems to be adaptive, helping to ensure that new skills will not be interrupted before they strengthen (Carey & Markman, 1999). Piaget considered revisions in the circular reaction so important that, as Table 5.1 shows, he named the sensorimotor substages after them.

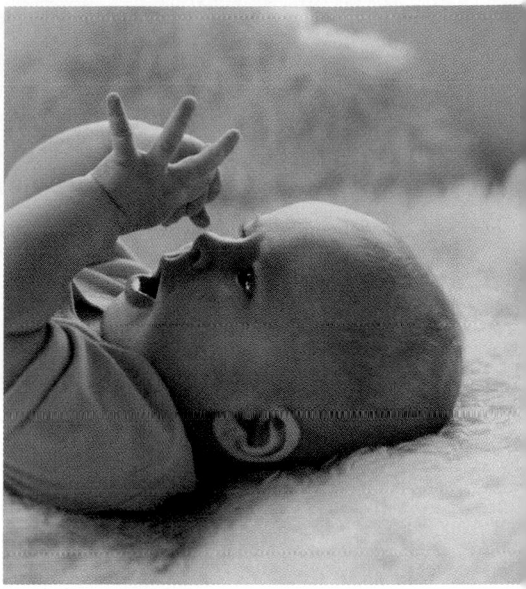

This 3-month-old sees his hands touch, open, and close. He tries to repeat these movements, in a primary circular reaction that helps him gain voluntary control over his behavior.

■ **REPEATING CHANCE BEHAVIORS.** Piaget saw newborn reflexes as the building blocks of sensorimotor intelligence. In Substage 1, babies suck, grasp, and look in much the same way, no matter what experiences they encounter. In one amusing example, Carolyn described how 2-week-old Caitlin lay on the bed next to her sleeping father. Suddenly, he awoke with a start. Caitlin had latched on and begun to suck on his back!

Around 1 month, as babies enter Substage 2, they start to gain voluntary control over their actions through the *primary circular reaction*, by repeating chance behaviors largely motivated by basic needs. This leads to some simple motor habits, such as sucking their fists or thumbs. Babies of this substage also begin to vary their behavior in response to environmental demands. For example, they open their mouths differently for a nipple than for a spoon. And they start to anticipate events. At 3 months, when Timmy awoke from his nap, he cried out with hunger. But as soon as Vanessa entered the room, he stopped crying. He knew that feeding time was near.

■ **TABLE 5.1** ■ ***Summary of Piaget's Sensorimotor Stage***

SENSORIMOTOR SUBSTAGE	TYPICAL ADAPTIVE BEHAVIORS
1. Reflexive schemes (birth–1 month)	Newborn reflexes (see Chapter 3, page 107)
2. Primary circular reactions (1–4 months)	Simple motor habits centered around the infant's own body; limited anticipation of events
3. Secondary circular reactions (4–8 months)	Actions aimed at repeating interesting effects in the surrounding world; imitation of familiar behaviors
4. Coordination of secondary circular reactions (8–12 months)	Intentional, or goal-directed, behavior; ability to find a hidden object in the first location in which it is hidden (object permanence); improved anticipation of events; imitation of behaviors slightly different from those the infant usually performs
5. Tertiary circular reactions (12–18 months)	Exploration of the properties of objects by acting on them in novel ways; imitation of novel behaviors; ability to search in several locations for a hidden object (accurate *A–B* search)
6. Mental representation (18 months–2 years)	Internal depictions of objects and events, as indicated by sudden solutions to problems; ability to find an object that has been moved while out of sight (invisible displacement); deferred imitation; and make-believe play

During Substage 3, from 4 to 8 months, infants sit up and reach for and manipulate objects. These motor achievements strengthen the *secondary circular reaction,* through which babies try to repeat interesting events in the surrounding environment that are caused by their own actions. For example, 4-month-old Caitlin accidentally knocked a toy hung in front of her, producing a fascinating swinging motion. Over the next three days, Caitlin tried to repeat this effect and, when she succeeded, gleefully repeated her new "hitting" scheme. Improved control over their own behavior permits infants to imitate others' behavior more effectively. However, 4- to 8-month-olds cannot adapt flexibly and quickly enough to imitate novel behaviors (Kaye & Marcus, 1981). Therefore, although they enjoy watching an adult demonstrate a game of pat-a-cake, they are not yet able to participate.

■ **INTENTIONAL BEHAVIOR.** In Substage 4, 8- to 12-month-olds combine schemes into new, more complex action sequences. As a result, actions that lead to new schemes no longer have a hit-or-miss quality—*accidentally* bringing the thumb to the mouth or *happening* to hit the toy. Instead, 8- to 12-month-olds can engage in **intentional,** or **goal-directed, behavior,** coordinating schemes deliberately to solve simple problems. Consider Piaget's famous object-hiding task, in which he shows the baby an attractive toy and then hides it behind his hand or under a cover. Infants of this substage can find the object by coordinating two schemes—"pushing" aside the obstacle and "grasping" the toy. Piaget regarded these action sequences as the foundation for all problem solving.

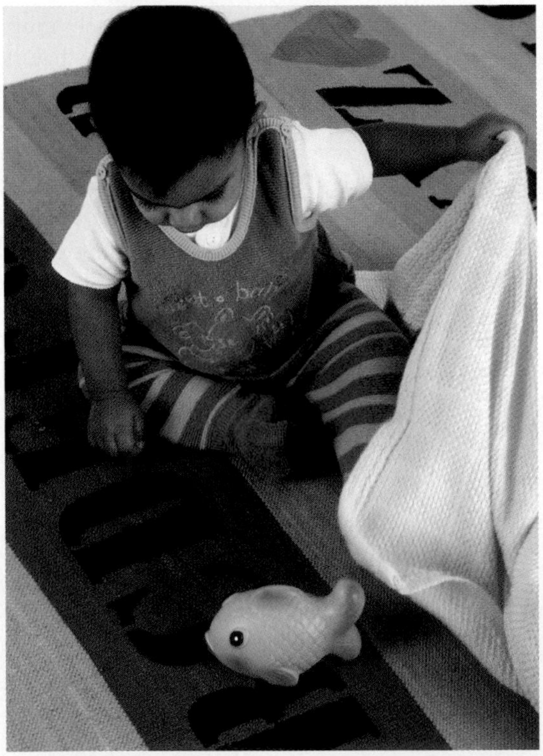

The capacity to search for and find hidden objects between 8 and 12 months of age marks a major advance in cognitive development.

Retrieving hidden objects reveals that infants have begun to master **object permanence,** the understanding that objects continue to exist when out of sight. But awareness of object permanence is not yet complete. Babies still make the *A-not-B search error:* If they reach several times for an object at a first hiding place *(A),* then see it moved to a second *(B),* they still search for it in the first hiding place *(A).* Consequently, Piaget concluded, they do not have a clear image of the object as persisting when hidden from view.

Infants of Substage 4, who can better anticipate events, sometimes use their capacity for intentional behavior to try to change those events. At 10 months, Timmy crawled after Vanessa when she put on her coat, whimpering to keep her from leaving. Also, babies can now imitate behaviors slightly different from those they usually perform. After watching someone else, they try to stir with a spoon, push a toy car, or drop raisins into a cup. Again, they draw on intentional behavior, purposefully modifying schemes to fit an observed action (Piaget, 1945/1951).

In Substage 5, from 12 to 18 months, the *tertiary circular reaction,* in which toddlers repeat behaviors with variation, emerges. Recall how Timmy dropped objects over the basement steps, trying first this action, then that, then another. Because they approach the world in this deliberately exploratory way, 12- to 18-month-olds become better problem solvers. For example, Grace figured out how to fit a shape through a hole in a container by turning and twisting it until it fell through and how to use a stick to get toys that were out of reach. According to Piaget, this capacity to experiment leads to a more advanced understanding of object permanence. Toddlers look for a hidden toy in several locations, displaying an accurate *A–B* search. Their more flexible action patterns also permit them to imitate many more behaviors, such as stacking blocks, scribbling on paper, and making funny faces.

■ **MENTAL REPRESENTATION.** Substage 6 brings the ability to create **mental representations**—internal depictions of information that the mind can manipulate. Our most powerful mental representations are of two kinds: (1) *images,* or mental pictures of objects, people, and spaces; and (2) *concepts,* or categories in which similar objects or events are grouped together. We can use a mental image to retrace our steps when we've misplaced something or to imitate someone's behavior long after we've observed it. And by thinking in concepts and labeling them (for example, "ball" for all rounded, movable objects used in play), we become more efficient thinkers, organizing our diverse experiences into meaningful, manageable, and memorable units.

Piaget noted that 18- to 24-month-olds arrive at solutions suddenly rather than through trial-and-error behavior. In doing so, they seem to experiment with actions inside their heads—evidence that they can mentally represent their experiences. For example, at 19 months, Grace—after bumping her new push toy against a wall—paused for a moment as if to "think," then immediately turned the toy in a new direction.

Representation also enables older toddlers to solve advanced object permanence problems involving *invisible displacement*—finding a toy moved while out of sight, such as into a small box while under a cover. It permits **deferred imitation**—the ability to remember and copy the behavior of models who are not present. And it makes possible **make-believe play,** in which children act out everyday and imaginary activities. As the sensorimotor stage draws to a close, mental symbols have become major instruments of thinking.

Follow-Up Research on Infant Cognitive Development

Many studies suggest that infants display a wide array of understandings earlier than Piaget believed. Recall the operant conditioning research reviewed in Chapter 4, in which newborns sucked vigorously on a nipple to gain access to interesting sights and sounds. This behavior, which closely resembles Piaget's secondary circular reaction, shows that infants explore and control the external world long before 4 to 8 months. In fact, they do so as soon as they are born.

To discover what infants know about hidden objects and other aspects of physical reality, researchers often use the **violation-of-expectation method.** They may *habituate* babies to a physical event (expose them to the event until their looking declines) to familiarize them with a situation in which their knowledge will be tested. Or they may simply show babies an *expected event* (one that follows physical laws) and an *unexpected event* (a variation of the first event that violates physical laws). Heightened attention to the unexpected event suggests that the infant is "surprised" by a deviation from physical reality and, therefore, is aware of that aspect of the physical world.

The violation-of-expectation method is controversial. Some researchers believe that it indicates only limited awareness of physical events, not the full-blown, conscious understanding that was Piaget's focus in requiring infants to act on their surroundings, as in searching for hidden objects (Munakata, 2001; Thelen & Smith, 1994). Others maintain that the method reveals only babies' perceptual preference for novelty, not their understanding of experience (Bremner & Mareschal, 2004; Hood, 2004; Kagan, 2008). Let's examine this debate in light of recent evidence.

■ **OBJECT PERMANENCE.** In a series of studies using the violation-of-expectation method, Renée Baillargeon and her collaborators claimed to have found evidence for object permanence in the first few months of life. One of Baillargeon's studies is illustrated in Figure 5.1 (Aguiar & Baillargeon, 2002; Baillargeon & DeVos, 1991). After habituating to a short and a tall carrot moving behind a screen, infants were given two test events: (1) an *expected event,* in which the short carrot moved behind a screen, could not been seen in its window, and reappeared on the other side; and (2) an *unexpected event,* in which the tall carrot moved behind a screen, could not be seen in its window (although it was taller than the window's lower edge), and reappeared. Infants as young as 2½ to 3½ months looked longer at the unexpected event, suggesting that they had some awareness that an object moved behind a screen would continue to exist.

Additional violation-of-expectation studies yielded similar results (Baillargeon, 2004; Wang, Baillargeon, & Paterson, 2005). But several researchers using similar procedures failed to confirm some of Baillargeon's findings (Bogartz, Shinskey, & Schilling,

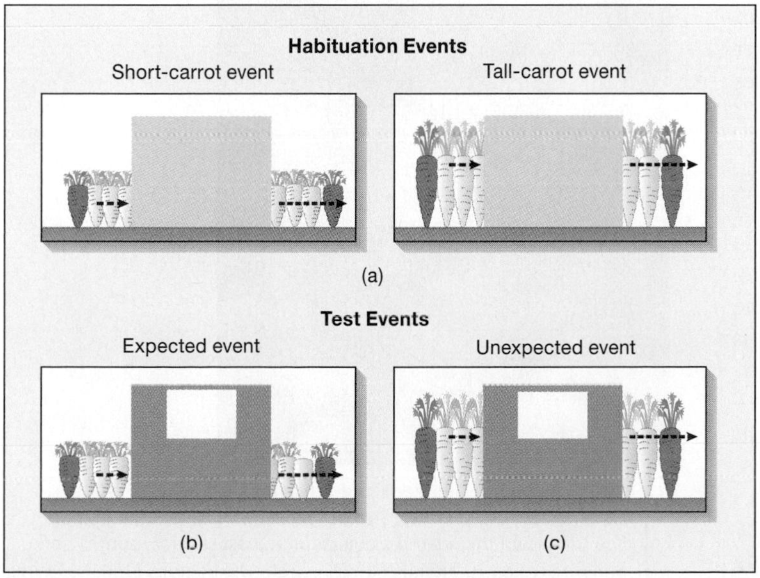

■ **FIGURE 5.1** ■ **Testing young infants for understanding of object permanence using the violation-of-expectation method.** (a) First, infants were habituated to two events: a short carrot and a tall carrot moving behind a yellow screen, on alternate trials. Next, the researchers presented two test events. The color of the screen was changed to help infants notice its window. (b) In the *expected event,* the carrot shorter than the window's lower edge moved behind the blue screen and reappeared on the other side. (c) In the *unexpected event,* the carrot taller than the window's lower edge moved behind the screen and did not appear in the window, but then emerged intact on the other side. Infants as young as 2½ to 3½ months recovered to (looked longer at) the *unexpected event,* suggesting that they had some understanding of object permanence. (From R. Baillargeon and J. DeVos, 1991, "Object Permanence in Young Infants: Further Evidence," *Child Development, 62,* p. 1230. © The Society for Research in Child Development. Adapted with permission.)

2000; Cashon & Cohen, 2000; Rivera, Wakeley, & Langer, 1999). Baillargeon and others maintain that these opposing investigations did not include crucial controls. They emphasize that infants look longer at a wide variety of unexpected events involving hidden objects (Newcombe, Sluzenski, & Huttenlocher, 2005; Wang, Baillargeon, & Paterson, 2005). Still, critics question what babies' looking preferences tell us about what they actually know.

But another type of looking behavior suggests that young infants are aware that objects persist when out of view. Four- and 5-month-olds will track a ball's path of movement as it disappears and reappears from behind a barrier, even gazing ahead to where they expect it to emerge (Bertenthal, Longo, & Kenny, 2007; Rosander & von Hofsten, 2004). With age, babies are more likely to fixate on the predicted place of the ball's reappearance and wait for it—evidence of an increasingly secure grasp of object permanence.

In related research, investigators recorded 6-month-olds' ERP brain-wave activity as the babies watched two events on a computer screen. In one, a black square moved until it covered an object, then moved away to reveal the object (object permanence). In the other, as a black square began to move across an object, the object disintegrated (object disappearance) (Kaufman, Csibra, & Johnson, 2005). Only while watching the first event did infants show a particular brain-wave pattern in the right temporal lobe—the same pattern adults exhibit when told to sustain a mental image of an object.

If young infants do have some notion of object permanence, which strengthens with age, how do we explain Piaget's finding that even babies who are capable of reaching do not try to search for hidden objects? Consistent with Piaget's theory, searching for hidden objects is a true cognitive advance because infants solve some object-hiding tasks before others. Ten-month-olds search for an object placed on a table and covered by a cloth before they search for an object that a hand deposits under a cloth (Moore & Meltzoff, 1999). In the second, more difficult task, infants seem to expect the object to reappear in the hand from which it initially disappeared. When the hand emerges without the object, they conclude that there is no other place the object could be. Not until 14 months can most babies infer that the hand deposited the object under the cloth.

Once 8- to 12-month-olds search for hidden objects, they make the *A*-not-*B* search error. Some research suggests that they search at *A* (where they found the object previously) instead of *B* (its most recent location) because they have trouble inhibiting a previously rewarded response (Diamond, Cruttenden, & Neiderman, 1994). Another possibility is that after finding the object several times at *A*, they do not attend closely when it is hidden at *B* (Ruffman & Langman, 2002). A more comprehensive explanation is that a complex, dynamic system of factors—having built a habit of reaching toward *A*, continuing to look at *A*, having the hiding place at *B* appear similar to the one at *A*, and maintaining a constant body posture—increases the chances that the baby will make the *A*-not-*B* search error. Disrupting any one of these factors increases 10-month-olds' accurate searching at *B* (Thelen et al., 2001).

In sum, mastery of object permanence is a gradual achievement. According to one view, younger babies presented with a simple object-hiding task and older babies presented with an *A–B* search task have a remarkable appreciation of an object's continued existence and location, but at first they have difficulty translating what they know into a successful search strategy (Baillargeon, 2000; Berthier et al., 2001). Another view is that babies' understanding becomes increasingly complex with age: They must distinguish the object from the barrier concealing it, keep track of its whereabouts, and use this knowledge to find it (Cohen & Cashon, 2006; Munakata & Stedron, 2002). Success at object search tasks coincides with rapid development of the frontal lobes of the cerebral cortex (Bell, 1998). Also crucial are a wide variety of experiences perceiving, acting on, and remembering objects.

■ **MENTAL REPRESENTATION.** In Piaget's theory, infants lead purely sensorimotor lives, unable to mentally represent experience until about 18 months of age. Yet 8-month-olds' ability to recall the location of a hidden object after delays of more than a minute, and 14-month-olds' recall after delays of a day or more, indicate that babies construct mental representations of objects and their whereabouts (McDonough, 1999; Moore & Meltzoff, 2004). And in studies of deferred imitation and problem solving, representational thought is evident even earlier.

Deferred Imitation. Piaget studied imitation by noting when his three children demonstrated it in their everyday behavior. Under these conditions, a great deal must be known about the infant's daily life to be sure that deferred imitation—

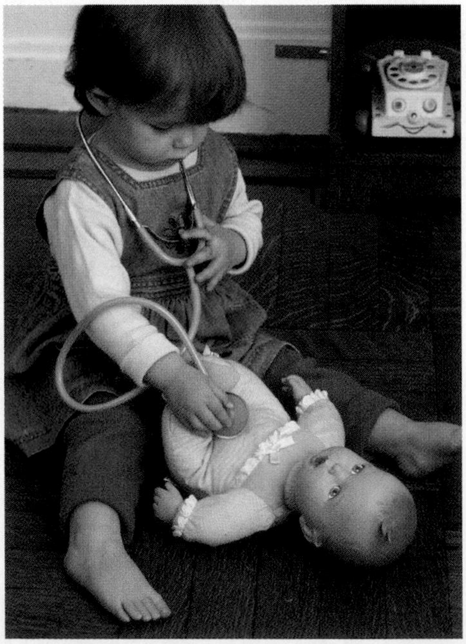
© LAURA DWIGHT/CORBIS

As this 18-month-old reenacts a procedure she herself has experienced, she demonstrates her capacity for deferred imitation. She can retain modeled behaviors for at least several months and imitate across situational changes—from the doctor's office to home.

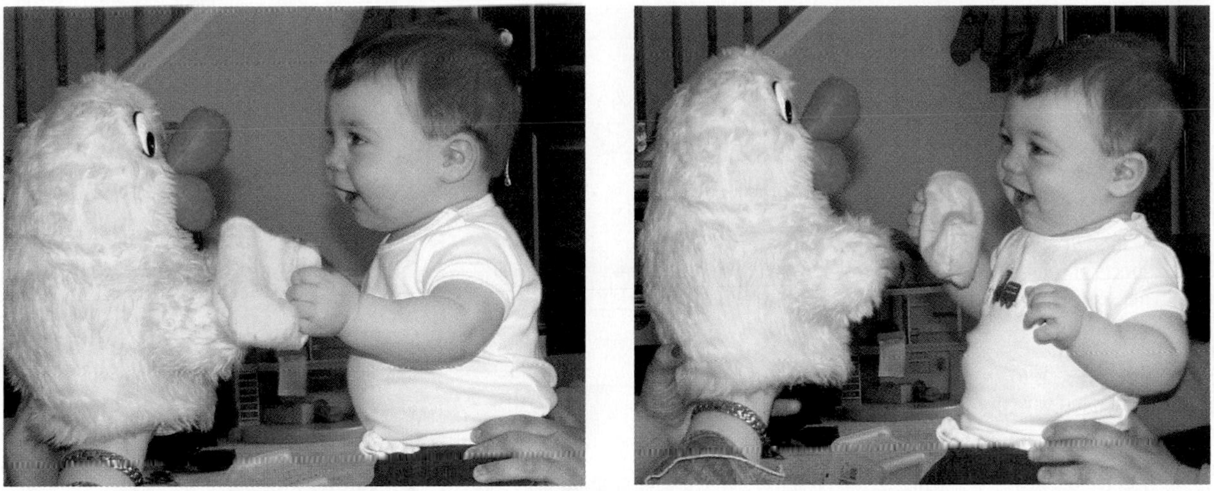

COURTESY OF CAROLYN ROVEE-COLLIER

■ **FIGURE 5.2** ■ **Testing infants for deferred imitation.** After researchers performed a novel series of actions with a puppet, this 6-month-old imitated the actions a day later—at left, removing the glove; at right, shaking the glove to ring a bell inside. During the second half-year, gains in recall are evident in deferred imitation of others' behaviors over longer delays.

which requires infants to represent a model's past behavior—has occurred.

Laboratory research suggests that deferred imitation is present at 6 weeks of age! Infants who watched an unfamiliar adult's facial expression imitated it when exposed to the same adult the next day (Meltzoff & Moore, 1994). As motor capacities improve, infants copy actions with objects. In one study, an adult showed 6- and 9-month-olds a novel series of actions with a puppet: taking its glove off, shaking the glove to ring a bell inside, and replacing the glove. When tested a day later, infants who had seen the novel actions were far more likely to display them (see Figure 5.2). And when researchers paired a second, motionless puppet with the first puppet a day before the demonstration, infants generalized the novel actions to a new, very different-looking puppet (Barr, Marrott, & Rovee-Collier, 2003).

Between 12 and 18 months, toddlers use deferred imitation skillfully to enrich their range of sensorimotor schemes. They retain modeled behaviors for at least several months, copy the actions of peers as well as adults, and imitate across a change in context—for example, enact at home a behavior learned at child care or on TV (Barr & Hayne, 1999; Hayne, Boniface, & Barr, 2000; Klein & Meltzoff, 1999). Over the second year, toddlers also gain in ability to imitate an adult's action on toys in the order in which those actions occurred (Bauer, 2002b, 2006). And when toddlers imitate in correct sequence, they remember more modeled behaviors (Knopf, Kraus, & Kressley-Mba, 2006).

Toddlers even imitate rationally, by inferring others' intentions! Fourteen-month-olds are more likely to imitate purposeful than accidental behaviors (Carpenter, Akhtar, & Tomasello, 1998). And they adapt their imitative acts to a model's goals. If 12-month-olds see an adult perform an unusual action for fun (make a toy dog enter a miniature house by jumping through the chimney, even though its door is wide open), they copy the behavior. But if the adult engages in the odd behavior because she *must* (she makes the dog go through the chimney only after first trying to use the door and finding it locked), 12-month-olds typically imitate the more efficient action (putting the dog through the door) (Schwier et al., 2006).

Around 18 months, toddlers can imitate actions an adult *tries* to produce, even if these are not fully realized (Meltzoff, 1995). On one occasion, Ginette attempted to pour some raisins into a bag but missed, spilling them onto the counter. A moment later, Grace began dropping the raisins into the bag, indicating that she had inferred Ginette's goal (Falck-Ytter, Gredebäck, & von Hofsten, 2006). By age 2, children mimic entire social roles—mommy, daddy, baby—during make-believe play.

Problem Solving. As Piaget indicated, around 7 to 8 months, infants develop intentional action sequences, which they use to solve simple problems, such as pulling on a cloth to obtain a toy resting on its far end (Willatts, 1999). Soon after, infants' representational skills permit more effective problem solving than Piaget's theory suggests.

By 10 to 12 months, infants can *solve problems by analogy*—apply a solution strategy from one problem to other relevant problems. In one study, babies were given three similar problems, each requiring them to overcome a barrier, grasp a string, and pull it to get an attractive toy. The problems differed in all aspects of their superficial features (see Figure 5.3 on page 158). For the first problem, the parent demonstrated the solution and encouraged the baby to imitate. Infants obtained the toy more readily with each additional problem (Chen, Sanchez, & Campbell, 1997). In another study, 12-month-olds who were repeatedly presented with a spoon in the same orientation (handle to one side) readily adapted their motor actions when the spoon was presented with the handle to the other side, successfully transporting food to their mouths most of the time (McCarty & Keen, 2005). These findings suggest that at the end of the first year, infants form flexible mental representations of how to use tools to get objects.

■ **FIGURE 5.3** ■ **Analogical problem solving by 10- to 12-month-olds.** After the parent demonstrated the solution to problem (a), infants solved problems (b) and (c) with increasing efficiency, even though these problems differed from problem (a) in all aspects of their superficial features. (From Z. Chen, R. P. Sanchez, & T. Campbell, 1997, "From Beyond to Within Their Grasp: The Rudiments of Analogical Problem Solving in 10- to 13-Month-Olds," *Developmental Psychology, 33,* p. 792. Copyright © 1997 by the American Psychological Association. Adapted with permission of the American Psychological Association.)

With age, children become better at reasoning by analogy, applying relevant strategies across increasingly dissimilar situations (Goswami, 1996). But even in the first year, infants have some ability to move beyond trial-and-error experimentation, represent solutions mentally, and use them in new contexts.

Evaluation of the Sensorimotor Stage

Table 5.2 summarizes the remarkable cognitive attainments we have just considered. ***TAKE A MOMENT...*** Compare this table with Piaget's description of the sensorimotor substages in Table 5.1 on page 153. You will see that infants anticipate events, actively search for hidden objects, master the *A–B* object search, flexibly vary their sensorimotor schemes, and engage in make-believe play within Piaget's time frame. Yet other capacities—including secondary circular reactions, understanding of object properties, first signs of object permanence, deferred imitation, and problem solving by analogy—emerge earlier than Piaget expected. These findings show that the cognitive attainments of infancy do not develop together in the neat, stepwise fashion that Piaget assumed.

Recent research raises questions about Piaget's view of how infant development takes place. Consistent with Piaget's ideas, sensorimotor action helps infants construct some forms of knowledge. For example, in Chapter 4, we saw that crawling enhances depth perception and ability to find hidden objects,

■ **TABLE 5.2** ■ ***Some Cognitive Attainments of Infancy and Toddlerhood***

AGE	COGNITIVE ATTAINMENTS
Birth–1 month	Secondary circular reactions using limited motor skills, such as sucking a nipple to gain access to interesting sights and sounds
1–4 months	Possible awareness of object permanence, object solidity, and gravity, as suggested by violation-of-expectation findings; deferred imitation of an adult's facial expression over a short delay (one day)
4–8 months	Improved knowledge of object properties and of basic numerical knowledge, as suggested by violation-of-expectation findings; deferred imitation of an adult's novel actions on objects over a short delay (one day)
8–12 months	Ability to search for a hidden object when covered by a cloth; ability to solve simple problems by analogy to a previous problem
12–18 months	Ability to search for a hidden object when a hand deposits it under a cloth and when it is moved from one location to another (accurate *A–B* search). Deferred imitation of an adult's novel actions on an object over a long delay (at least several months) and across a change in situation (from child care to home, from TV to everyday life); rational imitation, taking into account the model's intentions
18 months–2 years	Deferred imitation of actions an adult tries to produce, again indicating a capacity to infer others' intentions; imitation of everyday behaviors in make-believe play

TAKE A MOMENT... Which of the capacities listed in the table indicate that mental representation emerges earlier than Piaget believed?

and handling objects fosters awareness of object properties. Yet we have also seen that infants comprehend a great deal before they are capable of the motor behaviors that Piaget assumed led to those understandings. How can we account for babies' amazing cognitive accomplishments?

■ **ALTERNATIVE EXPLANATIONS.** Unlike Piaget, who thought young babies constructed all mental representations out of sensorimotor activity, most researchers now believe that infants have some built-in cognitive equipment for making sense of experience. But intense disagreement exists over the extent of this initial understanding. As we have seen, much evidence on young infants' cognition rests on the violation-of-expectation method. Researchers who lack confidence in this method argue that babies' cognitive starting point is limited (Campos et al., 2008; Cohen & Cashon, 2006; Kagan, 2008). For example, some believe that newborns begin life with a set of biases for attending to certain information and with general-purpose learning procedures, such as powerful techniques for analyzing complex perceptual information. Together, these capacities enable infants to construct a wide variety of schemes (Bahrick, Lickliter, & Flom, 2004; Huttenlocher, 2002; Mandler, 2004; Quinn, 2008).

Others, convinced by violation-of-expectation findings, believe that infants start out with impressive understandings. According to this **core knowledge perspective,** babies are born with a set of innate knowledge systems, or *core domains of thought.* Each of these prewired understandings permits a ready grasp of new, related information and therefore supports early, rapid development (Carey & Markman, 1999; Leslie, 2004; Spelke, 2004; Spelke & Kinzler, 2007). Core knowledge theorists argue that infants could not make sense of the complex stimulation around them without having been genetically "set up" in the course of evolution to comprehend its crucial aspects.

Researchers have conducted many studies of infants' *physical knowledge,* including object permanence, object solidity (that one object cannot move through another), and gravity (that an object will fall without support). Violation-of-expectation findings suggest that in the first few months, infants have some awareness of all these basic object properties and quickly build on this knowledge (Baillargeon, 2004; Hespos & Baillargeon, 2001; Luo & Baillargeon, 2005; Spelke, 2000). Core knowledge theorists also assume that an inherited foundation of *linguistic knowledge* enables swift language acquisition in early childhood—a possibility we will consider later in this chapter. Further, these theorists argue, infants' early orientation toward people initiates rapid development of *psychological knowledge*—in particular, understanding of mental states, such as intentions, emotions, desires, and beliefs, which we will address further in Chapter 6.

Researchers have even examined infants' *numerical knowledge!* In the best-known study, 5-month-olds saw a screen raised to hide a single toy animal, then watched a hand place a second toy behind the screen. Finally the screen was removed to reveal either one or two toys. If infants kept track of the two objects (requiring them to add one object to another), then they should look longer at the unexpected, one-toy display—which is what they did (see Figure 5.4) (Wynn, Bloom, &

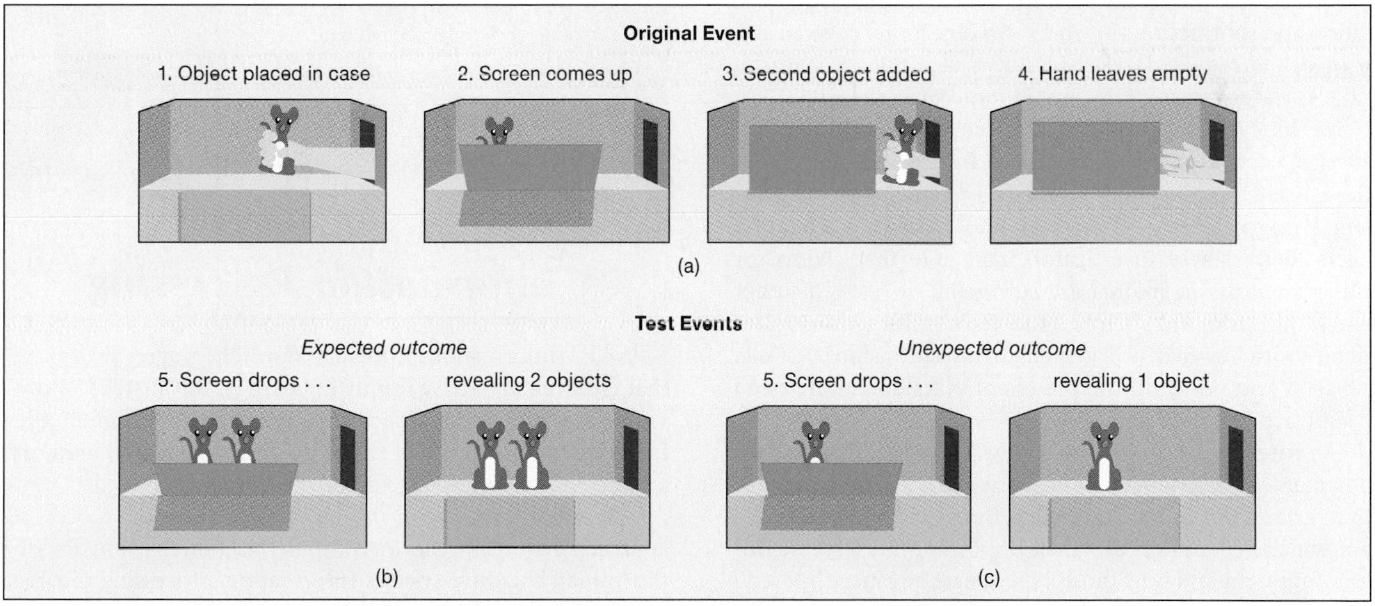

■ **FIGURE 5.4** ■ **Testing infants for basic number concepts.** (a) First, infants saw a screen raised in front of a toy animal. Then an identical toy was added behind the screen. Next, the researchers presented two outcomes. (b) In the *expected outcome,* the screen dropped to reveal two toy animals. (c) In the *unexpected outcome,* the screen dropped to reveal one toy animal. Five-month-olds shown the unexpected outcome looked longer than did 5-month-olds shown the expected outcome. The researchers concluded that infants can discriminate the quantities "one" and "two" and use that knowledge to perform simple addition: 1 + 1 = 2. A variation of this procedure suggested that 5-month-olds could also do simple subtraction: 2 – 1 = 1. (From K. Wynn, 1992, "Addition and Subtraction by Human Infants," *Nature, 358,* p. 749. © 1992 by Nature Publishing Group. Reprinted by permission of Nature Publishing Group. Adapted by permission of Macmillan Publishers, Ltd.)

Did this toddler acquire the knowledge to build a block tower by repeatedly acting on objects, as Piaget assumed? Or did he begin life with innate physical knowledge that enables him to understand objects and their relationships quickly, with little hands-on exploration?

Chiang, 2002). These findings and those of similar investigations suggest that babies can discriminate quantities up to three and use that knowledge to perform simple arithmetic—both addition and subtraction (in which two objects are covered and one object is removed) (Kobayashi et al., 2004; Kobayashi, Hiraki, & Hasegawa, 2005; Wynn, Bloom, & Chiang, 2002).

But like other violation-of-expectation results, babies' numerical capacities are controversial. In experiments similar to those just described, infants' looking preferences were inconsistent (Langer, Gillette, & Arriaga, 2003; Wakeley, Rivera, & Langer, 2000). These investigators also note that claims for number concepts in infants are surprising, in view of other research indicating that before 14 to 16 months, toddlers have difficulty with less-than and greater-than relationships between small sets. And not until the preschool years do children add and subtract small sets correctly.

The core knowledge perspective, while emphasizing native endowment, acknowledges that experience is essential for children to extend this initial knowledge. But so far, it has said little about which experiences are most important in each core domain of thought and how those experiences advance children's thinking. Despite ongoing challenges from critics, who take issue with the assumption that infants' looking behaviors indicate that they are endowed with *knowledge,* core knowledge research has sharpened the field's focus on clarifying the starting point of human cognition and on carefully tracking the changes that build on it.

PIAGET'S LEGACY. Current research on infant cognition yields broad agreement on two issues: First, many cognitive changes of infancy are not abrupt and stagelike but gradual and continuous (Bjorklund, 2004; Courage & Howe, 2002). Second, rather than developing together, various aspects of infant cognition change unevenly because of the challenges posed by different types of tasks and infants' varying experience with them. These ideas serve as the basis for another major approach to cognitive development—*information processing.*

Before turning to this alternative point of view, let's recognize Piaget's enormous contributions. Piaget's work inspired a wealth of research on infant cognition, including studies that challenged his theory. Although his account of development is no longer fully accepted, contemporary theorists are far from consensus on how to modify or replace it. Piaget's observations also have been of great practical value. Teachers and caregivers continue to look to the sensorimotor stage for guidelines on how to create developmentally appropriate environments for infants and toddlers.

ASK YOURSELF

REVIEW
Using the text discussion on pages 155–158, construct an age-related list of infant and toddler cognitive attainments. Which ones are consistent with Piaget's sensorimotor stage? Which develop earlier than Piaget anticipated?

APPLY
Several times, after her father hid a teething biscuit under a red cup, 12-month-old Mimi retrieved it easily. Then Mimi's father hid the biscuit under a nearby yellow cup. Why did Mimi persist in searching for it under the red cup?

REFLECT
Which explanation of infants' cognitive competencies do you prefer, and why?

Information Processing

Information-processing researchers agree with Piaget that children are active, inquiring beings. But instead of providing a single, unified theory of cognitive development, they focus on many aspects of thinking, from attention, memory, and categorization skills to complex problem solving.

Recall from Chapter 1 that the information-processing approach frequently relies on computerlike flowcharts to describe the human cognitive system. Information-processing theorists are not satisfied with general concepts, such as assimilation and accommodation, to describe how children think. Instead, they want to know exactly what individuals of different ages do when faced with a task or problem (Birney et al., 2005; Halford, 2002). The computer model of human thinking is attractive because it is explicit and precise.

Structure of the Information-Processing System

Most information-processing researchers assume that we hold information in three parts of the mental system for processing: *the sensory register; working,* or *short-term, memory;* and *long-term memory* (see Figure 5.5). As information flows through each, we can use **mental strategies** to operate on and transform it, increasing the chances that we will retain information, use it efficiently, and think flexibly, adapting the information to changing circumstances. To understand this more clearly, let's look at each aspect of the mental system.

First, information enters the **sensory register,** where sights and sounds are represented directly and stored briefly. ***TAKE A MOMENT...*** Look around you, and then close your eyes. An image of what you saw persists for a few seconds, but then it decays, or disappears, unless you use mental strategies to preserve it. For example, by *attending to* some information more carefully than to other information, you increase the chances that it will transfer to the next step of the information-processing system.

In the second part of the mind, **working,** or **short-term, memory,** we actively apply mental strategies as we "work" on a limited amount of information. For example, if you are studying this book effectively, you are taking notes, repeating information to yourself, or grouping pieces of information together. Why do you apply these strategies? The sensory register, though limited, can take in a wide panorama of information. The capacity of working memory is more restricted. By meaningfully connecting pieces of information into a single representation, we reduce the number of pieces we must attend to, thereby making room in working memory for more. Also, the more thoroughly we learn information, the more *automatically* we use it. Automatic processing expands working memory by permitting us to focus on other information simultaneously.

To manage its complex activities, a special part of working memory—called the **central executive**—directs the flow of information. It decides what to attend to, coordinates incoming information with information already in the system, and selects, applies, and monitors strategies (Baddeley, 1993, 2000; Pressley & Hilden, 2006). The central executive is the conscious, reflective part of our mental system. It works closely with working memory to direct such activities as comprehension, reasoning, and problem solving.

The longer we hold information in working memory, the more likely it will transfer to the third, and largest, storage area—**long-term memory,** our permanent knowledge base, which is unlimited. In fact, we store so much in long-term memory that *retrieval*—getting information back from the system—can be problematic. To aid retrieval, we apply strategies, just as we do in working memory. Information in long-term memory is *categorized* according to a master plan based on content, much like a library shelving system that allows us to retrieve items easily by following the same network of associations used to store them in the first place.

Information-processing researchers believe that the basic structure of the mental system remains similar throughout life. But the *capacity* of the system—the amount of information that can be retained and processed at once—and the speed with which it can be processed increases, making more complex forms of thinking possible with age (Case, 1998; Kail, 2003). Gains in information-processing capacity are due in part to brain development and in part to improvements in

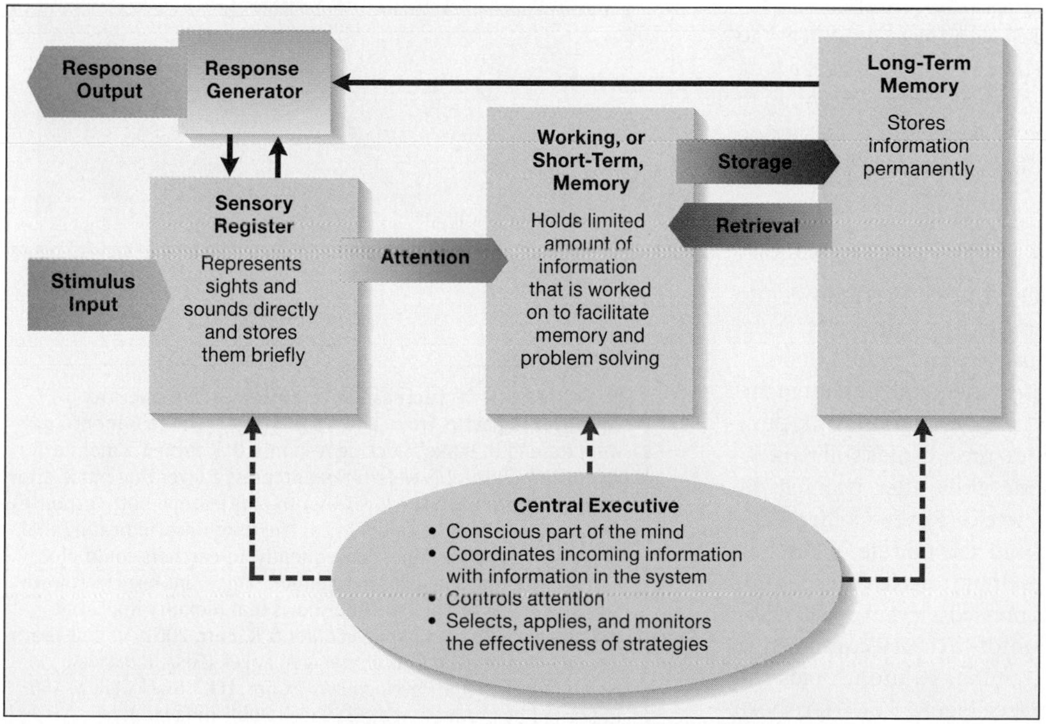

■ **FIGURE 5.5** ■ **Model of the human information-processing system.** Information flows through three parts of the mental system: the *sensory register; working,* or *short-term, memory;* and *long-term memory*. In each, mental strategies can be used to manipulate information, increasing the efficiency and flexibility of thinking and the chances that information will be retained. The *central executive* is the conscious, reflective part of working memory. It coordinates incoming information already in the system, decides what to attend to, and oversees the use of strategies.

strategies—such as attending to information and categorizing it effectively—that are already developing in the first two years of life.

Attention

Recall from Chapter 4 that between 1 and 2 months of age, infants shift from focusing on single, high-contrast features to exploring objects and patterns more thoroughly. Besides attending to more aspects of the environment, infants gradually take in information more quickly. Habituation research reveals that preterm and newborn babies require a long time to habituate and recover to novel visual stimuli—about 3 or 4 minutes. But by 4 or 5 months, infants require as little as 5 to 10 seconds to take in a complex visual stimulus and recognize it as different from a previous one (Rose, Feldman, & Janowski, 2001; Slater et al., 1996).

One reason that very young babies' habituation times are so long is that they have difficulty disengaging their attention from interesting stimuli (Colombo, 2002). When Carolyn held up a doll dressed in red-and-white checked overalls, 2-month-old Caitlin stared intently until, unable to break her gaze, she burst into tears. The ability to shift attention from one stimulus to another is just as important as attending to a stimulus. By 4 months, infants' attention becomes more flexible—a change believed to be due to development of structures in the cerebral cortex controlling eye movements (Blaga & Colombo, 2006; Posner & Rothbart, 2007).

During the first year, infants attend to novel and eye-catching events. With the transition to toddlerhood, children become increasingly capable of intentional behavior (refer back to Piaget's Substage 4). Consequently, attraction to novelty declines (but does not disappear) and *sustained attention* improves, especially when children play with toys. A toddler who engages even in simple goal-directed behavior, such as stacking blocks or putting them in a container, must sustain attention to reach the goal. As plans and activities become more complex, so does the duration of attention (Ruff & Capozzoli, 2003).

Memory

Operant conditioning and habituation provide windows into early memory. Both methods show that retention of visual events increases dramatically over infancy and toddlerhood.

Using operant conditioning, researchers study infant memory by teaching 2- to 6-month-olds to move a mobile by kicking a foot tied to it with a long cord. Three-month-olds still remember how to activate the mobile one week after training. By 6 months, memory increases to two weeks (Rovee-Collier, 1999; Rovee-Collier & Bhatt, 1993). Around the middle of the first year, babies can manipulate switches or buttons to control stimulation. When 6- to 18-month-olds pressed a lever to make a toy train move around a track, duration of memory continued to increase with age; 13 weeks after training, 18-month-olds still remembered how to press the lever (see Figure 5.6) (Hartshorn et al., 1998).

Even after 3- to 6-month-olds forget an operant response, they need only a brief prompt—an adult who shakes the mobile—to reinstate the memory (Hildreth & Rovee-Collier, 2002). And when 6-month-olds are given a chance to reactivate the response themselves for just a couple of minutes, their memory not only returns but extends dramatically, to about 17 weeks (Hildreth, Sweeney, & Rovee-Collier, 2003). Perhaps permitting the baby to generate the previously learned behavior strengthens memory because it reexposes the child to more aspects of the original learning situation.

Habituation/recovery research shows that infants learn and retain a wide variety of information just by watching objects and events, without being physically active. Sometimes, they do so for much longer time spans than in operant conditioning studies. Babies are especially attentive to the movements of objects and people. In one investigation, 5½-month-olds remembered a woman's captivating action (such as blowing bubbles or brushing hair) seven weeks later, as indicated by a *familiarity preference* (see page 135 in Chapter 4) (Bahrick, Gogate, & Ruiz, 2002). The babies were so attentive to the woman's action that they did not remember her face, even when tested 1 minute later for a *novelty preference.*

In Chapter 4, we saw that 3- to 5-month-olds are excellent at discriminating faces. But their memory for the faces of unfamiliar people and for other static patterns is short-lived—at

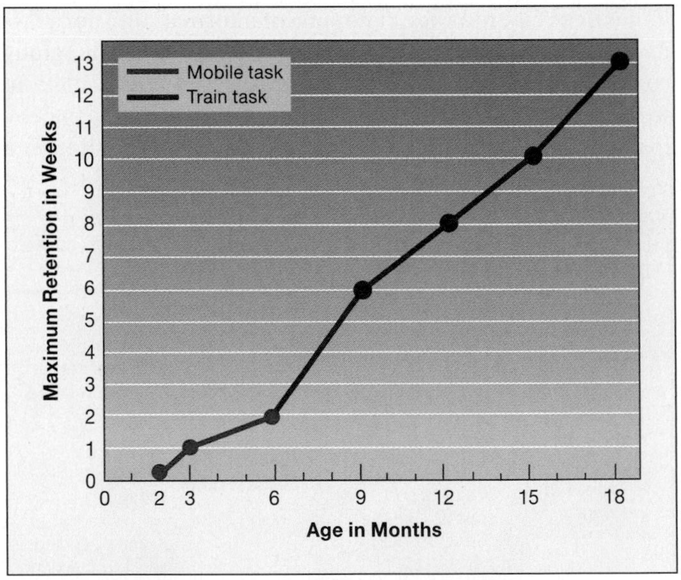

■ **FIGURE 5.6** ■ **Increase in retention in two operant conditioning tasks from 2 to 18 months.** Two- to 6-month-olds were trained to make a kicking response that turned a mobile. Six- to 18-month-olds were trained to press a lever that made a toy train move around a track. Six-month-olds learned both responses and retained them for an identical length of time, indicating that the tasks are comparable. Consequently, researchers could plot a single line tracking gains in retention of operant responses from 2 to 18 months of age. The line shows that memory improves dramatically. (From C. Rovee-Collier & R. Barr, 2001, "Infant Learning and Memory," in G. Bremner & A. Fogel, (Eds.), *Blackwell Handbook of Infant Development,* Oxford, U.K.: Blackwell, p. 150. Reprinted by permission of Blackwell Publishing Ltd.)

3 months, only about 24 hours, and at the end of the first year, several days to a few weeks (Fagan, 1973; Pascalis, de Haan, & Nelson, 1998). In comparison, 3-month-olds' memory for the unusual movements of objects (such as a metal nut swinging on the end of a string) persists for at least three months (Bahrick, Hernandez-Reif, & Pickens, 1997).

By 10 months, infants remember both novel actions and features of objects involved in those actions equally well (Horst, Oakes, & Madole, 2005). Thus, over the second half-year, sensitivity to object appearance increases. This change, as noted earlier, is fostered by infants' increasing ability to manipulate objects, which helps them learn about objects' observable properties.

So far, we have discussed only **recognition**—noticing when a stimulus is identical or similar to one previously experienced. It is the simplest form of memory: All babies have to do is indicate (by kicking, pressing a lever, or looking) that a new stimulus is identical or similar to a previous one. **Recall** is more challenging because it involves remembering something not present. But by the end of the first year, infants are capable of recall, as indicated by their ability to find hidden objects and to imitate others' actions long after observing the behavior (see page 156).

Long-term recall depends on connections among multiple regions of the cerebral cortex, especially with the frontal lobes. During the second year, these neural circuits start to increase rapidly (Bauer et al., 2006; Nelson, Thomas, & de Haan, 2006). Yet a puzzling finding is that older children and adults no longer recall their earliest experiences. The Lifespan Vista box on page 164 helps explain this puzzling finding.

Categorization

Even young infants can *categorize,* grouping similar objects and events into a single representation. Categorization helps infants reduce the enormous amount of new information they encounter every day so they can learn and remember (Cohen, 2003; Oakes & Madole, 2003).

Some creative variations of operant conditioning research with mobiles have been used to investigate infant categorization. One such study, of 3-month-olds, is described and illustrated in Figure 5.7. Similar investigations reveal that in the first few months, babies categorize stimuli on the basis of shape, size, color, and other physical properties (Wasserman & Rovee-Collier, 2001). By 6 months of age, they can categorize on the basis of two correlated features—for example, the shape and color of the alphabet letter (Bhatt et al., 2004). This ability to categorize using clusters of features prepares babies for acquiring many complex everyday categories.

Habituation/recovery has also been used to study infant categorization. Researchers show babies a series of pictures belonging to one category and then see whether they recover to (look longer at) a picture that does not belong to the category. Findings reveal that 6- to 12-month-olds structure objects into an impressive array of meaningful categories—food items, furniture, birds, animals, plants, vehicles, kitchen utensils, and spatial location ("above" and "below," "on" and "in") (Casasola, Cohen, & Chiarello, 2003; Mandler & McDonough, 1998; Oakes, Coppage, & Dingel, 1997). Besides organizing the physical world, infants of this age categorize their emotional and social worlds. Their looking response reveals that they sort people and their voices by gender and age, have begun to distinguish emotional expressions, and can separate people's natural movements from other motions (see Chapter 4, pages 145–146).

Babies' earliest categories are *perceptual*—based on similar overall appearance or prominent object parts: legs for animals, wheels for vehicles. But by the second half of the first year, more categories are *conceptual*—based on common functions or behaviors (Cohen, 2003; Mandler, 2004; Quinn, 2008).

In the second year, toddlers become active categorizers. Around 12 months, they touch objects that go together. As their knowledge of categories and verbal labels expands, toddlers start to categorize flexibly: When 14-month-olds are given four balls and four blocks, some made of soft rubber and some of rigid plastic, their sequence of object touching reveals that after classifying by shape, they can switch to classifying by material

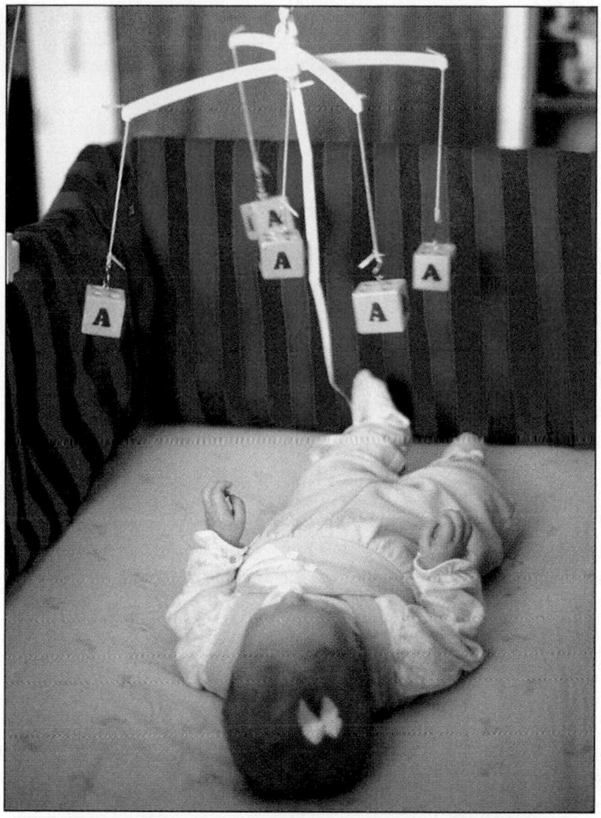

■ FIGURE 5.7 ■ Investigating infant categorization using operant conditioning. Three-month-olds were taught to kick to move a mobile that was made of small blocks, all with the letter *A* on them. After a delay, kicking returned to a high level only if the babies were shown a mobile whose elements were labeled with the same form (the letter *A*). If the form was changed (from *A*s to *2*s), infants no longer kicked vigorously. While making the mobile move, the babies had grouped together its features. They associated the kicking response with the category *A* and, at later testing, distinguished it from the category *2*. (Bhatt, Rovee-Collier, & Weiner, 1994; Hayne, Rovee-Collier, & Perris, 1987.)

■ A LIFESPAN VISTA: Looking Forward, Looking Back ■

Infantile Amnesia

If toddlers remember many aspects of their everyday lives, how do we explain **infantile amnesia**—that most of us cannot retrieve events that happened to us before age 3? The reason we forget cannot be merely the passage of time because we can recall many personally meaningful one-time events from both the recent and the distant past: the day a sibling was born, a birthday party, or a move to a new house—recollections known as **autobiographical memory.**

Several explanations of infantile amnesia exist. One theory credits brain development, suggesting that vital changes in the frontal lobes of the cerebral cortex may pave the way for an *explicit* memory system—one in which children remember deliberately rather than *implicitly,* without conscious awareness (Boyer & Diamond, 1992). But a growing number of researchers argue that even young infants remember consciously: Their memory processing is not fundamentally different from that of children and adults (Bauer, 2006; Rovee-Collier & Barr, 2001).

Another conjecture is that older children and adults often use verbal means for storing information, whereas infants' and toddlers' memory processing is largely nonverbal—an incompatibility that may prevent long-term retention of early experiences. To test this idea, researchers sent two adults to the homes of 2- to 4-year-olds with an unusual toy that the children were likely to remember: The Magic Shrinking Machine, shown in Figure 5.8. One adult showed the child how, after inserting an object in an opening on top of the machine and turning a crank that activated flashing lights and musical sounds, the child could retrieve a smaller, identical object from behind a door on the front of the machine. (The second adult discreetly dropped the smaller object down a chute leading to the door.) The child was encouraged to participate as the machine "shrank" additional objects.

A day later, the researchers tested the children to see how well they recalled the event. Their nonverbal memory—based on acting out the "shrinking" event and recognizing the "shrunken" objects in photos—was excellent. But even when they had the vocabulary, children younger than age 3 had trouble describing features of the "shrinking" experience. Verbal recall increased sharply between ages 3 and 4—the period during which children "scramble over the amnesia barrier" (Simcock & Hayne, 2003, p. 813). In a second study, preschoolers could not translate their nonverbal memory for the game into language six months to one year later, when their language had improved dramatically. Their verbal reports were "frozen in time," reflecting their limited language skill at the time they played the game (Simcock & Hayne, 2002).

These findings help us reconcile infants' and toddlers' remarkable memory skills with infantile amnesia. During the first few years, children remember largely with nonverbal techniques, such as visual images and motor actions. As language develops, preschoolers can use it to refer to preverbal memories. But their ability to do so is fragile, requiring strong contextual cues, such as direct exposure to the physical setting of the to-be-recalled experience (Morris & Baker-Ward, 2007). Only after age 3 do children often represent events verbally and participate in elaborate conversations with adults about them. As children encode autobiographical events in verbal form, they can use language-based cues to retrieve them, increasing the accessibility of these memories at later ages (Hayne, 2004).

Other findings suggest that the advent of a clear self-image contributes to the end of infantile amnesia. Toddlers who were advanced in development of a sense of self demonstrated better verbal memories a year later while conversing about past events with their mothers (Harley & Reese, 1999). Very likely, both biology and social experience contribute to the decline of infantile amnesia. Brain development and adult–child interaction may jointly foster self-awareness, language, and improved memory, which enable children to talk with adults about significant past experiences (Bauer, 2007; Nelson & Fivush, 2004). As a result, preschoolers begin to construct a long-lasting autobiographical narrative of their lives and enter into the history of their family and community.

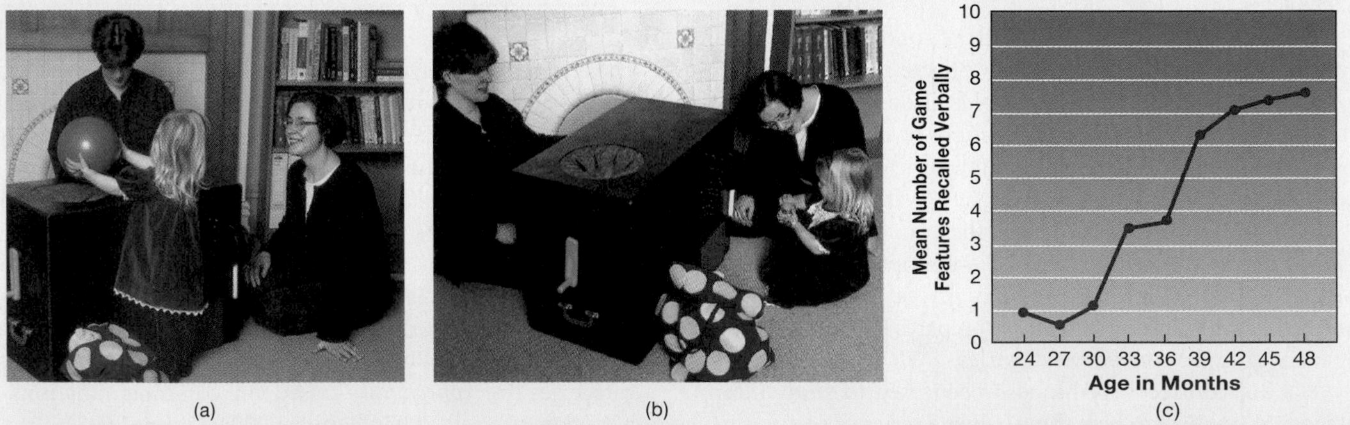

■ **FIGURE 5.8** ■ **The Magic Shrinking Machine, used to test young children's verbal and nonverbal memory of an unusual event.** After being shown how the machine worked, the child participated in selecting objects from a polka-dot bag, dropping them into the top of the machine (a) and turning a crank, which produced a "shrunken" object (b). When tested the next day, 2- to 4-year-olds' nonverbal memory for the event was excellent. But below 36 months, verbal recall was poor, based on the number of features recalled about the game during an open-ended interview (c). Recall improved between 36 and 48 months, the period during which infantile amnesia subsides. (From G. Simcock & H. Hayne, 2003, "Age-Related Changes in Verbal and Nonverbal Memory During Early Childhood," *Developmental Psychology, 39,* pp. 807, 809. Copyright © 2003 by the American Psychological Association. Reprinted with permission of the American Psychological Association. Photos: Ross Coombes/Courtesy of Harlene Hayne.)

(soft versus hard) if an adult calls their attention to the new basis for grouping (Ellis & Oakes, 2006). At 16 months, toddlers can arrange objects into a single category—grouping all the balls together. And around 18 months, they can sort objects into two classes (Gopnik & Meltzoff, 1987).

Compared with habituation/recovery, touching, sorting, and other play behaviors better reveal the meanings that toddlers attach to categories. After watching an adult give a toy dog a drink from a cup, 14-month-olds shown a rabbit and a motorcycle usually offer the drink only to the rabbit (Mandler & McDonough, 1998). They clearly understand that certain actions are appropriate for some categories of items (animals) and not others (vehicles).

By the end of the second year, toddlers' grasp of the animate–inanimate distinction expands. Nonlinear motions are typical of animates (a person or a dog jumping), linear motions of inanimates (a car or a table pushed along a surface). At 18 months, toddlers more often imitate a nonlinear motion with a toy that has animate-like parts (legs), even if it represents an inanimate (a bed). At 22 months, displaying a much fuller understanding, they imitate a nonlinear motion only with toys in the animate category (a cat but not a bed) (Rakison, 2005). They seem to grasp that whereas animates are self-propelled and, therefore, have varied paths of movement, inanimates move only when acted on, in highly restricted ways (Rakison, 2006).

How does this perceptual-to-conceptual change in categorization occur? Although researchers disagree on whether this shift requires a new approach to analyzing experience, all acknowledge that exploration of objects and expanding knowledge of the world contribute to older infants' capacity to group objects by their functions and behaviors (Mandler, 2004; Oakes & Madole, 2003). In addition, adult labeling of objects ("This one's a car, and that one's a bicycle") calls babies' attention to commonalities among objects while also promoting vocabulary growth (Waxman & Braun, 2005). Toddlers' advancing vocabulary, in turn, fosters categorization (Gelman & Kalish, 2006; Waxman, 2003).

Variations among languages lead to cultural differences in conceptual development. Korean toddlers, who learn a language in which object names are often omitted from sentences, develop object-sorting skills later than their English-speaking counterparts (Gopnik & Choi, 1990). At the same time, Korean contains a common work, *kkita*, with no English equivalent, referring to a tight fit between objects in contact—a ring on a finger, a cap on a pen—and Korean toddlers are advanced in forming the spatial category "tight fit" (Choi et al., 1999).

Evaluation of Information-Processing Findings

The information-processing perspective underscores the continuity of human thinking from infancy into adult life. In attending to the environment, remembering everyday events, and categorizing objects, Caitlin, Grace, and Timmy think in ways that are remarkably similar to our own, though their mental processing is far from proficient. Findings on infant memory and categorization join other evidence that challenges Piaget's view of early cognitive development. If 3-month-olds can remember events for as long as three months and can categorize stimuli, then they must have some ability to represent their experiences.

Information-processing research has contributed greatly to our view of young babies as sophisticated cognitive beings. But its central strength—analyzing cognition into its components, such as perception, attention, and memory—is also its greatest drawback. Information processing has had difficulty putting these components back together into a broad, comprehensive theory.

One approach to overcoming this weakness has been to combine Piaget's theory with the information-processing approach, an effort we will explore in Chapter 9. A more recent trend has been the application of a *dynamic systems view* (see Chapter 4, page 138). Researchers analyze each cognitive attainment to see how it results from a complex system of prior accomplishments and the child's current goals (Courage & Howe, 2002; Spencer & Perone, 2008; Thelen & Smith, 2006). Once these ideas are fully tested, they may move the field closer to a more powerful view of how the minds of infants and children develop.

The Social Context of Early Cognitive Development

Recall the description at the beginning of this chapter of Grace dropping shapes into a container. Notice that she learns about the toy with Ginette's help. With adult support, Grace will gradually become better at matching shapes to openings and dropping them into the container. Then she will be able to perform this and similar activities on her own.

Vygotsky's sociocultural theory emphasizes that children live in rich social and cultural contexts that affect the way their cognitive world is structured (Bodrova & Leong, 2007; Rogoff, 2003). Vygotsky believed that complex mental activities have their origins in social interaction. Through joint activities with more mature members of their society, children master activities and think in ways that have meaning in their culture.

A special Vygotskian concept explains how this happens. The **zone of proximal** (or potential) **development** refers to a range of tasks that the child cannot yet handle alone but can do with the help of more skilled partners. To understand this idea, think about how a sensitive adult (such as Ginette) introduces a child to a new activity. The adult picks a task that the child can master but that is challenging enough that the child cannot do it alone, or perhaps capitalizes on an activity chosen by the child. As the adult guides and supports, the child joins in the interaction and picks up mental strategies. As her competence increases, the adult steps back, permitting the child to take more responsibility for the task. This form of teaching—known as *scaffolding*—promotes learning at all ages, and we will consider it further in Chapter 7.

Vygotsky's ideas have been applied mostly to older children, who are more skilled in language and social communication. Recently, however, his theory has been extended to infancy and

© JAMES SHAFFER/PHOTOEDIT

Using simple words and gestures, this father brings a challenging task within his toddler's zone of proximal development. By adjusting his communication to suit the child's needs, the father transfers mental strategies to the child and promotes learning.

toddlerhood. Recall that babies are equipped with capacities that ensure that caregivers will interact with them. Then adults adjust the environment and their communication in ways that promote learning adapted to their cultural circumstances.

A study by Barbara Rogoff and her collaborators (1984) illustrates this process. Placing a jack-in-the-box nearby, the researchers watched how several adults played with Rogoff's son and daughter over the first two years. In the early months, the adults tried to focus the baby's attention by working the toy and, as the bunny popped out, saying something like "My, what happened?" By the end of the first year, when the baby's cognitive and motor skills had improved, interaction centered on how to use the toy. The adults guided the baby's hand in turning the crank and putting the bunny back in the box. During the second year, adults helped from a distance, using gestures and verbal prompts, such as making a turning motion with the hand near the crank. Research indicates that this fine-tuned support is related to advanced play, language, and problem solving in toddlerhood and early childhood (Bornstein et al., 1992; Charman et al., 2001; Tamis-LeMonda & Bornstein, 1989).

As early as the first year, cultural variations in social experiences affect mental strategies. In the jack-in-the-box example, adults and children focused their attention on a single activity. This strategy, common in Western middle-SES homes, is well-suited to lessons in which children master skills apart from the everyday situations in which they will later use those skills. In contrast, Guatemalan Mayan adults and babies often attend to several events at once. For example, one 12-month-old skillfully put objects in a jar while also watching a passing truck and blowing a toy whistle (Chavajay & Rogoff, 1999). Processing several competing events simultaneously may be vital in cultures where children learn largely through keen observation of others' ongoing activities. Mexican children from low-SES families continue to display this style of attention well into middle childhood (Correa-Chavez, Rogoff, & Mejía-Arauz, 2005).

Earlier we saw how infants and toddlers create new schemes by acting on the physical world (Piaget) and how certain skills become better developed as children represent their experiences more efficiently and meaningfully (information processing). Vygotsky adds a third dimension to our understanding by emphasizing that many aspects of cognitive development are socially mediated. The Cultural Influences box on the following page presents additional evidence for this idea, and we will see even more in the next section.

ASK YOURSELF

REVIEW
What impact does toddlers' more advanced play with toys have on the development of attention?

APPLY
When Timmy was 18 months old, his mother stood behind him, helping him throw a large ball into a box. As his skill improved, she stepped back, letting him try on his own. Using Vygotsky's ideas, explain how Timmy's mother is supporting his cognitive development.

CONNECT
Review the research on pages 157–158, indicating that by age 10 to 12 months, infants can solve problems by analogy. How might this attainment be related to the shift from perceptual to conceptual categorization (less emphasis on similar appearance, more on common functions or behaviors) over the second half-year?

REFLECT
Describe your earliest autobiographical memory. How old were you when the event occurred? Do your responses fit with research on infantile amnesia?

Individual Differences in Early Mental Development

Because of Grace's deprived early environment, Kevin and Monica had a psychologist give her one of many tests available for assessing mental development in infants and toddlers. Worried about Timmy's progress, Vanessa also arranged for him to be tested. At age 22 months, he had only a handful of words in his vocabulary, played in a less mature way than Caitlin and Grace, and seemed restless and overactive.

The cognitive theories we have just discussed try to explain the *process* of development—how children's thinking changes. Mental tests, in contrast, focus on cognitive *products.* Their goal

CULTURAL INFLUENCES

Social Origins of Make-Believe Play

One of the activities my husband, Ken, used to do with our two sons when they were young was to bake pineapple upside-down cake, a favorite treat. One Sunday afternoon when a cake was in the making, 21-month-old Peter stood on a chair at the kitchen sink, busily pouring water from one cup to another.

"He's in the way, Dad!" complained 4-year-old David, trying to pull Peter away from the sink.

"Maybe if we let him help, he'll give us room," Ken suggested. As David stirred the batter, Ken poured some into a small bowl for Peter, moved his chair to the side of the sink, and handed him a spoon.

"Here's how you do it, Petey," instructed David, with a superior air. Peter watched as David stirred, then tried to copy his motion. When it was time to pour the batter, Ken helped Peter hold and tip the small bowl.

"Time to bake it," said Ken.

"Bake it, bake it," repeated Peter, watching Ken slip the pan into the oven.

Several hours later, we observed one of Peter's earliest instances of make-believe play. He got his pail from the sandbox and, after filling it with a handful of sand, carried it into the kitchen and put it down on the floor in front of the oven. "Bake it, bake it," Peter called to Ken. Together, father and son placed the pretend cake in the oven.

Piaget and his followers concluded that toddlers discover make-believe independently, once they are capable of representational schemes. Vygotsky's theory has challenged this view. He believed that society provides children with opportunities to represent culturally meaningful activities in play. Make-believe, like other complex mental activities, is first learned under the guidance of experts (Berk, Mann, & Ogan, 2006). In the example just described, Peter extended his capacity to represent daily events when Ken drew him into the baking task and helped him act it out in play.

Current evidence supports the idea that early make-believe is the combined result of children's readiness to engage in it and social experiences that promote it. In one observational study of U.S. middle-SES toddlers, 75 to 80 percent of make-believe involved mother–child interaction (Haight & Miller, 1993). At 12 months, almost all play episodes were initiated by mothers, but by the end of the second year, half of pretend episodes were initiated by each.

© CAROLINE PENN/PANOS PICTURES

In cultures where sibling caregiving is common, make-believe play is more frequent and complex with older siblings than with mothers. These Kenyan brothers pretend with sand and rocks—"toys" that are plentiful in their surroundings. The older boy easily engages his toddler sibling, teaching him how to play.

During make-believe, mothers offer toddlers a rich array of cues that they are pretending—looking and smiling at the child more, making more exaggerated movements, and using more "we" talk (acknowledging that pretending is a joint endeavor) than they do during the same real-life event (Lillard, 2007). When adults participate, toddlers' make-believe is more elaborate (Keren et al., 2005). They are more likely to combine schemes into complex sequences, as Peter did when he put sand in the bucket ("making the batter"), carried it into the kitchen, and, with Ken's help, put it in the oven ("baking the cake"). The more parents pretend with their toddlers, the more time their children devote to make-believe. In certain collectivist societies, such as Argentina and Japan, mother–toddler other-directed pretending, as in feeding or putting a doll to sleep, is particularly rich in maternal expressions of affection and praise (Bornstein et al., 1999).

In some cultures, such as those of Indonesia and Mexico, where extended-family households and sibling caregiving are common, make-believe is more frequent and more complex with older siblings than with mothers. As early as age 3 to 4, children provide rich, challenging stimulation to their younger brothers and sisters, take these teaching responsibilities seriously, and, with age, become better at them (Zukow-Goldring, 2002). In a study of Zinacanteco Indian children of southern Mexico, by age 8, sibling teachers were highly skilled at showing 2-year-olds how to play at everyday tasks, such as washing and cooking. They often guided toddlers verbally and physically and provided feedback (Maynard, 2002).

In Western middle-SES families, older siblings less often teach deliberately but still serve as influential models of playful behavior. In a study of New Zealand families of Western European descent, when both a parent and an older sibling were available, toddlers more often imitated the actions of the sibling, especially when siblings engaged in make-believe or in routines (like answering the phone or raking leaves) that could inspire pretending (Barr & Hayne, 2003).

As we will see in Chapter 7, make-believe is a major means through which children extend their cognitive skills and learn about important activities in their culture. Vygotsky's theory, and the findings that support it, tell us that providing a stimulating physical environment is not enough to promote early cognitive development. In addition, toddlers must be invited and encouraged by more skilled members of their culture to participate in the social world around them. Parents and teachers can enhance early make-believe by playing often with toddlers, guiding and elaborating on their make-believe themes.

is to measure behaviors that reflect development and to arrive at scores that *predict* future performance, such as later intelligence, school achievement, and adult vocational success. This concern with prediction arose nearly a century ago, when French psychologist Alfred Binet designed the first successful intelligence test, which predicted school achievement (see Chapter 1). It inspired the design of many new tests, including ones that measure intelligence at very early ages.

A trained examiner administers the Bayley Scales of Infant Development to a 1-year-old sitting in her mother's lap. Compared with earlier editions, the Bayley-III Cognitive and Language Scales better predict preschool mental test performance.

Infant and Toddler Intelligence Tests

Accurately measuring infants' intelligence is a challenge because babies cannot answer questions or follow directions. All we can do is present them with stimuli, coax them to respond, and observe their behavior. As a result, most infant tests emphasize perceptual and motor responses. But new tests are being developed that also tap early language, cognition, and social behavior, especially with older infants and toddlers.

One commonly used test, the *Bayley Scales of Infant and Toddler Development,* is suitable for children between 1 month and 3½ years. The most recent edition, the Bayley-III, has three main subtests: (1) the Cognitive Scale, which includes such items as attention to familiar and unfamiliar objects, looking for a fallen object, and pretend play; (2) the Language Scale, which assesses understanding and expression of language—for example, recognition of objects and people, following simple directions, and naming objects and pictures; and (3) the Motor Scale, which includes gross and fine motor skills, such as grasping, sitting, stacking blocks, and climbing stairs (Bayley, 2005).

Two additional Bayley-III scales depend on parental report: (4) the Social-Emotional Scale, which asks caregivers about such behaviors as ease of calming, social responsiveness, and imitation in play; and (5) the Adaptive Behavior Scale, which asks about adaptation to the demands of daily life, including communication, self-control, following rules, and getting along with others.

COMPUTING INTELLIGENCE TEST SCORES. Intelligence tests for infants, children, and adults are scored in much the same way—by computing an **intelligence quotient (IQ),** which indicates the extent to which the raw score (number of items passed) deviates from the typical performance of same-age individuals. To make this comparison possible, test designers engage in **standardization**—giving the test to a large, representative sample and using the results as the *standard* for interpreting scores. The standardization sample for the Bayley-III included 1,700 infants, toddlers, and young preschoolers, reflecting the U.S. population in SES and ethnic diversity.

Within the standardization sample, performances at each age level form a **normal distribution** in which most scores cluster around the mean, or average, with progressively fewer falling toward the extremes (see Figure 5.9). This *bell-shaped* distribution results whenever researchers measure individual differences in large samples. When intelligence tests are standardized, the mean IQ is set at 100. An individual's IQ is higher or lower than 100 by an amount that reflects how much his or her test performance deviates from the standardization-sample mean.

The IQ offers a way of finding out whether an individual is ahead, behind, or on time (average) in mental development compared with others of the same age. For example, if Timmy's score is 100, then he did better than 50 percent of his agemates. A child with an IQ of 85 did better than only 16 percent, whereas a child with an IQ of 130 outperformed 98 percent. The IQs of 96 percent of individuals fall between 70 and 130; only a few achieve higher or lower scores.

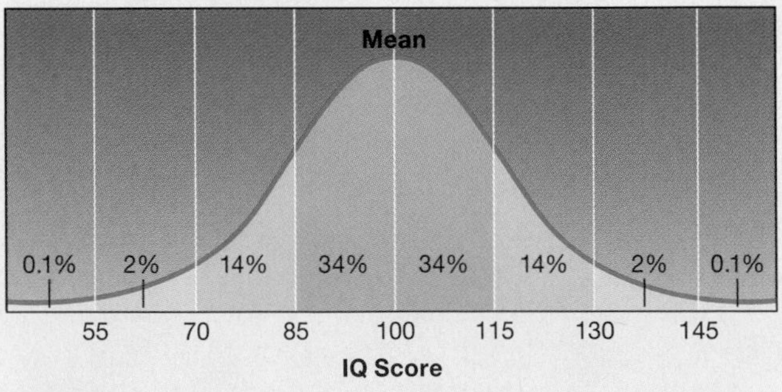

■ FIGURE 5.9 ■ Normal distribution of intelligence test scores. To determine what percentage of same-age individuals in the population a person with a certain IQ outperformed, add the figures to the left of that IQ score. For example, an 8-year-old child with an IQ of 115 scored better than 84 percent of the population of 8-year-olds.

Applying What We Know

Features of a High-Quality Home Life: The HOME Infant–Toddler Subscales

Home Subscale	Sample Item
Emotional and verbal responsiveness of the parent	Parent caresses or kisses child at least once during observer's visit. Parent spontaneously speaks to child twice or more (excluding scolding) during observer's visit.
Parental acceptance of the child	Parent does not interfere with child's actions or restrict child's movements more than three times during observer's visit.
Organization of the physical environment	Child's play environment appears safe and free of hazards.
Provision of appropriate play materials	Parent provides toys or interesting activities for child during observer's visit.
Parental involvement with the child	Parent tends to keep child within visual range and to look at child often during observer's visit.
Opportunities for variety in daily stimulation	Child eats at least one meal per day with mother and/or father, according to parental report. Child frequently has a chance to get out of house (for example, accompanies parent on trips to grocery store).

Sources: Bradley, 1994; Bradley et al., 2001.

PREDICTING LATER PERFORMANCE FROM INFANT TESTS. Despite careful construction, most infant tests—including previous editions of the Bayley—predict later intelligence poorly. Longitudinal research reveals that the majority of children show substantial fluctuations in IQ between toddlerhood and adolescence—typically 10 to 20 points, and sometimes much more (McCall, 1993; Weinert & Hany, 2003).

Infants and toddlers easily become distracted, fatigued, or bored during testing, so their scores often do not reflect their true abilities. And infant perceptual and motor items differ from the tasks given to older children, which increasingly emphasize verbal, conceptual, and problem-solving skills. In contrast, the Bayley-III Cognitive and Language Scales, which better dovetail with childhood tests, are good predictors of preschool mental test performance (Albers & Grieve, 2007). But because most infant scores do not tap the same dimensions of intelligence measured at older ages, they are conservatively labeled **developmental quotients (DQs)** rather than IQs.

Infant tests are somewhat better at making long-term predictions for extremely low-scoring babies. Today, they are largely used for *screening*—helping to identify for further observation and intervention babies who are likely to have developmental problems.

As an alternative to infant tests, some researchers have turned to information-processing measures, such as habituation, to assess early mental progress. Their findings show that speed of habituation and recovery to novel visual stimuli are among the best available infant predictors of IQ from early childhood through early adulthood (Fagan, Holland, & Wheeler, 2007; Kavsek, 2004; McCall & Carriger, 1993). Habituation and recovery seem to be especially effective early indexes of intelligence because they assess memory as well as quickness and flexibility of thinking, which underlie intelligent behavior at all ages (Colombo, 1995; Rose & Feldman, 1997). The consistency of these findings has prompted designers of the Bayley-III to include items that tap such cognitive skills as habituation/recovery, object permanence, and categorization.

Early Environment and Mental Development

In Chapter 2, we indicated that intelligence is a complex blend of hereditary and environmental influences. Many studies have examined the relationship of environmental factors to infant and toddler mental test scores. As we consider this evidence, you will encounter findings that highlight the role of heredity as well.

HOME ENVIRONMENT. The **Home Observation for Measurement of the Environment (HOME)** is a checklist for gathering information about the quality of children's home lives through observation and parental interview (Caldwell & Bradley, 1994). Applying What We Know above lists factors measured by HOME during the first three years. Each is positively related to toddlers' mental test performance. Regardless of SES and ethnicity, an organized, stimulating physical setting and parental affection, involvement, and encouragement of new skills repeatedly predict better language and IQ scores in toddlerhood and early childhood (Fuligni, Han, & Brooks-Gunn, 2004; Linver, Martin, & Brooks-Gunn, 2004; Tamis-LeMonda et al., 2004). The extent to which parents talk to infants and toddlers is particularly important. It contributes strongly to early language progress, which, in turn, predicts intelligence and academic achievement in elementary school (Hart & Risley, 1995).

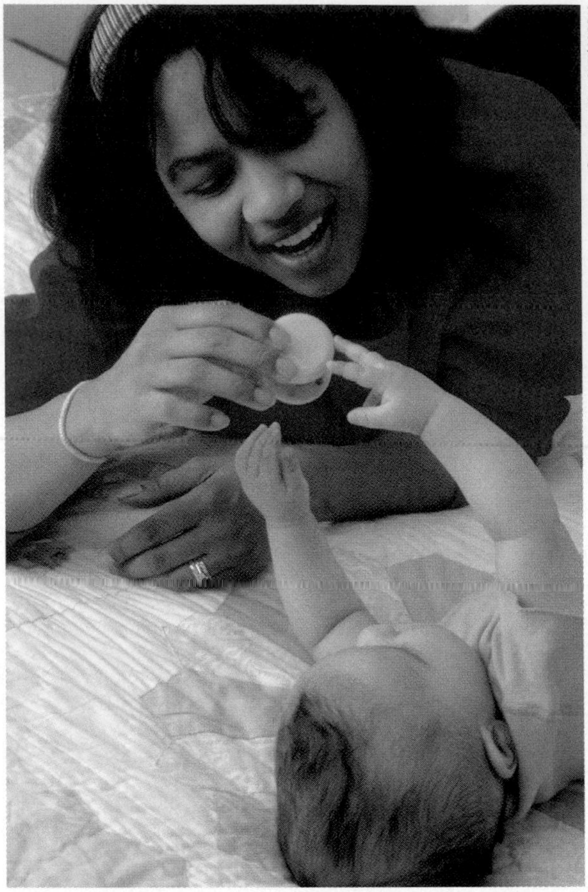

A mother plays affectionately with her 5-month-old baby. Parental warmth, attention, and verbal communication in infancy predict better language and IQ scores in toddlerhood and early childhood.

Yet we must interpret these correlational findings cautiously. In all the studies, children were reared by their biological parents, with whom they share not just a common environment but also a common heredity. Parents who are genetically more intelligent may provide better experiences while also giving birth to genetically brighter children, who evoke more stimulation from their parents. Research supports this hypothesis, which refers to *genetic–environmental correlation* (see Chapter 2, pages 72–73) (Saudino & Plomin, 1997). But heredity does not account for the entire association between home environment and mental test scores. Family living conditions—both HOME scores and affluence of the surrounding neighborhood—continue to predict children's IQ beyond the contribution of parental IQ and education (Chase-Lansdale et al., 1997; Klebanov et al., 1998).

How can the research summarized so far help us understand Vanessa's concern about Timmy's development? Ben, the psychologist who tested Timmy, found that he scored only slightly below average. Ben talked with Vanessa about her child-rearing practices and watched her play with Timmy. A single parent who worked long hours, Vanessa had little energy for Timmy at the end of the day. Ben also noticed that Vanessa, anxious about Timmy's progress, tended to pressure him, dampening his active behavior and bombarding him with directions: "That's enough ball play. Stack these blocks."

Ben explained that when parents are intrusive in these ways, infants and toddlers are likely to be distractible, play immaturely, and do poorly on mental tests (Bono & Stifter, 2003; Stilson & Harding, 1997). He coached Vanessa in how to interact sensitively with Timmy, while also assuring her that Timmy's current performance need not forecast his future development. Warm, responsive parenting that builds on toddlers' current capacities is a much better indicator than an early mental test score of how children will do later.

■ **INFANT AND TODDLER CHILD CARE.** Today, more than 60 percent of U.S. mothers with a child under age 2 are employed (U.S. Census Bureau, 2009b). Child care for infants and toddlers has become common, and its quality has a major impact on mental development. Research consistently shows that infants and young children exposed to poor-quality child care—whether they come from middle-class or from low-SES homes—score lower on measures of cognitive and social skills (Hausfather et al., 1997; NICHD Early Child Care Research Network, 2000b, 2001, 2003b, 2006).

In contrast, good child care can reduce the negative impact of a stressed, poverty-stricken home life, and it sustains the benefits of growing up in an economically advantaged family (Lamb & Ahnert, 2006; McCartney et al., 2007; NICHD Early Child Care Research Network, 2003b). In Swedish longitudinal research, entering high-quality child care in infancy and toddlerhood was associated with cognitive, emotional, and social competence in middle childhood and adolescence (Andersson, 1989, 1992; Broberg et al., 1997).

TAKE A MOMENT... Visit several child-care settings, and take notes on what you see. In contrast to most European countries and to Australia and New Zealand, where child care is nationally regulated and funded to ensure its quality, U.S. child care is cause for concern. Standards are set by the states and vary widely. In studies of U.S. child-care quality, only 20 to 25 percent of child-care centers and family child-care settings (in which a caregiver cares for children in her home) provided infants and toddlers with sufficiently positive, stimulating experiences to promote healthy psychological development. Most settings offered substandard care (NICHD Early Childhood Research Network, 2000a, 2004).

Unfortunately, many U.S. children from low-income families experience inadequate child care (Brooks-Gunn, 2004). But U.S. settings providing the very worst care tend to serve middle-SES families. These parents are especially likely to place their children in for-profit centers, where quality tends to be lowest. Low-SES children more often attend publicly subsidized, nonprofit centers, which have smaller group sizes and better teacher–child ratios (Lamb & Ahnert, 2006). Still, child-care quality for low-SES children varies widely. And probably because of greater access to adult stimulation, infants and toddlers in high-quality family child care score higher than those in center care in cognitive and language development (NICHD Early Child Care Research Network, 2000b).

Applying What We Know

Signs of Developmentally Appropriate Infant and Toddler Child Care

Program Characteristics	Signs of Quality
Physical setting	Indoor environment is clean, in good repair, well-lit, and well-ventilated. Fenced outdoor play space is available. Setting does not appear overcrowded when children are present.
Toys and equipment	Play materials are appropriate for infants and toddlers and are stored on low shelves within easy reach. Cribs, highchairs, infant seats, and child-sized tables and chairs are available. Outdoor equipment includes small riding toys, swings, slide, and sandbox.
Caregiver–child ratio	In child-care centers, caregiver–child ratio is no greater than one to three for infants and one to six for toddlers. Group size (number of children in one room) is no greater than six infants with two caregivers and 12 toddlers with two caregivers. In family child care, caregiver is responsible for no more than six children; within this group, no more than two are infants and toddlers. Staffing is consistent, so infants and toddlers can form relationships with particular caregivers.
Daily activities	Daily schedule includes times for active play, quiet play, naps, snacks, and meals. It is flexible rather than rigid, to meet the needs of individual children. Atmosphere is warm and supportive, and children are never left unsupervised.
Interactions among adults and children	Caregivers respond promptly to infants' and toddlers' distress; hold, talk to, sing to, and read to them; and interact with them in a manner that respects the individual child's interests and tolerance for stimulation.
Caregiver qualifications	Caregiver has some training in child development, first aid, and safety.
Relationships with parents	Parents are welcome anytime. Caregivers talk frequently with parents about children's behavior and development.
Licensing and accreditation	Child-care setting, whether a center or a home, is licensed by the state. In the United States, voluntary accreditation by the National Academy of Early Childhood Programs *(www.naeyc.org/accreditation)* or the National Association for Family Child Care *(www.nafcc.org)* is evidence of an especially high-quality program.

Sources: Copple & Bredekamp, 2009.

See Applying What We Know above for signs of high-quality care for infants and toddlers, based on standards for **developmentally appropriate practice.** These standards, devised by the U.S. National Association for the Education of Young Children, specify program characteristics that serve young children's developmental and individual needs, based on both current research and expert consensus. Caitlin, Grace, and Timmy are fortunate to be in family child care that meets these standards.

© ELLEN B. SENISI PHOTOGRAPHY

High-quality child care, with a generous caregiver–infant ratio, well-trained caregivers, and developmentally appropriate activities, can be especially beneficial to children from low-SES homes.

Child care in the United States is affected by a macrosystem of individualistic values and weak government regulation and funding. Furthermore, many parents think that their children's child-care experiences are better than they really are. Unable to identify good care, they do not demand it (Helburn, 1995). In recent years, recognizing that child care is in a state of crisis, the U.S. federal government and some states have allocated additional funds to subsidize its cost, especially for low-income families. Though far from meeting the need, this increase in resources has had a positive impact on child-care quality and accessibility (Children's Defense Fund, 2008).

Good child care is a cost-effective means of protecting children's well-being. And much like the programs we are about to consider, it can serve as effective early intervention for children whose development is at risk.

Early Intervention for At-Risk Infants and Toddlers

Children living in poverty are likely to show gradual declines in intelligence test scores and to achieve poorly when they reach school age (Bradley et al., 2001; Gutman, Sameroff, & Cole, 2003). These problems are largely due to stressful home environments that undermine children's ability to learn and that increase their likelihood of remaining poor throughout their lives (McLoyd, Aikens, & Burton, 2006). A variety of intervention programs have been developed to break this tragic cycle of poverty. Although most begin in the preschool years (we will discuss these in Chapter 7), a few start during infancy and continue through early childhood.

In center-based interventions, children attend an organized child-care or preschool program where they receive educational, nutritional, and health services, and their parents receive child-rearing and other social-service supports. In home-based interventions, a skilled adult visits the home and works with parents, teaching them how to stimulate young children's development. In most programs of either type, participating children score higher than untreated controls on mental tests by age 2. The earlier intervention begins, the longer it lasts, and the greater its scope and intensity, the better participants' cognitive and academic performance is throughout childhood and adolescence (Brooks-Gunn, 2004; Ramey, Ramey, & Lanzi, 2006; Sweet & Appelbaum, 2004).

The Carolina Abecedarian Project illustrates these favorable outcomes. In the 1970s, more than 100 infants from poverty-stricken families, ranging in age from 3 weeks to 3 months, were randomly assigned to either a treatment group or a control group. Treatment infants were enrolled in full-time, year-round child care through the preschool years. There they received stimulation aimed at promoting motor, cognitive, language, and social skills and, after age 3, literacy and math concepts. Special emphasis was placed on rich, responsive adult–child verbal communication. All children received nutrition and health services; the primary difference between treatment and control groups was the intensive child-care experience.

As Figure 5.10 shows, by 12 months of age, the IQs of the two groups diverged. Treatment children sustained their advantage until last tested—at age 21. In addition, throughout their school years, treatment youths achieved considerably better in reading and math. These gains translated into more years of schooling completed, higher rates of college enrollment and employment in skilled jobs, and lower rates of drug use and adolescent parenthood (Campbell et al., 2001, 2002; Ramey & Ramey, 1999).

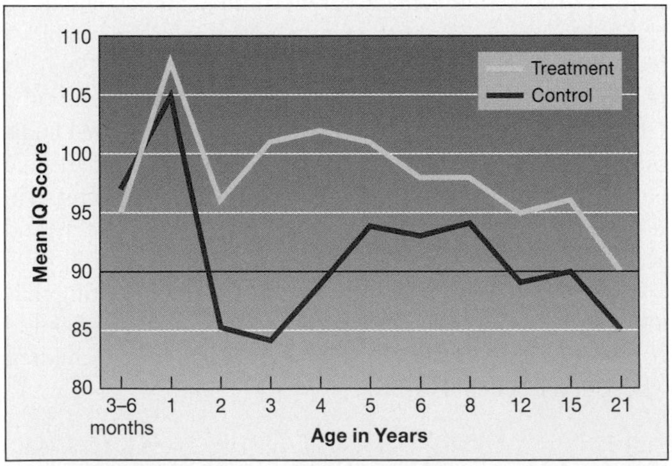

■ **FIGURE 5.10** ■ **IQ scores of treatment and control children from infancy to 21 years in the Carolina Abecedarian Project.** At 1 year, treatment children outperformed controls, an advantage consistently maintained through age 21. The IQ scores of both groups declined gradually during childhood and adolescence—a trend probably due to the damaging impact of poverty on mental development. (Adapted from Campbell et al., 2001.)

Without early intervention, many children born into economically disadvantaged families will not reach their potential. Recognition of this reality led the U.S. Congress to provide limited funding for intervention directed at infants and toddlers at risk for developmental problems. Early Head Start, begun in 1995, currently has 700 sites serving 65,000 low-income families. A recent evaluation, conducted when children reached age 3, showed that intervention led to warmer, more stimulating parenting, a reduction in harsh discipline, gains in cognitive and language development, and lessening of child aggression (Love et al., 2005; Love, Chazan-Cohen, & Raikes, 2007). The strongest effects occurred at sites offering a mix of center- and home-based services. Though not yet plentiful enough to meet the need, such programs are a promising beginning.

ASK YOURSELF

REVIEW
What probably accounts for the finding that speed of habituation and recovery to novel visual stimuli predicts later IQ better than most infant mental test scores?

APPLY
Fifteen-month-old Joey's developmental quotient (DQ) is 115. His mother wants to know exactly what this means and what she should do to support his mental development. How would you respond?

CONNECT
Using what you learned about brain development in Chapter 4, explain why it is best to initiate intervention for poverty-stricken children in the first two years rather than later.

REFLECT
Suppose you were seeking a child-care setting for your baby. What would you want it to be like, and why?

Language Development

Improvements in perception and cognition during infancy pave the way for an extraordinary human achievement—language. In Chapter 4, we saw that by the second half of the first year, infants make dramatic progress in distinguishing the basic sounds of their language and in segmenting the flow of speech into word and phrase units. They also start to comprehend some word meanings and, around 12 months of age, say their first word. Sometime between 1½ and 2 years, toddlers combine two words (MacWhinney, 2005). By age 6, children have a vocabulary of about 10,000 words, speak in elaborate sentences, and are skilled conversationalists.

To appreciate this awesome task, think about the many abilities involved in your own flexible use of language. When you speak, you must select words that match the underlying concepts you want to convey. To be understood, you must pronounce words correctly. Then you must combine them into phrases and sentences using a complex set of grammatical rules. Finally, you must follow the rules of everyday conversation—taking turns, making comments relevant to what your partner just said, and using an appropriate tone of voice.

How do infants and toddlers make such remarkable progress in launching these skills? To address this question, let's examine several prominent theories of language development.

Theories of Language Development

In the 1950s, researchers did not take seriously the idea that very young children might be able to figure out important properties of language. As a result, the first two theories of how children acquire language were extreme views. One, *behaviorism,* regards language development as entirely due to environmental influences. The second, *nativism,* assumes that children are "prewired" to master the intricate rules of their language.

■ **THE BEHAVIORIST PERSPECTIVE.** Behaviorist B. F. Skinner (1957) proposed that language, like any other behavior, is acquired through *operant conditioning* (see Chapter 4, page 134). As the baby makes sounds, parents reinforce those that are most like words with smiles, hugs, and speech in return. For example, at 12 months, my older son, David, often babbled like this: "book-a-book-a-dook-a-dook-a-book-a-nook-a-book-aaa." One day as he babbled away, I held up his picture book and said, "Book!" Soon David was saying "book-aaa" in the presence of books.

Some behaviorists believe that children rely on *imitation* to rapidly acquire complex utterances, such as whole phrases and sentences (Moerk, 2000). Imitation can combine with reinforcement to promote language, as when a parent coaxes, "Say, 'I want a cookie,'" and delivers praise and a treat after the toddler responds, "Wanna cookie!"

Although reinforcement and imitation contribute to early language development, they are best viewed as supporting rather than fully explaining it. "It's amazing how creative Caitlin is with language," Carolyn remarked one day. "She combines words in ways she's never heard before, like 'needle it' when she wants me to sew up her teddy bear and 'allgone outside' when she has to come in."

Carolyn's observations are accurate: Young children create many novel utterances that are not reinforced by or copied from others. And when they do imitate others' language, they do so selectively, focusing mainly on building their vocabularies and on refining aspects of language that they are working on at the moment (Owens, 2005).

■ **THE NATIVIST PERSPECTIVE.** Linguist Noam Chomsky (1957) proposed a nativist theory that regards the young child's amazing language skill as etched into the structure of the human brain. Focusing on grammar, Chomsky reasoned that the rules of sentence organization are too complex to be directly taught to or discovered by even a cognitively adept young child. Rather, he argued, all children have a **language acquisition device (LAD),** an innate system that contains a *universal grammar,* or set of rules common to all languages. It enables children, no matter which language they hear, to understand and speak in a rule-oriented fashion as soon as they pick up enough words.

Are children biologically primed to acquire language? Recall from Chapter 4 that newborn babies are remarkably sensitive to speech sounds. And children the world over reach major language milestones in a similar sequence (Gleitman & Newport, 1996). Also, the ability to master a grammatically complex language system seems unique to humans, as efforts to teach language to nonhuman primates—using either specially devised artificial symbol systems or sign language—have met with limited success. Even after extensive training, chimpanzees (who are closest to humans in terms of evolution) master only a basic vocabulary and short word combinations, and they produce these far less consistently than human preschoolers (Tomasello, Call, & Hare, 2003).

Furthermore, evidence that childhood is a *sensitive period* for language acquisition is consistent with Chomsky's idea of a biologically based language program. Researchers have examined the language competence of deaf adults who acquired their first language—American Sign Language (ASL), a gestural system used by the deaf—at different ages. The late learners, whose parents chose to educate them through speech and lip-reading, did not acquire spoken language because of their profound deafness. Consistent with the sensitive period notion, those who learned ASL in adolescence or adulthood never became as proficient as those who learned in childhood (Mayberry, 1994; Newport, 1991; Singleton & Newport, 2004).

But challenges to Chomsky's theory suggest that it, too, provides only a partial account of language development. First, researchers have had great difficulty identifying the single system of grammar that Chomsky believes underlies all languages (Maratsos, 1998; Tomasello, 2003, 2005). Second, children do not acquire language as quickly as nativist theory suggests. They refine and generalize many grammatical forms gradually, engaging in much piecemeal learning and making errors along the way. This suggests that more experimentation and learning are involved than Chomsky assumed (Tomasello, 2003, 2006).

Finally, recall from Chapter 4 that for most people, language is housed largely in the left hemisphere of the cerebral cortex, consistent with Chomsky's notion of a brain prepared to process language. But our discussion also revealed that language areas in the cortex *develop* as children acquire language. Although the left hemisphere is biased for language processing, if it is injured in the early years, other regions take over (see pages 125–126 in Chapter 4). So localization of language in the left hemisphere is not necessary for effective language use. Furthermore, brain-imaging research shows that many regions of the cerebral cortex participate in language activities to differing degrees, depending on the language skill and the individual's mastery of that skill (Shafer & Garrido-Nag, 2007).

THE INTERACTIONIST PERSPECTIVE. Recent ideas about language development emphasize *interactions* between inner capacities and environmental influences. One type of interactionist theory applies the information-processing perspective to language development. A second type emphasizes social interaction.

Some information-processing theorists assume that children make sense of their complex language environments by applying powerful cognitive capacities of a general kind (Bates, 2004; Elman, 2001; Munakata, 2006). These theorists note that brain regions housing language also govern similar perceptual and cognitive abilities, such as the capacity to analyze musical and visual patterns (Koelsch et al., 2002; Saygin et al., 2004).

Other theorists blend this information-processing view with Chomsky's nativist perspective. They agree that infants are amazing analyzers of speech and other information. But, they argue, these capacities probably are not sufficient to account for mastery of higher-level aspects of language, such as intricate grammatical structures (Newport & Aslin, 2000). They also point out that grammatical competence may depend more on specific brain structures than the other components of language. When 2- to 2½-year-olds and adults listened to short sentences—some grammatically correct, others with phrase-structure violations—both groups showed similarly distinct ERP brain-wave patterns for each sentence type in the left frontal and temporal lobes of the cerebral cortex (Oberecker & Friederici, 2006; Oberecker, Friedrich, & Friederici, 2005). This suggests that 2-year-olds process sentence structures using the same neural system as adults do. Furthermore, in studies of older children and adults with left-hemispheric brain damage, grammar is more impaired than other language functions (Baynes & Gazzaniga, 1988; Stromswold, 2000).

Still other interactionists emphasize that children's social skills and language experiences are centrally involved in language development. In this social-interactionist view, an active child, well-endowed for making sense of language, strives to communicate. In doing so, she cues her caregivers to provide appropriate language experiences, which help her relate the content and structure of language to its social meanings (Bohannon & Bonvillian, 2009; Chapman, 2000, 2006).

Among social interactionists, disagreement continues over whether or not children are equipped with specialized language abilities (Lidz, 2007; Shatz, 2007; Tomasello, 2003, 2006). Nevertheless, as we chart the course of language development, we will encounter much support for their central premise—that children's social competencies and language experiences greatly affect their language progress. In reality, native endowment, cognitive-processing strategies, and social experience probably operate in different balances with respect to each aspect of language. Table 5.3 provides an overview of early language milestones that we will examine in the next few sections.

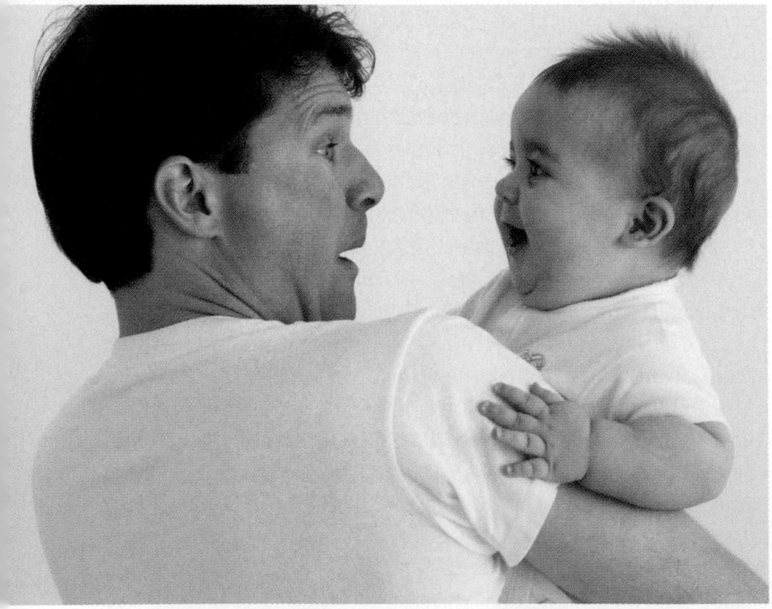

Infants communicate from the very beginning of life, as seen in this interchange between a father and his baby. How will this child accomplish the impressive task of becoming a fluent speaker of his native language within just a few years? Theorists disagree sharply on answers to this question.

Getting Ready to Talk

Before babies say their first word, they make impressive progress toward understanding and speaking their native tongue. They listen attentively to human speech, and they make speechlike sounds. As adults, we can hardly help but respond.

COOING AND BABBLING. Around 2 months, babies begin to make vowel-like noises, called **cooing** because of their pleasant "oo" quality. Gradually, consonants are added, and around 6 months, **babbling** appears, in which infants repeat consonant–vowel combinations in long strings, such as "babababababa" or "nanananana."

Babies everywhere (even those who are deaf) start babbling at about the same age and produce a similar range of early sounds. But for babbling to develop further, infants must be able to hear human speech. In hearing-impaired babies, these speechlike sounds are greatly delayed. And a deaf infant not exposed to sign language will stop babbling entirely (Oller, 2000).

As infants listen to spoken language, babbling expands to include a broader range of sounds. Around 7 months, it includes many sounds common in spoken languages. By 10 months, it reflects the sound and intonation patterns of infants' language community, some of which are transferred to their first words (Boysson-Bardies & Vihman, 1991).

Deaf infants exposed to sign language from birth babble with their hands much as hearing infants do through speech (Petitto & Marentette, 1991). Furthermore, hearing babies who have deaf, signing parents produce babblelike hand motions with the rhythmic patterns of natural sign languages (Petitto et al., 2001, 2004). This sensitivity to language rhythm—evident in both spoken and signed babbling—supports both discovery and production of meaningful language units.

TABLE 5.3 Milestones of Language Development During the First Two Years

APPROXIMATE AGE	MILESTONE
2 months	Infants coo, making pleasant vowel sounds.
4 months on	Infants observe with interest as the caregiver plays turn-taking games, such as pat-a-cake and peekaboo.
6 months on	Infants babble, adding consonants to their cooing sounds and repeating syllables. By 7 months, babbling starts to include many sounds of spoken languages. Infants begin to comprehend a few commonly heard words.
8–12 months	Infants become more accurate at establishing joint attention with the caregiver, who often verbally labels what the baby is looking at. Infants actively participate in turn-taking games, trading roles with the caregiver. Infants use preverbal gestures, such as showing and pointing, to influence the behavior of others.
12 months	Babbling includes sound and intonation patterns of the child's language community. Speed and accuracy of word comprehension increase rapidly. Toddlers say their first recognizable word.
18–24 months	Spoken vocabulary expands from about 50 to 200 words. Toddlers combine two words.

BECOMING A COMMUNICATOR. At birth, infants are prepared for some aspects of conversational behavior. For example, they initiate interaction through eye contact and terminate it by looking away. By 3 to 4 months, infants start to gaze in the same direction adults are looking, a skill that becomes more accurate at 10 to 11 months, as babies realize that others' focus provides information about their communicative intentions (Amano, Kezuka, & Yamamoto, 2004; Brooks & Meltzoff, 2005). Adults also follow the baby's line of vision and comment on what the infant sees. This **joint attention,** in which the child attends to the same object or event as the caregiver, contributes greatly to early language development. Infants and toddlers who often experience it sustain attention longer, comprehend more language, produce meaningful gestures and words earlier, and show faster vocabulary development (Carpenter, Nagell, & Tomasello, 1998; Flom & Pick, 2003; Silvén, 2001).

Between 4 and 6 months, interactions between caregivers and babies begin to include *give-and-take,* as in pat-a-cake and peekaboo games. At first, the parent starts the game, and the baby is an amused observer. But even 4-month-olds are sensitive to the structure and timing of these interactions, smiling more at an organized than a disorganized peekaboo exchange (Rochat, Querido, & Striano, 1999). By 12 months, babies participate actively, trading roles with the parent. In this way, they practice the turn-taking pattern of conversation—a vital context for acquiring language and communication skills. Infants' play maturity and vocalizations during games predict advanced language progress in the second year (Rome-Flanders & Cronk, 1995).

At the end of the first year, babies extend their joint attention and social interaction skills. They use *preverbal gestures* to influence others' behavior (Liszkowski et al., 2004). For example, while looking at her mother, Caitlin held up a toy to show it and pointed to the cupboard when she wanted a cookie. Carolyn responded to these gestures and also labeled them ("Oh, you want a cookie!"). In this way, toddlers learn that using language leads to desired results. Soon they integrate words with gestures, using the gesture to expand their verbal

© S. FELD/ROBERTSTOCK

This baby uses a preverbal gesture to draw his father's attention to the birdhouse. His father's verbal response promotes the baby's transition to spoken language.

message, as in pointing to a toy while saying "give" (Capirci et al., 2005). Gradually, gestures recede, and words become dominant. But the earlier toddlers form word–gesture combinations, the sooner they produce two-word utterances at the end of the second year (Goldin-Meadow & Butcher, 2003; Özçaliskan & Goldin-Meadow, 2005).

First Words

In the second half of the first year, infants begin to understand word meanings. When 6-month-olds listened to the word "Mommy" or "Daddy" while looking at side-by-side videos of their parents, they looked longer at the video of the named parent (Tincoff & Jusczyk, 1999). First spoken words, around 1 year, build on the sensorimotor foundations Piaget described and on categories children form during their first two years. Usually they refer to important people ("Mama," "Dada"), animals ("doggie," "kitty,"), objects that move ("car," "ball,"), foods ("milk," "apple"), familiar actions ("bye-bye," "more"), or outcomes of familiar actions ("wet," "hot") (Hart, 2004; Nelson, 1973). In their first 50 words, toddlers rarely name things that just *sit there,* like "table" or "vase."

When toddlers first learn words, they often apply them too narrowly, an error called **underextension.** At 16 months, Caitlin used "bear" only to refer to the worn and tattered bear she carried nearly constantly. As vocabulary expands, a more common error is **overextension**—applying a word to a wider collection of objects and events than is appropriate. For example, Grace used "car" for buses, trains, trucks, and fire engines. Toddlers' overextensions reflect their sensitivity to categories (MacWhinney, 2005). They apply a new word to a group of similar experiences: "car" to wheeled objects, "open" to opening a door, peeling fruit, and undoing shoelaces. This suggests that children often overextend deliberately because they have difficulty recalling or have not acquired a suitable word. And when a word is hard to pronounce, toddlers are likely to substitute a related one they can say (Bloom, 2000). As vocabulary and pronunciation improve, overextensions disappear.

Overextensions illustrate another important feature of language development: the distinction between language *production* (the words children use) and language *comprehension* (the words they understand). At all ages, comprehension develops ahead of production. A 2-year-old who refers to trucks, trains, and bikes as "car" may look at or point to these objects correctly when given their names (Naigles & Gelman, 1995). Still, the two capacities are related. The speed and accuracy of toddlers' comprehension of spoken language increase dramatically over the second year. And toddlers who are faster and more accurate in comprehension tend to show more rapid growth in words understood and produced as they approach age 2 (Fernald, Perfors, & Marchman, 2006). Quick comprehension frees space in working memory for picking up new words and for the more demanding task of using them to communicate.

The Two-Word Utterance Phase

Young toddlers add to their spoken vocabularies at a rate of one to three words per week. Because gains in word production between 18 and 24 months are so impressive (one or two words per day), many researchers concluded that toddlers undergo a *spurt in vocabulary*—a transition from a slower to a faster learning phase. But recent evidence indicates that most children show a steady, continuous increase in rate of word learning that continues through the preschool years (Ganger & Brent, 2004).

How do toddlers build their vocabularies so quickly? In the second year, they improve in ability to categorize experience, recall words, and grasp others' social cues to meaning, such as eye gaze, pointing, and handling objects (Dapretto & Bjork, 2000; Golinkoff & Hirsh-Pasek, 2006; Liszkowski, Carpenter, & Tomasello, 2007). In Chapter 7, we will consider young children's specific strategies for word learning.

Once toddlers produce about 200 words, they start to combine two words: "Mommy shoe," "go car," "more cookie." These two-word utterances are called **telegraphic speech** because, like a telegram, they focus on high-content words, omitting smaller, less important ones. Children the world over use them to express an impressive variety of meanings.

Two-word speech consists largely of simple formulas ("more + *X*," "eat + *X*"), with different words inserted in the *X* position. Toddlers rarely make gross grammatical errors, such as saying "chair my" instead of "my chair." But their word-order regularities are usually copies of adult word pairings, as when the parent says, "How about *more sandwich?*" or "That's *my book.*" These findings indicate that young children first acquire "concrete pieces of language" from frequent word pairings they hear. Only gradually do they generalize from those pieces to construct word-order and other grammatical rules (Tomasello, 2003, 2006). As we will see in Chapter 7, children master grammar steadily over the preschool years.

Individual and Cultural Differences

Although, on average, children produce their first word around their first birthday, the range is large, from 8 to 18 months—variation due to a complex blend of genetic and environmental influences. Earlier we saw that Timmy's spoken language was delayed, in part because of Vanessa's tense, directive communication with him. But Timmy is also a boy, and many studies show that girls are slightly ahead of boys in early vocabulary growth (Fenson et al., 1994). The most common explanation is girls' faster rate of physical maturation, believed to promote earlier development of the left cerebral hemisphere.

Temperament matters, too. Shy toddlers often wait until they understand a great deal before trying to speak. Once they do speak, their vocabularies increase rapidly, although they remain slightly behind their agemates (Spere et al., 2004). Temperamentally negative toddlers also acquire language more slowly because their high emotional reactivity diverts them from processing linguistic information (Salley & Dixon, 2007).

The surrounding environment also plays a role: The more words caregivers use, the more children learn (Weizman & Snow, 2001). Mothers talk much more to toddler-age girls than to boys, and parents converse less often with shy than with sociable children (Leaper, Anderson, & Sanders, 1998; Patterson & Fisher, 2002). Low-SES children, who receive less verbal stimulation in their homes than higher-SES children, usually have smaller vocabularies (Hoff, 2006). Limited parent–child book reading is a major factor. On average, a middle-SES child is read to for 1,000 hours between 1 and 5 years, a low-SES child for only 25 hours (Neuman, 2003). As a result, low-SES kindergartners have vocabularies only one fourth as large as those of their higher SES agemates (Lee & Burkam, 2002).

Young children have distinct styles of early language learning. Caitlin and Grace, like most toddlers, used a **referential style;** their vocabularies consisted mainly of words that refer to objects. A smaller number of toddlers use an **expressive style;** compared with referential children, they produce many more social formulas and pronouns ("thank you," "done," "I want it"). These styles reflect early ideas about the functions of language. Grace, for example, thought words were for naming things. In contrast, expressive-style children believe words are for talking about people's feelings and needs. The vocabularies of referential-style toddlers grow faster because all languages contain many more object labels than social phrases (Bates et al., 1994).

What accounts for a toddler's language style? Rapidly developing referential-style children often have an especially active interest in exploring objects. They also eagerly imitate their parents' frequent naming of objects, and their parents imitate back—a strategy that supports swift vocabulary growth by helping children remember new labels (Masur & Rodemaker, 1999). Expressive-style children tend to be highly sociable, and their parents more often use verbal routines ("How are you?" "It's no trouble") that support social relationships (Goldfield, 1987).

The two language styles are also linked to culture. Object words are particularly common in the vocabularies of English-speaking toddlers, but Chinese, Japanese, and Korean toddlers have more words for social routines. Mothers' speech in each culture reflects this difference: Asian mothers, perhaps because of a cultural emphasis on the importance of group membership, teach social routines as soon as their children begin to speak (Choi & Gopnik, 1995; Fernald & Morikawa, 1993; Tardif, Gelman, & Xu, 1999).

At what point should parents be concerned if their child talks very little or not at all? If a toddler's language is greatly delayed when compared with the norms in Table 5.3 (page 175), then parents should consult the child's doctor or a speech and language therapist. Late babbling may be a sign of slow language development that can be prevented with early intervention (Fasolo, Marjorano, & D'Odorico, 2008). Some toddlers who do not follow simple directions or who, after age 2, have difficulty putting their thoughts into words may suffer from a hearing impairment or a language disorder that requires immediate treatment.

Supporting Early Language Development

Consistent with the interactionist view, a rich social environment builds on young children's natural readiness to acquire language. For a summary of how caregivers can consciously support early language development, see Applying What We Know on page 178. Caregivers also do so unconsciously—through a special style of speech.

Adults in many cultures speak to young children in **child-directed speech (CDS),** a form of communication made up of short sentences with high-pitched, exaggerated expression, clear pronunciation, distinct pauses between speech segments, and repetition of new words in a variety of contexts ("See the ball," "The ball bounced!") (Fernald et al., 1989; O'Neill et al., 2005). Deaf parents use a similar style of communication when

© ELLEN B. SENISI PHOTOGRAPHY

This mother speaks to her baby in short, clearly pronounced sentences with high-pitched, exaggerated intonation. Adults' use of child-directed speech eases language learning for infants and toddlers.

Applying What We Know

Supporting Early Language Learning

Strategy	Consequence
Respond to coos and babbles with speech sounds and words.	Encourages experimentation with sounds that can later be blended into first words. Provides experience with turn-taking pattern of human conversation.
Establish joint attention and comment on what child sees.	Predicts earlier onset of language and faster vocabulary development.
Play social games, such as pat-a-cake and peekaboo.	Provides experience with the turn-taking pattern of human conversation.
Engage toddlers in joint make-believe play.	Promotes all aspects of conversational dialogue.
Engage toddlers in frequent conversations.	Predicts faster early language development and academic success during the school years.
Read to toddlers often, engaging them in dialogues about picture books.	Provides exposure to many aspects of language, including vocabulary, grammar, communication skills, and information about written symbols and story structures.

signing to their deaf babies (Masataka, 1996). CDS builds on several communicative strategies we have already considered: joint attention, turn-taking, and caregivers' sensitivity to toddlers' preverbal gestures. In this example, Carolyn uses CDS with 18-month-old Caitlin:

Caitlin: "Go car."

Carolyn: "Yes, time to go in the car. Where's your jacket?"

Caitlin: *[Looks around, walks to the closet.]* "Dacket!" *[Points to her jacket.]*

Carolyn: "There's that jacket! *[She helps Caitlin into the jacket.]* On it goes! Let's zip up. *[Zips up the jacket.]* Now, say bye-bye to Grace and Timmy."

Caitlin: "Bye-bye, G-ace."

Carolyn: "What about Timmy? Bye to Timmy?"

Caitlin: "Bye-bye, Te-te."

Carolyn: "Where's your bear?"

Caitlin: *[Looks around.]*

Carolyn: *[Pointing.]* "See? Go get the bear. By the sofa." *[Caitlin gets the bear.]*

From birth on, infants prefer CDS over other adult talk, and by 5 months they are more emotionally responsive to it (Aslin, Jusczyk, & Pisoni, 1998). Parents constantly fine-tune the length and content of their utterances to fit their children's needs—adjustments that foster word learning and enable toddlers to join in (Cameron-Faulkner, Lieven, & Tomasello, 2003; Fernald & Hurtado, 2006). As we saw earlier, parent–toddler conversation—especially, reading and talking about picture books—strongly predicts language development and academic success during the school years. And as the Biology and Environment box on the following page makes clear, when a child's disability makes it difficult for parents to engage in the sensitive communication of CDS, language and cognitive development are drastically delayed.

Do social experiences that promote language development remind you of those that strengthen cognitive development in general? CDS and parent–child conversation create a *zone of proximal development* in which children's language skills expand. In contrast, impatience with and rejection of children's efforts to talk lead them to stop trying and result in immature language skills (Baumwell, Tamis-LeMonda, & Bornstein, 1997; Cabrera, Shannon, & Tamis-LeMonda, 2007). In the next chapter, we will see that sensitivity to children's needs and capacities supports their emotional and social development as well.

ASK YOURSELF

REVIEW
Why is the social interactionist perspective attractive to many investigators of language development? Cite evidence that supports it.

APPLY
Fran frequently corrects her 17-month-old son Jeremy's attempts to talk and—fearing that he won't use words—refuses to respond to his gestures. How might Fran be contributing to Jeremy's slow language progress?

CONNECT
Cognition and language are interrelated. List examples of how cognition fosters language development. Next, list examples of how language fosters cognitive development.

REFLECT
Find an opportunity to speak to an infant or toddler. How did your manner of speaking differ from the way you typically speak to an adult? What features of your speech are likely to promote early language development, and why?

BIOLOGY AND ENVIRONMENT

Parent–Child Interaction: Impact on Language and Cognitive Development of Deaf Children

About one in every 1,000 North American infants is born profoundly or fully deaf (Deafness Research Foundation, 2005). When a deaf child cannot participate fully in communication with caregivers, development is severely compromised. Yet the consequences of deafness for children's language and cognition vary with social context, as comparisons of deaf children of hearing parents with deaf children of deaf parents reveal.

Over 90 percent of deaf children have hearing parents who are not fluent in sign language. In toddlerhood and early childhood, these children often are delayed in development of language and make-believe play. In middle childhood, many achieve poorly in school, are deficient in social skills, and display impulse-control problems (Arnold, 1999; Edmondson, 2006). Yet deaf children of deaf parents escape these difficulties! Their language (use of sign) and play maturity are on a par with hearing children's. After school entry, deaf children of deaf parents learn easily and get along well with adults and peers (Bornstein et al., 1999; Spencer & Lederberg, 1997).

These differences can be traced to early parent–child communication. Beginning in infancy, hearing parents of deaf children are less positive, less responsive to the child's efforts to communicate, less effective at achieving joint attention and turn-taking, less involved in play, and more directive and intrusive (Spencer, 2000; Spencer & Meadow-Orlans, 1996). In contrast, the quality of interaction between deaf children and deaf parents is similar to that of hearing children and hearing parents.

Hearing parents are not to blame for their deaf child's problems. Rather, they lack experience with visual communication, which enables deaf parents to respond readily to a deaf child's needs. Deaf parents know they must wait for the child to turn toward them before interacting (Loots & Devise, 2003). Hearing parents tend to speak or gesture while the child's attention is directed elsewhere—a strategy that works with a hearing but not with a deaf partner. When the child is confused or unresponsive, hearing parents often feel overwhelmed and become overly controlling (Jamieson, 1995).

The impact of deafness on language and cognitive development can best be understood by considering its impact on parents and other significant people in the child's life. Deaf children need access to language models—deaf adults and peers—to experience natural language learning. And their hearing parents benefit from social support along with training in how to interact sensitively with a nonhearing partner.

Screening techniques can now identify deaf babies at birth. Many U.S. states and an increasing number of Western nations require that every newborn be tested, enabling immediate enrollment in programs aimed at fostering effective parent–child interaction. When children with profound hearing loss start to receive intervention within the first year of life, they show much better language, cognitive, and social development (Vohr et al., 2008; Yoshinaga-Itano, 2003).

When the mother signs "eat" to her 11-month-old child, who is deaf, he responds with babblelike hand motions, similar to the babbling that hearing infants do through speech. This "babbling" supports his production of meaningful language.

Summary

Piaget's Cognitive-Developmental Theory

According to Piaget, how do schemes change over the course of development?

» By acting on the environment, children move through four stages in which psychological structures, or **schemes,** achieve a better fit with external reality.

» Schemes change in two ways: through **adaptation,** which is made up of two complementary activities—**assimilation** and **accommodation**—and through **organization**, the internal rearrangement of schemes into a strongly interconnected cognitive system.

Describe the major cognitive achievements of the sensorimotor stage.

» In the **sensorimotor stage**, the **circular reaction** provides a means of adapting first schemes, and the newborn's reflexes are gradually transformed into the flexible action patterns of the older infant. Around 8 months, infants develop **intentional, or goal-directed, behavior** and begin to understand **object permanence.** Between 18 and 24 months, **mental representation** is evident in sudden solutions to sensorimotor problems, mastery of object permanence problems involving invisible displacement, **deferred imitation,** and **make-believe play.**

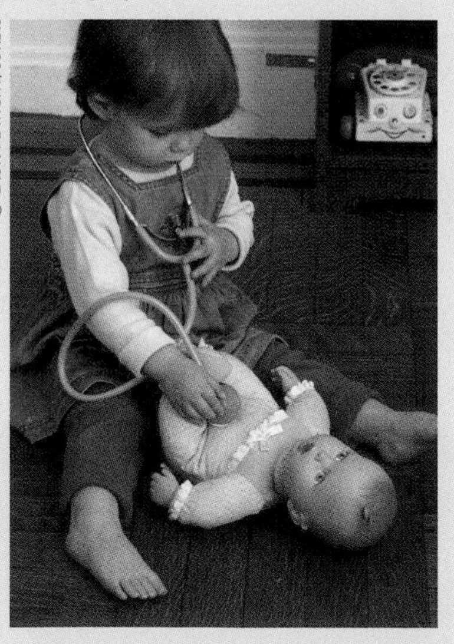

© LAURA DWIGHT/CORBIS

What does follow-up research reveal about the accuracy of Piaget's sensorimotor stage?

» Many studies suggest that infants display certain understandings earlier than Piaget believed. Some awareness of object permanence, as revealed by the **violation-of-expectation method** and object-tracking research, may be evident in the first few months. In addition, young infants display deferred imitation and analogical problem solving, which suggests that they are capable of mental representation in the first year.

» Today, researchers believe that newborns have more built-in equipment for making sense of their world than Piaget assumed, although they disagree on how much initial understanding infants have. According to the **core knowledge perspective,** infants begin life with core domains of thought that support early, rapid cognitive development. Although findings on early, ready-made knowledge are mixed, there is broad agreement that many cognitive changes of infancy are continuous rather than stagelike and that various aspects of cognition develop unevenly rather than in an integrated fashion.

Information Processing

Describe the information-processing view of cognitive development.

» Information-processing researchers regard development as gradual and continuous and many aspects of thinking. Most assume that we hold information in three parts of the system, the **sensory register; working,** or **short-term, memory;** and **long-term memory.** As information flows through the system, **mental strategies** operate on it so that it can be retained and used efficiently. To manage the complex activities of working memory, the **central executive** directs the flow of information.

What changes in attention, memory, and categorization take place during the first two years?

» With age, infants attend to more aspects of the environment and take information in more quickly. In the second year, attention to novelty declines and sustained attention improves, especially during play with toys.

» Young infants are capable of **recognition** memory. By the end of the first year, they can **recall** past events.

» During the first year, infants group stimuli into increasingly complex categories, and categorization shifts from a *perceptual* to a *conceptual* basis. By the second year, children become active categorizers, spontaneously sorting objects during play.

Describe contributions and limitations of the information-processing approach to our understanding of early cognitive development.

» Information-processing findings challenge Piaget's view of babies as purely sensorimotor beings who cannot mentally represent experiences. But information processing has not yet provided a broad, comprehensive theory of children's thinking.

The Social Context of Early Cognitive Development

How does Vygotsky's concept of the zone of proximal development expand our understanding of early cognitive development?

» Vygotsky believed that infants master tasks within the **zone of proximal development**—that is, tasks just ahead of their current capacities—through the support and guidance of more skilled partners. As early as the first year, cultural variations in social experiences affect mental strategies.

© JAMES SHAFFER/PHOTOEDIT

Individual Differences in Early Mental Development

Describe the mental testing approach and the extent to which infant tests predict later performance.

» The mental testing approach measures intellectual development in an effort to predict future performance. Scores are arrived at by computing an **intelligence quotient (IQ),** which compares an individual's test performance with that of a **standardization** sample of same-age individuals.

» Infant tests, which consist largely of perceptual and motor responses, predict later intelligence poorly. As a result, scores on infant tests are called **developmental quotients (DQs),** rather than IQs. Speed of habituation and recovery to visual stimuli are better predictors of future performance.

Discuss environmental influences on early mental development, including home, child care, and early intervention for at-risk infants and toddlers.

» Research with the **Home Observation for Measurement of the Environment (HOME)** shows that an organized, stimulating home environment and parental encouragement, involvement, and affection repeatedly predict early mental test scores. Although the HOME–IQ relationship is partly due to heredity, family living conditions also affect mental development.

» Infant and toddler child care is increasingly common, and its quality has a major impact on mental development. Standards for **developmentally appropriate practice** specify program characteristics that meet young children's developmental needs.

» Intensive intervention beginning in infancy and extending through early childhood can prevent the gradual declines in intelligence and the poor academic performance seen in many poverty-stricken children.

Language Development

Describe theories of language development, and indicate how much emphasis each places on innate abilities and environmental influences.

» According to the *behaviorist* perspective, parents train children in language skills through operant conditioning and imitation. Behaviorism, however, has difficulty accounting for children's novel utterances.

» In contrast, Chomsky's *nativist* view regards children as naturally endowed with a **language acquisition device (LAD).** Although evidence that mastery of a complex language system is unique to humans and that childhood is a *sensitive period* for language acquisition is supportive, Chomsky's theory provides only a partial account of language development.

» Recent theories suggest that language development results from *interactions* between inner capacities and environmental influences. Some interactionists apply the information-processing perspective to language development. Others emphasize the importance of children's social skills and language experiences.

Describe major language milestones in the first two years, individual differences, and ways adults can support early language development.

» Infants begin **cooing** at 2 months and **babbling** at about 6 months. Around 10 to 11 months, their skill at establishing **joint attention** improves. Adults can encourage language progress by responding to infants' coos and babbles, establishing joint attention and labeling what babies see, playing turn-taking games, and acknowledging infants' preverbal gestures.

» In the second half of the first year, infants begin to understand word meanings. At the end of the first year, they use *preverbal gestures*, such as pointing, to influence others' behavior.

» Around 12 months, toddlers say their first word. Young children often make errors of **underextension** and **overextension.** Rate of word learning increases steadily, and once vocabulary reaches about 200 words, two-word utterances called **telegraphic speech** appear. At all ages, language *comprehension* is ahead of *production*.

» Individual and cultural differences in early language development exist. Girls show faster progress than boys, and reserved, cautious toddlers may wait before trying to speak. Most toddlers use a **referential style** of language learning; their early words consist largely of names for objects. A few use an **expressive style,** in which pronouns and social formulas are common and vocabulary grows more slowly.

» Adults in many cultures speak to young children in **child-directed speech (CDS),** a simplified form of language that is well suited to their learning needs. Conversation between parent and toddler is one of the best predictors of early language development and academic success during the school years.

Important Terms and Concepts

accommodation (p. 152)
adaptation (p. 152)
assimilation (p. 152)
autobiographical memory (p. 164)
babbling (p. 174)
central executive (p. 161)
child-directed speech (CDS) (p. 177)
circular reaction (p. 153)
cooing (p. 174)
core knowledge perspective (p. 159)
deferred imitation (p. 155)
developmentally appropriate practice (p. 171)
developmental quotient (DQ) (p. 169)
expressive style of language learning (p. 177)
Home Observation for Measurement of the Environment (HOME) (p. 169)
infantile amnesia (p. 164)
intelligence quotient (IQ) (p. 168)
intentional, or goal-directed, behavior (p. 154)
joint attention (p. 175)
language acquisition device (LAD) (p. 173)
long-term memory (p. 161)
make-believe play (p. 155)
mental representation (p. 154)
mental strategies (p. 161)
normal distribution (p. 168)
object permanence (p. 154)
organization (p. 152)
overextension (p. 176)
recall (p. 163)
recognition (p. 163)
referential style of language learning (p. 177)
scheme (p. 152)
sensorimotor stage (p. 152)
sensory register (p. 161)
standardization (p. 168)
telegraphic speech (p. 176)
underextension (p. 176)
violation-of-expectation method (p. 155)
working, or short-term, memory (p. 161)
zone of proximal development (p. 165)

© BLEND IMAGES/SUPERSTOCK

Separations—a fact of life in military families—are highly stressful, especially during wartime. Nevertheless, the time this father takes to build a strong, affectionate bond with his baby will engender feelings of security in the child—a vital foundation for all aspects of early development.

CHAPTER 6

Emotional and Social Development in Infancy and Toddlerhood

As Caitlin reached 8 months of age, her parents noticed that she had become more fearful. One evening, when Carolyn and David left her with a baby-sitter, she wailed as they headed for the door—an experience she had accepted easily a few weeks earlier. Caitlin and Timmy's caregiver Ginette also observed an increasing wariness of strangers. When Ginette turned to go to another room, both babies dropped their play to crawl after her. At the mail carrier's knock at the door, they clung to Ginette's legs, reaching out to be picked up.

At the same time, each baby seemed more willful. Removing an object from the hand produced little response at 5 months. But at 8 months, when Timmy's mother, Vanessa, took away a table knife he had managed to reach, he burst into angry screams and could not be consoled or distracted.

All Monica and Kevin knew about Grace's first year was that she had been deeply loved by her destitute, homeless mother. Separation from her, followed by a long journey to an unfamiliar home, had left Grace in shock. At first she was extremely sad, turning away when Monica or Kevin picked her up. But as Grace's new parents held her close, spoke gently, and satisfied her craving for food, Grace returned their affection. Two weeks after her arrival, her despondency gave way to a sunny, easy-going disposition. She burst into a wide grin, reached out at the sight of Monica and Kevin, and laughed at her brother Eli's funny faces. As her second birthday approached, she pointed to herself, exclaiming "Gwace!" and laid claim to treasured possessions. "Gwace's chicken!" she would announce at mealtimes, sucking the marrow from the drumstick, a practice she had brought with her from Cambodia.

Taken together, the children's reactions reflect two related aspects of personality development during the first two years: close ties to others and a sense of self. We begin with Erikson's psychosocial theory, which provides an overview of personality development during infancy and toddlerhood. Then, as we chart the course of emotional development, we will discover why fear and anger became more apparent in Caitlin's and Timmy's range of emotions by the end of the first year. Our attention then turns to individual differences in temperament. We will examine biological and environmental contributions to these differences and their consequences for future development.

Next, we take up attachment to the caregiver, the child's first affectionate tie. We will see how the feelings of security that grow out of this important bond support the child's sense of independence and expanding social relationships.

Finally, we focus on early self-development. By the end of toddlerhood, Grace recognized herself in mirrors and photographs, labeled herself as a girl, and showed the beginnings of self-control. "Don't touch!" she instructed herself one day as she resisted the desire to pull a lamp cord out of its socket. Cognitive advances combine with social experiences to produce these changes during the second year.

Erikson's Theory of Infant and Toddler Personality

Our discussion of major theories in Chapter 1 revealed that psychoanalytic theory is no longer in the mainstream of human development research. But one of its lasting contributions is its ability to capture the essence of personality during each period of development. Recall that Sigmund Freud believed that psychological health and maladjustment could be traced to the early years—in particular, to the quality of the child's relationships with parents. Although Freud's preoccupation with the channeling of instincts and his neglect of important experiences beyond infancy and early childhood came to be heavily criticized, the basic outlines of his theory were accepted and elaborated in several subsequent theories. The most influential is Erik Erikson's *psychosocial theory,* also introduced in Chapter 1.

Basic Trust versus Mistrust

Erikson accepted Freud's emphasis on the importance of the parent–infant relationship during feeding, but he expanded and enriched Freud's view. A healthy outcome during infancy, Erikson believed, does not depend on the *amount* of food or oral stimulation offered but rather on the *quality* of caregiving: relieving discomfort promptly and sensitively, holding the infant gently, waiting patiently until the baby has had enough milk, and weaning when the infant shows less interest in breast or bottle.

Erikson recognized that no parent can be perfectly in tune with the baby's needs. Many factors affect parental of personal happiness, current life conditions (for example, additional young children in the family), and culturally valued child-rearing practices. But when the *balance of care* is sympathetic and loving, the psychological conflict of the first year—**basic trust versus mistrust**—is resolved on the positive side. The trusting infant expects the world to be good and gratifying, so he feels confident about venturing out and exploring it. The mistrustful baby cannot count on the kindness and compassion of others, so she protects herself by withdrawing from people and things around her.

Autonomy versus Shame and Doubt

With the transition to toddlerhood, Freud viewed the parents' manner of toilet training as decisive for psychological health. But in Erikson' view, toilet training is only one of many influential experiences. The familiar refrains of newly walking, talking toddlers—"No!" "Do it myself!"—reveal that they have entered a period of budding selfhood. They want to decide for themselves not just in toileting but also in other situations. The conflict of toddlerhood, **autonomy versus shame and doubt,** is resolved favorably when parents provide young children with suitable guidance and reasonable choices. A self-confident, secure 2-year-old has parents who do not criticize or attack him when he fails at new skills—using the toilet, eating with a spoon, or putting away toys. And they meet his assertions of independence with tolerance and understanding—for example, by giving him an extra five minutes to finish his play before leaving for the grocery store. In contrast, when parents are over- or undercontrolling, the outcome is a child who feels forced and shamed or who doubts his ability to control his impulses and act competently on his own.

© GERI ENGBERG/THE IMAGE WORKS

At a community Earth Day festival, this father gently encourages his 1-year-old daughter as she examines a strange object—a turtle shell. The more sensitive he is in this and other situations, the more likely she is to view the world as good and gratifying and to confidently explore it.

In sum, basic trust and autonomy grow out of warm, sensitive parenting and reasonable expectations for impulse control starting in the second year. If children emerge from the first few years without sufficient trust in caregivers and without a healthy sense of individuality, the seeds are sown for adjustment problems. Adults who have difficulty establishing intimate ties, who are overly dependent on a loved one, or who continually doubt their own ability to meet new challenges may not have fully mastered the tasks of trust and autonomy during infancy and toddlerhood.

Emotional Development

TAKE A MOMENT... Observe several infants and toddlers, noting the emotions each displays, the cues you rely on to interpret the baby's emotional state, and how caregivers respond. Researchers have conducted many such observations to find out how babies convey their emotions and interpret those of others. They have discovered that emotions play powerful roles in organizing the attainments that Erikson regarded as so important: social relationships, exploration of the environment, and discovery of the self (Halle, 2003; Saarni et al., 2006).

Think back to the *dynamic systems perspective* introduced in Chapters 1 and 5. As you read about early emotional development in the following sections, notice how emotions are an integral part of young children's dynamic systems of action. Emotions energize development. At the same time, they are an aspect of the system that develops, becoming more varied and complex as children reorganize their behavior to attain new goals (Campos, Frankel, & Camras, 2004; Witherington, Campos, & Hertenstein, 2001).

Because infants cannot describe their feelings, determining exactly which emotions they are experiencing is a challenge. Although vocalizations and body movements provide some information, facial expressions offer the most reliable cues. Cross-cultural evidence reveals that people around the world associate photographs of different facial expressions with emotions in the same way (Ekman, 2003; Ekman & Friesen, 1972). These findings inspired researchers to analyze infants' facial patterns to determine the range of emotions they display at different ages.

Development of Basic Emotions

Basic emotions—happiness, interest, surprise, fear, anger, sadness, and disgust—are universal in humans and other primates and have a long evolutionary history of promoting survival. Do infants come into the world with the ability to express basic emotions? Although signs of some emotions are present, babies' earliest emotional life consists of little more than two global arousal states: attraction to pleasant stimulation and withdrawal from unpleasant stimulation (Camras et al., 2003; Fox, 1991). Only gradually do emotions become clear, well-organized signals.

According to one view, sensitive, contingent caregiver communication, in which parents selectively mirror aspects of the baby's diffuse emotional behavior, helps infants construct emotional expressions that closely resemble those of adults (Gergely & Watson, 1999). Around 6 months, face, voice, and posture form organized patterns that vary meaningfully with environmental events. For example, Caitlin typically responded to her parents' playful interaction with a joyful face, pleasant babbling, and a relaxed posture, as if to say, "This is fun!" In contrast, an unresponsive parent often evokes a sad face, fussy vocalizations, and a drooping body (sending the message, "I'm despondent") or an angry face, crying, and "pick-me-up" gestures (as if to say, "Change this unpleasant event!") (Weinberg & Tronick, 1994; Yale et al., 1999). By the middle of the first year, emotional expressions are well-organized and specific—and therefore able to tell us a great deal about the infant's internal state.

Four basic emotions—happiness, anger, sadness, and fear—have received the most research attention. Let's see how they develop.

■ HAPPINESS.

Happiness—expressed first in blissful smiles and later through exuberant laughter—contributes to many aspects of development. When infants achieve new skills, they smile and laugh, displaying delight in motor and cognitive mastery. As the smile encourages caregivers to be affectionate and stimulating, the baby smiles even more (Aksan & Kochanska, 2004). Happiness binds parent and baby into a warm, supportive relationship that fosters the infant's developing competences.

During the early weeks, newborn babies smile when full, during REM sleep, and in response to gentle touches and sounds, such as stroking of the skin, rocking, and the mother's soft, high-pitched voice. By the end of the first month, infants smile at dynamic, eye-catching sights, such as a bright object jumping suddenly across their field of vision. Between 6 and 10 weeks, the parent's communication evokes a broad grin called the **social smile** (Lavelli & Fogel, 2005; Sroufe & Waters, 1976). These changes in smiling parallel the development of infant perceptual capacities—in particular, babies' increasing sensitivity to visual patterns, including the human face (see Chapter 4). And social smiling becomes better organized and stable as babies learn to use it to evoke and sustain pleasurable face-to-face interaction with the parent.

Laughter, which appears around 3 to 4 months, reflects faster processing of information than smiling. But, as with smiling, the first laughs occur in response to very active stimuli, such as the parent saying playfully, "I'm gonna get you!" and kissing the baby's tummy. As infants understand more about their world, they laugh at events with subtler elements of surprise, such as a silent game of peekaboo (Sroufe & Wunsch, 1972).

Around the middle of the first year, infants smile and laugh more when interacting with familiar people, a preference that strengthens the parent–child bond. Between 8 and 10 months, the smile becomes a deliberate social signal: Infants more often interrupt their play with an interesting toy to relay their delight to an attentive adult (Venezia et al., 2004). And like adults,

10- to 12-month-olds have several smiles, which vary with context—a broad, "cheek-raised" smile in response to a parent's greeting; a reserved, muted smile for a friendly stranger; and a "mouth-open" smile during stimulating play (Bolzani et al., 2002; Dickson, Fogel, & Messinger, 1998).

© CHRISTINA KENNEDY/ALAMY

When an unfamiliar adult attempts to hold her, an 8-month-old makes it clear that she prefers her mother! Fear rises during the second half of the first year. Its most frequent expression is stranger anxiety.

■ **ANGER AND SADNESS.** Newborn babies respond with generalized distress to a variety of unpleasant experiences, including hunger, painful medical procedures, changes in body temperature, and too much or too little stimulation. From 4 to 6 months into the second year, angry expressions increase in frequency and intensity. Older infants react with anger in a wider range of situations—when an object is taken away, their arms are restrained, the caregiver leaves for a brief time, they are put down for a nap, or they cannot control an expected outcome—for example, a toy that previously produced interesting sounds but no longer does so (Camras et al., 1992; Stenberg & Campos, 1990; Sullivan & Lewis, 2003).

Cognitive and motor development contribute to this rise in angry reactions. As infants become capable of intentional behavior (see Chapter 5), they want to control their own actions and the effect they produce. They are also more persistent about obtaining desired objects (Mascolo & Fischer, 2007). Furthermore, older infants are better at identifying who caused them pain or removed a toy. The rise in anger is also adaptive. New motor capacities enable an angry infant to defend herself or overcome an obstacle (Izard & Ackerman, 2000). Finally, anger motivates caregivers to relieve the infant's distress and, in the case of separation, may discourage them from leaving again soon.

Although expressions of sadness also occur in response to pain, removal of an object, and brief separations, they are less frequent than anger (Alessandri, Sullivan, & Lewis, 1990; Izard, Hembree, & Huebner, 1987). But when caregiver–infant communication is seriously disrupted, infant sadness is common—a condition that impairs all aspects of development (see the Lifespan Vista box on the following page).

■ **FEAR.** Like anger, fear rises during the second half of the first year. Older infants often hesitate before playing with a new toy, and newly crawling infants soon show fear of heights (see Chapter 4). But the most frequent expression of fear is to unfamiliar adults, a response called **stranger anxiety.** Many infants and toddlers are quite wary of strangers, although the reaction does not always occur. It depends on several factors: temperament (some babies are generally more fearful), past experiences with strangers, and the current situation (Thompson & Limber, 1991). When an unfamiliar adult picks up the infant in a new setting, stranger anxiety is likely. But if the adult sits still while the baby moves around and a parent is nearby, infants often show positive and curious behavior (Horner, 1980). The stranger's style of interaction—expressing warmth, holding out an attractive toy, playing a familiar game, and approaching slowly rather than abruptly—reduces the baby's fear.

Cross-cultural research reveals that infant-rearing practices can modify stranger anxiety. Among the Efe hunters and gatherers of Congo, West Africa, where the maternal death rate is high, infant survival is safeguarded by a collective caregiving system in which, starting at birth, Efe babies are passed from one adult to another. Consequently, Efe infants show little stranger anxiety (Tronick, Morelli, & Ivey, 1992). In contrast, among infants in Israeli kibbutzim (cooperative agricultural settlements), who live in isolated communities vulnerable to terrorist attacks, wariness of strangers is widespread. By the end of the first year, when infants look to others for cues about how to respond emotionally, kibbutz babies display greater stranger anxiety than their city-reared counterparts (Saarni et al., 2006).

The rise in fear after age 6 months keeps newly mobile babies' enthusiasm for exploration in check. Once wariness develops, babies use the familiar caregiver as a **secure base,** or point from which to explore, venturing into the environment and then returning for emotional support. As part of this adaptive system, encounters with strangers lead to two conflicting tendencies: approach (indicated by interest and friendliness) and avoidance (indicated by fear). The infant's behavior is a balance between the two.

As cognitive development enables toddlers to discriminate more effectively between threatening and nonthreatening people and situations, stranger anxiety and other fears of the

A LIFESPAN VISTA: Looking Forward, Looking Back

Parental Depression and Children's Development

About 8 to 10 percent of women experience chronic depression—mild to severe feelings of sadness and withdrawal that continue for months or years. Often, the beginnings of this emotional state cannot be pinpointed. In other instances, depression emerges or strengthens after childbirth but fails to subside as the new mother adjusts to hormonal changes in her body and gains confidence in caring for her baby. Julia experienced this type—called *postpartum depression*.

Although less recognized and studied, fathers, too, experience chronic depression. About 3 to 5 percent of fathers report symptoms after the birth of a child (Madsen & Juhl, 2007; Spector, 2006). Parental depression can interfere with effective parenting and seriously impair children's development. Genetic makeup increases the risk of depressive illness, but social and cultural factors are also involved.

Maternal Depression

During Julia's pregnancy, her husband, Kyle, showed so little interest in the baby that Julia worried that having a child might be a mistake. Then, shortly after Lucy was born, Julia's mood plunged. She became anxious and weepy, overwhelmed by Lucy's needs, and angry at loss of control over her own schedule. When Julia approached Kyle about her own fatigue and his unwillingness to help with the baby, he snapped that she was overreacting. Julia's childless friends stopped by just once to see Lucy but did not call again.

Julia's depressed mood quickly affected her baby. In the weeks after birth, infants of depressed mothers sleep poorly, are less attentive to their surroundings, and have elevated levels of the stress hormone cortisol (Field, 1998). The more extreme the depression and the greater the number of stressors in a mother's life (such as marital discord, little or no social support, and poverty), the more the parent–child relationship suffers (Simpson et al., 2003). Julia rarely smiled at, comforted, or talked to Lucy, who responded to her mother's sad, vacant gaze by turning away, crying, and often looking sad or angry herself (Herrera, Reissland, & Shepherd, 2004; Stanley, Murray, & Stein, 2004). Julia, in turn, felt guilty and inadequate, and her depression deepened. By age 6 months, Lucy showed mental and emotional symptoms common in babies of depressed mothers—delays in development, an irritable mood, and attachment difficulties (Cornish et al., 2005; McMahon et al., 2006).

When maternal depression persists, the parent–child relationship worsens. Depressed mothers view their infants more negatively than independent observers do (Forman et al., 2007). And they use inconsistent discipline sometimes lax, at other times too forceful. As we will see in later chapters, children who experience these maladaptive parenting practices often have serious adjustment problems. Some withdraw into a depressed mood themselves; others become impulsive and aggressive. In several studies, infants and preschoolers of depressed mothers showed atypical EEG brain-wave patterns—reduced activation of the left hemisphere (which governs positive emotion) and increased activation of the right hemisphere (which governs negative emotion). These alterations, a sign of difficulty controlling negative emotional arousal, are associated with increased behavior problems (Dawson et al., 2003; Jones, Field, & Davalos, 2000).

Paternal Depression

Paternal depression is also linked to dissatisfaction with marriage and family life after childbirth and to other life stressors, including job loss and divorce (Bielawska-Batorowicz & Kossakowska-Petrycka, 2006). In a study of a large representative sample of British parents and babies, researchers assessed depressive symptoms of fathers shortly after birth and again the following year. Then they tracked the children's development into the preschool years. Persistent paternal depression was a strong predictor of child behavior problems—especially overactivity, defiance, and aggression in boys—even after many other factors, including family SES and maternal depression, had been controlled (Ramchandani et al., 2005).

Paternal depression is linked to frequent father–child conflict as children grow older (Kane & Garber, 2004). Over time, children subjected to parental negativity develop a pessimistic world view—one in which they lack self-confidence and perceive their parents and other people as threatening. Children who constantly feel endangered are especially likely to become overly aroused in stressful situations, easily losing control in the face of cognitive and social challenges (Cummings & Davies, 1994). Although children of depressed parents may inherit a tendency toward emotional and behavior problems, quality of parenting is a major factor in their adjustment.

Interventions

Early treatment is vital to prevent parental depression from interfering with the relationship. Julia's doctor referred her to a therapist, who helped Julia and Kyle with their marital problems. At times, antidepressant medication is prescribed.

In addition to alleviating parental depression, therapy that encourages depressed mothers to revise their negative views of their babies and to engage in emotionally positive, responsive caregiving is vital for reducing young children's attachment and other developmental problems (Forman et al., 2007). When a depressed parent does not respond easily to treatment, a warm relationship with the other parent or another caregiver can safeguard children's development (Mezulis, Hyde, & Clark, 2004).

This depressed mother appears completely uninterested in her infant. If her disengagement continues, the baby is likely to become negative and irritable, eventually withdraw, and develop serious emotional and behavior problems.

first two years decline. Fear also wanes as toddlers acquire more strategies for coping with it, as you will see when we discuss emotional self-regulation.

Understanding and Responding to the Emotions of Others

Infants' emotional expressions are closely tied to their ability to interpret the emotional cues of others. We have seen that in the first few months, babies match the feeling tone of the caregiver in face-to-face communication. Some researchers claim that infants respond in kind to others' emotions through a fairly automatic process of *emotional contagion,* just as we tend to feel happy or sad when we sense these emotions in others (Stern, 1985). Others, however, believe that infants acquire these emotional contingencies through operant conditioning—for example, learning that a smile generally triggers pleasurable feedback and that distress prompts a comforting response (Saarni et al., 2006).

Around 3 to 4 months, infants become sensitive to the structure and timing of face-to-face interactions. When they gaze, smile, or vocalize, they now expect their social partner to respond in kind, and they reply with positive vocal and emotional reactions (Markova & Legerstee, 2006; Rochat, Striano, & Blatt, 2002). Within these exchanges, babies become increasingly aware of the range of emotional expressions (Montague & Walker-Andrews, 2001). According to some researchers, out of this early imitative communication, infants start to view others as "like me"—an awareness believed to lay the foundation for understanding others' thoughts and feelings (Gergely & Watson, 1996; Meltzoff, 2007).

From 5 months on, infants perceive facial expressions as organized patterns and can match the emotion in a voice with the appropriate face of a speaking person (see Chapter 4). Responding to emotional expressions as organized wholes indicates that these signals have become meaningful to babies. As skill at establishing joint attention improves, infants realize that an emotional expression not only has meaning but is also a meaningful reaction to a specific object or event (Moses et al., 2001; Tomasello, 1999).

Once these understandings are in place, beginning at 8 to 10 months, infants engage in **social referencing**—actively seeking emotional information from a trusted person in an uncertain situation (Mumme et al., 2007). Many studies show that the caregiver's emotional expression (happy, angry, or fearful) influences whether a 1-year-old will be wary of strangers, play with an unfamiliar toy, or cross the deep side of the visual cliff (see page 143 in Chapter 4) (Repacholi, 1998; Stenberg, 2003; Striano & Rochat, 2000). The adult's voice, either alone or combined with a facial expression, is more effective than a facial expression alone (Vaish & Striano, 2004). The voice conveys both emotional and verbal information, and the baby need not turn toward the adult but, instead, can focus on evaluating the novel event.

Parents can take advantage of social referencing to teach their baby how to react to many everyday events. And around the middle of the second year, as toddlers begin to appreciate that others' emotional reactions may differ from their own, social referencing allows them to compare their own and others' assessments of events. In one study, an adult showed 14- and 18-month-olds broccoli and crackers and acted delighted with one food but disgusted with the other. When asked to share the food, 18-month-olds gave the adult whichever food she appeared to like, regardless of their own preferences (Repacholi & Gopnik, 1997).

In sum, social referencing helps young children move beyond simply reacting to others' emotional messages. They use those signals to guide their own actions and to find out about others' intentions and preferences. These experiences, along with cognitive and language development, help toddlers refine the meanings of emotions—for example, happiness versus surprise, anger versus fear—during the second year.

Emergence of Self-Conscious Emotions

Besides basic emotions, humans are capable of a second, higher-order set of feelings, including guilt, shame, embarrassment, envy, and pride. These are called **self-conscious emotions** because each involves injury to or enhancement of our sense of self. We feel guilt when we have harmed someone and want to correct the wrongdoing. When we are ashamed or embarrassed, we have negative feelings about our behavior, and we

A mother applauds her toddler's success at tower-building. To experience self-conscious emotions, such as pride, babies need self-awareness as well as adult instruction.

want to retreat so others will no longer notice our failings. In contrast, pride reflects delight in the self's achievements, and we are inclined to tell others what we have accomplished (Saarni et al., 2006).

Self-conscious emotions appear at the end of the second year, as 18- to 24-month-olds become firmly aware of the self as a separate, unique individual. Toddlers show shame and embarrassment by lowering their eyes, hanging their heads, and hiding their faces with their hands. They show guiltlike reactions, too: One 22-month-old returned a toy she had grabbed and patted her upset playmate. Pride also emerges around this time, and envy by age 3 (Barrett, 2005; Garner, 2003; Lewis et al., 1989).

Besides self-awareness, self-conscious emotions require an additional ingredient: adult instruction in when to feel proud, ashamed, or guilty. Parents begin this tutoring early when they say, "Look how far you can throw that ball!" or "You should feel ashamed for grabbing that toy!" Self-conscious emotions play important roles in children's achievement-related and moral behaviors. The situations in which adults encourage these feelings vary from culture to culture. In Western individualistic nations, most children are taught to feel pride in personal achievement—throwing a ball the farthest, winning a game, and (later on) getting good grades. In collectivist cultures such as China and Japan, calling attention to individual success evokes embarrassment and self-effacement. And violating cultural standards by failing to show concern for others—a parent, a teacher, or an employer—sparks intense shame (Akimoto & Sanbonmatsu, 1999; Lewis, 1992).

Beginnings of Emotional Self-Regulation

Besides expressing a wider range of emotions, infants and toddlers begin to manage their emotional experiences. **Emotional self-regulation** refers to the strategies we use to adjust our emotional state to a comfortable level of intensity so we can accomplish our goals (Eisenberg & Spinrad, 2004; Thompson & Goodvin, 2007). When you remind yourself that an anxiety-provoking event will be over soon, suppress your anger at a friend's behavior, or decide not to see a scary horror film, you are engaging in emotional self-regulation.

Emotional self-regulation requires voluntary, effortful management of emotions. This capacity for *effortful control* improves gradually, as a result of development of the cerebral cortex and the assistance of caregivers, who help children manage intense emotion and teach them strategies for doing so (Fox & Calkins, 2003; Rothbart, Posner, & Kieras, 2006). Individual differences in control of emotion are evident in infancy and, by early childhood, play such a vital role in children's adjustment that—as we will see later—effortful control is considered a major dimension of temperament. A good start in regulating emotion during the first two years contributes greatly to autonomy and mastery of cognitive and social skills (Eisenberg et al., 2004; Lawson & Ruff, 2004).

In the early months, infants have only a limited capacity to regulate their emotional states. When their feelings get too intense, they are easily overwhelmed. They depend on the soothing interventions of caregivers—lifting the distressed baby to the shoulder, rocking, and talking softly.

Rapid development of the frontal lobes of the cerebral cortex increases the baby's tolerance for stimulation. Between 2 and 4 months, caregivers build on this capacity by initiating face-to-face play and attention to objects. In these interactions, parents arouse pleasure in the baby while adjusting the pace of their behavior so the infant does not become overwhelmed and distressed. As a result, the baby's tolerance for stimulation increases further (Kopp & Neufeld, 2003).

By 4 to 6 months, the ability to shift attention helps infants control emotion. Babies who more readily turn away from unpleasant events or engage in self-soothing are less prone to distress (Axia, Bonichini, & Benini, 1999; Crockenberg & Leerkes, 2003). At the end of the first year, crawling and walking enable infants to regulate feelings by approaching or retreating from various situations.

Infants whose parents "read" and respond contingently and sympathetically to their emotional cues tend to be less fussy, to express more pleasurable emotion, to be more interested in exploration, and to be easier to soothe (Crockenberg & Leerkes, 2004; Volling et al., 2002). In contrast, parents who respond impatiently or angrily or who wait to intervene until the infant has become extremely agitated reinforce the baby's rapid rise to intense distress. When caregivers do not regulate stressful experiences for babies, brain structures that buffer stress may fail to develop properly, resulting in an anxious, reactive child with a reduced capacity for regulating emotion and at increased risk of later behavior problems (Crockenberg & Leerkes, 2000; Feldman, 2007; Little & Carter, 2005).

Caregivers also provide lessons in socially approved ways of expressing feelings. From the first few months, parents encourage infants to suppress negative emotion by imitating their expressions of interest, happiness, and surprise more often than their expressions of anger and sadness. Boys get more of this training than girls, in part because boys have a harder time regulating negative emotion (Else-Quest et al., 2006; Malatesta et al., 1986). As a result, the well-known sex difference—females as emotionally expressive and males as emotionally controlled—is promoted at a tender age. Collectivist cultures place particular emphasis on socially appropriate emotional behavior. Compared with North Americans, Japanese and Chinese adults discourage the expression of strong emotion in babies (Fogel, 1993; Kuchner, 1989). By the end of the first year, Chinese and Japanese infants smile and cry less than American infants (Camras et al., 1998).

Toward the end of the second year, a vocabulary for talking about feelings—"happy," "surprised," "scary," "yucky," "mad"—develops rapidly (Bretherton et al., 1986). But toddlers are not yet good at using language to manage their emotions. Temper tantrums tend to occur when an adult rejects their demands, particularly when toddlers are fatigued or hungry (Mascolo & Fischer, 2007). When parents are emotionally sympathetic but set limits (by not giving in to tantrums), distract the child from prohibited activities by offering acceptable alternatives, and later suggest better ways to handle adult refusals, children acquire more effective anger-regulation strategies and social skills during the preschool years (Laible & Thompson, 2002; Lecuyer & Houck, 2006).

Parents who offer such sensitive support encourage toddlers to describe their internal states. Then, when 2-year-olds feel distressed, they can guide caregivers in helping them. For example, while listening to a story about monsters, Grace whimpered, "Mommy, scary." Monica put the book down and gave Grace a comforting hug.

ASK YOURSELF

» REVIEW
Why do many infants show stranger anxiety in the second half of the first year? What factors can increase or decrease wariness of strangers?

» APPLY
At age 14 months, Reggie built a block tower and gleefully knocked it down. But at age 2, he called to his mother and pointed proudly at his tall block tower. What explains this change in Reggie's emotional behavior?

» CONNECT
Why do children of depressed mothers have difficulty regulating emotion (see page 187)? What implications do their weak self-regulatory skills have for their response to cognitive and social challenges?

» REFLECT
How do you typically manage negative emotion? Describe several recent examples. How might your early experiences, gender, and cultural background have influenced your style of emotional self-regulation?

Temperament and Development

From early infancy, Caitlin's sociability was unmistakable. She smiled and laughed while interacting with adults and, in her second year, readily approached other children. Meanwhile, Monica marveled at Grace's calm, relaxed disposition. At 19 months, she sat contented in a highchair through a two-hour family celebration at a restaurant. In contrast, Timmy was active and distractible. Vanessa found herself chasing him as he dropped one toy, moved on to the next, and climbed on chairs and tables.

When we describe one person as cheerful and "upbeat," another as active and energetic, and still others as calm, cautious, or prone to angry outbursts, we are referring to **temperament**—early-appearing, stable individual differences in reactivity and self-regulation. *Reactivity* refers to quickness and intensity of emotional arousal, attention, and motor activity. *Self-regulation,* as we have seen, refers to strategies that modify that reactivity (Rothbart & Bates, 2006). The psychological traits that make up temperament are believed to form the cornerstone of the adult personality.

In 1956, Alexander Thomas and Stella Chess initiated the New York Longitudinal Study, a groundbreaking investigation of the development of temperament that followed 141 children from early infancy well into adulthood. Results showed temperament can increase a child's chances of experiencing psychological problems or, alternatively, protect a child from the negative effects of a highly stressful home life. At the same time, Thomas and Chess (1977) discovered that parenting practices can modify children's temperaments considerably.

These findings stimulated a growing body of research on temperament, including its stability, biological roots, and interaction with child-rearing experiences. Let's begin to explore these issues by looking at the structure, or makeup, of temperament and how it is measured.

The Structure of Temperament

Thomas and Chess's nine dimensions, listed in Table 6.1, served as the first influential model of temperament, inspiring all others that followed. When detailed descriptions of infants' and children's behavior obtained from parent interviews were rated on these dimensions, certain characteristics clustered together, yielding three types of children:

- The **easy child** (40 percent of the sample) quickly establishes regular routines in infancy, is generally cheerful, and adapts easily to new experiences.
- The **difficult child** (10 percent of the sample) is irregular in daily routines, is slow to accept new experiences, and tends to react negatively and intensely.
- The **slow-to-warm-up child** (15 percent of the sample) is inactive, shows mild, low-key reactions to environmental stimuli, is negative in mood, and adjusts slowly to new experiences.

Note that 35 percent of the children did not fit any of these categories. Instead, they showed unique blends of temperamental characteristics.

The "difficult" pattern places children at high risk for adjustment problems—both anxious withdrawal and aggressive behavior in early and middle childhood (Bates, Wachs, & Emde, 1994; Ramos et al., 2005; Thomas, Chess, & Birch, 1968). Compared with difficult children, slow-to-warm-up children present fewer problems in the early years. However, they tend to show excessive fearfulness and slow, constricted behavior in the late preschool and school years, when they are expected to respond actively and quickly in classrooms and peer groups (Chess & Thomas, 1984; Schmitz et al., 1999).

Table 6.1 also shows a second model of temperament, devised by Mary Rothbart, which combines overlapping dimen-

■ **TABLE 6.1** ■ ***Two Models of Temperament***

THOMAS AND CHESS

DIMENSION	DESCRIPTION
Activity level	Ratio of active periods to inactive ones
Rhythmicity	Regularity of body functions, such as sleep, wakefulness, hunger, and excretion
Distractibility	Degree to which stimulation from the environment alters behavior—for example whether crying stops when a toy is offered
Approach/withdrawal	Response to a new object, food, or person
Adaptability	Ease with which child adapts to changes in the environment, such as sleeping or eating in a new place
Attention span and persistence	Amount of time devoted to an activity, such as watching a mobile or playing with a toy
Intensity of reaction	Energy level of response, such as laughing, crying, talking, or gross motor activity
Threshold of responsiveness	Intensity of stimulation required to evoke a response
Quality of mood	Amount of friendly, joyful behavior as opposed to unpleasant, unfriendly behavior

ROTHBART

DIMENSION	DESCRIPTION
REACTIVITY	
Activity level	Level of gross motor activity
Attention span/ persistence	Duration of orienting or interest
Fearful distress	Wariness and distress in response to intense or novel stimuli, including time to adjust to new situations
Irritable distress	Extent of fussing, crying, and distress when desires are frustrated
Positive affect	Frequency of expression of happiness and pleasure
SELF-REGULATION	
Effortful control	Capacity to voluntarily suppress a dominant, reactive response in order to plan and execute a more adaptive response

Sources: Left: Thomas & Chess, 1977; Right: Rothbart, Ahadi, & Evans, 2000; Rothbart & Mauro, 1990.

sions of Thomas and Chess and other researchers. For example, "distractibility" and "attention span and persistence" are considered opposite ends of the same dimension, labeled "attention span/persistence." This model also includes a dimension not identified by Thomas and Chess, "irritable distress," which distinguishes between reactivity triggered by frustration and reactivity due to fear. And it omits overly broad dimensions such as "rhythmicity," "intensity of reaction," and "threshold of responsiveness" (Rothbart, Ahadi, & Evans, 2000; Rothbart & Mauro, 1990). A child who is rhythmic in sleeping is not necessarily rhythmic in eating or bowel habits. And a child who smiles and laughs quickly and intensely is not necessarily quick and intense in fear, irritability, or motor activity.

According to Rothbart, individuals differ not just in their reactivity on each dimension, but also in the self-regulatory dimension of temperament, **effortful control**—the capacity to voluntarily suppress a dominant response in order to plan and execute a more adaptive response (Rothbart, 2003; Rothbart & Bates, 2006). Variations in effortful control are evident in how effectively a child can focus and shift attention, inhibit impulses, and manage negative emotion.

Measuring Temperament

Temperament is often assessed through interviews or questionnaires given to parents. Behavior ratings by pediatricians, teachers, and others familiar with the child and laboratory observations by researchers have also been used. Parental reports are convenient and take advantage of parents' depth of knowledge about their child (Gartstein & Rothbart, 2003). Although information from parents has been criticized as biased, parental reports are moderately related to researchers' observations of children's behavior (Mangelsdorf, Schoppe, & Buur, 2000). And parent perceptions are useful for understanding how parents view and respond to their child.

Observations by researchers in the home or laboratory avoid the subjectivity of parental reports but can lead to other inaccuracies. In homes, observers find it hard to capture rare but important events, such as infants' response to frustration. And in an unfamiliar lab, fearful children who calmly avoid certain experiences at home may become too upset to complete the session (Wachs & Bates, 2001). Still, researchers can better control children's experiences in the lab. And they can conveniently combine observations of behavior with physiological measures to gain insight into the biological bases of temperament.

Most physiological research has focused on children who fall at opposite extremes of the positive-affect and fearful-distress dimensions of temperament (refer again to Table 6.1): **inhibited,** or **shy, children,** who react negatively to and withdraw from novel stimuli, and **uninhibited,** or **sociable, children,** who display positive emotion to and approach novel stimuli. As the Biology and Environment box on the following page reveals,

BIOLOGY AND ENVIRONMENT

Development of Shyness and Sociability

Two 4-month-old babies, Larry and Mitch, visited the laboratory of Jerome Kagan, who observed their reactions to various unfamiliar experiences. When exposed to new sights and sounds, such as a moving mobile decorated with colorful toys, Larry tensed his muscles, moved his arms and legs with agitation, and began to cry. In contrast, Mitch remained relaxed and quiet, smiling and cooing.

As toddlers, Larry and Mitch returned to the laboratory, where they experienced procedures designed to induce uncertainty. Electrodes were placed on their bodies and blood pressure cuffs on their arms to measure heart rate; toy robots, animals, and puppets moved before their eyes; and unfamiliar people behaved in unexpected ways or wore novel costumes. While Larry whimpered and quickly withdrew, Mitch watched with interest, laughed, and approached the toys and strangers.

On a third visit, at age 4½, Larry barely talked or smiled during an interview with an unfamiliar adult. In contrast, Mitch asked questions and communicated his pleasure at each new activity. In a playroom with two unfamiliar peers, Larry pulled back and watched, while Mitch made friends quickly.

In longitudinal research on several hundred Caucasian children, Kagan found that about 20 percent of 4-month-old babies were, like Larry, easily upset by novelty; 40 percent, like Mitch, were comfortable, even delighted, with new experiences. About 20 to 30 percent of these groups retained their temperamental styles as they grew older (Kagan, 2003; Kagan & Saudino, 2001; Kagan et al., 2007). But most children's dispositions became less extreme over time. Biological makeup and child-rearing experiences jointly influenced stability and change in temperament.

Physiological Correlates of Shyness and Sociability

Kagan believes that individual differences in arousal of the *amygdala,* an inner brain structure that controls avoidance reactions, contribute to these contrasting temperaments. In shy, inhibited children, novel stimuli easily excite the amygdala and its connections to the cerebral cortex and the sympathetic nervous system, which prepares the body to act in the face of threat. In sociable, uninhibited children, the same level of stimulation evokes minimal neural excitation (Kagan & Fox, 2006). While viewing photos of unfamiliar faces, adults who had been classified as inhibited in the second year of life showed greater fMRI activity in the amygdala than adults who had been uninhibited as toddlers (Schwartz et al., 2003). And additional physiological reponses mediated by the amygdala distinguish these two emotional styles:

- *Heart rate.* From the first few weeks of life, the heart rates of shy children are consistently higher than those of sociable children, and they speed up further in response to unfamiliar events (Schmidt et al., 2007; Snidman et al., 1995).
- *Cortisol.* Saliva concentrations of the stress hormone cortisol tend to be higher, and to rise more in response to a stressful event, in shy than in sociable children (Schmidt et al., 1997, 1999; Zimmermann & Stansbury, 2004).
- *Pupil dilation, blood pressure, and skin surface temperature.* Compared with sociable children, shy children show greater pupil dilation, rise in blood pressure, and cooling of the fingertips when faced with novelty (Kagan et al., 1999, 2007).

Another physiological correlate of approach–withdrawal to people and objects is the pattern of brain waves in the frontal lobes of the cerebral cortex. Shy infants and preschoolers show greater EEG activity in the right frontal lobe, which is associated with negative emotional reactivity; sociable children show the opposite pattern (Kagan & Snidman, 2004; Kagan et al., 2007). Neural activity in the amygdala, which is transmitted to the frontal lobes, probably contributes to these differences. Inhibited children also show greater generalized activation of the cerebral cortex, an indicator of high emotional arousal and monitoring of new situations for potential threats (Henderson et al., 2004).

Child-Rearing Practices

According to Kagan, extremely shy or sociable children inherit a physiology that biases them toward a particular temperamental style. Yet heritability research indicates that genes contribute only modestly to shyness and sociability (Kagan & Fox, 2006).

Child-rearing practices affect the chances that an emotionally reactive baby will become a fearful child. Warm, supportive parenting reduces shy infants' and preschoolers' intense physiological reaction to novelty, whereas cold, intrusive parenting heightens anxiety (Rubin, Burgess, & Hastings, 2002). And if parents protect infants who dislike novelty from minor stresses, they make it harder for the child to overcome an urge to retreat. Parents who make appropriate demands for their baby to approach new experiences help the child overcome fear (Rubin et al., 1997).

When inhibition persists, it leads to excessive cautiousness, low self-esteem, and loneliness. In adolescence, persistent shyness increases the risk of severe anxiety, especially social phobia—intense fear of being humiliated in social situations (Kagan & Fox, 2006). To acquire effective social skills, inhibited children need parenting tailored to their temperaments—a theme we will encounter again in this and later chapters.

A strong physiological response to unfamiliar situations prompts this toddler to cling to his older sister. With patient but insistent encouragement, the family can help the child overcome the urge to retreat.

biologically based reactivity—evident in heart rate, hormone levels, and EEG brain waves—differentiates children with inhibited and uninhibited temperaments.

Stability of Temperament

Young children who score low or high on attention span, irritability, sociability, shyness, or effortful control tend to respond similarly when assessed again several months to a few years later and, occasionally, even into the adult years (Caspi et al., 2003; Kochanska & Knaack, 2003; Komsi et al., 2006; Majdandžić & van den Boom, 2007; Rothbart, Ahadi, & Evans, 2000). However, the overall stability of temperament is only low to moderate.

A major reason is that temperament itself develops with age. To illustrate, let's look at irritability and activity level. Recall from Chapter 3 that the early months are a period of fussing and crying for most babies. As infants can better regulate their attention and emotions, many who initially seemed irritable become calm and content. In the case of activity level, the meaning of the behavior changes. At first, an active, wriggling infant tends to be highly aroused and uncomfortable, whereas an inactive baby is often alert and attentive. Once infants move on their own, the reverse is so! An active crawler is usually alert and interested in exploration, whereas an inactive baby may be fearful and withdrawn.

These discrepancies help us understand why long-term prediction from early temperament is best achieved after age 3, when styles of responding are better established (Roberts & DelVecchio, 2000). In line with this idea, between age 2½ and 3, children improve substantially and also perform more consistently across a wide range of tasks requiring effortful control, such as waiting for a reward, lowering their voice to a whisper, and selectively attending to one stimulus while ignoring competing stimuli (Kochanska, Murray, & Harlan, 2000; Li-Grining, 2007). Researchers believe that around this time, areas in the frontal lobes involved in suppressing impulses develop rapidly (Gerardi-Caulton, 2000; Rothbart & Bates, 2006).

Nevertheless, the ease with which children manage their reactivity in early childhood depends on the type and strength of the reactive emotion involved. Preschoolers who were highly fearful as toddlers score slightly better than their agemates in effortful control. In contrast, angry, irritable toddlers tend to be less effective at effortful control at later ages (Kochanska & Knaack, 2003; Kochanska, Murray, & Harlan, 2000).

In sum, many factors affect the extent to which a child's temperament remains stable, including development of the biological systems on which temperament is based, the child's capacity for effortful control, and the success of her efforts, which depend on the quality and intensity of her emotional reactivity. When we consider the evidence as a whole, the low to moderate stability of temperament makes sense. It also confirms that experience can modify biologically based temperamental traits considerably, although children rarely change from one extreme to another—that is, a shy toddler practically never becomes highly sociable. With these ideas in mind, let's turn to genetic and environmental contributions to temperament and personality.

Genetic Influences

The word *temperament* implies a genetic foundation for individual differences in personality. Research indicates that identical twins are more similar than fraternal twins across a wide range of temperamental and personality traits (Bouchard, 2004; Bouchard & Loehlin, 2001; Caspi & Shiner, 2006; Goldsmith, Pollak, & Davidson, 2008). In Chapter 2, we noted that heritability estimates suggest a moderate role for heredity in temperament and personality: On average, half of individual differences have been attributed to differences in genetic makeup.

Consistent ethnic and sex differences in early temperament exist, again implying a role for heredity. Compared with North American Caucasian infants, Japanese and Chinese babies tend to be less active, irritable, and vocal, more easily soothed when upset, and better at quieting themselves (Kagan et al., 1994; Lewis, Ramsay, & Kawakami, 1993). Grace's capacity to remain contentedly seated in her highchair through a long family dinner certainly fits with this evidence.

Timmy's high rate of activity illustrates a typical sex difference (Gartstein & Rothbart, 2003). From an early age, boys are more active and daring, more irritable when frustrated, and slightly more impulsive—factors that contribute to boys' higher injury rates throughout childhood and adolescence. And girls' large advantage in effortful control undoubtedly contributes to their greater compliance, better school performance, and lower incidence of behavior problems (Eisenberg et al., 2004; Else-Quest et al., 2006).

Nevertheless, genetic influences vary with the temperamental trait and with the age of individuals studied. For example, heritability estimates are higher for expressions of negative emotion than for positive emotion. And the role of heredity is considerably less in infancy than in childhood and later years, when temperament becomes more stable (Wachs & Bates, 2001).

Environmental Influences

Environment also has a powerful influence on temperament. For example, persistent nutritional and emotional deprivation profoundly alters temperament, resulting in maladaptive emotional reactivity. Recall from Chapter 4 that even after dietary improvement, children exposed to severe, early malnutrition remain more distractible and fearful than their agemates. And infants reared in deprived orphanages are easily overwhelmed by stressful events. Their poor regulation of emotion results in inattention and weak impulse control, including frequent expressions of anger (see pages 127 and 132).

Other research shows that heredity and environment often combine to influence temperament, since a child's approach to the world affects the experiences to which she is exposed. To see how this works, let's take a second look at ethnic and sex differences in temperament. Japanese mothers usually say that babies come into the world as independent beings who must learn to rely on their mothers through close physical contact. North American mothers typically believe just the opposite—that they must wean babies away from dependency toward autonomy. Consistent with these beliefs, Asian mothers interact gently, soothingly, and gesturally with their babies, whereas Caucasian mothers use a more active, stimulating, verbal approach (Rothbaum et al., 2000a). These differences enhance early ethnic differences in temperament.

A similar process seems to contribute to sex differences in temperament. Within 24 hours after birth (before they have had much experience with the baby), parents perceive boys and girls differently. They rate sons as larger, better coordinated, more alert, and stronger, daughters as softer, weaker, and more delicate and awkward (Stern & Karraker, 1989; Vogel et al., 1991). These gender-stereotyped beliefs influence parents' treatment of infants and toddlers. Parents more often encourage their young sons to be physically active and their daughters to seek help and physical closeness (Ruble, Martin, & Berenbaum, 2006).

In families with several children, an additional influence on temperament is at work. ***TAKE A MOMENT...*** Ask several parents to describe each of their children's personalities. You will see that they often look for differences between siblings: "She's a lot more active," "He's more sociable," "She's far more persistent." As a result, parents often view siblings as more distinct than other observers do. In a large study of 1- to 3-year-old twin pairs, parents rated identical twins as resembling each other less in temperament than researchers' ratings indicated. And whereas researchers rated fraternal twins as moderately similar, parents viewed them as somewhat opposite in temperamental style (Saudino, 2003).

Parents' tendency to emphasize each child's unique qualities affects their child-rearing practices. In an investigation of identical-twin toddlers, mothers' differential treatment predicted differences in psychological adjustment. The twin who received more warmth and less harshness was more positive in mood and social behavior (Deater-Deckard et al., 2001). Each child, in turn, evokes responses from caregivers that are consistent with parental beliefs and the child's developing temperament.

Besides different experiences within the family, siblings have distinct experiences with teachers, peers, and others in their community that affect personality development. And in middle childhood and adolescence, they often seek ways to differ from one another. In adulthood, both identical and fraternal twins tend to become increasingly dissimilar (Loehlin & Martin, 2001; McCartney, Harris, & Bernieri, 1990). The less contact twins have with each other, the stronger this effect. In sum, temperament and personality can be understood only in terms of complex interdependencies between genetic and environmental factors.

Temperament and Child Rearing: The Goodness-of-Fit Model

If a child's disposition interferes with learning or getting along with others, adults must gently but consistently counteract the child's maladaptive style. Thomas and Chess (1977) proposed a **goodness-of-fit model** to describe how temperament and environment together can produce favorable outcomes. Goodness of fit involves creating child-rearing environments that recognize each child's temperament while encouraging more adaptive functioning.

Difficult children (who withdraw from new experiences and react negatively and intensely) frequently experience parenting that fits poorly with their dispositions, putting them at high risk for later adjustment problems. By the second year, parents of difficult children often resort to angry, punitive discipline, which undermines the development of effortful control. As the child reacts with defiance and disobedience, parents

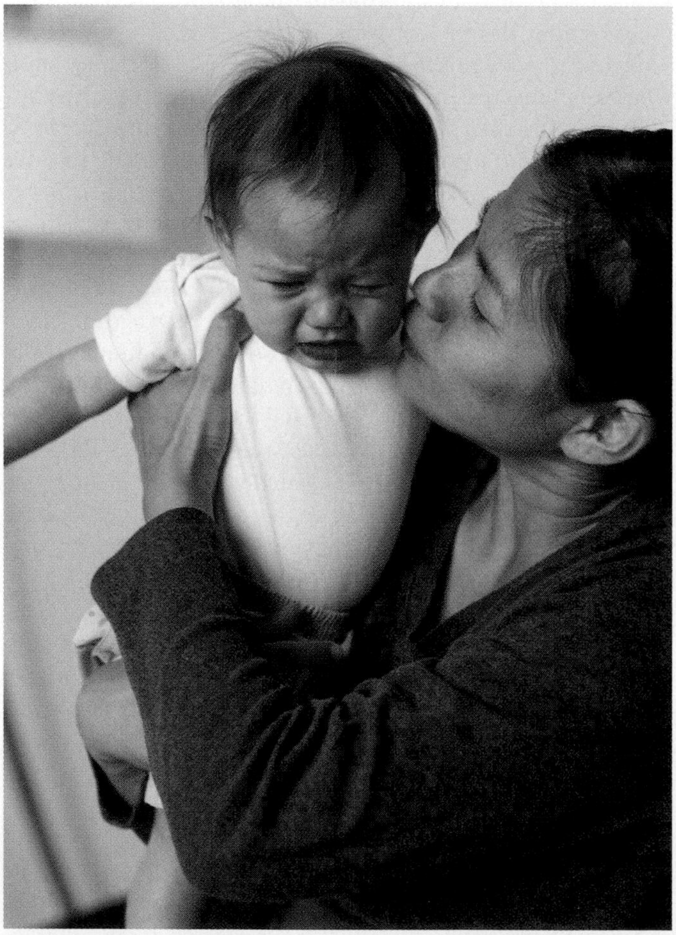

"Goodness-of-fit" describes the interaction between a child's biologically based temperament and the child-rearing environment. This mother's calm, soothing response to her baby's fussiness will help the child regulate intense emotions and develop more adaptive responses to frustration.

become increasingly stressed (Coplan, Bowker, & Cooper, 2003; Paulussen-Hoogeboom et al., 2007). As a result, they continue their coercive tactics and also discipline inconsistently, at times rewarding the child's noncompliance by giving in to it (Calkins, 2002). These practices sustain and even increase the child's irritable, conflict-ridden style. In contrast, when parents are positive and sensitive, which helps infants and toddlers regulate emotion, difficultness declines by age 2 or 3 (Feldman, Greenbaum, & Yirmiya, 1999; Raikes et al., 2007).

Effective parenting, however, depends on life conditions—good parental mental health, marital happiness, and favorable economic conditions (Schoppe-Sullivan et al., 2007). In a comparison of Russian and U.S. babies, Russian infants were more emotionally negative, fearful, and upset when frustrated (Gartstein, Slobodskaya, & Kinsht, 2003). Faced with a depressed national economy, which resulted in financial worries and longer work hours, Russian parents may have lacked time and energy for the patient parenting that protects against difficultness.

Cultural values also affect the fit between parenting and child temperament, as research in China illustrates. In the past, collectivist values, which discourage self-assertion, led Chinese adults to evaluate shy children positively. Several studies showed that Chinese children of a decade or two ago appeared well-adjusted, academically and socially (Chen, Rubin, & Li, 1995; Chen et al., 1998). But rapid expansion of a competitive economy in China, which requires assertiveness and sociability for success, may be responsible for a recent change in Chinese parents' and teachers' attitudes toward childhood shyness (Chen, Wang, & DeSouza, 2006; Yu, 2002). Among Shanghai fourth graders, the association between shyness and adjustment also changed over time. Whereas shyness was positively correlated with teacher-rated competence, peer acceptance, leadership, and academic achievement in 1990, these relationships weakened in 1998 and reversed in 2002, when they mirrored findings of Western research (see Figure 6.1) (Chen et al., 2005). Cultural context makes a difference in whether shy children receive support or disapproval and whether they adjust well or poorly.

An effective match between rearing conditions and child temperament is best accomplished early, before unfavorable temperament–environment relationships produce maladjustment. Both difficult and shy children benefit from warm, accepting parenting that makes firm but reasonable demands for mastering new experiences. With reserved, inactive toddlers, highly stimulating parental behavior—encouraging, questioning, and pointing out objects—fosters exploration. Yet for highly active babies, this approach is too directive, dampening their play and curiosity (Miceli et al., 1998).

The goodness-of-fit model reminds us that infants have unique dispositions that adults must accept. Parents can neither take full credit for their children's virtues nor be blamed for all their faults. But parents can turn an environment that exaggerates a child's problems into one that builds on the child's strengths. As we will see, goodness of fit is also at the heart of infant–caregiver attachment. This first intimate relationship grows out of interaction between parent and baby, to which the emotional styles of both partners contribute.

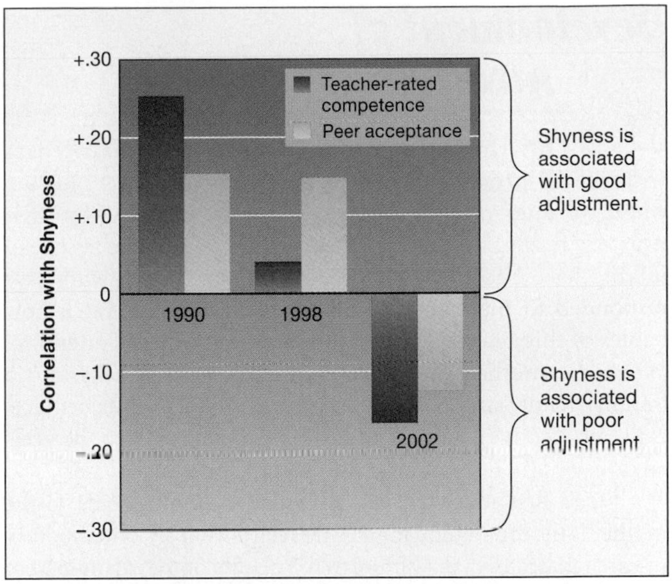

■ **FIGURE 6.1** ■ **Changes over time in correlations between shyness and adjustment among Chinese fourth graders.** In 1990, shy Chinese children appeared well-adjusted. But as China's market economy expanded and valuing of self-assertion and sociability increased, the direction of the correlations shifted. In 2002, shyness was negatively associated with adjustment. These findings are for teacher-rated competence and peer acceptance. Those for leadership (holding offices in student organizations) and academic achievement changed similarly. (Adapted from Chen et al., 2005.)

ASK YOURSELF

» REVIEW
How do genetic and environmental factors work together to influence temperament? Cite several examples from research.

» APPLY
Mandy and Jeff are parents of 2-year-old inhibited Sam and 3-year-old difficult Maria. Explain the importance of effortful control to Mandy and Jeff, and suggest ways they can strengthen it in each of their children.

» CONNECT
Do findings on ethnic and sex differences in temperament illustrate genetic–environmental correlation, discussed on page 72 in Chapter 2? Explain.

» REFLECT
How would you describe your temperament as a young child? Do you think your temperament has remained stable, or has it changed? What factors might be involved?

Development of Attachment

Attachment is the strong affectionate tie we have with special people in our lives that leads us to feel pleasure when we interact with them and to be comforted by their nearness in times of stress. By the second half of the first year, infants have become attached to familiar people who have responded to their needs. ***TAKE A MOMENT...*** Watch how babies of this age single out their parents for special attention. When the mother enters the room, the baby breaks into a broad, friendly smile. When she picks him up, he pats her face, explores her hair, and snuggles against her. When he feels anxious or afraid, he crawls into her lap and clings closely.

Freud first suggested that the infant's emotional tie to the mother is the foundation for all later relationships. Contemporary research indicates that—although the quality of the infant–parent bond is vitally important—later development is influenced not just by early attachment experiences but also by the continuing quality of the parent–child relationship.

Attachment has also been the subject of intense theoretical debate. Turn back to the description of Erikson's theory at the beginning of this chapter, and notice how the *psychoanalytic perspective* regards feeding as the primary context in which caregivers and babies build this emotional bond. *Behaviorism,* too, emphasizes the importance of feeding, but for different reasons. According to a well-known behaviorist explanation, infants learn to prefer the mother's soft caresses, warm smiles, and tender words of comfort because these events are paired with tension relief as she satisfies the baby's hunger.

Although feeding is an important context for building a close relationship, attachment does not depend on hunger satisfaction. In the 1950s, a famous experiment showed that rhesus monkeys reared with terry-cloth and wire-mesh "surrogate mothers" clung to the soft terry-cloth substitute, even though the wire-mesh "mother" held the bottle and infants had to climb onto it to be fed (Harlow & Zimmerman, 1959). Human infants, too, become attached to family members who seldom feed them, including fathers, siblings, and grandparents. And toddlers in Western cultures who sleep alone and experience frequent daytime separations from their parents sometimes develop strong emotional ties to cuddly objects, such as blankets and teddy bears, that have never played a role in infant feeding!

Baby monkeys reared with "surrogate mothers" preferred to cling to a soft terry-cloth "mother" over a wire-mesh "mother" that held a bottle. These findings contradict both psychoanalytic and behaviorist views of feeding as central to building infant–caregiver attachment.

Ethological Theory of Attachment

Today, **ethological theory of attachment,** which recognizes the infant's emotional tie to the caregiver as an evolved response that promotes survival, is the most widely accepted view. John Bowlby (1969), who first applied this idea to the infant–caregiver bond, was inspired by Konrad Lorenz's studies of imprinting (see Chapter 1). Bowlby believed that the human infant, like the young of other animal species, is endowed with a set of built-in behaviors that help keep the parent nearby to protect the infant from danger and to provide support for exploring and mastering the environment (Waters & Cummings, 2000). Contact with the parent also ensures that the baby will be fed, but Bowlby pointed out that feeding is not the basis for attachment. Rather, attachment can best be understood in an evolutionary context in which survival of the species—through ensuring both safety and competence—is of utmost importance.

According to Bowlby, the infant's relationship with the parent begins as a set of innate signals that call the adult to the baby's side. Over time, a true affectionate bond develops, supported by new cognitive and emotional capacities as well as by a history of warm, sensitive care. Attachment develops in four phases:

1. *Preattachment phase* (birth to 6 weeks). Built-in signals—grasping, smiling, crying, and gazing into the adult's eyes—help bring newborn babies into close contact with other humans, who comfort them. Babies of this age recognize their own mother's smell and voice (see Chapter 3). But they are not yet attached to her, since they do not mind being left with an unfamiliar adult.
2. *"Attachment-in-the-making" phase* (6 weeks to 6–8 months). During this phase, infants respond differently to a familiar caregiver than to a stranger. For example, at 4 months, Timmy smiled, laughed, and babbled more freely when interacting with his mother and quieted more quickly when she picked him up. As infants learn that their own actions affect the behavior of those around them, they begin to develop a *sense of trust*—the expectation that the care-

giver will respond when signaled—but they still do not protest when separated from her.

3. *"Clear-cut" attachment phase* (6–8 months to 18 months–2 years). Now attachment to the familiar caregiver is evident. Babies display **separation anxiety,** becoming upset when their trusted caregiver leaves. Like stranger anxiety (see page 186), separation anxiety does not always occur; it depends on infant temperament and the current situation. But in many cultures, separation anxiety increases between 6 and 15 months. Besides protesting the parent's departure, older infants and toddlers try hard to maintain her presence. They approach, follow, and climb on her in preference to others. And they use the familiar caregiver as a secure base from which to explore.
4. *Formation of a reciprocal relationship* (18 months–2 years and on). By the end of the second year, rapid growth in representation and language permits toddlers to understand some of the factors that influence the parent's coming and going and to predict her return. As a result, separation protest declines. Now children negotiate with the caregiver, using requests and persuasion to alter her goals. For example, at age 2, Caitlin asked Carolyn and David to read a story before leaving her with a baby-sitter. The extra time with her parents, along with a better understanding of where they were going ("to have dinner with Uncle Sean") and when they would be back ("right after you go to sleep"), helped Caitlin withstand her parents' absence.

According to Bowlby (1980), out of their experiences during these four phases, children construct an enduring affectionate tie to the caregiver that they can use as a secure base in the parents' absence. This image serves as an **internal working model,** or set of expectations about the availability of attachment figures and their likelihood of providing support during times of stress. The internal working model becomes a vital part of personality, serving as a guide for all future close relationships (Bretherton & Munholland, 1999).

Separation anxiety increases as clear-cut infant–caregiver attachment develops. But the occurrence of separation anxiety depends on infant temperament, context, and adult behavior. Here, the child's distress at his mother's departure will probably be short-lived because his caregiver is supportive and sensitive.

Consistent with these ideas, as early as the second year, toddlers form attachment-related expectations about parental comfort and support. In one study, securely attached 12- to 16-month-olds looked longer at a video of an unresponsive caregiver (inconsistent with their expectations) than a video of a responsive caregiver. Insecurely attached toddlers, in contrast, did not distinguish between the two (see Figure 6.2) (Johnson, Dweck, & Chen, 2007).

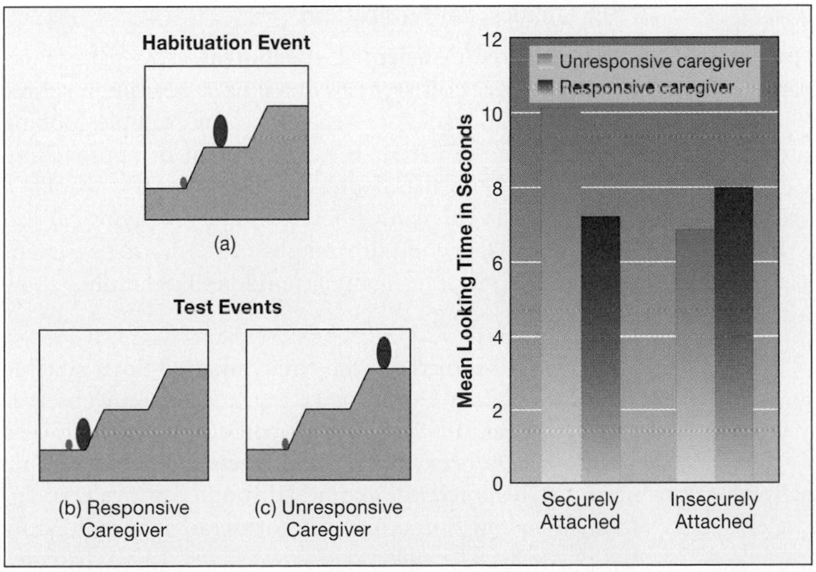

■ **FIGURE 6.2** ■ **Testing toddlers for internal working models of attachment.** (a) First, 12- to 16-month-olds were habituated to a video of two animated shapes, one large (the "caregiver") and one small (the "child"). The caregiver traveled halfway up an incline to a plateau, and the child began to "cry," depicted by pulsing and bouncing accompanied by an infant cry. Next the researchers presented two test events: (b) In the *responsive caregiver outcome,* the caregiver returned to the child. (c) In the *unresponsive caregiver outcome,* the caregiver continued up the slope away from the child. Securely attached toddlers looked longer at the unresponsive outcome, depicting caregiver behavior inconsistent with their expectations. Insecurely attached toddlers did not differentiate between the two test events. (Adapted from Johnson, Dweck, & Chen, 2007.)

■ TABLE 6.2 ■ *Episodes in the Strange Situation*

EPISODE	EVENTS	ATTACHMENT BEHAVIOR OBSERVED
1	Researcher introduces parent and baby to playroom and then leaves.	
2	Parent is seated while baby plays with toys.	Parent as a secure base
3	Stranger enters, is seated, and talks to parent.	Reaction to unfamiliar adult
4	Parent leaves room. Stranger responds to baby and offers comfort if baby is upset.	Separation anxiety
5	Parent returns, greets baby, and offers comfort if necessary. Stranger leaves room.	Reaction to reunion
6	Parent leaves room.	Separation anxiety
7	Stranger enters room and offers comfort.	Ability to be soothed by stranger
8	Parent returns, greets baby, offers comfort if necessary, and tries to reinterest baby in toys.	Reaction to reunion

Note: Episode 1 lasts about 30 seconds; each of the remaining episodes lasts about 3 minutes. Separation episodes are cut short if the baby becomes very upset. Reunion episodes are extended if the baby needs more time to calm down and return to play.
Source: Ainsworth et al., 1978.

With cognitive development and continuing experiences in close relationships, this budding internal working model expands into a broader, more complex representation. Children revise it as they interact with parents and form other bonds with adults, siblings, and friends.

Measuring the Security of Attachment

Although virtually all family-reared babies become attached to a familiar caregiver by the second year, the quality of this relationship varies. Some children appear secure—certain that the caregiver will provide affection and support. Others seem anxious and uncertain.

A widely used laboratory procedure for assessing the quality of attachment between 1 and 2 years of age is the **Strange Situation,** which takes the baby through eight short episodes in which brief separations from and reunions with the parent occur (see Table 6.2 above). In designing it, Mary Ainsworth and her colleagues reasoned that securely attached infants and toddlers should use the parent as a secure base from which to explore an unfamiliar playroom. In addition, when the parent leaves, an unfamiliar adult should be less comforting than the parent.

Observing infants' responses to these episodes, researchers have identified a secure attachment pattern and three patterns of insecurity; a few babies cannot be classified (Ainsworth et al., 1978; Barnett & Vondra, 1999; Main & Solomon, 1990; Thompson, 2006). ***TAKE A MOMENT...*** From the description at the beginning of this chapter, which pattern do you think Grace displayed after adjusting to her adoptive family?

- **Secure attachment.** These infants use the parent as a secure base. When separated, they may or may not cry, but if they do, it is because the parent is absent and they prefer her to the stranger. When the parent returns, they actively seek contact, and their crying is reduced immediately. About 60 percent of North American infants in middle-SES families show this pattern. (In low-SES families, a smaller proportion of babies show the secure pattern, with higher proportions falling into the insecure patterns.)
- **Avoidant attachment.** These infants seem unresponsive to the parent when she is present. When she leaves, they usually are not distressed, and they react to the stranger in much the same way as to the parent. During reunion, they avoid or are slow to greet the parent, and when picked up, they often fail to cling. About 15 percent of North American infants in middle-SES families show this pattern.
- **Resistant attachment.** Before separation, these infants seek closeness to the parent and often fail to explore. When the parent leaves, they are usually distressed, and on her return they combine clinginess with angry, resistive behavior, sometimes hitting and pushing. Many continue to cry after being picked up and cannot be comforted easily. About 10 percent of North American infants in middle-SES families show this pattern.
- **Disorganized/disoriented attachment.** This pattern reflects the greatest insecurity. At reunion, these infants show confused, contradictory behaviors—for example, looking away while the parent is holding them or approaching the parent with flat, depressed emotion. Most display a dazed facial expression. A few cry out after having calmed down or display odd, frozen postures. About 15 percent of North American infants in middle-SES families show this pattern.

An alternative method, the **Attachment Q-Sort,** suitable for children between 1 and 4 years, depends on home observation (Waters et al., 1995). Either the parent or a highly trained observer sorts 90 behaviors ("Child greets mother with a big smile when she enters the room," "If mother moves very far, child follows along") into nine categories ranging from highly descriptive to not at all descriptive of the child. Then a score, ranging from high to low in security, is computed.

The Q-Sort is time-consuming, requiring a nonparent observer to spend several hours observing the child before sorting. And it does not indicate patterns of insecurity. But it may better reflect the parent–infant relationship in everyday life. The Q-Sort responses of expert observers correspond well with babies' secure-base behavior in the Strange Situation, but parents' Q-Sorts do not (van IJzendoorn et al., 2004). Parents of insecure children, especially, may have difficulty accurately reporting their child's attachment behaviors.

Stability of Attachment

Research on the stability of attachment patterns between 1 and 2 years of age yields a wide range of findings (Thompson, 2000, 2006). A close look at which babies stay the same and which ones change yields a more consistent picture. Quality of attachment is usually secure and stable for middle-SES babies experiencing favorable life conditions. And infants who move from insecurity to security typically have well-adjusted mothers with positive family and friendship ties. Perhaps many became parents before they were psychologically ready but, with social support, grew into the role.

In contrast, in low-SES families with many daily stresses and little social support, attachment generally moves away from security or changes from one insecure pattern to another (Belsky et al., 1996; Fish, 2004; Vondra, Hommerding, & Shaw, 1999; Vondra et al., 2001). In one long-term follow-up of a poverty-stricken sample, many securely attached infants ended up insecure when reassessed in early adulthood. Child maltreatment, maternal depression, and poor family functioning in adolescence distinguished these young people from the few who stayed securely attached (Weinfield, Sroufe, & Egeland, 2000; Weinfield, Whaley, & Egeland, 2004).

These findings indicate that securely attached babies more often maintain their attachment status than insecure babies. The exception is disorganized/disoriented attachment, an insecure pattern that is as stable as attachment security: Nearly 70 percent retain this classification over time (Hesse & Main, 2000; Weinfield, Whaley, & Egeland, 2004). As you will soon see, many disorganized/disoriented babies experience extremely negative caregiving, which may disrupt emotional self-regulation so severely that confused, ambivalent feelings toward parents persist.

Among the Dogon people of Mali, Africa, mothers stay close to their babies and respond promptly and gently to infant distress. Dogon mothers are almost never overly stimulating or intrusive—practices linked to avoidant attachment. And none of their infants were avoidantly attached to their mothers.

Cultural Variations

Cross-cultural evidence indicates that attachment patterns may have to be interpreted differently in certain cultures. For example, as Figure 6.3 on page 200 reveals, German infants show considerably more avoidant attachment than American babies do. But German parents value independence and encourage their infants to be nonclingy (Grossmann et al., 1985). In contrast, a study of infants of the Dogon people of Mali, Africa, revealed that none showed avoidant attachment to their mothers (True, Pisani, & Oumar, 2001). Even when grandmothers are primary caregivers (as they are with firstborn sons), Dogon mothers remain available, holding their babies close and nursing promptly in response to hunger and distress.

Japanese infants, as well, rarely show avoidant attachment (refer again to Figure 6.3) Rather, many are resistantly attached, but this reaction may not represent true insecurity. Japanese mothers seldom leave their babies in others' care, so the Strange Situation probably induces greater stress in them than in infants who frequently experience maternal separations (Takahashi, 1990). Also, Japanese parents view the infant attention seeking that is part of resistant attachment as a normal indicator of infant dependency (Rothbaum et al., 2000b). Despite such cultural variations, the secure pattern is still the most common attachment quality in all societies studied (van IJzendoorn & Sagi, 1999).

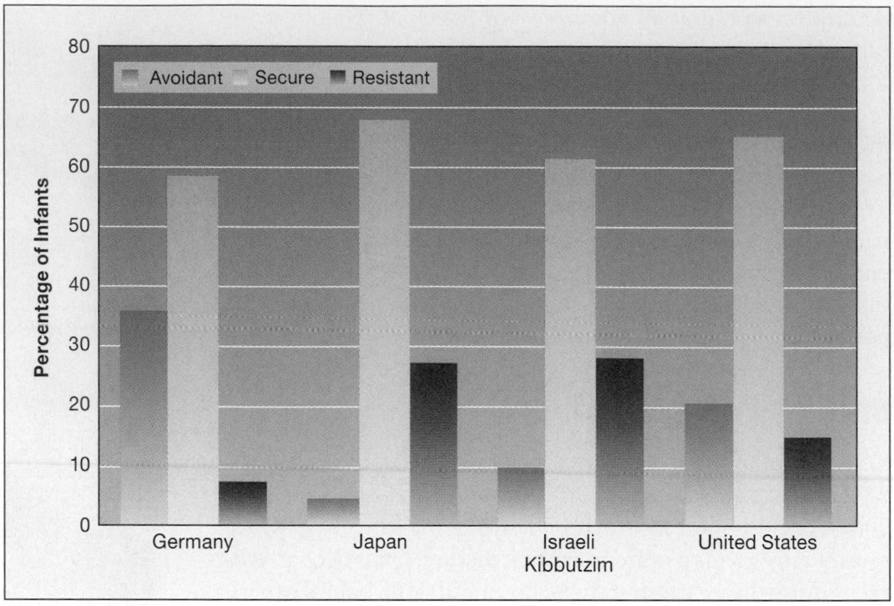

■ **FIGURE 6.3** ■ **A cross-cultural comparison of infants' reactions in the Strange Situation.** A high percentage of German babies seem avoidantly attached, whereas a substantial number of Japanese infants appear resistantly attached. Note that these responses may not reflect true insecurity. Instead, they are probably due to cultural differences in values and child-rearing practices. (Adapted from van IJzendoorn & Kroonenberg, 1988.)

Factors That Affect Attachment Security

What factors might influence attachment security? Researchers have looked closely at four important influences: (1) opportunity to establish a close relationship, (2) quality of caregiving, (3) the baby's characteristics, and (4) family context.

■ **OPPORTUNITY FOR ATTACHMENT.** What happens when a baby does not have the opportunity to establish a close tie to a caregiver? In a series of studies, René Spitz (1946) observed institutionalized infants whose mothers had given them up between 3 and 12 months of age. After being placed in a large ward where each shared a nurse with at least seven others, the babies lost weight, wept, and withdrew from their surroundings. If a consistent caregiver did not replace the mother, the depression deepened rapidly.

These institutionalized babies had emotional problems because they were prevented from forming a bond with one or a few adults (Rutter, 1996). Another study supports this conclusion. Researchers followed the development of infants in an institution with a good caregiver–child ratio and a rich selection of books and toys. However, staff turnover was so rapid that the average child had 50 caregivers by age 4½! Many of these children became "late adoptees" who were placed in homes after age 4. Most developed deep ties with their adoptive parents, indicating that a first attachment bond can develop as late as 4 to 6 years of age (Hodges & Tizard, 1989; Tizard & Rees, 1975). But these children were more likely to display attachment difficulties, including an excessive desire for adult attention, "overfriendliness" to unfamiliar adults and peers, failure to check back with the parent in anxiety-arousing situations, and few friendships.

Adopted children who spent their first 6 to 8 months or more in deprived Romanian orphanages often display these same difficulties (O'Connor et al., 2003). Symptoms typically persist and are associated with wide-ranging mental health problems in middle childhood, including cognitive impairments, peer rejection, inattention and hyperactivity, and disruptive behavior (O'Connor et al., 2003; Rutter et al., 2007). Furthermore, as early as 7 months, Romanian orphanage children show reduced ERP brain waves in response to facial expressions of emotion and have trouble discriminating such expressions—outcomes that suggest disrupted formation of neural structures involved in "reading" emotions (Parker et al., 2005). Taken together, the evidence indicates that fully normal development depends on establishing close ties with caregivers early in life.

■ **QUALITY OF CAREGIVING.** Dozens of studies report that **sensitive caregiving**—responding promptly, consistently, and appropriately to infants and holding them tenderly and carefully—is moderately related to attachment security in diverse cultures and SES groups (De Wolff & van IJzendoorn, 1997; Posada et al., 2002, 2004; van IJzendoorn et al., 2004). In contrast, insecurely attached infants tend to have mothers who engage in less physical contact, handle them awkwardly or "routinely," and are sometimes resentful and rejecting, particularly in response to infant distress (Ainsworth et al., 1978; Isabella, 1993; McElwain & Booth-LaForce, 2006; Pederson & Moran, 1996).

Also, in several studies of North American infants, a special form of communication called **interactional synchrony** separated the experiences of secure and insecure babies. It is best described as a sensitively tuned "emotional dance," in which the caregiver responds to infant signals in a well-timed, rhythmic, appropriate fashion. In addition, both partners match emotional states, especially the positive ones (Feldman, 2003; Isabella & Belsky, 1991). Earlier we saw that sensitive face-to-face play, in which interactional synchrony occurs, helps infants regulate emotion. But moderate adult–infant coordination predicts attachment security, not "tight" coordination in which the

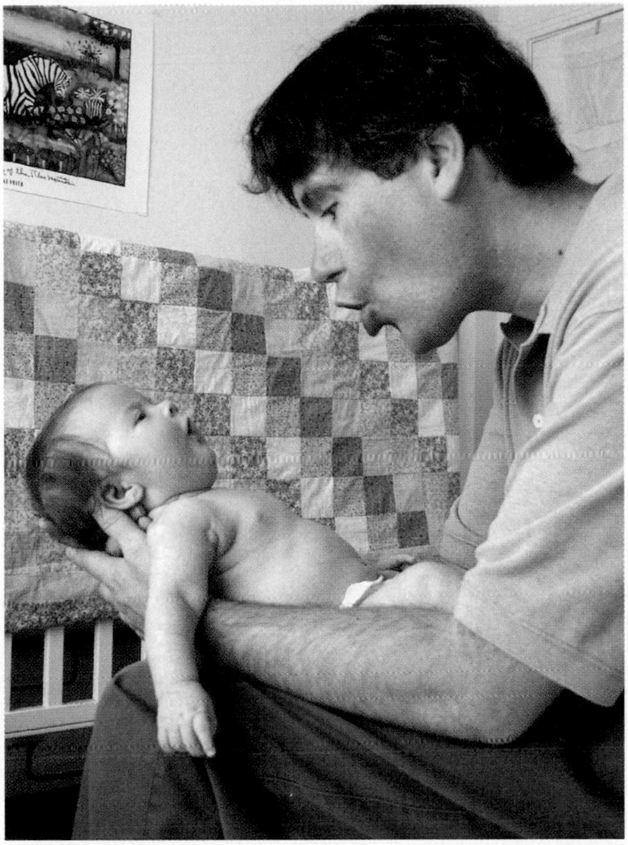

This father and baby are engaged in a sensitively tuned form of communication called interactional synchrony, in which they match emotional states, especially positive ones. Interactional synchrony may support secure attachment, but it does not characterize parent–infant interaction in all cultures.

adult responds to most infant cues (Jaffe et al., 2001). Perhaps warm, sensitive caregivers use a relaxed, flexible style of communication in which they comfortably accept and repair emotional mismatches, returning to a synchronous state.

Cultures vary in their view of sensitivity toward infants. Among the Gusii people of Kenya, for example, mothers rarely cuddle, hug, or interact playfully with their babies, although they are very responsive to their infants' needs. Yet most Gusii infants appear securely attached (LeVine et al., 1994). This suggests that security depends on attentive caregiving, not necessarily on moment-by-moment contingent interaction. Puerto Rican mothers, who highly value obedience and socially appropriate behavior, often physically direct and limit their babies' actions—a caregiving style linked to attachment security in Puerto Rican culture. Yet in many Western cultures, such physical control predicts insecurity (Carlson & Harwood, 2003).

Compared with securely attached infants, avoidant babies tend to receive overstimulating, intrusive care. Their mothers might, for example, talk energetically to them while they are looking away or falling asleep. By avoiding the mother, these infants try to escape from overwhelming interaction. Resistant infants often experience inconsistent care. Their mothers are unresponsive to infant signals. Yet when the baby begins to explore, these mothers interfere, shifting the infant's attention back to themselves. As a result, the baby is overly dependent as well as angry at the mother's lack of involvement (Cassidy & Berlin, 1994; Isabella & Belsky, 1991).

Highly inadequate caregiving is a powerful predictor of disruptions in attachment. Child abuse and neglect (topics we will consider in Chapter 8) are associated with all three forms of attachment insecurity. Among maltreated infants, disorganized/disoriented attachment is especially high (van IJzendoorn, Schuengel, & Bakermans-Kranenburg, 1999). Persistently depressed mothers, mothers with very low marital satisfaction, and parents suffering from a traumatic event, such as loss of a loved one, also tend to promote the uncertain behaviors of this pattern (Campbell et al., 2004; Moss et al., 2005; van IJzendoorn, 1995). Some of these mothers display frightening, contradictory, and unpleasant behaviors—looking scared, teasing the baby, holding the baby stiffly at a distance, pulling the baby by the arm, or seeking reassurance from the upset child (Goldberg et al., 2003; Lyons-Ruth, Bronfman, & Parsons, 1999; Madigan, Moran, & Pederson, 2006).

■ **INFANT CHARACTERISTICS.** Because attachment is the result of a *relationship* between two partners, infant characteristics should affect how easily it is established. In Chapter 3, we saw that prematurity, birth complications, and newborn illness make caregiving more taxing. In families under stress, these difficulties are linked to attachment insecurity (Poehlmann & Fiese, 2001). But at-risk newborns whose parents have the time and patience to care for them fare quite well in attachment security (Brisch et al., 2005; Cox, Hopkins, & Hans, 2000).

Babies whose temperament is emotionally reactive and difficult are more likely to develop later insecure attachments (Kagan & Fox, 2006; van IJzendoorn et al., 2004). Again, however, caregiving is involved. In a study extending from birth to age 2, difficult infants more often had highly anxious mothers—a combination that, by the second year, often resulted in a "disharmonious relationship" characterized by both maternal insensitivity and attachment insecurity (Symons, 2001).

If children's temperaments determined attachment quality, we would expect attachment, like temperament, to be at least moderately heritable. Yet the heritability of attachment is virtually nil (O'Connor & Croft, 2001). In fact, about two-thirds of siblings—whether identical twins, fraternal twins, nontwin siblings, unrelated siblings, or foster infants—establish similar attachment patterns with their parent. Yet these siblings often differ in temperament (Cole, 2006; Dozier et al., 2001; van IJzendoorn, 1995). This suggests that most parents try to adjust their caregiving to each child's individual needs.

Why don't infant characteristics show strong relationships with attachment quality? Their influence probably depends on goodness of fit. From this perspective, *many* child attributes can lead to secure attachment as long as the caregiver behaves sensitively (Seifer & Schiller, 1995). Interventions that teach parents to interact with difficult-to-care-for infants are highly successful in enhancing both sensitive care and attachment security (Velderman et al., 2006). But when parents' capacity is strained—by their own personalities or by stressful living conditions—then infants with illnesses, disabilities, and difficult temperaments are at risk for attachment problems.

■ **FAMILY CIRCUMSTANCES.** Shortly after Timmy's birth, his parents divorced and his father moved to a distant city. Anxious and distracted, Vanessa placed 1-month-old Timmy in Ginette's child-care home and began working 50- to 60-hour weeks to make ends meet. On days Vanessa stayed late at the office, a babysitter picked Timmy up, gave him dinner, and put him to bed. Once or twice a week, Vanessa went to get Timmy from child care. As he neared his first birthday, Vanessa noticed that unlike the other children, who reached out, crawled, or ran to their parents, Timmy ignored her.

Timmy's behavior reflects a repeated finding: Job loss, a failing marriage, and financial difficulties can undermine attachment by interfering with parental sensitivity. These stressors can also affect babies' sense of security directly, by exposing them to angry adult interactions or unfavorable child-care arrangements (Raikes & Thompson, 2005; Thompson & Raikes, 2003). (See the Social Issues box on the following page to find out how child care affects early emotional development.) Social support, especially assistance with parenting, reduces parental stress and fosters attachment security. Ginette's sensitivity was helpful, as was the advice Vanessa received from Ben, a psychologist. As Timmy turned 2, his relationship with his mother seemed warmer.

Parents bring to the family context their own history of attachment experiences, from which they construct internal working models that they apply to the bonds they establish with their babies. Monica, who recalled her mother as tense and preoccupied, expressed regret that they had not had a closer relationship. Is her image of parenthood likely to affect Grace's attachment security?

To assess parents' internal working models, researchers have asked them to evaluate childhood memories of attachment experiences (Main & Goldwyn, 1998). Parents who discuss their childhoods with objectivity and balance, regardless of whether their experiences were positive or negative, tend to have securely attached infants. In contrast, parents who either dismiss the importance of early relationships or describe them in angry, confused ways usually have insecurely attached babies (Slade et al., 1999; van IJzendoorn, 1995). And parents of disorganized/disoriented infants often express extremely negative feelings—either hostile or fearful—about their early attachment bonds, while also viewing themselves as "bad" and deserving of unkind treatment (Lyons-Ruth et al., 2005).

But we must not assume any direct transfer of parents' childhood experiences to quality of attachment with their own children. Internal working models are *reconstructed memories* affected by many factors, including relationship experiences over the life course, personality, and current life satisfaction. Longitudinal research shows that negative life events can weaken the link between an individual's own attachment security in infancy and a secure internal working model in adulthood. And insecurely attached babies who become adults with insecure internal working models often have lives that, based on self-reports in adulthood, are filled with family crises (Waters et al., 2000; Weinfield, Sroufe, & Egeland, 2000).

In sum, our early rearing experiences do not destine us to become sensitive or insensitive parents. Rather, the way we *view* our childhoods—our ability to come to terms with negative events, to integrate new information into our working models, and to look back on our own parents in an understanding, forgiving way—is much more influential in how we rear our children than the actual history of care we received (Main, 2000).

Multiple Attachments

Babies develop attachments to a variety of familiar people—not just mothers but also fathers, siblings, grandparents, and professional caregivers. Although Bowlby (1969) acknowledged the existence of multiple attachments, he believed that infants are predisposed to direct their attachment behaviors to a single special person, especially when they are distressed. Consistent with this view, when anxious or unhappy, most babies prefer to be comforted by their mother. But this preference declines over the second year. And when babies are not distressed, they approach, vocalize to, and smile at both parents equally (Bornstein, 2006; Parke, 2002).

■ **FATHERS.** Fathers' sensitive caregiving and interactional synchrony with infants, like mothers', predict attachment security (Lundy, 2003; van IJzendoorn et al., 2004). But in many cultures, including Australia, Canada, India, Israel, Italy, Japan, and the United States, mothers and fathers tend to interact differently with babies. Mothers devote more time to physical care and expressing affection, fathers to playful interaction (Roopnarine et al., 1990).

Mothers and fathers also play differently. Mothers more often provide toys, talk to infants, and gently play conventional games like pat-a-cake and peekaboo. In contrast, fathers—especially with their infant sons—tend to engage in highly arousing physical play with bursts of excitement that increase as play progresses (Feldman, 2003). This stimulating, surprising play style may help prepare babies to venture confidently into their surrounding world and to approach unfamiliar situations, such as play with peers (Paquette, 2004).

In cultures such as Japan, where long work hours prevent most fathers from sharing in infant caregiving, play is a vital context in which fathers build secure attachments (Hewlett, 2004; Shwalb et al., 2004). In many Western nations, however, a strict division of parental roles—mother as caregiver, father as playmate—has changed over the past several decades in response to women's workforce participation and to cultural valuing of gender equality. Recent surveys indicate that in dual-earner families, U.S. fathers devote 85 percent as much time as mothers do to children—on average, about 3½ hours per day (Pleck & Masciadrelli, 2004; Sandberg & Hofferth, 2001). Paternal time availability to children is fairly similar across SES

SOCIAL ISSUES

Does Child Care in Infancy Threaten Attachment Security and Later Adjustment?

Research suggests that infants placed in full-time child care before 12 months of age are more likely than infants who remain at home to display insecure attachment—especially avoidance—in the Strange Situation (Belsky, 2001, 2005). Does this mean that infants who experience daily separations from their employed parents and early placement in child care are at risk for developmental problems? Let's look closely at the evidence.

Attachment Quality

In U.S. studies reporting an association between child care and attachment quality, the rate of insecurity among child-care infants is somewhat higher than among non-child-care infants—about 36 versus 29 percent (Lamb, Sternberg, & Prodromidis, 1992). But not all investigations find this difference (NICHD Early Child Care Research Network, 1997; Roggman et al., 1994). Rather, the relationship between child care and emotional well-being depends on both family and child-care experiences.

Family Circumstances

We have seen that family conditions affect attachment security. For many employed women, handling two full-time jobs—work and motherhood—is stressful. Some mothers, fatigued and anxious because they receive little help from the child's father, may respond less sensitively to their babies, thereby risking the infants' security (Stifter, Coulehan, & Fish, 1993). Other employed parents probably value and encourage their infants' independence. Or their babies may be unfazed by the Strange Situation because they are used to separating from their parents. In these cases, avoidance in the Strange Situation may represent healthy autonomy, not insecurity (Clarke-Stewart, Althusen, & Goosens, 2001).

Quality and Extent of Child Care

Long periods spent in poor-quality child care may contribute to a higher rate of insecure attachment. In the U.S. National Institute of Child Health and Human Development (NICHD) Study of Early Child Care—the largest longitudinal study to date, including more than 1,300 infants and their families—child care alone did not contribute to attachment insecurity. But when babies were exposed to combined home and child-care risk factors—insensitive caregiving at home along with insensitive caregiving in child care, long hours in child care, or more than one child-care arrangement—the rate of insecurity increased. Overall, mother–child interaction was more favorable when children attended higher-quality child care and also spent fewer hours in child care (NICHD Early Child Care Research Network, 1997, 1999).

Furthermore, when these children reached age 3, a history of higher-quality child care predicted better social skills (NICHD Early Child Care Research Network, 2002b). However, at age 4½ to 5, children averaging more than 30 child-care hours per week displayed more behavior problems, especially defiance, disobedience, and aggression (NICHD Early Child Care Research Network, 2003, 2006). This does not necessarily mean that child care causes behavior problems. Rather, heavy exposure to substandard care, which is widespread in the United States, may promote these difficulties. In Australia, infants enrolled full-time in government-funded, high-quality child care have a higher rate of secure attachment than infants informally cared for by relatives, friends, or baby-sitters (Love et al., 2003). And in the Canadian province of Quebec, time in high quality child care is associated with fewer behavior problems (Palacio-Quintin, 2000).

Still, some children may be particularly stressed by long child-care hours. Many infants, toddlers, and preschoolers attending child-care centers for full days show a mild increase in saliva concentrations of the stress hormone cortisol across the day—a pattern not evident on days they spend at home. In one study, children rated as highly fearful by their caregivers experienced an especially sharp increase in cortisol levels (Watamura et al., 2003). Inhibited children may find the constant company of large numbers of peers particularly stressful.

Conclusions

Taken together, research suggests that some infants may be at risk for attachment insecurity and adjustment problems due to inadequate child care, long hours in child care, and the joint pressures their mothers experience from full-time employment and parenthood. But it is inappropriate to use these findings to justify a reduction in child-care services. When family incomes are limited or mothers who want to work are forced to stay at home, children's emotional security is not promoted.

Instead, it makes sense to increase the availability of high-quality child care, to provide paid employment leave so parents can limit the hours their children spend in child care (see page 104), and to educate parents about the vital role of sensitive caregiving and child-care quality in early emotional development. Return to Chapter 5, page 171, to review signs of developmentally appropriate child care for infants and toddlers. When caregiver–child ratios are generous, group sizes are small, and caregivers are educated about child development and child rearing, caregivers' interactions are more positive and children develop more favorably (McCartney et al., 2007; NICHD Early Child Care Research Network, 2000b, 2002a, 2006). Child care with these characteristics can become part of an ecological system that relieves rather than intensifies parental and child stress, thereby promoting healthy attachment and development.

At the end of her day in child care, an 11-month-old eagerly greets her mother. High-quality child care and fewer hours in child care are associated with attachment security.

CULTURAL INFLUENCES

The Powerful Role of Paternal Warmth in Development

Research in diverse cultures demonstrates that fathers' warmth contributes greatly to children's long-term favorable development. In studies of many societies and ethnic groups around the world, researchers coded paternal expressions of love and nurturance—evident in such behaviors as cuddling, hugging, comforting, playing, verbally expressing love, and praising the child's behavior. Fathers' sustained affectionate involvement predicted later cognitive, emotional, and social competence as strongly as did mothers' warmth—and occasionally more strongly (Rohner & Veneziano, 2001; Veneziano, 2003). And in Western cultures, paternal warmth protected children against a wide range of difficulties, including childhood emotional and behavior problems and adolescent substance abuse and delinquency (Grant et al., 2000; Rohner & Brothers, 1999; Tacon & Caldera, 2001).

Fathers who devote little time to physical caregiving express warmth through play. In a German study, fathers' play sensitivity—accepting toddlers' play initiatives, adapting play behaviors to toddlers' capacities, and responding appropriately to toddlers' expressions of emotion—predicted a secure father–child relationship in childhood and adolescence (Grossmann et al., 2002). Through play, fathers seemed to transfer to young children a sense of confidence about parental support, which may strengthen their capacity to master many later challenges.

What factors promote paternal warmth? Cross-cultural research reveals a consistent association between the amount of time fathers spend near infants and toddlers and their expressions of caring and affection (Rohner & Veneziano, 2001). Consider the Aka hunters and gatherers of Central Africa, where fathers spend more time in physical proximity to their babies than in any other known society. Observations reveal that Aka fathers are within arm's reach of infants more than half the day. They pick up, cuddle, and play with their babies at least five times as often as fathers in other hunting-and-gathering societies. Why are Aka fathers so involved? The bond between Aka husband and wife is unusually cooperative and intimate. Throughout the day, couples share hunting, food preparation, and social and leisure activities. The more time Aka parents spend together, the greater the father's loving interaction with his baby (Hewlett, 1992).

In Western cultures as well, fathers in gratifying marriages spend more time with and interact more effectively with infants. In contrast, marital dissatisfaction is associated with insensitive paternal care (Grych & Clark, 1999; Lundy, 2002). Clearly mothers' and fathers' warm interactions with each other and with their babies are closely linked. But paternal warmth promotes long-term favorable development, beyond the influence of maternal warmth (Rohner & Veneziano, 2001). Evidence for the power of fathers' affection, reported in virtually every culture and ethnic group studied, is reason to encourage more men to engage in nurturing care of young children.

© BLEND IMAGES/GETTY IMAGES

In both Western and non-Western nations, fathers' warmth predicts long-term, favorable cognitive, emotional, and social development.

and ethnic groups, with one exception: Hispanic fathers spend more time engaged, probably because of the particularly high value that Hispanic cultures place on family involvement (Cabrera & Garcia-Coll, 2004; Parke et al., 2004).

Mothers in dual-earner families tend to engage in more playful stimulation of their babies than mothers who are at home full-time (Cox et al., 1992). But fathers who are primary caregivers retain their arousing play style (Lamb & Oppenheim, 1989). These highly involved fathers typically are less gender-stereotyped in their beliefs; have sympathetic, friendly personalities; often had fathers who were more involved in rearing them; and regard parenthood as an especially enriching experience (Cabrera et al., 2000; Levy-Shiff & Israelashvili, 1988).

Fathers' involvement with babies unfolds within a complex system of family attitudes and relationships. When both mothers and fathers believe that men are capable of nurturing infants, fathers devote more time to caregiving (Beitel & Parke, 1998). A warm marital bond supports both parents' involvement with babies, but it is especially important for fathers (Lamb & Lewis, 2004). See the Cultural Influences box above for cross-cultural evidence documenting this conclusion—and also highlighting the powerful role of paternal warmth in children's development.

SIBLINGS. Despite declines in family size, 80 percent of North American and European children grow up with at least one sibling (Dunn, 2004). The arrival of a new baby is a difficult experience for most preschoolers, who—realizing that they must now share their parents' attention and affection—often become demanding, clingy, and deliberately naughty for a time. Attachment security also declines, especially for children over age 2 (old enough to feel threatened and displaced) and for those with mothers under stress (Baydar, Greek, & Brooks-Gunn, 1997; Teti et al., 1996).

Applying What We Know

Encouraging Affectionate Ties Between Infants and Their Preschool Siblings

Suggestion	Description
Spend extra time with the older child.	To minimize the older child's feelings of being deprived of affection and attention, set aside time to spend with her. Fathers can be especially helpful, planning special outings with the preschooler and taking over care of the baby so the mother can be with the older child.
Handle sibling misbehavior with patience.	Respond patiently to the older sibling's misbehavior and demands for attention, recognizing that these reactions are temporary. Give the preschooler opportunities to feel proud of being more grown-up than the baby. For example, encourage the older child to assist with feeding, bathing, dressing, and offering toys and show appreciation for these efforts.
Discuss the baby's wants and needs.	By helping the older sibling understand the baby's point of view, parents can promote friendly, considerate behavior. Say, for example, "He's so little that he just can't wait to be fed," or "He's trying to reach his rattle and can't."

Yet resentment is only one feature of a rich emotional relationship that starts to build between siblings after a baby's birth. Older children also show affection and concern—kissing and patting the baby and calling out, "Mom, he needs you" when the infant cries. By the end of the first year, babies typically spend much time with older siblings and are comforted by the presence of a preschool-age brother or sister during short parental absences. And in the second year, toddlers often imitate and join in play with older siblings (Barr & Hayne, 2003).

The arrival of a baby brother or sister is a difficult experience for most preschoolers. Maternal warmth toward both children assures the older sibling of continuing parental love, models affectionate caring, and is related to positive sibling interaction.

Nevertheless, individual differences in sibling relationships emerge soon after the new baby's arrival. Temperament plays an important role. For example, conflict is greater when one sibling is emotionally intense or highly active (Brody, Stoneman, & McCoy, 1994; Dunn, 1994). And maternal warmth toward both children is related to positive sibling interaction and to preschoolers' support of a distressed younger sibling (Volling, 2001; Volling & Belsky, 1992). In contrast, maternal harshness and lack of involvement are linked to antagonistic sibling relationships (Howe, Aquan-Assee, & Bukowski, 2001). Finally, a good marriage is correlated with older preschool siblings' capacity to cope adaptively with jealousy and conflict (Volling, McElwain, & Miller, 2002). Perhaps good communication between parents serves as a model of effective problem solving. It may also foster a generally happy family environment, giving children less reason to feel jealous.

Refer to Applying What We Know above for ways to promote positive sibling relationships between babies and preschoolers. Siblings offer a rich social context in which young children learn and practice a wide range of skills, including affectionate caring, conflict resolution, and control of hostile and envious feelings.

Attachment and Later Development

According to psychoanalytic and ethological theories, the inner feelings of affection and security that result from a healthy attachment relationship support all aspects of psychological development. Consistent with this view, an extensive longitudinal study found that preschoolers who were securely attached as babies were rated by their teachers as higher in self-esteem, social skills, and empathy than were their avoidantly and resistantly attached counterparts. Studied again at age 11 in summer camp, children who had been secure infants continued to be more socially competent, as judged by camp counselors. And as these well-functioning school-age children became adolescents and young adults, they continued to benefit from more supportive social networks, formed happier and more stable romantic relationships, and attained higher levels of education (Elicker, Englund, & Sroufe, 1992; Sroufe, 2002; Sroufe et al., 2005).

For some researchers, these findings indicate that secure attachment in infancy causes better development in later years. Yet contrary evidence exists. In other longitudinal research, secure infants sometimes developed more favorably than avoidant and resistant infants—but not always (Lewis, 1997; McCartney et al., 2004; Schneider, Atkinson, & Tardif, 2001; Stams, Juffer, & van IJzendoorn, 2002).

What accounts for this inconsistency? Mounting evidence indicates that *continuity of caregiving* determines whether attachment security is linked to later development (Lamb et al., 1985; Thompson, 2006). Parents who respond sensitively not just in infancy but also during later years promote many aspects of development: a more confident self-concept, more advanced understanding of others' perspectives (including emotions and beliefs), more favorable relationships with teachers and peers, a stronger sense of moral responsibility, and higher motivation to achieve in school (Repacholi & Trapolini, 2004; Thompson, Easterbrooks, & Padilla-Walker, 2003). In contrast, children of parents who react insensitively over a long period are at risk for a wide array of developmental difficulties.

Evidence on disorganized/disoriented attachment—a pattern associated with persistent insensitive caregiving—is consistent with this interpretation. This insecure pattern uniformly predicts both internalizing problems (fear and anxiety) and externalizing problems (anger and aggression) during the preschool and school years (Lyons-Ruth, 1996; Lyons-Ruth, Easterbrooks, & Cibelli, 1997; Moss et al., 2004, 2006; Moss, Cyr, & Dubois-Comtois, 2004).

Although a secure attachment in infancy does not guarantee good parenting, it does launch the parent–child relationship on a positive path. But the effects of early attachment security are *conditional*—dependent on the quality of the baby's future relationships. A child who experiences tender care in infancy but lacks sympathetic ties later is at risk for problems. In contrast, a child whose parental caregiving improves or who has other compensating ties outside the immediate family is likely to display *resilience,* or recovery from adversity (Belsky & Fearon, 2002).

As we conclude our discussion of attachment, consider the diverse factors that affect the parent–child bond: infant and parent characteristics, parents' marital relationship, stressors outside the family, availability of social supports, parents' views of their own attachment history, and child-care arrangements. Although attachment builds within the warmth and intimacy of caregiver–infant interactions, it can be fully understood only from an ecological systems perspective (Cummings & Cummings, 2002). ***TAKE A MOMENT...*** Return to Chapter 1, page 24, to review ecological systems theory. Notice how research confirms the contribution of each level of the environment to attachment security.

ASK YOURSELF

» REVIEW
What factors explain stability in attachment pattern for some children and change for others? Are these factors also involved in the link between attachment in infancy and later development? Explain.

» APPLY
What attachment pattern did Timmy display when Vanessa picked him up from child care? What factors probably contributed to his response?

» CONNECT
Review research on emotional self-regulation on page 189. How do the caregiving experiences of securely attached infants promote development of emotional self-regulation?

» REFLECT
How would you characterize your internal working model? What factors, in addition to your relationship with your parents, might have influenced it?

Self-Development During the First Two Years

Infancy is a rich formative period for the development of both physical and social understanding. In Chapter 5, you learned that infants develop an appreciation of the permanence of objects. And in this chapter, we have seen that over the first year, infants recognize and respond appropriately to others' emotions and distinguish familiar from unfamiliar people. That both objects and people achieve an independent, stable existence for the infant implies that knowledge of the self as a separate, permanent entity is also emerging.

Self-Awareness

After Caitlin's bath, Carolyn often held her in front of the bathroom mirror. As early as the first few months, Caitlin smiled and returned friendly behaviors to her image. At what age did she realize that the charming baby gazing and grinning back was herself?

■ BEGINNINGS OF SELF-AWARENESS. At birth, infants sense that they are physically distinct from their surroundings. For example, newborns display a stronger rooting reflex in response to external stimulation (an adult's finger touching their cheek) than to self-stimulation (their own hand contacting their cheek) (Rochat & Hespos, 1997). Newborns' remarkable capacity for *intermodal perception* (see page 146 in Chapter 4) supports the beginnings of self-awareness (Rochat, 2003). As they feel their own touch, feel and watch their limbs move, and feel and hear themselves cry, babies experience intermodal matches that differentiate their own body from surrounding bodies and objects.

This 22-month-old, seeing his changed appearance in a mirror as a result of wearing a new hat, reaches for the hat—an indication that he recognizes his unique physical features. He is well aware of himself as a separate being, distinct from other people and objects.

Over the first few months, infants distinguish their own visual image from other stimuli, although self-awareness is still limited—expressed only in perception and action. When shown two side-by-side video images of their kicking legs, one from their own perspective (camera behind the baby) and one from an observer's perspective (camera in front of the baby), 3-month-olds looked longer at the unfamiliar, observer's view (Rochat, 1998). By 4 months, infants look and smile more at video images of others than at video images of themselves, indicating that they treat another person (as opposed to the self) as a social partner (Rochat & Striano, 2002).

■ SELF-RECOGNITION. During the second year, toddlers become consciously aware of the self's physical features. In several studies, 9- to 28-month-olds were placed in front of a mirror. Then, under the pretext of wiping the baby's face, each mother rubbed red dye on her child's nose or forehead. Younger babies touched the mirror as if the red mark had nothing to do with themselves. But those older than 20 months touched or rubbed their strange-looking noses, indicating awareness of their unique appearance (Bard et al., 2006; Lewis & Brooks-Gunn, 1979).

Around age 2, **self-recognition**—identification of the self as a physically unique being—is well under way. Children point to themselves in photos and refer to themselves by name or with a personal pronoun ("I" or "me"). And soon they will identify themselves in images with less detail and fidelity than mirrors. Around age 2½, most reach for a sticker surreptitiously placed on top of their heads when shown themselves in a live video, and around age 3 most recognize their own shadow (Cameron & Gallup, 1988; Suddendorf, Simcock, & Nielsen, 2007).

According to many theorists, self-awareness develops as infants and toddlers increasingly realize that their own actions cause objects and people to react in predictable ways (Harter, 1998). In support of this idea, babies whose parents respond sensitively to their signals and encourage exploration tend to be advanced in self-development (Pipp, Easterbrooks, & Harmon, 1992). As infants act on the environment, they notice effects that help them sort out self, other people, and objects (Nadel, Prepin, & Okanda, 2005; Rochat, 2001). For example, batting a mobile and seeing it swing in a pattern different from the infant's own actions informs the baby about the relation between self and physical world. Smiling and vocalizing at a caregiver who smiles and vocalizes back helps clarify the relation between self and social world. The contrast between these experiences helps infants build an image of the self as separate from, but vitally connected to, external reality.

Cultural variations exist in early self-development. Urban German and Greek toddlers attain mirror self-recognition earlier than toddlers of the Nso people of Cameroon, a collectivist rural farming society that highly values social harmony and responsibility to others (Keller et al., 2004, 2005). Compared to their German and Greek counterparts, Nso mothers engage in less face-to-face communication and object stimulation and more body contact and physical stimulation of their babies. German and Greek practices reflect a *distal parenting style* common in cultures that emphasize independence; the Nso practice a *proximal parenting style* typical in cultures that promote interdependence. In line with these differences, Nso proximal parenting predicts later attainment of self-recognition but earlier emergence of toddlers' compliance with adult requests (see Figure 6.4).

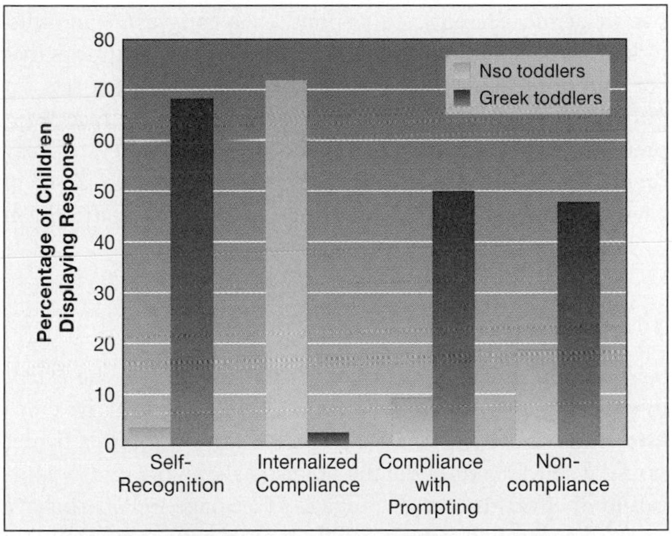

■ FIGURE 6.4 ■ Self-recognition and compliance among Nso and Greek toddlers. At 10 and 20 months, toddlers were tested for mirror self-recognition and for compliance (they were told not to open a transparent container with an attractive food). Among Greek toddlers, whose culture values independence, many more had attained self-recognition. But Nso toddlers, reared in an interdependent culture, were greatly advanced in compliance. The majority displayed internalized compliance (following directions without prompting), whereas Greek toddlers either needed reminders or did not comply. (Adapted from Keller et al., 2004.)

SELF-AWARENESS AND EARLY EMOTIONAL AND SOCIAL DEVELOPMENT. Self-awareness quickly becomes a central part of children's emotional and social lives. Recall that self-conscious emotions depend on a strengthening sense of self. Self-awareness also leads to first efforts to appreciate others' perspectives. Toddlers show the beginnings of **empathy**—the ability to understand another's emotional state and *feel with* that person, or respond emotionally in a similar way. For example, they start to give to others what they themselves find comforting—a hug, a reassuring comment, or a favorite doll or blanket (Hoffman, 2000). At the same time, toddlers demonstrate clearer awareness of how to upset others. One 18-month-old heard her mother talking to another adult about an older sibling: "Anny is really frightened of spiders" (Dunn, 1989, p. 107). The innocent-looking toddler ran to the bedroom, returned with a toy spider, and pushed it in front of Anny's face!

Categorizing the Self

By the end of the second year, language becomes a powerful tool in self-development. Because it permits children to represent the self more clearly, it greatly enhances self-awareness.

Between 18 and 30 months, children develop a **categorical self** as they classify themselves and others on the basis of age ("baby," "boy," or "man"), sex ("boy" or "girl"), physical characteristics ("big," "strong"), and even goodness versus badness ("I a good girl," "Tommy mean!") (Stipek, Gralinski, & Kopp, 1990). Toddlers use their limited understanding of these social categories to organize their own behavior. For example, children's ability to label their own gender is associated with a sharp rise in gender-stereotyped responses. As early as 18 months, toddlers select and play in a more involved way with toys that are stereotyped for their own gender—dolls and tea sets for girls, trucks and cars for boys. Parents then encourage these preferences by responding positively when toddlers display them (Ruble, Martin, & Berenbaum, 2006). As we will see in Chapter 8, gender-typed behavior increases dramatically in early childhood.

Self-Control

Self-awareness also contributes to *effortful control,* the extent to which children can inhibit impulses, manage negative emotion, and behave in socially acceptable ways. Indeed, a firmer sense of self may underlie the increasing stability and organization of effortful control after age 2 (see page 193). To behave in a self-controlled fashion, children must have some ability to think of themselves as separate, autonomous beings who can direct their own actions. And they must have the representational and memory capacities to recall a caregiver's directive ("Caitlin, don't touch that light socket!") and apply it to their own behavior.

As these capacities emerge between 12 and 18 months, toddlers first become capable of **compliance.** They show clear awareness of caregivers' wishes and expectations and can obey simple requests and commands. And as every parent knows, they can also decide to assert their autonomy and do just the opposite! But for most, opposition is far less common than compliance with an eager, willing spirit, which suggests that the child is beginning to adopt the adult's directives as his own (Kochanska, Murray, & Harlan, 2000). Compliance quickly leads to toddlers' first consciencelike verbalizations—for example, correcting the self by saying "No, can't" before touching a delicate object or jumping on the sofa.

Researchers often study the early emergence of self-control by giving children tasks that, like the situations just mentioned, require **delay of gratification**—waiting for an appropriate time and place to engage in a tempting act. Between ages 1½ and 3, children show an increasing capacity to wait before eating a treat, opening a present, or playing with a toy (Vaughn, Kopp, & Krakow, 1984). Children who are advanced in development of

This father is encouraging compliance and the beginnings of self-control. The toddler joins in the task with a willing spirit, which suggests he is adopting the adult's directive as his own.

Applying What We Know

Helping Toddlers Develop Compliance and Self-Control

Suggestion	Rationale
Respond to the toddler with sensitivity and encouragement.	Toddlers whose parents are sensitive and supportive are more compliant and self-controlled.
Provide advance notice when the toddler must stop an enjoyable activity.	Toddlers find it more difficult to stop a pleasant activity already under way than to wait before engaging in a desired action.
Offer many prompts and reminders.	Toddlers' ability to remember and comply with rules is limited; they need continuous adult oversight.
Respond to self-controlled behavior with verbal and physical approval.	Praise and hugs reinforce appropriate behavior, increasing its likelihood of occurring again.
Encourage sustained attention (see Chapter 5, page 162).	Development of attention is related to self-control. Children who can shift attention from a captivating stimulus and focus on a less attractive alternative are better at controlling their impulses.
Support language development (see Chapter 5, page 178).	Early language development is related to self-control. In the second year, children begin to use language to remind themselves of adult expectations and to delay gratification.
Gradually increase rules in accord with the toddler's developing capacities.	As cognition and language improve, toddlers can follow more rules related to safety, respect for people and property, family routines, manners, and simple chores.

attention and language tend to be better at delaying gratification—findings that help explain why girls are typically more self-controlled than boys (Else-Quest et al., 2006). Some toddlers already use verbal and other attention-diverting techniques—talking to themselves, singing, or looking away—to keep from engaging in prohibited acts.

Like effortful control in general, young children's capacity to delay gratification is influenced by both biologically based temperament and quality of caregiving (Kochanska & Aksan, 2006; Kochanska & Knaack, 2003). Inhibited children find it easier to wait than angry, irritable children do. But toddlers who experience parental warmth and gentle encouragement are more likely to be cooperative and to resist temptation. Such parenting—which encourages and models patient, nonimpulsive behavior—is particularly important for temperamentally reactive babies. In one study, anger-prone 7-month-olds with gentle, responsive mothers became eagerly compliant 15-month-olds, whereas angry infants with insensitive mothers developed into uncooperative toddlers (Kochanska, Aksan, & Carlson, 2005).

As self-control improves, parents gradually expand the rules they expect toddlers to follow, from safety and respect for property and people to family routines, manners, and responsibility for simple chores (Gralinski & Kopp, 1993). Still, toddlers' control over their own actions depends on constant parental oversight and reminders. Several prompts ("Remember, we're going to go in just a minute") and gentle insistence were usually necessary to get Caitlin to stop playing so that she and her parents could go on an errand. Applying What We Know above summarizes ways to help toddlers develop compliance and self-control.

As the second year of life drew to a close, Carolyn, Monica, and Vanessa were delighted at their children's readiness to learn the rules of social life. As we will see in Chapter 8, advances in cognition and language, along with parental warmth and reasonable maturity demands, lead preschoolers to make tremendous strides in this area.

ASK YOURSELF

>> REVIEW
Why is insisting that infants comply with parental directives inappropriate? What competencies are necessary for the emergence of compliance and self-control?

>> APPLY
Len, a caregiver of 1- and 2-year-olds, wonders whether toddlers recognize themselves. List signs of self-recognition in the second year that Len can observe.

>> CONNECT
What type of early parenting fosters development of emotional self-regulation, secure attachment, and self-control? Why, in each instance, is it effective?

Summary

Erikson's Theory of Infant and Toddler Personality

According to Erikson's psychosocial theory, how do infants and toddlers resolve the psychological conflicts of the first two years?

» Warm, responsive caregiving leads infants to resolve the psychological conflict of **basic trust versus mistrust** on the positive side. During toddlerhood, **autonomy versus shame and doubt** is resolved favorably when parents provide appropriate guidance and reasonable choices. If children emerge from the first few years without sufficient trust and autonomy, the seeds are sown for adjustment problems.

© GERI ENGBERG/THE IMAGE WORKS

Emotional Development

Describe changes in happiness, anger, and fear over the first year, noting the adaptive function of each.

» During the first half-year, **basic emotions** gradually become clear, well-organized signals. The **social smile** appears between 6 and 10 weeks, laughter around 3 to 4 months. Happiness strengthens the parent–child bond and both reflects and supports physical and cognitive mastery.

» Anger and fear, especially in the form of **stranger anxiety,** increase in the second half of the first year as infants' cognitive and motor capacities improve. Newly mobile babies use the familiar caregiver as a **secure base** from which to explore. Sadness is common when caregiver–infant communication is seriously disrupted.

Summarize changes during the first two years in understanding others' emotions, expression of self-conscious emotions, and emotional self-regulation.

» As infants' ability to detect the meaning of emotional expressions improves over the first year, **social referencing** appears; in uncertain situations, 8- to -10-month-olds begin actively seeking emotional information from caregivers, relying especially on the caregiver's voice. By the middle of the second year, infants appreciate that others' emotional reactions may differ from their own.

» During toddlerhood, self-awareness and adult instruction provide the foundation for **self-conscious emotions,** such as guilt, shame, embarrassment, envy, and pride. **Emotional self-regulation** emerges as the frontal lobes of the cerebral cortex develop and as caregivers sensitively assist infants in adjusting their emotional reactions. In the second year, growth in representation and language leads to more effective ways of regulating emotion.

Temperament and Development

What is temperament, and how is it measured?

» Children differ greatly in **temperament**—early-appearing, stable individual differences in reactivity and self-regulation. Thomas and Chess's New York Longitudinal Study identified three patterns of temperament: the **easy child,** the **difficult child,** and the **slow-to-warm-up child.** Another model of temperament, devised by Mary Rothbart, includes **effortful control,** the ability to regulate one's reactivity.

» Temperament is assessed using parental reports, behavior ratings by others familiar with the child, and laboratory observations. Most physiological research has focused on distinguishing **inhibited,** or **shy, children** from **uninhibited,** or **sociable, children.**

» Stability of temperament is generally low to moderate. Temperament has a genetic foundation, but child rearing and cultural beliefs and practices have much to do with maintaining or changing it. The **goodness-of-fit model** describes how temperament and environment work together to affect later development. Parenting practices that create a good fit with the child's temperament help difficult and shy children achieve more adaptive functioning.

Development of Attachment

Describe the development of attachment during the first two years.

» The most widely accepted perspective on development of **attachment** is **ethological theory,** which recognizes the infant's emotional tie to the caregiver as an evolved response that promotes survival. In early infancy, a set of built-in behaviors encourages the parent to remain close to the baby.

» Around 6 to 8 months, **separation anxiety** and use of the parent as a secure base indicate that a true attachment bond has formed. As representation and language develop, toddlers try to alter the parent's coming and going through requests and persuasion. Out of early caregiving experiences, children construct an **internal working model** that serves as a guide for all future close relationships.

© DAVID YOUNG-WOLFF/PHOTOEDIT

Describe the Strange Situation and the Attachment Q-Sort, along with factors that affect attachment security.

» The **Strange Situation** is a laboratory technique for assessing the quality of attachment between 1 and 2 years. Using it, researchers have identified four attachment patterns: **secure attachment, avoidant attachment, resistant attachment,** and **disorganized/disoriented attachment.** The **Attachment Q-Sort,** a home observation method suitable for 1- to 4-year- olds, yields a score ranging from high to low in security.

» Securely attached babies in middle-SES families experiencing favorable life conditions more often maintain their attachment pattern than do insecure babies. An exception is the disorganized/disoriented pattern, which is highly stable. Cultural conditions must be considered in interpreting the meaning of attachment patterns.

» Attachment quality is influenced by **sensitive caregiving,** the fit between the baby's temperament and parenting practices, and family circumstances. In some (but not all) cultures, **interactional synchrony** characterizes the experiences of securely attached babies. Parents' internal working models are good predictors of infant attachment patterns, but parents' childhood experiences do not transfer directly to quality of attachment with their own children.

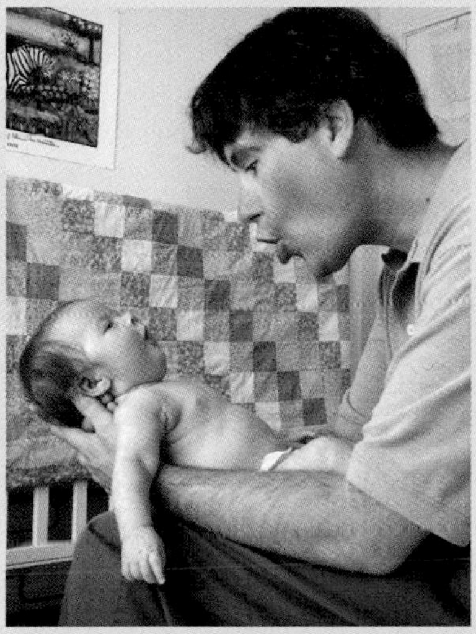

© GERI ENGBERG/THE IMAGE WORKS

» Infants develop strong affectionate ties to fathers, who tend to engage in more exciting, physical play with babies than do mothers. Early in the first year, infants begin to build rich emotional relationships with siblings that mix affection and caring with rivalry and resentment. Individual differences in the quality of sibling relationships are influenced by temperament and parenting practices.

» Continuity of caregiving is the crucial factor that determines whether attachment security is linked to later development. Children can recover from an insecure attachment history if caregiving improves.

Self-Development During the First Two Years

Describe the development of self-awareness in infancy and toddlerhood, along with the emotional and social capacities it supports.

» At birth, infants sense that they are physically distinct from their surroundings, an awareness that is promoted by their capacity for intermodal perception. Around age 2, **self-recognition**—identification of the self as a physically unique being—is well under way. Two-year-olds refer to themselves by name or with a personal pronoun and point to themselves in photos.

» Self-awareness is associated with the beginnings of **empathy,** the ability to feel with another person. As language strengthens and toddlers compare themselves to others, between 18 and 30 months they develop a **categorical self** based on age, sex, physical characteristics, and goodness and badness.

» Self-awareness also provides the foundation for the emergence of **compliance** between 12 and 18 months, and an increasing capacity for **delay of gratification** between ages 1½ and 3 years. Children who are advanced in development of attention and language and who have warm, encouraging parents tend to be more self-controlled.

© W PRODUCTIONS/GETTY IMAGES/PHOTODISC GREEN

Important Terms and Concepts

attachment (p. 196)
Attachment Q-Sort (p. 198)
autonomy versus shame and doubt (p. 184)
avoidant attachment (p. 198)
basic emotions (p. 185)
basic trust versus mistrust (p. 184)
categorical self (p. 208)
compliance (p. 208)
delay of gratification (p. 208)
difficult child (p. 190)
disorganized/disoriented attachment (p. 198)
easy child (p. 190)
effortful control (p. 191)
emotional self-regulation (p. 189)
empathy (p. 208)
ethological theory of attachment (p. 196)
goodness-of-fit model (p. 194)
inhibited, or shy, child (p. 191)
interactional synchrony (p. 200)
internal working model (p. 197)
resistant attachment (p. 198)
secure attachment (p. 198)
secure base (p. 186)
self-conscious emotions (p. 188)
self-recognition (p. 207)
sensitive caregiving (p. 200)
separation anxiety (p. 197)
slow-to-warm-up child (p. 190)
social referencing (p. 188)
social smile (p. 185)
stranger anxiety (p. 186)
Strange Situation (p. 198)
temperament (p. 190)
uninhibited, or sociable, child (p. 191)

Milestones
Development in Infancy and Toddlerhood

Birth–6 months

PHYSICAL

- Height and weight increase rapidly. (120–121)
- Newborn reflexes decline. (107–108)
- Distinguishes basic tastes and odors; shows preference for sweet-tasting foods. (112)
- Responses can be classically and operantly conditioned. (133–134)
- Habituates to unchanging stimuli; recovers to novel stimuli. (134–135)
- Sleep is increasingly organized into a night–day schedule. (128)
- Holds head up, rolls over, and grasps objects. (137, 139)
- Perceives auditory and visual stimuli as organized patterns. (141, 145)
- Shows sensitivity to motion and binocular depth cues. (143)
- Recognizes and prefers human facial pattern; recognizes features of mother's face. (145–146)
- By end of this period, moves from relying on motion and spatial arrangement to using shape, color, and texture to visually identify objects. (146)
- Masters a wide range of intermodal (visual, auditory, and tactile) relationships. (146)

COGNITIVE

- Engages in immediate and deferred imitation of adults' facial expressions. (135–136, 155)
- Repeats chance behaviors that lead to pleasurable and interesting results. (153–154)
- Violation-of-expectation tasks suggest some awareness of many physical properties (including object permanence) and basic numerical knowledge. (155, 159)
- Recognition memory for visual events improves. (162)
- Attention becomes more efficient and flexible. (162)
- Forms perceptual categories based on objects' similar features. (163, 165)

LANGUAGE

- Coos and, by end of this period, babbles. (174)
- Begins to establish joint attention with caregiver, who labels objects and events. (175)

EMOTIONAL/SOCIAL

- Social smile and laughter emerge. (185)
- Matches feeling tone of caregiver in face-to-face communication; later, expects matched responses. (188)
- Emotional expressions become well-organized and meaningfully related to environmental events. (185)

- Regulates emotion by shifting attention and self-soothing. (189)
- Awareness of self as physically distinct from surroundings increases. (206–207)

7–12 months

PHYSICAL

- Approaches adultlike sleep–wake schedule. (128)
- Sits alone, crawls, and walks. (137)

- Reaching and grasping improve in flexibility and accuracy; shows refined pincer grasp. (140)
- Develops sensitivity to pictorial depth cues. (143)
- Intermodal perception continues to improve. (146–147)

COGNITIVE

- Engages in intentional, or goal-directed, behavior. (154)
- Finds object hidden in an initial location. (154)
- Engages in deferred imitation of adults' actions with objects. (156–157)
- Solves simple problems by analogy to a previous problem. (157)
- Categorizes objects conceptually, by similar function and behavior. (163)

LANGUAGE

- Babbling expands to include sounds of spoken languages and patterns of the child's language community. (174)
- Joint attention with caregiver becomes more accurate. (175)

Note: Numbers in parentheses indicate the page or pages on which each milestone is discussed.

- Takes turns in games, such as pat-a-cake and peekaboo. (175)
- Comprehends some word meanings. (176).
- Uses preverbal gestures (showing, pointing) to influence others' behavior. (175)

- Around end of this period, says first words. (176)

EMOTIONAL/SOCIAL

- Smiling and laughter increase in frequency and expressiveness. (185–186)
- Anger and fear increase in frequency and intensity. (186)
- Stranger anxiety and separation anxiety appear. (186)
- Uses caregiver as a secure base for exploration. (186)
- Shows "clear-cut" attachment to familiar caregivers. (197)
- Increasingly detects the meaning of others' emotional expressions and engages in social referencing. (188)
- Regulates emotion by approaching and retreating from stimulation. (189)

13–18 months

PHYSICAL

- Height and weight gain are rapid, but not as great as in first year. (120)
- Walking is better coordinated. (138)
- Manipulates small objects with improved coordination. (140)

COGNITIVE

- Explores the properties of objects by acting on them in novel ways. (153)
- Searches in several locations for a hidden object. (154)
- Engages in deferred imitation of adults' actions with objects over longer delays and across a change in context—for example, from child care to home. (156–157)
- Sustained attention improves. (162)
- Recall memory for people, places, and objects improves. (163)
- Sorts objects into categories. (163, 165)

LANGUAGE

- Steadily adds to vocabulary. (175, 176)
- Comprehends 50 words at 13 months; produces 50 words at 18 months. (175)

EMOTIONAL/SOCIAL

- Joins in play with familiar adults and siblings. (202, 204–205)
- Realizes that others' emotional reactions may differ from one's own. (188)
- Shows signs of empathy. (208)
- Complies with simple directives. (208–209)

19–24 months

PHYSICAL

- Jumps, walks on tiptoe, runs, and climbs. (137)
- Manipulates small objects with good coordination. (139–140)

COGNITIVE

- Solves simple problems suddenly, through representation. (154–155)
- Finds a hidden object that has been moved while out of sight. (154)
- Engages in make-believe play, using simple actions experienced in everyday life. (155)

- Engages in deferred imitation of actions an adult tries to produce, even if not fully realized. (156–157)
- Sorts objects into categories more effectively. (163, 165)

LANGUAGE

- Produces about 200 words. (175, 176)
- Combines two words. (176)

EMOTIONAL/SOCIAL

- Self-conscious emotions (shame, embarrassment, guilt, envy, and pride) emerge. (188–189)
- Acquires a vocabulary for talking about feelings. (189)
- Begins to use language to assist with emotional self-regulation. (189–190)
- Begins to tolerate caregiver's absences more easily; separation anxiety declines. (197)
- Recognizes image of self and, by end of this period, uses own name or personal pronoun to refer to self. (207)
- Categorizes self and others on the basis of age, sex, physical characteristics, and goodness and badness. (208)
- Shows gender-stereotyped toy preferences. (208)
- Self-control, as indicated by delay of gratification, emerges. (208–209)

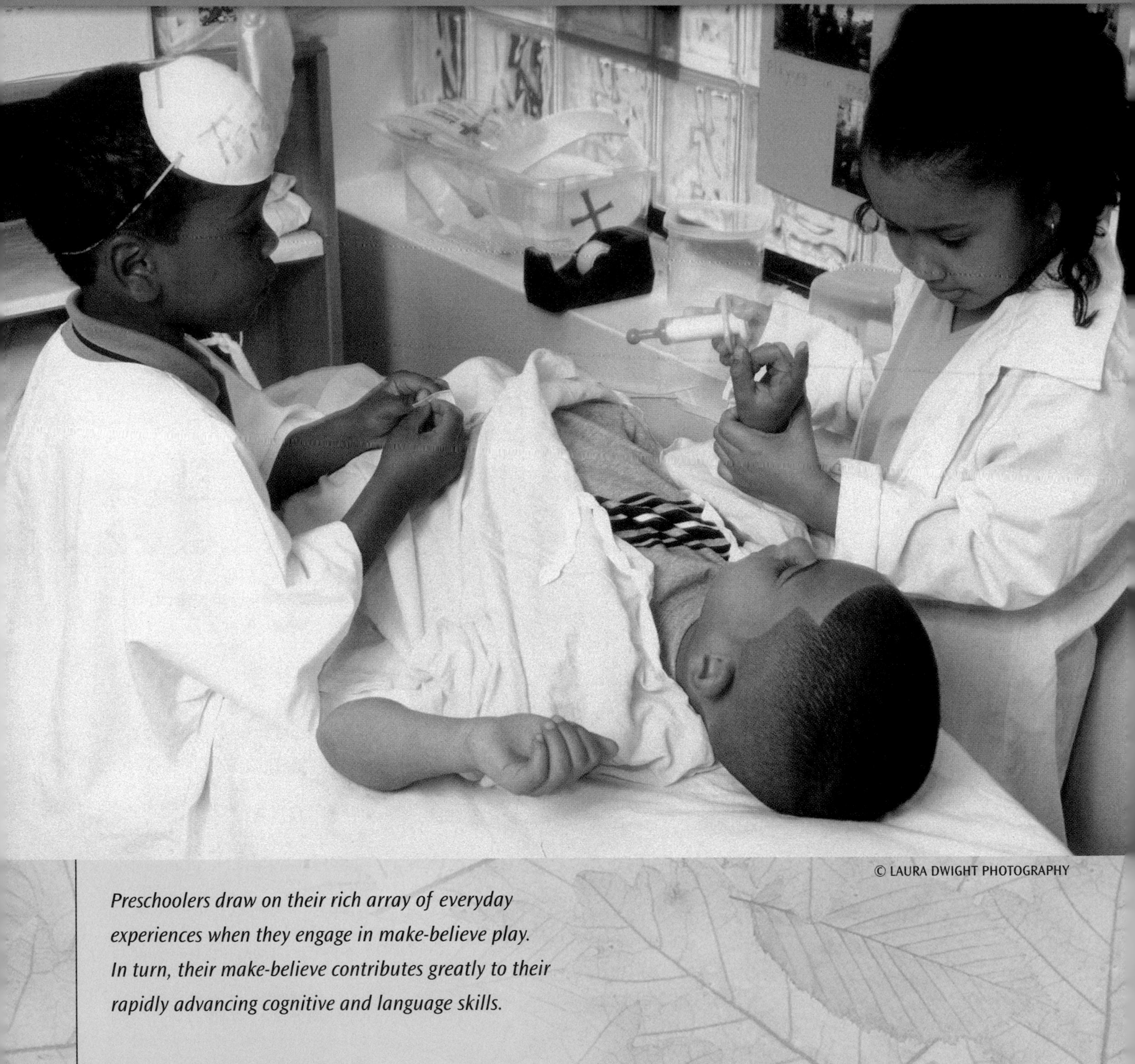

© LAURA DWIGHT PHOTOGRAPHY

Preschoolers draw on their rich array of everyday experiences when they engage in make-believe play. In turn, their make-believe contributes greatly to their rapidly advancing cognitive and language skills.

CHAPTER 7

Physical and Cognitive Development in Early Childhood

For more than a decade, my fourth-floor office window overlooked the preschool and kindergarten play yard of our university laboratory school. On mild fall and spring mornings, the doors of the classrooms swung open, and sand table, easels, and large blocks spilled out into a small courtyard. Alongside the building was a grassy area with jungle gyms, swings, a playhouse, and a flower garden planted by the children; beyond it, a circular path lined with tricycles and wagons. Each day, the setting was alive with activity.

The years from 2 to 6 are often called "the play years"—aptly so, since play blossoms during this time and supports every aspect of development. Our discussion opens with the physical achievements of early childhood—growth in body size and improvements in motor coordination. We look at biological and environmental factors that support these changes and at their intimate connection with other domains of development.

© DAVID YOUNG-WOLFF/PHOTOEDIT

Then we explore early childhood cognition, beginning with Piaget's preoperational stage. Recent research, along with Vygotsky's sociocultural theory and information processing, extends our understanding of preschoolers' cognitive competencies. Next, we turn to factors that contribute to early childhood mental development—the home environment, the quality of preschool and child care, and educational media. We conclude with the most awesome achievement of early childhood—language development.

Physical Development

A Changing Body and Brain

In early childhood, body growth tapers off from the rapid rate of the first two years. On average, children add 2 to 3 inches in height and about 5 pounds in weight each year. Boys continue to be slightly larger than girls. As "baby fat" drops off further, children gradually become thinner, although girls retain somewhat more body fat than boys, who are slightly more muscular. As Figure 7.1 shows, by age 5 the top-heavy, bowlegged, potbellied toddler has become a more streamlined, flat-tummied, longer-legged child with body proportions similar to those of adults. Consequently, posture and balance improve—changes that support gains in motor coordination.

Individual differences in body size are even more apparent during early childhood than in infancy and toddlerhood. Speeding around the bike path in the play yard, 5-year-old Darryl—at 48 inches tall and 55 pounds—towered over his kindergarten classmates. (The average North American 5-year-old boy is 43 inches tall and weighs 42 pounds.) Priti, an Asian-Indian child, was unusually small because of genetic factors linked to her cultural ancestry. Lynette and Hal, two Caucasian children with impoverished home lives, were well below average for reasons we will discuss shortly.

■ **FIGURE 7.1** ■ **Body growth during early childhood.** During the preschool years, children grow more slowly than in infancy and toddlerhood. Chris and Mariel's bodies became more streamlined, flat-tummied, and longer-legged. Boys continue to be slightly taller, heavier, and more muscular than girls. But generally, the two sexes are similar in body proportions and physical capacities.

Skeletal Growth

The skeletal changes of infancy continue throughout early childhood. Between ages 2 and 6, approximately 45 new *epiphyses,* or growth centers in which cartilage hardens into bone, emerge in various parts of the skeleton. X-rays of these growth centers enable doctors to estimate children's *skeletal age,* or progress toward physical maturity (see page 121 in Chapter 4)—information helpful in diagnosing growth disorders.

By the end of the preschool years, children start to lose their primary, or "baby," teeth. Genetic factors heavily influence the age at which they do so. For example, girls, who are ahead of boys in physical development, lose teeth earlier. Environmental influences also matter: Prolonged malnutrition delays the appearance of permanent teeth, whereas overweight and obesity accelerate it (Hilgers et al., 2006).

Diseased baby teeth can affect the health of permanent teeth, so preventing decay in primary teeth is essential—by brushing consistently, avoiding sugary foods, drinking fluoridated water, and getting topical fluoride treatments and sealants (plastic coatings that protect tooth surfaces). Another factor is exposure to tobacco smoke, which suppresses children's immune system, including the ability to fight bacteria responsible for tooth decay. Young children in homes with regular smokers are three times as likely as their agemates to have decayed teeth (Shenkin et al., 2004).

Unfortunately, an estimated 30 percent of U.S. preschoolers have tooth decay, a figure that rises to 60 percent by age 18. Causes include poor diet and inadequate health care—factors more likely to affect low-SES children. About 12 percent of U.S. children living in poverty have untreated tooth decay (U.S. Department of Health and Human Services, 2007g).

Brain Development

Between ages 2 and 6, the brain increases from 70 percent of its adult weight to 90 percent. By age 4, many parts of the cerebral cortex have overproduced synapses, and fMRI evidence indicates that cerebral blood flow peaks, signifying a high energy need (Huttenlocher, 2002; Nelson, Thomas, & de Haan, 2006). As *formation of synapses, cell death, myelination,* and *synaptic pruning* occur (see Chapter 4), preschoolers improve in a wide variety of skills—physical coordination, perception, attention, memory, language, logical thinking, and imagination.

EEG and fMRI measures of neural activity in various cortical regions reveal especially rapid growth from early to middle childhood in frontal-lobe areas devoted to inhibiting impulses and planning and organizing behavior (Bartgis, Lilly, & Thomas, 2003; Diamond, 2004). Furthermore, for most children, the left cerebral hemisphere is especially active between 3 and 6 years and then levels off. In contrast, activity in the right hemisphere increases steadily throughout early and middle childhood (Thatcher, Walker, & Giudice, 1987; Thompson et al., 2000a).

These findings fit nicely with what we know about several aspects of cognitive development. Early childhood is a time of marked gains on tasks that depend on the frontal cortex—ones that require inhibiting impulses and substituting thoughtful responses (Diamond, 2004; Rothbart & Bates, 2006). Further, language skills (typically housed in the left hemisphere) increase at an astonishing pace in early childhood, and they support children's increasing control over behavior. In contrast, spatial skills (usually located in the right hemisphere), such as giving directions, drawing pictures, and recognizing geometric shapes, develop gradually over childhood and adolescence. Differences in rate of development between the two hemispheres suggest that they are continuing to *lateralize* (specialize in cognitive functions). Let's take a closer look at brain lateralization in early childhood by focusing on handedness.

HANDEDNESS. On one visit to the preschool, I observed 3-year-old Moira drawing pictures, eating a snack, and playing outside. Unlike most of her classmates, Moira does most things—drawing, eating, and zipping her jacket—with her left hand. But she uses her right hand for a few activities, such as throwing a ball. Research on handedness, along with other evidence covered in Chapter 4, supports the joint contribution of nature and nurture to brain lateralization.

By age 6 months, infants typically display a smoother, more efficient movement when reaching with their right than their left arm—a difference, believed to be biologically based, that may contribute to the right-hand preference evident in most children by the end of the first year (Hinojosa, Sheu, & Michael, 2003; Rönnqvist & Domellöf, 2006). Gradually, handedness extends to additional skills.

Handedness reflects the greater capacity of one side of the brain—the individual's **dominant cerebral hemisphere**—to carry out skilled motor action. Other important abilities are generally located on the dominant side as well. For right-handed people—in Western nations, 90 percent of the population—language is housed in the left hemisphere with hand control. For the left-handed 10 percent, language is occasionally located

Twins are more likely than ordinary siblings to differ in hand preference, perhaps because twins usually lie in opposite orientations in the uterus.

in the right hemisphere or, more often, shared between the hemispheres (Szaflarski et al., 2002). This indicates that the brains of left-handers tend to be less strongly lateralized than those of right-handers.

Left-handed parents show only a weak tendency to have left-handed children. One genetic theory proposes that most children inherit a gene that *biases* them for right-handedness and a left-dominant cerebral hemisphere, but this bias is not strong enough to overcome experiences that might sway children toward a left-hand preference (Annett, 2002). Even prenatal events may profoundly affect handedness. Both identical and fraternal twins are more likely than ordinary siblings to differ in hand preference, probably because twins usually lie in opposite orientations in the uterus (Derom et al., 1996). The orientation of most singleton fetuses—facing toward the left—is believed to promote greater control over movements on the body's right side (Previc, 1991).

Handedness also involves practice. Newborns' bias in head position causes them to spend more time looking at and using one hand, which contributes to greater skillfulness of that hand (Hinojosa, Sheu, & Michael, 2003). Also, wide cultural differences exist: In Tanzania, Africa, where children are physically restrained and punished for favoring their left hand, less than 1 percent of adults are left-handed (Provins, 1997).

Although left-handedness occurs more frequently among severely retarded and mentally ill people than in the general population, atypical lateralization is probably not responsible for these individuals' problems. Rather, early damage to the left hemisphere may have caused their disabilities while also leading to a shift in handedness. In support of this idea, left-handedness is associated with prenatal and birth difficulties that can result in brain damage, including prolonged labor, prematurity, Rh incompatibility, and breech delivery (O'Callaghan et al., 1993; Powls et al., 1996).

Most left-handers, however, have no developmental problems. In fact, left- and mixed-handed youngsters are more likely than their right-handed agemates to develop outstanding verbal and mathematical talents (Flannery & Liederman, 1995). More even distribution of cognitive functions across both hemispheres may be responsible.

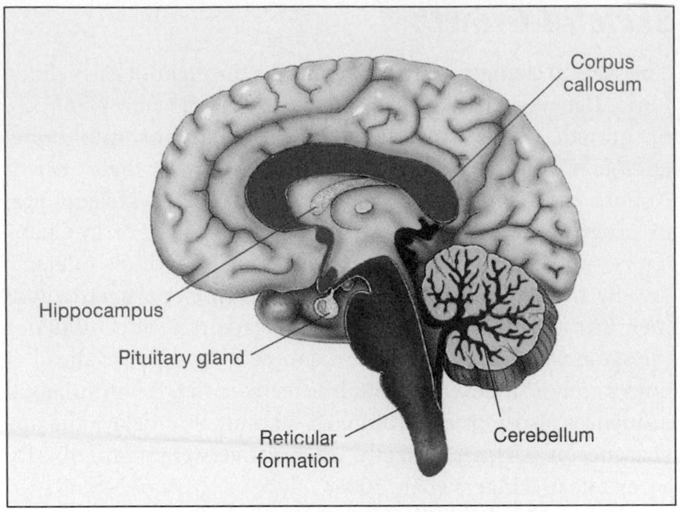

■ **FIGURE 7.2 ■ Cross-section of the human brain, showing the location of the cerebellum, the reticular formation, the hippocampus, and the corpus callosum.** These structures undergo considerable development during early childhood. Also shown is the pituitary gland, which secretes hormones that control body growth (see page 219).

■ **OTHER ADVANCES IN BRAIN DEVELOPMENT.** In addition to the cerebral cortex, other parts of the brain make strides during early childhood (see Figure 7.2). All of these changes involve establishing links between parts of the brain, increasing the coordinated functioning of the central nervous system.

At the rear and base of the brain is the **cerebellum,** a structure that aids in balance and control of body movement. Fibers linking the cerebellum to the cerebral cortex grow and myelinate from birth through the preschool years, contributing to dramatic gains in motor coordination: By the end of the preschool years, children can play hopscotch, throw a ball with well-coordinated movements, and print letters of the alphabet. Connections between the cerebellum and cerebral cortex also support thinking (Diamond, 2000): Children with damage to the cerebellum usually display both motor and cognitive deficits, including problems with memory, planning, and language (Noterdaeme et al., 2002; Riva & Giorgi, 2000).

The **reticular formation,** a structure in the brain stem that maintains alertness and consciousness, generates synapses and myelinates throughout childhood and into adolescence. Neurons in the reticular formation send out fibers to the frontal lobes of the cortex, contributing to improvements in sustained, controlled attention.

An inner-brain structure called the **hippocampus,** which plays a vital role in memory and in images of space that help us find our way, undergoes rapid synapse formation and myelination in the second half of the first year, when recall memory and independent movement emerge. Over the preschool and school years, the hippocampus and surrounding areas of the cerebral cortex continue to develop swiftly, establishing connections with one another and with the frontal lobes (Nelson, Thomas, & de Haan, 2006). These changes support the dramatic gains in memory and spatial understanding of early and middle childhood (Nelson, Thomas, & de Haan, 2006).

The **corpus callosum** is a large bundle of fibers connecting the two cerebral hemispheres. Production of synapses and myelination of the corpus callosum peak between 3 and 6 years, then continue more slowly through adolescence (Thompson et al., 2000a). The corpus callosum supports smooth coordination of movements on both sides of the body and integration of many aspects of thinking, including perception, attention, memory, language, and problem solving. The more complex the task, the more essential is communication between the hemispheres.

In early childhood, changes in the corpus callosum and other brain structures enhance communication between parts of the brain, enabling children to perform increasingly complex tasks—like this board game—that require integration of attention, memory, language, and problem solving.

ASK YOURSELF

REVIEW
What aspects of brain development underlie the tremendous gains in language, thinking, and motor control of early childhood?

APPLY
Dental checkups revealed a high incidence of untreated tooth decay in a U.S. preschool program serving low-income children. Using findings presented in this and previous chapters, list possible contributing factors.

CONNECT
What stand on the nature–nurture issue do findings on development of handedness support? Explain, using research findings.

REFLECT
How early, and to what extent, did you experience tooth decay in childhood? What factors might have been responsible?

Influences on Physical Growth and Health

As we consider factors affecting growth and health in early childhood, you will encounter some familiar themes. Heredity remains important, but environmental factors—including emotional well-being, good nutrition, relative freedom from disease, and physical safety—also are essential. And as the Biology and Environment box on page 220 illustrates, environmental pollutants can threaten children's healthy development. The extent to which low-level lead—one of the most common—undermines children's mental and emotional functioning is the focus of intensive research.

Heredity and Hormones

The impact of heredity on physical growth is evident throughout childhood. Children's physical size and rate of growth are related to those of their parents (Bogin, 2001). Genes influence growth by controlling the body's production of hormones. The **pituitary gland,** located at the base of the brain, plays a critical role by releasing two hormones that induce growth.

The first, **growth hormone (GH),** is necessary for development of all body tissues except the central nervous system and the genitals. Children who lack GH reach an average mature height of only 4 feet, 4 inches. When treated early with injections of GH, such children show catch-up growth and then grow at a normal rate, becoming much taller than they would have without treatment (Saenger, 2003).

A second pituitary hormone, **thyroid-stimulating hormone (TSH),** prompts the thyroid gland in the neck to release *thyroxine,* which is necessary for brain development and for GH to have its full impact on body size. Infants born with a deficiency of thyroxine must receive it at once, or they will be mentally retarded. Once the most rapid period of brain development is complete, children with too little thyroxine grow at a below-average rate, but the central nervous system is no longer affected. With prompt treatment, such children catch up in body growth and eventually reach normal size (Salerno et al., 2001).

Emotional Well-Being

In childhood as in infancy, emotional well-being can profoundly affect growth and health. Children with stressful home lives (due to divorce, financial difficulties, or parental job loss) suffer more respiratory and intestinal illnesses and more unintentional injuries than others (Cohen & Herbert, 1996; Kemeny, 2003).

In addition, high stress suppresses the release of GH (Deltondo et al., 2008). Consequently, extreme emotional deprivation can lead to **psychosocial dwarfism,** a growth disorder that usually appears between ages 2 and 15. Typical characteristics include decreased GH secretion, very short stature, immature skeletal age, and serious adjustment problems, which help distinguish psychosocial dwarfism from normal shortness (Tarren-Sweeney, 2006). Lynette, the 4-year-old mentioned earlier in this chapter, was diagnosed with this condition. She was placed in foster care after child welfare authorities discovered that she spent most of the day home alone, unsupervised, and might also have been physically abused. When such children are removed from their emotionally inadequate environments, their GH levels quickly return to normal, and they grow rapidly. But if treatment is delayed, the dwarfism can be permanent.

BIOLOGY AND ENVIRONMENT

Low-Level Lead Exposure and Children's Development

Lead is a highly toxic element that, at blood levels exceeding 60 μg/dL (micrograms per deciliter), causes brain swelling and hemorrhaging. Risk of death rises as blood-lead level exceeds 100 μg/dL. Before 1980, lead exposure resulted from use of lead-based paints in residences (where infants and young children often ate paint flakes) and from use of leaded gasoline (car exhaust resulted in a highly breathable form of lead). Laws limiting the lead content of paint and mandating lead-free gasoline led to a sharp decline in children's lead levels, from an average of 15 μg/dL in 1980 to 1.8 μg/dL today (Jones et al., 2009; Meyer et al., 2003).

But in neighborhoods near industries that use lead production processes, or where lead-based paint remains in older homes, children's blood levels are still markedly elevated. About 15 percent of low-income children living in large central cities, and 19 percent of African-American children, have blood-lead levels exceeding 10 μg/dL (the official "level of concern"), warranting immediate efforts to reduce exposure (Jones et al., 2009).

How much lead exposure is too much? Is lead contamination a "silent epidemic," impairing children's mental functioning even in small quantities? Until recently, answers were unclear. Studies reporting a negative relationship between children's current lead levels and cognitive performance often failed to control for factors associated with both blood-lead levels and mental test scores (such as SES, home environmental quality, and nutrition) that might account for the findings.

Over the past two decades, seven longitudinal studies of the developmental consequences of lead have been conducted—three in the United States, two in Australia, one in Mexico City, and one in Yugoslavia. Some focused on inner-city, low-SES minority children; others on middle- and upper-middle-SES suburban children; and one on children living close to a lead smelter. Each tracked children's lead exposure over an extended time and included relevant controls.

Five sites reported negative relationships between lead exposure and children's IQs (Hubbs-Tait et al., 2005). Higher blood levels were also associated with verbal and visual-motor skill deficits, distractibility, overactivity, poor organization, and behavior problems. And an array of findings suggested that persistent childhood lead exposure contributes to antisocial behavior in adolescence (Dietrich et al., 2001; Needleman et al., 2002; Nevin, 2000; Stretesky & Lynch, 2001).

AP IMAGES/MOHAMED EL-DAKHAKNY

These children play near a factory in Cairo, Egypt, ranked among the world's most polluted cities in levels of lead and other toxins. Studies consistently show lasting negative effects of lead exposure, including learning and behavior problems.

The investigations disagreed on an age period of greatest vulnerability. In some, relationships were strongest in toddlerhood and early childhood; in others, at the most recently studied age—suggesting cumulative effects over time. Still other studies reported similar lead-related cognitive deficits from infancy through adolescence. Overall, poorer mental test scores associated with lead exposure persisted over time and seemed to be permanent. Children given drugs to induce excretion of lead (chelation) did not improve (Dietrich et al., 2004; Rogan et al., 2001). And negative cognitive consequences were evident at all levels of exposure—even below 10 μg/dL (Lamphear et al., 2005).

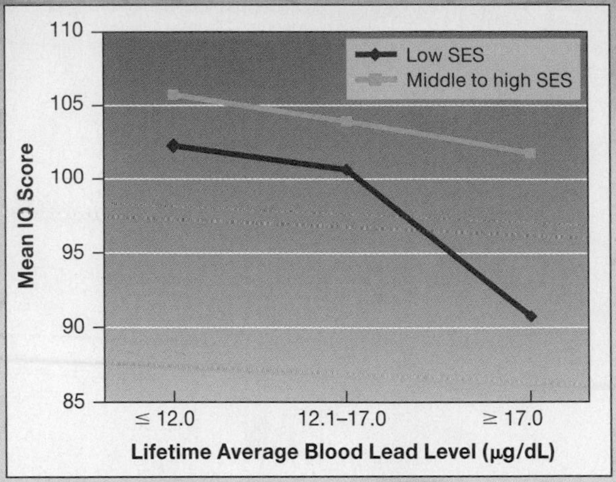

FIGURE 7.3 **Relationship of lifetime average lead exposure to 11- to-13-year-old IQ by SES.** In this study, conducted in the lead-smelting city of Port Pirie, Australia, blood-lead levels of 375 children were measured repeatedly from birth to age 11 to 13. The lead-exposure-related drop in IQ was much greater for low-SES than higher-SES children. (Adapted from Tong, McMichael, & Baghurst, 2000.)

Although the overall impact of low-level lead exposure on all outcomes is modest, in three longitudinal investigations, cognitive consequences were greatest for low-SES children (see, for example, Figure 7.3) (Bellinger, Leviton, & Sloman, 1990; Ris et al., 2004; Tong, McMichael, & Baghurst, 2000). A stressed, disorganized home life seems to heighten lead-induced damage. Dietary factors can also magnify lead's toxic effects. Iron deficiency, common in low-SES children, increases lead concentration in the blood, whereas iron supplements decrease it. Similarly, exposed children absorb less lead when their diets contain enough zinc (Noonan et al., 2003; Wolf, Jimenez, & Lozoff, 2003; Wright et al., 2003).

In sum, lead impairs learning and contributes to behavior problems. Low-SES children are more likely both to live in lead-contaminated areas and to experience additional risks that magnify lead-induced damage. Because lead is a stable element, its release into the air and soil is difficult to reverse. Therefore, in addition to laws that control lead pollution and limit children's exposure, interventions that reduce the negative impact of lead—through involved parenting, better schools, and dietary enrichment—are vital.

Nutrition

With the transition to early childhood, many children become unpredictable, picky eaters. One father I know wistfully recalled how his son, as a toddler, eagerly sampled Chinese food: "Now, at age 3, the only thing he'll try is the ice cream!"

Preschoolers' appetites decline because their growth has slowed. Their wariness of new foods is also adaptive. If they stick to familiar foods, they are less likely to swallow dangerous substances when adults are not around to protect them (Birch & Fisher, 1995). Parents need not worry about variations in amount eaten from meal to meal. Preschoolers compensate for a meal in which they eat little by eating more at a later meal (Hursti, 1999).

Though they eat less, preschoolers require a high-quality diet, including the same foods adults need, but in smaller amounts. Fats, oils, and salt should be kept to a minimum because of their link to high blood pressure and heart disease in adulthood. Foods high in sugar should also be avoided to prevent tooth decay and protect against overweight and obesity—a topic we will take up in Chapter 9.

Children tend to imitate the food choices of people they admire, both adults and peers. For example, in Mexico, where children often see family members enjoying peppery foods, preschoolers enthusiastically eat chili peppers, whereas most North American children reject them (Birch, Zimmerman, & Hind, 1980). Repeated, unpressured exposure to a new food also increases acceptance (Fuller et al., 2005). Serving broccoli or tofu increases children's liking for these healthy foods. In contrast, offering sweet fruit or soft drinks promotes "milk avoidance" (Black et al., 2002).

Although children's healthy eating depends on a wholesome food environment, too much parental control limits children's opportunities to develop self-control. Offering bribes ("Finish your vegetables, and you can have an extra cookie") causes children to like the healthy food less and the treat more (Birch, Fisher, & Davison, 2003).

Finally, as indicated in earlier chapters, many children in North America and in developing countries lack access to sufficient high-quality food to support healthy development. Five-year-old Hal rode a bus from a poor neighborhood to our laboratory preschool. His mother's welfare check barely covered her rent, let alone food. Hal's diet was deficient in protein and in essential vitamins and minerals—iron (to prevent anemia), calcium (to support development of bones and teeth), vitamin A (to help maintain eyes, skin, and a variety of internal organs), and vitamin C (to facilitate iron absorption and wound healing). These are the most common deficiencies of the preschool years (Ganji, Hampl, & Betts, 2003). Not surprisingly, Hal was thin, pale, and tired. By the school years, low-SES North American children are, on average, ½ to 1 inch shorter than their economically advantaged counterparts (Cecil et al., 2005; Yip, Scanlon, & Trowbridge, 1993).

© MARC GARANGER/CORBIS

This Quechua child of the Peruvian highlands enthusiastically accepts a spoonful of soup made from bitter-tasting potatoes. She has already acquired a taste for the foods that are commonly served in her culture.

Infectious Disease

One day, I noticed that Hal had been absent from the play yard for several weeks, so I asked Leslie, his preschool teacher, what was wrong. "Hal's been hospitalized with the measles," she explained. "He's had difficulty recovering—lost weight when there wasn't much to lose in the first place." In well-nourished children, ordinary childhood illnesses have no effect on physical growth. But when children are poorly fed, disease interacts with malnutrition in a vicious spiral, with potentially severe consequences.

INFECTIOUS DISEASE AND MALNUTRITION. Hal's reaction to the measles is commonplace in developing nations, where a large proportion of the population lives in poverty and children do not receive routine immunizations. Illnesses such as measles and chicken pox, which typically do not appear until after age 3 in industrialized nations, occur much earlier. Poor diet depresses the body's immune system, making children far more susceptible to disease. Of the 10 million annual deaths of children under age 5 worldwide, 98 percent are in developing countries and 70 percent are due to infectious diseases (World Health Organization, 2008a).

Disease, in turn, is a major contributor to malnutrition, hindering both physical growth and cognitive development. Illness reduces appetite and limits the body's ability to absorb foods, especially in children with intestinal infections. In developing countries, widespread diarrhea, resulting from unsafe water and contaminated foods, leads to growth stunting and nearly two million childhood deaths each year (World Health Organization, 2008a). Studies carried out in the slums and shantytowns of Brazil and Peru reveal that the more persistent diarrhea is in early childhood, the shorter children are in height and the lower they score on mental tests during the school years (Checkley et al., 2003; Niehaus et al., 2002).

Most developmental impairments and deaths due to diarrhea can be prevented with nearly cost-free *oral rehydration therapy (ORT),* in which sick children are given a solution of glucose, salt, and water that quickly replaces fluids the body loses. Since 1990, public health workers have taught nearly half the families in the developing world how to administer ORT. Also, supplements of zinc (essential for immune system functioning), which cost only 30 cents for a month's supply, substantially reduce the incidence of severe diarrhea (Aggarwal, Sentz, & Miller, 2007). Through these interventions, the lives of millions of children are saved each year.

IMMUNIZATION. In industrialized nations, childhood diseases have declined dramatically during the past half-century, largely as a result of widespread immunization of infants and young children. Hal got the measles because, unlike classmates from advantaged homes, he did not receive a full program of immunizations. About 23 percent of U.S. preschoolers lack essential immunizations. The rate rises to 26 percent for poverty-stricken children, who do not receive full protection until age 5 or 6, when it is required for school entry (U.S. Department of Health and Human Services, 2007d). In contrast, fewer than 10 percent of preschoolers lack immunizations in Denmark and Norway, and fewer than 7 percent in Great Britain, Canada, the Netherlands, and Sweden (United Nations, 2002; UNICEF, 2008).

Why does the United States lag behind these countries in immunization? As noted in earlier chapters, many U.S. children do not have access to the health care they need. In 1994, all medically uninsured children in the United States were guaranteed free immunizations, a program that has led to a steady improvement in immunization rates.

Inability to pay for vaccines is only one cause of inadequate immunization. Parents with stressful daily lives or without health benefits of their own often fail to schedule vaccination appointments, and those without a primary care physician do not want to endure long waits in crowded public health clinics. Some parents have been influenced by media reports suggesting a link between the measles–mumps–rubella vaccine and a rise in the number of children diagnosed with autism, although large-scale studies show no such association (Dales, Hammer, & Smith, 2001; Richler et al., 2006; Stehr-Green et al., 2003). In areas where many parents have refused to immunize their children, disease outbreaks of whooping cough and rubella have occurred, with life-threatening consequences (Kennedy & Gust, 2008; Tuyen & Bisgard, 2003). Public education programs to increase parental knowledge about the importance and safety of timely immunizations are badly needed.

Childhood Injuries

More than any other child in the preschool classroom, 3-year-old Tommy had trouble sitting still and paying attention. Instead, he darted from one place and activity to another. One day, he narrowly escaped serious injury when he put his mother's car into gear while she was outside scraping ice from its windows. The vehicle rolled through a guardrail and over the side of a 10-foot concrete underpass, where it hung until rescue workers arrived. Police charged Tommy's mother with failure to use a restraint seat for a child younger than age 8.

Unintentional injuries are the leading cause of childhood mortality in industrialized nations. As Figure 7.4 reveals, the United States ranks poorly in these largely preventable events. Nearly 35 percent of U.S. childhood deaths and 50 percent of adolescent deaths result from injuries (Children's Defense Fund, 2008). And among injured children and youths who survive, thousands suffer pain, brain damage, and permanent physical disabilities.

Auto and traffic accidents, drownings, and burns are the most common injuries during early and middle childhood. Motor vehicle collisions are by far the most frequent source of injury across all ages, ranking as the leading cause of death among children more than 1 year old.

FACTORS RELATED TO CHILDHOOD INJURIES. The common view of childhood injuries as "accidental" suggests they are due to chance and cannot be prevented (Sleet & Mercy, 2003). In fact, these injuries occur within a complex *ecological system* of individual, family, community, and societal influences—and we can do something about them.

Because of their higher activity level and greater impulsivity and risk taking, boys are 1.5 times more likely to be injured than

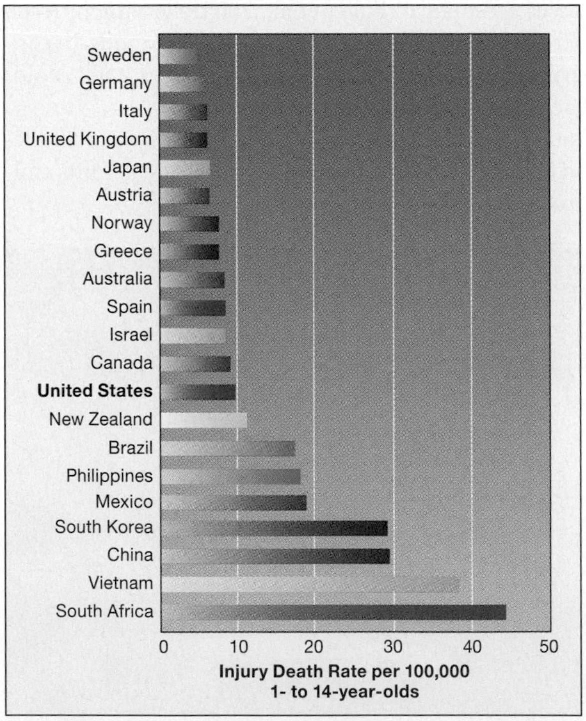

FIGURE 7.4 **International death rates due to unintentional injury among 1- to 14-year-olds.** Compared with other industrialized nations, the United States has a high injury rate, largely because of widespread childhood poverty and shortages of high-quality child care. Injury death rates are many times higher in developing nations, where poverty, rapid population growth, overcrowding in cities, and inadequate safety measures endanger children's lives. (Adapted from World Health Organization, 2008c.)

girls (National Safe Kids Campaign, 2005). Children with certain temperamental and personality characteristics—inattentiveness, overactivity, irritability, defiance, and aggression—are also at greater risk (Ordonana, Caspi, & Moffitt, 2008; Schwebel & Gaines, 2007). As we saw in Chapter 6, these children present child-rearing challenges. They are likely to protest when placed in auto seat restraints or refuse to take a companion's hand when crossing the street—even after repeated instruction and discipline.

Poverty, single parenthood, and low parental education are also strongly associated with injury (Schwebel & Brezausek, 2007; World Health Organization, 2008c). Parents who must cope with many daily stresses often have little energy to monitor the safety of their children. And their rundown homes and neighborhoods pose further risks (Dal Santo et al., 2004).

Broad societal conditions also affect childhood injury. In developing countries, the rate of death from injury before age 15 is five times higher than in developed nations and soon may exceed disease as the leading cause of childhood mortality (World Health Organization, 2008c). Rapid population growth, overcrowding in cities, and heavy road traffic combined with weak safety measures are major causes. Safety devices, such as car safety seats and bicycle helmets, are neither readily available nor affordable.

Childhood injury rates are high in the United States because of extensive poverty, shortages of high-quality child care (to supervise children in their parents' absence), and a high rate of births to teenagers, who are not ready for parenthood. But U.S. children from advantaged families are also at considerably greater risk for injury than children in Western Europe (World Health Organization, 2008c). This indicates that besides reducing poverty and teenage pregnancy and upgrading the status of child care, additional steps are needed to ensure children's safety.

PREVENTING CHILDHOOD INJURIES. Childhood injuries have many causes, so a variety of approaches are needed to reduce them. Laws prevent many injuries by requiring car safety seats, child-resistant caps on medicine bottles, flameproof clothing, and fencing around backyard swimming pools (the site of 50 percent of early childhood drownings) (Brenner & Committee on Injury, Violence, and Poison Protection, 2003). Communities can help by modifying their physical environments. Playgrounds, a common site of injury, can be covered with protective surfaces (National Safe Kids Campaign, 2005). Free, easily installed window guards can be given to families in high-rise apartment buildings to prevent falls. And media campaigns can inform parents and children about safety issues.

But even though they know better, many parents and children behave in ways that compromise safety. About 40 percent of U.S. parents (like Tommy's mother) fail to place their preschoolers in car safety seats. And when parents do use safety seats, 82 percent either install or use them incorrectly (Howard, 2002; National Safe Kids Campaign, 2005). American parents, especially, seem willing to ignore familiar safety practices, perhaps because of the high value they place on individual rights and personal freedom (Damashek & Peterson, 2002).

Furthermore, many parents begin relying on children's knowledge of safety rules, rather than controlling access to hazards, as early as 2 or 3 years of age—a premature transition associated with a rise in home injuries (Morrongiello, Ondejko, & Littlejohn, 2004). But even older preschoolers spontaneously recall only about half the safety rules their parents teach them. Even with well-learned rules, they need supervision to ensure they comply (Morrongiello, Midgett, & Shields, 2001).

Parent interventions that highlight risk factors and that model and reinforce safety practices are effective in reducing home hazards and childhood injuries (Kendrick et al., 2008). But such efforts focus narrowly on specific risks. Attention must also be paid to family conditions that can prevent childhood injury: relieving crowding in the home, providing social supports to ease parental stress, and teaching parents to use effective discipline—a topic we take up in Chapter 8.

This Thai family—like many others—rides unprotected on the only form of transportation it has. In developing countries, heavy road traffic and weak safety measures contribute to an injury death rate before age 15 that is five times higher than in developed nations.

ASK YOURSELF

» REVIEW
How can psychosocial dwarfism caused by extreme emotional deprivation be distinguished from ordinary shortness?

» APPLY
One day, Leslie prepared a new snack to serve at preschool: celery stuffed with ricotta cheese. The first time she served it, few children touched it. How can Leslie encourage her students to accept the snack? What tactics should she avoid?

» CONNECT
Using research on malnutrition or on unintentional injuries, show how physical growth and health in early childhood result from a continuous, complex interplay between heredity and environment.

» REFLECT
Ask a parent or other family member whether, as a preschooler, you were a picky eater, suffered from many infectious diseases, or sustained any serious injuries. In each instance, what factors might have been responsible?

Motor Development

TAKE A MOMENT... Observe several 2- to 6-year-olds at play in a neighborhood park, preschool, or child-care center. You will see that an explosion of new motor skills occurs in early childhood, each of which builds on the simpler movement patterns of toddlerhood.

During the preschool years, children continue to integrate previously acquired skills into more complex, *dynamic systems.* Then they revise each new skill as their bodies grow larger and stronger, their central nervous systems develop, and their environments present new challenges.

Gross-Motor Development

As children's bodies become more streamlined and less top-heavy, their center of gravity shifts downward, toward the trunk. As a result, balance improves greatly, paving the way for new motor skills involving large muscles of the body. By age 2, preschoolers' gaits become smooth and rhythmic—secure enough that soon they leave the ground, at first by running and later by jumping, hopping, galloping, and skipping.

As children become steadier on their feet, their arms and torsos are freed to experiment with new skills—throwing and catching balls, steering tricycles, and swinging on horizontal bars and rings. Then upper- and lower-body skills combine into more refined actions. Five- and 6-year-olds simultaneously steer and pedal a tricycle and flexibly move their whole body when throwing, catching, hopping, and jumping. By the end of the preschool years, all skills are performed with greater speed and endurance. Table 7.1 provides a closer look at gross-motor development in early childhood.

As preschoolers' bodies become more streamlined, their balance improves greatly, enabling children to combine upper- and lower-body skills into more refined actions.

Fine-Motor Development

Fine-motor skills, too, take a giant leap forward in the preschool years. As control of the hands and fingers improves, young children put puzzles together, build with small blocks, cut and paste, and string beads. To parents, fine-motor progress is most apparent in two areas: (1) children's care of their own bodies, and (2) the drawings and paintings that fill the walls at home, child care, and preschool.

■ **SELF-HELP SKILLS.** As Table 7.1 shows, young children gradually become self-sufficient at dressing and feeding. But parents must be patient about these abilities: When tired and in a hurry, young children often revert to eating with their fingers. And the 3-year-old who dresses himself may end up with his shirt on inside out, his pants on backward, and his left snow boot on his right foot! Perhaps the most complex self-help skill of early childhood is shoe tying, mastered around age 6. Success requires a longer attention span, memory for an intricate series of hand movements, and the dexterity to perform them. Shoe tying illustrates the close connection between motor and cognitive development, as do two other skills: drawing and writing.

■ **DRAWING.** When given crayon and paper, even toddlers scribble in imitation of others. As preschoolers' ability to mentally represent the world expands, marks on the page take on meaning. A variety of factors combine with fine-motor control to influence changes in children's artful representations (Golomb, 2004). These include the realization that pictures can serve as symbols, improved planning and spatial understanding, and the emphasis that the child's culture places on artistic expression.

Typically, drawing progresses through the following sequence:

1. *Scribbles.* At first, children's gestures rather than the resulting scribbles contain the intended representation. For example, one 18-month-old made her crayon hop and, as it produced a series of dots, explained, "Rabbit goes hop-hop" (Winner, 1986).
2. *First representational forms.* Around age 3, children's scribbles start to become pictures. Often children make a gesture with the crayon, notice that they have drawn a recognizable shape, and then label it (Winner, 1986). Few 3-year-olds spontaneously draw so others can tell what their picture represents. But when adults draw with children and point out the resemblances between drawings and objects, preschoolers' pictures become more comprehensible and detailed (Braswell & Callanan, 2003).

■ **TABLE 7.1** ■ ***Changes in Gross- and Fine-Motor Skills During Early Childhood***

AGE	GROSS-MOTOR SKILLS	FINE-MOTOR SKILLS
2–3 years	Walks more rhythmically; hurried walk changes to run Jumps, hops, throws, and catches with rigid upper body Pushes riding toy with feet; little steering	Puts on and removes simple items of clothing Zips and unzips large zippers Uses spoon effectively
3–4 years	Walks up stairs, alternating feet, and downstairs, leading with one foot Jumps and hops, flexing upper body Throws and catches with slight involvement of upper body; still catches by trapping ball against chest Pedals and steers tricycle	Fastens and unfastens large buttons Serves self food without assistance Uses scissors Copies vertical line and circle Draws first picture of person, using tadpole image
4–5 years	Walks downstairs, alternating feet Runs more smoothly Gallops and skips with one foot Throws ball with increased body rotation and transfer of weight on feet; catches ball with hands Rides tricycle rapidly, steers smoothly	Uses fork effectively Cuts with scissors following line Copies triangle, cross, and some letters
5–6 years	Increases running speed Gallops more smoothly; engages in true skipping Displays mature throwing and catching patterns Rides bicycle with training wheels	Uses knife to cut soft food Ties shoes Draws person with six parts Copies some numbers and simple words

Sources: Cratty, 1986; Haywood & Getchell, 2005; Malina & Bouchard, 1991.

A major milestone in drawing occurs when children use lines to represent the boundaries of objects, enabling 3- and 4-year-olds to draw their first picture of a person. Fine-motor and cognitive limitations lead the preschooler to reduce the figure to the simplest form that still looks human: a circular shape with lines attached—the universal "tadpole" image shown on the left in Figure 7.5.

3. *More realistic drawings.* Greater realism in drawings develops gradually, as perception, language (ability to describe visual details), memory, and fine-motor capacities improve (Toomela, 2002). Five- and 6-year-olds create more complex drawings, like the one on the right in Figure 7.5, containing more conventional human and animal figures, with the head and body differentiated. Older preschoolers' drawings still contain perceptual distortions because they have just begun to represent depth (Cox & Littlejohn, 1995). This free depiction of reality makes their artwork look fanciful and inventive. Accomplished artists often must work hard to achieve what they did effortlessly as 5- and 6-year-olds.

■ **FIGURE 7.5** ■ **Examples of young children's drawings.** The universal tadpolelike shape that children use to draw their first picture of a person is shown on the left. The tadpole soon becomes an anchor for greater details that sprout from the basic shape. By the end of the preschool years, children produce more complex, differentiated pictures like the one on the right, drawn by a 6-year-old child. (*Left:* From H. Gardner, 1980, *Artful Scribbles: The Significance of Children's Drawings,* New York: Basic Books, p. 64. Reprinted by permission of Basic Books, a member of Perseus Books Group. *Right:* From E. Winner, "Where Pelicans Kiss Seals," *Psychology Today, 20*[8], August 1986, p. 35. Reprinted by permission from the collection of Ellen Winner.)

CULTURAL VARIATIONS IN DEVELOPMENT OF DRAWING. In cultures with rich artistic traditions, children create elaborate drawings that reflect the conventions of their culture. Adults encourage young children in drawing activities by offering suggestions, modeling ways to draw, and commenting on children's pictures (Boyatzis, 2000). Parents and teachers frequently ask children to label their pictures, emphasizing the representational function of drawing. Peers, as well, discuss one another's pictures and copy from one another's work (Braswell, 2006). All of these cultural practices enhance young children's drawing progress.

But in cultures with little interest in art, even older children and adolescents produce simple forms. In the Jimi Valley, a remote region of Papua New Guinea with no indigenous pictorial art, many children do not attend school and therefore have little opportunity to develop drawing skills. When a Western researcher asked nonschooled Jimi 10- to 15-year-olds to draw a human figure for the first time, most produced nonrepresentational scribbles and shapes or simple "stick" or "contour" images (see Figure 7.6) (Martlew & Connolly, 1996). These forms, which resemble those of preschoolers, seem to be a universal beginning in drawing. Once children realize that lines must evoke human features, they find solutions to figure drawing that vary somewhat from culture to culture but, overall, follow the sequence described earlier.

EARLY PRINTING. When preschoolers first try to write, they scribble, making no distinction between writing and drawing. Around age 4, writing shows some distinctive features of print, such as separate forms arranged in a line on the page. But children often include picturelike devices—for example, using a circular shape to write "sun" (Levin & Bus, 2003). Only gradually, between ages 4 and 6, do children realize that writing stands for language.

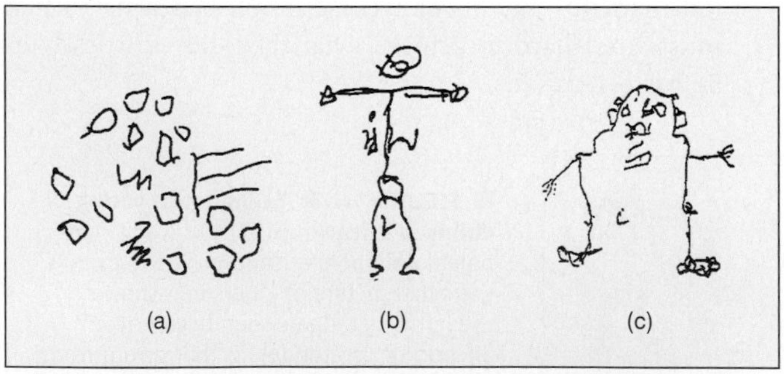

FIGURE 7.6 Drawings produced by nonschooled 10- to 15-year-olds of the Jimi Valley of Papua New Guinea when asked to draw a human figure for the first time. Many produced nonrepresentational scribbles and shapes (a), "stick" figures (b), or "contour" figures (c). Compared with the Western tadpole form, the Jimi "stick" and "contour" figures emphasize the hands and feet. Otherwise, the drawings of these older children resemble those of young preschoolers. (From M. Martlew and K. J. Connolly, 1996, "Human Figure Drawings by Schooled and Unschooled Children in Papua New Guinea," *Child Development, 67,* pp. 2750–2751. © The Society for Research in Child Development. Adapted by permission.)

Preschoolers' first attempts to print often involve their name, generally using a single letter. "How do you make a *D?*" my older son, David, asked at age 3. When I printed a large uppercase *D,* he tried to copy. "*D* for David," he proclaimed, quite satisfied with his backward, imperfect creation. By age 5, David printed his name clearly enough for others to read but, like many children, continued to reverse some letters until well into second grade. Until children start to read, they do not find it useful to distinguish between mirror-image forms, such as *b* and *d* and *p* and *q* (Bornstein & Arterberry, 1999; Casey, 1986).

Individual Differences in Motor Skills

Wide individual differences exist in the ages at which children reach motor milestones. A tall, muscular child tends to move more quickly and to acquire certain skills earlier than a short, stocky youngster. And as in other domains, parents and teachers probably provide more encouragement to children with biologically based motor-skill advantages.

Sex differences in motor skills are evident in early childhood. Boys are ahead of girls in skills that emphasize force and power. By age 5, they can jump slightly farther, run slightly faster, and throw a ball about five feet farther. Girls have an edge in fine-motor skills and in certain gross-motor skills that require a combination of good balance and foot movement, such as hopping and skipping (Fischman, Moore, & Steele, 1992; Haywood & Getchell, 2005). Boys' greater muscle mass and, in the case of throwing, slightly longer forearms contribute to their skill advantages. And girls' greater overall physical maturity may be partly responsible for their better balance and precision of movement.

From an early age, boys and girls are usually encouraged into different physical activities. For example, fathers are more likely to play catch with their sons than with their daughters. Sex differences in motor skills increase with age, but they remain small throughout childhood. This suggests that social pressures for boys, more than girls, to be active and physically skilled exaggerate small, genetically based sex differences (Greendorfer, Lewko, & Rosengren, 1996).

Children master the motor skills of early childhood during everyday play. Aside from throwing (where direct instruction is helpful), preschoolers exposed to gymnastics, tumbling, and other formal lessons do not make faster progress. When children have access to play spaces appropriate for running, climbing, jumping, and throwing and are encouraged to use them, they respond eagerly to these challenges. Similarly, fine-motor skills can be supported through daily routines, such as pouring juice and dressing, and through play that involves puzzles, construction sets, drawing, painting, sculpting, cutting, and pasting.

Finally, the social climate created by adults can enhance or dampen preschoolers' motor development. When parents and teachers criticize a child's performance, push specific motor skills, or promote a competitive attitude, they risk undermining children's self-confidence and, in turn, their motor progress (Berk, Mann, & Ogan, 2006). Adults involved in young children's motor activities should focus on fun rather than on winning or perfecting the "correct" technique.

ASK YOURSELF

REVIEW
Describe typical changes in children's drawings during early childhood, along with factors that contribute to those changes.

APPLY
Mabel and Chad want to do everything they can to support their 3-year-old daughter's motor development. What advice would you give them?

CONNECT
How are experiences that best support preschoolers' motor development consistent with experience-expectant brain growth of the early years? (Return to page 127 in Chapter 4 to review.)

Cognitive Development

One rainy morning, as I observed in our laboratory preschool, Leslie, the children's teacher, joined me at the back of the room for a moment. "Preschoolers' minds are such a blend of logic, fantasy, and faulty reasoning," Leslie reflected. "Every day, I'm startled by the maturity and originality of what they say and do. Yet at other times, their thinking seems limited and inflexible."

Leslie's comments sum up the puzzling contradictions of early childhood cognition. That day, for example, 3-year-old Sammy looked up, startled, after a loud crash of thunder outside. "A magic man turned on the thunder!" he pronounced. Even when Leslie patiently explained that thunder is caused by lightning, not by a person turning it on or off, Sammy persisted: "Then a magic lady did it."

In other respects, Sammy's thinking was surprisingly advanced. At snack time, he accurately counted, "One, two, three, four!" and then got four cartons of milk, one for each child at his table. But when his snack group included more than four children, Sammy's counting broke down. And after Priti dumped out her raisins, scattering them in front of her on the table, Sammy asked, "How come you got lots, and I only got this little bit?" He didn't realize that he had just as many raisins; his were simply all bunched up in a tiny red box.

To understand Sammy's reasoning, we turn first to Piaget's and Vygotsky's theories and evidence highlighting the strengths and limitations of each. Then we consider additional research on young children's cognition, inspired by the information-processing perspective, and look at the dramatic expansion of language in early childhood.

Piaget's Theory: The Preoperational Stage

As children move from the sensorimotor to the **preoperational stage,** which spans the years 2 to 7, the most obvious change is an extraordinary increase in representational, or symbolic, activity. Recall that infants and toddlers have some ability to represent their world. During early childhood, this capacity blossoms.

Mental Representation

Piaget acknowledged that language is our most flexible means of mental representation. By detaching thought from action, language permits far more efficient thinking than was possible earlier. When we think in words, we overcome the limits of our momentary experiences. We can deal with past, present, and future at once and combine concepts in unique ways, as when we imagine a hungry caterpillar eating bananas or monsters flying through the forest at night.

But Piaget did not regard language as the primary ingredient in childhood cognitive change. Instead, he believed that sensorimotor activity leads to internal images of experience, which children then label with words (Piaget, 1936/1952). In support of Piaget's view, recall from Chapter 5 that children's first words have a strong sensorimotor basis. In addition, infants and toddlers acquire an impressive range of categories long before they use words to label them (see page 163). But as we will see, other theorists regard Piaget's account of the link between language and thought as incomplete.

Make-Believe Play

Make-believe play is another excellent example of the development of representation in early childhood. Piaget believed that through pretending, young children practice and strengthen newly acquired representational schemes. Drawing on his ideas, several investigators have traced the development of make-believe during the preschool years.

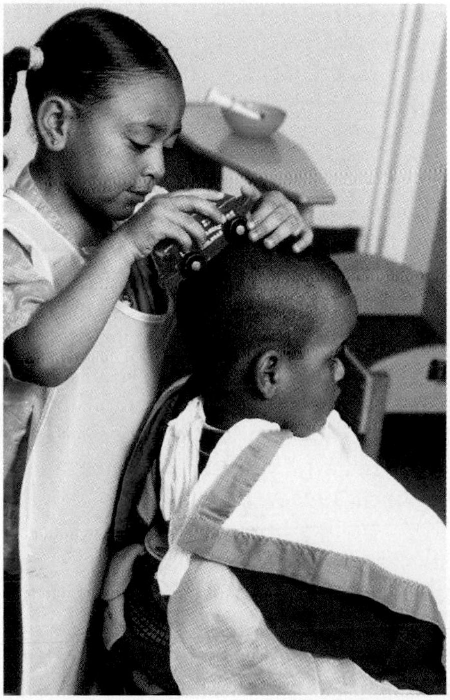

© LAURA DWIGHT PHOTOGRAPHY

Make-believe play increases in sophistication during the preschool years. Children pretend with less realistic toys, so a toy truck can stand for an electric hair clipper. And children increasingly coordinate make-believe roles.

■ **DEVELOPMENT OF MAKE-BELIEVE.** One day, Sammy's 18-month-old brother, Dwayne, visited the classroom. Dwayne wandered around, picked up a toy telephone receiver, said, "Hi, Mommy," and then dropped it. Next, he found a cup, pretended to drink, and then toddled off again. Meanwhile, Sammy joined Vance and Lynette in the block area for a space shuttle launch.

"That can be our control tower," Sammy suggested, pointing to a corner by a bookshelf. "Countdown!" he announced, speaking into his "walkie-talkie"—a small wooden block. "Five, six, two, four, one, blastoff!" Lynette made a doll push a pretend button, and the rocket was off!

Comparing Dwayne's pretend play with Sammy's, we see three important changes that reflect the preschool child's growing symbolic mastery:

- *Play detaches from the real-life conditions associated with it.* In early pretending, toddlers use only realistic objects—a toy telephone to talk into, a cup to drink from. Their first pretend acts imitate adults' actions and are not yet flexible. Children younger than age 2, for example, will pretend to drink from a cup but refuse to pretend a cup is a hat (Tomasello, Striano, & Rochat, 1999). They have trouble using an object (cup) that already has an obvious use as a symbol of another object (hat).

  After age 2, children pretend with less realistic toys—a block might stand for a telephone receiver. Gradually, they can flexibly imagine objects and events without any support from the real world, as Sammy's imaginary control tower illustrates (O'Reilly, 1995; Striano, Tomasello, & Rochat, 2001).
- *Play becomes less self-centered.* At first, make-believe is directed toward the self—for example, Dwayne pretends to feed only himself. Soon, children begin to direct pretend actions toward other objects, as when a child feeds a doll. Early in the third year, they become detached participants who make a doll feed itself or (in Lynette's case) push a button to launch a rocket. Make-believe becomes less self-centered as children realize that agents and recipients of pretend actions can be independent of themselves (McCune, 1993).
- *Play includes more complex combinations of schemes.* Dwayne can pretend to drink from a cup, but he does not yet combine pouring and drinking. Later, children combine schemes with those of peers in **sociodramatic play,** the make-believe with others that is under way around age 2 and increases rapidly during the next few years (Kavanaugh, 2006). Already, Sammy and his classmates can create and coordinate several roles in an elaborate plot. By the end of early childhood, children have a sophisticated understanding of story lines (Göncü, 1993).

In sociodramatic play, children display awareness that make-believe is a representational activity—an understanding that improves steadily over early childhood (Lillard, 2003; Rakoczy, Tomasello, & Striano, 2004; Sobel, 2006). ***TAKE A MOMENT...*** Listen closely to a group of preschoolers as they assign roles and negotiate make-believe plans: "You *pretend to be* the astronaut, I'll *act like* I'm operating the control tower!" In communicating about pretend, children think about their own and others' fanciful representations—evidence that they have begun to reason about people's mental activities.

■ **BENEFITS OF MAKE-BELIEVE.** Today, Piaget's view of make-believe as mere practice of representational schemes is regarded as too limited. Play not only reflects but also contributes to children's cognitive and social skills. Compared with social nonpretend activities (such as drawing or putting puzzles together), during sociodramatic play preschoolers' interactions last longer, show more involvement, draw more children into the activity, and are more cooperative (Creasey, Jarvis, & Berk, 1998).

It is not surprising, then, that preschoolers who spend more time at sociodramatic play are seen as more socially competent by their teachers (Connolly & Doyle, 1984). And many studies reveal that make-believe strengthens a wide variety of mental abilities, including sustained attention, memory, logical reasoning, language and literacy skills, imagination, creativity, understanding of emotions, and the ability to reflect on one's own thinking, control one's own behavior, and take another's perspective (Bergen & Mauer, 2000; Berk, Mann, & Ogan, 2006; Elias & Berk, 2002; Hirsh-Pasek et al., 2009; Lindsey & Colwell, 2003; Ruff & Capozzoli, 2003). We will return to the topic of early childhood play in this and the next chapter.

Symbol–Real-World Relations

To make believe and draw—and to understand other forms of representation, such as photographs, models, and maps—preschoolers must realize that each symbol corresponds to something specific in everyday life. When do children comprehend symbol–real-world relations?

Children who experience a variety of symbols come to understand that one object, such as this play village, can stand for another—a full-sized real village that people live in.

In one study, 2½ - and 3-year-olds watched an adult hide a small toy (Little Snoopy) in a scale model of a room and then were asked to retrieve it. Next, they had to find a larger toy (Big Snoopy) hidden in the room that the model represented. Not until age 3 could most children use the model as a guide to finding Big Snoopy in the real room (DeLoache, 1987). The 2½-year-olds did not realize that the model could be both *a toy room* and *a symbol of another room.* They had trouble with **dual representation**—viewing a symbolic object as both an object in its own right and a symbol. In support of this interpretation, when researchers made the model room less prominent as an object, by placing it behind a window and preventing children from touching it, more 2½-year-olds succeeded at the search task (DeLoache, 2000, 2002).

Recall that in make-believe play, 1½- to 2-year-olds cannot use an object with an obvious use (cup) to stand for another object (hat). Likewise, 2-year-olds do not yet grasp that a drawing—an object in its own right—also represents real-world objects.

How do children grasp the dual representation of symbolic objects? When adults point out similarities between models and real-world spaces, 2½-year-olds perform better on the find-Snoopy task (Peralta de Mendoza & Salsa, 2003). Also, insight into one type of symbol–real-world relation helps preschoolers master others. For example, children regard photos and pictures in books as symbols early, around 1½ to 2 years, because a picture's primary purpose is to stand for something; it is not an interesting object in its own right (Preissler & Carey, 2004; Simcock & DeLoache, 2006). And 3-year-olds who can use a model of a room to locate Big Snoopy readily transfer their understanding to a simple map (Marzolf & DeLoache, 1994). In sum, experiences with diverse symbols—photos, picture books, make-believe, and maps—help preschoolers appreciate that one object can stand for another.

■ **FIGURE 7.7** ■ **Piaget's three-mountains problem.** Each mountain is distinguished by its color and by its summit. One has a red cross, another a small house, and the third a snow-capped peak. Children at the preoperational stage respond egocentrically. They cannot select a picture that shows the mountains from the doll's perspective. Instead, they simply choose the photo that reflects their own vantage point.

Limitations of Preoperational Thought

Aside from gains in representation, Piaget described preschoolers in terms of what they *cannot* understand (Beilin, 1992). As the term *pre*operational suggests, he compared them to older, more competent children who have reached the concrete operational stage. According to Piaget, young children are not capable of *operations*—mental actions that obey logical rules. Rather, their thinking is rigid, limited to one aspect of a situation at a time, and strongly influenced by the way things appear at the moment.

■ **EGOCENTRISM.** For Piaget, the most fundamental deficiency of preoperational thinking is **egocentrism**—failure to distinguish the symbolic viewpoints of others from one's own. He believed that when children first mentally represent the world, they tend to focus on their own viewpoint and simply assume that others perceive, think, and feel the same way they do.

Piaget's most convincing demonstration of egocentrism involves his *three-mountains problem,* described in Figure 7.7. Egocentrism is responsible for preoperational children's **animistic thinking**—the belief that inanimate objects have lifelike qualities, such as thoughts, wishes, feelings, and intentions (Piaget, 1926/1930). Recall Sammy's firm insistence that someone must have turned on the thunder. According to Piaget, because young children egocentrically assign human purposes to physical events, magical thinking is common during the preschool years.

Piaget argued that preschoolers' egocentric bias prevents them from *accommodating,* or reflecting on and revising their faulty reasoning in response to their physical and social worlds. To understand this shortcoming, let's consider some additional tasks that Piaget gave to children.

■ **INABILITY TO CONSERVE.** Piaget's famous conservation tasks reveal a variety of deficiencies of preoperational thinking. **Conservation** refers to the idea that certain physical characteristics of objects remain the same, even when their outward appearance changes. At snack time, Priti and Sammy had identical boxes of raisins, but when Priti spread her raisins out on the table, Sammy was convinced that she had more.

In another conservation task involving liquid, the child is shown two identical tall glasses of water and asked if they contain equal amounts. Once the child agrees, the water in one glass is poured into a short, wide container, changing its appearance but not its amount. Then the child is asked whether or not the amount of water has changed. Preoperational children think the quantity has changed. They explain, "There is less now because the water is way down here" (that is, its level is so low) or, "There is more now because it is all spread out." Figure 7.8 on page 230 illustrates other conservation tasks that you can try with children.

The inability to conserve highlights several related aspects of preoperational children's thinking. First, their understanding is *centered,* or characterized by **centration.** They focus on

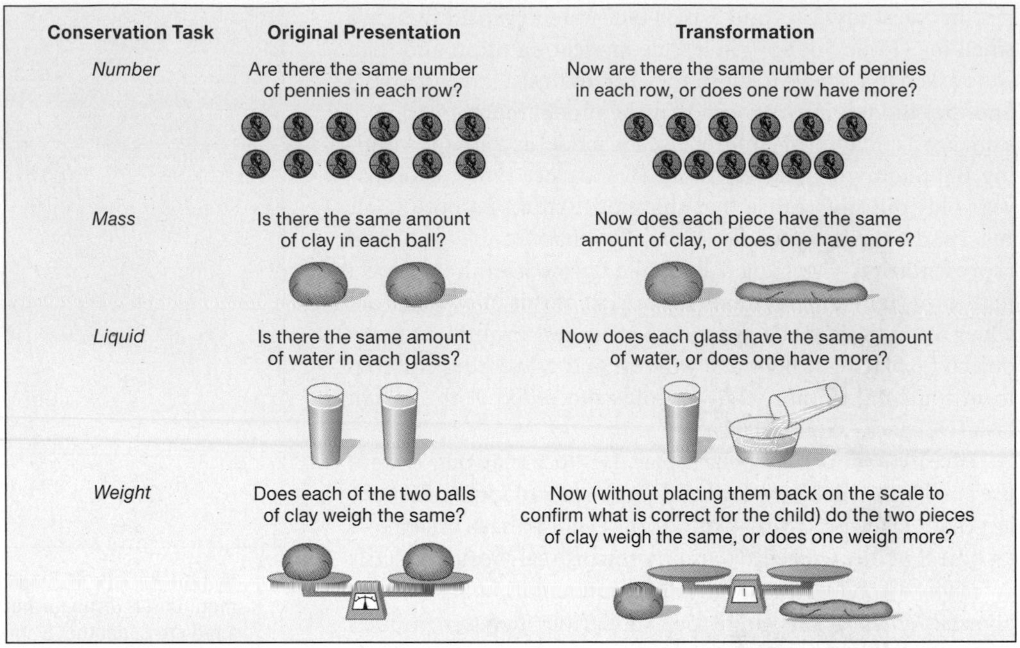

■ **FIGURE 7.8** ■ **Some Piagetian conservation tasks.** Children at the preoperational stage cannot yet conserve. These tasks are mastered gradually over the concrete operational stage. Children in Western nations typically acquire conservation of number, mass, and liquid sometime between 6 and 7 years and of weight between 8 and 10 years.

one aspect of a situation, neglecting other important features. In conservation of liquid, the child *centers* on the height of the water, failing to realize that changes in width compensate for changes in height. Second, children are easily distracted by the *perceptual appearance* of objects. Third, children treat the initial and final states of the water as unrelated events, ignoring the *dynamic transformation* (pouring of water) between them.

The most important illogical feature of preoperational thought is its **irreversibility,** an inability to mentally go through a series of steps in a problem and then reverse direction, returning to the starting point. *Reversibility* is part of every logical operation. After Priti spills her raisins, Sammy cannot reverse by thinking, "I know that Priti doesn't have more raisins than I do. If we put them back in that little box, her raisins and my raisins would look just the same."

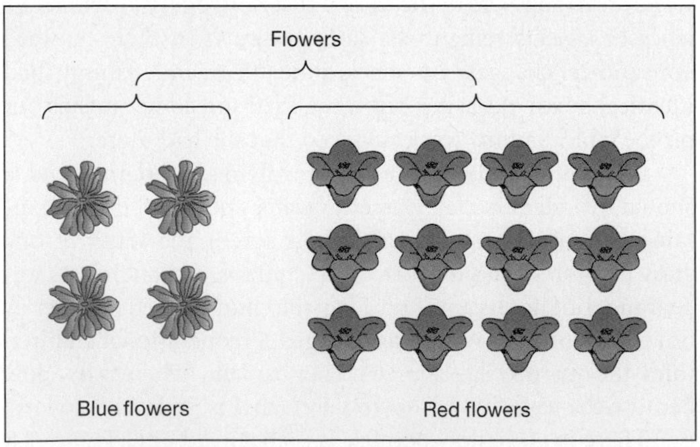

■ **FIGURE 7.9** ■ **A Piagetian class inclusion problem.** Children are shown 16 flowers, 4 of which are blue and 12 of which are red. Asked, "Are there more red flowers or flowers?" the preoperational child responds, "More red flowers," failing to realize that both red and blue flowers are included in the category "flowers."

■ **LACK OF HIERARCHICAL CLASSIFICATION.** Preoperational children have difficulty with **hierarchical classification**—the organization of objects into classes and subclasses on the basis of similarities and differences. Piaget's famous *class inclusion problem*, illustrated in Figure 7.9, demonstrates this limitation. Preoperational children center on the overriding feature, red. They do not think reversibly by moving from the whole class (flowers) to the parts (red and blue) and back again.

Follow-Up Research on Preoperational Thought

Over the past three decades, researchers have challenged Piaget's view of preschoolers as cognitively deficient. Because many Piagetian problems contain unfamiliar elements or too many pieces of information for young children to handle at once, preschoolers' responses do not reflect their true abilities. Piaget also missed many naturally occurring instances of effective reasoning by preschoolers.

■ **EGOCENTRIC, ANIMISTIC, AND MAGICAL THINKING.** Do young children really believe that a person standing elsewhere in a room sees the same thing they see? When researchers adapt the three-mountains problem to include familiar objects and use methods other than picture selection (which is difficult even for 10-year-olds), 4-year-olds show clear awareness of others' vantage points (Borke, 1975; Newcombe & Huttenlocher, 1992). Even 2-year-olds realize that what they see sometimes differs from what another person sees. When asked to help an adult looking for a lost object, 24-month-olds—but not 18-month-olds—handed her a toy resting behind a bucket that was within the child's line of sight but not the adult's (Moll & Tomasello, 2006).

Nonegocentric responses also appear in young children's conversations. For example, preschoolers adapt their speech to fit the needs of their listeners. Four-year-olds use shorter, simpler expressions when talking to 2-year-olds than to age-mates or adults (Gelman & Shatz, 1978). And in describing objects, children do not use such words as "big" and "little" in a rigid, egocentric fashion. Rather, they *adjust* their descriptions to allow for context. By age 3, children judge a 2-inch shoe as small when seen by itself (because it is much smaller than most shoes) but as big for a tiny 5-inch-tall doll (Ebeling & Gelman, 1994).

In Chapter 5, we saw that toddlers have already begun to infer others' intentions (see page 157). And in his later writings, Piaget (1945/1951) did describe preschoolers' egocentrism as a tendency rather than an inability. As we revisit the topic of perspective taking, we will see that it develops gradually throughout childhood and adolescence.

Piaget also overestimated preschoolers' animistic beliefs. Even young infants have begun to distinguish animate from inanimate, as indicated by their developing categorical distinctions between living and nonliving things (see page 163). By age 2½, children give psychological explanations ("he likes to"; "she wants to") for people and occasionally for animals, but rarely for objects (Hickling & Wellman, 2001). They do make errors when questioned about vehicles, such as trains and airplanes, which appear to be self-moving and have other lifelike features—for example, headlights that resemble eyes (Gelman & Opfer, 2002). But their responses result from incomplete knowledge, not from a belief that inanimate objects are alive.

The same is true for other fantastic beliefs of the preschool years. Most 3- and 4-year-olds believe in the supernatural powers of fairies, goblins, and other enchanted creatures. They think that magic accounts for events that they cannot explain, as in 3-year-old Sammy's magical explanation of thunder in the opening to this chapter (Rosengren & Hickling, 2000). Furthermore, older 3-year-olds and 4-year-olds think that violations of physical laws (walking through a wall) and mental laws (turning on the TV just by thinking about it) require magic more than violations of social conventions (taking a bath with shoes on) (Browne & Woolley, 2004). These responses indicate that preschoolers' notions of magic are flexible and appropriate.

Between ages 4 and 8, as children gain familiarity with physical events and principles, their magical beliefs decline. They figure out who is really behind Santa Claus and the Tooth Fairy, and they realize that the antics of magicians are due to trickery (Subbotsky, 2004). Religion and culture also play a role. Jewish children are more likely than their Christian age-mates to express disbelief in Santa Claus and the Tooth Fairy. Having learned at home that Santa is unreal, they seem to generalize this attitude to other magical figures (Woolley, 1997). And cultural myths about wishing—for example, the custom of making a wish before blowing out birthday candles—probably underlie the conviction of most 3- to 6-year-olds that by wishing, you can sometimes make your desires come true (Woolley, 2000).

■ **ILLOGICAL THOUGHT.** Many studies show that when preschoolers are given tasks that are simplified and relevant to their everyday lives, they do not display the illogical characteristics that Piaget saw in the preoperational stage. For example, when a conservation-of-number task is scaled down to include only three items instead of six or seven, 3-year-olds perform well (Gelman, 1972). And when preschoolers are asked carefully worded questions about what happens to substances (such as sugar) after they are dissolved in water, they give accurate explanations. Most 3- to 5-year-olds know that the substance is conserved—that it continues to exist, can be tasted, and makes the liquid heavier, even though it is invisible in the water (Au, Sidle, & Rollins, 1993; Rosen & Rozin, 1993).

Preschoolers' ability to reason about transformations is evident on other problems. They can engage in impressive *reasoning by analogy* about physical changes. Presented with the picture-matching problem "Play dough is to cut-up play dough as apple is to . . . ?," even 3-year-olds choose the correct answer (a cut-up apple) from a set of alternatives, several of which (a bitten apple, a cut-up loaf of bread) share physical features with the right choice (Goswami, 1996). These findings indicate that in familiar contexts, preschoolers can overcome appearances and think logically about cause and effect.

Finally, even without detailed biological knowledge, preschoolers understand that the insides of animals are responsible for cause–effect sequences (such as willing oneself to move) that are impossible for nonliving things (Gelman, 2003; Keil & Lockhart, 1999). Preschoolers seem to use illogical reasoning only when grappling with unfamiliar topics, too much information, or contradictory facts that they cannot reconcile (Ruffman, 1999).

■ **CATEGORIZATION.** Although preschoolers have difficulty with Piagetian class inclusion tasks, they organize their everyday knowledge into nested categories at an early age. By the second half of the first year, children have formed a variety of global categories—furniture, animals, vehicles, plants, and kitchen utensils—each of which includes objects varying widely in perceptual features (Mandler, 2004). The objects go together because of their common function or behavior, challenging Piaget's assumption that preschoolers' thinking is wholly governed by appearances. Indeed, 2- to 5-year-olds readily draw inferences about nonobservable characteristics shared by category members (Gopnik & Nazzi, 2003). For example, after being told that a bird has warm blood and that a stegosaurus (dinosaur) has cold blood, preschoolers infer that a pterodactyl (labeled a dinosaur) has cold blood, even though it closely resembles a bird.

During the second and third years, and perhaps earlier, children's global categories differentiate. They form many *basic-level categories*—ones at an intermediate level of generality, such as "chairs," "tables," and "beds." By the third year, children easily move back and forth between basic-level categories and *general categories,* such as "furniture." And they break down basic-level categories into *subcategories,* such as "rocking chairs" and "desk chairs," "bluebirds" and "cardinals" (Mervis, Pani, & Pani, 2003).

© LAURA DWIGHT/PHOTOEDIT

Preschoolers devise many categories based on nonobservable characteristics that members share. This 4-year-old knows that despite wide variations in size and appearance, all dinosaurs share common inner features, such as cold blood.

Preschoolers' rapidly expanding vocabularies and general knowledge support their impressive skill at categorizing (Gelman & Koenig, 2003). As they learn more about their world, they devise ideas about underlying characteristics that category members share—for example, that a combination of physical features, internal organs, and behaviors determines an animal's identity (Gelman & Koenig, 2003). Also, adults label and explain categories to children, and picture-book reading is a rich context for doing so (Gelman & Kalish, 2006). While looking at books, parents make categorical statements ("Penguins live at the South Pole, swim, catch fish, and have thick layers of fat and feathers that help them stay warm") that guide children's construction of categories.

In sum, preschoolers' category systems are not yet very complex. But they already have capacity to classify hierarchically and on the basis of nonobvious properties. And preschoolers use logical, causal reasoning to identify the interrelated features that form the basis of a category and to classify new members.

■ APPEARANCE VERSUS REALITY. What happens when preschoolers encounter objects that have two identities—a real one and an apparent one? Can they distinguish appearance from reality? In a series of studies, John Flavell and his colleagues presented children with objects that were disguised in various ways and asked what each "looks like" and what each "is really and truly." Preschoolers had difficulty. For example, when asked whether a candle that looks like a crayon "is really and truly" a crayon, they often responded, "Yes!" Not until age 6 or 7 did children do well on these tasks (Flavell, Green, & Flavell, 1987).

Younger children's poor performance, however, is not due to a general difficulty in distinguishing appearance from reality, as Piaget suggested. Rather, they have trouble with the *language* of these tasks (Deák, Ray, & Brenneman, 2003). When permitted to solve appearance–reality problems nonverbally, by choosing from an array of objects the one that "really" has a particular identity, most 3-year-olds perform well (Sapp, Lee, & Muir 2000).

Note how the appearance–reality distinction involves an attainment discussed earlier: *dual representation*—the realization that an object can be one thing (a candle) while symbolizing another (a crayon). At first, however, children's understanding is fragile. After putting on a Halloween mask, young preschoolers may be frightened when they see themselves in a mirror. Performing well on verbal appearance–reality tasks signifies a more secure understanding and is related to further progress in representational ability (Bialystok & Senman, 2004).

Evaluation of the Preoperational Stage

Table 7.2 provides an overview of the cognitive attainments of early childhood. ***TAKE A MOMENT...*** Compare them with Piaget's description of the preoperational child on pages 229–230. The evidence as a whole indicates that Piaget was partly wrong and partly right about young children's cognitive capacities. When given simplified tasks based on familiar experiences, preschoolers show the beginnings of logical thinking, which suggests that they attain logical operations gradually.

Evidence that preschoolers can be trained to perform well on Piagetian problems also supports the idea that operational thought is not absent at one point in time and present at another (Ping & Goldin-Meadow, 2008; Siegler & Svetina, 2006). Over time, children rely on increasingly effective mental (as opposed to perceptual) approaches to solving problems. For example, children who cannot use counting to compare two sets of items do not conserve number (Rouselle, Palmers, & Noël, 2004; Sophian, 1995). Once preschoolers can count, they apply this skill to conservation-of-number tasks involving just a few items. As counting improves, they extend the strategy to problems with more items. By age 6, they understand that number remains the same after a transformation as long as nothing is added or taken away. Consequently, they no longer need to count to verify their answer (Halford & Andrews, 2006).

That logical operations develop gradually poses yet another challenge to Piaget's stage concept, which assumes abrupt change toward logical reasoning around age 6 or 7. Does a preoperational stage really exist? Some no longer think so. Recall from Chapter 5 that according to the information-processing perspective, children work out their understanding of each type of task separately, and their thought processes are basically the same at all ages—just present to a greater or lesser extent.

Other experts think the stage concept is valid but must be modified. For example, some *neo-Piagetian theorists* combine Piaget's stage approach with the information-processing empha-

■ **TABLE 7.2** ■ ***Some Cognitive Attainments of Early Childhood***

APPROXIMATE AGE	COGNITIVE ATTAINMENTS
2–4 years  © ELLEN B. SENISI/THE IMAGE WORKS	Shows a dramatic increase in representational activity, as reflected in the development of language, make-believe play, drawing, understanding of dual representation, and categorization Takes the perspective of others in simplified, familiar situations and in everyday, face-to-face communication Distinguishes animate beings from inanimate objects; denies that magic can alter everyday experiences Grasps conservation, notices transformations, reverses thinking, and understands many cause-and-effect relationships in familiar contexts Categorizes objects on the basis of common function and behavior and devises ideas about underlying characteristics that category members share Sorts familiar objects into hierarchically organized categories Distinguishes appearance from reality
4–7 years  © STEVE STARR/CORBIS	Becomes increasingly aware that make-believe (and other thought processes) are representational activities Replaces magical beliefs about fairies, goblins, and events that violate expectations with plausible explanations Solves verbal appearance–reality problems, signifying a more secure understanding

sis on task-specific change (Case, 1998; Halford & Andrews, 2006). They believe that Piaget's strict stage definition must be transformed into a less tightly knit concept, one in which a related set of competencies develops over an extended time period, depending on brain development and specific experiences. These investigators point to findings indicating that as long as the complexity of tasks and children's exposure to them are carefully controlled, children approach those tasks in similar, stage-consistent ways (Andrews & Halford, 2002; Case & Okamoto, 1996). For example, in drawing pictures, preschoolers depict objects separately, ignoring their spatial arrangement. In understanding stories, they grasp a single story line but have trouble with a main plot plus one or more subplots.

This flexible stage notion recognizes the unique qualities of early childhood thinking. At the same time, it provides a better account of why, as Leslie put it, "Preschoolers' minds are such a blend of logic, fantasy, and faulty reasoning."

Piaget and Education

Three educational principles derived from Piaget's theory continue to have a major impact on both teacher training and classroom practices, especially during early childhood:

- *Discovery learning.* In a Piagetian classroom, children are encouraged to discover for themselves through spontaneous interaction with the environment. Instead of presenting ready-made knowledge verbally, teachers provide a rich variety of materials designed to promote exploration—art supplies, puzzles, table games, dress-up clothing, building blocks, books, measuring tools, musical instruments, and more.
- *Sensitivity to children's readiness to learn.* In a Piagetian classroom, teachers introduce activities that build on children's current thinking, challenging their incorrect ways of viewing the world and enabling them to practice newly discovered schemes. But they do not try to hasten development by imposing new skills before children indicate interest or readiness.
- *Acceptance of individual differences.* Piaget's theory assumes that all children go through the same sequence of development, but at different rates. Therefore, teachers must plan activities for individual children and small groups, not just for the whole class. In addition, teachers evaluate educational progress in relation to the child's previous development, rather than on the basis of normative standards, or average performance of same-age peers.

Like his stages, educational applications of Piaget's theory have met with criticism. Perhaps the greatest challenge has to do with his insistence that young children learn mainly through acting on the environment (Brainerd, 2003). In the next section, we will see that young children also rely on language-based routes to knowledge.

ASK YOURSELF

REVIEW
Select two of the following features of preoperational thought: egocentrism, a focus on perceptual appearances, difficulty reasoning about transformations, and lack of hierarchical classification. Present evidence indicating that preschoolers are more capable thinkers than Piaget assumed.

APPLY
Three-year-old Will understands that his tricycle isn't alive and can't feel or move on its own. But at the beach, while watching the sun dip below the horizon, Will exclaimed, "The sun is tired. It's going to sleep!" What explains this apparent contradiction in Will's reasoning?

CONNECT
Make-believe play promotes both cognitive and social development (see page 228). Explain why this is so.

REFLECT
On the basis of what you have read, do you accept Piaget's claim for a preoperational stage of cognitive development? Explain.

Vygotsky's Sociocultural Theory

Piaget's deemphasis on language as a source of cognitive development brought on yet another challenge, this time from Vygotsky's sociocultural theory, which stresses the social context of cognitive development. During early childhood, rapid growth of language broadens preschoolers' participation in social dialogues with more knowledgeable individuals, who encourage them to master culturally important tasks. Soon children start to communicate with themselves in much the same way they converse with others. This greatly enhances their thinking and ability to control their own behavior. Let's see how this happens.

Private Speech

TAKE A MOMENT... Watch preschoolers as they play and explore the environment, and you will see that they frequently talk out loud to themselves. For example, as Sammy worked a puzzle, he said, "Where's the red piece? Now, a blue one. No, it doesn't fit. Try it here."

Piaget (1923/1926) called these utterances *egocentric speech,* reflecting his belief that young children have difficulty taking the perspectives of others. Their talk, he said, is often "talk for self" in which they express thoughts in whatever form they happen to occur, regardless of whether a listener can understand. Piaget believed that cognitive development and certain social experiences eventually bring an end to egocentric speech. Specifically, through disagreements with peers, children see that others hold viewpoints different from their own. As a result, egocentric speech declines.

Vygotsky (1934/1987) disagreed with Piaget's conclusions. Because language helps children think about their mental activities and behavior and select courses of action, Vygotsky saw it as the foundation for all higher cognitive processes, including controlled attention, deliberate memorization and recall, categorization, planning, problem solving, and self-reflection. In Vygotsky's view, children speak to themselves for self-guidance. As they get older and find tasks easier, their self-directed speech is internalized as silent, *inner speech*—the internal verbal dialogues we carry on while thinking and acting in everyday situations.

Over the past three decades, almost all studies have supported Vygotsky's perspective (Berk & Harris, 2003; Winsler, 2009). As a result, children's self-directed speech is now called **private speech** instead of egocentric speech. Research shows that children use more of it when tasks are appropriately challenging (neither too easy nor too hard), after they make errors, or when they are confused about how to proceed. With age, as Vygotsky predicted, private speech goes underground, changing into whispers and silent lip movements. Furthermore, children who freely use private speech during a challenging activity are more attentive and involved and show better task peformance than their less talkative agemates (Al-Namlah, Fernyhough, & Meins, 2006; Berk & Spuhl, 1995; Fernyhough & Fradley, 2005; Winsler, Naglieri, & Manfra, 2006).

© LAURA DWIGHT PHOTOGRAPHY

This 4-year-old talks to himself as he explores a collection of shells, pine cones, and other natural objects. Research supports Vygotsky's theory that children use private speech to guide their own thinking and behavior.

Social Origins of Early Childhood Cognition

Where does private speech come from? Recall from Chapter 5 that Vygotsky believed that children's learning takes place within the *zone of proximal development*—a range of tasks too difficult for the child to do alone but possible with the help of adults and more skilled peers. Consider the joint activity of Sammy and his mother, who helps him put together a difficult puzzle:

Sammy: I can't get this one in. *[Tries to insert a piece in the wrong place.]*

Mother: Which piece might go down here? *[Points to the bottom of the puzzle.]*

Sammy: His shoes. *[Looks for a piece resembling the clown's shoes but tries the wrong one.]*

Mother: Well, what piece looks like this shape? *[Points again to the bottom of the puzzle.]*

Sammy: The brown one. *[Tries it, and it fits; then attempts another piece and looks at his mother.]*

Mother: Try turning it just a little. *[Gestures to show him.]*

Sammy: There! *[Puts in several more pieces while his mother watches.]*

Sammy's mother keeps the puzzle within his zone of proximal development, at a manageable level of difficulty. To do so, she engages in **scaffolding**—adjusting the support offered during a teaching session to fit the child's current level of performance. When the child has little notion of how to proceed, the adult uses direct instruction, breaking the task into manageable units, suggesting strategies, and offering rationales for using them. As the child's competence increases, effective scaffolders gradually and sensitively withdraw support, turning over responsibility to the child. Then children take the language of these dialogues, make it part of their private speech, and use this speech to organize their independent efforts.

What evidence supports Vygotsky's ideas on the social origins of cognitive development? In several studies, children whose parents were effective scaffolders used more private speech, were more successful when attempting difficult tasks on their own, and were advanced in overall cognitive development (Berk & Spuhl, 1995; Conner & Cross, 2003; Mulvaney et al., 2006). Adult cognitive support—teaching in small steps and offering strategies—predicts gains in children's thinking. And adult emotional support—offering encouragement and allowing the child to take over the task—predicts children's effort (Neitzel & Stright, 2003).

Other research shows that although children benefit from working on tasks with same-age peers, their planning and problem solving improve more when their partner is either an "expert" peer (especially capable at the task) or an adult. And peer disagreement (emphasized by Piaget) seems less important in fostering cognitive development than the extent to which children resolve differences of opinion and cooperate (Kobayashi, 1994; Tudge, 1992).

Vygotsky and Education

Both Piagetian and Vygotskian classrooms emphasize active participation and acceptance of individual differences. But a Vygotskian classroom goes beyond independent discovery to promote *assisted discovery.* Teachers guide children's learning, tailoring their interventions to each child's zone of proximal development. Assisted discovery is also aided by *peer collaboration* as children of varying abilities work in groups, teaching and helping one another.

Vygotsky (1933/1978) saw make-believe play as the ideal social context for fostering cognitive development in early childhood. As children create imaginary situations, they learn to follow internal ideas and social rules rather than their immediate impulses. For example, a child pretending to go to sleep follows the rules of bedtime behavior. A child imagining himself as a father and a doll as a child conforms to the rules of parental behavior. According to Vygotsky, make-believe play is a unique, broadly influential zone of proximal development in which children try out a wide variety of challenging activities and acquire many new competencies.

Turn back to page 228 to review findings that make-believe play enhances a diverse array of cognitive and social skills. Pretending is also rich in private speech—a finding that supports its role in helping children bring action under the control of thought (Krafft & Berk, 1998). And preschoolers who spend

In this Vygotsky-inspired classroom, 4- and 5-year-olds benefit from peer collaboration. As they jointly make music, their conductor ensures that each player stays on beat.

CULTURAL INFLUENCES

Children in Village and Tribal Cultures Observe and Participate in Adult Work

In Western societies, the role of equipping children with the skills they need to become competent workers is assigned to school. In early childhood, middle-SES parents' interactions with children dwell on preparing the children for school success through child-focused activities—especially adult–child conversations and play that enhance language, literacy, and other academic knowledge. In village and tribal cultures, children receive little or no schooling, spend their days in contact with adult work, and start to assume mature responsibilities in early childhood (Rogoff et al., 2003). Consequently, parents have little need to rely on conversation and play to teach children.

A study comparing 2- and 3-year-olds' daily lives in four cultures—two U.S. middle-SES suburbs, the Efe hunters and gatherers of the Republic of Congo, and a Mayan agricultural town in Guatemala—documented these differences (Morelli, Rogoff, & Angelillo, 2003). In the U.S. communities, young children had little access to adult work and spent much time conversing and playing with adults. In contrast, the Efe and Mayan children rarely engaged in these child-focused activities. Instead, they spent their days close to—and frequently observing—adult work, which often took place in or near the Efe campsite or the Mayan family home.

An ethnography of a remote Mayan village in Yucatán, Mexico, shows that when young children are legitimate onlookers and participants in a daily life structured around adult work, their competencies differ from those of Western preschoolers (Gaskins, 1999; Gaskins, Haight, & Lancy, 2007). Yucatec Mayan adults are subsistence farmers. Men tend cornfields, aided by sons age 8 and older. Women prepare meals, wash clothes, and care for the livestock and garden, assisted by daughters and by sons too young to work in the fields. Children join in these activities from the second year on. When not participating, they are expected to be self-sufficient. Young children make many nonwork decisions for themselves—how much to sleep and eat, what to wear, and even when to start school. As a result, Yucatec Mayan preschoolers are highly competent at self-care. In contrast, their make-believe play is limited; when it occurs, they usually enact adult work. Otherwise, they watch others—for hours each day.

Yucatec Mayan parents rarely converse or play with preschoolers or scaffold their learning. Rather, when children imitate adult tasks, parents conclude that they are ready for more responsibility. Then they assign chores, selecting tasks the child can do with little help so that adult work is not disturbed. If a child cannot do a task, the adult takes over and the child observes, reengaging when able to contribute.

Expected to be autonomous and helpful, Yucatec Mayan children seldom ask others for something interesting to do. From an early age, they can sit quietly for long periods—through a long religious service or a ride to town. And when an adult directs them to do a chore, they respond eagerly to the type of command that Western children frequently resent. By age 5, Yucatec Mayan children spontaneously take responsibility for tasks beyond those assigned.

A Mayan 3-year-old imitates her mother in balancing a basin of water on her head, while her younger sibling prepares to attempt the skill. Children in Yucatec Mayan culture join in the work of their community from an early age, spending many hours observing adults.

more time engaged in sociodramatic play are better at taking personal responsibility for following classroom rules and at regulating emotion (Berk, Mann, & Ogan, 2006; Lemche et al., 2003). These findings support the role of make-believe in children's increasing self-control.

Evaluation of Vygotsky's Theory

In granting social experience a fundamental role in cognitive development, Vygotsky's theory underscores the vital role of teaching and helps us understand the wide cultural variation in children's cognitive skills. Nevertheless, it has not gone unchallenged. Verbal communication may not be the only means through which children's thinking develops—or even, in some cultures, the most important means. When Western parents scaffold their young children's mastery of challenging tasks, their verbal communication resembles the teaching that takes place in school, where their children will spend years preparing for adult life. In cultures that place less emphasis on schooling and literacy, parents often expect children to take greater responsibility for acquiring new skills through keen observation and participation in community activities (see the Cultural Influences box above).

To account for children's diverse ways of learning through involvement with others, Barbara Rogoff (1998, 2003) suggests the term **guided participation,** a broader concept than scaffolding. It refers to shared endeavors between more expert and less expert participants, without specifying the precise features of communication. Consequently, it allows for variations across situations and cultures.

Finally, Vygotsky's theory says little about how basic motor, perceptual, attention, memory, and problem-solving skills, discussed in Chapters 4 and 5, contribute to socially transmitted higher cognitive processes. For example, his theory does not address how these elementary capacities spark changes in children's social experiences, from which more advanced cognition springs (Miller, 2001; Moll, 1994). Piaget paid far more attention than Vygotsky to the development of basic cognitive processes. It is intriguing to speculate about the broader theory that might exist today if Piaget and Vygotsky—the two twentieth-century giants of cognitive development—had had a chance to meet and weave together their extraordinary accomplishments.

ASK YOURSELF

» REVIEW
Describe characteristics of social interaction that support children's cognitive development. How does such interaction create a zone of proximal development?

» APPLY
Tanisha sees her 5-year-old son Toby talking aloud to himself as he plays. She wonders whether she should discourage this behavior. Using Vygotsky's theory and related research, explain why Toby talks to himself. How would you advise Tanisha?

» CONNECT
Explain how Piaget's and Vygotsky's theories complement each other. How would classroom practices inspired by these theories be similar? How would they be different?

» REFLECT
When do you use private speech? Does it serve a self-guiding function for you, as it does for children? Explain.

Information Processing

Return to the model of information processing discussed on page 161 in Chapter 5. Recall that information processing focuses on *mental strategies* that children use to transform stimuli flowing into their mental systems. During early childhood, advances in representation and in children's ability to guide their own behavior lead to more efficient ways of attending, manipulating information, and solving problems. Preschoolers also become more aware of their own mental life and begin to acquire academically relevant knowledge important for school success.

Attention

As parents and teachers know, preschoolers—compared with school-age children—spend shorter times involved in tasks and are easily distracted. But recall from Chapter 5 that sustained attention improves in toddlerhood, a trend that continues during the preschool years.

■ **INHIBITION.** A major reason is a steady gain in children's ability to inhibit impulses and keep their mind on a competing goal. Consider a task in which the child must tap once when the adult taps twice and tap twice when the adult taps once or must say "night" to a picture of the sun and "day" to a picture of the moon with stars. As Figure 7.10 shows, 3- and 4-year-olds make many errors. But by age 6 to 7, children find such tasks easy (Johnson, Im-Bolter, & Pascual-Leone, 2003; Kirkham, Cruess, & Diamond, 2003; Zelazo et al., 2003). They can resist the "pull" of their attention toward a dominant stimulus—a skill that, as early as age 3 to 5, predicts reading and math achievement from kindergarten through high school (Blair & Razza, 2007; Duncan et al., 2007).

Gains in inhibition are linked to development of the cerebral cortex, especially the frontal lobes (see page 217). But relevant experiences are crucial. In *Tools of the Mind*—a preschool curriculum inspired by Vygotsky's theory scaffolding of attentional skills is woven into virtually all classroom activities. For example, teachers provide external aids to support attention (a child might hold a drawing of an ear as a reminder to listen during story time); lead games requiring frequent shifts in attention; and encourage make-believe play, which helps children follow rules and use thought to guide behavior (Bodrova & Leong, 2007). When preschoolers from low-income families were randomly assigned to either Tools of the Mind or comparison classrooms, Tools children performed substantially better on end-of-year tasks assessing inhibition and other attentional capacities (Diamond et al., 2007).

■ **PLANNING.** During early childhood, children also become better at *planning*—thinking out a sequence of acts ahead of time and allocating attention accordingly to reach a goal. As long as tasks are familiar and not too complex, preschoolers can generate and follow a plan. For example, 4-year-olds can search

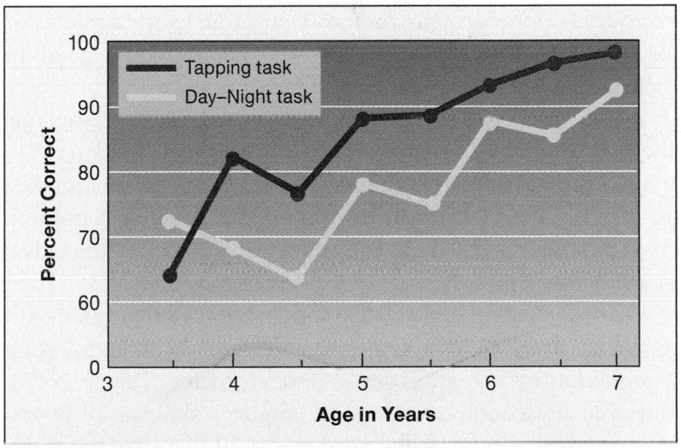

■ **FIGURE 7.10** ■ **Gains between ages 3 and 7 in performance on tasks requiring children to inhibit an impulse and focus on a competing goal.** In the tapping task, children had to tap once when the adult tapped twice and tap twice when the adult tapped once. In the day–night task, children had to say "night" to a picture of the sun and "day" to a picture of the moon with stars. (From A. Diamond, 2004, "Normal Development of Prefrontal Cortex from Birth to Young Adulthood: Cognitive Functions, Anatomy, and Biochemistry," as appeared in D. T. Stuff and R. T. Knight, (Eds.), *Principles of Frontal Lobe Function,* New York: Oxford University Press, p. 474. Reprinted by permission of Adele Diamond.)

for a lost object in a play area systematically if possible locations are few (McColgan & McCormack, 2008). But when asked to compare detailed pictures, preschoolers fail to search thoroughly. And on tasks with several steps, they rarely decide what to do first and what to do next in an orderly fashion (Friedman & Scholnick, 1997; Ruff & Rothbart, 1996).

Children learn much from cultural tools that support planning—directions for playing games, patterns for construction, and recipes for cooking—especially when they collaborate with more expert planners. When 4- to 7-year-olds were observed jointly constructing a toy with their mothers, the mothers provided basic information about the usefulness of plans and how to implement specific steps: "Do you want to look at the picture and see what goes where? What piece do you need first?" After working with their mothers, younger children more often referred to the plan when building on their own (Gauvain, 2004; Gauvain, de la Ossa, & Hurtado-Ortiz, 2001). When parents encourage planning in everyday activities, from loading the dishwasher to packing for a vacation, they help children plan more effectively.

Memory

Unlike infants and toddlers, preschoolers have the language skills to describe what they remember, and they can follow directions on memory tasks. As a result, memory becomes easier to study in early childhood.

RECOGNITION AND RECALL. ***TAKE A MOMENT...*** Show a young child a set of 10 pictures or toys. Then mix them up with some unfamiliar items, and ask the child to point to the ones in the original set. You will find that preschoolers' *recognition* memory—ability to tell whether a stimulus is the same as or similar to one they have seen before—is remarkably good. In fact, 4- and 5-year-olds perform nearly perfectly.

Now keep the items out of view, and ask the child to name the ones she saw. This more demanding task requires *recall*—that the child generate a mental image of an absent stimulus. Young children's recall is much poorer than their recognition. At age 2, they can recall no more than one or two of the items, at age 4 only about three or four (Perlmutter, 1984).

Better recall in early childhood is strongly associated with language development, which greatly enhances long-lasting representations of past experiences (Simcock & Hayne, 2003). But even preschoolers with good language skills recall poorly because they are not skilled at using **memory strategies,** deliberate mental activities that improve our chances of remembering. Preschoolers do not yet *rehearse,* or repeat items over and over to remember. Nor do they *organize,* grouping together items that are alike (all the animals together, all the vehicles together) so they can easily retrieve the items by thinking of their similar characteristics—even when they are trained to do so (Gathercole, Adams, & Hitch, 1994).

Why do young children seldom use memory strategies? One reason is that strategies tax their limited working memories. *Digit span* tasks, in which children try to repeat an adult-provided string of numbers, assess the size of working memory, which improves slowly, from an average of two digits at age 2½ to five digits at age 7 (Kail, 2003). With such limits, preschoolers have difficulty holding on to pieces of information and applying a strategy at the same time.

MEMORY FOR EVERYDAY EXPERIENCES. Think about the difference between your recall of listlike information and your memory for everyday experiences. In remembering lists, you recall isolated bits, reproducing them exactly as you originally learned them. In remembering everyday experiences, you recall complex, meaningful events.

Memory for Familiar Events. Like adults, preschoolers remember familiar, repeated events—what you do when you go to preschool or have dinner—in terms of **scripts,** general descriptions of what occurs and when it occurs in a particular situation. Young children's scripts begin as a structure of main acts. For example, when asked to tell what happens at a restaurant, a 3-year-old might say, "You go in, get the food, eat, and then pay." Although first scripts contain only a few acts, they are almost always recalled in correct sequence (Bauer, 2002a, 2006). With age, scripts become more elaborate, as in this 5-year-old's account of going to a restaurant: "You go in. You can sit in a booth or at a table. Then you tell the waitress what you want. You eat. If you want dessert, you can have some. Then you pay and go home." (Hudson, Fivush, & Kuebli, 1992).

Scripts help children (and adults) organize and interpret everyday experiences. Once formed, they can be used to predict what will happen in the future. Children rely on scripts in make-believe play and when listening to and telling stories. Scripts also support children's earliest efforts at planning by helping them represent sequences of actions that lead to desired goals (Hudson, Sosa, & Shapiro, 1997).

Memory for One-Time Events. In Chapter 5, we considered a second type of everyday memory—*autobiographical memory,* or representations of personally meaningful, one-time events. As preschoolers' cognitive and conversational skills improve, their descriptions of special events become better organized in time, more detailed, and related to the larger context of their lives (Fivush, 2001).

Adults use two styles to elicit children's autobiographical narratives. In the *elaborative style,* they follow the child's lead, ask varied questions, add information to the child's statements, and volunteer their own recollections and evaluations of events. For example, after a trip to the zoo, the parent might say, "What was the first thing we did?" "Why weren't the parrots in their cages?" "I thought the lion was scary. What did you think?" In contrast, adults who use the *repetitive style* provide little information and keep repeating the same questions, regardless of the child's interest: "Do you remember the zoo? What did we do at the zoo?" Preschoolers who experience the elaborative style recall more information about past events, and they also produce more organized and detailed personal stories when followed up one to two years later (Cleveland & Reese, 2005; Farrant & Reese, 2000).

© TINA MANLEY/CHILDREN/ALAMY

As she converses with her father about past experiences, this young child in Shanghai builds an autobiographical memory. Perhaps because Asian parents tend to discourage children from talking about themselves, Asian adults' autobiographical memories focus less on their own roles than on the roles of others.

As children talk with adults about the past, they not only improve their autobiographical memory but also create a shared history that strengthens close relationships and self-understanding. Parents and preschoolers with secure attachment bonds engage in more elaborate reminiscing (Bost et al., 2006; Fivush & Reese, 2002). And children of elaborative-style parents describe themselves in clearer, more consistent ways (Bird & Reese, 2006). When, in past-event conversations, a child discovers that she finds swimming, getting together with friends, and going to the zoo fun, she can begin to connect these specific experiences into a general understanding of "what I enjoy," yielding a clearer image of herself (Farrant & Reese, 2000).

Girls produce more organized and detailed narratives than boys. And Western children include more comments about their own thoughts, emotions, and preferences than do Asian children. These differences fit with variations in parent–child conversations. Parents reminisce in more detail with daughters (Bruce, Dolan, & Phillips-Grant, 2000). And collectivist cultural values lead many Asian parents to discourage children from talking about themselves. Chinese parents, for example, engage in less detailed and evaluative past-event dialogues with their preschoolers (Fivush & Wang, 2005; Wang, 2006a). Consistent with these early experiences, women report an earlier age of first memory and more vivid early memories than men. And Western adults' autobiographical memories include earlier, more detailed events that focus more on their own roles than do the memories of Asians, who tend to highlight the roles of others (Wang, 2006b).

The Young Child's Theory of Mind

As representation of the world, memory, and problem solving improve, children start to reflect on their own thought processes. They begin to construct a *theory of mind,* or coherent set of ideas about mental activities. This understanding is also called **metacognition,** or "thinking about thought" (the prefix *meta-* means "beyond" or "higher"). As adults, we have a complex appreciation of our inner mental worlds, which we use to interpret our own and others' behavior and to improve our performance on various tasks. How early are children aware of their mental lives, and how complete and accurate is their knowledge?

AWARENESS OF MENTAL LIFE. At the end of the first year, babies view people as intentional beings who can share and influence one another's mental states, a milestone that opens the door to new forms of communication—joint attention, social referencing, preverbal gestures, and spoken language. These interactive skills, in turn, enhance toddlers' mental understandings (Tomasello & Rakoczy, 2003). As they approach age 2, children display a clearer grasp of others' emotions and desires, evident in their realization that people often differ from one another and from themselves in likes, dislikes, wants, needs, and wishes ("Mommy like broccoli. Daddy like carrots. I no like carrots.").

As 2-year-olds' vocabularies expand, their first verbs include such words as *think, remember,* and *pretend* (Wellman, 2002). By age 3, children realize that thinking takes place inside their heads and that a person can think about something without seeing, touching, or talking about it (Flavell, Green, & Flavell, 1995). But 2- to 3-year-olds have only a beginning grasp of the distinction between mental life and behavior. They think that people always behave in ways consistent with their desires and do not understand that less obvious, more interpretive mental states, such as beliefs, also affect behavior.

Between ages 3 and 4, children increasingly refer to their own and others' thoughts and beliefs (Wellman, 2002). And from age 4 on, they realize that both *beliefs* and *desires* determine behavior. Dramatic evidence for this new understanding comes from games that test whether preschoolers realize that *false beliefs*—ones that do not represent reality accurately—can guide people's actions.

TAKE A MOMENT... For example, show a child two small closed boxes—a familiar Band-Aid box and a plain, unmarked box (see Figure 7.11 on page 240). Then say, "Pick the box you think has the Band-Aids in it." Children usually pick the marked container. Next, open the boxes and show the child that, contrary to her own belief, the marked one is empty and the unmarked one contains the Band-Aids. Finally, introduce the child to a hand puppet and explain, "Here's Pam. She has a cut, see? Where do you think she'll look for Band-Aids? Why would she look in there? Before you looked inside, did you think that the plain box contained Band-Aids? Why?" (Bartsch & Wellman, 1995). Only a handful of 3-year-olds can explain Pam's—and their own—false beliefs, but many 4-year-olds can.

Among children of diverse cultural and SES backgrounds, false-belief understanding strengthens after age 3½, becoming

■ **FIGURE 7.11** ■ **Example of a false-belief task.** (a) An adult shows a child the contents of a Band-Aid box and of an unmarked box. The Band-Aids are in the unmarked container. (b) The adult introduces the child to a hand puppet named Pam and asks the child to predict where Pam would look for the Band-Aids and to explain Pam's behavior. The task reveals whether children understand that without having seen that the Band-Aids are in the unmarked container, Pam will hold a false belief.

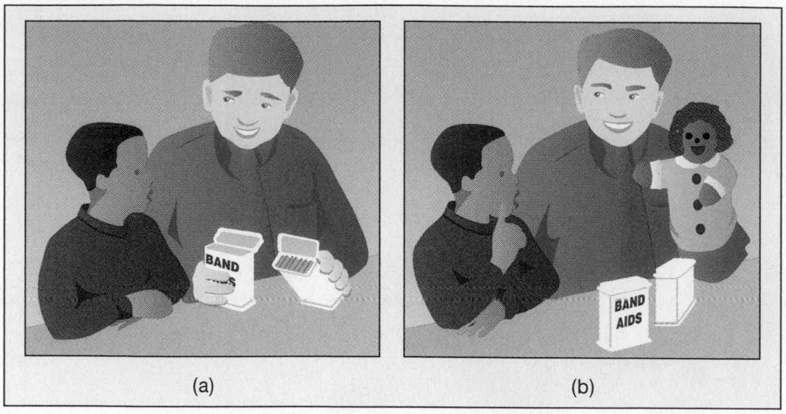

more secure between ages 4 and 6 (Amsterlaw & Wellman, 2006; Callaghan et al., 2005; Flynn, 2006). During that time, it becomes a powerful tool for understanding oneself and others and a good predictor of social skills (Harwood & Farrar, 2006; Watson et al., 1999). It is also associated with early reading ability, probably because it helps children comprehend story narratives (Astington & Pelletier, 2005).

■ **FACTORS CONTRIBUTING TO PRESCHOOLERS' THEORY OF MIND.** How do children develop a theory of mind at such a young age? Language, cognitive abilities, make-believe play, and social experiences all contribute.

Understanding the mind requires the ability to reflect on thoughts, which language makes possible. Many studies indicate that language ability strongly predicts preschoolers' grasp of false belief (Milligan, Astington, & Dack, 2007). Children who spontaneously use, or who are trained to use, complex sentences with mental-state words are especially likely to pass false-belief tasks (de Villiers & de Villiers, 2000; Hale & Tager-Flusberg, 2003). Among the Quechua of the Peruvian highlands, whose language lacks mental-state terms, children have difficulty with false-belief tasks for years after children in industrialized nations have mastered them (Vinden, 1996). Chinese languages, in contrast, have verb markers that can label the word *believe* as decidedly false. When adults use those markers within false-belief tasks, Chinese preschoolers perform better (Tardif, Wellman, & Cheung, 2004).

The ability to inhibit inappropriate responses, think flexibly, and plan fosters mastery of false belief (Hughes, 1998; Sabbagh et al., 2006). Gains in inhibition are strongly related to mastery of false belief, perhaps because to do well on false-belief tasks, children must suppress an irrelevant response—the tendency to assume that others share their own knowledge and beliefs (Birch & Bloom, 2003; Carlson, Moses, & Claxton, 2004).

Social experience also promotes understanding of the mind. In longitudinal research, mothers of securely attached babies were more likely to comment appropriately on their infants' mental states: "Do you *remember* Grandma?" "You really *like* that swing!" These mothers continued to describe their children, when they reached preschool age, in terms of mental characteristics: "She's got a mind of her own!" This maternal "mind-mindedness" was positively associated with later performance on false-belief and other theory-of-mind tasks (Meins et al., 1998, 2003; Ruffman et al., 2006). Secure attachment is also related to more elaborative parent–child narratives, including discussions of mental states—conversations that expose preschoolers to concepts and language that help them think about their own and others' mental lives (Ontai & Thompson, 2008; Taumoepeau & Ruffman, 2006).

Also, preschoolers with siblings who are children (but not infants)—especially older siblings or two or more siblings—tend to be more aware of false belief because they are exposed to more family talk about others' perspectives (Jenkins et al., 2003; McAlister & Peterson, 2006, 2007). Similarly, preschool friends who often engage in mental-state talk—as children do during make-believe play—are ahead in false-belief understanding (de Rosnay & Hughes, 2006). Interacting with more mature members of society contributes, too. In a study of Greek preschoolers, daily contact with many adults and older children predicted mastery of false belief (Lewis et al., 1996). All these encounters offer extra opportunities to observe different viewpoints and talk about inner states.

Core knowledge theorists (see Chapter 5, page 159) believe that to profit from the social experiences just described, children must be biologically prepared to develop a theory of mind. They claim that children with *autism,* for whom mastery of false belief is either greatly delayed or absent, are deficient in the brain mechanism that enables humans to detect mental states. See the Biology and Environment box on the following page to find out more about the biological basis of reasoning about the mind.

■ **LIMITATIONS OF PRESCHOOLERS' UNDERSTANDING OF MENTAL LIFE.** Though surprisingly advanced, preschoolers' awareness of mental activities is far from complete. For example, 3- and 4-year-olds are unaware that people continue to think while they wait, look at pictures, listen to stories, or read books—when there are no obvious cues that they are thinking (Flavell, Green, & Flavell, 1993, 1995, 2000). And children younger than age 6 pay little attention to the *process* of thinking. When asked about subtle distinctions between mental states, such as *know* and *forget,* they express confusion (Lyon & Flavell, 1994). And they believe that all events must be directly observed to be known. They do not understand that *mental inferences* can be a source of knowledge (Miller, Hardin, & Montgomery, 2003).

These findings suggest that preschoolers view the mind as a passive container of information. Consequently, they greatly

BIOLOGY AND ENVIRONMENT

"Mindblindness" and Autism

Michael stood at the water table in Leslie's classroom, repeatedly filling a plastic cup and dumping out its contents—dip–splash, dip–splash—until Leslie came over and redirected his actions. Without looking at Leslie's face, Michael moved to a new repetitive pursuit: pouring water from one cup into another and back again. As other children entered the play space and conversed, Michael hardly noticed.

Michael has *autism* (a term that means "absorbed in the self"), the most severe behavior disorder of childhood. Like other children with autism, by age 3 he displayed deficits in three core areas of functioning. First, he had only limited ability to engage in nonverbal behaviors required for successful social interaction, such as eye gaze, facial expressions, gestures, and give-and-take. Second, his language was delayed and stereotyped. He used words to echo what others said and to get things he wanted, not to exchange ideas. Third, he engaged in much less make-believe play than other children (Frith, 2003; Walenski, Tager-Flusberg, & Ullman, 2006). And Michael showed another typical feature of autism: His interests were narrow and overly intense. For example, one day he sat for more than an hour spinning a toy Ferris wheel.

Researchers agree that autism stems from abnormal brain functioning, usually due to genetic or prenatal environmental causes. From the first year on, children with the disorder have larger-than-average brains, perhaps due to massive overgrowth of synapses and lack of synaptic pruning, which accompanies normal development of cognitive and language skills (Courchesne, Carper, & Akshoomoff, 2003). Furthermore, fMRI studies reveal that autism is associated with reduced activity in areas of the cerebral cortex known to mediate emotional and social responsiveness and thinking about mental activities, including mirror neurons, discussed in Chapter 4 (see page 136) (Mundy, 2003; Théoret et al., 2005).

Growing evidence reveals that children with autism have a deficient theory of mind. Long after they reach the intellectual level of an average 4-year-old, they have great difficulty with false-belief tasks. Most find it hard to attribute mental states to themselves or others (Steele, Joseph, & Tager-Flusberg, 2003). They rarely use mental-state words, such as *believe, think, know, feel,* and *pretend*.

As early as the second year, children with autism show deficits in capacities believed to contribute to an understanding of mental life. Compared with other children, they less often establish joint attention, engage in social referencing, or imitate an adult's novel behaviors (Mundy & Stella, 2000; Vivanti et al., 2008). Furthermore, they are relatively insensitive to eye gaze as a cue to what a speaker is talking about. Instead, they often assume that another person's language refers to what they themselves are looking at—a possible reason for their frequent nonsensical expressions (Baron-Cohen, Baldwin, & Crowson, 1997).

This child, who has autism, is barely aware of his teacher and classmates. Researchers disagree on whether the "mindblindness" accompanying autism results from a specific deficit in social understanding or a general impairment in executive processing.

Do these findings indicate that autism is due to impairment of an innate, core brain function, which leaves the child "mindblind" and therefore deficient in human sociability? Some researchers think so (Baron-Cohen & Belmonte, 2005; Scholl & Leslie, 2000). But others point out that individuals with mental retardation but not autism also do poorly on tasks assessing mental understanding (Yirmiya et al., 1998). This suggests that some kind of general intellectual impairment may be involved.

One conjecture is that children with autism are impaired in *executive processing* (refer to the *central executive* in the information-processing model on page 161 in Chapter 5). This leaves them deficient in skills involved in flexible, goal-oriented thinking, including shifting attention to relevant aspects of a situation, inhibiting irrelevant responses, applying strategies to hold information in working memory, and generating plans (Geurts et al., 2004; Joseph & Tager-Flusberg, 2004). Another possibility is that children with autism display a peculiar style of information processing, preferring to process the parts of stimuli over patterns and coherent wholes (Frith & Happé, 1994). Deficits in thinking flexibly and in holistic processing of stimuli would each interfere with understanding the social world, since social interaction requires quick integration of information from various sources and evaluation of alternative possibilities.

It is not clear which of these hypotheses is correct. Some research suggests that impairments in social awareness, flexible thinking, processing coherent wholes, and verbal ability contribute independently to autism (Morgan, Maybery, & Durkin, 2003; Pellicano et al., 2006). Perhaps several biologically based deficits underlie the tragic social isolation of children like Michael.

underestimate the amount of mental activity that people engage in and are poor at inferring what people know or are thinking about. In contrast, older children view the mind as an active, constructive agent—a change we will consider further in Chapter 9.

Early Childhood Literacy

One week, Leslie's students created a make-believe grocery store. They brought empty food boxes from home, placed them on shelves in the classroom, labeled items with prices, and made paper money for use at the cash register. A sign at the entrance announced the daily specials: "APLS BNS 5¢" ("apples bananas 5¢").

As such play reveals, preschoolers understand a great deal about written language long before they learn to read or write in conventional ways. This is not surprising: Children in industrialized nations live in a world filled with written symbols. Each day, they observe and participate in activities involving storybooks, calendars, lists, and signs and, while doing so, try to figure out how written symbols convey meaning. Children's active efforts to construct literacy knowledge through informal experiences are called **emergent literacy.**

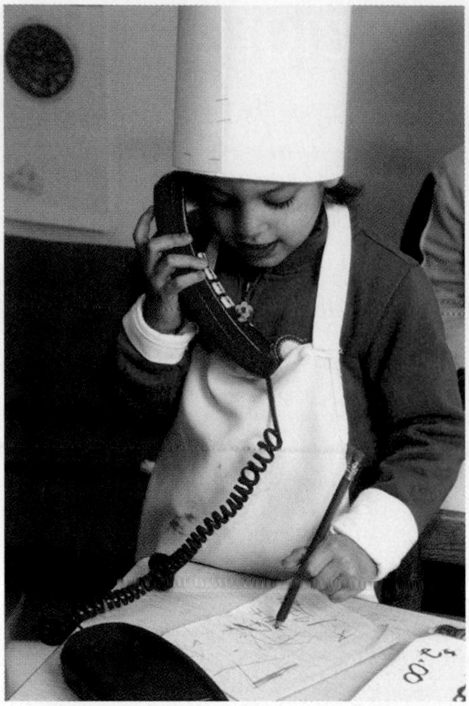

Preschoolers acquire literacy knowledge informally through participating in everyday activities involving written symbols. Here a young chef "jots down" a phone order for a take-out meal.

Young preschoolers search for units of written language as they "read" memorized versions of stories and recognize familiar signs, such as "PIZZA." But they do not yet understand the symbolic function of the elements of print (Bialystok & Martin, 2003). Many preschoolers think that a single letter stands for a whole word or that each letter in a person's signature represents a separate name. Children revise these ideas as their cognitive capacities improve, as they encounter writing in many contexts, and as adults help them with written communication. Gradually, they notice more features of written language and depict writing that varies in function, as in the "story" and "grocery list" in Figure 7.12.

Eventually, children figure out that letters are parts of words and are linked to sounds in systematic ways, as seen in the invented spellings that are typical between ages 5 and 7. At first, children rely on sounds in the names of letters, as in "ADE LAFWTS KRMD NTU A LAVATR" ("eighty elephants crammed into a[n] elevator"). Over time, they grasp sound–letter correspondences and learn that some letters have more than one common sound (McGee & Richgels, 2008).

Literacy development builds on a broad foundation of spoken language and knowledge about the world. Over time, children's language and literacy progress facilitate one another. **Phonological awareness**—the ability to reflect on and manipulate the sound structure of spoken language, as indicated by sensitivity to changes in sounds within words, to rhyming, and to incorrect pronunciation—is a strong predictor of emergent literacy knowledge (Dickinson et al., 2003; Paris & Paris, 2006). When combined with sound–letter knowledge, it enables children to isolate speech segments and link them with their written symbols. Vocabulary and grammatical skills are also influential.

The more informal literacy-related experiences young children have, the better their language and emergent literacy development and their later reading skills (Dickinson & McCabe, 2001; Speece et al., 2004). Pointing out letter–sound correspondences and playing language–sound games enhance children's awareness of the sound structure of language and how it is represented in print (Foy & Mann, 2003). *Interactive* reading, in which adults discuss storybook content with preschoolers, promotes many aspects of language and literacy development. And adult-supported writing activities that focus on narrative, such as preparing a letter or a story, also have wide-ranging benefits (Purcell-Gates, 1996; Wasik & Bond, 2001).

Preschoolers from low-SES families have fewer home and preschool language and literacy learning opportunities—a major reason that they are behind in reading achievement throughout the school years (Foster et al., 2005; Foster & Miller, 2007). In a program that "flooded" child-care centers with children's books and provided training to caregivers on how to get 3- and 4-year-olds to spend time with books, children showed much greater gains in emergent literacy than a no-intervention control group (Neuman, 1999). Providing low-SES parents with children's books, along with guidance in how to stimulate literacy learning in preschoolers, greatly enhances literacy activities in the home (High et al., 2000).

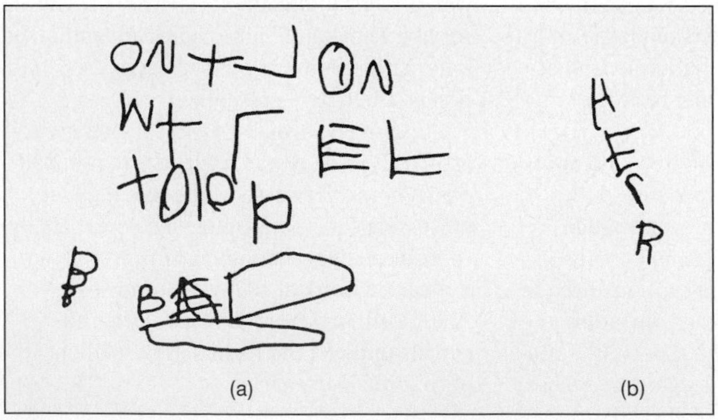

■ **FIGURE 7.12** ■ **A story (a) and a grocery list (b) written by a 4-year-old child.** This child's writing has many features of real print. It also reveals an awareness of different kinds of written expression. (From L. M. McGee & D. J. Richgels, *Literacy's Beginnings: Supporting Young Readers and Writers, 4/e.* Published by Allyn and Bacon, Boston, MA. Copyright © 2004 by Pearson Education. Reprinted by permission of the publisher.)

Young Children's Mathematical Reasoning

Mathematical reasoning, like literacy, builds on informally acquired knowledge. Between 14 and 16 months, toddlers display a beginning grasp of **ordinality,** or order relationships between quantities—for example, that 3 is more than 2, and 2 is more than 1. Soon they attach verbal labels *(lots, little, big, small)* to amounts and sizes. Sometime in the third year, they begin to count. By the time children turn 3, most can count rows of about five objects, although they do not yet know exactly what the words mean. For example, when asked for *one,* they give one item, but when asked for *two, three, four,* or *five,* they usually give a larger, but incorrect, amount. Nevertheless, 2½- to 3½-year-olds realize that a number word refers to a unique quantity—that when a number label changes (for example, from *five* to *six*), the number of items should also change (Sarnecka & Gelman, 2004).

By age 3½ to 4, most children have mastered the meaning of numbers up to ten, count correctly, and grasp the vital principle of **cardinality**—that the last number in a counting sequence indicates the quantity of items in a set (Geary, 2006a). Mastery of cardinality increases the efficiency of children's counting.

Around age 4, children use counting to solve arithmetic problems. At first, their strategies are tied to the order of numbers as presented; to add 2 + 4, they count on from 2 (Bryant & Nunes, 2002). But soon they experiment with other strategies and eventually arrive at the most efficient, accurate approach—in this example, beginning with the higher digit. Around this time, children realize that subtraction cancels out addition. Knowing, for example, that 4 + 3 = 7, they can infer without counting that 7 − 3 = 4 (Rasmussen, Ho, & Bisanz, 2003). Grasping basic arithmetic rules facilitates rapid computation, and with enough practice, children recall answers automatically.

When adults provide many occasions for counting, comparing quantities, and talking about number concepts, children acquire these understandings sooner (Ginsburg, Lee, & Boyd, 2008; Klibanoff et al., 2006). In an early childhood math curriculum, called *Building Blocks,* materials that promote math concepts and skills through three types of media—computers, manipulatives, and print—enable teachers to weave math into many preschool daily activities, from building blocks to art and stories. Compared with agemates randomly assigned to other preschool programs, low-SES preschoolers experiencing Building Blocks showed substantially greater year-end gains in math concepts and skills, including counting, sequencing, arithmetic computation, and geometric shapes (Clements & Sarama, 2008). Solid, secure early childhood math knowledge is essential for the wide variety of mathematical skills children will be taught in school.

Preschoolers construct basic arithmetic understandings sooner when they have many opportunities to count, compare quantities, and talk about number concepts.

ASK YOURSELF

» REVIEW
Describe a typical 4-year-old's understanding of mental activities, noting both strengths and limitations.

» APPLY
Lena, mother of 4-year-old Gregor, wonders why his preschool teacher provides extensive playtime in learning centers instead of formal lessons in literacy and math skills. Explain to Lena why adult-supported play is the best way for preschoolers to develop academically.

» CONNECT
Cite evidence on the development of preschoolers' memory, theory of mind, and literacy and mathematical understanding that is consistent with Vygotsky's sociocultural theory.

» REFLECT
Describe informal experiences important for literacy and math development that you experienced while growing up. How do you think those experiences contributed to your academic progress in school?

Individual Differences in Mental Development

Five-year-old Hal sat in a testing room while Sarah gave him an intelligence test. Some of Sarah's questions were *verbal.* For example, she showed him a picture of a shovel and said, "Tell me what this is"—an item measuring vocabulary. She tested his memory by asking him to repeat sentences and lists of numbers back to her. To assess Hal's spatial reasoning, Sarah

Applying What We Know

Features of a High-Quality Home Life for Preschoolers: The HOME Early Childhood Subscales

Subscale	Sample Item
Cognitive stimulation through toys, games, and reading material	Home includes toys that teach colors, sizes, and shapes.
Language stimulation	Parent teaches child about animals through books, games, and puzzles.
Organization of the physical environment	All visible rooms are reasonably clean and minimally cluttered.
Emotional support	Parent spontaneously praises child's qualities or behavior twice during observer's visit. Parent caresses, kisses, or hugs child at least once during observer's visit.
Stimulation of academic behavior	Child is encouraged to learn colors.
Modeling and encouragement of social maturity	Parent introduces interviewer to child.
Opportunities for variety in daily stimulation	Family member takes child on one outing at least every other week (picnic, shopping).
Avoidance of physical punishment	Parent neither slaps nor spanks child during observer's visit.

Sources: Bradley, 1994; Bradley et al., 2001.

used *nonverbal* tasks: Hal copied designs with special blocks, figured out the pattern in a series of shapes, and indicated what a piece of paper folded and cut would look like when unfolded (Roid, 2003; Wechsler, 2002).

Sarah knew that Hal came from an economically disadvantaged family. When low-SES and certain ethnic minority preschoolers are bombarded with questions by an unfamiliar adult, they sometimes react with anxiety. Also, such children may not define the testing situation in achievement terms. Instead, they may look for attention and approval from the adult and may settle for lower performance than their abilities allow. Sarah spent time playing with Hal before she began testing and encouraged him while testing was in progress. Under these conditions, low-SES preschoolers improve in performance (Bracken, 2000).

The questions Sarah asked Hal tap knowledge and skills that not all children have equal opportunity to learn. In Chapter 9, we will take up the hotly debated issue of *cultural bias* in mental testing. For now, keep in mind that intelligence tests do not sample all human abilities, and performance is affected by cultural and situational factors (Sternberg, 2005). Nevertheless, test scores remain important: By age 6 to 7, they are good predictors of later IQ and academic achievement, which are related to vocational success in industrialized societies. Let's see how the environments in which preschoolers spend their days—home, preschool, and child care—affect mental test performance.

Home Environment and Mental Development

A special version of the *Home Observation for Measurement of the Environment (HOME),* covered in Chapter 5, assesses aspects of 3- to 6-year-olds' home lives that support mental development (see Applying What We Know above). Preschoolers who develop well intellectually have homes rich in educational toys and books. Their parents are warm and affectionate, stimulate language and academic knowledge, and arrange interesting outings. They also make reasonable demands for socially mature behavior—for example, that the child perform simple chores and behave courteously toward others. And these parents resolve conflicts with reason instead of physical force and punishment (Bradley & Caldwell, 1982; Espy, Molfese, & DiLalla, 2001; Roberts, Burchinal, & Durham, 1999).

As we saw in Chapter 2, these characteristics are less often seen in poverty-stricken families. When low-SES parents manage, despite daily pressures, to obtain high HOME scores, their preschoolers do substantially better on tests of intelligence and emergent literacy skills (Foster et al., 2005; Klebanov et al., 1998). And in a study of low-SES African-American 3- and 4-year-olds, HOME cognitive stimulation and emotional support subscales predicted reading achievement four years later (Zaslow et al., 2006). These findings highlight the vital role of home environmental quality in children's mental development.

Preschool, Kindergarten, and Child Care

Children between ages 2 and 6 spend even more time away from their homes and parents than infants and toddlers do. Largely because of the rise in maternal employment, over the past several decades the number of young children enrolled in preschool or child care has steadily increased to more than 60 percent in the United States (U.S. Census Bureau, 2009b).

A *preschool* is a program with planned educational experiences aimed at enhancing the development of 2- to 5-year-olds. In contrast, *child care* refers to a variety of arrangements for supervising children. With age, children tend to shift from home-based to center programs. Many children, however, experience several types of arrangements at once (Federal Interagency Forum on Child and Family Statistics, 2008).

The line between preschool and child care is fuzzy. Responding to the needs of employed parents, many U.S. preschools, as well as public school kindergartens, have increased their hours from half to full days (U.S. Department of Education, 2009). At the same time, good child care means more than simply keeping children safe and adequately fed. It should provide the same high-quality educational experiences that an effective preschool does.

■ TYPES OF PRESCHOOL AND KINDERGARTEN. Preschool and kindergarten programs range along a continuum, from child-centered to teacher-directed. In **child-centered programs,** teachers provide a variety of activities from which children select, and much learning takes place through play. In contrast, in **academic programs,** teachers structure children's learning, teaching letters, numbers, colors, shapes, and other academic skills through formal lessons, often using repetition and drill.

Despite evidence that formal academic training in early childhood undermines motivation and emotional well-being, preschool and kindergarten teachers have felt increased pressure to take this approach. Preschoolers and kindergartners who spend much time passively sitting and completing worksheets display more stress behaviors (such as wiggling and rocking), have less confidence in their abilities, prefer less challenging tasks, and are less advanced in motor, academic, language, and social skills at the end of the school year (Marcon, 1999a; Stipek et al., 1995). Follow-ups reveal lasting effects through elementary school in poorer study habits and achievement (Burts et al., 1992; Hart et al., 1998, 2003). These outcomes are strongest for low-SES children.

A special type of child-centered approach is Montessori education, devised a century ago by Italian physician and child development researcher Maria Montessori, who originally applied her method to poverty-stricken children. Features of Montessori schooling include materials designed to promote exploration and discovery, child-chosen activities, and equal emphasis on academic and social development (Lillard, 2007). In an evaluation of public preschools serving mostly urban minority children in Milwaukee, researchers compared students randomly assigned to either Montessori or other classrooms (Lillard & Else-Quest, 2006). Five-year-olds who had completed two years of Montessori education outperformed controls in literacy and math skills, false-belief understanding, concern with fairness in solving conflicts with peers, and cooperative play with classmates.

■ EARLY INTERVENTION FOR AT-RISK PRESCHOOLERS. In the 1960s, as part of the "War on Poverty" in the United States, many intervention programs for low-SES preschoolers were initiated in an effort to address learning problems before formal schooling begins. The most extensive of these federal programs, **Project Head Start,** began in 1965. A typical Head Start center provides children with a year or two of preschool, along with nutritional and health services. Parent involvement is central to the Head Start philosophy. Parents serve on policy councils, contribute to program planning, work directly with children in classrooms, attend special programs on parenting and child development, and receive services directed at their own emotional, social, and vocational needs. Currently, more than 18,000 U.S. Head Start centers serve about 908,000 children (Head Start Bureau, 2008).

More than two decades of research have established the long-term benefits of preschool intervention. The most extensive of these studies combined data from seven interventions implemented by universities or research foundations. Results showed that poverty-stricken children who attended programs scored higher in IQ and achievement than controls during the first two to three years of elementary school. After that, differences declined (Lazar & Darlington, 1982). But on real-life measures of school adjustment, children and adolescents who had received intervention remained ahead. They were less likely to be placed in special education or retained in grade, and a greater number graduated from high school.

A separate report on one program—the High/Scope Perry Preschool Project—revealed benefits lasting well into adulthood. Two years' exposure to cognitively enriching preschool was associated with increased employment and reduced pregnancy and delinquency rates in adolescence. At age 27, those who had attended preschool were more likely than no-preschool controls to have graduated from high school and college, have higher earnings, be married, and own their own home—and less likely to have been involved with the criminal justice system (see Figure 7.13 on page 246) (Weikart, 1998). In the most recent follow-up, at age 40, the intervention group

Project Head Start provides preschoolers from poverty-stricken families with preschool education and nutritional and health services. High-quality, early educational intervention has benefits lasting into adulthood.

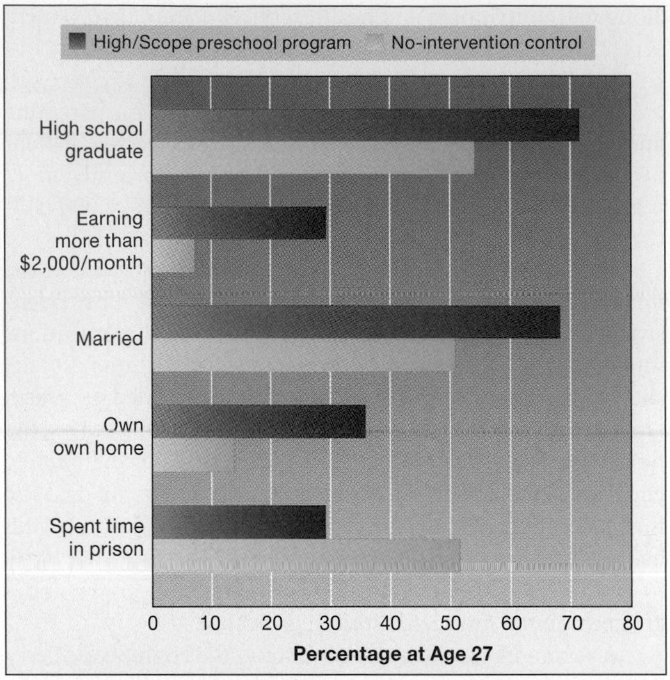

■ **FIGURE 7.13** ■ **Some outcomes of the High/Scope Perry Preschool Project on follow-up at age 27.** Although two years of a cognitively enriching preschool program did not eradicate the effects of growing up in poverty, children who received intervention were advantaged over no-intervention controls on all measures of life success when they reached adulthood. (Adapted from Schweinhart et al., 2005.)

sustained its advantage on all measures of life success, including education, income, family life, and law-abiding behavior (Schweinhart et al., 2005).

Do the effects of these well-designed and well-delivered programs generalize to Head Start and other community-based preschool interventions? Gains are similar, though not as strong. Head Start preschoolers, who are more economically disadvantaged than children in other programs, have more severe learning and behavior problems. And quality of services is more variable across community programs (Barnett, 2004; NICHD Early Child Care Research Network, 2001). But interventions of high quality are associated with diverse favorable outcomes, including greater year-end gains in academic skills and—in the long term—higher rates of high school graduation and college enrollment and lower rates of adolescent drug use and delinquency (Garces, Thomas, & Currie, 2002; Love et al., 2006; Mashburn, 2008).

A consistent finding is that gains in IQ and achievement test scores from attending Head Start and other interventions quickly dissolve. These children typically enter inferior public schools in poverty-stricken neighborhoods, an experience that undermines the benefits of preschool education (Brooks-Gunn, 2003; Ramey, Ramey, & Lanzi, 2006). An exception is the Chicago Child–Parent Centers—a program emphasizing literacy intervention and parent involvement that began at age 3 and continued through third grade—in which gains in academic achievement were still evident in junior high school (Reynolds & Temple, 1998).

Still, the gains in school adjustment that result from attending a one- or two-year Head Start program are impressive. Program effects on parents may contribute: The more involved parents are in Head Start, the better their child-rearing practices and the more stimulating their home learning environments—factors positively related to preschoolers' task persistence and year-end academic, language, and social skills (Marcon, 1999b; McLoyd, Aikens, & Burton, 2006; Parker et al., 1999).

Head Start is highly cost-effective when compared with the cost of providing special education, treating criminal behavior, and supporting unemployed adults. Economists estimate a lifetime return to society of more than $250,000 on an investment of $15,000 per preschool child—a potential savings of many billions of dollars if every poverty-stricken preschooler in the United States were enrolled (Heckman & Masterov, 2004; Temple & Reynolds, 2006). Because of funding shortages, however, many eligible children do not receive services.

■ **CHILD CARE.** We have seen that high-quality early intervention can enhance the development of economically disadvantaged children. As noted in Chapter 5, however, much U.S. child care lacks quality. Preschoolers exposed to substandard child care, especially for long hours, score lower in cognitive and social skills and higher in behavior problems (Belsky, 2006; Lamb & Ahnert, 2006; NICHD Early Child Care Research Network, 2003b, 2006). Psychological well-being also declines when children experience the instability of several child-care settings. The emotional problems of temperamentally difficult preschoolers worsen considerably (De Schipper, van IJzendoorn, & Tavecchio, 2004; De Schipper et al., 2004).

In contrast, good child care enhances cognitive, language, and social development, especially for low-SES children—effects that persist into the early school years (Lamb & Ahnert, 2006; NICHD Early Child Care Research Network, 2006; Peisner-Feinberg et al., 2001). In an investigation that followed very-low-income children over the preschool years, center-based care was more strongly associated with cognitive gains than were other child-care arrangements, probably because centers are more likely to provide a systematic educational program. At the same time, better-quality experiences in all types of child care predicted modest improvements in cognitive, emotional, and social development (Loeb et al., 2004).

Applying What We Know on the following page summarizes characteristics of high-quality early childhood programs, based on standards for developmentally appropriate practice devised by the U.S. National Association for the Education of Young Children. These standards offer a set of worthy goals as the United States strives to upgrade child-care and educational services for young children.

Educational Media

Besides home and preschool, young children spend much time in another learning environment: electronic media, including both television and computers. In the United States and other industrialized nations, nearly all homes have at least one televi-

Applying What We Know

Signs of Developmentally Appropriate Early Childhood Programs

Program Characteristics	Signs of Quality
Physical setting	Indoor environment is clean, in good repair, and well-ventilated. Classroom space is divided into richly equipped activity areas, including make-believe play, blocks, science, math, games and puzzles, books, art, and music. Fenced outdoor play space is equipped with swings, climbing equipment, tricycles, and sandbox.
Group size	In preschools and child-care centers, group size is no greater than 18 to 20 children with two teachers.
Caregiver–child ratio	In child-care centers, teacher is responsible for no more than eight to ten children. In child-care homes, caregiver is responsible for no more than six children.
Daily activities	Children mainly work individually or in small groups, selecting many of their own activities and learning through experiences relevant to their own lives. Teachers facilitate children's involvement, accept individual differences, and adjust expectations to children's developing capacities.
Interactions between adults and children	Teachers move among groups and individuals, asking questions, offering suggestions, and adding more complex ideas. Teachers use positive guidance techniques, such as modeling and encouraging expected behavior and redirecting children to more acceptable activities.
Teacher qualifications	Teachers have college-level specialized preparation in early childhood development, early childhood education, or a related field.
Relationships with parents	Parents are encouraged to observe and participate. Teachers talk frequently with parents about children's behavior and development.
Licensing and accreditation	Child-care setting, whether a center or a home, is licensed by the state or province. In the United States, voluntary accreditation by the National Academy of Early Childhood Programs *(www.naeyc.org/accreditation)* or the National Association for Family Child Care *(www.nafcc.org)* is evidence of a high-quality program.

Source: Copple & Bredekamp, 2009.

sion set, and most have two or more. And about 85 percent of U.S. children live in homes with one or more computers, two-thirds of which have an Internet connection (Roberts, Foehr, & Rideout, 2005; U.S. Census Bureau, 2009b).

■ **EDUCATIONAL TELEVISION.** Sammy's favorite TV program, *Sesame Street,* uses lively visual and sound effects to stress basic literacy and number concepts and puppet and human characters to teach general knowledge, emotional and social understanding, and social skills. Today, *Sesame Street* is broadcast in more than 120 countries, making it the most widely viewed children's program in the world (Sesame Workshop, 2008).

Time devoted to watching children's educational programs is associated with gains in early literacy and math skills and academic progress in elementary school (Ennemoser & Schneider, 2007; Linebarger et al., 2004; Wright et al., 2001). Consistent with these findings, one study reported a link between preschool viewing of *Sesame Street* and other similar educational programs and getting higher grades, reading more books, and placing more value on achievement in high school (Anderson et al., 2001). In recent years, *Sesame Street* has modified its rapid-paced format in favor of more leisurely episodes with a clear story line. Watching children's programs with slow-paced action and easy-to-follow narratives, such as *Barney and Friends,* leads to more elaborate make-believe play than viewing programs that present quick, disconnected bits of information (Singer & Singer, 2005).

Despite the spread of computers, television remains the dominant form of youth media, with children first becoming viewers in early infancy. About 40 percent of U.S. 3-month-olds regularly watch either TV or videos, a figure that rises to 90 percent by age 2 (Zimmerman, Christakis, & Meltzoff, 2007). The average U.S 2- to 6-year-old watches TV programs and videos from 1½ to 2 hours a day. In middle childhood, viewing time increases to an average of 3½ hours a day, then declines slightly in adolescence (Rideout & Hamel, 2006; Scharrer & Comstock, 2003).

Low-SES children are more frequent viewers, perhaps because few alternative forms of entertainment are available in their neighborhoods or affordable for their parents. Also, parents with limited education are more likely to engage in practices that heighten TV viewing, including eating family meals in front of the set and failing to limit children's TV access (Hesketh et al., 2007). About one-third of U.S. preschoolers and two-thirds of school-age children and adolescents have a TV set in their bedroom; these children spend from 40 to 90 more minutes per day watching than agemates without one (Rideout & Hamel, 2006). And if parents watch a lot of TV, their children do, too.

Does extensive TV viewing take children away from worthwhile activities? The more preschool and school-age children watch prime-time shows and cartoons, the less time they spend reading and interacting with others and the poorer their academic skills (Ennemoser & Schneider, 2007; Huston et al., 1999; Wright et al., 2001). Whereas educational programs can be beneficial, watching entertainment TV—especially heavy viewing—detracts from children's school success and social experiences.

LEARNING WITH COMPUTERS. Because computers can have rich educational benefits, many early childhood classrooms include computer learning centers. Word-processing programs can support emergent literacy, enabling preschool and young school-age children to experiment with letters and words without having to struggle with handwriting and to easily revise their text and check their spelling. When children worry less about making mistakes, their written products tend to be longer and of higher quality (Clements & Sarama, 2003).

Simplified computer languages that children can use to make designs or build structures introduce them to programming skills. As long as adults support children's efforts, computer programming promotes improved problem solving and metacognition because children must plan and reflect on their thinking to get their programs to work. Furthermore, while programming, children are especially likely to help one another and to persist in the face of challenge (Nastasi & Clements, 1994; Resnick & Silverman, 2005).

As with television, children spend much time using computers for entertainment purposes, especially game playing. Both media are rife with gender stereotypes and violence. We will consider their impact on emotional and social development in the next chapter.

ASK YOURSELF

REVIEW
What findings indicate that child-centered rather than academic preschools and kindergartens are better suited to fostering academic development?

APPLY
Your senator has heard that IQ gains resulting from Head Start do not last, so he plans to vote against additional funding. Write a letter explaining why he should support Head Start.

CONNECT
Compare outcomes resulting from preschool intervention programs with those from interventions beginning in infancy (see pages 171–172 in Chapter 5). Which are more likely to lead to lasting cognitive gains? Explain.

REFLECT
How much and what kinds of TV viewing and computer use did you engage in as a child? How do you think your home media environment influenced your development?

Language Development

Language is intimately related to virtually all the cognitive changes discussed in this chapter. Between ages 2 and 6, children make momentous advances in language. Their remarkable achievements, as well as their mistakes along the way, reveal their active, rule-oriented approach to mastering language.

Vocabulary

At age 2, Sammy had a spoken vocabulary of 200 words. By age 6, he will have acquired around 10,000 words (Bloom, 1998). To accomplish this feat, Sammy will learn about five new words each day. How do children build their vocabularies so quickly? Research shows that they can connect new words with their underlying concepts after only a brief encounter, a process called **fast-mapping.** Preschoolers can even fast-map two or more new words encountered in the same situation (Wilkinson, Ross, & Diamond, 2003).

TYPES OF WORDS. Children in many Western and non-Western language communities fast-map labels for objects especially rapidly because these refer to concepts that are easy to perceive. When adults point to, label, and talk about an object, they help the child figure out the word's meaning (Gershoff-Stowe & Hahn, 2007). Soon children add verbs *(go, run, broke)*, which require more complex understandings of relationships between objects and actions. Children learning Chinese, Japanese, and Korean—languages in which nouns are often omitted from adult sentences, while verbs are stressed—acquire verbs especially quickly (Kim, McGregor, & Thompson, 2000; Tardif, 2006). Gradually, preschoolers add modifiers *(red, round, sad)*. Among those that are related in meaning, general distinctions (which are easier) appear before specific ones. Thus, children first acquire *big–small,* then *tall–short, high–low,* and *wide–narrow* (Stevenson & Pollitt, 1987).

To fill in for words they have not yet learned, children as young as age 3 coin new words using ones they already know—for example, "plant-man," for a gardener, "crayoner" for a child using crayons. Preschoolers also extend language meanings through metaphor—like the 3-year-old who described a stomachache as a "fire engine in my tummy" (Winner, 1988). Young preschoolers' metaphors involve concrete sensory comparisons: "Clouds are pillows," "Leaves are dancers." Once vocabulary and general knowledge expand, children also appreciate nonsensory comparisons: "Friends are like magnets," "Time flies by" (Keil, 1986; Özçaliskan, 2005). As a result, young children sometimes communicate in amazingly vivid and memorable ways.

STRATEGIES FOR WORD LEARNING. Preschoolers figure out the meanings of new words by contrasting them with words they already know. But exactly how they discover which concept each word picks out is not yet fully understood. One speculation is that early in vocabulary growth, children adopt a *mutual exclusivity bias;* they assume that words refer to entirely separate (nonoverlapping) categories (Markman, 1992). Consistent with this idea, when 2-year-olds hear the labels for two distinct novel objects (for example, *clip* and *horn*), they assign each word correctly, to the whole object and not just a part of it (Waxman & Senghas, 1992).

Indeed, children's first several hundred nouns refer mostly to objects well-organized by shape. And learning of nouns based on the perceptual property of shape heightens young children's attention to the distinctive shapes of other objects

(Smith et al., 2002; Yoshida & Smith, 2003). This *shape bias* helps preschoolers master additional names of objects, and vocabulary accelerates.

But mutual exclusivity and object shape cannot account for preschoolers' remarkably flexible responses when objects have more than one name. In these instances, children often call on other components of language. According to one proposal, they figure out many word meanings by observing how words are used in the structure of sentences (Gleitman et al., 2005; Naigles & Swenson, 2007). Consider an adult who says, "This is a *citron* one," while showing the child a yellow car. Two- and 3-year-olds conclude that a new word used as an adjective for a familiar object (car) refers to a property of that object (Hall & Graham, 1999; Imai & Haryu, 2004). As preschoolers hear the word in various sentence structures ("That lemon is bright *citron*"), they refine its meaning.

Young children also take advantage of the rich social information that adults frequently provide when they introduce new words. For example, they often draw on their expanding ability to infer others' intentions, desires, and perspectives (Akhtar & Tomasello, 2000). In one study, an adult performed an action on an object and then used a new label while looking back and forth between the child and the object, as if inviting the child to play. Two-year-olds concluded that the label referred to the action, not the object (Tomasello & Akhtar, 1995). By age 3, children can even use a speaker's recently expressed desire (which of two novel objects the adult said she liked) to figure out a word's meaning ("I really want to play with the *riff*") (Saylor & Troseth, 2006).

© SYRACUSE NEWSPAPERS/THE IMAGE WORKS

Young children rely on any useful information available to add to their vocabularies. As his father prepares a hook, this 3-year-old attends to a variety of perceptual, social, and linguistic cues to grasp the meanings of unfamiliar fishing words, such as bait, line, bobber, and sinker.

Adults also inform children directly about which of two or more words to use—by saying, for example, "You can call it a sea creature, but it's better to say *dolphin*." Parents who provide such clarifying information have preschoolers whose vocabularies grow more quickly (Callanan & Sabbagh, 2004).

■ EXPLAINING VOCABULARY DEVELOPMENT. Children acquire vocabulary so efficiently and accurately that some theorists believe that they are innately biased to induce word meanings using certain principles, such as mutual exclusivity (Lidz, Gleitman, & Gleitman, 2004; Woodward & Markman, 1998). But critics point out that a small set of built-in, fixed principles cannot account for the varied, flexible manner in which children master vocabulary (Deák, 2000). And many word-learning strategies cannot be innate because children acquiring different languages use different approaches to mastering the same meanings.

An alternative perspective is that vocabulary growth is governed by the same cognitive strategies that children apply to nonlinguistic information. According to one account, children draw on a *coalition* of cues—perceptual, social, and linguistic—which shift in importance with age (Golinkoff & Hirsh-Pasek, 2006). Infants rely solely on perceptual features. Toddlers and young preschoolers, while still sensitive to perceptual features (such as object shape), increasingly attend to social cues—the speaker's direction of gaze, gestures, and expressions of desire and intention (Hollich, Hirsh-Pasek, & Golinkoff, 2000; Pruden et al., 2006). And as language develops further, linguistic cues—sentence structure and intonation (stress, pitch, and loudness)—play larger roles.

Preschoolers are most successful at figuring out new word meanings when several kinds of information are available (Saylor, Baldwin, & Sabbagh, 2005). Researchers have just begun to study the multiple cues that children use for different kinds of words and how their combined strategies change with development.

Grammar

Between ages 2 and 3, English-speaking children use simple sentences that follow a subject–verb–object word order. Children learning other languages adopt the word orders of the adult speech to which they are exposed.

■ BASIC RULES. Studies of children acquiring diverse languages reveal that their first use of grammatical rules is piecemeal—limited to just a few verbs. As children listen for familiar verbs in adults' speech, they expand their own utterances containing those verbs, relying on adult speech as their model (Gathercole, Sebastián, & Soto, 1999; Lieven, Pine, & Baldwin, 1997). Sammy, for example, added the preposition *with* to the verb *open* ("You open with scissors") but not to the word *hit* ("He hit me stick").

To test preschoolers' ability to generate novel sentences that conform to basic English grammar, researchers had them use a new verb in the subject–verb–object form after hearing it in a different construction, such as passive: "Ernie is getting *gorped* by the dog." The percentage of children who, when asked what the dog was doing, could respond, "He's *gorping* Ernie," rose steadily with age. But not until 3½ to 4 could the majority of children apply the subject–verb–object structure broadly, to newly acquired verbs (Tomasello, 2003, 2006).

As soon as children form three-word sentences, they make small additions and changes to words that enable them to express meanings flexibly and efficiently. For example, they add *-s* for plural *(cats),* use prepositions (*in* and *on*), and form various tenses of the verb *to be (is, are, were, has been, will).* All English-speaking children master these grammatical markers in a regular sequence, starting with those that involve the simplest meanings and structures (Brown, 1973; de Villiers & de Villiers, 1973).

Once children acquire these markers, they sometimes overextend the rules to words that are exceptions—a type of error called **overregularization.** "My toy car *breaked*" and "We each have two *feets*" are expressions that appear between ages 2 and 3 (Maratsos, 2000; Marcus, 1995).

■ COMPLEX STRUCTURES. Gradually, preschoolers master more complex grammatical structures, although they do make mistakes. In first creating questions, 2- to 3-year-olds use many formulas: "Where's *X?*" "Can I *X?*" (Dabrowska, 2000; Tomasello, 1992, 2003). Question asking remains variable for the next couple of years. An analysis of one child's questions revealed that he inverted the subject and verb when asking certain questions but not others ("What she will do?" "Why he can go?") The correct expressions were the ones he heard most often in his mother's speech (Rowland & Pine, 2000). And sometimes children produce errors in subject–verb agreement ("Where does the dogs play?") and in subject case ("Where can me sit?") (Rowland, 2007).

Similarly, children have trouble with some passive sentences. When told, "The car was pushed by the truck," young preschoolers often make a toy car push a truck. By age 5, they understand such expressions, but full mastery of the passive form is not complete until the end of middle childhood (Horgan, 1978; Lempert, 1990).

Nevertheless, preschoolers' grasp of grammar is remarkable. By age 4 to 5, they form embedded sentences ("I think *he will come*"), tag questions ("Dad's going to be home soon, *isn't he?*"), and indirect objects ("He showed *his friend* the present"). As the preschool years draw to a close, children use most of the grammatical constructions of their language competently (Tager-Flusberg & Zukowski, 2009).

■ EXPLAINING GRAMMATICAL DEVELOPMENT. Evidence that grammatical development is an extended process has raised questions about Chomsky's nativist theory (to review, see page 173 in Chapter 5). Some experts believe that grammar is a product of general cognitive development—children's tendency to search consistencies and patterns of all sorts (Bloom, 1999; Chang, Dell, & Bock, 2006; Tomasello, 2003). These *information-processing theorists* believe that children notice which words appear in the same positions in sentences and are similarly combined with other words. Over time, they group words into grammatical categories and use them appropriately in sentences.

Still other theorists, while also focusing on how children process language, agree with Chomsky that children are specially tuned to acquire grammar. One idea proposes that the grammatical categories into which children group word meanings are innate—present at the outset (Pinker, 1999). But critics point out that children's early word combinations do not show a grasp of grammar. According to another view, rather than starting with innate knowledge, children have built-in procedures for analyzing language that support discovery of grammatical regularities (Slobin, 1985, 1997). Controversy persists over whether a universal language-processing device exists or whether children hearing different languages devise unique strategies (Lidz, 2007; Marchman & Thal, 2005).

Conversation

Besides acquiring vocabulary and grammar, children must learn to engage in effective and appropriate communication. This practical, social side of language is called **pragmatics,** and preschoolers make considerable headway in mastering it.

As early as age 2, children are skilled conversationalists. In face-to-face interaction, they take turns and respond appropriately to their partners' remarks (Pan & Snow, 1999). With age, the number of turns over which children can sustain interaction and their ability to maintain a topic over time increase. By age 4, children adjust their speech to fit the age, sex, and social status of their listeners. For example, in acting out roles with hand puppets, they use more commands when playing socially dominant and male roles (teacher, doctor, father) but speak more politely and use more indirect requests when playing less dominant and female roles (student, patient, mother) (Anderson, 2000).

Preschoolers' conversational skills occasionally do break down—for example, when talking on the phone. Here is an

Preschool children are skilled conversationalists. In face-to-face interaction, they take turns and respond appropriately to their partners' remarks.

excerpt from one 4-year-old's phone conversation with his grandfather:

Grandfather: How old will you be?
John: Dis many. *[Holding up four fingers.]*
Grandfather: Huh?
John: Dis many. *[Again holding up four fingers.]*
(Warren & Tate, 1992, pp. 259–260)

Young children's conversations appear less mature in highly demanding situations in which they cannot see their listeners' reactions or rely on typical conversational aids, such as gestures and objects to talk about. But when asked to tell a listener how to solve a simple puzzle, 3- to 6-year-olds give more specific directions over the phone than in person, indicating that they realize the need for more verbal description on the phone (Cameron & Lee, 1997). Between ages 4 and 8, both conversing and giving directions over the phone improve greatly. Telephone talk provides yet another example of how preschoolers' competencies depend on the demands of the situation.

Supporting Language Development in Early Childhood

How can adults foster preschoolers' language development? As in toddlerhood, interaction with more skilled speakers is vital. Conversational give-and-take with adults, either at home or in preschool, is consistently related to language progress (Hart & Risley, 1995; NICHD Early Child Care Research Network, 2000b).

Sensitive, caring adults use additional techniques that promote early language skills. When children use words incorrectly or communicate unclearly, they give helpful, explicit feedback, such as, "I can't tell which ball you want. Do you mean the large red one?" But they do not overcorrect, especially when children make grammatical mistakes. Criticism discourages children from freely using language in ways that lead to new skills.

Instead, adults often provide indirect feedback about grammar by using two strategies, often in combination: **recasts**—restructuring inaccurate speech into correct form, and **expansions**—elaborating on children's speech, increasing its complexity (Bohannon & Stanowicz, 1988; Chouinard & Clark, 2003). For example, if a child says, "I gotted new red shoes," the parent might respond, "Yes, you got a pair of new red shoes." In one study, after such corrective input, 2- to 4-year-olds often shifted to correct forms—improvements still evident several months later (Saxton, Backley, & Galloway, 2005). However, the impact of such feedback has been challenged. The techniques are not used in all cultures and, in a few investigations, had no impact on children's grammar (Strapp & Federico, 2000; Valian, 1999). Rather than eliminating errors, perhaps expansions and recasts model grammatical alternatives and encourage children to experiment with them.

Do the findings just described remind you once again of Vygotsky's theory? In language, as in other aspects of intellectual growth, parents and teachers gently prompt children to take the next step forward. Children strive to master language because they want to connect with other people. Adults, in turn, respond to children's desire to become competent speakers by listening attentively, elaborating on what children say, modeling correct usage, and stimulating children to talk further. In the next chapter, we will see that this combination of warmth and encouragement of mature behavior is at the heart of early childhood emotional and social development as well.

ASK YOURSELF

» REVIEW
Provide a list of recommendations for supporting language development in early childhood, noting research that supports each.

» APPLY
Sammy's mother explained to him that the family would take a vacation in Miami. The next morning, Sammy announced, "I gotted my bags packed. When are we going to Your-ami?" What explains Sammy's error?

» CONNECT
Explain how children's strategies for word learning support the interactionist perspective on language development, described on page 174 in Chapter 5.

Summary

PHYSICAL DEVELOPMENT

A Changing Body and Brain

Describe body growth and brain development during early childhood.

» Children grow more slowly in early childhood than they did in the first two years, and they become longer and leaner. New growth centers appear in the skeleton, and by the end of early childhood, children start to lose their primary teeth.

» Frontal-lobe areas of the cerebral cortex devoted to planning and organizing behavior develop rapidly. The left cerebral hemisphere shows more neural activity than the right, supporting preschoolers' expanding language skills.

» Hand preference strengthens during early and middle childhood, indicating that lateralization is increasing. Handedness reflects an individual's **dominant cerebral hemisphere.** One theory proposes that most children are genetically biased for right-handedness but that experience can sway them toward a left-hand preference.

- In early childhood, fibers linking the **cerebellum** to the cerebral cortex myelinate, enhancing balance, motor control, and thinking. The **reticular formation,** responsible for alertness and consciousness; the **hippocampus,** which plays a vital role in memory and spatial orientation; and the **corpus callosum,** connecting the two cerebral hemispheres, also develop rapidly.

Influences on Physical Growth and Health

Describe the effects of heredity, emotional well-being, nutrition, and infectious disease on physical growth in early childhood.

- Heredity influences physical growth by controlling the release of hormones from the **pituitary gland.** Two hormones are especially influential: **growth hormone (GH)** and **thyroid-stimulating hormone (TSH).**
- Emotional well-being continues to influence body growth. An emotionally inadequate home life can lead to a disorder called **psychosocial dwarfism.**
- As growth rate slows, preschoolers' appetites decline, and many become picky eaters. Repeated exposure to new foods and a positive mealtime atmosphere encourages healthy, varied eating.

© MARC GARANGER/CORBIS

- Dietary deficiencies, especially in protein, vitamins and minerals, can affect growth and resistance to disease. In the developing world, disease often contributes to malnutrition and growth stunting, especially when intestinal infections cause persistent diarrhea.
- Immunization rates are lower in the United States than in other industrialized nations because many economically disadvantaged children lack access to health care. Parental stress and misconceptions about vaccine safety also contribute.

What factors increase the risk of unintentional injuries, and how can childhood injuries be prevented?

- Unintentional injuries are the leading cause of childhood mortality in industrialized countries. Injury victims are more likely to be boys; to be temperamentally irritable, inattentive, and negative; and to be growing up in stressed, poverty-stricken inner-city families.
- Effective injury prevention includes reducing poverty and other sources of family stress; passing laws that promote child safety; creating safer home, travel, and play environments; improving public education; and changing parent and child behaviors.

Motor Development

Cite major milestones of gross- and fine-motor development in early childhood.

- As the child's center of gravity shifts toward the trunk, balance improves, paving the way for many gross-motor achievements. Preschoolers run, jump, hop, gallop, eventually skip, throw and catch, and generally become better coordinated.
- Increasing control of the hands and fingers leads to dramatic improvements in fine-motor skills. Preschoolers gradually become self-sufficient at dressing and using a knife and fork.
- By age 3, children's scribbles become pictures. With age, their drawings increase in complexity and realism, influenced by schooling and by their culture's artistic traditions. Preschoolers also try to print alphabet letters and, later, words.
- Body build and opportunity for physical play affect motor development. Sex differences that favor boys in skills requiring force and power and girls in skills requiring balance and fine movements are partly genetic, but environmental pressures exaggerate them. Children master the motor skills of early childhood through informal play experiences.

COGNITIVE DEVELOPMENT

Piaget's Theory: The Preoperational Stage

Describe cognitive advances and limitations during the preoperational stage.

- Rapid advances in mental representation mark the beginning of Piaget's **preoperational stage.** With age, make-believe becomes increasingly complex, evolving into **sociodramatic play** with others. Preschoolers' make-believe supports many aspects of development. Gradually, children become capable of **dual representation**—viewing a symbolic object as both an object in its own right and a symbol.
- Piaget also described preoperational children as egocentric, often failing to imagine others' perspectives. **Egocentrism** contributes to **animistic thinking, centration,** a focus on perceptual appearances, and **irreversibility.** These difficulties cause preschoolers to fail **conservation** and **hierarchical classification** tasks.

What does follow-up research reveal about the accuracy of Piaget's preoperational stage?

- When young children are given simplified problems relevant to their everyday lives, their performance appears more mature than Piaget assumed. Preschoolers recognize differing perspectives, distinguish animate from inanimate objects, reason by analogy about physical transformations, understand cause-and-effect relationships, and organize knowledge into hierarchical categories, including categories based on nonobvious features.
- Evidence that operational thinking develops gradually over the preschool years challenges Piaget's stage concept. Some theorists propose a more flexible view of stages.

What educational principles can be derived from Piaget's theory?

- A Piagetian classroom promotes discovery learning, sensitivity to children's readiness to learn, and acceptance of individual differences.

Vygotsky's Sociocultural Theory

Explain Vygotsky's perspective on children's private speech, describe applications of his theory to education, and note how cross-cultural research has expanded his ideas.

- Unlike Piaget, Vygotsky regarded language as the foundation for all higher cognitive processes. According to Vygotsky, **private speech,** or language used for self-guidance, emerges out of social communication as adults and more skilled peers help children master challenging tasks. Private speech is gradually internalized as inner, verbal thought. **Scaffolding** is a form of social interaction that promotes the transfer of cognitive processes to children.
- A Vygotskian classroom emphasizes assisted discovery—verbal guidance from teachers and peer collaboration. Make-believe play is a vital zone of proximal development that promotes many competencies.

© ELLEN B. SENISI PHOTOGRAPHY

- **Guided participation,** a broader term than scaffolding, recognizes cultural and situational variations in adult support of children's efforts.

Information Processing

How do attention and memory change during early childhood?

- Attention gradually becomes more sustained, and planning improves. Nevertheless, compared with older children, preschoolers spend relatively short periods involved in tasks and are less systematic in planning.

» Preschoolers' recognition memory is very accurate, but their recall for listlike information is poor because they use **memory strategies** less effectively than older children.

» Like adults, preschoolers remember recurring experiences in terms of **scripts,** which become more elaborate with age. When adults use an elaborative style of conversing with children about the past, their autobiographical memory becomes better organized and detailed.

Describe the young child's theory of mind.

» Preschoolers begin to construct a theory of mind, indicating that they are capable of **metacognition.** Around age 4, they understand that people can hold false beliefs. Language, cognitive abilities, make-believe play, and diverse social experiences with adults, siblings, and peers all contribute to the development of a theory of mind. Preschoolers regard the mind as a passive container of information rather than as an active, constructive agent.

Summarize children's literacy and mathematical knowledge during early childhood.

» Young children in industrialized nations attempt to figure out how written symbols convey meaning—an active effort known as **emergent literacy.** Preschoolers gradually revise incorrect ideas about the meaning of written symbols as their cognitive and language capacities improve, as they encounter writing in many different contexts, and as adults help them with written communication. **Phonological awareness** is a strong predictor of emergent literacy knowledge.

» In the second year, children have a beginning grasp of **ordinality.** Soon they discover additional mathematical principles, including **cardinality,** and experiment with counting strategies to solve arithmetic problems, eventually arriving at the most efficient, accurate techniques. Many occasions for counting, comparing quantities, and talking about number promote mathematical knowledge.

Individual Differences in Mental Development

Describe early childhood intelligence tests and the impact of home, educational programs, child care, and media on preschoolers' mental development.

» By age 5 to 6, intelligence test scores are good predictors of later IQ and academic achievement. Children growing up in warm, stimulating homes with parents who make reasonable demands for mature behavior score higher on mental tests.

» Preschool and kindergarten programs include both **child-centered programs,** in which much learning takes place through play, and **academic programs,** in which teachers train children in academic skills, often through repetition and drill. Emphasizing formal academic instruction undermines young children's motivation and negatively influences later school achievement.

» **Project Head Start** is the largest U.S. federally funded preschool program for low-income children. High-quality preschool intervention results in immediate IQ and achievement gains and long-term improvements in school adjustment. The more parents are involved in Head Start, the higher children's year-end academic, language, and social skills. Regardless of SES, poor-quality child care undermines preschoolers' cognitive and social development.

» Children pick up many cognitive skills from educational television programs. Programs with slow-paced action and easy-to-follow story lines foster more elaborate make-believe play. But heavy viewing of prime-time shows and cartoons takes children away from reading and interacting with others and is related to weaker academic skills.

» Computer word-processing programs can support preschoolers' emergent literacy. Introducing young children to simplified computer languages fosters problem solving and metacognition.

Language Development

Trace the development of vocabulary, grammar, and conversational skills in early childhood.

» Supported by **fast-mapping,** preschoolers' vocabularies grow dramatically. On hearing a new word, children contrast it with words they know and often assume that words refer to entirely separate categories. When adults call an object by more than one name, preschoolers figure out word meanings from diverse cues—perceptual, social, and lingustic. They also extend language meanings by coining new words and creating metaphors.

» Between ages 2 and 3, children adopt the basic word order of their language. As they master grammatical rules, they sometimes overextend them in a type of error called **overregularization.** By the end of early childhood, children have acquired complex grammatical forms.

» **Pragmatics** refers to the practical, social side of language. Two-year-olds are already skilled conversationalists in face-to-face interaction. By age 4, children adapt their speech to their listeners in culturally accepted ways.

Cite factors that support language learning in early childhood.

» Conversational give-and-take with more skilled speakers fosters language progress. Adults often provide explicit feedback on the clarity of children's language and indirect feedback about grammar through **recasts** and **expansions.**

Important Terms and Concepts

academic programs (p. 245)
animistic thinking (p. 229)
cardinality (p. 243)
centration (p. 229)
cerebellum (p. 218)
child-centered programs (p. 245)
conservation (p. 229)
corpus callosum (p. 218)
dominant cerebral hemisphere (p. 217)
dual representation (p. 229)
egocentrism (p. 229)
emergent literacy (p. 242)
expansions (p. 251)
fast-mapping (p. 248)
growth hormone (GH) (p. 219)
guided participation (p. 236)
hierarchical classification (p. 230)
hippocampus (p. 218)
irreversibility (p. 230)
memory strategies (p. 238)
metacognition (p. 239)
ordinality (p. 243)
overregularization (p. 250)
phonological awareness (p. 242)
pituitary gland (p. 219)
pragmatics (p. 250)
preoperational stage (p. 227)
private speech (p. 234)
Project Head Start (p. 245)
psychosocial dwarfism (p. 219)
recasts (p. 251)
reticular formation (p. 218)
scaffolding (p. 235)
scripts (p. 238)
sociodramatic play (p. 228)
thyroid-stimulating hormone (TSH) (p. 219)

During the preschool years, children make great strides in understanding the thoughts and feelings of others, and they build on these skills as they form first friendships—special relationships marked by attachment and common interests.

CHAPTER 8

Emotional and Social Development in Early Childhood

As the children in Leslie's classroom moved through the preschool years, their personalities took on clearer definition. By age 3, they voiced firm likes and dislikes as well as new ideas about themselves. "Stop bothering me," Sammy said to Mark, who had reached for Sammy's beanbag as Sammy aimed it toward the mouth of a large clown face. "See, I'm great at this game," Sammy announced with confidence, an attitude that kept him trying, even though he missed most of the throws.

The children's conversations also revealed early notions about morality. Often they combined adults' statements about right and wrong with forceful attempts to defend their own desires. "You're 'posed to share," stated Mark, grabbing the beanbag out of Sammy's hand.

"I was here first! Gimme it back," demanded Sammy, pushing Mark. The two boys struggled until Leslie intervened, provided another beanbag, and showed them how both could play.

As the interaction between Sammy and Mark reveals, preschoolers quickly become complex social beings. Young children argue, grab, and push, but cooperative exchanges are far more frequent. Between ages 2 and 6, first friendships form, in which children converse, act out complementary roles, and learn that their own desires for companionship and toys are best met when they consider others' needs and interests.

The children's developing understanding of their social world was especially evident in their growing attention to the dividing line between male and female. While Lynette and Karen cared for a sick baby doll in the housekeeping area, Sammy, Vance, and Mark transformed the block corner into a busy intersection. "Green light, go!" shouted police officer Sammy as Vance and Mark pushed large wooden cars and trucks across the floor. Already, the children preferred same-sex peers and, in their play, mirrored their culture's gender stereotypes.

This chapter is devoted to the many facets of early childhood emotional and social development. We begin with Erik Erikson's theory, which provides an overview of personality change in the preschool years. Then we consider children's concepts of themselves, their insights into their social and moral worlds, their gender typing, and their increasing ability to manage their emotional and social behaviors. Finally, we ask, What is effective child rearing? And we discuss the complex conditions that support good parenting or lead it to break down.

Erikson's Theory: Initiative versus Guilt

Erikson (1950) described early childhood as a period of "vigorous unfolding." Once children have a sense of autonomy, they become less contrary than they were as toddlers. Their energies are freed for tackling the psychological conflict of the preschool years: **initiative versus guilt.** As the word *initiative* suggests, young children have a new sense of purposefulness. They are eager to tackle new tasks, join in activities with peers, and discover what they can do with the help of adults. They also make strides in conscience development.

Erikson regarded play as a means through which young children learn about themselves and their social world. Play permits preschoolers to try out new skills with little risk of criticism and failure. It also creates a small social organization of children who must cooperate to achieve common goals. Around the world, children act out family scenes and highly visible occupations—police officer, doctor, and nurse in Western societies, rabbit hunter and potter among the Hopi Indians, hut builder and spear maker among the Baka of West Africa (Göncü, Patt, & Kouba, 2004).

© DORANNE JACOBSON

This 3-year-old in India pretends to do the laundry on the washing stone outside her family's home. Around the world, young children act out family scenes and highly visible occupations, developing a sense of initiative as they gain insight into what they can do.

Recall that Erikson's theory builds on Freud's psychosexual stages (see Chapter 1, page 15). In Freud's Oedipus and Electra conflicts, to avoid punishment and maintain the affection of parents, children form a *superego,* or conscience, by identifying with the same-sex parent. As a result, they adopt the moral and gender-role standards of their society. Each time the child disobeys standards of conscience, painful feelings of guilt occur. For Erikson, the negative outcome of early childhood is an overly strict superego that causes children to feel too much guilt because they have been threatened, criticized, and punished excessively by adults. When this happens, preschoolers' exuberant play and bold efforts to master new tasks break down.

Although Freud's ideas are no longer accepted as satisfactory explanations of conscience development, Erikson's image of initiative captures the diverse changes in young children's emotional and social lives. Early childhood is, indeed, a time when children develop a confident self-image, more effective control over their emotions, new social skills, the foundations of morality, and a clear sense of themselves as boy or girl.

Self-Understanding

The development of language enables young children to talk about their own subjective experience of being. In Chapter 7, we noted that young children acquire a vocabulary for talking about their inner mental lives and refine their understanding of mental states. As self-awareness strengthens, preschoolers focus more intently on qualities that make the self unique. They begin to develop a **self-concept,** the set of attributes, abilities, attitudes, and values that an individual believes defines who he or she is.

Foundations of Self-Concept

Ask a 3- to 5-year-old to tell you about himself, and you are likely to hear something like this: "I'm Tommy. See, I got this new red T-shirt. I'm 4 years old. I can wash my hair all by myself. I have a new Tinkertoy set, and I made this big, big tower." Preschoolers' self-concepts are very concrete. Usually, they mention observable characteristics, such as their name, physical appearance, possessions, and everyday behaviors (Harter, 2006; Watson, 1990).

By age 3½, preschoolers also describe themselves in terms of typical emotions and attitudes—"I'm happy when I play with my friends"; "I don't like being with grownups"—suggesting a beginning understanding of their unique psychological characteristics (Eder & Mangelsdorf, 1997). Furthermore, when given a trait label ("shy" or "mean"), 4-year-olds infer appropriate motives and feelings. For example, they know that a shy person doesn't like to be with unfamiliar people (Heyman & Gelman, 1999). But preschoolers do not say, "I'm helpful" or "I'm shy." Direct references to personality traits must wait for greater cognitive maturity.

CULTURAL INFLUENCES

Cultural Variations in Personal Storytelling: Implications for Early Self-Concept

Preschoolers of many cultural backgrounds participate in personal storytelling with their parents. Striking cultural differences exist in parents' selection and interpretation of events in these narratives, affecting the way children view themselves.

In one study, researchers spent hundreds of hours studying the storytelling practices of six middle-SES Irish-American families in Chicago and six middle-SES Chinese families in Taiwan. From extensive videotapes of adults' conversations with 2½-year-olds, the investigators identified personal stories and coded them for content, quality of their endings, and evaluation of the child (Miller, Fung, & Mintz, 1996; Miller et al., 1997).

Parents in both cultures discussed pleasurable holidays and family excursions in similar ways and with similar frequency. But Chinese parents more often told long stories about the child's misdeeds—using impolite language, writing on the wall, or playing in an overly rowdy way. These narratives were conveyed with warmth and caring, stressed the impact of misbehavior on others ("You made Mama lose face"), and often ended with direct teaching of proper behavior ("Saying dirty words is not good"). By contrast, in the few instances in which Irish-American stories referred to transgressions, parents downplayed their seriousness, attributing them to the child's spunk and assertiveness.

Early narratives about the child launch preschoolers' self-concepts on culturally distinct paths (Miller, Fung, & Koven, 2007). Influenced by Confucian traditions of strict discipline and social obligations, Chinese parents integrated these values into their stories, affirming the importance of not disgracing the family and explicitly conveying expectations in the story's conclusion. Although Irish-American parents disciplined their children, they rarely dwelt on misdeeds in storytelling. Rather, they cast the child's shortcomings in a positive light, perhaps to promote self-esteem.

Whereas most North Americans believe that favorable self-esteem is crucial for healthy development, Chinese adults generally see it as unimportant or even negative—as impeding the child's willingness to listen and be corrected (Miller et al., 2002). Consistent with this view, the Chinese parents did little to cultivate their child's individuality. Instead, they used storytelling to guide the child toward socially responsible behavior. Hence, the Chinese child's self-image emphasizes obligations to others, whereas the North American child's is more autonomous.

A Chinese mother speaks gently to her children about proper behavior. Chinese parents often tell preschoolers stories that point out the negative impact on others of the child's misdeeds. The Chinese child's self-concept, in turn, emphasizes social obligations.

In fact, very young preschoolers' concepts of themselves are so bound up with specific possessions and actions that they spend much time asserting their rights to objects ("Mine!"), as Sammy did in the beanbag incident at the beginning of this chapter. The stronger children's self-definition, the more possessive they tend to be (Fasig, 2000; Levine, 1983). A firmer sense of self also enables children to cooperate in resolving disputes over objects, playing games, and solving simple problems (Brownell & Carriger, 1990; Caplan et al., 1991). Accordingly, when trying to promote friendly peer interaction, parents and teachers can accept young children's possessiveness as a sign of self-assertion ("Yes, that's your toy") and then encourage compromise ("but in a little while, would you give someone else a turn?"), rather than simply insisting on sharing.

Recall from Chapter 7 that adult–child conversations about personally experienced events contribute to the development of an autobiographical memory—a life-story narrative that is more coherent and lasting than the isolated memories of the first few years (see page 238). In one study, the richness of mothers' emotional communication about the past (evaluations of positive events, explanations of children's negative feelings and their resolution) helped children understand themselves: It predicted greater consistency in 5- and 6-year-olds' reports of their personal characteristics (Bird & Reese, 2006).

And as early as age 2, parents use these narratives to impart rules, standards for behavior, evaluative information about the child: "You added the milk when we made the mashed potatoes. That's a very important job!" (Nelson, 2003). As the Cultural Influences box above reveals, these self-evaluative narratives are a major means through which caregivers imbue the young child's self-concept with cultural values.

As they talk about personally significant events and as their cognitive skills advance, preschoolers gradually come to view themselves as persisting over time. Around age 4, children first become certain that a video image of themselves replayed a few minutes after it was filmed is still "me" (Povinelli, 2001). Similarly, when researchers asked 3- to 5-year-olds to imagine a future event (walking next to a waterfall) and to envision a future personal state by choosing from three items (a raincoat, money, a blanket) the one they would need to bring with them, performance—along with future-state justifications ("I'm gonna get wet")—increased sharply from age 3 to 4 (Atance & Meltzoff, 2005).

Emergence of Self-Esteem

Another aspect of self-concept emerges in early childhood: **self-esteem,** the judgments we make about our own worth and the feelings associated with those judgments. ***TAKE A MOMENT...*** Make a list of your own self-judgments. Notice that, besides a global appraisal of your worth as a person, you have a variety of separate self-evaluations concerning how well you perform at different activities. These evaluations are among the most important aspects of self-development because they affect emotional experiences, future behavior, and long-term psychological adjustment.

By age 4, preschoolers have several self-judgments—for example, about learning things in school, making friends, getting along with parents, and treating others kindly (Marsh, Ellis, & Craven, 2002). But because preschoolers cannot distinguish between their desired and their actual competence, they usually rate their own ability as extremely high and underestimate task difficulty, as when Sammy asserted, despite his many misses, that he was great at beanbag throwing (Harter, 2003, 2006).

High self-esteem contributes greatly to preschoolers' initiative during a period in which they must master many new skills. By age 3, children with a history of parental criticism of their worth and performance give up easily when faced with a challenge and express shame and despondency after failing (Kelley, Brownell, & Campbell, 2000). When preschool nonpersisters use dolls to act out an adult's reaction to failure, they anticipate disapproval—saying, for example, "He's punished because he can't do the puzzle." They also report that their parents berate them for small mistakes (Burhans & Dweck, 1995; Heyman, Dweck, & Cain, 1992). Adults can avoid promoting these self-defeating reactions by adjusting their expectations to children's capacities, scaffolding children's attempts at difficult tasks (see Chapter 7, page 235), and pointing out effort and improvement in children's behavior.

A preschooler proudly displays a string of beads she has assembled. Her high self-esteem contributes greatly to her initiative in mastering many new skills.

Emotional Development

Gains in representation, language, and self-concept support emotional development in early childhood. Between ages 2 and 6, children make strides in emotional abilities that, collectively, researchers refer to as *emotional competence* (Halberstadt, Denham, & Dunsmore, 2001; Saarni et al., 2006). First, preschoolers gain in emotional understanding, becoming better able to talk about feelings and to respond appropriately to others' emotional signals. Second, they become better at emotional self-regulation—in particular, at coping with intense negative emotion. Finally, preschoolers more often experience *self-conscious emotions* and *empathy,* which contribute to their developing sense of morality.

Parenting strongly influences preschoolers' emotional competence. Emotional competence, in turn, is vital for successful peer relationships and overall mental health.

Understanding Emotion

Early in the preschool years, children refer to causes, consequences, and behavioral signs of emotion, and over time their understanding becomes more accurate and complex (Stein & Levine, 1999). By age 4 to 5, children correctly judge the causes of many basic emotions ("He's happy because he's swinging very high"; "He's sad because he misses his mother"). Preschoolers' explanations tend to emphasize external factors over internal states, a balance that changes with age (Levine, 1995). After age 4, children better understand that both desires and beliefs motivate behavior (see page 239 in Chapter 7). Then their grasp of how internal factors can trigger emotion expands.

Preschoolers can also predict what a playmate expressing a certain emotion might do next. Four-year-olds know that an angry child might hit someone and that a happy child is more likely to share (Russell, 1990). And they realize that thinking and feeling are interconnected—that a person reminded of a previous sad experience is likely to feel sad (Lagattuta, Wellman, & Flavell, 1997). Furthermore, they come up with effective ways to relieve others' negative feelings, such as hugging to reduce sadness (Fabes et al., 1988). Overall, preschoolers have an impressive ability to interpret, predict, and change others' feelings.

At the same time, preschoolers have difficulty interpreting situations that offer conflicting cues about how a person is feeling. When shown a picture of a happy-faced child with a broken bicycle, 4- and 5-year-olds tended to rely on the emotional expression: "He's happy because he likes to ride his bike." Older children more often reconciled the two cues: "He's happy because his father promised to help fix his broken bike" (Gnepp, 1983; Hoffner & Badzinski, 1989). As in their approach to Piagetian tasks, preschoolers focus on the most obvious aspect of an emotional situation to the neglect of other relevant information.

Preschoolers whose parents frequently acknowledge their emotional reactions and talk about diverse emotions are better able to judge others' emotions when tested at later ages (Denham & Kochanoff, 2002). In one study, mothers who explained feelings and who negotiated and compromised during conflicts with their 2½-year-olds had children who, at age 3, were advanced in emotional understanding and used similar strategies to resolve disagreements (Laible & Thompson, 2002). Furthermore, 3- to 5-year-olds who are securely attached to their mothers better understand emotion. Attachment security is related to warmer and more elaborative parent–child narratives, including discussions of feelings that highlight the emotional significance of events (Laible, 2004; Laible & Song, 2006; Raikes & Thompson, 2006).

As preschoolers learn about emotion from interacting with adults, they engage in more emotion talk with siblings and friends, especially during make-believe play (Brown, Donelan-McCall, & Dunn, 1996; Hughes & Dunn, 1998). Make-believe, in turn, contributes to emotional understanding, especially when children play with siblings (Youngblade & Dunn, 1995). The intense nature of the sibling relationship, combined with frequent acting out of feelings, makes pretending an excellent context for learning about emotions. Also, the more preschoolers refer to feelings when interacting with playmates, the better liked they are by their peers (Fabes et al., 2001). Children seem to recognize that acknowledging others' emotions and explaining their own enhance the quality of relationships.

Emotional Self-Regulation

Language also contributes to preschoolers' improved *emotional self-regulation.* By age 3 to 4, children verbalize a variety of strategies for adjusting their emotional arousal to a more comfortable level. For example, they know they can blunt emotions by restricting sensory input (covering their eyes or ears to block out a scary sight or sound), talking to themselves ("Mommy said she'll be back soon"), or changing their goals (deciding that they don't want to play anyway after being excluded from a game) (Thompson & Goodvin, 2007). As children use these strategies, emotional outbursts decline. *Effortful control*—in particular, inhibiting impulses and shifting attention—also continues to be vital in managing emotion during early childhood. Three-year-olds who can distract themselves when frustrated tend to become cooperative school-age children with few problem behaviors (Gilliom et al., 2002a).

Temperament affects the development of emotional self-regulation. Children who experience negative emotion intensely find it harder to inhibit feelings and shift attention away from disturbing events. They are more likely to be anxious and fearful, respond with irritation to others' distress, react angrily or aggressively when frustrated, and get along poorly with teachers and peers (Chang et al., 2003; Denham et al., 2002; Eisenberg et al., 2005).

To avoid social difficulties, emotionally reactive children must develop effective emotion-regulation strategies (Rothbart & Bates, 2006). By watching parents manage their feelings, children learn strategies for regulating their own. When parents rarely express positive emotion, dismiss children's feelings as unimportant, and have difficulty controlling their own anger, children have continuing problems managing emotion (Gilliom et al., 2002; Katz & Windecker-Nelson, 2004). And because emotionally reactive children become increasingly difficult to rear, they are often targets of ineffective parenting, which compounds their poor self-regulation.

Adults' conversations with preschoolers also foster emotional self-regulation (Thompson, 2006). Parents who prepare children for difficult experience by describing what to expect and ways to handle anxiety offer strategies that children can apply. Preschoolers' vivid imaginations and incomplete grasp of the distinction between appearance and reality make fears common in early childhood. Consult Applying What We Know on page 260 for ways adults can help young children manage fears.

Self-Conscious Emotions

One morning in Leslie's classroom, a group of children crowded around for a bread-baking activity. Leslie asked them to wait patiently while she got a baking pan. But Sammy reached over to feel the dough, and the bowl tumbled off the table. When Leslie returned, Sammy looked at her, then covered his eyes with his hands and said, "I did something bad." He felt ashamed and guilty.

As their self-concepts develop, preschoolers become increasingly sensitive to praise and blame or to the possibility of such feedback. They more often experience *self-conscious emotions*—feelings that involve injury to or enhancement of their sense of self (see Chapter 6). By age 3, self-conscious emotions are clearly linked to self-evaluation (Stipek, 1995; Thompson, Meyer, & McGinley, 2006). But because preschoolers are still developing standards of excellence and conduct, they depend on the messages of parents, teachers, and others who matter to them to know *when* to feel proud, ashamed, or guilty, often viewing adult expectations as obligatory rules ("Dad said you're 'posed to take turns") (Stipek, 1995; Thompson, Meyer, & McGinley, 2006).

When parents repeatedly comment on the worth of the child and her performance ("That's a bad job! I thought you were a good girl!"), children experience self-conscious emotions

Applying What We Know

Helping Children Manage Common Fears of Early Childhood

Fear	Suggestion
Monsters, ghosts, and darkness	Reduce exposure to frightening stories in books and on TV until the child is better able to sort out appearance from reality. Make a thorough "search" of the child's room for monsters, showing him that none are there. Leave a night-light burning, sit by the child's bed until he falls asleep, and tuck in a favorite toy for protection.
Preschool or child care	If the child resists going to preschool but seems content once there, then the fear is probably separation. Provide a sense of warmth and caring while gently encouraging independence. If the child fears being at preschool, find out what is frightening—the teacher, the children, or perhaps a crowded, noisy environment. Provide extra support by accompanying the child and gradually lessening the amount of time you are present.
Animals	Do not force the child to approach a dog, cat, or other animal that arouses fear. Let the child move at her own pace. Demonstrate how to hold and pet the animal, showing the child that when treated gently, the animal is friendly. If the child is larger than the animal, emphasize this: "You're so big. That kitty is probably afraid of you!"
Intense fears	If a child's fear is intense, persists for a long time, interferes with daily activities, and cannot be reduced in any of the ways just suggested, it has reached the level of a *phobia.* Sometimes phobias are linked to family problems, and counseling is needed to reduce them. At other times, phobias diminish without treatment as the child's capacity for emotional self-regulation improves.

intensely—more shame after failure, more pride after success. In contrast, parents who focus on how to improve performance ("You did it this way; now try doing it that way") induce moderate, more adaptive levels of shame and pride and greater persistence on difficult tasks (Kelley, Brownell, & Campbell, 2000; Lewis, 1998).

Among Western children, intense shame is associated with feelings of personal inadequacy ("I'm stupid"; "I'm a terrible person") and with maladjustment—withdrawal and depression as well as intense anger and aggression toward those who participated in the shame-evoking situation (Lindsay-Hartz, de Rivera, & Mascolo, 1995; Mills, 2005). In contrast, guilt—when it occurs in appropriate circumstances and is not accompanied by shame—is related to good adjustment. Guilt helps children resist harmful impulses, and it motivates a misbehaving child to repair the damage and behave more considerately (Mascolo & Fischer, 2007; Tangney, 2001).

The consequences of shame for children's adjustment, however, may vary across cultures. As illustrated in the Cultural Influences box on page 257 and on page 189 in Chapter 6, people in Asian collectivist societies, who define themselves in relation to their social group, view shame as an adaptive reminder of an interdependent self and of the importance of others' judgments (Bedford, 2004).

Empathy

In early childhood, another emotional capacity, *empathy,* becomes more common and serves as an important motivator of **prosocial,** or **altruistic, behavior**—actions that benefit another person without any expected reward for the self (Eisenberg, Fabes, & Spinrad, 2006). Compared with toddlers, preschoolers rely more on words to communicate empathic feelings, a change that indicates a more reflective level of empathy. And as the ability to take another's perspective improves, empathic responding increases. When a 4-year-old received a Christmas gift that she hadn't included on her list for Santa, she assumed it belonged to another little girl and pleaded with her parents, "We've got to give it back—Santa's made a big mistake. I think the girl's crying 'cause she didn't get her present!"

Yet empathy—*feeling with* another person and responding emotionally in a similar way—does not always yield acts of kindness and helpfulness. For some children, empathizing with an upset adult or peer escalates into personal distress. In trying to reduce these feelings, the child focuses on his own anxiety rather than the person in need. As a result, empathy does not lead to **sympathy**—feelings of concern or sorrow for another's plight.

As children's language skills and ability to take the perspective of others improve, empathy also increases, motivating prosocial, or altruistic, behavior.

Temperament plays a role in whether empathy prompts sympathetic, prosocial behavior or self-focused personal distress. Children who are sociable, assertive, and good at regulating emotion are more likely to help, share, and comfort others in distress. But poor emotion regulators less often display sympathetic concern and prosocial behavior (Bengtsson, 2005; Eisenberg et al., 1998). When faced with someone in need, they react with facial and physiological distress—frowning, lip biting, a rise in heart rate, and a sharp increase in EEG brain-wave activity in the right cerebral hemisphere (which houses negative emotion)—indications that they are overwhelmed by their feelings (Jones, Field, & Davalos, 2000; Pickens, Field, & Nawrocki, 2001).

As with emotional self-regulation, parenting affects empathy and sympathy. When parents are warm, encourage emotional expressiveness, and show sensitive, empathic concern for their preschoolers' feelings, children are likely to react in similar fashion to others' distress—relationships that persist into adolescence and early adulthood (Koestner, Franz, & Weinberger, 1990; Michalik et al., 2007; Strayer & Roberts, 2004). Besides modeling sympathy, parents can teach children the importance of kindness and can intervene when they display inappropriate emotion—strategies that predict high levels of sympathetic responding (Eisenberg, 2003).

In contrast, angry, punitive parenting disrupts empathy and sympathy at an early age (Valiente et al., 2004). In one study, physically abused preschoolers at a child-care center rarely expressed concern at a peer's unhappiness but, rather, reacted with fear, anger, and physical attacks (Klimes-Dougan & Kistner, 1990). The children's behavior resembled their parents' insensitive responses to the suffering of others.

Peer Relations

As children become increasingly self-aware and better at communicating and understanding the thoughts and feelings of others, their skill at interacting with peers improves rapidly. Peers provide young children with learning experiences they can get in no other way. Because peers interact on an equal footing, children must keep a conversation going, cooperate, and set goals in play. With peers, children form friendships—special relationships marked by attachment and common interests. Let's look at how peer interaction changes over the preschool years.

Advances in Peer Sociability

Mildred Parten (1932), one of the first to study peer sociability among 2- to 5-year-olds, noticed a dramatic rise with age in joint, interactive play. She concluded that social development proceeds in a three-step sequence. It begins with **nonsocial activity**—unoccupied, onlooker behavior and solitary play Then it shifts to **parallel play,** in which a child plays near other children with similar materials but does not try to influence their behavior. At the highest level are two forms of true social interaction. In **associative play,** children engage in separate activities but exchange toys and comment on one another's behavior. Finally, in **cooperative play,** a more advanced type of interaction, children orient toward a common goal, such as acting out a make-believe theme.

■ **FOLLOW-UP RESEARCH ON PEER SOCIABILITY.** Longitudinal evidence indicates that these play forms emerge in the order suggested by Parten but that later-appearing ones do not replace earlier ones in a developmental sequence (Rubin, Bukowski, & Parker, 2006). Rather, all types coexist in early childhood.

TAKE A MOMENT... Watch preschoolers move from one type of play to another in a play group or preschool classroom, and you will see that they often transition from onlooker to parallel to cooperative play and back again (Robinson et al., 2003). Preschoolers seem to use parallel play as a way station—a respite from the demands of complex social interaction and a crossroad to new activities. And although nonsocial activity declines with age, it is still the most frequent form among 3- to 4-year-olds and accounts for a third of kindergartners' free-play

© LAURA DWIGHT PHOTOGRAPHY

© ELLEN B. SENISI PHOTOGRAPHY

These 4-year-olds (left) engage in parallel play. Cooperative play (right) develops later than parallel play, but preschool children continue to move back and forth between the two types of sociability, sometimes using parallel play as a respite from the complex demands of cooperation.

TABLE 8.1 ■ *Developmental Sequence of Cognitive Play Categories*

PLAY CATEGORY	DESCRIPTION	EXAMPLES
Functional play	Simple, repetitive motor movements with or without objects, especially common during the first two years	Running around a room, rolling a car back and forth, kneading clay with no intent to make something
Constructive play	Creating or constructing something, especially common between 3 and 6 years	Making a house out of toy blocks, drawing a picture, putting together a puzzle
Make-believe play	Acting out everyday and imaginary roles, especially common between 2 and 6 years	Playing house, school, or police officer; acting out storybook or television characters

Source: Rubin, Fein, & Vandenberg, 1983.

time. Also, both solitary and parallel play remain fairly stable from 3 to 6 years, accounting for as much of the child's play as cooperative interaction (Rubin, Fein, & Vandenberg, 1983).

We now understand that the *type,* not the amount, of solitary and parallel play changes in early childhood. In studies of preschoolers' play in Taiwan and the United States, researchers rated the *cognitive maturity* of nonsocial, parallel, and cooperative play, using the categories shown in Table 8.1 above. Within each play type, older children displayed more cognitively mature behavior than younger children (Pan, 1994; Rubin, Watson, & Jambor, 1978).

Often parents wonder if a preschooler who spends much time playing alone is developing normally. But only *certain types* of nonsocial activity—aimless wandering, hovering near peers, and functional play involving repetitive motor action—are cause for concern. Children who watch peers without playing are usually temperamentally inhibited—high in social fearfulness (Coplan et al., 2004; Rubin, Burgess, & Hastings, 2002). And preschoolers who engage in solitary, repetitive behavior (banging blocks, making a doll jump up and down) tend to be immature, impulsive children who find it difficult to regulate anger and aggression (Coplan et al., 2001). In the classroom, both reticent and impulsive children are at risk for rejection by their peers.

But most preschoolers with low rates of peer interaction simply like to play alone, and their solitary activities are positive and constructive. Children who prefer solitary play with art materials, puzzles, and building toys are typically well-adjusted youngsters who, when they do play with peers, show socially skilled behavior (Rubin & Coplan, 1998). Still, a few preschoolers who engage in such age-appropriate solitary play (mostly boys) are rebuffed by peers. Perhaps because their behavior is inconsistent with the "masculine" gender role, boys who play quietly are at risk for negative reactions from both parents and peers and, eventually, for adjustment problems (Coplan et al., 2001, 2004).

■ **CULTURAL VARIATIONS.** Peer sociability in collectivist societies, which stress group harmony, differs from that in individualistic cultures. For example, children in India generally play in large groups that require high levels of cooperation. Much of their behavior is imitative, occurs in unison, and involves close physical contact. In a game called Bhatto Bhatto, children act out a script about a trip to the market, touching one another's elbows and hands as they pretend to cut and share a tasty vegetable (Roopnarine et al., 1994).

Furthermore, unlike North American preschoolers, who tend to reject reticent classmates, Chinese preschoolers are more willing to include a quiet, reserved child in play (Chen et al., 2006). In Chapter 6, we saw that until recently, collectivist values, which discourage self-assertion, led to a positive attitude toward shyness in China (see page 195). Apparently, this benevolent stance is still evident in the play behaviors of Chinese young children.

Village children in India, varying widely in age, play a "circle tapping" game to help one another learn that requires high levels of cooperation. The child in the center recites a poem, the alphabet, or numbers, then walks around the outside of the circle, saying, "Whomever I tap, whomever I tap, it will be their turn." The tapped child moves to the center to recite.

Cultural beliefs about the importance of play also affect early peer associations. Adults who view play as mere entertainment are less likely to provide props or to encourage pretend than those who value its cognitive and social benefits (Farver & Wimbarti, 1995). Preschoolers of Korean-American parents, who emphasize task persistence as vital for learning, spend less time than Caucasian-American children in joint make-believe and more time unoccupied and in parallel play (Farver, Kim, & Lee, 1995).

Recall the description of children's daily lives in village and tribal cultures, described on page 236 in Chapter 7. Mayan parents, for example, do not promote children's play—yet Mayan children are socially competent (Gaskins, 2000). Perhaps Western-style sociodramatic play, with its elaborate materials and wide-ranging themes, is particularly important for social development in societies where child and adult worlds are distinct. It may be less crucial when children participate in adult activities from an early age.

First Friendships

As preschoolers interact, first friendships form that serve as important contexts for emotional and social development. To adults, friendship is a mutual relationship involving companionship, sharing, understanding of thoughts and feelings, and caring for one another in times of need. In addition, mature friendships endure over time and survive occasional conflicts.

Preschoolers understand something about the uniqueness of friendship. They say that a friend is someone "who likes you" and with whom you spend a lot of time playing. Yet their ideas about friendship are far from mature. Four- to 7-year-olds regard friendship as pleasurable play and sharing of toys. As yet, friendship does not have a long-term, enduring quality based on mutual trust (Damon, 1988a; Hartup, 2006). Indeed, Sammy would declare, "Mark's my best friend," on days when the boys got along well. But when a dispute arose, he would reverse himself: "Mark, you're not my friend!"

Nevertheless, interactions between young friends are unique. Preschoolers give far more reinforcement—greetings, praise, and compliance—to children they identify as friends and also receive more from them. Friends are more emotionally expressive—talking, laughing, and looking at each other more often than nonfriends do (Hartup, 2006; Vaughn et al., 2001). Furthermore, children who begin kindergarten with friends in their class or readily make new friends adjust to school more favorably (Ladd, Birch, & Buhs, 1999; Ladd & Price, 1987). Perhaps the company of friends serves as a secure base from which to develop new relationships, enhancing children's feelings of comfort in the new classroom.

The ease with which kindergartners make new friends and are accepted by their classmates predicts cooperative participation in classroom activities and self-directed completion of learning tasks—behaviors linked to gains in achievement (Ladd, Birch, & Buhs, 1999; Ladd, Buhs, & Seid, 2000). The capacity to form friendships enables kindergartners to integrate themselves into classroom environments in ways that foster both academic and social competence. In a longitudinal follow-up of more than 900 4-year-olds, children of average intelligence but with above-average social skills fared better in academic achievement in first grade than children of equal mental ability who were socially below average (Konold & Pianta, 2005).

Because social maturity in early childhood contributes to later academic performance, a growing number of experts propose that kindergarten readiness be assessed in terms of not just academic skills but also social skills (Ladd, Herald, & Kochel, 2006; Thompson & Raikes, 2007). Preschool interventions, too, should attend to these vital social prerequisites.

Parental Influences on Early Peer Relations

Children first acquire skills for interacting with peers within the family. Parents influence children's peer sociability both *directly*, through attempts to influence children's peer relations, and *indirectly*, through their child-rearing practices and play behaviors (Ladd & Pettit, 2002; Rubin et al., 2005).

Parents influence preschoolers' peer interaction skills by offering advice, guidance, and examples of how to behave. These children receive a lesson in how to greet a friend by shaking hands.

DIRECT PARENTAL INFLUENCES. Preschoolers whose parents frequently arrange informal peer play activities tend to have larger peer networks and to be more socially skilled (Ladd, LeSieur, & Profilet, 1993). In providing play opportunities, parents show children how to initiate their own peer contacts. And parents' skillful suggestions for entering play groups and managing conflict are associated with preschoolers' social competence and peer acceptance (Mize & Pettit, 1997; Parke et al., 2004b).

INDIRECT PARENTAL INFLUENCES. Many parenting behaviors not directly aimed at promoting peer sociability nevertheless influence it. For example, secure attachments to parents are linked to more responsive, harmonious peer interaction, larger peer networks, and warmer, more supportive friendships during the preschool and school years (Laible, 2007; Lucas-Thompson & Clarke-Stewart, 2007; Wood, Emmerson, & Cowan, 2004). The sensitive, emotionally expressive communication that contributes to attachment security may be responsible.

Parent–child play is a particularly effective context for promoting peer-interaction. During play, parents interact with their child on a "level playing field," much as peers do. And perhaps because parents play more with children of their own sex, mothers' play is more strongly linked to daughters' competence, fathers' play to sons' competence (Lindsey & Mize, 2000; Pettit et al., 1998).

Some preschoolers already have great difficulty with peer relations. In Leslie's classroom, Robbie was one of them. Wherever he happened to be, comments like "Robbie ruined our block tower" and "Robbie hit me for no reason" could be heard. As we take up moral development in the next section, you will learn more about how parenting contributed to Robbie's peer problems.

ASK YOURSELF

>> REVIEW
Among children who spend much time playing alone, what factors distinguish those who are likely to have adjustment difficulties from those who are well-adjusted and socially skilled?

>> APPLY
Three-year-old Ben lives in the country, with no other preschoolers nearby. His parents wonder whether it is worth driving Ben into town once a week to participate in a peer play group. What advice would you give Ben's parents, and why?

>> CONNECT
How does emotional self-regulation affect the development of empathy and sympathy? Why are these emotional capacities vital for positive peer relations?

>> REFLECT
What did your parents do, directly and indirectly, that might have influenced your earliest peer relationships?

Foundations of Morality

Children's conversations and behavior provide many examples of their developing moral sense. By age 2, they use words to evaluate behavior as "good" or "bad" and react with distress to acts that are aggressive or that otherwise might do harm (Kochanska, Casey, & Fukumoto, 1995). And we have seen that children of this age share toys, help others, and cooperate in games—early indicators of considerate, responsible prosocial attitudes.

Adults everywhere take note of this budding capacity to distinguish right from wrong. Some cultures have special terms for it. The Utku Indians of Hudson Bay say the child develops *ihuma* (reason). The Fijians believe that *vakayalo* (sense) appears. In response, parents hold children more responsible for their behavior (Dunn, 2005). By the end of early childhood, children can state many moral rules: "Don't take someone's things without asking!" "Tell the truth!" In addition, they argue over matters of justice: "You sat there last time, so it's my turn." "It's not fair. He got more!"

All theories of moral development recognize that conscience begins to take shape in early childhood. And most agree that at first, the child's morality is *externally controlled* by adults. Gradually, it becomes regulated by *inner standards.* Truly moral individuals do not do the right thing just to conform to others' expectations. Rather, they have developed compassionate concerns and principles of good conduct, which they follow in many situations.

Each major theory emphasizes a different aspect of morality. Psychoanalytic theory stresses the *emotional side* of conscience development—in particular, identification and guilt as motivators of good conduct. Social learning theory focuses on how *moral behavior* is learned through reinforcement and modeling. Finally, the cognitive-developmental perspective emphasizes *thinking*—children's ability to reason about justice and fairness.

The Psychoanalytic Perspective

Recall that according to Freud, young children form a *superego,* or conscience, by *identifying* with the same-sex parent, whose moral standards they adopt. Children obey the superego to avoid *guilt,* a painful emotion that arises each time they are tempted to misbehave. Moral development, Freud believed, is largely complete by 5 to 6 years of age.

Today, most researchers disagree with Freud's view of conscience development. In his theory (see page 256), fear of punishment and loss of parental love motivate conscience formation and moral behavior (Tellings, 1999). Yet children whose parents frequently use threats, commands, or physical force tend to violate standards often and feel little guilt, whereas parental warmth and responsiveness predict greater guilt following transgressions (Kochanska et al., 2002, 2005, 2008). And if a parent withdraws love after misbehavior—for example, refuses to speak to or states a dislike for the child—children often respond with high levels of self-blame, thinking "I'm no good," or "Nobody loves me." Eventually, to protect themselves from overwhelming guilt, these children may deny the emotion and, as a result, also develop a weak conscience (Kochanska, 1991; Zahn-Waxler et al., 1990).

INDUCTIVE DISCIPLINE. In contrast, conscience formation is promoted by a type of discipline called **induction,** in which an adult helps the child notice feelings by pointing out the effects of the child's misbehavior on others. For example, a parent might say, "She's crying because you won't give back her doll" (Hoffman, 2000). When generally warm parents provide explanations that match the child's capacity to understand while firmly insisting that the child listen and comply, induction is effective as early as age 2. Preschoolers whose parents use it are more likely to refrain from wrongdoing, confess and repair damage after misdeeds, and display prosocial behavior (Kerr et al., 2004; Zahn-Waxler, Radke-Yarrow, & King, 1979).

The success of induction may lie in its power to motivate children's active commitment to moral standards. Induction gives children information about how to behave that they can use in future situations. By emphasizing the impact of the child's actions on others, it encourages empathy and sympathy (Krevans & Gibbs, 1996). And giving children reasons for changing their behavior encourages them to adopt moral standards because they make sense.

In contrast, discipline that relies too heavily on threats of punishment or withdrawal of love makes children so anxious and frightened that they cannot think clearly enough to figure out what they should do. As a result, these practices do not get children to internalize moral rules (Eisenberg, Fabes, & Spinrad, 2006).

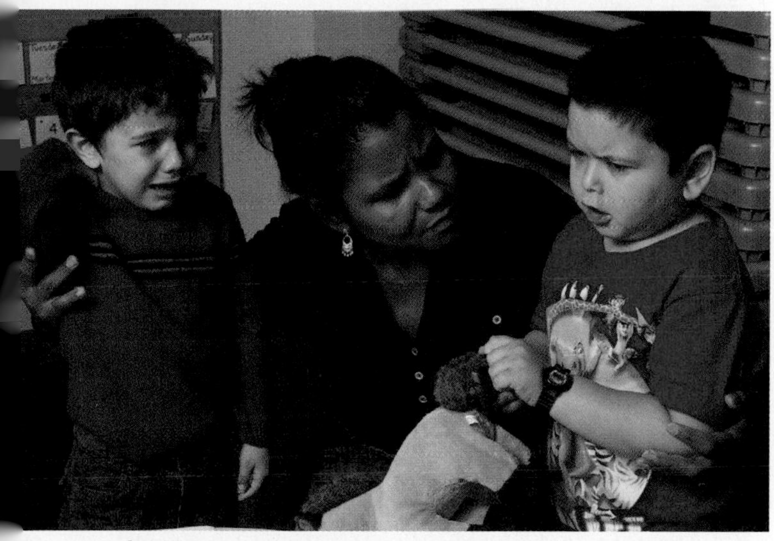

© LAURA DWIGHT PHOTOGRAPHY

This teacher uses inductive discipline to explain to a child the impact of his transgression on others. She indicates how the child should behave, encouraging empathy and sympathetic concern.

THE CHILD'S CONTRIBUTION. Although good discipline is crucial, children's characteristics also affect the success of parenting techniques. Twin studies suggest a modest genetic contribution to empathy (Knafo & Plomin, 2006; Zahn-Waxler et al., 2001). More empathic children require less power assertion and are more responsive to induction.

Temperament is also influential. Mild, patient tactics—requests, suggestions, and explanations—are sufficient to prompt guilt reactions in anxious, fearful preschoolers (Kochanska et al., 2002). But with fearless, impulsive children, gentle discipline has little impact. Power assertion also works poorly. It undermines the child's capacity for effortful control, which strongly predicts good conduct, empathy, sympathy, and prosocial behavior (Kochanska & Aksan, 2006; Kochanska & Knaack, 2003). Parents of impulsive children can foster conscience development by ensuring a secure attachment relationship and combining firm correction with induction (Kochanska, Aksan, & Joy, 2007). When children are so low in anxiety that parental disapproval causes them little discomfort, a close parent–child bond motivates them to listen to parents as a means of preserving an affectionate, supportive relationship.

THE ROLE OF GUILT. Although little support exists for Freudian ideas about conscience development, Freud was correct that guilt is an important motivator of moral action. Inducing *empathy-based guilt* (expressions of personal responsibility and regret, such as "I'm sorry I hurt him") by explaining that the child is harming someone and has disappointed the parent is a means of influencing children without using coercion. Empathy-based guilt reactions are associated with stopping harmful actions, repairing damage caused by misdeeds, and engaging in future prosocial behavior (Baumeister, 1998). At the same time, parents must help children deal with guilt feelings constructively—by guiding them to make up for immoral behavior rather than minimizing or excusing it.

But contrary to what Freud believed, guilt is not the only force that compels us to act morally. Nor is moral development complete by the end of early childhood. Rather, it is a gradual process, extending into adulthood.

Social Learning Theory

According to social learning theory, morality does not have a unique course of development. Rather, moral behavior is acquired just like any other set of responses: through reinforcement and modeling.

THE IMPORTANCE OF MODELING. Operant conditioning—reinforcement for good behavior, in the form of approval, affection, and other rewards—is not enough for children to acquire moral responses. To be reinforced, a behavior must first occur spontaneously. Yet many prosocial acts, such as sharing, helping, or comforting an unhappy playmate, occur so rarely at first that reinforcement cannot explain their rapid development in early childhood. Rather, social learning theorists believe that children learn to behave morally largely through *modeling*—observing and imitating people who demonstrate appropriate behavior (Bandura, 1977; Grusec, 1988). Once children acquire a moral response, such as sharing or telling the truth, reinforcement in the form of praise increases its frequency (Mills & Grusec, 1989).

Many studies show that having helpful or generous models increases young children's prosocial responses. And certain characteristics of models affect children's willingness to imitate:

- *Warmth and responsiveness.* Preschoolers are more likely to copy the prosocial actions of a warm, responsive adult than those of a cold, distant adult (Yarrow, Scott, & Waxler, 1973). Warmth seems to make children more attentive and receptive to the model and is itself an example of a prosocial response.
- *Competence and power.* Children admire and therefore tend to imitate competent, powerful models—especially older peers and adults (Bandura, 1977).
- *Consistency between assertions and behavior.* When models say one thing and do another—for example, announce that "it's important to help others" but rarely engage in helpful acts—children generally choose the most lenient standard of behavior that adults demonstrate (Mischel & Liebert, 1966).

Models are most influential in the early years. In one study, toddlers' eager, willing imitation of their mothers' behavior predicted moral conduct (not cheating in a game) and guilt following transgressions at age 3 (Forman, Aksan, & Kochanska, 2004). At the end of early childhood, children who have had consistent exposure to caring adults have internalized prosocial rules and follow them whether or not a model is present (Mussen & Eisenberg-Berg, 1977).

THE EFFECTS OF PUNISHMENT. Many parents know that yelling at, slapping, and spanking children for misbehavior are ineffective disciplinary tactics. A sharp reprimand or physical force to restrain or move a child is justified when immediate obedience is necessary—for example, when a 3-year-old is about to run into the street. In fact, parents are most likely to use forceful methods under these conditions. But to foster long-term goals, such as acting kindly toward others, they tend to rely on warmth and reasoning (Kuczynski, 1984). And in response to very serious transgressions, such as lying and stealing, they often combine power assertion with reasoning (Grusec, 2006; Grusec & Goodnow, 1994).

Frequent punishment, however, promotes only immediate compliance, not lasting changes in behavior. For example, Robbie's parents often hit, criticized, and shouted at him. But as soon as they were out of sight, Robbie usually engaged in the unacceptable behavior again. The more harsh threats, angry physical control, and physical punishment children experience, the more likely they are to develop serious, lasting mental health problems. These include weak internalization of moral rules; depression, aggression, antisocial behavior, and poor academic performance in childhood and adolescence; and depression, alcohol abuse, criminality, and partner and child abuse in adulthood (Afifi et al., 2006; Bender et al., 2007; Gershoff, 2002a; Kochanska, Aksan, & Nichols, 2003; Lynch et al., 2006).

Parents with conflict-ridden marriages and with mental health problems (who are depressed or aggressive) are more likely to be punitive and also to have hard-to-manage children, whose disobedience evokes more parental harshness (Erath et al., 2006; Knafo & Plomin, 2006). These parent–child similarities suggest that heredity contributes to the link between punitive discipline and children's adjustment difficulties. But heredity is not a complete explanation. Return to page 74 in Chapter 2 to review findings indicating that good parenting can shield children who are genetically at risk for aggression and antisocial activity from developing those behaviors. Furthermore, parental harshness and corporal punishment predict emotional and behavior problems in children of diverse temperaments (Mulvaney & Mebert, 2007). Negative outcomes are simply more pronounced among temperamentally difficult children.

In view of these findings, the widespread use of corporal punishment by American parents is cause for concern. A survey of a nationally representative sample of U.S. households revealed that although corporal punishment increases from infancy to age 5 and then declines, it is high at all ages (see Figure 8.1) (Straus & Stewart, 1999). Repeated use of physical punishment is more common with toddlers and preschoolers. And more than one-fourth of physically punishing parents report having used a hard object, such as a brush or a belt (Gershoff, 2002b).

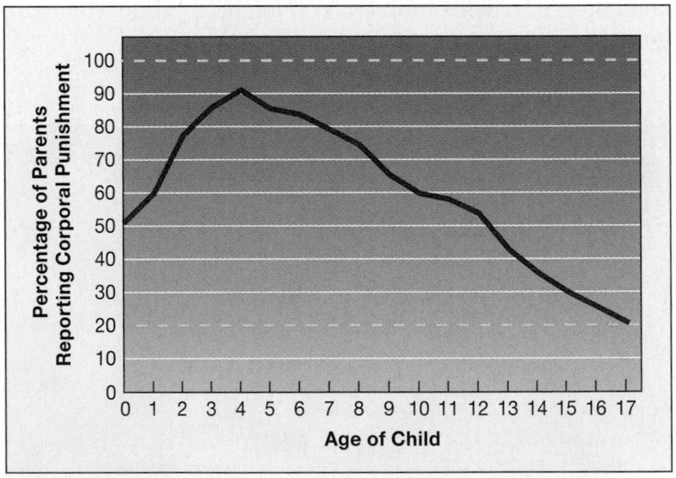

■ FIGURE 8.1 ■ Prevalence of corporal punishment by children's age. Estimates are based on the percentage of parents in a nationally representative U.S. sample of nearly 1,000 reporting one or more instances of spanking, slapping, pinching, shaking, or hitting with a hard object in the past year. Physical punishment increases sharply during early childhood and then declines, but it is high at all ages. (From M. A. Straus & J. H. Stewart, 1999, "Corporal Punishment by American Parents: National Data on Prevalence, Chronicity, Severity, and Duration, in Relation to Child and Family Characteristics," *Clinical Child and Family Psychology Review, 2,* p. 59. Adapted with kind permission from Springer Science and Business Media and Murray Straus.)

CULTURAL INFLUENCES

Ethnic Differences in the Consequences of Physical Punishment

In an African-American community, six elders, who had volunteered to serve as mentors for parents facing child-rearing challenges, met to discuss parenting issues at a social service agency. Their attitudes toward discipline were strikingly different from those of the white social workers who had brought them together. Each elder argued that successful child rearing required the use of appropriate physical tactics. At the same time, they voiced strong disapproval of screaming or cursing at children, calling such out-of-control parental behavior "abusive." Ruth, the oldest and most respected member of the group, characterized good parenting as a complex combination of warmth, teaching, talking nicely, and disciplining physically. She related how an older neighbor advised her to handle her own children when she was a young parent:

> She said to me says, don't scream . . . you talk to them real nice and sweet and when they do something ugly . . . she say you get a nice little switch and you won't have any trouble with them and from that day that's the way I raised 'em. (Mosby et al., 1999, pp. 511–512)

Use of physical punishment is highest among low SES ethnic minority parents, who are more likely than middle-SES white parents to advocate slaps and spankings (Pinderhughes et al., 2000; Straus & Stewart, 1999). And although corporal punishment is linked to a wide array of negative child outcomes, exceptions do exist.

In one longitudinal study, researchers followed several hundred families for 12 years, collecting information from mothers on disciplinary strategies in early and middle childhood and from both mothers and their children on youth problem behaviors in adolescence. Even after many child and family characteristics were controlled, the findings were striking: In Caucasian American families, physical punishment was positively associated with adolescent aggression and antisocial behavior. In African-American families, by contrast, the more mothers had disciplined physically in childhood, the less their teenagers displayed angry, acting-out behavior and got in trouble at school and with the police (Lansford et al., 2004).

African-American and Caucasian-American parents seem to mete out physical punishment differently. In black families, such discipline is typically culturally approved, mild, delivered in a context of parental warmth, and aimed at helping children become responsible adults. White parents, in contrast, typically consider physical punishment to be wrong, so when they resort to it, they are often highly agitated and rejecting of the child (Dodge, McLoyd, & Lansford, 2006). As a result, most black children may view spanking as a practice carried out with their best interests in mind, whereas white children may regard it as an "act of personal aggression" (Gunnoe & Mariner, 1997, p. 768).

In support of this view, when several thousand ethnically diverse children were followed from the preschool through the early school years, spanking was associated with a rise in behavior problems if parents were cold and rejecting, but not if they were warm and supportive (McLoyd & Smith, 2002). And in another study, spanking predicted depressive symptoms only among a minority of African-American children whose mothers disapproved of the practice and, as a result, tended to use it when they were highly angry and frustrated (McLoyd et al., 2007).

These findings are not an endorsement of physical punishment. Other forms of discipline, including time out, withdrawal of privileges, and the positive strategies listed on page 268, are far more effective. But it is noteworthy that the meaning and impact of physical discipline vary sharply with cultural context.

© JOSE LUIS PELAEZ INC./BLEND IMAGES/PHOTOLIBRARY

In African-American families, physical discipline is typically culturally approved, mild, and delivered in a context of parental warmth. As a result, African-American children may view spanking as a practice carried out with their best interests in mind, not as an act of aggression.

A prevailing North American belief is that corporal punishment, if implemented by caring parents, is harmless, perhaps even beneficial. But as the Cultural Influences box above reveals, this assumption is valid only under conditions of limited use in certain social contexts.

Repeated harsh punishment has wide-ranging, undesirable side effects:

- Parents often spank in response to children's aggression (Holden, Coleman, & Schmidt, 1995). Yet the punishment itself models aggression!
- Harshly treated children develop a chronic sense of being personally threatened, which prompts a focus on their own distress rather than a sympathetic orientation to others' needs.
- Children who are frequently punished soon learn to avoid the punishing adult, who, as a result, has little opportunity to teach desirable behaviors.
- By stopping children's misbehavior temporarily, harsh punishment gives adults immediate relief. For this reason, a punitive adult is likely to punish with greater frequency over time, a course of action that can spiral into serious abuse.
- Adults whose parents used corporal punishment are more accepting of such discipline (Bower-Russa, Knutson, & Winebarger, 2001; Deater-Deckard et al., 2003). In this way, use of physical punishment may transfer to the next generation.

Applying What We Know

Using Positive Discipline

Strategy	Explanation
Use transgressions as opportunities to teach.	When a child engages in harmful or unsafe behavior, intervene firmly, and then use induction, which motivates children to make amends and behave prosocially.
Reduce opportunities for misbehavior.	On a long car trip, bring back-seat activities that relieve children's restlessness. At the supermarket, converse with children and let them help with shopping. As a result, children learn to occupy themselves constructively when options are limited.
Provide reasons for rules.	When children appreciate that rules are fair to all concerned, not arbitrary, they strive to follow the rules because these are reasonable and rational.
Arrange for children to participate in family routines and duties.	By joining with adults in preparing a meal, washing dishes, or raking leaves, children develop a sense of responsible participation in family and community life and acquire many practical skills.
When children are obstinate, try compromising and problem solving.	When a child refuses to obey, express understanding of the child's feelings ("I know it's not fun to clean up"), suggest a compromise ("You put those away, I'll take care of these"), and help the child think of ways to avoid the problem in the future. Responding firmly but kindly and respectfully increases the likelihood of willing cooperation.
Encourage mature behavior.	Express confidence in children's capacity to learn and appreciation for effort and cooperation, as in "You gave that your best!" "Thanks for helping!" Adult encouragement fosters pride and satisfaction in succeeding, thereby inspiring children to improve further.

ALTERNATIVES TO HARSH PUNISHMENT. Alternatives to criticism, slaps, and spankings can reduce the side effects of punishment. A technique called **time out** involves removing children from the immediate setting—for example, by sending them to their rooms—until they are ready to act appropriately. When a child is out of control, a few minutes in time out can be enough to change behavior while also giving angry parents a cooling-off period. Another approach is *withdrawal of privileges,* such as watching a favorite TV program. Like time out, removing privileges allows parents to avoid harsh techniques that can easily intensify into violence.

When parents decide to use punishment, they can increase its effectiveness in three ways:

- *Consistency.* Permitting children to act inappropriately on some occasions but scolding them on others confuses them, and the unacceptable act persists (Acker & O'Leary, 1996).
- *A warm parent–child relationship.* Children of involved, caring parents find the interruption in parental affection that accompanies punishment especially unpleasant. They want to regain parental warmth and approval as quickly as possible.
- *Explanations.* Providing reasons for mild punishment helps children relate the misdeed to expectations for future behavior. This approach leads to a far greater reduction in misbehavior than using punishment alone (Larzelere et al., 1996).

POSITIVE DISCIPLINE. The most effective forms of discipline encourage good conduct—by building a mutually respectful bond with the child, letting the child know ahead of time how to act, and praising mature behavior (Zahn-Waxler & Robinson, 1995). When sensitivity, cooperation, and shared positive emotion are evident in joint activities between parents and preschoolers, children show firmer conscience development—expressing empathy after transgressions, playing fairly in games, and considering others' welfare (Kochanska et al., 2005, 2008). Parent–child closeness leads children to heed parental demands because the child feels a sense of commitment to the relationship.

Consult Applying What We Know above for ways to discipline positively. Parents who use these strategies focus on long-

Parents who engage in positive discipline encourage good conduct and reduce opportunities for misbehavior. By bringing along toys and joining in his make-believe, this mother helps her young child behave appropriately during a long wait at the airport.

term social and life skills—cooperation, problem solving, and consideration for others. As a result, they greatly reduce the need for punishment.

The Cognitive-Developmental Perspective

The psychoanalytic and behaviorist approaches to morality focus on how children acquire ready-made standards of good conduct from adults. In contrast, the cognitive-developmental perspective regards children as *active thinkers* about social rules. As early as the preschool years, children make moral judgments, deciding what is right or wrong on the basis of concepts they construct about justice and fairness (Gibbs, 2010; Turiel, 2006).

Young children have some well-developed ideas about morality. As long as researchers emphasize people's intentions, 3-year-olds say that a person with bad intentions—someone who deliberately frightens, embarrasses, or otherwise hurts another—is more deserving of punishment than a well-intentioned person (Helwig, Zelazo, & Wilson, 2001; Jones & Thompson, 2001). Around age 4, children know that a person who expresses an insincere intention—says, "I'll come over and help you rake leaves" but doesn't intend to do so—is lying (Maas, 2008). And 4-year-olds approve of telling the truth and disapprove of lying, even when a lie remains undetected (Bussey, 1992).

Furthermore, preschoolers distinguish **moral imperatives,** which protect people's rights and welfare, from two other types of rules and expectations: **social conventions,** customs determined solely by consensus, such as table manners and politeness rituals (saying "please," "thank you"); and **matters of personal choice,** such as choice of friends, hairstyle, and leisure activities, which do not violate rights and are up to the individual (Killen, Margie, & Sinno, 2006; Nucci, 1996; Smetana, 2006). Interviews with 3- and 4-year-olds reveal that they judge moral violations (stealing an apple) as more wrong than violations of social conventions (eating ice cream with your fingers). And preschoolers' concern with personal choice, conveyed through such statements as "I'm gonna wear *this* shirt," serves as the springboard for moral concepts of individual rights, which will expand greatly in middle childhood and adolescence (Nucci, 2005).

Within the moral domain, however, preschool and young school-age children tend to reason *rigidly,* making judgments based on salient features and consequences while neglecting other important information. For example, they are more likely than older children to claim that stealing and lying are always wrong, even when a person has a morally sound reason for engaging in these acts (Lourenco, 2003). They view inflicting physical damage (breaking a peer's toy) as a more serious transgression than treating others unfairly (not sharing) (Nucci, 2002). And their focus on outcomes means that they fail to realize that a promise is still a promise, even if it is unfulfilled (Maas, 2008; Maas & Abbeduto, 2001).

Still, preschoolers' ability to distinguish moral imperatives from social conventions is impressive. How do they do so? According to cognitive-developmental theorists, they *actively make sense* of their experiences (Turiel, 2006). They observe that after a moral offense, peers respond with strong negative emotion, describe their own injury or loss, tell another child to stop, or retaliate. And an adult who intervenes is likely to call attention to the rights and feelings of the victim. In contrast, violations of social convention elicit less intense peer reactions. And in these situations, adults usually demand obedience without explanation or point to the importance of keeping order.

Cognition and language support preschoolers' moral understanding, but social experiences are vital. Disputes with siblings and peers over rights, possessions, and property allow preschoolers to negotiate, compromise, and work out their first ideas about justice and fairness (Killen & Nucci, 1995). Children also learn by observing the way adults handle rule violations and discuss moral issues. Children who are advanced in moral thinking tend to have parents who adapt their communications about fighting, honesty, and ownership to what their children can understand, tell stories with moral implications, encourage prosocial behavior, and gently stimulate the child to think further, without being hostile or critical (Janssens & Deković, 1997; Walker & Taylor, 1991a).

Preschoolers who verbally and physically assault others, often with little or no provocation, are already delayed in moral reasoning (Helwig & Turiel, 2004; Sanderson & Siegal, 1988). Without special help, such children show long-term disruptions in moral development, deficits in self-control, and ultimately an antisocial lifestyle.

The Other Side of Morality: Development of Aggression

Beginning in late infancy, all children display aggression at times. As interactions with siblings and peers increase, so do aggressive outbursts (Dodge, Coie, & Lynam, 2006; Tremblay, 2004). By the second year, two general types of aggression emerge. Initially, the most common is **proactive** (or *instrumental*) **aggression,** in which children act to fulfill a need or desire—obtain an object, privilege, space, or social reward, such as adult or peer attention—and unemotionally attack a person to achieve their goal. The other type, **reactive** (or *hostile*) **aggression,** is an angry, defensive response to provocation or a blocked goal and is meant to hurt another person (Dodge, Coie, & Lynam, 2006; Little et al., 2003).

Proactive and reactive aggression come in three forms, which are the focus of the majority of research:

- **Physical aggression** harms others through physical injury—pushing, hitting, kicking, or punching others or destroying another's property.
- **Verbal aggression** harms others through threats of physical aggression, name-calling, or hostile teasing.
- **Relational aggression** damages another's peer relationships through social exclusion, malicious gossip, or friendship manipulation.

Although verbal aggression is always direct, physical and relational aggression can be either *direct* or *indirect.* For example, hitting injures a person directly, whereas destroying property indirectly inflicts physical harm. Similarly, saying, "Do what I say, or I won't be your friend," conveys relational aggression directly, while spreading rumors, refusing to talk to a peer, or manipulating friendships by saying behind someone's back, "Don't play with her; she's a nerd," does so indirectly.

In early childhood, verbal aggression gradually replaces physical aggression (Alink et al., 2006; Tremblay et al., 1999). And proactive aggression declines as preschoolers' improved capacity to delay gratification enables them to avoid grabbing others' possessions. But reactive aggression in verbal and relation forms tends to rise over early and middle childhood (Côté et al., 2007; Tremblay, 2000). Older children are better able to recognize malicious intentions and, as a result, more often respond in hostile ways.

By age 17 months, boys are more physically aggressive than girls—a difference found throughout childhood in many cultures (Baillargeon et al., 2007; Card et al., 2008). The sex difference is due in part to biology—in particular, to male sex hormones (androgens) and temperamental traits (activity level, irritability, impulsivity) on which boys score higher. Gender-role conformity is also important. As soon as preschoolers are aware of gender stereotypes—that males and females are expected to behave differently—physical aggression drops off more sharply in girls than in boys (Fagot & Leinbach, 1989). Parents also respond far more negatively to physical fighting in girls (Arnold, McWilliams, & Harvey-Arnold, 1998).

Although girls have a reputation for being both more verbally and relationally aggressive than boys, the sex difference is small (Crick et al., 2004, 2006; Crick, Ostrov, & Werner, 2006). Beginning in the preschool years, girls concentrate most of their aggressive acts in the relational category. Boys inflict harm in more variable ways: Physically and verbally aggressive boys also tend to be relationally aggressive (Card et al., 2008). Therefore, boys display overall rates of aggression that are much higher than girls'.

© LAURA DWIGHT PHOTOGRAPHY

As early as 17 months of age, boys are more physically aggressive than girls—a difference found throughout childhood in many cultures.

At the same time, girls more often use indirect relational tactics that—in disrupting intimate bonds especially important to girls—can be particularly mean. Whereas physical attacks are usually brief, acts of indirect relational aggression may extend for hours, weeks, or even months (Nelson, Robinson, & Hart, 2005; Underwood, 2003). In one instance, a 6-year-old girl formed a "pretty-girls club" and—for nearly an entire school year—convinced its members to exclude several classmates by saying they were "dirty and smelly."

An occasional aggressive exchange between preschoolers is normal. But children who are emotionally negative, impulsive, and disobedient are prone to early, high rates of physical or relational aggression (or both) that often persist, resulting in serious conduct problems in middle childhood and adolescence (Côté et al., 2007; Vaillancourt et al., 2003). These negative outcomes, however, depend on child-rearing conditions.

THE FAMILY AS TRAINING GROUND FOR AGGRESSIVE BEHAVIOR. "I can't control him, he's impossible," Robbie's mother, Nadine, complained to Leslie one day. When Leslie asked if Robbie might be troubled by something happening at home, she discovered that his parents fought constantly and resorted to harsh, inconsistent discipline. The same child-rearing practices that undermine moral internalization—love withdrawal, power assertion, physical punishment, and inconsistency—are linked to aggression from early childhood through adolescence, in children of both sexes and in many cultures, with most of these practices predicting both physical and relational forms (Bradford et al., 2003; Côté et al., 2007; Nelson et al., 2006a; Rubin et al., 2003; Yang et al., 2004).

In families like Robbie's, anger and punitiveness quickly create a conflict-ridden family atmosphere and an "out-of-control" child. The pattern begins with forceful discipline, which occurs more often with stressful life experiences, a parent with an unstable personality, or a difficult child (Dodge, Coie, & Lynam, 2006). Typically, the parent threatens, criticizes, and punishes, and the child whines, yells, and refuses until the parent "gives in." As these cycles become more frequent, they generate anxiety and irritability among other family members, who soon join in the hostile interactions. Compared with siblings in typical families, preschool siblings who have critical, punitive parents are more aggressive to one another. Destructive sibling conflict, in turn, quickly spreads to peer relationships, contributing to poor impulse control and antisocial behavior by the early school years (Garcia et al., 2000; Ostrov, Crick, & Stauffacher, 2006).

Boys are more likely than girls to be targets of harsh, inconsistent discipline because they are more active and impulsive and therefore harder to control. Children who are products of these family processes come to view the world from a violent perspective, seeing hostile intent where it does not exist (Lochman & Dodge, 1998; Orbio de Castro et al., 2002). As a result, they make many unprovoked attacks and soon conclude that aggression "works" to control others.

Highly aggressive children tend to be rejected by peers, to fail in school, and (by adolescence) to seek out deviant peer groups that lead them toward violent delinquency and adult criminality. We will consider this life-course path of antisocial activity in Chapter 12.

■ **VIOLENT MEDIA AND AGGRESSION.** In the United States, 57 percent of television programs between 6 A.M. and 11 P.M. contain violent scenes, often portraying repeated aggressive acts that go unpunished. TV victims of violence are rarely shown experiencing serious harm, and few programs condemn violence or depict other ways of solving problems. Violent content is 9 percent above average in children's programming, and cartoons are the most violent (Center for Communication and Social Policy, 1998).

Reviewers of thousands of studies have concluded that TV violence increases the likelihood of hostile thoughts and emotions and of verbally, physically, and relationally aggressive behavior (Comstock & Scharrer, 2006; Ostrov, Gentile, & Crick, 2006). And a growing number of studies show that playing violent video and computer games has similar effects (Anderson, 2004). Although young people of all ages are susceptible, preschool and young school-age children are especially likely to imitate TV violence because they believe much TV fiction is real and accept what they see uncritically.

Violent programming not only creates short-term difficulties in parent and peer relations but also has lasting negative consequences. In several longitudinal studies, time spent watching TV in childhood and adolescence predicted aggressive behavior in adulthood, after other factors linked to TV viewing (such as prior child and parent aggression, IQ, parent education, family income, and neighborhood crime) were controlled (see Figure 8.2) (Graber et al., 2006; Huesmann, 1986; Huesmann et al., 2003; Johnson et al., 2002). Aggressive children and adolescents have a greater appetite for violent TV and computer games. And boys devote more time to violent media than girls, in part because of male-oriented themes of conquest and adventure and use of males as lead characters. But even in nonaggressive children, violent TV sparks hostile thoughts and behavior; its impact is simply less intense (Bushman & Huesmann, 2001).

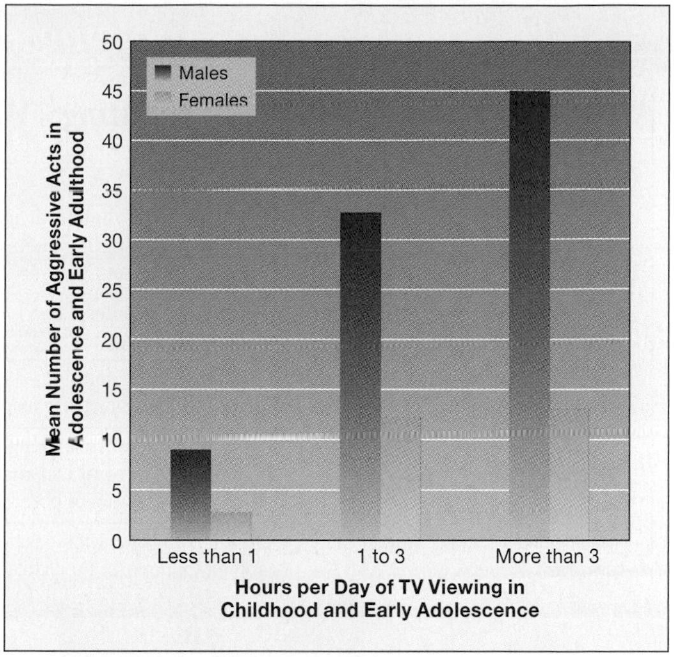

■ **FIGURE 8.2** ■ **Relationship of television viewing in childhood and early adolescence to aggressive acts in adolescence and early adulthood.** Interviews with more than 700 parents and youths revealed that the more TV watched in childhood and early adolescence, the greater the annual number of aggressive acts committed by the young person, as reported in follow-up interviews at ages 16 and 22. (Adapted from Johnson et al., 2002.)

TV violence increases the likelihood of hostile thoughts and emotions and tolerance of real-world aggression. And playing violent video and computer games has similar effects.

Furthermore, media violence "hardens" children to aggression. Viewers quickly habituate, responding with reduced arousal to real-world instances and tolerating more aggression in others (Anderson et al., 2003). Heavy viewers believe that there is much more violence in society than actually exists—an effect that is especially strong for children who perceive media violence to be relevant to their own lives (Donnerstein, Slaby, & Eron, 1994). As these responses indicate, exposure to violent media modifies children's attitudes toward social reality so they increasingly match media images.

The ease with which television and computer games can manipulate children's beliefs and behavior has led to strong public pressure to improve its content. In the United States, the First Amendment right to free speech has hampered efforts to regulate TV content. Instead, all programs must be rated for violent and sexual content, and all new TV sets are required to contain the V-chip, which allows parents to block undesired material. In contrast, Canada's nationwide broadcasting code bans from children's shows realistic scenes of violence that minimize

Applying What We Know

Regulating TV and Computer Use

Strategy	Description
Limit TV viewing and computer use.	Provide clear rules limiting what children can view on TV and do on the computer, and stick to them. Avoid using the TV or the computer as a babysitter for children. Do not place a TV or a computer in a child's bedroom; doing so substantially increases use and makes the child's activity hard to monitor.
Avoid using TV or computer time as a reward.	When TV or computer access is used to reward or withheld as a punishment, children become increasingly attracted to it.
When possible, watch TV with children.	When adults raise questions about realism in TV depictions, express disapproval of on-screen behavior, and encourage discussion, they help children understand and evaluate TV content.
Link TV content to everyday learning experiences.	Parents can extend TV learning in ways that encourage children to engage actively with their surroundings. For example, a program on animals might spark a trip to the zoo, a visit to the library for a book about animals, or new ways of observing and caring for the family pet.
Model good TV and computer practices.	Parents' media behavior—avoiding excessive TV and computer use and limiting exposure to harmful content—influences their children's media behavior.

consequences and cartoons with violence as the central theme. Further, violent programming intended for adults cannot be shown on Canadian channels before 9 P.M. (Canadian children, however, can access violent TV fare on U.S. channels.)

At present, parents bear most responsibility for regulating their children's exposure to media violence and other inappropriate content. Besides TV and computer games, the Internet poses risks. As with the V-chip for TV, parents can control children's Internet access by using filters or programs that monitor website visits. Yet surveys of U.S. parents indicate that 20 to 30 percent of preschoolers and 40 percent of school-age children experience no limits on TV or computer use at home. Some children begin accessing websites without parental supervision as early as age 4 (Rideout & Hamel, 2006; Roberts, Foehr, & Rideout, 2005; Varnhagen, 2007). Applying What We Know above lists strategies parents can use to protect their children from undesirable TV and computer fare.

■ **HELPING CHILDREN AND PARENTS CONTROL AGGRESSION.** Treatment for aggressive children is best begun early, before their antisocial behavior becomes well-practiced and difficult to change. Breaking the cycle of hostilities between family members and promoting effective ways of relating to others are crucial.

Leslie suggested that Robbie's parents see a family therapist, who observed their inept practices and coached them in alternatives. They learned not to give in to Robbie, to pair commands with reasons, and to replace verbal insults and harsh physical punishment with more effective strategies, such as time out and withdrawal of privileges. After several weeks of such training, children's aggression declines, and parents view their children more positively—benefits still evident one to four years later (Kazdin, 2003; Patterson & Fisher, 2002).

Leslie also began coaching Robbie in emotional competence (see page 258) and in how to interact successfully with peers. When opportunities arose, she encouraged Robbie to talk about a playmate's feelings and to express his own. As Robbie practiced taking the perspective of others and feeling sympathetic concern, his angry lashing out at peers declined (Izard et al., 2004). Robbie participated in social problem-solving training as well. Over several months, he met with Leslie and a small group of classmates to act out common conflicts using puppets, discuss alternatives for resolving disputes, and practice successful strategies. Children who receive such training show gains in social competence still present several months later (Shure & Aberson, 2005).

Finally, Robbie's parents sought counseling for their marital problems. When parents receive help in coping with stressors in their own lives, interventions aimed at reducing children's aggression are even more effective (Kazdin & Whitley, 2003).

ASK YOURSELF

» REVIEW
What experiences help children differentiate moral imperatives, social conventions, and matters of personal choice?

» APPLY
Alice and Wayne want their two children to become morally mature, caring individuals. List some parenting practices they should use and some they should avoid.

» CONNECT
What must parents do to foster conscience development in fearless, impulsive children? Does this remind you of the concept of goodness of fit (see page 194 in Chapter 6)? Explain.

» REFLECT
Which types of punishment for a misbehaving preschooler do you endorse, and which types do you reject? Why?

Gender Typing

Gender typing refers to any association of objects, activities, roles, or traits with one sex or the other in ways that conform to cultural stereotypes (Liben & Bigler, 2002). In Leslie's classroom, girls spent more time in the housekeeping, art, and reading corners, while boys gathered more often in spaces devoted to blocks, woodworking, and active play. Already, the children had acquired many gender-linked beliefs and preferences and tended to play with peers of their own sex.

The same theories that provide accounts of morality have been used to explain children's gender typing: *social learning theory,* with its emphasis on modeling and reinforcement, and *cognitive-developmental theory,* with its focus on children as active thinkers about their social world. We will see that neither is adequate by itself. *Gender schema theory,* a third perspective that combines elements of both, has gained favor. In the following sections, we consider the early development of gender typing.

Gender-Stereotyped Beliefs and Behavior

Even before children can label their own sex consistently, they have begun to acquire common associations with gender—men as rough and sharp, women as soft and round. In one study, 18-month-olds linked such items as fir trees and hammers with males, although they had not yet learned comparable feminine associations (Eichstedt et al., 2002). Recall from Chapter 6 that around age 2, children use such words as *boy, girl, lady,* and *man* appropriately. As soon as gender categories are established, children sort out what they mean in terms of activities and behavior.

Preschoolers associate toys, articles of clothing, tools, household items, games, occupations, colors (blue and pink), and behaviors (physical and relational aggression) with one sex or the other (Giles & Heyman, 2005; Poulin-Dubois et al., 2002; Ruble, Martin, & Berenbaum, 2006). And their actions reflect their beliefs, not only in play preferences but in personality traits as well. As we have seen, boys tend to be more active, impulsive, assertive, and physically aggressive. Girls tend to be more fearful, dependent, emotionally sensitive, compliant, advanced in effortful control, and skilled at understanding self-conscious emotions and at inflicting indirect relational aggression (Bosacki & Moore, 2004; Else-Quest et al., 2006; Underwood, 2003).

During early childhood, children's gender-stereotyped beliefs strengthen—so much so that many children apply them as blanket rules rather than as flexible guidelines. When children were asked whether gender stereotypes could be violated, half or more of 3- and 4-year-olds answered "no" to clothing, hairstyle, and play with certain toys (such as Barbie dolls and GI Joes) (Blakemore, 2003). Furthermore, most 3- to 6-year-olds are firm about not wanting to be friends with a child who violates a gender stereotype (a boy who wears nail polish, a girl who plays with trucks) or to attend a school where such violations are allowed (Ruble et al., 2007).

The rigidity of preschoolers' gender stereotypes helps us understand some commonly observed everyday behaviors. When Leslie showed her class a picture of a Scottish bagpiper wearing a kilt, the children insisted, "Men don't wear skirts!" During free play, they often exclaimed that girls can't be police officers and boys don't take care of babies. These one-sided judgments are a joint product of gender stereotyping in the environment and young children's cognitive limitations (Trautner et al., 2005). Most preschoolers do not yet realize that characteristics *associated with* being male or female—activities, toys, occupations, hairstyle, and clothing—do not *determine* a person's sex.

Genetic Influences on Gender Typing

The sex differences just described appear in many cultures around the world (Munroe & Romney, 2006; Whiting & Edwards, 1988). Certain ones—male activity level and physical aggression, female emotional sensitivity, and preference for same-sex playmates—are widespread among mammalian species (de Waal, 1993, 2001). According to an evolutionary perspective, the adult life of our male ancestors was largely oriented toward competing for mates, that of our female ancestors toward rearing children. Therefore, males became genetically primed for dominance and females for intimacy, responsiveness, and cooperativeness. Evolutionary theorists claim that family and cultural forces can influence the intensity of biologically based sex differences. But experience cannot eradicate those aspects of gender typing that served adaptive functions in human history (Geary, 1999; Maccoby, 2002).

© LAURA DWIGHT PHOTOGRAPHY

Early in the preschool years, gender typing is well under way. Girls tend to play with girls and are drawn to toys and activities that emphasize nurturance, cooperation, and physical attractiveness.

Experiments with animals reveal that prenatally administered androgens increase active play and aggression and suppress maternal caregiving in both male and female mammals (Sato et al., 2004). Eleanor Maccoby (1998) argues that hormones also affect human play styles, leading to rough, noisy movements among boys and calm, gentle actions among girls. Then, as children interact with peers, they choose partners whose interests and behaviors are compatible with their own. Preschool girls increasingly seek out other girls and like to play in pairs because they share a preference for quieter activities involving cooperative roles. Boys come to prefer larger-group play with other boys, who share a desire to run, climb, play-fight, compete, and build up and knock down (Fabes, Martin, & Hanish, 2003). At age 4, children spend three times as much time with same-sex as with other-sex playmates. By age 6, this ratio has climbed to 11 to 1 (Martin & Fabes, 2001).

Even stronger support for the role of biology in human gender typing comes from research on girls exposed prenatally to high levels of androgens, due either to normal variation in hormone levels or to a genetic defect. In both instances, these girls showed more "masculine" behavior—a preference for trucks and blocks over dolls, for active over quiet play, and for boys as playmates—even when parents encouraged them to engage in gender-typical play (Cohen-Bendahan, van de Beek, & Berenbaum, 2005; Pasterski et al., 2005).

And additional evidence for the role of biology in gender typing comes from a case study of a boy who experienced serious sexual-identity and adjustment problems because his biological makeup and sex of rearing were at odds. Turn to the Lifespan Vista box on the following page to find out about David's development.

Environmental Influences on Gender Typing

In a study following almost 14,000 British children from ages 2½ to 8, gender-typed behavior rose steadily over early childhood, with the most gender-typed young preschoolers showing the sharpest increase (Golombok et al., 2008). A wealth of evidence reveals that environmental forces—at home, at school, and in the community—build on genetic influences to promote vigorous gender typing in early childhood.

■ PARENTS. Beginning at birth, parents have different expectations of sons than of daughters. Many parents prefer that their children play with "gender-appropriate" toys. And they tend to describe achievement, competition, and control of emotion as important for sons and warmth, "ladylike" behavior, and closely supervised activities as important for daughters (Brody, 1999; Turner & Gervai, 1995).

Actual parenting practices reflect these beliefs. Parents give their sons toys that stress action and competition (guns, cars, tools, footballs) and their daughters toys that emphasize nurturance, cooperation, and physical attractiveness (dolls, tea sets, jewelry) (Leaper, 1994; Leaper & Friedman, 2007). Parents also actively reinforce independence in boys and closeness and dependency in girls. For example, parents react more positively when a son plays with cars and trucks, demands attention, runs and climbs, or tries to take toys from others. When interacting with daughters, they more often direct play activities, provide help, encourage participation in household tasks, make supportive statements (approval, praise, and agreement), and refer to emotions (Clearfield & Nelson, 2006; Fagot & Hagan, 1991; Kuebli, Butler, & Fivush, 1995; Leaper et al., 1995). Gender-typed play contexts amplify these communication differences. For example, when playing housekeeping, mothers engage in high rates of supportive, emotion talk with girls (Leaper, 2000).

Furthermore, parents provide children with indirect cues about gender categories and stereotypes through the language they use. In one study, researchers observed mothers talking about picture books with their 2- to 6-year-olds (Gelman, Taylor, & Nguyen, 2004). Mothers often labeled gender, even when they did not have to do so ("That's a boy." "Is that a she?"). And they frequently expressed *generic utterances,* which referred to many, or nearly all, males or females as alike, ignoring exceptions: "Boys can be sailors." "Most girls don't like trucks." As Figure 8.3 shows, with age, both mothers and children produced more of these generic statements. At age 2, mothers introduced these sweeping generalizations nearly three times as often as children. By age 6, children were producing these generics more often than mothers, suggesting that children picked up many of these expressions from parental speech. And 4- to 6-year-olds frequently made stereotyped generic statements, which their mothers often affirmed (*Child:* "Only boys can drive trucks." *Mother:* "OK.").

Of the two sexes, boys are more gender-typed. Fathers, especially, are more insistent that boys conform to gender roles. They place more pressure to achieve on sons than on daughters

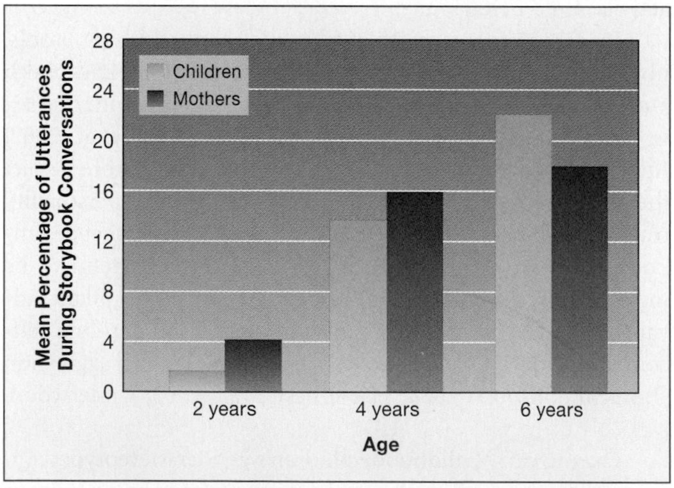

■ FIGURE 8.3 ■ Mothers' and children's use of generic reference to gender during storybook conversations. Mothers' and children's use of generics increased dramatically between ages 2 and 6. At age 2, mothers produced more generics than children. By age 6, children produced more generics than mothers. (From S. A. Gelman, M. G. Taylor, & S. P. Nguyen, "Mother–Child Conversations About Gender," *Monographs of the Society for Research in Child Development, 69*[1, Serial No. 275], p. 46. Reprinted by permission of Wiley-Blackwell Publishers.)

A LIFESPAN VISTA: Looking Forward, Looking Back

David: A Boy Who Was Reared as a Girl

As a married man and father in his mid-thirties, David Reimer talked freely about his everyday life: his problems at work and the challenges of child rearing. But when asked about his first 15 years, he distanced himself, speaking as if the child of his early life were another person. In essence, she was.

David—named Bruce at birth—underwent the first infant sex reassignment ever reported on a genetically and hormonally normal child. To find out about David's development, researchers interviewed him intensively and studied his medical and psychotherapy records (Colapinto, 2001; Diamond & Sigmundson, 1999).

When Bruce was 8 months old, his penis was accidentally severed during circumcision. Soon afterward, his desperate parents heard about psychologist John Money's success in assigning a sex to children born with ambiguous genitals. They traveled from their home in Canada to Johns Hopkins University in Baltimore, where, under Money's oversight, 22-month-old Bruce had surgery to remove his testicles and sculpt his genitals to look like those of a girl. The operation complete, Bruce's parents named their daughter Brenda.

Brenda's upbringing was tragic. From the outset, she resisted her parents' efforts to steer her in a "feminine" direction. A dominant, rough-and-tumble child, Brenda picked fights with other children and usually won. Brian (Brenda's identical twin brother) recalled that Brenda looked like a delicate, pretty girl—until she moved or spoke: "She walked like a guy. Sat with her legs apart. She talked about guy things. . . . She played with my toys: Tinkertoys, dump trucks" (Colapinto, 2001, p. 57).

At school, Brenda's boyish behavior led classmates to taunt and tease her. When she played with girls, she tried organizing large-group, active games, but they weren't interested. Friendless and uncomfortable as a girl, Brenda increasingly displayed behavior problems. During periodic medical follow-ups, she drew pictures of herself as a boy and refused additional surgery to create a vagina.

As adolescence approached, Brenda's parents moved her from school to school and from therapist to therapist in an effort to help her fit in socially and accept a female identity—pressures that only increased Brenda's anxiety and conflict with her parents. At puberty, when Brenda's shoulders broadened and her body added muscle, her parents insisted that she begin estrogen therapy to feminize her appearance. Soon she grew breasts and added fat around her waist and hips. Repelled by her feminizing shape, Brenda began overeating to hide it. Her classmates reacted to her confused appearance with stepped-up brutality.

COURTESY OF DAVID REIMER

Because of a medical accident when he was a baby, David Reimer underwent the first sex reassignment on a genetically and hormonally normal child: He was reared as a girl. David's case shows the overwhelming impact of biology on gender identity. At age 36, as shown here, he was a married man and father. But two years later, the troubled life that sprang from David's childhood ended tragically, in suicide.

At last, Brenda was transferred to a therapist who recognized her despair and encouraged her parents to tell her about her infancy. When Brenda was 14, her father explained the circumcision accident. David recalled reacting with relief. Deciding to return to his biological sex immediately, he chose for himself the name David, after the biblical lad who slew a giant and overcame adversity. David soon started injections of the androgen hormone testosterone to masculinize his body, and he underwent surgery to remove his breasts and to construct a penis. Although his adolescence continued to be troubled, in his twenties he fell in love with Jane, a single mother of three children, and married her.

David's case confirms the impact of genetic sex and prenatal hormones on a person's sense of self as male or female. His gender reassignment failed because his male biology overwhelmingly demanded a consistent sexual identity. At the same time, his childhood highlights the importance of experience. David expressed outrage at adult encouragement of dependency in girls—after all, he had experienced it firsthand.

Although David tried to surmount his tragic childhood, the troubled life that sprang from it persisted. When David was in his mid-thirties, his twin brother, Brian, committed suicide. Then, after David had lost his job and had been swindled out of his life savings in a shady investment deal, his wife left him, taking the children with her. Grief-stricken, David sank into a deep depression. On May 4, 2004, at age 38, he shot himself.

---

and are less tolerant of "cross-gender" behavior in sons—more concerned when a boy acts like a "sissy" than when a girl acts like a "tomboy" (Sandnabba & Ahlberg, 1999; Wood, Desmarais, & Gugula, 2002). Parents who hold nonstereotyped values and consciously avoid behaving in these ways have children who are less gender-typed (Tenenbaum & Leaper, 2002; Weisner & Wilson-Mitchell, 1990).

TEACHERS. Teachers often act in ways that extend gender-role learning. Several times, Leslie caught herself emphasizing gender distinctions when she called out, "Will the girls line up on one side and the boys on the other?" or pleaded, "Boys, I wish you'd quiet down like the girls!"

Like parents, preschool teachers give girls more encouragement to participate in adult-structured activities. Girls frequently cluster around the teacher, following directions, while boys are attracted to areas of the classroom where teachers are minimally involved (Campbell, Shirley, & Candy, 2004; Powlishta, Serbin, & Moller, 1993). As a result, boys and girls engage in different social behaviors. Compliance and bids for help occur more often in adult-structured contexts; assertiveness, leadership, and creative use of materials in unstructured pursuits.

© ALTRENDO IMAGES/GETTY IMAGES

Gender-typed behavior rises steadily over early childhood, due to a mix of genetic and environmental forces. On the environmental side, fathers, especially, are more insistent that boys conform to gender roles. This father shows his son how to cut shavings of wood for kindling a campfire.

Teachers also use more disapproval and controlling discipline with boys. When girls misbehave, teachers tend to negotiate, coming up with a joint plan to improve behavior (Erden & Wolfgang, 2004). Teachers seem to expect boys to misbehave more often—a belief based partly on boys' actual behavior and partly on gender stereotypes.

■ **PEERS.** Children's same-sex peer associations make the peer context a potent source of gender-role learning. The more preschoolers play with same-sex partners, the more their behavior becomes gender-typed—in toy choices, activity level, aggression, and adult involvement (Martin & Fabes, 2001). By age 3, same-sex peers positively reinforce one another for gender-typed play by praising, imitating, or joining in. In contrast, when preschoolers engage in "cross-gender" activities—for example, when boys play with dolls or girls with cars and trucks—peers criticize them. Boys are especially intolerant of cross-gender play in other boys (Fagot, 1984). A boy who frequently crosses gender lines is likely to be ignored by other boys even when he does engage in "masculine" activities!

Children also develop different styles of social influence in gender-segregated peer groups. To get their way in large-group play, boys often rely on commands, threats, and physical force. Girls' preference for playing in pairs leads to greater concern with a partner's needs, evident in girls' use of polite requests, persuasion, and acceptance. Girls soon find that these tactics succeed with other girls but not with boys, who ignore their courteous overtures (Leaper, 1994; Leaper, Tenenbaum, & Shaffer, 1999). Boys' unresponsiveness gives girls another reason to stop interacting with them.

Over time, children come to believe in the "correctness" of gender-segregated play, which further strengthens gender segregation and gender-stereotyped activities (Martin et al., 1999). As boys and girls separate, *in-group favoritism*—more positive evaluations of members of one's own gender—becomes another factor that sustains the separate social worlds of boys and girls, resulting in "two distinct subcultures" of knowledge, beliefs, interests, and behaviors (Maccoby, 2002).

■ **THE BROADER SOCIAL ENVIRONMENT.** Finally, although children's everyday environments have changed to some degree, they continue to present many examples of gender-typed behavior—in occupations, leisure activities, media portrayals, and achievements of men and women. As we will see next, children soon come to view not just their social surroundings but also themselves through a "gender-biased lens"—a perspective that can seriously restrict their interests and learning opportunities.

Gender Identity

As adults, each of us has a **gender identity**—an image of oneself as relatively masculine or feminine in characteristics. By middle childhood, researchers can measure gender identity by asking children to rate themselves on personality traits. A child or adult with a "masculine" identity scores high on traditionally masculine items (such as *ambitious, competitive,* and *self-sufficient*) and low on traditionally feminine items (such as *affectionate, cheerful,* and *soft-spoken*). Someone with a "feminine" identity does the reverse. And a substantial minority (especially females) have a gender identity called **androgyny,** scoring high on both masculine and feminine personality characteristics.

Gender identity is a good predictor of psychological adjustment. "Masculine" and androgynous children and adults have higher self-esteem than "feminine" individuals, perhaps because many typically feminine traits are not highly valued by society (Boldizar, 1991; Bronstein, 2006; Harter, 2006). Also, androgynous individuals are more adaptable—able to show masculine independence or feminine sensitivity, depending on the situation (Huyck, 1996; Taylor & Hall, 1982). The existence of an androgynous identity demonstrates that children can acquire a mixture of positive qualities traditionally associated with each gender—an orientation that may best help them realize their potential.

■ **EMERGENCE OF GENDER IDENTITY.** How do children develop a gender identity? According to *social learning theory,* behavior comes before self-perceptions. Preschoolers first acquire gender-typed responses through modeling and reinforcement and only later organize these behaviors into gender-linked ideas about themselves. In contrast, *cognitive-developmental theory* maintains that self-perceptions come before behavior. Over the preschool years, children acquire a cognitive appreciation of the permanence of their sex. They develop **gender constancy**—a full understanding of the biologically based permanence of their gender, including the realization that sex remains the same even if clothing, hairstyle, and play activities change. Then children use this knowledge to guide their behavior (Kohlberg, 1966).

Children younger than age 6 who watch an adult dress a doll in "other-gender" clothing typically insist that the doll's sex has also changed (Chauhan, Shastri, & Mohite, 2005; Fagot, 1985). Attainment of gender constancy is strongly related to ability to pass Piagetian conservation and verbal appearance–reality tasks (see page 232 in Chapter 7) (De Lisi & Gallagher, 1991; Trautner, Gervai, & Nemeth, 2003). Indeed, gender constancy tasks can be considered a type of appearance–reality problem, in that children must distinguish what a person looks like from who he or she really is.

In many cultures, young children do not have access to basic biological knowledge about gender because they rarely see members of the other sex naked. But giving preschoolers information about genital differences does not result in gender constancy. Preschoolers who have such knowledge usually say changing a doll's clothing will not change its sex, but when asked to justify their responses, they do not refer to sex as an innate, unchanging quality of people (Szkrybalo & Ruble, 1999). This suggests that cognitive immaturity, not social experience, is responsible for preschoolers' difficulty grasping the permanence of sex.

Is cognitive-developmental theory correct that gender constancy is responsible for children's gender-typed behavior? Evidence for this assumption is weak. "Gender-appropriate" behavior appears so early in the preschool years that its initial appearance must result from modeling and reinforcement, as social learning theory suggests. Although outcomes are not entirely consistent, some evidence suggests that gender constancy actually contributes to the emergence of more flexible gender-role attitudes during the school years (Ruble et al., 2007). But overall, the impact of gender constancy on gender typing is not great. As research in the following section reveals, gender-role adoption is more powerfully affected by children's beliefs about how close the connection must be between their own gender and their behavior.

■ **GENDER SCHEMA THEORY.** **Gender schema theory** is an information-processing approach to gender typing that combines social learning and cognitive-developmental features. It explains how environmental pressures and children's cognitions work together to shape gender-role development (Martin & Halverson, 1987; Martin, Ruble, & Szkrybalo, 2002). At an early age, children pick up gender-typed preferences and behaviors from others. At the same time, they organize their experiences into *gender schemas,* or masculine and feminine categories, that they use to interpret their world. As soon as preschoolers can label their own sex, they select gender schemas consistent with it ("Only boys can be doctors" or "Cooking is a girl's job") and apply those categories to themselves. Their self-perceptions then become gender-typed and serve as additional schemas that children use to process information and guide their own behavior.

We have seen that individual differences exist in the extent to which children endorse gender-typed views. Figure 8.4 shows different cognitive pathways for children who often apply gender schemas to their experiences and those who rarely do (Liben & Bigler, 2002). Consider Billy, who encounters a doll. If Billy is a *gender-schematic child,* his *gender-salience filter* immediately makes gender highly relevant. Drawing on his prior learning, he asks himself, "Should boys play with dolls?" If he answers "yes" and the toy interests him, he will approach

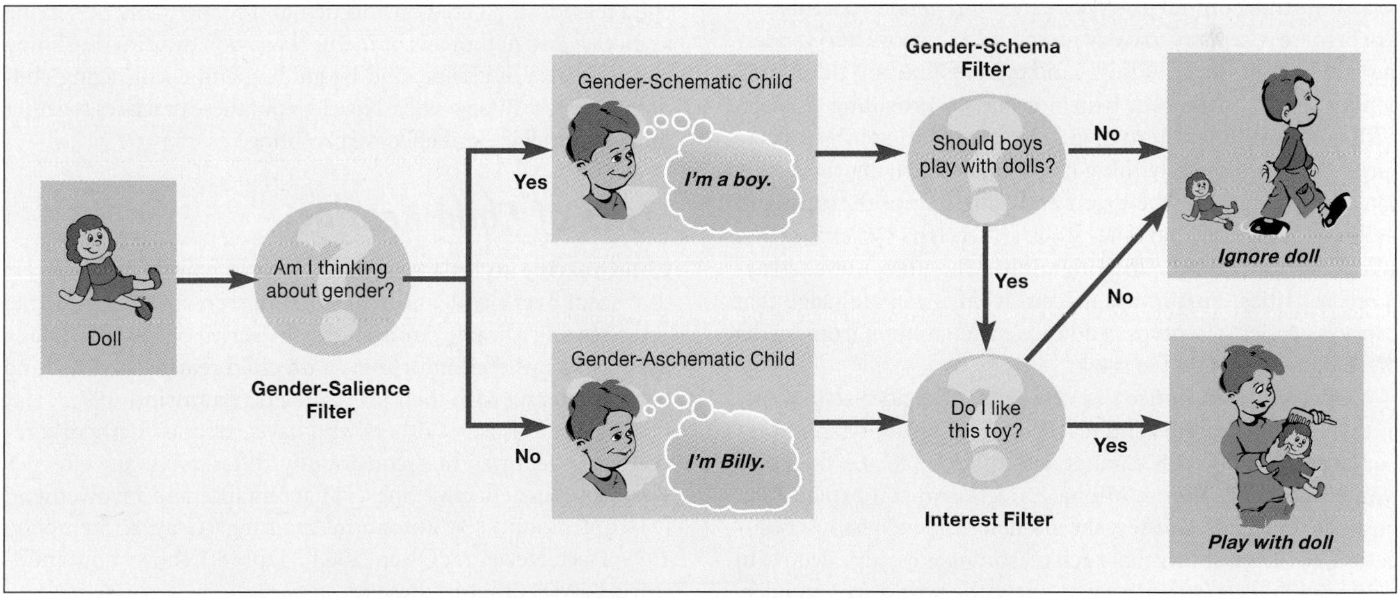

■ **FIGURE 8.4** ■ **Cognitive pathways for gender-schematic and gender-aschematic children.** In *gender-schematic children,* the gender-salience filter immediately makes gender highly relevant: Billy sees a doll and thinks, "I'm a boy. Should boys play with dolls?" Drawing on his experiences, he answers "yes" or "no." If he answers "yes" and the doll interests him, he plays with the doll. If he answers "no," he avoids the "gender-inappropriate" toy. *Gender-aschematic children* rarely view the world in gender-linked terms: Billy simply asks, "Do I like this toy?" and responds on the basis of his interests. (Reprinted by permission of Rebecca Bigler.)

it, explore it, and learn more about it. If he answers "no," he will respond by avoiding the "gender-inappropriate" toy. But if Billy is a *gender-aschematic child*—one who seldom views the world in gender-linked terms—he simply asks himself, "Do I like this toy?" and responds on the basis of his interests.

Gender schemas are powerful: When children see others behaving in "gender-inconsistent" ways, they often cannot remember the information or distort it to make it "gender-consistent." For example, when shown a picture of a male nurse, they may remember him as a doctor (Liben & Signorella, 1993; Martin & Ruble, 2004). And because gender-schematic preschoolers typically conclude, "What I like, children of my own sex will also like," they often use their own preferences to add to their gender biases! For example, a girl who dislikes oysters may conclude that only boys like oysters even though she has never actually been given information promoting such a stereotype (Liben & Bigler, 2002).

Reducing Gender Stereotyping in Young Children

How can we help young children avoid rigid gender schemas that restrict their behavior and learning opportunities? No easy recipe exists. Biology clearly affects children's gender typing, channeling boys toward active, competitive play and girls toward quieter, more intimate interaction. But most aspects of gender typing are not built into human nature (Maccoby, 2000). Furthermore, a long human childhood ensures that experiences can greatly influence biologically based sex differences (Ruble, Martin, & Berenbaum, 2006).

Because young children's cognitive limitations lead them to assume that cultural practices determine gender, parents and teachers are wise to try to delay preschoolers' exposure to gender-stereotyped messages. Adults can begin by limiting traditional gender roles in their own behavior and by providing children with nontraditional alternatives. For example, parents can take turns making dinner, bathing children, and driving the family car, and they can give their sons and daughters both trucks and dolls and both pink and blue clothing. Teachers can ensure that all children spend time in both adult-structured and unstructured activities. Finally, adults can avoid using language that conveys gender stereotypes and can shield children from media presentations that do the same.

Once children notice the vast array of gender stereotypes in their society, parents and teachers can point out exceptions. For example, they can arrange for children to see men and women pursuing nontraditional careers and can explain that interests and skills, not sex, should determine a person's occupation. Research shows that such reasoning is highly effective in reducing children's tendency to view the world in a gender-biased fashion. By middle childhood, children who hold flexible beliefs about what boys and girls can do are more likely to notice instances of gender discrimination (Bigler & Liben, 1992; Brown & Bigler, 2004). And, as we will see next, a rational approach to child rearing promotes healthy, adaptable functioning in many other areas as well.

ASK YOURSELF

» REVIEW
Explain how the social environment and young children's cognitive limitations contribute to rigid gender stereotyping in early childhood.

» APPLY
List findings indicating that language and communication—between parents and children, between teachers and children, and between peers—powerfully affect children's gender typing. What recommendations would you make to counteract these influences?

» CONNECT
What other cognitive changes are associated with gender constancy? What do these attainments have in common?

» REFLECT
Would you describe your own gender identity as "masculine," "feminine," or androgynous? What biological and social factors might have influenced your gender identity?

Child Rearing and Emotional and Social Development

In this and previous chapters, we have seen how parents can foster children's competence—by building a parent–child relationship based on affection and cooperation, by serving as models and reinforcers of mature behavior, by using reasoning and inductive discipline, and by guiding and encouraging children's mastery of new skills. Now let's put these practices together into an overall view of effective parenting.

Styles of Child Rearing

Child-rearing styles are combinations of parenting behaviors that occur over a wide range of situations, creating an enduring child-rearing climate. In a landmark series of studies, Diana Baumrind gathered information on child rearing by watching parents interact with their preschoolers (Baumrind, 1971). Her findings, and those of others who have extended her work, reveal three features that consistently differentiate an effective style from less effective ones: (1) acceptance and involvement, (2) control, and (3) autonomy granting (Gray & Steinberg, 1999; Hart, Newell, & Olsen, 2003). Table 8.2 shows how child-rearing styles differ in these features.

■ **AUTHORITATIVE CHILD REARING.** The **authoritative child-rearing style**—the most successful approach—involves high acceptance and involvement, adaptive control techniques,

■ TABLE 8.2 ■ *Features of Child-Rearing Styles*

CHILD-REARING STYLE	ACCEPTANCE AND INVOLVEMENT	CONTROL	AUTONOMY GRANTING
Authoritative	Is warm, responsive, attentive, patient, and sensitive to the child's needs	Makes reasonable demands for maturity and consistently enforces and explains them	Permits the child to make decisions in accord with readiness Encourages the child to express thoughts, feelings, and desires When parent and child disagree, engages in joint decision making when possible
Authoritarian	Is cold and rejecting and frequently degrades the child	Makes many demands coercively, using force and punishment Often uses psychological control, withdrawing love and intruding on the child's individuality	Makes decisions for the child Rarely listens to the child's point of view
Permissive	Is warm but overindulgent or inattentive	Makes few or no demands	Permits the child to make many decisions before the child is ready
Uninvolved	Is emotionally detached and withdrawn	Makes few or no demands	Is indifferent to the child's decision making and point of view

and appropriate autonomy granting. Authoritative parents are warm, attentive, and sensitive to their child's needs. They establish an enjoyable, emotionally fulfilling parent–child relationship that draws the child into close connection. At the same time, authoritative parents exercise firm, reasonable control. They insist on mature behavior, give reasons for their expectations, and use disciplinary encounters as "teaching moments" to promote the child's self-regulation. Finally, authoritative parents engage in gradual, appropriate autonomy granting, allowing the child to make decisions in areas where he is ready to do so (Kuczynski & Lollis, 2002; Russell, Mize, & Bissaker, 2004).

Throughout childhood and adolescence, authoritative parenting is linked to many aspects of competence—an upbeat mood, self-control, task persistence, cooperativeness, high self-esteem, social and moral maturity, and favorable school performance (Amato & Fowler, 2002; Aunola, Stattin, & Nurmi, 2000; Gonzalez & Wolters, 2006; Mackey, Arnold, & Pratt, 2001; Milevsky et al., 2007; Steinberg, Darling, & Fletcher, 1995).

■ **AUTHORITARIAN CHILD REARING.** The **authoritarian child-rearing style** is low in acceptance and involvement, high in coercive control, and low in autonomy granting. Authoritarian parents appear cold and rejecting. To exert control, they yell, command, criticize, and threaten. "Do it because I said so!" is their attitude. They make decisions for their child and expect the child to accept their word unquestioningly. If the child resists, authoritarian parents resort to force and punishment.

Children of authoritarian parents are anxious, unhappy, and low in self-esteem and self-reliance. When frustrated, they tend to react with hostility and, like their parents, resort to force when they do not get their way. Boys, especially, show high rates of anger and defiance. Although girls also engage in acting-out behavior, they are more likely to be dependent, lacking interest in exploration, and overwhelmed by challenging tasks (Hart, Newell, & Olsen, 2003; Nix et al., 1999; Thompson, Hollis, & Richards, 2003). Children and adolescents exposed to the authoritarian style typically do poorly in school, but because of their parents' concern with control, they tend to achieve better and to commit fewer antisocial acts than peers with undemanding parents—that is, whose parents use one of the type styles we will consider next (Steinberg, Blatt-Eisengart, & Cauffman, 2006).

In addition to unwarranted direct control, authoritarian parents engage in a more subtle type called **psychological control**—behaviors that intrude on and manipulate children's verbal expression, individuality, and attachments to parents. In an attempt to decide virtually everything for the child, these parents frequently interrupt or put down the child's ideas, decisions, and choice of friends. When they are dissatisfied, they withdraw love, making their affection or attention contingent on the child's compliance. They also hold excessively high expectations that do not fit the child's developing capacities. Children and adolescents subjected to psychological control exhibit adjustment problems involving both anxious, withdrawn and defiant, aggressive behaviors (Barber & Harmon, 2002; Silk et al., 2003).

■ **PERMISSIVE CHILD REARING.** The **permissive child-rearing style** is warm and accepting but uninvolved. Permissive parents are either overindulging or inattentive and, thus, engage in little control. Instead of gradually granting autonomy, they allow children to make many of their own decisions at an age when they are not yet capable of doing so. Their children can eat meals and go to bed whenever they wish and can watch as much television as they want. They do not have to learn good manners or do any household chores. Although some permissive parents truly believe in this approach, many others simply lack confidence in their ability to influence their child's behavior (Oyserman et al., 2005).

Children of permissive parents are impulsive, disobedient, and rebellious. Compared with children whose parents exert more control, they are also overly demanding and dependent on adults, and they show less persistence on tasks, poorer school achievement, and more antisocial behavior. The link between permissive parenting and dependent, nonachieving behavior is especially strong for boys (Barber & Olsen, 1997; Baumrind, 1971; Steinberg, Blatt-Eisengart, & Cauffman, 2006).

■ **UNINVOLVED CHILD REARING.** The **uninvolved child-rearing style** combines low acceptance and involvement with little control and general indifference to issues of autonomy. Often these parents are emotionally detached and depressed, so overwhelmed by life stress that they have little time and energy for children. At its extreme, uninvolved parenting is a form of child maltreatment called *neglect*. Especially when it begins early, it disrupts virtually all aspects of development (see Chapter 6, page 187). Even with less extreme parental disengagement, children and adolescents display many problems—poor emotional self-regulation, school achievement difficulties, and antisocial behavior (Aunola, Stattin, & Nurmi, 2000; Kurdek & Fine, 1994).

What Makes Authoritative Child Rearing Effective?

Like all correlational findings, the relationship between the authoritative style and children's competence is open to interpretation. Perhaps parents of well-adjusted children are authoritative because their youngsters have especially cooperative dispositions. But longitudinal research indicates that authoritative child rearing promotes maturity and adjustment in children of diverse temperaments (Hart, Newell, & Olson, 2003; Olson et al., 2000; Rubin, Burgess, & Coplan, 2002). It seems to create a positive emotional context for parental influence in the following ways:

- Warm, involved parents who are secure in the standards they hold for their children provide models of caring concern as well as confident, self-controlled behavior.
- Children are far more likely to comply with and internalize control that appears fair and reasonable, not arbitrary.
- By making demands and engaging in autonomy granting that matches children's ability to take responsibility for their own behavior, authoritative parents let children know that they are competent individuals who can do things successfully for themselves. In this way, parents foster favorable self-esteem and cognitive and social maturity.
- Supportive aspects of the authoritative style, including parental acceptance, involvement, and rational control, help protect children from the negative effects of family stress and poverty (Beyers et al., 2003).

Over time, the relationship between parenting and children's attributes becomes increasingly bidirectional (Kuczynski, 2003). When parents intervene patiently but firmly, they promote favorable adjustment, setting the stage for a positive parent–child relationship.

Cultural Variations

Although authoritative child rearing is broadly advantageous, ethnic groups often have distinct parenting beliefs and practices that reflect cultural values. Let's take some examples.

Compared with Western parents, Chinese parents describe their parenting as more controlling. They are more directive in teaching and scheduling their children's time, as a way of fostering self-control and high achievement. Chinese parents may appear less warm than Western parents because they withhold praise, which they believe results in self-satisfied, poorly motivated children (Chao, 1994; Chen et al., 2001). Chinese parents report expressing affection and using induction and other reasoning-oriented discipline as much as North American parents do, but they more often shame a misbehaving child (see page 257), withdraw love, and use physical punishment (Jose et al., 2000; Shwalb et al., 2004; Wu et al., 2002). When these practices become excessive, Chinese children display the same negative outcomes seen in Western children: anxiety, depression, and aggression (Nelson et al., 2005, 2006a, 2006b; Wang, Pomerantz, & Chen, 2007).

In Hispanic families, Asian Pacific Island families, and Caribbean families of African and East Indian origins, firm insistence on respect for parental authority is paired with high parental warmth—a combination suited to promoting competence and family loyalty (Harrison et al., 1994; Roopnarine & Evans, 2007). Hispanic fathers typically spend much time with their children and are warm and sensitive (Cabrera & Garcia-Coll, 2004; Jambunathan, Burts, & Pierce, 2000). In Caribbean

© GERI ENGBERG/THE IMAGE WORKS

This father encourages his daughter to help with recycling. By letting children know they are competent individuals, authoritative parents foster high self-esteem and social maturity.

families that have immigrated to the United States, fathers' authoritativeness—but not mothers—predicted preschoolers' literacy and math skills, probably because Caribbean fathers take a larger role in guiding their children's academic progress (Roopnarine et al., 2006).

Although wide variation exists, low-SES African-American parents tend to expect immediate obedience, regarding strictness as fostering self-control and a watchful attitude in risky surroundings. Consistent with these beliefs, African-American parents who use more controlling strategies tend to have more cognitively and socially competent children (Brody & Flor, 1998). Recall, also, that a history of physical punishment is associated with a reduction in antisocial behavior among African-American youths but with an increase among Caucasian Americans (see page 267). Most African-American parents who use strict, "no-nonsense" discipline use physical punishment sparingly and combine it with warmth and reasoning.

These cultural variations remind us that child-rearing styles must be viewed in their larger context. As we have seen, many factors contribute to good parenting: personal characteristics of the child and parent, SES, access to extended family and community supports, cultural values and practices, and public policies.

As we turn to the topic of child maltreatment, our discussion will underscore, once again, that effective child rearing is sustained not just by the desire of mothers and fathers to be good parents. Almost all want to be. Unfortunately, when vital supports for parenting break down, children—as well as parents—can suffer terribly.

Child Maltreatment

Child maltreatment is as old as human history, but only recently has the problem been widely acknowledged and research aimed at understanding it. Perhaps public concern has increased because child maltreatment is especially common in large industrialized nations. In the most recently reported year, 905,000 U.S. children (12 out of every 1,000) were identified as victims (U.S. Department of Health and Human Services, 2008e). Most cases go unreported, so the true figures are much higher.

Child maltreatment takes the following forms:

- *Physical abuse:* Assaults, such as kicking, biting, shaking, punching, or stabbing, that inflict physical injury
- *Sexual abuse:* Fondling, intercourse, exhibitionism, commercial exploitation through prostitution or production of pornography, and other forms of exploitation
- *Neglect:* Failure to meet a child's basic needs for food, clothing, medical attention, or supervision
- *Emotional abuse:* Acts that could cause serious mental or behavioral disorders, including social isolation, repeated unreasonable demands, ridicule, humiliation, intimidation, or terrorizing

Parents commit more than 80 percent of abusive incidents. Other relatives account for about 7 percent. The remainder are perpetrated by parents' unmarried partners, school officials, camp counselors, and other adults. Mothers engage in neglect more often than fathers, whereas fathers engage in sexual abuse more often than mothers. Maternal and paternal rates of physical and emotional abuse are fairly similar. Infants and young preschoolers are at greatest risk for neglect, preschool and school-age children for physical, emotional, and sexual abuse (Trocomé & Wolfe, 2002; U.S. Department of Health and Human Services, 2008e). Because most sexual abuse victims are identified in middle childhood, we will pay special attention to this form of maltreatment in Chapter 10.

ORIGINS OF CHILD MALTREATMENT. Early findings suggested that child maltreatment was rooted in adult psychological disturbance (Kempe et al., 1962). But although child maltreatment is more common among disturbed parents, no

Each year, fourth to sixth graders across Los Angeles County enter a poster contest to celebrate Child Abuse Prevention Month. This 2008 winner appeals to parents to treat children with warmth and caring. (Lisa Valicente and Madeline Zauss, 6th Grade, Jefferson Elementary School, Redondo Beach, CA. Courtesy ICAN Associates, Los Angeles County InterAgency Council on Child Abuse & Neglect, ican4kids.org.)

■ TABLE 8.3 ■ *Factors Related to Child Maltreatment*

FACTOR	DESCRIPTION
Parent characteristics	Psychological disturbance; alcohol and drug abuse; history of abuse as a child; belief in harsh, physical discipline; desire to satisfy unmet emotional needs through the child; unreasonable expectations for child behavior; young age (most under 30); low educational level
Child characteristics	Premature or very sick baby; difficult temperament; inattentiveness and overactivity; other developmental problems
Family characteristics	Low income; poverty; homelessness; marital instability; social isolation; physical abuse of mother by husband or boyfriend; frequent moves; large families with closely spaced children; overcrowded living conditions; disorganized household; lack of steady employment; other signs of high life stress
Community	Characterized by violence and social isolation; few parks, child-care centers, preschool programs, recreation centers, or religious institutions to serve as family supports
Culture	Approval of physical force and violence as ways to solve problems

Sources: Wekerle & Wolfe, 2003; Whipple, 2006.

single "abusive personality type" exists. Parents who were abused as children do not necessarily become abusers (Buchanan, 1996; Simons et al., 1991). And sometimes even "normal" parents harm their children!

For help in understanding child maltreatment, researchers turned to ecological systems theory (see Chapters 1 and 2). They discovered that many interacting variables—at the family, community, and cultural levels—contribute. The more risks present, the greater the likelihood of abuse or neglect (see Table 8.3 above).

The Family. Within the family, children whose characteristics make them more challenging to rear are more likely to become targets of abuse. These include premature or very sick babies and children who are temperamentally difficult, are inattentive and overactive, or have other developmental problems (Sidebotham et al., 2003). But whether such children actually are maltreated depends on parents' characteristics.

Maltreating parents are less skillful than other parents in handling discipline confrontations. They also suffer from biased thinking about their child. For example, they often attribute their baby's crying or their child's misdeeds to a stubborn or bad disposition, evaluate child transgressions as worse than they are, and feel powerless in parenting—perspectives that lead them to move quickly toward physical force (Bugental & Happaney, 2004; Crouch et al., 2008).

Once abuse begins, it quickly becomes part of a self-sustaining relationship. The small irritations to which abusive parents react—a fussy baby, a preschooler who knocks over her milk, a child who will not mind immediately—soon become bigger ones. Then the harshness increases. By the preschool years, abusive and neglectful parents seldom interact with their children. When they do, the communication is almost always negative (Wolfe, 2005).

Most parents have enough self-control not to respond with abuse to their child's misbehavior or developmental problems. Other factors combine with these conditions to prompt an extreme response. Abusive parents react to stressful situations with high emotional arousal. And low income, low education (less than a high school diploma), unemployment, young maternal age, alcohol and drug use, marital conflict, overcrowded living conditions, frequent moves, and extreme household disorganization are common in abusive homes (Wekerle & Wolfe, 2003; Wekerle et al., 2007). These conditions increase the chances that parents will be too overwhelmed to meet basic child-rearing responsibilities or will vent their frustrations by lashing out at their children.

The Community. The majority of abusive and neglectful parents are isolated from both formal and informal social supports. Because of their life histories, many have learned to mistrust and avoid others and are poorly skilled at establishing and maintaining positive relationships. Also, maltreating parents are more likely to live in unstable, rundown neighborhoods that provide few links between family and community, such as parks, child-care centers, preschool programs, recreation centers, and religious institutions (Coulton et al., 2007; Zielinski & Bradshaw, 2006). They lack "lifelines" to others and have no one to turn to for help during stressful times.

The Larger Culture. Cultural values, laws, and customs profoundly affect the chances that child maltreatment will occur when parents feel overburdened. Societies that view violence as an appropriate way to solve problems set the stage for child abuse.

Although the United States has laws to protect children from maltreatment, widespread support exists for use of physical force with children (refer back to page 266). Many countries—including Austria, Croatia, Cyprus, Denmark, Finland, Germany, Israel, Italy, Latvia, Norway, and Sweden—have outlawed physical punishment, a measure that dampens both physical discipline and abuse (Bugental & Grusec, 2006). Furthermore, every industrialized nation except the United States and Canada now prohibits corporal punishment in schools (Center for Effective Discipline,

2005). The U.S. Supreme Court has twice upheld the right of school officials to use corporal punishment. Fortunately, some U.S. states and Canadian provinces have passed laws that ban it.

CONSEQUENCES OF CHILD MALTREATMENT. The family circumstances of maltreated children impair the development of emotional self-regulation, empathy and sympathy, self-concept, social skills, and academic motivation. Over time, these youngsters show serious learning and adjustment problems, including academic failure, severe depression, aggressive behavior, peer difficulties, substance abuse, and delinquency, including violent crime (Cicchetti & Toth, 2006; Shonk & Cicchetti, 2001; Wolfe et al., 2001).

How do these damaging consequences occur? Think back to our earlier discussion of hostile cycles of parent–child interaction. For abused children, these are especially severe. Indeed, a family characteristic strongly associated with child abuse is partner abuse (Cox, Kotch, & Everson, 2003). Clearly, the home lives of abused children overflow with opportunities to learn to use aggression as a way of solving problems.

Furthermore, demeaning parental messages, in which children are ridiculed, humiliated, rejected, or terrorized, result in low self-esteem, high anxiety, self-blame, depression, and efforts to escape from extreme psychological pain—at times severe enough to lead to attempted suicide in adolescence (Wolfe, 2005). At school, maltreated children present serious discipline problems. Their noncompliance, poor motivation, and cognitive immaturity interfere with academic achievement, further undermining their chances for life success (Wekerle & Wolfe, 2003).

Finally, repeated abuse is associated with central nervous system damage, including abnormal EEG brain-wave activity, fMRI-detected reduced size and impaired functioning of the cerebral cortex and corpus callosum, and atypical production of the stress hormone cortisol—initially too high but, after months of abuse, often too low. Over time, the massive trauma of persistent abuse seems to blunt children's normal physiological response to stress (Cicchetti, 2007; Teicher et al., 2004; Watts-English et al., 2006). These effects increase the chances that cognitive and emotional problems will endure.

PREVENTING CHILD MALTREATMENT. Because child maltreatment is embedded in families, communities, and society as a whole, efforts to prevent it must be directed at each of these levels. Suggested approaches include teaching high-risk parents effective child-rearing strategies, providing direct experience with children in high school child development courses, and developing broad social programs aimed at improving economic conditions for low-SES families.

We have seen that providing social supports to families is effective in easing parental stress. This approach sharply reduces child maltreatment. A trusting relationship with another person is the most important factor in preventing mothers with childhood histories of abuse from repeating the cycle with their own children (Egeland, Jacobvitz, & Sroufe, 1988). Parents Anonymous, a U.S. organization with affiliate programs around the world, helps child-abusing parents learn constructive parenting practices, largely through social supports. Its local chapters offer self-help group meetings, daily phone calls, and regular home visits to relieve social isolation and teach child-rearing skills.

Early intervention aimed at strengthening both child and parent competencies can reduce child maltreatment substantially. Healthy Families America, a program that began in Hawaii and has spread to 440 sites across the United States and Canada, identifies at-risk families during pregnancy or at birth. Each receives three years of home visitation, in which a trained worker helps parents manage crises, encourages effective child rearing, and puts parents in touch with community services (PCA America, 2009). In an evaluation its effectiveness, Healthy Families home visitation alone reduced only neglect, not abuse (Duggan et al., 2004). But adding a *cognitive component* dramatically increased its impact. When home visitors helped parents change negative appraisals of their children—by countering inaccurate interpretations (for example, that the baby is behaving with malicious intent) and by working on solving child-rearing problems—physical punishment and abuse dropped sharply after one year of intervention (Bugental et al., 2002).

Even with intensive treatment, some adults persist in their abusive acts. An estimated 1,500 U.S. children, most of them infants and preschoolers, die from maltreatment each year (U.S. Department of Health and Human Services, 2008e). When parents are unlikely to change their behavior, the drastic step of separating parent from child and legally terminating parental rights is the only justifiable course of action.

Child maltreatment is a sad note on which to end our discussion of a period of childhood that is so full of excitement, awakening, and discovery. But there is reason to be optimistic. Great strides have been made over the past several decades in understanding and preventing child maltreatment.

ASK YOURSELF

» REVIEW
Summarize findings on ethnic variations in child-rearing styles. Is the concept of authoritative parenting useful for understanding effective parenting across cultures? Explain.

» APPLY
Chandra heard a news report about ten severely neglected children, living in squalor in an inner-city tenement. She wondered, "Why would parents mistreat their children?" How would you answer Chandra?

» CONNECT
Which child-rearing style is most likely to be associated with inductive discipline, and why?

» REFLECT
How would you classify your parents' child-rearing styles? What factors might have influenced their approach to parenting?

Summary

Erikson's Theory: Initiative versus Guilt

What personality changes take place during Erikson's stage of initiative versus guilt?

» Erikson's image of **initiative versus guilt** captures the emotional and social changes of early childhood. A healthy sense of initiative depends on exploring the social world through play, forming a conscience through identification with the same-sex parent, and receiving supportive child rearing.

Self-Understanding

Describe preschoolers' self-concepts and self-esteem.

» As preschoolers think more intently about themselves, they construct a **self-concept,** or set of beliefs about their own characteristics, that consists largely of observable characteristics and typical emotions and attitudes. Their increasing self-awareness underlies struggles over objects as well as first efforts to cooperate.

» During early childhood, high **self-esteem** contributes to a mastery-oriented approach to the environment. But even a little adult disapproval can undermine a young child's self-esteem and enthusiasm for learning.

© MYRLEEN FERGUSON CATE/PHOTOEDIT

Emotional Development

Cite changes in understanding and expression of emotion during early childhood, along with factors that influence those changes.

» Preschoolers have an impressive understanding of the causes, consequences, and behavioral signs of basic emotions, supported by secure attachment and conversations about feelings. By age 3 to 4, children are aware of various strategies for emotional self-regulation. Temperament and parental modeling influence preschoolers' capacity to handle negative emotion.

» As their self-concepts develop, preschoolers experience self-conscious emotions more often. Parental messages affect the intensity of these emotions and the situations in which they occur. Empathy also becomes more common. Temperament and parenting affect the extent to which empathy leads to **sympathy** and to **prosocial,** or **altruistic, behavior.**

Peer Relations

Describe peer sociability and friendship in early childhood, along with cultural and parental influences on early peer relations.

» During early childhood, peer interaction increases, as children move from **nonsocial activity** to **parallel play,** then to **associative** and **cooperative play.** But even as associative and cooperative play increase, both solitary and parallel play remain common.

» In collectivist societies, play occurs in large groups and is highly cooperative. Sociodramatic play seems especially important in societies where child and adult worlds are distinct.

» Preschoolers view friendship in concrete, activity-based terms. Parents affect peer sociability both directly, through attempts to influence their child's peer relations, and indirectly, through their child-rearing practices.

Foundations of Morality

What are the central features of psychoanalytic, social learning, and cognitive-developmental approaches to moral development?

» Psychoanalytic and social learning approaches to morality focus on how children acquire ready-made standards held by adults. Contrary to the claims of Freud's psychoanalytic theory, discipline based on fear of punishment and loss of parental love does not foster conscience development. Instead, **induction** is far more effective in encouraging self-control and prosocial behavior.

» Social learning theory regards reinforcement and modeling as the basis for moral action. Adults who are warm, powerful, and practice what they preach provide effective models of morality. Alternatives such as **time out** and withdrawal of privileges can help parents avoid the undesirable side effects of harsh punishment. Punishment is more effective when parents are consistent, have a warm relationship with the child, and offer explanations.

© STOCK4B/GETTY IMAGES

» The cognitive-developmental perspective views children as active thinkers about social rules. Although preschoolers tend to reason rigidly about moral matters, by age 4 they can consider people's intentions in making moral judgments and can distinguish truthfulness from lying. Preschoolers also distinguish **moral imperatives** from **social conventions** and **matters of personal choice.**

Describe the development of aggression in early childhood, including family and television as major influences.

» Aggression first appears by the second year. During early childhood, **proactive aggression** declines, while **reactive aggression** increases. Proactive and reactive aggression come in at least three forms: **physical aggression, verbal aggression,** and **relational aggression.** Preschoolers gradually replace physical with verbal aggression. By the second year, boys are more physically aggressive than girls.

» Ineffective discipline and a conflict-ridden family atmosphere promote and sustain aggression in children. Media violence, both on TV and in computer games, also triggers childhood aggression. Teaching parents effective child-rearing practices, providing children with social problem-solving training, reducing family hostility, and shielding children from violent media can reduce aggressive behavior.

Gender Typing

Discuss genetic and environmental influences on preschoolers' gender-stereotyped beliefs and behavior.

» **Gender typing** is well under way in the preschool years. Prenatal male sex hormone (androgen) levels contribute to sex differences in play styles and, in turn, to preference for same-sex peers. But parents, teachers, peers, and the broader social environment also encourage many gender-typed responses.

© LAURA DWIGHT PHOTOGRAPHY

Describe and evaluate the accuracy of major theories that explain the emergence of gender identity.

» Although most people have a traditional **gender identity,** some exhibit **androgyny,** combining both masculine and feminine characteristics. Masculine and androgynous identities are linked to better psychological adjustment.

» According to social learning theory, preschoolers first acquire gender-typed responses through modeling and reinforcement and then organize them into gender-linked ideas about themselves. Cognitive-developmental theory suggests that **gender constancy** must precede gender-typed behavior, though evidence for this assumption is weak.

» **Gender schema theory** combines features of social learning and cognitive-developmental perspectives. As children acquire gender-stereotyped preferences and behaviors, they form masculine and feminine categories that they apply to themselves and use to interpret their world.

Child Rearing and Emotional and Social Development

Describe the impact of child-rearing styles on children's development, and note cultural variations in child rearing.

» Three features distinguish major **child-rearing styles:** (1) acceptance and involvement, (2) control, and (3) autonomy granting. In contrast to the **authoritarian, permissive,** and **uninvolved** styles, the **authoritative style** promotes cognitive, emotional, and social competence. Warmth, explanations, and reasonable demands for mature behavior account for the effectiveness of this style.

© GERI ENGBERG/THE IMAGE WORKS

» Certain ethnic groups, including Chinese, Hispanic, Asian Pacific Island, and African-American, combine parental warmth with high levels of control. But when control becomes harsh and excessive, it impairs academic and social competence.

Discuss the multiple origins of child maltreatment, its consequences for development, and effective prevention.

» Maltreating parents use ineffective discipline, hold a negatively biased view of their child, and feel powerless in parenting. Unmanageable parental stress and social isolation greatly increase the chances of abuse and neglect. Societal approval of physical force as a means of solving problems promotes child abuse.

» Maltreated children are impaired in emotional self-regulation, empathy and sympathy, self-concept, social skills, and academic motivation. The trauma of repeated abuse is associated with central nervous system damage and serious adjustment problems. Successful prevention requires efforts at the family, community, and societal levels.

Important Terms and Concepts

androgyny (p. 276)
associative play (p. 261)
authoritarian child-rearing style (p. 279)
authoritative child-rearing style (p. 278)
child-rearing styles (p. 278)
cooperative play (p. 261)
gender constancy (p. 276)
gender identity (p. 276)
gender schema theory (p. 277)
gender typing (p. 273)
induction (p. 265)
initiative versus guilt (p. 256)
matters of personal choice (p. 269)
moral imperatives (p. 269)
nonsocial activity (p. 261)
parallel play (p. 261)
permissive child-rearing style (p. 279)
physical aggression (p. 269)
proactive aggression (p. 269)
prosocial, or altruistic, behavior (p. 260)
psychological control (p. 279)
reactive aggression (p. 269)
relational aggression (p. 269)
self-concept (p. 256)
self-esteem (p. 258)
social conventions (p. 269)
sympathy (p. 260)
time out (p. 268)
uninvolved child-rearing style (p. 280)
verbal aggression (p. 269)

Milestones

Development in Early Childhood

2 years

PHYSICAL

- Throughout early childhood, height and weight increase more slowly than in toddlerhood. (216)
- Balance improves; walks more rhythmically; hurried walk changes to run. (224, 225)
- Jumps, hops, throws, and catches with rigid upper body. (224, 225)
- Puts on and removes simple items of clothing. (224, 225)
- Uses spoon effectively. (225)
- First drawings are gestural scribbles. (224)

COGNITIVE

- Make-believe becomes less dependent on realistic objects, less self-centered, and more complex. (228); sociodramatic play increases. (228)
- Understands the symbolic function of photos and pictures in books. (229)
- Takes the perspective of others in simplified, familiar situations and in face-to-face communication. (230–231)
- Recognition memory is well-developed. (238)
- Shows awareness of the distinction between inner mental and outer physical events. (239)
- Begins to count. (243)

LANGUAGE

- Vocabulary increases rapidly. (248)
- Uses a coalition of cues—perceptual and, increasingly, social and linguistic—to figure out word meanings. (249)
- Speaks in simple sentences that follow basic word order of native language. (249)
- Adds grammatical markers. (250)
- Displays effective conversational skills. (250)

EMOTIONAL/SOCIAL

- Understands causes, consequences, and behavioral signs of basic emotions. (258)
- Begins to develop self-concept and self-esteem. (256–258)
- Shows early signs of developing moral sense—verbal evaluations of own and others' actions and distress at harmful behaviors. (264)
- May display proactive (instrumental) aggression. (269)
- Gender-stereotyped beliefs and behavior increase. (273)

3–4 years

PHYSICAL

- Running, jumping, hopping, throwing, and catching become better coordinated. (225)

- Galloping and one-foot skipping appear. (225)
- Pedals and steers tricycle. (225)
- Uses scissors. (225)
- Fastens and unfastens large buttons. (225)
- Uses fork effectively. (225)
- Draws first picture of a person, using tadpole image. (225)

COGNITIVE

- Understands the symbolic function of drawings and of models of real-world spaces. (229)
- Grasps conservation, reasons about transformations, reverses thinking, and understands cause-and-effect relationships in familiar contexts. (231)
- Distinguishes appearance from reality. (232)
- Sorts familiar objects into hierarchically organized categories. (233)
- Uses private speech to guide behavior during challenging tasks. (234)
- Sustained attention and planning improve. (237–238)
- Uses scripts to recall familiar experiences. (238)
- Understands that both beliefs and desires determine behavior. (239)
- Knows meaning of numbers up to ten, counts correctly, grasps principle of cardinality. (243)

Note: Numbers in parentheses indicate the page or pages on which each milestone is discussed.

LANGUAGE

- Aware of some meaningful features of written language. (242)
- Coins new words based on known words; extends language meanings through metaphor. (248)
- Masters increasingly complex grammatical structures. (250)
- Occasionally overextends grammatical rules to exceptions. (250)
- Adjusts speech to fit the age, sex, and social status of listeners. (250)

EMOTIONAL/SOCIAL

- Describes self in terms of observable characteristics and typical emotions and attitudes. (256)
- Has several self-esteems, such as learning things in school, making friends, and getting along with parents. (258)
- Emotional self-regulation improves. (259)
- Experiences self-conscious emotions more often. (259)
- Relies more on language to express empathy. (260)
- Engages in associative and cooperative play with peers, in addition to parallel play. (261)
- Forms first friendships, based on pleasurable play and sharing of toys. (263)

- Distinguishes truthfulness from lying. (269)
- Distinguishes moral imperatives from social conventions and matters of personal choice. (269)
- Proactive aggression declines, while reactive aggression (verbal and relational) increases. (270)
- Preference for same-sex playmates strengthens. (274)

5–6 years

PHYSICAL

- Starts to lose primary teeth. (217)
- Increases running speed, gallops more smoothly, and engages in true skipping. (224, 225)
- Displays mature throwing and catching patterns. (225)

- Uses knife to cut soft foods. (225)
- Ties shoes. (224, 225)
- Draws more complex pictures. (225)
- Copies some numbers and simple words. (225)

COGNITIVE

- Magical beliefs decline. (231, 233)
- Ability to distinguish appearance from reality improves. (232)
- Attention and planning continue to improve. (237–238)
- Recognition, recall, scripted memory, and autobiographical memory improve. (238–239)
- Understanding of false belief strengthens. (239–240)

LANGUAGE

- Understands that letters and sounds are linked in systematic ways. (242)
- Uses invented spellings. (242)
- By age 6, vocabulary reaches about 10,000 words. (248)
- Uses most grammatical constructions competently. (250)

EMOTIONAL/SOCIAL

- Emotional understanding (ability to interpret, predict, and influence others' emotional reactions) improves. (258–259)
- Empathic responding increases. (260)
- Has acquired many morally relevant rules and behaviors. (265–266)
- Gender-stereotyped beliefs and behavior and preference for same-sex playmates continue to strengthen. (273–274)
- Understands gender constancy. (276)

Photo credits appear on p. ii.

On a bird-watching field trip, fourth-grade classmates collaborate to identify an unfamiliar species. An improved capacity to remember, reason, and reflect on one's own thinking makes middle childhood a time of dramatic advances in academic learning and problem solving.

CHAPTER 9

Physical and Cognitive Development in Middle Childhood

"I'm on my way, Mom!" hollered 10-year-old Joey as he stuffed the last bite of toast into his mouth, slung his book bag over his shoulder, dashed out the door, jumped on his bike, and headed down the street for school. Joey's 8-year-old sister Lizzie followed, kissing her mother good-bye and pedaling furiously until she caught up with Joey. Rena, the children's mother and one of my colleagues at the university, watched from the front porch as her son and daughter disappeared in the distance.

"They're branching out," Rena told me over lunch that day, as she described the children's expanding activities and relationships. Homework, household chores, soccer teams, music lessons, scouting, friends at school and in the neighborhood, and Joey's new paper route were all part of the children's routine. "It seems as if the basics are all there. I don't have to monitor Joey and Lizzie constantly anymore. Being a parent is still very challenging, but it's more a matter of refinements—helping them become independent, competent, and productive individuals."

Joey and Lizzie have entered middle childhood—the years from 6 to 11. Around the world, children of this age are assigned new responsibilities. For children in industrialized nations, middle childhood is often called the "school years" because its onset is marked by the start of formal schooling. In village and tribal cultures, the school may be a field or a jungle. But universally, children in this period are guided by mature members of society toward real-world tasks that increasingly resemble those they will perform as adults.

This chapter focuses on physical and cognitive development in middle childhood. By age 6, the brain has reached 90 percent of its adult weight, and the body continues to grow slowly. In this way, nature gives school-age children the mental powers to master challenging tasks as well as added time to acquire the knowledge and skills essential for life in a complex social world.

We begin by reviewing typical growth trends, gains in motor skills, and special health concerns. Then we return to Piaget's theory and the information-processing approach for an overview of cognitive changes during the school years. Next, we examine the genetic and environmental roots of IQ scores, which often enter into educational decisions. Our discussion continues with the further blossoming of language. Finally, we turn to the importance of schools in children's learning and development.

Physical Development

Body Growth

Physical growth during the school years continues at the slow, regular pace of early childhood. At age 6, the average North American child weighs about 45 pounds and is 3½ feet tall. Over the next few years, children add about 2 to 3 inches in height and 5 pounds in weight each year (see Figure 9.1). Between ages 6 and 8, girls are slightly shorter and lighter than boys. By age 9, this trend reverses as girls approach the dramatic adolescent growth spurt, which occurs two years earlier in girls than in boys.

Because the lower portion of the body is growing fastest, Joey and Lizzie appeared longer-legged than they had in early childhood. They grew out of their jeans more quickly than their jackets and frequently needed larger shoes. As in early childhood, girls have slightly more body fat and boys more muscle. After age 8, girls begin accumulating fat at a faster rate, and they will add even more during adolescence (Siervogel et al., 2000).

During middle childhood, the bones of the body lengthen and broaden. But ligaments are not yet firmly attached to bones, and this, combined with increasing muscle strength, gives children the unusual flexibility needed to perform cartwheels and handstands. As their bodies become stronger, many children experience a greater desire for physical exercise. Nighttime "growing pains"—stiffness and aches in the legs—are common as muscles adapt to an enlarging skeleton (Evans & Scutter, 2004).

Between ages 6 and 12, all 20 primary teeth are lost and replaced by permanent ones, with girls losing their teeth slightly earlier than boys. For a while, the permanent teeth seem much too large. Gradually, growth of facial bones, especially the jaw and chin, causes the child's face to lengthen and mouth to widen, accommodating the newly erupting teeth.

PHOTOS COURTESY OF PATRICIA SELFE

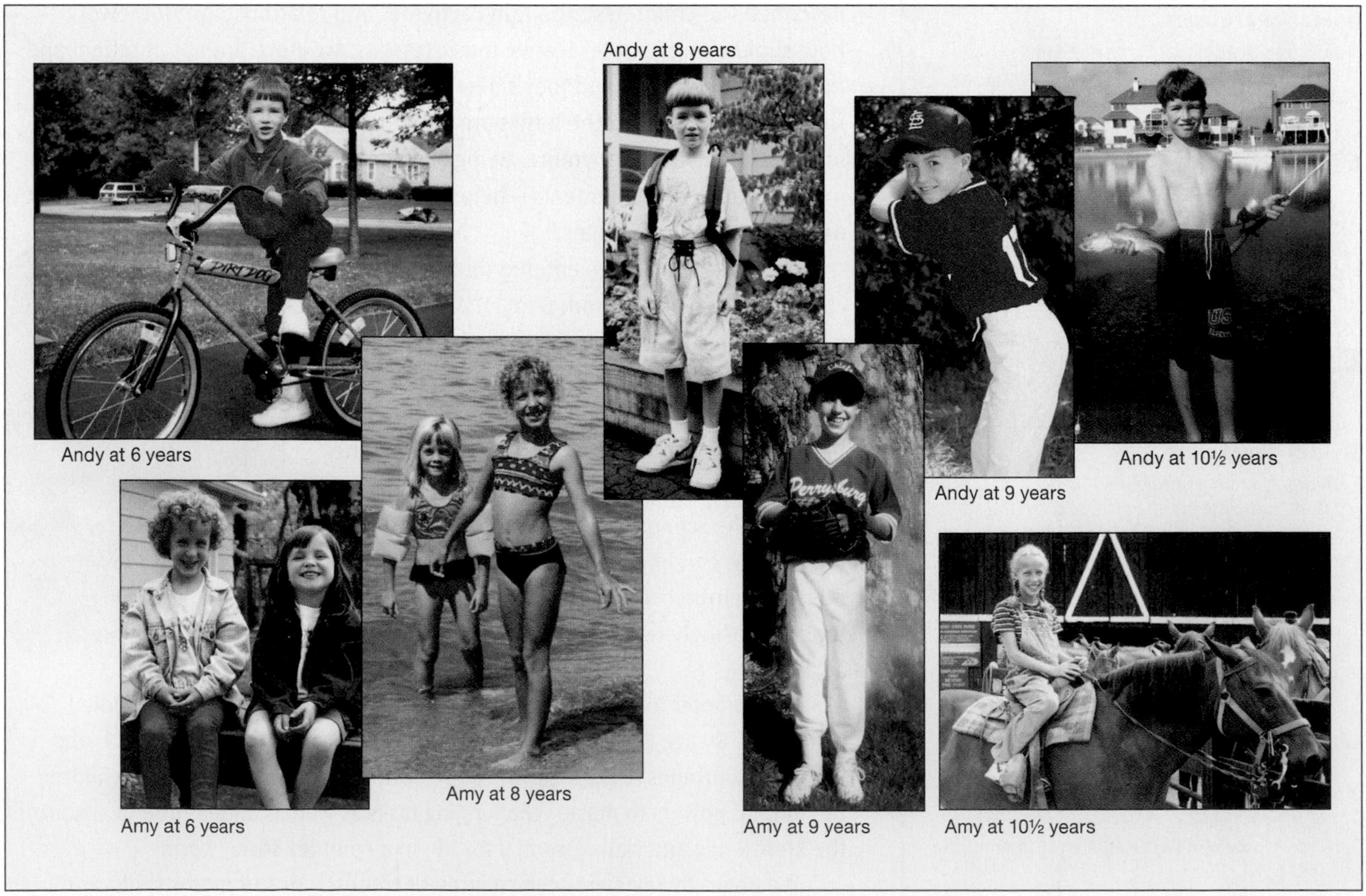

■ **FIGURE 9.1** ■ **Body growth during middle childhood.** School-age children continue the slow, regular pattern of growth they showed in early childhood. But around age 9, girls begin to grow at a faster rate than boys. At age 10½, Amy was taller, heavier, and more mature looking than Andy.

Common Health Problems

Children from economically advantaged homes, like Joey and Lizzie, are at their healthiest in middle childhood, full of energy and play. The cumulative effects of good nutrition, combined with rapid development of the body's immune system, offer greater protection against disease. At the same time, growth in lung size permits more air to be exchanged with each breath, so children are better able to exercise vigorously without tiring.

Not surprisingly, poverty continues to be a powerful predictor of ill health during the school years. Because economically disadvantaged U.S. families often lack health insurance (see Chapter 7), many children do not have regular access to a doctor. A substantial number also lack such basic necessities as a comfortable home and regular meals.

Vision and Hearing

The most common vision problem in middle childhood is *myopia,* or nearsightedness. By the end of the school years, it affects nearly 25 percent of children—a rate that rises to 60 percent by early adulthood. Heredity plays a role: Identical twins are more likely than fraternal twins to share the condition (Pacella et al., 1999). And worldwide, it occurs far more frequently in Asian than in Caucasian populations (Feldkámper & Schaeffel, 2003). Early biological trauma also can induce myopia. School-age children with low birth weights show an especially high rate, believed to result from immaturity of visual structures, slower eye growth, and a greater incidence of eye disease (O'Connor et al., 2002).

© LAURA DWIGHT PHOTOGRAPHY

Heredity contributes to myopia, or nearsightedness—the most common vision problem in middle childhood. Identical twins are more likely than fraternal twins to share the condition.

When parents warn their children not to read in dim light or sit too close to the TV or computer screen, their concern ("You'll ruin your eyes!") is well-founded. In diverse cultures, the more time children spend reading, writing, using the computer, and doing other close work, the more likely they are to be myopic (Mutti et al., 2002; Rose et al., 2008). Consequently, myopia is one of the few health conditions to increase with SES. Fortunately, it can be overcome easily with corrective lenses.

During middle childhood, the Eustachian tube (canal that runs from the inner ear to the throat) becomes longer, narrower, and more slanted, preventing fluid and bacteria from traveling so easily from the mouth to the ear. As a result, middle-ear infections, common in infancy and early childhood, become less frequent. Still, about 3 to 4 percent of the school-age population, and as many as 20 percent of low-SES children, develop permanent hearing loss as a result of repeated infections (Ryding et al., 2002). With regular screening for both vision and hearing, defects can be corrected before they lead to serious learning difficulties.

Nutrition

School-age children need a well-balanced, plentiful diet to provide energy for successful learning in school and increased physical activity. With their increasing focus on play, friendships, and new activities, many children spend little time at the table, and the percentage who eat dinner with their families drops sharply between ages 9 and 14. Family dinnertimes have waned in general over the past two decades. Yet eating an evening meal with parents leads to a diet higher in fruits and vegetables and lower in fried foods and soft drinks (Fiese & Schwartz, 2008; Neumark-Sztainer et al., 2003).

School-age children say that they "feel better" and "focus better" after eating healthy foods and that they feel sluggish, "like a blob," after eating junk foods (O'Dea, 2003). Consistent with these informal reports, even mild nutritional deficits can affect cognitive functioning. Among school-age children from middle- to high-SES families, insufficient dietary iron and folate predicted slightly lower mental test performance (Arija et al., 2006).

As we saw in earlier chapters, many poverty-stricken children in developing countries and in North America suffer from serious and prolonged malnutrition. Unfortunately, malnutrition that persists from infancy or early childhood into the school years usually leads to permanent physical and mental damage (Grantham-McGregor, Walker, & Chang, 2000; Liu et al., 2003). Government-sponsored supplementary food programs from the early years through adolescence can prevent these effects. In studies carried out in Egypt, Kenya, and Mexico, quality of food (protein, vitamin, and mineral content) strongly predicted favorable cognitive development in middle childhood (Sigman, 1995; Watkins & Pollitt, 1998).

Obesity

Mona, a very heavy child in Lizzie's class, often watched from the sidelines during recess. When she did join in games, she was slow and clumsy, the target of unkind comments: "Move it, Tubs!" Most afternoons, she walked home from school alone while the other children gathered in groups, talking, laughing, and chasing. At home, Mona sought comfort in high-calorie snacks.

Mona suffers from **obesity,** a greater-than-20-percent increase over healthy weight, based on *body mass index (BMI)*—a ratio of weight to height associated with body fat. (A BMI above the 85th percentile for a child's age and sex is considered overweight, a BMI above the 95th percentile obese.) During the past several decades, a rise in overweight and obesity has occurred in many Western nations, with large increases in Canada, Finland, Greece, Great Britain, Ireland, New Zealand, and the United States. Today, 32 percent of U.S. children and adolescents are overweight, and 11 percent are obese (Ogden, Carroll, & Flegal, 2008; Shields, 2005).

Obesity rates are also increasing rapidly in developing countries, as urbanization shifts the population toward sedentary lifestyles and diets high in meats and refined foods (World Press Review, 2004; Wrotniak et al., 2004). In China, for example, where obesity was nearly nonexistent a generation ago, today 15 percent of children and adolescents are overweight, and 3 percent are obese—a fourfold increase over the past two decades, with boys affected more than girls (Wu, 2006). In addition to lifestyle changes, a prevailing belief in Chinese culture that excess body fat signifies prosperity and health—carried over from a half-century ago, when famine caused millions of deaths—has contributed to this alarming upsurge. High valuing of sons may induce Chinese parents to offer boys especially generous portions of energy-dense foods that were once scarce but now are widely available.

© JEFF GREENBERG/THE IMAGE WORKS

These children consume a snack of cheesy fries with joyous abandon. High-calorie, fatty foods are prominent in the family diets provided by overweight parents, leaving their children at high risk for excessive weight gain.

Overweight rises with age, from 24 percent among U.S. preschoolers to nearly 34 percent among teenagers (Ogden, Carroll, & Flegal, 2008). More than 80 percent of affected children become overweight adults. Besides serious emotional and social difficulties, obese children are at risk for lifelong health problems. Symptoms that begin to appear in the early school years—high blood pressure, high cholesterol levels, respiratory abnormalities, and insulin resistance—are powerful predictors of heart disease, circulatory difficulties, type 2 diabetes, gallbladder disease, sleep and digestive disorders, many forms of cancer, and early death (Krishnamoorthy, Hart, & Jelalian, 2006; World Cancer Research Fund, 2007). Furthermore, obesity has caused a dramatic rise in cases of diabetes in children, sometimes leading to early, severe complications, including stroke, kidney failure, and circulatory problems that heighten the risk of eventual blindness and leg amputation (Hannon, Rao, & Arslanian, 2005).

CAUSES OF OBESITY. Not all children are equally at risk for excessive weight gain. Overweight children tend to have overweight parents, and identical twins are more likely to share the disorder than fraternal twins. But heredity accounts only for a *tendency* to gain weight (Salbe et al., 2002). The importance of environment is seen in the consistent relationship of low SES to obesity in industrialized nations, especially among ethnic minorities, including African-American, Hispanic, and Native-American children and adults (Anand et al., 2001; Ogden et al., 2006). Factors responsible include lack of knowledge about healthy diet; a tendency to buy high-fat, low-cost foods; and family stress, which can prompt overeating. Recall, also, that children who were malnourished in their early years are at increased risk for becoming overweight later (see page 132 in Chapter 4).

Parental feeding practices also play a role. Some parents anxiously overfeed, interpreting almost all their child's discomforts as a desire for food. Others are overly controlling, restricting when, what, and how much their child eats and constantly worrying about weight gain (Moens, Braet, & Soetens, 2007). Both types of parents fail to help children learn to regulate their own energy intake. Also, parents of overweight children often use high-fat, sugary foods to reinforce other behaviors—a practice that leads children to attach greater value to treats (Sherry et al., 2004).

Because of these experiences, obese children soon develop maladaptive eating habits. They are more responsive than normal-weight individuals to external stimuli associated with food—taste, sight, smell, time of day, and food-related words—and less responsive to internal hunger cues (Jansen et al., 2003; Temple et al., 2007). They also eat faster and chew their food less thoroughly, a behavior pattern that appears as early as 18 months of age (Drabman et al., 1979).

Another behavior pattern implicated in weight gain involves sleep. A follow-up of more than 2,000 U.S. 3- to 12-year-olds revealed that children who got less nightly sleep were more likely to be overweight five years later (Snell, Adam, & Duncan,

2007). Reduced sleep may increase time available for eating, leave children too fatigued for physical activity, or disrupt the brain's regulation of hunger and metabolism.

Overweight children are less physically active than their normal-weight peers. Inactivity is both cause and consequence of excessive weight gain. Research reveals that the rise in childhood obesity is due in part to the many hours U.S. children spend watching television. In a study that tracked children's TV viewing from ages 4 to 11, the more TV children watched, the more body fat they added: Children who devoted more than 3 hours per day to TV accumulated 40 percent more fat than those devoting less than 1¾; hours (see Figure 9.2) (Proctor et al., 2003). Watching TV reduces time spent in physical exercise, and TV ads encourage children to eat fattening, unhealthy snacks. Children permitted to have a TV in their bedroom—a practice linked to especially high TV viewing—are at even further risk for overweight (Adachi-Mejia et al., 2007).

Finally, the broader food environment affects the incidence of obesity. Compared with a half-century ago, new communities today are designed for automobile use, with fewer sidewalks and other walkways—a change that has contributed to reduced physical activity (Krishnamoorthy, Hart, & Jelalian, 2006). And over the past two to three decades, the number of families who frequently eat meals outside the home has risen dramatically. Eating in restaurants or at relatives', neighbors', or friends' homes, as opposed to at home, substantially increases children's overall food consumption, including high-calorie drinks and snacks, and risk of weight gain (Ayala et al., 2008; French, Story, & Jeffrey, 2001).

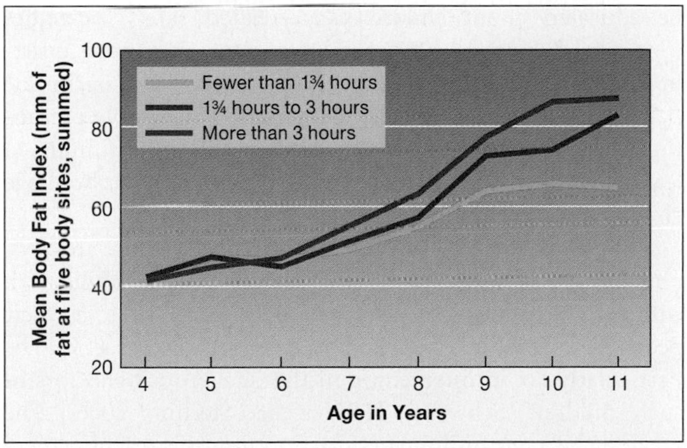

■ **FIGURE 9.2** ■ **Relationship of television viewing to gains in body fat from ages 4 to 11.** Researchers followed more than 100 children longitudinally, collecting information on hours per day of television viewing and on body fat, measured in millimeters of skinfold thickness at five body sites (upper arms, shoulders, abdomen, trunk, and thighs). The more TV children watched, the greater the gain in body fat. At ages 10 to 11, the difference between children watching fewer than 1¾ hours and those watching more than 3 hours had become large. (From M. H. Proctor et al., 2003, "Television Viewing and Change in Body Fat from Preschool to Early Adolescence: The Framingham Children's Study," *International Journal of Obesity, 27,* p. 831. © 2003 Nature Publishing Group. Adapted by permission of Macmillan Publishers, Ltd.)

■ **CONSEQUENCES OF OBESITY.** Unfortunately, physical attractiveness is a powerful predictor of social acceptance. In Western societies, both children and adults rate obese youngsters as less likable than other children, stereotyping them as lazy, sloppy, ugly, stupid, self-doubting, and deceitful (Kilpatrick & Sanders, 1978; Penny & Haddock, 2007; Tiggemann & Anesbury, 2000). By middle childhood, obese children are often socially isolated, and they report more emotional, social, and school difficulties and display more behavior problems than normal-weight agemates. Persistent obesity from childhood into adolescence predicts serious disorders, including defiance, aggression, and severe depression (Schwimmer, Burwinkle, & Varni, 2003; Young-Hyman et al., 2006). As we will see in Chapter 13, these psychological consequences combine with continuing discrimination to result in reduced life chances in close relationships and employment.

■ **TREATING OBESITY.** In Mona's case, the school nurse suggested that Mona and her obese mother enter a weight-loss program together. But Mona's mother, unhappily married for many years, had her own reasons for overeating and rejected this idea. In one study, only one-fourth of overweight parents judged their overweight children to have a weight problem (Jeffrey, 2004). Consistent with these findings, fewer than 20 percent of obese children get any treatment.

The most effective interventions are family-based and focus on changing behaviors (Kitzmann & Beech, 2006). In one program, both parent and child revised eating patterns, exercised daily, and reinforced each other with praise and points for progress, which they exchanged for special activities and times together. The more weight parents lost, the more their children lost (Wrotniak et al., 2004). Follow-ups after five and ten years showed that children maintained their weight loss more effectively than adults, a finding that underscores the importance of early intervention (Epstein, Roemmich, & Raynor, 2001). Treatment programs that focus on diet and lifestyle can yield substantial, long-lasting weight reduction among children and adolescents. But these interventions work best when parents' and children's weight problems are not severe (Eliakim et al., 2004; Nemet et al., 2005).

Children consume one-third of their daily caloric intake at school. Therefore, schools can also help reduce obesity by serving healthier meals, ensuring regular physical activity, and offering weight reduction programs.

Illnesses

Children experience a somewhat higher rate of illness during the first two years of elementary school than later because of exposure to sick children and an immune system that is still developing. About 15 to 20 percent of North American children have chronic diseases and conditions (including physical disabilities). By far the most common—accounting for about one-third of childhood chronic illness and the most frequent cause of school absence and childhood hospitalization—is *asthma,* in which the bronchial tubes (passages that connect the throat and lungs) are highly sensitive (Bonilla et al., 2005). In response to a variety of stimuli, such as cold weather, infection, exercise, allergies, and emotional stress, they fill with mucus and contract, leading to coughing, wheezing, and serious breathing difficulties.

During the past three decades, the number of children with asthma has more than doubled, and asthma-related deaths have also risen. Although heredity contributes to asthma, researchers believe that environmental factors are necessary to spark the illness. Boys, African-American children, and children who were born underweight, whose parents smoke, or who live in poverty are at greatest risk (Federico & Liu, 2003; Pearlman et al., 2006). For African-American and poverty-stricken youngsters, pollution in inner-city areas (which triggers allergic reactions), stressful home lives, and lack of access to good health care are implicated. Childhood obesity is also related to asthma in middle childhood, perhaps due to high levels of blood-circulating inflammatory substances associated with body fat (Saha, Riner, & Liu, 2005).

About 2 percent of North American youngsters have more severe chronic illnesses, such as sickle cell anemia, cystic fibrosis, diabetes, arthritis, cancer, and AIDS. Painful medical treatments, physical discomfort, and changes in appearance often disrupt the sick child's daily life, making it difficult to concentrate in school and separating the child from peers. As the illness worsens, family stress increases (LeBlanc, Goldsmith, & Patel, 2003). For these reasons, chronically ill children are at risk for academic, emotional, and social difficulties.

A strong link between good family functioning and child well-being exists for chronically ill children, just as it does for physically healthy children (Drotar et al., 2006). Interventions that foster positive family relationships help parent and child cope with the disease and improve children's adjustment. These include health education, counseling, social support, and disease-specific summer camps, which teach children self-help skills and give parents time off from the demands of caring for a chronically ill youngster.

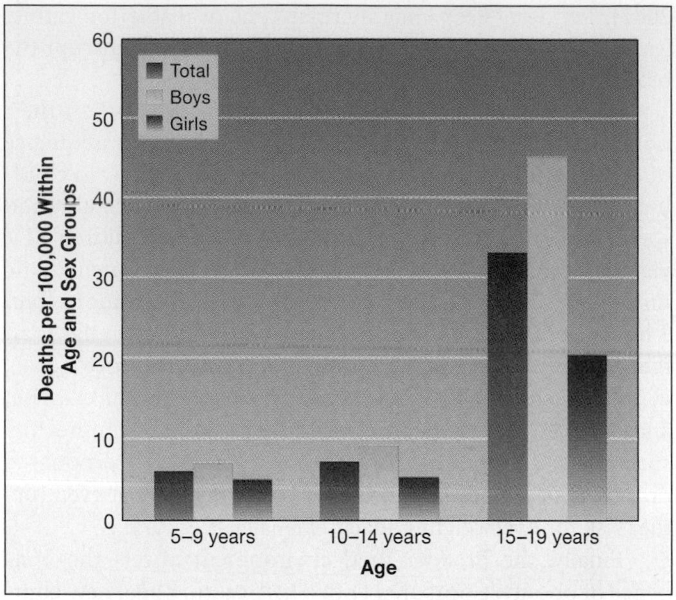

■ FIGURE 9.3 ■ U.S. rates of injury mortality from middle childhood to adolescence. Injury fatalities increase with age, and the gap between boys and girls expands. Motor vehicle (passenger and pedestrian) accidents are the leading cause, with bicycle injuries next in line. (From U.S. Department of Health and Human Services, 2008d.)

Unintentional Injuries

As we conclude our discussion of threats to school-age children's health, let's return to the topic of unintentional injuries (discussed in detail in Chapter 7). As Figure 9.3 shows, injury fatalities increase from middle childhood into adolescence, with rates for boys rising considerably above those for girls.

Motor vehicle accidents, involving children as passengers or pedestrians, continue to be the leading cause of injury, followed by bicycle accidents (U.S. Department of Health and Human Services, 2008d). Pedestrian injuries most often result from mid-block dart-outs, bicycle accidents from disobeying traffic signals and rules. When many stimuli impinge on them at once, young school-age children often fail to think before they act (Tuchfarber, Zins, & Jason, 1997). They need frequent reminders, supervision, and prohibitions against venturing into busy traffic on their own—especially as they begin to range farther from home.

Effective school-based intervention programs use extensive modeling and rehearsal of safety practices, give children feedback about their performance along with praise and tangible rewards for acquiring safety skills, and provide occasional booster sessions (Zins et al., 1994). Parents, who often overestimate their child's safety knowledge and physical abilities, must be educated about children's age-related safety capacities (Schwebel & Bounds, 2003). One vital safety measure is insisting that children wear protective helmets while bicycling, in-line skating, skateboarding, or using scooters. This simple precaution leads to an 85 percent reduction in risk of head injury, a leading cause of permanent disability and death in school-age children (Schieber & Sacks, 2001).

Highly active, impulsive children, many of whom are boys, remain especially susceptible to injury in middle childhood. Although they have just as much safety knowledge as their peers, they are far less likely to implement it. Parents tend to be particularly lax in intervening in the dangerous behaviors of such children (Schwebel, Hodgens, & Sterling, 2006). The greatest challenge for injury control programs is reaching these children and reducing their exposure to hazardous situations.

Motor Development and Play

TAKE A MOMENT... Visit a park on a pleasant weekend afternoon, and watch several preschool and school-age children at play. You will see that gains in body size and muscle strength support improved motor coordination in middle childhood. And greater cognitive and social maturity enables older children to use their new motor skills in more complex ways. A major change in children's play takes place at this time.

Gross-Motor Development

During the school years, running, jumping, hopping, and ball skills become more refined. Third to sixth graders burst into sprints as they race across the playground, jump quickly over rotating ropes, engage in intricate hopscotch patterns, kick and dribble soccer balls, bat at balls pitched by their classmates, and balance adeptly as they walk heel-to-toe across narrow ledges. These diverse skills reflect gains in four basic motor capacities:

- *Flexibility.* Compared with preschoolers, school-age children are physically more pliable and elastic, a difference that can be seen as they swing bats, kick balls, jump over hurdles, and execute tumbling routines.
- *Balance.* Improved balance supports many athletic skills, including running, hopping, skipping, throwing, kicking, and the rapid changes of direction required in many team sports.
- *Agility.* Quicker and more accurate movements are evident in the fancy footwork of dance and cheerleading and in the forward, backward, and sideways motions used to dodge opponents in tag and soccer.
- *Force.* Older youngsters can throw and kick a ball harder and propel themselves farther off the ground when running and jumping than they could at earlier ages (Haywood & Getchell, 2005).

© MICHAEL NEWMAN/PHOTOEDIT

A fancy twist of the rope following each revolution complicates this game of jump rope. During the school years, improved physical flexibility, balance, agility, and force combine with more efficient information processing to promote gains in many gross motor skills.

Along with body growth, more efficient information processing plays a vital role in improved motor performance. During middle childhood, the capacity to react only to relevant information increases. And steady gains in reaction time occur, with 11-year-olds responding twice as quickly as 5-year-olds (Band et al., 2000; Kail, 2003). Because 6- and 7-year-olds are seldom successful at batting a thrown ball, T-ball is more appropriate than baseball at this age. Likewise, handball, four-square, and kickball should precede instruction in tennis, basketball, and football.

Fine-Motor Development

Fine-motor development also improves over the school years. On rainy afternoons, Joey and Lizzie experimented with yo-yos, built model airplanes, and wove potholders on small looms. Like many children, they took up musical instruments, which demand considerable fine-motor control.

By age 6, most children can print the alphabet, their first and last names, and the numbers from 1 to 10 with reasonable clarity. Their writing is large, however, because they make strokes with the entire arm rather than just the wrist and fingers. Children usually master uppercase letters first because their horizontal and vertical motions are easier to control than the small curves of the lowercase alphabet. Legibility of writing gradually increases as children produce more accurate letters with uniform height and spacing. These improvements prepare children for mastering cursive writing by third grade.

Children's drawings show dramatic gains in middle childhood. By the end of the preschool years, children can accurately copy many two-dimensional shapes, and they integrate these into their drawings. Some depth cues have also begun to appear, such as making distant objects smaller than near ones (Braine et al., 1993). Around 9 to 10 years, the third dimension is clearly evident through overlapping objects, diagonal placement, and converging lines. Furthermore, as Figure 9.4 on page 296 shows, school-age children not only depict objects in considerable detail but also relate them to one another as part of an organized whole (Case, 1998; Case & Okamoto, 1996).

Sex Differences

Sex differences in motor skills that appeared during the preschool years extend into middle childhood and, in some instances, become more pronounced. Girls have an edge in fine-motor skills of handwriting and drawing and in gross-motor capacities that depend on balance and agility, such as hopping and skipping. But

■ **FIGURE 9.4** ■ **Increase in organization, detail, and depth cues in school-age children's drawings.** ***TAKE A MOMENT...*** Compare both drawings to the one by a 6-year-old on page 225. In the drawing on the left, an 8-year-old represents her family at the dinner table. Notice how all parts are depicted in relation to one another, and with greater detail. Integration of depth cues increases dramatically over the school years, as shown in the drawing on the right, by a 10-year-old artist from Singapore. Here, depth is indicated by overlapping objects, diagonal placement, and converging lines, as well as by making distant objects smaller than near ones.

boys outperform girls on all other gross-motor skills and, in throwing and kicking, the gender gap is large (Cratty, 1986; Haywood & Getchell, 2005).

School-age boys' genetic advantage in muscle mass is not large enough to account for their gross-motor superiority. Rather, the social environment plays a larger role. Research confirms that parents hold higher expectations for boys' athletic performance, and children readily absorb these messages. From first through twelfth grades, girls are less positive than boys about the value of sports and their own sports ability—differences explained in part by parental beliefs (Fredricks & Eccles, 2002). In one study, boys more often stated that it was vital to their parents that they participate in athletics. These attitudes affected children's self-confidence and behavior. Girls saw themselves as having less talent at sports and, by sixth grade, devoted less time than boys to athletics (Eccles & Harold, 1991). But girls and older school-age children regard boys' advantage in sports as unjust. They indicate, for example, that coaches should spend equal time with children of each sex and that female sports should command just as much media attention as male sports (Solomon & Bredemeier, 1999).

Educating parents about the minimal differences between school-age boys' and girls' physical capacities and sensitizing them to unfair biases against promotion of girls' athletic ability may help increase girls' self-confidence and participation in athletics. And greater emphasis on skill training for girls, along with increased attention to their athletic achievements, is also likely to help. As a positive sign, compared with a generation ago, many more girls now participate in individual and team sports such as gymnastics and soccer (National Council of Youth Sports, 2008). Middle childhood is a crucial time to encourage girls' sports participation because during this time, children start to discover what they are good at and make some definite skill commitments.

Games with Rules

The physical activities of school-age children reflect an important advance in the quality of their play: Games with rules become common. Children around the world engage in an enormous variety of informally organized games, including variants on popular sports such as soccer, baseball, and basketball. In addition to the best-known childhood games, such as tag, jacks, and hopscotch, children have also invented hundreds of other games, including red rover, statues, leapfrog, kick the can, and prisoner's base (Kirchner, 2000).

Gains in perspective taking—in particular, the ability to understand the roles of several players in a game—permit this transition to rule-oriented games. These play experiences, in turn, contribute greatly to emotional and social development. Child-invented games usually rely on simple physical skills and a sizable element of luck. As a result, they rarely become contests of individual ability. Instead, they permit children to try out different styles of cooperating, competing, winning, and losing with little personal risk. Also, in their efforts to organize a game, children discover why rules are necessary and which ones work well. As we will see in Chapter 10, these experiences help children construct more mature concepts of fairness and justice.

Partly because of parents' concerns about safety and because of the attractions of TV, video games, and the Internet,

Applying What We Know

Providing Developmentally Appropriate Organized Sports in Middle Childhood

Suggestion	Description
Build on children's interests.	Permit children to select from among appropriate activities the ones that suit them best. Do not push children into sports they do not enjoy.
Teach age-appropriate skills.	For children younger than age 9, emphasize basic skills, such as kicking, throwing, and batting, and simplified games that grant all participants adequate playing time.
Emphasize enjoyment.	Permit children to progress at their own pace and to play for the fun of it, whether or not they become expert athletes.
Limit the frequency and length of practices.	Adjust practice time to children's attention spans and need for unstructured time with peers, with family, and for homework. Two practices a week, each no longer than 30 minutes for younger school-age children and 60 minutes for older school-age children, are sufficient.
Focus on personal and team improvement.	Emphasize effort, skill gains, and teamwork rather than winning. Avoid criticism for errors and defeat, which promotes anxiety and avoidance of athletics.
Discourage unhealthy competition.	Avoid all-star games and championship ceremonies that recognize individuals. Instead, acknowledge all participants.
Permit children to contribute to rules and strategies.	Involve children in decisions aimed at ensuring fair play and teamwork. To strengthen desirable responses, reinforce compliance rather than punishing noncompliance.

today's children devote less time to informal outdoor play. At the same time, organized sports, such as Little League baseball and soccer and hockey leagues, have expanded tremendously, filling many hours that children used to devote to spontaneous play. About half of U.S. children—66 percent of boys and 37 percent of girls—participate in organized sports at some time between ages 5 and 18 (National Council of Youth Sports, 2008).

For most children, playing on a community athletic team is associated with increased self-esteem and social competence (Daniels & Leaper, 2006; Fletcher, Nickerson, & Wright, 2003). And children who view themselves as good at sports are more likely to continue playing on teams in adolescence, which predicts greater participation in sports and other physical fitness activities in early adulthood (Marsh et al., 2007; McHale et al., 2005).

With their coach's encouragement, these young softball players are likely to evaluate their own sports ability positively and to continue playing, thereby narrowing the gender gap in athletic participation.

In some cases, though, the arguments of critics—that youth sports overemphasize competition and substitute adult control for children's natural experimentation with rules and strategies—are valid. Children who join teams so early that the necessary skills are beyond their abilities soon lose interest. Coaches and parents who criticize rather than encourage and who react angrily to defeat can prompt intense anxiety in some children, setting the stage for emotional difficulties and early athletic dropout, not elite performance (Tofler, Knapp, & Drell, 1998; Wall & Côté, 2007). See Applying What We Know above for ways to ensure that athletic leagues provide children with positive learning experiences.

Shadows of Our Evolutionary Past

TAKE A MOMENT... While watching children in your neighborhood park, notice how they sometimes wrestle, roll, hit, and run after one another, alternating roles while smiling and laughing. This friendly chasing and play-fighting is called **rough-and-tumble play.** It emerges in the preschool years and peaks in middle childhood, and children in many cultures engage in it with peers whom they like especially well (Pellegrini, 2004).

Children's rough-and-tumble play resembles the social behavior of many other young mammals. It seems to originate in parents' physical play with babies, especially fathers with sons (see page 202 in Chapter 6). And it is more common among boys, probably because prenatal exposure to androgens (male sex hormones) predisposes boys toward active play (see Chapter 8).

SOCIAL ISSUES

School Recess—A Time to Play, a Time to Learn

When 7-year-old Whitney's family moved to a new city, she left a school with three daily recess periods for one with just a single 15-minute break per day, which her second-grade teacher cancelled if any child misbehaved. Whitney, who had previously enjoyed school, complained daily of headaches and an upset stomach. Her mother, Jill, thought, "My child is stressing out because she can't move all day!" After Jill and other parents successfully appealed to the school board to add a second recess period, Whitney's symptoms vanished (Rauber, 2006).

In recent years, recess—with its rich opportunities for child-organized play and peer interaction—has diminished or disappeared in many U.S. elementary schools (Pellegrini, 2005; Pellegrini & Holmes, 2006). Under the assumption that extra time for academics will translate into achievement gains, 7 percent of U.S. schools no longer provide recess to students as young as second grade. And over half of schools that do have recess now schedule it just once a day (U.S. Department of Education, 2009).

Yet rather than subtracting from classroom learning, recess periods boost it! Research dating back more than a century confirms that distributing cognitively demanding tasks over a longer time by introducing regular breaks, rather than consolidating intensive effort within one period, enhances attention and performance at all ages. Such breaks are particularly important for children. In a series of studies, elementary school students were more attentive in the classroom after recess than before it—an effect that was greater for second than fourth graders (Pellegrini, Huberty, & Jones, 1995).

In other research, kindergartners' and first graders' engagement in peer conversation and games during recess predicted gains in academic achievement, even after other factors that might explain the relationship (such as previous achievement) were controlled (Pellegrini, 1992; Pellegrini et al., 2002). Recall from Chapter 8 that children's social maturity contributes substantially to academic competence. Recess is one of the few remaining contexts devoted to child-organized games that provide practice in vital social skills—cooperation, leadership, followership, and inhibition of aggression—under adult supervision rather than adult direction. As children transfer these skills to the classroom, they may participate in discussions, collaborate, follow rules, and enjoy academic pursuits more—factors that enhance motivation and achievement.

© MICHAEL NEWMAN/PHOTOEDIT

Recess offers rich opportunities for child-organized play and games that promote academic achievement and social competence.

In our evolutionary past, rough-and-tumble play may have been important for developing fighting skill (Power, 2000). It also helps children form a **dominance hierarchy**—a stable ordering of group members that predicts who will win when conflict arises. Observations of arguments, threats, and physical attacks between children reveal a consistent lineup of winners and losers that becomes increasingly stable in middle childhood, especially among boys. Once school-age children establish a dominance hierarchy, hostility is rare (Pellegrini & Smith, 1998; Roseth et al., 2007). Children seem to use play-fighting as a safe context to assess the strength of a peer before challenging that peer's dominance.

© EASTCOTT/MOMATIUK/THE IMAGE WORKS

On an Alaskan beach, these 6- and 7-year-old brothers engage in rough-and-tumble play, which can be distinguished from aggression by its good-natured quality.

As children reach puberty, individual differences in strength become apparent, and rough-and-tumble play declines. When it does occur, its meaning changes: Adolescent boys' rough-and-tumble is linked to aggression (Pellegrini, 2003). Unlike children, teenage rough-and-tumble players "cheat," hurting their opponent. In explanation, boys often say that they are retaliating, apparently to reestablish dominance. Thus, a play behavior that limits aggression in childhood becomes a context for hostility in adolescence.

Physical Education

Physical activity supports many aspects of children's development—health, sense of self-worth, and the cognitive and social skills necessary for getting along with others. Yet to devote more time to academic instruction, U.S. elementary schools have cut back on recess, despite its contribution to all domains of development (see the Social Issues box above). Similarly, only 15 percent of U.S. elementary and middle schools provide students with physical education at least three days a week, a figure that drops to 3 percent in high school (Lee et al., 2007). Not surprisingly, physical inactivity among school-age children is pervasive: Only 42 percent of boys and 11 percent of girls are active enough for good health—that is, engage in at least moderate-intensity exercise for one hour or more per day (Metcalf et al., 2008).

Many experts believe that schools should not only offer more frequent physical education classes but also change the content of these programs. Training in competitive sports, often a high priority, is unlikely to reach the least physically fit youngsters, who avoid activities demanding a high level of skill. Instead, programs should emphasize enjoyable, informal games and individual exercise—pursuits most likely to endure.

Physically fit children tend to become active adults who reap many benefits (Dennison et al., 1998; Tammelin et al., 2003). These include greater physical strength, resistance to many illnesses (from colds and flu to cancer, diabetes, and heart disease), enhanced psychological well-being, and a longer life.

ASK YOURSELF

» REVIEW
Explain the adaptive value of rough-and-tumble play and dominance hierarchies.

» APPLY
Nine-year-old Allison thinks she isn't good at sports, and she doesn't like physical education class. Suggest some strategies her teacher can use to improve her pleasure and involvement in physical activity.

» CONNECT
Select one of the following health problems of middle childhood: myopia, obesity, asthma, or unintentional injuries. Explain how both genetic and environmental factors contribute to it.

» REFLECT
Did you participate in organized sports as a child? If so, what kind of climate for learning did coaches and parents create? What impact do you think your experiences had on your development?

Cognitive Development

"Finally!" 6-year-old Lizzie exclaimed the day she entered first grade. "Now I get to go to real school, just like Joey!" Lizzie walked into her classroom confidently, pencils, crayons, and writing pad in hand, ready for a more disciplined approach to learning than she had experienced in early childhood.

Lizzie was entering a whole new world of challenging mental activities. In a single morning, she and her classmates wrote in journals, met in reading groups, worked on addition and subtraction, and sorted leaves gathered for a science project. As Lizzie and Joey moved through the elementary school grades, they tackled increasingly complex tasks and became more accomplished at reading, writing, math skills, and general knowledge of the world. To understand the cognitive attainments of middle childhood, we turn to research inspired by Piaget's theory and by the information-processing perspective. And we look at expanding definitions of intelligence that help us appreciate individual differences. Our discussion continues with language, which blossoms further in these years. Finally, we consider the role of schools in children's development.

Piaget's Theory: The Concrete Operational Stage

When Lizzie visited my child development class as a 4-year-old, Piaget's conservation problems confused her (see Chapter 7, page 229). For example, when water was poured from a tall, narrow container into a short, wide one, she insisted that the amount of water had changed. But when Lizzie returned at age 8, she found these tasks easy. "Of course it's the same!" she exclaimed. "The water's shorter, but it's also wider. Pour it back," she instructed the college student who was interviewing her. "You'll see, it's the same amount!"

Concrete Operational Thought

Lizzie has entered Piaget's **concrete operational stage,** which extends from about 7 to 11 years and marks a major turning point in cognitive development. Thought is far more logical, flexible, and organized than it was earlier.

■ **CONSERVATION.** The ability to pass *conservation tasks* provides clear evidence of *operations*—mental actions that obey logical rules. Notice how Lizzie is capable of *decentration,* focusing on several aspects of a problem and relating them, rather than centering on just one. Lizzie also demonstrates **reversibility,** the capacity to think through a series of steps and then mentally reverse direction, returning to the starting point. Recall from Chapter 7 that reversibility is part of every logical operation. It is solidly achieved in middle childhood.

■ **CLASSIFICATION.** Between ages 7 and 10, children pass Piaget's *class inclusion problem* (see page 230). This indicates that they are more aware of classification hierarchies and can focus on relations between a general category and two specific categories at the same time—that is, on three relations at once (Hodges & French, 1988; Ni, 1998). Collections—stamps, coins, baseball cards, rocks, and bottle caps—become common in middle childhood. At age 10, Joey spent hours sorting and resorting his baseball cards, grouping them first by league and team, then by playing position and batting average. He could separate the players into a variety of classes and subclasses and easily rearrange them.

■ **SERIATION.** The ability to order items along a quantitative dimension, such as length or weight, is called **seriation.** To test for it, Piaget asked children to arrange sticks of different lengths from shortest to longest. Older preschoolers can put the sticks in a row, but they do so haphazardly, making many errors. In

An improved ability to categorize underlies children's interest in collecting objects during middle childhood. Here, an 8-year-old sorts and organizes buttons in her extensive collection.

contrast, 6- to 7-year-olds create the series efficiently, moving in an orderly sequence from the smallest stick, to the next largest, and so on.

The concrete operational child can also seriate mentally, an ability called **transitive inference.** In a well-known transitive inference problem, Piaget showed children pairings of sticks of different colors. From observing that Stick A is longer than Stick B and Stick B is longer than Stick C, children must infer that A is longer than C. Like Piaget's class inclusion task, transitive inference requires children to integrate three relations at once—in this instance, A–B, B–C, and A–C. When researchers take steps to ensure that children remember the premises (A–B and B–C), 7-year-olds can grasp transitive inference (Andrews & Halford, 1998; Wright, 2006).

■ **SPATIAL REASONING.** Piaget found that school-age children's understanding of space is more accurate than that of preschoolers. Let's consider children's **cognitive maps**—their mental representations of familiar large-scale spaces, such as their neighborhood or school. Drawing a map of a large-scale space requires considerable perspective-taking skill. Because the entire space cannot be seen at once, children must infer its overall layout by relating its separate parts.

Preschoolers and young school-age children include *landmarks* on the maps they draw, but their arrangement is not always accurate. They do better when asked to place stickers showing the location of desks and people on a map of their classroom. But if the map is rotated to a position other than the orientation of the classroom, they have difficulty (Liben & Downs, 1993).

Around age 8 to 10, maps become better organized, showing landmarks along an *organized route of travel.* At the same time, children become able to give clear, well-organized instructions for getting from one place to another by using a "mental walk" strategy—imagining another person's movements along a route (Gauvain & Rogoff, 1989). At the end of middle childhood, children form an *overall view of a large-scale space.* And they readily draw and read maps, even when the orientation of the map and the space it represents do not match (Liben, 1999). Ten- to 12-year-olds also grasp the notion of *scale*—the proportional relation between a space and its representation on a map (Liben, 2006).

Cultural frameworks influence children's map making. In many non-Western communities, people rarely use maps for way-finding but rely on information from neighbors, street vendors, and shopkeepers. Also, compared to their Western agemates, non-Western children less often ride in cars and more often walk, which results in intimate neighborhood knowledge. When a researcher had older school-age children in small cities in India and in the United States draw maps of their neighborhoods, the Indian children represented a rich array of landmarks and aspects of social life, such as people and vehicles, in a small area surrounding their home. The U.S. children, in contrast, drew a more formal, extended space, highlighting main streets and key directions (north–south, east–west) but including few landmarks (see Figure 9.5) (Parameswaran, 2003). Although the U.S. children's maps scored higher in cognitive maturity, this difference reflected cultural interpretations of the task. When asked to create a map to "help people find their way," the Indian children drew spaces as far-reaching and organized as the U.S. children's.

Limitations of Concrete Operational Thought

As the name of this stage suggests, concrete operational thinking suffers from one important limitation: Children think in an organized, logical fashion only when dealing with concrete information they can perceive directly. Their mental operations work poorly with abstract ideas—ones not apparent in the real world. Consider children's solutions to transitive inference problems. When shown pairs of sticks of unequal length, Lizzie easily engaged in transitive inference. But she had difficulty with a hypothetical version of this task: "Susan is taller than Sally, and Sally is taller than Mary. Who is the tallest?" Not until age 11 or 12 can children solve this problem.

That logical thought is at first tied to immediate situations helps account for a special feature of concrete operational reasoning: School-age children master concrete operational tasks step by step, not all at once. For example, they usually grasp conservation of number first, followed by conservation of length, liquid, and mass, and then weight. This *continuum of acquisition* (or gradual mastery) of logical concepts is another indication of

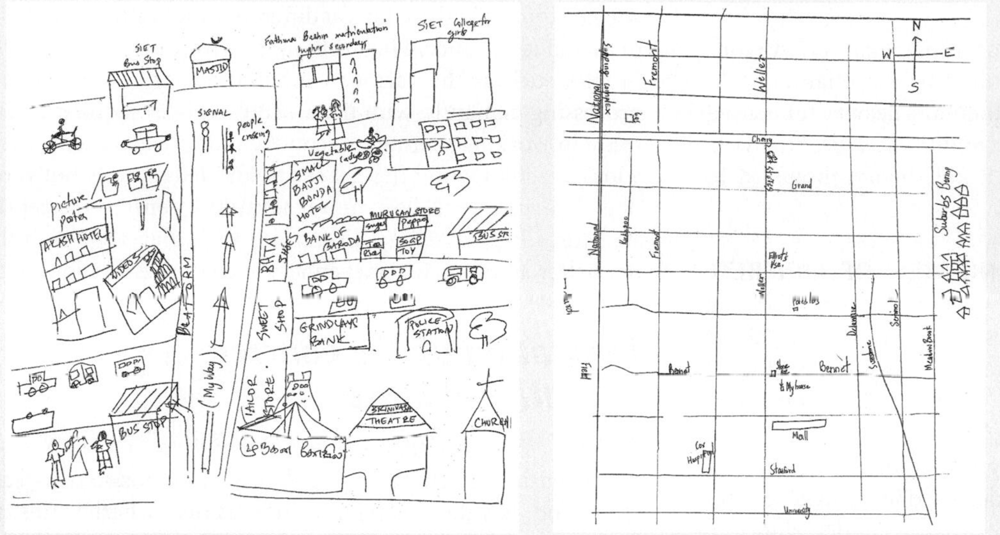

(a) (b)

■ **FIGURE 9.5** ■ **Maps drawn by older school-age children from India and the United States.** (a) The Indian child depicted many landmarks and features of social life in a small area near her home. (b) The U.S. child drew a more extended space and highlighted main streets and key directions but included few landmarks and people. (From G. Parameswaran, 2003, "Experimenter Instructions as a Mediator in the Effects of Culture on Mapping One's Neighborhood," *Journal of Environmental Psychology, 23,* pp. 415–416. Copyright © 2003, reprinted with permission from Elsevier.)

the limitations of concrete operational thinking (Fischer & Bidell, 1991). Rather than coming up with general logical principles that they apply to all relevant situations, school-age children seem to work out the logic of each problem separately.

Follow-Up Research on Concrete Operational Thought

According to Piaget, brain development combined with experience in a rich and varied external world should lead children everywhere to reach the concrete operational stage at about the same time. Yet recent evidence indicates that specific cultural and school practices have much to do with mastery of Piagetian tasks (Rogoff, 2003; Rogoff & Chavajay, 1995). And information-processing research helps explain the gradual mastery of logical concepts in middle childhood.

■ **THE IMPACT OF CULTURE AND SCHOOLING.** In tribal and village societies, conservation is often delayed. For example, among the Hausa of Nigeria, who live in small agricultural settlements and rarely send their children to school, even the most basic conservation tasks—number, length, and liquid—are not understood until age 11 or later (Fahrmeier, 1978). This suggests that taking part in relevant everyday activities helps children master conservation and other Piagetian problems. Joey and Lizzie, for example, think of fairness in terms of equal distribution—a value emphasized in their culture. They frequently divide materials, such as crayons or treats, equally among their friends. Because they often see the same quantity arranged in different ways, they grasp conservation early.

The very experience of going to school seems to promote mastery of Piagetian tasks. When children of the same age are tested, those who have been in school longer do better on transitive inference problems (Artman & Cahan, 1993). Opportunities to seriate objects, to learn about order relations, and to remember the parts of complex problems are probably responsible. Yet certain informal nonschool experiences can also foster operational thought. Around age 7 to 8, Zinacanteco Indian girls of southern Mexico, who learn to weave elaborately designed fabrics as an alternative to schooling, engage in mental transformations to figure out how a warp strung on a loom will turn out as woven cloth—reasoning expected at the concrete operational stage. North American children of the same age, who do much better than Zinacanteco children on Piagetian tasks,

This Zinacanteco Indian girl of southern Mexico learns the centuries-old practice of backstrap weaving, which requires complex mental transformations. Although North American children perform better on Piaget's tasks, Zinacanteco children are far more adept at figuring out how to transform warp strung on a loom into woven cloth.

have great difficulty with these weaving problems (Maynard & Greenfield, 2003).

On the basis of such findings, some investigators have concluded that the forms of logic required by Piagetian tasks do not emerge spontaneously but, rather, are heavily influenced by training, context, and cultural conditions. Does this view remind you of Vygotsky's sociocultural theory, discussed in earlier chapters?

AN INFORMATION-PROCESSING VIEW OF CONCRETE OPERATIONAL THOUGHT. The gradual mastery of logical concepts in middle childhood raises a familiar question about Piaget's theory: Is an abrupt stagewise transition to logical thought the best way to describe cognitive development in middle childhood?

Some *neo-Piagetian theorists* argue that the development of operational thinking can best be understood in terms of gains in information-processing speed rather than a sudden shift to a new stage. For example, Robbie Case (1996, 1998) proposed that, with practice, cognitive schemes demand less attention and become more automatic. This frees up space in *working memory* (see page 161) so children can focus on combining old schemes and generating new ones. For instance, the child who sees water poured from one container to another recognizes that the height of the liquid changes. As this understanding becomes routine, the child notices that the width of the water changes as well. Soon children coordinate these observations, and they conserve liquid. Then, as this logical idea becomes well-practiced, the child transfers it to more demanding situations.

Once the schemes of a Piagetian stage are sufficiently automatic, enough working memory is available to integrate them into an improved representation. As a result, children acquire *central conceptual structures*—networks of concepts and relations that permit them to think more effectively about a wide range of situations (Case, 1996, 1998). The central conceptual structures that emerge from integrating concrete operational schemes are broadly applicable principles that result in increasingly complex, systematic reasoning, which we will discuss in Chapter 11 in the context of formal operational thought.

Case and his colleagues—along with other information-processing researchers—have examined children's performance on a wide variety of tasks, including solving arithmetic problems, understanding stories, drawing pictures, and interpreting social situations. In each task, preschoolers typically focus on only one dimension. In understanding stories, for example, they grasp only a single story line. In drawing pictures, they depict objects separately. By the early school years, children coordinate two dimensions—two story lines in a single plot and drawings that show both the features of objects and their relationships. Around 9 to 11 years, children integrate multiple dimensions (Case, 1998; Halford & Andrews, 2006). Children tell coherent stories with a main plot and several subplots. And their drawings follow a set of rules for representing perspective and, therefore, include several points of reference, such as near, midway, and far.

Case's theory helps explain why many understandings appear in specific situations at different times rather than being mastered all at once. First, different forms of the same logical insight, such as the various conservation tasks, vary in their processing demands, with those acquired later requiring more space in working memory. Second, children's experiences vary widely. A child who often listens to and tells stories but rarely draws pictures displays more advanced central conceptual structures in storytelling. Compared with Piaget's, Case's theory better accounts for unevenness in cognitive development.

Evaluation of the Concrete Operational Stage

Piaget was correct that school-age children approach many problems in organized, rational ways not possible in early childhood. But disagreement continues over whether this difference occurs because of *continuous* improvement in logical skills or *discontinuous* restructuring of children's thinking (as Piaget's stage idea assumes). Many researchers think that both types of change may be involved (Carey, 1999; Case, 1998; Demetriou et al., 2002; Fischer & Bidell, 2006; Halford & Andrews, 2006).

During the school years, children apply logical schemes to many more tasks. In the process, their thought seems to undergo qualitative change—toward a comprehensive grasp of the underlying principles of logical thought. Piaget himself seems to have recognized this possibility in evidence for gradual mastery of conservation and other tasks. So perhaps some blend of Piagetian and information-processing ideas holds the greatest promise for understanding cognitive development in middle childhood.

ASK YOURSELF

>> REVIEW
Children's performance on conservation tasks illustrates a continuum of acquisition of logical concepts. Review the preceding sections, and list additional examples of gradual development of logical reasoning.

>> APPLY
Nine-year-old Adrienne spends many hours helping her father build furniture in his woodworking shop. How might this experience facilitate Adrienne's performance on Piagetian seriation problems?

>> CONNECT
Explain how advances in perspective taking contribute to school-age children's improved ability to draw and use maps.

>> REFLECT
Which aspects of Piaget's description of the concrete operational child do you accept? Which do you doubt? Explain, citing research evidence.

Information Processing

In contrast to Piaget's focus on overall cognitive change, the information-processing perspective examines separate aspects of thinking. Attention and memory, which underlie every act of cognition, are central concerns in middle childhood, just as they were during infancy and the preschool years. Advances in metacognition and opportunities for self-regulation aid development. Also, increased understanding of how school-age children process information is being applied to their academic learning—in particular, to reading and mathematics.

Researchers believe that brain development contributes to the following basic changes in information processing that facilitate diverse aspects of thinking:

- *Increases in information-processing speed and capacity.* Time needed to process information on a wide variety of cognitive tasks declines rapidly between ages 6 and 12 (Kail & Park, 1992, 1994). This suggests a biologically based gain in speed of thinking, possibly due to myelination and synaptic pruning in the brain (Kail, 2003). Some researchers believe this greater efficiency contributes to more complex, effective thinking because a faster thinker can hold on to and operate on more information in working memory (Halford & Andrews, 2006; Luna et al., 2004). Indeed, *digit span,* which assesses the basic capacity of working memory (see page 238), improves from about five digits at age 7 to seven digits at age 12 (Kail, 2003).
- *Gains in inhibition.* As indicated in earlier chapters, inhibition—the ability to control internal and external distracting stimuli—improves from infancy on. But additional strides occur in middle childhood as the frontal lobes of the cerebral cortex develop further (Luna et al., 2004; Nelson, Thomas, & de Haan, 2006). Individuals skilled at inhibition can prevent their minds from straying to irrelevant thoughts, an ability that supports many information-processing skills by preserving space in working memory for the task at hand (Dempster & Corkill, 1999; Klenberg, Korkman, & Lahti-Nuuttila, 2001).

Besides brain development, strategy use contributes to more effective information processing. As we will see, school-age children think far more strategically than preschoolers.

Attention

In middle childhood, attention becomes more selective, adaptable, and planful. First, children become better at deliberately attending to just those aspects of a situation that are relevant to their goals. Researchers study this increasing selectivity of attention by introducing irrelevant stimuli into a task and seeing how well children attend to its central elements. Performance improves sharply between ages 6 and 10 (Goldberg, Maurer, & Lewis, 2001; Gomez-Perez & Ostrosky-Solis, 2006; Tabibi & Pfeffer, 2007).

Second, older children flexibly adapt their attention to task requirements. When asked to sort cards with pictures that vary in both color and shape, children age 5 and older can switch their basis of sorting from color to shape when asked to do so; younger children typically persist in sorting in just one way (Brooks et al., 2003; Zelazo, Frye, & Rapus, 1996). And when studying for a spelling test, 10-year-old Joey was much more likely than Lizzie to devote most attention to the words he knew least well (Masur, McIntyre, & Flavell, 1973).

Finally, planning improves greatly in middle childhood (Gauvain, 2004; Scholnick, 1995). School-age children scan detailed pictures and written materials for similarities and differences more thoroughly than preschoolers. And on tasks with many parts, they make decisions about what to do first and what to do next in an orderly fashion. As Chapter 7 revealed, children learn much about planning by collaborating with more expert planners. In one study of family interactions, discussions involving planning at ages 4 and 9 predicted planning competence in adolescence (Gauvain & Huard, 1999). The demands of school tasks—and teachers' explanations of how to plan—also contribute to gains in planning.

The attentional strategies just considered are crucial for success in school. Unfortunately, some children have great difficulty paying attention. See the Biology and Environment box on pages 304–305 for a discussion of the serious learning and behavior problems of children with attention-deficit hyperactivity disorder.

Memory Strategies

As attention improves, so do *memory strategies,* deliberate mental activities we use to store and retain information. When Lizzie had a list of things to learn—for example, the state capitals of the United States—she immediately used **rehearsal**—repeating the information to herself. This memory strategy first appears in the early grade school years. Soon after, a second strategy becomes common: **organization**—grouping related items together (for example, all state capitals in the same part of the country), an approach that improves recall dramatically (Schneider, 2002).

Perfecting memory strategies requires time and effort. Eight-year-old Lizzie rehearsed in a piecemeal fashion. After being given the word *cat* in a list of items, she said, "Cat, cat, cat." But 10-year-old Joey used a more effective approach: He combined previous words with each new item, saying, "Desk, man, yard, cat, cat" (Kunzinger, 1985). Joey also organized more skillfully, grouping items into fewer categories. And he used organization in a wide range of memory tasks, whereas Lizzie used it only when categorical relations among items were obvious (Bjorklund et al., 1994).

Furthermore, Joey often combined several strategies—for example, organizing items, then stating the category names, and finally rehearsing. The more strategies children apply simultaneously and consistently, the better they remember (Hock, Park, & Bjorklund, 1998; DeMarie et al., 2004). Younger

BIOLOGY AND ENVIRONMENT

Children with Attention-Deficit Hyperactivity Disorder

While the other fifth graders worked quietly at their desks, Calvin squirmed, dropped his pencil, looked out the window, and fiddled with his shoelaces. "Hey Joey," he yelled across the room, "wanna play ball after school?" But the other children weren't eager to play with Calvin, who was physically awkward and failed to follow the rules of the game. He had trouble taking turns at bat. In the outfield, he tossed his mitt up in the air and looked elsewhere when the ball came his way. Calvin's desk was a chaotic mess. He often lost pencils, books, and other school materials, and he had difficulty remembering assignments and due dates.

Symptoms of ADHD

Calvin is one of 3 to 6 percent of school-age children with **attention-deficit hyperactivity disorder (ADHD)**, which involves inattention, impulsivity, and excessive motor activity resulting in academic and social problems (American Psychiatric Association, 1994; Barkley, 2006). Boys are diagnosed about four times as often as girls. However, many girls with ADHD seem to be overlooked, either because their symptoms are less flagrant or because of a gender bias: A disruptive boy is more likely to be referred for treatment (Abikoff et al., 2002; Biederman et al., 2005).

Children with ADHD cannot stay focused on a task requiring mental effort for more than a few minutes. They often act impulsively, ignoring social rules and lashing out with hostility when frustrated. Many, though not all, are *hyperactive,* exhausting parents and teachers and irritating other children with their excessive motor activity. For a child to be diagnosed with ADHD, these symptoms must have appeared before age 7 as a persistent problem.

Because of their difficulty concentrating, children with ADHD score 7 to 15 points lower than other children on intelligence tests (Barkley, 2002a). Researchers agree that deficient executive processing (see page 161 in Chapter 5) underlies ADHD symptoms. According to one view, children with ADHD are impaired in capacity to inhibit action in favor of thought (Barkley, 2003a). Another hypothesis is that ADHD results from a cluster of executive processing problems that interfere with ability to guide one's own actions (Brown, 2005, 2006). Research confirms that children with ADHD do poorly on tasks requiring sustained attention; find it hard to ignore irrelevant information; have difficulty with memory, planning, reasoning, and problem solving in academic and social situations; and often fail to manage frustration and intense emotion (Barkley, 2003b, 2006).

Origins of ADHD

ADHD runs in families and is highly heritable: Identical twins share it more often than fraternal twins (Rasmussen et al., 2004; Rietvelt et al., 2004). Children with ADHD show abnormal brain functioning, including reduced electrical and blood-flow activity and structural abnormalities in the frontal lobes of the cerebral cortex and in other areas involved in attention, inhibition of behavior, and other aspects of motor control (Mackie et al., 2007; Sowell et al., 2003). Also, the brains of children with ADHD grow more slowly and are about 3 percent smaller in overall volume than those of unaffected agemates (Durston et al., 2004; Shaw et al., 2007). Several genes affecting neural communication have been implicated in the disorder (Biederman & Spencer, 2000; Quist & Kennedy, 2001).

At the same time, ADHD is associated with environmental factors. Prenatal teratogens—particularly those involving long-term exposure, such as illegal drugs, alcohol, and tobacco—are linked to inattention and hyperactivity (Milberger et al., 1997). Furthermore, children with ADHD are more likely to come from homes in which marriages are unhappy and family stress is high (Bernier & Siegel, 1994). But a stressful home life rarely causes

school-age children often try out various memory strategies, but they use them less systematically and with less success than older children. Still, the tendency to experiment allows younger children to discover which strategies work best and how to combine them effectively. Indeed, children experiment with strategies when faced with many cognitive challenges—an approach that enables them to gradually "home in" on the most effective techniques (Siegler, 1996, 2007).

By the end of middle childhood, children start to use **elaboration**—creating a relationship, or shared meaning, between two or more pieces of information that do not belong to the same category. For example, if two of the words you must learn are *fish* and *pipe,* you might generate the verbal statement or mental image, "The fish is smoking a pipe." This highly effective memory technique, which requires considerable effort and space in working memory, becomes increasingly common in adolescence and early adulthood (Schneider & Pressley, 1997).

Because organization and elaboration combine items into *meaningful chunks,* they permit children to hold onto much more information and, as a result, further expand working memory. In addition, when children link a new item to information they already know, they can *retrieve* it easily by thinking of other items associated with it. As we will see, this also contributes to improved memory during the school years.

The Knowledge Base and Memory Performance

During middle childhood, the long-term knowledge base grows larger and becomes organized into increasingly elaborate, hierarchically structured networks. This rapid growth of knowledge helps children use strategies and remember (Schneider, 2002). In other words, knowing more about a topic makes new information more meaningful and familiar so it is easier to store and retrieve.

To test this idea, researchers classified fourth graders as either experts or novices in knowledge of soccer, then gave both groups lists of soccer and nonsoccer items to learn. Experts remembered far more items on the soccer list (but not on the nonsoccer list) than novices. And during recall, experts' listing of items was better organized, as indicated by clustering of items into categories (Schneider & Bjorklund, 1992). This better

ADHD. Rather, these children's behaviors can contribute to family problems, which intensify the child's preexisting difficulties.

Treating ADHD

Calvin's doctor eventually prescribed stimulant medication, the most common treatment for ADHD. As long as dosage is carefully regulated, these drugs reduce symptoms in 70 percent of children who take them (Greenhill, Halperin, & Abikoff, 1999). Stimulant medication seems to increase activity in the frontal lobes, thereby improving the child's capacity to sustain attention and to inhibit off-task behavior.

In 2006, an advisory panel convened by the U.S. Food and Drug Administration warned that stimulants might impair heart functioning, even causing sudden death in a few individuals, and advocated warning labels describing these potential risks. Debate over the safety of medication for ADHD is likely to intensify. In any case, medication is not enough. Drugs cannot teach children to compensate for inattention and impulsivity. The most effective treatment approach combines medication with interventions that model and reinforce appropriate academic and social behavior (American Academy of Pediatrics, 2005a; Smith, Barkley, & Shapiro, 2006).

Family intervention is also important. Inattentive, overactive children strain the patience of parents, who are likely to react punitively and inconsistently—a child-rearing style that strengthens defiant, aggressive behavior. In fact, in 45 to 65 percent of cases, these two sets of behavior problems occur together (Barkley, 2002b).

Some media reports suggest that the number of U.S. children diagnosed with ADHD has increased greatly. But two large surveys yielded similar overall prevalence rates 20 years ago and today. Nevertheless, the incidence of ADHD is much higher in some communities than others. At times, children are overdiagnosed and unnecessarily medicated because their parents and teachers are impatient with inattentive, active behavior within normal range. In Hong Kong, where academic success is particularly prized, children are diagnosed at more than twice the rate seen in North America. But in Great Britain, where doctors are hesitant to label a child with ADHD or to prescribe medication, children are underdiagnosed and often do not receive the treatment they need (Taylor, 2004).

ADHD is usually a lifelong disorder. Affected individuals are at risk for persistent antisocial behavior, depression, and other problems (Kessler et al., 2005, 2006). Adults with ADHD continue to need help in structuring their environments, regulating negative emotion, selecting appropriate careers, and understanding their condition as a biological deficit rather than a character flaw.

This child frequently engages in disruptive behavior at school. Children with ADHD have great difficulty staying on task and often act impulsively, ignoring social rules.

organization at retrieval suggests that highly knowledgeable children organize information in their area of expertise with little or no effort. Consequently, experts can devote more working-memory resources to using recalled information for reasoning and problem solving (Bjorklund & Douglas, 1997).

But knowledge is not the only important factor in children's strategic memory processing. Children who are expert in an area are usually highly motivated. As a result, they not only acquire knowledge more quickly but also *actively use what they know* to add more. In contrast, academically unsuccessful children fail to ask how previously stored information can clarify new material. This, in turn, interferes with the development of a broad knowledge base (Schneider & Bjorklund, 1998). So by the end of the school years, extensive knowledge and use of memory strategies support one another.

Culture, Schooling, and Memory Strategies

Rehearsal, organization, and elaboration are techniques that people usually use when they need to remember information for its own sake. On many other occasions, memory occurs as a natural byproduct of participation in daily activities (Rogoff, 2003).

A repeated finding is that people in non-Western cultures who lack formal schooling do not use or benefit from instruction in memory strategies because they see no practical reason to use these techniques (Rogoff & Chavajay, 1995). Tasks that require children to recall isolated bits of information, which are common in classrooms, strongly motivate use of memory strategies. In fact, Western children get so much practice with this type of learning that they do not refine techniques relying on cues available in everyday life, such as spatial location and arrangement of objects. For example, Guatemalan Mayan 9-year-olds do slightly better than their North American agemates when told to remember the placement of 40 familiar objects in a play scene. North American children often rehearse object names when it would be more effective to keep track of spatial relations (Rogoff & Wadell, 1982). The development of memory strategies, then, is not just a product of a more competent information-processing system. It also depends on task demands and cultural circumstances.

A mother and daughter of the Colombian U'wa people, who have no written tradition, make "cocara" leaf hats, which girls wear from puberty until marriage. Although this child demonstrates keen memory for how to select, cut, and assemble the leaves, she may have difficulty recalling the isolated bits of information that school tasks often require.

The School-Age Child's Theory of Mind

During middle childhood, children's *theory of mind,* or set of ideas about mental activities, becomes more elaborate and refined. Recall from Chapter 7 that this awareness of thought is often called *metacognition.* School-age children's improved ability to reflect on their own mental life is another reason that their thinking advances.

Unlike preschoolers, who view the mind as a passive container of information, older children regard it as an active, constructive agent that selects and transforms information (Kuhn, 2000). Consequently, they have a much better understanding of cognitive processes and the impact of psychological factors on performance. School-age children, for example, know that doing well on a task depends on focusing attention—concentrating and exerting effort (Miller & Bigi, 1979). With age, they also become increasingly aware of effective memory strategies and why they work (Alexander et al., 2003). And children gradually grasp relationships between mental activities—for example, that remembering is crucial for understanding and that understanding strengthens memory (Schwanenflugel, Henderson, & Fabricius, 1998).

Furthermore, school-age children's understanding of sources of knowledge expands. They realize that people can extend their knowledge not just by directly observing events and talking to others but also by making *mental inferences* (Miller, Hardin, & Montgomery, 2003). This grasp of inference enables knowledge of *false belief* to expand. In several studies, researchers told children complex stories involving one character's belief about a second character's belief. Then the children answered questions about what the first character thought the second character would do (see Figure 9.6). By age 7, children were aware that people form beliefs about other people's beliefs and that these second-order beliefs can be wrong! Appreciation of *second-order false belief* enables children to pinpoint the reasons that another person arrived at a certain belief (Astington, Pelletier, & Homer, 2002; Naito & Seki, 2009). This assists them greatly in understanding others' perspectives.

School-age children's capacity for more complex thinking contributes greatly to their more reflective, process-oriented view of the mind. But experiences that foster awareness of mental activities are also involved. In a study of rural children of Cameroon, Africa, those who attended school performed much better on theory-of-mind tasks (Vinden, 2002). In school, teachers often call attention to the workings of the mind when they remind children to pay attention, remember mental steps, and evaluate their reasoning. And as children engage in reading,

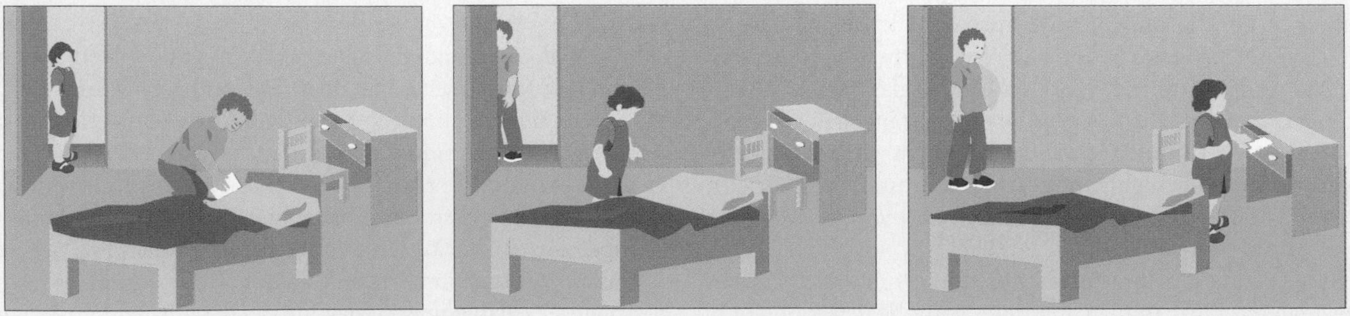

(a) Jason has a letter from a friend. Lisa wants to read the letter, but Jason doesn't want her to. Jason puts the letter under his pillow.

(b) Jason leaves the room to help his mother.

(c) While Jason is gone, Lisa takes the letter and reads it. Jason returns and watches Lisa, but Lisa doesn't see Jason. Then Lisa puts the letter in Jason's desk.

■ **FIGURE 9.6** ■ **A second-order false-belief task.** After relating the story in the sequence of pictures, the researcher asks a second-order false-belief question: "Where does Lisa think Jason will look for the letter? Why?" Around age 7, children answer correctly—that Lisa thinks Jason will look under his pillow because Lisa doesn't know that Jason saw her put the letter in the desk. (Adapted from Astington, Pelletier, & Homer, 2002.)

writing, and math, they often use *private speech,* at first speaking out loud and then silently to themselves. As they "hear themselves think," they probably detect many aspects of mental life.

Cognitive Self-Regulation

Although metacognition expands, school-age children often have difficulty putting what they know about thinking into action. They are not yet good at **cognitive self-regulation,** the process of continuously monitoring progress toward a goal, checking outcomes, and redirecting unsuccessful efforts. For example, Lizzie knows she should group items when memorizing and that she should reread a complicated paragraph to make sure she understands. But she does not always engage in these activities.

To study cognitive self-regulation, researchers sometimes look at the impact that children's awareness of memory strategies has on how well they remember. By second grade, the more children know about memory strategies, the more they recall—a relationship that strengthens over middle childhood (Pierce & Lange, 2000). And when children apply a strategy consistently, their knowledge of strategies strengthens, resulting in a bidirectional association between metacognition and strategy use that enhances self-regulation (Schlagmüller & Schneider, 2002).

Why does cognitive self-regulation develop gradually? Monitoring learning outcomes is cognitively demanding, requiring constant evaluation of effort and progress. By adolescence, self-regulation is a strong predictor of academic success (Joyner & Kurtz-Costes, 1997). Students who do well in school know when their learning is going well. If they encounter obstacles, they take steps to address them—for example, organize the learning environment, review confusing material, or seek support from more expert adults or peers. This active, purposeful approach contrasts sharply with the passive orientation of students who achieve poorly (Zimmerman & Risemberg, 1997).

Parents and teachers can foster self-regulation. In one study, researchers observed parents helping their children with problem solving during the summer before third grade. Parents who patiently pointed out important features of the task and suggested strategies had children who, in the classroom, more often discussed ways to approach problems and monitored their own performance (Stright et al., 2002). Explaining the effectiveness of strategies is particularly helpful because it provides a rationale for future action.

Children who acquire effective self-regulatory skills develop a sense of *academic self-efficacy*—confidence in their own ability, which supports future self-regulation (Schunk & Pajares, 2005). Unfortunately, some children receive messages from parents and teachers that seriously undermine their academic self-esteem and self-regulatory skills. We will consider these *learned-helpless* children, along with ways to help them, in Chapter 10.

Applications of Information Processing to Academic Learning

Fundamental discoveries about the development of information processing have been applied to children's learning of reading and mathematics. Researchers are identifying the cognitive ingredients of skilled performance, tracing their development, and pinpointing differences in cognitive skills between good and poor readers. They hope, as a result, to design teaching methods that will improve children's learning.

■ **READING.** Reading makes use of many skills at once, taxing all aspects of our information-processing systems. Joey and Lizzie must perceive single letters and letter combinations, translate them into speech sounds, recognize the visual appearance of many common words, hold chunks of text in working memory while interpreting their meaning, and combine the meanings of various parts of a text passage into an understandable whole. And because reading is so demanding, most or all of these skills must be done automatically. If one or more are poorly developed, they will compete for space in our limited working memories, and reading performance will decline.

As children make the transition from emergent literacy to conventional reading, *phonological awareness* continues to facilitate their progress (see page 242 in Chapter 7). Other information-processing activities also contribute. Gains in processing speed foster children's rapid conversion of visual symbols into sounds (McBride-Chang & Kail, 2002). And visual scanning and discrimination are also important and improve with reading experience (Rayner, Pollatsek, & Starr, 2003). Performing all these skills efficiently releases working memory for higher-level activities involved in comprehending the text's meaning.

Until recently, researchers were involved in an intense debate over how to teach beginning reading. Those who took a **whole-language approach** argued that reading should be taught in a way that parallels natural language learning. From the beginning, children should be exposed to text in its complete form—stories, poems, letters, posters, and lists—so that they can appreciate the communicative function of written language. According to this view, as long as reading is kept whole and meaningful, children will be motivated to discover the specific skills they need (Watson, 1989). Other experts advocated a **phonics approach,** believing that children should first be coached on *phonics*—the basic rules for translating written symbols into sounds. Only after mastering these skills should they get complex reading material (Rayner & Pollatsek, 1989).

Many studies show that, in fact, children learn best with a mixture of both approaches. In kindergarten, first, and second grades, teaching that includes phonics boosts reading scores, especially for children who lag behind in reading progress (Stahl & Miller, 2006; Xue & Meisels, 2004). And when teachers combine real reading and writing with teaching of phonics and engage in other excellent teaching practices—encouraging children to tackle reading challenges and integrating reading into all school subjects—first graders show far greater literacy progress (Pressley et al., 2002).

Why might combining phonics with whole language work best? Learning relationships between letters and sounds enables children to decipher words they have never seen before. Consequently, it promotes children's belief that they can succeed at challenging reading tasks (Tunmer & Chapman, 2002). Yet too much emphasis on basic skills may cause children to lose sight of the goal of reading: understanding. Children who read aloud fluently without registering meaning know little about effective reading strategies—for example, that they must read more carefully if they will be tested than if they are reading for pleasure, or that explaining a passage in their own words is a good way to assess comprehension. Providing instruction aimed at increasing knowledge and use of reading strategies enhances reading performance from third grade on (Paris & Paris, 2006; Van Keer, 2004).

■ **MATHEMATICS.** Mathematics teaching in elementary school builds on and greatly enriches children's informal knowledge of number concepts and counting. Written notation systems and formal computational procedures enhance children's ability to represent numbers and compute. Over the early elementary school years, children acquire basic math facts through a combination of frequent practice, experimentation with diverse computational procedures (through which they discover faster, more accurate techniques), reasoning about number concepts, and teaching that conveys effective strategies (Alibali, 1999; Siegler, 2007). For example, when first graders realize that regardless of the order in which two sets are combined, they yield the same result ($2 + 6 = 8$ and $6 + 2 = 8$), they more often start with the higher digit (6) and count on (7, 8), a strategy that minimizes the work involved. Eventually children retrieve answers automatically and apply this knowledge to more complex problems.

Arguments about how to teach mathematics resemble those about reading, pitting drill in computing against "number sense," or understanding. Again, a blend of both approaches is most beneficial. In learning basic math, poorly performing students use cumbersome techniques or try to retrieve answers from memory too soon. They have not sufficiently experimented with strategies to see which are most effective and to reorganize their observations in logical, efficient ways—for example, noticing that multiplication problems involving 2 (2×8) are equivalent to addition doubles ($8 + 8$). On tasks that assess their understanding of math concepts, their performance is weak (Canobi, 2004; Canobi, Reeve, & Pattison, 2003). This suggests that encouraging students to apply strategies and making sure they understand why certain strategies work well are essential for solid mastery of basic math.

A similar picture emerges for more complex skills, such as carrying in addition, borrowing in subtraction, and operating with decimals and fractions. When taught by rote, children cannot apply the procedure to new problems. Instead, they persistently make mistakes, following a "math rule" that they recall incorrectly because they do not understand it (Carpenter et al., 1999). Consider the following subtraction errors:

$$\begin{array}{r} 427 \\ -\ 138 \\ \hline 311 \end{array} \qquad \begin{array}{r} 7{,}002 \\ -\ 5{,}445 \\ \hline 1{,}447 \end{array}$$

In the first problem, the child subtracts a smaller from a larger digit, regardless of which is on top. In the second, the child skips columns with zeros in a borrowing operation, and the bottom digit is written as the answer.

© LAURA DWIGHT PHOTOGRAPHY

Arguments about how to teach mathematics pit drill in computing against "number sense," or understanding. A blend of both approaches is most beneficial, including opportunities to experiment with problem solving, grasp the reasons behind strategies, and evaluate solution techniques.

Children who are given rich opportunities to experiment with problem solving, to grasp the reasons behind strategies, and to evaluate solution techniques seldom make such errors. In one study, second graders taught in these ways not only mastered correct procedures but even invented their own successful strategies, some of which were superior to standard, school-taught methods (Fuson & Burghard, 2003).

In Asian countries, students receive a variety of supports for acquiring mathematical knowledge and often excel at math computation and reasoning. Use of the metric system helps Asian children grasp place value. The consistent structure of number words in Asian languages (*ten-two* for 12, *ten-three* for 13) also makes this idea clear (Miura & Okamoto, 2003). And because Asian number words are shorter and more quickly pronounced, more digits can be held in working memory at once, increasing the speed of thinking. Furthermore, Chinese parents provide their preschoolers with extensive practice in counting and adding—experiences that contribute to the superiority of Chinese over U.S. children's math knowledge even before school entry (Siegler & Mu, 2008; Zhou et al., 2006). Finally, as we will see later in this chapter, compared with lessons in North America, those in Asian classrooms devote more time to exploring math concepts and less to drill and repetition.

ASK YOURSELF

» REVIEW
Cite evidence that school-age children view the mind as an active, constructive agent.

» APPLY
After viewing a slide show on endangered species, second and fifth graders were asked to remember as many animals as they could. Explain why fifth graders recalled much more than second graders.

» APPLY
Lizzie knows that if you have difficulty learning part of a task, you should devote extra attention to that part. But she plays each of her piano pieces from beginning to end instead of practicing the hard parts. What explains Lizzie's failure to engage in cognitive self-regulation?

» REFLECT
In your own elementary school math education, how much emphasis was placed on computational drill and how much on understanding of concepts? How do you think that balance affected your interest and performance in math?

Individual Differences in Mental Development

Around age 6, IQ becomes more stable than it was at earlier ages, and it correlates moderately well with academic achievement, typically around .50 to .60. And children with higher IQs are more likely when they grow up to attain higher levels of education and enter more prestigious occupations (Brody, 1997; Deary et al., 2007). Because IQ predicts school performance and educational attainment, it often enters into educational decisions. Do intelligence tests accurately assess the school-age child's ability to profit from academic instruction? Let's look closely at this controversial issue.

Defining and Measuring Intelligence

Virtually all intelligence tests provide an overall score (the IQ), which represents *general intelligence,* or reasoning ability, along with an array of separate scores measuring specific mental abilities (see page 168 in Chapter 5). But intelligence is a collection of many capacities, not all of which are included on currently available tests (Carroll, 2005; Sternberg, 2005). Test designers use a complicated statistical technique called *factor analysis* to identify the various abilities that intelligence tests measure. It identifies which sets of test items cluster together, meaning that test-takers who do well on one item in a cluster tend to do well on the others. Distinct clusters are called *factors,* each of which represents an ability. See Figure 9.7 for items typically included in intelligence tests for children.

The intelligence tests given from time to time in classrooms are *group-administered tests.* They permit large numbers of students to be tested at once and are useful for instructional planning and for identifying children who require more extensive evaluation with *individually administered tests.* Unlike group tests, which teachers can give with minimal training, individually administered tests demand considerable training and experience to give well. The examiner not only considers the child's answers but also observes the child's behavior, noting such reactions as attention to and interest in the tasks and wariness of the adult. These observations provide insight into whether the test results accurately reflect the child's abilities. Two individual tests—the Stanford-Binet and the Wechsler—

TYPICAL VERBAL ITEMS

Vocabulary Tell me what *carpet* means.

General Information What day of the week comes right after Thursday?

Verbal Comprehension Why do we need police officers?

Similarities How are a ship and a train alike?

Arithmetic If a $60 jacket is 25% off, how much does it cost?

TYPICAL PERCEPTUAL- AND SPATIAL-REASONING ITEMS

Block Design Make these blocks look just like the picture.

Picture Concepts Choose one object from each row to make a group of objects that goes together.

Spatial Visualization Which of the boxes on the right can be made from the pattern on the left?

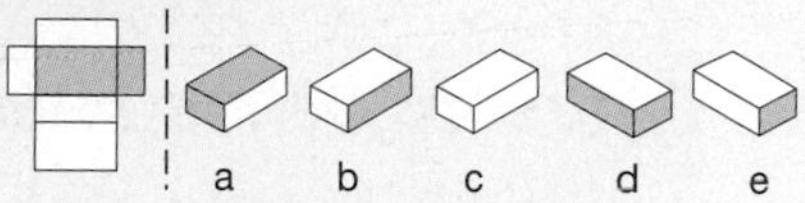

TYPICAL WORKING-MEMORY ITEMS

Digit Span Repeat these digits in the same order. Now repeat these digits (a similar series) backward.
2, 6, 4, 7, 1, 8

Letter–Number Sequencing Repeat these numbers and letters, first giving the numbers, then the letters, each in correct sequence.
8 G 4 B 5 N 2

TYPICAL PROCESSING-SPEED ITEM

Symbol Search If the shape on the left is the same as any of those on the right, mark YES. If the shape is not the same, mark NO. Work as quickly as you can without making mistakes.

■ **FIGURE 9.7** ■ **Test items like those on commonly used intelligence tests for children.** The verbal items emphasize culturally loaded, fact-oriented information. The perceptual- and spatial-reasoning, working-memory, and processing-speed items emphasize aspects of information processing and are assumed to assess more biologically based skills.

are often used to identify highly intelligent children and to diagnose children with learning problems.

The modern descendant of Alfred Binet's first successful intelligence test is the *Stanford-Binet Intelligence Scales,* Fifth Edition, for individuals from age 2 to adulthood. It assesses general intelligence and five intellectual factors: knowledge, quantitative reasoning, visual–spatial processing, working memory, and basic information processing (such as speed of analyzing information). Each factor includes both a verbal mode and a nonverbal mode of testing, yielding 10 subtests in all (Roid, 2003). The nonverbal subtests, which do not require spoken language, are especially useful when assessing individuals with limited English, hearing impairments, or communication disorders. The knowledge and quantitative reasoning factors emphasize culturally loaded, fact-oriented information, such as vocabulary and arithmetic problems. In contrast, the visual–spatial processing, working-memory, and basic information-processing factors are assumed to be less culturally biased because they require little specific information (see the spatial visualization item in Figure 9.7).

The *Wechsler Intelligence Scale for Children (WISC-IV)* is the fourth edition of a widely used test for 6- through 16-year-olds (Wechsler, 2003). It measures general intelligence and four broad factors: verbal reasoning, perceptual (or visual–spatial) reasoning, working memory, and processing speed. Each factor is made up of two or three subtests, yielding 10 separate scores in all. The WISC-IV was designed to downplay culturally dependent knowledge, which is emphasized on only one factor (verbal reasoning). According to the test designers, the result is the most "culture-fair" intelligence test available (Williams, Weis, & Rolfhus, 2003). The WISC was also the first test to be standardized on children representing the total population of the United States, including ethnic minorities.

Recent Efforts to Define Intelligence

As we have seen, mental tests now tap important aspects of information processing. In line with this trend, some researchers are combining the mental testing approach to defining intelligence with the information-processing approach. They believe that once we identify the processing skills that separate individuals who test well from those who test poorly, we will know more about how to intervene to improve performance. These investigators conduct *componential analyses* of children's test scores. This means that they look for relationships between aspects (or components) of information processing and children's intelligence test scores.

Measures of basic working-memory capacity (such as digit span) correlate well with mental test scores (de Ribaupierre & Lecerf, 2006). And processing speed, assessed in terms of reaction time on diverse cognitive tasks, is moderately related to IQ (Deary, 2001; Li et al., 2004). Individuals whose nervous systems function efficiently, permitting them to take in more information and manipulate it quickly, appear to have an edge in intellectual skills.

But flexible attention, memory, and reasoning strategies are as important as efficient thinking in predicting IQ, and they explain some of the association between response speed and good test performance (Lohman, 2000; Miller & Vernon, 1992). Children who apply strategies effectively acquire more knowledge and can retrieve it rapidly—advantages that carry over to mental test performance. Similarly, recall that available space in working memory depends in part on effective inhibition (see page 303). Inhibition and sustained and selective attention are among a wide array of attentional skills that are good predictors of IQ (Schweizer, Moosbrugger, & Goldhammer, 2006).

The componential approach has one major shortcoming: It regards intelligence as entirely due to causes within the child. Yet throughout this book, we have seen how cultural and situational factors affect children's thinking. Robert Sternberg has expanded the componential approach into a comprehensive theory that regards intelligence as a product of inner and outer forces.

■ STERNBERG'S TRIARCHIC THEORY OF SUCCESSFUL INTELLIGENCE. As Figure 9.8 shows, Sternberg's (2001, 2002, 2005) **triarchic theory of successful intelligence** identifies three broad, interacting intelligences: (1) *analytical intelligence,* or information-processing skills; (2) *creative intelligence,* the capacity to solve novel problems; and (3) *practical intelligence,* application of intellectual skills in everyday situations. Intelligent behavior involves balancing all three intelligences to achieve success in life according to one's personal goals and the requirements of one's cultural community.

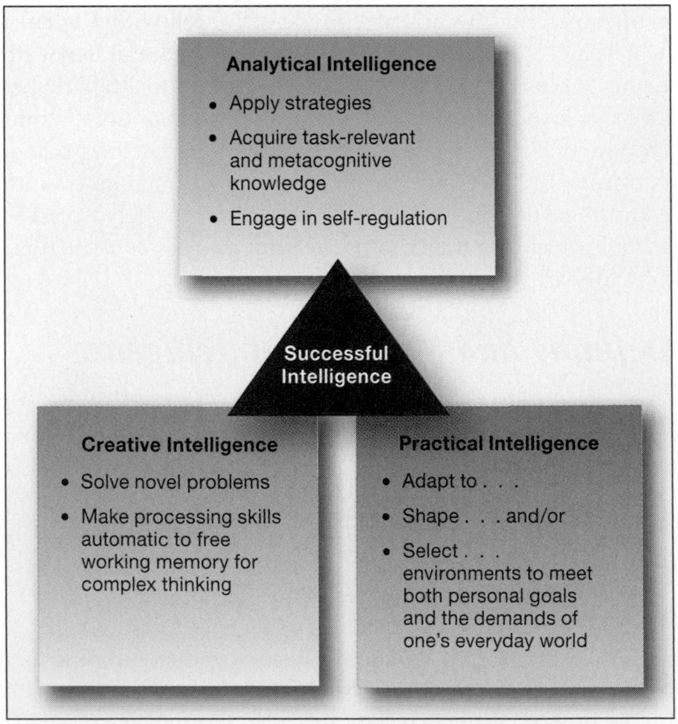

■ FIGURE 9.8 ■ Sternberg's triarchic theory of successful intelligence. People who behave intelligently balance three interrelated intelligences—analytical, creative, and practical—to achieve success in life, defined by their personal goals and the requirements of their cultural communities.

Analytical Intelligence. *Analytical intelligence* consists of the information-processing components that underlie all intelligent acts: applying strategies, acquiring task-relevant and metacognitive knowledge, and engaging in self-regulation. On mental tests, however, processing skills are used in only a few of their potential ways, resulting in a far too narrow view of intelligent behavior. As we have seen, children in tribal and village societies do not necessarily perform well on measures of "school" knowledge but thrive when processing information in out-of-school situations that most Westerners would find highly challenging.

Creative Intelligence. In any context, success depends not only on processing familiar information but also on generating useful solutions to new problems. People who are *creative* think more skillfully than others when faced with novelty. Given a new task, they apply their information-processing skills in exceptionally effective ways, rapidly making these skills automatic so that working memory is freed for more complex aspects of the situation. Consequently, they quickly move to high-level performance. Although all of us are capable of some creativity, only a few individuals excel at generating novel solutions.

Practical Intelligence. Finally, intelligence is a *practical,* goal-oriented activity aimed at *adapting to, shaping,* or *selecting environments.* Intelligent people skillfully *adapt* their thinking to fit with both their desires and the demands of their everyday worlds. When they cannot adapt to a situation, they try to *shape,* or change, it to meet their needs. If they cannot shape it, they *select* new contexts that better match their skills, values, or goals. Practical intelligence reminds us that intelligent behavior is never culture-free. Children with certain life histories do well at the behaviors required for success on intelligence tests and adapt easily to the testing conditions. Others, with different backgrounds, may misinterpret or reject the testing context. Yet such children often display sophisticated abilities in daily life—for example, telling stories, engaging in complex artistic activities, or interacting skillfully with other people.

The triarchic theory highlights the complexity of intelligent behavior and the limitations of current intelligence tests in assessing that complexity. For example, out-of-school, practical forms of intelligence are vital for life success and help explain why cultures vary widely in the behaviors they regard as intelligent (Sternberg et al., 2000). When researchers asked ethnically diverse parents to describe an intelligent first grader, Caucasian Americans mentioned cognitive traits. In contrast, ethnic minorities (Cambodian, Filipino, Vietnamese, and Mexican immigrants) identified noncognitive capacities—motivation, self-management, and social skills (Okagaki & Sternberg, 1993). According to Sternberg, mental tests can easily underestimate, and even overlook, the intellectual strengths of some children, especially ethnic minorities.

■ **GARDNER'S THEORY OF MULTIPLE INTELLIGENCES.** In yet another view of how information-processing skills underlie intelligent behavior, Howard Gardner's (1983, 1993, 2000) **theory of multiple intelligences** defines intelligence in terms of distinct sets of processing operations that permit individuals to engage in a wide range of culturally valued activities. Dismissing the idea of general intelligence, Gardner proposes at least eight independent intelligences (see Table 9.1).

■ **TABLE 9.1** ■ ***Gardner's Multiple Intelligences***

INTELLIGENCE	PROCESSING OPERATIONS	END-STATE PERFORMANCE POSSIBILITIES
Linguistic	Sensitivity to the sounds, rhythms, and meaning of words and the functions of language	Poet, journalist
Logico-mathematical	Sensitivity to, and capacity to detect, logical or numerical patterns; ability to handle long chains of logical reasoning	Mathematician
Musical	Ability to produce and appreciate pitch, rhythm (or melody), and aesthetic quality of the forms of musical expressiveness	Instrumentalist, composer
Spatial	Ability to perceive the visual–spatial world accurately, to perform transformations on those perceptions, and to re-create aspects of visual experience in the absence of relevant stimuli	Sculptor, navigator
Bodily-kinesthetic	Ability to use the body skillfully for expressive as well as goal-directed purposes; ability to handle objects skillfully	Dancer, athlete
Naturalist	Ability to recognize and classify all varieties of animals, minerals, and plants	Biologist
Interpersonal	Ability to detect and respond appropriately to the moods, temperaments, motivations, and intentions of others	Therapist, salesperson
Intrapersonal	Ability to discriminate complex inner feelings and to use them to guide one's own behavior; knowledge of one's own strengths, weaknesses, desires, and intelligences	Person with detailed, accurate self-knowledge

Sources: Gardner, 1993, 1998a, 2000.

According to Gardner, children are capable of at least eight distinct intelligences. As this child learns pottery skills under the guidance of an expert potter, she enriches her spatial intelligence.

Gardner believes that each intelligence has a unique biological basis, a distinct course of development, and different expert, or "end-state," performances. At the same time, he emphasizes that a lengthy process of education is required to transform any raw potential into a mature social role (Connell, Sheridan, & Gardner, 2003). Cultural values and learning opportunities affect the extent to which a child's intellectual strengths are realized and the ways they are expressed.

Gardner's list of abilities has yet to be firmly grounded in research. Neurological evidence for the independence of his abilities is weak. Some exceptionally gifted individuals have abilities that are broad rather than limited to a particular domain (Goldsmith, 2000). And research with mental tests suggests that several of Gardner's intelligences (linguistic, logico-mathematical, and spatial) have common features. Nevertheless, Gardner calls attention to several abilities not measured by intelligence tests. For example, his interpersonal and intrapersonal intelligences include a set of capacities for dealing with people and understanding oneself. As the Lifespan Vista box on the following page indicates, researchers are attempting to define, measure, and foster these abilities, which are vital for a satisfying, successful life.

Explaining Individual and Group Differences in IQ

When we compare individuals in terms of academic achievement, years of education, and occupational status, it quickly becomes clear that certain sectors of the population are advantaged over others. In trying to explain these differences, researchers have compared the IQ scores of ethnic and SES groups. American black children score, on average, 12 to 13 IQ points below American white children, although the difference has been shrinking (Dickens & Flynn, 2006; Edwards & Oakland, 2006; Hedges & Nowell, 1998). Hispanic children fall midway between black and white children (Ceci, Rosenblum, & Kumpf, 1998).

The IQ gap between middle-SES and low-SES children—about 9 points—accounts for some of the ethnic differences in IQ, but not all. When black children and white children are matched on parental education and income, the black–white IQ gap is reduced by a third to a half (Brooks-Gunn et al., 2003; Smith, Duncan, & Lee, 2003). Of course, considerable variation exists within each ethnic and SES group. Still, these group differences in IQ are large enough and their consequences serious enough that they cannot be ignored.

In the 1970s, the IQ nature–nurture controversy escalated after psychologist Arthur Jensen (1969) published a controversial monograph entitled, "How Much Can We Boost IQ and Scholastic Achievement?" Jensen argued—and still maintains—that heredity is largely responsible for individual, ethnic, and SES variations in intelligence (Jensen, 1998, 2001; Rushton & Jensen, 2005, 2006). His work sparked an outpouring of research studies and responses, including ethical challenges reflecting deep concern that his conclusions would fuel social prejudices. Richard Herrnstein and Charles Murray rekindled the controversy with *The Bell Curve* (1994). Like Jensen, they argued that heredity contributes substantially to individual and SES differences in IQ, and they implied that heredity plays a sizable role in the black–white IQ gap. Let's look closely at some important evidence.

NATURE VERSUS NURTURE. In Chapter 2, we introduced the *heritability estimate.* Recall that heritabilities are obtained from *kinship studies,* which compare family members. The most powerful evidence on the role of heredity in IQ involves twin comparisons. The IQ scores of identical twins (who share all their genes) are more similar than those of fraternal twins (who are genetically no more alike than ordinary siblings). On the basis of this and other kinship evidence, researchers estimate that about half the differences in IQ among children can be traced to their genetic makeup.

Recall, however, that heritabilities risk overestimating genetic influences and underestimating environmental influences. Although these measures offer convincing evidence that genes contribute to IQ, disagreement persists over how large the role of heredity really is (Grigorenko, 2000; Plomin, 2003). And heritability estimates do not reveal the complex processes through which genes and experiences influence intelligence as children develop.

Compared with heritabilities, adoption studies offer a wider range of information. Findings consistently reveal that when young children are adopted into caring, stimulating homes, their IQs rise substantially compared with the IQs of nonadopted children who remain in economically deprived families (van IJzendoorn, Juffer, & Poelhuis, 2005). But adopted children benefit to varying degrees. In one investigation, children of two extreme groups of biological mothers—those with

A LIFESPAN VISTA: Looking Forward, Looking Back

Emotional Intelligence

During recess, Muriel handed a birthday party invitation to every fifth-grade girl except Claire, who looked on sadly as her classmates chattered about the party. But one of Muriel's friends, Jessica, looked troubled. Pulling Muriel aside, she exclaimed, "Why'd you do that? You hurt Claire's feelings—you embarrassed her! If you bring invitations to school, you've got to give everybody one!" And after school, Jessica comforted Claire, saying, "If you aren't invited, I'm not going, either!"

Jessica's IQ is only slightly above average, but she excels at *emotional intelligence*—a term that has captured public attention because of popular books suggesting that it is an overlooked set of skills that can greatly improve life success (Goleman, 1995, 1998). According to one influential definition, **emotional intelligence** refers to a set of emotional abilities that enable individuals to process and adapt to emotional information (Salovey & Pizzaro, 2003). To measure it, researchers have devised items tapping emotional skills that enable people to manage their own emotions and interact competently with others. One test requires people to identify and rate the strength of emotions expressed in photographs of faces (emotional perception), to reason about emotions in social situations (emotional understanding), to identify which emotions promote certain thoughts and activities (emotional facilitation), and to evaluate the effectiveness of strategies for controlling negative emotions (emotion regulation). Factor analyses of the scores of hundreds of test-takers identified several emotional capacities as well as a higher-order general factor (Mayer, Salovey, & Caruso, 2003).

Emotional intelligence is modestly related to IQ. And in school-age children, adolescents, and adults, it is positively associated with self-esteem, empathy, prosocial behavior, cooperation, leadership skills, and life satisfaction and negatively related to drug and alcohol use, dependency, depression, and aggressive behavior (Brackett, Mayer, & Warner, 2004; Mavroveli et al., 2007; Petrides et al., 2006). In the workplace, emotional intelligence predicts many aspects of success, including managerial effectiveness, productive co-worker relationships, and job performance (Mayer, Roberts, & Barsade, 2008; Mayer, Salovey, & Caruso, 2008).

Only a few assessments of emotional intelligence are available for children. These require careful training of teachers in observing and recording children's emotional skills during everyday activities, gathering information from parents, and taking ethnic backgrounds into account (Denham, 2005; Denham & Burton, 2003). As more and better measures are devised, they may help identify children with weak social and emotional competencies who would profit from intervention (Denham, 2006; Stewart-Brown & Edmunds, 2007).

The concept of emotional intelligence has increased teachers' awareness that providing experiences that meet students' social and emotional needs can improve their adjustment. Lessons that teach emotional understanding, respect and caring for others, strategies for regulating emotion, and resistance to unfavorable peer pressure—using active learning techniques that provide skill practice both in and out of the classroom—are becoming more common (Goetz et al., 2005).

© ELLEN B. SENISI PHOTOGRAPHY

The 7-year-old on the right displays high emotional intelligence as she accurately reads her friend's sadness and offers comfort.

IQs below 95 and those with IQs above 120—were adopted at birth by parents who were well above average in income and education. During the school years, the children of the low-IQ biological mothers scored above average in IQ, indicating that test performance can be greatly improved by an advantaged home life. But they did not do as well as children of high-IQ biological mothers placed in similar adoptive families (Loehlin, Horn, & Willerman, 1997). Adoption research confirms that heredity and environment contribute jointly to IQ.

Adoption research also sheds light on the black–white IQ gap. In two studies, African-American children adopted into economically well-off white homes during the first year of life scored high on intelligence tests, attaining mean IQs of 110 and 117 by middle childhood—20 to 30 points higher than the typical scores of children growing up in low-income black communities (Moore, 1986; Scarr & Weinberg, 1983). In one investigation, the IQs of black adoptees declined in adolescence, perhaps because of the challenges faced by minority teenagers in forming an ethnic identity that blends birth and adoptive backgrounds (DeBerry, Scarr, & Weinberg, 1996). When this process is filled with emotional turmoil, it can dampen motivation on tests and in school. Still, the black adoptees remained above the IQ average for low-SES African Americans.

Adoption findings do not completely resolve questions about ethnic differences in IQ. Nevertheless, the IQ gains of black children "reared in the culture of the tests and schools" are consistent with a wealth of evidence that poverty severely depresses the intelligence of ethnic minority children.

CULTURAL INFLUENCES. A controversial question raised about ethnic differences in IQ has to do with whether they result from *test bias*. If a test samples knowledge and skills that not all groups of children have had equal opportunity to learn, or if the testing situation impairs the performance of some groups but not others, then the resulting score is a biased, or unfair, measure.

Some experts reject the idea that intelligence tests are biased, claiming that they are intended to represent success in the common culture. According to this view, because IQ predicts academic achievement equally well for majority and minority children, IQ tests are fair to both groups (Edwards & Oakland, 2006; Jensen, 2002). Others believe that lack of exposure to certain communication styles and knowledge, along with negative stereotypes about the test-taker's ethnic group, can undermine children's performance (Ceci & Williams, 1997; Sternberg, 2005). Let's look at the evidence.

Communication Styles. Ethnic minority families often foster unique language skills that do not match the expectations of most classrooms and testing situations. In one study, a researcher spent many hours observing in low-SES black homes in a southeastern U.S. city (Heath, 1990). She found that African-American parents rarely asked their children the knowledge-training questions typical of middle-SES white parents and of tests and classrooms ("What color is it?" "What's this story about?"). Instead, the black parents asked only "real" questions, ones they themselves could not answer. Often these were analogy questions ("What's that like?") or story-starter questions ("Didja hear Miss Sally this morning?") that called for elaborate responses about everyday events and had no "right" answer.

These experiences lead low-SES black children to develop complex verbal skills at home, such as storytelling and exchanging quick-witted remarks. But their language emphasizes emotional and social concerns rather than facts about the world. Not surprisingly, black children may be confused by the "objective" questions they encounter on tests and in classrooms.

Furthermore, many ethnic minority parents without extensive schooling prefer a *collaborative style of communication* when completing tasks with children. They work together in a coordinated, fluid way, each focused on the same aspect of the problem. This pattern of adult–child engagement has been observed in Native-American, Canadian Inuit, Hispanic, and Guatemalan Mayan cultures (Chavajay & Rogoff, 2002; Crago, Annahatak, & Ningiuruvik, 1993; Delgado-Gaitan, 1994). With increasing education, parents establish a *hierarchical style of communication,* like that of classrooms and tests. The parent directs each child to carry out an aspect of the task, and children work independently (Greenfield, Suzuki, & Rothstein-Fish, 2006). This sharp discontinuity between home and school practices may contribute to low-SES minority children's lower IQ and school performance.

Test Content. Many researchers argue that IQ scores are affected by specific information acquired as part of majority-culture upbringing. Consistent with this view, low-SES African-American children often miss vocabulary words on mental tests that have alternative meanings in their cultural community—for example, interpreting the word *frame* as "physique" and *wrapping* as "rapping," a popular style of music (Champion, 2003a).

Unfortunately, attempts to change tests by eliminating verbal, fact-oriented items and relying only on spatial reasoning tasks (believed to be less culturally loaded) have not raised the scores of low-SES minority children much (Reynolds & Kaiser, 1990). Yet even these nonverbal test items depend on learning opportunities. For example, using small blocks to duplicate designs and playing video games increase success on spatial tasks (Dirks, 1982; Maynard, Subrahmanyam, & Greenfield, 2005). Low-income minority children, who often grow up in more "people-oriented" than "object-oriented" homes, may lack toys and games that promote certain intellectual skills.

Furthermore, the sheer amount of time a child spends in school predicts IQ. When children of the same age enrolled in different grades are compared, those who have been in school longer score higher on intelligence tests (Ceci, 1991, 1999). Taken together, these findings indicate that children's exposure to the factual knowledge and ways of thinking valued in classrooms has a sizable impact on their intelligence test performance.

Stereotypes. Imagine trying to succeed at an activity when the prevailing attitude is that members of your group are incompetent. **Stereotype threat**—the fear of being judged on the basis of a negative stereotype—can trigger anxiety that interferes with performance (Steele, 1997). Mounting evidence confirms that stereotype threat undermines test taking in children and adults. For example, researchers gave African-American, Hispanic-American, and Caucasian 6- to 10-year-olds verbal tasks. Some children were told that the tasks were "not a test." Others were told they were "a test of how good children are at school problems" (McKown & Weinstein, 2003). Among children who were aware of ethnic stereotypes (such as "black people aren't smart"), African Americans and Hispanics performed far

© ELLEN B. SENISI PHOTOGRAPHY

School-age children become increasingly conscious of ethnic stereotypes, and those from stigmatized groups are especially mindful of them. The fear of being judged on the basis of a negative stereotype may be behind this child's hands-off attitude toward his schoolwork.

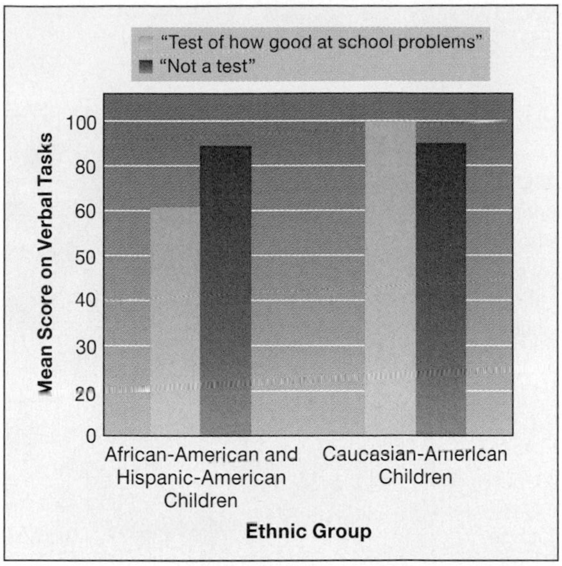

■ **FIGURE 9.9** ■ **Effect of stereotype threat on test performance.** Among African-American and Hispanic-American children who were aware of ethnic stereotypes, being told that verbal tasks were a "test of how good children are at school problems" led to far worse performance than being told the tasks were "not a test." These statements had little impact on the performance of Caucasian-American children. (Adapted from McKown & Weinstein, 2003.)

worse in the "test" condition than in the "not a test" condition. Caucasian children, in contrast, performed similarly in both conditions (see Figure 9.9).

Over middle childhood, children become increasingly conscious of ethnic stereotypes, and those from stigmatized groups are especially mindful of them. By junior high school, many low-SES minority students start to say that doing well in school is not important to them (Major et al., 1998; Osborne, 1994). Self-protective disengagement, sparked by stereotype threat, may be responsible. This weakening of motivation can have serious, long-term consequences. Research shows that self-discipline—effort and delay of gratification—predicts school performance at least as well as, and sometimes better than, IQ does (Duckworth & Seligman, 2005).

Reducing Cultural Bias in Testing. Although not all experts agree, many acknowledge that IQ scores can underestimate the intelligence of culturally different children. A special concern exists about incorrectly labeling minority children as slow learners and assigning them to remedial classes, which are far less stimulating than regular school experiences. To avoid this danger, test scores need to be combined with assessments of children's adaptive behavior—their ability to cope with the demands of their everyday environments. The child who does poorly on an intelligence test yet plays a complex game on the playground or figures out how to rewire a broken TV is unlikely to be mentally deficient.

In addition, culturally relevant testing procedures enhance minority children's test performance. In an approach called **dynamic assessment,** an innovation consistent with Vygotsky's zone of proximal development, an adult introduces purposeful teaching into the testing situation to find out what the child can attain with social support. Research shows that children's receptivity to teaching and their capacity to transfer what they have learned to novel problems contribute substantially to gains in test performance (Lidz, 2001; Sternberg & Grigorenko, 2002). In one study, Ethiopian 6- and 7-year-olds who had recently immigrated to Israel scored well below their Israeli-born agemates on spatial reasoning tasks. The Ethiopian children had little experience with this type of thinking. After several dynamic assessment sessions in which the adult suggested effective strategies, the Ethiopian children's scores rose sharply, nearly equaling those of the Israeli-born children (Tzuriel & Kaufman, 1999). They also transferred their learning to new test items.

But rather than adapting testing to support ethnic minority children's learning needs, North American education is placing greater emphasis on traditional test scores. To upgrade the academic achievement of poorly performing students, a *high-stakes testing* movement has arisen, making progress through school contingent on test performance. As the Social Issues box on pages 316–317 indicates, this stepped-up emphasis on passing standardized tests has narrowed the focus of instruction, and it may widen SES and ethnic differences in educational attainment.

In view of its many problems, should intelligence testing in schools be suspended? Most experts reject this solution. Without testing, important educational decisions would be based only on subjective impressions, perhaps increasing discriminatory placement of minority children. Intelligence tests are useful when interpreted carefully by psychologists and educators who are sensitive to cultural influences on test performance. And despite their limitations, IQ scores continue to be fairly accurate measures of school learning potential for the majority of Western children.

© JANINE WIEDEL PHOTOLIBRARY/ALAMY

This teacher uses dynamic assessment, tailoring instruction to students' individual needs—an approach that reveals what a child can learn with social support.

SOCIAL ISSUES

High-Stakes Testing

To better hold schools accountable for educating students, during the past two decades many U.S. states have mandated that students pass exams for high school graduation. As these high-stakes achievement tests spread, schools stepped up their testing programs, extending them downward to elementary school. Some states and school districts also made grade promotion (in New York City, as early as the third grade) and secondary-school academic course credits contingent on test scores (Gootman, 2005).

The U.S. No Child Left Behind Act, authorized by Congress in 2002, broadens high-stakes testing to the identification of "passing" and "failing" schools. The law mandates that each state evaluate every public school's performance through annual achievement testing and publicize the results. Schools that consistently perform poorly (have a high percentage of failing students) must give parents options for upgrading their children's education, such as transfers to nearby, higher-performing schools or enrollment in remedial classes. Some states offer schoolwide rewards for high scores, including official praise and financial bonuses to school staff. Penalties imposed for low scores include withdrawal of accreditation, state takeover, and closure.

Proponents of high-stakes testing believe that it introduces greater rigor into classroom teaching, improves student motivation and achievement, and either turns around poor-performing schools or protects students from being trapped in them. But accumulating evidence indicates that high-stakes testing often undermines, rather than upgrades, the quality of education.

In a Canadian study, researchers examined the impact of requiring students to pass a high school exit exam on eighth-, tenth-, and twelfth-grade science teaching. They found that twelfth grade teachers narrowed the scope of what they taught to strings of facts to be memorized for the test. As a result, eighth and tenth graders, in some respects, were doing more advanced work than twelfth graders—conducting more experiments, exploring topics in greater depth, and engaging in more critical thinking (Wideen et al., 1997).

Because the main goal of high-stakes testing is to upgrade the test performance of poorly performing students, low-income and ethnic minority children are especially likely to be exposed to narrowly focused, regimented teaching. Simultaneously, the education needs of gifted students are neglected (Mondoza, 2006).

An additional concern is that high-stakes testing promotes fear—a poor motivator for upgrading teaching and learning. Principals and teachers worry about losing funding and their jobs if students do poorly—punishments that have sparked unprecedented levels of adult cheating and other educationally detrimental behaviors. These range from giving students answers, changing students' scores,

© ELLEN B. SENISI PHOTOGRAPHY

In many U.S. classrooms, high-stakes testing has narrowed the focus of the curriculum to test preparation and promoted a one-size-fits-all education.

ASK YOURSELF

REVIEW
Using Sternberg's triarchic theory and Gardner's theory of multiple intelligences, explain the limitations of current intelligence tests in assessing the diversity of human intelligence.

APPLY
Josefina, a Hispanic fourth grader, does well on homework assignments. But when her teacher announces, "It's time for a test to see how much you've learned," Josefina usually does poorly. How might stereotype threat explain this inconsistency?

CONNECT
Explain how dynamic assessment is consistent with Vygotsky's zone of proximal development and with scaffolding. (See Chapter 7, page 235.)

REFLECT
Do you think that intelligence tests are culturally biased? What observations and evidence influenced your conclusions?

Language Development

Vocabulary, grammar, and pragmatics continue to develop in middle childhood, although less obviously than at earlier ages. In addition, school-age children's attitude toward language undergoes a fundamental shift. They develop language awareness.

Schooling contributes greatly to these language competencies. Reflecting on language is extremely common during reading instruction. And fluent reading is a major new source of language learning (Ravid & Tolchinsky, 2002). In the following sections, we will see how an improved ability to reflect on language grows out of literacy and supports language skills.

Vocabulary

During the elementary school years, vocabulary increases fourfold, eventually exceeding 40,000 words. On average, children learn about 20 new words each day, a rate of growth exceeding that in early childhood. In addition to the word-learning strategies discussed in Chapter 7, school-age children add to their

and offering students rewards (money, sweets, and expensive toys) for earning high scores to suspending or expelling students likely to perform poorly just before test administration (Nichols & Berliner, 2007).

Furthermore, many students who get passing school grades, even high grades, fail exams because a time-limited test can tap only a small sample of skills covered in the classroom (Hursh, 2007). Students most likely to score poorly are minority youths living in poverty. When they are punished with course failure and grade retention, their self-esteem and motivation drop sharply. Research confirms that high-stakes testing requirements have contributed to the high U.S. dropout rates among inner-city minority youths (Balfanz et al., 2007; Hursh, 2007).

The trend toward teaching to tests induced by high-stakes testing contrasts sharply with the emphasis on teaching for deeper understanding in countries that rank at the top in cross-cultural comparisons of academic achievement (see pages 324–325).

Even after hundreds of hours of class time devoted to test preparation, tens of thousands of U.S. students fail school-exit exams and do not graduate. Although most retake these exams, some fail repeatedly, with potentially dire consequences for the course of their lives.

Clearly, serious issues remain for lawmakers and educators to resolve about the use of high-stakes tests. These include their questionable power to spark school reforms that make students better learners.

vocabularies by analyzing the structure of complex words. From *happy* and *decide,* they quickly derive the meanings of *happiness* and *decision* (Larsen & Nippold, 2007). They also figure out many more word meanings from context (Nagy & Scott, 2000).

As at earlier ages, children benefit from conversation with more expert speakers, especially when their partners use complex words and explain them (Weizman & Snow, 2001). But because written language contains a far more diverse and complex vocabulary than spoken language, reading contributes enormously to vocabulary growth in middle childhood and adolescence. Children who engage in as little as 21 minutes of independent reading per day are exposed to nearly 2 million words per year (Cunningham & Stanovich, 1998).

As their knowledge expands and becomes better organized, older school-age children think about and use words more precisely: In addition to the verb *fall,* for example, they also use *topple, tumble,* and *plummet* (Berman, 2007). Word definitions also illustrate this change. Five- and 6-year-olds offer concrete descriptions referring to functions or appearance: *knife:* "when you're cutting carrots"; *bicycle:* "it's got wheels, a chain, and handlebars." By the end of elementary school, synonyms and explanations of categorical relationships appear—for example, *knife:* "something you could cut with. A saw is like a knife. It could also be a weapon" (Wehren, De Lisi, & Arnold, 1981). This advance reflects older children's ability to deal with word meanings on an entirely verbal plane. They can add new words to their vocabulary simply by being given a definition.

School-age children's more reflective and analytical approach to language permits them to appreciate the multiple meanings of words—to recognize, for example, that many words, such as *cool* or *neat,* have psychological as well as physical meanings: "What a cool shirt!" or "That movie was really neat!" This grasp of double meanings permits 8- to 10-year-olds to comprehend subtle metaphors, such as "sharp as a tack" and "spilling the beans" (Nippold, Taylor, & Baker, 1996; Wellman & Hickling, 1994). It also leads to a change in children's humor. Riddles and puns that alternate between different meanings of a key word are common: "Hey, did you take a bath?" "Why, is one missing?"

Grammar

During the school years, mastery of complex grammatical constructions improves. For example, English-speaking children use the passive voice more frequently, and they more often extend it from an abbreviated form ("It broke") into full statements ("The glass was broken by Mary") (Israel, Johnson, & Brooks, 2000; Tomasello, 2006). Although the passive form is challenging, language input makes a difference. When adults speak a language that emphasizes full passives, such as Inukitut (spoken by the Inuit people of Arctic Canada), children produce them earlier (Allen & Crago, 1996).

Another grammatical achievement of middle childhood is advanced understanding of infinitive phrases—the difference between "John is eager to please" and "John is easy to please" (Chomsky, 1969). Like gains in vocabulary, appreciation of these subtle grammatical distinctions is supported by an improved ability to analyze and reflect on language.

Pragmatics

Improvements in *pragmatics,* the communicative side of language, also occur. Conversational strategies become more refined. For example, school-age children are better at phrasing things to get their way. When an adult refuses to hand over a desired object, 9-year-olds, but not 5-year-olds, state their second requests more politely (Axia & Baroni, 1985).

Furthermore, as a result of improved memory and ability to take the perspective of listeners, children's narratives increase in organization, detail, and expressiveness. A typical 4- or 5-year-old's narrative states what happened: "We went to the lake. We fished and waited. Paul caught a huge catfish." Six- and 7-year-olds, in contrast, include orienting information (time, place, and participants) and many connectives that lend coherence to the story ("next," "then," "so," "finally"). Gradually, narratives lengthen into a *classic form* in which events not only build to a high point but resolve: "After Paul reeled in the catfish, Dad cleaned and cooked it. Then we ate it all up!" And evaluative comments rise dramatically, becoming common by age 8 to 9:

© JUPITERIMAGES/COMSTOCK IMAGES/ALAMY

In families who regularly eat meals together, children are advanced in language and literacy development. Mealtimes offer many opportunities to relate complex, extended personal stories.

"The catfish tasted great. Paul was so proud!" (Melzi & Ely, 2009; Ukrainetz et al., 2005).

Because children pick up the narrative styles of significant adults in their lives, their narrative forms vary widely across cultures. For example, instead of the *topic-focused style* of most North American school-age children, who describe an experience from beginning to end, African-American children often use a *topic-associating style* in which they blend several similar anecdotes. One 9-year-old related having a tooth pulled, then described seeing her sister's tooth pulled, next told how she had removed one of her baby teeth, and concluded, "I'm a pullin-teeth expert . . . call me, and I'll be over" (McCabe, 1997, p. 164). As a result, African-American children's narratives are usually longer and more complex than those of white children (Champion, 2003b).

The ability to generate clear oral narratives enhances reading comprehension and prepares children for producing longer, more explicit written narratives. In families who regularly eat meals together, children are advanced in language and literacy development because mealtimes offer many opportunities to relate complex, extended personal stories (Snow & Beals, 2006).

Learning Two Languages at a Time

Joey and Lizzie speak only one language—English, their native tongue. Yet throughout the world, many children grow up *bilingual,* learning two languages, and sometimes more than two, in childhood. An estimated 15 percent of U.S. children—6 million in all—speak a language other than English at home (U.S. Census Bureau, 2009b).

BILINGUAL DEVELOPMENT. Children can become bilingual in two ways: (1) by acquiring both languages at the same time in early childhood or (2) by learning a second language after mastering the first. Children of bilingual parents who teach them both languages in infancy and early childhood separate the language systems from the start and attain early language milestones according to a typical timetable (Bosch & Sebastian-Galles, 2001; Conboy & Thal, 2006; Holowka, Brosseau-Lapré, & Petitto, 2002). When school-age children acquire a second language after they already speak a first language, they generally take five to seven years to attain speaking and writing skills on a par with those of native-speaking agemates (Paradis, 2007).

As with first-language development, a *sensitive period* for second-language development exists. Mastery must begin sometime in childhood for most second-language learners to attain full proficiency. But a precise age cutoff for a decline in second-language learning has not been established (Hakuta, Bialystok, & Wiley, 2003). Rather, a continuous age-related decrease from childhood to adulthood occurs.

A large body of research shows that bilingualism has positive consequences for development. Children who are fluent in two languages do better than others on tests of selective attention, analytical reasoning, concept formation, and cognitive flexibility (Bialystok, 2001; Bialystok & Martin, 2004). They are also advanced in certain aspects of language awareness, such as detection of errors in grammar and meaning. And children readily transfer their phonological awareness skills in one language to the other (Bialystok, McBride-Chang, & Luk, 2005; Snow & Kang, 2006). These capacities, as noted earlier, enhance reading achievement.

BILINGUAL EDUCATION. The advantages of bilingualism provide strong justification for bilingual education programs in schools. In Canada, about 7 percent of elementary school students are enrolled in *language immersion programs,* in which English-speaking children are taught entirely in French for several years. This strategy has been successful in developing children who are proficient in both languages and who, by grade 6, achieve as well in reading, writing, and math as their counterparts in the regular English program (Harley & Jean, 1999; Holobow, Genesee, & Lambert, 1991; Turnbull, Hart, & Lapkin, 2003).

In the United States, fierce disagreement exists over the question of how best to educate ethnic minority children with limited English proficiency. Some believe that time spent communicating in the child's native tongue detracts from English-language achievement, which is crucial for success in school and at work. Other educators, committed to developing minority children's native language while fostering mastery of English, note that providing instruction in the native tongue lets minority children know that their heritage is respected. In addition, it prevents inadequate proficiency in both languages. Minority children who gradually lose the first language as a result of being taught the second end up limited in both languages for a time (Ovando & Collier, 1998). This circumstance leads to serious academic difficulties and is believed to contribute to high rates of school failure and dropout among low-SES Hispanic young people, who make up 50 percent of the U.S. language-minority population.

At present, public opinion and educational practice favor English-only instruction. Many U.S. states have passed laws declaring English to be their official language, creating conditions in which schools have no obligation to teach minority students in languages other than English. Yet in classrooms where

© ROBIN SACHS/PHOTOEDIT

In this English–Spanish bilingual classroom, children are more involved in learning, participate more actively in class discussions, and acquire the second language more easily.

both languages are integrated into the curriculum, minority children are more involved in learning and acquire the second language more easily. In contrast, when teachers speak only in a language children can barely understand, minority children display frustration, boredom, and withdrawal (Crawford, 1997).

Supporters of U.S. English-only education often point to the success of Canadian language immersion programs, in which classroom lessons are conducted in the second language. But Canadian parents enroll their children in immersion classrooms voluntarily, and both French and English are majority languages that are equally valued in Canada. For American non-English-speaking minority children, whose native languages are not valued by the larger society, a different strategy seems necessary: one that promotes children's native-language skills while they learn English.

ASK YOURSELF

» REVIEW
Cite examples of how language awareness fosters school-age children's language progress.

» APPLY
Ten-year-old Shana arrived home from soccer practice and remarked, "I'm wiped out!" Megan, her 5-year-old sister, looked puzzled. "What did'ya wipe out, Shana?" Megan asked. Explain Shana's and Megan's different understandings of this expression.

» CONNECT
How can bilingual education promote ethnic minority children's cognitive and academic development?

» REFLECT
Did you acquire a second language at home or study one in school? When did you start, and how proficient are you in the second language? Considering research on bilingualism, what changes would you make in your own second-language learning, and why?

Learning in School

Evidence cited throughout this chapter indicates that schools are vital forces in children's cognitive development. How do schools exert such a powerful influence? Research looking at schools as complex social systems—class size, educational philosophies, teacher–student relationships, and larger cultural context—provides important insights. As you read about these topics, refer to Applying What We Know on page 320, which summarizes characteristics of high-quality education in elementary school.

Class Size

As each school year began, Rena telephoned the principal's office to ask, "How large will Joey's and Lizzie's classes be?" Her concern is well-founded. In a large field experiment, more than 6,000 Tennessee kindergartners were randomly assigned to three class types: "small" (13 to 17 students), "regular" (22 to 25 students) with only a teacher, and regular with a teacher plus a full-time teacher's aide. These arrangements continued into third grade. Small-class students—especially ethnic minority children—scored higher in reading and math achievement each year (Mosteller, 1995). Placing teacher's aides in regular-size classes had no impact. Rather, being in small classes from kindergarten through third grade predicted substantially higher achievement from fourth through ninth grades, after children had returned to regular-size classes. It also predicted greater likelihood of graduating from high school (Finn, Gerber, & Boyd-Zaharias, 2005; Nye, Hedges, & Konstantopoulos, 2001).

Why is small class size beneficial? With fewer children, teachers spend less time disciplining and more time teaching and giving individual attention. Also, children who learn in smaller groups show better concentration, higher-quality class participation, and more favorable attitudes toward school (Blatchford et al., 2003, 2007; Blatchford, Bassett, & Brown, 2005).

Educational Philosophies

Each teacher brings to the classroom an educational philosophy that plays a major role in children's learning. Two philosophical approaches have received most research attention. They differ in what children are taught, the way they are believed to learn, and how their progress is evaluated.

■ TRADITIONAL VERSUS CONSTRUCTIVIST CLASSROOMS. In a **traditional classroom,** the teacher is the sole authority for knowledge, rules, and decision making and does most of the talking. Students are relatively passive—listening, responding when called on, and completing teacher-assigned tasks. Their progress is evaluated by how well they keep pace with a uniform set of standards for their grade.

A **constructivist classroom,** in contrast, encourages students to *construct* their own knowledge. Although constructivist approaches vary, many are grounded in Piaget's theory,

Applying What We Know

Signs of High-Quality Education in Elementary School

Classroom Characteristics	Signs of Quality
Class size	Optimum class size is no larger than 18 children.
Physical setting	Space is divided into richly equipped activity centers—for reading, writing, playing math or language games, exploring science, working on construction projects, using computers, and engaging in other academic pursuits. Spaces are used flexibly for individual and small-group activities and whole-class gatherings.
Curriculum	The curriculum helps children both achieve academic standards and make sense of their learning. Subjects are integrated so that children apply knowledge in one area to others. The curriculum is implemented through activities responsive to children's interests, ideas, and everyday lives, including their cultural backgrounds.
Daily activities	Teachers provide challenging activities that include opportunities for small-group and independent work. Groupings vary in size and makeup of children, depending on the activity and on children's learning needs. Teachers encourage cooperative learning and guide children in attaining it.
Interactions between teachers and children	Teachers foster each child's progress and use intellectually engaging strategies, including posing problems, asking thought-provoking questions, discussing ideas, and adding complexity to tasks. They also demonstrate, explain, coach, and assist in other ways, depending on each child's learning needs.
Evaluations of progress	Teachers regularly evaluate children's progress through written observations and work samples, which they use to enhance and individualize teaching. They help children reflect on their work and decide how to improve it. They also seek information and perspectives from parents on how well children are learning and include parents' views in evaluations.
Relationship with parents	Teachers forge partnerships with parents. They hold periodic conferences and encourage parents to visit the classroom anytime, to observe and volunteer.

Source: Copple & Bredekamp, 2009.

which views children as active agents who reflect on and coordinate their own thoughts rather than absorbing those of others. A glance inside a constructivist classroom reveals richly equipped learning centers, small groups and individuals solving self-chosen problems, and a teacher who guides and supports in response to children's needs. Students are evaluated by considering their progress in relation to their own prior development.

In the United States, the pendulum has swung back and forth between these two views. In the 1960s and early 1970s, constructivist classrooms gained in popularity. Then, as concern arose over the academic progress of children and youths, a "back-to-basics" movement arose. Classrooms returned to traditional instruction, a style still prevalent today.

Although older elementary school children in traditional classrooms have a slight edge in achievement test scores, constructivist settings are associated with many other benefits—gains in academic motivation, critical thinking, social and moral maturity, and positive attitudes toward school (DeVries, 2001; Rathunde & Csikszentmihalyi, 2005; Walberg, 1986). And as noted in Chapter 7, when teacher-directed instruction is emphasized in preschool and kindergarten, it actually undermines academic motivation and achievement, especially in low-SES children.

The heavy emphasis on knowledge absorption as early as kindergarten has contributed to a growing trend among parents to delay their child's school entry—especially if the child is a boy with a birth date close to the cutoff for kindergarten enrollment. But research has not revealed any long-term benefits, either academic or social (Lincove & Painter, 2006; Stipek, 2002). To the contrary, younger first graders reap achievement gains from on-time enrollment, outperforming same-age children a year behind them (Stipek & Byler, 2001). An alternative perspective is that school readiness can be cultivated through classroom experiences that foster children's individual progress.

■ **NEW PHILOSOPHICAL DIRECTIONS.** New approaches to education, grounded in Vygotsky's sociocultural theory, capitalize on the rich social context of the classroom to spur children's learning. In these **social-constructivist classrooms,** children participate in a wide range of challenging activities with teachers and peers, with whom they jointly construct understandings. As children acquire knowledge and strategies from working together, they become competent, contributing members of their classroom community and advance in cognitive and social development (Bodrova & Leong, 2007; Palincsar, 2003). Vygotsky's emphasis on the social origins of higher cognitive processes has inspired the following educational themes:

- *Teachers and children as partners in learning.* A classroom rich in both teacher–child and child–child collaboration transfers culturally valued ways of thinking to children.

- *Experiences with many types of symbolic communication in meaningful activities.* As children master reading, writing, and mathematics, they become aware of their culture's communication systems, reflect on their own thinking, and bring it under voluntary control. ***TAKE A MOMENT...*** Can you identify research presented earlier in this chapter that supports this theme?
- *Teaching adapted to each child's zone of proximal development.* Assistance that both responds to current understandings and encourages children to take the next step helps ensure that each child makes the best progress possible.

According to Vygotsky, besides teachers, more expert peers can spur children's learning, as long as they adjust the help they provide to fit the less mature child's zone of proximal development. Consistent with this idea, mounting evidence confirms that peer collaboration promotes development only under certain conditions. A crucial factor is **cooperative learning,** in which small groups of classmates work toward common goals—by resolving differences of opinion, sharing responsibilities, and providing one another with sufficient explanations to correct misunderstandings. And children profit more when their peer partner is an "expert"—especially capable at the task. When older or more expert students assist younger or less expert students, both benefit in achievement and self-esteem (Ginsburg-Block, Rohrbeck, & Fantuzzo, 2006; Renninger, 1998).

Because Western cultural-majority children regard competition and independent work as natural, they typically require extensive guidance to succeed at cooperative learning. In several studies, groups of students trained in collaborative processes displayed more cooperative behavior, gave clearer explanations, and enjoyed learning more than did untrained groups (Gillies, 2000, 2003; Terwel et al., 2001). In other research, the quality of children's collaborative discussions predicted gains in diverse cognitive skills that persisted for weeks beyond the cooperative learning experience (Fleming & Alexander, 2001). Notice how teaching through cooperative learning broadens Vygotsky's concept of the zone of proximal development, from a single child collaborating with an expert partner (adult or peer) to multiple partners with diverse expertises, stimulating and encouraging one another.

© DORANNE JACOBSON

These children attending a rural school in India cooperate easily while completing a reading assignment. Their Western cultural-majority agemates, in contrast, typically require extensive guidance to succeed at cooperative learning.

Teacher–Student Interaction

Elementary school students describe good teachers as caring, helpful, and stimulating—behaviors associated with gains in motivation, achievement, and positive peer relations (Daniels, Kalkman, & McCombs, 2001; Hughes & Kwok, 2006, 2007; Hughes, Zhang, & Hill, 2006). But too many U.S. teachers emphasize repetitive drill over higher-level thinking, such as grappling with ideas and applying knowledge to new situations (Sacks, 2005). In a longitudinal investigation of middle-school students, those in more academically demanding classrooms showed better attendance and larger gains in math achievement over the following two years (Phillips, 1997).

Of course, teachers do not interact in the same way with all children. Well-behaved, high-achieving students typically get more encouragement and praise, whereas unruly students have more conflicts with teachers and receive more criticism from them (Henricsson & Rydell, 2004). Caring teacher–student relationships have an especially strong impact on the achievement and social behavior of low-SES minority students (Baker, 2006; Crosno, Kirkpatrick, & Elder, 2004). But overall, higher-SES students—who tend to be higher-achieving and to have fewer discipline problems—have more supportive relationships with teachers (Pianta, Hamre, & Stuhlman, 2003).

Unfortunately, once teachers' attitudes toward students are established, they can become more extreme than is warranted by students' behavior. Of special concern are **educational self-fulfilling prophecies:** Children may adopt teachers' positive or negative views and start to live up to them. This effect is especially strong when teachers emphasize competition and publicly compare children, regularly favoring the best students (Kuklinski & Weinstein, 2001; Weinstein, 2002).

Teacher expectations have a greater impact on low achievers than high achievers (Madon, Jussim, & Eccles, 1997). When a teacher is critical, high achievers can fall back on their history of success. Low-achieving students' sensitivity to self-fulfilling prophecies can be beneficial when teachers believe in them. But biased teacher judgments are usually slanted in a negative direction. In one study, African-American children were especially responsive to negative teacher expectations in reading, and girls were especially responsive to negative teacher expectations in math (McKown & Weinstein, 2002). Recall our discussion of *stereotype threat.* A child in the position of confirming a negative stereotype may respond with anxiety and reduced motivation, increasing the likelihood of a negative self-fulfilling prophecy.

© G.J.Y CALI/THE STOCK CONNECTION

These second and third graders learn together during a visit to their school library. Compared to children in single-grade classrooms, children in multigrade classrooms are usually advantaged in academic achievement, self-esteem, and attitudes toward school.

Grouping Practices

In many schools, students are assigned to *homogeneous groups* or classes, in which children of similar ability levels are taught together. Homogeneous grouping can be a potent source of self-fulfilling prophecies. Low-group students—who as early as first grade are more likely to be low-SES, minority, and male—get more drill on basic facts and skills, engage in less discussion, and progress at a slower pace. Gradually, they decline in self-esteem and motivation (Chorzempa & Graham, 2006; Condron, 2007; Trautwein et al., 2006). Not surprisingly, homogeneous grouping widens the gap between high and low achievers (Ross & Harrison, 2006).

Partly because of this finding, some schools have increased the *heterogeneity* of classes by combining two or three adjacent grades. In *multigrade classrooms,* academic achievement, self-esteem, and attitudes toward school are usually more favorable than in the single-grade arrangement (Lloyd, 1999; Ong, Allison, & Haladyna, 2000). Perhaps multigrade grouping decreases competition and promotes *cooperative learning,* which also fosters these positive outcomes (see page 321).

Teaching Children with Special Needs

We have seen that effective teachers flexibly adjust their teaching strategies to accommodate students with a wide range of characteristics. These adjustments are especially challenging at the very low and high ends of the ability distribution. How do schools serve children with special learning needs?

CHILDREN WITH LEARNING DIFFICULTIES. U.S. legislation mandates that schools place children who require special supports for learning in the "least restrictive" (as close to normal as possible) environments that meet their educational needs. In **inclusive classrooms,** students with learning difficulties are placed in regular classrooms for all or part of the school day, a practice designed to prepare them for participation in society and to combat prejudices against individuals with disabilities (Kugelmass & Ainscow, 2004). Largely as the result of parental pressures, an increasing number of students experience *full inclusion*—full-time placement in regular classrooms.

Some students in inclusive classrooms have *mild mental retardation:* Their IQs fall between 55 and 70, and they also show problems in adaptive behavior, or skills of everyday living (American Psychiatric Association, 1994). But the largest number—5 to 10 percent of school-age children—have **learning disabilities,** great difficulty with one or more aspects of learning, usually reading. As a result, their achievement is considerably behind what would be expected on the basis of their IQ. Sometimes deficits express themselves in other ways—for example, as severe inattention, which depresses both IQ and achievement (recall our discussion of ADHD on page 304). The problems of students with learning disabilities cannot be traced to any obvious physical or emotional difficulty or to environmental disadvantage. Instead, subtle deficits in brain functioning seem to be involved (Berninger, 2006). In many instances, the cause is unknown.

Although some included students benefit academically, many do not. Achievement gains depend on both the severity of the disability and the support services available (Klingner et al., 1998). Furthermore, children with disabilities are often rejected by regular-classroom peers. Students with mental retardation are overwhelmed by the social skills of their classmates; they cannot interact adeptly in a conversation or game. And the processing deficits of some students with learning disabilities lead to problems in social awareness and responsiveness (Kelly & Norwich, 2004; Sridhar & Vaughn, 2001).

Does this mean that students with special needs cannot be served in regular classrooms? Not necessarily. Often these children do best when they receive instruction in a resource room for part of the day and in the regular classroom for the remainder (Weiner & Tardif, 2004). In the resource room, a special education teacher works with students on an individual and small-group basis. Then, depending on their progress, children join regular classmates for different subjects and amounts of time.

Special steps must to be taken to promote peer relations in inclusive classrooms. Cooperative learning and peer-tutoring experiences in which teachers guide children with learning difficulties and their classmates in working together lead to friendly interaction, improved peer acceptance, and achievement gains (Fuchs et al., 2002a, 2002b). Teachers can also prepare their class for the arrival of a student with special needs. Under these conditions, inclusion may foster emotional sensitivity and prosocial behavior among regular classmates.

In this inclusive second-grade classroom, a teacher encourages a special-needs child to listen to his classmate read a story. The child is likely to do well if he receives support from a special education teacher and if his classroom teacher minimizes comparisons and promotes cooperative learning.

■ **GIFTED CHILDREN.** In Joey and Lizzie's school, some children are **gifted,** displaying exceptional intellectual strengths. One or two students in every grade have IQ scores above 130, the standard definition of giftedness based on intelligence test performance (Gardner, 1998b). High-IQ children, as we have seen, have keen memories and an exceptional capacity to solve challenging academic problems. Yet recognition that intelligence tests do not sample the entire range of human mental skills has led to an expanded conception of giftedness.

Creativity and Talent. **Creativity** is the ability to produce work that is original yet appropriate—something others have not thought of that is useful in some way (Lubart, 2003; Sternberg, 2003b). A child with high potential for creativity can be designated as gifted. Tests of creative capacity tap **divergent thinking**—the generation of multiple and unusual possibilities when faced with a task or problem. Divergent thinking contrasts with **convergent thinking,** which involves arriving at a single correct answer and is emphasized on intelligence tests (Guilford, 1985).

Because highly creative children (like high-IQ children) are often better at some tasks than others, a variety of tests of divergent thinking are available (Runco, 1992; Torrance, 1988). A verbal measure might ask children to name uses for common objects (such as a newspaper). A figural measure might ask them to create drawings based on a circular motif (see Figure 9.10). A "real-world problem" measure requires students to suggest solutions to everyday problems. Responses can be scored for the number of ideas generated and their originality.

Yet critics point out that these measures are poor predictors of creative accomplishment in everyday life because they tap only one of the complex cognitive contributions to creativity. Also involved are defining new and important problems, evaluating divergent ideas, choosing the most promising, and calling on relevant knowledge to understand and solve problems (Sternberg, 2003b; Guignard & Lubart, 2006).

Consider these ingredients, and you will see why people usually demonstrate creativity in only one or a few related areas. Even individuals designated as gifted by virtue of high IQ often show uneven ability across academic subjects. Partly for this reason, definitions of giftedness have been extended to include **talent**—outstanding performance in a specific field. Case studies reveal that excellence in writing, mathematics, science, music, visual arts, athletics, or leadership has roots in specialized interests and skills that first appear in childhood (Moran & Gardner, 2006; Winner, 2003). Highly talented children are biologically prepared to master their domain of interest, and they display a passion for doing so.

But talent must be nurtured. Studies of the backgrounds of talented children and highly accomplished adults often reveal parents who are warm and sensitive, provide a stimulating home life, are devoted to developing their child's abilities, and provide models of hard work. These parents are reasonably demanding but not driving or overambitious (Winner, 1996, 2000). They arrange for caring teachers while the child is young and for more rigorous master teachers as the talent develops.

Many gifted children and adolescents are socially isolated, partly because their highly driven, nonconforming, and

■ **FIGURE 9.10** ■ **Responses of an 8-year-old who scored high on a figural measure of divergent thinking.** This child was asked to make as many pictures as she could from the circles on the page. The titles she gave her drawings, from left to right, are as follows: "Dracula," "one-eyed monster," "pumpkin," "Hula-Hoop," "poster," "wheelchair," "earth," "stop-light," "planet," "movie camera," "sad face," "picture," "beach ball," "the letter *O*," "car," "glasses." Tests of divergent thinking tap only one of the complex cognitive contributions to creativity. (Reprinted by permission of Laura Berk.)

independent styles leave them out of step with peers and partly because they enjoy solitude, which is necessary to develop their talents. Still, gifted children desire gratifying peer relationships, and some—more often girls than boys—try to become better liked by hiding their abilities. Compared with their ordinary agemates, gifted youths, especially girls, report more emotional and social difficulties, including low self-esteem and depression (Reis, 2004; Winner, 2000).

Finally, whereas many talented youths become experts in their fields, few become highly creative. Rapidly mastering an existing field requires different skills than innovating in that field (Moran & Gardner, 2006). The world, however, needs both experts and creators.

Educating the Gifted. Debate about the effectiveness of school programs for the gifted typically focuses on factors irrelevant to giftedness—whether to provide enrichment in regular classrooms, pull children out for special instruction (the most common practice), or advance brighter students to a higher grade. Overall, gifted children fare well academically and socially within each of these models (Moon & Feldhusen, 1994). Yet the extent to which programs foster creativity and talent depends on opportunities to acquire relevant skills.

Gardner's theory of multiple intelligences has inspired several model programs that provide enrichment to all students in diverse disciplines. Meaningful activities, each tapping a specific intelligence or set of intelligences, serve as contexts for assessing strengths and weaknesses and, on that basis, teaching new knowledge and original thinking (Gardner, 1993, 2000). For example, linguistic intelligence might be fostered through storytelling or playwriting; spatial intelligence through drawing, sculpting, or taking apart and reassembling objects; and kinesthetic intelligence through dance or pantomime.

Evidence is still needed on how effectively these programs nurture children's talent and creativity. But they have already succeeded in one way—by highlighting the strengths of some students who previously had been considered unexceptional or even at risk for school failure (Kornhaber, 2004). Consequently, they may be especially useful in identifying talented, low-SES ethnic minority children, who are underrepresented in school programs for the gifted (McBee, 2006).

How Well-Educated Are North American Children?

Our discussion of schooling has largely focused on how teachers can support the education of children. Yet many factors—both within and outside schools—affect children's learning. Societal values, school resources, quality of teaching, and parental encouragement all play important roles. Nowhere are these multiple influences more apparent than when schooling is examined in cross-cultural perspective.

In international studies of reading, mathematics, and science achievement, young people in Hong Kong, Korea, Japan, and Taiwan are consistently top performers. Among Western nations, Canada, Finland, Netherlands, and Switzerland are also in the top tier. But U.S. students typically perform at the international average, and sometimes below it (see Figure 9.11) (Programme for International Student Assessment, 2003, 2006).

Why do U.S. youths fall behind in academic accomplishment? In the Programme for International Student Assessment, which periodically assesses academic achievement of 15-year-olds in many countries, students were asked about their study habits. Compared with students in the top-achieving nations, many more U.S. students reported studying by memorizing rather than by relating information to previously acquired knowledge. Also, achievement varies much more among U.S. schools, suggesting that the United States is less equitable in the quality of education it provides (Programme for International Student Assessment, 2005).

Researchers have conducted in-depth research on learning environments in Asian nations, such as Japan, Korea, and

	Country	Average Math Achievement Score
High-Performing Nations	Taiwan	549
	Finland	548
	Hong Kong	547
	Korea, Republic of	547
	Netherlands	531
	Switzerland	530
	Canada	527
	Macao, China	525
	Japan	523
	New Zealand	522
	Belgium	520
	Australia	520
Intermediate-Performing Nations	Denmark	513
	Czech Republic	510
	Iceland	506
	Austria	505
	Germany	504
	Sweden	502
	Ireland	501
International Average = 498		
	France	496
	United Kingdom	495
	Poland	495
	Hungary	491
	Luxembourg	491
	Norway	490
	Spain	480
	United States	**474**
Low-Performing Nations	Portugal	466
	Italy	462
	Greece	459
	Turkey	424

■ **FIGURE 9.11** ■ **Average mathematics scores of 15-year-olds by country.** The Programme for International Student Assessment measured achievement in many nations around the world. Taiwan, Hong Kong, Korea, and Japan were among the top performers in mathematics, whereas the United States performed below the international average. Similar outcomes occurred in reading and science. (Adapted from Programme for International Student Assessment, 2006.)

Taiwan, to clarify the factors that support high achievement. A variety of social forces combine to foster a strong commitment to learning in Asian families and schools:

- *Emphasis on effort.* Whereas North American parents and teachers tend to regard native ability as key to academic success, Japanese, Korean, and Taiwanese parents and teachers believe that all children can succeed academically with enough effort. Asian parents devote many more hours to helping their children with homework (Stevenson, Lee, & Mu, 2000). Furthermore, Asian youths, influenced by collectivist values, typically view striving to achieve as a moral obligation—a responsibility to family and community. North American young people view working hard in individualistic terms—as a personal choice (Bempechat & Drago-Severson, 1999).
- *High-quality education for all.* Ability grouping is absent from Japanese, Korean, and Taiwanese elementary schools. All students receive the same nationally mandated, high-quality education, delivered by teachers who are better paid than in the United States (U.S. Department of Education, 2008). Academic lessons are particularly well-organized and presented in ways that capture children's attention and encourage high-level thinking (Grow-Maienza, Hahn, & Joo, 2001). And Japanese elementary school teachers are three times as likely as U.S. teachers to work outside class with students who need extra help (Woodward & Ono, 2004).
- *More time devoted to instruction.* In Japan, Hong Kong, and Taiwan, the school year is more than 50 days longer than in the United States (World Education Services, 2007). And on a day-to-day basis, Asian teachers devote much more time to academic pursuits (Stevenson, Lee, & Mu, 2000). Yet Asian schools are not regimented: An eight-hour school day allows time for extra recesses as well as field trips and extracurricular activities, which contribute to children's capacity to learn (see page 298).

The Asian examples underscore the need for families, schools, and the larger society to work together to upgrade education. Currently, the United States is investing more tax dollars in elementary and secondary education and strengthening teacher preparation. In addition, many schools are taking steps to increase parent involvement. Children whose parents create stimulating learning environments at home, monitor their child's academic progress, help with homework, and communicate often with teachers consistently show superior achievement (Hill & Taylor, 2004; Jeynes, 2005). The results of these efforts can be seen in recent national assessments of educational progress (U.S Department of Education, 2003, 2005). After two decades of decline, U.S. students' overall academic achievement has risen, although not enough to enhance their standing internationally.

ASK YOURSELF

» REVIEW
List some teaching practices that foster children's achievement and some that undermine it. Provide a brief explanation of each practice.

» APPLY
Sandy wonders why her daughter Mira's teacher often has students work on assignments in small, cooperative groups. Explain the benefits of this approach to Sandy. What must Mira's teacher do to ensure that cooperative learning succeeds?

» CONNECT
Review research on child-rearing styles on pages 278–280 in Chapter 8. What style do gifted children who realize their potential typically experience? Explain.

» REFLECT
What grouping practices were used in your elementary education—homogeneous, heterogeneous, or a combination? What impact do you think those practices had on your motivation and achievement?

Summary

PHYSICAL DEVELOPMENT

Body Growth

Describe major trends in body growth during middle childhood.

» Gains in body size during middle childhood continue at a slow, regular pace. Bones lengthen and broaden, and permanent teeth replace all 20 primary teeth. By age 9, girls overtake boys in physical size.

Common Health Problems

What vision and hearing problems are common in middle childhood?

» The most common vision problem is myopia, or nearsightedness. It is influenced by heredity, early biological trauma, and time spent doing close work. Myopia is one of the few health conditions that increase with SES.

» Middle-ear infections become less frequent. But repeated infections lead to permanent hearing loss in as many as 20 percent of low-SES children.

Describe the causes and consequences of serious nutritional problems in middle childhood, giving special attention to obesity.

» Many poverty-stricken children in developing countries and North America continue to suffer from serious and prolonged malnutrition, which can permanently impair physical and mental development.

- Overweight and **obesity** are growing problems in Western and developing nations, posing long-term health risks. Although heredity contributes to obesity, reduced sleep, parental feeding practices, maladaptive eating habits, and lack of exercise also play important roles.
- Obese children are rated as less likable by peers and adults and have serious adjustment problems. Family-based interventions to change parents' and children's eating patterns and lifestyles are the most effective treatment approaches.

© JEFF GREENBERG/THE IMAGE WORKS

What factors contribute to illness during the school years, and how can these health problems be reduced?

- Children experience more illnesses during the first two years of elementary school than later because of exposure to sick children and an immature immune system.
- The most common cause of school absence and childhood hospitalization is asthma. Although heredity contributes to asthma, environmental factors—pollution, stressful home lives, lack of access to good health care, and the rise in childhood obesity—have led to an increase in the disease, especially among African-American and poverty-stricken children.
- Children with severe chronic illnesses are at risk for academic, emotional, and social difficulties, but positive family relationships improve adjustment.

Describe changes in unintentional injuries in middle childhood.

- Unintentional injuries increase over middle childhood and adolescence, especially for boys, with auto and bicycle accidents accounting for most of the rise. School-based programs that use modeling, rehearsal, and rewards for following safety practices help prevent injuries.

Motor Development and Play

Cite major changes in motor development and play during middle childhood.

- Gains in flexibility, balance, agility, and force, along with more efficient information processing, contribute to school-age children's improved motor performance.
- Fine-motor development also improves. Children's writing becomes more legible, and their drawings increase in organization, detail, and representation of depth.
- While girls outperform boys in fine-motor skills, boys outperform in all gross-motor skills except those requiring balance and agility. Higher expectations by parents for boys' athletic performance play a large role.
- Games with rules become common during the school years, contributing to emotional and social development. Children, especially boys, also engage in **rough-and-tumble play,** friendly play-fighting that helps establish a **dominance hierarchy** among group members.
- Most U.S. school-age children are not active enough for good health. With cutbacks in recess and physical education, they do not reap the health and social benefits of physical fitness.

COGNITIVE DEVELOPMENT

Piaget's Theory: The Concrete Operational Stage

What are the major characteristics of concrete operational thought?

- Children in the **concrete operational stage** can reason logically about concrete, tangible information. Mastery of conservation demonstrates **reversibility** in thinking. School-age youngsters are also better at hierarchical classification and **seriation,** including **transitive inference.** Their spatial reasoning improves, as seen in their ability to give directions and to create **cognitive maps** representing familiar large-scale spaces.
- School-age children master logical ideas gradually, not all at once. Concrete operational thought is limited in that children do not come up with general logical principles.

Discuss follow-up research on concrete operational thought.

- Specific cultural practices, especially those associated with schooling, affect children's mastery of Piagetian tasks.
- Some researchers attribute the gradual development of operational thought to gains in information-processing speed. According to Case's neo-Piagetian theory, with practice, cognitive schemes demand less attention and become more automatic, freeing up space in working memory for combining old schemes and generating new ones. Eventually, children consolidate schemes into highly efficient, central conceptual structures, becoming increasingly able to coordinate and integrate multiple dimensions.

Information Processing

Cite basic changes in information processing, and describe the development of attention and memory in middle childhood.

- Brain development contributes to increases in processing speed and capacity and to gains in inhibition, which facilitate many aspects of thinking.
- During the school years, attention becomes more selective, adaptable, and planful. The serious symptoms of **attention-deficit hyperactivity disorder (ADHD)** lead to both academic and social problems.
- Memory strategies also improve. **Rehearsal** appears first, followed by **organization** and then **elaboration.** With age, children combine memory strategies.
- Development of the long-term knowledge base makes new information easier to store and retrieve. Children's motivation to use what they know also contributes to memory development. Memory strategies are promoted by learning activities in school.

Describe the school-age child's theory of mind and capacity to engage in self-regulation.

- Metacognition expands over middle childhood. School-age children regard the mind as an active, constructive agent, and they develop an integrated theory of mind. **Cognitive self-regulation**—putting what one knows about thinking into action—develops slowly over middle childhood and adolescence. It improves with instructions to monitor cognitive activity.

Discuss current controversies in teaching reading and mathematics to elementary school children.

- Skilled reading draws on all aspects of the information-processing system. Research showing that a mixture of **whole language** and **phonics** is most effective in teaching beginning reading has resolved a long-standing debate. Teaching that blends practice in basic skills with conceptual understanding also is best in mathematics.

© LAURA DWIGHT PHOTOGRAPHY

Individual Differences in Mental Development

Describe major approaches to defining and measuring intelligence.

- Most intelligence tests yield an overall score as well as scores for separate intellectual factors. During the school years, IQ becomes more stable, and it correlates moderately well with academic achievement.

» The componential approach to defining intelligence seeks to identify the inner, information-processing skills that contribute to mental test performance. Memory span, speed of thinking, and effective strategy use are positively related to IQ.

» Sternberg's **triarchic theory of successful intelligence** views intelligence as an interaction of inner and outer forces—analytical intelligence (information-processing skills), creative intelligence (capacity to solve novel problems), and practical intelligence (ability to succeed in one's everyday world).

» Gardner's **theory of multiple intelligences** identifies at least eight mental abilities, each with a distinct biological basis and course of development. It has stimulated efforts to define, measure, and foster **emotional intelligence.**

Describe evidence indicating that both heredity and environment contribute to intelligence.

» Heritability estimates and adoption research indicate that intelligence is a product of both heredity and environment. Studies of black children adopted into well-to-do homes during the first year of life indicate that the black–white IQ gap is substantially influenced by environment.

» IQ scores are affected by cultural forces, including exposure to certain communication styles and knowledge and ways of thinking sampled by the test. Among children aware of ethnic stereotypes, **stereotype threat** can trigger anxiety that interferes with test performance. **Dynamic assessment** helps many minority children perform more competently on mental tests.

Language Development

Describe changes in school-age children's vocabulary, grammar, and pragmatics, and cite the advantages of bilingualism for development.

» During middle childhood, vocabulary continues to grow rapidly, and children have a more precise and flexible understanding of word meanings. They also use more complex grammatical constructions and conversational strategies, and their narratives increase in organization, detail, and expressiveness. Language awareness contributes to school-age children's language progress.

» Mastery of a second language must begin in childhood for full proficiency to occur. Bilingualism has positive consequences for cognitive development and certain aspects of language awareness. In Canada, language immersion programs are highly successful in making children proficient in both English and French. In the United States, bilingual education that combines instruction in the native tongue and in English supports ethnic minority children's academic learning.

Learning in School

Describe the impact of class size and educational philosophies on children's motivation and academic achievement.

» Smaller classes in the early elementary grades promote lasting gains in academic achievement. Older elementary school students in **traditional classrooms** have a slight edge in academic achievement over those in **constructivist classrooms,** who gain in academic motivation, critical thinking, social and moral maturity, and positive attitudes toward school.

» Students in **social-constructivist classrooms** benefit from working collaboratively in meaningful activities and from teaching adapted to each child's zone of proximal development. **Cooperative learning** promotes achievement and self-esteem.

Discuss the role of teacher–student interaction and grouping practices in academic achievement.

» Caring, helpful, and stimulating teaching fosters children's motivation, academic achievement, and peer relations. **Educational self-fulfilling prophecies** have a greater impact on low than high achievers and are especially likely to occur in classrooms that emphasize competition and public evaluation. Heterogeneous grouping in multigrade classrooms promotes favorable self-esteem and school attitudes and higher achievement.

Under what conditions is placement of children with learning difficulties in regular classrooms successful?

» Students with mild mental retardation and **learning disabilities** are often placed in **inclusive classrooms.** The success of regular-classroom placement depends on meeting individual learning needs and positive peer relations.

Describe the characteristics of gifted children and current efforts to meet their educational needs.

» **Giftedness** includes high IQ, **creativity,** and **talent.** Tests of creativity that tap **divergent** rather than **convergent thinking** focus on only one of the ingredients of creativity. Highly talented children have parents and teachers who nurture their exceptional abilities. Gifted children are best served by educational programs that build on their special strengths.

How well are North American children achieving compared with children in other industrialized nations?

» In international studies, young people in Asian nations are consistently top performers, whereas American students typically display an average or below-average performance. Asian parents and teachers emphasize effort over native ability, and Asian schools provide the same high-quality education to all students and devote more time to instruction.

Important Terms and Concepts

attention-deficit hyperactivity disorder (ADHD) (p. 304)
cognitive maps (p. 300)
cognitive self-regulation (p. 307)
concrete operational stage (p. 299)
constructivist classroom (p. 319)
convergent thinking (p. 323)
cooperative learning (p. 321)
creativity (p. 323)
divergent thinking (p. 323)
dominance hierarchy (p. 298)
dynamic assessment (p. 315)
educational self-fulfilling prophecies (p. 321)
elaboration (p. 304)
emotional intelligence (p. 313)
gifted (p. 323)
inclusive classrooms (p. 322)
learning disabilities (p. 322)
obesity (p. 292)
organization (p. 303)
phonics approach (p. 307)
rehearsal (p. 303)
reversibility (p. 299)
rough-and-tumble play (p. 297)
seriation (p. 299)
social-constructivist classroom (p. 320)
stereotype threat (p. 314)
talent (p. 323)
theory of multiple intelligences (p. 311)
traditional classroom (p. 319)
transitive inference (p. 300)
triarchic theory of successful intelligence (p. 310)
whole-language approach (p. 307)

Social understanding expands greatly in middle childhood. Like others their age around the world, these Turkish children select friends based on personal qualities, and they become more responsive to one another's needs and desires.

CHAPTER 10

Emotional and Social Development in Middle Childhood

Late one afternoon, Rena heard her son Joey burst through the front door, run upstairs, and phone his best friend Terry. "Terry, gotta talk to you," Joey pleaded breathlessly. "Everything was going great until that word I got—*porcupine,*" Joey went on, referring to the fifth-grade spelling bee at school that day. "Just my luck! *P-o-r-k,* that's how I spelled it! I can't believe it. Maybe I'm not so good at social studies," Joey confided, "but I *know* I'm better at spelling than that stuck-up Belinda Brown. I knocked myself out studying those spelling lists. Then *she* got all the easy words. If I *had* to lose, why couldn't it be to a nice person?"

Joey's conversation reflects his new emotional and social capacities. By entering the spelling bee, he shows *industriousness,* the energetic pursuit of meaningful achievement in his culture—a major change of middle childhood. Joey's social understanding has also expanded: He can size up strengths, weaknesses, and personality characteristics. Furthermore, friendship means something different to Joey than it did earlier—he counts on his best friend, Terry, for understanding and emotional support.

© BLEND IMAGES/ALAMY

For an overview of personality change in middle childhood, we return to Erikson's theory. Then we look at children's views of themselves and of others, their moral understanding, and their peer relationships. Each increases in complexity as children reason more effectively and spend more time in school and with agemates.

Despite changing parent–child relationships, the family remains powerfully influential in middle childhood. Today, family lifestyles are more diverse than ever before. Through Joey and his younger sister Lizzie's experiences with parental divorce, we will see that family functioning is far more important than family structure in ensuring children's well-being. Finally, we look at some common emotional problems of middle childhood.

Erikson's Theory: Industry versus Inferiority

According to Erikson (1950), children whose previous experiences have been positive enter middle childhood prepared to redirect their energies from the make-believe of early childhood into realistic accomplishment. Erikson believed that the combination of adult expectations and children's drive toward mastery sets the stage for the psychological conflict of middle childhood, **industry versus inferiority,** which is resolved positively when children develop a sense of competence at useful skills and tasks. In cultures everywhere, adults respond to children's improved physical and cognitive capacities by making new demands, and children are ready to benefit from those challenges.

In industrialized nations, the beginning of formal schooling marks the transition to middle childhood. With it comes literacy training, which prepares children for a vast array of specialized careers. In school, children discover their own and others' unique capacities, learn the value of division of labor, and develop a sense of moral commitment and responsibility. The danger at this stage is *inferiority,* reflected in the pessimism of children who have little confidence in their ability to do things well. This sense of inadequacy can develop when family life has not prepared children for school life or when teachers and peers destroy children's feelings of competence and mastery with negative responses.

Erikson's sense of industry combines several developments of middle childhood: a positive but realistic self-concept, pride in accomplishment, moral responsibility, and cooperative participation with agemates. How do these aspects of self and social relationships change over the school years?

© TOM & DEE ANN MCCARTHY/CORBIS

The industriousness of middle childhood involves mastery of useful skills. As these young musicians participate in their school orchestra, they gain awareness of others' unique capacities and come to view themselves as responsible, capable, and cooperative.

Self-Understanding

In middle childhood, children become able to describe themselves in terms of psychological traits, to compare their own characteristics with those of their peers, and to speculate about the causes of their strengths and weaknesses. These transformations in self-understanding have a major impact on children's self-esteem.

Self-Concept

During the school years, children refine their self-concept, organizing their observations of behaviors and internal states into general dispositions. A major change takes place between ages 8 and 11, as the following self-description by an 11-year-old illustrates:

> My name is A. I'm a human being. I'm a girl. I'm a truthful person. I'm not pretty. I do so-so in my studies. I'm a very good cellist. I'm a very good pianist. I'm a little bit tall for my age. I like several boys. I like several girls. I'm old-fashioned. I play tennis. I am a very good swimmer. I try to be helpful. I'm always ready to be friends with anybody. Mostly I'm good, but I lose my temper. I'm not well-liked by some girls and boys. I don't know if I'm liked by boys or not. (Montemayor & Eisen, 1977, pp. 317–318)

Instead of specific behaviors, this child emphasizes competencies: "I'm a very good cellist" (Damon & Hart, 1988). She also describes her personality, mentioning both positive and negative traits: "truthful" but short-tempered. Older school-age children are far less likely than younger children to describe themselves in extreme, all-or-none ways (Harter, 2003, 2006).

These evaluative self-descriptions result from school-age children's frequent **social comparisons**—judgments of their appearance, abilities, and behavior in relation to those of others. For example, Joey observed that he was "better at spelling" than his peers but "not so good at social studies." Whereas 4- to 6-year-olds can compare their own performance to that of one peer, older children can compare multiple individuals, including themselves (Butler, 1998; Harter, 2006).

What factors account for these revisions in self-concept? Cognitive development affects the changing *structure* of the self. School-age children, as we saw in Chapter 9, can better coordinate several aspects of a situation in reasoning about their physical world. Similarly, in the social realm, they combine typical experiences and behaviors into psychological dispositions, blend positive and negative characteristics, and compare their own characteristics with those of many peers (Harter, 2003, 2006).

The changing *content* of self-concept is a product of both cognitive capacities and feedback from others. Sociologist George Herbert Mead (1934) proposed that a well-organized psychological self emerges when children adopt a view of the self that resembles others' attitudes toward the child. Mead's ideas indicate that *perspective-taking skills*—in particular, an improved ability to infer what other people are thinking—are crucial for developing a self-concept based on personality traits. School-age children become better at "reading" others' messages and internalizing their expectations. As they do so, they form an *ideal self* that they use to evaluate their real self. As we will see shortly, a large discrepancy between the two can undermine self-esteem.

In middle childhood, children look to more people beyond the family for information about themselves as they enter a wider range of settings in school and community. And self-descriptions now include frequent reference to social groups: "I'm a Boy Scout, a paperboy, and a Prairie City soccer player," said Joey. And as children move into adolescence, although parents and other adults remain influential, self-concept is increasingly vested in feedback from close friends (Oosterwegel & Oppenheimer, 1993).

But recall that the content of self-concept varies from culture to culture. In earlier chapters, we noted that Asian parents stress harmonious interdependence, whereas Western parents stress independence and self-assertion. When asked to recall personally significant past experiences (their last birthday, a time their parent scolded them), U.S. children gave longer accounts including more personal preferences, skills, and opinions. Chinese children, in contrast, more often referred to social interactions and to others. Similarly in their self-descriptions, U.S. children listed more personal attributes ("I'm smart," "I like hockey"), Chinese children more attributes involving group membership and relationships ("I'm in second grade," "My friends are crazy about me") (Wang, 2004, 2006b).

Development of Self-Esteem

Recall that most preschoolers have extremely high self-esteem. But as children enter school and receive much more feedback about how well they perform compared with their peers, self-esteem differentiates and also adjusts to a more realistic level.

■ **A HIERARCHICALLY STRUCTURED SELF-ESTEEM.** Researchers have asked children to indicate the extent to which statements such as "I am good at homework" or "I'm usually the one chosen for games" are true of themselves. By age 6 to 7, children have formed at least four broad self-evaluations—academic competence, social competence, physical/athletic competence, and physical appearance. Within these are more refined categories that become increasingly distinct with age (Marsh, 1990; Marsh & Ayotte, 2003; Van den Bergh & De Rycke, 2003). Furthermore, the capacity to view the self in terms of stable dispositions permits school-age children to combine their separate self-evaluations into a general psychological image of themselves—an overall sense of self-esteem (Harter, 2003, 2006). As a result, self-esteem takes on the hierarchical structure shown in Figure 10.1.

Children attach greater importance to certain self-evaluations than to others. Although individual differences exist, during

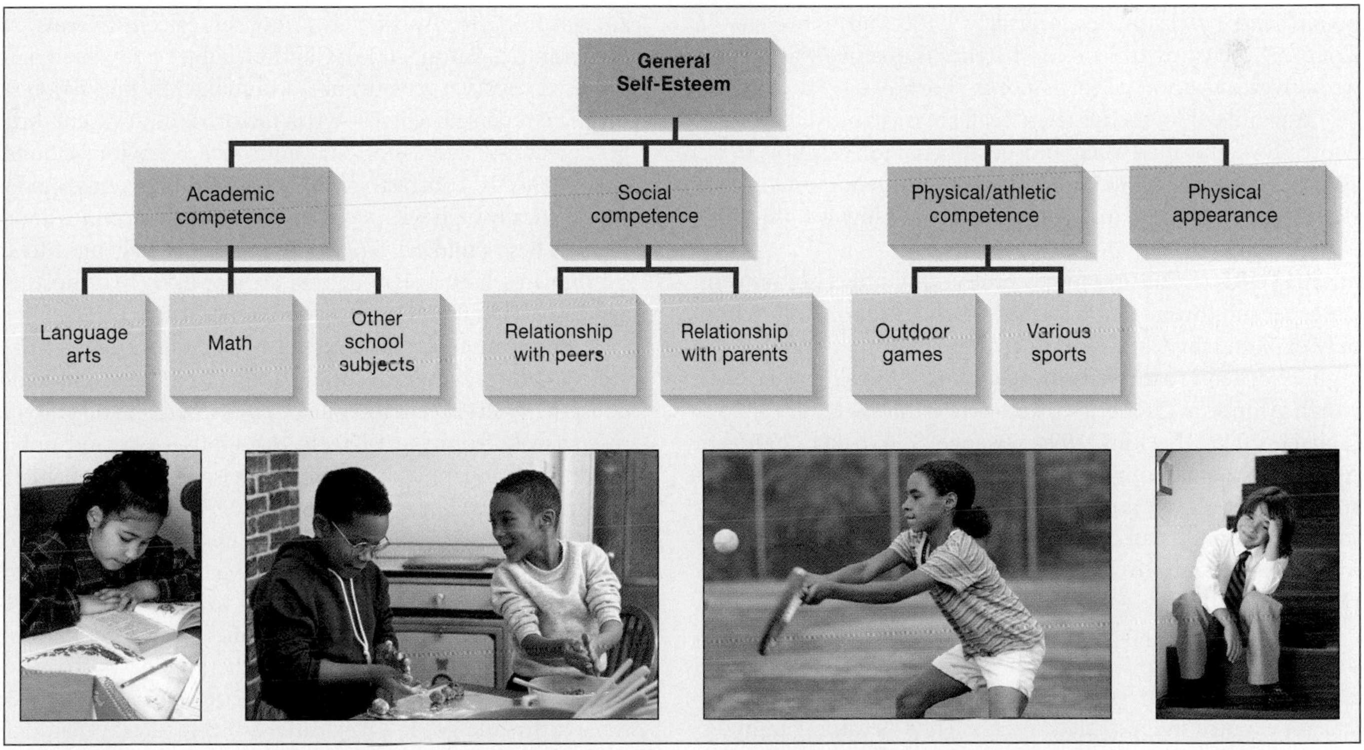

PHOTOS FROM LEFT TO RIGHT: © LAJRA DWIGHT PHOTOGRAPHY; © GEORGE DISARIO/CORBIS; © MITCH WOJNAROWICZ/THE IMAGE WORKS; © SIRI STAFFORD/GETTY IMAGES/DIGITAL VISION

■ **FIGURE 10.1** ■ **Hierarchical structure of self-esteem in the mid-elementary school years.** From their experiences in different settings, children form at least four separate self-esteems: academic competence, social competence, physical/athletic competence, and physical appearance. These differentiate into additional self-evaluations and combine to form a general sense of self-esteem.

childhood and adolescence, perceived physical appearance correlates more strongly with overall self-worth than any other self-esteem factor (Klomsten, Skaalvik, & Espnes, 2004; Shapka & Keating, 2005). Emphasis on appearance, in the media and in society, has major implications for young people's overall satisfaction with themselves.

CHANGES IN LEVEL OF SELF-ESTEEM. Self-esteem declines during the first few years of elementary school as children evaluate themselves in various areas (Marsh, Craven, & Debus, 1998; Wigfield et al., 1997). Typically, the drop is not great enough to be harmful. Most (but not all) children appraise their characteristics and competencies realistically while maintaining an attitude of self-respect. Then, from fourth grade on, self-esteem rises for the majority of young people, who feel especially good about their peer relationships and athletic capabilities (Cole et al., 2001; Twenge & Campbell, 2001).

Influences on Self-Esteem

From middle childhood on, individual differences in self-esteem become increasingly stable (Trzesniewski, Donnellan, & Robins, 2003). And positive relationships among self-esteem, valuing of various activities, and success at those activities emerge and strengthen. Academic self-esteem predicts how important, useful, and enjoyable children judge school subjects to be, their willingness to try hard, and their achievement (Denissen, Zarrett, & Eccles, 2007; Valentine, DuBois, & Cooper, 2004). Children with high social self-esteem are consistently better-liked by classmates (Harter, 1999). And as we saw in Chapter 9, sense of athletic competence is positively associated with investment and performance in sports.

A profile of low self-esteem in all areas is linked to anxiety, depression, and increasing antisocial behavior (DuBois et al., 1999; Robins et al., 2001). What social influences might lead self-esteem to be high for some children and low for others?

CULTURE. Cultural forces profoundly affect self-esteem. An especially strong emphasis on social comparison in school may explain why Chinese and Japanese children, despite their higher academic achievement, score lower in self-esteem than North American children—a difference that widens with age (Harter, 2006; Hawkins, 1994; Twenge & Crocker, 2002). In Asian classrooms, competition is tough and achievement pressure is high. At the same time, because their culture values social harmony, Asian children tend to be reserved about judging themselves positively but generous in their praise of others (Falbo et al., 1997).

Gender-stereotyped expectations also affect self-esteem. In one study, the more 5- to 8-year-old girls talked with friends about the way people look, watched TV shows focusing on physical appearance, and perceived their friends as valuing thinness, the lower their physical self-esteem and overall self-worth a year later (Dohnt & Tiggemann, 2006). In academic self-judgments, girls score higher in language arts self-esteem, whereas boys have higher math, science, and physical/athletic self-esteem—even when children of equal skill levels are compared (Fredricks & Eccles, 2002; Jacobs et al., 2002; Tennenbaum & Leaper, 2003). At the same time, girls exceed boys in self-esteem dimensions of close friendship and social acceptance. And despite a widely held assumption that boys' overall self-worth is much higher than girls', the difference is slight (Marsh & Ayotte, 2003; Young & Mroczek, 2003). Girls may think less well of themselves because they internalize this negative cultural message.

Compared with their Caucasian agemates, African-American children tend to have slightly higher self-esteem, possibly because of warm, extended families and a stronger sense of ethnic pride (Gray-Little & Hafdahl, 2000). Finally, children and adolescents who attend schools or live in neighborhoods where their SES and ethnic groups are well-represented feel a stronger sense of belonging and have fewer self-esteem problems (Gray-Little & Carels, 1997).

CHILD-REARING PRACTICES. Children whose parents use an *authoritative* child-rearing style (see Chapter 8) feel especially good about themselves (Carlson, Uppal, & Prosser, 2000; Rudy & Grusec, 2006; Wilkinson, 2004). Warm, positive parenting lets children know that they are accepted as competent and worthwhile. And firm but appropriate expectations, backed up with explanations, help them evaluate their own behavior against reasonable standards.

Controlling parents—those who too often help or make decisions for their child—communicate a sense of inadequacy to children. Having parents who are repeatedly disapproving and insulting is also linked to low self-esteem (Kernis, 2002; Pomerantz & Eaton, 2000). Children subjected to such parenting need constant reassurance, and many rely heavily on peers to affirm their self-worth—a risk factor for adjustment difficulties, including aggression and antisocial behavior (Donnellan et al., 2005). In contrast, indulgent parenting is correlated with unrealistically high self-esteem, which also undermines development. These children tend to lash out at challenges to their overblown self-images and, thus, are also likely to be hostile and aggressive (Hughes, Cavell, & Grossman, 1997).

American cultural values have increasingly emphasized a focus on the self that may lead parents to indulge children and boost their self-esteem too much. The self-esteem of U.S. youths rose sharply from the 1970s to the 1990s—a period in which much popular parenting literature advised promoting children's self-esteem (Twenge & Campbell, 2001). Yet compared with previous generations, American youths are achieving less well and displaying more antisocial behavior and other adjustment problems (Berk, 2005). Research confirms that children do not benefit from compliments ("You're terrific") that have no basis in real attainment (Damon, 1995). Rather, the best way to foster a positive, secure self-image is to encourage children to strive for worthwhile goals. Over time, a bidirectional relationship emerges: Achievement fosters self-esteem, which contributes to further effort and gains in performance (Gest, Domitrovich, & Welsh, 2005; Guay, Marsh, & Boivin, 2003).

What can adults do to promote, and to avoid undermining, this mutually supportive relationship between motivation and self-esteem? Some answers come from research on the precise content of adults' messages to children in achievement situations. Let's look first at the meanings children assign to their successes and failures.

MAKING ACHIEVEMENT-RELATED ATTRIBUTIONS. *Attributions* are our common, everyday explanations for the causes of behavior—our answers to the question, "Why did I or another person do that?" Notice how Joey, in talking about the spelling bee at the beginning of this chapter, attributes his disappointing performance to *luck* (Belinda got all the easy words) and his usual success to *ability* (he *knows* he's a better speller than Belinda). Joey also appreciates that *effort* matters: "I knocked myself out studying those spelling lists."

Cognitive development permits school-age children to separate all these variables in explaining performance (Dweck, 2002). Those who are high in academic self-esteem and motivation make **mastery-oriented attributions,** crediting their successes to ability—a characteristic they can improve through trying hard and can count on when facing new challenges. And they attribute failure to factors that can be changed or controlled, such as insufficient effort or a very difficult task (Heyman & Dweck, 1998). So whether these children succeed or fail, they take an industrious, persistent approach to learning.

In contrast, children who develop **learned helplessness** attribute their failures, not their successes, to ability. When they succeed, they conclude that external factors, such as luck, are responsible. Unlike their mastery-oriented counterparts, they believe that ability is fixed and cannot be improved by trying hard (Cain & Dweck, 1995). When a task is difficult, these children experience an anxious loss of control—in Erikson's terms, a pervasive sense of inferiority. They give up without really trying.

Children's attributions affect their goals. Mastery-oriented children seek information on how best to increase their ability through effort. Hence, their performance improves over time (Blackwell, Trzesniewski, & Dweck, 2007). In contrast, learned-helpless children focus on obtaining positive and avoiding negative evaluations of their fragile sense of ability. Over time, their ability no longer predicts how well they do (Pomerantz & Saxon, 2001). Because they fail to connect effort with success, learned-helpless children do not develop the metacognitive and self-regulatory skills necessary for high achievement (see Chapter 9). Lack of effective learning strategies, reduced persistence, low performance, and a sense of loss of control sustain one another in a vicious cycle (Chan & Moore, 2006).

INFLUENCES ON ACHIEVEMENT-RELATED ATTRIBUTIONS. What accounts for the different attributions of mastery-oriented and learned-helpless children? Adult communication plays a key role. Children with a learned-helpless style often have parents who believe that their child is not very capable and must work harder than others to succeed. When the child fails, the parent might say, "You can't do that, can you? It's OK if you quit" (Hokoda & Fincham, 1995). After the child succeeds, the parent might give feedback that evaluates the child's traits ("You're so smart"). Trait statements promote a fixed view of ability, leading children to question their competence in the face of setbacks and to retreat from challenge (Mueller & Dweck, 1998).

© LAURA DWIGHT PHOTOGRAPHY

Mastery-oriented children credit their successes to ability, and they seek information on how best to increase their ability through effort. Hence, their performance improves over time.

Teachers' messages also affect children's attributions. Teachers who are caring and helpful and emphasize learning over getting good grades tend to have mastery-oriented students (Anderman et al., 2001). In contrast, students with unsupportive teachers often regard their performance as externally controlled (by teachers or luck), withdraw from learning activities, and decline in achievement—outcomes that lead children to doubt their ability (Skinner, Zimmer-Gembeck, & Connell, 1998).

For some children, performance is especially likely to be undermined by adult feedback. Despite their higher achievement, girls more often than boys blame poor performance on ability. Girls tend to receive messages from teachers and parents that their ability is at fault when they do not do well, and negative stereotypes (for example, that girls are weak at math) reduce their interest and effort (Bleeker & Jacobs, 2004; Cole et al., 1999). And as Chapter 9 revealed, low-SES ethnic minority students often receive less favorable feedback from teachers, especially when assigned to homogeneous groups of poorly achieving students—conditions that result in a drop in academic self-esteem and achievement (Harris and Graham, 2007).

Finally, cultural values affect the likelihood that children will develop learned helplessness. Because of the high value their

Applying What We Know

Fostering a Mastery-Oriented Approach to Learning

Strategy	Description
Provision of tasks	Select tasks that are meaningful, responsive to a diversity of student interests, and appropriately matched to current competence so that the child is challenged but not overwhelmed.
Parent and teacher encouragement	Communicate warmth, confidence in the child's abilities, the value of achievement, and the importance of effort in success. Model high effort in overcoming failure. (For teachers) Communicate often with parents, suggesting ways to foster children's effort and progress. (For parents) Monitor schoolwork; provide scaffolded assistance that promotes knowledge of effective strategies and self-regulation.
Performance evaluations	Make evaluations private; avoid publicizing success or failure through wall posters, stars, privileges for "smart" children, or prizes for "best" performance. Emphasize individual progress and self-improvement.
School environment	Offer small classes, which permit teachers to provide individualized support for mastery. Provide for cooperative learning and peer tutoring, in which children assist one another; avoid ability grouping, which makes evaluations of children's progress public. Accommodate individual and cultural differences in learning styles. Create an atmosphere that values academics and sends a clear message that all students can learn.

Sources: Hilt, 2004; Wigfield et al., 2006.

culture places on effort and self-improvement, Asians attend more to failure than to success, because failure indicates where corrective action is needed. Americans, in contrast, focus more on success because it enhances self-esteem. When researchers observed U.S. and Chinese mothers' responses to their fourth and fifth graders' puzzle solutions, the U.S. mothers offered more praise after success, whereas the Chinese mothers more often pointed out the child's inadequate performance. And regardless of success or failure, Chinese mothers made more task-relevant statements aimed at ensuring that children exerted sufficient effort to do well ("You concentrated on it": "You got only 6 out of 12"). When children continued with the task after mothers left the room, the Chinese children showed greater gains in performance (Ng, Pomerantz, & Lam, 2007).

■ **FOSTERING A MASTERY-ORIENTED APPROACH.** Attribution research suggests that well-intended messages from adults sometimes undermine children's competence. An intervention called *attribution retraining* encourages learned-helpless children to believe that they can overcome failure by exerting more effort. Children are given tasks difficult enough that they will experience some failure, followed by repeated feedback that helps them revise their attributions: "You can do it if you try harder." After they succeed, children receive additional feedback—"You're really good at this" or "You really tried hard on that one"—so that they attribute their success to both ability and effort, not chance. Another approach is to encourage low-effort students to focus less on grades and more on mastering a task for its own sake (Hilt, 2004; Horner & Gaither, 2004). Instruction in effective strategies and self-regulation is also vital, to compensate for development lost in this area and to ensure that renewed effort pays off (Wigfield et al., 2006).

Attribution retraining is best begun early, before children's views of themselves become hard to change. An even better approach is to prevent learned helplessness, using the strategies summarized in Applying What We Know above.

ASK YOURSELF

» REVIEW
How does level of self-esteem change in middle childhood, and what accounts for these changes?

» APPLY
Should parents promote children's self-esteem by telling them they're "smart" or "wonderful"? Are children harmed if they do not feel good about everything they do? Why or why not?

» CONNECT
What cognitive changes, described in Chapter 9, support the transition to a self-concept emphasizing competencies, personality traits, and social comparisons?

» REFLECT
Recall your own attributions for academic successes and failures when you were in elementary school. What are those attributions like now? What messages from others may have contributed to your attributions?

Emotional Development

Greater self-awareness and social sensitivity support gains in emotional competence in middle childhood. Changes take place in experience of self-conscious emotions, emotional understanding, and emotional self-regulation.

Self-Conscious Emotions

In middle childhood, the self-conscious emotions of pride and guilt become clearly governed by personal responsibility. Children experience pride in a new accomplishment and guilt over a transgression, even when no adult is present (Harter & Whitesell, 1989). Also, children no longer report guilt for any mishap, as they did earlier, but only for intentional wrongdoing, such as ignoring responsibilities, cheating, or lying (Ferguson, Stegge, & Damhuis, 1991).

Pride motivates children to take on further challenges, whereas guilt prompts them to make amends and to strive for self-improvement. But harsh, insensitive reprimands from adults ("Everyone else can do it! Why can't you?") can lead to intense shame, which (as noted in Chapter 8) is particularly destructive. A shame-induced, sharp drop in self-esteem can trigger withdrawal, depression, and intense anger at those who participated in the shame-evoking situation (Lindsay-Hartz, de Rivera, & Mascolo, 1995; Mills, 2005).

AP IMAGES/ELAINE THOMPSON

These 8-year-old twin brothers raised over $5,000 for victims of the devastating tsunami of 2005. Their gains in emotional understanding and perspective taking enable them to respond with empathy to people's immediate distress as well as to their general life condition.

Emotional Understanding

School-age children's understanding of mental activity means that, unlike preschoolers, they are likely to explain emotion by referring to internal states, such as happy or sad thoughts, than to external events (Flavell, Flavell, & Green, 2001). Also, around age 8, children become aware that they can experience more than one emotion at a time, each of which may be positive or negative and differ in intensity (Pons et al., 2003). For example, recalling the birthday present he received from his grandmother, Joey reflected, "I was very happy that I got something but a little sad that I didn't get just what I wanted."

Appreciating mixed emotions helps children realize that people's expressions may not reflect their true feelings (Misailidi, 2006; Saarni, 1999). It also fosters awareness of self-conscious emotions. For example, between ages 6 and 7, children improve sharply in ability to distinguish pride from happiness and surprise (Tracy, Robins, & Lagattuta, 2005). And 8- and 9-year-olds understand that pride combines two sources of happiness—joy in accomplishment and joy that a significant person recognized that accomplishment (Harter, 1999). Furthermore, children of this age can reconcile contradictory facial and situational cues in figuring out another's feelings (see page 259 in Chapter 8). And they can use information about "what might have happened" to predict how people will feel in a new situation—realizing, for example, that someone will feel a sense of relief when an actual outcome is more favorable than what could have occurred (Guttentag & Ferrell, 2004).

As with self-understanding, gains in emotional understanding are supported by cognitive development and social experiences, especially adults' sensitivity to children's feelings and willingness to discuss emotions. Together, these factors lead to a rise in empathy as well. As children move closer to adolescence, advances in perspective taking permit an empathic response not just to people's immediate distress but also to their general life condition (Hoffman, 2000). As Joey and Lizzie imagined how people who are chronically ill or hungry feel and evoked those emotions in themselves, they gave part of their allowance to charity and joined in fundraising projects through school, community center, and scouting.

Emotional Self-Regulation

Rapid gains in emotional self-regulation occur in middle childhood. As children engage in social comparison and care more about peer approval, they must learn to manage negative emotion that threatens their self-esteem.

By age 10, most children shift adaptively between two general strategies for managing emotion. In **problem-centered coping,** they appraise the situation as changeable, identify the difficulty, and decide what to do about it. If problem solving does not work, they engage in **emotion-centered coping,** which is internal, private, and aimed at controlling distress when little can be done about an outcome (Kliewer, Fearnow, & Miller, 1996;

Lazarus & Lazarus, 1994). For example, when faced with an anxiety-provoking test or an angry friend, older school-age children view problem solving and seeking social support as the best strategies. But when outcomes are beyond their control—for example, after receiving a bad grade—they opt for distraction or try to redefine the situation: "Things could be worse. There'll be another test." School-age children's improved ability to reflect on thoughts and feelings means that, compared with preschoolers, they more often use these internal strategies to manage emotion (Brenner & Salovey, 1997).

Furthermore, through interacting with parents, teachers, and peers, school-age children become more knowledgeable about socially approved ways to display negative emotion. They increasingly prefer verbal strategies ("Please stop pushing and wait your turn") to crying, sulking, or aggression (Shipman et al., 2003). Young school-age children justify these more mature displays of emotion by mentioning avoidance of punishment or adult approval but, by third grade, they begin to emphasize concern for others' feelings. Children with this awareness are rated as especially helpful, cooperative, and socially responsive by teachers and as better-liked by peers (Garner, 1996; McDowell & Parke, 2000).

When emotional self-regulation has developed well, school-age children acquire a sense of *emotional self-efficacy*—a feeling of being in control of their emotional experience (Saarni, 2000). This fosters a favorable self-image and an optimistic outlook, which further help children face emotional challenges. As at younger ages, school-age children whose parents respond sensitively and helpfully when the child is distressed are emotionally well-regulated—generally upbeat in mood and also empathic and prosocial. In contrast, poorly regulated children often experience hostile, dismissive parental reactions to distress (Davidov & Grusec, 2006; Zeman, Shipman, & Suveg, 2002). These children are overwhelmed by negative emotion, a response that interferes with empathy and prosocial behavior.

Understanding Others: Perspective Taking

We have seen that middle childhood brings major advances in **perspective taking,** the capacity to imagine what other people may be thinking and feeling. These changes support self-concept and self-esteem, understanding of others, and a wide variety of social skills. Robert Selman's five-stage sequence describes changes in perspective-taking skill, based on children's and adolescents' responses to social dilemmas in which characters have differing information and opinions about an event.

As Table 10.1 indicates, at first children have only a limited idea of what other people might be thinking and feeling. Over time, they become more aware that people can interpret the same event quite differently. Soon, they can "step into another person's shoes" and reflect on how that person might regard their own thoughts, feelings, and behavior, as when they say something like, "I *thought you would think* I was just kidding when I said that." (Note the similarity between this level of perspective taking and second-order false belief, described on page 306 in Chapter 9.) Finally, older children and adolescents can evaluate two people's perspectives simultaneously, at first from the vantage point of a disinterested spectator and later by referring to societal values (Gurucharri & Selman, 1982). The following explanation reflects this ability: "I know why Joey hid the stray kitten in the basement, even though his mom was against keeping it. He believes in not hurting animals. If you put the kitten outside or give it to the pound, it might die."

Experiences in which adults and peers explain their viewpoints contribute greatly to children's perspective taking. Good perspective takers, in turn, are more likely to display empathy and sympathy and to handle difficult social situations effectively—among the reasons they are better-liked by peers (FitzGerald & White, 2003). Children with poor social skills, especially the angry, aggressive styles discussed in Chapter 8, have great dif-

■ **TABLE 10.1** ■ ***Selman's Stages of Perspective Taking***

STAGE	APPROXIMATE AGE RANGE	DESCRIPTION
Level 0: Undifferentiated perspective taking	3–6	Children recognize that self and other can have different thoughts and feelings, but they frequently confuse the two.
Level 1: Social-informational perspective taking	4–9	Children understand that different perspectives may result because people have access to different information.
Level 2: Self-reflective perspective taking	7–12	Children can "step into another person's shoes" and view their own thoughts, feelings, and behavior from the other person's perspective. They also recognize that others can do the same.
Level 3: Third-party perspective taking	10–15	Children can step outside a two-person situation and imagine how the self and other are viewed from the point of view of a third, impartial party.
Level 4: Societal perspective taking	14–adult	Individuals understand that third-party perspective taking can be influenced by one or more systems of larger societal values.

Sources: Selman, 1976; Selman & Byrne, 1974.

ficulty imagining others' thoughts and feelings. They often mistreat adults and peers without feeling the guilt and remorse prompted by awareness of another's viewpoint. Interventions that provide coaching and practice in perspective taking help reduce antisocial behavior and increase empathy and prosocial responding (Chalmers & Townsend, 1990).

Moral Development

Recall from Chapter 8 that preschoolers pick up many morally relevant behaviors through modeling and reinforcement. By middle childhood, they have had time to internalize rules for good conduct: "It's good to help others in trouble" or "It's wrong to take something that doesn't belong to you." This change leads children to become considerably more independent and trustworthy.

In Chapter 8, we also saw that children do not just copy their morality from others. As the cognitive-developmental approach emphasizes, they actively think about right and wrong. An expanding social world, the capacity to consider more information when reasoning, and perspective taking lead moral understanding to advance greatly in middle childhood.

© JEFF GREENBERG/ALAMY

School-age children recognize that certain social conventions have a clear purpose—such as separating recyclables from trash to prevent waste. And they regard violations of these kinds of conventions as closer to moral transgressions.

Moral and Social-Conventional Understanding

During the school years, children construct a flexible appreciation of moral rules. By age 7 to 8, they no longer say truth telling is always good and lying is always bad but also consider prosocial and antisocial intentions. They evaluate certain types of truthfulness very negatively—for example, bluntly telling a classmate that you don't like her drawing (Bussey, 1999). And although both Chinese and North American schoolchildren consider lying about antisocial acts "very naughty," Chinese children—influenced by collectivist values—more often rate lying favorably when the intention is modesty, as when a student who has thoughtfully picked up litter from the playground says, "I didn't do it" (Lee et al., 1997, 2001). Similarly, Chinese children are more likely to favor lying to support the group at the expense of the individual (saying you're sick so, as a poor singer, you won't harm your class's chances of winning a singing competition). In contrast, North American children more often favor lying to support the individual at the expense of the group (claiming that a friend who is a poor speller is actually a good speller because he wants to participate in a spelling competition) (Fu et al., 2007).

As children's ideas about justice take into account an increasing number of variables, they clarify and link moral imperatives and social conventions. School-age children, for example, distinguish social conventions with a clear *purpose* (not running in school hallways to prevent injuries) from ones with no obvious justification (crossing a "forbidden" line on the playground). They regard violations of purposeful social conventions as closer to moral transgressions (Buchanan-Barrow & Barrett, 1998). With age, they also realize that people's *intentions* and the *contexts* of their actions affect the moral implications of violating a social convention. In one study, 8- to 10-year-olds stated that because of a flag's symbolic value, burning it to express disapproval of a country or to start a cooking fire is worse than burning it accidentally. But they recognized that flag burning is a form of freedom of expression, and most agreed that it would be acceptable in a country that treated its citizens unfairly (Helwig & Prencipe, 1999).

Children in Western and non-Western cultures reason similarly about moral and social-conventional concerns (Neff & Helwig, 2002; Nucci, 2002, 2005). When a directive is fair and caring, such as telling children to stop fighting or to share candy, school-age children view it as right, regardless of who states it—a principal, a teacher, or a child with no authority. In contrast, even in Korean culture, which places a high value on deference to authority, 7- to 11-year-olds evaluate negatively a teacher's or principal's order to engage in immoral acts, such as stealing or refusing to share—a response that strengthens with age (Kim, 1998; Kim & Turiel, 1996).

Understanding Individual Rights

When children in diverse cultures challenge adult authority, they typically do so within the personal domain. As their grasp of moral imperatives and social conventions strengthens, so does their conviction that certain choices, such as hairstyle, friends, and leisure activities, are up to the individual. A Colombian child illustrated this passionate defense of personal control when asked if a teacher had the right to tell a student where to sit during circle time. In the absence of a moral reason from the teacher, the child declared, "She should be able to sit wherever she wants" (Ardila-Rey & Killen, 2001, p. 249).

Notions of personal choice, in turn, enhance children's moral understanding. As early as age 6, children view freedom of speech and religion as individual rights, even if laws exist that deny those rights (Helwig, 2006). And they regard laws that discriminate against individuals—for example, denying certain people access to medical care or education—as wrong and worthy of violating (Helwig & Jasiobedzka, 2001). In justifying their responses, children appeal to personal privileges and, by the end of middle childhood, to the importance of individual rights for maintaining a fair society.

At the same time, older school-age children place limits on individual choice. Fourth graders faced with conflicting moral and personal concerns—such as whether or not to befriend a classmate of a different race or gender—typically decide in favor of kindness and fairness (Killen et al., 2002). Partly for this reason, prejudice usually declines in middle childhood.

Understanding Diversity and Inequality

By the early school years, children associate power and privilege with white people and poverty and inferior status with people of color. They do not necessarily acquire these views directly from parents or friends (Aboud & Doyle, 1996). Rather, they seem to pick up prevailing societal attitudes from implicit messages in the media and elsewhere in their environments.

IN-GROUP AND OUT-GROUP BIASES: DEVELOPMENT OF PREJUDICE. Studies in diverse Western nations confirm that by age 5 to 7, white children generally evaluate their own racial group favorably and other racial groups less favorably or negatively (Aboud, 2003; Nesdale et al., 2004). Many minority children of this age, in a reverse pattern, assign positive characteristics to the privileged white majority and negative characteristics to their own group (Averhart & Bigler, 1997; Corenblum, 2003).

But recall that with age, children pay more attention to inner traits. The capacity to classify the social world in multiple ways enables school-age children to understand that people who look different need not think, feel, or act differently (Aboud & Amato, 2001). Consequently, voicing of negative attitudes toward minorities declines. After age 7 or 8, both majority and minority children express in-group favoritism, and white children's prejudice against out-group members often weakens (Nesdale et al., 2005; Ruble et al., 2004).

Yet even in children aware of the injustice of discrimination, prejudice may operate unintentionally and without awareness—as it does in many white adults (Dunham, Baron, & Banaji, 2006). Consider a study in which white school-age children were asked to divide fairly among three child artists—two white and one black—money that had been earned from selling the children's art. In each version of the task, one artist was labeled "productive" (making more art works), one as "the oldest," and one as "poor and needing money for lunch." By age 8 to 9, most children recognize that special consideration should be given to children who either perform exceptionally or are at a disadvantage. But racial stereotypes interfered with fourth graders' evenhanded application of these principles. They gave more money to a productive black artist (who countered the racial stereotype of "low achiever") than to a productive white artist and less money to a needy black artist (who conformed to the racial stereotype of "poor") than to a needy white artist (see Figure 10.2) (McGillicuddy-De Lisi, Daly, & Neal, 2006).

Nevertheless, the extent to which children hold racial and ethnic biases varies, depending on the following factors:

- *A fixed view of personality traits.* Children who believe that people's personality traits are fixed rather than changeable often judge others as either "good" or "bad." Ignoring motives and circumstances, they readily form prejudices on the basis of limited information. For example, they might infer that "a new child at school who tells a lie to get other kids to like her" is simply a bad person (Levy & Dweck, 1999).
- *Overly high self-esteem.* Children (and adults) with very high self-esteem are more likely to hold racial and ethnic prejudices (Baumeister et al., 2003; Bigler, Brown, & Markell, 2001). These individuals seem to belittle disadvantaged individuals or groups to justify their own extremely favorable

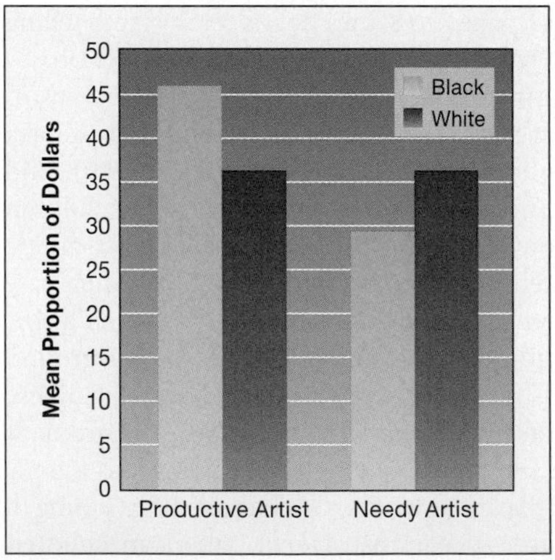

FIGURE 10.2 White fourth graders' racially biased distribution of money to child artists. When dividing money earned from selling children's art among three child artists—two white and one black—the fourth graders gave more money to a productive black artist (who countered a stereotype) than to a productive white artist and less money to a needy black artist (who conformed to a stereotype) than to a needy white artist. In both instances, the fourth graders seemed to engage in subtle, unintentional prejudice. (From A. V. McGillicuddy-De Lisi, M. Daly, & A. Neal, 2006, "Children's Distributive Justice Judgments: Aversive Racism in Euro-American Children?" *Child Development, 77,* p. 1072. © The Society for Research in Child Development, Inc. Adapted by permission of Blackwell Publishing Ltd. and A. V. McGillicuddy-De Lisi.)

© MICHAEL J. DOOLITTLE/THE IMAGE WORKS

Children perform a Polynesian song on the playground of their culturally diverse school. Collaboration with members of other ethnic groups and traditions can reduce the tendency to classify the social world on the basis of race and ethnicity and to view one's own group positively and other groups negatively.

self-evaluation. Furthermore, children who say their own ethnicity makes them feel especially "good"—and thus perhaps socially superior—are more likely to display in-group favoritism and out-group prejudice (Pfeifer et al., 2007).

- *A social world in which people are sorted into groups.* The more adults highlight group distinctions for children and the less interracial contact children experience, the more likely white children are to display prejudice (Bigler, Brown, & Markell, 2001; McGlothlin & Killen, 2006).

REDUCING PREJUDICE. Research confirms that an effective way to reduce prejudice is through intergroup contact, in which racially and ethnically different children work toward common goals and become personally acquainted (Tropp & Pettigrew, 2005). Children assigned to cooperative learning groups with peers of diverse backgrounds, for example, form more cross-race friendships. Sharing thoughts and feelings with close, cross-race friends, in turn, reduces even subtle, unintentional prejudices (Turner, Hewstone, & Voci, 2007). But these positive effects seem not to generalize to relationships beyond the group.

Long-term contact and collaboration in neighborhoods, schools, and communities may be the best way to reduce prejudice. Classrooms that expose children to ethnic diversity, teach them to value those differences, directly address the damage caused by prejudice, and encourage perspective taking and empathy both prevent children from forming negative biases and reduce already acquired biases (Pfeifer, Brown, & Juvonen, 2007).

Finally, inducing children to view others' traits as changeable, by discussing with them the many possible influences on those traits, is helpful. The more children believe that people can change their personalities, the more they report liking and perceiving themselves as similar to members of disadvantaged groups. Furthermore, children who believe in the changeability of human attributes spend more time volunteering to help the needy (Karafantis & Levy, 2004). Volunteering, in turn, may promote a changeable view of others by helping children take the perspective of the underprivileged and appreciate the social conditions that lead to disadvantage.

ASK YOURSELF

REVIEW
How does emotional self-regulation improve in middle childhood? What implications do these changes have for children's self-esteem?

APPLY
Ten-year-old Marla says her classmate Bernadette will never get good grades because she's lazy. Jane believes that Bernadette tries but can't concentrate because her parents are divorcing. Why is Marla more likely than Jane to develop prejudices?

CONNECT
Cite examples of how older children's capacity to take more information into account enhances their emotional and moral understanding.

REFLECT
Did you attend an integrated elementary school? Why is school integration vital for reducing racial and ethnic prejudice?

Peer Relations

In middle childhood, the society of peers becomes an increasingly important context for development. Peer contact, as we have seen, contributes to perspective taking and understanding of self and others. These developments, in turn, enhance peer interaction. Compared with preschoolers, school-age children resolve conflicts more effectively, using persuasion and compromise (Mayeux & Cillessen, 2003). Sharing, helping, and other prosocial acts also increase. In line with these changes, aggression declines. But the drop is greatest for physical attacks (Côte et al., 2007; Tremblay, 2000). As we will see, verbal and relational aggression continue as children form peer groups.

Peer Groups

TAKE A MOMENT... Watch children in the schoolyard or neighborhood, and notice how often they gather in groups of three to a dozen or more. In what ways are members of the same group noticeably alike?

By the end of middle childhood, children display a strong desire for group belonging. They form **peer groups,** collectives that generate unique values and standards for behavior and a social structure of leaders and followers. Peer groups organize on the basis of proximity (being in the same classroom) and similarity in sex, ethnicity, popularity, and aggression (Rubin, Bukowski, & Parker, 2006).

The practices of these informal groups lead to a "peer culture" that typically consists of a specialized vocabulary, dress code, and place to "hang out." As children develop these exclusive associations, the codes of dress and behavior that grow out of them become more broadly influential. Schoolmates who deviate—by "kissing up" to teachers, wearing the wrong kind of shirt or shoes, or tattling on classmates—are often rebuffed, becoming targets of critical glances and comments. These customs bind peers together, creating a sense of group identity. Within the group, children acquire many social skills—cooperation, leadership, followership, and loyalty to collective goals.

Most school-age children believe a group is wrong to exclude a peer (Killen, Crystal, & Watanabe, 2002). Nevertheless, children do exclude, often using relationally aggressive tactics. Peer groups—at the instigation of their leaders, who can be skillfully aggressive—frequently oust no longer "respected" children. Some, whose own previous behavior toward outsiders reduces their chances of being included elsewhere, turn to other low-status peers with poor social skills (Werner & Crick, 2004). Socially anxious children, when ousted, often become increasingly peer-avoidant and thus more isolated (Gazelle & Rudolph, 2004). In either case, opportunities to acquire socially competent behavior diminish.

School-age children's desire for group membership can also be satisfied through formal group ties such as scouting, 4-H, and religious youth groups. Adult involvement holds in check the negative behaviors associated with children's informal peer groups. And through working on joint projects and helping in their communities, children gain in social and moral maturity (Vandell & Shumow, 1999).

These girls have probably established a peer-group structure of leaders and followers as they gather for joint activities. Their relaxed body language and similar way of dressing suggest their strong sense of group belonging.

Friendships

Whereas peer groups provide children with insight into larger social structures, friendships contribute to the development of trust and sensitivity. During the school years, friendship becomes more complex and psychologically based. Consider the following 8-year-old's ideas:

> *Why is Shelly your best friend?* Because she helps me when I'm sad, and she shares. . . . *What makes Shelly so special?* I've known her longer, I sit next to her and got to know her better. . . . *How come you like Shelly better than anyone else?* She's done the most for me. She never disagrees, she never eats in front of me, she never walks away when I'm crying, and she helps me with my homework. . . . *How do you get someone to like you?* . . . If you're nice to [your friends], they'll be nice to you. (Damon, 1988b, pp. 80–81)

As these responses show, friendship has become a mutually agreed-on relationship in which children like each other's personal qualities and respond to one another's needs and desires. And once a friendship forms, *trust* becomes its defining feature. School-age children state that a good friendship is based on acts of kindness that signify that each person can be counted on to support the other (Hartup & Abecassis, 2004; Selman, 1980). Consequently, older children regard violations of trust, such as not helping when others need help, breaking promises, and gossiping behind the other's back, as serious breaches of friendship.

Because of these features, school-age children's friendships are more selective. Whereas preschoolers say they have lots of friends, by age 8 or 9, children name only a handful of good friends. Girls, who demand greater closeness than boys, are more exclusive in their friendships (Markovitz, Benenson, & Dolensky, 2001).

In addition, children tend to select friends similar to themselves in age, sex, race, ethnicity, and SES. Friends also resemble one another in personality (sociability, aggression), popularity, academic achievement, prosocial behavior, and judgments (including biased perceptions) of other people (Hartup, 2006; Mariano & Harton, 2005). But friendship opportunities offered by children's environments also affect their choices. As noted earlier, in integrated classrooms with mixed-race collaborative learning groups, students form more cross-race friendships.

Over middle childhood, friendships remain fairly stable, with about 50 to 70 percent enduring over a school year, and some for several years (Berndt, 2004). Through them, children come to realize that close relationships can survive disagreements if friends are secure in their liking for one another (Rose & Asher, 1999). In this way, friendship provides an important context in which children learn to tolerate criticism and resolve disputes.

Yet the impact of friendships on children's development depends on the nature of those friends. Children who bring kindness and compassion to their friendships strengthen each

School-age children tend to select friends similar to themselves in age, sex, race, ethnicity, and SES. However, in integrated classrooms with mixed-race collaborative learning groups, students form more cross-race friendships.

other's prosocial tendencies and form more lasting ties. When aggressive children make friends, the relationship is often riddled with hostile interaction and is at risk for breakup, especially when just one member of the pair is aggressive (Ellis & Zarbatany, 2007). Aggressive girls' friendships are high in exchange of private feelings but full of jealousy, conflict, and betrayal (Werner & Crick, 2004). Aggressive boys' friendships involve frequent expressions of anger, coercive statements, physical attacks, and enticements to rule-breaking behavior (Bagwell & Coie, 2004; Crick & Nelson, 2002; Dishion, Andrews, & Crosby, 1995). These findings indicate that the social problems of aggressive children operate within their closest peer ties.

Peer Acceptance

Peer acceptance refers to likability—the extent to which a child is viewed by a group of agemates, such as classmates, as a worthy social partner. Unlike friendship, likability is not a mutual relationship but a one-sided perspective, involving the group's view of an individual. Nevertheless, certain social skills that contribute to friendship also enhance peer acceptance. Better-accepted children tend to have more friends and more positive relationships with them (Lansford et al., 2006).

To assess peer acceptance, researchers usually use self-reports that measure *social preferences*—for example, asking children to identify classmates whom they "like very much" or "like very little." Another approach assesses *social prominence*—children's judgments of whom most of their classmates admire. The classmates children identify as prominent (looked up to by many others) show only moderate correspondence with those they say they personally prefer (LaFontana & Cillessen, 1999).

Children's self-reports yield four general categories of peer acceptance:

- **Popular children,** who get many positive votes (are well-liked)
- **Rejected children,** who get many negative votes (are disliked)
- **Controversial children,** who get a large number of positive and negative votes (are both liked and disliked)
- **Neglected children,** who are seldom mentioned, either positively or negatively

About two-thirds of students in a typical elementary school classroom fit one of these categories (Coie, Dodge, & Coppotelli, 1982). The remaining one-third, who do not receive extreme scores, are *average* in peer acceptance.

Peer acceptance is a powerful predictor of psychological adjustment. Rejected children, especially, are anxious, unhappy, disruptive, and low in self-esteem. Both teachers and parents rate them as having a wide range of emotional and social problems. Peer rejection in middle childhood is also strongly associated with poor school performance, absenteeism, dropping out, substance use, depression, antisocial behavior, and delinquency in adolescence and with criminality in early adulthood (Laird et al., 2001; Parker et al., 1995; Rubin, Bukowski, & Parker, 2006).

However, earlier influences—children's characteristics combined with parenting practices—may largely explain the link between peer acceptance and adjustment. School-age children with peer-relationship problems are more likely to have experienced family stress due to low income, insensitive child rearing, and coercive discipline (Cowan & Cowan, 2004). Nevertheless, as we will see, rejected children evoke reactions from peers that contribute to their unfavorable development.

■ **DETERMINANTS OF PEER ACCEPTANCE.** Why is one child liked while another is rejected? A wealth of research reveals that social behavior plays a powerful role.

Popular Children. The majority of **popular-prosocial children** combine academic and social competence, performing well in school and communicating with peers in sensitive, friendly, and cooperative ways (Cillessen & Bellmore, 2004). But other popular children are admired for their socially adept yet belligerent behavior. This smaller subtype, **popular-antisocial children,** includes "tough" boys—athletically skilled but poor students who cause trouble and defy adult authority—and relationally aggressive boys and girls who enhance their own status by ignoring, excluding, and spreading rumors about other children (Cillessen & Mayeux, 2004; Rodkin et al., 2000; Rose, Swenson, & Waller, 2004).

Despite their aggressiveness, peers view these youths as "cool," perhaps because of their athletic ability and sophisticated but devious social skills. Although peer admiration gives these children some protection against lasting adjustment difficulties, their antisocial acts require intervention (Prinstein & La Greca, 2004; Rodkin et al., 2006). With age, peers like these high-status, aggressive youths less and less, a trend that is stronger for relationally aggressive girls. The more socially prominent and controlling these girls become, the more they engage in relational aggression (Cillessen & Mayeux, 2004). Eventually peers condemn their nasty tactics and reject them.

Rejected Children. Rejected children display a wide range of negative social behaviors. Most are **rejected-aggressive children,** who show high rates of conflict, physical and relational aggression, and hyperactive, inattentive, and impulsive behavior. These children are also deficient in perspective taking and emotion regulation. For example, they tend to misinterpret the innocent behaviors of peers as hostile and to blame others for their social difficulties (Crick, Casas, & Nelson, 2002; Dodge, Coie, & Lynam, 2006; Hoza et al., 2005). Compared with popular-aggressive children, they are more extremely antagonistic. In contrast, **rejected-withdrawn children,** a smaller subtype, are passive and socially awkward. These timid children are overwhelmed by social anxiety, hold negative expectations for treatment by peers, and worry about being scorned and attacked (Hart et al., 2000; Ladd & Burgess, 1999; Troop-Gordon & Asher, 2005).

Rejected children are excluded by peers as early as kindergarten. Soon their classroom participation declines, their feelings of loneliness rise, their academic achievement falters, and they want to avoid school (Buhs & Ladd, 2001). Most have few friends, and some have none—a circumstance that predicts severe adjustment difficulties (Ladd & Troop-Gordon, 2003).

Both types of rejected children are at risk for peer harassment. But as the Biology and Environment box on the following page reveals, rejected-aggressive children also act as bullies, and rejected-withdrawn children are especially likely to be victimized (Putallaz et al., 2007; Sandstrom & Cillessen, 2003).

Controversial and Neglected Children. Consistent with the mixed peer opinion they engender, controversial children display a blend of positive and negative social behaviors. They are hostile and disruptive, but they also engage in positive, prosocial acts. Even though some peers dislike them, they have qualities that protect them from social exclusion. They have as many friends as popular children and are happy with their peer relationships (Newcomb, Bukowski, & Pattee, 1993). But like their popular-antisocial counterparts, they often bully others and engage in calculated relational aggression to sustain their dominance (DeRosier & Thomas, 2003; Putallaz et al., 2007).

Perhaps the most surprising finding is that neglected children, once thought to be in need of treatment, are usually well-adjusted. Although they engage in low rates of interaction, most are just as socially skilled as average children. They do not report feeling lonely or unhappy, and when they want to, they can break away from their usual pattern of playing by themselves (Harrist et al., 1997; Ladd & Burgess, 1999). Neglected children remind us that an outgoing, gregarious personality style is not the only path to emotional well-being.

■ **HELPING REJECTED CHILDREN.** A variety of interventions exist to improve the peer relations and psychological adjustment of rejected children. Most involve coaching, modeling, and reinforcing positive social skills, such as how to initiate interaction with a peer, cooperate in play, and respond to another child with friendly emotion and approval. Several of these programs have produced lasting gains in social competence and peer acceptance (Asher & Rose, 1997; DeRosier, 2007). Combining social-skills training with other treatments increases their effectiveness. Rejected children are often poor students, whose low academic self-esteem magnifies negative reactions to teachers and classmates. Intensive academic tutoring improves both school achievement and social acceptance (O'Neill et al., 1997).

Still another approach focuses on training in perspective taking and in solving social problems. But many rejected-aggressive children are unaware of their poor social skills and do not take responsibility for their social failures (Mrug, Hoza, & Gerdes, 2001). Rejected-withdrawn children, in contrast, are likely to develop a *learned-helpless* approach to peer difficulties—concluding, after repeated rebuffs, that they will never be liked (Wichmann, Coplan, & Daniels, 2004). Both types of children need help attributing their peer difficulties to internal, changeable causes.

Finally, because rejected children's socially incompetent behaviors often originate in harsh, intrusive, authoritarian parenting, interventions that focus on the child alone may not be sufficient (Rubin, Bukowski, & Parker, 2006). If parent–child interaction does not change, children may soon return to their old behavior patterns.

Gender Typing

Children's understanding of gender roles broadens in middle childhood, and their gender identities (views of themselves as relatively masculine or feminine) change as well. We will see that development differs for boys and girls, and it can vary considerably across cultures.

Gender-Stereotyped Beliefs

Research in many countries reveals that stereotyping of personality traits increases steadily in middle childhood, becoming adultlike around age 11 (Best, 2001; Heyman & Legare, 2004). For example, children regard "tough," "aggressive," "rational," and "dominant" as masculine and "gentle," "sympathetic," and "dependent" as feminine (Serbin, Powlishta, & Gulko, 1993).

Children derive these distinctions from observing sex differences in behavior as well as from adult treatment. When helping a child with a task, for example, parents (especially fathers) behave in a more mastery-oriented fashion with sons, setting higher

BIOLOGY AND ENVIRONMENT

Bullies and Their Victims

Follow the activities of aggressive children over a school day, and you will see that they reserve their hostilities for certain peers. A particularly destructive form of interaction is **peer victimization,** in which certain children become targets of verbal and physical attacks or other forms of abuse. What sustains these repeated assault–retreat cycles between pairs of children?

About 10 to 20 percent of children are bullies, while 15 to 30 percent are repeatedly victimized. Most bullies are boys who use both physical and verbal attacks, but girls sometimes bombard a vulnerable classmate with verbal and relational hostility (Rigby, 2004). And in a study of several hundred middle school students, about one in four reported experiencing "cyberbullying" through text messages, e-mail, or other electronic tools (Li, 2006).

Some bullies are high-status youngsters who may be liked for their leadership or athletic abilities. But most are disliked, or become so, because of their cruelty (Vaillancourt, Hymel, & McDougall, 2003). Nevertheless, peers rarely intervene to help victims, and about 20 to 30 percent of onlookers actually encourage bullies, even joining in (Salmivalli & Voeten, 2004).

Chronic victims tend to be passive when active behavior is expected. On the playground, they hang around chatting or wander on their own. When bullied, they give in, cry, and assume defensive postures (Boulton, 1999). Biologically based traits—an inhibited temperament and a frail physical appearance—contribute to victimization. But victims also have histories of resistant attachment, overly controlling child rearing, and maternal overprotection—parenting that prompts anxiety, low self-esteem, and dependency, resulting in a fearful demeanor that marks these children as vulnerable (Snyder et al., 2003). Persistent bullying, in turn, further impairs victims' emotional self-regulation and social skills—outcomes that heighten victimization (Hoglund & Leadbeater, 2007; Rosen, Milich, & Harris, 2007). Victims' adjustment problems include depression, loneliness, poor school performance, disruptive behavior, and school avoidance (Paul & Cillessen, 2003).

Aggression and victimization are not polar opposites. One-third to one-half of victims are also aggressive. Occasionally, they retaliate against powerful bullies, who respond by abusing them again—a cycle that sustains their victim status (Kochenderfer-Ladd, 2003). Among rejected children, these bully/victims are the most despised. They often have histories of extremely maladaptive parenting, including child abuse. This combination of highly negative home and peer experiences places them at severe risk for maladjustment (Schwartz, Proctor, & Chien, 2001).

Interventions that change victimized children's negative opinions of themselves and that teach them to respond in nonreinforcing ways to their attackers are helpful. Another way to assist victimized children is to help them form and maintain a gratifying friendship. When children have a close friend to whom they can turn for help, bullying episodes usually end quickly. Anxious, withdrawn children with a best friend have fewer adjustment problems than victims with no close friends (Bollmer et al., 2005; Fox & Boulton, 2006).

Although modifying victimized children's behavior can help, this does not mean they are to blame. The best way to reduce bullying is to change youth environments (including school, sports programs, recreation centers, and neighborhoods), promoting prosocial attitudes and behaviors. Effective approaches include developing school and community codes against bullying, teaching child bystanders to intervene, enlisting parents' assistance in changing bullies' behaviors, and (if necessary) moving socially prominent bullies to another class or school (Leadbeater & Hoglund, 2006; Smith, Ananiadou, & Cowie, 2003).

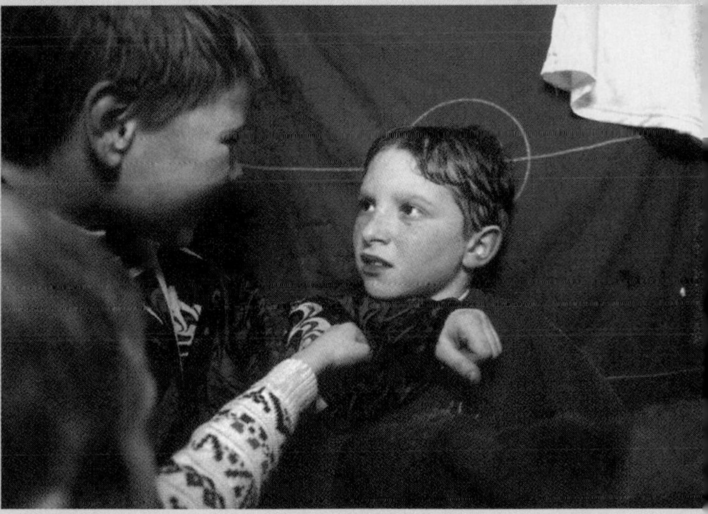

© PAUL BALDESARE/PHOTOFUSION

Some bullies are high-status youngsters, but most are disliked, or become so, because of their cruelty. Chronic victims tend to be physically weak, rejected by peers, and afraid to defend themselves—characteristics that make them easy targets.

standards, explaining concepts, and pointing out important features of tasks—particularly during gender-typed pursuits, such as science activities (Tenenbaum & Leaper, 2003; Tenenbaum et al., 2005). Furthermore, parents less often encourage girls to make their own decisions. And both parents and teachers more often praise boys for knowledge and accomplishment, girls for obedience (Good & Brophy, 2003; Leaper, Anderson, & Sanders, 1998; Pomerantz & Ruble, 1998).

Also in line with adult stereotypes, school-age children quickly figure out which academic subjects and skill areas are "masculine" and which are "feminine." They often regard reading, spelling, art, and music as more for girls and mathematics, athletics, and mechanical skills as more for boys (Eccles, Jacobs, & Harold, 1990; Jacobs & Weisz, 1994). These attitudes influence children's preferences for and sense of competence at certain subjects. For example, boys tend to feel more competent than girls at math and science, whereas girls feel more competent than boys at language arts—even when children of equal skill level are compared (Bhanot & Jovanovic, 2005; Freedman-Doan et al., 2000; Hong, Veach, & Lawrenz, 2003). As we will see in Chapter 11, these beliefs become realities for many young people in adolescence.

Although school-age children are aware of many stereotypes, they also develop a more open-minded view of what males and females *can do* (Trautner et al., 2005). As with racial stereotypes (see page 338), the ability to classify flexibly underlies this change. School-age children realize that a person can belong to more than one social category—for example, be a "boy" yet "like to play house" (Bigler, 1995). By the end of middle childhood, children regard gender typing as socially rather than biologically influenced (Taylor, 1996). Nevertheless, acknowledging that people *can* cross gender lines does not mean that children always *approve* of doing so. They take a harsh view of certain violations—boys playing with dolls and wearing girls' clothing, girls acting noisily and roughly. They are especially intolerant when boys engage in "cross-gender" acts, which children regard as nearly as bad as moral transgressions (Blakemore, 2003; Levy, Taylor, & Gelman, 1995).

Gender Identity and Behavior

From third to sixth grade, boys strengthen their identification with "masculine" personality traits, whereas girls' identification with "feminine" traits declines. Girls often describe themselves as having some "other-gender" characteristics (Serbin, Powlishta, & Gulko, 1993). Whereas boys usually stick to "masculine" pursuits, girls now experiment with a wider range of options—from cooking and sewing to sports and science fairs—and more often consider traditionally male future work roles, such as firefighter or astronomer (Liben & Bigler, 2002).

These changes are due to a mixture of cognitive and social forces. School-age children of both sexes are aware that society attaches greater prestige to "masculine" characteristics. For example, they rate "masculine" occupations as having higher status than "feminine" occupations (Liben, Bigler, & Krogh, 2001). Messages from adults and peers are also influential. In Chapter 8, we saw that parents (especially fathers) are far less tolerant when sons, as opposed to daughters, cross gender lines. Similarly, a tomboyish girl can make her way into boys' activities without losing the approval of her female peers, but a boy who hangs out with girls is likely to be ridiculed and rejected.

© PETER HVIZDAK/THE IMAGE WORKS

This 9-year-old girl enjoys karate lessons. Whereas school-age boys usually stick to "masculine" pursuits, girls experiment with a wider range of options.

As school-age children make social comparisons and characterize themselves in terms of stable dispositions, their gender identity expands to include the following self-evaluations, which greatly affect their adjustment:

- *Gender typicality*—the degree to which the child feels similar to others of the same gender. Although children need not be highly gender-typed to view themselves as gender-typical, their psychological well-being depends, to some degree, on feeling that they "fit in" with their same-sex peers (Egan & Perry, 2001).
- *Gender contentedness*—the degree to which the child feels satisfied with his or her gender assignment, which also promotes happiness.
- *Felt pressure to conform to gender roles*—the degree to which the child feels parents and peers disapprove of his or her gender-related traits. Because such pressure reduces the likelihood that children will explore options related to their interests and talents, children who feel strong gender-typed pressure are often distressed.

In a longitudinal study of third through seventh graders, *gender-typical* and *gender-contented* children gained in self-esteem over the following year. In contrast, children who were *gender-atypical* and *gender-discontented* declined in self-worth. Furthermore, gender-atypical children who reported *intense pressure to conform to gender roles* experienced serious difficulties—withdrawal, sadness, disappointment, and anxiety (Yunger, Carver, & Perry, 2004).

Clearly, how children feel about themselves in relation to their gender group becomes vitally important in middle childhood, and those who experience rejection because of their gender-atypical traits suffer profoundly. ***TAKE A MOMENT...*** Return to the case of David, the boy who was reared as a girl, on page 275 in Chapter 8. Note how David's dissatisfaction with his gender assignment joined with severe peer condemnation to severely impair his adjustment.

Currently, researchers and therapists are debating how best to help children who feel gender-atypical. Some advocate making them more gender-typical, through therapy that reinforces such children for engaging in traditional gender-role activities so they will feel more compatible with same-sex peers (Zucker, 2006). Others oppose this approach on grounds that it is likely to heighten felt pressure to conform (which predicts maladjustment) and—for children who fail to change—may result in parental rejection. These experts advocate intervening with parents and peers to help them become more accepting of children's gender-atypical interests and behaviors (Bigler, 2007; Conway, 2007; Crawford, 2003). ***TAKE A MOMENT...*** In view of what you have learned about the development of children's gender typing, which approach do you think would be more successful, and why?

ASK YOURSELF

REVIEW
How does friendship change in middle childhood?

APPLY
What changes in parent–child relationships are probably necessary to help rejected children?

CONNECT
Return to page 276 in Chapter 8, and review the concept of androgyny. Which of the two sexes is more androgynous in middle childhood, and why?

REFLECT
As a school-age child, did you have classmates you would classify as popular-aggressive? What were they like, and why do you think peers admired them?

Family Influences

As children move into school, peer, and community contexts, the parent–child relationship changes. At the same time, children's well-being continues to depend on the quality of family interaction. In the following sections, we will see that contemporary changes in families—high rates of divorce, remarriage, and maternal employment—can have positive as well as negative effects on children. In later chapters, we take up other family structures, including gay and lesbian families, never-married single-parent families, and the increasing numbers of grandparents rearing grandchildren.

Parent–Child Relationships

In middle childhood, the amount of time children spend with parents declines dramatically. The child's growing independence means that parents must deal with new issues. "I've struggled with how many chores to assign, how much allowance to give, whether their friends are good influences, and what to do about problems at school," Rena remarked. "And then there's the challenge of keeping track of them when they're out—or even when they're home and I'm not there to see what's going on."

Despite these new concerns, child rearing becomes easier for those parents who established an authoritative style in the early years. Reasoning is more effective with school-age children because of their greater capacity for logical thinking and their increased respect for parents' expert knowledge (Collins, Madsen, & Susman-Stillman, 2002).

As children demonstrate that they can manage daily activities and responsibilities, effective parents gradually shift control from adult to child. They do not let go entirely but, rather, engage in **coregulation,** a form of supervision in which parents exercise general oversight while letting children take charge of moment-by-moment decision making. Coregulation grows out of a warm, cooperative relationship between parent and child based on give-and-take and mutual respect. Parents must guide and monitor from a distance and effectively communicate expectations when they are with their children. And children must inform parents of their whereabouts, activities, and problems so parents can intervene when necessary (Maccoby, 1984). Coregulation supports and protects children while preparing them for adolescence, when they will make many important decisions themselves.

As at younger ages, mothers spend more time than fathers with school-age children. Mothers also are more knowledgeable about children's everyday activities. Still, fathers are often highly involved. Each parent, however, tends to devote more time to children of their own sex (Crouter et al., 1999; Lamb & Lewis, 2004). In parents' separate activities with children, mothers are more concerned with caregiving and ensuring that children meet responsibilities in homework, after-school lessons, and chores. Fathers, especially those with sons, focus on achievement-related and recreational pursuits (Collins & Russell, 1991). But when both parents are present, fathers engage in as much caregiving as mothers.

Although school-age children often press for greater independence, they know how much they need their parents' continuing support. In one study, fifth and sixth graders described parents as the most influential people in their lives (Furman & Buhrmester, 1992). They often turned to mothers and fathers for affection, advice, enhancement of self-worth, and assistance with everyday problems.

Siblings

In addition to parents and friends, siblings continue to be important sources of support. Yet sibling rivalry tends to increase in middle childhood. As children participate in a wider range of activities, parents often compare siblings' traits and accomplishments. The child who gets less parental affection, more disapproval, or fewer material resources is likely to be resentful (Dunn, 2004; Tamrouti-Makkink et al., 2004).

For same-sex siblings who are close in age, parental comparisons are more frequent, resulting in more quarreling and antagonism and poorer adjustment. This effect is particularly strong when parents are under stress as a result of financial worries, marital conflict, or single parenthood (Jenkins, Rasbash, & O'Connor, 2003). Parents whose energies are drained become less careful about being fair.

To reduce this rivalry, siblings often strive to be different from one another. For example, two brothers I know deliberately selected different athletic pursuits and musical instruments. If the older one did especially well at an activity, the younger one did not want to try it. Parents can limit these effects by making an effort not to compare children, but some feedback about their competencies is inevitable. As siblings

© MICHAEL NEWMAN/PHOTOEDIT

Although sibling rivalry tends to increase in middle childhood, siblings also provide one another with emotional support and help with difficult tasks.

Only Children

Although sibling relationships bring many benefits, they are not essential for healthy development. Contrary to popular belief, only children are not spoiled, and in some respects, they are advantaged. U.S. children growing up in one-child and multichild families do not differ in self-rated personality traits (Mottus, Indus, & Allik, 2008). And compared to children with siblings, only children are higher in self-esteem and achievement motivation, do better in school, and attain higher levels of education. One reason may be that only children have somewhat closer relationships with parents, who may exert more pressure for mastery and accomplishment (Falbo, 1992). However, only children tend to be less well-accepted in the peer group, perhaps because they have not had opportunities to learn effective conflict resolution strategies through sibling interaction (Kitzmann, Cohen, & Lockwood, 2002).

Favorable development also characterizes only children in China, where a one-child family policy has been strictly enforced in urban areas for more than two decades to control population growth (Yang, 2008). Compared with agemates who have siblings, Chinese only children are advanced in cognitive development and academic achievement. They also feel more emotionally secure, perhaps because government disapproval promotes tension in families with more than one child (Falbo & Poston, 1993; Jiao, Ji, & Jing, 1996; Yang et al., 1995). Chinese mothers usually ensure that their children have regular contact with first cousins (who are considered siblings). Perhaps as a result, Chinese only children do not differ from agemates with siblings in social skills and peer acceptance (Hart, Newell, & Olsen, 2003). The next generation of Chinese only children, however, will have no first cousins.

strive to win recognition for their own uniqueness, they shape important aspects of each other's development.

Although conflict rises, school-age siblings continue to rely on each other for companionship and assistance. When researchers asked siblings about shared daily activities, children mentioned that older siblings often helped younger siblings with academic and peer challenges. And both offered each other help with family issues (Tucker, McHale, & Crouter, 2001).

But for siblings to reap these benefits, parental encouragement of warm, considerate sibling ties is vital. Providing parents with training in mediation—how to get siblings to lay down ground rules, clarify their points of disagreement and common ground, and discuss possible solutions—increases siblings' awareness of each other's perspectives and reduces animosity (Smith & Ross, 2007). When siblings get along well, the older sibling's academic and social competence tends to "rub off on" the younger sibling, fostering more favorable achievement and peer relations (Brody & Murry, 2001; Lamarche et al., 2006). But older siblings with conflict-ridden peer relations tend to transmit their physically or relationally aggressive styles to their younger brothers and sisters (Ostrov, Crick, & Staffacher, 2006).

© PHOTOALTO/JAMES HARDY/JUPITER IMAGES

In China, a one-child family policy has been strictly enforced in urban areas for more than two decades to control population growth. However, Chinese only children do not differ from agemates with siblings in social skills and peer acceptance.

Divorce

Children's interactions with parents and siblings are affected by other aspects of family life. Joey and Lizzie's relationship, Rena told me, had been particularly negative only a few years before. Joey pushed, hit, and taunted Lizzie and called her names. Although she tried to retaliate, she was no match for Joey's larger size. The arguments usually ended with Lizzie running in tears to her mother. Joey and Lizzie's fighting coincided with their parents' growing marital unhappiness. When Joey was 8 and Lizzie 5, their father, Drake, moved out.

Between 1960 and 1985, divorce rates in Western nations rose dramatically before stabilizing in most countries. The United States has the highest divorce rate in the world (see Figure 10.3). Of the 45 percent of American marriages that end in divorce, half involve children. At any given time, one-fourth of U.S. children live in single-parent households. Although most reside with their mothers, the percentage in father-headed households has increased steadily, to about 12 percent (Federal Interagency Forum on Child and Family Statistics, 2008).

Children of divorce spend an average of five years in a single-parent home—almost a third of childhood. For many, divorce leads to new family relationships. About two-thirds of divorced parents marry again. Half their children eventually experience a third major change—the end of a parent's second marriage (Hetherington & Kelly, 2002).

These figures reveal that divorce is not a single event in the lives of parents and children. Instead, it is a transition that leads to a variety of new living arrangements, accompanied by changes in housing, income, and family roles and responsibilities. Since the 1960s, many studies have reported that marital breakup is stressful for children. But the research also reveals great individual differences (Hetherington, 2003). How well children fare depends on many factors: the custodial parent's psychological health, the child's characteristics, and social supports within the family and surrounding community.

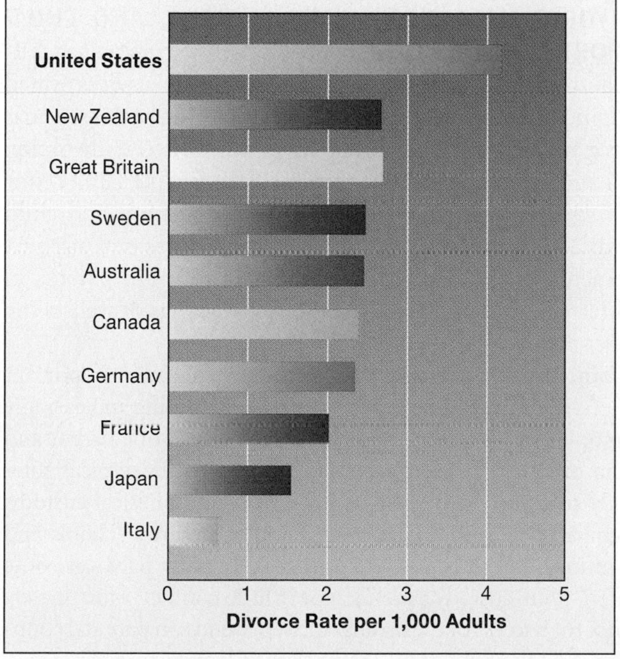

■ **FIGURE 10.3** ■ **Divorce rates in ten industrialized nations.** The U.S. divorce rate is the highest in the industrialized world, far exceeding divorce rates in other countries. (Adapted from U.S. Census Bureau, 2008c; United Nations, 2002.)

■ **IMMEDIATE CONSEQUENCES.** "Things were worst during the period Drake and I decided to separate," Rena reflected. "We fought over division of our belongings and the custody of the children, and the kids suffered. Sobbing, Lizzie told me she was 'sorry she made Daddy go away.' Joey kicked and threw things at home and didn't do his work at school. In the midst of everything, I could hardly deal with their problems. We had to sell the house; I couldn't afford it alone. And I needed a better-paying job."

Family conflict often rises in newly divorced households as parents try to settle disputes over children and possessions. Once one parent moves out, additional events threaten supportive interactions between parents and children. Mother-headed households typically experience a sharp drop in income. In the United States, the majority of single mothers with young children live in poverty, getting less than the full amount of child support from the absent father or none at all (Children's Defense Fund, 2009). They often have to move to lower-cost housing, reducing supportive ties to neighbors and friends.

The transition from marriage to divorce typically leads to high maternal stress, depression, and anxiety and to a disorganized family situation. Declines in well-being are greatest for mothers of young children (Williams & Dunne-Bryant, 2006). "Meals and bedtimes were at all hours, the house didn't get cleaned, and I stopped taking Joey and Lizzie on weekend outings," said Rena. As children react with distress and anger to their less secure home lives, discipline may become harsh and inconsistent. Contact with noncustodial fathers often decreases over time (Hetherington & Kelly, 2002). Fathers who see their children only occasionally are inclined to be permissive and indulgent, making the mother's task of managing the child even more difficult.

The more parents argue and fail to provide children with warmth, involvement, and consistent guidance, the poorer children's adjustment. About 20 to 25 percent of children in divorced families display severe problems, compared with about 10 percent in nondivorced families (Gerard, Krishnakumar, & Buehler, 2006; Strohschein, 2005). At the same time, reactions vary with children's age, temperament, and sex.

Children's Age. Five-year-old Lizzie's fear that she had caused her father to leave is not unusual. Preschool and young school-age children often blame themselves for a marital breakup and fear that both parents may abandon them (Pryor & Rodgers, 2001). Even many older children, with the cognitive maturity to understand that they are not responsible for their parents' divorce, react strongly, declining in school performance, becoming unruly, and escaping into undesirable peer activities, especially when family conflict is high and supervision of children is low (D'Onofrio et al., 2006; Lansford et al., 2006). But some older children—especially the oldest child in the family—display more mature behavior, willingly taking on extra family and household tasks as well as emotional support of a depressed, anxious mother. But if these demands are too great, these children may eventually become resentful, withdraw from the family, and engage in angry, acting-out behavior (Hetherington, 1999).

Children's Temperament and Sex. Exposure to stressful life events and inadequate parenting magnifies the problems of temperamentally difficult children. In contrast, easy children are less often targets of parental anger and also cope more effectively with adversity.

These findings help explain sex differences in response to divorce. Girls sometimes respond as Lizzie did, with internalizing reactions such as crying, self-criticism, and withdrawal. More often, children of both sexes show demanding, attention-getting, acting-out behavior. But in mother-custody families, boys are at greater risk for serious adjustment problems (Amato, 2001). Recall from Chapter 8 that boys are more active and noncompliant—behaviors that increase with exposure to parental conflict and inconsistent discipline. Coercive maternal behavior and defiance on the part of sons are common in divorcing households.

Perhaps because their behavior is so unruly, boys receive less emotional support from mothers, teachers, and peers. And as Joey's behavior toward Lizzie illustrates, the coercive cycles of interaction between boys and their divorced mothers soon spread to sibling relationships, compounding adjustment difficulties (Hetherington & Kelly, 2002; Sheehan et al., 2004). After divorce, children who are challenging to rear generally get worse.

■ **LONG-TERM CONSEQUENCES.** Rena eventually found better-paying work and gained control over the daily operation of the household. Her own feelings of anger and rejection also declined. And after several meetings with a counselor, Rena and Drake realized the harmful impact of their quarreling on Joey and Lizzie. Drake visited regularly and handled Joey's unruliness with firmness and consistency. Soon Joey's school performance improved, his behavior problems subsided, and both children seemed calmer and happier.

Most children show improved adjustment by two years after divorce. Yet overall, children and adolescents of divorced parents continue to score slightly lower than children of continuously married parents in academic achievement, self-esteem, and social competence and emotional adjustment (Amato, 2001). Children with difficult temperaments are especially likely to drop out of school, to be depressed, and to display antisocial behavior. And divorce is linked to problems with adolescent sexuality and development of intimate ties. Young people who experienced parental divorce—especially more than once—display higher rates of early sexual activity and adolescent parenthood (Wolfinger, 2000). Some experience other lasting difficulties—reduced educational attainment, troubled romantic relationships and marriages, divorce in adulthood, and unsatisfying parent–child relationships (Amato, 2006; Amato & Cheadle, 2005; Wallerstein & Lewis, 2004).

The overriding factor in positive adjustment following divorce is effective parenting—shielding the child from family conflict and using authoritative child rearing (Leon, 2003; Wolchik et al., 2000). Where the custodial parent is the mother, contact with fathers is important. The more paternal contact and the warmer the father–child relationship, the less children react with defiance and aggression (Dunn et al., 2004). For girls, a good father–child relationship protects against early sexual activity and unhappy romantic involvements. For boys, it seems to affect overall psychological well-being. In fact, several studies indicate that outcomes for sons are better when the father is the custodial parent (Clarke-Stewart & Hayward, 1996; McLanahan, 1999). Fathers' greater economic security and image of authority seem to help them engage in effective parenting with sons. And boys in father-custody families may benefit from greater involvement of both parents because noncustodial mothers participate more than noncustodial fathers in their children's lives.

Although divorce is painful for children, remaining in an intact but high-conflict family is much worse than making the transition to a low-conflict, single-parent household (Greene et al., 2003; Strohschein, 2005). Divorcing parents who set aside their disagreements and support each other in their child-rearing roles greatly improve their children's chances of growing up competent, stable, and happy. Caring extended-family members, teachers, siblings, and friends also reduce the likelihood that divorce will result in long-term difficulties (Hetherington, 2003; Lussier et al., 2002).

■ **DIVORCE MEDIATION, JOINT CUSTODY, AND CHILD SUPPORT.** Awareness that divorce is highly stressful for children and families has led to community-based services aimed at helping them through this difficult time. One such service is **divorce mediation,** a series of meetings between divorcing adults and a trained professional aimed at reducing family conflict, including legal battles over property division and child custody. Research reveals that mediation increases out-of-court settlements, cooperation and involvement of both parents in child rearing, and parents' and children's feelings of well-being (Emery, Sbarra, & Grover, 2005).

Joint custody, which grants parents equal say in important decisions about the child's upbringing, is becoming increasingly common. In most instances, children reside with one parent and see the other on a fixed schedule, similar to the typical sole-custody situation. In other cases, parents share physical custody, and children move between homes and sometimes schools and peer groups. These transitions can be especially hard on some children. Joint-custody parents report little conflict—fortunately so, since the success of the arrangement depends on parental cooperation. And their children—regardless of living arrangements—tend to be better-adjusted than children in sole-maternal-custody homes (Bauserman, 2002).

Finally, many single-parent families depend on child support from the noncustodial parent to relieve financial strain. All

Applying What We Know

Helping Children Adjust to Their Parents' Divorce

Suggestion	Rationale
Shield children from conflict.	Witnessing intense parental conflict is very damaging to children. If one parent insists on expressing hostility, children fare better if the other parent does not respond in kind.
Provide children with as much continuity, familiarity, and predictability as possible.	Children adjust better during the period surrounding divorce when their lives have some stability—for example, the same school, bedroom, babysitter, playmates, and daily schedule.
Explain the divorce, and tell children what to expect.	Children are more likely to develop fears of abandonment if they are not prepared for their parents' separation. They should be told that their parents will not be living together anymore, which parent will be moving out, and when they will be able to see that parent. If possible, parents should explain the divorce together. Parents should provide a reason for the divorce that the child can understand and assure children that they are not to blame.
Emphasize the permanence of the divorce.	Fantasies of parents getting back together can prevent children from accepting the reality of their current life. Children should be told that the divorce is final and that they cannot change this fact.
Respond sympathetically to children's feelings.	Children need a supportive and understanding response to their feelings of sadness, fear, and anger. For children to adjust well, their painful emotions must be acknowledged, not denied or avoided.
Engage in authoritative parenting.	Parents should provide children with affection and acceptance, reasonable demands for mature behavior, and consistent, rational discipline. Parents who engage in authoritative parenting greatly reduce their children's risk of maladjustment following divorce.
Promote a continuing relationship with both parents.	When parents disentangle their lingering hostility toward the former partner from the child's need for a continuing relationship with the other parent, children adjust well. Grandparents and other extended-family members can help by not taking sides.

Source: Teyber, 2001.

U.S. states have procedures for withholding wages from parents who fail to make these payments. Although child support is usually not enough to lift a single-parent family out of poverty, it can ease its burdens substantially. Noncustodial fathers who have generous visitation schedules and who often see their children are more likely to pay child support regularly (Amato & Sobolewski, 2004). Applying What We Know above summarizes ways to help children adjust to their parents' divorce.

Blended Families

"If you get married to Wendell, and Daddy gets married to Carol," Lizzie wondered aloud to Rena, "then I'll have two sisters and one more brother. And let's see, how many grandmothers and grandfathers? A lot!" exclaimed Lizzie.

About 60 percent of divorced parents remarry within a few years. Others *cohabit,* or share a sexual relationship and a residence with a partner outside of marriage. Parent, stepparent, and children form a new family structure called the **blended,** or **reconstituted, family.** For some children, this expanded family network is positive, bringing more adult attention. But most have more problems than children in stable, first-marriage families. Switching to stepparents' new rules and expectations can be stressful, and children often view steprelatives as intruders. How well they adapt is, again, related to the quality of family functioning (Hetherington & Kelly, 2002). This depends on which parent forms a new relationship, the child's age and sex, and the complexity of blended-family relationships. As we will see, older children and girls seem to have the hardest time.

■ **MOTHER–STEPFATHER FAMILIES.** Because mothers generally retain custody of children, the most common form of blended family is a mother–stepfather arrangement. Boys tend to adjust quickly, welcoming a stepfather who is warm, who refrains from exerting his authority too quickly, and who offers relief from coercive cycles of mother–son interaction. Mothers' friction with sons also declines as a result of greater economic security, another adult to share household tasks, and an end to loneliness (Visher, Visher, & Pasley, 2003). Stepfathers who marry rather than cohabit are more involved in parenting, perhaps because men who choose to marry a mother with children are more interested in and skilled at child rearing (Hofferth & Anderson, 2003). Girls, however, often have difficulty with their custodial mother's remarriage. Stepfathers disrupt the close ties many girls have established with their mothers, and girls often react with sulky, resistant behavior (Bray, 1999).

But age affects these findings. Older school-age children and adolescents of both sexes display more irresponsible, acting-out behavior than their peers not in stepfamilies (Hetherington & Stanley-Hagan, 2000). Some parents are warmer and more involved with their biological children than with their stepchildren. Older children are more likely to notice and challenge unfair treatment. And adolescents often view the new stepparent as a threat to their freedom, especially if they experienced little

Adapting to life in a blended family can be stressful for children. But the transition can be eased if stepparents move into their new roles gradually, first building warm relationships with children.

parental monitoring in the single-parent family. Still, when teenagers have affectionate, cooperative relationships with their mothers, many eventually develop good relations with their stepfathers—a circumstance linked to better adjustment (Yuan & Hamilton, 2006).

■ **FATHER–STEPMOTHER FAMILIES.** Remarriage of noncustodial fathers often leads to reduced contact with their biological children, as these fathers tend to withdraw from their "previous" families (Dunn, 2002). When fathers have custody, children typically react negatively to remarriage. One reason is that children living with fathers often start out with more problems. Perhaps the biological mother could no longer handle the difficult child (usually a boy), so the father and his new partner are faced with a youngster who has behavior problems. In other instances, the father has custody because of a very close relationship with the child, and his remarriage disrupts this bond (Buchanan, Maccoby, & Dornbusch, 1996).

Girls, especially, have a hard time getting along with their stepmothers, either because the remarriage threatens the girl's bond with her father or because she becomes entangled in loyalty conflicts between the two mother figures. But the longer girls live in father–stepmother households, the more positive their interaction with stepmothers becomes (Hetherington & Jodl, 1994). With time and patience, most girls benefit from the support of a second mother figure.

■ **SUPPORT FOR BLENDED FAMILIES.** Family life education and therapy can help parents and children adapt to the complexities of blended families. Effective approaches encourage stepparents to move into their new roles gradually by first building a warm relationship with the child (Visher, Visher, & Pasley, 2003). Counselors can help couples form a cooperative "parenting coalition" to limit loyalty conflicts and provide consistency in child rearing. This allows children to benefit from the increased diversity that stepparent relationships bring to their lives.

Unfortunately, the divorce rate for second marriages is even higher than for first marriages. Parents with antisocial tendencies and poor child-rearing skills are particularly likely to have several divorces and remarriages. And the more marital transitions children experience, the greater their difficulties (Dunn, 2002). These families usually require prolonged, intensive therapy.

Maternal Employment and Dual-Earner Families

Today, U.S. single and married mothers are in the labor market in nearly equal proportions, and more than three-fourths of those with school-age children are employed (U.S. Census Bureau, 2009a). In previous chapters, we saw that the impact of maternal employment on early development depends on the quality of child care and the continuing parent–child relationship. The same is true in middle childhood.

■ **MATERNAL EMPLOYMENT AND CHILD DEVELOPMENT.** Children whose mothers enjoy their work and remain committed to parenting show favorable adjustment—higher self-esteem, more positive family and peer relations, less gender-stereotyped beliefs, and better grades in school. Girls, especially, profit from the image of female competence. Regardless of SES, daughters of employed mothers perceive women's roles as involving more freedom of choice and satisfaction and are more achievement- and career-oriented (Hoffman, 2000).

Parenting practices contribute to these benefits. Employed mothers who value their parenting role are more likely to use authoritative child rearing and coregulation. Also, children in dual-earner households devote more daily hours to doing homework under parental guidance and participate more in household chores. And maternal employment leads fathers—especially those who believe in the importance of the paternal role and who feel successful at parenting—to take on greater child-rearing responsibilities, with a small but increasing number staying home full-time (Gottfried, Gottfried, & Bathurst, 2002; Jacobs & Kelley, 2006). Paternal involvement is associated with higher intelligence and achievement, more mature social behavior, and a flexible view of gender roles in childhood and adolescence, and with generally better mental health in adulthood (Coltrane, 1996; Pleck & Masciadrelli, 2004).

But when employment places heavy demands on a mother's schedule or is stressful for other reasons, children are at risk for ineffective parenting. Working many hours or experiencing a negative workplace atmosphere is associated with reduced parental sensitivity, fewer joint parent–child activities, and poorer cognitive development in children throughout childhood and adolescence (Brooks-Gunn, Han, & Waldfogel, 2002; Bumpus,

Crouter, & McHale, 2006; Strazdins et al., 2006). Negative consequences are magnified when low-SES mothers spend long days at low-paying, physically exhausting jobs—conditions linked to maternal depression and harsh, inconsistent discipline (Raver, 2003). In contrast, part-time employment and flexible work schedules are associated with good child adjustment (Frederiksen-Goldsen & Sharlach, 2000; Hill et al., 2006). By preventing work–family role conflict, these arrangements help parents meet children's needs.

■ SUPPORT FOR EMPLOYED PARENTS AND THEIR FAMILIES. In dual-earner families, the father's willingness to share responsibilities is a crucial factor. If he helps little or not at all, the mother carries a double load, at home and at work, leading to fatigue, distress, and little time and energy for children.

Employed mothers and dual-earner parents need assistance from work settings and communities in their child-rearing roles. Part-time employment, flexible schedules, job sharing, and paid leave when children are ill help parents juggle the demands of work and child rearing. Equal pay and employment opportunities for women are also important. Because these policies enhance financial status and morale, they improve the way mothers feel and behave when they arrive home at the end of the working day.

■ CHILD CARE FOR SCHOOL-AGE CHILDREN. High-quality child care is vital for parents' peace of mind and children's well-being, even in middle childhood. An estimated 7 million 5- to 13-year-olds in the United States are **self-care children,** who are without adult supervision for some period of time after school (Durlak & Weissberg, 2007). Self-care increases with age and also with SES, perhaps because of the greater safety of higher-income neighborhoods. But when lower-SES parents lack alternatives to self-care, their children spend more hours on their own (Casper & Smith, 2002).

Some studies report that self-care children suffer from adjustment problems, whereas others show no such effects. Children's maturity and the way they spend their time seem to explain these contradictions. Among younger school-age children, those who spend more hours alone have more emotional and social difficulties (Vandell & Posner, 1999). As children become old enough to look after themselves, those who have a history of authoritative child rearing, are monitored by parental telephone calls, and have regular after-school chores appear responsible and well-adjusted. In contrast, children left to their own devices are more likely to bend to peer pressures and engage in antisocial behavior (Coley, Morris, & Hernandez, 2004; Vandell et al., 2006).

Before age 8 or 9, most children need supervision because they are not yet competent to handle emergencies (Galambos & Maggs, 1991). But throughout middle childhood, attending after-school programs with well-trained staffs, generous adult–child ratios, and skill-building activities is linked to good school performance and emotional and social adjustment (Durlak & Weissberg, 2007; Granger, 2008). Low-SES children who participate in "after-care" programs offering academic assistance and enrichment activities (scouting, music and art lessons, clubs) show special benefits. They exceed their self-care counterparts in classroom work habits, academic achievement, and prosocial behavior and display fewer behavior problems (Lauer et al., 2006; Vandell et al., 2006).

Unfortunately, good after-care is in especially short supply in low-income neighborhoods (Afterschool Alliance, 2004). A special need exists for well-planned programs in these areas—ones that provide safe environments, warm relationships with adults, and enjoyable, goal-oriented activities.

© BOB DAEMMRICH/PHOTOEDIT

In this after-school program, children learn about fossils from an AmeriCorps volunteer. Attending high-quality after-school programs is linked to good school performance and emotional and social adjustment.

ASK YOURSELF

» REVIEW
Describe and explain changes in sibling relationships during middle childhood.

» APPLY
Steve and Marissa are in the midst of an acrimonious divorce. Their 9-year-old son Dennis has become hostile and defiant. How can Steve and Marissa help Dennis adjust?

» CONNECT
How does each level in Bronfenbrenner's ecological systems theory—microsystem, mesosystem, exosystem, and macrosystem—contribute to the effects of maternal employment on children's development?

» REFLECT
What after-school child-care arrangements did you experience in elementary school? How do you think they influenced your development?

Some Common Problems of Development

We have considered a variety of stressful experiences that place children at risk for future problems. Next, we address two more areas of concern: school-age children's fears and anxieties and the consequences of child sexual abuse. Finally, we sum up factors that help children cope effectively with stress.

Fears and Anxieties

Although fears of the dark, thunder and lightning, and supernatural beings persist into middle childhood, older children's anxieties are also directed toward new concerns. As children begin to understand the realities of the wider world, the possibility of personal harm (being robbed, stabbed, or shot) and media events (war and disasters) often trouble them. Other common worries include academic failure, parents' health, physical injuries, and peer rejection (Muris et al., 2000; Weems & Costa, 2005).

Children in Western nations mention exposure to negative information in the media as the most common source of their fears, followed by direct exposure to frightening events (Muris et al., 2001). Nevertheless, as we saw in Chapter 8, many parents have no rules about their children's TV viewing or computer use, including Internet access.

As long as fears are not too intense, most children handle them constructively, using the more sophisticated emotional regulation strategies that develop in middle childhood. Consequently, fears decline with age, especially for girls, who express more fears than boys throughout childhood and adolescence (Gullone, 2000). But about 5 percent of school-age children develop an intense, unmanageable fear called a **phobia.** Children with inhibited temperaments are at high risk, displaying phobias five to six times more often than other children (Ollendick, King, & Muris, 2002).

For example, in *school phobia,* children feel severe apprehension about attending school, often accompanied by physical complaints (dizziness, nausea, stomachaches, and vomiting). About one-third of children with school phobia are 5- to 7-year-olds for whom the real fear is maternal separation. Family therapy helps these children, whose difficulty can often be traced to parental overprotection (Elliott, 1999). Most cases of school phobia appear around age 11 to 13. These children usually find a particular aspect of school frightening—an overcritical teacher, a school bully, or too much parental pressure to achieve. A change in school environment or parenting practices may be needed. Firm insistence that the child return to school, along with training in how to cope with difficult situations, is also helpful (Silverman & Pina, 2008).

Severe childhood anxieties may arise from harsh living conditions. In inner-city ghettos and in war-torn areas of the world, large numbers of children live in the midst of constant danger, chaos, and deprivation. As the Lifespan Vista box on the following page reveals, these youngsters are at risk for long-term emotional distress and behavior problems. Finally, as we saw in our discussion of child abuse in Chapter 8, too often violence and other destructive acts become part of adult–child relationships. During middle childhood, child sexual abuse increases.

Child Sexual Abuse

Until recently, child sexual abuse was considered rare, and adults often dismissed children's claims of abuse. In the 1970s, efforts by professionals and media attention led to recognition of child sexual abuse as a serious and widespread problem. About 90,000 cases in the United States were confirmed in the most recently reported year (U.S. Department of Health and Human Services, 2008e).

CHARACTERISTICS OF ABUSERS AND VICTIMS. Sexual abuse is committed against children of both sexes, but more often against girls. Most cases are reported in middle childhood, but for some victims, abuse begins early in life and continues for many years (Hoch-Espada, Ryan, & Deblinger, 2006; Trickett & Putnam, 1998).

Typically, the abuser is male—a parent or someone the parent knows well—a father, stepfather, or live-in boyfriend, somewhat less often an uncle or older brother. But in about 25 percent of cases, mothers are the offenders, more often with sons (Boroughs, 2004). If the abuser is a nonrelative, the person is usually someone the child has come to know and trust. However, the Internet and mobile phones have become avenues through which other adults commit sexual abuse—for example, by exposing children and adolescents to pornography and online sexual advances as a way of "grooming" them for sexual acts offline (Wolak et al., 2008).

Abusers make the child comply in a variety of distasteful ways, including deception, bribery, verbal intimidation, and physical force. You may wonder how any adult—especially a parent or close relative—could violate a child sexually. Many offenders deny their own responsibility, blaming the abuse on the willing participation of a seductive youngster. Yet children are not capable of making a deliberate, informed decision to enter into a sexual relationship! Even older children and adolescents are not free to say yes or no. Rather, the responsibility lies with abusers, who tend to have characteristics that predispose them toward sexual exploitation of children. They have great difficulty controlling their impulses and may suffer from psychological disorders, including alcohol and drug abuse. Often they pick out children who are unlikely to defend themselves or to be believed—those who are physically weak, emotionally deprived, socially isolated, or affected by disabilities (Bolen, 2001).

Reported cases of child sexual abuse are linked to poverty, marital instability, and resulting weakening of family ties. Children who live in homes with a constantly changing cast of characters—repeated marriages, separations, and new partners—are especially vulnerable. But children in economically advantaged, stable families are also victims, although their abuse is more likely to escape detection (Putnam, 2003).

A LIFESPAN VISTA: Looking Forward, Looking Back

Impact of Ethnic and Political Violence on Children

Around the world, many children live with armed conflict, terrorism, and other acts of violence stemming from ethnic and political tensions. Some children may participate in fighting, either because they are forced or because they want to please adults. Others are kidnapped, assaulted, and tortured. Those who are bystanders often come under direct fire and may be killed or physically maimed. And many watch in horror as family members, friends, and neighbors flee, are wounded, or die. In the past decade, wars have left 6 million children physically disabled, 20 million homeless, and more than 1 million separated from their parents (Ursano & Shaw, 2007; Wexler, Branski, & Kerem, 2006).

When war and social crises are temporary, most children can be comforted and do not show long-term emotional difficulties. But chronic danger requires children to make substantial adjustments that can seriously disrupt their psychological functioning. Many children of war lose their sense of safety, become desensitized to violence, are haunted by terrifying memories, are impaired in moral reasoning, and build a pessimistic view of the future. Anxiety and depression increase, as do aggression and antisocial behavior—outcomes seen in every war zone studied, from Bosnia, Angola, Rwanda, and the Sudan to the West Bank, Afghanistan, and Iraq (Barenbaum, Ruchkin, & Schwab-Stone, 2004; Klingman, 2006).

Parental affection and reassurance are the best protection against lasting problems. When parents offer security and serve as role models of calm emotional strength, most children can withstand even extreme war-related violence (Smith et al., 2001). Children who are separated from parents must rely on help from their communities. Orphans in Eritrea who were placed in residential settings where they could form close emotional ties with an adult showed less emotional stress five years later than orphans placed in impersonal settings (Wolff & Fesseha, 1999). Education and recreation programs are powerful safeguards, too, providing children with consistency in their lives along with teacher and peer supports.

With the September 11, 2001, terrorist attacks on the World Trade Center, some U.S. children experienced extreme wartime violence firsthand. Children in Public School 31 in Brooklyn, New York, for example, watched through classroom windows as the planes struck the towers and were engulfed in flames and as the towers crumbled. Many worried about the safety of family members, and some lost them. In the aftermath, most expressed intense fears—for example, that terrorists were infiltrating their neighborhoods and that planes flying overhead might smash into nearby buildings.

Unlike many war-traumatized children in the developing world, Public School 31 students received immediate intervention—a "trauma curriculum" in which they expressed their emotions through writing, drawing, and discussion and participated in experiences aimed at restoring trust and tolerance (Lagnado, 2001). Older children learned about the feelings of their Muslim classmates, the dire condition of children in Afghanistan, and ways to help victims as a means of overcoming a sense of helplessness.

When wartime drains families and communities of resources, international organizations must step in and help children. Efforts to preserve children's physical, psychological, and educational well-being may be the best way to stop transmission of violence to the next generation.

AP IMAGES/ANJA NIEDRINGHAUS

A trauma counselor comforts a child standing amid the rubble of her neighborhood in the Gaza Strip. Many children of war lose their sense of safety, and without special support from caring adults, they are likely to have lasting emotional problems.

CONSEQUENCES. The adjustment problems of child sexual abuse victims—including anxiety, depression, low self-esteem, mistrust of adults, and anger and hostility—are often severe and can persist for years after the abusive episodes. Younger children frequently react with sleep difficulties, loss of appetite, and generalized fearfulness. Adolescents may run away and show suicidal reactions, substance abuse, and delinquency. At all ages, persistent abuse accompanied by force, violence, and a close relationship to the perpetrator (incest) has a greater impact (Feiring, Taska, & Lewis, 1999; Wolfe, 2006). And repeated sexual abuse, like physical abuse, is associated with central nervous system damage (Cicchetti, 2007).

Sexually abused children frequently display precocious sexual knowledge and behavior. In adolescence, abused young people often become promiscuous, and as adults, they show increased arrest rates for sex crimes (mostly against children) and prostitution (Salter et al., 2003; Whipple, 2006). Furthermore, women who were sexually abused are likely to choose partners who abuse them and their children. As mothers, they often engage in irresponsible and coercive parenting, including child abuse and neglect (Pianta, Egeland, & Erickson, 1989). In all these ways, the harmful impact of sexual abuse is transmitted to the next generation.

PREVENTION AND TREATMENT. Because sexual abuse typically appears in the midst of other serious family problems, long-term therapy with both children and parents is usually needed (Olafson & Boat, 2000). The best way to reduce

COURTESY OF THE NEW ZEALAND POLICE

Keeping Ourselves Safe is New Zealand's school-based child abuse prevention program. It involves teachers, police officers, and parents in protecting children by teaching them to recognize and respond to abusive adult behaviors.

the suffering of victims is to prevent sexual abuse from continuing. Today, courts are prosecuting abusers more vigorously and taking children's testimony more seriously (see the Social Issues box on the following page).

Educational programs that teach children to recognize inappropriate sexual advances and whom to turn to for help reduce the risk of abuse (Hebert & Tourigny, 2004). Yet because of controversies over educating children about sexual abuse, few schools offer these interventions. New Zealand is the only country with a national, school-based prevention program targeting sexual abuse. In Keeping Ourselves Safe, children and adolescents learn that abusers are rarely strangers. Parent involvement ensures that home and school collaborate in teaching children self-protection skills. Evaluations reveal that virtually all New Zealand parents and children support the program and that it has helped many children avoid or report abuse (Sanders, 2006).

Fostering Resilience in Middle Childhood

Throughout middle childhood—and other periods of development—children encounter challenging and sometimes threatening situations that require them to cope with psychological stress. In this and the previous chapter, we have considered such topics as chronic illness, learning disabilities, achievement expectations, divorce, wartime trauma, and sexual abuse. Each taxes children's coping resources, creating serious risks for development.

Nevertheless, only a modest relationship exists between stressful life experiences and psychological disturbance in childhood (Masten & Reed, 2002). In our discussion in Chapter 3 of the long-term consequences of birth complications, we noted that some children manage to overcome the combined effects of birth trauma, poverty, and troubled family life. The same is true for school difficulties, family transitions, and child maltreatment. Recall from Chapter 1 that four broad factors protect against maladjustment: (1) the child's personal characteristics, including an easy temperament and a mastery-oriented approach to new situations; (2) a warm parental relationship; (3) an adult outside the immediate family who offers a support system; and (4) community resources, such as good schools, social services, and youth organizations and recreation centers (Commission on Children at Risk, 2008; Wright & Masten, 2005).

Any one of these ingredients of resilience can account for why one child fares well and another poorly. Usually, however, personal and environmental factors are interconnected: Each resource favoring resilience strengthens others. For example, safe, stable neighborhoods with family-friendly community services reduce parents' daily hassles and stress, thereby promoting good parenting (Pinderhughes et al., 2001). In contrast, unfavorable home and neighborhood experiences increase the chances that children will act in ways that expose them to further hardship. And when negative conditions pile up, such as marital discord, poverty, crowded living conditions, neighborhood violence, and abuse, the rate of maladjustment multiplies (Wright & Masten, 2005).

Rather than a preexisting attribute, *resilience* is a capacity that develops, enabling children to use internal and external resources to cope with adversity (Roberts & Masten, 2004; Yates, Egeland, & Sroufe, 2003). Throughout our discussion, we have seen how families, schools, communities, and society as a whole can enhance or undermine school-age children's supportive relationships and sense of competence. As the next two chapters will reveal, young people whose childhood experiences helped them learn to overcome obstacles, strive for self-direction, and respond considerately and sympathetically to others meet the challenges of the next period—adolescence—quite well.

ASK YOURSELF

REVIEW
When children must testify in court cases, what factors increase the chances of accurate reporting?

APPLY
Claire told her 6-year-old daughter never to talk to or take candy from strangers. Why will Claire's warning not protect her daughter from sexual abuse?

CONNECT
Explain how factors that promote resilience contribute to favorable adjustment following divorce.

REFLECT
Describe a challenging time during your childhood. What aspects of the experience increased stress? What resources helped you cope with adversity?

SOCIAL ISSUES

Children's Eyewitness Testimony

Increasingly, children are being called on to testify in court cases involving child abuse and neglect, child custody, and similar matters. The experience can be difficult and traumatic, requiring children to report on highly stressful events and sometimes to speak against a parent or other relative to whom they feel loyal. In some family disputes, they may fear punishment for telling the truth. In addition, child witnesses are faced with an unfamiliar situation—at the very least an interview in the judge's chambers and at most an open courtroom with judge, jury, spectators, and the possibility of unsympathetic cross-examination. Not surprisingly, these conditions can compromise the accuracy of children's recall.

Age Differences

Until recently, children younger than age 5 were rarely asked to testify, and not until age 10 were they assumed fully competent to do so. As a result of societal reactions to rising rates of child abuse and the difficulty of prosecuting perpetrators, legal requirements for child testimony have been relaxed in the United States (Sandler, 2006). Children as young as age 3 frequently serve as witnesses.

Compared with preschoolers, school-age children are better at giving accurate, detailed narrative accounts of past experiences and correctly inferring others' motives and intentions. Older children are also more resistant to misleading questions that attorneys may ask when probing for more information or, in cross-examination, trying to influence the child's response (Roebers & Schneider, 2001). But when properly questioned, even 3-year-olds can recall recent events accurately (Peterson & Rideout, 1998).

Suggestibility

Court testimony, however, often involves repeated interviews. When biased adults lead witnesses by suggesting incorrect "facts," interrupt children's denials, reinforce them for giving desired answers, or use a confrontational questioning style, they increase the likelihood of incorrect reporting by preschoolers and school-age children alike (Bruck & Ceci, 2004; Owen-Kostelnik, Rappucci, & Meyer, 2006).

In one study, 4- to 7-year-olds were asked to recall details about a visitor who had come to their classroom a week earlier. Half the children received a low-pressure interview containing leading questions that implied abuse ("He took your clothes off, didn't he?"). The other half received a high-pressure interview in which an adult told the child that her friends had said "yes" to the leading questions, praised the child for agreeing ("You're doing great"), and, if the child did not agree, repeated the question. Children were far more likely to give false information—even to fabricate quite fantastic events—in the high-pressure condition (Finnilä et al., 2003).

By the time children appear in court, weeks, months, or even years have passed since the target events. When a long delay is combined with biased interviewing and with stereotyping of the accused ("He's in jail because he's been bad"), children can easily be misled into giving false information (Gilstrap & Ceci, 2005; Quas et al., 2007). The more distinctive and personally relevant an event is, the more likely children are to recall it accurately over time. For example, a year later, even when exposed to misleading information, children correctly reported details of an injury that required emergency room treatment (Peterson, Parsons, & Dean, 2004).

In many sexual abuse cases, anatomically correct dolls are used to prompt children's recall. Although this method helps older children provide more detail about experienced events, it increases the suggestibility of preschoolers, who report physical and sexual contact that never happened (Goodman et al., 1999).

Interventions

Adults must prepare child witnesses so they understand the courtroom process and know what to expect. In some places, "court schools" take children through the setting and give them an opportunity to role-play court activities. Practice interviews—in which children learn to provide the most accurate, detailed information possible and to admit not knowing rather than agreeing or guessing—are helpful (Saywitz, Goodman, & Lyon, 2002).

At the same time, legal professionals must use interviewing procedures that increase children's accurate reporting. Unbiased, open-ended questions that prompt children to disclose details—"Tell me what happened" or "You said there was a man; tell me about the man"—reduce suggestibility (Holliday, 2003). Also, a warm, supportive interview tone fosters accurate recall, perhaps by easing children's fears so they feel freer to disagree with an interviewer's false suggestions (Ceci, Bruck, & Battin, 2000).

If children are likely to experience emotional trauma or later punishment (as in a family dispute), courtroom procedures can be adapted to protect them. For example, children can testify over closed-circuit TV so they do not have to face an abuser. When it is not wise for a child to participate directly, impartial expert witnesses can provide testimony that reports on the child's psychological condition and includes important elements of the child's story.

When interviewed for their eyewitness accounts, school-age children are better able than preschoolers to give accurate, detailed descriptions and correctly infer others' motives and intentions. This police officer can promote accurate recall by using a warm, supportive tone and avoiding leading questions.

Summary

Erikson's Theory: Industry versus Inferiority

What personality changes take place during Erikson's stage of industry versus inferiority?

» According to Erikson, children who successfully resolve the psychological conflict of **industry versus inferiority** develop a sense of competence at skills and tasks, a positive but realistic self-concept, pride in accomplishment, moral responsibility, and the ability to work cooperatively with agemates.

© TOM & DEE ANN MCCARTHY/CORBIS

Self-Understanding

Describe school-age children's self-concept and self-esteem and how they make achievement-related attributions.

» During middle childhood, children's self-concepts include competencies, personality traits, and **social comparisons.**

» Self-esteem differentiates further and becomes hierarchically organized and more realistic. Authoritative parenting is linked to favorable self-esteem.

» Children who make **mastery-oriented attributions** credit success to ability and failure to controllable factors, such as insufficient effort. In contrast, children who receive negative feedback about their ability are likely to develop **learned helplessness,** attributing success to external factors, such as luck, and failure to low ability.

Emotional Development

Cite changes in self-conscious emotions and in understanding and management of emotion in middle childhood.

» In middle childhood, the self-conscious emotions of pride and guilt become clearly governed by personal responsibility. Experiencing intense shame can shatter self-esteem.

» School-age children recognize that people can experience more than one emotion at a time. They also reconcile contradictory cues in interpreting another's feelings. Empathy increases and includes sensitivity to both people's immediate distress and their general life condition.

» By age 10, most children can shift adaptively between **problem-centered** and **emotion-centered coping** in regulating emotion. Emotionally well-regulated children are upbeat, empathic, and prosocial.

Understanding Others: Perspective Taking

How does perspective taking change in middle childhood?

» As Selman's five-stage sequence indicates, **perspective taking,** the capacity to imagine others' thoughts and feelings, improves greatly, supported by cognitive maturity and experiences in which others explain their viewpoints. Good perspective takers have more positive social skills.

Moral Development

Describe changes in moral understanding during middle childhood.

» By middle childhood, children have internalized rules for good conduct. They clarify and link moral imperatives and social conventions, considering the purpose of the rule, people's intentions, and the context of their actions. They also better understand individual rights.

© JEFF GREENBERG/ALAMY

» Though children of all races pick up prevailing societal attitudes about race and ethnicity, school-age children understand that people who look different need not think, feel, or act differently, and prejudice typically declines. Children most likely to hold biases are those who believe that personality traits are fixed, who have inflated self-esteem, and who live in a social world that highlights group distinctions. Long-term, intergroup contact is most effective at reducing prejudice.

Peer Relations

How do peer sociability and friendship change in middle childhood?

» In middle childhood, prosocial acts increase while physical aggression declines. By the end of the school years, children organize themselves into **peer groups.**

» Friendships develop into mutual relationships based on trust. Children tend to select friends similar to themselves in many ways.

Describe categories of peer acceptance and ways to help rejected children.

» On measures of **peer acceptance, popular children** are well-liked by many agemates; **rejected children** are actively disliked; **controversial children** are both liked and disliked; and **neglected children** are seldom chosen, either positively or negatively.

» Two subtypes of popular children exist: **popular-prosocial children,** who are academically and socially competent, and **popular-antisocial children,** who are aggressive but admired. Rejected children also divide into two subtypes: **rejected-aggressive children,** who are especially high in conflict and hostility, and **rejected-withdrawn children,** who are passive, socially awkward, and at risk for **peer victimization.**

» Rejected children often experience lasting adjustment difficulties. Interventions involving coaching in social skills, academic tutoring, and training in perspective taking and solving social problems produce gains in social competence and peer acceptance.

Gender Typing

What changes in gender-stereotyped beliefs and gender identity occur during middle childhood?

» School-age children extend their awareness of gender stereotypes to personality traits and academic subjects. But they also develop a more open-minded view of what males and females can do.

» Boys strengthen their identification with the masculine role, whereas girls often experiment with "other-gender" activities. Gender identity includes self-evaluations based on typicality, contentedness, and felt pressure to conform to gender roles, each of which affects adjustment.

© PETER HVIZDAK/THE IMAGE WORKS

Family Influences

How do parent–child communication and sibling relationships change in middle childhood?

» Despite declines in time spent with parents, effective **coregulation** allows parents to exercise general oversight over children, who increasingly make their own decisions.

» Sibling rivalry tends to increase with greater participation in diverse activities and more frequent parental comparisons. Only children do not differ from children with siblings in self-rated personality traits and are higher in self-esteem, school performance, and educational attainment.

What factors influence children's adjustment to divorce and remarriage?

» Although marital breakup is often quite stressful for children, individual differences exist based on parental psychological health, child characteristics (age, temperament, and sex), and social supports. Boys and children with difficult temperaments are at greater risk for adjustment problems. In both sexes, divorce is linked to early sexual activity, adolescent parenthood, and relationship difficulties.

» The overriding factor in positive adjustment following divorce is effective parenting. Positive father–child relationships have protective value, as do extended-family supports.

» **Divorce mediation** can be beneficial in the period surrounding divorce. The success of **joint custody** depends on a cooperative relationship between divorcing parents.

» When divorced parents enter new relationships and form **blended,** or **reconstituted, families,** girls, older children, and children in father–stepmother families display the greatest adjustment problems. Stepparents who move into their roles gradually and form a "parenting coalition" help children adjust.

© ARIEL SKELLEY/GETTY IMAGES/BLEND IMAGES

How do maternal employment and life in dual-earner families affect school-age children?

» When mothers enjoy their work and remain committed to parenting, their children benefit from higher self-esteem, more positive family and peer relations, less gender-stereotyped beliefs, and better school grades. In dual-earner families, the father's willingness to share in household responsibilities is linked to many positive child outcomes Workplace supports help parents in their child-rearing roles.

» Authoritative child rearing, parental monitoring, and regular after-school chores lead **self-care children** to be responsible and well-adjusted. Good "after-care" programs also aid school performance and emotional and social adjustment.

Some Common Problems of Development

Cite common fears and anxieties in middle childhood.

» School-age children's fears are directed toward new concerns, including personal harm, media events, academic failure, parents' health, and peer rejection. Children with inhibited temperaments are at higher risk of developing a **phobia.** Harsh living conditions can also cause severe anxiety.

Discuss factors related to child sexual abuse and its consequences for children's development.

» Child sexual abuse is generally committed by male family members, more often against girls than boys. Abusers have characteristics that predispose them toward sexual exploitation of children. Reported cases are strongly associated with poverty and marital instability. Abused children often have severe adjustment problems.

Cite factors that foster resilience in middle childhood.

» Overall, only a modest relationship exists between stressful life experiences and psychological disturbance in childhood. The child's personal characteristics, a warm parental relationship, other supportive adults, and community resources predict resilience. But when negative factors pile up, the rate of maladjustment multiplies.

Important Terms and Concepts

Milestones

Development in Middle Childhood

6–8 years

PHYSICAL

- Slow gains in height and weight continue until adolescent growth spurt. (290)
- Permanent teeth gradually replace primary teeth. (290)
- Legibility of writing increases, preparing children to master cursive writing. (295)
- Drawings become more organized and detailed and include some depth cues. (295)
- Games with rules and rough-and-tumble play become common. (296, 297–298)
- Dominance hierarchies become more stable, especially among boys. (298)

COGNITIVE

- Thought becomes more logical, as shown by the ability to pass Piagetian conservation, class inclusion, and seriation problems. (299–300)

- Spatial reasoning improves; gives clear, well-organized directions and draws coherent cognitive maps. (300)
- Attention becomes more selective, adaptable, and planful. (303)
- Uses memory strategies of rehearsal and then organization. (303)
- Views the mind as an active, constructive agent, capable of transforming information. (306)
- Awareness of memory strategies and the impact of psychological factors (such as focusing attention) on task performance improves. (306)
- Appreciates second-order false beliefs. (306)
- Uses informal knowledge of number concepts and counting to master more complex mathematical skills. (308)

LANGUAGE

- Vocabulary increases rapidly throughout middle childhood, eventually exceeding 40,000 words. (316)
- Word definitions are concrete, referring to functions and appearance. (317)
- Narratives increase in organization, detail, and expressiveness. (317)
- Transitions from emergent literacy to conventional reading. (307)
- Language awareness improves. (316)
- Conversational strategies become more refined. (317)

EMOTIONAL/SOCIAL

- Self-concept begins to include personality traits and social comparisons. (330)
- Self-esteem differentiates, becomes hierarchically organized, and declines to a more realistic level. (331–332)
- Self-conscious emotions of pride and guilt are governed by personal responsibility. (335)
- Understands that people may have different perspectives because they have access to different information. (336)
- Recognizes that individuals can experience more than one emotion at a time and that people's expressions may not reflect their true feelings. (335)
- Empathy increases. (335)
- Reconciles contradictory facial and situational cues in understanding another's feelings. (335)
- Becomes more independent and trustworthy. (337)
- Constructs a flexible appreciation of moral rules, taking prosocial and antisocial intentions into account. (337)
- Physical aggression declines; verbal and relational aggression continue. (339)
- Resolves conflicts more effectively. (339)

9–11 years

PHYSICAL

- Adolescent growth spurt begins two years earlier in girls than in boys. (290)
- Executes gross motor skills of running, jumping, throwing, catching, kicking, batting, and dribbling more quickly and with better coordination. (295)

Note: Numbers in parentheses indicate the page or pages on which each milestone is discussed.

- Steady gains in reaction time contribute to improved motor performance. (295)
- Representation of depth in drawings expands. (295)

COGNITIVE

- Continues to master Piagetian tasks in a step-by-step fashion. (299)
- Spatial reasoning further improves; readily draws and reads maps, and grasps the notion of scale. (300)
- Selective attention and planning improve further. (303)
- Uses memory strategies of rehearsal and organization more effectively. (303)

- Applies several memory strategies simultaneously; begins to use elaboration. (303–304)
- Long-term knowledge base grows larger and becomes better organized. (304)
- Theory of mind becomes more elaborate and refined. (306)
- Cognitive self-regulation improves. (307)

LANGUAGE

- Thinks about and uses words more precisely; word definitions emphasize synonyms and categorical relations. (317)
- Grasps double meanings of words, as reflected in comprehension of metaphors and humor. (317)
- Continues to master complex grammatical constructions. (317)
- Continues to refine conversational strategies. (317)
- Narratives lengthen, become more coherent, and include more evaluative comments. (317–318)

EMOTIONAL/SOCIAL

- Self-esteem tends to rise (332)
- Distinguishes ability, effort, and external factors in attributions for success and failure. (333)
- Becomes more knowledgeable about socially approved ways to display negative emotion. (335–336)
- Empathic responding extends to general life conditions. (335)

- Shifts adaptively between problem-centered and emotion-centered strategies in regulating emotion. (335–336)
- Can "step into another's shoes" and view the self from that person's perspective; later, can view the relationship between self and other from the perspective of a third, impartial party. (336)
- Clarifies and links moral rules and social conventions. (337–338)
- Convictions about matters of personal choice strengthen, and understanding of individual rights expands. (338)

- Friendships become more selective and are based on mutual trust. (340)
- Peer groups emerge. (339)
- Becomes aware of more gender stereotypes, including personality traits and achievement, but has a flexible appreciation of what males and females can do. (343–344)
- Gender identity expands to include self-evaluations of typicality, contentedness, and pressure to conform. (344–345)
- Sibling rivalry tends to increase. (345)

Adolescence brings momentous advances. A flood of biological events leads to an adult-sized body and sexual maturity. Cognitive changes allow teenagers to grasp complex scientific principles, grapple with political issues, and detect the deep meaning of a poem or story.

CHAPTER 11

Physical and Cognitive Development in Adolescence

On Sabrina's eleventh birthday, her friend Joyce gave her a surprise party, but Sabrina seemed somber during the celebration. Although Sabrina and Joyce had been close friends since third grade, their relationship was faltering. Sabrina was a head taller and some 20 pounds heavier than most girls in her sixth-grade class. Her breasts were well-developed, her hips and thighs had broadened, and she had begun to menstruate. In contrast, Joyce still had the short, lean, flat-chested body of a school-age child.

Ducking into the bathroom while the other girls put candles on the cake, Sabrina frowned at her image in the mirror. "I'm so big and heavy," she whispered. At church youth group on Sunday evenings, Sabrina broke away from Joyce and joined the eighth-grade girls. Around them, she didn't feel so large and awkward.

Once a month, parents gathered at Sabrina's and Joyce's school to discuss child-rearing concerns. Sabrina's parents, Franca and Antonio, attended whenever they could. "How you know they are becoming teenagers is this," volunteered Antonio. "The bedroom door is closed, and they want to be alone. Also, they contradict and disagree. I tell Sabrina, 'You have to go to Aunt Gina's on Saturday for dinner with the family.' The next thing I know, she is arguing with me."

© DAVID YOUNG-WOLFF/PHOTOEDIT

Sabrina has entered **adolescence**, the transition between childhood and adulthood. In industrialized societies, the skills young people must master are so complex and the choices confronting them so diverse that adolescence is greatly extended. But around the world, the basic tasks of this period are much the same. Sabrina must accept her full-grown body, acquire adult ways of thinking, attain greater independence from her family, develop more mature ways of relating to peers of both sexes, and begin to construct an identity—a secure sense of who she is in terms of sexual, vocational, moral, ethnic, religious, and other life values and goals.

The beginning of adolescence is marked by **puberty**, a flood of biological events leading to an adult-sized body and sexual maturity. As Sabrina's reactions suggest, entry into adolescence can be an especially trying time for some young people. In this chapter, we trace the events of puberty and take up a variety of health concerns—physical exercise, nutrition, sexual activity, substance abuse, and other problems affecting teenagers who encounter difficulties on the path to maturity.

Adolescence also brings with it vastly expanded powers of reasoning. Teenagers can grasp complex scientific and mathematical principles, grapple with social and political issues, and delve deeply into the meaning of a poem or story. The second part of this chapter traces these extraordinary changes from both Piaget's and the information-processing perspective. Next, we examine sex differences in mental abilities. Finally, we turn to the main setting in which adolescent thought takes shape: the school.

Physical Development

Conceptions of Adolescence

Why is Sabrina self-conscious, argumentative, and in retreat from family activities? Historically, theorists explained the impact of puberty on psychological development by resorting to extremes—either a biological or a social explanation. Today, researchers realize that biological and social forces jointly determine adolescent psychological change.

The Biological Perspective

TAKE A MOMENT... Ask several parents of young children what they expect their sons and daughters to be like as teenagers. You will probably get answers like these: "Rebellious and irresponsible," "Full of rages and tempers" (Buchanan & Holmbeck, 1998). This widespread storm-and-stress view dates back to major early-twentieth-century theorists. The most influential, G. Stanley Hall, based his ideas about development on Darwin's theory of evolution. Hall (1904) described adolescence as a period so turbulent that it resembled the era in which humans evolved from savages into civilized beings. Similarly, Anna Freud (1969), who expanded the focus on adolescence of her father Sigmund Freud's theory, viewed the teenage years as a biologically based, universal "developmental disturbance." In Freud's *genital stage,* sexual impulses reawaken, triggering psychological conflict and volatile behavior. As adolescents find intimate partners, inner forces gradually achieve a new, mature harmony, and the stage concludes with marriage, birth, and child rearing. In this way, young people fulfill their biological destiny: sexual reproduction and survival of the species.

The Social Perspective

Contemporary research suggests that the storm-and-stress notion of adolescence is exaggerated. Certain problems, such as eating disorders, depression, suicide, and lawbreaking, do occur more often than earlier (Farrington, 2004; Graber, 2004). But the overall rate of psychological disturbance rises only slightly, by about 3 percent, from childhood to adolescence, when it is nearly the same as in the adult population—about 15 percent (Roberts, Attkisson, & Rosenblatt, 1998). Although some teenagers encounter serious difficulties, emotional turbulence is not routine.

The first researcher to point out the wide variability in adolescent adjustment was anthropologist Margaret Mead (1928). She returned from the Pacific islands of Samoa with a startling conclusion: Because of the culture's relaxed social relationships and openness toward sexuality, adolescence "is perhaps the pleasantest time the Samoan girl (or boy) will ever know" (p. 308). Mead offered an alternative view in which the social environment is entirely responsible for the range of teenage experiences, from erratic and agitated to calm and stress-free. Later researchers found that Samoan adolescence was not as untroubled as Mead had assumed (Freeman, 1983). Still, she showed that to understand adolescent development, researchers must pay greater attention to social and cultural influences.

A Balanced Point of View

Today we know that biological, psychological, and social forces combine to influence adolescent development (Magnusson, 1999; Susman & Rogol, 2004). Biological changes are universal—found in all primates and all cultures. These internal stresses and the social expectations accompanying them—that the young person give up childish ways, develop new interpersonal relationships, and take on greater responsibility—are likely to prompt moments of uncertainty, self-doubt, and disappointment in all teenagers. Adolescents' prior and current experiences affect their success in surmounting these challenges.

At the same time, the length of adolescence and its demands and pressures vary substantially among cultures. Most tribal and village societies have only a brief intervening phase between childhood and full assumption of adult roles (Schlegel & Barry, 1991; Weisfield, 1997). In industrialized nations, young people face prolonged dependence on parents and postponement of sexual gratification while they prepare for a productive work life. As a result, adolescence is greatly extended—so much so that researchers commonly divide it into three phases:

1. *Early adolescence* (11–12 to 14 years): This is a period of rapid pubertal change.
2. *Middle adolescence* (14 to 16 years): Pubertal changes are now nearly complete.
3. *Late adolescence* (16 to 18 years): The young person achieves full adult appearance and anticipates assumption of adult roles.

The more the social environment supports young people in achieving adult responsibilities, the better they adjust. For all the biological tensions and uncertainties about the future that teenagers feel, most negotiate this period successfully. With this in mind, let's look closely at puberty, the dawning of adolescent development.

Puberty: The Physical Transition to Adulthood

The changes of puberty are dramatic: Within a few years, the body of the school-age child is transformed into that of a full-grown adult. Genetically influenced hormonal processes regulate pubertal growth. Girls, who have been advanced in physical maturity since the prenatal period, reach puberty, on average, two years earlier than boys.

Hormonal Changes

The complex hormonal changes that underlie puberty occur gradually and are under way by age 8 or 9. Secretions of *growth hormone (GH)* and *thyroxine* (see Chapter 7, page 219) increase, leading to tremendous gains in body size and to attainment of skeletal maturity.

Sexual maturation is controlled by the sex hormones. Although we think of *estrogens* as female hormones and *androgens* as male hormones, both types are present in each sex but in different amounts. The boy's testes release large quantities of the androgen *testosterone,* which leads to muscle growth, body and facial hair, and other male sex characteristics. Androgens (especially testosterone for boys) also contribute greatly to gains in body size. Because the testes secrete small amounts of estrogen as well, 50 percent of boys experience temporary breast enlargement. In both sexes, estrogens also increase GH secretion, adding to the growth spurt and, in combination with androgens, stimulating gains in bone density, which continue into early adulthood (Cooper, Sayer, & Dennison, 2006; Styne, 2003).

Estrogens released by girls' ovaries cause the breasts, uterus, and vagina to mature, the body to take on feminine proportions, and fat to accumulate. Estrogens also contribute to regulation of the menstrual cycle. *Adrenal androgens,* released from the adrenal glands on top of each kidney, influence girls' height spurt and stimulate growth of underarm and pubic hair. They have little impact on boys, whose physical characteristics are influenced mainly by androgen and estrogen secretions from the testes.

As you can see, pubertal changes are of two broad types: (1) overall body growth and (2) maturation of sexual characteristics. We have seen that the hormones responsible for sexual maturity also affect body growth, making puberty the time of greatest sexual differentiation since prenatal life.

© LAURA DWIGHT PHOTOGRAPHY

Sex differences in pubertal growth are obvious among these sixth graders. Although the children are the same age, the boy is much shorter and less mature looking than the girls.

Body Growth

The first outward sign of puberty is the rapid gain in height and weight known as the **growth spurt.** On average, it is under way for North American girls shortly after age 10, for boys around age 12½. Because estrogens trigger and then restrain GH secretion more readily than androgens, the typical girl is taller and heavier during early adolescence (Archibald, Graber, & Brooks-Gunn, 2006; Bogin, 2001). At age 14, however, she is surpassed by the typical boy, whose adolescent growth spurt has now started, whereas hers is almost finished. Growth in body size is complete for most girls by age 16 and for boys by age 17½, when the epiphyses at the ends of the long bones close completely (see Chapter 7, page 217). Altogether, adolescents add 10 to 11 inches in height and 50 to 75 pounds—nearly 50 percent of adult body weight. Figure 11.1 on page 364 illustrates pubertal changes in general body growth.

■ **BODY PROPORTIONS.** During puberty, the cephalocaudal growth trend of infancy and childhood reverses. The hands, legs, and feet accelerate first, followed by the torso, which accounts for most of the adolescent height gain (Sheehy et al., 1999). This pattern helps explain why early adolescents often appear awkward and out of proportion—long-legged, with giant feet and hands.

Large sex differences in body proportions also appear, caused by the action of sex hormones on the skeleton. Boys' shoulders broaden relative to the hips, whereas girls' hips broaden relative to the shoulders and waist. Of course, boys also end up larger than girls, and their legs are longer in relation to the rest of the body—mainly because boys have two extra years of preadolescent growth, when the legs are growing the fastest.

■ **MUSCLE–FAT MAKEUP AND OTHER INTERNAL CHANGES.** Sabrina worried about her weight because compared with her later-developing girlfriends, she had accumulated much more fat. Around age 8, girls start to add fat on their arms, legs, and trunk, a trend that accelerates between ages 11 and 16. In

■ **FIGURE 11.1** ■ **Body growth during adolescence.** Because the pubertal growth spurt takes place earlier for girls than for boys, Kate reached her adult body size earlier than Steven. During puberty, adolescents show large sex differences in body proportions.

contrast, arm and leg fat decreases in adolescent boys. Although both sexes gain in muscle, this increase is much greater in boys, who develop larger skeletal muscles, hearts, and lung capacity (Rogol, Roemmich, & Clark, 2002). Also, the number of red blood cells—and therefore the ability to carry oxygen from the lungs to the muscles—increases in boys but not in girls. Altogether, boys gain far more muscle strength than girls, a difference that contributes to teenage boys' superior athletic performance (Ramos et al., 1998).

Motor Development and Physical Activity

Puberty brings steady improvement in gross motor performance, but the pattern of change differs for boys and girls. Girls' gains are slow and gradual, leveling off by age 14. In contrast, boys show a dramatic spurt in strength, speed, and endurance that continues through the teenage years. By midadolescence, few girls perform as well as the average boy in running speed, broad jump, and throwing distance, and practically no boys score as low as the average girl (Haywood & Getchell, 2005; Malina & Bouchard, 1991).

Because girls and boys are no longer well-matched physically, gender-segregated physical education usually begins in middle or junior high school. At the same time, athletic options for both sexes expand as new sports—including track and field, wrestling, tackle football, weight lifting, floor hockey, archery, tennis, and golf—are added to the curriculum.

Among boys, athletic competence is strongly related to peer admiration and self-esteem. Some adolescents are so obsessed with physical prowess that they turn to performance-enhancing drugs. In recent large-scale studies, about 8 percent of U.S. high school seniors, mostly boys, reported using creatine, an over-the-counter substance that enhances short-term muscle power but carries a risk of serious side effects, including muscle tissue disease, brain seizures, and heart irregularities (Castillo & Comstock, 2007). About 2 percent of seniors, again mostly boys, have taken anabolic steroids or a related substance, androstenedione—powerful prescription medications that boost muscle mass and strength (Johnston et al., 2007). Teenagers usually obtain steroids illegally, ignoring side effects, which range from acne, excess body hair, and high blood pressure to mood swings, aggressive behavior, and damage to the liver, circulatory system, and reproductive organs (Casavant et al., 2007).

AP IMAGES/THE ALBUQUERQUE JOURNAL, MARLA BROSE

Although high school girls' participation in sports has increased, it still falls far short of boys'. Yet intraschool and intramural athletics yield many benefits—not just gains in motor skills but important lessons in teamwork, problem solving, assertiveness, and competition.

Coaches and health professionals should inform teenagers of the dangers of these performance-enhancing substances.

In 1972, the U.S. federal government required schools receiving public funds to provide equal opportunities for males and females in all educational programs, including athletics. Since then, high school girls' sports participation has increased, although it still falls far short of boys'. According to a recent survey of all 50 U.S. state high school athletic associations, 41 percent of sports participants are girls, 59 percent boys (National Federation of State High School Associations, 2008). In Chapter 9, we saw that girls get less encouragement and recognition for athletic achievement, a pattern that starts early and clearly persists into the teenage years (see page 296).

Furthermore, when researchers followed a large, representative sample of U.S. youths from ages 9 to 15, physical activity declined by about 40 minutes per day each year until, at age 15, less than one-third met the U.S. government recommendation of at least 60 minutes of moderate to strenuous physical activity per day (see Figure 11.2) (Nader et al., 2008). In high school, only 58 percent of U.S. boys and 49 percent of girls are enrolled in any physical education, with less than 30 percent of all students experiencing a daily physical education class (U.S. Department of Health and Human Services, 2008k).

Besides improving motor performance, sports and exercise influence cognitive and social development. Interschool and intramural athletics provide important lessons in teamwork, problem solving, assertiveness, and competition. And regular, sustained physical activity—which required physical education can ensure—is associated with lasting health benefits and enjoyment of sports and exercise. In one study, participating in team or individual sports at age 14 at least once a week for girls and twice a week for boys predicted high physical activity rates at age 31. Endurance sports, such as running and cycling—activities that do not require expensive equipment or special facilities—were especially likely to continue into adulthood (Tammelin et al., 2003). And adolescent exertion during exercise, defined as sweating and breathing heavily, is one of the best predictors of adult physical exercise, perhaps because it fosters high *physical self-efficacy*—belief in one's ability to sustain an exercise program (Motl et al., 2002; Telama et al., 2005).

Sexual Maturation

Accompanying rapid body growth are changes in physical features related to sexual functioning. Some, called **primary sexual characteristics,** involve the reproductive organs (ovaries, uterus, and vagina in females; penis, scrotum, and testes in males). Others, called **secondary sexual characteristics,** are visible on the outside of the body and serve as additional signs of sexual maturity (for example, breast development in females and the appearance of underarm and pubic hair in both sexes). As Table 11.1 on page 366 shows, these characteristics develop in a fairly standard sequence, although the ages at which each begins and is completed vary greatly. Typically, pubertal development takes about four years, but some adolescents complete it in two years, whereas others take five to six years.

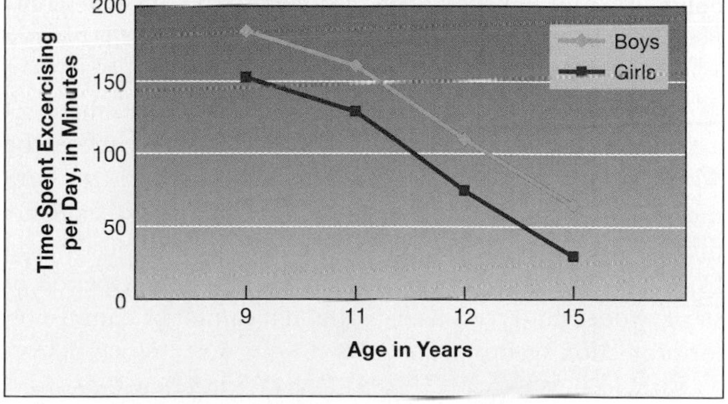

■ **FIGURE 11.2** ■ **Decline in physical activity from ages 9 to 15 among U.S. boys and girls.** In a large representative sample of youths followed over six years, time spent exercising dropped sharply until, at age 15, most youths did not meet government recommendations of at least 60 minutes of moderate to vigorous physical activity per day. At all ages, boys spent more time exercising than girls. (Adapted from Nader et al., 2008.)

■ **TABLE 11.1** ■ ***Pubertal Development in North American Girls and Boys***

GIRLS	AVERAGE AGE ATTAINED	AGE RANGE	BOYS	AVERAGE AGE ATTAINED	AGE RANGE
Breasts begin to "bud"	10	(8–13)	Testes begin to enlarge	11.5	(9.5–13.5)
Height spurt begins	10	(8–13)	Pubic hair appears	12	(10–15)
Pubic hair appears	10.5	(8–14)	Penis begins to enlarge	12	(10.5–14.5)
Peak strength spurt	11.6	(9.5–14)	Height spurt begins	12.5	(10.5–16)
Peak height spurt	11.7	(10–13.5)	Spermarche (first ejaculation) occurs	13.5	(12–16)
Menarche (first menstruation) occurs	12.5	(10.5–14)	Peak height spurt	14	(12.5–15.5)
Peak weight spurt	12.7	(10–14)	Peak weight spurt	14	(12.5–15.5)
Adult stature reached	13	(10–16)	Facial hair begins to grow	14	(12.5–15.5)
Pubic hair growth completed	14.5	(14–15)	Voice begins to deepen	14	(12.5–15.5)
Breast growth completed	15	(10–17)	Penis and testes growth completed	14.5	(12.5–16)
			Peak strength spurt	15.3	(13–17)
			Adult stature reached	15.5	(13.5–17.5)
			Pubic hair growth completed	15.5	(14–17)

Sources: Chumlea et al., 2003; Herman-Giddens, 2006; Rogol, Roemmich, & Clark, 2002; Wu, Mendola, & Buck, 2002.
Photos: (left) © David Young-Wolff/PhotoEdit; (right) © Rob Melnychuk/Getty Images/Taxi

■ **SEXUAL MATURATION IN GIRLS.** Female puberty usually begins with the budding of the breasts and the growth spurt. **Menarche,** or first menstruation, typically occurs around age 12½ for North American girls, 13 for Western Europeans. But the age range is wide, from 10½ to 15½ years. Following menarche, breast and pubic hair growth are completed, and underarm hair appears (Archibald, Graber, & Brooks-Gunn, 2006).

Notice in Table 11.1 that nature delays sexual maturity until the girl's body is large enough for childbearing; menarche takes place after the peak of the height spurt. As an extra measure of security, for 12 to 18 months following menarche, the menstrual cycle often occurs without the release of an ovum from the ovaries (Bogin, 2001). But this temporary period of sterility does not occur in all girls, and it cannot be counted on for protection against pregnancy.

■ **SEXUAL MATURATION IN BOYS.** The first sign of puberty in boys is the enlargement of the testes (glands that manufacture sperm), accompanied by changes in the texture and color of the scrotum. Pubic hair emerges soon after, about the same time the penis begins to enlarge (Rogol, Roemmich, & Clark, 2002).

As Table 11.1 reveals, the growth spurt occurs much later in the sequence of pubertal events for boys than for girls. When it reaches its peak around age 14, enlargement of the testes and penis is nearly complete, and underarm hair appears. So do facial and body hair, which increase gradually for several years. Another landmark of male physical maturity is the deepening of the voice as the larynx enlarges and the vocal cords lengthen. (Girls' voices also deepen slightly.) Voice change usually takes place at the peak of the male growth spurt and is often not complete until puberty is over (Archibald, Graber, & Brooks-Gunn, 2006).

While the penis is growing, the prostate gland and seminal vesicles (which together produce semen, the fluid containing sperm) enlarge. Then, around age 13½, **spermarche,** or first ejaculation, occurs (Rogol, Roemmich, & Clark, 2002). For a while, the semen contains few living sperm. So, like girls, boys have an initial period of reduced fertility.

Individual Differences in Pubertal Growth

Heredity contributes substantially to the timing of pubertal changes: Identical twins are more similar than fraternal twins in attainment of most pubertal milestones (Eaves et al., 2004; Mustanski et al., 2004). Nutrition and exercise also make a difference. In females, a sharp rise in body weight and fat may trigger sexual maturation. Fat cells release a protein called *leptin,* which is believed to signal the brain that a girl's energy stores are sufficient for puberty—a likely reason that breast and pubic hair growth and menarche occur earlier for heavier and, especially, obese girls. In contrast, girls who begin rigorous athletic training at an early age or who eat very little (both of which reduce the percentage of body fat) usually experience later puberty (Anderson, Dallal, & Must, 2003; Lee et al., 2007; Slyper, 2006).

Variations in pubertal growth also exist among regions of the world and among SES and ethnic groups. Physical health plays a major role. In poverty-stricken regions where malnutrition and infectious disease are common, menarche is greatly delayed, occurring as late as age 14 to 16 in many parts of Africa. Within developing countries, girls from higher-income families reach menarche 6 to 18 months earlier than those living in economically disadvantaged homes (Parent et al., 2003).

But in industrialized nations where food is abundant, the joint roles of heredity and environment in pubertal growth are apparent. For example, breast and pubic hair growth begin, on average, around age 9 in African-American girls—a year earlier than in Caucasian-American girls. And African-American girls reach menarche about six months earlier, around age 12. Although widespread overweight and obesity in the black population contribute, a genetically influenced faster rate of physical maturation is also involved. Black girls usually reach menarche before white girls of the same age and body weight (Anderson, Dallal, & Must, 2003; Chumlea et al., 2003; Herman-Giddens, 2006).

Early family experiences may also affect pubertal timing. One theory suggests that humans have evolved to be sensitive to the emotional quality of their childhood environments. When children's safety and security are at risk, it is adaptive for them to reproduce early. Research indicates that girls and (less consistently) boys with a history of family conflict, harsh parenting, or parental separation tend to reach puberty early. In contrast, those with warm, stable family ties reach puberty relatively late (Belsky et al., 2007; Bogaert, 2005; Ellis, 2004; Ellis & Essex, 2007; Mustanski et al., 2004; Tremblay & Frigon, 2005). But critics offer an alternative explanation—that mothers who reached puberty early are more likely to bear children earlier, which increases the risk of marital conflict and separation (Mendle et al., 2006). Children of these mothers also inherit a genetic tendency toward early puberty.

In the research we have considered, threats to emotional health accelerate puberty, whereas threats to physical health delay it. A **secular trend,** or generational change, in pubertal timing lends added support to the role of physical well-being in pubertal development. In industrialized nations, age of menarche declined steadily—by about three to four months per decade—from 1900 to 1970, a period in which nutrition, health care, sanitation, and control of infectious disease improved greatly. Boys, too, have reached puberty earlier in recent decades (Karpati et al., 2002). In North America and a few European countries, soaring rates of overweight and obesity are responsible for a modest, continuing trend toward earlier menarche (Kaplowitz, 2006; Parent et al., 2003). A worrisome consequence is that girls who reach sexual maturity at age 10 or 11 will feel pressure to act much older than they are. As we will see shortly, early-maturing girls are at risk for unfavorable peer involvements, including sexual activity.

Brain Development

The physical transformations of adolescence include major changes in the brain. Brain-imaging research reveals continued pruning of unused synapses in the cerebral cortex, especially in the frontal lobes—the "governor" of thought and action. In addition, growth and myelination of stimulated neural fibers accelerate, strengthening connections among various brain regions. In particular, linkages between the two cerebral hemispheres through the corpus callosum, and between the frontal lobes and other brain areas, expand and attain rapid communication (Blakemore & Choudhury, 2006; Keating, 2004; Lenroot & Giedd, 2006). This sculpting of the adolescent brain supports diverse cognitive skills, including improved processing speed, attention, memory, planning, capacity to integrate information, and self-regulation.

In addition, sensitivity of neurons to certain chemical messages changes. In humans and other mammals, neurons become more responsive to excitatory neurotransmitters during puberty. As a result, adolescents react more strongly to stressful events and experience pleasurable stimuli more intensely—but have not yet acquired the capacity to control these powerful impulses (Casey, Getz, & Galvan, 2008; Spear, 2004, 2008). These changes probably contribute to teenagers' drive for novel experiences, including drug taking, especially among those who engage in reward seeking to counteract chronic emotional pain. Alterations in neurotransmitter activity may also be involved in adolescents' increased susceptibility to certain disorders, such as depression and eating disturbances.

© SW PRODUCTIONS/GETTY IMAGES/PHOTODISC

During puberty, neurons become more responsive to excitatory neurotransmitters. As a result, adolescents react more strongly to stressful events, such as disagreements with parents. This mother must try to be patient with her son, despite his intense resistance.

To what extent are the hormonal changes of puberty responsible for adolescent brain growth and reorganization? Researchers do not yet have a ready answer. But the transformations that occur—much greater than previously thought—enhance our understanding of both the cognitive advances and the troubling behaviors of adolescence, along with teenagers' need for adult patience, oversight, and guidance.

Changing States of Arousal

At puberty, revisions occur in the way the brain regulates the timing of sleep, perhaps because of increased neural sensitivity to evening light. As a result, adolescents go to bed much later than they did as children. Yet they need almost as much sleep as they did in middle childhood—about nine hours. When the school day begins early, their sleep needs are not satisfied.

This sleep "phase delay" strengthens with pubertal growth. But today's teenagers often have evening social activities and part-time jobs, as well as TVs, computers, and phones in their bedrooms. As a result, they get much less sleep than teenagers of previous generations (Carskadon, Acebo, & Jenni, 2004; Carskadon et al., 2002). Sleep-deprived adolescents perform especially poorly on cognitive tasks during morning hours. And they are more likely to achieve less well in school, suffer from depressed mood, and engage in high-risk behaviors, including drinking and reckless driving (Dahl & Lewin, 2002; Hansen et al., 2005). Sleep rebound on weekends sustains the pattern by leading to difficulty falling asleep on subsequent evenings (Laberge et al., 2001). Later school start times ease but do not eliminate sleep loss. Educating teenagers about the importance of sleep is vital.

The Psychological Impact of Pubertal Events

TAKE A MOMENT... Think back to your late elementary and middle school days. As you reached puberty, how did your feelings about yourself and your relationships with others change? Research reveals that pubertal events affect adolescents' self-image, mood, and interaction with parents and peers. Some outcomes are a response to dramatic physical change, whenever it occurs. Others have to do with pubertal timing.

Reactions to Pubertal Changes

Two generations ago, menarche was often traumatic. Today, girls commonly react with "surprise," undoubtedly due to the sudden onset of the event. Otherwise, they typically report a mixture of positive and negative emotions (DeRose & Brooks-Gunn, 2006). Yet wide individual differences exist that depend on prior knowledge and support from family members, which in turn are influenced by cultural attitudes toward puberty and sexuality.

For girls who have no advance information, menarche can be shocking and disturbing. In the 1950s, up to 50 percent received no prior warning, and of those who did, many were given "grin-and-bear-it" messages (Costos, Ackerman, & Paradis, 2002; Shainess, 1961). Today, few girls are uninformed, a shift that is probably due to parents' greater willingness to discuss sexual matters and to the spread of health education classes (Omar, McElderry, & Zakharia, 2003). Almost all girls get some information from their mothers. And some evidence suggests that compared with Caucasian-American families, African-American families may better prepare girls for menarche, treat it as an important milestone, and express less conflict over girls reaching sexual maturity—factors that lead African-American girls to react more favorably (Martin, 1996; Scott et al., 1989).

Like girls' reactions to menarche, boys' responses to spermarche reflect mixed feelings. Virtually all boys know about ejaculation ahead of time, but many say that no one spoke to them before or during puberty about physical changes (Omar, McElderry, & Zakharia, 2003). Usually they get their information from reading material. Even boys who had advance information often say that their first ejaculation occurred earlier than they expected and that they were unprepared for it. As with girls, boys who feel better prepared tend to react more positively (Stein & Reiser, 1994). But whereas almost all girls eventually tell a friend that they are menstruating, far fewer boys tell anyone about spermarche (DeRose & Brooks-Gunn, 2006; Downs & Fuller, 1991). Overall, boys get much less social support than girls for the physical changes of puberty. They might benefit, especially, from opportunities to ask questions and discuss feelings with a sympathetic parent or health professional.

Many tribal and village societies celebrate the onset of puberty with an *initiation ceremony,* a ritualized announcement to the community that marks an important change in privilege and responsibility. Consequently, young people know that reaching puberty is valued in their culture. In contrast, Western societies grant little formal recognition to movement from childhood to adolescence or from adolescence to adulthood. Ceremonies such as the Jewish bar or bat mitzvah and the *quinceañera* in Hispanic communities (celebrating a 15-year-old girl's sexual maturity and marriage availability), resemble initiation ceremonies, but only within the ethnic or religious subculture. They do not mark a significant change in social status in the larger society.

Instead, Western adolescents are granted partial adult status at many different ages—for example, an age for starting employment, for driving, for leaving high school, for voting, and for drinking. And in some contexts (at home and at school), they may still be regarded as children. The absence of a widely accepted marker of physical and social maturity makes the process of becoming an adult more confusing.

Pubertal Change, Emotion, and Social Behavior

A common belief is that puberty has something to do with adolescent moodiness and the desire for greater physical and

In Hispanic communities, the *quinceañera,* celebrated at age 15, is a rite of passage honoring a girl's journey from childhood to maturity. It usually begins with a mass in which the priest blesses gifts presented to the girl.

psychological separation from parents. Let's see what research says about these relationships.

ADOLESCENT MOODINESS. Higher pubertal hormone levels are linked to greater moodiness, but only modestly so (Buchanan, Eccles, & Becker, 1992; Graber, Brooks-Gunn, & Warren, 2006). What other factors might contribute? In several studies, the moods of children, adolescents, and adults were monitored by having them carry electronic pagers. Over a one-week period, they were beeped at random intervals and asked to write down what they were doing, whom they were with, and how they felt.

As expected, adolescents reported less favorable moods than school-age children and adults (Larson et al., 2002; Larson & Lampman-Petraitis, 1989). But negative moods were linked to a greater number of negative life events, such as difficulty getting along with parents, disciplinary actions at school, and breaking up with a boyfriend or girlfriend. Negative events increased steadily from childhood to adolescence, and teenagers also seemed to react to them with greater emotion than children (Larson & Ham, 1993). (Recall that stress reactivity is heightened by changes in brain neurotransmitter activity during adolescence.)

Compared with the moods of older adolescents and adults, those of younger adolescents (ages 12 to 16) were less stable, often shifting from cheerful to sad and back again. These mood swings were strongly related to situational changes. High points of adolescents' days were times spent with peers and in self-chosen leisure activities. Low points tended to occur in adult-structured settings—class, job, and religious services. Furthermore, emotional highs coincided with Friday and Saturday evenings, especially in high school (see Figure 11.3). Going out with friends and romantic partners increases so dramatically during adolescence that it becomes a "cultural script" for what is *supposed* to happen. Consequently, teenagers who spend weekend evenings at home often feel profoundly lonely (Larson & Richards, 1998).

In sum, biological, psychological, and social forces combine to make adolescence a time of deeper valleys and higher peaks in emotional experience. This explanation is consistent with the balanced view presented earlier in this chapter.

PARENT–CHILD RELATIONSHIPS. Sabrina's father noticed that as his children entered adolescence, they kept their bedroom doors closed, resisted spending time with the family, and became more argumentative. Sabrina and her mother squabbled over Sabrina's messy room ("It's *my* room, Mom. You don't have to live in it!"). And Sabrina resisted the family's regular weekend visit to Aunt Gina's ("Why do I have to go *every* week?"). Research in cultures as diverse as the United

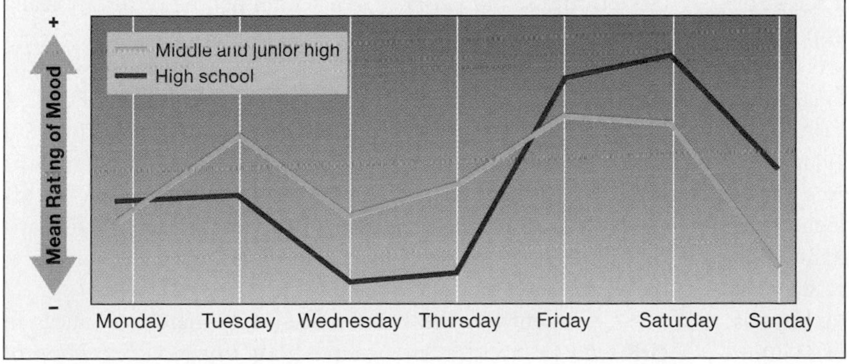

FIGURE 11.3 **Younger and older adolescents' emotional experiences across the week.** Adolescents' reports revealed that emotional high points are on Fridays and Saturdays. Mood drops on Sunday, before returning to school, and during the week, as students spend much time in adult-structured settings in school. (From R. Larson & M. Richards, 1998, "Waiting for the Weekend: Friday and Saturday Night as the Emotional Climax of the Week," in A. C. Crouter & R. Larson (Eds.), *Temporal Rhythms in Adolescence: Clocks, Calendars, and the Coordination of Daily Life.* San Francisco: Jossey-Bass, p. 41. Reprinted with permission from John Wiley & Sons, Inc.)

States and Turkey shows a rise in parent–child conflict at puberty (Gure, Ucanok, & Sayil, 2006; Laursen, Coy, & Collins, 1998; Steinberg & Morris, 2001). Frequency of arguing is surprisingly similar across North American subcultures, occurring as often in families of European descent as in immigrant Asian and Hispanic families whose traditions emphasize respect for parental authority (Fuligni, 1998).

Why should a youngster's more adultlike appearance trigger these disputes? The association may have adaptive value. Among nonhuman primates, the young typically leave the family group around the time of puberty. The same is true in many nonindustrialized cultures (Caine, 1986; Schlegel & Barry, 1991). Departure of young people discourages sexual relations between close blood relatives. But adolescents in industrialized nations, who are still economically dependent on parents, cannot leave the family. Consequently, a modern substitute seems to have emerged: psychological distancing.

As children become physically mature, they demand to be treated in adultlike ways. And as we will see, adolescents' new powers of reasoning may also contribute to a rise in family tensions. Parent–adolescent disagreements focus largely on everyday matters such as driving, dating partners, and curfews (Adams & Laursen, 2001). But beneath these disputes lie serious concerns: parental efforts to protect teenagers from substance use, auto accidents, and early sex. The larger the gap between parents' and adolescents' views of teenagers' readiness for new responsibilities, the more quarreling (Deković, Noom, & Meeus, 1997).

Parent–daughter conflict tends to be more intense than conflict with sons, perhaps because parents place more restrictions on girls (Allison & Schultz, 2004). But this gender disparity varies with culture; for example, it is less evident in Canada than in Italy, where gender-role attitudes are more traditional (Claes et al., 2003). But most disputes are mild. Parents and teenagers display both conflict and affection, and they usually agree on important values, such as honesty and the importance of education. Although separation from parents is adaptive, both generations benefit from warm, protective family bonds throughout the lifespan.

Pubertal Timing

"All our children were early maturers," said Franca during the parents' discussion group. "The three boys were tall by age 12 or 13, but it was easier for them. They felt big and important. Sabrina was skinny as a little girl, but now she says she is too fat and needs to diet. She thinks about boys and doesn't concentrate on her schoolwork."

Findings of several studies match the experiences of Sabrina and her brothers. Both adults and peers viewed early-maturing boys as relaxed, independent, self-confident, and physically attractive. Popular with agemates, they tended to hold leadership positions in school and to be athletic stars. In contrast, both adults and peers viewed late-maturing boys as anxious, overly talkative, and attention-seeking (Brooks-Gunn, 1988; Clausen, 1975). However, early-maturing boys, though viewed as well-adjusted, report slightly more psychological stress and problem behaviors (sexual activity, smoking, drinking, delinquency) than their later-maturing agemates (Ge, Conger, & Elder, 2001; Huddleston & Ge, 2003).

© BOB DAEMMRICH/PHOTOEDIT

African-American early-maturing girls seem to escape the adjustment difficulties commonly associated with early pubertal timing. Their families and friends tend to be welcoming of menarche, and they are more likely to report a positive body image than their Caucasian counterparts.

In contrast, early-maturing girls were unpopular, withdrawn, lacking in self-confidence, anxious, and prone to depression, and they held few leadership positions (Ge, Conger, & Elder, 1996; Graber et al., 1997; Graber, Brooks-Gunn, & Warren, 2006; Jones & Mussen, 1958). They were more involved in deviant behavior (getting drunk, participating in early sexual activity) and achieved less well in school (Caspi et al., 1993; Dick et al., 2000; Ge et al., 2006). In contrast, their later-maturing counterparts were regarded as physically attractive, lively, sociable, and leaders at school. In one study of several hundred eighth graders, however, negative effects were not evident among early-maturing African-American girls, whose families—and perhaps friends as well—tend to be more unconditionally welcoming of menarche (see page 368) (Michael & Eccles, 2003).

Two factors largely account for these trends: (1) how closely the adolescent's body matches cultural ideals of physical attractiveness, and (2) how well young people fit in physically with their peers.

■ THE ROLE OF PHYSICAL ATTRACTIVENESS. ***TAKE A MOMENT...*** Flip through your favorite popular magazine. You will see evidence of our society's view of an attractive female as thin and long-legged and a good-looking male as tall, broad-shouldered, and muscular. The female image is a girlish shape that favors the late developer. The male image fits the early-maturing boy.

Consistent with these preferences, early-maturing Caucasian girls tend to report a less positive **body image**—conception of and attitude toward their physical appearance—than their on-time and late-maturing agemates. Compared with African-American and Hispanic girls, Caucasian girls are more likely to have internalized the cultural ideal of female attractiveness: Most want to be thinner (Rosen, 2003; Stice, Presnell, & Bearman, 2001; Williams & Currie, 2000). Although boys are less consistent, early, rapid maturers are more likely to be satisfied with their physical characteristics (Alsaker, 1995; Sinkkonen, Anttila, & Siimes, 1998).

Body image is a strong predictor of young people's self-esteem (Harter, 2006). But the negative effects of pubertal timing on body image and—as we will see next—emotional adjustment are greatly amplified when accompanied by other stressors (Stice, 2003).

■ THE IMPORTANCE OF FITTING IN WITH PEERS. Physical status in relation to peers also explains differences in adjustment between early and late maturers. From this perspective, early-maturing girls and late-maturing boys have difficulty because they fall at the extremes of physical development and feel "out of place" when with their agemates. Not surprisingly, adolescents feel most comfortable with peers who match their own level of biological maturity (Stattin & Magnusson, 1990).

Because few agemates of the same pubertal status are available, early-maturing adolescents of both sexes seek out older companions, who often encourage them into activities they are not ready to handle emotionally, including sexual activity, drug and alcohol use, and minor delinquent acts (Ge et al., 2002). Perhaps as a result, early maturers of both sexes report feeling emotionally stressed and show declines in academic performance (Graber, 2003; Mendle, Turkheimer, & Emery, 2007).

At the same time, the young person's context greatly increases the likelihood that early pubertal timing will lead to negative outcomes. Early maturers in economically disadvantaged neighborhoods are especially vulnerable to establishing ties with deviant peers, which heightens their defiant, hostile behavior. And because families in such neighborhoods tend to be exposed to chronic, severe stressors and to have few social supports, these early maturers are also more likely to experience harsh, inconsistent parenting, which predicts both deviant peer associations and antisocial behavior (Conger et al., 2002; Ge et al., 2002).

■ LONG-TERM CONSEQUENCES. Do the effects of pubertal timing last? Follow-ups reveal that early-maturing girls, especially, are prone to lasting difficulties. In one study, depression subsided by age 13 in early-maturing boys but tended to persist in early-maturing girls (Ge et al., 2003). In another study, which followed young people from ages 14 to 24, early-maturing boys again showed good adjustment. But early-maturing girls reported poorer-quality relationships with family and friends, smaller social networks, and lower life satisfaction into early adulthood than their on-time counterparts (Graber et al., 2004).

Recall that childhood family conflict and harsh parenting are linked to earlier pubertal timing, more so for girls than for boys (see page 367). Perhaps many early-maturing girls enter adolescence with emotional and social difficulties. As the stresses of puberty interfere with school performance and lead to unfavorable peer pressures, poor adjustment extends and deepens (Graber, 2003). Clearly, interventions that target at-risk early-maturing youths are needed. These include educating parents and teachers and providing adolescents with counseling and social supports so they will be better prepared to handle the emotional and social challenges of this transition.

ASK YOURSELF

» REVIEW
Summarize the impact of pubertal timing on adolescent development.

» APPLY
As a school-age child, Chloe enjoyed leisure activities with her parents. Now, at age 14, she spends hours in her room and resists going on weekend family excursions. Explain Chloe's behavior.

» CONNECT
How might adolescent moodiness contribute to psychological distancing between parents and adolescents? (*Hint:* Think about bidirectional influences in parent–child relationships.)

» REFLECT
Recall your own reactions to the physical changes of puberty. Are they consistent with research findings? Explain.

Health Issues

The arrival of puberty brings new health issues related to the young person's efforts to meet physical and psychological needs. As adolescents attain greater autonomy, their personal decision making becomes important, in health as well as other areas. Yet none of the health concerns we are about to discuss can be traced to a single cause. Rather, biological, psychological, family, peer, and cultural factors jointly contribute.

Nutritional Needs

When their sons reached puberty, Franca and Antonio reported a "vacuum cleaner effect" in the kitchen as the boys routinely emptied the refrigerator. Rapid body growth leads to a dramatic rise in food intake. During the growth spurt, boys require about 2,700 calories a day and much more protein than they did earlier, girls about 2,200 calories but somewhat less protein than boys because of their smaller size and muscle mass (Cortese & Smith, 2003).

This increase in nutritional requirements comes at a time when the diets of many young people are the poorest. Of all age groups, adolescents are the most likely to skip breakfast (a practice linked to obesity), eat on the run, and consume empty calories rather than nutrient-rich fruits and vegetables

(Stockman et al., 2005; Striegel-Moore & Franko, 2006). Fast-food restaurants, where teenagers often gather, have begun to offer some healthy menu options. But adolescents need guidance in choosing these alternatives. Eating fast food and school purchases from snack bars and vending machines is strongly associated with consumption of high-fat foods and soft drinks, indicating that teenagers often make unhealthy food choices (Bowman et al., 2004; Kubik et al., 2003).

The most common nutritional problem of adolescence is iron deficiency. Iron requirements increase to a maximum during the growth spurt and remain high among girls because of iron loss during menstruation. A tired, irritable teenager may be suffering from anemia rather than unhappiness and should have a medical checkup. Most teenagers get too little calcium and are also deficient in riboflavin (vitamin B_2) and magnesium, both of which support metabolism (Cavadini, Siega-Riz, & Popkin, 2000).

Frequency of family meals is strongly associated with greater intake of fruits, vegetables, grains, and calcium-rich foods and reduced soft drink consumption by teenagers (Fiese & Schwartz, 2008). But compared to families with younger children, those with adolescents eat fewer meals together. In addition to their other benefits (see page 61 in Chapter 2 and page 318 in Chapter 9), family meals can greatly improve teenagers' diets.

Adolescents—especially girls concerned about their weight—tend to be attracted to fad diets. Unfortunately, most are too limited in nutrients and calories to be healthy for fast-growing, active teenagers (Donatelle, 2009). Parents should encourage young people to consult a doctor or dietitian before trying any special diet.

Eating Disorders

Sabrina's desire to lose weight worried Franca. She explained to her daughter that Sabrina was really quite average in build for an adolescent girl and reminded her that her Italian ancestors had considered a plump female body more beautiful than a thin one. Girls who reach puberty early, who are very dissatisfied with their body image, and who grow up in homes where concern with weight and thinness is high are at risk for serious eating problems. Severe dieting is the strongest predictor of the onset of an eating disorder in adolescence (Lock & Kirz, 2008). The two most serious are anorexia nervosa and bulimia nervosa.

■ **ANOREXIA NERVOSA.** **Anorexia nervosa** is a tragic eating disturbance in which young people starve themselves because of a compulsive fear of getting fat. About 1 percent of North American and Western European teenage girls are affected. During the past half-century, cultural admiration of female thinness has fueled a sharp increase in cases. Anorexia nervosa is equally common in all SES groups, but Asian-American, Caucasian-American, and Hispanic girls are at greater risk than African-American girls, who tend to be more satisfied with their size and shape (Fairburn & Harrison, 2003; Granillo, Jones-Rodriguez, & Carvajal, 2005; Steinhausen, 2006). Boys account for about 10 percent of cases of anorexia; about half of these are homosexual or bisexual young people who are uncomfortable with a strong, muscular appearance (Robb & Dadson, 2002).

Aiva, age 16, an anorexia nervosa patient, is shown at left on the day she entered treatment. She weighed just 77 pounds—69 percent of her normal body weight. At right, Aiva appears 10 weeks later, on her last day of treatment. Only about 50 percent of young people with anorexia fully overcome the disorder.

Anorexics have an extremely distorted body image. Even after they have become severely underweight, they see themselves as too heavy. Most go on self-imposed diets so strict that they struggle to avoid eating in response to hunger. To enhance weight loss, they exercise strenuously.

In their attempt to reach "perfect" slimness, anorexics lose between 25 and 50 percent of their body weight. Because a normal menstrual cycle requires about 15 percent body fat, either menarche does not occur or menstrual periods stop. Malnutrition causes pale skin, brittle discolored nails, fine dark hairs all over the body, and extreme sensitivity to cold. If it continues, the heart muscle can shrink, the kidneys can fail, and irreversible brain damage and loss of bone mass can occur. About 6 percent of anorexics die of the disorder, as a result of either physical complications or suicide (Katzman, 2005).

Forces within the person, the family, and the larger culture give rise to anorexia nervosa. Identical twins share the disorder more often than fraternal twins, indicating a genetic influence. Abnormalities in neurotransmitters in the brain, linked to anxiety and impulse control, may make some individuals more susceptible (Kaye, 2008; Lock & Kirz, 2008). Many anorexics have extremely high standards for their own behavior and performance, are emotionally inhibited, and avoid intimate ties outside the family. Consequently, they are often excellent students who are responsible and well-behaved. But as we have also seen, the societal image of "thin is beautiful" contributes to the poor body image of many girls—especially early-maturing girls, who are at greatest risk for anorexia nervosa (Tyrka, Graber, & Brooks-Gunn, 2000).

In addition, parent–adolescent interactions reveal problems related to adolescent autonomy. Often the mothers of these girls have high expectations for physical appearance, achievement, and social acceptance and are overprotective and controlling. Fathers tend to be emotionally distant. These parental attributes may contribute to anorexic girls' persistent anxiety and fierce pursuit of perfection in achievement, respectable behavior, and thinness (Kaye, 2008). Nevertheless, it remains unclear whether maladaptive parent–child relationships precede the disorder, emerge in response to it, or both.

Because anorexic girls typically deny or minimize the seriousness of their disorder, treating it is difficult (Couturier & Lock, 2006). Hospitalization is often necessary to prevent life-threatening malnutrition. The most successful treatment is family therapy and medication to reduce anxiety and neurotransmitter imbalances (Fairburn, 2005; Treasure & Schmidt, 2005). Still, only about 50 percent of anorexics fully recover. For many, eating problems continue in less extreme form. About 10 percent show signs of a less severe, but nevertheless debilitating, disorder: bulimia nervosa.

■ **BULIMIA NERVOSA.** When Sabrina's 16-year-old brother, Louis, brought his girlfriend Cassie to the house, Sabrina admired her good figure. "What willpower!" Sabrina thought. "Cassie hardly touches food. But what's the matter with her teeth?"

Cassie's secret was not willpower. She actually had great difficulty controlling her appetite. Cassie suffered from **bulimia nervosa,** an eating disorder in which young people (again, mainly girls, but gay and bisexual boys are also vulnerable) engage in strict dieting and excessive exercise accompanied by binge eating, often followed by deliberate vomiting and purging with laxatives (Herzog, Eddy, & Beresin, 2006; Wichstrøm, 2006). When she was alone, Cassie often felt anxious and unhappy. She responded with eating rampages, consuming thousands of calories in an hour or two, followed by vomiting that eroded the enamel on her teeth. In some cases, life-threatening damage to the throat and stomach occurs.

Bulimia is more common than anorexia nervosa, affecting about 2 to 4 percent of teenage girls, only 5 percent of whom have previously been anorexic. Twin studies show that bulimia, like anorexia, is influenced by heredity (Klump, Kaye, & Strober, 2001). Overweight and early menarche increase the risk. Some bulimics, like anorexics, are perfectionists. But most are impulsive, sensation-seeking young people who lack self-control in many areas, engaging in petty shoplifting, alcohol abuse, and other risky behaviors (Kaye, 2008). And although bulimics share with anorexics pathological anxiety about gaining weight, they may have experienced their parents as disengaged and emotionally unavailable rather than controlling (Fairburn & Harrison, 2003).

Unlike anorexics, bulimics usually feel depressed and guilty about their abnormal eating habits and desperately want help. As a result, bulimia is usually easier to treat than anorexia, through support groups, nutrition education, training in changing eating habits, and anti-anxiety, antidepressant, and appetite-control medication (Hay & Bacaltchuk, 2004).

Sexuality

Louis and Cassie hadn't planned to have intercourse—it "just happened." But before and after, a lot of things passed through their minds. After they had dated for three months, Cassie began to wonder, "Will Louis think I'm normal if I don't have sex with him? If he wants to and I say no, will I lose him?" Both young people knew their parents wouldn't approve. In fact, when Franca and Antonio noticed how attached Louis was to Cassie, they talked to him about the importance of waiting and the dangers of pregnancy. But that Friday evening, Louis and Cassie's feelings for each other seemed overwhelming. "If I don't make a move," Louis thought, "will she think I'm a wimp?"

With the arrival of puberty, hormonal changes—in particular, the production of androgens in young people of both sexes—lead to an increase in sex drive (Halpern, Udry, & Suchindran, 1997). In response, adolescents become very concerned about managing sexuality in social relationships. New cognitive capacities involving perspective taking and self-reflection affect

© JEFF GREENBERG/PHOTOEDIT

Adolescence is an especially important time for the development of sexuality, as these two young people demonstrate. But North American teenagers receive contradictory and confusing messages about the appropriateness of sex.

Applying What We Know

Communicating with Adolescents About Sexual Issues

Strategy	Explanation
Foster open communication.	Let the teenager know you are a willing and trustworthy resource by stating that you are available when questions arise and will answer fully and accurately.
Use correct terms for body parts.	Correct vocabulary gives the young person a basis for future discussion and also indicates that sex is not a secretive topic.
Use effective discussion techniques.	Listen, encourage the adolescent to participate, ask open-ended rather than yes/no questions, and give supportive responses. Avoid dominating and lecturing, which cause teenagers to withdraw.
Reflect before speaking.	When the adolescent asks questions or offers opinions about sex, remain nonjudgmental. If you differ with the teenager's views, convey your perspective in a nonthreatening manner, emphasizing that although you disagree, you are not attacking his or her character. Trying to dictate the young person's behavior generally results in alienation.
Keep conversations going.	Many parents regard their job as finished once they have had the "big talk" in early adolescence. But young people are more likely to be influenced by an accumulation of smaller discussions. If open communication is sustained, the teenager is more likely to return with thoughts and questions.

Source: Berkowitz, 2004.

their efforts to do so. Yet like the eating behaviors we have just discussed, adolescent sexuality is heavily influenced by the young person's social context.

THE IMPACT OF CULTURE. ***TAKE A MOMENT...*** When did you first learn the "facts of life"—and how? Was sex discussed openly in your family, or was it treated with secrecy? Exposure to sex, education about it, and efforts to limit the sexual curiosity of children and adolescents vary widely around the world.

Despite the prevailing image of sexually free adolescents, sexual attitudes in North America are relatively restrictive. Typically, parents provide little or no information about sex, discourage sex play, and rarely talk about sex in children's presence. When young people become interested in sex, only about half report getting information from parents about intercourse, pregnancy prevention, and sexually transmitted disease. Many parents, fearing embarrassment or concerned that their teenager will not take them seriously, avoid meaningful discussions about sex. Yet warm, open give-and-take, as described in Applying What We Know above, is associated with teenagers' adoption of parents' views and with reduced sexual risk taking (Jaccard, Dodge, & Dittus, 2003; Miller, Forehand, & Kotchick, 1999).

Adolescents who do not get information about sex from their parents are likely to learn from friends, books, magazines, movies, TV, and the Internet (Jaccard, Dodge, & Dittus, 2002; Sutton et al., 2002). On prime-time TV shows, which adolescents watch more than other TV offerings, 80 percent of programs contain sexual content. Most depict partners as spontaneous and passionate, taking no steps to avoid pregnancy or sexually transmitted disease, and experiencing no negative consequences (Roberts, Henriksen, & Foehr, 2004). In several studies, media exposure to sexual content predicted teenagers' current sexual activity, intentions to be sexually active in the future, and subsequent pregnancies, even after many other relevant factors were controlled (Chandra et al., 2008; Friedman, 2006; Pardum, L'Engle, & Brown, 2005).

The Internet is an especially hazardous "sex educator." In a survey of a large sample of U.S. 10- to 17-year-old Web users, 42 percent said they had viewed online pornographic websites (images of naked people or people having sex) while surfing the Internet in the past 12 months. Of these, 66 percent indicated they had encountered the images accidentally and did not want to view them. Youths who felt depressed, had been bullied by peers, or were involved in delinquent activities had more encounters with Internet pornography, which may have intensified their adjustment problems (Wolak, Mitchell, & Finkelhor, 2007).

Consider the contradictory messages young people receive. On one hand, adults express disapproval of sex at a young age and outside of marriage. On the other hand, the broader social environment extols the excitement and romanticism of sex. North American teenagers are left bewildered, poorly informed about sexual facts, and with little sound advice on how to conduct their sex lives responsibly.

ADOLESCENT SEXUAL ATTITUDES AND BEHAVIOR. Although differences between subcultural groups exist, sexual attitudes of U.S. adolescents and adults have become more liberal over the past 40 years. Compared with a generation ago, more people believe that sexual intercourse before marriage is all right, as long as two people are emotionally committed to each other (ABC News, 2004; Michael et al., 1994). During the past decade, adolescents have swung back slightly toward more conservative sexual beliefs, largely in response to the risk of sexually transmitted disease, especially AIDS, and to teenage sexual abstinence programs sponsored by schools and religious organizations (Ali & Scelfo, 2002; Cope-Farrar & Kunkel, 2002).

Trends in adolescents' sexual behavior are consistent with their attitudes. Rates of extramarital sex among U.S. young people rose for several decades but have recently declined (U.S. Department of Health and Human Services, 2008k). Nevertheless, as Figure 11.4 illustrates, a substantial percentage of U.S. young people are sexually active quite early, by ninth grade (ages 14 to 15). Males tend to have their first intercourse earlier than females.

Overall teenage sexual activity rates are similar in the United States and other Western countries: About half of adolescents have had intercourse. But quality of sexual experiences differs. U.S. youths become sexually active earlier than their Canadian and European counterparts (Boyce et al., 2006; U.S. Department of Health and Human Services, 2008k). And about 18 percent of adolescent boys in the United States—more than twice the percentage in Canada, France, and Great Britain—have had sexual relations with three or more partners in the past year (Alan Guttmacher Institute, 2004). Most teenagers, however, have had only one or two sexual partners by the end of high school.

CHARACTERISTICS OF SEXUALLY ACTIVE ADOLESCENTS.

Early and frequent teenage sexual activity is linked to personal, family, peer, and educational characteristics. These include childhood impulsivity, weak sense of personal control over life events, early pubertal timing, parental divorce, single-parent and stepfamily homes, large family size, little or no religious involvement, weak parental monitoring, disrupted parent–child communication, sexually active friends and older siblings, poor school performance, lower educational aspirations, and tendency to engage in norm-violating acts, including alcohol and drug use and delinquency (Crockett, Raffaelli, & Shen, 2006; Howard & Wang, 2004; Manlove et al., 2006; Siebenbruner, Zimmer-Gembeck, & Egeland, 2007; Silver & Bauman, 2006).

Because many of these factors are associated with growing up in a low-income family, it is not surprising that early sexual activity is more common among young people from economically disadvantaged homes. Living in a neighborhood high in physical deterioration, crime, and violence also increases the likelihood that teenagers will be sexually active (Ge et al., 2002). In such neighborhoods, social ties are weak, adults exert little oversight and control over adolescents' activities, and negative peer influences are widespread. In fact, the high rate of sexual activity among African-American teenagers—67 percent report having had sexual intercourse, compared with 48 percent of all U.S. young people—is largely accounted for by widespread poverty in the black population (Darroch, Frost, & Singh, 2001; U.S. Department of Health & Human Services, 2008k).

CONTRACEPTIVE USE.

Although adolescent contraceptive use has increased in recent years, about 20 percent of sexually active teenagers in the United States are at risk for unintended pregnancy because they do not use contraception consistently (see Figure 11.5 on page 376) (Alan Guttmacher Institute, 2002, 2005). Why do so many fail to take precautions? Typically, teenagers respond, "I wasn't planning to have sex," or, "I didn't want to spoil the moment." As we will see when we take up adolescent cognitive development, although adolescents can consider multiple possibilities when faced with a problem, they often fail to apply this reasoning to everyday situations.

One reason is that advances in perspective taking lead teenagers, for a time, to be extremely concerned about others' opinions of them. Recall how Cassie and Louis each worried about what the other would think if they decided not to have sex. Furthermore, in the midst of everyday social pressures, adolescents often overlook the consequences of engaging in risky behaviors (Beyth-Marom & Fischhoff, 1997). And many teenagers—especially those from troubled, low-SES families—do not have realistic expectations about the impact of early parenthood on their current and future lives (Stevens-Simon, Sheeder, & Harter, 2005).

As these findings suggest, the social environment also contributes to teenagers' reluctance to use contraception. Those without the rewards of meaningful education and work are especially likely to engage in irresponsible sex, sometimes within relationships characterized by exploitation. About 11 percent of U.S. girls and 5 percent of boys say they were pressured to have intercourse when they were unwilling (U.S. Department of Health and Human Services, 2008k).

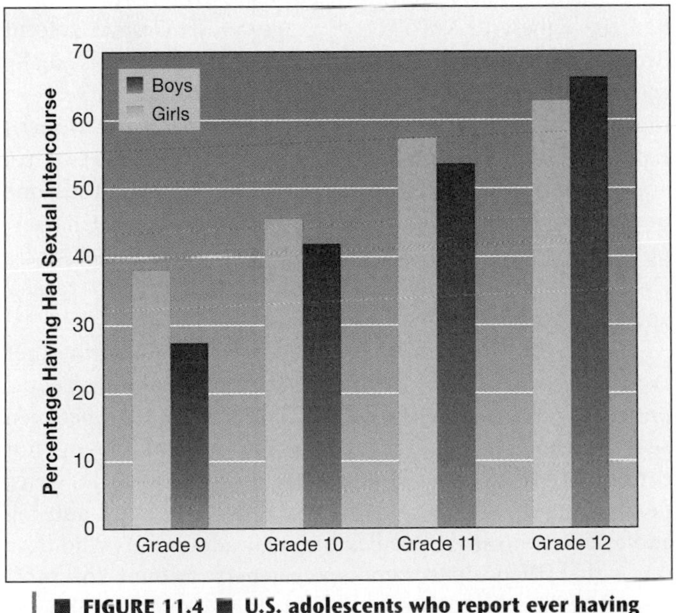

FIGURE 11.4 **U.S. adolescents who report ever having had sexual intercourse.** Many young adolescents are sexually active—more than in other Western nations. Boys tend to have their first intercourse earlier than girls. By the end of high school, rates of boys and girls having had sexual intercourse are similar. (From U.S. Department of Health and Human Services, 2008k.)

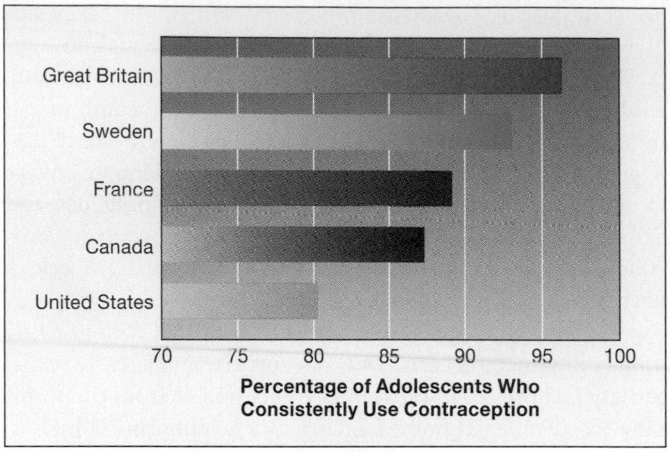

■ **FIGURE 11.5** ■ **Adolescent contraceptive use in five industrialized nations.** Sexually active U.S. teenagers are less likely to use contraception consistently than teenagers in other industrialized nations. (Adapted from Darroch, Frost, & Singh, 2001; U.S. Department of Health and Human Services, 2008k.)

In contrast, teenagers who report good relationships with parents and who talk openly with them about sex and contraception are more likely to use birth control (Henrich et al., 2006; Kirby, 2002a). But few adolescents believe their parents would be understanding and supportive. School sex education classes, as well, often leave teenagers with incomplete or incorrect knowledge. Some do not know where to get birth control counseling and devices; those who do often worry that a doctor or family planning clinic might not keep their visits confidential. About 20 percent of adolescents using health services say that if their parents were notified, they would still have sex, but without contraception (Jones et al., 2005).

■ **SEXUAL ORIENTATION.** So far, we have focused only on heterosexual behavior. About 2 to 3 percent of young people identify as lesbian, gay, or bisexual (Bailey, Dunne, & Martin, 2000; Savin-Williams & Diamond, 2004). An unknown number experience same-sex attraction but have not come out to friends or family (see the Social Issues box on the following page). Adolescence is an equally crucial time for the sexual development of these young people, and societal attitudes, again, loom large in how well they fare.

Heredity makes an important contribution to homosexuality: Identical twins of both sexes are much more likely than fraternal twins to share a homosexual orientation; so are biological (as opposed to adoptive) relatives (Kendler et al., 2000; Kirk et al., 2000). Furthermore, male homosexuality tends to be more common on the maternal than on the paternal side of families, suggesting that it might be X-linked (see Chapter 2). Indeed, one gene-mapping study found that among 40 pairs of homosexual brothers, 33 (82 percent) had an identical segment of DNA on the X chromosome. One or several genes in that region might predispose males to become homosexual (Hamer et al., 1993).

How might heredity lead to homosexuality? According to some researchers, certain genes affect the level or impact of prenatal sex hormones, which modify brain structures in ways that induce homosexual feelings and behavior (Bailey et al., 1995; LeVay, 1993). Keep in mind, however, that environmental factors can also alter prenatal hormones. Girls exposed prenatally to very high levels of androgens or estrogens—either because of a genetic defect or from drugs given to the mother to prevent miscarriage—are more likely to become homosexual or bisexual (Meyer-Bahlburg et al., 1995). Furthermore, homosexual men tend to be later in birth order and to have a higher-than-average number of older brothers (Blanchard & Bogaert, 2004). Perhaps mothers with several male children sometimes produce antibodies to androgens, which reduces the prenatal impact of male sex hormones on the brains of later-born boys.

Stereotypes and misconceptions about homosexuality persist. For example, contrary to common belief, most homosexual adolescents are not "gender-deviant" in dress or behavior. And attraction to members of the same sex is not limited to gay, lesbian, and bisexual teenagers. About 50 to 60 percent of adolescents who report having engaged in homosexual acts identify as heterosexual (Savin-Williams & Diamond, 2004).

The evidence to date suggests that genetic and prenatal biological influences are largely responsible for homosexuality. In our evolutionary past, homosexuality may have served the adaptive function of reducing aggressive competition for other-sex mates (Rahman & Wilson, 2003).

Sexually Transmitted Diseases

Sexually active adolescents, both homosexual and heterosexual, are at risk for sexually transmitted diseases (STDs). Adolescents have the highest rates of STDs of all age groups. Despite a recent decline in STDs in the United States, one out of six sexually active teenagers contracts one of these illnesses each year—a rate three or more times as high as that of Canada and Western Europe (Health Canada, 2006; U.S. Centers for Disease Control and Prevention, 2007). Teenagers at greatest risk are the same ones most likely to engage in irresponsible sexual behavior: poverty-stricken young people who feel a sense of hopelessness (Niccolai et al., 2004). Left untreated, STDs can lead to sterility and life-threatening complications.

By far the most serious STD is AIDS. In contrast to other Western nations, where the incidence of AIDS among people under age 30 is low, one-fifth of U.S. AIDS cases occur between ages 20 and 29. Because AIDS symptoms typically do not emerge until 8 to 10 years after infection with the HIV virus, nearly all these cases originated in adolescence. Drug-abusing adolescents who share needles and male adolescents who have sex with HIV-positive same-sex partners account for most cases, but heterosexual spread of the disease remains high, especially among teenagers with more than one partner in the previous 18 months (Kelley et al., 2003). It is at least twice as easy for a male to infect a female with any STD, including HIV, as for a female to infect a male. Currently, females account for about 37 percent of new U.S. cases among adolescents and young adults (Rangel et al., 2006).

SOCIAL ISSUES

Gay, Lesbian, and Bisexual Youths: Coming Out to Oneself and Others

Cultures vary as much in their acceptance of homosexuality as in their approval of extramarital sex. In North America, homosexuals are stigmatized, as shown by the degrading language often used to describe them. This makes forming a sexual identity a much greater challenge for gay, lesbian, and bisexual youths than for their heterosexual counterparts.

Wide variations in sexual identity formation exist, depending on personal, family, and community factors. Yet interviews with gay and lesbian adolescents and adults reveal that many (though not all) move through a three-phase sequence in coming out to themselves and others.

Feeling Different

Many gay men and lesbians recall feeling different from other children when they were young. Typically, this first sense of their biologically determined sexual orientation appears between ages 6 and 12, in play interests more like those of the other gender (Rahman & Wilson, 2003). Boys may find that they are less interested in sports, more drawn to quieter activities, and more emotionally sensitive than other boys; girls may find that they are more athletic and active than other girls.

By age 10, many of these children start to engage in *sexual questioning*—wondering why the typical heterosexual orientation does not apply to them. Often, they experience their sense of being different as deeply distressing. Compared with children who are confident of their homosexuality, sexual-questioning children report greater anxiety about peer relationships and greater dissatisfaction with their biological gender over time (Carver, Egan, & Perry, 2004).

Confusion

With the arrival of puberty, feeling different clearly encompasses feeling sexually different. In research on ethnically diverse gay, lesbian, and bisexual youths, awareness of a same-sex physical attraction occurred, on average, between ages 11 and 12 for boys and 14 and 15 for girls, perhaps because adolescent social pressures toward heterosexuality are particularly intense for girls (D'Augelli, 2006; Diamond, 1998).

Realizing that homosexuality has personal relevance generally sparks additional confusion. A few adolescents resolve their discomfort by crystalizing a gay, lesbian, or bisexual identity quickly, with a flash of insight into their sense of being different. But most experience an inner struggle and a deep sense of isolation—outcomes intensified by lack of role models and social support (D'Augelli, 2002; Safren & Pantalone, 2006).

COURTESY OF GLSEN.ORG

These teens prepare to celebrate ALLY week, designed to encourage students to be allies against anti-lesbian, gay, bisexual, and transgender language, bullying, and harassment in America's schools. When peers react with acceptance, coming out strengthens the young person's view of homosexuality as a valid and fulfilling identity.

Some throw themselves into activities they associate with heterosexuality. Boys may go out for athletic teams; girls may drop softball and basketball in favor of dance. And many homosexual youths (more females than males) try heterosexual dating, sometimes to hide their sexual orientation and at other times to develop intimacy skills that they later apply to same-sex relationships (D'Augelli, 2006; Dubé, Savin-Williams, & Diamond, 2001). Those who are extremely troubled and guilt-ridden may escape into alcohol, drugs, and suicidal thinking. Suicide attempts are unusually high among gay, lesbian, and bisexual young people (McDaniel, Purcell, & D'Augelli, 2001; Morrow, 2006).

Self-Acceptance

By the end of adolescence, the majority of gay, lesbian, and bisexual teenagers accept their sexual identity. But they face another crossroad: whether to tell others. Powerful stigma against their sexual orientation leads some to decide that disclosure is impossible: While self-defining as gay, they otherwise "pass" as heterosexual (Savin-Williams, 2001). When homosexual youths do come out, they often face intense hostility. In a study of over 500 gay, lesbian, and bisexual youths in Canada, New Zealand, and the United States, 75 percent reported being verbally abused, and 15 percent physically attacked, because of their sexual orientation (D'Augelli, 2002).

Nevertheless, many young people eventually acknowledge their sexual orientation publicly, usually by telling trusted friends first. Once teenagers establish a same-sex sexual or romantic relationship, many come out to parents. Few parents respond with severe rejection; most are either positive or slightly negative and disbelieving (Savin-Williams & Ream, 2003a). Parental understanding is the strongest predictor of favorable adjustment—including reduced *internalized homophobia*, or societal prejudice turned against the self (D'Augelli, Grossman, & Starks, 2005; Savin-Williams, 2003).

When people react positively, coming out strengthens the young person's view of homosexuality as a valid, meaningful, and fulfilling identity. Contact with other gays and lesbians is important for reaching this phase, and changes in society permit many adolescents in urban areas to attain it earlier than their counterparts did a decade or two ago. Gay and lesbian communities exist in large cities, but teenagers in small towns and rural areas may have difficulty meeting other homosexuals and finding a supportive environment. These adolescents have a special need for caring adults and peers who can help them find self- and social acceptance.

Gay, lesbian, and bisexual youths who succeed in coming out to themselves and others integrate their sexual orientation into a broader sense of identity, a process we will address in Chapter 12. As a result, they no longer need to focus so heavily on their homosexual self, and energy is freed for other aspects of psychological growth. In sum, coming out can foster many aspects of adolescent development, including self-esteem, psychological well-being, and relationships with family and friends.

As the result of school courses and media campaigns, about 60 percent of U.S. middle-school students and 90 percent of high school students are aware of basic facts about AIDS. But most have limited understanding of other STDs, underestimate their own susceptibility, and are poorly informed about how to protect themselves (Coholl et al., 2001; Ethier et al., 2003). Furthermore, high school students report engaging in oral sex much more often than intercourse, and with more partners. But few report consistently using STD protection during oral sex, which is a significant mode of transmission of several STDs (Prinstein, Meade, & Cohen, 2003). Concerted efforts are needed to educate young people about the full range of STDs and risky sexual behaviors.

Adolescent Pregnancy and Parenthood

Cassie didn't get pregnant after having sex with Louis, but some of her classmates were less fortunate. An estimated 750,000 to 850,000 teenage girls in the United States—20 percent of those who have sexual intercourse—become pregnant annually, about 25,000 of them younger than age 15. Despite a steady decline since 1991, the U.S. adolescent pregnancy rate is much higher than that of any other industrialized country (see Figure 11.6). Three factors heighten the incidence of adolescent pregnancy: (1) Effective sex education reaches too few teenagers; (2) convenient, low-cost contraceptive services for adolescents are scarce; and (3) many families live in poverty, which encourages young people to take risks without considering the future implications of their behavior.

Because 40 percent of U.S. adolescent pregnancies end in abortion, the number of American teenage births is actually lower than it was 50 years ago (U.S. Department of Health and Human Services, 2007a). But teenage parenthood is a much greater problem today because adolescents are far less likely to marry before childbirth. In 1960, only 15 percent of teenage births were to unmarried females, compared with 86 percent today (Child Trends, 2008). Increased social acceptance of single motherhood, along with the belief of many teenage girls that a baby might fill a void in their lives, means that very few girls give up their infants for adoption.

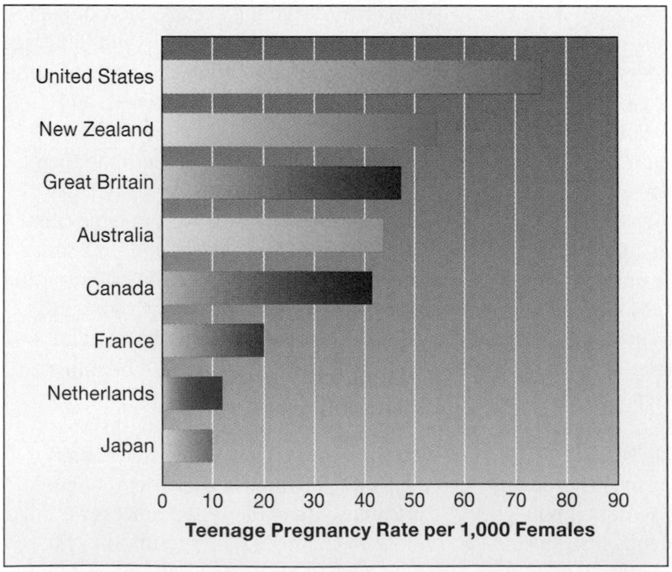

■ **FIGURE 11.6** ■ **Pregnancy rates among 15- to 19-year-olds in eight industrialized nations.** U.S. teenagers have the highest pregnancy rate. (Adapted from Alan Guttmacher Institute, 2001, 2006.)

CORRELATES AND CONSEQUENCES OF ADOLESCENT PARENTHOOD. Becoming a parent is especially challenging for adolescents, who have not yet established a clear sense of direction for their own lives. Both life conditions and personal attributes jointly contribute to adolescent childbearing and also interfere with teenagers' capacity to parent effectively (Jaffee et al., 2001).

Teenage parents are far more likely to be poor than agemates who postpone parenthood. Their backgrounds often include low parental warmth and involvement, domestic violence and child abuse, repeated parental divorce and remarriage, adult models of early unmarried parenthood, and residence in neighborhoods where other adolescents also display these risks. Girls at risk for early pregnancy do poorly in school, engage in alcohol and drug use, have a childhood history of aggressive and antisocial behavior, associate with deviant peers, and experience high rates of depression (Elfenbein & Felice, 2003; Hillis et al., 2004; Luster & Haddow, 2005). A high percentage of out-of-wedlock births are to low-income ethnic minority teenagers. Many turn to early parenthood as a way to move into adulthood when educational and career avenues are unavailable.

After a baby is born, adolescents' lives often worsen in several respects:

- *Educational attainment.* Giving birth before age 18 reduces the likelihood of finishing high school. Only about 70 percent of U.S. adolescent mothers graduate, compared with 95 percent of girls who wait to become parents (National Women's Law Center, 2007).
- *Marital patterns.* Teenage motherhood reduces the chances of marriage and, for those who do marry, increases the likelihood of divorce compared with peers who delay childbearing (Moore & Brooks-Gunn, 2002). Consequently, teenage mothers spend more of their parenting years as single parents. About 35 percent become pregnant again within two years. Of these, about half go on to deliver a second child (Child Trends, 2008).
- *Economic circumstances.* Because of low educational attainment, marital instability, and poverty, many teenage mothers are on welfare. Limited education restricts many others to unsatisfying, low-paid jobs. Many adolescent fathers, too, are unemployed or work at unskilled jobs, usually earning too little to provide their children with basic necessities (Bunting & McAuley, 2004). And an estimated 50 percent have committed illegal offenses resulting in imprisonment (Elfenbein & Felice, 2003).

Because many pregnant teenage girls have inadequate diets, smoke, use alcohol and other drugs, and do not receive early prenatal care, their babies often experience prenatal and birth complications—especially low birth weight (Dell, 2001). And compared with adult mothers, adolescent mothers know less about child development, have unrealistically high expectations of infants, perceive their babies as more difficult, and interact less effectively with them (Moore & Florsheim, 2001; Pomerleau, Scuccimarri, & Malcuit, 2003). Their children tend to score low on intelligence tests, achieve poorly in school, and engage in disruptive social behavior.

Furthermore, teenage parents tend to pass on their personal attributes as well as create unfavorable child-rearing conditions. Consequently, their offspring are at risk for irresponsible sexual activity when they reach puberty. As the Lifespan Vista box on page 380 indicates, adolescent parenthood frequently is repeated in the next generation (Brooks-Gunn, Schley, & Hardy, 2002). Even when children born to teenage mothers do not become early child bearers, their development is often compromised, in terms of likelihood of high school graduation, financial independence in adulthood, and long-term physical and mental health (Moore, Morrison, & Green, 1997; Pogarsky, Thornberry, & Lizotte, 2006).

Still, outcomes vary widely. If a teenage parent finishes high school, secures gainful employment, avoids additional births, and finds a stable marriage partner, long-term disruptions in her own and her child's development will be less severe.

PREVENTION STRATEGIES. Preventing teenage pregnancy means addressing the many factors underlying early sexual activity and lack of contraceptive use. Too often, sex education courses are given late (after sexual activity has begun), last only a few sessions, and are limited to a catalog of facts about anatomy and reproduction. Sex education that goes beyond this minimum does not encourage early sex, as some opponents claim (Kirby, 2002c). It does improve awareness of sexual facts—knowledge that is necessary for responsible sexual behavior.

Knowledge, however, is not enough: Sex education must also help teenagers build a bridge between what they know and what they do. Effective sex education programs combine several key elements:

- They teach techniques for handling sexual situations—including refusal skills for avoiding risky sexual behaviors and communication skills for improving contraceptive use—through role-playing and other activities.
- They deliver clear, accurate messages that are appropriate in view of participating adolescents' culture and sexual experiences.
- They last long enough to have an impact.
- They provide specific information about contraceptives and ready access to them.

Many studies show that sex education with these components can delay the initiation of sexual activity, increase contraceptive use, change attitudes (for example, strengthen future orientation), and reduce pregnancy rates (Kirby, 2002b; Manlove et al., 2006; Thomas & Dimitrov, 2007).

Proposals to increase access to contraceptives are the most controversial aspect of adolescent pregnancy prevention. Many adults argue that placing birth control pills or condoms in the hands of teenagers is equivalent to approving of early sex. Yet sex education programs focusing on abstinence have little or no impact on delaying teenage sexual activity or on preventing pregnancy (Bennett & Assefi, 2005; Underhill, Montgomery, & Operario, 2007). And in Canada and Western Europe, where community- and school-based clinics offer adolescents contraceptives and where universal health insurance helps pay for them, teenage sexual activity is no higher than in the United States—but pregnancy, childbirth, and abortion rates are much lower (Schalet, 2007). Radio and TV campaigns promoting contraceptive use—used widely in Africa, Europe, India, and South America—are associated with a reduction in early sexual activity and with an increase in teenagers' use of birth control (Keller & Brown, 2002).

Efforts to prevent adolescent pregnancy and parenthood must go beyond improving sex education and access to contraception to build academic and social competence (Allen, Seitz, & Apfel, 2007). In one study, researchers randomly assigned at-risk high school students either to a year-long community service class, called Teen Outreach, or to regular classroom experiences in health or social studies. In Teen Outreach, adolescents spent at least 20 hours per week in volunteer work tailored to their interests. They returned to school for discussions that focused on enhancing their community service skills and their ability to cope with everyday challenges. At the end of the school year, pregnancy, school failure, and school suspension were substantially lower among participants in Teen Outreach, which fostered social skills, connection to the community, and self-respect (Allen et al., 1997).

Finally, teenagers who look forward to a promising future are far less likely to engage in early and irresponsible sex. By expanding educational, vocational, and employment opportunities, society can give young people good reasons to postpone childbearing.

INTERVENING WITH ADOLESCENT PARENTS. The most difficult and costly way to deal with adolescent parenthood is to wait until it happens. Young parents need health care, encouragement to stay in school, job training, instruction in parenting and life-management skills, and high-quality, affordable child care. Schools that provide these services reduce the incidence of low-birth-weight babies, increase educational success, and prevent additional childbearing (Barnet et al., 2004; Seitz & Apfel, 2005).

Adolescent mothers also benefit from relationships with family members who are sensitive to their developmental needs. Older teenage mothers display more effective parenting when they establish their own residence with the help of relatives—an arrangement that offers a balance of autonomy and support

A LIFESPAN VISTA: Looking Forward, Looking Back

Like Parent, Like Child: Intergenerational Continuity in Adolescent Parenthood

Does adolescent parenthood increase the chances of teenage childbearing in the next generation? To find out, researchers have conducted several unique studies of mothers (first generation)—some who gave birth as teenagers and some who postponed parenting—and their children (second generation), who were followed longitudinally for several decades (Barber, 2001b; Campa & Eckenrode, 2006; Hardy et al., 1998; Manlove, 1997).

First-generation mothers' age at first childbirth strongly predicted the age at which second-generation young people—both daughters and sons—became parents. Yet becoming a second-generation teenage parent is not inevitable for individuals born to an adolescent mother. Rather, adolescent parenthood is linked to a set of related, unfavorable family conditions and personal characteristics, which negatively influence development over an extended time and, therefore, often transfer to the next generation:

- *Home environmental quality and parenting skills.* The long-term poverty and unstable marital patterns linked to adolescent parenthood reduce the quality of the home environment—in terms of organization, play and learning materials, and parental warmth, encouragement, verbal stimulation, and acceptance of the child (as opposed to punitiveness and abuse). Compared with daughters in other families, the daughters of unmarried adolescent mothers live in families that obtain lower early childhood HOME scores (see page 244 in Chapter 7), even after mothers' prebirth SES is controlled (Campa & Eckenrode, 2006). Low HOME scores are associated with poorer language and IQ scores, which, in turn, contribute to the poor school performance and decision making associated with early sexual activity, laxity in use of contraceptives, and adolescent childbearing.
- *Intelligence and education.* Younger mothers' cognitive deficits and reduced educational attainment contribute to the likelihood their children will experience long-term, poor-quality home environments and, thus, in adolescence will engage in the maladaptive behaviors just mentioned (Barber, 2001b; Hardy et al., 1998).
- *Father absence.* In several studies, intergenerational continuity in adolescent parenthood—especially for daughters—was far greater when teenage mothers remained unmarried (Barber, 2001b; Campa & Eckenrode, 2006). Marriage may limit the negative impact of teenage childbearing on development by strengthening parental financial resources and involvement and reducing family stress. It may be particularly protective for girls because unmarried fathers are less likely to remain in regular contact with daughters than with sons. Recall from Chapter 10 that a warm, involved noncustodial father is linked to reduced early sexual activity in girls (see page 348).

Will the child of this teenage mother also become an adolescent parent? Negative family conditions and personal characteristics associated with early childbearing increase the likelihood that adolescent parenthood will recur in the next generation.

In sum, a life course of adversity—poverty, depleted and disorganized home environments, poor parenting, father absence, intellectual deficits, poor academic performance, and limited educational opportunities—contributes to intergenerational continuity in adolescent pregnancy and parenthood.

(East & Felice, 1996). In one study, African-American teenage mothers who had a long-term "mentor" relationship—an aunt, neighbor, or teacher who provided emotional support and guidance—were far more likely than those without a mentor to stay in school and graduate (Klaw, Rhodes, & Fitzgerald, 2003).

Programs focusing on fathers attempt to increase their financial and emotional commitment to the baby. Although nearly half of young fathers visit their children during the first few years, contact usually diminishes. By the time the child starts school, fewer than one-fourth have regular paternal contact. As with teenage mothers, support from family members helps fathers stay involved (Bunting & McAuley, 2004). Teenage mothers who receive financial and child-care assistance and emotional support from their child's father are less distressed and more likely to sustain a relationship with him (Cutrona et al., 1998; Gee & Rhodes, 2003). And infants with lasting ties to their teenage fathers show better long-term adjustment (Florsheim & Smith, 2005; Furstenberg & Harris, 1993).

Substance Use and Abuse

At age 14, Louis waited until he was alone at home, took some cigarettes from his uncle's pack, and smoked. At an unchaperoned party, he and Cassie drank several cans of beer and lit up marijuana joints. Louis got little physical charge out of these experiences. A good student, who was well-liked by peers and got along well with his parents, he did not need drugs as an escape valve. But he knew of other teenagers who started with

Encouragement from friends contributes to teenagers' alcohol and drug use and—among young people with family difficulties—increases the risk of drug abuse.

alcohol and cigarettes, moved on to harder substances, and eventually were hooked.

Teenage alcohol and drug use is pervasive in industrialized nations. According to the most recent, nationally representative survey of U.S. high school students, by tenth grade, 40 percent of U.S. young people have tried cigarette smoking, 63 percent drinking, and 38 percent at least one illegal drug (usually marijuana). At the end of high school, 17 percent smoke cigarettes regularly, 28 percent have engaged in heavy drinking during the past two weeks, and 40 percent have experimented with illegal drugs. About 20 percent have tried at least one highly addictive and toxic substance, such as amphetamines, cocaine, phencyclidine (PCP), Ecstasy (MDMA), inhalants, heroin, sedatives (including barbiturates), or OxyContin (a narcotic painkiller) (Johnston et al., 2008).

These figures represent a substantial decline since the mid-1990s, probably resulting from greater parent, school, and media focus on the hazards of drug use. But use of inhalants, sedatives, and OxyContin has risen in recent years (Johnston et al., 2008). Other drugs, such as LSD, PCP, and Ecstasy, have made a comeback as adolescents' knowledge of their risks faded.

In part, drug taking reflects the sensation seeking of the teenage years. But adolescents also live in drug-dependent cultural contexts. They see adults relying on caffeine to stay alert, alcohol and cigarettes to cope with daily hassles, and other remedies to relieve stress, depression, and physical discomfort. And compared to a decade or two ago, today doctors more often prescribe—and parents frequently seek—medication to treat children's problems (Brody, 2006). In adolescence, these young people may readily "self-medicate" when stressed. Furthermore, over 90 percent of teenagers say they are aware of cigarette and alcohol ads specifically targeting them, and most say these ads influence their behavior (Alcohol Concern, 2007).

The majority of teenagers who dabble in alcohol, tobacco, and marijuana are not headed for a life of addiction. These *minimal experimenters* are usually psychologically healthy, sociable, curious young people (Shedler & Block, 1990). As Figure 11.7 shows, tobacco and alcohol use is somewhat greater among European than U.S. adolescents, perhaps because European adults more often smoke and drink. But illegal drug use is far more prevalent among U.S. teenagers (Hibell, 2001). A greater percentage of American young people live in poverty, which is linked to family and peer contexts that promote illegal drug use. At the same time, use of diverse drugs is lower among African Americans than among Hispanic and Caucasian Americans; Native-American youths rank highest in drug taking (Johnston et al., 2008; Wallace et al., 2003). Researchers have yet to explain these variations.

Adolescent experimentation with any drug should not be taken lightly. Because most drugs impair perception and thought processes, a single heavy dose can lead to permanent injury or death. And a worrisome minority of teenagers move from substance use to abuse—taking drugs regularly, requiring increasing amounts to achieve the same effect, moving on to harder substances, and using enough to interfere with their ability to meet daily responsibilities.

■ **CORRELATES AND CONSEQUENCES OF ADOLESCENT SUBSTANCE ABUSE.** Unlike experimenters, drug abusers are seriously troubled young people. Their impulsive, disruptive, hostile style is often evident in early childhood, and they are inclined to express their unhappiness through antisocial acts. Compared with other young people, their drug taking starts

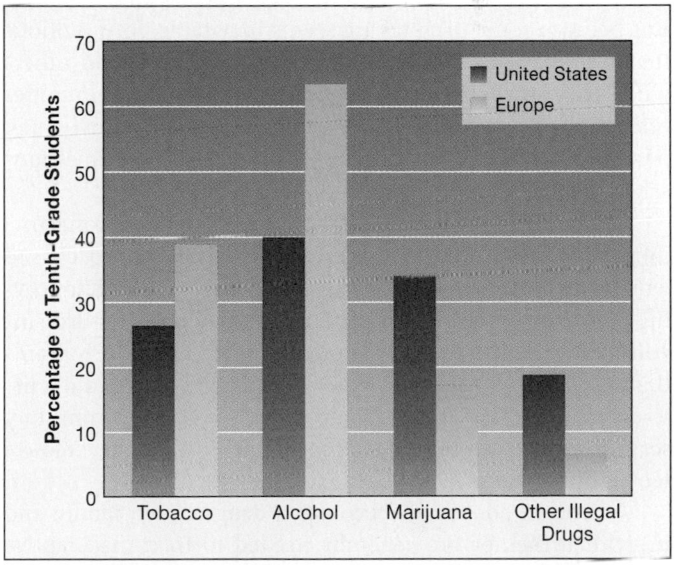

■ **FIGURE 11.7** ■ **Tenth-grade students in the United States and Europe who have used various substances.** Rates for tobacco and alcohol are based on any use in the past 30 days. Rates for marijuana and other illegal drugs are based on any lifetime use. Tobacco use and alcohol use are greater for European adolescents, whereas illegal drug use is greater for U.S. adolescents. (Adapted from Hibell, 2001; Johnston et al., 2008.)

earlier and may have genetic roots (Chassin et al., 2004; Ellickson et al., 2005). But environmental factors also contribute. These include low SES, family mental health problems, parental and older sibling drug abuse, lack of parental warmth and involvement, physical and sexual abuse, and poor school performance. Especially among teenagers with family difficulties, encouragement from friends who use and provide drugs increases substance abuse (Goldstein, Davis-Kean, & Eccles, 2005; Prinstein, Boergers, & Spirito, 2001).

Teenagers who depend on alcohol and hard drugs to deal with daily stresses fail to learn responsible decision-making skills and alternative coping techniques. They show serious adjustment problems, including chronic anxiety, depression, and antisocial behavior, that are both cause and consequence of heavy drug taking (Kassel et al., 2005; Simons-Morton & Haynie, 2003). And they often enter into marriage, childbearing, and the work world prematurely and fail at them—painful outcomes that further promote addictive behavior.

PREVENTION AND TREATMENT. School and community programs that reduce drug experimentation typically combine several components:

- They promote effective parenting, including monitoring of teenagers' activities.
- They teach skills for resisting peer pressure.
- They reduce the social acceptability of drug taking by emphasizing health and safety risks.
- They get adolescents to commit to not using drugs (Cuijpers, 2002; Griffin et al., 2003).

But because some drug taking seems inevitable, interventions that prevent teenagers from harming themselves and others when they do experiment are essential. Many communities offer weekend on-call transportation services that any young person can contact for a safe ride home, with no questions asked.

Because drug abuse has different roots than occasional use, different prevention strategies are required. One approach is to work with parents early, reducing family adversity and improving parenting skills, before children are old enough for drug involvement (Velleman, Templeton, & Copello, 2005). Programs that teach at-risk teenagers effective strategies for handling life stressors and that build competence through community service reduce alcohol and drug abuse, just as they reduce teenage pregnancy.

When an adolescent becomes a drug abuser, family and individual therapy are generally needed to treat maladaptive parent–child relationships, impulsivity, low self-esteem, anxiety, and depression. Academic and vocational training to improve life success also helps. But even comprehensive programs have alarmingly high relapse rates—from 35 to 85 percent (Brown & Ramo, 2005; Waldron, Turner, & Ozechowski, 2005). One recommendation is to start treatment gradually, through support-group sessions that focus on reducing drug taking (Myers et al., 2001). Modest improvements may increase young people's motivation to make longer-lasting changes through intensive treatment.

ASK YOURSELF

REVIEW
Compare risk factors for anorexia nervosa and bulimia nervosa. How do treatments and outcomes differ for the two disorders?

APPLY
After 17-year-old Veronica gave birth to Ben, her parents told her they didn't have room for the baby. Veronica dropped out of school and moved in with her boyfriend, who soon left. Why are Veronica and Ben likely to experience long-term hardships?

CONNECT
What unfavorable life experiences do teenagers who engage in early and frequent sexual activity have in common with those who abuse drugs?

REFLECT
Describe your experiences with peer pressure to experiment with alcohol and drugs. What factors influenced your response?

Cognitive Development

One mid-December evening, a knock at the front door announced the arrival of Franca and Antonio's oldest son, Jules, home for vacation after the fall semester of his sophomore year at college. The family gathered around the kitchen table. "How did it all go, Jules?" asked Antonio as he served slices of apple pie.

"Well, physics and philosophy were awesome," Jules responded with enthusiasm. "The last few weeks, our physics prof introduced us to Einstein's theory of relativity. Boggles my mind, it's so incredibly counterintuitive."

"Counter-what?" asked 11-year-old Sabrina.

"Counterintuitive. Unlike what you'd normally expect," explained Jules. "Imagine you're on a train, going unbelievably fast, like 160,000 miles a second. The faster you go, approaching the speed of light, the slower time passes and the denser and heavier things get relative to on the ground. The theory revolutionized the way we think about time, space, matter—the entire universe."

Sabrina wrinkled her forehead, baffled by Jules's otherworldly reasoning. "Time slows down when I'm bored, like right now, not on a train when I'm going somewhere exciting. No speeding train ever made me heavier, but this apple pie will if I eat any more of it," Sabrina announced, leaving the table.

Sixteen-year-old Louis reacted differently. "Totally cool, Jules. So what'd you do in philosophy?"

"It was a course in philosophy of technology. We studied the ethics of futuristic methods in human reproduction. For example, we argued the pros and cons of a world in which all embryos develop in artificial wombs."

"What do you mean?" asked Louis. "You order your kid at the lab?"

"That's right. I wrote my term paper on it. I had to evaluate it in terms of principles of justice and freedom. I can see some advantages but also lots of dangers. . . ."

As this conversation illustrates, adolescence brings with it vastly expanded powers of reasoning. At age 11, Sabrina finds it difficult to move beyond her firsthand experiences to a world of possibilities. Over the next few years, her thinking will acquire the complex qualities that characterize the cognition of her older brothers. Jules considers multiple variables simultaneously and thinks about situations that are not easily detected in the real world or that do not exist at all. As a result, he can grasp advanced scientific and mathematical principles and grapple with social and political issues. Compared with school-age children's thinking, adolescent thought is more enlightened, imaginative, and rational.

Systematic research on adolescent cognitive development began with testing of Piaget's ideas (Keating, 2004). Recently, information-processing research has greatly enhanced our understanding.

■ **FIGURE 11.8** ■ **Piaget's pendulum problem.** Adolescents who engage in hypothetico-deductive reasoning think of variables that might possibly affect the speed with which a pendulum swings through its arc. Then they isolate and test each variable, as well as testing the variables in combination. Eventually they deduce that the weight of the object, the height from which it is released, and how forcefully it is pushed have no effect on the speed with which the pendulum swings through its arc. Only string length makes a difference.

Piaget's Theory: The Formal Operational Stage

According to Piaget, around age 11 young people enter the **formal operational stage,** in which they develop the capacity for abstract, systematic, scientific thinking. Whereas concrete operational children can "operate on reality," formal operational adolescents can "operate on operations." They no longer require concrete things and events as objects of thought. Instead, they can come up with new, more general logical rules through internal reflection (Inhelder & Piaget, 1955/1958). Let's look at two major features of the formal operational stage.

Hypothetico-Deductive Reasoning

Piaget believed that at adolescence, young people first become capable of **hypothetico-deductive reasoning.** When faced with a problem, they start with a *hypothesis,* or prediction about variables that might affect an outcome, from which they *deduce* logical, testable inferences. Then they systematically isolate and combine variables to see which of these inferences are confirmed in the real world. Notice how this form of problem solving begins with possibility and proceeds to reality. In contrast, concrete operational children start with reality—with the most obvious predictions about a situation. When these are not confirmed, they usually cannot think of alternatives and fail to solve the problem.

Adolescents' performance on Piaget's famous *pendulum problem* illustrates this approach. Suppose we present several school-age children and adolescents with strings of different lengths, objects of different weights to attach to the strings, and a bar from which to hang the strings (see Figure 11.8). Then we ask each of them to figure out what influences the speed with which a pendulum swings through its arc.

Formal operational adolescents hypothesize that four variables might be influential: (1) the length of the string, (2) the weight of the object hung on it, (3) how high the object is raised before it is released, and (4) how forcefully the object is pushed. By varying one factor at a time while holding the other three constant, they test each variable separately and, if necessary, also in combination. Eventually they discover that only string length makes a difference.

In contrast, concrete operational children cannot separate the effects of each variable. They may test for the effect of string length without holding weight constant—comparing, for example, a short, light pendulum with a long, heavy one. Also, they typically fail to notice variables that are not immediately suggested by the concrete materials of the task—for example, how high the object is raised or how forcefully it is released.

Propositional Thought

A second important characteristic of Piaget's formal operational stage is **propositional thought**—adolescents' ability to evaluate the logic of propositions (verbal statements) without referring to real-world circumstances. In contrast, children can evaluate the logic of statements only by considering them against concrete evidence in the real world.

In Piaget's formal operational stage, adolescents engage in propositional thought. As these students discuss problems in a science class, they show that they can reason with symbols that do not necessarily represent objects in the real world.

In a study of propositional reasoning, a researcher showed children and adolescents a pile of poker chips and asked whether statements about the chips were true, false, or uncertain (Osherson & Markman, 1975). In one condition, the researcher hid a chip in her hand and presented the following propositions:

> "*Either* the chip in my hand is green or it is not green."
> "The chip in my hand is green *and* it is not green."

In another condition, the experimenter made the same statements while holding either a red or a green chip in full view.

School-age children focused on the concrete properties of the poker chips. When the chip was hidden, they replied that they were uncertain about both statements. When it was visible, they judged both statements to be true if the chip was green and false if it was red. In contrast, adolescents analyzed the logic of the statements. They understood that the "either-or" statement is always true and the "and" statement is always false, regardless of the chip's color.

Although Piaget did not view language as playing a central role in children's cognitive development (see Chapter 7), he acknowledged its importance in adolescence. Formal operations require language-based and other symbolic systems that do not stand for real things, such as those in higher mathematics. Secondary school students use such systems in algebra and geometry. Formal operational thought also involves verbal reasoning about abstract concepts. Jules was thinking in this way when he pondered relationships among time, space, and matter in physics and wondered about justice and freedom in philosophy.

Follow-Up Research on Formal Operational Thought

Research on formal operational thought poses questions similar to those we discussed with respect to Piaget's earlier stages: Does formal operational thinking appear earlier than Piaget expected? Do all individuals reach formal operations during their teenage years?

■ ARE CHILDREN CAPABLE OF HYPOTHETICO-DEDUCTIVE AND PROPOSITIONAL THINKING? School-age children show the glimmerings of hypothetico-deductive reasoning, although they are less competent at it than adolescents. In simplified situations—ones involving no more than two possible causal variables—6-year-olds understand that hypotheses must be confirmed by appropriate evidence (Ruffman et al., 1993). But school-age children cannot sort out evidence that bears on three or more variables at once. And as we will see when we take up information-processing research, children have difficulty explaining why a pattern of observations supports a hypothesis, even when they recognize the connection between the two.

With respect to propositional thought, when a simple set of premises defies real-world knowledge ("All cats bark. Rex is a cat. Does Rex bark?"), 4- to 6-year-olds can reason logically in make-believe play. To justify their answer, they are likely to say, "We can pretend cats bark!" (Dias & Harris, 1988, 1990). But in an entirely verbal mode, children have great difficulty reasoning from premises that contradict reality or their own beliefs.

Consider this set of statements: "If dogs are bigger than elephants and elephants are bigger than mice, then dogs are bigger than mice." Children younger than 10 judge this reasoning to be false because some of the relations specified do not occur in real life (Moshman & Franks, 1986; Pillow, 2002). They have more difficulty than adolescents inhibiting activation of well-learned knowledge ("Elephants are larger than dogs") that casts doubt on the truthfulness of the premises (Klaczynski, Schuneman, & Daniel, 2004; Simoneau & Markovits, 2003). Partly for this reason, they fail to grasp the *logical necessity* of propositional reasoning—that the accuracy of conclusions drawn from premises rests on the rules of logic, not on real-world confirmation.

As with hypothetico-deductive reasoning, in early adolescence, young people become better at analyzing the *logic* of propositions irrespective of their *content.* And as they get older, they handle problems requiring increasingly complex mental operations. In justifying their reasoning, they more often explain the logical rules on which it is based (Müller, Overton, & Reese, 2001; Venet & Markovits, 2001). But these capacities do not appear suddenly at puberty. Rather, gains occur gradually from childhood on—findings that call into question the emergence of a discrete new stage of cognitive development at adolescence (Keating, 2004; Kuhn & Franklin, 2006; Moshman, 2005).

■ DO ALL INDIVIDUALS REACH THE FORMAL OPERATIONAL STAGE? ***TAKE A MOMENT...*** Try giving one or two of the formal operational tasks just described to your friends. How well do they do? Even many well-educated adults fail hypothetico-deductive tasks and have difficulty reasoning with sets of propositions that contradict real-world facts (Keating, 1979; Markovits & Vachon, 1990).

Why are so many adults not fully formal operational? One reason is that people are most likely to think abstractly and systematically on tasks in which they have had extensive guidance and practice in using such reasoning. This conclusion is supported by evidence that taking college courses leads to improvements in formal reasoning related to course content. Math and science prompt gains in propositional thought, social science in methodological and statistical reasoning (Lehman & Nisbett, 1990). Like concrete reasoning in children, formal operations do not emerge in all contexts at once but are specific to situation and task (Keating, 1990, 2004).

Individuals in tribal and village societies rarely master formal operational tasks (Cole, 1990). Piaget acknowledged that without the opportunity to solve hypothetical problems, people in some societies might not display formal operations. Still, these findings raise further questions about Piaget's stage sequence. Does formal operational thought largely result from children's and adolescents' independent efforts to make sense of their world, as Piaget claimed? Or is it a culturally transmitted way of thinking that is specific to literate societies and taught in school? In an Israeli study of middle school students, after controlling for participants' age, researchers found that years of schooling fully accounted for gains in propositional thought (Artman, Cahan, & Avni-Babad, 2006). School tasks, the investigators speculated, provide crucial experiences in setting aside the "if . . . then" logic of everyday conversations that is often used to convey intentions, promises, and threats ("If you don't do your chores, then you won't get your allowance") but that conflicts with the logic of academic reasoning. In school, then, adolescents encounter rich opportunities to realize their neurological potential to think more effectively.

An Information-Processing View of Adolescent Cognitive Development

Information-processing theorists refer to a variety of specific mechanisms, supported by brain development and experience, that underlie cognitive change in adolescence. Each was discussed in previous chapters (Case, 1998; Kuhn & Franklin, 2006; Luna et al., 2004). Now let's draw them together:

- *Attention* becomes more selective (focused on relevant information) and better-adapted to the changing demands of tasks.
- *Inhibition*—both of irrelevant stimuli and of well-learned responses in situations where they are inappropriate—improves, supporting gains in attention and reasoning.
- *Strategies* become more effective, improving storage, representation, and retrieval of information.
- *Knowledge* increases, easing strategy use.
- *Metacognition* (awareness of thought) expands, leading to new insights into effective strategies for acquiring information and solving problems.
- *Cognitive self-regulation* improves, yielding better moment-by-moment monitoring, evaluation, and redirection of thinking.
- *Speed of thinking* and *processing capacity* increase. As a result, more information can be held at once in working memory and combined into increasingly complex, efficient representations, "opening possibilities for growth" in the capacities just listed and also improving as a result of gains in those capacities (Demetriou et al., 2002, p. 97).

As we look at influential findings from an information-processing perspective, we will see some of these mechanisms of change in action. And we will discover that researchers regard one of them—*metacognition*—as central to adolescent cognitive development.

Scientific Reasoning: Coordinating Theory with Evidence

During a free moment in physical education class, Sabrina wondered why more of her tennis serves and returns passed the net and dropped into her opponent's court when she used a particular brand of balls. "Is it something about their color or size?" she asked herself. "Hmm . . . or maybe it's their surface texture—that might affect their bounce."

The heart of scientific reasoning is coordinating theories with evidence. Deanna Kuhn (2002) has conducted extensive research into the development of scientific reasoning, using problems that, like Piaget's tasks, involve several variables that might affect an outcome. In one series of studies, third, sixth, and ninth graders and adults were first given evidence—sometimes consistent and sometimes conflicting with theories—and then questioned about the accuracy of each theory.

For example, participants were given a problem much like the one Sabrina posed. They were asked to theorize about which of several features of sports balls—size (large or small), color (light or dark), texture (rough or smooth), or presence or absence of ridges on the surface—influences the quality of a player's serve. Next, they were told about the theory of Mr. (or Ms.) S, who believes that the ball's size is important, and the theory of Mr. (or Ms.) C, who thinks color makes a difference. Finally, the interviewer presented evidence by placing balls with certain characteristics in two baskets, labeled "good serve" and "bad serve" (see Figure 11.9 on page 386).

The youngest participants often ignored conflicting evidence or distorted it in ways consistent with their preferred theory. Instead of viewing evidence as separate from and bearing on a theory, children often blend the two into a single representation of "the way things are." They are especially likely to overlook evidence that does not match their prior beliefs when a causal variable is implausible (like color affecting the performance of a sports ball) and when task demands (number of variables to be evaluated) are high (Zimmerman, 2005, 2007). The ability to distinguish theory from evidence and to use logical rules to examine their relationship improves steadily from childhood into adolescence, continuing into adulthood (Kuhn & Dean, 2004; Kuhn & Pearsall, 2000).

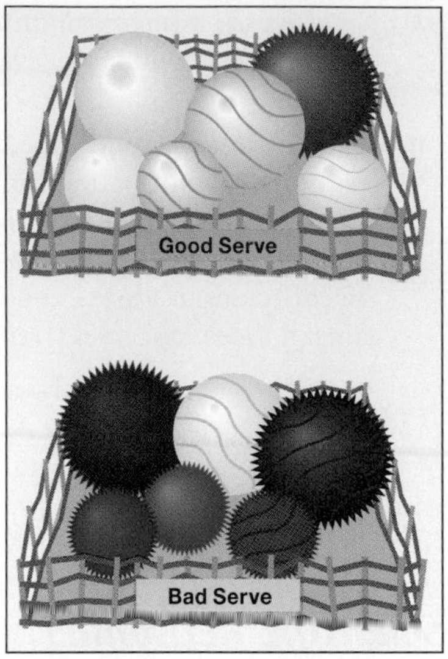

■ **FIGURE 11.9** ■ **Which features of these sports balls—size, color, surface texture, or presence or absence of ridges—influence the quality of a player's serve?** This set of evidence suggests that color might be important, since light-colored balls are largely in the good-serve basket and dark-colored balls in the bad-serve basket. But the same is true for texture! The good-serve basket has mostly smooth balls; the bad-serve basket, rough balls. Since all light-colored balls are smooth and all dark-colored balls are rough, we cannot tell whether color or texture makes a difference. But we can conclude that size and presence or absence of ridges are not important, since these features are equally represented in the good-serve and bad-serve baskets. (Adapted from Kuhn, Amsel, & O'Loughlin, 1988.)

How Scientific Reasoning Develops

What factors support skill at coordinating theory with evidence? Greater working-memory capacity, permitting a theory and the effects of several variables to be compared at once, is vital. Adolescents also benefit from exposure to increasingly complex problems and to teaching that highlights critical features of scientific reasoning—for example, why a scientist's expectations in a particular situation are inconsistent with everyday beliefs and experiences (Chinn & Malhotra, 2002). This explains why scientific reasoning is strongly influenced by years of schooling, whether individuals grapple with traditional scientific tasks (like the sports-ball problem) or engage in informal reasoning—for example, justifying a theory about what causes children to fail in school (Amsel & Brock, 1996).

Researchers believe that sophisticated *metacognitive understanding* is vital for scientific reasoning (Kuhn, 1999; Moshman, 1999). When adolescents regularly pit theory against evidence over many weeks, they experiment with various strategies, reflect on and revise them, and become aware of the nature of logic. Then they apply their appreciation of logic to an increasingly wide variety of situations. The ability to *think about* theories, *deliberately isolate* variables, and *actively seek* disconfirming evidence is rarely present before adolescence (Kuhn, 2000; Moshman, 1998).

But adolescents and adults vary widely in scientific reasoning skills. Many continue to show a self-serving bias, applying logic more effectively to ideas they doubt than to ideas they favor (Klaczynski, 1997; Klaczynski & Narasimham, 1998). Reasoning scientifically requires the metacognitive capacity to evaluate one's objectivity—to be fair-minded rather than self-serving (Moshman, 1999). As we will see in Chapter 12, this flexible, open-minded approach is not just a cognitive attainment but a personality trait—one that assists teenagers greatly in forming an identity and developing morally.

Adolescents develop scientific reasoning skills in a similar step-by-step fashion on different types of tasks. In a series of studies, 10- to 20-year-olds were given sets of problems graded in difficulty. One set consisted of quantitative-relational tasks like the pendulum problem in Figure 11.8. Another contained propositional tasks like the poker chip problem on page 384. Still another set were causal-experimental tasks like the sports-ball problem in Figure 11.9 (Demetriou et al., 1993, 1996, 2002).

In each type of task, adolescents mastered component skills in sequential order by expanding their metacognitive awareness. For example, on causal-experimental tasks, they first became aware of the many variables that—separately and in combination—could influence an outcome. This enabled them to formulate and test hypotheses. Over time, adolescents combined separate skills into a smoothly functioning system, constructing a general model that they could apply to many instances of a given type of problem. In the researcher's words, young people seem to form a "hypercognitive system," or supersystem, that understands, organizes, and influences other aspects of cognition (Demetriou & Kazi, 2001).

Piaget underscored the role of metacognition in formal operational thought when he spoke of "operating on operations" (see page 383). But information-processing findings confirm that scientific reasoning does not result from an abrupt, stagewise change. Instead, it develops gradually out of many specific experiences that require children and adolescents to match theories against evidence and reflect on and evaluate their thinking.

Consequences of Adolescent Cognitive Changes

The development of increasingly complex, effective thinking leads to dramatic revisions in the way adolescents see themselves, others, and the world in general. But just as adolescents are occasionally awkward in using their transformed bodies, they initially falter in their abstract thinking. Teenagers' self-concern, idealism, criticism, and indecisiveness, though perplexing to adults, are usually beneficial in the long run. Applying What We Know on the following page suggests ways to handle the everyday consequences of teenagers' newfound cognitive capacities.

Self-Consciousness and Self-Focusing

Adolescents' ability to reflect on their own thoughts, combined with physical and psychological changes, leads them to think more about themselves. Piaget believed that a new form of egocentrism arises, in which adolescents again have difficulty distinguishing their own and others' perspectives (Inhelder & Piaget, 1955/1958). Piaget's followers suggest that two distorted images of the relation between self and other appear.

Applying What We Know

Handling Consequences of Teenagers' New Cognitive Capacities

Thought expressed as . . .	Suggestion
Sensitivity to public criticism	Refrain from finding fault with the adolescent in front of others. If the matter is important, wait until you can speak to the teenager alone.
Exaggerated sense of personal uniqueness	Acknowledge the adolescent's unique characteristics. At opportune times, encourage a more balanced perspective by pointing out that you had similar feelings as a teenager.
Idealism and criticism	Respond patiently to the adolescent's grand expectations and critical remarks. Point out positive features of targets, helping the teenager see that all societies and people are blends of virtues and imperfections.
Difficulty making everyday decisions	Refrain from deciding for the adolescent. Model effective decision making and offer diplomatic suggestions about the pros and cons of alternatives, the likelihood of various outcomes, and learning from poor choices.

The first is called the **imaginary audience,** adolescents' belief that they are the focus of everyone else's attention and concern (Elkind & Bowen, 1979). As a result, they become extremely self-conscious. When Sabrina woke up one Sunday morning with a large pimple on her chin, her first thought was, "I can't possibly go to church! Everyone will notice how ugly I look." The imaginary audience helps explain why adolescents spend long hours inspecting every detail of their appearance and why they are so sensitive to public criticism. To teenagers, who believe that everyone is monitoring their performance, a critical remark from a parent or teacher can be mortifying.

A second cognitive distortion is the **personal fable.** Certain that others are observing and thinking about them, teenagers develop an inflated opinion of their own importance—a feeling that they are special and unique. Many adolescents view themselves as reaching great heights of omnipotence and also sinking to unusual depths of despair—experiences that others cannot possibly understand (Elkind, 1994). One teenager wrote in her diary, "My parents' lives are so ordinary, so stuck in a rut. Mine will be different. I'll realize my hopes and ambitions." Another, upset when a boyfriend failed to return her affections, rebuffed her mother's comforting words: "Mom, you don't know what it's like to be in love!"

Although imaginary-audience and personal-fable ideation is common in adolescence, these distorted visions of the self do not result from egocentrism, as Piaget suggested. Rather, they are partly an outgrowth of advances in perspective taking, which cause young teenagers to be more concerned with what others think (Vartanian & Powlishta, 1996).

In fact, certain aspects of the imaginary audience may serve positive, protective functions. When asked why they worry about the opinions of others, adolescents responded that others' evaluations have important *real* consequences—for self-esteem, peer acceptance, and social support (Bell & Bromnick, 2003). The idea that others care about their appearance and behavior also has emotional value, helping teenagers hold onto important relationships as they struggle to establish an independent sense of self (Vartanian, 1997).

With respect to the personal fable, in a study of sixth through tenth graders, sense of omnipotence predicted self-esteem and overall positive adjustment. Viewing the self as highly capable and influential may help young people cope with challenges of adolescence. In contrast, sense of personal uniqueness was modestly associated with depression and suicidal thinking (Aalsma, Lapsley, & Flannery, 2006). Focusing on the distinctiveness of one's own experiences may interfere with forming close, rewarding relationships, which provide social support in stressful times. And when combined with a sensation-seeking personality, the personal fable seems to contribute to adolescent risk taking by reducing teenagers' sense of vulnerability. Young people with high personal-fable and sensation-seeking scores tend to take more sexual risks, more often use drugs, and commit more delinquent acts than their agemates (Greene et al., 2000).

The personal fable leads adolescents to view themselves as special and unique. When combined with a sensation-seeking personality, it seems to reduce teenagers' sense of vulnerability and contribute to risky behaviors.

Idealism and Criticism

Adolescents' capacity to think about possibilities opens up the world of the ideal. Teenagers can imagine alternative family, religious, political, and moral systems, and they want to explore them. They often construct grand visions of a world with no injustice, discrimination, or tasteless behavior. The disparity between teenagers' idealism and adults' greater realism creates tension between parent and child. Envisioning a perfect family against which their parents and siblings fall short, adolescents become fault-finding critics.

Overall, however, teenage idealism and criticism are advantageous. Once adolescents come to see other people as having both strengths and weaknesses, they have a much greater capacity to work constructively for social change and to form positive and lasting relationships (Elkind, 1994).

© BOB DAEMMRICH/THE IMAGE WORKS

These high school students attending a college fair will face many choices over the next few years. In unfamiliar situations, teenagers are more likely than adults to fall back on intuitive judgments rather than to use sound decision-making strategies.

Decision Making

Adolescents handle many cognitive tasks more effectively than they did when younger. But in their everyday decision making, they often do not think rationally: (1) identifying the pros and cons of each alternative, (2) assessing the likelihood of various outcomes, (3) evaluating their choice in terms of whether their goals were met and, if not, (4) learning from the mistake and making a better future decision. In one study of decision making, researchers gave adolescents and adults hypothetical dilemmas—whether to have cosmetic surgery, which parent to live with after divorce—and asked them to explain how they would decide. Adults outperformed adolescents, more often considering alternatives, weighing benefits and risks, and suggesting advice seeking (Halpern-Felsher & Cauffman, 2001).

Furthermore, in making decisions, adolescents, more often than adults (who also have difficulty), fall back on well-learned intuitive judgments (Jacobs & Klaczynski, 2002). Consider a hypothetical problem requiring a choice, on the basis of two arguments, between taking a traditional lecture class and taking a computer-based class. One argument contains large-sample information: course evaluations from 150 students, 85 percent of whom liked the computer class. The other argument contains small-sample personal reports: complaints of two honor-roll students who both hated the computer class and enjoyed the traditional class. Most adolescents, even those who knew that selecting the large-sample argument was "more intelligent," based their choice on the small-sample argument, which resembled the informal opinions they depend on in everyday life (Klaczynski, 2001).

Why is decision making so challenging for adolescents? As "first-timers" at many experiences, they do not have sufficient knowledge to predict potential outcomes. They also face many complex situations involving competing goals, such as how to maintain social status while avoiding getting drunk at a party. In unfamiliar circumstances and when making a good decision would mean inhibiting "feel-good" behavior (smoking, overeating, unsafe sex), adolescents are far more likely than adults to emphasize short-term over long-term goals (Amsel et al., 2005; Boyer, 2006; Reyna & Farley, 2006). Furthermore, teenagers often feel overwhelmed by their expanding range of options—abundant school courses, extracurricular activities, social events, and material goods. As a result, their efforts to choose frequently break down, and they resort to habit, act on impulse, or postpone decisions.

Over time, young people learn from their successes and failures, gather information from others about factors that affect decision making, and reflect on the decision-making process (Byrnes, 2003; Jacobs & Klaczynski, 2002). Consequently, their confidence and performance improve. Still, errors in decision making remain common in adulthood.

ASK YOURSELF

» REVIEW
Describe research findings that challenge Piaget's notion of a new, discrete stage of cognitive development at adolescence.

» APPLY
Clarissa, age 14, is convinced that no one appreciates how hurt she feels at not being invited to the homecoming dance. Meanwhile, 15-year-old Justine, alone in her room, pantomimes being sworn in as student body president with her awestruck parents looking on. Which aspect of the personal fable is each girl displaying? Which girl is more likely to be well-adjusted, which poorly adjusted? Explain.

» CONNECT
How does evidence on adolescent decision making help us understand teenagers' risk taking in sexual activity and drug use?

» REFLECT
Do you recall engaging in idealistic thinking or poor decision making as a teenager? Cite examples.

Sex Differences in Mental Abilities

Sex differences in mental abilities have sparked almost as much controversy as the ethnic and SES differences in IQ considered in Chapter 9. Although boys and girls do not differ in general intelligence, they do vary in specific mental abilities.

Verbal Abilities

Throughout the school years, girls attain higher scores in reading achievement and account for a lower percentage of children referred for remedial reading instruction. Girls continue to score slightly higher on tests of verbal ability in middle childhood and adolescence in every country in which assessments have been conducted (Halpern, 2000, 2004; Mullis et al., 2007). And when verbal tests are heavily weighted with writing, girls' advantage is large (Halpern et al., 2007).

A special concern is that girls' advantage in reading and writing achievement increases in adolescence, with boys doing especially poorly in writing—trends evident in the United States and other industrialized nations (see Figure 11.10) (OECD, 2008a; Statistics Canada, 2006a; U.S. Department of Education, 2007c, 2007d). These differences are believed to be major contributors to a widening gender gap in college enrollments. Thirty years ago, males accounted for 60 percent of North American undergraduate students; today, they are in the minority, at 42 percent (Statistics Canada, 2006a; U.S. Department of Education, 2009).

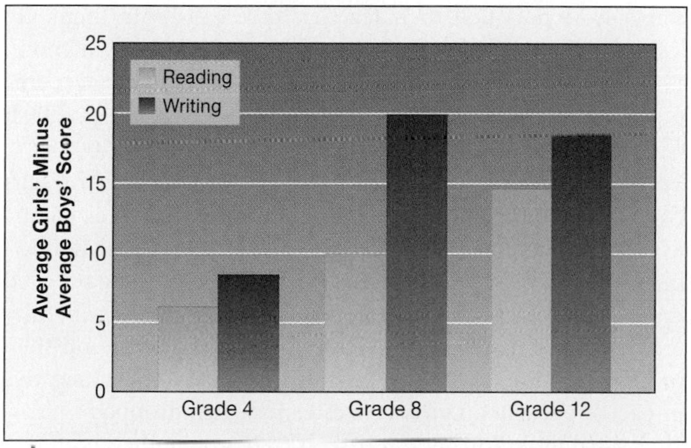

■ **FIGURE 11.10** ■ **Reading and writing achievement score gaps favoring girls at grades 4, 8, and 12.** Findings are based on the U.S. National Assessment of Educational Progress. The bars represent the average girls' score minus the average boys' score. Thus, the height of the bar indicates the extent to which girls outperform boys, a difference that increases in adolescence. By grades 8 and 12, girls have an especially large advantage in writing skill. Similar trends are evident in other industrialized nations. (Adapted from U.S. Department of Education, 2007c, 2007d.)

Recall from Chapter 5 that girls show a biological advantage in earlier development of the left hemisphere of the cerebral cortex, where language is usually localized. And fMRI research indicates that in tackling language tasks (such as deciding whether two spoken or written words rhyme), 9- to 15-year-old girls show concentrated activity in language-specific brain areas. Boys, in contrast, display more widespread activation—in addition to language areas, considerable activity in auditory and visual areas, depending on how words are presented (Burman, Bitan, & Booth, 2007). This suggests that girls are more efficient linguistic processors than boys, who rely heavily on sensory brain regions and process spoken and written words differently.

Girls also receive more verbal stimulation from mothers from the preschool years through adolescence (Peterson & Roberts, 2003). Furthermore, children view language arts as a "feminine" subject. And as a result of the high-stakes testing movement, students today spend more time at their desks being taught in a regimented way—an approach particularly at odds with boys' higher activity level, assertiveness, and incidence of learning problems.

Finally, high divorce and out-of-wedlock birth rates mean that more children today grow up without the continuous presence of a father who models and encourages good work habits and skill at reading and writing. Both maternal and paternal involvement contributes to the achievement and educational attainment of adolescents of both genders (Flouri & Buchanan, 2004). But some research suggests that high-achieving African-American boys are particularly likely to come from homes in which fathers are warm, verbally communicative, and demanding of achievement (Grief, Hrabowski, & Maton, 1998). Clearly, reversing boys' weakening literacy skills is a high priority, requiring a concerted effort by families, schools, and communities.

Mathematics

Studies of mathematical abilities in the early school grades are inconsistent. Some find no sex differences, others slight disparities depending on the skill assessed (Lachance & Mazzocco, 2006). Girls tend to be advantaged in arithmetic computation, perhaps because of their better verbal skills and more methodical approach to problem solving. But around early adolescence, when math concepts become more abstract and spatial, boys start to outperform girls. The difference is especially evident on tests of complex reasoning and geometry (Bielinski & Davison, 1998). In science achievement, too, boys' advantage increases as problems become more difficult (Penner, 2003).

This male advantage is evident in virtually every country where males and females have equal access to secondary education, but the gap is small and has diminished over the past 30 years (Bussière, Knighton, & Pennock, 2007; Halpern, Wai, & Saw, 2005; U.S. Department of Education, 2007a). Among the most capable, however, the gender gap is greater. In widely publicized research on more than 100,000 bright seventh and eighth graders invited to take the Scholastic Assessment Test (SAT), boys outscored girls on the mathematics subtest year after year. Yet even this disparity has been shrinking. A quarter-century ago, 13 times as many boys as girls scored over 700 (out of a possible 800) on the math portion of the SAT; today, the ratio is 2.8 to 1 (Benbow & Stanley, 1983; Monastersky, 2005).

Some researchers believe that heredity contributes substantially to the gender gap in math, especially to the tendency for more boys to be extremely talented. Accumulating evidence indicates that boys' advantage originates in two skill areas: (1) their more rapid numerical memory, which permits them to devote more energy to complex mental operations; and (2) their superior spatial reasoning, which enhances their mathematical problem solving (Geary et al., 2000; Halpern et al., 2007). (See the Biology and Environment box on the following page for discussion of this issue.)

Social pressures are also influential. Long before sex differences in math achievement appear, many children view math as a "masculine" subject. Also, many parents think boys are better at it—an attitude that encourages girls to blame their errors on lack of ability and to consider math less useful for their future lives. These beliefs, in turn, reduce girls' confidence and interest in math and their willingness to consider math- or science-related careers (Bhanot & Jovanovic, 2005; Bleeker & Jacobs, 2004; Kenney-Benson et al., 2006). Furthermore, *stereotype threat*—fear of being judged on the basis of a negative stereotype (see page 314 in Chapter 9)—causes females to do worse than their abilities allow on difficult math problems (Ben-Zeev et al., 2005; Muzzatti & Agnoli, 2007). As a result of these influences, even girls who are highly talented are less likely to develop effective math reasoning skills.

A positive sign is that today, boys and girls reach advanced levels of high school math and science study in equal proportions—a crucial factor in reducing sex differences in knowledge and skill (Gallagher & Kaufman, 2005). But boys spend more time than girls with computers, and they tend to use them differently. Whereas girls typically focus on e-mail, instant messaging, and gathering information for homework assignments, boys more often write computer programs, analyze data, and use graphics programs (Freeman, 2004; Looker & Thiessen, 2003). As a result, boys acquire more specialized computer knowledge.

Clearly, extra steps must be taken to promote girls' interest in and confidence at math and science. When parents hold nonstereotyped beliefs, daughters are less likely to avoid math and science and more likely to achieve well (Updegraff, McHale, & Crouter, 1996). And a math curriculum beginning in kindergarten that teaches children how to apply effective spatial strategies—drawing diagrams, mentally manipulating visual images, searching for numerical patterns, and graphing—is vital (Nuttal, Casey, & Pezaris, 2005). Because girls are biased toward verbal processing, they may not realize their math and science potential unless they are taught how to think spatially.

Learning in School

In complex societies, adolescence coincides with entry into secondary school. Most young people move into either a middle or a junior high school and then into a high school. With each change, academic achievement increasingly determines higher education options and job opportunities. In the following sections, we take up various aspects of secondary school life.

School Transitions

When Sabrina started junior high, she left a small, intimate, self-contained sixth-grade classroom for a much larger school. "I don't know most of the kids in my classes, and my teachers don't know me," Sabrina complained to her mother at the end of the first week. "Besides, there's too much homework. I get assignments in all my classes at once. I can't do all this!" she shouted, bursting into tears.

IMPACT OF SCHOOL TRANSITIONS. As Sabrina's reactions suggest, school transitions can create adjustment problems. With each school change—from elementary to middle or junior high and then to high school—adolescents' grades decline. The drop is partly due to tighter academic standards. At the same time, the transition to secondary school often means less personal attention, more whole-class instruction, and less chance to participate in classroom decision making (Seidman, Aber, & French, 2004).

It is not surprising, then, that students rate their middle or junior high school learning experiences less favorably than their elementary school experiences (Wigfield & Eccles, 1994). They also report that their teachers care less about them, are less friendly, grade less fairly, and stress competition more. Consequently, many young people feel less academically competent, and their motivation declines (Barber & Olsen, 2004; Gutman & Midgley, 2000; Otis, Grouzet, & Pelletier, 2005).

Inevitably, students must readjust their feelings of self-confidence and self-worth as they encounter revised academic expectations and a more complex social world. A study following more than 300 students from sixth to tenth grade revealed that grade point average declined and feelings of anonymity increased after each school change—to junior high and then to high school. But the earlier transition had a more negative impact, especially on girls' self-esteem, which dropped sharply after starting junior high and then only gradually rebounded (Simmons & Blyth, 1987). Girls fared less well, the researchers argued, because movement to junior high tended to coincide with other life changes: the onset of puberty and dating. Adolescents facing added strains—family disruption, poverty, low parental involvement, or learned helplessness on academic tasks—are at greatest risk for self-esteem and academic difficulties (de Bruyn, 2005; Rudolph et al., 2001; Seidman et al., 2003).

BIOLOGY AND ENVIRONMENT

Sex Differences in Spatial Abilities

Spatial skills are a key focus of researchers' efforts to explain sex differences in mathematical reasoning. The gender gap favoring males is large for *mental rotation tasks,* in which individuals must rotate a three-dimensional figure rapidly and accurately inside their heads (see Figure 11.11). Males also do considerably better on *spatial perception tasks,* in which people must determine spatial relationships by considering the orientation of the surrounding environment. Sex differences on *spatial visualization tasks,* involving analysis of complex visual forms, are weak or nonexistent. Because many strategies can be used to solve these tasks, both sexes may come up with effective procedures (Collaer & Hill, 2006; Voyer, Voyer, & Bryden, 1995).

Sex differences in spatial abilities emerge in early childhood, persist throughout the lifespan, and are evident in many cultures (Levine et al., 1999; Silverman, Choi, & Peters, 2007). The pattern is consistent enough to suggest a biological explanation. One hypothesis is that heredity, perhaps through exposure to androgen hormones, enhances right hemispheric functioning, giving males a spatial advantage. (Recall that for most people, spatial skills are housed in the right hemisphere of the cerebral cortex.) In support of this idea, girls and women whose prenatal androgen levels were abnormally high show superior performance on spatial rotation tasks (Berenbaum, 2001; Halpern & Collaer, 2005). And in some studies, spatial performance varies with daily and annual androgen levels in both men and women (Temple & Carney, 1995; Van Goozen et al., 1995).

Why might a biologically based sex difference in spatial abilities exist? Evolutionary theorists point out that mental rotation skill predicts rapid, accurate map drawing and interpretation, areas in which boys and men do better than girls and women. Over the course of human evolution, the cognitive abilities of males became adapted for hunting, which required generating mental representations of large-scale spaces to find one's way (Jones, Braithwaite, & Healy, 2003). But this explanation is controversial: Critics point out that female gatherers also needed to travel long distances to find fruits and vegetables that ripened in different seasons (Newcombe, 2007).

PHOTO COURTESY OF SIEMENS FOUNDATION

When provided with the necessary encouragement and educational experiences, girls are capable of top-level achievement in math and science. In 2007, high school senior Isha Jain won first prize in the prestigious Siemens Competition in Math, Science, and Technology for her breakthrough discovery of a cellular mechanism that underlies bone growth spurts. She aspires to lead a research lab focusing on biology and math.

Experience also contributes to males' superior spatial performance. Children who engage in manipulative activities, such as block play, model building, and carpentry, do better on spatial tasks (Baenninger & Newcombe, 1995). Furthermore, playing video games that require rapid mental rotation of visual images enhances spatial scores (Subrahmanyam & Greenfield, 1996; Terlecki & Newcombe, 2005). Boys spend far more time than girls at these pursuits.

In studies of middle and high school students, *both* spatial abilities and self-confidence at doing math were related to performance on complex math problems, with spatial skills being the stronger predictor (Casey, Nuttall, & Pezaris, 1997, 2001). Boys are advantaged in both spatial performance and math self-confidence. Still, spatial skills respond readily to training, with improvements often larger than the sex differences themselves. But because boys and girls show similar training effects, sex differences persist (Newcombe & Huttenlocher, 2006). In sum, biology and environment *jointly* explain variations in spatial and math performance—both within and between the sexes.

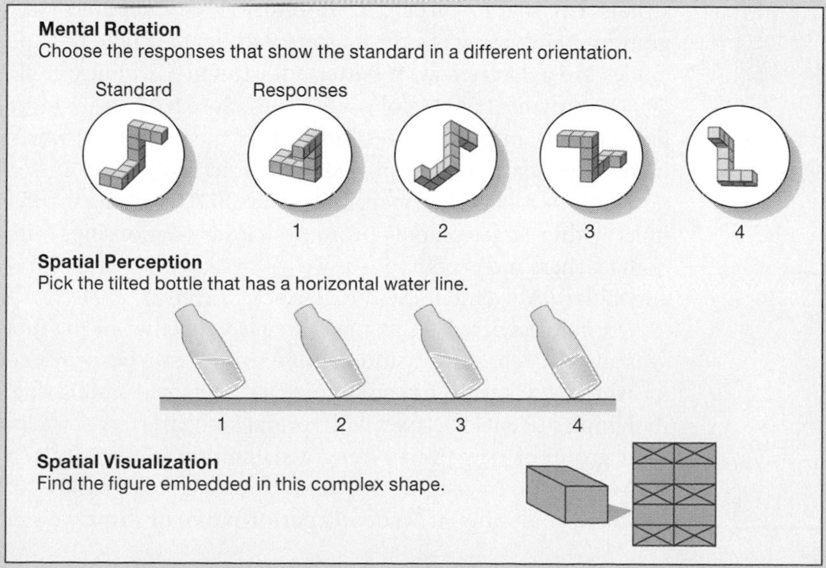

■ **FIGURE 11.11** ■ **Types of spatial tasks.** Large sex differences favoring males appear on mental rotation, and males do considerably better than females on spatial perception. In contrast, sex differences on spatial visualization are weak or nonexistent. (From M. C. Linn & A. C. Petersen, 1985, "Emergence and Characterization of Sex Differences in Spatial Ability: A Meta-Analysis," *Child Development, 56,* pp. 1482, 1483, 1485. © The Society for Research in Child Development. Reprinted with permission.)

Distressed young people whose school performance either remains low or drops sharply after school transition often show a persisting pattern of poor self-esteem, motivation, and achievement. In another study, researchers compared "multiple-problem" youths (those having both academic and mental health problems), youths having difficulties in just one area (either academic or mental health), and well-adjusted youths (those doing well in both areas) across the transition to high school. Although all groups declined in grade point average, well-adjusted students continued to get high marks and multiple-problem youths low marks, with the others falling in between. And as Figure 11.12 shows, the multiple-problem youths showed a far greater rise in truancy and out-of-school problem behaviors (Roeser, Eccles, & Freedman-Doan, 1999). For some, school transition initiates a downward spiral in academic performance and school involvement that leads to dropping out.

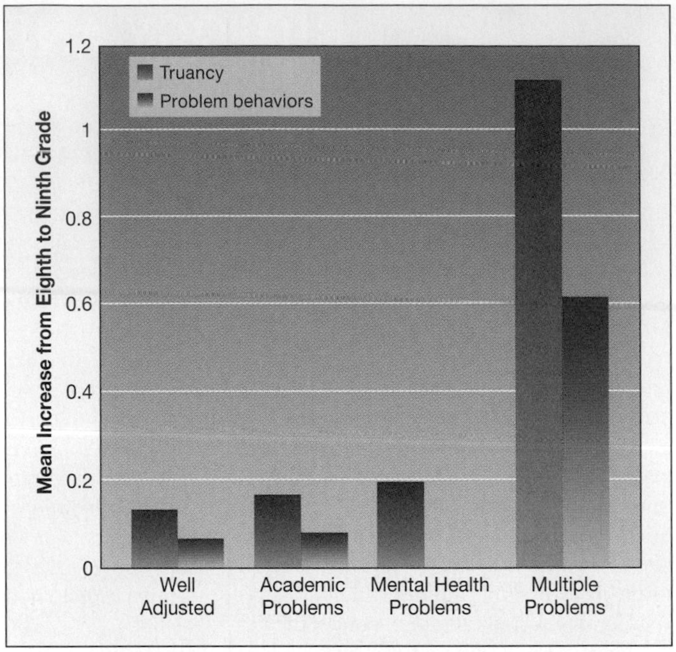

■ **FIGURE 11.12** ■ **Increase in truancy and out-of-school problem behaviors across the transition to high school in four groups of students.** Well-adjusted students, students with only academic problems, and students with only mental health problems showed little change. (Good students with mental health problems actually declined in problem behaviors, so no purple bar is shown for them.) In contrast, multiple-problem students—with both academic and mental health difficulties—increased sharply in truancy and problem behaviors after changing schools from eighth to ninth grade. (Adapted from Roeser, Eccles, & Freedman-Doan, 1999.)

■ **HELPING ADOLESCENTS ADJUST TO SCHOOL TRANSITIONS.** As these findings reveal, school transitions often lead to environmental changes that fit poorly with adolescents' developmental needs (Eccles, 2004). They disrupt close relationships with teachers at a time when adolescents need adult support. They emphasize competition during a period of heightened self-focusing. They reduce decision making and choice as the desire for autonomy is increasing. And they interfere with peer networks as young people become more concerned with peer acceptance.

This seventh grader hurries at his locker so he won't be late for class at his new middle school. Moving from a small, self-contained elementary school classroom to a large, impersonal secondary school is stressful for adolescents.

Support from parents, teachers, and peers can ease these strains. Parental involvement, monitoring, gradual autonomy granting, and emphasis on mastery rather than merely good grades are associated with better adjustment (Grolnick et al., 2000; Gutman, 2006). Adolescents with close friends are more likely to sustain these friendships across the transition, which increases social integration and academic motivation in the new school (Aikens, Bierman, & Parker, 2005). Forming smaller units within larger schools promotes closer relationships with both teachers and peers and—as we will see later—greater extracurricular involvement (Seidman, Aber, & French, 2004).

Other, less extensive changes are also effective. In the first year after a school transition, homerooms can be provided in which teachers offer academic and personal counseling. Assigning students to classes with several familiar peers or a constant group of new peers strengthens emotional security and social support. In schools that took these steps, students were less likely to decline in academic performance or display other

Applying What We Know

Supporting High Achievement During Adolescence

Factor	Description
Child-rearing practices	Authoritative parenting Joint parent–adolescent decision making Parent involvement in the adolescent's education
Peer influences	Peer valuing of and support for high achievement
School characteristics	Teachers who are warm and supportive, develop personal relationships with parents, and show them how to support their teenager's learning Learning activities that encourage high-level thinking Active student participation in learning activities and classroom decision making
Employment schedule	Job commitment limited to less than 15 hours per week High-quality vocational education for non-college-bound adolescents

adjustment problems, including low self-esteem, substance abuse, delinquency, and dropping out (Felner et al., 2002).

Finally, teenagers' perceptions of the sensitivity and flexibility of their school learning environments contribute substantially to successful school transitions. When schools minimize competition and differential treatment based on ability, middle school students are less likely to feel angry and depressed, to be truant, or to show declines in academic values, self-esteem, and achievement (Roeser, Eccles, & Sameroff, 2000).

Academic Achievement

Adolescent achievement is the result of a long history of cumulative effects. Early on, positive educational environments, both family and school, lead to personal traits that support achievement—intelligence, confidence in one's own abilities, the desire to succeed, and high educational aspirations. Nevertheless, improving an unfavorable environment can foster resilience among poorly performing young people. See Applying What We Know above for a summary of environmental factors that enhance achievement during the teenage years.

■ **CHILD-REARING PRACTICES.** Authoritative parenting is linked to higher grades in school among adolescents varying widely in SES, just as it predicts mastery-oriented behavior in childhood. In contrast, authoritarian and permissive styles are associated with lower grades (Collins & Steinberg, 2006; Vazsonyi, Hibbert, & Snider, 2003). Uninvolved parenting (low in both warmth and maturity demands) predicts the poorest grades and worsening school performance over time (Glasgow et al., 1997; Kaisa, Stattin, & Nurmi, 2000).

The link between authoritative parenting and adolescents' academic competence has been confirmed in countries with diverse value systems, including Argentina, Australia, China, Hong Kong, Pakistan, and Scotland (de Bruhn, Deković, & Meijnen, 2003; Steinberg, 2001). In Chapter 8, we noted that authoritative parents adjust their expectations to children's capacity to take responsibility for their own behavior. Adolescents whose parents engage in joint decision making, gradually permitting more autonomy with age, achieve especially well (Spera, 2005; Wang, Pomerantz, & Chen, 2007). Warmth, open discussion, firmness, and monitoring of the adolescents' whereabouts and activities make young people feel cared about and valued, encourage reflective thinking and self-regulation, and increase awareness of the importance of doing well in school. These factors, in turn, are related to mastery-oriented attributions, effort, achievement, and high educational aspirations (Aunola, Stattin, & Nurmi, 2000; Gregory & Weinstein, 2004; Trusty, 1999).

■ **PARENT–SCHOOL PARTNERSHIPS.** High-achieving students typically have parents who keep tabs on their child's progress, communicate with teachers, and make sure that their child is enrolled in challenging, well-taught classes. These efforts are just as important during middle and high school as they were earlier (Hill & Taylor, 2004). In a large, nationally representative sample of U.S. adolescents, parents' school involvement in eighth grade strongly predicted students' grade point average in tenth grade, beyond the influence of SES and previous academic achievement. This relationship held for each ethnic group included—black, white, Native-American, and Asian (Keith et al., 1998). Parents who are in frequent contact with the school send their teenager a message about the value of educa-

© ROYALTY-FREE/CORBIS

This parent is involved in his adolescent son's schooling. By keeping tabs on his progress, the father sends a message to his child about the importance of education and teaches skills for solving academic problems.

tion, model constructive solutions to academic problems, and promote wise educational decisions.

The daily stresses of living in low-income, high-risk neighborhoods reduce parents' energy for school involvement (Bowen, Bowen, & Ware, 2002). Yet stronger home–school links could relieve some of this stress. Schools can build parent–school partnerships by strengthening personal relationships between teachers and parents, tapping parents' talents to improve the quality of school programs, and including parents in school governance so they remain invested in school goals.

PEER INFLUENCES. Peers play an important role in adolescent achievement, in a way that relates to both family and school. Teenagers whose parents value achievement generally choose friends who share those values (Rubin, Bukowski, & Parker, 2006). For example, when Sabrina began to make new friends in junior high, she often studied with her girlfriends. Each girl wanted to do well and reinforced this desire in the others.

Peer support for high achievement also depends on the overall climate of the peer culture, which, for ethnic minority youths, is powerfully affected by the surrounding social order. In one study, integration into the school peer network predicted higher grades among Caucasians and Hispanics but not among Asians and African Americans (Faircloth & Hamm, 2005). Asian cultural values stress respect for family and teacher expectations over close peer ties (Chao & Tseng, 2002; Chen, 2005). African-American minority adolescents may observe that their ethnic group is worse off than the white majority in educational attainment, jobs, income, and housing. And discriminatory treatment by teachers and peers, often resulting from stereotypes that they are "not intelligent," triggers anger, anxiety, self-doubt, declines in achievement, association with peers who are not interested in school, and increases in problem behaviors (Wong, Eccles, & Sameroff, 2003).

Yet not all economically disadvantaged minority students respond this way. Case studies of inner-city, poverty-stricken African-American adolescents who were high-achieving and optimistic about their future revealed that they were intensely aware of oppression but believed in striving to alter their social position (O'Connor, 1997). How did they develop this sense of agency? Parents, relatives, and teachers had convinced them through discussion and example that injustice should not be tolerated and that, together, African Americans could overcome it—a perspective that encouraged both strong ethnic identity and high academic motivation, even in the face of peer pressures against excelling academically.

SCHOOL CHARACTERISTICS. Adolescents need school environments that are responsive to their expanding powers of reasoning and their emotional and social needs. Without appropriate learning experiences, their cognitive potential is unlikely to be realized.

Classroom Learning Experiences. As noted earlier, in large, departmentalized secondary schools, many adolescents report that their classes lack warmth and supportiveness—a circumstance that dampens their motivation. One study tracked changes in students' academic orientation in math classes from seventh to eighth grade. Those who entered classrooms high in teacher support, encouragement of student interaction about academic work, and promotion of mutual respect among classmates gained in academic motivation and cognitive self-regulation (reflected in whether they understood concepts and in their willingness to check their work). In classrooms emphasizing competition and public comparison of students, declines in motivation and self-regulation occurred (Ryan & Patrick, 2001).

Of course, an important benefit of separate classes in each subject is that adolescents can be taught by experts, who are more likely to encourage high-level thinking, teach effective learning strategies, and emphasize content relevant to students' experiences—factors that promote interest, effort, and achievement (Eccles, 2004). But many secondary school classrooms do not consistently provide interesting, challenging teaching. Because of the uneven quality of instruction, many seniors graduate from high school deficient in basic academic skills. Although the achievement gap separating African-American, Hispanic, and Native-American students from white students has declined since the 1970s, mastery of reading, writing, mathematics, and science by low-SES ethnic minority students remains disappointing (U.S. Department of Education, 2007b, 2007c, 2007d). Too often these young people attend underfunded schools with rundown buildings, outdated equipment, and textbook shortages. In some, crime and discipline problems receive more attention than teaching and learning. By middle school, many low-SES minority students have been placed in low academic tracks, compounding their learning difficulties.

Tracking. Ability grouping, as we saw in Chapter 9, is detrimental during the elementary school years. At least into middle or junior high school, mixed-ability classes are desirable. They effectively support the motivation and achievement of students who vary widely in academic progress (Gillies, 2003; Gillies & Ashman, 1996).

By high school, some grouping is unavoidable because certain aspects of education must dovetail with the young person's future educational and vocational plans. In the United States, high school students are counseled into college preparatory, vocational, or general education tracks. Unfortunately, low-SES minority students are assigned in large numbers to noncollege tracks, perpetuating educational inequalities of earlier years.

Longitudinal research following thousands of U.S. students from eighth to twelfth grade reveals that assignment to a college preparatory track accelerates academic progress, whereas assignment to a vocational or general education track decelerates it (Hallinan & Kubitschek, 1999). Even in secondary schools with no formal tracking program, low-SES minority students tend to be assigned to lower course levels in most or all academic subjects, resulting in *de facto* (unofficial) *tracking* (Lucas & Behrends, 2002).

Breaking out of a low academic track is difficult. Track or course enrollment is generally based on past performance, which is limited by placement history. Interviews with African-American students in one high school revealed that many thought their previous performance did not reflect their ability. Yet teachers and counselors, overburdened with other responsibilities, had little time to reconsider individual cases (Ogbu, 2003). And compared to students in higher tracks, those in low tracks exert substantially less effort—a difference due in part to less stimulating classroom experiences (Carbonaro, 2005).

High school students are separated into academic and vocational tracks in virtually all industrialized nations. In China, Japan, and most Western European countries, students' placement in high school is determined by their performance on a national exam. The outcome usually fixes the young person's future possibilities. In the United States, students who are not assigned to a college preparatory track or who do poorly in high school can still attend college. Ultimately, however, many young people do not benefit from the more open U.S. system. By adolescence, SES differences in quality of education and academic achievement are greater in the United States than in most other industrialized countries (Marks, Cresswell, & Ainley, 2006). And the United States has a higher percentage of young people who see themselves as educational failures and drop out of high school (see Figure 11.13).

■ **PART-TIME WORK.** In high school, nearly half of U.S. adolescents are employed—a greater percentage than in other developed countries (Bowlby & McMullen, 2002; Children's Defense Fund, 2008). Most are middle-SES adolescents in pursuit of spending money rather than vocational exploration and training. Low-income teenagers who need to contribute to family income or to support themselves find it harder to get jobs (U.S. Department of Education, 2009).

Adolescents typically hold jobs that involve low-level, repetitive tasks and provide little contact with adult supervisors. A heavy commitment to such jobs is harmful. The more hours students work, the poorer their school attendance, the lower their grades, the less likely they are to participate in extracurricular activities, and the more likely they are to drop out (Marsh & Kleitman, 2005). Students who spend many hours at such jobs also tend to feel more distant from their parents and report more drug and alcohol use and delinquent acts (Kouvonen & Kivivuori, 2001; Staff & Uggen, 2003).

In contrast, participation in work–study programs or other jobs that provide academic and vocational learning opportunities is related to positive school and work attitudes, improved achievement, and reduced delinquency (Hamilton & Hamilton, 2000; Staff & Uggen, 2003). Yet high-quality vocational preparation for non-college-bound U.S. adolescents is scarce. Unlike some European nations, the United States has no widespread training system to prepare youths for skilled business and industrial occupations and manual trades. Although U.S. federal and state governments support some job-training programs, most are brief to make a difference. Poorly skilled adolescents need intensive training and academic remediation before they are ready to enter the job market. And at present, these programs serve only a small minority of young people who need assistance.

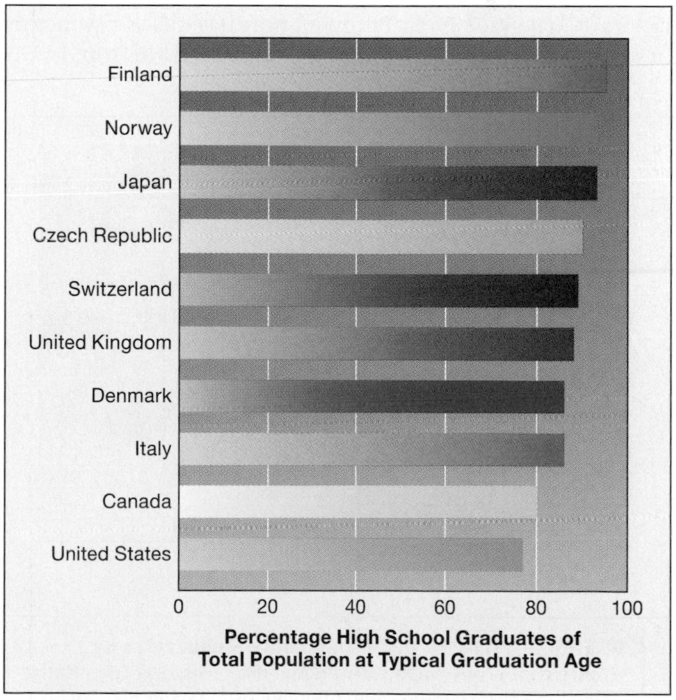

■ **FIGURE 11.13** ■ **High school graduation rates in ten industrialized nations.** The United States ranks below many other developed countries. (From OECD, 2008a.)

Dropping Out

Across the aisle from Louis in math class sat Norman, who daydreamed, crumpled his notes into his pocket after class, and rarely did his homework. On test days, he twirled a rabbit's foot for good luck but left most questions blank. Louis and Norman had been classmates since fourth grade, but they had little to do with each other. To Louis, who was quick at schoolwork, Norman seemed to live in another world. Once or twice a week, Norman cut class; one spring day, he stopped coming altogether.

Norman is one of about 10 percent of U.S. 16- to 24-year-olds who dropped out of high school and remain without a diploma or a GED (U.S. Department of Education, 2009). The dropout rate is higher among boys than girls and is particularly high among low-SES ethnic minority youths, especially Native-American and Hispanic teenagers (see Figure 11.14). The decision to leave school has dire consequences. Youths without upper secondary education have much lower literacy scores than high school graduates; they lack the skills employers value in today's knowledge-based economy. Consequently, dropouts have much lower employment rates than high school graduates. Even when employed, dropouts are far more likely to remain in menial, low-paying jobs and to be out of work from time to time.

FACTORS RELATED TO DROPPING OUT. Although many dropouts achieve poorly and show high rates of norm-violating acts, a substantial number are like Norman—young people with few behavior problems who simply experience academic difficulties and quietly disengage from school (Janosz et al., 2000; Newcomb et al., 2002). The pathway to dropping out starts early. Risk factors in first grade predict dropout nearly as well as risk factors in secondary school (Entwisle, Alexander, & Olson, 2005).

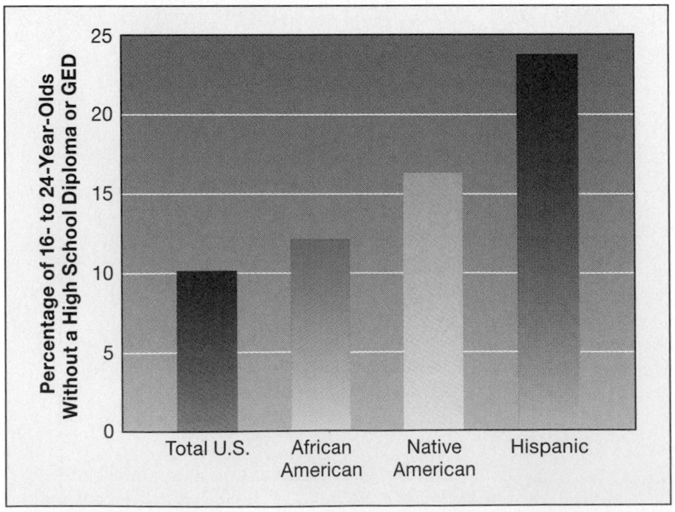

FIGURE 11.14 U.S. high school dropout rates by ethnicity. Because many African-American, Hispanic, and Native-American young people come from low-income and poverty-stricken families and attended underfunded, poor-quality schools, their dropout rates are above the national average. Rates for Native-American and Hispanic youths are especially high. (From U.S. Department of Education, 2009.)

Norman had a long history of marginal-to-failing school grades and low academic self-esteem. Faced with a challenging task, he gave up, relying on luck—his rabbit's foot—to get by. As Norman got older, he attended class less regularly, paid little attention when he was there, and rarely did his homework. He didn't join school clubs or participate in sports. As a result, few teachers or students got to know him well. By the day he left, Norman felt alienated from all aspects of school life.

As with other dropouts, Norman's family background contributed to his problems. Compared with other students, even those with the same grade profile, dropouts are more likely to have parents who are uninvolved in their teenager's education and engage in little monitoring of their youngster's daily activities. Many are single parents, never finished high school themselves, and are unemployed (Englund, Egeland, & Collins, 2008; Pagani et al., 2008).

Academically marginal students who drop out often have school experiences that undermine their chances for success: grade retention, which marks them as academic failures; large, impersonal secondary schools; and classes with unsupportive teachers and few opportunities for active participation (Hardre & Reeve, 2003; Lee & Burkam, 2003). In such schools, rule breaking is common and often results in suspension, which—by excluding students from classes—contributes further to academic failure (Christie, Jolivette, & Nelson, 2007). Recent reports indicate that over 60 percent of adolescents in some U.S. inner-city high schools do not graduate. Students in general education and vocational tracks, where teaching tends to be the least stimulating, are three times as likely to drop out as those in a college preparatory track (U.S. Department of Education, 2009).

PREVENTION STRATEGIES. Among the diverse strategies available for helping teenagers at risk of dropping out, several common themes are related to success:

- *Remedial instruction and counseling that offer personalized attention.* Most potential dropouts need intensive remedial instruction in small classes that foster warm, caring teacher–student relationships. To overcome the negative psychological effects of repeated school failure, academic assistance must be combined with social support (Christenson & Thurlow, 2004). In one successful approach, at-risk students are matched with retired adults, who serve as tutors, mentors, and role models in addressing academic and vocational needs (Prevatt, 2003).
- *High-quality vocational training.* For many marginal students, the real-life nature of vocational education is more comfortable and effective than purely academic work. To work well, vocational education must carefully integrate academic and job-related instruction so students see the relevance of classroom experiences to their future goals (Harvey, 2001).
- *Efforts to address the many factors in students' lives related to leaving school early.* Programs that strengthen parent involvement, offer flexible work–study arrangements, and provide on-site child care for teenage parents can make staying in school easier for at-risk adolescents.

AP IMAGES/CAROLYN KASTER

A baking and pastry student puts the finishing touches on a cake at a technical high school in Pennsylvania. High-quality vocational education, integrated with academic instruction, helps students at risk for dropping out see the relevance of school learning to their future goals.

- *Participation in extracurricular activities.* Another way of helping marginal students is to draw them into the community life of the school. The most powerful influence on extracurricular involvement is small school size (Barker & Gump, 1964; Feldman & Matjasko, 2007). In high schools of 500 to 700 students or less, potential dropouts are far more likely to be needed to help staff and operate school activities. In large schools, creation of smaller "schools within schools" has the same effect.

  Participation focusing on the arts, community service, and vocational development promotes diverse aspects of adjustment, including improved academic performance, reduced antisocial behavior, more favorable self-esteem and initiative, and increased peer acceptance (Fredricks & Eccles, 2005, 2006; Mahoney, 2000). Adolescents with academic, emotional, and social problems are especially likely to benefit (Marsh & Kleitman, 2002).

As we conclude our discussion of academic achievement, let's place the school dropout problem in historical perspective. Over the past half-century, the percentage of U.S. young people completing high school by age 24 increased steadily, from less than 50 percent to 90 percent. College attendance also rose during this period: Today, nearly 40 percent of U.S. young people earn college degrees. Despite the worrisome decline in male college enrollment noted earlier, U.S. higher education rates continue to rank among the highest in the world (U.S. Department of Education, 2007a).

Finally, although many dropouts get caught in a vicious cycle in which their lack of self-confidence and skills prevents them from seeking further education and training, about one-third return to finish their secondary education within a few years (U.S. Department of Education, 2008). And some extend their schooling further, realizing how essential education is for a rewarding job and a satisfying adult life.

ASK YOURSELF

>> REVIEW
List ways that parents can promote their adolescent's academic achievement. Explain why each is effective.

>> APPLY
Tanisha is finishing sixth grade. She can either continue in her current school through eighth grade or switch to a much larger seventh- to ninth-grade middle school. Which choice would you suggest, and why?

>> CONNECT
How are educational practices that prevent school dropout similar to those that improve learning for adolescents in general?

>> REFLECT
Describe your own experiences in making the transition to middle or junior high school and then to high school. What did you find stressful? What helped you adjust?

Summary

PHYSICAL DEVELOPMENT

Conceptions of Adolescence

How have conceptions of adolescence changed over the past century?

>> **Adolescence** is the period of transition between childhood and adulthood. Early theorists viewed adolescence as either a biologically determined period of storm and stress or entirely influenced by the social environment. Contemporary research shows that adolescence is a product of biological, psychological, and social forces.

Puberty: The Physical Transition to Adulthood

Describe pubertal changes in body size, proportions, motor performance, and sexual maturity.

>> Hormonal changes beginning in middle childhood initiate **puberty,** on average, two years earlier for girls than for boys. The first outward sign is the **growth spurt.** As the body enlarges, girls' hips and boys' shoulders broaden. Girls add more fat, boys more muscle. Puberty brings improvement in gross motor performance—slow and gradual for girls, more dramatic for boys. Nevertheless, the number of adolescents participating in regular physical activity declines sharply with age.

AP IMAGES/THE ALBUQUERQUE JOURNAL, MARLA BROSE

>> At puberty, changes in **primary** and **secondary sexual characteristics** accompany rapid body growth. **Menarche** occurs late in the girl's sequence of pubertal events, after the growth spurt peaks. In boys, the peak in growth occurs later, preceded by enlargement of the sex organs and **spermarche.**

What factors influence the timing of puberty?

>> Heredity, nutrition, exercise, and overall physical health contribute to pubertal timing. A **secular trend** toward earlier menarche has occurred in industrialized nations as physical well-being increased.

What changes in the brain take place during adolescence?

>> Pruning of unused synapses in the cerebral cortex continues in adolescence, and growth and myelination of stimulated neural fibers accelerate, supporting cognitive advances. Also, neurons become more responsive to excitatory neurotransmitters, a change that probably contributes to teenagers' drive for novel experiences.

>> Changes also occur in brain regulation of sleep timing, leading to a sleep "phase delay." Sleep deprivation increases, contributing to poorer achievement, depressed mood, and behavior problems.

The Psychological Impact of Pubertal Events

Explain adolescents' reactions to the physical changes of puberty.

>> Girls generally react to menarche with mixed emotions, although those who receive advance information and support from family members respond more positively. Although boys usually know ahead of time about spermarche, they also react with mixed feelings. Boys receive less social support for pubertal changes than girls.

>> Besides higher hormone levels, negative life events and adult-structured situations are associated with adolescents' negative moods. In contrast, teenagers feel upbeat when with peers and in self-chosen leisure activities.

>> Psychological distancing between parent and child accompanies puberty. It may be a modern substitute for physical departure from the family, which typically occurs at sexual maturity in primate species.

Describe the impact of pubertal timing on adolescent adjustment, noting sex differences.

>> Early-maturing boys and late-maturing girls, whose appearance closely matches cultural standards of physical attractiveness, have a more positive **body image** and usually adjust well in adolescence. In contrast, early-maturing girls and late-maturing boys, who fit in least well with peers, experience emotional and social difficulties, which—for girls—persist into early adulthood.

Health Issues

Describe nutritional needs during adolescence, and cite factors that contribute to eating disorders.

>> Nutritional requirements increase with rapid body growth. Poor eating habits lead to vitamin and mineral deficiencies in many adolescents. Frequency of family meals is associated with healthy eating.

>> Early puberty, certain personality traits, maladaptive family interactions, and societal emphasis on thinness heighten risk of eating disorders such as **anorexia nervosa** and **bulimia nervosa.**

Discuss factors that influence adolescent sexual attitudes and behavior.

>> North American attitudes toward adolescent sex remain relatively restrictive, and the social environment—parents, schools, and mass media—delivers contradictory messages. Compared with a generation ago, U.S. adolescents' sexual attitudes and behavior have become more liberal, with a slight swing back recently.

© JEFF GREENBERG/PHOTOEDIT

>> Early, frequent sexual activity is linked to factors associated with economic disadvantage. Many sexually active teenagers do not practice contraception consistently. Adolescent cognitive processes and a lack of social support for responsible sexual behavior, including access to birth control, underlie this failure to take precautions against pregnancy.

>> Biological factors, including heredity and prenatal hormone levels, play an important role in homosexuality. Lesbian and gay teenagers face special challenges in developing a positive sexual identity.

>> Early sexual activity combined with inconsistent contraceptive use results in high rates of sexually transmitted diseases (STDs) among U.S. adolescents.

Discuss factors related to adolescent pregnancy and parenthood.

>> Adolescent pregnancy and parenthood rates are higher in the United States than in any other industrialized nation. Life conditions linked to economic disadvantage, along with personal attributes, contribute to adolescent childbearing. Adolescent parenthood is associated with school dropout, reduced chances of marriage, greater likelihood of divorce, and poverty.

>> Effective sex education, access to contraceptives, and programs that build academic and social competence help prevent early pregnancy. Adolescent mothers need school programs that provide job training, instruction in life-management skills, child care, and family support that is sensitive to their needs. When teenage fathers stay involved, children develop more favorably.

What personal and social factors are related to adolescent substance use and abuse?

>> Teenage alcohol and drug use is pervasive in industrialized nations, reflecting the sensation seeking of adolescence as well as a drug-dependent cultural context. The minority who move to substance abuse often start drug-taking early, display other antisocial behaviors, and come from families with mental health problems. Effective prevention programs work with parents early, to reduce family adversity and strengthen parenting skills, and build teenagers' competence.

COGNITIVE DEVELOPMENT

Piaget's Theory: The Formal Operational Stage

What are the major characteristics of formal operational thought?

>> During Piaget's **formal operational stage,** adolescents engage in **hypothetico-deductive reasoning.** When faced with a problem, they start with a hypothesis about variables that might affect an outcome, deduce logical, testable inferences, and systematically isolate and combine variables to see which inferences are confirmed.

>> **Propositional thought** also develops. Adolescents can evaluate the logic of verbal statements apart from real-world circumstances.

Discuss follow-up research on formal operational thought and its implications for the accuracy of Piaget's formal operational stage.

» Adolescents and adults are most likely to think abstractly and systematically in situations in which they have had extensive guidance and practice in using such reasoning. Individuals in tribal and village societies rarely master formal operational tasks. Piaget's highest stage seems to depend on specific learning opportunities made available in school.

An Information-Processing View of Adolescent Cognitive Development

How do information-processing researchers account for cognitive changes in adolescence?

» Information-processing researchers believe that a variety of specific mechanisms underlie cognitive gains in adolescence: improved attention and inhibition, more effective strategies, greater knowledge, improved cognitive self-regulation, gains in speed of thinking and processing capacity, and, especially, advances in metacognition.

» Research on scientific reasoning indicates that the ability to coordinate theory with evidence improves as adolescents solve increasingly complex problems and reflect on their thinking, acquiring more mature metacognitive understanding.

Consequences of Adolescent Cognitive Changes

Describe typical reactions of adolescents that result from their advancing cognition.

» As adolescents reflect on their own thoughts, they think more about themselves, and two distorted images of the relation between self and other appear—the **imaginary audience** and the **personal fable.** Teenagers' capacity to think about possibilities prompts idealistic visions at odds with everyday reality, and they often become fault-finding critics.

» Compared with adults, adolescents have difficulty with decision making. They more often fall back on well-learned, intuitive judgments and emphasize short-term over long-term goals.

© BOB DAEMMRICH/THE IMAGE WORKS

Sex Differences in Mental Abilities

What factors contribute to sex differences in mental abilities during adolescence?

» Girls score slightly better than boys on tests of verbal ability, and their advantage in reading and writing achievement increases, probably due to earlier development of the left hemisphere of the cerebral cortex and greater maternal verbal stimulation. Gender-stereotyping of language arts as "feminine" and regimented teaching may weaken boys' literacy skills.

» Boys surpass girls in complex mathematical reasoning. Overall, the gender difference is small, but it is greater among the most capable students. Boys' biologically based superior spatial skills enhance their mathematical problem solving. Gender stereotyping of math as "masculine" and self-confidence and interest in doing math contribute to boys' spatial and math advantages.

Learning in School

Discuss the impact of school transitions on adolescent adjustment.

» Girls experience more adjustment difficulties than boys after transitioning to middle or junior high school because other life changes (puberty and the beginning of dating) also occur at that time. Teenagers coping with added stresses—especially those with both academic and mental health difficulties—are at greatest risk for adjustment problems following school transition.

Discuss family, peer, school, and employment influences on academic achievement during adolescence.

» Authoritative parenting and parents' school involvement promote high achievement. Teenagers whose parents encourage achievement are likely to choose friends from similar families.

» Warm, supportive learning environments with activities that emphasize high-level thinking enable adolescents to reach their academic potential.

» By high school, separate educational tracks that dovetail with students' future plans are necessary. But high school tracking in the United States often extends the educational inequalities of earlier years.

» The more hours students devote to a part-time job, the poorer their school attendance, academic performance, and extracurricular participation. In contrast, work–study programs that provide academic and vocational learning opportunities predict positive school and work attitudes and better academic achievement among non-college-bound teenagers.

What factors increase the risk of high school dropout?

» About 10 percent of U.S. young people leave high school and remain without a diploma, many of whom are low-SES minority youths. Contributing factors include a long history of poor school performance, lack of parental support for academic achievement, large impersonal classes, and unstimulating teaching.

Important Terms and Concepts

© ROLF BRUDERER/CORBIS

As adolescents spend less time with family, peer groups become more tightly knit into cliques. Mixed-sex cliques provide boys and girls with models of how to interact and a chance to do so without having to be intimate.

CHAPTER 12

Emotional and Social Development in Adolescence

Louis sat on the grassy hillside overlooking the high school, waiting for his best friend, Darryl, to arrive from his fourth-period class. The two boys often met at noontime and had lunch together. Watching as hundreds of students poured onto the school grounds, Louis reflected on what he had learned in government class that day. "Suppose I *had* been born in the People's Republic of China. I'd be sitting here, speaking a different language, being called by a different name, and thinking about the world in different ways. Wow," Louis pondered. "I am who I am through some quirk of fate."

Louis awoke from his thoughts with a start to see Darryl standing in front of him. "Hey, dreamer! I've been shouting and waving from the bottom of the hill for five minutes. How come you're so spaced out lately, Louis?"

"Oh, just wondering about stuff—what I want, what I believe in. My older brother Jules—I envy him. He seems to know more about where he's going. I'm up in the air about it. You ever feel that way?"

"Yeah, a lot," Darryl admitted, looking at Louis seriously. "I wonder, what am I really like? Who will I become?"

© MARY KATE DENNY/PHOTOEDIT

Louis and Darryl's introspective remarks are signs of a major reorganization of the self at adolescence: the development of identity. Both young people are attempting to formulate who they are—their personal values and the directions they will pursue in life.

We begin this chapter with Erikson's account of identity development and the research it has stimulated on teenagers' thoughts and feelings about themselves. The quest for identity extends to many aspects of development. We will see how a sense of cultural belonging, moral understanding, and masculine and feminine self-images are refined during adolescence. And as parent–child relationships are revised and young people become increasingly independent of the family, friendships and peer networks become crucial contexts for bridging the gap between childhood and adulthood. Our chapter concludes with a discussion of several serious adjustment problems of adolescence: depression, suicide, and delinquency.

Erikson's Theory: Identity versus Role Confusion

Erikson (1950, 1968) was the first to recognize **identity** as the major personality achievement of adolescence and as a crucial step toward becoming a productive, content adult. Constructing an identity involves defining who you are, what you value, and the directions you choose to pursue in life. One expert described it as an explicit theory of oneself as a rational agent—one who acts on the basis of reason, takes responsibility for those actions, and can explain them (Moshman, 2005). This search for what is true and real about the self drives many choices—vocation, interpersonal relationships, community involvement, ethnic-group membership, and expression of one's sexual orientation, as well as moral, political, and religious ideals.

Although the seeds of identity formation are planted early, not until late adolescence and early adulthood do young people become absorbed in this task. According to Erikson, in complex societies, teenagers experience an *identity crisis*—a temporary period of distress as they experiment with alternatives before settling on values and goals. They go through a process of inner soul-searching, sifting through characteristics that defined the self in childhood and combining them with emerging traits, capacities, and commitments. Then they mold these into a solid inner core that provides a mature identity—a sense of self-continuity as they move through various roles in daily life. Once formed, identity continues to be refined in adulthood as people reevaluate earlier commitments and choices.

Erikson called the psychological conflict of adolescence **identity versus role confusion.** If young people's earlier conflicts were resolved negatively or if society limits their choices to ones that do not match their abilities and desires, they may appear shallow, directionless, and unprepared for the challenges of adulthood.

Current theorists agree with Erikson that questioning of values, plans, and priorities is necessary for a mature identity, but they no longer describe this process as a "crisis" (Grotevant, 1998; Kroger, 2005). For most young people, identity development is not traumatic and disturbing but, rather, a process of *exploration* followed by *commitment.* As young people try out life possibilities, they gather important information about themselves and their environment and move toward making enduring decisions. In doing so, they forge an organized self-structure (Arnett, 2000, 2006; Moshman, 2005). In the following sections, we will see that adolescents go about the task of defining the self in ways that closely match Erikson's description.

Self-Understanding

During adolescence, the young person's vision of the self becomes more complex, well-organized, and consistent. Compared with younger children, adolescents have more or less positive feelings about an increasing variety of aspects of the self. Over time, they form a balanced, integrated representation of their strengths and limitations (Harter, 2003, 2006). Changes in self-concept and self-esteem set the stage for developing a unified personal identity.

Changes in Self-Concept

Recall that by the end of middle childhood, children can describe themselves in terms of personality traits. In early adolescence, they unify separate traits ("smart," "talented") into more abstract descriptors ("intelligent"). But these generalizations are not interconnected and are often contradictory. For example, 12- to 14-year-olds might mention opposing traits—"intelligent" and "dork," "shy" and "outgoing." These disparities result from the expansion of adolescents' social world, which creates pressure to display different selves in different contexts—self with mother, father, close friends, and romantic partner; self as student, athlete, and employee. As teenagers become increasingly aware of inconsistencies, they agonize over "which is the real me" (Harter, 1998, 2003, 2006).

From middle to late adolescence, cognitive changes enable teenagers to combine their traits into an organized system. Their use of qualifiers ("I have a *fairly* quick temper," "I'm not *thoroughly* honest") reveals their awareness that psychological qualities can vary from one situation to the next. Older adolescents also add integrating principles that make sense out of formerly troublesome contradictions. "I'm very adaptable," said one young person. "When I'm around my friends, who think what I say is important, I'm talkative; but around my family I'm quiet because they're never interested enough to really listen to me" (Damon, 1990, p. 88).

Compared with school-age children, teenagers place more emphasis on social virtues, such as being friendly, considerate, kind, and cooperative—traits that reflect adolescents' increasing concern with being viewed positively by others. Among older adolescents, personal and moral values also appear as key themes. As young people revise their views of themselves to include enduring beliefs and plans, they move toward the unity of self that is central to identity development.

Changes in Self-Esteem

Self-esteem, the evaluative side of self-concept, continues to differentiate in adolescence. Teenagers add several new dimensions of self-evaluation—close friendship, romantic appeal, and job competence—to those of middle childhood (see Chapter 10, page 331) (Harter, 1999, 2003, 2006).

Level of self-esteem also changes. Though some adolescents experience temporary or persisting declines after school transitions (see Chapter 11, pages 390 and 392), self-esteem rises for most young people, who report feeling especially good about their peer relationships and athletic capabilities (Cole et al., 2001; Twenge & Campbell, 2001). Teenagers often assert that they have become more mature, capable, personable, and attractive than in the past. In a study of adolescents in 13 industrialized nations, most were optimistic, felt a sense of control over their personal and vocational futures, and expressed

During adolescence, self-esteem rises for most young people, who feel especially good about their peer relationships and athletic capabilities.

confidence in their ability to cope with life's problems (Grob & Flammer, 1999).

At the same time, individual differences in self-esteem become increasingly stable in adolescence (Trzesniewski, Donnellan, & Robins, 2003). And positive relationships among self-esteem, valuing of various activities, and success at those activities strengthen. For example, academic self-esteem is a powerful predictor of teenagers' judgments of the importance and usefulness of school subjects, willingness to exert effort, achievement, and eventual career choice (Bleeker & Jacobs, 2004; Denissen, Zarrett, & Eccles, 2007; Valentine, DuBois, & Cooper, 2004; Whitesell et al., 2009).

Across SES and ethnic groups, individuals with mostly favorable self-esteem profiles tend to be well-adjusted, sociable, and conscientious. In contrast, low self-esteem in all areas is linked to adjustment difficulties (DuBois et al., 1999; Robins et al., 2001). But certain self-esteem factors are more strongly related to adjustment. Teenagers who feel highly dissatisfied with parental relationships often are aggressive and antisocial. Those with poor academic self-esteem tend to be anxious and unfocused. And those with negative peer relationships are likely to be anxious and depressed (Marsh, Parada, & Ayotte, 2004; Rudolph, Caldwell, & Conley, 2005).

In adolescence as in childhood, authoritative parenting predicts high self-esteem, as does encouragement from teachers (Carlson, Uppal, & Prosser, 2000; McKinney, Donnelly, & Renk, 2008; Wilkinson, 2004). In contrast, teenagers whose parents are critical and insulting have unstable and generally low self-esteem (Kernis, 2002). Feedback that is negative, inconsistent, or not contingent on performance triggers, at best, uncertainty about the self's capacities and, at worst, a sense of being incompetent and unloved. Teenagers who experience such parenting tend to rely only on peers, not on adults, to affirm their self-esteem—a risk factor for adjustment difficulties (DuBois et al., 1999, 2002).

Paths to Identity

Adolescents' well-organized self-descriptions and differentiated sense of self-esteem provide the cognitive foundation for forming an identity. Using a clinical interviewing procedure devised by James Marcia (1980) or briefer questionnaire measures, researchers commonly evaluate progress in identity development on two key criteria derived from Erikson's theory: *exploration* and *commitment.* Their various combinations yield four *identity statuses,* summarized in Table 12.1 on page 404: **identity achievement,** commitment to values, beliefs, and goals following a period of exploration; **identity moratorium,** exploration without having reached commitment; **identity foreclosure,** commitment in the absence of exploration; and **identity diffusion,** an apathetic state characterized by lack of both exploration and commitment.

Identity development follows many paths. Some young people remain in one status, whereas others experience many status transitions. And the pattern often varies across *identity domains,* such as sexual orientation, vocation, and religious and political values. Most young people change from "lower" statuses (foreclosure or diffusion) to higher ones (moratorium or achievement) between their mid-teens and mid-twenties, but some move in the reverse direction (Kroger, 2001, 2005; Meeus, 1996).

Because attending college provides opportunities to explore career options and lifestyles, college students make more identity progress than they did in high school (Montgomery & Côté, 2003). After college, they often sample a broad range of life experiences before choosing a life course. Those who go to work immediately after high school graduation settle on a self-definition earlier. But if they encounter obstacles to realizing their occupational goals because of lack of training or vocational choices, they are at risk for identity foreclosure or diffusion (Cohen et al., 2003; Eccles et al., 2003).

At one time, researchers thought that adolescent girls postponed establishing an identity and instead focused on Erikson's next stage, intimacy development. Some girls do show more sophisticated reasoning than boys in identity domains related to intimacy, such as sexuality and family versus career priorities. Otherwise, adolescents of both sexes typically make progress on identity concerns before experiencing genuine intimacy in relationships (Berman et al., 2006; Kroger, 2000).

Identity Status and Psychological Well-Being

A wealth of research verifies that both identity achievement and moratorium are psychologically healthy routes to a mature self-definition. Long-term foreclosure and diffusion, in contrast, are maladaptive.

■ TABLE 12.1 ■ *The Four Identity Statuses*

IDENTITY STATUS	DESCRIPTION	EXAMPLE
Identity achievement	Having already explored alternatives, identity-achieved individuals are committed to a clearly formulated set of self-chosen values and goals. They feel a sense of psychological well-being, of sameness through time, and of knowing where they are going.	When asked how willing she would be to give up going into her chosen occupation if something better came along, Lauren responded, "Well, I might, but I doubt it. I've thought long and hard about law as a career. I'm pretty certain it's for me."
Identity moratorium	*Moratorium* means "delay or holding pattern." These individuals have not yet made definite commitments. They are in the process of exploring—gathering information and trying out activities, with the desire to find values and goals to guide their lives.	When asked whether he had ever had doubts about his religious beliefs, Ramón said, "Yes, I guess I'm going through that right now. I just don't see how there can be a God and yet so much evil in the world."
Identity foreclosure	Identity-foreclosed individuals have committed themselves to values and goals without exploring alternatives. They accept a ready-made identity chosen for them by authority figures—usually parents but sometimes teachers, religious leaders, or romantic partners.	When asked if she had ever reconsidered her political beliefs, Hillary answered, "No, not really, our family is pretty much in agreement on these things."
Identity diffusion	Identity-diffused individuals lack clear direction. They are neither committed to values and goals nor actively trying to reach them. They may never have explored alternatives or may have found the task too threatening and overwhelming.	When asked about his attitude toward nontraditional gender roles, Joel responded, "Oh, I don't know. It doesn't make much difference to me. I can take it or leave it."

Adolescents in moratorium resemble identity-achieved individuals in using an active, *information-gathering cognitive style* when making personal decisions and solving problems: They seek out relevant information, evaluate it carefully, and critically reflect on and revise their views (Berzonsky, 2003; Berzonsky & Kuk, 2000). Young people who are identity-achieved or exploring have higher self-esteem, feel more in control of their own lives, are more likely to view school and work as feasible avenues for realizing their aspirations, and are more advanced in moral reasoning (Adams & Marshall, 1996; Kroger, 2007; Serafini & Adams, 2002).

Adolescents stuck in either foreclosure or diffusion are passive in the face of identity concerns and have adjustment difficulties. Foreclosed individuals display a *dogmatic, inflexible cognitive style,* internalizing the values and beliefs of parents and others without deliberate evaluation and resisting information that threatens their position (Berzonsky & Kuk, 2000). Most fear rejection by people on whom they depend for affection and self-esteem. A few foreclosed teenagers who are alienated from their families and society may join cults or other extremist groups, uncritically adopting a way of life different from their past.

Long-term diffused individuals are the least mature in identity development. They typically use a *diffuse-avoidant cognitive style* in which they avoid dealing with personal decisions and problems and, instead, allow current situational pressures to dictate their reactions (Berzonsky & Kuk, 2000; Krettenauer, 2005). Taking an "I don't care" attitude, they entrust themselves to luck or fate and tend to go along with the crowd. As a result, they experience time management and academic difficulties and, of all young people, are most likely to use and abuse drugs (Archer & Waterman, 1990; Schwartz et al., 2005). Often at the heart of their apathy is a sense of hopelessness about the future.

Factors Affecting Identity Development

Adolescent identity formation begins a lifelong, dynamic process in which a change in either the individual or the context opens up the possibility of reformulating identity (Kunnen & Bosma, 2003). A wide variety of factors influence identity development.

Identity status, as we have just seen, is both cause and consequence of personality characteristics. Adolescents who assume that absolute truth is always attainable tend to be foreclosed, while those who doubt that they will ever feel certain about anything are more often identity-diffused. Young people who appreciate that they can use rational criteria to choose among alternatives are likely to be in a state of moratorium or identity achievement (Berzonsky & Kuk, 2000; Boyes & Chandler, 1992).

Teenagers' identity development is enhanced when their families serve as a "secure base" from which they can confidently move out into the wider world. Adolescents who feel attached to their parents but also free to voice their own opinions tend to be in a state of moratorium or identity achievement (Berzonsky, 2004; Luyckx, Goossens, & Soenens, 2006; Schwartz et al., 2005). Foreclosed teenagers usually have close bonds with parents but lack opportunities for healthy separation. And diffused young people report the lowest levels of parental support and of warm, open communication (Reis & Youniss, 2004; Zimmerman & Becker-Stoll, 2002).

Interaction with diverse peers through school and community activities encourages adolescents to explore values and role possibilities (Barber et al., 2005). And close friends, like parents, can act as a secure base, providing emotional support, assistance, and models of identity development. In one study, 15-year-olds with warm, trusting peer ties were more involved

Applying What We Know

Supporting Healthy Identity Development

Strategy	Explanation
Engage in warm, open communication.	Provides both emotional support and freedom to explore values and goals
Initiate discussions that promote high-level thinking at home and at school.	Encourages rational and deliberate selection among beliefs and values
Provide opportunities to participate in extracurricular activities and vocational training programs.	Permits young people to explore the real world of adult work
Provide opportunities to talk with adults and peers who have worked through identity questions.	Offers models of identity achievement and advice on how to resolve identity concerns
Provide opportunities to explore ethnic heritage and learn about other cultures in an atmosphere of respect.	Fosters identity achievement in all areas and ethnic tolerance, which supports the identity explorations of others

in exploring relationship issues—for example, thinking about what they valued in close friends and in a life partner (Meeus, Oosterwegel, & Vollebergh, 2002). In another study, young people's attachment to friends predicted progress in choosing a career (Felsman & Blustein, 1999).

Identity development also depends on schools and communities that offer rich and varied opportunities for exploration. Supportive experiences include classrooms that promote high-level thinking, extracurricular activities that enable teenagers to take on responsible roles, teachers and counselors who encourage low-SES students to go to college, and vocational training that immerses young people in the real world of adult work (Coatsworth et al., 2005; McIntosh, Metz, & Youniss, 2005).

Culture strongly influences an aspect of mature identity not captured by the identity-status approach: constructing a sense of self-continuity despite major personal changes. In one study, researchers asked Native Canadian and cultural-majority 12- to 20-year-olds to describe themselves in the past and in the present and then to justify why they were the same continuous person (Lalonde & Chandler, 2005). Most cultural-majority adolescents used an individualistic approach: They described an *enduring personal essence,* a core self that remained the same despite change. In contrast, Native Canadian youths took an interdependent approach that emphasized a *constantly transforming self,* resulting from new roles and relationships. They typically constructed a *coherent narrative* in which they linked together various time slices of their life with a thread that explained how they had changed in meaningful ways.

Finally, societal forces also are responsible for the special challenges faced by gay, lesbian, and bisexual youths (see Chapter 11) and by ethnic minority adolescents in forming a secure identity (see the Cultural Influences box on page 406). Applying What We Know above summarizes ways that adults can support adolescents in their quest for identity.

This adolescent feels attached to her father but also free to voice her own opinions—circumstances that foster healthy identity development.

ASK YOURSELF

» REVIEW
List personal and contextual factors that promote identity development.

» APPLY
Return to the conversation between Louis and Darryl in the opening of this chapter. Which identity status best characterizes each of the two boys, and why?

» CONNECT
Explain the close link between adolescent identity development and cognitive processes.

» REFLECT
Does your identity status vary across the domains of sexuality, close relationships, vocation, religious beliefs, and political values? Describe factors that may have influenced your identity development in an important domain.

CULTURAL INFLUENCES

Identity Development Among Ethnic Minority Adolescents

Most adolescents are aware of their cultural ancestry but relatively unconcerned about it. However, for teenagers who are members of minority groups, **ethnic identity**—a sense of ethnic-group membership and attitudes and feelings associated with that membership—is central to the quest for identity. As they develop cognitively and become more sensitive to feedback from the social environment, minority youths become painfully aware that they are targets of discrimination and inequality. This discovery complicates their efforts to develop a sense of cultural belonging and a set of personally meaningful goals.

In many immigrant families from collectivist cultures, adolescents' commitment to obeying their parents and fulfilling family obligations lessens the longer the family has been in the immigrant-receiving country—a circumstance that induces **acculturative stress,** psychological distress resulting from conflict between the minority and the host culture (Phinney, Ong, & Madden, 2000). When immigrant parents tightly restrict their teenagers through fear that assimilation into the larger society will undermine their cultural traditions, their youngsters often rebel, rejecting aspects of their ethnic background.

At the same time, discrimination can interfere with the formation of a positive ethnic identity. In one study, Mexican-American youths who had experienced more discrimination were less likely to explore their ethnicity and to report feeling good about it. Those with low ethnic pride showed a sharp drop in self-esteem in the face of discrimination (Romero & Roberts, 2003).

With age, some ethnic minority young people progress from ethnic-identity diffusion or foreclosure through moratorium to ethnic-identity achievement. But because the process of forging an ethnic identity can be painful and confusing, others show no change, and still others regress (Seaton, Scottham, & Sellers, 2006). Young people with parents of different ethnicities face extra challenges. In a large survey of high school students, part-black biracial teenagers reported as much discrimination as their monoracial black counterparts, yet they felt less positively about their ethnicity. And compared with monoracial minorities, many biracials—including black–white, black–Asian, white–Asian, black–Hispanic, and white–Hispanic—regarded ethnicity as less central to their identities (Herman, 2004). Perhaps these adolescents encountered fewer opportunities in their homes and communities to forge a strong sense of belonging to either culture.

When family members encourage adolescents to disprove ethnic stereotypes of low achievement or antisocial behavior, young people typically surmount the threat that discrimination poses to a favorable ethnic identity. These young people manage experiences of unfair treatment effectively, by seeking social support and engaging in direct problem solving (Phinney & Chavira, 1995; Scott, 2003). Also, adolescents whose families taught them the history, traditions, values, and language of their ethnic group and who frequently interact with same-ethnicity peers are more likely to forge a favorable ethnic identity (Hughes et al., 2006; McHale et al., 2006).

How can society help minority adolescents resolve identity conflicts constructively? Here are some relevant approaches:

- Promote effective parenting, in which children and adolescents benefit from family ethnic pride yet are encouraged to explore the meaning of ethnicity in their own lives.
- Ensure that schools respect minority youths' native languages, unique learning styles, and right to high-quality education.
- Foster contact with peers of the same ethnicity, along with respect between ethnic groups (García Coll & Magnuson, 1997).

A strong, secure ethnic identity is associated with higher self-esteem, optimism, and sense of mastery over the environment, and with more positive attitudes toward one's ethnicity (St. Louis & Liem, 2005; Umana-Taylor & Updegraff, 2007; Worrell & Gardner-Kitt, 2006). For these reasons, adolescents with a positive connection to their ethnic group are better adjusted. They cope more effectively with stress, show higher achievement in school, and have fewer emotional and behavior problems than agemates who identify only weakly with their ethnicity (Greene, Way, & Pahl, 2006; Seaton, Scottham, & Sellers, 2006; Umana-Taylor & Alfaro, 2006; Yip, Seaton, & Sellers, 2006).

Forming a **bicultural identity** by exploring and adopting values from both the adolescent's subculture and the dominant culture—offers additional benefits. Biculturally identified adolescents tend to be achieved in other areas of identity as well and to have especially favorable relations with members of other ethnic groups (Phinney, 2007; Phinney et al., 2001). In sum, achievement of ethnic identity enhances many aspects of emotional and social development.

© DAVID GROSSMAN/THE IMAGE WORKS

These adolescents celebrate their cultural heritage by participating in a Filipino parade in New York City. When minority youths encounter respect for their ethnic heritage in schools and communities, they are more likely to retain ethnic values and customs as an important part of their identity.

Moral Development

Eleven-year-old Sabrina sat at the kitchen table reading the Sunday newspaper, her eyes wide with interest. "You gotta see this," she said to 16-year-old Louis, who sat munching cereal. Sabrina held up a page of large photos showing a 70-year-old woman standing in her home. The floor and furniture were piled with stacks of newspapers, cardboard boxes, tin cans, glass containers, food, and clothing. The accompanying article described crumbling plaster on the walls, frozen pipes, and nonfunctioning sinks, toilet, and furnace. The headline read: "Loretta Perry: My Life Is None of Their Business."

"Look what they're trying to do to this poor lady," exclaimed Sabrina. "They wanna throw her out of her house and tear it down! Those city inspectors must not care about anyone. Here it says, 'Mrs. Perry has devoted much of her life to doing favors for people.' Why doesn't someone help *her?*"

"Sabrina, you're missing the point," Louis responded. "Mrs. Perry is violating 30 building code standards. The law says you're supposed to keep your house clean and in good repair."

"But Louis, she's old, and she needs help. She says her life will be over if they destroy her home."

"The building inspectors aren't being mean, Sabrina. Mrs. Perry is stubborn. She's refusing to obey the law. And she's not just a threat to herself—she's a danger to her neighbors, too. Suppose her house caught on fire. You can't live around other people and say your life is nobody's business."

"You don't just knock someone's home down," Sabrina replied angrily. "Why aren't her friends and neighbors over there fixing up that house? You're just like those building inspectors, Louis. You've got no feelings!"

As Louis and Sabrina's disagreement over Mrs. Perry's plight illustrates, cognitive development and expanding social experiences permit adolescents to better understand larger social structures—societal institutions and law-making systems—that govern moral responsibilities. As their grasp of social arrangements expands, adolescents construct new ideas about what should be done when the needs and desires of people conflict. As a result, they move toward increasingly just, fair, and balanced solutions to moral problems.

Kohlberg's Theory of Moral Development

Early work by Piaget on the moral judgment of the child inspired Lawrence Kohlberg's more comprehensive cognitive-developmental theory of moral understanding. Kohlberg used a clinical interviewing procedure in which he presented a sample of 10- to 16-year-old boys with hypothetical *moral dilemmas*—stories presenting a conflict between two moral values—and asked them what the main actor should do and why. Then he followed the participants longitudinally, reinterviewing them at 3- to 4-year intervals over the next 20 years. The best known of Kohlberg's dilemmas, the "Heinz dilemma," pits the value of obeying the law (not stealing) against the value of human life (saving a dying person):

> In Europe a woman was near death from cancer. There was one drug the doctors thought might save her. A druggist in the same town had discovered it, but he was charging ten times what the drug cost him to make. The sick woman's husband, Heinz, went to everyone he knew to borrow the money, but he could only get together half of what it cost. The druggist refused to sell the drug for less or let Heinz pay later. So Heinz became desperate and broke into the man's store to steal the drug for his wife. Should Heinz have done that? Why or why not? (paraphrased from Colby et al., 1983, p. 77)

Kohlberg emphasized that it is *the way an individual reasons* about the dilemma, not *the content of the response* (whether or not to steal), that determines moral maturity. Individuals who believe Heinz should take the drug and those who think he should not can be found at each of Kohlberg's first four stages. Only at the two highest stages do moral reasoning and content come together in a coherent ethical system (Kohlberg, Levine, & Hewer, 1983). Given a choice between obeying the law and preserving individual rights, the most advanced moral thinkers support individual rights (in the Heinz dilemma, stealing the drug to save a life). ***TAKE A MOMENT...*** Does this remind you of adolescents' efforts to formulate a sound, well-organized set of personal values in constructing an identity? According to some theorists, the development of identity and moral understanding are part of the same process (Bergman, 2004; Blasi, 1994).

■ KOHLBERG'S STAGES OF MORAL UNDERSTANDING. Kohlberg organized moral development into three levels, each with two stages, yielding six stages in all. He believed that moral understanding is promoted by the same factors Piaget thought were important for cognitive development: (1) actively grappling with moral issues and noticing weaknesses in one's current reasoning, and (2) gains in perspective taking, which permit individuals to resolve moral conflicts in more effective ways. ***TAKE A MOMENT...*** As we examine Kohlberg's developmental sequence in light of possible responses to the Heinz dilemma, look for changes in perspective taking that each stage assumes.

The Preconventional Level. At the **preconventional level,** morality is externally controlled. Children accept the rules of authority figures and judge actions by their consequences. Behaviors that result in punishment are viewed as bad, those that lead to rewards as good.

- *Stage 1: The punishment and obedience orientation.* Children at this stage find it difficult to consider two points of view in a moral dilemma. As a result, they overlook people's intentions. Instead, they focus on fear of authority and avoidance of punishment as reasons for behaving morally.

  Prostealing: "If you let your wife die, you will . . . be blamed for not spending the money to help her and there'll be an investigation of you and the druggist for your wife's death." (Kohlberg, 1969, p. 381)

If the 12-year-old on the right expects a favor in return for carrying her injured friend's backpack, she is at Kohlberg's preconventional level. If she is guided by the Golden Rule, "Do unto others as you would have them do unto you," then she understands ideal reciprocity and has advanced to the conventional level.

Antistealing: "You shouldn't steal the drug because you'll be caught and sent to jail if you do. If you do get away, [you'd be scared that] the police would catch up with you any minute." (Kohlberg, 1969, p. 381)

- ***Stage 2: The instrumental purpose orientation.*** Children become aware that people can have different perspectives in a moral dilemma, but at first this understanding is concrete. They view right action as flowing from self-interest and understand reciprocity as equal exchange of favors: "You do this for me and I'll do that for you."

  Prostealing: "[I]f Heinz decides to risk jail to save his wife, it's his life he's risking; he can do what he wants with it. And the same goes for the druggist; it's up to him to decide what he wants to do." (Rest, 1979, p. 26)

  Antistealing: "[Heinz] is running more risk than it's worth [to save a wife who is near death]." (Rest, 1979, p. 27)

The Conventional Level. At the **conventional level,** individuals continue to regard conformity to social rules as important, but not for reasons of self-interest. They believe that actively maintaining the current social system ensures positive relationships and societal order.

- ***Stage 3: The "good boy–good girl" orientation, or the morality of interpersonal cooperation.*** The desire to obey rules because they promote social harmony first appears in the context of close personal ties. Stage 3 individuals want to maintain the affection and approval of friends and relatives by being a "good person"—trustworthy, loyal, respectful, helpful, and nice. The capacity to view a two-person relationship from the vantage point of an impartial, outside observer supports this new approach to morality. At this stage, individuals understand *ideal reciprocity:* They express the same concern for the welfare of another as they do for themselves—a standard of fairness summed up by the Golden Rule: "Do unto others as you would have them do unto you."

  Prostealing: "No one will think you're bad if you steal the drug, but your family will think you're an inhuman husband if you don't. If you let your wife die, you'll never be able to look anyone in the face again." (Kohlberg, 1969, p. 381)

  Antistealing: "It isn't just the druggist who will think you're a criminal, everyone else will too. . . . [Y]ou'll feel bad thinking how you've brought dishonor on your family and yourself." (Kohlberg, 1969, p. 381)

- ***Stage 4: The social-order-maintaining orientation.*** At this stage, the individual takes into account a larger perspective—that of societal laws. Moral choices no longer depend on close ties to others. Instead, rules must be enforced in the same evenhanded fashion for everyone, and each member of society has a personal duty to uphold them. The Stage 4 individual believes that laws should never be disobeyed because they are vital for ensuring societal order and cooperative relations between individuals.

  Prostealing: "Heinz has a duty to protect his wife's life; it's a vow he took in marriage. But it's wrong to steal, so he would have to take the drug with the idea of paying the druggist for it and accepting the penalty for breaking the law later."

  Antistealing: "Even if his wife is dying, it's still [Heinz's] duty as a citizen to obey the law. . . . If everyone starts breaking the law in a jam, there'd be no civilization, just crime and violence." (Rest, 1979, p. 30)

The Postconventional or Principled Level. Individuals at the **postconventional level** move beyond unquestioning support for their own society's rules and laws. They define morality in terms of abstract principles and values that apply to all situations and societies.

- ***Stage 5: The social contract orientation.*** At Stage 5, individuals regard laws and rules as flexible instruments for furthering human purposes. They can imagine alternatives to their own social order, and they emphasize fair procedures for interpreting and changing the law. When laws are consistent with individual rights and the interests of the majority, each person follows them because of a *social* *contract orientation*—free and willing participation in the system because it brings about more good for people than if it did not exist.

> *Prostealing:* "Although there is a law against stealing, the law wasn't meant to violate a person's right to life. . . . If Heinz is prosecuted for stealing, the law needs to be reinterpreted to take into account situations in which it goes against people's natural right to keep on living."

- ***Stage 6: The universal ethical principle orientation.*** At this highest stage, right action is defined by self-chosen ethical principles of conscience that are valid for all people, regardless of law and social agreement. These values are abstract, not concrete moral rules like the Ten Commandments. Stage 6 individuals typically mention such principles as respect for the worth and dignity of each person.

> *Prostealing:* "It doesn't make sense to put respect for property above respect for life itself. [People] could live together without private property at all. Respect for human life and personality is absolute and accordingly [people] have a mutual duty to save one another from dying." (Rest, 1979, p. 37)

RESEARCH ON KOHLBERG'S STAGE SEQUENCE. Kohlberg's original research and other longitudinal studies provide the most convincing evidence for his stage sequence. With few exceptions, individuals move through the first four stages in the predicted order (Colby et al., 1983; Dawson, 2002; Walker & Taylor, 1991b). Moral development is slow and gradual: Reasoning at Stages 1 and 2 decreases in early adolescence, while Stage 3 increases through midadolescence and then declines. Stage 4 reasoning rises over the teenage years until, by early adulthood, it is the typical response.

Few people move beyond Stage 4. In fact, postconventional morality is so rare that no clear evidence exists that Kohlberg's Stage 6 actually follows Stage 5. This poses a key challenge to Kohlberg's theory: If people must reach Stages 5 and 6 to be considered truly morally mature, few individuals anywhere would measure up! According to one reexamination of Kohlberg's stages, moral maturity can be found in a revised understanding of Stages 3 and 4 (Gibbs, 1991, 2010). These stages are not "conventional"—based on social conformity—as Kohlberg assumed. Rather, they require profound moral constructions—an understanding of ideal reciprocity as the basis for relationships (Stage 3) and for widely accepted moral standards, set forth in rules and laws (Stage 4). In this view, "postconventional" morality is a highly reflective endeavor limited to a handful of people who have attained advanced education, usually in philosophy.

TAKE A MOMENT... Think of an actual moral dilemma you faced recently. How did you solve it? Did your reasoning fall at the same stage as your thinking about Heinz? Real-life conflicts often elicit moral reasoning below a person's actual capacity because they involve practical considerations and mix cognition with intense emotion (Carpendale, 2000). Although adolescents and adults mention reasoning as their most frequent strategy for resolving these dilemmas, they also refer to other strategies—talking through issues with others, relying on intuition, and calling on notions of religion and spirituality. And they report feeling drained, confused, and torn by temptation—an emotional side of moral judgment not tapped by hypothetical situations, which evoke the upper limits of moral thought because they allow reflection without the interference of personal risk (Walker, 2004).

The influence of situational factors on moral judgments indicates that like Piaget's cognitive stages, Kohlberg's moral stages are loosely organized and overlapping. Rather than developing in a neat, stepwise fashion, people draw on a range of moral responses that vary with context. With age, this range shifts upward as less mature moral reasoning is gradually replaced by more advanced moral thought.

Are There Sex Differences in Moral Reasoning?

As we have seen, real-life moral dilemmas often highlight the role of emotion in moral judgment. In the discussion at the beginning of this section, notice how Sabrina's moral argument focuses on caring and commitment to others.

Carol Gilligan (1982) is the best-known of those who have argued that Kohlberg's theory—originally formulated on the basis of interviews with males—does not adequately represent the morality of girls and women. Gilligan believes that feminine morality emphasizes an "ethic of care" that Kohlberg's system devalues. Sabrina's reasoning falls at Stage 3 because it is based on mutual trust and affection, whereas Louis's is at Stage 4 because he emphasizes following the law. According to Gilligan, a concern for others is a *different* but no less valid basis for moral judgment than a focus on impersonal rights.

Many studies have tested Gilligan's claim that Kohlberg's approach underestimates the moral maturity of females, and most do not support it (Turiel, 2006; Walker, 2006). On hypothetical dilemmas as well as everyday moral problems, adolescent and adult females display reasoning at the same stage as their male agemates and often at a higher stage. Themes of justice and caring appear in the responses of both sexes, and when girls do raise interpersonal concerns, they are not downgraded in Kohlberg's system (Jadack et al., 1995; Kahn, 1992; Walker, 1995). These findings suggest that although Kohlberg emphasized justice rather than caring as the highest moral ideal, his theory taps both sets of values.

Still, Gilligan makes a powerful claim that research on moral development has been limited by too much attention to rights and justice (a "masculine" ideal) and too little to care and responsiveness (a "feminine" ideal). Some evidence shows that although the morality of males and females taps both orientations, females do tend to emphasize care, whereas males either stress justice or focus equally on justice and care (Jaffee & Hyde, 2000; Wark & Krebs, 1996; Weisz & Black, 2002). This difference in emphasis, which appears more often in real-life dilemmas than in hypothetical ones, may reflect women's greater involvement in daily activities involving care and concern for others.

Indeed, both cultural and situational contexts profoundly affect use of a care orientation. In one study, U.S. and Canadian 17- to 26-year-old females exceeded their male counterparts in complex reasoning about care issues. But Norwegian males were just as advanced as Norwegian females in care-based understanding (Skoe, 1998). Perhaps Norwegian culture, which explicitly endorses gender equality, induces boys and men to think deeply about interpersonal obligations. And in an Australian investigation, researchers presented 18- to 38-year-old university students with one of three versions of a moral dilemma, in which the main character varied in familiarity: (1) a close friend in class, (2) a person "known only vaguely" from class, or (3) a classmate whose relationship was unspecified (Ryan, David, & Reynolds, 2004). When asked whether they would permit the character, who was in danger of failing the course, to borrow a copy of their recently completed assignment despite risk of cheating, both males and females gave more care responses when considering a close friend than a socially distant classmate. As Figure 12.1 shows, gender differences emerged only in the unspecified condition, where women—who tend to forge closer relationships—may have assumed greater familiarity.

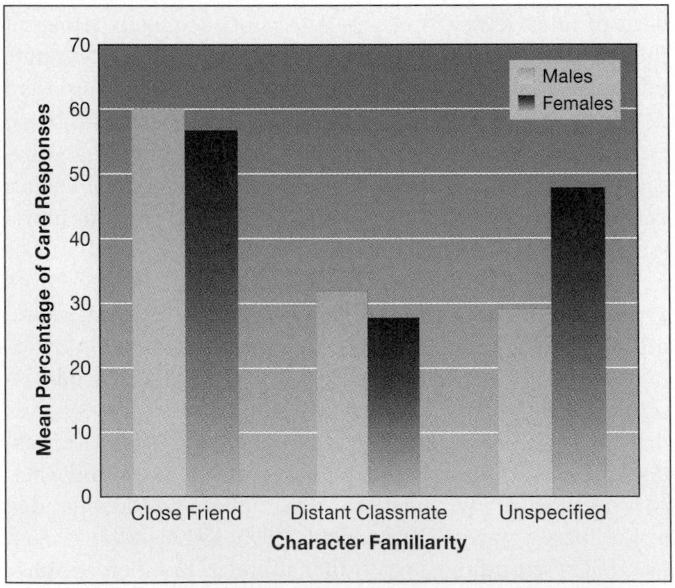

■ **FIGURE 12.1** ■ **Relationship of familiarity of the main character in a moral dilemma to care responses.** Australian university students were presented with one of three versions of a moral dilemma in which familiarity of the main character varied: close friend, distant classmate, and unspecified. Both male and female participants gave more care responses when considering a close friend than a distant classmate. Sex differences appeared only in the unspecified condition, where females may have assumed greater familiarity. (From M. K. Ryan, B. David, & K. J. Reynolds, 2004, "Who Cares? The Effect of Gender and Context on the Self and Moral Reasoning," *Psychology of Women Quarterly, 28,* 246–255. Copyright © 2004 by the American Psychological Association. Reprinted with permission of the American Psychological Association.)

Coordinating Moral, Social-Conventional, and Personal Concerns

Adolescents' moral advances are also evident in their reasoning about situations that raise competing moral, social-conventional, and personal issues. In diverse Western and non Western cultures, teenagers express great concern with matters of personal choice—a reflection of their quest for identity and strengthening independence (Neff & Helwig, 2002; Nucci, 2002). More firmly than at younger ages, they assert that dress, hairstyle, diary records, and friendships are solely the province of the individual and not subject to control by authority figures (such as parents) (Nucci, 2001, 2005). As adolescents enlarge the range of issues they regard as personal, they think more intently about conflicts between personal choice and community obligation—for example, whether, and under what conditions, it is permissible for laws to restrict speech, religion, marriage, childbearing, group membership, and other individual rights (Helwig, 1995; Wainryb, 1997).

Teenagers display more subtle thinking than school-age children on such issues. When asked if it is OK to exclude a child from a peer group on the basis of race or gender, fourth graders usually say exclusion is always unfair. But by tenth grade, young people, though increasingly mindful of fairness, indicate that under certain conditions—within friendship more often than peer groups, and on the basis of gender more often than race—exclusion is OK (Killen et al., 2002). In explaining, they mention the right to personal choice as well as concerns about effective group functioning. Justifying her opinion that members of an all-boys music club need not let a girl join, one tenth grader said, "It's not nice . . . but it's their club." Another commented, "[The girl and the boys] probably wouldn't relate on very many things" (p. 62).

As adolescents integrate personal rights with ideal reciprocity, they demand that protections they want for themselves extend to others. For example, with age, adolescents are more likely to defend the government's right to limit the personal right to engage in risky health behaviors such as smoking and drinking, in the interest of the larger public good (Flanagan, Stout, & Gallay, 2008). Similarly, they are increasingly mindful of the overlap between moral imperatives and social conventions. Eventually they realize that violating strongly held conventions—showing up at a wedding in a T-shirt, talking out of turn at a student council meeting—can harm others, either by inducing distress or by undermining fair treatment. Over time, as their grasp of fairness deepens, young people realize that many social conventions have moral implications: They are vital for maintaining a just and peaceful society (Nucci, 2001). Notice how this understanding is central to Kohlberg's Stage 4, which is typically attained as adolescence draws to a close.

Influences on Moral Reasoning

Many factors influence moral understanding, including child-rearing practices, schooling, peer interaction, and culture. Growing evidence suggests that, as Kohlberg believed, these

© JEFF GREENBERG/ALAMY

These teenagers are making signs for an anti-war demonstration. Adolescent moral development involves thinking more intently about conflicts between personal choice and community obligation—for example, whether, and under what conditions, it is permissible to challenge a decision by one's country to go to war.

experiences work by presenting young people with cognitive challenges, which stimulate them to think about moral problems in more complex ways.

■ **PARENTING PRACTICES.** As in childhood, parenting practices associated with moral maturity in adolescence combine warmth, exchange of ideas, and appropriate demands for maturity. Adolescents who gain most in moral understanding have parents who engage in moral discussions, encourage prosocial behavior, and create a supportive atmosphere by listening sensitively, asking clarifying questions, and presenting higher-level reasoning (Pratt, Skoe, & Arnold, 2004; Wyatt & Carlo, 2002). In one study, 11-year-olds were asked what they thought an adult would say to justify a moral rule, such as not lying, stealing, or breaking a promise. Those with warm, demanding, communicative parents were far more likely than their agemates to point to the importance of ideal reciprocity: "You wouldn't like it if I did it to you" (Leman, 2005). In contrast, when parents lecture, use threats, or make sarcastic remarks, adolescents show little or no change in moral reasoning over time (Walker & Taylor, 1991a).

■ **SCHOOLING.** Years of schooling is a powerful predictor of movement to Kohlberg's Stage 4 or higher (Dawson et al., 2003; Gibbs et al., 2007). Higher education introduces young people to social issues that extend beyond personal relationships to entire political or cultural groups. Consistent with this idea, college students who report more perspective-taking opportunities (for example, classes that emphasize open discussion of opinions, friendships with others of different cultural backgrounds) and who indicate that they have become more aware of social diversity tend to be advanced in moral reasoning (Comunian & Gielen, 2006; Mason & Gibbs, 1993a, 1993b).

■ **PEER INTERACTION.** Interaction among peers who present differing viewpoints promotes moral understanding. When young people negotiate and compromise with agemates, they realize that social life can be based on cooperation between equals rather than authority relations (Killen & Nucci, 1995). Teenagers who report more close friendships and who more often participate in conversations with their friends are advanced in moral reasoning (Schonert-Reichl, 1999). The mutuality and intimacy of friendship, which fosters decisions based on consensual agreement, may be particularly important for moral development.

Peer discussions and role playing of moral problems have provided the basis for interventions aimed at improving high school and college students' moral understanding. For these discussions to be effective, young people must be highly engaged—confronting, critiquing, and attempting to clarify one another's viewpoints, as Sabrina and Louis did when they argued over Mrs. Perry's plight (Berkowitz & Gibbs, 1983; Comunian & Gielen, 2006). And because moral development occurs gradually, many peer interaction sessions over weeks or months typically are needed to produce moral change.

■ **CULTURE.** Individuals in industrialized nations move through Kohlberg's stages more quickly and advance to a higher level than individuals in village societies, who rarely move beyond Stage 3. One explanation of these cultural differences is that in village societies, moral cooperation is based on direct relations between people and does not allow for the development of advanced moral understanding (Stages 4 to 6), which depends on appreciating the role of larger social structures, such as laws and government institutions (Gibbs et al., 2007).

A second possible reason for cultural variation is that responses to moral dilemmas in collectivist cultures (including village societies) are often more other-directed than in Western Europe and North America (Miller, 2006). In both village and industrialized cultures that highly value interdependency, statements portraying the individual as vitally connected to the social group are common. In one study, Japanese male and female adolescents, who almost always integrated caring and justice-based reasoning, placed greater weight on caring, which they regarded as a communal responsibility (Shimizu, 2001). Similarly, in research conducted in India, even highly educated people (expected to have attained Kohlberg's Stages 4 and 5) viewed solutions to moral dilemmas as the responsibility of the entire society, not of a single person (Miller & Bersoff, 1995).

These findings raise the question of whether Kohlberg's highest level represents a culturally specific way of thinking—one limited to Western societies that emphasize individualism

© EARL & NAZIMA KOWALL/CORBIS

Growing up in a small village in the Pamir Mountains of China, these adolescents view moral cooperation as based on direct relations between people. Consequently, their moral reasoning is unlikely to advance beyond Kohlberg's Stage 3.

and an appeal to an inner, private conscience. At the same time, a review of over 100 studies confirmed an age-related trend consistent with Kohlberg's Stages 1 to 4 across diverse societies (Gibbs et al., 2007). A common justice morality is clearly evident in the dilemma responses of people from vastly different cultures.

Moral Reasoning and Behavior

A central assumption of the cognitive-developmental perspective is that moral understanding should affect moral action. According to Kohlberg, mature moral thinkers realize that behaving in line with their beliefs is vital for creating and maintaining a just social world (Gibbs, 2010). Consistent with this idea, higher-stage adolescents more often act prosocially by helping, sharing, and defending victims of injustice (Carlo et al., 1996; Comunian & Gielen, 2000, 2006). Also, they less often engage in cheating, aggression, and other antisocial behaviors (Gregg, Gibbs, & Fuller, 1994; Raaijmakers, Engels, & Van Hoof, 2005; Stams et al., 2006).

Yet the connection between mature moral reasoning and action is only modest. As we have seen, moral behavior is influenced by many factors besides cognition, including the emotions of empathy, sympathy, and guilt; individual differences in temperament; and a long history of experiences that affect moral decision making. **Moral self-relevance**—the degree to which morality is central to self-concept—also affects moral behavior (Walker, 2004). In a study of low-SES African-American and Hispanic teenagers, those who emphasized moral traits and goals in their self-descriptions displayed exceptional levels of community service (Hart & Fegley, 1995). But they did not differ from their agemates in moral reasoning.

Research has yet to identify the origins of a sense of moral self-relevance, or just how thought combines with other influences to foster moral commitment. Close relationships with parents, teachers, and friends may play a vital role by modeling prosocial behavior and fostering morally relevant emotions of empathy and guilt, which combine with moral cognition to powerfully motivate moral action (Arsenio, 2006; Hoffman, 2000). Another possibility is that *just educational environments*—in which teachers guide students in democratic decision making and rule setting, resolving disputes civilly, and taking responsibility for others' welfare—are influential (Atkins, Hart, & Donnelly, 2004). A compassionate and just school climate may be particularly important for poverty-stricken ethnic minority students. For many, meaningful participation in their school community may be crucial in preventing them from concluding that prejudice and diminished opportunity are so pervasive in society as to be insurmountable (Hart & Atkins, 2002).

Schools may also foster students' moral self-relevance by expanding opportunities for civic engagement. As the Social Issues box on the following page reveals, encouraging civic responsibility in young people can help them see the connection between their personal interests and the public interest—an insight that may foster all aspects of morality.

Religious Involvement and Moral Development

Recall that in resolving real-life moral dilemmas, many people voice notions of religion and spirituality. Religion is especially important in U.S. family life. In recent national polls, nearly two-thirds of Americans reported being religious, compared with one-half of those in Canada, one-third of those in Great Britain and Italy, and even fewer elsewhere in Europe (Gallup News Service, 2006; Jones, 2003). People who regularly attend religious services include many parents with children. But as adolescents search for a personally meaningful identity, formal religious involvement declines—for U.S. youths, from 55 percent at ages 13 to 15 to 40 percent at ages 17 to 18 (Donahue & Benson, 1995; Kerestes & Youniss, 2003).

Nevertheless, teenagers who remain part of a religious community are advantaged in moral values and behavior. Compared with nonaffiliated youths, they are more involved in community service activities aimed at helping the less fortunate (Kerestes, Youniss, & Metz, 2004). And religious involvement promotes responsible academic and social behavior and discourages misconduct (Dowling et al., 2004). It is associated with lower levels of drug and alcohol use, early sexual activity, and delinquency (Regnerus, Smith, & Fritsch, 2003).

A variety of factors probably contribute to these favorable outcomes. In a study of inner-city high school students, religiously involved young people were more likely to report trusting relationships with parents, other adults, and friends who hold similar worldviews. The more activities they shared with this network, the higher they scored in empathy and prosocial behavior (King & Furrow, 2004). Furthermore, religious

SOCIAL ISSUES

Development of Civic Responsibility

On Thanksgiving Day, Jules, Louis, and Sabrina joined their parents at a soup kitchen to serve a holiday dinner to poverty-stricken people. Throughout the year, Sabrina volunteered on Saturday mornings at a nursing home, conversing with bedridden elders. During a congressional election campaign, all three adolescents raised questions about issues at special youth meetings with candidates. At school, Louis and his girlfriend, Cassie, formed an organization devoted to promoting ethnic and racial tolerance.

These young people show a strong sense of *civic responsibility*—a complex combination of cognition, emotion, and behavior. Civic responsibility involves knowledge of political issues, a desire to make a difference in the community, and skills for achieving civic goals, such as how to resolve differing views fairly and conduct meetings so all participants have a voice (Flanagan & Faison, 2001).

When young people engage in community service that exposes them to people in need or to public issues, they are especially likely to express a commitment to future service. And youth volunteers—who tend to be advanced in moral reasoning—gain further in moral maturity as a result of participating (Gibbs et al., 2007; Hart, Atkins, & Donnelly, 2006). Family, school, and community experiences contribute to adolescents' civic responsibility.

Family Influences

Teenagers whose parents encourage their children to form opinions about controversial issues are more knowledgeable about civic issues and better able to see them from more than one perspective (Santoloupo & Pratt, 1994). Also, adolescents whose parents engage in community service and stress compassion for the less fortunate tend to hold socially responsible values. When asked what causes unemployment or poverty, they more often mention situational and societal factors (lack of education, government policies, or the state of the economy) than individual factors (low intelligence or personal problems). Youths who endorse situational and societal causes, in turn, have more altruistic life goals, such as working to eradicate poverty or to preserve the earth for future generations (Flanagan & Tucker, 1999). And they engage in more civic activities into early adulthood (Zaff, Malanchuk, & Eccles, 2008).

School and Community Influences

A democratic climate at school in which teachers promote discussion of controversial issues, while insisting that students listen to and respect one another, fosters critical analysis of political issues and commitment to social causes (Flanagan & Faison, 2001). Participation in extracurricular activities at school and in youth organizations is also associated with civic commitment that persists into adulthood (Obradović & Masten, 2007).

Two aspects of these involvements seem to account for their lasting impact. First, they introduce adolescents to the vision and skills required for mature civic engagement. Within student government, clubs, teams, and other groups, young people see how their actions affect the wider school and community. They realize that collectively they can achieve results greater than any one person can achieve alone. And they learn to work together, balancing strong convictions with compromise (Atkins, Hart, & Donnelly, 2004; Youniss, McLellan, & Yates, 1997). Second, while producing a weekly newspaper or implementing a service project, young people explore political and moral ideals. Often they redefine their identities to include a responsibility to combat others' misfortunes (Wheeler, 2002).

The power of family, school, and community to promote civic responsibility may lie in discussions, educational practices, and activities that jointly foster moral thought, emotion, and behavior. In a comparison of nationally representative samples of 14-year-olds in 28 nations, U.S. young people excelled at community service, with 50 percent of students reporting membership in organizations devoted to volunteering (Torney-Purta, 2002).

Currently, 66 percent of U.S. public schools provide students with community service opportunities. Nearly half of these have *service-learning programs,* which integrate service activities into the academic curriculum, and about one-third of students enroll. High school students who are required to serve their communities express as strong a desire to remain engaged as do students who volunteer. And when they reach early adulthood, they are equally likely to vote and participate in community organizations (Hart et al., 2007; Metz & Youniss, 2005).

Still, most U.S. schools offering service learning do not have policies encouraging or mandating such programs (Scales & Roehlkepartain, 2004). Furthermore, low-SES, inner-city youths—although they express high interest in contributing to society—score substantially lower than higher-SES youths in civic knowledge and participation (Balsano, 2005). A broad societal commitment to fostering civic character must pay special attention to supportive school and community experiences for these young people, so their eagerness to make a difference can be realized.

© JIM WEST/THE IMAGE WORKS

Adolescents paint a mural on a wall once filled with graffiti in a low-income, inner-city neighborhood. Family, school, and community experiences contribute to their sense of civic responsibility.

© JIM WEST/THE IMAGE WORKS

These teenagers gather with other religious groups to voice their support for world peace. Involvement in a religious community promotes teens' moral values and behavior, encouraging responsible academic work and community service.

education and youth activities directly teach concern for others and provide opportunities for moral discussions and civic engagement. And adolescents who feel connected to a higher being may develop certain inner strengths, including moral self-relevance and prosocial values, that help them translate their thinking into action (Hardy & Carlo, 2005; Sherrod & Spiewak, 2008).

Because most teenagers, regardless of formal affiliation, identify with a religious denomination and say they believe in a higher being, religious institutions may be uniquely suited to foster moral and prosocial commitments. For inner-city youths with few alternative sources of social support, outreach by religious institutions can lead to life-altering involvement (Jang & Johnson, 2001). An exception is seen in religious cults, where rigid indoctrination into the group's beliefs, suppression of individuality, and estrangement from society all work against moral maturity (Richmond, 2004).

Further Challenges to Kohlberg's Theory

Although much evidence is consistent with the cognitive-developmental approach to morality, Kohlberg's theory has faced major challenges. The most radical opposition comes from researchers who—referring to wide variability in moral reasoning across situations—claim that Kohlberg's stage sequence inadequately accounts for morality in everyday life (Krebs and Denton, 2005). These investigators favor abandoning Kohlberg's stages for a *pragmatic approach to morality.* They assert that each person makes moral judgments at varying levels of maturity, depending on the individual's current context and motivations: Conflict over a business deal is likely to evoke Stage 2 (instrumental purpose) reasoning, a friendship or romantic dispute Stage 3 (ideal reciprocity) reasoning, and a breach of contract Stage 4 (social-order-maintaining) reasoning (Krebs et al., 1991).

According to the pragmatic view, everyday moral judgments—rather than being efforts to arrive at just solutions—are practical tools that people use to achieve their goals. To benefit personally, they often must advocate cooperation with others. But people often act first and then invoke moral judgments to rationalize their actions, regardless of whether their behavior is self-centered or prosocial (Haidt, 2001). And sometimes people use moral judgments for immoral purposes—for example, to excuse their transgressions.

Is the pragmatic approach correct that people strive to resolve moral conflicts fairly only when they themselves have nothing to lose? Supporters of the cognitive-developmental perspective point out that people frequently rise above self-interest to defend others' rights. For example, moral leaders in business—rather than resorting to Stage 2 reasoning—endorse trust, integrity, good faith, and just laws and codes of conduct (Damon, 2004; Gibbs, 2006). Also, when presented with moral justifications varying in maturity, adolescents and adults are well aware of the greater adequacy of higher-stage thinking, which some people act on despite highly corrupt environments. Furthermore, individuals who engage in sudden altruistic action may have previously considered relevant moral issues so thoroughly that their moral judgment activates automatically, triggering an immediate response (Gibbs et al., 2009a; Pizzaro & Bloom, 2003). In these instances, people who appear to be engaging in after-the-fact moral justification are actually behaving with great forethought.

In sum, the cognitive-developmental approach to morality has done much to clarify our profound moral potential. And despite opposition, Kohlberg's central assumption—that with age, humans everywhere construct a deeper understanding of fairness and justice that guides moral action—remains powerfully influential.

Gender Typing

As Sabrina entered adolescence, she began to place more emphasis on excelling in literature, art, and music—traditionally feminine subjects. When with peers, she worried about walking, talking, eating, dressing, laughing, and competing in ways consistent with gender roles.

Early adolescence is a period of **gender intensification**—increased gender stereotyping of attitudes and behavior and movement toward a more traditional gender identity (Basow & Rubin, 1999; Galambos, Almeida, & Petersen, 1990). Both sexes experience gender intensification, but it is stronger for girls, who feel less free to experiment with "other-gender" activities and behavior than they did in middle childhood (Huston & Alvarez, 1990).

What accounts for gender intensification? Biological, social, and cognitive factors are involved. As puberty magnifies sex differences in appearance, teenagers spend more time thinking about themselves in gender-linked ways. Pubertal changes also prompt gender-typed pressures from others. Parents—especially those with traditional gender-role beliefs—may encourage "gender-appropriate" activities and behavior more than they did earlier (Crouter, Manke, & McHale, 1995;

© LWA-DANN TARDIF/CORBIS

In early adolescence, young people, especially girls, move toward more traditional gender identities. By the late teens, gender intensification declines, especially among adolescents encouraged to explore non-gender-typed options.

Shanahan et al., 2007). And when adolescents start to date, they often become more gender-typed as a way of increasing their attractiveness (Maccoby, 1998). Finally, cognitive changes—in particular, greater concern with what others think—make young teenagers more responsive to gender-role expectations.

Gender intensification declines by middle to late adolescence, but not all young people move beyond it to the same degree. Teenagers who are encouraged to explore non-gender-typed options and to question the value of gender stereotypes for themselves and society are more likely to build an androgynous gender identity (see Chapter 8, page 276). Overall, androgynous adolescents, especially girls, tend to be psychologically healthier—more self-confident, more willing to speak their own mind, better-liked by peers, and identity-achieved (Bronstein, 2006; Dusek, 1987; Harter, 2006).

ASK YOURSELF

» REVIEW
How does an understanding of ideal reciprocity contribute to moral development? Why are Kohlberg's Stages 3 and 4 morally mature constructions?

» APPLY
Tam grew up in a small village culture, Lydia in a large industrial city. At age 15, Tam reasons at Kohlberg's Stage 3, Lydia at Stage 4. What factors might account for the difference?

» CONNECT
How might the exploration of values and goals associated with healthy identity development contribute to the eventual decline in adolescent gender intensification?

» REFLECT
Do you favor a cognitive-developmental or a pragmatic approach to morality, or both? What research evidence and personal experiences influenced your viewpoint?

The Family

Franca and Antonio remember their son Louis's freshman year of high school as a difficult time. Because of a demanding project at work, Franca was away from home many evenings and weekends. In her absence, Antonio took over, but when business declined and he had to cut costs at his hardware store, he, too, had less time for the family. That year, Louis and two friends used their computer know-how to crack the code of a long-distance telephone service. From the family basement, they made calls around the country. Louis's grades fell, and he often left the house without saying where he was going. Franca and Antonio began to feel uncomfortable about the long hours Louis was spending in the basement and their lack of contact with him. Finally, when the telephone company traced the illegal calls to their phone number, they knew they had cause for concern.

Development at adolescence involves striving for **autonomy**—a sense of oneself as a separate, self-governing individual. Teenagers strive to rely more on themselves and less on parents for decision making (Collins & Laursen, 2004; Steinberg & Silk, 2002). Nevertheless, parent–child relationships remain vital for helping adolescents become autonomous, responsible individuals.

Parent–Child Relationships

A variety of changes within the adolescent support autonomy. In Chapter 11, we saw that puberty triggers psychological distancing from parents. In addition, as young people look more mature, parents give them more independence and responsibility. Cognitive development also paves the way toward autonomy: Gradually, adolescents solve problems and make decisions more effectively. And an improved ability to reason about social relationships leads teenagers to *deidealize* their parents, viewing them as "just people." Consequently, they no longer bend as easily to parental authority as they did when younger.

Yet as Franca and Antonio's episode with Louis reveals, teenagers still need guidance and, at times, protection from dangerous situations. In diverse ethnic groups, SES levels, nations, and family structures (including single-parent, two-parent, and stepparent), warm, supportive parent–adolescent ties that permit young people to explore ideas and social roles foster autonomy, predicting high self-reliance, work orientation, academic competence, favorable self-esteem, and ease of separation in the transition to college (Bean, Barber, & Crane, 2007; Eisenberg et al., 2005b; Vazsonyi, Hibbert, & Snider, 2003; Wang, Pomerantz, & Chen, 2007). Conversely, parents who are coercive or psychologically controlling interfere with the development of autonomy. These tactics are consistently linked to low self-esteem, depression, drug and alcohol use, and antisocial behavior among teenagers—outcomes that often persist into early adulthood (Barber, Stolz, & Olsen, 2005; Bronte-Tinkew, Moore, & Carrano, 2006; Wissink, Deković, & Meijer, 2006).

In Chapter 2, we described the family as a *system* that must adapt to changes in its members. The rapid physical and psychological changes of adolescence trigger conflicting expectations

© DEX IMAGES/CORBIS

This teenager and his father share an affectionate moment. Adolescents may resist parental authority, especially in matters of personal choice such as dress. But most maintain close family ties, particularly when parents give them the freedom to explore ideas and social roles.

in parent–child relationships—a major reason that many parents find rearing teenagers to be stressful.

Earlier we noted that interest in making choices about personal matters strengthens in adolescence. Yet parents and teenagers—especially young teenagers—differ sharply on the appropriate age for granting certain privileges, such as control over clothing, school courses, going out with friends, and dating (Smetana, 2002). Consistent parental monitoring of the young person's daily activities, through a cooperative relationship in which the adolescent willingly discloses information, is linked to a variety of positive outcomes—prevention of delinquency, reduction in sexual activity, improved school performance, and positive psychological well-being (Crouter & Head, 2002; Jacobson & Crockett, 2000).

Parents' own development can also lead to friction with teenagers. While their children face a boundless future and a wide array of choices, middle-aged parents must accept the fact that their own possibilities are narrowing (Holmbeck, 1996). Often they can't understand why the adolescent wants to skip family activities to be with peers. And teenagers fail to appreciate that parents want the family to spend as much time together as possible because an important period in their adult life—child rearing—will soon end.

Immigrant parents from cultures that highly value family closeness and obedience to authority have greater difficulty adapting to their teenagers' push for autonomy, often reacting more strongly to adolescent disagreement (Phinney & Ong, 2001). And as adolescents acquire the host culture's language and are increasingly exposed to its individualistic values, immigrant parents may become even more critical, causing teenagers to rely less on the family network for social support. The resulting acculturative stress is associated with a rise in deviant behavior, including alcohol use and delinquency (Crane et al., 2005; Warner et al., 2006).

Throughout adolescence, the quality of the parent–child relationship is the single most consistent predictor of mental health. In well-functioning families, teenagers remain attached to parents and seek their advice, but they do so in a context of greater freedom (Collins & Steinberg, 2006). The mild conflict that arises facilitates adolescent identity and autonomy by helping family members express and tolerate disagreement. Conflicts also inform parents of teenagers' changing needs and expectations, signaling a need for adjustments in the parent–child relationship.

By middle to late adolescence, most parents and children achieve this mature, mutual relationship, and harmonious interaction is on the rise. The reduced time that Western teenagers spend with parents—for U.S. youths, a drop from 33 percent of waking hours in fifth grade to 14 percent in twelfth grade—has little to do with conflict (Larson et al., 1996). Rather, it results from the large amount of unstructured time available to teenagers in North America and Western Europe—on average, nearly half their waking hours (Larson, 2001). Young people tend to fill these hours with activities that take them away from home—part-time jobs, leisure and volunteer pursuits, and time with friends.

But this drop in family time is not universal. In one study, urban low- and middle-SES African-American youths showed no decline in hours spent with family—a pattern typical in cultures with collectivist values (Larson et al., 2001). Furthermore, teenagers living in risky neighborhoods tend to have more trusting relationships with parents and adjust more favorably when parents maintain tighter control and pressure them not to engage in worrisome behaviors (McElhaney & Allen, 2001). In harsh surroundings, young people seem to interpret more measured granting of autonomy as a sign of parental caring.

Family Circumstances

As Franca and Antonio's experience with Louis reminds us, adult life stress can interfere with warm, involved parenting and, in turn, with children's adjustment at any period of development. But parents who are financially secure, not overloaded with job pressures, and content with their marriages usually find it easier to grant teenagers appropriate autonomy and experience less conflict with them (Cowan & Cowan, 2002; Crouter & Bumpass, 2001). When Franca and Antonio's work stress eased and they recognized Louis's need for more involvement and guidance, his problems subsided.

Less than 10 percent of families with adolescents have seriously troubled relationships. Of these, most have difficulties that began in childhood (Collins & Laursen, 2004). Table 12.2 summarizes family conditions considered in earlier chapters that pose challenges for adolescents. Teenagers who develop well despite family stresses continue to benefit from factors that fostered resilience in earlier years: an appealing, easy-going disposition; a parent who combines warmth with high expectations; and (especially if parental supports are lacking) bonds with prosocial adults outside the family who care deeply about the adolescent's well-being (Masten, 2001; Masten & Shaffer, 2006).

■ **TABLE 12.2** ■ ***Family Circumstances with Implications for Adolescent Adjustment***

FAMILY CIRCUMSTANCE	TO REVIEW, TURN TO . . .
TYPE OF FAMILY	
Adoptive	Chapter 2, pages 57–59
Divorced single-parent	Chapter 10, pages 347–349
Blended	Chapter 10, pages 349–350
Employed mother and dual-earner	Chapter 10, pages 350–351
FAMILY CONDITIONS	
Economic hardship	Chapter 2, page 63
Child maltreatment	Chapter 8, pages 281–283 Chapter 10, pages 352–354
Adolescent parenthood	Chapter 11, pages 378–380

Siblings

Like parent–child relationships, sibling interactions adapt to development at adolescence. As younger siblings become more self-sufficient, they accept less direction from their older brothers and sisters, and sibling influence declines. Also, as teenagers become more involved in friendships and romantic relationships, they invest less time and energy in siblings, who are part of the family from which they are trying to establish autonomy. As a result, sibling relationships often become less intense, in both positive and negative feelings (Hetherington, Henderson, & Reiss, 1999; Kim et al., 2006).

Nevertheless, attachment between siblings remains strong for most young people. Brothers and sisters who established a positive bond in early childhood continue to express affection and caring—an outcome linked to more favorable emotional and social adjustment (Branje et al., 2004; Kim et al., 2007). Also, mild sibling differences in perceived parental affection no longer trigger jealousy but, instead, predict greater sibling warmth (Feinberg et al., 2003). Perhaps adolescents interpret a unique relationship with parents, as long as it is generally accepting, as a gratifying sign of their own individuality.

Peer Relations

As adolescents spend less time with family members, peers become increasingly important. In industrialized nations, young people spend most of each weekday with agemates in school. Teenagers also spend much out-of-class time together, more in some cultures than others. For example, U.S. young people have about 50 hours of free time per week, Europeans about 45 hours, and East Asians about 33 hours (Larson, 2001). A shorter school year and less demanding academic standards, which lead American youths to devote much less time to schoolwork, account for this difference.

In the following sections, we will see that adolescent peer relations can be both positive and negative. At their best, peers serve as critical bridges between the family and adult social roles.

Friendships

Number of "best friends" declines from about four to six in early adolescence to one or two in adulthood (Hartup & Stevens, 1999). At the same time, the nature of the relationship changes.

■ **CHARACTERISTICS OF ADOLESCENT FRIENDSHIPS.** When asked about the meaning of friendship, teenagers stress three characteristics. The most important is *intimacy,* or psychological closeness, which is supported by *mutual understanding* of each other's values, beliefs, and feelings. In addition, more than younger children, teenagers want their friends to be *loyal*—to stick up for them and not to leave them for somebody else (Buhrmester, 1996; Hartup & Abecassis, 2004).

As frankness and faithfulness increase, *self-disclosure* (sharing of private thoughts and feelings) between friends rises steadily over the adolescent years (see Figure 12.2 on page 418). As a result, teenage friends get to know each other better as personalities. In addition to the many characteristics that school-age friends share (see page 340 in Chapter 10), adolescent friends tend to be alike in identity status, educational aspirations, political beliefs, and willingness to try drugs and engage in lawbreaking acts. Over time, they become more similar in these ways (Akers, Jones, & Coyl, 1998; Berndt & Murphy, 2002). Occasionally, however, teenagers choose friends with differing attitudes and values, which permits them to explore new perspectives within the security of a compatible relationship.

During adolescence, cooperation and mutual affirmation between friends increase—changes that reflect greater skill at preserving the relationship and sensitivity to a friend's needs and desires (Phillipsen, 1999). Adolescents also are less possessive of their friends than they were in childhood (Parker et al., 2005). Desiring a certain degree of autonomy for themselves, they recognize that friends need this, too.

■ **SEX DIFFERENCES IN FRIENDSHIPS.** ***TAKE A MOMENT...*** Ask several adolescents to describe their close friendships. You are likely to find a consistent sex difference: Emotional closeness is more common between girls than between boys (Markovits, Benenson, & Dolensky, 2001). Girls frequently get together to "just talk," and their interactions contain more self-disclosure and supportive statements. In contrast, boys more often gather for an activity—usually sports and competitive games. Boys' discussions usually focus on accomplishments and involve more competition and conflict (Brendgen et al., 2001; Rubin, Bukowski, & Parker, 2006).

Because of gender-role expectations, girls' friendships typically focus on communal concerns, boys' on achievement and status. Boys do form close friendship ties, but the quality of their friendships is more variable. Gender identity plays a role:

■ **FIGURE 12.2** ■ **Age changes in reported self-disclosure to parents and peers, based on findings of several studies.** Self-disclosure to friends increases steadily during adolescence, reflecting intimacy as a major basis of friendship. Self-disclosure to romantic partners also rises. However, not until the college years does it surpass intimacy with friends. Self-disclosure to parents declines in early adolescence, a time of mild parent–child conflict. As family relationships readjust to the young person's increasing autonomy, self-disclosure to parents rises. (From D. Buhrmester, 1996, "Need Fulfillment, Interpersonal Competence, and the Developmental Contexts of Early Adolescent Friendship," in W. M. Bukowski, A. F. Newcomb, & W. W. Hartup (Eds.), *The Company They Keep: Friendship During Childhood and Adolescence,* New York: Cambridge University Press, p. 168. Reprinted with the permission of Cambridge University Press.)

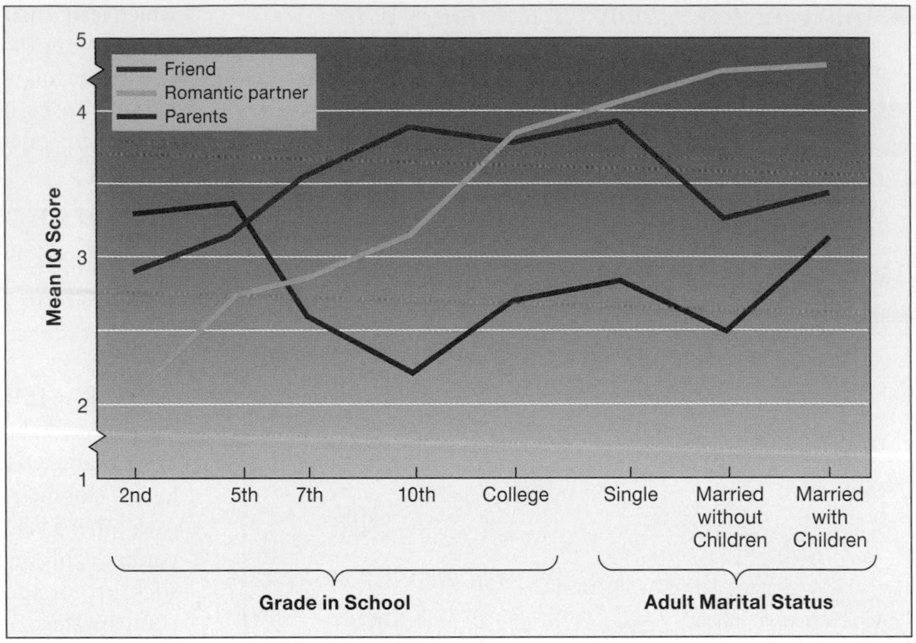

Androgynous boys are just as likely as girls to form intimate same-sex ties, whereas highly "masculine" boys are less likely to do so (Jones & Dembo, 1989).

Friendship closeness, though usually beneficial, can have costs. When focusing on deeper thoughts and feelings, adolescent friends tend to *coruminate,* or repeatedly mull over problems and negative emotions. Corumination, while contributing to high friendship quality, also triggers anxiety and depression—symptoms more common among girls than among boys (Rose, Carlson, & Waller, 2007). And when conflicts arise between intimate friends, more potential exists for one party to harm the other through relational aggression—for example, by divulging sensitive personal information to outsiders. For this reason, girls' closest same-sex friendships tend to be of shorter duration than boys' (Benenson & Christakos, 2003).

Compared to boys, girls place a higher value on emotional closeness, engaging in more self-disclosure and mutually supportive statements with friends.

■ **FRIENDSHIPS ON THE INTERNET.** Teenagers frequently use the Internet to communicate with friends. Instant messaging—their preferred means of online interaction—seems to support friendship closeness. As amount of instant messaging between preexisting friends increases, so do young people's perceptions of intimacy in the relationship and feelings of well-being (Hu et al., 2004; Valkenburg & Peter, 2007a, 2007b).

Although mostly communicating with friends they know, teenagers are also drawn to meeting new people over the Internet. Chat rooms, blogs, message boards, and social networking sites such as MySpace open up vast alternatives beyond their families, schools, and communities. Through these online ties, young people explore central adolescent issues—sexuality, challenges in parent and peer relationships, and attitudes and values—in contexts that may feel less threatening than similar everyday conversations (Subrahmanyam, Smahel, & Greenfield, 2006). Online interactions with strangers also offer some teenagers vital social support. Young people suffering from eating disorders, depression, and other problems can access message boards where participants provide mutual assistance, including a sense of group belonging and acceptance (Whitlock, Powers, & Eckenrode, 2006).

But online communication also poses dangers. In unmonitored chat rooms, teenagers are likely to encounter degrading racial and ethnic slurs and sexually obscene and harassing remarks (Tynes, Reynolds, & Greenfield, 2004). Furthermore, in a survey of a nationally representative sample of U.S. 10- to 17-year-olds, 14 percent reported online close friendships or romances (Wolak, Mitchell, & Finkelhor, 2003). Although some well-adjusted adolescents formed these bonds, many were youths who reported high levels of conflict with parents, peer victimization, depression, and delinquency, and who spent extensive time on the Internet (see Figure 12.3). They also more often had been asked by online friends for face-to-face meetings and had attended those meetings—without telling their parents.

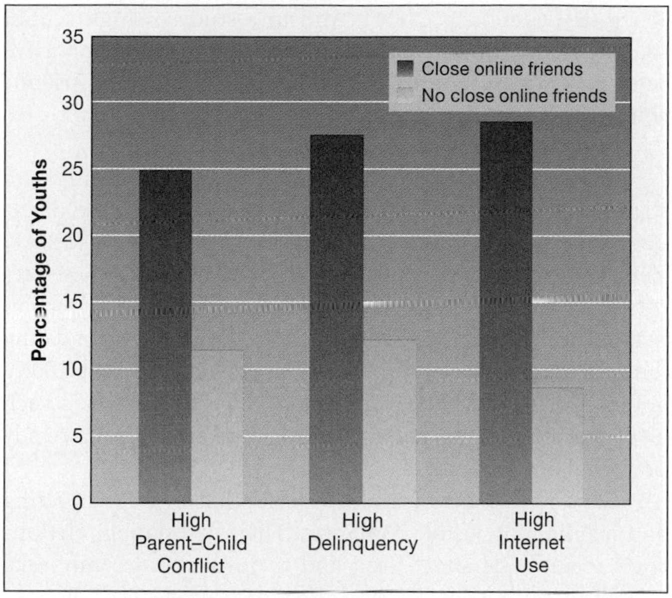

■ **FIGURE 12.3** ■ **Association of close online friendships with parent–child conflict, delinquency, and high Internet use.** In this survey of a nationally representative sample of 1,500 U. S. Internet-using 10- to 17-year-olds, those who reported that they had formed close online friendships or romances were more likely to be troubled youths who spent much time on the Internet. (Adapted from Wolak, Mitchell, & Finkelhor, 2003.)

The Internet's value for enabling convenient and satisfying communication among teenage friends must be weighed against its potential for facilitating harmful social experiences. Parents are wise to point out the risks of Internet communication, including harassment and exploitation, and to insist that teenagers follow Internet safety rules (see *www.safeteens.com*).

FRIENDSHIPS AND ADJUSTMENT. As long as adolescent friendships are not characterized by jealousy, relational aggression, or attraction to antisocial behavior, they are related to many aspects of psychological health and competence into early adulthood (Bagwell et al., 2001; Bukowski, 2001), for several reasons:

- *Close friendships provide opportunities to explore the self and develop a deep understanding of another.* Through open, honest communication, friends become sensitive to each other's strengths and weaknesses, needs and desires—a process that supports the development of self-concept, perspective taking, and identity.
- *Close friendships provide a foundation for future intimate relationships.* Recall from Figure 12.2 that self-disclosure to friends precedes disclosure to romantic partners. Conversations with teenage friends about sexuality and romance, along with the intimacy of friendship itself, may help adolescents establish and work out problems in romantic partnerships (Connolly & Goldberg, 1999).
- *Close friendships help young people deal with the stresses of adolescence.* By enhancing sensitivity to and concern for another, supportive friendships promote empathy, sympathy, and prosocial behavior. As a result, friendships contribute to involvement in constructive youth activities, avoidance of antisocial acts, and psychological well-being (Lansford et al., 2003; Wentzel, Barry, & Caldwell, 2004).
- *Close friendships can improve attitudes toward and involvement in school.* When teenagers enjoy interacting with friends at school, they may begin to view all aspects of school life more positively (Berndt & Murphy, 2002).

Cliques and Crowds

In early adolescence, *peer groups* (see Chapter 10) become increasingly common and tightly knit. They are organized into **cliques,** groups of about five to seven members who are friends and, therefore, usually resemble one another in family background, attitudes, and values. At first, cliques are limited to same-sex members. Among girls but not boys, being in a clique predicts academic and social competence. Clique membership is more important to girls, who use it as a context for expressing emotional closeness (Henrich et al., 2000). By midadolescence, mixed-sex cliques are common.

Often several cliques with similar values form a larger, more loosely organized group called a **crowd.** Unlike the more intimate clique, membership in a crowd is based on reputation and stereotype, granting the adolescent an identity within the larger social structure of the school. Prominent crowds in a typical high school might include "brains" (nonathletes who enjoy academics), "jocks" (who are very involved in sports), "populars" (class leaders who are highly social and involved in activities), "partyers" (who value socializing but care little about schoolwork), "nonconformists" (who like unconventional clothing and music), and "burnouts" (who cut school and get into trouble) (Kinney, 1999; Stone & Brown, 1999).

What influences the sorting of teenagers into cliques and crowds? Crowd affiliations are linked to strengths in adolescents' self-concepts, which reflect their abilities and interests (Prinstein & La Greca, 2002). Family factors are important, too. In a study of 8,000 ninth to twelfth graders, adolescents who described their parents as authoritative were members of "brain," "jock," and "popular" groups that accepted both adult and peer reward systems. In contrast, boys with permissive parents aligned themselves with the "partyers" and "burnouts," suggesting lack of identification with adult reward systems (Durbin et al., 1993).

These findings indicate that many peer-group values are extensions of ones acquired at home. Once adolescents join a clique or crowd, it can modify their beliefs and behavior. But the positive impact of having academically and socially skilled peers is greatest for teenagers whose own parents are authoritative. And the negative impact of having antisocial, drug-using friends is strongest for teenagers whose parents use less effective child-rearing styles (Mounts & Steinberg, 1995). In sum, family experiences affect the extent to which adolescents become like their peers over time.

As interest in dating increases, boys' and girls' cliques come together. Mixed-sex cliques provide boys and girls with models of how to interact and a chance to do so without having to be

Members of this Ultimate Frisbee team form a crowd. Unlike the more intimate clique, the larger, more loosely organized crowd grants the adolescent an identity within the larger social structure of the school.

intimate (Connolly et al., 2004). By late adolescence, when boys and girls feel comfortable enough about approaching each other directly, the mixed-sex clique disappears (Connolly & Goldberg, 1999).

Crowds also decline in importance. As adolescents settle on personal values and goals, they no longer feel a need to broadcast, through dress, language, and activities, who they are. From tenth to twelfth grade, about half of young people switch crowds, mostly in favorable directions (Strouse, 1999). "Brains" and "normal" crowds grow and deviant crowds lose members as teenagers focus more on their future.

Dating

The hormonal changes of puberty increase sexual interest, but cultural expectations determine when and how dating begins. Asian youths start dating later and have fewer dating partners than young people in Western societies, which tolerate and even encourage romantic involvements from middle school on (see Figure 12.4). At age 12 to 14, these relationships last only briefly, but by age 16 they continue, on average, for nearly two years (Carver, Joyner, & Udry, 2003). Young adolescents tend to mention recreation and achieving peer status as reasons for dating. By late adolescence, as young people are ready for greater psychological intimacy, they look for someone who offers companionship, affection, and social support (Brown, 2004; Collins & van Dulmen, 2006c).

The achievement of intimacy between dating partners typically lags behind that between friends. Recall from Chapter 6 that according to ethological theory, early attachment bonds lead to an *internal working model,* or set of expectations about attachment figures, that guides later close relationships. Consistent with this idea, secure attachment to parents in infancy and childhood—together with recollections of that security in adolescence—predicts quality of teenagers' friendship and romantic ties (Collins & van Dulmen, 2006a; Weimer, Kerns, & Oldenburg, 2004). And in a study of high school seniors, secure models of parental attachment and supportive interactions with parents predicted secure models of friendship, which, in turn, were related to the security of romantic relationships (Furman et al., 2002).

Perhaps because early adolescent dating relationships are shallow and stereotyped, early dating is related to drug use, delinquency, and poor academic achievement (Eaton et al., 2007; Zimmer-Gembeck, Siebenbruner, & Collins, 2001). These factors, along with a history of uninvolved parenting and aggression in family and peer relationships, increase the likelihood of dating violence (Arriaga & Foshee, 2004; Cyr, McDuff, & Wright, 2006). Young teenagers are better off sticking with group activities, such as parties and dances, before becoming involved with a steady boyfriend or girlfriend.

Gay and lesbian youths face special challenges in initiating and maintaining visible romances. Their first dating relationships seem to be short-lived and to involve little emotional commitment, but for reasons different from those of heterosexuals: They fear peer harassment and rejection (Diamond & Lucas, 2004). Recall from Chapter 11 that because of intense prejudice, homosexual adolescents often retreat into heterosexual dating. In addition, many have difficulty finding a same-sex partner because their homosexual peers have not yet come out. Often their first contacts with other sexual minority youths occur in support groups, where they are free to date publicly and can discuss concerns about coming out (Diamond, 2003).

As long as it does not begin too soon, dating provides lessons in cooperation, etiquette, and dealing with people in a wide range of situations. Among older teenagers, close romantic ties promote sensitivity, empathy, self-esteem, social support, and identity development (Collins, 2003; Furman & Shaffer, 2003). Still, about half of first romances do not survive high school graduation, and those that do usually become less

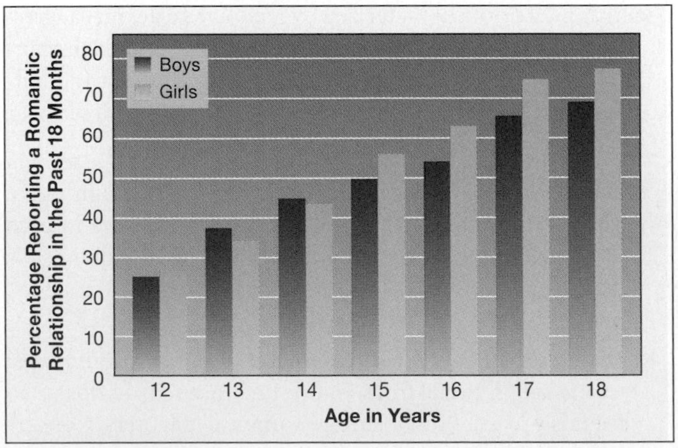

■ **FIGURE 12.4** ■ **Increase in romantic relationships in adolescence.** More than 16,000 U.S. youths responded to an interview in which they indicated whether they had been involved in a romantic relationship during the past 18 months. At age 12, about one-fourth of young people reported them, a figure that rose to about three-fourths at age 18. (Adapted from Carver, Joyner, & Udry, 2003.)

As long as dating does not begin too soon, it extends the benefits of adolescent friendships. Besides being fun, dating promotes sensitivity, empathy, and identity development as teenagers relate to someone whose needs differ from their own.

satisfying (Shaver, Furman, & Buhrmester, 1985). Because young people are still forming their identities, high school couples often find that they have little in common later.

Peer Conformity

When Franca and Antonio discovered Louis's lawbreaking during his freshman year of high school, they began to worry about the negative side of adolescent peer networks. Although conformity to peer pressure is greater during adolescence than in childhood or early adulthood, it is a complex process, varying with the young person's age, current situation, need for social approval, and culture.

A study of several hundred U.S. youths revealed that adolescents felt greatest pressure to conform to the most obvious aspects of the peer culture—dress, grooming, and participation in social activities. Peer pressure to engage in proadult behavior, such as cooperating with parents and getting good grades, was also strong (Brown, Lohr, & McClenahan, 1986). Many teenagers said that their friends actively discouraged antisocial acts. In research conducted in Singapore, a culture that emphasizes family loyalty, outcomes were similar, except that peer pressure to meet family and school obligations exceeded pressure to join in peer-culture pursuits (Sim & Koh, 2003). As these findings show, peers and parents often act in concert, toward desirable ends!

Perhaps because of greater concern with what their friends think of them, early adolescents are more likely than younger or older individuals to give in to peer pressure to engage in drug taking and delinquent acts (Brown, Clasen, & Eicher, 1986; McIntosh, MacDonald, & McKeganey, 2006). But although peers exert more influence on teenagers' day-to-day personal choices, parents have more impact on basic life values and educational plans (Steinberg, 2001). And young people who feel competent and worthwhile are less likely to fall in line behind peers.

Finally, authoritative child rearing is related to resistance to peer pressure. When parents are supportive and exert appropriate oversight, teenagers respect them and, therefore, usually follow their rules and consider their advice. In contrast, adolescents whose parents exert either too much or too little control tend to be highly peer-oriented (Allen, Porter, & McFarland, 2006). They more often rely on friends for advice about their personal lives and future and are more willing to break their parents' rules, ignore their schoolwork, and engage in other problem behaviors.

ASK YOURSELF

» REVIEW
Describe the distinct positive functions of friendships, cliques, and crowds in adolescence. What factors lead some friendships and peer-group ties to be harmful?

» APPLY
Thirteen-year-old Mattie's parents are warm, firm in their expectations, and consistent in monitoring her activities. At school, Mattie met some girls who want her to tell her parents she's going to a friend's house and then, instead, join them at the beach for a party. Is Mattie likely to comply? Explain.

» CONNECT
How might gender intensification contribute to the shallow quality of early adolescent dating relationships?

» REFLECT
How did family experiences influence your crowd membership in high school? How did your crowd membership influence your behavior?

Problems of Development

Most young people move through adolescence with little disturbance. But as we have seen, some encounter major disruptions in development, such as early parenthood, substance abuse, and school failure. In each instance, biological and psychological changes, families, schools, peers, communities, and culture combine to yield particular outcomes. Serious difficulties rarely occur in isolation but are usually interrelated—as is apparent in three additional problems of the teenage years: depression, suicide, and delinquency.

Depression

Depression—feeling sad, frustrated, and hopeless about life, accompanied by loss of pleasure in most activities and disturbances in sleep, appetite, concentration, and energy—is the most common psychological problem of adolescence. About 15 to 20 percent of teenagers have had one or more major depressive episodes, a rate comparable to that of adults. From 2 to 8 percent are chronically depressed—gloomy and self-critical for many months and sometimes years (Rushton, Forcier, & Schectman, 2002).

Serious depression affects only 1 to 2 percent of children, many of whom remain depressed in adolescence. In addition, depression increases sharply from ages 12 to 16 in industrialized nations, with many more girls than boys displaying adolescent onset. Teenage girls are twice as likely as boys to report persistent depressed mood—a difference sustained throughout the lifespan (Dekker et al., 2007; Hankin & Abela, 2005; Nolen-Hoeksema, 2002). If allowed to continue, depression seriously impairs social, academic, and vocational functioning. Unfortunately, the stereotypical view of adolescence as a period of "storm and stress" leads many adults to minimize the seriousness of adolescent depression, misinterpreting it as just a passing phase.

© DAVID GROSSMAN/THE IMAGE WORKS

In industrialized nations, stressful life events and gender-typed coping styles—passivity, dependency, and rumination—make adolescent girls more susceptible to depression than boys.

FACTORS RELATED TO DEPRESSION. The precise combination of biological and environmental factors leading to depression varies from one individual to the next. Kinship studies reveal that heredity plays an important role (Glowinski et al., 2003). Genes can induce depression by affecting the balance of neurotransmitters in the brain, the development of brain regions involved in inhibiting negative emotion, or the body's hormonal response to stress.

But experience can also activate depression, promoting any of these biological changes. A high incidence of depression and other psychological disorders is seen in parents of depressed children and adolescents. Although a genetic risk may be passed from parent to child, in earlier chapters we saw that depressed or otherwise stressed parents often engage in maladaptive parenting. As a result, their child's emotional self-regulation, attachment, and self-esteem may be impaired, with serious consequences for many cognitive and social skills (Abela et al., 2005; Yap, Allen, & Ladouceur, 2008). Depressed youths usually display a learned-helpless attributional style (see Chapter 10) (Graber, 2004). In a vulnerable young person, numerous events can spark depression—for example, failing at something important, parental divorce, or the end of a close friendship or romantic partnership.

SEX DIFFERENCES. Why are girls more prone to depression than boys? Biological changes associated with puberty cannot be responsible because the gender difference is limited to industrialized nations. In developing countries, rates of depression are similar for males and females and occasionally higher in males (Culbertson, 1997). Even when females do exceed males in depression, the size of the difference varies. For example, it is smaller in China than in North America, perhaps because of decades of efforts by the Chinese government to eliminate gender inequalities (Greenberger et al., 2000).

Instead, stressful life events and gender-typed coping styles seem to be responsible. Early-maturing girls are especially prone to depression (see Chapter 11). And the gender intensification of early adolescence often strengthens girls' passivity, dependency, and tendency to ruminate on their anxieties and problems—maladaptive approaches to tasks expected of teenagers in complex cultures. Consistent with this explanation, adolescents who identify strongly with "feminine" traits ruminate more and are more depressed, regardless of their sex (Broderick & Korteland, 2004; Papadakis et al., 2006). Girls who repeatedly feel overwhelmed develop an overly reactive physiological stress response and cope more poorly with future challenges (Nolen-Hoeksema, 2006). In this way, stressful experiences and stress reactivity feed on one another, sustaining depression. Profound depression can lead to suicidal thoughts, which all too often are translated into action.

Suicide

The suicide rate increases over the lifespan, from childhood to old age, but it jumps sharply at adolescence. Currently, suicide is the third-leading cause of death among American youths (after motor vehicle collisions and homicides) (U.S. Census Bureau, 2009b). Perhaps because U.S. teenagers experience more stress and fewer supports than in the past, the adolescent suicide rate tripled between the mid-1960s and mid-1990s, followed by a slight decline (Spirito & Esposito-Smythers, 2006). At the same time, rates of adolescent suicide vary widely among industrialized nations—low in Greece, Italy, the Netherlands, and Spain; intermediate in Australia, Canada, Japan, and the United States; and high in Finland, New Zealand, and Singapore (Bridge, Goldstein, & Brent, 2006). These international differences remain unexplained.

FACTORS RELATED TO ADOLESCENT SUICIDE. Despite girls' higher rates of depression, the number of boys who kill themselves exceeds the number of girls by a ratio of 3 or 4 to 1. Girls make more unsuccessful suicide attempts and use methods from which they are more likely to be revived, such as a sleeping pill overdose. In contrast, boys tend to choose techniques that lead to instant death, such as firearms or hanging. Gender-role expectations may contribute; less tolerance exists for feelings of helplessness and failed efforts in males than in females (Canetto & Sakinofsky, 1998).

Perhaps because of greater extended-family support, African Americans and Hispanics have lower suicide rates than

Caucasian Americans. Recently, however, suicide has risen among African-American adolescent males; the current rate approaches that of Caucasian-American males. And Native-American youths commit suicide at rates two to six times national averages (U.S. Census Bureau, 2009b). High rates of profound family poverty, school failure, alcohol and drug use, and depression probably underlie these trends.

Gay, lesbian, and bisexual youths are also at high risk, attempting suicide three times as often as other adolescents. Those who have tried to kill themselves report more family conflict over their gender-atypical behavior, inner turmoil about their sexuality, and peer victimization due to their sexual orientation (D'Augelli et al., 2005).

Suicide tends to occur in two types of young people. The first group includes adolescents who are highly intelligent but solitary, withdrawn, and unable to meet their own standards or those of important people in their lives. Members of a second, larger group show antisocial tendencies and express their unhappiness through bullying, fighting, stealing, increased risk taking, and drug abuse (Evans, Hawton, & Rodham, 2004). Besides being hostile and destructive, they turn their anger and disappointment inward.

Suicidal adolescents often have a family history of emotional and antisocial disorders. In addition, they are likely to have experienced multiple stressful life events, including economic disadvantage, parental divorce, frequent parent–child conflict, and abuse and neglect. Stressors typically increase during the period preceding a suicide attempt or completion (Beautrais, 2003; Pfeffer, 2006). Triggering events include parental blaming of the teenager for family problems, the breakup of an important peer relationship, or the humiliation of having been caught engaging in antisocial acts.

Public policies resulting in cultural disintegration have amplified suicide rates among Native-American youths. From the late 1800s to the 1970s, Native-American families were forced to enroll their children in government-run residential boarding schools designed to erase tribal affiliations. From the moment children arrived, they were not allowed to "be Indian" in any way—culturally, linguistically, artistically, or spiritually (Goldston et al., 2008). These repressive schools left many young people academically unprepared and emotionally scarred, contributing to family and community disorganization in current and succeeding generations. Consequently, youth crime and suicide rates increased (Barnes, Josefowitz, & Cole, 2006; Howell & Yuille, 2004).

Why does suicide increase in adolescence? One factor seems to be teenagers' improved ability to plan ahead. Although some act impulsively, many young people take purposeful steps toward killing themselves. Other cognitive changes also contribute. Belief in the personal fable leads many depressed young people to conclude that no one could possibly understand their intense pain. As a result, their despair and hopelessness deepen.

PREVENTION AND TREATMENT. To prevent suicides, parents and teachers must be trained to pick up on the signals that a troubled teenager sends (see Table 12.3). Schools and recreational and religious organizations can provide counseling and support (Spirito et al., 2003). Once a teenager takes steps toward suicide, staying with the young person, listening, and expressing compassion and concern until professional help can be obtained are essential.

TABLE 12.3 *Warning Signs of Suicide*

Efforts to put personal affairs in order—smoothing over troubled relationships, giving away treasured possessions
Verbal cues—saying goodbye to family members and friends, making direct or indirect references to suicide ("I won't have to worry about these problems much longer"; "I wish I were dead")
Feelings of sadness, despondency, "not caring" anymore
Extreme fatigue, lack of energy, boredom
No desire to socialize; withdrawal from friends
Easily frustrated
Emotional outbursts—spells of crying or laughing, bursts of energy
Inability to concentrate, distractible
Decline in grades, absence from school, discipline problems
Neglect of personal appearance
Sleep change—loss of sleep or excessive sleepiness
Appetite change—eating more or less than usual
Physical complaints—stomachaches, backaches, headaches

Treatments for depressed and suicidal adolescents range from antidepressant medication to individual, family, and group therapy. Until the adolescent improves, removing weapons, knives, razors, scissors, and drugs from the home is vital. On a broader scale, gun-control legislation that limits adolescents' access to the most frequent and deadly suicide method in the United States would greatly reduce both the number of suicides and the high teenage homicide rate (Commission on Adolescent Suicide Prevention, 2005).

After a suicide, family and peer survivors need support to help them cope with grief, anger, and guilt over not having been able to help the victim. Teenage suicides often occur in clusters, with one death increasing the likelihood of others among depressed peers who knew the young person or heard about the suicide through the media (Bearman & Moody, 2004; Gould, Jamieson, & Romer, 2003). In view of this trend, a watchful eye must be kept on vulnerable adolescents after a suicide happens. Restraint by journalists in publicizing teenage suicides also aids prevention.

Delinquency

Juvenile delinquents are children or adolescents who engage in illegal acts. Although youth crime has declined in the United States since the mid-1990s, 12- to 17-year-olds account for about 15 percent of police arrests, although they constitute only

8 percent of the population (U.S. Department of Justice, 2008). When asked directly and confidentially about lawbreaking, almost all teenagers admit to having committed some sort of offense—usually a minor crime, such as petty stealing or disorderly conduct (Flannery et al., 2003).

Both police arrests and self-reports show that delinquency rises over the early teenage years, remains high in middle adolescence, and then declines (Farrington, 2004; U.S. Department of Justice, 2008). Recall that among young teenagers, antisocial behavior increases as a result of desire for peer approval. Over time, peers become less influential, moral reasoning improves, and young people enter social contexts (such as higher education, work, marriage, and career) that are less conducive to lawbreaking.

For most adolescents, a brush with the law does not forecast long-term antisocial behavior. But repeated arrests are cause for concern. Teenagers are responsible for 18 percent of violent offenses in the United States (U.S. Department of Justice, 2008). A small percentage become recurrent offenders, who commit most of these crimes, and some enter a life of crime. As the Lifespan Vista box on the following page reveals, childhood-onset conduct problems are far more likely to persist than conduct problems that first appear in adolescence.

© ACE STOCK LIMITED/ALAMY

Delinquency rises during the early teen years and remains high during middle adolescence. Although most of the time it involves petty stealing and disorderly conduct, a small percentage of young people engage in repeated, serious offenses and are at risk for a life of crime.

FACTORS RELATED TO DELINQUENCY. In adolescence, the gender gap in physical aggression widens (Chesney-Lind, 2001). Although girls account for about one in five adolescent arrests for violence, their offenses are largely limited to simple assault (such as pushing or spitting). Violent crime is mostly the domain of boys (Dahlberg & Simon, 2006). SES and ethnicity are strong predictors of arrests but only mildly related to teenagers' self-reports of antisocial acts. The difference is due to the tendency to arrest, charge, and punish low-SES ethnic minority youths more often than their higher-SES white and Asian counterparts (Farrington, 2004; U.S. Department of Justice, 2008).

Difficult temperament, low intelligence, poor school performance, peer rejection in childhood, and association with antisocial peers are linked to delinquency (Laird et al., 2005). How do these factors fit together? One of the most consistent findings about delinquent youths is that their families are low in warmth, high in conflict, and characterized by harsh, inconsistent discipline and low monitoring (Barnes et al., 2006; Capaldi et al., 2002a). Because marital transitions often contribute to family discord and disrupted parenting, boys who experience parental separation and divorce are especially prone to delinquency (Farrington, 2004). And youth crime peaks on weekdays between 2:00 and 8:00 P.M., when many teenagers are unsupervised (U.S. Department of Justice, 2008).

Our discussion on page 270 in Chapter 8 explained how ineffective parenting can promote and sustain children's aggression. Boys are more likely than girls to be targets of angry, inconsistent discipline because they are more active and impulsive and therefore harder to control. When children who are extreme in these characteristics are exposed to emotionally negative, inept parenting, aggression rises during childhood, leads to violent offenses in adolescence, and persists into adulthood (again, see the Lifespan Vista box).

Teenagers commit more crimes in poverty-stricken neighborhoods with limited recreational and employment opportunities and high adult criminality (Kroneman, Loeber, & Hipwell, 2004). In such neighborhoods, adolescents have easy access to deviant peers, drugs, and firearms and are likely to be recruited into antisocial gangs, whose members commit the vast majority of violent delinquent acts. Furthermore, schools in these locales typically fail to meet students' developmental needs (Flannery et al., 2003). Large classes, weak instruction, and lax enforcement of rules increase teenagers' inclination toward aggression and violence.

PREVENTION AND TREATMENT. Because delinquency has roots in childhood and results from events in several contexts, prevention must start early and take place at multiple levels (Frey et al., 2009). Positive family relationships, authoritative parenting, high-quality teaching in schools, and communities with healthy economic and social conditions go a long way toward reducing adolescent antisocial acts.

Lacking resources for effective prevention, many U.S. schools have implemented *zero tolerance policies,* which severely punish all disruptive and threatening behavior, major and minor, usually with suspension or expulsion. Yet often they are implemented inconsistently: Low-SES minority students are two to three times as likely to be punished, especially for minor misbehaviors (Goode & Goode, 2007; Skiba & Rausch, 2006). No evidence exists that zero tolerance achieves its objective of reducing youth aggression and other forms of misconduct (Stinchcomb, Bazemore, & Riestenberg, 2006). To the contrary, some studies find that by excluding students from school, zero tolerance heightens high school dropout and antisocial behavior.

A LIFESPAN VISTA: Looking Forward, Looking Back

Two Routes to Adolescent Delinquency

Persistent adolescent delinquency follows two paths of development, one involving a small number of youths with an onset of conduct problems in childhood, the second a larger number with an onset in adolescence. The early-onset type is far more likely to lead to a life-course pattern of aggression and criminality (Moffitt, 2006). The late-onset type usually does not persist beyond the transition to early adulthood.

Both childhood-onset and adolescent-onset youths engage in serious offenses; associate with deviant peers; participate in substance abuse, unsafe sex, and dangerous driving; and spend time in correctional facilities. Why does antisocial activity more often continue and escalate into violence in the first group? Longitudinal studies yield similar answers to this question. Most research has focused on boys, but several investigations report that girls who were physically aggressive in childhood are also at risk for later problems—occasionally violent delinquency but more often other norm-violating behaviors and psychological disorders (Broidy et al., 2003; Chamberlain, 2003).

Early-Onset Type

Early-onset youngsters seem to inherit traits that predispose them to aggressiveness (Pettit, 2004). For example, violence-prone boys are emotionally negative, restless, willful, and physically aggressive as early as age 2. They also show subtle deficits in cognitive functioning that seem to contribute to disruptions in the development of language, memory, and cognitive and emotional self-regulation (Moffitt, 2006; Shaw et al., 2003). Some have attention-deficit hyperactivity disorder (ADHD), which compounds their learning and self-control problems (see Chapter 9, page 304).

Yet these biological risks are not sufficient to sustain antisocial behavior: Most early-onset boys decline in aggression over time. Among those who follow the life-course path, inept parenting transforms their undercontrolled style into defiance and persistent aggression (Brame, Nagin, & Tremblay, 2001; Broidy et al., 2003). As they fail academically and are rejected by peers, they befriend other deviant youths, who facilitate one another's violent behavior while relieving loneliness (see Figure 12.5) (Lacourse et al., 2003). Limited cognitive and social skills result in high rates of school dropout and unemployment, contributing further to antisocial involvements. Often these boys experience their first arrest before age 14—a good indicator that they will be chronic offenders by age 18 (Patterson & Yoerger, 2002).

Preschoolers high in relational aggression also tend to be hyperactive and frequently in conflict with peers and adults (Willoughby, Kupersmidt, & Bryant, 2001). As these behaviors trigger peer rejection, relationally aggressive girls befriend other girls high in relational hostility, and their relational aggression rises (Werner & Crick, 2004). Adolescents high in relational aggression are often angry, vengeful, and defiant of adult rules. Among teenagers who combine physical and relational hostility, these oppositional reactions intensify, increasing the likelihood of serious antisocial activity (Harachi et al., 2006; Prinstein, Boergers, & Vernberg, 2001).

Late-Onset Type

Other youths first display antisocial behavior around the time of puberty, gradually increasing their involvement. Their conduct problems arise from the peer context of early adolescence, not from biological deficits and a history of unfavorable development. For some, quality of parenting may decline for a time, perhaps due to family stresses or the challenges of disciplining an unruly teenager (Moffitt, 2006). When age brings gratifying adult privileges, these youths draw on prosocial skills mastered before adolescence and abandon their antisocial ways.

A few late-onset youths do continue to engage in antisocial acts. The seriousness of their adolescent offenses seems to trap them in situations that close off opportunities for responsible behavior. Being employed or in school and forming positive, close relationships predict an end to criminal offending by age 20 to 25 (Clingempeel & Henggeler, 2003; Stouthamer-Loeber et al., 2004). In contrast, the longer antisocial young people spend in prison, the more likely they are to sustain a life of crime.

These findings suggest a need for a fresh look at policies aimed at stopping youth crime. Keeping youth offenders locked up for many years disrupts their vocational lives and access to social support during a crucial period of development, condemning them to a bleak future.

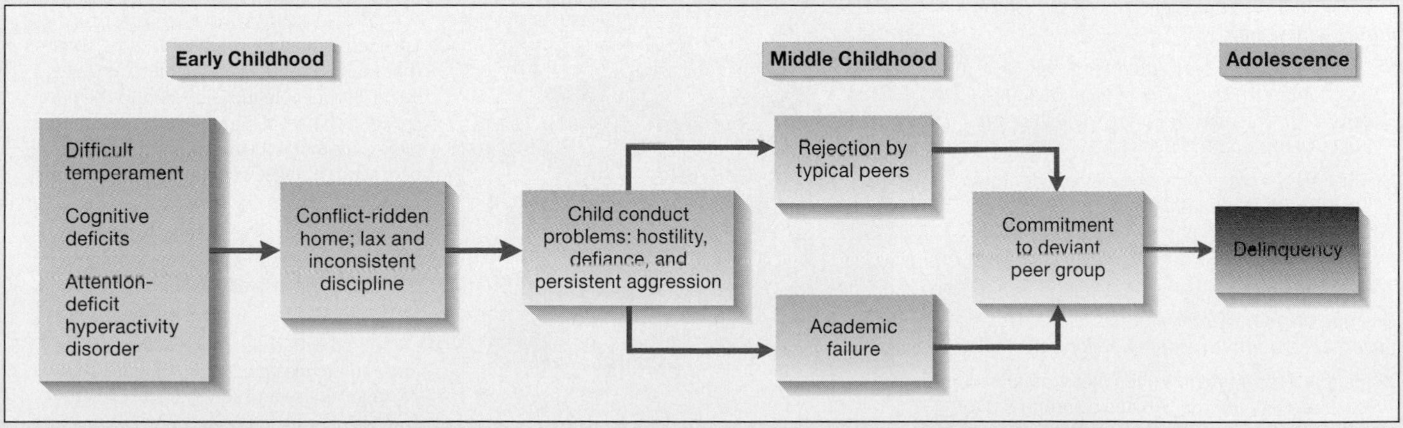

■ **FIGURE 12.5** ■ **Path to chronic delinquency for adolescents with childhood-onset antisocial behavior.** Difficult temperament and cognitive deficits characterize many of these youths in early childhood; some have attention-deficit hyperactivity disorder. Inept parenting transforms biologically based self-control difficulties into hostility and defiance.

Treating serious offenders requires an intensive, often lengthy approach, also directed at the multiple determinants of delinquency. The most effective methods include training parents in communication, monitoring, and discipline strategies and providing youths with experiences that improve cognitive and social skills, moral reasoning, and anger management and other aspects of emotional self-regulation (Gibbs et al., 2009b; Heilbrun, Lee, & Cottle, 2005).

Yet even these multidimensional treatments can fall short if young people remain embedded in hostile home lives, antisocial peer groups, and fragmented neighborhoods. In a program called *multisystemic therapy,* counselors combined family intervention with integrating violent youths into positive school, work, and leisure activities and disengaging them from deviant peers. Compared with conventional services or individual therapy, the intervention led to greater improvement in parent–child relations and school performance and a dramatic and sustained drop in number of arrests (Borduin, 2007; Henggeler, Sheidow, & Lee, 2007). Efforts to create nonaggressive environments—at the family, community, and cultural levels—are needed to help delinquent youths and to foster healthy development of all young people.

ASK YOURSELF

» REVIEW
Why are adolescent girls at greater risk for depression and adolescent boys at greater risk for suicide?

» APPLY
Zeke had been well-behaved in elementary school, but at age 13 he started spending time with the "wrong crowd." At age 16, he was arrested for property damage. Is Zeke likely to become a long-term offender? Why or why not?

» CONNECT
Reread the sections on adolescent pregnancy and substance abuse in Chapter 11. What factors do these problems have in common with suicide and delinquency?

Summary

Erikson's Theory: Identity versus Role Confusion

According to Erikson, what is the major personality achievement of adolescence?

» Erikson's theory regards **identity** as the major personality achievement of adolescence. Young people who successfully resolve the psychological conflict of **identity versus role confusion** construct a solid self-definition consisting of self-chosen values and goals.

Self-Understanding

Describe changes in self-concept and self-esteem during adolescence.

» Cognitive changes lead adolescents' self-descriptions to become more organized and consistent. Personal and moral values appear as key themes.

» Self-esteem further differentiates and, for most adolescents, rises. Authoritative parenting and schools and neighborhoods that respect the young person's ethnicity support positive self-esteem.

Describe the four identity statuses, along with factors that promote identity development.

» Identity development is often measured by exploration of alternatives and commitment to self-chosen values and goals. **Identity achievement** (commitment, preceded by exploration) and **identity moratorium** (exploration without having reached commitment) are psychologically healthy identity statuses.

» Long-term **identity foreclosure** (commitment without exploration) and **identity diffusion** (lack of both exploration and commitment) are related to adjustment difficulties.

» An information-gathering cognitive style, healthy parental attachment, interaction with diverse peers, close friendships, and schools and communities that provide rich and varied opportunities promote healthy identity development. Similarly, supportive parents, peers, and schools can foster a strong, secure **ethnic identity** among minority adolescents. A **bicultural identity** offers additional emotional and social benefits.

© DAVID GROSSMAN/THE IMAGE WORKS

Moral Development

Describe Kohlberg's theory of moral development, and evaluate its accuracy.

» According to Kohlberg, moral reasoning develops gradually through three levels, each of which contains two stages: At the **preconventional level,** morality is externally controlled by rewards, punishments, and authority figures; at the **conventional level,** conformity to laws and rules preserves positive human relationships and societal order; and at the **postconventional level,** morality is defined by abstract, universal principles of justice.

» A reexamination of Kohlberg's stages suggests that moral maturity can be found at Stages 3 and 4; few people move beyond to the postconventional level. The influence of situational factors on moral judgment suggests that Kohlberg's moral stages are best viewed as loosely organized and overlapping.

» Contrary to Gilligan's claim, Kohlberg's theory does not underestimate the moral reasoning of females but instead taps both justice and caring moralities.

» Compared with children, teenagers display more subtle reasoning about conflicts between personal choice and community obligation. They are also increasingly aware of the moral implications of following social conventions.

Describe influences on moral reasoning and its relationship to moral behavior.

» Experiences contributing to moral maturity include warm, rational child-rearing practices, years of schooling, and peer discussions of moral issues. In village societies, where moral cooperation is based on direct relations between people, moral reasoning rarely moves beyond Kohlberg's Stage 3. In collectivist cultures, dilemma responses often are more other-directed than in Western societies.

» Maturity of moral reasoning is only modestly related to moral behavior. Moral action is also influenced by the individual's empathy and guilt, temperament, history of morally relevant experiences, and **moral self-relevance.**

© JIM WEST/THE IMAGE WORKS

» Despite declines in formal religious involvement in adolescence, most religiously affiliated teenagers are advantaged in moral values and behavior.

Gender Typing

Why is early adolescence a period of gender intensification?

» Biological, social, and cognitive factors jointly contribute to **gender intensification.** As pubertal changes occur and concern with what others think strengthens, teenagers focus on gender-linked attributes. Also, parents and dating partners encourage gender-appropriate behavior.

The Family

Discuss changes in parent–child and sibling relationships during adolescence.

» In their quest for **autonomy,** adolescents strive to rely more on themselves and less on parents for decision making. As teenagers deidealize their parents, they often question parental authority. During a time of major life transitions, adolescents and parents approach situations with conflicting expectations and from different perspectives. Warm, supportive parenting and consistent monitoring predict favorable outcomes, even in the face of reduced time spent with parents.

» Sibling relationships become less intense as adolescents separate from the family and turn toward peers. Still, attachment to siblings remains strong for most young people.

Peer Relations

Describe adolescent friendships, peer groups, and dating relationships and their consequences for development.

» Adolescent friendships are based on greater intimacy, mutual understanding, and loyalty and contain more self-disclosure. Girls' friendships place greater emphasis on emotional closeness, boys' on shared activities and accomplishments.

» As long as they are not characterized by jealousy, relational aggression, or attraction to antisocial behavior, adolescent friendships promote self-concept, perspective taking, identity, and the capacity for intimate relationships. They also help young people deal with stress and can improve attitudes toward school.

» Adolescent peer groups are organized into more intimate **cliques,** particularly important to girls, and **crowds,** which grant teenagers an identity within the larger social structure of the school. Parenting styles influence the assortment of teenagers into cliques and crowds. With interest in dating, mixed-sex cliques grow in importance and then decline. Crowds also diminish, as teenagers settle on personal values and goals.

» Intimacy in dating relationships lags behind that of same-sex friendships. Positive relationships with parents and friends contribute to secure romantic ties, which enhance emotional and social development in older teenagers.

© NICO KAI/ICONICA/GETTY IMAGES

Discuss conformity to peer pressure in adolescence.

» Peer conformity is greater during adolescence than earlier or later. Young teenagers are most likely to give in to peer pressure for antisocial behavior. Yet most peer pressure is not in conflict with important adult values. Authoritative parenting is related to resistance to unfavorable peer pressure.

Problems of Development

What factors are related to adolescent depression and suicide?

» Depression is the most common psychological problem of the teenage years, with girls at greater risk in industrialized nations. Various combinations of biological and environmental factors are implicated—heredity, maladaptive parenting, learned-helpless attributional style, and negative life events.

» The suicide rate increases dramatically at adolescence. Boys account for most teenage deaths by suicide, while girls make more unsuccessful suicide attempts. Teenagers at risk for suicide may be intelligent, solitary, and withdrawn, but more often, they are antisocial. Family turmoil is common in the backgrounds of suicidal adolescents.

Discuss factors related to delinquency.

» Although almost all teenagers engage in some delinquent activity, only a few are serious repeat offenders. Most are boys with a childhood history of conduct problems.

» A consistent factor related to delinquency is a family environment low in warmth, high in conflict, and characterized by inconsistent discipline and low monitoring. Poverty-stricken neighborhoods with high crime rates and ineffective schools also promote lawbreaking.

Important Terms and Concepts

acculturative stress (p. 406)
autonomy (p. 415)
bicultural identity (p. 406)
clique (p. 419)
conventional level (p. 408)
crowd (p. 419)
ethnic identity (p. 406)
gender intensification (p. 414)
identity (p. 402)
identity achievement (p. 403)
identity diffusion (p. 403)
identity foreclosure (p. 403)
identity moratorium (p. 403)
identity versus role confusion (p. 402)
moral self-relevance (p. 412)
postconventional level (p. 408)
preconventional level (p. 407)

Milestones

Development in Adolescence

Early Adolescence: 11–14

PHYSICAL

- If a girl, reaches peak of growth spurt. (363)
- If a girl, adds more body fat than muscle. (363–364)
- If a girl, starts to menstruate. (366)
- If a boy, begins growth spurt. (363)
- If a boy, starts to ejaculate seminal fluid. (366)
- Is likely to be aware of sexual orientation. (376)
- If a girl, motor performance increases gradually, leveling off by age 14. (364)
- Shows heightened stress response and novelty-seeking. (367)

COGNITIVE

- Shows gains in hypothetico-deductive reasoning and propositional thought. (383–384)
- Improves in scientific reasoning—coordinating theory with evidence—on complex, multivariable tasks. (385)
- Becomes more self-conscious and self-focused. (386–387)
- Becomes more idealistic and critical. (388)
- Metacognition and self-regulation continue to improve. (385)

EMOTIONAL/SOCIAL

- Self-concept includes abstract descriptors unifying separate personality traits, but these are are often contradictory and not interconnected. (402)
- Shows gender intensification—increased gender stereotyping of attitudes and behavior. (414)
- In striving for autonomy, spends less time with parents and siblings, more time with peers. (417)
- Friendships decline in number and are based on intimacy, mutual understanding, and loyalty. (417)
- Peer groups become organized around same-sex cliques. (419)
- Cliques with similar values form crowds. (419–420)
- Conformity in response to peer pressure increases. (421)

Middle Adolescence: 14–16

PHYSICAL

- If a girl, completes growth spurt. (363)
- If a boy, reaches peak of growth spurt. (363)
- If a boy, voice deepens. (366)
- If a boy, adds muscle while body fat declines. (364)
- If a boy, motor performance improves dramatically. (364)
- May have had sexual intercourse. (375)

COGNITIVE

- Continues to improve in hypothetico-deductive reasoning and propositional thought. (383–384)

Note: Numbers in parentheses indicate the page or pages on which each milestone is discussed.

- Continues to improve in scientific reasoning, following a similar sequential order on different types of tasks. (386)
- Becomes less self-conscious and self-focused. (387)
- Improves in everyday decision making. (388)

EMOTIONAL/SOCIAL

- Combines features of the self into an organized self-concept. (402)
- Self-esteem differentiates further and tends to rise. (402–403)

- In most cases, begins to move from "lower" to "higher" identity statuses. (403–404)
- Is likely to engage in societal perspective taking. (336, 408)
- Increasingly emphasizes ideal reciprocity and societal laws as the basis for resolving moral dilemmas. (408)
- Engages in more subtle reasoning about conflicts between moral, social-conventional, and personal-choice issues. (410)
- Gender intensification declines. (415)
- Mixed-sex cliques become common. (419–420)
- Has probably started dating. (420)
- Conformity to peer pressure may decline. (421)

Late Adolescence: 16–18

PHYSICAL

- If a boy, completes growth spurt. (363)
- If a boy, gains in motor performance continue. (364)

COGNITIVE

- Continues to improve in metacognition, scientific reasoning, and decision making. (385–386, 388)

EMOTIONAL/SOCIAL

- Self-concept emphasizes personal and moral standards. (402)
- Continues to construct an identity, typically moving to higher identity statuses. (403–405)
- Continues to advance in maturity of moral reasoning. (407–409)
- Cliques and crowds decline in importance. (419–420)
- Seeks psychological intimacy in romantic ties, which last longer. (420)

Photo credits appear on p. ii.

© DANIEL LECLAIR/REUTERS/CORBIS

Early adulthood brings momentous changes—among them, selecting a vocation, starting full-time work, and attaining economic independence. Once young adults embark on a career path, as this young Guatemalan archaeologist has, strong ties with mentors are vital for success.

CHAPTER 13

Physical and Cognitive Development in Early Adulthood

The back seat and trunk piled high with belongings, 23-year-old Sharese hugged her mother and brother goodbye, jumped in the car, and headed toward the interstate with a sense of newfound freedom mixed with apprehension. Three months earlier, the family had watched proudly as Sharese received her bachelor's degree in chemistry from a small university 40 miles from her home. Her college years had been a time of gradual release from economic and psychological dependency on her family. She returned home periodically on weekends and lived there during the summer months. Her mother supplemented Sharese's loans with a monthly allowance. But this day marked a turning point. She was moving to her own apartment in a city 800 miles away, with plans to work on a master's degree. With a teaching assistantship and a student loan, Sharese felt more "on her own" than at any previous time in her life.

During her college years, Sharese made lifestyle changes and settled on a vocational direction. Overweight throughout high school, she lost 20 pounds in her sophomore year, revised her diet, and began an exercise regimen by joining the university's Ultimate Frisbee team, eventually becoming its captain. A summer spent as a counselor at a camp for chronically ill children helped convince Sharese to apply her background in science to a career in public health.

Still, two weeks before she was to leave, Sharese confided in her mother that she was having doubts about her decision. "Sharese," her mother advised, "we never know if our life choices are going to suit us just right, and most times they aren't perfect. It's what we make of them—how we view and mold them—that turns them into successes." So Sharese embarked on her journey and found herself face-to-face with a multitude of exciting challenges and opportunities.

In this chapter, we take up the physical and cognitive sides of early adulthood, which extends from about age 18 to 40. As noted in Chapter 1, the adult years are difficult to divide into discrete periods because the timing of important milestones varies greatly among individuals—much more so than in childhood and adolescence. But for most people, early adulthood involves a common set of tasks: leaving home, completing education, beginning full-time work, attaining economic independence, establishing a long-term sexually and emotionally intimate relationship, and starting a family. These are energetic decades filled with momentous decisions that—more than any other time of life—offer the potential for living to the fullest.

Physical Development

We have seen that throughout childhood and adolescence, the body grows larger and stronger, coordination improves, and sensory systems gather information more effectively. Once body structures reach maximum capacity and efficiency, **biological aging,** or **senescence,** begins—genetically influenced declines in the functioning of organs and systems that are universal in all members of our species. Like physical growth, however, biological aging varies widely across parts of the body, and individual differences are great—variation that the *lifespan perspective* helps us understand. A host of contextual factors—including each person's unique genetic makeup, lifestyle, living environment, and historical period—influence biological aging, each of which can accelerate or slow age-related declines (Arking, 2006). As a result, the physical changes of the adult years are, indeed, *multidimensional* and *multidirectional* (see page 9 in Chapter 1).

In the following sections, we examine the process of biological aging. Then we turn to physical and motor changes already under way in early adulthood. As you will see, biological aging is not fixed and immutable. It can be modified substantially through behavioral and environmental interventions. Over the past century, improved nutrition, medical treatment, sanitation, and safety have added 25 to 30 years to *average life expectancy* in industrialized nations (see Chapter 1, page 8). We will take up life expectancy in greater depth in Chapter 17.

This rock climber, in her early twenties, is at her peak in strength, endurance, sensory acuteness, and immune system responsiveness.

Biological Aging Is Under Way in Early Adulthood

At an intercollegiate tournament, Sharese dashed across the playing field for hours, leaping high to catch Frisbees sailing her way. In her early twenties, she is at her peak in strength, endurance, sensory acuteness, and immune system responsiveness. Yet over the next two decades, she will age and, as she moves into middle and late adulthood, will show more noticeable declines.

Biological aging is the combined result of many causes, some operating at the level of DNA, others at the level of cells, and still others at the level of tissues, organs, and the whole organism. Hundreds of theories exist, indicating that our understanding is still in an early stage (Arking, 2006). For example, one popular idea—the *"wear-and-tear" theory*—is that the body wears out from use. But no relationship exists between physical activity and early death. To the contrary, regular, moderate-to-vigorous exercise predicts a healthier, longer life for people differing widely in SES and ethnicity (Cockerham et al., 2004; Stessman et al., 2005). We now know that this "wear-and-tear" theory is an oversimplification.

Aging at the Level of DNA and Body Cells

Current explanations of biological aging at the level of DNA and body cells are of two types: (1) those that emphasize the *programmed effects of specific genes* and (2) those that emphasize the *cumulative effects of random events* that damage genetic and cellular material. Support for both views exists, and a combination may eventually prove to be correct.

Genetically programmed aging receives some support from kinship studies indicating that longevity is a family trait. People whose parents had long lives tend to live longer themselves. And greater similarity exists in the lifespans of identical than fraternal twins. But the heritability of longevity is modest, ranging from .15 to .25 for age at death and from .27 to .57 for various measures of current biological age, such as strength of hand grip, respiratory capacity, blood pressure, and bone density (Cevenini et al., 2008; Kerber et al., 2001; Mitchell et al., 2001). Rather than inheriting longevity directly, people probably

BIOLOGY AND ENVIRONMENT

Telomere Length: A New Marker of the Impact of Life Circumstances on Biological Aging

In the not-too-distant future, your annual physical exam may include an assessment of the length of your *telomeres*—DNA at the ends of chromosomes, which safeguard the stability of your cells. Telomeres shorten with each cell duplication; when they drop below a critical length, the cell can no longer divide and becomes senescent. Although telomeres shorten with age, the rate at which they do so varies greatly. An enzyme called *telomerase* prevents shortening and can even reverse the trend, causing telomeres to lengthen and, thus, protecting the aging cell.

Over the past decade, research examining the influence of life circumstances on telomere length has exploded. A well-established finding is that chronic illnesses, such as cardiovascular disease and cancer, hasten telomere shortening in white blood cells, which play a vital role in the immune response (see page 437). Telomere shortening, in turn, predicts more rapid disease progression and earlier death (Fuster & Andres, 2006).

Accelerated telomere shortening has been linked to a variety of unhealthy behaviors, including cigarette smoking and the physical inactivity and overeating that lead to obesity and to insulin resistance, which often precedes type 2 diabetes (Epel et al., 2006; Gardner et al., 2005). Unfavorable health conditions may alter telomere length as early as the prenatal period, with possible long-term negative consequences for biological aging. In research on rats, poor maternal nutrition during pregnancy resulted in low birth weight and development of shorter telomeres in kidney and heart tissue (Jennings et al., 1999; Tarry-Adkins et al., 2008). In a related human investigation, preschoolers who had been low-birth-weight as infants had shorter telomeres in their white blood cells than did their normal-birth-weight agemates (Raqib et al., 2007).

Persistent psychological stress—parenting a child with a chronic illness, caring for an elder with dementia, or severe depression—is linked to reduced telomerase activity and telomere shortness in white blood cells (Damjanovic et al., 2007; Epel et al., 2004; McEwen, 2007; Simon et al., 2006). Can stress actually modify telomeres? In a laboratory experiment, researchers exposed human white blood cells to the stress hormone cortisol. The cells responded by decreasing production of telomerase (Choi, Fauce, & Effros, 2008).

Fortunately, when adults make positive lifestyle changes, telomeres seem to respond accordingly. In one study, declines in psychological stress were associated with telomere lengthening in white blood cells (Epel et al., 2009). In another investigation of men with low-risk prostate cancer, three months of intensive improvement in diet and exercise led to decreased blood cholesterol and psychological stress, along with increased white blood cell telomerase activity (Ornish et al., 2008).

Currently, researchers are working on identifying sensitive periods of telomere change—times when telomeres are most susceptible to modification. Early intervention—for example, enhanced prenatal care and interventions to reduce obesity in childhood—may be particularly powerful. But telomeres are changeable well into late adulthood (Epel et al., 2009). As our understanding of predictors and consequences of telomere length expands, it may become an important index of health and aging throughout life.

© THINKSTOCK/GETTY IMAGES

Accelerated telomere shortening has been linked to a variety of unhealthy behaviors. Fortunately, positive lifestyle changes, including healthy diet and exercise, seem to trigger a positive response in telomeres.

inherit one or more risk factors, which influence their chances of dying earlier or later.

One "genetic programming" theory proposes the existence of "aging genes" that control certain biological changes, such as menopause, gray hair, and deterioration of body cells. The strongest evidence for this view comes from research showing that human cells allowed to divide in the laboratory have a lifespan of 50 divisions, plus or minus 10 (Hayflick, 1998). With each duplication, a special type of DNA called **telomeres**—located at the ends of chromosomes, serving as a "cap" to protect the ends from destruction—shortens. Eventually, so little remains that the cells no longer duplicate at all. Telomere shortening acts as a brake against somatic mutations (such as those involved in cancer), which become more likely as cells duplicate (Wright & Shay, 2005). But an increase in the number of senescent cells (ones with short telomeres) also contributes to age-related disease, loss of function, and earlier mortality (Epel et al., 2009; Shin et al., 2006). As the Biology and Environment box above reveals, researchers have begun to identify health behaviors and psychological states that accelerate telomere shortening—powerful biological evidence that certain life circumstances compromise longevity.

According to an alternative, "random events" theory, DNA in body cells is gradually damaged through spontaneous or externally caused mutations. As these accumulate, cell repair and replacement become less efficient, and abnormal cancerous cells are often produced. Animal studies confirm an increase in DNA breaks and deletions and damage to other cellular material with age. Similar evidence is accruing for humans (Schumacher, Garinis, & Hoeijmakers, 2007).

© RONNIE KAUFMAN/LARRY HIRSHOWITZ/GETTY IMAGES/BLEND IMAGES

Kinship studies indicate that longevity is a family trait. In addition to favorable heredity, these grandsons will likely benefit from the model of a fit, active grandfather who buffers stress by enjoying life.

One probable cause of age-related DNA and cellular abnormalities is the release of **free radicals**—naturally occurring, highly reactive chemicals that form in the presence of oxygen. (Radiation and certain pollutants and drugs can trigger similar effects.) When oxygen molecules break down within the cell, the reaction strips away an electron, creating a free radical. As it seeks a replacement from its surroundings, it destroys nearby cellular material, including DNA, proteins, and fats essential for cell functioning. Free radicals are thought to be involved in more than 60 disorders of aging, including cardiovascular disease, neurological disorders, cancer, cataracts, and arthritis (Barja, 2004; Cutler & Mattson, 2006). Although our bodies produce substances that neutralize free radicals, some harm occurs, and it accumulates over time.

Animal species with longer life expectancies display slower rates of free-radical damage to DNA (Sanz, Pamplona, & Barja, 2006). Some researchers believe that genes for longevity work by defending against free radicals. In this way, a programmed genetic response may limit random DNA and cellular deterioration. Foods rich in vitamins C and E and beta-carotene also forestall free-radical damage—a reason that improved diet contributes to gains in life expectancy (Milbury & Richer, 2008).

Aging at the Level of Tissues and Organs

What consequences might the DNA and cellular deterioration just described have for the structure and functioning of organs and tissues? There are many possibilities. Among those with clear support is the **cross-linkage theory of aging.** Over time, protein fibers that make up the body's connective tissue form bonds, or links, with one another. When these normally separate fibers cross-link, tissue becomes less elastic, leading to many negative outcomes, including loss of flexibility in the skin and other organs, clouding of the lens of the eye, clogging of arteries, and damage to the kidneys. Like other aspects of aging, cross-linking can be reduced by external factors, including regular exercise and a vitamin-rich, low-fat diet (Schneider, 1992; Wickens, 2001).

Gradual failure of the endocrine system, which produces and regulates hormones, is yet another route to aging. An obvious example is decreased estrogen production in women, which culminates in menopause. Because hormones affect many body functions, disruptions in the endocrine system can have widespread effects on health and survival. For example, a gradual drop in growth hormone (GH) is associated with loss of muscle and bone mass, addition of body fat, thinning of the skin, and decline in cardiovascular functioning. In adults with abnormally low levels of GH, hormone therapy can slow these symptoms, but it has serious side effects, including increased risk of fluid retention in tissues, muscle pain, and cancer (Harman & Blackman, 2004; Toogood, 2004). So far, diet and physical activity are safer ways to limit these aspects of biological aging.

Finally, declines in immune system functioning contribute to many conditions of aging, including increased susceptibility to infectious disease and cancer and changes in blood vessel walls associated with cardiovascular disease. Decreased vigor of the immune response seems to be genetically programmed, but other aging processes we have considered (such as weakening of the endocrine system) can intensify it (Hawkley & Cacioppo, 2004; Malaguarnera et al., 2001). Indeed, combinations of theories—the ones just reviewed as well as others—are needed to explain the complexities of biological aging. With this in mind, let's turn to physical signs and other characteristics of aging.

Physical Changes

During the twenties and thirties, changes in physical appearance and declines in body functioning are so gradual that most are hardly noticeable. Later, they will accelerate. The physical changes of aging are summarized in Table 13.1. We will examine several in detail here and take up others in later chapters. Before we begin, let's note that these trends are derived largely from cross-sectional studies. Because younger cohorts have experienced better health care and nutrition, cross-sectional evidence can exaggerate impairments associated with aging. Fortunately, longitudinal evidence is expanding, helping to correct this picture.

Cardiovascular and Respiratory Systems

During her first month in graduate school, Sharese pored over research articles on cardiovascular functioning. In her African-American extended family, her father, an uncle, and three aunts had died of heart attacks in their forties and fifties. These tragedies prompted Sharese to reconsider her own health-related behaviors. She also decided to enter the field of public health in hopes of finding ways to relieve health problems among black Americans. *Hypertension,* or high blood pressure, occurs 12 percent more often in the U.S. black than in the U.S. white population;

TABLE 13.1 ■ *Physical Changes of Aging*

ORGAN OR SYSTEM	TIMING OF CHANGE	DESCRIPTION
Sensory		
Vision	From age 30	As the lens stiffens and thickens, ability to focus on close objects declines. Yellowing of the lens, weakening of muscles controlling the pupil, and clouding of the vitreous (gelatin-like substance that fills the eye) reduce light reaching the retina, impairing color discrimination and night vision. Visual acuity, or fineness of discrimination, decreases, with a sharp drop between ages 70 and 80.
Hearing	From age 30	Sensitivity to sound declines, especially at high frequencies but gradually extending to all frequencies. Change is more than twice as rapid for men as for women.
Taste	From age 60	Sensitivity to the four basic tastes—sweet, salty, sour, and bitter—is reduced. This may be due to factors other than aging, since number and distribution of taste buds do not change.
Smell	From age 60	Loss of smell receptors reduces ability to detect and identify odors.
Touch	Gradual	Loss of touch receptors reduces sensitivity on the hands, particularly the fingertips.
Cardiovascular	Gradual	As the heart muscle becomes more rigid, maximum heart rate decreases, reducing the heart's ability to meet the body's oxygen requirements when stressed by exercise. As artery walls stiffen and accumulate plaque, blood flow to body cells is reduced.
Respiratory	Gradual	Under physical exertion, respiratory capacity decreases and breathing rate increases. Stiffening of connective tissue in the lungs and chest muscles makes it more difficult for the lungs to expand to full volume.
Immune	Gradual	Shrinking of the thymus limits maturation of T cells and disease-fighting capacity of B cells, impairing the immune response.
Muscular	Gradual	As nerves stimulating them die, fast-twitch muscle fibers (responsible for speed and explosive strength) decline in number and size to a greater extent than slow-twitch fibers (which support endurance). Tendons and ligaments (which transmit muscle action) stiffen, reducing speed and flexibility of movement.
Skeletal	Begins in the late thirties, accelerates in the fifties, slows in the seventies	Cartilage in the joints thins and cracks, leading bone ends beneath it to erode. New cells continue to be deposited on the outer layer of the bones, and mineral content of bone declines. The resulting broader but more porous bones weaken the skeleton and make it more vulnerable to fracture. Change is more rapid in women than in men.
Reproductive	In women, accelerates after age 35; in men, begins after age 40	Fertility problems (including difficulty conceiving and carrying a pregnancy to term) and risk of having a baby with a chromosomal disorder increase.
Nervous	From age 50	Brain weight declines as neurons lose water content and die, mostly in the cerebral cortex, and as ventricles (spaces) within the brain enlarge. Development of new synapses and limited generation of new neurons can, in part, compensate for these declines.
Skin	Gradual	Epidermis (outer layer) is held less tightly to the dermis (middle layer); fibers in the dermis and hypodermis (inner layer) thin; fat cells in the hypodermis decline. As a result, the skin becomes looser, less elastic, and wrinkled. Change is more rapid in women than in men.
Hair	From age 35	Grays and thins.
Height	From age 50	Loss of bone strength leads to collapse of disks in the spinal column, leading to a height loss of as much as 2 inches by the seventies and eighties.
Weight	Increases to age 50; declines from age 60	Weight change reflects a rise in fat and a decline in muscle and bone mineral. Since muscle and bone are heavier than fat, the resulting pattern is weight gain followed by loss. Body fat accumulates on the torso and decreases on the extremities.

Sources: Arking, 2006; Whalley, 2001; Whitbourne, 1996.

the rate of death from heart disease among African Americans is 30 percent higher (American Heart Association, 2009).

Sharese was surprised to learn that fewer age-related changes occur in the heart than we might expect, given that heart disease is a leading cause of death throughout adulthood, responsible for as many as 10 percent of U.S. male and 5 percent of U.S. female deaths between ages 20 and 34—figures that more than double in the following decade and, thereafter, continue to rise steadily with age (Lloyd-Jones et al., 2009). In healthy individuals, the heart's ability to meet the body's oxygen requirements under typical conditions (as measured by heart rate in relation to volume of blood pumped) does not change during adulthood. Only during stressful exercise does heart performance decline with age—a change due to a decrease in maximum heart rate and greater rigidity of the heart muscle (Arking, 2006). Consequently, the heart has difficulty delivering enough oxygen to the body during high activity and bouncing back from strain.

One of the most serious diseases of the cardiovascular system is *atherosclerosis,* in which heavy deposits of plaque containing cholesterol and fats collect on the walls of the main arteries. If present, it usually begins early in life, progresses during middle adulthood, and culminates in serious illness. Atherosclerosis is multiply determined, making it hard to separate the contributions of biological aging from individual genetic and environmental influences. The complexity of causes is illustrated by animal research indicating that before puberty, a high-fat diet produces only fatty streaks on the artery walls (Olson, 2000). In sexually mature adults, however, it leads to serious plaque deposits, suggesting that sex hormones may heighten the insults of a high-fat diet.

Heart disease has decreased considerably since the mid-twentieth century, with a larger drop in the last 20 years due to a decline in cigarette smoking, to improved diet and exercise among at-risk individuals, and to better medical detection and treatment of high blood pressure and cholesterol (American Heart Association, 2008). And as longitudinal research on more than 17,000 Chicago-area 18- to 39-year-olds revealed, young adults at low risk for heart disease—defined by not smoking, absence of diabetes, and normal blood cholesterol, blood pressure, and body weight—had much lower death rates than their higher-risk agemates over the succeeding three decades (Daviglus et al., 2004; Stamler et al., 1999). Later, when we consider health and fitness, we will see why heart attacks were so common in Sharese's family—and why they occur at especially high rates in the African-American population.

Like the heart, the lungs show few age-related changes in functioning at rest, but during physical exertion, respiratory volume decreases and breathing rate increases with age. Maximum vital capacity (amount of air that can be forced in and out of the lungs) declines by 10 percent per decade after age 25 (Mahanran et al., 1999). Connective tissue in the lungs, chest muscles, and ribs stiffens with age, making it more difficult for the lungs to expand to full volume (Smith & Cotter, 2008). Fortunately, under normal conditions, we use less than half our vital capacity. Nevertheless, aging of the lungs contributes to older adults' difficulty in meeting the body's oxygen needs while exercising.

Motor Performance

Declines in heart and lung functioning under conditions of exertion, combined with gradual muscle loss, lead to changes in motor performance. In most people, the impact of biological aging on motor skills is difficult to separate from decreases in motivation and practice. Therefore, researchers study outstanding athletes, who try to attain their very best performance in real life (Tanaka & Seals, 2003). As long as athletes continue intensive training, their attainments at each age approach the limits of what is biologically possible.

Many athletic skills peak between ages 20 and 35, then gradually decline. In several investigations, the mean ages for best performance of Olympic and professional athletes in a variety of sports were charted over time. Absolute performance in most events improved over the past century. Athletes continually set new world records, suggesting improved training methods. But ages of best performance remained relatively constant. Athletic tasks that require speed of limb movement, explosive strength, and gross-motor coordination—sprinting, jumping, and tennis—typically peak in the early twenties. Those that depend on endurance, arm–hand steadiness, and aiming—long-distance running, baseball, and golf—usually peak in the late twenties and early thirties. Because these skills require either stamina or precise motor control, they take longer to perfect (Schulz & Curnow, 1988).

Research on outstanding athletes tells us that the upper biological limit of motor capacity is reached in the first part of early adulthood. How quickly do athletic skills weaken in later years? Longitudinal research on master runners reveals that as long as practice continues, speed drops only slightly from the mid-thirties into the sixties, when performance falls off at an accelerating pace (see Figure 13.1) (Tanaka & Higuchi, 1998; Trappe, 2007). In the case of long-distance swimming—a non-weight-bearing exercise with a low incidence of injury—the decline in speed is even more gradual: The accelerating performance drop-off is delayed until the seventies (Tanaka & Seals, 1997).

In 2009, 37-year-old Lance Armstrong attempted the near-impossible by going for an eighth victory in the Tour de France, the world's toughest cycling race. He scored an impressive third place; first and second place went to cyclists more than ten years younger. Sustained training leads to adaptations in body structures that minimize motor decline into the sixties.

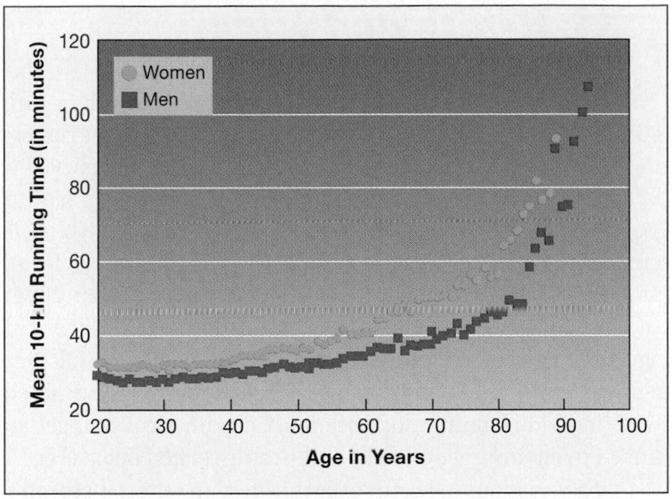

■ **FIGURE 13.1** ■ **Ten-kilometer running times with advancing age, based on longitudinal performances of hundreds of master athletes.** Runners maintain their speed into the mid-thirties, followed by modest increases in running times into the sixties, with a progressively steeper increase thereafter. (From H. Tanaka & D. R. Seals, 2003, "Dynamic Exercise Performance in Masters Athletes: Insight into the Effects of Primary Human Aging on Physiological Functional Capacity," *Journal of Applied Physiology, 5,* p. 2153. Adapted with permission of The American Physiological Society.)

Indeed, sustained training leads to adaptations in body structures that minimize motor decline. For example, vital capacity is one-third greater in both younger and older people who participate actively in sports than in healthy inactive agemates (Pimentel et al., 2003; Tanaka et al., 1997). Training also slows muscle loss, increases speed and force of muscle contraction, and leads fast-twitch muscle fibers to be converted into slow-twitch fibers, which support excellent long-distance running performance and other endurance skills (Faulkner et al., 2007; Trappe, 2001).

In sum, although athletic skills are at their best in early adulthood, biological aging accounts for only a small part of age-related decline until advanced old age. Lower levels of performance by healthy people into their sixties and seventies largely reflect reduced capacities resulting from adaptation to a less physically demanding lifestyle.

Immune System

The immune response is the combined work of specialized cells that neutralize or destroy antigens (foreign substances) in the body. Two types of white blood cells play vital roles. *T cells,* which originate in the bone marrow and mature in the thymus (a small gland located in the upper part of the chest), attack antigens directly. *B cells,* manufactured in the bone marrow, secrete antibodies into the bloodstream that multiply, capture antigens, and permit the blood system to destroy them. Since receptors on their surfaces recognize only a single antigen, T and B cells come in great variety. They join with additional cells to produce immunity.

The capacity of the immune system to offer protection against disease increases through adolescence and declines after age 20. The trend is partly due to changes in the thymus, which is largest during the teenage years, then shrinks until it is barely detectable by age 50. As a result, production of thymic hormones is reduced, and the thymus is less able to promote full maturity and differentiation of T cells. Because B cells release far more antibodies when T cells are present, the immune response is compromised further (Weng, 2008).

Withering of the thymus is not the only reason that the body gradually becomes less effective in warding off illness. The immune system interacts with the nervous and endocrine systems. For example, psychological stress can weaken the immune response (Coe & Laudenslager, 2007; Larbi et al., 2008). During final exams, for example, Sharese was less resistant to colds. And in the month after her father died, she had great difficulty recovering from the flu. Divorce, caring for an ill aging parent, sleep deprivation, and chronic depression can also reduce immunity (Hamer, Wolvers, & Albers, 2004; Robles & Kiecolt-Glaser, 2003). And physical stress—from pollution, allergens, poor nutrition, and rundown housing—undermines immune functioning throughout adulthood. When physical and psychological stress combine, the risk of illness is magnified (Friedman & Lawrence, 2002).

The link between stress and illness makes sense when we consider that stress hormones mobilize the body for action, whereas the immune response is fostered by reduced activity. But this also means that increased difficulty coping with physical and psychological stress can contribute to age-related declines in immune system functioning.

Reproductive Capacity

Sharese was born when her mother was in her early twenties. At the same age a generation later, Sharese was still single and entering graduate school. Many people believe that pregnancy during the twenties is ideal, not only because of lower risk of miscarriage and chromosomal disorders (see Chapter 2) but also because younger parents have more energy to keep up with active children. As Figure 13.2 on page 438 reveals, however, first births to women in their thirties have increased greatly over the past three decades. Many people are delaying childbearing until their education is complete, their careers are well-established, and they know they can support a child.

Nevertheless, reproductive capacity does decline with age. Fertility problems among women increase from age 15 to 50. Between ages 15 and 29, 8 percent of U.S. women surveyed report difficulties, a figure that rises to 14 percent among 30- to 34-year-olds and 18 percent among 35- to 44-year-olds, when the success of reproductive technologies drops sharply (see page 54 in Chapter 2) (U.S. Department of Health and Human Services, 2009a). Since the uterus shows no consistent changes from the late thirties through the forties, the decline in female fertility is largely due to reduced number and quality of ova. In many mammals, including humans, a certain level of reserve ova in the ovaries is necessary for conception. Some women have normal menstrual cycles but do not conceive because their reserve of ova is too low—the major cause of the female age-related decline in fertility (Djahanbakhch, Ezzati, & Zosmer, 2007).

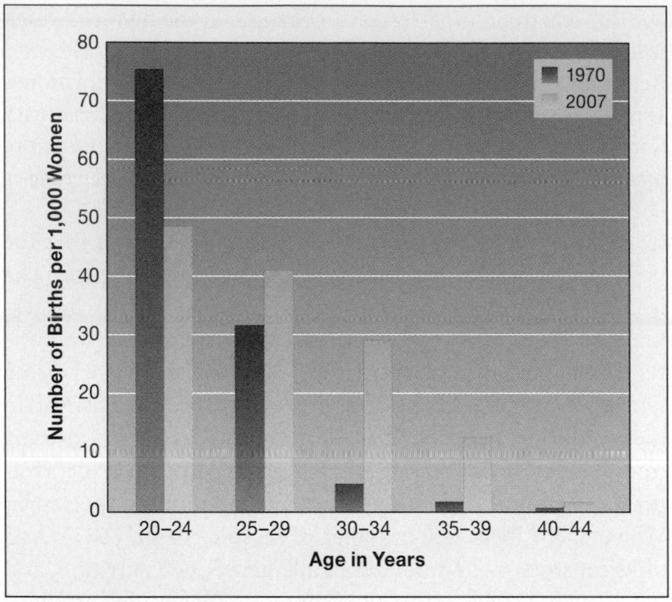

■ **FIGURE 13.2** ■ **First births to American women of different ages in 1970 and 2007.** The birthrate decreased during this period for women 20 to 24 years of age, whereas it increased for women 25 years of age and older. For women in their thirties, the birthrate more than doubled. Similar trends have occurred in other industrialized nations. (From U.S. Census Bureau, 2009b.)

In males, semen volume, sperm motility, and percentage of normal sperm decrease gradually after age 35, contributing to reduced fertility rates in older men (Lambert, Masson, & Fisch, 2006). Although there is no best time in adulthood to begin parenthood, individuals who postpone childbearing until their late thirties or their forties risk having fewer children than they desired or none at all.

ASK YOURSELF

» REVIEW
How does research on life conditions that accelerate telomere shortening illustrate the joint influence of heredity and environment on biological aging?

» APPLY
Penny is a long-distance runner for her college track team. She wonders what her running performance will be like 30 years from now. What factors will affect Penny's future athletic skill?

» CONNECT
How do heredity and environment jointly contribute to age-related changes in cardiovascular, respiratory, and immune system functioning?

» REFLECT
Before reading this chapter, had you thought of early adulthood as a period of aging? Why is it important for young adults to be conscious of factors that contribute to biological aging?

Health and Fitness

Figure 13.3 displays leading causes of death in early adulthood in the United States. Death rates for all causes exceed those of other industrialized nations—a difference believed to be due to a combination of factors, including higher rates of poverty and extreme obesity, more lenient gun-control policies, and lack of universal, government-sponsored health insurance in the United States (OECD, 2008b; Torrey & Haub, 2004). In later chapters, we will see that homicide rates decline with age, while disease and physical disability rates rise. Biological aging clearly contributes to this trend. But, as we have noted, wide individual and group differences in physical changes are linked to environmental risks and health-related behaviors.

SES variations in health over the lifespan reflect these influences. Income, education, and occupational status show strong and continuous relationships with almost every disease and health indicator (Adler & Newman, 2002; Alwin & Wray, 2005; Geiger, 2007). Furthermore, when a nationally representative sample of 3,600 Americans were asked about health-related limitations on their daily lives, SES differences widened over early and middle adulthood but contracted during old age, when individuals in the poorest health had died (see Figure 13.4) (House, Lantz, & Herd, 2005). Longitudinal evidence confirms these trends: Economically advantaged and well-educated individuals sustain better health over most of their adult lives, whereas the health of lower-income individuals with limited education steadily declines (Lantz et al., 1998, 2001).

SES differences in health-related circumstances and habits—stressful life events, crowding, pollution, diet, exercise, overweight and obesity, substance abuse, jobs with numerous health risks, availability of supportive social relationships, and (in the United States) access to affordable health care—are largely responsible (Brand et al., 2007; Evans & Kantrowitz, 2002; Wray, Alwin, & McCammon, 2005). Further, poor health in childhood, which is linked to low SES, affects health in adulthood. The overall influence of childhood factors lessens if SES improves. But in most instances, child and adult SES remain fairly consistent, exerting a cumulative impact that amplifies SES health disparities with age (Luo & Waite, 2005; Strand & Kunst, 2007).

Why are SES disparities in health and mortality larger in the United States than in other industrialized nations (Mackenbach, 2002)? Besides the lack of universal health insurance, poverty-stricken U.S. families have lower incomes than those classified as poor in other countries. In addition, SES groups are more likely to be segregated by neighborhood in the United States, resulting in greater inequalities in environmental factors that affect health, such as housing, pollution, education, and community services.

These findings reveal, once again, that the living conditions that nations and communities provide combine with those that people create for themselves to affect physical aging. Because the incidence of health problems is much lower during the twenties and thirties than later on, early adulthood is an excellent time to

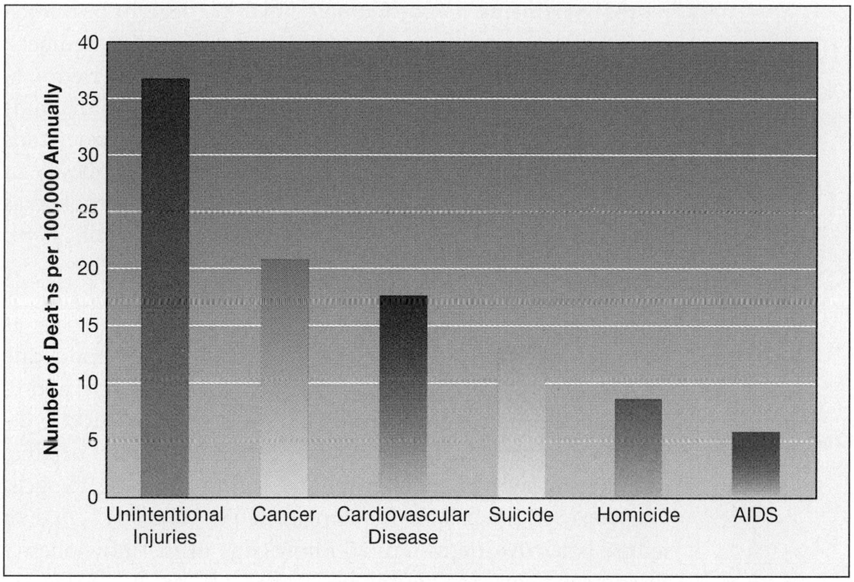

■ **FIGURE 13.3** ■ **Leading causes of death between 25 and 44 years of age in the United States.** Nearly half of unintentional injuries are motor vehicle accidents. As later chapters will reveal, unintentional injuries remain a leading cause of death at older ages, rising sharply in late adulthood. Rates of cancer and cardiovascular disease rise steadily over middle and late adulthood. (Adapted from U.S. Census Bureau, 2009b.)

prevent later problems. In the following sections, we take up a variety of major health concerns—nutrition, exercise, substance abuse, sexuality, and psychological stress.

Nutrition

Bombarded with advertising claims and an extraordinary variety of food choices, adults find it increasingly difficult to make wise dietary decisions. An abundance of food, combined with a heavily scheduled life, means that most Americans eat because they feel like it or because it is time to do so rather than to maintain the body's functions (Donatelle, 2009). As a result, many eat the wrong types and amounts of food. Overweight and obesity and a high-fat diet are widespread nutritional problems with long-term consequences for health in adulthood.

■ **OVERWEIGHT AND OBESITY.** In Chapter 9, we noted that obesity (a greater than 20 percent increase over average body weight, based on age, sex, and physical build) has increased dramatically in many Western nations. Among adults, a body mass index (BMI) of 25 to 29 constitutes overweight, a BMI of 30 or greater (amounting to 30 or more excess pounds) constitutes obesity. Today, 34 percent of U.S. adults are obese. The rate rises to 35 percent among Native Americans, 36 percent among Hispanics, and 45 percent among African Americans. In the United States and Western Europe, 5 to 7 percent more women than men suffer from obesity (Tjepkema, 2005; U.S. Department of Health and Human Services, 2009a, 2009c).

Overweight—a less extreme but nevertheless unhealthy condition—affects an additional 33 percent of Americans. Combine the rates of overweight and obesity and the total,

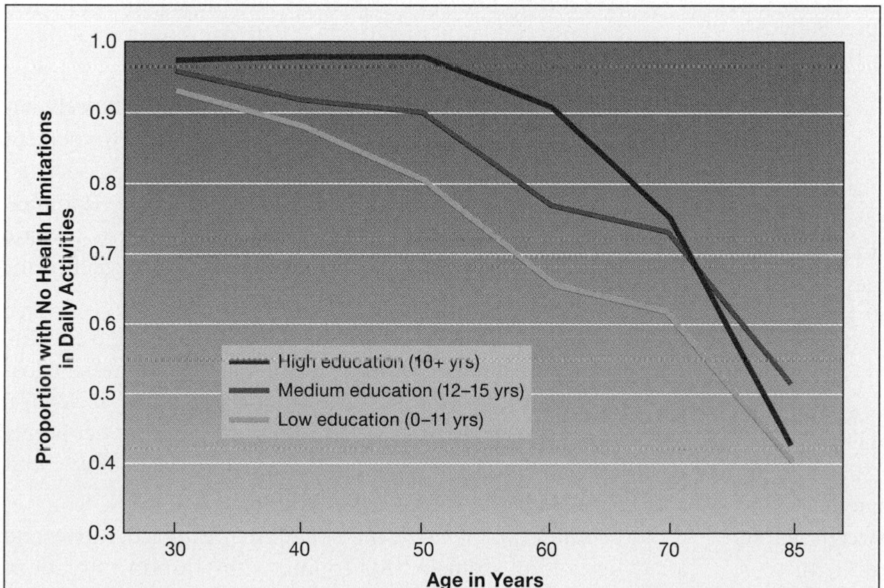

■ **FIGURE 13.4** ■ **Age differences in self-reported health status by socioeconomic status (SES), as indexed by education.** The figure shows cross-sectional trends. In longitudinal research as well, SES differences in health increase over early and middle adulthood and then contract in old age as people in the poorest health die earlier. Environmental risks and poor health habits contribute to earlier declining health among low-SES adults. (From J. S. House, P. M. Lantz, & P. Herd, 2005, "Continuity and Change in the Social Stratification of Aging and Health Over the Life Course: Evidence from a Nationally Representative Longitudinal Study from 1986 to 2001/2002," *Journal of Gerontology, 60B,* p. 16. Copyright © 2005 The Gerontological Society of America. Adapted by permission of Oxford University Press and James S. House.)

Overweight adults suffer enormous social discrimination. Which of these two young career women is more likely to find a mate, successfully vie for a new job, and be treated kindly by others?

67 percent, makes Americans the heaviest people in the world. ***TAKE A MOMENT...*** Notice in these figures that the U.S. obesity rate now exceeds its rate of overweight, a blatant indicator of the growing severity of the problem.

Recall from Chapter 9 that overweight children are very likely to become overweight adults. But a substantial number of people show large weight gains in adulthood, most often between ages 25 and 40. And young adults who were already overweight or obese typically get heavier, leading obesity rates to rise steadily between ages 20 and 60 (Tjepkema, 2005; U.S. Department of Health and Human Services, 2009a).

Causes and Consequences. As noted in Chapter 9, heredity makes some people more vulnerable to obesity than others. But environmental pressures underlie the rising rates of obesity in industrialized nations: With the decline in need for physical labor in the home and workplace, our lives have become more sedentary. Meanwhile, the average number of calories and amount of sugar and fat consumed by Americans rose over most of the twentieth and early twenty-first century, with a sharp increase after 1970 (see the Lifespan Vista box on pages 442–443).

Adding some weight between ages 25 and 50 is a normal part of aging because **basal metabolic rate (BMR),** the amount of energy the body uses at complete rest, gradually declines as the number of active muscle cells (which create the greatest energy demand) drops off. But excess weight is strongly associated with serious health problems (see page 292 in Chapter 9)—including type 2 diabetes, heart disease, and many forms of cancer—and with early death. Furthermore, overweight adults suffer enormous social discrimination. Compared with their normal-weight agemates, they are less likely to find mates, be rented apartments, receive financial aid for college, or be offered jobs. And they report frequent mistreatment by family members, peers, co-workers, and health professionals (Carr & Friedman, 2005; Puhl & Brownell, 2006). From the mid-1990s to the mid-2000s, discrimination experienced by overweight Americans increased, perhaps because of greater attention to obesity in national news coverage, which typically frames the problem as simply a personal choice (Andreyeva, Puhl, & Brownell, 2008).

Treatment. Because obesity climbs in early and middle adulthood, treatment for adults should begin as soon as possible—preferably in the early twenties. Even moderate weight loss reduces health problems substantially (Orzano & Scott, 2004). But successful intervention is difficult. Most individuals who start a weight loss program return to their original weight, and often to a higher weight, within two years (Vogels, Diepvens, & Westerterp-Plantenga, 2005). The high rate of failure is partly due to limited knowledge of just how obesity disrupts the complex neural, hormonal, and metabolic factors that maintain a normal body-weight set point. Until more information is available, researchers are examining the features of treatments and participants associated with greater success. The following elements promote lasting behavior change:

- *A well-balanced diet lower in calories and fat, plus exercise.* To lose weight, Sharese sharply reduced calories, sugar, and fat in her diet and exercised regularly. The precise balance of dietary protein, carbohydrates, and fats that best helps adults lose weight is a matter of heated debate. Although scores of diet books offer different recommendations, no clear-cut evidence exists for the long-term superiority of one approach over others (Tsai & Wadden, 2005). Research does confirm that a lifestyle alteration that restricts calorie intake and fat (to no more than 20 to 30 percent of calories) and increases physical activity is essential for reducing the impact of a genetic tendency toward overweight (Franz et al., 2007). In addition (as we will see shortly), exercise offers physical and psychological benefits that help prevent overeating.
- *Training participants to keep an accurate record of what they eat.* About 30 to 35 percent of obese people sincerely believe they eat less than they do, and from 25 to 45 percent report problems with binge eating—a behavior associated with weight-loss treatment failure (Blaine & Rodman, 2007; Wadden & Foster, 2000). When Sharese became aware of how often she ate when she was not actually hungry, she was better able to limit her food intake.
- *Social support.* Group or individual counseling and encouragement from friends and relatives help sustain weight-loss efforts by fostering self-esteem (Dansinger et al., 2007). Once Sharese decided to act, with the support of her family and a weight-loss counselor, she began to feel better about herself even before the first pounds were shed.
- *Teaching problem-solving skills.* Acquiring cognitive and behavioral strategies for coping with tempting situations and periods of slowed progress is associated with long-

term change. Weight-loss maintainers are more likely than individuals who relapse to be conscious of their behavior, to use social support, and to confront problems directly (Cooper & Fairburn, 2002).

- *Extended intervention.* Longer treatments (from 25 to 40 weeks) that include the components listed here grant people time to develop new habits.

Although many Americans on weight-reduction diets are overweight, about one-third are within normal range (Mokdad et al., 2001). Recall from Chapter 11 that the high value placed on thinness creates unrealistic expectations about desirable body weight and contributes to anorexia and bulimia, dangerous eating disorders that remain common in early adulthood (see pages 372–373). Throughout adulthood, both underweight and obesity are associated with increased mortality (Flegal et al., 2005). A sensible body weight—neither too low nor too high—predicts physical and psychological health and longer life.

DIETARY FAT. During college, Sharese altered the diet of her childhood and adolescent years, sharply limiting red meat, eggs, butter, and fried foods. U.S. national dietary recommendations include reducing dietary fat to 30 percent of total caloric intake, with no more than 10 percent made up of saturated fat, which generally comes from meat and dairy products and is solid at room temperature (U.S. Department of Health and Human Services, 2009a). Many researchers believe that fat consumption plays a role in breast cancer and (when it includes large amounts of red meat) is linked to colon cancer (Blackburn & Wang, 2007; Kono, 2004). But the main reasons for limiting dietary fat are the strong connection of total fat with obesity and of saturated fat with cardiovascular disease

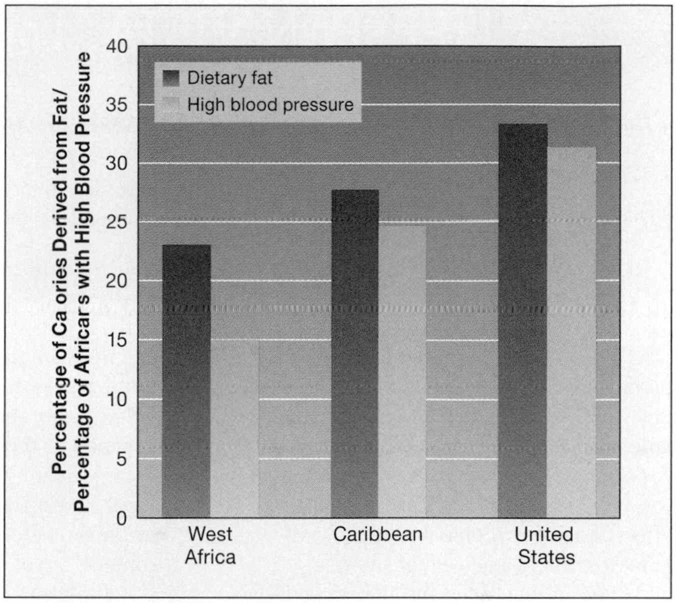

FIGURE 13.5 Dietary fat and prevalence of high blood pressure among Africans in West Africa, the Caribbean, and the United States. The three regions represent the historic path of the slave trade and, therefore, have genetically similar populations. As dietary fat increases, high blood pressure and heart disease rise. Both are particularly high among African Americans. (Adapted from Luke et al., 2001.)

(Bruner et al., 2007). Nevertheless, despite a slight drop in fat consumption, most American adults eat too much.

Moderate fat consumption is essential for normal body functioning. But when we consume too much fat, especially saturated fat, some is converted to cholesterol, which accumulates as plaque on the arterial walls in atherosclerosis. Earlier in this chapter, we noted that atherosclerosis is determined by multiple biological and environmental factors. But excess fat consumption (along with other societal conditions) is a major contributor to the high rate of heart disease in the U.S. black population. When researchers compare Africans in West Africa, the Caribbean, and the United States (the historic path of the slave trade), dietary fat increases, and so do high blood pressure and heart disease (see Figure 13.5) (Luke et al., 2001). Indeed, West Africans have one of the lowest rates of heart disease in the world.

The best rule of thumb is to eat less fat of all kinds and to substitute unsaturated fat, which is derived from vegetables or fish and liquid at room temperature, for saturated fat when possible. Furthermore, regular exercise can reduce the harmful influence of dietary fat because it creates chemical byproducts that help eliminate cholesterol from the body.

A balanced, low-fat diet promotes physical and psychological well-being and contributes to a normal body weight.

Exercise

Three times a week, over the noon hour, Sharese delighted in running, making her way to a wooded trail that cut through a picturesque area of the city. Regular exercise kept her fit and slim, and she noticed that she caught fewer respiratory illnesses than in the days when she had been sedentary and overweight. As

A LIFESPAN VISTA: Looking Forward, Looking Back

The Obesity Epidemic: How Americans Became the Heaviest People in the World

In the late 1980s, obesity in the United States started to soar. As the maps in Figure 13.6 show, it quickly engulfed the nation and has continued to expand. The epidemic also spread to other Western nations and, more recently, to developing countries. For example, as noted in Chapter 9, obesity was rare in China 30 years ago, but today it affects 3 percent of Chinese children and adolescents and 6 percent of adults; an additional 23 percent of the Chinese population is overweight (Levine, 2007). Yet China is a low-prevalence country! Worldwide, overweight afflicts more than 1 billion adults, 300 million of whom are obese. Samoa leads the globe in overweight and obesity, with more than 75 percent of people affected (World Health Organization, 2009b). Among industrialized nations, no country matches the United States in prevalence of this life-threatening condition.

A Changing Food Environment and Lifestyle

Several societal factors have encouraged widespread rapid weight gain:

- *Availability of cheap commercial fat and sugar.* The 1970s saw two massive changes in the U.S. food economy: (1) the discovery and mass production of high-fructose corn syrup, a sweetener six times as sweet as ordinary sugar, and therefore far less expensive; and (2) the importing from Malaysia of large quantities of palm oil, which is lower in cost and tastier than other vegetable oils because of its high saturated fat content. Use of corn syrup and palm oil in soft drinks and calorie-dense convenience foods lowered production costs for these items, inaugurating a new era of "cheap, abundant, and tasty calories" (Critser, 2003).
- *Portion supersizing.* Fast-food chains discovered a successful strategy for attracting customers: increasing portion sizes substantially and prices just a little for foods that had become inexpensive to produce. Customers thronged to buy "value meals," jumbo burgers and burritos, and 20-ounce Cokes (Critser, 2003). And research revealed that when presented with larger portions, individuals 2 years and older increased their intake, on average, by 25 to 30 percent (Fisher, Rolls, & Birch, 2003; Rolls, Morris, & Roe, 2002).
- *Increasingly busy lives.* Between the 1970s and 1990s, women entered the labor force in record numbers, and the average amount of time Americans worked increased by 15 percent, or about 350 hours per year (Higgins & Duxbury, 2002; Schor, 2002). As time became scarce, eating out increased. In addition, Americans became frequent snackers, aided by a growing diversity of high-calorie snack foods on supermarket shelves. During this period, the number of calories Americans consumed away from home nearly doubled, and dietary fat increased from 19 to 38 percent. Overall, average daily food intake rose by almost 200 calories—enough to add an extra pound every 20 days (Nielsen & Popkin, 2003).
- *Declining rates of physical activity.* During the 1980s, physical activity, which had risen since the 1960s, started to fall as Americans spent more time in sedentary transportation and jobs—driving to and

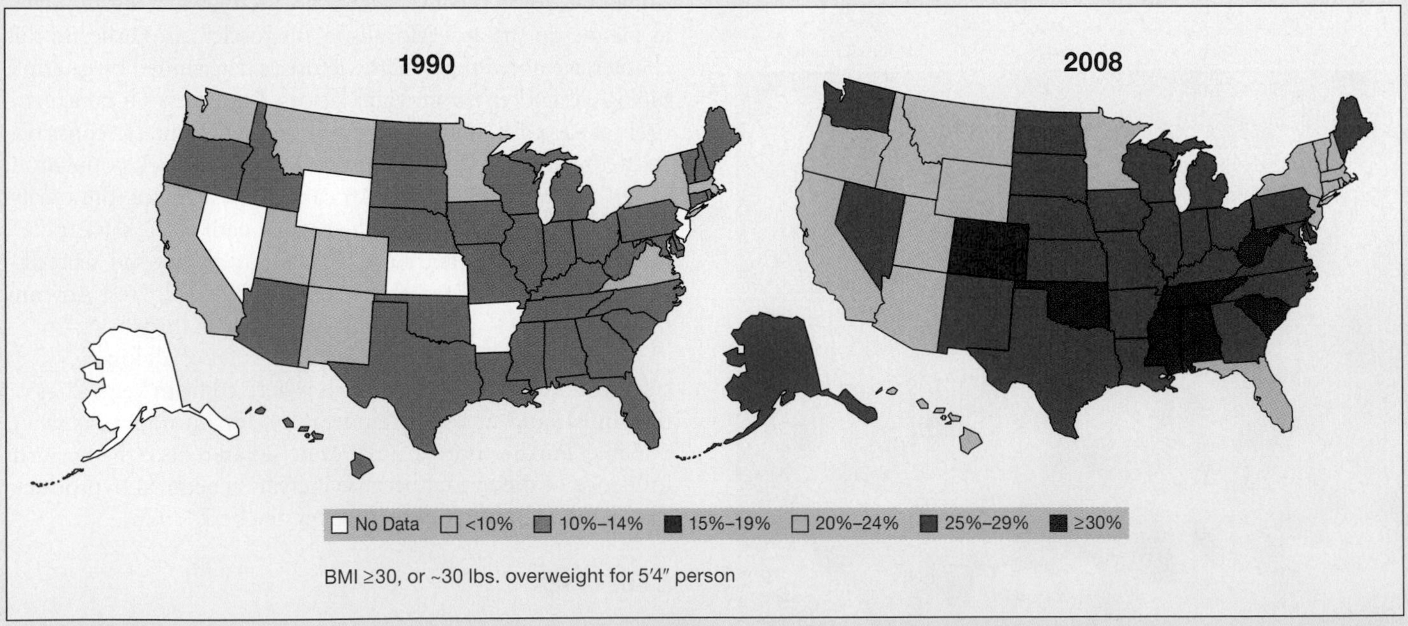

■ **FIGURE 13.6** ■ **Obesity trends among U.S. adults, 1990 and 2008.** The maps show that obesity has increased sharply. In 2008, only one state (Colorado) had an obesity rate less than 20 percent. Thirty-two states had rates equal to or greater than 25 percent; six of these states (Alabama, Mississippi, Oklahoma, South Carolina, Tennessee, and West Virginia) had rates equal to or greater than 30 percent. (CDC Behavioral Risk Factor Surveillance System, U.S. Department of Health and Human Services, 2009e.)

from work and sitting throughout the work day, often behind a computer. At home, a rise in TV viewing to an average of more than four hours per day has been linked to weight gain in adults and children alike (Foster, Gore, & West, 2006).

Combating the Obesity Epidemic

Obesity is responsible for $150 billion in health expenditures and 300,000 premature deaths per year in the United States alone (Levine, 2007; Manson et al., 2004). Broad societal efforts are needed to combat this epidemic. Suggestions include

- Government funding to support massive public education about healthy eating and physical activity
- A high priority placed on building parks and recreation centers in low-income neighborhoods, where overweight and obesity are highest
- Laws that mandate prominent posting of the calorie, sugar, and fat content of foods sold in restaurants, movie theaters, and convenience stores
- A special tax on foods high in calories, sugar, or fat
- Incentives to schools and workplaces for promoting healthy eating and daily exercise and for offering weight-management programs

Sharese explained to a friend, "Exercise gives me a positive outlook and calms me down. Afterward, I feel a burst of energy that gets me through the day. If I don't do it, I get tired in the afternoon."

Although most Americans are aware of the health benefits of exercise, only 30 percent engage in at least moderate leisure-time physical activity for 20 minutes or more at least five times a week. And about 40 percent are inactive, with no regular brief sessions of even light activity (U.S. Department of Health and Human Services, 2009a). More women than men are inactive. And inactivity is greater among low-SES adults, who live in less safe neighborhoods, have more health problems, experience less social support for exercising regularly, and feel less personal control over their health (Grzywacz & Marks, 2001; Wilson et al., 2004).

Besides reducing body fat and building muscle, exercise fosters resistance to disease. Frequent bouts of moderate-intensity exercise enhance the immune response, lowering the risk of colds or flu and promoting faster recovery from these illnesses (Donatelle, 2009). Furthermore, in several longitudinal studies extending over 10 to 20 years, physical activity was linked to reduced incidence of cancer at all body sites except the skin, with the strongest findings for cancer of the rectum and colon (Albanes, Blair, & Taylor, 1989; Tardon et al., 2005; Wannamethee, Shaper, & Macfarlane, 1993). Physically active people are also less likely to develop diabetes and cardiovascular disease (Bassuk & Manson, 2005). If they do, these illnesses typically occur later and are less severe than among their inactive agemates.

How does exercise help prevent these serious illnesses? First, it reduces the incidence of obesity—a risk factor for heart disease, diabetes, and several forms of cancer. In addition, people who exercise probably adopt other healthful behaviors, thereby lowering the risk of diseases associated with high-fat diets, alcohol consumption, and smoking. In animal studies, exercise directly inhibits growth of cancerous tumors—beyond the impact of diet, body fat, and the immune response (de Lima et al., 2008). Exercise also promotes cardiovascular functioning by strengthening the heart muscle, decreasing blood pressure, and producing a form of "good cholesterol" (high-density lipoproteins, or HDLs) that helps remove "bad cholesterol" (low-density lipoproteins, or LDLs) from the artery walls (Donatelle, 2009).

Yet another way that exercise may guard against illness is through its mental health benefits. Physical activity reduces anxiety and depression and improves mood, alertness, and energy.

Regular, moderate-to-vigorous exercise predicts a healthier, longer life. Participants in this kickboxing class reap both physical and mental health benefits.

Furthermore, as EEG and fMRI evidence indicates, exercise enhances neural activity in the cerebral cortex and improves overall cognitive functioning (Hillman, Erickson, & Kramer, 2008; Johnson & Krueger, 2007; Mutrie & Faulkner, 2004; Penedo & Dahn, 2005). The impact of exercise on a "positive outlook" as Sharese expressed it, is most obvious just after a workout and can last for several hours (Chollar, 1995). The stress-reducing properties of exercise undoubtedly strengthen immunity to disease. And as physical activity enhances cognitive functioning and psychological well-being, it promotes on-the-job productivity, self-esteem, ability to cope with stress, and life satisfaction.

When we consider the evidence as a whole, it is not surprising that physical activity is associated with substantially lower death rates from all causes. The contribution of exercise to longevity cannot be accounted for by preexisting illness in inactive people. In a Danish longitudinal study of a nationally representative sample of 7,000 healthy 20- to 79-year-olds followed over several decades, mortality was lower among those who increased their leisure-time physical activity from low to either moderate or high than among those who remained consistently inactive (Schnohr, Scharling, & Jensen, 2003).

How much exercise is recommended for a healthier, happier, and longer life? Moderately intense physical activity—for example, 30 minutes of brisk walking—on most days leads to health benefits for previously inactive people. Adults who exercise at greater intensity—enough to build up a sweat—derive even greater protection against cardiovascular disease, diabetes, colon cancer, and obesity (Hu & Manson, 2001; Yu et al., 2003). Currently, the U.S. government recommends 30 minutes of moderate-intensity physical activity on five or more days per week or 20 or more minutes of vigorous-intensity exercise (for example, jogging, biking uphill, fast swimming) on three or more days per week (U.S. Department of Health and Human Services, 2009d).

Substance Abuse

Drug taking peaks among U.S. 19- to 22-year-olds and then declines over the decade of the twenties. Eager to try a wide range of experiences before settling down to the responsibilities of adulthood, young people of this age are more likely than younger or older individuals to smoke cigarettes, chew tobacco, use marijuana, and take stimulants to enhance cognitive or physical performance (U.S. Department of Health and Human Services, 2009b). Binge drinking and experimentation with prescription drugs (such as OxyContin, a highly addictive painkiller) and "party drugs" (such as LSD and MDMA, or Ecstasy) also increase, at times with tragic consequences. Risks include brain damage, lasting impairments in mental functioning, and unintentional injury and death (Burgess, O'Donohoe, & Gill, 2000; Montoya et al., 2002).

Furthermore, when alcohol and drug taking become chronic, they intensify the psychological problems that underlie addiction. As many as 20 percent of U.S. 21- to 25-year-olds are substance abusers (U.S. Department of Health and Human Services, 2009b). Return to Chapter 11, pages 381–382, to review the factors that lead to alcohol and drug abuse in adolescence. The same personal and situational conditions are predictive in the adult years. Cigarette smoking and alcohol consumption are the most commonly abused substances.

CIGARETTE SMOKING. Dissemination of information on the harmful effects of cigarette smoking has helped reduce its prevalence among U.S. adults from 40 percent in 1965 to 24 percent in 2007 (U.S. Department of Health and Human Services, 2009b). Still, smoking has declined very slowly, and most of the drop is among college graduates, with very little change for those who did not finish high school. Furthermore, although more men than women smoke, the gender gap is much smaller today than in the past, reflecting a sharp increase in smoking among young women who did not finish high school. Smoking among college students has also risen—for students of both sexes and of diverse ethnicities. More than 90 percent of men and 85 percent of women who smoke started before age 21 (U.S. Department of Health and Human Services, 2009b). And the earlier people start smoking, the greater their daily cigarette consumption and likelihood of continuing, an important reason that preventive efforts with adolescents and young adults are vital.

The ingredients of cigarette smoke—nicotine, tar, carbon monoxide, and other chemicals—leave their damaging mark throughout the body. As smokers inhale, oxygen delivery to tissues is reduced, and heart rate and blood pressure rise. Over time, exposure to toxins and insufficient oxygen result in damage to the retina of the eye; skin abnormalities, including premature aging, poor wound healing, and hair loss; a decline in bone mass; a decrease in reserve ova and earlier menopause in women; and a reduced sperm count and higher rate of sexual impotence in men (American Society for Reproductive Medicine, 2004; Freiman et al., 2004; Thornton et al., 2005). Other deadly outcomes include increased risk of heart attack, stroke, acute leukemia, melanoma, and cancer of the mouth, throat, larynx, esophagus, lungs, stomach, pancreas, kidneys, and bladder.

Cigarette smoking is the single most important preventable cause of death in industrialized nations. One of every three young people who become regular smokers will die from a smoking-related disease (U.S. Department of Health and Human Services, 2008a). The chances of premature death rise with the number of cigarettes consumed. At the same time, the benefits of quitting include return of most disease risks to nonsmoker levels within three to eight years. Although millions of people have stopped smoking without help, those who enter treatment programs or use cessation aids (for example, nicotine gum, nasal spray, or patches, designed to reduce dependency gradually) often fail: After one year, 70 to 90 percent start smoking again (Ludvig, Miner, & Eisenberg, 2005). Unfortunately, too few treatments last long enough or teach skills for avoiding relapse.

■ **ALCOHOL.** National surveys reveal that about 11 percent of men and 3 percent of women in the United States are heavy drinkers (U.S. Department of Health and Human Services, 2009b). About one-third of this group are *alcoholics*—people who cannot limit their alcohol use. In men, alcoholism usually begins in the teens and early twenties and worsens over the following decade. In women, its onset is typically later, in the twenties and thirties, and its course is more variable. Many alcoholics are also addicted to other drugs. About 80 percent are heavy cigarette smokers (John et al., 2003).

Twin studies support a genetic contribution to alcoholism (Tsuang et al., 2001). But whether a person comes to deal with life's problems through drinking is greatly affected by personal characteristics and circumstances: Half of hospitalized alcoholics have no family history of problem drinking (Hawkins, Catalano, & Miller, 1992). Alcoholism crosses SES and ethnic lines but is higher in some groups than others. In cultures where alcohol is a traditional part of religious or ceremonial activities, people are less likely to abuse it. Where access to alcohol is carefully controlled and viewed as a sign of adulthood, dependency is more likely—factors that may, in part, explain why college students drink more heavily than young people not enrolled in college (Slutske et al., 2004). Poverty and hopelessness also promote excessive drinking (Donatelle, 2009; U.S. Department of Health and Human Services, 2009b).

Alcohol acts as a depressant, impairing the brain's ability to control thought and action. In a heavy drinker, it relieves anxiety at first but then induces it as the effects wear off, so the alcoholic drinks again. Chronic alcohol use does widespread physical damage. Its best-known complication is liver disease, but it is also linked to cardiovascular disease, inflammation of the pancreas, irritation of the intestinal tract, bone marrow problems, disorders of the blood and joints, and some forms of cancer. Over time, alcohol causes brain damage, leading to confusion, apathy, inability to learn, and impaired memory (Brun & Andersson, 2001). The costs to society are enormous. About 40 percent of fatal motor vehicle crashes in the United States involve drivers who have been drinking (Pickrell, 2006). Nearly half of convicted felons are alcoholics, and about half of police activities in large cities involve alcohol-related offenses (McKim, 2002). Alcohol frequently plays a part in sexual coercion, including date rape, and in domestic violence.

The most successful treatments combine personal and family counseling, group support, and aversion therapy (use of medication that produces a physically unpleasant reaction to alcohol, such as nausea and vomiting). Alcoholics Anonymous, a community support approach, helps many people exert greater control over their lives through the encouragement of others with similar problems. Nevertheless, breaking an addiction that has dominated a person's life is difficult; about 50 percent of alcoholics relapse within a few months (Volpicelli, 2001).

Sexuality

At the end of high school, about 65 percent of U.S. young people have had sexual intercourse; by age 25, nearly all have done so, and the gender and SES differences that were apparent in adolescence (see page 375 in Chapter 11) have diminished (U.S. Department of Health and Human Services, 2008k). Compared with earlier generations, contemporary adults display a wider range of sexual choices and lifestyles, including cohabitation, marriage, extramarital experiences, and orientation toward a heterosexual or homosexual partner. In this chapter, we explore the attitudes, behaviors, and health concerns that arise as sexual activity becomes a regular event in young people's lives. In Chapter 14, we focus on the emotional side of close relationships.

In cultures where alcohol is a traditional part of religious or ceremonial activities, people are less likely to abuse it. This Jewish grandfather teaches his grandson the customs of the Passover Seder, which include blessing and drinking wine.

■ **HETEROSEXUAL ATTITUDES AND BEHAVIOR.** One Friday evening, Sharese accompanied her roommate Heather to a young singles bar. Shortly after they arrived, two young men joined them. Faithful to her boyfriend, Ernie, whom she had met in college and who worked in another city, Sharese remained aloof for the next hour. In contrast, Heather was talkative and gave one of the men, Rich, her phone number. The next weekend, Heather went out with Rich. On the second date, they had intercourse, but the romance lasted only a few weeks. Aware of Heather's more adventurous sex life, Sharese wondered whether her own was normal. Only after several months of dating exclusively had she and Ernie slept together.

Since the 1950s, public display of sexuality in movies, newspapers, magazines, and books has steadily increased, fostering the impression that Americans are more sexually active than ever before. What are contemporary adults' sexual attitudes and behaviors really like? Answers were difficult to find until the National Health and Social Life Survey, the first in-depth study of U.S. adults' sex lives based on a nationally representative sample, was carried out in the early 1990s. Nearly four out of

Sexual partners tend to be similar in age, education, ethnicity, and religion. And those who establish lasting relationships usually meet through family members or friends, or at work, school, or social events where people similar to themselves congregate.

five randomly chosen 18- to 59-year-olds agreed to participate—3,400 in all. Findings were remarkably similar to those of surveys conducted at about the same time in France, Great Britain, and Finland, and to a more recent U.S. survey (Langer, 2004; Laumann et al., 1994; Michael et al., 1994).

Recall from Chapter 11 that the sex lives of most teenagers do not dovetail with exciting media images. The same is true of adults in Western nations. Although their sexual practices are diverse, they are far less sexually active than we have come to believe. Monogamous, emotionally committed couples like Sharese and Ernie are more typical (and more satisfied) than couples like Heather and Rich.

Sexual partners, whether dating, cohabiting, or married, usually do not select each other arbitrarily. They tend to be similar in age (within five years), education, ethnicity, and (to a lesser extent) religion. In addition, people who establish lasting relationships usually meet in conventional ways—either through family members or friends, or at work, school, or social events where people similar to themselves congregate. The powerful influence of social networks on sexual choice is adaptive. Sustaining an intimate relationship is easier when adults share interests and values and people they know approve of the match.

Over the past decade, Internet dating services have become an increasingly popular and widely accepted way to initiate relationships. According to one estimate, over 40 percent of single U.S. adults visit these matchmaking websites (Mazzarella, 2007). By creating a personal profile and describing the type of person they want to meet, users hope to find a compatible partner quickly. Although success rates are lower than with conventional strategies, adults who form an online relationship and then meet face-to-face often go on to see each other again, with 18 percent of such ties lasting for more than a year (Gavin, Scott, & Duffield, 2005).

Consistent with popular belief, Americans today have more sexual partners over their lifetimes than they did a generation ago. For example, one-third of adults over age 50 have had five or more partners, whereas half of 30- to 50-year-olds have accumulated that many in much less time. And although women are more opposed to casual sex then men, after excluding a small number of men (less than 3 percent) with a great many sexual partners, contemporary men and women differ little in average number of lifetime sexual partners (Langer, 2004). Why is this so? From an evolutionary perspective, contemporary effective contraception has permitted sexual activity with little risk of pregnancy, enabling women to have as many partners as men without risking the welfare of their offspring.

But when adults of any age are asked how many partners they have had in the past year, the usual reply (for about 70 percent) is one. What explains the trend toward more relationships in the context of sexual commitment? In the past, dating several partners was followed by marriage. Today, dating more often gives way to cohabitation, which leads either to marriage or to breakup. In addition, people are marrying later, and the divorce rate remains high. Together, these factors create more opportunities for new partners. Still, surveys of college students reveal that almost all want to settle down with a mutually exclusive sexual partner eventually (Pedersen et al., 2002). In line with this goal, most people spend the majority of their lives with one partner.

How often do Americans have sex? Not nearly as frequently as the media would suggest. One-third of 18- to 59-year-olds have intercourse as often as twice a week, another third have it a few times a month, and the remaining third have it a few times a year or not at all. Three factors affect frequency of sexual activity: age, whether people are cohabiting or married, and how long the couple has been together. Single people have more partners, but this does not translate into more sex! Sexual activity increases through the twenties as people either cohabit or marry. Then, around age 30, it declines, even though hormone levels have not changed much. The demands of daily life—working, commuting, taking care of home and children—are probably responsible. Despite the common assumption that sexual practices vary greatly across social groups, the patterns just described are unaffected by education, SES, or ethnicity.

Most adults say they are happy with their sex lives. For those in committed relationships, more than 80 percent report feeling "extremely physically and emotionally satisfied," a figure that rises to 88 percent for married couples. In contrast, as number of sex partners increases, satisfaction declines sharply. These findings challenge two stereotypes—that marriage is sexually dull and that people with many partners have the "hottest" sex.

Only a minority of adults—women more often than men—report persistent sexual problems. For women, the two most frequent difficulties are lack of interest in sex (33 percent) and inability to achieve orgasm (24 percent); for men, climaxing too early (29 percent) and anxiety about performance (16 percent). Sexual difficulties are linked to low SES and psychological stress, and are more common among people who are not married, have had more than five partners, and have experienced sexual abuse during childhood or (for women) sexual coercion in adulthood (Laumann, Paik, & Rosen, 1999). As these findings suggest, a history of unfavorable personal relationships and sexual experiences increases the risk of sexual dysfunction.

But overall, a completely untroubled physical experience is not essential for sexual happiness. Surveys of adults repeatedly show that satisfying sex involves more than technique; it is attained in the context of love, affection, and fidelity. In sum, happiness with partnered sex is linked to an emotionally fulfilling relationship, good mental health, and overall contentment with life (Bancroft, 2002; Santtila et al., 2008).

■ **HOMOSEXUAL ATTITUDES AND BEHAVIOR.** The majority of Americans support civil liberties and equal employment opportunities for gay men, lesbians, and bisexuals (Brooks, 2000). And attitudes toward sexual relations between two adults of the same sex have gradually become more accepting: In one survey, 55 to 65 percent of U.S. 18- to 65-year-olds agreed "it is OK" (Langer, 2004). Homosexuals' political activism and greater openness about their sexual orientation have contributed to slow gains in acceptance. Exposure and interpersonal contact reduce negative attitudes. But perhaps because they are especially concerned with gender-role conformity, heterosexual men judge homosexuals (and especially gay men) more harshly than do heterosexual women (Kite & Whitley, 2003; Lim, 2002).

In the National Health and Social Life Survey, 2.8 percent of men and 1.4 percent of women identified themselves as homosexual or bisexual—figures similar to those of other national surveys conducted in the United States, France, and Great Britain (Black, Gates, & Sanders, 2000; Mercer et al., 2007; Mosher, Chandra, & Jones, 2005; Spira, 1992). But an estimated 30 percent of same-sex couples do not report themselves as such in survey research. This unwillingness to answer questions, engendered by a climate of persecution, has limited researchers' access to information about the sex lives of gay men and lesbians. The little evidence available indicates that homosexual sex follows many of the same rules as heterosexual sex: People tend to seek out partners similar in education and background to themselves; partners in committed relationships have sex more often and are more satisfied; and the overall frequency of sex is modest (Laumann et al., 1994; Michael et al., 1994).

Homosexuals tend to live in large cities, where many others share their sexual orientation, or in college towns, where attitudes are more accepting. Living in small communities where prejudice is intense and no social network exists through which to find compatible homosexual partners is isolating, lonely, and predictive of mental health problems (Meyer, 2003).

People who identify themselves as gay or lesbian also tend to be well-educated (Black, Gates, & Sanders, 2000; Mercer et al., 2007). In the National Health and Social Life Survey, twice as many college-educated as high-school-educated men and eight times as many college-educated as high-school-educated women stated they were homosexual. Although the reasons for these findings are not clear, they probably reflect greater social and sexual liberalism among the more highly educated and therefore greater willingness to disclose homosexuality.

■ **SEXUALLY TRANSMITTED DISEASES.** In the United States, one in every four individuals is likely to contract a sexually transmitted disease (STD) at some point in life (U.S. Department of Health and Human Services, 2009a). Although the incidence is highest in adolescence, STDs continue to be prevalent in early adulthood. During the teens and twenties, people accumulate most of their sexual partners, and they often do not take appropriate precautions to prevent the spread of STDs (see page 376 in Chapter 11). The overall rate of STDs is higher among women than men because it is at least twice as easy for a man to infect a woman with any STD, including AIDS, than for a woman to infect a man.

Although AIDS, the most deadly STD, remains concentrated among gay men and intravenous drug abusers, many homosexuals have responded to its spread by changing their sexual practices—limiting number of sexual partners, choosing partners more carefully, and using latex condoms consistently and correctly. Heterosexuals at high risk due to a history of many partners have done the same. As a result, the number of infections is lower among gay and heterosexual men today than it was in the early 1980s. Still, AIDS remains the sixth-leading cause of death among U.S. young adults (refer to Figure 13.3 on page 439). The incidence of HIV-positive adults is higher in the United States than in any other industrialized nation (OECD, 2008b). AIDS is spreading most rapidly through heterosexual contact in poverty-stricken minority groups, among whom high rates of intravenous drug abuse coexist with poor health, inadequate education, high life stress, and hopelessness. People overwhelmed by these problems are least likely to take preventive measures (Capaldi et al., 2002b).

Yet AIDS can be contained and reduced—through sex education extending from childhood into adulthood and through access to health services, condoms, and clean needles and syringes for high-risk individuals. In view of the dramatic rise in AIDS among women, who currently account for one-fourth of cases in North America, Western Europe, and East Asia, one-third in Latin America, and slightly over half in Africa, a special need exists for female-controlled preventive measures (Quinn & Overbaugh, 2005). A recent redesign of the female condom for comfort and ease of use offers some promise. But it is more expensive than the male condom, and its effectiveness and acceptability are not yet established.

■ **SEXUAL COERCION.** After a long day of classes, Sharese flipped on the TV and caught a talk show discussion on sex without consent. Karen, a 25-year-old woman, described her husband Mike pushing, slapping, verbally insulting, and forcing her to have sex. "It was a control thing," Karen explained tearfully. "He complained that I wouldn't always do what he wanted. I was confused and blamed myself. I didn't leave because I was sure he'd come after me and get more violent."

One day, as Karen was speaking long distance to her mother on the phone, Mike grabbed the receiver and shouted, "She's not the woman I married! I'll kill her if she doesn't shape up!" Alarmed, Karen's parents arrived by plane the next day to rescue her, then helped her start divorce proceedings and get treatment.

An estimated 15 to 20 percent of U.S. women have endured *rape,* legally defined as intercourse by force, by threat of harm, or when the victim is incapable of giving consent (because of mental illness, mental retardation, or alcohol consumption). From 22 to 57 percent of women have experienced other forms of sexual aggression. The majority of victims (eight out of ten) are under age 30 (Schewe, 2007; Testa et al., 2003; U.S. Department of Health and Human Services, 2009a). Women are vulnerable to partners, acquaintances, and strangers, but in most instances their abusers are men they know well. Sexual coercion crosses SES and ethnic lines; people of all walks of life are offenders and victims.

Personal characteristics of the man with whom a woman is involved are far better predictors of her chances of becoming a victim than her own characteristics. Men who engage in sexual assault tend to believe in traditional gender roles, approve of violence against women, and accept rape myths (for example, "Women really want to be raped"). Perpetrators also tend to interpret women's social behavior inaccurately, viewing friendliness as seductiveness, assertiveness as hostility, and resistance as desire. Frequently reasoning that "she brought it on herself," they express little remorse (Abbey & McAuslan, 2004; Scully & Marolla, 1998). Furthermore, sexual abuse in childhood, promiscuity in adolescence, and alcohol abuse in adulthood are associated with sexual coercion. Approximately half of all sexual assaults take place while people are intoxicated (Abbey et al., 2004; Kalof, 2000).

Cultural forces also contribute. When men are taught from an early age to be dominant, competitive, and aggressive and women to be submissive, cooperative, and passive, the themes of rape are reinforced. Under these conditions, men may view a date not as a chance to get to know a partner but as a potential sexual conquest. Societal acceptance of violence also sets the stage for rape, which typically occurs in relationships in which other forms of aggression are commonplace. Exposure to sexually aggressive pornography and other media images, which portray women desiring and enjoying the assault, also promote sexual coercion by dulling sensitivity to its harmful consequences.

A counselor and client talk at a rape crisis center. A variety of community services, including safe houses, crisis hotlines, and support groups, help women take refuge from abusive partners.

About 15 to 30 percent of U.S. young adult samples report female-initiated coercive sexual behavior against men, with 3 to 10 percent of male respondents indicating threats of physical force or actual force. Victimized men often say that women who committed these acts encouraged them to get drunk and threatened to end the relationship unless they complied (Anderson & Savage, 2005). Unfortunately, authorities rarely recognize female-initiated forced sex as illegal, and few men report these crimes.

Consequences. Women's psychological reactions to rape resemble those of survivors of extreme trauma. Immediate responses—shock, confusion, withdrawal, and psychological numbing—eventually give way to chronic fatigue, tension, disturbed sleep, depression, substance abuse, social anxiety, and suicidal thoughts (Schewe, 2007; Stein et al., 2004). Victims of ongoing sexual coercion may fall into a pattern of extreme passivity and fear of taking any action. A woman who has a history of sexual abuse or who received negative feedback after trying to tell someone is more likely to blame herself, which strengthens helpless reactions (Briere & Jordan, 2004).

One-third to one-half of female rape victims are physically injured. From 4 to 30 percent contract sexually transmitted diseases, and pregnancy results in 5 to 20 percent of cases. Furthermore, women victimized by rape (and other crimes) report more symptoms of illness across almost all body systems. And they are more likely to engage in negative health behaviors, including smoking and alcohol use (McFarlane et al., 2005; Schewe, 2007).

Like their female counterparts, some male victims report psychological and physical consequences, including long-term depression (Struckman-Johnson & Struckman-Johnson, 1998). But female-initiated coercion and its effects are far less often studied.

Prevention and Treatment. Many female rape victims are less fortunate than Karen because anxiety about provoking another attack keeps them from confiding even in trusted family members and friends. If they seek help for other problems, conflict over issues surrounding sexuality may lead a sensitive health professional to detect a possible rape. A variety of community services, including safe houses, crisis hotlines, support groups, and legal assistance, exist to help women take refuge from abusive partners, but most are underfunded and cannot reach out to everyone in need. Practically no services are available for victimized men, who are often too embarrassed to come forward (Anderson & Savage, 2005).

The trauma induced by rape is severe enough that therapy is important—both individual treatment to reduce anxiety and depression and group sessions where contact with other survivors

Applying What We Know

Preventing Sexual Coercion

Suggestion	Description
Reduce gender stereotyping and gender inequalities.	The roots of men's sexual coercion of women lie in the historically subordinate status of women. Unequal educational and employment opportunities keep many women economically dependent on men and therefore poorly equipped to avoid partner violence. At the same time, there is a need for increased public awareness that women sometimes commit sexually aggressive acts.
Mandate treatment for men and women who physically or sexually assault their partners.	Ingredients of effective intervention include combating rape myths and inducing personal responsibility for violent behavior; teaching social awareness, social skills, and anger management; and developing a support system to prevent future attacks.
Expand interventions for children and adolescents who have witnessed violence between their parents.	Although most child witnesses to parental violence do not become involved in abusive relationships as adults, they are at increased risk.
Teach both men and women to take precautions that lower the risk of sexual assault.	Risk of sexual assault can be reduced by communicating sexual limits clearly to a date and, among women, developing neighborhood ties to other women; increasing the safety of the immediate environment (for example, installing deadbolt locks, checking the back seat of the car before entering); avoiding deserted areas; not walking alone after dark; and leaving parties where alcohol use is high.
Broaden definitions of rape to be gender-neutral.	In some U.S. states, where the definition of rape is limited to vaginal or anal penetration, a woman legally cannot rape a man. A broader definition is needed to encompass women as both receivers and perpetrators of sexual aggression.

Sources: Anderson & Savage, 2005; Schewe, 2007.

helps counter isolation and self-blame (Neville & Heppner, 2002). Other critical features that foster recovery include

- *Routine screening for victimization* during health-care visits to ensure referral to community services and protection from future harm
- *Validation of the experience,* by acknowledging that many others have been physically and sexually assaulted by intimate partners; that such assaults lead to a wide range of persisting symptoms, are illegal and inappropriate, and should not be tolerated; and that the trauma can be overcome
- *Safety planning,* even when the abuser is no longer present, to prevent recontact and reassault. This includes information about how to obtain police protection, legal intervention, a safe shelter, and other aid should a rape survivor be at risk again.

Finally, many steps can be taken at the level of the individual, the community, and society to prevent sexual coercion. Some are listed in Applying What We Know above.

MENSTRUAL CYCLE. The menstrual cycle is central to women's lives and presents unique health concerns. Although almost all women experience some discomfort during menstruation, others have more severe difficulties. **Premenstrual syndrome (PMS)** refers to an array of physical and psychological symptoms that usually appear six to ten days prior to menstruation. The most common are abdominal cramps, fluid retention, diarrhea, tender breasts, backache, headache, fatigue, tension, irritability, and depression; the precise combination varies from person to person. Nearly 40 percent of women have some form of PMS, usually beginning sometime after age 20. For most, symptoms are mild, but for 10 to 20 percent, PMS is severe enough to interfere with academic, occupational, and social functioning. PMS affects women of all SES levels and is a worldwide phenomenon—just as common in Italy and the Islamic nation of Bahrain as it is in the United States (Brody, 1992; Halbreich, 2004).

The causes of PMS are not well-established, but evidence for a genetic predisposition is accumulating. Identical twins are twice as likely as fraternal twins to share the syndrome (Freeman & Halbreich, 1998; Treloar, Heath, & Martin, 2002). PMS is related to hormonal changes that follow ovulation and precede menstruation. But hormone therapy is not consistently effective, suggesting that sensitivity of brain centers to these hormones, rather than the hormones themselves, is probably responsible (Dickerson, Mazyck, & Hunter, 2003; Indusekhar, Usman, & O'Brien, 2007). Common treatments include analgesics for pain, antidepressant medication, diuretics for fluid buildup, limiting caffeine intake (which can intensify symptoms), a low-fat, high-fiber diet, vitamin/mineral supplements, exercise, and other strategies for reducing stress. Although each of these approaches is helpful in certain cases, no method has been devised for curing PMS.

Psychological Stress

A final health concern, threaded throughout previous sections, has such a broad impact that it merits a comment of its own. Psychological stress, measured in terms of adverse social conditions,

Applying What We Know

Fostering a Healthy Adult Life

Suggestion	Description
Engage in healthy eating behavior.	Educate yourself and those with whom you live about the makeup of a healthy diet. Eat in moderation, and learn to distinguish true hunger from eating due to boredom or stress.
Maintain a reasonable body weight.	If you need to lose weight, make a commitment to a lifelong change in the way you eat, not just a temporary diet. Select a sensible, well-balanced dietary plan, and exercise regularly.
Keep physically fit.	Choose a specific time to exercise, and stick with it. To help sustain physical activity and make it more enjoyable, exercise with your partner or a friend, and encourage each other. Set reasonable expectations, and allow enough time to reach your fitness goals; many people become exercise dropouts because their expectations were too high.
Control alcohol intake and do not smoke cigarettes.	Drink moderately or not at all. Do not allow yourself to feel you must drink to be accepted or to enjoy a social event. If you smoke, choose a time that is relatively stress-free to quit. Seek the support of your partner or a friend.
Engage in responsible sexual behavior.	Identify attitudes and behaviors that you need to change to develop a healthy intimate relationship. Educate yourself about sexual anatomy and functioning so you can make sound decisions about contraception and protect yourself against sexually transmitted disease.
Manage stress.	Seek a reasonable balance among work, family, and leisure. Become more aware of stressors, and identify effective ways of coping with them so you are better-prepared when they arise. Engage in regular exercise, and find time each day for relaxation and quiet reflection.

Source: Donatelle, 2009.

negative life events, or daily hassles, is related to a wide variety of unfavorable health outcomes—both unhealthy behaviors and clear physical consequences.

Chronic stress resulting from economic hardship and inner-city living is consistently linked to hypertension, a relationship that contributes to the high incidence of heart disease in low-income groups, especially African Americans. As it mobilizes the body for action, stress elevates blood pressure. Compared with higher-SES individuals, low-SES adults show a stronger cardiovascular response to stress, perhaps because they more often perceive stressors as unsolvable (Almeida et al., 2005; Carroll et al., 2007). Earlier we mentioned that psychological stress interferes with immune system functioning, a link that may underlie its relationship to several forms of cancer. And by reducing digestive activity as blood flows to the brain, heart, and extremities, stress can cause gastrointestinal difficulties, including constipation, diarrhea, colitis, and ulcers (Donatelle, 2009).

The many challenging tasks of early adulthood make it a particularly stressful time of life. Young adults more often report depressive feelings than middle-aged people, many of whom have attained vocational success and financial security and are enjoying more free time as parenting responsibilities decline (Schieman, Gundy, & Taylor, 2001; Wade & Cairney, 1997). Also, as we will see in Chapters 15 and 16, middle-aged adults are better than young adults at coping with stress (Aldwin & Levenson, 2002). Because of their longer life experience and greater sense of personal control over their lives, they are more likely to engage in problem-centered coping when stressful conditions can be changed and emotion-centered coping when nothing can be done.

In previous chapters, we repeatedly noted the stress-buffering effect of social support, which continues throughout life. Helping stressed young adults establish and maintain satisfying social ties is as important a health intervention as any we have mentioned. Before we turn to the cognitive side of early adulthood, consult Applying What We Know above for strategies that foster a healthy adult life.

ASK YOURSELF

» REVIEW
List as many factors as you can that may have contributed to heart attacks and early death among Sharese's African-American relatives.

» REVIEW
Why are people in committed relationships likely to be more sexually active and satisfied than those who are dating several partners?

» APPLY
Tom had been going to a health club three days a week after work, but job pressures convinced him that he no longer had time for regular exercise. Explain to Tom why he should keep up his exercise regimen, and suggest ways to fit it into his busy life.

» CONNECT
Describe history-graded influences that have contributed to the obesity epidemic. (To review this aspect of the lifespan perspective, refer to page 13 in Chapter 1.)

Cognitive Development

The cognitive changes of early adulthood are supported by further development of the cerebral cortex, especially the frontal lobes. Pruning of synapses along with growth and myelination of stimulated neural fibers continue, though at a slower pace than in adolescence (Nelson, Thomas, & De Haan, 2006). As we will see, cognitive advances (and underlying brain growth) are promoted by major life events, including attaining higher education, establishing a career, and grappling with the demands of marriage and child rearing. fMRI evidence reveals that as young adults become increasingly proficient in a field of endeavor, cortical regions specialized for those activities undergo further *experience-dependent brain growth* (see page 127 in Chapter 4). In addition to functioning more efficiently, structural changes may occur as skill refinement results in increased cortical tissue devoted to the task and, at times, reorganization of brain areas governing the activity (Hill & Schneider, 2006).

How does cognition change in early adulthood? Lifespan theorists have examined this question from three familiar vantage points. First, they have proposed transformations in the structure of thought—new, qualitatively distinct ways of thinking that extend the cognitive-developmental changes of childhood and adolescence. Second, adulthood is a time of attaining advanced knowledge in a particular area, an accomplishment that has important implications for information processing and creativity. Finally, researchers have been interested in the extent to which the diverse mental abilities assessed by intelligence tests remain stable or change during the adult years—a topic we will address in Chapter 15.

Changes in the Structure of Thought

Sharese described her first year in graduate school as a "cognitive turning point." As part of her internship in a public health clinic, she observed firsthand the many factors that affect human health-related behaviors. For a time, the realization that everyday dilemmas did not have clear-cut solutions made her intensely uncomfortable. "Working in this messy reality is so different from the problem solving I did in my undergraduate classes," she told her mother over the phone one day.

Piaget (1967) acknowledged the possibility that important advances in thinking follow the attainment of formal operations. He observed that adolescents prefer an idealistic, internally consistent perspective on the world to one that is vague, contradictory, and adapted to particular circumstances (see Chapter 11, page 388). Sharese's reflections fit the observations of researchers who have studied **postformal thought**—cognitive development beyond Piaget's formal operations. To clarify how thinking is restructured in adulthood, let's look at some influential theories, along with supportive research. Together, they show how personal effort and social experiences spark increasingly rational, flexible, and practical ways of thinking that accept uncertainties and vary across situations.

Perry's Theory: Epistemic Cognition

The work of William Perry (1981, 1970/1998) provided the starting point for an expanding research literature on the development of *epistemic cognition. Epistemic* means "of or about knowledge," and **epistemic cognition** refers to our reflections on how we arrived at facts, beliefs, and ideas. When mature, rational thinkers reach conclusions that differ from those of others, they consider the justifiability of their conclusions. When they cannot justify their approach, they revise it, seeking a more balanced, adequate route to acquiring knowledge.

DEVELOPMENT OF EPISTEMIC COGNITION. Perry wondered why young adults respond in dramatically different ways to the diversity of ideas they encounter in college. To find out, he interviewed Harvard University undergraduates at the end of each of their four years, asking "what stood out" during the previous year. Responses indicated that students' reflections on knowing changed as they experienced the complexities of university life and moved closer to adult roles—findings confirmed in many subsequent studies (King & Kitchener, 1994, 2002; Magolda, 2002; Moore, 2002).

Younger students regarded knowledge as made up of separate units (beliefs and propositions), whose truth could be determined by comparing them to objective standards—standards that exist apart from the thinking person and his or her situation.

© ERIK DREYER/GETTY IMAGES/STONE

When college students challenge one another's reasoning while tackling realistic, ambiguous problems, they are likely to gain in epistemic cognition.

As a result, they engaged in **dualistic thinking,** dividing information, values, and authority into right and wrong, good and bad, we and they. As one college freshman stated, "When I went to my first lecture, what the man said was just like God's word. I believe everything he said because he is a professor . . . and this is a respected position" (Perry, 1981, p. 81). And when asked, "If two people disagree on the interpretation of a poem, how would you decide which one is right?" a sophomore replied, "You'd have to ask the poet. It's his poem" (Clinchy, 2002, p. 67).

Older students, in contrast, had moved toward **relativistic thinking**—viewing all knowledge as embedded in a framework of thought. Aware of a diversity of opinions on many topics, they gave up the possibility of absolute truth in favor of multiple truths, each relative to its context. As a result, their thinking became more flexible and tolerant. As one college senior put it, "Just seeing how [famous philosophers] fell short of an all-encompassing answer, [you realize] that ideas are really individualized. And you begin to have respect for how great their thought could be, without its being absolute" (Perry, 1970/1998, p. 90). Relativistic thinking leads to the realization that one's own beliefs are often subjective, since several frameworks may satisfy the criterion of internal logical consistency (Moore, 2002; Sinnott, 2003). Thus, the relativistic thinker is acutely aware that each person, in arriving at a position, creates her own "truth."

Eventually, the most mature individuals progress to **commitment within relativistic thinking.** Instead of choosing between opposing views, they try to formulate a more satisfying perspective that synthesizes contradictions. When considering which of two theories studied in a college course is better, or which of several movies most deserves an Oscar, the individual moves beyond the stance that everything is a matter of opinion and generates rational criteria against which options can be evaluated (Moshman, 2003, 2005). Few college students reach this extension of relativism. Adults who attain it generally display a more sophisticated approach to learning, in which they actively seek out differing perspectives to advance their knowledge and understanding.

■ **IMPORTANCE OF PEER INTERACTION AND REFLECTION.** Advances in epistemic cognition depend on further gains in metacognition, which are likely to occur in situations that challenge young peoples' perspectives and induce them to consider the rationality of their thought processes (Moshman, 2005). In a study of the college learning experiences of seniors who scored low and high in Perry's scheme, high-scoring students frequently reported activities that encouraged them to struggle with realistic but ambiguous problems in a supportive environment, in which faculty offered encouragement and guidance. For example, an engineering major, describing an airplane-design project that required advanced epistemic cognition, noted his discovery that "you can design 30 different airplanes and each one's going to have its benefits and there's going to be problems with each one" (Marra & Palmer, 2004, p. 116). The low-scoring students rarely mentioned such experiences.

When students tackle challenging, ill-structured problems, interaction among individuals who are roughly equal in knowledge and authority is beneficial because it prevents acceptance of another's reasoning simply because of greater power or expertise. When college students were asked to devise the most effective solution to a difficult logical problem, only 3 out of 32 students (9 percent) in a "work alone" condition succeeded. But in an "interactive" condition, 15 out of 20 small groups (75 percent) arrived at the correct solution following extensive discussion (Moshman & Geil, 1998). Whereas few students working alone reflected on their solution strategies, most groups engaged in a process of "collective rationality" in which members challenged one another to justify their reasoning and collaborated in working out the most defensible strategy.

Of course, reflection on one's own thinking can also occur individually. But peer interaction fosters the necessary type of individual reflection: arguing with oneself over competing ideas and strategies and coordinating opposing perspectives into a new, more effective structure. ***TAKE A MOMENT...*** Return to page 321 in Chapter 9 to review how peer collaboration fosters cognitive development in childhood. It remains a highly effective basis for education in early adulthood.

Perry's theory and the research it stimulated are based on samples of highly educated young adults. These investigators acknowledge that movement from dualism to relativism is probably limited to people confronting the multiplicity of viewpoints typically encountered during a college education, and that the most advanced attainment—commitment within relativism—may require advanced graduate study (King & Kitchener, 2002). But the underlying theme—thought less constrained by the need to find one answer to a question and more responsive to its context—is also evident in another theory of adult cognition.

Labouvie-Vief's Theory: Pragmatic Thought and Cognitive-Affective Complexity

Gisella Labouvie-Vief's (1980, 1985) portrait of adult cognition echoes features of Perry's theory. Adolescents, she points out, operate within a world of possibility. Adulthood involves movement from hypothetical to **pragmatic thought,** a structural advance in which logic becomes a tool for solving real-world problems.

According to Labouvie-Vief, the need to specialize motivates this change. As adults select one path out of many alternatives, they become more aware of the constraints of everyday life. And in the course of balancing various roles, they accept contradictions as part of existence and develop ways of thinking that thrive on imperfection and compromise. Sharese's friend Christy, a student and mother of two young children, illustrates:

> I've always been a feminist, and I wanted to remain true to my beliefs in family and career. But this is Gary's first year of teaching high school, and he's saddled with four preparations and coaching the school's basketball team. At least

for now, I've had to settle for "give-and-take feminism"—going to school part-time and shouldering most of the responsibility for the kids while he gets used to his new job. Otherwise, we'd never make it financially.

Labouvie-Vief (2003, 2006) also points out that young adults' enhanced reflective capacities alter the dynamics of their emotional lives: They become more adept at integrating cognition with emotion and, in doing so, again make sense of discrepancies. Examining the self-descriptions of several hundred 10- to 80-year-olds diverse in SES, Labouvie-Vief found that from adolescence through middle adulthood, people gained in **cognitive-affective complexity**—awareness of positive and negative feelings and coordination of them into a complex, organized structure (see Figure 13.7) (Labouvie-Vief, 2008; Labouvie-Vief et al., 1995; Labouvie-Vief, DeVoe, & Bulka, 1989). For example, one 34-year-old combined roles, traits, and diverse emotions into this coherent self-description: "With the recent birth of our first child, I find myself more fulfilled than ever, yet struggling in some ways. My elation is tempered by my gnawing concern over meeting all my responsibilities in a satisfying way while remaining an individualized person with needs and desires."

Cognitive-affective complexity promotes greater awareness of one's own and others' perspectives and motivations. As Labouvie-Vief (2003) notes, it is a vital aspect of adult *emotional intelligence* (see page 313 in Chapter 9) and is valuable in solving many pragmatic problems. Individuals high in cognitive-affective complexity view events and people in a tolerant, open-minded fashion. And because cognitive-affective complexity involves accepting and making sense of both positive and negative feelings, it helps people regulate intense emotion and, therefore, think rationally about real-world dilemmas, even those that are laden with negative information (Labouvie-Vief & Gonzalez, 2004).

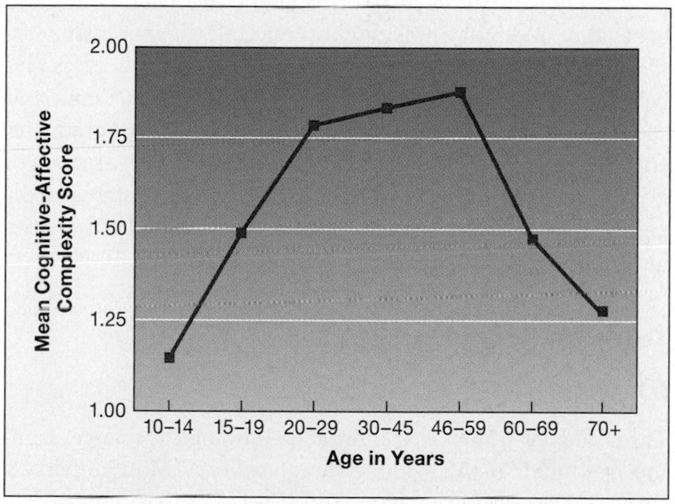

■ **FIGURE 13.7** ■ **Changes in cognitive-affective complexity from adolescence to late adulthood.** Performance, based on participants' descriptions of their roles, traits, and emotions, increased steadily from adolescence through early adulthood, peaked in middle age, and fell off in late adulthood when (as we will see in later chapters) basic information-processing skills decline. (From G. Labouvie-Vief, 2004, "Dynamic Integration: Affect, Cognition, and the Self in Adulthood," *Current Directions in Psychological Science, 12,* p. 203. Reprinted by permission of Blackwell Publishing Ltd.)

Awareness of multiple truths, integration of logic with reality, and cognitive-affective complexity sum up qualitative transformations in thinking under way in early adulthood (Sinnott, 1998, 2003, 2008). As we will see next, adults' increasingly specialized and context-bound thought, although it closes off certain options, opens new doors to higher levels of competence.

Expertise and Creativity

In Chapter 9, we noted that children's expanding knowledge improves their ability to remember new information related to what they already know. For young adults, **expertise**—acquisition of extensive knowledge in a field or endeavor—is supported by the specialization that begins with selecting a college major or an occupation, since it takes many years for a person to master any complex domain. Once attained, expertise has a profound impact on information processing.

Compared with novices, experts remember and reason more quickly and effectively. The expert knows more domain-specific concepts and represents them in richer ways—at a deeper and more abstract level and as having more features that can be linked to other concepts. As a result, unlike novices, whose understanding is superficial, experts approach problems with underlying principles in mind. For example, a highly trained physicist notices when several problems deal with conservation of energy and can therefore be solved similarly. In contrast, a beginning physics student focuses only on surface features—whether the problem contains a disk, a pulley, or a coiled spring (Chi, 2006; Chi, Glaser, & Farr, 1988). Experts can use what they know to arrive at many solutions automatically—through quick and easy remembering. And when a problem is challenging, they tend to plan ahead, systematically analyzing and categorizing elements and selecting the best from many possibilities, while the novice proceeds more by trial and error.

Expertise is necessary for creativity as well as problem solving (Weissberg, 2006). The creative products of adulthood differ from those of childhood in that they are not just original but also directed at a social or aesthetic need. Mature creativity requires a unique cognitive capacity—the ability to formulate new, culturally meaningful problems and to ask significant questions that have not been posed before. According to Patricia Arlin (1989), movement from *problem solving* to *problem finding* is a core feature of postformal thought evident in highly accomplished artists and scientists.

Case studies support the 10-year rule in development of master-level creativity—a decade between initial exposure to a field and sufficient expertise to produce a creative work (Simonton, 2000; Winner, 2003). Furthermore, a century of research reveals that creative accomplishment rises in early adulthood, peaks in the late thirties or early forties, and gradually declines, though rarely so substantially as to turn a creative person into a noncreative person (Dixon, 2003). And exceptions to this pattern exist. Those who get an early start in creativity tend to peak and drop off sooner, whereas "late bloomers" reach their full stride at older ages. This suggests that creativity is more a function of "career age" than of chronological age.

The course of creativity also varies across disciplines (Simonton, 1991, 2006). For example, artists and musicians typically show an early rise in creativity, perhaps because they do not need extensive formal education before they begin to produce. Academic scholars and scientists, who must earn higher academic degrees and spend years doing research to make worthwhile contributions, usually display their achievements later and over a longer time.

Though creativity is rooted in expertise, not all experts are creative. Creativity also requires other qualities—an innovative thinking style, tolerance of ambiguity, a special drive to succeed, and a willingness to experiment and try again after failure (Lubart, 2003; Sternberg & Lubart, 1996). And creativity demands time and energy. For women especially, it may be postponed or disrupted by child rearing, divorce, or an unsupportive partner (Vaillant & Vaillant, 1990). In sum, creativity is multiply determined. When personal and situational factors jointly promote it, creativity can continue for many decades, well into old age.

© BORDERLANDS/ALAMY

A sculptor works on a statue to honor those who died in the Asian tsunami of 2004. The creative products of adulthood differ from those of childhood in that they are not just original but also directed at a social or aesthetic need.

ASK YOURSELF

>> REVIEW
How does expertise affect information processing? Why is expertise necessary for, but not the same as, creativity?

>> APPLY
For her human development course, Marcia wrote a paper in which she discussed differing implications of Piaget's and Vygotsky's theories for education. Then she presented evidence that combining both perspectives yields a more effective approach than either position by itself. Explain how Marcia's reasoning illustrates advanced epistemic cognition.

>> CONNECT
Our discussion in Chapter 9 noted that emotional intelligence is associated with life satisfaction and success in the workplace. How might cognitive-affective complexity contribute to these favorable outcomes?

>> REFLECT
Describe a classroom experience or assignment in one of your college courses that promoted relativistic thinking.

The College Experience

Looking back at the trajectory of their lives, many people view the college years as formative—more influential than any other period of adulthood. This is not surprising. College serves as a "developmental testing ground," a time for devoting full attention to exploring alternative values, roles, and behaviors. To facilitate this exploration, college exposes students to a form of "culture shock"—encounters with new ideas and beliefs, new freedoms and opportunities, and new academic and social demands. About two-thirds of U.S. high school graduates enroll in an institution of higher education (U.S. Department of Education, 2009). Besides offering a route to a high-status career and its personal and monetary rewards, colleges and universities have a transforming impact on young people.

Psychological Impact of Attending College

Thousands of studies reveal broad psychological changes from the freshman to the senior year of college (Montgomery & Côté, 2003; Pascarella & Terenzini, 1991). As research inspired by Perry's theory indicates, students become better at reasoning about problems that have no clear solution, identifying the strengths and weaknesses of opposing sides of complex issues, and reflecting on the quality of their thinking. Their attitudes and values also broaden. They show increased interest in literature, the performing arts, and philosophical and historical issues and greater tolerance for ethnic and cultural diversity. Also, as noted in Chapter 12, college leaves its mark on moral reasoning by fostering concern with individual rights and human welfare.

© JAMES MARSHALL/THE IMAGE WORKS

Interacting with other college students in academic and extracurricular settings yields rich benefits. Residence hall living in particular predicts cognitive change because it maximizes involvement in the educational and social systems of the institution.

Finally, exposure to multiple worldviews encourages young people to look more closely at themselves. During the college years, students develop greater self-understanding, enhanced self-esteem, and a firmer sense of identity.

How do these interrelated changes come about? The type of four-year institution attended—public versus private, highly selective versus relatively open in enrollment—makes little difference in psychological outcomes or even in ultimate career success and earnings (Montgomery & Côté, 2003). And cognitive growth is just as great at two-year community colleges as at four-year institutions (Bohr et al., 1994).

Rather, the impact of college is jointly influenced by the person's involvement in academic and nonacademic activities and the richness and diversity of the campus environment. The more students interact with peers in academic and extracurricular settings, the more they benefit. Residence hall living is one of the most consistent predictors of cognitive change because it maximizes involvement in the educational and social systems of the institution (Terenzini, Pascarella, & Blimling, 1999). These findings underscore the importance of programs that integrate commuting students into out-of-class campus life. Quality of academic experiences also affects college outcomes. Psychological benefits increase with students' effort and willingness to participate in class and with challenging teaching that integrates learning in separate courses, offers extensive contact with faculty, and connects course work with real workplace activities (Franklin, 1995).

Dropping Out

Completing a college education has enduring effects on people's postcollege opportunities and worldview. Yet 45 percent of U.S. students at two-year institutions and 30 percent of students at four-year institutions drop out, most within the first year and many within the first six weeks (ACT, 2008). Dropout rates are higher in colleges with less selective admission requirements; in some, first-year dropout approaches 50 percent. And ethnic minority students from low-SES families are at increased risk for dropping out (Montgomery & Côté, 2003).

Both personal and institutional factors contribute to college leaving. Most entering freshmen have high hopes for college life but find the transition difficult. Those who have trouble adapting—because of lack of motivation, poor study skills, financial pressures, or emotional dependence on parents—quickly develop negative attitudes toward the college environment. Often these exit-prone students do not meet with their advisers or professors. At the same time, colleges that do little to help high-risk students, through developmental courses and other support services, have a higher percentage of dropouts (Moxley, Najor-Durack, & Dumbrigue, 2001). And when students report experiencing "disrespect" on campus because of their ethnicity or religion, their desire to continue plummets (Zea et al., 1997).

Beginning to prepare young people in early adolescence with the necessary visions and skills can do much to improve college success. In a study that followed up nearly 700 young people from sixth grade until two years after high school graduation, a set of factors—grade point average, academic self-concept, persistence in the face of challenge, parental SES and valuing of a college education, and the individual's plans to attend college—predicted college enrollment at age 20 (Eccles, Vida, & Barber, 2004). Although parental SES is difficult to modify, improving parents' attitudes and behaviors and students' academic motivation and educational aspirations is within reach, through a wide array of strategies considered in Chapters 11 and 12.

Once young people enroll in college, reaching out to them, especially during the early weeks and throughout the first year, is crucial. Programs that forge bonds between teachers and students and that provide academic support, part-time work opportunities, and meaningful extracurricular roles increase retention. Membership in campus-based social and religious organizations is especially helpful in strengthening minority students' sense of belonging (Fashola & Slavin, 1998). Young people who feel that they have entered a college community that is concerned about them as individuals are far more likely to graduate.

Vocational Choice

Young adults, college-bound or not, face a major life decision: the choice of a suitable work role. Being a productive worker calls for many of the same qualities as being an active citizen and a nurturant family member—good judgment, responsibility, dedication, and cooperation. What influences young people's decisions about careers? What is the transition from school to work like, and what factors make it easy or difficult?

Selecting a Vocation

In societies with an abundance of career possibilities, occupational choice is a gradual process that begins long before adolescence. Major theorists view the young person as moving through several periods of vocational development (Gottfredson, 2005; Super, 1990, 1994):

1. The **fantasy period:** In early and middle childhood, children gain insight into career options by fantasizing about them. Their preferences, guided largely by familiarity, glamour, and excitement, bear little relation to the decisions they will eventually make.
2. The **tentative period:** Between ages 11 and 16, adolescents think about careers in more complex ways, at first in terms of their *interests,* and soon—as they become more aware of personal and educational requirements for different vocations—in terms of their *abilities* and *values.* "I like science and the process of discovery," Sharese thought as she neared high school graduation. "But I'm also good with people, and I'd like to do something to help others. So maybe teaching or medicine would suit my needs."
3. The **realistic period:** By the late teens and early twenties, with the economic and practical realities of adulthood just around the corner, young people start to narrow their options. A first step is often further *exploration*—gathering more information about possibilities that blend with their personal characteristics. In the final phase, *crystallization,* they focus on a general vocational category and experiment for a time before settling on a single occupation. As a college sophomore, Sharese pursued her interest in science, but she had not yet selected a major. Once she decided on chemistry, she considered whether to pursue teaching, medicine, or public health.

Factors Influencing Vocational Choice

Most, but not all, young people follow this pattern of vocational development. A few know from an early age just what they want to be and follow a direct path to a career goal. Some decide and later change their minds, and still others remain undecided for an extended period. College students are granted added time to explore various options. In contrast, the life conditions of many low-SES youths restrict their range of choices.

Making an occupational choice is not simply a rational process in which young people weigh abilities, interests, and values against career options. Like other developmental milestones, it is the result of a dynamic interaction between person and environment (Gottfredson & Duffy, 2008). A great many influences feed into the decision, including personality, family, teachers, and gender stereotypes, among others.

■ **PERSONALITY.** People are attracted to occupations that complement their personalities. John Holland (1985, 1997) identified six personality types that affect vocational choice:

- The *investigative person,* who enjoys working with ideas, is likely to select a scientific occupation (for example, anthropologist, physicist, or engineer).
- The *social person,* who likes interacting with people, gravitates toward human services (counseling, social work, or teaching).
- The *realistic person,* who prefers real-world problems and working with objects, tends to choose a mechanical occupation (construction, plumbing, or surveying).
- The *artistic person,* who is emotional and high in need for individual expression, looks toward an artistic field (writing, music, or the visual arts).
- The *conventional person,* who likes well-structured tasks and values material possessions and social status, has traits well suited to certain business fields (accounting, banking, or quality control).
- The *enterprising person,* who is adventurous, persuasive, and a strong leader, is drawn to sales and supervisory positions or to politics.

TAKE A MOMENT... Does one of these personality types describe you? Or do you have aspects of more than one type? Research confirms a relationship between personality and vocational choice in diverse cultures, but it is only moderate. Many people are blends of several personality types and can do well at more than one kind of occupation (Holland, 1997; Spokane & Cruza-Guet, 2005). Furthermore, career decisions are made in the context of family influences, educational opportunities, and current life circumstances. For example, Sharese's friend Christy scored high on Holland's investigative dimension. But when she married and had children early, she postponed her dream of becoming a college professor and chose a human services career that required fewer years of education. As Christy's case illustrates, personality takes us only partway in understanding vocational choice.

■ **FAMILY INFLUENCES.** Young people's vocational aspirations correlate strongly with their parents' jobs. Individuals who grew up in higher-SES homes are more likely to select high-status, white-collar occupations, such as doctor, lawyer, scientist, or engineer. In contrast, those with lower-SES backgrounds tend to choose less prestigious, blue-collar careers—for example, plumber, construction worker, food service employee, or secretary. Parent–child vocational similarity is partly a function of similarity in personality, intellectual abilities, and—especially—educational attainment (Ellis & Bonin, 2003; Schoon & Parsons, 2002). More today than in past generations, number of years of schooling completed powerfully predicts occupational status.

Other factors also promote family resemblance in occupational choice. Higher-SES parents are more likely to give their children important information about the world of work and to have connections with people who can help the young person obtain a high-status position (Kalil, Levine, & Ziol-Guest, 2005). In a study of African-American mothers' influence on their

© PBNJ PRODUCTIONS/GETTY IMAGES/BLEND IMAGES

This young man has followed his father's career path to become an emergency medical technician. Parent–child vocational similarity is partly a function of similarity in personality, intellectual abilities, and—especially—educational attainment.

daughters' academic and career goals, college-educated mothers engaged in a wider range of strategies to promote their daughters' progress, including gathering information on colleges and areas of study and identifying knowledgeable professionals who could help (Kerpelman, Shoffner, & Ross-Griffin, 2002). Parenting practices also shape work-related values. Recall from Chapter 2 that higher-SES parents tend to promote curiosity and self-direction, which are required in many high-status careers. Lower-SES parents, in contrast, are more likely to emphasize conformity and obedience. Eventually, young people may choose careers that dovetail with these differences.

Still, parents can foster higher aspirations. Parental pressure to do well in school and encouragement toward high-status occupations predict vocational attainment beyond SES (Bryant, Zvonkovic, & Reynolds, 2006).

■ **TEACHERS.** Young adults preparing for or in careers requiring extensive education often report that teachers influenced their choice (Bright et al., 2005; Reddin, 1997). High school students who say that most of their teachers are caring and accessible, interested in their future, and expect them to work hard feel more confident about choosing a personally suitable career and succeeding at it (Metheny, McWhirter, & O'Neil, 2008). College-bound high school students tend to have closer relationships with teachers than do other students—relationships that are especially likely to foster high career aspirations in young women (Wigfield et al., 2002).

These findings provide yet another reason to promote positive teacher–student relations, especially for high school students from low-SES families. The power of teachers in offering encouragement and acting as role models can serve as an important source of resilience for these young people.

■ **GENDER STEREOTYPES.** Over the past three decades, young women have expressed increasing interest in occupations largely held by men (Gottfredson, 2005). Changes in gender-role attitudes, along with a dramatic rise in numbers of employed mothers who serve as career-oriented models for their daughters, are common explanations for women's attraction to nontraditional careers.

But women's progress in entering and excelling at male-dominated professions has been slow. As Table 13.2 shows, although the percentage of women engineers, lawyers, doctors, and business executives increased between 1983 and 2007 in the United States, it still falls far short of equal representation. Women remain concentrated in less well-paid, traditionally feminine professions, such as writing, social work, education, and nursing (U.S. Census Bureau, 2009b). In virtually all fields, their achievements lag behind those of men, who write more books, make more discoveries, hold more positions of leadership, and produce more works of art.

Ability cannot account for these dramatic sex differences. Recall from Chapter 11 that girls are advantaged in reading and writing achievement, and the gender gap favoring boys in math is small. Rather, gender-stereotyped messages play a key role. Although girls earn higher grades than boys, they reach secondary school less confident of their abilities, more likely to underestimate their achievement, and less likely to express interest in math and science careers (Wigfield et al., 2002). In college, the career aspirations of many women decline further as they question their capacity and opportunities to succeed in male-dominated fields and worry about combining a highly

■ **TABLE 13.2** ■ ***Percentage of Women in Various Professions in the United States, 1983 and 2007***

PROFESSION	1983	2007
Engineer	5.8	9.7
Lawyer	15.8	32.6
Doctor	15.8	30.0
Business executive	32.4	37.5[a]
Author, artist, entertainer	42.7	47.1
Social worker	64.3	82.0
Elementary or middle school teacher	93.5	80.9
Secondary school teacher	62.2	56.9
College or university professor	36.3	46.2
Librarian	84.4	83.2
Registered nurse	95.8	91.7
Psychologist	57.1	64.4

Source: U.S. Census Bureau, 2009b.

[a]This percentage includes executives and managers at all levels. Women make up only 25 percent of chief executive officers at large corporations, although that figure represents a sixfold increase over the past 25 years.

SOCIAL ISSUES

Masculinity at Work: Men Who Choose Nontraditional Careers

Ross majored in engineering through his sophomore year of college, when he startled his family and friends by switching to nursing. "I've never looked back," Ross said. "I love the work." He noted some benefits of being a male in a female work world, including the high regard of women colleagues and rapid advancement. "But as soon as they learn what I do," Ross remarked with disappointment, "guys on the outside question my abilities and masculinity."

What factors influence the small but increasing number of men who, like Ross, enter careers dominated by women? Compared to their traditional-career counterparts, these men are less gender-typed, less focused on the social status of their work, and more interested in working with people (Dodson & Borders, 2006; Jome, Surething, & Taylor, 2005). When several hundred men were assessed in their first year of college and again four years later, those who chose traditionally feminine occupations had more liberal social attitudes, including attitudes about gender roles, than those who chose traditionally masculine occupations. They also less often rated occupational prestige as important in their choice and were less likely to aspire to graduate education (Lease, 2003). Perhaps these men's gender-stereotype flexibility allowed them to choose occupations they found satisfying, even if those jobs were not typically regarded as appropriate for men.

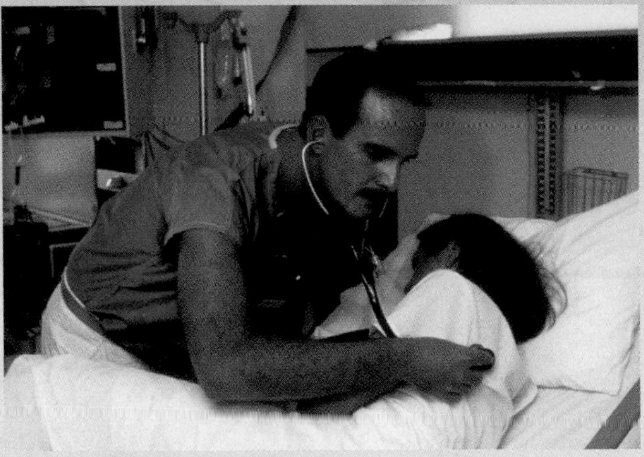
© PAUL CONKLIN/PHOTOEDIT

This nurse exemplifies the increasing number of men entering careers dominated by women. Compared with his traditional-career counterparts, he is likely to be less gender-typed, less focused on the social status of his work, and more interested in working with people.

In one study, 40 men who were primary school teachers, nurses, airline stewards, or librarians, when asked how they arrived at their choice, described diverse pathways (Simpson, 2005). Some actively sought the career, others happened on it while exploring possibilities, and still others first spent time in another occupation (usually male-dominated), found

---

demanding career with family responsibilities (Chhin, Bleeker, & Jacobs, 2008; Wigfield et al., 2006). Research indicates that many mathematically talented college women settle on nonscience majors. And those who remain in the sciences more often choose medicine or another health profession and less often choose engineering or a math or physical science career, than their male counterparts (Benbow et al., 2000; Halpern et al., 2007).

These findings reveal a pressing need for programs that sensitize high school and college personnel to the special problems women face in developing and maintaining high vocational aspirations and selecting nontraditional careers. Young women's aspirations rise in response to career guidance that encourages them to set goals that match their abilities, interests, and values. Those who continue to achieve usually have four experiences in common:

- A college environment that values women's accomplishments and attempts to enhance women's experiences in its curriculum
- Frequent interaction with faculty and professionals in their chosen fields
- The opportunity to test their abilities in a supportive environment
- Models of accomplished women who have successfully dealt with family–career role conflict (Swanson & Fouad, 1999; Zeldin & Pajares, 2000)

Compared to women, men have changed little in their interest in nontraditional occupations. See the Social Issues box above for research on the motivations and experiences of men who do choose female-dominated careers.

Vocational Preparation of Non-College-Bound Young Adults

Sharese's younger brother Leon graduated from high school in a vocational track. Like approximately one-third of American young people with a high school diploma, he had no current plans to go to college. While in school, Leon held a part-time job selling candy at the local shopping mall. He hoped to work in data processing after graduation, but six months later he was still a part-time sales clerk at the candy store. Although Leon had filled out many job applications, he got no interviews or offers. He soon despaired of discovering any relationship between his schooling and a career.

Leon's inability to find a job other than the one he held as a student is typical for U.S. non-college-bound high school graduates. Although they are more likely to find employment than youths who drop out, they have fewer work opportunities than high school graduates of several decades ago. About 20 percent of recent high school graduates who do not continue their education are unemployed (U.S. Department of Education, 2009). When they do find work, most hold low-paid, unskilled jobs. In addition, they have few alternatives for vocational counseling

it unsatisfying, and then settled into their current career.

The men also confirmed Ross's observations: Because of their male minority status, co-workers often assumed they were more knowledgeable than they actually were. They also had opportunities to move quickly into supervisory positions, although many did not seek advancement (Simpson, 2004). As one teacher commented, "I just want to be a good classroom teacher. What's wrong with that?" Furthermore, while in training and on the job, virtually all the men reported feeling socially accepted—relaxed and comfortable working with women.

But when asked to reflect on how others reacted to their choice, many men expressed anxiety about being stigmatized—by other men, not by women, whom they reported as generally accepting. To reduce these feelings, the men frequently described their job in ways that minimized its feminine image. Several librarians emphasized technical requirements by referring to their title as "information scientist" or "researcher." The teachers often highlighted the sports aspect of their work. And nurses sometimes distanced themselves from a feminine work identity by specializing in "adrenalin-charged" areas such as accident or emergency.

Despite these tensions, the men uniformly derived enjoyment and self-esteem from their nontraditional career choice. As with Ross, their high level of private comfort seemed to prevail over uneasiness about the feminine public image of their work.

and job placement as they transition from school to work (Shanahan, Mortimer, & Krüger, 2002).

American employers regard recent high school graduates as poorly prepared for skilled business and industrial occupations and manual trades. And there is some truth to this impression. As noted in Chapter 11, unlike European nations, the United States has no widespread training system for non-college-bound youths. As a result, most graduate without work-related skills and experience a "floundering period" that lasts for several years.

In Germany, young people who do not go to a Gymnasium (college-preparatory high school) have access to one of the most successful work–study apprenticeship systems in the world for entering business and industry. About two-thirds of German youths participate. After completing full-time schooling at age 15 or 16, they spend the remaining two years of compulsory education in the Berufsschule, combining part-time vocational courses with an apprenticeship that is jointly planned by educators and employers. Students train in work settings for more than 350 blue- and white-collar occupations (Deissinger, 2007). Apprentices who complete the program and pass a qualifying examination are certified as skilled workers and earn union-set wages. Businesses provide financial support because they know that the program guarantees a competent, dedicated work force (Heinz, 1999; Kerckhoff, 2002). Many apprentices are hired into well-paid jobs by the firms that train them. And young employees who excel are eligible for government financial aid to extend their vocational education in special promotion programs (Buchman, 2002).

The success of the German system—and of similar systems in Austria, Denmark, Switzerland, and several East European countries—suggests that a national apprenticeship program would improve the transition from high school to work for U.S. young people. The many benefits of bringing together the worlds of schooling and work include helping non-college-bound young people establish productive lives right after graduation, motivating at-risk youths to stay in school, and contributing to the nation's economic growth. Nevertheless, implementing an apprenticeship system poses major challenges: overcoming the reluctance of employers to assume part of the responsibility for vocational training, ensuring cooperation between schools and businesses, and preventing low-SES youths from being concentrated in the lowest-skilled apprenticeship placements, an obstacle that Germany itself has not yet fully overcome (Hamilton & Hamilton, 2000). Currently, small-scale school-to-work projects in the United States are attempting to solve these problems and build bridges between learning and working.

Although vocational development is a lifelong process, adolescence and early adulthood are crucial periods for defining occupational goals and launching a career. Young people who are well-prepared for an economically and personally satisfying work life are much more likely to become productive citizens, devoted family members, and contented adults. The support of families, schools, businesses, communities, and society as a whole can contribute greatly to a positive outcome. In Chapter 14, we will take up the challenges of establishing a career and integrating it with other life tasks.

ASK YOURSELF

» REVIEW
What student and college-environment characteristics contribute to favorable psychological changes during the college years?

» APPLY
Diane, a high school senior, knows that she wants to "work with people" but doesn't yet have a specific career in mind. Diane's father is a chemistry professor, her mother a social worker. What steps can Diane's parents take to broaden her awareness of the world of work and help her focus on an occupational goal?

» CONNECT
What have you learned in previous chapters about development of gender stereotypes that helps explain why women's progress in entering and excelling at male-dominated professions has been slow? (*Hint:* See Chapter 10, pages 342–343, and Chapter 11, page 390.)

» REFLECT
Describe your progress in choosing a vocation. What personal and environmental factors have been influential?

Summary

PHYSICAL DEVELOPMENT

Biological Aging Is Under Way in Early Adulthood

Describe current theories of biological aging, including those at the level of DNA and body cells and those at the level of tissues and organs.

- Once body structures reach maximum capacity and efficiency in the teens and twenties, **biological aging,** or **senescence,** begins.
- The programmed effects of specific genes may control certain age-related biological changes in DNA and body cells. For example, **telomere** shortening results in senescent cells, which contribute to disease and loss of function.

© THINKSTOCK/GETTY IMAGES

- DNA may also be damaged as random mutations accumulate, leading to less efficient cell repair and replacement and to abnormal cancerous cells. Release of highly reactive **free radicals** is a likely cause of age-related DNA and cellular damage.
- Genetic and cellular deterioration affects tissues and organs. The **cross-linkage theory of aging** suggests that over time, protein fibers form links and become less elastic, producing negative changes in many organs. Declines in the endocrine and immune systems may also contribute to aging.

Physical Changes

Describe the physical changes of aging, paying special attention to the cardiovascular and respiratory systems, motor performance, the immune system, and reproductive capacity.

- Gradual physical changes take place in early adulthood and later accelerate. Declines in heart and lung performance are evident during exercise. Heart disease is a leading cause of death in adults, although it has decreased considerably since the mid-twentieth century due to lifestyle changes and medical advances. Atherosclerosis is a serious, multiply determined cardiovascular disease involving fatty deposits on artery walls.
- Athletic skills requiring speed, strength, and gross-motor coordination peak in the early twenties; those requiring endurance, arm–hand steadiness, and aiming peak in the late twenties and early thirties. Less active lifestyles rather than biological aging account for most of the age-related decline in athletic skill and motor performance.
- The immune response declines after age 20. This trend is due to shrinking of the thymus gland and increased difficulty coping with physical and psychological stress.
- Women's reproductive capacity declines with age due to reduced quality and quantity of ova. Men show a gradual decrease in semen volume and sperm quality after age 35.

Health and Fitness

Describe the impact of SES, nutrition, and exercise on health, and discuss obesity in adulthood.

- Economically advantaged, well-educated adults tend to sustain good health, whereas the health of lower-income individuals with limited education declines. Health-related living conditions and habits are largely responsible.
- Today, Americans are the heaviest people in the world. Sedentary lifestyles and diets high in sugar and fat contribute to obesity, which is associated with serious health problems, social discrimination, and early death.
- Some weight gain between ages 25 and 50 results from a decrease in **basal metabolic rate (BMR),** but many young adults show large increases. Treatments for obesity involve a reduced-calorie, low-fat diet plus exercise, recording of food consumption, social support, and teaching problem-solving skills.
- Regular exercise reduces body fat, builds muscle, helps prevent illness (including cardiovascular disease), and enhances psychological well-being. Moderately intense exercise on most days leads to health benefits, which increase with greater intensity of exercise.

© LORI ADAMSKI PEEK/GETTY IMAGES/STONE

What are the two most commonly abused substances, and what health risks may result?

- Cigarette smoking and alcohol consumption are the two most common substance abuses. Smokers, most of whom began before age 21, are at increased risk for many health problems, including eye and skin abnormalities, decline in bone mass, heart attack, stroke, and numerous cancers.
- About one-third of heavy drinkers suffer from alcoholism, to which both heredity and environment contribute. Alcohol is implicated in liver and cardiovascular disease, certain cancers, numerous other physical disorders, and highway fatalities, crime, and sexual coercion.

Describe sexual attitudes and behavior of young adults, and discuss sexually transmitted diseases, sexual coercion, and premenstrual syndrome.

- Most adults are less sexually active than popular media images suggest, but they display a wider range of sexual choices and lifestyles and have had more sexual partners than earlier generations.

© SPENCER GRANT/PHOTOEDIT

- Adults in committed relationships report high satisfaction with their sex lives. Only a minority of adults report persistent sexual problems—difficulties linked to low SES and stress.
- Attitudes toward same-sex couples have gradually become more accepting. Homosexual relationships, like heterosexual relationships, are characterized by similarity between partners in education and background, greater satisfaction in committed relationships, and modest frequency of sexual activity.
- One-quarter of Americans are likely to contract a sexually transmitted disease (STD) during their lifetime; women are more vulnerable than men. Although AIDS remains concentrated among gay men and intravenous drug abusers, the incidence among homosexuals is declining. Currently, the disease is spreading most rapidly through heterosexual contact in poverty-stricken minority groups, with women at high risk.

- Most rape victims are under age 30 and have been harmed by men they know well. Men who commit sexual assault typically hold traditional gender roles, approve of violence against women, accept rape myths, and have difficulty interpreting women's social behavior accurately. Cultural acceptance of strong gender typing and of violence contributes to sexual coercion, which leads to psychological trauma. Female-initiated coercive sexual behavior also occurs, although it is less often reported and recognized by the legal system.

- Nearly 40 percent of women experience **premenstrual syndrome (PMS),** usually in mild form. For some, PMS is severe enough to interfere with daily life. Evidence for a genetic predisposition to PMS is accumulating.

How does psychological stress affect health?

- Chronic psychological stress induces physical responses that contribute to heart disease, several types of cancer, and gastrointestinal problems. Because the many challenges of early adulthood make it a highly stressful time of life, interventions that help stressed young people form supportive social ties are especially important.

COGNITIVE DEVELOPMENT

Changes in the Structure of Thought

Describe characteristics of adult thought, and explain how thinking changes in adulthood.

- Cognitive development beyond Piaget's formal operations is known as **postformal thought.** Adult cognition typically reflects an awareness of multiple truths, integrates logic with reality, and tolerates the gap between the ideal and the real.

- According to Perry's theory of **epistemic cognition,** college students move from **dualistic thinking,** dividing information into right and wrong, to **relativistic thinking,** awareness of multiple truths. Eventually, the most mature individuals progress to **commitment within relativistic thinking,** a perspective that synthesizes contradictions.

© ERIK DREYER/GETTY IMAGES/STONE

- Advances in epistemic cognition depend on gains in metacognition. Peer collaboration on challenging, ill-structured problems is especially beneficial.

- According to Labouvie-Vief's theory, the need to specialize motivates adults to progress from the ideal world of possibilities to **pragmatic thought,** which uses logic as a tool to solve real-world problems and accepts contradiction, imperfection, and the need to compromise. As a result of enhanced reflective capacities, adults also gain in **cognitive-affective complexity**—coordination of positive and negative feelings into a complex, organized structure.

Expertise and Creativity

What roles do expertise and creativity play in adult thought?

- Specialization in college and in an occupation leads to **expertise,** which enhances problem solving and is necessary for creativity. Mature creativity involves formulating meaningful new problems and questions. Although creativity tends to rise in early adulthood and to peak in the late thirties or early forties, its development varies across disciplines and individuals. In addition to expertise, diverse personal and situational factors jointly promote creativity.

The College Experience

Describe the impact of a college education on young people's lives, and discuss the problem of dropping out.

- Through involvement in academic programs and campus life, college students engage in exploration that produces gains in knowledge and reasoning ability, revised attitudes and values, enhanced self-understanding and self-esteem, and preparation for a high-status career.

- Dropout rates are higher in less selective colleges and for ethnic minority students from low-SES families. Personal and institutional factors contribute to college leaving, which is especially likely during the freshman year. High-risk students benefit from interventions that show concern for them as individuals.

Vocational Choice

Trace the development of vocational choice, and cite factors that influence it.

- Vocational choice moves through a **fantasy period,** in which children explore career options by fantasizing about them; a **tentative period,** in which teenagers weigh different careers against their interests, abilities, and values; and a **realistic period,** in which young people settle on a vocational category and then a specific occupation.

- Vocational choice is influenced by personality; parents' provision of educational opportunities, vocational information, and encouragement; and close relationships with teachers. Women's progress in male-dominated professions has been slow, and their achievements lag behind those of men in virtually all fields. Gender-stereotyped messages play a key role. Although some men choose careers in female-dominated fields, this is still uncommon.

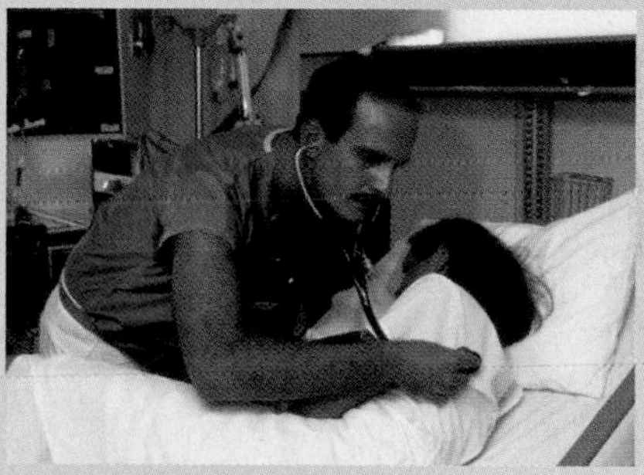

© PAUL CONKLIN/PHOTOEDIT

What problems do U.S. non-college-bound young people face in preparing for a vocation?

- U.S. non-college-bound high school graduates are poorly prepared for skilled business and industrial occupations and manual trades. Most are limited to low-paid, unskilled jobs, and too many are unemployed. Youth apprenticeships, like those widely available in European countries, would address the need for vocational training and improve the transition from school to work for these young people.

Important Terms and Concepts

basal metabolic rate (BMR) (p. 440)
biological aging, or senescence (p. 432)
cognitive-affective complexity (p. 453)
commitment within relativistic thinking (p. 452)
cross-linkage theory of aging (p. 434)
dualistic thinking (p. 452)
epistemic cognition (p. 451)
expertise (p. 453)
fantasy period (p. 456)
free radicals (p. 434)
postformal thought (p. 451)
pragmatic thought (p. 452)
premenstrual syndrome (PMS) (p. 449)
realistic period (p. 456)
relativistic thinking (p. 452)
telomeres (p. 433)
tentative period (p. 456)

COURTESY OF AMÉLIE GRYSOLE, HAITI 2009, AGRYSOLE@YAHOO.FR, CLOWNS WITHOUT BORDERS

For many young people in industrialized nations, the transition to early adulthood is a time of prolonged exploration of attitudes, values, and life possibilities. This young adult has interrupted his education to volunteer for Clowns Without Borders, an organization that brings joy to children living in refugee camps and conflict zones. Here he entertains a Sudanese audience, most of whom have lost family members and been left homeless due to ongoing civil war.

CHAPTER 14

Emotional and Social Development in Early Adulthood

After completing her master's degree at age 26, Sharese returned to her hometown, where she and Ernie would soon be married. During their year-long engagement, Sharese had vacillated about whether to follow through. At times, she looked with envy at Heather, still unattached and free to choose from an array of options before her. After graduating from college, Heather accepted a Peace Corps assignment in a remote region of Ghana, forged a romance with another Peace Corps volunteer that she ended at the conclusion of her tour of duty, and then traveled for eight months before returning to the United States to contemplate next steps.

Sharese also pondered the life circumstances of Christy and her husband, Gary—married their junior year in college and parents of two children born within the next few years. Despite his good teaching performance, Gary's relationship with the high school principal deteriorated, and he quit his job at the end of his first year. Financial pressures and the demands of parenthood had put Christy's education and career plans on hold. Sharese wondered whether it was really possible to combine family and career.

As her wedding approached, Sharese's ambivalence intensified, and she admitted to Ernie that she didn't feel ready to marry. Ernie's admiration for Sharese had strengthened over their courtship, and he reassured her of his love. His career had been under way for two years, he recently had received a company promotion, and at age 28, he looked forward to marriage and starting a family. Uncertain and conflicted, Sharese felt swept toward the altar as relatives, friends, and gifts began to arrive. On the appointed day, she walked down the aisle.

In this chapter, we take up the emotional and social sides of early adulthood. Notice that Sharese, Ernie, and Heather moved toward adult roles slowly, at times vacillating along the way. Not until their mid- to late twenties did they make lasting career and romantic choices and attain full economic independence—broadly accepted markers of adulthood that young people of previous generations reached considerably earlier. Each of these young people received financial and other forms of support from parents and other family members, which enabled them to postpone taking on adult roles. We consider whether prolonged exploration of life options has become so widespread that we must posit a new developmental period—*emerging adulthood*—to describe and understand it.

Recall from Chapter 12 that identity development continues to be a central focus from the late teens into the mid-twenties (see page 403). As they achieve a secure identity and independence from parents, young adults seek close, affectionate ties. Yet the decade of the twenties is accompanied by a sharp rise in the extent to which people feel they are personally in control of events in their lives. Indeed, 20- to 29-year-olds report a greater sense of control than they ever will again (Grob, Krings, & Bangerter, 2001). Perhaps for this reason, like Sharese, they often fear losing their freedom. Once this struggle is resolved, early adulthood leads to new family units and parenthood, accomplished in the context of diverse lifestyles. At the same time, young adults must master the skills and tasks of their chosen career.

Our discussion will reveal that identity, love, and work are intertwined. In negotiating these arenas, young adults do more choosing, planning, and changing course than any other age group. When their decisions are in tune with themselves and their social and cultural worlds, they acquire many new competencies, and life is full and rewarding.

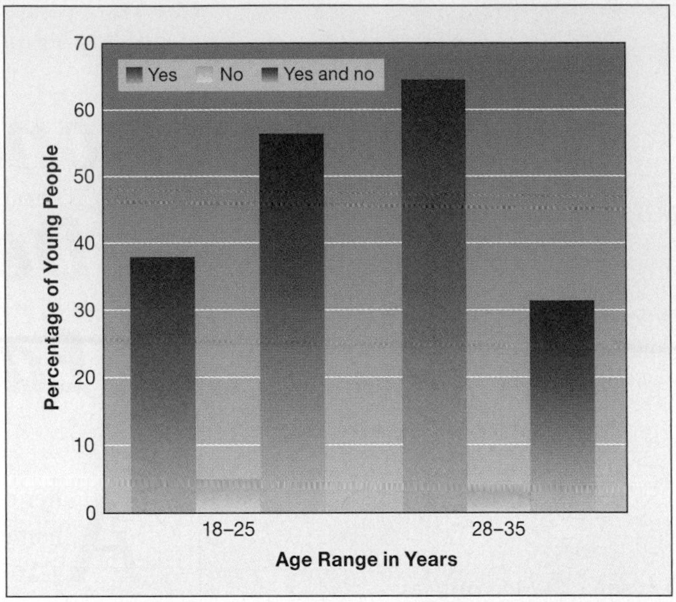

FIGURE 14.1 American young people's responses to the question, "Do you feel that you have reached adulthood?" Between ages 18 and 25, the majority answered "yes and no," reflecting their view that they had left adolescence but were not yet fully adult. Even in their late twenties and early thirties, about one-third of young people judged that they had not completed the transition to adulthood. (Adapted from Arnett, 2001.)

A Gradual Transition: Emerging Adulthood

TAKE A MOMENT... Think about your own development. Do you consider yourself to have reached adulthood? When a large sample of American 18- to 25-year-olds was asked this question, the majority gave an ambiguous answer: "yes and no" (see Figure 14.1). Only after reaching their late twenties and early thirties did most feel that they were truly adult—findings evident in a wide range of industrialized nations, including Argentina, Canada, the Czech Republic, Finland, Germany, Israel, Italy, and Spain (Arnett, 1997, 2001, 2003, 2007a; Buhl & Lanz, 2007; Macek, Bejček, & Vaníčková, 2007). The life pursuits and subjective judgments of many contemporary young people indicate that the transition to adult roles has become so delayed and prolonged that it has spawned a new transitional period, extending from the late teens to the mid-twenties, called **emerging adulthood**.

Unprecedented Exploration and Advances in Identity

The late teens and early twenties are a time of great challenge and uncertainty. Emerging adults have left adolescence but are some distance from taking on adult responsibilities, and their parents agree: In a survey of parents of a large sample of ethnically and religiously diverse U.S. undergraduate and graduate students, most viewed their children as not yet fully adult (Nelson et al., 2007). Rather, young people who have the economic resources to do so explore alternatives in education, work, personal beliefs and values, and love more intensively than they did as teenagers (Arnett, 2006, 2007b).

Notice how emerging adulthood greatly prolongs identity development. Released from the oversight of parents but not yet immersed in adult roles, 18- to 25-year-olds can engage in activities of the widest possible scope. Because so little is normative, or socially expected, routes to adult responsibilities are highly diverse in timing and order across individuals (Côté, 2006). For example, many more college students than in past generations pursue their education in a drawn-out, nonlinear way—changing majors as they explore career options, taking courses while working part-time, or interrupting school to work or travel. About one-third of U.S. college graduates enter graduate school, taking still more years to settle into their desired career track (U.S. Department of Education, 2009).

As a result of these experiences, young people's attitudes and values broaden. They express increased interest in philosophical, historical, and political issues and greater tolerance for ethnic and cultural diversity. And as discussed in Chapter 12, college leaves its mark on moral reasoning by fostering greater concern with individual rights and human welfare, sometimes expressed in political activism. Furthermore, exposure to multiple viewpoints encourages young people to look more closely at themselves. As a result, they develop a more complex self-concept that includes awareness of their own changing traits and values over time, along with enhanced self-esteem (Galambos, Barker, & Krahn, 2006; Labouvie-Vief, 2006; Montgomery & Côté, 2003). Together, these changes contribute to advances in identity.

During the college years, young people refine their approach to constructing an identity. Besides exploring in *breadth* (weighing multiple possibilities), they also explore in *depth*—evaluating existing commitments (Luyckx et al., 2006). For example, if you have not yet selected your major, you may be taking classes in a broad array of disciplines. Once you choose a major, you are likely to embark on an in-depth evaluation of your choice—reflecting on your interest, motivation, and performance and on your career prospects as you take additional classes in that field. Depending on the outcome of your evaluation, either your commitment to your major strengthens, or you return to a broad exploration of options.

In a longitudinal study extending over the first two years of college, most students cycled between making commitments and evaluating commitments in various identity domains. Fluctuations in students' certainty about their commitments sparked movement between these two states (Luyckx, Goossens, & Soenens, 2006). ***TAKE A MOMENT...*** Consider your own identity progress. Does it fit this *dual-cycle model,* in which identity formation is a lengthy process of feedback loops? Notice how the model helps explain the movement between identity statuses displayed by many young people, described in Chapter 12. College students who move toward exploration in depth and certainty of commitment are better-adjusted, academically and socially. Those who spend much time exploring in breadth without making commitments tend to be poorly adjusted—depressed and higher in drug use (Luyckx et al., 2006).

Identity development during the college years involves exploring in depth—evaluating current commitments. As these archaeology majors excavate a Mayan site in Belize, they mull over their interest, motivation, and career prospects as future archaeologists.

Many aspects of the life course that were once socially structured—marriage, parenthood, religious beliefs, and career paths—are increasingly left to individuals to decide on their own. During the college years, for example, attendance at religious services drops to its lowest level—about 30 percent in the United States—as young people continue to evaluate the beliefs they acquired in their families against alternatives. Many emerging adults work on constructing their own individualistic faith, often weaving together beliefs and practices from a variety of sources, including Eastern and Western religious traditions, science, and popular culture (Shipman et al., 2002).

Identity progress in emerging adulthood requires a sense of purpose, self-efficacy (belief in one's ability to succeed), determination to overcome obstacles, and responsibility for outcomes. Among young people of diverse ethnicities and SES levels, this set of qualities—called *personal agency*—is positively related to an information-gathering cognitive style and identity exploration and commitment, and negatively related to identity diffusion (Schwartz, Côté, & Arnett, 2005).

Cultural Change, Cultural Variation, and Emerging Adulthood

Rapid cultural change explains the recent appearance of this rich, complex bridge between adolescence and assumption of adult responsibilities. First, entry-level positions in many fields require more education than in the past, prompting young adults to seek higher education in record numbers and thus delaying financial independence and career commitment. Second, wealthy nations with longer-lived populations have no pressing need for young people's labor, freeing 18- to 25-year-olds for the extended exploration of emerging adulthood.

Indeed, emerging adulthood is limited to cultures that postpone entry into adult roles until the twenties. In developing nations such as China and India, only a privileged few—usually those from wealthier families who are admitted to universities—experience emerging adulthood, often for a shorter time span than their Western counterparts (Badger, Nelson, & Barry, 2006; Nelson & Chen, 2007). Furthermore, the overwhelming majority of young people in traditional non-Western countries—those who have few economic resources or who remain in rural regions where they grew up—have no "emerging adulthood." With limited education, they typically enter marriage, parenthood, and lifelong work early (UNICEF, 2009).

In industrialized countries, where many benefit from these transitional years, young people nevertheless vary in their beliefs about what it means to become an adult. Reflecting on the self-searching of these years, respondents from diverse cultures, ethnicities, and religious backgrounds emphasize psychological qualities, especially self-sufficiency—accepting responsibility for one's actions, deciding on personal beliefs and values, establishing an equal relationship with parents, and becoming financially independent (Facio & Micocci, 2003; Mayseless & Sharf, 2003; Nelson et al., 2007). Youths from collectivist minority groups also attach great importance to becoming more considerate of others, to attaining certain roles, and to self-control.

For example, African-American and Hispanic young people point to supporting and caring for a family as a major marker of adulthood (Arnett, 2003). Mormon college students believe that becoming less self-oriented and conducting oneself responsibly are as important as self-sufficiency, and they rate family commitments a close second (Nelson, 2003). And in a survey of Canadian Aboriginal university students (which includes Native Canadian and Inuit peoples, as well as Métis, or mixed blood people of both Native Canadian and European descent), those who identified strongly with their cultural heritage regarded "good control over emotions" and "capable of supporting parents financially" as more important than did those with less cultural identification. And both groups of Aboriginal students placed greater weight on financial self-sufficiency and on interdependent qualities (such as making lifelong commitments to others) than did Canadian white students (Cheah & Nelson, 2004).

Nevertheless, for low-SES young people in Western nations who are burdened by early parenthood, do not finish high school, are otherwise academically unprepared for college, or do not have access to vocational training, emerging adulthood is limited or nonexistent (see Chapters 11 and 13). Instead of excitement and personal expansion, these individuals encounter a "floundering period," during which they alternate between unemployment and dead-end, low-paying jobs (Cohen et al., 2003; Eccles et al., 2003).

As the Cultural Influences box on the following page indicates, because of its strong association with SES and higher education, some researchers reject the notion of emerging adulthood as a distinct period of development. Others disagree, predicting that emerging adulthood will become increasingly common as *globalization*—the exchange of ideas, information, trade, and immigration among nations—accelerates. Contact between industrialized and developing countries fosters economic progress. It also heightens awareness of events, lifestyles, and practices in faraway places. As globalization proceeds, gains in financial security and higher education and the formation of a common "global identity" among young people may lead to rapid spread of emerging adulthood (Arnett, 2007a; Nelson & Chen, 2007). Eventually, proponents claim, this period may become a typical experience on the path to adult life around the world.

Risk and Resilience in Emerging Adulthood

In grappling with momentous choices, emerging adults play a more active role in their own development than at any earlier time. They must choose and coordinate demanding life roles and acquire the skills necessary to succeed in those roles (Arnett, 2006; Eccles et al., 2003). As they experiment, they often encounter disappointments in love and work that require them to adjust, and sometimes radically change, their life path.

Emerging adults' vigorous explorations also extend earlier risks, including unprotected sexual activity, substance use, and hazardous driving behavior. And certain risks increase. For example, drug taking peaks between ages 19 and 22 (see Chapter 13). And as we will see later in this chapter, feelings of loneliness are higher than at any other time of life. As they move through school and employment settings, emerging adults must constantly separate from friends and forge new relationships.

Longitudinal research shows that the personal attributes and social supports listed in Applying What We Know on page 468 foster successful passage through these years, as indicated by completing a college education, forging a warm, stable intimate relationship, finding and keeping a well-paying job, and volunteering in one's community (Benson et al., 2006; Eccles & Gootman, 2002). Notice how factors in the table overlap with ones discussed in previous chapters that promote development through *resilience,* the capacity to overcome challenge and adversity. Young people with more of these resources—and with resources in all three categories—probably make an especially smooth transition to adulthood. But many emerging adults with only a few resources also fare well.

As in childhood, certain resources strengthen others. Relationships with parents have an especially wide-ranging influence. A secure, affectionate parent–emerging adult bond that extends the balance of connection and separation established in adolescence promotes many aspects of adaptive functioning: favorable self-esteem, identity progress, successful transition to college life, higher academic achievement, more rewarding friendships and romantic ties, and reduced anxiety, depression, loneliness, and drug abuse (Aquilino, 2006).

In addition, emerging adults who feel securely attached to parents and who view them as having used an authoritative child-rearing style are more likely to have integrated their parents' religious or spiritual beliefs into their own personal world view (Okagaki, Hammond, & Seamon, 1999). Then, as young people seek their place in an increasingly complex, ever-changing world, a religious or spiritual ideology helps anchor them. It serves as a reminder of social injustices, motivating—as it did in adolescence—community service. It also offers a transcendent system through which they can view stressful, confusing events and an image of ideal character traits toward which they can strive (Kerestes & Youniss, 2003).

CULTURAL INFLUENCES

Is Emerging Adulthood Really a Distinct Period of Development?

Although broad consensus exists that cultural change has prolonged the transition to adult roles for many young people, disagreement exists over whether these years of "emergence" merit the creation of a new developmental period (Hendry & Kloep, 2007). Critics of the concept of emerging adulthood offer the following arguments.

First, burgeoning higher education enrollment, delayed career entry, and later marriage and parenthood are cultural trends that began as early as the 1970s in industrialized nations, only gradually becoming more conspicuous. At no time has adulthood in complex societies been attained at a distinct moment. Rather, young people have in the past and continue today to reach adult status earlier in some domains, later in others. And they may reverse direction. For example, after finishing college or being laid off from a job, they might move back to the parental home to get their bearings (Cohen et al., 2003). In accord with the lifespan perspective, development is multidimensional and multidirectional, for 18- to 25-year-olds as it is for adults of all ages. Transitions occur during all periods of the lifespan, with societal conditions heavily influencing their length and complexity.

Second, emerging adulthood fails to describe the experiences of most of the world's youths (Bynner, 2005). In many developing countries, young people—particularly women—are limited in education and marry and have children early (see page 62 in Chapter 2). According to one estimate, nearly 1.5 billion individuals—86 percent of young people—follow this traditional route to adulthood, with no prospect of alternatives (Lloyd, 2005). And as we have seen, many low-SES young people in industrialized nations lack the academic preparation and financial resources to experience an emerging adulthood.

Third, research on emerging adulthood largely emphasizes its personal and societal benefits. But the extended exploration that defines this period, though opening opportunities, might be risky for those without the personal agency to make effective choices and acquire adult skills (Levine, 2005). These young people may remain uncommitted for too long—an outcome that would impede the focused learning required for a successful work life. A favorable emerging adulthood, then, depends on whether it is used effectively to acquire the competencies needed for modern living.

Proponents of emerging adulthood as a distinct developmental period respond that, though not universal, it applies to most young people in industrialized societies and is spreading rapidly in developing nations that play major roles in our global economy (Arnett, 2007a). Furthermore, the concept reminds us that the lives of many people in their early twenties differ vastly from those in their thirties, and of the need to clarify the contextual factors that contribute to their experiences. But—as skeptics note—age-graded influences have declined in favor of nonnormative influences throughout contemporary adulthood (see page 13 in Chapter 1 to review) (Hendry & Kloep, 2007). In their view, rather than being unique, emerging adults are part of a general trend toward blurring of age-related expectations, yielding multiple transitions and increased diversity in development across the adult years.

This married man and father living in a rural region of India has few economic resources. Like the majority of young people in developing countries, he has no emerging adulthood.

As one reviewer of research concluded, "What seems advantageous for emerging adults' achievement of independence is feeling connected, secure, understood, and loved in their families, and having the willingness to call on parental resources" (Aquilino, 2006, p. 201). In contrast, exposure to multiple negative life events—family conflict, abusive intimate relationships, repeated romantic breakups, academic or employment difficulties, and financial strain—undermines development, even in emerging adults whose childhood and adolescence prepared them well for this transition (Cui & Vaillant, 1996).

In sum, supportive family, school, and community environments are crucial, just as they were at earlier ages. The overwhelming majority of young people with access to these resources are highly optimistic about their future (Arnett, 2000, 2006). Although they worry about grim aspects of their world, such as crime, war, environmental destruction, and persistent economic recession, they remain convinced that they will eventually arrive at where they want to be in life: secure enough financially and happy in work and close relationships. Now let's turn to theories of psychosocial development in early adulthood.

Applying What We Know

Resources That Foster Resilience in Emerging Adulthood

Type of Resource	Description
Cognitive attributes	Effective planning and decision making Information-gathering cognitive style Good school performance Knowledge of vocational options and skills
Emotional and social attributes	Positive self-esteem Good emotional self-regulation and flexible coping strategies Good conflict-resolution skills Confidence in one's ability to reach one's goals Sense of personal responsibility for outcomes Persistence and good use of time Healthy identity development—movement toward exploration in depth and commitment certainty Strong moral character Sense of meaning and purpose in life, engendered by religion, spirituality, or other sources Desire to contribute meaningfully to one's community
Social supports	Positive relationships with parents, peers, teachers, and mentors Sense of connection to social institutions, such as school, church, workplace, and community center

Sources: Benson et al., 2006; Eccles and Gootman, 2002.

ASK YOURSELF

REVIEW
What cultural changes have led to the emergence of the period known as emerging adulthood?

APPLY
List supports that your college environment offers emerging adults in its health and counseling services, academic advising, residential living, and extracurricular activities. How does each help young people master the challenges of this period?

CONNECT
How are resources that foster resilience in emerging adulthood similar to those that promote resilience in childhood and adolescence? (See pages 10–11 in Chapter 1, page 354 in Chapter 10, and page 416 in Chapter 12.)

REFLECT
Should emerging adulthood be considered a distinct developmental period? Why or why not?

Erikson's Theory: Intimacy versus Isolation

Erikson's vision has influenced all contemporary theories of adult personality development. His psychological conflict of early adulthood is **intimacy versus isolation,** reflected in the young person's thoughts and feelings about making a permanent commitment to an intimate partner.

As Sharese discovered, establishing a mutually gratifying close relationship is challenging. Most young adults are still grappling with identity issues. Yet intimacy requires that they give up some of their independent self and redefine their identity to include both partners' values and interests. Those in their teens and early twenties frequently say they don't feel ready for a lasting tie (Collins & van Dulmen, 2006b). During their first year of marriage, Sharese separated from Ernie twice as she tried to reconcile her desire for self-determination with her desire for intimacy. Maturity involves balancing these forces. Without intimacy, young adults face the negative outcome of Erikson's early adulthood stage: loneliness and self-absorption. Ernie's patience and stability helped Sharese realize that committed love requires generosity and compromise but not total surrender of the self.

Research confirms that—as Erikson emphasized—a secure identity fosters attainment of intimacy. Commitment to personally meaningful values and goals prepares young adults for interpersonal commitments, which increase as early adulthood progresses (Kroger, 2007). Among large samples of college students, identity achievement was positively correlated with fidelity (loyalty in relationships) and love, for both men and women. In contrast, identity moratorium—a state of searching prior to commitment—was negatively associated with fidelity and love (Markstrom et al., 1997; Markstrom & Kalmanir, 2001). Other studies show that advanced identity development strongly predicts involvement in a deep, committed love partnership or readiness to establish such a partnership (Craig-Bray, Adams, & Dobson, 1988; Montgomery, 2005). Still, the coordination of identity and intimacy is more complex for women, who are more likely than men to consider the impact of their personal goals on important relationships (Archer, 2002).

In friendships and work ties, too, young people who have achieved intimacy are cooperative, tolerant, and accepting of differences in background and values. In contrast, people with a sense of isolation hesitate to form close ties because they fear loss of their own identity, tend to compete rather than cooperate, are not accepting of differences, and are easily threatened when others get too close (Hamachek, 1990; Marcia, 2002).

Erikson believed that successful resolution of intimacy versus isolation prepares the individual for the middle adulthood stage, which focuses on *generativity*—caring for the next generation and helping to improve society. But as noted previously, few adults follow a fixed series of tasks tied neatly to age. Some aspects of generativity—childbearing and child rearing, as well as contributions to society through work—are under way in the twenties and thirties. And many combinations of intimate partnership, parenting, and career exist, each with a unique pattern of timing and commitment.

In sum, identity, intimacy, and generativity are concerns of early adulthood, with shifts in emphasis that differ among individuals. Recognizing that Erikson's theory provides only a broad sketch of adult personality development, other theorists have expanded and modified his stage approach, adding detail and flexibility.

Other Theories of Adult Psychosocial Development

In the 1970s, growing interest in adult development led to several widely read books on the topic. Daniel Levinson's *The Seasons of a Man's Life* (1978) and George Vaillant's *Adaptation to Life* (1977) and *Aging Well* (2002) present psychosocial theories in the tradition of Erikson. Each is summarized in Table 14.1.

Levinson's Seasons of Life

Seeking an underlying order to the life course, Levinson (1978) conducted in-depth biographical interviews with 40 35- to 45-year-old men from four occupational subgroups: hourly workers in industry, business executives, university biologists, and novelists. Later he interviewed 45 women, also 35 to 45 years of age, from three subgroups: homemakers, business executives, and university professors. His results and those of others suggest a common path of change within which men and women approach developmental tasks in somewhat different ways (Levinson, 1996; Roberts & Newton, 1987).

Like Erikson, Levinson (1978, 1996) saw development as a sequence of qualitatively distinct eras (stages or seasons). Each begins with a *transition,* followed by a stable phase during which individuals build a life structure aimed at harmonizing inner personal and outer societal demands to enhance quality of life. Eventually people question the current structure, and a new transition ensues.

The **life structure,** a key concept in Levinson's theory, is the underlying design of a person's life, consisting of relationships with significant others—individuals, groups, and institutions. Of its many components, usually only a few, relating to marriage/family and occupation, are central. But wide individual differences exist in the weight of central and peripheral components.

Men's and women's accounts of their lives offer support for Levinson's description. They also reveal that early adulthood is the era of "greatest energy and abundance, contradiction and stress" (Levinson, 1986, p. 5). These years can bring rich satisfaction in love, sexuality, occupational advancement, family life, and realization of life goals. But they also involve serious decisions about work, marriage, children, and lifestyle before many people have enough experience to choose wisely.

TABLE 14.1 ■ ***Theories of Adult Psychosocial Development***

PERIOD OF DEVELOPMENT	ERIKSON	LEVINSON	VAILLANT
Early adulthood (18–40 years)	Intimacy versus isolation	Early adult transition: 17–22 years Entry life structure for early adulthood: 22–28 years Age-30 transition: 28–33 years Culminating life structure for early adulthood: 33–40 years	Intimacy Career consolidation
Middle adulthood (40–65 years)	Generativity versus stagnation	Midlife transition: 40–45 years Entry life structure for middle adulthood: 45–50 years Age-50 transition: 50–55 years Culminating life structure for middle adulthood: 55–60 years	Generativity Keeper of meaning
Late adulthood (65 years–death)	Ego integrity versus despair	Late adult transition: 60–65 years Late adulthood: 65 years–death	Ego integrity

© IMAGE 100/ALAMY

Although both of these young scientists are deeply committed to their careers, their images of their future lives may differ. Men more often see themselves as independent achievers in their occupational role, whereas women tend to have "split dreams" involving both marriage and career.

Levinson reported that during the early adult transition, most young people construct a *dream*—an image of themselves in the adult world that guides their decision making. For men, the dream usually emphasizes an independent achiever in an occupational role. In contrast, most career-oriented women display "split dreams" involving both marriage and career. Also, women's dreams tend to define the self in terms of relationships with husband, children, and colleagues. Men's dreams are usually more individualistic: They view significant others, especially wives, as vital supporters of their goals and less often see themselves as supporting others' goals.

Young adults also form a relationship with a *mentor* who facilitates realization of their dream—often a senior colleague at work but occasionally a more experienced friend, neighbor, or relative. As we will see when we take up vocational development, finding a supportive mentor is easier for men than for women. According to Levinson, men oriented toward high-status careers spend their twenties acquiring professional skills, values, and credentials. Although some women follow this path, for many others (and for men who serve as primary caregivers of their children), career development extends into middle age (Kogan & Vacha-Haase, 2002; Levinson, 1978, 1996).

During the age-30 transition, young people who had been preoccupied with career and are still single usually focus on finding a life partner, while women who had emphasized marriage and motherhood often develop more individualistic goals. For example, Christy, who had dreamed of becoming a professor, finally earned her doctoral degree in her mid-thirties and secured a college teaching position. Married women tend to demand that their husbands recognize and accommodate their interests and aspirations beyond the home. For young people without a satisfying intimate tie or vocational direction, this can be a time of crisis. For others who question the personal meaning of their life structure, it can bring considerable conflict and instability.

To create the culminating life structure of early adulthood, men usually "settle down" by focusing on certain relationships and aspirations, setting others aside. Their goal is to establish a stable niche in society that is consistent with their values, whether those be wealth, prestige, artistic or scientific achievement, or forms of family or community participation. In his thirties, Sharese's husband, Ernie, expanded his knowledge of real estate accounting, became a partner in his firm, coached his son's soccer team, and was elected treasurer of his church. He paid less attention to golf, travel, and playing the guitar than he had in his twenties.

Many women, however, remain unsettled in their thirties, often because they have added an occupational or relationship commitment. When her two children were born, Sharese felt torn between her research position in the state health department and her family. She took three months off after the arrival of each baby. When she returned to work, she did not pursue attractive administrative openings that required travel and time away from home. And shortly after Christy began teaching, she and Gary divorced. Becoming a single parent while starting her professional life introduced new strains. Not until middle age do many women attain the stability typical of men in their thirties—reaching career maturity and taking on more authority in the community (Levinson, 1996).

Vaillant's Adaptation to Life

Vaillant (1977) examined the development of nearly 250 men born in the 1920s, selected for study while they were students at a highly competitive liberal arts college, and followed as many as possible over the lifespan. In college, the participants underwent extensive interviews. During each succeeding decade, they answered lengthy questionnaires. Then Vaillant (2002) interviewed the men at ages 47, 60, and 70 about work, family, and physical and mental health.

Other than denying a strict age-related schedule of change, Vaillant's theory is compatible with Levinson's. Both agree that quality of relationships with important people shape the life course. In studying how the men altered themselves and their social world to adapt to life, Vaillant confirmed Erikson's stages but filled gaps between them. After a period in their twenties devoted to intimacy concerns, the men focused on career consolidation in their thirties. During their forties, they pulled back from individual achievement and became more generative—giving to and guiding others. In their fifties and sixties, they became "keepers of meaning," or guardians of their culture, expressing concern about the values of the younger generation and the state of their society. Many felt a deep need to preserve and pass on cultural traditions by teaching others what they had learned from life experience (Vaillant & Koury, 1994). Finally, in their seventies, the men became more spiritual and reflective, contemplating the meaning of life and accepting its finiteness.

Although Vaillant initially studied only men, eventually he examined the development of a sample of bright, well-educated women who were participants in another lifelong study. His findings, and those of others, suggest that women undergo a series of changes similar to those just described (Block, 1971; Oden & Terman, 1968; Vaillant, 2002).

Limitations of Levinson's and Vaillant's Theories

The patterns Levinson and Vaillant identified are based largely on interviews with people born in the first few decades of the twentieth century. As our discussion of emerging adulthood illustrates, young adults' development is more variable today than in past generations. Furthermore, Levinson's sample included only a few non-college-educated, low-income adults, and low-SES women remain almost entirely uninvestigated. Examining longitudinal archives on low-SES men who had grown up in the 1940s, Vaillant (1993) reported evidence for his stage sequence. Still, he acknowledged that the sample was limited.

Finally, Levinson's participants, interviewed in middle age, might not have remembered all aspects of their early adulthoods accurately. Studies of new generations—both men and women, of diverse backgrounds—are needed to discern the extent to which the developmental paths just described apply to most or all young people.

The Social Clock

As we have seen, changes in society from one generation to the next can affect the life course. Bernice Neugarten (1968a, 1979) identified an important cultural and generational influence on adult development: the **social clock**—age-graded expectations for major life events, such as beginning a first job, getting married, birth of the first child, buying a home, and retiring. All societies have such timetables. Being on time or off time can affect self-esteem because adults (like children and adolescents) make social comparisons, measuring their progress against that of agemates.

Conformity to or departure from the social clock can be a major source of adult personality change. In a study of college women born in the 1930s who were followed up at ages 27 and 43, researchers determined how closely participants followed a "feminine" social clock (marriage and parenthood in the early or mid-twenties) or a "masculine" one (entry into a high-status career and advancement by the late twenties). Those who started families on time became more responsible, self-controlled, tolerant, and caring but declined in self-esteem and felt more vulnerable as their lives progressed. Those who followed a "masculine" occupational timetable became more dominant, sociable, independent, and intellectually effective, a trend also found in a cohort born a decade later (Vandewater & Stewart, 1997). And women who had neither married nor begun a career by age 30 suffered from self-doubt, feelings of incompetence, and loneliness (Helson, 1992; Helson, Mitchell, & Moane, 1984).

As noted earlier, age-graded expectations for appropriate behavior have become increasingly flexible. Still, many adults experience psychological distress when they are substantially behind in timing of life events (Antonucci & Akiyama, 1997; Rook, Catalano, & Dooley, 1989). Following a social clock of some kind seems to foster confidence during early adulthood because it guarantees that young people will engage in the work of society, develop skills, and gain in understanding of the self and others (Helson, 1997; Hendry & Kloep, 2007). As Neugarten (1979) suggested, the stability of society depends on having people committed to social-clock patterns. With this in mind, let's take a closer look at how young men and women traverse the major tasks of young adulthood.

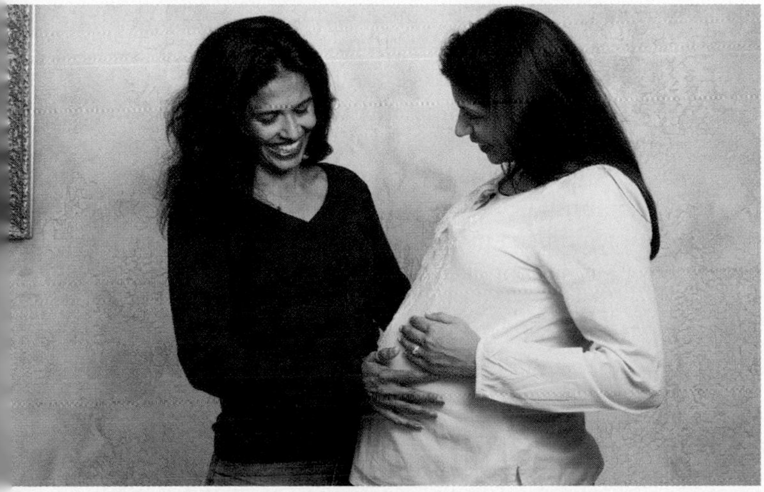

Being on time or off time for major life events, such as parenthood, can affect self-esteem because adults make social comparisons, measuring their progress against that of agemates.

ASK YOURSELF

» REVIEW
According to Levinson, how do the life structures of men and women differ?

» APPLY
Using the concept of the social clock, explain Sharese's conflicted feelings about marrying Ernie after she finished graduate school.

» CONNECT
Return to page 403 in Chapter 12 and review the contributions of exploration and commitment to a mature identity. Using the two criteria, explain why identity achievement is positively related to attainment of intimacy (fidelity and love), whereas identity moratorium is negatively predictive.

» REFLECT
Describe your early adulthood dream. Then ask a friend or classmate of the other gender to describe his or her dream, and compare the two. Are they consistent with Levinson's findings?

Close Relationships

To establish an intimate tie to another person, people must find a partner and build an emotional bond that they sustain over time. Although young adults are especially concerned with romantic love, the need for intimacy can also be satisfied through other relationships involving mutual commitment—with friends, siblings, and co-workers.

Romantic Love

At a party during her junior year of college, Sharese fell into conversation with Ernie, a senior and one of the top students in her government class. Sharese had already noticed Ernie in class, and as they talked, she discovered that he was as warm and interesting as he had seemed from a distance. Ernie found Sharese to be lively, intelligent, and attractive. By the end of the evening, the two realized that they had similar opinions on important social issues and liked the same leisure activities. They began dating steadily. Six years later, they married.

Finding a life partner is a major milestone of early adult development, with profound consequences for self-concept and psychological well-being (Meeus et al., 2007). As Sharese and Ernie's relationship reveals, it is also a complex process that unfolds over time and is affected by a variety of events.

■ **SELECTING A MATE.** Recall from Chapter 13 that intimate partners generally meet in places where they find people of their own age, ethnicity, SES, and religion or (somewhat less often) connect through Internet dating services. People usually select partners who resemble themselves in other ways—attitudes, personality, educational plans, intelligence, physical attractiveness, and even height (Keith & Schafer, 1991; Simpson & Harris, 1994). Romantic partners sometimes have complementary traits—for example, one more gregarious, the other more reserved. As long as these differences permit each person to satisfy personal preferences and goals, they can contribute to compatibility (Dryer & Horowitz, 1997). But overall, little support exists for the idea that "opposites attract." In fact, many studies confirm that the more similar partners are, the more satisfied they tend to be with their relationship and the more likely they are to stay together (Blackwell & Lichter, 2004; Lucas et al., 2004).

Nevertheless, in choosing a long-term partner, men and women differ in the importance they place on certain characteristics. In research carried out in diverse industrialized and developing countries, women assign greater weight to intelligence, ambition, financial status, and moral character, whereas men place more emphasis on physical attractiveness and domestic skills. In addition, women prefer a same-age or slightly older partner, men a younger partner (Buunk, 2002; Cramer, Schaefer, & Reid, 2003; Stewart, Stinnett, & Rosenfeld, 2000).

Evolutionary theory helps us understand these findings. Recall from Chapter 13 that because their capacity to reproduce is limited, women seek a mate with traits, such as earning power and emotional commitment, that help ensure children's survival and well-being. In contrast, men look for a mate with traits that signal youth, health, sexual pleasure, and ability to give birth to and care for offspring. As further evidence for this difference, men often want a relationship to move quickly toward physical intimacy, while women typically prefer to take the time to achieve psychological intimacy first (Buss, 2008).

From an alternative, social learning perspective, gender roles profoundly influence criteria for mate selection. Beginning in childhood, men learn to be assertive and independent—behaviors needed for success in the work world. Women acquire nurturant behaviors, which facilitate caregiving. Then each sex learns to value traits in the other that fit with a traditional division of labor (Eagly & Wood, 1999; Wood & Eagly, 2000). In support of this theory, in cultures and in younger generations experiencing greater gender equity, men and women are more alike in their mate preferences. For example, compared with men in China and Japan, American men place more emphasis on their mate's financial prospects, less on her domestic skills. Also, when either male or female young adults are asked to imagine themselves as a future homemaker, their preferences for a good provider and an older partner strengthen (Eagly, Eastwick, & Johannesen-Schmidt, 2009).

But neither men nor women put good looks, earning power, and mate's age relative to their own at the top of their wish list. They place a higher value on mutual attraction, caring, dependability, emotional maturity, and a pleasing disposition—that is, on relationship satisfaction (Buss et al., 2001; Toro-Morn & Sprecher, 2003). Nevertheless, men continue to value physical attractiveness more than women do, and women continue to value earning capacity more than men do. Furthermore, these gender differences—along with gender similarity in desire for a caring, sensitive partner—also characterize homosexual men and women (Impett & Peplau, 2006; Regan, Medina, & Joshi, 2001). In sum, both biological and social forces contribute to mate selection.

As the Lifespan Vista box on the following page reveals, young people's choice of an intimate partner and the quality of their relationship also are affected by memories of their early parent–child bond. Finally, for romance to lead to a lasting partnership, it must happen at the right time. Two people may be right for each other, but if one or both do not feel ready to marry, the relationship is likely to dissolve.

■ **THE COMPONENTS OF LOVE.** How do we know that we are in love? Robert Sternberg's (1988, 2000, 2006) **triangular theory of love** identifies three components—intimacy, passion, and commitment—that shift in emphasis as romantic relationships develop. *Intimacy,* the emotional component, involves warm, tender communication, expressions of concern about the other's well-being, and a desire for the partner to reciprocate. *Passion,* the desire for sexual activity and romance, is the physical- and psychological-arousal component. *Commitment*

A LIFESPAN VISTA: Looking Forward, Looking Back

Childhood Attachment Patterns and Adult Romantic Relationships

According to Bowlby's ethological theory of attachment, the early attachment bond leads to construction of an *internal working model,* or set of expectations about attachment figures, that serves as a guide for close relationships throughout life. Adults' evaluations of their early attachment experiences are related to their parenting behaviors—specifically, to the quality of attachments they build with their children (see page 202 in Chapter 6). Additional evidence indicates that recollections of childhood attachment patterns strongly predict romantic relationships in adulthood.

In studies carried out in Australia, Israel, and the United States, researchers asked people about their early parental bonds (attachment history), their attitudes toward intimate relationships (internal working model), and their actual experiences with romantic partners. In a few studies, investigators also observed couples' behaviors. Consistent with Bowlby's theory, adults' memories and interpretations of childhood attachment patterns were good indicators of internal working models and relationship experiences. (To review patterns of attachment, see page 198.)

Secure Attachment

Adults who described their attachment history as secure (warm, loving, and supportive parents) had internal working models that reflected this security. They viewed themselves as likable and easy to get to know, were comfortable with intimacy, and rarely worried about abandonment. They characterized their most important love relationship in terms of trust, happiness, and friendship (Cassidy, 2001). Their behaviors toward their partner were empathic and supportive and their conflict resolution strategies constructive. They were also at ease in turning to their partner for comfort and assistance and reported mutually initiated, enjoyable sexual activity (Collins et al., 2006; Creasey, 2002; Creasey & Ladd, 2004; Roisman et al., 2002).

Avoidant Attachment

Adults who reported an avoidant attachment history (demanding, disrespectful, and critical parents) displayed internal working models that stressed independence, mistrust of love partners, and anxiety about people getting too close. They were convinced that others disliked them and that romantic love is hard to find and rarely lasts. Jealousy, emotional distance, lack of support in response to their partner's distress, and little enjoyment of physical contact pervaded their most important love relationship (Collins et al., 2006). Avoidant adults often deny attachment needs through excessive work and brief sexual encounters and affairs (Feeney, 1998). They endorse many unrealistic beliefs about relationships—for example, that partners cannot change, that males' and females' needs differ, and that "mind reading" is expected (Stackert & Bursik, 2003).

Resistant Attachment

Adults recalling a resistant attachment history (parents who responded unpredictably and unfairly) presented internal working models in which they sought to merge completely with another person and fall in love quickly (Cassidy, 2001). At the same time, they worried that their intense feelings would overwhelm others, who really did not love them and would not want to stay with them. Their most important love relationship was riddled with jealousy, emotional highs and lows, and desperation about whether the partner would return their affection (Feeney, 1999). Resistant adults, though offering support, do so in ways that fit poorly with their partner's needs (Collins et al., 2006). They are also quick to express fear and anger, and they disclose information about themselves at inappropriate times (Brennan & Shaver, 1995).

Are adults' descriptions of their childhood attachment experiences accurate, or are they distorted or even completely invented? In several longitudinal studies, quality of parent–child interactions, observed or assessed through family interviews 5 to 23 years earlier, were good predictors of internal working models and romantic-relationship quality in early adulthood (Allen & Hauser, 1996; Donnellan, Larsen-Rife, & Conger, 2005; Ogawa et al., 1997; Roisman et al., 2001). These findings suggest that adult recollections bear some resemblance to actual parent–child experiences. However, quality of attachment to parents is not the only factor that influences later internal working models and intimate ties. Characteristics of the partner and current life conditions also are important. In one study, adults with an inner sense of security fostered security in their partners as well as in their adolescent and young adult children (Cook, 2000).

In sum, negative parent–child experiences can be carried forward into adult relationships. At the same time, internal working models are continuously "updated." When adults with unhappy love lives have a chance to form more satisfying intimate ties, they may revise their internal working models. As the new partner approaches the relationship with a secure state of mind and sensitive, supportive behavior, the insecure partner reappraises her expectations and responds in kind. This reciprocity creates a feedback loop through which a revised, more favorable internal working model, along with mutually gratifying interaction, is sustained over time.

COURTESY OF CAROL ALPER

How might the internal working model constructed by this baby, held tenderly by his father, have influenced the relationship he forged as a young adult with his wife? Research indicates that early attachment pattern is one among several factors that predicts the quality of later intimate ties.

Applying What We Know

Keeping Love Alive in a Romantic Partnership

Suggestion	Description
Make time for your relationship.	To foster relationship satisfaction and a sense of being "in love," plan regular times to be together.
Tell your partner of your love.	Express affection and caring, including the powerful words "I love you," at appropriate times. These messages increase perceptions of commitment and encourage your partner to respond in kind.
Be available to your partner in times of need.	Provide emotional support, giving of yourself when your partner is distressed.
Communicate constructively and positively about relationship problems.	When you or your partner is dissatisfied, suggest ways of overcoming difficulties and ask your partner to collaborate in choosing and implementing a course of action. Avoid the four enemies of a gratifying, close relationship: criticism, contempt, defensiveness, and stonewalling.
Show an interest in important aspects of your partner's life.	Ask about your partner's work, friends, family, and hobbies and express appreciation for his or her special abilities and achievements. In doing so, you grant your partner a sense of being valued.
Confide in your partner.	Share innermost feelings, keeping intimacy alive.
Forgive minor offenses and try to understand major offenses.	Whenever possible, overcome feelings of anger through forgiveness. In this way, you acknowledge unjust behavior but avoid becoming preoccupied with it.

Sources: Donatelle, 2009; McCarthy & McCarthy, 2004.

is the cognitive component, leading partners to decide that they are in love and to maintain that love.

At the beginning of a relationship, **passionate love**—intense sexual attraction—is strong. Gradually, passion declines in favor of intimacy and commitment, which form the basis for **companionate love**—warm, trusting affection and caregiving (Acker & Davis, 1992; Fehr, 1994). Each aspect of love, however, helps sustain the relationship. Early passionate love is a strong predictor of whether partners keep dating. But without the quiet intimacy, predictability, and shared attitudes and values of companionate love, most romances eventually break up (Hendrick & Hendrick, 2002).

An ongoing relationship requires effort from both partners. Research on newlyweds' feelings and behavior over the first year of marriage reveals that husbands and wives gradually felt less "in love" and less pleased with married life. A variety of factors contributed, including a sharp drop in time spent talking to each other and doing things that brought each other pleasure (for example, saying "I love you" or making the other person laugh). Joint leisure pursuits gave way to more household tasks and chores and, therefore, fewer enjoyable times together. Also, when discussing areas of conflict, partners declined in accurate reading of each other's thoughts and feelings. Perhaps after an increasing number of such interactions, they tried less hard to grasp the other's point of view and resorted to well-established habits, such as giving in or withdrawing (Huston, McHale, & Crouter, 1986; Kilpatrick, Bissonnette, & Rusbult, 2002).

But couples whose relationships endure generally report that they love each other more than they did earlier (Sprecher, 1999). In the transformation of romantic involvements from passionate to companionate, *commitment* may be the aspect of love that determines whether a relationship survives. Communicating that commitment—through warmth, attentiveness, empathy, caring, acceptance, and respect—strongly predicts relationship maintenance (Rusbult et al., 2006). For example, Sharese's doubts about getting married subsided largely because of Ernie's expressions of commitment. In the most dramatic of these, he painted a large sign, reading "I LOVE SHARESE," and placed it in their front yard on her birthday. Sharese returned Ernie's sentiments, and the intimacy of their bond deepened.

Intimate partners who consistently express their commitment report higher-quality and longer-lasting relationships (Fitzpatrick & Sollie, 1999). An important feature of their communication is constructive conflict resolution—directly expressing wishes and needs, listening patiently, asking for clarification, compromising, accepting responsibility, forgiving their partner, and avoiding the escalation of negative interaction sparked by criticism, contempt, defensiveness, and stonewalling (Johnson et al., 2005; Schneewind & Gerhard, 2002). In a longitudinal study, newlyweds' negative behavior and, especially, sharp rise in blood levels of stress hormones during conflict predicted eventual marital dissatisfaction and divorce over the following decade (Kiecolt-Glaser et al., 2003). Couples whose relationships dissolved did not show greater initial physiological reactivity. Rather, poor problem solving altered their stress hormone levels, which often remained elevated throughout the day.

How men handle conflict is particularly important because they tend to be less skilled than women at negotiating it, often avoiding discussion (Gayle, Preiss, & Allen, 2002). Applying What We Know above lists ways to help keep the embers of love aglow in a romantic partnership.

CULTURE AND THE EXPERIENCE OF LOVE. Passion and intimacy, which form the basis for romantic love, became the dominant basis for marriage in twentieth-century Western nations as the value of individualism strengthened. From this vantage point, mature love is based on autonomy, appreciation of the partner's unique qualities, and intense emotion. Trying to satisfy dependency needs through an intimate bond is regarded as immature (Hatfield, Rapson, & Martel, 2007).

This Western view contrasts sharply with the perspectives of Eastern cultures. In Japan, for example, lifelong dependency is accepted and viewed positively. The Japanese word *amae,* or love, means "to depend on another's benevolence." The traditional Chinese collectivist view defines the self through role relationships—son or daughter, brother or sister, husband or wife. Feelings of affection are distributed across a broad social network, reducing the intensity of any one relationship.

In choosing a mate, Chinese and Japanese young people are expected to consider obligations to others, especially parents. As one writer summarized, "An American asks, 'How does my heart feel?' A Chinese asks, 'What will other people say?'" (Hsu, 1981, p. 50). College students of Asian heritage are less likely than those of American or European descent to endorse a view of love based solely on physical attraction and deep emotion (Hatfield, Rapson, & Martel, 2007; Hatfield & Sprecher, 1995). Instead, compared to Westerners, they place greater weight on companionship and practical matters—similarity of background, career promise, and likelihood of being a good parent. Similarly, compared with American couples, dating couples in China report less passion but equally strong feelings of intimacy and commitment (Gao, 2001).

© EXOTIC EYE/ALAMY

In this Hindu wedding ceremony, a relative symbolizes the marriage knot by tying the groom's scarf to the bride's dress. Although arranged marriages are still common in India, parents and prospective brides and grooms usually consult one another before moving forward.

Still, even in countries where arranged marriages are still fairly common (including China, India, and Japan), parents and prospective brides and grooms consult one another before moving forward (Goodwin & Pillay, 2006). If parents try to force their children into an unappealing marriage, sympathetic extended family members may come to children's defense. In a study in which college students in diverse nations were asked if they were willing to marry someone they did not love, those from more affluent industrialized nations (such as Japan) said no. Only in developing countries were students willing to compromise on love (Levine et al., 1995). In sum, today young people in many countries consider love to be a prerequisite for marriage, though Westerners assign greater importance to it—especially, its passionate component.

Friendships

Like romantic partners and childhood friends, adult friends are usually similar in age, sex, and SES—factors that contribute to common interests, experiences, and needs and therefore to the pleasure derived from the relationship. As in earlier years, friends in adulthood enhance self-esteem through affirmation and acceptance and provide support in times of stress (Bagwell et al., 2005; Collins & Madsen, 2006). Friends also make life more interesting by expanding social opportunities and access to knowledge and points of view.

Trust, intimacy, and loyalty continue to be important in adult friendships, as they were in middle childhood and adolescence. Sharing thoughts and feelings is sometimes greater in friendship than in marriage, although commitment is less strong as friends come and go over the life course. Even so, some adult friendships continue for many years, at times throughout life. Female friends see one another more often, which contributes to greater friendship continuity for women (Sherman, de Vries, & Lansford, 2000).

SAME-SEX FRIENDSHIPS. Throughout life, women have more intimate same-sex friendships than men. Extending a pattern evident in childhood and adolescence, female friends often say they prefer to "just talk," whereas male friends say they like to "do something" such as play sports (see Chapter 12, page 417). Barriers to intimacy between male friends include competitiveness, which may make men unwilling to disclose weaknesses, and concern that if they tell about themselves, their friends will not reciprocate (Reid & Fine, 1992). Because a balance of power and give-and-take is basic to a good friendship, women generally evaluate their same-sex friendships more positively than men do (Veniegas & Peplau, 1997).

Of course, individual differences in friendship quality exist. The longer-lasting men's friendships are, the closer they become and the more they involve disclosure of personal information (Sherman, de Vries, & Lansford, 2000). Furthermore, involvement in family roles affects reliance on friends. For single adults, friends are the preferred companions and confidants. The more intimate young adults' same-sex friendships are in terms of warmth, exchange of social support, and self-disclosure, the more satisfying and longer-lasting the relationship and the greater its contribution to psychological well-being (Sanderson, Rahm, & Beigbeder, 2005; Sherman, Lansford, & Volling, 2006). Gay and lesbian romantic relationships often develop out of close same-sex friendships, with lesbians, especially, forging compatible friendships based on gratifying communication before becoming involved romantically (Diamond, 2006).

As they develop romantic ties and marry, young adults—especially men—direct more of their disclosures toward their partners (Carbery & Buhrmester, 1998; Kito, 2005). Still, friendships continue to be vital contexts for personal sharing throughout adulthood. Turn back to Figure 12.2 on page 410 to view developmental trends in self-disclosure to romantic partners and friends.

As young people marry and invest less time in developing romantic partnerships, siblings—especially sisters whose earlier bond was positive—become more frequent companions than in adolescence. Often, friend and sibling roles merge.

OTHER-SEX FRIENDSHIPS. During the college years, other-sex friendships are as common as romantic relationships. After marriage, they decline with age for men but increase for women, who tend to form them in the workplace. Highly educated, employed women have the largest number of other-sex friends. Through these relationships, young adults often gain in companionship and self-esteem and learn a great deal about masculine and feminine styles of intimacy (Bleske & Buss, 2000). Because men confide especially easily in their female friends, such friendships offer them a unique opportunity to broaden their expressive capacity. And women sometimes say male friends offer objective points of view on problems and situations—perspectives not available from female friends (Monsour, 2002).

Many people try to keep other-sex friendships platonic to safeguard their integrity (Messman, Canary, & Hause, 2000). Still, about half of college students engage in sexual activity with an other-sex friend whom they have no intention of dating. Men are more likely than women to feel sexually attracted to an other-sex friend (Kaplan & Keys, 1997). If these feelings persist, the relationship often changes into a romantic bond. Some friends sustain a platonic friendship that includes sexuality. Others find the platonic and sexual aspects incompatible, and the friendship disintegrates (Afifi & Faulkner, 2000). When a solid other-sex friendship does evolve into a romance, it may be more stable and enduring than a romantic relationship formed without a foundation in friendship (Hendrick & Hendrick, 1993).

SIBLINGS AS FRIENDS. Whereas intimacy is essential to friendship, commitment—willingness to maintain a relationship and care about the other—is the defining characteristic of family ties. As young people marry and invest less time in developing a romantic partnership, siblings—especially sisters whose earlier bond was positive—become more frequent companions than in adolescence. Often, friend and sibling roles merge. For example, Sharese described Heather's practical assistance—helping with moving and running errands during an illness—in kinship terms: "She's like a sister to me. I can always turn to her." And adult sibling ties resemble friendships, in which the main concerns are staying in contact, offering social support, and enjoying being together (O'Connor, 1992).

A childhood history of intense parental favoritism and sibling rivalry can disrupt sibling bonds in adulthood (Panish & Stricker, 2002). But when family experiences have been positive, relationships between adult same-sex siblings can be especially close. A shared background promotes similarity in values and perspectives and the possibility of deep mutual understanding.

Warm sibling relationships in adulthood are important sources of psychological well-being (Sherman, Lansford, & Volling, 2006). In Vaillant's (1977) study of well-educated men, a close sibling tie in early adulthood was the single best predictor of emotional health at age 65.

Loneliness

Young adults are at risk for **loneliness**—unhappiness resulting from a gap between the social relationships we currently have and those we desire—when they either do not have an intimate partner or lack gratifying friendships. Though both situations give rise to similar emotions, they are not interchangeable. For example, even though she had several enjoyable friendships, Heather sometimes felt lonely because she was not dating someone she cared about. And although Sharese and Ernie

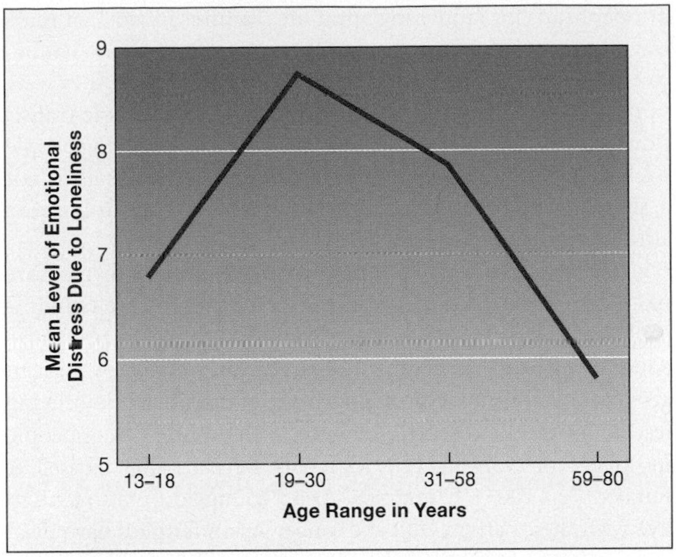

■ **FIGURE 14.2** ■ **Changes in emotional distress due to loneliness from adolescence to late adulthood.** More than 700 Canadian 13- to 80-year-olds responded to a questionnaire assessing the extent to which they experienced emotional distress due to loneliness. Loneliness rose sharply from the early teens to the late teens and early twenties and then declined. (Adapted from Rokach, 2001.)

were happily married, they felt lonely after moving to a new town where they did not know anyone.

Loneliness peaks in the late teens and early twenties, then declines steadily into the seventies. Figure 14.2 shows this trend, based on a large Canadian sample ranging in age from 13 to 80 (Rokach, 2001). The rise in loneliness during early adulthood is understandable. As young people move through school and employment settings, they must constantly develop new relationships. Also, young adults may expect more from their intimate ties than older adults, who have learned to live with imperfections. With age, people become better at accepting loneliness and using it for positive ends—to sharpen awareness of their personal fears and needs (Rokach, 2003).

Loneliness is intense after loss of an intimate tie: Separated, divorced, or widowed adults are lonelier than their married, cohabiting, or single counterparts. Men not involved in a romantic relationship feel lonelier than women, perhaps because they have fewer alternatives for satisfying intimacy needs (Stroebe et al., 1996). And immigrants from collectivist cultures report higher levels of loneliness than people born in the United States and Canada (DiTommaso, Brannen, & Burgess, 2005). Leaving a large, close-knit family system for an individualistic society seems to prompt intense feelings of isolation.

Personal characteristics also contribute to loneliness. Young adults who are socially anxious or who have insecure working models of attachment to parents are more often intensely lonely (Jackson et al., 2002). When extreme loneliness persists, it is associated with a wide variety of self-defeating attitudes and behaviors. Lonely people evaluate themselves and others more negatively, tend to be socially unresponsive and insensitive, and are slow to develop intimacy because they are reluctant to tell others about themselves (Jones, 1990). These responses, whether cause or consequence of loneliness, promote further isolation.

As long as loneliness is not overwhelming, it can motivate young people to reach out to others. It can also encourage them to find ways to be comfortably alone and to use this time to understand themselves better (Rokach & Neto, 2006). Healthy personality development involves striking this balance between gratifying relationships with others and contentment within ourselves.

MYRLEEN FERGUSON CATE/PHOTOEDIT

Loneliness peaks in the late teens and early twenties as young people frequently change school and employment settings. But loneliness can be used for positive ends—to deepen self-understanding.

ASK YOURSELF

» REVIEW
Describe gender differences in traits usually desired in a long-term partner. What findings indicate that *both* biological and social forces contribute to those differences?

» APPLY
After dating for two years, Mindy and Graham reported greater love and relationship satisfaction than during their first few months of dating. What features of communication probably deepened their bond, and why is it likely to endure?

» CONNECT
How might recollections and evaluations of childhood attachment history, discussed on page 473, affect intimate partners' readiness to develop companionate love?

» REFLECT
Do you have a nonromantic, close other-sex friendship? If so, how has it enhanced your emotional and social development?

The Family Life Cycle

For most young people, the life course takes shape within the **family life cycle**—a sequence of phases characterizing the development of most families around the world. In early adulthood, people typically live on their own, marry, and bear and rear children. In middle age, as their children leave home, their parenting responsibilities diminish. Late adulthood brings retirement, growing old, and (more often for women) death of one's spouse (Carter & McGoldrick, 2005).

But we must be careful not to view the family life cycle as a fixed progression. Today, wide variations exist in the sequence and timing of its phases—high rates of out-of-wedlock births, delayed marriage and childbearing, divorce, and remarriage, among others. And some people, voluntarily or involuntarily, do not experience all family life-cycle phases. Still, the family life-cycle model is useful. It offers an organized way of thinking about how the family system changes over time and the impact of each phase on the family unit and the individuals within it.

Leaving Home

During her first semester of college, Sharese noticed a change in how she related to her mother. She found it more enjoyable to discuss daily experiences and life goals, sought advice and listened with greater openness, and expressed affection more freely. Looking around her childhood bedroom before she moved out permanently, Sharese felt nostalgia for the warmth and security of her childhood days, coupled with a sense of pride at being on her own.

Departure from the parental home is a major step toward assuming adult responsibilities. The average age of leaving has decreased in recent years as more young people live independently before marriage. In 1940, over 80 percent of Americans in their twenties resided with their parents; today, only about 50 percent of 18- to 25-year-olds do. Residential independence rises steadily with age—a trend evident in most industrialized nations (Cohen et al., 2003).

Departures for education tend to occur at earlier ages, those for full-time work and marriage later. Because the majority of U.S. young adults enroll in higher education, many leave home around age 18. Other young people leave early to escape family friction (Stattin & Magnusson, 1996). Those from divorced, single-parent homes tend to be early leavers, perhaps because of family stress (Cooney & Mortimer, 1999). Compared with the previous generation, fewer North American and Western European young people leave home to marry; more do so just to be "independent"—to express their adult status. But difficult job markets and high housing costs mean that many must take undesirable work or remain financially dependent on parents (Lindsay, Almey, & Normand, 2002).

Nearly half of young adults return home for a brief time after initial leaving. Those who left to marry are least likely to return. But single, independent living is a fragile arrangement. As people encounter unexpected twists and turns on the road to independence, the parental home offers a safety net and base of operations for launching adult life. Failures in work or marriage can prompt a move back. Also, young people who left because of family conflict often return—largely because they were not ready for independent living. Usually, though, role transitions, such as the end of college or military service, bring people back. Contrary to popular belief, returning home usually is not a sign of weakness but a common event among unmarried adults (Ward & Spitze, 2007).

The extent to which young people live on their own before marriage varies with SES and ethnicity. Those who are economically well-off are more likely to establish their own residence. Among African-American, Hispanic, and Native-American groups, poverty and a cultural tradition of extended family living lead to lower rates of leaving home, even among young people in college or working (De Marco & Berzin, 2008; Fussell & Furstenberg, 2005). Unmarried Asian young adults also tend to live with their parents. But the longer Asian families have lived in the United States and thus been exposed to individualistic values, the more likely young people are to move out after finishing high school (Goldscheider & Goldscheider, 1999).

When young adults are prepared for independence and feel securely attached to their parents, departure from the home is linked to more satisfying parent–child interaction and successful transition to adult roles, even among ethnic minorities that strongly emphasize family loyalty and obligations. In a study of middle-SES African-American 17- to 20-year-olds, girls who had moved out of the home to attend college reported fewer negative interactions with their mothers than girls still living at home or in transition to independent living (Smetana, Metzger, & Campione-Barr, 2004). African-American boys (unlike their Caucasian counterparts in other studies) showed no systematic change in frequency of conflict with mothers as a result of autonomous living, perhaps because in adolescence, they had been granted considerably more freedom than teenagers of other ethnic groups (Bulcroft, Carmody, & Bulcroft, 1996).

Finally, leaving home very early can contribute to long-term disadvantage because it is associated with job seeking rather than education and with lack of parental financial and social support. Not surprisingly, non-college-bound youths who move out in their late teens have less successful marriages and work lives (White, 1994).

Joining of Families in Marriage

The average age of first marriage in the United States has risen from about 20 for women and 23 for men in 1950 to 25½ for women and 27½ for men today. The number of first and second marriages has declined over the last few decades as more people stay single, cohabit, or do not remarry after divorce. Still, nearly 90 percent of Americans marry at least once. At present, 58 percent of U.S. adults live together as married couples (U.S. Census Bureau, 2009b).

Same-sex marriages are recognized nationwide in Belgium, Canada, the Netherlands, Norway, South Africa, Spain, and Sweden. In the United States, Connecticut, Iowa, Massachusetts, and Vermont have legalized same-sex marriage. California,

Hawaii, Maine, New Hampshire, New Jersey, Washington, and the District of Columbia grant people in same-sex unions the same legal status as married couples. Because legalization is so recent, research on same-sex couples in the context of marriage is scant. But evidence on cohabiting same-sex couples suggests that the same factors that contribute to happiness in other-sex marriages do so in same-sex unions (Diamond, 2006).

Marriage is more than the joining of two individuals. It also requires that two systems—the spouses' families—adapt and overlap to create a new subsystem. Consequently, marriage presents complex challenges. This is especially so today because husband–wife roles have only recently moved in the direction of a true partnership—educationally, occupationally, and in emotional connectedness. Among same-sex couples, acceptance of the relationship by parents, inclusion of the partner in family events, and living in a supportive community where they can be open about their bond benefit relationship satisfaction and durability (Diamond, 2006; Elizur & Mintzer, 2003; Rostosky et al., 2007).

MARITAL ROLES. Their honeymoon over, Sharese and Ernie turned to a multitude of issues that they had previously decided individually or that their families of origin had prescribed—from everyday matters (when and how to eat, sleep, talk, work, relax, have sex, and spend money) to family traditions and rituals (which to retain, which to work out for themselves). And as they related to their social world as a couple, they modified relationships with parents, siblings, extended family, friends, and co-workers.

Contemporary alterations in the context of marriage, including changing gender roles and living farther away from family members, mean that couples must work harder than in the past to define their relationships. Although partners are usually similar in religious and ethnic background, "mixed" marriages are increasingly common today. For example, nearly half of American Jews who marry today select a non-Jewish spouse (Fishman, 2004). And other-race unions now account for nearly 4 percent of the married population in the United States (U.S. Census Bureau, 2009b). Couples whose backgrounds differ greatly face extra challenges in making the transition to married life.

Because many couples live together before marriage, it has become less of a turning point in the family life cycle. Still, defining marital roles can be difficult. Age of marriage is the most consistent predictor of marital stability. Young people who marry in their teens and early twenties are far more likely to divorce than those who marry later (Heaton, 2002). Most of those who marry early have not developed a secure identity or sufficient independence to form a mature marital bond. Both early marriage followed by childbirth and the reversal of family life-cycle events (childbirth before marriage) are more common among low-SES adults (Leonard & Roberts, 1998; U.S. Census Bureau, 2009b). This acceleration of family formation complicates adjustment to life as a couple.

Despite progress in the area of women's rights, **traditional marriages,** involving a clear division of husband's and wife's roles, still exist in Western nations. The man is the head of household; his primary responsibility is the economic well-being of his family. The woman devotes herself to caring for her husband and children and to creating a nurturant, comfortable home. In recent decades, however, these marriages have changed, with many women who focused on motherhood while their children were young returning to the work force later.

© ROLF BRUDERER/CORBIS

In an egalitarian marriage, husband and wife share power and authority. Both are equally concerned with the balance between work, children, and their relationship.

In **egalitarian marriages,** partners relate as equals, sharing power and authority. Both try to balance the time and energy they devote to their occupations, their children, and their relationship. Most well-educated, career-oriented women expect this form of marriage. And college-student couples who eventually intend to marry often plan in advance how they will coordinate work and family roles, especially if the woman intends to enter a male-dominated career (Botkin, Weeks, & Morris, 2000; Peake & Harris, 2002).

In Western nations, men in dual-earner marriages participate much more in child care than in the past. U.S. fathers in such marriages put in 85 percent as much time as mothers do (see page 202 in Chapter 6). But housework—cleaning, shopping, cooking, laundry, picking up clutter—reveals a different story. Recent surveys indicate that women in the United States and Canada spend nearly twice as much time as men on housework, women in Australia nearly three times as much (see Figure 14.3 on page 480). In Sweden, which places a high value on gender equality, men do more than in other nations. In contrast, men typically do little housework or child care in Japan, where corporate jobs typically demand long work hours (Institute for Social Research, 2002; Shwalb et al., 2004). In sum, true equality in marriage is still rare, and couples who strive for it usually attain a form of marriage in between traditional and egalitarian.

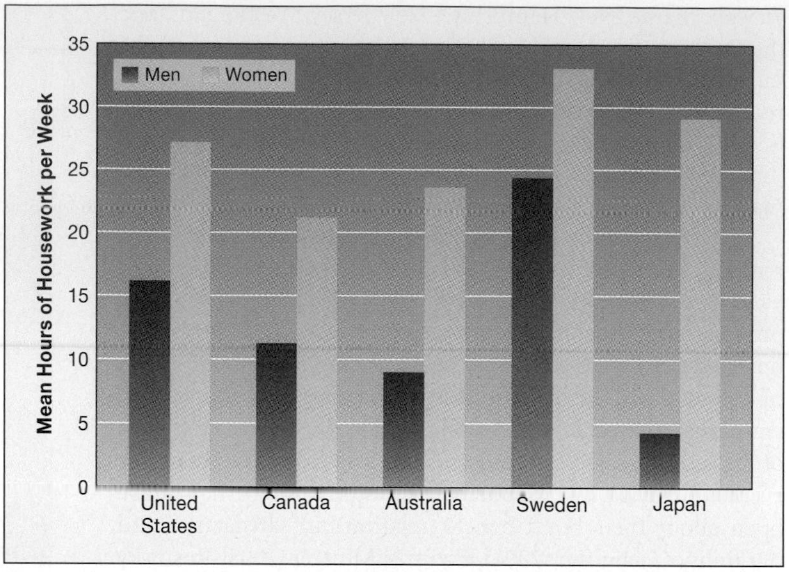

■ **FIGURE 14.3** ■ **Average hours per week of housework reported by men and women in five nations.** In each nation, women devote considerably more time than men to housework. Men's participation is greater in Sweden, which places a high value on gender equality. In Japan, where traditional gender roles prevail, men devote the least time to housework. (Data for the United States, Sweden, and Japan from Institute for Social Research, 2002; for Canada from Statistics Canada, 2006b; for Australia from Baxter, Hewett, & Haynes, 2008.)

■ **MARITAL SATISFACTION.** Despite its rocky beginnings, Sharese and Ernie's marriage grew to be especially happy. In contrast, Christy and Gary became increasingly discontented. What distinguishes satisfying marriages from less successful partnerships? Differences between these two couples mirror the findings of a large body of research on personal and contextual factors, summarized in Table 14.2.

Christy and Gary had a brief courtship, married and had children early, and struggled financially. Gary's negative, critical personality led him to get along poorly with Christy's parents and to feel threatened when he and Christy disagreed. Christy tried to offer Gary encouragement and support, but her own needs for nurturance and individuality were not being met. Gary felt threatened by Christy's career aspirations. As she came closer to attaining them, the couple grew further apart. In contrast, Sharese and Ernie married later, after their educations were complete. They postponed having children until their careers were under way and they had built a sense of togetherness that allowed each to thrive as an individual. Patience, caring, common values, enjoyment of each other's company, sharing of personal experiences through conversation, cooperating in household responsibilities, and good conflict-resolution skills contributed to their compatibility.

Men tend to report feeling slightly happier with their marriages than women do (Dillaway & Broman, 2001; Kurdek, 2005). In the past, quality of the marital relationship had a greater impact on women's psychological well-being, but today it predicts mental health similarly for both genders (Kurdek, 2005; Williams, 2003). Women, however, feel particularly dissatisfied with marriage when the demands of husband, children, housework, and career are overwhelming (Forry, Leslie, & Letiecq, 2007; Saginak & Saginak, 2005). Research in both Western and non-Western industrialized nations reveals that equal power in the relationship and sharing of family responsibilities usually enhance both men's and women's satisfaction, largely by strengthening marital harmony (Amato & Booth, 1995; Xu & Lai, 2004).

At their worst, marital relationships can become contexts for intense opposition, dominance–submission, and emotional and physical violence. As the Social Issues box on pages 482–483 explains, although women are more often targets of severe partner abuse, both men and women play both roles: perpetrator and victim.

■ **MARITAL EXPECTATIONS AND MYTHS.** In a study in which 50 happily married couples were interviewed about their marriages, each participant reported both good times and bad, and many admitted to having moments when they wanted out (Wallerstein & Blakeslee, 1995). Clearly, marital happiness was no "rose garden." Rather, it was grounded in mutual respect, pleasure and comfort in each other's company, and joint problem solving. All couples emphasized the need to reshape their relationship in response to new circumstances and to each partner's changing needs and desires.

Yet many young people have a mythical image of marital bliss, based more on TV romantic comedies and dramas than on reality (Segrin & Nabi, 2002). For example, a substantial number of young adults endorse these beliefs, all unsupported by facts:

- The best single predictor of marital satisfaction is the quality of a couple's sex life.
- If my spouse loves me, he or she should instinctively know what I want and need to be happy.
- No matter how I behave, my spouse should love me simply because he or she is my spouse. (Larson, 1988, p. 5; McCarthy & McCarthy, 2004)

As these myths are overturned, couples react with disappointment, and marriage becomes less satisfying and more conflict-ridden. Interestingly, young people who hold a religious view of marriage as sacred are less likely to enter it with unrealistic expectations and better able to cope with disagreement (Mahoney et al., 1999). Perhaps because of their reverence for the marital bond, they are highly invested in forging a well-functioning

■ TABLE 14.2 ■ *Factors Related to Marital Satisfaction*

FACTOR	HAPPY MARRIAGE	UNHAPPY MARRIAGE
Family backgrounds	Partners similar in SES, education, religion, and age	Partners very different in SES, education, religion, and age
Age at marriage	After age 23	Before age 23
Length of courtship	At least six months	Less than six months
Timing of first pregnancy	After first year of marriage	Before or within first year of marriage
Relationship to extended family	Warm and positive	Negative; wish to maintain distance
Marital patterns in extended family	Stable	Unstable; frequent separations and divorces
Financial and employment status	Secure	Insecure
Family responsibilities	Shared; perception of fairness	Largely the woman's responsibility; perception of unfairness
Personality characteristics	Emotionally positive; good conflict-resolution skills	Emotionally negative and impulsive; poor conflict-resolution skills

Note: The more factors present, the greater the likelihood of marital happiness or unhappiness.

Sources: Bradbury, Fincham, & Beach, 2000; Johnson et al., 2005; Waldinger et al., 2004.

relationship, engaging in more verbal collaboration and less conflict than other couples.

In view of its long-term implications, it is surprising that most couples spend little time before their wedding day reflecting on the decision to marry. High school and college courses in family life education can help dispel marital myths and promote better mate selection. And counseling aimed at helping couples discuss their desires openly and use positive, respectful conflict-resolution strategies are highly effective in easing adjustment to marriage and enhancing relationship quality (Christensen & Heavey, 1999; Gordon, Temple, & Adams, 2005).

Parenthood

For many adults, the decision to have children used to be "a biological given or an unavoidable cultural demand" (Michaels, 1988, p. 23). Today, in Western industrialized nations, parenthood is a matter of true individual choice. Effective birth control techniques enable adults to avoid having children in most instances. And changing cultural values allow people to remain childless with less fear of social criticism and rejection than a generation or two ago.

In 1950, 78 percent of American married couples were parents. Today, 70 percent bear children, and they tend to be older when they have their first child. Consistent with this pattern of delayed childbearing and with the decision of most women to divide their energies between family and work, family size in industrialized nations has declined. In 1950, the average number of children per couple was 3.1. Currently, it is 1.8 in the United States and Canada; 1.7 in Australia, Great Britain, and Sweden; 1.4 in Japan and Germany; and 1.3 in Italy (U.S. Census Bureau, 2009a, 2009b). Nevertheless, the vast majority of married people continue to embrace parenthood as one of life's most meaningful experiences. Why do they do so, and how do the challenges of child rearing affect the adult life course?

■ **THE DECISION TO HAVE CHILDREN.** The choice of parenthood is affected by a complex array of factors, including financial circumstances, personal and religious values, and health conditions. Women with traditional gender identities usually decide to have children. Whether a woman is employed has less impact on childbearing than her occupation. Women with high-status, demanding careers less often choose parenthood and, when they do, more often delay it than women with less consuming jobs (Barber, 2001a; Tangri & Jenkins, 1997).

When Americans are asked about their desire to have children, they mention a variety of advantages and disadvantages, listed in Table 14.3 on page 482. Some ethnic and regional differences exist, but in all groups, the most important reasons for having children include the warm, affectionate relationship and the stimulation and fun that children provide. Also frequently mentioned are growth and learning experiences that children bring to the lives of adults, the desire to have someone carry on after one's own death, and feelings of accomplishment and creativity that come from helping children grow (Cowan & Cowan, 2000; O'Laughlin & Anderson, 2001).

Most young adults also realize that having children means years of extra burdens and responsibilities. Among disadvantages of parenthood, they cite "loss of freedom" most often, followed by "financial strain." According to a conservative estimate, new parents in the United States today will spend about $200,000 to rear a child from birth to age 18, and many will incur substantial additional expense for higher education and financial dependency during emerging adulthood (U.S. Department of Agriculture, 2007).

Greater freedom to choose whether and when to have children makes family planning more challenging today than in the past. With each partner expecting an equal say, childbearing often becomes a matter of delicate negotiation (Cowan & Cowan, 2000). Yet carefully weighing the pros and cons of parenthood

SOCIAL ISSUES

Partner Abuse

Violence in families is a widespread health and human rights issue, occurring in all cultures and SES groups. Often one form of domestic violence is linked to others. Recall the story of Karen in Chapter 13. Her husband, Mike, not only assaulted her sexually and physically but also abused her psychologically—isolating, humiliating, and demeaning her (Dutton, 2007; Dutton & Nicholls, 2005). Violent adults also break their partner's favorite possessions, punch holes in walls, or throw objects. If children are present, they may become victims.

Partner abuse in which husbands are perpetrators and wives are physically injured is the type most likely to be reported to authorities. But many acts of family violence are not reported. When researchers ask American couples about fights that led to acts of hostility, men and women report similar rates of assault (Archer, 2002; Dutton, 2007). Women victims are more often physically injured, but sex differences in severity of abuse are not great (Archer, 2002; Ehrensaft, Moffitt, & Caspi, 2004). Partner abuse occurs at about the same rate in same-sex relationships as in heterosexual relationships (Schwartz & Waldo, 2004).

Although self-defense is a frequently reported cause of domestic assault by women, American men and women are equally likely to "strike first" (Carrado et al., 1996; Currie, 1999). "Getting my partner's attention," "gaining control," and "expressing anger" are reasons that partners typically give for abusing each other (Dutton, 2007).

Factors Related to Partner Abuse

In abusive relationships, dominance–submission sometimes proceeds from husband to wife, sometimes from wife to husband. In about one-third to one-half of cases, both partners are violent (Dutton, Nicholls, & Spidel, 2005). Marvin's and Pat's relationship helps us understand how partner abuse escalates. Shortly after their wedding, Pat began complaining about the demands of Marvin's work and insisted that he come home early to spend time with her. When he resisted, she hurled epithets, threw objects, and slapped him. One evening, Marvin became so angry at Pat's hostilities that he smashed a dish against the wall, threw his wedding ring at her, and left the house. The next morning, Pat apologized and promised not to attack again. But her outbursts became more frequent and desperate.

These violence–remorse cycles, in which aggression escalates, characterize many abusive relationships. Why do they occur? Personality and developmental history, family circumstances, and cultural factors combine to make partner abuse more likely (Dixon & Browne, 2003).

Many abusers are overly dependent on their spouses as well as jealous, possessive, and controlling. For example, the thought of Karen ever leaving induced such high anxiety in Mike that he monitored all her activities. Depression, anxiety, and low self-esteem also characterize abusers. And because they have great difficulty managing anger, trivial events—such as an unwashed shirt or a late meal—can trigger abusive episodes. When asked to explain their offenses, they attribute greater blame to their partner than to themselves (Henning, Jones, & Holdford, 2005).

A high proportion of spouse abusers grew up in homes where parents engaged in hostile interactions, used coercive discipline, and were abusive toward their children (Bevan & Higgins, 2002; Ehrensaft, Cohen, & Johnson, 2006). Perhaps this explains why conduct problems in childhood and violent delinquency in adolescence also predict partner abuse (Dutton, 2007). Adults with childhood exposure to domestic violence are not doomed to repeat it. But their parents provided them with negative expectations and behaviors that they often transfer to their close relationships. Stressful life events, such as job loss or financial difficulties, increase the likelihood of partner abuse (Emery & Laumann-Billings,

means that many more couples are making informed and personally meaningful choices—a trend that should increase the chances that they will have children when ready and will find parenting an enriching experience.

TRANSITION TO PARENTHOOD. The early weeks after a baby enters the family are full of profound changes: constant caregiving, added financial responsibilities, and less time for the couple's relationship. These demands usually cause the gen-

TABLE 14.3 *Advantages and Disadvantages of Parenthood Mentioned by Contemporary Couples*

ADVANTAGES	DISADVANTAGES
Giving and receiving warmth and affection	Loss of freedom, being tied down
Experiencing the stimulation and fun that children add to life	Financial strain
Being accepted as a responsible and mature member of the community	Role overload—not enough time for both family and work responsibilities
Experiencing new growth and learning opportunities that add meaning to life	Interference with mother's employment opportunities
Having someone carry on after one's own death	Risks of bringing up children in a world plagued by crime, war, and pollution
Gaining a sense of accomplishment and creativity from helping children grow	Worries over children's health, safety, and well-being
Learning to become less selfish and to sacrifice	Reduced time to spend with partner
Having offspring who help with parents' work or add their own income to the family's resources	Loss of privacy
	Fear that children will turn out badly, through no fault of one's own

Source: Cowan & Cowan, 2000; O'Laughlin & Anderson, 2001.

1998). Because of widespread poverty, African Americans and Native Americans report high rates of partner violence (Hoff, 2001). Alcohol abuse is another related factor.

At a societal level, cultural norms that endorse male dominance and female submissiveness promote partner abuse (World Health Organization, 2000, 2005). As Figure 14.4 shows, in countries with widespread poverty that also sanction gender inequality, partner violence against women is especially high, affecting nearly half or more of the female population.

Victims are chronically anxious and depressed and experience frequent panic attacks (Stuart et al., 2006). Why don't they simply leave these destructive relationships? A variety of situational factors discourage them from leaving. A victimized wife may depend on her husband's earning power or fear even worse harm to herself or her children. Extreme assaults, including homicide, tend to occur after partner separation. And victims of both sexes, but especially men, are deterred by the embarrassment of going to the police. Also, victims may falsely believe that their partner will change (Straus, 1999).

Intervention and Treatment

Community services available to battered women include crisis telephone lines that provide anonymous counseling and social support and shelters that offer protection and treatment (see page 448). Because many women return to their abusive partners several times before making their final move, community agencies usually offer therapy to male batterers. Most rely on several months to a year of group sessions that confront rigid gender stereotyping; teach communication, problem solving, and anger control; and use social support to motivate behavior change (Whitaker, Baker, & Arias, 2007).

Although existing treatments are better than none, most are not effective at dealing with relationship difficulties or alcohol abuse. Consequently, many treated perpetrators repeat their violent behavior with the same or a new partner (Schwartz & Waldo, 2004; Stuart, 2005). At present, few interventions acknowledge that men also are victims. Yet ignoring their needs perpetuates domestic violence. When victims do not want to separate from a violent partner, a whole-family treatment approach that focuses on changing partner interaction and reducing high life stress is crucial.

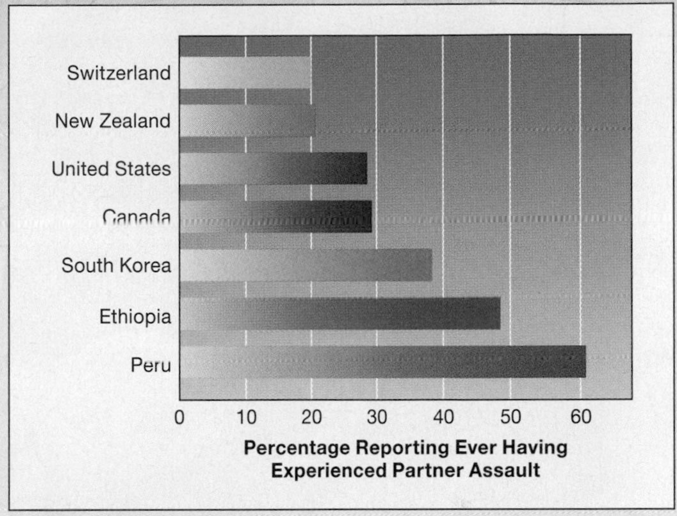

■ **FIGURE 14.4** ■ **Assaults by intimate partners against women in seven nations.** In each country, samples of women were asked to indicate whether they had ever experienced partner physical abuse. The incidence, always underreported, is high in all nations. It is especially high in countries that endorse traditional gender roles and suffer from widespread poverty. (From World Health Organization, 2000, 2005.)

der roles of husband and wife to become more traditional—even for couples like Sharese and Ernie who are strongly committed to gender equality (Cowan & Cowan, 2000; Salmela-Aro et al., 2001).

First and Second Births. For most new parents, however, the arrival of a baby does not cause significant marital strain. Marriages that are gratifying and supportive tend to remain so (Feeney et al., 2001; Miller, 2000). But troubled marriages usually become more unhappy and distressed (Houts et al., 2008; Kluwer & Johnson, 2007). In a study of newlyweds who were interviewed annually for six years, the husband's affection, expression of "we-ness" (values and goals similar to his wife's), and awareness of his wife's daily life predicted mothers' stable or increasing marital satisfaction after childbirth. In contrast, the husband's negativity and the couple's out-of-control conflict predicted a drop in mothers' satisfaction (Shapiro, Gottman, & Carrere, 2000). When expectant couples anticipate lack of partner support in parenting, their prediction generally becomes reality, yielding an especially difficult post-birth adjustment (McHale & Rotman, 2007).

Violated expectations about division of labor in the home powerfully affect new parents' well-being. In dual-earner marriages, the larger the difference in men's and women's caregiving responsibilities, the greater the decline in marital satisfaction after childbirth, especially for women—with negative consequences for parent–infant interaction. In contrast, sharing caregiving predicts greater parental happiness and sensitivity to the baby (McHale et al., 2004; Moller, Hwang, & Wickberg, 2008). An exception exists, however, for employed lower-SES women who endorse traditional gender roles. When their husbands take on considerable child-care responsibilities, these mothers tend to report more distress, perhaps because of disappointment at being unable to fulfill their desire to do most of the caregiving (Goldberg & Perry-Jenkins, 2003).

Postponing childbearing until the late twenties or thirties, as more couples do today, eases the transition to parenthood. Waiting permits couples to pursue occupational goals, gain life experience, and strengthen their relationship. Under these circumstances, men are more enthusiastic about becoming fathers and therefore more willing to participate. And women whose careers are well under way and whose marriages are happy are

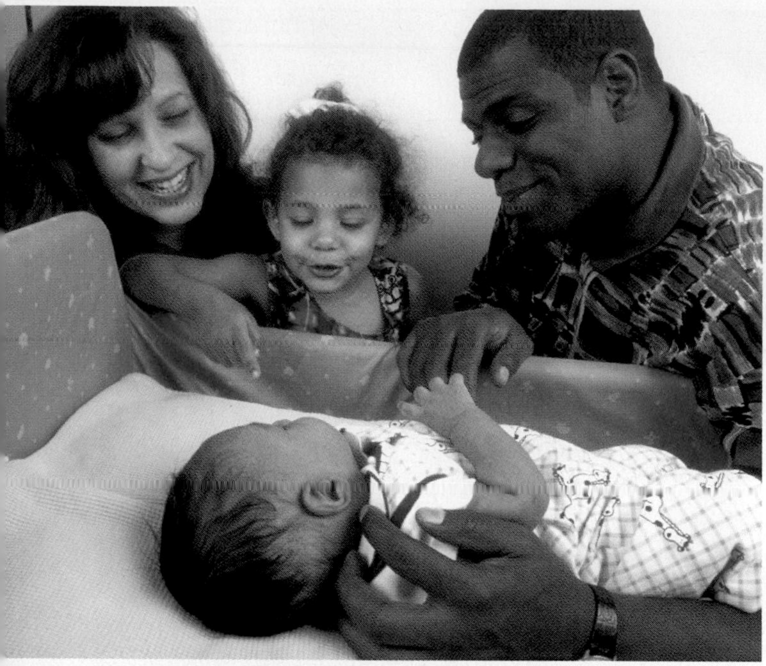

© MICHAEL NEWMAN/PHOTOEDIT

Compared to a first birth, a second birth typically requires that fathers become more actively involved in parenting, sharing in the high demands of tending to both a baby and a young child.

more likely to encourage their husbands to share housework and child care, which fosters fathers' involvement (Lee & Dougherty, 2007; Schoppe-Sullivan et al., 2008).

A second birth typically requires that fathers take an even more active role in parenting—by caring for the firstborn while the mother is recuperating and by sharing in the high demands of tending to both a baby and a young child. Consequently, well-functioning families with a newborn second child typically pull back from the traditional division of responsibilities that occurred after the first birth. In a study that tracked parents from the end of pregnancy through the first year after their second child's birth, fathers' willingness to place greater emphasis on the parenting role was strongly linked to mothers' adjustment after the arrival of a second baby (Stewart, 1990). And the support of family, friends, and spouse are crucial for fathers' well-being.

Interventions. Couples' groups led by counselors are highly effective in easing the transition to parenthood. In one program, first-time expectant couples gathered once a week for six months to discuss their dreams for the family and changes in relationships sparked by the baby's arrival. Eighteen months after the program ended, participating fathers described themselves as more involved with their child than did fathers in a no-intervention condition. Perhaps because of fathers' caregiving assistance, participating mothers maintained their prebirth satisfaction with family and work roles. Three years after the birth, the marriages of participating couples were intact and just as happy as they had been before parenthood. In contrast, 15 percent of couples receiving no intervention had divorced (Cowan & Cowan, 1997; Schulz, Cowan, & Cowan, 2006). For high-risk parents struggling with poverty or the birth of a child with disabilities, interventions must be more intensive, focusing on enhancing social support and parenting skills (Cowan & Cowan, 1995).

Generous, paid employment leave—widely available in industrialized nations but not in the United States—is crucial for parents of newborns (see Chapter 3, page 104). But financial pressures mean that many new mothers who are eligible for unpaid work leave take far less than they are guaranteed by U.S. federal law, while new fathers take little or none (Han & Waldfogel, 2003). When favorable workplace policies exist and parents take advantage of them, couples are more likely to support each other and experience family life as gratifying (Feldman, Sussman, & Zigler, 2004). As a result, the stress caused by the birth of a baby stays at manageable levels.

FAMILIES WITH YOUNG CHILDREN. A year after the birth of their first child, Sharese and Ernie received a phone call from Heather, who asked how they liked parenthood: "Is it a joy, a dilemma, a stressful experience—how would you describe it?"

Chuckling, Sharese and Ernie responded in unison, "All of the above!"

In today's complex world, men and women are less certain about how to rear children than in previous generations. Clarifying child-rearing values and implementing them in warm, involved, and appropriately demanding ways are crucial for the welfare of the next generation and society. Yet cultures do not always place a high priority on parenting, as indicated by the lack of many societal supports for children and families (see Chapter 2, pages 67–68). Furthermore, changing family forms mean that the lives of today's parents differ substantially from those of past generations.

In previous chapters, we discussed a wide variety of influences on child-rearing styles, including personal characteristics of children and parents, SES, and ethnicity. The couple's relationship is also vital. Parents who work together as a *coparenting team,* cooperating and showing solidarity and respect for each other in parenting roles, are more likely to gain in warm marital interaction, feel competent as parents, use effective child-rearing practices, and have children who are developing well (McHale et al., 2002; Schoppe-Sullivan et al., 2004). When parents forge this coparenting alliance within the first few months after childbirth, it is more likely to persist (Fivaz-Depeursinge & Corboz-Warnery, 1999).

For employed parents, a major struggle is finding good child care and, when their child is ill or otherwise in need of emergency care, taking time off from work or making other urgent arrangements. The younger the child, the greater parents' sense of risk and difficulty—especially low-income parents, who must work longer hours to pay bills; who often, in the United States, have no workplace benefits (health insurance or paid sick leave); and who typically cannot afford the cost of child care (Halpern, 2005b). When competent, convenient child care is not available, the woman usually faces added pressures. She must either curtail or give up her work, with profound financial consequences in low-income families, or endure unhappy children, missed workdays, and constant searches for new arrangements.

Despite its challenges, rearing young children is a powerful source of adult development. Parents report that it expands their emotional capacities and enriches their lives. For example, Ernie remarked that through sharing in child rearing, he felt "rounded out" as a person. Other involved parents say that parenthood helped them tune in to others' feelings and needs, required that they become more tolerant, self-confident, and responsible, and broadened their extended family, friendship, and community ties (Knoester & Eggebeen, 2006; Nomaguchi & Milkie, 2003).

FAMILIES WITH ADOLESCENTS. Adolescence brings sharp changes in parental roles. In Chapters 11 and 12, we noted that parents must establish a revised relationship with their adolescent children—blending guidance with freedom and gradually loosening control. As adolescents gain in autonomy and explore values and goals in their search for identity, parents often complain that their teenager is too focused on peers and no longer cares about being with the family. Heightened parent–child bickering over everyday issues takes a toll, especially on mothers, who do most of the negotiating with teenagers.

Overall, children seem to navigate the challenges of adolescence more easily than parents, many of whom report a dip in marital and life satisfaction. More people seek family therapy during this period of the family life cycle than during any other (Steinberg & Silk, 2002).

PARENT EDUCATION. In the past, family life changed little from one generation to the next, and adults learned what they needed to know about parenting through modeling and direct experience. Today's world confronts adults with a host of factors that impinge on their ability to succeed as parents.

Contemporary parents eagerly seek information on child rearing. New mothers often regard popular parenting books and magazines as particularly valuable. They also reach out to a network of other women for knowledge and assistance. Fathers, by contrast, rarely have social networks through which they can learn about child care and child rearing. Consequently, they frequently turn to mothers to figure out how to relate to their child, especially if they have a close, confiding marriage (Lamb & Lewis, 2004; McHale, Kuersten-Hogan, & Rao, 2004). Recall from Chapter 6 that marital harmony fosters both parents' positive engagement with babies, but it is especially important for fathers.

Parent education courses exist to help parents clarify child-rearing values, improve family communication, understand how children develop, and apply more effective parenting strategies. A variety of programs yield positive outcomes, including enhanced knowledge of effective parenting practices, improved parent–child interaction, and heightened awareness by parents of their role as educators of their children (Bert, Ferris, & Borkowski, 2008; Smith, Perou, & Lesesne, 2002). Another benefit is social support—opportunities to discuss concerns with experts and other dedicated parents, who share the view that no job is more important to the future of society than child rearing.

© JOHN BIRDSALL/THE IMAGE WORKS

Contemporary parents eagerly seek information on child rearing, and women often reach out to a network of friends for knowledge and assistance.

ASK YOURSELF

REVIEW
What strategies can couples use to ease the transition to parenthood?

APPLY
After her wedding, Sharese was convinced she had made a mistake. Cite factors that sustained her marriage and led it to become especially happy.

CONNECT
What aspects of adolescent development make rearing teenagers stressful for parents, leading to a dip in marital and life satisfaction? (See Chapter 11, pages 369–370 and 388, and Chapter 12, pages 415–416.)

REFLECT
Do you live with your parents or on your own? What factors contributed to your current living arrangements? If you live independently, has your relationship with your parents changed in ways that match the findings of research?

The Diversity of Adult Lifestyles

The current array of adult lifestyles dates back to the 1960s, when young people began to question the conventional wisdom of previous generations and to ask, "How can I find happiness? What kinds of commitments should I make to live a full and rewarding life?" As the public became more accepting of diverse lifestyles, choices such as staying single, cohabiting, remaining childless, and divorcing seemed more available.

Today, nontraditional family options have penetrated the American mainstream. Many adults experience not just one but several. As we will see, some adults make a deliberate decision to adopt a lifestyle, whereas others drift into it. The lifestyle may be imposed by society, as is the case for cohabiting same-sex couples in the United States, who cannot marry legally in most states. Or people may choose a certain lifestyle because they feel pushed away from another, such as a marriage gone sour. In sum, the adoption of a lifestyle can be within or beyond the person's control.

Compared with single men, single women more easily come to terms with their lifestyle, in part because of the greater social support available to women through intimate same-sex friendships.

Singlehood

On finishing her education, Heather joined the Peace Corps and spent four years in Ghana. Though open to a long-term relationship, she had only fleeting romances. After she returned to the United States, she accepted a management position with an insurance company. Professional challenge and travel preoccupied her. At age 35, over lunch with Sharese, she reflected on her life: "I was open to marriage, but after my career took off, it would have interfered. Now I'm so used to independence that I question whether I could adjust to living with another person. I like being able to pick up and go where I want, when I want, without having to ask anyone or think about caring for anyone. But there's a tradeoff: I sleep alone, eat most of my meals alone, and spend a lot of my leisure time alone."

Singlehood—not living with an intimate partner—has increased in recent years, especially among young adults. For example, rates of never-married American 30- to 34-year-olds have risen sixfold since 1970, to about one-third of males and one-fourth of females. More people marry later or not at all, and divorce has added to the numbers of single adults. In view of these trends, it is likely that most Americans will spend a substantial part of their adult lives single, and a growing minority—about 8 to 10 percent—will stay that way (U.S. Census Bureau, 2009b).

Because they marry later, more young adult men than women are single. But women are far more likely than men to remain single for many years or their entire life. With age, fewer men are available with characteristics that most women seek in a mate—the same age or older, equally or better educated, and professionally successful. In contrast, men can choose partners from a large pool of younger unmarried women. Because of the tendency for women to "marry up" and men to "marry down," men in blue-collar occupations and women in prestigious careers are overrepresented among singles after age 30.

Ethnic differences also exist. For example, the percentage of never-married African Americans is nearly twice as great as that of Caucasian Americans in early adulthood. As we will see later, high unemployment among black men interferes with marriage. Many African Americans eventually marry in their late thirties and forties, a period in which black and white marriage rates come closer together (U.S. Census Bureau, 2009b).

Singlehood can have a variety of meanings. At one extreme are people who choose it deliberately; at the other those who see themselves as single because of circumstances beyond their control. Most, like Heather, are in the middle—adults who wanted to marry but made choices that took them in a different direction. In interview studies of never-married women, some said they focused on occupational goals instead of marriage. Others reported that they found singlehood preferable to their disappointing intimate relationships. And still others commented that they just did not meet "the right person" (Baumbusch, 2004; Lewis, 2000).

The most commonly mentioned advantages of singlehood are freedom and mobility. But singles also recognize drawbacks—loneliness, the dating grind, limited sexual and social life, reduced sense of security, and feelings of exclusion from the world of married couples. Single men have more physical and mental health problems than single women, who more easily come to terms with their lifestyle, in part because of the greater social support available to women through intimate same-sex friendships (Pinquart, 2003). But overall, people who have always been single are content with their lives. Though not quite as happy as married people, they report feeling considerably happier than people recently widowed or divorced (Lucas et al., 2003; DePaulo & Morris, 2005).

Nevertheless, many single people go through a stressful period in their late twenties, when most of their friends have married. Widespread veneration of marriage, along with negative stereotyping of singles as socially immature and self-centered, probably contributes (DePaulo & Morris, 2006). For single women, the mid-thirties is another trying time, as the biological deadline for childbearing approaches. A few decide to become parents through artificial insemination or a love affair. And an increasing number are adopting, often from overseas countries.

Cohabitation

Cohabitation refers to the lifestyle of unmarried couples who have a sexually intimate relationship and who share a residence. Until the 1960s, cohabitation in Western nations was largely limited to low-SES adults. Since then, it has increased in all groups, with an especially dramatic rise among well-educated, economically advantaged young people. Today's young adults are much more likely than those of a generation ago to form their first conjugal union through cohabitation. Among Americans in their twenties, cohabitation is now the preferred mode of entry into a committed intimate partnership, chosen by more than 50 percent of couples (U.S. Census Bureau, 2009b). Cohabitation rates are even higher among adults with failed marriages. Half of cohabiting relationships in the United States involve at least one partner who is separated or divorced; one-third of these households include children (Cohan & Kleinbaum, 2002).

For some couples, cohabitation serves as *preparation for marriage*—a time to test the relationship and get used to living together. For others, however, it is an *alternative to marriage*, offering the rewards of sexual intimacy and companionship along with the possibility of easy departure if satisfaction declines. It is not surprising, then, that cohabiters vary greatly in the extent to which they share money and possessions and take responsibility for each other's children.

Although Americans are more open to cohabitation than in the past, their attitudes are not yet as positive as those of Western Europeans. In the Netherlands, Norway, and Sweden, cohabitation is thoroughly integrated into society. From 70 to 90 percent of young people cohabit in their first intimate partnership, and cohabiters are nearly as devoted to each other as married people (Fussell & Gauthier, 2005; Ramsøy, 1994). Whereas about 50 percent of American cohabiting unions break up within two years, only 6 to 16 percent dissolve in Western Europe (Brown, 2000; Kiernan, 2002). When they decide to marry, Dutch, Norwegian, and Swedish cohabiters more often do so to legalize their relationships, especially for the sake of children. American cohabiters typically marry to confirm their love and commitment—sentiments that Western Europeans attach to cohabitation.

Furthermore, American couples who cohabit before they are engaged to be married are more prone to divorce than couples who wait to live together until after they have made a commitment to each other. But this association is less strong or absent in Western European nations (Kiernan, 2001, 2002; Kline et al., 2004; Rhoades, Stanley, & Markman, 2006). U.S. young people who cohabit prior to engagement tend to have less conventional values. They have had more sexual partners and are more politically liberal, less religious, and more androgynous. In addition, a larger number have parents who divorced (Axinn & Barber, 1997; Cunningham & Antill, 1994; Kurdek, 2006).

These personal characteristics may contribute to the negative outcomes associated with cohabitation. But the cohabitation experience itself also plays a role. Cohabiters are less likely than married people to pool finances or jointly own a house. In addition, both preengagement cohabiters and formerly cohabiting married couples have poorer-quality relationships (Cohan & Kleinbaum, 2002; Kline et al., 2004). Perhaps the open-ended nature of the cohabiting relationship reduces motivation to develop effective conflict-resolution skills. When cohabiters carry negative communication into marriage, it undermines marital satisfaction. Finally, a history of parental divorce may increase cohabiters' willingness to dissolve a union when it becomes less satisfying.

Certain couples, however, are exceptions to the trends just described. People who cohabit after separation or divorce often test a new relationship carefully to prevent another failure, especially when children are involved. As a result, they cohabit longer and are less likely to move toward marriage (Smock & Gupta, 2002). Similarly, cohabitation is often an alternative to marriage among low-SES couples. Many regard their earning power as too uncertain for marriage and continue living together, sometimes giving birth to children and marrying when their financial status improves (Jayakody & Cabrera, 2002).

In the Netherlands, cohabitation is thoroughly integrated into society. Most Dutch young people cohabit in their first intimate partnership, and cohabiters are nearly as devoted to each other as married people.

Finally, cohabiting gay and lesbian couples report strong commitment, equal to that of married people. When their relationships become difficult, they end more often than marriages only because of fewer barriers to separating, including children in common, financial dependence on a partner, or concerns about the costs of divorce (Kurdek, 1998, 2006). In a study in which same-sex couples in Vermont were followed over three years, cohabiters were more likely than couples in civil unions to have ended their relationships (Balsam et al., 2008). Civil unions were as stable as heterosexual marriages.

For people not ready for marriage, cohabitation combines the rewards of a close relationship with the opportunity to avoid the legal obligations of marriage. But cohabiting couples can encounter difficulties precisely because they do not have these obligations (Mahoney, 2002). Bitter fights over property, money, rental contracts, and responsibility for children are the rule rather than the exception when unmarried couples split up.

Childlessness

At work, Sharese got to know Beatrice and Daniel. Married for seven years and in their mid-thirties, they did not have children and were not planning any. To Sharese, their relationship seemed especially caring and affectionate. "At first, we were open to becoming parents," Beatrice explained, "but eventually we decided to focus on our marriage."

Some people are *involuntarily childless* because they did not find a partner with whom to share parenthood or their efforts at fertility treatments did not succeed. Beatrice and Daniel are in another category—men and women who are *voluntarily childless.*

Childlessness in the United States has increased steadily, from 9 percent of women between ages 20 and 44 in 1975 to about 20 percent in the mid-2000s, with similar trends occurring in other Western nations (Rowland, 2007; Sewall & Burns, 2006). Current figures vary somewhat, perhaps because voluntary childlessness is not always a permanent condition. A few people decide early that they do not want to be parents and stick to their plans. But most, like Beatrice and Daniel, make their decision after they are married and have developed a lifestyle they do not want to give up. Later, some change their minds.

Besides marital satisfaction and freedom from child-care responsibilities, common reasons for not having children include the woman's career and economic security. Consistent with these motives, the voluntarily childless are usually college-educated, have prestigious occupations, and are highly committed to their work (Amba & Martinez, 2006; Kemkes-Grottenhaler, 2003).

Negative stereotypes of nonparenthood—as a sign of self-indulgence and irresponsibility—have weakened in Western nations as people have become more accepting of diverse lifestyles (Dykstra & Hagestad, 2007). Acceptance is greatest among highly educated women, who—while not necessarily embracing childlessness—may be more attuned to the demands of parenthood, which are still borne mostly by women (Koropeckyj-Cox & Pendell, 2007).

In line with this trend, voluntarily childless adults are just as content with their lives as parents who have warm relationships with their children. But adults who cannot overcome infertility are likely to be dissatisfied—some profoundly disappointed, others more ambivalent, depending on compensations in other areas of their lives (Letherby, 2002; Nichols & Pace-Nichols, 2000). Childlessness interferes with adjustment and life satisfaction only when it is beyond a person's control.

Divorce and Remarriage

Divorce rates have stabilized since the mid-1980s, partly because of rising age of marriage, which is linked to greater financial stability and marital satisfaction. In addition, the increase in cohabitation has curtailed divorce: Many relationships that once would have been marriages now break up before marriage (Bumpass, 2004; Heaton, 2002). Still, 45 percent of U.S. marriages dissolve. Because most divorces occur within seven years of marriage, many involve young children. Divorces are also common during the transition to midlife, when people have adolescent children—a period (as noted earlier) of reduced marital satisfaction.

About two-thirds of divorced people remarry. But marital failure is even greater during the first few years of second marriages—10 percent above that for first marriages. Afterward, the divorce rates for first and second marriages are similar (Coleman, Ganong, & Fine, 2000; U.S. Census Bureau, 2009b).

■ **FACTORS RELATED TO DIVORCE.** Why do so many marriages fail? As Christy and Gary's divorce illustrates, the most obvious reason is a disrupted husband–wife relationship. Christy and Gary did not argue more than Sharese and Ernie. But their problem-solving style was ineffective, and it weakened their attachment to each other. When Christy raised concerns, Gary reacted with contempt, resentment, defensiveness, and retreat—a demand–withdraw pattern found in many partners who split up (Haltzman, Holstein, & Moss, 2007). Another

© NOEL HENDRICKSON/PHOTODISC RED/GETTY IMAGES

An ineffective problem-solving style can lead to divorce. Many partners who split up follow a pattern in which one partner raises concerns, and the other reacts with resentment, anger, and retreat.

typical style involves little conflict, but partners increasingly lead separate lives because they have different expectations of family life and few shared interests, activities, or friends (Gottman & Levenson, 2000).

What problems underlie these maladaptive communication patterns? In a nine-year longitudinal study, researchers asked a U.S. national sample of 2,000 married people about marital problems and followed up three, six, and nine years later to find out who had separated or divorced (Amato & Rogers, 1997). Wives reported more problems than husbands, with the gender difference largely involving the wife's emotions, such as anger and hurt feelings. Husbands seemed to have difficulty sensing their wife's distress, which contributed to her view of the marriage as unhappy. Regardless of which spouse reported the problem or was judged responsible for it, the strongest predictors of divorce during the following decade were infidelity, spending money foolishly, drinking or using drugs, expressing jealousy, engaging in irritating habits, and moodiness.

Background factors that increase the chances of divorce are younger age at marriage, not attending religious services, being previously divorced, and having parents who had divorced—all of which are linked to marital difficulties. For example, couples who married at younger ages are more likely to report infidelity and jealousy. Low religious involvement subtracts an influential context for instilling positive marital attitudes and behaviors. And research following families over two decades reveals that parental divorce elevates risk of divorce in at least two succeeding generations, in part because it promotes child adjustment problems and reduces commitment to the norm of lifelong marriage (Amato & Cheadle, 2005; Wolfinger, 2005). As a result, when adult children marry, they are more likely to engage in inconsiderate behaviors and to have conflict-ridden relationships and less likely to try to work through these difficulties or (if they do try) to have the skills to do so. Marriage to a caring spouse from a stable family background reduces these negative outcomes.

Poorly educated, economically disadvantaged couples who suffer multiple life stresses are especially likely to split up (Clarke-Stewart & Brentano, 2006). But Christy's case represents another trend—rising marital breakup among well educated, career-oriented, economically independent women. When a woman's workplace status and income exceed her husband's, the risk of divorce increases—an association explained by differing gender-role beliefs between the spouses. A husband's lack of support for his wife's career can greatly heighten her unhappiness and, therefore, the chances that she will end the marriage (Popenoe, 2006). Overall, women are twice as likely as men to initiate divorce proceedings.

CONSEQUENCES OF DIVORCE. When Sharese learned that Christy and Gary's marriage had dissolved, she felt as if "someone had died." Her description is fitting: Divorce involves the loss of a way of life and therefore a part of the self sustained by that way of life. As a result, it provides opportunities for both positive and negative change.

Immediately after separation, both men and women experience disrupted social networks, a decline in social support, and increased anxiety, depression, and impulsive behavior (Amato, 2000). For most, these reactions subside within two years. Nonworking women who organized their identities around their husbands have an especially hard time. And some noncustodial fathers feel disoriented and rootless as a result of decreased contact with their children. Others distract themselves with a frenzy of social activity (Coleman, Ganong, & Leon, 2006).

Finding a new partner contributes most to the life satisfaction of divorced adults (Forste & Heaton, 2004; Wang & Amato, 2000). But it is more crucial for men, who adjust less well than women to living on their own. Despite loneliness and a drop in income (see Chapter 10), women tend to bounce back more easily from divorce. Christy, for example, developed new friendships and a sense of self-reliance that might not have emerged had she remained married to Gary. However, a few women—especially those who are anxious and fearful, who remain strongly attached to their ex-spouses, or who lack education and job skills—experience a drop in self-esteem and persistent depression and sometimes enter into unsuccessful relationships repeatedly (Amato, 2000; Coleman, Ganong, & Leon, 2006). Job training, continued education, career advancement, and social support from family and friends play vital roles in the economic and psychological well-being of many divorced women.

REMARRIAGE. On average, people remarry within four years of divorce, men somewhat faster than women. As noted earlier, remarriages are especially vulnerable to breakup, for several reasons. Practical matters—financial security, help in rearing children, relief from loneliness, and social acceptance—figure more heavily into a second marriage than a first. These concerns do not provide a sound footing for a lasting partnership. Second, some people transfer the negative patterns of interaction and problem solving learned in their first marriage to the second. Third, people with a failed marriage behind them are more likely to view divorce as an acceptable solution when marital difficulties resurface. Finally, remarried couples experience more stress from stepfamily situations (Coleman, Ganong, & Leon, 2006). As we will see, stepparent–stepchild ties are powerful predictors of marital happiness.

Blended families generally take three to five years to develop the connectedness and comfort of intact biological families (Ihinger-Tallman & Pasley, 1997). Family life education, couples counseling, and group therapy can help divorced and remarried adults adapt to the complexities of their new circumstances (Whiteside, 2006).

Variant Styles of Parenthood

Diverse family forms result in varied styles of parenthood. Each type of family—blended, never-married, gay or lesbian, among others—presents unique challenges to parenting competence and adult psychological well-being.

STEPPARENTS. Whether stepchildren live in the household or visit only occasionally, stepparents are in a difficult position. Stepparents enter the family as outsiders and, too often, move into their new parental role too quickly. Lacking a warm attachment bond to build on, their discipline is usually ineffective. Stepparents frequently criticize the biological parent for being too lenient, while the biological parent may view the stepparent as too harsh (Ganong & Coleman, 2004). Compared with first-marriage parents, remarried parents typically report higher levels of tension and disagreement, most centering on child-rearing issues. When both adults have children from prior marriages, rather than only one, more opportunities for conflict exist and relationship quality is poorer (Coleman, Ganong, & Fine, 2000).

Stepmothers are especially likely to experience conflict. Those who have not previously been married and had children may have an idealized image of family life, which is quickly shattered. Expected to be in charge of family relationships, stepmothers quickly find that stepparent–stepchild ties do not develop instantly. After divorce, biological mothers are frequently jealous, uncooperative, and possessive of their children. Even when their husbands do not have custody, stepmothers feel stressed. As stepchildren go in and out of the home, stepmothers find life easier without resistant children and then feel guilty about their "unmaternal" feelings (Church, 2004; MacDonald & DeMaris, 1996). No matter how hard a stepmother tries to build a close parent–child bond, her efforts are probably doomed to failure in the short run.

Stepfathers with children of their own tend to establish positive bonds with stepchildren relatively quickly, perhaps because they are experienced in building warm parent–child ties and feel less pressure than stepmothers to plunge into parenting. And stepchildren generally respond favorably to stepfathers' efforts to connect with them through enjoyable activities (Ganong et al., 1999). But stepfathers without biological children (like their stepmother counterparts) can have unrealistic expectations. Or their wives may push them into the father role, sparking negativity from children. After making several overtures that are ignored or rebuffed, these stepfathers often withdraw from parenting (Hetherington & Clingempeel, 1992).

A caring husband–wife relationship, cooperation from the biological parent, and children's willingness to accept their parent's new spouse are crucial for stepparent adjustment. Over time, many couples strengthen their relationship and build a coparenting partnership that improves interactions with stepchildren (Church, 2004). But because stepparent–stepchild bonds are hard to establish, the divorce rate is higher for remarried couples with stepchildren than for those without them.

■ **NEVER-MARRIED SINGLE PARENTS.** About 10 percent of U.S. children live with a single parent who has never married and does not have a partner. Of these parents, about 85 percent are mothers, 15 percent fathers (U.S. Census Bureau, 2009b). In recent years, more single women over age 30 in high-status occupations have become parents. But they are still few in number, and little is known about how they and their children fare.

In the United States, African-American young women make up the largest group of never-married parents. Over 60 percent of births to black mothers in their twenties are to women without a partner, compared with 13 percent of births to white women (U.S. Census Bureau, 2009b). African-American women postpone marriage more and childbirth less than women in other U.S. ethnic groups. Job loss, persisting unemployment, and consequent inability of many black men to support a family have contributed to the postponement of marriage.

Never-married black mothers tap the extended family, especially their own mothers and sometimes male relatives, for help in rearing their children (Gasden, 1999; Jayakody & Kalil, 2002). For about one-third, marriage—not necessarily to the child's biological father—occurs within nine years after birth of the first child (Wu, Bumpass, & Musick, 2001). These couples function much like other first-marriage parents. Their children are often unaware that the father is a stepfather, and parents do not report the child-rearing difficulties typical of blended families (Ganong & Coleman, 1994).

Still, for low-SES women, never-married parenthood generally increases financial hardship. Nearly 50 percent of white mothers and 60 percent of black mothers have a second child while unmarried. And they are far less likely than divorced mothers to receive paternal child support payments, although child support enforcement both reduces financial stress and increases father involvement (Huang, 2006).

Children of never-married mothers who lack father involvement achieve less well in school and display more antisocial behavior than children in low-SES, first-marriage families—problems that make life more difficult for mothers (Coley, 1998). But marriage to the child's biological father benefits children only when the father is a reliable source of economic and emotional support. When a mother pairs up with an antisocial father, her child is at greater risk for conduct problems than if she had reared the child alone (Jaffee et al., 2003). Strengthening social support, education, and employment opportunities for low-SES parents would greatly enhance the well-being of unmarried mothers and their children.

■ **GAY AND LESBIAN PARENTS.** Several million American gay men and lesbians are parents, most through previous heterosexual marriages, some through adoption, and a growing number through reproductive technologies (Ambert, 2005; Patterson, 2002). In the past, because of laws assuming that homosexuals could not be adequate parents, those who divorced a heterosexual partner lost custody of their children. Today, some U.S. states hold that sexual orientation by itself is irrelevant to custody. A few U.S. states, however, ban gay and lesbian couples from adopting children.

Most research on homosexual parents and children is limited to volunteer samples. Findings of these investigations indicate that gay and lesbian parents are as committed to and effective at child rearing as heterosexual parents and sometimes more so (Bos, van Balen, & van den Boom, 2007; Tasker, 2005). Also, whether born to or adopted by their parents or conceived through donor insemination, children in gay and lesbian families did not differ from the children of heterosexuals in mental health, peer relations, or gender identity (Allen & Burrell, 1996; Flaks et al., 1995; Golombok & Tasker, 1996). Two additional studies, which surmounted the potential bias associated with a volunteer sample by including all lesbian-mother families who had conceived children at a fertility clinic, also reported that children were developing favorably (Brewaeys et al., 1997; Chan, Raboy, & Patterson, 1998). Likewise, among participants drawn from a representative sample of British mothers and their 7-year-olds, children reared in lesbian-mother families did not differ from children reared in heterosexual families in adjustment and gender-role preferences (Golombok et al., 2003). Furthermore, children of gay and lesbian parents do not differ from other children in sexual orientation; the large majority are heterosexual (Tasker, 2005).

When extended-family members have difficulty accepting them, homosexual mothers and fathers often build "families of choice" through friends, who assume the roles of relatives. Usually, however, parents of gays and lesbians cannot endure a permanent rift (Fisher, Easterly, & Lazear, 2008). With time, interactions between homosexual parents and their families of origin become more positive and supportive.

Homosexual couples' joint involvement in parenting varies with the way children entered the family. When partners choose parenthood through adoption or reproductive technologies, they report fairly even division of child-care and household tasks (Chan, Raboy, & Patterson, 1998). When children resulted from a previous heterosexual relationship, the biological parent typically assumes a larger parenting role (Hare & Richards, 1993).

A major concern of gay and lesbian parents is that their children will be stigmatized by their parents' sexual orientation. Most studies indicate that incidents of teasing or bullying are rare because parents and children carefully manage the information they reveal to others (Tasker, 2005). But in an Australian study, even though most third to tenth graders were guarded about discussing their parents' relationship with peers, nearly half reported harassment (Ray & Gregory, 2001). Overall, families headed by homosexuals can be distinguished from other families only by issues related to living in a nonsupportive society.

Gay and lesbian parents are as committed to and effective at child rearing as heterosexual parents. Overall, families headed by same-sex partners can be distinguished from other families only by issues related to living in a nonsupportive society.

ASK YOURSELF

» REVIEW
Why is never-married single parenthood especially high among African Americans? What conditions affect parent and child well-being in these families?

» APPLY
After dating for a year, Wanda and Scott decided to live together. Their parents worried that cohabitation would reduce the couple's chances for a successful marriage. Is this fear justified? Why or why not?

» CONNECT
Return to Chapter 10, pages 347–348, and review the impact of divorce and remarriage on children and adolescents. How do those findings resemble outcomes for adults? What might account for the similarities?

» REFLECT
Do your own experiences or those of your friends match research findings on cohabitation, singlehood, never-married parents, or gay and lesbian parents? Select one instance and discuss.

Career Development

Besides family life, vocational life is a vital domain of social development in early adulthood. After choosing an occupation, young people must learn how to perform its tasks well, get along with co-workers, respond to authority, and protect their own interests. When work experiences go well, adults develop new competencies, feel a sense of personal accomplishment, make new friends, and become financially independent and secure. And as we have seen, especially for women but also for men who support their partner's career development, aspirations and accomplishments in the workplace and the family are interwoven.

Establishing a Career

Our discussion of Levinson's and Vaillant's theories highlighted diverse paths and timetables for career development. ***TAKE A MOMENT...*** Consider, once again, the wide variations among Sharese, Ernie, Christy, and Gary. Notice that, as is typical for men, Ernie's and Gary's career lives were long and *continuous,* from completion of formal education to retirement. Sharese and Christy, like many women, had *discontinuous* career paths—ones that were interrupted or deferred by child rearing and other family needs (Huang & Sverke, 2007; Moen & Roehling, 2005). Furthermore, not all people embark on the vocation of their dreams. In an Australian study that followed 1,200 young people after they finished their schooling, at any given time during the next seven years, only 20 percent were working in a field consistent with their greatest interest (Athanasou, 2002).

Even for those who enter their chosen field, initial experiences can be discouraging. At the health department, Sharese discovered that committee meetings and paperwork consumed much of her day. Because each project had a deadline, the pressure of productivity weighed heavily on her. Adjusting to unanticipated disappointments in salary, supervisors, and co-workers is difficult. As new workers become aware of the gap between their expectations and reality, resignations are common. On average, people in their twenties move to a new job every two years; five or six changes are not unusual (Petersen & Gonzales, 1999).

After a period of evaluation and adjustment, young adults generally settle into their work. In careers with opportunities for promotion, high aspirations must often be revised downward because the structure of most work settings resembles a pyramid, with few high-level executive and supervisory jobs. In a longitudinal study of more than 400 lower-level male managers at AT&T, the importance of work in men's lives varied with career advancement and age (Howard & Bray, 1988). For men who advanced very little, "work disengagement" occurred early; family, recreation, and community service assumed greater importance by the early thirties. Men with average levels of career success emphasized nonwork roles at a later age. In contrast, men who were highly successful became more involved in their jobs over time. Although the desire for advancement tends to decline with age, most people still seek challenges and find satisfaction in their work roles.

Besides opportunity, personal characteristics affect career progress. As we will see, a sense of self-efficacy is influential. Young people who are very anxious about on-the-job failure tend to set their career aspirations either too high or too low. When they encounter obstacles, they quickly conclude that career tasks are too hard and give up (Lent & Brown, 2002). As a result, they achieve far less than their abilities would permit.

Recall from our discussion of Levinson's theory that career success often depends on the quality of a mentoring relationship. Access to an effective mentor—a person with advanced experience and knowledge who is emotionally invested in the junior person's development and who fosters a bond of trust—is jointly affected by the availability of willing people and the individual's capacity to select an appropriate individual (Ramaswami & Dreher, 2007). The best mentors are seldom top executives, who tend to be preoccupied and therefore less helpful and sympathetic. Usually, young adults fare better with lower-level mentors—more experienced co-workers or members of their professional associations (Allen & Finkelstein, 2003).

Women and Ethnic Minorities

Although women and ethnic minorities have penetrated nearly all professions, their talents often are not developed to the fullest. Women, especially those who are members of economically disadvantaged minorities, remain concentrated in occupations that offer little opportunity for advancement, and they are underrepresented in executive and managerial roles (see Chapter 13, page 457). And although the overall difference between men's and women's earnings is smaller today than 30 years ago, it remains considerable. U.S. government surveys following 9,000 U.S. college-educated workers for a decade revealed that a year after receiving their bachelor's degrees, women working full time earned just 80 percent as much as men. The difference was largely (but not entirely) due to gender differences in college majors: Women more often chose education and service fields, men higher-paying scientific and technical fields. Ten years after graduation, the gender pay gap had widened: Women's pay was only 69 percent of men's, and in no profession did women's earnings equal men's (Dey & Hill, 2007). Gender disparities in career development accounted for about 90 percent of the gap, with the remaining 10 percent attributed to on-the-job discrimination.

Especially for women in traditionally feminine occupations, career planning is often short term and subject to change. Many enter and exit the labor market several times as they give birth to and rear children. Between ages 18 and 34, the typical woman has been out of the labor force 26 percent of the time, in contrast to 11 percent for the typical man (Furchtgott-Roth, 2009; U.S. Department of Labor, 2004). Time away from a career greatly hinders advancement—a major reason that women in prestigious, male-dominated careers tend to delay or avoid childbearing (Blair-Loy & DeHart, 2003). Yet an increasing number of accomplished professional women are leaving their jobs to devote themselves full-time to child rearing—a trend that has generated much media attention along with mistaken, gender-stereotyped interpretations of their "choice" (see the Social Issues box on the following page).

Ethnic minority women, such as this scientist, must surmount combined gender and racial discrimination to realize their career potential. Those who succeed often display an unusually high sense of self-efficacy.

SOCIAL ISSUES

Women in "Fast-Track" Careers Who Opt to Stay Home

Although the vast majority are employed, women with professional degrees opt out of the labor force at three to four times the rate of similarly accomplished men. In one national survey, ten years after graduation, 12 percent of women but only 4 percent of men in the field of law were not working. The figures for MDs were 11 versus 3 percent, for MBAs 8 versus 2 percent (Baker, 2002). Women often said they left their careers to attend to family responsibilities.

The apparent contradiction between these women's achievements and their decision to stay home has made them the focus of a growing number of newspaper and magazine features and on-air programs. Often their transformation into full-time mothers is interpreted in gender-stereotyped terms, as the exercise of a personal preference for a traditional role. In fact, it is almost always an agonizing decision—the outcome of multiple constraints in their lives.

In-depth interviews with 43 women—all of whom had left prestigious, well-paid careers after being employed for an average of 13 years to focus full-time on their families—revealed that over 90 percent were ambivalent about quitting (Stone & Lovejoy, 2004). Giving up a solid career identity, pride in accomplishment, and the intrinsic pleasure they derived from work was a painful, protracted process.

Two-thirds of the women had excelled in male-dominated professions such as law, business, medicine, or the sciences. Others had high-powered careers in publishing, marketing, banking, or health. Even though they were professionally and financially successful, a mix of work-, spouse-, and child-related factors led them to hand in their resignations.

Work

For 86 percent, work environments were the most significant reason for leaving. Many, with work weeks of 60 hours or more, had faced extreme time pressures even before they had children. And economic restructuring of their industries—mergers, takeovers, and expansions—often disrupted their existing work–family equilibrium. One former company executive commented after a merger: "I had to travel before, but this was just on a scale like [gesturing with her hands and making sounds to indicate a nuclear explosion]" (p. 71).

More than one-third, citing pervasive workplace inflexibility, characterized their jobs as "all or nothing." Requests to cut back to part-time were often denied. Of those who arranged part-time work, most ended up with part-time positions in name only: Their actual hours expanded. In workplaces where part-time employment was rare, women reported being labeled as on the "mommy track," losing interesting responsibilities, and watching their chances for promotion evaporate. They wondered, "Is this worth it?" and ultimately concluded, "No."

Women in fast-track careers may opt out of the labor force because their workplace thwarts their efforts to balance work with family. Requests to work part-time or spend some days working from home are often denied.

Spouses and Children

Because most participants were married to men in "high-octane" careers like their own, their husbands were usually minimally involved in child care and housework. But despite their own success, few entertained the possibility that their husbands would agree to cut back. Rather, these women implicitly assumed that when the pressures of the dual-earner lifestyle became excessive, they would need to sacrifice. Their husbands, while usually stating, "It's your choice," concurred.

Almost all the women had the financial means to hire in-home help. Yet having worked for a decade or more and (in many instances) postponed childbearing, they felt uncomfortable, sometimes anguished, about being away from their children. Several who had become first-time mothers in their early forties felt a strong desire to experience motherhood because they did not expect to have more children. Others wanted to be available to support their school-age children's increasingly complex lives—homework, lessons, sports, and other activities—or simply worried about "missing out." But though the pull of family was intense, for most, work-related issues cemented their decision.

Other investigations confirm that few professionally successful women freely chose to step off the career track (Rubin & Wooten, 2007). Rather, their highly demanding, inflexible workplaces thwart their efforts to balance work and family.

In addition, low self-efficacy with respect to male-dominated fields limits women's career progress. Women who pursue nontraditional careers usually have "masculine" traits—high achievement orientation, self-reliance, and belief that their efforts will result in success. But even those with high self-efficacy are less certain than their male counterparts that they can overcome barriers to career success (Lindley, 2005). In a study of women scientists on university faculties, those reporting a sexist work climate (sexual harassment or discrimination in salary, promotion, or resources) were less satisfied with their jobs and less productive (Settles et al., 2006). Gender-stereotyped images of women as followers rather than leaders slow advancement into top-level management positions. And because men dominate high-status fields, fewer women are available to serve as mentors (Stewart & Lavaque-Manty, 2008). Although amount of mentor support is similar in same-sex and other-sex mentoring relationships, women with female mentors tend to be more productive (O'Neill, Horton, & Crosby, 1999). Perhaps female mentors are more likely to be perceived as role models and to provide guidance on the unique problems women encounter in the workplace.

Despite laws guaranteeing equal opportunity, racial bias in the labor market remains strong. In one study, researchers responded to more than 1,300 help-wanted newspaper ads with fictitious résumés, some containing higher qualifications and some lower qualifications. Half the résumés were assigned a white-sounding name (Emily Walsh, Brendan Baker) and half a black-sounding name (Lakisha Washington, Jamal Jones). At all job levels, from clerical work to top management, résumés with "white" names evoked 50 percent more callbacks than résumés with "black" names. And although whites received substantially more callbacks in response to high-quality than to low-quality résumés, having a high-quality résumé made little difference for blacks (see Figure 14.5). As the researchers noted, "Discrimination appears to bite twice, making it harder for African Americans to find a job and to improve their employability" (Bertrand & Mullainathan, 2004, p. 3). Consistent with this conclusion, African Americans spend more time searching for work, experience less stable employment, and acquire less work experience than Caucasian Americans with equivalent job qualifications (Pager & Shepherd, 2008).

Ethnic minority women must surmount combined gender and racial discrimination to realize their career potential. Those who succeed often display an unusually high sense of self-efficacy, attacking problems head-on despite repeated obstacles to achievement (Byars & Hackett, 1998). In an interview study of African-American women who had become leaders in diverse fields, all reported intense persistence, fueled by supportive relationships with other women, including teachers, colleagues, and friends who countered their sense of professional isolation. Many described their mothers as inspiring role models who had set high standards for them. Others felt empowered by a deep sense of connection to their African-American communities (Richie et al., 1997).

Despite obstacles to success, young and middle-aged women who have developed rewarding careers generally report higher levels of psychological well-being and life satisfaction (Burke, 2001). This finding suggests that some of the discontent frequently expressed by married women may not be due to marriage per se but, rather, to lack of a gratifying work life. Consistent with this idea, most women prefer to blend work and family (Barnett & Hyde, 2001). And those in financially stressed families must do so.

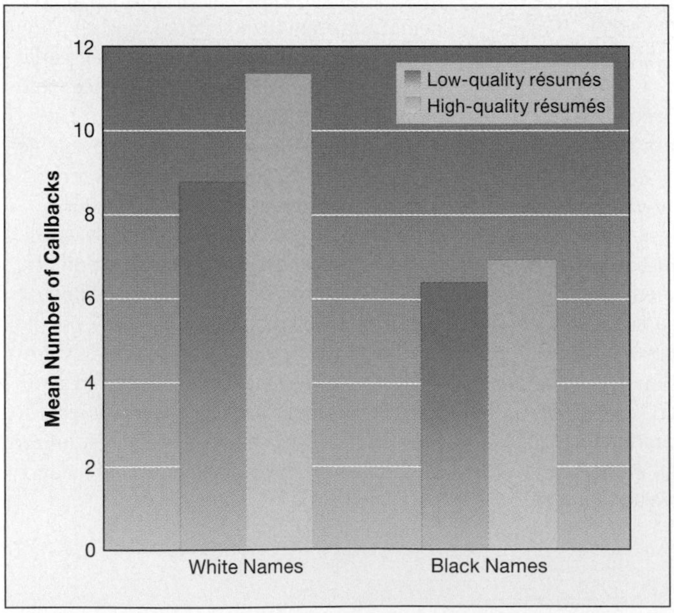

■ **FIGURE 14.5** ■ **Relationship of ethnicity of job applicant's name to employer callbacks.** Researchers responded to help-wanted newspaper ads with fictitious résumés, some having white-sounding names and others black-sounding names. Résumés with "white" names evoked many more callbacks than résumés with "black" names. When résumés were high in quality, callbacks to whites increased, but those to blacks showed little change. (Adapted from Bertrand & Mullainathan, 2004.)

Combining Work and Family

Whether women work because they want to or have to (or both), the dominant family form today is the dual-earner marriage. Most dual-earner couples are also parents, since the majority of women with children are in the work force (see page 350 in Chapter 10). But many more women than men experience moderate to high levels of stress in trying to meet both work and family responsibilities (Cinamon & Rich, 2002).

TAKE A MOMENT... Think about a dual-earner family you know well. What are the main sources of strain? When Sharese returned to her job after her children were born, she felt a sense of *role overload,* or conflict between work and family responsibilities. In addition to a demanding career, she also (like most employed women) shouldered most of the household and child-care tasks. And both Sharese and Ernie felt torn between the desire to excel at their jobs and the desire to spend more time with each other, their children, and their friends and relatives. Role overload is linked to increased psychological stress, poorer marital relations, less effective parenting, and child behavior problems (Perry-Jenkins, Repetti, & Crouter, 2000; Saginak & Saginak, 2005).

Role overload is greater for women than for men, especially for women in low-status work roles with rigid schedules and little autonomy (Marshall, 1997). Couples in prestigious careers have more control over both work and family domains. For example, Sharese and Ernie devised ways to spend more time with their children. They picked them up at child care early one day a week, compensating by doing certain occupational tasks on evenings and weekends. Like other career-oriented mothers, Sharese eased role pressures by setting priorities: She decreased the amount of time she spent on household chores, not child rearing (Institute for Social Research, 2002).

As Sharese and Ernie's strategies indicate, workplace supports can greatly reduce role overload, yielding substantial payoffs for employers. Among a large, nationally representative sample of U.S. working adults, the greater the number of time-flexible policies available in their work settings (for example,

Applying What We Know

Strategies That Help Dual-Earner Couples Combine Work and Family Roles

Strategy	Description
Devise a plan for sharing household tasks.	As soon as possible in the relationship, discuss relative commitment to work and family and division of household responsibilities. Decide who does a particular chore on the basis of who has the needed skill and time, not on the basis of gender. Schedule regular times to rediscuss your plan.
Begin sharing child care right after the baby's arrival.	For fathers, strive to spend equal time with the baby early. For mothers, refrain from imposing your standards on your partner. Instead, share the role of "child-rearing expert" by discussing parenting values and concerns often. Attend a parent education course together.
Talk over conflicts about decision making and responsibilities.	Face conflict through communication. Clarify your feelings and needs and express them to your partner. Listen and try to understand your partner's point of view. Then be willing to negotiate and compromise.
Establish a balance between work and family.	Critically evaluate the time you devote to work in view of your values and priorities. If it is too much, cut back.
Make sure your relationship receives regular loving care.	See Applying What We Know on page 474.
Press for workplace and public policies that assist dual-earner-family roles.	Difficulties faced by dual-earner couples are partly due to lack of workplace and societal supports. Encourage your employer to provide benefits that help combine work and family, such as flexible work hours, parental leave with pay, and on-site high-quality, affordable child care. Communicate with lawmakers and other citizens about improving public policies for children and families.

time off to care for a sick child, choice in start and stop times, and opportunities to work from home), the better their work performance (Halpern, 2005a). Employees with several time-flexible options missed fewer days of work, less often arrived at work late or left early, felt more committed to their employer, and worked harder. They also reported fewer stress-related health symptoms.

Effectively balancing work and family brings many benefits—a better standard of living, improved work productivity, enhanced psychological well-being, greater self-fulfillment, and happier marriages. Ernie took great pride in Sharese's career accomplishments, which contributed to his view of her as an interesting, capable helpmate. Multiple roles also granted both young people expanded contexts for experiencing success and greater similarity in everyday experiences, which fostered gratifying communication (Barnett & Hyde, 2001). Applying What We Know above lists strategies that help dual-earner couples combine work and family roles in ways that promote mastery and pleasure in both spheres of life.

Dual-earner couples can better balance work and family if they share both the pleasures and the burdens of child rearing.

ASK YOURSELF

REVIEW
Why do professionally accomplished women, especially those who are members of economically disadvantaged minorities, typically display high self-efficacy?

APPLY
Heather climbed the career ladder of her company quickly, reaching a top-level executive position by her early thirties. In contrast, Sharese and Christy did not attain managerial roles in early adulthood. What factors might account for this disparity in career progress?

CONNECT
Work and family life are inseparably intertwined. Explain how this is so in early adulthood.

REFLECT
Contact a major employer in your area and ask about its policies for helping employees combine work and family roles. What improvements would you suggest? Why are family-friendly policies "win-win" situations for both workers and employers?

Summary

A Gradual Transition: Emerging Adulthood

What is emerging adulthood, and how has cultural change contributed to it?

» In **emerging adulthood,** young adults from about age 18 to 25 have not yet taken on adult roles. During these years, they prolong identity development as they explore alternatives in breadth and depth.

© JIM WEST/THE IMAGE WORKS

» Increased education required for entry-level positions in many fields, gains in economic prosperity, reduced need for young people's labor, and globalization have prompted the appearance and spread of emerging adulthood.

» In trying out possibilities, emerging adults must adjust to disappointments in love and work, and their explorations also extend risky behaviors of adolescence. A wide array of personal attributes and social supports foster resilience.

Erikson's Theory: Intimacy versus Isolation

According to Erikson, what personality changes take place during early adulthood?

» In Erikson's theory, young adults must resolve the conflict of **intimacy versus isolation** as they form a close relationship with a partner. The negative outcome is loneliness and self-absorption.

» Young people also focus on aspects of generativity, including parenting and contributions to society through work.

Other Theories of Adult Psychosocial Development

Describe and evaluate Levinson's and Vaillant's psychosocial theories of adult personality development.

» Levinson described a series of eras, each consisting of a transition and a stable phase, in which people revise their **life structure.** Young adults usually construct a dream, typically involving career for men and both marriage and career for women, and form a relationship with a mentor to help them realize their dream. In their thirties, men tend to settle down, whereas many women remain unsettled into middle adulthood.

» Vaillant refined Erikson's stages, portraying the twenties as devoted to intimacy, the thirties to career consolidation, the forties to generativity, and the fifties and sixties to cultural values.

» The patterns Levinson and Vaillant identified are based on limited samples of people born in the first few decades of the twentieth century. Young adults' development is more variable today than in past generations.

What is the social clock, and how does it affect personality in adulthood?

» Conformity to or departure from the **social clock**—age-graded expectations for major life events—can be a major source of personality change in adulthood. Following a social clock grants confidence to young adults; deviating from it can bring psychological distress.

Close Relationships

Describe factors affecting mate selection and the role of romantic love in the young adult's quest for intimacy.

» Establishing an intimate bond is a major milestone of adult development. Romantic partners tend to resemble one another in age, ethnicity, SES, religion, and various personal and physical attributes.

» According to evolutionary theory, women seek a mate with traits that help ensure children's survival, while men look for characteristics signaling sexual pleasure and ability to bear offspring. An alternative, social learning perspective emphasizes that gender roles profoundly influence criteria for mate selection. Research suggests that both biological and social forces are involved.

© EXOTIC EYE/ALAMY

» According to the **triangular theory of love,** the balance among intimacy, passion, and commitment changes as romantic relationships move from the intense sexual attraction of **passionate love** toward more settled **companionate love.** Commitment is key to a satisfying, enduring relationship. The Western emphasis on romantic love in mate selection does not characterize all cultures.

Describe adult friendships and sibling relationships, and the role of loneliness in adult development.

» Adult friendships have characteristics and benefits similar to earlier friendships and are based on trust, intimacy, and loyalty. Women's same-sex friendships tend to be more intimate than men's. After college, other-sex friendships decline with age for men but increase for highly educated, employed women, who tend to form them in the workplace. Adult sibling relationships often resemble friendships, especially among sisters with positive early experiences.

» Young adults are vulnerable to **loneliness,** which declines with age as they form satisfying intimate ties. As long as it is not too intense, loneliness can encourage young people to reach out to others and better understand themselves.

The Family Life Cycle

Trace phases of the family life cycle that are prominent in early adulthood, and cite factors that influence these phases today.

» Wide variations exist in the sequence and timing of phases of the **family life cycle.** Leaving home is a major step in assuming adult responsibilities. Departures for education occur earlier than those for full-time work and marriage. SES and ethnicity influence the likelihood that a young person will live independently before marriage. Many unmarried young adults return home for a period of time.

» Nearly 90 percent of Americans marry, at later ages than in the past. Today, couples must work harder to define their marital roles. Both **traditional marriages** and **egalitarian marriages** are affected by women's participation in the work force. Even in dual-earner marriages, North American women spend nearly twice as much time as men on housework.

» Quality of the marital relationship predicts mental health similarly for both men and women. Women, however, feel particularly dissatisfied when the combined demands of work and family roles are overwhelming. Many young people enter marriage with unrealistic expectations.

» Effective birth control techniques and changing cultural values make parenthood a matter of choice in Western industrialized nations. Although most couples become parents, they do so at a later age and have fewer children than in the past.

» The arrival of a child requires couples to adjust to increased responsibilities and often prompts a shift to more traditional roles, though this may reverse after the birth of a second child. Marriages that are gratifying and supportive tend to remain so after childbirth, but troubled marriages usually become more distressed. Shared caregiving predicts greater parental happiness and positive parent–infant interaction.

© MICHAEL NEWMAN/PHOTOEDIT

» Families with young children face challenges of clarifying and implementing child-rearing values. Couples who work together as a coparenting team are more likely to gain in warm marital interaction, feel competent as parents, use effective child-rearing practices, and have children who are developing well.

» In families with adolescents, parents must establish new relationships with their increasingly autonomous teenagers, blending guidance with freedom and gradually loosening control. Marital satisfaction often declines in this phase.

» Parent education programs can help parents clarify their child-rearing values and use more effective strategies.

The Diversity of Adult Lifestyles

Discuss the diversity of adult lifestyles, focusing on singlehood, cohabitation, and childlessness.

» Singlehood has risen in recent years because of a trend toward later marriage and a high divorce rate. Despite certain drawbacks, singles appreciate their freedom and mobility. Women tend to adjust more favorably than men.

» **Cohabitation** has risen dramatically, especially among well-educated, economically advantaged young adults, for whom it is the preferred mode of entry into a committed intimate partnership. Cohabitation rates are especially high among separated and divorced adults. Compared with their Western European counterparts, American cohabiters tend to be less conventional in values and behavior and less committed to their partner, and their subsequent marriages are more likely to fail. However, gay and lesbian couples who cohabit because they cannot marry report commitment equal to that of married couples.

» Voluntarily childless adults tend to be well-educated and career-oriented and are as satisfied with their lives as parents who have good relationships with their children. But when childlessness is beyond a person's control, it interferes with adjustment and life satisfaction.

Discuss today's high rates of divorce and remarriage, and cite factors that contribute to them.

» Nearly half of U.S. marriages dissolve, often while children are at home. About two-thirds of divorced people remarry, and many divorce again. Maladaptive communication patterns, younger ages at marriage, a family history of divorce, poverty, and the changing status of women all contribute to divorce.

» Finding a new partner is important to many divorced adults, especially men. Remarriages break up for several reasons, including the prominence of practical concerns rather than love in the decision to remarry, the persistence of negative styles of communication, the acceptance of divorce as a solution to marital difficulties, and problems adjusting to a stepfamily.

Discuss the challenges associated with variant styles of parenthood, including stepparents, never-married parents, and gay and lesbian parents.

» Establishing stepparent–stepchild ties is difficult, especially for stepmothers and for stepfathers without children of their own. A caring husband–wife relationship, cooperation from the biological parent, and children's acceptance are crucial for stepparent adjustment.

» Never-married single parenthood is especially high among low-income African-American women in their twenties. Unemployment among black men contributes to this trend. Although these mothers often receive help from extended family members, they find it difficult to overcome poverty.

» Gay and lesbian parents are as committed to and effective at child rearing as heterosexual parents, and their children are as well-adjusted as those reared by heterosexual parents.

Career Development

Discuss patterns of career development, and cite difficulties faced by women, ethnic minorities, and couples seeking to combine work and family.

» Men's career paths are usually continuous, whereas women's are often discontinuous because of child rearing and other family needs. After adjusting to the realities of the work world, young adults settle into an occupation. Their progress is affected by opportunities for promotion, personal characteristics such as self-efficacy, and access to an effective mentor.

» Women and ethnic minorities have penetrated nearly all professions but have made limited progress in career advancement. Women are hampered by time away from the labor market, low self-efficacy and lack of mentoring in traditionally male-dominated fields, and gender stereotypes of women as followers rather than leaders. Racial bias in the labor market remains strong, and ethnic minority women who succeed display an unusually high sense of self-efficacy.

© NOEL HENDRICKSON/GETTY IMAGES/DIGITAL VISION

» Couples, particularly women, in dual-earner marriages often experience role overload. Effectively balancing work and family brings a better standard of living, enhanced psychological well-being, and happier marriages. Time-flexible workplace policies reduce stress while augmenting work performance.

Important Terms and Concepts

cohabitation (p. 487)
companionate love (p. 474)
egalitarian marriage (p. 479)
emerging adulthood (p. 464)
family life cycle (p. 478)
intimacy versus isolation (p. 468)
life structure (p. 469)
loneliness (p. 476)
passionate love (p. 474)
social clock (p. 471)
traditional marriage (p. 479)
triangular theory of love (p. 472)

Milestones

Development in Early Adulthood

18–30 years

PHYSICAL

- Athletic skills that require speed of limb movement, explosive strength, and gross motor coordination peak early in this decade, then decline. (436)
- Athletic skills that depend on endurance, arm–hand steadiness, and aiming peak at the end of this decade, then decline. (436)
- Declines in touch sensitivity, cardiovascular and respiratory capacity, immune system functioning, and skin elasticity begin and continue throughout adulthood. (435)
- As basal metabolic rate declines, gradual weight gain begins in the middle of this decade and continues through middle adulthood. (439–440)
- Sexual activity increases. (445–447)

COGNITIVE

- If college educated, dualistic thinking declines in favor of relativistic thinking. (452)

- Moves from hypothetical to pragmatic thought. (452)
- Narrows vocational options and settles on a specific career. (456)
- Shows gains in cognitive–affective complexity, which continue through middle adulthood. (453)
- Develops expertise in a field of endeavor, which enhances problem solving. (453)

- May increase in creativity. (453–454)

EMOTIONAL/SOCIAL

- In the first half of this decade, if life circumstances permit, may engage in the extended exploration that characterizes emerging adulthood. (464–465)
- Feels increasingly in control of life events. (464)
- Is likely to achieve a personally meaningful identity. (465)
- Leaves the parental home permanently. (478)

- Strives to make a permanent commitment to an intimate partner. (468–469, 472)
- Usually constructs a dream—an image of the self in the adult world that guides decision making. (470)

Note: Numbers in parentheses indicate the page or pages on which each milestone is discussed.

- Typically forms a relationship with a mentor. (470)
- If in a high-status career, acquires professional skills, values, and credentials. (470)
- Begins to develop mutually gratifying adult friendships and work ties. (475–476)
- May cohabit, marry, and bear children. (478–479, 481–484)

- Sibling relationships become more companionate. (476)
- Loneliness peaks early in this decade, then declines steadily throughout adulthood. (477)

30–40 years

PHYSICAL

- Declines in vision, hearing, and the skeletal system begin and continue throughout adulthood. (435)
- In women, reproductive capacity continues to decline, and fertility problems increase sharply after the middle of this decade. (437)

- In men, semen volume, sperm motility, and percentage of normal sperm decrease gradually in the second half of this decade. (438)
- Hair begins to gray and thin in the middle of this decade. (435)
- Sexual activity declines, probably as a result of the demands of daily life. (446)

COGNITIVE

- May develop commitment within relativistic thinking. (452)
- Creative accomplishment often peaks in the second half of this decade, although this varies across disciplines. (453–454)

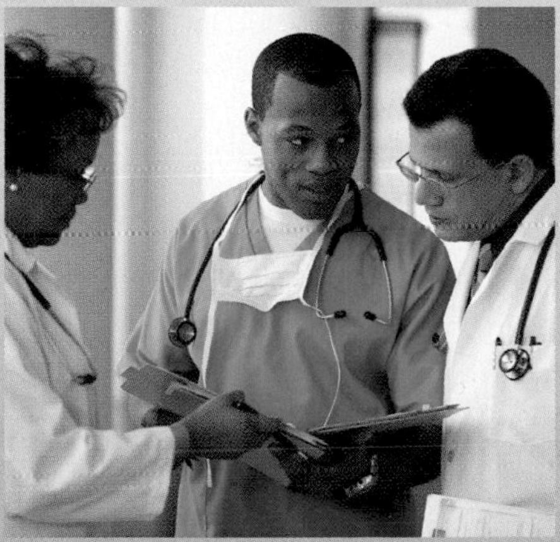

EMOTIONAL/SOCIAL

- Reevaluates life structure and tries to change components that are inadequate. (469–470)
- Establishes a stable niche in society through family, occupation, and community activities. (For women, career maturity and authority in the community may be delayed.) (470)

In middle adulthood, expertise—accumulated knowledge that supports high-level performance in vocational or leisure pursuits—reaches its height. As this master calligrapher shares his expertise with a young student, he transfers knowledge, skill, and passion for the art to a new generation.

CHAPTER 15

Physical and Cognitive Development in Middle Adulthood

On a snowy December evening, Devin and Trisha sat down to read the holiday cards piled high on the kitchen counter. Devin's 55th birthday had just passed; Trisha would turn 48 in a few weeks. During the past year, they had celebrated their 24th wedding anniversary. These milestones, along with the annual updates they received from friends, brought the changes of midlife into bold relief.

Instead of new births, children starting school, or a first promotion at work, holiday cards and letters sounded new themes. Jewel's recap of the past year reflected a growing awareness of a finite lifespan, one in which time had become more precious. She wrote:

> My mood has been lighter ever since my birthday. There was some burden I laid down by turning 49. My mother passed away when she was 48, so it all feels like a gift now. Blessed be!

George and Anya reported on their son's graduation from law school and their daughter Michelle's first year of university:

> Anya is filling the gap created by the children's departure by returning to college for a nursing degree. After enrolling this fall, she was surprised to find herself in the same psychology class as Michelle. At first, Anya worried about handling the academic work, but after a semester of success, she's feeling more confident.

Tim's message reflected continuing robust health, acceptance of physical changes, and a new burden: caring for aging parents—a firm reminder of the limits of the lifespan:

> I used to be a good basketball player in college, but recently I noticed that my 20-year-old nephew, Brent, can dribble and shoot circles around me. It must be my age! But I ran our city marathon in September and came in seventh in the over-50 division. Brent ran, too, but he opted out a few miles short of the finish line to get some pizza while I pressed on. That must be my age, too!

The saddest news is that my dad had a bad stroke. His mind is clear, but his body is partially paralyzed. It's really upsetting because he was getting to enjoy the computer I gave him, and it was so upbeat to talk with him about it in the months before the stroke.

Middle adulthood, which begins around age 40 and ends at about 65, is marked by narrowing life options and a shrinking future as children leave home and career paths become more determined. In other ways, middle age is hard to define because wide variations in attitudes and behaviors exist. Some individuals seem physically and mentally young at age 65—active and optimistic, with a sense of serenity and stability. Others feel old at age 40—as if their lives had peaked and were on a downhill course.

Another reason middle adulthood eludes definition is that it is a contemporary phenomenon. Before the twentieth century, only a brief interval separated the tasks of early adulthood from those of old age. Women were often widows by their mid-fifties, before their youngest child left home. And harsh living conditions led people to accept a ravaged body as a natural part of life. As life expectancy—and, with it, health and vigor—increased over the past century, adults became more aware of their own aging and mortality.

In this chapter, we trace physical and cognitive development from the fifth into the seventh decade of life. In both domains, we will encounter not just progressive declines but also sustained performance and compensating gains. As in earlier chapters, we will see that change occurs in manifold ways. Besides heredity and biological aging, our personal approach to passing years combines with family, community, and cultural contexts to affect the way we age.

Physical Development

Physical development in midlife is a continuation of the gradual changes under way in early adulthood. Even the most vigorous adults notice an older body when looking in the mirror or at family photos. Hair grays and thins, new lines appear on the face, and a fuller, less youthful body shape is evident. During midlife, most individuals begin to experience life-threatening health episodes—if not in themselves, then in their partners and friends. And a change in time orientation, from "years since birth" to "years left to live," adds to consciousness of aging (Neugarten, 1968b).

These factors lead to a revised physical self-image, with somewhat less emphasis on hoped-for gains and more on feared declines (Bybee & Wells, 2003). Prominent concerns among 40- to 65-year-olds include getting a fatal disease, being too ill to maintain independence, and losing mental capacities. Unfortunately, many middle-aged adults fail to embrace realistic alternatives—becoming more physically fit and developing into healthy, energetic older adults. Although certain aspects of aging cannot be controlled, people can do much to promote physical vigor and good health in midlife.

Physical Changes

As she dressed for work one morning, Trisha remarked jokingly to Devin, "I think I'll leave the dust on the mirror so I can't see the wrinkles and gray hairs." Catching sight of her image, she continued in a more serious tone. "And look at this fat—it just doesn't want to go! I need to figure out how to fit some regular exercise into my life." In response, Devin glanced down soberly at his own enlarged midriff.

At breakfast, Devin took his glasses on and off and squinted while reading the paper. "Trish—what's the eye doctor's phone number? I've gotta get these bifocals adjusted again." As they conversed between the kitchen and the adjoining den, Devin sometimes asked Trisha to repeat herself. And he kept turning up the radio and TV volume. "Does it need to be that loud?" Trisha frequently asked. Apparently Devin couldn't hear as clearly as before.

In the following sections, we look closely at the major physical changes of midlife. As we do so, you may find it helpful to refer back to Table 13.1 on page 435, which provides a summary.

Vision

By the forties, difficulty reading small print is common, due to thickening of the lens combined with weakening of the muscle that enables the eye to *accommodate* (adjust its focus) to nearby objects. As new fibers appear on the surface of the lens, they compress older fibers toward the center, creating a thicker, denser, less pliable structure that eventually cannot be transformed at all. By age 50, the accommodative ability of the lens is one-sixth of what it was at age 20. Around age 60, the lens loses its capacity to adjust to objects at varying distances entirely, a condition called **presbyopia** (literally, "old eyes"). As the lens enlarges, the eye rapidly becomes more farsighted between ages 40 and 60 (Charman, 2008). Corrective lenses—or, for nearsighted people, bifocals—ease reading problems.

A second set of changes limits ability to see in dim light, which declines at twice the rate of daylight vision (Jackson & Owsley, 2000). Throughout adulthood, the size of the pupil shrinks and the lens yellows. In addition, starting at age 40, the *vitreous* (transparent gelatin-like substance that fills the eye) develops opaque areas, reducing the amount of light reaching the retina. Changes in the lens and vitreous also cause light to scatter within the eye, increasing sensitivity to glare. Devin had always enjoyed driving at night, but now he sometimes had trouble making out signs and moving objects. And his vision was more disrupted by bright light sources, such as headlights of oncoming cars (Owsley et al., 1998). Yellowing of the lens and increasing density of the vitreous also limit color discrimination, especially at the green–blue–violet end of the spectrum (Kraft & Werner, 1999). Occasionally, Devin had to ask whether his sport coat, tie, and socks matched.

Besides structural changes in the eye, neural changes in the visual system occur. Gradual loss of rods and cones (light- and color-receptor cells) in the retina and of neurons in the optic nerve (the pathway between the retina and the cerebral cortex) contributes to visual declines. By midlife, half the *rods* (which enable vision in dim light) are lost. And because rods secrete substances necessary for survival of *cones* (which enable daylight and color vision), gradual loss of cones follows (Bonnel, Mohand-Said, & Sahel, 2003).

Middle-aged adults are at increased risk of **glaucoma,** a disease in which poor fluid drainage leads to a buildup of pressure within the eye, damaging the optic nerve. Glaucoma affects nearly 2 percent of people over age 40, more often women than men. It typically progresses without noticeable symptoms and is a leading cause of blindness. Glaucoma runs in families: Siblings of people with glaucoma have a tenfold increased risk, and the disease occurs three to four times as often in African Americans and Hispanics as in Caucasians (Friedman, 2006; Kwon et al., 2009). Starting in midlife, eye exams should include a glaucoma test. Drugs that promote release of fluid and surgery to open blocked drainage channels prevent vision loss.

Hearing

An estimated 14 percent of Americans between ages 45 and 64 suffer from hearing loss, often resulting from adult-onset hearing impairments. Although some conditions run in families and may be hereditary, most are age-related, a condition called **presbycusis** ("old hearing") (Gratton & Vásquez, 2003).

As we age, inner-ear structures that transform mechanical sound waves into neural impulses deteriorate through natural cell death or reduced blood supply caused by atherosclerosis. Processing of neural messages in the auditory cortex also declines. The first sign, at around age 50, is a noticeable hearing loss at high frequencies, which gradually extends to all frequencies. Late in life, human speech becomes more difficult to make out (Liu & Yan, 2007). Still, throughout middle adulthood, most people hear reasonably well across a wide frequency range. And African tribal peoples display little age-related hearing loss (Jarvis & van Heerden, 1967; Rosen, Bergman, & Plester, 1962). These findings suggest factors other than biological aging are involved.

Men's hearing declines earlier and more rapidly than women's, a difference associated with cigarette smoking, intense noise and chemical pollutants in some male-dominated occupations, and (at older ages) high blood pressure and cerebrovascular disease, or strokes that damage brain tissue (Heltzner et al., 2005; Van Eyken, Van Camp, & Van Laer, 2007). Government regulations requiring industries to implement such safeguards as noise monitoring, provision of earplugs, pollution control, and regular hearing tests have greatly reduced hearing damage, but some employers do not comply fully (Daniell et al., 2006; Ohlemiller, 2008).

© MICHAEL J. DOOLITTLE/THE IMAGE WORKS

Welders prepare a drill bit to penetrate bedrock. Men's hearing declines more rapidly than women's, a difference associated with several factors, including intense noise in some male-dominated occupations.

Most middle-aged and elderly people with hearing difficulties benefit from sound amplification with hearing aids. When perception of the human voice is affected, speaking to the person patiently, clearly, and with good eye contact aids understanding.

Skin

Our skin consists of three layers: (1) the *epidermis,* or outer protective layer, where new skin cells are constantly produced; (2) the *dermis,* or middle supportive layer, consisting of connective tissue that stretches and bounces back, giving the skin flexibility; and (3) the *hypodermis,* an inner fatty layer that adds to the soft lines and shape of the skin. As we age, the epidermis becomes less firmly attached to the dermis, fibers in the dermis thin, cells in both the epidermis and dermis decline in water content, and fat in the hypodermis diminishes, leading the skin to wrinkle, loosen, and feel dry.

In the thirties, lines develop on the forehead as a result of smiling, furrowing the brow, and other facial expressions. In the forties, these become more pronounced, and "crow's-feet" appear around the eyes. Gradually, the skin loses elasticity and begins to sag, especially on the face, arms, and legs. After age 50, "age spots," collections of pigment under the skin, increase. Blood vessels in the skin become more visible as the fatty layer thins.

Because sun exposure hastens wrinkling and spotting, individuals who have spent much time outdoors without proper skin protection look older than their contemporaries (Landau, 2007). And partly because the dermis of women is not as thick as that of men, women's skin ages more quickly (Makrantonaki & Xouboulis, 2007).

Muscle–Fat Makeup

As Trisha and Devin make clear, weight gain—"middle-age spread"—is a concern for both men and women. A common pattern of change is an increase in body fat and a loss of lean body mass (muscle and bone). The rise in fat largely affects the torso and occurs as fatty deposits within the body cavity; as noted earlier, fat beneath the skin on the limbs declines. On average, the size of the abdomen increases 6 to 16 percent in men, 25 to 35 percent in women from early through middle adulthood (Whitbourne, 1996). Sex differences in fat distribution also appear. Men accumulate more on the back and upper abdomen, women around the waist and upper arms (Sowers et al., 2007). Muscle mass declines very gradually in the forties and fifties, largely due to atrophy of fast-twitch fibers, responsible for speed and explosive strength.

Yet, as indicated in Chapter 13, large weight gain and loss of muscle power are not inevitable. With age, people must gradually reduce caloric intake to adjust for the age-related decline in basal metabolic rate (see page 440). In a longitudinal study of nearly 30,000 U.S. 50- to 79-year-old women diverse in SES and ethnicity, a low-fat diet involving increased consumption of vegetables, fruits, and grains was associated with greater initial weight loss and success at maintaining that loss over a seven-year period (Howard et al., 2006). In nonhuman animals, dietary restraint dramatically increases longevity while sustaining health and vitality. Currently, researchers are identifying the biological mechanisms involved and studying their relevance to humans (see the Biology and Environment box on the following page).

Furthermore, weight-bearing exercise that includes resistance training (a strength-training routine that places a moderately stressful load on the muscles) offsets both excess weight and muscle loss. Within the same individual, strength varies between often-used and little-used muscles (Macaluso & De Vito, 2004; Rivlin, 2007). Consider Devin's 57-year-old friend Tim, who for years has ridden his bike to and from work and jogged on weekends, averaging an hour of vigorous activity per day. Like many endurance athletes, he maintained the same weight and muscular physique throughout early and middle adulthood.

Skeleton

As new cells accumulate on their outer layers, the bones broaden, but their mineral content declines, so they become more porous. This leads to a gradual loss in bone density that begins in the late thirties and accelerates in the fifties, especially among women (Chan & Duque, 2002). Women's reserve of bone minerals is lower than men's to begin with. And following menopause, the favorable impact of estrogen on bone mineral absorption is lost. Reduction in bone density during adulthood is substantial—about 8 to 12 percent in men and 20 to 30 percent in women (Seeman, 2002, 2008).

Loss of bone strength causes the disks in the spinal column to collapse. Consequently, height may drop by as much as 1 inch by age 60, a change that will hasten thereafter. In addition, the weakened bones cannot support as much load: They fracture more easily and heal more slowly. A healthy lifestyle—including weight-bearing exercise, adequate calcium and vitamin D intake, and avoidance of smoking and heavy alcohol consumption—can slow bone loss in postmenopausal women by as much as 30 to 50 percent (Borer, 2005; Cooper et al., 2009).

When bone loss is very great, it leads to a debilitating disorder called *osteoporosis.* We will take up this condition shortly when we consider illness and disability.

Reproductive System

The midlife transition in which fertility declines is called the **climacteric.** In women, it brings an end to reproductive capacity; in men, by contrast, fertility diminishes but is retained.

REPRODUCTIVE CHANGES IN WOMEN. The changes involved in women's climacteric occur gradually over a 10-year period, during which the production of estrogen drops. As a result, the number of days in a woman's monthly cycle shortens from about 28 in her twenties and thirties to perhaps 23 by her late forties, and her cycles become more irregular. In some, ova are not released; when they are, more are defective (see Chapter 2, page 54). The climacteric concludes with **menopause,** the end of menstruation and reproductive capacity. This occurs, on average, in the early fifties among North American, European, and East Asian women, although the age range extends from the late thirties to the late fifties. Women who smoke or who have not borne children tend to reach menopause earlier (Avis, Crawford, & Johannes, 2002; Rossi, 2005).

Following menopause, estrogen declines further, causing the reproductive organs to shrink in size, the genitals to be less easily stimulated, and the vagina to lubricate more slowly during arousal. As a result, complaints about sexual functioning increase, with about 35 to 40 percent of women reporting difficulties, especially among those with health problems or whose partners have sexual performance difficulties (Lindau et al., 2007; Walsh & Berman, 2004). The drop in estrogen also contributes to decreased elasticity of the skin and loss of bone mass. Also lost is estrogen's ability to help protect against accumulation of plaque on the walls of the arteries, by boosting "good cholesterol" (high-density lipoprotein).

The period leading up to and following menopause is often accompanied by emotional and physical symptoms, including mood fluctuations and *hot flashes*—sensations of

BIOLOGY AND ENVIRONMENT

Anti-Aging Effects of Dietary Calorie Restriction

For nearly 70 years, scientists have known that dietary calorie restriction in nonhuman animals slows aging while maintaining good health and body functions. Rats and mice fed 30 to 40 percent fewer calories than they would freely eat beginning in early life show various physiological health benefits, lower incidence of chronic diseases, and a 60 percent increase in length of life (Fontana, 2009). Mild to moderate calorie restriction begun after rodents reach physical maturity also slows aging and extends longevity, though to a lesser extent. Other studies reveal similar dietary-restriction effects in mice, fleas, spiders, worms, fish, and yeast.

Primate Research

Would primates, especially humans, also benefit from a restricted diet? Researchers are tracking health indicators in rhesus monkeys and squirrel monkeys ranging from 1 to 20 years of age, after placing some on regimens of 30 percent reduced calories, supplemented with vitamins and minerals to ensure a healthy diet. More than a decade of longitudinal findings reveals that, compared with freely eating controls, dietary-restricted monkeys are smaller but not overly thin. They accumulate body fat differently—less on the torso, a type of fat distribution that reduces middle-aged humans' risk of heart disease.

Calorie-restricted monkeys also have a lower body temperature and basal metabolic rate—changes that suggest they shift physiological processes away from growth to life-maintaining functions. Consequently, like calorie-restricted rodents, they seem better able to withstand severe physical stress, such as surgery and infectious disease, perhaps because their bodies more easily repair damaged cells (Weindruch et al., 2001).

Among physiological processes mediating the benefits of calorie restriction, three seem most powerful. First, calorie restriction inhibits production of free radicals, thereby limiting cellular deterioration, which contributes to many diseases of aging (see page 434 in Chapter 13) (Carter et al., 2007; Yu, 2006). Second, calorie restriction reduces blood glucose and insulin levels, which protects against diabetes and cardiovascular disease. Lower blood pressure and cholesterol and a high ratio of "good" to "bad" cholesterol in calorie-restricted primates strengthen these effects (Fontana, 2008). Third, calorie restriction combined with limited consumption of dietary protein reduces levels of IGF-1, an insulin-like hormone produced primarily in the liver, by 30 to 40 percent—a physiological effect consistently linked to increased longevity (Fontana et al., 2009).

The earlier monkeys are placed on calorie restriction, the more favorable its physiological consequences. Because most monkeys in the study are still alive, we do not know whether calorie restriction grants them an exceptionally long lifespan (Mattison et al., 2003). But so far, early death rates for calorie-restricted monkeys have been lower than for fully fed controls.

Human Parallels

The laboratory experimental strategies used to study calorie restriction in animals cannot be applied to humans. But natural experiments indicate that people who limit their food intake may benefit similarly.

Compared with mainland Japanese citizens, residents of the island of Okinawa consume an average of 20 percent fewer calories, while maintaining a healthy diet. This restricted diet is associated with a 60 to 70 percent reduction in incidence of deaths due to cancer and cardiovascular disease and a two- to forty-fold increase in seniors living to age 100 over other regions of Japan (Kagawa, 1978). Although other differences between Okinawans and mainland Japanese may play a role, Okinawans who move away from the island and, presumably, give up their calorie-limited lifestyle show increased mortality rates (Mizushima & Yapori, 1992).

In the early 1990s, eight American men and women ranging in age from 25 to 67 entered the Biosphere, an enclosed three-acre natural habitat, where they lived and raised their own food for two years. Eating 1,800 calories a day and engaging in three to four hours of daily heavy labor, the Biospherians experienced physiological changes similar to those observed in calorie-restricted rodents and monkeys, including reduced blood glucose, insulin, cholesterol, and blood pressure; a stronger immune-system response; and decreased fat mass (Heilbronn & Ravussin, 2003). Measures taken on normal and overweight people placed on high-quality, energy-restricted diets show the same effects (Fontana, 2009; Redman et al., 2008).

Why might calorie restriction be an anti-aging strategy? Researchers speculate that the body's response to food scarcity evolved to increase the chances of surviving adversity.

Residents of Okinawa—like this elderly street vendor preparing dumplings for the day's customers—consume 20 percent fewer calories, on average, than mainland Japanese citizens. Their diet is associated with longer life.

Nevertheless, calorie restriction may add only two to three years to the extended longevity already conferred by human improvements in living conditions and medical treatment (de Grey, 2005). Also, to be effective, calorie restriction in humans may need to involve substantial reductions in protein intake to induce the decline in IGF-1 consistently linked to longevity in animal research. Yet ethical considerations, including insufficient energy to meet requirements of daily life and risks of malnutrition, argue against trying to get people to modify the quantity and makeup of their food intake substantially. Finally, very few people would be willing to maintain a drastically reduced diet for most of their lifespan. As a result, scientists have begun to explore *calorie-restriction mimetics*—agents such as natural food substances, herbs, and vigorous exercise regimens—that might yield the same benefits as calorie restriction, without dieting (Barzilai & Bartke, 2009; Ingram et al., 2006). These investigations are still in their early stages.

warmth accompanied by a rise in body temperature and redness in the face, neck, and chest, followed by sweating. Hot flashes—which may occur during the day and also, as *night sweats,* during sleep—affect more than 50 percent of women in Western industrialized nations (Nelson, 2008). Typically, they are not severe: Only about 1 woman in 12 experiences them every day.

Although menopausal women tend to report increased irritability and less satisfying sleep, research using EEG and other physiological measures finds no links between menopause and changes in quantity or quality of sleep (Lamberg, 2007; Young et al., 2002). Also, many studies reveal no association between menopause and depression in the general population (Avis, 2003; Soares, 2007; Vesco et al., 2007). Rather, women who have a previous history of depression, are physically inactive, have financial difficulties, or are experiencing other highly stressful life events are more likely to experience depressive episodes during the climacteric. In view of these findings, sleep difficulties or depression should not be dismissed as temporary byproducts of menopause: These problems merit serious evaluation and treatment.

As Figure 15.1 illustrates, compared with North American, European, African, and Middle Eastern women, Asian women report fewer menopausal complaints, including hot flashes. Asian diets, which are low in fat and high in soy-based foods (a rich source of plant estrogen) may be involved (Obermeyer, 2000).

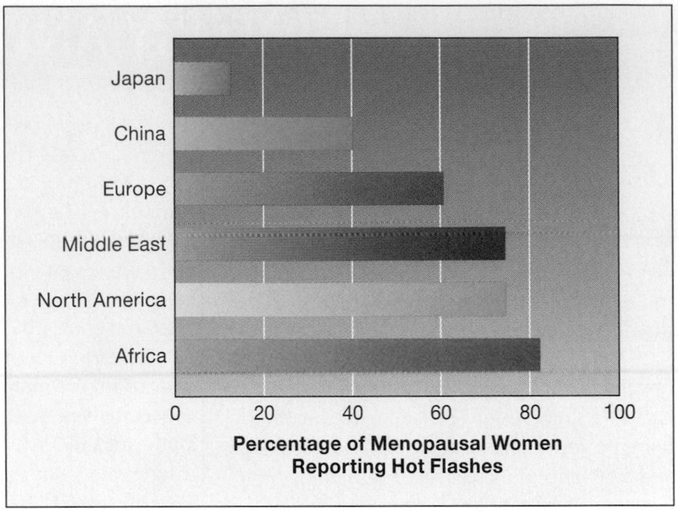

■ FIGURE 15.1 ■ Percentage of menopausal women in different regions of the world reporting hot flashes. Findings are derived from interviews with large samples in each region. Women in Asian nations, especially Japanese women, are less likely to suffer from hot flashes, perhaps because they eat soy-based foods, a rich source of plant estrogen. See the Cultural Influences box on page 508 for additional evidence on the low rates of menopausal symptoms among Japanese women. (Adapted from Obermeyer, 2000; Shea, 2006.)

■ **HORMONE THERAPY.** To reduce the physical discomforts of menopause, doctors may prescribe **hormone therapy,** or low daily doses of estrogen. Hormone therapy comes in two types: (1) estrogen alone, or *estrogen replacement therapy (ERT),* for women who have had hysterectomies (surgical removal of the uterus); and (2) estrogen plus progesterone, or *hormone replacement therapy (HRT),* for other women. Combining estrogen with progesterone lessens the risk of cancer of the endometrium (lining of the uterus), which has long been known as a serious side effect of hormone therapy.

Hormone therapy is highly successful at counteracting hot flashes and vaginal dryness. Although it has no clear impact on the moods of nondepressed women, for women diagnosed with depression, it may add to the effectiveness of antidepressant medication (Miller, 2003). Hormone therapy also offers some protection against bone deterioration and colon cancer (Nelson et al., 2002).

Nevertheless, a large-scale experiment, in which more than 16,000 50- to 79-year-olds randomly assigned to take HRT or a sugar pill were followed for five years, revealed two negative consequences. First, HRT caused a mild increase in heart attacks, stroke, and blood clots. Second, HRT taken for more than four years slightly elevated the incidence of breast cancer (Women's Health Initiative, 2002, 2004). In other studies, ERT, as well, increased the risk of breast cancer and blood clots (Bhavnani & Strickler, 2005; Prentice et al., 2008). Furthermore, an additional experiment involving 4,500 65- to 79-year-olds indicated that HRT slightly elevated the risk of mild cognitive declines and nearly doubled the risk of Alzheimer's disease and other dementias (Rapp et al., 2003; Shumaker et al., 2003).

But timing of intervention may make a difference. Hormone therapy begun before menopausal age may actually reduce the risk of cardiovascular disease. And hormone therapy begun around the time of menopause, rather than a decade or two later, may reduce the risk of Alzheimer's (Henderson, 2009; Rossouw et al., 2007).

On the basis of available evidence, women and their doctors should make decisions about hormone therapy carefully. Women with family histories of cardiovascular disease or breast cancer are generally advised against it. Fortunately, the number of alternative treatments is increasing. A relatively safe migraine-headache medication, gabapentin, substantially reduces hot flashes, perhaps by acting on the brain's temperature regulation center. At high doses, which still appear safe, gabapentin is nearly as effective as hormone therapy (Reddy et al., 2006). Several antidepressant drugs and black cohosh, an herbal medication, are helpful as well (Oktem et al., 2007; Osmers et al., 2005; Uebelhack et al., 2006). Alternative medications are also available to protect the bones, although their long-term safety is not yet clear.

At present, however, hormone therapy continues to provide the most reliable relief from menopausal symptoms. Therefore, some experts argue that prescribing it to low-risk women on a short-term basis (no longer than five years) is justified because it improves quality of life (Col et al., 2004).

■ WOMEN'S PSYCHOLOGICAL REACTIONS TO MENOPAUSE. How do women react to menopause—a clear-cut signal that their childbearing years are over? The answer lies in how they interpret the event in relation to their past and future lives.

For Jewel, who had wanted marriage and family but never attained these goals, menopause was traumatic. Her sense of physical competence was still bound up with the ability to have children. Physical symptoms can also make menopause a difficult time (Elavsky & McAuley, 2007). And in a society that values a youthful appearance, some women respond to the climacteric with disappointment about a loss of sex appeal (Howell & Beth, 2002).

Many women, however, find menopause to be little or no trouble, regard it as a new beginning, and report improved quality of life (George, 2002; Mishra & Kuh, 2006). When more than 2,000 U.S. women were asked what their feelings were about no longer menstruating, nearly 50 percent of those currently experiencing changes in their menstrual cycles, and 60 percent of those whose periods had ceased, said they felt relieved (Rossi, 2005). Most do not want more children and are thankful to be freed from worry about birth control. And highly educated, career-oriented Caucasian-American women with fulfilling lives outside the home usually have more positive attitudes toward menopause than those with less education (Theisen et al., 1995).

Compared with previous generations, the baby-boom generation seems more accepting of menopause (Avis & Crawford, 2006). Their strong desire to cast aside old, gender-stereotyped views (such as menopause as a sign of decay and disease), their more active approach to seeking health information, and their greater willingness to openly discuss sexual topics may contribute to their generally positive adaptation.

Other research suggests that African-American and Mexican-American women hold especially favorable views. In several studies, African-American women experienced less irritability and moodiness than Caucasian Americans (Melby, Lock, & Kaufert, 2005). They rarely spoke of menopause in terms of physical aging but, instead, regarded it as normal, inevitable, even welcome (Holmes-Rovner et al., 1996; Sampselle et al., 2002, p. 359). Several African Americans expressed exasperation at society's readiness to label as "crazy" middle-aged women's authentic reactions to work- or family-based stressors that often coincide with menopause. Among Mexican-American women who have not yet adopted the language (and perhaps certain beliefs) of the larger society, attitudes toward menopause are especially positive (Bell, 1995). And in an investigation of more than 13,000 40- to 55-year-old U.S. women diverse in ethnicity, other factors—SES, physical health, lifestyle factors (smoking, diet, exercise, weight gain), and especially psychological stress—overshadowed menopausal status and three common symptoms (hot flashes, night sweats, and vaginal dryness) in impact on self-rated quality of life (Avis et al., 2004).

The wide variation in physical symptoms and attitudes indicates that menopause is not just a hormonal event; it is also affected by cultural beliefs and practices. The Cultural Influences box on page 508 provides a cross-cultural look at women's experience of menopause.

African-American women generally speak of menopause as normal, inevitable, even welcome. They also experience less irritability and moodiness during this transition than Caucasian-American women.

■ REPRODUCTIVE CHANGES IN MEN. Although men also experience a climacteric, no male counterpart to menopause exists. Both quantity and motility of sperm decrease from the twenties on, and quantity of semen diminishes after age 40, negatively affecting fertility in middle age (Sloter et al., 2006). Still, sperm production continues throughout life, and men in their nineties have fathered children. Testosterone production also declines with age, but the change is minimal in healthy men who continue to engage in sexual activity, which stimulates cells that release testosterone (Hermann et al., 2000).

Nevertheless, because of reduced blood flow to and changes in connective tissue in the penis, more stimulation is required for an erection, and it may be harder to maintain. The inability to attain an erection when desired can occur at any age, but it becomes more common in midlife, affecting about 30 percent of men by age 60 (Lindau et al., 2007).

An episode or two of impotence is not serious, but frequent bouts can lead some men to fear that their sex life is over and undermine their self-image. Viagra and other drugs that increase blood flow to the penis offer temporary relief from erectile dysfunction. Publicity surrounding these drugs

CULTURAL INFLUENCES

Menopause as a Biocultural Event

Biology and culture join forces to influence women's response to menopause, making it a *biocultural event.* In Western industrialized nations, menopause is "medicalized"—assumed to be a syndrome requiring treatment. Many women experience physical and emotional symptoms (Chrisler, 2008; Houck, 2006). The more symptoms they report, the more negative their attitude toward menopause tends to be.

Yet change the circumstances in which menopause is evaluated, and attitudes change as well. In one study, nearly 600 men and women between ages 19 and 85 described their view of menopause in one of three contexts—as a medical problem, as a life transition, or as a symbol of aging. The medical context evoked many more negative statements than the other contexts (Gannon & Ekstrom, 1993).

Research in non-Western cultures reveals that middle-aged women's social status also affects the experience of menopause. In societies where older women are respected and the mother-in-law and grandmother roles bring new privileges and responsibilities, complaints about menopausal symptoms are rare (Fuh et al., 2005). Perhaps in part for this reason, women in Asian nations report fewer discomforts (Shea, 2006). And their symptoms usually differ from those of Western women.

For example, though they rarely complain of hot flashes, a small number of Japanese women report shoulder stiffness, back pain, headaches, and fatigue. In midlife, a Japanese woman attains peak respect and responsibility. Typically her days are filled with monitoring the household economy, attending to grandchildren, caring for dependent parents-in-law, and part-time employment (Lock & Kaufert, 2001). The rare woman who experiences menopausal distress seems to interpret it in light of these socially valued commitments. Neither Japanese women nor their doctors consider menopause to be a significant marker of female middle age. Rather, midlife is viewed as an extended period of "socially recognized, productive maturity" (Menon, 2002, p. 58).

A comparison of rural Mayan women of the Yucatán with rural Greek women on the island of Evia reveals additional biocultural influences on the menopausal experience (Beyene, 1992; Beyene & Martin, 2001; Mahady et al., 2008). In both societies, old age is a time of increased status, and menopause brings freedom from child rearing and more time for leisure activities. Otherwise, Mayan and Greek women differ greatly.

Mayan women marry as teenagers. By 35 to 40, they have given birth to many children but rarely menstruated because of repeated pregnancies and breastfeeding, and they experience menopause up to 10 years earlier than their counterparts in developed nations, perhaps because of added factors, such as poor nutrition and heavy physical work. Eager for childbearing to end, they welcome menopause, describing it with such phrases as "being happy" and "free like a young girl again." None report hot flashes or any other symptoms.

Like North Americans, rural Greek women use birth control to limit family size, and most report hot flashes and sweating at menopause. But they regard these as temporary discomforts that will stop on their own, not as medical symptoms requiring treatment. When asked what they do about hot flashes, the Greek women reply, "Pay no attention," "Go outside for fresh air," and "Throw off the covers at night."

Does frequency of childbearing affect menopausal symptoms, as this contrast between Mayan and Greek women suggests? More research is needed to be sure. At the same time, the difference between North American and Greek women in attitudes toward and management of hot flashes is striking. This—along with other cross-cultural findings—highlights the combined impact of biology and culture on menopausal experiences (Melby, Lock, & Kaufert, 2005).

For these rural Mayan women of the Yucatán, menopause brings freedom. After decades of childbearing, Mayan women welcome menopause, describing it as "being happy" and "free like a young girl again."

has prompted open discussion of erectile dysfunction and encouraged more men to seek treatment (Berner et al., 2008). But those taking the medications are often not adequately screened for the host of factors besides declining testosterone that contribute to impotence, including disorders of the nervous, circulatory, and endocrine systems; anxiety and depression; pelvic injury; and loss of interest in one's sexual partner (Montorsi, 2005). Although drugs for impotence are generally safe, a few users have experienced serious vision loss. In men with high blood pressure or atherosclerosis, the medications heighten the risk of constricting blood vessels in the optic nerve, permanently damaging it (O'Malley, 2006).

ASK YOURSELF

» **REVIEW**
Describe cultural influences on the experience of menopause.

» **APPLY**
At age 42, Stan began to wear bifocals, and over the next 10 years, he required an adjustment to his corrective lenses almost every year. What physical changes account for his recurring need for new eyewear?

» **APPLY**
Between ages 40 and 50, Nancy gained 20 pounds. She also began to have trouble opening tightly closed jars, and her calf muscles ached after she climbed a flight of stairs. "Exchanging muscle for fat must be an inevitable part of aging," Nancy thought. Is she correct? Why or why not?

» **REFLECT**
In view of the benefits and risks of hormone therapy, what factors would you consider, or advise others to consider, before taking such medication?

Health and Fitness

In midlife, nearly 85 percent of Americans rate their health as either "excellent" or "good"—still a large majority, but lower than the 95 percent figure in early adulthood (U.S. Department of Health and Human Services, 2009a). Whereas younger people usually attribute health complaints to temporary infections, middle-aged adults more often point to chronic diseases. As we will see, among those who rate their health unfavorably, men are more likely to suffer from fatal illnesses, women from nonfatal, limiting health problems.

In addition to typical negative indicators—major diseases and disabling conditions—our discussion takes up sexuality as a positive indicator of health. Before we begin, it is important to note that our understanding of health in middle and late adulthood is limited by insufficient research on women and ethnic minorities. Most studies of illness risk factors, prevention, and treatment have been carried out on men. Fortunately, this situation is changing. For example, the Women's Health Initiative (WHI)—a commitment by the U.S. federal government, extending from 1993 to 2005, to study the impact of various lifestyle and medical prevention strategies on the health of nearly 162,000 postmenopausal women of all ethnic groups and SES levels—has led to important findings, including health risks associated with hormone therapy, discussed earlier. A five-year extension, involving annual health updates from 115,000 WHI participants, continues to yield vital information.

Sexuality

Frequency of sexual activity among married couples tends to decline in middle adulthood, but for most, the drop is slight. Longitudinal research reveals that stability of sexual activity is far more typical than dramatic change. Couples who have sex often in early adulthood continue to do so in midlife (Dennerstein & Lehert, 2004; Walsh & Berman, 2004). And the best predictor of sexual frequency is marital happiness, an association that is probably bidirectional (Edwards & Booth, 1994). Sex is more likely to occur in the context of a good marriage, and couples who have sex often probably view their relationship more positively.

Nevertheless, *intensity* of sexual response declines in midlife due to physical changes of the climacteric. Both men and women take longer to feel aroused and to reach orgasm (Bartlik & Goldstein, 2001; Walsh & Berman, 2004). If partners perceive each other as less attractive, this may contribute to a drop in sexual desire. Yet in the context of a positive outlook, sexual activity can become more satisfying. Devin and Trisha, for example, viewed each other's aging bodies with acceptance and affection—as a sign of their enduring and deepening relationship. And with greater freedom from the demands of work and family, their sex life became more spontaneous. The majority of married people over age 50 say that their sex life is an important component of their relationship, and most find ways to overcome difficulties with sexual functioning. One happily married 52-year-old woman commented, "We know what we are doing, we've had plenty of practice (laughs), and I would never have believed that it gets better as you get older, but it does" (Gott & Hinchliff, 2003, p. 1625; Kingsberg, 2002).

When surveys include both married and unmarried people, a striking gender difference in age-related sexual activity appears. The proportion of U.S. men with no sexual partners in the previous year increases only slightly, from 8 percent in the thirties to 12 percent in the late fifties. In contrast, the rise for women is dramatic, from 9 percent to 40 percent—a gender gap that becomes even greater in late adulthood (Lindau et al., 2007; Laumann & Mahay, 2002). A higher male mortality rate and the value women place on affection and continuity in sexual relations make partners less available to them. Taken as a whole, the evidence reveals that sexual activity in midlife, as in earlier periods, is the combined result of biological, psychological, and social forces.

Illness and Disability

As Figure 15.2 on page 510 shows, cancer and cardiovascular disease are the leading causes of death in middle age. Unintentional injuries, though still a major health threat, occur at a lower rate than in early adulthood, largely because motor vehicle collisions decline. Despite a rise in vision problems, older adults' many years of driving experience and greater cautiousness may reduce these deaths. In contrast, falls resulting in bone fractures and death nearly double from early to middle adulthood (U.S. Census Bureau, 2009).

Men are more vulnerable than women to most health problems. Among middle-aged men, cancer deaths exceed cardiovascular disease deaths by a small margin; among women, cancer is by far the leading cause of death (refer again to

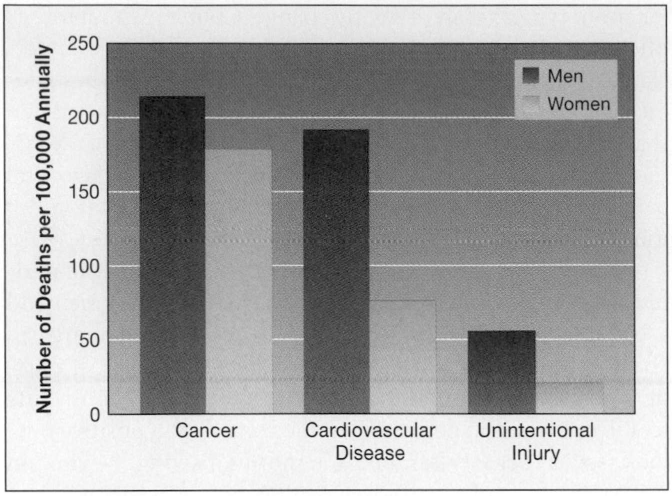

■ **FIGURE 15.2 ■ Leading causes of death among people age 45 to 64 in the United States.** Men are more vulnerable than women to each leading cause of death. Cancer is the leading killer of both sexes, by a far smaller margin over cardiovascular disease for men than for women. (Adapted from U.S. Census Bureau, 2009.)

Figure 15.2). As in earlier decades, economic disadvantage is a strong predictor of poor health and premature death in midlife. And largely because of more severe poverty and lack of universal health insurance, the United States continues to exceed most other industrialized nations in death rates from major causes (OECD, 2008b). Finally, as we take a closer look at illness and disability in the following sections, we will encounter yet another familiar theme: the close connection between psychological and physical well-being. Personality traits that magnify stress—especially hostility and anger—are serious threats to health in midlife.

■ **CANCER.** From early to middle adulthood, the death rate due to cancer multiplies tenfold, accounting for about one-third of all midlife deaths in the United States. Although the incidence of many types of cancer is currently leveling off or declining, cancer mortality was on the rise for many decades, largely because of a dramatic increase in lung cancer due to cigarette smoking. In the last 15 years, the incidence of lung cancer has dropped in men; 50 percent fewer smoke today than in the 1950s. In contrast, lung cancer has increased in women, many of whom took up smoking in the decades after World War II (U.S. Department of Health and Human Services, 2009a).

Cancer occurs when a cell's genetic program is disrupted, leading to uncontrolled growth and spread of abnormal cells that crowd out normal tissues and organs. Why does this happen? Mutations of three main kinds contribute to cancer. Some result in *oncogenes* (cancer genes) that directly undergo abnormal cell duplication. Others interfere with the activity of *tumor suppressor genes* so they fail to keep oncogenes from multiplying. And a third type of mutation disrupts the activity of *stability genes,* which normally keep genetic alterations to a minimum by repairing subtle DNA mistakes that occur either during normal cell duplication or as a result of environmental agents (Vogelstein & Kinzler, 2004). When stability genes do not function, mutations in many other genes occur at a higher rate.

Each of these cancer-linked mutations can be either *germline* (due to an inherited predisposition) or *somatic* (occurring in a single cell, which then multiplies) (see pages 51–52 in Chapter 2 to review). Recall from Chapter 13 that according to one theory, error in DNA duplication increases with age, either occurring spontaneously or resulting from the release of free radicals or breakdown of the immune system. Environmental toxins may initiate or intensify this process.

Figure 15.3 shows the incidence of the most common types of cancer. For cancers that affect both sexes, men are generally more vulnerable than women. The difference may be due to genetic makeup, exposure to cancer-causing agents as a result of lifestyle or occupation, and a tendency to delay going to the doctor. Although the relationship of SES to cancer varies with site (for example, lung and stomach cancers are linked to lower SES, breast and prostate cancers to higher SES), cancer death rates increase sharply as SES decreases and are especially high among low-income ethnic minorities (Jemal et al., 2008).

■ **FIGURE 15.3 ■ Incidence of ten leading cancer types among men and women in the United States.** (From A. Jemal et al., 2008, "Cancer Statistics, 2008," *CA: A Cancer Journal for Clinicians, 58,* p. 76. Reprinted by permission of Lippincott Williams & Wilkins, http://lww.com.)

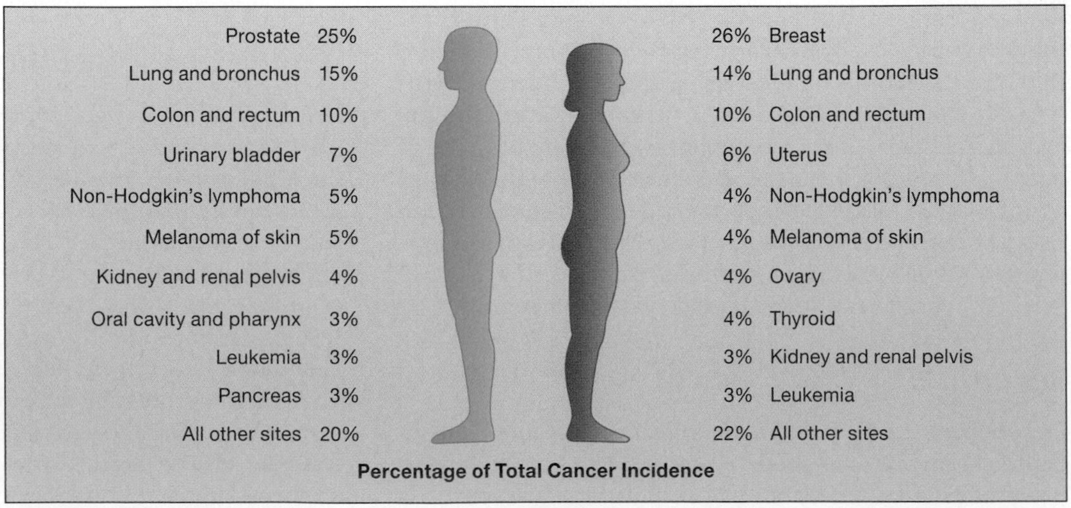

Applying What We Know

Reducing Cancer Incidence and Deaths

Intervention	Description
Know the seven warning signs of cancer.	The signs are change in bowel or bladder habits, sore that does not heal, unusual bleeding or discharge, thickening or lump in a breast or elsewhere in your body, indigestion or swallowing difficulty, obvious change in a wart or mole, nagging cough or hoarseness. If you have any of these signs, consult your doctor immediately.
Do self-examination.	Women should self-examine the breasts and men the testicles for lumps and other changes once a month. If detected early, breast and testicular cancers usually can be cured.
Schedule regular medical checkups and cancer-screening tests.	Women should have a mammogram and Pap test every one to two years. Beginning at age 50, men should have an annual prostate screening test. Both men and women should be screened periodically for colon cancer, as recommended by their doctor.
Avoid tobacco.	Cigarette smoking causes 90 percent of lung cancer deaths and 30 percent of all cancer deaths. Smokeless (chewing) tobacco increases risk of cancers of the mouth, larynx, throat, and esophagus.
Limit alcohol consumption.	Consuming more than one drink per day for women or two drinks per day for men increases risk of cancers of the breast, kidney, liver, head, and neck.
Avoid excessive sun exposure.	Sun exposure causes many cases of skin cancer. When in the sun for an extended time, use a sun blocker and cover exposed skin.
Avoid unnecessary X-ray exposure.	Excessive exposure to X-rays increases risk of many cancers. Most medical X-rays are adjusted to deliver the lowest possible dose but should not be used unnecessarily.
Avoid exposure to industrial chemicals and other pollutants.	Exposure to nickel, chromate, asbestos, vinyl chloride, and other industrial agents increases risk of various cancers.
Weigh the benefits versus risks of hormone therapy.	Because estrogen replacement increases risk of uterine and breast cancers, carefully consider hormone therapy with your doctor.
Maintain a healthy diet.	Eating vegetables and foods rich in fiber and vitamins A and C, while avoiding excess dietary fat and salt-cured, smoked, and nitrite-cured foods, reduces risk of colon and rectal cancers.
Avoid excessive weight gain.	Overweight and obesity increase risk of cancers of the breast, colon, esophagus, uterus, and kidney.
Adopt a physically active lifestyle.	Physical activity offers protection against cancers at all body sites except the skin, with the strongest evidence for cancers of the breast, rectum, and colon.

Sources: Demark-Wahnefried et al., 2008; Smith, Cokkinides, & Brawley, 2008.

Poorer medical care and reduced ability to fight the disease, due to inadequate diet and high life stress, underlie this trend.

Overall, a complex interaction of heredity, biological aging, and environment contributes to cancer. For example, many patients with familial breast cancer who respond poorly to treatment have defective forms of particular tumor-suppressor genes (either BRCA1 or BRCA2). Genetic screening for these mutations is available, permitting prevention efforts to begin early. Even though women with one of these faulty genes are at much greater risk for breast cancer than other women, only 35 to 50 percent actually develop the disease. Other genes and lifestyle factors—including alcohol consumption, overweight, greater number of pregnancies, use of oral contraceptives, and hormone therapy to treat menopausal symptoms—heighten their risk. Women with BRCA1 or BRCA2 mutations are especially likely to develop early-onset breast cancer, before age 30 (Ripperger et al., 2009). But their risk remains elevated throughout middle and late adulthood, when breast cancer rises among women in general.

People often fear cancer because they believe it is incurable. Yet 40 percent of affected individuals are cured—free of the disease for five years or longer. Survival rates, however, vary widely with type of cancer (Jemal et al., 2008). For example, they are relatively high for breast and prostate cancers, intermediate for cervical and colon cancers, and low for lung and pancreatic cancers.

Breast cancer is the leading malignancy for women, prostate cancer for men. Lung cancer—largely preventable through avoiding tobacco—ranks second for both sexes, followed closely by colon and rectal cancer. Scheduling annual medical checkups that screen for these and other forms of cancer and taking the additional steps listed in Applying What We Know above can reduce cancer illness and death rates considerably. An increasing number of cancer-promoting mutations are being identified, and promising new therapies targeting these genes are being tested.

Surviving cancer is a triumph, but it also brings emotional challenges. During cancer treatment, relationships focus on the

Applying What We Know

Reducing the Risk of Heart Attack

Intervention	Risk Reduction
Quit smoking.	↓ 70% Five years after quitting, up to 70 percent lower risk compared to current smokers
Reduce blood cholesterol level.	↓ 60% 2 to 3 percent decline in risk for each 1 percent reduction in blood cholesterol. Reductions in cholesterol average 10 percent with diet therapy and can exceed 20 percent with drug therapy.
Treat high blood pressure.	↓ 60% Combined diet and drug therapy can lower blood pressure substantially, leading to as much as a 60 percent risk reduction.
Maintain ideal weight.	↓ 55% Up to 55 percent lower risk for people who maintain ideal body weight compared to those who are obese
Exercise regularly.	↓ 45% 45 percent lower risk for people who maintain an active rather than a sedentary lifestyle
Drink an occasional glass of wine or beer.[a]	↓ 30% Up to 30 percent lower risk for people who consume small-to-moderate amounts of alcohol; believed to promote high-density lipoproteins (a form of "good cholesterol" that reduces "bad cholesterol") and to reduce the risk of clot formation
Take low-dose aspirin.	↓ 20% Up to 20 percent lower risk for people who take 72 to 162 mg (¼ to ½ tablet) daily or every other day; reduces the likelihood of blood clots (should be medically recommended; long-term use can have serious side effects)
Reduce hostility and other forms of psychological stress.	Extent of risk reduction not yet known.

[a]Recall from Chapter 13 that heavy alcohol use increases the risk of cardiovascular disease as well as many other diseases.

Sources: American Heart Association, 2009; Collins et al., 2009; Ho, Hankey, & Eikelboom, 2004.

illness. Afterward, they must refocus on health and full participation in daily life. Unfortunately, stigmas associated with cancer exist. Friends, family, and co-workers may need reminders that cancer is not contagious and that with patience and support from supervisors and co-workers, cancer survivors regain their on-the-job productivity (Mains et al., 2005).

■ **CARDIOVASCULAR DISEASE.** Despite a decline over the last few decades (see Chapter 13), each year about 25 percent of middle-aged Americans who die succumb to cardiovascular disease (U.S. Department of Health and Human Services, 2009a). We associate cardiovascular disease with heart attacks, but Devin, like many middle-aged and older adults, learned of the condition during an annual checkup. His doctor detected high blood pressure, high blood cholesterol, and *atherosclerosis*—a buildup of plaque in his coronary arteries, which encircle the heart and provide its muscles with oxygen and nutrients. These indicators of cardiovascular disease are known as "silent killers" because they often have no symptoms.

When symptoms *are* evident, they take different forms. The most extreme is a *heart attack*—blockage of normal blood supply to an area of the heart, usually brought on by a blood clot in one or more plaque-filled coronary arteries. Intense pain results as muscle in the affected region dies. A heart attack is a medical emergency; over 50 percent of victims die before reaching the hospital, another 15 percent during treatment, and an additional 15 percent over the next few years (American Heart Association, 2009). Among other, less extreme symptoms of cardiovascular disease are *arrhythmia,* or irregular heartbeat. When it persists, it can prevent the heart from pumping enough blood and result in faintness. It can also allow clots to form within the heart's chambers, which may break loose and travel to the brain. In some individuals, indigestion-like pain or crushing chest pain, called *angina pectoris,* reveals an oxygen-deprived heart.

Today, cardiovascular disease can be treated in many ways—including coronary bypass surgery, medication, and pacemakers to regulate heart rhythm. To relieve arterial blockage, Devin had *angioplasty,* a procedure in which a surgeon threaded a needle-thin catheter into his arteries and inflated a balloon at its tip, which flattened fatty deposits to allow blood to flow more freely. Unless Devin took other measures to reduce his risk, his doctor warned, the arteries would clog again within a year. As Applying What We Know above indicates, adults can do much to prevent heart disease or slow its progress.

Some risks, such as heredity, advanced age, and being male, cannot be changed. But cardiovascular disease is so disabling and deadly that people must be alert for it where they least expect it—for example, in women. Because men account for over 70 percent of cases in middle adulthood, doctors often view a heart condition as a "male problem" and frequently overlook women's symptoms, which tend to be milder, more often taking the form of angina than a heart attack (Mosca et al., 2005). In one study, researchers had male and female actors present identical symptoms of angina to a sample of over 700 doctors. The doctors were far less likely to suspect heart problems in women—especially African-American women, who are at greater risk for heart disease than Caucasian-American women (Schulman et al., 1999). In follow-ups of victims of full-blown heart attacks, once again women—and especially African-American women—were less likely to be offered costly, invasive treatments, such as angioplasty and bypass surgery (Dey et al., 2009; Jneid et al., 2008; Steiner & Miller, 2008). As a result, treatment outcomes—including rehospitalization and death—tend to be worse for women.

■ **OSTEOPOROSIS.** When age-related bone loss is severe, a condition called **osteoporosis** develops. The disorder, affecting about 10 million U.S. adults, 80 percent of whom are women, greatly magnifies the risk of bone fractures. An estimated 55 percent of people over age 50 are at risk for osteoporosis because they have bone density levels low enough to be of concern, and 12 percent have been diagnosed with it (National Osteoporosis Foundation, 2008). After age 70, osteoporosis affects the majority of people of both sexes (Donatelle, 2009). Although we associate it with a slumped-over posture, a shuffling gait, and a "dowager's hump" in the upper back, this extreme is rare. Because the bones gradually become more porous over many years, osteoporosis may not be evident until fractures—typically in the spine, hips, and wrist—occur or are discovered through X-rays.

A major factor related to osteoporosis is the decline in estrogen associated with menopause. In middle and late adulthood, women lose about 50 percent of their bone mass, about half of it in the first 10 years following menopause—a decline that, by the late sixties, is two to five times greater than in men (Bonnick, 2008). The earlier a woman reaches menopause, the greater her chances of developing osteoporosis related to estrogen loss. In men, the age-related decrease in testosterone—though much more gradual than estrogen loss in women—contributes to bone loss because the body converts some to estrogen.

Heredity plays an important role. A family history of osteoporosis increases risk, with identical twins more likely than fraternal twins to share the disorder (Williams & Spector, 2006). People with thin, small-framed bodies are more likely to be affected because they typically attain a lower peak bone mass in adolescence. In contrast, higher bone density makes African Americans less susceptible than Asian Americans, Caucasians, Hispanics, and Native Americans (Pothiwala, Evans, & Chapman-Novakofski, 2006). An unhealthy lifestyle also contributes: A calcium-deficient diet, excess intake of sodium and caffeine, and physical inactivity reduce bone mass, as do cigarette smoking and alcohol consumption, which interfere with the replacement of bone cells (National Osteoporosis Foundation, 2008).

When major bone fractures (such as the hip) occur, 10 to 20 percent of patients die within a year (Reginster & Burlet, 2006). Because osteoporosis usually develops earlier in women than in men, it has become known as a "women's disease," and men are far less likely to be screened and treated for it, even after a hip fracture (Bonnick, 2008; Kiebzak et al., 2002). Compared with women, men with hip fractures tend to be older and to lack a history of interventions aimed at preserving bone density. Probably for these reasons, the one-year mortality rate after hip fracture is nearly twice as great for men as for women—a gap that widens with age (Campion & Maricic, 2003; Gennari & Bilezikian, 2007).

To treat osteoporosis, doctors recommend a diet enriched with calcium and vitamin D (which promotes calcium absorption), weight-bearing exercise (walking rather than swimming), strength training (weight lifting), and bone-strengthening medications (National Osteoporosis Foundation, 2008). A better way to reduce lifelong risk is through early prevention: maximizing peak bone density by increasing calcium and vitamin D intake and engaging in regular exercise in childhood, adolescence, and early adulthood.

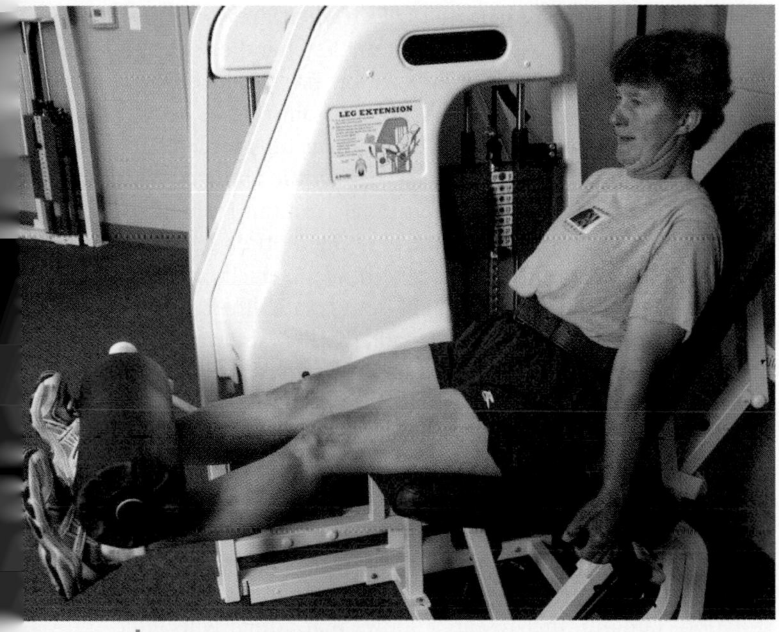

Physical inactivity increases the chances of osteoporosis. More than half of people over age 50, mostly women, are at risk. Weight-bearing exercise and strength training are recommended for both prevention and treatment.

Hostility and Anger

Whenever Trisha's sister Dottie called, she seemed like a powder keg ready to explode. Dottie was critical of her boss at work and dissatisfied with the way Trisha, a lawyer, had handled the family's affairs after their father died. Inevitably, Dottie's anger surfaced, exploding in hurtful remarks: "Any lawyer knows that, Trisha. How could you be so stupid! I should have called a *real* lawyer." "You and Devin are so stuck in your privileged lives that you can't think of anyone else. You don't know what work *is*."

After listening as long as she could bear, Trisha would warn, "Dottie, if you continue, I'm going to hang up. . . . Dottie, I'm ending this right now!"

At age 53, Dottie had high blood pressure, difficulty sleeping, and back pain. In the past five years, she had been hospitalized five times—twice for treatment of digestive problems, twice for an irregular heartbeat, and once for a benign tumor on her thyroid gland. Trisha often wondered whether Dottie's personal style was partly responsible for her array of health problems.

That hostility and anger might have negative effects on health is a centuries-old idea. Several decades ago, researchers first tested this notion by identifying 35- to 59-year-old men who displayed the **Type A behavior pattern**—extreme competitiveness, ambition, impatience, hostility, angry outbursts, and a sense of time pressure. They found that within the next eight years, Type As were more than twice as likely as Type Bs (people with a more relaxed disposition) to develop heart disease (Rosenman et al., 1975).

Later studies, however, often failed to confirm these results. Type A is actually a mix of behaviors, only one or two of which affect health. Current evidence pinpoints hostility as a "toxic" ingredient of Type A, since isolating it from global Type A consistently predicts heart disease and other health problems in both men and women (Aldwin et al., 2001; Eaker et al., 2004; Matthews et al., 2004; Smith et al., 2004). The risks of high blood pressure, atherosclerosis, and stroke are several times greater in adults scoring high on hostility measures than in those scoring low (Räikkönen et al., 2004; Yan et al., 2003; Williams et al., 2002).

Expressed hostility in particular—frequent angry outbursts; rude, disagreeable behavior; critical and condescending nonverbal cues during social interaction, including glares; and expressions of contempt and disgust—leads to greater cardiovascular arousal, health complaints, and illness (Chesney et al., 1997; Julkunen & Ahlström, 2006). As people get angry, heart rate, blood pressure, and stress hormones escalate until the body's response is extreme.

Of course, people who are repeatedly enraged are more likely to be depressed and dissatisfied with their lives, to lack social supports, and to engage in unhealthy behaviors. But hostility predicts health problems even after such factors as smoking, alcohol consumption, overweight, general unhappiness, and negative life events are controlled (Smith & Mackenzie, 2006).

Another unhealthy feature of the Type A pattern, which also predicts heart disease, is a socially dominant style, evident in rapid, loud, insistent speech and a tendency to cut off and talk over others (Smith, 2006; Smith, Gallo, & Ruiz, 2003). And because men score higher in hostility and dominance than women (Dottie is an exception), emotional style may contribute to the sex differences in heart disease described earlier.

Can Dottie preserve her health by bottling up her hostility instead of expressing it? Repeatedly suppressing overt anger or ruminating about past anger-provoking events is also associated with high blood pressure and heart disease (Hogan & Linden, 2004; Julkunen, 1996). A better alternative, as we will see, is to develop effective ways of handling stress and conflict.

Adapting to the Physical Challenges of Midlife

Middle adulthood is often a productive time of life, when people attain their greatest accomplishments and satisfactions. Nevertheless, it takes considerable stamina to cope with the full array of changes this period can bring. Devin responded to his expanding waistline and cardiovascular symptoms by leaving his desk twice a week to attend a low-impact aerobics class and by reducing job-related stress through daily 10-minute meditation sessions. Aware of her sister Dottie's difficulties, Trisha resolved to handle her own hostile feelings more adaptively. And her generally optimistic outlook enabled her to cope successfully with the physical changes of midlife, the pressures of her legal career, and Devin's cardiovascular disease.

Stress Management

TAKE A MOMENT... Turn back to Chapter 13, pages 449–450, and review the negative consequences of psychological stress on the cardiovascular, immune, and gastrointestinal systems. As adults encounter problems at home and at work, daily hassles can add up to a serious stress load. Stress management is important at any age, but in middle adulthood it can limit the age-related rise in illness and, when disease strikes, reduce its severity.

Applying What We Know on the following page summarizes effective ways to reduce stress. Even when stressors cannot be eliminated, people can change how they handle some and view others. At work, Trisha focused on problems she could control—not on her boss's irritability but on ways to delegate routine tasks to her staff so she could focus on problems that required her knowledge and skills. When Dottie phoned, Trisha learned to distinguish normal emotional reactions from unreasonable self-blame. Instead of interpreting Dottie's anger as a sign of her own incompetence, she reminded herself of Dottie's difficult temperament and hard life. And greater life experience helped her accept change as inevitable, so that she was better-equipped to deal with the jolt of sudden events, such as Devin's hospitalization for treatment of heart disease.

Notice how Trisha called on two general strategies for coping with stress, discussed in Chapter 10: (1) *problem-centered coping,* in which she appraised the situation as changeable, identified the difficulty, and decided what to do about it; and (2) *emotion-centered coping,* which is internal, private, and aimed at controlling distress when little can be done about a situation. Longitudinal research shows that adults who effectively reduce stress move flexibly between problem-centered and emotion-centered techniques, depending on the situation (Zakowski et al., 2001). Their approach is deliberate, thoughtful,

Applying What We Know

Managing Stress

Strategy	Description
Reevaluate the situation.	Learn to differentiate normal reactions from those based on irrational beliefs.
Focus on events you can control.	Don't worry about things you cannot change or that may never happen; focus on strategies for handling events under your control.
View life as fluid.	Expect change and accept it as inevitable; then many unanticipated changes will have less emotional impact.
Consider alternatives.	Don't rush into action; think before you act.
Set reasonable goals for yourself.	Aim high, but be realistic about your capacities, motivation, and the situation.
Exercise regularly.	A physically fit person can better handle stress, both physically and emotionally.
Master relaxation techniques.	Relaxation helps refocus energies and reduce the physical discomfort of stress. Classes and self-help books teach these techniques.
Use constructive approaches to anger reduction.	Delay responding ("Let me check into that and get back to you"); use mentally distracting behaviors (counting to 10 backwards) and self-instruction (a covert "Stop!") to control anger arousal; then engage in calm, self-controlled problem solving ("I should call him rather than confront him personally").
Seek social support.	Friends, family members, co-workers, and organized support groups can offer information, assistance, and suggestions for coping with stressful situations.

and respectful of both themselves and others. In contrast, ineffective coping is largely emotion-centered and either impulsive or escapist (Brennan, Schutte, & Moos, 2006; Lazarus, 1999).

Constructive approaches to anger reduction are a vital health intervention (refer again to Applying What We Know). Teaching people to be assertive rather than hostile and to negotiate rather than explode interrupts the intense physiological response that intervenes between psychological stress and illness. Sometimes it is best to delay responding by simply leaving a provocative situation, as Trisha did when she told Dottie that she would hang up after one more insult.

As noted in Chapter 13, people tend to cope with stress more effectively as they move from early to middle adulthood. They may become more realistic about their ability to change situations and more skilled at anticipating stressful events and at preparing to manage them (Aldwin & Levenson, 2002). Furthermore, when middle-aged adults surmount a highly stressful experience, they often report lasting personal benefits—for some, a greater sense of mastery as they look back with amazement at what they were able to accomplish under extremely trying conditions. A serious illness and brush with death commonly brings changes in values and perspectives, such as rediscovery of the importance of health-promoting behaviors and of family relationships (Aldwin, Sutton, & Lachman, 1996). In these ways, managing intense stress can serve as a context for positive development.

But for people who do have difficulty handling midlife's challenges, communities provide fewer social supports than for young adults or senior citizens. For example, Jewel had little knowledge of what to expect during the climacteric. "It would have helped to have a support group so I could have learned about menopause and dealt with it more easily," she told Trisha. Community programs addressing typical midlife concerns, such as those of adult learners returning to college and caregivers of elderly parents, can reduce stress during this period.

Stress management is important at any age, but in middle adulthood, it can limit the age-related rise in illness. This midlifer reduces stress by periodically leaving her high-pressure office environment to work in a tranquil, picturesque setting.

Exercise

Regular exercise, as noted in Chapter 13, has a range of physical and psychological benefits—among them, equipping adults to handle stress more effectively and reducing the risk of many diseases. Heading for his first aerobics class, Devin wondered, Can starting to exercise at age 50 counteract years of physical inactivity? His question is important: Nearly 70 percent of U.S. middle-aged adults are sedentary, and half of those who begin an exercise program discontinue it within the first six months. Even among those who stay active, fewer than 20 percent exercise at levels that lead to health benefits (U.S. Department of Health and Human Services, 2009a).

A person beginning to exercise in midlife must overcome initial barriers and ongoing obstacles—lack of time and energy, inconvenience, work conflicts, and health factors (such as overweight). *Self-efficacy*—belief in one's ability to succeed—is just as vital in adopting, maintaining, and exerting oneself in an exercise regimen as it is in career progress (see Chapter 14). An important outcome of starting an exercise program is that sedentary adults gain in self-efficacy, which further promotes physical activity (McAuley & Elavsky, 2008; Wilbur et al., 2005). Enhanced physical fitness, in turn, prompts middle-aged adults to feel better about their physical selves. Over time, their physical self-esteem—sense of body conditioning and attractiveness—rises (Elavsky & McAuley, 2007; McAuley, Mihalko, & Bane, 1997).

CAPITAL CRESCENT TRAIL, D.C. © JON LOWENSTEIN/RAILS-TO-TRAILS CONSERVANCY

In some areas of the United States, barriers to exercise have been overcome through creation of attractive, safe parks and trails, like this hiking and biking trail built on a former rail line in Washington, D.C. Frequent opportunities to observe others exercising can promote physical activity.

The exercise format that works best depends on the beginning exerciser's characteristics. Normal-weight adults are more likely to stick with group classes than are overweight adults, who may feel embarrassed and struggle to keep up with the pace. Overweight people do better with an individualized, home-based routine planned by a consultant (King, 2001). However, adults with highly stressful lives are more likely to persist in group classes, which offer a regular schedule and the face-to-face support of others, than in a home-based program (King et al., 1997). Yet when stressed people do manage to sustain a home-based program, it substantially reduces stress—more so than the group format (King, Taylor, & Haskell, 1993). Perhaps succeeding on their own helps stressed adults gain better control over their lives.

Accessible, attractive, and safe exercise environments—parks, walking and biking trails, and community recreation centers—and frequent opportunities to observe others using them also promote physical activity (King et al., 2000). Besides health problems and daily stressors, low-SES adults often mention inconvenient access to facilities, expense, unsafe neighborhoods, and unclean streets as barriers to exercise—important reasons that activity level declines sharply with SES (Taylor et al., 2007; Wilbur et al., 2003). Interventions aimed at increasing physical activity among low-SES adults must address these issues in addition to lifestyle and motivational factors.

An Optimistic Outlook

What type of individual is likely to cope adaptively with stress brought on by the inevitable changes of life? Researchers interested in this question have identified a set of three personal qualities—control, commitment, and challenge—that, together, they call **hardiness** (Maddi, 1999, 2005, 2007).

Trisha fit the pattern of a hardy individual. First, she regarded most experiences as *controllable.* "You can't stop all bad things from happening," she advised Jewel after hearing about her menopausal symptoms, "but you can try to do something about them." Second, Trisha displayed a *committed,* involved approach to daily activities, finding interest and meaning in almost all of them. Finally, she viewed change as a *challenge*—a normal part of life and a chance for personal growth.

Hardiness influences the extent to which people appraise stressful situations as manageable, interesting, and enjoyable. These optimistic appraisals, in turn, predict health-promoting behaviors, tendency to seek social support, and fewer physical symptoms (Maddi, 2006; Smith, Young, & Lee, 2004). Furthermore, high-hardy individuals are likely to use active, problem-centered coping strategies in situations they can control. In contrast, low-hardy people more often use emotion-centered and avoidant coping strategies—for example, saying, "I wish I could change how I feel," denying that the stressful event occurred, or eating and drinking to forget about it (Maddi, 2007; Maddi & Hightower, 1999; Soderstrom et al., 2000).

In some studies, hardiness-related optimistic appraisals were associated with lower physiological arousal to stress—a major means by which hardiness is believed to protect against illness. This link does not always appear, perhaps because a hardy person's active coping sometimes leads to greater physiological arousal. But over time, this increase may be offset by a calm that comes with effective stress management (Wiebe & Williams, 1992). In support of this idea, the optimistic component of hardiness predicts lower average blood pressure, measured over a three-day period (Räikkönen et al., 1999). And in a longitudinal study of more than 400 medical-clinic patients, optimism was positively related to self-reported physical and mental health 30 years later (Maruta et al., 2002).

In this and previous chapters, we have seen that many factors act as stress-resistant resources—among them heredity, diet, exercise, social support, and coping strategies. Research on hardiness adds yet another ingredient: a generally optimistic outlook and zest for life.

Gender and Aging: A Double Standard

Negative stereotypes of aging, which lead many middle-aged adults to fear physical changes, are more likely to be applied to women than to men, yielding a double standard. Though many women in midlife say they have "hit their stride"—feel assertive, confident, versatile, and capable of resolving life's problems—people often rate them as less attractive and as having more negative personality characteristics than middle-aged men (Canetto, Kaminski, & Felicio, 1995; Denmark & Klara, 2007; Kite et al., 2005). And the sex of the person doing the rating makes a difference: Men tend to judge an aging female more harshly than women do (Kogan & Mills, 1992).

These effects appear more often when people rate photos as opposed to verbal descriptions of men and women. The ideal of a sexually attractive woman—smooth skin, good muscle tone, lustrous hair—may be at the heart of the double standard of aging. Some evidence suggests that the end of a woman's ability to bear children contributes to negative judgments of physical appearance, especially by men (Marcus-Newhall, Thompson, & Thomas, 2001). Yet societal forces exaggerate this view. For example, middle-aged people in media ads are usually male executives, fathers, and grandfathers—handsome images of competence and security. And many more cosmetic products designed to hide signs of aging are offered for women than for men.

At one time in our evolutionary history, this double standard may have been adaptive. Today, as many couples limit childbearing and devote more time to career and leisure pursuits, it has become irrelevant. And new surveys suggest that the double standard is declining—that more people are viewing middle age as a potentially upbeat, satisfying time for both genders, sometimes even more so for women than for men (Menon, 2002; Narayan, 2008). Models of older women with lives full of intimacy, accomplishment, hope, and imagination are promoting acceptance of physical aging and a new vision of growing older—one that emphasizes gracefulness, fulfillment, and inner strength.

ASK YOURSELF

» REVIEW
Cite evidence that biological aging, individual heredity, and environmental factors contribute to osteoporosis.

» APPLY
During a routine physical exam, Dr. Furrow gave 55-year-old Bill a battery of tests for cardiovascular disease but did not assess his bone density. In contrast, when 60-year-old Cara complained of chest pains, Dr. Furrow opted to "wait and see" before initiating further testing. What might account for Dr. Furrow's different approaches to Cara and Bill?

» CONNECT
According to the lifespan perspective, development is multidimensional—affected by biological, psychological, and social forces. Provide examples of how this assumption characterizes health at midlife.

» REFLECT
Which midlife health problem is of greatest personal concern to you? What steps can you take now to help prevent it?

Cognitive Development

In middle adulthood, the cognitive demands of everyday life extend to new and sometimes more challenging situations. Consider a typical day in the lives of Devin and Trisha. Recently appointed dean of faculty at a small college, Devin was at his desk by 7:00 A.M. In between strategic-planning meetings, he reviewed files of applicants for new positions, worked on the coming year's budget, and spoke at an alumni luncheon. Meanwhile, Trisha prepared for a civil trial, participated in jury selection, and then joined the other top lawyers at her firm for a conference about management issues. That evening, Trisha and Devin advised their 20-year-old son, Mark, who had dropped by to discuss his uncertainty over whether to change his college major. By 7:30 P.M., Trisha was off to an evening meeting of the local school board. And Devin left for a biweekly gathering of an amateur quartet in which he played the cello.

Middle adulthood is a time of expanding responsibilities—on the job, in the community, and at home. To juggle diverse roles effectively, Devin and Trisha called on a wide array of intellectual abilities, including accumulated knowledge, verbal fluency, memory, rapid analysis of information, reasoning, problem solving, and expertise in their areas of specialization. What changes in thinking take place in middle adulthood? How does vocational life—a major arena in which cognition is expressed—influence intellectual skills? And what can be done to support the rising tide of adults who are returning to college in hopes of enhancing their knowledge and quality of life?

Changes in Mental Abilities

At age 50, when he occasionally couldn't recall a name or had to pause in the middle of a lecture or speech to think about what to say next, Devin wondered, Are these signs of an aging mind? Twenty years earlier, he had taken little notice of the same events. His questioning stems from widely held stereotypes of older adults as forgetful and confused. Most cognitive aging research has focused on deficits while neglecting cognitive stability and gains.

As we examine changes in thinking in middle adulthood, we will revisit the theme of diversity in development. Different aspects of cognitive functioning show different patterns of change. Although declines occur in some areas, most people display cognitive competence, especially in familiar contexts, and some attain outstanding accomplishment. As we will see, some apparent decrements in cognitive aging result from weaknesses in the research itself! Overall, the evidence supports an optimistic view of adult cognitive potential.

The research we are about to consider illustrates core assumptions of the lifespan perspective: development as *multidimensional,* or the combined result of biological, psychological, and social forces; development as *multidirectional,* or the joint expression of growth and decline, with the precise mix varying across abilities and individuals; and development as *plastic,* or open to change, depending on how a person's biological and environmental history combines with current life conditions. You may find it helpful to return to pages 9–10 in Chapter 1 to review these ideas.

Cohort Effects

Research using intelligence tests sheds light on the widely held belief that intelligence inevitably declines in middle and late adulthood as the brain deteriorates. Many early cross-sectional studies showed this pattern—a peak in performance at age 35 followed by a steep drop into old age. But widespread testing of college students and soldiers in the 1920s provided a convenient opportunity to conduct longitudinal research, retesting participants in middle adulthood. These findings revealed an age-related increase! To explain this contradiction, K. Warner Schaie (1998, 2005) used a sequential design, combining longitudinal and cross-sectional approaches (see pages 36–37 in Chapter 1) in the Seattle Longitudinal Study.

In 1956, people ranging in age from 22 to 70 were tested cross-sectionally. Then, at regular intervals, longitudinal follow-ups were conducted and new samples added, yielding a total of 5,000 participants, five cross-sectional comparisons, and longitudinal data spanning more than 60 years. Findings on five mental abilities showed the typical cross-sectional drop after the mid-thirties. But longitudinal trends for those abilities revealed modest gains in midlife, sustained into the fifties and the early sixties, after which performance decreased gradually.

Figure 15.4 illustrates Schaie's cross-sectional and longitudinal outcomes for just one intellectual factor: verbal ability. How can we explain the seeming contradiction in findings? *Cohort effects* are largely responsible for this difference. In cross-sectional research, each new generation experienced better health and education than the one before it. Also, the tests given may tap abilities less often used by older individuals, whose lives no longer require that they learn information for its own sake but, instead, skillfully solve real-world problems.

Crystallized and Fluid Intelligence

A close look at diverse mental abilities shows that only certain ones follow the longitudinal pattern identified in Figure 15.4. To appreciate this variation, let's consider two broad mental abilities, each of which includes an array of specific intellectual factors.

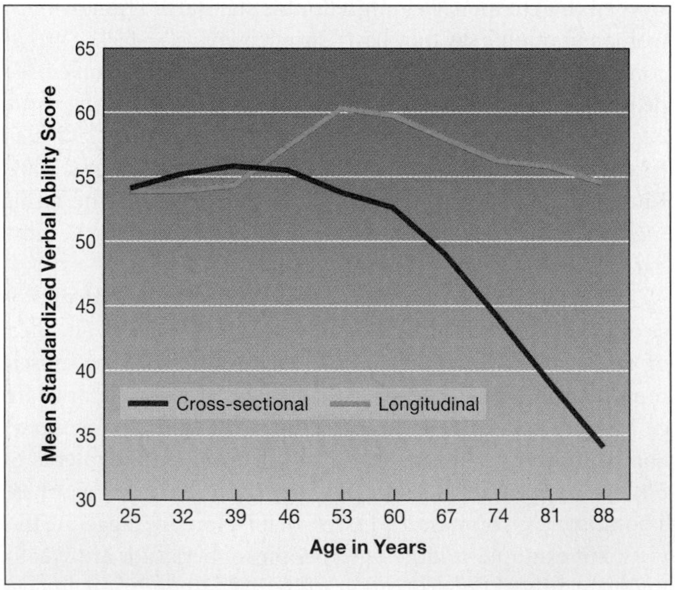

■ **FIGURE 15.4** ■ **Cross-sectional and longitudinal trends in verbal ability, illustrating cohort effects.** The steep cross-sectional decline is largely due to better health and education in younger generations. When adults are followed longitudinally, their verbal scores rise during early and middle adulthood and gradually decline during later years. However, this longitudinal trend does not hold for all abilities. (From K. W. Schaie, 1988, "Variability in Cognitive Functioning in the Elderly," in M. A. Bender, R. C. Leonard, & A. D. Woodhead (Eds.), *Phenotypic Variation in Populations,* p. 201. Adapted with kind permission from Springer Science and Business Media and the author.)

In 2009, 58-year-old Chesley "Sully" Sullenberger successfully landed a distressed commercial airliner in the Hudson River just off-shore of New York City, saving all its passengers and crew. As his extraordinary skill illustrates, midlife is a time when some of the most complex mental abilities are at their peak.

The first of these broad abilities, **crystallized intelligence,** refers to skills that depend on accumulated knowledge and experience, good judgment, and mastery of social conventions—abilities acquired because they are valued by the individual's culture. Devin made use of crystallized intelligence when he expressed himself articulately at the alumni luncheon and suggested effective ways to save money in budget planning. On intelligence tests, vocabulary, general information, verbal comprehension, and logical reasoning items measure crystallized intelligence.

In contrast, **fluid intelligence** depends more heavily on basic information-processing skills—ability to detect relationships among visual stimuli, speed of analyzing information, and capacity of working memory. Though fluid intelligence often combines with crystallized intelligence to support effective reasoning and problem solving, it is believed to be influenced less by culture than by conditions in the brain and by learning unique to the individual (Horn & Noll, 1997). Intelligence test items reflecting fluid abilities include spatial visualization, digit span, letter–number sequencing, and symbol search. (Refer to page 309 in Chapter 9 for examples.)

Many cross-sectional studies show that crystallized intelligence increases steadily through middle adulthood, whereas fluid intelligence begins to decline in the twenties. These trends have been found repeatedly in investigations in which younger and older participants had similar education and general health status, largely correcting for cohort effects (Horn, Donaldson, & Engstrom, 1981; Kaufman & Horn, 1996; Park et al., 2002). In one such investigation, including nearly 2,500 mentally and physically healthy 16- to 85-year-olds, verbal (crystallized) IQ peaked between ages 45 and 54 and did not decline until the eighties! Nonverbal (fluid) IQ, in contrast, dropped steadily over the entire age range (Kaufman, 2001).

The midlife rise in crystallized abilities makes sense because adults are constantly adding to their knowledge and skills at work, at home, and in leisure activities. In addition, many crystallized skills are practiced almost daily. But does longitudinal evidence confirm the progressive falloff in fluid intelligence? And if so, how can we explain it?

■ **SCHAIE'S SEATTLE LONGITUDINAL STUDY.** Figure 15.5 shows Schaie's longitudinal findings in detail. The five factors that gained in early and middle adulthood—verbal ability, inductive reasoning, verbal memory, spatial orientation, and numeric ability—include both crystallized and fluid skills. Their paths of change confirm that midlife is a time when some of the most complex mental abilities are at their peak (Willis & Schaie, 1999). According to these findings, middle-aged adults are intellectually "in their prime," not—as stereotypes would have it—"over the hill."

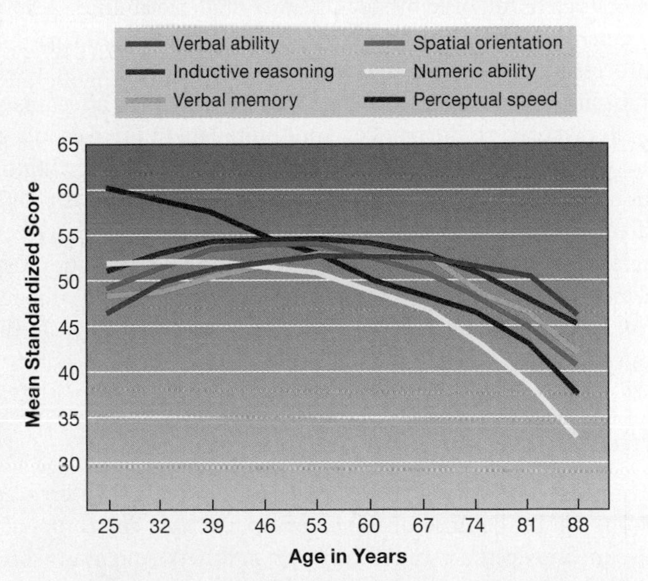

■ **FIGURE 15.5** ■ **Longitudinal trends in six mental abilities, from the Seattle Longitudinal Study.** In five abilities, modest gains occurred into the fifties and early sixties, followed by gradual declines. The sixth ability—perceptual speed—decreased steadily from the twenties to the late eighties. And late in life, fluid factors (spatial orientation, numeric ability, and perceptual speed) showed greater decrements than crystallized factors (verbal ability, inductive reasoning, and verbal memory). (From K. W. Schaie, 1994, "The Course of Adult Intellectual Development," *American Psychologist, 49,* p. 308. Copyright © 1994 by the American Psychological Association. Reprinted with permission of American Psychological Association.)

Figure 15.5 also shows a sixth ability, *perceptual speed*—a fluid skill in which participants must, for example, identify within a time limit which of five shapes is identical to a model or whether pairs of multidigit numbers are the same or different. Perceptual speed decreased from the twenties to the late eighties—a pattern that fits with a wealth of research indicating that cognitive processing slows as people get older (Schaie, 1998, 2005). Also notice in Figure 15.5 how, late in life, fluid factors (spatial orientation, numeric ability, and perceptual speed) show greater decrements than crystallized factors (verbal ability, inductive reasoning, and verbal memory). These trends have been confirmed in short-term longitudinal follow-ups of individuals varying widely in age (McArdle et al., 2002).

EXPLAINING CHANGES IN MENTAL ABILITIES. Some theorists believe that a general slowing of central nervous system functioning underlies nearly all age-related declines in cognitive performance (Salthouse, 1996, 2006). Many studies offer at least partial support for this idea. For example, Kaufman (2001) reported that scores on speeded tasks mirror the regular, age-related decline in fluid-task performance. Researchers have also identified other important changes in information processing, some of which may be triggered by declines in speed.

Before we turn to this evidence, let's clarify why research reveals gains followed by stability in crystallized abilities, despite a much earlier decline in fluid intelligence, or basic information-processing skills. First, the decrease in basic processing, while substantial after age 45, may not be great enough to affect many well-practiced performances until quite late in life. Second, as we will see, adults can often compensate for cognitive limitations by drawing on their cognitive strengths. Finally, as people discover that they are no longer as good as they once were at certain tasks, they accommodate, shifting to activities that depend less on cognitive efficiency and more on accumulated knowledge. Thus, the basketball player becomes a coach, the once quick-witted salesperson a manager.

Individual and Group Differences

The age trends just described mask large individual differences. Some adults, because of illness or unfavorable environments, decline intellectually much earlier than others. And many show full functioning, even in fluid abilities, at an advanced age (Schaie, 1989).

Adults who use their intellectual skills seem to maintain them longer. In the Seattle Longitudinal Study, declines were delayed for people with above-average education, complex occupations, and stimulating leisure pursuits that included reading, traveling, attending cultural events, and participating in clubs and professional organizations. People with flexible personalities, lasting marriages (especially to a cognitively high-functioning partner), and absence of cardiovascular and other chronic diseases were also likely to maintain mental abilities well into late adulthood. And being economically well-off was linked to favorable cognitive development, undoubtedly because SES is associated with many of the factors just mentioned (Schaie, 1996, 2000).

Several sex differences also emerged, consistent with those found in childhood and adolescence. In early and middle adulthood, women outperformed men on verbal tasks and perceptual speed, while men excelled at spatial skills (Maitland et al., 2000). Overall, however, changes in mental abilities over the adult years were remarkably similar for the two sexes, defying the stereotype that older women are less competent than older men.

Furthermore, when the baby-boom generation, now middle-aged, was compared with the previous generation at the same age, cohort effects were evident. On verbal memory, inductive reasoning, and spatial orientation, baby boomers performed substantially better, reflecting generational advances in education, technology, environmental stimulation, and health care (Willis & Schaie, 1999). These gains are expected to continue: Today's children, adolescents, and adults of all ages attain substantially higher mental test scores than same-age individuals born just a decade or two earlier—differences that are largest for fluid-ability tasks (Flynn, 1999, 2007; Rodgers & Wänström, 2007; Zelinski & Kennison, 2007).

Finally, adults who maintained higher levels of perceptual speed tended to be advantaged in other cognitive capacities. As we turn to information processing in midlife, we will pay special attention to the impact of processing speed on other aspects of cognitive functioning.

Information Processing

Information-processing researchers interested in adult development usually use the model of the mental system introduced in Chapter 5 (see page 161) to guide their exploration of different aspects of thinking. As processing speed slows, certain aspects of attention and memory decline. Yet midlife is also a time of great expansion in cognitive competence as adults apply their vast knowledge and life experience to problem solving in the everyday world.

Speed of Processing

Devin watched with fascination as his 20-year-old son, Mark, played a computer game, responding to multiple on-screen cues in rapid-fire fashion. When Devin tried it, although he practiced over several days, his performance remained well behind Mark's. Similarly, on a family holiday in Australia, Mark adjusted quickly to driving on the left side of the road, but after a week, Trisha and Devin still felt confused at intersections, where rapid responses were needed.

These real-life experiences fit with laboratory findings. On both simple reaction-time tasks (pushing a button in response to a light) and complex ones (pushing a left-hand button to a blue light, a right-hand button to a yellow light), response time increases steadily from the early twenties into the nineties. The more complex the situation, the more disadvantaged older adults are. Though small—less than 1 second in most studies—the decline in speed is nevertheless of practical significance (Deary & Der, 2005; Der & Deary, 2006).

What causes this age-related slowing of cognitive processing? Researchers agree that changes in the brain are responsible but disagree on the precise explanation (Hartley, 2006; Salthouse & Caja, 2000). According to the **neural network view,** as neurons in the brain die, breaks in neural networks occur. The brain adapts by forming bypasses—new synaptic connections that go around the breaks but are less efficient (Cerella, 1990). Another hypothesis, the **information-loss view,** suggests that older adults experience greater loss of information as it moves through the cognitive system. As a result, the whole system must slow down to inspect and interpret the information. Imagine making a photocopy, then using it to make another copy. Each subsequent copy is less clear. Similarly, with each step of thinking, information degrades. The older the adult, the more exaggerated this effect. Complex tasks, which have more processing steps, are more affected by information loss (Myerson et al., 1990).

At present, researchers are not sure whether just one or two neural changes, or multiple changes that vary across individuals, underlie declines in processing speed (Hartley, 2006). What is clear is that processing speed predicts adults' performance on many tests of complex abilities. The slower their reaction time, the lower people's scores on memory, reasoning, and problem-solving tasks, with relationships greater for fluid- than crystallized-ability items (Finkel et al., 2007; Salthouse, 2005, 2006). Indeed, as adults get older, correlations between processing speed and other cognitive performances strengthen (see Figure 15.6). This suggests that processing speed contributes broadly to declines in cognitive functioning, which become more widespread and pronounced with aging (Li et al., 2004).

Yet as Figure 15.6 shows, processing speed correlates only moderately with older adults' performances, including fluid-ability tasks. And it is not the only major predictor of age-related cognitive changes. Other factors—declines in vision and hearing and in attentional resources, inhibition, working-memory capacity, and use of memory strategies—also predict diverse age-related cognitive performances (Hartley, 2006; Luo & Craik, 2008). Nevertheless, processing speed, as we will see in the following sections, does contribute to the decrements in attention and memory just mentioned (Levitt, Fugelsang, & Crossley, 2006; Salthouse, Fristoe, & Rhee, 1996). But disagreement persists over whether age-related cognitive changes have just one common cause, best represented by processing speed, or multiple independent causes.

Furthermore, processing speed is a weak predictor of the skill with which older adults perform complex, familiar tasks in everyday life, which they continue to do with considerable proficiency. Devin, for example, played a Mozart quartet on his cello with great speed and dexterity, keeping up with three other players 10 years his junior. How did he manage? Compared with the others, he more often looked ahead in the score (Krampe & Charness, 2007). Using this compensatory approach, he could prepare a response in advance, thereby minimizing the importance of speed. In one study, researchers asked 19- to 72-year-olds to perform a variety of typing tasks and also tested their reaction time. Although reaction time slowed with age, typing speed did not change (Salthouse, 1984). Like Devin, older typists look further ahead in the material to be typed, anticipating their next keystrokes. Knowledge and experience can also compensate for impairments in processing speed. Devin's many years of playing the cello undoubtedly supported his ability to play swiftly and fluidly.

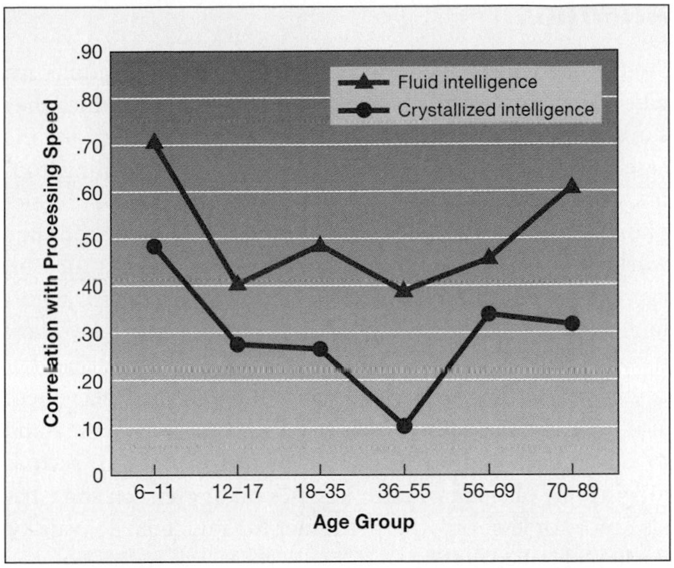

■ **FIGURE 15.6** ■ **Age-related changes in correlations of processing speed with measures of fluid and crystallized intelligence.** Correlations are higher at younger and at older ages. During childhood, gains in processing speed support development of other abilities and are related to mental test performance (see Chapter 9, page 310). As people age, declines in processing speed limit many abilities, but more so for fluid than crystallized skills. Note, however, that even at the oldest ages, correlations between processing speed and other abilities are moderate. (From S.-C. Li et al., 2004, "Transformations in the Couplings Among Intellectual Abilities and Constituent Cognitive Processes Across the Life Span," *Psychological Science, 15,* p. 160. © Association of Psychological Science. Reprinted by permission of Blackwell Publishing Ltd.)

Because older adults find ways to compensate for cognitive slowing on familiar tasks, their reaction time is considerably better on verbal items (indicating as quickly as possible whether a string of letters forms a word) than on nonverbal items (responding to a light or other signal) (Hultsch, MacDonald, & Dixon, 2002; Wingfield & Stine-Morrow, 2000). Finally, as we will see in Chapter 17, older adults' processing speed can be improved through training, though age differences remain.

Attention

Studies of attention focus on how much information adults can take into their mental systems at once; the extent to which they can attend selectively, ignoring irrelevant information; and the ease with which they can adapt their attention, switching from one task to another as the situation demands. When Dottie telephoned, Trisha sometimes tried to prepare dinner or continue working on a legal brief while talking on the phone. But with age, she found it harder to engage in the two activities simultaneously. Consistent with Trisha's experience, laboratory research reveals that sustaining two complex tasks at once becomes more challenging with age. An age-related decrement also occurs in the ability to focus on relevant information and to switch back and forth between mental operations, such as judging one of a pair of numbers as "odd or even" on some trials, "more or less" on others (Kramer & Kray, 2006; Radvansky, Zacks, & Hasher, 2005).

These declines in attention might be due to the slowdown in information processing described earlier, which limits the amount of information a person can attend to at once (Kramer & Madden, 2008; Plude & Hoyer, 1985). Reduced processing speed may also contribute to a related finding: a decrement with age in the ability to combine many pieces of visual information into a meaningful pattern. When the mind inspects stimuli slowly, they are more likely to remain disconnected (Plude & Doussard-Roosevelt, 1989). This problem, in turn, can intensify attentional difficulties.

As adults get older, *inhibition*—resistance to interference from irrelevant information—is also harder (Gazzaley et al., 2005; Hasher, Zacks, & May, 1999). On *continuous performance tasks,* in which participants are shown a series of stimuli on a computer screen and asked to press the space bar only after a particular sequence occurs (for example, the letter *K* immediately followed by the letter *A*), performance declines steadily from the thirties into old age, with older adults making more errors of commission (pressing the space bar in response to incorrect letter sequences). And when extraneous noise is introduced, errors of omission (not pressing the space bar after a *K–A* sequence) also rise with age (Mani, Bedwell, & Miller, 2005). In everyday life, inhibitory difficulties cause older adults to appear distractible—inappropriately diverted from the task at hand by a thought or a feature of the environment.

Again, adults can compensate for these changes. People highly experienced in attending to critical information and performing several tasks at once, such as air traffic controllers and pilots, know exactly what to look for. As a result, they show smaller age-related attentional declines (Tsang & Shaner, 1998). Similarly, older adults focus on relevant information and handle two tasks proficiently when they have extensively practiced those activities over their lifetimes (Kramer & Madden, 2008).

Finally, practice can improve the ability to divide attention between two tasks, selectively focus on relevant information, and switch back and forth between mental operations. When older adults receive training in these skills, their performance improves as much as that of younger adults, although training does not close the gap between age groups (Bherer et al., 2006; Erickson et al., 2007; Kramer, Hahn, & Gopher, 1998).

ELLIOTT FRANKS/© AFENAPAL/TOPHAM/THE IMAGE WORKS

Conductors and teachers must focus on relevant information within a complex field of stimulation and divide their attention among competing tasks—well-practiced skills that may help slow age-related declines in attention.

Memory

Memory is crucial for all aspects of information processing—an important reason that we place great value on a good memory in middle and late adulthood. From the twenties into the sixties, the amount of information people can retain in working memory diminishes. Whether given lists of words or digits or meaningful prose passages to learn, middle-aged and older adults recall less than young adults, although memory for prose suffers less than memory for list items (Hultsch et al., 1998; Old & Naveh-Benjamin, 2008a).

This change is largely due to a decline in use of memory strategies on these tasks. Older individuals rehearse less than younger individuals—a difference believed to be due to a slower rate of thinking (Salthouse, 1996). Older people cannot repeat new information to themselves as quickly as younger people. Reduced working-memory capacity is another likely influence, leading to difficulties in retaining to-be-remembered items and processing them at the same time (Park & Payer, 2006).

Memory strategies of organization and elaboration, which require people to link incoming information with already stored information, are also applied less often and less effectively with age (Dunlosky & Hertzog, 2001; Troyer et al., 2006). An additional reason older adults are less likely to use these techniques is that they find it harder to retrieve information from long-term memory that would help them recall. For example, given a list of words containing *parrot* and *blue jay,* they don't immediately access the category "bird," even though they know it well (Hultsch et al., 1998). Why does this happen? Greater difficulty keeping one's attention on relevant information seems to be involved. As irrelevant stimuli take up space in working memory, less is available for the memory task at hand (O'Connor & Kaplan, 2003; Radvansky, Zacks, & Hasher, 2005).

But keep in mind that the memory tasks given by researchers require strategies that many adults seldom use and may not be motivated to use, since most are not in school (see Chapter 9, page 305). When a word list has a strong category-based structure, older adults organize as well as younger adults do (Naveh-Benjamin, 2000; Naveh-Benjamin et al., 2005). And when given training in strategic memorizing, middle-aged and older people use strategies willingly, and they show improved performance over long periods, though age differences remain (Derwinger, Neely, & Bäckman, 2005).

Furthermore, tasks can be designed to help older people compensate for age-related declines in working memory—for example, by slowing the pace at which information is presented or cuing the link between new and previously stored information ("To learn these words, try thinking of the category 'bird'") (Hay & Jacoby, 1999). In one study, adults ranging in age from 19 to 68 were shown a video and immediately tested on its content (a pressured, classroomlike condition). Then they were given a packet of information on the same topic as the video to study at their leisure and told to return three days later to be tested (a self-paced condition) (Beier & Ackerman, 2005). Performance declined with age only in the pressured condition, not in the self-paced condition. And although topic-relevant knowledge predicted better recall in both conditions, it did so more strongly in the self-paced condition, which granted participants ample time to retrieve and apply what they already knew.

© JESSE FOLKS

Age-related changes in memory vary widely across tasks and individuals. Bringing decades of experience to the task, these actors in a community theater production retain the ability to memorize hundreds of lines and perform demanding roles.

As these findings illustrate, assessing older adults in highly structured, constrained conditions substantially underestimates what they can remember when given an opportunity to pace their own learning. When we consider the variety of memory skills we call on in daily life, the decrements just described are limited in scope. General *factual knowledge* (such as historical events), *procedural knowledge* (such as how to drive a car or solve a math problem), and knowledge related to one's occupation either remain unchanged or increase into midlife. Furthermore, middle-aged people who have trouble recalling something often draw on decades of accumulated *metacognitive knowledge* about how to maximize performance—reviewing major points before an important presentation, organizing notes and files so information can be found quickly, and parking the car in the same area of the parking lot each day. Research suggests that aging has little impact on metacognition (Berg, 2000; Schwartz & Frazier, 2005).

In sum, age-related changes in memory vary widely across tasks and individuals as people use their cognitive capacities to meet the requirements of their everyday worlds. ***TAKE A MOMENT...*** Does this remind you of Sternberg's *theory of successful intelligence,* described in Chapter 9—in particular, his notion of *practical intelligence* (see page 311)? Intelligent people adapt their information-processing skills to fit with their personal desires and the demands of their environments. Therefore, to understand memory development (and other aspects of cognition) in adulthood, we must view it in context. As we turn to problem solving, expertise, and creativity, we will encounter this theme again.

Practical Problem Solving and Expertise

One evening, as Devin and Trisha sat in the balcony of the Chicago Opera House awaiting curtain time, the announcement came that 67-year-old Ardis Krainik, the opera company's general director and "life force," had died. After a shocked hush, members of the audience began turning to one another, asking about the woman who had made the opera company into one of the world's greatest.

Starting as a chorus singer and clerk typist, Ardis rose rapidly through the ranks, becoming assistant to the director and developing a reputation for tireless work and unmatched organizational skill. When the opera company fell deeply in debt, Ardis—now the newly appointed general director—erased the deficit within a year and restored the company's sagging reputation. She charmed donors into making large contributions, attracted world-class singers, and filled the house to near capacity. On her office wall hung a sign she had received as a gift. It read, "Wonder Woman" (Rhein, 1997).

Ardis's story is a dramatic one, but all middle-aged adults encounter opportunities to display continued cognitive growth in the realm of **practical problem solving,** which requires people to size up real-world situations and analyze how best to achieve goals that have a high degree of uncertainty. Gains in *expertise*—an extensive, highly organized, and integrated knowledge base that can be used to support a high level of performance—help us understand why practical problem solving takes this leap forward.

The development of expertise is under way in early adulthood and reaches its height in midlife, leading to highly efficient and effective approaches to solving problems that are organized around abstract principles and intuitive judgments. Saturated with experience, the expert intuitively feels when an approach to a problem will work and when it will not. This rapid, implicit application of knowledge is the result of years of learning, experience, and effortful practice (Krampe & Charness, 2007; Wagner, 2000). It cannot be assessed by laboratory tasks or mental tests that do not call on this knowledge.

Expertise is not just the province of the highly educated and of those who rise to the top of administrative ladders. In a study of food service workers, researchers identified the diverse ingredients of expert performance in terms of physical skills (strength and dexterity); technical knowledge (of menu items, ordering, and food presentation); organizational skills (setting priorities, anticipating customer needs); and social skills (confident presentation and a pleasant, polished manner). Next, 20- to 60-year-olds with fewer than two to more than ten years of experience were evaluated on these qualities. Although physical strength and dexterity declined with age, job knowledge and organizational and social skills increased (Perlmutter, Kaplan, & Nyquist, 1990). Compared to younger adults with similar years of experience, middle-aged employees performed more competently, serving customers in especially adept, attentive ways.

Age-related advantages are also evident in solutions to everyday problems (Denney, 1990; Denney & Pearce, 1989). ***TAKE A MOMENT...*** Consider the following dilemma:

> What would you do if you had a landlord who refused to make some expensive repairs you want done because he or she thinks they are too costly?
>
> **a.** Try to make the repairs yourself.
> **b.** Try to understand your landlord's view and decide whether they are necessary repairs.
> **c.** Try to get someone to settle the dispute between you and your landlord.
> **d.** Accept the situation and don't dwell on it. (Cornelius & Caspi, 1987, p. 146)

In this example, the preferred choice is (b), a problem-centered approach that involves seeking information and using it to guide action. From middle age on, adults place greater emphasis on thinking through a practical problem—trying to understand it better, interpreting it from different perspectives, and solving it through logical analysis. On tasks like this one, middle-aged and older adults select strategies that are at least as good as and sometimes better than (as rated by independent judges) those of young adults (Kim & Hasher, 2005). Perhaps for this reason, they are more rational decision makers—less likely than young adults to select attractive-looking options that, on further reflection, are not the best.

Creativity

As noted in Chapter 13, creative accomplishment tends to peak in the late thirties or early forties and then decline, but with considerable variation across individuals and disciplines. Some people produce highly creative works in later decades: In her early sixties, Martha Graham choreographed *Clytemnestra,*

© BRIANA ©RR

In middle adulthood, creativity becomes more thoughtful, integrative, and altruistic. Author Masha Hamilton's travels to northeastern Kenya to research her novel, *The Camel Bookmobile,* led her to help organize the Camel Book Drive. It has funded the purchase of camels, books, and equipment for nomadic schools in the area.

recognized as one of the great full-length modern-dance dramas. Igor Stravinsky composed his last major musical work at age 84. Charles Darwin finished *On the Origin of Species* at age 50 and continued to write groundbreaking books and papers in his sixties and seventies. After abandoning a career in embroidery because of arthritis, Anna Mary Robertson Moses (known as Grandma Moses) began painting scenes of country life in her seventies, producing about 1,600 works between ages 75 and 101 (Antonini et al., 2008; Tahir & Gruber, 2003). And as with problem solving, the *quality* of creativity may change with advancing age—in at least three ways.

First, youthful creativity in literature and the arts is often spontaneous and intensely emotional, while creative works produced after age 40 often appear more deliberately thoughtful (Lubart & Sternberg, 1998). Perhaps for this reason, poets produce their most frequently cited works at younger ages than do authors of fiction and nonfiction (Cohen-Shalev, 1986). Poetry depends more on language play and "hot" expression of feelings, whereas story- and book-length works require extensive planning and molding.

Second, with age, many creators shift from generating unusual products to combining extensive knowledge and experience into unique ways of thinking (Abra, 1989; Sasser-Coen, 1993). Creative works by older adults more often sum up or integrate ideas. Mature academics typically devote less energy to new discoveries in favor of writing memoirs, histories of their field, and other reflective works. And in older creators' novels, scholarly writings, paintings, and musical compositions, living with old age and facing death are common themes (Beckerman, 1990; Sternberg & Lubart, 2001).

Finally, creativity in middle adulthood frequently reflects a transition from a largely egocentric concern with self-expression to more altruistic goals (Tahir & Gruber, 2003). As the middle-aged person overcomes the youthful illusion that life is eternal, the desire to give to humanity and enrich the lives of others increases.

Taken together, these changes may contribute to an overall decline in creative output in later decades. In reality, however, creativity takes new forms.

Information Processing in Context

Cognitive gains in middle adulthood are especially likely in areas involving experience-based buildup and transformation of knowledge and skills. As the evidence just reviewed confirms, processing speed varies with the situation. When given challenging real-world problems related to their expertise, middle-aged adults are likely to win out in both efficiency and excellence of thinking. Furthermore, on tasks and test items relevant to their real-life endeavors, intelligent, cognitively active midlifers respond as quickly and competently as their younger counterparts do!

By middle age, people's past and current experiences vary enormously—more so than in previous decades—and thinking is characterized by an increase in specialization as people branch out in various directions. Yet to reach their cognitive potential, adults must have opportunities for continued growth. Let's see how vocational and educational environments can support cognition in midlife.

ASK YOURSELF

» REVIEW
How do slowing of cognitive processing, reduced working-memory capacity, and difficulties with inhibition affect memory in midlife? What can older adults do to compensate for these declines?

» APPLY
Asked about hiring older sales personnel, a department store manager replied, "They're my best employees!" Why does this manager find older employees desirable, despite the age-related decline in speed of processing?

» CONNECT
In which aspects of cognition did Devin decline, and in which did he gain? How do changes in Devin's thinking reflect assumptions of the lifespan perspective?

Vocational Life and Cognitive Development

Vocational settings are vital contexts for maintaining previously acquired skills and learning new ones. Yet work environments vary in the degree to which they are cognitively stimulating and promote autonomy. And inaccurate, negative stereotypes of age-related problem-solving and decision-making skills can result in older employees being assigned less challenging work.

Recall from Chapter 13 that cognitive and personality characteristics affect occupational choice. Once a person is immersed in a job, it influences cognition. In a study of over 600 U.S. men representing a wide range of occupations, researchers asked about the task complexity and self-direction of their jobs. During the interview, they also assessed cognitive flexibility, based on logical reasoning, awareness of both sides of an issue, and independence of judgment. A decade later, the job and cognitive variables were remeasured, permitting a look at their effects on each other. As expected, cognitively flexible men sought work that offered challenge and autonomy. But the relationship was reciprocal—complex work also led to gains in cognitive flexibility (Kohn & Schooler, 1978).

These same findings emerged in large-scale studies carried out in Japan and Poland—cultures quite different from the United States (Kohn, 2006; Kohn et al., 1990; Kohn & Slomczynski, 1990). In each nation, having a stimulating, nonroutine job helped explain the relationship between SES and flexible, abstract thinking. And people who do intellectually demanding work seek out stimulating leisure pursuits, which also foster cognitive flexibility (Kohn et al., 2000). Finally, because flexible thinkers come to value self-direction, for themselves and also for their children, they are likely to pass on their cognitive preferences to the next generation.

Is the impact of a challenging job on cognitive growth greatest for young adults, who are in the early phase of career development? In fact, research shows that people in their fifties and early sixties gain as much as those in their twenties and thirties. The relationship also holds for people of different generations and, therefore, widely varying life experiences (Avolio & Sosik, 1999; Miller, Slomczynski, & Kohn, 1985). Once again, we are reminded of the plasticity of development. Cognitive flexibility is responsive to vocational experience well into middle adulthood and perhaps beyond. This means that more jobs should be designed to promote intellectual stimulation and challenge—factors linked to higher cognitive functioning later in the lifespan.

© JIM WEST/ALAMY

In this Wayne State University labor studies class for union members, students benefit from an approachable teacher who uses small-group discussion. Active engagement with the subject matter and personal relationships with faculty and other students help middle-aged learners succeed.

Adult Learners: Becoming a Student in Midlife

Adults are returning to undergraduate and graduate study in record numbers. During the past quarter-century, students over age 25 in U.S. colleges and universities increased from 27 to 45 percent of total enrollment, with an especially sharp rise in those over age 35 (U.S. Department of Education, 2009). Life transitions often trigger a return to formal education, as with Devin and Trisha's friend Anya, who entered a nursing program after her last child left home. Divorce, widowhood, a job layoff, a family move, and a youngest child reaching school age are examples of other changes that commonly precede reentry (Moen & Roehling, 2005). Among a sample of African-American women, additional motivations included serving as a role model for children and enriching their ethnic community as a whole (Coker, 2003).

Characteristics of Returning Students

About 60 percent of adult learners are women (U.S. Department of Education, 2009). As Anya's fear of not being able to handle class work suggests (see page 501), first-year reentry women report feeling more self-conscious, inadequate, and hesitant to talk in class than either returning men or traditional-age students (under age 25) (Wilke & Thompson, 1993). Their anxiety is due in part to not having practiced academic learning for many years but is also prompted by negative aging and gender stereotypes—erroneous beliefs that traditional-age students are smarter or that men are more logical and therefore more academically capable. And for minority students, ethnic stereotypes about ability to learn and prejudicial treatment are also factors (Coker, 2003).

Role demands outside of school—from spouses, children, other family members, friends, and employers—pull many returning women in conflicting directions. Those reporting high psychological stress typically have career rather than enrichment goals, young children, limited financial resources, and nonsupportive husbands (Padula & Miller, 1999). When couples fail to rework divisions of household and child-care responsibilities to accommodate the woman's return to school, marital satisfaction declines (Sweet & Moen, 2007). As a classmate told Anya one day, "I tried keeping the book open and reading, cooking, and talking to the kids. It didn't work. So I had to say to my husband, 'Can't you put in a load of laundry once in a while, get home earlier on just some nights?' He forgets—I went through his going to graduate school!"

Because of multiple demands on their time, mature-age women tend to take fewer credits, experience more interruptions in their academic programs, and progress at a slower pace than mature-age men. Role overload is the most common reason for not completing their degrees (Jacobs & King, 2002). But many express high motivation to work through those difficulties, referring to the excitement of learning, to the fulfillment academic success brings, and to their hope that a college education will improve both their work and family lives (Kinser & Deitchman, 2007).

Supporting Returning Students

As these findings suggest, social supports for returning students can make the difference between continuing in school and dropping out. Adult students need family members and friends who encourage their efforts and enable them to find time for uninterrupted study. Anya's classmate explained, "My doubts subsided when one day, my husband volunteered, 'You take your books and do what you need to do. I can cook dinner and do the laundry.'" Institutional services for returning students are also essential. Personal relationships with faculty, peer networks enabling adults to get to know one another, conveniently

Applying What We Know

Facilitating Adult Reentry to College

Sources of Support	Description
Partner and children	Value and encourage educational efforts. Help with household tasks to permit time for uninterrupted study.
Extended family and friends	Value and encourage educational efforts.
Educational institution	Provide orientation programs and literature that inform adult students about services and social supports. Provide counseling and intervention addressing academic weaknesses, self-doubts about success, and matching courses to career goals. Facilitate peer networks through regular meetings or phone contacts. Promote personal relationships with faculty. Encourage active engagement and discussion in classes and integration of course content with real-life experiences. Offer evening, Saturday, and off-campus classes and online courses. Provide financial aid for part-time students. Initiate campaigns to recruit returning students, including those from low-income families and ethnic minority groups. Help students with young children find child-care arrangements and provide on-campus child care.
Workplace	Value and encourage educational efforts. Offer flexible work schedules to make possible coordination of work, class, and family responsibilities.

scheduled evening and Saturday classes, online courses, and financial aid for part-time students increase the chances of academic success.

Although nontraditional students rarely require assistance in settling on career goals, they report a strong desire for help in choosing the most appropriate courses and in exploring jobs related to their talents (Luzzo, 1999). Academic advising and professional internship opportunities responsive to their needs are vital. Low-income students often need special assistance, such as academic tutoring, sessions in confidence building and assertiveness, and—in the case of ethnic minorities—help adjusting to styles of learning that are at odds with their cultural background.

Applying What We Know above suggests ways to facilitate adult reentry to college. When support systems are in place, most returning students reap great personal benefits and do well academically. Succeeding at coordinating education, family, and work demands leads to gains in self-efficacy and admiration from family members, friends, and co-workers (Chao & Good, 2004). Nontraditional students especially value forming new relationships, sharing opinions and experiences, and relating subject matter to their own lives. Their greater ability to integrate knowledge results in an enhanced appreciation of classroom experiences and assignments. And their presence in college classes provides valuable intergenerational contact. As younger students observe the capacities and talents of older classmates, unfavorable stereotypes of aging decline.

After finishing her degree, Anya secured a position as a parish nurse with creative opportunities to counsel members of a large congregation about health concerns. Education granted her new life options, financial rewards, and higher self-esteem as she reevaluated her own competencies. Sometimes (though not in Anya's case) these revised values and increased self-reliance can spark other changes, such as a divorce or a new intimate partnership (Esterberg, Moen, & Dempster-McClain, 1994). In middle adulthood as in earlier years, education transforms development, often powerfully reshaping the life course.

ASK YOURSELF

» REVIEW
In view of the impact of vocational and educational experiences on midlife cognitive development, evaluate the saying "You can't teach an old dog new tricks."

» APPLY
Marcella completed one year of college in her twenties. Now, at age 42, she has returned to earn a degree. Plan a set of experiences for Marcella's first semester that will increase her chances of success.

» CONNECT
Most high-level government and corporate positions are held by middle-aged and older adults rather than by young adults. What cognitive capacities enable mature adults to perform these jobs well?

» REFLECT
Interview a nontraditional student in one of your classes about the personal challenges and rewards of working toward a degree at a later age. What services does your institution offer to support returning students?

Summary

PHYSICAL DEVELOPMENT

Physical Changes

Describe the physical changes of middle adulthood, paying special attention to vision, hearing, the skin, muscle–fat makeup, and the skeleton.

» The gradual physical changes begun in early adulthood continue in midlife, contributing to a revised physical self-image, with less emphasis on hoped-for gains and more on feared declines.

» Vision is affected by **presbyopia,** or loss of the accommodative ability of the lens, reduced ability to see in dim light, increased sensitivity to glare, and diminished color discrimination. After age 40, risk of **glaucoma,** a buildup of pressure in the eye that damages the optic nerve, increases.

» Hearing loss, or **presbycusis,** first affects detection of high frequencies and then spreads to other tones. Presbycusis begins earlier and is more rapid for men, due in part to cigarette smoking and exposure to intense workplace noise.

» The skin wrinkles, loosens, dries, and starts to develop age spots, especially in women and in people exposed to the sun.

» Muscle mass declines and fat deposits increase, with notable sex differences in fat distribution. A low-fat diet and regular exercise that includes resistance training can offset excess weight and muscle loss.

© CHRIS WILLSON/ALAMY

» Bone density declines in both sexes, but to a greater extent in women, especially after menopause. Height loss and bone fractures can result.

Describe reproductive changes in women during middle adulthood, and discuss women's psychological reactions to menopause.

» The **climacteric** in women, which occurs gradually over a 10-year period as estrogen production drops, concludes with **menopause,** sometimes accompanied by emotional and physical symptoms.

» Though **hormone therapy** is successful in reducing the discomforts of menopause, it remains controversial because of increased risks of cardiovascular disease, certain cancers, and cognitive declines.

» Menopause is a biocultural event—affected by societal beliefs and practices as well as hormonal changes. Physical symptoms and psychological reactions vary widely.

Describe reproductive changes in men during middle adulthood.

» Though sperm production continues throughout life, quantity of semen diminishes after age 40. Erections become harder to attain and maintain, but drugs are available to combat impotence.

Health and Fitness

Discuss sexuality in middle adulthood and its association with psychological well-being.

» Frequency of sexual activity among married couples declines only slightly in middle adulthood and is associated with marital happiness. Intensity of sexual response declines more, due to physical changes of the climacteric. Most married people over age 50 find ways to overcome difficulties with sexual functioning.

Discuss cancer, cardiovascular disease, and osteoporosis, noting risk factors and interventions.

» The death rate from cancer increases tenfold from early to middle adulthood. A complex interaction of heredity, biological aging, and environment contributes to cancer. Today 40 percent of affected people are cured. Annual screenings and various preventive steps can reduce the incidence of cancer and cancer deaths.

» Although cardiovascular disease has declined in recent decades, it remains a major cause of death in middle adulthood, especially among men. Symptoms include high blood pressure, high blood cholesterol, atherosclerosis, heart attack, arrhythmia, and angina pectoris. Quitting smoking, reducing blood cholesterol through diet and drug therapy, exercising, and reducing stress can decrease risk and aid in treatment.

» **Osteoporosis** affects 12 percent of people over age 50, most of whom are postmenopausal women. Adequate calcium and vitamin D, weight-bearing and strength-training exercise, and bone-strengthening medications can help prevent and treat osteoporosis.

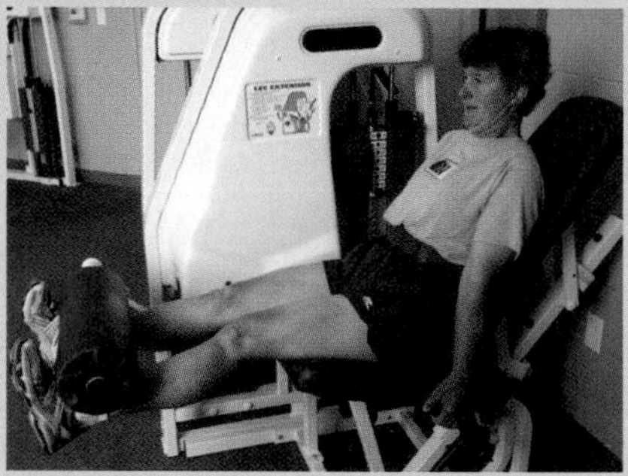
© JEFF GREENBERG/PHOTOEDIT

Discuss the association of hostility and anger with heart disease and other health problems.

» Expressed hostility is a component of the **Type A behavior pattern** that predicts heart disease and other health problems, largely due to physiological arousal associated with anger. Because anger suppression is also related to health problems, a better alternative is to develop effective ways of handling stress and conflict.

Adapting to the Physical Challenges of Midlife

Discuss the benefits of stress management, exercise, and an optimistic outlook in dealing effectively with the physical challenges of midlife.

» Effective stress management includes both problem-centered and emotion-centered coping, depending on the situation; constructive approaches to anger reduction; and social support. In middle adulthood, people tend to cope with stress more effectively, and when they do, they often report lasting personal benefits.

» Regular exercise confers many physical and psychological advantages, making it worthwhile for sedentary middle-aged people to begin exercising. Developing a sense of self-efficacy, choosing an appropriate exercise format, and making exercise environments accessible, attractive, and safe promote physical activity.

» **Hardiness** is made up of three personal qualities: control, commitment, and challenge. By inducing a generally optimistic outlook on life, hardiness helps people cope with stress adaptively.

Explain the double standard of aging.

» Although negative stereotypes of aging discourage older adults of both sexes, middle-aged women are more likely to be viewed unfavorably, especially by men. New surveys suggest that the double standard of aging is declining as both genders view middle age more positively.

COGNITIVE DEVELOPMENT

Changes in Mental Abilities

Describe cohort effects on intelligence revealed by Schaie's Seattle Longitudinal Study.

» Early cross-sectional research showed a peak in intelligence test performance around age 35 followed by a steep decline, whereas longitudinal evidence revealed modest gains in midlife. Using a sequential design, Schaie found that the cross-sectional, steep drop-off largely resulted from cohort effects, as each new generation experienced better health and education.

Describe changes in crystallized and fluid intelligence in middle adulthood, and discuss individual and group differences in intellectual development.

» In cross-sectional studies that correct for cohort effects, **crystallized intelligence** (which depends on accumulated knowledge and experience) gains steadily through middle adulthood. In contrast, **fluid intelligence** (which depends more on basic information-processing skills) declines starting in the twenties.

» In the Seattle Longitudinal Study, perceptual speed follows a pattern of steady, continuous decline. But other fluid skills, in addition to crystallized abilities, increase through middle adulthood, confirming that midlife is a time of peak performance on a variety of complex abilities.

» Large individual differences among middle-aged adults remind us that intellectual development is multidimensional, multidirectional, and plastic. Illness and unfavorable environments are linked to intellectual declines, while stimulating occupations and leisure pursuits, flexible personalities, lasting marriages, good health, and economic advantage predict favorable cognitive development.

» Women outperform men on verbal tasks and perceptual speed, whereas men excel at spatial skills. Generational gains in certain intellectual skills reflect advances in education, technology, environmental stimulation, and health care.

Information Processing

How does information processing change in midlife?

» Speed of cognitive processing slows with age, a change explained by either the **neural network view** or the **information-loss view.** As reaction time slows, people perform less well on complex memory, reasoning, and problem-solving tasks, and especially on fluid-ability items. But other factors also predict diverse, age-related cognitive performances.

» Middle-aged people show declines in ability to divide their attention, focus on relevant stimuli, and switch from one task to another as the situation demands. Cognitive inhibition becomes more difficult, at times prompting distractibility.

ELLIOTT FRANKS/© ARENAPAL/TOPHAM/THE IMAGE WORKS

» Adults in midlife retain less information in working memory, largely due to a decline in use of memory strategies. But training, improved design of tasks, and metacognitive knowledge enable older adults to compensate for age-related decrements.

Discuss the development of practical problem solving, expertise, and creativity in middle adulthood.

» Middle-aged adults in all walks of life often become good at **practical problem solving,** largely due to development of expertise. In midlife, creativity becomes more deliberately thoughtful. It also shifts from generating unusual products to integrating ideas and from concern with self-expression to more altruistic goals.

Vocational Life and Cognitive Development

Describe the relationship between vocational life and cognitive development.

» At all ages and in different cultures, the relationship between vocational life and cognitive development is reciprocal. Stimulating, complex work and flexible, abstract, autonomous thinking support each other.

Adult Learners: Becoming a Student in Midlife

Discuss the challenges that adults face in returning to college, ways to support returning students, and benefits of earning a degree in midlife.

» Adults are returning to college and graduate school in record numbers. The majority are women, who are often motivated by life transitions. Returning students must cope with a lack of recent practice at academic work, stereotypes of aging and ethnicity, and demands of multiple roles.

» Social support from family and friends and institutional services suited to their needs can help returning students succeed. Further education results in enhanced competencies, new relationships, intergenerational contact, and reshaped life paths.

Important Terms and Concepts

climacteric (p. 504)
crystallized intelligence (p. 519)
fluid intelligence (p. 519)
glaucoma (p. 503)
hardiness (p. 516)
hormone therapy (p. 506)
information-loss view (p. 521)
menopause (p. 504)
neural network view (p. 521)
osteoporosis (p. 513)
practical problem solving (p. 524)
presbycusis (p. 503)
presbyopia (p. 502)
Type A behavior pattern (p. 514)

© JIM WEST/PHOTOEDIT

Midlife is a time of increased generativity—giving to and guiding younger generations. As these volunteers build a playground for children in a low-income neighborhood, their exuberance conveys the deep sense of satisfaction they derive from generative activities.

CHAPTER 16

Emotional and Social Development in Middle Adulthood

One weekend when Devin, Trisha, and their 24-year-old son, Mark, were vacationing together, the two middle-aged parents knocked on Mark's hotel room door. "Your dad and I are going off to see a crafts exhibit," Trisha explained. "Feel free to stay behind," she offered, recalling Mark's antipathy toward attending such events as an adolescent. "We'll be back around noon for lunch."

"That exhibit sounds great!" Mark replied. "I'll meet you in the lobby. We've got so little time together as it is."

"Sometimes I forget he's an adult!" exclaimed Trisha as she and Devin returned to their room to grab their coats. "It's been great to have Mark with us these few days—like spending time with a good friend."

In their forties and fifties, Trisha and Devin built on earlier strengths and intensified their commitment to leaving a legacy for those who would come after them. As Mark graduated from college, took his first job, fell in love, and married, they felt a sense of pride at having escorted a member of the next generation into responsible adult roles. Family activities, which had declined during Mark's adolescent and college years, now increased as Trisha and Devin related to their son and daughter-in-law not just as kin but as enjoyable adult companions. Challenging work and more time for community involvement, leisure pursuits, and each other contributed to a richly diverse and gratifying time of life.

The midlife years were not as smooth for two of Trisha and Devin's friends. Fearing that she might grow old alone, Jewel frantically pursued her quest for an intimate partner. She attended singles events, registered with dating services, and traveled in hopes of meeting a like-minded companion. "I can't stand the thought of turning 50," she lamented in a letter to Trisha. Jewel also had compensating satisfactions—friendships that had grown more meaningful, a warm relationship with a nephew and niece, and a successful consulting business.

Tim, Devin's best friend from graduate school, had been divorced for over 15 years. Recently, he had met Elena and had come to love her deeply. But

Elena was in the midst of major life changes. In addition to her own divorce, she was dealing with a troubled daughter, a career change, and a move away from the city that served as a constant reminder of her unhappy past. Whereas Tim had reached the peak of his career and was ready to enjoy life, Elena wanted to recapture much of what she had missed in earlier decades—not just a gratifying intimate relationship, but opportunities to realize her talents. "I don't know where I fit into Elena's plans," Tim wondered aloud on the phone with Trisha.

With the arrival of middle adulthood, half or more of the lifespan is over. Increasing awareness of limited time ahead prompts adults to reevaluate the meaning of their lives, refine and strengthen their identities, and reach out to future generations. Most middle-aged people make modest adjustments in their outlook, goals, and daily lives. But a few experience profound inner turbulence and initiate major changes, often in an effort to make up for lost time. Together with advancing years, family and work transitions contribute greatly to emotional and social development.

More midlifers are addressing these tasks than ever before, now that the baby boomers have reached their forties, fifties, and early sixties. Indeed, 45- to 54-year-olds are currently the largest age sector of the U.S. population (U.S. Census Bureau, 2009b). As our discussion will reveal, the baby boomers have brought increased self-confidence, social consciousness, and vitality—along with great developmental diversity—to this period of the lifespan.

A monumental survey called *Midlife Development in the United States (MIDUS),* conducted in the mid-1990s, has contributed enormously to our understanding of midlife emotional and social development. Conceived by a team of researchers spanning diverse fields, including psychology, sociology, anthropology, and medicine, the aim of MIDUS was to generate new knowledge on the challenges faced by middle-aged adults. Its nationally representative sample included nearly 3,500 U.S. 25- to 75-year-olds, enabling those in the middle years to be compared with younger and older individuals. Through telephone interviews and self-administered questionnaires, participants responded to over 1,100 items addressing wide-ranging psychological, health, and background factors, yielding unprecedented breadth of information in a single study (Brim, Ryff, & Kessler, 2005). The research endeavor also included "satellite" studies, in which subsamples of respondents were questioned in greater depth on key topics. And it is now being extended longitudinally.

MIDUS has greatly expanded our knowledge of the *multidimensional* and *multidirectional* nature of midlife change, and it promises to be a rich source of information about middle adulthood and beyond for many years to come. Hence, our discussion repeatedly draws on MIDUS, at times delving into its findings, at other times citing them alongside those of other investigations. Let's turn now to Erikson's theory and related research, to which MIDUS has contributed.

Erikson's Theory: Generativity versus Stagnation

Erikson's psychological conflict of midlife is called **generativity versus stagnation.** Generativity involves reaching out to others in ways that give to and guide the next generation. Recall from Chapter 14 that generativity is under way in early adulthood, typically through childbearing and child rearing and establishing a niche in the occupational world. It expands greatly in midlife, when commitment extends beyond oneself (identity) and one's life partner (intimacy) to a larger group—family, community, or society. The generative adult combines the need for self-expression with the need for communion, integrating personal goals with the welfare of the larger social world (McAdams & Logan, 2004). The resulting strength is the capacity to care for others in a broader way than in previous stages.

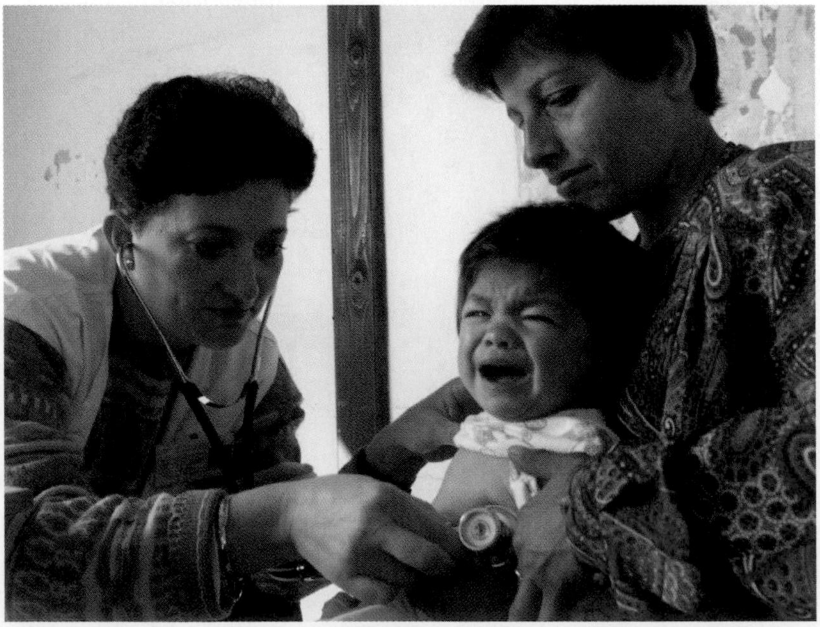

AP IMAGES/LAURENT REBOURS

Albanian doctor Besa Basha works in Kosovo for Doctors Without Borders, a Nobel Prize–winning organization that treats patients, distributes food and medicine, and builds medical facilities in troubled regions throughout the world. Her generative work integrates personal goals with concern for societal welfare.

Erikson (1950) selected the term *generativity* to encompass everything generated that can outlive the self and ensure society's continuity and improvement: children, ideas, products, works of art. Although parenting is a major means of realizing generativity, it is not the only means: Adults can be generative in other family relationships (as Jewel was with her nephew and niece), as mentors in the workplace, in volunteer endeavors, and through many forms of productivity and creativity.

Notice, from what we have said so far, that generativity brings together personal desires and cultural demands. On the personal side, middle-aged adults feel a need to be needed—to attain symbolic immortality by making a contribution that will survive their death (Kotre, 1999; McAdams, Hart, & Maruna, 1998). This desire may stem from a deep-seated evolutionary urge to protect and advance the next generation. On the cultural side, society imposes a social clock for generativity in midlife, requiring adults to take responsibility for the next generation through their roles as parents, teachers, mentors, leaders, and coordinators (McAdams & Logan, 2004). And according to Erikson, a culture's "belief in the species"—the conviction that life is good and worthwhile, even in the face of human destructiveness and deprivation—is a major motivator of generative action. Without this optimistic worldview, people would have no hope of improving humanity.

The negative outcome of this stage is stagnation: Once people attain certain life goals, such as marriage, children, and career success, they may become self-centered and self-indulgent. Adults with a sense of stagnation express their self-absorption in many ways—through lack of interest in young people (including their own children), through a focus on what they can get from others rather than what they can give, and through taking little interest in being productive at work, developing their talents, or bettering the world in other ways.

Some researchers study generativity by assessing personality traits, such as assertiveness, nurturance, and responsibility. Others ask people to rate themselves on generative characteristics, such as feelings of duty to help others in need or obligation to be an involved citizen. Still others look for generative themes in people's narrative descriptions of themselves (Keyes & Ryff, 1998a, 1998b; McAdams, 2006; McAdams et al., 1997). Whichever method is used, generativity tends to increase in midlife (Keyes & Ryff, 1998a; Rossi, 2001, 2004). For example, in longitudinal and cross-sectional studies of college-educated women, and in an investigation of middle-aged adults diverse in SES, self-rated generativity rose from the thirties into the forties and fifties (see Figure 16.1). At the same time, participants expressed greater concern about aging, increased security with their identities, and a stronger sense of competence (Miner-Rubino, Winter, & Stewart, 2004; Stewart, Ostrove, & Helson, 2001; Zucker, Ostrove, & Stewart, 2002). As the Lifespan Vista box on page 534 illustrates, generativity is also a major unifying theme in middle-aged adults' life stories.

Just as Erikson's theory suggests, highly generative people appear especially well-adjusted—low in anxiety and depression; high in autonomy, self-acceptance, and life satisfaction; and more likely to have successful marriages and close friends (Ackerman, Zuroff, & Moskowitz, 2000; An & Cooney, 2006; Grossbaum & Bates, 2002; Westermeyer, 2004). They are also more open to differing viewpoints, possess leadership qualities, desire more from work than financial rewards, and care greatly about the welfare of their children, their partner, their aging parents, and the wider society (Peterson, 2002; Peterson, Smirles, & Wentworth, 1997). Furthermore, generativity is associated with more effective child rearing—higher valuing of trust, open communication, transmission of values to children, and an authoritative style (Hart et al., 2001; Peterson & Duncan, 2007; Pratt et al., 2008). Generative midlifers are also more involved in political activities, including voting, campaigning, and contacting public officials (Cole & Stewart, 1996).

Although these findings characterize adults of all backgrounds, individual differences in contexts for generativity exist. Having children seems to foster men's generative development more than women's. In several studies, including the MIDUS survey, fathers scored higher in generativity than childless men (Marks, Bumpass, & Jun, 2004; McAdams & de St. Aubin, 1992; Snarey et al., 1987). Perhaps parenting awakens in men a tender, caring attitude toward the next generation that women have opportunities to develop in other ways. And for low-SES men with troubled pasts as sons, students, workers, and intimate partners, fatherhood can provide a context for highly generative, positive life change (Roy & Lucas, 2006). At times, these fathers express this generativity as a refusal to pass on their own history of suffering. As one former gang member, who earned an associate's degree and struggled to keep his teenage sons off the streets, explained, "I came through the depths of hell to try to be a father. I let my sons know, 'You're never without a daddy, don't you let anybody tell you that.' I tell them that if me and your mother separate, I make sure that wherever I go, I build something for you to come to" (p. 153).

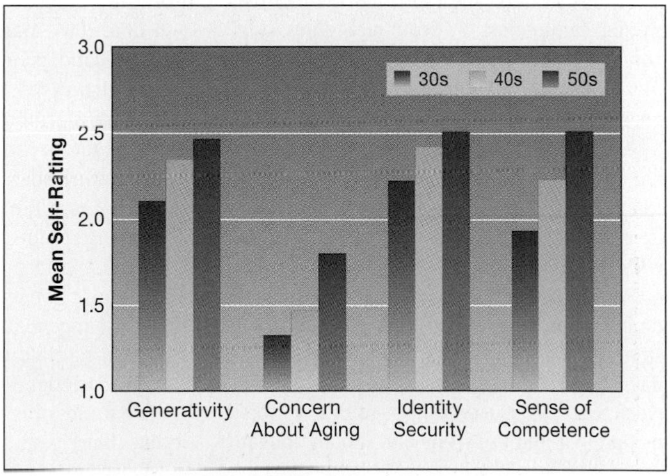

■ **FIGURE 16.1** ■ **Age-related changes in self-rated generativity, concern about aging, identity security, and sense of competence.** In a longitudinal study of over 300 college-educated women, self-rated generativity increased from the thirties to the fifties, as did concern about aging. The rise in generativity was accompanied by other indicators of psychological health—greater security with one's identity and sense of competence. (Adapted from Stewart, Ostrove, & Helson, 2001.)

A LIFESPAN VISTA: Looking Forward, Looking Back

Generative Adults Tell Their Life Stories

In research aimed at understanding how highly generative adults make sense of their lives, Dan McAdams and his colleagues (1997, 2001) interviewed two groups of midlifers: those who often behave generatively and those who seldom do. Participants were asked to relate their life stories, including a high point, a low point, a turning point, and important scenes from childhood, adolescence, and adulthood. Analyses of story lines and themes revealed that adults high and low in generativity reconstruct their past and anticipate their future in strikingly different ways.

Narratives of highly generative people usually contained an orderly sequence of events that the researchers called a commitment story, in which adults give to others as a means of giving back to family, community, and society (McAdams, 1993, 2006). The generative storyteller typically describes an early special advantage (such as a good family or a talent), along with early awareness of the suffering of others. This clash between blessing and suffering motivates the person to view the self as "called," or committed, to being good to others. In commitment stories, the theme of redemption is prominent. Highly generative adults frequently describe scenes in which extremely negative life events, involving frustration, failure, loss, or death, are followed by good outcomes—personal renewal, improvement, and enlightenment. That is, bad scenes are redeemed, or made better, by what follows.

Consider a story related by Diana, a 49-year-old fourth-grade teacher. Born in a small town to a minister and his wife, Diana was a favorite among the parishioners, who showered her with attention and love. When she was 8, however, her life hit its lowest point: As she looked on in horror, her younger brother ran into the street and was hit by a car; he died later that day. Afterward, Diana, sensing her father's anguish, tried—unsuccessfully—to be the "son" he had lost. But the scene ends on an upbeat note, with Diana marrying a man who forged a warm bond with her father and who became accepted "as his own son." One of Diana's life goals was to improve her teaching, because "I'd like to give something back . . . to grow and help others grow" (McAdams et al., 1997, p. 689). Her interview overflowed with expressions of generative commitment.

Whereas highly generative adults tell stories in which bad scenes turn good, less generative adults relate stories with themes of contamination, in which good scenes turn bad. For example, a child gets a treasured musical instrument, which is immediately stolen. A good first year of college turns sour when a professor grades unfairly. A young woman loses weight and looks good but can't overcome her low self-esteem.

Why is generativity connected to life-story redemption events, in which bad gives way to good? First, some adults may view their generative activities as a way to redeem negative aspects of their lives. In a study of the life stories of ex-convicts who turned away from crime, many spoke of a strong desire to do good works as penance for their transgressions (Maruna, 2001; Maruna, LeBel, & Lanier, 2004). Second, generativity seems to entail the conviction that the imperfections of today can be transformed into a better tomorrow. Through guiding and giving to the next generation, mature adults increase the chances that the mistakes of the past will not happen again. Finally, interpreting one's own life in terms of redemption offers hope that hard work will lead to future benefits—an expectation that may sustain generative efforts of all kinds, from rearing children to advancing communities and societies (Kotre, 1999).

Life stories offer insight into how people imbue their lives with meaning and purpose. Adults high and low in generativity do not differ in the number of positive and negative events included in their narratives. Rather, they interpret those events differently. Commitment stories, filled with redemption, involve a way of thinking about the self that fosters a caring, compassionate approach to others (McAdams & Logan, 2004). Such stories help people realize that although their own personal story will someday end, other stories will follow, due in part to their own generative efforts.

The more redemptive events adults include in their life stories, the higher their life satisfaction, self-esteem, and certainty that the challenges of life are meaningful, manageable, and rewarding (McAdams, 2001). Researchers still have much to learn about factors that lead people to view good as emerging from adversity.

© ANNA CORORATON/THE DAILY PENNSYLVANIAN

Harold Wilson was falsely convicted of murder and—after almost 18 years on death row in Pennsylvania—was exonerated due to advances in DNA evidence. He travels the United States to tell his story of redemption. Saying, "I have a long, hard road ahead of me to rebuild my life after what I suffered through," he is committed to educating the public about flaws in the criminal justice system.

Finally, compared with Caucasians, African Americans more often engage in certain types of generativity. They are more involved in religious groups and activities, offer more social support to members of their community, and are more likely to view themselves as role models and sources of wisdom for their children (Hart et al., 2001). A life history of strong support from church and extended family may strengthen these generative values and actions. In samples of Caucasian Americans, religiosity and spirituality are also linked to greater generative activity (Dillon & Wink, 2004; Wink & Dillon,

2003). Highly generative middle-aged adults often indicate that as children and adolescents, they internalized moral values rooted in a religious tradition and sustained their commitment to those values, which provided lifelong encouragement for generative action (McAdams, 2006; McAdams et al., 1997). Especially in individualistic societies, belonging to a religious community or believing in a higher being may help preserve generative commitments.

Other Theories of Psychosocial Development in Midlife

Erikson's theory provides only a broad sketch of adult personality development. For a closer look at psychosocial change in midlife, let's revisit Levinson's and Vaillant's theories, which were introduced in Chapter 14.

Levinson's Seasons of Life

Return to page 469 to review Levinson's eras (stages or seasons). Like early adulthood, middle adulthood begins with a transitional period (age 40 to 45), during which people evaluate their success in meeting early adulthood goals. Realizing that from now on, more time will lie behind than ahead, they regard the remaining years as increasingly precious. Consequently, some make drastic revisions in their life structure: divorcing, remarrying, changing careers, or displaying enhanced creativity. Others make smaller changes while staying in the same marriage, surroundings, occupation, and workplace.

Whether these years bring a gust of wind or a storm, most people turn inward for a time, focusing on personally meaningful living (Neugarten, 1968b). One reason is that for many middle-aged adults, only limited career advancement and personal growth remain possible. Those who have not fully realized their early adulthood dream may seek a more satisfying path before it is too late. And those who have achieved their goals ask, What good are these accomplishments to others, to society, and to myself?

According to Levinson, for middle-aged adults to reassess their relation to themselves and the external world and rebuild their life structure, they must confront four developmental tasks. Each requires the individual to reconcile two opposing tendencies within the self, attaining greater internal harmony.

- *Young–old:* The middle-age person must seek new ways of being both young and old. This means giving up certain youthful qualities, retaining and transforming others, and finding positive meaning in being older. Perhaps because of the double standard of aging (see page 517 in Chapter 15), most middle-aged women express concern about appearing less attractive as they grow older (Rossi, 2005). But middle-aged men—particularly non-college-educated men, who often hold blue-collar jobs requiring physical strength and stamina—are also highly sensitive to physical aging. In one study, they were more concerned about physical changes than both college- and non-college-educated women, who exceeded college-educated men (see Figure 16.2) (Miner-Rubino, Winter, & Stewart, 2004). Compared with previous midlife cohorts, the baby boomers are especially interested in controlling physical changes—a desire that has helped energize a huge industry of anti-aging cosmetic products and medical procedures (Lachman, 2004; Jones, Whitbourne, & Skultety, 2006).
- *Destruction–creation:* With greater awareness of mortality, the middle-aged person focuses on ways he or she has acted destructively and how others have done the same. Past hurtful acts toward parents, intimate partners, children, friends, and co-workers are countered by a strong desire to participate in activities that advance human welfare, thereby leaving a legacy for future generations. The image of a legacy can be satisfied in many ways—through charitable gifts, creative products, volunteer service, or mentoring young people.
- *Masculinity–femininity:* The middle-aged person must create a better balance between masculine and feminine parts of the self. For men, this means greater acceptance of "feminine" traits of nurturance and caring, which enhance close relationships and compassionate exercise of authority

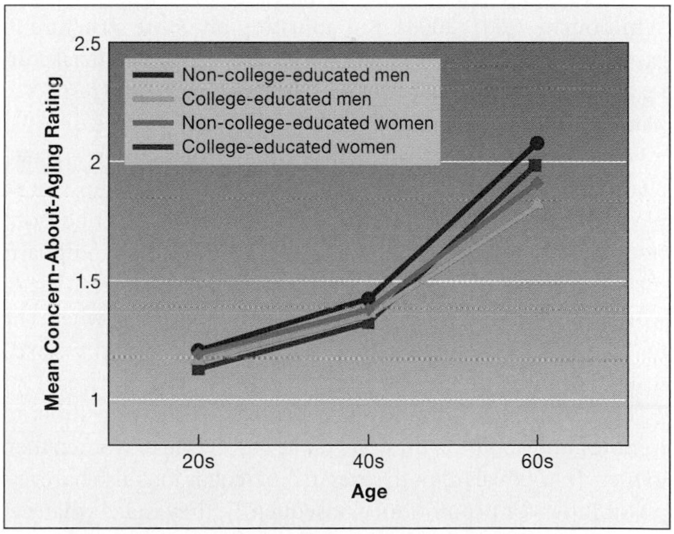

■ FIGURE 16.2 ■ Age-related change in concern about physical aging, by sex and level of education. More than 250 men and women in their early sixties retrospectively rated their degree of concern over physical aging in their forties, fifties, and sixties, using a three-point scale. Non-college-educated men reported the greatest rise in sensitivity to physical changes, followed by women, both college- and non-college-educated, and finally college-educated men. (From K. Miner-Rubino, D. G. Winter, & A. J. Stewart, 2004, "Gender, Social Class, and the Subjective Experience of Aging: Self-Perceived Personality Change from Early Adulthood to Midlife," *Personality and Social Psychology Bulletin, 30,* p. 1605. Copyright 2004 by Sage Publications. Reprinted by permission of Sage Publications.)

in the workplace. For women, it generally means being more open to "masculine" characteristics of autonomy and assertiveness (Gilligan, 1982; Harris, Ellicott, & Holmes, 1986). Recall from Chapter 8 that people who combine masculine and feminine traits have an androgynous gender identity. Later we will see that androgyny is associated with favorable personality traits and adjustment.

- *Engagement–separateness:* The middle-aged person must forge a better balance between engagement with the external world and separateness. For many men, and for women who have had successful careers, this may mean reducing concern with ambition and achievement and attending more fully to the self. But women who have been devoted to child rearing or an unfulfilling job often feel compelled to move in the other direction (Levinson, 1996). At age 48, Elena left her position as a reporter for a small-town newspaper, pursued an advanced degree in creative writing, accepted a college teaching position, and began writing a novel. Tim, in contrast, recognized his overwhelming desire for a gratifying romantic partnership. By scaling back his own career, he realized he could grant Elena the time and space she needed to build a rewarding work life—and that doing so might deepen their attachment to each other.

People who flexibly modify their identities in response to age-related changes yet maintain a sense of self-continuity are more aware of their own thoughts and feelings and are higher in self-esteem (Jones, Whitbourne, & Skultety, 2006; Sneed & Whitbourne, 2001, 2003). But adjusting one's life structure to incorporate the effects of aging requires supportive social contexts. When poverty, unemployment, and lack of a respected place in society dominate the life course, energies are directed toward survival rather than realistically approaching age-related changes. Even adults whose jobs are secure and who live in pleasant neighborhoods may find that employment conditions restrict possibilities for growth by placing too much emphasis on productivity and profit and too little on the meaning of work. In her early forties, Trisha left a large law firm, where she felt constant pressure to bring in high-fee clients and received little acknowledgment of her efforts, for a small practice.

Opportunities for advancement ease the transition to middle adulthood. Yet these are far less available to women than to men. Individuals of both sexes in blue-collar jobs also have few possibilities for promotion. Consequently, they make whatever vocational adjustments they can—becoming active union members, shop stewards, or mentors of younger workers. Many men find compensating rewards in moving to the senior generation of their families (Christensen & Larsen, 2008; Levinson, 1978).

Vaillant's Adaptation to Life

Whereas Levinson interviewed 35- to 45-year-olds, Vaillant (1977, 2002)—in his longitudinal research on well-educated men and women—followed participants past the half-century mark. Recall from Chapter 14 how adults in their late forties and fifties take on peak responsibility for the functioning of society, eventually becoming "keepers of meaning," or guardians of their culture (see page 470). Vaillant reported that the most-successful and best-adjusted entered a calmer, quieter time of life. "Passing the torch"—concern that the positive aspects of their culture survive—became a major preoccupation.

In societies around the world, older people are guardians of traditions, laws, and cultural values. This stabilizing force holds in check too-rapid change sparked by the questioning and challenging of adolescents and young adults. As people approach the end of middle age, they focus on longer-term, less personal goals, such as the state of human relations in their society. And they become more philosophical, accepting the fact that not all problems can be solved in their lifetime.

Is There a Midlife Crisis?

Levinson (1978, 1996) reported that most men and women in his samples experienced substantial inner turmoil during the transition to middle adulthood. Yet Vaillant (1977, 2002) saw few examples of crisis but, rather, slow and steady change. These contrasting findings raise the question of how much personal upheaval actually accompanies entry to midlife. Are self-doubt and stress especially great during the forties, and do they prompt major restructuring of the personality, as the term **midlife crisis** implies?

Consider the reactions of Trisha, Devin, Jewel, Tim, and Elena to middle adulthood. Trisha and Devin moved easily into this period, whereas Jewel, Tim, and Elena displayed greater questioning of their situations and sought alternative life paths. Clearly, wide individual differences exist in response to midlife. ***TAKE A MOMENT...*** Now ask several individuals in their twenties and thirties whether they expect to encounter a midlife crisis between ages 40 and 50. You are likely to find that Americans often anticipate it, perhaps because of culturally induced apprehension of aging (Menon, 2001; Wethington, Kessler, & Pixley, 2005). Yet little evidence supports this view of middle age as a turbulent time.

When MIDUS participants were asked to describe "turning points" (major changes in the way they felt about an important aspect of their lives) that had occurred during the past five years, most of the ones reported concerned work. Women's work-related turning points peaked in early adulthood, when many adjusted their work lives to accommodate marriage and childrearing (see Chapter 14). The peak for men, in contrast, came at midlife, a time of increased career responsibility and advancement. Other common turning points in early and middle adulthood were positive: They involved fulfilling a dream and learning something good about oneself (Wethington, Kessler, & Pixley, 2004). Overall, turning points rarely resembled midlife crises. Even negative work-related turning points generally led to personal growth—for example, a layoff that sparked a positive career change or a shift in energy from career to personal life.

Asked directly if they had ever experienced something they would consider a midlife crisis, only one-fourth of the MIDUS respondents said yes. And they defined such events much more loosely than researchers do. Some reported a crisis well before age 40, others well after age 50. And most attributed it not to age but rather to challenging life events (Wethington, 2000). Consistent with this view, Elena had considered both a divorce and a new career long before she initiated these changes. In her thirties, she separated from her husband; later she reconciled with him and told him that she desired to return to school, which he firmly opposed. She put her own life on hold because of her daughter's academic and emotional difficulties and her husband's resistance.

Another way of exploring midlife questioning is to ask adults about life regrets—attractive opportunities for career or other life-changing activities they did not pursue or lifestyle changes they did not make. In two investigations of women in their early forties, those who acknowledged regret without making life changes, compared to those who modified their lives, reported less favorable psychological well-being and poorer physical health over time (Landman et al., 1995; Stewart & Vandewater, 1999). The two groups did not differ in social or financial resources available to effect change. Rather, they differed in personality: Those who made changes were higher in confidence and assertiveness.

By late midlife, with less time ahead to make life changes, people's interpretation of regrets plays a major role in their well-being. Mature, contented adults acknowledge a past characterized by some losses, have thought deeply about them, and feel stronger because of them. At the same time, they are able to disengage from them, investing in current, personally rewarding goals (King & Hicks, 2007). Among a sample of several hundred 60- to 65-year-olds diverse in SES, about half expressed at least one regret. Compared to those who had not resolved their disappointments, those who had come to terms with them (accepted and identified some eventual benefits) or had "put the best face on things" (identified benefits but still had some lingering regret) reported better physical health and greater life satisfaction (Torges, Stewart, & Miner-Rubino, 2005).

In sum, life evaluation is common during middle age. Most people make changes that are best described as turning points rather than drastic alterations of their lives. Those who cannot modify their life paths often look for the "silver lining" in life's difficulties (Lachman & James, 1997; Wethington, Kessler, & Pixley, 2004). The few midlifers who are in crisis typically have had early adulthoods in which gender roles, family pressures, or low income and poverty severely limited their ability to fulfill personal needs and goals, at home or in the wider world.

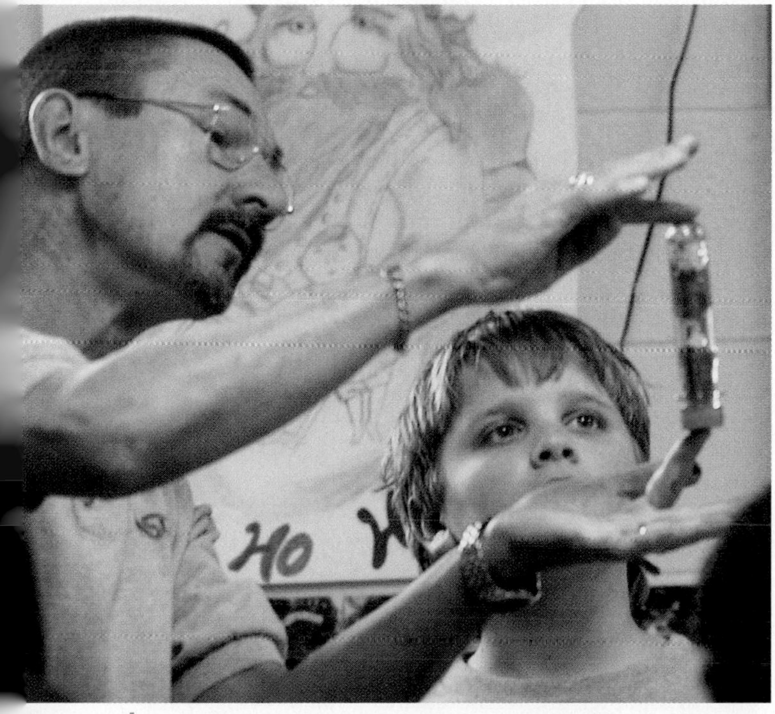

AP IMAGES/THE REPORTER, KEITH VANDERVORT

As is typical for midlifers, elementary school teacher Jaime Malwitz modified his career in ways that resemble a turning point, not a crisis. He designed a scientist-in-residence program, which is currently being implemented in many school districts. Here he serves as a resident physicist, discussing a density experiment with a fifth grader.

Stage or Life Events Approach

If crisis and major restructuring in midlife are rare, is middle adulthood actually a stage of development, as Erikson's, Levinson's, and Vaillant's theories indicate? Some researchers believe the midadult transition is not stagelike (McCrae & Costa, 2003; Srivastava et al., 2003). Rather, they regard it as simply an adaptation to normative life events, such as children growing up, reaching the crest of a career, and impending retirement.

Yet recall from earlier chapters that life events are no longer as age-graded as they were in the past. Their timing is so variable that they cannot be the sole cause of midlife change. Furthermore, in several studies, people were asked to trace their thoughts, feelings, attitudes, and hopes during early and middle adulthood. Psychosocial change, in terms of personal disruption followed by reassessment, coincided with both family life cycle events and chronological age. For this reason, most experts regard adaptation during midlife as the combined result of growing older and social experiences (Lachman, 2004; Sneed, Whitbourne, & Culang, 2006). ***TAKE A MOMENT...*** Return to our discussion of generativity and the midlife transition, and notice how both factors are involved.

Finally, in describing their lives, the large majority of middle-aged people report troubling moments that prompt new understandings and goals—a finding consistent with the stage approach. As we look closely at emotional and social development in middle adulthood, we will see that this period, like others, is characterized by both continuity and stagewise change. With this in mind, let's turn to the diverse inner concerns and outer experiences that contribute to psychological well-being and decision making in midlife.

ASK YOURSELF

>> REVIEW
What personal and cultural forces motivate generativity? Why does it increase and contribute vitally to favorable adjustment in midlife?

>> APPLY
After years of experiencing little personal growth at work, 42-year-old Mel looked for a new job and received an attractive offer in another city. Although he felt torn between leaving close friends and pursuing a long-awaited career opportunity, after several weeks of soul searching, he took the new job. Was Mel's dilemma a midlife crisis? Why or why not?

>> CONNECT
How might the approach of many middle-aged adults to handling life regrets prevent the occurrence of midlife crises?

>> REFLECT
Think of a middle-aged adult whom you admire. Describe the various ways that individual expresses generativity.

Stability and Change in Self-Concept and Personality

Midlife changes in self-concept and personality reflect growing awareness of a finite lifespan, longer life experience, and generative concerns. Yet certain aspects of personality remain stable, revealing the persistence of individual differences established during earlier periods.

Possible Selves

On a business trip, Jewel found a spare afternoon to visit Trisha. Sitting in a coffee shop, the two women reminisced about the past and thought aloud about the future. "It's been tough living on my own and building the business," Jewel said. "What I hope for is to become better at my work, to be more community-oriented, and to stay healthy and available to my friends. Of course, I would rather not grow old alone, but if I don't find that special person, I suppose I can take comfort in the fact that I'll never have to face divorce or widowhood."

Jewel is discussing **possible selves,** future-oriented representations of what one hopes to become and what one is afraid of becoming. Possible selves are the temporal dimension of self-concept—what the individual is striving for and attempting to avoid. To lifespan researchers, these hopes and fears are just as vital in explaining behavior as people's views of their current characteristics. Indeed, possible selves may be an especially strong motivator of action in midlife, as more meaning becomes attached to time (Frazier & Hooker, 2006). As we age, we may rely less on social comparisons in judging our self-worth and more on temporal comparisons—how well we are doing in relation to what we had planned.

Throughout adulthood, the personality traits people assign to their current selves show considerable stability. A 30-year-old who says he is cooperative, competent, outgoing, or successful is likely to report a similar picture at a later age. But reports of possible selves change greatly. Adults in their early twenties mention many possible selves, and their visions are lofty and idealistic—being "perfectly happy," "rich and famous," "healthy throughout life," and not being "down and out" or "a person who does nothing important." With age, possible selves become fewer in number and more modest and concrete. Most middle-aged people no longer desire to be the best or the most successful. Instead, they are largely concerned with performance of roles and responsibilities already begun—"being competent at work," "being a good husband and father," "putting my children through the colleges of their choice," "staying healthy," and not being "a burden to my family" or "without enough money to meet my daily needs" (Bybee & Wells, 2003; Cross & Markus, 1991; Ryff, 1991).

What explains these shifts in possible selves? Because the future no longer holds limitless opportunities, adults preserve mental health by adjusting their hopes and fears. To stay motivated, they must maintain a sense of unachieved possibility, yet they must still manage to feel good about themselves and their lives despite disappointments (Lachman & Bertrand, 2002). For example, Jewel no longer desired to be an executive in a large company, as she had in her twenties. Instead, she wanted to grow in her current occupation. And although she feared loneliness in old age, she reminded herself that marriage can lead to equally negative outcomes, such as divorce and widowhood—possibilities that made not having attained an important interpersonal goal easier to bear.

Unlike current self-concept, which is constantly responsive to others' feedback, possible selves (though influenced by others) can be defined and redefined by the individual, as needed. Consequently, they permit affirmation of the self, even when things are not going well (Cross & Markus, 1991). Researchers believe that possible selves may be the key to continued well-being in adulthood, as people revise these future images to achieve a better match between desired and achieved goals. Many studies reveal that the self-esteem of middle-aged and older individuals equals or surpasses that of younger people, perhaps because of the protective role of possible selves (Robins & Trzesniewski, 2005).

Self-Acceptance, Autonomy, and Environmental Mastery

An evolving mix of competencies and experiences leads to changes in certain aspects of personality during middle adulthood. In Chapter 15, we noted that midlife brings gains in expertise and practical problem solving. Middle-aged adults also offer more complex, integrated descriptions of themselves than do younger and older individuals (Labouvie-Vief, 2003). Furthermore, midlife is typically a period in which the number of social roles peaks—spouse, parent, worker, and engaged community member. And status at work and in the community typically rises, as adults take advantage of opportunities for leadership and other complex responsibilities (Helson, Soto, & Cate, 2006).

These changes in cognition and breadth of roles undoubtedly contribute to other gains in personal functioning. In research on well-educated adults ranging in age from the late teens into the seventies, three qualities increased from early to middle adulthood and then leveled off:

- *Self-acceptance:* More than young adults, middle-aged people acknowledged and accepted both their good and bad qualities and felt positively about themselves and life.
- *Autonomy:* Middle-aged adults saw themselves as less concerned about others' expectations and evaluations and more concerned with following self-chosen standards.
- *Environmental mastery:* Middle-aged people saw themselves as capable of managing a complex array of tasks easily and effectively (Ryff, 1991, 1995).

As these findings indicate, midlife is generally a time of increased comfort with the self, independence, assertiveness, commitment to personal values, and life satisfaction (Helson, Jones, & Kwan, 2002; Helson & Wink, 1992; Keyes, Shmotkin, & Ryff, 2002; Mitchell & Helson, 1990). Perhaps because of these personal attributes, people sometimes refer to middle age as "the prime of life."

At the same time, factors contributing to psychological well-being differ substantially among cohorts, as self-reports gathered from 25- to 65-year-old MIDUS survey respondents reveal (Carr, 2004). Among women who were born during the baby-boom years or later, and who thus benefited from the women's movement, balancing career with family predicted greater self-acceptance and environmental mastery. But also consider that women born before or during World War II who sacrificed career to focus on child rearing—expected of young mothers in the 1950s and 1960s—were similarly advantaged in self-acceptance. Likewise, men who were in step with prevailing social expectations scored higher in well-being. Baby-boom and younger men who modified their work schedules to make room for family responsibilities—who fit their cohort's image of the "good father"—were more self-accepting. But older men who made this accommodation scored much lower in self-acceptance than those who focused on work and thus conformed to the "good provider" ideal of their times. (See the Biology and Environment box on pages 540–541 for additional influences on midlife psychological well-being.)

Notions of happiness, however, vary among cultures. In a comparison of Korean adults in their fifties with same-age U.S. MIDUS participants, the Koreans reported lower levels of psychological well-being, largely because they were less willing than the Americans to endorse individualistic traits, such as self-acceptance and autonomy, as characteristic of themselves (Keyes & Ryff, 1998b). Consistent with their collectivist orientation, Koreans' highest well-being scores were on positive relations with others. They viewed personal fulfillment as achieved through family, especially the success of children. Americans also regarded family relations as relevant to well-being but placed greater emphasis on their own traits and accomplishments than on their children's.

Coping with Daily Stressors

In Chapter 15, we discussed the importance of stress management in preventing illness. It is also vital for psychological well-being. In a MIDUS satellite study in which more than 1,000 participants were interviewed on eight consecutive evenings, researchers found an early- to mid-adulthood plateau in frequency of daily stressors, followed by a decline as work and family responsibilities ease and leisure time increases (see Figure 16.3) (Almeida & Horn, 2004). Women reported more frequent role overload (conflict among employment, spouse, parent, and elder-care roles) and family-network and child-related stressors, men more work-related stressors, but both genders experienced all varieties. Compared with older people, young and midlife adults also perceived their stressors as more disruptive and unpleasant, perhaps because they often experienced several at once, and many involved financial risks and children.

But recall, also, from Chapter 15 that midlife brings an increase in effective coping strategies. Middle-aged individuals

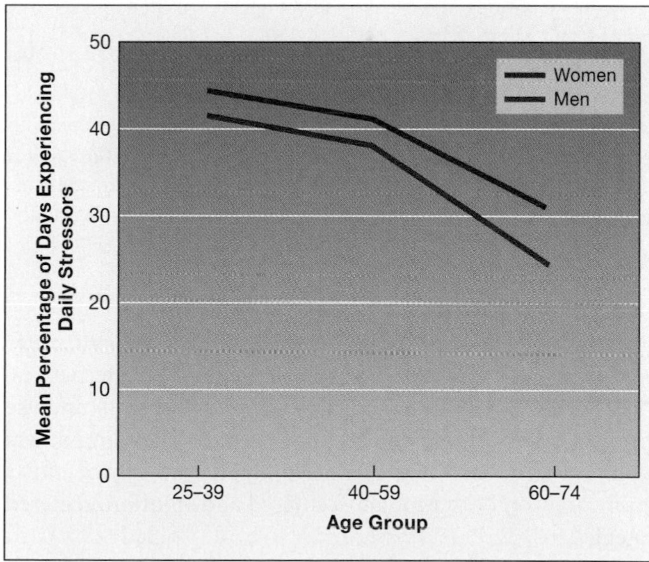

■ **FIGURE 16.3** ■ **Age-related change in daily stressors among men and women.** In a MIDUS satellite study, researchers interviewed more than 1,000 adults on eight consecutive evenings. Findings revealed an early- to mid-adulthood plateau, followed by a decline as work and family responsibilities ease and leisure time increases. (From D. M. Almeida & M. C. Horn, 2004, "Is Daily Life More Stressful During Middle Adulthood?" in O. G. Brim, C. D. Ruff, and R. C. Kessler (Eds.), *How Healthy Are We? A National Study of Well-Being at Midlife,* Chicago: The University of Chicago Press, p. 438. Adapted by permission of The University of Chicago Press.)

▪ BIOLOGY AND ENVIRONMENT ▪

What Factors Promote Psychological Well-Being in Midlife?

For Trisha and Devin, midlife brought contentment and high life satisfaction. But the road to happiness was rockier for Jewel, Tim, and Elena. What factors contribute to individual differences in psychological well-being at midlife? Consistent with the lifespan perspective, biological, psychological, and social forces are involved, and their effects are interwoven.

Good Health and Exercise

Good health affects energy and zest for life at any age. But during middle and late adulthood, taking steps to improve health and prevent disability becomes a better predictor of psychological well-being. Among a large, nationally representative sample of U.S. 20- to 64-year-olds, engaging in regular exercise—walking, dancing, jogging, or swimming—was more strongly associated with self-rated health and a positive outlook in older than in younger individuals (Ransford & Palisi, 1996). Middle-aged adults who maintain an exercise regimen are likely to perceive themselves as particularly active for their age and, therefore, to feel a special sense of accomplishment (Netz et al., 2005). As an extra psychological benefit, exercise may reduce feelings of vulnerability to chronic illness and disability—a strong contributor to poor psychological well-being at midlife (Barsky, Cleary, & Klerman, 1992).

Sense of Control and Personal Life Investment

Middle-aged adults who report a high sense of control over events in various aspects of their lives—health, family, and work—also report more favorable psychological well-being, as MIDUS and other survey findings reveal. A sense of control fosters self-efficacy—a belief in one's ability to surmount challenges—and, consequently, helps sustain a positive outlook in the face of health, family, and work difficulties (Lachman & Firth, 2004; Smith et al., 2000).

Personal life investment—firm commitment to goals and involvement in pursuit of those goals—also adds to mental health and life satisfaction (Staudinger, Fleeson, & Baltes, 1999). According to Mihaly Csikszentmihalyi, a vital wellspring of happiness is *flow*—the psychological state of being so engrossed in a demanding, meaningful activity that one loses all sense of time and self-awareness. People describe flow as the height of enjoyment, even as an ecstatic state. The more people experience flow, the more they judge their lives to be gratifying (Nakamura & Csikszentmihalyi, 2002). Although flow is common in people engaged in creative endeavors, many others report it—students who love studying, employees who like their jobs, adults involved in challenging leisure pursuits, and parents and grandparents engaged in pleasurable learning activities with children. Flow depends on perseverance and skill at complex endeavors that offer potential for growth. These qualities are well-developed in middle adulthood.

© JEFF GREENBERG/PHOTOEDIT

After crossing a marathon finish line, these middle-aged runners express a joyful sense of accomplishment. Maintaining an exercise regimen contributes greatly to midlife psychological well-being.

are more likely to identify the positive side of difficult situations, postpone action to permit evaluation of alternatives, anticipate and plan ways to handle future discomforts, and use humor to express ideas and feelings without offending others (Diehl, Coyle, & Labouvie-Vief, 1996). Notice how these efforts flexibly draw on both problem-centered and emotion-centered strategies.

Why might effective coping increase in middle adulthood? Other personality changes seem to support it. In one study, complex, integrated self-descriptions—which increase in midlife, indicating an improved ability to blend strengths and weaknesses into an organized picture—predicted good coping strategies (Labouvie-Vief & Diehl, 2000). Midlife gains in emotional stability and confidence in handling life's problems may also contribute (Roberts et al., 2007; Roberts & Mroczek, 2008). These attributes predict work and relationship effectiveness—outcomes that reflect the sophisticated, flexible coping of middle age.

Gender Identity

In her forties and early fifties, Trisha appeared more assertive at work. She spoke out more freely at meetings and took a leadership role when a team of lawyers worked on an especially complex case. She was also more dominant in family relationships, expressing her opinions to her husband and son more readily than she had 10 or 15 years earlier. In contrast, Devin's sense of empathy and caring became more apparent, and he was less assertive and more accommodating to Trisha's wishes than before.

Many studies report an increase in "masculine" traits in women and "feminine" traits in men across middle age (Huyck, 1990; James et al., 1995). Women become more confident, self-sufficient, and forceful, men more emotionally sensitive, caring, considerate, and dependent. These trends appear in cross-sectional and longitudinal research, in people varying in SES, and in diverse cultures—not just Western industrialized nations but also village societies such as the Maya

Positive Social Relationships

Developing gratifying social ties is closely linked to midlife psychological well-being. In a longitudinal study of 90 men selected for good physical and mental health as college students and followed over 32 years, a good mentor relationship in early adulthood (which fosters high career achievement) and favorable peer ties were among the best predictors of well-being in the late forties and early fifties (Westermeyer, 1998). In a survey of college alumni, those who preferred occupational prestige and high income to close friends were twice as likely as other respondents to describe themselves as "fairly" or "very" unhappy (Perkins, 1991, as cited by Myers, 2000).

Enjoyable social ties can strengthen the impact of an exercise regimen on well-being. Among an ethnically diverse sample of women using a private gym or an African Caribbean community center, exercising with likeminded companions contributed to their happiness and life satisfaction (Wray, 2007). The social side of going to the gym appeared especially important to minority women, who were less concerned with physical-appearance benefits than their Caucasian agemates.

A Good Marriage

Although friendships and positive relationships with co-workers are important, a good marriage boosts psychological well-being even more. The role of marriage in mental health increases with age, becoming a powerful predictor by late midlife (Marks, Bumpass, & Jun, 2004; Westermeyer, 1998).

Longitudinal studies tracking people as they move in and out of intimate relationships suggest that marriage actually brings about well-being. For example, when interviews with over 13,000 U.S. adults were repeated five years later, people who remained married reported greater happiness than those who remained single. Those who separated or divorced became less happy, reporting considerable depression. Men and women who married for the first time experienced a sharp increase in happiness, those who entered their second marriage a modest increase (Marks & Lambert, 1998).

Although not everyone is better off married, the link between marriage and well-being is similar in many nations, suggesting that marriage changes people's behavior in ways that make them better off (Diener et al., 2000; Lansford et al., 2005). Married partners monitor each other's health and offer care in times of illness. They also earn and save more money than single people, and higher income is modestly linked to psychological well-being (Myers, 2000; Waite, 1999). Furthermore, sexual satisfaction predicts mental health, and married couples have more satisfying sex lives than unmarried couples and singles (see Chapter 14).

Mastery of Multiple Roles

Finally, success in handling multiple roles is linked to psychological well-being. In a study of nearly 300 middle-aged women, researchers asked about feelings of competence and control in four roles: wife, mother, caregiver of an impaired parent, and employee. Participants experienced the highest levels of mastery in their work roles. But competence and control in all four roles predicted life satisfaction and reduced depression (Christensen, Stephens, & Townsend, 1998). And women who occupied several roles—in work and family arenas—seemed to benefit from added opportunities to enhance their sense of mastery.

In the MIDUS survey, as role involvement increased, both men and women reported greater environmental mastery, more rewarding social relationships, heightened sense of purpose in life, and more positive emotion. Once again, adults who occupied multiple roles and who also reported high control (suggesting effective role management) scored especially high in well-being—an outcome that was stronger for less-educated adults (Ahrens & Ryff, 2006). Control over roles may be vital for individuals with lower educational attainment, whose role combinations may be particularly stressful and who have fewer economic resources.

of Guatemala, the Navajo of the United States, and the Druze of the Middle East (Fry, 1985; Gutmann, 1977; Turner, 1982). Consistent with Levinson's theory, gender identity in midlife becomes more androgynous—a mixture of "masculine" and "feminine" characteristics.

Although the existence of these changes is well-accepted, explanations for them are controversial. A well-known evolutionary view, **parental imperative theory,** holds that identification with traditional gender roles is maintained during the active parenting years to help ensure the survival of children. Men become more goal-oriented, while women emphasize nurturance. After children reach adulthood, parents are free to express the "other-gender" side of their personalities (Gutmann & Huyck, 1994).

But these biological accounts have been criticized. As we discussed in earlier chapters, parents need both warmth and assertiveness (in the form of firmness and consistency) to rear children effectively. And although children's departure from the home is related to men's openness to the "feminine" side of their

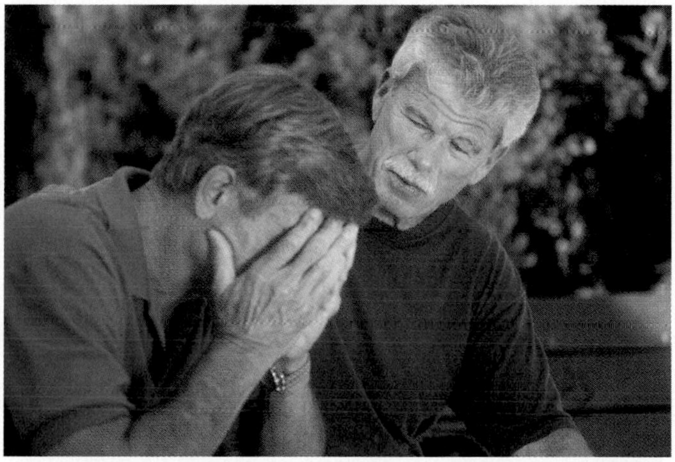

In middle age, gender identity becomes more androgynous for both sexes. Men tend to show an increase in "feminine" traits, becoming more emotionally sensitive, caring, considerate, and dependent.

■ TABLE 16.1 ■ *The "Big Five" Personality Traits*

TRAIT	DESCRIPTION
Neuroticism	Individuals who are high on this trait are worrying, temperamental, self-pitying, self-conscious, emotional, and vulnerable. Individuals who are low are calm, even-tempered, self-content, comfortable, unemotional, and hardy.
Extroversion	Individuals who are high on this trait are affectionate, talkative, active, fun-loving, and passionate. Individuals who are low are reserved, quiet, passive, sober, and emotionally unreactive.
Openness to experience	Individuals who are high on this trait are imaginative, creative, original, curious, and liberal. Individuals who are low are down-to-earth, uncreative, conventional, uncurious, and conservative.
Agreeableness	Individuals who are high on this trait are soft-hearted, trusting, generous, acquiescent, lenient, and good-natured. Individuals who are low are ruthless, suspicious, stingy, antagonistic, critical, and irritable.
Conscientiousness	Individuals who are high on this trait are conscientious, hard-working, well-organized, punctual, ambitious, and persevering. Individuals who are low are negligent, lazy, disorganized, late, aimless, and nonpersistent.

Source: McCrae & Costa, 2006.

personalities, the link to a rise in "masculine" traits among women is less apparent (Huyck, 1996, 1998). In longitudinal research, college-educated women in the labor force became more independent by their early forties, regardless of whether they had children; those who were homemakers did not. Women attaining high status at work gained most in dominance, assertiveness, and outspokenness by their early fifties (Helson & Picano, 1990; Wink & Helson, 1993). Furthermore, cohort effects can contribute to this trend: In one study, middle-aged women of the baby-boom generation—who experienced new career opportunities as a result of the women's movement—more often described themselves as having masculine and androgynous traits than did older women (Strough et al., 2007).

Additional demands of midlife may prompt a more androgynous orientation. For example, among men, a need to enrich a marital relationship after children have departed, along with reduced chances for career advancement, may be involved in the awakening of emotionally sensitive traits. Compared with men, women are far more likely to face economic and social disadvantages. A greater number remain divorced, are widowed, and encounter discrimination in the workplace. Self-reliance and assertiveness are vital for coping with these circumstances.

In sum, androgyny in midlife results from a complex combination of social roles and life conditions. In Chapter 8, we noted that androgyny predicts high self-esteem. In adulthood, it is also associated with advanced moral reasoning and psychosocial maturity (Prager & Bailey, 1985; Waterman & Whitbourne, 1982). People who do not integrate the masculine and feminine sides of their personalities tend to have mental health problems, perhaps because they are unable to adapt flexibly to the challenges of aging (Huyck, 1996).

Individual Differences in Personality Traits

Although Trisha and Jewel both became more self-assured and assertive in midlife, in other respects they differed. Trisha had always been more organized and hard-working, Jewel more gregarious and fun-loving. Once, the two women traveled together. At the end of each day, Trisha was disappointed if she had not kept to a schedule and visited every tourist attraction. Jewel liked to "play it by ear"—wandering through streets and stopping to talk with shopkeepers and residents.

In previous sections, we considered personality changes common to many middle-aged adults, but stable individual differences also exist. The hundreds of personality traits on which people differ have been organized into five basic factors, called the **"big five" personality traits:** neuroticism, extroversion, openness to experience, agreeableness, and conscientiousness. Table 16.1 provides a description of each. Notice that Trisha is high in conscientiousness, whereas Jewel is high in extroversion.

Longitudinal and cross-sectional studies of U.S. men and women reveal that agreeableness and conscientiousness increase from the teenage years through middle age, whereas neuroticism declines, and extroversion and openness to experience do not change or decrease slightly—changes that reflect "settling down" and greater maturity. Similar trends have been identified in many other countries varying widely in cultural traditions, including Canada, Germany, Italy, Japan, Russia, and South Korea (McCrae & Costa, 2006; Roberts et al., 2003; Roberts, Walton, & Viechtbauer, 2006; Srivastava et al., 2003). The consistency of these cross-cultural findings has led some researchers to conclude that adult personality change is genetically influenced. They note that individual differences in the "big five" traits are large and highly stable: A person who scores high or low at one age is likely to do the same at another, over intervals ranging from 3 to 30 years (McCrae & Costa, 2006). In a reanalysis of more than 150 longitudinal studies including more than 50,000 participants, personality-trait stability increased from early to middle adulthood, reaching a peak in the decade of the fifties (see Figure 16.4) (Roberts & DelVecchio, 2000).

How can there be high stability in personality traits, yet significant changes in aspects of personality discussed earlier? Studies of the "big five" traits include very large samples and typically do not examine the impact of a host of contextual factors—including life events, the social clock, and cultural values—that shape aspirations, goals, and expectations for appropriate behavior (Caspi & Roberts, 2001). Look closely at the traits in Table 16.1, and you will see that they differ from the attributes considered in previous sections: They do not take into account motivations, preferred tasks, and coping styles, nor do they consider how certain aspects of personality, such as masculinity and femininity, are integrated (Block, 1995; Helson & Stewart, 1994). Theorists concerned with change due to experience focus on how personal needs and life events induce new strategies and goals. In contrast, those who emphasize stability due to heredity measure personality traits on which individuals can easily be compared and that are present at any time of life.

To resolve this apparent contradiction, we can think of adults as changing in overall organization and integration of personality but doing so on a foundation of basic, enduring dispositions that support a coherent sense of self as people adapt to changing life circumstances. When more than 2,000 individuals in their forties were asked to reflect on their personalities during the previous six years, 52 percent said they had "stayed the same," 39 percent said they had "changed a little," and 9 percent said they had "changed a lot" (Herbst et al., 2000). Again, these findings contradict a view of middle adulthood as a period of great turmoil and change. But they also underscore that personality remains an "open system," responsive to the pressures of life experiences. Indeed, certain midlife personality changes may strengthen trait consistency! Improved self-understanding, self-acceptance, and skill at handling challenging situations may result in less need to modify basic personality dispositions over time.

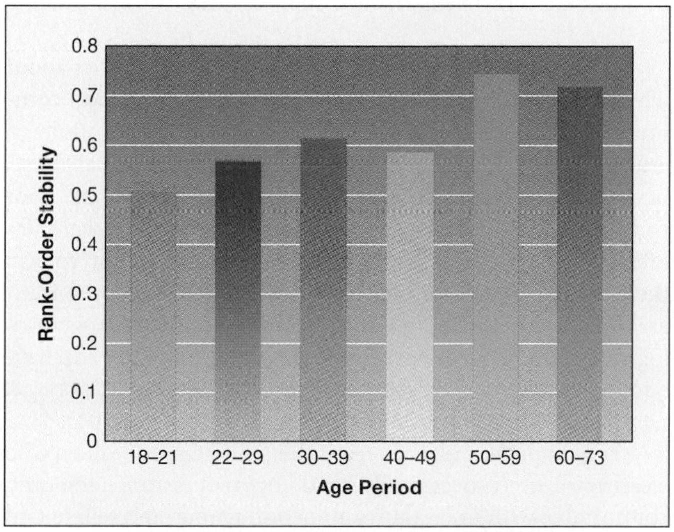

■ **FIGURE 16.4** ■ **Increase in stability of the "big five" personality traits across early and middle adulthood.** In a reanalysis of more than 150 longitudinal studies, stability of personality traits was strong at all ages; adults who scored high or low in certain traits largely retained that pattern when retested. Stability reached a peak in the fifties. (Adapted from Roberts & DelVecchio, 2000.)

ASK YOURSELF

» REVIEW
Summarize personality changes at midlife. How can these changes be reconciled with increasing stability of the "big five" personality traits?

» APPLY
Jeff, age 46, suggested to his wife, Julia, that they set aside time once a year to discuss their relationship—both positive aspects and ways to improve. Julia was surprised because Jeff had never before expressed interest in working on their marriage. What developments at midlife probably fostered this new concern?

» CONNECT
List cognitive gains that typically occur during middle adulthood. (See Chapter 15, pages 519 and 523–525.) How might they support midlife personality changes?

» REFLECT
List your hoped-for and feared possible selves. Then ask family members in the early and middle adulthood periods to do the same. Are their reports consistent with age-related research findings? Explain.

Relationships at Midlife

The emotional and social changes of midlife take place within a complex web of family relationships and friendships. Although a few middle-aged people live alone, the vast majority—90 percent in the United States—live in families, most with a spouse (U.S. Census Bureau, 2009b). Partly because they have ties to older and younger generations in their families and partly because their friendships are well-established, people tend to have a larger number of close relationships during midlife than at any other period (Antonucci, Akiyama, & Takahashi, 2004).

The middle adulthood phase of the family life cycle is often referred to as "launching children and moving on." In the past, it was often called the "empty nest," but this phrase implies a negative transition, especially for women. When adults devote themselves entirely to their children, the end of active parenting can trigger feelings of emptiness and regret. But for many people, middle adulthood is a liberating time, offering a sense of completion and an opportunity to strengthen existing ties and build new ones.

A century ago, most parents reared children for almost all of their active adulthood. A declining birthrate and longer life expectancy mean that many contemporary parents launch children a decade or more before retirement, then seek other rewarding activities. Because this period has lengthened, it is marked by the greatest number of exits and entries of family members. As adult children leave home and marry, middle-aged people must adapt to new roles of parent-in-law and grandparent. At the same time, they must establish a different type of relationship with their aging parents, who may become ill or infirm and die. Let's see how ties within and beyond the family change during this time of life.

Marriage and Divorce

Although not all couples are financially comfortable, middle-aged households are well-off economically compared with other age groups. Americans between 45 and 54 have the highest average annual income. And the baby boomers—more of whom have earned college and postgraduate degrees and live in dual-earner families—are financially better off than previous midlife generations (Eggebeen & Sturgeon, 2006; U.S. Census Bureau, 2009b). Partly because of increased education and financial security, the contemporary social view of marriage in midlife is one of expansion and new horizons.

These forces strengthen the need to review and adjust the marital relationship. For Devin and Trisha, this shift was gradual. By middle age, their marriage had permitted satisfaction of family and individual needs, endured many changes, and culminated in deeper feelings of love. Elena's marriage, in contrast, became more conflict-ridden as her teenage daughter's problems introduced added strains and as departure of children made marital difficulties more obvious. Tim's failed marriage revealed yet another pattern. With passing years, the number of problems declined, but so did the love expressed. As less happened in the relationship, good or bad, the couple had little to keep them together (Rokach, Cohen, & Dreman, 2004).

As the Biology and Environment box on pages 540–541 revealed, marital satisfaction is a strong predictor of midlife psychological well-being. Middle-aged men who have focused only on career often realize the limited nature of their pursuits. At the same time, their wives may insist on a more gratifying relationship. And children fully engaged in adult roles remind middle-aged parents that they are in the latter part of their lives, prompting many to decide that the time for improving their marriages is now (Berman & Napier, 2000).

As in early adulthood, divorce is one way of resolving an unsatisfactory marriage in midlife. Although most divorces occur within five to ten years of marriage, about 10 percent take place after 20 years or more (U.S. Department of Health and Human Services, 2002). Divorce at any age takes a heavy psychological toll, but midlifers seem to adapt more easily than younger people. A survey of more than 13,000 Americans revealed that following divorce, middle-aged men and women reported less decline in psychological well-being than their younger counterparts (Marks & Lambert, 1998). Midlife gains in practical problem solving and effective coping strategies may reduce the stressful impact of divorce.

Because the divorce rate is more than twice as great among remarried couples as among those in first marriages, a substantial number of midlife divorces involve people who have had one or more previous unsuccessful marriages. Highly educated middle-aged adults are more likely to divorce, probably because their more comfortable economic circumstances make it easier to leave an unhappy marriage (Skaff, 2006; Wu & Penning,

© JEFF GREENBERG/PHOTOEDIT

For many middle-aged couples, having forged a relationship that permits satisfaction of both family and individual needs results in deep feelings of love.

1997). Nevertheless, for many women, marital breakup—especially when it is repeated—severely reduces standard of living (see page 347 in Chapter 10). For this reason, in midlife and earlier, it is a strong contributor to the **feminization of poverty**—a trend in which women who support themselves or their families have become the majority of the adult population living in poverty, regardless of age and ethnic group. Because of weak public policies safeguarding families (see Chapter 2), the gender gap in poverty is higher in the United States than in other Western industrialized nations (U.S. Census Bureau, 2009b).

What do recently divorced middle-aged people say about why their marriages ended? Women frequently mention communication problems, inequality in the relationship, adultery, gradual distancing, substance abuse, physical and verbal abuse, or their own desire for autonomy. Men also bring up poor communication and sometimes admit that their "workaholic" lifestyle or emotional inattentiveness played a major role in their marital failure. Women are more likely than men to initiate divorce, and those who do fare somewhat better in psychological well-being. Men who initiate a split often already have another romantic involvement to turn to (Rokach, Cohen, & Dreman, 2004; Sakraida, 2005; Schneller & Arditti, 2004).

Longitudinal evidence reveals that middle-aged women who weather divorce successfully tend to become more tolerant, comfortable with uncertainty, nonconforming, and self-reliant in personality—factors believed to be fostered by divorce-forced independence. And both men and women reevaluate what they consider important in a healthy relationship, placing greater weight on equal friendship and less on passionate love than they had the first time. As in earlier periods, divorce represents both a time of trauma and a time of growth (Baum, Rahav, & Sharon, 2005; Schneller & Arditti, 2004). Little is known about long-term adjustment following divorce among middle-aged men, perhaps because most enter new relationships and remarry within a short time.

Changing Parent–Child Relationships

Parents' positive relationships with their grown children are the result of a gradual process of "letting go," starting in childhood, gaining momentum in adolescence, and culminating in children's independent living. As mentioned earlier, most parents "launch" adult children sometime in midlife. But because more people are delaying having children to their thirties and even forties (see page 438 in Chapter 13), the age at which midlifers experience their children's departure varies widely. Most parents adjust well; only a minority have difficulty. Investment in nonparental relationships and roles, children's characteristics, parents' marital and economic circumstances, and cultural forces affect the extent to which this transition is expansive and rewarding or sad and distressing.

After moving their son Mark into his college dormitory at the start of his freshman year, Devin and Trisha felt a twinge of nostalgia. Driving home, they recalled his birth, first day of school, and high school graduation and commented on their suddenly tranquil household. Beyond this, they returned to rewarding careers and community participation and delighted in having more time for each other. Parents who have developed gratifying alternative activities typically welcome their children's adult status (Dennerstein, Dudley, & Guthrie, 2002). A strong work orientation, especially, predicts gains in life satisfaction after children depart from the home (Seltzer & Ryff, 1994; Silverberg, 1996).

Whether or not they reside with parents, adolescent and young adult children who are "off-time" in development—not showing expected signs of independence and accomplishment—can prompt parental strain (Aquilino, 1996; Pillemer & Suitor, 2002). Consider Elena, whose daughter was frequently truant from high school and in danger of not graduating. The need for greater parental oversight and guidance caused anxiety and unhappiness for Elena, who was ready to complete the active parenting phase and focus on her own personal and vocational development.

However, wide variations exist in the social clock for children's departure. Recall from Chapter 13 that many young people from low-SES homes and with cultural traditions of extended-family living do not leave home early. In the Southern European countries of Greece, Italy, and Spain, parents often actively delay their children's leaving. In Italy, for example, parents believe that moving out without a "justified" reason signifies that something is wrong in the family. Hence, many more Italian young adults reside with their parents until marriage than in other Western nations. At the same time, Italian adults grant their grown children extensive freedom within the parental home (Rusconi, 2004). Parent–adult-child relationships are usually positive, making living with parents attractive.

With the end of parent–child coresidence comes a substantial decline in parental authority. Devin and Trisha no longer knew of Mark's daily comings and goings or expected him to inform them. Nevertheless, Mark telephoned at regular intervals to report on events in his life and seek advice about major decisions. Although the parental role changes, its continuation is important to middle-aged adults. Departure of children is a relatively minor event when parent–child contact and affection are sustained. When it results in little or no communication, parents' life satisfaction declines (White, 1994). In a large longitudinal study of New Zealand families, parents' relations with adult children were linked to quality of parenting years before. Parents who had been warm and supportive in middle childhood and adolescence were more likely to experience contact and closeness with their child in early adulthood (Belsky et al., 2001).

Throughout middle adulthood, parents continue to give more assistance to children than they receive, especially while children are unmarried or when they face difficulties, such as marital breakup or unemployment (Ploeg et al., 2004; Zarit & Eggebeen, 2002). Providing emotional and financial support while children get their lives under way is related to midlife psychological well-being. Because of their own disrupted relationships and economic need, divorced and remarried parents are less likely than parents in first marriages to offer adult children support, and they are also less content (Marks, 1995). Children's psychological adjustment is more important than their educational and occupational success for midlife parental adjustment (Ryff, Schmutte, & Lee, 1996). When young adult children are relatively free of emotional and social problems, they relate more positively to their parents. Favorable adaptation to the launching phase depends on feeling successful as a parent and on not being estranged from one's children.

When children marry, parents face additional challenges in enlarging the family network to include in-laws. Difficulties occur when parents do not approve of their child's partner or when the young couple adopts a way of life inconsistent with the parents' values. But as MIDUS findings confirm, when warm, supportive relationships endure, intimacy between parents and children increases over the adult years, with great benefits for parents' life satisfaction (Ryff, Singer, & Seltzer, 2002). Once young adults strike out on their own, members of the middle generation, especially mothers, usually take on the role of **kinkeeper,** gathering the family for celebrations and making sure everyone stays in touch.

As children become adults, parents expect a mature relationship with them, marked by tranquility and contentment. Yet many factors—on the child's and the adult's side—affect whether that goal is achieved. Applying What We Know on page 546 suggests ways middle-aged parents can increase the chances that bonds with adult children will be loving and rewarding and serve as contexts for personal growth.

Grandparenthood

Two years after Mark married, Devin and Trisha were thrilled to learn that a granddaughter was on the way. Although the stereotypical image of grandparents as elderly persists, today the average age of becoming a grandparent is 50 years for American women, 52 for American men (Legacy Project, 2009). A longer

Applying What We Know

Ways Middle-Aged Parents Can Promote Positive Ties with Their Adult Children

Suggestion	Description
Emphasize positive communication.	Let adult children know of your respect, support, and interest. This not only communicates affection but also permits conflict to be handled in a constructive context.
Avoid unnecessary comments that are a holdover from childhood.	Adult children, like younger children, appreciate an age-appropriate relationship. Comments that have to do with safety, eating, and self-care ("Be careful on the freeway," "Don't eat those foods," "Make sure you wear a sweater—it's cold out today") annoy adult children and can stifle communication.
Accept the possibility that some cultural values and practices and aspects of lifestyle will be modified in the next generation.	In constructing a personal identity, most adult children have gone through a process of evaluating the meaning of cultural values and practices for their own lives. Traditions and lifestyles cannot be imposed on adult children.
When an adult child encounters difficulties, resist the urge to "fix" things.	Accept the fact that no meaningful change can take place without the willing cooperation of the adult child. Stepping in and taking over communicates a lack of confidence and respect. Find out whether the adult child wants your help, advice, and decision-making skills.
Be clear about your own needs and preferences.	When it is difficult to arrange for a visit, babysit, or provide other assistance, say so and negotiate a reasonable compromise rather than letting resentment build.

life expectancy means that many adults will spend one-third or more of their lifespan in the grandparent role.

MEANINGS OF GRANDPARENTHOOD. Middle-aged adults typically rate grandparenthood as highly important, following closely behind the roles of parent and spouse but ahead of worker, son or daughter, and sibling (Reitzes & Mutran, 2002). Why did Trisha and Devin, like many others their age, greet the announcement of a grandchild with such enthusiasm? Most people experience grandparenthood as a significant milestone, mentioning one or more of the following gratifications:

- *Valued elder*—being perceived as a wise, helpful person
- *Immortality through descendants*—leaving behind not just one but two generations after death
- *Reinvolvement with personal past*—being able to pass family history and values to a new generation
- *Indulgence*—having fun with children without major child-rearing responsibilities (AARP, 2002; Miller & Cavanaugh, 1990)

GRANDPARENT–GRANDCHILD RELATIONSHIPS. Grandparents' styles of relating to grandchildren vary as widely as the meanings they derive from their new role. The grandparent's and grandchild's age and sex make a difference. When their granddaughter was young, Trisha and Devin enjoyed an affectionate, playful relationship with her. As she got older, she looked to them for information and advice in addition to warmth and caring. By the time their granddaughter reached adolescence, Trisha and Devin had become role models, family historians, and conveyers of social, vocational, and religious values.

Living nearby is the strongest predictor of frequent, face-to-face interaction with young grandchildren. Despite high family mobility in Western industrialized nations, most grandparents live close enough to at least one grandchild to enable

© GARY WALTS/THE IMAGE WORKS

Many grandparents derive great joy from an affectionate, playful relationship with young grandchildren. As this grandchild gets older, he may look to his grandmother for advice, as a role model, and for family history in addition to warmth and caring.

regular visits. But because time and resources are limited, number of "grandchild sets" (households with grandchildren) reduces grandparent visits, though frequent contact with at least one set is more likely when grandparents have multiple sets (Uhlenberg & Hammill, 1998). A strong desire to affect the development of grandchildren can motivate grandparents' involvement. As grandchildren get older, distance becomes less influential and relationship quality more so: The extent to which adolescent or young adult grandchildren believe their grandparent values contact is a good predictor of a close bond (Brussoni & Boon, 1998).

As Figure 16.5 shows, maternal grandmothers report more frequent visits with grandchildren than do paternal grandmothers, who are slightly advantaged over both maternal and paternal grandfathers (Uhlenberg & Hammill, 1998). Typically, relationships are closer between grandparents and grandchildren of the same sex and, especially, between maternal grandmothers and granddaughters—a pattern found in many countries (Brown & Rodin, 2004). Grandmothers also report higher satisfaction with the grandparent role than grandfathers, perhaps because grandmothers are more likely to participate in recreational, religious, and family activities with grandchildren (Silverstein & Marenco, 2001; Somary & Stricker, 1998). The grandparent role may be a vital means through which women satisfy their kinkeeping function.

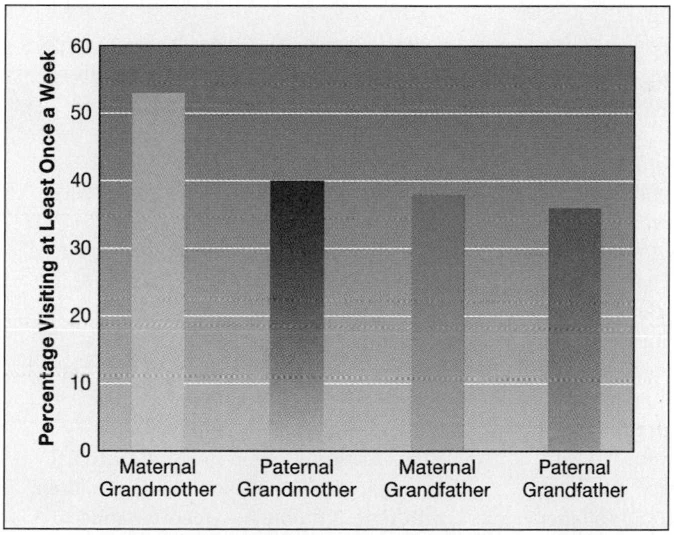

FIGURE 16.5 **Influence of grandparent sex and lineage on frequent visiting of grandchildren.** When a nationally representative sample of 4,600 U.S. grandparents were asked how often they visited a particular set of grandchildren, maternal grandmothers were especially likely to report visiting frequently (at least once a week). Paternal grandmothers slightly exceeded both maternal and paternal grandfathers. (From P. Uhlenberg & B. G. Hammill, 1998, "Frequency of Grandparent Contact with Grandchild Sets: Six Factors That Make a Difference," *Gerontologist, 38,* p. 281. Copyright © 1998 The Gerontological Society of America. Reprinted by permission of Oxford University Press and Peter Uhlenberg.

SES and ethnicity also influence grandparent–grandchild ties. In higher-income families, where the grandparent role is not central to family maintenance and survival, it is fairly unstructured and takes many forms. In low-income families, by contrast, grandparents often perform essential activities. For example, many single parents live with their families of origin and depend on grandparents' financial and caregiving assistance to reduce the impact of poverty. Compared with grandchildren in intact families, grandchildren in single-parent and stepparent families report engaging in more diverse, higher-quality activities with their grandparents (Kennedy & Kennedy, 1993). As children experience the stress of family transition, bonds with grandparents take on increasing importance.

In some cultures, grandparents are absorbed into an extended-family household and become actively involved in child rearing. When a Chinese, Korean, or Mexican-American maternal grandmother is a homemaker, she is the preferred caregiver while parents of young children are at work (Kamo, 1998; Williams & Torrez, 1998). Similarly, involvement in child care is high among Native-American grandparents. In the absence of a biological grandparent, an unrelated elder may be integrated into the family to serve as a mentor and disciplinarian for children (Werner, 1991). (See Chapter 2, page 66, for a description of the grandmother's role in the African-American extended family.)

RECENT TRENDS IN GRANDPARENTING. Increasingly, grandparents have stepped in as primary caregivers in the face of serious family problems. As the Social Issues box on page 548 reveals, a rising number of North American children live apart from their parents in grandparent-headed households. Despite their willingness to help and their competence at child rearing, grandparents who take full responsibility for young children experience considerable emotional and financial strain. They need much more assistance from community and government agencies than is currently available.

Because parents usually serve as gatekeepers of grandparents' contact with grandchildren, relationships between grandparents and their daughter-in-law or son-in-law strongly affect the closeness of grandparent–grandchild ties. A positive bond with a daughter-in-law seems particularly important in the relationship between grandparents and their son's children (Fingerman, 2004). And after a marital breakup, grandparents related to the custodial parent (typically the mother) have more frequent contact with grandchildren (Johnson, 1998).

A growing concern among grandparents—especially those on the noncustodial side—is maintaining relationships with grandchildren after parental divorce. Currently, all 50 U.S. states permit grandparents to seek legal visitation judgments. Yet grandparent visitation rights can add to family difficulties. When parents are divorcing, grandparents' behavior varies greatly, from constructive help to entanglement in parental battles. Unfortunately, intense conflict usually lies behind the legal petitions of grandparents who fail to work out visitation informally (Smith & Drew, 2002). Consequently, courts are wise to exercise restraint in awarding grandparents visitation privileges.

SOCIAL ISSUES

Grandparents Rearing Grandchildren: The Skipped-Generation Family

Nearly 2.4 million U.S. children—4 to 5 percent of the child population—live with grandparents but apart from parents, in **skipped-generation families** (U.S. Census Bureau, 2009b). The number of grandparents rearing grandchildren has increased over the past two decades. The arrangement occurs in all ethnic groups, though more often in African-American, Hispanic, and Native-American families than in Caucasian families (Fuller-Thomson & Minkler, 2005, 2007; Minkler & Fuller-Thomson, 2005). Although grandparent caregivers are more likely to be women than men, many grandfathers participate. Often these families take in two or more children.

One grandmother's account illustrates the circumstances in which skipped-generation families form:

> I think [the child's mother] is doing an awful lot of drugs. I don't know if it's serious drugs, but enough that she wasn't doing a good job. They were doing an awful lot of partying, and I just finally went to her one day and said, "Your life is messed up, let me take the baby for a while so you can get your life together." And it was just because we wanted her [the granddaughter] out of there. She had become our main priority. (Jendrek, 1994, p. 209)

In about half of skipped-generation families, grandparents step in because substance-abuse problems prevent parents, usually the child's mother, from engaging in competent child rearing. In most other instances, parental emotional or physical illness is involved (Pruchno & McKenney, 2000; Weber & Waldrop, 2000). Child abuse and neglect is often a factor. Occasionally child welfare authorities, out of a preference for placing the child with relatives rather than in a foster home, approach the grandparent, who assumes temporary or permanent legal custody. More often, grandparents offer their assistance, sometimes with and sometimes without legal responsibility. Most say they took action to protect the child only when the parents' situation became intolerable.

Because the skipped-generation family structure is not freely chosen, many custodial grandparents face highly stressful life circumstances. Unfavorable child-rearing experiences have left their mark on the children, who show high rates of learning difficulties, depression, and antisocial behavior. Absent parents' adjustment difficulties strain family relationships. Parents may interfere by violating the grandparents' behavioral limits, taking grandchildren away without permission, or making promises to children that they do not keep. These youngsters also introduce financial burdens into households that often are already low-income (Mills, Gomez-Smith, & De Leon, 2005; Williamson, Softas-Nall, & Miller, 2003). All these factors heighten grandparents' emotional distress.

© JIM WEST PHOTOGRAPHY

A custodial grandmother helps her 8-year-old granddaughter with homework. Grandparents in skipped-generation families face shattered dreams of freedom and considerable emotional and financial strain. But most find compensating rewards in rearing grandchildren.

Grandparents struggle with daily dilemmas—wanting to be grandparents, not parents; wanting the parent to be present in the child's life but fearing for the child's well-being if the parent returns and does not provide good care. Child-rearing tasks leave grandparents with less time for spouses, friends, and leisure when they had expected to have more time. Many report feeling emotionally drained, depressed, and worried about what will happen to the children if their own health fails (Hayslip & Kaminski, 2005; Kolomer & McCallion, 2005). Some families are extremely burdened. Native-American caregiving grandparents are especially likely to be unemployed, to have a disability, to be caring for several grandchildren, and to be living in extreme poverty (Fuller-Thomson & Minkler, 2005).

Despite great hardship, these grandparents seem to realize their widespread image as "silent saviors," often forging close emotional bonds with their grandchildren and using effective child-rearing practices (Fuller-Thomson & Minkler, 2000; Gibson, 2005). A survey of a large, representative sample of U.S. families revealed that compared with children in divorced, single-parent families or in blended families, children reared by grandparents were better-behaved in school, less susceptible to physical illness, and doing just as well academically (Solomon & Marx, 1995).

Skipped-generation families have a tremendous need for social and financial support and intervention services for troubled children. But although their daily existence is often stressful, custodial grandparents—even those rearing children with serious problems—report as much satisfaction with the grandparent role as typical grandparents (Hayslip et al., 2002). Many mention joy from sharing children's lives and feelings of pride at children's progress, which help compensate for difficult circumstances. And some grandparents view the rearing of grandchildren as a "second chance"—an opportunity to make up for earlier, unfavorable parenting experiences and "do it right" (Dolbin-MacNab, 2006; Waldrop & Weber, 2001).

When family relationships are positive, grandparenthood provides an important means of fulfilling personal and societal needs in midlife and beyond. Typically, grandparents are a frequent source of pleasure, support, and knowledge for children, adolescents, and young adults. They also provide the young with firsthand experience in how older people think and function. In return, grandchildren become deeply attached to grandparents and keep them abreast of social change. Clearly, grandparenthood is a vital context for sharing between generations.

Middle-Aged Children and Their Aging Parents

The percentage of middle-aged Americans with living parents has risen dramatically—from 10 percent in 1900 to 50 percent at the beginning of the twenty-first century (U.S. Census Bureau, 2009b). A longer life expectancy means that adult children and their parents are increasingly likely to grow old together. What are middle-aged children's relationships with their aging parents like? And how does life change for adult children when an aging parent's health declines?

FREQUENCY AND QUALITY OF CONTACT. A widespread myth is that adults of past generations were more devoted to their aging parents than are today's adults. Although adult children spend less time in physical proximity to their parents, the reason is not neglect or isolation. Fewer aging adults live with younger generations now than in the past because of a desire to be independent, made possible by gains in health and financial security. Nevertheless, approximately two-thirds of older adults in the United States live close to at least one of their children, and frequency of contact is high through both visits and telephone calls (U.S. Census Bureau, 2009b). Proximity increases with age: Elders who move usually do so in the direction of kin, and younger people tend to move in the direction of their aging parents.

Middle age is a time when adults reassess relationships with their parents, just as they rethink other close ties. Many adult children become more appreciative of their parents' strengths and generosity and mention positive changes in the quality of the relationship, even after parents show physical declines (Fingerman et al., 2007). Trisha, for example, felt closer to her parents and made an effort to learn more about their early lives. And she recalled her mother's sound advice just before her marriage to Devin nearly three decades earlier: "Build a life together, but also forge your own life. You'll be happier." At several turning points, that advice influenced Trisha's decisions.

As Trisha's rapport with her mother conveys, mother–daughter relationships tend to be closer than other parent–child ties (Fingerman, 2001b). As the tensions of the adolescent years ease, many young-adult daughters and mothers build rewarding, intimate bonds. Daughters benefit greatly from maternal support, and many describe the relationship in glowing terms. As daughters move into middle age, their descriptions of the mother–daughter bond become more complex, reflecting both positive and negative aspects—a change that may stem from daughters' more mature perspective and from growing relationship tensions (Fingerman, 2000). Although middle-aged daughters love their aging mothers, they face many competing demands on their time and energy (Fingerman, 1996). Consequently, older mothers (especially those who are widowed) may be more emotionally invested in their daughters than their middle-aged daughters are able to be in their mothers (Fingerman, 2001a).

In collectivist cultures, older adults most often live with their married children. For example, traditionally, Chinese, Japanese, and Korean elderly moved in with a son and his wife and children; today, many live with a daughter and her family, too. This tradition of coresidence, however, is declining in some parts of Asia and in the United States, as more Asian and Asian-American elders choose to live on their own (Takagi, Silverstein, & Crimmins, 2007; Zhan & Montgomery, 2003; Zhang, 2004). Whether or not coresidence and daily contact are typical, relationship quality usually reflects patterns established earlier: Positive parent–child ties generally remain so, as do conflict-ridden interactions.

Help exchanged between adult children and their aging parents is responsive to past and current family circumstances. The more positive the history of the parent–child tie, the more help given and received (Whitbeck, Hoyt, & Huck, 1994). Also, parents give more help to unmarried children and to children with disabilities. Children give more to widowed parents and parents in poor health—usually emotional support and practical help, less often financial assistance. At the same time, a shift in helping occurs over the adult years. Parent-to-child assistance

© IMAGE SOURCE/GETTY IMAGES

In midlife, many adults become more appreciative of their parents' strengths and generosity. They also mention positive changes in relationship quality—feeling closer and desiring to learn more about their parents' early lives.

declines, while child-to-parent aid increases (Kunemund, Motel-Klingebiel, & Kohli, 2005; Rossi & Rossi, 1990; Zarit & Eggebeen, 2002).

Even when parent–child relationships have been emotionally distant, adult children offer more support as their parents age, out of a sense of altruism and family duty (Silverstein et al., 2002). And although the baby-boom generation is often described as self-absorbed, in surveys of large samples of U.S. adults repeated over time, baby-boom midlifers actually expressed a stronger commitment to caring for their aging parents than did the preceding middle-aged generation (Gans & Silverstein, 2006).

■ **CARING FOR AGING PARENTS.** About 16 percent of the U.S. adult population provides unpaid care to an aging adult, and 25 to 35 percent of those in the work force report doing so (AARP, 2004; Family Caregiver Alliance, 2009). The burden of caring for aging parents can be great. In Chapter 2, we noted that as birthrates have declined, the family structure has become more "top-heavy," with more generations alive but fewer younger members. Consequently, more than one older family member is likely to need assistance, with fewer younger adults available to provide it.

The term **sandwich generation** is widely used to refer to the idea that middle-aged adults must care for multiple generations above and below them at the same time (Riley & Bowen, 2005). Although only a minority of contemporary middle-aged adults who care for elderly parents have children younger than age 18 at home, many are providing assistance to young-adult children and to grandchildren—obligations that, when combined with work and community responsibilities, can lead middle-aged caregivers to feel "sandwiched," or squeezed, between the pressures of older and younger generations. As the baby boomers move into late adulthood and as their adult children continue to delay childbearing, the number of sandwiched midlifers who are working, rearing young children, and caring for aging parents will increase.

Middle-aged adults living far from aging parents who are in poor health often substitute financial help for direct care, if they have the means. But when parents live nearby and have no spouse to meet their needs, adult children usually engage in direct care. Regardless of family income level, African-American, Asian-American, and Hispanic adults give aging parents more direct care and financial support than Caucasian-American adults do (AARP, 2004; Shuey & Hardy, 2003). Minority families typically build a large and strong support network, with African Americans often drawing on close, family-like relationships with friends and neighbors for financial or caregiving assistance.

In all ethnic groups, responsibility for providing care to aging parents falls more on daughters than on sons. Why are women usually the principal caregivers? Families turn to the person who seems most available—living nearby and with fewer commitments regarded as interfering with the ability to assist. These unstated rules, in addition to parents' preference for same-sex caregivers (aging mothers live longer), lead more women to fill the role. Daughters also feel more obligated than sons to care for aging parents (Gans & Silverstein, 2006). And although couples strive to be fair to both sides of the family, they tend to provide more direct care for the wife's parents. This bias, however, is weaker in ethnic minority families and is nonexistent in Asian nations where cultural norms specify that daughters-in-law provide care to their husband's parents (Shuey & Hardy, 2003; Zhan & Montgomery, 2003).

About 50 percent of American women caregivers are employed; another 10 to 30 percent quit their jobs to provide care. And the time they devote to caring for a disabled aging parent is substantial, averaging 10 to 20 hours per week (AARP, 2004; Takamura & Williams, 2002). Nevertheless, men—although doing less than women—do contribute. In one investigation, employed men spent an average of 7½ hours per week caring for parents or parents-in-law (Neal & Hammer, 2007). Tim, for example, looked in on his father, a recent stroke victim, every evening, reading to him, running errands, making household repairs, and taking care of finances. His sister, however, provided more hands-on care—cooking, feeding, bathing, managing medication, and doing laundry. The care sons and daughters provide tends to be divided along gender-role lines. About 10 percent of the time—generally when no other family member can do so—sons become primary caregivers, heavily involved in basic-care tasks (Harris, 1998; Pinquart & Sörensen, 2006).

As adults move from early to later middle age, the sex difference in parental caregiving declines. Perhaps as men reduce their vocational commitments and feel less need to conform to a "masculine" gender role, they grow more able and willing to provide basic care (Marks, 1996). At the same time, parental caregiving may contribute to men's greater openness to the "feminine" side of their personalities. A man who cared for his mother, severely impaired by Alzheimer's disease, commented on how the experience altered his outlook:

> Having to do personal care, becoming a male nurse, was a great adjustment. It was so difficult to do these tasks; things a man, a son, is not supposed to do. But, I had to alter, since charity must come before maintaining a selfish, conventional view. I have definitely modified my views on conventional expectations. (Hirsch, 1996, p. 112)

Although most adult children help willingly, caring for a chronically ill or disabled parent is highly stressful—and radically different from caring for a young child. The need for parental care typically arises suddenly, after a heart attack, fall, stroke, or diagnosis of cancer, leaving little time for preparation. Whereas children become increasingly independent, the parent usually gets worse, and the caregiving task and its cost escalate. As Tim explained to Devin and Trisha, "One of the hardest aspects is the emotional strain of seeing my father's physical and mental decline up close." Tim also felt a sense of grief over the loss of a cherished relationship, as his father no longer seemed to be his former self. Because duration of caregiving is uncertain, caregivers often feel they no longer have control over their lives (Gatz, Bengtson, & Blum, 1990).

Adults who share a household with ill parents—about 10 percent of American caregivers—experience the most stress. When a parent and child who have lived separately for years must

Caring for a chronically ill or disabled aging parent is highly stressful. But social support reduces physical and emotional strain, enabling adult children to find satisfactions and rewards in tending to parents' needs.

move in together, conflicts generally arise over routines and lifestyles. But the greatest source of stress is problem behavior, especially for caregivers of parents who have deteriorated mentally (Alzheimer's Association, 2009). Tim's sister reported that their father would wake during the night, ask repetitive questions, follow her around the house, and become agitated and combative.

Parental caregiving often has emotional and physical health consequences. It leads to role overload, high job absenteeism, exhaustion, inability to concentrate, feelings of hostility, anxiety about aging, and rates of depression as high as 30 to 50 percent (Killian, Turner, & Cain, 2005; Neal & Hammer, 2007). In cultures and subcultures where adult children feel an especially strong sense of obligation to care for aging parents, the toll tends to be greater. In research on Korean, Korean-American, and Caucasian-American caregivers of parents with mental disabilities, the Koreans and Korean Americans reported higher levels of family obligation and care burden—and also higher levels of anxiety and depression—than the Caucasian Americans (Lee & Farran, 2004; Youn et al., 1999). And among African-American caregivers, women who strongly endorsed cultural reasons for providing care ("It's what my people have always done") fared less well in mental health two years later than women who moderately endorsed cultural reasons (Dilworth-Anderson, Goodwin, & Williams, 2004).

Social support is highly effective in reducing caregiver stress. Tim's encouragement, assistance, and willingness to listen helped his sister cope with in-home care of their father so that she could find satisfactions and rewards in it. Despite having more time to care for an ill parent, women who quit work generally fare poorly, probably because of social isolation and financial strain (Pohl et al., 1994). Positive experiences at work can actually reduce the stress of parental care as caregivers bring a favorable self-evaluation and a positive mood home with them (Neal & Hammer, 2007).

In Denmark, Sweden, and Japan, a government-sponsored home helper system eases the burden of parental care by making specially trained nonfamily caregivers available, based on the elder's needs (Blomberg, Edebalk, & Petersson, 2000; Lechner & Neal, 1999). In the United States, in-home care by a nonfamily caregiver is too costly for most families; only 10 to 20 percent arrange it (Family Caregiver Alliance, 2009). And unless they must, few people want to place their parents in formal care, such as nursing homes, which also are expensive. Applying What We Know on page 552 summarizes ways to relieve the stress of caring for an aging parent—at the individual, family, community, and societal levels. We will address additional elder care options, along with interventions for caregivers, in Chapter 17.

Siblings

As Tim's relationship with his sister reveals, siblings are ideally suited to provide social support. Nevertheless, a survey of a large sample of ethnically diverse Americans revealed that sibling contact and support decline from early to middle adulthood, rebounding only after age 70 for siblings living near one another (White, 2001). Decreased midlife contact is probably due to the demands of middle-aged adults' diverse roles. However, most adult siblings report getting together or talking on the phone at least monthly (Antonucci, Akiyama, & Merline, 2002).

Despite reduced contact, many siblings feel closer in midlife, often in response to major life events (Stewart et al., 2001). Launching and marriage of children seem to prompt siblings to think more about one another. As Tim commented, "It helped our relationship when my sister's children were out of the house and married. I'm sure she cared about me. I think she just didn't have time!" When a parent becomes seriously ill, brothers and sisters who previously had little to do with one another may find themselves in touch about parental care. And when parents die, adult children realize they have become the oldest generation and must look to one another to sustain family ties (Gold, 1996).

Not all sibling bonds improve, of course. Recall Trisha's negative encounters with her sister, Dottie (see Chapter 15, page 513). Dottie's difficult temperament had made her hard to get along with since childhood, and her temper flared when their father died and problems arose over family finances. When siblings do not help with parental caregiving, the child shouldering the burden can unleash powerful negative feelings (Merrill, 1997). As one expert expressed it, "As siblings grow older, good relationships [often] become better and rotten relationships get worse" (Moyer, 1992, p. 57).

As in early adulthood, sister–sister relationships are closer than sister–brother and brother–brother ties, a difference apparent in many industrialized nations (Cicirelli, 1995; Fowler, 2009). But a comparison of middle-aged men of the baby-boom

Applying What We Know

Relieving the Stress of Caring for an Aging Parent

Strategy	Description
Use effective coping strategies.	Use problem-centered coping to manage the parent's behavior and caregiving tasks. Delegate responsibilities to other family members, seek assistance from friends and neighbors, and recognize the parent's limits while calling on capacities the parent does have. Use emotion-centered coping to reinterpret the situation in a positive way, such as emphasizing the opportunity it offers for personal growth and for giving to parents in the last years of their lives. Avoid denial of anger, depression, and anxiety in response to the caregiver work burden, which heightens stress.
Seek social support.	Confide in family members and friends about the stress of caregiving, seeking their encouragement and help. So far as possible, avoid quitting work to care for an ill parent, because doing so leads to social isolation and loss of financial resources.
Make use of community resources.	Contact community organizations to seek information and assistance, in the form of caregiver support groups, in-home respite help, home-delivered meals, transportation, and adult day care.
Press for workplace and public policies that relieve the emotional and financial burdens of caring for an aging parent.	Encourage your employer to provide elder care benefits, such as flexible work hours and employment leave for caregiving. Communicate with lawmakers and other citizens about the need for additional government funding to help pay for elder care. Emphasize the need for improved health insurance plans that reduce the financial strain of elder care on middle- and low-income families.

generation with those of the preceding cohort revealed warmer, more expressive ties between baby-boom brothers (Bedford & Avioli, 2006). A contributing factor may be baby boomers' more flexible gender-role attitudes.

In industrialized nations, sibling relationships are voluntary. In village societies, they are generally involuntary and basic to family functioning. For example, among Asian Pacific Islanders, family social life is organized around strong brother–sister attachments. A brother–sister pair is often treated as a unit in exchange marriages with another family. After marriage, brothers are expected to protect sisters, and sisters serve as spiritual mentors to brothers. Families not only include biological siblings but also grant other relatives, such as cousins, the status of brother or sister, creating an unusually large network of lifelong sibling support (Cicirelli, 1995).

In village societies, cultural norms reduce sibling conflict, thereby ensuring family cooperation. In industrialized nations, promoting positive sibling interaction in childhood is vital for warm, supportive sibling bonds in later years.

Friendships

As family responsibilities declined in middle age, Devin found he had more time to spend with friends. On Friday afternoons, he met several male friends at a coffee house, and they chatted for a couple of hours. But most of Devin's friendships were couple-based—relationships he shared with Trisha. Compared with Devin, Trisha more often got together with friends on her own.

Middle-aged friendships reflect the same trends discussed in Chapter 14. At all ages, friendships between men are less intimate than those between women. Men tend to talk about sports, politics, and business, whereas women focus on feelings and life problems. Women report a greater number of close friends and say they both receive and provide their friends with more emotional support (Antonucci, 1994).

Nevertheless, for both sexes, number of friends declines with age, probably because people become less willing to invest in nonfamily ties unless they are very rewarding (Carbery & Buhrmester, 1998). As selectivity of friendship increases, older adults try harder to get along with friends (Antonucci & Akiyama, 1995). Having chosen a friend, middle-aged people attach great value to the relationship and take extra steps to protect it.

Friendships become more selective in midlife. Compared with younger people, middle-aged adults are less willing to invest in friendships unless they are very rewarding.

By midlife, family relationships and friendships support different aspects of psychological well-being. Family ties protect against serious threats and losses, offering security within a long-term timeframe. In contrast, friendships serve as current sources of pleasure and satisfaction, with women benefiting somewhat more than men (Antonucci, Akiyama, & Merline, 2002). As middle-aged couples renew their sense of companionship, they may combine the best of family and friendship. Indeed, research indicates that viewing a spouse as a best friend contributes greatly to marital happiness (Bengtson, Rosenthal, & Burton, 1990).

ASK YOURSELF

REVIEW
How do age, sex, proximity, and culture affect grandparent–grandchild ties?

APPLY
Raylene and her brother Walter live in the same city as their aging mother, Elsie. When Elsie could no longer live independently, Raylene took primary responsibility for her care. What factors probably contributed to Raylene's involvement in caregiving and Walter's lesser role?

CONNECT
Cite evidence that early family relationships affect middle-aged adults' bonds with adult children, aging parents, and siblings.

REFLECT
Ask a middle-aged couple you know well to describe the number and quality of their friendships today compared to their friendships in early adulthood. Does their report match research findings? Explain.

Vocational Life

As we have seen, the midlife transition typically involves vocational adjustments. For Devin, it resulted in a move up the career ladder to a demanding administrative post as college dean. Trisha reoriented her career from a large to a small law firm, where she felt her efforts were appreciated. Recall from Chapter 15 that after her oldest child left home, Anya earned a college degree and entered the work force for the first time. Jewel strengthened her commitment to an already successful business, while Elena changed careers. Finally, Tim reduced his career obligations as he prepared for retirement.

Work continues to be a salient aspect of identity and self-esteem in middle adulthood. More so than in earlier or later years, people attempt to increase the personal meaning and self-direction of their vocational lives. At the same time, certain aspects of job performance improve. Middle-aged employees have lower rates of absenteeism, turnover, and accidents. And because of their greater knowledge and experience, their work productivity typically equals or exceeds that of younger workers (Warr, 1994, 2001). Consequently, an older employee ought to be as valuable as a younger employee, and possibly more so.

The large tide of baby boomers currently moving through midlife and (as we will see in Chapter 18) the desire of most to work longer than the previous generation means that the number of older workers will rise dramatically over the next few decades (HSBC & Oxford Institute of Ageing, 2007). Yet a favorable transition from adult worker to older worker is hindered by negative stereotypes of aging—incorrect beliefs about limited learning capacity, slower decision making, and resistance to change and supervision (Maurer, 2007). Furthermore, gender discrimination continues to restrict the career attainments of many women. Let's take a close look at middle-aged work life.

Job Satisfaction

Job satisfaction has both psychological and economic significance. If people are dissatisfied at work, the consequences include absenteeism, turnover, grievances, and strikes, all of which are costly to employers.

Research shows that job satisfaction increases in midlife in diverse nations and at all occupational levels, from executives to hourly workers (see Figure 16.6). The relationship is weaker for women than for men, probably because women's reduced chances for advancement result in a sense of unfairness. It is also weaker for blue-collar than for white-collar workers, perhaps because blue-collar workers have less control over their own work schedules and activities (Avolio & Sosik, 1999). When different aspects of jobs are considered, intrinsic satisfaction—happiness with the work itself—shows a strong age-related gain. Extrinsic satisfaction—contentment with supervision, pay, and

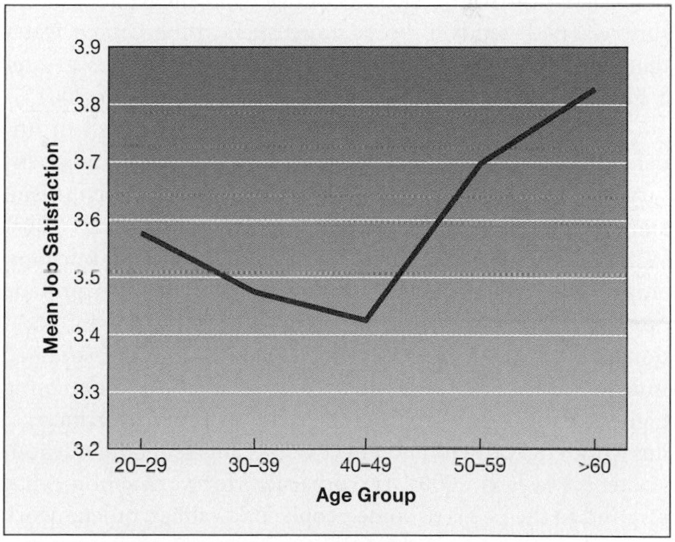

■ **FIGURE 16.6** ■ **Age-related change in job satisfaction.** In this study of more than 2,000 university employees at all levels, from secretary to university president, job satisfaction dropped slightly in early adulthood as people encountered some discouraging experiences (see Chapter 14). In middle age, job satisfaction showed a steady rise. (From W. A. Hochwarter et al., 2001, "A Note on the Nonlinearity of the Age–Job-Satisfaction Relationship," *Journal of Applied Social Psychology, 31,* p. 1232. Reprinted by permission of Blackwell Publishing Ltd.)

promotions—changes very little (Barnes-Farrell & Matthews, 2007).

What explains the rise in job satisfaction during middle adulthood? An improved capacity to cope effectively with difficult situations and a broader time perspective probably contribute. "When I first started teaching, I complained about a lot of things," remarked Devin. "From my current vantage point, I can tell a big problem from a trivial one." Moving out of unrewarding work roles, as Trisha did, can also boost morale. Key characteristics that predict job well-being include involvement in decision making, reasonable workloads, and good physical working conditions. Older people may have greater access to jobs that are attractive in these ways. Furthermore, having fewer alternative positions into which they can move, older workers generally reduce their career aspirations (Barnes-Farrell & Matthews, 2007). As the perceived gap between actual and possible achievements narrows, job involvement—importance of one's work to self-esteem—increases (Warr, 1994, 2001).

Although emotional engagement with work is usually seen as psychologically healthy, it can also result in **burnout**—a condition in which long-term job stress leads to mental exhaustion, a sense of loss of personal control, and feelings of reduced accomplishment. Burnout occurs more often in the helping professions, including health care, human services, and teaching, which place high emotional demands on employees. Although people in interpersonally demanding jobs are as psychologically healthy as other people, sometimes a worker's dedication exceeds his or her coping skills, especially in an unsupportive work environment (Schmidt, Neubach, & Heuer, 2007; Zapf et al., 2001). Burnout is associated with excessive work assignments for available time and lack of encouragement and feedback from supervisors. It tends to occur more often in the United States than in Western Europe, perhaps because of Americans' greater achievement orientation (Maslach, Schaufeli, & Leiter, 2001).

Burnout is a serious occupational hazard, linked to impaired attention and memory, severe depression, on-the-job injuries, physical illnesses, poor job performance, absenteeism, and turnover (Melamed et al., 1999; Sandström et al., 2005; Wang, 2005; Wright & Bonett, 1997). To prevent burnout, employers can make sure workloads are reasonable, provide opportunities for workers to take time out from stressful situations, limit hours of stressful work, and offer social support. Interventions that enlist employees' participation in designing higher-quality work environments show promise for increasing work engagement and effectiveness and reducing burnout (Leiter & Maslach, 2000). And provisions for work at home may respond to the needs of some people for a calmer, quieter work atmosphere.

Career Development

After several years as a parish nurse, Anya felt a need for additional training to do her job better. Trisha appreciated her firm's generous support of workshop and course attendance, which helped her keep abreast of new legal developments. And as college dean, Devin took several seminars each year on management effectiveness and instructional technology. As these experiences reveal, career development is vital throughout work life.

This project team, consisting of two young and two middle-aged adults, works on a challenging assignment. Age-balanced work groups foster communication and, in turn, on-the-job learning and enhanced performance.

■ **JOB TRAINING.** Anya's 35-year-old supervisor, Roy, was surprised when she asked for time off to upgrade her skills. "You're in your fifties," he replied. "What're you going to do with so much new information at this point in your life?"

Roy's insensitive, narrow-minded response, though usually unspoken, is unfortunately all too common among managers—even some who are older themselves! Research suggests that training and on-the-job career counseling are less available to older workers. And when career development activities are offered, older employees may be less likely to volunteer for them (Barnes-Farrell & Matthews, 2007; Hedge, Borman, & Lammlein, 2006). What influences willingness to engage in job training and updating?

Personal characteristics are important, starting with the degree to which an individual wants to change. With age, growth needs give way somewhat to security needs. Consequently, learning and challenge may have less intrinsic value to many older workers. Perhaps for this reason, older employees depend more on co-worker and supervisor encouragement for vocational development. Yet as we have seen, they are less likely to have supportive supervisors. Furthermore, negative stereotypes of aging reduce older workers' self-efficacy, or confidence that they can renew and expand their skills. Self-efficacy is a powerful predictor of employees' efforts to improve career-relevant skills (Maurer, 2001; Maurer, Wrenn, & Weiss, 2003).

Workplace characteristics matter, too. An employee given work that requires new learning must pursue that learning to complete the assignment. Unfortunately, older workers sometimes receive more routine tasks than younger workers. Therefore, some of their reduced motivation to engage in career-relevant learning may be due to the type of assignments they receive. Interaction among co-workers can also have a profound impact. Within project teams, people similar in age communicate more often. Age-balanced work groups (with more than one person in each age range) foster on-the-job learning and engagement because communication is a source of support as well as a means of acquiring job-relevant information (Avery, McKay, & Wilson, 2007; Zenger & Lawrence, 1989).

■ **GENDER AND ETHNICITY: THE GLASS CEILING.** In her thirties, Jewel became a company president by starting her own business. She had concluded that, as a woman, her chances of rising to a top executive position in a large corporation were low, so she didn't even try. In a longitudinal study of 1,500 U.S. adults, the probability of attaining a managerial position climbed substantially over 30 years of career experience for white men. By contrast, it rose modestly for white women and black men, and hardly at all for black women. Inequalities at career entry became more pronounced over time—findings that held after work skills and work productivity factors were controlled (see Figure 16.7) (Maume, 2004). When the most prestigious high-level management positions are considered, white men are even more advantaged: They account for 75 percent of chief executive officers at large corporations and 98 percent at Fortune 500 companies (U.S. Census Bureau, 2009b).

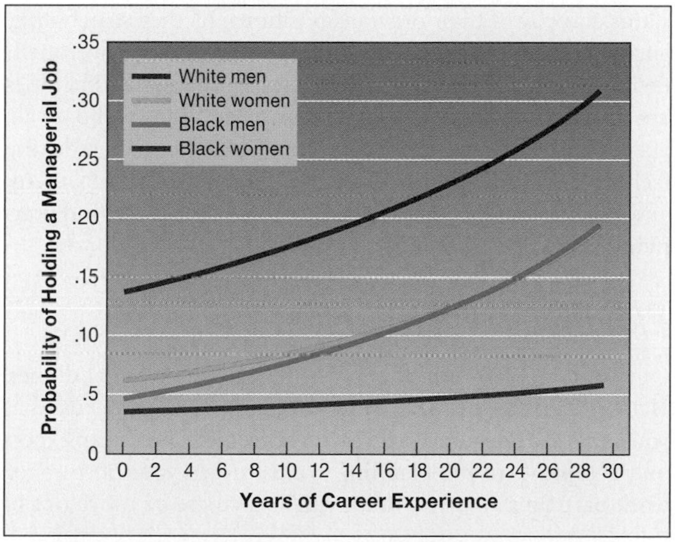

■ **FIGURE 16.7** ■ **Probability of attaining a managerial position over 30 years of career experience, by sex and ethnicity.** In a longitudinal study of 1,500 U.S. adults, chances of promotion to a managerial position increased steadily with experience for white men. In comparison, women and black men lagged behind in attainment of managerial authority, with black women nearly shut out of managerial jobs. The trends confirm the existence of a glass ceiling for women and ethnic minorities. (From D. J. Maume, 2004, "Is the Glass Ceiling a Unique Form of Inequality?" *Work and Occupations, 31,* p. 266. Copyright 2004 by Sage Publications. Reprinted by permission of Sage Publications, Inc.)

Indra K. Nooyi, CEO of PepsiCo, is among a handful of women who have shattered the glass ceiling at Fortune 500 companies, attaining the top leadership position. The recipient of numerous honors and awards, she has amassed an outstanding record in advancing PepsiCo's international business operations and in humanitarian service.

Women and ethnic minorities face a **glass ceiling,** or invisible barrier to advancement up the corporate ladder. Why is this so? Management is an art and skill that must be taught. Yet women and members of ethnic minorities have less access to mentors, role models, and informal networks that serve as training routes. And because of stereotyped doubts about women's career commitment and ability to become strong managers, large companies spend less money on formal training programs for their female employees. Furthermore, challenging, high-risk, high-visibility assignments that require leadership and open the door to advancement, such as startup ventures, international experience, and troubleshooting, are less often granted to women and minorities (Lyness & Thompson, 1997).

Finally, women who demonstrate qualities linked to leadership and advancement—assertiveness, confidence, forcefulness, and ambition—encounter prejudice because they deviate from traditional gender roles. They are evaluated more negatively than men with these traits (Carli & Eagly, 2000; Eagly & Karau, 2002). To overcome this bias, women in line for top positions must demonstrate greater competence than their male counterparts. In an investigation of several hundred senior managers at a multinational financial services corporation, promoted female managers had earned higher performance ratings than promoted male managers (Lyness & Heilman, 2006). In contrast, no gender difference existed in performance of managers not selected for promotion.

Like Jewel, many women have dealt with the glass ceiling by going around it. Largely because of lack of advancement opportunities, nearly twice as many female as male middle managers quit their jobs in large corporations, with most going into business for themselves (Mergenhagen, 1996). Today, more than half of all startup businesses in the United States are owned and operated by women. Most are successful entrepreneurs: 72 percent achieve or exceed their expansion and earnings goals (Ahuja, 2005; U.S. Census Bureau, 2009b). But when women and ethnic minorities leave the corporate world to further their careers, companies not only lose valuable talent but also fail to address the leadership needs of an increasingly diverse work force.

Career Change at Midlife

Although most people remain in the same vocation through middle age, career change does occur, as with Elena's shift from journalism to teaching and creative writing. Recall that circumstances at home and at work motivated Elena's decision to pursue a new vocation. Like other career changers, she wanted a more satisfying life—a goal she attained by ending an unhappy marriage and initiating a long-awaited vocational move at the same time.

As noted earlier, midlife career changes are seldom radical; they typically involve leaving one line of work for a related one. Elena sought a more stimulating, involving job. But other people move in the reverse direction—to careers that are more relaxing, free of painful decisions, and less demanding in terms of responsibility for others (Juntunen, Wegner, & Matthews, 2002). The decision to change is often difficult. The individual must weigh years invested in one set of skills, current income, and job security against present frustrations and hoped-for gains from a new vocation.

An extreme career shift, by contrast, usually signals a personal crisis (Young & Rodgers, 1997). In a study of professionals who abandoned their well-paid, prestigious positions for routine, poorly paid, semiskilled work, nonwork problems influenced the break with an established career. An eminent 55-year-old TV producer became a school bus driver, a New York banker a waiter in a ski resort. Each was responding to feelings of personal meaninglessness—escaping from family conflict, difficult relationships with colleagues, and work that had become unsatisfying into a freer, more independent lifestyle (Sarason, 1977).

Unemployment

Devin and Trisha's friend George worked in a corporate retirement-planning office, counseling retirees on how to enjoy leisure time or find new work. When he lost his job at age 54, George had to apply his counseling skills to himself. He found unemployment to be a culture shock. For the first two weeks, he spent most of his days in bed, didn't shave, and drank heavily. Even after this initial phase, George was depressed and had frequent bouts of illness.

As companies downsize, eliminating jobs, the majority of people affected are middle-aged and older. Although unemployment is difficult at any time, middle-aged workers show a sharper decline in physical and mental health than their younger counterparts (Breslin & Mustard, 2003). Older workers affected by layoffs remain jobless longer, suffering substantial income loss. In addition, people over age 40 who must reestablish occupational security find themselves "off-time" in terms of the social clock. Consequently, job loss can disrupt major tasks of midlife, including generativity and reappraisal of life goals and accomplishments (Broomhall & Winefield, 1990). Finally, having been more involved in and committed to an occupation, the older unemployed worker has also lost something of greater value.

After a despondent period, George began to follow the advice he had given his clients. He made a list of things he really liked to do, things he didn't want to do again, and the risks he could take given his current financial and life circumstances. He formed his own small business and continued to advise retirees, write articles, and give speeches on all aspects of retirement—but working from home in a T-shirt instead of from an office in a business suit. Effective problem-centered coping strategies enabled George to reestablish a satisfying work life (Kinicki, Prussia, & McKee-Ryan, 2000).

Social support is vital for reducing stress and reassuring middle-aged job seekers of their worth. But not all forms of social support work equally well. Recognition of one's abilities and communication with others who share interests and values—experiences that occur often in relations with co-workers—help the most (Mallinckrodt & Fretz, 1988).

People who lose their jobs in midlife seldom duplicate the status and pay of their previous positions. As they search, they encounter age discrimination and find that they are overqualified for many openings. Those also facing financial difficulties are at risk for deepening depression over time (Gallo et al., 2006). Counseling that focuses on financial planning, reducing feelings of humiliation due to the stigma of unemployment, and encouraging personal flexibility can help people find gratifying alternative work roles.

Planning for Retirement

One evening, Devin and Trisha met George and Anya for dinner. Halfway through the meal, Devin inquired, "George, tell us what you and Anya are going to do about retirement. You're an expert on the topic—are you planning to close down your business or work part-time? Do you think you'll stay here or move out of town?"

Three or four generations ago, the two couples would not have had this conversation. In 1900, about 70 percent of American men age 65 and over were in the labor force. By 1970, however, the figure had dropped to 27 percent, and in the early twenty-first century it declined to 16 percent (U.S. Census Bureau, 2009b). Because of government-sponsored retirement benefits (begun in the United States in 1935), retirement is no longer a privilege reserved for the wealthy. The federal government pays Social Security to the majority of the aged, and others are covered by employer-based private pension plans.

Applying What We Know

Ingredients of Effective Retirement Planning

Issue	Description
Finances	Ideally, financial planning for retirement should start with the first paycheck; at a minimum, it should begin 10 to 15 years before retirement, since most people spend more than 20 years retired.
Fitness	Starting a fitness program in middle age is important because good health is crucial for well-being in retirement.
Role adjustment	Retirement is harder for people who strongly identify with their work role. Preparing for a radical role adjustment reduces stress.
Where to live	The pros and cons of moving should be considered carefully because where one lives affects access to health care, friends, family, recreation, entertainment, and part-time employment.
Leisure and volunteer activities	A retiree typically gains an additional 50 hours per week of free time. Careful planning of what to do with that time has a major impact on psychological well-being.
Health insurance	Finding out about government-sponsored health insurance options helps protect quality of life after retirement.
Legal affairs	The preretirement period is an excellent time to finalize a will and begin estate planning.

As the trend just noted suggests, the average age of retirement declined during the past several decades. Currently, it is age 62 in the United States and hovers between 60 and 63 in other Western nations (U.S. Census Bureau, 2009b). As indicated earlier, the healthy, active, long-lived baby-boom generation is expected to work longer. Still, up to one-fourth of their lives may lie ahead after they leave their career jobs.

Retirement is a lengthy, complex process that begins as soon as the middle-aged person first thinks about it (Kim & Moen, 2002b). Planning is important because retirement leads to a loss of two important work-related rewards—income and status—and to a change in many other aspects of life. Like other life transitions, retirement can be stressful.

"Retirement planning helps you evaluate your options, learn about the availability of resources, and prepare emotionally for the changes ahead," George explained at one of his retirement seminars. Nearly half of middle-aged people engage in no concrete retirement planning, yet research consistently shows that clarifying goals for the future and acquiring financial-planning knowledge result in better retirement savings, adjustment, and satisfaction (Hershey et al., 2007; Jacobs-Lawson, Hershey, & Neukam, 2004; Quick & Moen, 1998).

Applying What We Know above lists the variety of issues addressed in a typical retirement preparation program. Financial planning is especially vital in the United States where (unlike Western European nations) the federal government does not offer a pension system that guarantees an adequate standard of living (see page 68 in Chapter 2). Hence, U.S. retirees' income typically drops by 50 percent. But although more people engage in financial planning than in other forms of preparation, even those who attend financial education programs often fail to look closely at their financial well-being and to make wise decisions (Hershey et al., 1998). Many could benefit from an expert's financial analysis and counsel.

Retirement leads to ways of spending time that are largely guided by one's interests rather than one's obligations. Individuals who have not thought carefully about how to fill this time may find their sense of purpose in life seriously threatened. Research reveals that planning for an active life has an even greater impact on happiness after retirement than financial planning. Participation in activities promotes many factors essential for psychological well-being, including a structured time schedule, social contact, and self-esteem (Schlossberg, 2004). Carefully considering whether or not to relocate at retirement is related to an active life, since it affects access to health care, friends, family, recreation, entertainment, and part-time work.

Devin retired at age 62, George at age 66. Though several years younger, Trisha and Anya—like many married women—coordinated their retirements with those of their husbands (Ruhm, 1996). In contrast, Jewel—in good health but without an intimate partner to share her life—kept her consulting business going until age 75. Tim took early retirement and moved to be near Elena, where he devoted himself to public service—tutoring second graders in a public school, transporting inner-city children to museums, and coaching after-school and weekend youth sports. For Tim, retirement offered a new opportunity to give generously to his community.

Unfortunately, less well-educated people with lower lifetime earnings are least likely to attend retirement preparation programs—yet they stand to benefit the most. Although baby boomers as a whole are financially better off than their agemates of the previous generation, the lowest-income quartile are actually worse off than their predecessors (Lusardi &

Mitchell, 2007). And compared with men, women do less planning for retirement. They often depend on their husband's preparations—a finding that may change as women increasingly become equal, rather than secondary, family earners (Han & Moen, 1999). Employers must take extra steps to encourage lower-paid workers and women to participate in planning activities (Jacobs-Lawson, Hershey, & Neukam, 2004). In addition, enhancing retirement adjustment among the economically disadvantaged depends on access to better health care, vocational training, and jobs at early ages. Clearly, a lifetime of opportunities and experiences affects the transition to retirement. In Chapter 18, we will consider the decision to retire and retirement adjustment in greater detail.

ASK YOURSELF

» REVIEW
What factors lead job satisfaction to increase with age?

» APPLY
An executive wonders how his large corporation can foster advancement of women and ethnic minorities to upper management positions. What strategies would you recommend?

» CONNECT
Supervisors sometimes assign only the more routine tasks to older workers, believing that they can no longer handle complex assignments. Cite evidence from this and the previous chapter indicating that this assumption is incorrect.

Summary

Erikson's Theory: Generativity versus Stagnation

According to Erikson, how does personality change in middle age?

» Generativity expands greatly as middle-aged adults face Erikson's psychological conflict of **generativity versus stagnation.** Highly generative people find fulfillment as they make contributions to society through parenthood, other family relationships, the workplace, and volunteer activities.

» Personal desires and cultural demands jointly shape adults' generative activities. Highly generative people appear especially well-adjusted. The negative outcome, stagnation, occurs when people become self-centered and self-indulgent in midlife.

Other Theories of Psychosocial Development in Midlife

Describe Levinson's and Vaillant's views of psychosocial development in middle adulthood, and discuss similarities and differences between men and women.

» According to Levinson, middle-aged adults reassess their relation to themselves and the external world. They confront four developmental tasks, each requiring them to reconcile two opposing tendencies within the self: young–old, destruction–creation, masculinity–femininity, and engagement–separateness.

» Perhaps because of the double standard of aging, women express concern about appearing less attractive. But non-college-educated men, even more than women, show a rise in sensitivity to physical aging in midlife.

» Middle-aged men may adopt "feminine" traits of nurturance and caring, while women may take on "masculine" traits of autonomy and assertiveness. Men and successful career-oriented women often reduce their focus on ambition and achievement, whereas women who have devoted themselves to child rearing or an unfulfilling job typically focus outward, on rewarding work or community engagement.

» Vaillant found that adults in their late forties and fifties become guardians of their culture, seeking to "pass the torch" to later generations.

Does the term midlife crisis *fit most people's experience of middle adulthood?*

» Most people respond to midlife with changes that are better described as "turning points" than as a crisis. Only a minority experience a **midlife crisis** characterized by intense self-doubt and stress that lead to drastic life alterations.

Characterize middle adulthood using a life events approach and a stage approach.

» In middle adulthood, some changes are adaptations to external life events (such as the family life cycle) that are less age-graded than in the past. Most middle-aged adults also report stagelike development, in which troubling moments prompt new understandings and goals.

Stability and Change in Self-Concept and Personality

Describe changes in self-concept and personality in middle adulthood.

» Middle-aged individuals maintain self-esteem and stay motivated by revising their **possible selves,** which become fewer in number as well as more modest and concrete as people adjust their hopes and fears to their life circumstances.

» Midlife typically leads to greater self-acceptance, autonomy, and environmental mastery—changes that lead to greater psychological well-being and life satisfaction. As a result, middle age is sometimes called the "prime of life." Factors contributing to well-being, however, vary widely among cohorts and cultures.

» Daily stressors plateau from early to middle adulthood, then decline as work and family responsibilities ease. Coping with daily stressors becomes more effective with midlife gains in emotional stability and confidence in handling life's problems.

Describe changes in gender identity in midlife.

» Both men and women become more androgynous in middle adulthood. Biological explanations, such as **parental imperative theory,** are controversial. A complex combination of social roles and life conditions is more likely responsible. For men, these changes are often linked to children's departure from the home; for women, to workplace experiences.

Discuss stability and change in the "big five" personality traits in adulthood.

» Among the **"big five" personality traits,** neuroticism, extroversion, and openness to experience show stability or modest declines during adulthood, while agreeableness and conscientiousness increase. But individual differences in the "big five" traits are large and highly stable: Although adults change in overall organization and integration of personality, they do so on a foundation of basic, enduring dispositions.

Relationships at Midlife

Describe the middle adulthood phase of the family life cycle.

» "Launching children and moving on" is the midlife phase of the family life cycle. Adults must adapt to many entries and exits of family members as their children leave, marry, and produce grandchildren, and as their own parents age and die.

» Midlife changes prompt many adults to adjust their marriages. When divorce occurs, middle-aged adults seem to adapt more easily than younger people. For women, marital breakup usually brings significant economic disadvantage, contributing to the **feminization of poverty.**

» Most middle-aged parents adjust well to launching adult children, especially if parent–child contact and affection are sustained. As children marry, middle-aged parents, especially mothers, often become **kinkeepers.**

© JIM WEST PHOTOGRAPHY

» Grandparenthood is an important means of fulfilling personal and societal needs. Proximity, number of grandchild sets, sex of grandparent and grandchild, and in-law relationships affect grandparent–grandchild contact and closeness. In low-income families and in some ethnic groups, grandparents provide essential financial and child-care assistance. When serious family problems exist, grandparents may become primary caregivers in **skipped-generation families.**

» Middle-aged adults reassess their relationships with aging parents, often becoming more appreciative. Mother–daughter relationships tend to be closer than other parent–child ties. Yet quality of the early parent–child relationship—positive or conflict-ridden—usually persists, affecting help exchanged.

» Middle-aged adults, often caught between caring for ill or frail parents, assisting young-adult children and grandchildren, and meeting work and community responsibilities, are called the **sandwich generation.** The burden of caring for aging parents falls most heavily on adult daughters, though in later middle age, the sex difference declines.

» Parental caregiving has emotional and health consequences. The toll is greatest in cultures and subcultures where adult children feel an especially strong obligation to provide care. Social support is highly effective in relieving caregiver stress.

Describe midlife sibling relationships and friendships.

» Sibling contact and support decline from early to middle adulthood, probably because of the demands of diverse roles. However, most middle-aged siblings tend to feel closer, often in response to major life events, such as launching of children and parents' illness and death. Sister–sister ties are typically closest in industrialized nations. In nonindustrialized societies, where sibling relationships are basic to family functioning, other attachments (such as brother–sister) may be stronger.

» In midlife, friendships become fewer, more selective, and more deeply valued. Men continue to be less expressive with their friends than women, who have more close friendships. Viewing a spouse as a best friend can contribute greatly to marital happiness.

Vocational Life

Discuss job satisfaction and career development in middle adulthood, with special attention to sex differences and experiences of ethnic minorities.

» Vocational readjustments are common as middle-aged people seek to increase the personal meaning and self-direction of their work lives. Certain aspects of job performance improve. Job satisfaction increases at all occupational levels, more so for men than for women.

» **Burnout** is a serious occupational hazard, especially for those in helping professions. It can be prevented by ensuring reasonable workloads, limiting hours of stressful work, providing workers with social support, and enlisting employees' participation in designing higher-quality work environments.

» Older workers engage in less career development because of negative stereotypes of aging, which impair self-efficacy; lack of encouragement from supervisors; and less challenging work assignments.

» Women and ethnic minorities face a **glass ceiling** because of limited access to management training and prejudice against women who demonstrate qualities linked to leadership and advancement. Many women further their careers by leaving the corporate world, often to start their own businesses.

© WORLD ECONOMIC FORUM (WWW.WEFORUM.ORG). SWISS-IMAGE.CH/PHOTO BY REMY STEINEGGER

Discuss career change and unemployment in middle adulthood.

» Midlife career change typically involves leaving one line of work for a related one. Radical career change often signals a personal crisis.

» Unemployment is especially difficult for middle-aged adults, who constitute the majority of workers affected by corporate downsizing and layoffs. Counseling can help them find alternative, gratifying work roles, but these rarely duplicate their previous status or pay.

Discuss the importance of planning for retirement.

» An increasing number of workers in the United States and Western nations are retiring from full-time work in midlife. Retirement brings major life changes, including loss of income and status and an increase in free time. Besides financial planning, planning for an active life is vital, with an especially strong impact on happiness after retirement. Low-paid workers and women need extra encouragement to participate in retirement planning activities.

Important Terms and Concepts

"big five" personality traits (p. 542)
burnout (p. 554)
feminization of poverty (p. 544)
generativity versus stagnation (p. 532)
glass ceiling (p. 555)
kinkeeper (p. 545)
midlife crisis (p. 536)
parental imperative theory (p. 541)
possible selves (p. 538)
sandwich generation (p. 550)
skipped-generation family (p. 548)

Milestones
Development in Middle Adulthood

40–50 years

PHYSICAL

- Accommodative ability of the lens of the eye, ability to see in dim light, and color discrimination decline; sensitivity to glare increases. (502–503)
- Hearing loss at high frequencies occurs. (503)
- Hair grays and thins. (502)
- Lines on the face become more pronounced; skin loses elasticity and begins to sag. (503)
- Weight gain continues, accompanied by a rise in fatty deposits in the torso, while fat beneath the skin declines. (504)
- Loss of lean body mass (muscle and bone) occurs. (504)
- In women, production of estrogen drops, leading to shortening and irregularity of the menstrual cycle. (504, 506)

- In men, quantity of semen and sperm declines. (507)
- Intensity of sexual response declines, but frequency of sexual activity drops only slightly. (509)
- Rates of cancer and cardiovascular disease increase. (509–513)

COGNITIVE

- Consciousness of aging increases. (502, 535)
- Crystallized intelligence increases; fluid intelligence declines. (518–519)

- Cognitive-processing speed declines, but adults can compensate through experience and practice. (520–521)
- On complex tasks, ability to divide and control attention declines, but adults can compensate through experience and practice. (522)
- Amount of information retained in working memory declines, largely because of reduced use of memory strategies. (522–523)
- Retrieving information from long-term memory becomes more difficult. (522–523)

- General factual knowledge, procedural knowledge, and knowledge related to one's occupation remain unchanged or may increase. (523)
- Practical problem solving and expertise increase. (524)
- Creativity may emphasize integrating ideas and shift from self-expression to more altruistic goals. (524–525)

- If occupation offers challenge and autonomy, may show gains in cognitive flexibility. (525–526)

EMOTIONAL/SOCIAL

- Generativity increases. (532–533)
- Focus shifts toward personally meaningful living. (533, 535)

Note: Numbers in parentheses indicate the page or pages on which each milestone is discussed.

- Possible selves become fewer in number and more modest and concrete. (538)
- Self-acceptance, autonomy, and environmental mastery increase. (538–539)
- Strategies for coping with stressors become more effective. (539–540)
- Gender identity becomes more androgynous; "masculine" traits increase in women, "feminine" traits in men. (535–536, 540–542)
- Agreeableness and conscientiousness increase, while neuroticism declines. (542)
- May launch children. (543)
- May become a kinkeeper, especially if a mother. (545)

- May become a parent-in-law and a grandparent. (545–547, 549)
- May care for a parent with a disability or chronic illness. (550–551)
- Siblings may feel closer. (551–552)
- Number of friends generally declines. (552)
- Job satisfaction typically increases. (553–554)

50–65 years

PHYSICAL

- Lens of the eye loses its capacity to adjust to objects at varying distances entirely. (502)
- Hearing loss extends to all frequencies but remains greatest for high frequencies. (503)
- Skin continues to wrinkle and sag, "age spots" increase, and blood vessels in the skin become more visible. (503)
- In women, menopause occurs; as estrogen declines further, genitals are less easily stimulated, and the vagina lubricates more slowly during arousal. (504)

- In men, inability to attain an erection when desired becomes more common. (507)
- Loss of bone mass continues; rates of osteoporosis rise. (504, 513)
- Collapse of disks in the spinal column causes height to drop by as much as 1 inch. (504)

- Rates of cancer and cardiovascular disease continue to increase. (510–513)

COGNITIVE

- Cognitive changes previously listed continue.

EMOTIONAL/SOCIAL

- Emotional and social changes previously listed continue.

- Parent-to-child help-giving declines, and child-to-parent aid increases. (549–551)
- May retire. (556–558)

Cultures around the world connect age with wisdom. Elders' extensive life experience enhances their ability to solve human problems and fill leadership positions, both of which are endeavors of South African anti-Apartheid activist Archbishop Desmond Tutu. Here, he gives high fives to students after an honorary degree ceremony at Edinburgh University.

CHAPTER 17

Physical and Cognitive Development in Late Adulthood

At age 67, Walt gave up his photography business and looked forward to more spare time with 64-year-old Ruth, who retired from her position as a social worker at the same time. For Walt and Ruth, this culminating period of life was filled with volunteer work, golfing three times a week, and joint vacations with Walt's older brother Dick and his wife, Goldie. Walt also took up activities he had always loved but had little time to pursue—writing poems and short stories, attending theater performances, enrolling in a class on world politics, and cultivating a garden that became the envy of the neighborhood. Ruth read voraciously, served on the board of directors of an adoption agency, and had more time to visit her sister Ida in a nearby city.

Over the next 20 years, Walt and Ruth amazed nearly everyone who met them with their energy and vitality. Their warmth, concern for others, and generosity with their time led not just their own children and grandchildren, but also nieces, nephews, children of friends, and former co-workers, to seek them out. On weekends, their home was alive with visitors.

Then, in their early eighties, the couple's lives changed profoundly. Walt had surgery to treat a cancerous prostate gland and within 3 months was hospitalized again after a heart attack. He lingered for 6 weeks with Ruth at his side and then died. Ruth's grieving was interrupted by the need to care for Ida. Alert and spry at age 78, Ida deteriorated mentally in her seventy-ninth year, despite otherwise excellent physical health. Meanwhile, Ruth's arthritis worsened, and her vision and hearing weakened.

As Ruth turned 85, certain activities had become difficult—but not impossible. "It just takes a little adjustment!" Ruth exclaimed in her usual upbeat manner. Reading was harder, so she checked out "talking books" from her local library. Her gait was slower and her eyesight less reliable, so she hesitated to go out alone. At dinner in a noisy restaurant with her daughter and family, Ruth felt overwhelmed and participated little in the fast-moving conversation. But in one-to-one interactions in a calm environment, she showed the same intelligence, wit, and astute insights that she had displayed all her life.

Late adulthood stretches from age 65 to the end of the lifespan. Unfortunately, popular images fail to capture the quality of these final decades. Instead, many myths prevail—that the elderly have entered a period of deterioration and dependency; that they are no longer able to learn; and that their families isolate them in nursing homes. Young people who have little contact with older adults are often surprised that elders like Walt and Ruth even exist—active and involved in the world around them.

As we trace physical and cognitive development in late adulthood, we will see that the balance of gains and declines shifts as death approaches. But in industrialized nations, the typical 65-year-old can anticipate nearly two healthy, rewarding decades before this shift affects everyday life. And as Ruth illustrates, even after older adults become frail, many find ways to surmount physical and cognitive challenges.

Late adulthood is best viewed as an extension of earlier periods, not a break with them. As long as social and cultural contexts give elders support, respect, and purpose in life, these years are a time of continued potential.

Physical Development

TAKE A MOMENT... Do you know an older person who "seems young" or "seems old" for his or her age? In using these descriptors, we acknowledge that chronological age is an imperfect indicator of **functional age,** or actual competence and performance. Because people age biologically at different rates, some 80-year-olds appear younger than many 65-year-olds (Neugarten & Neugarten, 1987). Also, recall from Chapter 13 that within each person, change differs across parts of the body. For example, Ruth became infirm physically but remained active mentally, whereas Ida, though physically fit for her age, found it hard to carry on a conversation, keep appointments, or complete familiar tasks.

Two friends enjoy a stroll and conversation in Tokyo, Japan. How old are they? How old do they look and feel? Because people age biologically at different rates, the elder on the right appears younger than the elder on the left, though they are both in their early eighties.

So much variation exists between and within individuals that researchers have not yet identified any single biological measure that predicts the overall rate at which an elderly person will age. But we do have estimates of how much longer older adults can expect to live, and our knowledge of factors affecting longevity in late adulthood has increased rapidly.

Life Expectancy

"I wonder how many years I have left," Ruth asked herself each time a major life event, such as retirement or widowhood, occurred. Dramatic gains in **average life expectancy**—the number of years that an individual born in a particular year can expect to live, starting at any given age—provide powerful support for the multiplicity of factors considered in previous chapters that slow biological aging, including improved nutrition, medical treatment, sanitation, and safety. Recall from Chapter 1 that a U.S. baby born in 1900 had an average life expectancy of just under 50 years. In 2008, this figure reached 78.1 in the United States (75 for men and nearly 81 for women). Twentieth-century gains in life expectancy were extraordinary—equal to those of the previous 5,000 years! Steady declines in infant mortality (see Chapter 3) are a major factor, but death rates among adults have decreased as well. For example, heart disease, the leading cause of overall adult death in the United States, has dropped by more than 60 percent in the past 50 years, due to declines in risk factors (such as high blood pressure and cigarette smoking) and, mostly, advances in medical treatment (U.S. Department of Health and Human Services, 2009a).

Variations in Life Expectancy

Consistent group differences in life expectancy underscore the joint contribution of heredity and environment to biological aging. In almost all cultures, women can look forward to 4 to 7 more years of life than men—an advantage that also characterizes females of several animal species, including rats, mice, and dogs (Shock, 1977). The protective value of the female's extra X chromosome (see Chapter 2) is believed to be responsible. Yet since the early 1970s, the gender gap in life expectancy has narrowed in industrialized nations (Conti et al., 2003; Leung, Zhang, & Zhang, 2004). Because men are at higher risk for disease and early death, they reap somewhat larger generational gains from positive lifestyle changes and new medical discoveries.

Life expectancy varies substantially with SES, ethnicity, and nationality. As education and income increase, so does length

These spry veterans tie a rope around a cherry tree to honor Japanese citizens who died in World War II. Japan's low-fat diet, which contributes to its low rates of obesity and heart disease, along with its favorable health-care policies, makes it the world's leader in average healthy life expectancy.

of life (De Vogli et al., 2005). In the United States, a white child born in 2007 is likely to live 5 to 7 years longer than an African-American child and 4 to 5 years longer than a Native-American child (U.S. Department of Health and Human Services, 2009a). Accounting for these differences are higher rates of infant mortality, unintentional injuries, life-threatening disease, poverty-linked stress, and violent death in low-SES minority groups.

Length of life—and, even more important, *quality of life* in old age—can be predicted by a country's health care, housing, and social services, along with lifestyle factors. When researchers estimate **average healthy life expectancy,** the number of years a person born in a particular year can expect to live in full health, without disease or injury, Japan ranks first, the United States a disappointing twenty-ninth (see Figure 17.1). Japan's low rates of obesity and heart disease, linked to its low-fat diet, along with its favorable health-care policies, are largely responsible for its leading status. Because the United States falls short of other industrialized nations in these respects, Americans spend somewhat more time disabled and die earlier than elders in most other developed countries. In developing nations with widespread poverty, malnutrition, disease, and armed conflict, average life expectancy hovers around 50 years, and healthy life expectancy is reduced by three to four decades compared with the industrialized world—for example, 75 years in Japan, 73 years in Sweden, 70 years in the United States, but only 44 in Haiti, 38 in Rwanda, 36 in Afghanistan, and 29 in Sierra Leone (World Health Organization, 2009a).

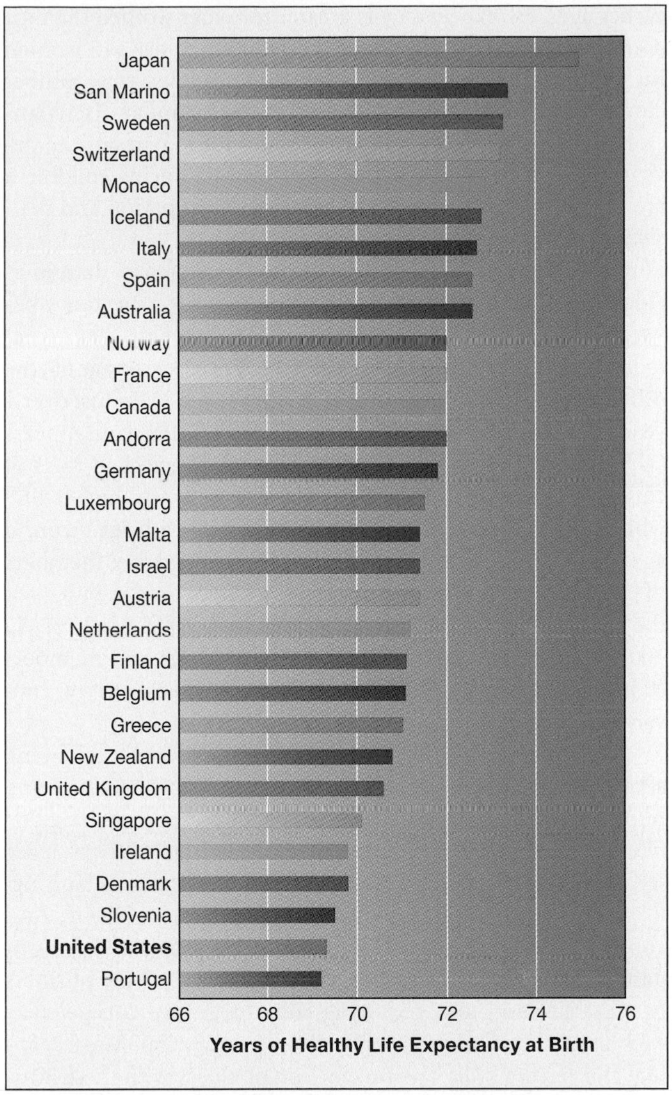

■ **FIGURE 17.1** ■ **Average healthy life expectancy at birth in 30 nations.** The United States ranks a disappointing twenty-ninth in the world. In each nation, women's healthy life expectancy is 2 to 3 years longer, men's 2 to 3 years shorter, than the average depicted. (From World Health Organization, 2009a.)

Life Expectancy in Late Adulthood

Although poverty-stricken groups lag behind the economically advantaged, the number of people age 65 and older has risen dramatically in the industrialized world. From 1900 to 2008, the elderly increased from 4 percent to nearly 13 percent of the U.S. population. And because the baby-boom generation makes 45- to 54-year-olds the currently fastest-growing segment of the population, older adults are projected to rise to 18 percent by 2025. The second fastest-growing segment is the 85-and-older group, who currently make up nearly 2 percent of Americans. By 2050, they will more than double, reaching 4.3 percent (U.S. Census Bureau, 2009b).

Americans reaching age 65 in the early twenty-first century can look forward, on average, to 19 more years of life. As at earlier ages, life expectancy is greater for older women than for men. Today, the 65- to 69-year age group includes 115 women for every 100 men; for people age 85 and older, this number climbs to 210 (U.S. Census Bureau, 2009b). Similar discrepancies exist in all developed countries but not in parts of the developing world where death rates of women during childbirth are high or women experience severe discrimination and deprivation (World Health Organization, 2009a).

Although women outnumber men by a greater margin as elders advance in age, differences in average life expectancy between the sexes decline. An American newborn girl can expect to live about 5½ years longer than a newborn boy. At age 65, the difference narrows to just under 3 years; at age 85, to just over 1 year. Over age 100, the gender gap in life expectancy disappears (U.S. Census Bureau, 2009b). Similarly, differences in rates of chronic illness and in life expectancy between higher-SES whites and low-SES ethnic minorities decline with age. Around age 85, a *life expectancy crossover* occurs—surviving members of low-SES ethnic minority groups live longer than members of the white majority (House, Lantz, & Herd, 2005; Liang et al., 2002). Researchers speculate that among males and members of low-SES groups, only the biologically sturdiest survive into very old age.

Most Americans age 65 and older are capable of living active, independent, productive lives, but with age, growing numbers need assistance. After age 75, about 9 percent have difficulty carrying out **activities of daily living (ADLs)**—basic self-care tasks required to live on one's own, such as bathing, dressing, getting in and out of bed or a chair, or eating. And about 17 percent cannot carry out **instrumental activities of daily living (IADLs)**—tasks necessary to conduct the business of daily life and also requiring some cognitive competence, such as telephoning, shopping, food preparation, housekeeping, and paying bills. The proportion of elders with these limitations rises sharply with age (U.S. Department of Health and Human Services, 2009a).

Throughout this book, we have seen that genetic and environmental factors jointly affect aging. With respect to heredity, identical twins typically die within 3 years of each other, whereas fraternal twins of the same sex differ by more than 6 years. Also, longevity runs in families. When both parents survive to age 70 or older, the chances that their children will live to 90 or 100 are double that of the general population (Cevenini et al., 2008; Hayflick, 1994; Mitchell et al., 2001). At the same time, evidence from twin studies suggests that once people pass 75 to 80 years, the contribution of heredity to length of life decreases in favor of environmental factors—a healthy diet; normal body weight; regular exercise; little or no tobacco, alcohol, and drug use; an optimistic outlook; low psychological stress; and social support (Yates et al., 2008; Zaretsky, 2003). As the Lifespan Vista box on pages 568–569 reveals, the study of centenarians—people who cross the 100-year mark—offers special insights into how biological, psychological, and social influences work together to promote a long, satisfying life.

Maximum Lifespan

Finally, perhaps you are wondering: What is the **maximum lifespan,** or the genetic limit to length of life for a person free of external risk factors? According to current estimates, it varies between 70 and 110 for most people, with 85 about average (Harman, 2002). As the Lifespan Vista box indicates, the oldest verified age to which an individual has lived is 122 years.

Do these figures reflect the upper bound of human longevity, or can our lifespans be extended further? Some scientists believe that about 85 or 90 years is as much as most humans can expect, since gains in average life expectancy are largely the result of reducing health risks in the first 20 or 30 years. Expected life for people age 65 and older has increased very little—only about 5 months—over the past decade (U.S. Census Bureau, 2009b). But others think we have not yet identified the human genetic limit. They note that the lifespans of several species have been stretched in the laboratory through selective breeding, genetic engineering, and (as we saw in Chapter 15) dietary calorie restriction (Arking, Novoseltsev, & Novoseltseva, 2004).

The possibility of similar achievements in humans raises another issue: *Should* the lifespan be increased as far as possible? ***TAKE A MOMENT...*** How would you answer this question? Many people respond that quality, not just quantity, of life is the important goal—that is, doing everything possible to extend healthy life expectancy. Most experts agree that only after reducing the high rates of preventable illness and disability among low-SES individuals and wiping out age-related diseases should we invest in lengthening the maximum lifespan.

Physical Changes

The programmed effects of specific genes and the random cellular events believed to underlie biological aging (see Chapter 13) make physical declines more apparent in late adulthood. Nevertheless, most body structures can last into our eighties and beyond, if we take good care of them. For an overview of the physical changes we are about to discuss, return to Table 13.1 on page 435.

Nervous System

On a routine office visit, 80-year-old Ruth's doctor asked her how she was getting along. "I think I might be losing my mind," Ruth replied anxiously. "Yesterday, I forgot the name of the family who just moved in next door. And the day before, I had trouble finding the right words to explain to a delivery service how to get to my house."

"Ruth, everyone forgets those sorts of things from time to time," Dr. Wiley reassured her. "When we were young and had a memory lapse, we reprimanded ourselves for being scatterbrained and thought no more about it. Now, when we do the same thing, we attribute it to having 'a senior moment,' and we worry."

Ruth also wondered why extremes of hot and cold weather felt more uncomfortable than in earlier years. And she needed more time to coordinate a series of movements and had become less sure of her balance.

Aging of the central nervous system affects a wide range of complex activities. Although brain weight declines throughout adulthood, brain-imaging research and after-death autopsies reveal that the loss becomes greater starting in the sixties and may amount to as much as 5 to 10 percent by age 80, due to death of neurons and enlargement of ventricles (spaces) within the brain (Vinters, 2001).

Neuron loss occurs throughout the cerebral cortex but at different rates among different regions and often inconsistently within parts of those regions. In longitudinal studies, the frontal lobes (responsible for integration of information, judgment, and reflective thought) and the corpus callosum (which connects the two cortical hemispheres) tended to show greater shrinkage than the parietal and temporal lobes, with the occipital lobes changing little (see page 124 in Chapter 4 for a visual image of these regions) (Resnick et al., 2003; Smith et al., 2007). The cerebellum (which controls balance and coordination) also loses neurons—in all, about 25 percent. Glial cells, which myelinate neural fibers, decrease as well (Raz, 2005). And EEG measures reveal gradual slowing and reduced intensity of brain waves—signs of diminished efficiency of the central nervous system (Kramer, Fabiani, & Colcombe, 2006).

But the brain can overcome some of these declines. In several studies, growth of neural fibers in the brains of older adults unaffected by illness took place at the same rate as in middle-aged people. Aging neurons established new synapses after other neurons had degenerated (Flood & Coleman, 1988). Furthermore, the aging cerebral cortex can, to some degree, generate new neurons (Gould, 2007; Gould et al., 1999). And fMRI evidence reveals that compared with younger adults, elders who do well on memory and other cognitive tasks show more widely distributed activity across areas of the cerebral cortex, particularly in the frontal lobes and in regions mirroring typically active sites but located in the opposite hemisphere (Reuter-Lorenz & Cappell, 2008). This suggests that one way older adults compensate for neuron loss is to call on additional brain regions to support cognitive processing (Reuter-Lorenz & Mikels, 2005).

The autonomic nervous system, involved in many life-support functions, also performs less well, putting the elderly at risk during heat waves and cold spells. For example, Ruth's reduced tolerance for hot weather was due to decreased sweating. And her body found it harder to raise its core temperature during cold exposure. However, among physically fit elders who are free of disease, these declines are mild (Whitbourne, 2001). The autonomic nervous system also releases higher levels of stress hormones into the bloodstream than it did earlier, perhaps to arouse body tissues that have become less responsive to these hormones over the years (Whitbourne, 2002). As we will see, this change may contribute to decreased immunity and to sleep problems.

Sensory Systems

Changes in sensory functioning become increasingly noticeable in late life. Older adults see and hear less well, and their taste, smell, and touch sensitivity may also decline. As Figure 17.2 shows, in late life, hearing impairments are more common than visual impairments. Extending trends for middle adulthood, more women than men report being visually impaired, more men than women hearing impaired.

■ **VISION.** In Chapter 15 (see pages 502–503), we noted that structural changes in the eye make it harder to focus on nearby objects, see in dim light, and perceive color. In late adulthood, vision diminishes further. The cornea (clear covering of the eye) becomes more translucent and scatters light, which blurs images and increases sensitivity to glare. The lens continues to yellow, leading to further impairment in color discrimination. The number of individuals with **cataracts**—cloudy areas in the lens, resulting in foggy vision and (without surgery) eventual blindness—increases tenfold from middle to late adulthood, affecting 25 percent of people in their seventies and 50 percent of those in their eighties (Harvey, 2003; U.S. Census Bureau, 2009b). Besides biological aging, heredity, sun exposure, cigarette smoking, and certain diseases (such as diabetes) increase the risk of cataracts (Hammond et al., 2000; Klein et al., 2003). Fortunately, removal of the lens and replacement with an artificial lens implant or corrective eyewear are highly successful in restoring vision.

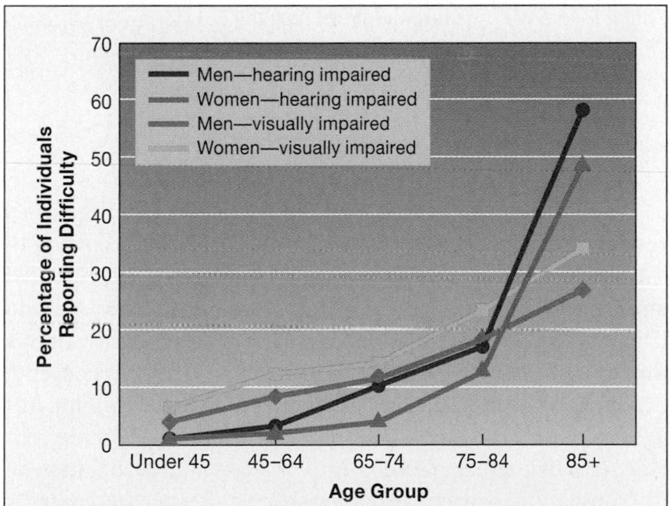

■ **FIGURE 17.2** ■ **Rates of visual and hearing impairments among U.S. men and women by age.** Among a large, nationally representative sample, those reporting that they had trouble seeing, even when wearing glasses or contact lenses, were judged visually impaired; those reporting "a lot of trouble" hearing were judged hearing impaired. Women report more visual impairments; men report more hearing impairments, a gap that widens considerably in late adulthood. In late life, hearing impairments become more common than visual impairments. (Adapted from U.S. Department of Health and Human Services, 2008i.)

A LIFESPAN VISTA: Looking Forward, Looking Back

What Can We Learn About Aging from Centenarians?

Jeanne Louise Calment, listed in *Guinness World Records* as the longest-lived person whose age could be documented, was born in Arles, France, in 1875 and died there in 1997, 122 years later. Heredity may have contributed to her longevity: Her father lived to age 94, her mother to 86. Her family was middle-SES, and in her twenties, she married a prosperous merchant (Robine & Allard, 1999). As a young woman, she was healthy and energetic; she bicycled, swam, roller-skated, played tennis, and ran up the steps of the cathedral to attend daily Mass.

Jeanne attributed her longevity to a diet rich in olive oil and an occasional glass of port wine. Others credit her easy-going disposition and resistance to stress. "If you can't do anything about it," she once said, "don't worry about it." Jeanne took up fencing at age 85 and rode a bicycle until age 100. Shortly thereafter, she moved into assisted living (see page 589), where she blossomed, becoming a celebrity because of both her age and her charming personality. Alert and quick-witted until her final year, she recommended laughter as the best recipe for long life. Asked once about the effects of aging, she quipped, "I've only one wrinkle, and I am sitting on it."

Because of stereotypes of aging and researchers' focus on the very old with the heaviest burden of illness and disability, we tend to picture the most elderly humans as extremely frail. Yet the past 40 years have seen a tenfold increase in centenarians in the industrialized world—a trend expected to accelerate. Currently, American centenarians number about 80,000—a figure that is expected to be 7 to 8 times as great in 2050 and to double every decade thereafter (U.S. Census Bureau, 2009b).

Among centenarians, women outnumber men by five to one. About 60 to 70 percent have physical and mental impairments that interfere with independent functioning. But the rest lead active, autonomous lives (Hagberg et al., 2001; Perls & Terry, 2003). These robust centenarians are of special interest because they represent the ultimate potential of the human species. What are they like? Results of several longitudinal studies reveal that they are diverse in years of education (none to postgraduate), economic well-being (very poor to very rich), and ethnicity. At the same time, their physical condition and life stories reveal common threads.

Jeanne Louise Calment, shown here at age 121, took up fencing at age 85, rode a bicycle until age 100, and maintained a quick wit until her final year. The longest-lived person on record, she died at age 122.

Impaired eyesight in late adulthood largely results from a reduction in light reaching the retina (caused by yellowing of the lens, shrinking of the pupil, and clouding of the vitreous) and from cell loss in the retina and optic nerve (refer again to Chapter 15). Dark adaptation—moving from a brightly lit to a dim environment, such as a movie theater—becomes harder. A decline in binocular vision (the brain's ability to combine images received from both eyes) makes depth perception less reliable (Brabyn et al., 2001). And visual acuity (fineness of discrimination) worsens, dropping sharply after age 70 (Fozard & Gordon-Salant, 2001).

When light-sensitive cells in the *macula,* or central region of the retina, break down, older adults may develop **macular degeneration,** in which central vision blurs and gradually is lost. Macular degeneration is the leading cause of blindness among older adults. About 10 percent of 65- to 74-year-olds, and 30 percent of 75- to 85-year-olds, have symptoms. If diagnosed early, macular degeneration can sometimes be treated with laser therapy. As with cataracts, heredity (including several identified genes) increases risk, especially when combined with cigarette smoking or obesity (Chu et al., 2008; Rhone & Basu, 2008; Wysong, Lee, & Sloan, 2009). Atherosclerosis also contributes by constricting blood flow to the retina. Protective factors—believed to exert their effects by shielding cells in the macula from free-radical damage—include regular, brisk physical activity and a diet rich in green, leafy vegetables, which are excellent sources of vitamins A, C, E, and carotenoids (yellow and red plant pigments) (Feret et al., 2007). But vitamin pills, once thought to help reduce the incidence of both cataracts and macular degeneration, show no consistent benefits in carefully designed, experimental studies (Evans, 2008).

Visual difficulties have a profound impact on older people's self-confidence and everyday behavior. As she approached age 80, Ruth gave up driving, and she worried about Walt, who found it hard to shift focus between the road and the dashboard or to make out pedestrians at dusk and at night (Wood, 2002). On foot, problems with depth perception and dark adaptation increase older adults' chances of stumbling.

When vision loss is extensive, it can affect leisure pursuits and be very isolating. Because of her poor vision, Ruth could no longer enjoy museums, movies, playing bridge, or working crossword puzzles, and she depended on others for help with

Health

Centenarians usually have grandparents, parents, and siblings who reached very old age, suggesting a genetically based survival advantage. Likewise, their children, who are typically in their seventies and eighties, appear physically young for their age (Coles, 2004; Perls et al., 2002). Some centenarians share with their siblings a segment of identical DNA on the fourth chromosome, suggesting that a certain gene, or several genes, may increase the likelihood of exceptionally long life (Perls & Terry, 2003).

Most robust centenarians escape age-related chronic illnesses. Genetic testing reveals a low incidence of genes associated with immune-deficiency disorders, cancer, and Alzheimer's disease. Consistent with these findings, robust centenarians usually have efficiently functioning immune systems, and after-death examinations reveal few brain abnormalities (Silver & Perls, 2000). Others live successfully despite underlying chronic illness—typically atherosclerosis and other cardiovascular problems (Berzlanovich et al., 2005). Compared with the general population, about four times as many centenarian women gave birth to healthy children after age 40 (Perls et al., 2000). Late childbearing may indicate that the body, including the reproductive system, is aging slowly.

As a group, robust centenarians are of average or slender build and practice moderation in eating. Many have most or all of their own teeth—another sign of unusual physical health. The large majority have never smoked, and most report lifelong physical activity extending past age 100 (Kropf & Pugh, 1995).

Personality

In personality, these very senior citizens appear highly optimistic (Jopp & Rott, 2006). In a study in which robust centenarians retook personality tests after 18 months, they reported more fatigue and depression, perhaps in response to increased frailty at the very end of their lives. But they also scored higher in toughmindedness, independence, emotional security, and openness to experience—traits that may be vital for surviving beyond 100 (Martin, Long, & Poon, 2002).When asked about contributors to their longevity, these extremely long-lived elders often mention close family bonds and a long and happy marriage. An unusually large percentage of centenarian men—about one-fourth—are still married (Velkoff, 2000).

Activities

Robust centenarians have a history of community involvement—working for just causes that are central to their growth and happiness. Their current activities often include stimulating work, leisure pursuits, and learning, which may help sustain their good cognition and life satisfaction (Samuelsson et al., 1997). Writing letters, poems, plays, and memoirs; making speeches; teaching music lessons and Sunday school; nursing the sick; chopping wood; selling merchandise, bonds, and insurance; painting; practicing medicine; and preaching sermons are among robust centenarians' varied involvements. In several cases, illiterate centenarians learned to read and write. One 105-year-old woman enrolled in classes four nights a week and, within a short time, could read road signs, newspaper headlines, and sections of the Bible (Beard, 1991).

As their numbers increase, robust centenarians are likely to be viewed less as curiosities and more as examples of typical development at its best. These independent, mentally alert, happy 100-year-olds illustrate how a healthy lifestyle, personal resourcefulness, and close ties to family and community can build on biological strengths, thereby pushing the limits of an active, fulfilling life.

housekeeping and shopping. But even among people age 85 and older, only 30 percent experience visual impairment severe enough to interfere with daily living (U.S. Department of Health and Human Services, 2009a). For many, however, reduced vision goes undetected (Evans & Rowlands, 2004). Treatment is vital for sustaining quality of life.

■ **HEARING.** "Mom, I'd like you to meet Joe's cousin Leona," said Ruth's daughter Sybil at a Thanksgiving gathering. But in the clamor of boisterous children, television sounds, and nearby conversations, 85-year-old Ruth didn't catch Leona's name or her relationship to Sybil's husband, Joe.

"Tell me your name again?" Ruth asked, adding, "Let's go into the other room, where it's quieter, so we can speak a bit."

Reduced blood supply and natural cell death in the inner ear and auditory cortex, discussed in Chapter 15, along with stiffening of membranes (such as the eardrum), cause hearing to decline in late adulthood. Decrements are greatest at high frequencies, although detection of soft sounds diminishes throughout the frequency range (see page 503). In addition, responsiveness to startling noises lessens, and discriminating complex tone patterns becomes harder (Fitzgibbons & Gordon-Salant, 1998; Hietanen et al., 2004).

Although hearing loss has less impact on self-care than vision loss, it affects safety and enjoyment of life. In the din of city traffic, 80-year-old Ruth didn't always correctly interpret warnings, whether spoken ("Watch it, don't step out yet") or nonspoken (the beep of a horn). And when she turned up the radio or television volume, she sometimes missed the ring of the telephone or a knock at the door.

As hearing declines, the elderly report lower self-efficacy, more loneliness and depressive symptoms, and a smaller social network than their normally hearing peers (Kramer et al., 2002). Of all hearing difficulties, the age-related decline in speech perception has the greatest impact on life satisfaction. After age 70, ability to detect the content and emotionally expressive features of conversation declines, especially in noisy settings (Schneider et al., 2000).

Although Ruth used problem-centered coping to increase her chances of hearing conversation, she wasn't always successful. At the family's Thanksgiving reunion, fewer relatives took time to talk with Ruth, and she felt some pangs of loneliness. And

© JEFF GREENBERG/THE IMAGE WORKS

This adult son's patient guidance helps his elderly father feel included at a boisterous family reunion. Declines in hearing make it difficult for elders to socialize in noisy settings.

sometimes people were inconsiderate. On a dinner outing, when Ruth asked Joe to repeat himself, he turned to Sybil and said loudly, "Be honest, Syb, Ruth's going deaf, isn't she?" In one study, elders' adoption of such negative stereotypes of aging predicted greater hearing loss over a three-year period (Levy, Slade, & Gill, 2006).

As with vision, most older adults do not suffer from hearing loss great enough to disrupt their daily lives. For those who do, compensating with a hearing aid and minimizing background noise are helpful. Furthermore, recall from Chapter 4 (page 146) that beginning at birth, our perception is *intermodal* (combines information from more than one sensory system). By attending to facial expressions, gestures, and lip movements, older adults can use vision to help interpret the spoken word. When family members and others speak in quiet environments, older people are far more likely to convey an image of alertness and competence than of reduced sensitivity to the surrounding world.

■ **TASTE AND SMELL.** Walt's brother Dick was a heavy smoker. In his sixties, he poured salt and pepper over his food, took his coffee with extra sugar, and asked for "extra hot" in Mexican and Indian restaurants.

Dick's reduced sensitivity to the four basic tastes—sweet, salty, sour, and bitter—is evident in many adults after age 60. Older adults also have greater difficulty recognizing familiar foods by taste alone (Fukunaga, Uematsu, & Sugimoto, 2005; Mojet, Christ-Hazelhof, & Heidema, 2001). But no change in the number or distribution of taste buds occurs late in life, so this drop in taste sensitivity may be due to factors other than aging. Cigarette smoking, dentures, medications, and environmental pollutants can affect taste perception. When taste is harder to detect, food is less enjoyable, increasing the likelihood of deficiencies in the elderly person's diet. Flavor additives can help make food more attractive (Drewnowski & Shultz, 2001).

Besides enhancing food enjoyment, smell has a self-protective function. An aging person who has difficulty detecting rancid food, gas fumes, or smoke may be in a life-threatening situation. A decrease in the number of smell receptors after age 60 contributes to declines in odor sensitivity. Researchers believe that odor perception not only wanes but becomes distorted, a change that may promote complaints that "food no longer smells and tastes right" (Seiberling & Conley, 2004).

But other factors may make this decline appear greater than it actually is. For example, older adults experiencing greater difficulty with verbal recall, including retrieval of odor labels, have greater difficulty with odor recognition tasks (Larsson & Bäckman, 1998; Larsson, Öberg, & Bäckman, 2005). Furthermore, practicing odor discriminations affects their maintenance (Engen, 1982). In his early eighties, Walt, a lifelong wine enthusiast, could still distinguish the aromas of fine wines.

■ **TOUCH.** Touch sensitivity is especially crucial for certain adults, such as the severely visually impaired who must read in Braille and people who must make fine judgments about texture in their occupations or leisure pursuits—for example, in art and handicraft activities. After age 70, nearly all elders experience a decline in touch perception on the hands, especially the fingertips, believed to be due to loss of touch receptors in certain regions of the skin and slowing of blood circulation to the extremities (Stevens & Cruz, 1996).

The elements of Braille letters are so closely spaced that nearly all elderly people have difficulty interpreting them (Stevens, Foulke, & Patterson, 1996). Just as the sighted need new visual aids for reading as they age, so the visually impaired may need new tactile aids—an important consideration in responding to diversity in the aging population.

Cardiovascular and Respiratory Systems

Aging of the cardiovascular and respiratory systems proceeds gradually and usually unnoticed in early and middle adulthood. In late adulthood, changes become more apparent. In their sixties, Ruth and Walt noticed that they felt more physically stressed after running to catch a bus or to cross a street before the light changed.

As the years pass, the heart muscle becomes more rigid, and some of its cells die while others enlarge, leading the walls of the left ventricle (the largest heart chamber, from which blood is pumped to the body) to thicken. In addition, artery walls stiffen and accumulate some plaque (cholesterol and fats) due to normal aging (much more in those with atherosclerosis). Finally, the heart muscle becomes less responsive to signals from pacemaker cells within the heart, which initiate each contraction (Smith & Cotter, 2008).

As a combined result of these changes, the heart pumps with less force, maximum heart rate decreases, and blood flow throughout the circulatory system slows. This means that suffi-

After an uphill stretch, this biker needs a rest to catch his breath and feel re-energized. Aging of the cardiovascular and respiratory systems means that sufficient oxygen may not be delivered to body tissues during physical exertion.

cient oxygen may not be delivered to body tissues during high physical activity. (Recall from Chapter 13 that a healthy heart supports typical levels of exertion well into old age.)

Changes in the respiratory system compound the effects of reduced oxygenation. Because lung tissue gradually loses its elasticity, vital capacity (amount of air that can be forced in and out of the lungs) is reduced by half between ages 25 and 80. As a result, the lungs fill and empty less efficiently, causing the blood to absorb less oxygen and give off less carbon dioxide. This explains why older people increase their breathing rate more and feel more out of breath while exercising.

Cardiovascular and respiratory deficiencies are more extreme in lifelong smokers and in people who have failed to reduce dietary fat or have had many years of exposure to environmental pollutants. As we have seen in previous chapters, exercise is a powerful means of slowing cardiovascular aging. Exercise also facilitates respiratory functioning, as we will see later when we discuss health and fitness.

Immune System

As the immune system ages, T cells, which attack antigens (foreign substances) directly, become less effective (see Chapter 13, page 437). In addition, the immune system is more likely to malfunction by turning against normal body tissues in an **autoimmune response.** A less competent immune system can increase the elderly person's risk for a variety of illnesses, including infectious diseases (such as the flu), cardiovascular disease, certain forms of cancer, and various autoimmune disorders, such as rheumatoid arthritis and diabetes (Hasler & Zouali, 2005). But an age-related decline in immune functioning is not the cause of most illnesses among the elderly. It merely permits disease to progress, whereas a stronger immune reaction would have stamped out the disease agent.

Older adults vary greatly in immunity. A few have sturdy immune systems that continue to respond nearly as well as in early adulthood. But most experience some loss of function, ranging from partial to profound (Pawelec et al., 1999). The strength of the aging person's immune system seems to be a sign of overall physical vigor. Certain immune indicators, such as high T cell activity, predict survival over the next two years in very old people (Wikby et al., 1998).

In Chapter 13, we emphasized that other physical changes contribute to impaired immune functioning. Recall that stress hormones undermine immunity. With age, the autonomic nervous system releases higher levels of these into the bloodstream (refer back to page 567). As the immune response declines with age, stress-induced susceptibility to infection rises dramatically (Butcher & Lord, 2004). A healthy diet and exercise help protect the immune response in old age, whereas obesity aggravates the age-related decline (Chandra, 2002b; Drela, Kozdron, & Szczypiorski, 2004; Senchina & Kohut, 2007).

Sleep

When Walt went to bed at night, he usually lay awake for a half-hour to an hour before falling asleep, remaining in a drowsy state longer than when he was younger. During the night, he spent less time in the deepest phase of NREM sleep (see Chapter 3, page 108) and awoke several times—again sometimes lying awake for a half-hour or more before drifting back to sleep.

Older adults require about as much total sleep as younger adults: around 7 hours per night. Yet as people age, they have more difficulty falling asleep, staying asleep, and sleeping deeply. Insomnia affects nearly half of older adults at least a few nights per month. The timing of sleep tends to change as well, toward earlier bedtime and earlier morning awakening (Wolkove et al., 2007). Changes in brain structures controlling sleep and higher levels of stress hormones in the bloodstream, which have an alerting effect on the central nervous system, are believed to be responsible.

Until age 70 or 80, men experience more sleep disturbances than women, for several reasons. First, enlargement of the prostate gland, which occurs in almost all aging men, constricts the urethra (the tube draining the bladder) and leads to a need to urinate more often, including during the night. Second, men—especially those who are overweight and use alcohol heavily—are more prone to **sleep apnea,** a condition in which breathing ceases for 10 seconds or longer, resulting in many brief awakenings. An estimated 45 to 60 percent of the elderly are affected (Wolcove et al., 2007). Finally, periodic rapid movement of the legs sometimes accompanies sleep apnea but also occurs at other times of night. Called "restless legs," these movements may be due to muscle tension, reduced circulation, or age-related changes in motor areas of the brain (Chasens, Williams, & Umlauf, 2008). Though common among the elderly and not dangerous, they do disrupt sleep.

Poor sleep can feed on itself. Walt's nighttime wakefulness led to daytime fatigue and short naps, which made it harder to fall asleep the following evening. And because Walt expected to have trouble sleeping, he worried about it, which also interfered with sleep.

Fortunately, there are ways to foster restful sleep, such as establishing a consistent bedtime and waking time, exercising regularly, and using the bedroom only for sleep (not for eating, reading, or watching TV) (McCurry et al., 2007). Explaining that even very healthy older adults have trouble sleeping lets people know that age-related changes in the sleep–wake pattern are normal. The elderly receive more prescription sedatives for sleep complaints than do 40- to 60-year-olds. Used briefly, these drugs can help relieve temporary insomnia. But long-term medication can make matters worse by increasing the frequency and severity of sleep apnea and by inducing rebound insomnia after the drug is discontinued (Feinsilver, 2003). Finally, discomfort due to an enlarged prostate, including frequent urination at night, can be corrected with new laser surgical procedures that relieve symptoms without complications (Van Cleynenbreugel, Srirangam, & Van Poppel, 2009).

Physical Appearance and Mobility

In earlier chapters, we saw that changes leading to an aged appearance are under way as early as the twenties and thirties. Because these occur gradually, older adults may not notice their elderly appearance until it has become obvious. Each year during their summer travels, Walt and Ruth observed that Dick's and Goldie's skin appeared more wrinkled. Their hair turned from gray to white as all pigment was lost; their bodies grew rounder and their arms and legs thinner. When they returned home, Walt and Ruth also were more aware that they themselves had aged.

Creasing and sagging of the skin, described in Chapter 15, extends into old age. In addition, oil glands that lubricate the skin become less active, leading to dryness and roughness. "Age spots" increase; in some individuals, the arms, backs of the hands, and face may be dotted with these pigmented marks. Moles and other small skin growths may also appear. Blood vessels can be seen beneath the more transparent skin, which has largely lost its layer of fatty support (Whitbourne, 2002). This loss further limits the older adult's ability to adapt to hot and cold temperatures.

The face is especially likely to show these effects because it is frequently exposed to the sun, which accelerates aging. Other factors that contribute to facial wrinkling and age spots include long-term alcohol use, cigarette smoking, and stress. In a study of identical twins, those who had been divorced appeared almost two years older than their married or widowed siblings (Guyuron et al., 2009). Additional facial changes occur: The nose and ears broaden as new cells are deposited on the outer layer of the skeleton. And especially in elders with a history of poor dental care, teeth may be yellowed, cracked, and chipped, and gums may have receded. As hair follicles under the skin's surface die, hair on the head thins in both sexes, and the scalp may be visible. In men with hereditary pattern baldness, follicles do not die but, instead, begin to produce fine, downy hair (Whitbourne, 2002).

Changes in appearance that accompany aging are evident in these portraits of Jimmy Carter—former U.S. president—at ages 52, 63, and 85. The skin creases and sags, "age spots" increase, the nose and ears broaden as new cells are deposited on the outer layer of the skeleton, and hair follicles die, causing hair on the head to thin.

Body build changes as well. Height continues to decline, especially in women, as loss of bone mineral content leads to further collapse of the spinal column. Weight generally drops after age 60 because of additional loss of lean body mass (bone density and muscle), which is heavier than the fat deposits accumulating on the torso.

Several factors affect mobility. The first is muscle strength, which generally declines at a faster rate in late adulthood than in middle age. On average, by 60 to 70 years of age, 10 to 20 percent of muscle power has been lost, a figure that climbs to 30 to 50 percent after age 70 to 80 (Whitbourne, 2001, 2002). Second, bone strength deteriorates because of reduced bone mass, and tiny cracks in response to stress weaken the bones further. Third, strength and flexibility of the joints and the ligaments and tendons (which connect muscle to bone) diminish. In her eighties, Ruth's reduced ability to support her body, flex her limbs, and rotate her hips made walking at a steady, moderate pace, climbing stairs, and rising from a chair difficult.

In Chapter 13, we noted that endurance athletes who continue training throughout adulthood retain their muscular physiques and much of their strength into their sixties and seventies. These especially active people, like other aging individuals, lose fast-twitch muscle fibers, but they compensate by strengthening remaining slow-twitch fibers so they work more efficiently. A history of regular physical activity translates into greater mobility in late life (Koster et al., 2007; Patel et al., 2006). At the same time, a carefully planned exercise program can enhance elders' joint flexibility and range of movement. When Ruth complained of joint stiffness and pain, her doctor recommended certain rhythmic and flexing exercises, as well as exercises that strengthen muscles supporting the joints.

Adapting to Physical Changes of Late Adulthood

Great diversity exists in older adults' adaptation to the physical changes of aging. People who are more anxious about growing older monitor their physical state more closely and are more concerned about their appearance (Montepare, 2006). Dick and Goldie took advantage of an enormous industry designed to stave off outward signs of old age, including cosmetics, wigs, and plastic surgery, plus various "anti-aging" dietary supplements, herbal products, and hormonal medications offered by "longevity" clinics—none with any demonstrated benefits and some of them harmful (Olshansky, Hayflick, & Perls, 2004). In contrast, Ruth and Walt were relatively unconcerned about their thinning white hair and wrinkled skin. Their identities were less bound up with their appearance than with their ability to remain actively engaged in their surroundings. Like Ruth and Walt, most elders say they feel younger than they look and than they actually are—self-evaluations that promote satisfaction with growing older (Kleinspehn-Ammerlahn, Kotter-Grühn, & Smith, 2008; Rubin & Berntsen, 2006).

People also vary in the aspects of physical aging that matter most to them. And because parts of the body age at different rates, older adults' sense of physical aging is multidimensional: They view themselves as physically older in some domains than in others. Compared with Dick and Goldie, Ruth and Walt approached aging with a more positive outlook and greater peace of mind, resolving to intervene in those aspects that could be changed and to accept those that could not.

Research shows that the most obvious outward signs of aging—graying hair, facial wrinkles, and baldness—bear no relationship to sensory, cognitive, and motor functioning or to longevity (Schnohr et al., 1998). In contrast, neurological, sensory, cardiovascular, respiratory, immune-system, and skeletal and muscular health strongly predict cognitive performance and both quality and length of later life (Anstey, Luszcz, & Sanchez, 2001; Bergman, Blomberg, & Almkvist, 2007; Reyes-Ortiz et al., 2005). Furthermore, people can do more to prevent declines in the functioning of these internal body systems than they can do to prevent gray hair and baldness!

■ **EFFECTIVE COPING STRATEGIES.** Think back to our discussion of problem-centered and emotion-centered coping in Chapter 15. It applies here as well. As Walt and Ruth prevented and compensated for age-related changes through diet, exercise, environmental adjustments, and an active, stimulating lifestyle, they felt a sense of personal control over their fates. This prompted additional positive coping and improved physical functioning.

In one study, elders who generated new, problem-centered coping strategies for dealing with vision loss—such as relying on sound to recognize people, acting more cautiously in risky situations, and exchanging ideas with other visually impaired individuals—adapted more favorably to everyday challenges and felt less depressed (Brennan & Cardinali, 2000). In contrast, older adults who consider age-related declines inevitable and uncontrollable, and who ruminate about their damaging effects, tend to be passive when faced with them and to report more physical and psychological adjustment difficulties (Kraaij, Pruymboom, & Garnefski, 2002; Morrison, 2008).

■ **ASSISTIVE TECHNOLOGY.** A rapidly expanding **assistive technology,** or array of devices that permit people with disabilities to improve their functioning, is available to help older people cope with physical declines. Computers are the greatest source of these innovative products. People with sensory impairments can use special software to enlarge text or have it read aloud. Phones that can be dialed and answered by voice commands help elders who have difficulty pushing buttons or getting across a room to answer the phone. And for elders who take multiple medications, a tiny computer chip called a "smart cap" can be placed on medicine bottles. It beeps on a programmed schedule to remind the older person to take the drug and tracks how many and at what time pills have been taken.

Architects are also designing homes that can adapt to changing physical needs—equipping them with movable walls that expand and contract, plumbing that enables a full bathroom to be added on the main floor, and "smart-home" technologies

AP IMAGES/STEVEN SENNE

Erez Lieberman, Massachusetts Institute of Technology graduate student, displays the "iShoe" insole he invented. The device, designed to prevent catastrophic falls in the elderly, contains sensors that detect a wearer's balance. Data collected can be reported to the elder's doctor. The iShoe also can be outfitted with an alarm that alerts family members when a fall occurs.

that promote safety and mobility, such as sensors in floors that activate room lights when an older person gets up at night and alarm systems that detect falls. Another remarkable device is a bathroom scale that helps monitor health status. It sends a signal to a control box, which reads the person's weight aloud.

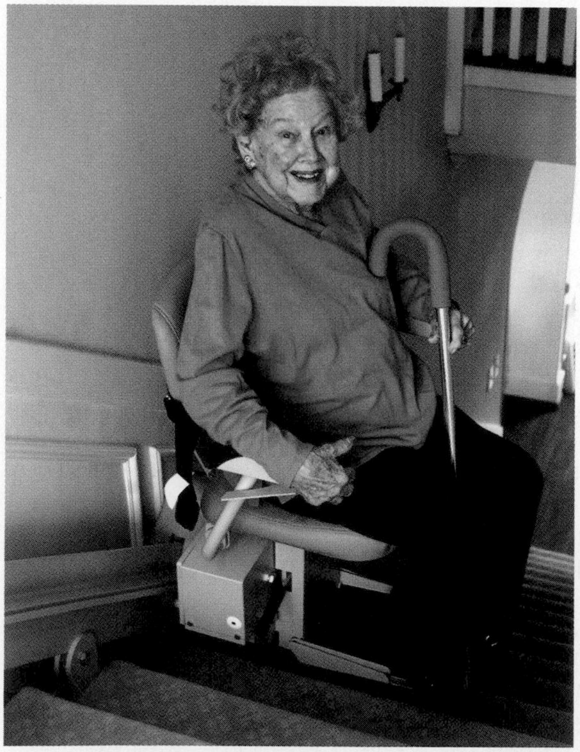

© ERIN MORONEY LABELLE/THE IMAGE WORKS

A motorized chair allows this 90-year-old to remain in her own home despite its long staircase.

After comparing weight with previous readings, the box asks relevant questions—"Are you more tired than usual?" "Are you having trouble sleeping?"—that can be answered by pressing a "yes" or "no" button. The box also works with equipment that measures blood pressure, activity level, and other health indicators. Data collected are sent electronically to whomever the older adult gives access.

Elders with disabilities who use assistive devices require fewer hours of personal caregiving (Hoenig, Taylor, & Sloan, 2003). Do they regard some technologies as invasions of privacy? The overwhelming majority weigh privacy concerns against potential benefits—saying for example, "If this [monitoring system] would keep me independent longer, I wouldn't mind" (Melenhorst et al., 2004; Rogers & Fisk, 2005).

At present, smart-home technologies are beyond the means of most elders; U.S. government-sponsored health care coverage is largely limited to essential medical equipment. Sweden's health care system, in contrast, covers many assistive devices that promote function and safety, and its building code requires that new homes include a full bathroom on the main floor (Hooyman & Kiyak, 2008). In this way, Sweden helps older adults remain as independent as possible.

OVERCOMING STEREOTYPES OF AGING. Stereotypes of late adulthood, which view "deterioration as inevitable," are widespread in Western nations. Overcoming this pessimistic picture is vital for helping people adapt favorably to late-life physical changes. In a survey of older adults diverse in SES, many reported experiencing prejudice and discrimination. For example, 30 to 40 percent had been ignored, talked down to, or assumed to be unable to hear or understand well because of their age (Palmore, 2001).

Like gender stereotypes, aging stereotypes often operate automatically, without awareness; people "see" elders in stereotypical ways, even when they appear otherwise. As seniors encounter these negative messages, they experience *stereotype threat,* which results in diminished performance on tasks related to the stereotype (see page 314 in Chapter 9). In several studies, researchers exposed older adults to words associated with either negative aging stereotypes ("decrepit," "confused") or positive aging stereotypes ("sage," "enlightened"). Those in the negative-stereotype condition displayed a more intense physiological response to stress along with worse handwriting, memory performance, self-efficacy, and will to live (Hess & Hinson, 2006; Hess, Hinson, & Statham, 2004; Levy & Banaji, 2002; Levy et al., 2000). ***TAKE A MOMENT...*** How might stereotype threat explain the hearing loss linked to negative stereotypes of aging, mentioned on page 570?

As the findings just reviewed indicate, negative stereotypes have a stressful, disorganizing impact on elders' functioning. Positive stereotypes, in contrast, reduce stress and foster competence (Levy, 2003). In a longitudinal investigation, people with positive self-perceptions of aging—who, for example, agreed with such statements as "As I get older, things are better than I thought they'd be"—lived, on average, 7½ years longer than those with negative self-perceptions. This survival advantage remained after gender, SES, loneliness, and physical health status were controlled (Levy et al., 2002). Adults with less education are especially susceptible to the detrimental effects of aging stereotypes, perhaps because they tend to accept those messages uncritically (Andreoletti & Lachman, 2004).

Elders rarely appear in television programs and, when they do, typically play minor roles. But a positive sign is that negative portrayals of seniors on TV and in other media are rare. TV commercials featuring older adults usually depict them in stereotypically positive roles, most commonly as an "adventurous golden ager" (fun-loving, sociable, and active), "perfect grandparent" (family-oriented, kind, and generous), or "productive golden ager" (intelligent, capable, and successful). Still, the products promoted in such ads are mostly medications and medical services, "anti-aging" beauty products, and financial services—images that reinforce negative views of older adults as preoccupied with physical declines, dissatisfied with their appearance, and feeling financially vulnerable (Lee, Carpenter, & Meyers, 2006).

In cultures where the elderly are treated with deference and respect, an aging appearance can be a source of pride. In one study, Chinese adults diverse in age were less likely than Canadian adults to stereotype elders, either positively or negatively (Ryan et al., 2004). In the native language of the Inuit people of Canada, the closest word to "elder" is *isumataq*, or "one who knows things"—a high status that begins when a couple becomes head of the extended family unit. When Inuit older adults were asked for their thoughts on aging well, they mentioned attitudes—a positive approach to life, interest in transmitting cultural knowledge to young people, and community involvement—nearly twice as often as physical health (Collings, 2001).

Japan honors its elderly citizens with an annual celebration, Respect for the Aged Day. Also, a ritual called *kanreki* recognizes the older person's new freedoms and competencies and senior place in the family and society. Japanese extended families in the United States often plan the kanreki as a surprise sixtieth birthday party, incorporating elements of both the traditional ritual (such as dress) and the Western birthday (a special cake). Cultural valuing of aging prompts a welcoming approach to late adulthood, including some of its physical transitions.

Despite inevitable declines, physical aging can be viewed with either optimism or pessimism. As Walt commented, "You can think of your glass as half full or half empty." As the Cultural Influences box on page 576 makes clear, cultural valuing of elders greatly increases the likelihood that they will adopt the "half full" alternative.

© EASTCOTT-MOMATIUK/THE IMAGE WORKS

This Inuit elder of northern Canada enjoys a visit with her daughter. In Inuit culture, aging is associated with expert knowledge and high status. Hence, changes in physical appearance can be a source of pride.

ASK YOURSELF

» REVIEW
Cite examples of how older adults can compensate for age-related physical declines.

» APPLY
"The best way to adjust to this is to learn to like it," thought 65-year-old Herman, inspecting his thinning hair in the mirror. "I remember reading that bald older men are regarded as leaders." What type of coping is Herman using, and why is it effective?

» CONNECT
Review research on stereotype threat on page 314 in Chapter 9. How do stereotypes of aging similarly affect elders' behavior?

» REFLECT
While watching TV during the coming week, keep a log of portrayals of older adults in commercials. How many images were positive? How many negative? Compare your observations with research findings.

Health, Fitness, and Disability

At Walt and Ruth's fiftieth wedding anniversary, 77-year-old Walt thanked a roomful of well-wishers for joining in the celebration. Then, with emotion, he announced, "I'm so grateful Ruth and I are in good health and still able to give to our family, friends, and community."

As Walt's remarks affirm, health is central to psychological well-being in late life. When researchers ask the elderly about possible selves (see Chapter 16, page 538), number of hoped-for physical selves declines with age and number of feared physical selves increases. Nevertheless, because older adults compare themselves to same-age peers, the majority rate their health favorably (U.S. Department of Health and Human Services, 2009a). In an investigation of more than 500 70- to 100-year-olds living in Berlin, Germany, subjective evaluations of one's own health rose in late life, while objective health

CULTURAL INFLUENCES

Cultural Variations in Sense of Usefulness in Late Life

A wealth of evidence confirms that older adults fare best when they retain social status and opportunities for community participation, even after they become frail (Fry et al., 1997; Rossi, 2004). Yet cultures vary widely in the extent to which they include their oldest members in meaningful social roles.

Consider the Herero, a pastoral people of Botswana, Africa. Elders who are strong and active spend their days just as younger adults do, tending the cattle and performing other chores. When older adults decline physically, they retain positions of seniority and are treated with respect. A status hierarchy makes the oldest man and his wife village leaders. They are responsible for preserving the sacred flame of the ancestors, who remain significant family members after death. Children are sent to live in the homes of frail elders to provide care—an assignment that is a source of great pride and prestige.

Old age is also a gratifying time of life in Momence, Illinois, a small, working-class farming and manufacturing town. The population is highly stable, so elders hold positions of authority because of their length of residence and intimate knowledge of the community. Town, church, and club leaders tend to be older, and past leaders are included in decision making. And because frail elders are embedded in family, neighborhood, and church networks that have persisted for many years, other community members often inquire about them, visit them, and monitor their condition.

The Herero and the residents of Momence seldom refer to older adults in terms of their age. Rather, they mention knowledge and social position (Keith et al., 1994). But in most of the Western world, old age is a salient attribute that readily triggers negative stereotypes, including the label "useless." For example, after a young anthropologist who was studying life at a senior center introduced several of his contemporaries to an 80-year-old man, one remarked, "He has outlived his usefulness. He would be happier dead" (Tsuji, 2005, p. 3). In line with this view, compared with younger and middle-aged adults, older adults typically score lower on measures of sense of purpose in life (Ryff & Singer, 2002).

Yet contributing to making life better for others, as we will see in Chapter 18, is an important component of older adults' life goals. It also affects their health and survival. Studies in diverse nations—Finland, France, Japan, and the United States—reveal that elders who often felt useless were more likely to display increasing disability and to die in the ensuing 4 to 10 years than those who felt needed, after initial health status, SES, and other relevant factors were controlled (Gruenewald et al., 2007; Okamoto & Tanaka, 2004; Pitkala et al., 2004).

Fortunately, only a minority of Western older adults report feeling useless most or all of the time—6 percent in a U.S sample. But another 35 percent said that they sometimes feel that way (Gruenewald et al., 2007). Providing elders with opportunities to assume important roles readily combats this harmful self-perception. In one instance, seniors with arthritis were trained to become lay leaders, who delivered courses on coping with disease symptoms. Six months later, they reported a changed outlook: They highly valued their newly acquired status, felt more self-confident, better managed their own symptoms, and were more willing "to get on with life" (Hainsworth & Barlow, 2001). As one lay leader remarked, "It's almost as if I've stopped aging and started to get younger!"

Among the Herero people of Botswana, Africa, elders continue to participate actively in their community. When they decline physically, children are assigned the prestigious task of living in their homes to provide care. And the oldest man and woman will be named leaders of the village.

assessments declined (see Figure 17.3) (Baltes & Smith, 2003). As for protecting their health, elders' sense of self-efficacy is as high as that of young adults and higher than that of middle-aged people (Frazier, 2002; Hooker, 1992).

The stronger elders' sense of control in coping with physical challenges, and the more optimistic they are about health outcomes, the better they are at overcoming threats to health, which promotes further optimism and continued health-enhancing behaviors (Kubzansky et al., 2002; Morrison, 2008). Disability need not inevitably lead to further disability and dependency. In several longitudinal studies, 10 to 50 percent of elders with disabilities showed substantial improvement two to six years later (Johnston et al., 2004; Ostir et al., 1999). Furthermore, good health permits older adults to remain socially active, thereby fostering psychological well-being (Fiori, Smith, & Antonucci, 2007).

As mentioned earlier, SES and ethnic variations in health diminish in late adulthood. Nevertheless, before age 85, SES continues to predict physical functioning (House, Lantz, & Herd, 2005; Yao & Robert, 2008). African-American and Hispanic

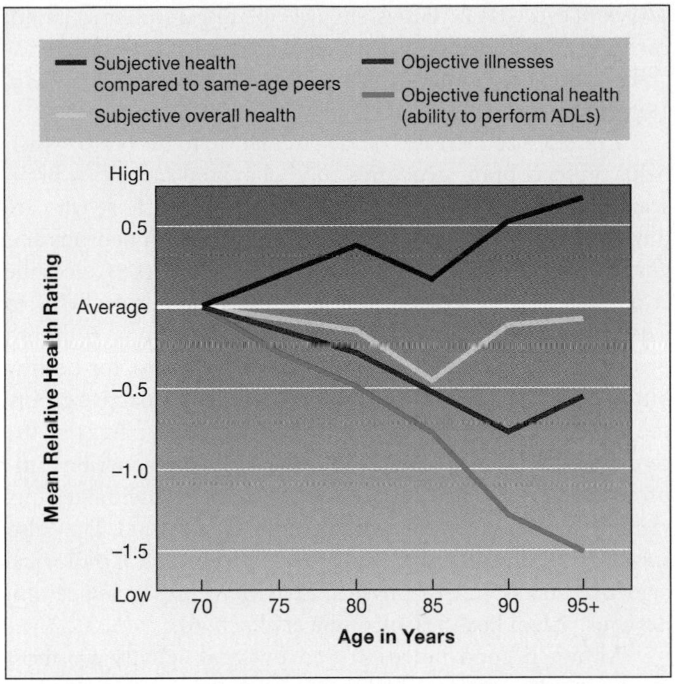

■ **FIGURE 17.3** ■ **Changes in subjective and objective health evaluations with age.** In the Berlin Aging Study, 500 70- to 100-year-olds both evaluated their own health and received examinations and assessments by health professionals. Despite declines in objective health, ratings of subjective health—especially comparisons with same-age peers—rose with age. Older adults are generally optimistic about their health, an attitude that helps them cope with physical challenges. (From Paul B. Baltes and Karl Ulrich Mayer, (Eds.), *The Berlin Aging Study: Aging from 70 to 100,* © Paul B. Baltes and Karl Ulrich Mayer 1999. Reprinted with the permission of Cambridge University Press.)

elderly (one-fifth of whom live in poverty) remain at greater risk for various health problems, including cardiovascular disease, diabetes, and certain cancers. Native-American older adults are even worse off. The majority are poor, and chronic health conditions—including diabetes, kidney disease, liver disease, tuberculosis, and hearing and vision impairments—are so widespread that in the United States, the federal government grants Native Americans special health benefits. These begin as early as age 45, reflecting a much harder and shorter lifespan. Unfortunately, low-SES elders are less likely than their higher-SES counterparts to seek medical treatment. When they do, they often do not comply with the doctor's directions because they feel less in control of their health and less optimistic that treatment will work (Hopper, 1993). Their low sense of self-efficacy further impairs their physical condition.

The sex differences noted in Chapter 15 extend into late adulthood: Men are more prone to fatal diseases, women to non-life-threatening disabling conditions. By very old age (80 to 85 and beyond), women are more impaired than men because only the sturdiest men have survived (Murtagh & Hubert, 2004; Morrison, 2008). In addition, with fewer physical limitations, older men are better able to remain independent and to engage in exercise, hobbies, and involvement in the social world, all of which promote better health.

Widespread health-related optimism among the elderly suggests that substantial inroads into preventing disability can be made even in the last few decades of life. Ideally, as life expectancy extends, we want the average period of diminished vigor before death to decrease—a public health goal called the **compression of morbidity.** Several large-scale studies indicate that over the past two decades, compression of morbidity has occurred in industrialized nations despite rising rates of obesity and sedentary lifestyles, suggesting that medical advances and improved socioeconomic conditions are largely responsible (Fries, 2003; Hessler et al., 2003).

Yet the impact of good health habits on postponement of disability is large, indicating that compression of morbidity can be greatly extended. In a longitudinal investigation following university alumni from their late sixties on, disability was delayed by nearly eight years in those who were lean, who exercised, and who did not smoke compared with those who were obese, sedentary, or addicted to tobacco. Elders with these risks surged to extremely high levels of disability in the two years before death (Hubert et al., 2002; Vita et al., 1998). Researchers believe that the most promising route to further compression of morbidity in developed countries is to reduce negative lifestyle factors. Improved prevention and treatment of chronic diseases, starting early and continuing throughout life, are also vital (Barondess, 2005). As we look closely at health, fitness, and disability in late adulthood, we will add to our discussion of health promotion in earlier chapters, taking up additional routes to this objective.

More comprehensive strategies are needed in the developing world, where 70 percent of older people will reside by 2025. In these nations, poverty is rampant, chronic diseases occur earlier, even routine health interventions are unavailable or too costly for all but a few, and most public health programs do not focus on the elderly (Kalache, Aboderin, & Hoskins, 2002). As a result, disability rates among old people are especially high, and as yet, no progress has been made in compression of morbidity.

Nutrition and Exercise

The physical changes of late life lead to an increased need for certain nutrients—calcium and vitamin D to protect the bones; zinc and vitamins B_6, C, and E to protect the immune system; and vitamins A, C, and E to prevent free radicals (see Chapter 13, page 434). Yet declines in physical activity, in the senses of taste and smell, and in ease of chewing (because of deteriorating teeth) can reduce the quantity and quality of food eaten (Morley, 2001). Furthermore, the aging digestive system has greater difficulty absorbing certain nutrients, such as protein, calcium, and vitamin D. And older adults who live alone may have problems shopping or cooking and may feel less like eating by themselves. Together, these physical and environmental conditions increase the risk of dietary deficiencies, which affect 10 to 25 percent of U.S. elders (High, 2001).

In several studies, a daily vitamin–mineral tablet resulted in an enhanced immune response and a 50 percent drop in days of infectious illness (Chandra, 2002a; Wintergest, Maggini, & Hornig, 2007). But growing evidence indicates that vitamin–mineral supplements do not reduce the incidence of cardiovascular disease or cancer (Huang et al., 2006; Lee et al., 2005; Neuhouser et al., 2009). Furthermore, supplemental nutrients and herbs identified as "cognitive enhancers"—including B and E vitamins, folic acid, and ginkgo biloba—do not improve elders' cognitive functioning and neither prevent nor slow the progression of Alzheimer's disease (Aisen et al., 2008; DeKosky et al., 2008; McDaniel, Maier, & Einstein, 2002; Morris et al., 2006). At the same time, several surveys suggest that regularly eating fish high in polyunsaturated fatty acids (which promote vascular health) offers some protection against mental disabilities (Issa et al., 2006; Morris et al., 2005).

In addition to a healthy diet, exercise continues to be a powerful health intervention. Sedentary healthy older adults up to age 80 who begin endurance training (walking, cycling, aerobic dance) show gains in vital capacity that compare favorably with those of much younger individuals. And weight-bearing exercise begun in late adulthood—even as late as age 90—promotes muscle size and strength, blood flow to muscles, and ability of muscles to extract oxygen from blood. This translates into improved walking speed, balance, posture, and ability to carry out everyday activities, such as opening a stubborn jar lid, carrying an armload of groceries, or lifting a 30-pound grandchild (deJong & Franklin, 2004; Goldberg, Dengel, & Hagberg, 1996; Pyka et al., 1994).

© BOB DAEMMRICH/PHOTOEDIT

This spectacularly fit woman, participating in the Senior Olympics, has likely been exercising for most of her life. However, even exercise programs begun in late adulthood can promote muscle size and strength and preservation of brain structures and behavioral capacities.

Exercise also increases blood circulation to the brain, which helps preserve brain structures and behavioral capacities. Brain scans show that, compared with inactive elders, those who are physically fit experienced less tissue loss—in both neurons and glial cells—in diverse areas of the cerebral cortex (Colcombe et al., 2003). In a series of studies, researchers used fMRI to assess changes in brain activity resulting from a 6-month program of regular, moderate to vigorous exercise for healthy but sedentary seniors. Compared to a physically inactive group, the new exercisers displayed increased activity in areas of the cerebral cortex governing control of attention, as well as improved sustained and selective attention during mental testing, yielding better performance (Colcombe et al., 2004). They also showed gains in volume of the cerebral cortex—clear biological evidence for the role of physical activity in preserving central nervous system health (Colcombe et al., 2006).

Although good nutrition and physical activity are most beneficial when they are lifelong, it is never too late to change. Beginning in his sixties and until his death at age 94, Walt's Uncle Louie played tennis for an hour or two every day and went ballroom dancing three nights a week. Exercise led Louie to sustain a high sense of physical self-esteem. As a dancer, he dressed nattily and moved gracefully. He often commented on how dance and other sports could transform an older person's appearance from dowdy to elegant, expressing the beauty of the inner self.

Elders who come to value the intrinsic benefits of exercise—feeling stronger, healthier, and more energetic—are likely to engage in it regularly (Caserta & Gillett, 1998). Yet 75 percent of elderly men and 80 percent of elderly women are not active enough (Stewart et al., 2001). Often, those with chronic disease symptoms think "taking it easy" is the best treatment and believe that exercise actually will do harm. In planning exercise programs for older adults, it is important to instill a sense of control over the aging process—by stressing the health-enhancing rewards of physical activity and by changing negative beliefs that interfere with sustained effort (Lachman et al., 1997). Active seniors can serve as positive role models and sources of encouragement.

Sexuality

When Walt turned 60, he asked his 90-year-old Uncle Louie at what age sexual desire and activity cease. Walt's question stemmed from a widely held myth that sex drive disappears among the elderly (Hillman, 2000). Louie corrected this impression. "My sexual interest has never gone away," he explained to Walt. "I can't do it as often, and it's a quieter experience than it was in my youth. But Rachella and I have led a happy intimate life, and it's still that way."

As in previous cross-sectional studies, a recent survey of a large, nationally representative sample of U.S. 57- to 85-year-olds reported a decline in frequency of sexual activity in older people—especially among women, who are less likely than men to be in a marital or other intimate relationship. At the same time, the majority of respondents attributed at least some importance to sex, and those who had been sexually active in the previous year mostly rated sex as "very" or "extremely" important. Consistent with these attitudes, most healthy couples reported continued, regular sexual enjoyment. More than half of the oldest respondents with an intimate partner indicated that they engaged in some type of sexual activity (usually intercourse) at least two to three times per month (see Figure 17.4) (Lindau et al., 2007). Note that these trends are probably influenced by cohort effects: A new generation of elders, accustomed to viewing sexuality positively, will probably be more sexually active.

The same generalization we discussed for midlife applies to late life: Good sex in the past predicts good sex in the future. Furthermore, using intercourse as the only measure of sexual activity promotes a narrow view of pleasurable sex. Even at the most advanced ages, there is more to sexuality than the sex act itself—feeling sensual, enjoying close companionship, and being loved and wanted. Both older men and older women report that the male partner is usually the one who ceases to interact sexually (Burgess, 2004; DeLamater & Moorman, 2007; Lindau et al., 2007). In a culture that emphasizes an erection as necessary for being sexual, a man may withdraw from all erotic activity when he finds that erections are harder to achieve and more time must elapse between them.

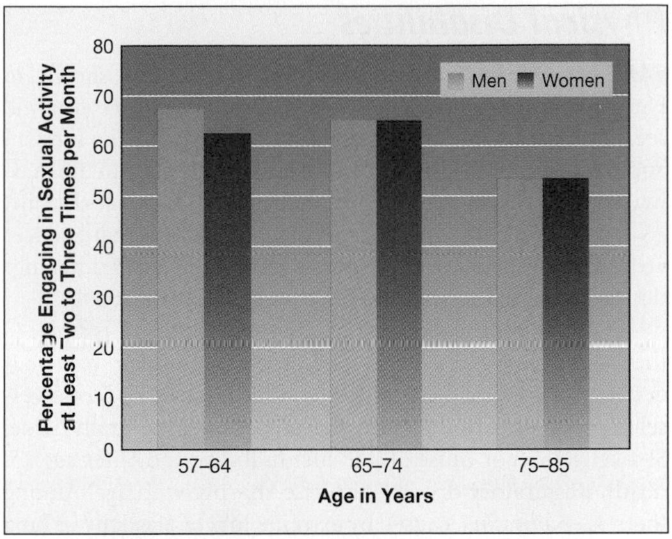

■ FIGURE 17.4 ■ Age-related changes in sexual activity among adults with an intimate partner. In a nationally representative sample of more than 3,000 U.S. 57- to 85-year-olds, most men and women with an intimate partner reported engaging in sexual activity (usually intercourse) at least two to three times per month. Sexual activity declined during late adulthood. Still, more than half of partnered 75- to 85-year-olds reported regular sexual activity. (Adapted from Lindau et al., 2007.)

Most healthy older couples report continued, regular sexual enjoyment. In addition to intercourse, feeling sensual, enjoying close companionship, and being loved and wanted all are part of sexuality at the most advanced ages.

Disabilities that disrupt blood flow to the penis—most often, disorders of the autonomic nervous system, cardiovascular disease, and diabetes—are largely responsible for dampening sexuality in older men. But as noted in Chapter 15, availability of drug treatments, such as Viagra, has increased men's willingness to discuss erectile dysfunction with their doctors. Cigarette smoking, excessive alcohol intake, and a variety of prescription medications also lead to diminished sexual performance. Among women, poor health and absence of a partner are major factors that reduce sexual activity (Gott & Hinchliff, 2003; Lindau et al., 2007). Because the sex ratio increasingly favors females, aging heterosexual women have fewer and fewer opportunities for sexual encounters. Older adults who lack partners for an extended time tend to drift into a state of sexual disinterest.

In most tribal and village cultures, sexual activity among elders is expected and is common for both men and women until very late life (Winn & Newton, 1982). But in Western nations, sex in old age often meets with disapproval. Educational programs informing older adults about normal, age-related changes in sexual functioning and fostering a view of sex as extending throughout adulthood promote positive sexual attitudes (Hillman & Stricker, 1994). In nursing homes, education for caregivers is vital for ensuring residents' rights to privacy and other living conditions that permit sexual expression (Hajjar & Kamel, 2004).

Physical Disabilities

TAKE A MOMENT... Compare the death rates shown in Figure 17.5 with those in Figure 15.2 on page 510. You will see that illness and disability climb as the end of the lifespan approaches. Cardiovascular disease and cancer remain the leading causes of death, increasing dramatically from mid- to late life. As before, death rates from cardiovascular disease and cancer are higher for men than for women, although the sex difference declines with advancing age (U.S. Census Bureau, 2009b).

The third most common killer among the aged is *stroke*—the only leading cause that is more prevalent among women. It occurs when a blood clot blocks a blood vessel or a blood vessel hemorrhages in the brain, causing damage to brain tissue. Stroke is a major cause of late-life disability and, after age 75, death. Respiratory diseases also rise sharply with age. Among them is *emphysema,* caused by extreme loss of elasticity in lung tissue, which results in serious breathing difficulty. Although a few cases of emphysema are inherited, most result from long-term cigarette smoking. In addition, as the longest-lived people escape chronic diseases or weaken because of them, the immune system eventually encounters an infection it cannot fight. Consequently, many of the very old succumb to one of the more than 50 lung inflammations classified as *pneumonia.* Doctors recommend that people age 65 and older be vaccinated against the most common type.

Other diseases are less frequent killers, but they limit older adults' ability to live fully and independently. We have already noted the increase after age 65 in macular degeneration, which severely impairs vision and leads to blindness (see page 568). Osteoporosis, discussed in Chapter 15, continues to rise in late adulthood; recall that it affects the majority of men and women after age 70. Yet another bone disorder—*arthritis*—adds to the physical limitations of many elders. And *type 2 diabetes* and *unintentional injuries* also multiply in late adulthood. In the following sections, we take up these last three conditions.

Finally, an important point must be kept in mind as we discuss physical and mental disabilities of late adulthood: The fact that these conditions are *related to age* does not mean that they are *entirely caused by aging.* To clarify this distinction, experts distinguish between **primary aging** (another term for *biological aging*), or genetically influenced declines that affect all members of our species and take place even in the context of overall good health, and **secondary aging,** declines due to hereditary defects and negative environmental influences, such as poor diet, lack of exercise, disease, substance abuse, environmental pollution, and psychological stress.

Throughout this book, we have seen that it is difficult to distinguish primary from secondary aging. Undoubtedly you have, at one time or another, encountered a *frail elder*—a person of extreme infirmity who displays wasted muscle mass and strength, weight loss, severe mobility problems, and perhaps cognitive impairment. **Frailty** involves weakened functioning of diverse organs and body systems, which profoundly interferes with everyday competence and leaves the older adult highly vulnerable in the face of an infection, extremely hot or cold weather, or an injury (Walston et al., 2006). Although primary aging contributes to frailty, researchers agree that secondary aging plays a larger role, through genetic disorders, unhealthy lifestyle, and chronic disease (Bergman et al., 2007; Hogan, MacKnight, & Bergman, 2003). The serious conditions we are about to discuss are major sources of frailty in the elderly.

■ **ARTHRITIS.** Beginning in her fifties, Ruth felt a slight morning stiffness in her neck, back, hips, and knees. In her sixties, she developed bony lumps on the end joints of her fingers. As the years passed, she experienced periodic joint swelling and some loss of flexibility—changes that affected her ability to move quickly and easily.

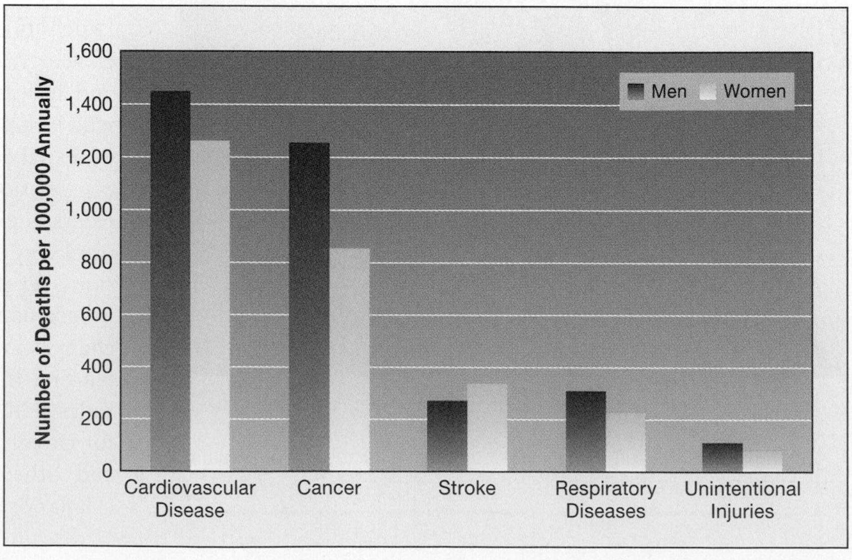

■ **FIGURE 17.5** ■ **Leading causes of death among people age 65 and older in the United States.** In late adulthood, cardiovascular disease is the leading cause of death, followed by cancer. Stroke (unique in being more prevalent among women), respiratory diseases, and unintentional injuries also claim the lives of many elders. (Adapted from U.S. Census Bureau, 2009b.)

© MONIKA GRAFF/THE IMAGE WORKS

This frail elder, working with a physical therapist, suffers from wasted muscle mass and strength, weight loss, severe mobility problems, and perhaps cognitive impairment. Although biological aging contributes to his frailty, secondary aging—through genetic disorders, unhealthy lifestyle, and chronic disease—plays a larger role.

Arthritis, a condition of inflamed, painful, stiff, and sometimes swollen joints and muscles, becomes more common in late adulthood. It occurs in several forms. Ruth has **osteoarthritis,** the most common type, which involves deteriorating cartilage on the ends of bones of frequently used joints. Otherwise known as "wear-and-tear arthritis" or "degenerative joint disease," it is one of the few age-related disabilities in which years of use make a difference. Although a genetic proneness seems to exist, the disease usually does not appear until the forties or fifties. In frequently used joints, cartilage on the ends of the bones, which reduces friction during movement, gradually deteriorates. Or obesity places abnormal pressure on the joints and damages cartilage. Almost all older adults show some osteoarthritis on X-rays, although wide individual differences in severity exist (Fajardo & Di Cesare, 2005).

Unlike osteoarthritis, which is limited to certain joints, **rheumatoid arthritis** involves the whole body. An autoimmune response leads to inflammation of connective tissue, particularly the membranes that line the joints, resulting in overall stiffness, inflammation, and aching. Tissue in the cartilage tends to grow, damaging surrounding ligaments, muscles, and bones. The result is deformed joints and often serious loss of mobility. Sometimes other organs, such as the heart and lungs, are affected. Worldwide, about 2 percent of older adults have rheumatoid arthritis (Rasch et al., 2003).

Overall, disability due to arthritis affects 45 percent of U.S. men over age 65 and rises modestly with age. Among women, the incidence is higher and increases sharply with age: About 50 percent of 65- to 84-year-olds and 70 percent of those over age 85 are affected (U.S. Census Bureau, 2009b). Although rheumatoid arthritis can strike at any age, it rises after age 60. Twin studies support a strong hereditary contribution. Presence of certain genes heightens disease risk, possibly by triggering a late-life defect in the immune system (Turesson & Matteson, 2006). However, identical twins differ widely in disease severity, indicating that environment makes a difference. So far, cigarette smoking is the only confirmed lifestyle influence (Klareskog et al., 2006). Early treatment with powerful anti-inflammatory medications helps slow the course of the disease.

Managing arthritis requires a balance of rest when the disease flares, pain relief, and physical activity involving gentle stretching of all muscles to maintain mobility. Twice a week, 84-year-old Ruth attended a water-based exercise class. Within two months, her symptoms lessened, and she no longer needed a walker (Kettunen & Kujala, 2004). In obese people, weight loss is helpful. Although osteoarthritis responds to these interventions more easily than rheumatoid arthritis, the course of each varies greatly. With proper analgesic medication, joint protection, and lifestyle changes, many people with either form of the illness lead long, productive lives. If hip or knee joints are badly damaged or deformed, they can be surgically rebuilt or replaced with plastic or metal devices.

■ **DIABETES.** After a meal, the body breaks down the food, releasing glucose (the primary energy source for cell activity) into the bloodstream. Insulin, produced by the pancreas, keeps the blood concentration of glucose within set limits by stimulating muscle and fat cells to absorb it. When this balance system fails, either because not enough insulin is produced or because body cells become insensitive to it, *type 2 diabetes* (otherwise known as *diabetes mellitus*) results. Over time, abnormally high blood glucose damages the blood vessels, increasing the risk of stroke, heart attack, circulatory problems in the legs, and injury to the eyes, kidneys, and nerves.

Excessive blood glucose also reduces blood flow to the hippocampus, a brain structure that plays an important role in memory (see page 218 in Chapter 7) (Wu et al., 2008). In several longitudinal studies, diabetes was associated with more rapid cognitive declines in the elderly and an elevated risk of Alzheimer's disease—an association we will soon revisit when we take up Alzheimer's (Arvanitakis et al., 2004; Logroscino, Kang, & Grodstein, 2004; Yaffe et al., 2004).

From middle to late adulthood, the incidence of type 2 diabetes doubles; it affects 10 percent of the elderly in the United States (U.S. Census Bureau, 2009b). Diabetes runs in families, suggesting that heredity is involved. But inactivity and abdominal fat deposits greatly increase the risk. Higher rates of type 2 diabetes are found among African-American, Mexican-American, and Native-American minorities for both genetic and environmental reasons, including high-fat diets and obesity associated with poverty.

Treating type 2 diabetes requires lifestyle changes, including a carefully controlled diet, regular exercise, and weight loss

(Meneilly, 2006). By promoting glucose absorption and reducing abdominal fat, physical activity lessens disease symptoms.

UNINTENTIONAL INJURIES. At age 65 and older, the death rate from unintentional injuries is at an all-time high—more than twice as great as in adolescence and early adulthood. Motor vehicle collisions and falls are largely responsible.

Motor Vehicle Accidents. Motor vehicle collisions account for only one-fourth of injury mortality in late life, compared with one-half in middle adulthood. But a look at individual drivers tells a different story. Older adults have higher rates of traffic violations, accidents, and fatalities per mile driven than any other age group, with the exception of drivers under age 25. The high rate of injury persists, even though many elders, especially women, limit their driving after noticing that their ability to drive safely is slipping. Deaths due to injuries—motor vehicle and otherwise—continue to be much higher for men than for women in late adulthood (Silvi, 2004; U.S. Census Bureau, 2009b).

Recall that visual declines led Walt to have difficulty seeing the dashboard and identifying pedestrians at night. The greater elders' visual processing difficulties, the higher their rate of moving violations and crashes (Wood, 2002). Compared with young drivers, the elderly are less likely to drive quickly and recklessly but more likely to fail to heed signs, yield the right of way, and turn appropriately. They often try to compensate for their difficulties by being more cautious. Slowed reaction time and indecisiveness pose hazards, too. In Chapter 15, we noted that with age, adults find it harder to attend selectively, engage in two activities at once, and switch back and forth between tasks—skills essential for safe driving. Yet elders' speed of response slows dramatically in the face of such demands (Makishita & Matsunaga, 2008). Hence, they are at high risk for collisions at busy intersections and in other complex traffic situations.

Nevertheless, older adults usually try to drive as long as possible. Giving up driving results in loss of freedom, control over one's life, and self-esteem (Wood, 2002). Specially trained driver rehabilitation consultants—affiliated with hospitals, drivers licensing agencies, or U.S. Area Agencies on Aging (see page 68 in Chapter 2)—can help assess an elder's capacity to continue driving, provide driver retraining, or counsel elders to retire from driving and to arrange other transportation options.

The elderly also make up more than 30 percent of all pedestrian deaths (U.S. Census Bureau, 2009b). Confusing intersections, especially crossing signals that do not allow older people enough time to get to the other side of the street, are often involved.

Falls. One day, Ruth fell down the basement steps and lay there with a broken ankle until Walt arrived home an hour later. Ruth's tumble represents the leading type of accident among the elderly. About 30 percent of adults over age 65 and 50 percent over age 80 have experienced a fall within the last year. Declines in vision, hearing, mobility, muscle strength, and cognitive functioning; depressed mood; use of medications that affect mental processing; and development of certain chronic illnesses (such as arthritis)—all of which make it harder to avoid hazards and keep one's balance—increase the risk of falling in late adulthood. The more of these factors that are present, the greater the risk of falling (Rubenstein, Stevens, & Scott, 2008).

Because of weakened bones and difficulty breaking a fall, serious injury results about 10 percent of the time. Among the most common is hip fracture. It increases twentyfold from age 65 to 85 and is associated with a 20 percent increase in mortality. Of those who survive, half never regain the ability to walk without assistance (U.S. Department of Health and Human Services, 2008i).

Falling can also impair health indirectly, by promoting fear of falling. Almost half of older adults who have fallen admit that they purposefully avoid activities because they are afraid of falling again (Health and Disability Research Institute, 2006). In this way, a fall can limit mobility and social contact, undermining both physical and psychological well-being. Although an active lifestyle may expose the elderly to more situations that can cause a fall, the health benefits of activity far outweigh the risk of serious injury due to falling.

Preventing Unintentional Injuries. Many steps can be taken to reduce unintentional injury in late adulthood. Designing motor vehicles and street signs to accommodate the visual needs of the elderly is a goal for the future. Meanwhile, training that enhances visual and cognitive skills essential for safe driving and that helps older adults avoid high-risk situations (such as busy intersections and rush hour) can save lives.

Similarly, efforts to prevent falls must address risks within the person and the environment—through corrective eyewear, strength and balance training, and improved safety in homes and communities. Applying What We Know on the following page summarizes ways to protect the elderly from injury.

Mental Disabilities

Normal age-related cell death in the brain, described earlier, does not lead to loss of ability to engage in everyday activities. But when cell death and structural and chemical abnormalities are profound, serious deterioration of mental and motor functions occurs.

Dementia refers to a set of disorders occurring almost entirely in old age in which many aspects of thought and behavior are so impaired that everyday activities are disrupted. Dementia strikes 13 percent of adults over age 65, both sexes about equally. Approximately 1 percent of people in their sixties are affected; the rate increases with age, rising sharply after age 80 until it reaches about 50 percent after age 85—trends that apply to the United States and other Western nations (Berr, Wancata, & Ritchie, 2005; Matthews & Brayne, 2005; Plassman et al., 2007). Although dementia rates are similar across most ethnic groups, African Americans have an elevated incidence—a difference explained by associated risk factors, not by race, as we will see shortly (Alzheimer's Association, 2009).

Applying What We Know

Preventing Unintentional Injury in Late Adulthood

Suggestion	Description
Motor Vehicle Collisions and Pedestrian Accidents	
Modify driving behavior in accord with visual and other limitations.	Drive fewer miles; reduce or eliminate driving during rush hour, at night, through busy intersections, or in bad weather.
Modify pedestrian behavior in accord with visual and other limitations.	Wear light-colored clothing at night; allow extra time to cross streets; walk with a companion.
Attend training classes for older drivers; if not available, press for them in your community.	Practice tracking vehicles and pedestrians in dim light, judging vehicle speed, and reading signs and dashboard displays; review rules of the road.
Falls	
Schedule regular medical checkups.	Have eye exams to ensure that corrective lenses are up to date, and physical exams to identify health risks that increase the chances of falling; do a review of medications for effects on attention and coordination.
Engage in regular exercise.	Take part in strength and balance training to promote coordination and counteract fear of falling.
Use safe footwear and necessary walking aids.	Wear low-heeled shoes with a firm sole. Use canes and walkers to compensate for poor balance and unsteady gait.
Improve safety of the living environment.	Install extra lighting in dim areas, such as entrances, hallways, and staircases; put handrails in hallways and grab bars in bathrooms; make sure loose rugs are secured to floor or moved and that furniture and other objects are arranged so they are not obstacles.
Be alert, and plan ahead in risky situations.	Watch for slippery pavement; carry a flashlight at night; allow extra time to cross streets; become familiar with new settings before moving about freely.

Sources: Menant et al., 2008; Rubenstein & Josephson, 2006.
Note: Consult the National Resource Center for Safe Aging, *www.safeaging.org,* for a wealth of information on senior safety.

About a dozen types of dementia have been identified. Some are reversible with proper treatment, but most are irreversible and incurable. A few forms, such as Parkinson's disease,[1] involve deterioration in subcortical brain regions (primitive structures below the cortex) that often extends to the cerebral cortex and, in many instances, results in brain abnormalities resembling Alzheimer's disease. Some researchers believe that Parkinson's and Alzheimer's are related (Gallardo, Schlüter, & Südhoff, 2008). But in the large majority of dementia cases, subcortical brain regions are intact, and progressive damage occurs only to the cerebral cortex. *Cortical dementia* comes in two varieties: Alzheimer's disease and cerebrovascular dementia.

ALZHEIMER'S DISEASE. When Ruth took 79-year-old Ida to the ballet, an occasion the two sisters anticipated eagerly each year, she noticed a change in Ida's behavior. Ida, who had forgotten the engagement, reacted angrily when Ruth arrived unannounced at her door. Driving to the theater, which was in a familiar part of town, Ida got lost—all the while insisting that she knew the way perfectly well. As the lights dimmed and the music began, Ida talked loudly and dug noisily in her purse.

"Shhhhhh," responded a dozen voices from surrounding seats.

"It's just the music!" Ida snapped at full volume. "You can talk all you want until the dancing starts." Ruth was astonished and embarrassed at the behavior of her once socially sensitive sister.

Six months later, Ida was diagnosed with **Alzheimer's disease,** the most common form of dementia, in which structural and chemical brain deterioration is associated with gradual loss of many aspects of thought and behavior. Alzheimer's accounts for 60 percent of all dementia cases and, at older ages, for an even higher percentage. Approximately 8 to 10 percent of people over age 65—about 5.1 million Americans—have the disorder. Of those over age 85, close to 45 percent are affected.

[1]In Parkinson's disease, neurons in the part of the brain that controls muscle movements deteriorate. Symptoms include tremors, shuffling gait, loss of facial expression, rigidity of limbs, difficulty maintaining balance, and stooped posture.

In 2030, when all baby boomers will have reached late adulthood, the number of Americans with Alzheimer's is expected to rise to 7.7 million—an increase of more than 50 percent. About 5 percent of all deaths among the elderly involve Alzheimer's, making it a significant cause of late-life mortality (Alzheimer's Association, 2009).

Symptoms and Course of the Disease. The earliest symptoms are often severe memory problems—forgetting names, dates, appointments, familiar routes of travel, or the need to turn off the kitchen stove. At first, recent memory is most impaired, but as serious disorientation sets in, recall of distant events and such basic facts as time, date, and place evaporates. Faulty judgment puts the person in danger. For example, Ida insisted on driving after she was no longer competent to do so. Personality changes occur—loss of spontaneity and sparkle, anxiety in response to uncertainties created by mental problems, aggressive outbursts, reduced initiative, and social withdrawal. Depression often appears in the early phase of Alzheimer's and other forms of dementia and seems to be part of the disease process (Yaari & Corey-Bloom, 2007; Zubenko et al., 2003). However, depression may worsen as the older adult reacts to disturbing mental changes.

As the disease progresses, skilled and purposeful movements disintegrate. When Ruth took Ida into her home, she had to help her dress, bathe, eat, brush her teeth, and (eventually) walk and use the bathroom. Ida's sleep was disrupted by delusions and imaginary fears. She often awoke in the night and banged on the wall, insisting that it was dinnertime, or cried out that someone was choking her. Over time, Ida lost the ability to comprehend and produce speech. And when her brain ceased to process information, she could no longer recognize objects and familiar people. In the final months, Ida became increasingly vulnerable to infections, lapsed into a coma, and died.

The course of Alzheimer's varies greatly, from a year to as long as 15 years. The average life expectancy for a 70-year-old man with the disease is about 4½ years, for a 70-year-old woman about 8 years (Larson et al., 2004).

Brain Deterioration. A diagnosis of Alzheimer's disease is made through exclusion, after ruling out other causes of dementia by a physical examination and psychological testing—an approach that is more than 90 percent accurate. To confirm Alzheimer's, doctors inspect the brain after death for a set of abnormalities that either cause or result from the disease (Yaari & Corey-Bloom, 2007). In nearly 90 percent of cases, however, brain-imaging techniques (MRI and PET), which yield three-dimensional pictures of brain volume and activity, predict whether elders who do not yet show symptoms will receive an after-death confirmation of Alzheimer's (Mosconi et al., 2007; Vitali et al., 2008). Researchers are also tracking changes in the chemical makeup of the blood and cerebrospinal fluid to see which ones predict Alzheimer's (Hampel et al., 2008). These procedures offer hope of very early diagnosis, opening the door to more successful interventions.

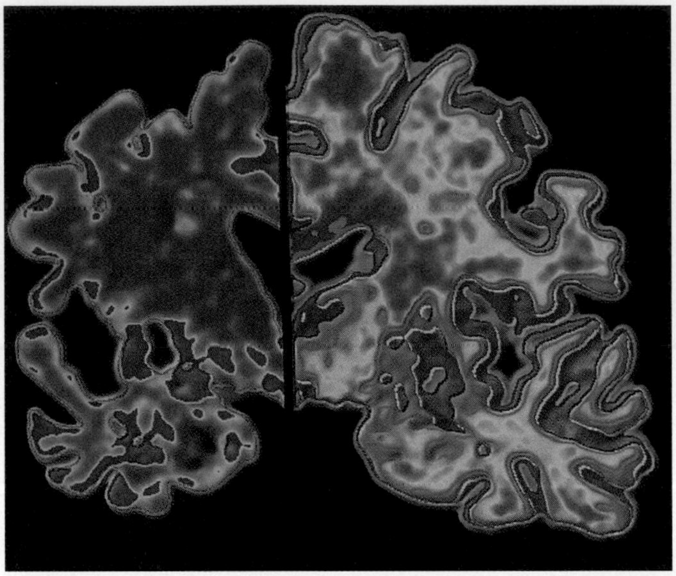

Computer images compare a brain scan of an Alzheimer's patient (left) with one of a healthy older adult (right). The Alzheimer's brain is shrunken, due to massive degeneration and death of neurons. Activity and blood flow (marked by yellow and green coding in the right scan) are also greatly reduced in the Alzheimer's brain.

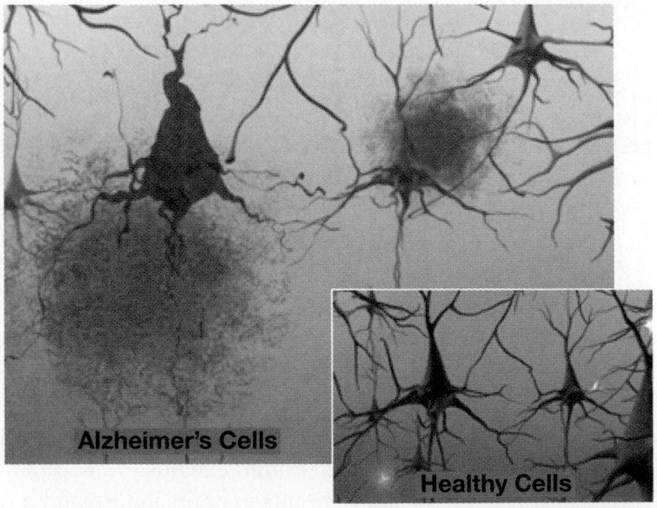

An image of tissue in the Alzheimer's brain (left) reveals amyloid plaques between neurons, dead and dying neurons containing neurofibrillary tangles, and far fewer neurons and synapses than in the healthy brain (right).

Two major structural changes in the cerebral cortex, especially in memory and reasoning areas, are associated with Alzheimer's. Inside neurons, **neurofibrillary tangles** appear—bundles of twisted threads that are the product of collapsed neural structures and that contain abnormal forms of a protein called *tau.* Outside neurons, **amyloid plaques,** dense deposits of a deteriorated protein called *amyloid,* surrounded by clumps of dead nerve and glial cells, develop. Although some neurofibrillary tangles and amyloid plaques are present in the brains of normal middle-aged and older people and increase with age, they are far more abundant in Alzheimer's victims.

Researchers once thought that plaques contributed to the neuronal damage of Alzheimer's. But recent findings suggest that they actually reflect the brain's effort to get harmful amyloid away from neurons. Instead, a major culprit is abnormal breakdown of amyloid remaining *within* neurons (Cleary et al., 2005; National Institute on Aging, 2008). In both Alzheimer's disease and Parkinson's disease, disruptions occur in a key neuronal structure responsible for chopping up and disposing of abnormal proteins (Ding et al., 2004). These damaged proteins (including amyloid) build to toxic levels, causing cell damage and death.

A major thrust of current research is understanding exactly how amyloid damages neurons, so treatments can be developed to slow or block this process. Several studies suggest that amyloid causes synapses—tiny gaps between neurons essential for neuronal communication—to malfunction (Lacor et al., 2007). Amyloid also induces heightened, abnormal electrical activity throughout the brain, contributing to neural network malfunctioning (Palop et al., 2007). And new evidence suggests that abnormal tau in neurofibrillary tangles facilitates amyloid-induced damage (Roberson et al., 2007)

As synapses deteriorate, levels of neurotransmitters—vital for sustaining neuronal communication—decline, neurons die in massive numbers, and brain volume shrinks. Destruction of neurons that release the neurotransmitter acetylcholine, involved in transporting messages between distant brain regions, further disrupts neuronal networks. As a result, many complex functions, including perception, memory, reasoning, and judgment, are impaired. A drop in serotonin, a neurotransmitter that regulates arousal and mood, may contribute to sleep disturbances, aggressive outbursts, and depression (Lanctot et al., 2002; Mintzer, 2001).

Risk Factors. Alzheimer's disease comes in two types: *familial,* which runs in families, and *sporadic,* which has no obvious family history. Familial Alzheimer's generally has an early onset (before age 65) and progresses more rapidly than the later-appearing sporadic type. Researchers have identified genes on chromosomes 1, 14, and 21, involved in generation of harmful amyloid, that are linked to familial Alzheimer's. In each case, the abnormal gene is dominant; if it is present in only one of the pair of genes inherited from parents, the person will develop early-onset Alzheimer's (Ertekin-Tanner, 2007; National Institute on Aging, 2008). Recall that chromosome 21 is involved in Down syndrome. Individuals with this chromosomal disorder who live past age 40 almost always have the brain abnormalities and symptoms of Alzheimer's.

Heredity plays a different role in sporadic Alzheimer's, through somatic mutation. About half of people with this form of the disease have an abnormal gene on chromosome 19, which results in excess levels of *ApoE4,* a blood protein that carries cholesterol throughout the body. Researchers believe that a high blood concentration of ApoE4 affects the expression of a gene involved in regulating insulin. Deficient insulin and resulting glucose buildup in the bloodstream (conditions that, when extreme, lead to diabetes) are linked to brain damage, especially in areas regulating memory, and to abnormally high buildup of amyloid in brain tissue (National Institute on Aging, 2008; Neumann et al., 2008). In line with these findings, elders with diabetes have a 65 percent increased risk of developing Alzheimer's (Arvanitakis et al., 2004).

At present, the abnormal ApoE4 gene is the most commonly known risk factor for sporadic Alzheimer's. But genetic testing has revealed other genes that seem to make an equal or greater contribution. For example, in older adults with Alzheimer's, genes involved in clearing amyloid from neurons often are altered, enabling excessive amyloid buildup (Weeraratna et al., 2007).

Nevertheless, many sporadic Alzheimer's victims show no currently known genetic marker, and some individuals with the ApoE4 gene do not develop the disease. Evidence is increasing for the role of a variety of other factors in susceptibility to Alzheimer's, including excess dietary fat, physical inactivity, overweight and obesity, chronic psychological stress, cardiovascular disease, stroke, and (as just noted) diabetes (Kivipelto et al., 2008; Pasinetti & Eberstein, 2008; Whitmer et al., 2007, Wilson et al., 2006). Head injury, by accelerating deterioration of amyloid, may also increase Alzheimer's risk, especially among people with the ApoE4 gene (Jellinger, 2004). The age-related rise in free radicals can also trigger toxic alterations in amyloid (Siegel et al., 2007).

Still, some older adults with an abundance of amyloid in their brains never develop Alzheimer's (Bennett et al., 2006a; Mintun et al., 2006; Rowe et al., 2007). The disease probably results from different combinations of genetic and environmental factors, each leading to a somewhat different course of the disease. The high incidence of Alzheimer's and other forms of dementia among African-American elderly illustrates the complexity of potential causes.

Compared with African Americans, Yoruba village dwellers of Nigeria show a much lower Alzheimer's incidence and no association between the ApoE4 gene and the disease (Gureje et al., 2006). Some investigators speculate that intermarriage with Caucasians heightened genetic risk among African Americans and that environmental factors translated that risk into reality (Hendrie, 2001). Whereas the Yoruba of Nigeria eat a low-fat diet, the African-American diet is high in fat. Eating fatty foods may increase the chances that the ApoE4 gene will lead to Alzheimer's. And even for Yoruba and African Americans without the ApoE4 gene, a high-fat diet is risky. The more fat consumed and the higher the blood level of "bad" cholesterol (low-density lipoproteins), the greater the incidence of Alzheimer's (Hall et al., 2006).

Protective Factors. Researchers are testing both drug and nondrug approaches to preventing or slowing the progress of

SOCIAL ISSUES

Interventions for Caregivers of Elders with Dementia

Margaret, wife and caregiver of a 71-year-old Alzheimer's patient, sent a desperate plea to an advice columnist at her local newspaper: "My husband can't feed or bathe himself, or speak to anyone or ask for assistance. I must constantly anticipate his needs and try to meet them. Please help me. I'm at the end of my rope."

The effects of Alzheimer's disease are devastating not just to elderly victims but also to family members who provide care with little or no outside assistance. Caregiving under these conditions has been called the "36-hour day" because of its constant demands. Although the majority of home caregivers are middle-aged, an estimated 15 to 25 percent are elders caring for a spouse or an aging parent. One-third of them are in poor health themselves, yet the number of hours dedicated to caregiving increases with the age of the caregiver (Chappell et al., 2003; Family Caregiver Alliance, 2005). Family members who exceed their caregiving capacities suffer greatly in physical and mental health and are at risk for early mortality (Schultz & Beach, 1999; Sörensen & Pinquart, 2005). Severity of cognitive impairments and behavior problems in care recipients is a strong predictor of weakening caregiver health.

Most communities offer interventions designed to support family caregivers, but these need to be expanded and made more cost-effective. Those that work best begin before caregivers become overwhelmed and address multiple needs: knowledge, coping strategies, caregiving skills, and respite.

© ALAN ODDIE/PHOTOEDIT

This daughter cares for her father, who has Alzheimer's disease. Although the task has compensating rewards, it is physically demanding and emotionally draining. A great need exists for interventions that support caregivers.

Knowledge

Virtually all interventions try to enhance knowledge about the disease, caregiving challenges, and available community assistance. Knowledge is usually delivered through classes, but websites with wide-ranging information on caregiving, and online message boards and chat rooms through which caregivers can share information, also exist. Gains in knowledge, however, must be combined with other approaches to improve caregivers' well-being.

Coping Strategies

Many interventions teach caregivers everyday problem-solving strategies for managing the dependent elder's behavior, along with techniques for dealing with their own negative thoughts and feelings, such as resentment about having to provide constant care. Modes of delivery include support groups, individual therapy, and "coping with frustration" classes. All yield improvements in caregivers'

Alzheimer's. Although hormone therapy was previously believed to offer women protection against Alzheimer's, rigorously designed research yielded contrary findings (see Chapter 15, page 506). Vitamins B and E and folate supplements, also once regarded as protective, do not reduce the incidence of the disease or its symptoms (see page 578). Similarly, anti-inflammatory drugs, administered to reduce inflammation of brain tissue caused by amyloid and other abnormalities, did not delay progression of the disease in carefully designed experiments (National Institute on Aging, 2005).

But a "Mediterranean diet" emphasizing fish, unsaturated fat (olive oil), and moderate consumption of red wine is linked to a 13 percent reduced incidence of Alzheimer's disease, to slower disease progression in diagnosed individuals, and also to a reduction in cerebrovascular dementia (which we will turn to next) (Scarmeas et al., 2007; Sofi et al., 2008). These foods contain fatty acids and other substances that help maintain the cardiovascular system, and they also promote the health of neural structures and neurotransmitter activity.

Education and an active lifestyle are beneficial as well. The rate of Alzheimer's is reduced by more than half in elders with higher education, though this protective effect is not as great for those with the ApoE4 gene (Qiu et al., 2001; Seeman et al., 2005). Some researchers speculate that education leads to more synaptic connections, which act as a *cognitive reserve,* giving the aging brain greater tolerance for injury before it crosses the threshold into mental disability. In support of this view, compared to their less educated counterparts, highly educated elders show a faster rate of decline following an Alzheimer's diagnosis, suggesting that they show symptoms only after very advanced brain deterioration (Andel et al., 2006; Hall et al., 2007). Late-life engagement in social and leisure activities also reduces the risk of Alzheimer's and of dementia in general, perhaps by stimulating synaptic growth (Bennett et al., 2006b; Verghese et al., 2003).

adjustment and in patients' disturbing behaviors, both immediately and in follow-ups more than a year later (Selwood et al., 2007). Individual approaches are most effective because assistance can be tailored to the specific caregiver–patient situation.

Caregiving Skills

Caregivers benefit from lessons in how to communicate with elders who can no longer express thoughts and emotions clearly and handle everyday tasks—for example, sustaining good eye contact to convey interest and caring; speaking slowly, with short, simple words; using gestures to reinforce meaning; waiting patiently for a response; refraining from interrupting, correcting, and criticizing; distracting rather than scolding when the person repeatedly asks the same question; and introducing pleasant activities, such as music and slow-paced children's TV programs, that relieve agitation (Alzheimer's Association, 2005). Interventions that teach communication skills through active practice reduce elders' troublesome behavior and, as a result, lessen caregivers' distress and boost their sense of self-efficacy (Done & Thomas, 2001; Irvine, Ary, & Bourgeois, 2003).

Respite

Although caregivers usually say that *respite*—time away from providing care—is the assistance they most desire, they may be reluctant to use available services, such as adult day care or temporary placement in a care facility, because of cost, worries about the elder's adjustment, and guilt. Yet respite at least twice a week for several hours improves physical and mental health by permitting caregivers to maintain friendships, engage in enjoyable activities, and sustain a balanced life (Jeon, Brodaty, & Chesterson, 2005; Lund, Wright, & Caserta, 2005).

Recognizing caregivers' need for relief from unrelenting in-home care, one group of researchers devised a unique tool called Video Respite—a series of videotapes suited to the interests of Alzheimer's patients that provide caregivers with a half-hour to an hour break. On each tape, a professional actor conducts a friendly, slow-paced, simple conversation about familiar experiences, people, and objects, pausing occasionally for the impaired elder to respond. Evaluations show that the videos not only capture the attention of people with Alzheimer's but also reduce problem behaviors, such as wandering, agitation, repeated questioning, and aggression (Lund et al., 1995).

No single magic bullet exists for eliminating caregiver stress. But multifaceted interventions that begin early in the caregiving process, that continue for many weeks or months, and that are tailored to caregivers' individual needs make a substantial difference in caregivers' lives. And they usually delay placement of dementia patients in institutions as well.

The Resources for Enhancing Alzheimer's Caregiver Health (REACH) initiative is an evaluation of nine "active" intervention programs, each including some or all of the ingredients just described, versus five "passive" interventions providing only information and referral to community agencies. Among more than 1,200 participating caregivers, those receiving six months of active intervention declined more in self-reported burden. And one program providing family therapy in the home—through a telephone system facilitating frequent communication among therapist, caregiver, family members, and other support systems—substantially reduced caregiver depressive symptoms (Gitlin et al., 2003; Schultz et al., 2003). Caregivers with greater care responsibility—women versus men, lower-SES versus higher-SES, spouses versus nonspouses—benefited most from active intervention. In an additional evaluation with more than 600 participants, REACH active intervention programs enhanced quality of life among caregivers of diverse ethnicities—African American, Caucasian, and Hispanic (Belle et al., 2006).

Finally, persistence, intensity, and variety of physical activity are associated with decreased risk for Alzheimer's and cerebrovascular dementia, but again, benefits are limited for elders with the ApoE4 gene (Podewils et al., 2005). In two studies, exercising regularly in midlife predicted reduced late-life dementia, after many other dementia-linked lifestyle factors were controlled (Andel et al., 2008; Rovio et al., 2005). Beginning regular exercise in late life is also protective (Larson et al., 2006; van Gelder et al., 2004). In one investigation, older adults with mild cognitive impairment and therefore judged to be at risk for Alzheimer's were randomly assigned to either a 24-week home-based physical activity program or to a usual home-care control group (Lautenschlager et al., 2008). At a six-month follow-up, those experiencing the intervention continued to engage in regular exercise and showed slight cognitive improvement, whereas controls had declined in cognitive functioning.

Helping Alzheimer's Victims and Their Caregivers. As Ida's Alzheimer's worsened, the doctor prescribed a mild sedative and an antidepressant to help control her behavior. Drugs that increase levels of the neurotransmitters acetylcholine and serotonin show promise in limiting challenging dementia symptoms—especially agitation and disruptive behaviors, which are particularly stressful for caregivers (National Institute on Aging, 2008).

But with no cure available, family interventions ensure the best adjustment possible for the Alzheimer's victim, spouse, and other relatives. Dementia caregivers devote substantially more time to caregiving and experience more stress than do people caring for elders with physical disabilities (Alzheimer's Association, 2009). They need assistance and encouragement from extended-family members, friends, and community agencies. The Social Issues box above describes a variety of helpful interventions for family caregivers. In addition to these strategies, avoiding dramatic changes in living conditions, such as moving to a new location, rearranging furniture, or modifying daily routines, helps elders with Alzheimer's disease feel as secure as possible in a cognitive world that is gradually disintegrating.

■ CEREBROVASCULAR DEMENTIA. In **cerebrovascular dementia,** a series of strokes leaves areas of dead brain cells, producing step-by-step degeneration of mental ability, with each step occurring abruptly after a stroke. About 20 percent of all cases of dementia in Western nations are cerebrovascular, and about 10 percent are due to a combination of Alzheimer's and repeated strokes (Knopman, 2006).

Cerebrovascular dementia results from a combination of genetic and environmental forces. The effects of heredity are indirect, through high blood pressure, cardiovascular disease, and diabetes, each of which increases the risk of stroke. And environmental influences—including cigarette smoking, heavy alcohol use, high salt intake, very low dietary protein, obesity, inactivity, and psychological stress—also heighten stroke risk (Román, 2003).

Because of their susceptibility to cardiovascular disease, more men than women have cerebrovascular dementia by their late sixties. Women are not at great risk until after age 75 (Sachdev, Brodaty, & Looi, 1999). The disease also varies among countries. For example, deaths due to stroke are high in Japan. Although a low-fat diet reduces Japanese adults' risk of cardiovascular disease, high intake of alcohol and salt and a diet very low in animal protein increase the risk of stroke. As Japanese consumption of alcohol and salt declined and intake of meat rose in recent decades, rates of cerebrovascular dementia and stroke-caused deaths dropped (Goldman & Takahashi, 1996; Jellinger, 2008). However, they remain higher than in other developed nations.

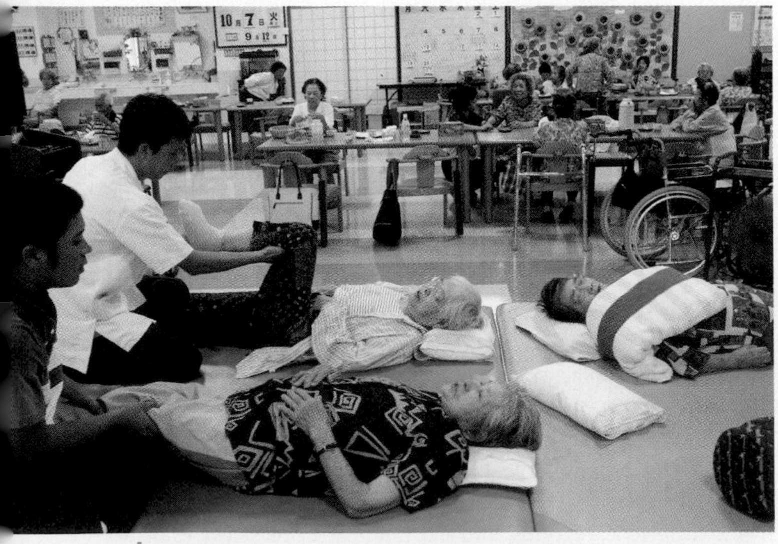

In this Japanese rehabilitation center, staff provide care for elderly stroke patients. High intake of alcohol and salt, coupled with low intake of animal protein, increases the risk of stroke among the Japanese.

Although Japan presents a unique, contradictory picture (there, cardiovascular disease is low, and stroke is high), in most cases cerebrovascular dementia is caused by atherosclerosis. Prevention is the only effective way to stop the disease. The incidence of cerebrovascular dementia has dropped in the last two decades, largely as a result of the decline in heart disease and more effective stroke prevention methods (Manton, Gu, & Ukraintseva, 2005; U.S. Department of Health and Human Services, 2009a). Signs that a stroke might be coming are weakness, tingling, or numbness in an arm, a leg, or the face; sudden vision loss or double vision; speech difficulty; and severe dizziness and imbalance. Doctors may prescribe drugs to reduce the tendency of the blood to clot. Once strokes occur, paralysis and loss of speech, vision, coordination, memory, and other mental abilities are common.

■ MISDIAGNOSED AND REVERSIBLE DEMENTIA. Careful diagnosis of dementia is crucial because other disorders can be mistaken for it. And some forms of dementia can be treated and a few reversed.

Depression is the disorder most often misdiagnosed as dementia. The depressed (but not demented) older adult is likely to exaggerate his or her mental difficulties, whereas the demented person minimizes them and is not fully aware of cognitive declines. About 1 to 2 percent of people over age 65 are severely depressed, and another 2 percent are moderately depressed—rates lower than those for young and middle-aged adults (Nordhus, 2008). As we will see in Chapter 18, however, depression rises with age. It is often related to physical illness and pain and can lead to cognitive deterioration. As at younger ages, the support of family members and friends, antidepressant medication, and individual, family, and group therapy can help relieve depression. However, U.S. older adults often do not receive the mental health services they need—partly because Medicare offers reduced coverage for treating mental health problems and partly because doctors rarely refer elders to mental health specialists (Knight et al., 2006). These circumstances increase the chances that depression will deepen and be confused with dementia.

The older we get, the more likely we are to be taking drugs that may have side effects resembling dementia. For example, some medications for coughs, diarrhea, and nausea inhibit the neurotransmitter acetylcholine, leading to Alzheimer's-like symptoms. Because tolerance for drugs decreases with age, these reactions intensify in late adulthood. In addition, some diseases can cause temporary memory loss and mental symptoms, especially among the elderly, who often become confused and withdrawn when ill (Fong, Tulevaev, & Inouye, 2009). Treatment of the underlying illness relieves the problem. Finally, environmental changes and social isolation can trigger mental declines (Maynard, 2003). When supportive ties are restored, cognitive functioning usually bounces back.

Health Care

Health-care professionals and lawmakers in industrialized nations worry about the economic consequences of rapid increase in the elderly population. Rising government-supported health care costs and demand for certain health care services, particularly long-term care, are of greatest concern.

■ COST OF HEALTH CARE FOR THE ELDERLY. Adults age 65 and older make up just under 13 percent of the North American population but account for over 40 percent of U.S. government health-care expenditures in the United States (U.S. Department of Health and Human Services, 2008h). According to current estimates, the cost of government-sponsored health insurance, or Medicare, for the elderly will double by 2025 and nearly triple by 2050, outpacing growth of the overall economy as the baby-boom generation enters late adulthood and average life expectancy extends further (Social Security and Medicare Board of Trustees, 2009).

Medicare expenses rise steeply with age. People age 75 and older receive, on average, 70 percent more benefits than younger senior citizens. Most of this increase reflects the need for long-term care—in hospitals and nursing homes—resulting from an age-related rise in disabling chronic diseases and acute illnesses. Because U.S. Medicare funds only about half of older adults' medical needs, American elders devote nearly 13 percent of their annual expenditures to health care—several times the proportion spent by older adults in other industrialized nations (OECD, 2008b; U.S. Department of Labor, 2008). And Medicare provides far less support for long-term care than elders with severe disabilities need.

■ LONG-TERM CARE. When Ida moved into Ruth's home, Ruth promised never to place Ida in an institution. But as Ida's condition worsened and Ruth faced health problems of her own, she couldn't keep her word. Ida needed round-the-clock monitoring. Reluctantly, Ruth placed her in a nursing home.

Advancing age is strongly associated with use of long-term care services, especially nursing homes. Nearly half of U.S. nursing home residents are age 85 and older (U.S. Department of Health and Human Services, 2004). Among disorders of aging, dementia—especially Alzheimer's disease—most often leads to nursing home placement, followed by arthritis, hip fracture, and stroke (Agüero-Torres et al., 2001). Greater use of nursing homes is also prompted by loss of informal caregiving support through widowhood—which mostly affects women—and aging of adult children and other relatives.

Overall, only 5 percent of Americans age 65 and older are institutionalized, about half the rate in other industrialized nations, such as the Netherlands and Sweden, which provide more generous public financing of institutional care (OECD, 2008b). Unless nursing home placement follows hospitalization for an acute illness, older adults must pay for it until their resources are exhausted. At that point, Medicaid (health insurance for the poor) takes over. Consequently, the largest users of nursing homes in the United States are people with either very low or high incomes. Middle-income elderly and their families are more likely to try to protect their savings from being drained by high nursing home costs.

Nursing home residents exercise together in physical therapy. Unless nursing home placement follows hospitalization for an acute illness, U.S. Medicare does not cover it. Hence, American elders with severe disabilities must pay nursing home costs until their resources are exhausted.

Nursing home use also varies across ethnic groups. For example, Caucasian Americans are nearly twice as likely as African Americans to be institutionalized. African-American older adults are more likely to have large, close-knit extended families. As a result, over 70 percent of them do not live alone, and over one-third reside with their adult children. Similarly, Asian, Hispanic, and Native-American elders use nursing homes less often than Caucasian Americans because of families' strong sense of caregiving responsibility (Yaffe et al., 2002). Overall, families provide at least 60 to 80 percent of all long-term care in Australia, Canada, New Zealand, the United States, and Western Europe. As we have seen, families of diverse ethnic and SES backgrounds willingly step in to care for elders in times of need.

To reduce institutionalized care of the elderly and its associated high cost, experts advocate alternatives, such as publicly funded in-home help for family caregivers (see Chapter 16, page 551). Another option rapidly becoming more widely available is **assisted living**—a homelike housing arrangement for seniors who require more care than can be provided at home but less than is usually provided in nursing homes. Assisted living is a cost-effective alternative to nursing homes that prevents unnecessary institutionalization (Stone & Reinhard, 2007).

It also can enhance residents' autonomy, social life, community involvement, and life satisfaction—benefits that we will take up in Chapter 18.

In Denmark, the combination of a government-sponsored home-helper system and expansion of assisted-living housing resulted in a 30 percent reduction in the need for nursing home beds over a 15-year period. At the same time, the Danish government saved money: Public expenditures for long-term care declined by 8 percent (Hastrup, 2007; Stuart & Weinrich, 2001). Strengthening caregiving and health-care services in U.S. assisted-living facilities would result in similarly favorable outcomes, while also enhancing elders' happiness. In a survey of a nationally representative sample of U.S. assisted-living residents, 98 percent said they expected to remain there for as long as they wished (Phillips et al., 2000). But within a seven-month period, 12 percent were moved to nursing homes because assisted living could no longer meet their health-care needs (Phillips et al., 2003).

When nursing home placement is necessary, steps can be taken to improve its quality. For example, the Netherlands has established separate facilities designed to meet the different needs of patients with mental and physical disabilities. And every elderly person, no matter how disabled, benefits from opportunities to maintain existing strengths and acquire new skills that can compensate for declines. Institutionalized elderly—like older people everywhere—desire a sense of personal control, gratifying social relationships, and meaningful and enjoyable daily activities (Alkema, Wilber, & Enguidanos, 2007). As Chapter 18 will reveal, designing nursing homes to meet these needs promotes both physical and psychological well-being.

© JOHN WALKER/MCT/LANDOV

A resident greets a server in the dining room of an assisted living facility. This homelike environment enhances older adults' autonomy, social life, community involvement, and life satisfaction.

ASK YOURSELF

» REVIEW
Cite evidence that both genetic and environmental factors contribute to Alzheimer's disease and cerebrovascular dementia.

» APPLY
Marissa complained to a counselor that at age 68, her husband, Wendell, no longer initiated sex or cuddled her. Why might Wendell have ceased to interact sexually? What interventions—both medical and educational—could be helpful to Marissa and Wendell?

» CONNECT
Explain how each level of ecological systems theory (Chapter 1, pages 24–25) contributes to caregiver well-being and quality of home care for elders with dementia.

» REFLECT
What care and living arrangements have been made for elders needing assistance in your family? How did culture, personal values, financial means, health, and other factors influence those decisions?

Cognitive Development

Ruth's complaints to her doctor about difficulties with memory and verbal expression reflect common concerns about cognitive functioning in late adulthood. Decline in speed of processing, under way throughout the adult years, is believed to affect many aspects of cognition in old age. In Chapter 15, we noted that reduced efficiency of thinking compromises attention, the amount of information that can be held in working memory, the use of memory strategies, and retrieval from long-term memory. These decrements continue in the final decades of life.

TAKE A MOMENT... Return to Figure 15.5 on page 519, and note that the more a mental ability depends on fluid intelligence (biologically based information-processing skills), the earlier it starts to decline. In contrast, mental abilities that rely on crystallized intelligence (culturally based knowledge) are sustained longer. But maintenance of crystallized intelligence depends on continued opportunities to enhance cognitive skills. When these are available, crystallized abilities—general information and expertise in specific endeavors—can offset losses in fluid intelligence.

Look again at Figure 15.5. In advanced old age, decrements in fluid intelligence limit what people can accomplish even with cultural supports, including a rich background of experience, knowledge of how to remember and solve problems, and a stimulating daily life (Berg & Sternberg, 2003; Kaufman, 2001). Consequently, crystallized intelligence shows a modest decline.

Overall, loss outweighs improvement and maintenance as people approach the end of life, but plasticity is still possible (Baltes & Smith, 2003). Research reveals greater individual variation in cognitive functioning in late adulthood than at any other time of life (Hultsch, MacDonald, & Dixon, 2002; Riediger et al., 2006). Besides fuller expression of genetic and lifestyle influences, increased freedom to pursue self-chosen courses of action—some that enhance and others that undermine cognitive skills—may be responsible.

How can older adults make the most of their cognitive resources? According to one view, elders who sustain high levels of functioning engage in **selective optimization with compensation:** Narrowing their goals, they *select* personally valued activities to *optimize* (or maximize) returns from their diminishing energy. They also find new ways to *compensate* for losses (Baltes, 1997; Freund & Baltes, 2000).

One day, Ruth and Walt watched a public television rebroadcast of an interview with 80-year-old concert pianist Arthur Rubinstein. Asked how he managed to sustain such extraordinary piano playing at his advanced age, Rubinstein replied that he was *selective;* he played fewer pieces. This enabled him to *optimize* his energy; he could practice each piece more. Finally, he developed new, *compensatory* techniques for a decline in playing speed. For example, before a fast passage, he played extra slowly, so the fast section appeared to his audience to move more quickly.

Research confirms that in late adulthood, personal goals—while still including gains—increasingly focus on maintaining abilities and preventing losses (Freund & Ebner, 2005). In one study, researchers asked people to rate their most important physical and cognitive goals for emphasis on growth ("With this goal, I want to improve something or achieve something new") and maintenance/prevention of losses ("With this goal, I want to maintain something or prevent a loss"). As Figure 17.6 shows, compared with young adults, older adults accentuated maintenance and loss prevention (Ebner, Freund, & Baltes, 2006). Additional evidence revealed that the high-energy demands of growth goals induced this shift toward balancing losses—an orientation that predicted elders' greater satisfaction with goal attainment and psychological well-being.

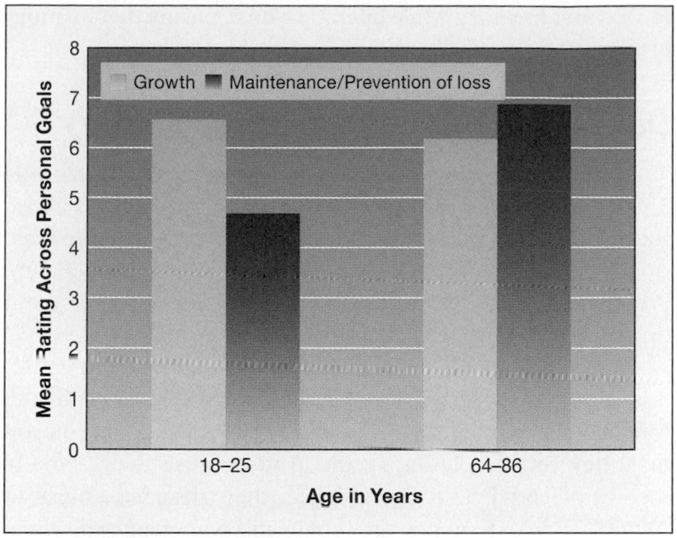

■ **FIGURE 17.6** ■ **Personal goal orientation toward growth and maintenance/prevention of loss in young and older adults.** Participants were asked to list two physical and two cognitive goals and then to rate each for emphasis on growth and on maintenance or prevention of loss, using an 8-point scale. Elders—while continuing to pursue growth—placed much greater emphasis on maintenance and loss prevention than did young adults. (From N. C. Ebner, A. M. Freund, & P. B. Baltes, 2006, "Developmental Changes in Personal Goal Orientation from Young to Late Adulthood: From Striving for Gains to Maintenance and Prevention of Losses," *Psychology and Aging, 21,* p. 671. Adapted by permission of American Psychological Association.)

© JOURNAL-COURIEE/STEVE WARMOWSKI/THE IMAGE WORKS

Elders can sustain high levels of functioning through selective optimization with compensation. This retired theater teacher has done so by creating a studio at home where he focuses on composing music.

As we review major changes in memory, language processing, and problem solving, we will consider ways that older adults optimize and compensate in the face of declines. We will also see that certain abilities that depend on extensive life experience, not processing efficiency, are sustained or increase in old age. Last, we take up programs that recognize the elderly as lifelong learners empowered by new knowledge, just as they were at earlier periods of development.

Memory

As older adults take in information more slowly and find it harder to apply strategies, inhibit irrelevant information, and retrieve relevant knowledge from long-term memory, the chances of memory failure increase (Luo & Craik, 2008; Old & Naveh-Benjamin, 2008b). A reduced capacity to hold material in working memory while operating on it means that memory problems are especially evident on complex tasks.

Deliberate versus Automatic Memory

"Ruth, you know that movie we saw—the one with the little 5-year-old boy who did such a wonderful acting job. I'd like to suggest it to Dick and Goldie. But what was it called?" asked Walt.

"I can't think of it, Walt. We've seen a few movies lately. Which theater was it at? Who'd we go with? Tell me more about the little boy—maybe it'll come to me."

Although we all occasionally have memory failures like this, difficulties with recall rise in old age. When Ruth and Walt watched the movie, their slower cognitive processing meant that they retained fewer details. And because their working memories could hold less at once, they attended poorly to *context*—where they saw the movie and who went with them (Wegesin et al., 2000; Zacks & Hasher, 2006). When we try to remember, context serves as an important retrieval cue.

Because older adults take in less about a stimulus and its context, their recall is reduced in relation to that of younger people. For example, they sometimes cannot distinguish an experienced event from one they imagined (Rybash & Hrubi-Bopp, 2000). They also have difficulty remembering the source of information, particularly when potential sources are similar—which member of their bridge club made a certain statement, in what magazine they read about a particular news event, and to whom and on which occasion they previously told a certain joke or story (Simons et al., 2004). Temporal memory—recall of the order in which events occurred or how recently they happened—suffers as well (Dumas & Hartman, 2003; Hartman & Warren, 2005).

A few days later, when Ruth saw an ad for the movie on TV, she recognized its title immediately. Recognition—a fairly automatic type of memory that demands little mental effort—suffers less than recall in late adulthood because a multitude of environmental supports for remembering are present. Age-related memory declines are greatest on tasks that require deliberate processing (Hoyer & Verhagen, 2006).

Consider another automatic form of memory: **implicit memory,** or memory without conscious awareness. In a typical implicit memory task, you would be shown a list of words, then asked to fill in a word fragment (such as *t− −k*). You would probably complete the sequence with a word you had just seen *(task)* rather than another word (*took* or *teak*). Without trying to do so, you would engage in recall.

Age differences in implicit memory are much smaller than in explicit, or deliberate, memory. Memory that depends on familiarity rather than on conscious use of strategies is largely spared in old age (Fleischman et al., 2004; Hudson, 2008). The memory problems elders report—for names of people, places where they put important objects, directions for getting from one place to another, and (as we will see) appointments and medication schedules—all place substantial demands on their more limited working memories.

Associative Memory

The memory deficits just described are part of a general, age-related decline in binding information into complex memories. Researchers call this an **associative memory deficit,** or difficulty creating and retrieving links between pieces of information—for example, two items or an item and its context, such as Ruth's attempt to remember the name of the movie with the child actor or where she had seen the movie.

To find out whether older adults have greater difficulty with associative memory than younger adults, researchers showed them pairs of unrelated words or pictures of objects (such as *table–overcoat* or *sandwich–radio*) and asked that they study the pairs for an upcoming memory test. During the test, one group of participants was given a page of *single items,* some that had appeared in the study phase and some that had not, and asked to circle the ones they had studied. The other group was given a page of *item pairs,* some intact from the study phase *(table–overcoat)* and some that had been rearranged *(overcoat–radio),* and asked to circle pairs they had studied. As Figure 17.7 shows, older adults did almost as well as younger adults on the single-item memory test. But they performed far worse on the item-pair test—findings that support an associative memory deficit (Naveh-Benjamin, 2000; Naveh-Benjamin et al., 2003).

Notice that the memory tasks in this study relied on recognition. Because recognition memory usually requires only that we recognize single pieces of information, elders perform well.

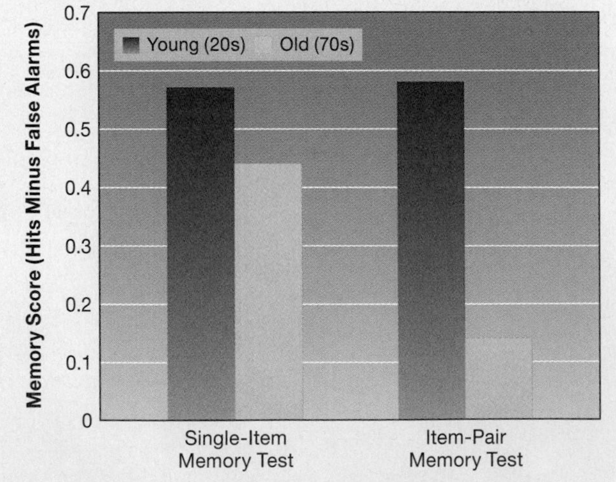

■ **FIGURE 17.7** ■ **Young and older adults' performance on single-item and item-pair memory tests, supporting an associative memory deficit in late adulthood.** After studying pairs of unrelated words or pictures, some participants were asked to identify single items they had seen. Others were asked to identify item pairs they had seen. Older adults performed almost as well as young adults on the single-item memory test. But they did far worse on the item-pair memory test. These findings support an associative memory deficit in late adulthood. (Adapted from Naveh-Benjamin, 2000.)

When researchers complicate recognition tasks by making them depend on associative memory, elders have difficulty with widely varying associations, including face–name, face–face, word–voice, and person–action pairings (Naveh-Benjamin et al., 2004; Old & Naveh-Benjamin, 2008b, 2008c). Providing older adults with repeated presentations of information to be learned and more memory cues improves their associative memory (Naveh-Benjamin et al., 2003; Simons et al., 2004). For example, to associate names with faces, elders profit from mention of relevant facts about those individuals. When older adults are directed to use the memory strategy of *elaboration* (relating word pairs by generating a sentence linking them) during both study and retrieval, the young–old difference in memory nearly disappears (Naveh-Benjamin, Brav, & Levy, 2007). Clearly, elders' associative deficits are greatly affected by lack of spontaneous use of strategies that help bind information into integrated wholes.

Remote Memory

Although older people often say that their **remote memory,** or very long-term recall, is clearer than their memory for recent events, research does not support this conclusion. In several studies, adults ranging in age from their twenties to their seventies were asked to recall names of grade school teachers and high school classmates and Spanish vocabulary from high school—information very well learned early in life. Memory declined rapidly for the first 3 to 6 years, then changed little for the next 20 years. After that, additional modest forgetting occurred (Bahrick, 1984; Bahrick, Bahrick, & Wittlinger, 1975).

How about *autobiographical memory,* or memory for personally meaningful events, such as what you did on your first date or how you celebrated your college graduation? To test for this type of memory, researchers typically give a series of words (such as *book, machine, sorry, surprised*) and ask adults to report a personal memory cued by each. Or they present participants with a time line on a piece of paper, representing birth to present age, and ask them to place important life events on the line and note the age at which each occurred. People between ages 50 and 90 recall both remote and recent events more frequently than intermediate events, with recent events mentioned most often in the word-cue studies (see Figure 17.8). Among remote events recalled using either word-cue or time-line procedures, most happened between ages 10 and 30 (Rubin, 2002; Rubin & Schulkind, 1997; Schroots, van Dijkum, & Assink, 2004).

Why do older adults recall their adolescent and early adulthood experiences more readily than their mid-adulthood lives? Youthful events occur during a period of rapid life change filled with novel experiences that stand out from the humdrum of daily life. Adolescence and early adulthood are also times of identity development, when many personally significant experiences occur. Recall from Chapter 5 that such events are likely to become a lasting part of the individual's life story. Even public events linked to this period—World Series champions, Academy Award winners, and current events—are especially salient to elders (Rubin, Rahhal, & Poon, 1998).

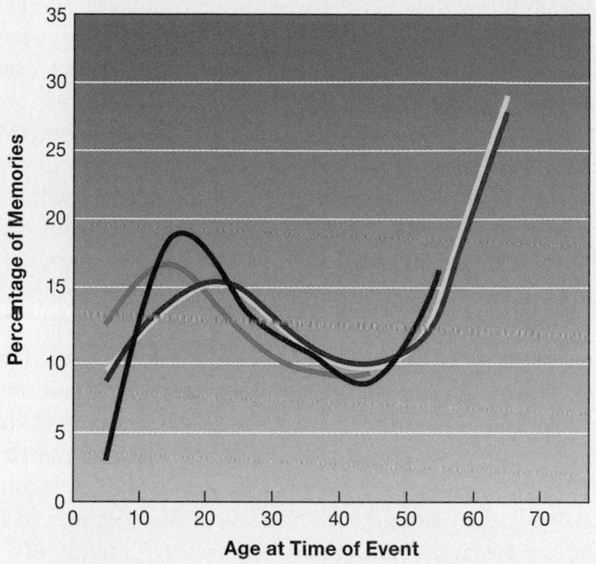

■ **FIGURE 17.8** ■ **Distribution of older adults' autobiographical memories by reported age at time of the event.** In the four studies of 50- to 90-year-olds represented here, later events were remembered better than early events. Among early events, most of those recalled occurred between ages 10 and 30. (From D. C. Rubin, T. A. Rahhal, & L. W. Poon, 1998, "Things Learned in Early Adulthood Are Remembered Best," *Memory and Cognition, 26,* p. 4. Copyright © 1998 by the Psychonomic Society, Inc. Adapted by permission.)

Nevertheless, older adults recall recent personal experiences more readily than remote ones, probably because of interference produced by years of additional experience (Kausler, 1994). As we accumulate more memories, some inevitably resemble others. As a result, certain early memories become less clear than they once were. However, even when asked to recall an important event of the previous year, elders—because of their recall difficulties—provide considerably fewer details than do young adults (Levine et al., 2002).

Prospective Memory

Elderly people often complain that they have become more absent-minded about daily events. Because Ruth and Walt knew they were prone to forget appointments, they asked about them repeatedly. "Sybil, what time is our dinner engagement?" Walt queried several times during the preceding two days. His questioning was not a sign of dementia. He simply wanted to be sure to remember an important date.

So far, we have considered various aspects of *retrospective memory* (remembrance of things past). **Prospective memory** refers to remembering to engage in planned actions in the future. The amount of mental effort required determines whether older adults have trouble with prospective memory. Remembering the dinner date was challenging for Walt because he typically ate dinner with his daughter on Thursday evenings at 6 P.M., but this time, dinner was set for Tuesday at 7:15 P.M.

In the laboratory, older adults do better on *event-based* than on *time-based* prospective memory tasks. In an event-based task, an event (such as a certain word appearing on a computer screen) serves as a cue for remembering to do something (pressing a key) while the participant engages in an ongoing activity (reading paragraphs). As long as the event-based task is not complex, older adults do as well as younger adults. But when researchers introduce extra memory demands (for example, press the key when any one of four cues appears), older adults' performance worsens (Einstein et al., 2000; Kliegel, Jäger, & Phillips, 2008; McDaniel, Einstein, & Rendell, 2007). In time-based tasks, the adult must engage in an action after a certain time interval has elapsed, without any obvious external cue (for example, pressing a key every 10 minutes). Time-based prospective memory requires considerable initiative to keep the planned action in mind, and declines in late adulthood are large (Park et al., 1997; West & Craik, 1999).

But difficulties with prospective memory seen in the laboratory do not appear in real life, where adults are highly motivated to remember and good at setting up reminders for themselves, such as a buzzer ringing in the kitchen or a note tacked up prominently (Henry et al., 2004). In trying to remember a future activity, younger adults rely more on strategies like rehearsal, older adults on external memory aids (Dixon, de Frias, & Bäckman, 2001). In this way, the elderly compensate for their reduced-capacity working memories and the challenge of dividing attention between what they are doing now and what they must do in the future.

Language Processing

Language and memory skills are closely related. In language comprehension (understanding the meaning of spoken or written prose), we recollect what we have heard or read without conscious awareness. Like implicit memory, language comprehension changes very little in late life, as long as conversational partners do not speak too quickly and elders are given enough time to process written text accurately (Stine-Morrow et al., 2008; Thornton & Light, 2006). Successful older readers make a variety of adjustments to ensure comprehension, such as attending more closely to features of text prose, pausing more often to integrate information, and making good use of story organization to help them recall both main ideas and details.

Two aspects of language production do show age-related losses. The first is retrieving words from long-term memory (Connor et al., 2004). When conversing with others, Ruth and Walt sometimes had trouble finding the right words to convey their thoughts—even well-known words they had used many times in the past. Consequently, their speech contained more pronouns and other unclear references than it did at younger ages. They also spoke more slowly and paused more often, partly because they needed time to search their memories for certain words. And compared to younger people, they more often reported a *tip-of-the-tongue state*—certainty that they knew a word accompanied by an inability to produce it (Burke & Shafto, 2004).

Second, planning what to say and how to say it is harder in late adulthood. As a result, Walt and Ruth displayed slightly more hesitations, false starts, word repetitions, and sentence fragments as they aged (Bortfeld et al., 2001). Their statements were also less well-organized than before (Kemper, Kynette, & Norman, 1992).

What explains these changes? Whereas the meanings elders want to convey have many "mental connections" with other meanings, the sound of a word has only one mental connection to the word's underlying concept. Consequently, as associative memory declines with age, memory difficulties in everyday conversation are especially apparent in word retrieval (Burke & Shafto, 2004). Also, diminished working-memory capacity is involved. Because less information can be held at once, older adults have difficulty coordinating the multiple tasks required to produce coherent speech.

As with memory, older adults develop compensatory techniques for their language production problems. For example, they speak more slowly and simplify their grammatical structures so they can devote more effort to retrieving words and organizing their thoughts. Sacrificing efficiency for greater clarity, they use more sentences to convey their message (Griffin & Spieler, 2006; Kemper, Thompson, & Marquis, 2001). As elders monitor their word-retrieval failures and try hard to overcome them, they show a greater frequency of tip-of-the-tongue states—but they resolve tip-of-the-tongues at a higher rate than do younger people (Schwartz & Frazier, 2005).

© CHUCK SAVAGE/CORBIS

Older adults compensate for their language-production problems: They speak more slowly, simplify their grammatical structures, and represent information in terms of gist rather than details. These strategies enable them to extract the essence of a message and enrich it with personal interpretations.

Furthermore, the elderly often compensate by representing information they want to communicate in terms of gist rather than details (Jepson & Labouvie-Vief, 1992). For example, when Walt told his granddaughter Marci fairytales, he left out many concrete facts while substituting personal inferences and a moral lesson—elements that appear less often in the storytelling of younger adults. Here is Walt's rendition of "Sleeping Beauty": "An evil fairy condemns Sleeping Beauty to death. But a kind fairy changes the curse from death to sleep. Then a handsome prince awakens the girl with a kiss. So you see, Marci, both good and bad exist in the world. The bad things instill in us the need to care for others."

Older adults often make the most of their limited working memories by extracting the essence of a message. Then, drawing on their extensive life experience, they enrich it with symbolic interpretations.

Problem Solving

Problem solving is yet another cognitive skill that illustrates how aging brings not only deterioration but also adaptive changes. Problem solving in the laboratory declines in late adulthood (Finucane et al., 2005). Older adults' memory limitations make it hard to keep all relevant facts in mind when dealing with a complex hypothetical problem.

Yet the everyday problems the elderly encounter differ from hypothetical problems devised by researchers—and also from the problems they experienced at earlier ages. After retirement, older adults do not have to deal with workplace problems. Their children are typically grown and living on their own, and their marriages have endured long enough to have fewer difficulties (Berg et al., 1998). With age, major concerns involve dealing with extended-family relationships (for example, expectations of adult children that they babysit grandchildren) and managing IADLs, such as preparing nutritious meals, handling finances, and attending to health concerns.

How do the elderly solve problems of daily living? Their strategies extend the adaptive problem solving of midlife. As long as they perceive problems as under their control and as important, elders are active and effective in solving them (Artistico, Cervone, & Pezzuti, 2003; Berg, 2008). Perhaps because older adults are especially concerned with maintaining positive relationships, they usually do what they can to avoid interpersonal conflicts (Blanchard-Fields, 2007; Blanchard-Fields, Chen, & Norris, 1997). As we will see in Chapter 18, this strategy also fits with elders' desire to conserve energy and limit stress.

The health arena, especially salient for elders, illustrates the adaptiveness of everyday problem solving in late adulthood (Sansone & Berg, 1993). Older adults make faster decisions about whether they are ill, seek medical care sooner, and select treatments more quickly. In contrast, young and middle-aged adults are more likely to adopt a "wait and see" approach in favor of gathering more facts, even when the health problem is serious (Leventhal et al., 1993; Meyer, Russo, & Talbot, 1995). This swift response of the elderly is interesting in view of their slower cognitive processing. Research reveals that they have accumulated more health-related knowledge, which enables them to move ahead with greater certainty (Meyer, Talbot, & Ranalli, 2007). Acting decisively when faced with health risks is sensible in old age.

Finally, older adults report that they often consult others—generally spouses and adult children, but also friends, neighbors, and members of their religious congregation—for advice about everyday problems (Strough et al., 2003). And compared with younger married couples, older married couples more often collaborate in problem solving, and researchers judge their jointly generated strategies as highly effective (Meegan & Berg, 2002). In jointly solving problems, elders seem to compensate for moments of cognitive difficulty, yielding enhanced accomplishment of life tasks.

Wisdom

We have seen that a wealth of life experience enhances the storytelling and problem solving of the elderly. It also underlies another capacity believed to reach its height in old age: **wisdom.** When researchers ask people to describe wisdom, most mention breadth and depth of practical knowledge, ability to reflect on and apply that knowledge in ways that make life more bearable and worthwhile; emotional maturity, including the ability to listen, evaluate, and give advice; and the altruistic form of creativity discussed in Chapter 15 that involves contributing to humanity and enriching others' lives. One group of researchers summed up the multiple cognitive and personality traits that make up wisdom as "expertise in the conduct and meaning of life" (Baltes & Smith, 2008; Baltes & Staudinger, 2000, p. 124; Staudinger, Dörner, & Mickler, 2005).

During her college years, Ruth and Walt's granddaughter Marci telephoned with a pressing personal dilemma. Ruth's advice reflected the features of wisdom just mentioned. After her boyfriend Ken moved to another city to attend medical school, Marci, unsure whether her love for Ken would endure, had begun dating another student. "I can't stand being pulled in two directions," she exclaimed. "I'm thinking of calling Ken and telling him about Steve. Do you think I should?"

"This is not a good time, Marci," Ruth advised. "You'll break Ken's heart before you've had a chance to size up your feelings for Steve. And you said Ken's taking some important exams in two weeks. If you tell him now and he's distraught, it could affect the rest of his life."

Wisdom—whether applied to personal problems or to community, national, and international concerns—requires the "pinnacle of insight into the human condition" (Baltes & Staudinger, 2000; Birren, 2009). Not surprisingly, cultures around the world assume that age and wisdom go together. In village and tribal societies, the most important social positions, such as chieftain and shaman (religious leader), are reserved for the old. Similarly, in industrialized nations, older adults are chief executive officers of large corporations, high-level religious leaders, members of legislatures, and supreme court justices.

© NAJLAH FEANNY/CORBIS SABA

Beaming as she hosts the annual conference for the Children's Defense Fund, Maya Angelou—revered author, teacher, and activist—exemplifies wisdom. She embodies the altruistic form of creativity that involves contributing to humanity and enriching others' lives. Her work on behalf of women and African Americans has continuously challenged sexism and racism.

What explains this widespread trend? According to an evolutionary view, the genetic program of our species grants health, fitness, and strength to the young. Culture tames this youthful advantage in physical power with the insights of the old, ensuring balance and interdependence between generations (Assmann, 1994; Csikszentmihalyi & Rathunde, 1990).

In the most extensive research to date on development of wisdom, adults ranging in age from 20 to 89 responded to uncertain real-life situations—for example, what to consider and do if a good friend is about to commit suicide or if, after reflecting on your life, you discover that you have not achieved your goals (Staudinger, Dörner, & Mickler, 2005). Responses were rated for five ingredients of wisdom:

- Knowledge about fundamental concerns of life, including human nature, social relations, and emotions
- Effective strategies for applying that knowledge to making life decisions, handling conflict, and giving advice
- A view of people that considers the multiple demands of their life contexts
- A concern with ultimate human values, such as the common good, as well as respect for individual differences in values
- Awareness and management of the uncertainties of life—that many problems have no perfect solution

Results revealed that age is no guarantee of wisdom. A small number of adults of diverse ages ranked among the wise. But type of life experience made a difference. People in human-service careers who had extensive training and practice in grappling with human problems tended to attain high wisdom scores. Other high-scorers held leadership positions (Staudinger, Smith, & Baltes, 1992; Staudinger, 1996). And when age and relevant life experiences were considered together, more older than younger people scored in the top 20 percent. Consistent with this finding, a panel of citizens asked to nominate public figures high in wisdom mostly selected older adults ranging in age from 50 to 70, with an average age of 64 (Baltes et al., 1995).

In addition to age and life experience, having faced and overcome adversity appears to be an important contributor to late-life wisdom (Brugman, 2006; Linley, 2003). In a longitudinal study of people who were young adults during the Great Depression of the 1930s, those who experienced economic hardship and surmounted it scored especially high in wisdom nearly 40 years later, as indicated by thoughtful interview responses to life events, insights into their own motives and behavior, and warmth and compassion (Ardelt, 1998).

Compared to their agemates, older adults with the cognitive, reflective, and emotional qualities that make up wisdom are better educated and physically healthier, forge more positive relations with others, and score higher on the personality dimension of openness to experience (Kramer, 2003). Wisdom is also a strong predictor of psychological well-being (Peterson & Seligman, 2004). Wise elders seem to flourish, even when faced with physical and cognitive challenges. This suggests that finding ways to promote wisdom would be a powerful means of both contributing to human welfare and fostering a gratifying old age.

Factors Related to Cognitive Change

As in middle adulthood, a mentally active life—above-average education; frequent, supportive contact with family members and friends; stimulating leisure pursuits; community participation; and a flexible personality—predicts maintenance of mental abilities into advanced old age (Hughes et al., 2008; Schaie, 2005). Today's elders in industrialized nations are better educated than any previous generation. Since 1950, the rate of high school completion among U.S. adults age 65 and older has quadrupled, reaching 76 percent. Those with at least a bachelor's degree have increased more than fivefold, to 19 percent (National Institute on Aging, 2008). As the baby boomers enter late adulthood, these trends are expected to continue, forecasting improved preservation of cognitive functions.

As noted earlier, health status powerfully predicts elders' intellectual performance. In several longitudinal studies, cigarette smokers declined cognitively at a faster rate than their nonsmoking counterparts, even after initial health status, SES, and mental test performance were controlled (Ott et al., 2004; Starr et al., 2007). And a wide variety of chronic conditions, including vision and hearing impairments, cardiovascular disease, diabetes, osteoporosis, and arthritis, are strongly associated with cognitive declines (Anstey & Christensen, 2000; Baltes, Lindenberger, & Staudinger, 2006). But we must be cautious in interpreting this link between physical and cognitive deterioration. The relationship may be exaggerated by the fact that brighter adults are more likely to engage in health-protective behaviors, which postpone the onset of serious disease.

Retirement also affects cognitive change, both positively and negatively. When people leave routine jobs for stimulating leisure activities, outcomes are favorable. In contrast, retiring from a highly complex job without developing challenging substitutes accelerates intellectual declines (Schaie, 1996). In fact, complex, challenging work in late adulthood has an even stronger, facilitating impact on intellectual functioning than in middle adulthood (see page 525 in Chapter 15) (Schooler, Mulatu, & Oates, 1999).

As elders grow older, their scores on cognitive tasks show larger fluctuations from one occasion to the next. This rising instability of performance—especially in speed of response—accelerates in the seventies and is associated with cognitive declines. Researchers speculate that it signals end-of-life degeneration in wide-ranging areas of the brain (Hultsch, MacDonald, & Dixon, 2002; McDonald, Hultsch, & Dixon, 2003).

In the year before Walt died, those close to him noticed that he had become less active and more withdrawn. In the company of friends, he talked and moved less. At home, he spent more time looking out the window instead of immersing himself in creative writing and gardening. **Terminal decline** refers to marked acceleration in deterioration of cognitive functioning prior to death. Some longitudinal studies indicate that it is limited to a few aspects of intelligence, others that it occurs generally, across many abilities. Findings also differ greatly in its estimated length. Some report that it lasts only 1 to 3 years, others that it extends for as long as 14 years. The average is 4 to 5 years (Hassing et al., 2002; Lövdén et al., 2005; Rabbitt, Lunn, & Wong, 2008; Wilson et al., 2003). In one investigation, a sharp drop in life satisfaction predicted mortality. The downturn appeared, on average, four years in advance of death, was especially steep in people age 85 and older, and showed only a weak relationship to mental deterioration or chronic illnesses (Gerstorf et al., 2008).

Perhaps different kinds of terminal decline exist—one type arising from disease processes, another as part of a general biological breakdown due to normal aging. What we know for sure is that an extended, steep falloff in cognitive performance or in emotional investment in life is a sign of loss of vitality and impending death.

Cognitive Interventions

For most of late adulthood, cognitive declines are gradual. Although aging of the brain contributes to them, recall from our earlier discussion that the brain can compensate by growing new neural fibers. Furthermore, some cognitive decrements may be due to disuse of particular skills rather than biological aging. If plasticity of development is possible in old age, then interventions that train the elderly in cognitive strategies should at least partially reverse the age-related declines we have discussed.

The Adult Development and Enrichment Project (ADEPT) is the most extensive cognitive intervention program conducted to date. By using participants in the Seattle Longitudinal Study (see Chapter 15, page 518), researchers were able to do what no other investigation has done: assess the effects of cognitive training on long-term development (Schaie, 2005).

Intervention began with adults over age 64, some of whom had maintained their scores on two mental abilities (inductive reasoning and spatial orientation) over the previous 14 years and others who had shown declines. After just five one-hour training sessions in one of two types of mental test items, two-thirds of participants improved their performance on the trained skill. Gains for decliners were dramatic. Forty percent returned to the level at which they had been functioning 14 years earlier! A follow-up after 7 years revealed that although scores dropped somewhat, elders remained advantaged in their trained skill over agemates trained in the other ability. Finally, "booster" training at this time led to further gains, although these were smaller than the earlier gains.

In another large-scale intervention study called ACTIVE (Advanced Cognitive Training for Independent and Vital Elderly), more than 2,800 65- to 84-year-olds were randomly assigned to a ten-session training program focusing on one of three abilities—speed of processing, memory, or reasoning—or to a no-intervention control group. Again, trained elders showed an immediate advantage in the trained skill over controls that was still evident—though smaller in magnitude—at one- and two-year follow-ups (Ball et al., 2002). Five years after intervention, cognitive training was associated with reduced declines in general health and ability to engage in social and leisure pursuits—outcomes that were strongest for the speed-of-processing group (Wolinsky et al., 2006). The investigators speculated that speed-of-processing training induces a broad pattern of brain activation, affecting many regions.

Clearly, many cognitive skills can be enhanced in old age. A vital goal is to transfer intervention from the laboratory to the community, weaving it into the daily experiences of elderly people. As we will see in the next section, a promising approach is to provide older adults with well-designed, highly interesting learning experiences in which cognitive training is an integral part.

Lifelong Learning

Think about the competencies that older adults need to live in our complex, changing world. They are the same as those of younger people—communicating effectively through spoken and written systems; locating information, sorting through it, and selecting what is needed; using math strategies, such as estimation; planning and organizing activities, including making good use of time and resources; mastering new technologies; and understanding past and current events and the relevance of each to their own lives. The elderly also need to develop new, problem-centered coping strategies—ways to sustain health and operate their households efficiently and safely—and updated vocational skills, for those who continue to work.

Applying What We Know

Increasing the Effectiveness of Instruction for Older Adults

Technique	Description
Provide a positive learning environment.	Some elders have internalized negative stereotypes of their abilities and come to the learning environment with low self-esteem. A supportive group atmosphere, in which the instructor acts as a colleague, helps convince older adults that they can learn.
Allow ample time to learn new information.	Rate of learning varies widely among older adults, and some master new material at a fairly slow rate. Presenting information over several sessions or allowing for self-paced instruction aids mastery.
Present information in a well-organized fashion.	Older adults do not organize information as effectively as younger adults. Material that is outlined, presented, and then summarized enhances memory and understanding. Digressions make a presentation harder to comprehend.
Relate information to elders' experiences.	Relating new material to what elders have already learned, by drawing on their experiences and giving many vivid examples, enhances recall.

Source: Illeris, 2004.

Participation of the elderly in continuing education has increased substantially over the past few decades. Successful programs include a wide variety of offerings responsive to the diversity of senior citizens and teaching methods suited to their developmental needs.

Types of Programs

One summer, Walt and Ruth attended an Elderhostel at a nearby university. After moving into a dormitory room, they joined 30 other seniors for two weeks of morning lectures on Shakespeare, afternoon visits to points of interest, and evening performances of plays at a nearby Shakespeare festival.

Elderhostel programs and their Canadian counterpart, Routes to Learning, attract over a quarter million North American older adults annually. Local educational institutions serve as hosts, combining stimulating one- to three-week courses with recreational pursuits. Some programs make use of community resources through classes on local ecology or folk life. Others involve travel abroad. Still others focus on innovative topics and experiences—writing one's own life story, discussing contemporary films with screenwriters, whitewater rafting, Chinese painting and calligraphy, and acquiring French language skills.

Other similar educational programs have sprung up in North America and elsewhere. The Bernard Osher Foundation collaborates with more than 120 U.S. universities to establish Osher Lifelong Learning Institutes on campuses. Each offers older adults a wide array of stimulating learning experiences, from auditing regular courses, to forming learning communities that address common interests, to helping to solve community problems. Originating in France, the University of the Third Age[2] provides Western European, British, and Australian elders with university- and community-sponsored courses, workshops on special topics, and excursions, with elders often doing the teaching. Some programs foster intergenerational relations. In Austria, for example, training in academic subjects is offered to grandparents so they can help their grandchildren with schoolwork.

Participants in the programs just mentioned tend to be active, well-educated, and financially well-off (Abraham, 1998). Much less is available for elders with little education and limited income. Community senior centers with inexpensive offerings related to everyday living attract more low-SES people than programs such as Elderhostel. Regardless of course content and which seniors attend, using the techniques summarized in Applying What We Know above increases the effectiveness of instruction.

© JEFF GREENBERG/PHOTOEDIT

Elderhostel programs, like this class on U.S. folk cultures, respond to older adults' intense desire to learn. Besides acquiring new knowledge and skills, participants often make new friends and abandon stereotypes of aging as they see that they can still engage in complex learning.

[2]The term *Third Age,* as we will see in Chapter 18, refers to the period after the "Second Age" of midlife, when older people are freed from responsibilities of earning a living and rearing children to focus on personal fulfillment.

Benefits of Continuing Education

Elderly participants in continuing education report a rich array of benefits—learning interesting facts, understanding new ideas in many disciplines, making new friends, and developing a broader perspective on the world (Kim & Merriam, 2004; Preece & Findsen, 2007). Furthermore, seniors come to see themselves differently. Many abandon their own ingrained stereotypes of aging when they realize that adults in late life—including themselves—can still engage in complex learning. In Elderhostel courses, participants with the least education report learning the most, an argument for recruiting less economically privileged people into these programs (Brady, 1984).

The educational needs of seniors are likely to be given greater attention in coming decades, as their numbers grow and they assert their right to lifelong learning. Once this happens, false stereotypes—"the elderly are too old to learn" or "education is for the young"—are likely to weaken and, perhaps, disappear.

ASK YOURSELF

» REVIEW
Describe cognitive functions that are maintained or improve in late adulthood. What aspects of aging contribute to them?

» APPLY
Estelle complained that she had recently forgotten two of her regular biweekly hair appointments and sometimes had trouble finding the right words to convey her thoughts. What cognitive changes account for Estelle's difficulties? What can she do to compensate?

» CONNECT
What processes in brain development contribute to the success of elders' efforts to compensate for cognitive declines? (See page 567.)

» REFLECT
Interview an older adult in your family, asking about ways the individual engages in selective optimization with compensation to make the most of declining cognitive resources. Describe several examples.

Summary

PHYSICAL DEVELOPMENT

Life Expectancy

Distinguish between chronological age and functional age, and discuss changes in life expectancy over the past century.

» Because people age biologically at different rates, chronological age is an imperfect indicator of **functional age,** or actual competence and performance. Dramatic twentieth-century gains in **average life expectancy**—resulting from declines in both infant mortality and death rates among adults—confirm that biological aging can be modified by environmental factors, including improved nutrition, medical treatment, sanitation, and safety.

© BORDERLANDS/ALAMY

» Length of life and, even more important, **average healthy life expectancy,** can be predicted by a country's health care, housing, and social services, along with lifestyle factors. In developing nations, both are shortened by poverty, malnutrition, disease, and armed conflict.

» With advancing age, the gender gap in average life expectancy declines as do differences between higher-SES whites and low-SES ethnic minorities. Around age 85, a life-expectancy cross-over occurs, with longer life expectancy for low-SES minority groups.

» About 9 percent of Americans over age 75 have difficulty carrying out **activities of daily living (ADLs),** or basic self-care tasks, and about 17 percent cannot perform **instrumental activities of daily living (IADLs),** which are tasks requiring some cognitive competence. The proportion of elders with these limitations increases sharply with age.

» Longevity runs in families, but environmental factors become increasingly important with age. Scientists disagree on whether **maximum lifespan** can be extended beyond about 85 to 90 years.

Physical Changes

Describe changes in the nervous system and the senses in late adulthood.

» Loss of neurons occurs throughout the cerebral cortex, with greater shrinkage in the frontal lobes and the corpus callosum. The cerebellum also loses neurons. But the brain compensates by forming new synapses and, to some extent, generating new neurons. The autonomic nervous system functions less well in old age and releases more stress hormones.

» Older adults—more women than men—tend to suffer from impaired vision and may experience **cataracts** and **macular degeneration.** Visual deficits affect elders' self-confidence and everyday behavior and can lead to isolation.

» In late life, hearing impairments are more common than visual impairments, especially in men, and can lead to reduced self-efficacy and social interaction, loneliness, and depressive symptoms. Impaired speech perception has the greatest impact on life satisfaction.

» Taste and odor sensitivity decline, making food less appealing. Touch sensitivity also deteriorates, particularly on the fingertips.

Describe cardiovascular, respiratory, and immune system changes in late adulthood.

- Reduced capacity of the cardiovascular and respiratory systems becomes more apparent in late adulthood. As at earlier ages, not smoking, reducing dietary fat, avoiding environmental pollutants, and exercising can slow aging of these systems.
- The immune system functions less effectively in late life, permitting diseases to progress and making **autoimmune responses** and stress-induced infection more likely.

Discuss sleep difficulties in late adulthood.

- Older adults find it harder to fall asleep, stay asleep, and sleep deeply. Until age 70 or 80, men have more trouble sleeping than women because of prostate enlargement (initiating frequent urination), **sleep apnea,** and "restless legs."

Describe changes in physical appearance and mobility in late adulthood, along with effective adaptations to these changes.

- Outward signs of aging, such as white hair, wrinkled and sagging skin, age spots, and decreased height and weight, become more noticeable. Mobility diminishes as muscle and bone strength and joint flexibility decline.
- "Anti-aging" dietary supplements, herbal products, and hormonal medications have shown no demonstrated benefits and may cause harm. Instead, problem-centered coping strategies yield improved physical functioning in the elderly. A rapidly expanding **assistive technology** is available to help older people cope with physical declines.

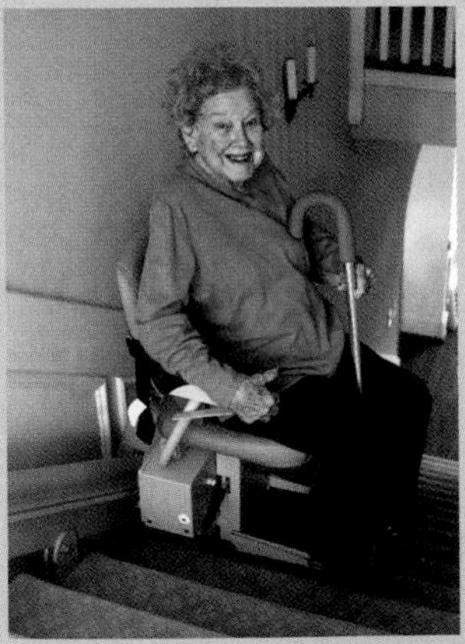

© ERIN MORONEY LABELLE/THE IMAGE WORKS

- Negative stereotypes of aging have a stressful, disorganizing impact on elders' functioning, whereas positive ones reduce stress and foster competence.

Health, Fitness, and Disability

Discuss health and fitness in late life, paying special attention to nutrition, exercise, and sexuality.

- Most elders rate their health favorably and, with respect to protecting it, have a high sense of self-efficacy. Low-SES ethnic minority elders remain at greater risk for certain health problems and are less likely to believe they can control their health.
- In late life, men continue to be more prone to fatal diseases and women to disabling conditions. By very old age, women are more impaired than surviving men. In industrialized nations, **compression of morbidity** has occurred, largely as a result of medical advances and improved socioeconomic conditions. Further gains are possible, especially in the developing world.
- Because risk of dietary deficiencies increases, a daily vitamin–mineral supplement is beneficial, preventing infectious illness. But supplements do not reduce the incidence of cardiovascular disease and cancer, and those labeled as "cognitive enhancers" show no positive effects. Exercise, even when begun in late adulthood, continues to be a powerful health intervention.
- Though sexual activity declines, especially among women, most elder couples report continued, regular sexual enjoyment.

Discuss physical disabilities common in late adulthood.

- Illness and disability increase toward the end of life. Cardiovascular disease, cancer, stroke, and respiratory diseases claim many lives. **Primary aging** (species-wide genetically influenced declines) contributes to **frailty** in the elderly. But **secondary aging** (declines due to hereditary defects and negative environmental influences) plays a larger role.
- **Osteoarthritis** and **rheumatoid arthritis** are widespread among older adults, especially women. Type 2 diabetes also increases.
- The death rate from unintentional injuries reaches an all-time high in those age 65 and older, largely due to motor vehicle collisions, pedestrian accidents, and falls. Visual declines and slowed reaction time often contribute.

Discuss mental disabilities common in late adulthood.

- **Alzheimer's disease** is the most common form of **dementia.** Often starting with severe memory problems, it brings personality changes, depression, disintegration of purposeful movements, loss of ability to comprehend and produce speech, and death. Underlying these changes are abundant **neurofibrillary tangles** and **amyloid plaques** and lowered neurotransmitter levels in the brain.
- Familial Alzheimer's generally has an early onset, progresses rapidly, and is linked to dominant genes on chromosomes 1, 14, and 21. About half of sporadic Alzheimer's victims have an abnormal ApoE4 gene on chromosome 19, resulting in insulin deficiency linked to brain damage.
- Diverse environmental factors, including a high-fat diet, physical inactivity, chronic psychological stress, and cardiovascular disease, increase the risk of Alzheimer's. A "Mediterranean diet," education, and an active lifestyle are associated with lower incidence.
- Heredity contributes to **cerebrovascular dementia** indirectly, through high blood pressure, cardiovascular disease, and diabetes. Many environmental influences also heighten stroke risk. Because of their greater susceptibility to cardiovascular disease, men are affected more than women.
- Treatable problems, such as depression, side effects of medication, and reactions to social isolation, can be mistaken for dementia.

Discuss health-care issues that affect senior citizens.

- Only a small percentage of American seniors are institutionalized, a rate about half that of other industrialized nations that offer more generous public financing of nursing home care. Though ethnic differences exist, family members provide most long-term care in Western nations. Publicly funded in-home help and **assisted living** can reduce the high costs of institutional placement and increase elders' life satisfaction.

COGNITIVE DEVELOPMENT

Describe overall changes in cognitive functioning in late adulthood.

- Individual differences in cognitive functioning are greater in late adulthood than at any other time of life. With opportunities to enhance cognitive skills, crystallized intelligence can offset losses in fluid intelligence. Older adults can make the most of their cognitive resources through **selective optimization with compensation.** Personal goals increasingly focus on maintenance of abilities and prevention of loss over growth.

© JOURNAL-COURIER/STEVE WARMOWKSI/THE IMAGE WORKS

Memory

How does memory change in late life?

» Memory failures become more apparent, especially on tasks that are complex and require deliberate processing. Recall of context, source, and temporal order of events declines. Automatic forms of memory, such as recognition and **implicit memory,** suffer less. In general, an **associative memory deficit,** or difficulty creating and retrieving links between pieces of information, seems to characterize older adults' memory problems.

» Contrary to what older people often report, **remote memory** is not clearer than recent memory. Autobiographical memory is best for recent experiences, followed by personally meaningful events that happened between ages 10 and 30, a period of rapid life change and identity development. In the laboratory, older adults do better on event-based than on time-based **prospective memory** tasks. In everyday life, they compensate for declines in prospective memory by using external memory aids.

Language Processing

Describe changes in language processing in late adulthood.

» Although language comprehension changes little in late life, age-related losses occur in two aspects of language production: retrieving words from long-term memory and planning what to say and how to say it. Elders compensate by simplifying their grammatical structures and communicating gist rather than details.

Problem Solving

How does problem solving change in late life?

» Hypothetical problem solving declines in late adulthood. But in everyday problem solving, older adults are active and effective as long as they perceive problems as important and under their control. In matters of health, elders make quicker decisions than younger people. And they more often consult others about everyday problems.

Wisdom

What capacities make up wisdom, and how is it affected by age and life experience?

» **Wisdom** involves extensive practical knowledge, ability to reflect on and apply that knowledge in ways that make life more bearable and worthwhile, emotional maturity, and altruistic creativity. When age and life experience in grappling with human problems are combined, more older than younger people rank among the wise. Having faced and overcome adversity seems to foster late-life wisdom.

Factors Related to Cognitive Change

List factors related to cognitive change in late adulthood.

» Mentally active people are likely to maintain their cognitive abilities into advanced old age. A wide array of chronic conditions are associated with cognitive decline. Retirement can bring about either positive or negative changes. Stimulating leisure activities and complex, challenging work facilitate intellectual functioning.

» As elders grow older, their scores on cognitive tasks become increasingly unstable. As death approaches, **terminal decline**—a marked acceleration in deterioration of cognitive functioning—often occurs.

Cognitive Interventions

Can cognitive interventions help older adults sustain their mental abilities?

» Large-scale interventions like ADEPT and ACTIVE demonstrate that training can enhance cognitive skills in older adults, with large benefits for those who had experienced cognitive declines.

Lifelong Learning

Discuss types of continuing education and benefits of such programs in late life.

» Increasing numbers of older people continue their education through university courses, community offerings, and programs such as Elderhostel and Osher Lifelong Learning Institutes. Participants acquire new knowledge, new friends, a broader perspective on the world, and an image of themselves as more competent. Unfortunately, fewer continuing-education opportunities are available to low-SES seniors.

Important Terms and Concepts

© SEAN SPRAGUE/THE IMAGE WORKS

As family responsibilities and vocational pressures lessen, friendships—like the close tie between these Honduran elders—take on increasing importance. Having friends is an especially strong predictor of mental health in late adulthood.

CHAPTER 18

Emotional and Social Development in Late Adulthood

With Ruth at his side, Walt spoke to the guests at their sixtieth-anniversary party. "Even when things were hard," he reflected, "the time of life I liked best always seemed to be the one I was currently experiencing. When I was a kid, I adored playing baseball. In my twenties, I loved learning the photography business. And of course," Walt continued, glancing affectionately at Ruth, "our wedding was the most memorable day of all."

He went on: "Then came the Depression, when professional picture taking was a luxury few people could afford. But we found ways to have fun without money—singing in the church choir and acting in community theater. And then Sybil was born. It meant so much to me to be a father—and now a grandfather and a great-grandfather. Looking back at my parents and grandparents and forward at Sybil, Marci, and Marci's son Jamel, I feel a sense of unity with past and future generations."

Walt and Ruth greeted old age with calm acceptance, grateful for the gift of long life and loved ones. Yet not all older adults find such peace of mind. Walt's brother Dick was contentious, complaining about petty issues and major disappointments alike: "Goldie, why'd you serve cheesecake? No one eats cheesecake on birthdays!" "Know why we've got financial worries? Uncle Louie wouldn't lend me the money to keep the bakery going, so I *had* to retire."

A mix of gains and losses characterizes these twilight years, extending the multidirectionality of development begun early in life. On one hand, old age is a time of pleasure and tranquility, when children are grown, life's work is nearly done, and responsibilities are lightened. On the other hand, it brings concerns about declining physical functions, unwelcome loneliness, and the growing specter of imminent death.

In this chapter, we consider how older adults reconcile these opposing forces. Although some are weary and discontented, most traverse this period with poise and calm composure. They attach deeper significance to life and reap great benefits from family and friendship bonds, leisure activities, and community involvement. We will see how personal attributes and life history combine with home, neighborhood, community, and societal conditions to mold emotional and social development in late life.

Erikson's Theory: Ego Integrity versus Despair

The final psychological conflict of Erikson's (1950) theory, **ego integrity versus despair,** involves coming to terms with one's life. Adults who arrive at a sense of integrity feel whole, complete, and satisfied with their achievements. They have adapted to the mix of triumphs and disappointments that are an inevitable part of love relationships, child rearing, work, friendships, and community participation. They realize that the paths they followed, abandoned, and never selected were necessary for fashioning a meaningful life course.

The capacity to view one's life in the larger context of all humanity—as the chance combination of one person and one segment in history—contributes to the serenity and contentment that accompany integrity. "These last few decades have been the happiest," Walt murmured, clasping Ruth's hand—only weeks before the heart attack that would end his life. At peace with himself, his wife, and his children, Walt had accepted his life course as something that had to be the way it was.

Erik Erikson and his wife Joan exemplified the ideal of Erikson's final stage. They aged gracefully, felt satisfied with their achievements, and could often be seen walking hand in hand, deeply in love.

In a study that followed a sample of women diverse in SES throughout adulthood, midlife generativity predicted ego integrity in late adulthood. Ego integrity, in turn, was associated with more favorable psychological well-being—a more upbeat mood, greater self-acceptance, higher marital satisfaction, closer relationships with adult children, greater community involvement, and increased ease in accepting help from others when it is needed (James & Zarrett, 2007). As Erikson's theory indicates, psychosocial maturity in late life brings increased contentment, affectionate, enjoyable bonds with others, and continued service to society.

Scanning the newspaper, Walt pondered, "I keep reading these percentages: One out of five people will get heart disease, one out of three will get cancer. But the truth is, one out of one will die. We are all mortal and must accept this fate." The year before, Walt had given his granddaughter, Marci, his collection of prized photos, which had absorbed him for over half a century. With the realization that the integrity of one's own life is part of an extended chain of human existence, death loses its sting (Vaillant, 1994, 2002).

The negative outcome of this stage, despair, occurs when elders feel they have made many wrong decisions, yet time is too short to find an alternate route to integrity. Without another chance, the despairing person finds it hard to accept that death is near and is overwhelmed with bitterness, defeat, and hopelessness. According to Erikson, these attitudes are often expressed as anger and contempt for others, which disguise contempt for oneself. Dick's argumentative, fault-finding behavior, tendency to blame others for his personal failures, and regretful view of his own life reflect this deep sense of despair.

Other Theories of Psychosocial Development in Late Adulthood

As with Erikson's stages of early and middle adulthood, other theorists have clarified and refined his vision of late adulthood, specifying the tasks and thought processes that contribute to a sense of ego integrity. All agree that optimal development involves greater integration and deepening of the personality.

Peck's Tasks of Ego Integrity and Joan Erikson's Gerotranscendence

According to Robert Peck (1968), attaining ego integrity involves three distinct tasks:

- *Ego differentiation:* For those who invested heavily in their careers, finding other ways to affirm self-worth—through family, friendship, and community life.
- *Body transcendence:* Surmounting physical limitations by emphasizing the compensating rewards of cognitive, emotional, and social powers.

- *Ego transcendence:* As contemporaries die, facing the reality of death constructively through efforts to make life more secure, meaningful, and gratifying for younger generations.

In Peck's theory, ego integrity requires older adults to move beyond their life's work, their bodies, and their separate identities by investing in a future that extends beyond their own lifespan. Research suggests that as elders grow older, both *body transcendence* (focusing on psychological strengths) and *ego transcendence* (orienting toward a larger, more distant future) increase. In a study of elderly women, those in their eighties and nineties stated with greater certainty than those in their sixties that they "accept the changes brought about by aging," "have moved beyond fear of death," "have a clearer sense of the meaning of life," and "have found new, positive spiritual gifts to explore" (Brown & Lowis, 2003).

Erikson's widow Joan Erikson suggested that these attainments actually represent development beyond ego integrity (which requires satisfaction with one's past life) to an additional psychosocial stage that she calls **gerotranscendence**—a cosmic and transcendent perspective directed forward and outward, beyond the self. Drawing on her own experience of aging, her observations of her husband's final years, and the work of others on the positive potential of the years shortly before death, Joan Erikson speculated that success in attaining gerotranscendence is apparent in heightened inner calm and contentment and additional time spent in quiet reflection (Erikson, 1998; Tornstam, 1997, 2000).

Although interviews with people in their ninth and tenth decades reveal that many (but not all) experience this peaceful, contemplative state, more research is needed to confirm the existence of a distinct, transcendent late-life stage. Besides focusing more intently on life's meaning, many of the very old continue to report investments in the real world—visiting friends, keeping up with current events, striving to be a good neighbor, and engaging in rewarding leisure and volunteer pursuits (Adams, 2004).

Labouvie-Vief's Emotional Expertise

In Chapter 13, we discussed Gisella Labouvie-Vief's research on development of adults' reasoning about emotion (see page 453). Recall that cognitive-affective complexity (awareness and coordination of positive and negative feelings into an organized self-description) increases from adolescence through middle adulthood, then declines as basic information-processing skills diminish in late adulthood.

But elders display a compensating emotional strength: They improve in **affect optimization,** the ability to maximize positive emotion and dampen negative emotion, which contributes to their remarkable resilience (Labouvie-Vief, 2003, 2005; Labouvie-Vief et al., 2007; Labouvie-Vief & Medler, 2002). Despite physical declines, increased health problems, a restricted future, and death of loved ones, most older adults sustain a sense of optimism and good psychological well-being

© JULIA CUMES/THE IMAGE WORKS

Although she suffers from serious medical problems, this older adult asserted, "Being an invalid does not invalidate your life." She adopted this rescue dog, who gives her great pleasure. The ability of elders to maximize positive emotion and dampen negative emotion contributes to their remarkable resilience.

(Diehl, Coyle, & Labouvie-Vief, 1996; Mroczek & Kolarz, 1998). And about 30 to 40 percent of elders not only are high in affect optimization but also retain considerable capacity for cognitive-affective complexity—a combination related to especially effective emotional self-regulation.

Furthermore, when asked to relate personal experiences in which they were happy, angry, fearful, or sad and to indicate how they knew they felt that emotion, many middle-aged and elderly individuals gave more vivid accounts than those of younger people—evidence that they were more in touch with their feelings. Consider this example:

> You have sunshine in your heart. During the wedding the candles were glowing. And that's just how I felt. I was glowing too. It was kind of dull outside. But that isn't how I felt. Everybody in the church felt like they were glowing. It was that kind of feeling. (Labouvie-Vief, DeVoe, & Bulka, 1989, p. 429)

Older adults' emotional perceptiveness helps them separate interpretations from objective aspects of situations. Consequently, their coping strategies often include making sure they fully understand their own feelings before deciding on a course of action. And they readily use emotion-centered coping strategies (controlling distress internally) in negatively charged situations (Blanchard-Fields, 2007). In sum, a significant late-life psychosocial attainment is becoming expert at reflecting on one's own feelings and regulating negative affect (Labouvie-Vief & Diehl, 1999; Lawton, 2001b).

Reminiscence

We often think of the elderly as engaged in **reminiscence**—telling stories about people and events from their past and reporting associated thoughts and feelings. Indeed, the widespread image of a reminiscing elder ranks among negative stereotypes of aging. In this common view, older people live in the past to escape the realities of a shortened future and the nearness of death. Although we do not yet fully understand why older people reminisce more often than younger people do, current theory and research indicate that reflecting on the past can be positive and adaptive.

In his comments on major events in his life at the beginning of this chapter, Walt was engaging in a special form of reminiscence called *life review*—calling up past experiences with the goal of achieving greater self-understanding. According to Robert Butler (1968), most older adults engage in life review as part of attaining ego integrity—a notion that has led many therapists to encourage life-review reminiscence. Older adults who participate in counselor-led life review report increased self-esteem, greater sense of purpose in life, and reduced depression (Watt & Cappeliez, 2000; Westerhof, Bohlmeijer, & Valenkamp, 2004). Life-review interventions can also help bereaved adults find a place for lost loved ones in their emotional lives, reinvest energy in other relationships, and move on with life (Worden, 2009).

But many elders who are high in self-acceptance and life satisfaction spend little time evaluating their pasts (Wink, 2007; Wink & Schiff, 2002). Indeed, in several studies in which older adults were asked what they considered to be the best time of life, 10 to 30 percent identified one of the decades of late adulthood. Early and middle adulthood received especially high marks, whereas childhood and adolescence ranked as less satisfying (Field, 1997; Mehlson, Platz, & Fromholt, 2003). These findings challenge the widespread belief that older adults inevitably focus on the past and wish to be young again. To the contrary, today's elders in industrialized nations are largely present- and future-oriented: They seek avenues for personal growth and fulfillment (see the Lifespan Vista box on the following page).

Clearly, life review is not essential for adapting well to late adulthood. Indeed, reminiscence that is *self-focused*, engaged in to reduce boredom and revive bitter events, is linked to adjustment problems. Despairing elders tend to ruminate, sustaining their negative emotion by dwelling on painful past experiences (Cully, LaVoie, & Gfeller, 2001). In contrast, extraverted elders tend to engage in *other-focused* reminiscence directed at social goals, such as solidifying family and friendship ties and reliving relationships with lost loved ones. And at times, older adults—especially those who score high in openness to experience—engage in *knowledge-based* reminiscence, drawing on their past for effective problem-solving strategies and for teaching younger people. These socially engaged, mentally stimulating forms of reminiscence help make life rich and rewarding (Cappeliez & O'Rourke, 2002). Perhaps because of their strong storytelling traditions, African-American and Chinese immigrant elders are more likely than their Caucasian counterparts to use reminiscence to teach others about the past (Merriam, 1993; Webster, 2002).

For young and old alike, reminiscence often occurs during times of life transition (Parker, 1995). Older adults who have recently retired, been widowed, or moved to a new residence may turn temporarily to the past to sustain a sense of personal continuity. As long as they do not get stuck in mulling over unresolved difficulties, reminiscence probably helps them recapture a sense of meaning.

Stability and Change in Self-Concept and Personality

Longitudinal research reveals continuing stability of the "big five" personality traits from mid- to late life (see Chapter 16, page 542). Yet the ingredients of ego integrity—wholeness, contentment, and image of the self as part of a larger world order—are reflected in several significant late-life changes in both self-concept and personality.

Secure and Multifaceted Self-Concept

Elders have accumulated a lifetime of self-knowledge, leading to more secure and complex conceptions of themselves than at earlier ages (Labouvie-Vief & Diehl, 1999). Ruth, for example, knew with certainty that she was good at growing a flower garden, budgeting money, counseling others, giving dinner parties, and figuring out who could be trusted and who couldn't. Furthermore, when young and older adults were asked for several life-defining memories, 65- to 85-year-olds were more likely to mention events with a consistent theme—such as the importance of relationships or personal independence—and to explain how the events were interrelated (McLean, 2008). Their autobiographical selves emphasized coherence and consistency, despite physical, cognitive, and occupational changes. As Ruth remarked humorously, "I know who I am. I've had plenty of time to figure it out!"

The firmness, stability, and multifaceted nature of Ruth's self-concept enabled her to compensate for lack of skill in domains she had never tried, had not mastered, or could no longer perform as well as before. Consequently, it allowed for self-acceptance—a key feature of integrity. In a study of old (70 to 84 years) and very old (85 to 103 years) German elders asked to respond to the question "Who am I?," participants mentioned a broad spectrum of life domains, including hobbies, interests, social participation, family, health, and personality traits. Adults in both age groups expressed more positive than negative self-evaluations, although a slight increase in negative comments occurred in the older group. Positive, multifaceted self-definitions predicted psychological well-being (Freund & Smith, 1999).

As the future shortens, most elders, into their eighties and nineties, continue to mention—and actively pursue—hoped-for

A LIFESPAN VISTA: Looking Forward, Looking Back

The New Old Age

After retiring, pediatrician Jack McConnell tried a relaxing lifestyle near a lake and golf course, but it worked poorly for the energetic 64-year-old. As his desire for a more fulfilling retirement grew, he noticed that outside his comfortable, gated community were many people serving community needs as gardeners, laborers, fast-food workers, and the like, yet who lived in or near poverty. The contrast galvanized Jack to found Volunteers in Medicine, a free clinic for working-poor adults and their families who lack health insurance (Croker, 2007). Five years later, at age 69, Jack was overseeing a highly cost-effective operation involving 200 retired doctors, nurses, and lay volunteers, who treat 6,000 patients a year.

Jack exemplifies a new approach to late adulthood: Increasingly, older adults are using their newfound freedom from work and parenting responsibilities to pursue personally enriching interests and goals. In doing so, they are giving back to their communities in significant ways and serving as role models for younger generations.

Added years of longevity and health plus financial stability have granted this active, opportunistic time of life to so many contemporary seniors that some experts believe a new phase of late adulthood has evolved called the **Third Age**—a term originating over a decade ago in France that spread through Western Europe and recently has stretched to North America. According to this view, the First Age is childhood, the Second Age is the adult period of earning a living and rearing children, and the Third Age—extending from ages 65 to 79, and sometimes longer—is a time of personal fulfillment (James & Wink, 2007). The Fourth Age brings physical decline and need for care.

The baby boomers—healthier and financially better off than any preceding aging generation—are approaching late life with the conviction that their old age will not begin until 80 (Gergen & Gergen, 2003). This self-perception has helped define the Third Age as a time of self-realization and high life satisfaction. But even people a decade ahead of the oldest baby boomers are experiencing the Third Age as a phase of new goal setting and purpose rather than as an extended vacation (Winter et al., 2007). As we will see later in this chapter, retirement is no longer a one-way, age-graded event. In one survey of 300 older Americans, very few self-identified as retired (Trafford, 2004). Instead, they were building hybrid lives—leaving career jobs to work at different jobs that utilized their skills, and devoting themselves to community service that they experienced as more meaningful than the paid work they left behind (Moen & Altobelli, 2007).

Although policy makers often express concern about the huge, impending baby-boomer burden on Social Security and Medicare, this large pool of vigorous, publicly minded future seniors has the potential to make enormous economic and social contributions. Today's Third Agers donate billions to the global economy in volunteer work, continue to participate in the work force in large numbers, and give generously to their families through monetary support and other forms of help—far more than they receive (see page 625).

But as midlife roles shrink and terminate, too few alternatives are available for the many aging adults eager to make a difference (Freedman, 1999; Wink & James, 2007). Societies need to provide abundant volunteer, national service, and other public interest opportunities, thereby harnessing their rich elder resources to solve pressing problems. The U.S. Serve America Act, signed into law in 2009, offers expanded service incentives and options to American adults of all ages and, thus, is a major step in that direction.

COURTESY OF VOLUNTEERS IN MEDICINE, WWW.VOLUNTEERSINMEDICINE.ORG

Retired pediatrician Jack McConnell founded Volunteers in Medicine, a free clinic for uninsured working-poor adults and their families. Added years of longevity and health plus financial stability have made late adulthood a time of personal enrichment and new goal-setting for many older adults.

Finally, although the majority of U.S. adults in their sixties and seventies have more energy and choice than ever before, others—more often ethnic minorities, women, and those who live alone—suffer from financial hardship and distress and, thus, have little chance for new beginnings (Sorensen, 2007). When social security, health care, and housing policies ensure a comfortable Third Age to all retiring adults, benefits accrue to the entire nation.

selves in the areas of physical health, cognitive functioning, personal characteristics, relationships, and social responsibility (Frazier, 2002; Markus & Herzog, 1992). At the same time, possible selves reorganize well into old age. When the German 70- to 103-year-olds just mentioned were followed longitudinally for four years, the majority deleted some possible selves and replaced them with new ones (Smith & Freund, 2002). Elders often characterize hoped-for selves in terms of "improving," "achieving," or "attaining." Consistent with this view, those who hold hoped-for goals usually take concrete steps to attain them. Engaging in hope-related activities, in turn, is associated with gains in life satisfaction and with longer life (Hoppmann et al., 2007). Clearly, late adulthood is not a time of withdrawal from future planning!

Resilience: Agreeableness and Acceptance of Change

During late adulthood, shifts occur in personality characteristics that, once again, defy aging stereotypes. Old age is not a time in which the personality inevitably becomes rigid and morale declines. Rather, a flexible, optimistic approach to life, which fosters resilience in the face of adversity, is common.

Both open-ended interviews and personality tests reveal that elders gain in *agreeableness,* becoming increasingly generous, acquiescent, and good-natured well into late life (Allemand, Zimprich, & Martin, 2008; Field & Millsap, 1991; Weiss et al., 2005). Agreeableness seems to characterize people who have come to terms with life despite its imperfections.

At the same time, elders show modest age-related dips in *extraversion* and *openness to experience* (Allemand, Zimprich, & Martin, 2008; Roberts, Walton, & Viechtbauer, 2006). Perhaps this reflects a narrowing of social contacts as people become more selective about relationships and as family members and friends die—trends we will take up in a later section. Still, older adults who were extraverted and open to experience throughout their lives tend to remain so—personality traits associated with greater life satisfaction (Mroczek & Spiro, 2005).

A related development is greater *acceptance of change*—an attribute the elderly frequently mention as important to psychological well-being (Ryff, 1989). When asked about dissatisfactions in their lives, many older adults respond that they are not unhappy about anything! Acceptance of change is also evident in most elders' effective coping with the loss of loved ones, including death of a spouse, which they describe as the most stressful event they ever experienced (Lund, Caserta, & Dimond, 1993). The capacity to accept life's twists and turns, many of which are beyond one's control, is vital for adaptive functioning in late adulthood.

Most older adults are resilient, bouncing back in the face of adversity—especially if they did so earlier in their lives. And elders' heightened capacity for positive emotion contributes greatly to their resilience. In one study, older adults kept diaries for a two-week period, in which they recorded their experience of positive and negative emotions as well as the most stressful event that occurred each day. Experiencing higher levels of positive emotion dampened the experience of negative emotion during times of stress, an effect that was strongest for participants with a generally positive outlook on life—who often looked for the "silver lining in the clouds" (Ong et al., 2006).

As these findings illustrate, older adults' general cheerfulness strengthens their physiological resistance to stress, enabling them to conserve physical and mental resources needed for effective coping (Ong & Allaire, 2005). The minority of elders who are high in neuroticism—emotionally negative, short-tempered, and dissatisfied—tend to cope poorly with stressful events, experience mounting negative affect, and are at risk for health problems and earlier death (Mroczek & Spiro, 2007; Ong, Edwards, & Bergeman, 2006).

Spirituality and Religiosity

How do older adults manage to accept declines and losses yet still feel whole and complete and anticipate death with calm composure? One possibility, consistent with Peck's and Erikson's emphasis on a transcendent perspective among the elderly, is the development of a more mature sense of spirituality. Spirituality is not the same as religion: An inspirational sense of life's meaning can be found in art, nature, and social relationships. But for many people, religion provides beliefs, symbols, and rituals that guide this quest for meaning.

Older adults attach great value to religious beliefs and behaviors. According to a recent national survey, 72 percent of Americans age 65 and older say that religion is very important in their lives—the highest of any age group (Gallup New Service, 2006). Over half of U.S. elders attend religious services or other events weekly, nearly two-thirds watch religious TV programs, and about one-fourth pray at least three times a day (Princeton Religion Research Center, 1999).

Although health and transportation difficulties reduce organized religious participation in advanced old age, U.S. elders generally become more religious or spiritual as they age (Argue, Johnson, & White, 1999; Wink & Dillon, 2002). But this trend is far from universal. In a British 20-year longitudinal study, the majority of elders showed stability in religiosity over time, with nearly half indicating that religion was very important to them. One-fourth, however, said they had become less religious, with some citing disappointment at the support they had received from their religious institution during stressful times (such as bereavement) as the reason (Coleman, Ivani-Chalian, & Robinson, 2004). Wide cultural variation also exists that has yet to be explained. For example, the late-life rise in religiosity is even stronger in Japan than in the United States, but in the Netherlands it is minimal (Sasaki & Suzuki, 1987).

Despite these differences, spirituality and faith may advance to a higher level in late adulthood—away from prescribed beliefs toward a more reflective approach that emphasizes links to others and is at ease with mystery and uncertainty. According to James Fowler's theory of faith development, many mature adults forge new faith capacities, including awareness of their own belief system as just one of many possible worldviews, contemplation of the deeper significance of religious symbols and rituals, openness to other religious perspectives as sources of inspiration, and (especially in late life) an enlarged vision of a common good that serves the needs of all humanity (Fowler & Dell, 2006; McFadden, 1996). For example, as a complement to his Catholicism, Walt became intensely interested in Buddhism, especially its focus on attaining perfect peace and happiness by mastering thoughts and feelings, never harming others, and resisting attachment to worldly objects.

Involvement in both organized and informal religious activities is especially high among low-SES ethnic minority elders, including African-American, Hispanic, and Native-American groups. In African-American communities, churches not only provide contexts for deriving meaning from life but also are

This minister takes time to offer a senior parishioner emotional support. African-American elders often look to religion as a powerful resource for the inner strength to withstand the challenges of late life.

centers for education, health, social welfare, and political activities aimed at improving life conditions. African-American elders look to religion as a powerful resource for social support beyond the family and for the inner strength to withstand daily stresses and physical impairments (Armstrong & Crowther, 2002; Husaini, Blasi, & Miller, 1999). Compared with their Caucasian agemates, more African-American older adults report collaborating with God to overcome life problems (Krause, 2005; Lee & Sharpe, 2007).

Sex differences in religious involvement and spirituality are also evident throughout adulthood. Women are more likely than men to report that religion is very important to them, to participate in religious activities, and to engage in a personal quest for connectedness with a higher power (Gallup News Service, 2006; Levin, Taylor, & Chatters, 1994; Wink & Dillon, 2002). Women's higher rates of poverty, widowhood, and participation in caregiving, including caring for chronically ill family members, expose them to higher levels of stress and anxiety. As with ethnic minorities, they turn to religion for social support and for a larger vision of community that places life's challenges in perspective.

Religious involvement is associated with diverse benefits, including better physical and psychological well-being, more time devoted to exercising and leisure activities, greater sense of closeness to family and friends, and greater generativity (care for others) (Boswell, Kahana, & Dilworth-Anderson, 2006; Idler & Kasl, 1997; Lee, 2007; Wink, 2006, 2007). In longitudinal research, both organized and informal religious participation predicted longer survival, after family background, health, social, and psychological factors known to affect mortality were controlled (Helm et al., 2000; Strawbridge et al., 2001).

But aspects of religious connection that make a difference in elders' lives are not always clear. In two investigations of Caucasian older adults, religious *activity*—not religiosity or membership in a congregation—was associated with favorable adjustment following loss of a spouse (Lund, Caserta, & Dimond, 1993). The researchers found that increased social engagement brought about by religious participation, rather than the specifically religious nature of the activity, was the influential factor. Other evidence, however, indicates that belief in God's powers contributes substantially to the self-esteem, optimism, and life satisfaction of low-SES, ethnic minority elders (Krause, 2005; Schieman, Pudrovska, & Milkie, 2005). Older adults who have experienced social and economic disadvantages often turn to their personal relationship with God for help in coping with hardships.

Contextual Influences on Psychological Well-Being

As we have seen in this and the previous chapter, most adults adapt well to old age, yet some feel dependent, incompetent, and worthless. Personal and situational factors often combine to affect psychological well-being. Identifying these contextual influences is vital for designing interventions that foster positive adjustment.

Control versus Dependency

As Ruth's eyesight, hearing, and mobility declined in her eighties, Sybil visited daily to help with self-care and household tasks. During the hours mother and daughter were together, Sybil interacted most often with Ruth when she asked for help with activities of daily living. When Ruth handled tasks on her own, Sybil usually withdrew.

Observations of people interacting with older adults in both private homes and institutions reveal two highly predictable, complementary behavior patterns. In the first, called the **dependency–support script,** dependent behaviors are attended to immediately. In the second, the **independence–ignore script,** independent behaviors are mostly ignored. Notice how these sequences reinforce dependent behavior at the expense of independent behavior, regardless of the older person's competencies. Even a self-reliant elder like Ruth did not always resist Sybil's unnecessary help because it brought about social contact (Baltes, 1995, 1996).

Among elders who experience no difficulty with daily activities, opportunities to interact with others are related to high satisfaction with everyday life. In contrast, among elders who have trouble performing daily activities, social contact is linked to a less positive everyday existence (Lang & Baltes, 1997). This suggests that social interaction while assisting elders with physical care, household chores, and errands is often not meaningful and rewarding but, rather, demeaning and unpleasant.

© JOSE GALVEZ/PHOTOEDIT

Will this Apache elder become too dependent by letting his son help with grocery shopping? Not necessarily. When older adults assume personal control over areas of dependency, they can conserve their strength and invest it in highly valued activities.

Consider these typical reactions of care recipients to a spouse's help with daily activities: "felt dependent," "felt indebted," "felt like a weak, incapable person" (Newsom, 1999).

Longitudinal research shows that negative reactions to caregiving can result in persisting depression (Newsom & Schulz, 1998). But whether assistance from others undermines well-being depends on many factors, including the quality of help, the caregiver–elder relationship, and the social and cultural context in which helping occurs. Why do family members and other caregivers often respond in ways that promote excessive dependency in old age? A stereotype of the elderly as passive and incompetent appears to be responsible. Older adults seem well aware of others' low expectations for them. They frequently attribute their dependency to overresponsive social partners (Wahl, 1991).

In Western societies, which highly value independence, many elders fear relinquishing control and becoming dependent on others. This is especially so for older adults with a high need for self-determination (Curtiss, Hayslip, & Dolan, 2007; Frazier, 2002). Does this mean we should encourage elders to be as independent as possible? According to Mary Baltes (1996), this alternative is as counterproductive as promoting passivity and incompetence. Aging brings diminished energy at a time when people confront many challenging developmental tasks. Dependency can be adaptive if it permits older people to remain in control by choosing those areas in which they desire help. In this way, they can conserve their strength by investing it in highly valued activities, using a set of strategies we considered in Chapter 17: *selective optimization with compensation.*

Physical Health

As noted in Chapter 16, physical health is a powerful predictor of psychological well-being. Physical declines and chronic disease can lead to a sense of loss of personal control—a major factor in adult mental health. Furthermore, physical illness resulting in disability is among the strongest risk factors for late-life depression (Morrison, 2008; Schieman & Plickert, 2007). Although fewer older than young and middle-aged adults are depressed (see Chapter 17), profound feelings of hopelessness rise with age as physical disability and consequent social isolation increase. But more than actual physical limitations, *perceived negative physical health* predicts depressive symptoms (Jang et al., 2007). This helps explain the stronger physical impairment–depression relationship among higher-SES elders (Schieman & Plickert, 2007). Because of their lifetime of better physical health, they probably experience physical limitations as more unexpected and challenging.

The relationship between physical and mental health problems can become a vicious cycle, each intensifying the other. In survey research conducted in 15 countries, adults of all ages reported that mental health problems actually interfered more than physical disabilities with activities of daily living, including home management and social life (Ormel et al., 2008). At times, despondency and "giving up" trigger rapid physical decline in a sick elder (Penninx et al., 2000). This downward spiral can be hastened by a move to a nursing home, requiring the older person to adjust to diminished control over daily life and greater distance from family and friends. In the months after admission, many residents judge their quality of life to have worsened substantially, become severely anxious and depressed, and deteriorate rapidly. The stress of illness together with institutionalization is associated with escalating physical and mental health problems and with mortality (Scocco, Rapattoni, & Fantoni, 2006; Tobin, 1989).

Depression in old age is often lethal. People age 65 and older have the highest suicide rate of all age groups (see the Social Issues box on pages 612–613). What factors enable elders like Ruth to surmount the physical impairment–depression relationship, remaining content? Personal characteristics discussed in this and earlier chapters—optimism, effective coping, and a sense of self-efficacy—are vitally important (Morrison, 2008). But for frail elders to display these attributes, families and caregivers must grant them autonomy by avoiding the dependency–support script. When older adults remain in charge of personally important areas of their lives, they retain essential aspects of their identity in the face of change, view their past and future more favorably, and are emotionally more upbeat (Kunzmann, Little, & Smith, 2002).

Unfortunately, elders generally do not get the mental health care they need—even in nursing homes, where depression and other mental health problems are widespread (Gruber-Baldini et al., 2004; Watson et al., 2006). More than half of U.S. nursing home residents receive no regular mental health intervention.

Negative Life Changes

Ruth lost Walt to a heart attack, cared for his sister Ida as her Alzheimer's symptoms worsened, and faced health problems of her own—all within a span of a few years. Elders are at risk for a variety of negative life changes—death of loved ones, illness and physical disabilities, declining income, and greater dependency. Negative life changes are difficult for everyone but may actually evoke less stress and depression in older than in younger adults (Gatz, Kasl-Godley, & Karel, 1996). Many elders have learned to cope with hard times, to appraise negative changes as common and expected in late life, and to accept loss as part of human existence.

Still, when negative changes pile up, they test the coping skills of older adults (Kraaij, Arensman, & Spinhoven, 2002). In very old age, such changes are greater for women than for men. Women over age 75 are far less likely to be married, more often have lower incomes, and suffer from more illnesses—especially ones that restrict mobility. Furthermore, elderly women (as at younger ages) more often say that others depend on them for caregiving and emotional support. Thus, their social relations, even in very old age, are more often a source of stress (Antonucci, Ajrouch, & Birditt, 2008). And because of failing health, older women may not be able to meet others' needs for care, with negative consequences for their self-esteem. Not surprisingly, women of very advanced age tend to report a lower sense of psychological well-being than men (Pinquart & Sörensen, 2001).

Social Support

In late adulthood, social support continues to reduce stress, thereby promoting physical health and psychological well-being. Availability of social support increases the odds of living longer (Fry & Debats, 2006; Liang et al., 1999; Temkin-Greener et al., 2004). And it may help explain the relationship of religious participation to survival, noted earlier. Usually, elders receive informal assistance with tasks of daily living from family members—first from their spouse or, if none exists, from children and then from siblings. If these individuals are not available, other relatives and friends may step in.

Nevertheless, many older adults place such high value on independence that they do not want a great deal of help from people close to them unless they can reciprocate. When assistance is excessive or cannot be returned, it often results in psychological distress (Liang, Krause, & Bennett, 2001). Perhaps for this reason, adult children express a deeper sense of obligation toward their aging parents than their parents expect from them (see Chapter 16, page 549). Formal support—a paid home helper or agency-provided services—as a complement to informal assistance not only helps relieve caregiving burden but also spares elders from feeling overly dependent in their close relationships (Krause, 1990).

Ethnic minority elders do not readily accept formal assistance. But they are more willing to do so when home helpers are connected to a familiar neighborhood organization, especially the church. Although African-American seniors say they rely more on their families than on the church for assistance, those with support and meaningful roles in both contexts score highest in mental health (Coke, 1992; Taylor, Lincoln, & Chatters, 2005; Walls & Zarit, 1991). Support from religious congregants has psychological benefits for elders of all backgrounds, perhaps because recipients feel that it is motivated by genuine care and concern, not just obligation (Krause, 2001). Also, the warm atmosphere of religious organizations fosters a sense of social acceptance and belonging.

Overall, for social support to foster well-being, elders need to assume personal control of it. This means consciously giving up primary control in some areas to remain in control of other, highly valued pursuits. For example, although she could handle dressing, financial matters, shopping, and food preparation for herself, Ruth allowed her daughter Sybil to assist with these activities, leaving Ruth with more stamina for pleasurable reading. To optimize her energies, Ruth selected certain domains in which to become dependent. This permitted her to compensate for poor eyesight by taking extra time to use a magnifying glass while reading or to listen to a book on tape. In this way, social support granted Ruth autonomy—a means for managing her own aging.

When we intervene with older adults, we must ask ourselves, What kind of assistance are we providing? Help that is not wanted or needed or that exaggerates weaknesses can undermine mental health, and—if existing skills fall into disuse—can also accelerate physical disability. In contrast, help that frees up energy for endeavors that are personally satisfying and that lead to growth enhances elders' quality of life. These findings clarify why *perceived social support* (elders' sense of being able to count on family or friends in times of need) is associated with a positive outlook in older adults with disabilities, whereas sheer *amount* of help family and friends provide has little impact (Taylor, Lynch, & Scott, 2004).

Finally, besides tangible assistance, elders benefit from social support that offers affection, affirmation of their self-worth, and sense of belonging. Extraverted elders are more likely to take advantage of opportunities to engage with others, thereby reducing loneliness and depression and fostering self-esteem and life satisfaction (Mroczek & Spiro, 2005). But as we will see in the next section, supportive social ties in old age have little to do with quantity of contact. Instead, high-quality relationships, involving expressions of kindness, encouragement, respect, and emotional closeness, have the greatest impact on mental health in late life.

SOCIAL ISSUES

Elder Suicide

When 65-year-old Abe's wife died, he withdrew from life. Living far from his two daughters, he spent his nonworking days alone, watching television and reading mystery novels. As grandchildren were born, Abe visited his daughters' homes from time to time, carrying his despondent behavior with him. "Look at my new pajamas, Grandpa!" Abe's 6-year-old grandson Tony exclaimed on one occasion, but Abe did not respond.

After arthritis made walking difficult, Abe retired. With more empty days, his depression deepened. Gradually, he developed painful digestive difficulties, but he refused to see a doctor. "Don't need to," he said abruptly when one of his daughters begged him to get medical attention. Answering her invitation to Tony's tenth birthday party, Abe wrote, "Maybe—if I'm still around next month. By the way, when I go, I want my body cremated." Two weeks later, Abe died from an intestinal blockage. His body was found in the living room chair where he habitually spent his days. Although it may seem surprising, Abe's self-destructive acts are a form of suicide.

Factors Related to Elder Suicide

Recall from Chapter 12 that suicide increases over the lifespan. It continues to climb during the elder years, reaching its highest rate among people age 75 and older. Although the incidence of suicide varies among nations, older adults are at increased risk around the world (World Health Organization, 2002).

The higher suicide rate among males persists through late adulthood. Five times as many U.S. elderly men as women take their own lives (U.S. Census Bureau, 2009). Compared with the white majority, most ethnic minority elders have low suicide rates.

What explains these trends? Despite the lifelong pattern of higher rates of depression and more suicide attempts among females, elderly women's closer ties to family and friends, greater willingness to seek social support, and religiosity prevent many from taking their own lives. High levels of social support through extended families and church affiliations may also prevent suicide among ethnic minorities. And within certain groups, such as Alaskan Natives, deep respect for and reliance on older adults to teach cultural traditions foster self-esteem and social integration (Kettl, 1998). This reduces elder suicide, making it nonexistent after age 80.

As in earlier years, the methods favored by elderly males (firearms, hanging) offer less chance of revival than those by elder females (poisoning or drug overdose). Nevertheless, failed suicides are much rarer in old age than in adolescence. The ratio of attempts to completions for the young is as high as 300 to 1; for the elderly, it is 4 to 1 or lower (Conwell, Duberstein, & Caine, 2002). When elders decide to die, they seem especially determined to succeed.

Underreporting of suicides probably occurs at all ages, but it is more common in old age. Medical examiners are less likely to pursue suicide as a cause of death when a person is old. And many elders, like Abe, engage in indirect self-destructive acts rarely classified as suicide—deciding not to go to a doctor when ill or refusing to eat or take prescribed medications. Among institutionalized elders, these efforts to hasten death are widespread (Reiss & Tishler, 2008b). Consequently, elder suicide is an even larger problem than official statistics indicate.

Two types of events prompt suicide in late life. Losses—retirement from a highly valued occupation, widowhood, or social isolation—place elders who have difficulty coping with change at risk for persistent depression. Risks of another type arise when chronic and terminal

ASK YOURSELF

REVIEW
Many elders adapt effectively to negative life changes. List personal and situational factors that facilitate this generally positive outcome.

APPLY
At age 85, Miriam took a long time to get dressed. Joan, her home helper, suggested, "Don't get dressed until I get there. Then I can help you, and it won't take so long." What impact is Joan's approach likely to have on Miriam's personality? What alternative approach would you recommend?

CONNECT
Why is it important to understand older adults' *perceptions* of their circumstances—physical changes (see page 574 in Chapter 17), health, negative life changes, and social support? How do most elders' perceptions contribute to their psychological well-being?)

REFLECT
Among elders you know, do any fit the description of a Third Ager? Explain.

A Changing Social World

Walt and Ruth's outgoing personalities led many family members and friends to seek them out, and they often reciprocated. In contrast, Dick's stubborn nature meant that he and Goldie, for many years, had had a far more restricted network of social ties.

As noted earlier, extraverts (like Walt and Ruth) continue to interact with a wider range of people than do introverts and people (like Dick) with poor social skills. Nevertheless, both cross-sectional and longitudinal research reveals that size of social networks and, therefore, amount of social interaction decline for virtually everyone (Antonucci, Akiyama, & Takahashi, 2004; Lang, Staudinger, & Carstensen, 1998). This finding presents a curious paradox: If social interaction and social support are essential for mental health, how is it possible for elders to interact less yet be generally satisfied with life and less depressed than younger adults?

illnesses severely reduce physical functioning or cause intense pain (Woods, 2008). As comfort and quality of life diminish, feelings of hopelessness and helplessness deepen. Very old people, especially men, are particularly likely to take their own lives under these conditions. The chances are even greater when a sick elder is socially isolated—living alone or in a nursing home with high staff turnover, minimal caregiver support, and little opportunity for personal control over daily life (Reiss & Tishler, 2008a).

Prevention and Treatment

Warning signs of suicide in late adulthood, like those at earlier ages, include efforts to put personal affairs in order, statements about dying, despondency, and sleep and appetite changes. But family members, friends, and caregivers must also watch for indirect self-destructive acts that are unique to old age, such as refusing food or medical treatment. Too often, people in close touch with the elderly incorrectly assume that these symptoms are a "natural" consequence of aging. More than 70 percent of older suicide victims visited their doctors within a month of taking their lives, and 30 percent did so the same week (Pearson & Brown, 2000). Yet their suicidal risk was not recognized.

When suicidal elders are depressed, the most effective treatment combines antidepressant medication with therapy, including help in coping with role transitions, such as retirement, widowhood, and dependency brought about by illness. Distorted ways of thinking ("I'm old, and nothing can be done about my problems") must be countered and revised. Meeting with the family to find ways to reduce loneliness and desperation is also helpful.

Although youth suicide has risen (see Chapter 12, page 422), elder suicide has declined during the past 50 years, as a result of increased economic security among older adults, improved medical care and social services, and more favorable cultural attitudes toward retirement. Communities are beginning to recognize the importance of additional preventive steps, such as telephone hot lines with trained volunteers who provide emotional support and agencies that arrange for regular home visitors or "buddy system" phone calls. In institutions, providing residents with privacy, autonomy, and space helps prevent self destructive behavior (Conwell & Duberstein, 2001).

Finally, elder suicide raises a controversial ethical issue: Do people with incurable illnesses have the right to take their own lives? We will take up this topic in Chapter 19.

Suicide reaches its highest rate among people age 75 and older. Warning signs include efforts to put personal affairs in order, statements about dying, despondency, and sleep and appetite changes.

Social Theories of Aging

Social theories of aging offer explanations for changes in elders' social activity. Two older perspectives—disengagement theory and activity theory—interpret declines in social interaction in opposite ways. More recent approaches—continuity theory and socioemotional selectivity theory—account for a wider range of findings.

■ **DISENGAGEMENT THEORY.** According to **disengagement theory,** mutual withdrawal between elders and society takes place in anticipation of death (Cumming & Henry, 1961). Older people decrease their activity levels and interact less frequently, becoming more preoccupied with their inner lives. At the same time, society frees elders from employment and family responsibilities. The result is viewed as beneficial for both sides. Elders are granted a life of tranquility. And once they disengage, their deaths are less disruptive to society.

Clearly, however, not everyone disengages! As we saw in Chapter 17 when we discussed wisdom, older adults in many cultures move into new positions of prestige and power because of their long life experience. Even after retirement, many people sustain aspects of their work; others develop new, rewarding roles in their communities. Disengagement by the elderly, then, may represent not their personal preference but, rather, a failure of the social world to provide opportunities for engagement. The more social opportunities elders report, the more strongly they believe they can create worthwhile social experiences for themselves (Lang, Featherman, & Nesselroade, 1997).

As we will see shortly, older adults' retreat from interaction is more complex than disengagement theory implies. Instead of disengaging from all social ties, they let go of unsatisfying contacts and maintain satisfying ones. And sometimes, they put up with less than satisfying relationships to remain engaged! For example, though Ruth often complained about Dick's insensitive behavior, she reluctantly agreed to travel with Dick and Goldie because she wanted to share the experience with Walt.

■ **ACTIVITY THEORY.** Attempting to overcome the flaws of disengagement theory, **activity theory** states that social barriers to engagement, not the desires of elders, cause declining rates of interaction. When older people lose certain roles (for example, through retirement or widowhood), they try to find others in an effort to stay about as active and busy as they were in middle age. In this view, elders' life satisfaction depends on conditions that permit them to remain engaged in roles and relationships (Maddox, 1963).

Although people do seek alternative sources of meaning and gratification in response to social losses, activity theory fails to acknowledge any psychological change in old age. Many studies show that merely offering elders opportunities for social contact does not lead to greater social activity. In nursing homes, for example, where social partners are abundant, social interaction is very low, even among the healthiest residents—a circumstance we will examine when we discuss housing arrangements for the elderly. Especially troubling for activity theory is the repeated finding that when health status is controlled, elders who have larger social networks and engage in more activities are not necessarily happier (Lee & Markides, 1990; Ritchey, Ritchey, & Dietz, 2001). Recall that quality, not quantity, of relationships predicts psychological well-being in old age.

■ **CONTINUITY THEORY.** Unlike activity theory, **continuity theory** does not view elders' efforts to remain active in terms of simple replacement of lost social roles with new ones. Rather, according to this view, most aging adults strive to maintain a personal system—an identity and a set of personality dispositions, interests, roles, and skills—that promotes life satisfaction by ensuring consistency between their past and anticipated future. This striving for continuity does not mean that elders' lives are static. To the contrary, aging produces inevitable change, but most older adults try to minimize stress and disruptiveness by integrating those changes into a coherent, consistent life path. As much as possible, they choose to use familiar skills and engage in familiar activities with familiar people—preferences that provide a secure sense of routine and direction in life.

Research on the daily lives of older adults confirms a high degree of continuity in everyday pursuits and relationships. For most, friends and family members with whom they interact remain much the same, as do work, volunteer, leisure, and social activities. Even after a change (such as retirement), people usually make choices that extend the previous direction of their lives, engaging in new activities but often within familiar domains. For example, a retired manager of a children's bookstore collaborated with friends to build a children's library and donate it to an overseas orphanage. A musician who, because of arthritis, could no longer play the violin arranged regular get-togethers with musically inclined friends to listen to and talk about music. Robert Atchley (1989), originator of continuity theory, noted, "Everyday life for most older people is like long-running improvisational theater in which . . . changes are mostly in the form of new episodes [rather] than entirely new plays" (p. 185).

Elders' reliance on continuity has many benefits. Participation in familiar activities with familiar people provides repeated practice that helps preserve physical and cognitive functioning, fosters self-esteem and mastery, and affirms identity (Finchum & Weber, 2000). Investing in long-standing, close relationships provides comfort, pleasure, and a network of social support. Finally, striving for continuity is essential for attaining Erikson's sense of ego integrity, which depends on preserving a sense of personal history (Atchley, 1999).

As we explore social contexts and relationships of aging, we will encounter many examples of how elders use continuity to experience aging positively, as a "gentle slope." We will also address ways that communities can help them do so.

■ **SOCIOEMOTIONAL SELECTIVITY THEORY.** A final perspective addresses how people's social networks sustain continuity while also narrowing as they age. According to **socioemotional selectivity theory,** social interaction extends lifelong selection processes. In middle adulthood, marital relationships deepen, siblings feel closer, and number of friendships declines. In old age, contacts with family and long-term friends are sustained until the eighties, when they diminish

© DAVID M. GROSSMAN/THE IMAGE WORKS

These sisters—ages 93 and 89—greet each other with enthusiasm. The one on the right traveled from Poland to New York City to make possible this reunion. To preserve emotional equilibrium and reduce stress, elders increasingly emphasize familiar, emotionally rewarding relationships.

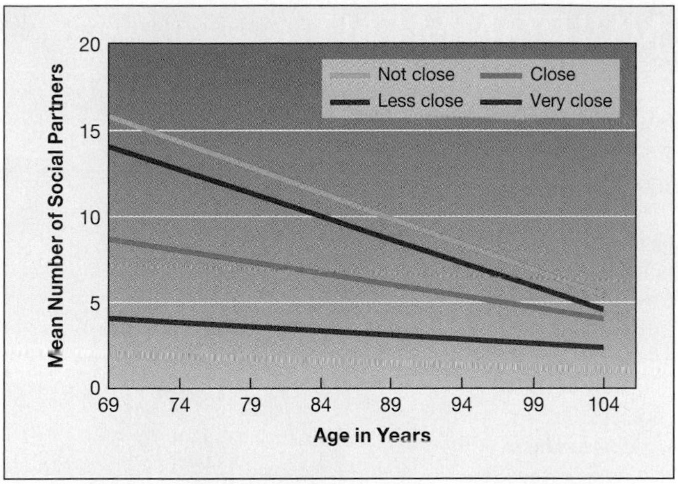

■ **FIGURE 18.1** ■ **Age-related change in number of social partners varying in closeness.** In interviews with over 500 elders ranging in age from 69 to 104, the number of "not close" and "less close" partners fell off steeply with age, whereas the number of "close" and "very close" partners declined minimally. (From F. R. Lang, U. M. Staudinger, & L. L. Carstensen, 1998, "Perspectives on Socioemotional Selectivity in Late Life: How Personality and Social Context Do (and Do Not) Make a Difference," *Journal of Gerontology, 53B,* p. 24. Copyright © 1998 The Gerontological Society of America. Adapted by permission of Oxford University Press and F. R. Lang.)

gradually in favor of a few very close relationships. In contrast, as Figure 18.1 shows, contacts with acquaintances and willingness to form new social ties fall off steeply from middle through late adulthood (Carstensen, Fung, & Charles, 2003; Fung, Carstensen, & Lang, 2001).

What explains these changes? Socioemotional selectivity theory states that physical and psychological aspects of aging lead to changes in the functions of social interaction. ***TAKE A MOMENT...*** Consider the reasons you interact with members of your social network. At times, you approach them to get information. At other times, you seek affirmation of your worth as a person. You also choose social partners to regulate emotion, approaching those who evoke positive feelings and avoiding those who make you feel sad, angry, or uncomfortable. For older adults, who have gathered a lifetime of information, the information-gathering function becomes less significant. And elders realize it is risky to approach people they do not know for self-affirmation: Stereotypes of aging increase the odds of receiving a condescending, hostile, or indifferent response.

Instead, as physical fragility makes it more important to avoid stress, older adults emphasize the emotion-regulating function of interaction. In one study, younger and older adults were asked to categorize their social partners. Younger people more often sorted them on the basis of information seeking and future contact, while older people emphasized anticipated feelings (Frederickson & Carstensen, 1990). They appeared highly motivated to approach pleasant relationships and avoid unpleasant ones. Interacting mostly with relatives and friends increases the chances that elders' emotional equilibrium will be preserved.

Within these close bonds, older adults apply their emotional expertise to promote harmony. They are less likely than younger people to respond to tensions with destructive tactics (yelling, arguing) and more likely to use constructive strategies, such as expressing affection or calmly letting the situation blow over (Birditt & Fingerman, 2005; Carstensen, Gottman, & Levenson, 1995). Elders also reinterpret conflict in less stressful ways—often by identifying something positive in the situation (Labouvie-Vief, 2003). Consequently, despite their smaller social networks, they are happier than younger people with their number of friends and report fewer problematic relationships (Akiyama et al., 2003; Fingerman & Birditt, 2003). As the Biology and Environment box on page 614 reveals, people's perception of time is strongly linked to their social goals. When remaining time is limited, adults of all ages place more emphasis on the emotional quality of their social experiences.

This emphasis on *relationship quality* in late life helps explain an exception to the restriction of social relationships just described. In collectivist cultures, where people value an interdependent self and, thus, attach great importance to remaining embedded in their social group, elders may be motivated to sustain high-quality ties with all partners! In line with this prediction, in a Hong Kong study, older adults scoring high in interdependence both expanded their number of emotionally close social partners and sustained the same number of peripheral social partners into advanced old age (Yeung, Fung, & Lang, 2008). In contrast, Hong Kong elders scoring low in interdependence resembled their Western counterparts: They gradually limited their social ties to a few close relationships.

In sum, socioemotional selectivity theory views elders' preference for high-quality, emotionally fulfilling relationships to result from changing life conditions. But the meaning of relationship quality and, therefore, the number and variety of people to whom elders turn for pleasurable interaction and self-affirmation vary with culture.

Social Contexts of Aging: Communities, Neighborhoods, and Housing

The physical and social contexts in which elders live affect their social experiences and, consequently, their development and adjustment. Communities, neighborhoods, and housing arrangements vary in the extent to which they enable aging residents to satisfy their social needs.

■ **COMMUNITIES AND NEIGHBORHOODS.** About half of U.S. ethnic minority older adults live in cities, compared with only one-third of Caucasians. The majority of senior citizens reside in suburbs, where they moved earlier in their lives and usually remain after retirement. Suburban elders have higher incomes and report better health than inner-city elders do. But

BIOLOGY AND ENVIRONMENT

Aging, Time Perception, and Social Goals

With whom would you spend time if you knew you would soon be moving away from your community? When asked this question, young people typically choose close friends and relatives, with whom they have enduring, positive relationships. Their response resembles that of older people. Elders view time as precious and perceive it as flying by rapidly (Kennedy, Fung, & Carstensen, 2001). Aware that time is "running out," they don't waste it on unlikely future payoffs. Instead, they opt for emotionally gratifying social experiences in the here and now.

Socioemotional selectivity theory underscores the crucial role our time perspective plays in the social goals we select and pursue (Carstensen, Isaacowitz, & Charles, 1999). People who perceive future time as limited search for meaningful social experiences. Yet tests of the theory documenting an age-related rise in time spent with familiar, highly rewarding social partners do not permit us to separate the influences of age and time orientation on people's social goals. Is time perspective really at the heart of elders' focus on old friends and family members as desired social partners?

To find out, Laura Carstensen and her colleagues uncoupled age from time. In a study that held age constant but varied time left in life, the researchers compared three groups of men in their late thirties. The first group was HIV-negative, the second HIV-positive without AIDS symptoms, and the third HIV-positive and experiencing deadly symptoms of AIDS (Carstensen & Fredrickson, 1998). When asked to categorize a variety of potential social partners, each successive group increasingly emphasized the emotional rewards of the relationship. The men with AIDS symptoms, who had the least time left, focused nearly exclusively on the emotional quality of social ties, just as very old people do.

In another investigation, the researchers permitted age to vary but held time perspective constant by giving participants a hypothetical situation in which their future had expanded. People between ages 11 and 92 were asked to imagine that they had just received a telephone call from their doctor, who told them of a new medical breakthrough that would add 20 years to their life (Fung, Carstensen, & Lutz, 1999). Under these conditions, older people's strong bias for familiar, emotionally close social partners disappeared! Their social preferences were just as diverse as those of younger people.

The preference for close partners when time is short actually stems from increased desire for emotionally meaningful interactions, not from a need for social support during difficult times. Adults of all ages explain their choice by referring to the emotionally fulfilling quality of the relationship (Fung & Carstensen, 2004). They also say they would take special steps to promote positive interaction if they knew a relationship would be short-lived—for example, treat a social partner who had behaved inappropriately more gently, by avoiding confrontation (Fingerman, Miller, & Charles, 2008).

© KEVIN DODGE/CORBIS

Elders view time as precious and perceive it as flying by rapidly—an important reason this grandmother savors this joyous moment with her young granddaughter.

In sum, the social preferences of old age are an active adaptation to shrinking longevity. When days are numbered, present-oriented goals—social connectedness and gratifying relationships—become high priorities.

inner-city elders are better off in terms of transportation and proximity to social services, and they are not as disadvantaged in terms of health, income, and availability of services as the one-fifth of American seniors who live in small towns and rural areas (U.S. Department of Health and Human Services, 2007a). In addition, small-town and rural elderly are less likely to live near their children, who often leave these communities in early adulthood.

Yet small-town and rural elderly compensate for distance from children and social services by establishing closer relationships with nearby extended family and by interacting more with neighbors and friends (Schilling & Wahl, 2002; Shaw, 2005). Smaller communities have features that foster gratifying relationships—stability of residents, shared values and lifestyles, willingness to exchange social support, and frequent social visits as country people "drop in" on one another. And many suburban and rural communities have responded to elder residents' needs by developing transportation programs (such as special buses and vans) to take elders to health and social services, senior centers, and shopping centers.

Both urban and rural older adults report greater life satisfaction when many senior citizens reside in their neighborhood and are available as like-minded companions. Presence of family is less crucial when neighbors and nearby friends provide social support (Gabriel & Bowling, 2004). This does not mean that neighbors replace family relationships. But elders are content as long as their children and other relatives who live far away arrange occasional visits (Hooyman & Kiyak, 2008).

Like many older adults, these Spanish men reap great satisfaction from residing in a neighborhood with like-minded senior residents. Presence of family is less crucial when neighbors and nearby friends provide social support.

Compared with older adults in urban areas, those in quiet neighborhoods in small and midsized communities are more satisfied with life. A major reason is that smaller communities have lower crime rates (AARP, 2006; Scheidt & Windley, 1985). As we will see next, fear of crime has profound, negative consequences for elders' sense of security and comfort.

VICTIMIZATION AND FEAR OF CRIME. Walt and Ruth's single-family home stood in an urban neighborhood, five blocks from the business district where Walt's photography shop had been prior to his retirement. When leaving home for more than a few hours, Walt and Ruth telephoned their next-door neighbor and asked her to keep an eye on the property. As the neighborhood aged, some homes fell into disrepair, and the population became more transient. Shops were open Thursday and Friday evenings, but Walt and Ruth saved their errands for daylight hours. Although they had never been victimized, crime was on their minds and affected their behavior.

Media attention has led to a widely held belief that crime against the elderly is common. In reality, older adults are less often targets of crime, especially violent crime, than other age groups. In urban areas, however, purse snatching and pickpocketing are more often committed against elders (especially women) than younger people, probably because perpetrators feel that they can easily overpower older and female victims (U.S. Department of Justice, 2008). A single incident can strike intense anxiety into the hearts of seniors because of its potential for physical injury and its financial consequences for those with low incomes.

Among frail elders living alone and in inner-city areas, fear of crime, which is sometimes greater than worries about income, health, and housing, restricts activities and undermines morale (Beaulieu, Leclerc, & Dube, 2003). Even one event can have serious, long-term consequences. In one study, older adults who had experienced a violent crime were more likely than those with physical and cognitive impairments to enter a nursing home (Lachs et al., 2006). Neighborhood Watch and other programs that encourage residents to look out for one another reduce fear and feelings of isolation from the community. Some cities have established special police units to investigate and prevent crimes against seniors.

HOUSING ARRANGEMENTS. Elders' housing preferences reflect a strong desire for **aging in place**—remaining in a familiar setting where they have control over their everyday life. Overwhelmingly, older adults in Western nations want to stay in the neighborhoods where they spent their adult lives; in fact, 90 percent remain in or near their old home. In the United States, fewer than 5 percent relocate to other communities (U.S. Department of Health and Human Services, 2007b). These moves are usually motivated by a desire to live closer to children or, among the more economically advantaged and healthy, a desire for a more temperate climate and a place to pursue leisure interests.

Most elder relocations occur within the same town or city and are prompted by declining health, widowhood, or disability (Sergeant, Ekerdt, & Chapin, 2008). As we look at housing arrangements for older adults, we will see that the more a setting deviates from home life, the harder it is for elders to adjust.

Ordinary Homes. For the majority of elders, who are not physically impaired, staying in their own homes affords the greatest possible personal control—freedom to arrange space and schedule daily events as one chooses. More elders in Western countries live on their own today than ever before—a trend due to improved health and economic well-being (U.S. Department of Health and Human Services, 2009a). But when health and mobility problems appear, independent living poses risks. Most homes are designed for younger people. They are seldom modified to suit the physical capacities of their elder residents. And living alone in ill health is linked to social isolation and loneliness (Victor et al., 2000).

When Ruth reached her mid-eighties, Sybil begged her to move into her home. Like many adult children of Southern, Central, and Eastern European descent (Greek, Italian, Polish, and others), Sybil felt an especially strong obligation to care for her frail mother. Older adults of these cultural backgrounds, as well as African Americans, Asians, Hispanics, and Native Americans, more often live in extended families (Gabrel, 2000; Hays & George, 2002).

Yet increasing numbers of ethnic minority elders want to live on their own, although poverty often prevents them from doing so. For example, two decades ago, most Asian-American older adults were living with their children, whereas today half live independently—a trend also evident in certain Asian nations, such as Japan (Takagi, Silverstein, & Crimmins, 2007; Wilmoth, 2001). With sufficient income to keep her home, Ruth refused to move in with Sybil. Continuity theory helps us understand why many elders react this way, even after health

© MICHAEL NEWMAN/PHOTOEDIT

This Chinese-American elder lives in her son and daughter-in-law's home, helping to rear their children—a traditional arrangement common in China. But increasingly, Asian-American older adults are choosing to live independently.

problems accumulate. As the site of memorable life events, the home strengthens continuity with the past, sustaining elders' sense of identity in the face of physical declines and social losses. And it permits older adults to adapt to their surroundings in familiar, comfortable ways (Atchley, 1999). Elders also value their independence, privacy, and network of nearby friends and neighbors.

During the past half century, the number of unmarried, divorced, and widowed elders living alone has risen dramatically. Approximately 30 percent of U.S. elders live by themselves, a figure that rises to nearly 50 percent for those age 85 and older. This trend, though evident in all segments of the elderly population, is less pronounced among men, who are far more likely than women to be living with a spouse into advanced old age (U.S. Census Bureau, 2009).

Over 40 percent of American elders who live alone are poverty-stricken—rates many times greater than among elderly couples. More than 70 percent are widowed women. Because of lower earnings in earlier years, some entered old age this way. Others became poor for the first time, often because they outlived a spouse who suffered a lengthy, costly illness. With age, their financial status worsens as their assets shrink and their own health-care costs rise (Biegel & Liebbrant, 2006; U.S. Census Bureau, 2009). Under these conditions, isolation, loneliness, and depression can pile up. Poverty among lone elderly women is deeper in the United States than in other Western nations because of less generous government-sponsored income and health benefits. Consequently, the feminization of poverty deepens in old age.

Residential Communities. About 15 percent of U.S. senior citizens live in residential communities, which come in great variety (Schafer, 1999; U.S. Department of Health and Human Services, 2007b). Housing developments for the aged, either single-dwelling or apartment complexes, differ from ordinary homes only in that they have been modified to suit elders' capacities (featuring, for example, single-level living space and grab bars in bathrooms). Some are federally subsidized units for the elderly poor, but most are privately developed retirement villages with adjoining recreational facilities.

For elders who need more help with everyday tasks, *assisted-living* arrangements are available (see Chapter 17, page 589). **Congregate housing**—an increasingly popular long-term care option—provides a variety of support services, including meals in a common dining room, along with watchful oversight of residents with physical and mental disabilities. **Life-care communities** offer a range of housing alternatives, from independent or congregate housing to full nursing home care. For a large initial payment and additional monthly fees, life care guarantees that elders' changing needs will be met within the same facility as they age.

Unlike Ruth and Walt, who remained in their own home, Dick and Goldie decided in their late sixties to move to nearby congregate housing. For Dick, the move was a positive turn of events that permitted him to relate to peers on the basis of their current life together, setting aside past failures in the outside world. Dick found gratifying leisure pursuits—leading an exercise class, organizing a charity drive with Goldie, and using his skills as a baker to make cakes for birthday and anniversary celebrations.

Studies of diverse residential options for older adults reveal that they can have positive effects on physical and mental health. A specially designed physical space and care on an as-needed basis help elders overcome mobility limitations, thereby enabling greater social participation and a more active lifestyle (Fonda, Clipp, & Maddox, 2002; Jenkins, Pienta, & Horgas, 2002). And in societies where old age leads to reduced status, age-segregated living is gratifying to most elders who choose it. It may open up useful roles and leadership opportunities (Ball et al., 2000). The more older adults perceive the environment as socially supportive, the more they collaborate with one another in coping with stressors of aging and in providing assistance to other residents (Lawrence & Schigelone, 2002). Congregate housing appears to be well-suited to promoting mutually supportive relationships among elder residents.

Nevertheless, no U.S. federal regulations govern assisted-living facilities, which vary widely in quality. Low-income ethnic minority elders are less likely to use assisted living and, when they do, usually enter lower-quality settings. And in some states, assisted-living facilities are prohibited from providing any nursing care and monitoring, requiring elders to move when their health declines (Hawes & Phillips, 2007; Hernandez & Newcomer, 2007). Yet physical designs and support services that enable aging in place are vital for elders' well-being. These include homelike surroundings, division of large environments into smaller units to facilitate meaningful activities, social roles and relationships, and the latest assistive technologies to permit adaptation to elders' changing health needs (Cutler, 2007).

Shared values and goals among residents with similar backgrounds also enhance life satisfaction. Older adults who feel socially integrated into the setting are more likely to consider it their home. But those who lack like-minded companions are unlikely to characterize it as home and are at high risk for loneliness and depression (Adams, Sanders, & Auth, 2004; Young, 1998).

Nursing Homes. The 5 percent of Americans age 65 and older who live in nursing homes experience the most extreme restriction of autonomy and social integration. Although potential companions are abundant, interaction is low. To regulate emotion in social interaction (so important to elders), personal control over social experiences is vital. Yet nursing home residents have little opportunity to choose their social partners, and timing of contact is generally determined by staff rather than by elders' preferences. Social withdrawal is an adaptive response to these often overcrowded, hospital-like settings. Although interaction with people in the outside world predicts nursing home residents' life satisfaction, interaction within the institution does not (Baltes, Wahl, & Reichert, 1992). Not surprisingly, nursing home residents with physical but not mental impairments are far more depressed, anxious, and lonely than their community-dwelling counterparts (Guildner et al., 2001).

Designing more homelike nursing homes could help increase residents' sense of security and control. U.S. nursing homes, usually operated for profit, are often packed with residents and institutional in their operation. In contrast, European facilities are liberally supported by public funds and resemble high-quality assisted living.

In a radically changed U.S. nursing-home concept called THE GREEN HOUSE® model, a large, outdated nursing home in Mississippi was replaced by ten small, self-contained houses (Rabig et al., 2006). Each is limited to ten or fewer residents, who live in private bedroom-bathroom suites that surround a family-style communal space. Besides providing personal care, a stable staff of nursing assistants fosters elders' control and independence. Residents determine their own daily schedules and are invited to join in both recreational and household activities, including planning and preparing meals, cleaning, gardening, and caring for pets. A professional support team—including licensed nurses, therapists, social workers, physicians, and pharmacists—visits regularly to serve residents' health needs. In a comparison of Green House residents with traditional nursing home residents, Green House elders reported substantially better quality of life, and they also showed less decline over time in ability to carry out activities of daily living (ADLs) (Kane et al., 2007).

The Green House model—and other models like it—is blurring distinctions among nursing home, assisted living, and "independent" living. By making the home a central, organizing principle, The Green House approach includes all the aging-in-place features that ensure late-life well-being: physical and emotional comfort, enjoyable daily pursuits, functional competence, and meaningful relationships.

THE GREEN HOUSE® model blurs distinctions among nursing home, assisted living, and "independent" living. In this homelike setting, residents determine their own daily schedules and are invited to help with household tasks. Green House living environments, including this one in San Angelo, Texas, now exist in more than 20 U.S. states.

ASK YOURSELF

REVIEW
Cite features of neighborhoods and residential communities that enhance elders' life satisfaction.

APPLY
Sam lives alone in the same home he has occupied for over 30 years. His adult children cannot understand why he won't move across town to a modern apartment. Using continuity theory, explain why Sam prefers to stay where he is.

CONNECT
According to socioemotional selectivity theory, when time is limited, adults focus on the emotional quality of their social relationships. How do elders apply their emotional expertise (discussed on page 605) to attain this goal?

REFLECT
Imagine yourself as an elderly resident in an assisted-living facility. List all the features you would want your living environment to have, explaining how each helps ensure your well-being.

Relationships in Late Adulthood

The **social convoy** is an influential model of changes in our social networks as we move through life. ***TAKE A MOMENT...*** Picture yourself in the midst of a cluster of ships traveling together, granting one another safety and support. Ships in the inner circle represent people closest to you, such as a spouse, best friend, parent, or child. Those less close but still important travel on the outside. With age, ships exchange places in the convoy, and some drift off while others join the procession (Antonucci, Akiyama, & Takahashi, 2004). As long as the convoy continues to exist, you adapt positively.

In the following sections, we examine the ways elders with diverse lifestyles sustain social networks of family members and friends. As ties are lost, older adults draw others closer and occasionally add replacements, though not at the rate they did at younger ages. Although the size of the convoy decreases as agemates die, elders are rarely left without people in their inner circle who contribute to their well-being—a testament to their resilience in maintaining effective social networks (Fiori, Smith, & Antonucci, 2007). But tragically, for some older adults the social convoy breaks down. We will also explore the circumstances in which elders experience abuse and neglect at the hands of those close to them.

© DAVID YOUNG-WOLFF/PHOTOEDIT

After retirement, men's increased participation in household tasks results in a greater sense of equity in marriage, contributing to the rise in marital satisfaction from middle to late adulthood.

Marriage

Even with the high U.S. divorce rate, one in every four or five first marriages is expected to last at least 50 years. Walt's comment to Ruth that "the last few decades have been the happiest" characterizes the attitudes and behaviors of many elderly couples who have spent their adult lives together. Marital satisfaction rises from middle to late adulthood, when it is at its peak (Ko et al., 2007; Levenson, Carstensen, & Gottman, 1993). Several changes in life circumstance and couples' communication underlie this trend.

First, late-life marriages involve fewer stressful responsibilities that can negatively affect relationships, such as rearing children and balancing demands of career and family (Kemp & Kemp, 2002). Second, perceptions of fairness in the relationship increase as men participate more in household tasks after retirement. For elders who experienced little social pressure for gender equality in their youth, division of labor in the home still reflects traditional roles. Men take on more home maintenance projects, whereas women's duties—cooking, cleaning, laundry, and shopping—continue as before. Among adults retiring today, "feminine" tasks are more equally shared than they were during work life (Kulik, 2001). In either case, men's increased involvement at home often results in a greater sense of equity in marriage than before. Third, with extra time together, the majority of couples engage in more joint leisure activities, which—especially for women—enhances sense of marital closeness (Trudel et al., 2008).

Fourth, greater emotional understanding and emphasis on regulating emotion in relationships lead to more positive interactions between spouses. Compared to younger couples, elderly couples rate their relationship as higher in quality, disagree less often, and resolve their differences in more constructive ways. Even in unhappy marriages, elders are less likely to let their disagreements escalate into expressions of anger and resentment (Carstensen, Isaacowitz, & Charles, 1999; Hatch & Bulcroft, 2004). For example, when Dick complained about Goldie's cooking, Goldie tried to appease him: "All right, Dick, next birthday I won't make cheesecake." And when Goldie brought up Dick's bickering and criticism, Dick usually said, "I know, dear," and retreated to another room. As in other relationships, the elderly protect themselves from stress by molding marital ties to make them as pleasant as possible.

Finally, compared to their single agemates, married elders generally have larger social networks of both family members and friends, with whom they interact more frequently. As long as older adults report mostly high-quality ties, this relationship profile provides for social engagement and support from a variety of sources and is linked to higher psychological well-being (Birditt & Antonucci, 2007; Fiori, Smoth, & Antonucci, 2007).

When marital dissatisfaction exists, however, even having close, high-quality friendships cannot reduce its profoundly negative impact on adjustment. A poor marriage often takes a greater toll on women than on men (Birditt & Antonucci, 2007; Whisman et al., 2006). Recall from Chapter 14 that women more often try to work on a troubling relationship. In old age, expending energy in this way is especially taxing, both physically and mentally. Men, in contrast, often protect themselves by avoiding discussion (Levenson, Carstensen, & Gottman, 1993).

Gay and Lesbian Partnerships

Elderly gays and lesbians in long-term partnerships have sustained their relationships through a historical period of hostility and discrimination toward homosexuals. Nevertheless, most report happy, highly fulfilling relationships, pointing to their partner as their most important source of social support. And compared with homosexual elders who live alone, homosexual partners rate their physical and mental health more favorably (Grossman, D'Augelli, & Hershberger, 2000; Wojciechowski, 1998).

A lifetime of effective coping with an oppressive social environment may have strengthened homosexuals' skill at dealing with late-life physical and social changes, thereby contributing to a satisfying partnership (Gabbay & Wahler, 2002). And changing social conditions, including the greater ease with which younger generations embrace their sexual minority identities and "come out," may have encouraged more older adults to do the same, with benefits for their well-being. Also, greater gender-role flexibility enables gay and lesbian couples to adapt easily to sharing household tasks following retirement (Cohler & Hostetler, 2007).

Because of imagined or real strain in family relationships when they told others about their homosexuality, gays and lesbians less often assume that family members will provide support in old age. Consequently, many have forged strong friendships to replace or supplement family ties (Kimmel, 2004; Richard & Brown, 2006). Homosexual couples with gratifying friendship networks report high life satisfaction and less fear of aging (Slusher, Mayer, & Dunkle, 1996).

Nevertheless, because of continuing prejudice and lack of societal recognition of their partnerships, aging gays and lesbians face unique challenges (Woolf, 2001). Health-care systems are often unresponsive to their unique needs. And where gay and lesbian unions are not legally recognized (in most U.S. states), if one partner becomes frail or ill, the other may not be welcome in hospitals or nursing homes or be allowed to participate in health-care decisions—an issue we will return to in Chapter 19. These circumstances can make late-life declines and losses especially painful.

Divorce, Remarriage, and Cohabitation

When Walt's uncle Louie was 61, he divorced his wife Sandra after 17 years of marriage. Although she knew the marriage was far from perfect, Sandra had lived with Louie long enough that the divorce came as a shock. A year later, Louie married Rachella, a divorcée who shared his enthusiasm for sports and dance.

Couples who divorce in late adulthood constitute less than 1 percent of all divorces in any given year. But the divorce rate among people age 65 and older is increasing as new generations of elders become more accepting of marital breakup and as the divorce risk rises for second and subsequent marriages. When asked about the reasons for divorce, elderly men typically mention lack of shared interests and activities, whereas women frequently cite emotional distance and their partner's refusal to communicate (Weingarten, 1988). "We never talked," Sandra said. "I felt isolated."

Compared with younger adults, longtime married elders have given their adult lives to the relationship. Following divorce, they find it harder to separate their identity from that of their former spouse, and they suffer more from a sense of personal failure. Relationships with family and friends shift at a time when close bonds are crucial for psychological well-being. Women, overall, suffer more than men because they are more likely to spend their remaining years living alone. The financial consequences are severe—greater than for widowhood because many accumulated assets are lost in property settlements (McDonald & Robb, 2004; Miller, Hemesath, & Nelson, 1997).

In younger individuals, divorce often leads to greater awareness of negative patterns of behavior and determination to change. In contrast, self-criticism in divorced elders heightens guilt and depression because their self-worth depends more on past than on future accomplishments. Louie and Sandra blamed each other. "I was always miserable with Sandra," Louie claimed, even though the couple's earlier days had been reasonably happy. Although blaming the partner may distort the marital history, it is a common coping strategy that enables older adults to preserve integrity and self-esteem (Weingarten, 1989).

Remarriage rates are low in late adulthood and decline with age, although they are considerably higher among divorced than widowed elders. Older men's opportunities for remarriage are far greater than women's. Nevertheless, the gender gap in elder remarriage is much smaller after divorce than after widowhood. Perhaps because their previous relationship was disappointing, divorcées find it easier than widows to enter a new relationship. Also, divorced older women may be more motivated to remarry because of their more extreme economic circumstances. Finally, some divorced elders (like Louie and Rachella) leave their marriages only after a new bond is forming (Huyck, 1995).

Compared with younger people who remarry, elders who do so enter more stable relationships, as their divorce rate is much lower. In Louie and Rachella's case, the second marriage lasted for 32 years! Perhaps late-life remarriages are more successful because they involve more maturity, patience, and a better balance of romantic with practical concerns (Kemp & Kemp, 2002). Older couples who remarry are generally very satisfied with their new relationships, although men tend to be more content than women (Brubaker, 1985). With fewer potential mates, perhaps women who remarry in late life settle for less desirable partners.

Rather than remarrying, today more elders who enter a new relationship choose cohabitation, a trend expected to continue as the baby boomers—the first generation to cohabit at high rates in early adulthood—reach late life. Also, divorce rates have been relatively high among the baby boomers, yielding more unmarried aging adults available for partnering.

Like elder remarriages, cohabitation in late adulthood results in more stable relationships and higher relationship quality than it did at younger ages. But compared with younger people, fewer cohabiting elders have plans to marry. Reasons frequently given are concerns about acceptance of the new partner by adult children and negative financial consequences with respect to taxes, social security or pension benefits, and adult children's inheritance (King & Scott, 2005; Kemp & Kemp, 2002). In addition, older divorced and widowed women often mention unwillingness to give up their newfound independence (Lopata, 1996). Finally, like younger cohabiters, U.S. cohabiting elders tend to have less conventional values—for example, are less religious—than their married agemates (Brown, Lee, & Bulanda, 2006).

Widowhood

Walt died shortly after Ruth turned 80. Like over 70 percent of widowed elders, Ruth described the loss of her spouse as the most stressful event of her life. As two researchers noted, being widowed means that the survivor has "lost the role and identity of being a spouse (being married and doing things as a couple), which is potentially one of the most pervasive, intense, intimate, and personal roles that they have ever had in their life" (Lund & Caserta, 2004a, p. 29). Ruth felt lonely, anxious, and depressed for several months after the funeral.

Widows make up about one-third of the elderly population in industrialized nations. Because women live longer than men and are less likely to remarry, more than 40 percent of U.S. women age 65 and older are widowed, compared with only 13 percent of men. Ethnic minorities with high rates of poverty and chronic disease are more likely to be widowed (U.S. Census Bureau, 2009).

Earlier we mentioned that most widows and widowers live alone rather than in extended families, a trend that is stronger for whites than for ethnic minorities. Though less well-off financially than married elders, most want to retain control over their time and living space and to avoid disagreements with their adult children. Widowed elders who relocate because they cannot make mortgage payments or keep up their homes usually move closer to family but not into the same residence (Lopata, 1996).

© PETER ARNOLD, INC./ALAMY

Most men rely on their wives for social connectedness, household tasks, and promotion of healthy behaviors, so they are less prepared than women for the challenges of widowhood. This man, however, appears to be managing well—in part because he is skilled at preparing nutritious meals.

The greatest problem for recently widowed elders is profound loneliness (Lund, 1993). But adaptation varies widely, depending on age, social support, and personality. Elders have fewer lasting problems than younger individuals who are widowed, probably because death in later life is viewed as less unfair (Stroebe & Stroebe, 1993). And most widowed elders—especially those with outgoing personalities and high self-esteem—are resilient in the face of loneliness (Moore & Stratton, 2002; van Baarsen, 2002). To sustain continuity with their past, they try to preserve social relationships that were important before the spouse's death and report that relatives and friends respond in kind, contacting them at least as often as before (Utz et al., 2002). Also, the stronger elders' sense of self-efficacy in handling tasks of daily living, the more favorably they adjust (Fry, 2001).

Nevertheless, widowed individuals must reorganize their lives, reconstructing an identity that is separate from the deceased spouse. Wives whose roles depended on their husbands' typically find this harder than those who developed rewarding roles of their own. But overall, men show more physical and mental health problems and greater risk of mortality than women, for several reasons (Bennett, Smith, & Hughes, 2005; Pinquart, 2003). First, because most men relied on their wives for social connectedness, household tasks, promotion of healthy behaviors, and coping with stressors, they are less prepared than women for the challenges of widowhood. Second, because of gender-role expectations, men feel less free to express their emotions or to ask for help with meals, household tasks, and social relationships (Bennett, 2007; Lund & Caserta, 2004b). Finally, men tend to be less involved in religious activities—a vital source of social support and inner strength (Lee et al., 2001).

In two studies of older widowers, those in their seventies reported the most depression and showed the slowest rate of improvement over the following two years. The death of their wives occurred around the time they were adjusting to retirement, resulting in two major changes at once, with widowhood highly unexpected because most wives outlive their husbands (Lund & Caserta, 2001, 2004a). African-American widowers, however, show no elevated risk of mortality over African-American married elders, and they report less depression than Caucasian widowers (Balaswamy & Richardson, 2001; Elwert & Christakis, 2006). Perhaps greater support from extended family and church is responsible.

Sex differences in the experience of widowhood contribute to men's higher remarriage rate. Women's kinkeeper role (see Chapter 16, page 545) and ability to form close friendships may lead them to feel less need to remarry. In addition, because many elderly women share the widowed state, they probably offer one another helpful advice and sympathy. In contrast, men often lack skills for maintaining family relationships, forming emotionally satisfying ties outside marriage, and handling the chores of their deceased wives.

Still, most widowed elders fare well within a few years, resembling their married counterparts in psychological well-being.

Applying What We Know

Fostering Adaptation to Widowhood in Late Adulthood

Suggestion	Description
Family and Friends	
Social support and interaction	Social support and interaction must extend beyond the grieving period to ongoing assistance and caring relationships. Family members and friends can help most by making support available while encouraging the widowed elder to use effective coping strategies.
Community	
Senior centers	Senior centers offer communal meals and other social activities, enabling widowed and other elders to connect with people in similar circumstances and to gain access to other community resources, such as listings of part-time employment and available housing.
Support groups	Support groups can be found in senior centers, religious institutions, and other agencies. Besides new relationships, they offer an accepting atmosphere for coming to terms with loss, effective role models, and assistance with developing skills for daily living.
Religious activities	Involvement in a church, synagogue, or mosque can help relieve the loneliness associated with loss of a spouse and offer social support, new relationships, and meaningful roles.
Volunteer activities	One of the best ways for widowed elders to find meaningful roles is through volunteer activities. Some are sponsored by formal service organizations, such as the Red Cross or the Retired and Senior Volunteer Program. Other volunteer programs exist in hospitals, senior centers, schools, and charitable organizations.

Those who arrive at this traumatic event with high self-esteem and a sense of purpose in life have less difficulty adapting to loss of a spouse (Lund & Caserta, 2001). Older widows and widowers who participated in several months of weekly classes providing information and support in acquiring daily living skills felt better prepared to manage the challenges of widowed life (Caserta, Lund, & Obray, 2004). Applying What We Know above suggests a variety of ways to foster adaptation to widowhood in old age.

Never-Married, Childless Older Adults

Shortly after Ruth and Walt's marriage in their twenties, Ruth's father died. Her sister Ida continued to live with and care for their mother, who was in ill health until she died 16 years later. When, at age 25, Ida received a marriage proposal, she responded, "I can't marry anybody while my mother is still living. I'm expected to look after her." Ida's decision was not unusual for a daughter of her day. She never married or had children.

About 5 percent of older Americans have remained unmarried and childless throughout their lives. Almost all are conscious of being different from the norm, but most have developed alternative meaningful relationships. Ida, for example, formed a strong bond with a neighbor's son. In his childhood, she provided emotional support and financial assistance, which helped him overcome a stressful home life. He included Ida in family events and visited her regularly until she died. Other nonmarried elders also speak of the centrality of younger people—often nieces and nephews—in their social networks and of influencing them in enduring ways (Rubinstein et al., 1991). In addition, same-sex friendships are key in never-married elderly women's lives (McDill, Hall, & Turell, 2006). These tend to be unusually close and often involve joint travel, periods of coresidence, and associations with one another's extended families.

Nonmarried, childless men are more likely than women to feel lonely and depressed. And without pressure from a spouse to maintain a healthy lifestyle, they engage in more unhealthy behaviors. Hence, their physical and mental health is poor compared with their married counterparts (Kendig et al., 2007). Never-married elderly women report a level of well-being equivalent to that of married elders and greater than that of divorcées and recently widowed elders. Only when they agree with the stereotype that "life is empty without a partner," or when they cannot maintain social contacts because of declining health, do they report feeling lonely (Baumbusch, 2004; Dykstra, 1995). These single women often state that they avoided many problems associated with being a wife and mother, and they view their enhanced friendships as an advantage of not marrying. At the same time, they realize that friendships are not the same as blood ties when it comes to caregiving in old age. And because their close ties tend to be weighted toward friends, they lose more network members with increasing age (Dykstra, 2006).

Though they have smaller social networks than married elders with children, most unmarried, childless elders say that support is still available (Wenger, 2001; Wu & Pollard, 1998). Never-married elderly women are more likely than other older adults to have relatives and nonrelatives living in their households, with whom they form mutually supportive relationships (Stull & Scarisbrick-Hauser, 1989).

Siblings

Nearly 80 percent of Americans over age 65 have at least one living sibling. Most elder siblings live within 100 miles of each other, communicate regularly, and visit at least several times a year. Both men and women perceive bonds with sisters to be closer than bonds with brothers. Perhaps because of women's greater emotional expressiveness and nurturance, the closer the tie to a sister, the higher elders' psychological well-being (Cicirelli, 1989; Van Volkom, 2006).

Elderly siblings in industrialized nations are more likely to socialize than to provide one another with direct assistance because most older adults turn first to their spouse and children. Nevertheless, siblings seem to be an important "insurance policy" in late adulthood. Figure 18.2 shows the extent to which, in a large, nationally representative U.S. survey, individuals ranging in age from 16 to 85 reported giving or receiving aid from a sibling. As we saw in earlier chapters, sibling support rises in early adulthood and then declines in middle adulthood. After age 70, it increases for siblings living within 25 miles of each other (White, 2001). Most elders say they would turn to a sibling for help in a crisis, less often in other situations (Connidis, 1994).

Widowed and never-married elders have more contacts with siblings, perhaps because they have fewer competing family relationships. They are also more likely to receive sibling support during illness (Connidis & Campbell, 1995). For example, when Ida's Alzheimer's symptoms worsened, Ruth came to her aid. Although Ida had many friends, Ruth was her only living relative.

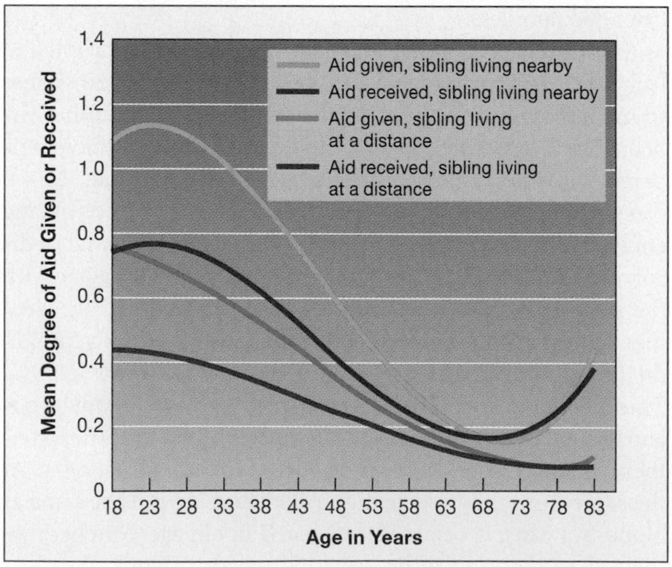

■ **FIGURE 18.2** ■ **Age-related changes in aid given to or received from a sibling.** In a large, nationally representative American survey, adults reported a rise in sibling aid in early adulthood, a decline during middle adulthood, and then a rise after age 70 for siblings living near one another (within 25 miles). In late life, siblings seem to be an important "insurance policy" when help is not available from a spouse or child. (From L. White, 2001, "Sibling Relationships over the Life Course: A Panel Analysis," *Journal of Marriage and the Family, 63,* p. 564. Adapted by permission of Blackwell Publishing Ltd., publisher and Lynn K. White.)

Friendships

As family responsibilities and vocational pressures lessen, friendships take on increasing importance. Having friends is an especially strong predictor of mental health among the elderly (Nussbaum, 1994; Rawlins, 2004). Older adults report more favorable experiences with friends than with family members, in part because of the pleasurable leisure activities they share with friends (Larson, Mannell, & Zuzanek, 1986). Unique qualities of friendship interaction—openness, spontaneity, mutual caring, and common interests—are also influential.

FUNCTIONS OF ELDER FRIENDSHIPS. The diverse functions of friendship in late adulthood clarify its profound significance:

- *Intimacy and companionship are basic to meaningful elder friendships.* As Ida and her best friend, Rosie, took walks, went shopping, or visited each other, they disclosed their deepest sources of happiness and worry. They also engaged in pleasurable conversation, laughed, and had fun (Crohan & Antonucci, 1989). When elders are asked to describe qualities of their close friendships, their responses reveal that mutual interests, feelings of belongingness, and opportunities to express feelings and confide in another sustain these bonds over time (Field, 1999).
- *Elderly women mention acceptance as a primary aspect of close friendship.* Late-life friends shield one another from others' negative judgments about their capabilities and worth as a person, which frequently stem from stereotypes of aging (Adams, 1985–1986). "Where's your cane, Rosie?" Ida asked when the two women were about to leave for a restaurant. "Come on, don't be self-conscious. When y'get one of those 'you're finished' looks from someone, just remember: In the Greek village where my mother grew up, there was no separation between generations, so the young ones got used to wrinkled skin and weak knees and recognized older women as the wise ones. Why, they were midwives, matchmakers, experts in herbal medicine; they knew about everything!" (Deveson, 1994).
- *Friendships link elderly people to the larger community.* For elders who cannot go out as often, interactions with friends can keep them abreast of events in the wider world. "Rosie," Ida reported, "did you know the Thompson girl was named high school valedictorian . . . and the business community is supporting Jesse for mayor?" Friends can also open up new experiences that older adults might not take part in alone. Often a first trip to a senior citizens' center takes place within the context of friendship (Nussbaum, 1994).
- *Friendships help protect elders from the psychological consequences of loss.* Older adults in declining health who remain in contact with friends through phone calls and visits show improved psychological well-being. Similarly, when close relatives die, friends offer compensating social supports (Fiori, Smith, & Antonucci, 2007).

These men often meet to chat on a village street on the Greek island of Corfu. Even after physical mobility declines, many elders find ways to sustain ties with friends, who offer companionship, links to the larger community, and social support in the face of loss.

CHARACTERISTICS OF ELDER FRIENDSHIPS. Although older adults prefer familiar, established relationships over new ones, friendship formation continues throughout life. Ties to old and dear friends who live far away are maintained, but practical restrictions promote more frequent interaction with friends in the immediate environment. With age, elders report that the friends they feel closest to are fewer in number and live in the same community. Nevertheless, close elder friendships are not affected by patterns of daily life, such as participation in social groups or volunteerism (Dugan & Kivett, 1998). Many elders find ways to sustain links with friends, even after declining health restricts their mobility.

As in earlier years, elders tend to choose friends whose age, sex, race, ethnicity, and values are like their own. Compared with younger people, fewer report other-sex friendships. But some have them—usually longstanding ones dating back several decades. Elders continue to benefit uniquely from these ties, obtaining an insider's view of the thoughts, feelings, and behavior of members of the other sex (Monsour, 2002). As agemates die, the very old report more intergenerational friends—both same- and other-sex (Johnson & Troll, 1994). In her eighties, Ruth spent time with Margaret, a 55-year-old widow she met while serving on the board of directors of an adoption agency. Two or three times a month, Margaret came to Ruth's home for tea and lively conversation.

Sex differences in friendship, discussed in previous chapters, extend into late adulthood. Women are more likely to have intimate friends; men depend on their wives and, to a lesser extent, their sisters for warm, open communication. Also, older women have more **secondary friends**—people who are not intimates but with whom they spend time occasionally, such as a group that meets for lunch, bridge, or museum tours. Through these associates, elders meet new people, remain socially involved, and gain in psychological well-being (Adams, Bleiszner, & De Vries, 2000).

In elder friendships, affection and emotional support are both given and received to maintain balance in the relationship (Ikkink & van Tilburg, 1998). Although friends call on each other for help with tasks of daily living, they generally do so only in emergencies or for occasional, limited assistance. Elders with physical limitations whose social networks consist mainly of friends and who therefore must rely frequently on them for help tend to report low psychological well-being (Fiori, Smith, & Antonucci, 2007). Feelings of excessive dependency and of helplessness at being unable to reciprocate are probably responsible.

Relationships with Adult Children

About 80 percent of older adults in Western nations are parents of living children, most of whom are middle-aged. In Chapter 16, we noted that exchanges of help vary with the closeness of the parent–child bond and the needs of the parent and adult child. Recall, also, that over time, parent-to-child help declines, whereas child-to-parent assistance increases. Elders and their adult children are often in touch, even when they live far from each other. But as with other ties, quality rather than quantity of interaction affects older adults' life satisfaction. In diverse ethnic groups and cultures, warm bonds with adult children reduce the negative impact of physical impairments and other losses (such as death of a spouse) on psychological well-being. Alternatively, conflict or unhappiness with adult children contributes to poor physical and mental health (Ajrouch, 2007; Milkie, Bierman, & Schieman, 2008; Silverstein & Bengtson, 1991).

Although aging parents and adult children in Western nations provide each other with various forms of help, level of assistance is typically modest. Older adults in their sixties and seventies—especially those who own their own home and who are married or widowed as opposed to divorced—are more likely to be providers than recipients of help, suggesting SES variations in the balance of support (Grundy, 2005). This balance shifts as elders age, but well into late adulthood, elders in Western nations give more than they receive, especially in financial support but also in practical assistance—a circumstance that contradicts stereotypes of older adults as "burdens" on younger generations (HSBC & Oxford Institute of Ageing, 2007).

Interviews with parents age 75 and older in five Western nations revealed that in all countries, aid received from adult children most often took the form of emotional support. Fewer than one-third said their children assisted with household chores and errands. Elders who provided more help of various kinds than they received scored highest in life satisfaction, those receiving more help than they gave scored lowest, while those in a balanced exchange fell in between (Lowenstein, Katz, & Gur-Yaish, 2007). To avoid dependency, older parents usually do not seek children's practical assistance in the absence of a pressing need, and they express annoyance when children are overprotective or help unnecessarily (Spitze & Gallant, 2004). Moderate support, with many opportunities to reciprocate, is beneficial, fostering self-esteem and sense of family connection. Again, extensive support that cannot be returned is linked to poor well-being.

Sex differences in older parent–adult child interaction are evident. Both mothers and fathers feel ambivalent toward adult offspring with problematic lives—who are financially needy, emotionally troubled, or experiencing marital problems. But mothers are more likely to have adult children who feel similarly ambivalent toward them, perhaps because mothers more often express their mixed feelings (Fingerman et al., 2006). Nevertheless, aging parents' ambivalence toward children is typically low. Consistent with socioemotional selectivity theory, older parents are more likely to describe their family ties as solely close rather than ambivalent (Fingerman, Hay, & Birditt, 2004; Willson et al., 2006). Mother–daughter ties are particularly warm, although competing demands in middle-aged daughters' lives may leave less time to devote to the relationship than each would like (see page 549 in Chapter 16).

As social networks shrink in size, relationships with adult children become more important sources of family involvement. Elders 85 years and older with children have substantially more contacts with relatives than do those without children (Hooyman & Kiyak, 2008). Why is this so? Consider Ruth, whose daughter Sybil linked her to grandchildren, great-grandchildren, and relatives by marriage. When childless elders reach their eighties, siblings, other same-age relatives, and close friends may have become frail or died and hence may no longer be available as companions.

Relationships with Adult Grandchildren and Great-Grandchildren

Older adults with adult grandchildren and great-grandchildren benefit from a wider potential network of support. Ruth and Walt saw their granddaughter, Marci, and their great-grandson, Jamel, at family gatherings. At other times, Marci telephoned, visited, and sent greeting cards, expressing deep affection for her aging grandparents.

In developed nations, slightly more than half of elders over age 65 have a grandchild who is at least 18 years old (AARP, 2002). In the few studies available on grandparent–adult grandchild relationships, the overwhelming majority of grandchildren felt obligated to assist grandparents in need. Grandparents expected affection (but not practical help) from grandchildren, and in most cases they received it. They regarded the adult grandchild tie as very gratifying—a vital link between themselves and the future (Langer, 1990).

Grandparents regard ties with adult grandchildren as a vital link between themselves and the future. And great-grandparents comment that this new role reaffirms the continuity of their families.

Still, grandparent–adult grandchild relationships vary greatly. Degree of grandparent involvement during childhood strongly predicts the quality of the current relationship. Often, the tie with one grandchild is "special," characterized by more frequent contact, mutual expressions of affection, and enjoyable times together—factors that enhance elders' psychological well-being (Fingerman, 1998). However, longitudinal research reveals that as grandparents and grandchildren move through life, contact declines. Many grandchildren establish distant homes and become immersed in work and family roles that compete for time with extended-family members.

But despite less contact, grandparents' affection for their adult grandchildren strengthens with age, usually exceeding grandchildren's expressed closeness toward their grandparents (which is still strong) (Giarrusso et al., 2001; Harwood, 2001; Silverstein & Long, 1998). This difference in emotional investment reflects each generation's distinct needs and goals—adult grandchildren in establishing independent lives, grandparents in preserving closeness of family relationships and continuity of values across generations. When with their adult grandchildren, grandparents frequently convey information and engage in activities related to family cultural heritage—telling stories about earlier times and discussing family traditions and customs (Wiscott & Kopera-Frye, 2000). Grandchildren become increasingly important sources of emotional meaning for elders in the last decade or two of life.

About 40 percent of older adults have great-grandchildren (Hooyman & Kiyak, 2008). Although most describe their new role as limited and a sign of advancing age, they welcome it with enthusiasm, commenting that it reaffirms the continuity of their families. Parents mediate contact with great-grandchildren, as they did with young grandchildren (see Chapter 16).

Elder Maltreatment

Although the majority of older adults enjoy positive relationships with family members, friends, and professional caregivers, some suffer maltreatment at the hands of these individuals. Through recent media attention, elder maltreatment has become a serious public concern.

Reports from many industrialized nations reveal widely varying rates of maltreatment, from 3 to 28 percent in general population studies. Overall, more than 6 percent of elders say they were targets during the past month, amounting to about 2 million victims in the United States (Cooper, Selwood, & Livingston, 2008). Elder maltreatment crosses ethnic lines, although it is lower in Asian, Hispanic, and Native-American groups with strong traditions of respect for and obligation to the aged and highly disapproving attitudes toward harming them (Rittman, Kuzmeskus, & Flum, 2000; Sherman, Rosenblatt, & Antonucci, 2008). Yet all figures underestimate the actual incidence, because most abusive acts take place in private, and victims are often unable or unwilling to complain.

Elder maltreatment usually takes the following forms:

- *Physical abuse.* Intentional infliction of pain, discomfort, or injury, through hitting, cutting, burning, physical force, restraint, sexual assault, and other acts
- *Physical neglect.* Intentional or unintentional failure to fulfill caregiving obligations, resulting in lack of food, medication, or health services or in the elderly person being left alone or isolated
- *Emotional abuse.* Verbal assaults (such as name calling), humiliation (being treated as a child), and intimidation (threats of isolation or placement in a nursing home)
- *Sexual abuse.* Unwanted sexual contact of any kind
- *Financial abuse.* Illegal or improper exploitation of the elder's property or financial resources, through theft or use without the elder's consent

Financial abuse, emotional abuse, and neglect are the most frequently reported types. Often several forms occur in combination (Anetzberger, 2005; World Health Organization, 2002). The perpetrator is usually a person the older adult trusts and depends on for care and assistance. Most abusers are family members—spouses (usually men), followed by children of both sexes and then by other relatives. Some are friends, neighbors, and in-home caregivers (U.S. Administration on Aging, 2009). Abuse in nursing homes is a major concern. In one survey, one-third of nurses indicated that they had observed it, while 10 percent admitted to at least one act of physical abuse and 40 percent to at least one act of emotional abuse (Wilber & McNeilly, 2001).

Over the past several decades, another form of neglect—referred to in the media as "granny dumping"—has increased: abandonment of elders with severe disabilities by family caregivers, usually at hospital emergency rooms (Fulmer, 2008). According to one U.S. hospital survey, between 100,000 and 200,000 older adults—most suffering from dementia—are left in hospital waiting rooms each year (Tanne, 1992). Overwhelmed, their caregivers seem to have concluded that they have no other option but to take this drastic step. (See pages 550–551 in Chapter 16 and pages 586–587 in Chapter 17 for related research.)

© SIMON RAWLES/ALAMY

This older adult, who suffers from depression and physical disabilities, lives in a dilapidated rooming house. When conditions are ripe for elder maltreatment, those with physical or cognitive impairments are least able to protect themselves.

RISK FACTORS. Characteristics of the victim, the abuser, their relationship, and its social context are related to the incidence and severity of elder maltreatment. The more of the following risk factors that are present, the greater the likelihood that abuse and neglect will occur.

Dependency of the Victim. Very old, frail, and mentally and physically impaired elders are more vulnerable to maltreatment (Reay & Browne, 2008). This does not mean that declines in functioning cause abuse; most older adults with disabilities do not experience it. Rather, when other conditions are ripe for maltreatment, elders with severe disabilities are least able to protect themselves. Those with physical or cognitive impairments may also have personality traits that make them vulnerable—a tendency to lash out when angry or frustrated, a passive or avoidant approach to handling problems, and a low sense of self-efficacy (Comijs et al., 1999).

Dependency of the Perpetrator. Many abusers are dependent, emotionally or financially, on their victims. This dependency, experienced as powerlessness, can lead to aggressive, exploitative behavior. Often the perpetrator–victim relationship is one of mutual dependency (Henderson, Buchanan, & Fisher, 2002). The abuser needs the older person for money or housing, and the older person needs the abuser for assistance with everyday tasks or to relieve loneliness.

Psychological Disturbance and Stress of the Perpetrator. Abusers are more likely than other caregivers to have psychological problems and to be dependent on alcohol or other drugs (Pillemer et al., 2007). Often they are socially isolated, have difficulties at work, or are unemployed, with resulting financial worries. These factors increase the likelihood that they will lash out when caregiving is highly demanding or the behavior of an elder with dementia is irritating or hard to manage.

History of Family Violence. Elder abuse is often part of a long history of family violence. Adults who were abused as children are at increased risk of harming elders (Reay & Browne, 2008). In Chapter 8, we showed how aggressive cycles between family members can easily become self-sustaining, leading to the development of individuals who cope with anger through hostility toward others. In many instances, elder abuse is an extension of years of partner abuse (Walsh et al., 2007).

Institutional Conditions. Elder maltreatment is more likely to occur in nursing homes that are rundown and overcrowded and that have staff shortages, minimal staff supervision, high staff turnover, and few visitors (Payne & Fletcher, 2005). Highly stressful work conditions combined with minimal oversight of caregiving quality set the stage for abuse and neglect.

■ **PREVENTING ELDER MALTREATMENT.** Preventing elder maltreatment by family members is especially challenging. Victims may fear retribution; wish to protect abusers who are spouses, sons, or daughters; or feel embarrassed that they cannot control the situation. And they may be intimidated into silence or not know where to turn for help (Summers & Hoffman, 2006). Once abuse is discovered, intervention involves immediate protection and provision of unmet needs for the elder and of mental health services and social support for the spouse or caregiver.

Prevention programs offer caregivers counseling, education, and respite services, such as elder day care and in-home help. Trained volunteer "buddies" who make visits to the home can combat social isolation among elders and assist them with problem solving to avoid further harm. Support groups help seniors identify abusive acts, practice appropriate responses, and form new relationships. And agencies that provide informal financial services to older adults who are unable to manage on their own, such as writing and cashing checks and holding valuables in a safe, reduce financial abuse (Rabiner, O'Keeffe, & Brown, 2004).

When elder abuse is extreme, legal action offers elders the best protection, yet it is rare. Many victims are reluctant to initiate court procedures or, because of mental impairments, cannot do so. In these instances, social service professionals must help caregivers rethink their role, even if it means that the aging person might be institutionalized. In nursing homes, improving staff selection, training, and working conditions can greatly reduce abuse and neglect.

Combating elder maltreatment also requires efforts at the level of the larger society, including public education to encourage reporting of suspected cases and improved understanding of the needs of older people. As part of this effort, elders benefit from information on where to go for help (U.S. Administration on Aging, 2009). Finally, countering negative stereotypes of aging reduces maltreatment because recognizing elders' dignity, individuality, and autonomy is incompatible with acts of physical and psychological harm.

ASK YOURSELF

» REVIEW
Why is adjustment to late-life divorce usually more difficult for women and adjustment to widowhood more difficult for men?

» APPLY
At age 51, Mae lost her job and couldn't afford to pay rent. She moved in with her 78-year-old widowed mother, Beryl. Although Beryl welcomed Mae's companionship, Mae grew depressed and drank heavily. When Beryl complained about Mae's failure to look for work, Mae pushed and slapped her. Explain why this mother–daughter relationship led to elder abuse.

» CONNECT
After reviewing sections on sibling relationships in Chapter 14 (page 476) and Chapter 16 (page 551), explain lifespan trends in sibling support, shown in Figure 18.2 on page 624.

» REFLECT
If you have living elderly grandparents, describe your relationship with one or more of them. How have you and your grandparent contributed to each other's development?

Retirement

In Chapter 16, we noted that the period of retirement has lengthened because of increased life expectancy and a steady decline in average age of retirement—trends occurring in all Western industrialized nations. These changes have also led to a blurring of the distinction between work and retirement. Because mandatory retirement no longer exists for most workers in Western countries, older adults have more choices about when to retire and how they spend their time.

Indeed, the trend toward earlier retirement may soon reverse, and not just because of a decline in older adults' retirement savings due to the recent global economic recession. According to a survey of 21,000 adults in 21 countries, most baby boomers say they want to work longer, over 40 percent as long as possible—an inclination already evident among older adults in industrialized nations and in many urban areas of developing countries (HSBC & Oxford Institute of Ageing, 2007). Currently, 45 percent of U.S. adults in their sixties, and nearly 20 percent of those in their seventies, are still working in some capacity.

As these figures suggest, the contemporary retirement process is highly variable: It may include a planning period, the decision itself, diverse acts of retiring, and continuous adjustment and readjustment of activities for the rest of the life course. The majority of U.S. older adults with career jobs retire gradually by cutting down their hours and responsibilities. Many take *bridge jobs* (new part-time jobs or full-time jobs of shorter duration) that serve as transitions between full-time career and retirement (Moen & Altobelli, 2007). Others leave their jobs but later return to paid work to introduce interest and challenge into the retirement years, to supplement limited financial resources, or both.

In the following sections, we examine factors that affect the decision to retire, happiness during the retirement years, and leisure and volunteer pursuits. We will see that the process of retirement and retired life reflect an increasingly diverse retired population.

The Decision to Retire

When Walt and Ruth retired, both had worked long enough to be eligible for comfortable income-replacement benefits—Walt's through the government-sponsored Social Security program, Ruth's through a private pension plan. In addition, they had planned for retirement (see Chapter 16, pages 556–558) and decided on a date for leaving the work force. They wanted to retire early enough to pursue leisure activities while they were both in good health and could enjoy them together. In contrast, Walt's brother Dick was forced to retire as the operating costs of his bakery rose and his clientele dropped off. He looked for temporary employment in sales while his wife, Goldie, kept her part-time job as a bookkeeper to help cover living expenses.

Affordability of retirement is usually the first consideration in the decision to retire. Yet despite economic concerns, many preretirees decide to let go of a steady work life in favor of alternative, personally meaningful work, leisure, or volunteer activities. "I was working since I was 10 years old," said one retired auto worker. "I wanted a rest." Exceptions to this favorable outlook are people like Dick—forced into retirement or earning very low wages—who often take bridge jobs reluctantly to make ends meet (Cahill, Giandrea, & Quinn, 2006; Warr et al., 2004).

Figure 18.3 summarizes personal and workplace factors in addition to income that influence the decision to retire. People in good health, for whom vocational life is central to self-esteem, and whose work environments are pleasant and interesting are likely to keep on working. For these reasons, individuals in high-earning professional occupations usually retire later than those in blue-collar or clerical positions. And when they do retire, they more often shift to stimulating bridge jobs (Cahill, Giandrea, & Quinn, 2006; Siegrist et al., 2007). Self-employed elders also stay with their jobs longer, probably because they can flexibly adapt their working hours to changing needs (Helson & Cates, 2007). In contrast, people in declining health, who are engaged in routine, boring work, and who have compelling leisure interests often opt for retirement.

Societal factors also affect retirement decisions. When many younger, less costly workers are available to replace older workers, industries are likely to offer added incentives for people to retire, such as increments to pension plans and earlier benefits—a trend that has, until recently, contributed to many early retirements in Western nations. But when concern increases about the burden on younger generations of an expanding population of retirees, eligibility for retirement benefits may be postponed to a later age.

Retirement decisions vary with gender. On average, women retire earlier than men, largely because family events—a husband's retirement or the need to care for an ill spouse or

© JEFF GREENBERG/THE IMAGE WORKS

A recent retiree enjoys an adult-education class in bookbinding.

Retire

- Adequate retirement benefits
- Compelling leisure interests
- Low work commitment
- Declining health
- Spouse retiring
- Routine, boring job

© GETTY IMAGES/BLEND IMAGES

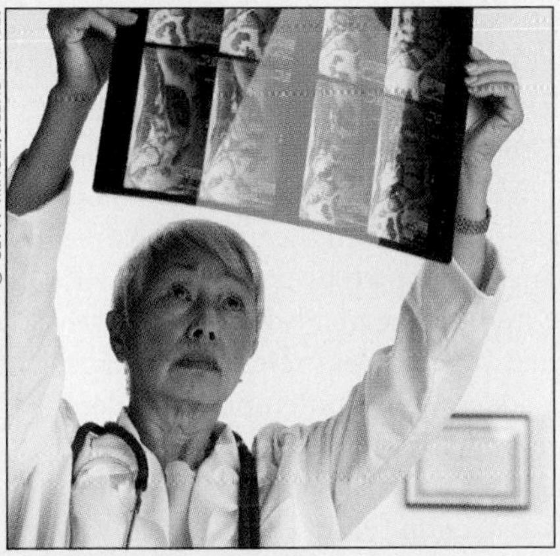

This doctor, in her 60s, plans to keep practicing medicine indefinitely.

Continue Working

- Limited or no retirement benefits
- Few leisure interests
- High work commitment
- Good health
- Spouse working
- Flexible work schedule
- Pleasant, stimulating work environment

■ **FIGURE 18.3** ■ **Personal and workplace factors that influence the decision to retire.**

parent—play larger roles in their decisions (Chappell et al., 2003; Moen et al., 2006). Women in or near poverty, however, are an exception. Lacking financial resources to retire, many continue working into old age. This trend is especially pronounced among African-American women, who are more likely to have minimal retirement benefits and to be caring for other family members (DeVaney, 2008; Hogan & Perrucci, 2007).

In most Western nations, generous social security benefits make retirement feasible for the economically disadvantaged and sustain the standard of living of most workers after they retire. The United States is an exception: Many U.S. retirees, especially those who held low-income jobs without benefits, experience falling living standards (Hungerford, 2003). Denmark, France, Germany, Finland, and Sweden have gradual retirement programs in which older employees reduce their work hours, receive a partial pension to make up income loss, and continue to accrue pension benefits. Besides strengthening financial security, this approach introduces a transitional phase that fosters retirement planning and well-being (Reday-Mulvey, 2000). And some countries' retirement policies are sensitive to women's more interrupted work lives. In Canada, France, and Germany, for example, time devoted to child rearing is given some credit when figuring retirement benefits (Service Canada, 2009).

In sum, individual preferences shape retirement decisions. At the same time, older adults' opportunities and limitations greatly affect their choices.

Adjustment to Retirement

Because retirement involves giving up roles that are a vital part of identity and self-esteem, it usually is assumed to be a stressful process that contributes to declines in physical and mental health. Consider Dick, who reacted to the closing of his bakery with anxiety and depression. His adjustment difficulties resembled those of younger people experiencing job loss (see Chapter 16, page 556). But recall that Dick had a cranky, disagreeable personality. In this respect, his psychological well-being after retirement was similar to what it had been before!

We must be careful not to assume a cause-and-effect relationship each time retirement is paired with an unfavorable reaction. For example, a wealth of evidence confirms that physical health problems lead elders to retire, rather than the reverse (Shultz & Wang, 2007). And for most people, mental health and perceived quality of life are fairly stable from the pre- to postretirement years, with little change prompted by retirement itself. The widely held belief that retirement inevitably leads to adjustment problems is contradicted by countless research findings indicating that most people adapt well. Contemporary elders view retirement as a time of opportunity and personal growth and describe themselves as active and socially involved—major determinants of retirement satisfaction (HSBC & Oxford Institute of Ageing, 2007; Kloep & Hendry, 2007). Still, about 10 to 30 percent mention some adjustment difficulties.

Workplace factors—especially financial worries and having to give up one's job—predict stress following retirement. Pressures at work also make a difference. Moving out of a high-stress job is associated with gains in psychological well-being following retirement, whereas leaving a pleasant, low-stress job or a highly satisfying job before one is ready is linked to greater difficulties during the retirement transition, typically followed by recovery (Wang, 2007). And especially for women, a continuous work life leading to consistency between career expectations and actual achievements enhances retirement quality (Quick & Moen, 1998). Perhaps because fewer women than men have continuous careers, women whose husbands heavily influenced their retirement decision are less satisfied. In contrast, men whose wives encourage them to retire are generally happy with retirement (Smith & Moen, 2004).

Among psychological factors, a sense of personal control over life events, including deciding to retire for internally motivated reasons (to do other things), is strongly linked to retirement satisfaction (Quine et al., 2007; Kim & Moen, 2002c). At the same time, those who find it hard to give up the predictable schedule and social contacts of the work setting experience discomfort with their less structured way of life. Overall, however, well-educated people in high-status careers adjust more favorably, perhaps because the satisfactions derived from challenging, meaningful work readily transfer to nonwork pursuits (Kim & Moen, 2002a).

As with other major life events, social support reduces stress associated with retirement. Although social-network size typically shrinks as relationships with co-workers decline, quality of relationships remains fairly stable. And many elders add to their social networks through leisure and volunteer pursuits (Kloep & Hendry, 2007). In Dick's case, entering congregate housing eased a difficult postretirement period, leading to new friends and rewarding leisure activities, some of which he shared with Goldie.

Finally, earlier in this chapter we noted that marital happiness tends to rise after retirement. When a couple's relationship is positive, it can buffer the uncertainty of retirement. And retirement can enhance marital satisfaction by granting husband and wife more time for companionship (Kim & Moen, 2002a; van Solinge & Henkens, 2008). Consequently, a good marriage not only promotes adjustment to retirement but also benefits from the greater freedom of the retirement years.

In line with continuity theory, people try to sustain earlier lifestyle patterns, self-esteem, and values following retirement and, in favorable economic and social contexts, usually succeed in doing so (Atchley, 2003). Return to Chapter 16, page 557, for ways adults can plan ahead to increase the chances of a positive transition to retirement.

Leisure and Volunteer Activities

With retirement, most older adults have more time for leisure and volunteer activities than ever before. After a "honeymoon period" of trying out new options, many find that interests and skills do not develop suddenly. Instead, meaningful leisure and community service pursuits are usually formed earlier and

Volunteering grants elders a gratifying sense of making valuable contributions to society. These older adults, who range in age from 65 to 80, traveled to Thailand to help rebuild homes along the seacoast after the devastating tsunami of 2005.

sustained or expanded during retirement (HSBC & Oxford Institute of Ageing, 2007; Mannell, 1999). For example, Walt's fondness for writing, theater, and gardening dated back to his youth. And Ruth's strong focus on her vocation of social work led her to become an avid community volunteer.

Involvement in leisure activities and, especially, volunteer service is related to better physical and mental health and reduced mortality (Avlund et al., 2004; Cutler & Hendricks, 2001; Moen, 2003). But simply participating does not explain this relationship. Instead, elders select these pursuits because they permit self-expression, new achievements, the rewards of helping others, pleasurable social interaction, and a structured daily life. And those high in sense of self-efficacy are more engaged (Diehl & Berg, 2007). These factors account for gains in well-being.

With age, the frequency and variety of leisure pursuits tend to decline, especially travel, outdoor recreation, and exercise. After age 75, mobility limitations lead leisure activities to become more sedentary and home based (Strain et al., 2002). Elders in residential communities participate more than those in ordinary homes because activities are conveniently available. But regardless of living arrangements, older adults do not spend much time in programs designed just for them. Rather, they choose activities on the basis of whether they are personally gratifying. Partly for this reason, organized activities in community senior centers attract only about 15 percent of elders who live nearby (Krout, Cutler, & Coward, 1990). Nevertheless, these structured opportunities are important for elders who have limited incomes or who lack daily companionship.

Older adults contribute enormously to society through volunteer work, a trend that is strengthening. About one-third of 60- and 70-year-olds in industrialized nations report volunteering. Of those who do, over half give 200 or more hours per year (HSBC & Oxford Institute of Ageing, 2007; Kloep & Hendry, 2007). And a survey of U.S. baby boomers revealed that half plan to incorporate service into later life (Freedman, 2007). Younger, better-educated, and financially secure elders with social interests are more likely to volunteer, women more often than men. Although most extend an earlier pattern of civic engagement, nonvolunteers are especially receptive to volunteer activities in the first few years after retiring—a prime time to recruit them into these personally rewarding and socially useful pursuits (Mutchler, Burr, & Caro, 2003).

Volunteering grants elders a continuing sense of making valuable contributions to society, and most sustain high commitment through their seventies. In a survey of a large, nationally representative U.S. sample, time spent volunteering did not decline until the eighties (see Figure 18.4) (Hendricks & Cutler, 2004). Even then, it remained higher than at any other time of life! In accord with socioemotional selectivity theory, older adults eventually narrowed their volunteering to fewer roles, concentrating on one or two that meant the most to them. They seemed to recognize that excessive volunteering reduces its emotional rewards and, thus, its benefits to well-being (Windsor, Anstey, & Rodgers, 2008).

Finally, when Walt and Ruth got together with Dick and Goldie, the two couples often discussed politics. Older adults report greater awareness of and interest in public affairs and

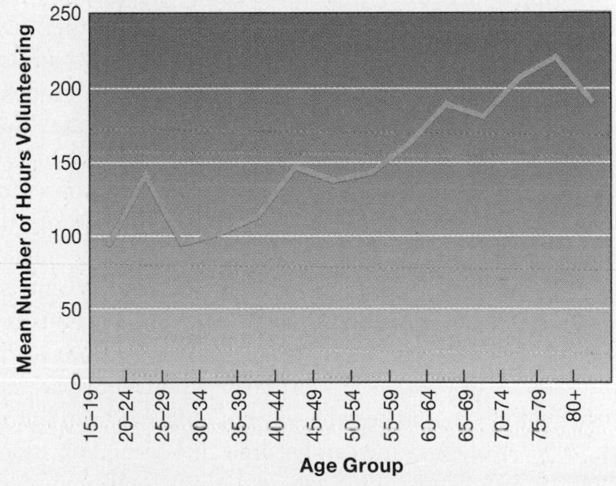

■ **FIGURE 18.4** ■ **Age-related change in number of hours spent volunteering during the past year.** A nationally representative sample of nearly 29,000 U.S. adolescents and adults reported on the amount of time they devoted to each of their volunteer activities. Time devoted to volunteering increased sharply in the early twenties, dipped in the late twenties and thirties as young people focused on establishing families and careers, then rose steadily, peaking in the seventies. Even in the eighties, when volunteering declined slightly, it remained higher than at any other time of life. (From J. Hendricks and S. J. Cutler, 2004, "Volunteerism and Socioemotional Selectivity in Later Life," *Journal of Gerontology, 59B*, p. S255. Copyright © 2004 The Gerontological Society of America. Adapted by permission of Oxford University Press and Jon Hendricks.)

vote at a higher rate than any other age group. Even in late old age, their political knowledge shows no sign of decline. After retiring, elders have more time to keep abreast of current events through reading and watching TV. They also have a major stake in political debates over policies central to their welfare. But elders' political concerns are far broader than those that serve their own age group, and their voting behavior is not driven by self-interest (Binstock & Quadagno, 2001). Rather, their political involvement may stem from a deep desire for a safer, more secure world for future generations.

Optimal Aging

Walt, Ruth, Dick, Goldie, and Ida, and the research findings they illustrate, reveal great diversity in development during the final decades of life. Walt and Ruth fit contemporary experts' view of **optimal aging,** in which gains are maximized and losses minimized. Both were actively engaged with their families and communities, coped well with negative life changes, enjoyed a happy intimate partnership and other close relationships, and led daily lives filled with gratifying activities. Ida, too, experienced optimal aging until the onset of Alzheimer's symptoms overwhelmed her ability to manage life's challenges. As a single adult, she built a rich social network that sustained her into old age, despite the hardship of having spent many years caring for her ailing mother. In contrast, Dick and Goldie reacted with despondency to physical aging and other losses (such as Dick's forced retirement). And Dick's angry outbursts restricted their social contacts, although the couple's move to congregate housing eventually led to an improved social life.

People age optimally when their growth, vitality, and striving limit and, at times, overcome physical, cognitive, and social declines. Researchers want to know more about factors that contribute to optimal aging so they can help more seniors experience it. Yet theorists disagree on the precise ingredients of a satisfying old age. Some focus on easily measurable outcomes, such as excellent cardiovascular functioning, absence of disability, superior cognitive performance, and creative achievements. But this view has been heavily criticized (Aldwin, Spiro, & Park, 2006). Not everyone can become an outstanding athlete, an innovative scientist, or a talented artist. And many older adults do not want to keep on accomplishing and producing—the main markers of success in Western nations. Each of us is limited by our genetic potential as it combines with a lifetime of environments we encounter and select for ourselves. Furthermore, outcomes valued in one culture may not be valued in others.

Recent views of a contented, fulfilling late adulthood have turned away from specific achievements toward processes people use to reach personally valued goals (Freund & Baltes, 1998; Lund, 1998; Kahana et al., 2005). Instead of identifying one set of standards as "successful," this perspective focuses on how people minimize losses while maximizing gains. In recent research on three samples of adults followed over the lifespan, George Vaillant looked at how various life-course factors contributed to late-life physical and psychological well-being. His findings revealed that factors people could control to some degree (such as health habits, coping strategies, marital stability, and years of education) far outweighed uncontrollable factors (parental SES, family warmth in childhood, early physical health, and longevity of family members) in predicting a happy, active old age (Vaillant & Mukamal, 2001).

Consider the following description of one participant, who in childhood had experienced low SES, parental discord, a depressed mother, and seven siblings crowded into a tenement apartment. Despite these early perils, he became happily married and, through the GI bill, earned an accounting degree. At 70, he was aging well:

> Anthony Pirelli may have been *ill* considering his heart attack and open-heart surgery, but he did not feel *sick.* He was physically active as ever, and he continued to play tennis. Asked what he missed about his work, he exulted, "I'm so busy doing other things that I don't have time to miss work. . . . Life is not boring for me." He did not smoke or abuse alcohol; he loved his wife; he used mature [coping strategies]; he obtained 14 years of education; he watched his waistline; and he exercised regularly. (Adapted from Vaillant, 2002, pp. 12, 305.)

Vaillant concluded, "The past often predicts but never determines our old age" (p. 12). Optimal aging is an expression of remarkable resilience during this final phase of the lifespan.

In this and the previous chapter, we have considered the many ways that older adults realize their goals. ***TAKE A MOMENT...*** Look back and review the most important ones:

- Optimism and sense of self-efficacy in improving health and physical functioning (pages 575–576)
- Selective optimization with compensation to make the most of limited physical energies and cognitive resources (pages 591 and 610)
- Strengthening of self-concept, which promotes self-acceptance and pursuit of hoped-for possible selves (pages 606–607)
- Enhanced emotional understanding and emotional self-regulation, which support meaningful, rewarding social ties (page 605)
- Acceptance of change, which fosters life satisfaction (page 608)
- A mature sense of spirituality and faith, permitting anticipation of death with calmness and composure (page 608)
- Personal control over domains of dependency and independence (pages 609–610, 611)
- High-quality relationships, which offer social support and pleasurable companionship (pages 615–616)

Optimal aging is facilitated by societal contexts that permit elders to manage life changes effectively. Older adults need well-funded social security plans, good health care, safe housing, and diverse social services. (See, for example, the description of the U.S. Area Agencies on Aging in Chapter 2, page 68.) Yet because of inadequate funding and difficulties reaching rural communities, many older adults' needs remain unmet. Isolated elders with little education may not know how to gain access to available assistance. Furthermore, the U.S. Medicare system of sharing health-care costs with senior citizens strains their financial resources. And housing that adjusts to changes in elders' capacities, permitting them to age in place without disruptive and disorienting moves, is available only to the economically well-off.

Besides improving policies that meet older adults' basic needs, new future-oriented approaches must prepare for increased aging of the population. More emphasis on lifelong learning for workers of all ages would help people maintain and even increase skills as they grow older. Also, reforms that prepare for expected growth in the number of frail elders are vital, including affordable help for family caregivers, adapted housing, and sensitive nursing home care.

All these changes involve recognizing, supporting, and enhancing the contributions that seniors make to society—both the elders of today and those of tomorrow. A nation that takes care of its senior citizens and grants them a multitude of opportunities for personal growth maximizes the chances that each of us, when our time comes to be old, will age optimally.

ASK YOURSELF

» REVIEW
What psychological and workplace factors predict favorable adjustment to retirement?

» APPLY
Nate, happily married to Gladys, adjusted well to retirement, and his marriage became even happier. How can a good marriage ease the transition to retirement? How can retirement enhance marital satisfaction?

» CONNECT
Leisure and volunteer interests and skills usually form early and persist over the lifespan. Referring back to earlier parts of this book, cite examples of childhood, adolescent, and early adulthood experiences that are likely to foster meaningful pursuits after retirement.

» REFLECT
Think of someone you know who is aging optimally. What personal qualities led you to select that person?

Summary

Erikson's Theory: Ego Integrity versus Despair

According to Erikson, how does personality change in late adulthood?

» The final psychological conflict of Erikson's theory, **ego integrity versus despair,** involves coming to terms with one's life. Adults who arrive at a sense of integrity feel whole and satisfied with their achievements. Despair occurs when elders feel time is too short to find an alternate route to integrity.

Other Theories of Psychosocial Development in Late Adulthood

Describe Peck's, Joan Erikson's, and Labouvie-Vief's views of psychosocial development in late adulthood, and discuss reminiscence in older adults' lives.

» According to Robert Peck, attaining ego integrity involves three distinct tasks: ego differentiation, body transcendence, and ego transcendence.

» Joan Erikson believes these attainments represent an additional psychosocial stage, **gerotranscendence,** evident in inner calm and quiet reflection.

» Gisella Labouvie-Vief points out that older adults improve in **affect optimization**—the ability to maximize positive emotion and dampen negative emotion. Full understanding of their own feelings contributes to expertise in processing emotional information and regulating negative affect.

© JULIA CUMES/THE IMAGE WORKS

» **Reminiscence**—telling stories about people and events from one's past—can be positive and adaptive for older people. But many well-adjusted elders spend little time in life review to achieve greater self-understanding. Rather, as the term **Third Age** conveys, they are largely present- and future-oriented, seeking opportunities for personal fulfillment.

Stability and Change in Self-Concept and Personality

Cite stable and changing aspects of self-concept and personality, and discuss spirituality and religiosity in late adulthood.

» The "big five" personality traits show continuing stability from mid- to late life. With the accumulation of a lifetime of self-knowledge, elders have more secure and complex self-concepts. Those who continue to strive toward hoped-for possible selves improve in life satisfaction. In late adulthood, resilience is fostered by gains in agreeableness and acceptance of change.

» While U.S. elders generally become more religious or spiritual as they age, this trend is not universal: Some elders decline in religiosity. Faith and spirituality may advance to a higher level, toward a more reflective approach that emphasizes links to others and that accepts uncertainty. Religious involvement is especially high among low-SES ethnic minority elders and women and is linked to improved physical and psychological well-being and longer survival.

© HILL STREET STUDIOS/BLEND IMAGES/PHOTOLIBRARY

Contextual Influences on Psychological Well-Being

Discuss the influence of control versus dependency, physical health, negative life changes, and social support on older adults' psychological well-being.

» Friends, family members, and caregivers often promote excessive dependency in elders. In patterns of behavior called the **dependency–support script** and the **independence–ignore script,** older adults' dependency behaviors are attended to immediately while their independent behaviors are ignored. But dependency can be adaptive if older adults remain in control by selecting areas in which they desire help. This enables them to conserve their strength for highly valued activities.

» Physical health is a powerful predictor of late-life psychological well-being. The relationship between physical and mental health problems can become a vicious cycle, each intensifying the other. Older adults have the highest suicide rate of all age groups.

» Although elders are at risk for a variety of negative life changes, these events actually evoke less stress and depression in older than in younger adults. But when negative changes pile up, they test elders' coping resources.

» Social support eases stress, thereby fostering older adults' physical health and psychological well-being. But if assistance is excessive or cannot be returned, it often sparks feelings of dependency and distress. Consequently, perceived social support, rather than sheer amount of help, is associated with a positive outlook.

A Changing Social World

Describe social theories of aging, including disengagement theory, activity theory, continuity theory, and socioemotional selectivity theory.

» **Disengagement theory** holds that social interaction declines because of mutual withdrawal between elders and society in anticipation of death. However, not everyone disengages, and elders' retreat from interaction is more complex than this theory implies.

» According to **activity theory,** social barriers to engagement, not the desires of elders, cause declining rates of interaction. Yet opportunities for social contact do not guarantee greater social activity.

» **Continuity theory** proposes that most aging adults strive to maintain consistency between their past and anticipated future. By using familiar skills and engaging in familiar activities with familiar people, elders minimize stress and disruptiveness by integrating late-life changes into a coherent, consistent life path.

» **Socioemotional selectivity theory** states that social networks become more selective as we age. Older adults emphasize the emotion-regulating function of interaction, preferring high-quality, emotionally fulfilling relationships.

How do communities, neighborhoods, and housing arrangements affect elders' social lives and adjustment?

» Suburban elders are better off in terms of income and health, whereas inner-city elders have easier access to social services. Small-town and rural elders are least well-off in these ways. Older adults living in neighborhoods with many like-minded seniors and in smaller communities report greater life satisfaction. For urban elders living alone, fear of crime restricts activities and undermines morale.

» Most elders prefer **aging in place,** remaining in a familiar setting where they have control over everyday life. For healthy elders, staying in one's own home offers the greatest personal control. But for those with health and mobility problems, independent living poses risks. Many older adults who live alone, especially widowed women, are poverty-stricken and suffer from unmet needs.

» Residential communities for seniors come in great variety. Among assisted-living arrangements, **congregate housing** offers a variety of support services, including meals in a common dining room, and is well-suited to promoting social participation. **Life-care communities** offer a range of options, from independent or congregate housing to full nursing home care.

» The small number of U.S. elders who live in nursing homes experience extreme restriction of autonomy. Typically, social interaction among residents is low. Designing homelike nursing homes with aging-in-place features fosters late-life competence, control, and well-being.

Relationships in Late Adulthood

Describe changes in social relationships in late adulthood, including marriage, gay and lesbian partnerships, divorce, remarriage, and widowhood, and discuss never-married, childless older adults.

» As we move through life, a **social convoy,** or cluster of family members and friends, provides safety and support. Though relationships change with age, elders do their best to sustain close, high-quality ties, which predicts positive adaptation.

» Marital satisfaction peaks in late adulthood as stressful responsibilities decline and gains in perceptions of relationship fairness, shared leisure activities, and positive communication increase. Most gay and lesbian elders also report happy, highly fulfilling relationships.

» When divorce occurs, stress is higher for older than for younger adults. Because of greater financial hardship and less likelihood of remarrying, women suffer more than men from late-life divorce.

» Although elders' remarriage rates are low, those who do remarry enter into more stable relationships. Increasingly, older adults are choosing cohabitation over remarriage, for financial and personal reasons.

» Wide variation exists in adaptation to widowhood, with age, social support, and personality making a difference. Elders fare better than younger individuals, and women better than men. Efforts to maintain social ties, an outgoing personality, high self-esteem, and a sense of self-efficacy in handling tasks of daily living foster adjustment.

© PETER ARNOLD, INC./ALAMY

» Most older adults who remain unmarried and childless throughout their lives develop alternative meaningful relationships. Never-married childless women are better-adjusted than men, but—despite smaller social networks—both find social support.

How do sibling relationships and friendships change in late life?

» In late adulthood, most siblings live nearby, communicate regularly, and visit several times a year. Socialization is more common than direct assistance, though siblings provide an important "insurance policy." Sibling support increases for siblings living very near.

» Friendships grow in importance in late adulthood and serve a variety of functions: intimacy and companionship, acceptance, a link to the larger community, and protection from the psychological consequences of loss. Elders prefer familiar, established relationships over new ones, and fewer older than younger people have other-sex friendships. Women are more likely than men to have both intimate friends and **secondary friends**—people with whom they spend time occasionally.

Describe older adults' relationships with adult children, adult grandchildren, and great-grandchildren.

» Elders are often in touch with their adult children, who more often provide emotional support than direct assistance. Older adults often give more help than they receive, especially financial and practical assistance—an arrangement that is psychologically beneficial to elders.

» Seniors with adult grandchildren and great-grandchildren benefit from a wider network of support. Most often, grandparents expect and receive affection rather than practical help from their grandchildren. Although grandparent–grandchild contact declines over time, affection remains high.

Discuss elder maltreatment, including risk factors and strategies for prevention.

» Some elders suffer maltreatment at the hands of family members, friends, or professional caregivers. Risk factors include a dependent perpetrator–victim relationship, perpetrator psychological disturbance and stress, a history of family violence, and inadequate nursing homes. In recent years, abandonment of elders with severe disabilities by family caregivers has increased.

» Elder-abuse prevention programs offer caregivers counseling, education, and respite services. Elders benefit from trained volunteers and support groups that help them avoid future harm. Societal efforts, including public education to encourage reporting of suspected cases and improved understanding of the needs of older people, are also vital.

Retirement

Discuss the decision to retire, adjustment to retirement, and involvement in leisure and volunteer activities.

» The decision to retire depends on affordability, health status, nature of the work environment, opportunities to pursue meaningful activities, societal factors such as retirement benefits, and gender. On average, women retire earlier than men because family events play a larger role in their decisions.

» Most older adults adapt well to retirement, especially those who view it as a time of personal growth and remain active and socially involved. Factors affecting adjustment include health status, financial stability, satisfactions previously derived from work, a sense of personal control over life events (including the retirement decision), social support, and marital happiness.

» Meaningful leisure and community service pursuits are typically formed earlier and sustained or expanded during retirement. Involvement is related to better physical and mental health and to reduced mortality.

Optimal Aging

Discuss the meaning of optimal aging.

» Elders who experience **optimal aging** have developed many ways to minimize losses and maximize gains. Societal contexts that permit older adults to manage life changes effectively foster optimal aging. These include well-funded social security plans, good health care, safe housing that adjusts to changes in elders' capacities, social services, and opportunities for lifelong learning.

Important Terms and Concepts

activity theory (p. 614)
affect optimization (p. 605)
aging in place (p. 617)
congregate housing (p. 618)
continuity theory (p. 614)
dependency–support script (p. 609)
disengagement theory (p. 613)
ego integrity versus despair (p. 604)
gerotranscendence (p. 605)
independence–ignore script (p. 609)
life-care communities (p. 618)
optimal aging (p. 632)
reminiscence (p. 606)
secondary friends (p. 625)
social convoy (p. 619)
socioemotional selectivity theory (p. 614)
Third Age (p. 607)

Milestones

Development in Late Adulthood

65–80 years

PHYSICAL

- Performance of autonomic nervous system declines, impairing tolerance for extremes of heat and cold. (567)
- Declines in vision continue, with increased sensitivity to glare and impaired color discrimination, dark adaptation, depth perception, and visual acuity. (567–568)
- Declines in hearing continue throughout the frequency range. (569)
- Sensitivity to taste and odor may decline. (570)
- Touch sensitivity declines on the hands, especially the fingertips. (570)
- Declines in cardiovascular and respiratory functioning lead to greater physical stress during exercise. (570–571)

- Aging of the immune system increases risk for a variety of illnesses, including infectious diseases, cardiovascular disease, certain forms of cancer, and several autoimmune disorders. (571)
- Sleep difficulties increase, especially in men. (571)
- Graying and thinning of the hair continue; the skin wrinkles further and becomes more transparent as it loses its fatty layer of support; "age spots" increase. (572)
- Height and weight decline because of loss of lean body mass. (573)

- Continued loss of bone mass leads to rising rates of osteoporosis. (573, 580)
- Intensity of sexual response and sexual activity decline, although most healthy married couples report regular sexual enjoyment. (579)

COGNITIVE

- Processing speed continues to decline, but crystallized intelligence is largely sustained. (590)
- Ability to control and divide attention continues to decline. (590)

- Amount of information that can be held in working memory, use of memory strategies, and retrieval from long-term memory diminish further; problems are greatest on tasks requiring deliberate processing and associative memory. (591–594)
- Modest forgetting of remote memories occurs. (593)

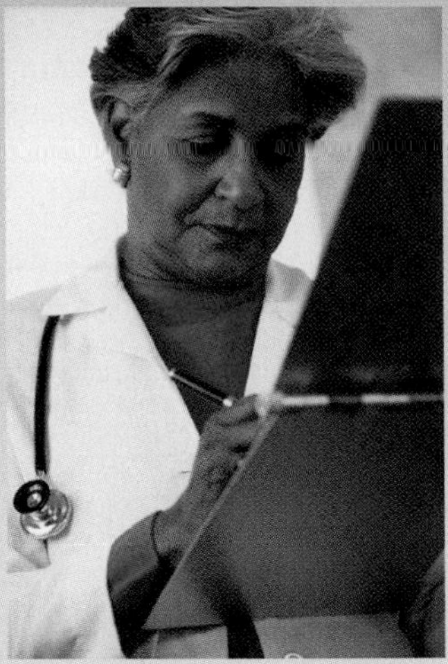

- Use of external aids for prospective memory increases. (593–594)
- Retrieving words from long-term memory and planning what to say and how to say it become more difficult. (594)
- Information is more likely to be represented in terms of gist rather than details. (595)
- Hypothetical problem solving declines, but everyday problem solving remains adaptive. (595)

Note: Numbers in parentheses indicate the page or pages on which each milestone is discussed.

- May hold an important position of leadership in society, such as chief executive officer, religious leader, or supreme court justice. (595)
- May develop wisdom. (595–596)
- Can improve a wide range of cognitive skills through training. (597)

EMOTIONAL/SOCIAL

- Comes to terms with life, developing ego integrity. (604–605)
- Cognitive-affective complexity declines as basic information-processing skill diminish. (605)

- Affect optimization, the ability to maximize positive emotion and dampen negative emotion, increases. (605)
- May engage in reminiscence and life review, but continues to seek avenues for personal growth and fulfillment. (606)
- Self-concept strengthens, becoming more secure and complex. (606)
- Agreeableness and acceptance of change increase, while extroversion and openness to experience decline modestly. (608)
- Spirituality and faith may advance to a higher level, away from prescribed beliefs toward a more reflective approach. (608–609)

- Perceived negative physical health may lead to depression. (610)
- Size of social network and amount of social interaction decline. (612–615)
- Selection of social partners is based on anticipated feelings, including pursuit of pleasant relationships and avoidance of unpleasant ones. (614–615)
- Marital satisfaction increases, peaking in late adulthood. (620)

- May be widowed. (622)
- Sibling closeness and mutual support may increase. (624)
- Number of friends generally declines. (625)
- May become a great-grandparent. (626)
- May retire. (628–630)
- Likely to increase involvement in leisure and volunteer activities (630–631)
- More likely to be knowledgeable about politics and to vote. (631–632)

80 years and older

PHYSICAL

- Physical changes previously listed continue.

- Mobility diminishes as muscle and bone strength and joint flexibility decline. (573)

COGNITIVE

- Cognitive changes previously listed continue.

- Fluid abilities decline further; crystallized abilities drop as well, though only modestly. (590)

EMOTIONAL/SOCIAL

- Emotional and social changes previously listed continue.
- May develop gerotranscendence, a cosmic perspective directed beyond the self. (605)
- Relationships with adult children become more important. (625–626)

- Frequency and variety of leisure and volunteer activities decline. (631)

© CHRISTOPHE BOISVIEUX/CORBIS

All cultures have rituals for celebrating the end of life and helping the bereaved cope with profound loss. Here, community members perform a lion dance in front of a coffin during a traditional Han funeral in China. In Buddhist lore, the lion is a guardian, ensuring peace and good luck to those who cross its path.

CHAPTER 19

Death, Dying, and Bereavement

As every life is unique, so each death is unique. The final forces of the human spirit separate themselves from the body in manifold ways.

My mother Sofie's death was the culmination of a five-year battle against cancer. In her last months, the disease invaded organs throughout her body, attacking the lungs in its final fury. She withered slowly, with the mixed blessing of time to prepare against certain knowledge that death was just around the corner. My father, Philip, lived another 18 years. At age 80, he was outwardly healthy, active, and about to depart on a long-awaited vacation when a heart attack snuffed out his life suddenly, without time for last words or deathbed reconciliations.

As I set to work on this chapter, my 65-year-old neighbor Nicholas gambled for a higher quality of life. To be eligible for a kidney transplant, he elected bypass surgery to strengthen his heart. Doctors warned that his body might not withstand the operation. But Nicholas knew that without taking a chance, he would live only a few years, in debilitated condition. Shortly after the surgery, infection set in, traveling throughout his system and so weakening him that only extreme measures—a respirator to sustain breathing and powerful drugs to elevate his fading blood pressure—could keep him alive.

"Come on, Dad, you can do it," encouraged Nicholas's daughter Sasha, standing by his bedside and stroking his hand. But Nicholas could not. After two months in intensive care, he experienced brain seizures and slipped into a coma. Three doctors met with his wife, Giselle, to tell her there was no hope. She asked them to disconnect the respirator, and within half an hour Nicholas drifted away.

Death is essential for the survival of our species. We die so that our own children and the children of others may live. When it comes to this fate, nature treats humankind, with all its unique capabilities, just as it treats every other living creature (Nuland, 1993). As hard as it is to accept the reality that we too will die, our greatest solace lies in the knowledge that death is part of ongoing life.

In this chapter, we address the culmination of lifespan development. Over the past century, technology has provided us with so many means to keep death at bay that many people regard it as a forbidden topic. But pressing social and economic dilemmas that are an outgrowth of the dramatic increase in life expectancy are forcing us to attend to life's end—its quality, its timing, and ways to help people adjust to their own and others' final leave taking. The interdisciplinary field of **thanatology,** devoted to the study of death and dying, has expanded tremendously over the past 20 years.

Our discussion addresses the physical changes of dying; understanding of and attitudes toward death in childhood, adolescence, and adulthood; the thoughts and feelings of people as they stand face to face with death; where people die; hopelessly ill patients' right to die; and coping with the death of a loved one. The experiences of Sofie, Philip, Nicholas, their families, and others illustrate how each person's life history joins with social and cultural contexts to shape death and dying, lending great diversity to this universal experience.

How We Die

Our vast literature on death is largely aimed at helping people cope with the emotional trauma of dying and its aftermath. In industrialized countries, opportunities to witness the physical aspects of death are less available today than in previous generations. Most people in the developed world die in hospitals, where doctors and nurses, not loved ones, typically attend their last moments. Nevertheless, many want to know how we die, either to anticipate their own end or grasp what is happening to a dying loved one.

Physical Changes

My father's fatal heart attack came suddenly during the night. When I heard the news, I longed for reassurance that his death had been swift and without suffering.

When asked how they would like to die, most people say they want "death with dignity"—either a quick, agony-free end during sleep or a clear-minded final few moments in which they can say farewell and review their lives. In reality, death is the culmination of a straightforward biological process. For about 20 percent of people, it is gentle—especially when narcotic drugs ease pain and mask the destructive events taking place (Nuland, 1993). But most of the time it is not.

Recall that unintentional injuries are the leading cause of death in childhood and adolescence, cardiovascular disease and cancer in adulthood. Of the one-quarter of people in industrialized nations who die suddenly, within a few hours of experiencing symptoms, 80 to 90 percent are victims of heart attacks (Winslow, Mehta, & Fuster, 2005). My yearning for a painless death for my father was probably not fulfilled. Undoubtedly he felt the sharp, crushing sensation of a heart deprived of oxygen. As his heart twitched uncontrollably (called *fibrillation*) or stopped entirely, blood circulation slowed and ceased, and he was thrust into unconsciousness. A brain starved of oxygen for more than two to four minutes is irreversibly damaged—an outcome indicated by the pupils of the eyes becoming unresponsive to light and widening into large, black circles. Other oxygen-deprived organs stop functioning as well.

Death is long and drawn out for three-fourths of people—many more than in times past, as a result of life-saving medical technology. They succumb in different ways. Of those with heart disease, most have congestive heart failure, the cause of Nicholas's death (Gruenewald & White, 2006). His scarred heart could no longer contract with the force needed to deliver enough oxygen to his tissues. As it tried harder, its muscle weakened further. Without sufficient blood pressure, fluid backed up in Nicholas's lungs. This hampered his breathing and created ideal conditions for inhaled bacteria to multiply, enter the bloodstream, and run rampant in his system, leading many organs to fail.

Cancer also chooses diverse paths to inflict its damage. When it metastasizes, bits of tumor travel through the bloodstream and implant and grow in vital organs, disrupting their functioning. Medication made my mother's final days as comfortable as possible, granting a relatively easy death. But the preceding weeks involved physical suffering, including impaired breathing and digestion and turning and twisting to find a comfortable position in bed.

In the days or hours before death, activity declines; the person moves and communicates less and shows little interest in food, water, and surroundings. At the same time, body temperature, blood pressure, and circulation to the limbs fall, so the hands and feet feel cool and skin color changes to a duller, grayish hue (Hospice Foundation of America, 2005). When the transition from life to death is imminent, the person moves through three phases:

1. The **agonal phase.** The Greek word *agon* means "struggle." Here agonal refers to gasps and muscle spasms during the first moments in which the regular heartbeat disintegrates (Manole & Hickey, 2006).
2. **Clinical death.** A short interval follows in which heartbeat, circulation, breathing, and brain functioning stop, but resuscitation is still possible.
3. **Mortality.** The individual passes into permanent death. Within a few hours, the newly lifeless being appears shrunken, not at all like the person he or she was when alive.

Defining Death

TAKE A MOMENT... Consider what we have said so far, and note the dilemma of identifying just when death occurs. Death is not an event that happens at a single point in time but, rather,

© MICHAEL S. YAMASHITA/CORBIS

A monk prays with mourners during a Shinto funeral in Japan. Shinto beliefs, which stress ancestor worship and time for the spirit to leave the corpse, may be partly responsible for the Japanese discomfort with the brain death standard and organ donation.

a process in which organs stop functioning in a sequence that varies from person to person. Because the dividing line between life and death is fuzzy, societies need a definition of death to help doctors decide when life-saving measures should be terminated, to signal survivors that they must begin to grieve their loss and reorganize their lives, and to establish when donated organs can be removed.

Several decades ago, loss of heartbeat and respiration signified death. But these criteria are no longer adequate because resuscitation techniques frequently permit vital signs to be restored. Today, **brain death,** irreversible cessation of all activity in the brain and the brain stem (which controls reflexes), is used in most industrialized nations.

But not all countries accept this standard. In Japan, for example, doctors rely on traditional criteria—absence of heartbeat and respiration. This approach stands in the way of a national organ transplant program because few organs can be salvaged from bodies without artificially maintaining vital signs. Buddhist, Confucian, and Shinto beliefs about death, which stress ancestor worship and time for the spirit to leave the corpse, may be partly responsible for the Japanese discomfort with brain death and organ donation. Marring the body to harvest organs violates respect for the deceased. Today, Japanese law allows people who want to be organ donors to choose the standard of brain death, as long as their families do not object (Bagheri, 2007). Otherwise, they are considered to be alive until the heart stops beating.

Often the brain death standard does not solve the problem of when to halt treatment. Consider Nicholas, who, though not brain dead, had entered a **persistent vegetative state,** in which the cerebral cortex no longer registered electrical activity but the brain stem remained active. Doctors were certain they could not restore consciousness or body movement. Because thousands of people in the United States and other nations are in a persistent vegetative state, with health-care costs totaling many millions of dollars annually, some experts believe that absence of activity in the cerebral cortex should be sufficient to declare a person dead. But others point to a few cases in which patients who had been vegetative for months regained cortical responsiveness and consciousness, though usually with very limited functioning (Kotchoubey et al., 2005; Laureys & Boly, 2007). In still other instances of illness, a fully conscious but suffering person refuses life-saving measures—an issue we will consider later when we take up the right to die.

Death with Dignity

We have seen that nature rarely delivers the idealized, easy end most people want, nor can medical science guarantee it. Therefore, the greatest dignity in death is in the integrity of the life that precedes it—an integrity we can foster by the way we communicate with and care for the dying person.

First, we can assure the majority of dying people, who succumb gradually, that we will support them through their physical and psychological distress. We can do everything possible to provide the utmost in humane and compassionate care. And we can treat them with esteem and respect—for example, by taking interest in those aspects of their lives that they most value and by addressing their greatest concerns (Chochinov, 2006).

Second, we can be candid about death's certainty. Unless people are aware that they are dying and understand (as far as possible) the likely circumstances of their death, they cannot plan for end-of-life care and decision making and share the sentiments that bring closure to relationships they hold most dear. Because Sofie knew how and when her death would probably take place, she chose a time when she, Philip, and her children could express what their lives had meant to one another. Among those precious bedside exchanges was Sofie's memorable last

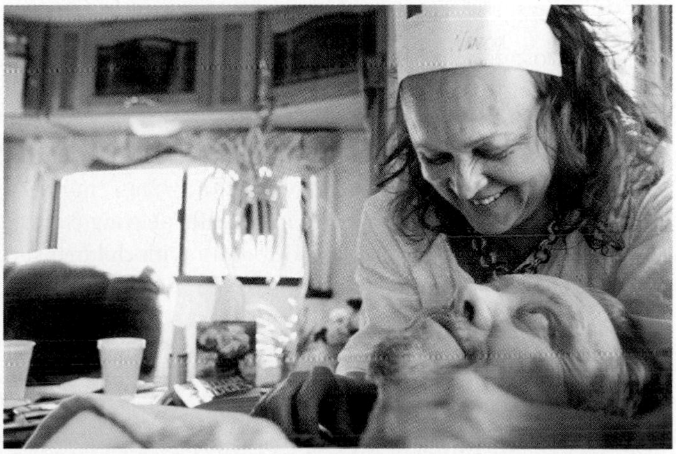

AP IMAGES/CCEUR D'ALENE PRESS, JEROME A. POLLOS

In Post Falls, Idaho, dying patient Dick Warner's wife Nancy wears a nurse's hat she crafted from paper to symbolize her dual roles as medical and emotional caregiver. The evening of this photo, Nancy heard Dick's breaths shortening. She kissed him and whispered, "It's time to let go." He smiled and died the way he wanted, with the gentle support of his wife at his bedside.

wish that Philip remarry after her death so he would not live out his final years alone. Openness about impending death granted Sofie a final generative act, helped her let go of the person closest to her, and offered comfort as she faced death.

Finally, doctors and nurses can help dying people learn enough about their condition to make reasoned choices about whether to fight on or say no to further treatment. An understanding of how the normal body works simplifies comprehension of how disease affects it—education that can begin as early as the childhood years.

In sum, when the conditions of illness do not permit a graceful, serene death, we can still ensure the most dignified exit possible by offering the dying person care, affection, and companionship; the truth about diagnosis; and the maximum personal control over this final phase of life (American Hospice Foundation, 2009). These are essential ingredients of a "good death," and we will revisit them throughout this chapter.

Understanding of and Attitudes Toward Death

A century ago, when most deaths occurred at home, people of all ages, including children, helped with care of the dying family member and were present at the moment of death. They saw their loved one buried on family property or in the local cemetery, where the grave could be visited regularly. Because infant and childhood mortality rates were high, all people were likely to know someone their own age, or even younger, who had died. And it was common for children to experience the death of a parent.

Compared with earlier generations, today more young people reach adulthood without having experienced the death of someone they know well. When a death does occur, professionals in hospitals and funeral homes take care of most tasks that involve confronting it directly (Morgan & Laungani, 2005).

This distance from death undoubtedly contributes to a sense of uneasiness about it. Despite frequent images of death in television shows, movies, and news reports of accidents, murders, wars, and natural disasters, we live in a death-denying culture. Adults are often reluctant to talk about death with children and adolescents. And substitute expressions, such as "passing away," "going out," or "departing," permit us to avoid acknowledging it candidly. In the following sections, we examine the development of conceptions of and attitudes toward death, along with ways to foster increased understanding and acceptance.

Childhood

Five-year-old Miriam arrived at our university laboratory preschool the day after her dog Pepper died. Instead of joining the other children, she stayed close to her teacher, Leslie, who noticed Miriam's discomfort. "What's wrong?" Leslie asked.

"Daddy said Pepper was so sick the vet had to put him to sleep." For a moment, Miriam looked hopeful. "When I get home, Pepper might wake up."

Leslie answered directly, "No, Pepper won't get up again. He's not asleep. He's dead, and that means he can't sleep, eat, run, or play anymore."

Miriam wandered off but later returned to Leslie and, sobbing, confessed, "I chased Pepper too hard."

Leslie put her arm around Miriam. "Pepper didn't die because you chased him," she explained. "He was very old and sick."

Over the next few days, Miriam asked many questions: "When I go to sleep, will I die?" "Can a tummy ache make you die?" "Does Pepper feel better now?" "Will Mommy and Daddy die?"

DEVELOPMENT OF THE DEATH CONCEPT. An understanding of death is based on five ideas:

1. *Permanence.* Once a living thing dies, it cannot be brought back to life.
2. *Inevitability.* All living things eventually die.
3. *Cessation.* All living functions, including thought, feeling, movement, and bodily processes, cease at death.
4. *Applicability.* Death applies only to living things.
5. *Causation.* Death is caused by a breakdown of bodily functioning.

To understand death, children must acquire some basic notions of biology—that animals and plants contain body parts (brain, heart, stomach; leaf, stem, roots) essential for maintaining life. They must also break down their global category of *not alive* into *dead, inanimate, unreal,* and *nonexistent* (Carey, 1999). Until children grasp these ideas, they interpret death in terms of familiar experiences—as a change in behavior. Consequently, they may believe that they caused a relative's or pet's death; that having a stomachache can cause someone to die; that dead people eat, go to the bathroom, see, and think; and that death is like sleep (Slaughter, Jaakkola, & Carey, 1999; Slaughter & Lyons, 2003).

Permanence is the first understood component of the death concept. Preschoolers accept this fact quickly, perhaps because they have seen it in other situations—for example, in the dead butterflies and beetles they pick up and inspect while playing outside. Appreciation of *inevitability* soon follows. At first, children think that certain people do not die—themselves, people like themselves (other children), and people with whom they have close emotional ties. *Cessation, applicability,* and *causation* are more challenging ideas (Kenyon, 2001). Preschoolers and kindergartners realize that the dead lose the capacity for body processes and perception. But the majority of 10- to 12-year-olds continue to say that the dead are able to think and feel (Bering & Bjorklund, 2004). Many adults, too, believe in some form of personal consciousness after death.

© GIANNI GIANSANTI/SYGMA/CORBIS

Because of exposure to the realities of death, these children in El Salvador—carrying the coffin of an infant during the funeral—likely exceed many agemates in their grasp of what death means.

■ **INDIVIDUAL AND CULTURAL VARIATIONS.** Although children typically attain an adultlike understanding of death in middle childhood, wide individual differences exist (Speece & Brent, 1996). Terminally ill children under age 6 often have a well-developed concept of death. If parents and health professionals have not been forthright, they discover that they are deathly ill in other ways—through nonverbal communication, eavesdropping, and talking with other child patients (O'Halloran & Altmaier, 1996). Children growing up on Israeli kibbutzim (agricultural settlements) who have witnessed terrorist attacks, family members' departure on army tours, and parental anxiety about safety express an adultlike grasp of death by age 5 (Mahon, Goldberg, & Washington, 1999).

Ethnic variations suggest that religious teachings affect children's understanding. In a comparison of four ethnic groups in Israel, Druze and Moslem children's death concepts differed from those of Christian and Jewish children (Florian & Kravetz, 1985). The Druze emphasis on reincarnation and the greater religiosity of both Druze and Moslem groups may have led more of their children to deny that death is permanent and that the body stops functioning. Similarly, children of U.S. Southern Baptist families, who believe in an afterlife, were less likely to endorse permanence than were children of Unitarian families, who do not dwell on an afterlife (Candy-Gibbs, Sharp, & Petrun, 1985).

■ **ENHANCING CHILDREN'S UNDERSTANDING.** Parents often worry that discussing death candidly with children will fuel their fears. But children with a good grasp of the facts of death express less anxiety about it (Slaughter & Griffiths, 2007). Direct explanations, like Leslie's, that fit the child's capacity to understand, work best. When adults use clichés or make misleading statements, children may take these literally and react with confusion. For example, when a parent told her 5-year-old daughter, "Grandpa went on a long trip," the child wondered, "Why didn't he take me?" (Wolfelt, 1997). Sometimes children ask difficult questions, such as "Will I die?" "Will you die?" Parents can be truthful as well as comforting by taking advantage of the child's sense of time. "Not for many, many years," they can say. "First I'm going to enjoy you as a grownup and be a grandparent."

Another way to foster an accurate appreciation of death is to teach young children about human biology. Three- to 5-year-olds given lessons in the role of the heart, brain, lungs, stomach, and other organs in sustaining life have more advanced death concepts than children not given such lessons (Slaughter & Lyons, 2003).

Adult–child discussions should also be culturally sensitive. Rather than presenting scientific evidence as negating religious beliefs, parents and teachers can help children blend the two sources of knowledge. Older children often combine their appreciation of the death concept with religious and philosophical views, which offer solace in times of bereavement (Cuddy-Casey & Orvaschel, 1997). As we will see later, open, honest discussions not only contribute to a realistic understanding of death but also facilitate grieving after a child has experienced a loss.

Adolescence

Recall that teenagers have difficulty integrating logical insights with the realities of everyday life. In this sense, their understanding of death is not yet fully mature, as both their reasoning and behavior reveal.

■ **THE GAP BETWEEN LOGIC AND REALITY.** Teenagers can explain the permanence and cessation aspects of death, but they are attracted to alternatives. For example, adolescents often describe death as an enduring abstract state—"darkness," "eternal light," "transition," or "nothingness" (Brent et al., 1996). They also formulate personal theories about life after death. Besides images of heaven and hell influenced by their religious background, they speculate about reincarnation, transmigration of souls, and spiritual survival on earth or at another level (Noppe & Noppe, 1997; Yang & Chen, 2002).

Although mortality in adolescence is low compared with that in infancy and adulthood, teenage deaths are typically sudden and human-induced; unintentional injuries, homicide, and suicide are leading causes. Adolescents are clearly aware that death happens to everyone and can occur at any time. But as their high-risk activities suggest, they do not take death personally. In one study, the lower adolescent boys' consciousness of personal mortality, the more they engaged in risky behavior (Word, 1996).

What explains teenagers' difficulty integrating logic with reality in the domain of death? First, adolescence is a period of rapid growth and onset of reproductive capacity—attainments

Applying What We Know

Discussing Concerns About Death with Children and Adolescents

Suggestion	Description
Take the lead.	Be alert to the child's or adolescent's nonverbal behaviors, bringing up the subject sympathetically, especially after a death-related situation has occurred.
Listen perceptively.	Give full attention to the child or adolescent and the feelings underlying his or her words. When adults pretend to listen while thinking about other things, young people quickly pick up this sign of indifference and withdraw their confidence.
Acknowledge feelings.	Accept the child's or adolescent's emotions as real and important; avoid being judgmental. For example, paraphrase sentiments you detect, such as "I see you're very puzzled about that. Let's talk more about it."
Provide factual information in a candid, culturally sensitive fashion.	For children who do not yet have a realistic understanding of death, provide simple, direct, and accurate explanations. Avoid misleading statements, such as "Grandpa went away on a long trip." Do not contradict the young person's religious beliefs. Rather, assist him or her in blending scientific with religious sources of knowledge.
Engage in joint problem solving.	When questions do not have easy answers, such as "Where does your soul go when you die?," convey your belief in the young person's worth by indicating that you do not want to impose a point of view but rather to help him or her come to personally satisfying conclusions. To questions you cannot answer, say, "I don't know." Such honesty shows a willingness to generate and evaluate solutions jointly.

© DENNIS MCDONALD/PHOTOEDIT

This teenager knows that death happens to everyone and can occur at any time, but his risk taking suggests otherwise. Wrapped up in their own uniqueness, adolescents may conclude they are beyond reach of death.

that are the opposite of death! Second, recall the adolescent personal fable: Wrapped up in their own uniqueness, teenagers may conclude they are beyond reach of death. Finally, as teenagers construct a personal identity and experience their first freely chosen love relationships, they may be strongly attracted to romantic notions of death, which challenge logic (Noppe & Noppe, 1996). Not until early adulthood are young people capable of the relativistic thinking needed to reconcile these conflicting ideas (see Chapter 13, page 452).

ENHANCING ADOLESCENTS' UNDERSTANDING. By encouraging adolescents to discuss concerns about death, adults can help them build a bridge between death as a logical concept and their personal experiences. In Chapter 12, we noted that teenagers with authoritative parents are more likely to turn to adults for guidance on important issues. In one study of 12- to 15-year-olds, most wanted to talk with parents rather than peers about the "meaning of life and death" and "what happens when you die." But 60 percent thought that their parents would not be genuinely interested, and the majority of parents felt inadequately prepared for the task (McNeil, 1986).

Taking up adolescents' thoughts and feelings about death can be part of everyday conversation, sparked by a news report or the death of an acquaintance. Parents can capitalize on these moments to express their own views, listen closely, accept teenagers' feelings, and correct misconceptions. Such mutual sharing deepens bonds of love and provides the basis for further exploration when the need arises. Applying What We Know above suggests ways to discuss concerns about death with children and adolescents.

Adulthood

In early adulthood, many people brush aside thoughts of death (Gresser, Wong, & Reker, 1987). This avoidance may be prompted by death anxiety, which we will consider in the next section. Alternatively, it may be due to relative lack of interest in death-related issues, given that young adults typically do not know very many people who have died and (like adolescents) think of their own death as a long way off.

In Chapters 15 and 16, we described midlife as a time of stock taking in which people begin to view the lifespan in terms of time left to live and focus on tasks to be completed. Middle-aged people no longer have a vague conception of their own death. They know that in the not-too-distant future, it will be their turn to grow old and die.

In late adulthood, adults think and talk more about death because it is much closer. Increasing evidence of mortality comes from physical changes, higher rates of illness and disability, and loss of relatives and friends (see Chapter 17). Compared with middle-aged people, older adults spend more time pondering the process and circumstances of dying than the state of death. Nearness to death seems to lead to a practical concern with how and when it might happen (de Vries, Bluck, & Birren, 1993; Kastenbaum, 2009).

Finally, although we have traced overall age-related changes, large individual differences exist. Some adults focus on life and death issues early on; others are less reflective, moving into old age without giving these matters much attention.

Death Anxiety

TAKE A MOMENT... As you read the following statements, do you find yourself agreeing, disagreeing, or reacting neutrally?

> "Never feeling anything again after I die upsets me."
>
> "I hate the idea that I will be helpless after I die."
>
> "The total isolation of death is frightening to me."
>
> "The feeling that I will be missing out on so much after I die disturbs me." (Thorson & Powell, 1994, pp. 38–39)

Items like these appear on questionnaires used to measure **death anxiety**—fear and apprehension of death. Even people who clearly accept the reality of death may fear it.

What predicts whether thoughts of our own demise trigger intense distress, relative calm, or something in between? To answer this question, researchers measure both general death anxiety and specific factors—fear of no longer existing, loss of control, a painful death, decay of the body, separation from loved ones, and the unknown (Neimeyer, 1994). Findings reveal large individual and cultural variations in aspects of death that arouse fear. For example, in a study of devout Islamic Saudi Arabians, certain factors that appear repeatedly in the responses of Westerners, such as fear of the body decaying and of the unknown, were entirely absent (Long, 1985).

Among Westerners, spirituality—a sense of life's meaning—seems to be more important than religious commitment in limiting death anxiety (Rasmussen & Johnson, 1994). People with a well-developed personal philosophy of death are also less fearful. And in two studies, Christian older adults whose religious beliefs and behavior were contradictory—who believed in a rewarding afterlife but rarely prayed or attended services, or who regularly prayed and attended services but doubted the existence of an afterlife—reported higher death anxiety (Wink, 2006; Wink & Scott, 2005). Together, these findings indicate that both firmness of beliefs and consistency between beliefs and practices, rather than religiousness itself, reduce fear of death. Death anxiety is especially low among adults with deep faith in some form of higher force or being—faith that may or may not be influenced by religion (Cicirelli, 1999, 2002).

TAKE A MOMENT... From what you have learned about adult psychosocial development, how do you think death anxiety might change with age? If you predicted it would decline, reaching its lowest level in late adulthood, you are correct (see Figure 19.1) (Russac et al., 2007; Tomer, Eliason, & Smith, 2000). This age-related drop has been found in many cultures and ethnic groups. Recall from Chapter 18 that older adults are especially effective at regulating negative emotion. As a result, most cope with anxieties, including fear of death, effectively. Furthermore, attainment of ego integrity reduces death anxiety. Elders have had more time to develop symbolic immortality—the belief that one will continue to live on through one's children or through one's work or personal influence (see Chapter 16, page 533).

As long as it is not overly intense, death anxiety can motivate people to strive to live up to internalized cultural values—for example, to be kind to others and to work hard to reach one's goals. These efforts increase adults' sense of self-esteem,

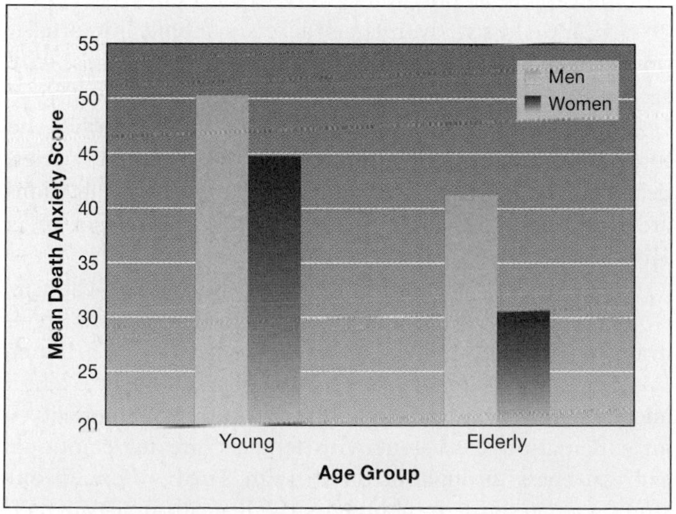

■ **FIGURE 19.1** ■ **Relationship of age and gender to death anxiety.** In this study comparing young and elderly adults, death anxiety declined with age. At both ages, women expressed greater fear of death than men. Many other studies show similar findings. (Adapted from Tomer, Eliason, & Smith, 2000.)

© MICHEL PORRO/GETTY IMAGES

Death anxiety declines in old age, and this 81-year-old from the Netherlands seems to have very little! She had this coffin made to serve as a bookshelf because, she said, "It's a waste to use a coffin just for burial." The pillow on the top will support her head after she dies.

self-efficacy, and purpose in life—powerful antidotes against the terrifying thought that, in the overall scheme of things, they "are no more important or enduring than any individual potato, pineapple, or porcupine" (Fry, 2003; Pyszczynski et al., 2004, p. 436). In a study of Israeli adults, symbolic immortality predicted reduced fear of death, especially among those with secure attachments (Florian & Mikulincer, 1998). Gratifying, close interpersonal ties seem to help people feel worthwhile and forge a sense of symbolic immortality. And people who view death as an opportunity to pass a legacy to future generations are less likely to fear it (Cicirelli, 2001; Mikulincer, Florian, & Hirschberger, 2003).

Regardless of age, in both Eastern and Western cultures, women appear more anxious about death than men do (refer again to Figure 19.1) (Madnawat & Kachhawa, 2007; Tomer, Eliason, & Smith, 2000). Women may be more likely to admit and men more likely to avoid troubled feelings about mortality—an explanation consistent with females' greater emotional expressiveness throughout the lifespan. Furthermore, in one study, women showed a temporary rise in death anxiety in their early fifties not seen in men (Russac et al., 2007). Perhaps menopause, in marking the end of reproductive capacity, provides women with a stark reminder of their mortality.

Experiencing some anxiety about death is normal and adaptive. But like other fears, very intense death anxiety can undermine effective adjustment. Although physical health in adulthood is not related to death anxiety, mental health clearly is. In cultures as different as China and the United States, people who are depressed or generally anxious are likely to have more severe death concerns (Neimeyer & Van Brunt, 1995; Wu, Tang, & Kwok, 2002). In contrast, people who are good at inhibition (keeping their minds from straying to irrelevant thoughts) and at emotional self-regulation report less death anxiety (Gailliot, Schmeichel, & Baumeister, 2006). They are better able to manage their concerns about death.

Death anxiety is largely limited to adolescence and adulthood. Children rarely display it unless they live in high-crime neighborhoods or war-torn areas where they are in constant danger (see the Lifespan Vista box on the impact of ethnic and political violence on children on page 353 in Chapter 10). Terminally ill children are also at risk for high death anxiety. Compared with other same-age patients, children with cancer express more destructive thoughts and negative feelings about death (Malone, 1982). For those whose parents make the mistake of not telling them they are going to die, loneliness and death anxiety can be extreme (O'Halloran & Altmaier, 1996).

ASK YOURSELF

REVIEW
Explain why older adults think and talk more about death than do younger people but feel less anxious about it.

APPLY
When 4-year-old Chloe's aunt died, Chloe asked, "Where's Aunt Susie?" Her mother explained, "Aunt Susie is taking a long, peaceful sleep." For the next two weeks, Chloe refused to go to bed, and, when finally coaxed into her room, lay awake for hours. What is the likely reason for Chloe's behavior? What might be a better way of answering her question?

CONNECT
How do advances in cognition contribute to adolescents' concepts of death? (Refer to Chapter 11, pages 383–384 and 387.)

REFLECT
Ask members of earlier generations in your family about their childhood experiences with death. Compare these to your own experiences. What differences did you find, and how would you explain them?

Thinking and Emotions of Dying People

In the year before her death, Sofie did everything possible to surmount her illness. In between treatments to control the cancer, she tested her strength. She continued to teach high school, traveled to visit her children, cultivated a garden, and took weekend excursions with Philip. Hope pervaded Sofie's approach to her deadly condition, and she spoke often about the disease—so much so that her friends wondered how she could confront it so directly.

As Sofie deteriorated physically, she moved in and out of various mental and emotional states. She was frustrated, and at times angry and depressed, about her inability to keep on fighting. I recall her lamenting anxiously on a day when she was in pain, "I'm sick, so very sick! I'm trying so hard, but I can't keep on." Once she asked when my husband and I, who were newly married, would have children. "If only I could live long enough to hold them in my arms!" she cried. In the last week, she appeared tired but free of struggle. Occasionally, she spoke of her love for us and commented on the beauty of the hills outside her window. But mostly, she looked and listened, rather than actively participating in conversation. One afternoon, she fell permanently unconscious.

Do Stages of Dying Exist?

As dying people move closer to death, are their reactions predictable? Do they go through a series of changes that are the same for everyone, or are their thoughts and feelings unique?

KÜBLER-ROSS'S THEORY. Although her theory has been heavily criticized, Elisabeth Kübler-Ross (1969) is credited with awakening society's sensitivity to the psychological needs of dying patients. From interviews with over 200 terminally ill people, she devised a theory of five typical responses—initially proposed as stages—to the prospect of death and the ordeal of dying:

- *Denial.* On learning of the terminal illness, the person denies its seriousness to escape from the prospect of death. While the patient still feels reasonably well, denial is self-protective, allowing the individual to deal with the illness at his or her own pace. Most people move in and out of denial, making great plans one day and, the next, acknowledging that death is near (Smith, 1993). Kübler-Ross recommends that family members and health professionals not prolong denial by distorting the truth about the person's condition. In doing so, they prevent the dying person from adjusting to impending death and hinder necessary arrangements—for social support, for bringing closure to relationships, and for making decisions about medical interventions.

- *Anger.* Recognition that time is short promotes anger at having to die without having had a chance to do all one wants to do. Family members and health professionals may be targets of the patient's rage, resentment, and envy. Even so, they must tolerate rather than lash out at the patient's behavior, recognizing that the underlying cause is the unfairness of death.

- *Bargaining.* Realizing the inevitability of death, the terminally ill person attempts to bargain for extra time—a deal he or she may try to strike with family members, friends, doctors, nurses, or God. The best response to these efforts to sustain hope is to listen sympathetically, as one doctor did to the pleas of a young AIDS-stricken father, whose wish was to live long enough to dance with his daughter—then 8 years old—at her wedding (Selwyn, 1996). Sometimes, bargains are altruistic acts. Tony, a 15-year-old leukemia patient, expressed to his mother:

  > I don't want to die yet. Gerry [youngest brother] is only 3 and not old enough to understand. If I could live just one more year, I could explain it to him myself and he will understand. Three is just too young. (Komp, 1996, pp. 69–70)

  Although many dying patients' bargains are unrealistic and impossible to fulfill, Tony lived for exactly one year—a gift to those who survived him.

- *Depression.* When denial, anger, and bargaining fail to postpone the illness, the person becomes depressed about the loss of his or her life. Unfortunately, many experiences associated with dying, including physical and mental deterioration, pain, lack of control, and being hooked to machines, intensify despondency (Maier & Newman, 1995). Health care that responds humanely to the patient's wishes can limit hopelessness and despair.

- *Acceptance.* Most people who reach acceptance, a state of peace and quiet about upcoming death, do so only in the last weeks or days. The weakened patient yields to death, disengaging from all but a few family members, friends, and caregivers. Some dying people, in an attempt to pull away from all they have loved, withdraw into themselves for long periods of time. "I'm getting my mental and emotional house in order," one patient explained (Samarel, 1995, p. 101).

EVALUATION OF KÜBLER-ROSS'S THEORY. Kübler-Ross cautioned that her five stages should not be viewed as a fixed sequence and that not all people display each response. But her use of the term *stages* has made it easy for her theory to be interpreted simplistically, as the series of steps a "normal" dying person follows. Some health professionals, unaware of diversity in dying experiences, have insensitively tried to push patients through Kübler-Ross's sequence. And caregivers, through callousness or ignorance, can too easily dismiss a dying patient's legitimate complaints about treatment as "just what you would expect in Stage 2" (Corr, 1993; Kastenbaum, 2009).

Research confirms that, in line with Kübler-Ross's observations, dying people are more likely to display denial after learning of their condition and acceptance shortly before death (Kalish, 1985). But rather than stages, the five reactions Kübler-Ross observed are best viewed as coping strategies that anyone may call on in the face of threat. Furthermore, dying people react in many additional ways—for example, through efforts to conquer the disease, as Sofie displayed; through an overwhelming need to control what happens to their bodies during the dying process; through acts of generosity and caring, as seen in Tony's concern for his 3-year-old brother, Gerry; and through shifting their focus to living in a fulfilling way—"seizing the day" because so little time is left (Silverman, 2004; Wright, 2003).

As these examples suggest, the most serious drawback to Kübler-Ross's theory is that it looks at dying patients' thoughts and feelings outside the contexts that give them meaning. As we will see next, people's adaptations to impending death can be understood only in relation to the multidimensional influences that have contributed to their life course and that also shape this final phase.

Contextual Influences on Adaptations to Dying

From the moment of her diagnosis, Sofie spent little time denying the deadliness of her disease. Instead, she met it head on, just as she had dealt with other challenges of life. Her impassioned plea to hold her grandchildren in her arms was less a bargain with fate than an expression of profound defeat that on the threshold of late adulthood, she would not live to enjoy its rewards. At the end, her quiet, withdrawn demeanor was probably resignation, not acceptance. All her life, she had been a person with a fighting spirit, unwilling to give in to challenge.

According to recent theorists, a single strategy, such as acceptance, is not best for every dying patient. Rather, an **appropriate death** is one that makes sense in terms of the individual's pattern of living and values and, at the same time, preserves or restores significant relationships and is as free of suffering as possible (Samarel, 1995; Worden, 2000). When asked about a "good death," most patients are clear about what, ideally, they would like to happen. They mention the following goals:

- Maintaining a sense of identity, or inner continuity with one's past
- Clarifying the meaning of one's life and death
- Maintaining and enhancing relationships
- Achieving a sense of control over the time that remains
- Confronting and preparing for death (Goldsteen et al., 2006; Kleespies, 2004; Proulx & Jacelon, 2004)

On September 18, 2007, Carnegie Mellon University computer science professor Randy Pausch, diagnosed with pancreatic cancer, gave his final lecture to a packed house. His message, which focused on achieving one's childhood dreams and enabling the dreams of others, can be viewed at *www.cmu.edu/homepage/multimedia/randy-pausch-lecture.shtml*. He died nine months later, at age 47, having approached his death in a way that suited his pattern of living and deepest values.

Research reveals that biological, psychological, and social and cultural forces affect people's coping with dying and, therefore, the extent to which they attain these goals. Let's look at some important influences on how people fare.

NATURE OF THE DISEASE. The course of the illness and its symptoms affect the dying person's reactions. For example, the extended nature of Sofie's illness and her doctor's initial optimism about achieving a remission undoubtedly contributed to her attempts to try to conquer the disease. During the final month, when cancer had spread to Sofie's lungs and she could not catch her breath, she was agitated and fearful until oxygen and medication relieved her uncertainty about being able to breathe. In contrast, Nicholas's weakened heart and failing kidneys so depleted his strength that he responded only with passivity.

Because of the toll of the disease, about one-third of cancer patients experience severe depression—reactions distinct from the sadness, grief, and worry that typically accompany the dying process. Profound depression amplifies pain, impairs the immune response, interferes with the patient's capacity for pleasure, meaning, and connection, and is associated with poorer survival (Williams & Dale, 2006). It requires immediate treatment—through therapy, antidepressant medication, and patient and family education.

PERSONALITY AND COPING STYLE. Understanding the way individuals view stressful life events and have coped with them in the past helps us appreciate the way they manage the dying process. In a study in which terminally ill patients discussed their images of dying, responses varied greatly. For example,

- Beth regarded *dying as imprisonment:* "I felt like the clock started ticking . . . like the future has suddenly been taken. . . . In a way, I feel like I'm already dead."
- To Faith, dying was *a mandate to live ever more fully:* "I have a saying . . . 'You're not ready to live until you're ready to die' . . . It never meant much to me until I . . . looked death in the eye, and now I'm living. . . . This life is a lot better than the one before."
- Dawn viewed dying as *part of life's journey:* "I learned all about my disease . . . I would read, read, read . . . I wanted to know as much as I can about it, and I don't think hiding . . . behind the door . . . could help me at all. And, I realized for the first time in my life—*really, really, really realized* that I could handle anything."
- Patty approached dying as *an experience to be transformed* so as to make it more bearable: "I am an avid, rabid fan of *Star Trek*, a trekkie like there never has been . . . I watch it to the point that I've memorized it . . . [In my mind, I play the various characters so] I'm not [always] thinking about cancer or dying . . . I think that's how I get through it." (Wright, 2003, pp. 442–444, 447)

Each patient's view of dying helps explain her responses to worsening illness. Poorly adjusted individuals—those with conflict-ridden relationships and many disappointments in life—are usually more distressed (Kastenbaum, 2009).

■ **FAMILY MEMBERS' AND HEALTH PROFESSIONALS' BEHAVIOR.** Earlier we noted that a candid approach, in which everyone close to and caring for the dying person acknowledges the terminal illness, is best. Yet this also introduces the burden of participating in the work of dying with the patient—bringing relationships to closure, reflecting on life, and dealing with fears and regrets.

People who find it hard to engage in these tasks may pretend that the disease is not as bad as it is. In patients inclined toward denial, a "game" can be set in motion in which participants are aware that the patient is dying but act as though it were not so. Though this game softens psychological pain for the moment, it makes dying much more difficult. Besides impeding communication, it frequently leads to futile medical interventions, in which the patient has little understanding of what is happening and is subjected to great physical and emotional suffering. One attending physician provided this account of a cancer patient's death:

> The problem was that she had a young husband and parents who were pretty much in complete denial. We were trying to be aggressive up to the end. To the point that we actually hung a new form of chemotherapy about four hours before she died, even though everybody knew except her immediate family that she was going to die within the next four to eight hours. (Jackson et al., 2005, p. 653)

At other times, the patient suspects what he or she has not been told. In one instance, a terminally ill child flew into a rage because his doctor and a nurse spoke to him in ways that denied the fact that he would not grow up. Trying to get the child to cooperate with a medical procedure, the doctor said,

> "I thought you would understand, Sandy. You told me once you wanted to be a doctor."
>
> He screamed back, "I'm not going to be anything!" and threw an empty syringe at her.
>
> The nurse standing nearby asked, "What are you going to be?"
>
> "A ghost," said Sandy, and turned away from them. (Bluebond-Langner, 1977, p. 59)

The behavior of health professionals impeded Sandy's efforts to form a realistic time perspective and intensified his anger at the injustice of his premature death.

When doctors do want to inform patients of their prognosis, they may encounter resistance, especially within certain ethnic groups. Withholding information is common in Southern and Eastern Europe, Central and South America, much of Asia, and the Middle East. Japanese terminally ill cancer patients are seldom told the truth about their condition, partly because dying disrupts important interdependent relationships (Yamamoto, 2004). Many Mexican Americans and Korean Americans believe that informing patients is wrong and will hasten death (Blackhall et al., 1995, 2001). In these instances, providing information is complex. When a family insists that a patient not be told, the doctor can first offer information to the patient and then, if the patient refuses, ask who should receive information and make health-care decisions. The patient's preference can be honored and reassessed at regular intervals (Zane & Yeh, 2002).

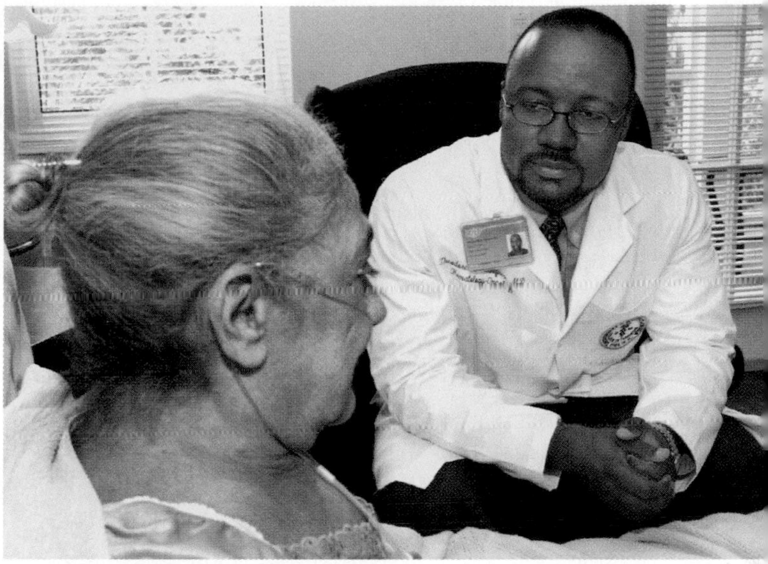

AP IMAGES

When doctors communicate openly and sensitively with terminally ill patients, they help them prepare for death by bringing relationships to closure, reflecting on life, and dealing with fears and regrets.

Care of the terminally ill is demanding and stressful. In one study, nurses trained to respond to the psychological needs of dying patients and their families consistently provided empathetic care. Keys to their success were staff meetings aimed at strengthening interpersonal skills, day-to-day mutual support among staff, and development of a personal philosophy of living and dying, which ensured that each nurse did not feel especially threatened by his or her own death (Samarel, 1991). Extensive experience working with dying patients in a sensitive, supportive environment is associated with low death anxiety, perhaps because such caregivers observe their patients' distress decline and, thus, gradually learn that their own previous fears are less founded (Bluck et al., 2008).

Social support from family members also affects adaptation to dying. Dying patients who feel they have much unfinished business to attend to are more anxious about impending death. But family contact reduces their sense of urgency to prolong life, perhaps because it permits patients to work through at least some incomplete tasks (Mutran et al., 1997).

Effective communication with the dying person is honest, fostering a trusting relationship, yet also oriented toward maintaining hope. Many dying patients move through a hope trajectory—at first, hope for a cure; later, hope for prolonging life; and finally, hope for a peaceful death with as few burdens

Applying What We Know

Communicating with Dying People

Suggestion	Description
Be truthful about the diagnosis and course of the disease.	Be honest about what the future is likely to hold, thereby permitting the dying person to bring closure to his or her life by expressing sentiments and wishes and participating in decisions about treatment.
Listen perceptively and acknowledge feelings.	Be truly present, focusing full attention on what the dying person has to say and accepting the patient's feelings. Patients who sense another's presence and concern are more likely to relax physically and emotionally and express themselves.
Maintain realistic hope.	Assist the dying person in maintaining hope by encouraging him or her to focus on a realistic goal that might yet be achieved—for example, resolution of a troubled relationship or special moments with a loved one. Knowing the dying person's hope, family members and health professionals can often help fulfill it.
Assist in the final transition.	Assure the dying person that he or she is not alone, offering a sympathetic touch, a caring thought, or just a calm presence. Some patients who struggle may benefit from being given permission to die—the message that giving up and letting go is all right.

Source: Lugton, 2001.

as possible (Fanslow, 1981). Once patients near death stop expressing hope, those close to them must accept this. Family members who find letting go very difficult may benefit from expert guidance. Applying What We Know above offers suggestions for communicating with the dying.

■ **SPIRITUALITY, RELIGION, AND CULTURE.** Earlier we noted that a sense of spirituality reduces fear of death. Informal reports from health professionals suggest that this is as true for dying patients as for people in general. One experienced nurse commented,

> At the end, those [patients] with a faith—it doesn't really matter in what, but a faith in something—find it easier. Not always, but as a rule. I've seen people with faith panic and I've seen those without faith accept it [death]. But, as a rule, it's much easier for those with faith. (Samarel, 1991, pp. 64–65)

Vastly different cultural beliefs, guided by religious ideas, also shape people's dying experiences:

- Buddhism, widely practiced in China, India, and Southeast Asia, fosters acceptance of death. By reading sutras (teachings of Buddha) to the dying person to calm the mind and emphasizing that dying leads to rebirth in a heaven of peace and relaxation, Buddhists believe that it is possible to reach Nirvana, a state beyond the world of suffering (Kubotera, 2004; Yeung, 1996).
- In many Native-American groups, death is met with stoic self-control, an approach taught at an early age through stories that emphasize a circular, rather than linear, relationship between life and death and the importance of making way for others (Cox, 2002).
- For African Americans, a dying loved one signals a crisis that unites family members in caregiving. The terminally ill person remains an active and vital force within the family until he or she can no longer carry out this role—an attitude of respect that undoubtedly eases the dying process (Sullivan, 1995).
- Among the Maori of New Zealand, relatives and friends gather around the dying person to give spiritual strength and comfort. Elders, clergy, and other experts in tribal customs conduct a *karakia* ceremony, in which they recite prayers asking for peace, mercy, and guidance from the creator. After the ceremony, the patient is encouraged to discuss important matters with those closest to her—giving away of personal belongings, directions for interment, and completion of other unfinished tasks (Ngata, 2004).

In sum, dying prompts a multitude of thoughts, emotions, and coping strategies. Which ones are emphasized depends on a wide array of contextual influences. A vital assumption of the lifespan perspective—that development is multidimensional and multidirectional—is just as relevant to this final phase as to each earlier period.

A Place to Die

Whereas in the past most deaths occurred at home, in the United States today about 50 percent take place in hospitals and another 20 percent in long-term care facilities, mostly nursing homes (U.S. Department of Health and Human Services, 2008f). In the large, impersonal hospital environment, meeting the human needs of dying patients and their families is secondary, not because professionals lack concern, but because the work to be done focuses on saving lives. A dying patient represents a failure.

In the 1960s, a death awareness movement arose as a reaction to hospitals' death-avoiding practices—attachment of complicated machinery to patients with no chance of survival and avoidance of communication with dying patients. This movement soon led to medical care better suited to the needs of dying people and also to hospice programs, which have spread to many countries in the industrialized world. Let's visit each of these settings for dying.

Home

Had Sofie and Nicholas been asked where they wanted to die, undoubtedly each would have responded, "At home"—the preference of 80 to 90 percent of Americans (NHPCO, 2005a; O'Connor, 2003). The reason is clear: The home offers an atmosphere of intimacy and loving care in which the terminally ill person is unlikely to feel abandoned or humiliated by physical decline or dependence on others.

However, only about one-fourth of Americans experience home death (U.S. Department of Health and Human Services, 2008f). And it is important not to romanticize dying at home. Because of dramatic improvements in medicine, dying people tend to be sicker or much older than in the past. Consequently, their bodies may be extremely frail, making ordinary activities—eating, sleeping, taking a pill, toileting, and bathing—major ordeals (Singer et al., 2005). Health problems of elderly spouses, work and other responsibilities of family members, and the physical, psychological, and financial strain of providing home care can make it difficult to honor a terminally ill person's wish to die at home.

For many people, the chance to be with the dying person until the very end is a rewarding tradeoff for the high demands of caregiving. But the advantages and disadvantages of home death should be carefully weighed before undertaking it. Adequate support for the caregiver is essential (Germino, 2003). A home health aide is often necessary—a service (as we will see shortly) that hospice programs have made more accessible. Still, when family relationships are conflict-ridden, a dying patient introduces additional strains, negating the benefits of home death. Finally, even with professional help, most homes are poorly equipped to handle the medical and comfort-care needs of the dying. To make home death possible, hospital-based equipment and technical support often must be transported to the home.

For all these reasons, older adults—although they view home as their ideal place to die—express concerns about quality of care, about burdening family and friends, and about the need for children to engage in unduly intimate caregiving tasks (Gott et al., 2004). And 10 months after a home death, family members continue to report more psychological stress than do family members whose loved one died elsewhere (Addington-Hall, 2000).

Hospital

Hospital dying takes many forms. Each is affected by the physical state of the dying person, the hospital unit in which it takes place, and the goal and quality of care.

Sudden deaths, due to injury or critical illness, typically occur in emergency rooms. Doctors and nurses must evaluate the problem and take action quickly. Little time is available for contact with family members. When staff break the news of death in a sympathetic manner and provide explanations, family members are grateful. Otherwise, feelings of anger, frustration, and confusion can add to their grief. Crisis intervention services are needed to help survivors cope with sudden death (Walsh & McGoldrick, 2004).

Nicholas died on an intensive care ward focused on preventing death in patients whose condition can worsen quickly. Privacy and communication with the family were secondary to monitoring his condition. To prevent disruption of nurses' activities, Giselle and Sasha could be at Nicholas's side only at scheduled times. Dying in intensive care—an experience unique to technologically sophisticated societies—is especially depersonalizing for patients like Nicholas, who linger between life and death while hooked to machines often for months.

Cancer patients, who account for most cases of prolonged dying, typically die in general or specialized cancer care hospital units. When hospitalized for a long time, they reach out for help with physical and emotional needs, usually with mixed success. In these hospital settings, as in intensive care, a conflict of values is apparent (Costello, 2006; Hanson, Danis, & Garrett, 1997). The tasks associated with dying must be performed efficiently so that all patients can be served and health professionals are not drained emotionally by repeated attachments and separations.

Only one-fourth of U.S. hospitals have comprehensive treatment programs aimed at easing physical, emotional, and spiritual suffering at the end of life (Medina & Puntillo, 2006). Although the majority of U.S. teaching hospitals have pain management programs, only 40 percent of public hospitals and 20 percent of for-profit hospitals do (Goldsmith et al., 2008). And less than 1 percent of doctors and nurses are specially

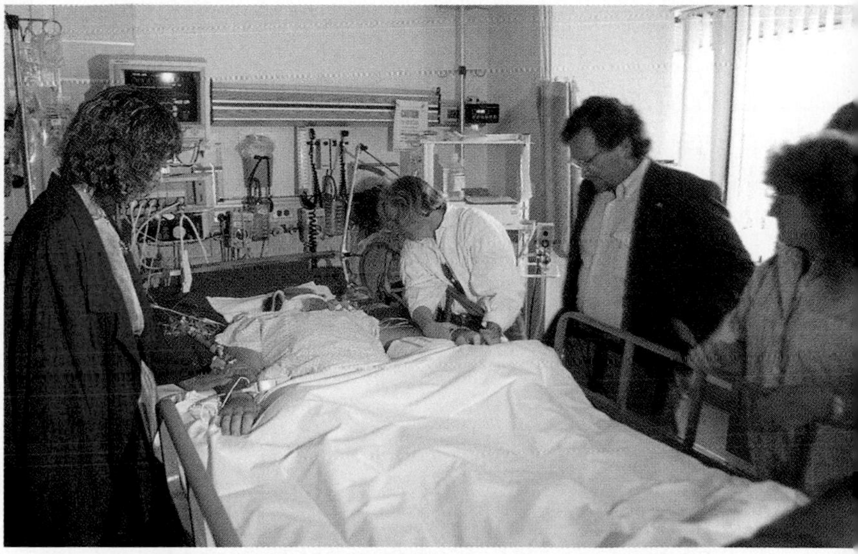

© MARK RICHARDS/PHOTOEDIT

Dying in intensive care is a depersonalizing experience unique to technologically sophisticated societies. In such settings, medical responses supersede privacy and communication.

trained in managing pain in chronically ill and dying people. In 2006, such education became a formal medical subspecialty in the United States, an event that eventually may improve hospital care of the dying (Hallenbeck, 2006). But at present, many people die in painful, frightening, and depersonalizing hospital conditions, without their wishes being met.

Nursing Home

Though deaths in U.S. nursing homes—mostly elderly patients—are common, care emphasizes rehabilitation rather than high-quality terminal care. At times, residents' end-of-life preferences are not gathered and recorded in medical records (Bradley, Peiris, & Wetle, 1998). The few studies that have addressed what it is like to die in nursing homes concur that patients suffer from high levels of untreated pain (Bernabei et al., 1998; Ferrell, 1995).

In one investigation, researchers conducted after-death interviews with nursing staff and family members of all residents who died during a 1-year period in two large North Carolina nursing homes (Reynolds et al., 2002). More than 50 percent had been in moderate to severe pain, 40 percent "very sad or depressed," 30 percent "very anxious or agitated," and 20 percent "very lonely" during their final three months. For the majority, "emotional and spiritual needs" had not been met. More than one-fourth of nursing staff and one-third of family members reported a need for improved communication about treatment decisions. As evidence of limited contact, more than one-third of family members could not identify the doctor in charge of their relative's care, and over half could not identify a nurse or nursing assistant.

The hospice approach—which we consider next—aims to reduce profound caregiving failures in hospitals and nursing homes. When combined with hospice, nursing home care of the dying improves greatly in pain management and in family satisfaction (Baer & Hanson, 2000; Miller et al., 2002).

The Hospice Approach

In medieval times, a *hospice* was a place where travelers could find rest and shelter. In the nineteenth and twentieth centuries, the word referred to homes for dying patients. Today, **hospice** is not a place but a comprehensive program of support services for terminally ill people and their families. It aims to provide a caring community sensitive to the dying person's needs so patients and family members can prepare for death in ways that are satisfying to them. Quality of life is central to the hospice approach, which includes these main features:

- The patient and family as a unit of care
- Emphasis on meeting the patient's physical, emotional, social, and spiritual needs, including controlling pain, retaining dignity and self-worth, and feeling cared for and loved
- Care provided by an interdisciplinary team: the patient's doctor, a nurse or nurse's aide, a chaplain, a counselor or social worker, and a pharmacist
- The patient kept at home or in an inpatient setting with a homelike atmosphere where coordination of care is possible
- Focus on protecting the quality of remaining life with **palliative,** or **comfort, care** that relieves pain and other symptoms (nausea, breathing difficulties, insomnia, and depression) rather than prolonging life
- In addition to regularly scheduled home care visits, on-call services available 24 hours a day, 7 days a week
- Follow-up bereavement services offered to families in the year after a death

Because hospice care is a philosophy, not a facility, it can be applied in diverse ways. In Great Britain, care in a special inpatient unit, sometimes associated with a hospital, is typical. In the United States, home care has been emphasized: About 50 percent of hospice patients die in their own home, 20 percent in nursing homes, 20 percent in special inpatient units, and 10 percent in typical hospital rooms (NHPCO, 2008).

But hospice programs everywhere have expanded to include a continuum of care, from home to inpatient options, including hospitals and nursing homes. Central to the hospice approach is that the dying person and his or her family be offered choices that guarantee an appropriate death. Some programs offer hospice day care, which permits caregivers to continue working or be relieved of the stresses of long-term care (Kernohan et al.,

AP IMAGES

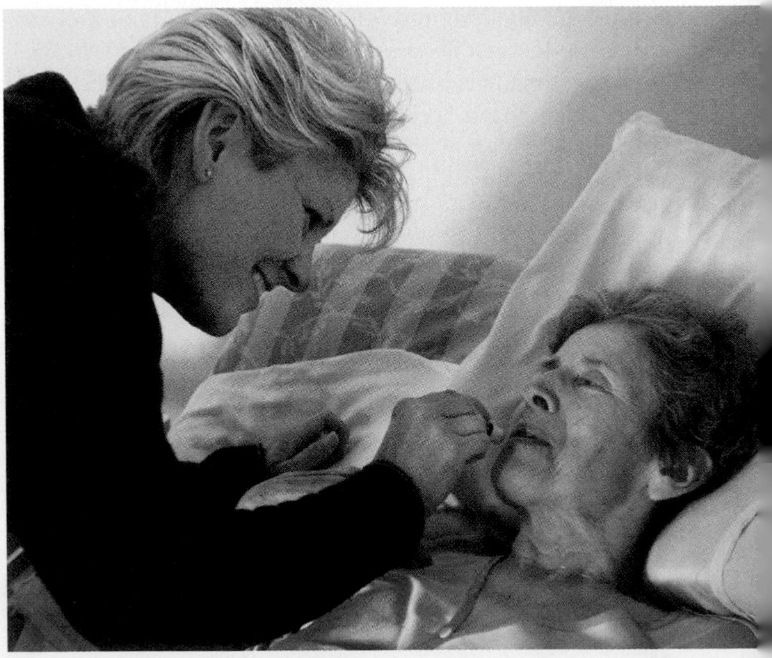

Hospice protects quality of life rather than extending it. This daughter applies lip balm for her mother—an act that increases her mother's comfort and enhances a sense of closeness and connection.

BIOLOGY AND ENVIRONMENT

Music as Palliative Care for Dying Patients

When Peter visits 82-year-old Stuart to play the harp, Stuart reports being transported to an idyllic place with water, children, and trees—far from the lung tumors that will soon take his life. "When Peter plays for me . . . I am no longer frightened," Stuart says.

Peter is a specialist in *music thanatology,* an emerging specialty in music therapy that focuses on providing palliative care to the dying through music. He uses his harp, and sometimes his voice, to induce calm and give solace to the dying, their families, and their caregivers. Peter applies music systematically—matching it to each patient's breathing patterns and other responses, delivering different sounds to uplift or comfort, depending on his assessment of the patient's moment-by-moment needs.

Chaplains and counselors informally report that after music vigils, patients' conversations indicate that they more easily come to terms with their own death (Fyfe, 2006). And in a study of 65 dying patients in which pre- and postintervention physiological measures were compared, music vigils averaging an hour in length resulted in decreased agitation and wakefulness and slower, deeper, less effortful breathing (Freeman et al., 2006). These physiological benefits extended to patients who, on the basis of their behavior, were clearly in pain.

Why is music effective in easing the distress of those who are dying? In patients close to death, hearing typically functions longer than other senses. Thus, responsiveness to music may persist until the individual's final moments. Besides reducing anxiety, music can, in some instances, enhance the effects of medication administered to control pain (Starr, 1999). For these reasons, music vigils may be an especially effective end-of-life therapy.

© SIMON CDWYER/THE AGE PHOTO SALES

Music thanatology focuses on providing palliative care for the dying through music. This practitioner uses his harp, and sometimes his voice, to induce calm and provide solace.

2006). Contact with others facing terminal illness is a supportive byproduct of many hospice arrangements. And to find out about a comforting musical intervention for patients near death, consult the Biology and Environment box above.

Currently, the United States has over 4,700 hospices serving approximately 1.4 million terminally ill patients annually. About 40 percent of hospice patients have cancer. The top noncancer diagnoses are heart disease (12 percent), extreme frailty in the elderly (11 percent), dementia (10 percent), and lung disease (8 percent) (NHPCO, 2008). Because hospice care is a cost-effective alternative to expensive life-saving treatments, U.S. government health-care benefits (Medicare and Medicaid) cover it, as do most private insurance plans. In addition, community and foundation contributions allow many hospices to provide free services to uninsured patients who cannot pay (Hospice Foundation of America, 2009). Consequently hospice is affordable for most dying patients and their families. Hospices also serve dying children—a tragedy so devastating that social support and bereavement intervention are vital.

Besides reducing patient physical suffering, hospice contributes to improved family functioning. The majority of patients and families report improved coping, increased social support, and increased feelings of family closeness after receiving hospice services (Godkin, Krant, & Doster, 1984). In one study, family members experiencing hospice scored higher than nonhospice family members in psychological well-being one to two years after their loved one's death (Ragow-O'Brien, Hayslip, & Guarnaccia, 2000).

As a long-range goal, hospice organizations are striving for broader acceptance of their patient- and family-centered approach. The majority of North Americans are still unfamiliar with the philosophy, although when it is described to them, nearly 90 percent say it is the type of end-of-life care they want (NHPCO, 2004). Recently, Canada launched a Web-based hospice outreach service, the Canadian Virtual Hospice *(www.virtualhospice.ca),* to support patients, families, and care providers with information, resources, and connections to others with similar concerns. Culturally sensitive approaches are needed to reach more ethnic minority patients, who are much less likely than white patients to participate in hospice (Crawley et al., 2000; Ngo-Metzger, Phillips, & McCarthy, 2007).

In developing countries, where millions die of cancer, AIDS, and other devastating illnesses each year, community-based teams working under a nurse's supervision sometimes deliver palliative care. But they face many obstacles, including lack of funding, pain-relieving drugs, and professional and public education about hospice. As a result, they are small "islands of excellence," accessible to only a few families (Wright et al., 2008).

ASK YOURSELF

» REVIEW
Why is the stage notion an inaccurate account of dying patients' mental and emotional reactions?

» APPLY
When 5-year-old Timmy's kidney failure was diagnosed as terminal, his parents could not accept the tragic news. Their hospital visits became shorter, and they evaded his anxious questions. Eventually, Timmy blamed himself. He died with little physical pain, but alone, and his parents suffered prolonged guilt. How could hospice care have helped Timmy and his family?

» CONNECT
Reread the description of Sofie's mental and emotional reactions to dying on pages 646–647. Then review the story of Sofie's life on pages 3–5 in Chapter 1. How were Sofie's responses consistent with her personality and lifelong style of coping with adversity?

» REFLECT
If you were terminally ill, where would you want to die? Explain.

The Right to Die

In 1976, the parents of Karen Ann Quinlan, a young woman who had fallen into an irreversible coma after taking drugs at a party, sued to have her respirator turned off. The New Jersey Supreme Court, invoking Karen's right to privacy and her parents' power as guardians, complied with this request. Although Karen was expected to die quickly, she breathed independently, continued to be fed intravenously, and lived another 10 years in a persistent vegetative state.

In 1990, 26-year-old Terri Schiavo's heart stopped briefly, temporarily cutting off oxygen to her brain. Like Karen, Terri lay in a persistent vegetative state. Her husband and guardian, Michael, claimed that she had earlier told him she would not want to be kept alive artificially, but Terri's parents disagreed. In 1998, the Florida Circuit Court granted Michael's petition to have Terri's feeding tube removed. In 2001, after her parents had exhausted their appeals, the tube was taken out. But on the basis of contradictory medical testimony, Terri's parents convinced a circuit court judge to order the feeding tube reinserted, and the legal wrangling continued. In 2002, Michael won a second judgment to remove the tube.

By that time, publicity over the case and its central question—who should make end-of-life decisions when the patient's wishes are unclear—had made Terri a political issue. In 2003, the Florida legislature passed a law allowing the governor to stay the circuit court's order to keep Terri alive, but on appeal, the law was declared unconstitutional. In 2005, the U.S. Congress entered the fray, passing a bill that transferred Terri's fate to the U.S. District Court. When the judge refused to intervene, the feeding tube was removed for a third time. In 2005—15 years after losing consciousness—Terri Schiavo died. The autopsy confirmed the original persistent vegetative state diagnosis: Her brain was half normal size.

Before the 1950s, the right to die was of little concern, because medical science could do little to extend the lives of terminally ill patients. Today, medical advances mean that the same procedures that preserve life can prolong inevitable death, diminishing both quality of life and personal dignity.

The Quinlan and Schiavo cases—and others like them—have brought right-to-die issues to the forefront of public attention. Today, all U.S. states have laws that honor patients' wishes concerning withdrawal of treatment in cases of terminal illness and, sometimes, in cases of a persistent vegetative state. But no uniform right-to-die policy exists, and heated controversy persists over how to handle the diverse circumstances in which patients and family members make requests.

Euthanasia is the practice of ending the life of a person suffering from an incurable condition. Its various forms are summarized in Table 19.1. As we will see, public acceptance of euthanasia is high, except when it involves ending the life of an anguished, terminally ill patient without his or her expressed permission.

Passive Euthanasia

In **passive euthanasia,** life-sustaining treatment is withheld or withdrawn, permitting a patient to die naturally. ***TAKE A MOMENT...*** Do you think Terri Schiavo should have been allowed to die sooner? Was it right for Nicholas's doctors to

■ **TABLE 19.1** ■ ***Forms of Euthanasia***

FORM	DESCRIPTION
Passive euthanasia	At the patient's request, the doctor withholds or withdraws treatment, thereby permitting the patient to die naturally. For example, the doctor does not perform surgery or administer medication that could prolong life, or the doctor turns off the respirator of a patient who cannot breathe independently.
Voluntary active euthanasia	The doctor ends a suffering patient's life at the patient's request. For example, the doctor administers a lethal dose of drugs.
Assisted suicide	The doctor helps a suffering patient take his or her own life. For example, the doctor enables the patient to swallow or inject a lethal dose of drugs.
Involuntary active euthanasia	The doctor ends a suffering patient's life without the patient's permission. For example, without obtaining the patient's consent, the doctor administers a lethal dose of drugs.

turn off his respirator at Giselle's request? When an Alzheimer's victim has lost all awareness and bodily functions, should life support be withheld?

In recent polls, more than three-fourths of Americans supported the right of patients or family members to end treatment when there is no hope of recovery (Pew Research Center, 2006). In 1986, the American Medical Association endorsed withdrawing all forms of treatment from the terminally ill when death is imminent and from those in a permanent vegetative state. Consequently, passive euthanasia is widely practiced as part of ordinary medical procedure, in which doctors exercise professional judgment.

Still, a minority of citizens do not endorse passive euthanasia. Religious denomination has surprisingly little effect on people's opinions. For example, most Catholics hold favorable views, despite slow official church acceptance because of fears that passive euthanasia might be a first step toward government-approved mercy killing. However, ethnicity makes a difference: Nearly twice as many African Americans as Caucasian Americans desire all medical means possible, regardless of the patient's condition, and African Americans more often receive life-sustaining intervention, such as feeding tubes (Bayer et al., 2006; Johnson et al., 2008). Their reluctance to forgo treatment reflects strong cultural and religious beliefs in overcoming adversity and in the power of God to promote healing (Johnson, Elbert-Avila, & Tulsky, 2005).

Because of controversial court cases like Terri Schiavo's, some doctors and health-care institutions are unwilling to end treatment without legal protection. In the absence of national consensus on passive euthanasia, people can best ensure that their wishes will be followed by preparing an **advance medical directive**—a written statement of desired medical treatment should they become incurably ill. U.S. states recognize two types of advance directives: a *living will* and a *durable power of attorney for health care* (U.S. Living Will Registry, 2005). Sometimes these are combined into one document.

In a **living will,** people specify the treatments they do or do not want in case of a terminal illness, coma, or other near-death situation (see Figure 19.2). For example, a person might state that without reasonable expectation of recovery, he or she should not be kept alive through medical intervention of any kind. In addition, a living will sometimes specifies that pain-relieving medication be given, even though it might shorten life. In Sofie's case, her doctor administered a powerful narcotic to relieve labored breathing and quiet her fear of suffocation. The narcotic suppressed respiration, causing death to occur hours or days earlier than if the medication had not been prescribed, but without distress. Such palliative care is accepted as appropriate and ethical medical practice.

Although living wills help ensure personal control, they do not guarantee it. Recognition of living wills is usually limited to patients who are terminally ill or are otherwise expected to die shortly. Only a few U.S. states cover people in a persistent vegetative state or elders who linger with many chronic problems, including Alzheimer's disease, because these conditions are not classified as terminal. Even when terminally ill patients have living wills, doctors often do not follow them for a variety of reasons, including fear of lawsuits, their own moral beliefs, failure to inquire about patients' directives, and inaccessibility of those directives—for example, located in the family safe or

LIVING WILL

THIS DECLARATION is made this ________ day of ________________, 20 ____.

I, ____________________, being of sound mind, willfully and voluntarily make known my desires that my moment of death shall not be artificially postponed. If at any time I should have an incurable and irreversible injury, disease, or illness judged to be a terminal condition by my attending physician who has personally examined me and has determined that my death is imminent except for death delaying procedures, I direct that such procedures which would only prolong the dying process be withheld or withdrawn, and that I be permitted to die naturally with only the administration of medication, sustenance, or the performance of any medical procedure deemed necessary by my attending physician to provide me with comfort care.

In the absence of my ability to give directions regarding the use of such death delaying procedures, it is my intention that this declaration shall be honored by my family and physician as the final expression of my legal right to refuse medical or surgical treatment and accept the consequences from such refusal.

Signed: ______________________________

City, County and State of Residence: ______________________________

____

____

The declarant is personally known to me and I believe him or her to be of sound mind. I saw the declarant sign the declaration in my presence (or the declarant acknowledged in my presence that he or she had signed the declaration) and I signed the declaration as a witness in the presence of the declarant. At the date of this instrument, I am not entitled to any portion of the estate of the declarant according to the laws of intestate succession or, to the best of my knowledge and belief, under any will of declarant or other instrument taking effect at declarant's death, or directly financially responsible for declarant's medical care.

Witness: ______________________________

Witness: ______________________________

■ **FIGURE 19.2** ■ **Example of a living will.** This document is legal in the State of Illinois. Each person completing a living will should use a form specific to the U.S. state or Canadian province in which he or she resides because laws vary widely. (Courtesy of Office of the Attorney General, State of Illinois.)

© DAVID YOUNG-WOLFF/PHOTOEDIT

This couple discusses a durable power of attorney with a hospital chaplain. This advance directive authorizes a trusted spokesperson to make health care decisions and helps ensure that one's desires will be granted.

family members unaware of them (Gorman et al., 2005; van Asselt, 2006).

Because living wills cannot anticipate all future medical conditions and can easily be ignored, a second form of advance directive has become common. The **durable power of attorney for health care** authorizes appointment of another person (usually, though not always, a family member) to make health-care decisions on one's behalf. It generally requires only a short signed and witnessed statement like this:

> I hereby appoint [name] as my attorney-in-fact (my "agent") to act for me and in my name (in any way I could act in person) to make any and all decisions for me concerning my personal care, medical treatment, hospitalization, and health care and to require, withhold, or withdraw any type of medical treatment or procedure, even though my death may ensue. (Courtesy of Office of the Attorney General, State of Illinois)

The durable power of attorney for health care is more flexible than the living will because it permits a trusted spokesperson to confer with the doctor as medical circumstances arise. Because authority to speak for the patient is not limited to terminal illnesses, more latitude exists for dealing with unexpected situations. And in gay and lesbian and other close relationships not sanctioned by law, the durable power of attorney can ensure the partner's role in decision making and in advocating for the patient's health-care needs.

Whether or not a person supports passive euthanasia, it is important to have a living will, durable power of attorney, or both, because most deaths occur in hospitals. Yet fewer than 30 percent of Americans have executed such documents, perhaps because of widespread uneasiness about bringing up the topic of death, especially with relatives (Pew Research Center, 2006). To encourage people to make decisions about potential treatment while they are able, U.S. federal law now requires that all medical facilities receiving federal funds provide information at admission about state laws and institutional policies on patients' rights and advance directives.

As happened with Karen Quinlan and Terri Schiavo, health-care professionals—unclear about a patient's intent and fearing liability—will probably decide to continue treatment regardless of cost and a person's prior oral statements. Perhaps for this reason, some U.S. states permit appointment of a health-care proxy, or substitute decision maker, if a patient failed to provide an advance medical directive while competent. Proxies are an important means of covering children and adolescents, who cannot legally execute advance medical directives.

Voluntary Active Euthanasia

In recent years, the right-to-die debate has shifted from withdrawal of treatment for the hopelessly ill to more active alternatives. In **voluntary active euthanasia,** doctors or others act directly, at a patient's request, to end suffering before a natural end to life. The practice, a form of mercy killing, is a criminal offense in most countries, including almost all U.S. states. But support for voluntary active euthanasia is growing. As Figure 19.3 shows, about 70 to 90 percent of people in Western nations

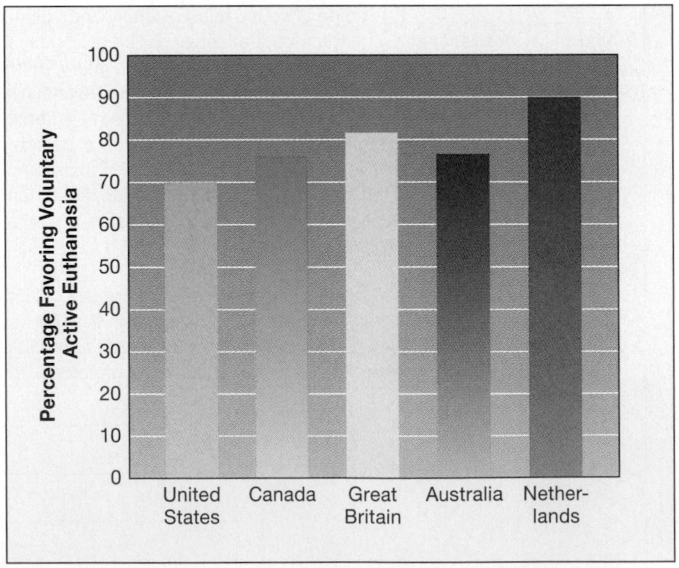

■ **FIGURE 19.3** ■ **Public opinion favoring voluntary active euthanasia in five nations.** A struggle exists between public opinion, which has increasingly favored voluntary active euthanasia over the past 30 years, and legal statutes, which prohibit it. The majority of people in Western nations believe that a hopelessly ill, suffering patient who asks for a lethal injection should be granted that request. Public support for voluntary active euthanasia is highest in the Netherlands—the only nation in the world where the practice is legal under certain conditions. (From Pew Research Center, 2006, *Right to Die Societies.* Reprinted by permission.)

approve of it (World Federation of Right to Die Societies, 2006). In these countries, religiosity has little impact on acceptance. But in Eastern European nations where most of the population is religious, such as Croatia, Poland, Romania, and Turkey, approval rates tend to be lower (Cohen et al., 2006). In the United States and other Western nations, when doctors engage in voluntary active euthanasia, judges are usually lenient, granting suspended sentences or probation—a trend reflecting rising public interest in self-determination in death as in life.

Nevertheless, attempts to legalize voluntary active euthanasia have prompted heated controversy. Supporters believe it represents the most compassionate option for terminally ill people in severe pain. Opponents stress the moral difference between "letting die" and "killing" and point out that at times, even very sick patients recover. They also argue that involving doctors in taking the lives of suffering patients may impair people's trust in health professionals. Finally, a fear exists that legalizing this practice—even when strictly monitored to make sure it does not arise out of depression, loneliness, coercion, or a desire to diminish the burden of illness on others—could lead to a broadening of euthanasia (Loewy, 2004). Initially limited to the terminally ill, it might be applied involuntarily to the frail, demented, or disabled—outcomes that most people find unacceptable and immoral.

Will legalizing voluntary active euthanasia lead us down a "slippery slope" to the killing of vulnerable people who did not ask to die? The Social Issues box on page 658 presents lessons from the Australian state of the Northern Territory, where a law allowing voluntary active euthanasia was passed in 1996, and from the Netherlands, where doctors have practiced it for years, even before its recent legalization.

Assisted Suicide

After checking Diane's blood count, Dr. Timothy Quill gently broke the news: leukemia. If she were to have any hope of survival, a strenuous course of treatment with only a 25 percent success rate would have to begin immediately. Convinced that she would suffer unspeakably from side effects and lack of control over her body, Diane chose not to undergo chemotherapy and a bone marrow transplant.

Dr. Quill made sure that Diane understood her options. As he adjusted to her decision, Diane raised another issue: She wanted no part of a lingering death. She calmly insisted that when the time came, she desired to take her own life in the least painful way possible—a choice she had discussed with her husband and son, who respected it. Realizing that Diane could get the most out of the time she had left only if her fears of prolonged pain were allayed, Dr. Quill granted her request for sleeping pills, making sure she knew the amounts needed for both sleep and suicide.

Diane's next few months were busy and fulfilling. Her son took leave from college to be with her, and her husband worked at home as much as possible. Gradually, bone pain, fatigue, and fever set in. Saying goodbye to her family and friends, Diane asked to be alone for an hour, took a lethal dose of medication, and died at home (Quill, 1991).

Assisting a suicide is illegal in Canada and in many, but not all, U.S. states. In Western Europe, doctor-assisted suicide is legal in Belgium, Germany, the Netherlands, and Switzerland and is tacitly accepted in many other countries (Hill, 2003; Scherer & Simon, 1999). In the United States, Oregon's 1997 Death with Dignity Act explicitly allows physicians to prescribe drugs so terminally ill patients can end their lives. To get a prescription, patients must have two doctors agree that they have less than six months to live and must request the drugs at least twice, with an interval of at least 15 days. In January 2006, the U.S. Supreme Court rejected a challenge to the Oregon law, but the Court has also upheld the right of other states to ban assisted suicide. In 2008, the state of Washington passed legislation—similar to Oregon's—permitting assisted suicide.

Only 46 percent of Americans approve of assisted suicide (Pew Research Center, 2006). And a survey of nearly 1,000 terminally ill U.S. patients ranging in age from 22 to 109 revealed that although they largely endorsed the practice, just one-tenth seriously considered asking for it; in a follow-up, many of them had changed their minds (Emanuel, Fairclough, & Emanuel, 2000). People who say they would choose assisted suicide if they were terminally ill tend to be higher in SES and more often Caucasian than African American (Cicirelli, 1997).

The number of Oregon residents dying by assisted suicide has increased since passage of the law, from 16 in 1998 to 60 in 2008. Most had cancer, a few Lou Gehrig's disease, chronic heart or respiratory disease, or AIDS. Still, assisted suicide accounts for only one-tenth of 1 percent of Oregon deaths (Oregon Department of Human Services, 2009). Ten times as many terminally ill people initiate the qualification process for assisted suicide as engage in it. But thousands of Oregonians say they find comfort in knowing the option is available should they suffer

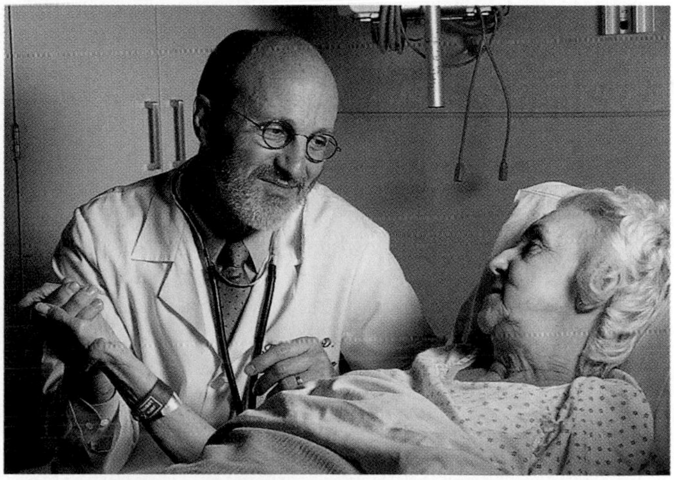

© BOB MAHONEY/THE IMAGE WORKS

In a prestigious medical journal, Dr. Timothy Quill explained how and why he assisted a terminally ill patient in taking her own life. Doctor-assisted suicide is legal in the states of Oregon and Washington and in several Western European countries.

SOCIAL ISSUES

Voluntary Active Euthanasia: Lessons from Australia and the Netherlands

In 1996, Australia's Northern Territory passed legislation allowing a terminally ill patient of sound mind and suffering from pain or other distress to ask a doctor to end his or her life. Two other doctors had to agree that the patient could not be cured, and a psychiatrist had to confirm the absence of treatable depression.

In the months that followed, four deaths occurred under the Northern Territory euthanasia statute, and it was heavily criticized. The Aborigines, valuing harmony and balance with nature, regarded it as culturally inappropriate. Their leaders claimed the law would discourage Aboriginal elders, many of whom have experienced a lifetime of persecution at the hands of European settlers, from seeking medical care (Fleming, 2000). Others considered the law to be a national issue because patients traveled from other states to make use of it. In 1997, the Northern Territory legislation was overturned by the Australian Parliament, which claimed that assemblies do not have the right to legislate intentional killing.

The episode placed Australia at the center of the debate over euthanasia—an issue that continues to spark high passions across the country. Opponents question the mental condition of patients seeking euthanasia and worry about error and abuse of the practice (Fickling, 2004). Supporters emphasize compassion and the right of individuals to control the course of their own lives. June Burns, an Australian woman with bladder cancer who participated in TV ads documenting the course of her illness, responded, "If I were a dog, they would have put me down by now. I feel life is very precious and . . . I wish I could go on, but I can't and I'd like to die with dignity." Eventually, she took her own life with a lethal dose of a barbiturate, which she had kept for the purpose for nearly a decade (Voluntary Euthanasia Society of New South Wales, 2008).

For the past several decades, doctors in the Netherlands have engaged in voluntary active euthanasia without criminal prosecution. In 2001, the practice became legal under the following conditions: when physical or mental suffering is severe, with no prospect of relief; when no doubt exists about the patient's desire to die; when the patient's decision is voluntary, well-informed, and stable over time; when all other options for care have been exhausted or refused; and when another doctor has been consulted.

Australian Aboriginal peoples regard voluntary active euthanasia as contrary to the values of their culture. The priority they place on harmony with nature is reflected in natural images that permeate their artwork.

Over 50 percent of Dutch doctors say they perform euthanasia, most often with cancer patients. Despite safeguards, both voluntary and involuntary (without patient permission) active euthanasia have occurred. A small minority of doctors admit granting the euthanasia requests of physically healthy patients—usually elders who felt "weary of life" (Rurup et al., 2005). And some say they actively caused a death when a patient did not ask for it, defending their action by referring to the impossibility of treating pain, a low quality of life, or drawn-out dying in a patient near death. Although doctors judged most of these patients incompetent to decide for themselves, an estimated 37 percent were deemed competent (Hendin, 1999). When asked why they did not discuss the decision with competent patients, doctors usually said they had previously done so; they did not express a need to check how the patient felt currently.

Voluntary active euthanasia in the Netherlands has risen steadily over the past decade. Currently, doctors report about 2,300 cases annually to medical examiners—1.7 percent of all deaths. But anonymous surveys reveal additional cases—as many as 20 percent of all such deaths—that probably were voluntary active euthanasia but were not reported. In most of these, attending doctors said that they had not perceived their act (sedation to relieve pain) as ending a life. But for some, they expressed doubts about whether they had properly followed legal standards of practice, such as ascertaining patient consent or consulting a second doctor (Onwuteaka-Philipsen et al., 2005; van der Heide et al., 2007).

The Northern Territory and Dutch examples reveal that legalizing voluntary active euthanasia can spark both the fear and the reality of death without consent. And the Dutch experience highlights the difficulties in monitoring euthanasia practices. Nevertheless, terminally ill individuals in severe pain continue to plead for such laws. Probably all would agree that when doctors feel compelled to relieve suffering and honor self-determination by assisting a patient in dying, they should be subject to the most stringent professional and legal oversight possible.

while dying (Hedberg, Hopkins, & Kohn, 2003). Doctors report that the most common reasons for assisted-suicide requests are decreasing ability to participate in activities that make life enjoyable, loss of dignity, loss of autonomy, and loss of control of bodily functions (Oregon Department of Human Services, 2009).

Public interest in assisted suicide was sparked in the 1990s by Dr. Jack Kevorkian, a vigorous proponent of euthanasia who devised "suicide machines" that permitted more than 100 terminally ill patients, after brief counseling, to self-administer lethal drugs and carbon monoxide. Less publicity surrounded

Dr. Quill's decision to assist Diane—a patient he knew well after serving for years as her personal doctor. After he told her story in a prestigious medical journal, reactions were mixed, as they are toward assisted suicide in general. Some view doctors who help suffering people who want to die as compassionate and respectful of patients' personal choices. Others oppose assisted suicide on religious and moral grounds or believe that the role of doctors should be limited to saving, not taking, lives.

Like euthanasia, assisted suicide poses grave dilemmas. Analyzing the practice, the American Academy of Hospice and Palliative Medicine (2007) advises great caution on the part of doctors practicing in regions where assisted suicide is legal, including making sure before engaging in it that the following conditions are met:

- The patient has access to the best possible palliative care and will continue to receive such care throughout the dying process.
- The patient has full decision-making capacity and requests assisted suicide voluntarily; health-care financial pressures and coercive influences from family members play no role.
- All reasonable alternatives to assisted suicide have been considered and implemented, if acceptable to the patient.
- The practice is consistent with the doctor's fundamental values, and he or she is willing to participate. (If not, the doctor should recommend transfer of care.)

Juries have seldom returned guilty verdicts in cases involving doctor-assisted suicide. Yet in April 1999, Kevorkian—after giving a terminally ill man a lethal injection, videotaping the death, and permitting the event to be broadcast on the CBS television program *60 Minutes*—was sentenced to 10 to 25 years in prison for second-degree murder and delivery of a controlled substance. The murder indictment prevented Kevorkian from introducing evidence indicating that the man wanted to kill himself—evidence that would have been permissible had the charge been assisted suicide or voluntary active euthanasia.

Public opinion consistently favors voluntary active euthanasia over assisted suicide. Yet in assisted suicide, the final act is solely the patient's, reducing the possibility of coercion. For this reason, some experts believe that legalizing assisted suicide is preferable to legalizing voluntary active euthanasia. However, in an atmosphere of high family caregiving burdens and intense pressure to contain health-care costs (see Chapter 17), legalizing either practice poses risks. The American Medical Association opposes both voluntary active euthanasia and assisted suicide. In a recent survey of 1,140 U.S. doctors, only 18 percent objected to sedating a dying patient to unconsciousness if pain can be controlled in no other way, whereas nearly 70 percent opposed assisted suicide (Curlin et al., 2008). Helping incurable, suffering patients who yearn for death poses profound moral and legal problems.

ASK YOURSELF

» REVIEW
What benefits and risks does legalizing voluntary active euthanasia pose?

» APPLY
Thinking ahead to the day she dies, Noreen imagines a peaceful scene in which she says goodbye to loved ones. What social and medical practices are likely to increase Noreen's chances of dying in the manner she desires?

» APPLY
Ramón is certain that, if he ever became terminally ill, he would want doctors to halt life-saving treatment. To best ensure that his wish will be granted, what should Ramón do?

» REFLECT
Do you approve of passive euthanasia, voluntary active euthanasia, or assisted suicide? If you were terminally ill, would you consider any of these practices? Explain.

Bereavement: Coping with the Death of a Loved One

Loss is an inevitable part of existence throughout the lifespan. Even when change is for the better, we must let go of some aspects of experience so we can embrace others. In this way, our development prepares us for profound loss.

Bereavement is the experience of losing a loved one by death. The root of this word means "to be robbed," suggesting unjust and injurious theft of something valuable. Consistent with this image, we respond to loss with **grief**—intense physical and psychological distress. When we say someone is grief-stricken, we imply that his or her total way of being is affected.

Because grief can be overwhelming, cultures have devised ways of helping their members move beyond it to deal with the life changes demanded by death of a loved one. **Mourning** is the culturally specified expression of the bereaved person's thoughts and feelings. Customs—such as gathering with family and friends, dressing in black, attending the funeral, and observing a prescribed mourning period with special rituals—vary greatly among societies and ethnic groups. But all have in common the goal of helping people work through their grief and learn to live in a world that does not include the deceased.

Clearly, grief and mourning are closely linked—in everyday language, we often use the two words interchangeably. Let's look closely at how people respond to the death of a loved one.

Grief Process

Theorists formerly believed that bereaved individuals—both children and adults—moved through three phases of grieving, each characterized by a different set of responses (Bowlby, 1980;

Rando, 1995). In reality, however, people vary greatly in behavior and timing and often move back and forth between these reactions. A more accurate account compares grief to a roller-coaster ride, with many ups and downs and, over time, gradual resolution (Lund, 1996). Rather than phases, the grieving process can be conceived as a set of *tasks*—actions the person must take to recover and return to a fulfilling life: (1) to accept the reality of the loss; (2) to work through the pain of grief; (3) to adjust to a world without the loved one; and (4) to develop an inner bond with the deceased and move on with life (Worden, 2009). According to this view, people can take active steps to overcome grief—a powerful remedy for the overwhelming feelings of vulnerability that the bereaved often experience.

■ **AVOIDANCE.** On hearing the news, the survivor experiences shock followed by disbelief, which may last from hours to weeks. A numbed feeling serves as "emotional anesthesia" while the person begins the first task of grieving: becoming painfully aware of the loss.

■ **CONFRONTATION.** As the mourner confronts the reality of the death, grief is most intense. The person often experiences a cascade of emotional reactions, including anxiety, sadness, protest, anger, helplessness, frustration, abandonment, and yearning for the loved one. Common responses include obsessively reviewing the circumstances of death, asking how it might have been prevented, and searching for meaning in it (Neimeyer, 2001b). In addition, the grief-stricken person may be absentminded, unable to concentrate, and preoccupied with thoughts of the deceased, and may experience loss of sleep and appetite. Self-destructive behaviors, such as taking drugs or driving too fast, may occur. Most of these responses are symptoms of depression—an invariable component of grieving.

Although confrontation is difficult, it enables the mourner to grapple with the second task: working through the pain of grief. Each surge of anguish that results from an unmet wish to be reunited with the deceased brings the mourner closer to acceptance that the loved one is gone. After hundreds, perhaps thousands, of these painful moments, the grieving person comprehends that a cherished relationship must be transformed from a physical presence to an inner representation. As a result, the mourner makes progress on the third task: adjusting to a world in which the deceased is missing.

■ **RESTORATION.** Adjusting to the loss is more than an internal, emotional task. The bereaved must also deal with stressors that are secondary outcomes of the death—overcoming loneliness by reaching out to others; mastering skills (such as finances or cooking) that the deceased had performed; reorganizing daily life without the loved one; and revising one's identity from "spouse" to "widow" or from "parent" to "parent of a deceased child."

According to a recent perspective, called the **dual-process model of coping with loss,** effective coping requires people to oscillate between dealing with the emotional consequences of loss and attending to life changes, which—when handled successfully—have restorative, or healing, effects (Hansson & Stroebe, 2007; Stroebe & Schut, 1999). Moving back and forth offers temporary distraction and relief from painful grieving. Much research indicates that confronting grief without relief has severe negative consequences for physical and mental health (Corr & Corr, 2007). Consistent with the dual-process model, in a study that assessed widowed older adults at 6, 18, and 48 months after the death of their spouses, both loss-oriented and restoration-oriented activities occurred throughout bereavement. As predicted, restoration-oriented events—such as visiting friends, attending religious services, and volunteering—reduced the stress of grieving (Richardson, 2007). Using the dual-process approach, one 14-session intervention for older adults grieving the loss of a spouse addresses both emotional and life-change issues, alternating between them (Lund et al., 2004).

As grief subsides, emotional energies increasingly shift toward the fourth task—forging a symbolic bond with the deceased and moving on with life by meeting everyday responsibilities, investing in new activities and goals, strengthening old ties, and building new relationships. On certain days, such as family celebrations or the anniversary of death, grief reactions may resurface and require attention, but they do not interfere with a healthy, positive approach to life.

How long does grieving last? There is no single answer. Sometimes confrontation continues for a few months, at other times for several years. An occasional upsurge of grief may persist for a lifetime and is a common response to losing a much-loved spouse, partner, child, or friend (Sanders, 1999).

Personal and Situational Variations

Like dying, grieving is affected by many factors, including personality, coping style, and religious and cultural background. Sex differences are also evident. Compared with women, men typically express distress and depression less directly and seek social support less readily—factors that may contribute to the much higher mortality rate among bereaved men than women (Doka & Martin, 2000; Lund & Caserta, 2004b; McGoldrick, 2004).

Furthermore, the quality of the mourner's relationship with the deceased is important. An end to a loving, fulfilling bond may lead to anguished grieving, but it is unlikely to leave the residue of anger, guilt, and regret that often follows dissolution of a conflict-ridden, ambivalent tie. And end-of-life care makes a difference: Widowed older adults whose spouses experienced a painful death reported more anxiety, intrusive thoughts, and yearning for the loved one six months later (Carr, 2003).

Circumstances surrounding the death—whether it is sudden and unanticipated or follows a prolonged illness—also shape mourners' responses. The nature of the lost relationship and the timing of the death within the life course make a difference as well.

■ SUDDEN, UNANTICIPATED DEATHS VERSUS PROLONGED, EXPECTED DEATHS. In instances of sudden, unexpected deaths—usually the result of murder, suicide, war, accident, or natural disaster—avoidance may be especially pronounced and confrontation highly traumatic because shock and disbelief are extreme. In a survey of a representative sample of 18- to 45-year-old adults in a large U.S. city, the trauma most often reported as prompting an intense, debilitating stress reaction was the sudden, unanticipated death of a loved one (Breslau et al., 1998). In contrast, during prolonged dying, the bereaved person has had time to engage in **anticipatory grieving**—acknowledging that the loss is inevitable and preparing emotionally for it. Survivors may feel less overwhelmed immediately following the death. But they may display more persistent anxiety due to long-term stressors, such as highly demanding caregiving and having watched a loved one suffer from a debilitating illness (Carr et al., 2001).

Adjusting to a sudden death is easier when the survivor understands the reasons for it. This barrier to confronting loss is tragically apparent in cases of sudden infant death syndrome (SIDS), in which doctors cannot tell parents exactly why their apparently healthy baby died (see Chapter 3, page 110). That death seems "senseless" also complicates grieving after suicides, terrorist attacks, school and drive-by shootings, and natural disasters. In Western societies, people tend to believe that momentous events should be comprehensible and nonrandom (Lukas & Seiden, 2007). A death that is sudden and unexpected can threaten basic assumptions about a just, benevolent, and controllable world.

Suicide, particularly that of a young person, is especially hard to bear. Compared with survivors of other sudden deaths, people grieving a suicidal loss are more likely to conclude that they contributed to or could have prevented it—self-blame that can trigger profound guilt and shame. These reactions are likely to be especially intense and persisting when a mourner's culture or religion condemns suicide as immoral (Dunne & Dunne-Maxim, 2004). Individuals who have survived a suicide typically score higher than those who have experienced other types of losses in feelings of guilt and shame, sense of rejection by the deceased, and desire to conceal the cause of death (Sveen & Walby, 2008). Typically, recovery from grief after a suicide is prolonged.

■ PARENTS GRIEVING THE LOSS OF A CHILD. The death of a child, whether unexpected or foreseen, is the most difficult loss an adult can face (Dent & Stewart, 2004). Children are extensions of parents' feelings about themselves—the focus of hopes and dreams, including parents' sense of immortality. Also, because children depend on, admire, and appreciate their parents in a deeply gratifying way, they are an unmatched source of love. Finally, the death of a child is unnatural: Children are not supposed to die before their parents.

Parents who have lost a child often report considerable distress many years later, along with frequent thoughts of the deceased. The guilt triggered by outliving their child frequently becomes a tremendous burden, even when parents "know" better (Murphy, 2008). For example, a psychologist who understood that his daughter's cancer was not hereditary nevertheless said to a therapist, "Her genes allowed her to develop cancer. I gave her her genes. Therefore, I killed my daughter" (Rando, 1991, p. 239).

Although a child's death sometimes leads to marital breakup, this is likely to happen only when the relationship was already unsatisfactory (Wheeler, 2001). If parents can reorganize the family system and reestablish a sense of life's meaning through valuing the lost child's impact on their lives and investing in other children and activities, then the result can be firmer family commitments and personal growth. The process, which often takes years, is associated with improved physical and mental health and gains in marital satisfaction (Murphy, 2008). Five years after her son's death, one parent reflected on her progress:

> I was afraid to let go [of my pain, which was] a way of loving him. . . . Finally I had to admit that his life meant more than pain, it also meant joy and happiness and fun—and living. . . . When we release pain we make room for happiness in our lives. My memories of S. became lighter and more spontaneous. Instead of hurtful, my memories brought comfort, even a chuckle. . . . I realized S. was still teaching me things. (Klass, 2004, p. 87)

AP IMAGES/DANIEL LUNA

Grieving parents find their children in a hospital morgue in Buenos Aires, Argentina, after a fire raced through a packed nightclub. The death of a child, whether unexpected or foreseen, is the most difficult loss an adult can face.

CHILDREN AND ADOLESCENTS GRIEVING THE LOSS OF A PARENT OR SIBLING. The loss of an attachment figure has long-term consequences for children. When a parent dies, children's basic sense of security and being cared for is threatened. And the death of a sibling not only deprives children of a close emotional tie but also informs them, often for the first time, of their own vulnerability.

Children grieving a family loss describe frequent crying, trouble concentrating in school, sleep difficulties, headaches, and other physical symptoms several months to years after a death. And clinical studies reveal that persistent depression, anxiety, angry outbursts, social withdrawal, and worries about dying themselves are common (Dowdney, 2000; Luecken, 2008). At the same time, many children say they have actively maintained mental contact with their dead parent or sibling, dreaming about and speaking to them regularly. In a follow-up seven to nine years after sibling loss, thinking about the deceased brother or sister at least once a day was common (Martinson, Davies, & McClowry, 1987; Silverman & Nickman, 1996). These images, reported by bereaved adults as well, seem to facilitate coping with loss.

Cognitive development contributes to the ability to grieve. For example, children with an immature understanding of death may believe the dead parent left voluntarily, perhaps in anger, and that the other parent may also disappear. For these reasons, young children need careful, repeated explanations assuring them that the parent did not want to die and was not angry at them (Christ, Siegel, & Christ, 2002). Keeping the truth from children isolates them and often leads to profound regrets. One 8-year-old who learned only a half-hour in advance that his sick brother was dying reflected, "If only I'd known, I could have said goodbye."

Regardless of children's level of understanding, honesty, affection, and reassurance help them tolerate painful feelings of loss. Grief-stricken school-age children are usually more willing than adolescents to confide in parents. To appear normal, teenagers tend to keep their grieving from both adults and peers. Consequently, they are more likely than children to become depressed or to escape from grief through acting-out behavior (Granot, 2005). Overall, effective parenting—warmth combined with rational discipline—fosters adaptive coping and positive long-term adjustment in both children and adolescents (Luecken, 2008).

ADULTS GRIEVING THE LOSS OF AN INTIMATE PARTNER. Recall from Chapter 18 that after the death of a spouse, adaptation to widowhood varies greatly, with age, social support, and personality making a difference. After a period of intense grieving, most widowed elders in Western nations fare well, while younger individuals display more negative outcomes (see page 622 to review). Older widows and widowers have many more contemporaries in similar circumstances. And most have already attained important life goals or adjusted to the fact that some goals will not be attained.

In contrast, loss of a spouse or partner in early or middle adulthood is a nonnormative event that profoundly disrupts life plans. Interviews with a large, U.S. nationally representative sample of adults who had been widowed from less than 1 to 64 years previously (typically in middle adulthood) revealed that thoughts about and conversations with the lost spouse occurred often in the first few years, then declined gradually (Carnelley et al., 2006). But they did not reach their lowest level for several decades, when the typical respondent still thought about the deceased partner once every week or two and conversed with him or her about once a month.

In addition to dealing with feelings of loss, young and middle-aged widows and widowers often must assume a greater role in comforting others, especially children (Lopata, 1996). They also face the stresses of single parenthood and rapid shrinking of the social network established during their life as a couple. The death of an intimate partner in a gay or lesbian relationship presents unique challenges. When relatives limit or bar the partner from participating in funeral services, the survivor experiences *disenfranchised grief*—a sense of loss without the opportunity to mourn publicly and benefit from others' support—which can profoundly disrupt the grieving process (Lund & Caserta, 2004a). Fortunately, gay and lesbian communities provide helpful alternative support in the form of memorial services and other rituals.

BEREAVEMENT OVERLOAD. When a person experiences several deaths at once or in close succession, bereavement overload can occur. Multiple losses deplete the coping resources

AP IMAGES/PIER PAOLO CITO

In the aftermath of the massive 2009 earthquake in L'Aquila, Italy, with a death toll of nearly 300, a couple mourns during the funeral service for quake victims. A public tragedy like this can spark bereavement overload, leaving mourners at risk for prolonged, overwhelming grief.

Applying What We Know

Suggestions for Resolving Grief After a Loved One Dies

Suggestion	Description
Give yourself permission to feel the loss.	Permit yourself to confront all thoughts and emotions associated with the death. Make a conscious decision to overcome your grief, recognizing that this will take time.
Accept social support.	In the early part of grieving, let others reach out to you by making meals, running errands, and keeping you company. Be assertive; ask for what you need so people who would like to help will know what to do.
Be realistic about the course of grieving.	Expect to have some negative and intense reactions, such as feeling anguished, sad, and angry, that last from weeks to months and may occasionally resurface years after the death. There is no one way to grieve, so find the best way for you.
Remember the deceased.	Review your relationship to and experiences with the deceased, permitting yourself to see that you can no longer be with him or her as before. Form a new relationship based on memories, keeping it alive through photographs, commemorative donations, prayers, and other symbols and actions.
When ready, invest in new activities and relationships, and master new tasks of daily living.	Determine which roles you must give up and which ones you must assume as a consequence of the death, and take deliberate steps to incorporate these into your life. Set small goals at first, such as a night at the movies, a dinner date with a friend, a cooking or household repair class, or a week's vacation.

of even well-adjusted people, leaving them emotionally overwhelmed and unable to resolve their grief (Lattanzi-Licht & Doka, 2003). In a study of over 700 gay men with partners or friends who had died of AIDS, those experiencing two or more losses in close succession reported more distress, suicidal thoughts, and substance use than did those with a single loss (Martin & Dean, 1993). Fear of discrimination may prevent sexual minorities overwhelmed by grief from seeking treatment, especially if they are unaware of psychological services, including counseling and social support networks, in the gay community (Springer & Lease, 2000).

Because old age often brings the death of spouse, siblings, and friends in close succession, elders are also at risk for bereavement overload. But recall from Chapter 18 that compared with young people, older adults are often better equipped to handle these losses. They know that decline and death are expected in late adulthood, and they have had a lifetime of experience through which to develop effective coping strategies.

Finally, public tragedies—random murders in schools, terrorist attacks, natural disasters (such as Hurricane Katrina in August 2005), or widely publicized kidnappings—can spark bereavement overload (Corr, 2003). Many survivors who lost loved ones, co-workers, or friends in the September 11, 2001, terrorist attacks (including an estimated 15,000 children who lost a parent) experienced repeated images of horror and destruction, which impeded coming to terms with loss. Children and adolescents suffered profoundly—from intense shock, prolonged grief, frequent mental replays of the vicious attack and gruesome outcomes, and fear of the settings in which those events occurred (Nader, 2002; Webb, 2002). The greater the bereaved individual's exposure to the catastrophic death scene, the more severe these reactions.

Funerals and other bereavement rituals, illustrated in the Cultural Influences box on page 664, assist mourners of all ages in resolving grief with the help of family and friends. Bereaved individuals who remain preoccupied with loss and who have difficulty resuming interest in everyday activities benefit from special interventions designed to help them adjust.

Bereavement Interventions

Sympathy and understanding are sufficient to enable most people to undertake the tasks necessary to recover from grief (see Applying What We Know above). Yet effective support is often difficult to provide, and relatives and friends can benefit from training in how to respond. Sometimes they give advice aimed at hastening recovery, an approach that most bereaved people dislike (Lehman, Ellard, & Wortman, 1986). Listening patiently and "just being there" are among the best ways to help.

Bereavement interventions typically encourage people to draw on their existing social network, while providing additional social support through group or individual counseling. Controversy exists over whether grief counseling benefits most bereaved people, or whether it helps only those experiencing profound difficulties (Allumbaugh & Hoyt, 1999; CFAH, 2003; Jordan & Neimeyer, 2003). A recent analysis of research expressed optimism about broadly favorable effects (Larson & Hoyt, 2007).

Self-help groups that bring together mourners who have experienced the same type of loss seem highly effective in reducing stress. In a program for recently widowed elders in

CULTURAL INFLUENCES

Cultural Variations in Mourning Behavior

The Balinese of Indonesia believe they must remain calm in the face of death so the gods can hear their prayers. While acknowledging their grief, these Balinese mourners work hard to maintain their composure as they participate in a cremation procession.

The ceremonies that commemorated Sofie's and Nicholas's deaths—the first Jewish, the second Quaker—were strikingly different. Yet they served common goals: announcing that a death has occurred, ensuring social support, commemorating the deceased, and conveying a philosophy of life after death.

At the funeral home, Sofie's body was washed and shrouded, a Jewish ritual signifying return to a state of purity. Then it was placed in a plain wooden (not metal) coffin, so as not to impede the natural process of decomposition. To underscore the finality of death, Jewish tradition does not permit viewing of the body; it remains in a closed coffin. Traditionally, the coffin is not left alone until burial; in honor of the deceased, the community maintains a day-and-night vigil.

To return the body quickly to the life-giving earth from which it sprang, Sofie's funeral was scheduled as soon as relatives could gather—just three days after death. Sofie's husband and children symbolized their anguish by cutting a black ribbon and pinning it to their clothing. The rabbi recited psalms of comfort, followed by a eulogy. The service continued at the graveside. Once the coffin had been lowered into the ground, relatives and friends took turns shoveling earth onto it, each participating in the irrevocable act of burial. The service concluded with the *Kaddish* prayer, which affirms life while accepting death.

At home, the family lit a memorial candle, which burned throughout *shiva,* the seven-day mourning period (Hazell, 2001). A meal of consolation prepared by others followed, creating a warm feeling of community. Jewish custom prescribes that after 30 days, life should gradually return to normal. When a parent dies, the mourning period is extended to 12 months.

In the Quaker tradition of simplicity, Nicholas was cremated promptly. During the next week, relatives and close friends gathered with Giselle and Sasha at their home. Together, they planned a memorial service to celebrate Nicholas's life.

When people arrived on the appointed day, a clerk of the Friends (Quaker) Meeting welcomed them and explained to newcomers the Quaker custom of worshipping silently, with those who feel moved to speak rising at any time to share thoughts and feelings. Many mourners offered personal statements about Nicholas or read poems and selections from Scripture. After concluding comments from Giselle and Sasha, everyone joined hands to close the service. A reception for the family followed.

Variations in mourning behavior are vast, both within and across societies. At African-American funerals, for example, grief is expressed freely: Eulogies and music are usually designed to trigger release of deep emotion (McGoldrick et al., 2004). In contrast, the Balinese of Indonesia believe they must remain calm in the face of death so that the gods can hear their prayers. While acknowledging their underlying grief, Balinese mourners work hard to maintain their composure (Rosenblatt, 1993, 2008).

Religions also render accounts of the aftermath of death that console both dying and bereaved individuals. Beliefs of tribal and village cultures typically include an elaborate world of ancestor spirits and customs designed to ease the journey of the deceased to this afterlife (Rosenblatt, 2008). Jewish tradition, while affirming personal survival, emphasizes how one lives on by granting life and care to others. Unlike other Christian groups, Quakers give little attention to hope of heaven or fear of hell, focusing mainly on "salvation by character"—working for peace, justice, and a loving community.

In recent years, a new ritual has arisen: "virtual cemeteries" on the Internet, which allow postings whenever bereaved individuals feel ready to convey their thoughts and feelings, creation of tributes at little or no cost, and continuous, easy access to the memorial. Most creators of Web tributes choose to tell personal stories, highlighting a laugh, a favorite joke, or a touching moment (Roberts & Vidal, 1999–2000). Some survivors use Web memorials to grieve openly, others to converse with the lost loved one. Cemetery guestbooks offer a place for visitors to connect with other mourners. Web cemeteries also provide a means for people excluded from traditional death rituals to engage in public mourning (Roberts, 2006; Stroebe, van der Houwen, & Schut, 2008). The following "gravesite" message captures the unique qualities of this highly flexible medium for mourning:

> I wish I could maintain contact with you, to keep alive the vivid memories of your impact on my life. . . . Because I cannot visit your grave today, I use this means to tell you how much you are loved.

which group members helped one another resolve grief and master tasks of daily living, participants readily bonded with one another and gained in sense of self-efficacy at managing their own lives (Caserta, Lund, & Rice, 1999). A widow expressed the many lasting benefits:

> We shared our anger at being left behind, . . . our fright of that aloneness. We shared our favorite pictures, so each of us could know the others' families and the fun we used to have. We shared our feelings of guilt if we had fun . . . and found out that it was okay to keep on living! . . . We cheered when one of us accomplished a new task. We also tried to lend a helping hand and heart when we would have one of our bad days! . . . This group will always be there for me and I will always be there for them. I love you all! (Lund, 2005)

Effective interventions for children and adolescents following violent deaths protect them from unnecessary reexposure, help parents and teachers with their own distress so they can effectively offer comfort, and are culturally sensitive. After shootings on the grounds of one school, administrators arranged for a ceremony that removed "angry dead souls." Only then did the large number of Vietnamese Buddhist students return to their classrooms (Nader, Dubrow, & Stamm, 1999).

A sudden, violent, and unexplainable death; the loss of a child; a death that the mourner feels he or she could have prevented; or an ambivalent or dependent relationship with the deceased makes it harder for bereaved people to overcome their loss. In these instances, grief therapy, or individual counseling with a specially trained professional, can be helpful. One successful approach is to assist bereaved adults in finding some value in the grieving experience—for example, gaining insight into the meaning of relationships, discovering their own capacity to cope with adversity, or crystallizing a sense of purpose in their lives (Neimeyer, 2001a).

Nevertheless, most bereaved individuals do not participate in bereavement interventions, even when readily available to them. One study reported that only 30 percent of family members who had been caregivers for hospice patients made use of hospice bereavement services—consisting of phone support, onsite support groups, and referrals for counseling (Cherlin et al., 2007). Many who refused these services were severely distressed yet did not realize that intervention could be helpful.

Death Education

Preparatory steps can help people of all ages cope with death more effectively. The death awareness movement that sparked increased sensitivity to the needs of dying patients has also led to the rise of college and university courses in death, dying, and bereavement. Instruction has been integrated into the training of doctors, nurses, psychologists, and social workers, although most professional offerings are limited to only a few lectures (Wass, 2004). Death education is also found in adult education programs in many communities and even in a few elementary and secondary schools.

Death education at all levels has the following goals:

- Increasing students' understanding of the physical and psychological changes that accompany dying
- Helping students learn how to cope with the death of a loved one
- Preparing students to be informed consumers of medical and funeral services
- Promoting understanding of social and ethical issues involving death

Educational format varies widely. Some programs simply convey information. Others are experiential and include activities such as role playing, discussions with the terminally ill, visits to mortuaries and cemeteries, and personal awareness exercises. Research reveals that although using a lecture style leads to gains in knowledge, it often leaves students more uncomfortable about death than when they entered. In contrast, experiential programs that help people confront their own mortality are less likely to heighten death anxiety and may sometimes reduce it (Durlak & Riesenberg, 1991; Maglio & Robinson, 1994).

Whether acquired in the classroom or in our daily lives, our thoughts and feelings about death are forged through interactions with others. Becoming more aware of how we die and of our own mortality, we encounter our greatest loss, but we also gain. Dying people have at times confided in those close to them that awareness of the limits of their lifespan permitted them to dispense with superficial distractions and wasted energies and focus on what is truly important in their lives. As one terminally ill patient summed up, "[It's] kind of like life, just speeded up"—an accelerated process in which, over a period of weeks to months, one grapples with issues that normally would have taken years or decades to resolve (Selwyn, 1996, p. 36). Applying this lesson to ourselves, we learn that by being in touch with death and dying, we can live ever more fully.

ASK YOURSELF

» REVIEW
What circumstances are likely to induce bereavement overload? Cite examples.

» APPLY
List features of self-help groups that contribute to their effectiveness in helping people cope with loss.

» CONNECT
Compare grieving individuals' reactions with terminally ill patients' thoughts and feelings as they move closer to death, described on page 647. Can a dying person's reactions be viewed as a form of grieving? Explain.

» REFLECT
Visit a Web cemetery, such as Virtual Memorials *(virtualmemorials.com)*. Select examples of Web tributes, guestbook entries, and testimonials that illustrate the unique ways in which virtual cemeteries help people cope with death.

Summary

How We Die

Describe the physical changes of dying, along with their implications for defining death and the meaning of death with dignity.

- Death is long and drawn-out for three-fourths of people—many more than in times past, as a result of life-saving medical technology. Among those who die suddenly, 80 to 90 percent are victims of heart attacks.
- In general, dying takes place in three phases: the **agonal phase,** in which regular heartbeat disintegrates; **clinical death,** a short interval in which resuscitation is still possible; and **mortality,** or permanent death.
- In most industrialized nations, **brain death** is accepted as the definition of death. But for the thousands of incurable patients who remain in a **persistent vegetative state,** the brain death standard does not always solve the dilemma of when to halt treatment.
- We can best ensure death with dignity by supporting dying patients through their physical and psychological distress, being candid about death's certainty, and helping them learn enough about their condition to make reasoned choices about treatment.

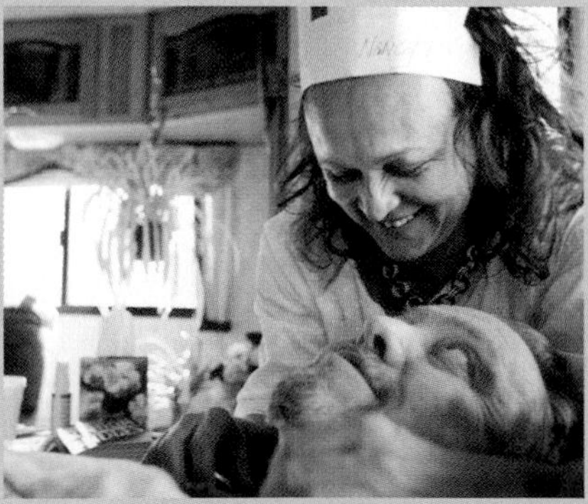
AP IMAGES/COEUR D'ALENE PRESS, JEROME A. POLLOS

Understanding of and Attitudes Toward Death

Discuss age-related changes in conceptions of and attitudes toward death, and cite factors that influence death anxiety.

- Compared with earlier generations, more young people reach adulthood having had little contact with death, contributing to a sense of unease about it.
- To understand death, children must have some basic notions of biology and must be able to distinguish between "dead," "inanimate," "unreal," and "nonexistent." Most children attain an adultlike concept of death in middle childhood, gradually mastering concepts of permanence, inevitability, cessation, applicability, and causation. Experiences with death and religious teachings affect children's understanding, as do open, honest discussions.
- Adolescents often fail to apply their understanding of death to everyday life. Though aware that death happens to everyone and can occur at any time, teenagers nevertheless seek alternative views, are high risk takers, and do not take death personally. Candid discussions with adolescents can help them build a bridge between death as a logical concept and their personal experiences.
- In early adulthood, many people avoid thinking about death, but in midlife, they become more conscious that their own lives are finite. In late adulthood, as death nears, people are more apt to ponder the process of dying than the state of death.
- Wide individual and cultural variations exist in **death anxiety.** People with a sense of spirituality. a well-developed personal philosophy of death, and deep faith in a higher force or being experience less fear of death. With greater ability to regulate negative emotion and a sense of symbolic immortality, older adults are less anxious about death than younger adults. Across cultures, women exhibit more death anxiety than men.

Thinking and Emotions of Dying People

Describe and evaluate Kübler-Ross's theory of typical responses to dying, citing factors that influence dying patients' responses.

- According to Elisabeth Kübler-Ross's theory, dying people typically express five responses, initially proposed as "stages": denial, anger, bargaining, depression, and acceptance. These reactions do not occur in fixed sequence, and dying people often display other coping strategies.
- An **appropriate death** is one that makes sense in terms of the individual's pattern of living and values, preserves or restores significant relationships, and is as free of suffering as possible. Many contextual variables—nature of the disease; personality and coping style; family members' and health professionals' truthfulness and sensitivity; and spirituality, religion, and cultural background—affect the way people respond to their own dying and, therefore, the extent to which they attain an appropriate death.

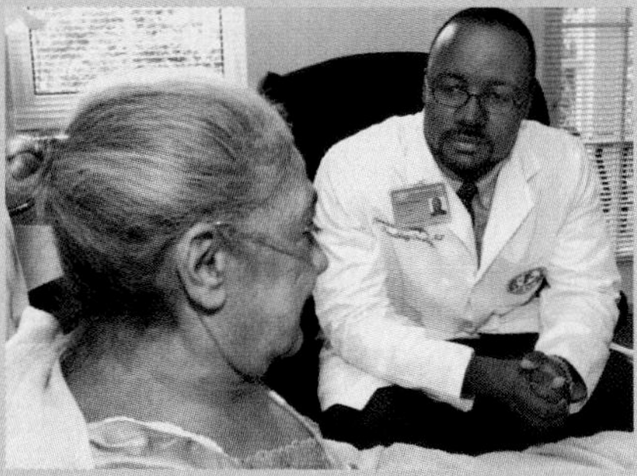
AP IMAGES

A Place to Die

Evaluate the extent to which homes, hospitals, nursing homes, and the hospice approach meet the needs of dying people and their families.

- Although most people say they want to die at home, only about one-fourth of Americans do. Even with professional help and hospital-supplied equipment, caring for a dying patient is highly demanding.
- Sudden deaths typically occur in hospital emergency rooms, where sympathetic explanations from staff can reduce family members' anger, frustration, and confusion. Intensive care is especially depersonalizing for patients, lingering between life and death while hooked to machines. Most U.S. hospitals still do not have comprehensive treatment programs aimed at easing suffering at the end of life.
- Though deaths in U.S. nursing homes are common, high-quality terminal care is lacking. Too many patients die in pain without having their needs met.

» Whether a person dies at home or in an institution, the **hospice** approach strives to meet the dying person's physical, emotional, social, and spiritual needs by providing **palliative,** or **comfort, care** focused on protecting the quality of remaining life rather than on prolonging life. Besides reducing patient physical suffering, hospice care contributes to improved family functioning and better psychological well-being among family survivors.

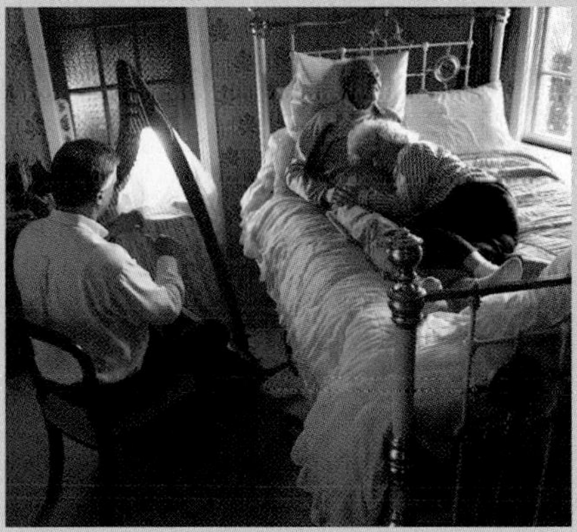
© SIMON ODWYER/THE AGE PHOTO SALES

The Right to Die

Discuss controversies surrounding euthanasia and assisted suicide.

» Modern medical procedures that preserve life can also prolong inevitable death, diminishing quality of life and personal dignity. **Euthanasia**—ending the life of a person suffering from an incurable condition—takes various forms.

» **Passive euthanasia,** withholding or withdrawing life-sustaining treatment from a hopelessly ill patient, is widely accepted and practiced. But in the absence of consensus on end-of-life health care, people can best ensure that their wishes will be followed by preparing a written **advance medical directive.** A **living will** contains instructions for treatment, whereas the **durable power of attorney for health care** names another person to make health care decisions on one's behalf.

» Public support for **voluntary active euthanasia,** in which doctors or others comply with a suffering patient's request to die before a natural end to life, is high. Nevertheless, the practice remains a criminal offense in most countries and has sparked heated controversy, fueled by fears that it will lead us down a slippery slope to the killing of vulnerable people who did not ask to die.

» Less public support exists for assisted suicide. But because the final act is solely the patient's, some experts believe that legalizing assisted suicide is preferable to legalizing voluntary active euthanasia.

Bereavement: Coping with the Death of a Loved One

Describe the phases of grieving, factors that underlie individual variations, and bereavement interventions.

» **Bereavement** refers to the experience of losing a loved one by death, **grief** to the intense physical and psychological distress that accompanies loss. **Mourning** customs are culturally prescribed expressions of thoughts and feelings designed to help people work through their grief.

» Although theorists previously regarded grieving as taking place in orderly phases—avoidance, confrontation, and finally restoration—a more accurate image is a roller-coaster ride, with the mourner completing a set of tasks to overcome grief. According to the **dual-process model of coping with loss,** effective coping involves oscillating between dealing with the emotional consequences of loss and attending to life changes, which offer temporary distraction and relief from painful grieving.

» Like dying, grieving is affected by many personal and situational factors. Bereaved men express grief less directly than bereaved women. After a sudden, unanticipated death, avoidance may be especially pronounced and confrontation highly traumatic. In contrast, a prolonged, expected death grants the bereaved person time to engage in **anticipatory grieving.**

» When a parent loses a child or a child loses a parent or sibling, grieving is generally intense and prolonged. Because loss of a spouse or partner in early or middle adulthood is a nonnormative event with a major impact on life plans, younger widowed individuals usually fare less well than widowed elders. Disenfranchised grief can profoundly disrupt the process of grieving.

AP IMAGES/DANIEL LUNA

» People who experience several deaths at once or in close succession may suffer from bereavement overload. Among those at risk are individuals who have lost partners and friends to AIDS, the elderly, and people who have witnessed unexpected, violent deaths.

» Sympathy and understanding are sufficient for most people to recover from grief. Self-help groups can provide extra social support. Professional bereavement interventions can be helpful for those experiencing severe distress.

Death Education

Explain how death education can help people cope with death more effectively.

» Today, instruction in death, dying, and bereavement can be found in colleges and universities; in training programs for doctors, nurses, and helping professionals; in adult education programs; and in a few elementary and secondary schools. Courses are more likely to reach students cognitively and emotionally when, in addition to conveying information, they include an experiential component.

Important Terms and Concepts

Glossary

A

academic programs Preschool and kindergarten programs in which teachers structure children's learning, teaching academic skills through formal lessons that often involve repetition and drill. Distinguished from *child-centered programs.* (p. 245)

accommodation In Piaget's theory, that part of adaptation in which new schemes are created and old ones adjusted to produce a better fit with the environment. Distinguished from *assimilation.* (p. 152)

acculturative stress Psychological distress resulting from conflict between an individual's minority culture and the host culture. (p. 406)

activities of daily living (ADLs) Basic self-care tasks required to live on one's own, such as bathing, dressing, getting in and out of bed or a chair, and eating. (p. 566)

activity theory A social theory of aging that states that declining rates of interaction in late adulthood reflect social barriers to engagement, not the desires of elders. Older people will try to preserve life satisfaction by finding roles that allow them to remain about as active and busy as they were in middle age. Distinguished from *disengagement theory, continuity theory,* and *socioemotional selectivity theory.* (p. 614)

adaptation In Piaget's theory, the process of building schemes through direct interaction with the environment. Consists of two complementary activities: *assimilation* and *accommodation.* (p. 152)

adolescence The transition between childhood and adulthood that begins with puberty. It involves accepting one's full-grown body, acquiring adult ways of thinking, attaining greater independence from one's family, developing more mature ways of relating to peers of both sexes, and beginning to construct an identity. (p. 361)

advance medical directive A written statement of desired medical treatment should a person become incurably ill. (p. 655)

affect optimization The ability to maximize positive emotion and dampen negative emotion. An emotional strength of late adulthood. (p. 605)

age-graded influences Influences on lifespan development that are strongly related to age and therefore fairly predictable in when they occur and how long they last. (p. 11)

age of viability The age at which the fetus can first survive if born early. Occurs sometime between 22 and 26 weeks. (p. 84)

aging in place In late adulthood, remaining in a familiar setting where one has control over one's everyday life. (p. 617)

agonal phase The phase of dying in which gasps and muscle spasms occur during the first moments in which the regular heart beat disintegrates. Distinguished from *clinical death* and *mortality.* (p. 640)

alcohol-related neurodevelopmental disorder (ARND) The least severe form of fetal alcohol spectrum disorder, involving brain injury but with typical physical growth and absence of facial abnormalities. Distinguished from *fetal alcohol syndrome (FAS)* and *partial fetal alcohol syndrome (p-FAS).* (p. 90)

allele Each of two or more forms of a gene located at the same place on corresponding pairs of chromosomes. (p. 48)

Alzheimer's disease The most common form of dementia, in which structural and chemical brain deterioration is associated with gradual loss of many aspects of thought and behavior, including memory, skilled and purposeful movements, and comprehension and production of speech. (p. 583)

amnion The inner membrane that encloses the developing organism in amniotic fluid, which helps keep temperature constant and provides a cushion against jolts caused by the mother's movements. (p. 82)

amyloid plaques A structural change in the cerebral cortex associated with Alzheimer's disease, in which dense deposits of a deteriorated protein called *amyloid* develop, surrounded by clumps of dead nerve and glial cells. (p. 584)

androgyny The gender identity held by individuals who score high on both traditionally masculine and traditionally feminine personality characteristics. (p. 276)

animistic thinking The belief that inanimate objects have lifelike qualities, such as thoughts, wishes, feelings, and intentions. (p. 229)

anorexia nervosa An eating disorder in which young people, mainly females, starve themselves because of a compulsive fear of getting fat and an extremely distorted body image. (p. 372)

anoxia Inadequate oxygen supply during labor and delivery. (p. 100)

anticipatory grieving Before a prolonged, expected death, acknowledging and preparing emotionally for the inevitable loss. (p. 661)

Apgar Scale A rating system used to assess a newborn baby's physical condition immediately after birth on the basis of five characteristics: heart rate, respiratory effort, reflex irritability, muscle tone, and color. (p. 98)

appropriate death A death that makes sense in terms of the individual's pattern of living and values, preserves or restores significant relationships, and is as free of suffering as possible. (p. 648)

assimilation In Piaget's theory, that part of adaptation in which the external world is interpreted in terms of current schemes. Distinguished from *accommodation.* (p. 152)

assisted living A homelike housing arrangement for elders who require more care than can be provided at home but less than is usually provided in nursing homes. (p. 589)

assistive technology An array of devices that permits people with disabilities, including older adults, to improve their functioning. (p. 573)

associative memory deficit Age-related difficulty creating and retrieving links between pieces of information—for example, two items or an item and its context. (p. 592)

associative play A form of social interaction in which children engage in separate activities but interact by exchanging toys and commenting on one another's behavior. Distinguished from *nonsocial activity, parallel play,* and *cooperative play.* (p. 261)

attachment The strong, affectionate tie that humans have with special people in their lives, which leads them to feel pleasure when interacting with those people and to be comforted by their nearness in times of stress. (p. 196)

Attachment Q-Sort A method for assessing the quality of attachment in children between 1 and 4 years of age through home observations of a variety of attachment-related behaviors. (p. 198)

attention-deficit hyperactivity disorder (ADHD) A childhood disorder involving inattentiveness, impulsivity, and excessive motor activity. Often leads to academic and social problems. (p. 304)

authoritarian child-rearing style A child-rearing style that is low in acceptance and involvement, high in coercive and psychological control, and low in autonomy granting. Distinguished from *authoritative, permissive,* and *uninvolved child-rearing styles.* (p. 279)

authoritative child-rearing style A child-rearing style that is high in acceptance and involvement, emphasizes adaptive control techniques, and includes gradual, appropriate autonomy granting. Distinguished from *authoritarian, permissive,* and *uninvolved child-rearing styles.* (p. 278)

autobiographical memory Long-lasting representations of personally meaningful one-time events from both the recent and the distant past. (p. 164)

autoimmune response A malfunction of the immune system in which it turns against normal body tissues. (p. 571)

autonomy At adolescence, a sense of oneself as a separate, self-governing individual. Involves relying more on oneself and less on parents for support and guidance and engaging in careful, well-reasoned decision making. (p. 415)

autonomy versus shame and doubt In Erikson's theory, the psychological conflict of toddlerhood, which is resolved favorably when parents provide young children with suitable guidance and reasonable choices. (p. 184)

autosomes The 22 matching chromosome pairs in each human cell. (p. 47)

average healthy life expectancy The number of years a person born in a particular year can expect to live in full health, without disease or injury. (p. 565)

average life expectancy The number of years an individual born in a particular year can expect to live, starting at any given age. Distinguished from *maximum lifespan* and *average healthy life expectancy.* (p. 564)

avoidant attachment The attachment pattern characterizing infants who seem unresponsive to the parent when she is present, are usually not distressed by parental separation, and avoid or are slow to greet the parent when she returns. Distinguished from *secure, resistant,* and *disorganized/disoriented attachment.* (p. 198)

B

babbling Repetition of consonant–vowel combinations in long strings, beginning around 6 months of age. (p. 174)

basal metabolic rate (BMR) The amount of energy the body uses at complete rest. (p. 440)

basic emotions Emotions such as happiness, interest, surprise, fear, anger, sadness, and disgust that are universal in humans and other primates and have a long evolutionary history of promoting survival. (p. 185)

basic trust versus mistrust In Erikson's theory, the psychological conflict of infancy, which is resolved positively when the balance of care is sympathetic and loving. (p. 184)

behaviorism An approach that regards directly observable events—stimuli and responses—as the appropriate focus of study and views the development of behavior as taking place through classical and operant conditioning. (p. 17)

behavior modification Procedures that combine conditioning and modeling to eliminate undesirable behaviors and increase desirable responses. (p. 18)

bereavement The experience of losing a loved one by death. (p. 659)

bicultural identity The identity constructed by individuals who explore and adopt values from both their family's subculture and the dominant culture. (p. 406)

"big five" personality traits Five basic factors into which hundreds of personality traits have been organized: neuroticism, extroversion, openness to experience, agreeableness, and conscientiousness. (p. 542)

biological aging, or **senescence** Genetically influenced, age-related declines in the functioning of organs and systems that are universal in all members of our species. Sometimes called *primary aging.* (p. 432)

blended, or reconstituted, family A family structure resulting from cohabitation or remarriage that includes parent, child, and steprelatives. (p. 349)

body image Conception of and attitude toward one's physical appearance. (p. 370)

brain death Irreversible cessation of all activity in the brain and the brain stem. The definition of death accepted in most industrialized nations. (p. 641)

brain plasticity The capacity of various parts of the cerebral cortex to take over functions of damaged regions. Declines as hemispheres of the cerebral cortex lateralize. (p. 124)

breech position A position of the baby in the uterus that would cause the buttocks or feet to be delivered first. (p. 100)

bulimia nervosa An eating disorder in which individuals, mainly females, engage in strict dieting and excessive exercise accompanied by binge eating, often followed by deliberate vomiting and purging with laxatives. (p. 373)

burnout A condition in which long-term job stress leads to mental exhaustion, a sense of loss of personal control, and feelings of reduced accomplishment. (p. 554)

C

canalization The tendency of heredity to restrict the development of some characteristics to just one or a few outcomes. (p. 72)

cardinality The mathematical principle specifying that the last number in a counting sequence indicates the quantity of items in the set. (p. 243)

carrier A heterozygous individual who can pass a recessive trait to his or her offspring. (p. 48)

cataracts Cloudy areas in the lens of the eye that increase from middle to old age, resulting in foggy vision and (without surgery) eventual blindness. (p. 567)

categorical self Classification of the self according to prominent ways in which people differ, such as age, sex, physical characteristics, and goodness and badness. Develops between 18 and 30 months. (p. 208)

central executive In information processing, the conscious part of working memory that directs the flow of information through the mental system by deciding what to attend to, coordinating incoming information with information already in the system, and selecting, applying, and monitoring strategies. (p. 161)

centration In Piaget's theory, the tendency of preoperational children to focus on one aspect of a situation while neglecting other important features. (p. 229)

cephalocaudal trend An organized pattern of physical growth and motor control that proceeds from head to tail. Distinguished from *proximodistal trend.* (p. 121)

cerebellum A structure at the rear and base of the brain that aids in balance and control of body movements. (p. 218)

cerebral cortex The largest, most complex structure of the human brain, containing the greatest number of neurons and synapses, which accounts for the highly developed intelligence of the human species. (p. 124)

cerebrovascular dementia A form of dementia that develops when a series of strokes leaves areas of dead brain cells, producing step-by-step degeneration of mental ability, with each step occurring abruptly after a stroke. (p. 588)

cesarean delivery A surgical delivery in which the doctor makes an incision in the mother's abdomen and lifts the baby out of the uterus. (p. 101)

child-centered programs Preschool and kindergarten programs in which teachers provide a variety of activities from which children select, and much learning takes place through play. Distinguished from *academic programs.* (p. 245)

child-directed speech (CDS) A form of language used by adults to speak to infants and toddlers, consisting of short sentences with high-pitched, exaggerated expression, clear pronunciation, distinct pauses between speech segments, and repetition of new words in a variety of contexts. (p. 177)

child-rearing styles Combinations of parenting behaviors that occur over a wide range of situations, creating an enduring child-rearing climate. (p. 278)

chorion The outer membrane that forms a protective covering around the prenatal organism. It sends out tiny hairlike villi, from which the placenta begins to develop. (p. 82)

chromosomes Rodlike structures in the cell nucleus that store and transmit genetic information. (p. 46)

chronosystem In ecological systems theory, temporal changes in environments, either externally imposed or arising from within the person, that produce new conditions affecting development. Distinguished from *microsystem, mesosystem, exosystem,* and *macrosystem.* (p. 26)

circular reaction In Piaget's theory, a means of building schemes in which infants try to repeat a chance event caused by their own motor activity. (p. 153)

classical conditioning A form of learning that involves associating a neutral stimulus with a stimulus that leads to a reflexive response. Once the nervous system makes the connection between the two stimuli, the neutral stimulus alone will produce the behavior. (p. 133)

climacteric The midlife transition in which fertility declines, bringing an end to reproductive capacity in women and diminished fertility in men. (p. 504)

clinical death The phase of dying in which heartbeat, circulation, breathing, and brain functioning stop, but resuscitation is still possible. Distinguished from *agonal phase* and *mortality.* (p. 640)

clinical interview An interview method in which the researcher uses a flexible, conversational style to probe for the participant's point of view. Distinguished from *structured interview.* (p. 29)

clinical, or **case study, method** A research method in which the aim is to obtain as complete a picture as possible of one individual's psychological functioning by bringing together interview data, observations, and sometimes test scores. (p. 30)

clique A group of about five to seven members who are good friends and, therefore, usually resemble one another in family background, attitudes, values, and interests. (p. 419)

cognitive-affective complexity A form of thinking that increases from adolescence through middle adulthood, involving awareness of positive and negative feelings and coordination of them into a complex, organized structure that integrates cognition with emotion. (p. 453)

cognitive-developmental theory An approach introduced by Piaget that views children as actively constructing knowledge as they manipulate and explore their world and that regards cognitive development as taking place in stages. (p. 19)

cognitive maps Mental representations of familiar large-scale spaces, such as neighborhood or school. (p. 300)

cognitive self-regulation The process of continuously monitoring progress toward a goal, checking outcomes, and redirecting unsuccessful efforts. (p. 307)

cohabitation The lifestyle of unmarried couples who have a sexually intimate relationship and who share a residence. (p. 487)

cohort effects Cultural–historical influences on the accuracy of longitudinal and cross-sectional research findings. Results based on one cohort—individuals developing in the same time period, who are influenced by particular historical and cultural conditions—may not apply to other cohorts. (p. 35)

collectivist societies Societies in which people define themselves as part of a group and stress group goals over individual goals. Distinguished from *individualistic societies.* (p. 66)

commitment within relativistic thinking In Perry's theory, the cognitive approach of the most mature adults, who, instead of choosing between opposing views, try to formulate a more satisfying perspective that synthesizes contradictions. (p. 452)

companionate love Love based on warm, trusting affection and caregiving. Distinguished from *passionate love.* (p. 474)

compliance Voluntary obedience to requests and commands. (p. 208)

compression of morbidity The public health goal of reducing the average period of diminished vigor before death as life expectancy extends. Medical advances, improved socioeconomic conditions, and good health habits all promote this goal. (p. 577)

concrete operational stage Piaget's third stage of cognitive development, extending from about 7 to 11 years of age, during which thought becomes logical, flexible, and organized in its application to concrete information, but the capacity for abstract thinking is not yet present. (p. 299)

conditioned response (CR) In classical conditioning, a new response produced by a conditioned stimulus (CS) that is similar to the unconditioned, or reflexive, response (UCR). (p. 133)

conditioned stimulus (CS) In classical conditioning, a neutral stimulus that through pairing with an unconditioned stimulus (UCS) leads to a new, conditioned response. (CR). (p. 133)

congregate housing Housing for the elderly that provides a variety of support services, including meals in a common dining room, along with watchful oversight of elders with physical and mental disabilities. (p. 618)

conservation The understanding that certain physical characteristics of objects remain the same, even when their outward appearance changes. (p. 229)

constructivist classroom A classroom grounded in Piaget's view of children as active agents who construct their own knowledge. Features include richly equipped learning centers, small groups and individuals solving self-chosen problems, a teacher who guides and supports in response to children's needs, and evaluation based on individual students' progress in relation to their own prior development. Distinguished from *traditional* and *social-constructivist classrooms.* (p. 319)

contexts Unique combinations of personal and environmental circumstances that can result in different paths of development. (p. 6)

continuity theory A social theory of aging that states that most aging adults, in their choice of everyday activities and social relationships, strive to maintain a personal system—an identity and a set of personality dispositions, interests, roles, and skills—that promotes life satisfaction by ensuring consistency between their past and anticipated future. Distinguished from *disengagement theory, activity theory,* and *socioemotional selectivity theory.* (p. 614)

continuous development The view that development is a process of gradually adding more of the same types of skills that were there to begin with. Distinguished from *discontinuous development.* (p. 6)

contrast sensitivity A general principle accounting for early pattern preferences, which states that if babies can detect a difference in contrast between two patterns, they will prefer the one with more contrast. (p. 144)

controversial children Children who receive many votes, both positive and negative, on self-report measures of peer acceptance, indicating that they are both liked and disliked. Distinguished from *popular, neglected,* and *rejected children.* (p. 341)

conventional level Kohlberg's second level of moral development, in which moral understanding is based on conforming to social rules to ensure positive human relationships and maintain societal order. (p. 408)

convergent thinking The type of cognition emphasized on intelligence tests, which involves arriving at a single correct answer to a problem. Distinguished from *divergent thinking.* (p. 323)

cooing Pleasant vowel-like noises made by infants beginning around 2 months of age. (p. 174)

cooperative learning Collaboration on a task by a small group of classmates who work toward common goals by resolving differences of opinion, sharing responsibilities, and providing one another with sufficient explanation to correct misunderstandings. (p. 321)

cooperative play A form of social interaction in which children orient toward a common goal, such as acting out a make-believe theme. Distinguished from *nonsocial activity, parallel play,* and *associative play.* (p. 261)

coregulation A form of supervision in which parents exercise general oversight while permitting children to take charge of moment-by-moment decision making. (p. 345)

core knowledge perspective A perspective that states that infants are born with a set of innate knowledge systems, or core domains of thought, each of which permits a ready grasp of new, related information and therefore supports early, rapid development of certain aspects of cognition. (p. 159)

corpus callosum The large bundle of fibers connecting the two hemispheres of the cerebral cortex. (p. 218)

correlational design A research design in which the investigator gathers information on individuals without altering their experiences and then examines relationships between participants' characteristics and their behavior or development. Does not permit inferences about cause and effect. (p. 31)

correlation coefficient A number, ranging from +1.00 to –1.00, that describes the strength and direction of the relationship between two variables. (p. 33)

creativity The ability to produce work that is original yet appropriate—something others have not thought of that is useful in some way. (p. 323)

cross-linkage theory of aging A theory of biological aging asserting that the formation of bonds, or links, between normally separate protein fibers causes the body's connective tissue to become less elastic over time, leading to many negative physical outcomes. (p. 434)

cross-sectional design A research design in which groups of participants of different ages are studied at the same point in time. Distinguished from *longitudinal design.* (p. 36)

crowd A large, loosely organized social group consisting of several cliques with similar values. Membership is based on reputation and stereotype. (p. 419)

crystallized intelligence Intellectual skills that depend on accumulated knowledge and experience, good judgment, and mastery of social conventions—abilities acquired because they are valued by the individual's culture. Distinguished from *fluid intelligence.* (p. 519)

D

death anxiety Fear and apprehension of death. (p. 645)

deferred imitation The ability to remember and copy the behavior of models who are not present. (p. 155)

delay of gratification The ability to wait for an appropriate time and place to engage in a tempting act. (p. 208)

dementia A set of disorders occurring almost entirely in old age in which many aspects of thought and behavior are so impaired that everyday activities are disrupted. (p. 582)

deoxyribonucleic acid (DNA) Long, double-stranded molecules that make up chromosomes. (p. 46)

dependency–support script A typical pattern of interaction in which caregivers attend to elders' dependent behaviors immediately, thereby reinforcing those behaviors. Distinguished from *independence–ignore script.* (p. 609)

dependent variable The variable the researcher expects to be influenced by the independent variable in an experiment. Distinguished from *independent variable.* (p. 33)

developmental cognitive neuroscience An area of investigation that brings together researchers from psychology, biology, neuroscience, and medicine to study the relationship between changes in the brain and the developing person's cognitive processing and behavior patterns. (p. 22)

developmentally appropriate practice A set of standards devised by the National Association for the Education of Young Children, specifying program characteristics that meet the developmental and individual needs of young children of varying ages, based on current research and the consensus of experts. (p. 171)

developmental quotient (DQ) A score on an infant intelligence test, computed in the same manner as an IQ but labeled more conservatively because it does not tap the same dimensions of intelligence measured in older children. (p. 169)

developmental science An interdisciplinary field devoted to the study of all changes humans experience throughout the lifespan. (p. 5)

differentiation theory The view that perceptual development involves the detection of increasingly fine-grained, invariant features in the environment. (p. 147)

difficult child A child whose temperament is characterized by irregular daily routines, slow acceptance of new experiences, and a tendency to react negatively and intensely. Distinguished from *easy child* and *slow-to-warm-up child.* (p. 190)

discontinuous development The view that development is a process in which new ways of understanding and responding to the world emerge at specific times. Distinguished from *continuous development.* (p. 6)

disengagement theory A social theory of aging that states that declines in social interaction in late adulthood are due to mutual withdrawal between elders and society in anticipation of death. Distinguished from *activity theory, continuity theory,* and *socioemotional selectivity theory.* (p. 613)

disorganized/disoriented attachment The attachment pattern reflecting the greatest insecurity, characterizing infants who show confused, contradictory responses when reunited with the parent after a separation. Distinguished from *secure, avoidant,* and *resistant attachment.* (p. 198)

divergent thinking The type of cognition associated with creativity, which involves generating multiple and unusual possibilities when faced with a task or problem. Associated with creativity. Distinguished from *convergent thinking.* (p. 323)

divorce mediation A series of meetings between divorcing adults and a trained professional that are aimed at reducing family conflict, including legal battles over property division and child custody. (p. 348)

dominance hierarchy A stable ordering of group members that predicts who will win when conflict arises. (p. 298)

dominant cerebral hemisphere The hemisphere of the cerebral cortex responsible for skilled motor action and other important abilities. In right-handed individuals, the left hemisphere is dominant; in left-handed individuals, motor and language skills are often shared between the hemispheres. (p. 217)

dominant–recessive inheritance A pattern of inheritance in which, under heterozygous conditions, the influence of only one allele is apparent. (p. 48)

dualistic thinking In Perry's theory, the cognitive approach typical of younger college students, who divide information, values, and authority into right and wrong, good and bad, we and they. Distinguished from *relativistic thinking.* (p. 452)

dual-process model of coping with loss A perspective that assumes that people cope most effectively with loss when they oscillate between dealing with the emotional consequences of loss and attending to life changes, which—when handled successfully—have restorative, or healing, effects. (p. 660)

dual representation The ability to view a symbolic object as both an object in its own right and a symbol. (p. 229)

durable power of attorney for health care A written statement authorizing appointment of another person (usually, though not always, a family member) to make health care decisions on one's behalf. (p. 656)

dynamic assessment An approach to testing consistent with Vygotsky's zone of proximal development, in which purposeful teaching is introduced into the testing situation to find out what the child can attain with social support. (p. 315)

dynamic systems theory of motor development A theory that views new motor skills as reorganizations of previously mastered skills, which lead to more effective ways of exploring and controlling the environment. Each new skill is a joint product of central nervous system development, the body's movement possibilities, environmental supports for the skill, and the child's goal. (p. 138)

E

easy child A child whose temperament is characterized by establishment of regular routines in infancy, general cheerfulness, and easy adaptation to new experiences. Distinguished from *difficult child* and *slow-to-warm-up child.* (p. 190)

ecological systems theory Bronfenbrenner's approach, which views the person as developing within a complex system of relationships affected by multiple levels of the surrounding environment, from immediate settings of family and school to broad cultural values and programs. (p. 24)

educational self-fulfilling prophecies Teachers' positive or negative views of individual children, who tend to adopt and start to live up to those views. (p. 321)

effortful control The self-regulatory dimension of temperament, involving voluntary suppression of a dominant response in order to plan and execute a more adaptive response. (p. 191)

egalitarian marriage A form of marriage in which partners relate as equals, sharing power and authority. Both try to balance the time and energy they devote to their occupations, their children, and their relationship. Distinguished from *traditional marriage.* (p. 479)

egocentrism Failure to distinguish the symbolic viewpoints of others from one's own. (p. 229)

ego integrity versus despair In Erikson's theory, the psychological conflict of late adulthood, which is resolved positively when elders come to terms with their lives and feel whole, complete, and satisfied with their achievements, recognizing that the paths they followed, abandoned, or never selected were necessary for fashioning a meaningful life course. (p. 604)

elaboration A memory strategy that involves creating a relationship, or shared meaning, between two or more items of information that do not belong to the same category in order to improve recall. (p. 304)

embryo The prenatal organism from 2 to 8 weeks after conception—the period when the groundwork for all body structures and internal organs is laid down. (p. 82)

emergent literacy Children's active efforts to construct literacy knowledge through informal experiences. (p. 242)

emerging adulthood A new transitional period of development, extending from the late teens to the mid-twenties, during which young people have typically left adolescence but have not yet assumed adult responsibilities. Rather, they continue to explore alternatives in education, work, personal beliefs and values, and love. (p. 464)

emotional intelligence A set of emotional abilities that enable individuals to process and adapt to emotional information. Measured by tapping the emotional skills people use to manage their own emotions and interact competently with others. (p. 313)

emotional self-regulation Strategies for adjusting our emotional state to a comfortable level of intensity so we can accomplish our goals. (p. 189)

emotion-centered coping A strategy for managing emotion that is internal, private, and aimed at controlling distress when little can be done to change an outcome. Distinguished from *problem-centered coping.* (p. 335)

empathy The ability to understand another's emotional state and to *feel with* that person, or respond emotionally in a similar way. (p. 208)

epigenesis Development resulting from ongoing, bidirectional exchanges between heredity and all levels of the environment. (p. 74)

epistemic cognition Reflections on how one arrived at facts, beliefs, and ideas. (p. 451)

ethnic identity A sense of ethnic group membership and attitudes and feelings associated with that membership, as an enduring aspect of the self. (p. 406)

ethnography A method in which the researcher attempts to understand the unique values and social processes of a culture or a distinct social group through participant observation—living with its members and taking field notes for an extended time. (p. 30)

ethological theory of attachment Bowlby's theory, the most widely accepted view of attachment, which regards the infant's emotional tie to the caregiver as an evolved response that promotes survival. (p. 196)

ethology An approach concerned with the adaptive, or survival, value of behavior and its evolutionary history. (p. 22)
euthanasia The practice of ending the life of a person suffering from an incurable condition. (p. 654)
evolutionary developmental psychology An approach that seeks to understand the adaptive value of species-wide cognitive, emotional, and social competencies as those competencies change with age. (p. 23)
exosystem In ecological systems theory, social settings that do not contain the developing person but nevertheless affect experiences in immediate settings. Distinguished from *microsystem, mesosystem, macrosystem,* and *chronosystem.* (p. 25)
expansions Adult responses that elaborate on children's speech, increasing its complexity. (p. 251)
experience-dependent brain growth Growth and refinement of established brain structures as a result of specific learning experiences that vary widely across individuals and cultures. Distinguished from *experience-expectant brain growth.* (p. 127)
experience-expectant brain growth The young brain's rapidly developing organization, which depends on ordinary experiences—opportunities to see and touch objects, to hear language and other sounds, and to move about and explore the environment. Distinguished from *experience-dependent brain growth.* (p. 127)
experimental design A research design in which the investigator randomly assigns participants to two or more treatment conditions and studies the effect that manipulating an independent variable has on a dependent variable. Permits inferences about cause and effect. (p. 33)
expertise Acquisition of extensive knowledge in a field or endeavor. (p. 453)
expressive style of language learning A style of early language learning in which toddlers use language mainly to talk about their own and others' feelings and needs, with an initial vocabulary emphasizing social formulas and pronouns. Distinguished from *referential style of language learning.* (p. 177)
extended-family household A household in which one or more adult relatives live with the parent–child nuclear family. (p. 66)

F

family life cycle A sequence of phases characterizing the development of most families around the world. In early adulthood, people typically live on their own, marry, and bear and rear children. In middle age, parenting responsibilities diminish. Late adulthood brings retirement, growing old, and (more often for women) death of one's spouse. (p. 478)
fantasy period Period of vocational development in which children gain insight into career options by fantasizing about them. Distinguished from *tentative period* and *realistic period.* (p. 456)
fast-mapping Children's ability to connect new words with their underlying concepts after only a brief encounter. (p. 248)
feminization of poverty A trend in which women who support themselves or their families have become the majority of the adult population living in poverty, regardless of age and ethnic group. (p. 544)
fetal alcohol spectrum disorder (FASD) A range of physical, mental, and behavioral outcomes caused by prenatal alcohol exposure, including *fetal alcohol syndrome (FAS), partial fetal alcohol syndrome (p-FAS),* and *alcohol-related neurodevelopmental disorder (ARND).* (p. 89)
fetal alcohol syndrome (FAS) The most severe form of fetal alcohol spectrum disorder, distinguished by slow physical growth, facial abnormalities, and brain injury. Usually seen in children whose mothers consumed large amounts of alcohol during most or all of pregnancy. Distinguished from *partial fetal alcohol syndrome (p-FAS)* and *alcohol-related neurodevelopmental disorder (ARND).* (p. 89)
fetal monitors Electronic instruments that track the baby's heart rate during labor. (p. 100)
fetus The prenatal organism from the ninth week to the end of pregnancy—the period during which body structures are completed and dramatic growth in size occurs. (p. 83)
fluid intelligence Intellectual skills that largely depend on basic information-processing skills—ability to detect relationships among visual stimuli, speed of analyzing information, and capacity of working memory. Influenced less by culture than by conditions in the brain and by learning unique to the individual. Distinguished from *crystallized intelligence.* (p. 519)
formal operational stage Piaget's highest stage, beginning around 11 years of age, in which adolescents develop the capacity for abstract, systematic, scientific thinking. (p. 383)
frailty Weakened functioning of diverse organs and body systems, which profoundly interferes with everyday competence and leaves the older adult highly vulnerable in the face of an infection, extremely hot or cold weather, or an injury. (p. 580)
fraternal, or **dizygotic, twins** Twins resulting from the release and fertilization of two ova. They are genetically no more alike than ordinary siblings. Distinguished from *identical,* or *monozygotic, twins.* (p. 47)
free radicals Naturally occurring, highly reactive chemicals that form in the presence of oxygen and destroy nearby cellular material, including DNA, proteins, and fats essential for cell functioning. Believed to be involved in many disorders of aging. (p. 434)
functional age Actual competence and performance of an older adult, as distinguished from chronological age. (p. 564)

G

gametes Sex cells, or sperm and ova, which contain half as many chromosomes as regular body cells. (p. 46)
gender constancy A full understanding of the biologically based permanence of one's gender, including the realization that sex remains the same even if clothing, hairstyle, and play activities change. (p. 276)
gender identity An image of oneself as relatively masculine or feminine in characteristics. (p. 276)
gender intensification Increased gender stereotyping of attitudes and behavior and movement toward a more traditional gender identity, typical of early adolescence. (p. 414)
gender schema theory An information-processing approach to gender typing that explains how environmental pressures and children's cognitions work together to shape gender-role development. (p. 277)
gender typing Any association of objects, roles, or traits with one sex or the other in ways that conform to cultural stereotypes. (p. 273)
gene A segment of a DNA molecule that contains instructions for production of various proteins that contribute to growth and functioning of the body. (p. 46)
generativity versus stagnation In Erikson's theory, the psychological conflict of midlife, which is resolved positively if the adult can integrate personal goals with the welfare of the larger social world. The resulting strength is the capacity to give to and guide the next generation. (p. 532)
genetic counseling A communication process designed to help couples assess their chances of giving birth to a baby with a hereditary disorder and choose the best course of action in view of risks and family goals. (p. 53)
genetic–environmental correlation The idea that heredity influences the environments to which individuals are exposed. (p. 72)
genomic imprinting A pattern of inheritance in which alleles are imprinted, or chemically marked, in such a way that one pair member is activated, regardless of its makeup. (p. 51)
genotype An individual's genetic makeup. Distinguished from *phenotype.* (p. 45)
gerotranscendence According to Joan Erikson, a psychosocial stage characterizing the very old and representing development beyond ego integrity. Involves a cosmic, transcendent perspective directed forward and outward, beyond the self. Apparent in heightened inner calm and contentment and in additional time spent in quiet reflection. (p. 605)
gifted Displaying exceptional intellectual strengths. Includes high IQ, high creativity, and specialized talent. (p. 323)
glass ceiling Invisible barrier to advancement up the corporate ladder, faced by women and ethnic minorities. (p. 555)
glaucoma A disease in which poor fluid drainage leads to a buildup of pressure within the eye, damaging the optic nerve. A leading cause of blindness among older adults. (p. 503)
glial cells Cells that are responsible for myelination of neural fibers, improving the efficiency of message transfer. (p. 122)
goodness-of-fit model A model that describes how favorable adjustment depends on an effective match between a child's temperament and the child-rearing environment. (p. 194)
grief Intense physical and psychological distress following the death of a loved one. (p. 659)

growth hormone (GH) A pituitary hormone that affects the development of all body tissues except the central nervous system and the genitals. (p. 219)

growth spurt Rapid gain in height and weight that is the first outward sign of puberty. (p. 363)

guided participation Shared endeavors between more expert and less expert participants, without specifying the precise features of communication in order to allow for variations across situations and cultures. A broader concept than *scaffolding.* (p. 236)

H

habituation A gradual reduction in the strength of a response due to repetitive stimulation. (p. 134)

hardiness A set of three personal qualities—control, commitment, and challenge—that help people cope adaptively with stress brought on by inevitable life change. (p. 516)

heritability estimate A statistic that measures the extent to which individual differences in complex traits, such as intelligence or personality, in a specific population are due to genetic factors. (p. 70)

heterozygous Having two different alleles at the same place on a pair of chromosomes. Distinguished from *homozygous.* (p. 48)

hierarchical classification The organization of objects into classes and subclasses on the basis of similarities and differences between the groups. (p. 230)

hippocampus An inner-brain structure that plays a vital role in memory and in images of space we use to help us find our way. (p. 218)

history-graded influences Influences on lifespan development that are unique to a particular historical era and explain why people born around the same time (called a *cohort*) tend to be alike in ways that set them apart from people born at other times. (p. 13)

Home Observation for Measurement of the Environment (HOME) A checklist for gathering information about the quality of children's home lives through observation and parental interview. (p. 169)

homozygous Having two identical alleles at the same place on a pair of chromosomes. Distinguished from *heterozygous.* (p. 48)

hormone therapy Low daily doses of estrogen, either alone or in combination with progesterone, aimed at reducing the physical discomforts of menopause. (p. 506)

hospice A comprehensive program of support services for terminally ill people and their families, which regards the patient and family as a unit of care and emphasizes meeting the patient's physical, emotional, social, and spiritual needs while also providing follow-up bereavement services to the family. (p. 652)

hypothetico-deductive reasoning A formal operational problem-solving strategy in which adolescents begin with a *hypothesis,* or prediction, about variables that might affect an outcome. From the hypothesis, they *deduce* logical, testable inferences. Then they systematically isolate and combine variables to see which of those inferences are confirmed in the real world. (p. 383)

I

identical, or **monozygotic, twins** Twins that result when a zygote, during early cell duplication, separates into two clusters of cells that have the same genetic makeup. Distinguished from *fraternal,* or *dizygotic, twins.* (p. 48)

identity A well-organized conception of the self, consisting of values, beliefs, and goals, to which the individual is solidly committed. (p. 402)

identity achievement The identity status of individuals who, after a period of exploration, have committed themselves to a clearly formulated set of self-chosen values and goals. Distinguished from *identity moratorium, identity foreclosure,* and *identity diffusion.* (p. 403)

identity diffusion The identity status of individuals who do not engage in exploration and are not committed to values and goals. Distinguished from *identity achievement, identity moratorium,* and *identity foreclosure.* (p. 403)

identity foreclosure The identity status of individuals who do not engage in exploration but, instead are committed to ready-made values and goals chosen for them by authority figures. Distinguished from *identity achievement, identity moratorium,* and *identity diffusion.* (p. 403)

identity moratorium The identity status of individuals who are exploring but not yet committed to self-chosen values and goals. Distinguished from *identity achievement, identity foreclosure,* and *identity diffusion.* (p. 403)

identity versus role confusion In Erikson's theory, the psychological conflict of adolescence, which is resolved positively when adolescents achieve an identity after a period of exploration and inner soul-searching. (p. 402)

imaginary audience Adolescents' belief that they are the focus of everyone else's attention and concern. (p. 387)

imitation Learning by copying the behavior of another person. Also called *modeling* or *observational learning.* (p. 135)

implantation Attachment of the blastocyst to the uterine lining, which occurs 7 to 9 days after fertilization. (p. 82)

implicit memory Memory without conscious awareness. (p. 592)

inclusive classrooms Classrooms in which students with learning difficulties learn alongside typical students in a regular educational setting for part or all of the school day. (p. 322)

incomplete dominance A pattern of inheritance in which both alleles are expressed in the phenotype, resulting in a combined trait, or one that is intermediate between the two. (p. 50)

independence–ignore script A typical pattern of interaction in which elders' independent behaviors are mostly ignored and, as a result, occur less often. Distinguished from *dependency–support script.* (p. 609)

independent variable In an experiment, the variable the investigator expects to cause changes in another variable and that the researcher manipulates by randomly assigning participants to treatment conditions. Distinguished from *dependent variable.* (p. 33)

individualistic societies Societies in which people think of themselves as separate entities and are largely concerned with their own personal needs. Distinguished from *collectivist societies.* (p. 66)

induction A type of discipline in which an adult helps the child notice feelings by pointing out the effects of the child's misbehavior on others. (p. 265)

industry versus inferiority In Erikson's theory, the psychological conflict of middle childhood, which is resolved positively when experiences lead children to develop a sense of competence at useful skills and tasks. (p. 330)

infantile amnesia The inability of most older children and adults to remember events that happened before age 3. (p. 164)

infant mortality The number of deaths in the first year of life per 1,000 live births. (p. 104)

information-loss view A view that attributes age-related slowing of cognitive processing to greater loss of information as it moves through the system. As a result, the whole system must slow down to inspect and interpret the information. Distinguished from *neural network view.* (p. 521)

information processing An approach that views the human mind as a symbol-manipulating system through which information flows and that regards cognitive development as a continuous process. (p. 21)

inhibited, or **shy, child** A child whose temperament is such that he or she reacts negatively to and withdraws from novel stimuli. Distinguished from *uninhibited,* or *sociable, child.* (p. 191)

initiative versus guilt In Erikson's theory, the psychological conflict of early childhood, which is resolved positively through play experiences that foster a healthy sense of initiative and through development of a superego, or conscience, that is not overly strict and guilt-ridden. (p. 256)

instrumental activities of daily living (IADLs) Tasks that are necessary to conduct the business of daily life and that also require some cognitive competence, such as telephoning, shopping, food preparation, housekeeping, and paying bills. (p. 566)

intelligence quotient (IQ) A score that permits an individual's performance on an intelligence test to be compared to the performances of other individuals of the same age. (p. 168)

intentional, or **goal-directed, behavior** A sequence of actions in which schemes are deliberately coordinated to solve a problem. (p. 154)

interactional synchrony A form of communication in which the caregiver responds to infant signals in a well-timed, rhythmic, appropriate fashion and both partners match emotional states, especially positive ones. (p. 200)

intermodal perception Perception that combines information from more than one modality, or sensory system, resulting in an integrated whole. (p. 146)

internal working model A set of expectations about the availability of attachment figures and the likelihood that they will provide support in times of stress. It becomes a vital part of personality, serving as a guide for all future close relationships. (p. 197)

intimacy versus isolation In Erikson's theory, the psychological conflict of early adulthood, reflected in the young person's thoughts and feelings about making a permanent commitment to an intimate partner. (p. 468)

irreversibility The inability to mentally go through a series of steps in a problem and then reverse direction, returning to the starting point. Distinguished from *reversibility.* (p. 230)

J

joint attention A state in which the child and the caregiver attend to the same object or event and the caregiver comments verbally about what the child sees. Supports language development. (p. 175)

joint custody A child custody arrangement following divorce in which parents are granted equal say in important decisions about the child's upbringing. (p. 348)

K

kinkeeper Role assumed by members of the middle generation, especially mothers, who take responsibility for gathering the family for celebrations and making sure everyone stays in touch. (p. 545)

kinship studies Studies comparing the characteristics of family members to determine the importance of heredity in complex human characteristics. (p. 70)

kwashiorkor A disease caused by a diet low in protein that usually appears after weaning, between 1 and 3 years of age. Symptoms include an enlarged belly, swollen feet, hair loss, skin rash, and irritable, listless behavior. (p. 132)

L

language acquisition device (LAD) In Chomsky's theory, an innate system containing a universal grammar, or set of rules common to all languages, that enables children, no matter which language they hear, to understand and speak in a rule-oriented fashion as soon as they pick up enough words. (p. 173)

lanugo White, downy hair that covers the entire body of the fetus, helping the vernix stick to the skin. (p. 84)

lateralization Specialization of functions in the two hemispheres of the cerebral cortex. (p. 124)

learned helplessness Attribution of success to external factors, such as luck, and failure to low ability, which cannot be improved through effort. Distinguished from *mastery-oriented attributions.* (p. 333)

learning disabilities Great difficulty with one or more aspects of learning, usually reading, resulting in achievement considerably behind what would be expected on the basis of a child's IQ. (p. 322)

life-care communities Housing for the elderly that offers a range of alternatives, from independent or congregate housing to full nursing home care, guaranteeing that elders' needs will be met within the same facility as they age. (p. 618)

lifespan perspective A dynamic systems approach to development that assumes development is lifelong, multidimensional and multidirectional, highly plastic, and affected by multiple interacting forces. (p. 8)

life structure In Levinson's theory, the underlying design of a person's life, consisting of relationships with significant others—individuals, groups, and institutions. Includes both central components, such as marriage/family and occupation, and peripheral ones. (p. 469)

living will A written statement specifying the treatments a person does or does not want in case of a terminal illness, coma, or other near-death situation. (p. 655)

loneliness Unhappiness resulting from a gap between actual and desired social relationships. (p. 476)

longitudinal design A research design in which participants are studied repeatedly, and changes are noted as they get older. Distinguished from *cross-sectional design.* (p. 34)

long-term memory In information processing, the largest storage area in memory, containing our permanent knowledge base. (p. 161)

M

macrosystem In ecological systems theory, cultural values, laws, customs, and resources that influence experiences and interactions at inner levels of the environment. Distinguished from *microsystem, mesosystem, exosystem,* and *chronosystem.* (p. 25)

macular degeneration Blurring and eventual loss of central vision due to a breakdown of light-sensitive cells in the macula, or central region of the retina. (p. 568)

make-believe play A type of play in which children act out everyday and imaginary activities. (p. 155)

marasmus A disease caused by a diet low in all essential nutrients that usually appears in the first year of life and leads to a wasted condition of the body. (p. 132)

mastery-oriented attributions Attributions that credit success to ability, which can be improved through effort, and failure to insufficient effort. Distinguished from *learned helplessness.* (p. 333)

matters of personal choice Concerns that do not involve rights or the welfare of others and, therefore, are up to the individual, such as choice of friends, hairstyle, and leisure activities. Distinguished from *moral imperatives* and *social conventions.* (p. 269)

maximum lifespan The genetic limit to length of life for a person free of external risk factors. Distinguished from *average life expectancy* and *average healthy life expectancy.* (p. 566)

meiosis The process of cell division through which gametes are formed and in which the number of chromosomes in each cell is halved. (p. 47)

memory strategies Deliberate mental activities that improve the likelihood of remembering. (p. 238)

menarche First menstruation. (p. 366)

menopause The end of menstruation and, therefore, of a woman's reproductive capacity. (p. 504)

mental representation An internal depiction of information that the mind can manipulate, including images and concepts. (p. 154)

mental strategies In information processing, procedures that operate on and transform information, increasing the chances that we will retain information, use it efficiently, and think flexibly, adapting the information to changing circumstances. (p. 161)

mesosystem In ecological systems theory, connections between a person's microsystems, or immediate settings. Distinguished from *microsystem, exosystem, macrosystem,* and *chronosystem.* (p. 25)

metacognition Thinking about thought; a coherent set of ideas about mental activities. (p. 239)

microsystem In ecological systems theory, the innermost level of the environment, consisting of activities and interaction patterns in the person's immediate surroundings. Distinguished from *mesosystem, exosystem, macrosystem,* and *chronosystem.* (p. 24)

midlife crisis Inner turmoil and self-doubt that prompt major restructuring of the personality during the transition to middle adulthood. Characterizes the experience of only a minority of adults. (p. 536)

mirror neurons Specialized cells in motor areas of the cerebral cortex in primates that underlie the ability to imitate by firing identically when a primate hears or sees an action and when it carries out the action on its own. (p. 136)

mitosis The process of cell duplication, in which each new cell receives an exact copy of the original chromosomes. (p. 46)

moral imperatives Rules and expectations that protect people's rights and welfare. Distinguished from *social conventions* and *matters of personal choice.* (p. 269)

moral self-relevance The degree to which morality is central to an individual's self-concept. (p. 412)

mortality The phase of dying in which the individual passes into permanent death. Distinguished from *agonal phase* and *clinical death.* (p. 640)

mourning The culturally specified expression of the bereaved person's thoughts and feelings through funerals and other rituals. (p. 659)

mutation A sudden change in a segment of DNA. (p. 51)

myelination The coating of neural fibers with an insulating fatty sheath, called *myelin,* that improves the efficiency of message transfer. (p. 122)

N

naturalistic observation A research method in which the researcher goes into the natural environment to observe the behavior of interest. Distinguished from *structured observation.* (p. 27)

natural, or **prepared, childbirth** A group of techniques aimed at reducing pain and medical intervention and making childbirth as rewarding an experience as possible. Typically includes classes that provide information about the birth process, relaxation and breathing techniques designed to counteract the pain of uterine contractions, and a labor coach who offers encouragement and affection. (p. 99)

nature–nurture controversy Disagreement among theorists about whether genetic or environmental factors are more important influences on development. (p. 7)

neglected children Children who are seldom chosen, either positively or negatively, on self-report measures of peer acceptance. Distinguished from *popular, rejected,* and *controversial children.* (p. 341)

Neonatal Behavioral Assessment Scale (NBAS) A test used to assess the behavior of the newborn baby, including reflexes, muscle tone, state changes, and responsiveness to physical and social stimuli. (p. 113)

neural network view A view that attributes age-related slowing of cognitive processing to breaks in neural networks as neurons die. The brain adapts by forming bypasses—new synaptic connections that go around the breaks but are less efficient. Distinguished from *information-loss view.* (p. 521)

neural tube The primitive spinal cord that develops from the ectoderm, the top of which swells to form the brain. (p. 83)

neurofibrillary tangles A structural change in the cerebral cortex associated with Alzheimer's disease in which bundles of twisted threads appear that are the product of collapsed neural structures. (p. 584)

neurons Nerve cells that store and transmit information. (p. 121)

neurotransmitters Chemicals released by neurons that cross the synapse to send messages to other neurons. (p. 122)

niche-picking A type of genetic–environmental correlation in which individuals actively choose environments that complement their heredity. (p. 73)

nonnormative influences Influences on lifespan development that are irregular, in that they happen to just one or a few individuals and do not follow a predictable timetable. (p. 13)

nonorganic failure to thrive A growth disorder, usually present by 18 months of age, that is caused by lack of affection and stimulation. Affected infants show signs of marasmus although no organic cause exists for the failure to grow. (p. 133)

non-rapid-eye-movement (NREM) sleep A "regular" sleep state in which the body is almost motionless and heart rate, breathing, and brain wave activity are slow and regular. Distinguished from *rapid-eye-movement (REM) sleep.* (p. 108)

nonsocial activity Unoccupied, onlooker behavior and solitary play. Distinguished from *parallel, associative,* and *cooperative play.* (p. 261)

normal distribution The bell-shaped distribution that results when individual differences are measured in large samples. Most scores cluster around the mean, or average, with progressively fewer falling toward the extremes. (p. 168)

normative approach An approach in which measures of behavior are taken on large numbers of individuals and age-related averages are computed to represent typical development. (p. 14)

O

obesity A greater-than-20-percent increase over healthy body weight, based on the body mass index, a ratio of weight to height associated with body fat. (p. 292)

object permanence The understanding that objects continue to exist when they are out of sight. (p. 154)

operant conditioning A form of learning in which a spontaneous behavior is followed by a stimulus that changes the probability that the behavior will occur again. (p. 134)

optimal aging Aging in which gains are maximized and losses minimized. (p. 632)

ordinality The mathematical principle specifying order relationships between quantities, such as three is more than two and two is more than one. (p. 243)

organization In Piaget's theory, the internal rearrangement and linking together of schemes so that they form a strongly interconnected cognitive system. In information processing, a memory strategy that involves grouping related items together to improve recall. (p. 152, p. 303)

osteoarthritis A form of arthritis characterized by deteriorating cartilage on the ends of bones of frequently used joints, which leads to swelling, stiffness, and loss of flexibility. Otherwise known as "wear-and-tear" arthritis or "degenerative joint disease." Distinguished from *rheumatoid arthritis.* (p. 581)

osteoporosis Severe age-related bone loss, which greatly magnifies the risk of bone fractures. (p. 513)

overextension An early vocabulary error in which a word is applied too broadly, to a wider collection of objects and events than is appropriate. Distinguished from *underextension.* (p. 176)

overregularization Extension of regular grammatical rules to words that are exceptions. (p. 250)

P

palliative, or **comfort, care** Care for terminally ill, suffering patients that relieves pain and other symptoms (such as nausea, breathing difficulties, insomnia, and depression), with the goal of protecting the patient's quality of remaining life rather than prolonging life. (p. 652)

parallel play A form of limited social participation in which a child plays near other children with similar materials but does not interact with them. Distinguished from *nonsocial, associative,* and *cooperative play.* (p. 261)

parental imperative theory A theory that claims that identification with traditional gender roles is maintained during the active parenting years to help ensure the survival of children but that when children reach adulthood, parents are free to express the "other-gender" side of their personalities. (p. 541)

partial fetal alcohol syndrome (p-FAS) A form of fetal alcohol spectrum disorder characterized by facial abnormalities and brain injury, but less severe than fetal alcohol syndrome. Usually seen in children whose mothers drank alcohol in smaller quantities during pregnancy. (p. 90)

passionate love Love based on intense sexual attraction. Distinguished from *companionate love.* (p. 474)

passive euthanasia The practice of withholding or withdrawing life-sustaining treatment, permitting a patient to die naturally. Distinguished from *voluntary active euthanasia.* (p. 654)

peer acceptance Likability, or the extent to which a child is viewed by a group of agemates, such as classmates, as a worthy social partner. (p. 341)

peer group A collective of peers who generate unique values and standards for behavior and a social structure of leaders and followers. (p. 339)

peer victimization A destructive form of peer interaction in which certain children become frequent targets of verbal and physical attacks or other forms of abuse. (p. 343)

permissive child-rearing style A child-rearing style that is high in acceptance but overindulging or inattentive, low in control, and lenient rather than appropriate in autonomy granting. Distinguished from *authoritative, authoritarian,* and *uninvolved child-rearing styles.* (p. 279)

persistent vegetative state A state resulting from absence of brain-wave activity in the cerebral cortex in which the person is unconscious and displays no voluntary movements. (p. 641)

personal fable Adolescents' belief that they are special and unique. Leads them to conclude that others cannot possibly understand their thoughts and feelings and may promote a sense of invulnerability to danger. (p. 387)

perspective taking The capacity to imagine what other people may be thinking and feeling. (p. 336)

phenotype An individual's directly observable physical and behavioral characteristics, which are determined by both genetic and environmental factors. Distinguished from *genotype.* (p. 45)

phobia An intense, unmanageable fear that leads to persistent avoidance of the feared situation. (p. 352)

phonics approach An approach to beginning reading instruction that emphasizes coaching children on phonics—the basic rules for translating written symbols into sounds—before exposing them to complex reading material. Distinguished from the *whole-language approach.* (p. 307)

phonological awareness The ability to reflect on and manipulate the sound structure of spoken language, as indicated by sensitivity to changes in sounds within words, to rhyming, and to incorrect pronunciation. A strong predictor of emergent literacy. (p. 242)

physical aggression A form of aggression that harms others through physical injury to themselves or their property. Distinguished from *verbal aggression* and *relational aggression.* (p. 269)

pituitary gland A gland located at the base of the brain that releases hormones that induce physical growth. (p. 219)

placenta The organ that permits exchange of nutrients and waste products between the bloodstreams of the mother and the embryo, while also preventing the mother's and embryo's blood from mixing directly. (p. 82)

polygenic inheritance A pattern of inheritance in which many genes influence a characteristic. (p. 52)

popular-antisocial children A subgroup of popular children who are admired for their socially adept yet belligerent behavior. Includes "tough" boys who are athletically skilled, aggressive, and poor students, as well as relationally aggressive boys and girls. Distinguished from *popular-prosocial children.* (p. 341)

popular children Children who receive many positive votes on self-report measures of peer acceptance, indicating they are well-liked. Distinguished from *rejected, controversial,* and *neglected children.* (p. 341)

popular-prosocial children A subgroup of popular children who combine academic and social competence. Distinguished from *popular-antisocial children.* (p. 341)

possible selves Future-oriented representations of what one hopes to become and what one is afraid of becoming. The temporal dimension of self-concept. (p. 538)

postconventional level Kohlberg's highest level of moral development, in which individuals define morality in terms of abstract principles and values that apply to all situations and societies. (p. 408)

postformal thought Cognitive development beyond Piaget's formal operational stage. (p. 451)

practical problem solving Problem solving that requires people to size up real-world situations and analyze how best to achieve goals that have a high degree of uncertainty. (p. 524)

pragmatics The practical, social side of language, concerned with how to engage in appropriate and effective communication. (p. 250)

pragmatic thought In Labouvie-Vief's theory, a structural advance in thinking in adulthood, characterized by the use of logic as a tool for solving real-world problems and by the acceptance of contradictions as part of existence. (p. 452)

preconventional level Kohlberg's first level of moral development, in which children accept the rules of authority figures and judge actions by their consequences, viewing behaviors that result in punishment as bad and those that lead to rewards as good. (p. 407)

premenstrual syndrome (PMS) An array of physical and psychological symptoms that usually appear 6 to 10 days prior to menstruation. The most common are abdominal cramps, fluid retention, diarrhea, tender breasts, backache, headache, fatigue, tension, irritability, and depression. (p. 449)

prenatal diagnostic methods Medical procedures that permit detection of developmental problems before birth. (p. 56)

preoperational stage Piaget's second stage of cognitive development, spanning 2 to 7 years of age, characterized by an extraordinary increase in representational, or symbolic, activity, although thought is not yet logical. (p. 227)

presbycusis Age-related hearing impairment, beginning around age 50 with noticeable hearing loss at high frequencies, which gradually extends to all frequencies. (p. 503)

presbyopia A condition of aging in which, around age 60, the lens of the eye loses its capacity to adjust to objects at varying distances. (p. 502)

preterm infants Infants born several weeks or more before their due date. (p. 102)

primary aging Genetically influenced age-related declines in the functioning of organs and systems that affect all members of our species and occur even in the context of overall good health. Also called *biological aging.* Distinguished from *secondary aging.* (p. 580)

primary sexual characteristics Physical features that involve the reproductive organs (ovaries, uterus, and vagina in females; penis, scrotum, and testes in males). Distinguished from *secondary sexual characteristics.* (p. 365)

private speech Self-directed speech that children use to plan and guide their own behavior. (p. 234)

proactive aggression A type of aggression in which children act to fulfill a need or desire—obtain an object, privilege, space, or social reward, such as adult attention—and unemotionally attack a person to achieve their goal. Also called *instrumental aggression.* Distinguished from *reactive aggression.* (p. 269)

problem-centered coping A strategy for managing emotion in which the individual appraises the situation as changeable, identifies the difficulty, and decides what to do about it. Distinguished from *emotion-centered coping.* (p. 335)

Project Head Start A U.S. federal early intervention program that provides children from low-income families with a year or two of preschool education, along with nutritional and health services, and that encourages parent involvement in program planning and children's learning and development. (p. 245)

propositional thought A type of formal operational reasoning involving the ability to evaluate the logic of propositions (verbal statements) without referring to real-world circumstances. (p. 383)

prosocial, or **altruistic, behavior** Actions that benefit another person without any expected reward for the self. (p. 260)

prospective memory Recall that involves remembering to engage in planned actions in the future. (p. 593)

proximodistal trend An organized pattern of physical growth and motor control that proceeds from the center of the body outward. Distinguished from *cephalocaudal trend.* (p. 121)

psychoanalytic perspective An approach to personality development introduced by Freud that assumes people move through a series of stages in which they confront conflicts between biological drives and social expectations. The way these conflicts are resolved determines the person's ability to learn, to get along with others, and to cope with anxiety. (p. 15)

psychological control Parental behaviors that intrude on and manipulate children's verbal expressions, individuality, and attachments to parents. (p. 279)

psychosexual theory Freud's theory, which emphasizes that how parents manage children's sexual and aggressive drives in the first few years is crucial for healthy personality development. (p. 15)

psychosocial dwarfism A growth disorder, usually appearing between 2 and 15 years of age, caused by extreme emotional deprivation. It is characterized by decreased growth hormone secretion, very short stature, immature skeletal age, and serious adjustment problems, which help distinguish it from normal shortness. (p. 219)

psychosocial theory Erikson's theory, which emphasizes that at each Freudian stage, individuals not only develop a unique personality but also acquire attitudes and skills that help them become active, contributing members of their society. Recognizes the lifespan nature of development and the impact of culture. (p. 15)

puberty Biological changes at adolescence that lead to an adult-sized body and sexual maturity. (p. 361)

public policies Laws and government programs designed to improve current conditions. (p. 67)

punishment In operant conditioning, removal of a desirable stimulus or presentation of an unpleasant stimulus, either of which decreases the occurrence of a response. (p. 134)

R

random assignment An evenhanded procedure for assigning participants to treatment conditions in an experiment, such as drawing numbers out of a hat or flipping a coin. Increases the chances that participants' characteristics will be equally distributed across treatment groups. (p. 34)

range of reaction Each person's unique, genetically determined response to a range of environmental conditions. (p. 72)

rapid-eye-movement (REM) sleep An "irregular" sleep state in which brain wave activity is similar to that of the waking state; eyes dart beneath the lids; heart rate, blood pressure, and breathing are uneven; and slight body movements occur. Distinguished from *non-rapid-eye-movement (NREM) sleep.* (p. 108)

reactive aggression An angry, defensive response to provocation or a blocked goal that is meant to hurt another person. Also called *hostile aggression.* Distinguished from *proactive aggression.* (p. 269)

realistic period Period of vocational development in which older adolescents and young adults narrow their vocational options, engaging in further exploration before focusing on a general vocational category and, slightly later, settling on a single occupation. Distinguished from *fantasy period* and *tentative period.* (p. 456)

recall A type of memory that involves remembering a stimulus that is not present. Distinguished from *recognition.* (p. 163)

recasts Adult responses that restructure children's grammatically inaccurate speech into correct form. (p. 251)

recognition A type of memory that involves noticing whether a stimulus is identical or similar to one previously experienced. Distinguished from *recall.* (p. 163)

recovery Following habituation, an increase in responsiveness to a new stimulus. (p. 135)

referential style of language learning A style of early language learning in which toddlers use language mainly to name things, producing many words that refer to objects. Distinguished from *expressive style of language learning.* (p. 177)

reflex An inborn, automatic response to a particular form of stimulation. (p. 106)

rehearsal A memory strategy that involves repeating information to oneself to improve recall. (p. 303)

reinforcer In operant conditioning, a stimulus that increases the occurrence of a response. (p. 134)

rejected-aggressive children A subgroup of rejected children who show high rates of conflict, physical and relational aggression, and hyperactive, inattentive, and impulsive behavior. Distinguished from *rejected-withdrawn children.* (p. 342)

rejected children Children who receive many negative votes on self-report measures of peer acceptance, indicating they are actively disliked. Distinguished from *popular, controversial,* and *neglected children.* (p. 341)

rejected-withdrawn children A subgroup of rejected children who are passive and socially awkward. Distinguished from *rejected-aggressive children.* (p. 342)

relational aggression A form of aggression that damages another's peer relationships through social exclusion, malicious gossip, or friendship manipulation. Distinguished from *physical aggression* and *verbal aggression.* (p. 269)

relativistic thinking In Perry's theory, the cognitive approach typical of older college students, who view all knowledge as embedded in a framework of thought and, therefore, give up the possibility of absolute truth in favor of multiple truths, each relative to its context. Distinguished from *dualistic thinking.* (p. 452)

reminiscence The process of telling stories about people and events from the past and reporting associated thoughts and feelings. (p. 606)

remote memory Recall of events that happened long ago. (p. 593)

resilience The ability to adapt effectively in the face of threats to development. (p. 10)

resistant attachment The attachment pattern characterizing infants who remain close to the parent and fail to explore before separation, are usually distressed when the parent leaves, and combine clinginess with angry, resistive behavior when the parent returns. Distinguished from *secure, avoidant,* and *disorganized/disoriented attachment.* (p. 198)

reticular formation A structure in the brain stem that maintains alertness and consciousness. (p. 218)

reversibility The ability to think through a series of steps in a problem and then mentally reverse direction, returning to the starting point. Distinguished from *irreversibility.* (p. 299)

rheumatoid arthritis A form of arthritis in which an autoimmune response leads to inflammation of connective tissue, particularly the membranes that line the joints, resulting in overall stiffness, inflammation, aching, deformed joints, and serious loss of mobility. Distinguished from *osteoarthritis.* (p. 581)

Rh factor incompatibility A condition that arises when the Rh protein is present in the fetus's blood but not in the mother's, causing the mother to build up antibodies. If these enter the fetus's system, they destroy red blood cells, reducing the oxygen supply to organs and tissues. Mental retardation, miscarriage, heart damage, or infant death can occur. (p. 94)

rough-and-tumble play A form of peer interaction involving friendly chasing and play-fighting that emerges in the preschool years and peaks in middle childhood. In our evolutionary past, it may have been important for the development of fighting skills. (p. 297)

S

sandwich generation A term used to describe middle-aged adults who must care for multiple generations above and below them at the same time. (p. 550)

scaffolding Adjusting the support offered during a teaching session to fit the learner's current level of performance. Direct instruction is offered when a task is new; less help is provided as competence increases, thereby keeping the task within the zone of proximal development. (p. 235)

scheme In Piaget's theory, a specific psychological structure, or organized way of making sense of experience, that changes with age. (p. 152)

scripts General descriptions of what occurs and when it occurs in a particular situation, used to organize and interpret everyday experiences. (p. 238)

secondary aging Declines due to hereditary defects and environmental influences, such as poor diet, lack of exercise, disease, substance abuse, environmental pollution, and psychological stress. Distinguished from *primary aging.* (p. 580)

secondary friends People who are not intimates but with whom an individual spends time occasionally, such as a group that meets for lunch, bridge, or museum tours. (p. 625)

secondary sexual characteristics Physical features visible on the outside of the body that serve as signs of sexual maturity but do not involve the reproductive organs (for example, breast development in females, appearance of underarm and pubic hair in both sexes). Distinguished from *primary sexual characteristics.* (p. 365)

secular trend A change from one generation to the next in an aspect of development, such as body size or pubertal timing. (p. 367)

secure attachment The attachment pattern characterizing infants who use the parent as a secure base from which to explore, may be distressed by parental separation, but actively seek contact and are easily comforted by the parent when she returns. Distinguished from *avoidant, resistant,* and *disorganized/disoriented attachment.* (p. 198)

secure base The familiar caregiver as a point from which the baby explores, venturing into the environment and then returning for emotional support. (p. 186)

selective optimization with compensation A set of strategies used by elders who sustain high levels of functioning. They narrow their goals, *selecting* personally valued activities as a way of *optimizing* returns from their diminishing energy while also finding new ways of *compensating* for losses. (p. 591)

self-care children Children who are without adult supervision for some period of time after school. (p. 351)

self-concept The set of attributes, abilities, attitudes, and values that an individual believes defines who he or she is. (p. 256)

self-conscious emotions Emotions involving injury to or enhancement of the sense of self, such as guilt, shame, embarrassment, envy, and pride. (p. 188)

self-esteem An aspect of self-concept that involves judgments about one's own worth and the feelings associated with those judgments. (p. 258)

self-recognition Identification of the self as a physically unique being. (p. 207)

sensitive caregiving Caregiving that involves responding promptly, consistently, and appropriately to infants and holding them tenderly and carefully. (p. 200)

sensitive period A time that is optimal for certain capacities to emerge and in which the individual is especially responsive to environmental influences. (p. 23)

sensorimotor stage Piaget's first stage, spanning the first two years of life, during which infants and toddlers "think" with their eyes, ears, hands, and other sensorimotor equipment. (p. 152)

sensory register The part of the information-processing system in which sights and sounds are represented directly and stored briefly. (p. 161)

separation anxiety An infant's distressed reaction to the departure of the familiar caregiver. (p. 197)

seriation The ability to order items along a quantitative dimension, such as length or weight. (p. 299)

sequential designs Developmental designs in which investigators conduct several similar cross-sectional or longitudinal studies (called *sequences*) at varying times. Some sequential designs combine longitudinal and cross-sectional strategies. (p. 36)

sex chromosomes The twenty-third pair of chromosomes, which determines the sex of the individual. In females, it is called *XX*; in males, *XY*. (p. 47)

skipped-generation family A family structure in which children live with grandparents but apart from parents. (p. 548)

sleep apnea A condition in which breathing ceases for 10 seconds or longer during sleep, resulting in many brief awakenings. (p. 571)

slow-to-warm-up child A child whose temperament is characterized by inactivity; mild, low-key reactions to environmental stimuli; negative mood; and slow adjustment to new experiences. Distinguished from *easy child* and *difficult child.* (p. 190)

small-for-date infants Infants whose birth weight is below their expected weight considering the length of the pregnancy. Some are full term; others are preterm infants who are especially underweight. (p. 102)

social clock Age-graded expectations for major life events, such as beginning a first job, getting married, birth of the first child, buying a home, and retiring. (p. 471)

social comparisons Judgments of one's own appearance, abilities, and behavior in relation to those of others. (p. 330)

social-constructivist classroom A classroom grounded in Vygotsky's sociocultural theory, in which children participate in a wide range of challenging activities with teachers and peers, with whom they jointly construct understandings. Distinguished from *traditional* and *constructivist classrooms.* (p. 320)

social conventions Customs determined solely by consensus, such as table manners and politeness rituals. Distinguished from *moral imperatives* and *matters of personal choice.* (p. 269)

social convoy A model of age-related changes in social networks, which views the individual as moving through life within a cluster of relationships. Close ties are in the inner circle, less close ties on the outside. With age, people change places in the convoy, new ties are added, and some are lost entirely. (p. 619)

social learning theory An approach that emphasizes the role of modeling, otherwise known as imitation or observational learning, in the development of behavior. (p. 18)

social referencing Actively seeking emotional information from a trusted person in an uncertain situation. (p. 188)

social smile The infant's broad grin evoked by the parent's communication. First appears between 6 and 10 weeks of age. (p. 185)

sociocultural theory Vygotsky's theory, in which children acquire the ways of thinking and behaving that make up a community's culture through cooperative dialogues with more knowledgeable members of society. (p. 23)

sociodramatic play The make-believe play with others that is under way around age 2 and increases rapidly during the next few years. (p. 228)

socioeconomic status (SES) A measure of an individual's or a family's social position and economic well-being that combines three related, but not completely overlapping, variables: years of education, prestige of and skill required by one's job, and income. (p. 60)

socioemotional selectivity theory A social theory of aging that states that social interaction in late adulthood extends lifelong selection processes. According to this view, physical and psychological aspects of aging lead to an increased emphasis on the emotion-regulating function of social interaction. Consequently, older adults prefer familiar social partners with whom they have developed pleasurable relationships. Distinguished from *disengagement theory, activity theory,* and *continuity theory.* (p. 614)

spermarche First ejaculation of seminal fluid. (p. 366)

stage A qualitative change in thinking, feeling, and behaving that characterizes a specific period of development. (p. 6)

standardization The practice of giving a newly constructed test to a large, representative sample of individuals and using the results as the standard for interpreting individual scores. (p. 168)

states of arousal Different degrees of sleep and wakefulness. (p. 108)

statistical learning capacity Infants' ability to analyze the speech stream for regularly occurring sound sequences, through which they acquire a stock of speech structures for which they will later learn meanings. (p. 141)

stereotype threat The fear of being judged on the basis of a negative stereotype, which can trigger anxiety that interferes with performance. (p. 314)

stranger anxiety The infant's expression of fear in response to unfamiliar adults, which appears in many babies in the second half of the first year. (p. 186)

Strange Situation A laboratory procedure involving short separations from and reunions with the parent, designed to assess the quality of infant caregiver attachment between 1 and 2 years of age. (p. 198)

structured interview An interview method in which each participant is asked the same questions in the same way. Distinguished from *clinical interview.* (p. 29)

structured observation A method in which the investigator sets up a laboratory situation that evokes the behavior of interest so that every participant has an equal opportunity to display the response. Distinguished from *naturalistic observation.* (p. 28)

subculture A group of people with beliefs and customs that differ from those of the larger culture. (p. 66)

sudden infant death syndrome (SIDS) The unexpected death, usually during the night, of an infant under 1 year of age that remains unexplained after thorough investigation. (p. 110)

sympathy Feelings of concern or sorrow for another's plight. (p. 260)

synapses The gaps between neurons, across which chemical messages are sent. (p. 121)

synaptic pruning Loss of synapses by seldom-stimulated neurons, thereby returning them to an uncommitted state so they can support future development. (p. 122)

T

talent Outstanding performance in a specific field. (p. 323)

telegraphic speech Toddlers' two-word utterances that, like a telegram, focus on high-content words while omitting smaller, less important words. (p. 176)

telomeres A special type of DNA located at the ends of chromosomes—serving as a "cap" to protect the ends from destruction—that shortens with each cell duplication. Eventually so little remains that the cells no longer duplicate at all. (p. 433)

temperament Early-appearing, stable individual differences in reactivity (quickness and intensity of emotional arousal, attention, and motor activity) and self-regulation (strategies that modify that reactivity). (p. 190)

tentative period Period of vocational development in which adolescents think about careers in more complex ways, at first in terms of their interests and soon—as they become more aware of personal and educational requirements for different vocations—in terms of their abilities and values. Distinguished from *fantasy period* and *realistic period.* (p. 456)

teratogen Any environmental agent that causes damage during the prenatal period. (p. 85)

terminal decline Marked acceleration in deterioration of cognitive functioning prior to death. (p. 597)

thanatology An interdisciplinary field devoted to the study of death and dying. (p. 640)

theory An orderly, integrated set of statements that describes, explains, and predicts behavior. (p. 5)

theory of multiple intelligences Gardner's theory, which identifies eight independent intelligences on the basis of distinct sets of processing operations that permit individuals to engage in a wide range of culturally valued activities. (p. 311)

Third Age A new phase of late adulthood extending from ages 65 to 79 or longer, resulting from added years of longevity plus good health and financial stability, in which older adults pursue personally enriching interests and goals. (p. 607)

thyroid-stimulating hormone (TSH) A pituitary hormone that stimulates the thyroid gland to release thyroxine, which is necessary for brain development and for growth hormone to have its full impact on body size. (p. 219)

time out A form of mild punishment that involves removing children from the immediate setting until they are ready to act appropriately. (p. 268)

traditional classroom A classroom in which the teacher is the sole authority for knowledge, rules, and decision making. Students are relatively passive—listening, responding when called on, and completing teacher-assigned tasks. Their progress is evaluated by how well they keep up with a uniform set of standards for their grade. Distinguished from *constructivist* and *social-constructivist classrooms.* (p. 319)

traditional marriage A form of marriage involving clear division of husband's and wife's roles. The man is the head of household and economic provider. The woman devotes herself to caring for her husband and children and creating a nurturant, comfortable home. Distinguished from *egalitarian marriage.* (p. 479)

transitive inference The ability to seriate, or order items along a quantitative dimension, mentally. (p. 300)

triarchic theory of successful intelligence Sternberg's theory, in which intelligent behavior involves balancing three broad, interacting intelligences—analytical intelligence, creative intelligence, and practical intelligence—to achieve success in life, according to one's personal goals and the requirements of one's cultural community. (p. 310)

triangular theory of love Sternberg's view of love as including three components—intimacy, passion, and commitment—that shift in emphasis as romantic relationships develop. (p. 472)

trimesters Three equal time periods into which prenatal development is sometimes divided, each of which lasts three months. (p. 83)

Type A behavior pattern A behavior pattern characterized by extreme competitiveness, ambition, impatience, hostility, angry outbursts, and a sense of time pressure. (p. 514)

U

umbilical cord The long cord connecting the prenatal organism to the placenta that delivers nutrients and removes waste products. (p. 82)

unconditioned response (UCR) In classical conditioning, a reflexive response that is produced by an unconditioned stimulus (UCS). Distinguished from *conditioned response.* (p. 133)

unconditioned stimulus (UCS) In classical conditioning, a stimulus that leads to a reflexive response. Distinguished from *conditioned stimulus.* (p. 133)

underextension An early vocabulary error in which a word is applied too narrowly, to a smaller number of objects and events than is appropriate. Distinguished from *overextension.* (p. 176)

uninhibited, or sociable, child A child whose temperament is such that he or she displays positive emotion to and approaches novel stimuli. Distinguished from *inhibited,* or *shy, child.* (p. 191)

uninvolved child-rearing style A child-rearing style that combines low acceptance and involvement with little control and general indifference to issues of autonomy. Distinguished from *authoritative, authoritarian,* and *permissive child-rearing styles.* (p. 280)

V

verbal aggression A type of aggression that harms others through threats of physical aggression, name-calling, or hostile teasing. Distinguished from *physical aggression* and *relational aggression.* (p. 269)

vernix A white, cheeselike substance that covers the fetus, preventing the skin from chapping due to constant exposure to amniotic fluid. (p. 84)

violation-of-expectation method A method in which researchers show babies an expected event (one that follows physical laws) and an unexpected event (a variation of the first event that violates physical laws). Heightened attention to the unexpected event suggests that the infant is "surprised" by a deviation from physical reality and, therefore, is aware of that aspect of the physical world. (p. 155)

visual acuity Fineness of visual discrimination. (p. 113)

voluntary active euthanasia The practice of acting directly, at a patient's request, to end suffering before a natural end to life. Distinguished from *passive euthanasia.* (p. 656)

W

whole-language approach An approach to beginning reading instruction that parallels natural language learning by exposing children to text in its complete form, using reading materials that are whole and meaningful to promote appreciation of the communicative function of written language. Distinguished from *phonics approach.* (p. 307)

wisdom A capacity made up of multiple cognitive and personality traits, combining breadth and depth of practical knowledge; the ability to reflect on and apply that knowledge in ways that make life more bearable and worthwhile; emotional maturity, including the ability to listen, evaluate, and give advice; and altruistic creativity, which involves contributing to humanity and enriching others' lives. (p. 595)

working, or **short-term, memory** The part of the information-processing system in which we "work" on a limited amount of information, actively applying mental strategies so the information will be retained and used effectively. (p. 161)

X

X-linked inheritance A pattern of inheritance in which a recessive gene is carried on the X chromosome, so that males are more likely to be affected. (p. 50)

Z

zone of proximal development In Vygotsky's theory, a range of tasks too difficult for a child to do alone but possible with the help of more-skilled partners. (p. 165)

zygote The newly fertilized cell formed by the union of sperm and ovum at conception. (p. 47)

References

A

Aalsma, M., Lapsley, D. K., & Flannery, D. J. (2006). Personal fables, narcissism, and adolescent adjustment. *Psychology in the Schools, 43,* 481–491.

AARP (American Association of Retired Persons). (2002). *The Grandparent Study 2002 report.* Washington, DC: Author.

AARP (American Association of Retired Persons). (2004). *Caregiving in the U.S.* Washington, DC: Author.

AARP (American Association of Retired Persons). (2006). *The state of 50+ America 2006.* Washington, DC: AARP Public Policy Institute.

Abbey, A., & McAuslan, P. (2004). A longitudinal examination of male college students' perpetration of sexual assault. *Journal of Consulting and Clinical Psychology, 72,* 747–756.

Abbey, A., Zawacki, T., Buck, P. O., Clinton, A. M., & McAuslan, P. (2004). Sexual assault and alcohol consumption: What do we know about their relationship and what types of research are still needed? *Aggression and Violent Behavior, 9,* 271–303.

Abbott, S. (1992). Holding on and pushing away: Comparative perspectives on an eastern Kentucky child-rearing practice. *Ethos, 20,* 33–65.

ABC News. (2004). *The American Sex Survey: A peek beneath the sheets.* Retrieved from abcnews.go.com/images/Politics/959a1AmericanSexSurvey.pdf

Abel, E. (2004). Paternal contribution to fetal alcohol syndrome. *Addiction Biology, 9,* 127–133.

Abela, J. R. Z., Hankin, B. L., Haigh, E. A. P., Adams, P., Vinokuroff, T., & Trayhern, L. (2005). Interpersonal vulnerability to depression in high-risk children: The role of insecure attachment and reassurance seeking. *Journal of Clinical Child and Adolescent Psychology, 34,* 182–192.

Aber, J. L., Jones, S. M., & Raver, C. C. (2007). Poverty and child development: New perspectives on a defining issue. In J. L. Aber, S. J. Bishop-Josef, S. M. Jones, K. T. McLearn, & D. Phillips (Eds.), *Child development and social policy: Knowledge for action* (pp. 149–166). Washington, DC: American Psychological Association.

Abikoff, H. B., Jensen, P. S., Arnold, L. L., & Hoza, B. (2002). Observed classroom behavior of children with ADHD: Relationship to gender and comorbidity. *Journal of Abnormal Child Psychology, 30,* 349–359.

Aboud, F. E. (2003). The formation of in-group favoritism and out-group prejudice in young children: Are they distinct attitudes? *Developmental Psychology, 39,* 48–60.

Aboud, F. E., & Amato, M. (2001). Developmental and socialization influences on intergroup bias. In R. Brown & S. Gaertner (Eds.), *Blackwell handbook of social psychology: Intergroup processes* (pp. 65–85). Oxford, UK: Blackwell.

Aboud, F. E., & Doyle, A. (1996). Parental and peer influences on children's racial attitudes. *International Journal of Intercultural Relations, 20,* 371–383.

Abra, J. (1989). Changes in creativity with age: Data, explanations, and further predictions. *International Journal of Aging and Human Development, 28,* 105–126.

Abraham, S. (1998). Satisfaction of participants in university-administered elderhostel programs. *Educational Gerontology, 24,* 529–536.

Achenbach, T. M., Phares, V., Howell, C. T., Rauh, V. A., & Nurcombe, B. (1990). Seven-year outcome of the Vermont program for low-birthweight infants. *Child Development, 61,* 1672–1681.

Acker, M. M., & Davis, M. H. (1992). Intimacy, passion, and commitment in adult romantic relationships: A test of the triangular love theory. *Journal of Social and Personal Relationships, 9,* 21–50.

Acker, M. M., & O'Leary, S. G. (1996). Inconsistency of mothers' feedback and toddlers' misbehavior and negative affect. *Journal of Abnormal Child Psychology, 24,* 703–714.

Ackerman, S., Zuroff, D. C., & Moskowitz, D. S. (2000). Generativity in midlife and young adults: Links to agency, communion, and subjective well-being. *International Journal of Aging and Human Development, 50,* 17–41.

ACT. (2008). *2008 retention/completion summary tables.* Retrieved from www.act.org/research/policymakers/pdf/retain_trends.pdf

Adachi-Mejia, A. M., Longacre, M. R., Gibson, J. J., Beach, M. L., Titus-Ernstoff, L. T., & Dalton, M. A. (2007). Children with a TV in their bedroom at higher risk for being overweight. *International Journal of Obesity, 31,* 644–651.

Adams, G. R., & Marshall, S. (1996). A developmental social psychology of identity: Understanding the person in context. *Journal of Adolescence, 19,* 429–442.

Adams, K. B. (2004). Changing investment in activities and interests in elders' lives: Theory and measurement. *International Journal of Aging and Human Development, 58,* 87–108.

Adams, K. B., Sanders, S., & Auth, E. A. (2004). Loneliness and depression in independent living retirement communities: Risk and resilience factors. *Aging and Mental Health, 8,* 475–485.

Adams, R. G. (1985–1986). Emotional closeness and physical distance between friends: Implications for elderly women living in age-segregated and age-integrated settings. *International Journal of Aging and Human Development, 22,* 55–76.

Adams, R. G., Bleiszner, R., & De Vries, B. (2000). Definitions of friendship in the third age: Age, gender, and study location effects. *Journal of Aging Studies, 14,* 117–133.

Adams, R. G., & Laursen, B. (2001). The organization and dynamics of adolescent conflict with parents and friends. *Journal of Marriage and the Family, 63,* 97–110.

Adams, R. J., & Courage, M. L. (1998). Human newborn color vision: Measurement with chromatic stimuli varying in excitation purity. *Journal of Experimental Child Psychology, 68,* 22–34.

Addington-Hall, J. (2000). Do home deaths increase distress in bereavement? *Palliative Medicine, 14,* 161–162.

Adler, N. E., & Newman, K. (2002). Socioeconomic disparities in health: Pathways and policies. *Health Affairs, 21,* 60–76.

Adolph, K. E. (2000). Specificity of learning: Why infants fall over a veritable cliff. *Psychological Science, 11,* 290–295.

Adolph, K. E. (2002). Learning to keep balance. In R. V. Kail (Ed.), *Advances in child development and behavior* (Vol. 30, pp. 1–40). Boston: Academic Press.

Adolph, K. E., & Berger, S. E. (2006). Motor development. In D. Kuhn & R. Siegler (Eds.), *Handbook of child psychology: Vol. 2. Cognition, perception, and language* (6th ed., pp. 161–213). Hoboken, NJ: Wiley.

Adolph, K. E., & Eppler, M. A. (1998). Development of visually guided locomotion. *Ecological Psychology, 10,* 303–321.

Adolph, K. E., & Eppler, M. A. (1999). Obstacles to understanding: An ecological approach to infant problem solving. In E. Winograd, R. Fivush, & W. Hirst (Eds.), *Ecological approaches to cognition* (pp. 31–58). Mahwah, NJ: Erlbaum.

Adolph, K. E. A., Vereijken, B., & Shrout, P. E. (2003). What changes in infant walking and why. *Child Development, 74,* 475–497.

Affifi, W. A., & Faulkner, S. L. (2000). On being "just friends": The frequency and impact of sexual activity in cross-sex friendships. *Journal of Social and Personal Relationships, 17,* 205–222.

Afifi, T. O., Brownridge, D. A., Cox, B. J., & Sareen J. (2006). Physical punishment, childhood abuse and psychiatric disorders. *Child Abuse and Neglect, 30,* 1093–1103.

Afterschool Alliance. (2004). *America after 3 PM: A household survey on afterschool in America.* Retrieved from www.afterschoolalliance.org/researchFactSheets.cfm

Aggarwal, R., Sentz, J., & Miller, M. A. (2007). Role of zinc administration in prevention of childhood diarrhea and respiratory illnesses: A meta-analysis. *Pediatrics, 119,* 1120–1130.

Agüero-Torres, H., von Strauss, E., Viitanen, M., Winblad, B., & Fratiglioni, L. (2001). Institutionalization in the elderly: The role of chronic diseases and dementia. Cross-sectional and longitudinal data from a population-based study. *Journal of Clinical Epidemiology, 54,* 795–801.

Aguiar, A., & Baillargeon, R. (2002). Developments in young infants' reasoning about occluded objects. *Cognitive Psychology, 45,* 267–336.

Ahlgren, M., Melbye, M., Wohlfahrt, J., & Sørensen, T. I. (2004). Growth patterns and the risk of breast cancer in women. *New England Journal of Medicine, 351,* 1619–1626.

Ahrens, C. J. C., & Ryff, C. D. (2006). Multiple roles and well-being: Sociodemographic and psychological moderators. *Sex Roles, 55,* 801–815.

Ahuja, J. (2005). *Women's entrepreneurship in the United States.* Kansas City, MO: Kauffman Center for Entrepreneurial Leadership, Clearinghouse on Entrepreneurship Education. Retrieved from www.celcee.edu

Aikens, J. W., Bierman, K. L., & Parker, J. G. (2005). Navigating the transition to junior high school: The influence of pre-transition friendship and self-system characteristics. *Social Development, 14,* 42–60.

Ainsworth, M. D. S., Blehar, M. C., Waters, E., & Wall, S. (1978). *Patterns of attachment.* Hillsdale, NJ: Erlbaum.

Aisen, P. S., Schneider, L. S., Sano, M., Diaz-Arrastia, R., van Dyck, C. H., & Weiner, M. F. (2008). High-dose B vitamin supplementation and cognitive decline in Alzheimer disease: A randomized controlled trial. *Journal of the American Medical Association, 15,* 1774–1783.

Ajrouch, K. (2007). Health disparities and Arab-American elders: Does intergenerational support buffer the inequality–health link? *Journal of Social Issues, 63,* 745–758.

Akers, J. F., Jones, R. M., & Coyl, D. D. (1998). Adolescent friendship pairs: Similarities in identity status development, behaviors, attitudes, and intentions. *Journal of Adolescent Research, 13,* 178–201.

Akhtar, N., & Tomasello, M. (2000). The social nature of words and word learning. In R. Golinkoff & K. Hirsh-Pasek (Eds.), *Becoming a word learner: A debate on lexical acquisition.* Oxford, UK: Oxford University Press.

Akimoto, S. A., & Sanbonmatsu, D. M. (1999). Differences in self-effacing behavior between European and Japanese Americans: Effect on competence evaluations. *Journal of Cross-Cultural Psychology, 30,* 159–177.

Akiyama, H., Antonucci, T., Takahashi, K., & Langfahl, E. S. (2003). Negative interactions in close relationships across the lifespan. *Journal of Gerontology, 58B,* P70–P79.

Aksan, N., & Kochanska, G. (2004). Heterogeneity of joy in infancy. *Infancy, 6,* 79–94.

Akshoomoff, N. A., Feroleto, C. C., Doyle, R. E., & Stiles, J. (2002). The impact of early unilateral brain injury on perceptual organization and visual memory. *Neuropsychologia, 40,* 539–561.

Alan Guttmacher Institute. (2001). *Can more progress be made? Teenage sexual and reproductive behavior in developed countries.* New York: Author. Retrieved from www.guttmacher.org

Alan Guttmacher Institute. (2002). Teen pregnancy: Trends and lessons learned. Retrieved from http://www.agi-usa.org/pubs/ib_1-02.html

Alan Guttmacher Institute. (2004). Teen sexuality: Stats & facts. Retrieved from www.fotf.ca/familyfacts/issues/teensexuality/stats.html

Alan Guttmacher Institute. (2005). *Facts in brief: Contraceptive use.* Retrieved from www.guttmacher.org/pubs/fb_contr_use.html

Alan Guttmacher Institute. (2006). *U.S. teenage pregnancy statistics: National and state trends and trends by race and ethnicity.* New York: Author. Retrieved from www.guttmacher.org/pubs/2006/09/12/USTPstats.pdf

Albanes, D., Blair, A., & Taylor, P. R. (1989). Physical activity and risk of cancer in the NHANES I population. *American Journal of Public Health, 79,* 744–750.

Albers, C. A., & Grieve, A. J. (2007). Test review: Bayley, N. (2006). Bayley Scales of Infant and Toddler Development–Third Edition. San Antonio, TX: Harcourt Assessment. *Journal of Psychoeducational Assessment, 25,* 180–190.

Alcohol Concern. (2007). *Advertising alcohol.* Retrieved from www.alcoholconcern.org.uk

Aldridge, M. A., Stillman, R. D., & Bower, T. G. R. (2001). Newborn categorization of vowel-like sounds. *Developmental Science, 4,* 220–232.

Aldwin, C. M., & Levenson, M. (2002). Stress, coping, and health at midlife: A developmental perspective. In M. E. Lachman (Ed.), *Handbook of midlife development* (pp. 188–214). New York: Wiley.

Aldwin, C. M., Spiro, A., III, Levenson, M. R., & Cupertino, A. P. (2001). Longitudinal findings from The Normative Aging Study: III. Personality, individual health trajectories, and mortality. *Psychology and Aging, 16,* 450–465.

Aldwin, C. M., Spiro, A., III, & Park, C. L. (2006). Health, behavior, and optimal aging: A life span developmental perspective. In J. E. Birren & K. W. Schaie (Eds.), *Handbook of the psychology of aging* (6th ed., pp. 85–104). Burlington, MA: Elsevier Academic Press.

Aldwin, C. M., Sutton, K. J., & Lachman, M. (1996). The development of coping resources in adulthood. *Journal of Personality, 64,* 91–113.

Alessandri, S. M., Sullivan, M. W., & Lewis, M. (1990). Violation of expectancy and frustration in early infancy. *Developmental Psychology, 26,* 738–744.

Alexander, J. M., Fabricius, W. V., Fleming, V. M., Zwahr, M., & Brown, S. A. (2003). The development of metacognitive causal explanations. *Learning and Individual Differences, 13,* 227–238.

Ali, L., & Scelfo, J. (2002, December 9). Choosing virginity. *Newsweek,* pp. 60–65.

Alibali, M. W. (1999). How children change their minds: Strategy change can be gradual or abrupt. *Developmental Psychology, 35,* 127–145.

Alink, L. R. A., Mesman, J., van Zeijl, J., Stolk, M. N., Juffer, F., & Koot, H. M. (2006). The early childhood aggression curve: Development of physical aggression in 10- to 50-month-old children. *Child Development, 77,* 954–966.

Alkema, G. E., Wilber, K. H., & Enguidanos, S. M. (2007). Community- and facility-based care. In J. A. Blackburn & C. N. Dulmus (Eds.), *Handbook of gerontology: Evidence-based approaches to theory, practice, and policy* (pp. 455–497). Hoboken, NJ: Wiley.

Allemand, M., Zimprich, D., & Martin, M. (2000). Long-term correlated change in personality traits in old age. *Psychology and Aging, 23,* 545–557.

Allen, J. P., & Hauser, S. T. (1996). Autonomy and relatedness in adolescent–family interactions as predictors of young adults' states of mind regarding attachment. *Development and Psychopathology, 8,* 793–809.

Allen, J. P., Philliber, S., Herrling, S., & Kuperminc, G. P. (1997). Preventing teen pregnancy and academic failure: Experimental evaluation of a developmentally based approach. *Child Development, 64,* 729–742.

Allen, J. P., Porter, M. R., & McFarland, F. C. (2006). Leaders and followers in adolescent close friendships: Susceptibility to peer influence as a predictor of risky behavior, friendship instability, and depression. *Development and Psychopathology, 18,* 155–172.

Allen, J. P., Seitz, V., & Apfel, N. H. (2007). The sexually mature teen as a whole person. In J. L. Aber, S. J. Bishop-Josef, S. M. Jones, K. T. McLearn, & D. A. Phillips (Eds.), *New directions in prevention and intervention for teen pregnancy and parenthood* (pp. 185–199). Washington, DC: American Psychological Association.

Allen, M., & Burrell, N. (1996). Comparing the impact of homosexual and heterosexual parents on children: Meta-analysis of existing research. *Journal of Homosexuality, 32,* 19–35.

Allen, S. E. M., & Crago, M. B. (1996). Early passive acquisition in Inukitut. *Journal of Child Language, 23,* 129–156.

Allen, T. D., & Finkelstein, L. M. (2003). Beyond mentoring: Alternative sources and functions of developmental support. *Career Development Quarterly, 51,* 346–355.

Allison, B. N., & Schultz, J. B. (2004). Parent–adolescent conflict in early adolescence. *Adolescence, 39,* 101–119.

Allumbaugh, D. L., & Hoyt, W. T. (1999). Effectiveness of grief therapy: A meta-analysis. *Journal of Counseling Psychology, 46,* 370–380.

Almeida, D. M., & Horn, M. C. (2004). Is daily life more stressful during middle adulthood? In O. G. Brim, C. D. Ryff, & R. C. Kessler (Eds.), *How healthy are we? A national study of well-being at midlife* (pp. 425–451). Chicago: University of Chicago Press.

Almeida, D. M., Neupert, S. D., Banks, S. R., & Serido, J. (2005). Do daily stress processes account for socioeconomic health disparities? *Journal of Gerontology, 60B,* 34–39.

Al-Namlah, A. S., Fernyhough, C., & Meins, E. (2006). Sociocultural influences on the development of verbal mediation: Private speech and phonological recoding in Saudi Arabian and British samples. *Developmental Psychology, 42,* 117–131.

Alsaker, F. D. (1995). Timing of puberty and reactions to pubertal changes. In M. Rutter (Ed.), *Psychosocial disturbances in young people* (pp. 37–82). New York: Cambridge University Press.

Alter, J. (2008, September 29). It's not just about the boys. Get girls into school. *Newsweek,* pp. 50–51.

Althaus, J., & Wax, J. (2005). Analgesia and anesthesia in labor. *Obstetrics and Gynecology Clinics of North America, 32,* 231–244.

Alwin, D. F., & Wray, L. A. (2005). A life-span developmental perspective on social status and health. *Journal of Gerontology, 60B*(Special Issue II), 7–14.

Alzheimer's Association. (2005). *Communication: Best ways to interact with the person with dementia.* Chicago: Author.

Alzheimer's Association. (2009). 2009 *Alzheimer's di ease facts and figures.* Retrieved from http://www.alz.org/national/documents/report_alzfactsfigures2009.pdf

Amano, S., Kezuka, E., & Yamamoto, A. (2004). Infant shifting attention from an adult's face to an adult's hand: A precursor of joint attention. *Infant Behavior and Development, 27,* 64–80.

Amato, P. R. (2000). The consequences of divorce for adults and children. *Journal of Marriage and Family, 62,* 1269–1287.

Amato, P. R. (2001). Children of divorce in the 1990s: An update of the Amato and Keith (1991) meta-analysis. *Journal of Family Psychology, 15,* 355–370.

Amato, P. R. (2006). Marital discord, divorce, and children's well-being: Results from a 20-year longitudinal study of two generations. In A. Clarke-Stewart & J. Dunn (Eds.), *Families count: Effects on child and adolescent development* (pp. 179–202). New York: Cambridge University Press.

Amato, P. R., & Booth, A. (1995). Change in gender role attitudes and perceived marital quality. *American Sociological Review, 60,* 58–66.

Amato, P. R., & Cheadle, J. (2005). The long reach of divorce: Divorce and child well-being across three generations. *Journal of Marriage and Family, 67,* 191–206.

Amato, P. R., & Fowler, F. (2002). Parenting practices, child adjustment, and family diversity. *Journal of Marriage and the Family, 64,* 703–716.

Amato, P. R., & Rogers, S. J. (1997). A longitudinal study of marital problems and subsequent divorce. *Journal of Marriage and the Family, 59,* 612–624.

Amato, P. R., & Sobolewski, J. M. (2004). The effects of divorce on fathers and children: Nonresidential fathers and stepfathers. In M. E. Lamb (Ed.), *The role of the father in child development* (4th ed., pp. 341–367). Hoboken, NJ: Wiley.

Amba, J. C., & Martinez, G. M. (2006). Childlessness among older women in the United States: Trends and profiles. *Journal of Marriage and Family, 68,* 1045–1056.

Ambert, A.-M. (2005). *Same-sex couples and same-sex parent families: Relationships, parenting, and issues of marriage.* Ontario: Vanier Institute of the Family. Retrieved from www.vifamily.ca/library/publications/samesexd.html

American Academy of Hospice and Palliative Medicine. (2007). Position statement on physician-assisted death. *Journal of Pain and Palliative Care Pharmacotherapy, 21,* 55–57.

American Academy of Pediatrics. (2005a). Breastfeeding and the use of human milk. *Pediatrics, 115,* 496–506.

American Academy of Pediatrics, Subcommittee on Attention-Deficit Hyperactivity Disorder. (2005b). Treatment of attention-deficit hyperactivity disorder. *Pediatrics, 115,* e749–e757.

American Academy of Pediatrics. (2006). Folic acid for the prevention of neural tube defects. *Pediatrics, 104,* 325–327.

American Heart Association. (2008). *Heart and stroke death rates steadily decline; risks still too high.* Retrieved from www.americanheart.org/presenter.jhtml?identifier=3053235

American Heart Association. (2009). *Heart disease and stroke statistics: 2009 update-at-a-glance.* Dallas: Author.

American Hospice Foundation. (2009). *Talking about hospice: Tips for physicians.* Washington, DC: Author.

American Psychiatric Association. (1994). *Diagnostic and statistical manual of mental disorders* (4th ed.). Washington, DC: Author.

American Psychological Association. (2002). Ethical principles of psychologists and code of conduct. *American Psychologist, 57,* 1060–1073.

American Society for Reproductive Medicine. (2004). Smoking and infertility. *Fertility and Sterility, 81,* 1181–1186.

Amsel, E., & Brock, S. (1996). The development of evidence evaluation skills. *Cognitive Development, 11,* 523–550.

Amsel, E., Cottrell, J., Sullivan, J., & Bowden, T. (2005). Anticipating and avoiding regret as a model of adolescent decision-making. In J. Jacobs & P. Kaczynski (Eds.), *The development of judgment and decision-making in children and adolescents* (pp. 119–154). Mahwah, NJ: Erlbaum.

Amsterlaw, J., & Wellman, H. M. (2006). Theories of mind in transition: A micro-genetic study of the development of false belief understanding. *Journal of Cognition and Development, 7,* 139–172.

An, J. S., & Cooney, T. M. (2006). Psychological well-being in mid to late life: The role of generativity development and parent–child relationships across the lifespan. *International Journal of Behavioral Development, 30,* 410–421.

Anand, S. S., Yusuf, S., Jacobs, R., Davis, A. D., Yi, Q., & Gerstein, H. (2001). Risk factors, atherosclerosis, and cardiovascular disease among Aboriginal people in Canada: The study of health assessment and risk evaluation in Aboriginal peoples (SHARE-AP). *Lancet, 358,* 1147–1153.

Andel, R., Crowe, M., Pedersen, N. L., Fratiglioni, L., Johansson, B., & Gatz, M. (2008). Physical exercise at midlife and risk of dementia three decades later: A population-based study of Swedish twins. *Journal of Gerontology, 63,* 62–66.

Andel, R., Vigen, C., Mack, W. J., Clark, L. J., & Gatz, M. (2006). The effect of education and occupational complexity on rate of cognitive decline in Alzheimer's patients. *Journal of the International Neuropsychological Society, 12,* 147–152.

Anderman, E. M., Eccles, J. S., Yoon, K. S., Roeser, R., Wigfield, A., & Blumenfeld, P. (2001). Learning to value mathematics and reading: Relations to mastery and performance-oriented instructional practices. *Contemporary Educational Psychology, 26,* 76–95.

Anderson, C. A. (2004). An update on the effects of violent video games. *Journal of Adolescence, 27,* 113–122.

Anderson, C. A., Berkowitz, L., Donnerstein, E., Huesmann, R., Johnson, J. D., Linz, D., Malamuth, N. M., & Wartella, E. (2003). The influence of media violence on youth. *Psychological Science in the Public Interest, 4*(3), 81–106.

Anderson, D. M., Huston, A. C., Schmitt, K. L., Linebarger, D. L., & Wright, J. C. (2001). Early childhood television viewing and adolescent behavior. *Monographs of the Society for Research in Child Development, 66*(1, Serial No. 264).

Anderson, E. (2000). Exploring register knowledge: The value of "controlled improvisation." In L. Menn & N. B. Ratner (Eds.), *Methods for studying language production* (pp. 225–248). Mahwah, NJ: Erlbaum.

Anderson, J. L., Morgan, J. L., & White, K. S. (2003). A statistical basis for speech sound discrimination. *Language and Speech, 46,* 155–182.

Anderson, M. E., Johnson, D. C., & Batal, H. A. (2005). Sudden infant death syndrome and prenatal maternal smoking: Rising attributed risk in the Back to Sleep era. *BMC Medicine, 3,* 4.

Anderson, P. B., & Savage, J. S. (2005). Social, legal, and institutional context of heterosexual aggression by college women. *Trauma, Violence, and Abuse, 6,* 130–140.

Anderson, P. J., Wood, S. J., Francis, D. E., Coleman, L., Anderson, V., & Boneh, A. (2007). Are neuropsychological impairments in children with early-treated phenylketonuria (PKU) related to white matter abnormalities or elevated phenylalanine levels? *Developmental Neuropsychology, 32,* 645–668.

Anderson, S. E., Dallal, G. E., & Must, A. (2003). Relative weight and race influence average age at menarche: Results from two nationally representative surveys of U.S. girls studied 25 years apart. *Pediatrics, 111,* 844–850.

Anderson, V. A., Catroppa, C., Dudgeon, P., Morse, S. A., Haritou, F., & Rosenfeld, J. V. (2006). Understanding predictors of functional recovery and outcome 30 months following early childhood head injury. *Neuropsychology, 20,* 42–57.

Andersson, B.-E. (1989). Effects of public day care—A longitudinal study. *Child Development, 60,* 857–866.

Andersson, B.-E. (1992). Effects of day care on cognitive and socioemotional competence of thirteen-year-old Swedish schoolchildren. *Child Development, 63,* 20–36.

Andreoletti, C., & Lachman, M. E. (2004). Susceptibility and resilience to memory aging stereotypes: Education matters more than age. *Experimental Aging Research, 30,* 129–148.

Andrews, G., & Halford, G. S. (1998). Children's ability to make transitive inferences: The importance of premise integration and structural complexity. *Cognitive Development, 13,* 479–513.

Andrews, G., & Halford, G. S. (2002). A cognitive complexity metric applied to cognitive development. *Cognitive Psychology, 45,* 475–506.

Andreyeva, T., Puhl, R. M., & Brownell, K. D. (2008). Changes in perceived weight discrimination among Americans, 1995–1996 through 2004–2006. *Obesity, 16,* 1129–1134.

Anetzberger, G. J. (2005). The reality of elder abuse. *Clinical Gerontologist, 28,* 2–25.

Anisfeld, M., Turkewitz, G., Rose, S. A., Rosenberg, F. R., Shelber, F. J., Couturier-Fagan, D. A., Ger, J. S., & Sommer, I. (2001). No compelling evidence that newborns imitate oral gestures. *Infancy, 2,* 111–122.

Annett, M. (2002). *Handedness and brain asymmetry: The right shift theory.* Hove, UK: Psychology Press.

Anslow, P. (1998). Birth asphyxia. *European Journal of Radiology, 26,* 148–153.

Anson, D. S., & Fletcher, J. M. (2007). Gene therapy for disorders affecting children, progress and potential. *Journal of Paediatrics and Child Health, 43,* 323–330.

Anstey, K., & Christensen, H. (2000). Education, activity, health, blood pressure, and apolipoprotein E as predictors of cognitive change in old age: A review. *Gerontology, 46,* 163–177.

Anstey, K. J., Luszcz, M. A., & Sanchez, L. (2001). Two-year decline in vision but not hearing is associated with memory decline in very old adults in a population-based sample. *Gerontology, 47,* 289–293.

Antonini, F. M., Magnolfi, S. U., Petruzzi, E., Pinzani, P., Malentacchi, F., Petruzzi, I., & Masotti, G. (2008). Physical performance and creative activities of centenarians. *Archives of Gerontology and Geriatrics, 46,* 253–261.

Antonucci, T. C. (1994). A life-span view of women's social relations. In B. F. Turner & L. E. Troll (Eds.), *Women growing older* (pp. 239–269). Thousand Oaks, CA: Sage.

Antonucci, T. C., Ajrouch, K. J., & Birditt, K. (2008). Social relations in the Third Age: Assessing strengths and challenges using the convoy model. In J. B. James & P. Wink (Eds.), *Annual review of gerontology and geriatrics* (Vol. 26, pp. 193–209). New York: Springer.

Antonucci, T. C., & Akiyama, H. (1995). Convoys of social relations: Family and friendships within a life span context. In R. Blieszner & V. H. Bedford (Eds.), *Handbook of aging and the family* (pp. 355–371). Westport, CT: Greenwood Press.

Antonucci, T. C., & Akiyama, H. (1997). Concern with others at midlife: Care, comfort, or compromise? In M. E. Lachman & J. B. James (Eds.), *Multiple paths of midlife development* (pp. 145–169). Chicago: University of Chicago Press.

Antonucci, T. C., Akiyama, H., & Merline, A. (2002). Dynamics of social relationships in midlife. In M. E. Lachman (Ed.), *Handbook of midlife development* (pp. 571–598). New York: Wiley.

Antonucci, T. C., Akiyama, H., & Takahashi, K. (2004). Attachment and close relationships across the lifespan. *Attachment and Human Development, 6,* 353–370.

Apgar, V. (1953). A proposal for a new method of evaluation in the newborn infant. *Current Research in Anesthesia and Analgesia, 32,* 260–267.

Aquilino, W. S. (1996). The returning adult child and parental experience at midlife. In C. D. Ryff & M. M. Seltzer (Eds.), *The parental experience in midlife* (pp. 423–458). Chicago: University of Chicago Press.

Aquilino, W. S. (2006). Family relationships and support systems in emerging adulthood. In J. J. Arnett & J. L. Tanner (Eds.), *Emerging adults in America: Coming of age in the 21st century* (pp. 193–218). Washington, DC: American Psychological Association.

Archer, J. (2002). Sex differences in aggression between heterosexual partners: A meta-analytic review. *Psychological Bulletin, 126,* 651–681.

Archer, S. L. (2002). Commentary on "Feminist Perspectives on Erikson's Theory: Their Relevance for Contemporary Identity Development Research." *Identity, 2,* 267–270.

Archer, S. L., & Waterman, A. S. (1990). Varieties of identity diffusions and foreclosures: An exploration of subcategories of the identity statuses. *Journal of Adolescent Research, 5,* 96–111.

Archibald, A. B., Graber, J. A., & Brooks-Gunn, J. (2006). Pubertal processes and physiological growth in adolescence. In G. R. Adams & M. D. Berzonsky (Eds.), *Blackwell handbook of adolescence* (pp. 24–48). Malden, MA: Blackwell.

Ardelt, M. (1998). Social crisis and individual growth: The long-term effects of the Great Depression. *Journal of Aging Studies, 12,* 291–314.

Ardila-Rey, A., & Killen, M. (2001). Middle-class Colombian children's evaluations of personal, moral, and social-conventional interactions in the classroom. *International Journal of Behavioral Development, 25,* 246–255.

Argue, A., Johnson, D. R., & White, L. K. (1999). Age and religiosity: Evidence from a three-wave panel analysis. *Journal for the Scientific Study of Religion, 38,* 423–435.

Arija, V., Esparó, G., Fernández-Ballart, J., Murphy, M. M., Biarnés, E., & Canals, J. (2006). Nutritional status and performance in test of verbal and non-

verbal intelligence in 6 year old children. *Intelligence, 34,* 141–149.
Arking, R. (2006). *Biology of aging: Observations and principles* (3rd ed.). New York: Oxford University Press.
Arking, R., Novoseltsev, V., & Novoseltseva, J. (2004). The human life span is not that limited: The effect of multiple longevity phenotypes. *Journal of Gerontology, 59A,* 697–704.
Arlin, P. K. (1989). Problem solving and problem finding in young artists and young scientists. In M. L. Commons, J. D. Sinnott, F. A. Richards, & C. Armon (Eds.), *Adult development: Vol 1. Comparisons and applications of developmental models* (pp. 197–216). New York: Praeger.
Armstrong, T. D., & Crowther, M. R. (2002). Spirituality among older African Americans. *Journal of Adult Development, 9,* 3–12.
Arnett, J. J. (1997). Young people's conceptions of the transition to adulthood. *Youth and Society, 29,* 1–23.
Arnett, J. J. (2000). Emerging adulthood: A theory of development from the late teens through the twenties. *American Psychologist, 55,* 469–480.
Arnett, J. J. (2001). Conceptions of the transition to adulthood: Perspectives from adolescence to midlife. *Journal of Adult Development, 8,* 133–143.
Arnett, J. J. (2003). Conceptions of the transition to adulthood among emerging adults in American ethnic groups. In J. J. Arnett & N. L. Galambos (Eds.), *New directions for child and adolescent development* (No. 100, pp. 63–75). San Francisco: Jossey-Bass.
Arnett, J. J. (2006). Emerging adulthood: Understanding the new way of coming of age. In J. J. Arnett & J. L. Tanner (Eds.), *Emerging adults in America: Coming of age in the 21st century* (pp. 3–19). Washington, DC: American Psychological Association.
Arnett, J. J. (2007a). Emerging adulthood, a 21st century theory: A rejoinder to Hendry and Kloep. *Child Development Perspectives, 1,* 80–82.
Arnett, J. J. (2007b). Emerging adulthood: What is it and what is it good for? *Child Development Perspectives, 1,* 68–73.
Arnold, D. H., McWilliams, L., & Harvey-Arnold, E. (1998). Teacher discipline and child misbehavior in daycare: Untangling causality with correlational data. *Developmental Psychology, 34,* 276–287.
Arnold, P. (1999). Emotional disorders in deaf children. In V. L. Schwean & D. H. Saklofske (Eds.), *Handbook of psychosocial characteristics of exceptional children* (pp. 493–522). New York: Kluwer.
Arnon, S., Shapsa, A., Forman, L., Regev, R., Bauer, S., & Litmanovitz, I. (2006). Live music is beneficial to preterm infants in the neonatal intensive care unit. *Birth, 33,* 131–136.
Arriaga, X. B., & Foshee, V. A. (2004). Adolescent dating violence: Do adolescents follow in their friends' or their parents' footsteps? *Journal of Interpersonal Violence, 19,* 162–184.
Arsenio, W. F. (2006). Happy victimizers and moral responsibility: Sociocultural and developmental considerations. In M. Schleifer & C. Martiny (Eds.), *Talking to children about responsibility and control of emotions* (pp. 49–69). Calgary, Canada: Detselig Enterprises.
Artistico, D., Cervone, D., & Pezzuti, L. (2003). Perceived self-efficacy and everyday problem solving among young and older adults. *Psychology and Aging, 18,* 68–79.
Artman, L., & Cahan, S. (1993). Schooling and the development of transitive inference. *Developmental Psychology, 29,* 753–759.
Artman, L., Cahan, S., & Avni-Babad, D. (2006). Age, schooling, and conditional reasoning. *Cognitive Development, 21,* 131–145.
Arvanitakis, Z., Wilson, R. S., Bienias, J. L., Evans, D. A., & Bennett, D. A. (2004). Diabetes mellitus and risk of Alzheimer disease and decline in cognitive function. *Archives of Neurology, 61,* 661–666.
Asakawa, K. (2001). Family socialization practices and their effects on the internationalization of educational values for Asian and white American adolescents. *Applied Developmental Science, 5,* 184–194.
Asher, S. R., & Rose, A. J. (1997). Promoting children's social-emotional adjustment with peers. In P. Salovey & D. J. Sluyter (Eds.), *Emotional development and emotional intelligence* (pp. 193–195). New York: Basic Books.
Aslin, R. N., Jusczyk, P. W., & Pisoni, D. B. (1998). Speech and auditory processing during infancy: Constraints on and precursors to language. In D. Kuhn & R. S. Siegler (Eds.), *Handbook of child psychology: Vol. 2. Cognition, perception, and language* (5th ed., pp. 147–198). New York: Wiley.
Assmann, A. (1994). Wholesome knowledge: Concepts of wisdom in a historical and cross-cultural perspective. In D. L. Featherman, R. M. Lerner, & M. Perlmutter (Eds.), *Lifespan development and behavior* (pp. 187–224). Hillsdale, NJ: Erlbaum.
Astington, J. W., & Pelletier, J. (2005). Theory of mind, language, and learning in the early years: Developmental origins of school readiness. In B. D. Homer & C. S. Tamis-LeMonda (Eds.), *The development of social cognition and communication* (pp. 205–230). Mahwah, NJ: Erlbaum.
Astington, J. W., Pelletier, J., & Homer, B. (2002). Theory of mind and epistemological development: The relation between children's second-order false belief understanding and their ability to reason about evidence. *New Ideas in Psychology, 20,* 131–144.
Atance, C. M., & Meltzoff, A. N. (2005). My future self: Young children's ability to anticipate and explain future states. *Cognitive Development, 20,* 341–361.
Atchley, R. C. (1989). A continuity theory of normal aging. *Gerontologist, 29,* 183–190.
Atchley, R. C. (1999). *Continuity and adaptation in aging: Creating positive experiences.* Baltimore, MD: Johns Hopkins University Press.
Atchley, R. C. (2003). Why people cope well with retirement. In J. L. Ronch & J. A. Goldfield (Eds.), *Mental wellness in aging: Strengths-based approaches* (pp. 123–138). Baltimore, MD: Health Professions Press.
Athanasou, J. A. (2002). Vocational pathways in the early part of a career: An Australian study. *Career Development Quarterly, 52,* 78–88.
Atkins, R., Hart, D., & Donnelly, T. M. (2004). Moral identity development and school attachment. In D. Lapsley & D. Narvaez (Eds.), *Moral development, self, and identity* (pp. 65–82). Mahwah, NJ: Erlbaum.
Atkinson, R. C., & Shiffrin, R. M. (1968). Human memory: A proposed system and its control processes. In K. W. Spence & J. T. Spence (Eds.), *Advances in the psychology of learning and motivation* (Vol. 2, pp. 90–195). New York: Academic Press.
Au, T. K., Sidle, A. L., & Rollins, K. B. (1993). Developing an intuitive understanding of conservation and contamination: Invisible particles as a plausible mechanism. *Developmental Psychology, 29,* 286–299.
Aunola, K., Stattin, H., & Nurmi, J.-E. (2000). Parenting styles and adolescents' achievement strategies. *Journal of Adolescence, 23,* 205–222.
Averhart, C. J., & Bigler, R. S. (1997). Shades of meaning: Skin tone, racial attitudes, and constructive memory in African-American children. *Journal of Experimental Child Psychology, 67,* 368–388.
Avery, D. R., McKay, P. F., & Wilson, D. C. (2007). Engaging the aging workforce: The relationships between perceived age similarity, satisfaction with coworkers, and employee engagement. *Journal of Applied Psychology, 92,* 1542–1556.
Avis, N. E. (2003). Depression during the menopausal transition. *Psychology of Women Quarterly, 27,* 91–100.
Avis, N. E., Assmann, S. F., Kravitz, H. M., Ganz, P. A., & Ory, M. (2004). Quality of life in diverse groups of midlife women: Assessing the influence of menopause, health status and psychosocial and demographic factors. *Quality of Life Research, 13,* 933–946.
Avis, N. E., & Crawford, S. (2006). Menopause: Recent research findings. In S. K. Whitbourne & S. L. Willis (Eds.), *The baby boomers grow up: Contemporary perspectives on midlife* (pp. 75–109). Mahwah, NJ: Erlbaum.
Avis, N. E., Crawford, S., & Johannes, C. B. (2002). Menopause. In G. M. Wingood & R. J. DeClemente (Eds.), *Handbook of women's sexual and reproductive health* (pp. 367–391). New York: Kluwer.
Avlund, K., Lund, R., Holstein, B. E., & Due, P. (2004). The impact of structural and functional characteristics of social relations as determinants of functional decline. *Journal of Gerontology,* 59B, 44–56.
Avolio, B. J., & Sosik, J. J. (1999). A lifespan framework for assessing the impact of work on white-collar workers. In S. L. Willis & J. D. Reid (Eds.), *Life in the middle* (pp. 249–274). San Diego, CA: Academic Press.
Axelin, A., Salanterä, S., & Lehtonen, L. (2006). 'Facilitated tucking by parents' in pain management of preterm infants—a randomized crossover trial. *Early Human Development, 82,* 241–247.
Axia, G., & Baroni, R. (1985). Linguistic politeness at different age levels. *Child Development, 56,* 918–927.
Axia, G., Bonichini, S., & Benini, F. (1999). Attention and reaction to distress in infancy: A longitudinal study. *Developmental Psychology, 35,* 500–504.
Axinn, W. G., & Barber, J. S. (1997). Living arrangements and family formation attitudes in early adulthood. *Journal of Marriage and the Family, 59,* 595–611.
Ayala, G. X., Rogers, M., Arredondo, E. M., Campbell, N. R., Baquero, B., Duerksen, S. C., & Elder, J. P. (2008). Away-from-home food intake and risk for obesity: Examining the influence of context. *Obesity, 16,* 1002–1008.

B

Bacallao, M. L., & Smokowski, P. R. (2007). The costs of getting ahead: Mexican family system changes after immigration. *Family Relations, 56,* 52–66.
Bach-y-Rita, P. (2001). Theoretical and practical considerations in the restoration of function after stroke. *Topics in Stroke Rehabilitation, 8,* 1–15.
Baddeley, A. (1993). Working memory and conscious awareness. In A. F. Collins, S. E. Gathercole, M. A. Conway, & P. E. Morris (Eds.), *Theories of memory* (pp. 11–28). Hove, UK: Erlbaum.
Baddeley, A. (2000). Short-term and working memory. In E. Tulving & R. I. M. Craik (Eds.), *The Oxford handbook of memory* (pp. 77–92). New York: Oxford University Press.
Badger, S., Nelson, L. J., & Barry, C. M. (2006). Perceptions of the transition to adulthood among Chinese and American emerging adults. *Inter-*

national Journal of Behavioral Development, 30, 84–93.
Baenninger, M., & Newcombe, N. (1995). Environmental input to the development of sex-related differences in spatial and mathematical ability. *Learning and Individual Differences, 7,* 363–379.
Baer, W. M., & Hanson, L. C. (2000). Families' perception of the added value of hospice in the nursing home. *Journal of the American Geriatric Society, 48,* 879–882.
Bagheri, A. (2007). Individual choice in the definition of death. *Journal of Medical Ethics, 33,* 146–149.
Bagwell, C. L., Bender, S. E., Andreassi, C. L., Kinoshita, T. L., Montarello, S. A., & Muller, J. G. (2005). Friendship quality and perceived relationship changes predict psychosocial adjustment in early adulthood. *Journal of Social and Personal Relationships, 22,* 235–254.
Bagwell, C. L., & Coie, J. D. (2004). The best friendships of aggressive boys: Relationship quality, conflict management, and rule-breaking behavior. *Journal of Experimental Child Psychology, 88,* 5–24.
Bagwell, C. L., Schmidt, M. E., Newcomb, A. F., & Bukowski, W. M. (2001). Friendship and peer rejection as predictors of adult adjustment. In D. W. Nangle & C. A. Erdley (Eds.), *The role of friendship in psychological adjustment* (pp. 25–49). San Francisco: Jossey-Bass.
Bahrick, H. P. (1984). Semantic memory content in permastore: Fifty years of memory for Spanish learned in school. *Journal of Experimental Psychology: General, 113,* 1–29.
Bahrick, H. P., Bahrick, P. O., & Wittlinger, R. P. (1975). Fifty years of memory for names and faces: A cross-sectional approach. *Journal of Experimental Psychology: General, 104,* 54–75.
Bahrick, L. E., Gogate, L. J., & Ruiz, I. (2002). Attention and memory for faces and actions in infancy: The salience of actions over faces in dynamic events. *Child Development, 73,* 1629–1643.
Bahrick, L. E., Hernandez-Reif, M., & Flom, R. (2005). The development of infant learning about specific face–voice relations. *Developmental Psychology, 41,* 541–552.
Bahrick, L. E., Hernandez-Reif, M., & Pickens, J. N. (1997). The effect of retrieval cues on visual preferences and memory in infancy: Evidence for a four-phase attention function. *Journal of Experimental Child Psychology, 67,* 1–20.
Bahrick, L. E., Lickliter, R., & Flom, R. (2004). Intersensory redundancy guides the development of selective attention, perception, and cognition in infancy. *Current Directions in Psychological Science, 13,* 99–102.
Bahrick, L. E., Netto, D., & Hernandez-Reif, M. (1998). Intermodal perception of adult and child faces and voices by infants. *Child Development, 69,* 1263–1275.
Bahrick, L. E., & Pickens, J. N. (1995). Infant memory for object motion across a period of three months: Implications for a four-phase attention function. *Journal of Experimental Child Psychology, 59,* 343–371.
Bai, D. L., & Bertenthal, B. I. (1992). Locomotor status and the development of spatial search skills. *Child Development, 63,* 215–226.
Bailey, J. M., Bobrow, D., Wolfe, M., & Mikach, S. (1995). Sexual orientation of adult sons of gay fathers. *Developmental Psychology, 31,* 124–129.
Bailey, J. M., Dunne, M. P., & Martin, N. G. (2000). Genetic and environmental influences on sexual orientation and its correlates in an Australian twin sample. *Journal of Personality and Social Psychology, 78,* 524–536.
Baillargeon, R. (2000). Reply to Bogartz, Shinskey, and Schilling; Schilling; and Cashon and Cohen. *Infancy, 1,* 447–462.
Baillargeon, R. (2004). Infants' reasoning about hidden objects: Evidence for event-general and event-specific expectations. *Developmental Science, 7,* 391–424.
Baillargeon, R., & DeVos, J. (1991). Object permanence in young infants: Further evidence. *Child Development, 62,* 1227–1246.
Baillargeon, R. H., Zoccolillo, M., Keenan, K., Côté, S., Pérusse, D., Wu, H.-X., & Boivin, M. (2007). Gender differences in physical aggression: A prospective population-based survey of children before and after 2 years of age. *Developmental Psychology, 43,* 13–26.
Baker, J. A. (2006). Contributions of teacher–child relationships to positive school adjustment during elementary school. *Journal of School Psychology, 44,* 211–229.
Baker, J. G. (2002). The influx of women into legal professions: An economic analysis. *Monthly Labor Review, 125,* 14–24.
Balaswamy, S., & Richardson, V. E. (2001). The cumulative effects of life event, personal, and social resources on subjective well-being of elderly widowers. *International Journal of Aging and Human Development, 53,* 311–327.
Balfanz, R., Legters, N., West, T. C., & Weber, L. M. (2007). Are NCLB's measures, incentives, and improvement strategies the right ones for the nation's low-performing high schools? *American Educational Research Journal, 44,* 559–593.
Ball, H. (2006). Parent–infant bed-sharing behavior: Effects of feeding type and presence of father. *Human Nature, 17,* 301–318.
Ball, K., Berch, D. B., Helmers, K. F., Jobe, J. B., Leveck, M. D., & Marsiske, M. (2002). Effects of cognitive training interventions with older adults: A randomized controlled trial. *Journal of the American Medical Association, 288,* 2271–2281.
Ball, M. M., Whittington, F. J., Perkins, M. M., Patterson, V. L., Hollingsworth, C., King, S. V., & Combs, B. L. (2000). Quality of life in assisted living facilities: Viewpoints of residents. *Journal of Applied Gerontology, 19,* 304–325.
Balsam, K. F., Beauchaine, T. P., Rothblum, E. D., & Solomon, S. E. (2008). Three-year follow-up of same-sex couples who had civil unions in Vermont, same-sex couples not in civil unions, and heterosexual married couples. *Developmental Psychology, 44,* 102–116.
Balsano, A. B. (2005). Youth civic engagement in the United States: Understanding and addressing the impact of social impediments on positive youth and community development. *Applied Developmental Science, 9,* 188–201.
Baltes, M. M. (1995, February). Dependency in old age: Gains and losses. *Psychological Science, 4*(1), 14–19.
Baltes, M. M. (1996). *The many faces of dependency in old age.* New York: Cambridge University Press.
Baltes, M. M., Wahl, H.-W., & Reichert, M. (1992). Successful aging in long-term care institutions. In K. W. Schaie & M. P. Lawton (Eds.), *Annual review of gerontology and geriatrics* (pp. 311–337). New York: Springer.
Baltes, P. B. (1997). On the incomplete architecture of human ontogeny: Selection, optimization, and compensation as foundation of developmental theory. *American Psychologist, 52,* 366–380.
Baltes, P. B., Lindenberger, U., & Staudinger, U. M. (2006). Life span theory in developmental psychology. In R. M. Lerner (Ed.), *Handbook of child psychology: Vol. 1. Theoretical models of human development* (6th ed., pp. 569–664). Hoboken, NJ: Wiley.
Baltes, P. B., & Smith, J. (2003). New frontiers in the future of aging: From successful aging of the young old to the dilemmas of the fourth age. *Gerontology, 49,* 123–135.
Baltes, P. B., & Smith, J. (2008). The fascination of wisdom. *Perspectives on Psychological Science, 3,* 56–64.
Baltes, P. B., & Staudinger, U. M. (2000). Wisdom: A metaheuristic (pragmatic) to orchestrate mind and virtue toward excellence. *American Psychologist, 55,* 122–136.
Baltes, P. B., Staudinger, U. M., Maercker, A., & Smith, J. (1995). People nominated as wise: A comparative study of wisdom-related knowledge. *Psychology and Aging, 10,* 155–166.
Bancroft, J. (2002). The medicalization of female sexual dysfunction: The need for caution. *Archives of Sexual Behavior, 31,* 451–455.
Band, G. P. H., van der Molen, M. W., Overtoom, C. C. E., & Verbaten, M. N. (2000). The ability to activate and inhibit speeded responses: Separate developmental trends. *Journal of Experimental Child Psychology, 75,* 263–290.
Bandura, A. (1977). *Social learning theory.* Englewood Cliffs, NJ: Prentice-Hall.
Bandura, A. (1992). Perceived self-efficacy in cognitive development and functioning. *Educational Psychologist, 28,* 117–148.
Bandura, A. (1999). Social cognitive theory of personality. In L. A. Pervin (Ed.), *Handbook of personality: Theory and research* (2nd ed., pp. 154–196). New York: Guilford.
Bandura, A. (2001). Social cognitive theory: An agentic perspective. *Annual Review of Psychology, 52,* 1–26.
Banish, M. T., & Heller, W. (1998). Evolving perspectives on lateralization of function. *Current Directions in Psychological Science, 7,* 1–2.
Banks, M. S. (1980). The development of visual accommodation during early infancy. *Child Development, 51,* 646–666.
Banks, M. S., & Ginsburg, A. P. (1985). Early visual preferences: A review and new theoretical treatment. In H. W. Reese (Ed.), *Advances in child development and behavior* (Vol. 19, pp. 207–246). New York: Academic Press.
Barber, B. K., & Harmon, E. L. (2002). Violating the self: Parental psychological control of children and adolescents. In B. K. Barber (Ed.), *Intrusive parenting: How psychological control affects children and adolescents* (pp. 15–52). Washington, DC: American Psychological Association.
Barber, B. K., & Olsen, J. A. (1997). Socialization in context: Connection, regulation, and autonomy in the family, school, and neighborhood, and with peers. *Journal of Adolescent Research, 12,* 287–315.
Barber, B. K., & Olsen, J. A. (2004). Assessing the transitions to middle and high school. *Journal of Adolescent Research, 19,* 3–30.
Barber, B. K., Stolz, H. E., & Olsen, J. A. (2005). Parental support, psychological control, and behavioral control: Assessing relevance across time, culture, and method. *Monographs of the Society for Research in Child Development, 70*(4, Serial No. 282).
Barber, B. L., Stone, M. R., Hunt, J. E., & Eccles, J. S. (2005). Benefits of activity participation: The roles of identity affirmation and peer group norm sharing. In J. L. Mahoney, R. W. Larson, & J. S. Eccles (Eds.), *Organized activities as contexts of development: Extracurricular activities, after-school and community programs* (pp. 185–210). Mahwah, NJ: Erlbaum.
Barber, J. S. (2001a). Ideational influences on the transition to parenthood: Attitudes toward childbearing and competing alternatives. *Social Psychology Quarterly, 64,* 101–127.
Barber, J. S. (2001b). The intergenerational transmission of age at first birth among married and

unmarried men and women. *Social Sciences Research, 30,* 219–247.
Bard, K. A., Todd, B. K., Bernier, C., Love, J., & Leavens, D. A. (2006). Self-awareness in human and chimpanzee infants: What is measured and what is meant by the mark and mirror test? *Infancy, 9,* 191–219.
Barenbaum, J., Ruchkin, V., & Schwab-Stone, M. (2004). The psychosocial aspects of children exposed to war: Practice and policy initiatives. *Journal of Child Psychology and Psychiatry, 45,* 41–62.
Bar-Haim, Y., Ziv, T., Lamy, D., & Hodes, R. M. (2006). Nature and nurture in own-race face processing. *Psychological Science, 17,* 159–163.
Barja, G. (2004). Free radicals and aging. *Trends in Neuroscience, 27,* 595–600.
Barker, D. (2002). Fetal programming of coronary heart disease. *Trends in Endocrinology and Metabolism, 13,* 364.
Barker, R. G., & Gump, P. V. (1964). *Big school, small school: High school size and student behavior.* Stanford, CA: Stanford University Press.
Barkley, R. A. (2002a). Psychosocial treatments of attention-deficit/hyperactivity disorder in children. *Journal of Clinical Psychology, 63*(Suppl. 12), 36–43.
Barkley, R. A. (2002b). Major life activity and health outcomes associated with attention-deficit/hyperactivity disorder. *Journal of Clinical Psychiatry, 63*(Suppl. 12), 10–15.
Barkley, R. A. (2003a). Attention-deficit/hyperactivity disorder. In E. J. Mash & R. A. Barkley (Eds.), *Child psychopathology* (2nd ed., pp. 75–143). New York: Guilford Press.
Barkley, R. A. (2003b). Issues in the diagnosis of attention-deficit hyperactivity disorder in children. *Brain and Development, 25,* 77–83.
Barkley, R. A. (2006). Attention-deficit/hyperactivity disorder. In R. A. Barkley, D. A. Wolfe, & E. J. Mash (Eds.), *Behavioral and emotional disorders in adolescents: Nature, assessment, and treatment* (pp. 91–152). New York: Guilford.
Barnes, G. M., Hoffman, J. H., Welte, J. W., Farrell, M. P., & Dintcheff, B. A. (2006). Effects of parental monitoring and peer deviance on substance use and delinquency. *Journal of Marriage and Family, 68,* 1084–1104.
Barnes, J., Katz, I., Korbin, J. E., & O'Brien, M. (2007). *Children and families in communities: Theory, research, policy and practice.* Hoboken, NJ: Wiley.
Barnes, R., Josefowitz, N., & Cole, E. (2006). Residential schools: Impact on Aboriginal students' academic and cognitive development. *Canadian Journal of School Psychology, 21,* 18–32.
Barnes-Farrell, J., & Matthews, R. A. (2007). Age and work attitudes. In K. S. Shultz & G. A. Adams (Eds.), *Aging and work in the 21st century* (pp. 139–162). Mahwah, NJ: Erlbaum.
Barnet, B., Arroyo, C., Devoe, M., & Duggan, A. K. (2004). Reduced school dropout rates among adolescent mothers receiving school-based prenatal care. *Archives of Pediatric and Adolescent Medicine, 158,* 262–268.
Barnett, D., & Vondra, J. I. (1999). Atypical patterns of early attachment: Theory, research, and current directions. In J. I Vondra & D. Barnett (Eds.), Atypical attachment in infancy and early childhood among children at developmental risk. *Monographs of the Society for Research in Child Development, 64*(3, Serial No. 258), 1–24.
Barnett, R. C., & Hyde, J. S. (2001). Women, men, work, family: An expansionist theory. *American Psychologist, 56,* 781–796.
Barnett, W. S. (2004). Does Head Start have lasting cognitive effects? The myth of fade-out. In E. Zigler & S. J. Styfco (Eds.), *The Head Start debates* (pp. 221–250). Baltimore: Brookes.
Baron-Cohen, S., Baldwin, D. A., & Crowson, M. (1997). Do children with autism use the speaker's direction of gaze strategy to crack the code of language? *Child Development, 68,* 48–57.
Baron-Cohen, S., & Belmonte, M. K. (2005). Autism: A window onto the development of the social and the analytic brain. *Annual Review of Neuroscience, 28,* 109–126.
Barondess, J. A. (2005). On the preservation of health. *Journal of the American Medical Association, 294,* 3024–3026.
Barr, H. M., Bookstein, F. L., O'Malley, K. D., Connor, P. D., Huggins, J. E., & Streissguth, A. P. (2006). Binge drinking during pregnancy as a predictor of psychiatric disorders on the structured clinical interview for DSM-IV in young adult offspring. *American Journal of Psychiatry, 163,* 1061–1065.
Barr, H. M., Streissguth, A. P., Darby, B. L., & Sampson, P. D. (1990). Prenatal exposure to alcohol, caffeine, tobacco, and aspirin: Effects on fine and gross motor performance in 4-year-old children. *Developmental Psychology, 26,* 339–348.
Barr, R., & Hayne, H. (1999). Developmental changes in imitation from television during infancy. *Child Development, 70,* 1067–1081.
Barr, R., & Hayne, H. (2003). It's not what you know, it's who you know: Older siblings facilitate imitation during infancy. *International Journal of Early Years Education, 11,* 7–21.
Barr, R., Marrott, H., & Rovee-Collier, C. (2003). The role of sensory preconditioning in memory retrieval by preverbal infants. *Learning and Behavior, 31,* 111–123.
Barr, R. G. (2001). "Colic" is something infants do, rather than a condition they "have": A developmental approach to crying phenomena patterns, pacification and (patho)genesis. In R. G. Barr, I. St. James-Roberts, & M. R. Keefe (Eds.), *New evidence on unexplained infant crying* (pp. 87–104). St. Louis: Johnson & Johnson Pediatric Institute.
Barr, R. G., Paterson, J. A., MacMartin, L. M., & Lehtonen, L. (2005). Prolonged and unsoothable crying bouts in infants with and without colic. *Journal of Developmental and Behavioral Pediatrics, 26,* 14–23.
Barratt, M. S., Roach, M. A., & Leavitt, L. A. (1996). The impact of low-risk prematurity on maternal behaviour and toddler outcomes. *International Journal of Behavioral Development, 19,* 581–602.
Barrett, K. C. (2005). The origins of social emotions and self-regulation in toddlerhood: New evidence. *Cognition and Emotion, 19,* 953–979.
Barsky, A. J., Cleary, P. D., & Klerman, G. L. (1992). Determinants of perceived health status of medical outpatients. *Social Science and Medicine, 34,* 1147–1154.
Bartgis, J., Lilly, A. R., & Thomas, D. G. (2003). Event-related potential and behavioral measures of attention in 5-, 7-, and 9-year-olds. *Journal of General Psychology, 130,* 311–335.
Bartlik, B., & Goldstein, M. Z. (2001). Men's sexual health after midlife. *Practical Geriatrics, 52,* 291–306.
Bartocci, M., Berggvist, L. L., Lagercrantz, H., & Anand, K. J. (2006). Pain activates cortical areas in the preterm newborn brain. *Pain, 122,* 109–117.
Bartrip, J., Morton, J., & de Schonen, S. (2001). Responses to mother's face in 3-week- to 5-month-old infants. *British Journal of Developmental Psychology, 19,* 219–232.
Bartsch, K., & Wellman, H. (1995). *Children talk about the mind.* New York: Oxford University Press.
Barzilai, N., & Bartke, A. (2009). Biological approaches to mechanistically understand the healthy life span extension achieved by calorie restriction and modulation of hormones. *Journal of Gerontology, 64A,* S187–S191.
Basow, S. A., & Rubin, L. R. (1999). Gender influences on adolescent development. In N. G. Johnson & M. C. Roberts (Eds.), *Beyond appearance: A new look at adolescent girls* (pp. 25–52). Washington, DC: American Psychological Association.
Bassuk, S. S., & Manson, J. E. (2005). Epidemiological evidence for the role of physical activity in reducing risk of type 2 diabetes and cardiovascular disease. *Journal of Applied Physiology, 99,* 1193–1204.
Bates, E. (2004). Explaining and interpreting deficits in language development across clinical groups: Where do we go from here? *Brain and Language, 88,* 248–253.
Bates, E., Marchman, V., Thal, D., Fenson, L., Dale, P., Reznick, J. S., Reilly, J., & Hartung, J. (1994). Developmental and stylistic variation in the composition of early vocabulary. *Journal of Child Language, 21,* 85–123.
Bates, J. E., Wachs, T. D., & Emde, R. N. (1994). Toward practical uses for biological concepts. In J. E. Bates & T. D. Wachs (Eds.), *Temperament: Individual differences at the interface of biology and behavior* (pp. 275–306). Washington, DC: American Psychological Association.
Bauer, C. R., Langer, J. C., Shakaran, S., Bada, H. S., & Lester, B. (2005). Acute neonatal effects of cocaine exposure during pregnancy. *Archives of Pediatrics and Adolescent Medicine, 159,* 824–834.
Bauer, P. J. (2002a). Early memory development. In U. Goswami (Ed.), *Blackwell handbook of child cognitive development* (pp. 127–150). Malden, MA: Blackwell.
Bauer, P. J. (2002b). Long-term recall memory: Behavioral and neurodevelopmental changes in the first 2 years of life. *Current Directions in Psychological Science, 11,* 137–141.
Bauer, P. J. (2006). Event memory. In D. Kuhn & R. Siegler (Eds.), *Handbook of child psychology: Vol. 2. Cognition, perception, and language* (6th ed., pp. 373–425). Hoboken, NJ: Wiley.
Bauer, P. J. (2007). Recall in infancy: A neurodevelopmental account. *Current Directions in Psychological Science, 16,* 142–146.
Bauer, P. J., Wiebe, S. A., Carver, L. J., Lukowski, A. F., Haight, J. C., Waters, J. M., & Nelson, C. A. (2006). Electrophysiological indexes of encoding and behavioral indexes of recall: Examining relations and developmental change late in the first year of life. *Developmental Neuropsychology, 29,* 293–320.
Baum, N., Rahav, G., & Sharon, D. (2005). Changes in the self-concepts of divorced women. *Journal of Divorce and Remarriage, 43,* 47–67.
Baumbusch, J. L. (2004). Unclaimed treasures: Older women's reflections on lifelong singlehood. *Journal of Women and Aging, 16,* 105–121.
Baumeister, R. F. (1998). Inducing guilt. In J. Bybee (Ed.), *Guilt and children* (pp. 185–213). San Diego: Academic Press.
Baumeister, R. F., Campbell, J. D., Krueger, J. I., & Vohs, K. D. (2003). Does high self-esteem cause better performance, interpersonal success, happiness, or healthier lifestyles? *Psychological Science in the Public Interest, 4*(1), 1–44.
Baumrind, D. (1971). Current patterns of parental authority. *Developmental Psychology Monograph, 4*(No. 1, Pt. 2).
Baumwell, L., Tamis-LeMonda, C. S., & Bornstein, M. H. (1997). Maternal verbal sensitivity and child language comprehension. *Infant Behavior and Development, 20,* 247–258.
Bauserman, R. (2002). Child adjustment in joint-custody versus sole-custody arrangements: A

meta-analytic review. *Journal of Family Psychology, 16,* 91–102.
Baxter, J., Hewitt, B., & Haynes, M. (2008). Life course transitions and housework: Marriage, parenthood, and time on housework. *Journal of Marriage and Family, 70,* 259–272.
Baydar, N., Greek, A., & Brooks-Gunn, J. (1997). A longitudinal study of the effects of the birth of a sibling during the first 6 years of life. *Journal of Marriage and the Family, 59,* 939–956.
Bayer, A., & Tadd, W. (2000). Unjustified exclusion of elderly people from studies submitted to research ethics committee for approval: Descriptive study. *British Medical Journal, 321,* 992–993.
Bayer, W., Mallinger, J. B., Krishnan, A., & Shields, C. G. (2006). Attitudes toward life-sustaining interventions among ambulatory black and white patients. *Ethnicity and Disease, 16,* 914–919.
Bayless, S. (2007). Executive functions in school-age children born very prematurely. *Early Human Development, 83,* 247–254.
Bayley, N. (1969). *Bayley Scales of Infant Development.* New York: Psychological Corporation.
Bayley, N. (1993). *Bayley Scales of Infant Development* (2nd ed.). San Antonio, TX: Psychological Corporation.
Bayley, N. (2005). *Bayley Scales of Infant and Toddler Development, Third Edition* (Bayley-III). San Antonio, TX: Harcourt Assessment.
Baynes, K., & Gazzaniga, M. S. (1988). Right hemisphere language: Insights into normal language mechanisms. In F. Plum (Ed.), *Language, communication, and the brain* (pp. 117–126). New York: Raven.
Bean, R. A., Barber, B. K., & Crane, D. R. (2007). Parental support, behavioral control, and psychological control among African American youth: The relationships to academic grades, delinquency, and depression. *Journal of Family Issues, 27,* 1335–1355.
Beard, B. B. (1991). *Centenarians: The new generation.* New York: Greenwood Press.
Bearman, P. S., & Moody, J. (2004). Suicide and friendships among American adolescents. *American Journal of Public Health, 94,* 89–95.
Beaulieu, M., Leclerc, N., & Dube, M. (2003). Fear of crime among the elderly: An analysis of mental health issues. *Journal of Gerontological Social Work, 40,* 121–138.
Beautrais, A. L. (2003). Life course factors associated with suicidal behaviors in young people. *American Behavioral Scientist, 46,* 1137–1156.
Becker, G., Beyene, Y., Newsome, E., & Mayen, N. (2003). Creating continuity through mutual assistance: Intergenerational reciprocity in four ethnic groups. *Journal of Gerontology, 38B,* S151–S159.
Beckerman, M. B. (1990). Leos Janácek and "the late style" in music. *Gerontologist, 30,* 632–635.
Beckett, C., Maughan, B., Rutter, M., Castle, J., Colvert, E., & Groothues, C. (2006). Do the effects of early severe deprivation on cognition persist into early adolescence? Findings from the English and Romanian adoptees study. *Child Development, 77,* 696–711.
Bedford, O. A. (2004). The individual experience of guilt and shame in Chinese culture. *Culture and Psychology, 10,* 29–52.
Bedford, V. H., & Avioli, P. S. (2006). "Shooting the bull": Cohort comparisons of fraternal intimacy in midlife and old age. In V. H. Bedford & B. F. Turner (Eds.), *Men in relationships* (pp. 81–101). New York: Springer.
Behnke, M., Eyler, F. D., Garvan, C. W., & Wobie, K. (2001). The search for congenital malformations in newborns with fetal cocaine exposure. *Pediatrics, 107, e74.*
Behnke, M., Eyler, F. D., Warner, T. D., Garvan, C. W., Hou, W., & Wobie, K. (2006). Outcome from a prospective, longitudinal study of prenatal cocaine use: Preschool development at 3 years of age. *Journal of Pediatric Psychology, 31,* 41–49.
Beier, M. E., & Ackerman, P. L. (2005). Age, ability, and the role of prior knowledge on the acquisition of new domain knowledge: Promising results in a real-world learning environment. *Psychology and Aging, 20,* 341–355.
Beilin, H. (1992). Piaget's enduring contribution to developmental psychology. *Developmental Psychology, 28,* 191–204.
Beitel, A. H., & Parke, R. D. (1998). Paternal involvement in infancy: The role of maternal and paternal attitudes. *Journal of Family Psychology, 12,* 268–288.
Bell, J. H., & Bromnick, R. D. (2003). The social reality of the imaginary audience: A grounded theory approach. *Adolescence, 38,* 205–219.
Bell, M. A. (1998). Frontal lobe function during infancy: Implications for the development of cognition and attention. In J. E. Richards (Ed.), *Cognitive neuroscience of attention: A developmental perspective* (pp. 327–362). Mahwah, NJ: Erlbaum.
Bell, M. A., & Fox, N. A. (1996). Crawling experience is related to changes in cortical organization during infancy: Evidence from EEG coherence. *Developmental Psychobiology, 29,* 551–561.
Bell, M. L. (1995). Attitudes toward menopause among Mexican American women. *Health Care for Women International, 16,* 425–435.
Bellamy, C. (2004). *The state of the world's children: 2004.* New York: UNICEF.
Bellamy, C. (2005). *The state of the world's children: 2005.* New York: UNICEF.
Belle, S. H., Burgio, L., Burns, R., Coon, D., Czaja, S. J., Gallagher-Thompson, D., & Gitlin, L. N. (2006). Enhancing quality of life of dementia caregivers from different ethnic or racial groups: A randomized, controlled trial. *Annals of Internal Medicine, 145,* 727–738.
Bellinger, D. C. (2005). Teratogen update: Lead and pregnancy. *Birth Defects Research: Part A, Clinical and Molecular Teratology, 73,* 409–420.
Bellinger, D. C., Leviton, A., & Sloman, J. (1990). Antecedents and correlates of improved cognitive performance in children exposed in utero to low levels of lead. *Environmental Health Perspectives, 89,* 5–11.
Belsky, J. (2001). Developmental risks (still) associated with child care. *Journal of Child Psychology and Psychiatry, 42,* 845–859.
Belsky, J. (2005). Attachment theory and research in ecological perspective: Insights from the Pennsylvania Infant and Family Development Project and the NICHD Study of Early Child Care. In K. E. Grossmann, K. Grossmann, & E. Waters (Eds.), *Attachment from infancy to adulthood: The major longitudinal studies* (pp. 71–97). New York: Guilford.
Belsky, J. (2006). Early child care and early child development: Major findings of the NICHD Study of Early Child Care. *European Journal of Developmental Psychology, 3,* 95–110.
Belsky, J., Campbell, S. B., Cohn, J. F., & Moore, G. (1996). Instability of infant–parent attachment security. *Developmental Psychology, 32,* 921–924.
Belsky, J., & Fearon, R. M. P. (2002). Early attachment security, subsequent maternal sensitivity, and later child development: Does continuity in development depend on caregiving? *Attachment and Human Development, 4,* 361–387.
Belsky, J., Jaffee, S., Hsieh, K., & Silva, P. A. (2001). Child-rearing antecedents of intergenerational relations in young adulthood: A prospective study. *Developmental Psychology, 37,* 801–813.
Belsky, J., Steinberg, L. D., Houts, R. M., Friedman, S. L., DeHart, G., Cauffman, E., Roisman, G. I., & Halpern-Felsher, B. (2007). Family rearing antecedents of pubertal timing. *Child Development, 78,* 1302–1321.
Bempechat, J., & Drago-Severson, E. (1999). Cross-national differences in academic achievement: Beyond etic conceptions of children's understandings. *Review of Educational Research, 69,* 287–314.
Benarroch, F., Hirsch, H. J., Genstil, L., Landau, Y. E., & Gross-Tsur, V. (2007). Prader-Willi syndrome: Medical prevention and behavioral challenges. *Child and Adolescent Psychiatric Clinics of North America, 16,* 695–708.
Benbow, C. P., Lubinski, D., Shea, D. L., & Eftekhara-Sanjani, H. (2000). Sex differences in mathematical reasoning ability at age 13: Their status 20 years later. *Psychological Science, 11,* 474–480.
Benbow, C. P., & Stanley, J. C. (1983). Sex differences in mathematical reasoning: More facts. *Science, 222,* 1029–1031.
Bender, H. L., Allen, J. P., McElhaney, K. B., Antonishak, J., Moore, C. M., Kelly, H. L., & Davis, S. M. (2007). Use of harsh physical discipline and developmental outcomes in adolescence. *Development and Psychopathology, 19,* 227–242.
Benenson, J. F., & Christakos, A. (2003). The greater fragility of females' versus males' closest same-sex friendships. *Child Development, 74,* 1123–1129.
Bengtson, V. L., Rosenthal, C. L., & Burton, L. (1990). Families and aging: Diversity and heterogeneity. In R. H. Binstock & L. K. George (Eds.), *Handbook of aging and the social sciences* (3rd ed., pp. 263–287). San Diego: Academic Press.
Bengtsson, H. (2005). Children's cognitive appraisal of others' distressful and positive experiences. *International Journal of Behavioral Development, 29,* 457–466.
Bennett, D. A., Schneider, J. A., Arvanitakis, Z., Kelly, J. F., Aggarwal, N. T., Shah, R. C., & Wilson, R. S. (2006a). Neuropathology of older persons without cognitive impairment from two community-based studies. *Neurology, 66,* 1837–1844.
Bennett, D. A., Schneider, J. A., Tang, Y., Arnold, S. E., & Wilson, R. S. (2006b). The effect of social networks on the relation between Alzheimer's disease pathology and level of cognitive function in old people: A longitudinal cohort study. *Lancet Neurology, 5,* 406–412.
Bennett, K. M. (2007). "No sissy stuff": Toward a theory of masculinity and emotional expression in older widowed men. *Journal of Aging Studies, 21,* 347–356.
Bennett, K. M., Smith, P. T., & Hughes, G. M. (2005). Coping, depressive feelings and gender differences in late life widowhood. *Aging and Mental Health, 9,* 348–353.
Bennett, S. E., & Assefi, N. P. (2005). School-based teenage pregnancy prevention programs: A systematic review of randomized controlled trials. *Journal of Adolescent Health, 36,* 72–81.
Benson, P. L., Scales, P. C., Hamilton, S. F., & Sesma, A., Jr. (2006). Positive youth development: Theory, research, and applications. In R. M. Lerner (Ed.), *Handbook of child psychology: Vol. 1. Theoretical models of human development* (6th ed., pp. 894–941). Hoboken, NJ: Wiley.
Ben-Zeev, T., Carrasquillo, C. M., Ching, A. M. L., Patton, G. E., Stewart, T. D., & Stoddard, T. (2005). "Math is hard!" (Barbie™, 1994): Responses of threat vs. challenge-mediated arousal to stereotypes alleging intellectual inferiority. In A. M. Gallagher & J. C. Kaufman (Eds.), *Gender differences in mathematics: An integrative psychological*

approach (pp. 189–206). New York: Cambridge University Press.

Berenbaum, S. A. (2001). Cognitive function in congenital adrenal hyperplasia. *Endocrinology and Metabolism Clinics of North America, 30,* 173–192.

Berg, C. A. (2000). Intellectual development in adulthood. In R. J. Sternberg (Ed.), *Handbook of intelligence* (pp. 117–137). New York: Cambridge University Press.

Berg, C. A. (2008). Everyday problem solving in context. In S. M. Hofer & D. F. Alwin (Eds.), *Handbook of cognitive aging: Interdisciplinary perspectives* (pp. 207–223). Thousand Oaks, CA: Sage.

Berg, C. A., & Sternberg, R. J. (2003). Multiple perspectives on the development of adult intelligence. In J. Demick & C. Andreoletti (Eds.), *Handbook of adult development* (pp. 103–119). New York: Springer.

Berg, C. A., Strough, J., Calderone, K. S., Sansone, C., & Weir, C. (1998). The role of problem definitions in understanding age and context effects on strategies for solving everyday problems. *Psychology and Aging, 13,* 29–44.

Bergen, D., & Mauer, D. (2000). Symbolic play, phonological awareness, and literacy skills at three age levels. In K. A. Roskos & J. F. Christie (Eds.), *Play and literacy in early childhood: Research from multiple perspectives* (pp. 45–62). Mahwah, NJ: Erlbaum.

Berger, S. E., Theuring, C., & Adolph, K. E. (2007). How and when infants learn to climb stairs. *Infant Behavior and Development, 30,* 36–49.

Bergman, H., Ferrucci, L., Guralnik, J., Hogan, D. B., Hummel, S., Karunananthan, S., & Wolfson. C. (2007). Frailty: An emerging research and clinical paradigm—issues and controversies. *Journal of Gerontology, 62A,* 731–737.

Bergman, I., Blomberg, M., & Almkvist, O. (2007). The importance of impaired physical health and age in normal cognitive aging. *Scandinavian Journal of Psychology, 48,* 115–125.

Bergman, R. (2004). Identity as motivation. In D. K. Lapsley & D. Narvaez (Eds.), *Moral development, self, and identity* (pp. 21–46). Mahwah, NJ: Erlbaum.

Bering, J. M., & Bjorklund, D. F. (2004). The natural emergence of reasoning about the afterlife as a developmental regularity. *Developmental Psychology, 40,* 217–233.

Berk, L. E. (2005). Why parenting matters. In S. Olfman (Ed.), *Childhood lost: How American culture is failing our kids* (pp. 19–53). New York: Guilford.

Berk, L. E., & Harris, S. (2003). Vygotsky, Lev. In L. Nadel (Ed.), *Encyclopedia of cognitive science.* London: Macmillan.

Berk, L. E., Mann, T., & Ogan, A. (2006). Make-believe play: Wellspring for development of self-regulation. In D. Singer, K. Hirsh-Pasek, & R. Golinkoff (Eds.), *Play = learning.* New York: Oxford University Press.

Berk, L. E., & Spuhl, S. (1995). Maternal interaction, private speech, and task performance in preschool children. *Early Childhood Research Quarterly, 10,* 145–169.

Berkowitz, C. M. (2004). *Talking to your kids about sex.* Somerville, NJ: Somerset Medical Center. Retrieved from www.somersetmedicalcenter.com/1817.cfm

Berkowitz, M. W., & Gibbs, J. C. (1983). Measuring the developmental features of moral discussion. *Merrill-Palmer Quarterly, 29,* 399–410.

Berkowitz, R. L., Roberts, J., & Minkoff, H. (2006). Challenging the strategy of maternal age-based prenatal genetic counseling. *Journal of the American Medical Association, 295,* 1446–1448.

Berman, E., & Napier, A. Y. (2000). The midlife family: Dealing with adolescents, young adults, and the marriage in transition. In W. C. Nichols, M. A. Pace-Nichols, D. S. Becvar, & A. Y. Napier (Eds.), *Handbook of family development and intervention* (pp. 208–234). New York: Wiley.

Berman, P. W. (1980). Are women more responsive than men to the young? A review of developmental and situational variables. *Psychological Bulletin, 88,* 668–695.

Berman, R. A. (2007). Developing linguistic knowledge and language use across adolescence. In K. Hirsh-Pasek & R. M. Golinkoff (Eds.), *Action meets word: How children learn verbs* (pp. 347–367). New York: Oxford University Press.

Berman, S. L., Weems, C. F., Rodriguez, E. T., & Zamora, I. J. (2006). The relation between identity status and romantic attachment style in middle and late adolescence. *Journal of Adolescence, 29,* 737–748.

Bernabei, R., Gambassi, G., Lapane, K., Landi, F., Gatsonis, C., & Dunlop, R. (1998). Management of pain in elderly cancer patients. *Journal of the American Medical Association, 279,* 1877–1882.

Berndt, T. J. (2004). Children's friendships: Shifts over a half-century in perspectives on their development and effects. *Merrill-Palmer Quarterly, 50,* 206–223.

Berndt, T. J., & Murphy, L. M. (2002). Influences of friends and friendships: Myths, truths, and research recommendations. In R. V. Kail (Ed.), *Advances in child development and behavior* (Vol. 30, pp. 275–310). San Diego, CA: Academic Press.

Berner, M. M., Leiber, C., Kriston, L., Stodden, V., & Gunzler, C. (2008). Effects of written information material on help-seeking behavior in patients with erectile dysfunction: A longitudinal study. *Journal of Sexual Behavior, 5,* 436–447.

Bernier, J. C., & Siegel, D. H. (1994). Attention-deficit hyperactivity disorder: A family ecological systems perspective. *Families in Society, 75,* 142–150.

Berninger, V. W. (2006). A developmental approach to learning disabilities. In K. A. Renninger & I. E. Sigel (Eds.), *Handbook of child psychology: Vol. 4. Child psychology in practice* (6th ed., pp. 420–452). Hoboken, NJ: Wiley.

Berr, C., Wancata, J., & Ritchie, K. (2005). Prevalence of dementia in the elderly in Europe. *European Neuropsychopharmacology, 15,* 463–471.

Bert, S. C., Farris, J. R., & Borkowski, J. G. (2008). Parent training: Implementation strategies for adventures in parenting. *Journal of Primary Prevention, 29,* 243–261.

Bertenthal, B. I. (1993). Infants' perception of biomechanical motions: Instrinsic image and knowledge-based constraints. In C. Granrud (Ed.), *Visual perception and cognition in infancy* (pp. 175–214). Hillsdale, NJ: Erlbaum.

Bertenthal, B. I., & Longo, M. R. (2007). Is there evidence of a mirror neuron system from birth? *Developmental Science, 10,* 513–523.

Bertenthal, B. I., Longo, M. R., & Kenny, S. (2007). Phenomenal permanence and the development of predictive tracking in infancy. *Child Development, 78,* 350–363.

Berthier, N. E., Bertenthal, B. I., Seaks, J. D., Sylvia, M. R., Johnson, R. L., & Clifton, R. K. (2001). Using object knowledge in visual tracking and reaching. *Infancy, 2,* 257–284.

Bertrand, M., & Mullainathan, S. (2004). *Are Emily and Brendan more employable than Lakisha and Jamal? A field experiment on labor market discrimination.* Unpublished manuscript, University of Chicago.

Berzlanovich, A. M., Keil, W. W., Sim, T., Fasching, P., & Fazeny-Dorner, B. (2005). Do centenarians die healthy? An autopsy study. *Journal of Gerontology, 60A,* 862–865.

Berzonsky, M. D. (2003). Identity style and well-being: Does commitment matter? *Identity: An International Journal of Theory and Research, 3,* 131–142.

Berzonsky, M. D. (2004). Identity style, parental authority, and identity commitment. *Journal of Youth and Adolescence, 33,* 213–220.

Berzonsky, M. D., & Kuk, L. S. (2000). Identity status, identity processing style, and the transition to university. *Journal of Adolescent Research, 15,* 81–98.

Best, D. L. (2001). Gender concepts: Convergence in cross-cultural research and methodologies. *Cross-cultural Research: The Journal of Comparative Social Science, 35,* 23–43.

Betrán, A. P., Merialdi, M., Lauer, J. A., Bing-Shun, W., Thomas, J., Van Look, P., & Wagner, M. (2007). Rates of ceasarean section: Analysis of global, regional and national estimates. *Paediatric and Perinatal Epidemiology, 21,* 98–113.

Bevan, E., & Higgins, D. J. (2002). Is domestic violence learned? The contribution of child maltreatment to men's violence and adjustment. *Journal of Family Violence, 17,* 223–245.

Beyene, Y. (1992). Menopause: A biocultural event. In A. J. Dan & L. L. Lewis (Eds.), *Menstrual health in women's lives* (pp. 169–177). Urbana, IL: University of Illinois Press.

Beyene, Y., & Martin, M. C. (2001). Menopausal experiences and bone density of Mayan women in Yucatan, Mexico. *American Journal of Human Biology, 13,* 47–71.

Beyers, J. M., Bates, J. E., Pettit, G. S., & Dodge, K. A. (2003). Neighborhood structure, parenting processes, and the development of youths' externalizing behaviors: A multilevel analysis. *American Journal of Community Psychology, 31,* 35–53.

Beyth-Marom, R., & Fischhoff, B. (1997). Adolescents' decisions about risks: A cognitive perspective. In J. Schulenberg, J. L. Maggs, & K. Hurrelmann (Eds.), *Health risks and developmental transitions during adolescence* (pp. 110–135). New York: Cambridge University Press.

Bhanot, R., & Jovanovic, J. (2005). Parents' academic gender stereotypes influence whether they intrude on their children's work. *Sex Roles, 52,* 597–607.

Bhat, A., Heathcock, J., & Galloway, J. C. (2005). Toy-oriented changes in hand and joint kinematics during the emergence of purposeful reaching. *Infant Behavior and Development, 28,* 445–465.

Bhatt, R. S., Rovee-Collier, C., & Weiner, S. (1994). Developmental changes in the interface between perception and memory retrieval. *Developmental Psychology, 30,* 151–162.

Bhatt, R. S., Wilk, A., Hill, D., & Rovee-Collier, C. (2004). Correlated attributes and categorization in the first half-year of life. *Developmental Psychobiology, 44,* 103–115.

Bhavnani, B. R., & Strickler, R. C. (2005). Menopausal hormone therapy. *Journal of Obstetrics and Gynaecology Canada, 27,* 137–162.

Bherer, L., Kramer, A. F., Peterson, M. S., Colcombe, S., Erickson, K., & Becic, E. (2006). Training effects on dual-task performance: Are there age-related differences in plasticity of attentional control? *Psychology and Aging, 20,* 695–709.

Bialystok, E. (2001). *Bilingualism in development: Language, literacy, and cognition.* New York: Cambridge University Press.

Bialystok, E., & Martin, M. M. (2003). Notation to symbol: Development in children's understanding of print. *Journal of Experimental Child Psychology, 86,* 223–243.

Bialystok, E., & Martin, M. M. (2004). Attention and inhibition in bilingual children: Evidence from the dimensional change card sort task. *Developmental Science, 7,* 325–339.

Bialystok, E., McBride-Chang, C., & Luk, G. (2005). Bilingualism, language proficiency, and learning to read in two writing systems. *Journal of Educational Psychology, 97,* 580–590.
Bialystok, E., & Senman, L. (2004). Executive processes in appearance–reality tasks: The role of inhibition of attention and symbolic representation. *Child Development, 75,* 562–579.
Bianchi, D. W. (2005). Prenatal genetic diagnosis. In H. W. Taeusch, R. A. Ballard, & C. A. Gleason (Eds.), *Avery's diseases of the newborn* (8th ed., pp. 37–70). Philadelphia: Saunders.
Bianco, A., Stone, J., Lynch, L., Lapinski, R., Berkowitz, G., & Berkowitz, R. L. (1996). Pregnancy outcome at age 40 and older. *Obstetrics and Gynecology, 87,* 917–922.
Biederman, J., Kwon, A., Aleardi, M., Chouinard, V.-A., Marino, T., & Cole, H. (2005). Absence of gender effects on attention-deficit hyperactivity disorder: Findings in nonreferred subjects. *American Journal of Psychiatry, 162,* 1083–1089.
Biederman, J., & Spencer, T. J. (2000). Genetics of childhood disorders: XIX. ADHD, part 3: Is ADHD a noradrenergic disorder? *Journal of the American Academy of Child and Adolescent Psychiatry, 39,* 1330–1333.
Biegel, D., & Liebbrant, S. (2006). Elders living in poverty. In B. Berkman & S. D'Ambruoso (Eds.), *Handbook of social work in health and aging* (pp. 161–180). New York: Oxford University Press.
Bielawska-Batorowicz, E., & Kossakowska-Petrycka, K. (2006). Depressive mood in men after the birth of their offspring in relation to a partner's depression, social support, fathers' personality and prenatal expectations. *Journal of Reproductive and Infant Psychology, 24,* 21–29.
Bielinski, J., & Davison, M. L. (1998). Gender differences by item difficulty interactions in multiple-choice mathematics items. *American Educational Research Journal, 35,* 455–476.
Bigler, R. S. (1995). The role of classification skill in moderating environmental influences on children's gender stereotyping: A study of the functional use of gender in the classroom. *Child Development, 66,* 1072–1087.
Bigler, R. S. (2007, June). Personal communication.
Bigler, R. S., Brown, C. S., & Markell, M. (2001). When groups are not created equal: Effects of group status on the formation of intergroup attitudes in children. *Child Development, 72,* 1151–1162.
Bimmel, N., Juffer, F., van IJzendoorn, M. H., & Bakermans-Kranenburg, M. J. (2003). Problem behavior of internationally adopted adolescents: A review and meta-analysis. *Harvard Review of Psychiatry, 11,* 64–77.
Bigler, R. S., & Liben, L. S. (1992). Cognitive mechanisms in children's gender stereotyping: Theoretical and educational implications of a cognitive-based intervention. *Child Development, 63,* 1351–1363.
Binstock, R. H., & Quadagno, J. (2001). Aging and politics. In R. H. Binstock & L. K. George (Eds.), *Handbook of aging and the social sciences* (5th ed., pp. 333–351). San Diego, CA: Academic Press.
Bioethics Consultative Committee. (2003). *Comparison of ethics legislation in Europe.* Retrieved from www.synapse.net.mt/bioethics/euroleg1.htm
Birch, E. E. (1993). Stereopsis in infants and its developmental relation to visual acuity. In K. Simons (Ed.), *Early visual development: Normal and abnormal* (pp. 224–236). New York: Oxford University Press.
Birch, L. L., & Fisher, J. A. (1995). Appetite and eating behavior in children. *Pediatric Clinics of North America, 42,* 931–953.
Birch, L. L., Fisher, J. O., & Davison, K. K. (2003). Learning to overeat: Maternal use of restrictive feeding practices promotes girls' eating in the absence of hunger. *American Journal of Clinical Nutrition, 78,* 215–220.
Birch, L. L., Zimmerman, S., & Hind, H. (1980). The influence of social–affective context on preschool children's food preferences. *Child Development, 51,* 856–861.
Birch, S. A. J., & Bloom, P. (2003). Children are cursed: An asymmetric bias in mental-state attribution. *Psychological Science, 14,* 283–286.
Bird, A., & Reese, E. (2006). Emotional reminiscing and the development of an autobiographical self. *Developmental Psychology, 42,* 613–626.
Birditt, K. S., & Antonucci, T. C. (2007). Relationship quality profiles and well-being among married adults. *Journal of Family Psychology, 21,* 595–604.
Birditt, K. S., & Fingerman, K. L. (2005). Do we get better at picking our battles? Age group differences in descriptions of behavioral reactions to interpersonal tensions. *Journal of Gerontology, 60B,* P121–P128.
Biringen, Z., Emde, R. N., Campos, J. J., & Appelbaum, M. I. (1995). Affective reorganization in the infant, the mother, and the dyad: The role of upright locomotion and its timing. *Child Development, 66,* 499–514.
Birney, D. P., Citron-Pousty, J. H., Lutz, D. J., & Sternberg, R. J. (2005). The development of cognitive and intellectual abilities. In M. H. Bornstein & M. E. Lamb (Eds.), *Developmental science: An advanced textbook* (5th ed., pp. 327–358). Mahwah, NJ: Erlbaum.
Birren, J. E. (2009). Gifts and talents of elderly people: The persimmon's promise. In F. D. Horowitz, R. F. Subotnik, & D. J. Matthews (Eds.), *The development of giftedness and talent across the life span* (pp. 171–185). Washington, DC: American Psychological Association.
Bjorklund, D. F. (2004). *Children's thinking* (4th ed.). Belmont, CA: Wadsworth.
Bjorklund, D. F., & Blasi, C. (2005). Evolutionary developmental psychology. In D. Buss (Ed.), *Handbook of evolutionary psychology* (pp. 828–850). Hoboken, NJ: Wiley.
Bjorklund, D. F., & Douglas, R. N. (1997). The development of memory strategies. In N. Cowan (Ed.), *The development of memory in childhood* (pp. 83–111). Hove, UK: Psychology Press.
Bjorklund, D. F., Schneider, W., Cassel, W. S., & Ashley, E. (1994). Training and extension of a memory strategy: Evidence for utilization deficiencies in high-and low-IQ children. *Child Development, 65,* 951–965.
Black, D., Gates, G., & Sanders, S. (2000). Demographics of the gay and lesbian population in the United States: Evidence from available systematic data sources. *Demography, 37,* 139–154.
Black, M. M. (2005). Failure to thrive. In M. C. Roberts (Ed.), *Handbook of pediatric psychology and psychiatry* (3rd ed., pp. 499–511). New York: Guilford.
Black, R. E., Williams, S. M., Jones, I. E., & Goulding, A. (2002). Children who avoid drinking cow milk have low dietary calcium intakes and poor bone health. *American Journal of Clinical Nutrition, 76,* 675–680.
Blackburn, G. L., & Wang, K. A. (2007). Dietary fat reduction and breast cancer outcome: Results from the Women's Intervention Nutrition Study (WINS). *American Journal of Clinical Nutrition, 86,* s878–s881.
Blackhall, L. J., Frank, G., Murphy, S., & Michel, V. (2001). Bioethics in a different tongue: The case of truth-telling. *Journal of Urban Health, 78,* 59–71.
Blackhall, L. J., Murphy, S. T., Frank, G., Michel, V., & Azen, S. (1995). Ethnicity and attitudes toward patient autonomy. *Journal of the American Medical Association, 274,* 820–825.
Blackwell, D. L., & Lichter, D. T. (2004). Homogamy among dating, cohabiting, and married couples. *Sociological Quarterly, 45,* 719–737.
Blackwell, L. S., Trzesniewski, K. H., & Dweck, C. S. (2007). Implicit theories of intelligence predict achievement across an adolescent transition: A longitudinal study and an intervention. *Child Development, 78,* 246–263.
Blaga, O. M., & Colombo, J. (2006). Visual processing and infant ocular latencies in the overlap paradigm. *Developmental Psychology, 42,* 1069–1076.
Blaine, B., & Rodman, J. (2007). Responses to weight loss treatment among obese individuals with and without BED: A matched-study meta-analysis. *Eating and Weight Disorders, 12,* 54–60.
Blair, C., & Razza, R. P. (2007). Relating effortful control, executive function, and false belief understanding to emerging math and literacy ability in kindergarten. *Developmental Psychology, 78,* 647–663.
Blair-Loy, M., & DeHart, G. (2003). Family and career trajectories among African-American female attorneys. *Journal of Family Issues, 24,* 908–933.
Blakemore, J. E. O. (2003). Children's beliefs about violating gender norms: Boys shouldn't look like girls, and girls shouldn't act like boys. *Sex Roles, 48,* 411–419.
Blakemore, S.-J., & Choudhury, S. (2006). Development of the adolescent brain: Implications for executive function and social cognition. *Journal of Child Psychology and Psychiatry, 47,* 296–312.
Blanchard, R., & Bogaert, A. F. (2004). Proportion of homosexual men who owe their sexual orientation to fraternal birth order: An estimate based on two national probability samples. *American Journal of Human Biology, 16,* 151–157.
Blanchard-Fields, F. (2007). Everyday problem solving and emotion: An adult developmental perspective. *Current Directions in Psychological Science, 16,* 26–31.
Blanchard-Fields, F., Chen, Y., & Norris, L. (1997). Everyday problem solving across the adult life span: Influence of domain specificity and cognitive appraisal. *Psychology and Aging, 12,* 684–693.
Blasi, A. (1994). Moral identity: Its role in moral functioning. In B. Puka (Ed.), *Fundamental research in moral development: A compendium* (Vol. 2, pp. 123–167). New York: Garland.
Blasi, C. H., & Bjorklund, D. F. (2003). Evolutionary developmental psychology: A new tool for better understanding human ontogeny. *Human Development, 46,* 259–281.
Blass, E. M., Ganchrow, J. R., & Steiner, J. E. (1984). Classical conditioning in newborn humans 2–48 hours of age. *Infant Behavior and Development, 7,* 223–235.
Blatchford, P., Bassett, P., & Brown, P. (2005). Teachers' and pupils' behavior in large and small classes: A systematic observation study of pupils aged 10 and 11 years. *Journal of Educational Psychology, 97,* 454–467.
Blatchford, P., Bassett, P., Goldstein, H., & Martin, C. (2003). Are class size differences related to pupils' educational progress and classroom processes? Findings from the Institute of Education Class Size Study of Children Aged 5–7 years. *British Educational Research Journal, 29,* 709–730.
Blatchford, P., Russell, A., Bassett, P., Brown, P., & Martin, C. (2007). The effect of class size on the teaching of pupils aged 7–11 years. *School Effectiveness and School Improvement, 18,* 147–172.

Bleeker, M. M., & Jacobs, J. E. (2004). Achievement in math and science: Do mothers' beliefs matter 12 years later? *Journal of Educational Psychology, 96,* 97–109.

Bleske, A. L., & Buss, D. M. (2000). Can men and women be just friends? *Personal Relationships, 7,* 131–151.

Block, J. (1971). *Lives through time.* Berkeley, CA: Bancroft.

Block, J. (1995). A contrarian view of the five-factor approach to personality description. *Psychological Bulletin, 117,* 187–215.

Blomberg, S., Edebalk, P. G., & Petersson, J. (2000). The withdrawal of the welfare state: Elderly care in Sweden in the 1990s. *European Journal of Social Work, 3,* 151–163.

Bloom, L. (1998). Language acquisition in its developmental context. In D. Kuhn & R. S. Siegler (Eds.), *Handbook of child psychology: Vol. 2. Cognition, perception, and language* (5th ed., pp. 309–370). New York: Wiley.

Bloom, L. (2000). The intentionality model of language development: How to learn a word, any word. In R. Golinkoff, K. Hirsh-Pasek, N. Akhtar, L. Bloom, G. Hollich, L. Smith, M. Tomasello, & A. Woodward (Eds.*), Becoming a word learner: A debate on lexical acquisition.* New York: Oxford University Press.

Bloom, P. (1999). The role of semantics in solving the bootstrapping problem. In R. Jackendoff & P. Bloom (Eds.), *Language, logic, and concepts* (pp. 285–309). Cambridge, MA: Cambridge University Press.

Bluck, S., Dirk, J., Mackay, M. M., & Hux, A. (2008). Life experience with death: Relation to death attitudes and to the use of death-related memories. *Death Studies, 32,* 524–549.

Bluebond-Langner, M. (1977). Meanings of death to children. In H. Feifel (Ed.), *New meanings of death* (pp. 47–66). New York: McGraw-Hill.

Blumenfeld, P. C., Marx, R. W., & Harris, C. J. (2006). Learning environments. In K. A. Renninger & I. E. Sigel (Eds.), *Handbook of child psychology: Vol. 4. Child psychology in practice* (6th ed., pp. 297–342). Hoboken, NJ: Wiley.

Boardman, J. D. (2004). Stress and physical health: The role of neighborhoods as mediating and moderating mechanisms. *Social Science and Medicine, 58,* 2473–2483.

Bodrova, E., & Leong, D. J. (2007). *Tools of the mind: The Vygotskian approach to early childhood education* (2nd ed.). Upper Saddle River, NJ: Merrill/Prentice Hall.

Bogaert, A. F. (2005). Age at puberty and father absence in a national probability sample. *Journal of Adolescence, 28,* 541–546.

Bogartz, R. S., Shinskey, J. L., & Schilling, T. H. (2000). Object permanence in five-and-a-half-month-old infants. *Infancy, 1,* 403–428.

Bogin, B. (2001). *The growth of humanity.* New York: Wiley-Liss.

Bohannon, J. N., & Bonvillian, J. D. (2009). Theoretical approaches to language acquisition. In J. B. Gleason & B. Ratner (Ed.), *The development of language* (7th ed., pp. 227–284). Boston: Allyn and Bacon.

Bohannon, J. N., III, & Stanowicz, L. (1988). The issue of negative evidence: Adult responses to children's language errors. *Developmental Psychology, 24,* 684–689.

Bohr, L., Pascarella, E., Nora, A., Zusman, B., Jacobs, M., Desler, M., & Bulakowski, C. (1994). Cognitive effects of two-year and four-year institutions: A preliminary study. *Community College Review, 22,* 4–11.

Boldizar, J. P. (1991). Assessing sex typing and androgyny in children: The children's sex role inventory. *Developmental Psychology, 27,* 505–515.

Bolen, R. M. (2001). *Child sexual abuse.* New York: Kluwer Academic.

Bolisetty, S., Bajuk, B., Me, A.-L., Vincent, T., Sutton, L., & Lui, K. (2006). Preterm outcome table (POT): A simple tool to aid counselling parents of very preterm infants. *Australian and New Zealand Journal of Obstetrics and Gynaecology, 46,* 189–192.

Bollmer, J. M., Milich, R., Harris, M. J., & Maras, M. A. (2005). A friend in need: The role of friendship quality as a protective factor in peer victimization and bullying. *Journal of Interpersonal Violence, 20,* 701–712.

Bolzani, L. H., Messinger, D. S., Yale, M., & Dondi, M. (2002). Smiling in infancy. In M. H. Abel (Ed.), *An empirical reflection on the smile* (pp. 111–136). Lewiston, NY: Edwin Mellen Press.

Bonilla, S., Kehl, S., Kwong, K. Y., Morphew, T., Kachru, R., & Jones, C. A. (2005). School absenteeism in children with asthma in a Los Angeles inner-city school. *Journal of Pediatrics, 147,* 802–806.

Bonnel, S., Mohand-Said, S., & Sahel, J.-A. (2003). The aging of the retina. *Experimental Gerontology, 38,* 825–831.

Bonnick, S. L. (2008). Osteoporosis in men and women. *Management of Osteoporosis, 8,* 28–36.

Bono, M. A., & Stifter, C. A. (2003). Maternal attention-directing strategies and infant focused attention during problem solving. *Infancy, 4,* 235–250.

Borduin, C. M. (2007). Multisystemic treatment of violent youth and their families. In T. A. Cavell & K. T. Malcolm (Eds.), *Anger, aggression and interventions for interpersonal violence* (pp. 239–265). Mahwah, NJ: Erlbaum.

Borer, K. T. (2005). Physical activity in the prevention and amelioration of osteoporosis in women: Interaction of mechanical, hormonal and dietary factors. *Sports Medicine, 35,* 779–830.

Borke, H. (1975). Piaget's mountains revisited: Changes in the egocentric landscape. *Developmental Psychology, 11,* 240–243.

Bornstein, M. H. (1989). Sensitive periods in development: Structural characteristics and causal interpretations. *Psychological Bulletin, 105,* 179–197.

Bornstein, M. H. (2006). Parenting science and practice. In K. Renninger & I. E. Sigel (Eds.), *Handbook of child psychology: Vol. 4. Child psychology in practice* (6th ed., pp. 893–949). Hoboken, NJ: Wiley.

Bornstein, M. H., & Arterberry, M. E. (1999). Perceptual development. In M. H. Bornstein & M. E. Lamb (Eds.), *Developmental psychology: An advanced textbook* (pp. 231–274). Mahwah, NJ: Erlbaum.

Bornstein, M. H., & Arterberry, M. E. (2003). Recognition, discrimination, and categorization of smiling by 5-month-old infants. *Developmental Science, 6,* 585–599.

Bornstein, M. H., Selmi, A. M. Haynes, O. M., Painter, K. M., & Marx, E. S. (1999). Representational abilities and the hearing status of child/mother dyads. *Child Development, 70,* 833–852.

Bornstein, M. H., Vibbert, M., Tal, J., & O'Donnell, K. (1992). Toddler language and play in the second year: Stability, covariation, and influences of parenting. *First Language, 12,* 323–338.

Boroughs, D. S. (2004). Female sexual abusers of children. *Children and Youth Services Review, 26,* 481–487.

Borst, C. G. (1995). *Catching babies: The professionalization of childbirth, 1870–1920.* Cambridge, MA: Harvard University Press.

Bortfeld, H., Leon, S., Bloom, J., Schober, M., & Brennan, S. (2001). Disfluency rates in conversation: Effects of age, relationship, topic, role, and gender. *Language and Speech, 44,* 123–147.

Bos, H. M. W., van Balen, F., & van den Boom, D. C. (2007). Child adjustment and parenting in planned lesbian-parent families. *American Journal of Orthopsychiatry, 77,* 38–48.

Bosacki, S. L., & Moore, C. (2004). Preschoolers' understanding of simple and complex emotions: Links with gender and language. *Sex Roles, 50,* 659–675.

Bosch, L., & Sebastian-Galles, N. (2001). Evidence of early language discrimination abilities in infants from bilingual environments. *Infancy, 2,* 29–49.

Bost, K. K., Shin, N., McBride, B. A., Brown, G. L., Vaughn, B. E., & Coppola, G. (2006). Maternal secure base scripts, children's attachment security, and mother–child narrative styles. *Attachment and Human Development, 8,* 241–260.

Boswell, G. H., Kahana, E., & Dilworth-Anderson, P. (2006). Spirituality and healthy lifestyle behaviors: Stress counter-balancing effects on the well-being of older adults. *Journal of Religion and Health, 45,* 587–602.

Botkin, D. R., Weeks, M. O., & Morris, J. E. (2000). Changing marriage role expectations: 1961–1996. *Sex Roles, 42,* 933–942.

Botton, J., Heude, B., Maccario, J., Ducimetiére, P., & Charles, M. A. (2008). Postnatal weight and height growth velocities at different ages between birth and 5y and body composition in adolescent boys and girls. *American Journal of Clinical Nutrition, 87,* 1760–1768.

Bouchard, T. J. (2004). Genetic influence on human psychological traits: A survey. *Current Directions in Psychological Science, 13,* 148–151.

Bouchard, T. J., & Loehlin, J. C. (2001). Genes, evolution, and personality. *Behavior Genetics, 31,* 243–274.

Boukydis, C. F. Z., & Lester, B. M. (1998). Infant crying, risk status and social support in families of preterm and term infants. *Early Development and Parenting, 7,* 31–39.

Boulton, M. J. (1999). Concurrent and longitudinal relations between children's playground behavior and social preference, victimization, and bullying. *Child Development, 70,* 944–954.

Bowen, N. K., Bowen, G. L., & Ware, W. B. (2002). Neighborhood social disorganization, families, and the educational behavior of adolescents. *Journal of Adolescent Research, 17,* 468–490.

Bower-Russa, M. E., Knutson, J. F., & Winebarger, A. (2001). Disciplinary history, adult disciplinary attitudes, and risk for abusive parenting. *Journal of Community Psychology, 29,* 219–240.

Bowlby, J. (1969). *Attachment and loss: Vol. 1. Attachment.* New York: Basic Books.

Bowlby, J. (1980). *Attachment and loss: Vol. 3. Loss: Sadness and depression.* New York: Basic Books.

Bowlby, J. W., & McMullen, K. (2002). *At a crossroads: First results for the 18- to 20-year-old cohort of the Youth in Transition Survey.* Ottawa: Human Resources Development Canada.

Bowman, S. A., Gortmaker, S. L., Ebbeling, C. B., Pereira, M. A., & Ludwig, D. S. (2004). Effects of fast-food consumption on energy intake and diet quality among children in a national household survey. *Pediatrics, 113,* 112–113.

Boyatzis, C. J. (2000). The artistic evolution of mommy: A longitudinal case study of symbolic and social processes. In C. J. Boyatzis & M. W. Watson (Eds.), *Symbolic and social constraints on the development of children's artistic style* (pp. 5–29). San Francisco: Jossey-Bass.

Boyce, W., Doherty-Poirier, M., MacKinnon, D., Fortin, C., Saab, H., King, M., & Gallupe, O. (2006). Sexual health of Canadian youth: Findings from the Canadian Youth, Sexual Health and

HIV/AIDS Study. *Canadian Journal of Human Sexuality, 15,* 59–68.
Boyd-Franklin, N. (2006). *Black families in therapy* (2nd ed.). New York: Guilford.
Boyer, K., & Diamond, A. (1992). Development of memory for temporal order in infants and young children. In A. Diamond (Ed.), *Development and neural bases of higher cognitive function* (pp. 267–317). New York: New York Academy of Sciences.
Boyer, T. W. (2006). The development of risk-taking: A multi-perspective review. *Developmental Review, 26,* 291–345.
Boyes, M. C., & Chandler, M. (1992). Cognitive development, epistemic doubt, and identity formation in adolescence. *Journal of Youth and Adolescence, 21,* 277–304.
Boysson-Bardies, B. de, & Vihman, M. M. (1991). Adaptation to language: Evidence from babbling and first words in four languages. *Language, 67,* 297–319.
Brabyn, J., Schneck, M., Haegerstrom-Portnoy, G., & Lott, L. (2001). The Smith-Kettlewell Institute (SKI) longitudinal study of vision function and its impact among the elderly: An overview. *Optometry and Vision Science, 78,* 264–269.
Bracci, R., Perrone, S., & Buonocore, G. (2006). The timing of neonatal brain damage. *Biology of the Neonate, 90,* 145–155.
Brackbill, Y., McManus, K., & Woodward, L. (1985). *Medication in maternity: Infant exposure and maternal information.* Ann Arbor: University of Michigan Press.
Bracken, B. A. (2000). Maximizing construct relevant assessment: The optimal preschool testing situation. In B. A. Bracken (Ed.), *The psychoeducational assessment of preschool children* (3rd ed., pp. 33–44). Upper Saddle River, NJ: Prentice-Hall.
Brackett, M. A., Mayer, J. D., & Warner, R. M. (2004). Emotional intelligence and the prediction of behavior. *Personality and Individual Differences, 36,* 1387–1402.
Bradbury, T. N., Fincham, F. D., & Beach, S. R. H. (2000). Research on the nature and determinants of marital satisfaction: A decade in review. *Journal of Marriage and Family, 62,* 964–980.
Bradford, K., Barber, B. K., Olsen, J. A., Maughan, S. L., Erickson, L. D., Ward, D., & Stolz, H. E. (2003). A multi-national study of interparental conflict, parenting, and adolescent functioning: South Africa, Bangladesh, China, India, Bosnia, Germany, Palestine, Colombia, and the United States. *Marriage and Family Review, 35,* 107–137.
Bradley, E. H., Peiris, V., & Wetle, T. (1998). Discussions about end-of-life care in nursing homes. *Journal of the American Geriatric Society, 46,* 1235–1241.
Bradley, P. J., & Bray, K. H. (1996). The Netherlands' Maternal–Child Health Program: Implications for the United States. *Journal of Obstetric, Gynecologic, and Neonatal Nursing, 25,* 471–475.
Bradley, R. H. (1994). The HOME Inventory: Review and reflections. In H. W. Reese (Ed.), *Advances in child development and behavior* (Vol. 25, pp. 241–288). San Diego, CA: Academic Press.
Bradley, R. H., & Caldwell, B. M. (1982). The consistency of the home environment and its relation to child development. *International Journal of Behavioral Development, 5,* 445–465.
Bradley, R. H., & Corwyn, R. F. (2003). Age and ethnic variations in family process mediators of SES. In M. H. Bornstein & R. H. Bradley (Eds.), *Socioeconomic status, parenting, and child development* (pp. 161 –188). Mahwah, NJ: Erlbaum.
Bradley, R. H., Corwyn, R. F., McAdoo, H. P., & Garcia-Coll, C. (2001). The home environments of children in the United States. Part I: Variations by age, ethnicity, and poverty status. *Child Development, 72,* 1844–1867.
Bradley, R. H., Whiteside, L., Mundfrom, D. J., Casey, P. H., Kelleher, K. J., & Pope, S. K. (1994). Early indications of resilience and their relation to experiences in the home environments of low birthweight, premature children living in poverty. *Child Development, 65,* 346–360.
Bradshaw, R. A., & Burlingame, A. L. (2005). From proteins to proteomics. *IUBMB Life, 57,* 267–272.
Brady, E. M. (1984). Demographic and educational correlates of self-reported learning among older students. *Educational Gerontology, 10,* 27–38.
Braine, L. G., Schauble, L., Kugelmass, S., & Winter, A. (1993). Representation of depth by children: Spatial strategies and lateral biases. *Developmental Psychology, 29,* 466–479.
Brainerd, C. J. (2003). Jean Piaget, learning, research, and American education. In B. J. Zimmerman (Ed.), *Educational psychology: A century of contributions* (pp. 251–287). Mahwah, NJ: Erlbaum.
Brame, B., Nagin, D. S., & Tremblay, R. E. (2001). Developmental trajectories of physical aggression from school entry to late adolescence. *Journal of Child Psychology and Psychiatry, 42,* 503 –512.
Branca, F., & Ferrari, M. (2002). Impact of micronutrient deficiencies on growth: The stunting syndrome. *Annals of Nutrition and Metabolism, 46*(Suppl. 1), 8–17.
Brand, J. E., Warren, J. R., Carayon, P., & Hoonakker, P. (2007). Do job characteristics mediate the relationship between SES and health? Evidence from sibling models. *Social Science Research, 36, 222–253.*
Branje, S. J. T., van Lieshout, C. F. M., van Aken, M. A. G., & Haselager, G. J. T. (2004). Perceived support in sibling relationships and adolescent adjustment. *Journal of Child Psychology and Psychiatry, 45,* 1385–1396.
Braswell, G. S. (2006). Sociocultural contexts for the early development of semiotic production. *Psychological Bulletin, 132,* 877–894.
Braswell, G. S., & Callanan, M. A. (2003). Learning to draw recognizable graphic representations during mother–child interactions. *Merrill-Palmer Quarterly, 49,* 471–494.
Bratt, R. G. (2002). Housing: The foundation of family life. In F. Jacobs, D. Wertlieb, & R. M. Lerner (Eds.), *Handbook of applied developmental science* (Vol. 2, pp. 445–468). Thousand Oaks, CA: Sage.
Bray, J. H. (1999). From marriage to remarriage and beyond: Findings from the Developmental Issues in Stepfamilies Research Project. In E. M. Hetherington (Ed.), *Coping with divorce, single parenting, and remarriage: A risk and resiliency perspective* (pp. 295–319). Mahwah, NJ: Erlbaum.
Brazelton, T. B., Koslowski, B., & Tronick, E. (1976). Neonatal behavior among urban Zambians and Americans. *Journal of the American Academy of Child Psychiatry, 15,* 97–107.
Brazelton, T. B., & Nugent, J. K. (1995). *Neonatal Behavioral Assessment Scale.* London, Mac Keith Press.
Brazelton, T. B., Nugent, J. K., & Lester, B. M. (1987). Neonatal Behavioral Assessment Scale. In J. D. Osofsky (Ed.), *Handbook of infant development* (2nd ed., pp. 780–817). New York: Wiley.
Bremner, A. J., & Mareschal, D. (2004). Reasoning . . . what reasoning? *Developmental Science, 7,* 419–421.
Brendgen, M., Markiewicz, D., Doyle, A. B., & Bukowski, W. M. (2001). The relations between friendship quality, ranked-friendship preference, and adolescents' behavior with their friends. *Merrill-Palmer Quarterly, 47,* 395–415.
Brennan, K. A., & Shaver, P. R. (1995). Dimensions of adult attachment, affect regulation, and romantic relationship functioning. *Personality and Social Psychology Bulletin, 21,* 267–283.
Brennan, M., & Cardinali, G. (2000). The use of preexisting and novel coping strategies in adapting to age-related vision loss. *Gerontologist, 40,* 327–334.
Brennan, P. L., Schutte, K. K., & Moos, R. H. (2006). Long-term patterns and predictors of successful stressor resolution in later life. *International Journal of Stress Management, 13,* 253–272.
Brennan, W. M., Ames, E. W., & Moore, R. W. (1966). Age differences in infants' attention to patterns of different complexities. *Science, 151,* 354–356.
Brenner, E., & Salovey, P. (1997). Emotional regulation during childhood: Developmental, interpersonal, and individual considerations. In P. Salovey & D. Sluyter (Eds.), *Emotional literacy and emotional development* (pp. 168–192). New York: Basic Books.
Brenner, R. A., & Committee on Injury, Violence, and Poison Prevention. (2003). Prevention of drowning in infants, children, and adolescents. *Pediatrics, 112,* 440-445.
Brenner, R. A., Simons-Morton, B. G., Bhaskar, B., Revenis, M., Das, A., & Clemens, J. D. (2003). Infant–parent bed sharing in an inner-city population. *Archives of Pediatrics and Adolescent Medicine, 157,* 33–39.
Brent, S. B., Speece, M. W., Lin, C., Dong, Q., & Yang, C. (1996). The development of the concept of death among Chinese and U.S. children 3–17 years of age: From binary to "fuzzy" concepts? *Omega, 33,* 67–83.
Breslau, N., Kessler, R. C., Chilcoat, H. D., Schultz, L. R., Davis, G. C., & Andreski, P. (1998). Trauma and posttraumatic stress disorder in the community: The 1996 Detroit Area Survey of Trauma. *Archives of General Psychiatry, 55,* 626–632.
Breslin, F. C., & Mustard, C. (2003). Factors influencing the impact of unemployment on mental health among young and older adults in a longitudinal, population-based survey. *Scandinavian Journal of Work, Environment, and Health, 29,* 5–14.
Bretherton, I., Fritz, J., Zahn-Waxler, C., & Ridgeway, D. (1986). Learning to talk about emotions: A functionalist perspective. *Child Development, 57,* 529–548.
Bretherton, I., & Munholland, K. A. (1999). Internal working models in attachment relationships: A construct revisited. In J. Cassidy & P. R. Shaver (Eds.), *Handbook of attachment* (pp. 89–111). New York: Guilford.
Brewaeys, A., Ponjaert, I., Van Hall, E. V., & Golombok, S. (1997). Donor insemination: Child development and family functioning in lesbian mother families. *Human Reproduction, 12,* 1349–1359.
Bridge, J. A., Goldstein, T. R., & Brent, D. A. (2006). Adolescent suicide and suicidal behavior. *Journal of Child Psychology and Psychiatry, 47,* 372–394.
Briefel, R. R., Reidy, K., Karwe, V., & Devaney, B. (2004). Feeding Infants and Toddlers Study: Improvements needed in meeting infant feeding recommendations. *Journal of the American Dietetic Association, 104*(Suppl. 1), s31–s37.
Briere, J., & Jordan, C. E. (2004). Violence against women: Outcome complexity and implications for assessment and treatment. *Journal of Interpersonal Violence, 19,* 1252–1276.
Bright, J. E. H., Pryor, R. G. L., Wilkenfeld, S., & Earl, J. (2005). The role of social context and serendipitous events in career decision making. *International Journal for Educational and Vocational Guidance, 5,* 19–36.
Brim, O. G., Ryff, C. D., & Kessler, R. C. (2005). The MIDUS National Survey: An overview. In O. G. Brim, C. D. Ryff, & R. C. Kessler (Eds.), *How healthy are we? A national study of well-being at*

midlife (pp. 1–34). Chicago: University of Chicago Press.
Brisch, K. H., Bechinger, D., Betzler, S., Heineman, H., Kachele, H., Pohlandt, F., Schmucker, G., & Buchheim, A. (2005). Attachment quality in very low birth weight premature infants in relation to maternal attachment representations and neurological development. *Parenting: Science and Practice, 5,* 11–32.
Broberg, A. G., Wessels, H., Lamb, M. E., & Hwang, C. P. (1997). Effects of day care on the development of cognitive abilities in 8-year-olds: A longitudinal study. *Developmental Psychology, 33,* 62–69.
Broderick, P. C., & Korteland, C. (2004). A prospective study of rumination and depression in early adolescence. *Clinical Child Psychology and Psychiatry, 9,* 383–394.
Brody, G. H., & Flor, D. L. (1998). Maternal resources, parenting practices, and child competence in rural, single-parent African American families. *Child Development, 69,* 803–816.
Brody, G. H., Ge, X., Kim, S. Y., Murry, V. M., Simons, R. L., & Gibbons, F. X. (2003). Neighborhood disadvantage moderates associations of parenting and older sibling problem attitudes and behavior with conduct disorders in African American children. *Journal of Consulting and Clinical Psychology, 71,* 211–222.
Brody, G. H., & Murry, V. M. (2001). Sibling socialization of competence in rural, single-parent African American families. *Journal of Marriage and Family, 63,* 996–1008.
Brody, G. H., Stoneman, Z., & McCoy, J. K. (1994). Forecasting sibling relationships in early adolescence from child temperaments and family processes in middle childhood. *Child Development, 65,* 771–784.
Brody, J. E. (1992, November 11). PMS is a worldwide phenomenon. *The New York Times,* p. C14.
Brody, L. (1999). *Gender, emotion, and the family.* Cambridge, MA: Harvard University Press.
Brody, L. R. (1997). Gender and emotion: Beyond stereotypes. *Journal of Social Issues, 53,* 369–393.
Brody, M. (2006). Child psychiatry, drugs, and the corporation. In S. Olfman (Ed.), *No child left different* (pp. 89–105). Westport, CT: Praeger.
Brodzinsky, D. M., & Pinderhughes, E. (2002). Parenting and child development in adoptive families. In M. H. Bornstein (Ed.), *Handbook of parenting: Vol. 1* (2nd ed., pp. 279–311). Mahwah, NJ: Erlbaum.
Broidy, L. M., Nagin, D. S., Tremblay, R. E., Bates, J. E., Brame, B., Dodge, K. A., Fergusson, D., Horwood, J. L., Loeber, R., Laird, R., Lynam, D. R., Moffitt, T. E., Pettit, G. S., & Vitaro, F. (2003). Developmental trajectories of childhood disruptive behaviors and adolescent delinquency: A six-site, cross-national study. *Developmental Psychology, 39,* 222–245.
Bronfenbrenner, U. (Ed.). (2005). *Making human beings human.* Thousand Oaks, CA: Sage.
Bronfenbrenner, U., & Morris, P. A. (2006). The bioecological model of human development. In R. M. Lerner (Ed.), *Handbook of child psychology: Vol. 1. Theoretical models of human development* (6th ed., pp. 297–342). Hoboken, NJ: Wiley.
Bronson, G. W. (1994). Infants' transitions toward adult-like scanning. *Child Development, 65,* 1243–1261.
Bronstein, P. (2006). The family environment: Where gender role socialization begins. In J. Worell & C. D. Goodheart (Eds.), *Handbook of girls' and women's psychological health: Gender and well-being across the lifespan* (pp. 262–271). New York: Oxford University Press.
Bronte-Tinkew, J., Moore, K. A., & Carrano, J. (2006). The father–child relationship, parenting styles, and adolescent risk behaviors in intact families. *Journal of Family Issues, 27,* 850–881.
Brooks, C. (2000). Civil rights, liberalism, and the suppression of a Republican political realignment in the United States, 1972 to 1996. *American Sociological Review, 65,* 483–505.
Brooks, P. J., Hanauere, J. B., Padowska, B., & Rosman, H. (2003). The role of selective attention in preschoolers' rule use in a novel dimensional card sort. *Cognitive Development, 18,* 195–215.
Brooks, R., & Meltzoff, A. N. (2005). The development of gaze following and its relation to language. *Developmental Science, 8,* 535–543.
Brooks-Gunn, J. (1988). Antecedents and consequences of variations in girls' maturational timing. *Journal of Adolescent Health Care, 9,* 365–373.
Brooks-Gunn, J. (2003). Do you believe in magic? What we can expect from early childhood intervention programs. *Social Policy Report of the Society for Research in Child Development, 17,* 3–14.
Brooks-Gunn, J. (2004). Intervention and policy as change agents for young children. In P. L. Chase-Lansdale, K. Kiernan, & R. J. Friedman (Eds.), *Human development across lives and generations: The potential for change* (pp. 293–340). New York: Cambridge University Press.
Brooks-Gunn, J., Han, W.-J., & Waldfogel, J. (2002). Maternal employment and child cognitive outcomes in the first three years of life: The NICHD study of early child care. *Child Development, 73,* 1052–1072.
Brooks-Gunn, J., Klebanov, P. K., Smith, J., Duncan, G. J., & Lee, K. (2003). The black–white test score gap in young children. Contributions of test and family characteristics. *Applied Developmental Science, 7,* 239–252.
Brooks-Gunn, J., Schley, S., & Hardy, J. (2002). Marriage and the baby carriage: Historical change and intergenerational continuity in early parenthood. In L. J. Crockett & R. K. Sibereisen (Eds.), *Negotiating adolescence in times of social change* (pp. 36–57). New York: Cambridge University Press.
Broomhall, H. S., & Winefield, A. H. (1990). A comparison of the affective well-being of young and middle-aged unemployed men matched for length of employment. *British Journal of Medical Psychology, 63,* 43–52.
Brown, A. M., & Miracle, J. A. (2003). Early binocular vision in human infants: Limitations on the generality of the Superposition Hypothesis. *Vision Research, 43,* 1563–1574.
Brown, A. S. (2006). Prenatal infection as a risk factor for schizophrenia. *Schizophrenia Bulletin, 32,* 200–202.
Brown, B. B. (2004). Adolescents' relationships with peers. In R. Lerner & L. Steinberg (Eds.), *Handbook of adolescent psychology* (2nd ed., pp. 363–394). Hoboken, NJ: Wiley.
Brown, B. B., Clasen, D., & Eicher, S. (1986). Perceptions of peer pressure, peer conformity dispositions, and self-reported behavior among adolescents. *Developmental Psychology, 22,* 521–530.
Brown, B. B., Lohr, M. J., & McClenahan, E. L. (1986). Early adolescents' perceptions of peer pressure. *Journal of Early Adolescence, 6,* 139–154.
Brown, C., & Lowis, M. J. (2003). Psychosocial development in the elderly: An investigation into Erikson's ninth stage. *Journal of Aging Studies, 17,* 415–426.
Brown, C. S., & Bigler, R. S. (2004). Children's perceptions of gender discrimination. *Developmental Psychology, 40,* 714–726.
Brown, J. R., Donelan-McCall, N., & Dunn, J. (1996). Why talk about mental states? The significance of children's conversations with friends, siblings, and mothers. *Child Development, 67,* 836–849.
Brown, L. H., & Rodin, P. A. (2004). Grandparent–grandchild relationships and the life course perspective. In J. Demick & C. Andreoletti (Eds.), *Handbook of adult development* (pp. 459–474). New York: Springer.
Brown, R. W. (1973). *A first language: The early stages.* Cambridge, MA: Harvard University Press.
Brown, S. A., & Ramo, D. E. (2005). Clinical course of youth following treatment for alcohol and drug problems. In H. A. Liddle & C. L. Rowe (Eds.), *Adolescent substance abuse: Research and clinical advances* (pp. 79–103). Cambridge, UK: Cambridge University Press.
Brown, S. L. (2000). Union transitions among cohabitors: The significance of relationship assessments and expectations. *Journal of Marriage and the Family, 62,* 833–846.
Brown, S. L., Lee, G. R., & Bulanda, J. R. (2006). Cohabitation among older adults: A national portrait. *Journal of Gerontology, 61B,* S71–S79.
Brown, T. E. (2005). *Attention deficit disorder: The unfocused mind in children and adults.* New Haven, CT: Yale University Press.
Browne, C. A., & Woolley, J. D. (2004). Preschoolers' magical explanations for violations of physical, social, and mental laws. *Journal of Cognition and Development, 5,* 239–260.
Browne, J. V., & Talmi, A. (2005). Family-based intervention to enhance infant–parent relationships in the neonatal intensive care unit. *Journal of Pediatric Psychology, 30,* 667–677.
Brownell, C. A., & Carriger, M. S. (1990). Changes in cooperation and self-other differentiation during the second year. *Child Development, 61,* 1164–1174.
Brubaker, T. (1985). *Later life families.* Beverly Hills, CA: Sage.
Bruce, D., Dolan, A., & Phillips-Grant, K. (2000). On the transition from childhood amnesia to recall of personal memories. *Psychological Science, 11,* 360–364.
Bruck, M., & Ceci, S. J. (2004). Forensic developmental psychology: Unveiling four common misconceptions. *Current Directions in Psychological Science, 13,* 229–232.
Bruer, J. T. (1999). *The myth of the first three years.* New York: Free Press.
Brugman, G. M. (2006). Wisdom and aging. In J. E. Birren & K. W. Schaie (Eds.), *Handbook of the psychology of aging* (6th ed., pp. 445–476). Burlington, MA: Elsevier Academic Press.
Brun, A., & Andersson, J. (2001). Frontal dysfunction and frontal cortical synapse loss in alcoholism: The main cause of alcohol dementia? *Dementia and Geriatric Cognitive Disorders, 12,* 289–294.
Bruner, E. J., Rees, K., Burke, M., & Thorogood, M. (2007). Dietary advice for reducing cardiovascular risk. *Cochrane Database of Systematic Reviews, Issue 4,* Art. No.: CD0021278.
Bruschweiler-Stern, N. (2004). A multifocal neonatal intervention. In A. J. Sameroff, S. C. McDonough, & K. L. Rosenblum (Eds.), *Treating parent–infant relationship problems* (pp. 188–212). New York: Guilford.
Brussoni, M. J., and Boon, S. D. (1998). Grandparental impact in young adults' relationships with their closest grandparents: The role of relationship strength and emotional closeness. *International Journal of Aging and Human Development, 45,* 267–286.
Bruzzese, J.-M., & Fisher, C. B. (2003). Assessing and enhancing the research consent capacity of chil-

dren and youth. *Applied Developmental Science, 7,* 13–26.
Bryant, B. K., Zvonkovic, A. M., & Reynolds, P. (2006). Parenting in relation to child and adolescent vocational development. *Journal of Vocational Behavior, 69,* 149–175.
Bryant, P., & Nunes, T. (2002). Children's understanding of mathematics. In U. Goswami (Ed.), *Blackwell handbook of childhood cognitive development* (pp. 412–439). Malden, MA: Blackwell.
Buchanan, A. (1996). *Cycles of child maltreatment.* Chichester, UK: Wiley.
Buchanan, C. M., Eccles, J. S., & Becker, J. B. (1992). Are adolescents the victims of raging hormones? Evidence for activational effects of hormones on moods and behavior at adolescence. *Psychological Bulletin, 111,* 62–107.
Buchanan, C. M., & Holmbeck, G. N. (1998). Measuring beliefs about adolescent personality and behavior. *Journal of Youth and Adolescence, 27,* 609–629.
Buchanan, C. M., Maccoby, E. E., & Dornbusch, S. M. (1996). *Adolescents after divorce.* Cambridge, MA: Harvard University Press.
Buchanan-Barrow, E., & Barrett, M. (1998). Children's rule discrimination within the context of the school. *British Journal of Developmental Psychology, 16,* 539–551.
Buchman, M. (2002). Labour market entry and beyond: Some reflections on the changing structure of work. *Education + Training, 44,* 217–223.
Buescher, E. S. (2001). Anti-inflammatory characteristics of human milk: How, where, why. *Advances in Experimental Medicine and Biology, 501,* 207–222.
Bugental, D. B., Ellerson, P. C., Lin, E. K., Rainey, B., & Kokotovic, A. (2002). A cognitive approach to child abuse prevention. *Journal of Family Psychology, 16,* 243–258.
Bugental, D. B., & Grusec, J. E. (2006). Socialization processes. In N. Eisenberg (Ed.), *Handbook of child psychology: Vol. 3. Social, emotional, and personality development* (6th ed., pp. 366–428). Hoboken, NJ: Wiley.
Bugental, D. B., & Happaney, K. (2004). Predicting infant maltreatment in low-income families: The interactive effects of maternal attributions and child status at birth. *Developmental Psychology, 40,* 234–243.
Buhl, H. M., & Lanz, M. (2007). Emerging adulthood in Europe: Common traits and variability across five European countries. *Journal of Adolescent Research, 22,* 439–443.
Buhrmester, D. (1996). Need fulfillment, interpersonal competence, and the developmental contexts of early adolescent friendship. In W. M. Bukowski, A. F. Newcomb, & W. W. Hartup (Eds.), *The company they keep: Friendship during childhood and adolescence* (pp. 158–185). New York: Cambridge University Press.
Buhrmester, D., & Furman, W. (1990). Perceptions of sibling relationships during middle childhood and adolescence. *Child Development, 61,* 1387–1398.
Buhs, E. S., & Ladd, G. W. (2001). Peer rejection as antecedent of young children's school adjustment: An examination of mediating processes. *Developmental Psychology, 37,* 550–560.
Bukowski, W. M. (2001). Friendship and the worlds of childhood. In D. W. Nangle & C. A. Erdley (Eds.), *The role of friendship in psychological adjustment* (pp. 93–105). San Francisco: Jossey-Bass.
Bulcroft, R. A., Carmody, D. C., & Bulcroft, K. A. (1996). Patterns of independence giving to adolescents: Variations by race, age, and gender of child. *Journal of Marriage and the Family, 58,* 866–883.
Bumpass, L. L. (2004). Social change and the American family. *Annals of the New York Academy of Sciences, 1038,* 213–219.
Bumpus, M. F., Crouter, A. C., & McHale, S. M. (2006). Linkages between negative work-to-family spillover and mothers' and fathers' knowledge of their young adolescents' daily lives. *Journal of Early Adolescence, 26,* 36–59.
Bunting, L., & McAuley, C. (2004). Teenage pregnancy and parenthood: The role of fathers. *Child and Family Social Work, 9,* 295–303.
Burden, M. J., Jacobson, S. W., & Jacobson, J. L. (2005). Relation of prenatal alcohol exposure to cognitive processing speed and efficiency in childhood. *Alcoholism: Clinical and Experimental Research, 29,* 1473–1483.
Burgess, C., O'Donohoe, A., & Gill, M. (2000). Agony and ecstasy: A review of MDMA effects and toxicity. *European Psychiatry, 15,* 287–294.
Burgess, E. O. (2004). Sexuality in midlife and later life couples. In J. Harvey, A. Wenzel, & S. Sprecher (Eds.), *Handbook of sexuality in close relationships* (pp. 437–454). Mahwah, NJ: Erlbaum.
Burhans, K. K., & Dweck, C. S. (1995). Helplessness in early childhood: The role of contingent worth. *Child Development, 66,* 1719–1738.
Burke, D. M., & Shafto, M. A. (2004). Aging and language production. *Current Directions in Psychological Science, 13,* 21–24.
Burke, R. J. (2001). Organizational values, work experiences, and satisfactions among managerial and professional women. *Journal of Management Development, 20,* 346–354.
Burman, D. D., Bitan, T., & Booth, J. R. (2007). Sex differences in neural processing of language among some children. *Neuropsychologia, 46,* 1349–1362.
Burts, D.C., Hart, C. H., Charlesworth, R., Fleege, P. O., Mosely, J., & Thomasson, R. H. (1992). Observed activities and stress behaviors of children in developmentally appropriate and inappropriate kindergarten classrooms. *Early Childhood Research Quarterly, 7,* 297–318.
Bushman, B. J., & Huesmann, L. R. (2001). Effects of televised violence on aggression. In D. G. Singer & J. L. Singer (Eds.), *Handbook of children and the media* (pp. 223–254). Thousand Oaks, CA: Sage.
Bushnell, E. W., & Boudreau, J. P. (1993). Motor development and the mind: The potential role of motor abilities as a determinant of aspects of perceptual development. *Child Development, 64,* 1005–1021.
Buss, D. M. (2008). *Evolutionary psychology: The new science of the mind* (3rd ed.). Boston: Allyn and Bacon.
Buss, D. M., Shackelford, T. K., Kirkpatrick, L. A., & Larsen, R. J. (2001). A half century of mate preferences: The cultural evolution of values. *Journal of Marriage and Family, 63,* 491–503.
Bussey, K. (1992). Lying and truthfulness: Children's definitions, standards, and evaluative reactions. *Child Development, 63,* 129–137.
Bussey, K. (1999). Children's categorization and evaluation of different types of lies and truths. *Child Development, 70,* 1338–1347.
Bussière, P., Knighton, T., & Pennock, D. (2007). *Measuring up: Canadian results of the OECD PISA Study: The performance of Canada's youth in science, reading, and mathematics: 2006.* First results for Canadians aged 15. Catalogue No. 81-590-XPE—No. 3. Ottawa: Human Resources and Social Development Canada, Council of Ministers of Education, Canada and Statistics Canada. Retrieved from www.statcan.ca/english/freepub/81-590-XIE/81-590-XIE2007001.htm
Buswell, S. D., & Spatz, D. L. (2007). Parent–infant co-sleeping and its relationship to breastfeeding. *Journal of Pediatric Health Care, 21,* 22–28.
Butcher, S. K., & Lord, J. M. (2004). Stress responses and innate immunity: Aging as a contributory factor. *Aging Cell, 10,* 151–160.
Butler, M., & Meaney, J. (Eds.). (2005). *Genetics of developmental disabilities.* Boca Raton, FL: Taylor & Francis.
Butler, R. (1998). Age trends in the use of social and temporal comparison for self-evaluation: Examination of a novel developmental hypothesis. *Child Development, 69,* 1054–1073.
Butler, R. N. (1968). The life review: An interpretation of reminiscence in the aged. In B. Neugarten (Ed.), *Middle age and aging* (pp. 486–496). Chicago: University of Chicago Press.
Buunk, B. P. (2002). Age and gender differences in mate selection criteria for various involvement levels. *Personal Relationships, 9,* 271–278.
Byard, R. W., & Krous, H. F. (2003). Sudden infant death syndrome: Overview and update. *Perspectives on Pediatric Pathology, 6,* 112–127.
Byars, A. M., & Hackett, G. (1998). Applications of social cognitive theory to the career development of women of color. *Applied and Preventive Psychology, 7,* 255–267.
Bybee, J. A., & Wells, Y. V. (2003). The development of possible selves during adulthood. In J. Demick & C. Andreoletti (Eds.), *Handbook of adult development* (pp. 257–270). New York: Springer.
Bynner, J. (2005). Rethinking the youth phase of the life course: The case for emerging adulthood? *Journal of Youth Studies, 8,* 367–384.
Byrnes, J. P. (2003). Cognitive development during adolescence. In G. R. Adams & M. D. Berzonsky (Eds.), *Blackwell handbook of adolescence* (pp. 227–246). Malden, MA: Blackwell.

C

Cabrera, N. J., & Garcia-Coll, C. (2004). Latino fathers: Uncharted territory in need of much exploration. In M. E. Lamb (Ed.), *The role of the father in child development* (4th ed., pp. 98–120). Hoboken, NJ: Wiley.
Cabrera, N. J., Shannon, J. D., & Tamis-LeMonda, C. (2007). Fathers' influence on their children's cognitive and emotional development: From toddlers to pre-K. *Applied Developmental Science, 11,* 208–213.
Cabrera, N. J., Tamis-LeMonda, C. S., Bradley, R. H., Hoferth, S., & Lamb, M. E. (2000). Fatherhood in the twenty-first century. *Child Development, 71,* 127–136.
Cahill, K. E., Giandrea, M. D., & Quinn, J. F. (2006). Retirement patterns from career employment. *Gerontologist, 46,* 514–523.
Cain, K. M., & Dweck, C. S. (1995). The relation between motivational patterns and achievement cognitions through the elementary school years. *Merrill-Palmer Quarterly, 41,* 25–52.
Caine, N. (1986). Behavior during puberty and adolescence. In G. Mitchell & J. Erwin (Eds.), *Comparative primate biology: Vol. 2A. Behavior, conservation, and ecology* (pp. 327–361). New York: Liss.
Cairns, R. B., & Cairns, B. D. (2006). The making of developmental psychology. In R. M. Lerner (Ed.), *Handbook of child psychology: Vol. 1. Theoretical models of human development* (6th ed., pp. 89–165). Hoboken, NJ: Wiley.
Caldera, Y. M., & Lindsey, E. W. (2006). Coparenting, mother–infant interaction, and infant–parent attachment relationships in two-parent families. *Journal of Family Psychology, 20,* 275–283.
Caldwell, B. M., & Bradley, R. H. (1994). Environmental issues in developmental follow-up

research. In S. L. Friedman & H. C. Haywood (Eds.), *Developmental follow-up* (pp. 235–256). San Diego: Academic Press.

Calkins, S. D. (2002). Does aversive behavior during toddlerhood matter? The effects of difficult temperament on maternal perceptions and behavior. *Infant Mental Health Journal, 23,* 381–402.

Callaghan, T., Rochat, P., Lillard, A., Claux, M. L., Odden, H., Itakura, S., Tapanya, S., & Singh, S. (2005). Synchrony in the onset of mental-state reasoning: Evidence from five cultures. *Psychological Science, 16,* 378–384.

Callanan, M. A., & Sabbagh, M. A. (2004). Multiple labels for objects in conversations with young children: Parents' language and children's developing expectations about word meanings. *Developmental Psychology, 40,* 746–763.

Cameron, C. A., & Lee, K. (1997). The development of children's telephone communication. *Journal of Applied Developmental Psychology, 18,* 55–70.

Cameron, P. A., & Gallup, G. G. (1988). Shadow recognition in human infants. *Infant Behavior and Development, 11,* 465–471.

Cameron-Faulkner, T., Lieven, E., & Tomasello, M. (2003). A construction based analysis of child-directed speech. *Cognitive Science, 27,* 843–873.

Campa, M. J., & Eckenrode, J. J. (2006). Pathways to intergenerational adolescent childbearing in a high-risk sample. *Journal of Marriage and Family, 68,* 558–572.

Campbell, A., Shirley, L., & Candy, J. (2004). A longitudinal study of gender-related cognition and behaviour. *Developmental Science, 7,* 1–9.

Campbell, F. A., Pungello, E. P., Miller-Johnson, S., Burchinal, M., & Ramey, C. T. (2001). The development of cognitive and academic abilities: Growth curves from an early childhood educational experiment. *Developmental Psychology, 37,* 231–242.

Campbell, F. A., Ramey, C. T., Pungello, E. P., Sparling, J., & Miller-Johnson, S. (2002). Early childhood education: Young adult outcomes from the Abecedarian Project. *Applied Developmental Science, 6,* 42–57.

Campbell, S. B., Brownell, C. A., Hungerford, A., Spieker, S. J., Mohan, R., & Blessing, J. S. (2004). The course of maternal depressive symptoms and maternal sensitivity as predictors of attachment security at 36 months. *Development and Psychopathology, 16,* 231–252.

Campion, J. M., & Maricic, M. J. (2003). Osteoporosis in men. *American Family Physician, 67,* 1521–1526.

Campos, J. J., Anderson, D. I., Barbu-Roth, M. A., Hubbard, E. M., Hertenstein, J. J., & Witherington, D. (2000). Travel broadens the mind. *Infancy, 1,* 149–219.

Campos, J. J., Frankel, C. B., & Camras, L. (2004). On the nature of emotion regulation. *Child Development, 75,* 377–394.

Campos, J. J., Witherington, D., Anderson, D. I., Frankel, C. I., Uchiyama, I., & Barbu-Roth, M. (2008). Rediscovering development in infancy. *Child Development, 79,* 1625–1632.

Campos, R. G. (1989). Soothing pain-elicited distress in infants with swaddling and pacifiers. *Child Development, 60,* 781–792.

Camras, L. A., Oster, H., Campos, J. J., & Bakeman, R. (2003). Emotional facial expressions in European-American, Japanese, and Chinese infants. *Annals of the New York Academy of Sciences, 1000,* 1–17.

Camras, L. A., Oster, H., Campos, J. J., Campos, R., Ujie, T., Miyake, K., Wang, L., & Meng, Z. (1998). Production of emotional and facial expressions in European American, Japanese, and Chinese infants. *Developmental Psychology, 34,* 616–628.

Camras, L. A., Oster, H., Campos, J. J., Miyake, K., & Bradshaw, D. (1992). Japanese and American infants' responses to arm restraint. *Developmental Psychology, 28,* 578–583.

Canada Campaign 2000. (2007). *Oh Canada! Too many children in poverty for too long . . . 2006 report card on child poverty in Canada from Campaign 2000.* Retrieved from http://campaign2000.ca/rc/rc06/index.html

Candy-Gibbs, S., Sharp, K., & Petrun, C. (1985). The effects of age, object, and cultural/religious background on children's concepts of death. *Omega, 154,* 329–345.

Canetto, S. S., Kaminski, P. L., & Felicio, D. M. (1995). Typical and optimal aging in women and men: Is there a double standard? *International Journal of Aging and Human Development, 40,* 187–207.

Canetto, S. S., & Sakinofsky, I. (1998). The gender paradox in suicide. *Suicide and Life-Threatening Behavior, 28,* 1–23.

Canobi, K. H. (2004). Individual differences in children's addition and subtraction knowledge. *Cognitive Development, 19,* 81–93.

Canobi, K. H., Reeve, R. A., & Pattison, P. E. (2003). The role of conceptual understanding in children's addition problem solving. *Developmental Psychology, 39,* 521–534.

Capaldi, D., DeGarmo, D., Patterson, G. R., & Forgatch, M. (2002a). Contextual risk across the early life span and association with antisocial behavior. In J. B. Reid, G. R. Patterson, & J. Snyder (Eds.), *Antisocial behavior in children and adolescents* (pp. 123–145). Washington, DC: American Psychological Association.

Capaldi, D., Stoolmiller, M., Clark, S., & Owen, L. D. (2002b). Heterosexual risk behaviors in at-risk young men from early adolescence to young adulthood: Prevalence, prediction, and association with STD contraction. *Developmental Psychology, 38,* 394–406.

Capirci, O., Contaldo, A., Caselli, M. C., & Volterra, V. (2005). From action to language through gesture. *Gesture, 5,* 155–177.

Caplan, M., Vespo, J., Pedersen, J., & Hay, D. F. (1991). Conflict and its resolution in small groups of one- and two-year-olds. *Child Development, 62,* 1513–1524.

Cappeliez, P., & O'Rourke, N. (2002). Personality traits and existential concerns as predictors of the functions of reminiscence in older adults. *Journal of Gerontology, 57B,* P116–P123.

Carbery, J., & Buhrmester, D. (1998). Friendship and need fulfillment during three phases of young adulthood. *Journal of Social and Personal Relationships, 15,* 393–409.

Carbonaro, W. (2005). Tracking, students' effort, and academic achievement. *Sociology of Education, 78,* 27–49.

Card, N. A., Stucky, B. D., Sawalani, G. M., & Little, T. D. (2008). Direct and indirect aggression during childhood and adolescence: A meta-analytic review of gender differences, intercorrelations, and relations to maladjustment. *Child Development, 79,* 1185–1229.

CARE Study Group. (2008). Maternal caffeine intake during pregnancy and risk of fetal growth restriction: A large prospective observational study. *British Medical Journal, 337,* a2337.

Carey, S. (1999). Sources of conceptual change. In E. K. Scholnick, K. Nelson, S. A. Gelman, & P. H. Miller (Eds.), *Conceptual development: Piaget's legacy* (pp. 293–326). Mahwah, NJ: Erlbaum.

Carey, S., & Markman, E. M. (1999). Cognitive development. In B. M. Bly & D. E. Rumelhart (Eds.), *Cognitive science* (pp. 201–254). San Diego: Academic Press.

Carli, L. L., & Eagly, A. H. (2000). Gender effects on influence and emergent leadership. In G. N. Powell (Ed.), *Handbook of gender in organizations* (pp. 203–222). Newbury Park, CA: Sage.

Carlo, G., Koller, S. H., Eisenberg, N., Da Silva, M., & Frohlich, C. (1996). A cross-national study on the relations among prosocial moral reasoning, gender role orientations, and prosocial behaviors. *Developmental Psychology, 32,* 231–240.

Carlson, C., Uppal, S., & Prosser, E. (2000). Ethnic differences in processes contributing to the self-esteem of early adolescent girls. *Journal of Early Adolescence, 20,* 44–67.

Carlson, M., & Earls, F. (1997). Psychological and neuroendocrinological sequelae of early social deprivation in institutionalized children in Romania. *Annals of the New York Academy of Sciences, 807,* 419–428.

Carlson, S. M., Moses, L. J., & Claxton, S. J. (2004). Individual differences in executive functioning and theory of mind: An investigation of inhibitory control and planning ability. *Journal of Experimental Child Psychology, 87,* 299–319.

Carlson, V. J., & Harwood, R. L. (2003). Attachment, culture, and the caregiving system: The cultural patterning of everyday experiences among Anglo and Puerto Rican mother–infant pairs. *Infant Mental Health Journal, 24,* 53–73.

Carmichael, S. L., & Shaw, G M. (2000). Maternal life stress and congenital abnormalities. *Epidemiology, 11,* 30–35.

Carnelley, K. B., Wortman, C. B., Bolger, N., & Burke, C. T. (2006). The time course of grief reactions to spousal loss: Evidence from a national probability sample. *Journal of Personality and Social Psychology, 91,* 476–492.

Carpendale, J. I. M. (2000). Kohlberg and Piaget on stages and moral reasoning. *Developmental Review, 20,* 181–205.

Carpenter, M., Akhtar, N., & Tomasello, M. (1998). Fourteen- through eighteen-month-old infants differentially imitate intentional and accidental actions. *Infant Behavior and Development, 21,* 315–330.

Carpenter, M., Nagell, K., & Tomasello, M. (1998). Social cognition, joint attention, and communicative competence. *Monographs of the Society for Research in Child Development, 63*(4, Serial No. 255).

Carpenter, T. P., Fennema, E., Fuson, K., Hiebert, J., Human, P., & Murray, H. (1999). Learning basic number concepts and skills as problem solving. In E. Fennema & T. A. Romberg (Eds.), *Mathematics classrooms that promote understanding: Studies in mathematical thinking and learning series* (pp. 45–61). Mahwah, NJ: Erlbaum.

Carr, D. (2003). A "good death" for whom? Quality of spouse's death and psychological distress among older widowed persons. *Journal of Health and Social Behavior, 44,* 215–232.

Carr, D. (2004). Psychological well-being across three cohorts: A response to shifting work–family opportunities and expectations? In O. G. Brim, C. D. Ryff, & R. C. Kessler (Eds.), *How healthy are we? A national study of well-being at midlife* (pp. 452–484). Chicago: University of Chicago Press.

Carr, D., & Friedman, M. A. (2005). Is obesity stigmatizing? Body weight, perceived discrimination, and psychological well-being in the United States. *Journal of Health and Social Behavior, 46,* 244–259.

Carr, D., House, J. S., Wortman, C., Nesse, R., & Kessler, R. C. (2001). Psychological adjustment to sudden and anticipated spousal loss among older widowed persons. *Journal of Gerontology, 56B,* S237–S248.

Carr, J. (2002). Down syndrome. In P. Howlin & O. Udwin (Eds.), *Outcomes in neurodevelopmental and genetic disorders* (pp. 169–197). New York: Cambridge University Press.

Carrado, M., George, M. J., Loxam, E., Jones, L., & Templar, D. (1996). Aggression in British heterosexual relationships: A descriptive analysis. *Aggressive Behavior, 22,* 401–415.

Carroll, D., Phillips, A. C., Hunt, K., & Der, G. (2007). Symptoms of depression and cardiovascular reactions to acute psychological stress: Evidence from a population study. *Biological Psychology, 75,* 68–74.

Carroll, J. B. (2005). The three-stratum theory of cognitive abilities. In D. P. Flanagan & P. L. Harrison (Eds.), *Contemporary intellectual assessment: Theories, tests, and issues* (2nd ed., pp. 69–76). New York: Guilford.

Carskadon, M. A., Acebo, C., & Jenni, O. G. (2004). Regulation of adolescent sleep: Implications for behavior. In R. E. Dahl & L. P. Spear (Eds.), *Adolescent brain development: Vulnerabilities and opportunities* (pp. 276–291). New York: New York Academy of Sciences.

Carskadon, M. A., Harvey, K., Duke, P., Anders, T. F., Litt, I. F., & Dement, W. C. (2002). Pubertal changes in daytime sleepiness. *Sleep, 25,* 525–605.

Carstensen, L. L., & Fredrickson, B. F. (1998). Socioemotional selectivity in healthy older people and younger people living with the human immunodeficiency virus: The centrality of emotion when the future is constrained. *Health Psychology, 17,* 1–10.

Carstensen, L. L., Fung, H. H., & Charles, S. T. (2003). Socioemotional selectivity theory and the regulation of emotion in the second half of life. *Motivation and Emotion, 27,* 103–123.

Carstensen, L. L., Gottman, J. M., & Levenson, R. W. (1995). Emotional behavior in long-term marriage. *Psychology and Aging, 10,* 140–149.

Carstensen, L. L., Isaacowitz, D. M., & Charles, S. T. (1999). Taking time seriously: A theory of socioemotional selectivity. *American Psychologist, 54,* 165–181.

Carter, B., & McGoldrick, M. (2005). *The expanded family life cycle: Individual, family, and social perspectives* (3rd ed.), Boston: Allyn and Bacon.

Carter, C. S., Hofer, T., Seo, A. Y., & Leeuwenburgh, C. (2007). Molecular mechanisms of life- and health-span extension: Role of calorie restriction and exercise intervention. *Applied Physiology, Nutrition, and Metabolism, 32,* 954–966.

Carver, K., Joyner, K., & Udry, J. R. (2003). National estimates of adolescent romantic relationships. In P. Florsheim (Ed.), *Adolescent romantic relations and sexual behavior: Theory, research, and practical implications* (pp. 23–56). Mahwah, NJ: Erlbaum.

Carver, P. R., Egan, S. K., & Perry, D. G. (2004). Children who question their heterosexuality. *Developmental Psychology, 40,* 43–53.

Casasola, M., Cohen, L. B., & Chiarello, E. (2003). Six-month-old infants' categorization of containment spatial relations. *Child Development, 74,* 679–693.

Casavant, M. J., Blake, K., Griffith, J., Yates, A., & Copley, L. M. (2007). Consequences of use of anabolic androgenic steroids. *Pediatric Clinics of North America, 54,* 677–690.

Case, R. (1996). Introduction: Reconceptualizing the nature of children's conceptual structures and their development in middle childhood. In R. Case & Y. Okamoto (Eds.), The role of central conceptual structures in the development of children's thought. *Monographs of the Society for Research in Child Development, 246*(61, Serial No. 246), pp. 1–26.

Case, R. (1998). The development of central conceptual structures. In D. Kuhn & R. Siegler (Eds.), *Handbook of child psychology: Vol. 2. Cognition, perception, and language* (5th ed., pp. 745–800). New York: Wiley.

Case, R., & Okamoto, Y. (Eds.). (1996). The role of central conceptual structures in the development of children's thought. *Monographs of the Society for Research in Child Development, 61*(1–2, Serial No. 246).

Caserta, M. S., & Gillett, P. A. (1998). Older women's feelings about exercise and their adherence to an aerobic regimen over time. *Gerontologist, 30,* 602–609.

Caserta, M. S., Lund, D. A., & Obray, S. J. (2004). Promoting self-care and daily living skills among older widows and widowers: Evidence from the Pathfinders Demonstration Project. *Omega, 49,* 217–236.

Caserta, M. S., Lund, D. A., & Rice, S. J. (1999). Pathfinders: A self-care and health education program for older widows and widowers. *Gerontologist, 39,* 615–620.

Casey, B. J., Getz, S., & Galvan, A. (2008). The adolescent brain. *Developmental Review, 28,* 62–77.

Casey, M. B. (1986). Individual differences in selective attention among prereaders: A key to mirror-image confusions. *Developmental Psychology, 22,* 824–831.

Casey, M. B., Nuttall, R. L., & Pezaris, E. (1997). Mediators of gender differences in mathematics college entrance test scores: A comparison of spatial skills with internalized beliefs and anxieties. *Developmental Psychology, 33,* 669–680.

Casey, M. B., Nuttall, R. L., & Pezaris, E. (2001). Spatial-mechanical reasoning skills versus mathematics self-confidence as mediators of gender differences on mathematics subtests using cross-national gender-based items. *Journal for Research in Mathematics Education, 32,* 28–57.

Cashon, C. H., & Cohen, L. B. (2000). Eight-month-old infants' perceptions of possible and impossible events. *Infancy, 1,* 429–446.

Casper, L. M., & Smith, K. E. (2002). Dispelling the myths: Self-care, class, and race. *Journal of Family Issues, 23,* 716–727.

Caspi, A. (2000). The child is father of the man: Personality continuities from childhood to adulthood. *Journal of Personality and Social Psychology, 78,* 158–172.

Caspi, A., Elder, G. H., Jr., & Bem, D. J. (1987). Moving against the world: Life-course patterns of explosive children. *Developmental Psychology, 23,* 308–313.

Caspi, A., Elder, G. H., Jr., & Bem, D. J. (1988). Moving away from the world: Life-course patterns of shy children. *Developmental Psychology, 24,* 824–831.

Caspi, A., Harrington, H., Milne, B., Amell, J. W., Theodore, R. F., & Moffitt, T. E. (2003). Children's behavioral styles at age 3 are linked to their adult personality traits at age 26. *Journal of Personality, 71,* 495–513.

Caspi, A., Lynam, D., Moffitt, T. E., & Silva, P. A. (1993). Unraveling girls' delinquency: Biological, dispositional, and contextual contributions to adolescent misbehavior. *Developmental Psychology, 29,* 19–30.

Caspi, A., McClay, J., Moffitt, T. E., Mill, J., Martin, J., & Craig, I. W. (2002). Role of genotype in the cycle of violence in maltreated children. *Science, 297,* 851–854.

Caspi, A., Moffitt, T. E., Morgan, J., Rutter, M., Taylor, A., Kim-Cohen, J., & Polo-Tomas, M. (2004). Maternal expressed emotion predicts children's antisocial behavior problems: Using monozygotic-twin differences to identify environmental effects on behavioral development. *Developmental Psychology, 40,* 149–161.

Caspi, A., & Roberts, B. W. (2001). Personality development across the life course: The argument for change and continuity. *Psychological Inquiry, 12,* 49–66.

Caspi, A., & Shiner, R. L. (2006). Personality development. In N. Eisenberg (Ed.), *Handbook of child psychology: Vol. 3. Social, emotional, and personality development* (6th ed., pp. 300–365). Hoboken, NJ: Wiley.

Cassia, V. M., Turati, C., & Simion, F. (2004). Can a nonspecific bias toward top-heavy patterns explain newborns' face preference? *Psychological Science, 15,* 379–383.

Cassidy, J. (2001). Adult romantic attachments: A developmental perspective on individual differences. *Review of General Psychology, 4,* 111–131.

Cassidy, J., & Berlin, L. J. (1994). The insecure/ambivalent pattern of attachment: Theory and research. *Child Development, 65,* 971–991.

Castillo, E. M., & Comstock, R. D. (2007). Prevalence of use of performance-enhancing substances among United States adolescents. *Pediatric Clinics of North America, 54,* 663–675.

Catalano, R. A. (2003). Sex ratios in the two Germanies: A test of the economic stress hypothesis. *Human Reproduction, 18,* 1972–1975.

Catalano, R. A., Bruckner, T., Anderson, E., & Gould, J. B. (2005). Fetal death sex ratios: A test of the economic stress hypothesis. *International Journal of Epidemiology, 34,* 944–948.

Caton, D., Corry, M. P., Frigoletto, F. D., Hokins, D. P., Liberman, E., & Mayberry, L. (2002). The nature and management of labor pain: Executive summary. *American Journal of Obstetrics and Gynecology, 186,* S1–S15.

Cavadini, C., Siega-Riz, A. M., & Popkin, B. M. (2000). U.S. adolescent food intake trends from 1965 to 1996. *Archives of Diseases in Childhood, 83,* 18–24.

CBS News Canada. (2005). *Living wills: FAQs.* Retrieved from www.cbc.ca/news/background/wills

Ceci, S. J. (1991). How much does schooling influence general intelligence and its cognitive components? A reassessment of the evidence. *Developmental Psychology, 27,* 703–722.

Ceci, S. J. (1999). Schooling and intelligence. In S. J. Ceci & W. M. Williams (Eds.), *The nature–nurture debate: The essential readings* (pp. 168–175). Oxford, UK: Blackwell.

Ceci, S. J., Bruck, M., & Battin, D. B. (2000). The suggestibility of children's testimony. In D. F. Bjorklund (Ed.), *False-memory creation in children and adults* (pp. 169–201). Mahwah, NJ: Erlbaum.

Ceci, S. J., Rosenblum, T. B., & Kumpf, M. (1998). The shrinking gap between high- and low-scoring groups: Current trends and possible causes. In U. Neisser (Ed.), *The rising curve* (pp. 287–302). Washington, DC: American Psychological Association.

Ceci, S. J., & Williams, W. M. (1997). Schooling, intelligence, and income. *American Psychologist, 52,* 1051–1058.

Cecil, J. E., Watt, P., Murrie, I. S. L., Wrieden, W., Wallis, D. J., Hetherington, M. M., Bolton-Smith, C., & Palmer, C. N. A. (2005). Childhood obesity and socioeconomic status: A novel role for height growth limitation. *International Journal of Obesity, 29,* 1199–1203.

Center for Communication and Social Policy. (Ed.). (1998). *National Television Violence Study* (Vol. 2). Newbury Park, CA: Sage.

Center for Effective Discipline. (2005). *Worldwide bans on corporal punishment.* Retrieved from www.stophitting.com/disatschool/facts.php

Cerella, J. (1990). Aging and information processing rate. In J. E. Birren & K. W. Schaie (Eds.), *Handbook of the psychology of aging* (3rd ed.), (pp. 201–221). San Diego: Academic Press.

Cernoch, J. M., & Porter, R. H. (1985). Recognition of maternal axillary odors by infants. *Child Development 56,* 1593–1598.

Cevenini, E., Invidia, L., Lescai, F., Salvioli, S., Tieri, P., Castellani, G., & Franceschi, G. (2008). Human models of aging and longevity. *Expert Opinion on Biological Therapy, 8,* 1393–1405.

CFAH (Center for Advancement of Health). (2003). *Report on Phase 1 of the Grief Research Gaps, Needs and Actions Project.* Washington, DC: Author.

Chalmers, J. B., & Townsend, M. A. R. (1990). The effects of training in social perspective taking on socially maladjusted girls. *Child Development, 61,* 178–190.

Chamberlain, P. (2003). Antisocial behavior and delinquency in girls. In P. Chamberlain (Ed.), *Treating chronic juvenile offenders* (pp. 109–127). Washington, DC: American Psychological Association.

Champion, T. B. (2003a). "A matter of vocabulary": Performances of low-income African-American Head Start children on the Peabody Picture Vocabulary Test. *Communication Disorders Quarterly, 24,* 121–127.

Champion, T. B. (2003b). *Understanding storytelling among African-American children: A journey from Africa to America.* Mahwah, NJ: Erlbaum.

Chan, G. K., & Duque, G. (2002). Age-related bone loss: Old bone, new facts. *Gerontology, 48,* 62–71.

Chan, L. K. S., & Moore, P. J. (2006). Development of attributional beliefs and strategic knowledge in years 5–9: A longitudinal analysis. *Educational Psychology, 26,* 161–185.

Chan, R. W., Raboy, B., & Patterson, C. J. (1998). Psychosocial adjustment among children conceived via donor insemination by lesbian and heterosexual mothers. *Child Development, 69,* 443–457.

Chandra, A., Martino, S. C., Collins, R. L., Elliott, M. N., Berry, S. H., Kanouse, D. E., & Miu, A. (2008). Does watching sex on television predict teen pregnancy? Findings from a national longitudinal survey of youth. *Pediatrics, 122,* 1047–1054.

Chandra, R. K. (1991). Interactions between early nutrition and the immune system. In *Ciba Foundation Symposium No. 156* (pp. 77–92). Chichester, UK: Wiley.

Chandra, R. K. (2002a). Influence of multinutrient supplement on immune response and infection-related illness in 50–65 year old individuals. *Nursing Research, 22,* 5–11.

Chandra, R. K. (2002b). Nutrition and the immune system from birth to old age. *European Journal of Clinical Nutrition, 56*(Suppl. 3), S73–S76.

Chang, F., Dell, G. S., & Bock, K. (2006). Becoming syntactic. *Psychological Review, 113,* 234–272.

Chang, L., Schwartz, D., Dodge, D. A., & McBride-Chang, C. (2003). Harsh parenting in relation to child emotion regulation and aggression. *Journal of Family Psychology, 17,* 598–606.

Channon, S., Mockler, C., & Lee, P. (2005). Executive functioning and speed of processing in phenylketonuria. *Neuropsychology, 19,* 679–686.

Chao, R. K., & Good, G. E. (2004). Nontraditional students' perspectives on college education: A qualitative study. *Journal of College Counseling, 7,* 5–12.

Chao, R. K. (1994). Beyond parental control and authoritarian parenting style: Understanding Chinese parenting through the cultural notion of training. *Child Development, 65,* 1111–1119.

Chao, R. K., & Tseng, V. (2002). Parenting of Asians. In M. H. Bornstein (Ed.), *Handbook of parenting: Vol 4* (2nd ed., pp. 59–94). Mahwah, NJ: Erlbaum.

Chapman, R. S. (2006). Children's language learning: An interactionist perspective. In R. Paul (Ed.), *Language disorders from a developmental perspective* (pp. 1–53). Mahwah, NJ: Erlbaum.

Chappell, N., Gee, E., McDonald, L., & Stones, M. (2003). *Aging in contemporary Canada.* Toronto: Pearson Education Canada.

Charman, T., Baron-Cohen, S., Swettenham, J., Baird, G., Cox, A., & Drew, A. (2001). Testing joint attention, imitation, and play as infancy precursors to language and theory of mind. *Cognitive Development, 15,* 481–49.

Charman, W. N. (2008). The eye in focus: Accommodation and presbyopia. *Optometry, 91,* 207–225.

Charpak, N., Ruiz-Peláez, J. G., & Figueroa, Z. (2005). Influence of feeding patterns and other factors on early somatic growth of healthy, preterm infants in home-based kangaroo mother care: A cohort study. *Journal of Pediatric Gastroenterology and Nutrition, 41,* 430–437.

Chase-Lansdale, P. L., Brooks-Gunn, J., & Zamsky, E. S. (1994). Young African-American multigenerational families in poverty: Quality of mothering and grandmothering. *Child Development, 65,* 373–393.

Chase-Lansdale, P. L., Gordon, R., Brooks-Gunn, J., & Klebanov, P. K. (1997). Neighborhood and family influences on the intellectual and behavioral competence of preschool and early school-age children. In J. Brooks-Gunn, G. Duncan, & J. L. Aber (Eds.), *Neighborhood poverty: Context and consequences for development* (pp. 79–118). New York: Russell Sage Foundation.

Chasens, E. R., Williams, L. L., & Umlauf, M. G. (2008). Excessive sleepiness. In E. Capezuti, D. Zwicker, M. Mezey, T. Fulmer, D. Gray-Miceli, et al. (Eds.), *Evidence-based geriatric nursing protocols for best practice* (3rd ed.) (pp. 459–476). New York: Springer Publishing Co.

Chassin, L., Hussong, A., Barrera, M., Jr., Molina, B. S. G., Trim, R., & Ritter, J. (2004). Adolescent substance use. In R. M. Lerner & L. Steinberg (Eds.), *Handbook of adolescent psychology* (2nd ed., pp. 665–696). Hoboken, NJ: Wiley.

Chauhan, G. S., Shastri, J., & Mohite, P. (2005). Development of gender constancy in preschoolers. *Psychological Studies, 50,* 62–71.

Chavajay, P., & Rogoff, B. (1999). Cultural variation in management of attention by children and their caregivers. *Developmental Psychology, 35,* 1079–1090.

Chavajay, P., & Rogoff, B. (2002). Schooling and traditional collaborative social organization of problem solving by Mayan mothers and children. *Developmental Psychology, 38,* 55–66.

Chazottes, D. (2004). Use of memory compensation strategies is related to psychosocial and health indicators. *Journal of Gerontology, 58B,* P12–P22.

Cheah, C. S. L., & Nelson, L. J. (2004). The role of acculturation in the emerging adulthood of aboriginal college students. *International Journal of Behavioral Development, 28,* 495–507.

Checkley, W., Epstein, L. D., Gilman, R. H., Cabrera, L., & Black, R. E. (2003). Effects of acute diarrhea on linear growth in Peruvian children. *American Journal of Epidemiology, 157,* 166–175.

Chen, J. J. (2005). Relation of academic support from parents, teachers, and peers to Hong Kong adolescents' academic achievement: The mediating role of academic engagement. *Genetic, Social, and General Psychology Monographs, 131,* 77–127.

Chen, L.-C., Metcalfe, J. S., Jeka, J. J., & Clark, J. E. (2007). Two steps forward and one back: Learning to walk affects infants' sitting posture. *Infant Behavior and Development, 30,* 16–25.

Chen, M. (2003). Wombs for rent: An examination of prohibitory and regulatory approaches to governing preconception arrangements. *Health Law in Canada, 23,* 33–50.

Chen, X., Cen, G., Li, D., & He, Y. (2005). Social functioning and adjustment in Chinese children: The imprint of historical time. *Child Development, 76,* 182–195.

Chen, X., DeSouza, A. T., Chen, H., & Wang, L. (2006). Reticent behavior and experiences in peer interactions in Chinese and Canadian children. *Developmental Psychology, 42,* 656–665.

Chen, X., Hastings, P. D., Rubin, K. H., Chen, H., Cen, G., & Stewart, S. L. (1998). Childrearing attitudes and behavioral inhibition in Chinese and Canadian toddlers: A cross-cultural study. *Developmental Psychology, 34,* 677–686.

Chen, X., Rubin, K. H., & Li, Z. (1995). Social functioning and adjustment in Chinese children: A longitudinal study. *Developmental Psychology, 31,* 531–539.

Chen, X., Wang, L., & DeSouza, A. (2006). Temperament, socioemotional functioning, and peer relationships in Chinese and North American children. In X. Chen, D. C. French, & B. H. Schneider (Eds.), *Peer relationships in cultural context* (pp. 123–147). New York: Cambridge University Press.

Chen, X., Wu, H., Chen, H., Wang, L., & Cen, G. (2001). Parenting practices and aggressive behavior in Chinese children. *Parenting: Science and Practice, 1,* 159–184.

Chen, Y.-C., Yu, M.-L., Rogan, W., Gladen, B., & Hsu, C.-C. (1994). A 6-year follow-up of behavior and activity disorders in the Taiwan Yu-cheng children. *American Journal of Public Health, 84,* 415–421.

Chen, Y.-J., & Hsu, C.-C. (1994). Effects of prenatal exposure to PCBs on the neurological function of children: A neuropsychological and neurophysiological study. *Developmental Medicine and Child Neurology, 36,* 312–320.

Chen, Z., Sanchez, R. P., & Campbell, T. (1997). From beyond to within their grasp: The rudiments of analogical problem solving in 10- to 13-month-olds. *Developmental Psychology, 33,* 790–801.

Cherlin, E. J., Barry, C. L., Prigerson, H. G., Schulman-Green, D., Johnson-Hurzeler, R., Kasl, S. V., & Bradley, E. H. (2007). Bereavement services for family caregivers: How often used, why, and why not. *Journal of Palliative Medicine, 10,* 148–158.

Chesney, M. A., Ekman, P., Friesen, W. V., Black, G. W., & Hecker, M. H. L. (1997). Type A behavior pattern: Facial behavior and speech components. In P. Ekman & E. L. Rosenberg (Eds.), *What the face reveals* (pp. 453–468). New York: Oxford University Press.

Chesney-Lind, M. (2001). Girls, violence, and delinquency: Popular myths and persistent problems. In S. O. White (Ed.), *Handbook of youth and justice* (pp. 135–158). New York: Kluwer Academic.

Chess, S., & Thomas, A. (1984). *Origins and evolution of behavior disorders.* New York: Brunner/Mazel.

Chhin, C. S., Bleeker, M. M., & Jacobs, J. E. (2008). Gender-typed occupational choices: The long-term impact of parents' beliefs and expectations. In H. M. G. Watt & J. S. Eccles (Eds.), *Gender and occupational outcomes: Longitudinal assessments of individual, social, and cultural influences* (pp. 215–234). Washington, DC: American Psychological Association.

Chi, M. T. H. (2006). Laboratory methods for assessing experts' and novices' knowledge. In K. A. Ericsson, N. Charness, P. J. Feltovich, & R. R. Hoffman (Eds.), *The Cambridge handbook of expertise and expert performance* (pp. 167–184). New York: Cambridge University Press.

Chi, M. T. H., Glaser, R., & Farr, M. J. (Eds.). (1988). *The nature of expertise.* Hillsdale, NJ: Erlbaum.

Child Trends. (2007). *Late or no prenatal care.* Retrieved from www.childtrendsdatabank.org/indicators/25PrenatalCare.cfm

Child Trends. (2008). *Facts at a glance.* Retrieved from www.childtrends.org/_docdisp_page.cfm?LID=D6F165A5-00B3-4D76-ABACFD97F248817C

Children's Defense Fund. (2008). *Annual report 2007.* Washington, DC: Author.

Children's Defense Fund. (2009). *State of America's children: 2008.* Washington, DC: Author.

Chinn, C. A., & Malhotra, B. A. (2002). Children's responses to anomalous scientific data: How is conceptual change impeded? *Journal of Educational Psychology, 94,* 327–343.

Chochinov, H. M. (2006). Dying, dignity, and new horizons in palliative end-of-life care. *CA: A Cancer Journal for Clinicians, 56,* 84–103.

Choi, J., Fauce, S. R., & Effros, R. B. (2008). Reduced telomerase activity in human T lymphocytes exposed to cortisol. *Brain, Behavior, and Immunity, 22,* 600–605.

Choi, S., & Gopnik, A. (1995). Early acquisition of verbs in Korean: A cross-linguistic study. *Journal of Child Language, 22,* 497–529.

Choi, S., McDonough, L., Bowerman, M., & Mandler, J. M. (1999). Early sensitivity to language-specific spatial categories in English and Korean. *Cognitive Development, 14,* 241–268.

Chollar, S. (1995, June). The psychological benefits of exercise. *American Health, 14*(5), 72–75.

Chomsky, C. (1969). *The acquisition of syntax in children from five to ten.* Cambridge, MA: MIT Press.

Chomsky, N. (1957). *Syntactic structures.* The Hague: Mouton.

Chomtho, S., Wells, J. C., Williams, J. E., Davies, P. S., Lucas, A., & Fewtrell, M. S. (2008). Infant growth and later body composition: Evidence from the 4-component model. *American Journal of Clinical Nutrition, 87,* 1776–1784.

Chorzempa, B. F., & Graham, S. (2006). Primary-grade teachers' use of within-class ability grouping in reading. *Journal of Educational Psychology, 98,* 529–541.

Chouinard, M. M., & Clark, E. V. (2003). Adult reformulations of child errors as negative evidence. *Journal of Child Language, 30,* 637–669.

Chrisler, J. C. (2008). The menstrual cycle in a biopsychosocial context. In F. L. Denmark & M. Paludi (Eds.), *Psychology of women: A handbook of issues and theories* (2nd ed., pp. 400–439). Westport, CT: Praeger.

Christ, G. H., Siegel, K., & Christ, A. E. (2002). "It never really hit me . . . until it actually happened." *Journal of the American Medical Association, 288,* 1269–1278.

Christ, S. E., Steiner, R. D., Grange, D. K., Abrams, R. A., & White, D. A. (2006). Inhibitory control in children with phenylketonuria. *Developmental Neuropsychology, 30,* 845–864.

Christensen, A., & Heavey, C. L. (1999). Interventions for couples. *Annual Review of Psychology, 50,* 165–190.

Christensen, A.-D., & Larsen, J. E. (2008). Gender, class, and family: Men and gender equality in a Danish context. *Social Politics: International Studies in Gender, State and Society, 15,* 53–78.

Christensen, K. A., Stephens, M. A. P., & Townsend, A. L. (1998). Mastery in women's multiple roles and well-being: Adult daughters providing care to impaired parents. *Health Psychology, 17,* 163–171.

Christenson, S. L., & Thurlow, M. L. (2004). School dropouts: Prevention considerations, interventions, and challenges. *Current Directions in Psychological Science, 13,* 36–39.

Christie, C. A., Jolivette, K., & Nelson, M. (2007) School characteristics related to high school dropout rates. *Remedial and Special Education, 28,* 325–339.

Chu, J., Zhou, C. C., Lu, N., Zhang, X., & Dong, F. T. (2008). Genetic variants in three genes and smoking show strong associations with susceptibility to exudative age-related macular degeneration in a Chinese population. *Chinese Medical Journal, 121,* 2525–2533.

Chudley, A. E., Conry, J., Cook, J. L., Loock, C., Rosales, T., & LeBlanc, N. (2005). Fetal alcohol spectrum disorder: Canadian guidelines for diagnosis. *Canadian Medical Association Journal, 172,* S1–S21.

Chumlea, W. C., Schubert, C. M., Roche, A. F., Kulin, H. E., Lee, P. A., Himes, J. H., & Sun, S. S. (2003). Age at menarche and racial comparisons in U.S. girls. *Pediatrics, 111,* 110–113.

Church, E. (2004). *Understanding stepmothers: Women share their struggles, successes, and insights.* Toronto: HarperCollins.

Cicchetti, D. (2007). Intervention and policy implications of research on neurobiological functioning in maltreated children. In J. L. Aber, S. J. Bishop-Josef, S. M. Jones, K. T. McLearn, & D. A. Phillips (Eds.), *Child development and social policy* (pp. 167–184). Washington, DC: American Psychological Association.

Cicchetti, D., & Toth, S. L. (2006). Developmental psychopathology and preventive intervention. In K. A. Renninger & I. E. Sigel (Eds.), *Handbook of child psychology: Vol. 4. Child psychology in practice* (6th ed., pp. 497–547). Hoboken, NJ: Wiley.

Cicirelli, V. G. (1989). Feelings of attachment to siblings and well-being in later life. *Psychology and Aging, 4,* 211–216.

Cicirelli, V. G. (1995). *Sibling relationships across the life span.* New York: Plenum.

Cicirelli, V. G. (1997). Relationship of psychosocial and background variables to older adults' end-of-life decisions. *Psychology and Aging, 12,* 72–83.

Cicirelli, V. G. (1999). Personality and demographic factors in older adults' fear of death. *Gerontologist, 39,* 569–579.

Cicirelli, V. G. (2001). Personal meanings of death in older adults and young adults in relation to their fears of death. *Death Studies, 25,* 663–683.

Cicirelli, V. G. (2002). *Older adults' views on death.* New York: Springer.

Cillessen, A. H. N., & Bellmore, A. D. (2004). Social skills and interpersonal perception in early and middle childhood. In P. K. Smith & C. H. Hart (Eds.), *Blackwell handbook of childhood social development* (pp. 355–374). Malden, MA: Blackwell.

Cillessen, A. H. N., & Mayeux, L. (2004). From censure to reinforcement: Developmental changes in the association between aggression and social status. *Child Development, 75,* 147–163.

Cinamon, R. G., & Rich, Y. (2002). Gender differences in the importance of work and family roles: Implications for work–family conflict. *Sex Roles, 47,* 531–541.

Claes, M., Lacourse, E., Bouchard, C., & Perucchini, P. (2003). Parental practices in late adolescence, a comparison of three countries: Canada, France and Italy. *Journal of Adolescence, 26,* 387–399.

Clapp, J. F., III, Kim, H., Burciu, B., Schmidt, S., Petry, K., & Lopez, B. (2002). Continuing regular exercise during pregnancy: Effect of exercise volume on fetoplacental growth. *American Journal of Obstetrics and Gynecology, 186,* 142–147.

Clarke-Stewart, K. A., Althusen, V., & Goosens, F. (2001). Day care and the Strange Situation. In A. Göncu & E. L. Klein (Eds.), *Children in play, story, and school* (pp. 241–266). New York: Guilford.

Clarke-Stewart, K. A., & Brentano, C. (2006). *Divorce: Causes and consequences.* New Haven: Yale University Press.

Clarke-Stewart, K. A., & Hayward, C. (1996). Advantages of father custody and contact for the psychological well-being of school-age children. *Journal of Applied Developmental Psychology, 17,* 239–270.

Clarkson, T. W., Magos, L., & Myers, G. J. (2003). The toxicology of mercury—current exposures and clinical manifestations. *New England Journal of Medicine, 349,* 1731–1737.

Clausen, J. A. (1975). The social meaning of differential physical and sexual maturation. In S. E. Dragastin & G. H. Elder (Eds.), *Adolescence in the life cycle: Psychological change and the social context* (pp. 25–47). New York: Halsted.

Claxton, L. J., Keen, R., & McCarty, M. E. (2003). Evidence of motor planning in infant reaching behavior. *Psychological Science, 14,* 354–356.

Clearfield, M. W., & Nelson, N. M. (2006). Sex differences in mothers' speech and play behavior with 6-, 9-, and 14-month-old infants. *Sex Roles, 54,* 127–137.

Clearfield, M. W., Obsborn, C. N., & Mullen, M. (2008). Learning by looking: Infants' social looking behavior across the transition from crawling to walking. *Journal of Experimental Child Psychology, 100,* 297–307.

Cleary, J. P., Walsh, D. M., Hofmeister, J. J., Shankar, G. M., Kuskowski, M. A., Selkoe, D. J., & Ashe, K. H. (2005). Natural oligomers of the amyloid-beta protein specifically disrupt cognitive function. *Nature Neuroscience, 8,* 79–84.

Clements, D. H., & Sarama, J. (2003). Young children and technology: What does the research say? *Young Children, 58*(6), 34–40.

Clements, D. H., & Sarama, J. (2008). Experimental evaluation of the effects of a research-based preschool mathematics curriculum. *American Educational Research Journal, 45,* 443–494.

Cleveland, E. S., & Reese, E. (2005). Maternal structure and autonomy support in conversations about the past: Contributions to children's autobiographical memory. *Developmental Psychology, 41,* 376–388.

Clifton, R. K., Rochat, P., Robin, D. J., & Berthier, N. E. (1994). Multimodal perception in the control of infant reaching. *Journal of Experimental Psychology: Human Perception and Performance, 20,* 876–886.

Clinchy, B. M. (2002). Revisiting women's ways of knowing. In B. K. Hofer & P. R. Pintrich (Eds.), *Personal epistemology: The psychological beliefs about knowledge and knowing* (pp. 63–87). Mahwah, NJ: Erlbaum.

Clingempeel, W. G., & Henggeler, S. W. (2003). Aggressive juvenile offenders transitioning into emerging adulthood: Factors discriminating persistors and desistors. *American Journal of Orthopsychiatry, 73,* 310–323.

Coatsworth, J. D., Sharp, E. H., Palen, L., Darling, N., Cumsille, P., & Marta, M. (2005). Exploring adolescent self-defining leisure activities and identity experiences across three countries. *International Journal of Behavioral Development, 29,* 361–370.

Cockerham, W. C., Hinote, B. P., Abbott, P., & Haerpfer, C. (2004). Healthy lifestyles in central Asia: The case of Kazakhstan and Kyrgyzstan. *Social Science and Medicine, 59,* 1409–1421.

Coe, C. L., & Laudenslager, M. L. (2007). Psychosocial influences on immunity, including effects on immune maturation and sensecence. *Brain, Behavior, and Immunity, 21,* 1000–1008.

Cohan, C. L., & Kleinbaum, S. (2002). Toward a greater understanding of the cohabitation effect: Premarital cohabitation and marital communication. *Journal of Marriage and Family, 64,* 180–192.

Cohen, J., Marcoux, I., Bilsen, J., Deboosere, P., van der Wal, G., & Deliens, L. (2006). European public acceptance of euthanasia: Socio-demographic and cultural factors associated with the acceptance of euthanasia in 33 European countries. *Social Science and Medicine, 63,* 743–756.

Cohen, L. B. (2003). Commentary on Part I: Unresolved issues in infant categorization. In D. H. Rakison & L. M. Oakes (Eds.), *Early category and concept development: Making sense of the blooming, buzzing confusion* (pp. 193–209). New York: Oxford University Press.

Cohen, L. B., & Cashon, C. H. (2006). Infant cognition. In D. Kuhn & R. Siegler (Eds.), *Handbook of child psychology: Vol. 2. Cognition, perception, and language* (6th ed., pp. 214–251). Hoboken, NJ: Wiley.

Cohen, P., Kasen, S., Chen, H., Hartmark, C., & Gordon, K. (2003). Variations in patterns of developmental transitions in the emerging adulthood period. *Developmental Psychology, 39,* 657–669.

Cohen, S., & Herbert, T. B. (1996). Health psychology: Psychological factors and physical disease from the perspective of human psychoneuroimmunology. *Annual Review of Psychology, 47,* 113–142.

Cohen-Bendahan, C. C. C., van de Beek, C., & Berenbaum, S. A. (2005). Prenatal sex hormones effects on child and adult sex-typed behavior: Methods and findings. *Neuroscience and Biobehavioral Reviews, 29,* 353–384.

Cohen-Shalev, A. (1986). Artistic creativity across the adult life span: An alternative approach. *Interchange, 17*(4), 1–16.

Cohler, B. J., & Hostetler, A. J. (2007). Gay lives in the Third Age: Possibilities and paradoxes. In J. B. James & P. Wink (Eds.), *Annual review of gerontology and geriatrics* (Vol. 26, pp. 193–209). New York: Springer.

Coholl, A., Kassotis, J., Parks, R., Vaughan, R., Bannister, H., & Northridge, M. (2001). Adolescents in the age of AIDS: Myths, misconceptions, and misunderstandings regarding sexually transmitted diseases. *Journal of the National Medical Association, 93,* 64–69.

Coie, J. D., Dodge, K. A., & Coppotelli, H. (1982). Dimensions and types of social status: A cross-age perspective. *Developmental Psychology, 18,* 557–570.

Coke, M. M. (1992). Correlates of life satisfaction among elderly African Americans. *Journal of Gerontology, 47,* P316–P320.

Coker, A. D. (2003). African American female adult learners: Motivations, challenges, and coping strategies. *Journal of Black Studies, 33,* 654–674.

Col, N. F., Weber, G., Stiggelbout, A., Chuo, J., D'Agostino, R., & Corso, P. (2004). Short-term menopausal hormone therapy for symptom relief. *Archives of Internal Medicine, 164,* 1634–1640.

Colapinto, J. (2001). *As nature made him: The boy who was raised as a girl.* New York: Perennial.

Colby, A., Kohlberg, L., Gibbs, J., & Lieberman, M. (1983). A longitudinal study of moral judgment. *Monographs of the Society for Research in Child Development, 48*(1–2, Serial No. 200).

Colcombe, S. J., Erickson, K. I., Raz, N., Webb, A. G., Cohen, N. J., & McAuley, E. (2003). Aerobic fitness reduces brain tissue loss in aging humans. *Journal of Gerontology, 58,* M176–M180.

Colcombe, S. J., Erickson, K. I., Scalf, P. E., Kim, J. S., Prakash, R., & McAuley, E. (2006). Aerobic exercise training increases brain volume in aging humans. *Journal of Gerontology, 61A,* 1166–1170.

Colcombe, S. J., Kramer, A. F., Erickson, K. I., Scalf, P., McAuley, E., & Cohen, N. J. (2004). Cardiovascular fitness, cortical plasticity, and aging. *Proceedings of the National Academy of Sciences, 101,* 3316–3321.

Cole, D. A., Martin, J. M., Peeke, L. A., Seroczynski, A. D., & Fier, J. (1999). Children's over- and underestimation of academic competence: A longitudinal study of gender differences, depression, and anxiety. *Child Development, 70,* 459–473.

Cole, D. A., Maxwell, S. E., Martin, J. M., Peeke, L. G., Seroczynski, A. D., & Tram, J. M. (2001). The development of multiple domains of child and adolescent self-concept: A cohort sequential longitudinal design. *Child Development, 72,* 1723–1746.

Cole, E. R., & Stewart, A. J. (1996). Meanings of political participation among black and white women: Political identity and social responsibility. *Journal of Personality and Social Psychology, 71,* 130–140.

Cole, M. (1990). Cognitive development and formal schooling: The evidence from cross-cultural research. In L. C. Moll (Ed.), *Vygotsky and education* (pp. 89–110). New York: Cambridge University Press.

Cole, M. (2005). Culture in development. In M. H. Bornstein & M. E. Lamb (Eds.), *Developmental science: An advanced textbook* (5th ed., pp. 45–102). Mahwah, NJ: Erlbaum.

Cole, M. (2006). Culture and cognitive development in phylogenetic, historical, and ontogenetic perspective. In R. M. Lerner (Ed.), *Handbook of child psychology: Vol. 1. Theoretical models of human development* (6th ed., pp. 636–685). Hoboken, NJ: Wiley.

Coleman, M., Ganong, L., & Fine, M. (2000). Reinvestigating remarriage: Another decade of progress. *Journal of Marriage and Family, 62,* 1288–1307.

Coleman, M., Ganong, L., & Leon, K. (2006). Divorce and postdivorce relationships. In A. L. Vangelisti & D. Perlman (Eds.), *The Cambridge handbook of personal relationships* (pp. 157–173). New York: Cambridge University Press.

Coleman, P. G., Ivani-Chalian, C., & Robinson, M. (2004). Religious attitudes among British older people: Stability and change in a 20-year longitudinal study. *Ageing and Society, 24,* 167–188.

Coles, L. (2004). Demography of human supercentenarians. *Journal of Gerontology, 59A,* 579–586.

Coley, R. L. (1998). Children's socialization experiences and functioning in single-mother households: The importance of fathers and other men. *Child Development, 69,* 219–230.

Coley, R. L., Morris, J. E., & Hernandez, D. (2004). Out-of-school care and problem behavior trajectories among low-income adolescents: Individual, family, and neighborhood characteristics as added risks. *Child Development, 75,* 948–965.

Collaer, M. L., & Hill, E. M. (2006). Large sex difference in adolescents on a timed line judgment task: Attentional contributors and task relationship to mathematics. *Perception, 35,* 561–572.

Collings, P. (2001). "If you got everything, it's good enough": Perspectives on successful aging in a Canadian Inuit community. *Journal of Cross-Cultural Gerontology, 16,* 127–155.

Collins, M. A., Neafsey, E. J., Mukamal, K. J., Gray, M. O., Parks, D. A., & Das, D. K. (2009). Alcohol in moderation, cardioprotection, and neuroprotection: Epidemiological considerations and mechanistic studies. *Alcoholism, Clinical and Experimental Research, 33,* 206–219.

Collins, N. L., Guichard, A. C., Ford, M. B., & Feeney, B. C. (2006). Responding to need in intimate relationships: Normative processes and individual differences. In M. Mikulincer & G. S. Goodman (Eds.), *Dynamics of romantic love* (pp. 149–189). New York: Guilford.

Collins, W. A. (2003). More than myth: The developmental significance of romantic relationships during adolescence. *Journal of Research on Adolescence, 13,* 1–24.

Collins, W. A., & Laursen, B. (2004). Parent–adolescent relationships and influences. In R. M. Lerner & L. Steinberg (Eds.), *Handbook of adolescent psychology* (2nd ed., pp. 331–361). New York: Wiley.

Collins, W. A., Maccoby, E. E., Steinberg, L., Hetherington, E. M., & Bornstein, M. H. (2000). Contemporary research on parenting: The case for nature and nurture. *American Psychologist, 55,* 218–232.

Collins, W. A., & Madsen, S. D. (2006). Personal relationships in adolescence and early adulthood. In A. L. Vangelisti & D. Perlman (Eds.), *The Cambridge handbook of personal relationships* (pp. 191–209). New York: Cambridge University Press.

Collins, W. A., Madsen, S. D., & Susman-Stillman, A. (2002). Parenting during middle childhood. In M. H. Bornstein (Ed.), *Handbook of parenting: Vol. 1* (2nd ed., pp. 73–101). Mahwah, NJ: Erlbaum.

Collins, W. A., & Russell, G. (1991). Mother–child and father–child interactions in middle childhood and adolescence. *Developmental Review, 11,* 99–136.

Collins, W. A., & van Dulmen, M. (2006a). "The course of true love(s) . . .": Origins and pathways in the development of romantic relationships. In A. Booth & A. Crouter (Eds.), *Romance and sex in adolescence and emerging adulthood: Risks and opportunities* (pp. 63–86). Mahwah, NJ: Erlbaum.

Collins, W. A., & van Dulmen, M. (2006b). Friendships and romance in emerging adulthood: Assessing distinctiveness in close relationships. In J. J. Arnett & J. L. Tanner (Eds.), *Emerging adults in America: Coming of age in the 21st century* (pp. 219–234). Washington, DC: American Psychological Association.

Collins, W. A., & van Dulmen, M. (2006c). Friendships and romantic relationships in emerging adulthood: Continuities and discontinuities. In J. J. Arnett & J. Tanner (Eds.), *Emerging adults in America: Coming of age in the 21st century* (pp. 219–234). Washington, DC: American Psychological Association.

Collins, W. K., & Steinberg, L. (2006). Adolescent development in interpersonal context. In N. Eisenberg (Ed.), *Handbook of child psychology: Vol. 3. Social, emotional, and personality development* (6th ed., pp. 1003–1067). Hoboken, NJ: Wiley.

Colman, L. L., & Colman, A. D. (1991). *Pregnancy: The psychological experience.* New York: Noonday Press.

Colombo, J. (1995). On the neural mechanism underlying developmental and individual differences in visual fixation in infancy. *Developmental Review, 15,* 97–135.

Colombo, J. (2002). Infant attention grows up: The emergence of a developmental cognitive neuroscience perspective. *Current Directions in Psychological Science, 11,* 196–199.

Coltrane, S. (1996). *Family man.* New York: Oxford University Press.

Comijs, H. C., Jonker, C., van Tilberg, W., and Smit, J. H. (1999). Hostility and coping capacity as risk factors of elder mistreatment. *Social Psychiatry and Psychiatric Epidemiology, 34,* 48–52.

Commission on Adolescent Suicide Prevention. (2005). Targeted youth suicide prevention programs. In D. L. Evans, E. B. Foa, R. E. Gur, H. Hending, & C. P. O'Brien (Eds.), *Treating and preventing adolescent mental health disorders: What we know and what we don't know* (pp. 463–469). New York: Oxford University Press.

Commission on Children at Risk. (2008). Hardwired to connect: The new scientific case for authoritative communities. In K. K. Kline (Ed.), *Authoritative communities: The scientific case for nurturing the whole child* (pp. 3–68). New York: Springer.

Comstock, G., & Scharrer, E. (2006). Media and popular culture. In K. A. Renninger & I. E. Sigel (Eds.), *Handbook of child psychology: Vol. 4. Child psychology in practice* (6th ed., pp. 817–863). Hoboken, NJ: Wiley.

Comunian, A. L., & Gielen, U. P. (2000). Sociomoral reflection and prosocial and antisocial behavior: Two Italian studies. *Psychological Reports, 87,* 161–175.

Comunian, A. L., & Gielen, U. P. (2006). Promotion of moral judgment maturity through stimulation of social role-taking and social reflection: An Italian intervention study. *Journal of Moral Education, 35,* 51–69.

Conboy, B. T., & Thal, D. J. (2006). Ties between the lexicon and grammar: Cross-sectional and longitudinal studies of bilingual toddlers. *Child Development, 77,* 712–735.

Condron, D. J. (2007). Stratification and educational sorting: Explaining ascriptive inequalities in early childhood reading group placement. *Social Problems, 54,* 139–160.

Conger, R., Wallace, L., Sun, Y., Simons, L., McLoyd, V., & Brody, G. (2002). Economic pressure in African American families: A replication and extension of the family stress model. *Developmental Psychology, 38,* 179–193.

Conger, R. D., & Conger, K. J. (2002). Resilience in Midwestern families: Selected findings from the first decade of a prospective, longitudinal study. *Journal of Marriage and Family, 64,* 361–373.

Conger, R. D., & Donnellan, M. B. (2007). An interactionist perspective on the socioeconomic context of human development. *Annual Review of Psychology, 58,* 175–199.

Connell, M. W., Sheridan, K., & Gardner, H. (2003). On abilities and domains. In R. J. Sternberg & E. Grigorenko (Eds.), *Perspectives on the psychology of abilities, competencies, and expertise* (pp. 126–155). New York: Cambridge University Press.

Conner, D. B., & Cross, D. R. (2003). Longitudinal analysis of the presence, efficacy, and stability of maternal scaffolding during informal problem-solving interactions. *British Journal of Developmental Psychology, 21,* 315–334.

Connidis, I. A. (1994). Sibling support in older age. *Journal of Gerontology, 49,* S309–S317.

Connidis, I. A., & Campbell, L. D. (1995). Closeness, confiding, and contact among siblings in middle and late adulthood. *Journal of Family Issues, 16,* 722–745.

Connolly, J., Craig, W., Goldberg, A., & Pepler, D. (2004). Mixed-gender groups, dating, and romantic relationships in early adolescence. *Journal of Research on Adolescence, 14,* 185–207.

Connolly, J., & Goldberg, A. (1999). Romantic relationships in adolescence: The role of friends and peers in their emergence and development. In W. Furman, B. B. Brown, & C. Feiring (Eds.), *The development of romantic relationships in adolescence* (pp. 266–290). New York: Cambridge University Press.

Connolly, J. A., & Doyle, A. B. (1984). Relations of social fantasy play to social competence in preschoolers. *Developmental Psychology, 20,* 797–806.

Connor, L. T., Spiro, A., Obler, L. K., & Albert, M. L. (2004). Change in object naming ability during adulthood. *Journal of Gerontology, 59B,* P203–P209.

Connor, P. D., Sampson, P. D., Streissguth, A. P., Bookstein, F. L., & Barr, H. M. (2006). Effects of prenatal alcohol exposure on fine motor coordination and balance: A study of two adult samples. *Neuropsychologia, 44,* 744–751.

Conti, S., Farchi, G., Masocco, M., Minelli, G., Toccaceli, V., & Vichi, M. (2003). Gender differentials in life expectancy in Italy. *European Journal of Epidemiology, 18,* 107–112.

Conway, L. (2007, April 5). Drop the Barbie: Ken Zucker's reparatist treatment of gender-variant children. *Trans News Updates.* Retrieved from ai.eecs.umich.edu/people/conway/TS/News/Drop%20the%20Barbie.htm

Conwell, Y., & Duberstein, P. R. (2001). Suicide in elders. *Annals of the New York Academy of Sciences, 932,* 132–150.

Conwell, Y., Duberstein, P. R., & Caine, E. D. (2002). Risk factors for suicide in later life. *Biological Psychiatry, 52,* 193–204.

Conyers, C., Miltenberger, R., Maki, A., Barenz, R., Jurgens, M., Sailer, A., Haugen, M., & Kopp, B. (2004). A comparison of response cost and differential reinforcement of other behaviors to reduce disruptive behavior in a preschool classroom. *Journal of Applied Behavior Analysis, 37,* 411–415.

Cook, W. L. (2000). Understanding attachment security in family context. *Journal of Personality and Social Psychology, 78,* 285–294.

Cooney, T. M., & Mortimer, J. T. (1999). Family structure differences in the timing of leaving home: Exploring mediating factors. *Journal of Research on Adolescence, 9,* 367–393.

Cooper, C., Harvey, N., Cole, Z., Hanson, M., & Dennison, E. (2009). Developmental origins of osteoporosis: The role of maternal nutrition. In B. Koletzko, T. Decsi, D. Molnár, & A. de la Hunty (Eds.), *Early nutrition programming and health outcomes in later life: Obesity and beyond* (pp. 31–39). New York: Springer Science + Business Media.

Cooper, C., Sayer, A. A., & Dennison, E. M. (2006). The developmental environment: Clinical perspectives on effects on the musculoskeletal system. In P. Gluckman & M. Hanson (Eds.), *Developmental origins of health and disease* (pp. 392–405). Cambridge, UK: Cambridge University Press.

Cooper, C., Selwood, A., & Livingston, G. (2008). The prevalence of elder abuse and neglect: A systematic review. *Age and Ageing, 37,* 151–160.

Cooper, Z., & Fairburn, C. G. (2002). Cognitive-behavioral treatment of obesity. In T. A. Wadden & A. J. Stunkard (Eds.), *Handbook of obesity treatment* (3rd ed., pp. 465–479). New York: Guilford.

Cope-Farrar, K. M., & Kunkel, D. (2002). Sexual messages in teens' favorite prime-time television programs. In J. D. Brown, J. R. Steele, & K. Walsh-Childers (Eds.), *Sexual teens, sexual media* (pp. 59–78). Mahwah, NJ: Erlbaum.

Coplan, R. J., Bowker, A., & Cooper, S. M. (2003). Parenting daily hassles, child temperament, and social adjustment in preschool. *Early Childhood Research Quarterly, 18,* 376–395.

Coplan, R. J., Gavinsky-Molina, M. H., Lagace-Seguin, D., & Wichmann, C. (2001). When girls versus boys play alone: Gender differences in the associates of nonsocial play in kindergarten. *Developmental Psychology, 37,* 464–474.

Coplan, R. J., Prakash, K., O'Neil, K., & Armer, M. (2004). Do you "want" to play? Distinguishing between conflicted shyness and social disinterest in early childhood. *Developmental Psychology, 40,* 244–258.

Copple, C., & Bredekamp, S. (2009). *Developmentally appropriate practice in early childhood programs* (3rd ed.). Washington, DC: National Association for the Education of Young Children.

Corenblum, B. (2003). What children remember about ingroup and outgroup peers: Effects of stereotypes on children's processing of information about group members. *Journal of Experimental Child Psychology, 86,* 32–66.

Cornelius, S. W., & Caspi, A. (1987). Everyday problem solving in adulthood and old age. *Psychology and Aging, 2,* 144–153.

Cornish, A. M., McMahon, C. A., Ungerer, J. A., Barnett, B., Kowalenko, N., & Tennant, C. (2005). Postnatal depression and infant cognitive and motor development in the second postnatal year: The impact of depression chronicity and infant gender. *Infant Behavior and Development, 28,* 407–417.

Cornwell, A. C., & Feigenbaum, P. (2006). Sleep biological rhythms in normal infants and those at high risk for SIDS. *Chronobiology International, 23,* 935–961.

Corr, C. A. (1993). Coping with dying: Lessons that we should and should not learn from the work of Elisabeth Kübler-Ross. *Death Studies, 17,* 69–83.

Corr, C. A. (2003). Loss, grief, and trauma in public tragedy. In M. Lattanzi-Licht & K. J. Doka (Eds.), *Living with grief: Coping with public tragedy* (pp. 63–76). New York: Brunner-Routledge.

Corr, C. A., & Corr, D. M. (2007). Historical and contemporary perspectives on loss, grief, and mourning. In C. A. Corr & D. M. Corr (Eds.), *Handbook of thanatology* (pp. 131–142). New York: Routledge.

Correa-Chávez, M., Rogoff, B., & Mejía-Arauz, R. (2005). Cultural patterns in attending to two events at once. *Child Development, 76,* 664–678.

Cortese, D. A., & Smith, H. C. (2003). *Mayo Clinic family health book* (3rd ed.). New York: HarperCollins.

Cosden, M., Peerson, S., & Elliott, K. (1997). Effects of prenatal drug exposure on birth outcomes and early child development. *Journal of Drug Issues, 27,* 525–539.

Costello, J. (2006). Dying well: Nurses' experiences of 'good and bad' deaths in hospital. *Journal of Advanced Nursing, 54,* 594–601.

Costos, D., Ackerman, R., & Paradis, L. (2002). Recollections of menarche: Communication between mothers and daughters regarding menstruation. *Sex Roles, 46,* 49–59.

Côté, J. E. (2006). Emerging adulthood as an institutionalized moratorium: Risks and benefits to identity formation. In J. J. Arnett (Ed.), *Emerging adults in America: Coming of age in the 21st century* (pp. 85–116). Washington, DC: American Psychological Association.

Côté, S. M., Vaillancourt, T., Barker, E. D., Nagin, D., & Tremblay, R. E. (2007). The joint development of physical and indirect aggression: Predictors of continuity and change during childhood. *Development and Psychopathology, 19,* 37–55.

Coulton, C. J., Crampton, D. S., Irwin, M., Spilsbury, J. C., & Korbin, J. E. (2007). How neighborhoods influence child maltreatment: A review of the literature and alternative pathways. *Child Abuse and Neglect, 31,* 1117–1142.

Courage, M. L., & Howe, M. L. (1998). The ebb and flow of infant attentional preferences: Evidence for long-term recognition memory in 3-month-olds. *Journal of Experimental Child Psychology, 18,* 98–106.

Courage, M. L., & Howe, M. L. (2002). From infant to child: The dynamics of cognitive change in the second year of life. *Psychological Bulletin, 128,* 250–277.

Courage, M. L., Reynolds, G. D., & Richards, J. E. (2006). Infants' attention to patterned stimuli:

Developmental change from 3 to 12 months of age. *Child Development, 77,* 680–695.
Courchesne, E., Carper, R., & Akshoomoff, N. (2003). Evidence of brain overgrowth in the first year of life in autism. *Journal of the American Medical Association, 290,* 337–344.
Couturier, J. L., & Lock, J. (2006). Denial and minimization in adolescents with anorexia nervosa. *International Journal of Eating Disorders, 39,* 212–216.
Covington, C. Y., Nordstrom-Klee, B., Ager, J., Sokol, R., & Delaney-Black, V. (2002). Birth to age 7 growth of children prenatally exposed to drugs: A prospective cohort study. *Neurotoxicology and Teratology, 24,* 489–496.
Cowan, C. P., & Cowan, P. A. (1995). Interventions to ease the transition to parenthood: Why they are needed and what they can do. *Family Relations, 44,* 412–423.
Cowan, C. P., & Cowan, P. A. (1997). Working with couples during stressful transitions. In S. Dreman (Ed.), *The family on the threshold of the 21st century* (pp. 17–47). Mahwah, NJ: Erlbaum.
Cowan, C. P., & Cowan, P. A. (2000). *When partners become parents: The big life change for couples.* Mahwah, NJ: Erlbaum.
Cowan, P. A., & Cowan, C. P. (2002). Interventions as tests of family systems theories: Marital and family relationships in children's development and psychopathology. *Development and Psychopathology, 14,* 731–759.
Cowan, P. A., & Cowan, C. P. (2004). From family relationships to peer rejection to antisocial behavior in middle childhood. In J. B. Kupersmidt & K. A. Dodge (Eds.), *Children's peer relations: From development to intervention* (pp. 159–177). Washington, DC: American Psychological Association.
Cox, C. E., Kotch, J. B., & Everson, M. D. (2003). A longitudinal study of modifying influences in the relationship between domestic violence and child maltreatment. *Journal of Family Violence, 18,* 5–17.
Cox, G. (2002). The Native American patient. In R. B. Gilbert (Ed.), *Health care and spirituality: Listening, assessing, caring* (pp. 107–127). Amityville, NY: Baywood.
Cox, M., & Littlejohn, K. (1995). Children's use of converging obliques in their perspective drawings. *Educational Psychology, 15,* 127–139.
Cox, M. J., Owen, M. T., Henderson, V. K., & Margand, N. A. (1992). Prediction of infant–father and infant–mother attachment. *Developmental Psychology, 28,* 474–483.
Cox, M. J., Paley, B., & Harter, K. (2001). Interparental conflict and parent–child relationships. In J. H. Grych & F. D. Fincham (Eds.), *Interparental conflict and child development: Theory, research, and applications* (pp. 249–272). New York: Cambridge University Press.
Cox, S. M., Hopkins, J., & Hans, S. L. (2000). Attachment in preterm infants and their mothers: Neonatal risk status and maternal representations. *Infant Mental Health Journal, 21,* 464–480.
Crago, M. B., Annahatak, B., & Ningiuruvik, L. (1993). Changing patterns of language socialization in Inuit homes. *Anthropology and Education Quarterly, 24,* 205–223.
Craig, C. M., & Lee, D. N. (1999). Neonatal control of sucking pressure: Evidence for an intrinsic tau-guide. *Experimental Brain Research, 124,* 371–382.
Craig, W. M., Pepler, D., & Atlas, R. (2000). Observations of bullying in the playground and in the classroom. *School Psychology International, 21,* 22–36.
Craig-Bray, L., Adams, G. R., & Dobson, W. R. (1988). Identity formation and social relations during late adolescence. *Journal of Youth and Adolescence, 17,* 173–187.
Crain, W. (2005). *Theories of development* (5th ed.). Upper Saddle River, NJ: Prentice-Hall.
Crair, M. C., Gillespie, D. C., & Stryker, M. P. (1998). The role of visual experience in the development of columns in cat visual cortex. *Science, 279,* 566–570.
Cramer, R. E., Schaefer, J. T., & Reid, S. (2003). Identifying the ideal mate: More evidence for male–female convergence. In N. J. Pallone (Ed.), *Love, romance, sexual interaction: Research perspectives from current psychology* (pp. 61–73). New Brunswick, NJ: Transaction Publishers.
Crane, D. R., Ngai, S. W., Larson, J. H., & Hafen, M., Jr. (2005). The influence of family functioning and parent–adolescent acculturation on North American Chinese adolescent outcomes. *Family Relations, 54,* 400–410.
Cratty, B. J. (1986). *Perceptual and motor development in infants and children* (3rd ed.), Englewood Cliffs, NJ: Prentice-Hall.
Crawford, J. (1997). *Best evidence: Research foundations of the bilingual education act.* Washington, DC: National Clearinghouse for Bilingual Education.
Crawford, N. (2003, September). Understanding children's atypical gender behavior. *APA Monitor,* p. 40.
Crawley, L., Payne, R., Bolden, J., Payne, T., Washington, P., & Williams, S. (2000). Palliative and end-of-life care in the African American community. *Journal of the American Medical Association, 284,* 2518–2521.
Creasey, G. L. (2002). Associations between working models of attachment and conflict management behavior in romantic couples. *Journal of Counseling Psychology, 49,* 365–375.
Creasey, G. L., Jarvis, P. A., & Berk, L. E. (1998). Play and social competence. In O. N. Saracho & B. Spodek (Eds.), *Multiple perspectives on play in early childhood education* (pp. 116–143). Albany: State University of New York Press.
Creasey, G. L., & Ladd, A. (2004). Negative mood regulation expectancies and conflict behaviors in late adolescent college student romantic relationships: The moderating role of generalized attachment representations. *Journal of Research on Adolescence, 14,* 235–255.
Crick, N. R., Casas, J. F., & Nelson, D. A. (2002). Toward a more comprehensive understanding of peer maltreatment: Studies of relational victimization. *Current Directions in Psychological Science, 11,* 98–101.
Crick, N. R., & Nelson, D. A. (2002). Relational and physical victimization within friendships: Nobody told me there'd be friends like these. *Journal of Abnormal Child Psychology, 30,* 599–607.
Crick, N. R., Ostrov, J. M., Appleyard, K., Jansen, E., & Casas, J. F. (2004). Relational aggression in early childhood: You can't come to my birthday party unless. . . . In M. Putallaz & K. Bierman (Eds.), *Aggression, antisocial behavior, and violence among girls: A developmental perspective* (pp. 71–89). New York: Guilford.
Crick, N. R., Ostrov, J. M., Burr, J. E., Cullerton-Sen, C., Jansen-Yeh, E., & Ralston, P. (2006). A longitudinal study of relational and physical aggression in preschool. *Journal of Applied Developmental Psychology, 27,* 254–268.
Crick, N. R., Ostrov, J. M., & Werner, N. E. (2006). A longitudinal study of relational aggression, physical aggression, and social-psychological adjustment. *Journal of Abnormal Child Psychology, 34,* 131–142.
Critser, G. (2003). *Fat land.* Boston: Houghton Mifflin.
Crockenberg, S., & Leerkes, E. (2000). Infant social and emotional development in family context. In C. H. Zeanah, Jr., *Handbook of infant mental health* (2nd ed., pp. 60–90). New York: Guilford.
Crockenberg, S., & Leerkes, E. (2003). Infant negative emotionality, caregiving, and family relationships. In A. C. Crouter & A. Booth (Eds.), *Children's influence on family dynamics* (pp. 57–78). Mahwah, NJ: Erlbaum.
Crockenberg, S., & Leerkes, E. (2004). Infant and maternal behaviors regulate infant reactivity to novelty at 6 months. *Developmental Psychology, 40,* 1123–1132.
Crockett, L. J., Raffaelli, M., & Shen, Y.-L. (2006). Linking self-regulation and risk proneness to risky sexual behavior: Pathways through peer pressure and early substance use. *Journal of Research on Adolescence, 16,* 503–525.
Crohan, S. E., & Antonucci, T. C. (1989). Friends as a source of social support in old age. In R. G. Adams & R. Blieszner (Eds.), *Older adult friendship* (pp. 129–146). Newbury Park, CA: Sage.
Croker, R. (2007). *The boomer century: 1946–2046: How America's most influential generation changed everything.* New York: Springboard Press.
Crosno, R., Kirkpatrick, M., & Elder, G. H., Jr. (2004). Intergenerational bonding in school: The behavioral and contextual correlates of student–teacher relationships. *Sociology of Education, 77,* 60–81.
Cross, S., & Markus, H. (1991). Possible selves across the life span. *Human Development, 34,* 230–255.
Crouch, J. L., Skowronski, J. J., Milner, J. S., & Harris, B. (2008). Parental responses to infant crying: The influence of child physical abuse risk and hostile priming. *Child Abuse and Neglect, 32,* 702–710.
Crouter, A. C., & Bumpus, M. F. (2001). Linking parents' work stress to children's and adolescents' psychological adjustment. *Current Directions in Psychological Science, 10,* 156–159.
Crouter, A. C., & Head, M. R. (2002). Parental monitoring and knowledge of children. In M. H. Bornstein (Ed.), *Handbook of parenting: Vol. 3. Being and becoming a parent* (2nd ed., pp. 461–483). Mahwah, NJ: Erlbaum.
Crouter, A. C., Helms-Erikson, H., Updegraff, K., & McHale, S. M. (1999). Conditions underlying parents' knowledge about children's daily lives in middle childhood: Between- and within-family comparisons. *Child Development, 70,* 246–259.
Crouter, A. C., Manke, B. A., & McHale, S. M. (1995). The family context of gender intensification in early adolescence. *Child Development, 66,* 317–329.
Csikszentmihalyi, M., & Rathunde, K. (1990). The psychology of wisdom: An evolutionary interpretation. In R. J. Sternberg (Ed.), *Wisdom: Its nature, origins, and development* (pp. 25–51). New York: Cambridge University Press.
Cuddy-Casey, M., & Orvaschel, H. (1997). Children's understanding of death in relation to child suicidality and homicidality. *Clinical Psychology Review, 17,* 33–45.
Cui, X., & Vaillant, G. E. (1996). Antecedents and consequences of negative life events in adulthood: A longitudinal study. *American Journal of Psychiatry, 153,* 21–26.
Cuijpers, P. (2002). Effective ingredients of school-based drug prevention programs: A systematic review. *Addictive Behaviors, 27,* 1009–1023.
Culbertson, F. M. (1997). Depression and gender: An international review. *American Psychologist, 52,* 25–51.
Cully, J. A., LaVoie, D., & Gfeller, J. D. (2001). Reminiscence, personality, and psychological functioning in older adults. *Gerontologist, 41,* 89–95.
Culnane, M., Fowler, M. G., Lee, S. S., McSherry, G., Brady, M., & O'Donnell, K. (1999). Lack of long-

term effects of in utero exposure to zidovudine among uninfected children born to HIV-infected women. *Journal of the American Medical Association, 281,* 151–157.

Cumming, E., & Henry, W. E. (1961). *Growing old: The process of disengagement.* New York: Basic Books.

Cummings, E. M., & Cummings, J. S. (2002). Parenting and attachment. In M. H. Bornstein (Ed.), *Handbook of parenting* (2nd ed., pp. 35–58). Mahwah, NJ: Erlbaum.

Cummings, E. M., & Davies, P. T. (1994). Maternal depression and child development. *Journal of Child Psychology and Psychiatry, 35,* 73–112.

Cunningham, A. E., & Stanovich, K. E. (1998, Spring/Summer). What reading does for the mind. *American Educator,* 8–15.

Cunningham, J. D., & Antill, J. K. (1994). Cohabitation and marriage: Retrospective and predictive comparisons. *Journal of Social and Personal Relationships, 11,* 77–93.

Curlin, F. A., Nwodim, C., Vance, J. L., Chin, M. H., & Lantos, J. D. (2008). To die, to sleep: U.S. physicians' religious and other objections to physician-assisted suicide, terminal sedation, and withdrawal of life support. *American Journal of Hospice and Palliative Medicine, 25,* 112–120.

Currie, D. H. (1999). Violent men or violent women? Whose definition counts? In R. K. Bergen (Ed.), *Issues in intimate violence* (pp. 97–111). Thousand Oaks, CA: Sage.

Curtiss, K., Hayslip, B., Jr., & Dolan, D. C. (2007). Motivational style, length of residence, voluntariness, and gender as influences on adjustment to long term care: A pilot study. *Journal of Human Behavior in the Social Environment, 15,* 13–34.

Cutler, L. J. (2007). Physical environments of assisted living: Research needs and challenges. *Gerontologist, 47*(Special Issue III), 68–82.

Cutler, R. G., & Mattson, M. P. (2006). Introduction: The adversities of aging. *Ageing Research Reviews, 5,* 221–238.

Cutler, S. J., & Hendricks, J. (2001). Emerging social trends. In R. H. Binstock & L. K. George (Eds.), *Handbook of aging and the social sciences* (5th ed., pp. 462–480). San Diego, CA: Academic Press.

Cutrona, C. E., Hessling, R. M., Bacon, P. L., & Russell, D. W. (1998). Predictors and correlates of continuing involvement with the baby's father among adolescent mothers. *Journal of Family Psychology, 12,* 369–387.

Cutter, W. J., Daly, E. M., Robertson, D. M. W., Chitnis, X. A., van Amelsvoort, T. A. M. J., & Simmons, A. (2006). Influence of X chromosome and hormones on human brain development: A magnetic resonance imaging and proton magnetic resonance spectroscopy study of Turner syndrome. *Biological Psychiatry, 59,* 273–283.

Cyr, M., McDuff, P., & Wright, J. (2006). Prevalence and predictors of dating violence among adolescent female victims of child sexual abuse. *Journal of Interpersonal Violence, 21,* 1000–1017.

D

Dabrowska, E. (2000). From formula to schema: The acquisition of English questions. *Cognitive Linguistics, 11,* 1–20.

Dahl, R. E., & Lewin, D. S. (2002). Pathways to adolescent healthy sleep regulation and behavior. *Journal of Adolescent Health, 31,* 175–184.

Dahl, R.E., Scher, M. S., Williamson, D. E., Robles, N., & Day, N. (1995). A longitudinal study of prenatal marijuana use: Effects on sleep and arousal at age 3 years. *Archives of Pediatric and Adolescent Medicine, 149,* 145–150.

Dahlberg, L. L., & Simon, T. R. (2006). Predicting and preventing youth violence: Developmental pathways and risk. In L. L. Dahlberg & T. R. Simon (Eds.), *Preventing violence: Research and evidence-based intervention strategies* (pp. 97–124). Washington, DC: American Psychological Association.

Dales, L., Hammer, S. J., & Smith, N. J. (2001). Time trends in autism and MMR immunization coverage in California. *Journal of the American Medical Association, 285,* 1183–1185.

Dal Santo, J. A., Goodman, R. M., Glik, D., & Jackson, K. (2004). Childhood unintentional injuries: Factors predicting injury risk among preschoolers. *Journal of Pediatric Psychology, 29,* 273–283.

Damashek, A., & Peterson, L. (2002). Unintentional injury prevention efforts for young children: Levels, methods, types, and targets. *Developmental and Behavioral Pediatrics, 23,* 443–455.

Damjanovic, A. M., Yang, Y., Glaser, R., Kiecolt-Glaser, J. K., & Nguyen, H. (2007). Accelerated telomere erosion is associated with a declining immune function of caregivers of Alzheimer's disease patients. *Journal of Immunology, 179,* 4249–4254.

Damon, W. (1988a). *The moral child.* New York: Free Press.

Damon, W. (1988b). *Self-understanding in childhood and adolescence.* New York: Cambridge University Press.

Damon, W. (1990). Self-concept, adolescent. In R. M. Lerner, A. C. Petersen, & J. Brooks-Gunn (Eds.), *The encyclopedia of adolescence* (Vol. 2, pp. 87–91). New York: Garland.

Damon, W. (1995). *Greater expectations: Overcoming the culture of indulgence in America's homes and schools.* New York: Free Press.

Damon, W. (2004). *The moral advantage: How to succeed in business by doing the right thing.* San Francisco: Berrett-Koehler.

Damon, W., & Hart, D. (1988). *Self-understanding in childhood and adolescence.* New York: Cambridge University Press.

Daniell, W. E., Swan, S. S., McDaniel, M. M., Camp, J. E., Cohen, M. A., & Stebbins, J. G. (2006). Noise exposure and hearing loss prevention programs after twenty years of regulations in the United States. *Occupational and Environmental Medicine, 63,* 343–351.

Daniels, D. H., Kalkman, D. L., & McCombs, B. L. (2001). Young children's perspectives on learning and teacher practices in different classroom contexts: Implications for motivation. *Early Education and Development, 12,* 253–273.

Daniels, E., & Leaper, C. (2006). A longitudinal investigation of sport participation, peer acceptance, and self-esteem among adolescent girls and boys. *Sex Roles, 55,* 875–880.

Daniels, P., Noe, G. F., & Mayberry, R. (2006). Barriers to prenatal care among black women of low socioeconomic status. *American Journal of Health Behavior, 30,* 188–198.

Dannemiller, J. L., & Stephens, B. R. (1988). A critical test of infant pattern preference models. *Child Development, 59,* 210–216.

Dansinger, M. L., Tatsioni, A., Wong, J. B., Chung, M., & Balk, E. M. (2007). Meta-analysis: The effect of dietary counseling for weight loss. *Annals of Internal Medicine, 147,* 41–50.

Dapretto, M., & Bjork, E. L. (2000). The development of word retrieval abilities in the second year and its relation to early vocabulary growth. *Child Development, 71,* 635–648.

Darroch, J. E., Frost, J. J., & Singh, S. (2001). *Teenage sexual and reproductive behavior in developed countries: Can more progress be made?* New York: Alan Guttmacher Institute.

Darwin, C. (1936). *On the origin of species by means of natural selection.* New York: Modern Library. (Original work published 1859)

D'Augelli, A. R. (2002). Mental health problems among lesbian, gay, and bisexual youths ages 14 to 21. *Clinical Child Psychology and Psychiatry, 7,* 433–456.

D'Augelli, A. R. (2006). Developmental and contextual factors and mental health among lesbian, gay, and bisexual youths. In A. M. Omoto & H. S. Howard (Eds.), *Sexual orientation and mental health: Examining identity and development in lesbian, gay, and bisexual people* (pp. 37–53). Washington, DC: American Psychological Association.

D'Augelli, A. R., Grossman, A. H., Salter, N. P., Vasey, J. J., Starks, M. T., & Sinclair, K. O. (2005). Predicting the suicide attempts of lesbian, gay, and bisexual youth. *Suicide and Life-Threatening Behavior, 35,* 646–660.

D'Augelli, A. R., Grossman, A. H., & Starks, M. T. (2005). Parents' awareness of lesbian, gay, and bisexual youths' sexual orientation. *Journal of Marriage and Family, 67,* 474–482.

Davidov, M., & Grusec, J. E. (2006). Untangling the links of parental responsiveness to distress and warmth to child outcomes. *Child Development, 77,* 44–58.

Davidson, R. J. (1994). Asymmetric brain function, affective style, and psychopathology: The role of early experience and plasticity. *Development and Psychopathology, 6,* 741–758.

Davies, P. A., & Lindsay, L. L. (2004). Everyday marital conflict and child aggression. *Journal of Abnormal Child Psychology, 32,* 191–202.

Daviglus, M. L., Stamler, J., Pirzada, A., Yan, L. L., Garside, D. B., & Liu, K. (2004). Favorable cardiovascular risk profile in young women and long-term risk of cardiovascular and all-cause mortality. *Journal of the American Medical Association, 292,* 1588–1592.

Davis, K. F., Parker, K. P., & Montgomery, G. L. (2004). Sleep in infants and young children. Part 1: Normal sleep. *Journal of Pediatric Health Care, 18,* 65–71.

Dawson, G., Ashman, S. B., Panagiotides, H., Hessl, D., Self, J., Yamada, E., & Embry, L. (2003). Preschool outcomes of children of depressed mothers: Role of maternal behavior, contextual risk, and children's brain activity. *Child Development, 74,* 1158–1175.

Dawson, T. L. (2002). New tools, new insights: Kohlberg's moral judgment stages revisited. *International Journal of Behavioral Development, 26,* 154–166.

Deafness Research Foundation. (2005). Hear us: Incidence of deafness in newborns. Retrieved from www.hearinghealth.com

Deák, G. O. (2000). Hunting the fox of word learning: Why "constraints" fail to capture it. *Developmental Review, 20,* 29–80.

Deák, G. O., Ray, S. D., & Brenneman, K. (2003). Children's perseverative appearance–reality errors are related to emerging language skills. *Child Development, 74,* 944–964.

Dearing, E., McCartney, K., & Taylor, B. A. (2006). Within-child associations between family income and externalizing and internalizing problems. *Developmental Psychology, 42,* 237–252.

Deary, I. J. (2001). *g* and cognitive elements of information progressing: An agnostic view. In R. J. Sternberg & E. L. Grigorenko (Eds.), *The general factor of intelligence: How general is it?* (pp. 447–479). Mahwah, NJ: Erlbaum.

Deary, I. J., & Der, G. (2005). Reaction time, age, and cognitive ability: Longitudinal findings from age 16 to 63 years in representative population samples. *Aging, Neuropsychology, and Cognition, 12,* 187–215.

Deary, I. J., Strand, S., Smith, P., & Fernandes, C. (2007). Intelligence and educational achievement. *Intelligence, 35,* 13–21.

Deater-Deckard, K., Lansford, J. E., Dodge, K. A., Pettit, G. S., & Bates, J. E. (2003). The development of attitudes about physical punishment: An 8-year longitudinal study. *Journal of Family Psychology, 17,* 351–360.

Deater-Deckard, K., Pike, A., Petrill, S. A., Cutting, A. L., Hughes, C., & O'Connor, T. G. (2001). Nonshared environmental processes in social-emotional development: An observational study of identical twin differences in the preschool period. *Developmental Science, 4,* F1–F6.

DeBerry, K. M., Scarr, S., & Weinberg, R. (1996). Family racial socialization and ecological competence: Longitudinal assessments of African-American transracial adoptees. *Child Development, 67,* 2375–2399.

DeBoer, T., Scott, L. S., & Nelson, C. A. (2007). Methods for acquiring and analyzing infant event-related potentials. In M. de Haan (Ed.), *Infant EEG and event-related potentials* (pp. 5–37). New York: Psychology Press.

de Bruyn, E. H. (2005). Role strain, engagement and academic achievement in early adolescence. *Educational Studies, 31,* 15–27.

de Bruyn, E. H., Deković, M., & Meijnen, G. W. (2003). Parenting, goal orientations, classroom behavior, and school success in early adolescence. *Journal of Applied Developmental Psychology, 24,* 393–412.

DeCasper, A. J., & Spence, M. J. (1986). Prenatal maternal speech influences newborns' perception of speech sounds. *Infant Behavior and Development, 9,* 133–150.

de Grey, A. D. N. J. (2005). The unfortunate influence of the weather on the rate of ageing: Why human caloric restriction or its emulation may only extend life expectancy by 2–3 years. *Gerontology, 51,* 73–82.

de Haan, M., Bauer, P. J., Georgieff, M. K., & Nelson, C. A. (2000). Explicit memory in low-risk infants aged 19 months born between 27 and 42 weeks of gestation. *Developmental Medicine and Child Neurology, 42,* 304–312.

de Haan, M., & Johnson, M. H. (2003). Mechanisms and theories of brain development. In M. de Haan & M. H. Johnson (Eds.), *The cognitive neuroscience of development* (pp. 1–18). Hove, UK: Psychology Press.

Deissinger, T. (2007). "Making schools practical": Practice firms and their function in the full-time vocational school system in Germany. *Education + Training, 49,* 364–378.

deJong, A., & Franklin, B. A. (2004). Prescribing exercise for the elderly: Current research and recommendations. *Current Sports Medicine Reports, 3,* 337–343.

Dekker, M. C., Ferdinand, R. F., van Lang, D. J., Bongers, I. L., van der Ende, J., & Verhulst, F. C. (2007). Developmental trajectories of depressive symptoms from early childhood to late adolescence: Gender differences and adult outcome. *Journal of Child Psychology and Psychiatry, 48,* 657–666.

DeKosky, S. T., Williamson, J. D., Fitzpatrick, A. L., Kronmal, R. A., Ives, D. G., & Saxton, J. A. (2008). Ginkgo biloba for prevention of dementia: A randomized controlled trial. *Journal of the American Medical Association, 300,* 2253–2262.

Deković, M., & Buist, K. L. (2005). Multiple perspectives within the family: Family relationship patterns. *Journal of Family Issues, 26,* 467–490.

Deković, M., Noom, M. J., & Meeus, W. (1997). Expectations regarding development during adolescence: Parent and adolescent perceptions. *Journal of Youth and Adolescence, 26,* 253–271.

DeLamater, J., & Moorman, S. M. (2007). Sexual behavior in later life. *Journal of Aging and Health, 19,* 921–945.

Delgado-Gaitan, C. (1994). Socializing young children in Mexican-American families: An intergenerational perspective. In P. Greenfield & R. Cocking (Eds.), *Cross-cultural roots of minority child development* (p. 55–86). Hillsdale, NJ: Erlbaum.

de Lima, C., Alves, L. E., Iagher, F., Machado, A. F., Bonatto, S. J., & Kuczera, D. (2008). Anaerobic exercise reduces tumor growth, cancer cachexia and increases macrophage and lymphocyte response in Walker 256 tumor-bearing rats. *European Journal of Applied Physiology, 104,* 957–964.

De Lisi, R., & Gallagher, A. M. (1991). Understanding gender stability and constancy in Argentinean children. *Merrill-Palmer Quarterly, 37,* 483–502.

Dell, D. L. (2001). Adolescent pregnancy. In N. L. Stotland & D. E. Stewart (Eds.), *Psychological aspects of women's health care* (pp. 95–116). Washington, DC: American Psychiatric Association.

DeLoache, J. S. (1987). Rapid change in symbolic functioning of very young children. *Science, 238,* 1556–1557.

DeLoache, J. S. (2000). Dual representation and children's use of scale models. *Child Development, 71,* 329–338.

DeLoache, J. S. (2002). The symbol-mindedness of young children. In W. Hartup & R. A. Weinberg (Eds.), *Minnesota Symposia on Child Psychology* (Vol. 32, pp. 73–101). Mahwah, NJ: Erlbaum.

Deltondo, J., Por, I., Hu, W., Merchenthaler, I., Semeniken, K., Jojart, J., & Dudas, B. (2008). Associations between the human growth hormone-releasing hormone and neuropeptide-Y-immunoreactive systems in the human diencephalons: A possible morphological substrate of the impact of stress on growth. *Neuroscience, 153,* 1146–1152.

DeMarie, D., Miller, P. H., Ferron, J., & Cunningham, W. R. (2004). Path analysis tests of theoretical models of children's memory performance. *Journal of Cognition and Development, 5,* 461–492.

De Marco, A. C., & Berzin, S. C. (2008). The influence of family economic status on home-leaving patterns during emerging adulthood. *Families in Society, 89,* 208–218.

Demark-Wahnefried, W., Rock, C. L., Patrick, K., & Byers, T. (2008). Lifestyle interventions to reduce cancer risk and improve outcomes. *American Family Physician, 77,* 1573–1578.

Demetriou, A., Christou, C., Spanoudis, G., & Platsidou, M. (2002). The development of mental processing: Efficiency, working memory, and thinking. *Monographs of the Society for Research in Child Development, 67*(1, Serial No. 268).

Demetriou, A., Efklides, A., Papadaki, M., Papantoniou, G., & Economou, A. (1993). Structure and development of causal thought: From early adolescence to youth. *Developmental Psychology, 29,* 480–497.

Demetriou, A., & Kazi, S. (2001). *Unity and modularity in the mind and the self: Studies on the relationships between self-awareness, personality, and intellectual development from childhood to adolescence.* London: Routledge.

Demetriou, A., Pachaury, A., Metallidou, Y., & Kazi, S. (1996). Universals and specificities in the structure and development of quantitative-relational throught: A cross-cultural study in Greece and India. *International Journal of Behavioral Development, 19,* 255–290.

Dempster, F. N., & Corkill, A. J. (1999). Interference and inhibition in cognition and behavior: Unifying themes for educational psychology. *Educational Psychology Review, 11,* 1–88.

DeNavas-Walt, C., Proctor, B. D., & Smith, J. C. (2009). *Income, poverty, and health insurance coverage in the United States: 2008.* U.S. Census Bureau, Current Population Reports, P60–236. Washington, DC: U.S. Government Printing Office.

Denham, S. A. (2005). Emotional competence counts: Assessment as support for school readiness. In K. Hirsh-Pasek, A. Kochanoff, N. S. Newcombe, & J. de Villiers (Eds.), Using scientific knowledge to inform preschool assessment. *Social Policy Report of the Society for Research in Child Development, 19*(No.1), 12.

Denham, S. A. (2006). Emotional competence: Implications for social functioning. In J. L. Luby (Ed.), *Handbook of preschool mental health: Development, disorders, and treatment* (pp. 23–44). New York: Guilford.

Denham, S. A., Blair, K., Schmidt, M., & DeMulder, E. (2002). Compromised emotional competence: Seeds of violence sown early? *American Journal of Orthopsychiatry, 72,* 70–82.

Denham, S. A., & Burton, R. (2003). *Social and emotional prevention and intervention programming for preschoolers.* New York: Kluwer-Plenum.

Denham, S. A., & Kochanoff, A. T. (2002). Parental contributions to preschoolers' understanding of emotion. *Marriage and Family Review, 34,* 311–343.

Denissen, J. J. A., Zarrett, N. R., & Eccles, J. S. (2007). I like to do it, I'm able, and I know I am: Longitudinal couplings between domain-specific achievement, self-concept, and interest. *Child Development, 78,* 430–447.

Denmark, F. L., & Klara, M. D. (2007). Empowerment: A prime time for women over 50. In V. Mulhbauer & J. C. Chrisler (Eds.), *Women over 50* (pp. 182–203). New York: Springer.

Dennerstein, L., Dudley, E., & Guthrie, J. (2002). Empty nest or revolving door? A prospective study of women's quality of life in midlife during the phase of children leaving and re-entering the home. *Psychological Medicine, 32,* 545–550.

Dennerstein, L., & Lehert, P. (2004). Modeling mid-aged women's sexual functioning: A prospective, population-based study. *Journal of Sex and Marriage Therapy, 30,* 173–183.

Denney, N. W. (1990). Adult age differences in traditional and practical problem solving. *Advances in Psychology, 72,* 329–349.

Denney, N. W., & Pearce, K A. (1989). A developmental study of practical problem solving in adults. *Psychology and Aging, 4,* 438–442.

Dennis, T., Bendersky, M., Ramsay, D., & Lewis, M. (2006). Reactivity and regulation in children prenatally exposed to cocaine. *Developmental Psychology, 42,* 688–697.

Dennis, W. (1960). Causes of retardation among institutionalized children: Iran. *Journal of Genetic Psychology, 96,* 47–59.

Dennison, B. A., Straus, J. H., Mellits, D., & Charney, E. (1998). Childhood physical fitness tests: Predictor of adult physical activity levels? *Pediatrics, 82,* 342–350.

Dent, A., & Stewart, A. (2004). *Sudden death in childhood: Support for the bereaved family.* London: Butterworth-Heinemann.

DePaulo, B. M., & Morris, W. L. (2005). Singles in society and in science. *Psychological Inquiry, 16,* 142–149.

DePaulo, B. M., & Morris, W. L. (2006). The unrecognized stereotyping and discrimination against singles. *Current Directions in Psychological Science, 15,* 251–254.

Der, G., Batty, G. D., & Deary, I. J. (2006). Effect of breastfeeding on intelligence in children: Prospective study, sibling pairs analysis, and meta-analysis. *British Medical Journal, 333,* 945.

Der, G., & Deary, I. J. (2006). Age and sex differences in reaction time in adulthood: Results from the United Kingdom Health and Lifestyle Survey. *Psychology and Aging, 21,* 62–73.

de Ribaupierre, A., & Lecerf, T. (2006). Relationships between working memory and intelligence from a developmental perspective: Convergent evidence from a neo-Piagetian and a psychometric approach. *European Journal of Cognitive Psychology, 18,* 109–137.

Derom, C., Thiery, E., Vlietinck, R., Loos, R., & Derom, R. (1996). Handedness in twins according to zygosity and chorion type: A preliminary report. *Behavior Genetics, 26,* 407–408.

DeRose, L. M., & Brooks-Gunn, J. (2006). Transition into adolescence: The role of pubertal processes. In L. Balter & C. S. Tamis-LeMonda (Eds.), *Child psychology: A handbook of contemporary issues* (2nd ed., pp. 385–414). New York: Psychology Press.

DeRosier, M. E. (2007). Peer-rejected and bullied children: A safe schools initiative for elementary school students. In J. E. Zins, M. J. Elias, & C. A. Maher (Eds.), *Bullying, victimization, and peer harassment* (pp. 257–276). New York: Haworth.

DeRosier, M. E., & Thomas, J. M. (2003). Strengthening sociometric prediction: Scientific advances in the assessment of children's peer relations. *Child Development, 75,* 1379–1392.

de Rosnay, M., & Hughes, C. (2006). Conversation and theory of mind: Do children talk their way to socio-cognitive understanding? *British Journal of Developmental Psychology, 24,* 7–37.

Derwinger, A., Neely, A. S., & Bäckman, L. (2005). Design your own memory strategies! Self-generated strategy training versus mnemonic training in old age: An 8-month follow-up. *Neuropsychological Rehabilitation, 15,* 37–54.

De Schipper, J. C., Tavecchio, L. W. C., van IJzendoorn, M. H., & van Zeijl, J. (2004). Goodness-of-fit in center day care: Relations of temperament, stability, and quality of care with the child's adjustment. *Early Childhood Research Quarterly, 19,* 257–272.

De Schipper, J. C., van IJzendoorn, M. H., & Tavecchio, L. W. C. (2004). Stability in center day care: Relations with children's well-being and problem behavior in day care. *Social Development, 13,* 531–550.

Desrochers, S. (2008). From Piaget to specific Genevan developmental models. *Child Development Perspectives, 2,* 7–12.

DeVaney, S. A. (2008). Financial issues of older adults. In J. J. Xiao (Ed.), *Handbook of consumer finance research* (pp. 209–221). New York: Springer Science + Business Media.

Deveson, A. (1994). *Coming of age: Twenty-one interviews about growing older.* Newham, Australia: Scribe.

de Villiers, J. G., & de Villiers, P. A. (1973). A cross-sectional study of the acquisition of grammatical morphemes in child speech. *Journal of Psycholinguistic Research, 2,* 267–278.

de Villiers, J. G., & de Villiers, P. A. (2000). Linguistic determinism and the understanding of false beliefs. In P. Metchell & K. J. Riggs (Eds.), *Children's reasoning and the mind* (pp. 87–99). Hove, UK: Psychology Press.

De Vogli, R., Mistry, R., Gnesolto, R., & Cornia, G. A. (2005). Has the relation between income inequality and life expectancy disappeared? Evidence from Italy and top industrialized countries. *Journal of Epidemiology and Community Health, 59,* 158–162.

de Vries, B., Bluck, S., & Birren, J. E. (1993). The understanding of death and dying in a life-span perspective. *Gerontologist, 33,* 366–372.

DeVries, R. (2001). Constructivist education in preschool and elementary school: The sociomoral atmosphere as the first educational goal. In S. L. Golbeck (Ed.), *Psychological perspectives on early childhood education* (pp. 153–180). Mahwah, NJ: Erlbaum.

de Waal, F. B. M. (1993). Sex differences in chimpanzee (and human) behavior: A matter of social values? In M. Hechter, L. Nadel, & R. E. Michod (Eds.), *The origin of values* (pp. 285–303). New York: Aldine de Gruyter.

de Waal, F. B. M. (2001). *Tree of origin.* Cambridge, MA: Harvard University Press.

De Weerd, A. W., & van den Bossche, A. S. (2003). The development of sleep during the first months of life. *Sleep Medicine Reviews, 7,* 179–191.

de Weerth, C., & Buitelaar, J. K. (2005). Physiological stress reactivity in human pregnancy—a review. *Neuroscience and Biobehavioral Reviews, 29,* 295–312.

De Wolff, M. S., & van IJzendoorn, M. H. (1997). Sensitivity and attachment: A meta-analysis on parental antecedents of infant attachment. *Child Development, 68,* 571–591.

Dey, J. G., & Hill, C. (2007). *Behind the pay gap.* Washington, DC: American Association of University Women.

Dey, S., Flather, M. D., Devlin, G. P., Brieger, D., Gurfinkle, D. P., & Steg, P. G. (2009). Sex-related differences in the presentation, treatment and outcomes among patients with acute coronary syndromes. *Heart, 95,* 20–26.

Diamond, A. (2000). Close interrelation of motor development and cognitive development and of the cerebellum and prefrontal cortex. *Child Development, 71,* 44–56.

Diamond, A. (2004). Normal development of prefrontal cortex from birth to young adulthood: Cognitive functions, anatomy, and biochemistry. In D. T. Stuff & R. T. Knight (Eds.), *Principles of frontal lobe function* (pp. 466–503). New York: Oxford University Press.

Diamond, A., Barnett, W. S., Thomas, J., & Munro, S. (2007). Preschool program improves cognitive control. *Science, 318,* 1387–1388.

Diamond, A., Cruttenden, L., & Neiderman, D. (1994). AB with multiple wells: 1. Why are multiple wells sometimes easier than two wells? 2. Memory or memory + inhibition. *Developmental Psychology, 30,* 192–205.

Diamond, L. M. (1998). Development of sexual orientation among adolescent and young adult women. *Developmental Psychology, 34,* 1085–1095.

Diamond, L. M. (2003). Love matters: Romantic relationships among sexual-minority adolescents. In P. Florsheim (Ed.), *Adolescent romantic relations and sexual behavior* (pp. 85–108). Mahwah, NJ: Erlbaum.

Diamond, L. M. (2006). The intimate same-sex relationships of sexual minorities. In A. L. Vangelisti & D. Perlman (Eds.), *The Cambridge handbook of personal relationships* (pp. 293–312). New York: Cambridge University Press.

Diamond, L. M., & Lucas, S. (2004). Sexual-minority and heterosexual youths' peer relationships: Experiences, expectations, and implications for well-being. *Journal of Research on Adolescence, 14,* 313–340.

Diamond, M., & Sigmundson, H. K. (1999). Sex reassignment at birth. In S. J. Ceci & W. M. Williams (Eds.), *The nature–nurture debate* (pp. 55–75). Malden, MA: Blackwell.

Dias, M. G., & Harris, P. L. (1988). The effect of make-believe play on deductive reasoning. *British Journal of Developmental Psychology, 6,* 207–221.

Dias, M. G., & Harris, P. L. (1990). The influence of the imagination on reasoning by young children. *British Journal of Developmental Psychology, 8,* 305–318.

Dick, D. M., Rose, R. J., Viken, R. J., & Kaprio, J. (2000). Pubertal timing and substance use: Associations between and within families across late adolescence. *Developmental Psychology, 36,* 180–189.

Dickens, W. T., & Flynn, J. R. (2006). Black Americans reduce the racial IQ gap: Evidence from standardization samples. *Psychological Science, 17,* 913–920.

Dickerson, L. M., Mazyck, P. J., & Hunter, M. H. (2003). Premenstrual syndrome. *American Family Physician, 67,* 1743–1752.

Dickinson, D. K., & McCabe, A. (2001). Bringing it all together: The multiple origins, skills, and environmental supports of early literacy. *Learning Disabilities Research and Practice, 16,* 186–202.

Dickinson, D. K., McCabe, A., Anastasopoulos, L., Peisner-Feinberg, E. S., & Poe, M. D. (2003). The comprehensive language approach to early literacy: The interrelationships among vocabulary, phonological sensitivity, and print knowledge among preschool-age children. *Journal of Educational Psychology, 95,* 465–481.

Dick-Read, G. (1959). *Childbirth without fear.* New York: Harper & Row.

Dickson, K. L., Fogel, A., & Messinger, D. (1998). The development of emotion from a social process view. In M. F. Mascolo (Ed.), *What develops in emotional development?* (pp. 253–271). New York: Plenum.

Dickstein, M. (1992). After utopia: The 1960s today. In B. L. Tischler (Ed.), *Sights on the sixties* (pp. 13–24). New Brunswick, NJ: Rutgers University Press.

Diehl, M., & Berg, K. M. (2007). Personality and involvement in leisure activities during the Third Age: Findings from the Ohio Longitudinal Study. In J. B. James & P. Wink (Eds.), *Annual review of gerontology and geriatrics* (Vol. 26, pp. 211–226). New York: Springer.

Diehl, M., Coyle, N., & Labouvie-Vief, G. (1996). Age and sex differences in strategies of coping and defense across the life span. *Psychology and Aging, 11,* 127–139.

Diener, E., Gohm, C. L., Suh, E., & Oishi, S. (2000). Similarity of the relations between marital status and subjective well-being across cultures. *Journal of Cross-Cultural Psychology, 31,* 419–436.

Dietrich, K. N., Ris, M. D., Succop, P. A., Berger, O. G., & Bornschein, R. L. (2001). Early exposure to lead and juvenile delinquency. *Neurotoxicology and Teratology, 23,* 511–518.

Dietrich, K. N., Ware, J. H., Salganik, M., Radcliffe, J., Rogan, W. J., & Rhoads, G. C. (2004). Effect of chelation therapy on the neuropsychological and behavioral development of lead-exposed children after school entry. *Pediatrics, 114,* 19–26.

Dildy, G. A., Jackson, G. M., Fowers, G. K., Oshiro, B. T., Varner, M. W., & Clark, S. L. (1996). Very advanced maternal age. Pregnancy after age 45. *American Journal of Obstetrics and Gynecology, 175,* 668–674.

Dillaway, H., & Broman, C. (2001). Race, class, and gender differences in marital satisfaction and divisions of household labor among dual-earner couples. *Journal of Family Issues, 22,* 309–327.

Dillon, M., & Wink, P. (2004). American religion, generativity, and the therapeutic culture. In E. de St. Aubin & D. P. McAdams (Eds.), *The generative society: Caring for future generations* (pp. 15–31).

Washington, DC: American Psychological Association.

Dilworth-Anderson, P., Goodwin, P. Y., & Williams, S. W. (2004). Can culture help explain the physical health effects of caregiving over time among African American caregivers? *Journal of Gerontology, 59B,* S138–S145.

Ding, Q., Bruce-Keller, A. J., Chen, Q., & Keller, J. N. (2004). Analysis of gene expression in neural cells subject to chronic proteasome inhibition. *Free Radical Biology and Medicine, 36,* 445–455.

DiPietro, J. A., Bornstein, M. H., Costigan, K. A., Pressman, E. K., Hahn, C.-S., & Painter, K. (2002). What does fetal movement predict about behavior during the first two years of life? *Developmental Psychobiology, 40,* 358–371.

DiPietro, J. A., Caulfield, L. E., Irizarry, R. A., Chen, P., Merialdi, M., & Zavaleta, N. (2006). Prenatal development of intrafetal and maternal-fetal synchrony. *Behavioral Neuroscience, 120,* 687–701.

DiPietro, J. A., Hodgson, D. M., Costigan, K. A., & Hilton, S. C. (1996). Fetal neurobehavioral development. *Child Development, 67,* 2553–2567.

Dirks, J. (1982). The effect of a commercial game on children's Block Design scores on the WISC-R test. *Intelligence, 6,* 109–123.

Dishion, T. J., Andrews, D. W., & Crosby, L. (1995). Antisocial boys and their friends in early adolescence: Relationship characteristics, quality, and interactional processes. *Child Development, 66,* 139–151.

Dishion, T. J., Shaw, D., Connell, A., Gardner, F., Weaver, C., & Wilson, M. (2008). The Family Check-Up with high-risk indigent families: Preventing problem behavior by increasing parents' positive behavior support in early childhood. *Child Development, 79,* 1395–1414.

DiTommaso, E., Brannen, C., & Burgess, M. (2005). The universality of relationship characteristics: A cross-cultural comparison of different types of attachment and loneliness in Canadian and visiting Chinese students. *Social Behavior and Personality, 33,* 57–68.

Dixon, L., & Browne, K. (2003). The heterogeneity of spouse abuse: A review. *Aggression and Violent Behavior, 8,* 107–130.

Dixon, R. A. (2003). Themes in the aging of intelligence: Robust decline with intriguing possibilities. In R. J. Sternberg, J. Lautrey, & T. I. Lubart (Eds.), *Models of intelligence: International perspectives* (pp. 151–167). Washington, DC: American Psychological Association.

Dixon, R. A., de Frias, C. M., & Bäckman, L. (2001). Characteristics of self-reported memory compensation in older adults. *Journal of Clinical and Experimental Neuropsychology, 23,* 650–661.

Djahanbakhch, O., Ezzati, M., & Zosmer, A. (2007). Reproductive ageing in women. *Journal of Pathology, 211,* 219–231.

Dodd, V. L. (2005). Implications of kangaroo care for growth and development in preterm infants. *JOGNN, 34,* 218–232.

Dodge, K. A., Coie, J. D., & Lynam, D. (2006). Aggression and antisocial behavior in youth. In N. Eisenberg (Ed.), *Handbook of child psychology: Vol. 3. Social, emotional, and personality development* (6th ed., pp. 719–788). New York: Wiley.

Dodge, K. A., McLoyd, V. C., & Lansford, J. E. (2006). The cultural context of physically disciplining children. In V. C. McLoyd, N. E. Hill, & K. A. Dodge (Eds.), *African-American family life: Ecological and cultural diversity* (pp. 245–263). New York: Guilford.

Dodson, T. A., & Borders, L. D. (2006). Men in traditional and nontraditional careers: Gender role attitudes, gender role conflict, and job satisfaction. *Career Development Quarterly, 54,* 283–296.

Doherty, N. N., & Hepper, P. G. (2000). Habituation in fetuses of diabetic mothers. *Early Human Development, 59,* 85–93.

Dohnt, H., & Tiggemann, M. (2006). The contribution of peer and media influences to the development of body satisfaction and self-esteem in young girls: A prospective study. *Developmental Psychology, 42,* 929–936.

Doka, K., & Martin, T. (2000). Take it like a man: Masculine response to loss. In D. A. Lund (Ed.), *Men coping with grief* (pp. 37–47). Amityville, NY: Baywood.

Dolbin-MacNab, M. L. (2006). Just like raising your own? Grandmothers' perceptions of parenting a second time around. *Family Relations, 55,* 564–575.

Dombrowski, S. C., Noonan, K., & Martin, R. P. (2007). Low birth weight and cognitive outcomes: Evidence for a gradient relationship in an urban, poor, African American birth cohort. *School Psychology Quarterly, 22,* 26–43.

Donahue, M. J., & Benson, P. L. (1995). Religion and the well-being of adolescents. *Journal of Social Issues, 51,* 145–160.

Donatelle, R. J. (2009). *Health: The basics* (8th ed.). San Francisco: Benjamin Cummings.

Dondi, M., Simion, F., & Caltran, G. (1999). Can newborns discriminate between their own cry and the cry of another newborn infant? *Developmental Psychology, 35,* 418–426.

Done, D. J., & Thomas, J. A. (2001). Training in communication skills for informal carers of people suffering from dementia: A cluster randomized clinic trial comparing a therapist led workshop and booklet. *International Journal of Geriatric Psychiatry, 16,* 816–821.

Donnellan, M. B., Larsen-Rife, D., & Conger, R. D. (2005). Personality, family history, and competence in early adult romantic relationships. *Journal of Personality and Social Psychology, 88,* 562–576.

Donnellan, M. B., Trzesniewski, K. H., Robins, R. W., Moffitt, T. E., & Caspi, A. (2005). Low self-esteem is related to aggression, antisocial behavior, and delinquency. *Psychological Science, 16,* 328–335.

Donnerstein, E., Slaby, R. G., & Eron, L. D. (1994). The mass media and youth aggression. In L. D. Eron, J. H. Gentry, & P. Schlegel (Eds.), *Reason to hope: A psychosocial perspective on violence and youth* (pp. 219–250). Washington, DC: American Psychological Association.

D'Onofrio, B. M., Turkheimer, E., Emery, R. E., Slutske, W. S., Heath, A. C., Madden, P. A., & Martin, N. G. (2006). A genetically informed study of the processes underlying the association between parental marital instability and offspring adjustment. *Developmental Psychology, 42,* 486–499.

Dorris, M. (1989). *The broken cord.* New York: Harper & Row.

dos Santos Silva, I., De Stavola, B. L., Hardy, R. J., Kuh, D. J., McCormack, V. A., & Wadsworth, M. E. J. (2004). Is the association of birth weight with premenopausal breast cancer risk mediated through childhood growth? *British Journal of Cancer, 91,* 519–524.

Dowdney, L. (2000). Annotation: Childhood bereavement following parental death. *Journal of Child Psychology and Psychiatry and Allied Disciplines, 41,* 819–830.

Dowling, E. M., Gestsdottir, S., Anderson, P. M., von Eye, A., Almerigi, J., & Lerner, R. M. (2004). Structural relations among spirituality, religiosity, and thriving in adolescence. *Applied Developmental Psychology, 8,* 7–16.

Downs, A. C., & Fuller, M. J. (1991). Recollections of spermarche: An exploratory investigation. *Current Psychology: Research and Reviews, 10,* 93–102.

Dozier, M., Stovall, K. C., Albus, K. E., & Bates, B. (2001). Attachment for infants in foster care: The role of caregiver state of mind. *Child Development, 72,* 1467–1477.

Drabman, R. S., Cordua, G. D., Hammer, D., Jarvie, G. J., & Horton, W. (1979). Developmental trends in eating rates of normal and overweight preschool children. *Child Development, 50,* 211–216.

Drela, N., Kozdron, E., & Szczypiorski, P. (2004). Moderate exercise may attenuate some aspects of immunosenscence. *BMC Geriatrics, 4,* 8.

Drewett, R. F., Corbett, S. S., & Wright, C. M. (2006). Physical and emotional development, appetite and body image in adolescents who failed to thrive as infants. *Journal of Child Psychology and Psychiatry, 47,* 524–531.

Drewnowski, A., & Shultz, J. M. (2001). Impact of aging on eating behaviors, food choices, nutrition, and health status. *Journal of Nutrition, Health, and Aging, 5,* 75–79.

Driscoll, M. C. (2007). Sickle cell disease. *Pediatrics in Review, 28,* 259–268.

Drotar, D., Pallotta, J., & Eckerle, D. (1994). A prospective study of family environments of children hospitalized for nonorganic failure-to-thrive. *Developmental and Behavioral Pediatrics, 15,* 78–85.

Drotar, D., Witherspoon, D. O., Zebracki, K., & Peterson, C. C. (2006). *Psychological interventions in childhood chronic illness.* Washington, DC: American Psychological Association.

Dryer, D. C., & Horowitz, L. M. (1997). When do opposites attract? Interpersonal complementarity versus similarity. *Journal of Personality and Social Psychology, 72,* 592–603.

Dubé, E. M., Savin-Williams, R. C., & Diamond, L. M. (2001). Intimacy development, gender, and ethnicity among sexual-minority youths. In A. R. D'Augelli & C. J. Patterson (Eds.), *Lesbian, gay, and bisexual identities and youth* (pp. 129–152). New York: Oxford University Press.

DuBois, D. L., Burk-Braxton, C., Swenson, L. P., Tevendale, H. D., Lockerd, E. M., & Moran, B. L. (2002). Getting by with a little help from self and others: Self-esteem and social support as resources during early adolescence. *Developmental Psychology, 38,* 822–939.

DuBois, D. L., Felner, R. D., Brand, S., & George, G. R. (1999). Profiles of self-esteem in early adolescence: Identification and investigation of adaptive correlates. *American Journal of Community Psychology, 27,* 899–932.

Duckworth, A. L., & Seligman, M. E. P. (2005). Self-discipline outdoes IQ in predicting academic performance of adolescents. *Psychological Science, 12,* 939–944.

Dugan, E., & Kivett, V. R. (1998). Implementing the Adams and Blieszner conceptual model: Predicting interactive friendship processes of older adults. *Journal of Social and Personal Relationships, 15,* 607–622.

Duggan, A., McFarlane, E., Fuddy, L., Burrell, L., Higman, S. M., Windham, A., & Sia, C. (2004). Randomized trial of a statewide home visiting program: Impact in preventing child abuse and neglect. *Child Abuse and Neglect, 28,* 597–622.

Dumas, J. A., & Hartman, M. (2003). Age differences in temporal and item memory. *Psychology and Aging, 18,* 573–586.

Duncan, G. J., Dowsett, C. J., Claessens, A., Magnuson, K., Huston, A. C., Klebanov, P., et al. (2007). School readiness and later achievement. *Developmental Psychology, 43,* 1428–1446.

Duncan, G. J., & Magnuson, K. A. (2003). Off with Hollingshead: Socioeconomic resources, parenting, and child development. In M. H. Bornstein &

R. H. Bradley (Eds.), *Socioeconomic status, parenting, and child development* (pp. 83–106). Mahwah, NJ: Erlbaum.

Dunham, Y., Baron, A. S., & Banaji, M. R. (2006). From American city to Japanese village: A cross-cultural investigation of implicit race attitudes. *Child Development, 77,* 1129–1520.

Duniz, M., Scheer, P. J., Trojovsky, A., Kaschnitz, W., Kvas, E., & Macari, S. (1996). Changes in psychopathology of parents of NOFT (nonorganic failure to thrive) infants during treatment. *European Child and Adolescent Psychiatry, 5,* 93–100.

Dunlosky, J., & Hertzog, C. (2001). Measuring strategy production during associative learning: The relative utility of concurrent versus retrospective reports. *Memory and Cognition, 29,* 247–253.

Dunn, J. (1989). Siblings and the development of social understanding in early childhood. In P. G. Zukow (Ed.), *Sibling interaction across cultures* (pp. 106–116). New York: Springer-Verlag.

Dunn, J. (1994). Temperament, siblings, and the development of relationships. In W. B. Carey & S. C. McDevitt (Eds.), *Prevention and early intervention* (pp. 50–58). New York: Brunner/Mazel.

Dunn, J. (2002). The adjustment of children in stepfamilies: Lessons from community studies. *Child and Adolescent Mental Health, 7,* 154–161.

Dunn, J. (2004). Sibling relationships. In P. K. Smith & C. H. Hart (Eds.), *Handbook of childhood social development* (pp. 223–237). Malden, MA: Blackwell.

Dunn, J. (2005). Moral development in early childhood and social interaction in the family. In M. Killen & J. G. Smetana (Eds.), *Handbook of moral development* (pp. 331–350). Mahwah, NJ: Erlbaum.

Dunn, J., Cheng, H., O'Connor, T. G., & Bridges, L. (2004). Children's perspectives on their relationships with their nonresident fathers: Influences, outcomes and implications. *Journal of Child Psychology and Psychiatry, 45,* 553–566.

Dunne, E. J., & Dunne-Maxim, K. (2004). Working with families in the aftermath of suicide. In F. Walsh & M. McGoldrick (Eds.), *Living beyond loss: Death in the family* (2nd ed., pp. 272–284). New York: Norton.

Durbin, D. L., Darling, N., Steinberg, L., & Brown, B. B. (1993). Parenting style and peer group membership among European-American adolescents. *Journal of Research on Adolescence, 3,* 87–100.

Durlak, J. A., & Riesenberg, L. A. (1991). The impact of death education. *Death Studies, 15,* 39–58.

Durlak, J. A., & Weissberg, R. P. (2007). *The impact of after-school programs that promote personal and social skills.* Chicago: Collaborative for Academic, Social, and Emotional Learning.

Durston, S., Pol, H. E. H., Schnack, H. G., Buitelaar, J. K., Steenhuis, M. P., & Minderaa, R. B. (2004). Magnetic resonance imaging of boys with attention-deficit/hyperactivity disorder and their unaffected siblings. *Journal of the American Academy of Child and Adolescent Psychiatry, 43,* 332–340.

Dusek, J. B. (1987). Sex roles and adjustment. In D. B. Carter (Ed.), *Current conceptions of sex roles and sex typing* (pp. 211–222). New York: Praeger.

Dutton, D. G. (2007). *The abusive personality: Violence and control in intimate relationships* (2nd ed.). New York: Guilford.

Dutton, D. G., & Nicholls, T. L. (2005). The gender paradigm in domestic violence research and theory: Part 1. The conflict of theory and data. *Aggression and Violent Behavior, 10,* 680–714.

Dutton, D. G., Nicholls, T. L., & Spidel, A. (2005). Female perpetrators of intimate abuse. In F. P. Buttell & M. M. Carney (Eds.), *Women who perpetrate relationship violence: Moving beyond political correctness* (pp. 1–31). New York: Haworth Press.

Dweck, C. S. (2002). Messages that motivate: How praise molds students' beliefs, motivation, and performance (in surprising ways). In J. Aronson (Ed.), *Improving academic achievement: Impact of psychological factors on education* (pp. 37–60). San Diego, CA: Academic Press.

Dykman, R., Casey, P. H., Ackerman, P. T., & McPherson, W. B. (2001). Behavioral and cognitive status in school-aged children with a history of failure to thrive during early childhood. *Clinical Pediatrics, 40,* 63–70.

Dykstra, P. A. (1995). Loneliness among the never and formerly married: The importance of supportive friendships and a desire for independence. *Journal of Gerontology, 50B,* S321–S329.

Dykstra, P. A. (2006). Off the beaten track: Childlessness and social integration in late life. *Research on Aging, 28,* 749–767.

Dykstra, P. A., & Hagestad, G. O. (2007). Roads less taken: Developing a nuanced view of older adults without children. *Journal of Family Issues, 28,* 1275–1310.

Dzurova, D., & Pikhart, H. (2005). Down syndrome, paternal age and education: Comparison of California and the Czech Republic. *BMC Public Health, 5,* 69.

E

Eagly, A. H., Eastwick, P. W., & Johannesen-Schmidt, M. (2009). Possible selves in marital roles: The impact of the anticipated division of labor on mate preferences of women and men. *Personality and Social Psychology Bulletin, 35,* 403–414.

Eagly, A. H., & Karau, S. J. (2002). Role congruity theory of prejudice toward female leaders. *Psychological Review, 109,* 573–598.

Eagly, A. H., & Wood, W. (1999). The origins of sex differences in human behavior: Evolved dispositions versus social roles. *American Psychologist, 54,* 408–423.

Eaker, E.D., Sullivan. L. M., Kelly-Hayes, M., D'Agostino, R. B., & Benjamin, E. J. (2004). Anger and hostility predict the development of atrial fibrillation in men in the Framingham Offspring Study. *Circulation, 109,* 1267–1271.

East, P. L., & Felice, M. E. (1996). *Adolescent pregnancy and parenting: Findings from a racially diverse sample.* Mahwah, NJ: Erlbaum.

Eaton, D. K., Davis, K. S., Barrios, L., Brener, N. D., & Noonan, R. K. (2007). Associations of dating violence victimization with lifetime participation, co-occurrence, and early initiation of risk behaviors among U.S. high school students. *Journal of Interpersonal Violence, 22,* 585–602.

Eaves, L., Silberg, J., Foley, D., Bulik, C., Maes, H., & Erkanli, A. (2004). Genetic and environmental influences on the relative timing of pubertal change. *Twin Research, 7,* 471–481.

Ebeling, K. S., & Gelman, S. A. (1994). Children's use of context in interpreting "big" and "little." *Child Development, 65,* 1178–1192.

Eberhart-Phillips, J. E., Frederick, P. D., & Baron, R. C. (1993). Measles in pregnancy: A descriptive study of 58 cases. *Obstetrics and Gynecology, 82,* 797–801.

Ebner, N. C., Freund, A. M., & Baltes, P. B. (2006). Developmental changes in personal goal orientation from young to late adulthood: From striving for gains to maintenance and prevention of losses. *Psychology and Aging, 21,* 664–678.

Eccles, J. S. (2004). Schools, academic motivation, and stage–environment fit. In R. M. Lerner & L. Steinberg (Eds.), *Handbook of Adolescent Psychology* (2nd ed., pp. 125–154). Hoboken, N. J.: Wiley.

Eccles, J. S., & Gootman, J. (Eds.). (2002). *Community programs to promote youth development.* Washington, DC: National Academy Press.

Eccles, J. S., & Harold, R. D. (1991). Gender differences in sport involvement: Applying the Eccles' expectancy-value model. *Journal of Applied Sport Psychology, 3,* 7–35.

Eccles, J. S., Jacobs, J. E., & Harold, R. D. (1990). Gender-role stereotypes, expectancy effects, and parents' role in the socialization of gender differences in self-perceptions and skill acquisition. *Journal of Social Issues, 46,* 183–201.

Eccles, J. S., Templeton, J., Barber, B., & Stone, M. (2003). Adolescence and emerging adulthood: The critical passageways to adulthood. In M. H. Bornstein, L. Davidson, C. L. M., Keyes, K. A. Moore, & the Center for Child Well-Being (Eds.), *Well-being: Positive development across the life course* (pp. 383–406). Mahwah, NJ: Erlbaum.

Eccles, J. S., Vida, M. N., & Barber, B. (2004). The relation of early adolescents' college plans and both academic ability and task-value beliefs to subsequent college enrollment. *Journal of Early Adolescence, 24,* 63–77.

Eder, R. A., & Mangelsdorf, S. C. (1997). The emotional basis of early personality development: Implications for the emergent self-concept. In R. Hogan, J. Johnson, & S. Briggs (Eds.), *Handbook of personality psychology* (pp. 209–240). San Diego, CA: Academic Press.

Edmondson, P. (2006). Deaf children's understanding of other people's thought processes. *Educational Psychology in Practice, 22,* 159–169.

Edwards, J. N., & Booth, A. (1994). Sexuality, marriage, and well-being: The middle years. In A. S. Rossi (Ed.), *Sexuality across the life course* (pp. 233–259). Chicago: University of Chicago Press.

Edwards, O. W., & Oakland, T. D. (2006). Factorial invariance of Woodcock-Johnson III scores for African Americans and Caucasian Americans. *Journal of Psychoeducational Assessment, 24,* 358–366.

Egan, S. K., & Perry, D. G. (2001). Gender identity: A multidimensional analysis with implications for psychosocial adjustment. *Developmental Psychology, 37,* 451–463.

Egeland, B., Jacobvitz, D., & Sroufe, L. A. (1988). Breaking the cycle of abuse. *Child Development, 59,* 1080–1088.

Eggebeen, D. J., & Sturgeon, S. (2006). Demography of the baby boomers. In S. K. Whitbourne & S. L. Willis (Eds.), *The baby boomers grow up: Contemporary perspectives on midlife* (pp. 3–21). Mahwah, NJ: Erlbaum.

Ehrensaft, M. K., Cohen, P., & Johnson, J. G. (2006). Development of personality disorder symptoms and the risk for partner violence. *Journal of Abnormal Psychology, 115,* 474–483.

Ehrensaft, M. K., Moffitt, T. E., & Caspi, A. (2004). Clinically abusive relationships in an unselected birth cohort: Men's and women's participation and developmental antecedents. *Journal of Abnormal Psychology, 113,* 258–270.

Eichstedt, J. A., Serbin, L. A., Poulin-Dubois, D., & Sen, M. G. (2002). Of bears and men: Infants' knowledge of conventional and metaphorical gender stereotypes. *Infant Behavior and Development, 25,* 296–310.

Einstein, G. O., McDaniel, M. A., Manzi, M., Cochran, B., & Baker, M. (2000). Prospective memory and aging: Forgetting intentions over short delays. *Psychology and Aging, 15,* 671–683.

Eisenberg, N. (2003). Prosocial behavior, empathy, and sympathy. In M. H. Bornstein & L. Davidson (Eds.), *Well-being: Positive development across the life course* (pp. 253–265). Mahwah, NJ: Erlbaum.

Eisenberg, N., Fabes, R. A., Shepard, S. A., Murphy, B. C., Jones, S., & Guthrie, I. K. (1998). Contemporaneous and longitudinal prediction of children's sympathy from dispositional regulation and emotionality. *Developmental Psychology, 34,* 910–924.

Eisenberg, N., Fabes, R. A., & Spinrad, T. L. (2006). Prosocial development. In N. Eisenberg (Ed.), *Handbook of child psychology: Vol. 3. Social, emotional, and personality development* (6th ed., pp. 646–718). Hoboken, NJ: Wiley.

Eisenberg, N., Sadovsky, A., Spinrad, T. L., Fabes, R. A., Losoya, S., & Valiente, C. (2005a). The relations of problem behavior status to children's negative emotionality, effortful control, and impulsivity: Concurrent relations and prediction of change. *Developmental Psychology, 41,* 193–211.

Eisenberg, N., Smith, C. L., Sadovsky, A., & Spinrad, T. L. (2004). Effortful control: Relations with emotion regulation, adjustment, and socialization in childhood. In R. Baumeister & K. D. Vohs (Eds.), *Handbook of self-regulation: Research, theory, and applications* (pp. 259–282). New York: Guilford.

Eisenberg, N., & Spinrad, T. L. (2004). Emotion-related regulation: Sharpening the definition. *Child Development, 75,* 334–339.

Eisenberg, N., Zhou, Q., Spinrad, T. L., Valiente, C., Fabes, R. A., & Liew, J. (2005b). Relations among positive parenting, children's effortful control, and externalizing problems: A three-wave longitudinal study. *Child Development, 76,* 1055–1071.

Ekman, P. (2003). *Emotions revealed.* New York: Times Books.

Ekman, P., & Friesen, W. (1972). Constants across culture in the face of emotion. *Journal of Personality and Social Psychology, 17,* 124–129.

Elavsky, S., & McAuley, E. (2007). Physical activity and mental health outcomes during menopause: A randomized controlled trial. *Annals of Behavioral Medicine, 33,* 132–142.

Elder, G. H., Jr., & Conger, R. (2000). *Children of the land: Adversity and success in rural America.* Chicago: University of Chicago Press.

Elder, G. H., Jr., Nguyen, T. V., & Caspi, A. (1985). Linking family hardship to children's lives. *Child Development, 56,* 361–375.

Elder, G. H., Jr., & Shanahan, M. J. (2006). The life course and human development. In R. M. Lerner (Ed.), *Handbook of child psychology: Vol. 1. Theoretical models of human development* (6th ed., pp. 665–715). Hoboken, NJ: Wiley.

Elfenbein, D. S., & Felice, M. E. (2003). Adolescent pregnancy. *Pediatric Clinics of North America, 50,* 781–800.

Eliakim, A., Friedland, O., Kowen, G., Wolach, B., & Nemet, D. (2004). Parental obesity and higher pre-intervention BMI reduce the likelihood of a multidisciplinary childhood obesity program to succeed: A clinical observation. *Journal of Pediatric Endocrinology and Metabolism, 17,* 1055–1061.

Elias, C. L., & Berk, L. E. (2002). Self-regulation in young children: Is there a role for sociodramatic play? *Early Childhood Research Quarterly, 17,* 1–17.

Elicker, J., Englund, M., & Sroufe, L. A. (1992). Predicting peer competence and peer-relationships in childhood from early parent–child relationships. In R. D. Parke & G. W. Ladd (Eds.), *Family–peer relationships: Modes of linkage* (pp. 77–106). Hillsdale, NJ: Erlbaum.

Elizur, Y., & Mintzer, A. (2003). Gay males' intimate relationship quality: The roles of attachment security, gay identity, social support, and income. *Personal Relationships, 10,* 411–435.

Elkind, D. (1994). *A sympathetic understanding of the child: Birth to sixteen* (3rd ed.). Boston: Allyn and Bacon.

Elkind, D., & Bowen, R. (1979). Imaginary audience behavior in children and adolescents. *Developmental Psychology, 15,* 33–44.

Ellickson, P. L., D'Amico, E. J., Collins, R. L., & Klein, D. J. (2005). Marijuana use and later problems: When frequency of recent use explains age of initiation effects. *Substance Use and Misuse, 40,* 343–359.

Elliott, J. G. (1999). School refusal: Issues of conceptualization, assessment, and treatment. *Journal of Child Psychology and Psychiatry and Allied Disciplines, 40,* 1001–1012.

Ellis, A. E., & Oakes, L. M. (2006). Infants flexibly use different dimensions to categorize objects. *Developmental Psychology, 42,* 1000–1011.

Ellis, B. J. (2004). Timing of pubertal maturation in girls: An integrated life history approach. *Psychological Bulletin, 130,* 920–958.

Ellis, B. J., & Essex, M. J. (2007). Family environments, adrenarche, and sexual maturation: A longitudinal test of a life history model. *Child Development, 78,* 1799–1817.

Ellis, L., & Bonin, S. L. (2003). Genetics and occupation-related preferences: Evidence from adoptive and non-adoptive families. *Personality and Individual Differences, 35,* 929–937.

Ellis, W. E., & Zarbatany, L. (2007). Explaining friendship formation and friendship stability: The role of children's and friends' aggression and victimization. *Merrill-Palmer Quarterly, 53,* 79–104.

Elman, J. L. (2001). Connectionism and language acquisition. In M. Tomasello & E. Bates (Eds.), *Language development* (pp. 295–306). Oxford, UK: Blackwell.

Else-Quest, N. M., Hyde, J. S., Goldsmith, H. H., & Van Hulle, C. A. (2006). Gender differences in temperament: A meta-analysis. *Psychological Bulletin, 132,* 33–72.

El-Sheikh, M., Cummings, E. M., & Reiter, S. (1996). Preschoolers' responses to ongoing interadult conflict: The role of prior exposure to resolved versus unresolved arguments. *Journal of Abnormal Child Psychology, 24,* 665–679.

Eltzschig, H. K., Lieberman, E. S., & Camann, W. R. (2003). Regional anesthesia and analgesia for labor and delivery. *New England Journal of Medicine, 384,* 319–332.

Elwert, F., & Christakis, N. A. (2006). Widowhood and race. *American Sociological Review, 71,* 16–41.

Emanuel, E. J., Fairclough, D. L., & Emanuel, L. L. (2000). Attitudes and desires related to euthanasia and physician-assisted suicide among terminally ill patients and their caregivers. *Journal of the American Medical Association, 284,* 2460–2468.

Emery, R. E., & Laumann-Billings, L. (1998). An overview of the nature, causes, and consequences of abusive family relationships: Toward differentiating maltreatment and violence. *American Psychologist, 53,* 121–135.

Emery, R. E., Sbarra, D., & Grover, T. (2005). Divorce mediation: Research and reflections. *Family Court Review, 43,* 22–37.

Emory, E. K., Schlackman, L. J., & Fiano, K. (1996). Drug–hormone interactions on neurobehavioral responses in human neonates. *Infant Behavior and Development, 19,* 213–220.

Engen, T. (1982). *The perception of odors.* New York: Academic Press.

Englund, M. E., Egeland, B., & Collins, W. A. (2008). Exceptions to high school dropout predictions in a low-income sample: Do adults make a difference? *Journal of Social Issues, 64,* 77–93.

Ennemoser, M., & Schneider, W. (2007). Relations of television viewing and reading: Findings from a 4-year longitudinal study. *Journal of Educational Psychology, 99,* 349–368.

Entwisle, D. R., Alexander, K. L., & Olson, L. S. (2005). First grade and educational attainment by age 22: A new story. *American Journal of Sociology, 110,* 1458–1502.

Epel, E. S., Blackburn, E., Lin, J., Dhabhar, F., Adler, N., & Morrow, J. D. (2004). Accelerated telomere shortening in response to exposure to life stress. *Proceedings of the National Academy of Sciences, 101,* 17312–17315.

Epel, E. S., Linn, J., Wilhelm, F., Mendes, W., Adler, N., & Dolbier, C. (2006). Cell aging in relation to stress arousal and cardiovascular disease risk factors. *Psychoneuroendocrinology, 31,* 277–287.

Epel, E. S., Merkin, S. S., Cawthon, R., Blackburn, E. H., Adler, N. E., Pletcher, M. J., & Seeman, T. S. (2009). The rate of leukocyte telomere shortening predicts mortality from cardiovascular disease in elderly men: A novel demonstration. *Aging, 1,* 81–88.

Epstein, L. H., Roemmich, J. N., & Raynor, H. A. (2001). Behavioral therapy in the treatment of pediatric obesity. *Pediatric Clinics of North America, 48,* 981–983.

Erath, S. A., Bierman, K. L., & the Conduct Problems Prevention Research Group. (2006). Aggressive marital conflict, maternal harsh punishment, and child aggressive-disruptive behavior: Evidence for direct and mediate relations. *Journal of Family Psychology, 20,* 217–226.

Erden, F., & Wolfgang, C. H. (2004). An exploration of the differences in prekindergarten, kindergarten, and first-grade teachers' beliefs related to discipline when dealing with male and female students. *Early Child Development and Care, 174,* 3–11.

Erickson, K. L., Colcombe, S. J., Wadhwa, R., Bherer, L., Peterson, M. S., & Scalf, P. E. (2007). Training-induced plasticity in older adults: Effects of training on hemispheric asymmetry. *Neurobiology of Aging, 28,* 272–283.

Erikson, E. H. (1950). *Childhood and society.* New York: Norton.

Erikson, E. H. (1964). *Insight and responsibility.* New York: Norton.

Erikson, E. H. (1968). *Identity, youth, and crisis.* New York: Norton.

Erikson, E. H. (1998). *The life cycle completed. Extended version with new chapters on the ninth stage by Joan M. Erikson.* New York: Norton.

Ertekin-Tanner, N. (2007). Genetics of Alzheimer's disease: A centennial review. *Neurologic Clinics, 25,* 611–667.

Espy, K. A., Molfese, V. J., & DiLalla, L. F. (2001). Effects of environmental measures on intelligence in young children: Growth curve modeling of longitudinal data. *Merrill-Palmer Quarterly, 47,* 42–73.

Esterberg, K. G., Moen, P., & Dempster-McClain, D. (1994). Transition to divorce: A life-course approach to women's marital duration and dissolution. *Sociological Quarterly, 35,* 289–307.

Estourgie-van Burk, G. F., Bartels, M., van Beijsterveldt, T. C., Delemarre-van de Waal, H. A., & Boomsma, D. I. (2006). Body size in five-year-old twins: Heritability and comparison to singleton standards. *Twin Research and Human Genetics, 9,* 646–655.

Ethier, K. A., Kershaw, T., Niccolai, L., Lewis, J. B., & Ickovics, J. R. (2003). Adolescent women underestimate their susceptibility to sexually transmitted infections. *Sexually Transmitted Infections, 79,* 408–411.

Evanoo, G. (2007). Infant crying: A clinical conundrum. *Journal of Pediatric Health Care, 21,* 333–338.

Evans, A. M., & Scutter, S. D. (2004). How common are "growing pains" in young children? *Journal of Pediatrics, 145,* 255–258.

Evans, B. J., & Rowlands, G. (2004). Correctable visual impairment in older people: A major unmet need. *Ophthalmic and Physiological Optics, 24,* 161–180.

Evans, E., Hawton, K., & Rodham, K. (2004). Factors associated with suicidal phenomena in adolescents: A systematic review of population-based studies. *Clinical Psychology Review, 24,* 957–979.

Evans, G. W. (2004). The environment of child poverty. *American Psychologist, 59,* 77–92.

Evans, G. W. (2006). Child development and the physical environment. *Annual Review of Psychology, 57,* 424–451.

Evans, G. W., & Kantrowitz, E. (2002). Socioeconomic status and health: The potential role of environmental risk exposure. *Annual Review of Public Health, 23,* 303–331.

Evans, J. (2008). Antioxidant supplements to prevent or slow down the progression of AMD: A systematic review and meta-analysis. *Eye, 22,* 751–760.

Everman, D. B., & Cassidy, S. B. (2000). Genetics of childhood disorders: XII. Genomic imprinting: Breaking the rules. *Journal of the American Academy of Child and Adolescent Psychiatry, 38,* 386–389.

F

Fabes, R. A., Eisenberg, N., Hanish, L. D., & Spinrad, T. L. (2001). Preschoolers' spontaneous emotion vocabulary: Relations to likeability. *Early Education and Development, 12,* 11–27.

Fabes, R. A., Eisenberg, N., McCormick, S. E., & Wilson, M. S. (1988). Preschoolers' attributions of the situational determinants of others' naturally occurring emotions. *Developmental Psychology, 24,* 376–385.

Fabes, R. A., Martin, C. L., & Hanish, L. D. (2003). Young children's play qualities in same-, other-, and mixed-sex peer groups. *Child Development, 74,* 921–932.

Facio, A., & Micocci, F. (2003). Emerging adulthood in Argentina. *New Directions for Child and Adolescent Development, 100,* 21–31.

Fagan, J. F., III. (1973). Infants' delayed recognition memory and forgetting. *Journal of Experimental Child Psychology, 16,* 424–450.

Fagan, J. F., Holland, C. R., & Wheeler, K. (2007). The prediction, from infancy, of adult IQ and achievement. *Intelligence, 35,* 225–231.

Fagard, J., & Pezé, A. (1997). Age changes in interlimb coupling and the development of bimanual coordination. *Journal of Motor Behavior, 29,* 199–208.

Fagot, B. I. (1984). The child's expectations of differences in adult male and female interactions. *Sex Roles, 11,* 593–600.

Fagot, B. I. (1985). Changes in thinking about early sex role development. *Developmental Review, 5,* 83–98.

Fagot, B. I., & Hagan, R. I. (1991). Observations of parent reactions to sex-stereotyped behaviors: Age and sex effects. *Child Development, 62,* 617–628.

Fagot, B. I., & Leinbach, M. D. (1989). The young child's gender schema: Environmental input, internal organization. *Child Development, 60,* 663–672.

Fahrmeier, E. D. (1978). The development of concrete operations among the Hausa. *Journal of Cross-Cultural Psychology, 9,* 23–44.

Fairburn, C. G. (2005). Evidence-based treatment of anorexia nervosa. *International Journal of Eating Disorders, 37,* S26–S30.

Fairburn, C. G., & Harrison, P. J. (2003). Eating disorders. *Lancet, 361,* 407–416.

Faircloth, B. S., & Hamm, J. V. (2005). Sense of belonging among high school students representing four ethnic groups. *Journal of Youth and Adolescence, 34,* 293–309.

Fajardo, M., & Di Cesare, P. E. (2005). Disease-modifying therapies for osteoarthritis. *Drugs and Aging, 22,* 141–161.

Falbo, T. (1992). Social norms and the one-child family: Clinical and policy implications. In F. Boer & J. Dunn (Eds.), *Children's sibling relationships* (pp. 71–82). Hillsdale, NJ: Erlbaum.

Falbo, T., & Poston, D. L., Jr. (1993). The academic, personality, and physical outcomes of only children in China. *Child Development, 64,* 18–35.

Falbo, T., Poston, D. L., Jr., Triscari, R. S., & Zhang, X. (1997). Self-enhancing illusions among Chinese schoolchildren. *Journal of Cross-Cultural Psychology, 28,* 172–191.

Falck-Ytter, T., Gredebäck, G., & von Hofsten, C. (2006). Infants predict other people's action goals. *Nature Neuroscience, 9,* 878–879.

Family Caregiver Alliance. (2005). *Fact sheet: Selected caregiver statistics.* Retrieved from www.caregiver.org/factsheets/selected_caregiver_statisticsC.html

Family Caregiver Alliance. (2009). *Fact sheet: Selected caregiver statistics.* Retrieved from www.caregiver.org/caregiver/jsp/content_node.jsp?nodeid=439

Fanslow, C. A. (1981). Death: A natural facet of the life continuum. In D. Krieger (Ed.), *Foundations for holistic health nursing practices: The renaissance nurse* (pp. 249–272). Philadelphia: Lippincott.

Fantz, R. L. (1961, May). The origin of form perception. *Scientific American, 204* (5), 66–72.

Farrant, K., & Reese, E. (2000). Maternal style and children's participation in reminiscing: Stepping stones in children's autobiological memory development. *Journal of Cognition and Development, 1,* 193–225.

Farrington, D. P. (2004). Conduct disorder, aggression, and delinquency. In R. M. Lerner & L. Steinberg (Eds.), *Handbook of adolescent psychology* (2nd ed., pp. 627–664). New York: Wiley.

Farroni, T., Csibra, G., Simion, F., & Johnson, M. H. (2002). Eye contact detection in humans from birth. *Proceedings of the National Academy of Sciences, 99,* 9602–9605.

Farroni, T., Massaccesi, S., Menon, E., & Johnson, M. H. (2007). Direct gaze modulates face recognition in young infants. *Cognition, 102,* 396–404.

Farver, J. M., & Branstetter, W. H. (1994). Preschoolers' prosocial responses to their peers' distress. *Developmental Psychology, 30,* 334–341.

Farver, J. M., Kim, Y. K., & Lee, Y. (1995). Cultural differences in Korean-and Anglo-American preschoolers' social interaction and play behaviors. *Child Development, 66,* 1088–1099.

Farver, J. M., & Wimbarti, S. (1995). Indonesian toddlers' social play with their mothers and older siblings. *Child Development, 66,* 1493–1503.

Fashola, O. S., & Slavin, R. E. (1998). Effective dropout prevention and college attendance programs for students placed at risk. *Journal of Education for Students Placed at Risk, 3,* 159–183.

Fasig, L. G. (2000). Toddlers' understanding of ownership: Implications for self-concept development. *Social Development, 9,* 370–382.

Fasolo, M., Majorano, M., & D'Odorico, L. (2008). Babbling and first words in children with slow expressive development. *Clinical Linguistics and Phonetics, 22,* 83–94.

Fattibene, P., Mazzei, F., Nuccetelli, C., & Risica, S. (1999). Prenatal exposure to ionizing radiation: Sources, effects, and regulatory aspects. *Acta Paediatrica, 88,* 693–702.

Faulkner, J. A., Larkin, L. M., Claflin, D. R., & Brooks, S. V. (2007). Age-related changes in the structure and function of skeletal muscles. *Clinical and Experimental Pharmacology and Physiology, 34,* 1091–1096.

Federal Interagency Forum on Child and Family Statistics. (2006). *Family structure and children's living arrangements.* Retrieved from www.childstats.gov/americaschildren06/tables/pop6b.asp

Federal Interagency Forum on Child and Family Statistics. (2008). *America's children: Key national indicators of well-being, 2008.* Retrieved from www.childstats.gov/americaschildren/tables.asp

Federenko, I. S., & Wadhwa, P. D. (2004). Women's mental health during pregnancy influences fetal and infant developmental and health outcomes. *CNS Spectrums, 9,* 198–206.

Federico, M. J., & Liu, A. H. (2003). Overcoming childhood asthma disparities of the inner-city poor. *Pediatric Clinics of North America, 50,* 655–675.

Feeney, J. A. (1998). Adult attachment and relationship-centered anxiety: Responses to physical and emotional distancing. In J. A. Simpson & W. S. Rholes (Eds.), *Attachment theory and close relationships* (pp. 189–218). New York: Guilford.

Feeney, J. A. (1999). Adult romantic attachment and couple relationships. In J. Cassidy & P. R. Shaver (Eds.), *Handbook of attachment* (pp. 355–377). New York: Guilford.

Feeney, J. A., Hohaus, L., Noller, P., & Alexander, R. P. (2001). *Becoming parents: Exploring the bonds between mothers, fathers, and their infants.* New York: Cambridge University Press.

Fehr, B. (1994). Prototype based assessment of laypeoples' views of love. *Personal Relationships, 1,* 309–331.

Feinberg, M. E., McHale, S. M., Crouter, A. C., & Cumsille, P. (2003). Sibling differentiation: Sibling and parent relationship trajectories in adolescence. *Child Development, 74,* 1261–1274.

Feinsilver, S. H. (2003). Sleep in the elderly: What is normal? *Clinical Geriatric Medicine, 19,* 177–188.

Feiring, C., Taska, L., & Lewis, M. (1999). Age and gender differences in children's and adolescents' adaptation to sexual abuse. *Child Abuse and Neglect, 23,* 115–128.

Feldkámper, M., & Schaeffel, F. (2003). Interactions of genes and environment in myopia. *Developmental Ophthalmology, 37,* 34–49.

Feldman, A. F., & Matjasko, J. L. (2007). Profiles and portfolios of adolescent school-based extracurricular activity participation. *Journal of Adolescence, 30,* 313–332.

Feldman, D. H. (2004). Child prodigies: A distinctive form of giftedness. In R. J. Sternberg (Ed.), *Definitions and conceptions of giftedness* (pp. 133–144). Thousand Oaks, CA: Corwin Press.

Feldman, P. J., & Steptoe, A. (2004). How neighborhoods and physical functioning are related: The roles of neighborhood socioeconomic status, perceived neighborhood strain, and individual health risk factors. *Annals of Behavioral Medicine, 27,* 91–99.

Feldman, R. (2003). Infant–mother and infant–father synchrony: The coregulation of positive arousal. *Infant Mental Health Journal, 24,* 1–23.

Feldman, R. (2006). From biological rhythms to social rhythms: Physiological precursors of mother–infant synchrony. *Developmental Psychology, 42,* 175–188.

Feldman, R. (2007). Maternal versus child risk and the development of parent–child and family relationships in five high-risk populations. *Development and Psychopathology, 19,* 293–312.

Feldman, R., & Eidelman, A. I. (2003). Skin-to-skin contact (kangaroo care) accelerates autonomic and neurobehavioral maturation in preterm infants. *Developmental Medicine and Child Neurology, 45,* 274–281.

Feldman, R., Eidelman, A. I., & Rotenberg, N. (2004). Parenting stress, infant emotion regulation, maternal sensitivity, and the cognitive development of triplets: A model for parent and child influences in a unique ecology. *Child Development, 75,* 1774–1791.

Feldman, R., Eidelman, A. I., Sirota, L., & Weller, A. (2002). Comparison of skin-to-skin (kangaroo) and traditional care: Parenting outcomes and preterm infant development. *Pediatrics, 110,* 16–26.

Feldman, R., Greenbaum, C. W., & Yirmiya, N. (1999). Mother–infant affect synchrony as an antecedent of the emergence of self-control. *Developmental Psychology, 35,* 223–231.

Feldman, R., & Klein, P. S. (2003). Toddlers' self-regulated compliance to mothers, caregivers, and fathers: Implications for theories of socialization. *Developmental Psychology, 39,* 680–692.

Feldman, R., Sussman, A. L., & Zigler, E. (2004). Parental leave and work adaptation at the transition to parenthood: Individual, marital, and social correlates. *Applied Developmental Psychology, 25,* 459–479.

Feldman, R., Weller, A., Sirota, L., & Eidelman, A. I. (2003). Testing a family intervention hypothesis: The contribution of mother–infant skin-to-skin contact (kangaroo care) to family interaction, proximity, and touch. *Journal of Family Psychology, 17,* 94–107.

Felner, R. D., Favazza, A., Shim, M., Brand, S., Gu, K., & Noonan, N. (2002). Whole school improvement and restructuring as prevention and promotion: Lessons from STEP and the Project on High Performance Learning Communities. *Journal of School Psychology, 39,* 177–202.

Felsman, D. E., & Blustein, D. L. (1999). The role of peer relatedness in late adolescent career development. *Journal of Vocational Behavior, 54,* 279–295.

Feng, Q. (2005). Postnatal consequences of prenatal cocaine exposure and myocardial apoptosis: Does cocaine in utero imperil the adult heart? *British Journal of Pharmacology, 144,* 887–888.

Fenson, L., Dale, P. S., Reznick, J. S., Bates, E., Thal, D. J., & Pethick, S. J. (1994). Variability in early communicative development. *Monographs of the Society for Research in Child Development, 59*(5, Serial No. 242).

Feret, A., Steinweg, S., Griffin, H. C., & Glover, S. (2007). Macular degeneration: Types, causes, and possible interventions. *Geriatric Nursing, 28,* 387–392.

Fergus, M. A. (1995, March 19). 99 years and . . . a joy to be around. *The Pantagraph,* pp. C1–C2.

Ferguson, T. J., Stegge, H., & Damhuis, I. (1991). Children's understanding of guilt and shame. *Child Development, 62,* 827–839.

Fergusson, D. M., & Horwood, J. (2003). Resilience to childhood adversity: Results of a 21-year study. In S. S. Luthar (Ed.), *Resilience and vulnerability* (pp. 130–155). New York: Cambridge University Press.

Fergusson, D. M., & Woodward, L. J. (1999). Breastfeeding and later psychosocial adjustment. *Paediatric and Perinatal Epidemiology, 13,* 144–157.

Fernald, A., & Hurtado, N. (2006). Names in frames: Infants interpret words in sentence frames faster than words in isolation. *Developmental Science, 9,* F33–F40.

Fernald, A., & Morikawa, H. (1993). Common themes and cultural variations in Japanese and American mothers' speech to infants. *Child Development, 64,* 637–656.

Fernald, A., Perfors, A., & Marchman, V. A. (2006). Picking up speed in understanding: Speech processing efficiency and vocabulary growth across the 2nd year. *Developmental Psychology, 42,* 98–116.

Fernald, A., Taeschner, T., Dunn, J., Papousek, M., Boyssen-Bardies, B., & Fukui, I. (1989). A cross-language study of prosodic modifications in mothers' and fathers' speech to preverbal infants. *Journal of Child Language, 16,* 477–502.

Fernald, L. C., & Grantham-McGregor, S. M. (1998). Stress response in school-age children who have been growth-retarded since early childhood. *American Journal of Clinical Nutrition, 68,* 691–698.

Fernyhough, C., & Fradley, E. (2005). Private speech on an executive task: Relations with task difficulty and task performance. *Cognitive Development, 20,* 103–120.

Ferrell, B. A. (1995). Pain evaluation and management in the nursing home. *Annals of Internal Medicine, 123,* 681–687.

Ficca, G., Fagioli, I., Giganti, F., & Salzarulo, P. (1999). Spontaneous awakenings from sleep in the first year of life. *Early Human Development, 55,* 219–228.

Fickling, D. (2004). A happy ending? *Lancet, 364,* 831–832.

Field, D. (1997). "Looking back, what period of your life brought you the most satisfaction?" *International Journal of Aging and Human Development, 45,* 169–194.

Field, D. (1999). Stability of older women's friendships: A commentary on Roberto. *International Journal of Aging and Human Development, 48,* 81–83.

Field, D., & Millsap, R. E. (1991). Personality in advanced old age: Continuity or change? *Journal of Gerontology, 46,* 299–308.

Field, T. (1998). Massage therapy effects. *American Psychologist, 53,* 1270–1281.

Field, T. (2001). Massage therapy facilitates weight gain in preterm infants. *Current Directions in Psychological Science, 10,* 51–54.

Field, T., Diego, M., Hernandez-Reif, M., Figueiredo, B., Schanberg, S., & Kuhn, C. (2007). Sleep disturbances in depressed pregnant women and their newborns. *Infant Behavior and Development, 30,* 127–133.

Field, T., Hernandez-Reif, M., Feijo, L., & Freedman, J. (2006). Prenatal, perinatal and neonatal stimulation: A survey of neonatal nurseries. *Infant Behavior and Development, 29,* 24–31.

Field, T., Hernandez-Reif, M., & Freedman, J. (2004). Stimulation programs for preterm infants. *Social Policy Report of the Society for Research in Child Development, 18*(1).

Fiese, B. H., & Schwartz, M. (2008). Reclaiming the family table: Mealtimes and child health and wellbeing. *Social Policy Report of the Society for Research in Child Development, 22*(4), 3–18.

Finchum, T., & Weber, J. A. (2000). Applying continuity theory to elder adult friendships. *Journal of Aging and Identity, 5,* 159–168.

Fingerman, K. L. (1996). Sources of tension in the aging mother and adult daughter relationship. *Psychology and Aging, 11,* 591–606.

Fingerman, K. L. (1998). The good, the bad, and the worrisome: Emotional complexities in grandparents' experiences with individual grandchildren. *Family Relations, 47,* 403–414.

Fingerman, K. L. (2000). "We had a nice little chat": Age and generational differences in mothers' and daughters' descriptions of enjoyable visits. *Journal of Gerontology, 55B,* P95–P106.

Fingerman, K. L. (2001a). A distant closeness: Intimacy between parents and their children in later life. *Generations, 25,* 26–33.

Fingerman, K. L. (2001b). *Aging mothers and their adult daughters: A study in mixed emotions.* New York: Springer.

Fingerman, K. L. (2004). The role of offspring and in-laws in grandparents' ties to their grandchildren. *Journal of Family Issues, 25,* 1026–1049.

Fingerman, K. L., & Birditt, K. S. (2003). Do we get better at picking our battles? Age group differences in descriptions of behavioral reactions to interpersonal tensions. *Journal of Gerontology, 60B,* P121–P128.

Fingerman, K. L., Chen, P.-C., Hay, E., Cichy, K. E., & Lefkowitz, E. S. (2006). Ambivalent reactions in the parent and offspring relationship. *Journal of Gerontology, 61B,* P152–P160.

Fingerman, K. L., Hay, E. L., & Birditt, K. S. (2004). The best of ties, the worst of ties: Close, problematic, and ambivalent social relationships. *Journal of Marriage and Family, 66,* 792–808.

Fingerman, K. L., Hay, E. L., Dush, C. M. K., Cichy, K. E., & Hosterman, S. J. (2007). Parents' and offspring's perceptions of change and continuity when parents experience the transition to old age. *Advances in Life Course Research, 12,* 275–305.

Fingerman, K. L., Miller, L., & Charles, S. (2008). Saving the best for last: How adults treat social partners of different ages. *Psychology and Aging, 23,* 399–409

Finkel, D., Reynolds, C. A., McArdle, J. J., & Pedersen, N. L. (2007). Age changes in processing speed as a leading indicator of cognitive aging. *Psychology and Aging, 22,* 558–568.

Finn, J. D., Gerber, S. B., & Boyd-Zaharias, J. (2005). Small classes in the early grades, academic achievement, and graduating from high school. *Journal of Educational Psychology, 97,* 214–233.

Finnilä, K., Mahlberga, N., Santtilia, P., & Niemib, P. (2003). Validity of a test of children's suggestibility for predicting responses to two interview situations differing in degree of suggestiveness. *Journal of Experimental Child Psychology, 85,* 32–49.

Finucane, M. L., Mertz, C. K., Slovic, P., & Schmidt, E. S. (2005). Task complexity and older adults' decision-making competence. *Psychology and Aging, 20,* 71–84.

Fiori, K. L., Smith, J., & Antonucci, T. C. (2007). Social network types among older adults: A multidimensional approach. *Journal of Gerontology, 62B,* P322–P330.

Fisch, H., Hyun, G., Golden, R., Hensle, T. W., Olsson, C. A., & Liberson, G. L. (2003). The influence of paternal age on Down syndrome. *Journal of Urology, 169,* 2275–2278.

Fischer, K. W., & Bidell, T. (1991). Constraining nativist inferences about cognitive capacities. In S. Carey & R. Gelman (Eds.), *The epigenesis of mind: Essays on biology and cognition* (pp. 199–235). Hillsdale, NJ: Erlbaum.

Fischer, K. W., & Bidell, T. R. (2006). Dynamic development of action and thought. In R. M. Lerner (Ed.), *Handbook of child psychology: Vol. 1. Theoretical models of human development* (6th ed., pp. 313–399). Hoboken, NJ: Wiley.

Fischman, M. G., Moore, J. B., & Steele, K. H. (1992). Children's one-hand catching as a function of age, gender, and ball location. *Research Quarterly for Exercise and Sport, 63,* 349–355.

Fish, M. (2004). Attachment in infancy and preschool in low socioeconomic status rural Appalachian children: Stability and change and relations to preschool and kindergarten competence. *Development and Psychopathology, 16,* 293–312.

Fisher, C. B. (1993, Winter). Integrating science and ethics in research with high-risk children and youth. *Social Policy Report of the Society for Research in Child Development, 4*(4).

Fisher, C. B. (2005). Deception research involving children: Ethical practices and paradoxes. *Ethics and Behavior, 15,* 271–287.

Fisher, J. O., Rolls, B. J., & Birch, L. L. (2003). Children's bite size and intake of an entrée are greater with large portions than with age-appropriate or self-selected portions. *American Journal of Clinical Nutrition, 77,* 1164–1170.

Fisher, S. K., Easterly, S., & Lazear, K. J. (2008). Lesbian, gay, bisexual and transgender families and their children. In T. P. Gullotta & G. M. Blau (Eds.), *Family influences on child behavior and development: Evidence-based prevention and treatment approaches* (pp. 187–208). New York: Routledge.

Fishman, S. B. (2004). *Double or nothing: Jewish families and mixed marriage.* Waltham, MA: Brandeis University Press.

FitzGerald, D. P., & White, K. J. (2003). Linking children's social worlds: Perspective-taking in parent–child and peer contexts. *Social Behavior and Personality, 31,* 509–522.

Fitzgibbons, P. J., & Gordon-Salant, S. (1998). Auditory temporal order perception in younger and older adults. *Journal of Speech, Language, and Hearing Research, 41,* 1052–1060.

Fitzpatrick, J., & Sollie, D. L. (1999). Influence of individual and interpersonal factors on satisfaction and stability in romantic relationships. *Personal Relationships, 6,* 337–350.

Fivaz-Depeursinge, E., & Corboz-Warnery, A. (1999). *The primary triangle: A developmental systems view of mothers, fathers, and infants.* New York: Basic Books.

Fivush, R. (2001). Owning experience: Developing subjective perspective in autobiographical narratives. In C. Moore & K. Lemmon (Eds.), *The self in time: Developmental perspectives* (pp. 35–52). Mahwah, NJ: Erlbaum.

Fivush, R., & Reese, E. (2002). Reminiscing and relating: The development of parent–child talk about the past. In J. D. Webster & B. K. Haight (Eds.), *Critical advances in reminiscence work: From theory to application* (pp. 109–122). New York: Springer.

Fivush, R., & Wang, Q. (2005). Emotion talk in mother–child conversations of the shared past: The effects of culture, gender, and event valence. *Journal of Cognition and Development, 6,* 489–506.

Flake, A. W. (2003). Surgery in the human fetus: The future. *Journal of Physiology, 547,* 45–51.

Flaks, D. K., Ficher, I., Masterpasqua, F., & Joseph, G. (1995). Lesbians choosing motherhood: A comparative study of lesbian and heterosexual parents and their children. *Developmental Psychology, 31,* 105–114.

Flanagan, C. A., & Faison, N. (2001). Youth civic development: Implications of research for social policy and programs. *Social Policy Report of the Society for Research in Child Development, 15*(1).

Flanagan, C. A., Stout, M., & Gallay, L. S. (2008). It's my body and none of your business: Developmental changes in adolescents' perceptions of rights concerning health. *Journal of Social Issues, 64,* 815–834.

Flanagan, C. A., & Tucker, C. J. (1999). Adolescents' explanations for political issues: Concordance with their views of self and society. *Developmental Psychology, 35,* 1198–1209.

Flannery, D. J., Hussey, D. L., Biebelhausen, L., & Wester, K. L. (2003). Crime, delinquency, and youth gangs. In G. R. Adams & M. D. Berzonsky (Eds.), *Blackwell handbook of adolescence* (pp. 502–522). Malden, MA: Blackwell.

Flannery, K. A., & Liederman, J. (1995). Is there really a syndrome involving the co-occurrence of neurodevelopmental disorder, talent, non–right handedness and immune disorder among children? *Cortex, 31,* 503–515.

Flavell, J. H., Flavell, E. R., & Green, F. L. (2001). Development of children's understanding of connections between thinking and feeling. *Psychological Science, 12,* 430–432.

Flavell, J. H., Green, F. L., & Flavell, E. R. (1987). Development of knowledge about the appearance–reality distinction. *Monographs of the Society for Research in Child Development, 51*(1, Serial No. 212)

Flavell, J. H., Green, F. L., & Flavell, E. R. (1993). Children's understanding of the stream of consciousness. *Child Development, 64,* 387–398.

Flavell, J. H., Green, F. L., & Flavell, E. R. (1995). Young children's knowledge about thinking. *Monographs of the Society for Research in Child Development, 60*(1, Serial No. 243).

Flavell, J. H., Green, F. L., & Flavell, E. R. (2000). Development of children's awareness of their own thoughts. *Journal of Cognition and Development, 1,* 97–112.

Flegal, K. M., Graubard, B. I., Williamson, D. F., & Gail, M. H. (2005). Excess deaths associated with underweight, overweight, and obesity. *Journal of the American Medical Association, 293,* 1861–1867.

Fleischman, D. A., Wilson, R. S., Gabrieli, J. D. E., Bienias, J. L., & Bennett, D. A. (2004). A longitudinal study of implicit and explicit memory in old persons. *Psychology and Aging, 19,* 617–625.

Fleming, J. I. (2000). Death, dying, and euthanasia: Australia versus the Northern Territory. *Issues in Law and Medicine, 15,* 291–305.

Fleming, V., M., & Alexander, J. M. (2001). The benefits of peer collaboration: A replication with a delayed posttest. *Contemporary Educational Psychology, 26,* 588–601.

Fletcher, A. C., Nickerson, P., & Wright, K. L. (2003). Structured leisure activities in middle childhood: Links to well-being. *Journal of Community Psychology, 31,* 641–659.

Floccia, C., Christophe, A., & Bertoncini, J. (1997). High-amplitude sucking and newborns: The quest for underlying mechanisms. *Journal of Experimental Child Psychology, 64,* 175–198.

Flom, R., & Pick, A. D. (2003). Verbal encouragement and joint attention in 18-month-old infants. *Infant Behavior and Development, 26,* 121–134.

Flood, D. G., & Coleman, P. D. (1988). Cell type heterogeneity of changes in dendritic extent in the hippocampal region of the human brain in normal aging and in Alzheimer's disease. In T. L. Petit & G. O. Ivy (Ed.), *Neural plasticity: A lifespan approach* (pp. 265–281). New York: Alan R. Liss.

Florian, V., & Kravetz, S. (1985). Children's concepts of death: A cross-cultural comparison among Muslims, Druze, Christians, and Jews in Israel. *Journal of Cross-Cultural Psychology, 16,* 174–179.

Florian,V., & Mikulincer,M. (1998). Symbolic immortality and the management of the terror of death: The moderating role of attachment style. *Journal of Personality and Social Psychology, 74,* 725–734.

Florsheim, P., & Smith, A. (2005). Expectant adolescent couples' relations and subsequent parenting behavior. *Infant Mental Health Journal, 26,* 533–548.

Flouri, E., & Buchanan, A. (2004). Early father's and mother's involvement and child's later educational outcomes. *British Journal of Educational Psychology, 74,* 141–153.

Flynn, E. (2006). A microgenetic investigation of stability and continuity in theory of mind development. *British Journal of Developmental Psychology, 24,* 631–654.

Flynn, J. R. (1999). Searching for justice: The discovery of IQ gains over time. *American Psychologist, 54,* 5–20.

Flynn, J. R. (2007). *What is intelligence? Beyond the Flynn effect.* New York: Cambridge University Press.

Fogel, A. (1993). *Developing through relationships: Origins of communication, self and culture.* New York: Harvester Wheatsheaf.

Fomon, S. J., & Nelson, S. E. (2002). Body composition of the male and female reference infants. *Annual Review of Nutrition, 22,* 1–17.

Fonda, S. J., Clipp, E. C., & Maddox, G. L. (2002). Patterns in functioning among residents of an affordable assisted living housing facility. *Gerontologist, 42,* 178–187.

Fong, T. G., Tulebaev, S. R., & Inouye, S. K. (2009). Delirium in elderly adults: Diagnosis, prevention and treatment. *Nature Reviews Neurology, 5,* 210–220.

Fontana, L. (2008). Calorie restriction and cardiometabolic health. *European Journal of Cardiovascular Prevention and Rehabilitation, 15,* 3–9.

Fontana, L. (2009). The scientific basis of caloric restriction leading to longer life. *Current Opinion in Gastroenterology, 25,* 144–150.

Fontana, L., Weiss, E., Villareal, D. T., Klein, S., & Holloszy, J. O. (2009). IGF-1, nutrition and aging: The big picture. *Aging Cell, 8,* 215.

Forman, D. R., Aksan, N., & Kochanska, G. (2004). Toddlers' responsive imitation predicts preschool-age conscience. *Psychological Science, 15,* 699–704

Forman, D. R., O'Hara, M. W., Stuart, S., Gorman, L. L., Larsen, K. E., & Coy, K. C. (2007). Effective treatment for postpartum depression is not sufficient to improve the developing mother–child relationship. *Development and Psychopathology, 19,* 585–602.

Forry, N. D., Leslie, L. A., & Letiecq, B. L. (2007). Marital quality in interracial relationships: The role of sex role ideology and perceived fairness. *Journal of Family Issues, 28,* 1538–1552.

Forste, R., & Heaton, T. B. (2004). The divorce generation: Well-being, family attitudes, and socioeconomic consequences of marital disruption. *Journal of Divorce and Remarriage, 42,* 95–114.

Foster, J. A., Gore, S. A., & West, D. S. (2006). Altering TV viewing habits: An unexplored strategy for adult obesity intervention? *American Journal of Health Behavior, 30,* 3–14.

Foster, M. A., Lambert, R., Abbott-Shim, M., McCarty, F., & Franze, S. (2005). A model of home learning environment and social risk factors in relation to children's emergent literacy and social outcomes. *Early Childhood Research Quarterly, 20,* 13–36.

Foster, W. A., & Miller, M. (2007). Development of the literacy achievement gap: A longitudinal study of kindergarten through third grade. *Language, Speech, and Hearing Services in Schools, 38,* 173–181.

Fowden, A. L., Giussani, D. A., & Forhead, A. J. (2005). Endocrine and metabolic programming during intrauterine development. *Early Human Development, 81,* 723–734.

Fowler, C. (2009). Motives for sibling communication across the lifespan. *Communication Quarterly, 57,* 51–66.

Fowler, J. W., & Dell, M. L. (2006). Stages of faith from infancy through adolescence: Reflections on three decades of faith development theory. In E. C. Roehlkepartain, P. E. King, L. Wagener, & P. L. Benson (Eds.), *Handbook of spiritual development in childhood and adolescence* (pp. 34–45). Thousand Oaks, CA: Sage.

Fox, C. L., & Boulton, M. J. (2006). Friendship as a moderator of the relationship between social skills

problems and peer victimization. *Aggressive Behavior, 32,* 110–121.
Fox, N. A. (1991). If it's not left, it's right: Electroencephalograph asymmetry and the development of emotion. *American Psychologist, 46,* 863–872.
Fox, N. A., & Calkins, S. D. (2003). The development of self-control of emotion: Intrinsic and extrinsic influences. *Motivation and Emotion, 27,* 7–26.
Fox, N. A., & Davidson, R. J. (1986). Taste-elicited changes in facial signs of emotion and the asymmetry of brain electrical activity in newborn infants. *Neuropsychologia, 24,* 417–422.
Foy, J. G., & Mann, V. (2003). Home literacy environment and phonological awareness in preschool children: Differential effects for rhyme and phoneme awareness. *Applied Psycholinguistics, 24,* 59–88.
Fozard, J. L., & Gordon-Salant, S. (2001). Changes in vision and hearing with aging. In J. E. Birren & K. W. Schaie (Eds.), *Handbook of the psychology of aging* (pp. 241–266). San Diego: Academic Press.
Franco, M. C., Danias, A. P., Akamine, E. H., Kawamoto, E. M., Fortes, Z. B., Scavone, C., Tostes, R. C., Carvalho, M. H., & Nigro, D. (2002). Enhanced oxidative stress as a potential mechanism underlying the programming of hypertension in utero. *Journal of Cardiovascular Pharmacology, 40,* 501–509.
Franco, P., Chabanski, S., Szliwowski, H., Dramaiz, M., & Kahn, A. (2000). Influence of maternal smoking on autonomic nervous system in healthy infants. *Pediatric Research, 47,* 215–220.
Frank, D. A., Rose-Jacobs, R., Beeghly, M., Wilbur, M., Bellinger, D., & Cabral, H. (2005). Level of prenatal cocaine exposure and 48-month IQ: Importance of preschool enrichment. *Neurotoxicology and Teratology, 27,* 15–28.
Franklin, M. (1995). The effects of differential college environments on academic learning and student perceptions of cognitive development. *Research in Higher Education, 36,* 127–153.
Franz, M. J., VanWormer, J. J., Crain, A. L., Boucher, J. L., Histon, T., Caplan, W., Bowman, J. D., & Pronk, N. P. (2007). Weight-loss outcomes: A systematic review and meta-analysis of weight-loss clinical trials with a minimum 1-year follow-up. *Journal of the American Dietetic Association, 107,* 1755–1767.
Frazier, L. D. (2002). Perceptions of control over health: Implications for sense of self in healthy and ill older adults. In S. P. Shohov (Ed.), *Advances in psychology research* (Vol. 10, pp. 145–163). Huntington, NY: Nova Science Publishers.
Frazier, L. D., & Hooker, K. (2006). Possible selves in adult development: Linking theory and research. In C. Dunkel & J. Kerpelman (Eds.), *Possible selves: Theory, research and applications* (pp. 41–59). Hauppauge, NY: Nova Science.
Frederickson, B. L., & Carstensen, L. L. (1990). Relationship classification using grade of membership analysis: A typology of sibling relationships in later life. *Journal of Gerontology, 45,* S43–S51.
Frederiksen-Goldsen, K. I., & Sharlach, A. E. (2000). *Families and work: New directions in the twenty-first century.* New York: Oxford University Press.
Fredricks, J. A., & Eccles, J. S. (2002). Children's competence and value beliefs from childhood through adolescence: Growth trajectories in two male-sex-typed domains. *Developmental Psychology, 38,* 519–533.
Fredricks, J. A., & Eccles, J. S. (2005). Developmental benefits of extracurricular involvement: Do peer characteristics mediate the link between activities and youth outcomes? *Journal of Youth and Adolescence, 34,* 507–520.
Fredricks, J. A., & Eccles, J. S. (2006). Is extracurricular participation associated with beneficial outcomes? Concurrent and longitudinal relations. *Developmental Psychology, 42,* 698–713.
Freedman, M. (1999). *Prime time: How baby boomers will revolutionize retirement and transform America.* New York: Public Affairs.
Freedman, M. (2007). The social-purpose encore career: Baby boomers, civic engagement, and the next stage of work. *Generations, 30,* 43–46.
Freedman-Doan, C., Wigfield, A., Eccles, J. S., Blumenfeld, P., Arbreton, A., & Harold, R. D. (2000). What am I best at? Grade and gender differences in children's beliefs about ability improvement. *Journal of Applied Developmental Psychology, 21,* 379–402.
Freeman, C. E. (2004). *Trends in educational equity of girls and women: 2004.* U.S. Department of Education, National Center for Education Statistics. Washington, DC: U.S. Government Printing Office.
Freeman, D. (1983). *Margaret Mead and Samoa: The making and unmaking of an anthropological myth.* Cambridge, MA: Harvard University Press.
Freeman, E. W., & Halbreich, U. (1998). Premenstrual syndromes. *Psychopharmacological Bulletin, 34,* 291–295.
Freeman, L., Caserta, M., Lund, D., Rossa, S., Dowdy, A., & Partenheimer, A. (2006). Music thanatology: Prescriptive harp music as palliative care for the dying patient. *American Journal of Hospice and Palliative Care, 23,* 100–104.
Freiman, A., Bird, G., Metelitsa, A. I., Barankin, B., & Lauzon, G. J. (2004). Cutaneous effects of smoking. *Journal of Cutaneous Medicine and Surgery, 8,* 415–423.
French, S. A., Story, M., & Jeffrey, R. W. (2001). Environmental influences on eating and physical activity. *Annual Review of Public Health, 22,* 309–335.
Freud, A. (1969). Adolescence as a developmental disturbance. In G. Caplan & S. Lebovici (Eds.), *Adolescence* (pp. 5–10). New York: Basic Books.
Freud, S. (1973). *An outline of psychoanalysis.* London: Hogarth. (Original work published 1938)
Freud, S. (1974). *The ego and the id.* London: Hogarth. (Original work published 1923)
Freund, A. M., & Baltes, P. B. (1998). Selection, optimization, and compensation as strategies of life management: Correlations with subjective indicators of successful aging. *Psychology and Aging, 13,* 531–543.
Freund, A. M., & Baltes, P. B. (2000). The orchestration of selection, optimization and compensation: An action-theoretical conceptualization of a theory of developmental regulation. In W. J. Perrig & A. Grob (Eds.), *Control of human behavior, mental processes, and consciousness* (pp. 35–58). Mahwah, NJ: Erlbaum.
Freund, A. M., & Ebner, N. C. (2005). The aging self: Shifting from promoting gains to balancing losses. In W. Greve, K. Rothermund, & D. Wentura (Eds.), *The adaptive self: Personal continuity and intentional self-development* (pp. 185–202). New York: Hogrefe.
Freund, A. M., & Smith, J. (1999). Content and function of the self-definition in old and very old age. *Journal of Gerontology, 54B,* P55–P67.
Frey, A., Ruchkin, V., Martin, A., & Schwab-Stone, M. (2009). Adolescents in transition: School and family characteristics in the development of violent behaviors entering high school. *Child Psychiatry and Human Development, 40,* 1–13.
Fried, P. A. (1993). Prenatal exposure to tobacco and marijuana: Effects during pregnancy, infancy, and early childhood. *Clinical Obstetrics and Gynecology, 36,* 319–337.
Fried, P. A., Watkinson, B., & Gray, R. (2003). Differential effects on cognitive functioning in 13- to 16-year-olds prenatally exposed to cigarettes and marijuana. *Neurotoxicology and Teratology, 25* 427–436.
Friedman, D. S. (2006, January). Understanding who is at high risk of having glaucoma. *Gleams,* pp. 1–2. Retrieved from www.umm.edu/patiented/articles/who_gets_glaucoma_000025_5.htm
Friedman, E. M., & Lawrence, D. A. (2002). Environmental stress mediates changes in neuroimmunological interactions. *Toxicological Sciences, 67,* 4–10.
Friedman, J. M. (1996). *The effects of drugs on the fetus and nursing infant: A handbook for health care professionals.* Baltimore: Johns Hopkins University Press.
Friedman, J. M. (2006). *The effects of drugs on the fetus and nursing infant: A handbook for health care professionals.* Baltimore: Johns Hopkins University Press.
Friedman, S. L., & Scholnick, E. K. (1997). An evolving "blueprint" for planning: Psychological requirements, task characteristics, and social–cultural influences. In S. L. Friedman & E. K. Scholnick (Eds.), *The developmental psychology of planning: Why, how, and when do we plan?* (pp. 3–22). Mahwah, NJ: Erlbaum.
Fries, J. F. (2003). Measuring and monitoring success in compressing morbidity. *Annals of Internal Medicine, 139,* 455–459.
Frith, L. (2001). Gamete donation and anonymity: The ethical and legal debate. *Human Reproduction, 16,* 818–824.
Frith, U. (2003). *Autism: Explaining the enigma* (2nd ed.). Malden, MA: Blackwell.
Frith, U., & Happé, F. (1994). Austism: Beyond "theory of mind." *Cognition, 50,* 115–132.
Fry, C. L. (1985). Culture, behavior, and aging in the comparative perspective. In J. E. Birren & K. W. Schaie (Eds.), *Handbook of the psychology of aging* (2nd ed., pp. 216–244). New York: Van Nostrand Reinhold.
Fry, C. L., Dickerson-Putman, J., Draper, P., Ikels, C., Keith, J., Glascock, A. P., & Harpending, H. C. (1997). Culture and the meaning of a good old age. In J. Sokolovsky (Ed.), *The cultural context of aging: Worldwide perspectives* (2nd ed., pp. 99–124). New York: Bergin & Garvey.
Fry, P. M. (2001). Predictors of health-related quality of life perspectives, self-esteem, and life satisfactions of older adults following spousal loss: An 18-month follow-up study of widows and widowers. *Gerontologist, 41,* 787–798.
Fry, P. S. (2003). Perceived self-efficacy domains as predictors of fear of the unknown and fear of dying among older adults. *Psychology and Aging, 18,* 474–486.
Fry, P. S., & Debats, D. L. (2006). Sources of life strengths as predictors of late-life mortality and survivorship. *International Journal of Aging and Human Development, 62,* 303–334.
Fu, G., Xu, F., Cameron, C. A., Heyman, G., & Lee, K. (2007). Cross-cultural differences in children's choices, categorizations, and evaluations of truths and lies. *Developmental Psychology, 43,* 278–293.
Fuchs, D., Fuchs, L. S., Mathes, P. G., & Martinez, E. A. (2002a). Preliminary evidence on the standing of students with learning disabilities in PALS and no-PALS classrooms. *Learning Disabilities Research and Practice, 17,* 205–215.
Fuchs, L. S., Fuchs, D., Yazkian, L., & Powell, S. R. (2002b). Enhancing first-grade children's mathematical development with peer-assisted learning strategies. *School Psychology Review, 31,* 569–583.
Fuh, M.-H., Wang, S.-J., Wang, P.-H., & Fuh, J.-L. (2005). Attitudes toward menopause among middle-aged women: A community survey in an island of Taiwan. *Maturitas, 52,* 348–355.

Fukunaga, A., Uematsu, H., & Sugimoto, K. (2005). Influences of aging on taste perception and oral somatic sensation. *Journal of Gerontology, 60A,* 109–113.

Fulhan, J., Collier, S., & Duggan, C. (2003). Update on pediatric nutrition: Breastfeeding, infant nutrition, and growth. *Current Opinion in Pediatrics, 15,* 323–332.

Fuligni, A. J. (1998). The adjustment of children from immigrant families. *Current Directions in Psychological Science, 7,* 99–103.

Fuligni, A. J. (2004). The adaptation and acculturation of children from immigrant families. In U. P. Gielen & J. Roopnarine (Eds.), *Childhood and adolescence: Cross-cultural perspectives* (pp. 297–318). Westport, CT: Praeger.

Fuligni, A. J., Yip. T., & Tseng, V. (2002). The impact of family obligation on the daily activities and psychological well-being of Chinese-American adolescents. *Child Development, 73,* 302–314.

Fuligni, A. J., & Yoshikawa, H. (2003). Socioeconomic resources, parenting, and child development among immigrant families. In M. H. Bornstein & R. H. Bradley (Eds.), *Socioeconomic status, parenting, and child development* (pp. 107–124). Mahwah, NJ: Erlbaum.

Fuligni, A. S., Han, W.-J., & Brooks-Gunn, J. (2004). The Infant-Toddler HOME in the 2nd and 3rd years of life. *Parenting: Science and Practice, 4,* 139–159.

Fuller, C., Keller, L., Olson, J., Plymale, A., & Gottesman, M. (2005). Helping preschoolers become healthy eaters. *Journal of Pediatric Health Care, 19,* 178–182.

Fuller-Thomson, E., & Minkler, M. (2000). The mental and physical health of grandmothers who are raising their grandchildren. *Journal of Mental Health and Aging, 6,* 311–323.

Fuller-Thomson, E., & Minkler, M. (2005). Native American grandparents raising grandchildren: Findings from the Census 2000 Supplementary Survey and implications for social work practice. *Social Work, 50,* 131–139.

Fuller-Thomson, E., & Minkler, M. (2007). Mexican American grandparents raising grandchildren: Findings from the Census 2000 American Community Survey. *Families in Society, 88,* 567–574.

Fullerton, J. T., Navarro, A. M., & Young, S. H. (2007). Outcomes of planned home birth: An integrative review. *Journal of Midwifery and Women's Health, 52,* 323–333.

Fulmer, T. (2008). Screening for mistreatment of older adults. *American Journal of Nursing, 108,* 52–56.

Fung, H. H., & Carstensen, L. L. (2004). Motivational changes in response to blocked goals and foreshortened time: Testing alternatives to socioemotional selectivity theory. *Psychology and Aging, 19,* 68–78.

Fung, H. H., Carstensen, L. L., & Lang, F. R. (2001). Age-related patterns in social networks among European Americans and African Americans: Implications for socioemotional selectivity across the life span. *International Journal of Aging and Human Development, 52,* 185–206.

Fung, H. H., Carstensen, L. L., & Lutz, A. (1999). The influence of time on social preferences: Implications for life-span development. *Psychology and Aging, 14,* 595–604.

Furchtgott-Roth, D. (2009). *Testimony on the gender pay gap* (testimony before the Joint Economic Committee, U.S. House of Representatives). Washington, DC: Hudson Institute.

Furman, W., & Buhrmester, D. (1992). Age and sex differences in perceptions of networks of personal relationships. *Child Development, 63,* 103–115.

Furman, W., & Shaffer, L. (2003). The role of romantic relationships in adolescent development. In P. Florsheim (Ed.), *Adolescent romantic relations and sexual behavior* (pp. 3–22). Mahwah, NJ: Erlbaum.

Furman, W., Simon, V. A., Shaffer, L., & Bouchey, H. A. (2002). Adolescents' working models and styles for relationships with parents, friends, and romantic partners. *Child Development, 73,* 241–255.

Furstenberg, F. F., Jr., & Harris, K. M. (1993). When and why fathers matter: Impact of father involvement on children of adolescent mothers. In R. I. Lerman & T. J. Ooms (Eds.), *Young unwed fathers* (pp. 117–138). Philadelphia: Temple University Press.

Fuson, K. C., & Burghard, B. H. (2003). Multidigit addition and subtraction methods invented in small groups and teacher support of problem solving and reflection. In J. J. Baroody & A. Dowker (Eds.), *The development of arithmetic concepts and skills* (pp. 267–304). Mahwah, NJ: Erlbaum.

Fussell, E., & Furstenberg, F. F., Jr. (2005). The transition to adulthood during the twentieth century. In R. A. Settersten, Jr., F. F. Furstenberg, Jr., & R. G. Rumbaut (Eds.), *On the frontier of adulthood* (pp. 29–75). Chicago: University of Chicago Press.

Fussell, E., & Gauthier, A. H. (2005). American women's transition to adulthood in comparative perspective. In R. A. Settersten, Jr., F. F. Furstenberg, Jr., & R. G. Rumbaut (Eds.), *On the frontier of adulthood: Theory, research, and public policy* (pp. 76–109). Chicago: University of Chicago Press.

Fuster, J. J., & Andres, V. (2006). Telomere biology and cardiovascular disease. *Circulation Research, 99,* 1167–1180.

Fyfe, M. (2006, April). Music and love help defy the doctors. Retrieved from www.theage.com.au/news/national/music-and-love-help-dying-defy-the-doctors/2006/03/31/1143441339517.html

G

Gabbay, S. G., & Wahler, J. J. (2002). Lesbian aging: Review of a growing literature. *Journal of Gay and Lesbian Social Services, 14,* 1–21.

Gabrel, C. S. (2000). *Advance data from Vital and Health Statistics of the Centers for Disease Control and Prevention.* Washington, DC: U.S. Department of Health and Human Services.

Gabriel, Z., & Bowling, A. (2004). Quality of life from the perspectives of older people. *Ageing and Society, 24,* 675–691.

Gailliot, M. T., Schmeichel, B. J., & Baumeister, R. F. (2006). Self-regulatory processes defend against the threat of death: Effects of self-control depletion and trait self-control on thoughts and fears of dying. *Journal of Personality and Social Psychology, 91,* 49–62.

Galambos, N. L., Almeida, D. M., & Petersen, A. C. (1990). Masculinity, femininity, and sex role attitudes in early adolescence: Exploring gender intensification. *Child Development, 61,* 1905–1914.

Galambos, N. L., Barker, E. T., & Krahn, H. J. (2006). Depression, anger, and self-esteem in emerging adulthood: Seven-year trajectories. *Developmental Psychology, 42,* 350–365.

Galambos, N. L., & Maggs, J. L. (1991). Children in self-care: Figures, facts, and fiction. In J. V. Lerner & N. L. Galambos (Eds.), *Employed mothers and their children* (pp. 131–157). New York: Garland.

Gallagher, A. M., & Kaufman, J. C. (2005). Gender differences in mathematics: What we know and what we need to know. In A. M. Gallagher & J. C. Kaufman (Eds.), *Gender differences in mathematics: An integrative psychological approach* (pp. 316–331). New York: Cambridge University Press.

Gallardo, G., Schlüter, O. M., & Südhof, T. C. (2008). A molecular pathway of neurodegeneration linking alpha-synuclein to ApoE and Abeta pepites. *Nature Neuroscience, 11,* 301–308.

Galler, J. R., Ramsey, C. F., Morley, D. S., Archer, E., & Salt, P. (1990). The long-term effects of early kwashiorkor compared with marasmus. IV. Performance on the National High School Entrance Examination. *Pediatric Research, 28,* 235–239.

Gallo, W. T., Bradley, E. H., Dubin, J. A., Jones, R. N., Falba, T. A., Teng, H.-M., & Kasl, S. V. (2006). The persistence of depressive symptoms in older workers who experience involuntary job loss: Results from the Health and Retirement Survey. *Journal of Gerontology, 61B,* S221–S228.

Galloway, J., & Thelen, E. (2004). Feet first: Object exploration in young infants. *Infant Behavior and Development, 27,* 107–112.

Gallup News Service. (2006). *Religion most important to blacks, women, and older Americans.* Retrieved from www.gallup.com/poll/25585/Religion-Most-Important-Blacks-Women-Older-Americans.aspx?version=print

Ganger, J., & Brent, M. R. (2004). Reexamining the vocabulary spurt. *Developmental Psychology, 40,* 621–632.

Ganji, V., Hampl, J. S., & Betts, N. M. (2003). Race-, gender-, and age-specific differences in dietary micronutrient intakes of U.S. children. *International Journal of Food Sciences and Nutrition, 54,* 485–490.

Gannon, L., & Ekstrom, B. (1993). Attitudes toward menopause: The influence of sociocultural paradigms. *Psychology of Women Quarterly, 17,* 275–288.

Ganong, L. H., & Coleman, M. (1994). *Remarried family relationships.* Thousand Oaks, CA: Sage.

Ganong, L. H., & Coleman, M. (2004). *Stepfamily relationships: Development, dynamics, and interventions.* New York: Kluwer/Plenum.

Ganong, L., Coleman, M., Fine, M., & Martin, P. (1999). Stepparents' affinity-seeking and affinity-maintaining strategies with stepchildren. *Journal of Family Issues, 20,* 299–327.

Gans, D., & Silverstein, M. (2006). Norms of filial responsibility for aging parents across time and generations. *Journal of Marriage and Family, 68,* 961–976.

Gao, G. (2001). Intimacy, passion, and commitment in Chinese and U.S. American romantic relationships. *International Journal of Intercultural Relations, 25,* 329–342.

Garces, E., Thomas, D., & Currie, J. (2002). Longer-term effects of Head Start. *American Economic Review, 92,* 999–1012.

Garcia, M. M., Shaw, D. S., Winslow, E. B., & Yaggi, K. E. (2000). Destructive sibling conflict and the development of conduct problems in young boys. *Developmental Psychology, 36,* 44–53.

Garcia-Bournissen, F., Tsur, L., Goldstein, L. H., Staroselsky, A., Avner, M., & Asrar, F. (2008). Fetal exposure to isotretinoin—an international problem. *Reproductive Toxicology, 25,* 124–128.

García Coll, C., & Magnuson, K. (1997). The psychological experience of immigration: A developmental perspective. In A. Booth, A. C. Crouter, & N. Landale (Eds.), *Immigration and the family* (pp. 91–131). Mahwah, NJ: Erlbaum.

Gardner, H. (1983). *Frames of mind: The theory of multiple intelligences.* New York: Basic Books.

Gardner, H. (1993). *Multiple intelligences: The theory in practice.* New York: Basic Books.

Gardner, H. E. (1998a). Are there additional intelligences? The case of the naturalist, spiritual, and existential intelligences. In J. Kane (Ed.),

Educational information and transformation. Upper Saddle River, NJ: Prentice-Hall.

Gardner, H. E. (1998b). Extraordinary cognitive achievements (ECA): A symbol systems approach. In R. M. Lerner (Ed.), *Handbook of child psychology: Vol. 1. Theoretical models of human development* (5th ed., pp. 415–466). New York: Wiley.

Gardner, H. E. (2000). *Intelligence reframed: Multiple intelligences for the twenty-first century.* New York: Basic Books.

Gardner, J. P., Li, S., Srinivasan, S. R., Chen, W., Kimura, M., & Lu, X. (2005). Rise in insulin resistance is associated with escalated telomere attrition. *Circulation, 111,* 2171–2177.

Garmezy, N. (1993). Children in poverty: Resilience despite risk. *Psychiatry, 56,* 127–136.

Garner, P. W. (1996). The relations of emotional role taking, affective/moral attributions, and emotional display rule knowledge to low-income school-age children's social competence. *Journal of Applied Developmental Psychology, 17,* 19–36.

Garner, P. W. (2003). Child and family correlates of toddlers' emotional and behavioral responses to a mishap. *Infant Mental Health Journal, 24,* 580–596.

Gartstein, M. A., & Rothbart, M. K. (2003). Studying infant temperament via the revised infant behavior questionnaire. *Infant Behavior and Development, 26,* 64–86.

Gartstein, M. A., Slobodskaya, H. R., & Kinsht, I. A. (2003). Cross-cultural differences in temperament in the first year of life: United States of America (U.S.) and Russia. *International Journal of Behavioral Development, 27,* 316–328.

Gasden, V. (1999). Black families in intergenerational and cultural perspective. In M. E. Lamb (Ed.), *Parenting and child development in "nontraditional" families* (pp. 221–246). Mahwah, NJ: Erlbaum.

Gaskins, S. (1999). Children's daily lives in a Mayan village: A case study of culturally constructed roles and activities. In R. Göncü (Ed.), *Children's engagement in the world: Sociocultural perspectives* (pp. 25–61). Cambridge, UK: Cambridge University Press.

Gaskins, S. (2000). Children's daily activities in a Mayan village: A culturally grounded description. *Cross-Cultural Research, 34,* 375–389.

Gaskins, S., Haight, W., & Lancy, D. F. (2007). The cultural construction of play. In A. Göncü & S. Gaskins (Eds.), *Play and development: Evolutionary, sociocultural, and functional perspectives* (pp. 179–202). Mahwah, NJ: Erlbaum.

Gathercole, S. E., Adams, A.-M., & Hitch, G. (1994). Do young children rehearse? An individual-differences analysis. *Memory and Cognition, 22,* 201–207.

Gathercole, V., Sebastián, E., & Soto, P. (1999). The early acquisition of Spanish verb morphology: Across-the-board or piecemeal knowledge? *International Journal of Bilingualism, 3,* 133–182.

Gatz, M., Bengtson, V. L., & Blum, M. J. (1990). Caregiving families. In J. E. Birren & K. W. Schaie (Eds.), *Handbook of the psychology of aging* (3rd ed., pp. 404–426). San Diego, CA: Academic Press.

Gatz, M., Kasl-Godley, J. E., & Karel, M. J. (1996). Aging and mental disorders. In J. E. Birren & K. W. Schaie (Eds.), *Handbook of the psychology of aging* (pp. 365–382). Sand Diego: Academic Press.

Gauvain, M. (2004). Bringing culture into relief: Cultural contributions to the development of children's planning skills. In R. V. Kail (Ed.), *Advances in child development and behavior* (pp. 39–71). San Diego, CA: Elsevier.

Gauvain, M., de la Ossa, J. L., & Hurtado-Ortiz, M. T. (2001). Parental guidance as children learn to use cultural tools: The case of pictorial plans. *Cognitive Development, 16,* 551–575.

Gauvain, M., & Huard, R. D. (1999). Family interaction, parenting style, and the development of planning: A longitudinal analysis using archival data. *Journal of Family Psychology, 13,* 75–92.

Gauvain, M., & Rogoff, B. (1989). Ways of speaking about space: The development of children's skill in communicating spatial knowledge. *Cognitive Development, 4,* 295–307.

Gavin, J., Scott, A., & Duffield, J. (2005). *Internet dating more successful than thought.* Retrieved from www.sciencedaily.com/releases/2005/02/050218125144.htm

Gayle, B. M., Preiss, R. W., & Allen, M. (2002). A meta-analytic interpretation of nonintimate interpersonal conflict. In M. Allen & R. W. Preiss (Eds.), *Interpersonal communication research: Advances through meta-analysis* (pp. 345–368). Mahwah, NJ: Erlbaum.

Gazelle, H., & Rudolph, K. D. (2004). Moving toward and away from the world: Social approach and avoidance trajectories in anxious and solitary youth. *Child Development, 75,* 829–849.

Gazzaley, A., Cooney, J. W., Rissman, J., & D'Esposito, M. (2005). Top-down suppression deficit underlies working memory impairment in normal aging. *Nature Neuroscience, 8,* 1298–1300.

Ge, X., Brody, G. H., Conger, R. D., Simons, R. L., & Murry, V. (2002). Contextual amplification of the effects of pubertal transition on African American children's deviant peer affiliation and externalized behavioral problems. *Developmental Psychology, 38,* 42–54.

Ge, X., Conger, R. D., & Elder, G. H., Jr. (1996). Coming of age too early: Pubertal influences on girls' vulnerability to psychological distress. *Child Development, 67,* 3386–3400.

Ge, X., Conger, R. D., & Elder, G. H., Jr. (2001). The relation between puberty and psychological distress in adolescent boys. *Journal of Research on Adolescence, 11,* 49–70.

Ge, X., Jin, R., Natsuaki, M. N., Frederick, X., Brody, G. H., Cutrona, C. E., & Simons, R. L. (2006). Pubertal maturation and early substance use risks among African American children. *Psychology of Addictive Behaviors, 20,* 404–414.

Ge, X., Kim, I. J., Brody, G. H., Conger, R. D., & Simons, R. L. (2003). It's about timing and change: Pubertal transition effects on symptoms of major depression among African American youths. *Developmental Psychology, 39,* 430–439.

Geary, D. C. (1999). Evolution and developmental sex differences. *Current Directions in Psychological Science, 8,* 115–120.

Geary, D. C. (2006a). Development of mathematical understanding. In D. Kuhn & R. Siegler (Eds.), *Handbook of child psychology: Vol. 2. Cognition, perception, and language* (pp. 777–810). Hoboken, NJ: Wiley.

Geary, D. C. (2006b). Evolutionary developmental psychology: Current status and future directions. *Developmental Review, 26,* 113–119.

Geary, D. C., Saults, J. S., Liu, F., & Hoard, M. K. (2000). Sex differences in spatial cognition, computational fluency, and arithmetic reasoning. *Journal of Experimental Child Psychology, 77,* 337–353.

Gee, C. B., & Rhodes, J. E. (2003). Adolescent mothers' relationship with their children's biological fathers: Social support, social strain, and relationship continuity. *Journal of Family Psychology, 17,* 370–383.

Geiger, H. J. (2007). Health disparities: What do we know? What should we do? In A. J. Schulz & L. Mullings (Eds.), *Gender, race, class, and health: Intersectional approaches* (pp. 3–17). San Francisco: Jossey-Bass.

Gelman, R. (1972). Logical capacity of very young children: Number invariance rules. *Child Development, 43,* 75–90.

Gelman, R., & Shatz, M. (1978). Appropriate speech adjustments: The operation of conversational constraints on talk to two-year-olds. In M. Lewis & L. A. Rosenblum (Eds.), *Interaction, conversation, and the development of language* (pp. 27–61). New York: Wiley.

Gelman, S. A. (2003). *The essential child.* New York: Oxford University Press.

Gelman, S. A., & Kalish, C. W. (2006). Conceptual development. In D. Kuhn & R. Siegler (Eds.), *Handbook of child psychology: Vol. 2. Cognition, perception, and language* (6th ed., pp. 687–733). Hoboken, NJ: Wiley.

Gelman, S. A., & Koenig, M. A. (2003). Theory-based categorization in early childhood. In D. H. Rakison & L. M. Oakes (Eds.), *Early category and concept development* (pp. 330–359). New York: Oxford University Press.

Gelman, S. A., & Opfer, J. E. (2002). Development of the animate–inanimate distinction. In U. Goswami (Ed.), *Blackwell handbook of childhood cognitive development* (pp. 151–166). Malden, MA: Blackwell.

Gelman, S. A., Taylor, M. G., & Nguyen, S. P. (2004). Mother–child conversations about gender. *Monographs of the Society for Research in Child Development, 69*(1, Serial No. 275), pp. 1–127.

Gennari, L., & Bilezikian, J. P. (2007). Osteoporosis in men: Pathophysiology and treatment. *Current Rheumatology Reports, 9,* 71–77.

George, S. A. (2002). The menopause experience: A woman's perspective. *Journal of Obstetric, Gynecologic, and Neonatal Nursing, 31,* 71–85.

Gerard, J. M., Krishnakumar, A., & Buehler, C. (2006). Marital conflict, parent–child relations, and youth maladjustment: A longitudinal investigation of spillover effects. *Journal of Family Issues, 27,* 951–975.

Gerardi-Caulton, G. (2000). Sensitivity to spatial conflict and the development of self-regulation in children 24–36 months of age. *Developmental Science, 3,* 397–404.

Gergely, G., & Watson, J. (1996). The social biofeedback theory of parental affect-mirroring: The development of emotional self-awareness and self-control in infancy. *International Journal of Psychoanalysis, 77,* 1181–1212.

Gergely, G., & Watson, J. (1999). Early socio-emotional development: Contingency perception and the social-biofeedback model. In P. Rochat (Ed.), *Early social cognition: Understanding others in the first months of life* (pp. 101–136). Mahwah, NJ: Erlbaum.

Gergen, M., & Gergen, K. J. (2003). Positive aging. In J. F. Gubrim & J. A. Holstein (Eds.), *Ways of aging* (pp. 203–224). Malden: Blackwell Publishers Ltd.

Germino, B. B. (2003). Dying at home. In I. Corless, B. B. Germino, & M. A. Pittman (Eds.), *Dying, death, and bereavement: A challenge for the living* (pp. 105–116). New York: Springer.

Gershoff, E. T. (2002a). Corporal punishment by parents and associated child behaviors and experiences: A meta-analytic and theoretical review. *Psychological Bulletin, 128,* 539–579.

Gershoff, E. T. (2002b). Corporal punishment, physical abuse, and the burden of proof: Reply to Baumrind, Larzelere, and Cowan (2002), Holden (2002), and Parke (2002). *Psychological Bulletin, 128,* 602–611.

Gershoff, E. T., & Aber, J. L. (2006). Neighborhoods and schools: Contexts and consequences for the mental health and risk behaviors of children and youth. In L. Balter & C. S. Tamis-LeMonda (Eds.), *Child psychology: A handbook of contemporary*

issues (2nd ed., pp. 611–645). New York: Psychology Press.
Gershoff-Stowe, L., & Hahn, E. R. (2007). Fast mapping skills in the developing lexicon. *Journal of Speech, Language, and Hearing Research, 50,* 682–697.
Gerstorf, D., Ram, N., Estabrook, R., Schupp, J., Wagner, G. G., & Lindenberger, U. (2008). Life satisfaction shows terminal decline in old age: Longitudinal evidence from the German socio-economic panel study. *Developmental Psychology, 44,* 1148–1159.
Gerten, K. A., Coonrod, D. V., Bay, R. C., & Chambliss, L. R. (2005). Cesarean delivery and -respiratory distress syndrome: Does labor make a difference? *American Journal of Obstetrics and Gynecology, 193,* 1061–1064.
Gertner, S., Greenbaum, C. W., Sadeh, A., Dolfin, Z., Sirota, L., & Ben-Nun, Y. (2002). Sleep-wake patterns in preterm infants and 6 month's home environment: Implications for early cognitive development. *Early Human Development, 68,* 93–102.
Gesell, A. (1933). Maturation and patterning of behavior. In C. Murchison (Ed.), *A handbook of child psychology.* Worcester, MA: Clark University Press.
Gest, S. D., Domitrovich, C. E., & Welsh, J. A. (2005). Peer academic reputation in elementary school: Associations with changes in self-concept and academic skills. *Journal of Educational Psychology, 97,* 337–346.
Geurts, H. M., Verte, S., Oosterlaan, J., Roeyers, H., & Sergeant, J. A. (2004). How specific are executive functioning deficits in attention-deficit hyperactivity disorder and autism? *Journal of Child Psychology and Psychiatry, 45,* 836–854.
Ghim, H. R. (1990). Evidence for perceptual organization in infants: Perception of subjective contours by young infants. *Infant Behavior and Development, 13,* 221–248.
Giarrusso, R., Feng, D., Silverstein, M., & Bengtson, V. L. (2001). Grandparent–adult grandchild affection and consensus. *Journal of Family Issues, 22,* 456–477.
Gibbons, A. (1998). Which of our genes make us human? *Science, 281,* 1432–1434.
Gibbons, R., Dugaiczyk, L. J., Girke, T., Duistermars, B., Zielinski, R., & Dugaiczyk, A. (2004). Distinguishing humans from great apes with AluYb8 repeats. *Journal of Molecular Biology, 339,* 721–729.
Gibbs, J. C. (1991). Toward an integration of Kohlberg's and Hoffman's theories of morality. In W. M. Kurtines & J. L. Gewirtz (Eds.), *Handbook of moral behavior and development* (Vol. 1, pp. 183–222). Hillsdale, NJ: Erlbaum.
Gibbs, J. C. (2006). Should Kohlberg's cognitive developmental approach to morality be replaced with a more pragmatic approach? Comment on Krebs and Denton (2005). *Psychological Review, 113,* 666–671.
Gibbs, J. C. (2010). *Moral development and reality: Beyond the theories of Kohlberg and Hoffman* (2nd ed.). Boston: Pearson Allyn & Bacon.
Gibbs, J. C., Basinger, K. S., Grime, R. L., & Snarey, J. R. (2007). Moral judgment development across cultures: Revisiting Kohlberg's universality claims. *Developmental Review, 24,* 443–500.
Gibbs, J. C., Moshman, D., Berkowitz, M. W., Basinger, K. S., & Grime, R. L. (2009a). Taking development seriously: Critique of the 2008 *JME* special issue on moral functioning. *Journal of Moral Education, 38,* 271–282.
Gibbs, J. C., Potter, G. B., DiBiase, A.-M., & Devlin, R. (2009b). The EQUIP program: Social perspective-taking for responsible thought and behavior. In B. Glick (Ed.), *Cognitive behavioral interventions for at-risk youth* (2nd ed.). Kingston, NJ: Civic Research Institute.
Gibson, E. J. (1970). The development of perception as an adaptive process. *American Scientist, 58,* 98–107.
Gibson, E. J. (2000). Perceptual learning in development: Some basic concepts. *Ecological Psychology, 12,* 295–302.
Gibson, E. J. (2003). The world is so full of a number of things: On specification and perceptual learning. *Ecological Psychology, 15,* 283–287.
Gibson, E. J., & Walk, R. D. (1960). The "visual cliff." *Scientific American, 202,* 64–71.
Gibson, J. J. (1979). *The ecological approach to visual perception.* Boston: Houghton Mifflin.
Gibson, P. A. (2005). Intergenerational parenting from the perspective of American grandmothers. *Family Relations, 54,* 280–297.
Giles, J. W., & Heyman, G. D. (2005). Young children's beliefs about the relationship between gender and aggressive behavior. *Child Development, 76,* 107–121.
Gillies, R. M. (2000). The maintenance of cooperative and helping behaviours in cooperative groups. *British Journal of Educational Psychology, 70,* 97–111.
Gillies, R. M. (2003). The behaviors, interactions, and perceptions of junior high school students during small-group learning. *Journal of Educational Psychology, 95,* 137–147.
Gillies, R. M., & Ashman, A. F. (1996). Teaching collaborative skills to primary school children in classroom-based workgroups. *Learning and Instruction, 6,* 187–200.
Gilligan, C. F. (1982). *In a different voice.* Cambridge, MA: Harvard University Press.
Gilliom, M., Shaw, D. S., Beck, J. E., Schonberg, M. A., & Lukon, J. L. (2002). Anger regulation in disadvantaged preschool boys: Strategies, antecedents, and the development of self-control. *Developmental Psychology, 38,* 222–235.
Gilstrap, L. L., & Ceci, S. J. (2005). Reconceptualizing children's suggestibility: Bidirectional and temporal properties. *Child Development, 76,* 40–53.
Ginsburg, H. P. (1997). *Entering the child's mind: The clinical interview in psychological research and practice.* New York: Cambridge University Press.
Ginsburg, H. P., Lee, J. S., & Boyd, J. S. (2008). Mathematics education for young children: What it is and how to promote it. *Social Policy Report of the Society for Research in Child Development, 12*(1).
Ginsburg-Block, M. D., Rohrbeck, C. A., & Fantuzzo, J. W. (2006). A meta-analytic review of social, self-concept, and behavioral outcomes of peer-assisted learning. *Journal of Educational Psychology, 98,* 732–749.
Gitlin, L. N., Belle, S. H., Burgio, L. D., Szaja, S. J., Mahoney, D., & Gallagher-Thompson, D. (2003). Effect of multicomponent interventions on care giver burden and depression: the REACH multisite initiative at 6-month follow-up. *Psychology and Aging, 18,* 361–374.
Giuliani, A., Schöll, W. M., Basver, A., & Tasmussino, K. F. (2002). Mode of delivery and outcome of 699 term singleton breech deliveries at a single center. *American Journal of Obstetrics and Gynaecology, 187,* 1649–1698.
Gladstone, I. M., & Katz, V. L. (2004). The morbidity of the 34- to 35-week gestation: Should we re-examine the paradigm? *American Journal of Perinatology, 21,* 9–13.
Glasgow, K. L., Dornbusch, S. M., Troyer, L., Steinberg, L., & Ritter, P. L. (1997). Parenting styles, adolescents' attributions, and educational outcomes in nine heterogeneous high schools. *Child Development, 68,* 507–523.
Gleitman, L. R., Cassidy, K., Nappa, R., Papfragou, A., & Trueswell, J. C. (2005). Hard words. *Language Learning and Development, 1,* 23–64.
Gleitman, L. R., & Newport, E. (1996). *The invention of language by children.* Cambridge, MA: MIT Press.
Glowinski, A. L., Madden, P. A. F., Bucholz, K. K., Lynskey, M. T., & Heath, A. C. (2003). Genetic epidemiology of self-reported lifetime DSM-IV major depressive disorder in a population-based twin sample of female adolescents. *Journal of Child Psychology and Psychiatry and Allied Disciplines, 44,* 988–996.
Gluckman, P. D., Sizonenko, S. V., & Bassett, N. S. (1999). The transition from fetus to neonate—an endocrine perspective. *Acta Paediatrica Supplement, 88*(428), 7–11.
Gnepp, J. (1983). Children's social sensitivity: Inferring emotions from conflicting cues. *Developmental Psychology, 19,* 805–814.
Godfrey, K. M., & Barker, D. J. (2000). Fetal nutrition and adult disease. *American Journal of Clinical Nutrition, 71,* 1344S–1352S.
Godkin, M., Krant, M., & Doster, N. (1984). The impact of hospice care on families. *International Journal of Psychiatry in Medicine, 13,* 153–165.
Goering, J. (Ed.). (2003). *Choosing a better life? How public housing tenants selected a HUD experiment to improve their lives and those of their children: The Moving to Opportunity Demonstration Program.* Washington, DC: Urban Institute Press.
Goetz, T., Frenzel, A. C., Pekrun, R., & Hall, N. (2005). Emotional intelligence in the context of learning and achievement. In R. Schulze & R. D. Roberts (Eds.), *Emotional intelligence: An international handbook* (pp. 233–253). Göttingen, Germany: Hogrefe & Huber.
Gogate, L. J., & Bahrick, L. E. (2001). Intersensory redundancy and 7-month-old infants' memory for arbitrary syllable–object relations. *Infancy, 2,* 219–231.
Gold, D. T. (1996). Continuities and discontinuities in sibling relationships across the life span. In V. L. Bengtson (Ed.), *Adulthood and aging: Research on continuities and discontinuities* (pp. 228–243). New York: Springer.
Goldberg, A. E., & Perry-Jenkins, M. (2003). Division of labor and working-class women's well-being across the transition to parenthood. *Journal of Family Psychology, 18,* 225–236.
Goldberg, A. P., Dengel, D. R., & Hagberg, J. M. (1996). Exercise physiology and aging. In E. L. Schneider & J. W. Rowe (Eds.), *Handbook of the biology of aging* (pp. 331–354). San Diego: Academic Press.
Goldberg, M. C., Maurer, D., & Lewis, T. L. (2001). Developmental changes in attention: The effects of endogenous cueing and of distracters. *Developmental Science, 4,* 209–219.
Goldberg, S., Benoit, D., Blokland, K., & Madigan, S. (2003). Atypical maternal behavior, maternal representations, and infant disorganized attachment. *Development and Psychopathology, 15,* 239–257.
Goldbloom, R. B. (2004). *Screening for hemoglobinopathies in Canada.* Hamilton, Ontario: McMaster University Medical Centre.
Goldenberg, C., Gallimore, R., Reese, L., & Garnier, H. (2001). Cause or effect? Immigrant Latino parents' aspirations and expectations, and their children's school performance. *American Educational Research Journal, 38,* 547–582.
Goldfield, B. A. (1987). The contributions of child and caregiver to referential and expressive language. *Applied Psycholinguistics, 8,* 267–280.
Goldin-Meadow, S., & Butcher, S. (2003). Pointing toward two-word speech in young children. In S. Kita (Ed.), *Pointing: Where language, culture,*

and cognition meet (pp. 85–107). Mahwah, NJ: Erlbaum.

Goldman, N., & Takahashi, S. (1996). Old-age mortality in Japan: Demographic and epidemiological perspectives. In G. Caselli & A. D. Lopez (Eds.), *Health and mortality among elderly populations* (pp. 157–181). New York: Oxford University Press.

Goldscheider, F., & Goldscheider, C. (1999). *The changing transition to adulthood: Leaving and returning home.* Thousand Oaks, CA: Sage.

Goldschmidt, L., Richardson, G. A., Cornelius, M. D., & Day, N. L. (2004). Prenatal marijuana and alcohol exposure and academic achievement at age 10. *Neurotoxicology and Teratology, 26,* 521–532.

Goldsmith, B., Dietrich, J., Du, Q., & Morrison, R. S. (2008). Variability in access to hospital palliative care in the United States. *Journal of Palliative Medicine, 11,* 1094–1102.

Goldsmith, H. H., Pollak, S. D., & Davidson, R. J. (2008). Developmental neuroscience perspectives on emotion regulation. *Child Development Perspectives, 2,* 132–140.

Goldsmith, L. T. (2000). Tracking trajectories of talent: Child prodigies growing up. In R. C. Friedman & B. M. Shore (Eds.), *Talents unfolding: Cognition and development* (pp. 89–122). Washington, DC: American Psychological Association.

Goldsteen, M., Houtepen, R., Proot, I. M., Abu-Saad, H. H., Spreeuwenberg, C., & Widdershoven, G. (2006). What is a good death? Terminally ill patients dealing with normative expectations around death and dying. *Patient Education and Counseling, 64,* 378–386.

Goldstein, S. E., Davis-Kean, P. E., & Eccles, J. S. (2005). Parents, peers, and problem behavior: A longitudinal investigation of the impact of relationship perceptions and characteristics on the development of adolescent problem behavior. *Developmental Psychology, 41,* 401–413.

Goldston, D. B., Molock, S. D., Whitbeck, L. B., Murakami, J. L., Zayas, L. H., & Hall, G. C. N. (2008). Cultural considerations in adolescent suicide prevention and psychosocial treatment. *American Psychologist, 63,* 14–31.

Goleman, D. (1995). *Emotional intelligence.* New York: Bantam.

Goleman, D. (1998). *Working with emotional intelligence.* New York: Bantam.

Golinkoff, R. M., & Hirsh-Pasek, K. (2006). Baby wordsmith: From associationist to social sophisticate. *Current Directions in Psychological Science, 15,* 30–33.

Golomb, C. (2004). *The child's creation of a pictorial world* (2nd ed.). Mahwah, NJ: Erlbaum.

Golombok, S., Lycett, E., MacCallum, F., Jadva, V., Murray, C., Rust, J., Abdalla, H., Jenkins, J., & Margar, R. (2004). Parenting of infants conceived by gamete donation. *Journal of Family Psychology, 18,* 443–452.

Golombok, S., & MacCallum, F. (2003). Practitioner review: Outcomes for parents and children following non-traditional conception: What do clinicians need to know? *Journal of Child Psychology and Psychiatry, 44,* 303–315.

Golombok, S., Perry, B., Burston, A., Murray, C., Mooney-Somers, J., Stevens, M., & Golding, J. (2003). Children with lesbian parents: A community study. *Developmental Psychology, 39,* 20–33.

Golombok, S., Rust, J., Zervoulis, K., Croudace, T., Golding, J., & Hines, M. (2008). Developmental trajectories of sex-typed behavior in boys and girls: A longitudinal general population study of children aged 2.5–8 years. *Child Development, 79,* 1583–1593.

Golombok, S., & Tasker, F. L. (1996). Do parents influence the sexual orientation of their children? Findings from a longitudinal study of lesbian families. *Developmental Psychology, 32,* 3–11.

Gomez-Perez, E., & Ostrosky-Solis, F. (2006). Attention and memory evaluation across the life span: Heterogeneous effects of age and education. *Journal of Clinical and Experimental Neuropsychology, 28,* 477–494.

Göncü, A. (1993). Development of intersubjectivity in the dyadic play of preschoolers. *Early Childhood Research Quarterly, 8,* 99–116.

Göncü, A., Patt, M. B., & Kouba E. (2004). Understanding young children's pretend play in context. In P. K. Smith & C. H. Hart (Eds.), *Blackwell handbook of childhood social development* (pp. 418–437). Malden, MA: Blackwell.

Gonzales, N. A., Cauce, A. M., Friedman, R. J., & Mason, C. A. (1996). Family, peer, and neighborhood influences on academic achievement among African American adolescents: One-year prospective effects. *American Journal of Community Psychology, 24,* 365–387.

Gonzalez, A.-L., & Wolters, C. A. (2006). The relation between perceived parenting practices and achievement motivation in mathematics. *Journal of Research in Childhood Education, 21,* 203–217.

Good, T. L., & Brophy, J. (2003). *Looking in classrooms* (9th ed.). Boston: Allyn and Bacon.

Goode, V., & Goode, J. D. (2007). De facto zero tolerance: An exploratory study of race and safe school violations. In J. L. Kincheloe & K. Hayes (Eds.), *Teaching city kids: Understanding and appreciating them* (pp. 85–96). New York: Peter Lang.

Goodlin-Jones, B. L., Burnham, M. M., & Anders, T. F. (2000). Sleep and sleep disturbances: Regulatory processes in infancy. In A. J. Sameroff, M. Lewis, & S. M. Miller (Eds.), *Handbook of developmental psychology* (2nd ed., pp. 309–325). New York: Kluwer.

Goodlin-Jones, B. L., Tassone, F., Gane, L. W., & Hagerman, R. J. (2004). Autistic spectrum disorder and the fragile X permutation. *Journal of Developmental and Behavioral Pediatrics, 25,* 392–398.

Goodman, G. S., Quas, J. A., Bulkley, J., & Shapiro, C. (1999). Innovations for child witnesses: A national survey. *Psychology, Public Policy, and Law, 5,* 255, 281.

Goodwin, R., & Pillay, U. (2006). Relationships, culture, and social change. In A. L. Vangelisti & D. Perlman (Eds.), *The Cambridge handbook of personal relationships* (pp. 760–779). New York: Cambridge University Press.

Gootman, E. (2005, January 16). New York City: The politics of promotion. *New York Times.* Retrieved from www.nytimes.com/2005/01/16/education/edlife/EDGOOT.html

Gopnik, A., & Choi, S. (1990). Do linguistic differences lead to cognitive differences? A cross-linguistic study of semantic and cognitive development. *First Language, 11,* 199–215.

Gopnik, A., & Meltzoff, A. N. (1987). The development of categorization in the second year and its relation to other cognitive and linguistic developments. *Child Development, 58,* 1523–1531.

Gopnik, A., & Nazzi, T. (2003). Words, kinds, and causal powers: A theory theory perspective on early naming and categorization. In D. H. Rakison & L. M. Oakes (Eds.), *Early category and concept development* (p. 303–329). New York: Oxford University Press.

Gordon, L. H., Temple, R. R., & Adams, D. W. (2005). Premarital counseling from the PAIRS perspective. In M. Harway (Ed.), *Handbook of couples therapy* (pp. 7–27). Hoboken, NJ: Wiley.

Gordon, R. A., Chase-Lansdale, P. L., & Brooks-Gunn, J. (2004). Extended households and the life course of young mothers: Understanding the associations using a sample of mothers with premature, low-birth-weight babies. *Child Development, 75,* 1013–1038.

Gormally, S., Barr, R G., Wertheim, L., Alkawaf, R., Calinoiu, N., & Young, S. N. (2001). Contact and nutrient caregiving effects on newborn infant pain responses. *Developmental Medicine and Child Neurology, 43,* 28–38.

Gorman, T. E., Ahern, S. P., Wiseman, J., & Skrobik, Y. (2005). Residents' end-of-life decision making with adult hospitalized patients: A review of the literature. *Academic Medicine, 80,* 622–633.

Goswami, U. (1996). Analogical reasoning and cognitive development. In H. Reese (Ed.), *Advances in child development and behavior* (Vol. 26, pp. 91–138). New York: Academic Press.

Gott, M., & Hinchliff, S. (2003). How important is sex in later life? The views of older people. *Social Science and Medicine, 56,* 1617–1628.

Gott, M., Seymour, J., Bellamy, G., Clark, D., & Ahmedzai, S. (2004). Older people's views about home as a place of care at the end of life. *Palliative Medicine, 18,* 460–467.

Gottesman, I. I. (1963). Genetic aspects of intelligent behavior. In N. Ellis (Ed.), *Handbook of mental deficiency* (pp. 253–296). New York: McGraw-Hill.

Gottfredson, G. D., & Duffy, R. D. (2008). Using a theory of vocational personalities and work environments to explore subjective well-being. *Journal of Career Assessment, 16,* 44–59.

Gottfredson, L. S. (2005). Applying Gottfredson's theory of circumscription and compromise in career guidance and counseling. In S. D. Brown & R. W. Lent (Eds.), *Career development and counseling* (pp. 71–100). Hoboken, NJ: Wiley.

Gottfried, A. E., Gottfried, A. W., & Bathurst, K. (2002). Maternal and dual-earner employment status and parenting. In M. H. Bornstein (Ed.), *Handbook of parenting. Vol. 2: Biology and ecology of parenting* (2nd ed., pp. 207–229). Mahwah, NJ: Erlbaum.

Gottlieb, B., Beitel, L. K., & Trifiro, M. A. (2001). Somatic mosaicism and variable expressivity. *Trends in Genetics, 11,* 70–82.

Gottlieb, G. (1998). Normally occurring environmental and behavioral influences on gene activity: From central dogma to probabilistic epigenesis. *Psychological Review, 105,* 792–802.

Gottlieb, G. (2000). Environmental and behavioral influences on gene activity. *Current Directions in Psychological Science, 9,* 93–97.

Gottlieb, G. (2003). On making behavioral genetics truly developmental. *Human Development, 46,* 337–355.

Gottlieb, G. (2007). Probabilistic epigenesis. *Developmental Science, 10,* 1–11.

Gottlieb, G., Wahlsten, D., & Lickliter, R. (2006). The significance of biology for human development: A developmental psychobiological systems view. In R. M. Lerner (Ed.), *Handbook of child psychology: Vol. 1. Theoretical models of human development* (6th ed., pp. 210–257). Hoboken, NJ: Wiley.

Gottman, J. M., & Levenson, R. W. (2000). The timing of divorce: Predicting when a couple will divorce over a 14-year period. *Journal of Marriage and Family, 62,* 737–745.

Gould, E. (2007). How widespread is adult neurogenesis in mammals? *Nature Reviews: Neuroscience, 8,* 481–488.

Gould, E., Reeves, A. J., Graziano, M. S. A., & Gross, C. G. (1999). Neurogenesis in the neocortex of adult primates. *Science, 286,* 548–552.

Gould, J. L., & Keeton, W. T. (1996). *Biological science* (6th ed.). New York: Norton.

Gould, M., Jamieson, P., & Romer, D. (2003). Media contagion and suicide among the young. *American Behavioral Scientist, 46,* 1269–1284.

Graber, J. A. (2003). Puberty in context. In C. Hayward (Ed.), *Gender differences at puberty* (pp. 307–325). New York: Cambridge University Press.

Graber, J. A. (2004). Internalizing problems during adolescence. In R. M. Lerner & L. Steinberg (Eds.), *Handbook of adolescent psychology* (2nd ed., pp. 587–626). Hoboken, NJ: Wiley.

Graber, J. A., Brooks-Gunn, J., & Warren, M. P. (2006). Pubertal effects on adjustment in girls: Moving from demonstrating effects to identifying pathways. *Journal of Youth and Adolescence, 35,* 413–423.

Graber, J. A., Lewinsohn, P. M., Seeley, J. R., & Brooks-Gunn, J. (1997). Is psychopathology associated with timing of pubertal development? *Journal of the American Academy of Child and -Adolescent Psychiatry, 36,* 1768–1776.

Graber, J. A., Nichols, T., Lynne, S. D., Brooks-Gunn, J., & Botwin, G. J. (2006). A longitudinal examination of family, friend, and media influences on competent versus problem behaviors among urban minority youth. *Applied Developmental Science, 10,* 75–85.

Graber, J. A., Seeley, J. R., Brooks-Gunn, J., & Lewinsohn, P. M. (2004). Is pubertal timing associated with psychopathology in young adulthood? *Journal of the American Academy of Child and Adolescent Psychiatry, 43,* 718–726.

Gralinski, J. H., & Kopp, C. B. (1993). Everyday rules for behavior: Mothers' requests to young children. *Developmental Psychology, 29,* 573–584.

Granger, R. C. (2008). After-school programs and academics: Implications for policy, practice, and research. *Social Policy Report of the Society for Research in Child Development, 22*(2), 3–11.

Granier-Deferre, C., Bassereau, S., Ribeiro, A., Jacquet, A.-Y., & Lecanuet, J.-P. (2003). *Cardiac "orienting" response in fetuses and babies following in utero melody-learning.* Paper presented at the 11th European Conference on Developmental Psychology, Milan, Italy.

Granillo, T., Jones-Rodriguez, G., & Carvajal, S. C. (2005). Prevalence of eating disorders in Latina adolescents: Associations with substance use and other correlates. *Journal of Adolescent Health, 36,* 214–220.

Granot, M., Spitzer, A., Aroian, K. J., Ravid, C., Tamir, B., & Noam, R. (1996). Pregnancy and delivery practices and beliefs of Ethiopian immigrant women in Israel. *Western Journal of Nursing Research, 18,* 299–313.

Granot, T. (2005). *Without you: Children and young people growing up with loss and its effects.* London: Jessica Kingsley.

Grant, K., O'Koon, J., Davis, T., Roache, N., Poindexter, L., & Armstrong, M. (2000). Protective factors affecting low-income urban African American youth exposed to stress. *Journal of Early Adolescence, 20,* 388–418.

Grantham-McGregor, S., Powell, C., Walker, S., Chang, S., & Fletcher, P. (1994). The long-term follow-up of severely malnourished children who participated in an intervention program. *Child Development, 65,* 428–439.

Grantham-McGregor, S., Schofield, W., & Powell, C. (1987). Development of severely malnourished children who received psychosocial stimulation: Six-year follow-up. *Pediatrics, 79,* 247–254.

Grantham-McGregor, S., Walker, S. P., & Chang, S. (2000). Nutritional deficiencies and later behavioral development. *Proceedings of the Nutrition Society, 59,* 47–54.

Gratton, M. A., & Vásquez, A. E. (2003). Age-related hearing loss: Current research. *Current Opinion in Otolaryngology—Head and Neck Surgery, 11,* 367–371.

Gray, K. A., Day, N. L., Leech, S., & Richardson, G. A. (2005). Prenatal marijuana exposure: Effect on child depressive symptoms at ten years of age. *Neurotoxicology and Teratology, 27,* 439–448.

Gray, M. R., & Steinberg, L. (1999). Unpacking authoritative parenting: Reassessing a multidimensional construct. *Journal of Marriage and the Family, 61,* 574–587.

Gray-Little, B., & Carels, R. (1997). The effects of racial and socioeconomic consonance on self-esteem and achievement in elementary, junior high, and high school students. *Journal of Research on Adolescence, 7,* 109–131.

Gray-Little, B., & Hafdahl, A. R. (2000). Factors influencing racial comparisons of self-esteem: A quantitative review. *Psychological Bulletin, 126,* 26–54.

Green, G. E., Irwin, J. R., & Gustafson, G. E. (2000). Acoustic cry analysis, neonatal status and long-term developmental outcomes. In R. G. Barr, B. Hopkins, & J. A. Green (Eds.), *Crying as a sign, a symptom, and a signal* (pp. 137–156). Cambridge, UK: Cambridge University Press.

Greenberg, S. A. (2007). *A profile of older Americans: 2007.* Washington, DC: National Institute on Aging.

Greenberger, E., Chen, C., Tally, S. R., & Dong, Q. (2000). Family, peer, and individual correlates of depressive symptomatology among U.S. and Chinese adolescents. *Journal of Counseling and Clinical Psychology, 68,* 209–219.

Greenberger, E., O'Neil, R., & Nagel, S. K. (1994). Linking workplace and homeplace: Relations between the nature of adults' work and their parenting behavior. *Developmental Psychology, 30,* 990–1002.

Greendorfer, S. L., Lewko, J. H., & Rosengren, K. S. (1996). Family and gender-based socialization of children and adolescents. In F. L. Smoll & R. E. Smith (Eds.), *Children and youth in sport: A biopsychological perspective* (pp. 89–111). Dubuque, IA: Brown & Benchmark.

Greene, K., Krcmar, M., Walters, L. H., Rubin, D. L., Hale, J., & Hale, L. (2000). Targeting adolescent risk-taking behaviors: The contributions of egocentrism and sensation-seeking. *Journal of Adolescence, 23,* 439–461.

Greene, M. L., Way, N., & Pahl, K. (2006). Trajectories of perceived adult and peer discrimination among black, Latino, and Asian American adolescents: Patterns and psychological correlates. *Developmental Psychology, 42,* 218–238.

Greene, S. M., Anderson, E., Hetherington, E. M., Forgath, M. S., & DeGarmo, D. S. (2003). Risk and resilience after divorce. In R. Walsh (Ed.), *Normal family processes* (pp. 96–120). New York: Guilford.

Greenfield, P. (1992, June). *Notes and references for developmental psychology.* Conference on Making Basic Texts in Psychology More Culture-Inclusive and Culture-Sensitive, Western Washington University, Bellingham, WA.

Greenfield, P. M. (2004). *Weaving generations together: Evolving creativity in the Maya of Chiapas.* Santa Fe, NM: School of American Research.

Greenfield, P. M., Keller, H., Fuligni, A., & Maynard, A. (2003). Cultural pathways through universal development. *Annual Review of Psychology, 54,* 461–490.

Greenfield, P. M., Maynard, A. E., & Childs, C. P. (2000). History, culture, learning, and development. *Cross-Cultural Research, 34,* 351–374.

Greenfield, P. M., Suzuki, L. K., & Rothstein-Fish, C. (2006). Cultural pathways through human development. In K. A. Renninger & I. E. Sigel (Eds.), *Handbook of child psychology: Vol. 4. Child psychology in practice* (6th ed., pp. 655–699). Hoboken, NJ: Wiley.

Greenhill, L. L., Halperin, J. M., & Abikoff, H. (1999). Stimulant medications. *Journal of the American Academy of Child and Adolescent Psychiatry, 38,* 503–512.

Greenough, W. T., & Black, J. E. (1992). Induction of brain structure by experience: Substrates for cognitive development. In M. R. Gunnar & C. A. Nelson (Eds.), *Minnesota Symposia on Child Psychology* (pp. 155–200). Hillsdale, NJ: Erlbaum.

Greenspan, S. I., & Shanker, S. G. (2004). *The first idea: how symbols, language, and intelligence evolved from our primate ancestors to modern humans.* Cambridge, MA: Da Capo Press.

Gregg, V., Gibbs, J. C., & Fuller, D. (1994). Patterns of developmental delay in moral judgment by male and female delinquents. *Merrill-Palmer Quarterly, 40,* 538–553.

Gregory, A., & Weinstein, R. S. (2004). Connection and regulation at home and in school: Predicting growth in achievement for adolescents. *Journal of Adolescent Research, 19,* 405–427.

Gresser, G., Wong, P., & Reker, G. (1987). Death attitudes across the life-span: The development and validation of the Death Attitude Profile (DAP). *Omega, 18,* 113–128.

Grief, G. L., Hrabowski, F. A., & Maton, K. I. (1998). African-American fathers of high-achieving sons: Using outstanding members of an at-risk population to guide intervention. *Families in Society, 79,* 45–52.

Griffin, K. W., Botwin, G. J., Nichols, T. R., & Doyle, M. M. (2003). Effectiveness of a universal drug abuse prevention approach for youth at high risk for substance use initiation. *Preventive Medicine, 36,* 1–7.

Griffin, Z. M., & Spieler, D. H. (2006). Observing the what and when of language production for different age groups by monitoring speakers' eye movements. *Brain and Language, 99,* 272–288.

Grigorenko, E. L. (2000). Heritability and intelligence. In R. J. Sternberg (Ed.), *Handbook of intelligence* (pp. 53–91). Cambridge, UK: Cambridge University Press.

Grob, A., & Flammer, A. (1999). Macrosocial context and adolescents' perceived control. In F. D. Alsaker & A. Flammer (Eds.), *The adolescent experience* (pp. 99–114). Mahwah, NJ: Erlbaum.

Grob, A., Krings, F., & Bangerter, A. (2001). Life markers in biographical narratives of people from three cohorts: A life span perspective in its historical context. *Human Development, 44,* 171–190.

Grolnick, W. S., Kurowski, C. O., Dunlap, K. G., & Hevey, C. (2000). Parental resources and the transition to junior high. *Journal of Research on Adolescence, 10,* 466–488.

Grossbaum, M. F., & Bates, G. W. (2002). Correlates of psychological well-being at midlife: The role of generativity, agency and communion, and narrative themes. *International Journal of Behavioral Development, 26,* 120–127.

Grossman, A. H., D'Augelli, A. R., & Hershberger, S. L. (2000). Social support networks of lesbian, gay, and bisexual adults 60 years of age and older. *Journal of Gerontology, 55B,* P171–179.

Grossmann, K., Grossmann, K. E., Fremmer-Bombik, E., Kindler, H., Scheueueu-Englisch, H., & Zimmerman, P. (2002). The uniqueness of the child–father attachment relationship: Fathers' sensitive and challenging play as a pivotable variable in a 16-year longitudinal study. *Social Development, 11,* 307–331.

Grossmann, K., Grossmann, K. E., Spangler, G., Suess, G., & Unzner, L. (1985). Maternal sensitivity and newborns' orientation responses as related to quality of attachment in Northern Germany. In I. Bretherton & E. Waters (Eds.), Growing points of attachment theory and research. *Monographs of the Society for Research in Child Development, 50*(1–2, Serial No. 209).

Grotevant, H. D. (1998). Adolescent development in family contexts. In N. Eisenberg (Ed.), *Handbook of child psychology: Vol. 3. Social, emotional, and personality development* (5th ed., pp. 1097–1149). New York: Wiley.

Grow-Maienza, J., Hahn, D.-D., & Joo, C.-A. (2001). Mathematics instruction in Korean primary schools: Structure, processes, and a linguistic analysis of questioning. *Journal of Educational Psychology, 93,* 363–376.

Gruber-Baldini, A., Boustani, M., Sloane, P., & Zimmerman, S. (2004). Behavioral symptoms in residential care/assisted living facilities: Prevalence, risk factors, and medication management. *Journal of the American Geriatrics Society, 52,* 1610–1617.

Gruendel J., & Aber, J. L. (2007). Bridging the gap between research and child policy change: The role of strategic communications in policy advocacy. In J. L. Aber, S. J. Bishop-Josef, S. M. Jones, K. T. McLearn, & D. Phillips (Eds.), *Child development and social policy: Knowledge for action* (pp. 43–58). Washington, DC: American Psychological Association.

Gruenewald, D. A., & White, E. J. (2006). The illness experience of older adults near the end of life: A systematic review. *Anesthesiology Clinics of North America, 24,* 163–180.

Gruenewald, T. L., Karlamangla, A. S., Greendale, G. A., Singer, B. H., & Seeman, T. E. (2007). Feelings of mortality in older adults: The MacArthur Study of Successful Aging. *Journal of Gerontology, 62B,* P28–P37.

Grunau, R. E., Whitfield, M. F., & Fay, T. B. (2004). Psychosocial and academic characteristics of extremely low birth weight (<or=800g) adolescents who are free of major impairment compared with term-born control subjects. *Pediatrics, 114,* E725–E732.

Grundy, E. (2005). Reciprocity in relationships: Socio-economic and health influences on intergenerational exchanges between Third Age parents and their adult children in Great Britain. *British Journal of Sociology, 56,* 233–255.

Grusec, J. E. (1988). *Social development: History, theory, and research.* New York: Springer.

Grusec, J. E. (2006). The development of moral behavior and conscience from a socialization perspective. In M. Killen & J. Smetana (Eds.), *Handbook of moral development* (pp. 243–265). Philadelphia: Erlbaum.

Grusec, J. E., & Goodnow, J. J. (1994). Impact of parental discipline methods on the child's internalization of values: A reconceptualization of current points of view. *Developmental Psychology, 30,* 4–19.

Grych, J. H., & Clark, R. (1999). Maternal employment and development of the father–infant relationship in the first year. *Developmental Psychology, 35,* 893–903.

Grzywacz, J. G., & Marks, N. F. (2001). Social inequalities and exercise during adulthood: Toward an ecological perspective. *Journal of Health and Social Behavior, 42,* 202–220.

Guay, F., Marsh, H. W., & Boivin, M. (2003). Academic self-concept and academic achievement: Developmental perspectives on their causal ordering. *Journal of Educational Psychology, 95,* 124–136.

Guignard, J.-H., & Lubart, T. (2006). Is it reasonable to be creative? In J. C. Kaufman & J. Baer (Eds.), *Creativity and reason in cognitive development* (pp. 269–281). New York: Cambridge University Press.

Guildner, S. H., Loeb, S., Morris, D., Penrod, J., Bramlett, M., Johnston, L., & Schlotzhauer, P. (2001). A comparison of life satisfaction and mood in nursing home residents and community-dwelling elders. *Archives of Psychiatric Nursing, 15,* 232–240.

Guilford, J. P. (1985). The structure-of-intellect model. In B. B. Wolman (Ed.), *Handbook of intelligence* (pp. 225–266). New York: Wiley.

Gullone, E. (2000). The development of normal fear: A century of research. *Clinical Psychology Review, 20,* 429–451.

Gulotta, T. P. (2008). How theory influences treatment and prevention practice within the family. In T. P. Gulotta (Ed.), *Family influences on child behavior and development: Evidence-based prevention and treatment approaches* (pp. 1–20). New York: Routledge.

Gunnar, M. R., & Cheatham, C. L. (2003). Brain and behavior interfaces: Stress and the developing brain. *Infant Mental Health Journal, 24,* 195–211.

Gunnar, M. R., Morison, S. J., Chisholm, K., & Schuder, M. (2001). Salivary cortisol levels in children adopted from Romanian orphanages. *Development and Psychopathology, 13,* 611–628.

Gunnar, M. R., & Quevedo, K. (2007). The neurobiology of stress and development. *Annual Review of Psychology, 58,* 145–173.

Gunnar, M. R., & Vasquez, D. M. (2001). Low cortisol and a flattening of expected day-time rhythm: Potential indices of risk in human development. *Development and Psychopathology, 13,* 515–538.

Gunnoe, M. L., & Mariner, C. L. (1997). Toward a developmental-contextual model of the effects of parental spanking on children's aggression. *Archives of Pediatrics and Adolescent Medicine, 151,* 768–775.

Gure, A., Ucanok, Z., & Sayil, M. (2006). The associations among perceived pubertal timing, parental relations and self-perception in Turkish adolescents. *Journal of Youth and Adolescence, 35,* 541–550.

Gureje, O., Ogunniyi, A., Baiyewu, O., Price, B., Unverzagt, F. W., & Evans, R. M. (2006). APOE epsilon4 is not associated with Alzheimer's disease in elderly Nigerians. *Annals of Neurology, 59,* 182–185.

Gurucharri, C., & Selman, R. L. (1982). The development of interpersonal understanding during childhood, preadolescence, and adolescence: A longitudinal follow-up study. *Child Development, 53,* 924–927.

Gustafson, G. E., Green, J. A., & Cleland, J. W. (1994). Robustness of individual identity in the cries of human infants. *Developmental Psychobiology, 27,* 1–9.

Gustafson, G. E., Wood, R. M., & Green, J. A. (2000). Can we hear the causes of infants' crying? In R. G. Barr & B. Hopkins (Eds.), *Crying as a sign, a symptom, and a signal: Clinical, emotional, and developmental aspects of infant and toddler crying* (pp. 8–22). New York: Cambridge University Press.

Gutman, L. M. (2006). How student and parent goal orientations and classroom goal structures influence the math achievement of African Americans during the high school transition. *Contemporary Educational Psychology, 31,* 44–63.

Gutman, L. M., & Midgley, C. (2000). The role of protective factors in supporting the academic achievement of poor African-American students during the middle school transition. *Journal of Youth and Adolescence, 29,* 223–248.

Gutman, L. M., Sameroff, A. J., & Cole, R. (2003). Academic growth curve trajectories from 1st grade to 12th grade: Effects of multiple social risk factors and preschool child factors. *Developmental Psychology, 39,* 777–790.

Gutmann, D. (1977). The cross-cultural perspective: Notes toward a comparative psychology of aging. In J. E. Birren & K. W. Schaie (Eds.), *Handbook of the psychology of aging* (pp. 302–326). New York: Van Nostrand Reinhold.

Gutmann, D. L., & Huyck, M. H. (1994). Development and pathology in post-parental men: A community study. In E. Thompson, Jr. (Ed.), *Older men's lives* (pp. 65–84). Thousand Oaks, CA: Sage.

Gutteling, B. M., de Weerth, C., Zandbelt, N., Mulder, E. J. H., Visser, G. H. A., & Buitelaar, J. K. (2006). Does maternal prenatal stress adversely affect the child's learning and memory at age six? *Journal of Abnormal Child Psychology, 34,* 789–798.

Guttentag, R., & Ferrell, J. (2004). Reality compared with its alternatives: Age differences in judgments of regret and relief. *Developmental Psychology, 40,* 764–775.

Guyuron, B., Rose, D. J., Weinfeld, A. B., Eshraghi, Y., Fathi, A., & Iamphongsai, S. (2009). Factors contributing to the facial aging of identical twins. *Plastic and Reconstructive Surgery, 123,* 1321–1331.

Gwiazda, J., & Birch, E. E. (2001). Perceptual development: Vision. In E. B. Goldstein (Ed.), *Blackwell handbook of perception* (pp. 636–668). Oxford, UK: Blackwell.

H

Hack, M., & Klein, N. (2006). Young adult attainments of preterm infants. *Journal of the American Medical Association, 295,* 695–696.

Hagberg, B., Alfredson, B. B., Poon, L. W., & Homma, A. (2001). Cognitive functioning in centenarians: A coordinated analysis of results from three countries. *Journal of Gerontology, 56B,* P141–P151.

Hagekull, B., Bohlin, G., & Rydell, A. (1997). Maternal sensitivity, infant temperament, and the development of early feeding problems. *Infant Mental Health Journal, 18,* 92–106.

Haidt, J. (2001). The emotional dog and its rational tail: A social intuitionist approach to moral judgment. *Psychological Review, 108,* 814–834.

Haight, W. L., & Miller, P. J. (1993). *Pretending at home: Early development in a sociocultural context.* Albany, NY: State University of New York Press.

Hainline, L. (1998). The development of basic visual abilities. In A. Slater (Ed.), *Perceptual development: Visual, auditory, and speech perception in infancy* (pp. 37–44). Hove, UK: Psychology Press.

Hainsworth, J., & Barlow, J. (2001). Volunteers' experiences of becoming arthritis self-management lay leaders: "It's almost as if I've stopped aging and started to get younger!" *Arthritis and Rheumatism, 45,* 378–383.

Hajjar, R. R., & Kamel, H. K. (2004). Sexuality in the nursing home, Part 1: Attitudes and barriers to sexual expression. *Journal of the American Medical Directors Association,* 5, S43–S47.

Hakuta, K., Bialystok, E., & Wiley, E. (2003). Critical evidence: A test of the critical-period hypothesis for second-language acquisitions. *Psychological Science, 14,* 31–38.

Halberstadt, A., Denham, S. A., & Dunsmore, J. (2001). Affective social competence. *Social Development, 10,* 79–119.

Halbreich, U. (2004). The diagnosis of premenstrual syndromes and premenstrual dysphoric disorder—clinical procedures and research perspectives. *Gynecological Endocrinology, 19,* 320–334.

Hale, C. M., & Tager-Flusberg, H. (2003). The influence of language on theory of mind: A training study. *Developmental Science, 6,* 346–359.

Hales, C. N., & Ozanne, S. E. (2003). The dangerous road of catch-up growth. *Journal of Physiology, 547,* 5–10.

Halfon, N., & McLearn, K. T. (2002). Families with children under 3: What we know and implications for results and policy. In N. Halfon & K. T. McLearn (Eds.), *Child rearing in America:*

Challenges facing parents with young children (pp. 367–412). New York: Cambridge University Press.

Halford, G. S. (2002). Information-processing models of cognitive development. In U. Goswami (Ed.), *Blackwell handbook of childhood cognitive development* (pp. 555–574). Malden, MA: Blackwell.

Halford, G. S. (2005). Development of thinking. In K. J. Holyoak & R. G. Morrison (Eds.), *The Cambridge handbook of thinking and reasoning* (pp. 529–558). New York: Cambridge University Press.

Halford, G. S., & Andrews, G. (2006). Reasoning and problem solving. In D. Kuhn & R. Siegler (Eds.), *Handbook of child psychology: Vol. 2. Cognition, perception, and language* (6th ed., pp. 557–608). Hoboken, NJ: Wiley.

Hall, C. B., Derby, C., LeValley, A., Katz, M. J., Verghese, J., & Lipton, R. B. (2007). Education delays accelerated decline on a memory test in persons who develop dementia. *Neurology, 69,* 1657–1664.

Hall, D. G., & Graham, S. A. (1999). Lexical form class information guides word-to-object mapping in preschoolers. *Child Development, 70,* 78–91.

Hall, G. S. (1904). *Adolescence.* New York: Appleton.

Hall, K., Murrell, J., Ogunniyi, A., Deeg, M., Baiyewu, O., & Gao, S. (2006). Cholesterol, APOE genotype, and Alzheimer disease: An epidemiologic study of Nigerian Yoruba. *Neurology, 66,* 223–227.

Halle, T. G. (2003). Emotional development and well-being. In M. H. Bornstein, L. Davidson, C. L. M. Keyes, K. A. Moore, & the Center for Child Well-Being (Eds.), *Well-being: Positive development across the life course* (pp. 125–138). Mahwah, NJ: Erlbaum.

Hallenbeck, J. (2006). Palliative care training for the generalist: A luxury or a necessity? *Journal of General Internal Medicine, 21,* 1005–1006.

Haller, J. (2005). Vitamins and brain function. In H. R. Lieberman, R. B. Kanarek, & C. Prasad (2005). *Nutritional neuroscience* (pp. 207–233). Philadelphia: Taylor & Francis.

Hallett, M. (2000). Brain plasticity and recovery from hemiplegia. *Journal of Medical Speech-Language Pathology, 9,* 107–115.

Halliday, J. L., Watson, L. F., Lumley, J., Danks, D. M., & Sheffield, L. S. (1995). New estimates of Down syndrome risks of chorionic villus sampling, amniocentesis, and live birth in women of advanced maternal age from a uniquely defined population. *Prenatal Diagnosis, 15,* 455–465.

Hallinan, M. T., & Kubitschek, W. N. (1999). Curriculum differentiation and high school achievement. *Social Psychology of Education, 3,* 41–62.

Halpern, C. T., Udry, J. R., & Suchindran, C. (1997). Testosterone predicts initiation of coitus in adolescent females. *Psychosomatic Medicine, 59,* 161–171.

Halpern, D. F. (2000). *Sex differences in cognitive abilities* (3rd ed.). Mahwah, NJ: Erlbaum.

Halpern, D. F. (2004). A cognitive-process taxonomy for sex differences in cognitive abilities. *Current Directions in Psychological Science, 13,* 135–139.

Halpern, D. F. (2005a). How time-flexible work policies can reduce stress, improve health, and save money. *Stress and Health, 21,* 157–168.

Halpern, D. F. (2005b). Psychology at the intersection of work and family: Recommendations for employers, working families, and policymakers. *American Psychologist, 60,* 397–409.

Halpern, D. F., Benbow, C. P., Geary, D. C., Gur, R. C., Hyde, J. S., & Gernsbacher, M. A. (2007). The science of sex differences in science and mathematics. *Psychological Science in the Public Interest, 8,* 1–51.

Halpern, D. F., & Collaer, M. L. (2005). Sex differences in visuospatial abilities: More than meets the eye. In P. Shah & A. Miyake (Eds.), *Handbook of visuospatial thinking* (pp. 170–212). New York: Cambridge University Press.

Halpern, D. F., Wai, J., & Saw, A. (2005). A psychobiological model: Why females are sometimes greater than and sometimes less than males in math achievement. In D. F. Halpern, J. Wai, & A. Saw (Eds.), *Gender differences in mathematics: An integrative psychological approach* (pp. 48–72). New York: Cambridge University Press.

Halpern-Felsher, B. L., & Cauffman, E. (2001). Costs and benefits of a decision: Decision-making competence in adolescents and adults. *Journal of Applied Developmental Psychology, 22,* 257–273.

Haltzman, S., Holstein, N., & Moss, S. B. (2007). Men, marriage, and divorce. In J. E. Grant & M. N. Potenza (Eds.), *Textbook of men's mental health* (pp. 283–305). Washington, DC: American Psychiatric Publishing.

Hamachek, D. (1990). Evaluating self-concept and ego status in Erikson's last three psychosocial stages. *Journal of Counseling and Development, 68,* 677–683.

Hamer, D. H., Hu, S., Magnuson, V. L., Hu, N., & Pattatucci, A. M. L. (1993). A linkage between DNA markers on the X chromosome and male sexual orientation. *Science, 261,* 321–327.

Hamer, M., Wolvers, D., & Albers, R. (2004). Using stress models to evaluate immuno-modulating effects of nutritional intervention in healthy individuals. *Journal of the American College of Nutrition, 23,* 637–646.

Hamilton, H. A. (2005). Extended families and adolescent well-being. *Journal of Adolescent Health, 36,* 260–266.

Hamilton, S. F., & Hamilton, M. A. (2000). Research, intervention, and social change: Improving adolescents' career opportunities. In L. J. Crockett & R. K. Silbereisen (Eds.), *Negotiating adolescence in times of social change* (pp. 267–283). New York: Cambridge University Press.

Hammes, B., & Laitman, C. J. (2003). Diethylstilbestrol (DES) update: Recommendations for the identification and management of DES-exposed individuals. *Journal of Midwifery and Women's Health, 48,* 19–29.

Hammond, C. J., Snieder, H., Spector, T. D., & Gilbert, C. E. (2000). Genetic and environmental factors in age-related nuclear cataracts in monozygotic and dizygotic twins. *New England Journal of Medicine, 342,* 1786–1790.

Hampel, H., Bürger, K., Teipel, S. J., Bokde, A. L., Zetterberg, H., & Blennow, K. (2008). Core candidate neurochemical and imaging biomarkers of Alzheimer's disease. *Alzheimer's and Dementia, 4,* 38–48.

Han, S. K., & Moen, P. (1999). Clocking out: Temporal patterning of retirement. *American Journal of Sociology, 105,* 191–236.

Han, W.-J., & Waldfogel, J. (2003). Parental leave: The impact of recent legislation on parents' leave taking. *Demography, 40,* 191–200.

Hanke, W., Sobala, W., & Kalinka, J. (2004). Environmental tobacco smoke exposure among pregnant women: Impact on fetal biometry at 20–24 weeks of gestation and newborn child's birth weight. *International Archives of Occupational and Environmental Health, 77,* 47–52.

Hankin, B. L., & Abela, J. R. Z. (2005). Depression from childhood through adolescence and adulthood: A developmental vulnerability and stress perspective. In B. L. Hankin & J. R. Z. Abela (Eds.), *Development of psychopathology: A vulnerability-stress perspective* (pp. 245–288). Thousand Oaks, CA: Sage.

Hannon, E. E., & Johnson, S. P. (2004). Infants use meter to categorize rhythms and melodies: Implications for musical structure learning. *Cognitive Psychology, 50,* 354–377.

Hannon, E. E., & Trehub, S. E. (2005a). Metrical categories in infancy and adulthood. *Psychological Science, 16,* 48–55.

Hannon, E. E., & Trehub, S. E. (2005b). Tuning in to musical rhythms: Infants learn more readily than adults. *Proceedings of the National Academy of Sciences, 102,* 12639–12643.

Hannon, T. S., Rao, G., & Arslanian, S. A. (2005). Childhood obesity and type 2 diabetes mellitus. *Pediatrics, 116,* 473–480.

Hansen, M., Janssen, I., Schiff, A., Zee, P. C., & Dubocovich, M. L. (2005). The impact of school daily schedule on adolescent sleep. *Pediatrics, 115,* 1555–1561.

Hanson, L. C., Danis, M., & Garrett, J. (1997). What is wrong with end-of-life care? Opinions of bereaved family members. *Journal of the American Geriatric Society, 45,* 1339–1344.

Hansson, R. O., & Stroebe, M. S. (2007). The dual process model of coping with bereavement and development of an integrative risk factor framework. In R. O. Hansson & M. S. Stroebe (Eds.), *Bereavement in late life: Coping, adaptation, and developmental influences* (pp. 41–60). Washington, DC: American Psychological Association.

Harachi, T. W., Fleming, C. B., White, H. R., Ensminger, M. E., Abbott, R. D., Catalano, R. F., & Haggerty, K. P. (2006). Aggressive behavior among girls and boys during middle childhood: Predictors and sequelae of trajectory group membership. *Aggressive Behavior, 32,* 279–293.

Hardre, P. L., & Reeve, J. (2003). A motivational model of rural students' intentions to persist in, versus drop out of, high school. *Journal of Educational Psychology, 95,* 347–356.

Hardy, J. B., Astone, N. M., Brooks-Gunn, J., Shapiro, S., & Miller, T. L. (1998). Like mother, like child: Intergenerational patterns of age at first birth and associations with childhood and adolescent characteristics and adult outcomes in the second generation. *Developmental Psychology, 34,* 1220–1232.

Hardy, S. A., & Carlo, G. (2005). Religiosity and prosocial behaviours in adolescence: The mediating role of prosocial values. *Journal of Moral Education, 34,* 231–249.

Hare, J., & Richards, L. (1993). Children raised by lesbian couples: Does context of birth affect father and partner involvement? *Family Relations, 42,* 249–255.

Harley, B., & Jean, G. (1999). Vocabulary skills of French immersion students in their second language. *Zeitschrift für Interkulturellen Fremdsprachenunterricht, 4*(2). Retrieved from http://www.ualberta.ca

Harley, K., & Reese, E. (1999). Origins of autobiographical memory. *Developmental Psychology, 35,* 1338–1348.

Harlow, H. F., & Zimmerman, R. (1959). Affectional responses in the infant monkey. *Science, 130,* 421–432.

Harman, D. (2002). Aging: Overview. *Annals of the New York Academy of Sciences, 959,* 1–21.

Harman, S. M., & Blackman, M. R. (2004). Use of growth hormone for prevention or treatment of effects of aging. *Journal of Gerontology, 59,* 652–658.

Harold, G. T., Shelton, K. H., Goeke-Morey, M. C., & Cummings, E. M. (2004). Marital conflict, child emotional security about family relationships, and child adjustment. *Social Development, 13,* 350–376.

Harris, G. (1997). Development of taste perception and appetite regulation. In G. Bremner, A. Slater, & G. Butterworth (Eds.), *Infant development: Recent advances* (pp. 9–30). East Sussex, UK: Erlbaum.

Harris, J. R. (1998). *The nurture assumption: Why children turn out the way they do.* New York: Free Press.

Harris, P. B. (1998). Listening to caregiving sons: Misunderstood realities. *Gerontologist, 38,* 342–352.

Harris, R. L., Ellicott, A. M., & Holmes, D. S. (1986). The timing of psychosocial transitions and changes in women's lives: An examination of women aged 45 to 60. *Journal of Personality and Social Psychology, 51,* 409–416.

Harris, Y. R., & Graham, J. A. (2007). *The African American child: Development and challenges.* New York: Springer.

Harrison, A. O., Wilson, M. N., Pine, C. J., Chan, S. Q., & Buriel, R. (1994). Family ecologies of ethnic minority children. In G. Handel & G. G. Whitchurch (Eds.), *The psychosocial interior of the family* (pp. 187–210). New York: Aldine de Gruyter.

Harrison, Y. (2004). The relationship between daytime exposure to light and nighttime sleep in 6–12-week-old infants. *Journal of Sleep Research, 13,* 345–352.

Harrist, A. W., Zaia, A. F., Bates, J. E., Dodge, K. A., & Pettit, G. S. (1997). Subtypes of social withdrawal in early childhood: Sociometric status and social–cognitive differences across four years. *Child Development, 68,* 278–294.

Hart, B. (2004). What toddlers talk about. *First Language, 24,* 91–106.

Hart, B., & Risley, T. R. (1995). *Meaningful differences in the everyday experience of young American children.* Baltimore: Paul H. Brookes.

Hart, C. H., Burts, D. C., Durland, M. A., Charlesworth, R., DeWolf, M., & Fleege, P. O. (1998). Stress behaviors and activity type participation of preschoolers in more and less developmentally appropriate classrooms: SES and sex differences. *Journal of Research in Childhood Education, 13,* 176–196.

Hart, C. H., Newell, L. D., & Olsen, S. F. (2003). Parenting skills and social–communicative competence in childhood. In J. O. Greene & B. R. Burleson (Eds.), *Handbook of communication and social interaction skills* (pp. 753–797). Mahwah, NJ: Erlbaum.

Hart, C. H., Yang, C., Nelson, L. J., Robinson, C. C., Olsen, J. A., Nelson, D. A., Porter, C. L., Jin, S., Olsen, S. F., & Wu, P. (2000). Peer acceptance in early childhood and subtypes of socially withdrawn behavior in China, Russia, and the United States. *International Journal of Behavioral Development, 24,* 73–81.

Hart, D., & Atkins, R. (2002). Civic competence in urban youth. *Applied Developmental Science, 6,* 227–236.

Hart, D., Atkins, R., & Donnelly, T. M. (2006). Community service and moral development. In M. Killen & J. G. Smetana (Eds.), *Handbook of moral development* (pp. 633–656). Philadelphia: Erlbaum.

Hart, D., & Fegley, S. (1995). Prosocial behavior and caring in adolescence: Relations to self-understanding and social judgment. *Child Development, 66,* 1346–1359.

Hart, D., Donnelly, T. M., Youniss, J., & Atkins, R. (2007). High school community service as a predictor of adult voting and volunteering. *American Educational Research Journal, 44,* 197–219.

Hart, H. M., McAdams, D. P., Hirsch, B. J., & Bauer, J. J. (2001). Generativity and social involvement among African Americans and white adults. *Journal of Research in Personality, 35,* 208–230.

Harter, S. (1998). The development of self-representations. In N. Eisenberg (Ed.), *Handbook of child psychology: Vol. 3. Social, emotional, and personality development* (5th ed., pp. 553–618). New York: Wiley.

Harter, S. (1999). *The construction of self: A developmental perspective.* New York: Guilford.

Harter, S. (2003). The development of self-representations during childhood and adolescence. In M. R. Leary & J. P. Tangney (Eds.), *Handbook of self and identity* (pp. 610–642). New York: Guilford.

Harter, S. (2006). The self. In N. Eisenberg (Ed.), *Handbook of child psychology: Vol. 3. Social, emotional, and personality development* (6th ed., pp. 505–570). Hoboken, NJ: Wiley.

Harter, S., & Whitesell, N. (1989). Developmental changes in children's understanding of simple, multiple, and blended emotion concepts. In C. Saarni & P. Harris (Eds.), *Children's understanding of emotion* (pp. 81–116). Cambridge, UK: Cambridge University Press.

Hartley, A. (2006). Changing role of the speed of processing construct. In J. E. Birren & K. W. Schaie (Eds.), *Handbook of the psychology of aging* (6th ed., pp. 183–207). Burlington, MA: Academic Press.

Hartman, J., & Warren, L. H. (2005). Explaining age differences in temporal working memory. *Psychology and Aging, 20,* 645–656.

Hartshorn, K., Rovee-Collier, C., Gerhardstein, P., Bhatt, R. S., Wondoloski, T. L., Klein, P., Gilch, J., Wurtzel, N., & Campos-de-Carvalho, M. (1998). The ontogeny of long-term memory over the first year-and-a-half of life. *Developmental Psychobiology, 32,* 69–89.

Hartup, W. W. (2006). Relationships in early and middle childhood. In A. L. Vangelisti & D. Perlman (Eds.), *Cambridge handbook of personal relationships* (pp. 177–190). New York: Cambridge University Press.

Hartup, W. W., & Abecassis, M. (2004). Friends and enemies. In P. K. Smith & C. H. Hart (Eds.), *Blackwell handbook of childhood social development* (pp. 285–306). Malden, MA: Blackwell.

Hartup, W. W., & Stevens, N. (1999). Friendships and adaptation across the life span. *Current Directions in Psychological Science, 8,* 76–79.

Harvey, M. W. (2001). Vocational-technical education: A logical approach to dropout prevention for secondary special education. *Preventing School Failure, 45,* 108–113.

Harvey, P. T. (2003). Common eye diseases of elderly people: Identifying and treating causes of vision loss. *Gerontology, 49,* 1–11.

Harwood, J. (2001). Comparing grandchildren's and grandparents' stake in their relationship. *International Journal of Aging and Human Development, 53,* 195–210.

Harwood, M. D., & Farrar, M. J. (2006). Conflicting emotions: The connection between affective perspective taking and theory of mind. *British Journal of Developmental Psychology, 24,* 401–418.

Harwood, R., Leyendecker, B., Carlson, V., Asencio, M., & Miller, A. (2002). Parenting among Latino families in the U.S. In M. H. Bornstein (Ed.), *Handbook of parenting: Vol. 4. Social conditions and applied parenting* (4th ed., pp. 21–46). Mahwah, NJ: Erlbaum.

Hasher, L., Zacks, R. T., & May, C. P. (1999). Inhibitory control, circadian arousal, and age. In D. Gopher & A. Koriat (Eds.), *Attention and performance* (Vol. 17, pp. 653–675). Cambridge, MA: MIT Press.

Hasler, P., & Zouali, M. (2005). Immune receptor signaling, aging, and autoimmunity. *Cellular Immunology, 233,* 102–108.

Hassing, L. B., Johansson, B., Berg, S., Nilsson, S. E., Pedersen, N. L., Hofer, S. M., & McClearn, G. (2002). Terminal decline and markers of cerebro- and cardiovascular disease: Findings from a longitudinal study of the oldest old. *Journal of Gerontology, 57B,* P268–P276.

Hastrup, B. (2007). Healthy aging in Denmark? In M. Robinson, W. Novelli, C. Pearson, & L. Norris (Eds.), *Global health and global aging* (pp. 71–84). San Francisco: Jossey-Bass.

Hatch, L. R., & Bulcroft, K. (2004). Does long-term marriage bring less frequent disagreements? *Journal of Family Issues, 25,* 465–495.

Hatfield, E., Rapson, R. L, & Martel, L. D. (2007). Passionate love and sexual desire. In S. Kitayama & D. Cohen (Eds.), *Handbook of cultural psychology* (pp. 760–779). New York: Guilford.

Hatfield, E., & Sprecher, S. (1995). Men's and women's mate preferences in the United States, Russia, and Japan. *Journal of Cross-Cultural Psychology, 26,* 728–750.

Hauck, F. R., Herman, S. M., Donovan, M., Iyasu, S., Moore, C. M., & Donoghue, E. (2003). Sleep environment and the risk of sudden infant death syndrome in an urban population: The Chicago Infant Mortality Study. *Pediatrics, 111,* 1207–1214.

Hauf, P., Aschersleben, G., & Prinz, W. (2007). Baby do–baby see! How action production influences action perception in infants. *Cognitive Development, 22,* 16–32.

Hausfather, A., Toharia, A., LaRoche, C., & Engelsmann, F. (1997). Effects of age of entry, day-care quality, and family characteristics on preschool behavior. *Journal of Child Psychology and Psychiatry, 38,* 441–448.

Hawes, C., & Phillips, C. D. (2007). Defining quality in assisted living: Comparing apples, oranges, and broccoli. *Gerontologist, 47*(Special Issue III), 40–50.

Hawkins, J. D., Catalano, R. F., & Miller, J. Y. (1992). Risk and protective factors for alcohol and other drug problems in adolescence and early adulthood: Implications for substance abuse prevention. *Psychological Bulletin, 112,* 64–105.

Hawkins, J. N. (1994). Issues of motivation in Asian education. In H. F. O'Neil, Jr., & M. Drillings (Eds.), *Motivation: Theory and research* (pp. 101–115). Hillsdale, NJ: Erlbaum.

Hawkley, L. C., & Cacioppo, J. T. (2004). Stress and the aging immune system. *Brain, Behavior and Immunity, 18,* 114–119.

Hay, J. F., & Jacoby, L. L. (1999). Separating habit and recollection in young and older adults: Effects of elaborative processing and distinctiveness. *Psychology and Aging, 14,* 122–134.

Hay, P., & Bacaltchuk, J. (2004). Bulimia nervosa. *Clinical Evidence, 12,* 1326–1347.

Hayflick, L. (1994). *How and why we age.* New York: Ballantine.

Hayflick, L. (1998). How and why we age. *Experimental Gerontology, 33,* 639–653.

Hayne, H. (2002). Thoughts from the crib: Meltzoff and Moore (1994) alter our views of mental representation during infancy. *Infant Behavior and Development, 25,* 62–64.

Hayne, H. (2004). Infant memory development: Implications for childhood amnesia. *Developmental Review, 24,* 33–73.

Hayne, H., Boniface, J., & Barr, R. (2000). The development of declarative memory in human infants: Age-related changes in deferred imitation. *Behavioral Neuroscience, 114,* 77–83.

Hayne, H., Rovee-Collier, C., & Perris, E. E. (1987). Categorization and memory retrieval by three-month-olds. *Child Development, 58,* 750–767.

Hays, J. C., & George, L. K. (2002). The life-course trajectory toward living alone: Racial differences. *Research on Aging, 24,* 283–307.

Hayslip, B., Jr., Emick, M. A., Handerson, C. E., & Elias, K. (2002). Temporal variations in the experience of custodial grandparenting: A short-term longitudinal study. *Journal of Applied Gerontology, 21,* 139–156.

Hayslip, B., Jr., & Kaminski, P. L. (2005). Grandparents raising their grandchildren. *Marriage and Family Review, 37,* 147–169.

Haywood, K. M., & Getchell, N. (2005). *Life span motor development* (4th ed.). Champaign, IL: Human Kinetics.

Hazell, L. V. (2001). Multicultural aftercare issues. In O. D. Weeks & C. Johnson (Eds.), *When all the friends have gone: Guide for aftercare providers* (pp. 57–71). Amityville, NY: Baywood.

Head Start Bureau. (2008) *Head Start fact sheet.* Retrieved from www.acf.hhs.gov/programs/ohs/about/fy2008.html

Health and Disability Research Institute. (2006). *Fear of falling: A matter of balance.* Boston: Author.

Health Canada. (2006). *Sexually transmitted infections surveillance and epidemiology.* Retrieved from www.phac-aspc.gc.ca/sti-its-surv-epi/surveillance_e.html

Heath, S. B. (1990). The children of Trackton's children: Spoken and written in social change. In J. Stigler, G. Herdt, & R. A. Shweder (Eds.), *Cultural psychology: Essays on comparative human development* (pp. 496–519). New York: Cambridge University Press.

Heaton, T. B. (2002). Factors contributing to increasing marital stability in the United States. *Journal of Family Issues, 23,* 392–409.

Hebert, M., & Tourigny, M. (2004). Child sexual abuse prevention: A review of evaluative studies and recommendations for program development. In S. P. Serge (Ed.), *Advances in psychology research* (Vol. 29, pp. 123–155). Hauppauge, NY: Nova Science Publishers.

Heckman, J. J., & Masterov, D. V. (2004). *The productivity argument for investing in young children.* Working Paper 5, Invest in Kids Working Group, Committee for Economic Development. Retrieved from jenni.uchicago.edu/Invest

Hedberg, K., Hopkins, D., & Kohn, M. (2003). Five years of legal physician-assisted suicide in Oregon. *New England Journal of Medicine, 348,* 961–964.

Hedge, J. W., Borman, W. C., & Lammlein, S. E. (2006). *The aging workforce: Realities, myths, and implications for organizations.* Washington, DC: American Psychological Association.

Hedges, L. V., & Nowell, A. (1998). Black–white test score convergence since 1995. In C. Jencks & M. Phillips (Eds.), *The black–white test score gap* (pp.149–181). Washington, DC: Brookings Institution.

Hediger, M. L., Overpeck, M. D., Ruan, W. J., & Troendle, J. F. (2002). Birthweight and gestational age effects on motor and social development. *Paediatric and Perinatal Epidemiology, 16,* 33–46.

Heilbronn, L. K., & Ravussin, E. (2003). Calorie restriction and aging: Review of the literature and implications for studies in humans. *American Journal of Clinical Nutrition, 78,* 361–369.

Heilbrun, K., Lee, R., & Cottle, C. C. (2005). Risk factors and intervention outcomes: Meta-analyses of juvenile offending. In K. Heilbrun, N. E. S. Goldstein, & R. E. Redding (Eds.), *Juvenile delinquency: Prevention, assessment, and intervention* (pp. 111–133). New York: Oxford University Press.

Heiman, N., Stallings, M. C., Hofer, S. M., & Hewitt, J. K. (2003). Investigating age differences in the genetic and environmental structure of the tridimensional personality questionnaire in later adulthood. *Behavior Genetics, 33,* 171–180.

Heinz, W. R. (1999). Job entry patterns in life-course perspective. In W. R. Heinz (Ed.), *From education to work: Cross-national perspectives* (pp. 214–231). New York: Cambridge University Press.

Helburn, S. W. (Ed.). (1995). *Cost, quality and child outcomes in child care centers.* Denver: University of Colorado.

Helm, H. M., Hays, J. C., Flint, E. P., Koenig, H. G., & Blazer, D. G. (2000). Does private religious activity prolong survival? A six-year follow-up study of 3,851 older adults. *Journal of Gerontology, 55A,* M400–M405.

Helson, R. (1992). Women's difficult times and the rewriting of the life story. *Psychology of Women Quarterly, 16,* 331–347.

Helson, R. (1997). The self in middle age. In M. E. Lachman & J. B. James (Eds.), *Multiple paths of midlife development* (pp. 21–43). Chicago: University of Chicago Press.

Helson, R., & Cate, R. A. (2007). Late middle age: Transition to the Third Age. In J. B. James & P. Wink (Eds.), *Annual review of gerontology and geriatrics* (Vol. 26, pp. 83–101). New York: Springer.

Helson, R., Jones, C. J., & Kwan, V. S. Y. (2002). Personality change over 40 years of adulthood: Hierarchical linear modeling analyses of two longitudinal samples. *Journal of Personality and Social Psychology, 83,* 752–766.

Helson, R., Mitchell, V., & Moane, G. (1984). Personality and patterns of adherence and nonadherence to the social clock. *Journal of Personality and Social Psychology, 46,* 1079–1096.

Helson, R., & Picano, J. (1990). Is the traditional role bad for women? *Journal of Personality and Social Psychology, 59,* 311–320.

Helson, R., Soto, C. J., & Cate, R. A. (2006). From young adulthood through the middle ages. In D. K. Mroczek & T. D. Little (Eds.), *Handbook of personality development* (pp. 337–352). Mahwah, NJ: Erlbaum.

Helson, R., & Stewart, A. (1994). Personality change in adulthood. In T. F. Heatherton & J. L. Weinberger (Eds.), *Can personality change?* (pp. 201–225). Washington, DC: American Psychological Association.

Helson, R., & Wink, P. (1992). Personality change in women from the early 40s to the early 50s. *Psychology and Aging, 7,* 46–55.

Heltzner, E. P., Cauley, J. A., Pratt, S. R., Wisniewski, S. R., Zmuda, J. M., & Talbott, E. O. (2005). Race and sex differences in age-related hearing loss: The health, aging and body composition study. *Journal of the American Geriatrics Society, 53,* 2119–2127.

Helwig, C. C. (1995). Adolescents' and young adults' conceptions of civil liberties: Freedom of speech and religion. *Child Development, 66,* 152–166.

Helwig, C. C. (2006). Rights, civil liberties, and democracy across cultures. In M. Killen & J. G. Smetana (Eds.), *Handbook of moral development* (pp. 185–210). Philadelphia: Erlbaum.

Helwig, C. C., & Jasiobedzka, U. (2001). The relation between law and morality: Children's reasoning about socially beneficial and unjust laws. *Child Development, 72,* 1382–1393.

Helwig, C. C., & Prencipe, A. (1999). Children's judgments of flags and flag-burning. *Child Development, 70,* 132–143.

Helwig, C. C., & Turiel, E. (2004). Children's social and moral reasoning. In P. K. Smith & C. H. Hart (Eds.), *Blackwell handbook of childhood social development* (pp. 476–490). Malden, MA: Blackwell.

Helwig, C. C., Zelazo, P. D., & Wilson, M. (2001). Children's judgments of psychological harm in normal and canonical situations. *Child Development, 72,* 66–81.

Henderson, D., Buchanan, J. A., & Fisher, J. E. (2002). Violence and the elderly population: Issues for prevention. In P. A. Schewe (Ed.), *Preventing violence in relationships: Interventions across the life span* (pp. 223–245). Washington, DC: American Psychological Association.

Henderson, H. A., Marshall, P. J., Fox, N. A., & Rubin, K. H. (2004). Psychophysiological and behavioral evidence for varying forms and functions of nonsocial behavior in preschoolers. *Child Development, 75,* 251–263.

Henderson, V. W. (2009). Estrogens, episodic memory, and Alzheimer's disease: A critical update. *Seminars in Reproductive Medicine, 27,* 283–293.

Hendin, H. (1999). Suicide, assisted suicide, and euthanasia. In D. G. Jacobs (Ed.), *The Harvard Medical School guide to suicide assessment and intervention* (pp. 540–560). San Francisco: Jossey-Bass.

Hendrick, S. S., & Hendrick, C. (1993). Lovers as friends. *Journal of Social and Personal Relationships, 10,* 459–466.

Hendrick, S. S., & Hendrick, C. (2002). Love. In C. R. Snyder & S. J. Lopez (Eds.), *Handbook of positive psychology* (pp. 472–484). New York: Oxford University Press.

Hendricks, J., & Cutler, S. J. (2004). Volunteerism and socioemotional selectivity in later life. *Journal of Gerontology, 59B,* S251–S257.

Hendrie, H. H. (2001). Exploration of environmental and genetic risk factors for Alzheimer's disease: The value of cross-cultural studies. *Current Directions in Psychological Science, 10,* 98–101.

Hendry, L. B., & Kloep, M. (2007). Conceptualizing emerging adulthood: Inspecting the emperor's new clothes? *Child Development Perspectives, 1,* 74–79.

Henggeler, S., Sheidow, A. J., & Lee, T. (2007). Multisystemic treatment of serious clinical problems in youths and their families. In D. W. Springer & A. R. Roberts (Eds.), *Handbook of forensic mental health with victims and offenders* (pp. 315–345). New York: Springer.

Henning, K., Jones, A. R., & Holdford, R. (2005). Attributions of blame among male and female domestic violence offenders. *Journal of Family Violence, 20,* 131–139.

Henrich, C. C., Brookmeyer, K. A., Shrier, L. A., & Shahar, G. (2006). Supportive relationships and sexual risk behavior in adolescence: An ecological–transactional approach. *Journal of Pediatric Psychology, 31,* 286–297.

Henrich, C. C., Kuperminc, G. P., Sack, A., Blatt, S. J., & Leadbeater, B. J. (2000). Characteristics and homogeneity of early adolescent friendship groups: A comparison of male and female clique and nonclique members. *Applied Developmental Science, 4,* 15–26.

Henricsson, L., & Rydell, A.-M. (2004). Elementary school children with behavior problems: Teacher–child relations and self-perception. A prospective study. *Merrill-Palmer Quarterly, 50,* 111–138.

Henry, J. D., MacLeod, M. S., Phillips, L. H., & Crawford, J. R. (2004). A meta-analytic review of prospective memory and aging. *Psychology and Aging, 19,* 27–39.

Herbst, J. H., McCrae, R. R., Costa, P. T., Jr., Feaganes, J. R., & Siegler, I. C. (2000). Self-perceptions of stability and change in personality at midlife: The UNC Alumni Heart Study. *Assessment, 7,* 379–388.

Herman, M. (2004). Forced to choose: Some determinants of racial identification in multiracial adolescents. *Child Development, 75,* 730–748.

Herman-Giddens, M. E. (2006). Recent data on pubertal milestones in United States children: The secular trend toward earlier development. *International Journal of Andrology, 29,* 241–246.

Hermann, M., Untergasser, G., Rumpold, H., & Berger, P. (2000). Aging of the male reproductive system. *Experimental Gerontology, 35,* 1267–1279.

Hernandez, M., & Newcomer, R. (2007). Assisted living and special populations: What do we know about differences in use and potential access barriers? *Gerontologist, 47*(Special Issue III), 110–117.

Heron, M. P., Hoyert, D. L., Xu, J., Scott, C, & Tejada-Vera B. (2008). Deaths: Preliminary data for 2006. *National Vital Statistics Reports,* Vol. 56, No. 16. Hyattsville, MD: National Center for Health Statistics.

Herrera, E., Reissland, N., & Shepherd, J. (2004). Maternal touch and maternal child-directed speech: Effects of depressed mood in the postnatal period. *Journal of Affective Disorders, 81,* 29–39.

Herrnstein, R. J., & Murray, C. (1994). *The bell curve.* New York: Free Press.

Hershey, D. A., Jacobs-Lawson, J. M., McArdle, J. J., & Hamagami, F. (2007). Psychological foundations of financial planning for retirement. *Journal of Adult Development, 14,* 26–36.

Hershey, D. A., Walsh, D. A., Brougham, R., & Carter, S. (1998). Challenges of training pre-retirees to make sound financial planning decisions. *Educational Gerontology, 24,* 447–470.

Herz, B. K. (2004). *What works in girls' education: Evidence and policies from the developing world.* New York: Council on Foreign Relations.

Herzog, D. B., Eddy, K. T., & Beresin, E. V. (2006). Anorexia and bulimia nervosa. In M. K. Dulcan & J. M. Wiener (Eds.), *Essentials of child and adolescent psychiatry* (pp. 527–560). Washington, DC: American Psychiatric Publishing.

Hesketh, K., Ball, K., Crawford, D., Campbell, K., & Salmon, J. (2007). Mediators of the relationship between maternal education and children's TV viewing. *American Journal of Preventive Medicine, 33,* 41–47.

Hespos, S. J., & Baillargeon, R. (2001). Reasoning about containment events in very young infants. *Cognition, 78,* 207–245.

Hess, T. M., & Hinson, J. T. (2006). Age-related variation in the influences of aging stereotypes on memory in adulthood. *Psychology and Aging, 21,* 621–625.

Hess, T. M., Hinson, J. T., & Statham, J. A. (2004). Explicit and implicit stereotype activation effects on memory: Do age and awareness moderate the impact of priming? *Psychology and Aging, 19,* 495–505.

Hesse, E., & Main, M. (2000). Disorganized infant, child, and adult attachment: Collapse in behavioral and attentional strategies. *Journal of the American Psychoanalytic Association, 48,* 1097–1127.

Hessler, R. M., Eriksson, B. G., Dey, D., Steen, G., Sundh, V., & Steen, B. (2003). The compression of morbidity debate in aging: An empirical test using the gerontological and geriatric population studies in Göteborg, Sweden. *Archives of Gerontology and Geriatrics, 37,* 213–222.

Hetherington, E. M. (1999). Should we stay together for the sake of the children? In E. M. Hetherington (Ed.), *Coping with divorce, single-parenting, and remarriage: A risk and resiliency perspective* (pp. 93–116). Hillsdale, NJ: Erlbaum.

Hetherington, E. M. (2003). Social support and the adjustment of children in divorced and remarried families. *Childhood, 10,* 237–254

Hetherington, E. M., & Clingempeel, W. G. (1992). Coping with marital transitions: A family systems perspective. *Monographs of the Society for Research in Child Development, 57*(2–3, Serial No. 227).

Hetherington, E. M., Henderson, S. H., & Reiss, D. (1999). Adolescent siblings in stepfamilies: Family functioning and adolescent adjustment. *Monographs of the Society for Research in Child Development, 64*(4, Serial No. 259).

Hetherington, E. M., & Jodl, K. M. (1994). Stepfamilies as settings for child development. In A. Booth & J. Dunn (Eds.), *Stepfamilies: Who benefits? Who does not?* (pp. 55–79). Hillsdale, NJ: Erlbaum.

Hetherington, E. M., & Kelly, J. (2002). *For better or for worse: Divorce reconsidered.* New York: Norton.

Hetherington, E. M., & Stanley-Hagan, M. (2000). Diversity among stepfamilies. In D. H. Demo, K. R. Allen, & M. A. Fine (Eds.), *Handbook of family diversity* (pp. 173–196). New York: Oxford University Press.

Hewlett, B. S. (1992). Husband–wife reciprocity and the father–infant relationship among Aka pygmies. In B. S. Hewlett (Ed.), *Father–child relations: Cultural and biosocial contexts* (pp. 153–176). New York: Aldine de Gruyter.

Hewlett, B. S. (2004). Fathers in forager, farmer, and pastoral cultures. In M. E. Lamb (Ed.), *The role of the father in child development* (4th ed., pp. 182–195). Hoboken, NJ: Wiley.

Hewlett, S. (2003). *Creating a life.* New York: Miramax.

Heyes, C. (2005). Imitation by association. In S. Hurley & N. Chater (Eds.), *From neuroscience to social science: Vol. 1. Mechanisms of imitation and imitation in animals* (pp. 157–177). Cambridge, MA: MIT Press.

Heyman, G. D., & Dweck, C. S. (1998). Children's thinking about traits: Implications for judgments of the self and others. *Child Development, 69,* 391–403.

Heyman, G. D., Dweck, C. S., & Cain, K. M. (1992). Young children's vulnerability to self-blame and helplessness: Relationship to beliefs about goodness. *Child Development, 63,* 401–415.

Heyman, G. D., & Gelman, S. A. (1999). The use of trait labels in making psychological inferences. *Child Development, 70,* 604–619.

Heyman, G. D., & Legare, C. H. (2004). Children's beliefs about gender differences in the academic and social domains. *Sex Roles, 50,* 227–239.

Hibell, B. (2001). *European School Survey Project on Alcohol and Drugs.* Stockholm: Swedish Council for Information on Alcohol and Other Drugs.

Hickling, A. K., & Wellman, H. M. (2001). The emergence of children's causal explanations and theories: Evidence from everyday conversation. *Developmental Psychology, 37,* 668–683.

Hietanen, A., Era, P., Sorri, M., & Heikkinen, E. (2004). Changes in hearing in 80-year-old people: A 10-year follow-up study. *International Journal of Audiology, 43,* 126–135.

Higginbottom, G. M. A. (2006). 'Pressure of life': Ethnicity as a mediating factor in mid-life and older peoples' experience of high blood pressure. *Sociology of Health and Illness, 28,* 583–610.

Higgins, C., & Duxbury, L. (2002). *The 2001 National Work-Life Conflict Study: Report One.* Retrieved from www.phac-aspc.gc.ca/publicat/work-travail/report1/index.html

High, K. P. (2001). Nutritional strategies to boost immunity and prevent infection in elderly individuals. *Aging and Infectious Diseases, 33,* 1892–1900.

High, P. C., LaGasse, L., Becker, S., Ahlgren, I., & Gardner, A. (2000). Literacy promotion in primary care pediatrics: Can we make a difference? *Pediatrics, 105,* 927–934.

Hildreth, K., & Rovee-Collier, C. (2002). Forgetting functions of reactivated memories over the first year of life. *Developmental Psychobiology, 41,* 277–288.

Hildreth, K., Sweeney, B., & Rovee-Collier, C. (2003). Differential memory-preserving effects of reminders at 6 months. *Journal of Experimental Child Psychology, 84,* 41–62.

Hilgers, K. K., Akridge, M., Scheetz, J. P., & Kinance, D. E. (2006). Childhood obesity and dental development. *Pediatric Dentistry, 28,* 18–22.

Hill, D. (2003). *Europe: When dying seems better than living.* New York: Radio Free Europe. Retrieved from http://www.rferl.org/nca/features/2003/01/22012003154227.as

Hill, E. J., Mead, N. T., Dean, L. R., Hafen, D. M., Gadd, R., & Palmer, A. A. (2006). Researching the 60-hour dual-earner workweek. *American Behavioral Scientist, 49,* 1184–1203.

Hill, J. L., Brooks-Gunn, J., & Waldfogel, J. (2003). Sustained effects of high participation in an early intervention for low-birth-weight premature infants. *Developmental Psychology, 39,* 730–744.

Hill, N. E., & Taylor, L. C. (2004). Parental school involvement and children's academic achievement: Pragmatics and issues. *Current Directions in Psychological Science, 13,* 161–164.

Hill, N. M., & Schneider, W. (2006). Brain changes in the development of expertise: Neuroanatomical and neurophysiological evidence about skill-based adaptations. In K. A. Ericsson, N. Charness, P. J. Feltovich, & R. R. Hoffman (Eds.), *The Cambridge handbook of expertise and expert performance* (pp. 653–682). New York: Cambridge University Press.

Hillis, S. D., Anda, R. F., Dube, S. R., Felitti, V. J., Marchbanks, P. A., & Marks, J. S. (2004). The association between adverse childhood experiences and adolescent pregnancy, long-term psychosocial consequences, and fetal death. *Pediatrics, 113,* 320–327.

Hillman, C. H., Erickson, K. I., & Kramer, A. F. (2008). Be smart, exercise your heart: Exercise effects on brain and cognition. *Nature Reviews Neuroscience, 9,* 58–65.

Hillman, J. L. (2000). *Clinical perspectives on elderly sexuality.* New York: Kluwer Academic.

Hillman, J. L., & Stricker, G. (1994). A linkage of knowledge and attitudes toward elderly sexuality: Not necessarily a uniform relationship. *Gerontologist, 34,* 256–260.

Hilt, L. M. (2004). Attribution retaining for therapeutic change: Theory, practice, and future directions. *Imagination, Cognition, and Personality, 23,* 289–307.

Hinojosa, T., Sheu, C.-F., & Michael, G. F. (2003). Infant hand-use preference for grasping objects contributes to the development of a hand-use preference for manipulating objects. *Developmental Psychobiology, 43,* 328–334.

Hirsch, C. (1996). Understanding the influence of gender role identity on the assumption of family caregiving roles by men. *International Journal of Aging and Human Development, 42,* 103–121.

Hirsh-Pasek, K., & Burchinal, M. (2006). Mother and caregiver sensitivity over time: Predicting language and academic outcomes with variable- and person-centered approaches. *Merrill-Palmer Quarterly, 52,* 449–485.

Hirsh-Pasek, K., & Golinkoff, R. M. (2003). *Einstein never used flash cards.* New York: Rodale.

Hirsh-Pasek, K., Golinkoff, R. M., Berk, L. E., & Singer, D. G. (2009). *A mandate for playful learning in preschool: Presenting the evidence.* New York: Oxford University Press.

Ho, W. K., Hankey, G. J., & Eikelboom, J. W. (2004). Prevention of coronary heart disease with aspirin and clopidogrel: Efficacy, safety, and cost-effectiveness. *Expert Opinion on Pharmacotherapy, 5,* 493–503.

Hoch-Espada, A., Ryan, E., & Deblinger, E. (2006). Child sexual abuse. In J. E. Fisher & W. T. O'Donohue (Eds.), *Practitioner's guide to evidence-based psychotherapy* (pp. 177–188). New York: Springer.

Hochwarter, W. A., Ferris, G. R., Perrewe, P. L., Witt, L. A., & Kiewitz, C. (2001). A note on the nonlinearity of the age–job satisfaction relationship. *Journal of Applied Social Psychology, 31,* 1223–1237.

Hock, H. S., Park, C. L., & Bjorklund, D. F. (1998). Temporal organization in children's strategy formation. *Journal of Experimental Child Psychology, 70,* 187–206.

Hodges, J., & Tizard, B. (1989). Social and family relationships of ex-institutional adolescents. *Journal of Child Psychology and Psychiatry, 30,* 77–97.

Hodges, R. M., & French, L. A. (1988). The effect of class and collection labels on cardinality, class-inclusion, and number conservation tasks. *Child Development, 59,* 1387–1396.

Hoekstra, C., Zhao, Z. Z., Lambalk, C. B., Willemsen, G., Martin, N. G., Boomsma, D. I., & Montgomery, G. W. (2008). Dizygotic twinning. *Human Reproduction Update, 14,* 37–47.

Hoenig, H., Taylor, D. H., Jr., & Sloan, F. A. (2003). Does assistive technology substitute for personal assistance among the disabled elderly? *American Journal of Public Health, 93,* 330–337.

Hoff, B. (2001). *Full report of the prevalence, incidence, and consequences of violence against women.* Washington, DC: U.S. Department of Justice.

Hoff, E. (2003). The specificity of environmental influence: Socioeconomic status affects early vocabulary development via maternal speech. *Child Development, 74,* 1368–1378.

Hoff, E. (2006). How social contexts support and shape language development. *Developmental Review, 26,* 55–88.

Hoff, E., Laursen, B., & Tardif, T. (2002). Socioeconomic status and parenting. In M. H. Bornstein (Ed.), *Handbook of parenting* (pp. 231–252). Mahwah, NJ: Erlbaum.

Hofferth, S. L., & Anderson, K. G. (2003). Are all dads equal? Biology versus marriage as a basis for paternal investment. *Journal of Marriage and Family, 65,* 213–232.

Hoffman, L. W. (2000). Maternal employment: Effects of social context. In R. D. Taylor & M. C. Wang (Eds.), *Resilience across contexts: Family, work, culture, and community* (pp. 147–176). Mahwah, NJ: Erlbaum.

Hoffman, M. L. (2000*). Empathy and moral development.* New York: Cambridge University Press.

Hoffman, S., & Hatch, M. C. (1996). Stress, social support and pregnancy outcome: A reassessment based on research. *Paediatric and Perinatal Epidemiology, 10,* 380–405.

Hoffmann, W. (2001). Fallout from the Chernobyl nuclear disaster and congenital malformations in Europe. *Archives of Environmental Health, 56,* 478–483.

Hoffner, C., & Badzinski, D. M. (1989). Children's integration of facial and situational cues to emotion. *Child Development, 60,* 411–422.

Hogan, B. E., & Linden, W. (2004). Anger response styles and blood pressure: At least don't ruminate about it! *Annals of Behavioral Medicine, 27,* 38–49.

Hogan, D. B., MacKnight, C., & Bergman, H. (2003). Models, definitions, and criteria of frailty. *Aging Clinical and Experimental Research, 15*(Suppl. to No. 3), 3–29.

Hogan, R., & Perrucci, C. C. (2007). Black women: Truly disadvantaged in the transition from employment to retirement income. *Social Science Research, 36,* 1184–1199.

Hoglund, W. L., & Leadbeater, B. J. (2007). Managing threat: Do social-cognitive processes mediate the link between peer victimization and adjustment problems in early adolescence? *Journal of Research on Adolescence, 17,* 525–540.

Hokoda, A., & Fincham, F. D. (1995). Origins of children's helpless and mastery achievement patterns in the family. *Journal of Educational Psychology, 87,* 375–385.

Holden, G. W., Coleman, S. M., & Schmidt, K. L. (1995). Why 3-year-old children get spanked: Determinants as reported by college-educated mothers. *Merrill-Palmer Quarterly, 41,* 431–452.

Holditch-Davis, D., Belyea, M., & Edwards, L. J. (2005). Prediction of 3-year developmental outcomes from sleep development over the preterm period. *Infant Behavior and Development, 79,* 49–58.

Holland, A. L. (2004). Plasticity and development. *Brain and Language, 88,* 254–255.

Holland, J. L. (1985). *Making vocational choices: A theory of vocational personalities and work environments.* Englewood Cliffs, NJ: Prentice-Hall.

Holland, J. L. (1997). *Making vocational choices: A theory of vocational personalities and work environments* (3rd ed.). Odessa, FL: Psychological Assessment Resources.

Hollich, G. J., Hirsh-Pasek, K., & Golinkoff, R. M. (2000). Breaking the language barrier: An emergentist coalition model for the origins of word learning. *Monographs of the Society for Research in Child Development,* 65(3, Serial No. 262).

Holliday, R. E. (2003). Reducing misinformation effects in children with cognitive interviews: Dissociating recollection and familiarity. *Child Development, 74,* 728–751.

Holmbeck, G. N. (1996). A model of family relational transformations during the transition to adolescence: Parent–adolescent conflict and adaptation. In J. A. Graber, J. Brooks-Gunn, & A. C. Petersen (Eds.), *Transitions through adolescence* (pp. 167–199). Mahwah, NJ: Erlbaum.

Holmes-Rovner, M., Rovner, D. R., Padonu, G., Talarczyk, G., Kroll, J., Rothert, M., & Breer, L. (1996). African-American women's attitudes and expectations of menopause. *American Journal of Preventive Medicine, 12,* 420–423.

Holobow, N., Genesee, F., & Lambert, W. (1991). The effectiveness of a foreign language immersion program for children from different ethnic and social class backgrounds: Report 2. *Applied Psycholinguistics, 12,* 179–198.

Holowka, S., Brosseau-Lapré, F., & Petitto, L. A. (2002). Semantic and conceptual knowledge underlying bilingual babies' first signs and words. *Language Learning, 52,* 205–262.

Honein, M. A., Paulozzi, L. J., & Erickson, J. D. (2001). Continued occurrence of Accutane-exposed pregnancies. *Teratology, 64,* 142–147.

Hong, Z.-R., Veach, P. M., & Lawrenz, F. (2003). An investigation of the gender stereotyped thinking of Taiwanese secondary school boys and girls. *Sex Roles, 48,* 495–504.

Hood, B. M. (2004). Is looking good enough or does it beggar belief? *Developmental Science, 7,* 415–417.

Hooker, K. (1992). Possible selves and perceived health in older adults and college students. *Journal of Gerontology, 47,* P85–P89.

Hooyman, N. R., & Kiyak, H. A. (2008). *Social gerontology: A multidisciplinary perspective* (8th ed.). Boston: Allyn and Bacon.

Hopkins, B., & Butterworth, G. (1997). Dynamical systems approaches to the development of action. In G. Bremner, A. Slater, & G. Butterworth (Eds.), *Infant development: Recent advances* (pp. 75–100). East Sussex, UK: Psychology Press.

Hopkins, B., & Westra, T. (1988). Maternal handling and motor development: An intracultural study. *Genetic, Social and General Psychology Monographs, 14,* 377–420.

Hopper, S. V. (1993). The influence of ethnicity on the health of older women. *Clinics in Geriatric Medicine, 9,* 231–259.

Hoppmann, C. A., Gerstorf, D., Smith, J., & Klumb, P. L. (2007). Linking possible selves and behavior: Do domain-specific hopes and fears translate into daily activities in very old age? *Journal of Gerontology, 62B,* P104–P111.

Horgan, D. (1978). The development of the full passive. *Journal of Child Language, 5,* 65–80.

Horn, J. L., Donaldson, G., & Engstrom, R. (1981). Apprehension, memory, and fluid intelligence decline through the "vital years" of adulthood. *Research on Aging, 3,* 33–84.

Horn, J. L., & Noll, J. (1997). Human cognitive capabilities: Gf–Gc theory. In D. P. Flanagan, J. L., Genshaft, & P. L. Harrison (Eds.), *Beyond traditional intellectual assessment* (pp. 53–91). New York: Guilford.

Horner, S. L., & Gaither, S. M. (2004). Attribution retraining instruction with a second-grade class. *Early Childhood Education Journal, 31,* 165–170.

Horner, T. M. (1980). Two methods of studying stranger reactivity in infants: A review. *Journal of Child Psychology and Psychiatry, 21,* 203–219.

Horst, J. S., Oakes, L. M., & Madole, K. M. (2005). What does it look like and what can it do? Category structure influences how infants categorize. *Child Development, 76,* 614–631.

Hospice Foundation of America. (2005). *The dying process: A guide for caregivers.* Washington, DC: Author.

Hospice Foundation of America. (2009). *Hospice services and expenses.* Retrieved from www.hospicefoundation.org/hospiceInfo/services.asp

Houck, J. A. (2006). *Hot and bothered: Women, medicine, and menopause in modern America.* Cambridge, MA: Harvard University Press.

Houlihan, J., Kropp. T., Wiles, R., Gray, S., & Campbell, C. (2005). *Body burden: The pollution in newborns.* Washington, DC: Environmental Working Group.

House, J. S., Lantz, P. M., & Herd, P. (2005). Continuity and change in the social stratification of aging and health over the life course: Evidence from a nationally representative longitudinal study from 1986 to 2001/2002 (Americans' Changing Lives Study). *Journal of Gerontology, 60B*(Special Issue II), 15–26.

Houts, R. M., Barnett-Walker, K. C., Paley, B., & Cox, M. J. (2008). Patterns of couple interaction during the transition to parenthood. *Personal Relationships, 15,* 103–122.

Hoven, C. W., Duarte, C. S., Lucas, C. P., Wu, P., Mandell, D. J., & Goodwin, R. D. (2005). Psychopathology among New York City school children 6 months after September 11. *Archives of General Psychiatry, 62,* 545–552.

Howard, A., & Bray, D. W. (1988). *Managerial lives in transition: Advancing age and changing times.* New York: Guilford Press.

Howard, A. W. (2002). Automobile restraints for children: A review for clinicians. *Canadian Medical Association Journal, 167,* 769–773.

Howard, B. V., Manson, J. E., Stefanick, M. L., Beresford, S. A., Frank, G., & Jones, B. (2006). Low-fat dietary pattern and weight change over 7 years: The Women's Health Initiative Dietary Modification Trial. *Journal of the American Medical Association, 295,* 39–49.

Howard, D. E., & Wang, M. Q. (2004). Multiple sexual-partner behavior among sexually active U.S. adolescent girls. *American Journal of Health Behavior, 28,* 3–12.

Howe, N., Aquan-Assee, J., & Bukowski, W. M. (2001). Predicting sibling relations over time: Synchrony between maternal management styles and sibling relationship quality. *Merrill-Palmer Quarterly, 47,* 121–141.

Howell, K. K., Lynch, M. E., Platzman, K. A., Smith, G. H., & Coles, C. D. (2006). Prenatal alcohol exposure and ability, academic achievement, and school functioning in adolescence: A longitudinal follow-up. *Journal of Pediatric Psychology, 31,* 116–126.

Howell, L. C., & Beth, A. (2002). Midlife myths and realities: Women reflect on their experiences. *Journal of Women and Aging, 14,* 189–204.

Howell, T. M., & Yuille, J. C. (2004). Healing and treatment of Aboriginal offenders: A Canadian example. *American Journal of Forensic Psychology, 22,* 53–76.

Hoyer, W. J., & Verhaeghen, P. (2006). Memory aging. In J. E. Birren & K. W. Schaie (Eds.), *Handbook of the psychology of aging* (6th ed., pp. 209–232). Burlington, MA: Elsevier Academic Press.

Hoza, B., Gerdes, A. C., Hinshaw, S. P., Bukowski, W. M., Gold, J. A., Kraemer, H. C., Pelham, W. E., Jr., Wigal, T., & Arnold, L. E. (2005). What aspects of peer relationships are impaired in children with attention-deficit/hyperactivity disorder? *Journal of Consulting and Clinical Psychology, 73,* 411–423.

HSBC & Oxford Institute of Ageing. (2007). *The future of retirement.* London: HSBC Insurance.

Hsu, F. L. K. (1981). *Americans and Chinese: Passage to difference* (3rd ed.). Honolulu: University of Hawaii Press.

Hu, F. B., & Manson, J. E. (2001). Diet, lifestyle, and the risk of type 2 diabetes mellitus in women. *New England Journal of Medicine, 345,* 790–797.

Hu, Y., Wood, J. F., Smith, V., & Westbrook, N. (2004). Friendships through IM: Examining the relationship between instant messaging and intimacy. *Journal of Computer-Mediated Communication, 10*(1). Retrieved from jcmc.indiana.edu/vol10/issue1

Huang, C.-C. (2006). Child support enforcement and father involvement for children in never-married mother families. *Fathering, 4,* 97–111.

Huang, H. Y., Caballero, B., Chang, S., Alberg, A., Semba, R., & Schneyer, C. (2006, May). Multivitamin/mineral supplements and prevention of chronic disease. *Evidence Report/Techology Assessment, 139,* 1–117.

Huang, Q., & Sverke, M. (2007). Women's occupational career patterns over 27 years: Relations to family of origin, life careers, and wellness. *Journal of Vocational Behavior, 70,* 369–397.

Hubbs-Tait, L., Nation, J. R., Krebs, N. F., & Bellinger, D. C. (2005). Neurotoxicants, micronurtrients, and social environments: Individual and combined effects on children's development. *Psychological Science in the Public Interest, 6,* 57–121.

Hubert, H. B., Bloch, D. A., Oehlert, J. W., & Fries, J. F. (2002). Lifestyle habits and compression of morbidity. *Journal of Gerontology, 57A,* M347–351.

Huddleston, J., & Ge, X. (2003). Boys at puberty: Psychosocial implications. In C. Hayward (Ed.), *Gender differences at puberty* (pp. 113–134). New York: Cambridge University Press.

Hudson, J. A., Fivush, R., & Kuebli, J. (1992). Scripts and episodes: The development of event memory. *Applied Cognitive Psychology, 6,* 483–505.

Hudson, J. A., Sosa, B. B., & Shapiro, L. R. (1997). Scripts and plans: The development of preschool children's event knowledge and event planning. In S. L. Friedman & E. K. Scholnick (Eds.), *The developmental psychology of planning* (pp. 77–102). Mahwah, NJ: Erlbaum.

Hudson, J. M. (2008). Automatic memory processes in normal ageing and Alzheimer's disease. *Cortex, 44,* 345–349.

Huesmann, L. R. (1986). Psychological processes promoting the relation between exposure to media violence and aggressive behavior by the viewer. *Journal of Social Issues, 42,* 125–139.

Huesmann, L. R., Moise-Titus, J., Podolski, C. & Eron, L. D. (2003). Longitudinal relations between children's exposure to TV violence and their aggressive and violent behavior in young adulthood: 1977–1992. *Developmental Psychology, 39,* 201–221.

Hughes, C. (1998). Finding your marbles: Does preschoolers' strategic behavior predict later understanding of mind? *Developmental Psychology, 34,* 1326–1339.

Hughes, C., & Dunn, J. (1998). Understanding mind and emotion: Longitudinal associations with mental-state talk between young friends. *Developmental Psychology, 34,* 1026–1037.

Hughes, D., Rodriguez, J., Smith, E. P., Johnson, D. J., Stevenson, H. C., & Spicer, P. (2006). Parents' ethnic-racial socialization practices: A review of research and directions for future study. *Developmental Psychology, 42,* 747–770.

Hughes, J. N., Cavell, T. A., & Grossman, P. B. (1997). A positive view of self: Risk or protection for aggressive children? *Development and Psychopathology, 9,* 75–94.

Hughes, J. N., & Kwok, O. (2006). Classroom engagement mediates the effect of teacher–student support on elementary students' peer acceptance. *Journal of School Psychology, 43,* 465–480.

Hughes, J. N., & Kwok, O. (2007). Influence of student–teacher and parent–teacher relationships on lower achieving readers' engagement and achievement in the primary grades. *Journal of Educational Psychology, 99,* 39–51.

Hughes, J. N., Zhang, D., & Hill, C. R. (2006). Peer assessments of normative and individual teacher–student support predict social acceptance and engagement among low-achieving children. *Journal of School Psychology, 43,* 447–463.

Hughes, T. F., Andel, R., Small, B. J., Borenstein, A. R., & Mortimer, J. A. (2008). The association between social resources and cognitive change in older adults: Evidence from the Charlotte County Healthy Aging Study. *Journal of Gerontology, 63B,* P241–P244.

Huijbregts, S. C. J., Séguin, J. R., Zelazo, P. D., Parent, S., Japel, C., & Tremblay, R. E. (2006). Interrelations between maternal smoking during pregnancy, birth weight and sociodemographic factors in the prediction of early cognitive abilities. *Infant and Child Development, 15,* 593–607.

Huizink, A. C., & Mulder, E. J. (2006). Maternal smoking, drinking or cannabis use during pregnancy and neurobehavioral and cognitive functioning in human offspring. *Neuroscience and Biobehavioral Reviews, 30,* 24–41.

Hultman, C. M., Torrang, A., Tuvblad, C., Cnattingius, S., Larsson, J.-O., & Lichtenstein, P. (2007). Birth weight and attention-deficit/hyperactivity symptoms in childhood and early adolescence: A prospective Swedish twin study. *Journal of the American Academy of Child and Adolescent Psychiatry, 46,* 370–377.

Hultsch, D. F., Hertzog, C., Dixon, R. A., & Small, B. J. (1998). *Memory change in the aged.* New York: Cambridge University Press.

Hultsch, D. F., MacDonald, S. W. S., & Dixon, R. A. (2002). Variability in reaction time performance of younger and older adults. *Journal of Gerontology, 57B,* P101–P115.

Humphrey, T. (1978). Function of the nervous system during prenatal life. In U. Stave (Ed.), *Perinatal physiology* (pp. 651–683). New York: Plenum.

Hungerford, T. L. (2003). Is there an American way of aging? Income dynamics of the elderly in the United States and Germany. *Research on Aging, 25,* 435–455.

Hunnius, S., & Geuze, R. H. (2004a). Developmental changes in visual scanning of dynamic faces and abstract stimuli in infants: A longitudinal study. *Infancy, 6,* 231–255.

Hunnius, S., & Geuze, R. H. (2004b). Gaze shifting in infancy: A longitudinal study using dynamic faces and abstract stimuli. *Infant Behavior and Development, 27,* 397–416.

Hunt, C. E., & Hauck, F. R. (2006). Sudden infant death syndrome. *Canadian Medical Association Journal, 174,* 1861–1869.

Huotilainen, M., Kujala, A., Hotakainen, M., Parkkonen, L., Taulu, S., & Simola, J. (2005). Short-term memory functions of the human fetus recorded with magneto-encephalography. *NeuroReport, 16,* 81–84.

Hursh, D. (2007). Assessing No Child Left Behind and the rise of neoliberal education policies. *American Educational Research Journal, 44,* 493–518.

Hursti, U. K. (1999). Factors influencing children's food choice. *Annals of Medicine, 31, 26–32.*

Hurt, H., Brodsky, N. L., Roth, H., Malmud, E., & Giannetta, J. M. (2005). School performance of children with gestational cocaine exposure. *Neurotoxicology and Teratology, 27,* 203–211.

Husaini, B. A., Blasi, A. J., & Miller, O. (1999). Does public and private religiosity have a moderating effect on depression? A bi-racial study of elders in the American south. *International Journal of Aging and Human Development, 48,* 63–72.

Huston, A. C., & Alvarez, M. M. (1990). The socialization of gender role development in early adolescence. In R. Montemayor, G. R. Adams, & T. P. Gullotta (Eds.), *From childhood to adolescence: A transitional period?* (pp. 156–179). Newbury Park, CA: Sage.

Huston, A. C., Wright, J. C., Marquis, J., & Green, S. B. (1999). How young children spend their time: Television and other activities. *Developmental Psychology, 35,* 912–925.

Huston, P., McHale, S., & Crouter, A. (1986). When the honeymoon's over: Changes in the marriage relationship over the first year. In R. Gilmour & S. Duck (Eds.), *The emerging field of personal relationships* (pp. 109–132). Hillsdale, NJ: Erlbaum.

Huttenlocher, P. R. (2002). *Neural plasticity: The effects of environment on the development of the cerebral cortex.* Cambridge, MA: Harvard University Press.

Huyck, M. H. (1990). Gender differences in aging. In J. E. Birren & K. W. Schaie (Eds.), *Handbook of the psychology of aging* (3rd ed., pp. 124–134). New York: Academic Press.

Huyck, M. H. (1995). Marriage and close relationships of the marital kind. In R. Blieszner & V. H. Bedford (Eds.), *Handbook of aging and the family* (pp. 181–200). Westport, CT: Greenwood Press.

Huyck, M. H. (1996). Continuities and discontinuities in gender identity in midlife. In V. L. Bengtson (Ed.), *Adulthood and aging* (pp. 98–121). New York: Springer-Verlag.

Huyck, M. H. (1998). Gender roles and gender identity in midlife. In S. L. Willis & J. D. Reid (Eds.), *Life in the middle* (pp. 209–232). San Diego: Academic Press.

Hyde, J. S., Essex, M. J., Clark, R., & Klein, M. H. (2001). Maternity leave, women's employment,

and marital incompatibility. *Journal of Family Psychology, 15,* 476–491.
Hyde, T. B., Kruszon-Moran, D., McQuillan, G. M., Cossen, C., Forghani, B., & Reef, S. E. (2006). Rubella immunity levels in the United States population: has the threshold of viral elimination been reached? *Clinical Infectious Diseases, 43*(Suppl. 3), S146-S150.
Hyppönen, E., Power, C., & Smith, G. D. (2003). Prenatal growth, BMI, and risk of type 2 diabetes by early midlife. *Diabetes Care, 26,* 2512–2517.

I

Idler, E. L., & Kasl, S. V. (1997). Religion among disabled and nondisabled persons I: Cross-sectional patterns in health practices, social activities, and well-being. *Journal of Gerontology, 52B,* S294–S305.
Iglowstein, I., Jenni, O. G., Molinari, L., & Largo, R. H. (2003). Sleep duration from infancy to adolescence: Reference values and generational trends. *Pediatrics, 111,* 302–307.
Ihinger-Tallman, M., & Pasley, K. (1997). Stepfamilies in 1984 and today—A scholarly perspective. *Marriage and Family Review, 26,* 19–40.
Ikkink, K. K., & van Tilburg, T. (1998). Do older adults' network members continue to provide instrumental support in unbalanced relationships? *Journal of Social and Personal Relationships, 15,* 59–75.
Illeris, K. (2004). *Adult education and adult learning.* Melbourne, FL: Krieger Publishing.
Imai, M., & Haryu, E. (2004). The nature of word-learning biases and their roles for lexical development: From a cross-linguistic perspective. In D. G. Hall & S. R. Waxman (Eds.), *Weaving a lexicon* (pp. 411–444). Cambridge, MA: MIT Press.
Impett, E. A., & Peplau, L. A. (2006). "His" and "her" relationships? A review of the empirical evidence. In A. L. Vangelisti & D. Perlman (Eds.), *The Cambridge handbook of personal relationships* (pp. 273–292). New York: Cambridge University Press.
Indusekhar, R., Usman, S. B., & O'Brien, S. (2007). Psychological aspects of premenstrual syndrome. *Best Practice and Research Clinical Obstetrics and Gynecology, 21,* 207–210.
Ingram, D. K., Roth, G. S., Lane, M. A., Ottinger, M. A., Zou, S., de Cabo, R., & Mattison, J. A. (2006). The potential for dietary restriction to increase longevity in humans: Extrapolation from monkey studies. *Biogerontology, 7,* 143–148.
Inhelder, B., & Piaget, J. (1958). *The growth of logical thinking from childhood to adolescence: An essay on the construction of formal operational structures.* New York: Basic Books. (Original work published 1955)
Institute for Social Research. (2002). U.S. husbands do more housework. Ann Arbor: Author. Retrieved from: http://www.newswise.com/articles/2002/3/timeuse.umi.html
International Human Genome Sequencing Consortium. (2004). Finishing the euchronmatic sequence of the human genome. *Nature, 21,* 931–945.
Iocaboni, M., Molnar-Szakacs, I., Gallese, V., Buccino, G., & Mazziotta, J. C. (2005). Grasping the intentions of others with one's own mirror neuron system. *Public Library of Science: Biology, 3*(3), e79.
Irvine, A. B., Ary, D. V., & Bourgeois, M. S. (2003). An interactive multimedia program to train professional caregivers. *Journal of Applied Gerontology, 22,* 269–288.
Isabella, R. (1993). Origins of attachment: Maternal interactive behavior across the first year. *Child Development, 64,* 605–621.
Isabella, R., & Belsky, J. (1991). Interactional synchrony and the origins of infant–mother attachment: A replication study. *Child Development, 62,* 373–384.
Isasi, R. M., Nguyen, T. M., & Knoppers, B. M. (2006) *National regulatory frameworks regarding human genetic modification technologies (somatic and germline modification).* Montréal, Québec: Centre de Recherché en Droit Public (CRDP), Université de Montréal.
Ishihara, K., Warita, K., Tanida, T., Sugawara, T., Kitagawa, H., & Hoshi, N. (2007). Does paternal exposure to 2, 3, 7, 8-tetrachlorodibenzo-p-dioxin (TCDD) affect the sex ratio of offspring? *Journal of Veterinary Medical Science, 69,* 347–352.
Israel, M., Johnson, C., & Brooks, P. J. (2000). From states to events: The acquisition of English passive participles. *Cognitive Linguistics, 11,* 103–129.
Issa, A. M., Mojica, W. A., Morton, S. C., Traina, S., Newberry, S. J., Hilton, L. G., Garland, R. H., & MacLean, C. H. (2006). The efficacy of omega-3 fatty acids on cognitive function in aging and dementia: A systematic review. *Dementia and Geriatric Cognitive Disorders, 21,* 88–96.
Itti, E., Gaw, G. I. T., Pawlikowska-Haddal, A., Boone, K. B., Mlikotic, A., & Itti, L. (2006). The structural brain correlates of cognitive deficits in adults with Klinefelter's syndrome. *Journal of Clinical Endocrinology and Metabolism, 91,* 1423–1427.
Izard, C. E., & Ackerman, B. P. (2000). Motivational, organizational, and regulatory functions of discrete emotions. In M. Lewis & J. M. Haviland-Jones (Eds.), *Handbook of emotions* (2nd ed., pp. 253–264). New York: Guilford.
Izard, C. E., Hembree, E. A., & Huebner, R. R. (1987). Infants' emotional expressions to acute pain. *Developmental Psychology, 23,* 105–113.
Izard, C. E., Trentacosta, C. J., King, K. A., & Mostow, A. J. (2004). An emotion-based prevention program for Head Start children. *Early Education and Development, 15,* 407–422.

J

Jaakkola, J. J., & Gissler, M. (2004). Maternal smoking in pregnancy, fetal development, and childhood asthma. *American Journal of Public Health, 94,* 136–140.
Jaccard, J., Dodge, T., & Dittus, P. (2002). Parent–adolescent communication about sex and birth control: A conceptual framework. In S. S. Feldman & D. A. Rosenthal (Eds.), *Talking sexuality: Parent–adolescent communication* (pp. 9–41). San Francisco: Jossey-Bass.
Jaccard, J., Dodge, T., & Dittus, P. (2003). Maternal discussions about pregnancy and adolescents' attitudes toward pregnancy. *Journal of Adolescent Health, 33,* 84–87.
Jackson, G. R., & Owsley, C. (2000). Scotopic sensitivity during adulthood. *Vision Research, 40,* 2467–2473.
Jackson, R. A., Gibson, K. A., & Wu, Y. W. (2004). Perinatal outcomes in singletons following in vitro fertilization: A meta-analysis. *Obstetrics and Gynecology, 103,* 551–563.
Jackson, T., Fritch, A., Nagaska, T., & Gunderson, J. (2002). Towards explaining the association between shyness and loneliness: A path analysis with American college students. *Social Behavior and Personality, 30,* 263–270.
Jackson, V. A., Sullivan, A. M., Gadmer, N. M., Seltzer, D., Mitchell, A. M., & Lakoma, M. D. (2005). "It was haunting . . . ": Physicians' descriptions of emotionally powerful patient deaths. *Academic Medicine, 80,* 648–656.
Jacobs, J. A., & King, R. B. (2002). Age and college completion: A life-history analysis of women aged 15–44. *Sociology of Education, 75,* 211–230.
Jacobs, J. E., & Klaczynski, P. A. (2002). The development of judgment and decision making during childhood and adolescence. *Current Directions in Psychological Science, 11,* 145–149.
Jacobs, J. E., Lanza, S., Osgood, D. W., Eccles, J. S., & Wigfield, A. (2002). Changes in children's self-competence and values: Gender and domain differences across grades one through twelve. *Child Development, 73,* 509–527.
Jacobs, J. E., & Weisz, V. (1994). Gender stereotypes: Implications for gifted education. *Roeper Review, 16,* 152–155.
Jacobs, J. N., & Kelley, M. L. (2006). Predictors of paternal involvement in childcare in dual-earner families with young children. *Fathering, 4,* 23–47.
Jacobs-Lawson, J. M., Hershey, D. A., & Neukam, K. A. (2004). Gender differences in factors that influence time spent planning for retirement. *Journal of Women and Aging, 16,* 55–69.
Jacobson, J. L., & Jacobson, S. W. (2003). Prenatal exposure to polychlorinated biphenyls and attention at school age. *Journal of Pediatrics, 143,* 780–788.
Jacobson, K. C., & Crockett, L. J. (2000). Parental monitoring and adolescent adjustment: An ecological perspective. *Journal of Research on Adolescence, 10,* 65–97.
Jacobson, S. W., Jacobson, J. L., Sokol, R. J., Chiodo, L. M., & Corobana, R. (2004). Maternal age, alcohol abuse history, and quality of parenting as moderators of the effects of prenatal alcohol exposure on 7.5-year intellectual function. *Alcoholism: Clinical and Experimental Research, 28,* 1732–1745.
Jacquet, P. (2004). Sensitivity of germ cells and embryos to ionizing radiation. *Journal of Biological Regulators and Homeostatic Agents, 18,* 106–114.
Jadack, R. A., Hyde, J. S., Moore, C. F., & Keller, M. L. (1995). Moral reasoning about sexually transmitted diseases. *Child Development, 66,* 167–177.
Jaffe, J., Beebe, B., Feldstein, S., Crown, C. L., & Jasnow, M. D. (2001). Rhythms of dialogue in infancy. *Monographs of the Society for Research in Child Development, 66*(2, Serial No. 265).
Jaffee, S. R., Caspi, A., Moffitt, T. E., Belsky, J., & Silva, P. (2001). Why are children born to teen mothers at risk for adverse outcomes in young adulthood? Results of a 20-year longitudinal study. *Development and Psychopathology, 13,* 377–397.
Jaffee, S. R., & Hyde, J. S. (2000). Gender differences in moral orientation: A meta-analysis. *Psychological Bulletin, 126,* 703–706.
Jaffee, S. R., Moffitt, T. E., Caspi, A., & Taylor, A. (2003). Life with (or without) father: The benefits of living with two biological parents depend on the father's antisocial behavior. *Child Development, 74,* 109–126.
Jambunathan, S., Burts, D. C., & Pierce, S. (2000). Comparisons of parenting attitudes among five ethnic groups in the United States. *Journal of Comparative Family Studies, 31,* 395–406.
James, J. B., Lewkowicz, C., Libhaber, J., & Lachman, M. (1995). Rethinking the gender identity crossover hypothesis: A test of a new model. *Sex Roles, 32,* 185–207.
James, J. B., & Wink, P. (2007). The Third Age: A rationale for research. In J. B. James & P. Wink (Eds.), *Annual review of gerontology and geriatrics* (Vol. 26, pp. xix–xxxii). New York: Springer.
James, J. B., & Zarrett, N. (2007). Ego integrity in the lives of older women. *Journal of Adult Development, 13,* 61–75.

Jamieson, J. R. (1995). Interactions between mothers and children who are deaf. *Journal of Early Intervention, 19,* 108–117.

Jang, S. J., & Johnson, B. R. (2001). Neighborhood disorder, individual religiosity, and adolescent use of illicit drugs: A test of multilevel hypotheses. *Criminology, 39,* 109–143.

Jang, Y., Bergman, E., Schonfeld, L., & Molinari, V. (2007). The mediating role of health perceptions in the relation between physical and mental health: A study of older residents in assisted living facilities. *Journal of Aging and Health, 19,* 439–452.

Janosz, M., Le Blanc, M., Boulerice, B., & Tremblay, R. E. (2000). Predicting different types of school dropouts: A typological approach with two longitudinal samples. *Journal of Educational Psychology, 92,* 171–190.

Jansen, A., Theunissen, N., Slechten, K., Nederkoorn, C., Booth, B., Mulkens, S., & Roefs, A. (2003). Overweight children overeat after exposure to food cues. *Eating Behaviors, 4,* 197–209.

Janssens, J. M. A. M., & Deković, M. (1997). Child rearing, prosocial moral reasoning, and prosocial behaviour. *International Journal of Behavioral Development, 20,* 509–527.

Jarvis, J. F., & van Heerden, H. G. (1967). The acuity of hearing in the Kalahari Bushman: A pilot study. *Journal of Laryngology and Otology, 81,* 63–68.

Jayakody, R., & Cabrera, N. (2002). What are the choices for low-income families? Cohabitation, marriage, and remaining single. In A. Booth & A. C. Crouter (Eds.), *Just living together* (pp. 85–96). Mahwah, NJ: Erlbaum.

Jayakody, R., & Kalil, A. (2002). Social fathering in low-income, African-American families with preschool children. *Journal of Marriage and Family, 64,* 504–516.

Jeffrey, J. (2004, November). Parents often blind to their kids' weight. *British Medical Journal Online.* Retrieved from content.health.msn.com/content/article/97/104292.htm

Jellinger, K. A. (2004). Head injury and dementia. *Current Opinion in Neurology, 17,* 719–723.

Jellinger, K. A. (2008). Morphologic diagnosis of "vascular dementia"—a critical update. *Journal of the Neurological Sciences, 270,* 1–12.

Jemal, A., Siegel, R., Ward, E., Hao, Y., Xu, J., Murray, T., & Thun, M. J. (2008). Cancer statistics, 2008. *CA: Cancer Journal for Clinicians, 58,* 71–96.

Jendrek, M. P. (1994). Grandparents who parent their grandchildren: Circumstances and decisions. *Gerontologist, 34,* 206–216.

Jenkins, J. M., Rasbash, J., & O'Connor, T. G. (2003). The role of the shared family context in differential parenting. *Developmental Psychology, 39,* 99–113.

Jenkins, J. M., Turrell, S. L., Kogushi, Y., Lollis, S., & Ross, H. S. (2003). A longitudinal investigation of the dynamics of mental state talk in families. *Child Development, 74,* 905–920.

Jenkins, K. R., Pienta, A. M., & Horgas, A. L. (2002). Activity and health-related quality of life in continuing care retirement communities. *Research on Aging, 24,* 124–149.

Jennings, B. J., Ozanne, S. E., Dorling, M. W., & Hales, C. N. (1999). Early growth determines longevity in male rats and may be related to telomere shortening in the kidney. *FEBS Letters, 448,* 4–8.

Jensen, A. R. (1969). How much can we boost IQ and scholastic achievement? *Harvard Educational Review, 39,* 1–123.

Jensen, A. R. (1998). *The g factor: The science of mental ability.* New York: Praeger.

Jensen, A. R. (2001). Spearman's hypothesis. In J. M. Collis & S. Messick (Eds.), *Intelligence and personality: Bridging the gap in theory and measurement* (pp. 3–24). Mahwah, NJ: Erlbaum.

Jensen, A. R. (2002). Galton's legacy to research on intelligence. *Journal of Biosocial Science, 34,* 145–172.

Jeon, Y.-H., Brodaty, H., & Chesterson, J. (2005). Respite care for caregivers and people with severe mental illness: Literature review. *Journal of Advanced Nursing, 49,* 297–306.

Jepson, K. L., & Labouvie-Vief, G. (1992). Symbolic processing of youth and elders. In R. L. West and J. D. Sinnott (Eds.), *Everyday memory and aging* (pp. 124–137). New York: Springer.

Jeynes, W. H. (2005). A meta-analysis of the relation of parental involvement to urban elementary school student academic achievement. *Urban Education, 40,* 237–269.

Jiao, S., Ji, G., & Jing, Q. (1996). Cognitive development of Chinese urban only children and children with siblings. *Child Development, 67,* 387–395.

Jneid, H., Fonarow, G. C., Cannon, C. P., Hernandez, A. F., Palacios, I. F., & Maree, A. O. (2008). Sex differences in medical care and early death after acute myocardial infarction. *Circulation, 118,* 2803–2810.

Joh, A. S., & Adolph, K. E. (2006). Learning from falling. *Child Development, 77,* 89–102.

John, U., Meyer, C., Rumpf, H. J., & Hapke, U. (2003). Probabilities of alcohol high-risk drinking, abuse or dependence estimating on grounds of tobacco smoking and nicotine dependence. *Addiction, 98,* 805–814.

Johnson, C. L. (1998). Effects of adult children's divorce on grandparenthood. In M. E. Szinovacz (Ed.), *Handbook on grandparenthood* (pp. 87–96). Westport, CT: Greenwood Press.

Johnson, C. L., & Troll, L. E. (1994). Constraints and facilitators to friendships in late life. *Gerontologist, 34,* 79–87.

Johnson, D. E. (2000). Medical and developmental sequelae of early childhood institutionalization in Eastern European adoptees. In C. A. Nelson (Ed.), *Minnesota symposia on child psychology* (Vol. 31, pp. 113–162). Mahwah, NJ: Erlbaum.

Johnson, D. E. (2002). Adoption and the effect on children's development. *Early Human Development, 68,* 39–54.

Johnson, J. G., Cohen, P., Smailes, E. M., Kasen, S., & Brook, J. S. (2002). Television viewing and aggressive behavior during adolescence and adulthood. *Science, 295,* 2468–2471.

Johnson, J., Im-Bolter, N., & Pascual-Leone, J. (2003). Development of mental attention in gifted and mainstream children: The role of mental capacity, inhibition, and speed of processing. *Child Development, 74,* 1594–1614.

Johnson, K. C., & Daviss, B.-A. (2005). Outcomes of planned home births with certified professional midwives: Large prospective study in North America. *British Medical Journal, 330,* 1416.

Johnson, K. S., Elbert-Avila, K. I., & Tulsky, J. A. (2005). The influence of spiritual beliefs and practices on the treatment preferences of African Americans: A review of the literature. *Journal of the American Geriatrics Society, 53,* 711–719.

Johnson, K. S., Juchibhatla, M., Tanis, D., & Tulsky, J. A. (2008). Racial differences in hospice revocation to pursue aggressive care. *Archives of Internal Medicine, 168,* 218–224.

Johnson, M. D., Cohan, C. L., Davilla, J., Lawrence, E., Rogge, R. D., Karney, B. R., Sullivan, K. T., & Bradbury, T. N. (2005). Problem-solving skills and affective expressions as predictors of change in marital satisfaction. *Journal of Consulting and Clinical Psychology, 73,* 15–27.

Johnson, M. H. (1999). Ontogenetic constraints on neural and behavioral plasticity: Evidence from imprinting and face processing. *Canadian Journal of Experimental Psychology, 55,* 77–90.

Johnson, M. H. (2001). The development and neural basis of face recognition: Comment and speculation. *Infant and Child Development, 10,* 31–33.

Johnson, M. H. (2005). Developmental neuroscience, psychophysiology, and genetics. In M. H. Bornstein & M. E. Lamb (Eds.), *Developmental science: An advanced textbook* (5th ed., pp. 187–222). Mahwah, NJ: Erlbaum.

Johnson, S. C., Dweck, C. S., & Chen, F. S. (2007). Evidence for infants' internal working models of attachment. *Psychological Science, 18,* 501–502.

Johnson, S. P., Slemmer, J. A., & Amso, D. (2004). Where infants look determines how they see: Eye movements and object perception performance in 3-month-olds. *Infancy, 6,* 185–201.

Johnson, W., & Krueger, R. F. (2007). The psychological benefits of vigorous exercise: A study of discordant MZ twin pairs. *Twin Research and Human Genetics, 10,* 275–285.

Johnston, L. D., O'Malley, P. M., Bachman, J. G., & Schulenberg, J. E. (2008). *Monitoring the future: National results on adolescent drug use.* Bethesda: MD: U.S. Department of Health and Human Services.

Johnston, M. V., Nishimura, A., Harum, K., Pekar, J., & Blue, M. E. (2001). Sculpting the developing brain. *Advances in Pediatrics, 48,* 1–38.

Johnston, M., Pollard, B., Morrison, V., & MacWalter, R. (2004). Functional limitations and survival following stroke: Psychological and clinical predictors of 3 year outcome. *International Journal of Behavioral Medicine, 11,* 187–196.

Jome, L. M., Surething, N. A., & Taylor, K. K. (2005). Relationally oriented masculinity, gender nontraditional interests, and occupational traditionality of employed men. *Journal of Career Development, 32,* 183–197.

Jones, C. M., Braithwaite, V. A., & Healy, S. D. (2003). The evolution of sex differences in spatial ability. *Behavioral Neuroscience, 117,* 403–411.

Jones, E. F., & Thompson, N. R. (2001). Action perception and outcome valence: Effects on children's inferences of intentionality and moral and liking judgments. *Journal of Genetic Psychology, 162,* 154–166.

Jones, F. (2003). *Religious commitment in Canada, 1997 and 2000. Religious Commitment Monograph No. 3.* Ottawa: Christian Commitment Research Institute.

Jones, G. P., & Dembo, M. H. (1989). Age and sex role differences in intimate friendships during childhood and adolescence. *Merrill-Palmer Quarterly, 35,* 445–462.

Jones, H. E. (2006). Drug addiction during pregnancy: Advances in maternal treatment and understanding child outcomes. *Current Directions in Psychological Science, 15,* 126–130.

Jones, J., Lopez, A., & Wilson, M. (2003). Congenital toxoplasmosis. *American Family Physician, 67,* 2131–2137.

Jones, K. M., Whitbourne, S. K., & Skultety, K. M. (2006). Identity processes and the transition to midlife among the baby boomers. In S. K. Whitbourne & S. L. Willis (Eds.), *The baby boomers grow up: Contemporary perspectives on midlife* (pp. 149–164). Mahwah, NJ: Erlbaum.

Jones, M. C., & Mussen, P. H. (1958). Self-conceptions, motivations, and interpersonal attitudes of early- and late-maturing girls. *Child Development, 29,* 491–501.

Jones, N. A., Field, T., & Davalos, M. (2000). Right frontal EEG asymmetry and lack of empathy in preschool children of depressed mothers. *Child Psychiatry and Human Development, 30,* 189–204.

Jones, R. K., Purcell, A., Singh, S., & Finer, L. B. (2005). Adolescents' reports of parental knowledge of adolescents' use of sexual health services and

their reactions to mandated parental notification for prescription contraceptives. *Journal of the American Medical Association, 293,* 340–348.
Jones, R. L., Homa, D. M., Meyer, P. A., Brody, D. J., Caldwell, K. L., Pirkle J. L., et al. (2009). Trends in blood lead levels and blood lead testing among U.S. children aged 1 to 5 years: 1998–2004. *Pediatrics, 123,* e376 385.
Jones, W. H. (1990). Loneliness and social exclusion. *Journal of Social and Clinical Psychology, 9,* 214–220.
Jongbloet, P. H., Zielhuis, G. A., Groenewoud, H. M., & Pasker-De Jong, P. C. (2001). The secular trends in male: female ratio at birth in postwar industrialized countries. *Environmental Health Perspectives, 109,* 749–752.
Jopp, D., & Rott, C. (2006). Adaptation in very old age: Exploring the role of resources, beliefs, and attitudes for centenarians' happiness. *Psychology and Aging, 21,* 266–280.
Jordan, B. (1993). *Birth in four cultures.* Prospect Heights, IL: Waveland.
Jordon, J., & Neimeyer, R. (2003). Does grief counseling work? *Death Studies, 27,* 765–786.
Jose, P., Huntsinger, C., Huntsinger, P., & Liaw, F.-R. (2000). Parental values and practices relevant to young children's social development in Taiwan and the United States. *Journal of Cross-Cultural Psychology, 31,* 677–702.
Joseph, R. M., & Tager-Flusberg, H. (2004). The relationship of theory of mind and executive functions to symptom type and severity in children with autism. *Development and Psychopathology, 16,* 137–155.
Joyner, M. H., & Kurtz-Costes, B. (1997). Metamemory development. In W. Schneider & F. E. Weinert (Eds.), *Memory performance and competencies: Issues in growth and development* (pp. 275–300). Hillsdale, NJ: Erlbaum.
Julkunen, J. (1996). Suppressing your anger: Good manners, bad health? In C. D. Spielberger & I. G. Sarason (Eds.), *Stress and emotion: Anxiety, anger, and curiosity* (Vol. 16, pp. 227–240). Washington, DC: Taylor & Francis.
Julkunen, J., & Ahlström, R. (2006). Hostility, anger, and sense of coherence as predictors of health-related quality of life. Results of an ASCOT substudy. *Journal of Psychosomatic Research, 61,* 33–39.
Juntunen, C. L., Wegner, K. E., & Matthews, L. G. (2002). Promoting positive career change in midlife. In C. L. Juntunen & D. R. Atkinson (Eds.), *Counseling across the lifespan* (pp. 329–347). Thousand Oaks, CA: Sage.
Jusczyk, P. W. (2001). In the beginning, was the word. . . . In F. Lacerda & C. von Hofsten (Eds.), *Emerging cognitive abilities in early infancy* (pp. 173–192). Mahwah, NJ: Erlbaum.
Jusczyk, P. W. (2002). Some critical developments in acquiring native language sound organization. *Annals of Otology, Rhinology and Laryngology, 189,* 11–15.
Jusczyk, P. W., & Hohne, E. A. (1997). Infants' memory for spoken words. *Science, 277,* 1984–1986.
Jusczyk, P. W., & Luce, P. A. (2002). Speech perception. In H. Pashler & S. Yantis (Eds.), *Stevens' handbook of experimental psychology: Vol. 1. Sensation and perception* (3rd ed., pp. 493–536). New York: Wiley.

K

Kagan, J. (2003). Behavioral inhibition as a temperamental category. In R. J. Davidson, K. R. Scherer, & H. H. Goldsmith (Eds.), *Handbook of affective science* (pp. 320–331). New York: Oxford University Press.
Kagan, J. (2008). In defense of qualitative changes in development. *Child Development, 79,* 1606–1624.
Kagan, J., Arcus, D., Snidman, N., Feng, W. Y. Hendler, J., & Greene, S. (1994). Reactivity in infants: A cross-national comparison. *Developmental Psychology, 30,* 342–345.
Kagan, J., & Fox, N. A. (2006). Biology, culture, and temperamental biases. In N. Eisenberg (Ed.), *Handbook of child psychology: Vol. 3. Social, emotional, and personality development* (6th ed., pp. 167–225). Hoboken, NJ: Wiley.
Kagan, J., & Saudino, K. J. (2001). Behavioral inhibition and related temperaments. In R. N. Emde & J. K. Hewitt (Eds.), *Infancy to early childhood: Genetic and environmental influences on developmental change* (pp. 111–119). New York: Oxford University Press.
Kagan, J., & Snidman, N. (2004). *The long shadow of temperament.* Cambridge, MA: Belknap Press.
Kagan, J., Snidman, N., Kahn, V., & Towsley, S. (2007). The preservation of two infant temperaments into adolescence. *Monographs of the Society for Research in Child Development, 72*(2, Serial No. 287).
Kagan, J., Snidman, N., Zentner, M., & Peterson, E. (1999). Infant temperament and anxious symptoms in school-age children. *Development and Psychopathology, 11,* 209–224.
Kagawa, Y. (1978). Impact of westernization on the nutrition of Japanese: Changes in physique, cancer, longevity, and centenarians. *Preventive Medicine, 7,* 205–217.
Kahana, E., King, C., Kahana, B., Menne, H., Webster, N. J., & Dan, A. (2005). Successful aging in the face of chronic disease. In M. L. Wykle, P. J. Whitehouse, & D. L. Morris (Eds.), *Successful aging through the life span* (pp. 101–126). New York: Springer.
Kahn, P. H., Jr. (1992). Children's obligatory and discretionary moral judgments. *Child Development, 63,* 416–430.
Kail, R. V. (2003). Information processing and memory. In M. H. Bornstein, L. Davidson, C. L. M. Keyes, K. A. Moore, and the Center for Child Well-Being (Eds.), *Well-being: Positive development across the life course* (pp. 269–280). Mahwah, NJ: Erlbaum.
Kail, R. V., & Park, Y. (1992). Global developmental change in processing time. *Merrill-Palmer Quarterly, 38,* 525–541.
Kail, R. V., & Park, Y. (1994). Processing time, articulation time, and memory span. *Journal of Experimental Child Psychology, 57,* 281–291.
Kaisa, A., Stattin, H., & Nurmi, J. (2000). Parenting styles and adolescents' achievement strategies. *Journal of Adolescence, 23,* 205–222.
Kalache, A., Aboderin, I., & Hoskins, I. (2002). Compression of morbidity and active ageing: Key priorities for public health policy in the 21st century. *Bulletin of the World Health Organization, 80,* 243–244.
Kalies, H., Heinrich, J., Borte, N., Schaaf, B., von Berg, A., & von Kries, R. (2005). The effect of breastfeeding on weight gain in infants: Results of a birth cohort study. *European Journal of Medical Research, 10,* 36–42.
Kalil, A., Levine, J. A., & Ziol-Guest, K. M. (2005). Following in their parents' footsteps: How characteristics of parental work predict adolescents' interest in parents' working jobs. In B. Schneider & L. J. Waite (Eds.), *Being together, working apart: Dual-career families and the work–life balance* (pp. 422–442). New York: Cambridge University Press.
Kalish, R. A. (1985). The social context of death and dying. In R. H. Binstock & E. Shanas (Eds.), *Handbook of aging and the social sciences* (2nd ed., pp. 149–170). New York: Van Nostrand Reinhold.
Kalof, L. (2000). Ethnic differences in female sexual victimization. *Sexuality and Culture, 2,* 75–97.
Kamo, Y. (1998). Asian grandparents. In M. E. Szinovacz (Ed.), *Handbook on grandparenthood* (pp. 97–112). Westport, CT: Greenwood Press.
Kane, C. M. (2000). African-American family dynamics as perceived by family members. *Journal of Black Studies, 30,* 691–702.
Kane, P., & Garber, J. (2004). The relations among depression in fathers, children's psychopathology, and father–child conflict: A meta-analysis. *Clinical Psychology Review, 24,* 339–360.
Kane, R. A., Lum, T. Y., Cutler, L. J., Degenholtz, H. B., & Yu, T.-C. (2007). Resident outcomes in small-house nursing homes: A longitudinal evaluation of the initial Green House program. *Journal of the American Geriatrics Society, 55,* 836–839.
Kaplan, D. L., & Keys, C. B. (1997). Sex and relationship variables as predictors of sexual attraction in cross-sex platonic friendships between young heterosexual adults. *Journal of Social and Personal Relationships, 14,* 191–206.
Kaplowitz, P. (2006). Pubertal development in girls: Secular trends. *Current Opinion in Obstetrics and Gynecology, 18,* 487–491.
Karafantis, D. M., & Levy, S. R. (2004). The role of children's lay theories about the malleability of human attributes in beliefs about and volunteering for disadvantaged groups. *Child Development, 75,* 236–250.
Karger, H., & Stoesz, D. (2008). *American social welfare policy: A pluralist approach.* Boston: Allyn & Bacon.
Karpati, A. M., Rubin, C. H., Kieszak, S. M., Marcus, M., & Troiano, R. P. (2002). Stature and pubertal stage assessment in American boys: The 1988–1994 Third National Health and Nutrition Examination Survey. *Journal of Adolescent Health, 30,* 205–212.
Karpov, Y. (2005). *The neo-Vygotskian approach to child development.* New York: Cambridge University Press.
Kasmauski, K., & Jaret, P. (2003). *Impact: On the frontlines of global health.* Washington, DC: National Geographic.
Kassel, J. D., Weinstein, S., Skitch, S. A., Veilleux, J., & Mermelstein, R. (2005). The development of substance abuse in adolescence: Correlates, causes, and consequences. In J. D. Kassel, S. Weinstein, S. A. Skitch, J. Veilleux, & R. Mermelstein (Eds.), *Development of psychopathology: A vulnerability-stress perspective* (pp. 355–384). Thousand Oaks, CA: Sage.
Kastenbaum, R. J. (2009). *Death, society, and human experience* (10th ed.). Boston: Allyn and Bacon.
Kato, I., Franco, P., Groswasser, J., Scaillet, S., Kelmanson, I., Togari, H., & Kahn, A. (2003). Incomplete arousal processes in infants who were victims of sudden death. *American Journal of Respiratory and Critical Care, 168,* 1298–1303.
Katz, L. F., & Windecker-Nelson, B. (2004). Parental meta-emotion philosophy in families with conduct-problem children: Links with peer relations. *Journal of Abnormal Child Psychology, 32,* 385–398.
Katzman, D. K. (2005). Medical complications in adolescents with anorexia nervosa: A review of the literature. *International Journal of Eating Disorders, 37,* S52–S59.
Kaufman, A. S. (2001). WAIS-III IQs, Horn's theory, and generational changes from young adulthood to old age. *Intelligence, 29,* 131–167.
Kaufman, A. S., & Horn, J. L. (1996). Age changes on tests of fluid and crystallized intelligence for females and males on the Kaufman Adolescent and Adult Intelligence Test (KAIT) at ages 17 to 94

years. *Archives of Clinical Neuropsychology, 11,* 97–121.

Kaufman, J., Csibra, G., & Johnson, M. H. (2005). Oscillatory activity in the infant brain reflects object maintenance. *Proceedings of the National Academy of Sciences, 102,* 15271–15274.

Kausler, D. H. (1994). *Learning and memory in normal aging.* San Diego: Academic Press.

Kavanaugh, R. D. (2006). Pretend play. In B. Spodek & O. N. Saracho (Eds.), *Handbook of research on the education of young children* (2nd ed., pp. 269–278). Mahwah, NJ: Erlbaum.

Kavsek, M. (2004). Predicting later IQ from infant visual habituation and dishabituation: A meta-analysis. *Journal of Applied Developmental Psychology, 25,* 369–393.

Kaye, K., & Marcus, J. (1981). Infant imitation: The sensory-motor agenda. *Developmental Psychology, 17,* 258–265.

Kaye, W. (2008). Neurobiology of anorexia and bulimia nervosa. *Physiology and Behavior, 94,* 121–135.

Kazdin, A. E. (2003). Problem-solving skills training and parent management training for conduct disorder. In A. E. Kazdin & J. R. Weisz (Eds.), *Evidence-based psychotherapies for children and adolescents* (pp. 241–262). New York: Guilford.

Kazdin, A. E., & Whitley, M. E. (2003). Treatment of parental stress to enhance therapeutic change among children referred for aggressive and antisocial behavior. *Journal of Consulting and Clinical Psychology, 71,* 504–515.

Keating, D. P. (1979). Adolescent thinking. In J. Adelson (Ed.), *Handbook of adolescent psychology* (pp. 211–246). New York: Wiley.

Keating, D. P. (1990). Adolescent thinking. In S. S. Feldman & G. R. Elliott (Eds.), *At the threshold* (pp. 54–89). Cambridge, MA: Harvard University Press.

Keating, D. P. (2004). Cognitive and brain development. In R. M. Lerner & L. Steinberg (Eds.), *Handbook of adolescent psychology* (2nd ed., pp. 45–84). Hoboken, NJ: Wiley.

Keil, F. C. (1986). Conceptual domains and the acquisition of metaphor. *Cognitive Development, 1,* 73–96.

Keil, F. C., & Lockhart, K. L. (1999). Explanatory understanding in conceptual development. In E. K. Scholnick, K. Nelson, S. A. Gelman, & P. H. Miller (Eds.), *Conceptual development: Piaget's legacy* (pp. 103–130). Mahwah, NJ: Erlbaum.

Keith, J., Fry, C. L., Glascock, A. P., Ikels, C., Dickerson-Putman, J., Harpending, H. C., & Draper, P. (1994). *The aging experience: Diversity and commonality across cultures.* Thousand Oaks, CA: Sage.

Keith, P. M., & Schafer, R. B. (1991). *Relationships and well-being over the life stages.* New York: Praeger.

Keith, T. Z., Keith, P. B., Quirk, K. J., Sperduto, J., Santillo, S., & Killings, S. (1998). Longitudinal effects of parent involvement on high school grades: Similarities and differences across gender and ethnic groups. *Journal of School Psychology, 36,* 335–363.

Keller, H., Borke, Y. J., Kärtner, J., Jensen, H., & Papaligoura, Z. (2004). Developmental consequences of early parenting experiences: Self-recognition and self-regulation in three cultural communities. *Child Development, 75,* 1745–1760.

Keller, H., Kärtner, J., Borke, J., Yovsi, R., & Kleis, A. (2005). Parenting styles and the development of the categorical self: A longitudinal study on mirror self-recognition in Cameroonian Nso and German families. *International Journal of Behavioral Development, 29,* 496–504.

Keller, S. N., & Brown, J. D. (2002). Media interventions to promote responsible sexual behavior. *Journal of Sex Research, 39,* 67–72.

Kelley, S. A., Brownell, C. A., & Campbell, S. B. (2000). Mastery motivation and self-evaluative affect in toddlers: Longitudinal relations with maternal behavior. *Child Development, 71,* 1061–1071.

Kelley, S. S., Borawski, E. A., Flocke, S. A., & Keen, K. J. (2003). The role of sequential and concurrent sexual relationships in the risk of sexually transmitted diseases among adolescents. *Journal of Adolescent Health, 32,* 296–305.

Kellman, P. J., & Arterberry, M. E. (2006). Infant visual perception. In D. Kuhn & R. Siegler (Eds.), *Handbook of child psychology: Vol. 2. Cognition, perception, and language* (6th ed., pp. 109–160). Hoboken, NJ: Wiley.

Kelly, D. J., Liu, S., Ge, L., Quinn, P. C., Slater, A. M., Lee, K., Liu, Q., & Pascalis, O. (2007). Cross-race preferences for same-race faces extend beyond the African versus Caucasian contrast in 3-month-old infants. *Infancy, 11,* 87–95.

Kelly, N., & Norwich, B. (2004). Pupils' perceptions of self and of labels: Moderate learning difficulties in mainstream and special schools. *British Journal of Educational Psychology, 74,* 411–435.

Kemeny, M. E. (2003). The psychobiology of stress. *Current Directions in Psychological Science, 12,* 124–129.

Kemkes-Grottenhaler, A. (2003). Postponing or rejecting parenthood? Results of a survey among female academic professionals. *Journal of Biosocial Science, 35,* 213–226.

Kemp, E. A., & Kemp, J. E. (2002). *Older couples: New romances.* Berkeley, CA: Celestial Arts.

Kempe, C. H., Silverman, B. F., Steele, P. W., Droegemueller, P. W., & Silver, H. K. (1962). The battered-child syndrome. *Journal of the American Medical Association, 181,* 17–24.

Kemper, S., Kynette, D., & Norman, S. (1992). Age differences in spoken language. In R. L. West & J. D. Sinnott (Eds.), *Everyday memory and aging* (pp. 138–152). New York: Springer-Verlag.

Kemper, S., Thompson, M., & Marquis, J. (2001). Longitudinal change in language production: Effects of aging and dementia on grammatical complexity and prepositional content. *Psychology and Aging, 16,* 600–614.

Kendig, H., Dykstra, P. A., van Gaalen, R. I., & Melkas, T. (2007). Health of aging parents and childless individuals. *Journal of Family Issues, 28,* 1457–1486.

Kendler, K. S., Thornton, L. M., Gilman, S. E., & Kessler, R. C. (2000). Sexual orientation in a U.S. national sample of twin and non-twin sibling pairs. *American Journal of Psychiatry, 157,* 1843–1846.

Kendrick, D., Barlow, J., Hampshire, A., Stewart-Brown, S., & Polnay, L. (2008). Parenting interventions and the prevention of unintentional injuries in childhood: Systematic review and meta-analysis. *Child: Care, Health and Development, 34,* 682–695.

Kennedy, A. M., & Gust, D. A. (2008). Measles outbreak associated with a church congregation: A study of immunization attitudes of congregation members. *Public Health Reports, 123,* 126–134.

Kennedy, G. E., & Kennedy, C. E. (1993). Grandparents: A special resource for children in stepfamilies. *Journal of Divorce and Remarriage, 19,* 45–68.

Kennedy, Q., Fung, H. H., & Carstensen, L. L. (2001). Aging, time estimation, and emotion. In S. H. McFadden & R. C. Atchley (Eds.), *Aging and the meaning of time: A multidisciplinary exploration* (pp. 51–73). New York: Springer.

Kennell, J., Klaus, M., McGrath, S., Robertson, S., & Hinkley, C. (1991). Continuous emotional support during labor in a U.S. hospital. *Journal of the American Medical Association, 265,* 2197–2201.

Kenney-Benson, G. A., Pomerantz, E. M. Ryan, A. M., & Patrick, H. (2006). Sex differences in math performance: The role of children's approach to schoolwork. *Developmental Psychology, 42,* 11–26.

Kenyon, B. L. (2001). Current research in children's conceptions of death: A critical review. *Omega, 43,* 63–91.

Kerber, R. A., O'Brien, E., Smith, K. R., & Cawthon, R. M. (2001). Familial excess longevity in Utah genealogies. *Journals of Gerontology, 567,* B130–B139.

Kerckhoff, A. C. (2002). The transition from school to work. In J. T. Mortimer & R. Larson (Eds.), *The changing adolescent experience* (pp. 52–87). New York: Cambridge University Press.

Keren, M., Feldman, R., Namdari-Weinbaum, I., Spitzer, S., & Tyano, S. (2005). Relations between parents' interactive style in dyadic and triadic play and toddlers' symbolic capacity. *American Journal of Orthopsychiatry, 75,* 599–607.

Kerestes, M., & Youniss, J. E. (2003). Rediscovering the importance of religion in adolescent development. In R. M. Lerner, F. Jacobs, & D. Wertlieb (Eds.), *Handbook of applied developmental science* (Vol. 1, pp. 165–184). Thousand Oaks, CA: Sage.

Kerestes, M., Youniss, J., & Metz, E. (2004). Longitudinal patterns of religious perspective and civic integration. *Applied Developmental Science, 8,* 39–46.

Kernis, M. H. (2002). Self-esteem as a multifaceted construct. In T. M. Brinthaupt & R. P. Lipka (Eds.), *Understanding early adolescent self and identity* (pp. 57–88). Albany, NY: State University of New York Press.

Kernohan, W. G., Hasson, F., Hutchison, P., & Cochrane, B. (2006). Patient satisfaction with hospice day care. *Supportive Care in Cancer, 14,* 462–468.

Kerpelman, J. L., Shoffner, M. F., & Ross-Griffin, S. (2002). African American mothers' and daughters' beliefs about possible selves and their strategies for reaching the adolescent's future academic and career goals. *Journal of Youth and Adolescence, 31,* 289–302.

Kerr, D. C. R., Lopez, N. L., Olson, S. L., & Sameroff, A. J. (2004). Parental discipline and externalizing behavior problems in early childhood: The roles of moral regulation and child gender. *Journal of Abnormal Child Psychology, 32,* 369–383.

Kesler, S. R. (2007). Turner syndrome. *Child and Adolescent Psychiatric Clinics of North America, 16,* 709–722.

Kessler, R. C., Adler, L. A., Barkley R., Biederman, J., Conners, C. K., & Demler, O. (2006). The prevalence and correlates of adult ADHD in the United States: Results from the National Comorbidity Survey Replication. *American Journal of Psychiatry, 163,* 716–723.

Kessler, R. C., Adler, L. A., Barkley, R., Biederman, J., Conners, C. K., & Faraone, S. V. (2005). Patterns and predictors of attention-deficit/hyperactivity disorder persistence into adulthood: Results from the National Comorbidity Survey Replication. *Biological Psychiatry, 57,* 1442–1451.

Kettl, P. (1998). Alaska Native suicide: Lessons for elder suicide. *International Psychogeriatrics, 10,* 205–211.

Kettunen, J. A., & Kujala, U. M. (2004). Exercise therapy for people with rheumatoid arthritis and osteoarthritis. *Scandinavian Journal of Medicine and Science in Sports, 14,* 138–142.

Keyes, C. L. M., & Ryff, C. D. (1998a). Generativity and adult lives: Social structural contours and quality of life consequences. In D. P. McAdams & E. de St. Aubin (Eds.), *Generativity and adult development: How and why we care for the next generation* (pp. 227–263). Washington, DC: American Psychological Association.

Keyes, C. L. M., & Ryff, C. D. (1998b). Psychological well-being in midlife. In S. L. Willis & J. D. Reid (Eds.), *Life in the middle* (pp. 161–180). San Diego: Academic Press.

Keyes, C. L. M., Shmotkin, D., & Ryff, C. D. (2002). Optimizing well-being: The empirical encounter of two traditions. *Journal of Personality and Social Psychology, 82,* 1007–1022.

Kiebzak, G. M., Beinart, G. A., Perser, K., Ambrose, C. G., Siff, S. J., & Heggeness, M. H. (2002). Undertreatment of osteoporosis in men with hip fracture. *Archives of Internal Medicine, 162,* 2217–2222.

Kiecolt-Glaser, J. K., Bane, C., Glaser, R., & Malarkey, W. B. (2003). Love, marriage, and divorce: Newlyweds' stress hormones foreshadow relationship changes. *Journal of Consulting and Clinical Psychology, 71,* 176–188.

Kiernan, K. (2001). European perspectives on nonmarital childbearing. In L. L. Wu & B. Wolfe (Eds.), *Out of wedlock: Causes and consequences of nonmarital fertility* (pp. 77–108). New York: Russell Sage Foundation.

Kiernan, K. (2002). Cohabitation in Western Europe: Trends, issues, and implications. In A. Booth & A. C. Crouter (Eds.), *Just living together* (pp. 3–32). Mahwah, NJ: Erlbaum.

Killen, M., Crystal, D., & Watanabe, H. (2002). The individual and the group: Japanese and American children's evaluations of peer exclusion, tolerance of difference, and prescriptions for conformity. *Child Development, 73,* 1788–1802.

Killen, M., Lee-Kim, J., McGlothlin, H., & Stangor, C. (2002). How children and adolescents evaluate gender and racial exclusion. *Monographs of the Society for Research in Child Development, 67*(4, Serial No. 271).

Killen, M., Margie, N. G., & Sinno, S. (2006). Morality in the context of intergroup relationships. In M. Killen & J. G. Smetana (Eds.), *Handbook of moral development* (pp. 155–183). Mahwah, NJ: Erlbaum.

Killen, M., & Nucci, L. P. (1995). Morality, autonomy, and social conflict. In M. Killen & D. Hart (Eds.), *Morality in everyday life: Developmental perspectives* (pp. 52–86). Cambridge, UK: Cambridge University Press.

Killian, T., Turner, J., & Cain, R. (2005). Depressive symptoms of caregiving women in midlife: The role of physical health. *Journal of Women and Aging, 17,* 115–127.

Kilpatrick, S. D., Bissonnette, V. L., & Rusbult, C. E. (2002). Empathic accuracy and accommodative behavior among newly married couples. *Personal Relationships, 9,* 369–393.

Kilpatrick, S. W., & Sanders, D. M. (1978). Body image stereotypes: A developmental comparison. *Journal of Genetic Psychology, 132,* 87–95.

Kim, A., & Merriam, S. B. (2004). Motivations for learning among older adults in a learning retirement institute. *Educational Gerontology, 30,* 441–455.

Kim, J. E., & Moen, P. (2002a). Is retirement good or bad for subjective well-being? *Current Directions in Psychological Science, 10,* 83–86.

Kim, J. E., & Moen, P. (2002b). Moving into retirement: Preparation and transitions in late midlife. In M. E. Lachman (Ed.), *Handbook of midlife development* (pp. 487–527). New York: Wiley.

Kim, J. E., & Moen, P. (2002c). Retirement transitions, gender, and psychological well-being: A life-course, ecological model. *Journal of Gerontology, 57B,* P212–P222.

Kim, J. M. (1998). Korean children's concepts of adult and peer authority and moral reasoning. *Developmental Psychology, 34,* 947–955.

Kim, J. M., & Turiel, E. (1996). Korean children's concepts of adult and peer authority. *Social Development, 5,* 310–329.

Kim, J.-Y., McHale, S. M., Crouter, A. C., & Osgood, D. W. (2007). Longitudinal linkages between sibling relationships and adjustment from middle childhood through adolescence. *Developmental Psychology, 43,* 960–973.

Kim, J.-Y., McHale, S. M., Osgood, D. W., & Crouter, A. C. (2006). Longitudinal course and family correlates of sibling relationships from childhood through adolescence. *Child Development, 77,* 1746–1761.

Kim, M., McGregor, K. K., & Thompson, C. K. (2000). Early lexical development in English-and Korean-speaking children: Language-general and language-specific patterns. *Journal of Child Language, 27,* 225–254.

Kim, S. Y. H., Appelbaum, P. S. J., Olin, D. V., & Jason, T. (2004). Proxy and surrogate consent in geriatric neuropsychiatric research: Update and recommendations. *American Journal of Psychiatry, 161,* 797–806.

Kim, S., & Hasher, L. (2005). The attraction effect in decision making: Superior performance by older adults. *Quarterly Journal of Experimental Psychology, 58A,* 120–133.

Kimbro, R. T. (2006). On-the-job moms: Work and breastfeeding initiation and duration for a sample of low-income women. *Maternal and Child Health Journal, 10,* 19–26.

Kimmel, D. C. (2004). Issues to consider in studies of midlife and older sexual minorities. In G. Herdt & B. DeVires (Eds.), *Gay and lesbian aging: Research and future directions* (pp. 265–284). New York: Springer.

King, A. C. (2001). Interventions to promote physical activity by older adults. *Journal of Gerontology, 56A,* 36A–46A.

King, A. C., Castro, C., Wilcox, S., Eyler, A. A., Sallis, J. F., & Brownson, R. C. (2000). Personal and environmental factors associated with physical inactivity among different racial–ethnic groups of U.S. middle-aged and older-aged women. *Health Psychology, 19,* 354–364.

King, A. C., Kiernan, M., Oman, R. F., Kraemer, H., Hull, M., & Ahn, D. (1997). Can we identify who will adhere to long-term physical activity? Signal detection methodology as a potential aid to clinical decision making. *Health Psychology, 16,* 380–389.

King, A. C., Taylor, C. B., & Haskell, W. L. (1993). Effects of differing intensities and formats of 12 months of exercise training on psychological outcomes in older adults. *Health Psychology, 12,* 292–300.

King, E. M., & Mason, A. D. (2001). *Engendering development: Through gender equality in rights, resources, and voice.* Washington, DC: UNICEF.

King, L. A., & Hicks, J. A. (2007). Whatever happened to "What might have been"? *American Psychologist, 62,* 625–636.

King, P. E., & Furrow, J. L. (2004). Religion as a resource for positive youth development: Religion, social capital, and moral outcomes. *Developmental Psychology, 40,* 703–713.

King, P. M., & Kitchener, K. S. (1994). *Developing reflective judgment: Understanding and promoting intellectual growth and critical thinking in adolescents and adults.* San Francisco: Jossey-Bass.

King, P. M., & Kitchener, K. S. (2002). The reflective judgment model: Twenty years of research on epistemic cognition. In B. K. Hofer & P. R. Pintrich (Eds.), *Personal epistemology: The psychological beliefs about knowledge and knowing* (pp. 37–61). Mahwah, NJ: Erlbaum.

King, V., & Scott, M. E. (2005). A comparison of cohabiting relationships among older and younger adults. *Journal of Marriage and Family, 67,* 271–285.

Kingsberg, S. A. (2002). The impact of aging on sexual function in women and their partners. *Archives of Sexual Behavior, 31,* 431–437.

Kinicki, A. J., Prussia, G. E., & McKee-Ryan, F. M. (2000). A panel study of coping with involuntary job loss. *Academy of Management Journal, 43,* 90–100.

Kinney, D. (1999). From "headbangers" to "hippies": Delineating adolescents' active attempts to form an alternative peer culture. In J. A. McLellan & M. J. V. Pugh (Eds.), *The role of peer groups in adolescent social identity: Exploring the importance of stability and change* (pp. 21–35). San Francisco: Jossey-Bass.

Kinser, K., & Deitchman, J. (2007). Tenacious persisters: Returning adult students in higher education. *Journal of College Student Retention, 9,* 75–94.

Kirby, D. (2002a). Antecedents of adolescent initiation of sex, contraceptive use, and pregnancy. *American Journal of Health Behavior, 26,* 473–485.

Kirby, D. (2002b). Effective approaches to reducing adolescent unprotected sex, pregnancy, and childbearing. *Journal of Sex Research, 39,* 51–57.

Kirby, D. (2002c). The impact of schools and school programs upon adolescent sexual behavior. *Journal of Sex Research, 39,* 27–33.

Kirchner, G. (2000). *Children's games from around the world.* Boston: Allyn and Bacon.

Kirk, K. M., Bailey, J. M., Dunne, M. P., & Martin, N. G. (2000). Measurement models for sexual orientation in a community twin sample. *Behavior Genetics, 30,* 345–356.

Kirkham, N. Z., Cruess, L., & Diamond, A. (2003). Helping children apply their knowledge to their behavior on a dimension-switching task. *Developmental Science, 6,* 449–476.

Kirkham, N. Z., Slemmer, J. A., & Johnson, S. P. (2002). Visual statistical learning in infancy: Evidence for a domain general learning mechanism. *Cognition, 83,* B35–B42.

Kisilevsky, B. S., Hains, S. M. J., Lee, K., Xie, X., Huang, H., Ye, H. H., Zhang, K., & Wang, Z. (2003). Effects of experience on fetal voice recognition. *Psychological Science, 14,* 220–224.

Kisilevsky, B. S., & Low, J. A. (1998). Human fetal behvior: 100 years of study. *Developmental Review, 18,* 1–29.

Kite, M. E., & Whitley, B. E., Jr. (2003). Do heterosexual women and men differ in their attitudes toward homosexuality? A conceptual and methodological analysis. In L. D. Garnets & D. C. Kimmel (Eds.), *Psychological perspectives on lesbian, gay, and bisexual experiences* (2nd ed., pp. 165–187). New York: Columbia University Press.

Kite, M. E., Stockdale, G. D., Whitley, B. E., Jr., & Johnson, B. T. (2005). Attitudes toward younger and older adults: An updated meta-analytic review. *Journal of Social Issues, 61,* 241–266.

Kito, M. (2005). Self-disclosure in romantic relationships and friendships among American and Japanese college students. *Journal of Social Psychology, 145,* 127–145.

Kitzmann, K. M., & Beech, B. M. (2006). Family-based interventions for pediatric obesity: Methodological and conceptual challenges from family psychology. *Journal of Family Psychology, 20,* 175–189.

Kitzmann, K. M., Cohen, R., & Lockwood, R. L. (2002). Are only children missing out? Comparison of the peer-related social competence of only

children and siblings. *Journal of Social and Personal Relationships, 19,* 299–316.
Kivipelto, M., Rovio, S., Ngandu, T., Karenhold, I., Eskelinen, M., & Winblad, B. (2008). Apolipoprotein E epsilon4 magnifies lifestyle risks for dementia: A population-based study. *Journal of Cellular and Molecular Medicine, 12,* 2762–2771.
Klaczynski, P. A. (1997). Bias in adolescents' everyday reasoning and its relationships with intellectual ability, personal theories, and self-serving motivation. *Developmental Psychology, 33,* 273–283.
Klaczynski, P. A. (2001). Framing effects on adolescent task representations, analytic and heuristic processing, and decision making: Implications for the normative/descriptive gap. *Applied Developmental Psychology, 22,* 289–309.
Klaczynski, P. A., & Narasimham, G. (1998). Development of scientific reasoning biases: Cognitive versus ego-protective explanations. *Developmental Psychology, 34,* 175–187.
Klaczynski, P. A., Schuneman, M. J., & Daniel, D. B. (2004). Theories of conditional reasoning: A developmental examination of competing hypotheses. *Developmental Psychology, 40,* 559–571.
Klahr, D., & MacWhinney, B. (1998). Information processing. In D. Kuhn & R. S. Siegler (Eds.), *Handbook of child psychology: Vol. 2. Cognition, perception, and language* (5th ed., pp. 631–678). New York: Wiley.
Klahr, D., & Nigam, M. (2004). The equivalence of learning paths in early science instruction: Effects of direct instruction and discovery learning. *Psychological Science, 15,* 661–667.
Klareskog, L., Padyukov, L., Rönnelid, J., & Alfredsson, L. (2006). Genes, environment and immunity in the development of rheumatoid arthritis. *Current Opinion in Immunology, 18,* 650–655.
Klass, D. (2004). The inner representation of the dead child in the psychic and social narratives of bereaved parents. In R. A. Neimeyer (Ed.), *Meaning reconstruction and the experience of loss* (pp. 77–94). Washington, DC: American Psychological Association.
Klaw, E. L., Rhodes, J. E., & Fitzgerald, L. F. (2003). Natural mentors in the lives of African-American adolescent mothers: Tracking relationships over time. *Journal of Youth and Adolescence, 32,* 223–232.
Klebanov, P. K., Brooks-Gunn, J., McCarton, C., & McCormick, M. C. (1998). The contribution of neighborhood and family income to developmental test scores over the first three years of life. *Child Development, 69,* 1420–1436.
Kleespies, P. M. (2004). Concluding thoughts on suffering, dying and choice. In P. M. Kleespies (Ed.), *Life and death decisions: Psychological and ethical considerations in end-of-life care* (pp. 163–167). Washington, DC: American Psychological Association.
Klein, B. E., Klein, R., Lee, K. E., & Meuer, S. M. (2003). Socioeconomic and lifestyle factors and the 10-year incidence of age-related cataracts. *American Journal of Ophthalmology, 136,* 506–512.
Klein, M. C. (2006). Does epidural analgesia increase rate of cesarean section? *Canadian Family Physician, 52,* 419–421.
Klein, P. J., & Meltzoff, A. N. (1999). Long-term memory, forgetting, and deferred imitation in 12-month-old infants. *Developmental Science, 2,* 102–113.
Kleinspehn-Ammerlahn, A., Kotter-Grühn, D., & Smith, J. (2008). Self-perceptions of aging: Do subjective age and satisfaction with aging change during old age? *The Journals of Gerontology Series B: Psychological Sciences and Social Sciences, 63,* 377–385.
Klenberg, L., Korkman, M., & Lahti-Nuuttila, P. (2001). Differential development of attention and executive functions in 3- to 12-year-old Finnish children. *Developmental Neuropsychology, 20,* 407–428.
Klesges, L., M., Johnson, K. C., Ward, K. D., & Barnard, M. (2001). Smoking cessation in pregnant women. *Obstetrics and Gynecology Clinics of North America, 28,* 269–282.
Klibanoff, R. S., Levine, S. C., Huttenlocher, J., Vasilyeva, M., & Hedges, L. V. (2006). Preschool children's mathematical knowledge: The effect of teacher "math talk." *Developmental Psychology, 42,* 59–69.
Kliegel, M., Jäger, T., & Phillips, L. H. (2008). Adult age differences in event-based prospective memory: A meta-analysis on the role of focal versus nonfocal cues. *Psychology and Aging, 23,* 203–208.
Kliegman, R. M., Behrman, R. E., Jenson, H. B., & Stanton, B. F. (Eds.). (2008). *Nelson textbook of pediatrics e-dition.* Philadelphia: Saunders.
Kliewer, W., Fearnow, M. D., & Miller, P. A. (1996). Coping socialization in middle childhood: Tests of maternal and paternal influences. *Child Development, 67,* 2339–2357.
Klimes-Dougan, B., & Kistner, J. (1990). Physically abused preschoolers' responses to peers' distress. *Developmental Psychology, 26,* 599–602.
Kline, G. H., Stanley, S. M., Markman, H. J., Olmos-Gallo, P. A., St. Peters, M., Whitton, S. W., & Prado, L. M. (2004). Timing is everything: Preengagement cohabitation and increased risk for poor marital outcomes. *Journal of Family Psychology, 18,* 311–318.
Klingman, A. (2006). Children and war trauma. In K. A. Renninger & I. E. Sigel (Eds.), *Handbook of child psychology: Vol. 4. Child psychology in practice* (6th ed., pp. 619–652). Hoboken, NJ: Wiley.
Klingner, J. K., Vaughn, S., Hughes, M. T., Schumm, J. S., & Elbaum, B. (1998). Outcomes for students with and without learning disabilities in inclusive classrooms. *Learning Disabilities Research and Practice, 13,* 153–161.
Kloep, M., & Hendry, L. B. (2007). Retirement: A new beginning? The *Psychologist, 20,* 742–745.
Klomsten, A. T., Skaalvik, E. M., & Espnes, G. A. (2004). Physical self-concept and sports: Do gender differences exist? *Sex Roles, 50,* 119–127.
Klump, K. L., Kaye, W. H., & Strober, M. (2001). The evolving foundations of eating disorders. *Psychiatric Clinics of North America, 24,* 215–225.
Kluwer, E. S., & Johnson, M. D. (2007). Conflict frequency and relationship quality across the transition to parenthood. *Journal of Marriage and Family, 69,* 1089–1106.
Knafo, A., & Plomin, R. (2006). Parental discipline and affection and children's prosocial behavior: Genetic and environmental links. *Journal of Personality and Social Psychology, 90,* 147–164.
Knight, B. G., Kaskie, B., Robinson, G., & Dave, J. (2006). Improving the mental health of older adults. In J. E. Birren & K. Warner Schaie (Eds.), *Handbook of the psychology of aging* (6th ed., pp. 407–424). Burlington, MA: Elsevier Academic Press.
Knobloch, H., & Pasamanick, B. (Eds.). (1974). *Gesell and Amatruda's Developmental Diagnosis.* Hagerstown, MD: Harper & Row.
Knoester, C., & Eggebeen, D. J. (2006). The effects of the transition to parenthood and subsequent children on men's well-being and social participation. *Journal of Family Issues, 27,* 152–1560.
Knopf, M., Kraus, U., & Kressley-Mba, R. A. (2006). Relational information processing of novel unrelated actions by infants. *Infant Behavior and Development, 29,* 44–53.
Knopman, D. S. (2006). Dementia and cerebrovascular disease. *Mayo Clinics Proceedings, 81,* 223–230.
Ko, K. J., Berg, C. A., Butner, J., Uchino, B. N., & Smith, T. W. (2007). Profiles of successful aging in middle-age and older adult married couples. *Psychology and Aging, 22,* 705–718.
Kobayashi, T., Hiraki, K., & Hasegawa, T. (2005). Auditory-visual intermodal matching of small numerosities in 6-month-old infants. *Developmental Science, 8,* 409–419.
Kobayashi, T., Kazuo, H., Ryoko, M., & Hasegawa, T. (2004). Baby arithmetic: One object plus one tone. *Cognition, 91,* B23–B34.
Kobayashi, Y. (1994). Conceptual acquisition and change through social interaction. *Human Development, 37,* 233–241.
Kochanska, G. (1991). Socialization and temperament in the development of guilt and conscience. *Child Development, 62,* 1379–1392.
Kochanska, G., & Aksan, N. (2006). Children's conscience and self-regulation. *Journal of Personality, 74,* 1587–1617.
Kochanska, G., Aksan, N., & Carlson, J. J. (2005). Temperament, relationships, and young children's receptive cooperation with their parents. *Developmental Psychology, 41*(4), 648–660.
Kochanska, G., Aksan, N., & Joy, M. E. (2007). Children's fearfulness as a moderator of parenting in early socialization: Two longitudinal studies. *Developmental Psychology, 43,* 222–237.
Kochanska, G., Aksan, N., & Nichols, K. E. (2003). Maternal power assertion in discipline and moral discourse contexts: Commonalities, differences, and implications for children's moral conduct and cognition. *Developmental Psychology, 39,* 949–963.
Kochanska, G., Aksan, N., Prisco, T. R., & Adams, E. E. (2008). Mother–child and father–child mutually responsive orientation in the first 2 years and children's outcomes at preschool age: Mechanisms of influence. *Child Development, 79,* 30–44.
Kochanska, G., Casey, R. J., & Fukumoto, A. (1995). Toddlers' sensitivity to standard violations. *Child Development, 66,* 643–656.
Kochanska, G., Forman, D. R., Aksan, N., & Dunbar, S. B. (2005). Pathways to conscience: Early mother–child mutually responsive orientation and children's moral emotion, conduct, and cognition. *Journal of Child Psychology and Psychiatry, 46,* 19–34.
Kochanska, G., Gross, J. N., Lin, M.-H., & Nichols, K. E. (2002). Guilt in young children: Development, determinants, and relations with broader system standards. *Child Development, 73,* 461–482.
Kochanska, G., & Knaack, A. (2003). Effortful control as a personality characteristic of young children: Antecedents, correlates, and consequences. *Journal of Personality, 71,* 1087–1112.
Kochanska, G., Murray, K. T., & Harlan, E. T. (2000). Effortful control in early childhood: Continuity and change, antecedents, and implications for social development. *Developmental Psychology, 36,* 220–232.
Kochenderfer-Ladd, B. (2003). Identification of aggressive and asocial victims and the stability of their peer victimization. *Merrill-Palmer Quarterly, 49,* 401–425.
Koelsch, S., Gunter, T., von Cramon, D., Zysset, S., Lohmann, G., & Friederici, A. (2002). Bach speaks: A cortical "language-network" serves the processing of music. *NeuroImage, 17,* 956–966.
Koestner, R., Franz, C., & Weinberger, J. (1990). The family origins of empathic concern: A 26-year longitudinal study. *Journal of Personality and Social Psychology, 58,* 709–717.
Kogan, L. R., & Vacha-Haase, T. (2002). Supporting adaptation to new family roles in middle age. In C. L. Juntunen & D. R. Atkinson (Eds.),

Counseling across the life span (pp. 299–347). Thousand Oaks, CA: Sage.

Kogan, N., & Mills, M. (1992). Gender influences on age cognitions and preferences: Sociocultural or sociobiological? *Psychology and Aging, 7,* 98–106.

Kohen, D. E., Brooks-Gunn, J., Leventhal, T., & Hertzman, C. (2002). Neighborhood income and physical and social disorder in Canada: Associations with young children's competencies. *Child Development, 73,* 1844–1860.

Kohlberg, L. (1966). A cognitive-developmental analysis of children's sex-role concepts and attitudes. In E. E. Maccoby (Ed.), *The development of sex differences* (pp. 82–173). Stanford, CA: Stanford University Press.

Kohlberg, L. (1969). Stage and sequence: The cognitive-developmental approach to socialization. In D. A. Goslin (Ed.), *Handbook of socialization theory and research* (pp. 347–480). Chicago: Rand McNally.

Kohlberg, L., Levine, C., & Hewer, A. (1983). *Moral stages: A current formulation and a response to critics.* Basel, Switzerland: Karger.

Kohn, M. L. (2006). *Change and stability: A cross-national analysis of social structure and personality.* Greenbrae, CA: Paradigm Press.

Kohn, M. L., Naoi, A., Schoenbach, C., Schooler, C., & Slomczynski, K. M. (1990). Position in the class structure and psychological functioning in the United States, Japan, and Poland. *American Journal of Sociology, 95,* 964–1008.

Kohn, M. L., & Schooler, C. (1978). The reciprocal effects of the substantive complexity of work and intellectual flexibility: A longitudinal assessment. *American Journal of Sociology, 84,* 24–52.

Kohn, M. L., & Slomczynski, K. M. (1990). *Social structure and self-direction: A comparative analysis of the United States and Poland.* Cambridge, MA: Blackwell.

Kohn, M. L., Zaborowski, W., Janicka, K., Mach, B. W., Khmelko, V., Slomczynski, K. M., Heyman, C., & Podobnik, B. (2000). Complexity of activities and personality under conditions of radical social change: A comparative analysis of Poland and Ukraine. *Social Psychology Quarterly, 63,* 187–207.

Kolb, B., & Gibb, R. (2001). Early brain injury, plasticity, and behavior. In C. A. Nelson & M. Luciana (Eds.), *Handbook of developmental cognitive neuroscience* (pp. 175–190). Cambridge, MA: MIT Press.

Kolomer, S. R., & McCallion, P. (2005). Depression and caregiver mastery in grandfathers caring for their grandchildren. *International Journal of Aging and Human Development, 60,* 283–294.

Komp, D. M. (1996). The changing face of death in children. In H. M. Spiro, M. G. M. Curnen, & L. P. Wandel (Eds.), *Facing death: Where culture, religion, and medicine meet* (pp. 66–76). New Haven: Yale University Press.

Komsi, N., Räikkönen, K., Pesonen, A.-K., Heinonen, K., Keskivaara, P., Järvenpää, A.-L., & Strandberg, T. E. (2006). Continuity of temperament from infancy to middle childhood. *Infant Behavior and Development, 29,* 494–508.

Kono, S. (2004). Secular trend of colon cancer incidence and mortality in relation to fat and meat intake in Japan. *European Journal of Cancer Prevention, 13,* 127–132.

Konold, T. R., & Pianta, R. C. (2005). Empirically-derived, person-oriented patterns of school readiness in typically developing children: Description and prediction to first-grade achievement. *Applied Developmental Science, 9,* 174–187.

Kopp, C. B., & Neufeld, S. J. (2003). Emotional development during infancy. In R. Davidson, K. R. Scherer, & H. H. Goldsmith (Eds.), *Handbook of affective sciences* (pp. 347–374). Oxford, UK: Oxford University Press.

Korkman, M., Kettunen, S., & Autti-Raemoe, I. (2003). Neurocognitive impairment in early adolescence following prenatal alcohol exposure of varying duration. *Child Neurology, 9,* 117–128.

Kornhaber, M. L. (2004). Using multiple intelligences to overcome cultural barriers to identification for gifted education. In D. Boothe & J. C. Stanley (Eds.), *In the eyes of the beholder: Critical issues for diversity in gifted education* (pp. 215–225). Waco, TX: Prufrock Press.

Koropeckyj-Cox, T., & Pendell, G. (2007). The gender gap in attitudes about childlessness in the United States. *Journal of Marriage and Family, 69,* 899–915.

Koster, A., Penninx, B. W., Newman, A. B., Visser, M., van Gool, C. H., & Harris, T. B. (2007). Lifestyle factors and incident mobility limitation in obese and non-obese older adults. *Obesity, 15,* 3122–3132.

Kotchoubey, B., Lang, S., Mezger, G., Schmalohr, D., Schneck, M., & Semmler, A. (2005). Information processing in severe disorders of consciousness: Vegetative state and minimally conscious state. *Clinical Neurophysiology, 116,* 2441–2453.

Kotre, J. (1999). *Make it count: How to generate a legacy that gives meaning to your life.* New York: Free Press.

Kouvonen, A., & Kivivuori, J. (2001). Part-time jobs, delinquency, and victimization among Finnish adolescents. *Journal of Scandinavian Studies in Criminology and Crime Prevention, 2,* 191–212.

Kozer, E., Costei, A. M., Boskovic, R., Nulman, I., Nikfar, S., & Koren, G. (2003). Effects of aspirin consumption during pregnancy on pregnancy outcomes: Meta-analysis. *Birth Defects Research, Part B, Developmental and Reproductive Toxicology, 68,* 70–84.

Kozulin, A. (Ed.). (2003). *Vygotsky's educational theory in cultural context.* Cambridge, U.K.: Cambridge University Press.

Kraaij, V., Arensman, E., & Spinhoven, P. (2002). Negative life events and depression in elderly persons: A meta-analysis. *Journal of Gerontology, 57B,* P87–P94.

Kraaij, V., Pruymboom, E., & Garnefski, N. (2002). Cognitive coping and depressive symptoms in the elderly: A longitudinal study. *Aging and Mental Health, 6,* 275–281.

Krafft, K., & Berk, L. E. (1998). Private speech in two preschools: Significance of open-ended activities and make-believe play for verbal self-regulation. *Early Childhood Research Quarterly, 13,* 637–658.

Kraft, J. M., & Werner, J. S. (1999). Aging and the saturation of colors. 2. Scaling of color appearance. *Journal of the Optical Society of America, 16,* 231–235.

Kramer, A. F., Fabiani, M., & Colcombe, S. J. (2006). Contributions of cognitive neuroscience to the understanding of behavior and aging. In J. E. Birren & K. W. Schaie (Eds.), *Handbook of the psychology of aging* (6th ed., pp. 57–83). Burlington, MA: Elsevier Academic Press.

Kramer, A. F., Hahn, S., & Gopher, D. (1998). Task coordination and aging: Explorations of executive control processes in the task switching paradigm. *Acta Psychologica, 101,* 339–378.

Kramer, A. F., & Kray, J. (2006). Aging and attention. In E. Bialystok & F. I. M. Fergus (Eds.), *Lifespan cognition: Mechanisms of change* (pp. 57–69). New York: Oxford University Press.

Kramer, A. F., & Madden, D. J. (2008). Attention. In F. I. M. Craik & T. A. Salthouse (Eds.), *Handbook of aging and cognition* (pp. 189–249). New York: Psychology Press.

Kramer, D. A. (2003). The ontogeny of wisdom in its variations. In J. Demick & C. Andreoletti (Eds.), *Handbook of adult development* (pp. 131–151). New York: Springer.

Kramer, M. S., Guo, T., Platt, R. W., Sevkowskaya, Z., Dzikovich, I., & Collet, J. P. (2003). Infant growth and health outcomes associated with 3 compared with 6 mo. of exclusive breastfeeding. *American Journal of Clinical Nutrition, 78,* 291–295.

Kramer, M. S., Guo, T., Platt, R. W., Shapiro, S., Collet, J. P., & Chalmers, B. (2002). Breastfeeding and infant growth: Biology or bias? *Pediatrics, 110,* 343–347.

Kramer, S. E., Kapteyn, T. S., Kuik, D. J., & Deeg, D. J. (2002). The association of hearing impairment and chronic diseases with psychosocial health status in older age. *Journal of Aging and Health, 14,* 122–137.

Krampe, R. T., & Charness, N. (2007). Aging and expertise. In K. A. Ericsson, N. Charness, P. J. Feltovich, & R. R. Hoffman (Eds.), *Cambridge handbook of expertise and expert performance* (pp. 723–742). New York: Cambridge University Press.

Krause, N. (1990). Perceived health problems, formal/informal support, and life satisfaction among older adults. *Journal of Gerontology, 45,* S193–S205.

Krause, N. (2001). Social support. In R. H. Binstock & L. K. George (Eds.), *Handbook of aging and the social sciences* (5th ed., pp. 272–294). San Diego, CA: Academic Press.

Krause, N. (2005). God-mediated control and psychological well-being in late life. *Research on Aging, 27,* 136–164.

Krebs, D., & Denton, K. (2005). Toward a more pragmatic approach to morality: A critical evaluation of Kohlberg's model. *Psychological Review, 112,* 629–649.

Krebs, D. L., Vermeulen, S. C., Carpendale, J. I., & Denton, K. (1991). Structural and situational influences on moral judgment: The interaction between stage and dilemma. In W. Kurtines & J. Gewirtz (Eds.), *Handbook of moral behavior and development: Theory, research, and application* (pp. 139–169). Hillsdale, NJ: Erlbaum.

Kreppner, J. M., Rutter, M., Beckett, C., Castle, J., Colvert, E., Groothues, C., Hawkins, A., & O'Connor, T. G. (2007). Normality and impairment following profound early institutional deprivation: A longitudinal follow-up into early adolescence. *Developmental Psychology, 43,* 931–946.

Krettenauer, T. (2005). The role of epistemic cognition in adolescent identity formation: Further evidence. *Journal of Youth and Adolescence, 34,* 185–198.

Krevans, J., & Gibbs, J. C. (1996). Parents' use of inductive discipline: Relations to children's empathy and prosocial behavior. *Child Development, 67,* 3263–3277.

Krishnamoorthy, J. S., Hart, C., & Jelalian, E. (2006). The epidemic of childhood obesity: Review of research and implications for public policy. *Social Policy Report of the Society for Research in Child Development, 9*(2).

Kroger, J. (2000). *Identity development: Adolescence through adulthood.* Thousand Oaks, CA: Sage.

Kroger, J. (2001). What transits in an identity status transition: A rejoinder to commentaries. *Identity, 3,* 291–304.

Kroger, J. (2005). *Identity in adolescence: The balance between self and other.* New York: Routledge.

Kroger, J. (2007). *Identity development: Adolescence through adulthood* (2nd ed.). Thousand Oaks, CA: Sage.

Kroneman, L., Loeber, R., & Hipwell, A. E. (2004). Is neighborhood context differently related to externalizing problems and delinquency for girls

compared with boys? *Clinical Child and Family Psychology Review, 7,* 109–122.
Kropf, N. P., & Pugh, K. L. (1995). Beyond life expectancy: Social work with centenarians. *Journal of Gerontological Social Work, 23,* 121–137.
Krout, J., Cutler, S. J., & Coward, R. T. (1990). Correlates of senior center participation: A national analysis. *Gerontologist, 30,* 72–79.
Krumhansl, C. L., & Jusczyk, P. W. (1990). Infants' perception of phrase structure in music. *Psychological Science, 1,* 70–73.
Kubik, M. Y., Lytle, L. A., Hannan, P. J., Perry, C. L., & Story, M. (2003). The association of the school food environment with dietary behaviors of young adolescents. *American Journal of Public Health, 93,* 1168–1173.
Kübler-Ross, E. (1969). *On death and dying.* New York: Macmillan.
Kubotera, I. (2004). Japanese religion in changing society: The spirits of the dead. In J. D. Morgan & P. Laungani (Eds.), *Death and bereavement around the world: Vol. 4. Asia, Australia, and New Zealand* (pp. 95–99). Amityville, NY: Baywood Publishing Company.
Kubzansky, L. D., Wright, R. J., Cohen, S., Weiss, S., Rosner, B., & Sparrow, D. (2002). Breathing easy: A prospective study of optimism and pulmonary function in the Normative Aging Study. *Annals of Behavioral Medicine, 24,* 345–353.
Kuchner, J. (1989, April). *Chinese-American and European-American mothers and infants: Cultural influences in the first three months of life.* Paper presented at the biennial meeting of the Society for Research in Child Development, Kansas City, MO.
Kuczynski, L. (1984). Socialization goals and mother–child interaction: Strategies for long-term and short-term compliance. *Developmental Psychology, 20,* 1061–1073.
Kuczynski, L. (2003). Beyond bidirectionality. In L. Kuczynski (Ed.), *Handbook of dynamics in parent–child relations* (pp. 3–24). Thousand Oaks, CA: Sage.
Kuczynski, L., & Lollis, S. (2002). Four foundations for a dynamic model of parenting. In J. R. M. Gerris (Ed.), *Dynamics of parenting.* Hillsdale, NJ: Erlbaum.
Kuebli, J., Butler, S., & Fivush, R. (1995). Mother–child talk about past emotions: Relations of maternal language and child gender over time. *Cognition and Emotion, 9,* 265–283.
Kugelmass, J., & Ainscow, M. (2004). Leadership for inclusion: A comparison of international practices. *Journal of Research in Special Educational Needs, 4,* 133–141.
Kuhl, P. K., Tsao, F.-M., & Liu, H.-M. (2003). Foreign-language experience in infancy: Effects of short-term exposure and social interaction on phonetic learning. *Proceedings of the National Academy of Sciences, 100,* 9096–9101.
Kuhn, D. (1999). Metacognitive development. *Current Directions in Psychological Science, 9,* 178–181.
Kuhn, D. (2000). Theory of mind, metacognition, and reasoning: A life-span perspective. In P. Mitchell & K. J. Riggs (Eds.), *Children's reasoning and the mind* (pp. 301–326). Hove, UK: Psychology Press.
Kuhn, D. (2002). What is scientific thinking, and how does it develop? In U. Goswami (Ed.), *Blackwell handbook of childhood cognitive development* (pp. 371–393). Malden, MA: Blackwell.
Kuhn, D., Amsel, E., & O'Loughlin, M. (1988). *The development of scientific thinking skills.* Orlando, FL: Academic Press.
Kuhn, D., & Dean, D. (2004). Connecting scientific reasoning and causal inference. *Journal of Cognition and Development, 5,* 261–288.
Kuhn, D., & Franklin, S. (2006). The second decade: What develops (and how)? In D. Kuhn & R. S. Siegler (Eds.), *Handbook of child psychology: Vol. 2. Cognition, perception, and language* (6th ed.). Hoboken, NJ: Wiley.
Kuhn, D., & Pearsall, S. (2000). Developmental origins of scientific thinking. *Journal of Cognition and Development, 1,* 113–129.
Kuklinski, M. R., & Weinstein, R. S. (2001). Classroom and developmental differences in a path model of teacher expectancy effects. *Child Development, 72,* 1554–1578.
Kulik, K. (2001). Marital relationships in late adulthood: Synchronous versus asynchronous couples. *International Journal of Aging and Human Development, 52,* 323–339.
Kumar, S., & O'Brien, A. (2004). Recent developments in fetal medicine. *British Medical Journal, 328,* 1002–1006.
Kunemund, H., Motel-Klingebiel, A., & Kohli, M. (2005). Do intergenerational transfers from elderly parents increase social inequality among their middle-aged children? Evidence from the German Aging Survey. *Journal of Gerontology, 60B,* S30-S36.
Kunisaki, S. M., & Jennings, R. W. (2008). Fetal surgery. *Journal of Intensive Care Medicine, 23,* 33–51.
Kunnen, E. S., & Bosma, H. A. (2003). Fischer's skill theory applied to identity development: A response to Kroger. *Identity, 3,* 247–270.
Kunzinger, E. L., III. (1985). A short-term longitudinal study of memorial development during early grade school. *Developmental Psychology, 21,* 642–646.
Kunzmann, U., Little, T., & Smith, J. (2002). Perceiving control: A double-edged sword in old age. *Journal of Gerontology, 57B,* P484–P491.
Kurdek, L. A. (1998). Relationship outcomes and their predictors: Longitudinal evidence from heterosexual married, gay cohabiting, and lesbian cohabiting couples. *Journal of Marriage and the Family, 60,* 553–568.
Kurdek, L. A. (2005). Gender and marital satisfaction early in marriage: A growth curve approach. *Journal of Marriage and Family, 67,* 68–84.
Kurdek, L. A. (2006). Differences between partners from heterosexual, gay, and lesbian cohabiting couples. *Journal of Marriage and Family, 68,* 509–528.
Kurdek, L. A., & Fine, M. A. (1994). Family acceptance and family control as predictors of adjustment in young adolescents: Linear, curvilinear, or interactive effects? *Child Development, 65,* 1137–1146.
Kwon, Y. H., Fingert, J. H., Kuehn, M. H., & Alward, W. L. (2009). Primary open-angle glaucoma. *New England Journal of Medicine, 360,* 1113–1124.

L

Laberge, L., Petit, D., Simard, C., Vitaro, F., Tremblay, R. E., & Montplaisir, J. (2001). Development of sleep patterns in early adolescence. *Journal of Sleep Research, 10,* 59–67.
Labouvie-Vief, G. (1980). Beyond formal operations: Uses and limits of pure logic in life-span development. *Human Development, 23,* 141–160.
Labouvie-Vief, G. (1985). Logic and self-regulation from youth to maturity: A model. In M. Commons, F. Richards, & C. Armon (Eds.), *Beyond formal operations: Late adolescent and adult cognitive development* (pp. 158–180). New York: Praeger.
Labouvie-Vief, G. (2003). Dynamic integration: Affect, cognition, and the self in adulthood. *Current Directions in Psychological Science, 12,* 201–206.
Labouvie-Vief, G. (2005). Self-with-other representations and the organization of the self. *Journal of Research in Personality, 39,* 185–205.
Labouvie-Vief, G. (2006). Emerging structures of adult thought. In J. J. Arnett & J. L. Tanner (Eds.), *Emerging adults in America: Coming of age in the 21st century* (pp. 59–84). Washington, DC: American Psychological Association.
Labouvie-Vief, G. (2008). When differentiation and negative affect lead to integration and growth. *American Psychologist, 63,* 564–565.
Labouvie-Vief, G., Chiodo, L. M., Goguen, L. A., Diehl, M., & Orwoll, L. (1995). Representations of self across the life span. *Psychology and Aging, 10,* 404–415.
Labouvie-Vief, G., DeVoe, M., & Bulka, D. (1989). Speaking about feelings: Conceptions of emotion across the life span. *Psychology and Aging, 4,* 425–437.
Labouvie-Vief, G., & Diehl, M. (1999). Self and personality development. In J. C. Kavanaugh & S. K. Whitbourne (Eds.), *Gerontology: An interdisciplinary perspective* (pp. 238–268). New York: Oxford University Press.
Labouvie-Vief, G., & Diehl, M. (2000). Cognitive complexity and cognitive-affective integration: Related or separate domains of adult development? *Psychology and Aging, 15,* 490–504.
Labouvie-Vief, G., Diehl, M., Jain, E., & Zhang, F. (2007). Six-year change in affect optimization and affect complexity across the adult life span: A further examination. *Psychology and Aging, 22,* 738–751.
Labouvie-Vief, G., & Gonzalez, M. M. (2004). Dynamic integration: Affect optimization and differentiation in development. In D. Y. Dai & R. J. Sternberg (Eds.), *Motivation, emotion, and cognition: Integrative perspectives on intellectual functioning and development* (pp. 237–272). Mahwah, NJ: Erlbaum.
Labouvie-Vief, G., & Medler, M. (2002). Affect optimization and affect complexity: Modes and styles of regulation in adulthood. *Psychology and Aging, 17,* 571–588.
Lachance, J. A., & Mazzocco, M. M. M. (2006). A longitudinal analysis of sex differences in math and spatial skills in primary school age children. *Learning and Individual Differences, 16,* 195–216.
Lachman, M. E. (2004). Development in midlife. *Annual Review of Psychology, 55,* 305–331.
Lachman, M. E., & Bertrand, R. M. (2002). Personality and self in midlife. In M. E. Lachman (Ed.), *Handbook of midlife development* (pp. 279–309). New York: Wiley.
Lachman, M. E., & Firth, K. M. P. (2004). The adaptive value of feeling in control during midlife. In O. G. Brim, C. D. Ryff, & R. C. Kessler (Eds.), *How healthy are we? A national study of well-being at midlife* (pp. 320–349). Chicago: University of Chicago Press.
Lachman, M. E., & James, J. B. (1997). Charting the course of midlife development: An overview. In M. E. Lachman & J. B. James (Eds.), *Multiple paths of midlife development* (pp. 1–17). Chicago: University of Chicago Press.
Lachman, M. E., Jette, A., Tennstedt, S., Howland, J., Harris, B. A., & Peterson, E. (1997). A cognitive-behavioural model for promoting regular physical activity in older adults. *Psychology, Health and Medicine, 2,* 251–261.
Lachs, M., Bachman, R., Williams, C. S., Kossack, A., Bove, C., & O'Leary, J. (2006). Violent crime victimization increases the risk of nursing home placement in older adults. *Gerontologist, 46,* 583–589.
Lacor, P. N., Buniel, M. C., Furlow, P. W., Clemente, A. S., Velasco, P. T., & Wood, M. (2007). Abeta

oligomer-induced aberrations in synapse composition, shape, and density provide a molecular basis for loss of connectivity in Alzheimer's disease. *Journal of Neuroscience, 27,* 796–807.

Lacourse, E., Nagin, D., Tremblay, R. E., Vitaro, F., & Claes, M. (2003). Developmental trajectories of boys' delinquent group membership and facilitation of violent behaviors during adolescence. *Development and Psychopathology, 15,* 183–197.

Ladd, G. W., Birch, S. H., & Buhs, E. S. (1999). Children's social and scholastic lives in kindergarten: Related spheres of influence? *Child Development, 70,* 1373–1400.

Ladd, G. W., Buhs, E. S., & Seid, M. (2000). Children's initial sentiments about kindergarten: Is school liking an antecedent of early classroom participation and achievement? *Merrill-Palmer Quarterly, 46,* 255–279.

Ladd, G. W., & Burgess, K. B. (1999). Charting the relationship trajectories of aggressive, withdrawn, and aggressive/withdrawn children during early grade school. *Child Development, 70,* 910–929.

Ladd, G. W., Herald, S. L., & Kochel, K. P. (2006). School readiness: Are there social prerequisites? *Early Education and Development, 17,* 115–150.

Ladd, G. W., LeSieur, K., & Profilet, S. M. (1993). Direct parental influences on young children's peer relations. In S. Duck (Ed.), *Learning about relationships* (Vol. 2, pp. 152–183). London: Sage.

Ladd, G. W., & Pettit, G. S. (2002). Parenting and the development of children's peer relationships. In M. Bornstein (Ed.), *Handbook of parenting* (2nd ed.). Mahwah, NJ: Erlbaum.

Ladd, G. W., & Price, J. M. (1987). Predicting children's social and school adjustment following the transition from preschool to kindergarten. *Child Development, 58,* 1168–1189.

Ladd, G. W., & Troop-Gordon, W. (2003). The role of chronic peer difficulties in the development of children's psychological adjustment problems. *Child Development, 74,* 1344–1367.

LaFontana, K. M., & Cillessen, A. H. N. (1999). Children's interpersonal perceptions as a function of sociometric and peer perceived popularity. *Journal of Genetic Psychology, 160,* 225–242.

Lagattuta, K. H., Wellman, H. M., & Flavell, J. H. (1997). Preschoolers' understanding of the link between thinking and feeling: Cognitive cuing and emotional change. *Child Development, 68,* 1081–1104.

Lagercrantz, H., & Slotkin, T. A. (1986). The "stress" of being born. *Scientific American, 254,* 100–107.

Lagnado, L. (2001, November 2). Kids confront Trade Center trauma. *Wall Street Journal,* pp. B1, B6.

Laible, D. (2004). Mother–child discourse in two contexts: Links with child temperament, attachment security, and socioemotional competence. *Developmental Psychology, 40,* 979–992.

Laible, D. (2007). Attachment with parents and peers in late adolescence: Links with emotional competence and social behavior. *Personality and Individual Differences, 43,* 1185–1197.

Laible, D., & Song, J. (2006). Constructing emotional and relational understanding: The role of affect and mother–child discourse. *Merrill-Palmer Quarterly, 52,* 44–69.

Laible, D., & Thompson, R. A. (2002). Mother–child conflict in the toddler years: Lessons in emotion, morality, and relationships. *Child Development, 73,* 1187–1203.

Laird, R. D., Jordan, K. Y., Dodge, K. A., Pettit, G. S., & Bates, J. E. (2001). Peer rejection in childhood, involvement with antisocial peers in early adolescence, and the development of externalizing behavior problems. *Development and Psychopathology, 13,* 337–354.

Laird, R. D., Pettit, G. S., Dodge, K. A., & Bates, J. E. (2005). Peer relationship antecedents of delinquent behavior in late adolescence: Is there evidence of demographic group differences in developmental processes? *Development and Psychopathology, 17,* 127–144.

Lalonde, C., & Chandler, M. (2005). Culture, selves, and time: Theories of personal persistence in native and non-native youth. In C. Lightfoot, C. Lalonde, & M. Chandler (Eds.), *Changing conceptions of psychological life* (pp. 207–229). Mahwah, NJ: Erlbaum.

Lamarche, V., Brendgen, M., Boivin, M., Vitaro, F., Perusse, D., & Dionne, G. (2006). Do friendships and sibling relationships provide protection against peer victimization in a similar way? *Social Development, 15,* 373–393.

Lamaze, F. (1958). *Painless childbirth.* London: Burke.

Lamb, M. E., & Ahnert, L. (2006). Nonparental child care: Context, concepts, correlates, and consequences. In K. A. Renninger & I. E. Sigel (Eds.), *Handbook of child psychology: Vol. 4. Child psychology in practice* (6th ed., pp. 700–778). Hoboken, NJ: Wiley.

Lamb, M. E., & Lewis, C. (2004). The development and significance of father–child relationships in two-parent families. In M. E. Lamb (Ed.), *The role of the father in child development* (4th ed., pp. 272–306). Hoboken, NJ: Wiley.

Lamb, M. E., & Oppenheim, D. (1989). Fatherhood and father–child relationships: Five years of research. In S. H. Cath, A. Gurwitt, & L. Gunsberg (Eds.), *Fathers and their families* (pp. 11–26). Hillsdale, NJ: Erlbaum.

Lamb, M. E., Sternberg, K. J., & Prodromidis, M. (1992). Nonmaternal care and the security of infant–mother attachment: A reanalysis of the data. *Infant Behavior and Development, 15,* 71–83.

Lamb, M. E., Thompson, R. A., Gardner, W., Charnov, E. L., & Connell, J. P. (1985). Infant–mother attachment: The origins and developmental significance of individual differences in the Strange Situation: Its study and biological interpretation. *Behavioral and Brain Sciences, 7,* 127–147.

Lamberg, L. (2007). Menopause not always to blame for sleep problems in midlife women. *Journal of the American Medical Association, 297,* 1865–1866.

Lambert, S. M., Masson, P., & Fisch, H. (2006). The male biological clock. *World Journal of Urology, 24,* 611–617.

Lamphear, B. P., Hornung, R., Khoury, J., Yolton, K., Baghurst, P., & Bellinger, D. C. (2005). Low-level environmental lead exposure and children's intellectual function: An international pooled analysis. *Environmental Health Perspectives, 113,* 894–899.

Lampl, M. (1993). Evidence of saltatory growth in infancy. *American Journal of Human Biology, 5,* 641–652.

Lampl, M., Veldhuis, J. D., & Johnson, M. L. (1992). Saltation and stasis: A model of human growth. *Science, 258,* 801–803.

Lanctot, K. L., Herrmann, N., Eryavec, G., van Reekum, R., Reed, K., & Naranjo, C. A. (2002). Central serotonergic activity is related to the aggressive behaviors of Alzheimer's disease. *Neuropsychopharmacology, 27,* 646–654.

Landau, M. (2007). Exogenous factors in skin aging. *Current Problems in Dermatology, 35,* 1–13.

Landman, J., Vandewater, E. A., Stewart, A. J., & Malley, J. E. (1995). Missed opportunities: Psychological ramifications of counterfactual thought in midlife women. *Journal of Adult Development, 2,* 87–97.

Lang, F. R., & Baltes, M. M. (1997). Being with people and being alone in later life: Costs and benefits for everyday functioning. *International Journal of Behavioral Development, 21,* 729–749.

Lang, F. R., Featherman, D. L., & Nesselroade, J. R. (1997). Social self-efficacy and short-term variability in social relationships: The MacArthur Successful Aging Studies. *Psychology and Aging, 12,* 657–666.

Lang, F. R., Staudinger, U. M., & Carstensen, L. L. (1998). Perspectives on socioemotional selectivity in late life: How personality and social context do (and do not) make a difference. *Journal of Gerontology, 53B,* P21–P30.

Langer, G. (2004). *ABC New Prime Time Live Poll: The American Sex Survey.* Retrieved from abcnews.go.com/Primetime/News/story?id=174461&page=1

Langer, J., Gillette, P., & Arriaga, R. I. (2003). Toddlers' cognition of adding and subtracting objects in action and in perception. *Cognitive Development, 18,* 233–246.

Langer, N. (1990). Grandparents and adult grandchildren: What do they do for one another? *International Journal of Aging and Human Development, 31,* 101–110.

Lansford, J. E., Antonucci, T. C., Akiyama, H., & Takahashi, K. (2005). A quantitative and qualitative approach to social relationships and well-being in the United States and Japan. *Journal of Comparative Family Studies, 36,* 1–22.

Lansford, J. E., Criss, M. M., Pettit, G. S., Dodge, K. A., & Bates, J. E. (2003). Friendship quality, peer group affiliation, and peer antisocial behavior as moderators of the link between negative parenting and adolescent externalizing behavior. *Journal of Research on Adolescence, 13,* 161–184.

Lansford, J. E., Deater-Deckard, K., Dodge, K. A., Bates, J. E., & Pettit, G. S. (2004). Ethnic differences in the link between physical discipline and later adolescent externalizing behaviors. *Journal of Child Psychology and Psychiatry, 45,* 801–812.

Lansford, J. E., Malone, P. S., Castellino, D. R., Dodge, K. A., Pettit, G., & Bates, J. E. (2006). Trajectories of internalizing, externalizing, and grades for children who have and have not experienced their parents' divorce or separation. *Journal of Family Psychology, 20,* 292–301.

Lantz, P. M., House, J. S., Lepkowski, J. M., Williams, D. R., Mero, R. P., & Chen, J. (1998). Socioeconomic factors, health behaviors, and mortality. *Journal of the American Medical Association, 279,* 1703–1708.

Lantz, P. M., Lynch, J. W., House, J. S., Lepkowski, J. M., Mero, R. P., & Musick, M. (2001). Socioeconomic disparities in health change in a longitudinal study of U.S. adults: The role of health risk behaviors. *Social Science and Medicine, 53,* 29–40.

Larbi, A., Franceschi, C., Mazzatti, D., Solana, R., Wikby, A., & Pawelec, G. (2008). Aging of the immune system as a prognostic factor for human longevity. *Physiology, 23,* 64–74.

Larsen, J. A., & Nippold, M. A. (2007). Morphological analysis in school-age children: Dynamic assessment of a word learning strategy. *Language, Speech, and Hearing Services in Schools, 38,* 201–212.

Larson, D. G., & Hoyt, W. T. (2007). What has become of grief counseling? An evaluation of the empirical foundations of the new pessimism. *Professional Psychology: Research and Practice, 38,* 347–355.

Larson, E. B., Shadlen, M. F., Wang, L., McCormick, W. C., Bowen, J. D., Teri, L., & Kukull, W. A. (2004). Survival after initial diagnosis of Alzheimer disease. *Annals of Internal Medicine, 140,* 501–509.

Larson, E. B., Wang, L., Bowen, J. D., McCormick, W. C., & Teri, L. (2006). Exercise is associated with reduced risk for incident dementia among persons 65 years of age and older. *Annals of Internal Medicine, 144,* 73–81.

Larson, J. H. (1988). The marriage quiz: College students' beliefs in selected myths about marriage. *Family Relations, 37,* 3–11.

Larson, R. W. (2001). How U.S. children and adolescents spend time: What it does (and doesn't) tell us about their development. *Current Directions in Psychological Science, 10,* 160–164.

Larson, R. W., & Ham, M. (1993). Stress and "storm and stress" in early adolescence: The relationship of negative events with dysphoric affect. *Developmental Psychology, 29,* 130–140.

Larson, R. W., & Lampman-Petraitis, C. (1989). Daily emotional states as reported by children and adolescents. *Child Development, 60,* 1250–1260.

Larson, R. W., Mannell, R., & Zuzanek, J. (1986). Daily well-being of older adults with friends and family. *Psychology and Aging, 1,* 117–126.

Larson, R. W., Moneta, G., Richards, M. H., & Wilson, S. (2002). Continuity, stability, and change in daily emotional experience across adolescence. *Child Development, 73,* 1151–1165.

Larson, R. W., & Richards, M. (1998). Waiting for the weekend: Friday and Saturday night as the emotional climax of the week. In A. C. Crouter & R. Larson (Eds.), *Temporal rhythms in adolescence: Clocks, calendars, and the coordination of daily life* (pp. 37–51). San Francisco: Jossey-Bass.

Larson, R. W., Richards, M. H., Moneta, G., Holmbeck, G., & Duckett, E. (1996). Changes in adolescents' daily interactions with their families from ages 10 to 18: Disengagement and transformation. *Developmental Psychology, 32,* 744–754.

Larson, R. W., Richards, M. H., Sims, B., & Dworkin, J. (2001). How urban African-American young adolescents spend their time: Time budgets for locations, activities, and companionship. *American Journal of Community Psychology, 29,* 565–597.

Larsson, M., & Bäckman, L. (1998). Modality memory across the adult life span: Evidence for selective age-related olfactory deficits. *Experimental Aging Research, 24,* 63–82.

Larsson, M., Öberg, C., & Bäckman, L. (2005). Odor identification in old age: Demographic, sensory and cognitive correlates. *Aging, Neuropsychology, and Cognition, 12,* 231–244.

Larzelere, R. E., Schneider, W. N., Larson, D. B., & Pike, P. L. (1996). The effects of discipline responses in delaying toddler misbehavior recurrences. *Child and Family Behavior Therapy, 18,* 35–57.

Lashley, F. R. (2007). Essentials of clinical genetics in nursing practice. New York: Springer.

Lattanzi-Licht, M., & Doka, K. J. (Eds.). (2003). *Living with grief: Coping with public tragedy.* New York: Brunner-Routledge.

Latz, S., Wolf, A. W., & Lozoff, B. (1999). Sleep practices and problems in young children in Japan and the United States. *Archives of Pediatric and Adolescent Medicine, 153,* 339–346.

Laucht, M., Esser, G., & Schmidt, M. H. (1997). Developmental outcome of infants born with biological and psychosocial risks. *Journal of Child Psychology and Psychiatry, 38,* 843–853.

Lauer, J. A., Betrán, A. P., Victora, C. G., de Onís, M., & Barros, A. J. (2004). Breastfeeding patterns and exposure to suboptimal breastfeeding among children in developing countries: Review and analysis of nationally representative surveys. *BMC Medicine, 2,* 26.

Lauer, P. A., Akiba, M., Wilkerson, S. B., Apthorp, H. S., Snow, D., & Martin-Glenn, M. (2006). Out-of-school time programs: A meta-analysis of effects for at-risk students. *Review of Educational Research, 76,* 275–313.

Laumann, E. O., Gagnon, J. H., Michael, R. T., & Michaels, S. (1994). *The social organization of sexuality.* Chicago: University of Chicago Press.

Laumann, E. O., & Mahay, J. (2002). The social organization of woman's sexuality. In G. M. Wingood & R. J. DiClemente (Eds.), *Handbook of women's sexual and reproductive health* (pp. 43–70). New York: Springer.

Laumann, E. O., Paik, A., & Rosen, R. C. (1999). Sexual dysfunction in the United States: Prevalence and predictors. *Journal of the American Medical Association, 281,* 537–544.

Laureys, S., & Boly, M. (2007). What is it like to be vegetative or minimally conscious? *Current Opinion in Neurology, 20,* 609–613.

Laursen, B., Coy, K., & Collins, W. A. (1998). Reconsidering changes in parent–child conflict across adolescence: A meta-analysis. *Child Development, 69,* 817–832.

Lautenschlager, N. T., Cox, K. L., Flicker, L., Foster, J. K., van Bockxmeer, F. M., Xiao, J., Greenop, K. R., & Almeida, O. P. (2008). Effect of physical activity on cognitive function in older adults at risk for Alzheimer disease: A randomized trial. *Journal of the American Medical Association, 300,* 1027–1037.

Lavelli, M., & Fogel, A. (2005). Developmental changes in the relationship between the infant's attention and emotion during early face-to-face communication: The 2-month transition. *Developmental Psychology, 41,* 265–280.

Law, K. L., Stroud, L. R., Niaura, R., LaGasse, L. L., Giu, J., & Lester, B. M. (2003). Smoking during pregnancy and newborn neurobehavior. *Pediatrics, 111,* 1318–1323.

Lawrence, A. R., & Schigelone, A. R. S. (2002). Reciprocity beyond dyadic relationships: Aging-related communal coping. *Research on Aging, 24,* 684–704.

Lawrence, K., Kuntsi, J., Coleman, M., Campbell, R., & Skuse, D. (2003). Face and emotion recognition deficits in Turner syndrome: A possible role for X-linked genes in amygdala development. *Neuropsychology, 17,* 39–49.

Lawson, K. R., & Ruff, H. A. (2004). Early attention and negative emotionality predict later cognitive and behavioral function. *International Journal of Behavioral Development, 28,* 157–165.

Lawton, M. P. (2001). Emotion in later life. *Current Directions in Psychological Science, 10,* 120–123.

Lazar, I., & Darlington, R. (1982). Lasting effects of early education: A report from the Consortium for Longitudinal Studies. *Monographs of the Society for Research in Child Development, 47*(2–3, Serial No. 195).

Lazarus, R. S. (1999). *Stress and emotion: A new synthesis.* New York: Springer.

Lazarus, R. S., & Lazarus, B. N. (1994). *Passion and reason.* New York: Oxford University Press.

Le Grand, R., Mondloch, C. J., Maurer, D., & Brent, H. P. (2001). Early visual experience and face processing. *Nature, 410,* 890.

Le Grand, R., Mondloch, C. J., Maurer, D., & Brent, H. P. (2003). Expert face processing requires input to the right hemisphere during infancy. *Nature Neuroscience, 6,* 1108–1112.

Leadbeater, B., & Hoglund, W. (2006). Changing the social texts of peer victimization. *Journal of the Canadian Academy of Child and Adolescent Psychiatry, 15,* 21–26.

Leaper, C. (1994). Exploring the correlates and consequences of gender segregation: Social relationships in childhood, adolescence, and adulthood. In C. Leaper (Ed.), *New directions for child development* (No. 65, pp. 67–86). San Francisco: Jossey-Bass.

Leaper, C. (2000). Gender, affiliation, assertion, and the interactive context of parent–child play. *Developmental Psychology, 36,* 381–393.

Leaper, C., Anderson, K. J., & Sanders, P. (1998). Moderators of gender effects on parents' talk to their children: A meta-analysis. *Developmental Psychology, 34,* 3–27.

Leaper, C., & Friedman, C. K. (2007). The socialization of gender. In J. E. Grusec & P. D. Hastings (Eds.), *Handbook of socialization: Theory and research* (pp. 561–587). New York: Guilford.

Leaper, C., Leve, L., Strasser, T., & Schwartz, R. (1995). Mother–child communication sequences: Play activity, child gender, and marital status effects. *Merrill-Palmer Quarterly, 41,* 307–327.

Leaper, C., Tenenbaum, H. R., & Shaffer, T. G. (1999). Communication patterns of African-American girls and boys from low-income, urban backgrounds. *Child Development, 70,* 1489–1503.

Lease, S. H. (2003). Testing a model of men's nontraditional occupational choices. *Career Development Quarterly, 51,* 244–258.

LeBlanc, L. A., Goldsmith, T., & Patel, D. R. (2003). Behavioral aspects of chronic illness in children and adolescents. *Pediatric Clinics of North America, 50,* 859–878.

Lecanuet, J.-P., Granier-Deferre, C., Jacquet, A.-Y., Capponi, I., & Ledru, L. (1993). Prenatal discrimination of a male and female voice uttering the same sentence. *Early Development and Parenting, 2,* 217–228.

Lechner, V., & Neal, M. (1999). *Working and caring for the elderly: International perspectives.* New York: Routledge.

Lecuyer, E., & Houck, G. M. (2006). Maternal limit-setting in toddlerhood: Socialization strategies for the development of self-regulation. *Infant Mental Health Journal, 27,* 344–370.

Lee, C.-Y. S., & Doherty, W. J. (2007). Marital satisfaction and father involvement during the transition to parenthood. *Fathering, 5,* 75–96.

Lee, D. J., & Markides, K. S. (1990). Activity and morality among aged persons over an eight-year period. *Journal of Gerontology, 45,* S39–S42.

Lee, E. E., & Farran, C. J. (2004). Depression among Korean, Korean American, and Caucasian American family caregivers. *Journal of Transcultural Nurising, 15,* 18–25.

Lee, E. O. (2007). Religion and spirituality as predictors of well-being among Chinese American and Korean American older adults. *Journal of Religion, Spirituality and Aging, 19,* 77–100.

Lee, E. O., & Sharpe, T. (2007). Understanding religious/spiritual coping and support resources among African American older adults: A mixed method approach. *Journal of Religion, Sprituality and Aging, 19,* 55–75.

Lee, G. R., DeMaris, A., Bavin, S., & Sullivan, R. (2001). Gender differences in the depressive effect of widowhood in later life. *Journal of Gerontology, 56B,* S56–S61.

Lee, I. M., Cook, N. R., Gaziano, J. M., Gordon, D., Ridker, P. M. & Manson, J. E. (2005). Vitamin E in the primary prevention of cardiovascular disease and cancer: The Women's Health Study, a randomized controlled trial. *Journal of the American Medical Association, 294,* 56–65.

Lee, J. M., Appulgiese, D., Kaciroti, N., Corwyn, R. F., Bradley, R. H., & Lumeng, J. C. (2007). Weight status in young girls and the onset of puberty. *Pediatrics, 119,* e624–e630.

Lee, K., Cameron, C., Xu, F., Fu, G., & Board, J. (1997). Chinese and Canadian children's evaluations of lying and truth telling: Similarities and differences in the context of pro- and antisocial behaviors. *Child Development, 68,* 924–934.

Lee, K., Xu, F., Fu, G., Cameron, C. A., & Chen, S. (2001). Taiwan and Mainland Chinese and Canadian children's categorization and evaluation of lie- and truth-telling: A modesty effect. *British Journal of Developmental Psychology, 19,* 525–542.

Lee, M. M., Carpenter, B., & Meyers, L. S. (2006). Representations of older adults in television advertisements. *Journal of Aging Studies, 21,* 23–30.

Lee, S. J., Ralston, H. J., Partridge, J. C., & Rosen, M. A. (2005). Fetal pain: A systematic multidisciplinary review of the evidence. *Journal of the American Medical Association, 294,* 947–954.

Lee, S. M., Burgeson, C. R., Fulton, J. E., & Spain, C. G. (2007). Physical education and physical activity: Results from the School Health Policies and Programs Study, 2006. *Journal of School Health, 77,* 435–463.

Lee, V. E., & Burkam, D. T. (2002). *Inequality at the starting gate.* Washington, DC: Economic Policy Institute.

Lee, V. E., & Burkam, D. T. (2003). Dropping out of high school: The role of school organization and structure. *American Educational Research Journal, 40,* 353–393.

Lefebvre, F., Mazurier, E., & Tessier, R. (2005). Cognitive and educational outcomes in early adulthood for infants weighing 1000 grams or less at birth. *Acta Paediatrica, 94,* 733–740.

Legacy Project. (2009). *Fast facts on grandparenting and intergenerational mentoring.* Retrieved from www.legacyproject.org/specialreports/fastfacts .html

Lehman, D., Ellard, J., & Wortman, C. (1986). Social support for the bereaved: Recipients' and providers' perspectives on what is helpful. *Journal of Consulting and Clinical Psychology, 54,* 438–446.

Lehman, D. R., & Nisbett, R. E. (1990). A longitudinal study of the effects of undergraduate training on reasoning. *Developmental Psychology, 26,* 952–960.

Lehr, V. T., Zeskind, P. S., Ofenstein, J. P., Cepeda, E., Warrier, I., & Aranda, J. V. (2007). Neonatal facial coding system scores and spectral characteristics of infant crying during newborn circumcision. *Clinical Journal of Pain, 23,* 417–424.

Leiferman, J. A., & Evenson, K. R. (2003). The effect of regular leisure physical activity on birth outcomes. *Maternal and Child Health Journal, 7,* 59–64.

Leiter, M. P., & Maslach, C. (2000). *Preventing burnout and building engagement: A complete program for organizational renewal.* San Francisco: Jossey-Bass.

Leman, P. J. (2005). Authority and moral reasons: Parenting style and children's perceptions of adult rule justifications. *International Journal of Behavioral Development, 29,* 265–270.

Lemche, E., Lennertz, I., Orthmann, C., Ari, A., Grote, K., Hafker, J., & Klann-Delius, G. (2003). Emotion-regulatory process in evoked play narratives: Their relation with mental representations and family interactions. *Praxis der Kinderpsychologie und Kinderpsychiatrie, 52,* 156–171.

Lemme, B. H. (2006). *Development in adulthood* (4th ed.). Boston: Allyn & Bacon.

Lempert, H. (1990). Acquisition of passives: The role of patient animacy, salience, and lexical accessibility. *Journal of Child Language, 17,* 677–696.

Lenroot, R. K., & Giedd, J. N. (2006). Brain development in children and adolescents: Insights from anatomical magnetic resonance imaging. *Neuroscience and Biobehavioral Reviews, 30,* 718–729.

Lent, R. W., & Brown, S. D. (2002). Social cognitive career theory and adult career development. In R. W. Lent & S. D. Brown (Eds.), *Adult career development: Concepts, issues, and practices* (3rd ed., pp. 76–97). Columbus, OH: National Career Development Association.

Leon, K. (2003). Risk and protective factors in young children's adjustment to parental divorce: A review of the research. *Family Relations, 52,* 258–270.

Leonard, K. E., & Roberts, L. J. (1998). Marital aggression, quality, and stability in the first year of marriage: Findings from the Buffalo Newlywed Study. In T. N. Bradbury (Ed.), *The developmental course of marital dysfunction* (pp. 44–73). New York: Cambridge University Press.

Lepage, J.-F., & Théoret, H. (2007). The mirror neuron system: Grasping others' actions from birth? *Developmental Science, 10,* 513–523.

Lerner, R. M. (2006). Developmental science, developmental systems, and contemporary theories of human development. In R. M. Lerner (Ed.), *Handbook of child psychology: Vol. 1. Theoretical models of human development* (6th ed., pp. 1–17). Hoboken, NJ: Wiley.

Lerner, R. M., Fisher, C. B., & Weinberg, R. A. (2000). Toward a science for and of the people: Promoting civil society through the application of developmental science. *Child Development, 71,* 11–20.

Lerner, R. M., Rothbaum, F., Boulos, S., & Castellino, D. R. (2002). Developmental systems perspective on parenting. In M. H. Bornstein (Ed.), *Handbook of parenting: Vol. 2* (2nd ed., pp. 315–344). Mahwah, NJ: Erlbaum.

Lerner, R. M., Theokas, C., & Bobek, D. L. (2005). Concepts and theories of human development: Historical and contemporary dimensions. In M. H. Bornstein & M. E. Lamb (Eds.), *Developmental science: An advanced textbook* (pp. 3–43). Mahwah, NJ: Erlbaum.

Leslie, A. M. (2004). Who's for learning? *Developmental Science, 7,* 417–419.

Lester, B. M. (1985). Introduction: There's more to crying than meets the ear. In B. M. Lester & C. F. Z. Boukydis (Eds.), *Infant crying* (pp. 1–27). New York: Plenum.

Lester, B. M., LaGasse, L., Seifer, R., Tronick, E. Z., Bauer, C., & Shankaran, S. (2003). The maternal lifestyle study (MLS): Effects of prenatal cocaine and/or opiate exposure on auditory brain response at one month. *Journal of Pediatrics, 142,* 279–285.

Lester, B. M., Masten, A. S., & McEwen, B. (Eds.). (2006). *Resilience in children.* New York: Annals of the New York Academy of Sciences.

Lester, B. M., & Tronick, E. Z. (2004). *NICU Network Neurobehavioral Scale (NNNS).* Baltimore, MD: Brookes.

Letherby, G. (2002). Childless and bereft? Stereotypes and realities in relation to "voluntary" and "involuntary" childlessness and womanhood. *Sociological Inquiry, 72,* 7–20.

Leung, M. C. M., Zhang, J., & Zhang, J. (2004). An economic analysis of life expectancy by gender with application to the United States. *Journal of Health Economics, 23,* 737–759.

LeVay, S. (1993). *The sexual brain.* Cambridge, MA: MIT Press.

Levenson, R. W., Carstensen, L. L., & Gottman, J. M. (1993). Long-term marriage: Age, gender, and satisfaction. *Psychology and Aging, 8,* 301–313.

Leventhal, E. A., Leventhal, H., Schaefer, P. M., & Easterling, D. (1993). Conservation of energy, uncertainty reduction, and swift utilization of medical care among the elderly. *Journal of Gerontology, 48,* P78–P86.

Leventhal, T., & Brooks-Gunn, J. (2003). Children and youth in neighborhood contexts. *Current Directions in Psychological Science, 12,* 27–31.

Levin, I., & Bus, A. G. (2003). How is emergent writing based on drawing? Analyses of children's products and their sorting by children and mothers. *Developmental Psychology, 39,* 891–905.

Levin, J. S., Taylor, R. J., & Chatters, L. M. (1994). Race and gender differences in religiosity among older adults: Findings from four national surveys. *Journal of Gerontology, 49,* S137–S145.

Levine, B., Svoboda, E., Hay, J. F., Winocur, G., & Moscovitch, M. (2002). Aging and autobiographical memory: Dissociating episodic from semantic retrieval. *Psychology and Aging, 17,* 677–689.

Levine, J. A. (2007). Obesity in China: Causes and solutions. *Chinese Medical Journal, 120,* 1043–1050.

Levine, L. E. (1983). Mine: Self-definition in 2-year-old boys. *Developmental Psychology, 19,* 544–549.

Levine, L. J. (1995). Young children's understanding of the causes of anger and sadness. *Child Development, 66,* 697–709.

Levine, M. (2005). *Ready or not, here life comes.* New York: Simon & Schuster.

Levine, R., Sato, S., Hashimoto, T., & Verma, J. (1995). Love and marriage in eleven cultures. *Journal of Cross-Cultural Psychology, 26,* 554–571.

LeVine, R. A., Dixon, S., LeVine, S., Richman, A., Leiderman, P. H., Keefer, C. H., & Brazelton, T. B. (1994). *Child care and culture: Lessons from Africa.* New York: Cambridge University Press.

LeVine, R. A., LeVine, S. E., Richman, A., Tapia Uribe, M. R., Suderland Correa, C., & Miller, P. M. (1991). Women's schooling and child care in the demographic transition: A Mexican case study. *Population and Development Review, 17,* 459–496.

LeVine, R. A., LeVine, S. E., Rowe, M. L., & Schnell-Anzola, B. (2004). Maternal literacy and health behavior: A Nepalese case study. *Social Science and Medicine, 58,* 863–877.

LeVine, R. A., LeVine, S. E., & Schnell, B. (2001). "Improve the women": Mass schooling, female literacy, and worldwide social change. *Harvard Educational Review, 71,* 1 –50.

Levine, S. C., Huttenlocher, J., Taylor, A., & Langrock, A. (1999). Early sex differences in spatial skill. *Developmental Psychology, 35,* 940–949.

Levinson, D. J. (1978). *The seasons of a man's life.* New York: Knopf.

Levinson, D. J. (1986). A conception of adult development. *American Psychologist, 41,* 3–13.

Levinson, D. J. (1996). *The seasons of a woman's life.* New York: Knopf.

Levitt, T., Fugelsang, J., & Crossley, M. (2006). Processing speed, attentional capacity, and age-related memory change. *Experimental Aging Research, 32,* 263–295.

Levy, B. R. (2003). Mind matters: Cognitive and physical effects of aging self-stereotypes. *Journal of Gerontology, 58B,* P203–P211.

Levy, B. R., & Banaji, M. R. (2002). Implicit ageism. In T. D. Nelson (Ed.), *Ageism: Stereotyping and prejudice against older persons* (pp. 49–75). Cambridge, MA: MIT Press.

Levy, B. R., Hausdorff, J., Hencke, R., & Wei, J. Y. (2000). Reducing cardiovascular stress with positive self-stereotypes of aging. *Journal of Gerontology, 55B,* P205–P213.

Levy, B. R., Slade, M. D., & Gill, T. M. (2006). Hearing decline predicted by elders' stereotypes. *Journal of Gerontology, 61B,* P82–P87.

Levy, B. R., Slade, M. D., Kunkel, S. R., & Kasl, S. V. (2002). Longevity increased by positive self-perceptions of aging. *Journal of Personality and Social Psychology, 83,* 261–270.

Levy, G. D., Taylor, M. G., & Gelman, S. A. (1995). Traditional and evaluative aspects of flexibility in gender roles, social conventions, moral rules, and physical laws. *Child Development, 66,* 515–531.

Levy, S. R., & Dweck, C. S. (1999). The impact of children's static vs. dynamic conceptions of people on stereotype formation. *Child Development, 70,* 1163–1180.

Levy-Shiff, R., & Israelashvili, R. (1988). Antecedents of fathering: Some further exploration. *Developmental Psychology, 24,* 434–440.

Lewis, C., Freeman, N. H., Kyriadidou, C., Maridakikassotaki, K., & Berridge, D. M. (1996). Social influences on false belief access—specific sibling influences or general apprenticeship? *Child Development, 67,* 2930–2947.

Lewis, K. G. (2000). *With or without a man: Single women taking control of their lives.* New York: Bull Publishing.

Lewis, M. (1992). *Shame: The exposed self.* New York: Free Press.

Lewis, M. (1997). *Altering fate: Why the past does not predict the future.* New York: Guilford.

Lewis, M. (1998). Emotional competence and development. In D. Pushkar, W. M. Bukowski, A. E. Schwartzman, E. M. Stack, & D. R. White (Eds.), *Improving competence across the lifespan* (pp. 27–36). New York: Plenum.

Lewis, M., & Brooks-Gunn, J. (1979). *Social cognition and the acquisition of self.* New York: Plenum.

Lewis, M., Ramsay, D. S., & Kawakami, K. (1993). Differences between Japanese infants and Caucasian American infants in behavioral and cortisol response to inoculation. *Child Development, 64,* 1722–1731.

Lewis, M., Sullivan, M. W., Stanger, C., & Weiss, M. (1989). Self development and self-conscious emotions. *Child Development, 60,* 146–156.

Li, D.-K., Willinger, M., Petitti, D. B., Odouli, R., Liu, L., & Hoffman, H. J. (2006). Use of a dummy (pacifier) during sleep and risk of sudden infant death syndrome (SIDS): Population based case-control study. *British Medical Journal, 332,* 18–21.

Li, Q. (2006). Cyberbullying in schools: A research of gender differences. *School Psychology International, 27,* 157–170.

Li, S.-C., Lindenberger, U., Hommel, B., Aschersleben, G., Prinz, W., & Baltes, P. B. (2004). Transformation in the couplings among intellectual abilities and constituent cognitive processes across the life span. *Psychological Science, 15,* 155–163.

Liang, J., Bennett, J. M., Krause, N. M., Chang, M., Lin, S., Chuang, Y. L., & Wo, S. (1999). Stress, social relationships, and old age mortality in Taiwan. *Journal of Clinical Epidemiology, 52,* 983–995.

Liang, J., Bennett, J., Krause, N., Kobayashi, E., Kim, H., Brown, J. W., Akiyama, H., Sugiawa, H., & Jain, A. (2002). Old age mortality in Japan: Does the socioeconomic gradient interact with gender and age? *Journal of Gerontology, 57,* S294–S307.

Liang, J., Krause, N. M., & Bennett, J. M. (2001). Social exchange and well-being: Is giving better than receiving? *Psychology and Aging, 16,* 511–523.

Liben, L. S. (1999). Developing an understanding of external spatial representations. In I. E. Sigel (Ed.), *Development of mental representation* (pp. 297–321). Mahwah, NJ: Erlbaum.

Liben, L. S. (2006). Education for spatial thinking. In K. A. Renninger & I. E. Sigel (Eds.), *Handbook of child psychology: Vol. 4. Child psychology in practice* (6th ed., pp. 197–247). Hoboken, NJ: Wiley.

Liben, L. S., & Bigler, R. S. (2002). The developmental course of gender differentiation: Conceptualizing, measuring, and evaluating constructs and pathways. *Monographs of the Society for Research in Child Development, 6*(4, Serial No. 271).

Liben, L. S., Bigler, R. S., & Krogh, H. R. (2001). Pink and blue collar jobs: Children's judgments of job status and job aspirations in relation to sex of worker. *Journal of Experimental Child Psychology, 79,* 346–363.

Liben, L. S., & Downs, R. M. (1993). Understanding person–space–map relations: Cartographic and developmental perspectives. *Developmental Psychology, 29,* 739–752.

Liben, L. S., & Signorella, M. L. (1993). Gender-schematic processing in children: The role of initial interpretations of stimuli. *Developmental Psychology, 29,* 141–149.

Lickliter, R., & Bahrick, L. E. (2000). The development of infant intersensory perception: Advantages of a comparative convergent-operations approach. *Psychological Bulletin, 126,* 260–280.

Lidz, C. S. (2001). Multicultural issues and dynamic assessment. In L. A. Suzuki & J. G. Ponterotto (Eds.), *Handbook of multicultural assessment: Clinical, psychological, and educational applications* (2nd ed., pp. 523–539). San Francisco: Jossey-Bass.

Lidz, J. (2007). The abstract nature of syntactic representations. In E. Hoff & M. Shatz (Eds.), *Blackwell handbook of language development* (pp. 277–303). Malden, MA: Blackwell.

Lidz, J., Gleitman, H., & Gleitman, L. (2004). Kidz in the 'hood: Syntactic bootstrapping and the mental lexicon. In D. G. Hall & S. R. Waxman (Eds.), *Weaving a lexicon* (pp. 603–636). Cambridge, MA: MIT Press.

Lieven, E., Pine, J., & Baldwin, G. (1997). Lexically based learning and early grammatical development. *Journal of Child Language, 24,* 187–220.

Li-Grining, C. P. (2007). Effortful control among low-income preschoolers in three cities: Stability, change, and individual differences. *Developmental Psychology, 43,* 208–221.

Lillard, A. (2003). Pretend play and cognitive development. In U. Goswami (Ed.), *Blackwell handbook of childhood cognitive development* (pp. 189–205). Malden, MA: Blackwell.

Lillard, A. (2007). *Montessori: The science behind the genius.* New York: Oxford University Press.

Lillard, A., & Else-Quest, N. (2006). Evaluating Montessori education. *Science, 313,* 1893–1894.

Lim, V. K. G. (2002). Gender differences and attitudes toward homosexuality. *Journal of Homosexuality, 43,* 85–97.

Linares, T. J., Singer, L. T., Kirchner, H., Lester, H., Short, E. J., & Min, M. O. (2006). Mental health outcomes of cocaine-exposed children at 6 years of age. *Journal of Pediatric Psychology, 31,* 85–97.

Lincove, J. A., & Painter, G. (2006). Does the age that children start kindergarten matter? Evidence of long-term educational and social outcomes. *Educational Evaluation and Policy Analysis, 28,* 153–179.

Lindau, S. T., Schumm, L. P., Laumann, E. O., Levinson, W., O'Muircheartaigh, C. A., & Waite, L. J. (2007). A study of sexuality and health among older adults in the United States. *New England Journal of Medicine, 357,* 762–774.

Lindley, L. D. (2005). Perceived barriers to career development in the context of social-cognitive career theory. *Journal of Career Assessment, 13,* 271–287.

Lindsay, C., Almey, M., & Normand, J. (2002). *Youth in Canada.* Retrieved from http://www.statcan.ca/english/IPS/Data/85-511-XPE.htm

Lindsay-Hartz, J., de Rivera, J., & Mascolo, M. F. (1995). Differentiating guilt and shame and their effects on motivation. In J. P. Tangney & K. W. Fischer (Eds.), *Self-conscious emotions* (pp. 274–300). New York: Guilford.

Lindsey, E. W., & Colwell, M. J. (2003). Preschoolers' emotional competence: Links to pretend and physical play. *Child Study Journal, 33,* 39–52.

Lindsey, E. W., & Mize, J. (2000). Parent–child physical and pretense play: Links to children's social competence. *Merrill-Palmer Quarterly, 46,* 565–591.

Linebarger, D. L., Kosanic, A. Z., Greenwood, C. R., & Doku, N. S. (2004). Effects of viewing the television program *Between the Lions* on the emergent literacy skills of young children. *Journal of Educational Psychology, 96,* 297–308.

Linley, P. A. (2003). Positive adaptation to trauma: Wisdom as both process and outcome. *Journal of Traumatic Stress, 16,* 601–610.

Linn, M. C., & Petersen, A. C. (1985). Emergence and characterization of sex differences in spatial ability: A meta-analysis. *Child Development, 56,* 1479–1498.

Linscheid, T. R., Budd, K. S., & Rasnake, L. K. (2005). Pediatric feeding problems. In M. C. Roberts (Ed.), *Handbook of pediatric psychology and psychiatry* (3rd ed., pp. 481–488). New York: Guilford.

Linver, M. R., Martin, A., & Brooks-Gunn, J. (2004). Measuring infants' home environment: The IT-HOME for infants between birth and 12 months in four national data sets. *Parenting: Science and Practice, 4,* 115–137.

Lipsitt, L. P. (2003). Crib death: A biobehavioral phenomenon? *Psychological Science, 12,* 164–170.

Liszkowski, U., Carpenter, M., Henning, A., Striano, T., & Tomasello, M. (2004). Twelve-month-olds point to share attention and interest. *Developmental Science, 7,* 297–307.

Liszkowski, U., Carpenter, M., & Tomasello, M. (2007). Pointing out new news, old news, and absent referents at 12 months of age. *Developmental Science, 10,* F1–F7.

Little, C., & Carter, A. S. (2005). Negative emotional reactivity and regulation in 12-month-olds following emotional challenge: Contributions of maternal–infant emotional availability in a low-income sample, *Infant Mental Health Journal, 26,* 354–368.

Little, T. D., Jones, S. M., Henrich, C. C., & Hawley, P. H. (2003). Disentangling the "whys" from the "whats" of aggressive behavior. *International Journal of Behavioral Development, 27,* 122–133.

Liu, J., Raine, A., Venables, P. H., Dalais, C., & Mednick, S. A. (2003). Malnutrition at age 3 years and lower cognitive ability at age 11 years. *Archives of Paediatric and Adolescent Medicine, 157,* 593–600.

Liu, X. Z., & Yan, D. (2007). Ageing and hearing loss. *Journal of Pathology, 211,* 188–197.

Lloyd, C. B. (2005). *Growing up global: The changing transitions to adulthood in developing countries.* Washington, DC: National Academy Press.

Lloyd, L. (1999). Multi-age classes and high ability students. *Review of Educational Research, 69,* 187–212.

Lloyd-Jones, D., Adams, R., Carnethon, M., De Simone, G., Ferguson, B., & Flegal, K. (2009). Heart disease and stroke statistics—2009 update. *Circulation, 119,* e21–e181.

Lochman, J. E., & Dodge K. A. (1998). Distorted perceptions in dyadic interactions of aggressive and nonaggressive boys: Effects of prior expectations, context, and boys' age. *Development and Psychopathology, 10,* 495–512.

Lock, J., & Kirz, N. (2008). Eating disorders: Anorexia nervosa. In W. E. Graighead, D. J. Miklowitz, & L. W. Craighead (Eds.), *Psychopathology: History, diagnosis, and empirical foundations* (pp. 467–494). Hoboken, NJ: Wiley.

Lock, M., & Kaufert, P. (2001). Menopause, local biologies, and cultures of aging. *American Journal of Human Biology, 13,* 494–504.

Lockhart, R. S., & Craik, F. I. M. (1990). Levels of processing: A retrospective commentary on a framework for memory research. *Canadian Journal of Psychology, 44,* 87–112.

Loeb, S., Fuller, B., Kagan, S. L., & Carrol, B. (2004). Child care in poor communities: Early learning effects of type, quality, and stability. *Child Development, 75,* 47–65.

Loehlin, J. C., Horn, J. M., & Willerman, L. (1997). Heredity, environment, and IQ in the Texas Adoption Project. In R. J. Sternberg & E. L. Grigorenko (Eds.), *Intelligence, heredity, and environment* (pp. 105–125). New York: Cambridge University Press.

Loehlin, J. C., Jonsson, E. G., Gustavsson, J. P., Stallings, M. C., Gillespie, N. A., Wright, M. J., & Martin, N. G. (2005). Psychological masculinity–femininity via the gender diagnosticity approach: Heritability and consistency across ages and populations. *Journal of Personality, 73,* 1295–1319.

Loehlin, J. C., & Martin, N. G. (2001). Age changes in personality traits and their heritabilities during the adult years: Evidence from Australian twin registry samples. *Personality and Individual Differences, 30,* 1147–1160.

Loewy, E. H. (2004). Euthanasia, physician assisted suicide and other methods of helping along death. *Health Care Analysis, 12,* 181–191.

Loganovskaja, T. K., & Loganovsky, K. N. (1999). EEG, cognitive and psychopathological abnormalities in children irradiated in utero. *International Journal of Psychophysiology, 34,* 211–224.

Loganovsky, K. N., Loganovskaja, T. K., Nechayev, S. Y., Antipchuk, Y. Y., & Bomko, M. A. (2008). Disrupted devlopment of the dominant hemisphere following prenatal irradiation. *Journal of Neuropsychiatry and Clinical Neurosciences, 20,* 274–291.

Logroscino, G., Kang, J. H., & Grodstein, F. (2004). Prospective study of type 2 diabetes and cognitive decline in women aged 70–81 years. *British Medical Journal, 328,* 548.

Lohman, D. F. (2000). Measures of intelligence: Cognitive theories. In A. E. Kazdin (Ed.), *Encyclopedia of psychology: Vol. 5* (pp. 147–150). Washington, DC: American Psychological Association.

Long, D. D. (1985). A cross-cultural examination of fears of death among Saudi Arabians. *Omega, 16,* 43–50.

Loock, C., Conry, J., Cook, J. L., Chudley, A. E., & Rosales, T. (2005). Identifying fetal alcohol spectrum disorder in primary care. *Canadian Medical Association Journal, 172,* 628–630.

Looker, D., & Thiessen, V. (2003). *The digital divide in Canadian schools: Factors affecting student access to and use of information technology.* Ottawa: Canadian Education Statistics Council.

Loots, G., & Devise, I. (2003). The use of visual-tactile communication strategies by deaf and hearing fathers and mothers of deaf infants. *Journal of Deaf Studies and Deaf Education, 8,* 31–42.

Lopata, H. Z. (1996). *Current widowhood: Myths and realities.* Thousand Oaks, CA: Sage.

Lorenz, K. (1952). *King Solomon's ring.* New York: Crowell.

Louie, V. (2001). Parents' aspirations and investment: The role of social class in the educational experiences of 1.5- and second generation Chinese Americans. *Harvard Educational Review, 71,* 438–474.

Louis, J., Cannard, C., Bastuji, H., & Challemel, M. J. (1997). Sleep ontogenesis revisited: A longitudinal 24-hour home polygraphic study on 15 normal infants during the first two years of life. *Sleep, 20,* 323–333.

Lourenco, O. (2003). Making sense of Turiel's dispute with Kohlberg: The case of the child's moral competence. *New Ideas in Psychology, 21,* 43–68.

Lövdén, M., Bergman, L., Adolfsson, R., Lindenberger, U., & Nilsson, L.-G. (2005). Studying individual aging in an interindividual context: Typical paths of age-related, dementia-related, and mortality-related cognitive development in old age. *Psychology and Aging, 20,* 303–316.

Love, J. M., Chazan-Cohen, R., & Raikes, H. (2007). Forty years of research knowledge and use: From Head Start to Early Head Start and beyond. In. J. L. Aber, S. J. Bishop-Josef, S. M. Jones, K. T. McLearn, & D. Phillips (Eds.), *Child development and social policy: Knowledge for action* (pp. 79–95). Washington, DC: American Psychological Association.

Love, J. M., Harrison, L., Sagi-Schwartz, A., van IJzendoorn, M. H., Ross, C., & Ungerer, J. A. (2003). Child care quality matters: How conclusions may vary with context. *Child Development, 74,* 1021–1033.

Love, J. M., Kisker, E. E., Ross, C., Raikes, H., Constantine, J., Boller, K., & Brooks-Gunn, J. (2005). The effectiveness of early Head Start for 3-year-old children and their parents: Lessons for policy and programs. *Developmental Psychology, 41,* 885–901.

Love, J. M., Tarullo, L. B., Raikes, H., & Chazan-Cohen, R. (2006). Head Start: What do we know about its effectiveness? What do we need to know? In K. McCartney & D. Phillips (Eds.), *Blackwell handbook of early childhood development* (pp. 550–575). Malden, MA: Blackwell.

Lowenstein, A., Katz, R., & Gur-Yaish, N. (2007). Reciprocity in parent–child exchange and life satisfaction among the elderly: A cross-national perspective. *Journal of Social Issues, 63,* 865–883.

Lubart, T. I. (2003). In search of creative intelligence. In R. J. Sternberg, J. Lautrey, & T. I. Lubart (Eds.), *Models of intelligence: International perspectives* (pp. 279–292). Washington, DC: American Psychological Association.

Lubart, T. I., & Sternberg, R. J. (1998). Life span creativity: An investment theory approach. In C. E. Adams-Price (Ed.), *Creativity and successful aging.* New York: Springer.

Lucas, R. E., Clark, A. E., Georgellis, Y., & Diener, E. (2003). Reexamining adaptation and the set point model of happiness: Reactions to changes in marital status. *Journal of Personality and Social Psychology, 84,* 803–805.

Lucas, S. R., & Behrends, M. (2002). Sociodemographic diversity, correlated achievement, and de facto tracking. *Sociology of Education, 75,* 328–348.

Lucas, T. W., Wendorf, C. A., Imamoglu, E. O., Shen, J., Parkhill, M. R., Weisfeld, C. C. & Weisfeld, G. E. (2004). Marital satisfaction in four cultures as a function of homogamy, male dominance, and female attractiveness. *Sexualities, Evolution and Gender, 6,* 97–130.

Lucas-Thompson, R., & Clarke-Stewart, K. A. (2007). Forecasting friendship: How marital quality, maternal mood, and attachment security are linked to children's peer relationships. *Journal of Applied Developmental Psychology, 28,* 499–514.

Ludemann, P. M. (1991). Generalized discrimination of positive facial expressions by seven-and ten-month-old infants. *Child Development, 62,* 55–67.

Ludvig, J., Miner, B., & Eisenberg, M. J. (2005). Smoking cessation in patients with coronary artery disease. *American Heart Journal, 149,* 565–572.

Luecken, L. J. (2008). Long-term consequences of parental death in childhood: Psychological and physiological manifestations. In M. S. Stroebe, R. O. Hansson, H. Schut, & W. Stroebe (Eds.), *Handbook of bereavement research and practice* (pp. 397–416). Washington, DC: American Psychological Association.

Lugton, J. (2001). *Communicating with dying people.* Nijmegen, Netherlands: Radcliff Medical Press.

Lukas, C., & Seiden, H. M. (2007). *Silent grief: Living in the wake of suicide* (rev. ed.). London, U.K.: Jessica Kingsley.

Luke, A., Cooper, R. S., Prewitt, T. E., Adeyemo, A. A., & Forrester, T. E. (2001). Nutritional consequences of the African diaspora. *Annual Review of Nutrition, 21,* 47–71.

Luna, B., Garver, K. E., Urban, T. A., Lazar, N. A., & Sweeney, J. A. (2004). Maturation of cognitive processes from late childhood to adulthood. *Child Development, 75,* 1357–1372.

Luna, B., Thulborn, K. R., Monoz, D. P., Merriam, E. P., Garver, K. E., Minshew, N. J., Keshavan, M. S., Genovese, C. R., Eddy, W. F., & Sweeney, J. A. (2001). Maturation of widely distributed brain function subserves cognitive development. *Neuroimage, 13,* 786–793.

Lund, D. A. (1993). Widowhood: The coping response. In R. Kastenbaum (Ed.), *Encyclopedia of adult development* (pp. 537–541). Phoenix, AZ: Oryx Press.

Lund, D. A. (1996). Bereavement and loss. In J. E. Birren (Ed.), *Encyclopedia of gerontology* (pp. 173–183). San Diego: Academic Press.

Lund, D. A. (1998). Statements and perspectives from leaders in the field of aging in Utah. In *Utah sourcebook on aging.* Salt Lake City: Empire Publishing.

Lund, D. A. (2005). *My journey* [Sue's letter]. Unpublished document. Salt Lake City, UT: University of Utah.

Lund, D. A., & Caserta, M. S. (2001). When the unexpected happens: Husbands coping with the deaths of their wives. In D. Lund (Ed.), *Men coping with grief* (pp. 147–166). Amityville, NY: Baywood.

Lund, D. A., & Caserta, M. S. (2004a). Facing life alone: Loss of a significant other in later life. In D. Doda (Ed), *Living with grief: Loss in later life* (pp. 207–223). Washington, DC: Hospice Foundation of America.

Lund, D. A., & Caserta, M. S. (2004b). Older men coping with widowhood. *Geriatrics and Aging, 7*(6), 29–33.

Lund, D. A., Caserta, M. S., de Vries, B., & Wright, S. (2004). Restoration after bereavement. *Generations Review, 14,* 9–15.

Lund, D. A., Caserta, M. S., & Dimond, M. F. (1993). The course of spousal bereavement in later life. In M. S. Stroebe, W. Stroebe, & R. O. Hansson (Eds.), *Handbook of bereavement* (pp. 240–245). New York: Cambridge University Press.

Lund, D. A., Hill, R. D., Caserta, M. S., & Wright, S. D. (1995). Video Respite™: An innovative resource for family, professional cargivers, and persons with dementia. *Gerontologist, 35,* 683–687.

Lund, D. A., Wright, S. D., & Caserta, M. S. (2005). Respite services: Enhancing the quality of daily life for caregivers and persons with dementia. *Geriatrics and Aging, 8,* 60–65.

Lundy, B. L. (2002). Paternal socio-psychological factors and infant attachment: The mediating role of synchrony in father–infant interactions. *Infant Behavior and Development, 25,* 221–236.

Lundy, B. L. (2003). Father– and mother–infant face-to-face interactions: Differences in mind-related comments and infant attachment? *Infant Behavior and Development, 26,* 200–212.

Luo, L., & Craik, F. I. M. (2008). Aging and memory: A cognitive approach. *Canadian Journal of Psychiatry, 53,* 346–353.

Luo, Y., & Baillargeon, R. (2005). When the ordinary seems unexpected: Evidence for incremental physical knowledge in young infants. *Cognition, 95,* 297–328.

Luo, Y., & Waite, L. J. (2005). The impact of childhood and adult SES on physical, mental, and cognitive well-being in later life. *Journal of Gerontology, 60B,* S93–S101.

Lusardi, A., & Mitchell, O. S. (2007). Baby boomer retirement security: The roles of planning, financial literacy, and housing wealth. *Journal of Monetary Economics, 54,* 205–224.

Lussier, G., Deater-Deckard, K., Dunn, J., & Davies, L. (2002). Support across two generations: Children's closeness to grandparents following parental divorce and remarriage. *Journal of Family Psychology, 16,* 363–376.

Luster, T., & Haddow, J. L. (2005). Adolescent mothers and their children: An ecological perspective. In T. Luster & J. L. Haddow (Eds.), *Parenting: An ecological perspective* (2nd ed., pp. 73–101). Mahwah, NJ: Erlbaum.

Luthar, S. S. (2006). Resilience in development: A synthesis of research across five decades. In D. Cicchetti & D. J. Cohen (Eds.), *Developmental psychopathology: Vol. 3. Risk, disorder, and adaptation* (2nd ed., pp. 739–795). Hoboken, NJ: Wiley.

Luthar, S. S., & Becker, B. E. (2002). Privileged but pressured: A study of affluent youth. *Child Development, 73,* 1593–1610.

Luthar, S. S., & Latendresse, S. J. (2005a). Children of the affluent: Challenges to well-being. *Current Directions in Psychological Science, 14,* 49–53.

Luthar, S. S., & Latendresse, S. J. (2005b). Comparable "risks" at the socioeconomic status extremes: Preadolescents' perceptions of parenting. *Development and Psychopathology, 17,* 207–230.

Luthar, S. S., & Sexton, C. (2004). The high price of affluence. In R. V. Kail (Ed.), *Advances in child development* (Vol. 32, pp. 126–162). San Diego, CA: Academic Press.

Luxembourg Income Study. (2008). *LIS key figures.* Retrieved from www.lisproject.org/php/kf/kf.php

Luyckx, K., Goossens, L., & Soenens, B. (2006). A developmental contextual perspective on identity construction in emerging adulthood: Change dynamics in commitment formation and commitment evaluation. *Developmental Psychology, 42,* 366–380.

Luyckx, K., Goossens, L., Soenens, B., & Beyers, W. (2006). Unpacking commitment and exploration: Preliminary validation of an integrative model of late adolescent identity formation. *Journal of Adolescence, 29,* 361–378.

Luzzo, D. A. (1999). Identifying the career decision-making needs of nontraditional college students. *Journal of Counseling and Development, 77,* 135–140.

Lynch, S. K., Turkheimer, E., D'Onofrio, B. M., Mendle, J., Emery, R. E., Slutske, W. S., & Martin, N. G. (2006). A genetically informed study of the association between harsh punishment and offspring behavioral problems. *Journal of Family Psychology, 20,* 190–198.

Lyness, K. S., & Heilman, M. E. (2006). When fit is fundamental: Performance evaluations and promotions of upper-level female and male managers. *Journal of Applied Psychology, 90,* 777–785.

Lyness, K. S., & Thompson, D. (1997). Above the glass ceiling? A comparison of matched samples of female and male executives. *Journal of Applied Psychology, 82,* 359–375.

Lyon, T. D., & Flavell, J. H. (1994). Young children's understanding of "remember" and "forget." *Child Development, 65,* 1357–1371.

Lyons-Ruth, K. (1996). Attachment relationships among children with aggressive behavior problems: The role of disorganized early attachment patterns. *Journal of Consulting and Clinical Psychology, 64,* 64–73.

Lyons-Ruth, K., Bronfman, E., & Parsons, E. (1999). Maternal frightened, frightening, or atypical behavior and disorganized infant attachment patterns. *Monographs of the Society for Research in Child Development, 64*(3, Serial No. 258), 67–96.

Lyons-Ruth, K., Easterbrooks, A., & Cibelli, C. (1997). Infant attachment strategies, infant mental lag, and maternal depressive symptoms: Predictors of internalizing and externalizing problems at age 7. *Developmental Psychology, 33,* 681–692.

Lyons-Ruth, K., Yellin, C., Melnick, S., & Atwood, G. (2005). Expanding the concept of unresolved mental states: Hostile/helpless states of mind on the Adult Attachment Interview are associated with disrupted mother–infant communication and infant disorganization. *Development and Psychopathology, 27,* 1–23.

Lytton, H., & Gallagher, L. (2002). Parenting twins and the genetics of parenting. In M. H. Bornstein (Ed.), *Handbook of parenting* (Vol. 1, pp. 227–253). Mahwah, NJ: Erlbaum.

M

Maas, F. K. (2008). Children's understanding of promising, lying, and false belief. *Journal of General Psychology, 13,* 301–321.

Maas, F. K., & Abbeduto, L. J. (2001). Children's judgments about intentionally and unintentionally broken promises. *Journal of Child Language, 28,* 517–529.

Macaluso, A., & De Vito, G. (2004). Muscle strength, power and adaptations to resistance training in older people. *European Journal of Applied Physiology, 91,* 450–472.

Maccoby, E. E. (1984). Socialization and developmental change. *Child Development, 55,* 317–328.

Maccoby, E. E. (1998). *The two sexes: Growing up apart, coming together.* Cambridge, MA: Belknap.

Maccoby, E. E. (2000). Perspectives on gender development. *International Journal of Behavioral Development, 24,* 398–406.

Maccoby, E. E. (2002). Gender and group process: A developmental perspective. *Current Directions in Psychological Science, 11,* 54–58.

MacDonald, W. L., & DeMaris, A. (1996). The effects of stepparent's gender and new biological children. *Journal of Family Issues, 17,* 5–25.

Macek, P., Bejček, J., & Vaníčková, J. (2007). Contemporary Czech emerging adults: Generation growing up in the period of social changes. *Journal of Adolescent Research, 22,* 444–475.

Machin, G. A. (2005). Multiple birth. In H. W. Taeusch, R. A. Ballard, & C. A. Gleason (Eds.), *Avery's diseases of the newborn* (8th ed., pp. 57–62). Philadelphia: Saunders.

Mackenbach, J. P. (2002). Income inequality and population health. *British Medical Journal, 324,* 1–2.

Mackey, K., Arnold, M. K., & Pratt, M. W. (2001). Adolescents' stories of decision making in more and less authoritative families: Representing the voices of parents in narrative. *Journal of Adolescent Research, 16,* 243–268.

Mackie, S., Show, P., Lenroot, R., Pierson, R., Greenstein, D. K., & Nugent, T. F., III. (2007). Cerebellar development and clinical outcome in attention deficit hyperactivity disorder. *American Journal of Psychiatry, 164,* 647–655.

MacWhinney, B. (2005). Language development. In M. H. Bornstein & M. E. Lamb (Eds.), *Developmental science: An advanced textbook* (5th ed., pp. 359–387). Mahwah, NJ: Erlbaum.

Maddi, S. R. (1999). The personality construct of hardiness: I. Effects on experiencing, coping, and strain. *Consulting Psychology Journal: Practice and Research, 51,* 83–94.

Maddi, S. R. (2005). On hardiness and other pathways to resilience. *American Psychologist, 60,* 261–262.

Maddi, S. R. (2006). Hardiness: The courage to be resilient. In J. C. Thomas, D. L. Segal, & M. Hersen (Eds.), *Comprehensive handbook of personality and psychopathology: Vol. 1. Personality and everyday functioning* (pp. 306–321). Hoboken, NJ: Wiley.

Maddi, S. R. (2007). The story of hardiness: Twenty years of theorizing, research, and practice. In A. Monat, R. S. Lazarus, & G. Reevy (Eds.), *Praeger handbook on stress and coping* (Vol. 2, pp. 327–340). Wastport, CT: Praeger.

Maddi, S. R., & Hightower, M. (1999). Hardiness and optimism as expressed in coping patterns. *Consulting Psychology Journal: Practice and Research, 51,* 95–105.

Maddox, G. L. (1963). Activity and morale: A longitudinal study of selected elderly subjects. *Social Forces, 42,* 195–204.

Madigan, S., Moran, G., & Pederson, D. R. (2006). Unresolved states of mind, disorganized attachment relationships, and disrupted interactions of adolescent mothers and their infants. *Developmental Psychology, 42,* 293–304.

Madnawat, A. V. S., & Kachhawa, P. S. (2007). Age, gender, and living circumstances: Discriminating older adults on death anxiety. *Death Studies, 31,* 763–769.

Madon, S., Jussim, L., & Eccles, J. (1997). In search of the powerful self-fulfilling prophecy. *Journal of Personality and Social Psychology, 72,* 791–809.

Madsen, S. A., & Juhl, T. (2007). Paternal depression in the postnatal period assessed with traditional and male depression scales. *Journal of Men's Health and Gender, 4,* 26–31.

Maglio, C. J., & Robinson, S. E. (1994). The effects of death education on death anxiety: A meta-analysis. *Omega, 29,* 319–335.

Magnusson, D. (1999). Holistic interactionism: A perspective for research on personality development. In L. A. Pervin & O. P. John (Eds.), *Handbook of personality: Theory and research* (2nd ed., pp. 219–247). New York: Guilford.

Magolda, M. B. B. (2002). Epistemological reflection: The evolution of epistemological assumptions from age 18 to 30. In B. K. Hofer & P. R. Pintrich (Eds.), *Personal epistemology* (pp. 89–102). Mahwah, NJ: Erlbaum.

Mahady, G. B., Locklear, T. D., Doyle, B. J., Huang, Y., Perez, A. L., & Caceres, A. (2008). Menopause, a universal female experience: Lessons from Mexico and Central America. *Current Women's Health Reviews, 4,* 3–8.

Mahanran, L. G., Bauman, P. A., Kalman, D., Skolnik, H., & Pele, S. M. (1999). Master athletes: Factors affecting performance. *Sports Medicine, 28,* 273–285.

Mahon, M. M., Goldberg, E. Z., & Washington, S. K. (1999). Concept of death in a sample of Israeli kibbutz children. *Death Studies, 23,* 43–59.

Mahoney, A., Pargament, K. I., Jewell, T., Swank, A. B., Scott, E., Emery, E., & Rye, M. (1999). Marriage and the spiritual realm: The role of proximal and distal religious constructs in marital functioning. *Journal of Family Psychology, 13,* 321–338.

Mahoney, J. L. (2000). Participation in school extracurricular activities as a moderator in the development of antisocial patterns. *Child Development, 71,* 502–516.

Mahoney, M. M. (2002). The economic rights and responsibilities of unmarried cohabitants. In A. Booth & A. C. Crouter (Eds.), *Just living together* (pp. 247–254). Mahwah, NJ: Erlbaum.

Maier, D. M., & Newman, M. J. (1995). Legal and psychological considerations in the development of a euthanasia statute for adults in the United States. *Behavioral Sciences and the Law, 13,* 3–25.

Main, M. (2000). The organized categories of infant, child, and adult attachment: Flexible vs. inflexible attention under attachment-related stress. *Journal of the American Psychoanalytic Association, 48,* 1055–1096.

Main, M., & Goldwyn, R. (1998). *Adult attachment classification system.* London: University College.

Main, M., & Solomon, J. (1990). Procedures for identifying infants as disorganized/disoriented during the Ainsworth Strange Situation. In M. Greenberg, D. Cicchetti, & M. Cummings (Eds.), *Attachment in the preschool years: Theory, research, and intervention* (pp. 121–160). Chicago: University of Chicago Press.

Mains, D. S., Nowels, C. T., Cavender, T. A., Etschmaier, M., & Steiner, J. F. (2005). A qualitative study of work and work return in cancer survivors. *Psycho-Oncology, 14,* 992–1004.

Maitland, S. B., Intrieri, R. C., Schaie, K. W., & Willis, S. L. (2000). Gender differences and changes in cognitive abilities across the adult life span. *Aging, Neuropsychology, and Cognition, 7,* 32–53.

Majdandžić, M., & van den Boom, D. C. (2007). Multimethod longitudinal assessment of temperament in early childhood. *Journal of Personality, 75,* 12.

Majnemer, A., & Barr, R. G. (2005). Influence of supine sleep positioning on early motor milestone acquisition. *Developmental Medicine and Child Neurology, 47,* 370–376.

Major, B., Spencer, S., Schmader, T., Wolfe, C., & Crocker, J. (1998). Coping with negative stereotypes about intellectual performance: The role of psychological disengagement. *Personality and Social Psychology Bulletin, 24,* 34–50.

Makin, J., Fried, P. A., & Watkinson, B. (1991). A comparison of active and passive smoking during pregnancy: Long-term effects. *Neurotoxicology and Teratology, 13,* 5–12.

Makishita, H., & Matsunaga, K. (2008). Differences of drivers' reaction times according to age and mental workload. *Accident Analysis Prevention, 40,* 567–575.

Makrantonaki, E., & Xouboulis, C. C. (2007). Molecular mechanisms of skin aging: State of the art. *Annals of the New York Academy of Sciences, 1119,* 40–50.

Malaguarnera, L., Ferlito, L., Imbesi, R. M., Gulizia, G. S., Di Mauro, S., Maugeri, D., Malaguarnera, M., & Messina, A. (2001). Immunosenescence: A review. *Archives of Gerontology and Geriatrics, 32,* 1–14.

Malatesta, C. Z., Grigoryev, P., Lamb, C., Albin, M., & Culver, C. (1986). Emotion socialization and expressive development in preterm and full-term infants. *Child Development, 57,* 316–330.

Malina, R. M., & Bouchard, C. (1991). *Growth, maturation, and physical activity.* Champaign, IL: Human Kinetics.

Mallinckrodt, B., & Fretz, B. R. (1988). Social support and the impact of job loss on older professionals. *Journal of Counseling Psychology, 35,* 281–286.

Malone, M. M. (1982). Consciousness of dying and projective fantasy of young children with malignant disease. *Developmental and Behavioral Pediatrics, 3,* 55–60.

Mandler, J. M. (2004). Thought before language. *Trends in Cognitive Sciences, 8,* 508–513.

Mandler, J. M., & McDonough, L. (1998). On developing a knowledge base in infancy. *Developmental Psychology, 34,* 1274–1288.

Mangelsdorf, S. C., Schoppe, S. J., & Buur, H. (2000). The meaning of parental reports: A contextual approach to the study of temperament and behavior problems. In V. J. Molfese & D. L. Molfese (Eds.), *Temperament and personality across the life span* (pp. 121–140). Mahwah, NJ: Erlbaum.

Mani, T. M., Bedwell, J. S., & Miller, L. S. (2005). Age-related decrements in performance on a brief continuous performance task. *Archives of Clinical Neuropsychology, 20,* 575–586.

Manlove, J. S. (1997). Early motherhood in an intergenerational perspective: The experiences of a British cohort. *Journal of Marriage and the Family, 59,* 263–279.

Manlove, J. S., Terry-Humen, E., Ikramullah, E. N., & Moore, K. A. (2006). The role of parent religiosity in teens' transitions to sex and contraception. *Journal of Adolescent Health, 39,* 578–587.

Mannell, R. C. (1999). Older adults, leisure, and wellness. *Journal of Leisurability, 26*(2), 3–10.

Manole, M. D., & Hickey, R. W. (2006). Preterminal gasping and effects on the cardiac function. *Critical Care Medicine, 34*(Suppl.), S438–S441.

Manson, J. E., Skerrett, P. J., Greenland, P., & VanItallie, T. B. (2004). The escalating pandemics of obesity and sedentary lifestyle: A call to action for clinicians. *Archives of Internal Medicine, 164,* 249–258.

Manton, K. C., Gu, X. L., & Ukraintseva, S. V. (2005). Declining prevalence of dementia in the U.S. elderly population. *Advances in Gerontology, 16,* 30–37.

Mao, A., Burnham, M. M., Goodlin-Jones, B. L., Gaylor, E. E., & Anders, T. F. (2004). A comparison of the sleep–wake patterns of cosleeping and solitary-sleeping infants. *Child Psychiatry and Human Development, 35,* 95–105.

Maratsos, M. (1998). The acquisition of grammar. In D. Kuhn & R. S. Siegler (Eds.), *Handbook of child psychology: Vol. 2. Cognition, perception, and language* (5th ed., pp. 421–466). New York: Wiley.

Maratsos, M. (2000). More overregularizations after all: New data and discussion on Marcus, Pinker, Ullman, Hollander, Rosen, & Xu. *Journal of Child Language, 27,* 183–212.

Marchman, V. A., & Thal, D. J. (2005). Words and grammar. In M. Tomasello & D. I. Slobin (Eds.), *Beyond nature–nurture: Essays in honor of Elizabeth Bates* (pp. 141–164). Mahwah, NJ: Erlbaum.

Marcia, J. E. (1980). Identity in adolescence. In J. Adelson (Ed.), *Handbook of adolescent psychology* (pp. 159–187). New York: Wiley.

Marcia, J. E. (2002). Identity and psychosocial development in adulthood. *Identity, 2,* 7–28.

Marcon, R. A. (1999a). Differential impact of preschool models on development and early learning of inner-city children: A three-cohort study. *Developmental Psychology, 35,* 358–375.

Marcon, R. A. (1999b). Positive relationships between parent–school involvement and public school inner-city preschoolers' development and academic performance. *School Psychology Review, 28,* 395–412.

Marcus, G. F. (1995). Children's overregularization of English plurals: A quantitative analysis. *Journal of Child Language, 22,* 447–459.

Marcus-Newhall, A., Thompson, S., & Thomas, C. (2001). Examining a gender stereotype: Menopausal women. *Journal of Applied Social Psychology, 31,* 698–719.

Mardh, P. A. (2002). Influence of infection with *Chlamydia trachomatis* on pregnancy outcome, infant health and life-long sequelae in infected offspring. *Best Practice and Research in Clinical Obstetrics and Gynaecology, 16,* 847–964.

Mariano, K. A., & Harton, H. C. (2005). Similarities in aggression, inattention/hyperactivity, depression, and anxiety in middle childhood friendships. *Journal of Social and Clinical Psychology, 24,* 471–496.

Markman, E. M. (1992). Constraints on word learning: Speculations about their nature, origins, and domain specificity. In M. R. Gunnar & M. P. Maratsos (Eds.), *Minnesota Symposia on Child Psychology* (Vol. 25, pp. 59–101). Hillsdale, NJ: Erlbaum.

Markova, G., & Legerstee, M. (2006). Contingency, imitation, and affect sharing: Foundations of infants' social awareness. *Developmental Psychology, 42,* 132–141.

Markovits, H., Benenson, J., & Dolensky, E. (2001). Evidence that children and adolescents have internal models of peer interactions that are gender differentiated. *Child Development, 72,* 879–886.

Markovits, H., & Vachon, R. (1990). Conditional reasoning, representation, and level of abstraction. *Developmental Psychology, 26,* 942–951.

Marks, G. N., Cresswell, J., & Ainley, J. (2006). Explaining socioeconomic inequalities in student achievement: The role of home and school factors. *Educational Research and Evaluation, 12,* 105–128.

Marks, N. F. (1995). Midlife marital status differences in social support relationships with adult children and psychological well-being. *Journal of Family Issues, 16,* 5–28.

Marks, N. F. (1996). Caregiving across the lifespan: National prevalence and predictors. *Family Relations, 45,* 27–36.

Marks, N. F., Bumpass, L. L., & Jun, H. (2004). Family roles and well-being during the middle life course. In O. G. Brim, C. D. Ryff, & R.C. Kessler (Eds.), *How healthy are we? A national study of well-being at midlife* (pp. 514–549). Chicago: University of Chicago Press.

Marks, N. F., & Lambert, J. D. (1998). Marital status continuity and change among young and midlife adults. *Journal of Family Issues, 19,* 652–686.

Markstrom, C. A., & Kalmanir, H. M. (2001). Linkages between the psychosocial stages of identity and intimacy and the ego strengths of fidelity and love. *Identity, 1,* 179–196.

Markstrom, C. A., Sabino, V., Turner, B., & Berman, R. (1997). The Psychosocial Inventory of Ego Strengths: Development and validation of a new Eriksonian measure. *Journal of Youth and Adolescence, 26,* 705–732.

Markus, H. R., & Herzog, A. R. (1992). The role of self-concept in aging. In K. W. Schaie & M. P. Lawton (Eds.), *Annual review of gerontology and geriatrics* (pp. 110–143). New York: Springer.

Marlier, L., & Schaal, B. (2005). Human newborns prefer human milk: Conspecific milk odor is attractive without postnatal exposure. *Child Development, 76,* 155–168.

Marra, R., & Palmer, B. (2004). Encouraging intellectual growth: Senior college student profiles. *Journal of Adult Development, 11,* 111–122.

Marsh, H. W. (1990). The structure of academic self-concept: The Marsh/Shavelson model. *Journal of Educational Psychology, 82,* 623–636.

Marsh, H. W., & Ayotte, V. (2003). Do multiple dimensions of self-concept become more differentiated with age? The differential distinctiveness hypothesis. *Journal of Educational Psychology, 95,* 687–706.

Marsh, H. W., Craven, R., & Debus, R. (1998). Structure, stability, and development of young children's self-concepts: A multicohort–multioccasion study. *Child Development, 69,* 1030–1053.

Marsh, H. W., Ellis, L. A., & Craven, R. G. (2002). How do preschool children feel about themselves? Unraveling measurement and multidimensional self-concept structure. *Developmental Psychology, 38,* 376–393.

Marsh, H. W., Gerlach, E., Trautwein, U., Lüdtke, O., & Brettschneider, W.-D. (2007). Longitudinal study of predadolescent sport self-concept and performance: Reciprocal effects and causal ordering. *Child Development, 78,* 1640–1656.

Marsh, H. W., & Kleitman, S. (2002). Extracurricular school activities: The good, the bad, and the nonlinear. *Harvard Educational Review, 72,* 464–514.

Marsh, H. W., & Kleitman, S. (2005). Consequences of employment during high school: Character building, subversion of academic goals, or a threshold? *American Educational Research Journal, 42,* 331–369.

Marsh, M. W., Parada, R. H., & Ayotte, V. (2004). A multidimensional perspective of relations between self-concept (Self Description Questionnaire II) and adolescent mental health (Youth Self Report). *Psychological Assessment, 16,* 27–41.

Marshall, N. L. (1997). Combining work and family. In S. J. Gallant, G. P. Keita, & R. Royak-Schaler (Eds.), *Health care for women* (pp. 163–174). Washington, DC: American Psychological Association.

Marshall-Baker, A., Lickliter, R. & Cooper, R. P. (1998). Prolonged exposure to a visual pattern may promote behavioral organization in preterm infants. *Journal of Perinatal and Neonatal Nursing, 12,* 50–62.

Martin, C. L., & Fabes, R. A. (2001). The stability and consequences of young children's same-sex peer interactions. *Developmental Psychology, 37,* 431–446.

Martin, C. L., Fabes, R. A., Evans, S. M., & Wyman, H. (1999). Social cognition on the playground: Children's beliefs about playing with girls versus boys and their relations to sex segregated play. *Journal of Social and Personal Relationships, 16,* 751–771.

Martin, C. L., & Halverson, C. F. (1987). The role of cognition in sex role acquisition. In D. B. Carter (Ed.), *Current conceptions of sex roles and sex typing: Theory and research* (pp. 123–137). New York: Praeger.

Martin, C. L., & Ruble, D. (2004). Children's search for gender cues: Cognitive perspectives on gender development. *Current Directions in Psychological Science, 13,* 67–70.

Martin, C. L., Ruble, D. N., & Szkrybalo, J. (2002). Cognitive theories of early gender development. *Psychological Bulletin, 128,* 903–933.

Martin, G. L., & Pear, J. (2007). *Behavior modification: What it is and how to do it* (8th ed.). Upper Saddle River, NJ: Prentice-Hall.

Martin, J. E., & Dean, L. (1993). Bereavement following death from AIDS: Unique problems, reactions, and special needs. In M. S. Stroebe, W. Stroebe, & R. O. Hansson (Eds.), *Handbook of bereavement* (pp. 317–330). Cambridge, UK: Cambridge University Press.

Martin, K. A. (1996). *Puberty, sexuality and the self: Girls and boys at adolescence.* New York: Routledge.

Martin, P., Long, M. V., & Poon, L. W. (2002). Age changes and differences in personality traits and states of the old and very old. *Journal of Gerontology, 57B,* P144–P152.

Martinez-Frias, M. L., Bermejo, E., Rodríguez-Pinilla, E., & Frías, J. L. (2004). Risk for congenital anomalies associated with different sporadic and daily doses of alcohol consumption during pregnancy: A case-control study. *Birth Defects Research, Part A, Clinical and Molecular Teratology, 70,* 194–200.

Martins, P. A., Hoffman, D. J., Fernandes, M. T., Nascimento, C. R., Roberts, S. B., Sesso, R., & Sawaya, A. L. (2004). Stunted children gain less lean body mass and more fat mass than their nonstunted counterparts: A prospective study. *British Journal of Nutrition, 92,* 819–825.

Martinson, I. M., Davies, E., & McClowry, S. G. (1987). The long-term effect of sibling death on self-concept. *Journal of Pediatric Nursing, 2,* 227–235.

Martlew, M., & Connolly, K. J. (1996). Human figure drawings by schooled and unschooled children in Papua New Guinea. *Child Development, 67,* 2743–2762.

Martyn, C. N., Barker, D. J. P., & Osmond, C. (1996). Mothers' pelvic size, fetal growth, and death from stroke and coronary heart disease in men in the UK. *Lancet, 348,* 1264–1268.

Maruna, S. (2001). *Making good: How ex-convicts reform and rebuild their lives.* Washington, DC: American Psychological Association.

Maruna, S., LeBel, T. P., & Lanier, C. S. (2004). Generativity behind bars: Some "redemptive truths" about prison society. In E. de St. Aubin, D. P. McAdams, & T.-C. Kim (Eds.), *The generative society* (pp. 131–151). Washington, DC: American Psychological Association.

Maruta, T., Colligan, R. C., Malinchoc, M., & Offord, K. P. (2002). Optimism–pessimism assessed in the 1960s and self-reported health status 30 years later. *Mayo Clinic Proceedings, 77,* 748–753.

Marzolf, D. P., & DeLoache, J. S. (1994). Transfer in young children's understanding of spatial representations. *Child Development, 65,* 1–15.

Masataka, N. (1996). Perception of motherese in a signed language by 6-month-old deaf infants. *Developmental Psychology, 32,* 874–879.

Mascolo, M. F., & Fischer, K. W. (2007). The codevelopment of self and sociomoral emotions during the toddler years. In C. A. Brownell & C. B. Kopp (Eds.), *Socioemotional development in the toddler years: Transitions and transformations* (pp. 66–99). New York: Guilford.

Mashburn, A. J. (2008). Quality of social and physical environments in preschools and children's development of academic, language, and literacy skills. *Applied Developmental Science, 12,* 113–127.

Maslach, C., Schaufeli, W. B., & Leiter, M. P. (2001). Job burnout. *Annual Review of Psychology, 52,* 397–422.

Mason, M. G., & Gibbs, J. C. (1993a). Role-taking opportunities and the transition to advanced moral judgment. *Moral Education Forum, 18,* 1–12.

Mason, M. G., & Gibbs, J. C. (1993b). Social perspective taking and moral judgment among college students. *Journal of Adolescent Research, 8,* 109–123.

Masten, A. S. (2001). Ordinary magic: Resilience processes in development. *American Psychologist, 56,* 227–238.

Masten, A. S., Coatsworth, J. D., Neemann, J., Gest, S. D., Tellegen, A., & Garmezy, N. (1995). The structure and coherence of competence from childhood through adolescence. *Child Development, 66,* 1635–1659.

Masten, A. S., & Gewirtz, A. H. (2006). Vulnerability and resilience in early child development. In K. McCartney & D. Phillips (Eds.), *Blackwell handbook of early child development* (pp. 22–43). Malden, MA: Blackwell.

Masten, A. S., & Powell, J. L. (2003). A resilience framework for research, policy, and practice. In S. S. Luthar (Ed.), *Resilience and vulnerability* (pp. 1–25). New York: Cambridge University Press.

Masten, A. S., & Reed, M. J. (2002). Resilience in development. In C. R. Snyder & S. J. Lopez (Eds.), *Handbook of positive psychology* (pp. 74–88). New York: Oxford University Press.

Masten, A. S., & Shaffer, A. (2006). How families matter in child development: Reflections from research on risk and resilience. In A. S. Masten & A. Shaffer (Eds.), *Families count: Effects on child and adolescent development* (pp. 5–25). New York: Cambridge University Press.

Mastropieri, D., & Turkewitz, G. (1999). Prenatal experience and neonatal responsiveness to vocal expression of emotion. *Developmental Psychobiology, 35,* 204–214.

Masur, E. F., McIntyre, C. W., & Flavell, J. H. (1973). Developmental changes in apportionment of study time among items in a multi-trial free recall task. *Journal of Experimental Child Psychology, 15,* 237–246.

Masur, E. F., & Rodemaker, J. E. (1999). Mothers' and infants' spontaneous vocal, verbal, and action imitation during the second year. *Merrill-Palmer Quarterly, 45,* 392–412.

Mathews, T. J., & MacDorman, M. F. (2008). Infant mortality statistics from the 2005 period linked birth/infant death data set. *National Vital Statistics Reports, 57*(2), 1–32.

Mathiesen, K. S., & Prior, M. (2006). The impact of temperament factors and family functioning on resilience processes from infancy to school age. *European Journal of Developmental Psychology, 3,* 357–387.

Matthews, F., & Brayne, C. (2005). The incidence of dementia in England and Wales: Findings from the five identical sites of the MRC CFA Study. *PLoS Medicine, 2,* e193.mmg/sec5/ch40/ch40a.jsp

Matthews, K. A., Gump, B. B., Harris, K. F., Haney, T. L., & Barefoot, J. C. (2004). Hostile behaviors predict cardiovascular mortality among men enrolled in the Multiple Risk Factor Intervention Trial. *Circulation, 109,* 66–70.

Mattison, J. A., Lane, M. A., Roth, G. S., & Ingram, D. K. (2003). Calorie restriction in rhesus monkeys. *Experimental Gerontology, 38,* 35–46.

Mattson, S. N., Calarco, K. E., & Lang, A. R. (2006). Focused and shifting attention in children with heavy prenatal alcohol exposure. *Neuropsychology, 20,* 361–369.

Maume, D. J., Jr. (2004). Is the glass ceiling a unique form of inequality? *Work and Occupations, 31,* 250–274.

Maupin, R., Lyman, R., Fatsis, J., Prystowiski, E., Nguyen, A., & Wright, C. (2004). Characteristics of women who deliver with no prenatal care. *Journal of Maternal-Fetal and Neonatal Medicine, 16,* 45–50.

Maurer, D., Lewis, T. L., Brent, H. P., & Levin, A. V. (1999). Rapid improvement in the acuity of infants after visual input. *Science, 286,* 108–110.

Maurer, T. J. (2001). Career-relevant learning and development, worker age, and beliefs about self-efficacy for development. *Journal of Management, 27,* 123–140.

Maurer, T. J. (2007). Employee development and training issues related to the aging workforce. In K. S. Shultz & G. A. Adams (Eds.), *Aging and work in the 21st century* (pp. 163–178). Mahwah, NJ: Erlbaum.

Maurer, T. J., Wrenn, K. A., & Weiss, E. M. (2003). Toward understanding and managing stereotypical beliefs about older workers' ability and desire for learning and development. In J. J. Martocchio & G. R. Ferris (Eds.), *Research in personnel and human resources management* (Vol. 22, pp. 253–285). Stamford, CT: JAI Press.

Mavroveli, S., Petrides, K. V., Rieffe, C., & Bakker, F. (2007). Trait emotional intelligence, psychological well-being and peer-rated social competence in adolescence. *British Journal of Developmental Psychology, 25,* 263–275.

Mayberry, R. I. (1994). The importance of childhood to language acquisition: Evidence from American Sign Language. In J. C. Goodman & H. C. Nusbaum (Eds.), *The development of speech perception: The transition from speech sounds to spoken words* (pp. 57–90). Cambridge, MA: MIT Press.

Mayer, J. D., Roberts, R. D., & Barsade, S. G. (2008). Human abilities: Emotional intelligence. *Annual Review of Psychology, 59,* 507–536.

Mayer, J. D., Salovey, P., & Caruso, D. R. (2003). *Mayer–Salovey–Caruso Emotional Intelligence Test (MSCEIT): User's manual.* Toronto, Ontario: Multi-Health Systems.

Mayer, J. D., Salovey, P., & Caruso, D. R. (2008). Emotional intelligence: New ability or eclectic traits? *American Psychologist, 63,* 503–517.

Mayes, L. C. (1999). Reconsidering the concept of vulnerability in children using the model of prenatal cocaine exposure. In T. B. Cohen & E. M. Hossein (Eds.), The vulnerable child (Vol. 3, pp. 35–54). Madison, CT: International Universities Press.

Mayes, L. C., & Zigler, E. (1992). An observational study of the affective concomitants of mastery in infants. *Journal of Child Psychology and Psychiatry, 33,* 659–667.

Mayeux, L., & Cillessen, A. H. N. (2003). Development of social problem solving in early childhood: Stability, change, and associations with social competence. *Journal of Genetic Psychology, 164,* 153–173.

Maynard, A. E. (2002). Cultural teaching: The development of teaching skills in Maya sibling interactions. *Child Development, 73,* 969–982.

Maynard, A. E., & Greenfield, P. M. (2003). Implicit cognitive development in cultural tools and children: Lessons from Maya Mexico. *Cognitive Development, 18,* 489–510.

Maynard, A. E., Subrahmanyam, K., & Greenfield, P. M. (2005). Technology and the development of intelligence: From the loom to the computer. In R. J. Sternberg & D. D. Preiss (Eds.), *Intelligence and technology: The impact of tools in the nature and development of human abilities* (pp. 29–53). Mahwah, NJ: Erlbaum.

Maynard, C. K. (2003). Differentiate depression from dementia. *Nurse Practitioner, 28*(3), 27–29.

Mayseless, O., & Sharf, M. (2003). What does it mean to be an adult? The Israeli experience. *New Directions for Child and Adolescent Development, 100,* 33–49.

Mazzarella, S. R. (2007). Cyberdating success stories and the mythic narrative of living "happily-ever-after with the one." In M.-L. Galician & D. L. Merskin (Eds.), *Critical thinking about sex, love, and romance in the mass media* (pp. 23–37). Mahwah, NJ: Erlbaum.

McAdams, D. P. (1993). *The stories we live by: Personal myths and the making of the self.* New York: William Morrow.

McAdams, D. P. (2001). Generativity in midlife. In M. E. Lachman (Ed.), *Handbook of midlife development* (pp. 395–443). New York: Wiley.

McAdams, D. P. (2006). The redemptive self: Generativity and the stories Americans live by. *Research in Human Development, 3,* 81–100.

McAdams, D. P. (2008). Generativity, the redemptive self, and the problem of a noisy ego in American life. In H. A. Wayment & J. J. Bauer (Eds.), *Transcending self-interest: Psychological explorations of the quiet ego* (pp. 235–242). Washington, DC: American Psychological Association.

McAdams, D. P., & de St. Aubin, E. (1992). A theory of generativity and its assessment through self-report, behavioral acts, and narrative themes in autobiography. *Journal of Personality and Social Psychology, 62,* 1003–1015.

McAdams, D. P., Diamond, A., de St. Aubin, E., & Mansfield, E. (1997). Stories of commitment: The psychosocial construction of generative lives. *Journal of Personality and Social Psychology, 72,* 678–694.

McAdams, D. P., Hart, H. M., & Maruna, S. (1998). The anatomy of generativity. In D. P. McAdams & E. de St. Aubin (Eds.), *Generativity and adult development* (pp. 7–43). Washington, DC: American Psychological Association.

McAdams, D. P., & Logan, R. L. (2004). What is generativity? In E. de St. Aubin & D. P. McAdams (Eds.), *The generative society: Caring for future generations* (pp. 15–31). Washington, DC: American Psychological Association.

McAdams, D. P., Reynolds, J., Lewis, M., Patten, A. H., & Bowman, P. J. (2001). When bad things turn good and good things turn bad: Sequences of redemption and contamination in life narrative and their relation to psychosocial adaptation in midlife adults and children. *Personality and Social Psychology Bulletin, 27,* 474–485.

McAlister, A., & Peterson, C. C. (2006). Mental playmates: Siblings, executive functioning and theory of mind. *British Journal of Developmental Psychology, 24,* 733–751.

McAlister, A., & Peterson, C. C. (2007). A longitudinal study of child siblings and theory of mind development. *Cognitive Development, 22,* 258–270.

McArdle, J. J., Ferrer-Caja, E., Hamagami, F., & Woodcock, R. W. (2002). Comparative longitudinal structural analyses of the growth and decline of multiple intellectual abilities over the life span. *Developmental Psychology, 38,* 115–142.

McAuley, E., & Elavsky, S. (2008). Self-efficacy, physical activity, and cognitive function. In W. W. Spirduso, L. W. Poon, & W. Chodzko-Zajko (Eds.). *Exercise and its mediating effects on cognition* (pp. 69–84). Champaign, IL: Human Kinetics.

McAuley, E., Mihalko, S. L., & Bane, S. M. (1997). Exercise and self-esteem in middle-aged adults: Multidimensional relationships and physical fitness and self-efficacy influences. *Journal of Behavioral Medicine, 20,* 67–83.

McBee, M. T. (2006). A descriptive analysis of referral sources for gifted identification screening by race and socioeconomic status. *Journal of Secondary Gifted Education, 17,* 103–111.

McBride-Chang, C., & Kail, R. V. (2002). Cross-cultural similarities in the predictors of reading acquisition. *Child Development, 73,* 1392–1407.

McCabe, A. (1997). Developmental and cross-cultural aspects of children's narration. In M. Bamberg (Ed.), *Narrative development: Six approaches* (pp. 137–174). Mahwah, NJ: Erlbaum.

McCall, R. B. (1993). Developmental functions for general mental performance. In D. K. Detterman (Ed.), *Current topics in human intelligence* (Vol. 3, pp. 3–29). Norwood, NJ: Ablex.

McCall, R. B., & Carriger, M. S. (1993). A meta-analysis of infant habituation and recognition memory performance as predictors of later IQ. *Child Development, 64,* 57–79.

McCarthy, B., & McCarthy, E. J. (2004). *Getting it right the first time: Creating a healthy marriage.* New York: Brunner-Routledge.

McCartney, K., Dearing, E., Taylor, B., & Bub, K. (2007). Quality child care supports the achievement of low-income children: Direct and indirect pathways through caregiving and the home environment. *Journal of Applied Developmental Psychology, 28,* 411–426.

McCartney, K., Harris, M. J., & Bernieri, F. (1990). Growing up and growing apart: A developmental meta-analysis of twin studies. *Psychological Bulletin, 107,* 226–237.

McCartney, K., Owen, M., Booth, C., Clarke-Stewart, A., & Vandell, D. (2004). Testing a maternal attachment model of behavior problems in early childhood. *Journal of Child Psychology and Psychiatry, 45,* 765–778.

McCarton, C. (1998). Behavioral outcomes in low birth weight infants. *Pediatrics, 102,* 1293–1297.

McCarty, M. E., & Ashmead, D. H. (1999). Visual control of reaching and grasping in infants. *Developmental Psychology, 35,* 620–631.

McCarty, M. E., & Keen, R. (2005). Facilitating problem-solving performance among 9- and 12-month-old infants. *Journal of Cognition and Development, 6,* 209–228.

McClearn, G. E., Johansson, B., Berg, S., & Pedersen, N. L. (1997). Substantial genetic influence on cognitive abilities in twins 80 or more years old. *Science, 276,* 1560–1563.

McColgan, K. L., & McCormack, T. (2008). Searching and planning: Young children's reasoning about past and future event sequences. *Child Development, 79,* 1477–1479.

McCormack, V. A., dos Santos Silva, I., Koupil, I., Leon, D. A., & Lithell, H. O. (2005). Birth characteristics and adult cancer incidence: Swedish cohort of over 11,000 men and women. *International Journal of Cancer, 115,* 611–617.

McCrae, R., & Costa, P. T., Jr. (2003). *Personality in adulthood: A five-factor theory perspective* (2nd ed.). New York: Guilford.

McCrae, R., & Costa, P. T., Jr. (2006). Cross-cultural perspectives on adult personality trait development. In D. K. Mroczek & T. D. Little (Eds.), *Handbook of personality development* (pp. 129–146). Mahwah, NJ: Erlbaum.

McCune, L. (1993). The development of play as the development of consciousness. In M. H. Bornstein & A. O'Reilly (Eds.), *New directions for child development* (No. 59, pp. 67–79). San Francisco: Jossey-Bass.

McCurry, S. M., Logsdon, R. G., Teri, L., & Vitello, M. V. (2007). Evidence-based psychological treatments for insomnia in older adults. *Psychology and Aging, 22,* 18–27.

McDaniel, J., Purcell, D., & D'Augelli, A. R. (2001). The relationship between sexual orientation and risk for suicide: Research findings and future directions for research and prevention. *Suicide and Life-Threatening Behavior, 31,* 84–105.

McDaniel, M. A., Einstein, G. O., & Rendell, P. G. (2007). The puzzle of inconsistent age-related declines in prospective memory: A multiprocess explanation. In M. Kliegel, M. A. McDaniel, & G. O. Einstein (Eds.), *Prospective memory: Cognitive, neuroscience, developmental, and applied perspectives* (pp. 141–160). Mahwah, NJ: Erlbaum.

McDaniel, M. A., Maier, S. F., & Einstein, G. O. (2002). "Brain-specific" nutrients: A memory cure? *Psychological Science in the Public Interest, 3,* 12–38.

McDill, T., Hall, S. K., & Turell, S. C. (2006). Aging and creating families: Never-married heterosexual women over forty. *Journal of Women and Aging, 18,* 37–50.

McDonagh, M. S., Osterweil, P., & Guise, J. M. (2005). The benefits and risks of inducing labour in patients with prior cesarean delivery: A systematic review. *BJOG, 112,* 1007–1015.

McDonald, L., & Robb, A. L. (2004). The economic legacy of divorce and separation for women in old age. *Canadian Journal on Aging, 23*(Suppl. 1), S83–S97.

McDonald, S. W. S., Hultsch, D. F., & Dixon, R. A. (2003). Performance variability is related to change in cognition: Evidence from the Victoria Longitudinal Study. *Psychology and Aging, 18,* 510–523.

McDonough, L. (1999). Early declarative memory for location. *British Journal of Developmental Psychology, 17,* 381–402.

McDowell, D. J., & Parke, R. D. (2000). Differential knowledge of display rules for positive and negative emotions: Influences from parents, influences on peers. *Social Development, 9,* 415–432.

McElhaney, K. B., & Allen, J. P. (2001). Autonomy and adolescent social functioning: The moderating effect of risk. *Child Development, 72,* 220–235.

McElwain, N. L., & Booth-LaForce, C. (2006). Maternal sensitivity to infant distress and nondistress as predictors of infant–mother attachment security. *Journal of Family Psychology, 20,* 247–255.

McEwen, B. S. (2007). Physiology and neurobiology of stress an adaptation: Central role of the brain. *Physiological Reviews, 87,* 873–904.

McFadden, S. H. (1996). Religion, spirituality, and aging. In J. E. Birren & K. W. Schaie (Eds.), *Handbook of the psychology of aging* (pp.182–177). San Diego: Academic Press.

McFarlane, J., Malecha, A., Watson, K., Gist, J., Batten, E., Hall, I., & Smith, S. (2005). Intimate partner assault against women: Frequency, health consequences, and treatment outcomes. *Obstetrics and Gynecology, 105,* 99–108.

McGee, G. (1997). Legislating gestation. *Human Reproduction, 12,* 407–408.

McGee, L. M., & Richgels, D. J. (2004). *Literacy's beginnings* (4th ed.). Boston: Allyn and Bacon.

McGee, L. M., & Richgels, D. J. (2008). *Literacy's beginnings: Supporting young readers and writers* (5th ed.). Boston: Allyn and Bacon.

McGillicuddy-De Lisi, A. V., Daly, M., & Neal, A. (2006). Children's distributive justice judgments: Aversive racism in Euro-American children? *Child Development, 77,* 1063–1080.

McGlothlin, H., & Killen, M. (2006). Intergroup attitudes of European American children attending ethnically homogeneous schools. *Child Development, 77,* 1375–1386.

McGoldrick, M. (2004). Echoes from the past: Helping families deal with their ghosts. In F. Walsh & M. McGoldrick (Eds.), *Living beyond loss* (pp. 99–118). New York: Norton.

McGoldrick, M., Schlesinger, J. M., Lee, E., Hines, P. M., Chan, J., & Almeida, R. (2004). Mourning in different cultures. In F. Walsh & M. McGoldrick (Eds.), *Living beyond loss* (pp. 1119–160). New York: Norton.

McGue, M., & Christensen, K. (2002). The heritability of level and rate-of-change in cognitive functioning in Danish twins aged 70 years and older. *Experimental Aging Research, 28,* 435–451.

McHale, J. P., Kazali, C., Rotman, T., Talbot, J., Carleton, M., & Lieberson, R. (2004). The transition to coparenthood: Parents' prebirth expectations and early coparental adjustment at 3 months postpartum. *Development and Psychopathology, 16,* 711–733.

McHale, J. P., Khazan, I., Erera, P., Rotman, T., DeCourcey, W., & McConnell, M. (2002). Coparenting in diverse family systems. In M. H. Bornstein (Ed.), *Handbook of parenting: Vol. 3* (2nd ed., pp. 75–107). Mahwah, NJ: Erlbaum.

McHale, J. P., Kuersten-Hogan, R., & Rao, N. (2004). Growing points for coparenting theory and research. *Journal of Adult Development, 11,* 221–234.

McHale, J. P., Lauretti, A., Talbot, J., & Pouquette, C. (2002). Retrospect and prospect in the psychological study of coparenting and family group process. In J. P. McHale & W. S. Grolnick (Eds.), *Retrospect and prospect in the psychological study of families* (pp. 127–165). Mahwah, NJ: Erlbaum.

McHale, J. P., & Rotman, T. (2007). Is seeing believing? Expectant parents' outlooks on coparenting and later coparenting solidarity. *Infant Behavior and Development, 30,* 63–81.

McHale, J. P., Vinden, P. G., Bush, L., Richer, D., Shaw, D., & Smith, B. (2005). Patterns of personal and social adjustment among sport-involved and noninvolved urban middle-school children. *Sociology of Sport Journal, 22,* 119–136.

McHale, S. M., Crouter, A. C., Kim, J.-Y., Burton, L. M., Davis, K. D., Dotterer, A. M., & Swanson, D. P. (2006). Mothers' and fathers' racial socialization in African-American families: Implications for youth. *Child Development, 77,* 1387–1402.

McIntosh, H., Metz, E., & Youniss, J. (2005). Community service and identity formation in adolescents. In J. S. Mahoney, R. W. Larson, & J. S. Eccles (Eds.), *Organized activities as contexts of development: Extracurricular activities, after-school and community programs* (pp. 331–351). Mahwah, NJ: Erlbaum.

McIntosh, J., MacDonald, F., & McKeganey, N. (2006). Why do children experiment with illegal drugs? The declining role of peer pressure with increasing age. *Addiction Research and Theory, 14,* 275–287.

McKelvie, P., & Low, J. (2002). Listening to Mozart does not improve children's spatial ability: Final curtains for the Mozart effect. *British Journal of Developmental Psychology, 20,* 241–258.

McKenna, J. J. (2001). Why we never ask "Is it safe for infants to sleep alone?" *Academy of Breast Feeding Medicine News and Views, 7*(4), 32, 38.

McKenna, J. J. (2002, September/October). Breastfeeding and bedsharing still useful (and important) after all these years. *Mothering, 114.* Retrieved from www.mothering.com/articles/new_baby/sleep/mckenna.html

McKenna, J. J., & McDade, T. (2005). Why babies should never sleep alone: A review of the co-sleeping controversy in relation to SIDS, bedsharing, and breastfeeding. *Paediatric Respiratory Reviews, 6,* 134–152.

McKenna, J. J., & Volpe, L. E. (2007). Sleeping with baby: An Internet-based sampling of parental experiences, choices, perceptions, and interpretations in a Western industrialized context. *Infant and Child Development, 16,* 359–385.

McKim, W. A. (2002). *Drugs and behavior* (5th ed.). Upper Saddle River, NJ: Prentice-Hall.

McKinney, C., Donnelly, R., & Renk, K. (2008). Perceived parenting, positive and negative perceptions of parents, and late adolescent emotional adjustment. *Child and Adolescent Mental health, 13,* 66–73.

McKown, C., & Weinstein, R. S. (2002). Modeling the role of child ethnicity and gender in children's differential response to teacher expectations. *Journal of Applied Social Psychology, 32,* 159–184.

McKown, C., & Weinstein, R. S. (2003). The development and consequences of stereotype consciousness in middle childhood. *Child Development, 74,* 498–515.

McKusick, V. A. (2007). *Online Mendelian inheritance in man.* Retrieved from www.ncbi.nlm.nih.gov/sites/entrez?db=omim

McLanahan, S. (1999). Father absence and the welfare of children. In E. M. Hetherington (Ed.), *Coping with divorce, single parenting, and remarriage: A risk and resiliency perspective* (pp. 117–145). Mahwah, NJ: Erlbaum.

McLean, K. C. (2008). Stories of the young and the old: Personal continuity and narrative identity. *Developmental Psychology, 44,* 254–264.

McLoyd, V. C., Aikens, N. L., & Burton, L. M. (2006). Child poverty, policy, and practice. In K. A. Renninger & I. E. Sigel (Eds.), *Handbook of child psychology: Vol. 4. Child psychology in practice* (6th ed., pp. 700–778). Hoboken, NJ: Wiley.

McLoyd, V. C., Kaplan, R., Hardaway, C. R., & Wood, D. (2007). Does endorsement of physical discipline matter? Assessing moderating influences on the maternal and child psychological correlates of physical discipline in African-American families. *Journal of Family Psychology, 21,* 165–175.

McLoyd, V. C., & Smith, J. (2002). Physical discipline and behavior problems in African-American, European-American, and Hispanic children: Emotional support as a moderator. *Journal of Marriage and Family, 64,* 40–53.

McMahon, C. A., Barnett, B., Kowalenko, N. M., & Tennant, C. C. (2006). Maternal attachment state of mind moderates the impact of postnatal depression on infant attachment. *Journal of Child Psychology and Psychiatry, 47,* 660–669.

McNeil, J. N. (1986). Talking about death: Adolescents, parents, and peers. In C. A. Corr & J. N. McNeil (Eds.), *Adolescence and death* (pp. 185–201). New York: Springer.

MCR Vitamin Study Research Group. (1991). Prevention of neural tube defects: Results of the Medical Research Council Vitamin Study. *Lancet, 338,* 131–137.

Mead, G. H. (1934). *Mind, self, and society.* Chicago: University of Chicago Press.

Mead, M. (1928). *Coming of age in Samoa.* Ann Arbor, MI: Morrow.

Mead, M., & Newton, N. (1967). Cultural patterning of perinatal behavior. In S. Richardson & A. Guttmacher (Eds.), *Childbearing: Its social and psychological aspects* (pp. 142–244). Baltimore: Williams & Wilkins.

Medina, J., & Puntillo, K. A. (2006). *Palliative care and end-of-life issues in critical care.* New York: Jones & Bartlett.

Meegan, S. P., & Berg, C. A. (2002). Contexts, functions, forms, and processes of collaborative everyday problem solving in older adulthood. *International Journal of Behavioral Development, 26,* 6–15.

Meek, J. (2002). Basic principles of optical imaging and application to the study of infant development. *Developmental Science, 5,* 371–380.

Meeus, W. (1996). Studies on identity development in adolescence: An overview of research and some new data. *Journal of Youth and Adolescence, 25,* 569–598.

Meeus, W., Oosterwegel, A., & Vollebergh, W. (2002). Parental and peer attachment and identity development in adolescence. *Journal of Adolescence, 25,* 93–106.

Meeus, W. H. J., Branje, S. J. T., van der Valk, I., & de Wied, M. (2007). Relationships with intimate partner, best friend, and parents in adolescence and early adulthood: A study of the saliency of the intimate partnership. *International Journal of Behavioral Development, 31,* 569–580.

Mehlmadrona, L., & Madrona, M. M. (1997). Physician- and midwife-attended home births—effects of breech, twin, and post-dates outcome data on mortality rates. *Journal of Nurse-Midwifery, 42,* 91–98.

Mehlson, M., Platz, M., & Fromholt, P. (2003). Life satisfaction across the life course: Evaluations of the most and least satisfying decades of life. *International Journal of Aging and Human Development, 57,* 217–236.

Meins, E., Fernyhough, C., Russell, J., & Clark-Carter, D. (1998). Security of attachment as a predictor of symbolic and mentalizing abilities: A longitudinal study. *Social Development, 7,* 1–24.

Meins, E., Fernyhough, C., Wainwright, R., Clark-Carter, D., Gupta, M. D., Fradley, E., & Tucker, M. (2003). Pathways to understanding mind: Construct validity and predictive validity of maternal mind-mindedness. *Child Development, 74,* 1194–1211.

Melamed, S., Yekutieli, D., Froom, P., Kristal-Boneh, E., & Ribak, J. (1999). Adverse work and environmental conditions predict occupational injuries. The Israeli Cardiovascular Occupational Risk Factors Determination in Israel (CORDIS) Study. *American Journal of Epidemiology, 150,* 18–26.

Melby, M. K., Lock, M., & Kaufert, P. (2005). Culture and symptom reporting at menopause. *Human Reproduction Update, 11,* 495–512.

Melenhorst, A. S., Fisk, A. D., Mynatt, E. D., & Rogers, W. A. (2004). Potential intrusiveness of aware home technology: Perceptions of older adults. In *Proceedings of the Human Factors and Ergonomics*

Society 48th annual meeting (pp. 266–270). Santa Monica, CA: Human Factors and Ergonomics Society.

Meltzoff, A. N. (1995). Understanding the intentions of others: Re-enactment of intended acts by 18-month-old children. *Developmental Psychology, 31,* 838–850.

Meltzoff, A. N. (2007). 'Like me': A foundation for social cognition. *Developmental Science, 10,* 126–134.

Meltzoff, A. N., & Kuhl, P. K. (1994). Faces and speech: Intermodal processing of biologically relevant signals in infants and adults. In D. J. Lewkowicz & R. Lickliter (Eds.), *The development of intersensory perception* (pp. 335–369). Hillsdale, NJ: Erlbaum.

Meltzoff, A. N., & Moore, M. K. (1977). Imitation of facial and manual gestures by human neonates. *Science, 198,* 75–78.

Meltzoff, A. N., & Moore, M. K. (1994). Imitation, memory, and the representation of persons. *Infant Behavior and Development, 17,* 83–99.

Meltzoff, A. N., & Moore, M. K. (1999). Persons and representations: Why infant imitation is important for theories of human development. In J. Nadel & G. Butterworth (Eds.), *Imitation in infancy* (pp. 9–35). Cambridge, UK: Cambridge University Press.

Melzi, G., & Ely, R. (2009). Language development in the school years. In J. B. Gleason & N. B. Ratner (Eds.), *The development of language* (7th ed., pp. 391–435). Boston: Allyn and Bacon.

Menant, J. C., Steele, J. R., Menz, H. B., Munro, B. J., & Lord, S. R. (2008). Effects of footwear features on balance and stepping in older people. *Gerontology, 54,* 18–23.

Mendle, J., Turkheimer, E., D'Onofrio, B. M., Lynch, S., Emery, R. E., & Slutske, W. S. (2006). Family structure and age at menarche: A children-of-twins approach. *Developmental Psychology, 42,* 533–542.

Mendle, J., Turkheimer, E., & Emery, R. E. (2007). Detrimental psychological outcomes associated with early pubertal timing in adolescent girls. *Developmental Review, 27,* 151–171.

Meneilly, G. S. (2006). Diabetes in the elderly. *Medical Clinics of North America, 90,* 909–923.

Mennella, J. A., & Beauchamp, G. K. (1998). Early flavor experiences: Research update. *Nutrition Reviews, 56,* 205–211.

Menon, U. (2001). Middle adulthood in cultural perspective: The imagined and the experienced in three cultures. In M. E. Lachman (Ed.), *Handbook of midlife development* (pp. 40–74). New York: Wiley.

Ment, L. R., Vohr, B., Allan, W., Katz, K. H., Schneider, K. C., Westerveld, M., Cuncan, C. C., & Makuch, R. W. (2003). Change in cognitive function over time in very low-birth-weight infants. *Journal of the American Medical Association, 289,* 705–711.

Mercer, C. H., Bailey, J. V., Johnson, A. M., Erens, B., Wellings, K., Fenton, K., & Copas, A. J. (2007). Women who report having sex with women: British national probability data on prevalence, sexual behaviors, and health outcomes. *Research and Practice, 97,* 1126–1133.

Mergenhagen, P. (1996). Her own boss. *American Demographics, 18,* 36–41.

Merriam, S. B. (1993). The uses of reminiscence in older adulthood. *Educational Gerontology, 8,* 275–290.

Merrill, D. M. (1997). *Caring for elderly parents.* Westport, CT: Auburn House.

Mervis, C. B., Pani, J. R., & Pani, A. M. (2003). Transaction of child cognitive-linguistic abilities and adult input in the acquisition of lexical categories at the basic and subordinate levels. In D. H. Rakison & L. M. Oakes (Eds.), *Early category and concept development* (pp. 242–274). New York: Oxford University Press.

Messman, S. J., Canary, D. J., & Hause, K. S. (2000). Motives to remain platonic, equity, and the use of maintenance strategies in opposite-sex friendships. *Journal of Social and Personal Relationships, 17,* 67–94.

Metcalf, B. S., Voss, L. D., Hosking, J., Jeffery, A. N., & Wilkin, T. J. (2008). Physical activity at the government-recommended level and obesity-related health outcomes: A longitudinal study. *Archives of Disease in Childhood, 93,* 772–777.

Metheny, J., McWhirter, E. H., & O'Neil, M. E. (2008). Measuring perceived teacher support and its influence on adolescent career development. *Journal of Career Assessment, 16,* 218–237.

Metz, E. C., & Youniss, J. (2005). Longitudinal gains in civic development through school-based required service. *Political Psychology, 26,* 413–437.

Meyer, B. J. F., Russo, C., & Talbot, A. (1995). Discourse comprehension and problem solving: Decisions about the treatment of breast cancer by women across the lifespan. *Psychology and Aging, 10,* 84–103.

Meyer, B. J. F., Talbot, A. P., & Ranalli, C. (2007). Why older adults make more immediate treatment decisions about cancer than younger adults. *Psychology and Aging, 22,* 505–524.

Meyer, I. H. (2003). Prejudice, social stress, and mental health in lesbian, gay, and bisexual populations: Conceptual issues and research evidence. *Psychological Bulletin, 129,* 674–697.

Meyer, P. A., Pivetz, T., Dignam, T. A., Hma, D. M., Schoonover, J., & Brody, D. (2003). Surveillance for elevated blood lead levels among children—United States, 1997–2001. *Morbidity and Mortality Weekly Report, 52*(No. SS-10), 1–21.

Meyer-Bahlburg, H. F. L., Ehrhardt, A. A., Rosen, L. R., Gruen, R. S., Veridiano, N. P., Vann, F. H., & Neuwalder, H. F. (1995). Prenatal estrogens and the development of homosexual orientation. *Developmental Psychology, 31,* 12–21.

Meyers, C., Adam, R., Dungan, J., & Prenger, V. (1997). Aneuploidy in twin gestations: When is maternal age advanced? *Obstetrics and Gynecology, 89,* 248–251.

Mezulis, A. H., Hyde, J. S., & Clark, R. (2004). Father involvement moderates the effect of maternal depression during a child's infancy on child behavior problems in kindergarten. *Journal of Family Psychology, 18,* 575–588.

Miceli, P. J., Whitman, T. L., Borkowski, J. G., Braungart-Riekder, J., & Mitchell, D. W. (1998). Individual differences in infant information processing: The role of temperamental and maternal factors. *Infant Behavior and Development, 21,* 119–136.

Michael, A., & Eccles, J. S. (2003). When coming of age means coming undone: Links between puberty and psychosocial adjustment among European American and African American girls. In C. Hayward (Ed.), *Gender differences at puberty* (pp. 277–303). New York: Cambridge University Press.

Michael, R. T., Gagnon, J. H., Laumann, E. O., & Kolata, G. (1994). *Sex in America.* Boston: Little, Brown.

Michaels, G. Y. (1988). Motivational factors in the decision and timing of pregnancy. In G. Y. Michaels & W. A. Goldberg (Eds.), *The transition to parenthood: Current theory and research* (pp. 23–61). New York: Cambridge University Press.

Michalik, N. M., Eisenberg, N., Spinrad, T. L., Ladd, B., Thompson, M., & Valiente, C. (2007). Longitudinal relations among parental emotional expressivity and sympathy and prosocial behavior in adolescence. *Social Development, 16,* 286–309.

Mikulincer, M., Florian, V., & Hirschberger, G. (2003). The existential function of close relationships: Introducing death into the science of love. *Personality and Social Psychology Review, 7,* 20–40.

Milberger, S., Biederman, J., Faraone, S. V., Guite, J., & Tsuang, M. T. (1997). Pregnancy, delivery and infancy complications and attention deficit hyperactivity disorder: Issues of gene–environment interaction. *Biological Psychiatry, 41,* 65–75.

Milbury, P. E., & Richer, A. C. (2008). *Understanding the antioxidant controversy.* Wastport, CT: Praeger.

Milevsky, A., Schlechter, M., Netter, S., & Keehn, D. (2007). Maternal and paternal parenting styles in adolescents: Associations with self-esteem, depression, and life satisfaction. *Journal of Child and Family Studies, 16,* 39–47.

Milkie, M. A., Bierman, A., & Schieman, S. (2008). How adult children influence older parents' mental health: Integrating stress-process and life-course perspectives. *Social Psychology Quarterly, 71,* 86–105.

Miller, J., Slomczynski, K. M., & Kohn, M. L. (1985). Continuity of learning-generalization: The effect of job on men's intellective process in the United States and Poland. *American Journal of Sociology, 91,* 593–615.

Miller, J. G. (2006). Insights into moral development from cultural psychology. In M. Killen & J. Smetana (Eds.), *Handbook of moral development* (pp. 375–398). Philadelphia: Erlbaum.

Miller, J. G., & Bersoff, D. M. (1995). Development in the context of everyday family relationships: Culture, interpersonal morality, and adaptation. In M. Killen & D. Hart (Eds.), *Morality in everyday life: Developmental perspectives* (pp. 259–282). Cambridge: Cambridge University Press.

Miller, K. J. (2003). The other side of estrogen replacement therapy: Outcome study results of mood improvement in estrogen users and nonusers. *Current Psychiatry Reports, 5,* 439–444.

Miller, K. S., Forehand, R., & Kotchick, B. (1999). Adolescent sexual behavior in two ethnic minority samples: The role of family variables. *Journal of Marriage and the Family, 61,* 85–98.

Miller, L. T., & Vernon, P. A. (1992). The general factor in short-term memory, intelligence, and reaction time. *Intelligence, 16,* 5–29.

Miller, P. H. (2001). *Theories of developmental psychology* (4th ed.). New York: Worth.

Miller, P. H., & Bigi, L. (1979). The development of children's understanding of attention. *Merrill-Palmer Quarterly, 25,* 235–250.

Miller, P. J., Fung, H., & Koven, M. (2007). Narrative reverberations: How participation in narrative practices co-creates persons and cultures. In S. Kitayama & D. Cohen (Eds.), *Handbook of cultural psychology* (pp. 595–614). New York: Guilford.

Miller, P. J., Fung, H., & Mintz, J. (1996). Self-construction through narrative practices: A Chinese and American comparison of early socialization. *Ethos, 24,* 1–44.

Miller, P. J., Hengst, J. A., & Wang, S. (2003). Ethnographic methods: Applications from developmental cultural psychology. In P. M. Carnic & J. E. Rhodes (Eds.), *Qualitative research in psychology* (pp. 219–242). Washington, DC: American Psychological Association.

Miller, P. J., Wang, S., Sandel, T., & Cho, G. E. (2002). Self-esteem as folk theory: A comparison of European American and Taiwanese mothers' beliefs. *Parenting: Science and Practice, 2,* 209–239.

Miller, P. J., Wiley, A. R., Fung, H., & Liang, C. H. (1997). Personal storytelling as a medium of

socialization in Chinese and American families. *Child Development, 68,* 557–568.
Miller, R. B. (2000). Do children make a marriage unhappy? *Family Science Review, 13,* 60–73.
Miller, R. B., Hemesath, K., & Nelson, B. (1997). Marriage in middle and later life. In T. D. Hargrave & S. M. Hanna (Eds.), *The aging family* (pp. 178–198). New York: Brunner/Mazel.
Miller, S. A., Hardin, C. A., & Montgomery, D. E. (2003). Young children's understanding of the conditions for knowledge acquisition. *Journal of Cognition and Development, 4,* 325–356.
Miller, S. C., Mor, V., Wu, N., Gozalo, P., & Papane, K. (2002). Does receipt of hospice care in nursing homes improve the management of pain at the end of life? *Journal of the American Geriatrics Society, 50,* 507–515.
Miller, S. S., & Cavanaugh, J. C. (1990). The meaning of grandparenthood and its relationship to demographic, relationship, and social participation variables. *Journal of Gerontology, 45,* P244–P246.
Milligan, K., Astington, J. W., & Dack, L. A. (2007). Language and theory of mind: Meta-analysis of the relation between language ability and false-belief understanding. *Child Development, 78,* 622–646.
Mills, D., Plunkett, K., Prat, C., & Schafer, G. (2005). Watching the infant brain learn words: Effects of language and experience. *Cognitive Development, 20,* 19–31.
Mills, R. S. L. (2005). Taking stock of the developmental literature on shame. *Developmental Review, 25,* 26–63.
Mills, R., & Grusec, J. (1989). Cognitive, affective, and behavioral consequences of praising altruism. *Merrill-Palmer Quarterly, 35,* 299–326.
Mills, T. L., Gomez-Smith, Z., & De Leon, J. M. (2005). Skipped generation families: Sources of psychological distress among grandmothers of grandchildren who live in homes where neither parent is present. *Marriage and Family Review, 37,* 191–212.
Miner-Rubino, K., Winter, D. G., & Stewart, A. J. (2004). Gender, social class, and the subjective experience of aging: Self-perceived personality change from early adulthood to late midlife. *Personality and Social Psychology Bulletin, 30,* 1599–1610.
Minkler, M., & Fuller-Thomson, E. (2005). African American grandparents raising grandchildren: A national study using the Census 2000 American Community Survey. *Journal of Gerontology, 60B,* S82–S92.
Mintun, M. A., Larossa, G. N., Sheline, Y. I., Sence, C. S., Lee, S. Y., & Mach, R. H. (2006). PIB in a nondemented population: Potential antecedent marker of Alzheimer disease. *Neurology, 67,* 446–452.
Mintzer, J. E. (2001). Underlying mechanisms of psychosis and aggression in patients with Alzheimer's disease. *Journal of Clinical Psychiatry, 62*(Suppl. 21), 23–25.
Misailidi, P. (2006). Young children's display rule knowledge: Understanding the distinction between apparent and real emotions and the motives underlying the use of display rules. *Social Behavior and Personality, 34,* 1285–1296.
Mischel, W., & Liebert, R. M. (1966). Effects of discrepancies between observed and imposed reward criteria on their acquisition and transmission. *Journal of Personality and Social Psychology, 3,* 45–53.
Mishra, G., & Kuh, D. (2006). Perceived change in quality of life during the menopause. *Social Science and Medicine, 62,* 93–102.
Mitchell, A., & Boss, B. J. (2002). Adverse effects of pain on the nervous systems of newborns and young children: A review of the literature. *Journal of Neuroscience Nursing, 34,* 228–235.
Mitchell, B. D., Hsueh, W. C., King, T. M., Pollin, T. I., Sorkin, J., Agarwala, R., Schäffer, A. A., & Shuldiner, A. R. (2001). Heritability of life span in the Old Order Amish. *American Journal of Medical Genetics, 102,* 346–352.
Mitchell, V., & Helson, R. (1990). Women's prime of life. *Psychology of Women Quarterly, 14,* 451–470.
Miura, I. T., & Okamoto, Y. (2003). Language supports for mathematics understanding and performance. In A. J. Baroody & A. Dowker (Eds.), *The development of arithmetic concepts and skills* (pp. 229–242). Mahwah, NJ: Erlbaum.
Mize, J., & Pettit, G. S. (1997). Mothers' social coaching, mother–child relationship style, and children's peer competence: Is the medium the message? *Child Development, 68,* 312–332.
Mizushima, S., & Yapori, Y. (1992). Nutritional improvement, cardiovascular diseases and longevity in Japan. *Nutrition and Health, 8,* 97–105.
Mocarelli, P., Gerthoux, P., Ferrari, E., Patterson, D. G., Jr., Kieszak, S. M., & Brambilla, P. (2000). Paternal concentrations of dioxin and sex ratio of offspring. *Lancet, 355,* 1858–1862.
Moen, P. (2003). *It's about time: Couples and careers.* Ithaca, NY: Cornell University Press.
Moen, P., & Altobelli, J. (2007). Strategic selection as a retirement project: Will Americans develop hybrid arrangements? In J. B. James & P. Wink (Eds.), *Annual review of gerontology and geriatrics* (Vol. 26, pp. 61–82). New York: Springer.
Moen, P., & Roehling, P. V. (2005). *The career mystique.* Bolder, CO: Rowman & Littlefield.
Moen, P., Huang, Q., Plassmann, V., & Dentinger, E. (2006). Deciding the future: Do dual-earner couples plan together for retirement? *American Behavioral Scientist, 49,* 1422–1443.
Moens, E., Braet, C., & Soetens, B. (2007). Observation of family functioning at mealtime: A comparison between families of children with and without overweight. *Journal of Pediatric Psychology, 32,* 52–63.
Moerk, E. L. (2000). *The guided acquisition of first language skills.* Westport, CT: Ablex.
Moffitt, T. E. (2006). A review of research on the taxonomy of life-course persistent versus adolescence-limited antisocial behavior. In F. T. Cullen, J. P. Wright, & K . Blevins (Eds.), *Taking stock: The status of criminological theory* (pp. 277–311). New Brunswick, NJ: Transaction Publishers.
Mojet, J., Christ-Hazelhof, E., & Heidema, J. (2001). Taste perception with age: Generic or specific losses in threshold sensitivity to the five basic tastes? *Chemical Senses, 26,* 845–860.
Mokdad, A. H., Bowman, B. A., Ford, E. S., Vinicor, F., Marks, J. S., & Koplan, J. P. (2001). The continuing epidemics of obesity and diabetes in the United States. *Journal of the American Medical Association, 286,* 1195–1200.
Moll, H., & Tomasello, M. (2006). Level I perspective-taking at 24 months of age. *British Journal of Developmental Psychology, 24,* 603–613.
Moll, I. (1994). Reclaiming the natural line in Vygotsky's theory of cognitive development. *Human Development, 37,* 333–342.
Moller, K., Hwang, C. P., & Wickberg, B. (2008). Couple relationship and transition to parenthood: Does workload at home matter? *Journal of Reproductive and Infant Psychology, 26,* 57–68.
Monastersky, R. (2005, March 4). Primed for numbers: Are boys born better at math? Experts try to divide the influences of nature and nurture. *Chronicle of Higher Education,* pp. A1, A12–A14.
Mondloch, C. J., Lewis, T., Budreau, D. R., Maurer, D., Dannemillier, J. L., Stephens, B. R., & Kleiner-Gathercoal, K. A. (1999). Face perception during early infancy. *Psychological Science, 10,* 419–422.
Mondoza, C. (2006). Inside today's classrooms: Teacher voices on No Child Left Behind and the education of gifted children. *Roeper Review, 29,* 28–31.
Monk, C., Fifer, W. P., Myers, M. M., Sloan, R. P., Trien, L., & Hurtado, A. (2000). Maternal stress responses and anxiety during pregnancy: Effects on fetal heart rate. *Developmental Psychobiology, 36,* 67–77.
Monk, C., Myers, M. M., Sloan, R. P., Ellman, L. M., & Fifer, W. P. (2003). Effects of women's stress-elicited physiological activity and chronic anxiety on fetal heart rate. *Journal of Developmental and Behavioral Pediatrics, 24,* 32–38.
Monk, C., Sloan, R., Myers, M. M., Ellman, L., Werner, E., Jeon, J., Tager, F., & Fifer, W. P. (2004). Fetal heart rate reactivity differs by women's psychiatric status: An early marker for developmental risk? *Journal of the American Academy of Child and Adolescent Psychiatry, 43,* 283–290.
Monsour, M. (2002). *Women and men as friends.* Mahwah, NJ: Erlbaum.
Montague, D. P. F., & Walker-Andrews, A. S. (2001). Peekaboo: A new look at infants' perception of emotion expressions. *Developmental Psychology, 37,* 826–838.
Montemayor, R., & Eisen, M. (1977). The development of self-conceptions from childhood to adolescence. *Developmental Psychology, 37,* 826–838.
Montepare, J. M. (2006). Body consciousness across the adult years: Variations with actual and subjective age. *Journal of Adult Development, 13,* 102–107.
Montgomery, M. J. (2005). Psychosocial intimacy and identity: From early adolescence to emerging adulthood. *Journal of Adolescent Research, 20,* 346–374.
Montgomery, M. J., & Côté, J. E. (2003). College as a transition to adulthood. In G. R. Adams & M. D. Berzonsky (Eds.), *Blackwell handbook of adolescence* (pp. 149–172). Malden, MA: Blackwell.
Montorsi, F. (2005). Assessment, diagnosis, and investigation of erectile dysfunction. *Clinical Cornerstone, 7,* 29–35.
Montoya, A. G., Sorrentino, R., Lukas, S. E., & Price, B. H. (2002). Long-term neuropsychiatric consequences of "ecstasy" (MDMA): A review. *Harvard Review of Psychiatry, 10,* 212–220.
Moon, C., Cooper, R. P., & Fifer, W. P. (1993). Two-day-old infants prefer their native language. *Infant Behavior and Development, 16,* 495–500.
Moon, S. M., & Feldhusen, J. F. (1994). The Program for Academic and Creative Enrichment (PACE): A follow-up study ten years later. In R. F. Subotnik & K. D. Arnold (Eds.), *Beyond Terman: Contemporary longitudinal studies of giftedness and talent* (pp. 375–400). Norwood, NJ: Ablex.
Moore, A., & Stratton, D. C. (2002). *Resilient widowers.* New York: Springer.
Moore, D. R., & Florsheim, P. (2001). Interpersonal processes and psychopathology among expectant and nonexpectant adolescent couples. *Journal of Consulting and Clinical Psychology, 69,* 101–113.
Moore, E. G. J. (1986). Family socialization and the IQ test performance of traditionally and transracially adopted black children. *Developmental Psychology, 22,* 317–326.
Moore, K. A., Morrison, D. R., & Greene, A. D. (1997). Effects on the children born to adolescent mothers. In R. A. Maynard (Ed.), *Kids having kids* (pp. 145–180). Washington, DC: The Urban Institute.

Moore, K. L., & Persaud, T. V. N. (2008). *Before we are born* (7th ed.). Philadelphia: Saunders.

Moore, M. K., & Meltzoff, A. N. (1999). New findings on object permanence: A developmental difference between two types of occlusion. *British Journal of Developmental Psychology, 17,* 563–584.

Moore, M. K., & Meltzoff, A. N. (2004). Object permanence after a 24-hr delay and leaving the locale of disappearance: The role of memory, space, and identity. *Developmental Psychology, 40,* 606–620.

Moore, M. R., & Brooks-Gunn, J. (2002). Adolescent parenthood. In M. H. Bornstein (Ed.), *Handbook of parenting: Vol. 3* (2nd ed., pp. 173–214). Mahwah, NJ: Erlbaum.

Moore, W. S. (2002). Understanding learning in a postmodern world: Reconsidering the Perry scheme of ethical and intellectual development. In B. K. Hofer & P. R. Pintrich (Eds.), *Personal epistemology* (pp. 17–36). Mahwah, NJ: Erlbaum.

Moran, S., & Gardner, H. (2006). Extraordinary achievements: A developmental and systems analysis. In D. Kuhn & R. Siegler (Eds.), *Handbook of child psychology: Vol. 2. Cognition, perception, and language* (6th ed., pp. 905–949). Hoboken, NJ: Wiley.

Morelli, G., Rogoff, B., Oppenheim, D., & Goldsmith, D. (1992). Cultural variation in infants' sleeping arrangements: Questions of independence. *Developmental Psychology, 28,* 604–613.

Morelli, G. A., Rogoff, B., & Angelillo, C. (2003). Cultural variation in young children's access to work or involvement in specialized child-focused activities. *International Journal of Behavioral Development, 27,* 264–274.

Morgan, B., Maybery, M., & Durkin, K. (2003). Weak central coherence, poor joint attention, and low verbal ability: Independent deficits in early autism. *Developmental Psychology, 39,* 646–656.

Morgan, J. D., & Laungani, P. (2005). General introduction. In J. D. Morgan & P. Laungani (Eds.), *Death and bereavement around the world* (pp. 1–4). Amityville, NY: Baywood.

Morgane, P. J., Austin-LaFrance, R., Bronzino, J., Tonkiss, J., Diaz-Cintra, S., Cintra, L., Kemper, T., & Galler, J. R. (1993). Prenatal malnutrition and development of the brain. *Neuroscience and Biobehavioral Reviews, 17,* 91–128.

Morley, J. E. (2001). Decreased food intake with aging. *Journal of Gerontology, 56A,* 81–88.

Morris, G., & Baker-Ward, L. (2007). Fragile but real: Children's capacity to use newly acquired words to convey preverbal memories. *Child Development, 78,* 448–458.

Morris, M. C., Evans, D. A., Schneider, J. A., Tangney, C. C., Bienias, J. L., & Aggarwal, N. T. (2006). Dietary folate and vitamins B-12 and B-6 not associated with incident Alzheimer's disease. *Journal of Alzheimer's Disease, 9,* 435–443.

Morris, M. C., Evans, D. A., Tangney, C. C., Bienias, J. L., & Wilson, R. S. (2005). Fish consumption and cognitive decline with age in a large community study. *Archives of Neurology, 62,* 1849–1853.

Morrison, V. (2008). Ageing and physical health. In B. Woods & L. Clare (Eds.), *Handbook of the clinical psychology of ageing* (2nd ed., pp. 57–74). Chichester, UK: Wiley.

Morrongiello, B. A., Fenwick, K. D., & Chance, G. (1998). Crossmodal learning in newborn infants: Inferences about properties of auditory-visual events. *Infant Behavior and Development, 21,* 543–554.

Morrongiello, B. A., Midgett, C., & Shields, R. (2001). Don't run with scissors: Young children's knowledge of home safety rules. *Journal of Pediatric Psychology, 26,* 105–115.

Morrongiello, B. A., Ondejko, L., & Littlejohn, A. (2004). Understanding toddlers' in-home injuries: I. Context, correlates, and determinants. *Journal of Pediatric Psychology, 29,* 415–431.

Morrow, D. F. (2006). Gay, lesbian, and transgender adolescents. In D. F. Morrow & L. Messinger (Eds.), *Sexual orientation and gender expression in social work practice* (pp. 177–195). New York: Columbia University Press.

Mosby, L., Rawls, A. W., Meehan, A. J., Mays, E., & Pettinari, C. J. (1999). Troubles in interracial talk about discipline: An examination of African American child rearing narratives. *Journal of Comparative Family Studies, 30,* 489–521.

Mosca, L., Mochari, H., Christian, A., Berra, K., Taurbert, K., & Mills, T. (2005). National study of women's awareness, preventive action and barriers to cardiovascular health. *Circulation, 113,* 525–534.

Mosconi L., Brys, M., Glodzik-Sobanska, L., De Santi, S., Rusinek, H., & de Leon, M. J. (2007). Early detection of Alzheimer's disease using neuroimaging. *Experimental Gerontology, 42,* 129–138.

Mosely-Howard, G. S., & Evans, C. B. (2000). Relationships and contemporary experiences of the African-American family: An ethnographic case study. *Journal of Black Studies, 30,* 428–451.

Moses, L. J., Baldwin, D. A., Rosicky, J. G., & Tidball, G. (2001). Evidence for referential understanding in the emotions domain at twelve and eighteen months. *Child Development, 72,* 718–735.

Mosher, W. D., Chandra, A., & Jones, J. (2005). *Sexual behavior and selected health measures: Men and women 15–44 years of age, United States 2002,* Vol. 362. Atlanta: U.S. Centers for Disease Control and Prevention.

Moshman, D. (1998). Identity as a theory of oneself. *Genetic Epistemologist, 26*(3), 1–9.

Moshman, D. (1999). *Adolescent psychological development: Rationality, morality, and identity.* Mahwah, NJ: Erlbaum.

Moshman, D. (2003). Developmental change in adulthood. In J. Demick & C. Andreoletti (Eds.), *Handbook of adult development* (pp. 43–61). New York: Plenum.

Moshman, D. (2005). *Adolescent psychological development: Rationality, morality, and identity* (2nd ed.). Mahwah, NJ: Erlbaum.

Moshman, D., & Franks, B. A. (1986). Development of the concept of inferential validity. *Child Development, 57,* 153–165.

Moshman, D., & Geil, M. (1998). Collaborative reasoning: Evidence for collective rationality. *Thinking and Reasoning, 4,* 231–248.

Moss, E., Bureau, J.-F., Cyr, C., Mongeau, C., & St. Laurent, D. (2004). Correlates of attachment at age 3: Construct validity of the preschool attachment classification system. *Developmental Psychology, 40,* 323–334.

Moss, E., Cyr, C., Bureau, J.-F., Tarabulsy, G. M., & Dubois-Comtois, K. (2005). Stability of attachment during the preschool period. *Developmental Psychology, 41,* 773–783.

Moss, E., Cyr, C., & Dubois-Comtois, K. (2004). Attachment at early school age and developmental risk: Examining family contexts and behavior problems of controlling-caregiving, controlling-punitive, and behaviorally disorganized children. *Developmental Psychology, 40,* 519–532.

Moss, E., Smolla, N., Guerra, I., Mazzarello, T., Chayer, D., & Berthiaume, C. (2006). Attachment and self-reported internalizing and externalizing behavior problems in a school period. *Canadian Journal of Behavioural Science, 38,* 142–157.

Mosteller, F. (1995, Fall). The Tennessee Study of Class Size in the Early School Grades. *Future of Children, 5*(2), 113–127.

Motl, R. W., Dishman, R. K., Saunders, R. P., Dowda, M., Felton, G., Ward, D. S., & Pate, R. R. (2002). Examining social–cognitive determinants of intention and physical activity among black and white adolescent girls using structural equation modeling. *Health Psychology, 21,* 459–467.

Mottus, R., Indus, K., & Allik, J. (2008). Accuracy of only children stereotype. *Journal of Research in Personality, 42,* 1047–1052.

Mounts, N. S., & Steinberg, L. (1995). An ecological analysis of peer influence on adolescent grade point average and drug use. *Developmental Psychology, 31,* 915–922.

Mounts, N. S., Valentiner, D. P., Anderson, K. L., & Boswell, M. K. (2006). Shyness, sociability, and parental support for the college transition: Relation to adolescents' adjustment. *Journal of Youth and Adolescence, 35,* 71–80.

Moxley, D. P., Najor-Durack, A., & Dumbrigue, C. (2001). *Keeping students in higher education.* London: Kogan Page.

Moyer, M. S. (1992). Sibling relationships among older adults. *Generations, 16*(3), 55–58.

Mroczek, D. K., & Kolarz, C. M. (1998). The effect of age on positive and negative affect: A developmental perspective on happiness. *Journal of Personality and Social Psychology, 75,* 1333–1349.

Mroczek, D. K., & Spiro, A., III. (2005). Change in life satisfaction during adulthood: Findings from the Veterans Affairs Normative Aging Study. *Journal of Personality and Social Psychology, 88,* 189–202.

Mroczek, D. K., & Spiro, A., III. (2007). Personality change influences mortality in older men. *Psychological Science, 18,* 371–376.

Mrug, S., Hoza, B., & Gerdes, A. C. (2001). Children with attention-deficit/hyperactivity disorder: Peer relationships and peer-oriented interventions. In D. W. Nangle & C. A. Erdley (Eds.), *The role of friendship in psychological adjustment* (pp. 51–77). San Francisco: Jossey-Bass.

Mueller, C. M., & Dweck, C. S. (1998). Intelligence praise can undermine motivation and performance. *Journal of Personality and Social Psychology, 75,* 33–52.

Muenchow, S., & Marsland, K. W. (2007). Beyond baby steps: Promoting the growth and development of U.S. child-care policy. In J. L. Aber, S. J. Bishop-Josef, S. M. Jones, K. T. McLearn, & D. Phillips (Eds.), *Child development and social policy: Knowledge for action* (pp. 97–112). Washington, DC: American Psychological Association.

Mulder, E. J. H., Robles de Medina, P. G., Huizink, A. C., Van den Bergh, B. R. H., Buitelaar, J. K., & Visser, G. H. A. (2002). Prenatal maternal stress: Effects on pregnancy and the (unborn) child. *Early Human Development, 70,* 3–14.

Müller, O., & Krawinkel, M. (2005). Malnutrition and health in developing countries. *Canadian Medical Association Journal, 173,* 279–286.

Müller, U., Overton, W. F., & Reese, K. (2001). Development of conditional reasoning: A longitudinal study. *Journal of Cognition and Development, 2,* 27–49.

Mullis, I. V. S., Martin, M. O., Kennedy, A. M., & Foy, P. (2007). *PIRLS 2006 international report: IEA's Progress in International Reading Literacy Study.* Boston: TIMSS & PIRLS International Study Center.

Mulvaney, M. K., McCartney, K., Bub, K. L., & Marshall, N. L. (2006). Determinants of dyadic scaffolding and cognitive outcomes in first graders. *Parenting: Science and Practice, 6,* 297–310.

Mulvaney, M. K., & Mebert, C. J. (2007). Parental corporal punishment predicts behavior problems in early childhood. *Journal of Family Psychology, 21,* 389–397.

Mumme, D. L., Bushnell, E. W., DiCorcia, J. A., & Lariviere, L. A. (2007). Infants' use of gaze cues to interpret others' actions and emotional reactions. In R. Flom, K. Lee, & D. Muir (Eds.), *Gaze-following: Its development and significance* (pp. 143–170). Mahwah, NJ: Erlbaum.

Munakata, Y. (2001). Task-dependency in infant behavior: Toward an understanding of the processes underlying cognitive development. In F. Lacerda, C. von Hofsten, & M. Heimann (Eds.), *Emerging cognitive abilities in early infancy* (pp. 29–52). Mahwah, NJ: Erlbaum.

Munakata, Y. (2006). Information processing approaches to development. In D. Kuhn & R. S. Siegler (Eds.), *Handbook of child psychology: Vol. 3. Cognition, perception, and language* (6th ed., pp. 426–463). Hoboken, NJ: Wiley.

Munakata, Y., Casey, B. J., & Diamond, A. (2004). Developmental cognitive neuroscience: progress and potential. *Trends in Cognitive Sciences, 8,* 122–128.

Munakata, Y., & Stedron, J. M. (2002). Modeling infants' perception of object unity: What have we learned? *Developmental Science, 5,* 176.

Mundy, P. (2003). The neural basis of social impairments in autism: The role of the dorsal medial-frontal cortex and anterior cingulate system. *Journal of Child Psychology and Psychiatry and Allied Disciplines, 44,* 793–809.

Mundy, P., & Stella, J. (2000). Joint attention, social orienting, and nonverbal communication in autism. In A. M. Wetherby & B. M. Prizant (Eds.), *Autism spectrum disorders* (Vol. 9, pp. 55–77). Baltimore, MD: Paul H. Brookes.

Munroe, R. L., & Romney, A. K. (2006). Gender and age differences in same-sex aggregation and social behavior. *Journal of Cross-Cultural Psychology, 37,* 3–19.

Muret-Wagstaff, S., & Moore, S. G. (1989). The Hmong in America: Infant behavior and rearing practices. In J. K. Nugent, B. M. Lester, & T. B. Brazelton (Eds.), *Biology, culture, and development* (Vol. 1, pp. 319–339). Norwood, NJ: Ablex.

Muris, P., Merckelbach, H., Gadet, B., & Moulaert, V. (2000). Fears, worries, and scary dreams in 4- to 12-year-old children: Their content, developmental pattern, and origins. *Journal of Clinical Child Psychology, 29,* 43–52.

Muris, P., Merckelbach, H., Ollendick, T. H., King, N. J., & Bogie, N. (2001). Children's nighttime fears: Parent–child ratings of frequency, content, origins, coping behaviors, and severity. *Behaviour Research and Therapy, 39,* 13–28.

Murphy, S. A. (2008). The loss of a child: Sudden death and extended illness perspectives. In M. S. Stroebe, R. O. Hansson, H. Schut, & W. Stroebe (Eds.), *Handbook of bereavement research and practice* (pp. 375–396). Washington, DC: American Psychological Association.

Murray, A. D. (1985). Aversiveness is in the mind of the beholder. In B. M. Lester & C. F. Z. Boukydis (Eds.), *Infant crying* (pp. 217–239). New York: Plenum.

Murtagh, K. N., & Hubert, H. B. (2004). Gender differences in physical disability among an elderly cohort. *American Journal of Public Health, 94,* 1406–1411.

Mussen, P., & Eisenberg-Berg, N. (1977). *Roots of caring, sharing, and helping.* San Francisco: Freeman.

Mustanski, B. S., Viken, R. J., Kaprio, J., Pulkkinen, L., & Rose, R. J. (2004). Genetic and environmental influences on pubertal development: Longitudinal data from Finnish twins at ages 11 and 14. *Developmental Psychology, 40,* 1188–1198.

Mutchler, J. E., Burr, J. A., & Caro, F. G. (2003). From paid worker to volunteer: Leaving the paid workforce and volunteering in later life. *Social Forces, 81,* 1267–1293.

Mutran, E. J., Danis, M., Bratton, K. A., Sudha, S., & Hanson, L. (1997). Attitudes of the critically ill toward prolonging life: The role of social support. *Gerontologist, 37,* 192–199.

Mutrie, N., & Faulkner, G. (2004). Physical activity: Positive psychology in motion. In P. A. Linley & S. Joseph (Eds.), *Positive psychology in practice* (pp. 146–164). Hoboken, NJ: Wiley.

Mutti, D. O., Mitchell, G. L., Moeschberger, M. L., Jones, L. A., & Zadnik, K. (2002). Parental myopia, near work, school achievement, and children's refractive error. *Investigative Ophthalmology and Visual Science, 43,* 3633–3640.

Muzzatti, B., & Agnoli, F. (2007). Gender and mathematics: Attitudes and stereotype threat susceptibility in Italian children. *Developmental Psychology, 43,* 747–759.

Myers, D. G. (2000). The funds, friends, and faith of happy people. *American Psychologist, 55,* 56–67.

Myers, M. G., Brown, S. A., Tate, S., Abrantes, A., & Tomlinson, K. (2001). *Adolescents, alcohol, and substance abuse* (pp. 275–296). New York: Guilford.

Myerson, J., Hale, S., Wagstaff, D., Poon, L. W., & Smith, G. A. (1990). The information-loss model: A mathematical theory of age-related cognitive slowing. *Psychological Review, 97,* 475–487.

Myowa-Yamakoshi, M., Tomonaga, M., Tanaka, M., & Matsuzawa, T. (2004). Imitation in neonatal chimpanzees *(Pan troglodytes). Developmental Science, 7,* 437–442.

N

Nadel, J., Prepin, K., & Okanda, M. (2005). Experiencing contingency and agency: First step toward self-understanding in making a mind? *Interaction Studies, 6,* 447–462.

Nader, K. (2002). Treating children after violence in schools and communities. In N. B. Webb (Ed.), *Helping bereaved children: A handbook for practitioners* (pp. 214–244). New York: Guilford.

Nader, K., Dubrow, N., & Stamm, B. H. (1999). *Honoring differences: Cultural issues in the treatment of trauma and loss.* Washington, DC: Taylor & Francis.

Nader, P. R., Bradley, R. H., Houts, R. M., McRitchie, S. L., & O'Brien, M. (2008). Moderate-to-vigorous physical activity from ages 9 to 15 years. *Journal of the American Medical Association, 16,* 295–305.

Nagy, E., Compagne, H., Orvos, H., Pal, A., Molnar, P., & Janszky, I. (2005). Index finger movement imitation by human neonates: Motivation, learning, and left-hand preference. *Pediatric Research, 58,* 749–753.

Nagy, W. E., & Scott, J. A. (2000). Vocabulary processes. In M. L. Kamil & P. B. Mosenthal (Eds.), *Handbook of reading research* (Vol. 3, pp. 269–284). Mahwah, NJ: Erlbaum.

Naigles, L. G., & Gelman, S. A. (1995). Overextensions in comprehension and production revisited: Preferential-looking in a study of dog, cat, and cow. *Journal of Child Language, 22,* 19–46.

Naigles, L. R., & Swenson, L. D. (2007). Syntactic supports for word learning. In E. Hoff & M. Shatz (Eds.), *Blackwell handbook of language development* (pp. 212–231). Malden, MA: Blackwell.

Naito, M., & Seki, Y. (2009). The relationship between second-order false belief and display rules reasoning: Integration of cognitive and affective social understanding. *Developmental Science, 12,* 150–164.

Nakamura, J., & Csikszentmihalyi, M. (2002). The concept of flow. In C. R. Snyder & S. J. Lopez (Eds.), *Handbook of positive psychology* (pp. 89–105). New York: Oxford University Press.

Nánez, J., Sr., & Yonas, A. (1994). Effects of luminance and texture motion on infant defensive reactions to optical collision. *Infant Behavior and Development, 17,* 165–174.

Narayan, C. (2008). Is there a double standard of aging? Older men and women and ageism. *Educational Gerontology, 34,* 782–787.

Nastasi, B. K., & Clements, D. H. (1994). Effectance motivation, perceived scholastic competence, and higher-order thinking in two cooperative computer environments. *Journal of Educational Computing Research, 10,* 249–275.

Natale, R., & Dodman, N. (2003). Birth can be a hazardous journey: Electronic fetal monitoring does not help. *JOGC, 25,* 1007–1009.

National Center for Biotechnology Information. (2004). SNPs: Variations on a theme. Retrieved from www.ncbi.nlm.nih.gov/About/primer/snps.html

National Coalition for the Homeless. (2008). *Homeless families with children.* Washington, DC: Author.

National Council of Youth Sports. (2008). *Report on trends and participation in organized youth sports.* Stuart, FL: Author.

National Federation of State High School Associations. (2008). *2007–08 High School Athletics Participation Survey.* Retrieved from www.nfhs.org/web/2008/09/high_school_sports_participation.aspx

National Institute on Aging. (2005). *Progress report on Alzheimer's disease 2004–2005: New discoveries, new insights.* Bethesda, MD: Author.

National Institute on Aging, U. S. Department of Health and Human Services. (2008). 2007 Progress report on Alzheimer's disease. Retrieved from www.nia.nih.gov/Alzheimers/Publications/ADProgress2007

National Institutes of Health. (2008). *Genes and disease.* Retrieved from www.ncbi.nlm.nih.gov/books/bv.fcgi?rid=gnd.TOC&depth=2

National Osteoporosis Foundation. (2008). *Fast facts.* Retrieved from www.nof.org/professionals/Fast_Facts_Osteoporosis.pdf

National Safe Kids Campaign. (2005). *Report to the nation: Trends in unintentional childhood injury mortality: 1987–2000.* Washington, DC: Author.

National Women's Law Center. (2007). *When girls don't graduate we all fail.* Washington, DC: Author.

Navarrete, C., Martinez, I., & Salamanca, F. (1994). Paternal line of transmission in chorea of Huntington with very early onset. *Genetic Counseling, 5,* 175–178.

Naveh-Benjamin, M. (2000). Adult age differences in memory performance: Tests of an associative deficit hypothesis. *Journal of Experimental Psychology: Learning, Memory, and Cognition, 26,* 1170–1187.

Naveh-Benjamin, M., Brav, T. K., & Levy, D. (2007). The associative memory deficit of older adults: The role of strategy utilization. *Psychology and Aging, 22,* 202–208.

Naveh-Benjamin, M., Craik, F. I. M., Guez, J., & Kreuger, S. (2005). Divided attention in younger and older adults: Effects of strategy and relatedness on memory performance and secondary task costs. *Journal of Experimental Psychology: Learning, Memory, and Cognition, 31,* 520–537.

Naveh-Benjamin, M., Guez, J., Kilb, A., & Reedy, S. (2004). The associative memory deficit of older adults: Further support using face–name associations. *Psychology and Aging, 19,* 541–546.

Naveh-Benjamin, M., Hussain, Z., Guez, J., & Bar-On, M. (2003). Adult age differences in episodic memory: Further support for an associative-deficit hypothesis. *Journal of Experimental Psychology: Learning, Memory, and Cognition, 29,* 826–837.

Neal, M. B., & Hammer, L. B. (2007). *Working couples caring for children and aging parents.* Mahwah, NJ: Erlbaum.

Needleman, H. L., MacFarland, C., Ness, R. B., Reinberg, S., & Tobin, M. J. (2002). Bone lead levels in adjudicated delinquents: A case control study. *Neurotoxicology and Teratology, 24,* 711–717.

Neff, K. D., & Helwig, C. C. (2002). A constructivist approach to understanding the development of reasoning about rights and authority within cultural contexts. *Cognitive Development, 17,* 1429–1450.

Neimeyer, R. A. (Ed.). (1994). *Death anxiety handbook.* Washington, DC: Taylor & Francis.

Neimeyer, R. A. (2001a). Meaning reconstruction and loss. In R. A. Neimeyer (Ed.), *Meaning reconstruction and the experience of loss* (pp. 1–9). Washington, DC: American Psychological Association.

Neimeyer, R. A. (2001b). The language of loss: Grief therapy as a process of meaning reconstruction. In R. A. Neimeyer (Ed.), *Meaning reconstruction and the experience of loss* (pp. 261–292). Washington, DC: American Psychological Association.

Neimeyer, R. A., & Van Brunt, D. (1995). Death anxiety. In H. Waas & R. A. Neimeyer (Eds.), *Dying: Facing the facts* (3rd ed., pp. 49–88). Washington, DC: Taylor & Francis.

Neitzel, C., & Stright, A. D. (2003). Mothers' scaffolding of children's problem solving: Establishing a foundation of academic self-regulatory competence. *Journal of Family Psychology, 17,* 147–159.

Nelson, C. A. (2001). The development and neural bases of face recognition. *Infant and Child Development, 10,* 3–18.

Nelson, C. A. (2002). Neural development and lifelong plasticity. In R. M. Lerner, F. Jacobs, & D. Wertlieb (Eds.), *Handbook of applied developmental science* (Vol. 1, pp. 31–60). Thousand Oaks, CA: Sage.

Nelson, C. A., & Bosquet, M. (2000). Neurobiology of fetal and infant development: Implications for infant mental health. In C. H. Zeanah, Jr. (Ed.), *Handbook of infant mental health* (2nd ed., pp. 37–59). New York: Guilford.

Nelson, C. A., Thomas, K. M., & de Haan, M. (2006). Neural bases of cognitive development. In D. Kuhn & R. Siegler (Eds.), *Handbook of child psychology: Vol. 2. Cognition, perception, and language* (6th ed., pp. 3–57). Hoboken, NJ: Wiley.

Nelson, D. A., Nelson, L. J., Hart, C. H., Yang, C., & Jin, S. (2005). Parenting and peer-group behavior in cultural context. In X. Chen, B. Schneider, & D. French (Eds.), *Peer relations in cultural context.* New York Cambridge University Press.

Nelson, D. A., Hart, C. H., Yang, C., Olsen, J. A., & Jin, S. (2006a). Aversive parenting in China: Associations with child physical and relational aggression. *Child Development, 77,* 554–572.

Nelson, D. A., Nelson, L. J., Hart, C. H., Yang, C., & Jin, S. (2006b). Parenting and peer-group behavior in cultural context. In X. Chen, D. French, & B. Schneider (Eds.), *Peer relations in cultural context* (pp. 213–246). New York: Cambridge University Press.

Nelson, D. A., Robinson, C. C., & Hart, C. H. (2005). Relational and physical aggression of preschool-age children: Peer status linkages across informants. *Early Education and Development, 16,* 115–139.

Nelson, H. D. (2008). Menopause. *Lancet, 371,* 760–770.

Nelson, H. D., Humphrey, L. L., Nygren, P., Teutsch, S. M., & Allan, J. D. (2002). Postmenopausal hormone replacement therapy: Scientific review. *Journal of the American Medical Association, 288,* 872–881.

Nelson, K. (1973). Structure and strategy in learning to talk. *Monographs of the Society for Research in Child Development, 38*(1–2, Serial No. 149).

Nelson, K. (2003). Narrative and the emergence of a consciousness of self. In G. D. Fireman & T. E. McVay, Jr. (Eds.). *Narrative and consciousness: Literature, psychology, and the brain* (pp. 17–36). London: Oxford University Press.

Nelson, K., & Fivush, R. (2004). The emergence of autobiographical memory: A social cultural developmental theory. *Developmental Review, 111,* 486–511.

Nelson, L. J. (2003). Rites of passage in emerging adulthood: Perspectives of young Mormons. In J. J. Arnett & N. L. Galambos (Eds.), *New directions for child and adolescent development* (No. 100, pp. 33–49). San Francisco: Jossey-Bass.

Nelson, L. J., & Chen, X. (2007). Emerging adulthood in China: The role of social and cultural factors. *Child Development Perspectives, 1,* 86–91.

Nelson, L. J., Padilla-Walker, L. M., Carroll, J. S., Madsen, S. D., Barry, C. M., & Badger, S. (2007). "If you want me to treat you like an adult, start acting like one!" Comparing the criteria that emerging adults and their parents have for adulthood. *Journal of Family Psychology, 21,* 665–674.

Nemet, D., Barkan, S., Epstein, Y., Friedland, O., Kowen, G., & Eliakim, A. (2005). Short- and long-term beneficial effects of a combined dietary–behavioral–physical activity intervention for the treatment of childhood obesity. *Pediatrics, 115,* e443–e449.

Nesdale, D., Durkin, K., Maas, A., & Griffiths, J. (2004). Group status, outgroup ethnicity, and children's ethnic attitudes. *Applied Developmental Psychology, 25,* 237–251.

Nesdale, D., Durkin, K., Maas, A., & Griffiths, J. (2005). Threat, group identification, and children's ethnic prejudice. *Social Development, 14,* 189–205.

Netz, Y., Wu, M.-J., Becker, B. J., & Tenenbaum, G. (2005). Physical activity and psychological well-being in advanced age: A meta-analysis of intervention studies. *Psychology and Aging, 20,* 272–284.

Neugarten, B. L. (1968a). Adult personality: Toward a psychology of the life cycle. In B. Neugarten (Ed.), *Middle age and aging* (pp. 137–147). Chicago: University of Chicago Press.

Neugarten, B. L. (1968b). The awareness of middle aging. In B. L. Neugarten (Ed.), *Middle age and aging* (pp. 93–98). Chicago: University of Chicago Press.

Neugarten, B. L. (1979). Time, age, and the life cycle. *American Journal of Psychiatry, 136,* 887–894.

Neugarten, B. L., & Neugarten, D. A. (1987, May). The changing meanings of age. *Psychology Today, 21*(5), 29–33.

Neuhouser, M. L., Wasserthel-Smoller, S., Thomson, C., Aragaki, A., Anderson, G. L., & Manson, J. E. (2009). Multivitamin use and risk of cancer and cardiovascular disease in the Women's Health Initiative cohorts. *Archives of Internal Medicine, 169,* 294–304.

Neuman, S. B. (1999). Books make a difference: A study of access to literacy. *Reading Research Quarterly, 34,* 286–311.

Neuman, S. B. (2003). From rhetoric to reality: The case for high-quality compensatory prekindergarten programs. *Phi Delta Kappan, 85*(4), pp. 286–291.

Neumann, K. F., Rojo, L., Navarrete, L. P., Farias, G., Reyes, P., & Maccioni, R. B. (2008). Insulin resistance and Alzheimer's disease: Molecular links and clinical implications. *Current Alzheimer Research, 5,* 438–447.

Neumark-Sztainer, D., Hannan, P. J., Story, M., Croll, J., & Perry, C. (2003). Family meal patterns: Associations with sociodemographic characteristics and improved dietary intake among adolescents. *Journal of the American Dietetic Association, 103,* 317–322.

Neville, H. A., & Heppner, M. J. (2002). Prevention and treatment of violence against women: An examination of sexual assault. In C. L. Juntunen & D. R. Atkinson (Eds.), *Counseling across the life span: Prevention and treatment* (pp. 261–277). Thousand Oaks, CA: Sage.

Neville, H. J., & Bavelier, D. (2002). Human brain plasticity: Evidence from sensory deprivation and altered language experience. In M. A. Hofman, G. J. Boer, A. J. G. D. Holtmaat, E. J. W. van Someren, J. Berhaagen, & D. F. Swaab (Eds.), *Plasticity in the adult brain: From genes to neurotherapy* (pp. 177–188). Amsterdam: Elsevier Science.

Nevin, R. (2000). How lead exposure relates to temporal changes in IQ, violent crime, and unwed pregnancy. *Environmental Research, 83,* 1 22.

Newcomb, A. F., Bukowski, W. M., & Pattee, L. (1993). Children's peer relations: A meta-analytic review of popular, rejected, neglected, controversial, and average sociometric status. *Psychological Bulletin, 113,* 99–128.

Newcomb, M. D., Abbott, R. D., Catalano, R. F., Hawkins, J. D., Battin-Pearson, S., & Hill, K. (2002). Mediational and deviance theories of late high school failure: Process roles of structural strains, academic competence, and general versus specific problem behavior. *Journal of Counseling Psychology, 49,* 172–186.

Newcombe, N. S. (2007). Taking science seriously: Straight thinking about spatial sex differences. In S. J. Ceci & W. M. Williams (Eds.), *Why aren't more women in science?* (pp. 69–77). Washington, DC: American Psychological Association.

Newcombe, N. S., & Huttenlocher, J. (1992). Children's early ability to solve perspective-taking problems. *Developmental Psychology, 28,* 635–643.

Newcombe, N. S., & Huttenlocher, J. (2006). Development of spatial cognition. In D. Kuhn & R. Siegler (Eds.), *Handbook of child psychology: Vol. 2. Cognition, perception, and language* (6th ed., pp. 734–776). Hoboken, NJ: Wiley.

Newcombe, N. S., Sluzenski, J., & Huttenlocher, J. (2005). Preexisting knowledge versus on-line learning: What do young infants really know about spatial location? *Psychological Science, 16,* 222–227.

Newman, C., Atkinson, J., & Braddick, O. (2001). The development of reaching and looking preferences in infants to objects of different sizes. *Developmental Psychology, 37,* 561–572.

Newport, E. L. (1991). Contrasting conceptions of the critical period for language. In S. Cary & R. Gelman (Eds.), *The epigenesis of mind: Essays on biology and cognition* (pp. 111–130). Hillsdale, NJ: Erlbaum.

Newport, E. L., & Aslin, R. N. (2000). Innately constrained learning: Blending old and new approaches to language acquisition. In S. C. Howell, S. A. Fish, & T. Keith-Lucas (Eds.), *Proceedings of the 24th Annual Boston University Conference on Language Development* (pp. 1–21). Somerville, MA: Cascadilla Press.

Newsom, J. T. (1999). Another side to caregiving: Negative reactions to being helped. *Current Directions in Psychological Science, 8,* 183–187.

Newsom, J. T., & Schulz, R. (1996). Social support as a mediator in the relation between functional status and quality of life in older adults. *Psychology and Aging, 11,* 34–44.

Ng, F. F., Pomerantz, E. M., & Lam, S. (2007). European American and Chinese parents' responses to children's success and failure: Implications for children's responses. *Developmental Psychology, 43,* 1239–1255.

Ngata, P. (2004). Death, dying, and grief: A Maori perspective. In J. D. Morgan & P. Laungani (Eds.), *Death and bereavement around the world: Vol. 4. Asia, Australia, and New Zealand* (pp. 95–99). Amityville, NY: Baywood.

Ngo-Metzger, Q., Phillips, R. S., & McCarthy, E. P. (2007). Ethnic disparities in hospice use among Asian-American and Pacific Islander patients dying with cancer. *Journal of the American Geriatric Society, 56,* 139–144.

NHPCO (National Hospice and Palliative Care Organization). (2004). *Facts and figures.* Alexandria, VA: Author.

NHPCO (National Hospice and Palliative Care Organization). (2005). 83% of Americans want to die at home. Retrieved from www.nhpco.org/templates/1/homepage.cfm

NHPCO (National Hospice and Palliative Care Organization). (2008). *NHPCO facts and figures: Hospice care in America.* Alexandria, VA: Author.

Ni, Y. (1998). Cognitive structure, content knowledge, and classificatory reasoning. *Journal of Genetic Psychology, 159,* 280–296.

Niccolai, L. M., Ethier, K. A., Kershaw, T. S., Lewis, J. B., Meade, C. S., & Ickovics, J. R. (2004). New sex partner acquisition and sexually transmitted disease risk among adolescent females. *Journal of Adolescent Health, 34,* 216–223.

NICHD (National Institute of Child Health and Human Development) Early Child Care Research Network. (1997). The effects of infant child care on infant–mother attachment security: Results of the NICHD Study of Early Child Care. *Child Development, 68,* 860–879.

NICHD (National Institute of Child Health and Human Development) Early Child Care Research Network. (1999). Child care and mother–child interaction in the first 3 years of life. *Developmental Psychology, 35,* 1399–1413.

NICHD (National Institute of Child Health and Human Development) Early Child Care Research Network. (2000a). Characteristics and quality of child care for toddlers and preschoolers. *Applied Developmental Science, 4,* 116–135.

NICHD (National Institute of Child Health and Human Development) Early Child Care Research Network. (2000b). The relation of child care to cognitive and language development. *Child Development, 71,* 960–980.

NICHD (National Institute of Child Health and Human Development) Early Child Care Research Network. (2001). Before Head Start: Income and ethnicity, family characteristics, child care experiences, and child development. *Early Education and Development, 12,* 545–575.

NICHD (National Institute of Child Health and Human Development) Early Child Care Research Network. (2002a). Child-care structure → process → outcome: Direct and indirect effects of child-care quality on young children's development. *Psychological Science, 13,* 199–206.

NICHD (National Institute of Child Health and Human Development) Early Child Care Research Network. (2002b). The interaction of child care and family risk in relation to child development at 24 and 36 months. *Applied Developmental Science, 6,* 144–156.

NICHD (National Institute of Child Health and Human Development) Early Child Care Research Network. (2003a). Does amount of time spent in child care predict socioemotional adjustment during the transition to kindergarten? *Child Development, 74,* 976–1005.

NICHD (National Institute of Child Health and Human Development) Early Child Care Research Network. (2003b). Does quality of child care affect child outcomes at age 4½? *Developmental Psychology, 39,* 451–469.

NICHD (National Institute of Child Health and Human Development) Early Child Care Research Network. (2004). Trajectories of physical aggression from toddlerhood to middle childhood. *Monographs of the Society for Research in Child Development, 69*(4, Serial No. 278).

NICHD (National Institute of Child Health and Human Development) Early Child Care Research Network. (2006). Child-care effect sizes for the NICHD Study of Early Child Care and Youth Development. *American Psychologist, 61,* 99–116.

Nichols, S. L., & Berliner, D. C. (2007). The pressure to cheat in a high-stakes testing environment. In E. M. Anderman & T. B. Murdock (Eds.), *Psychology of academic cheating* (pp. 289–311). San Francisco: Jossey-Bass.

Nichols, W. C., & Pace-Nichols, M. A. (2000). Childless married couples. In W. C. Nichols, M. A. Pace-Nichols, D. S. Becvar, & A. Y. Napier (Eds.), *Handbook of family development and intervention* (pp. 171–188). New York: Wiley.

Nickman, S. L., Rosenfeld, A. A., Fine, P., MacIntyre, J. C., Pilowsky, D. J., & Howe, R. A. (2005). Children in adoptive families: Overview and update. *Journal of the American Academy of Child and Adolescent Psychiatry, 44,* 987–995.

Niehaus, M. D., Moore, S. R., Patrick, P. D., Derr, L. L., Lorntz, B., Lima, A. A., & Gurerrant, R. L. (2002). Early childhood diarrhea is associated with diminished cognitive function 4 to 7 years later in children in a northeast Brazilian shanty-town. *American Journal of Tropical Medicine and Hygiene, 66,* 590–593.

Nielsen, S. J., & Popkin, B. M. (2003). Patterns and trends in food portion sizes. *Journal of the American Medical Association, 289,* 450–453.

Nigg, J. T., & Breslau, N. (2007). Prenatal smoking exposure, low birth weight, and disruptive behavior disorders. *Journal of the American Academy of Child and Adolescent Psychiatry, 46,* 362–369.

Nippold, M. A., Taylor, C. L., & Baker, J. M. (1996). Idiom understanding in Australian youth: A cross-cultural comparison. *Journal of Speech and Hearing Research, 39,* 442–447.

Nix, R. L., Pinderhughes, E. E., Dodge, K. A., Bates, J. E., Pettit, G. S., & McFadyen-Ketchum, S. A. (1999). The relation between mothers' hostile attribution tendencies and children's externalizing behavior problems: The mediating role of mothers' harsh discipline practices. *Child Development, 70,* 896–909.

Noland, J. S., Singer, L. T., Short, E. J., Minnes, S., Arendt, R. E., & Krichner, H. L. (2005). Prenatal drug exposure and selective attention in preschoolers. *Neurotoxicology and Teratology, 27,* 429–438.

Nolen-Hoeksema, S. (2002). Gender differences in depression. In I. H. Gotlib & C. L. Hammen (Eds.), *Handbook of depression* (pp. 492–509). New York: Guilford.

Nolen-Hoeksema, S. (2006). The etiology of gender differences in depression. In C. M. Mazure & G. Puryear (Eds.), *Understanding depression in women: Applying empirical research to practice and policy* (pp. 9–43). Washington, DC: American Psychological Association.

Nomaguchi, K. M., & Milkie, M. A. (2003). Costs and rewards of children: The effects of becoming a parent on adults' lives. *Journal of Marriage and Family, 65,* 356–374.

Noonan, C. W., Kathman, S. J., Sarasua, S. M., & White, M. C. (2003). Influence of environmental zinc on the association between environmental and biological measures of lead in children. *Journal of Exposure Analysis and Environmental Epidemiology, 13,* 318–323.

Noppe, I. C., & Noppe, L. D. (1997). Evolving meanings of death during early, middle, and later adolescence. *Death Studies, 21,* 253–275.

Noppe, L. D., & Noppe, I. C. (1996). Ambiguity in adolescent understandings of death. In C. A. Corr & D. E. Balk (Eds.), *Handbook of adolescent death and bereavement* (pp. 25–41). New York: Springer.

Nordhus, I. H. (2008). Manifestations of depression and anxiety in older adults. In B. Woods & L. Clare (Eds.), *Handbook of the clinical psychology of ageing* (pp. 97–110). Hoboken, NJ: Wiley-Interscience.

Noterdaeme, M., Mildenberger, K., Minow, F., & Amorosa, H. (2002). Evaluation of neuromotor deficits in children with autism and children with a specific speech and language disorder. *European Child and Adolescent Psychiatry, 11,* 219–225.

Nucci, L. P. (1996). Morality and the personal sphere of action. In E. Reed, E. Turiel, & T. Brown (Eds.), *Values and knowledge* (pp. 41–60). Hillsdale, NJ: Erlbaum.

Nucci, L. P. (2001). *Education in the moral domain.* New York: Cambridge University Press.

Nucci, L. P. (2002). The development of moral reasoning. In U. Goswami (Ed.), *Blackwell handbook of childhood cognitive development* (pp. 303–325). Malden, MA: Blackwell.

Nucci, L. P. (2005). Culture, context, and the psychological sources of human rights concepts. In W. Edelstein & G. Nunner-Winkler (Eds.), *Morality in context* (pp. 365–394). Amsterdam, Netherlands: Elsevier.

Nuland, S. B. (1993). *How we die.* New York: Random House.

Nussbaum, J. F. (1994). Friendship in older adulthood. In M. L. Hummer, J. M. Wiemann, & J. F. Nussbaum (Eds.), *Interpersonal communication in older adulthood* (pp. 209–225). Thousand Oaks, CA: Sage.

Nuttall, R. L., Casey, M. B., & Pezaris, E. (2005). Spatial ability as a mediator of gender differences on mathematics tests: A biological–environmental framework. In A. M. Gallagher & J. C. Kaufman (Eds.), *Gender differences in mathematics: An integrated psychological approach* (pp. 121–142). New York: Cambridge University Press.

Nyberg, L. (2005). Cognitive training in healthy aging: A cognitive neuroscience perspective. In R. Cabeza, L. Nyberg, & D. Park (Eds.), *Cognitive neuroscience of aging: Linking cognitive and cerebral aging* (pp. 309–321). New York: Oxford University Press.

Nye, B., Hedges, L. V., & Konstantopoulos, S. (2001). Are effects of small classes cumulative? Evidence from a Tennessee experiment. *Journal of Educational Research, 94,* 336–345.

O

Oakes, L. M., & Madole, K. L. (2003). Principles of developmental change in infants' category formation. In D. H. Rakison & L. M. Oakes (Eds.), *Early category and concept development: Making sense of the blooming, buzzing confusion* (pp. 132–158). New York: Oxford University Press.

Oakes, L. M., Coppage, D. J., & Dingel, A. (1997). By land or by sea: The role of perceptual similarity in infants' categorization of animals. *Developmental Psychology, 33,* 396–407.

Oberecker, R., & Friederici, A. D. (2006). Syntactic event-related potential components in 24-month-olds' sentence comprehension. *NeuroReport, 17,* 1017–1021.

Oberecker, R., Friedrich, M., & Friederici, A. D. (2005). Neural correlates of syntactic processing in two-year-olds. *Journal of Cognitive Neuroscience, 17,* 1667–1678.

Oberlander, T. F., Warburton, W., Misri, S., Jaafar, A., & Hertzman, C. (2006). Neonatal outcomes after prenatal exposure to selective serotonin reuptake inhibitor antidepressants and maternal depression using population-based linked health data. *Archives of General Psychiatry, 63,* 898–906.

Obermeyer, C. M. (2000). Menopause across cultures: A review of the evidence. *Menopause, 7,* 184–192.

Obradović, J., & Masten, A. S. (2007). Developmental antecedents of young adult civic engagement. *Applied Developmental Science, 11,* 2–19.

O'Callaghan, M. J., Burn, Y. R., Mohay, H. A., Rogers, Y., & Tudehope, D. I. (1993). The prevalence and origins of left hand preference in high risk infants, and its implications for intellectual, motor, and behavioral performance at four and six years. *Cortex, 29,* 617–627.

O'Connor, A. R., Stephenson, T., Johnson, A., Tobin, M. J., Ratib, S., Ng, Y., & Fielder, A. R. (2002). Long-term ophthalmic outcome of low birth weight children with and without retinopathy of prematurity. *Pediatrics, 109,* 12–18.

O'Connor, C. (1997). Dispositions toward (collective) struggle and educational resilience in the inner city: A case analysis of six African-American high school students. *American Educational Research Journal, 34,* 593–629.

O'Connor, M. G., & Kaplan, E. F. (2003). Age-related changes in memory. In J. Demick & C. Andreoletti (Eds.), *Handbook of adult development* (pp. 121–130). New York: Springer.

O'Connor, P. (1992). *Friendships between women.* New York: Guilford.

O'Connor, P. (2003). Dying in the hospital. In I. Corless, B. B. Germino, & M. A. Pitman (Eds.), *Dying, death, and bereavement: A challenge for the living* (2nd ed., pp. 87–103). New York: Springer.

O'Connor, T. G., & Croft, C. M. (2001). A twin study of attachment in preschool children. *Child Development, 72,* 1501–1511.

O'Connor, T. G., Marvin, R. S., Rutter, M., Olrich, J. T., Britner, P. A., & the English and Romanian Adoptees Study Team. (2003). Child–parent attachment following early institutional deprivation. *Development and Psychopathology, 15,* 19–38.

O'Connor, T. G., Rutter, M., Beckett, C., Keaveney, L., Dreppner, J. M., & the English and Romanian Adoptees Study Team. (2000). The effects of global severe privation on cognitive competence: Extension and longitudinal follow-up. *Child Development, 71,* 376–390.

O'Dea, J. A. (2003). Why do kids eat healthful food? Perceived benefits of and barriers to healthful eating and physical activity among children and adolescents. *Journal of the American Dietetic Association, 103,* 497–501.

Oden, M. H., & Terman, L. M. (1968). The fulfillment of promise—40-year follow-up of the Terman gifted group. *Genetic Psychology Monographs, 77,* 3–93.

OECD (Organisation for Economic Cooperation and Development). (2006). *Starting strong II: Early childhood education and care.* Paris: OECD Publishing. Retrieved from www.sourceoecd.org/education/9264035451

OECD (Organisation for Economic Cooperation and Development). (2008a). *Education at a glance 2008: OECD indicators.* Paris: Author.

OECD (Organisation for Economic Cooperation and Development). (2008b). *OECD Health data: 2008.* Retrieved from secure.cihi.ca/cihiweb/dispPage.jsp?cw_page=media_26jun2008_e

OECD (Organisation for Economic Cooperation and Development). (2008c). *Statistics directorate: Information by country.* Retrieved from www.oecd.org/infobycountry/0,3380,en_2649_33715_1_1_1_1_1,00.html

Ogawa, J. R., Sroufe, L. A., Weinfield, N. S., Carlson, E. A., & Egeland, B. (1997). Development and the fragmented self: Longitudinal study of dissociative symptomatology in a nonclinical sample. *Development and Psychopathology, 9,* 855–879.

Ogbu, J. U. (2003). *Black American students in an affluent suburb: A study of academic disengagement.* Mahwah, NJ: Erlbaum.

Ogden, C. L., Carroll, M. D., & Flegal, K. M. (2008). High body mass index for age among U.S. children and adolescents, 2003–2006. *Journal of the American Medical Association, 299,* 2401–2405.

Ogden, C. L., Carroll, M. D., McDowell, M., Tabak, C. J., & Flegal, K. M. (2006). Prevalence of overweight and obesity in the United States, 1999–2004. *Journal of the American Medical Association, 295,* 1549–1555.

O'Halloran, C. M., & Altmaier, E. M. (1996). Awareness of death among children: Does a life-threatening illness alter the process of discovery? *Journal of Counseling and Development, 74,* 259–262.

Ohgi, S., Arisawa, K., Takahashi, T., Kusumoto, T., Goto, Y., Akiyama, T., & Saito, H. (2003a). Neonatal behavioral assessment scale as a predictor of later developmental disabilities of low-birth-weight and/or premature infants. *Brain and Development, 25,* 313–321.

Ohgi, S., Takahashi, T., Nugent, J. K., Arisawa, K., & Akiyama, T. (2003b). Neonatal behavioral characteristics and later behavioral problems. *Clinical Pediatrics, 42,* 679–686.

Ohlemiller, K. K. (2008). Recent findings and emerging questions in cochlear noise injury. *Hearing Research, 245,* 5–17.

Okagaki, L., Hammond, K. A., & Seamon, L. (1999). Socialization of religious beliefs. *Journal of Applied Developmental Psychology, 20,* 273–294.

Okagaki, L., & Sternberg, R. J. (1993). Parental beliefs and children's school performance. *Child Development, 64,* 36–56.

Okami, P., Weisner, T., & Olmstead, R. (2002). Outcome correlates of parent–child bedsharing: An eighteen-year longitudinal study. *Developmental and Behavioral Pediatrics, 23,* 244–253.

Okamoto, K., & Tanaka, Y. (2004). Subjective usefulness and 6-year mortality risks among elderly persons in Japan. *Journal of Gerontology, 59B,* P246–P249.

O'Keefe, M. J., O'Callaghan, M., Williams, G. M., Najman, J. M., & Bor, W. (2003). Learning, cognitive, and attentional problems in adolescents born small for gestational age. *Pediatrics, 112,* 301–307.

Oktem, M., Eroglu, D., Karahan, H. B., Taskintuna, N., Kuscu, E., & Zeyneloglu, H. B. (2007). Black cohosh and fluoxetine in the treatment of postmenopausal symptoms: A prospective, randomized trial. *Advances in Therapy, 24,* 448–461.

Olafson, E., & Boat, B. W. (2000). Long-term management of the sexually abused child: Considerations and challenges. In R. M. Reece (Ed.), *Treatment of child abuse: Common ground for mental health, medical, and legal practitioners* (pp. 14–35). Baltimore: Johns Hopkins University Press.

O'Laughlin, E. M., & Anderson, V. N. (2001). Perceptions of parenthood among young adults: Implications for career and family planning. *American Journal of Family Therapy, 29,* 95–108.

Old, S. R., & Naveh-Benjamin, M. (2008a). Age-related changes in memory: Experimental approaches. In S. M. Hofer & D. F. Alwin (Eds.), *Handbook of cognitive aging: Interdisciplinary perspectives* (pp. 151–167). Thousand Oaks, CA: Sage.

Old, S. R., & Naveh-Benjamin, M. (2008b). Differential effects of age on item and associative measures of memory: A meta-analysis. *Psychology and Aging, 23,* 104–118.

Old, S. R., & Naveh-Benjamin, M. (2008c). Memory for people and their actions: Further evidence for an age-related associative deficit. *Psychology and Aging, 23,* 467–472.

Ollendick, T. H., King, N. J., & Muris, P. (2002). Fears and phobias in children: Phenomenology, epidemiology, and aetiology. *Child and Adolescent Mental Health, 7,* 98–106.

Oller, D. K. (2000). *The emergence of the speech capacity.* Mahwah, NJ: Erlbaum.

Olshansky, S. J., Hayflick, L., & Perls, T. T. (2004). Antiaging medicine: The hype and the reality—Part II. *Journal of Gerontology, 59A, 649*–651.

Olson, R. E. (2000). Is it wise to restrict fat in the diets of children? *Journal of the American Dietetic Association, 100,* 28–32.

Olson, S. L., Bates, J. E., Sandy, J. M., & Lantheir, R. (2000). Early development precursors of externalizing behavior in middle childhood and adolescence. *Journal of Abnormal Child Psychology, 28,* 119–133.

O'Malley, P. (2006). Viagra and vision loss: What is known and unknown. *Clinical Nurse Specialist, 20,* 227–228.

Omar, H., McElderry, D., & Zakharia, R. (2003). Educating adolescents about puberty: What are we missing? *International Journal of Adolescent Medicine and Health, 15,* 79–83.

Ondrusek, N., Abramovitch, R., Pencharz, P., & Koren, G. (1998). Empirical examination of the ability of children to consent to clinical research. *Journal of Medical Ethics, 24,* 158–165.

O'Neill, M., Bard, K. A., Kinnell, M., & Fluck, M. (2005). Maternal gestures with 20-month-old infants in two contexts. *Developmental Science, 8,* 352–359.

O'Neill, R., Welsh, M., Parke, R. D., Wang, S., & Strand, C. (1997). A longitudinal assessment of the academic correlates of early peer acceptance and rejection. *Journal of Clinical Child Psychology, 26,* 290–303.

O'Neill, R. M., Horton, S., & Crosby, F. J. (1999). *Mentoring dilemmas* (pp. 63–80). Mahwah, NJ: Erlbaum.

Ong, A. D., & Allaire, J. C. (2005). Cardiovascular intraindividual variability in later life: The influence of social connectedness and positive emotions. *Psychology and Aging, 20,* 476–485.

Ong, A. D., Bergeman, C. S., Bisconti, T. L., & Wallace, K. A. (2006). Psychological resilience, positive emotions, and successful adaptation to stress in later life. *Journal of Personality and Social Psychology, 91,* 730–749.

Ong, A. D., Edwards, L. M., & Bergeman, C. S. (2006). Hope as a source of resilience in later adulthood. *Personality and Individual Differences, 41,* 1263–1273.

Ong, W., Allison, J., & Haladyna, T. M. (2000). Student achievement of third graders in comparable single-age and multiage classrooms. *Journal of Research in Childhood Education, 14,* 205–215.

Ontai, L. L., & Thompson, R. A. (2008). Attachment, parent–child discourse and theory-of-mind development. *Social Development, 17,* 47–60.

Onwuteaka-Philipsen, B. D., van der Heide, A., Muller, M. T., Rurup, M., Rietjens, J. A. C., & Georges, J.-J. (2005). Dutch experience of monitoring euthanasia. *British Medical Journal, 331,* 691–693.

Oosterwegel, A., & Oppenheimer, L. (1993). *The self-system: Developmental changes between and within self-concepts.* Hillsdale, NJ: Erlbaum.

O'Rahilly, R., & Müller, F. (2001). *Human embryology and teratology.* New York: Wiley-Liss.

Orbio de Castro, B., Veerman, J. W., Koops, W., Bosch, J. D., & Monshouwer, H. J. (2002). Hostile attribution of intent and aggressive behavior: A meta-analysis. *Child Development, 73,* 916–934.

Ordonana, J. R., Caspi, A., & Moffitt, T. E. (2008). Unintentional injuries in a twin study of preschool children: Environmental, not genetic risk factors. *Journal of Pediatric Psychology, 33,* 185–194.

Oregon Department of Human Services. (2009). *Death with Dignity Act annual report: 2008 summary.* Retrieved from oregon.gov/DHS/ph/pas/ar-index.shtml

O'Reilly, A. W. (1995). Using representations: Comprehension and production of actions with imagined objects. *Child Development, 66,* 999–1010.

Ormel, J., Petukhova, M., Chatterji, S., Aguilar-Gaxiola, S., Alonso, J., & Angermeyer, M. C. (2008). Disability and treatment of specific mental and physical disorders across the world. *British Journal of Psychiatry, 192,* 368–375.

Ornish, D., Lin, J., Daubenmier, J., Weidner, G., Epel, E. S., & Kemp, C. (2008). Increased telomerase activity and comprehensive lifestyle changes: A pilot study. *Lancet Oncology, 9,* 1048–1057.

Orzano, A. J., & Scott, J. G. (2004). Diagnosis and treatment of obesity in adults: An applied evidence-based review. *Journal of the American Board of Family Practice, 17,* 359–369.

Osborne, J. (1994). Academics, self-esteem, and race: A look at the underlying assumption of the disidentification hypothesis. *Personality and Social Psychology Bulletin, 21,* 449–455.

Osherson, D. N., & Markman, E. M. (1975). Language and the ability to evaluate contradictions and tautologies. *Cognition, 2,* 213–226.

Osmers, R., Friede, M., Liske, E., Schnitker, J., Freudenstein, J., & Henneicke-von Zepelin, H. H. (2005). Efficacy and safety of isopropanolic black cohosh extract for climacteric symptoms. *Obstetrics and Gynecology, 105,* 1074–1083.

Ostir, G. V., Carlson, J. E., Black, S. A., Rudkin, L., Goodwin, J. S., & Markides, K. S. (1999). Disability in older adults 1: Prevalence, causes, and consequences. *Behavioral Medicine, 24,* 147–156.

Ostrov, J. M., Crick, N. R., & Stauffacher, K. (2006). Relational aggression in sibling and peer relationships during early childhood. *Applied Developmental Psychology, 27,* 241–253.

Ostrov, J. M., Gentile, D. A., & Crick, N. R. (2006). Media exposure, aggression, and prosocial behavior during early childhood: A longitudinal study. *Social Development, 15,* 612–627.

Otis, N., Grouzet, F. M. E., & Pelletier, L. G. (2005). Latent motivational change in an academic setting: A three-year longitudinal study. *Journal of Educational Psychology, 97,* 170–183.

Ott, A., Andersen, K., Dewey, M. E., Letenneur, L., Brayne, C., & Copeland, J. R. (2004). Effect of smoking on global cognitive function in nondemented elderly. *Neurology, 23,* 920–924.

Ovando, C. J., & Collier, V. P. (1998). *Bilingual and ESL classrooms: Teaching in multicultural contexts.* Boston: McGraw-Hill.

Owen-Kostelnik, J., Reppucci, N. D., & Meyer, J. R. (2006). Testimony and interrogation of minors: Assumptions about maturity and morality. *American Psychologist, 61,* 286–304.

Owens, R. E. (2005). *Language development: An introduction.* Boston: Allyn and Bacon.

Owsley, C., Ball, K., McGwin, G., Jr., Sloane, M. E., Roenker, D. L., White, M. F., & Overley, E. T. (1998). Visual processing impairment and risk of motor vehicle crash among older adults. *Journal of the American Medical Association, 279,* 1083–1088.

Oyserman, D., Bybee, D., Mowbray, C., & Hart-Johnson, T. (2005). When mothers have serious mental health problems: Parenting as a proximal mediator. *Journal of Adolescence, 28,* 443–463.

Özçaliskan, S. (2005). On learning to draw the distinction between physical and metaphorical motion: Is metaphor an early emerging cognitive and linguistic capacity? *Journal of Child Language, 32,* 291–318.

Özçaliskan, S., & Goldin-Meadow, S. (2005). Gesture is at the cutting edge of early language development. *Cognition, 96,* B101–B113.

P

Pacella, R., McLellan, M., Grice, K., Del Bono, E. A., Wiggs, J. L., & Gwiazda, J. E. (1999). Role of genetic factors in the etiology of juvenile-onset myopia based on a longitudinal study of refractive error. *Optometry and Vision Science, 76,* 381–386.

Padula, M. A., & Miller, D. L. (1999). Understanding graduate women's reentry experiences. *Psychology of Women Quarterly, 23,* 327–343.

Pagani, L. S., Japel, C., Vitaro, F., Tremblay, R. E., Larose, S., & McDuff, P. (2008). When predictions fail: The case of unexpected pathways toward high school dropout. *Journal of Social Issues, 64,* 175–193.

Pager, D., & Shepherd, H. (2008). The sociology of discrimination: Racial discrimination in employment, housing, credit, and consumer markets. *Annual Review of Sociology, 34,* 181–209.

Palacio-Quintin, E. (2000). Les services de garde et le développement de l'enfant [The impact of day care on child development]. *ISUMA: Canadian Journal of Policy Research, 1*(2), 25–30.

Palincsar, A. S. (2003). Advancing a theoretical model of learning and instruction. In B. J. Zimmerman (Ed.), *Educational psychology: A century of contributions* (pp. 459–475). Mahwah, NJ: Erlbaum.

Palmer, J. R., Hatch, E. E., Rao, R. S., Kaufman, R. H., Herbst, A. L., & Noller, K. L. (2001). Infertility among women exposed prenatally to diethylstilbestrol. *American Journal of Epidemiology, 154,* 316–321.

Palmore, E. (2001). The ageism survey: First findings. *Gerontologist, 41,* 572–575.

Palop, J. J., Chin, J., Roberson, E. D., Wang, J., Thwin, M. T., & Bien-Ly, N. (2007). Aberrant excitatory neuronal activity and compensatory remodeling of inhibitory hippocampal circuits in mouse models of Alzheimer's disease. *Neuron, 55,* 697–711.

Pan, B. A., & Snow, C. E. (1999). The development of conversation and discourse skills. In M. Barrett (Ed.), *The development of language* (pp. 229–249). Hove, UK: Psychology Press.

Pan, H. W. (1994). Children's play in Taiwan. In J. L. Roopnarine, J. E. Johnson, & F. H. Hooper (Eds.), *Children's play in diverse cultures* (pp. 31–50). Albany, NY: SUNY Press.

Panish, J. B., & Stricker, G. (2002). Perceptions of childhood and adult sibling relationships. *NYS Psychologist, 14,* 33–36.

Papadakis, A. A., Prince, R. P., Jones, N. P., & Strauman, T. J. (2006). Self-regulation, rumination, and vulnerability to depression in adolescent girls. *Development and Psychopathology, 18,* 815–829.

Paquette, D. (2004). Theorizing the father–child relationship: Mechanisms and developmental outcomes. *Human Development, 47,* 193–219.

Paradis, J. (2007). Second language acquisition in childhood. In E. Hoff & M. Shatz (Eds.), *Blackwell handbook of language development* (pp. 387–405). Malden, MA: Blackwell.

Parameswaran, G. (2003). Experimenter instructions as a mediator in the effects of culture on mapping one's neighborhood. *Journal of Environmental Psychology, 23,* 409–417.

Pardeck, J. T. (2005). An exploration of child maltreatment among homeless families: Implications for family policy. *Early Child Development and Care, 175,* 335–342.

Pardum, C. J., L'Engle, K. L., & Brown, J. D. (2005). Linking exposure to outcomes: Early adolescents' consumption of sexual content in six media. *Mass Communication and Society, 87,* 75–91.

Parent, A., Teilmann, G., Juul, A., Skakkebaek, N. E., Toppari, J., & Bourguingnon, J. (2003). The timing of normal puberty and the age limits of sexual precocity: Variations around the world, secular trends, and changes after migration. *Endocrine Reviews, 24,* 668–693.

Paris, S. G., & Paris, A. H. (2006). Assessments of early reading. In K. A. Renninger & I. E. Sigel (Eds.), *Handbook of child psychology: Vol. 4. Child psychology in practice* (6th ed., pp. 48–74). Hoboken, NJ: Wiley.

Park, D. C., Hertzog, C., Kidder, D. P., Morrell, R. W., & Mayhorn, C. B. (1997). Effect of age on event-based and time-based prospective memory. *Psychology and Aging, 12,* 314–327.

Park, D. C., Lautenschlager, G., Hedden, T., Davidson, N. S., Smith, A. D., & Smith, P. K. (2002). Models of visuospatial and verbal memory across the adult life span. *Psychology and Aging, 17,* 299–320.

Park, D. C., & Payer, D. (2006). Working memory across the adult lifespan. In E. Bialystok & F. I. M. Craik (Eds.), *Lifespan cognition: Mechanisms of change* (pp. 128–142). New York: Oxford University Press.

Parke, R. D. (2002). Fathers and families. In M. H. Bornstein (Ed.), *Handbook of parenting: Vol. 3* (2nd ed., pp. 27–73). Mahwah, NJ: Erlbaum.

Parke, R. D., & Buriel, R. (2006). Socialization in the family: Ethnic and ecological perspectives. In N. Eisenberg (Ed.), *Handbook of child psychology: Vol. 3. Social, emotional, and personality development* (6th ed., pp. 429–504). Hoboken, NJ: Wiley.

Parke, R. D., Coltrane, S., Fabricius, W., Powers, J., & Adams, M. (2004a). Assessing father involvement in Mexican-American families. In R. Day & M. E. Lamb (Eds.), *Conceptualizing and measuring paternal involvement* (pp. 17–38). Mahwah, NJ: Erlbaum.

Parke, R. D., Simpkins, S. D., McDowell, D. J., Kim, M., Killian, C., Dennis, J., Flyr, M. L., Wild, M., & Rah, Y. (2004b). Relative contributions of families and peers to children's social development. In P. K. Smith & C. H. Hart (Eds.), *Blackwell handbook of childhood social development* (pp. 156–177). Malden, MA: Blackwell.

Parker, F. L., Boak, A. Y., Griffin, K. W., Ripple, C., & Peay, L. (1999). Parent–child relationship, home learning environment, and school readiness. *School Psychology Review, 28,* 413–425.

Parker, J. G., Low, C. M., Walker, A. R., & Gamm, B. K. (2005). Friendship jealousy in young adolescents: Individual differences and links to sex, self-esteem, aggression, and social adjustment. *Developmental Psychology, 41,* 235–250.

Parker, J. G., Rubin, K. H., Price, J., & DeRosier, M. E. (1995). Peer relationships, child development, and adjustment: A developmental psychopathology perspective. In D. Chicchetti & D. Cohen (Eds.), *Developmental psychopathology: Vol. 2. Risk, disorder, and adaptation* (pp. 96–161). New York: Wiley.

Parker, R. G. (1995). Reminiscence: A continuity theory framework. *Gerontologist, 35,* 515–525.

Parker, S. W., Nelson, C. A., & the Bucharest Early Intervention Project Core Group. (2005). The impact of early institutional rearing on the ability to discriminate facial expressions of emotion: An event-related potential study. *Child Development, 76,* 54–72.

Parmelee, P. A., & Lawton, M. P. (1990). The design of special environments for the aged. In J. E. Birren & K. W. Schaie (Eds.), *Handbook of the psychology of aging* (3rd ed., pp. 464–488). San Diego, CA: Academic Press.

Parten, M. (1932). Social participation among preschool children. *Journal of Abnormal and Social Psychology, 27,* 243–269.

Pascalis, O., de Haan, M., & Nelson, C. A. (1998). Long-term recognition memory for faces assessed by visual paired comparison in 3-and 6-month-old infants. *Journal of Experimental Psychology: Learning, Memory, and Cognition, 24,* 249–260.

Pascalis, O., de Haan, M., & Nelson, C. A. (2002). Is face processing species-specific during the first year of life? *Science, 296,* 1321–1323.

Pascarella, E. T., & Terenzini, P. T. (1991). *How college affects students.* San Francisco: Jossey-Bass.

Pasinetti, G. M., & Eberstein, J. A. (2008). Metabolic syndrome and the role of dietary lifestyles in Alzheimer's disease. *Journal of Neurochemistry, 106,* 1503–1514.

Pasterski, V. L., Geffner, M. E., Brain, C., Hindmarsh, P., & Brook, C. (2005). Prenatal hormones and postnatal socialization by parents as determinants of male-typical toy play in girls with congenital adrenal hyperplasia. *Child Development, 76,* 264–278.

Patel, K. V., Coppin, A. K., Manini, T. M., Lauretani, F., Bandinelli, S., Ferrucci, L., & Guralnik, J. M. (2006). Midlife physical activity and mobility in older age: The InCHIANTI Study. *American Journal of Preventive Medicine, 31,* 217–224.

Paterson, D. S., Trachtenberg, F. L., Thompson, E. G., Belliveau, R. A., Beggs, A. H., & Darnall, R. (2006). Multiple serotonergic brainstem abnormalities in sudden infant death syndrome. *Journal of the American Medical Association, 296,* 2124–2132.

Pattenden, S., Antova, T., Neuberger, M., Nikiforov, B., De Sario, M., Grize, L., & Heinrich, J. (2006). Parental smoking and children's respiratory health: Independent effects of prenatal and postnatal exposure. *Tobacco Control, 15,* 294–301.

Patterson, C. J. (2002). Lesbian and gay parenthood. In M. H. Bornstein (Ed.), *Handbook of parenting* (Vol. 3, pp. 317–338). Mahwah, NJ: Erlbaum.

Patterson, G. R., & Fisher, P. A. (2002). Recent developments in our understanding of parenting: Bidirectional effects, causal models, and the search for parsimony. In M. H. Bornstein (Ed.), *Handbook of parenting* (Vol. 5, pp. 59–88). Mahwah, NJ: Erlbaum.

Patterson, G. R., & Yoerger, K. (2002). A developmental model for early-and late-onset delinquency. In J. B. Reid & G. R. Patterson (Eds.), *Antisocial behavior in children and adolescents* (pp. 147–172). Washington, DC: American Psychological Association.

Patterson, M. L., & Werker, J. F. (2002). Infants' ability to match dynamic phonetic and gender information in the face and voice. *Journal of Experimental Child Psychology, 81,* 93–115.

Paul, J. J., & Cillessen, A. H. N. (2003). Dynamics of peer victimization in early adolescence: Results from a four-year longitudinal study. *Journal of Applied School Psychology, 19,* 25–43.

Paulussen-Hoogeboom, M. C., Stams, G. J. J. M., Hermanns, J. M. A., & Peetsma, T. T. D. (2007). Child negative emotionality and parenting from infancy to preschool: A meta-analytic review. *Developmental Psychology, 43,* 438–453.

Pawelec, G., Wagner, W., Adibzadeh, M., & Engel, A. (1999). T cell immunosenescence in vitro and in vivo. *Experimental Gerontology, 34,* 419–429.

Payne, B. K., & Fletcher, L. B. (2005). Elder abuse in nursing homes: Prevention and resolution strategies and barriers. *Journal of Criminal Justice, 33,* 119–125.

PCA America. (2009). *Healthy Families America FAQ.* Retrieved from www.healthyfamiliesamerica.org/about_us/findex.shtml

Peake, A., & Harris, K. L. (2002). Young adults' attitudes toward multiple role planning: The influence of gender, career traditionality, and marriage plans. *Journal of Vocational Behavior, 60,* 405–421.

Pearlman, D. N., Zierler, S., Meersman, S., Kim, H. K., Viner-Brown, S. I., & Caron, C. (2006). Race disparities in childhood asthma: Does where you live matter? *Journal of the National Medical Association, 98,* 239–247.

Pearson, J. L., & Brown, G. K. (2000). Suicide prevention in late life: Directions for science and practice. *Clinical Psychology Review, 20,* 685–705.

Peck, R. C. (1968). Psychological developments in the second half of life. In B. L. Neugarten (Ed.), *Middle age and aging* (pp. 88–92). Chicago: University of Chicago Press.

Pedersen, W. C., Miller, L. C., Putcha-Bhagavatula, A. D., & Yang, Y. (2002). Evolved sex differences in the number of partners desired? The long and the short of it. *Psychological Science, 13,* 157–161.

Pederson, D. R., & Moran, G. (1996). Expressions of the attachment relationship outside of the Strange Situation. *Child Development, 67,* 915–927.

Peisner-Feinberg, E. S., Burchinal, M. R., Clifford, R. M., Culkin, M. L., Howes, C., Kagan, S. L., & Yazijian, N. (2001). The relation of preschool child-care quality to children's cognitive and social developmental trajectories through second grade. *Child Development, 72,* 1534–1553.

Pellegrini, A. D. (1992). Kindergarten children's social cognitive status as a predictor of first grade success. *Early Childhood Research Quarterly, 7,* 565–577.

Pellegrini, A. D. (2003). Perceptions and functions of play and real fighting in early adolescence. *Child Development, 74,* 1522–1533.

Pellegrini, A. D. (2004). Rough-and-tumble play from childhood through adolescence: Development and possible functions. In P. K. Smith & C. H. Hart (Eds.), *Blackwell handbook of childhood social development* (pp. 438–453). Malden, MA: Blackwell.

Pellegrini, A. D. (2005). *Recess: Its role in development and education.* Mahwah, NJ: Erlbaum.

Pellegrini, A. D., & Holmes, R. M. (2006). The role of recess in primary school. In D. G. Singer, R. M. Golinkoff, & K. Hirsh-Pasek (Eds.), *Play = learning* (pp. 36–53). New York: Oxford University Press.

Pellegrini, A. D., Huberty, P. D., & Jones, I. (1995). The effects of recess timing on children's playground and classroom behaviors. *American Educational Research Journal, 32,* 845–864.

Pellegrini, A. D., Kato, K., Blatchford, P., & Baines, E. (2002). A short-term longitudinal study of children's playground games across the first year of school: Implications for social competence and adjustment to school. *American Educational Research Journal, 39,* 991–1015.

Pellegrini, A. D., & Smith, P. K. (1998). Physical activity play: The nature and function of a neglected aspect of play. *Child Development, 69,* 577–598.

Pellicano, E., Maybery, M., Durkin, K., & Maley, A. (2006). Multiple cognitive capabilities/deficits in children with an autism spectrum disorder: "Weak" central coherence and its relationship to theory of mind and executive control. *Development and Psychopathology, 18,* 77–98.

Peña, R., Wall, S., & Person, L. (2000). The effect of poverty, social inequality, and maternal education on infant mortality in Nicaragua, 1988–1993. *American Journal of Public Health, 90,* 64–69.

Penedo, F. J., & Dahn, J. R. (2005). Exercise and well-being: A review of mental and physical health benefits associated with physical activity. *Current Opinion in Psychiatry, 18,* 189–193.

Penner, A. M. (2003). International gender item difficulty interactions in mathematics and science achievement tests. *Journal of Educational Psychology, 95,* 650–655.

Penninx, B. W., Deeg, D. J., van Eijk, J. T., Beekman, A. T., & Guralnik, J. M. (2000). Changes in depression and physical decline in older adults: A longitudinal perspective. *Journal of Affective Disorders, 61,* 1–12.

Penny, H., & Haddock, G. (2007). Anti-fat prejudice among children: The 'mere proximity' effect in 5–10 year olds. *Journal of Experimental Social Psychology, 43,* 678–683.

Peralta de Mendoza, O. A., & Salsa, A. M. (2003). Instruction in early comprehension and use of a symbol–referent relation. *Cognitive Development, 18,* 269–284.

Perkins, H. W. (1991). Religious commitment, yuppie values, and well-being in post-collegiate life. *Review of Religious Research, 32,* 244–251.

Perlmutter, M. (1984). Continuities and discontinuities in early human memory: Paradigms, processes, and performances. In R. V. Kail, Jr., & N. R. Spear (Eds.), *Comparative perspectives on the development of memory* (pp. 253–287). Hillsdale, NJ: Erlbaum.

Perlmutter, M., Kaplan, M., & Nyquist, L. (1990). Development of adaptive competence in adulthood. *Human Development, 33,* 185–197.

Perls, T., Levenson, R., Regan, M., & Puca, A. (2002). What does it take to live to 100? *Mechanisms of Ageing and Development, 123,* 231–242.

Perls, T., & Terry, D. (2003). Understanding the determinants of exceptional longevity. *Annals of Internal Medicine, 139,* 445–449.

Perls, T., Terry, D. F., Silver, M., Shea, M., Bowen, J., & Joyce, E. (2000). Centenarians and the genetics of longevity. *Results and Problems in Cell Differentiation, 29,* 1–20.

Perone, S., Madole, K. L., Ross-Sheehy, S., Carey, M., & Oakes, L. M. (2008). The relation between infants' activity with objects and attention to object appearance. *Developmental Psychology, 44,* 1242–1248.

Perry, W. G., Jr. (1981). Cognitive and ethical growth. In A. Chickering (Ed.), *The modern American college* (pp. 76–116). San Francisco: Jossey-Bass.

Perry, W. G., Jr. (1998). *Forms of intellectual and ethical development in the college years: A scheme.* San Francisco: Jossey-Bass. (Originally published 1970)

Perry-Jenkins, M., Repetti, R. L., & Crouter, A. C. (2000). Work and family in the 1990s. *Journal of Marriage and the Family, 62,* 981–998.

Peshkin, A. (1997). *Places of memory: Whiteman's schools and Native American communities.* Mahwah, NJ: Erlbaum.

Peters, R. D. (2005). A community-based approach to promoting resilience in young children, their families, and their neighborhoods. In R. D. Paters, B. Leadbeater, & R. J. McMahon (Eds.), *Resilience in children, families, and communities: Linking context to practice and policy* (pp. 157–176). New York: Kluwer Academic.

Peters, R. D., Petrunka, K., & Arnold, R. (2003). The Better Beginnings, Better Futures Project: A universal, comprehensive, community-based prevention approach for primary school children and their families. *Journal of Clinical Child and Adolescent Psychology, 32,* 215–227.

Petersen, N., & Gonzales, R. C. (1999). *Career counseling models for diverse populations.* Belmont, CA: Wadsworth.

Peterson, B. E. (2002). Longitudinal analysis of midlife generativity, intergenerational roles, and caregiving. *Psychology and Aging, 17,* 161–168.

Peterson, B. E., & Duncan, L. E. (2007). Midlife women's generativity and authoritarianism:

Marriage, motherhood, and 10 years of aging. *Psychology and Aging, 22,* 411–419.

Peterson, B. E., Smirles, K. A., & Wentworth, P. A. (1997). Generativity and authoritarianism: Implications for personality, political involvement, and parenting. *Journal of Personality and Social Psychology, 72,* 1202–1216.

Peterson, C., Parsons, T., & Dean, M. (2004). Providing misleading and reinstatement information a year after it happened: Effects on long-term memory. *Memory, 12,* 1–13.

Peterson, C., & Rideout, R. (1998). Memory for medical emergencies experienced by 1- and 2-year-olds. *Developmental Psychology, 34,* 1059–1072.

Peterson, C., & Roberts, C. (2003). Like mother, like daughter: Similarities in narrative style. *Developmental Psychology, 39,* 551–562.

Peterson, C., & Seligman, M. E. (2004). *Character strengths and virtues.* New York: Oxford University Press.

Petitto, L. A., Holowka, S., Sergio, L. E., Levy, B., & Ostry, D. J. (2004). Baby hands that move to the rhythm of language: Hearing babies acquiring sign languages babble silently on the hands. *Cognition, 93,* 43–73.

Petitto, L. A., Holowka, S., Sergio, L. E., & Ostry, D. (2001, September 6). Language rhythms in babies' hand movements. *Nature, 413,* 35–36.

Petitto, L. A., & Marentette, P. F. (1991). Babbling in the manual mode: Evidence for the ontogeny of language. *Science, 251,* 1493–1496.

Petrides, K. V., Sangareau, Y., Furnham, A., & Fredrickson, N. (2006). Trait emotional intelligence and children's peer relations at school. *Social Development, 15,* 537–547.

Petrill, S. A., & Deater-Deckard, K. (2004). The heritability of general cognitive ability: A within-family adoption design. *Intelligence, 32,* 403–409.

Pettit, G. S. (2004). Violent children in developmental perspective. *Current Directions in Psychological Science, 13,* 194–197.

Pettit, G. S., Brown, E. G., Mize, J., & Lindsey, E. (1998). Mothers' and fathers' socializing behaviors in three contexts: Links with children's peer competence. *Merrill-Palmer Quarterly, 44,* 173–193.

Pew Research Center. (2006). *Strong public support for right to die.* Retrieved from http://people-press.org/reports

Pfeffer, C. R. (2006). Suicide and suicidality. In M. K. Dulcan & J. M. Wiener (Eds.), *Essentials of child and adolescent psychiatry* (pp. 621–632). Washington, DC: American Psychiatric Publishing.

Pfeffer, C. R., Altemus, M., Heo, M., & Jiang, H. (2007). Salivary cortisol and psychopathology in children bereaved by the September 11, 2001 terror attacks. *Biological Psychiatry, 61,* 957–965.

Pfeifer, J. H., Brown, C. S., & Juvonen, J. (2007). Fifty years since Brown vs. Board of Education: Lessons learned about the development and reduction of children's prejudice. *Social Policy Report 21*(2), 3–23.

Pfeifer, J. H., Ruble, D. N., Bachman, M. A., Alvarez, J. M., Cameron, J. A., & Fuligni, A. J. (2007). Social identities and intergroup bias in immigrant and nonimmigrant children. *Developmental Psychology, 43,* 496–507.

Phillips, C. D., Hawes, C., Spry, K., & Rose, M. (2000, June). *Residents leaving assisted living: Descriptive and analytic results from a national survey.* Retrieved from aspe.hhs.gov/daltcp/reports/alresid.htm

Phillips, C. D., Munoz, Y., Sherman, M., Rose, M., Spector, W., & Hawes, C. (2003). Effects of facility characteristics on departures from assisted living: Results from a national study. *Gerontologist, 43,* 690–696.

Phillips, M. (1997). What makes schools effective? A comparison of the relationships of communitarian climate and academic climate to mathematics achievement and attendance during middle school. *American Educational Research Journal, 34,* 633–662.

Phillipsen, L. C. (1999). Associations between age, gender, and group acceptance and three components of friendship quality. *Journal of Early Adolescence, 19,* 438–464.

Phinney, J. S. (2007). Ethnic identity exploration in emerging adulthood. In J. J. Arnett & J. L. Tanner (Eds.), *Emerging adults in America: Coming of age in the 21st century* (pp. 117–134). Washington, DC: American Psychological Association.

Phinney, J. S., & Chavira, V. (1995). Parental ethnic socialization and adolescent outcomes in ethnic minority families. *Journal of Research on Adolescence, 5,* 31–53.

Phinney, J. S., Horenczyk, G., Liebkind, K., & Vedder, P. (2001). Ethnic identity, immigration, and well-being: An interactional perspective. *Journal of Social Issues, 57,* 493–510.

Phinney, J. S., Ong, A., & Madden, T. (2000). Cultural values and intergenerational value discrepancies in immigrant and non-immigrant families. *Child Development, 71,* 528–539.

Phinney J. S., & Ong, A. (2002). Adolescent–parent disagreements and life satisfaction in families from Vietnamese and European American backgrounds. *International Journal of Behavioral Development, 26,* 556–561.

Piaget, J. (1926). *The language and thought of the child.* New York: Harcourt, Brace & World. (Original work published 1923)

Piaget, J. (1930). *The child's conception of the world.* New York: Harcourt, Brace, & World. (Original work published 1926)

Piaget, J. (1951). *Play, dreams, and imitation in childhood.* New York: Norton. (Original work published 1945)

Piaget, J. (1952). *The origins of intelligence in children.* New York: International Universities Press. (Original work published 1936)

Piaget, J. (1967). *Six psychological studies.* New York: Vintage.

Piaget, J. (1971). *Biology and knowledge.* Chicago: University of Chicago Press.

Pianta, R., Egeland, B., & Erickson, M. F. (1989). The antecedents of maltreatment: Results of the Mother–Child Interaction Research Project. In D. Cicchetti & V. Carlson (Eds.), *Child maltreatment* (pp. 203–253). New York: Cambridge University Press.

Pianta, R. C., Hamre, B., & Stuhlman, M. (2003). Relationships between teachers and children. In W. M. Reynolds & G. E. Miller (Eds.), *Handbook of psychology: Educational psychology* (Vol. 7, pp. 199–234). New York: Wiley.

Pickens, J., Field, T., & Nawrocki, T. (2001). Frontal EEG asymmetry in response to emotional vignettes in preschool age children. *International Journal of Behavioral Development, 25,* 105–112.

Pickett, K. E., Luo, Y., & Lauderdale, D. S. (2005). Widening social inequalities in risk for sudden infant death syndrome. *American Journal of Public Health, 95,* 1976–1981.

Pickrell, T. M. (2006, July). Driver alchohol involvement in fatal crashes by age group and vehicle type. *Traffic Safety Facts.* Washington, DC: U.S. Department of Transportation.

Pierce, S. H., & Lange, G. (2000). Relationships among metamemory, motivation and memory performance in young school-age children. *British Journal of Developmental Psychology, 18,* 121–135.

Pietz, J., Peter, J., Graf, R., Rauterberg, R. I., Rupp, A., & Sontheimer, D. (2004). Physical growth and neurodevelopmental outcome of nonhandicapped low-risk children born preterm. *Early Human Development, 79,* 131–143.

Pillemer, K. A., Mueller-Johnson, K. U., Mock, S. E., Suitor, J. J., & Lachs, M. S. (2007). Interventions to prevent elder mistreatment. In L. S. Doll, S. Bonzo, J. A. Mercy, & D. A. Sleet (Eds.), *Handbook of injury and violence prevention* (pp. 241–254). New York: Springer Science + Business Media.

Pillemer, K., & Suitor, J. (2002). Explaining mothers' ambivalence toward their adult children. *Journal of Marriage and the Family, 64,* 602–613.

Pillow, B. (2002). Children's and adults' evaluation of the certainty of deductive inferences, inductive inferences, and guesses. *Child Development, 73,* 779–792.

Pimentel, A. E., Gentiel, C. L., Tanaka, H., Seals, D. R., & Gates, P. E. (2003). Greater rate of decline in maximal aerobic capacity with age in endurance-trained vs. sedentary men. *Journal of Applied Physiology, 94,* 2406–2413.

Pinderhughes, E. E., Dodge, K. A., Bates, J. E., Pettit, G. S., & Zelli, A. (2000). Discipline responses: Influences of parents' socioeconomic status, ethnicity, beliefs about parenting, stress, and cognitive-emotional processes. *Journal of Family Psychology, 14,* 380–400.

Pinderhughes, E. E., Nix, R., Foster, E. M., Jones, D., & the Conduct Problems Prevention Research Group. (2001). Parenting in context: Impact of neighborhood poverty, residential stability, public services, social networks, and danger on parental behaviors. *Journal of Marriage and Family, 63,* 941–953.

Ping, R. M., & Goldin-Meadow, S. (2008). Hands in the air: Using ungrounded iconic gestures to teach children conservation of quantity. *Developmental Psychology, 44,* 1277–1287.

Pinker, S. (1999). *Words and rules: The ingredients of language.* New York: Basic Books.

Pinquart, M. (2003). Loneliness in married, widowed, divorced, and never-married older adults. *Journal of Social and Personal Relationships, 20,* 31–53.

Pinquart, M., & Sörensen, S. (2001). Gender differences in self-concept and psychological well-being in old age: A meta-analysis. *Journal of Gerontology, 56B,* P195–P213.

Pinquart, M., & Sörensen, S. (2006). Gender differences in caregiver stressor, social resources, and health: An updated meta-analysis. *Journal of Gerontology, 61B,* P33–P45.

Pipp, S., Easterbrooks, M. A., & Harmon, R. J. (1992). The relation between attachment and knowledge of self and mother in one-year-old infants to three-year-old infants. *Child Development, 63,* 738–750.

Pitkala, K. H., Laakkonen, M. L., Strandberg, T. E., & Tilvis, R. S. (2004). Positive life orientation as a predictor of 10-year outcome in an aged population. *Journal of Clinical Epidemiology, 57,* 409–414.

Pivarnik, J. M. (1998). Potential effects of maternal physical activity on birth weight: Brief review. *Medicine and Science in Sports and Exercise, 30,* 407–414.

Pizarro, D. A., & Bloom, P. (2003). The intelligence of the moral intuitions: Comment on Haidt (2001). *Psychological Review, 110,* 193–196.

Plassmana, B. L., Langa, K. M., Fisher, G. G., Heeringa, S. G., Weir, D. R., Ofstedal, M. B., Burke, J. R., Hurd M. D., Potter, G. G., Rodgers, W. L., Steffens, D. C., Willis, R. J., & Wallace, R. B. (2007). Prevalence of dementia in the United States: The aging, demographics, and memory study. *Neuroepidemiology, 29,* 125–132.

Pleck, J. H., & Masciadrelli, B. P. (2004). Paternal involvement by U.S. residential fathers: Levels, sources, and consequences. In M. E. Lamb (Ed.),

The role of the father in child development (4th ed., pp. 222–271). Hoboken, NJ: Wiley.

Ploeg, J., Campbell, L., Denton, M., Joshi, A., & Davies, S. (2004). Helping to build and rebuild secure lives and futures: Financial transfers from parents to adult children and grandchildren. *Canadian Journal on Aging, 23,* S131–S143.

Plomin, R. (1994). *Genetics and experience: The interplay between nature and nurture.* Thousand Oaks, CA: Sage.

Plomin, R. (2003). General cognitive ability. In R. Plomin & J. C. DeFries (Eds.), *Behavioral genetics in the postgenomic era* (pp. 183–201). Washington, DC: American Psychological Association.

Plomin, R. (2005). *Finding genes in child psychology and psychiatry: When are we going to be there?* Unpublished manuscript. London: King's College.

Plomin, R., DeFries, J. C., Craig, I. W., & McGuffin, P. (2003). Behavioral genomics. In R. Plomin, J. C. DeFries, I. W. Craig, & P. McGuffin (Eds.), *Behavioral genetics in the postgenomic era* (pp. 531–540). Washington, DC: American Psychological Association.

Plomin, R., DeFries, J. C., McClearn, G. E., & McGuffin, P. (2001). *Behavioral genetics* (4th ed.). New York: Worth.

Plomin, R., & Spinath, F. M. (2004). Intelligence: Genetics, genes, and genomics. *Journal of Personality and Social Psychology, 86,* 112–129.

Plude, D. J., & Doussard-Roosevelt, J. A. (1989). Aging, selective attention, and feature integration. *Psychology and Aging, 4,* 98–105.

Plude, D. J., & Hoyer, W. J. (1985). Attention and performance: Identifying and localizing age deficits. In N. Charness (Ed.), *Aging and human performance* (pp. 47–99). Chichester, UK: Wiley.

Podewils, L. J., Guallar, E., Kuller, L. H., Fried, L. P., Lopez, O. L., Carlson, M., & Lyketsos, C. G. (2005). Physical activity, APOE genotype, and dementia risk: Findings from the Cardiovascular Health Cognition Study. *American Journal of Epidemiology, 161,* 639–651.

Poehlmann, J., & Fiese, B. H. (2001). The interaction of maternal and infant vulnerabilities on developing attachment relationships. *Development and Psychopathology, 13,* 1–11.

Pogarsky, G., Thornberry, T. P., & Lizotte, A. J. (2006). Developmental outcomes for children of young mothers. *Journal of Marriage and Family, 68,* 332–344.

Pohl, J. M., Given, C. W., Collins, C. E., & Given, B. A. (1994). Social vulnerability and reactions to caregiving in daughters and daughters-in-law caring for disabled aging parents. *Health Care for Women International, 15,* 385–395.

Pohl, R. (2002). *Poverty in Canada.* Ottawa, ON: Innercity Ministries.

Polka, L., & Werker, J. F. (1994). Developmental changes in perception of non-native vowel contrasts. *Journal of Experimental Psychology: Human Perception and Performance, 20,* 421–435.

Pollitt, E. (1996). A reconceptualization of the effects of undernutrition on children's biological, psychosocial, and behavioral development. *Social Policy Report of the Society for Research in Child Development, 10*(5).

Pomerantz, E. M., & Eaton, M. M. (2000). Developmental differences in children's conceptions of parental control: "They love me, but they make me feel incompetent." *Merrill-Palmer Quarterly, 46,* 140–167.

Pomerantz, E. M., & Ruble, D. N. (1998). The multidimensional nature of control: Implications for the development of sex differences in self-evaluation. In J. Heckhausen & C. S. Dweck (Eds.), *Motivation and self-regulation across the lifespan* (pp. 159–184). New York: Cambridge University Press.

Pomerantz, E. M., & Saxon, J. L. (2001). Conceptions of ability as stable and self-evaluative processes: A longitudinal examination. *Child Development, 72,* 152–173.

Pomerleau, A., Scuccimarri, C., & Malcuit, G. (2003). Mother–infant behavioral interactions in teenage and adult mothers during the first six months postpartum: Relations with infant development. *Infant Mental Health Journal, 24,* 495–509.

Pons, F., Lawson, J., Harris, P. L., & de Rosnay, M. (2003). Individual differences in children's emotion understanding: Effects of age and language. *Scandinavian Journal of Psychology, 44,* 347–353.

Popenoe, D. (2006). *Debunking divorce myths.* Retrieved from health.discovery.com/centers/loverelationships/articles/divorce.html

Portes, A., & Rumbaut, R. G. (2005), Introduction: The second generation and the Children of Immigrants Longitudinal Study. *Ethnic and Racial Studies, 28,* 983–999.

Posada, G., Carbonell, O. A., Alzate, G., & Plata, S. J. (2004). Through Colombian lenses: Ethnographic and conventional analyses of maternal care and their associations with secure base behavior. *Developmental Psychology, 40,* 508–518.

Posada, G., Jacobs, A., Richmond, M. K., Carbonell, O. A., Alzate, G., Bustamante, M. R., & Quiceno, J. (2002). Maternal caregiving and infant security in two cultures. *Developmental Psychology, 38,* 67–78.

Posner, M. I., & Rothbart, M. K. (2007). *Educating the human brain.* Washington, DC: American Psychological Association.

Pothiwala, P., Evans, E. M., & Chapman-Novakofski, K. M. (2006). Ethnic variation in risk for osteoporosis among women: A review of biological and behavioral factors. *Journal of Women's Health, 15,* 709–719.

Poulin-Dubois, D., Serbin, L. A., Eichstedt, J. A., Sen, M. G., & Beissel, C. F. (2002). Men don't put on make-up: Toddlers' knowledge of the gender stereotyping of household activities. *Social Development, 11,* 166–181.

Povinelli, D. J. (2001). The self—Elevated in consciousness and extended in time. In C. Moore & K. Lemmon (Eds.), *The self in time: Developmental perspectives* (pp. 75–95). Mahwah, NJ: Erlbaum.

Power, T. G. (2000). *Play and exploration in children and animals.* Mahwah, NJ: Erlbaum.

Powlishta, K. K., Serbin, L. A., & Moller, L. C. (1993). The stability of individual differences in gender typing: Implications for understanding gender segregation. *Sex Roles, 29,* 723–737.

Powls, A., Botting, N., Cooke, R. W. I., & Marlow, N. (1996). Handedness in very-low-birthweight (VLBW) children at 12 years of age: Relation to perinatal and outcome variables. *Developmental Medicine and Child Neurology, 38,* 594–602.

Prager, K. J., & Bailey, J. M. (1985). Androgyny, ego development, and psychological crisis resolution. *Sex Roles, 13,* 525–535.

Pratt, M. W., Norris, J. E., Hebblethwaite, S., & Arnold, M. L. (2008). Intergenerational transmission of values: Family generativity and adolescents' narratives of parent and grandparent value teaching. *Journal of Personality, 76,* 171–198.

Pratt, M. W., Skoe, E. E., & Arnold, M. L. (2004). Care reasoning development and family socialization patterns in later adolescence: A longitudinal analysis. *International Journal of Behavioral Development, 28,* 139–147.

Prechtl, H. F. R., & Beintema, D. (1965). *The neurological examination of the full-term newborn infant.* London: Heinemann Medical Books.

Preece, J., & Findsen, B. (2007). Keeping people active: Continuing education programs that work. In M. Robinson, W. Novelli, C. Pearson, & L. Norris (Eds.), *Global health and global aging* (pp. 313–322). San Francisco: Jossey-Bass.

Preissler, M. A., & Carey, S. (2004). Do both pictures and words function as symbols for 18- and 24-month-old children? *Journal of Cognition and Development, 5,* 185–212.

Prentice, R. L., Chlebowski, R. T., Stefanick, M. L., Manson, J. E., Pettinger, M., & Hendrix, S. L. (2008). Estrogen plus progestin therapy and breast cancer in recently postmenopausal women. *American Journal of Epidemiology, 167,* 1207–1216.

Pressley, M., & Hilden, D. (2006). Cognitive strategies. In D. Kuhn & R. Siegler (Eds.), *Handbook of child psychology: Vol. 2. Cognition, perception, and language* (6th ed., pp. 511–556). Hoboken, NJ: Wiley.

Pressley, M., Wharton-McDonald, R., Raphael, L. M., Bogner, K., & Roehrig, A. (2002). Exemplary first-grade teaching. In B. M. Taylor & P. D. Pearson (Eds.), *Teaching reading: Effective schools, accomplished teachers* (pp. 73–88). Mahwah, NJ: Erlbaum.

Prevatt, F. (2003). Dropping out of school: A review of intervention programs. *Journal of School Psychology, 41,* 377–399.

Previc, F. H. (1991). A general theory concerning the prenatal origins of cerebral lateralization. *Psychological Review, 98,* 299–334.

Priddy, K. D. (2004). Is there logic behind fetal monitoring? *Journal of Obstetric, Gynecologic, and Neonatal Nursing, 33,* 550–553.

Princeton Religion Research Center. (1999). *Religious Practices in the United States.* Princeton, NJ: Author.

Prinstein, M. J., & La Greca, A. (2004). Childhood peer rejection and aggression as predictors of adolescent girls' externalizing and health risk behaviors: A 6-year longitudinal study. *Journal of Consulting and Clinical Psychology, 72,* 103–112.

Prinstein, M. J., Boergers, J., & Spirito, A. (2001). Adolescents' and their friends' health-risk behavior: Factors that alter or add to peer influences. *Journal of Pediatric Psychology, 26,* 287–298.

Prinstein, M. J., Boergers, J., & Vernberg, E. M. (2001). Overt and relational aggression in adolescents: Social–psychological adjustment of aggressors and victims. *Journal of Clinical Child Psychology, 30,* 479–491.

Prinstein, M. J., & La Greca, A. M. (2002). Peer crowd affiliation and internalizing distress in childhood and adolescence: A longitudinal follow-back study. *Journal of Research on Adolescence, 12,* 325–351.

Prinstein, M. J., Meade, C. S., & Cohen, G. L. (2003). Adolescent oral sex, peer popularity, and perceptions of best friends' sexual behavior. *Journal of Pediatric Psychology, 28,* 243–249.

Proctor, M. H., Moore, L. L., Gao, D., Cupples, L. A., Bradlee, M. L., Hood, M. Y., & Ellison, R. C. (2003). Television viewing and change in body fat from preschool to early adolescence: The Framingham Children's Study. *International Journal of Obesity, 27,* 827–833.

Programme for International Student Assessment. (2003). *Learning for tomorrow's world: First results from Programme for International Student Assessment 2003.* Retrieved from www.pisa.oecd.org

Programme for International Student Assessment. (2005). *School factors related to quality and equity.* Retrieved from www.pisa.oecd.org

Programme for International Student Assessment. (2006). *PISA 2006: Science competencies for tomorrow's world.* Retrieved from www.oecd.org

Pronczuk, J., & Surdu, S. (2008). Children's environmental health in the twenty-first century. *Annals of the New York Academy of Sciences, 1140,* 143–154.

Proulx, K., & Jacelon, C. (2004). Dying with dignity: The good patient versus the good death. *American Journal of Hospice and Palliative Care, 21,* 116–120.

Provins, K. A. (1997). Handedness and speech: A critical reappraisal of the role of genetic and environmental factors in the cerebral lateralization of function. *Psychological Review, 104,* 554–571.

Pruchno, R., & McKenney, D. (2000). The effects of custodial and coresident households on the mental health of grandmothers. *Journal of Mental Health and Aging, 6,* 291–310.

Pruden, S. M., Hirsh-Pasek, K., Golinkoff, R. M., & Hennon, E. A. (2006). The birth of words: Ten-month-olds learn words through perceptual salience. *Child Development, 77,* 266–280.

Pryor, J., & Rodgers, B. (2001). *Children in changing families: Life after parental separation.* Oxford, UK: Blackwell.

Prysak, M., Lorenz, R. P., & Kisly, A. (1995). Pregnancy outcome in nulliparous women 35 years and older. *Obstetrics and Gynecology, 85,* 65–70.

Puhl, R., & Brownell, K. D. (2006). Confronting and coping with weight stigma: An investigation of overweight and obese individuals. *Obesity, 14,* 1802–1815.

Pujol, J., Soriano-Mas, C., Ortiz, H., Sebastián-Gallés, N., Losilla, J. M., & Deus, J. (2006). Myelination of language-related areas in the developing brain. *Neurology, 66,* 339–343.

Punamaki, R. L. (2006). Ante-and perinatal factors and child characteristics predicting parenting experience among formerly infertile couples during the child's first year: A controlled study. *Journal of Family Psychology, 20,* 670–679.

Purcell-Gates, V. (1996). Stories, coupons, and the TV Guide: Relationships between home literacy experiences and emergent literacy knowledge. *Reading Research Quarterly, 31,* 406–428.

Putallaz, M., Grimes, C. L., Foster, K. J., Kupersmidt, J. B., Coie, J. D., & Dearing, K. (2007). Overt and relational aggression and victimization: Multiple perspectives within the school setting. *Journal of School Psychology, 45,* 523–547.

Putnam, F. W. (2003). Ten-year research update review: Child sexual abuse. *Journal of the American Academy of Child and Adolescent Psychiatry, 42,* 269–278.

Pyka, G., Lindenberger, E., Charette, S., & Marcus, R. (1994). Muscle strength and fiber adaptations to a year-long resistance training program in elderly men and women. *Journal of Gerontology, 49,* M22–27.

Pyszczynski, T., Greenberg, J., Solomon, S., Arndt, J., & Schimel, J. (2004). Why do people need self-esteem? A theoretical and empirical view. *Psychological Bulletin, 130,* 435–468.

Q

Qiu, C., Bäckman, L., Winblad, B., Agüero-Torres, H., & Fratiglioni, L. (2001). The influence of education on clinically diagnosed dementia incidence and mortality data from the Kungsholmen Project. *Archives of Neurology, 58,* 2034–2039.

Quas, J. A., Malloy, L. C., Melinder, A., Goodman, G. S., & D'Mello, M. (2007). Developmental differences in the effects of repeated interviews and interviewer bias on young children's event memory and false reports. *Developmental Psychology, 43,* 823–837.

Quick, H. E., & Moen, P. (1998). Gender, employment, and retirement quality: A life course approach to the differential experiences of men and women. *Journal of Occupational Health Psychology, 3,* 44–64.

Quill, T. E. (1991). Death and dignity: A case of individualized decision making. *New England Journal of Medicine, 324,* 691–694.

Quine, S., Wells, Y., de Vaus, D., & Kendig, H. (2007). When choice in retirement decisions is missing: Qualitative and quantitative findings of impact on well-being. *Australasian Journal on Ageing, 26,* 173–179.

Quinn, P. C. (2008). In defense of core competencies, quantitative change, and continuity. *Child Development, 79,* 1633–1638.

Quinn, T. C., & Overbaugh, J. (2005). HIV/AIDS in women: An expanding epidemic. *Science, 308,* 1582–1583.

Quist, J. F., & Kennedy, J. L. (2001). Genetics of childhood disorders: XXIII. ADHD, part 7: The serotonin system. *Journal of the American Academy of Child and Adolescent Psychiatry, 40,* 253–256.

R

Raaijmakers, Q. A. W., Engels, R. C. M. E., & Van Hoof, A. (2005). Delinquency and moral reasoning in adolescence and young adulthood. *International Journal of Behavioral Development, 29,* 247–258.

Rabbitt, P., Lunn, M., & Wong, D. (2008). Death, dropout, and longitudinal measurements of cognitive change in old age. *Journal of Gerontology, 63B,* P271–P278.

Rabig, J., Thomas, W., Kane, R., Cutler, L. J., & McAlilly, S. (2006). Radical redesign of nursing homes: Applying the Green House concept in Tupelo, Mississippi. *Gerontologist, 46,* 533–539.

Rabiner, D. J., O'Keeffe, J., & Brown, D. (2004). A conceptual framework of financial exploitation of older persons. *Journal of Elder Abuse and Neglect, 16,* 53–73.

Radvansky, G. A., Zacks, R. T., & Hasher, L. (2005). Age and inhibition: The retrieval of situation models. *Journal of Gerontology, 60B,* P276–P278.

Ragow-O'Brien, D., Hayslip, B., Jr., & Guarnaccia, C. A. (2000). The impact of hospice on attitudes toward funerals and subsequent bereavement adjustment. *Omega, 41,* 291–305.

Rahman, Q., & Wilson, G. D. (2003). Born gay? The psychobiology of human sexual orientation. *Personality and Individual Differences, 34,* 1337–1382.

Raikes, H. A., Robinson, J. L., Bradley, R. H., Raikes, H. H., & Ayoub, C. C. (2007). Developmental trends in self-regulation among low-income toddlers. *Social Development, 16,* 128–149.

Raikes, H. A., & Thompson, R. A. (2005). Links between risk and attachment security: Models of influence. *Journal of Applied Developmental Psychology, 26,* 440–455.

Raikes, H. A., & Thompson, R. A. (2006). Family emotional climate, attachment security, and young children's emotion knowledge in a high-risk sample. *British Journal of Developmental Psychology, 24,* 89–104.

Räikkönen, K., Matthews, K. A., Flory, J. D., Owens, J. F., & Gump, B. B. (1999). Effects of optimism, pessimism, and trait anxiety on ambulatory blood pressure and mood during everyday life. *Journal of Personality and Social Psychology, 76,* 104–113.

Räikkönen, K., Matthews, K. A., Sutton-Tyrrell, K., & Kuller, L. H. (2004). Trait anger and the metabolic syndrome predict progression of carotid atherosclerosis in healthy middle-aged women. *Psychosomatic Medicine, 66,* 903–908.

Rakison, D. H. (2005). Developing knowledge of objects' motion properties in infancy. *Cognition, 96,* 183–214.

Rakison, D. H. (2006). Make the first move: How infants learn about self-propelled objects. *Developmental Psychology, 42,* 900–912.

Rakoczy, H., Tomasello, M., & Striano, T. (2004). Young children know that trying is not pretending: A test of the "behaving-as-if" construal of children's early concept of pretense. *Developmental Psychology, 40,* 388–399.

Ramaswami, A., & Dreher, G. F. (2007). The benefits associated with workplace mentoring relationships. In T. D. Allen & L. T. Eby (Eds.), *Blackwell handbook of mentoring: A multiple perspectives approach* (pp. 211–231). Malden, MA: Blackwell.

Ramchandani, P., Stein, A., Evans, J., O'Connor, T. G., & the ALSPAC Study Team. (2005). Paternal depression in the postnatal period and child development: A prospective population study. *Lancet, 365,* 2201–2205.

Ramey, C. T., Ramey, S. L., & Lanzi, R. G. (2006). Children's health and education. In K. A. Renninger & I. E. Sigel (Eds.), *Handbook of child psychology: Vol. 4. Child psychology in practice* (6th ed., pp. 864–892). Hoboken, NJ: Wiley.

Ramey, S. L., & Ramey, C. T. (1999). Early experience and early intervention for children "at risk" for developmental delay and mental retardation. *Mental Retardation and Developmental Disabilities, 5,* 1–10.

Ramos, E., Frontera, W. R., Llorpart, A., & Feliciano, D. (1998). Muscle strength and hormonal levels in adolescents: Gender related differences. *International Journal of Sports Medicine, 19,* 526–531.

Ramos, M. C., Guerin, D. W., Gottfried, A. W., Bathurst, K., & Oliver, P. H. (2005). Family conflict and children's behavior problems: The moderating role of child temperament. *Structural Equation Modeling, 12,* 278–298.

Ramsøy, N. R. (1994). Non-marital cohabitation and change in norms: The case of Norway. *Acta Sociologica, 37,* 23–37.

Rando, T. A. (1991). Parental adjustment to the loss of a child. In D. Papadatou & C. Papadatos (Eds.), *Children and death* (pp. 233–253). New York: Hemisphere.

Rando, T. A. (1995). Grief and mourning: Accommodating to loss. In H. Wass & R. A. Neimeyer (Eds.), *Dying: Facing the facts* (3rd ed., pp. 211–241). Washington, DC: Taylor & Francis.

Rangel, M. C., Gavin, L., Reed, C., Fowler, M. G., & Lee, L. M. (2006). Epidemiology of HIV and AIDS among adolescents and young adults in the United States. *Journal of Adolescent Health, 39,* 156–163.

Ransford, H. E., & Palisi, B. J. (1996). Aerobic exercise, subjective health and psychological well-being within age and gender subgroups. *Social Science and Medicine, 42,* 1555–1559.

Rapp, S. R., Espeland, M. A., Shumaker, S. A., Henderson, V. W., Brunner, R. L., & Manson, J. E. (2003). Effect of estrogen plus progestin on global cognitive function in postmenopausal women: The Women's Health Initiative Memory Study: A randomized controlled trial. *Journal of the American Medical Association, 289,* 2663–2672.

Raqib, R., Alam, D. S., Sarker, P., Ahmad, S. M., Ara, G., & Yunus, M. (2007). Low birth weight is associated with altered immune function in rural Bangladeshi children: A birth cohort study. *American Journal of Clinical Nutrition, 85,* 845–852.

Rasch, E. K., Hirsch, R., Paulose-Ram, R., & Hochberg, M. C. (2003). Prevalence of rheumatoid arthritis in persons 60 years of age and older in the United States: Effect of different methods of classification. *Arthritis and Rheumatism, 48,* 917–926.

Rasmussen, C., Ho, E., & Bisanz, J. (2003). Use of the mathematical principle of inversion in young children. *Journal of Experimental Child Psychology, 85,* 89–102.

Rasmussen, C. H., & Johnson, M. E. (1994). Spirituality and religiosity: Relative relationships to death anxiety. *Omega, 29,* 313–318.

Rasmussen, E. R., Neuman, R. J., Heath, A. C., Levy, F., Hay, D. A., & Todd, R. D. (2004). Familial clustering of latent class and DSM-IV defined attention-deficit hyperactivity disorder (ADHD) subtypes. *Journal of Child Psychology and Psychiatry, 45,* 589–598.

Rathunde, K., & Csikszentmihalyi, M. (2005). The social context of middle school: Teachers, friends, and activities in Montessori and traditional school environments. *Elementary School Journal, 106,* 59–79.

Rauber, M. (2006, May 18). Parents aren't sitting still as recess disappears. *Parents in Action.* Retrieved from http://healthyschoolscampaign.org/news/media/food/2006-05_recess_disappears.php

Rauscher, F. H., Shaw, G. L., & Ky, K. N. (1993). Music and spatial task performance. *Nature, 365,* 611.

Raver, C. C. (2003). Does work pay psychologically as well as economically? The role of employment in predicting depressive symptoms and parenting among low-income families. *Child Development, 74,* 1720–1736.

Ravid, D., & Tolchinsky, L. (2002). Developing linguistic literacy: A comprehensive model. *Journal of Child Language, 29,* 417–447.

Rawlins, W. K. (2004). Friendships in later life. In J. F. Nussbaum & J. Coupland (Eds.), *Handbook of communication and aging research* (2nd ed., pp. 273–299). Mahwah, NJ: Erlbaum.

Ray, V., & Gregory, R. (2001). School experiences of the children of lesbian and gay parents. *Family Matters, 59,* 28–35.

Rayner, K., & Pollatsek, A. (1989). *The psychology of reading.* Englewood Cliffs, NJ: Prentice-Hall.

Rayner, K., Pollatsek, A., & Starr, M. S. (2003). Reading. In A. F. Healy & R. W. Proctor (Eds.), *Handbook of psychology: Experimental psychology* (Vol. 4, pp. 549–574). New York: Wiley.

Raz, N. (2005). The aging brain observed in vivo: Differential changes and their modifiers. In R. Cabeza, L. Nyberg, & D. Park (Eds.), *Cognitive neuroscience of aging: Linking cognitive and cerebral aging* (pp. 19–57). New York: Oxford University Press.

Reay, A. C., & Browne, K. D. (2008). Elder abuse and neglect. In B. Woods & L. Clare (Eds.), *Handbook of the clinical psychology of ageing* (pp. 311–322). Chichester, UK: Wiley.

Reday-Mulvey, G. (2000). Gradual retirement in Europe. *Journal of Aging and Social Policy, 11,* 49–60.

Reddin, J. (1997). High-achieving women: Career development patterns. In H. S. Farmer (Ed.), *Diversity and women's career development* (pp. 95–126). Thousand Oaks, CA: Sage.

Reddy, S. Y., Warner, H., Guttuso, T., Jr., Messing, S., DiGrazio, W., Thornburg, L., & Guzick, D. S. (2006). Gabapentin, estrogen, and placebo for treating hot flushes: A randomized controlled trial. *Obstetrics and Gynecology, 108,* 41–48.

Redman, L. M., Martin, C. K., Williamson, D. A., & Ravussin, E. (2008). Effect of caloric restriction in non-obese humans on physiological, psychological and behavioral outcomes. *Physiology and Behavior, 94,* 643–648.

Regan, P. C., Medina, R., Joshi, A. (2001). Partner preferences among homosexual men and women: What is desirable in a sex partner is not necessarily desirable in a romantic partner. *Social Behavior and Personality, 29,* 625–634.

Reginster, J. Y., & Burlet, N. (2006). Osteoporosis: A still increasing prevalence. *Bone, 38,* 4–9.

Regnerus, M., Smith, C., & Fritsch, M. (2003). *Religion in the lives of American adolescents: A review of the literature.* Chapel Hill, NC: National Study of Youth and Religion.

Reid, H. M., & Fine, A. (1992). Self-disclosure in men's friendships: Variations associated with intimate relations. In P. M. Nardi (Ed.), *Men's friendships* (pp. 153–171). Newbury Park, CA: Sage.

Reilly, J. S., Bates, E. A., & Marchman, V. A. (1998). Narrative discourse in children with early focal brain injury. *Brain and Language, 61,* 335–375.

Reilly, J. S., Losh, M., Bellugi, U., & Wulfeck, B. (2004). "Frog, where are you?" Narratives in children with specific language impairment, early focal brain injury, and Williams syndrome. *Brain and Language, 88,* 229–247.

Reis, O., & Youniss, J. (2004). Patterns in identity change and development in relationships with mothers and friends. *Journal of Adolescent Research, 19,* 31–44.

Reis, S. M. (2004). We can't change what we don't recognize: Understanding the special needs of gifted females. In S. Baum (Ed.), *Twice-exceptional and special populations of gifted students* (pp. 67–80). Thousand Oaks, CA: Corwin Press.

Reisman, J. E. (1987). Touch, motion, and proprioception. In P. Salapatek & L. Cohen (Eds.), *Handbook of infant perception: Vol. 1. From sensation to perception* (pp. 265–303). Orlando, FL: Academic Press.

Reiss, A. L., & Dant, C. C. (2003). The behavioral neurogenetics of fragile X syndrome: Analyzing gene–brain–behavior relationships in child developmental psychopathologies. *Development and Psychopathology, 15,* 927–968.

Reiss, D. (2003). Child effects on family systems: Behavioral genetic strategies. In A. C. Crouter & A. Booth (Eds.), *Children's influence on family dynamics: The neglected side of family relationships* (pp. 3–36). Mahwah, NJ: Erlbaum.

Reiss, N. S., & Tishler, C. L. (2008a). Suicidality in nursing home residents: Part I. Prevalence, risk factors, methods, assessment, and management. *Professional Psychology: Research and Practice, 39,* 264–270.

Reiss, N. S., & Tishler, C. L. (2008b). Suicidality in nursing home residents: Part II. Prevalence, risk factors, methods, assessment, and management. *Professional Psychology: Research and Practice, 39,* 271–275.

Reitzes, D. C., & Mutran, E. J. (2002). Self-concept as the organization of roles: Importance, centrality, and balance. *Sociological Quarterly, 43,* 647–667.

Renninger, K. A. (1998). Developmental psychology and instruction: Issues from and for practice. In I. Sigel & K. A. Renninger (Eds.), *Handbook of child psychology: Vol. 4. Child psychology and practice* (pp. 211–274). New York: Wiley.

Repacholi, B. M. (1998). Infants' use of attentional cues to identify the referent of another person's emotional expression. *Developmental Psychology, 33,* 12–21.

Repacholi, B. M., & Gopnik, A. (1997). Early reasoning about desires: Evidence from 14- and 18-month-olds. *Developmental Psychology, 33,* 12–21.

Repacholi, B. M., & Trapolini, T. (2004). Attachment and preschool children's understanding of maternal versus non-maternal psychological states. *British Journal of Developmental Psychology, 22,* 395–415.

Resnick, M., & Silverman, B. (2005). *Some reflections on designing construction kits for kids.* Proceedings of the Conference on Interaction Design and Children, Boulder, CO.

Resnick, M. B., Gueorguieva, R. V., Carter, R. L., Ariet, M., Sun, Y., Roth, J., Bucciarelli, R. L., Curran, J. S., & Mahan, C. S. (1999). The impact of low birth weight, perinatal conditions, and sociodemographic factors on educational outcome in kindergarten. *Pediatrics, 104,* e74.

Resnick, S. M., Pham, D. L., Kraut, M. A., Zonderman, A. B., & Davatzikos, C. (2003). Longitudinal magnetic resonance imaging studies of older adults: A shrinking brain. *Journal of Neuroscience, 23,* 3295–3301.

Rest, J. R. (1979). *Development in judging moral issues.* Minneapolis: University of Minnesota Press.

Resta, R., Biesecker, B. B., Bennett, R. L., Blum, S., Hahn, S. E., Strecker, M. N., & Williams, J. L. (2006). A new definition of genetic counseling: National Society of Genetic Counselors' Task Force Report. *Journal of Genetic Counseling, 15,* 77–83.

RESULTS. (2006). *The abolition of public school fees.* Retrieved from www.results.org/website/article.asp?id=1718

Reuter-Lorenz, P. A., & Cappell, K. A. (2008). Neurocognitive aging and the compensation hypothesis. *Current Directions in Psychological Science, 17,* 177–182.

Reuter-Lorenz, P. A., & Mikels, J. A. (2005). The aging mind and brain: Implictions of enduring plasticity for behavioral and cultural change. In P. Baltes, P. A. Reuter-Lorenz, & F. Roesler (Eds.), *Lifespan development and the brain: The perspective of biocultural co-constructivism.* London: Cambridge University Press.

Reyes-Ortiz, C. A., Kuo, Y.-F., DiNuzzo, A. R., Ray, L. A., Raji, M. A., & Markides, K. S. (2005). Near vision impairment predicts cognitive decline: Data from the Hispanic established populations for epidemiologic studies of the elderly. *Journal of the American Geriatric Society, 53,* 681–686.

Reyna, V. F., & Farley, F. (2006). Risk and rationality in adolescent decision making: Implications for theory, practice, and public policy. *Psychological Science in the Public Interest, 7,* 1–44.

Reynolds, A. J., & Temple, J. A. (1998). Extended early childhood intervention and school achievement: Age 13 findings from the Chicago Longitudinal Study. *Child Development, 69,* 231–246.

Reynolds, C. R., & Kaiser, S. M. (1990). Test bias in psychological assessment. In T. B. Gutkin & C. R. Reynolds (Eds.), *The handbook of school psychology* (pp. 487–525). New York: Wiley.

Reynolds, K., Henderson, M., Schulman, A., & Hanson, L. C. (2002). Needs of the dying in nursing homes. *Journal of Palliative Medicine, 5,* 895–901.

Rhein, J. von (1997, January 19). Ardis Krainik, Lyric Opera's life force, dies. *Chicago Tribune,* pp. 1, 16.

Rhoades, G. K., Stanley, S. M., & Markman, H. J. (2006). Pre-engagement cohabitation and gender asymmetry in marital commitment. *Journal of Family Psychology, 20,* 553–560.

Rhone, M., & Basu, A. (2008). Phytochemicals and age-related eye diseases. *Nutrition Reviews, 66,* 465–472.

Richard, C. A., & Brown, A. H. (2006). Configurations of informal social support among older lesbians. *Journal of Women and Aging, 18,* 49–65.

Richards, M. (2004). Assisted reproduction, genetic technologies, and family life. In J. Scott, J. Treas, & M. Richards (Eds.), *The Blackwell companion to the sociology of families* (pp. 478–498). Malden, MA: Blackwell.

Richardson, V. E. (2007). A dual process model of grief counseling: Findings from the changing lives of older couples (CLOC) study. *Journal of Gerontological Social Work, 48,* 311–329.

Richie, B. S., Fassinger, R. E., Linn, S. G., Johnson, J., Prosser, J., & Robinson, S. (1997). Persistence, connection, and passion: A qualitative study of the career development of highly achieving African American–black and white women. *Journal of Counseling Psychology, 44,* 133–148.

Richler, J., Luyster, R., Risi, S., Hsu, W.-L., Dawson, G., & Bernier, R. (2006). Is there a 'regressive phenotype' of autism spectrum disorder associated with the measles-mumps-rubella vaccine? A CPEA study. *Journal of Autism and Developmental Disorders, 36,* 299–316.

Richmond, L. J. (2004). When spirituality goes awry: Students in cults. *Professional School Counseling, 7,* 367–375.

Ridenour, T. A. (2000). Genetic epidemiology of antisocial behavior. In D. H. Fishbein (Ed.), *The science, treatment, and prevention of antisocial behaviors* (pp. 7.1–7.24). Kingston, NJ: Civic Research Institute.

Rideout, V., & Hamel, E. (2006). *The media family: Electronic media in the lives of infants, toddlers, preschoolers and their parents.* Menlo Park, CA: Henry J. Kaiser Family Foundation.

Riediger, M., Li, S.-C., & Lindenberger, U. (2006). Selection, optimization, and compensation as developmental mechanisms of adaptive resource allocation: Review and preview. In J. E. Birren & K. W., Schaire (Eds.), *Handbook of the psychology of aging* (6th ed.) (pp. 289–313). Burlington, MA: Academic Press.

Rietvelt, M. J. H., Hudziak, J. J., Bartels, M., van Beijsterveldt, C. E. M., & Boomsma, D. I. (2004). Heritability of attention problems in children: Longitudinal results from a study of twins, age 3 to 12. *Journal of Child Psychology and Psychiatry, 45,* 577–588.

Rigby, K. (2004). Bullying in childhood. In P. K. Smith & C. H. Hart (Eds.), *Blackwell handbook of childhood social development* (pp. 549–568). Malden, MA: Blackwell.

Riley, E. P., McGee, C. L., & Sowell, E. R. (2004). Teratogenic effects of alcohol: A decade of brain imaging. *American Journal of Medical Genetics: Part C, Seminars in Medical Genetics, 127,* 35–41.

Riley, L. D., & Bowen, C. P. (2005). The sandwich generation: Challenges and coping strategies of multigenerational families. *Counseling and Therapy for Couples and Families, 13,* 52–58.

Riordan, J., Gross, A., Angeron, J., Drumwiede, B., & Melin, J. (2000). The effect of labor pain relief medication on neonatal suckling and breastfeeding duration. *Journal of Human Lactation, 16,* 7–12.

Ripperger, T., Gadzicki, D., Meindl, A. & Schlegelberger, B. (2009). Breast cancer susceptibility: Current knowledge and implications for genetic counseling. *European Journal of Human Genetics, 17,* 722–731.

Ripple, C. H., & Zigler, E. (2003). Research, policy, and the federal role in prevention initiatives for children. *American Psychologist, 58,* 482–490.

Ris, M. D., Dietrich, K. N., Succop, P. A., Berger, O. G., & Bornschein, R. L. (2004). Early exposure to lead and neuropsychological outcome in adolescence. *Journal of the International Neuropsychological Society, 10,* 261–270.

Ritchey, L. H., Ritchey, P. N., & Dietz, B. E. (2001). Clarifying the measurement of activity. *Activities, Adaptation, and Aging, 26,* 1–21.

Rittman, M., Kuzmeskus, L. B., & Flum, M. A. (2000). A synthesis of current knowledge on minority elder abuse. In T. Tatara (Ed.), *Understanding elder abuse in minority populations* (pp. 221–238). Philadelphia: Brunner/Mazel.

Riva, D., & Giorgi, C. (2000). The cerebellum contributes to higher functions during development: Evidence from a series of children surgically treated for posterior fossa tumours. *Brain, 123,* 1051–1061.

Rivera, S. M., Wakeley, A., & Langer, J. (1999). The drawbridge phenomenon: Representational reasoning or perceptual preference? *Developmental Psychology, 35,* 427–435.

Rivkees, S. A. (2003). Developing circadian rhythmicity in infants. *Pediatrics, 112,* 373–381.

Rivlin, R. S. (2007). Keeping the young–elderly healthy: Is it too late to improve our health through nutrition? *American Journal of Clinical Nutrition, 86*(Suppl.), 1572S–1576S.

Rizzolatti, G., & Craighero, L. (2004). The mirror-neuron system. *Annual Review of Neuroscience, 27,* 169–192.

Robb, A. S., & Dadson, M. J. (2002). Eating disorders in males. *Child and Adolescent Psychiatric Clinics of North America, 11,* 399–418.

Roberson, E. D., Scearce-Livie, K., Palop, J. J., Yan, F., Cheng, I. H., & Wu, T. (2007). Reducing endogenous tau ameliorates amyloid beta-induced deficits in an Alzheimer's disease mouse model. *Science, 316,* 750–754.

Roberts, B. W., & DelVecchio, W. E. (2000). The rank-order consistency of personality traits from childhood to old age: A quantitative review of longitudinal studies. *Psychological Bulletin, 126,* 3–25.

Roberts, B. W., Kuncel, N., Shiner, R., Caspi, A., & Goldberg, L. R. (2007). The power of personality: A comparative analysis of the predictive validity of personality traits, SES, and IQ. *Perspectives on Psychological Science, 2,* 313–345.

Roberts, B. W., & Mroczek, D. (2008). Personality and trait change in adulthood. *Current Directions in Psychological Science, 17,* 31–35.

Roberts, B. W., Robins, R. W., Caspi, A., & Trzesniewski, K. H. (2003). Personality trait development in adulthood. In J. L. Mortimer & M. Shanahan (Eds.), *Handbook of the life course* (pp. 579–598). New York: Plenum.

Roberts, B. W., Walton, K. E., & Viechtbauer, W. (2006). Patterns of mean-level change in personality traits across the life course: A meta-analysis of longitudinal studies. *Psychological Bulletin, 132,* 3–25.

Roberts, D. F., Foehr, U. G., & Rideout, V. (2005). *Generation M: Media in the lives of 8–18 year olds.* Menlo Park, CA: Henry J. Kaiser Family Foundation.

Roberts, D. F., Henriksen, L., & Foehr, U. G. (2004). Adolescents and media. In R. M. Lerner & L. Steinberg (Eds.), *Handbook of adolescent psychology* (2nd ed., pp. 627–664). Hoboken, NJ: Wiley.

Roberts, J. E., Burchinal, M. R., & Durham, M. (1999). Parents' report of vocabulary and grammatical development of American preschoolers: Child and environment associations. *Child Development, 70,* 92–106.

Roberts, J. M., & Masten, A. S. (2004). Resilience in context. In R. D. Peters, R. McMahon, & B. Leadbeater (Eds.), *Resilience in children, families, and communities: Linking context to practice and policy* (pp. 13–25). New York: Kluwer Academic.

Roberts, P. (2006). From my space to our space: The functions of Web memorials in bereavement. *The Forum, 32,* 1–4.

Roberts, P., & Newton, P. M. (1987). Levinsonian studies of women's adult development. *Psychology and Aging, 2,* 154–163.

Roberts, P., & Vidal, L. A. (1999–2000). Perpetual care in cyberspace: A portrait of memorials on the Web. *Omega, 40,* 521–545.

Roberts, R. E., Attkisson, C. C., & Rosenblatt, A. (1998) Prevalence of psychopathology among children and adolescents. *American Journal of Psychiatry, 155,* 715–725.

Robine, J.-M., & Allard, M. (1999). Jeanne Louise Calment: Validation of the duration of her life. In B. Jeune & J. W. Vaupel (Ed.), *Validation of exceptional longevity.* Odense, Denmark: Odense University Press.

Robins, R. W., Tracy, J. L., Trzesniewski, K., Potter, J., & Gosling, S. D. (2001). Personality correlates of self-esteem. *Journal of Research in Personality, 35,* 463–482.

Robins, R. W., & Trzesniewski, K. H. (2005). Self-esteem development across the lifespan. *Current Directions in Psychological Science, 14,* 158–162.

Robinson, C. C., Anderson, G. T., Porter, C. L., Hart, C. H., & Wouden-Miller, M. (2003). Sequential transition patterns of preschoolers' social interactions during child-initiated play: Is parallel-aware play a bi-directional bridge to other play states? *Early Childhood Research Quarterly, 18,* 3–21.

Robinson, J. L., Lee, B. E., Preiksaitis, J. K., Plitt, S., & Tipplies, G. A. (2006). Prevention of congenital rubella syndrome—What makes sense in 2006? *Epidemiologic Reviews, 28,* 81–87.

Robles, T. F., & Kiecolt-Glaser, J. K. (2003). The physiology of marriage: Pathways to health. *Physiology and Behavior, 79,* 409–416.

Rochat, P. (1989). Object manipulation and exploration in 2- to 5-month-old infants. *Developmental Psychology, 25,* 871–884.

Rochat, P. (1998). Self-perception and action in infancy. *Experimental Brain Research, 123,* 102–109.

Rochat, P. (2001). *The infant's world.* Cambridge, MA: Harvard University Press.

Rochat, P. (2003). Five levels of self-awareness as they unfold early in life. *Consciousness and Cognition, 12,* 717–731.

Rochat, P., & Goubet, N. (1995). Development of sitting and reaching in 5- to 6-month-old infants. *Infant Behavior and Development, 18,* 53–68.

Rochat, P., & Hespos, S. J. (1997). Differential rooting responses by neonates: Evidence for an early sense of self. *Early Development and Parenting, 6,* 105–112.

Rochat, P., Querido, J. G., & Striano, T. (1999). Emerging sensitivity to the timing and structure of proto-conversation. *Developmental Psychology, 35,* 950–957.

Rochat, P., & Striano, T. (2002). Who's in the mirror? Self–other discrimination in specular images by four- and nine-month-old infants. *Infant and Child Development, 11,* 289–303.

Rochat, P., Striano, T., & Blatt, L. (2002). Differential effects of happy, neutral, and sad still-faces on 2-, 4-, and 6-month-old infants. *Infant and Child Development, 11,* 289–303.

Rodgers, J. L., & Wänström, L. (2007). Identification of a Flynn effect in the NLSY: Moving from the center to the boundaries. *Intelligence, 35,* 187–196.

Rodkin, P. C., Farmer, T. W., Pearl, R., & Van Acker, R. (2000). Heterogeneity of popular boys: Antisocial and prosocial configurations. *Developmental Psychology, 36,* 14–24.

Rodkin, P. C., Farmer, T. W., Pearl, R., & Van Acker, R. (2006). They're cool: Social status and peer group supports for aggressive boys and girls. *Social Development, 15,* 175–204.

Roebers, C. M., & Schneider, W. (2001). Individual differences in children's eyewitness recall: The influence of intelligence and shyness. *Applied Developmental Science, 5,* 9–20.

Roelfsema, N. M., Hop, W. C., Boito, S. M., & Wladimiroff, J. W. (2004). Three-dimensional sonographic measurement of normal fetal brain volume during the second half of pregnancy. *American Journal of Obstetrics and Gynecology, 190,* 275–280.

Roeser, R. W., Eccles, J. S., & Freedman-Doan, C. (1999). Academic functioning and mental health in adolescence: Patterns, progressions, and routes from childhood. *Journal of Adolescent Research, 14,* 135–174.

Roeser, R. W., Eccles, J. S., & Sameroff, A. J. (2000). School as a context of early adolescents' academic and social-emotional development: A summary of research findings. *Elementary School Journal, 100,* 443–471.

Rogan, W. J., Dietrich, K. N., Ware, J. H., Dockery, D. W., Salganik, M., & Radcliffe, J. (2001). The effect of chelation therapy with succimer on neuropsychological development in children exposed to lead. *New England Journal of Medicine, 344,* 1421–1426.

Rogers, L. J. (2000). Evolution of hemispheric specialization: Advantages and disadvantages. *Brain and Language, 73,* 236–253.

Rogers, W. A., & Fisk, A. D. (2005). Aware home technology: Potential benefits for older adults. *Public Policy and Aging Report, 15*(4), 28–30.

Roggman, L. A., Langlois, J. H., Hubbs-Tait, L., & Rieser-Danner, L. A. (1994). Infant day-care, attachment, and the "file drawer problem." *Child Development, 65,* 1429–1443.

Rogoff, B. (1998). Cognition as a collaborative process. In D. Kuhn & R. S. Siegler (Eds.), *Handbook of child psychology: Vol. 2. Cognition, perception, and language* (5th ed., pp. 679–744). New York: Wiley.

Rogoff, B. (2003). *The cultural nature of human development.* New York: Oxford University Press.

Rogoff, B., & Chavajay, P. (1995). What's become of research on the cultural basis of cognitive development? *American Psychologist, 50,* 859–877.

Rogoff, B., Malkin, C., & Gilbride, K. (1984). Interaction with babies as guidance in development. In B. Rogoff & J. V. Wertsch (Eds.), *Children's learning in the "zone of proximal development" (New directions for child development,* No. 23, pp. 31–44). San Francisco: Jossey-Bass.

Rogoff, B., Paradise, R., Arauz, R. M., Correa-Chávez, M., & Angelillo, C. (2003). Firsthand learning through intent participation. *Annual Review of Psychology, 54,* 175–203.

Rogoff, B., & Waddell, K. J. (1982). Memory for information organized in a scene by children from two cultures. *Child Development, 53,* 1224–1228.

Rogol, A. D., Roemmich, J. N., & Clark, P. A. (2002). Growth at puberty. *Journal of Adolescent Health, 31,* 192–200.

Rohner, R., & Brothers, S. (1999). Perceived parental rejection, psychological maladjustment, and borderline personality disorder. *Journal of Emotional Abuse, 1,* 81–95.

Rohner, R. P., & Veneziano, R. A. (2001). The importance of father love: History and contemporary evidence. *Review of General Psychology, 5,* 382–405.

Roid, G. (2003). *The Stanford-Binet Intelligence Scales, Fifth Edition, interpretive manual.* Itasca, IL: Riverside Publishing.

Roisman, G. I., Madsen, S. D., Hennighausen, K. H., Sroufe, L. A., & Collins, W. A. (2001). The coherence of dyadic behavior across parent–child and romantic relationships as mediated by the internalized representation of experience. *Attachment and Human Development, 3,* 156–172.

Roisman, G. I., Padron, E., Sroufe, L. A., & Egeland, B. (2002). Earned-secure attachment status in retrospect and prospect. *Child Development, 73,* 1204–1219.

Roizen, N. J., & Patterson, D. (2003). Down's syndrome. *Lancet, 361,* 1281–1289.

Rokach, A. (2001). Perceived causes of loneliness in adulthood. *Journal of Social Behavior and Personality, 15,* 67–84.

Rokach, A. (2003). Strategies of coping with loneliness throughout the lifespan. In N. J. Pallone (Ed.), *Love, romance, sexual interaction: Research perspectives from current psychology* (pp. 225–344). New Brunswick, NJ: Transaction.

Rokach, A., & Neto, F. (2006). Age, culture, and coping with loneliness. *Psychology and Education, 43,* 1–21.

Rokach, R., Cohen, O., & Dreman, S. (2004). Who pulls the trigger? Who initiates divorce among over 45-year-olds. *Journal of Divorce and Remarriage, 42,* 61–83.

Rolls, B. J., Morris, E. L., & Roe, L. S. (2002). Portion size of food affects energy intake in normal-weight and overweight men and women. *American Journal of Clinical Nutrition, 6,* 1207–1213.

Román, G. C. (2003). Vascular dementia: Distinguishing characteristics, treatment, and prevention. *Journal of the American Geriatrics Society, 51,* S296–S304.

Rome-Flanders, T., & Cronk, C. (1995). A longitudinal study of infant vocalizations during mother–infant games. *Journal of Child Language, 22,* 259–274.

Romero, A. J., & Roberts, R. E. (2003). The impact of multiple dimensions of ethnic identity on discrimination and adolescents' self-esteem. *Journal of Applied Social Psychology, 33,* 2288–2305.

Rönnqvist, L., & Domellöf, E. (2006). Quantitative assessment of right and left reaching movements in infants: A longitudinal study from 6 to 36 months. *Developmental Psychobiology, 48,* 444–459.

Rook, K. S., Catalano, R., & Dooley, D. (1989). The timing of major life events: Effects of departing from the social clock. *American Journal of Community Psychology, 17,* 233–258.

Roopnarine, J. L., & Evans, M. E. (2007). Family structural organization, mother–child and father–child relationships and psychological outcomes in English-speaking African Caribbean and Indo Caribbean families. In M. Sutherland (Ed.), *Psychological of development in the Caribbean.* Kingston, Jamaica: Ian Randle.

Roopnarine, J. L., Hossain, Z., Gill, P., & Brophy, H. (1994). Play in the East Indian context. In J. L. Roopnarine, J. E. Johnson, & F. H. Hooper (Eds.), *Children's play in diverse cultures* (pp. 9–30). Albany: State University of New York Press.

Roopnarine, J. L., Krishnakumar, A., Metindogan, A., & Evans, M. (2006). Links between parenting styles, parent–child academic interaction, parent–school interaction, and early academic skills and social behaviors in young children of English-speaking Caribbean immigrants. *Early Childhood Research Quarterly, 21,* 238–252.

Roopnarine, J. L., Talukder, E., Jain, D., Joshi, P., & Srivastav, P. (1990). Characteristics of holding, patterns of play, and social behaviors between parents and infants in New Delhi, India. *Developmental Psychology, 26,* 667–673.

Rosander, K., & von Hofsten, C. (2002). Development of gaze tracking of small and large objects. *Experimental Brain Research, 146,* 257–264.

Rosander, K., & von Hofsten, C. (2004). Infants' emerging ability to represent occluded object motion. *Cognition, 91,* 1–22.

Rose, A. J., & Asher, S. R. (1999). Children's goals and strategies in response to conflicts within a friendship. *Developmental Psychology, 35,* 69–79.

Rose, A. J., Carlson, W., & Waller, E. M. (2007). Prospective associations of co-rumination with friendship and emotional adjustment: Considering the socioemotional trade-offs of co-rumination. *Developmental Psychology, 43,* 1019–1031.

Rose, A. J., Swenson, L. P., & Waller, E. M. (2004). Overt and relational aggression and perceived popularity: Developmental differences in concurrent and prospective relations. *Developmental Psychology, 40,* 378–387.

Rose, K. A., Morgan, I. G., Ip, J., Kifley, A., Huynh, S., Smith, W., & Mitchell, P. (2008). Outdoor activity reduces the prevalence of myopia in children. *Ophthalmology, 115,* 1279–1285.

Rose, S. A., & Feldman, J. F. (1997). Memory and speed: Their role in the relation of infant information processing to later IQ. *Child Development, 68,* 610–620.

Rose, S. A., Feldman, J. F., & Janowski, J. J. (2001). Attention and recognition memory in the 1st year of life: A longitudinal study of preterm and full-term infants. *Developmental Psychology, 37,* 135–151.

Rose, S. A., Jankowski, J. J., & Senior, G. J. (1997). Infants' recognition of contour-deleted figures. *Journal of Experimental Psychology: Human Perception and Performance, 23,* 1206–1216.

Roseboom, T., de Rooij, S., & Painter, R. (2006). The Dutch famine and its long-term consequences for adult health. *Early Human Development, 82,* 485–491.

Rosen, A. B., & Rozin, P. (1993). Now you see it, now you don't: The preschool child's conception of invisible particles in the context of dissolving. *Developmental Psychology, 29,* 300–311.

Rosen, D. (2003). Eating disorders in children and young adolescents: Etiology, classification, clinical features, and treatment. *Adolescent Medicine: State of the Art Reviews, 14,* 49–59.

Rosen, P. J., Milich, R., & Harris, M. J. (2007). Victims of their own cognitions: Implicit social cognitions, emotional distress, and peer victimization. *Journal of Applied Developmental Psychology, 28,* 211–226.

Rosen, S., Bergman, M., & Plester, D. (1962). Presbycusis study of a relatively noise-free population in the Sudan. *Transactions of the American Otological Society, 50,* 135–152.

Rosenblatt, P. C. (1993). Cross-cultural variation in the experience, expression, and understanding of grief. In D. P. Irish, K. F. Lundquist, & V. J. Nelsen (Eds.), *Ethnic variations in dying, death, and grief* (pp. 13–19). Washington, DC: Taylor & Francis.

Rosenblatt, P. C. (2008). Grief across cultures: A review and research agenda. In M. S. Stroebe, R. O. Hansson, H. Schut, & W. Stroebe (Eds.), *Handbook of bereavement research and practice* (pp. 207–222). Washington, DC: American Psychological Association.

Rosengren, K. S., & Hickling, A. K. (2000). The development of children's thinking about possible events and plausible mechanisms. In K. S. Rosengren, C. N. Johnson, & P. L. Harris (Eds.), *Imagining the impossible* (pp. 75–98). Cambridge, UK: Cambridge University Press.

Rosenman, R. H., Brand, R. J., Jenkins, C. D., Friedman, M., Strauss, R., & Wurm, M. (1975). Coronary heart disease in the Western Collaborative Group Study: Final follow-up experience of 8½ years. *Journal of the American Medical Association, 223,* 872–877.

Roseth, C. J., Pellegrini, A. D., Bohn, C. M., van Ryzin, M., & Vance, N. (2007). Preschoolers' aggression, affiliation, and social dominance relationships: An observational, longitudinal study. *Journal of School Psychology, 45,* 479–497.

Ross, C. M., & Harrison, P. L. (2006). Ability grouping. In G. G. Bear & K. M. Minke (Eds.), *Children's needs III: Development, prevention, and intervention* (pp. 579–588). Washington, DC: National Association of School Psychologists.

Rossi, A. S. (2001). (Ed.). *Caring and doing for others: Social responsibility in the domains of family, work, and community.* Chicago: University of Chicago Press.

Rossi, A. S. (2004). Social responsibility to family and community. In O. G. Brim, C. D. Ryff, & R. C. Kessler (Eds.), *How healthy are we? A national study of well-being at midlife* (pp. 550–585). Chicago: University of Chicago Press.

Rossi, A. S. (2005). The menopausal transition and aging processes. In O. G. Brim, C. D. Ryff, & R. C. Kessler (Eds.), *How healthy are we? A national study of well-being at midlife* (pp. 153–201). Chicago: University of Chicago Press.

Rossi, A. S., & Rossi, P. H. (1990). *Of human bonding: Parent–child relations across the life course.* New York: Aldine de Gruyter.

Rostosky, S. S., Riggle, E. D. B., Gray, B. E., & Hatton, R. L. (2007). Minority stress experiences in committed same-sex couple relationships. *Professional Psychology: Research and Practice, 38,* 392–400.

Rothbart, M. K. (2003). Temperament and the pursuit of an integrated developmental psychology. *Merrill-Palmer Quarterly, 50,* 492–505.

Rothbart, M. K., Ahadi, S. A., & Evans, D. E. (2000). Temperament and personality: Origins and outcome. *Journal of Personality and Social Psychology, 78,* 122–135.

Rothbart, M. K., & Bates, J. E. (2006). Temperament. In N. Eisenberg (Ed.), *Handbook of child psychology: Vol. 3. Social, emotional, and personality development* (6th ed., pp. 99–166). Hoboken, NJ: Wiley.

Rothbart, M. K., & Mauro, J. A. (1990). Questionnaire approaches to the study of infant temperament. In J. W. Fagen & J. Colombo (Eds.), *Individual differences in infancy: Reliability, stability and prediction* (pp. 411–429). Hillsdale, NJ: Erlbaum.

Rothbart, M. K., Posner, M. I., & Kieras, J. (2006). Temperament, attention, and the development of self-regulation. In K. McCartney & D. Phillips (Eds.), *Blackwell handbook of early childhood development* (pp. 338–357). Malden, MA: Blackwell.

Rothbaum, F., Pott, M., Azuma, H., Miyake, K., & Weisz, J. (2000a). The development of close relationships in Japan and the United States: Paths of symbiotic harmony and generative tension. *Child Development, 71,* 1121–1142.

Rothbaum, F., Weisz, J., Pott, M., Miyake, K., & Morelli, G. (2000b). Attachment and culture: Security in the United States and Japan. *American Psychologist, 55,* 1093–1104.

Rouselle, L., Palmers, E., & Noël, M.-P. (2004). Magnitude comparison in preschoolers: What counts? Influence of perceptual variables. *Journal of Experimental Child Psychology, 87,* 57–84.

Rovee-Collier, C. K. (1999). The development of infant memory. *Current Directions in Psychological Science, 8,* 80–85.

Rovee-Collier, C. K., & Barr, R. (2001). Infant learning and memory. In G. Bremner & A. Fogel (Eds.), *Blackwell handbook of infant development* (pp. 139–168). Oxford, UK: Blackwell.

Rovee-Collier, C. K., & Bhatt, R. S. (1993). Evidence of long-term memory in infancy. *Annals of Child Development, 9,* 1–45.

Rovio, S., Karenhold, I., Helkala, E. L., Viitanen, M., Winblad, B., & Tuomilehto, J. (2005). Leisure-time physical activity at midlife and the risk of dementia and Alzheimer's disease. *Lancet Neurology, 4,* 705–711.

Rowe, C. C., Ng, S., Ackermann, U., Gong, S. J., Pike, K., & Savage, G. (2007). Hippocampal expression analyses reveal selective association of immediate-early, neuroenergetic, and myelinogenic pathways with cognitive impairment in aged rats. *Journal of Neuroscience, 27,* 3098–3110.

Rowe, D. C. (1994). *The limits of family influence: Genes, experience, and behavior.* New York: Guilford.

Rowe, S., & Wertsch, J. V. (2002). Vygotsky's model of cognitive development. In G. Bremner & A. Fogel (Eds.), *Blackwell handbook of infant development* (pp. 538–554). Oxford, UK: Blackwell.

Rowland, C. F. (2007). Explaining errors in children's questions. *Cognition, 104,* 106–134.

Rowland, C., & Pine, J. M. (2000). Subject-auxiliary inversion errors and wh-question acquisition: "What children do know?" *Journal of Child Language, 27,* 157–181.

Rowland, D. T. (2007). Historical trends in childlessness. *Journal of Family Issues, 28,* 1311–1337.

Roy, K. M., & Lucas, K. (2006). Generativity as second chance: Low-income fathers and transformation of the difficult past. *Research in Human Development, 3,* 139–159.

Rubenstein, L. Z., & Josephson, K. R. (2006). Falls and their prevention in elderly people: What does the evidence show? *Medical Clinics of North America, 90,* 807–824.

Rubenstein, L. Z., Stevens, J. A., & Scott, V. (2008). Interventions to prevent falls among older adults. In L. S. Doll, S. E. Bonzo, D. A. Sleet, J. A. Mercy, & E. N. Haas (Eds.), *Handbook of injury and violence prevention* (pp. 37–53). New York: Springer.

Rubin, D. C. (2002). Autobiographical memory across the lifespan. In P. Graf & N. Ohta (Eds.), *Lifespan development of human memory* (pp. 159–184). Cambridge, MA: MIT Press.

Rubin, D. C., & Berntsen, D. (2006). People over forty feel 20% younger than their age: Subjective age across the lifespan. *Psychonomic Bulletin and Review, 13,* 776–780.

Rubin, D. C., Rahhal, T. A., & Poon, L. W. (1998). Things learned in early adulthood are remembered best. *Memory and Cognition, 26,* 3–19.

Rubin, D. C., & Schulkind, M. D. (1997). Distribution of important and word-cued autobiographical memories in 20-, 35-, and 70-year-old adults. *Psychology and Aging, 12,* 524–535.

Rubin, K. H., Bukowski, W. M., & Parker, J. G. (2006). Peer interactions, relationships, and groups. In N. Eisenberg (Ed.), *Handbook of child psychology: Vol. 3. Social, emotional, and personality development* (6th ed., pp. 571–645). Hoboken, NJ: Wiley.

Rubin, K. H., Burgess, K. B., & Coplan, R. (2002). Social withdrawal and shyness. In P. K. Smith & C. H. Hart (Eds.), *Blackwell handbook of child social development* (pp. 329–352). Oxford, UK: Blackwell.

Rubin, K. H., Burgess, K. B., Dwyer, K. M., & Hastings, P. D. (2003). Predicting preschoolers' externalizing behaviors from toddler temperament, conflict, and maternal negativity. *Developmental Psychology, 39,* 164–176.

Rubin, K. H., Burgess, K. B., & Hastings, P. D. (2002). Stability and social-behavioral consequences of toddlers' inhibited temperament and parenting behaviors. *Child Development, 73,* 483–495.

Rubin, K. H., & Coplan, R. J. (1998). Social and nonsocial play in childhood: An individual differences perspective. In O. N. Saracho & B. Spodek (Eds.), *Multiple perspectives on play in early childhood education* (pp. 144–170). Albany: State University of New York Press.

Rubin, K. H., Coplan, J., Chen, X., Buskirk, A. A., & Wojslawowicz, J. C. (2005). Peer relationships in childhood. In M. H. Bornstein & M. E. Lamb (Eds.), *Developmental science: An advanced textbook* (pp. 469–512). Mahwah, NJ: Erlbaum.

Rubin, K. H., Fein, G. G., & Vandenberg, B. (1983). Play. In E. M. Hetherington (Ed.), *Handbook of child psychology: Vol. 4. Socialization, personality, and social development* (4th ed., pp. 693–744). New York: Wiley.

Rubin, K. H., Hastings, P. D., Stewart, S. L., Henderson, H. A., & Chen, X. (1997). The consistency and concomitants of inhibition: Some of the children, all of the time. *Child Development, 68,* 467–483.

Rubin, K. H., Watson, K. S., & Jambor, T. W. (1978). Free-play behaviors in preschool and kindergarten children. *Child Development, 49,* 539–536.

Rubin, S. E., & Wooten, H. R. (2007). Highly educated stay-at-home mothers: A study of commitment and conflict. *Counseling and Therapy for Couples and Families, 15,* 336–345.

Rubinstein, R. L., Alexander, B. B., Goodman, M., & Luborsky, M. (1991). Key relationships of never married, childless older women: A cultural analysis. *Journal of Gerontology, 46,* S270–S277.

Ruble, D. N., Alvarez, J., Bachman, M., Cameron, J., Fuligni, A., García Coll, C., & Rhee, E. (2004). The development of a sense of "we": The emergence and implications of children's collective identity. In M. Bennett & F. Sani (Eds.), *The development of the social self* (pp. 29–76). Hove, UK: Psychology Press.

Ruble, D. N., Martin, C. L., & Berenbaum, S. A. (2006). Gender development. In N. Eisenberg (Ed.), *Handbook of child psychology: Vol. 3. Social, emotional, and personality development* (6th ed., pp. 226–299). Hoboken, NJ: Wiley.

Ruble, D. N., Taylor, L. J., Cyphers, L., Greulich, F. K., Lurye, L. E., & Shrout, P. E. (2007). The role of gender constancy in early gender development. *Child Development, 78,* 1121–1136.

Rudolph, K. D., Caldwell, M. S., & Conley, C. S. (2005). Need for approval and children's well-being. *Child Development, 76,* 309–323.

Rudolph, K. D., Lambert, S. F., Clark, A. G., & Kurlakowsky, K. D. (2001). Negotiating the transition to middle school: The role of self-regulatory processes. *Child Development, 72,* 929–946.

Rudy, D., & Grusec, J. E. (2006). Authoritarian parenting in individualist and collectivist groups: Associations with maternal emotion and cognition and children's self-esteem. *Journal of Family Psychology, 20,* 68–78.

Ruff, H. A., & Capozzoli, M. C. (2003). Development of attention and distractibility in the first 4 years of life. *Developmental Psychology, 39,* 877–890.

Ruff, H. A., & Rothbart, M. K. (1996). *Attention in early development.* New York: Oxford University Press.

Ruffman, T. (1999). Children's understanding of logical inconsistency. *Child Development, 70,* 887–895.

Ruffman, T., & Langman, L. (2002). Infants' reaching in a multi-well A not B task. *Infant Behavior and Development, 25,* 237–246.

Ruffman, T., Perner, J., Olson, D. R., & Doherty, M. (1993). Reflecting on scientific thinking: Children's understanding of the hypothesis–evidence relation. *Child Development, 64,* 1617–1636.

Ruffman, T., Slade, L., Devitt, K., & Crowe, E. (2006). What mothers say and what they do: The relation between parenting, theory of mind, language, and conflict/cooperation. *British Journal of Developmental Psychology, 24,* 105–124.

Ruhm, C. J. (1996). Gender differences in employment behavior during late middle age. *Journal of Gerontology, 51B,* S11–S17.

Runco, M. A. (1992). Children's divergent thinking and creative ideation. *Developmental Review, 12,* 233–264.

Rurup, M. L., Muller, M. T., Onwuteaka-Philipsen, B. D., van der Heide, A., van der Wal, G., & van der Maas, P. J. (2005). Requests for euthanasia or physician-assisted suicide from older persons who do not have a severe disease: An interview study. *Psychological Medicine, 35,* 665–671.

Rusbult, C. E., Coolsen, M. K., Kirchner, J. L., & Clarke, J. A. (2006). Commitment. In A. L. Vangelisti & D. Perlman (Eds.), *The Cambridge handbook of personal relationships* (pp. 615–635). New York: Cambridge University Press.

Rusconi, A. (2004). Different pathways out of the parental home: A comparison of West Germany and Italy. *Journal of Comparative Family Studies, 35,* 627–649.

Rushton, J. L., Forcier, M., & Schectman, R. M. (2002). Epidemiology of depressive symptoms in the National Longitudinal Study of Adolescent Health. *Journal of the American Academy of Child and Adolescent Psychiatry, 41,* 199–205.

Rushton, J. P., & Bons, T. A. (2005). Mate choice and friendship in twins. *Psychological Science, 16,* 555–559.

Rushton, J. P., & Jensen, A. R. (2005). Thirty years of research on race differences in cognitive ability. *Psychology, Public Policy, and Law, 11,* 235–294.

Rushton, J. P., & Jensen, A. R. (2006). The totality of available evidence shows the race IQ gap still remains. *Psychological Science, 17,* 921–924.

Russac, R. J., Gatliff, C., Reece, M., & Spottswood, D. (2007). Death anxiety across the adult years: An examination of age and gender effects. *Death Studies, 31,* 549–561.

Russell, A., Mize, J., & Bissaker, K. (2004). Parent–child relationships. In P. K. Smith & C. H. Hart (Eds.), *Blackwell handbook of childhood social development* (pp. 204–222). Malden, MA: Blackwell.

Russell, J. A. (1990). The preschooler's understanding of the causes and consequences of emotion. *Child Development, 61,* 1872–1881.

Russell, J. A., Douglas, A. J., & Ingram, C. D. (2001). Brain preparations for maternity—adaptive changes in behavioral and neuroendocrine systems during pregnancy and lactation. *Progress in Brain Research, 133,* 1–38.

Russell, R. B., Petrini, J. R., Damus, K., Mattison, D. R., & Schwarz, R. H. (2003). The changing epidemiology of multiple births in the United States. *Obstetrics and Gynecology, 101,* 129–135.

Rutter, M. (1996). Maternal deprivation. In M. H. Bornstein (Ed.), *Handbook of parenting: Vol. 4. Applied and practical parenting* (pp. 3–31). Mahwah, NJ: Erlbaum.

Rutter, M. (2002). Nature, nurture, and development: From evangelism through science toward policy and practice. *Child Development, 73,* 1–21.

Rutter, M. (2006). *Genes and behavior: Nature nurture interplay explained.* Malden, MA: Blackwell.

Rutter, M. (2007). Gene–environment interdependence. *Developmental Science, 10,* 12–18.

Rutter, M., Colvert, E., Kreppner, J., Beckett, C., Castle, J., & Groothues, C. (2007). Early adolescent outcomes for institutionally deprived and non-deprived adoptees. I: Disinhibited attachment. *Journal of Child Psychology and Psychiatry, 48,* 17–30.

Rutter, M., & the English and Romanian Adoptees Study Team. (1998). Developmental catch-up, and deficit, following adoption after severe global early privation. *Journal of Child Psychology and Psychiatry, 39,* 465–476.

Rutter, M., O'Connor, T. G., and the English and Romanian Adoptees Study Team. (2004). Are there biological programming effects for psychological development? Findings from a study of Romanian adoptees. *Developmental Psychology, 40,* 81–94.

Rutter, M., Pickles, A., Murray, R., & Eaves, L. (2001). Testing hypotheses on specific environmental causal effects on behavior. *Psychological Bulletin, 127,* 291–324.

Ryan, A. M., & Patrick, H. (2001). The classroom social environment and changes in adolescents' motivation and engagement during middle school. *American Educational Research Journal, 38,* 437–460.

Ryan, E. B., Jin, Y., Anas, A. P., & Luh, J. J. (2004). Communication beliefs about youth and old age in Asia and Canada. *Journal of Cross-Cultural Gerontology, 19,* 343–360.

Ryan, M. K., David, B., & Reynolds, K. J. (2004). Who cares? The effect of gender and context on the self and moral reasoning. *Psychology of Women Quarterly, 28,* 246–255.

Ryan, R. M., Fauth, R. C., & Brooks-Gunn, J. (2006). Childhood poverty: Implications for school readiness and early childhood education In B. Spodek & O. N. Saracho (Eds.), *Handbook of research on the education of young children* (2nd ed., pp. 323–346). Mahwah, NJ: Erlbaum.

Rybash, J. M., & Hrubi-Bopp, K. L. (2000). Isolating the neural mechanisms of age-related changes in human working memory. *Nature Neuroscience, 3,* 509–515.

Ryding, M., Konradsson, K., Kalm, O., & Prellner, K. (2002). Auditory consequences of recurrent acute purulent otitis media. *Annals of Otology, Rhinology, and Laryngology, 111*(3, Pt. 1), 261–266.

Ryff, C. D. (1989). In the eye of the beholder: Views of psychological well-being among middle-aged and older adults. *Psychology and Aging, 4,* 195–210.

Ryff, C. D. (1991). Possible selves in adulthood and old age: A tale of shifting horizons. *Psychology and Aging, 6,* 286–295.

Ryff, C. D. (1995). Psychological well-being in adult life. *Current Directions in Psychological Science, 4,* 99–104.

Ryff, C. D., Schmutte, P. S., & Lee, Y. H. (1996). How children turn out: Implications for parental self-evaluation. In C. D. Ryff & M. M. Seltzer (Eds.), *The parental experience in midlife* (pp. 383–422). Chicago: University of Chicago Press.

Ryff, C. D., & Singer, B. H. (2002). From social structure to biology. In S. J. L. C. R. Snyder (Ed.), *Handbook of positive psychology* (pp. 541–555). Oxford: Oxford University Press.

Ryff, C. D., & Singer, B. H. (2005). Social environments and the genetics of aging: Advancing knowledge of protective health mechanisms. *Journal of Gerontology, 60B,* 12–23.

Ryff, C. D., Singer, B. H., & Seltzer, M. M. (2002). Pathways through challenge: Implications for well-being and health. In L. Pulkkinen & A. Caspi (Eds.), *Paths to successful development* (pp. 302–328). Cambridge, UK: Cambridge University Press.

S

Saarni, C. (1999). *The development of emotional competence.* New York: Guilford.

Saarni, C. (2000). Emotional competence: A developmental perspective. In R. Bar-On & J. D. A. Parker (Eds.), *Handbook of emotional intelligence* (pp. 68–91). San Francisco: Jossey-Bass.

Saarni, C., Campos, J. J., Camras, L. A., & Witherington, D. (2006). Emotional development: Action, communication, and understanding. In N. Eisenberg (Ed.), *Handbook of child psychology: Vol. 3. Social, emotional, and personality development* (6th ed., pp. 226–299). Hoboken, NJ: Wiley.

Sabbagh, M. A., Xu, F., Carlson, S. M., Moses, L. J., & Lee, K. (2006). The development of executive functioning and theory of mind: A comparison of Chinese and U.S. preschoolers. *Psychological Science, 17,* 74–81.

Sachdev, P. S., Brodaty, H., & Looi, J. C. L. (1999). Vascular dementia: Diagnosis, management, and possible prevention. *Medical Journal of Australia, 170,* 81–85.

Sacks, P. (2005). "No child left": What are schools for in a democratic society? In S. Olfman (Ed.), *Childhood lost: How American culture is failing our kids* (pp. 185–202). Westport, CT: Praeger.

Sadeh, A. (1997). Sleep and melatonin in infants: A preliminary study. *Sleep, 20,* 185–191.

Sadeh, A., Flint-Ofir, E., Tirosh, T., & Tikotzky, L. (2007). Infant sleep and parental sleep-related cognitions. *Journal of Family Psychology, 21,* 74–87.

Saenger, P. (2003). Dose effects of growth hormone during puberty. *Hormone Research, 60*(Suppl. 1), 52–57.

Saffran, J. R., Aslin, R. N., & Newport, E. L. (1996). Statistical learning by 8-month-old infants. *Science, 27,* 1926–1928.

Saffran, J. R., & Thiessen, E. D. (2003). Pattern induction by infant language learners. *Developmental Psychology, 39,* 484–494.

Saffran, J. R., & Thiessen, E. D. (2007). Domain-general learning capacities. In E. Hoff & M. Shatz (Eds.), *Blackwell handbook of language development* (pp. 68–86). Malden, MA: Blackwell.

Saffran, J. R., Werker, J. F., & Werner, L. A. (2006). The infant's auditory world: Hearing, speech, and the beginnings of language. In D. Kuhn & R. Siegler (Eds.), *Handbook of child psychology: Vol. 2. Cognition, perception, and language* (6th ed., pp. 58–108). Hoboken, NJ: Wiley.

Safren, S. A., & Pantalone, D. W. (2006). Social anxiety and barriers to resilience among lesbian, gay, and bisexual adolescents. In A. M. Omoto & H. S. Kurtzman (Eds.), *Sexual orientation and mental health: Examining identity and development in lesbian, gay, and bisexual young people* (pp. 55–71). Washington, DC: American Psychological Association.

Saginak, K. A., & Saginak, M. A. (2005). Balancing work and family: Equity, gender, and marital satisfaction. *Counseling and Therapy for Couples and Families, 13,* 162–166.

Saha, C., Riner, M. E., & Liu, G. (2005). Individual and neighborhood-level factors in predicting asthma. *Archives of Pediatrics and Adolescent Medicine, 159,* 759–763.

Saigal, S., Stoskopf, B., Streiner, D., Boyle, M., Pinelli, J., & Paneth, N. (2006). Transition of extremely low-birth-weight infants from adolescence to young adulthood. *Journal of the American Medical Association, 295,* 667–675.

Saitta, S. C., & Zackai, E. H. (2005). Specific chromosome disorders in newborns. In H. W. Taeusch, R. A. Ballard, & C. A. Gleason (Eds.), *Avery's diseases of the newborn* (8th ed., pp. 204–215). Philadelphia: Saunders.

Sakraida, T. J. (2005). Divorce transition differences of midlife women. *Issues in Mental Health Nursing, 26,* 225–249.

Salbe, A. D., Weyer, C., Lindsay, R. S., Ravussin, E., & Tataranni, P. A. (2002). Assessing risk factors for obesity between childhood and adolescence: I. Birth weight, childhood adiposity, parental obesity, insulin, and leptin. *Pediatrics, 110,* 299–306.

Salerno, M., Micillo, M., Di Maio, S., Capalbo, D., Ferri, P., & Lettiero, T. (2001). Longitudinal growth, sexual maturation and final height in patients with congenital hypothyroidism detected by neonatal screening. *European Journal of Endocrinology, 145,* 377–383.

Salihu, H. M., Shumpert, M. N., Slay, M., Kirby, R. S., & Alexander, G. R. (2003). Childbearing beyond maternal age 50 and fetal outcomes in the United States. *Obstetrics and Gynecology, 102,* 1006–1014.

Salley, B. J., & Dixon, W. E., Jr. (2007). Temperamental and joint attentional predictors of language development. *Merrill-Palmer Quarterly, 53,* 131–154.

Salmela-Aro, K., Nurmi, J.-E., Saisto, T., & Halmesmaki, E. (2001). Goal reconstruction and depressive symptoms during the transition to motherhood: Evidence from two cross-lagged longitudinal studies. *Journal of Personality and Social Psychology, 81,* 1144–1159.

Salmivalli, C., & Voeten, M. (2004). Connections between attitudes, group norms, and behaviour in bullying situations. *International Journal of Behavioral Development, 28,* 246–258.

Salovey, P., & Pizarro, D. A. (2003). The value of emotional intelligence. In R. J. Sternberg, J. Lautrey, & T. I. Lubart (Eds.), *Models of intelligence: International perspectives* (pp. 263–278). Washington, DC: American Psychological Association.

Salter, D., McMillan, D., Richards, M., Talbot, T., Hodges, J., Bentovim, A., & Hastings, R. (2003). Development of sexually abusive behavior in sexually victimized males: A longitudinal study. *Lancet, 361,* 471–476.

Salthouse, T. A. (1984). Effects of age and skill in typing. *Journal of Experimental Psychology: General, 113,* 345–371.

Salthouse, T. A. (1996). Constraints on theories of cognitive aging. *Psychonomic Bulletin and Review, 3,* 287–299.

Salthouse, T. A. (2005). Relations between cognitive abilities and measures of executive functioning. *Neuropsychology, 19,* 532–545.

Salthouse, T. A. (2006). Aging of thought. In E. Bialystok & F. I. M. Craik (Eds.), *Lifespan cognition: Mechanisms of change* (pp. 274–284). New York: Oxford University Press.

Salthouse, T. A., & Caja, S. J. (2000). Structural constraints on process explanations in cognitive aging. *Psychology and Aging, 15,* 44–55.

Salthouse, T. A., Fristoe, N., & Rhee, S. H. (1996). How localized are age-related effects on neuropsychological measures? *Neuropsychology, 10,* 272–285.

Salvioli, S., Capri, M., Santoro, A., Raule, N., Sevini, F., & Lukas, S. (2008). The impact of mitochondrial DNA on human lifespan: A view from studies on centenarians. *Biotechnology Journal, 3,* 740–749.

Samarel, N. (1991). *Caring for life and death.* Washington, DC: Hemisphere.

Samarel, N. (1995). The dying process. In H. Wass & R. A. Neimeyer (Eds.), *Dying: Facing the facts* (3rd ed., pp. 89–116). Washington, DC: Taylor & Francis.

Sameroff, A. (2006). Identifying risk and protective factors for healthy child development. In A. Clarke-Stewart & J. Dunn (Eds.), *Families count: Effects on child and adolescent development* (pp. 53–76). New York: Cambridge University Press.

Sampselle, C. M., Harris, V., Harlow, S. D., & Sowers, M. (2002). Midlife development and menopause in African-American and Caucasian women. *Health Care for Women International, 23,* 351–363.

Samuels, M. (2003). Viruses and sudden infant death. *Paediatric Respiratory Reviews, 4,* 178–183.

Samuelsson, S. M., Alfredson, B. B., Hagberg, B., Anonymous, Nordbeck, B., Brun, A., Gustafson, L., & Risberg, J. (1997). The Swedish Centenarian Study: A multidisciplinary study of five consecutive cohorts at the age of 100. *International Journal of Aging and Human Development, 45,* 223–253.

Sandberg, J. F., & Hofferth, S. L. (2001). Changes in children's time with parents: United States, 1981–1997. *Demography, 38,* 423–436.

Sanders, C. M. (1999). *Grief: The mourning after* (2nd ed.). New York: Wiley.

Sanders, O. (2006). *Evaluating the Keeping Ourselves Safe Programme.* Wellington, NZ: Youth Education Service, New Zealand Police. Retrieved from www.nzfvc.org.nz/accan/papers-presentations/abstract11v.shtml

Sanderson, C. A., Rahm, K. B., & Beigbeder, S. A. (2005). The link between the pursuit of intimacy goals and satisfaction in close same-sex friendships: An examination of the underlying processes. *Journal of Social and Personal Relationships, 22,* 75–98.

Sanderson, J. A., & Siegal, M. (1988). Conceptions of moral and social rules in rejected and nonrejected preschoolers. *Journal of Clinical Child Psychology, 17,* 66–72.

Sandler, J. C. (2006). Alternative methods of child testimony: A review of law and research. In C. R. Bartol & A. M. Bartol (Eds.), *Current perspectives in forensic psychology and criminal justice* (pp. 203–212). Thousand Oaks, CA: Sage.

Sandnabba, N. K., & Ahlberg, C. (1999). Parents' attitudes and expectations about children's cross-gender behavior. *Sex Roles, 40,* 249–263.

Sandström, A., Rhodin, N., Lundberg, M., Olsson, T., & Nyberg, L. (2005). Impaired cognitive performance in patients with chronic burnout syndrome. *Biological Psychology, 69,* 271–279.

Sandstrom, M. J., & Cillessen, A. H. N. (2003). Sociometric status and children's peer experiences: Use of the daily diary method. *Merrill-Palmer Quarterly, 49,* 427–452.

Sann, C., & Streri, A. (2007). Perception of object shape and texture in human newborns: Evidence from cross-modal transfer tasks. *Developmental Science, 10,* 399–410.

Sansavini, A., Bertoncini, J., & Giovanelli, G. (1997). Newborns discriminate the rhythm of multisyllabic stressed words. *Developmental Psychology, 33,* 3–11.

Sansone, C., & Berg, C. A. (1993). Adapting to the environment across the life span: Different process or different inputs? *International Journal of Behavioral Development, 16,* 215–241.

Santoloupo, S., & Pratt, M. (1994). Age, gender, and parenting style variations in mother–adolescent dialogues and adolescent reasoning about political issues. *Journal of Adolescent Research, 9,* 241–261.

Santtila, P., Wager, I., Witting, K., Harlaar, N., Jern, P., Johansson, A., Varjonen, M., & Sandnabba, K. (2008). Discrepancies between sexual desire and sexual activity: Gender differences and associations with relationship satisfaction. *Journal of Sex and Marital Therapy, 34,* 31–44.

Sanz, A., Pamplona, R., & Barja, G. (2006). Is the mitochondrial free radical theory of aging intact? *Antioxidants and Redox Signaling, 8,* 582–599.

Sapp, F., Lee, K., & Muir, D. (2000). Three-year-olds' difficulty with the appearance–reality distinction: Is it real or is it apparent? *Developmental Psychology, 36,* 547–560.

Sarason, S. B. (1977). *Work, aging, and social change.* New York: Free Press.

Sarnecka, B. W., & Gelman, S. A. (2004). Six does not just mean a lot: Preschoolers see number words as specific. *Cognition, 92,* 329–352.

Sasaki, M., & Suzuki, T. (1987). Changes in religious commitment in the United States, Holland and Japan. *American Journal of Sociology, 92,* 1055–1076.

Sasser-Coen, J. A. (1993). Qualitative changes in creativity in the second half of life: A life-span developmental perspective. *Journal of Creative Behavior, 27,* 18–27.

Sato, T., Matsumoto, T., Kawano, H., Watanabe, T., Uematsu, Y., & Semine, K. (2004). Brain masculinization requires androgen receptor function. *Proceedings of the National Academy of Sciences, 101,* 1673–1678.

Saucier, J. F., Sylvestre, R., Doucet, H., Lambert, J., Frappier, J. Y., Charbonneau, L., & Malus, M. (2002). Cultural identity and adaptation to adolescence in Montreal. In F. J. C. Azima & N. Grizenko (Eds.), *Immigrant and refugee children and their families: Clinical, research, and training issues* (pp. 133–154). Madison, WI: International Universities Press.

Saudino, K. J. (2003). Parent ratings of infant temperament: Lessons from twin studies. *Infant Behavior and Development, 26,* 100–107.

Saudino, K. J., & Plomin, R. (1997). Cognitive and temperamental mediators of genetic contributions to the home environment during infancy. *Merrill-Palmer Quarterly, 43,* 1–23.

Sauls, D. J. (2002). Effects of labor support on mothers, babies, and birth outcomes. *Journal of Obstetric, Gynecologic, and Neonatal Nursing, 31,* 733–741.

Savin-Williams, R. C. (2001). A critique of research on sexual-minority youths. *Journal of Adolescence, 24,* 5–13.

Savin-Williams, R. C. (2003). Lesbian, gay, and bisexual youths' relationships with their parents. In L. D. Garnets & D. C. Kimmel (Eds.), *Psychological perspectives on lesbian, gay, and bisexual experiences* (2nd ed., pp. 299–326). New York: Columbia University Press.

Savin-Williams, R. C., & Diamond, L. M. (2004). Sex. In R. M. Lerner & L. Steinberg (Eds.), *Handbook of adolescent development* (2nd ed., pp. 189–231). Hoboken, NJ: Wiley.

Savin-Williams, R. C., & Ream, G. L. (2003). Sex variations in the disclosure to parents of same-sex attractions. *Journal of Family Psychology, 17,* 429–438.

Saxe, G. B. (1988, August–September). Candy selling and math learning. *Educational Researcher, 17*(6), 14–21.

Saxton, M., Backley, P., & Gallaway, C. (2005). Negative input for grammatical errors: Effects after a lag of 12 weeks. *Journal of Child Language, 32,* 643–672.

Saygin, A. P., Wilson, S. M., Dronkers, N. F., & Bates, E. (2004). Action comprehension in aphasia: Linguistic and non-linguistic deficits and their lesion correlates. *Neuropsychologia, 42,* 1788–1804.

Saylor, C. F., Cowart, B. L., Lipovsky, J. A., Jackson, C., & Finch, A. J., Jr. (2003). Media exposure to September 11: Elementary school students' experiences and posttraumatic symptoms. *American Behavioral Scientist, 46,* 1622–1642.

Saylor, M. M., Baldwin, D. A., & Sabbagh, M. A. (2005). Word learning: A complex product. In G. Hall & S. Waxman (Eds.), *Weaving a lexicon.* Cambridge, MA: MIT Press.

Saylor, M. M., & Troseth, G. L. (2006). Preschoolers use information about speakers' desires to learn new words. *Cognitive Development, 21,* 214–231.

Saywitz, K. J., Goodman, G. S., & Lyon, T. D. (2002). Interviewing children in and out of court: Current research and practice implications. In J. E. B. Myers & L. Berliner (Eds.), *The APSAC handbook on child maltreatment* (2nd ed., pp. 349–377). Thousand Oaks, CA: Sage.

Scales, P. C., & Roehlkepartain, E. C. (2004). *Community service and service learning in U.S. public schools, 2004: Findings from a national survey.* St. Paul, MN: National Youth Leadership Council.

Scarmeas, N., Luchsinger, J. A., Mayeux, R., & Stern, Y. (2007). Mediterranean diet and Alzheimer disease mortality. *Neurology, 69,* 1084–1093.

Scarr, S., & McCartney, K. (1983). How people make their own environments: A theory of genotype environment effects. *Child Development, 54,* 424–435.

Scarr, S., & Weinberg, R. A. (1983). The Minnesota Adoption Studies: Genetic differences and malleability. *Child Development, 54,* 260–267.

Schaal, B., Marlier, L., & Soussignan, R. (2000). Human fetuses learn odours from their pregnant mother's diet. *Chemical Senses, 25,* 729–737.

Schafer, R. (1999). *Determinants of living arrangements of the elderly.* Boston: Joint Center for Housing Studies, Harvard University.

Schaie, K. W. (1989). Individual differences in rate of cognitive change in adulthood. In V. L. Bengtson & K. W. Schaie (Eds.), *The course of later life: Research and reflections* (pp. 68–83). New York: Springer.

Schaie, K. W. (1994). The course of adult intellectual development. *American Psychologist, 49,* 304–313.

Schaie, K. W. (1996). *Intellectual development in adulthood: The Seattle Longitudinal Study.* New York: Cambridge University Press.

Schaie, K. W. (1998). The Seattle Longitudinal Studies of Adult Intelligence. In M. P. Lawton & T. A. Salthouse (Eds.), *Essential papers on the psychology of aging* (pp. 263–271). New York: New York University Press.

Schaie, K. W. (2000). The impact of longitudinal studies on understanding development from young adulthood to old age. *International Journal of Behavioral Development, 24,* 257–266.

Schaie, K. W. (2005). *Developmental influences on adult intelligence: The Seattle Longitudinal Study.* New York: Oxford University Press.

Schalet, A. (2007). Adolescent sexuality viewed through two different cultural lenses. In M. S. Tepper & A. F. Owens (Eds.), *Sexual health: Vol. 3. Moral and cultural foundations* (pp. 365–387). Westport, CT: Praeger.

Scharrer, E., & Comstock, G. (2003). Entertainment televisual media: Content patterns and themes. In E. L. Palmer & B. M. Young (Eds.), *The faces of televisual media: Teaching, violence, selling to children* (pp. 161–193). Mahwah, NJ: Erlbaum.

Scheidt, R. J., & Windley, P. G. (1985). The ecology of aging. In J. E. Birren & K. W. Schaie (Eds.), *Handbook of the psychology of aging* (pp. 245–258). New York: Van Nostrand Reinhold.

Schellenberg, E. G. (2004). Music lessons enhance IQ. *Psychological Science, 15,* 511–514.

Schellenberg, E. G., Nakata, T., Hunter, P. G., & Tamoto, S. (2007). Exposure to music and cognitive performance: Tests of children and adults. *Psychology of Music, 35,* 5–19.

Scher, A., Epstein, R., & Tirosh, E. (2004). Stability and changes in sleep regulation: A longitudinal study from 3 months to 3 years. *International Journal of Behavioral Development, 28,* 268–274.

Scher, A., Tirosh, E., Jaffe, M., Rubin, L., Sadeh, A., & Lavie, P. (1995). Sleep patterns of infants and young children in Israel. *International Journal of Behavioral Development, 18,* 701–711.

Scherer, J. M., & Simon, R. J. (1999). *Euthanasia and the right to die: A comparative view.* Lanham, MD: Rowman & Littlefield.

Schewe, P. A. (2007). Interventions to prevent sexual violence. In L. S. Doll, S. E. Bonzo, D. A. Sleet, & J. A. Mercy (Eds.), *Handbook of injury and violence prevention* (pp. 223–240). New York: Springer Science + Business Media.

Schieber, R. A., & Sacks, J. J. (2001). Measuring community bicycle helmet use among children. *Public Health Reports, 116,* 113–121.

Schieman, S., Gundy, V., & Taylor, K. (2001). Status, role, and resource explanations for age patterns in psychological distress. *Journal of Health and Social Behavior, 42,* 80–96.

Schieman, S., & Plickert, G. (2007). Functional limitations and changes in levels of depression among older adults: A multiple-hierarchy stratification perspective. *Journal of Gerontology, 62B,* S36–S42.

Schieman, S., Pudrovska, T., & Milkie, M. A. (2005). The sense of divine control and the self-concept: A study of race differences in late life. *Research on Aging, 27,* 165–196.

Schilling, O., & Wahl, H.-W. (2002). Family networks and life satisfaction of older adults in rural and urban regions. *Kolner Zeitschrift fur Soziologie und Sozialpsychologie, 54,* 304–317.

Schlagmüller, M., & Schneider, W. (2002). The development of organizational strategies in children: Evidence from a microgenetic longitudinal study. *Journal of Experimental Child Psychology, 81,* 298–319.

Schlegel, A., & Barry, H., III. (1991). *Adolescence: An anthropological inquiry.* New York: Free Press.

Schlossberg, N. (2004). *Retire smart, retire happy: Finding your true path in life.* Washington, DC: American Psychological Association.

Schmidt, K.-H., Neubach, B., & Heuer, H. (2007). Self-control demands, cognitive control deficits, and burnout. *Work and Stress, 21,* 142–154.

Schmidt, L. A., Fox, N. A., Rubin, K. H., Sternberg, E. M., Gold, P. W., & Smith, C. C. (1997). Behavioral and neuroendocrine responses in shy children. *Developmental Psychobiology, 35,* 119–135.

Schmidt, L. A., Fox, N. A., Schulkin, J., & Gold, P. W. (1999). Behavioral and psychophysiological correlates of self-presentation in temperamentally shy children. *Developmental Psychobiology, 30,* 127–140.

Schmidt, L. A., Santesso, D. L., Schulkin, J., & Segalowitz, S. J. (2007). Shyness is a necessary but not sufficient condition for high salivary cortisol in typically developing 10-year-old children. *Personality and Individual Differences, 43,* 1541–1551.

Schmitz, S., Fulker, D. W., Plomin, R., Zahn-Waxler, C., Emde, R. N., & DeFries, J. C. (1999). Temperament and problem behaviour during early childhood. *International Journal of Behavioural Development, 23,* 333–355.

Schneewind, K. A., & Gerhard, A. (2002). Relationship personality, conflict resolution, and marital satisfaction in the first 5 years of marriage. *Family Relations, 51,* 63–71.

Schneider, B. A., Daneman, M., Murphy, D. R., & See, S. K. (2000). Listening to discourse in distracting settings: The effects of aging. *Psychology and Aging, 15,* 110–125.

Schneider, B. H., Atkinson, L., & Tardif, C. (2001). Child–parent attachment and children's peer relations: A quantitative review. *Developmental Psychology, 37,* 87–100.

Schneider, E. L. (1992). Biological theories of aging. *Generations, 16*(4), 7–10.

Schneider, W. (2002). Memory development in childhood. In U. Goswami (Ed.), *Blackwell handbook of childhood cognitive development* (pp. 236–256). Malden, MA: Blackwell.

Schneider, W., & Bjorklund, D. F. (1992). Expertise, aptitude, and strategic remembering. *Child Development, 63,* 461–473.

Schneider, W., & Bjorklund, D. F. (1998). Memory. In D. Kuhn & R. S. Siegler (Eds.), *Handbook of child psychology: Vol. 2. Cognition, perception, and language* (5th ed., pp. 467–521). New York: Wiley.

Schneider, W., & Pressley, M. (1997). *Memory development between two and twenty* (2nd ed.). Mahwah, NJ: Erlbaum.

Schneller, D. P., & Arditti, J.A. (2004). After the breakup: Interpreting divorce and rethinking intimacy. *Journal of Divorce and Remarriage, 42,* 1–37.

Schnohr, P., Nyboe, J., Lange, P., & Jensen, G. (1998). Longevity and gray hair, baldness, facial wrinkles, and arcus senilis in 13,000 men and women: The Copenhagen City Heart Study. *Journal of Gerontology, 53,* M347–350.

Schnohr, P., Scharling, H., & Jensen, J. S. (2003). Changes in leisure-time physical activity and risk of death: An observational study of 7,000 men and women. *American Journal of Epidemiology, 158,* 639–644.

Scholl, B. J., & Leslie, A. M. (2000). Minds, modules, and meta-analysis. *Child Development, 72,* 696–701.

Scholl, T. O., Heidiger, M. L., & Belsky, D. H. (1996). Prenatal care and maternal health during adolescent pregnancy: A review and meta-analysis. *Journal of Adolescent Health, 15,* 444–456.

Scholnick, E. K. (1995, Fall). Knowing and constructing plans. *SRCD Newsletter,* pp. 1–2, 17.

Schonert-Reichl, K. A. (1999). Relations of peer acceptance, friendship adjustment, and social behavior to moral reasoning during early adolescence. *Journal of Early Adolescence, 19,* 249–279.

Schooler, C., Mulatu, M. S., & Oates, G. (1999). The continuing effects of substantively complex work on the intellectual functioning of older workers. *Psychology and Aging, 14,* 483–506.

Schoon, L., & Parsons, S. (2002). Teenage aspirations for future careers and occupational outcomes. *Journal of Vocational Behavior, 60,* 262–288.

Schoppe-Sullivan, S. J., Brown, G. L., Cannon, E. A., Mangelsdorf, S. C., & Sokolowski, M. S. (2008). Maternal gatekeeping, coparenting quality, and fathering behavior in families with infants. *Journal of Family Psychology, 22,* 389–398.

Schoppe-Sullivan, S. J., Mangelsdorf, S. C., Brown, G. L., & Sokolowski, M. S. (2007). Goodness-of-fit in family context: Infant temperament, marital quality, and early coparenting behavior. *Infant Behavior and Development, 30,* 82–96.

Schoppe-Sullivan, S. J., Mangelsdorf, S. C., Frosch, C. A., & McHale, J. (2004). Associations between coparenting and marital behavior from infancy to the preschool years. *Journal of Family Psychology, 18,* 194–207.

Schor, J. B. (2002). Time crunch among American parents. In S. A. Hewlett, N. Rankin, & C. West (Eds.), *Taking parenting public* (pp. 83–102). Boston: Rowman & Littlefield.

Schott, J. M., & Rossor, M. N. (2003). The grasp and other primitive reflexes. *Journal of Neurological and Neurosurgical Psychiatry, 74,* 558–560.

Schroots, J. J. F., van Dijkum, C., & Assink, M. H. J. (2004). Autobiographical memory from a life span perspective. *International Journal of Aging and Human Development, 58,* 69–85.

Schuetze, P., & Eiden, R. D. (2006). The association between maternal cocaine use during pregnancy and physiological regulation in 4- to 8-week-old infants: An examination of possible mediators and moderators. *Journal of Pediatric Psychology, 31,* 15–26,

Schull, W. J. (2003). The children of atomic bomb survivors: A synopsis. *Journal of Radiological Protection, 23,* 369–394.

Schulman, K. A., Berlin, J. A., Harless, W., Kerner, J. F., Sistrunk, S., & Gersh, B. J. (1999). The effect of race and sex on physicians' recommendations for cardiac catheterization. *New England Journal of Medicine, 340,* 618–626.

Schulte-Ruther, M., Markowitsch, H. J., Fink, G. R., & Piefke, M. (2007). Mirror neuron and theory of mind mechanisms involved in face-to-face interactions: A functional magnetic resonance imaging approach to empathy. *Journal of Cognitive Neuroscience, 19,* 1354–1372.

Schultz, R., & Beach, S. (1999). Caregiving as a risk factor for mortality: The caregiver health effects study. *Journal of the American Medical Association, 282,* 2215–2219.

Schultz, R., Burgio, L., Burns, R., Eisdorfer, C., Gallagher-Thompson, D., Gitlin, L. N., & Mahoney, D. F. (2003). Resources for enhancing Alzheimer's caregiver health (REACH): Overview, site-specific outcomes, and future directions. *Gerontologist, 43,* 514–520.

Schulz, M. S., Cowan, C. P., & Cowan, P. A. (2006). Promoting healthy beginnings: A randomized controlled trial. *Journal of Consulting and Clinical Psychology, 74,* 20–31.

Schulz, R., & Curnow, C. (1988). Peak performance and age among superathletes: Track and field, swimming, baseball, tennis, and golf. *Journal of Gerontology, 43,* P113–P120.

Schumacher, B., Garinis, G. A., & Hoeijmakers, J. H. J. (2007). Age to survive: DNA damage and aging. *Trends in Genetics, 24,* 77–85.

Schunk, D. H., & Pajares, F. (2005). Competence perceptions and academic functioning. In A. J. Andrew & C. S. Dweck (Eds.), *Handbook of competence and motivation* (pp. 85–104). New York: Guilford.

Schwanenflugel, P. J., Henderson, R. L., & Fabricius, W. V. (1998). Developing organization of mental verbs and theory of mind in middle childhood: Evidence from extensions. *Developmental Psychology, 34,* 512–524.

Schwartz, B. L., & Frazier, L. D. (2005). Tip-of-the-tongue states and aging: Contrasting psycholinguistic and metacognitive perspectives. *Journal of General Psychology, 132,* 377–391.

Schwartz, C. E., Wright, C. I., Shin, L. M., Kagan, J., & Rauch, S. L. (2003). Inhibited and uninhibited infants "grown up": Adult amygdalar response to novelty. *Science, 300,* 1952–1953.

Schwartz, D., Proctor, L. J., & Chien, D. H. (2001). The aggressive victim of bullying: Emotional and behavioral dysregulation as a pathway to victimization by peers. In J. Juonen & S. Graham (Eds.), *Peer harassment in school: The plight of the vulnerable and victimized* (pp. 147–174). New York: Guilford.

Schwartz, J. P., & Waldo, M. (2004). Group work with men who have committed partner abuse. In J. L. DeLucia-Waack, D. A. Gerrity, C. R. Kalodner, & M. T. Riva (Eds.), *Handbook of group counseling and psychotherapy* (pp. 576–592). Thousand Oaks, CA: Sage.

Schwartz, S. J., Côté, J. E., & Arnett, J. J. (2005). Identity and agency in emerging adulthood: Two developmental routes in the individualization process. *Youth and Society, 37,* 201–229.

Schwartz, S. J., Pantin, H., Prado, G., Sullivan, S., & Szapocznik, J. (2005). Family functioning, identity, and problem behavior: Immigrant early adolescents. *Journal of Early Adolescence, 25,* 392–420.

Schwarz, N. (1999). Self-reports: How the questions shape the answers. *American Psychologist, 54,* 93–105.

Schwebel, D. C., & Bounds, M. L. (2003). The role of parents and temperament on children's estimation of physical ability: Links to unintentional injury prevention. *Journal of Pediatric Psychology, 28,* 505–516.

Schwebel, D. C., & Brezausek, C. M. (2007). Father transitions in the household and young children's injury risk. *Psychology of Men and Masculinity, 8,* 173–184.

Schwebel, D. C., & Gaines, J. (2007). Pediatric unintentional injury: Behavioral risk factors and implications for prevention. *Journal of Developmental and Behavioral Pediatrics, 28,* 245–254.

Schwebel, D. C., Hodgens, J. B., & Sterling, S. (2006). How mothers parent their children with behavior disorders: Implications for unintentional injury risk. *Journal of Safety Research, 37,* 167–173.

Schweiger, W. K., & O'Brien, M. (2005). Special needs adoption: An ecological systems approach. *Family Relations, 54,* 512–522.

Schweinhart, L. J., Montie, J., Xiang, Z., Barnett, W. S., Belfield, C. R., & Nores, M. (2005). *Lifetime effects: The High/Scope Perry Preschool Study through age 40.* Ypsilanti, MI: High/Scope Press.

Schweizer, K., Moosbrugger, H., & Goldhammer, F. (2006). The structure of the relationship between attention and intelligence. *Intelligence, 33,* 589–611.

Schwier, C., van Maanen, C., Carpenter, M., & Tomasello, M. (2006). Rational imitation in 12-month-old infants. *Infancy, 10,* 303–311.

Schwimmer, J. B., Burwinkle, T. M., & Varni, J. W. (2003). Health-related quality of life of severely obese children and adolescents. *Journal of the American Medical Association, 289,* 1813–1819.

Scocco, P., Rapattoni, M., & Fantoni, G. (2006). Nursing home institutionalization: A source of eustress or distress for the elderly? *International Journal of Geriatric Psychiatry, 21,* 281–287.

Scott, C. S., Arthur, D., Owen, R., & Panizo, M. I. (1989). Black adolescents' emotional response to menarche. *Journal of the National Medical Association, 81,* 285–290.

Scott, L. D. (2003). The relation of racial identity and racial socialization to coping with discrimination among African Americans. *Journal of Black Studies, 20,* 520–538.

Scrutton, D. (2005). Influence of supine sleep positioning on early motor milestone acquisition. *Developmental Medicine and Child Neurology, 47,* 364.

Scully, D., & Marolla, J. (1998). "Riding the bull at Gilley's": Convicted rapists describe the rewards of rape. In M. E. Odem & J. Clay-Warner (Eds.), *Confronting rape and sexual assault* (pp. 181–198). Wilmington, DE: Scholarly Resources.

Seaton, E. K., Scottham, K. M., & Sellers, R. M. (2006). The status model of racial identity development in African American adolescents: Evidence of structure, trajectories, and well-being. *Child Development, 77,* 1416–1426.

Seeman, E. (2002). Pathogenesis of bone fragility in women and men. *Lancet, 359,* 1841–1850).

Seeman, E. (2008). Structural basis of growth-related gain and age-related loss of bone strength. *Rheumatology, 47,* iv2–iv8.

Seeman, T. E., Huang, M.-H., Bretsky, P., Crimmins, E., Launer, L., & Guralnik, J. M. (2005). Education and APOE-e4 in longitudinal cognitive decline: MacAurthur Studies of Successful Aging. *Journal of Gerontology, 60B,* P74–P83.

Segrin, C., & Nabi, R. L. (2002). Does television viewing cultivate unrealistic expectations about marriage? *Journal of Communication, 52,* 247–263.

Seiberling, K. A., & Conley, D. B. (2004). Aging and olfactory and taste function. *Otolaryngologic Clinics of North America, 37,* 1209–1228.

Seidman, E., Aber, J. L., & French, S. E. (2004). Assessing the transitions to middle and high school. *Journal of Adolescent Research, 19,* 3–30.

Seidman, E., Lambert, L. E., Allen, L., & Aber, J. L. (2003). Urban adolescents' transition to junior high school and protective family transactions. *Journal of Early Adolescence, 23,* 166–193.

Seifer, R., & Schiller, M. (1995). The role of parenting sensitivity, infant temperament, and dyadic interaction in attachment theory and assessment. In E. Waters, B. E. Vaughn, G. Posada, & K. Kondo-Ikemura (Eds.), Caregiving, cultural, and cognitive perspectives on secure-base behavior and working models: New growing points of attachment theory and research. *Monographs of the Society for Research in Child Development, 60*(2–3, Serial No. 244).

Seitz, V., & Apfel, N. H. (2005). Creating effective school-based interventions for pregnant teenagers. In R. DeV. Peters, B. Leadbeater, & R. J. McMahon (Eds.), *Resilience in children, families, and communities: Linking context to practice and policy* (pp. 65–82). New York: Kluwer Academic.

Selman, R. L. (1976). Social-cognitive understanding: A guide to educational and clinical practice. In T. Lickona (Ed.), *Moral development and behavior: Theory, research, and social issues* (pp. 299–316). New York: Holt, Rinehart and Winston.

Selman, R. L. (1980). *The growth of interpersonal understanding.* New York: Academic Press.

Selman, R. L., & Byrne, D. F. (1974). A structural-developmental analysis of levels of role taking in middle childhood. *Child Development, 45,* 803–806.

Seltzer, M. M., & Ryff, C. D. (1994). Parenting across the life span: The normative and nonnormative cases. In D. L. Featherman, R. M. Lerner, & M. Perlmutter (Eds.), *Lifespan development and behavior* (pp. 1–40). Hillsdale, NJ: Erlbaum.

Selwood, A., Johnston, K., Katona, C., Lyketsos, C., & Livingston, G. (2007). Systematic review of the effect of psychological interventions on family caregivers of people with dementia. *Journal of Affective Disorders, 101,* 75–89.

Selwyn, P. A. (1996). Before their time: A clinician's reflections on death and AIDS. In H. M. Spiro, M. G. M. Curnen, & L. P. Wandel (Eds.), *Facing death: Where culture, religion, and medicine meet* (pp. 33–37). New Haven, CT: Yale University Press.

Sen, M. G., Yonas, A., & Knill, D. C. (2001). Development of infants' sensitivity to surface contour information for spatial layout. *Perception, 30,* 167–176.

Senchina, D. S., & Kohut, M. L. (2007). Immunological outcomes of exercise in older adults. *Clinical Interventions in Aging, 2,* 3–16.

Serafini, T. E., & Adams, G. R. (2002). Functions of identity: Scale construction and validation. *Identity: An International Journal of Theory and Research, 2,* 361–389.

Serbin, L. A., Powlishta, K. K., & Gulko, J. (1993). The development of sex typing in middle childhood. *Monographs of the Society for Research in Child Development, 58*(2, Serial No. 232).

Sergeant, J. F., Ekerdt, D. J., & Chapin, R. (2008). Measurement of late-life residential relocation: Why are rates for such a manifest event so varied? *Journal of Gerontology, 63B,* S92–S98.

Sermon, K., Van Steirteghem, A., & Liebaers, I. (2004). Preimplantation genetic diagnosis. *Lancet, 363,* 1633–1641.

Service Canada. (2009). *Guide to Canada Pension Plan disability benefits.* Retrieved from www.servicecanada.gc.ca/eng/isp/pub/cpp/disability/guide/sectionb.shtml

Sesame Workshop. (2008). *Sesame Street season 37 press kit.* Retrieved from www.sesameworkshop.org/aboutus/pressroom/presskits/season37/sesame_street.php

Settles, I. H., Cortina, L. M., Malley, J., & Stewart, A. J. (2006). The climate for women in academic science: The good, the bad, and the changeable. *Psychology of Women Quarterly, 30,* 47–58.

Sewall, G., & Burns, L. H. (2006). Involuntary childlessness. In S. N. Covington & L. H. Burns (Eds.), *Infertility counseling: A comprehensive handbook for clinicians* (2nd ed., pp. 411–427). New York: Cambridge University Press.

Seymour, S. C. (1999). *Women, family, and child care in India.* Cambridge, UK: Cambridge University Press.

Shafer, V. L., & Garrido-Nag, K. (2007). The neurodevelopmental bases of language. In E. Hoff & M. Shatz (Eds.), *Blackwell handbook of language development* (pp. 21–45). Malden, MA: Blackwell.

Shah, T., Sullivan, K., & Carter, J. (2006). Sudden infant death syndrome and reported maternal smoking during pregnancy. *American Journal of Public Health, 96,* 1757–1759.

Shainess, N. (1961). A re-evaluation of some aspects of femininity through a study of menstruation: A preliminary report. *Comparative Psychiatry, 2,* 20–26.

Shanahan, L., McHale, S. M., Crouter, A. C., & Osgood, D. W. (2007). Warmth with mothers and fathers from middle childhood to late adolescence: Within- and between-families comparisions. *Developmental Psychology, 43,* 551–563.

Shanahan, M. J., Mortimer, J. T., & Krüger, H. (2002). Adolescence and adult work in the twenty first century. *Journal of Research on Adolescence, 12,* 99–120.

Shapiro, A. E., Gottman, J. M., & Carrere, S. (2000). The baby and the marriage: Identifying factors that buffer against decline in marital satisfaction after the first baby arrives. *Journal of Family Psychology, 14,* 59–70.

Shapka, J. D., & Keating, D. P. (2005). Structure and change in self-concept during adolescence. *Canadian Journal of Behavioural Science, 37,* 83–96.

Shatz, M. (2007). On the development of the field. In E. Hoff & M. Shatz (Eds.), *Blackwell handbook of language development* (pp. 1–20). Malden, MA: Blackwell.

Shaver, P., Furman, W., & Buhrmester, D. (1985). Transition to college: Network changes, social skills, and loneliness. In S. Duck & D. Perlman (Eds.), *Understanding personal relationships: An interdisciplinary approach* (pp. 193–219). London: Sage.

Shaw, B. A. (2005). Anticipated support from neighbors and physical functioning during later life. *Research on Aging, 27,* 503–525.

Shaw, D. S., Gilliom, M., Ingoldsby, E. M., & Nagin, D. S. (2003). Trajectories leading to school-age conduct problems. *Developmental Psychology, 39,* 189–200.

Shaw, P., Eckstrand, K., Sharp, W., Blumenthal, J., Lerch, J. P., & Greenstein, D. (2007, November 16). Attention-deficit/hyperactivity disorder is characterized by a delay in cortical maturation. *Proceedings of the National Academy of Sciences Online.* Retrieved from www.pnas.org/cgi/content/abstract/0707741104v1

Shea, J. L. (2006). Cross-cultural comparison of women's midlife symptom-reporting: A China study. *Culture, Medicine, and Psychiatry, 30,* 331–362.

Shedler, J., & Block, J. (1990). Adolescent drug use and psychological health: A longitudinal inquiry. *American Psychologist, 45,* 612–630.

Sheehan, G., Darlington, Y., Noller, P., & Feeney, J. (2004). Children's perceptions of their sibling relationships during parental separation and divorce. *Journal of Divorce and Remarriage, 41,* 69–94.

Sheehy, A., Gasser, T., Molinari, L., & Largo, R. H. (1999). An analysis of variance of the pubertal and midgrowth spurts for length and width. *Annals of Human Biology, 26,* 309–331.

Shenkin, J. D., Broffitt, B., Levy, S. M., & Warren, J. J. (2004). The association between environmental tobacco smoke and primary tooth caries. *Journal of Public Health Dentistry, 64,* 184–186.

Sherman, A. M., de Vries, B., & Lansford, J. E. (2000). Friendship in childhood and adulthood: Lessons across the life span. *International Journal of Aging and Human Development, 51,* 31–51.

Sherman, A. M., Lansford, J. E., & Volling, B. L. (2006). Sibling relationships and best friendships in young adulthood: Warmth, conflict, and well-being. *Personal Relationships, 13,* 151–165.

Sherman, C. W., Rosenblatt, D. E., & Antonucci, T. C. (2008). Elder abuse and mistreatment: A life span and cultural context. *Indian Journal of Gerontology, 22.*

Sherman, S. L., Freeman, S. B., Allen, E. G., & Lamb, N. E. (2005). Risk factors for nondisjunction of trisomy 21. *Cytogenetic Genome Research, 111,* 273–280.

Sherrod, L. R., & Spiewak, G. S. (2008). Possible interrelationships between civic engagement, positive youth development, and spirituality/religiosity. In R. M. Lerner, R. W. Roeser, & E. Phelps (Eds.), *Positive youth development and spirituality: From theory to research* (pp. 322–338). West Conshohocken, PA: Templeton Foundation Press.

Sherry, B., McDivitt, J., Brich, L. L., Cook, F. H., Sanders, S., Prish, J. L., Francis, L. A., & Scanlon, K. S. (2004). Attitudes, practices, and concerns about child feeding and child weight status among socioeconomically diverse white, Hispanic, and African-American mothers. *Journal of the American Dietetic Association, 104,* 215–221.

Shields, G., King, W., Fulks, S., & Fallon, L. F. (2002). Determinants of perceived safety among the elderly: An exploratory study. *Journal of Gerontological Social Work, 38,* 73–83.

Shields, M. (2005). *Overweight Canadian children and adolescents.* Nutrition: Findings from the Canadian Community Health Survey. Statistics Canada Catalogue No. 82-620-MWE2005001. Retrieved from www.statcan.ca/english/research/82-620-MIE/2005001/pdf/cobesity.pdf

Shimada, S., & Hiraki, K. (2006). Infant's brain responses to live and televised action. *NeuroImage, 32,* 930–939.

Shimizu, H. (2001). Japanese adolescent boys' senses of empathy (omoiyari) and Carol Gilligan's perspectives on the morality of care: A phenomenological approach. *Culture and Psychology, 7,* 453–475.

Shin, J. S., Hong, A., Solomon, M. J., & Lee, C. S. (2006). The role of telomeres and telomerase in the pathology of human cancer and aging. *Pathology, 38,* 103–113.

Shinn, M., Schteingart, J. S., Williams, N. C., Carlin-Mathis, J., Bialo-Karagis, N., Becker-Klein, R., & Weitzman, B. C. (2008). Long-term associations of homelessness with children's well-being. *American Behavioral Scientist, 51,* 789–809.

Shipman, H. L., Brickhouse, N. W., Dagher, Z., & Letts, W. J., IV. (2002). Changes in student views of religion and science in a college astronomy course. *Science Education, 86,* 526–547.

Shipman, K. L., Zeman, J., Nesin, A. E., & Fitzgerald, M. (2003). Children's strategies for displaying anger and sadness: What works with whom? *Merrill-Palmer Quarterly, 49,* 100–122.

Shock, N. W. (1977). Biological theories of aging. In J. E. Birren & K. W. Schaie (Eds.), *Handbook of the psychology of aging* (pp. 103–115). New York: Van Nostrand Reinhold.

Shonk, S. M., & Cicchetti, D. (2001). Maltreatment, competency deficits, and risk for academic and behavioral maladjustment. *Developmental Psychology, 37,* 3–17.

Shonkoff, J., & Phillips, D. (Eds.). (2001). *Neurons to neighborhoods: The science of early childhood development.* Washington, DC: National Academy Press.

Shuey, K., & Hardy, M. A. (2003). Assistance to aging parents and parents-in-law: Does lineage affect family allocation decisions? *Journal of Marriage and Family, 65,* 418–431.

Shultz, K. S., & Wang, M. (2007). The influence of specific physical health conditions on retirement decisions. *International Journal of Aging and Human Development, 65,* 149–161.

Shumaker, S. A., Legault, C., Thal, L., Wallace, R. B., Ockene, J. K., & Hendrix, S. L. (2003). Estrogen plus progestin and the incidence of dementia and mild cognitive impairment in postmenopausal women: The Women's Health Initiative Memory Study: A randomized controlled trial. *Journal of the American Medical Association, 289,* 2651–2662.

Shure, M. B., & Aberson, B. (2005). Enhancing the process of resilience through effective thinking. In S. Goldstein & R. B. Brooks (Eds.), *Handbook of resilience in children* (pp. 373–394). New York: Kluwer Academic.

Shwalb, D. W., Nakawaza, J., Yamamoto, T., & Hyun, J.-H. (2004). Fathering in Japanese, Chinese, and Korean cultures: A review of the research literature. In M. E. Lamb (Ed.), *The role of the father in child development* (4th ed., pp. 146–181). Hoboken, NJ: Wiley.

Shweder, R. A., Goodnow, J. J., Hatano, G., LeVine, R. A., Markus, H. R., & Miller, P. J. (2006). The cultural psychology of development: One mind, many mentalities. In R. M. Lerner (Ed.), *Handbook of child psychology: Vol. 1. Theoretical models of human development* (6th ed., pp. 716–792). Hoboken, NJ: Wiley.

Sidebotham, P., Heron, J., & the ALSPAC Study Team. (2003). Child maltreatment in the "children of the nineties:" The role of the child. *Child Abuse and Neglect, 27,* 337–352.

Siebenbruner, J., Zimmer-Gembeck, M. J., & Egeland, B. (2007). Sexual partners and contraceptive use: A 16-year prospective study predicting abstinence and risk behavior. *Journal of Research on Adolescence, 17,* 179–206.

Siegel, S. J., Beschke, J., Powers, E. T., Kelly, J. W. (2007). The oxidative stress metabolite 4-hydroxynonenal promotes Alzheimer protofibril formation. *Biochemistry, 46,* 1503–1510.

Siegler, R. S. (1996). *Emerging minds: The process of change in children's thinking.* New York: Oxford University Press.

Siegler, R. S. (2007). Cognitive variability. *Developmental Science, 10,* 104–109.

Siegler, R. S., & Alibali, M. W. (2005). *Children's thinking* (4th ed.). Upper Saddle River, NJ: Prentice-Hall.

Siegler, R. S., & Mu, Y. (2008). Chinese children excel on novel mathematics problems even before elementary school. *Psychological Science, 19,* 759–763.

Siegler, R. S., & Svetina, M. (2006). What leads children to adopt new strategies? A microgenetic/cross-sectional study of class inclusion. *Child Development, 77,* 997–1015.

Siegrist, J., Wahrendorf, M., von dem Knesebeck, O., Jurges, H., & Borsch-Supan, A. (2007). Quality of work, well-being, and intended early retirement of older employees—Baseline results from the SHARE study. *European Journal of Public Health, 17,* 62–68.

Siervogel, R. M., Maynard, L. M., Wisemandle, W. A., Roche, A. F., Guo, S. S., Chumlea, W. C., & Towne, B. (2000). Annual changes in total body fat and fat-free mass in children from 8 to 18 years in relation to changes in body mass index: The Fels Longitudinal Study. *Annals of the New York Academy of Sciences, 904,* 420–423.

Sigman, M. (1995). Nutrition and child development: More food for thought. *Current Directions in Psychological Science, 4,* 52–55.

Silk, J. S., Morris, A. S., Kanaya, T., & Steinberg, L. (2003). Psychological control and autonomy granting: Opposite ends of a continuum or distinct constructs? *Journal of Research on Adolescence, 13,* 113–128.

Silvén, M. (2001). Attention in very young infants predicts learning of first words. *Infant Behavior and Development, 24,* 229–237.

Silver, E. J., & Bauman, L. J. (2006). The association of sexual experience with attitudes, beliefs, and risk behaviors of inner-city adolescents. *Journal of Research on Adolescence, 16,* 29–45.

Silver, M. H., & Perls, T. T. (2000). Is dementia the price of a long life? An optimistic report from centenarians. *Journal of Geriatric Psychiatry, 33,* 71–79.

Silverberg, S. B. (1996). Parents' well-being at their children's transition to adolescence. In C. D. Ryff & M. M. Seltzer (Eds.), *The parental experience in midlife* (pp. 215–254). Chicago: University of Chicago Press.

Silverman, I., Choi, J., & Peters, M. (2007). The hunter-gatherer theory of sex differences in spatial abilities. *Archives of Sexual behavior, 36,* 261–268.

Silverman, P. R. (2004). Dying and bereavement in historical perspective. In J. Berzoff & P. R. Silverman (Eds.), *Living with dying: A handbook for end-of-life healthcare practitioners* (pp. 128–149). New York: Columbia University Press.

Silverman, P. R., & Nickman, S. L. (1996). Children's construction of their dead parents. In D. Klass, P. R. Silverman, & S. L. Nickman (Eds.), *Continuing bonds: New understandings of grief* (pp. 73–86). Washington, DC: Taylor & Francis.

Silverman, W. K., & Pina, A. A. (2008). Psychosocial treatments for phobic and anxiety disorders in youth. In R. G. Steele, T. D. Elkin, & M. Roberts (Eds.), *Handbook of evidence-based therapies for children and adolescents: Bridging science and practice* (pp. 65–82). New York: Springer.

Silverstein, M., & Bengtson, V. L. (1991). Do close parent–child relations reduce the mortality risk of older parents? *Journal of Health and Social Behavior, 32,* 382–395.

Silverstein, M., Conroy, S., Wang, H., Giarrusso, R., & Bengtson, V. L. (2002). Reciprocity in parent–child relations over the adult life course. *Journal of Gerontology, 57B,* S3–S13.

Silverstein, M., & Long, J. D. (1998). Trajectories of grandparents' perceived solidarity with adult grandchildren: A growth curve analysis over 23 years. *Journal of Marriage and the Family, 60,* 912–923.

Silverstein, M., & Marenco, A. (2001). How Americans enact the grandparent role across the family life course. *Journal of Family Issues, 22,* 493–522.

Silvi, J. (2004). Deaths from motor vehicle traffic accidents in selected countries of the Americas, 1985–2001. *Epidemiological Bulletin, 25,* 2–5.

Sim, T. N., & Koh, S. F. (2003). A domain conceptualization of adolescent susceptibility to peer pressure. *Journal of Research on Adolescence, 13,* 57–80.

Simcock, G., & DeLoache, J. (2006). Get the picture? The effects of iconicity on toddlers' reenactment from picture books. *Developmental Psychology, 42,* 1352–1357.

Simcock, G., & Hayne, H. (2002). Breaking the barrier? Children fail to translate their preverbal memories into language. *Psychological Science, 13,* 225–231.

Simcock, G., & Hayne, H. (2003). Age-related changes in verbal and nonverbal memory during early childhood. *Developmental Psychology, 39,* 805–814.

Simmons, R. G., & Blyth, D. A. (1987). *Moving into adolescence.* New York: Aldine De Gruyter.

Simon, N. M., Smoller, J. W., McNamara, K. L., Maser, R. S., Zlata, A. K., & Pollack, M. H. (2006). Telomere shortening and mood disorders: Preliminary support for a chronic stress model of accelerated aging. *Biological Psychiatry, 60,* 432–435.

Simoneau, M., & Markovits, H. (2003). Reasoning with premises that are not empirically true: Evidence for the role of inhibition and retrieval. *Developmental Psychology, 39,* 964–975.

Simons, J. S., Dodson, C. S., Bell, D., & Schachter, D. L. (2004). Specific-and partial-source memory: Effects of aging. *Psychology and Aging, 19,* 689–694.

Simons, L. G., Chen, Y. F., Simons, R. L., Brody, G., & Cutrona, C. (2006). Parenting practices and child adjustment in different types of households: A study of African-American families. *Journal of Family Issues, 27,* 803–825.

Simons, R. L., Whitbeck, L. B., Conger, R. D., & Wu, C.-I. (1991). Intergenerational transmission of harsh parenting. *Developmental Psychology, 27,* 159–171.

Simons-Morton, B. G., & Haynie, D. L. (2003). Growing up drug free: A developmental challenge. In M. H. Bornstein, L. Davidson, C. L. M. Keyes, K. A. Moore, & the Center for Child Well-Being (Eds.), *Well-being: Positive development across the life course* (pp. 109–122). Mahwah, NJ: Erlbaum.

Simonton, D. K. (1991). Creative productivity through the adult years. *Generations, 15*(2), 13–16.

Simonton, D. K. (2000). Creativity: Cognitive, personal, developmental, and social aspects. *American Psychologist, 55,* 151–158.

Simonton, D. K. (2006). Historiometric methods. In K. A. Ericsson, N. Charness, P. J. Feltovich, & R. R. Hoffman (Eds.), *The Cambridge handbook of expertise and expert performance* (pp. 319–335). New York: Cambridge University Press.

Simpson, J. A., & Harris, B. A. (1994). Interpersonal attraction. In A. L. Weber & J. H. Harvey (Eds.), *Perspectives on close relationships* (pp. 45–66). Boston: Allyn and Bacon.

Simpson, J. A., Rholes, W. S., Campbell, L., Tran, S., & Wilson, C. L. (2003). Adult attachment, the transition to parenthood, and depressive symptoms. *Journal of Personality and Social Psychology, 84,* 1172–1187.

Simpson, J. L., de la Cruz, F., Swerdloff, R. S., Samango-Sprouse, C., Skakkebaek, N. E., & Graham, J. M., Jr. (2003). Klinefelter syndrome: Expanding the phenotype and identifying new research directions. *Genetic Medicine, 5,* 460–468.

Simpson, J. M. (2001). Infant stress and sleep deprivation as an aetiological basis for the sudden infant death syndrome. *Early Human Development, 61,* 1–43.

Simpson, R. (2004). Masculinity at work: The experiences of men in female dominated occupations. *Work, Employment and Society, 18,* 349–368.

Simpson, R. (2005). Men in non-traditional occupations: Career entry, career orientation and experience of role strain. *Gender, Work and Organization, 12,* 363–380.

Singer, D. G., & Singer, J. L. (2005). *Imagination and play in the electronic age.* Cambridge, MA: Harvard University Press.

Singer, L. T., Minnes, S., Short, E., Arendt, R., Farkas, K., Lewis, B., & Klein, N. (2004). Cognitive outcomes of preschool children with prenatal cocaine exposure. *Journal of the American Medical Association, 291,* 2448–2456.

Singer, Y., Bachner, Y. G., Shvartzman, P., & Carmel, S. (2005). Home death—the caregivers' experiences. *Journal of Pain and Symptom Management, 30,* 70–74.

Singleton, J. L., & Newport, E. L. (2004). When learners surpass their models: The acquisition of American Sign Language from inconsistent input. *Cognitive Psychology, 49,* 370–407.

Sinkkonen, J., Anttila, R., & Siimes, M. A. (1998). Pubertal maturation and changes in self-image in early adolescent Finnish boys. *Journal of Youth and Adolescence, 27,* 209–218.

Sinnott, J. D. (1998). *The development of logic in adulthood: Postformal thought and its applications.* New York: Plenum.

Sinnott, J. D. (2003). Postformal thought and adult development: Living in balance. In J. Demick & C. Andreoletti (Eds.), *Handbook of adult development* (pp. 221–238). New York: Kluwer Academic.

Sinnott, J. D. (2008). Cognitive and representational development in adults. In K. B. Cartwright (Ed.), *Literacy processes: Cognitive flexibility in learning and teaching* (pp. 42–61). New York: Guilford.

Skaff, M. M. (2006). The view from the driver's seat: Sense of control in the baby boomers at midlife. In. S. K. Whitbourne & S. L. Willis (Eds.), *The baby boomers grow up: Contemporary perspectives on midlife* (pp. 185–204). Mahwah, NJ: Erlbaum.

Skiba, R. J., & Rausch, M. K. (2006). Zero tolerance, suspension, and expulsion: Questions of equity and effectiveness. In C. M. Evertson & C. S. Weinstein (Eds.), *Handbook of classroom management: Research, practice, and contemporary issues* (pp. 1063–1089). Mahwah, NJ: Erlbaum.

Skinner, B. F. (1957). *Verbal behavior.* New York: Appleton-Century-Crofts.

Skinner, E. A., Zimmer-Gembeck, M. J., & Connell, J. P. (1998). Individual differences and the development of perceived control. *Monographs of the Society for Research in Child Development, 63*(2–3, Serial No. 254).

Skoe, E. E. A. (1998). The ethic of care: Issues in moral development. In E. E. A. Skoe & A. L. von der Lippe (Eds.), *Personality development in adolescence* (pp. 143–171). London: Routledge.

Slade, A., Belsky, J., Aber, J. L., & Phelps, J. L. (1999). Mothers' representations of their relationships with their toddlers: Links to adult attachment and observed mothering. *Developmental Psychology, 35,* 611–619.

Slater, A. (2001). Visual perception. In G. Bremner & A. Fogel (Eds.), *Blackwell handbook of infant development* (pp. 5–34). Malden, MA: Blackwell.

Slater, A., Bremner, G., Johnson, S. P., Sherwood, P., Hayes, R., & Brown, E. (2000). Newborn infants' preference for attractive faces: The role of internal and external facial features. *Infancy, 1,* 265–274.

Slater, A., Brown, E., Mattock, A., & Bornstein, M. H. (1996). Continuity and change in habituation in the first 4 months from birth. *Journal of Reproductive and Infant Psychology, 14,* 187–194.

Slater, A., & Quinn, P. C. (2001). Face recognition in the newborn infant. *Infant and Child Development, 10,* 21–24.

Slaughter, V., & Griffiths, M. (2007). Death understanding and fear of death in young children. *Clinical Child Psychology and Psychiatry, 12,* 525–535.

Slaughter, V., Jaakkola, R., & Carey, S. (1999). Constructing a coherent theory: Children's biological understanding of life and death. In M. Siegel & C. C. Petersen (Eds.), *Children's understanding of biology and health* (pp. 71–96). Cambridge, UK: Cambridge University Press.

Slaughter, V., & Lyons, M. (2003). Learning about life and death in early childhood. *Cognitive Psychology, 46,* 1–30.

Sleet, D. A., & Mercy, J. A. (2003). Promotion of safety, security, and well-being. In M. H. Bornstein, L. Davidson, C. M. M. Keyes, K. A. Moore, & the Center for Child Well-Being (Eds.), *Well-being: Positive development across the life course* (pp. 81–97). Mahwah, NJ: Erlbaum.

Sloan, S., Gildea, A., Stewart, M., Sneddon, H., & Iwaniec, D. (2008). Early weaning is related to weight and rate of weight gain in infancy. *Child: Care, Health and Development, 34,* 59–64.

Slobin, D. I. (1985). Crosslinguistic evidence for the language-making capacity. In D. I. Slobin (Ed.), *The crosslinguistic study of language acquisition: Vol. 2. Theoretical issues.* Hillsdale, NJ: Erlbaum.

Slobin, D. I. (1997). *The crosslinguistic study of language acquisition: Vol. 5. Expanding the contexts.* Mahwah, NJ: Erlbaum.

Slonims, V., & McConachie, H. (2006). Analysis of mother-infant interaction in infants with Down syndrome and typically developing infants. *American Journal of Mental Retardation, 111,* 273–289.

Sloter, E., Schmid, T. E., Marchetti, F., Eskenazi, B., & Nath, J. (2006). Quantitative effects of male age on sperm motion. *Human Reproduction, 21,* 2868–2875.

Slusher, M. P., Mayer, C. J., & Dunkle, R. E. (1996). Gays and lesbians older and wiser (GLOW): A support group for older gay people. *Gerontologist, 36,* 118–123.

Slutske, W. S., Hunt-Carter, E. E., Nabors-Oberg, R. E., Sher, K. J., Bucholz, K. K., & Madden, P. A. F. (2004). Do college students drink more than their non-college-attending peers? Evidence from a population-based longitudinal female twin study. *Journal of Abnormal Psychology, 113,* 530–540.

Slyper, A. H. (2006). The pubertal timing controversy in the USA, and a review of possible causative factors for the advance in timing of onset of puberty. *Clinical Endocrinology, 65,* 1–8.

Small, M. (1998). *Our babies, ourselves.* New York: Anchor.

Smart, J., & Hiscock, H. (2007). Early infant crying and sleeping problems: A pilot study of impact on parental well-being and parent-endorsed strategies for management. *Journal of Paediatrics and Child Health, 43,* 284–290.

Smetana, J. G. (2002). Culture, autonomy, and personal jurisdiction in adolescent–parent relationships. In R. V. Kail & H. W. Reese (Eds.), *Advances in child development and behavior* (Vol. 29, pp. 51–87). San Diego, CA: Academic Press.

Smetana, J. G. (2006). Social-cognitive domain theory: Consistencies and variations in children's moral and social judgments. In M. Killen & J. G. Smetana (Eds.), *Handbook of moral development* (pp. 119–154). Mahwah, NJ: Erlbaum.

Smetana, J. G., Metzger, A., & Campione-Barr, N. (2004). African-American late adolescents' relationships with parents: Developmental transitions and longitudinal patterns. *Child Development, 75,* 932–947.

Smith, B. H., Barkley, R. A., & Shapiro, C. J. (2006). Attention-deficit/hyperactivity disorder. In E. J. Mash & R. A. Barkley (Eds.), *Treatment of childhood disorders* (3rd ed., pp. 65–136). New York: Guilford.

Smith, C., Perou, R., & Lesesne, C. (2002). Parent education. M. H. Bornstein (Ed.), *Handbook of parenting* (Vol. 4, pp. 389–410). Mahwah, NJ: Erlbaum.

Smith, C. D., Chebrolu, H., Wekstein, D. R., Schmitt, F. A., & Markesbery, W. R. (2007). Age and gender effects on human brain anatomy: A voxel-based morphometric study in healthy elderly. *Neurobiology of Aging, 28,* 1075–1087.

Smith, C. L., Calkins, S. D., Keane, S. P., Anastopoulos, A. D., & Shelton, T. L. (2004). Predicting stability and change in toddler behavior problems: Contributions of maternal behavior and child gender. *Developmental Psychology, 40,* 29–42.

Smith, C. M., & Cotter, V. T. (2008). Age-related changes in health. In E. Capezuti, D. Zwicker, M. Mezey, T. T. Fulmer, & D. Gray-Miceli (Eds.), *Evidence-based geritric nursing protocols for best practice* (3rd ed., pp. 431–458). New York: Springer.

Smith, D. B., & Moen, P. (2004). Retirement satisfaction for retirees and their spouses: Do gender and the retirement decision-making process matter? *Journal of Family Issues, 25,* 262–285.

Smith, D. C. (1993). The terminally ill patient's right to be in denial. *Omega, 27,* 115–121.

Smith, G. C., Kohn, S. J., Savage-Stevens, S. E., Finch, J. J., Ingate, R., & Lim, Y. (2000). The effects of interpersonal and personal agency on perceived control and psychological well-being in adulthood. *Gerontologist, 40,* 458–468.

Smith, J., & Baltes, P. B. (1999). Life-span perspectives on development. In M. H. Bornstein & M. E. Lamb (Eds.), *Developmental psychology: An advanced textbook* (4th ed., pp. 275–311). Mahwah, NJ: Erlbaum.

Smith, J., Duncan, G. J., & Lee, K. (2003). The black–white test score gap in young children: Contributions of test and family characteristics. *Applied Developmental Science, 7,* 239–252.

Smith, J., & Freund, A. M. (2002). The dynamics of possible selves in old age. *Journal of Gerontology, 57B,* P492–P500.

Smith, J., & Ross, H. (2007). Training parents to mediate sibling disputes affects children's negotiation and conflict understanding. *Child Development, 78,* 790–805.

Smith, L. B., Jones, S. S., Gershkoff-Stowe, L., & Samuelson, L. (2002). Object name learning provides on-the-job training for attention. *Psychological Science, 13,* 13–19.

Smith, M. (Ed.). (2002). *Sex without consent.* New York: New York University Press.

Smith, N., Young, A., & Lee, C. (2004). Optimism, health-related hardiness and well-being among older Australian women. *Journal of Health Psychology, 9,* 741–752.

Smith, P., Perrin, S., Yule, W., & Rabe-Hesketh, S. (2001). War exposure and maternal reactions in the psychological adjustment of children from Bosnia-Hercegovina. *Journal of Child Psychology and Psychiatry and Allied Disciplines, 42,* 395–404.

Smith, P. K., Ananiadou, K., & Cowie, H. (2003). Interventions to reduce school bullying. *Canadian Journal of Psychiatry, 48,* 591–599.

Smith, P. K., & Drew, L. M. (2002). Grandparenthood. In M. H. Bornstein (Ed.), *Handbook of parenting, Vol. 3* (2nd ed., pp. 141–172). Mahwah, NJ: Erlbaum.

Smith, R. A., Cokkinides, V., & Brawley, O. W. (2008). Cancer screening in the United States, 2008: A review of current American Cancer Society Guidelines and Cancer Screening Issues. *CA: Cancer Journal for Clinicians, 58,* 161–179.

Smith, T. W. (2006). Personality as risk and resilience in physical health. *Current Directions in Psychological Science, 15,* 227–231.

Smith, T. W., Gallo, L. C., & Ruiz, J. M. (2003). Toward a social psychophysiology of cardiovascular reactivity: Interpersonal concepts and methods in the study of stress and coronary disease. In J. Suls & K. Wallston (Eds.), *Social psychological foundations of health and illness* (pp. 335–366). Oxford, U.K.: Blackwell.

Smith, T. W., Glazer, K., Ruiz, J. M., & Gallo, L. C. (2004). Hostility, anger, aggressiveness, and coronary heart disease: An interpersonal perspective on personality, emotion, and health. *Journal of Personality, 72,* 1217–1270.

Smith, T. W., & Mackenzie, J. (2006). Personality and risk of physical illness. *Annual Review of Clinical Psychology, 2,* 435–467.

Smock, P. J., & Gupta, S. (2002). *Cohabitation in contemporary North America.* In A. Booth & A. C. Crouter (Eds.), *Just living together* (pp. 53–84). Mahwah, NJ: Erlbaum.

Snarey, J., Son, L., Kuehne, V. S., Hauser, S., & Vaillant, G. (1987). The role of parenting in men's psychosocial development: A longitudinal study of early adulthood infertility and midlife generativity. *Developmental Psychology, 23,* 593–603.

Sneed, J. R., & Whitbourne, S. K. (2001). Identity processing styles and the need for self-esteem in middle-aged and older adults. *International Journal of Aging and Human Development, 52,* 311–321.

Sneed, J. R., & Whitbourne, S. K. (2003). Identity processing and self-consciousness in middle and later adulthood. *Journal of Gerontology, 58B,* P313–P319.

Sneed, J. R., Whitbourne, S. K., & Culang, M. E. (2006). Trust, identity, and ego integrity: Modeling Erikson's core stages over 34 years. *Journal of Adult Development, 13,* 148–157.

Snell, E. K., Adam, E. K., & Duncan, G. J. (2007). Sleep and the body mass index and overweight status of children and adolescents. *Child Development, 78,* 309–323.

Snidman, N., Kagan, J., Riordan, L., & Shannon, D. C. (1995). Cardiac function and behavioral reactivity. *Psychophysiology, 32,* 199–207.

Snow, C. E., & Beals, D. E. (2006). Mealtime talk that supports literacy development. In R. W. Larson, A. R. Wiley, & K. R. Branscomb (Eds.), *Family mealtime as a context of development and socialization* (pp. 51–66). San Francisco: Jossey-Bass.

Snow, C. E., & Kang, J. Y. (2006). Becoming bilingual, biliterate, and bicultural. In K. A. Renninger & I. E. Sigel (Eds.), *Handbook of child psychology: Vol. 4. Child psychology in practice* (6th ed., pp. 75–102). Hoboken, NJ: Wiley.

Snyder, J., Brooker, M., Patrick, M. R., Snyder, A., Schrepferman, L., & Stoolmiller, M. (2003). Observed peer victimization during early elementary school: Continuity, growth, and relation to risk for child antisocial and depressive behavior. *Child Development, 74,* 1881–1898.

Soares, C. N. (2007). Menopausal transition and depression: Who is at risk and how to treat it? *Expert Review of Neurotherapeutics, 7,* 1285–1293.

Sobel, D. M. (2006). How fantasy benefits young children's understanding of pretense. *Developmental Science, 9,* 63–75.

Social Security and Medicare Board of Trustees. (2009). *Status of the Social Security and Medicare program.* Retrieved from www.ssa.gov/OACT/TR

Society for Research in Child Development. (2007). *SRCD ethical standards for research with children.* Retrieved from www.srcd.org/index.php?option=com_content&task=view&id=68&Itemid=110

Society of Obstetricians and Gynaecologists. (2008). *Record high caesarean rate rasing concerns among Canada's obstetricians.* Retrieved from www.sogc.org/media/pdf/articles/artcaesareanrate080625.pdf

Soderstrom, M., Dolbier, C., Leiferman, J., & Steinhardt, M. (2000). The relationship of hardiness, coping strategies, and perceived stress to symptoms of illness. *Journal of Behavioral Medicine, 23,* 311–328.

Soderstrom, M., Seidl, A., Nelson, D. G. K., & Jusczyk, P. W. (2003). The prosodic bootstrapping of

phrases: Evidence from prelinguistic infants. *Journal of Memory and Language, 49,* 249–267.
Sofi, F., Cesari, F., Abbate, R., Gensini, G. F., & Casini, A. (2008). Adherence to Mediterranean diet and health status: Meta-analysis. *British Medical Journal, 337,* a1344.
Solomon, G. B., & Bredemeier, B. J. L. (1999). Children's moral conceptions of gender stratification in sport. *International Journal of Sport Psychology, 30,* 350–368.
Solomon, J. C., & Marx, J. (1995). "To grandmother's house we go": Health and school adjustment of children raised solely by grandparents. *Gerontologist, 35,* 386–394.
Somary, K., & Stricker, G. (1998). Becoming a grandparent: A longitudinal study of expectations and early experiences as a function of sex and lineage. *Gerontologist, 38,* 53–61.
Sondergaard, C., Henriksen, T. B., Obel, C., & Wisborg, K. (2002). Smoking during pregnancy and infantile colic. *Journal of the American Academy of Child and Adolescent Psychiatry, 41,* 147.
Sophian, C. (1995). Representation and reasoning in early numerical development: Counting, conservation, and comparisons between sets. *Child Development, 66,* 559–577.
Sorensen, A. (2007). The demography of the Third Age. In J. B. James & P. Wink (Eds.), *Annual review of gerontology and geriatrics* (Vol. 26, pp. 1–18). New York: Springer.
Sörensen, S., & Pinquart, M. (2005). Racial and ethnic differences in the relationship of caregiving stressors, resources, and sociodemographic variables to caregiver depression and perceived physical health. *Aging and Mental Health, 9,* 482–495.
Sørensen, T. I., Holst, C., & Stunkard, A. J. (1998). Adoption study of environmental modifications of the genetic influences on obesity. *International Journal of Obesity and Related Metabolic Disorders, 22,* 73–81.
Sosa, R., Kennell, J., Klaus, M., Robertson, S., & Urrutia, J. (1980). The effect of a supportive companion on perinatal problems, length of labor, and mother–infant interaction. *New England Journal of Medicine, 303,* 597–600.
Sowell, E. R., Thompson, P. M., Welcome, S. E., Henkenius, A. L., Toga, A. W., & Peterson, B. S. (2003). Cortical abnormalities in children and adolescents with attention-deficit hyperactivity disorder. *Lancet, 362,* 1699–1707.
Sowell, E. R., Trauner, D. A., Gamst, A., & Jernigan, T. (2002). Development of cortical and subcortical brain structures in childhood and adolescence: A structural MRI study. *Developmental Medicine and Child Neurology, 44,* 4–16.
Sowers, M. F., Zheng, H., Tomey, K., Karvonen-Gutierrez, M. J., Li, X., Matheos, Y., & Symons, J. (2007). Changes in body composition in women over six years at midlife: Ovarian and chronological aging. *Journal of Clinical Endocrinology and Metabolism, 92,* 895–901.
Spadoni, A. D., McGee, C. L., Frayer, S. L., & Riley, E. P. (2007). Neuroimaging and fetal alcohol spectrum disorders. *Neuroscience and Biobehavioral Reviews, 31,* 239–245.
Spear, L. P. (2004). Adolescent brain development and animal models. In R. E. Dahl & L. P. Spear (Eds.), *Adolescent brain development: Vulnerabilities and opportunities* (pp. 23–26). New York: New York Academy of Sciences.
Spear, L. P. (2008). The psychobiology of adolescence. In K. K. Kline (Ed.), *Authoritative communities: The scientific case for nurturing the whole child* (pp. 263–280). New York: Springer Science + Business Media.
Spector, A. Z. (2006). Fatherhood and depression: A review of risks, effects, and clinical application. *Issues in Mental Health Nursing, 27,* 867–883.
Speece, D. L., Ritchey, K. D., Cooper, D. H., Roth, F. P., & Schatschneider, C. (2004). Growth in early reading skills from kindergarten to third grade. *Contemporary Educational Psychology, 29,* 312–332.
Speece, M. W., & Brent, S. B. (1996). The development of children's understanding of death. In C. A. Corr & D. M. Corr (Eds.), *Handbook of childhood death and bereavement* (pp. 29–50). New York: Springer.
Spelke, E. S. (2000). Core knowledge. *American Psychologist, 55,* 1233–1242.
Spelke, E. S. (2004). Core knowledge. In N. Kanwisher & J. Duncan (Eds.), *Attention and performance* (Vol. 20, pp. 29–56). Oxford, UK: Oxford University Press.
Spelke, E. S., & Kinzler, K. D. (2007). Core knowledge. *Developmental Science, 10,* 89–96.
Spence, M. J., & DeCasper, A. J. (1987). Prenatal experience with low-frequency maternal voice sounds influences neonatal perception of maternal voice samples. *Infant Behavior and Development, 10,* 133–142.
Spencer, J. P., & Perone, S. (2008). Defending qualitative change: The view from dynamical systems theory. *Child Development, 79,* 1639–1647.
Spencer, J. P., Verejiken, B., Diedrich, F. J., & Thelen, E. (2000). Posture and the emergence of manual skills. *Developmental Science, 3,* 216–233.
Spencer, P. E. (2000). Looking without listening: Is audition a prerequisite for normal development of visual attention in infancy? *Journal of Deaf Studies and Education, 5,* 291–302.
Spencer, P. E., & Lederberg, A. (1997). Different modes, different models: Communication and language of young deaf children and their mothers. In L. B. Adamson & M. Romski (Eds.), *Communication and language acquisition: Discoveries from atypical development* (pp. 203–230). Baltimore, MD: Paul H. Brookes.
Spencer, P. E., & Meadow-Orlans, K. P. (1996). Play, language, and maternal responsiveness: A longitudinal study of deaf and hearing infants. *Child Development, 67,* 3176–3191.
Spera, C. (2005). A review of the relationship among parenting practices, parenting styles, and adolescent school achievement. *Educational Psychology Review, 17,* 125–146.
Spere, K. A., Schmidt, L. A., Theall-Honey, L. A., & Martin-Chang, S. (2004). Expressive and receptive language skills of temperamentally shy preschoolers. *Infant and Child Development, 13,* 123–133.
Spira, A. (1992). *Les comportements sexuels en France.* Paris: La documentation Française.
Spirito, A., & Esposito-Smythers, C. (2006). Attempted and completed suicide. *Annual Review of Clinical Psychology, 2,* 237–266.
Spirito, A., Valeri, S., Boergers, J., & Donaldson, D. (2003). Predictors of continued suicidal behavior in adolescents following a suicide attempt. *Journal of Clinical Child and Adolescent Psychology, 32,* 284–289.
Spitz, R. A. (1946). Anaclitic depression. *Psychoanalytic Study of the Child, 2,* 313–342.
Spitze, G., & Gallant, M. P. (2004). "The bitter with the sweet": Older adults' strategies for handling ambivalence in relations with their adult children. *Research on Aging, 26,* 387–412.
Spock, B., & Needlman, R. (2004). *Dr. Spock's baby and child care* (8th ed.). New York: Pocket.
Spokane, A. R., & Cruza-Guet, M. C. (2005). Holland's theory of vocational personalities in work environments. In S. D. Brown & R. W. Lent (Eds.), *Career development and counseling* (pp. 24–41). Hoboken, NJ: Wiley.
Sprecher, S. (1999). "I love you more today than yesterday": Romantic partners' perceptions of changes in love and related affect over time. *Journal of Personality and Social Psychology, 76,* 46–53.
Springer, C. A., & Lease, S. H. (2000). The impact of multiple AIDS-related bereavement in the gay male population. *Journal of Counseling and Development, 78,* 297–304.
Sridhar, D., & Vaughn, S. (2001). Social functioning of students with learning disabilities. In D. P. Hallahan & B. K. Keogh (Eds.), *Research and global perspectives in learning disabilities* (pp. 65–91). Mahwah, NJ: Erlbaum.
Srivastava, S., John, O. P., Gosling, S. D., & Potter, J. (2003). Development of personality in early and middle adulthood: Set like plaster or persistent change? *Journal of Personality and Social Psychology, 84,* 1041–1053.
Sroufe, L. A. (2002). From infant attachment to promotion of adolescent autonomy: Prospective, longitudinal data on the role of parents in development. In J. G. Borkowski & S. L. Ramey (Eds.), *Parenting and the child's world* (pp. 187–202). Mahwah, NJ: Erlbaum.
Sroufe, L. A. (2005). Attachment and development: A prospective, longitudinal study from birth to adulthood. *Attachment and Human Development, 7,* 349–367.
Sroufe, L. A., Egeland, B., Carlson, E., & Collins, W. (2005). *Minnesota Study of Risk and Adaptation from birth to maturity: The development of the person.* New York: Guilford.
Sroufe, L. A., & Waters, E. (1976). The ontogenesis of smiling and laughter: A perspective on the organization of development in infancy. *Psychological Review, 83,* 173–189.
Sroufe, L. A., & Wunsch, J. P. (1972). The development of laughter in the first year of life. *Child Development, 43,* 1324–1344.
St James-Roberts, I. (2007). Helping parents to manage infant crying and sleeping: A review of the evidence and its implications for services. *Child Abuse Review, 16,* 47–69.
St James-Roberts, I., Goodwin, J., Peter, B., Adams, D., & Hunt, S. (2003). Individual differences in responsivity to a neurobehavioural examination predict crying patterns of 1-week-old infants at home. *Developmental Medicine and Child Neurology, 45,* 400–407.
St. Louis, G. R., & Liem, J. H. (2005). Ego identity, ethnic identity, and the psychosocial well-being of ethnic minority and majority college students. *Identity, 5,* 227–246.
Stackert, R. A., & Bursik, K. (2003). Why am I unsatisfied? Adult attachment style, gendered irrational relationship beliefs, and young adult romantic relationship satisfaction. *Personality and Individual Differences, 34,* 1419–1429.
Staff, J., & Uggen, C. (2003). The fruits of good work: Early work experiences and adolescent deviance. *Journal of Research in Crime and Delinquency, 40,* 263–290.
Stahl, S. A., & Miller, P. D. (2006). Whole language and language experience approaches for beginning reading: A quantitative research synthesis. In K. A. Dougherty Stahl & M. C. McKenna (Eds.), *Reading research at work: Foundations of effective practice* (pp. 9–35). New York: Guilford.
Stamler, J., Stamler, R., Neaton, J. D., Wentworth, D., Daviglus, M. L., Garside, D., Dyer, A. R., Liu, K. A., & Greenland, P. (1999). Low risk-factor profile and

long-term cardiovascular and noncardiovascular mortality and life expectancy: Findings for five large cohorts of young adult and middle-aged men and women. *Journal of the American Medical Association, 282,* 2012–2018.

Stams, G. J. M., Brugman, D., Deković, M., van Rosmalen, L., van der Laan, P., & Gibbs, J. C. (2006). The moral judgment of juvenile delinquents: A meta-analysis. *Journal of Abnormal Child Psychology, 34,* 697–713.

Stams, G. J. M., Juffer, F., & van IJzendoorn, M. H. (2002). Maternal sensitivity, infant attachment, and temperament in early childhood predict adjustment in middle childhood: The case of adopted children and their biologically unrelated parents. *Developmental Psychology, 38,* 806–821.

Standley, J. M. (1998). The effect of music and multimodal stimulation on responses of premature infants in neonatal intensive care. *Pediatric Nursing, 24,* 532–538.

Stanley, C., Murray, L., & Stein, A. (2004). The effect of postnatal depression on mother–infant interaction, infant response to the still-face perturbation, and performance on an instrumental learning task. *Development and Psychopathology, 16,* 1–18.

Stanovich, K. E. (2007). *How to think straight about psychology* (8th ed.). Boston: Allyn and Bacon.

Starr, J. M., Deary, I. J., Fox, H. C., & Whalley, L. J. (2007). Smoking and cognitive change from age 11 to 66: A confirmatory investigation. *Addictive Behaviors, 32,* 63–68.

Starr, R. J. (1999). Music therapy in hospice care. *American Journal of Hospice and Palliative Care, 16,* 739–742.

Statistics Canada. (2006a). *Education indicators in Canada: Report of the Pan-Canadian Education Indicators Program 2005.* Retrieved from www.statcan.ca/english/freepub/81-582-XIE/81-582-XIE2006001.htm

Statistics Canada. (2006b). *Hours spent doing unpaid housework for the population 15 years and over of Canada, 2006 Census—20% sample data.* Retrieved from www12.statcan.ca/english/census06/data/topics/

Stattin, H., & Magnusson, D. (1990). *Pubertal maturation in female development.* Hillsdale, NJ: Erlbaum.

Stattin, H., & Magnusson, D. (1996). Leaving home at an early age among females. In J. A. Graber & J. S. Dubas (Eds.), *New directions for child development* (No. 71, pp. 53–69). San Francisco: Jossey-Bass.

Staudinger, U. M. (1996). Wisdom and the social-interactive foundation of the mind. In P. B. Baltes & U. M. Staudinger (Eds.), *Interactive minds: Life-span perspectives on the social foundation of cognition* (pp. 276–315). New York: Cambridge University Press.

Staudinger, U. M., Dörner, J., & Mickler, C. (2005). Wisdom and personality. In R. J. Sternberg & J. Jordan (Eds.), *A handbook of wisdom: Psychological perspectives* (pp 191–219). New York: Cambridge University Press.

Staudinger, U. M., Fleeson, W., & Baltes, P. B. (1999). Predictors of subjective physical health and global well-being: Similarities and differences between the United States and Germany. *Journal of Personality and Social Psychology, 76,* 305–319.

Staudinger, U. M., & Lindenberger, U. (2003). Understanding human development takes a metatheory and multiple disciplines. In U. M. Staudinger & U. Lindenberger (Eds.), *Understanding human development: Dialogues with life span psychology* (pp. 1–13). Norwell, MA: Kluwer.

Staudinger, U. M., Smith, J., & Baltes, P. B. (1992). Wisdom-related knowledge in a life review task: Age differences and the role of professional specialization. *Psychology and Aging, 7,* 271–281.

Steele, C. M. (1997). A threat in the air: How stereotypes shape intellectual identity and performance. *American Psychologist, 52,* 613–629.

Steele, S., Joseph, R. M., & Tager-Flusberg, H. (2003). Developmental change in theory of mind abilities in children with autism. *Journal of Autism and Developmental Disorders, 33,* 461–467.

Stehr-Green, P., Tull, P., Stellfeld, M., Mortenson, P. B., & Simpson, D. (2003). Autism and thimerosal-containing vaccines: Lack of consistent evidence for an association. *American Journal of Preventive Medicine, 25,* 101–106.

Stein, J. H., & Reiser, L. W. (1994). A study of white middle-class adolescent boys' responses to "semenarche" (the first ejaculation). *Journal of Youth and Adolescence, 23,* 373–384.

Stein, M. B., Lang, A. J., Laffaye, C., Satz, L. E., Lenox, R. J., & Dresselhaus, T. R. (2004). Relationship of sexual assault history to somatic symptoms and health anxiety in women. *General Hospital Psychiatry, 26,* 178–183.

Stein, N., & Levine, L. J. (1999). The early emergence of emotional understanding and appraisal: Implications for theories of development. In T. Dalgleish & M. J. Power (Eds.), *Handbook of cognition and emotion* (pp. 383–408). Chichester, UK: Wiley.

Steinberg, L., Blatt-Eisengart, I., & Cauffman, E. (2006). Patterns of competence and adjustment among adolescents from authoritative, authoritarian, indulgent, and neglectful homes: A replication in a sample of serious juvenile offenders. *Journal of Research on Adolescence, 16,* 47–58.

Steinberg, L. D. (2001). We know some things: Parent–adolescent relationships in retrospect and prospect. *Journal of Research on Adolescence, 11,* 1–19.

Steinberg, L. D., Darling, N. E., & Fletcher, A. C. (1995). Authoritative parenting and adolescent development: An ecological journey. In P. Moen, G. H. Elder, Jr., & K. Luscher (Eds.), *Examining lives in context* (pp. 423–466). Washington, DC: American Psychological Association.

Steinberg, L. D., & Morris, A. S. (2001). Adolescent development. *Annual Review of Psychology, 52,* 83–110.

Steinberg, L. D., & Silk, J. S. (2002). Parenting adolescents. In M. H. Bornstein (Ed.), *Handbook of parenting* (Vol. 1, pp. 103–134). Mahwah, NJ: Erlbaum.

Steiner, H. A., & Miller, J. M. (2008). Disparity in utilization of implantable cardioverter-defibrillators in treatment of heart failure based on sex and race. *Women's Health, 4,* 23–25.

Steiner, J. E. (1979). Human facial expression in response to taste and smell stimulation. In H. W. Reese & L. P. Lipsitt (Eds.), *Advances in child development and behavior* (Vol. 13, pp. 257–295). New York: Academic Press.

Steiner, J. E., Glaser, D., Hawilo, M. E., & Berridge, D. C. (2001). Comparative expression of hedonic impact: Affective reactions to taste by human infants and other primates. *Neuroscience and Biobehavioral Review, 25,* 53–74.

Steinhausen, C. (2006). Eating disorders: Anorexia nervosa and bulimia nervosa. In C. Gillberg, R. Harrington, & H. Steinhausen (Eds.), *A clinician's handbook of child and adolescent psychiatry* (pp. 272–303). New York: Cambridge University Press.

Steinlein, O. K. (2004). Genes and mutations in human idiopathic epilepsy. *Brain Development, 26,* 213–218.

Stenberg, C. (2003). Effects of maternal inattentiveness on infant social referencing. *Infant and Child Development, 12,* 399–419.

Stenberg, C., & Campos, J. (1990). The development of anger expressions in infancy. In N. Stein, B. Leventhal, & T. Trabasso (Eds.), *Psychological and biological approaches to emotion* (pp. 247–282). Hillsdale, NJ: Erlbaum.

Stern, D. (1985). *The interpersonal world of the infant.* New York: Basic Books.

Stern, M., & Karraker, K. H. (1989). Sex stereotyping of infants: A review of gender labeling studies. *Sex Roles, 20,* 501–522.

Sternberg, R. J. (1988). Triangulating love. In R. J. Sternberg & M. L. Barnes (Eds.), *The psychology of love* (pp. 119–138). New Haven, CT: Yale University Press.

Sternberg, R. J. (2000). *Cupid's arrow: The course of love through time.* Cambridge, UK: Cambridge University Press.

Sternberg, R. J. (2001). Why schools should teach for wisdom: The balance theory of wisdom in educational settings. *Educational Psychologist, 36,* 227–245.

Sternberg, R. J. (2002). Intelligence is not just inside the head: The theory of successful intelligence. In J. Aronson (Ed.), *Improving academic achievement* (pp. 227–244). San Diego, CA: Academic Press.

Sternberg, R. J. (2003). The development of creativity as a decision-making process. In R. K. Sawyer, V. John-Steiner, S. Moran, R. J. Sternberg, D. H. Feldman, J. Nakamura, & M. Csikszentmihalyi (Eds.), *Creativity and development* (pp. 91–138). New York: Oxford University Press.

Sternberg, R. J. (2005). The triarchic theory of successful intelligence. In D. P. Flanagan & P. L. Harrison (Eds.), *Contemporary intellectual assessment: Theories, tests, and issues* (pp. 103–119). New York: Guilford.

Sternberg, R. J. (2006). A duplex theory of love. In R. J. Sternberg & K. Weis (Eds.), *The new psychology of love* (pp. 184–199). New Haven: Yale University Press.

Sternberg, R. J., Forsythe, G. B., Hedlund, J., Horvath, J. A., Wagner, R. K., Williams, W. M., Snook, S. A., & Grigorenko, E. L. (2000). *Practical intelligence in everyday life.* Cambridge, UK: Cambridge University Press.

Sternberg, R. J., & Grigorenko, E. L. (2002). *Dynamic testing.* New York: Cambridge University Press.

Sternberg, R. J., & Lubart, T. I. (1996). Investing in creativity. *American Psychologist, 51,* 677–688.

Sternberg, R. J., & Lubart, T. I. (2001). Wisdom and creativity. In J. E. Birren & K. W. Schaie (Eds.), *Handbook of the psychology of aging* (pp. 500–522). San Diego: Academic Press.

Stessman, J., Hammerman-Rozenberg, R., Maaravi, Y., Azoulai, D., & Cohen, A. (2005). Strategies to enhance longevity and independent function: The Jerusalem Longitudinal Study. *Mechanisms of Ageing and Development, 126,* 327–331.

Stevens, J. C., & Cruz, L. A. (1996). Spatial acuity of touch: Ubiquitous decline with aging revealed by repeated threshold testing. *Somatosensory and Motor Research, 13,* 1–10.

Stevens, J. C., Foulke, E., & Patterson, M. Q. (1996). Tactile acuity, aging, and Braille reading in long-term blind adults. *Journal of Experimental Psychology: Applied, 2,* 91–106.

Stevenson, H. W., Lee, S., & Mu, X. (2000). Successful achievement in mathematics: China and the United States. In C. F. M. van Lieshout & P. G.

Heymans (Eds.), *Developing talent across the life span* (pp. 167–183). Philadelphia: Psychology Press.

Stevenson, R., & Pollitt, C. (1987). The acquisition of temporal terms. *Journal of Child Language, 14,* 533–545.

Stevens-Simon, C., Sheeder, J., & Harter, S. (2005). Teen contraceptive decisions: Childbearing intentions are the tip of the iceberg. *Women and Health, 42,* 55–73.

Steward, D. K. (2001). Behavioral characteristics of infants with nonorganic failure to thrive during a play interaction. *American Journal of Maternal Child Nursing, 26,* 79–85.

Stewart, A. J., & Lavaque-Manty, D. (2008). Advancing women faculty in science and engineering: An effort in institutional transformation. In H. M. G. Watt & J. S. Eccles (Eds.), *Gender and occupational outcomes* (pp. 299–322). Washington, DC: American Psychological Association.

Stewart, A. J., & Malley, J. E. (2004). Women of the greatest generation. In C. Daiute & C. Lightfoot (Eds.), *Narrative analysis: Studying the development of individuals in society* (pp. 223–244). Thousand Oaks, CA: Sage.

Stewart, A. J., & Ostrove, J. M. (1998). Women's personality in middle age: Gender, history and midcourse correction. *American Psychologist, 53,* 1185–1194.

Stewart, A. J., Ostrove, J. M., & Helson, R. (2001). Middle aging in women: Patterns of personality change from the 30s to the 50s. *Journal of Adult Development, 8,* 23–37.

Stewart, A. J., & Vandewater, E. A. (1999). "If I had to do over again . . .": Midlife review, midcourse corrections, and women's well-being in midlife. *Journal of Personality and Social Psychology, 76,* 270–283.

Stewart, A. L., Verboncoeur, C. J., McLellan, B. Y., Gillis, D. E., Rush, S., & Mills, K. M. (2001). Physical activity outcomes of CHAMPS II: A physical activity promotion program for older adults. *Journal of Gerontology, 56A,* M465–M470.

Stewart, R. B., Jr. (1990). *The second child: Family transition and adjustment.* Newbury Park, CA: Sage.

Stewart, R. B., Jr., Kozak, A. L., Tingley, L. M., Goddard, J. M., Blake, E. M., & Cassel, W. A. (2001). Adult sibling relationships: Validation of a typology. *Personal Relationships, 8,* 299–324.

Stewart, S., Stinnett, H., & Rosenfeld, L. B. (2000). Sex differences in desired characteristics of short-term and long-term relationship partners. *Journal of Social and Personal Relationships, 17,* 843–853.

Stewart-Brown, S., & Edmunds, L. (2007). *Educating people to be emotionally intelligent* (pp. 241–257). Westport, CT: Praeger.

Stice, E. (2003). Puberty and body image. In C. Hayward (Ed.), *Gender differences at puberty* (pp. 61–76). New York: Cambridge University Press.

Stice, E., Presnell, K., & Bearman, S. K. (2001). Relation of early menarche to depression, eating disorders, substance abuse, and comorbid psychopathology among adolescent girls. *Developmental Psychology, 37,* 608–619.

Stifter, C. A., Coulehan, C. M., & Fish, M. (1993). Linking employment to attachment: The mediating effects of maternal separation anxiety and interactive behavior. *Child Development, 64,* 1451–1460.

Stiles, J. (2001a). Neural plasticity in cognitive development. *Developmental Neuropsychology, 18,* 237–272.

Stiles, J. (2001b). Spatial cognitive development. In C. A. Nelson & M. Luciana (Eds.), *Handbook of developmental cognitive neuroscience* (pp. 399–414). Cambridge, MA: MIT Press.

Stiles, J., Bates, E. A., Thal, D., Trauner, D. A., & Reilly, J. (2002). Linguistic and spatial cognitive development in children with pre- and perinatal focal brain injury: A ten-year overview from the San Diego longitudinal project. In M. H. Johnson & Y. Munakata (Eds.), *Brain development and cognition: A reader* (2nd ed., pp. 272–291). Malden, MA: Blackwell.

Stiles, J., Moses, P., Roe, K., Akshoomoff, N. A., Trauner, D., & Hesselink, J. (2003). Alternative brain organization after prenatal cerebral injury: Convergent fMRI and cognitive data. *Journal of the International Neuropsychological Society, 9,* 604–622.

Stiles, J., Reilly, J., Paul, B., & Moses, P. (2005). Cognitive development following early brain injury: Evidence for neural adaptation. *Trends in Cognitive Sciences, 9,* 136–143.

Stilson, S. R., & Harding, C. G. (1997). Early social context as it relates to symbolic play: A longitudinal investigation. *Merrill-Palmer Quarterly, 43,* 682–693.

Stinchcomb, J. B., Bazemore, G., & Riestenberg, N. (2006). Beyond zero tolerance: Restoring justice in secondary schools. *Youth Violence and Juvenile Justice, 4,* 123–147.

Stine-Morrow, E. A. L., Soederberg Miller, L. M., Gagne, D. D., & Hertzog, C. (2008). Self-regulated reading in adulthood. *Psychology and Aging, 23,* 131–153.

Stipek, D. J. (1995). The development of pride and shame in toddlers. In J. P. Tangney & K. W. Fischer (Eds.), *Self-conscious emotions* (pp. 237–252). New York: Guilford.

Stipek, D. J. (2002). At what age should children enter kindergarten? A question for policy makers and parents. *Social Policy Report of the Society for Research in Child Development, 16*(3).

Stipek, D. J., & Byler, P. (2001). Academic achievement and social behaviors associated with age of entry into kindergarten. *Journal of Applied Developmental Psychology, 22,* 175–189.

Stipek, D. J., Feiler, R., Daniels, D., & Milburn, S. (1995). Effects of different instructional approaches on young children's achievement and motivation. *Child Development, 66,* 209–223.

Stipek, D. J., Gralinski, J. H., & Kopp, C. B. (1990). Self-concept development in the toddler years. *Developmental Psychology, 26,* 972–977.

Stoch, M. B., Smythe, P. M., Moodie, A. D., & Bradshaw, D. (1982). Psychosocial outcome and CT findings after growth undernourishment during infancy: A 20-year developmental study. *Developmental Medicine and Child Neurology, 24,* 419–436

Stocker, C. J., Arch, J. R., & Cawthorne, M. A. (2005). Fetal origins of insulin resistance and obesity. *Proceedings of the Nutrition Society, 64,* 143–151.

Stockman, N. K. A., Schenkel, T. C., Brown, J. N., & Duncan, A. M. (2005). Comparison of energy and nutrient intakes among meals and snacks of adolescent males. *Preventive Medicine, 41,* 203–210.

Stone, M. R., & Brown, B. B. (1999). Identity claims and projections: Descriptions of self and crowds in secondary school. In J. A. McLellan & M. J. V. Pugh (Eds.), *The role of peer groups in adolescent social identity: Exploring the importance of stability and change* (pp. 7–20). San Francisco: Jossey-Bass.

Stone, P., & Lovejoy, M. (2004). Fast-track women and the "choice" to stay home. *Annals of the American Academy of Political and Social Science, 596,* 62–83.

Stone, R. I., & Reinhard, S. C. (2007). The place of assisted living in long-term care and related service systems. *Gerontologist, 47,* 23–32.

Storey, A. E., Walsh, C. J., Quinton, R. L., & Wynn-Edwards, K. E. (2000). Hormonal correlates of paternal responsiveness in new and expectant fathers. *Evolution and Human Behavior, 21,* 79–95.

Stormshak, E. A., Bierman, K. L., McMahon, R. J., Lengua, L. J., & the Conduct Problems Prevention Research Group. (2000). Parenting practices and child disruptive behavior problems in early elementary school. *Journal of Clinical Child Psychology, 29,* 17–29.

Stouthamer-Loeber, M., Wei, E., Loeber, R., & Masten, A. S. (2004). Desistance from persistent serious delinquency in the transition to adulthood. *Development and Psychopathology, 16,* 897–918.

Strain, L. A., Grabusic, C. C., Searle, M. S., & Dunn, N. J. (2002). Continuing and ceasing leisure activities in later life: A longitudinal study. *Gerontologist, 42,* 217–223.

Strand, B. H., & Kunst, A. (2007). Childhood socioeconomic position and cause-specific mortality in early adulthood. *American Journal of Epidemiology, 165,* 85–93.

Strapp, C. M., & Federico, A. (2000). Imitations and repetitions: What do children say following recasts? *First Language, 20,* 273–290.

Straus, M. A. (1999). The controversy over domestic violence by women: A methodological, theoretical, and sociology of science analysis. In X. B. Arriaga & S. Oskamp (Eds.), *Violence in intimate relationships* (pp.17–44). Thousand Oaks, CA: Sage.

Straus, M. A., & Stewart, J. H. (1999). Corporal punishment by American parents: National data on prevalence, chronicity, severity, and duration, in relation to child and family characteristics. *Clinical Child and Family Psychology Review, 2,* 55–70.

Strawbridge, W. J., Shema, S. J., Cohen, R. D., & Kaplan, G. A. (2001). Religious attendance increases survival by improving and maintaining good health behaviors. *Annals of Behavioral Medicine, 23,* 68–74.

Strayer, J., & Roberts, W. (2004). Children's anger, emotional expressiveness, and empathy: Relations with parents' empathy, emotional expressiveness, and parenting practices. *Social Development, 13,* 229–254.

Strazdins, L., Clements, M. S., Korda, R. J., Broom, D. H., & D'Souza, R. M. (2006). Unsociable work? Nonstandard work schedules, family relationships, and children's well-being. *Journal of Marriage and the Family, 68,* 394–410.

Streissguth, A. P., Bookstein, F. L., Barr, H. M., Sampson, P. D., O'Malley, K., & Young, J. K. (2004). Risk factors for adverse life outcomes in fetal alcohol syndrome and fetal alcohol effects. *Journal of Developmental and Behavioral Pediatrics, 25,* 228–238.

Streissguth, A. P., Treder, R., Barr, H. M., Shepard, T., Bleyer, W. A., Sampson, P. D., & Martin, D. (1987). Aspirin and acetaminophen use by pregnant women and subsequent child IQ and attention decrements. *Teratology, 35,* 211–219.

Streri, A. (2005). Touching for knowing in infancy: The development of manual abilities in very young infants. *European Journal of Developmental Psychology, 2,* 325–343.

Stretesky, P. B., & Lynch, M. J. (2001). The relationship between lead exposure and homicide. *Archives of Pediatrics and Adolescent Medicine, 155,* 579–582.

Striano, T., & Rochat, P. (2000). Emergence of selective social referencing in infancy. *Infancy, 1,* 253–264.

Striano, T., Tomasello, M., & Rochat, P. (2001). Social and object support for early symbolic play. *Developmental Science, 4,* 442–455.

Striegel-Moore, R. H., & Franko, D. L. (2006). Adolescent eating disorders. In R. H. Striegel-Moore & D. L. Franko (Eds.), *Child and adolescent psychopathology: Theoretical and clinical implications* (pp. 160–183). New York: Routledge.

Stright, A. D., Neitzel, C., Sears, K. G., & Hoke-Sinex, L. (2002). Instruction begins in the home: Relations between parental instruction and children's self-regulation in the classroom. *Journal of Educational Psychology, 93,* 456–466.

Stroebe, M. S., & Schut, H. (1999). The dual process model of coping with bereavement: Rationale and description. *Death Studies, 23,* 197–224.

Stroebe, M. S., van der Houwen, K., & Schut, H. (2008). Bereavement support, intervention, and research on the Internet: A critical review. In M. S. Stroebe, R. O. Hansson, H. Schut, & W. Stroebe (Eds.), *Handbook of bereavement research and practice* (pp. 551–574). Washington, DC: American Psychological Association.

Stroebe, W., & Stroebe, M. S. (1993). Determinants of adjustment to bereavement in younger widows and widowers. In M. S. Stroebe, W. Stroebe, & R. O. Hansson (Eds.), *Handbook of bereavement* (pp. 208–226). New York: Cambridge University Press.

Stroebe, W., Stroebe, M., Abakoumkin, G., & Schut, H. (1996). The role of loneliness and social support in adjustment to loss: A test of attachment versus stress theory. *Journal of Personality and Social Psychology, 70,* 1241–1249.

Strohschein, L. (2005). Parental divorce and child mental health trajectories. *Journal of Marriage and Family, 67,* 1286–1300.

Stromquist, N. P. (2007). Gender equity education globally. In S. S. Klein, B. Richardson, D. A. Grayson, L. H. Fox, & C. Kramarae (Eds.), *Handbook for achieving gender equity through education* (2nd ed., pp. 33–42). Mahwah, NJ: Erlbaum.

Stromswold, K. (2000). The cognitive neuro-science of language acquisition. In M. S. Gazzaniga (Ed.), *The new cognitive neuro-sciences* (pp. 909–932). Boston: MIT Press.

Strough, J., Hicks, P. J., Swenson, L. M., Cheng, S., & Barnes, K. A. (2003). Collaborative everyday problem solving: Interpersonal relationships and problem dimensions. *International Journal of Aging and Human Development, 56,* 43–66.

Strough, J., Leszczynski, J. P., Neely, T. L., Flinn, J. A., & Margrett, J. (2007). From adolescence to later adulthood: Femininity, masculinity, and androgyny in six age groups. *Sex Roles, 57,* 385–396.

Strouse, D. L. (1999). Adolescent crowd orientations: A social and temporal analysis. In J. A. McLellan & M. J. V. Pugh (Eds.), *The role of peer groups in adolescent social identity: Exploring the importance of stability and change* (pp. 37–54). San Francisco: Jossey-Bass.

Struckman-Johnson, C. J., & Struckman-Johnson, D. L. (1998). The dynamics and impact of sexual coercion of men by women. In P. B. Anderson & C. J. Struckman-Johnson (Eds.), *Sexually aggressive women: Current perspectives and controversies* (pp. 121–143). New York: Guilford.

Stuart, G. L., Moore, T. M., Gordon, K. C., Ramsey, S. E., & Kahler, C. W. (2006). Psychopathology in women arrested for domestic violence. *Journal of Interpersonal Violence, 21,* 376–389.

Stuart, M., & Weinrich, M. (2001). Home- and community-based long-term care: Lessons from Denmark. *Gerontologist, 41,* 474–480.

Stuart, R. B. (2005). Treatment for partner abuse: Time for a paradigm shift. *Professional Psychology: Research and Practice, 36,* 254–263.

Studelska, J. V. (2006, Spring). At home in birth. *Midwifery Today,* pp. 32–33.

Stull, D., & Scarisbrick-Hauser, A. (1989). Never-married elderly. *Research on Aging, 11,* 124–139.

Styne, D. M. (2003). The regulation of pubertal growth. *Hormone Research, 60*(Suppl. 1), 22–26.

Subbotsky, E. (2004). Magical thinking in judgments of causation: Can anomalous phenomena affect ontological causal beliefs in children and adults? *British Journal of Developmental Psychology, 22,* 123–152.

Subrahmanyam, K., & Greenfield, P. M. (1996). Effect of video game practice on spatial skills in girls and boys. In P. M. Greenfield & R. R. Cocking (Eds.), *Interacting with video* (pp. 95–114). Norwood, NJ: Ablex.

Subrahmanyam, K., Smahel, D., & Greenfield, P. (2006). Connecting developmental constructions to the Internet: Identity presentation and sexual exploration in online teen chat rooms. *Developmental Psychology, 42,* 395–406.

Suddendorf, T., Simcock, G., & Nielsen, M. (2007). Visual self-recognition in mirrors and live videos: Evidence for a developmental asynchrony. *Cognitive Development, 22,* 185–196.

Sullivan, M. A. (1995). May the circle be unbroken: The African-American experience of death, dying, and spirituality. In J. K. Parry & A. S. Ryan (Eds.), *A cross-cultural look at death, dying, and religion* (pp. 160–171). Chicago: Nelson-Hall.

Sullivan, M. W., & Lewis, M. (2003). Contextual determinants of anger and other negative expressions in young infants. *Developmental Psychology, 39,* 693–705.

Summers, R. W., & Hoffman, A. M. (Eds.). (2006). *Elder abuse: A public health perspective.* Washington, DC: American Public Health Association.

Super, C. M. (1981). Behavioral development in infancy. In R. H. Monroe, R. L. Monroe, & B. B. Whiting (Eds.), *Handbook of cross-cultural human development* (pp. 181–270). New York: Garland.

Super, D. E. (1990). A life span, life space approach to career development. In D. Brown & L. Brooks (Eds.), *Career choice and development* (2nd ed., pp. 197–261). San Francisco: Jossey-Bass.

Super, D. E. (1994). A life span, life space perspective on convergence. In M. L. Savikas & R. W. Lent (Eds.), *Convergence in career development theories* (pp. 62–71). Palo Alto, CA: Consulting Psychologists Press.

Susman, E. J., & Rogol, A. (2004). Puberty and psychological development. In R. M. Lerner & L. Steinberg (Eds.), *Handbook of adolescent psychology* (2nd ed., pp.15–44). Hoboken, NJ: Wiley.

Sutton, M. J., Brown, J. D., Wilson, K. M., & Klein, J. D. (2002). Shaking the tree of forbidden fruit: Where adolescents learn about sexuality and contraception. In J. D. Brown, J. R. Steele, & K. Walsh-Childers (Eds.), *Sexual teens, sexual media* (pp. 25–55). Mahwah, NJ: Erlbaum.

Sveen, C.-A., & Walby, F. A. (2008). Suicide survivors' mental health and grief reactions: A systematic review of controlled studies. *Suicide and Life-Threatening Behavior, 38,* 13–29.

Swanson, J. L., & Fouad, N. A. (1999). Applying theories of personfit to the transition from school to work. *Career Development Quarterly, 47,* 337–347.

Sweet, M. A., & Appelbaum, M. L. (2004). Is home visiting an effective strategy? A meta-analytic review of home visiting programs for families with young children. *Child Development, 75,* 1435–1456.

Sweet, S., & Moen, P. (2007). Integrating educational careers in work and family. *Community, Work and Family, 10,* 231–250.

Swingley, D. (2005). Statistical clustering and the contents of the infant vocabulary. *Cognitive Psychology, 50,* 86–132.

Symons, D. K. (2001). A dyad-oriented approach to distress and mother–child relationship outcomes in the first 24 months. *Parenting: Science and Practice, 1,* 101–122.

Szaflarski, J. P., Binder, J. R., Possing, E. T., McKiernan, K. A., Ward, B. D., & Hammeke, T. A. (2002). Language lateralization in left-handed and ambidextrous people: fMRI data. *Neurology, 59,* 238–244.

Szkrybalo, J., & Ruble, D. N. (1999). "God made me a girl": Sex-category constancy judgments and explanations revisited. *Developmental Psychology, 35,* 392–402.

Szlemko, W. J., Wood, J. W., & Thurman, P. J. (2006). Native Americans and alcohol: Past, present, and future. *Journal of General Psychology, 133,* 435–451.

T

Tabibi, Z., & Pfeffer, K. (2007). Finding a safe place to cross the road: The effect of distractors and the role of attention in children's identification of safe and dangerous road-crossing sites. *Infant and Child Development, 16,* 193–206.

Tacon, A., & Caldera, Y. (2001). Attachment and parental correlates in late adolescent Mexican American women. *Hispanic Journal of Behavioral Sciences, 23,* 71–88.

Taga, G., Asakawa, K., Maki, A., Konishi, Y., & Koizumi, H. (2003). Brain imaging in awake infants by near-infrared optical topography. *Proceedings of the National Academy of Sciences, 100,* 10722–10727.

Tager-Flusberg, H., & Zukowski, A. (2009). Putting words together: Morphology and syntax in the preschool years. In J. B. Gleason & B. Ratner (Ed.), *The development of language* (7th ed., pp. 139–191). Boston: Allyn and Bacon.

Tahir, L., & Gruber, H. E. (2003). Developmental trajectories and creative work in late life. In J. Demick & C. Andreoletti (Eds.), *Handbook of adult development* (pp. 239–255). New York: Springer.

Takagi, E., Silverstein, M., & Crimmins, E. (2007). Intergenerational coresidence of older adults in Japan: Conditions for cultural plasticity. *Journal of Gerontology, 62B,* S330–S339.

Takahashi, K. (1990). Are the key assumptions of the "Strange Situation" procedure universal? A view from Japanese research. *Human Development, 33,* 23–30.

Takamura, J., & Williams, B. (2002). *Informal caregiving: Compassion in action.* Arlington, TX: Arc of the United States.

Tamis-LeMonda, C. S., & Bornstein, M. H. (1989). Habituation and maternal encouragement of attention in infancy as predictors of toddler language, play, and representational competence. *Child Development, 60,* 738–751.

Tamis-LeMonda, C. S., Shannon, J. D., Cabrera, N. J., & Lamb, M. E. (2004). Fathers and mothers at play with their 2- and 3-year-olds: Contributions to language and cognitive development. *Child Development, 75,* 1806–1820.

Tammelin, T., Näyhä, S., Hills, A. P., & Järvelin, M. (2003). Adolescent participation in sports and adult physical activity. *American Journal of Preventive Medicine, 24,* 22–28.

Tamrouti-Makkink, I. D., Dubas, J. S., Gerris, J. R. M., & van Aken, A. G. (2004). The relation between the absolute level of parenting and differential parental treatment with adolescent siblings' adjustment. *Journal of Child Psychology and Psychiatry, 45,* 1397–1406.

Tanaka, H., DeSouza, C. A., Jones, P. P., Stevenson, E. T., Davy, K. P., & Seals, D. R. (1997). Greater rate of decline in maximal aerobic capacity with age in physically active vs. sedentary healthy women. *Journal of Applied Physiology, 83,* 1947–1953.

Tanaka, H., & Higuchi, M. (1998). Age, exercise performance, and physiological functional capacities. *Advances in Exercise Sports Physiology, 4,* 51–56.

Tanaka, H., & Seals, D. R. (1997). Age and gender interactions in physiological functional capacity: Insight from swimming performance. *Journal of Applied Physiology, 82,* 846–851.

Tanaka, H., & Seals, D. R. (2003). Dynamic exercise performance in master athletes: Insight into the effects of primary human aging on physiological functional capacity. *Journal of Applied Physiology, 95,* 2152–2162.

Tangney, J. P. (2001). Constructive and destructive aspects of shame and guilt. In A. C. Bohart & D. J. Stipek (Eds.), *Constructive and destructive behavior* (pp. 127–145). Washington, DC: American Psychological Association.

Tangri, S. S., & Jenkins, S. R. (1997). Why expecting conflict is good. *Sex Roles, 36,* 725–746.

Tanne, J. H. (1992). "Granny dumping" in the U.S. *British Medical Journal, 304,* 333–334.

Tanner, J. M., Healy, M., & Cameron, N. (2001). *Assessment of skeletal maturity and prediction of adult height* (3rd ed.). Philadelphia: Saunders.

Tardif, T. (2006). But are they really verbs? Chinese words for action. In K. Hirsh-Pasek & R. M. Golinkoff (Eds.), *Action meets word: How children learn verbs* (pp. 477–498). New York: Oxford University Press.

Tardif, T., Gelman, S. A., & Xu, F. (1999). Putting the "noun bias" in context: A comparison of English and Mandarin. *Child Development, 70,* 620–635.

Tardif, T., Wellman, H. M., & Cheung, K. M. (2004). False belief understanding in Cantonese-speaking children. *Journal of Child Language, 31,* 779–800.

Tardon, A., Lee, W. J., Delgado-Rodriguez, M., Dosemeci, M., Albanese, D., Hoover, R., & Blair, A. (2005). Leisure-time physical activity and lung cancer: A meta-analysis. *Cancer Causes and Control, 16,* 389–397.

Tarren-Sweeney, M. (2006). Patterns of aberrant eating among preadolescent children in foster care. *Journal of Abnormal Child Psychology, 34,* 623–634.

Tarry-Adkins, J. L., Martin-Gronert, M. S., Chen, J. H., Cripps, R. L., & Ozanne, S. E. (2008). Maternal diet influences DNA damage, aortic telomere length, oxidative stress, and antioxidant defense capacity in rats. *FASEB Journal, 22,* 2037–2044.

Tarullo, A. R., & Gunnar, M. R. (2006). Child maltreatment and the developing HPA axis. *Hormones and Behavior, 50,* 632–639.

Tasker, F. (2005). Lesbian mothers, gay fathers, and their children: A review. *Developmental and Behavioral Pediatrics, 26,* 224–240.

Taumoepeau, M., & Ruffman, T. (2006). Mother and infant talk about mental states relates to desire language and emotion understanding. *Child Development, 77,* 465–481.

Taylor, E. (2004). ADHD is best understood as a cultural construct: Against, *British Journal of Psychiatry, 184,* 9.

Taylor, M. (1996). The development of children's beliefs about the social and biological aspects of gender differences. *Child Development, 67,* 1555–1571.

Taylor, M. C., & Hall, J. A. (1982). Psychological androgyny: Theories, methods, and conclusions. *Psychological Bulletin, 92,* 347–366.

Taylor, M. G., Lynch, S. M., & Scott, M. (2004). Trajectories of impairment, social support, and depressive symptoms in later life. *Journal of Gerontology, 59B,* S238–S246.

Taylor, R. J., Lincoln, K. D., & Chatters, L. M. (2005). Supportive relationships with church members among African Americans. *Family Relations, 54,* 501–511.

Taylor, R. L. (2000). Diversity within African-American families. In D. H. Demo & K. R. Allen (Eds.), *Handbook of family diversity* (pp. 232–251). New York: Oxford University Press.

Taylor, W. C., Sallis, J. F., Lees, E., Hepworth, J. T., Feliz, K., Volding, D. C., Cassels, A., & Tobin, J. N. (2007). Changing social and built environments to promote physical activity: Recommendations from low-income, urban women. *Journal of Physical Activity and Health, 4,* 54–65.

Teicher, M. H., Dumont, N. L., Ito, Y., Vaituzis, C., Giedd, J., & Andersen, S. L. (2004). Childhood neglect is associated with reduced corpus callosum area. *Biological Psychiatry, 56,* 80–85.

Telama, R., Yang, X., Viikari, J., Valimaki, I., Wanne, O., & Raitakari, O. (2005). Physical activity from childhood to adulthood: A 21-year tracking study. *American Journal of Preventive Medicine, 28,* 267–273.

Tellings, A. (1999). Psychoanalytical and genetic-structuralistic approaches to moral development: Incompatible views? *Psychoanalytic Review, 86,* 903–914.

Temkin-Greener, H., Bajorska, A., Peterson, D. R., Kunitz, S. J., Gross, D., & Williams, T. F. (2004). Social support and risk-adjusted mortality in a frail older population. *Medical Care, 42,* 779–788.

Temple, C. M., & Carney, R. A. (1995). Patterns of spatial functioning in Turner's syndrome. *Cortex, 31,* 109–118.

Temple, J. A., & Reynolds, A. J. (2006). Economic returns of investments in preschool education. In E. Zigler & S. Jones (Eds.), *A vision for universal prekindergarten* (pp. 37–68). New York: Cambridge University Press.

Temple, J. L., Giacomelli, A. M., Roemmich, J. N., & Epstein, L. H. (2007). Overweight children habituate slower than nonoverweight children to food. *Physiology and Behavior, 9,* 250–254.

Tenenbaum, H. R., & Leaper, C. (2002). Are parents' gender schemas related to their children's gender-related cognitions? A meta-analysis. *Developmental Psychology, 38,* 615–630.

Tenenbaum, H. R., & Leaper, C. (2003). Parent–child conversations about science: The socialization of gender inequities? *Developmental Psychology, 39,* 34–47.

Tenenbaum, H. R., Snow, C. E., Roach, K. A., & Kurland, B. (2005). Talking and reading science: Longitudinal data on sex differences in mother–child conversations in low-income families. *Journal of Applied Developmental Psychology, 26,* 1–19.

ten Tusscher, G. W., & Koppe, J. G. (2004). Perinatal dioxin exposure and later effects—a review. *Chemosphere, 54,* 1329–1336.

Terenzini, P. T., Pascarella, E. T., & Blimling, G. S. (1999). Students' out-of-class experiences and their influence on learning and cognitive development: A literature review. *Journal of College Student Development, 40,* 610–623.

Terlecki, M. S., & Newcombe, N. S. (2005). How important is the digital divide? The relations of computer and videogame usage to gender differences in mental rotation ability. *Sex Roles, 53,* 433–441.

Terwel, J., Gillies, R. M., van den Eeden, P., & Hoek, D. (2001). Cooperative learning processes of students: A longitudinal multilevel perspective. *British Journal of Educational Psychology, 71,* 619–645.

Tessier, R., Cristo, M., Velez, S., Giron, M., Nadeau, L., & Figueroa de Calume, Z. (2003). Kangaroo mother care: A method of protecting high-risk premature infants against developmental delay. *Infant Behavior and Development, 26,* 384–397.

Testa, M., Livingston, J. A., Vanzile-Tamsen, C., & Frone, M. R. (2003). The role of women's substance use in vulnerability to forcible and incapacitated rape. *Journal of Studies in Alcohol, 64,* 756–764.

Teti, D. M., Saken, J. W., Kucera, E., & Corns, K. M. (1996). And baby makes four: Predictors of attachment security among preschool-age firstborns during the transition to siblinghood. *Child Development, 67,* 579–596.

Teyber, E. (2001). *Helping children cope with divorce* (rev. ed.). San Francisco: Jossey-Bass.

Thacker, S. B., & Stroup, D. F. (2003). Revisiting the use of the electronic fetal monitor. *Lancet, 361,* 445–446.

Thapar, A., Fowler, T., Rice, F., Scourfield, J., van den Bree, M., Thomas, H., Harold, G., & Hay, D. (2003). Maternal smoking during pregnancy and attention deficit hyperactivity disorder symptoms in offspring. *American Journal of Psychiatry, 160,* 1985–1989.

Tharpe, A. M., & Ashmead, D. H. (2001). A longitudinal investigation of infant auditory sensitivity. *American Journal of Audiology, 10,* 104–112.

Thatcher, R. W., Lyon, G. R., Rumsey, J., & Krasnegor, J. (1996). *Developmental neuroimaging.* San Diego, CA: Academic Press.

Thatcher, R. W., Walker, R. A., & Giudice, S. (1987). Human cerebral hemispheres develop at different rates and ages. *Science, 236,* 1110–1113.

Theisen, S. C., Mansfield, P. K., Seery, B. L., & Voda, A. (1995). Predictors of midlife women's attitudes toward menopause. *Health Values, 19,* 22–31.

Thelen, E. (1989). The (re)discovery of motor development: Learning new things from an old field. *Developmental Psychology, 25,* 946–949.

Thelen, E., & Adolph, K. E. (1992). Arnold Gesell: The paradox of nature and nurture. *Developmental Psychology, 28,* 368–380.

Thelen, E., Fisher, D. M., & Ridley-Johnson, R. (1984). The relationship between physical growth and a newborn reflex. *Infant Behavior and Development, 7,* 479–493.

Thelen, E., Schšner, G., Scheier, C., & Smith, L. B. (2001). The dynamics of embodiment: A field theory of infant perseverative reaching. *Behavioral and Brain Sciences, 24,* 1–34.

Thelen, E., & Smith, L. B. (1994). *A dynamic systems approach to the development of cognition and action.* Cambridge, MA: Cambridge University Press.

Thelen, E., & Smith, L. B. (1998). Dynamic systems theories. In R. M. Lerner (Ed.), *Handbook of child psychology: Vol. 1. Theoretical models of human development* (5th ed., pp. 563–634). New York: Wiley.

Thelen, E., & Smith, L. B. (2006). Dynamic systems theories. In R. M. Lerner (Ed.), *Handbook of child psychology: Vol. 1. Theoretical models of human development* (6th ed., pp. 258–312). Hoboken, NJ: Wiley.

Théoret, E., Halligan, M., Kobayashi, F., Fregni, H., Tager-Flusberg, H., & Pascual-Leone, A. (2005). Impaired motor facilitation during action observation in individuals with autism spectrum disorder, *Current Biology, 15,* R84–R85.

Thomas, A., & Chess, S. (1977). *Temperament and development.* New York: Brunner/Mazel.

Thomas, A., Chess, S., & Birch, H. G. (1968). *Temperament and behavior disorders in children.* New York: New York University Press.

Thomas, C. L., & Dimitrov, D. M. (2007). Effects of a teen pregnancy prevention program on teens' attitudes toward sexuality: A latent trait modeling approach. *Developmental Psychology, 43,* 173–185.

Thomas, K. A., & Tessler, R. C. (2007). Bicultural socialization among adoptive families: Where there is a will, there is a way. *Journal of Family Issues, 28,* 1189–1219.

Thomas, R. M. (2005). *Comparing theories of child development* (6th ed.). Belmont, CA: Wadsworth.

Thompson, A., Hollis, C., & Richards, D. (2003). Authoritarian parenting attitudes as a risk for conduct problems: Results of a British national cohort study. *European Child and Adolescent Psychiatry, 12,* 84–91.

Thompson, P. M., Giedd, J. N., Woods, R. P., MacDonald, D., Evans, A. C., & Toga, A. W. (2000). Growth patterns in the developing brain detected by using continuum mechanical tensor maps. *Nature, 404,* 190–192.

Thompson, R. A. (2000). The legacy of early attachments. *Child Development, 71,* 145–152.

Thompson, R. A. (2006). The development of the person: Social understanding, relationships, conscience, self. In N. Eisenberg (Ed.), *Handbook of child psychology: Vol. 3. Social, emotional, and personality development* (6th ed., pp. 24–98). Hoboken, NJ: Wiley.

Thompson, R. A., Easterbrooks, M. A., & Padilla-Walker, L. M. (2003). Social and emotional development in infancy. In R. M. Lerner & M. A. Easterbrooks (Eds.), *Social and emotional development in infancy* (pp. 91–112). New York: Wiley.

Thompson, R. A., & Goodvin, R. (2007). Taming the tempest in the teapot. In C. A. Brownell & C. B. Kopp (Eds.), *Socioemotional development in the toddler years: Transitions and transformations* (pp. 320–341). New York: Guilford.

Thompson, R. A., & Leger, D. W. (1999). From squalls to calls: The cry as a developing socioemotional signal. In B. Lester, J. Newman, & F. Pedersen (Eds.), *Biological and social aspects of infant crying.* New York: Plenum.

Thompson, R. A., & Limber, S. (1991). "Social anxiety" in infancy: Stranger wariness and separation distress. In H. Leitenberg (Ed.), *Handbook of social and evaluation anxiety* (pp. 85–137). New York: Plenum.

Thompson, R. A., Meyer, S., & McGinley, M. (2006). Understanding values in relationships: The development of conscience. In M. Killen & J. G. Smetana (Eds.), *Handbook of moral development* (pp. 267–298). Mahwah, NJ: Erlbaum.

Thompson, R. A., & Nelson C. A. (2001). Developmental science and the media. *American Psychologist, 56,* 5–15.

Thompson, R. A., & Raikes, H. A. (2003). Toward the next quarter-century: Conceptual and methodological challenges for attachment theory. *Development and Psychopathology, 15,* 691–718.

Thompson, R. A., & Raikes, H. A. (2007). The social and emotional foundations of school readiness. In D. F. Perry, R. K. Kaufmann, & J. Knitzer (Eds.), *Social and emotional health in early childhood: Building bridges between services and systems* (pp. 13–35). Baltimore, MD: Paul H. Brookes.

Thornton, J., Edwards, R., Mitchell, P., Harrison, R. A., Buchan, I., & Kelly, S. P. (2005). Smoking and age-related macular degeneration: A review of association. *Eye, 19,* 935–944.

Thornton, R., & Light, L. L. (2006). Language comprehension and production in normal aging. In J. E. Birren & K. Warner Schaie (Eds.), *Handbook of the psychology of aging* (6th ed., pp. 261–287). Burlington, MA: Elsevier Academic Press.

Thornton, S. (1999). Creating conditions for cognitive change: The interaction between task structures and specific strategies. *Child Development, 70,* 588–603.

Tienari, P., Wahlberg, K. E., & Wynne, L. C. (2006). Finnish adoption study of schizophrenia: Implications for family interventions. *Families, Systems, and Health, 24,* 442–451.

Tienari, P., Wynne, L. C., Lasky, K., Moring, J., Nieminen, P., & Sorri, A. (2003). Genetic boundaries of the schizophrenia spectrum: Evidence from the Finnish adoptive family study of schizophrenia. *American Journal of Psychiatry, 160,* 1587–1594.

Tiggemann, M., & Anesbury, T. (2000). Negative stereotyping of obesity in children: The role of controllability beliefs. *Journal of Applied Social Psychology, 30,* 1977–1993.

Tincoff, R., & Jusczyk, P. W. (1999). Some beginnings of word comprehension in 6-month-olds. *Psychological Science, 10,* 172–175.

Tizard, B., & Rees, J. (1975). The effect of early institutional rearing on the behaviour problems and affectional relationships of four-year-old children. *Journal of Child Psychology and Psychiatry, 16,* 61–73.

Tjepkema, M. (2005). Insomnia. *Health Reports, 17,* 9–25.

Tobin, S. S. (1989). The effects of institutionalization. In K. S. Markides & C. L. Cooper (Eds.), *Aging, stress and health* (pp. 139–164). Chichester, UK: Wiley.

Tofler, I. R., Knapp, P. K., & Drell, M. J. (1998). The achievement by proxy spectrum in youth sports: Historical perspective and clinical approach to pressured and high-achieving children and adolescents. *Child and Adolescent Psychiatric Clinics of North America, 7,* 803–820.

Tomasello, M. (1992). *First verbs: A case study of early grammatical development.* New York: Cambridge University Press.

Tomasello, M. (1999). Having intentions, understanding intentions, and understanding communicative intentions. In P. D. Zelazo, J. W. Astington, & J. Wilde (Eds.), *Developing theories of intention: Social understanding and self-control* (pp. 63–75). Mahwah, NJ: Erlbaum.

Tomasello, M. (2003). *Constructing a language: A usage-based theory of language acquisition.* Cambridge, MA: Harvard University Press.

Tomasello, M. (2005). Beyond formalities: The case of language acquisition. *Linguistic Review, 22,* 183–197.

Tomasello, M. (2006). Acquiring linguistic constructions. In D. Kuhn & R. Siegler (Eds.), *Handbook of child psychology: Vol. 2: Cognition, perception, and language* (6th ed., pp. 255–298). Hoboken, NJ: Wiley.

Tomasello, M., & Akhtar, N. (1995). Two-year-olds use pragmatic cues to differentiate reference to objects and actions. *Cognitive Development, 10,* 201–2

Tomasello, M., Call, J., & Hare, B. (2003). Chimpanzees understand psychological states—the question is which ones and to what extent. *Trends in Cognitive Sciences, 7,* 153–156.

Tomasello, M., & Rakoczy, H. (2003). What makes human cognition unique? From individual to shared to collective intentionality. *Mind and Language, 18,* 121–147.

Tomasello, M., Striano, T., & Rochat, P. (1999). Do young children use objects as symbols? *British Journal of Developmental Psychology, 17,* 563–584.

Tomer, A., Eliason, G., & Smith, J. (2000). Beliefs about the self, life, and death: Testing aspects of a comprehensive model of death anxiety and death attitudes. *Death attitudes and the older adult: Theories, concepts, and applications* (pp. 109–122). Philadelphia: Taylor & Francis.

Tong, S., McMichael, A. J., & Baghurst, P. A. (2000). Interactions between environmental lead exposure and sociodemographic factors on cognitive development. *Archives of Environmental Health, 55,* 330–335.

Toogood, A. A. (2004). The somatopause: An indication for growth hormone therapy? *Treatments in Endocrinology, 3,* 201–209.

Toomela, A. (2002). Drawing as a verbally mediated activity: A study of relationships between verbal, motor, visuospatial skills and drawing in children. *International Journal of Behavioral Development, 26,* 234–247.

Torges, C. M., Stewart, A. J., & Miner-Rubino, K. (2005). Personality after the prime of life: Men and women coming to terms with regrets. *Journal of Research in Personality, 39,* 148–165.

Torney-Purta, J. (2002). The school's role in developing civic engagement: A study of adolescents in twenty-eight countries. *Applied Developmental Science, 6,* 203–212.

Tornstam, L. (1997). Gero-transcendence: A reformulation of disengagement theory. *Aging, 1,* 55–63.

Tornstam, L. (2000). Transcendence in later life. *Generations, 23*(10), 10–14.

Toro-Morn, M., & Sprecher, S. (2003). A cross-cultural comparison of mate preferences among university students: The United States vs. the People's Republic of China (PRC). *Journal of Comparative Family Studies, 34,* 151–170.

Torrance, E. P. (1988). The nature of creativity as manifest in its testing. In R. J. Sternberg (Ed.), *The nature of creativity: Contemporary psychological perspectives* (pp. 43–75). New York: Cambridge University Press.

Torrey, B. B., & Haub, C. (2004). A comparison of U.S. and Canadian mortality in 1998. *Population and Development Review, 30,* No. 3.

Tracy, J. L., Robins, R. W., & Lagattuta, K. H. (2005). Can children recognize pride? *Emotion, 5,* 251–257.

Trafford, A. (2004). *My time: Making the most of the rest of your life.* New York: Basic Books.

Trahms, C. M., & Pipes, P. L. (1997). *Nutrition in infancy and childhood* (6th ed.). New York: McGraw-Hill.

Trappe, S. (2001). Master athletes. *International Journal of Sport Nutrition and Exercise Metabolism, 11,* S196–S207.

Trappe, S. (2007). Marathon runners: How do they age? *Sports Medicine, 37,* 302–305.

Trautner, H. M., Gervai, J., & Nemeth, R. (2003). Appearance–reality distinction and development of gender constancy understanding in children. *International Journal of Behavioral Development, 27,* 275–283.

Trautner, H. M., Ruble, D. N., Cyphers, L., Kirsten, B., Behrendt, R., & Hartmann, P. (2005). Rigidity and flexibility of gender stereotypes in childhood: Developmental or differential? *Infant and Child Development, 14,* 365–381.

Trautwein, U., Ludtke, O., Marsh, H. W., Koller, O., & Baumert, J. (2006). Tracking, grading, and student motivation: Using group composition and status to predict self-concept and interest in ninth-grade mathematics. *Journal of Educational Psychology, 98,* 788–806.

Treasure, J., & Schmidt, U. (2005). Anorexia nervosa. *Clinical Evidence, 13,* 1148–1157.

Trehub, S. E. (2001). Musical predispositions in infancy. *Annals of the New York Academy of Sciences, 930,* 1–16.

Treloar, S. A., Heath, A. C., & Martin, N. G. (2002). Genetic and environmental influences on premenstrual symptoms in an Australian twin sample. *Psychological Medicine, 32,* 25–38.

Tremblay, L., & Frigon, J.-Y. (2005). Precocious puberty in adolescent girls: A biomarker of later psychosocial adjustment problems. *Child Psychiatry and Human Development, 36,* 73–94.

Tremblay, R. E. (2000). The development of aggressive behaviour during childhood: What have we learned in the past century? *International Journal of Behavioral Development, 24,* 129–141.

Tremblay, R. E. (2004). Decade of behavior distinguished lecture: Development of physical aggression during infancy. *Infant Mental Health Journal, 25,* 399–407.

Tremblay, R. E., Japel, C., Perusse, D., Voivin, M., Zoccolillo, M., Montplaisir, J., & McDuff, P. (1999). The search for the age of "onset" of physical aggression: Rousseau and Bandura revisited. *Criminal Behavior and Mental Health, 9,* 8–23.

Trent, K., & Harlan, S. L. (1994). Teenage mothers in nuclear and extended households. *Journal of Family Issues, 15,* 309–337.

Triandis, H. C. (1995). *Individualism and collectivism.* Boulder, CO: Westview Press.

Triandis, H. C. (2005). Issues in individualism and collectivism research. In R. M. Sorrentino, D. Cohen, J. M. Olson, & M. P. Zanna (Eds.), *Culture and social behavior: The Ontario Symposium* (Vol. 10, pp. 207–225). Mahwah, NJ: Erlbaum.

Triandis, H. C. (2007). Culture and psychology: A history of the study of their relationship. In S. Kitayama & D. Cohen (Eds.), *Handbook of cultural psychology* (pp. 59–76). New York: Guilford.

Trickett, P. K., & Putnam, F. W. (1998). Developmental consequences of child sexual abuse. In P. K. Trickett & C. J. Schellenbach (Eds.), *Violence against children in the family and community* (pp. 39–56). Washington, DC: American Psychological Association.

Trocomé, N., & Wolfe, D. (2002). *Child maltreatment in Canada: The Canadian Incidence Study of Reported Child Abuse and Neglect.* Retrieved from www.hc-sc.gc.ca/pphb-dgspsp/cm-vee

Tronick, E., Morelli, G., & Ivey, P. (1992). The Efe forager infant and toddler's pattern of social relationships: Multiple and simultaneous. *Developmental Psychology, 28,* 568–577.

Tronick, E. Z., Thomas, R. B., & Daltabuit, M. (1994). The Quechua manta pouch: A caretaking practice for buffering the Peruvian infant against the multiple stressors of high altitude. *Child Development, 65,* 1005–1013.

Troop-Gordon, W., & Asher, S. R. (2005). Modifications in children's goals when encountering obstacles to conflict resolution. *Child Development, 76,* 568–582.

Tropp, L. R., & Pettigrew, T. F. (2005). Relationships between intergroup contact and prejudice among minority and majority status groups. *Psychological Science, 16,* 951–957.

Troyer, A. K., Häfliger, A., Cadieux, M. J., & Craik, F. I. M. (2006). Name and face learning in older adults: Effects of level of processing, self-generation, and intention to learn. *Journal of Gerontology, 61B,* P67–P74.

Trudel, G., Villeneuve, V., Anderson, A., & Pilon, G. (2008). Sexual and marital aspects of old age: An update. *Sexual and Relationship Therapy, 23,* 161–169.

True, M. M., Pisani, L., & Oumar, F. (2001). Infant–mother attachment among the Dogon of Mali. *Child Development, 72,* 1451–1466.

Trusty, J. (1999). Effects of eighth-grade parental involvement on late adolescents' educational expectations. *Journal of Research and Development in Education, 32,* 224–233.

Trzesniewski, K. H., Donnellan, M. B., & Robins, R. W. (2003). Stability of self-esteem across the life span. *Journal of Personality and Social Psychology, 84,* 205–220.

Tsai, A. G., & Wadden, T. A. (2005). Systematic review: An evaluation of major commercial weight loss programs in the United States. *Annals of Internal Medicine, 142,* 56–66.

Tsang, P. S., & Shaner, T. L. (1998). Age, attention, expertise, and time-sharing performance. *Psychology and Aging, 13,* 323–347.

Tsuang, M. T., Bar, J. L., Harley, R. M., & Lyons, M. J. (2001). The Harvard Twin Study of Substance Abuse: What we have learned. *Harvard Review of Psychiatry, 9,* 267–279.

Tsuji, Y. (2005). Time is not up: Temporal complexity of older Americans' lives. *Journal of Cross-Cultural Gerontology, 20,* 3–26.

Tuchfarber, B. S., Zins, J. E., & Jason, L. A. (1997). Prevention and control of injuries. In R. Weissberg, T. P. Gullotta, R. L. Hampton, B. A. Ryan, & G. R. Adams (Eds.), *Enhancing children's wellness* (pp. 250–277). Thousand Oaks, CA: Sage.

Tucker, C. J., McHale, S. M., & Crouter, A. C. (2001). Conditions of sibling support in adolescence. *Journal of Family Psychology, 15,* 254–271.

Tudge, J. R. H. (1992). Processes and consequences of peer collaboration: A Vygotskian analysis. *Child Development, 63,* 1364–1397.

Tudge, J. R. H., Hogan, D. M., Snezhkova, I. A., Kulakova, N. N., & Etz, K. E. (2000). Parents' child-rearing values and beliefs in the United States and Russia: The impact of culture and social class. *Infant and Child Development, 9,* 105–121.

Tunmer, W. E., & Chapman, J. W. (2002). The relation of beginning readers' reported word identification strategies to reading achievement, reading-related skills, and academic self-perceptions. *Reading and Writing, 15,* 341–358.

Turati, C. (2004). Why faces are not special to newborns: An account of the face preference. *Current Directions in Psychological Science, 13,* 5–8.

Turesson, C., & Matteson, E. L. (2006). Genetics of rheumatoid arthritis. *Mayo Clinic Proceedings, 81,* 94–101.

Turiel, E. (2006). The development of morality. In N. Eisenberg (Ed.), *Handbook of child psychology: Vol. 3. Social, emotional, and personality development* (6th ed., pp. 789–857). Hoboken, NJ: Wiley.

Turkheimer, E., Haley, A., Waldron, M., D'Onofrio, B., & Gottesman, I. I. (2003). Socioeconomic status modifies heritability of IQ in young children. *Psychological Science, 14,* 623–628.

Turnbull, M., Hart, D., & Lapkin, S. (2003). Grade 6 French immersion students' performance on large-scale reading, writing, and mathematics tests: Building explanations. *Alberta Journal of Educational Research, 49,* 6–23.

Turner, B. F. (1982). Sex-related differences in aging. In B. B. Wolman (Ed.), *Handbook of developmental psychology* (pp. 912–936). Englewood Cliffs, NJ: Prentice-Hall.

Turner, P. J., & Gervai, J. (1995). A multidimensional study of gender typing in preschool children and their parents: Personality, attitudes, preferences, behavior, and cultural differences. *British Journal of Developmental Psychology, 11,* 323–342.

Turner, R. N., Hewstone, M., & Voci, A. (2007). Reducing explicit and implicit outgroup prejudice via direct and extended contact: The mediating role of self-disclosure and intergroup anxiety. *Journal of Personality and Social Psychology, 93,* 369–388.

Tuyen, J. M., & Bisgard, K. (2003). Community setting: Pertussis outbreak. Atlanta, GA: U.S. Centers for Disease Control and Prevention. Retrieved from www.cdc.gov/nip/publications/pertussis/chapter10.pdf

Twenge, J. M. (1997). Changes in masculine and feminine traits over time: A meta-analysis. *Sex Roles, 36,* 305–325.

Twenge, J. M. (2001). Changes in women's assertiveness in response to status and roles: A cross-temporal meta-analysis, 1931–1993. *Journal of Personality and Social Psychology, 81,* 133–145.

Twenge, J. M., & Campbell, W. K. (2001). Age and birth cohort differences in self-esteem: A cross-temporal meta-analysis. *Personality and Social Psychology Review, 5,* 321–344.

Twenge, J. M., & Crocker, J. (2002). Race and self-esteem: Meta-analyses comparing whites, blacks, Hispanics, Asians, and America Indians and comment on Gray-Little and Hafdahl (2000). *Psychological Bulletin, 128,* 371–408.

Tynes, B., Reynolds, L., & Greenfield, P. M. (2004). Adolescence, race and ethnicity on the Internet: A comparison of discourse in monitored vs. unmonitored chat rooms. *Journal of Applied Developmental Psychology, 25,* 667–684.

Tyrka, A. R., Graber, J. A., & Brooks-Gunn, J. (2000). The development of disordered eating: Correlates and predictors of eating problems in the context of adolescence. In A. J. Sameroff & M. Lewis (Eds.), *Handbook of developmental psychopathology* (2nd ed., pp. 607–624). New York: Kluwer.

Tzuriel, D., & Kaufman, R. (1999). Mediated learning and cognitive modifiability: Dynamic assessment of young Ethiopian immigrant children to Israel. *Journal of Cross-Cultural Psychology, 30,* 359–380.

U

Uebelhack, R., Blohmer, J. U., Graubaum, H. J., Busch, R., Gruenwald, J., & Wernecke, K. D. (2006). Black cohosh and St. John's wort for climacteric complaints: A randomized trial. *Obstetrics and Gynecology, 107,* 247–255.

Uhlenberg, P., & Hammill, B. G. (1998). Frequency of grandparent contact with grandchild sets: Six factors that make a difference. *Gerontologist, 38,* 276–285.

Ukrainetz, T. A., Justice, L. M., Kaderavek, J. N., Eisenberg, S. L., Gillam, R., & Harm, H. M. (2005). The development of expressive elaboration in fictional narratives. *Journal of Speech, Language, and Hearing Research, 48,* 1363–1377.

Umana-Taylor, A. J., & Alfaro, E. C. (2006). Ethnic identity among U.S. Latino adolescents: Measurement and implications for well-being. In F. A. Villarruel & T. Luster (Eds.), *The crisis in youth mental health: Critical issues and effective programs:*

Vol. 2. Disorders in adolescence (pp. 195–211). Westport, CT: Praeger.

Umana-Taylor, A. J., & Updegraff, K. A. (2007). Latino adolescents' mental health: Exploring the interrelations among discrimination, ethnic identity, cultural orientation, self-esteem, and depressive symptoms. *Journal of Adolescence, 30,* 549–567.

Underhill, K., Montgomery, P., & Operario, D. (2007). Sexual abstinence only programmes to prevent HIV infection in high-income countries: Systematic review. *British Medical Journal, 335,* 248.

Underwood, M. K. (2003). *Social aggression among girls.* New York: Guilford.

UNICEF (United Nations Children's Fund). (2005). *Child poverty in rich countries: 2005.* Report Card No. 6. Florence, Italy: UNICEF Innocenti Research Centre.

UNICEF (United Nations Children's Fund). (2006). *Immunization Summary 2006.* Geneva, Switzerland: World Health Organization.

UNICEF (United Nations Children's Fund). (2008). *Immunization summary: A statistical reference containing data through 2006.* Geneva, Switzerland: World Health Organization.

UNICEF (United Nations Children's Fund). (2009). *State of the world's children.* New York: Author.

United Nations. (2002). *Human development report 2001.* New York: Author.

United Nations. (2006a). *Preventing HIV in women and infants.* Retrieved from www.unfpa.org/hiv/transmission.htm

United Nations. (2006b). *World population prospects: The 2006 revision. Population database.* Retrieved from esa.un.org/unpp/index.asp?panel=2

U.S. Administration on Aging, National Center on Elder Abuse. (2009). *Frequently asked questions about elder abuse.* Retrieved from www.ncea.aoa.gov/ncearoot/Main_Site/FAQ/Questions.aspx

U.S. Census Bureau. (2008a). *Annual estimates of the population by sex and selected age groups for the United States: April 1, 2000 to July 1, 2007.* Retrieved from www.census.gov/popest/national/asrh/NC-EST2003/NC-EST2003-02.pdf

U.S. Census Bureau. (2008b). Food insecurity: Percentage of children ages 0–17 in food-insecure households by severity of food insecurity and selected characteristics. Retrieved from www.childstats.gov/americaschildren/tables/econ3a.asp

U.S. Census Bureau. (2008c). *International data base.* Retrieved from www.census.gov/ipc/www/idb

U.S. Census Bureau. (2009a). *International data base.* Retrieved from www.census.gov/ipc/www/idb

U.S. Census Bureau. (2009b). *Statistical abstract of the United States* (128th ed.). Washington, DC: U.S. Government Printing Office.

U.S. Centers for Disease Control and Prevention. (2005). *Preventing lead poisoning in young children.* Atlanta: Author.

U.S. Centers for Disease Control and Prevention. (2007). *Sexually transmitted disease surveillance: 2006.* Retrieved from www.cdc.gov/std/stats

U.S. Department of Agriculture. (2007). *Expenditures on children by families.* Miscellaneous Publication No. 1528-2007. Washington, DC: U.S. Government Printing Office.

U.S. Department of Agriculture. (2008). *Frequently asked questions about WIC.* Retrieved from www.fns.usda.gov/wic/FAQs/faq.htm

U.S. Department of Education. (2003). The Nation's Report Card: National Assessment of Educational Progress: 2003 results. Retrieved from nces.ed.gov/nationsreportcard/mathematics

U.S. Department of Education. (2005). *Trial urban district report cards in reading and mathematics, 2005.* Retrieved from nces.ed.gov/nationsreportcard/nrc/tuda_reading_mathematics_2005

U.S. Department of Education. (2007a). *Comparative indicators of education in the United States and other G-8 countries: 2006.* Washington, DC: National Center for Education Statistics.

U.S. Department of Education. (2007b). *The Nation's Report Card: Mathematics 2007.* Retrieved from nces.ed.gov/pubsearch/pubsinfo.asp?pubid=2007494

U.S. Department of Education. (2007c). *The Nation's Report Card: Reading 2007.* Retrieved from nces.ed.gov/pubSearch/pubsinfo.asp?pubid=2007496

U.S. Department of Education. (2007d). *The Nation's Report Card: Writing 2007.* Retrieved from nces.ed.gov/pubsearch/pubsinfo.asp?pubid=2008468

U.S. Department of Education. (2008). *The condition of education.* Retrieved from nces.ed.gov/programs/coe/list/i4.asp

U.S. Department of Education. (2009). *Digest of education statistics, 2008.* Washington, DC. U.S. Government Printing Office.

U.S. Department of Health and Human Services. (2002). Cohabitation, marriage, divorce, and remarriage in the United States. *Vital and Health Statistics,* Series Report 23, Number 22. Washington, DC: U.S. Government Printing Office.

U.S. Department of Health and Human Services. (2004). *National nursing home survey* (NNHS). Retrieved from www.cdc.gov/nchs/nnhs.htm

U.S. Department of Health and Human Services. (2007a). Abortion surveillance—United States, 2004. *Morbidity and Mortality Weekly Report, 56*(SS09), 1–33. Retrieved from www.cdc.gov/mmwr/preview/mmwrhtml/ss5609a1.htm

U.S. Department of Health and Human Services. (2007b). *Births: Preliminary data for 2005.* Retrieved from www.cdc.gov/nchs/products/pubs/pubd/hestats/prelimbirths05/prelimbirths05.htm

U.S. Department of Health and Human Services. (2007c). *Growing older in America: Health and retirement study.* Bethesda, MD: National Institute on Aging.

U.S. Department of Health and Human Services. (2007d). National, state, and local area vaccination coverage among children aged 19–35 months—United States, 2006. *Morbidity and Mortality Weekly Report, 56*(34), 880–885.

U.S. Department of Health and Human Services. (2007e). *Prenatal care.* Retrieved from www.cdc.gov/nchs/fastats/prenatal.htm

U.S. Department of Health and Human Services. (2007f). *A profile of older Americans: 2007.* Retrieved from www.aoa.gov/prof/Statistics/profile/2007/8.aspx

U.S. Department of Health and Human Services. (2007g, April). Trends in oral health status: United States, 1988–1994 and 1999–2004. *Vital and Health Statistics, 11*(No. 248).

U.S. Department of Health and Human Services. (2008a). Annual smoking-attributable mortality, years of potential life lost, and productivity losses—United States, 2000–2004. *Morbidity and Mortality Weekly Report, 57,* 1226–1228.

U.S. Department of Health and Human Services. (2008b). Births: Final data for 2006. *National Vital Statistics Report, 56.* Retrieved from www.cdc.gov/nchs/data/nvsr/nvsr56/nvsr56_07.pdf

U.S. Department of Health and Human Services. (2008c). Breastfeeding among U.S. children born 1999–2005, CDC National Immunization Survey. Retrieved from www.cdc.gov/breastfeeding/data/NIS_data/index.htm

U.S. Department of Health and Human Services. (2008d). *CDC childhood injury report: Patterns of unintentional injuries among 0–19 year olds in the United States, 2000–2006.* Atlanta, GA: National Center for Injury Control and Prevention.

U.S. Department of Health and Human Services. (2008e). *Child maltreatment, 2006.* Retrieved from www.acf.hhs.gov/programs/cb/pubs/cm06/index.htm

U.S. Department of Health and Human Services. (2008f). *Deaths by place of death, age, race, and sex: United States, 1999–2004.* Retrieved from www.cdc.gov/nchs/datawh/statab/unpubd/mortabs/gmwk309_10.htm

U.S. Department of Health and Human Services. (2008g). *FASTATS: Births—methods of delivery.* Retrieved from www.cdc.gov/nchs/fastats/delivery.htm

U.S. Department of Health and Human Services, Centers for Medicare and Medicaid Services. (2008h). *National health expenditure data.* Retrieved from www.cms.hhs.gov/NationalHealthExpendData/02_NationalHealthAccountsHistorical.asp#TopOfPage

U.S. Department of Health and Human Services. (2008i). *Profile of older Americans 2008.* Retrieved from www.aoa.gov/AoARoot/Aging_Statistics/Profile/2008/docs/2008profile.pdf

U.S. Department of Health and Human Services. (2008j). *Your Medicare coverage.* Retrieved from www.medicare.gov/coverage/Home.asp

U.S. Department of Health and Human Services. (2008k). Youth Risk Behavior Surveillance—United States, 2007. *Morbidity and Mortality Weekly Report, 57*(No. SS-4), Retrieved from www.cdc.gov/HealthyYouth/yrbs

U.S. Department of Health and Human Services. (2009a). *Health, United States, with chartbook on trends in the health of Americans.* Hyattsville, MD: National Center for Health Statistics.

U.S. Department of Health and Human Services. (2009b). *National Survey on Drug Use and Health.* Retrieved from www.drugabusestatistics.samhsa.gov/nhsda.htm

U.S. Department of Health and Human Services. (2009c). *Obesity and American Indians/Alaska Natives.* Retrieved from www.omhrc.gov/templates/content.aspx?lvl=3&lvlID=537&ID=6457

U.S. Department of Health and Human Services. (2009d). *Physical activity for everyone: Recommendations.* Retrieved from www.cdc.gov/nccdphp/dnpa/physical/recommendations/index.htm

U.S. Department of Health and Human Services. (2009e). *U.S. obesity trends 1985–2007.* Retrieved from www.cdc.gov/obesity/data.trends.html

U.S. Department of Justice. (2008). *Crime in the United States, 2007.* Retrieved from www.fbi.gov/ucr/cius2007/index.html

U.S. Department of Labor. (2004, August 25). Number of jobs held, labor market activity, and earnings growth among younger baby boomers: Recent results from a longitudinal survey. *News* USDL04-1678. Washington DC: Bureau of Labor Statistics.

U.S. Department of Labor, Bureau of Labor Statistics. (2008). *Consumer expenditure survey: 2007.* Retrieved from www.bls.gov/cex/csxstnd.htm

U.S. Living Will Registry. (2005). *Advance directive forms.* Retrieved from www.uslivingwillregistry.com/forms.shtm

Updegraff, K. A., McHale, S. M., & Crouter, A. C. (1996). Gender roles in marriage: What do they mean for girls' and boys' school achievement? *Journal of Youth and Adolescence, 25,* 73–88.

Ursano, R. J., & Shaw, J. A. (2007). Children of war and opportunities for peace. *Journal of the American Medical Association, 298,* 567.

Utz, R. L., Carr, D., Nesse, R., & Wortman, C. B. (2002). The effect of widowhood on older adults' social participation: An evaluation of activity, disengagement, and continuity theories. *Gerontologist, 42,* 522–533.

V

Vaillancourt, T., Brendgen, M., Boivin, M., & Tremblay, R. E. (2003). A longitudinal confirmatory factor analysis of indirect and physical aggression: Evidence of two factors over time? *Child Development, 74,* 1628–1638.

Vaillancourt, T., Hymel, S., & McDougall, P. (2003). Bullying is power: Implications for school-based intervention strategies. *Journal of Applied Social Psychology, 19,* 157–176.

Vaillant, G. E. (1977). *Adaptation to life.* Boston: Little, Brown.

Vaillant, G. E. (1993). *The wisdom of the ego.* Cambridge, MA: Harvard University Press.

Vaillant, G. E. (1994). "Successful aging" and psychosocial well-being. In E. H. Thompson, Jr. (Ed.), *Older men's lives* (pp. 22–41). Thousand Oaks, CA: Sage.

Vaillant, G. E. (2002). *Aging well.* Boston: Little, Brown.

Vaillant, G. E., & Koury, S. H. (1994). Late midlife development. In G. H. Pollock & S. I. Greenspan (Eds.), *The course of life* (pp. 1–22). Madison, CT: International Universities Press.

Vaillant, G. E., & Mukamal, K. (2001). Successful aging. *American Journal of Psychiatry, 158,* 839–847.

Vaillant, G. E., & Vaillant, C. O. (1990). Determinants and consequences of creativity in a cohort of gifted women. *Psychology of Women Quarterly, 14,* 607–616.

Vaish, A., & Striano, T. (2004). Is visual reference necessary? Contributions of facial versus vocal cues in 12-month-olds' social referencing behavior. *Developmental Science, 7,* 261–269.

Valdés, G. (1998). The world outside and inside schools: Language and immigrant children. *Educational Researcher, 27*(6), 4–18.

Valentine, J. C., DuBois, D. L., & Cooper, H. (2004). The relation between self-beliefs and academic achievement: A meta-analytic review. *Educational Psychologist, 39,* 111–133.

Valian, V. (1999). Input and language acquisition. In W. C. Ritchie & T. K. Bhatia (Eds.), *Handbook of child language acquisition* (pp. 497–530). San Diego: Academic Press.

Valiente, C., Eisenberg, N., Fabes, R. A., Shepard, S. A., Cumberland, A., & Losoya, S. H. (2004). Prediction of children's empathy-related responding from their effortful control and parents' expressivity. *Developmental Psychology, 40,* 911–926.

Valkenburg, P. M., & Peter, J. (2007a). Internet communication and its relation to well-being: Identifying some underlying mechanisms. *Media Psychology, 9,* 43–58.

Valkenburg, P. M., & Peter, J. (2007b). Preadolescents' and adolescents' online communication and their closeness to friends. *Developmental Psychology, 43,* 267–277.

van Asselt, D. (2006). Advance directives: Prerequisites and usefulness. *Zeitschrift für Gerontologie und Geriatrie, 39,* 371–375.

van Baarsen, B. (2002). Theories on coping with loss: The impact of social support and self-esteem on adjustment to emotional and social loneliness following a partner's death in later life. *Journal of Gerontology, 57B,* S33–S42.

Van Cleynenbreugel, B., Srirangam, S. J., & Van Poppel, H. (2009). High-performance system Green-Light laser: Indications and outcomes. *Current Opinion in Urology, 19,* 33 37.

Vandell, D. L., & Posner, J. K. (1999). Conceptualization and measurement of children's after-school environments. In S. L. Friedman & T. D. Wachs (Eds.), *Measuring environment across the life span* (pp. 167–196). Washington, DC: American Psychological Association.

Vandell, D. L., Reisner, E. R., Pierce, K. M., Brown, B. B., Lee, D., Bolt, D., & Pechman, E. M. (2006). *The study of promising after-school programs: Examination of longer term outcomes after two years of program experiences.* Madison, WI: University of Wisconsin. Retrieved from www.wcer.wisc.edu/childcare/statements.html

Vandell, D. L., & Shumow, L. (1999). After-school child care programs. *Future of Children, 9*(2), 64–80.

Van den Bergh, B. R. H. (2004). High antenatal maternal anxiety is related to ADHD symptoms, externalizing problems, and anxiety in 8- and 9-year-olds. *Child Development, 75,* 1085–1097.

Van den Bergh, B. R. H., & De Rycke, L. (2003). Measuring the multidimensional self-concept and global self-worth of 6- to 8-year-olds. *Journal of Genetic Psychology, 164,* 201–225.

van der Heide, A., Onwuteaka-Philipsen, B. D., Rurup, M. L., Buiting, H. M., van Delden, J. J. M., & Hanssen-de Wolf, J. E. (2007). End-of-life practices in the Netherlands under the Euthanasia Act. *New England Journal of Medicine, 356,* 1957–1965.

Vandewater, E. A., & Stewart, A. J. (1997). Women's career commitment patterns and personality development. In M. E. Lachman & J. B. James (Eds.), *Multiple paths of midlife development* (pp. 375–410). Chicago: University of Chicago Press.

Van Eyken, E., Van Camp, G., & Van Laer, L. (2007). The complexity of age-related hearing impairment: Contributing environmental and genetic factors. *Audiology and Neurotology, 12,* 345–358.

Van Gelder, B. M., Tijhuis, M. A. R., Kalmijn, S., Giampaoli, S., Nissinen, A., & Kromhout, D. (2004). Physical activity in relation to cognitive decline in elderly men: The FINE Study. *American Journal of Epidemiology, 161,* 639–651.

Van Goozen, S. H. M., Cohen-Kettenis, P. T., Gooren, I. J. G., Frijda, N. H., & Van De Poll, N. E. (1995). Gender differences in behaviour: Activating effects of cross-sex hormones. *Psychoneuroendocrinology, 20,* 171–177.

van IJzendoorn, M. H. (1995). Adult attachment representations, parental responsiveness, and infant attachment: A meta-analysis on the predictive validity of the Adult Attachment Interview. *Psychological Bulletin, 117,* 387–403.

van IJzendoorn, M. H., & Hubbard, F. O. A. (2000). Are infant crying and maternal responsiveness during the first year related to infant–mother attachment at 15 months? *Attachment and Human Development, 2,* 371–391.

van IJzendoorn, M. H., Juffer, F., & Poelhuis, C. W. K. (2005). Adoption and cognitive development: A meta-analytic comparison of adopted and non-adopted children's IQ and school performance. *Psychological Bulletin, 131,* 301–316.

van IJzendoorn, M. H., & Kroonenberg, P. M. (1988). Cross-cultural patterns of attachment: A meta-analysis of the Strange Situation. *Child Development, 59,* 147–156.

van IJzendoorn, M. H., & Sagi, A. (1999). Cross-cultural patterns of attachment. In J. Cassidy & P. R. Shaver (Eds.), *Handbook of attachment: Theory, research, and clinical applications* (pp. 713–734). New York: Guilford.

van IJzendoorn, M. H., Schuengel, C., & Bakermans-Kranenburg, M. J. (1999). Disorganized attachment in early childhood: Meta-analysis of precursors, concomitants, and sequelae. *Development and Psychopathology, 11,* 225–249.

van IJzendoorn, M. H., Vereijken, C. M. J. L., Bakermans-Kranenburg, M. J., & Riksen-Walraven, J. M. (2004). Assessing attachment security with the Attachment Q Sort: Meta-analytic evidence for the validity of the Observer AQS. *Child Development, 75,* 1188–1213.

Van Keer, H. (2004). Fostering reading comprehension in fifth grade by explicit instruction in reading strategies and peer tutoring. *British Journal of Educational Psychology, 74,* 37–70.

van Solinge, H., & Henkens, K. (2008). Adjustment to and satisfaction with retirement: Two of a kind? *Psychology and Aging, 23,* 422–434.

Van Volkom, M. (2006). Sibling relationships in middle and older adulthood: A review of the literature. *Marriage and Family Review, 40,* 151–170.

Varendi, H., & Porter, R. H. (2001). Breast odour as the only maternal stimulus elicits crawling toward the odour source. *Acta Paediactrica, 90,* 372–375.

Varnhagen, C. (2007). Children and the Internet. In J. Gackenbach (Ed.), *Psychology and the Internet* (2nd ed., pp, 37–54). Amsterdam: Elsevier.

Vartanian, L. R. (1997). Separation–individuation, social support, and adolescent egocentrism: An exploratory study. *Journal of Early Adolescence, 17,* 245–270.

Vartanian, L. R., & Powlishta, K. K. (1996). A longitudinal examination of the social-cognitive foundations of adolescent egocentrism. *Journal of Early Adolescence, 16,* 157–178.

Vatten, L. J., Maehle, B. O., Lund, N. T., Treti, S., Hsieh, C. C., Trichopoulos, D., & Stuver, S. O. (2002). Birth weight as a predictor of breast cancer: A case-control study in Norway. *British Journal of Cancer, 86,* 89–91.

Vaughn, B. E., Colvin, T. N., Azria, M. R., Caya, L., & Krzysik, L. (2001). Dyadic analyses of friendship in a sample of preschool-age children attending Head Start: Correspondence between measures and implications for social competence. *Child Development, 72,* 862–878.

Vaughn, B. E., Kopp, C. B., & Krakow, J. B. (1984). The emergence and consolidation of self-control from eighteen to thirty months of age: Normative trends and individual differences. *Child Development, 55,* 990–1004.

Vazsonyi, A. T., Hibbert, J. R., & Snider, J. B. (2003). Exotic enterprise no more? Adolescent reports of family and parenting processes from youth in four countries. *Journal of Research on Adolescence, 13,* 129–160.

Velderman, M. K., Bakermans-Kranenburg, M. J., Juffer, F., & van IJzendoorn, M. H. (2006). Effects of attachment-based interventions on maternal sensitivity and infant attachment: Differential susceptibility of highly reactive infants. *Journal of Family Psychology, 20,* 266–274.

Velkoff, V. (2000, January–March). Centenarians in the United States, 1990 and beyond. *Statistical Bulletin, U.S. Bureau of the Census.* Washington, DC: U.S. Government Printing Office.

Velleman, R. D. B., Templeton, L. J., & Copello, A. G. (2005). The role of the family in preventing and intervening with substance use and misuse: A comprehensive review of family interventions, with a focus on young people. *Drug and Alcohol Review, 24,* 93–109.

Venet, M., & Markovits, H. (2001). Understanding uncertainty with abstract conditional premises. *Merrill-Palmer Quarterly, 47,* 74–99.

Venezia, M., Messinger, D. S., Thorp, D., & Mundy, P. (2004). The development of anticipatory smiling. *Infancy, 6,* 397–406.

Veneziano, R. A. (2003). The importance of paternal warmth. *Cross-Cultural Research, 37,* 265–281.

Veniegas, R., & Peplau, L. A. (1997). Power and the quality of same-sex friendships. *Psychology of Women Quarterly, 21,* 279–297.

Vereijken, B., & Adolph, K. E. (1999). Transitions in the development of locomotion. In G. J. P. Savelsbergh, H. L. J. van der Maas, & P. C. L. van Geert (Eds.), *Non-linear analyses of developmental processes* (pp. 137–149). Amsterdam: Elsevier.

Verghese, J., Lipston, R. B., Katz, M. J., Hall, C. B., Derby, C. A., & Kuslansky, G. (2003). Leisure activities and the risk of dementia in the elderly. *New England Journal of Medicine, 348,* 2508–2516.

Veríssimo, M., & Salvaterra, F. (2006). Maternal secure-base scripts and children's attachment security in an adopted sample. *Attachment and Human Development, 8,* 261–273.

Vesco, K. K., Haney, E. M., Humphrey, L., Fu, R., & Nelson, H. D. (2007). Influence of menopause on mood: A systematic review of cohort studies. *Climacteric, 10,* 448–465.

Victor, C., Scambler, S., Bond, J., & Bowling, A. (2000). Being alone in later life: Loneliness, social isolation, and living alone. *Reviews in Clinical Gerontology, 10,* 407–417.

Vidaeff, A. C., Carroll, M. A., & Ramin, S. M. (2005). Acute hypertensive emergencies in pregnancy. *Critical Care Medicine, 33,* S307–S312.

Vinden, P. G. (1996). Junín Quechua children's understanding of mind. *Child Development, 67,* 1707–1716.

Vinden, P. G. (2002). Understanding minds and evidence for belief: A study of Mofu children in Cameroon. *International Journal of Behavioral Development, 26,* 445–452.

Vinters, H. V. (2001). Aging and the human nervous system. In J. E. Birren & K. W. Schaie (Eds.), *Handbook of the psychology of aging* (pp. 135–160). San Diego: Academic Press.

Visher, E. B., Visher, J. S., & Pasley, K. (2003). Remarriage, families and stepparenting. In F. Walsh (Ed.), *Normal family processes* (pp. 153–175). New York: Guilford.

Vita, A. J., Terry, R. B., Hubert, H. B., & Fries, J. F. (1998). Aging, health risks, and cumulative disability. *New England Journal of Medicine, 338,*1035–1041.

Vitali, P., Migliaccio, R., Agosta, F., Rosen, H. J., & Geschwind, M. D. (2008). Neuroimaging in dementia. *Seminars in Neurology, 28,* 467–483.

Vivanti, G., Nadig, A., Ozonoff, S., & Rogers, S. J. (2008). What do children with autism attend to during imitation tasks? *Journal of Experimental Psychology, 101,* 186–205.

Vogel, D. A., Lake, M. A., Evans, S., & Karraker, H. (1991). Children's and adults' sex-stereotyped perceptions of infants. *Sex Roles, 24,* 605–616.

Vogels, N., Diepvens, K., & Westerterp-Plantenga, M. S. (2005). Predictors of long-term weight maintenance. *Obesity Research, 13,* 2162–2168.

Vogelstein, B., & Kinzler, K. (2004). Cancer genes and the pathways they control. *Nature Medicine, 10,* 789–799.

Vohr, B., Jodoin-Krauzyk, J., Tucker, R., Johnson, M. J., Topol, D., & Ahlgren, M. (2008). Early language outcomes of early-identified infants with permanent hearing loss at 12 to 16 months of age. *Pediatrics, 122,* 535–544.

Volling, B. L. (2001). Early attachment relationships as predictors of preschool children's emotion regulation with a distressed sibling. *Early Education and Development, 12,* 185–207.

Volling, B. L., & Belsky, J. (1992). Contribution of mother–child and father–child relationships to the quality of sibling interaction: A longitudinal study. *Child Development, 63,* 1209–1222.

Volling, B. L., McElwain, N. L., & Miller, A. L. (2002). Emotion regulation in context: The jealousy complex between young siblings and its relations with child and family characteristics. *Child Development, 73,* 581–600.

Volling, B. L., McElwain, N. L., Notaro, P. C., & Herrera, C. (2002). Parents' emotional availability and infant emotional competence: Predictors of parent–infant attachment and emerging self-regulation. *Journal of Family Psychology, 16,* 447–465.

Volpicelli, J. R. (2001). Alcohol abuse and alcoholism. *Journal of Clinical Psychiatry, 62*(Suppl. 20), 4–10.

Voluntary Euthanasia Society of New South Wales. (2008). *Australian timeline.* Retrieved from www.vesnsw.org.au/articles/facts-Aust_timeline.php

Vondra, J. I., Hommerding, K. D., & Shaw, D. S. (1999). Stability and change in infant attachment in a low-income sample. In J. I. Vondra & D. Barnett (Eds.), Atypical attachment in infancy and early childhood among children at developmental risk. *Monographs of the Society for Research in Child Development, 64*(3, Serial No. 258), 119–144.

Vondra, J. I., Shaw, D. S., Searingen, L., Cohen, M., & Owens, E. B. (2001). Attachment stability and emotional and behavioral regulation from infancy to preschool age. *Development and Psychopathology, 13,* 13–33.

von Hofsten, C. (2004). An action perspective on motor development. *Trends in Cognitive Sciences, 8,* 266–272.

von Hofsten, C., & Rosander, K. (1998). The establishment of gaze control in early infancy. In S. Simion & S. G. Butterworth (Eds.), *The development of sensory, motor and cognitive capacities in early infancy* (pp. 49–66). Hove, UK: Psychology Press.

Vouloumanos, A., & Werker, J. F. (2004). Tuned to the signal: The privileged status of speech for young infants. *Developmental Science, 7,* 270–276.

Voyer, D., Voyer, S., & Bryden, M. P. (1995). Magnitude of sex differences in spatial abilities: A meta-analysis and consideration of critical variables. *Psychological Bulletin, 117,* 250–270

Vygotsky, L. S. (1978). *Mind in society: The development of higher mental processes.* Cambridge, MA: Harvard University Press. (Original works published 1930, 1933, and 1935)

Vygotsky, L. S. (1987). Thinking and speech. In R. W. Rieber, & A. S. Carton (Eds.), & N. Minick (Trans.), *The collected works of L. S. Vygotsky: Vol. 1. Problems of general psychology* (pp. 37–285). New York: Plenum. (Original work published 1934)

W

Wachs, T. D. (1999). The what, why, and how of temperament: A piece of the action. In L. Balter & C. S. Tamis-LeMonda (Eds.), *Child psychology: A handbook of contemporary issues* (pp. 23–44). Philadelphia: Psychology Press.

Wachs, T. D., & Bates, J. E. (2001). Temperament. In G. Bremner & A. Fogel (Eds.), *Blackwell handbook of infant development* (pp. 465–501). Oxford, UK: Blackwell.

Wadden, T. A., & Foster, G. D. (2000). Behavioral treatment of obesity. *Medical Clinics of North America, 84,* 441–461.

Waddington, C. H. (1957). *The strategy of the genes.* London: Allen & Unwin.

Wade, T. J., & Cairney, J. (1997). Age and depression in a nationally representative sample of Canadians: A preliminary look at the National Population Health Survey. *Canadian Journal of Public Health, 88,* 297–302.

Wadhwa, P. D., Sandman, C. A., & Garite, T. J. (2001). The neurobiology of stress in human pregnancy: Implications for prematurity and development of the fetal central nervous system. *Progress in Brain Research, 133,* 131–142.

Wagner, R. K. (2000). Practical intelligence. In R. J. Sternberg (Ed.), *Handbook of intelligence* (pp. 380–395). New York: Cambridge University Press.

Wahl, H.-W. (1991). Dependence in the elderly from an interactional point of view: Verbal and observational data. *Psychology and Aging, 6,* 238–246.

Wahlsten, D. (1994). The intelligence of heritability. *Canadian Psychology, 35,* 244–259.

Wainryb, C. (1997). The mismeasure of diversity: Reflections on the study of cross-cultural differences. In H. D. Saltzstein (Ed.), *New directions for child development* (No. 76, pp. 51–65). San Francisco: Jossey-Bass.

Waite, L. J. (1999, July). *Debunking the marriage myth: It works for women, too.* Paper presented at the annual Smart Marriages Conference, Washington, DC.

Wakeley, A., Rivera, S., & Langer, J. (2000). Can young infants add and subtract? *Child Development, 71,* 1477–1720.

Walberg, H. J. (1986). Synthesis of research on teaching. In M. C. Wittrock (Ed.), *Handbook of research on teaching* (3rd ed., pp. 214–229). New York: Macmillan.

Waldfogel, J. (2001). International policies toward parental leave and child care. *Future of Children 11,* 52–61.

Waldinger, R. J., Schulz, M. S., Hauser, S. T., Allen, J. P., & Crowell, J. A. (2004). Reading others' emotions: The role of intuitive judgments in predicting marital satisfaction, quality, and stability. *Journal of Family Psychology, 18,* 58–71.

Waldron, H. B., Turner, C. W., & Ozechowski, T. J. (2005). Profiles of change in behavioral and family interventions for adolescent substance abuse and dependence. In H. A. Liddle & C. L. Rowe (Eds.), *Adolescent substance abuse: Research and clinical advances* (pp. 357–374). Cambridge, UK: Cambridge University Press.

Waldrop, D. P., & Weber, J. A. (2001). From grandparent to caregiver: The stress and satisfaction of raising grandchildren. *Families in Society, 82,* 461–472.

Walenski, M., Tager-Flusberg, H., & Ullman, M. T. (2006). Language in autism. In S. O. Moldin & J. L. R. Rubenstein (Eds.), *Understanding autism: From basic neuroscience to treatment* (pp. 175–203). Boca Raton, FL: CRC Press.

Walker, A., Rosenberg, M., & Balaban-Gil, K. (1999). Neurodevelopmental and neurobehavioral sequelae of selected substances of abuse and psychiatric medications in utero. *Neurological Disorders: Developmental and Behavioral Sequelae, 8,* 845–867.

Walker, L. J. (1995). Sexism in Kohlberg's moral psychology? In W. M. Kurtines & J. L. Gewirtz (Eds.), *Moral development: An introduction* (pp. 83–107). Boston: Allyn and Bacon.

Walker, L. J. (2004). Progress and prospects in the psychology of moral development. *Merrill-Palmer Quarterly, 50,* 546–557.

Walker, L. J. (2006). Gender and morality. In M. Killen & J. G. Smetana (Eds.), *Handbook of moral development* (pp. 93–118). Philadelphia: Erlbaum.

Walker, L. J., & Taylor, J. H. (1991a). Family interactions and the development of moral reasoning. *Child Development, 62,* 264–283.

Walker, L. J., & Taylor, J. H. (1991b). Stage transitions in moral reasoning: A longitudinal study of developmental processes. *Developmental Psychology, 27,* 330–337.

Walker-Andrews, A. (1997). Infants' perception of expressive behaviors: Differentiation of multimodal information. *Psychological Bulletin, 121,* 437–456.

Walkowiak, J., Wiener, J., Fastabend, A., Heinzow, B., Krämer, U., & Schmidt, E. (2001). Environmental exposure to polychlorinated biphenyls and quality of the home environment: Effects on psychodevelopment in early childhood. *Lancet, 358,* 1602–1607.

Wall, M., & Côté, J. (2007). Developmental activities that lead to dropout and investment in sport. *Physical Education and Sport Pedagogy, 12,* 77–87.

Wallace, J. M., Jr., Bachman, J. G., O'Malley, P. M., Schulenberg, J. E., Cooper, S. M., & Johnston, L. D. (2003). Gender and ethnic differences in smoking, drinking, and illicit drug use among American 8th, 10th, and 12th grade students, 1976–2000. *Addiction, 98,* 225–234.

Wallerstein, J. S., & Blakeslee, S. (1995). *The good marriage.* Boston: Houghton Mifflin.

Wallerstein, J. S., & Lewis, J. M. (2004). The unexpected legacy of divorce: Report of a 25-year study. *Psychoanalytic Psychology, 21,* 353–370.

Walls, C. T., & Zarit, S. H. (1991). Informal support from black churches and the well-being of elderly blacks. *Gerontologist, 31,* 490–495.

Walsh, C. A., Ploeg, J., Lohfeld, L., Horne, J., MacMillan, H., & Lai, D. (2007). Violence across the lifespan: Interconnections among forms of abuse as described by marginalized Canadian elders and their caregivers. *British Journal of Social Work, 37,* 491–514.

Walsh, F., & McGoldrick, M. (2004). Loss and the family: A systemic perspective. In F. Walsh & M. McGoldrick (Eds.), *Living beyond loss: Death in the family* (2nd ed., pp. 3–26). New York: Norton.

Walsh, K. E., & Berman, J. R. (2004). Sexual dysfunction in the older woman: An overview of the current understanding and management. *Therapy in Practice, 21,* 655–675.

Walston, J., Hadley, E. C., Ferrucci, L., Guralnik, J. M., Newman, A. B., Studenski, S. A., Ershler, W. B., Harris, T., & Fried, L. P. (2006). Research agenda for fraily in older adults: Toward a better understanding of physiology and etiology: Summary from the American Geriatrics Society/National Institute on Aging Research Conference on Frailty in Older Adults. *Journal of the American Geriatrics Society, 54,* 991–1001.

Wang, H., & Amato, P. R. (2000). Predictors of divorce adjustment: Stressors, resources, and definitions. *Journal of Marriage and Family, 62,* 655–668.

Wang, J. (2005). Work stress as a risk factor for major depressive episode(s). *Psychological Medicine, 35,* 865–871.

Wang, M. (2007). Profiling retirees in the retirement transition and adjustment process: Examining the longitudinal change patterns of retirees' psychological well-being. *Journal of Applied Psychology, 92,* 455–474.

Wang, Q. (2004). The emergence of cultural self-construct: Autobiographical memory and self-description in American and Chinese children. *Developmental Psychology, 40,* 3–15.

Wang, Q. (2006a). Earliest recollections of self and others in European American and Taiwanese young adults. *Psychological Science, 17,* 708–714.

Wang, Q. (2006b). Relations of maternal style and child self-concept to autobiographical memories in Chinese, Chinese immigrant, and European American 3-year-olds. *Child Development, 77,* 1794–1809.

Wang, Q., Pomerantz, E. M., & Chen, H. (2007). The role of parents' control in early adolescents' psychological functioning: A longitudinal investigation in the United States and China. *Child Development, 78,* 1592–1610.

Wang, S., Baillargeon, R., & Paterson, S. (2005). Detecting continuity violations in infancy: A new account and new evidence from covering and tube events. *Cognition, 95,* 129–173.

Wannamethee, G., Shaper, A. G., & Macfarlane, P. W. (1993). Heart rate, physical activity, and mortality from cancer and other noncardiovascular diseases. *American Journal of Epidemiology, 137,* 735–748.

Ward, R. A., & Spitze, G. D. (2007). Nestleaving and coresidence by young adult children: The role of family relations. *Research on Aging, 29,* 257–277.

Wark, G. R., & Krebs, D. L. (1996). Gender and dilemma differences in real-life moral judgment. *Developmental Psychology, 32,* 220–230.

Warner, L. A., Valdez, A., Vega, W. A., de la Rosa, M., Turner, R. J., & Canino, G. (2006). Hispanic drug abuse in an evolving cultural context: An agenda for research. *Drug and Alcohol Dependence, 84*(Suppl. 1), S8–S16.

Warnock, F., & Sandrin, D. (2004). Comprehensive description of newborn distress behavior in response to acute pain (newborn male circumcision). *Pain, 107,* 242–255.

Warr, P. B. (1994). Age and employment. In M. D. Dunnette, L. Hough, & H. Triandis (Eds.), *Handbook of industrial and organizational psychology* (pp. 485–550). Palo Alto, CA: Consulting Psychologists Press.

Warr, P. (2001). Age and work behavior: Physical attributes, cognitive abilities, knowledge, personality traits, and motives. *International Review of Industrial and Organizational Psychology, 16,* 1–36.

Warr, P., Butcher, V., Robertson, I., & Callinan, M. (2004). Older people's well-being as a function of employment, retirement, environmental characteristics, and role preference. *British Journal of Psychology, 95,* 297–324.

Warren, A. R., & Tate, C. S. (1992). Egocentrism in children's telephone conversations. In R. M. Diaz & L. E. Berk (Eds.), *Private speech: From social interaction to self-regulation* (pp. 245–264). Hillsdale, NJ: Erlbaum.

Wasik, B. A., & Bond, M. A. (2001). Beyond the pages of a book: Interactive book reading and language development in preschool classrooms. *Journal of Educational Psychology, 93,* 243–250.

Wass, H. (2004). A perspective on the current state of death education. *Death Studies, 28,* 289–308.

Wasserman, E. A., & Rovee-Collier, C. (2001). Pick the flowers and mind your As and 2s! Categorization by pigeons and infants. In M. E. Carroll & J. B. Overmier (Eds.), *Animal research and human health: Advancing human welfare through behavioral science* (pp. 263–279). Washington, DC: American Psychological Association.

Watamura, S. E., Donzella, B., Alwin, J., & Gunnar, M. R. (2003). Morning-to-afternoon increases in cortisol concentrations for infants and toddlers at child care: Age differences and behavioral correlates. *Child Development, 74,* 1006–1020.

Waterman, A. S., & Whitbourne, S. K. (1982). Androgyny and psychosocial development among college students and adults. *Journal of Personality, 50,* 121–133.

Waters, E., & Cummings, E. M. (2000). A secure base from which to explore close relationships. *Child Development, 71,* 164–172.

Waters, E., Merrick, S., Treboux, D., Crowell, J., & Albersheim, L. (2000). Attachment security in infancy and early adulthood: A twenty-year longitudinal study. *Child Development, 71,* 684–689.

Waters, E., Vaughn, B. E., Posada, G., & Kondo-Ikemura, K. (Eds.). (1995). Caregiving, cultural, and cognitive perspectives on secure-base behavior and working models: New growing points of attachment theory and research. *Monographs of the Society for Research in Child Development, 60*(2–3, Serial No. 244).

Watkins, W. E., & Pollitt, E. (1998). Iron deficiency and cognition among school-age children. In S. G. McGregor (Ed.), *Recent advances in research on the effects of health and nutrition on children's development and school achievement in the Third World.* Washington, DC: Pan American Health Organization.

Watson, A. C., Nixon, C. L., Wilson, A., & Capage, L. (1999). Social interaction skills and theory of mind in young children. *Developmental Psychology, 35,* 386–391.

Watson, D. J. (1989). Defining and describing whole language. *Elementary School Journal, 90,* 129–141.

Watson, J. B., & Raynor, R. (1920). Conditioned emotional reactions. *Journal of Experimental Psychology, 3,* 1–14.

Watson, L. C., Lehmann, S., Mayer, L., Samus, Q., Baker, A., & Brandt, J. (2006). Depression in assisted living is common and related to physical burden. *American Journal of Geriatric Psychiatry, 14,* 676–883.

Watson, M. (1990). Aspects of self development as reflected in children's role playing. In D. Cicchetti & M. Beeghly (Eds.), *The self in transition: Infancy to childhood* (pp. 281–307). Chicago: University of Chicago Press.

Watt, L. M., & Cappeliez, P. (2000). Integrative and instrumental reminiscence therapies for depression in older adults: Intervention strategies and treatment effectiveness. *Aging and Mental Health, 4,* 166–177.

Watts-English, T., Fortson, B. L., Gibler, N., Hooper, S. R., & De Bellis, M. D. (2006). The psychobiology of maltreatment in childhood. *Journal of Social Issues, 62,* 717–736.

Waxman, S. R. (2003). Links between object categorization and naming: Origins and emergence in human infants. In D. H. Rakison & L. M. Oakes (Eds.), *Early category and concept development: Making sense of the blooming, buzzing confusion* (pp. 193–209). New York: Oxford University Press.

Waxman, S. R., & Braun, I. (2005). Consistent (but not variable) names as invitations to form object categories: New evidence from 12-month-old infants. *Cognition, 95,* B59–B68.

Waxman, S. R., & Senghas, A. (1992). Relations among word meanings in early lexical development. *Developmental Psychology, 28,* 862–873.

Webb, N. B. (2002). September 11, 2001. In N. B. Webb (Ed.), *Helping bereaved children: A handbook for practitioners* (pp. 365–384). New York: Guilford.

Webb, S. J., Monk, C. S., & Nelson, C. A. (2001). Mechanisms of postnatal neurobiological development: Implications for human development. *Developmental Neuropsychology, 19,* 147–171.

Weber, C., Hahne, A., Friedrich, M., & Friederici, A. (2004). Discrimination of word stress in early infant perception: Electrophysiological evidence. *Cognitive Brain Research, 18,* 149–161.

Weber, J. A., & Waldrop, D. P. (2000). Grandparents raising grandchildren: Families in transition. *Journal of Gerontological Social Work, 33,* 27–46.

Webster, J. D. (2002). Reminiscence function in adulthood: Age, ethnic, and family dynamics correlates. In J. D. Webster & B. K. Haight (Eds.), *Critical advances in reminiscence work* (pp. 140–142). New York: Springer.

Wechsler, D. (2002). *WPPSI-III: Wechsler Preschool and Primary Scale of Intelligence* (3rd ed.). San Antonio, TX: Psychological Corporation.

Wechsler, D. (2003). *WISC-IV: Wechsler Intelligence Scale for Children* (4th ed.). San Antonio, TX: Psychological Corporation.

Weems, C. F., & Costa, N. M. (2005). Developmental differences in the expression of childhood anxiety symptoms and fears. *Journal of the American Academy of Child and Adolescent Psychiatry, 44,* 656–663.

Weeraratna, A. T., Kalehua, A., Deleon, I., Bertak, D., Maher, G., & Wade, M. S. (2007). Alterations in immunological and neurological gene expression patterns in Alzheimer's disease tissues. *Experimental Cell Research, 313,* 450–461.

Wegesin, D. J., Jacobs, D. M., Zubin, N. R., & Ventura, P. R. (2000). Source memory and encoding strategy in normal aging. *Journal of Clinical and Experimental Neuropsychology, 22,* 455–464.

Wehren, A., De Lisi, R., & Arnold, M. (1981). The development of noun definition. *Journal of Child Language, 8,* 165–175.

Weikart, D. P. (1998). Changing early childhood development through educational intervention. *Preventive Medicine, 27,* 233–237.

Weimer, B. L., Kerns, K. A., & Oldenburg, C. M. (2004). Adolescents' interactions with a best friend: Associations with attachment style. *Journal of Experimental Child Psychology, 88,* 102–120.

Weinberg, M. K., & Tronick, E. Z. (1994). Beyond the face: An empirical study of infant affective configurations of facial, vocal, gestural, and regulatory behaviors. *Child Development, 65,* 1503–1515.

Weindruch, R., Keenan, K. P., Carney, J. M., Fernandes, G., Feuers, R. J., & Floyd, R. A. (2001). Caloric restriction mimetics: Metabolic interventions. *Journal of Gerontology, 56A,* 20–33.

Weiner, J., & Tardif, C. (2004). Social and emotional functioning of children with learning disabilities: Does special education placement make a difference? *Learning Disabilities Research and Practice, 19,* 20–32.

Weinert, F. E., & Hany, E. A. (2003). The stability of individual differences in intellectual development: Empirical evidence, theoretical problems, and new research questions. In R. J. Sternberg & J. Lautrey (Eds.), *Models of intelligence: International perspectives* (pp. 169–181). Washington, DC: American Psychological Association.

Weinfield, N. S., Sroufe, L. A., & Egeland, B. (2000). Attachment from infancy to early adulthood in a high-risk sample: Continuity, discontinuity, and their correlates. *Child Development, 71,* 695–702.

Weinfield, N. S., Whaley, G. J. L., & Egeland, B. (2004). Continuity, discontinuity, and coherence in attachment from infancy to late adolescence: Sequelae of organization and disorganization. *Attachment and Human Development, 6,* 73–97.

Weingarten, H. R. (1988). Late life divorce and the life review. *Journal of Gerontological Social Work, 12*(3–4), 83–97.

Weingarten, H. R. (1989). The impact of late life divorce: A conceptual and empirical study. *Journal of Divorce, 12,* 21–38.

Weinstein, R. S. (2002). *Reaching higher: The power of expectations in schooling.* Cambridge, MA: Harvard University Press.

Weisfield, G. E. (1997). Puberty rites as clues to the nature of human adolescence. *Cross-Cultural Research, 31,* 27–54.

Weisner, T. S., & Wilson-Mitchell, J. E. (1990). Nonconventional family life-styles and sex typing in six-year-olds. *Child Development, 61,* 1915–1933.

Weiss, A., Costa, P. T., Jr., Karuza, J., Duberstein, P. R., Friedman, B., & McCrae, R. M. (2005). Cross-sectional age differences in personality among Medicare patients aged 65 to 100. *Psychology and Aging, 20,* 182–185.

Weiss, K. M. (2005). Cryptic causation of human disease: Reading between the germ lines. *Trends in Genetics, 21,* 82–88.

Weissberg, R. W. (2006). Modes of expertise in creative thinking: Evidence from case studies. In K. A. Ericsson, N. Charness, P. J. Feltovich, & R. R. Hoffman (Eds.), *The Cambridge handbook of expertise and expert performance* (pp. 761–787). New York: Cambridge University Press.

Weisz, A. N., & Black, B. M. (2002). Gender and moral reasoning: African American youths respond to dating dilemmas. *Journal of Human Behavior in the Social Environment, 6,* 17–34.

Weizman, Z. O., & Snow, C. E. (2001). Lexical output as related to children's vocabulary acquisition: Effects of sophisticated exposure and support for meaning. *Developmental Psychology, 37,* 265–279.

Wekerle, C., Wall, A.-M., Leung, E., & Trocmé, N. (2007). Cumulative stress and substantiated maltreatment: The importance of caregiver vulnerability and adult partner violence. *Child Abuse and Neglect, 31,* 427–443.

Wekerle, C., & Wolfe, D. A. (2003). Child maltreatment. In E. J. Mash & R. A. Barkley (Eds.), *Child psychopathology* (2nd ed., pp. 632–684). New York: Guilford.

Wellman, H. M. (2002). Understanding the psychological world: Developing a theory of mind. In U. Goswami (Ed.), *Blackwell handbook of child cognitive development* (pp. 167–187). Malden, MA: Blackwell.

Wellman, H. M., & Hickling, A. K. (1994). The mind's "I": Children's conception of the mind as an active agent. *Child Development, 65,* 1564–1580.

Weng, N. (2008). Aging of the immune system: How much can the adaptive immune system adapt? *Immunity, 24,* 495–499.

Weng, X., Odouli, R., & Li, D.-K. (2008). Maternal caffeine consumption during pregnancy and the risk of miscarriage: A prospective cohort study. *American Journal of Obstetrics and Gynecology, 198,* 279e1–279e8.

Wenger, G. C. (2001). Ageing without children: Rural Wales. *Journal of Cross-Cultural Gerontology, 16,* 79–109.

Wentworth, N., Benson, J. B., & Haith, M. M. (2000). The development of infants' reaches for stationary and moving targets. *Child Development, 71,* 576–601.

Wentzel, K. R., Barry, C. M., & Caldwell, K. A. (2004). Friendships in middle school: Influences on motivation and school adjustment. *Journal of Educational Psychology, 96,* 195–203.

Werner, E. E. (1989, April). Children of the garden island. *Scientific American, 260*(4), 106–111.

Werner, E. E. (1991). Grandparent–grandchild relationships amongst U.S. ethnic groups. In P. K. Smith (Ed.), *The psychology of grandparenthood: An international perspective* (pp. 68–82). London: Routledge.

Werner, E. E. (2001). *Journeys from childhood to midlife: Risk, resilience, and recovery.* Ithaca, NY: Cornell University Press.

Werner, E. E. (2005). What can we learn about resilience from large-scale longitudinal studies? In S. Goldstein & R. B. Brooks (Eds.), *Handbook of resilience in children* (pp. 91–105). New York: Kluwer Academic.

Werner, E. E., & Smith, R. S. (1982). *Vulnerable but invincible.* New York: McGraw-Hill.

Werner, E. E., & Smith, R. S. (1992). *Overcoming the odds: High-risk children from birth to adulthood.* Ithaca, NY: Cornell University Press.

Werner, E. E., & Smith, R. S. (2001). *Journeys from childhood to midlife: Risk, resilience, and recovery.* Ithaca, NY: Cornell University Press.

Werner, N. E., & Crick, N. R. (2004). Maladaptive peer relationships and the development of relational and physical aggression during middle childhood. *Social Development, 13,* 495–514.

West, R. L., & Craik, F. I. M. (1999). Age-related decline in prospective memory: The roles of cue accessibility and cue sensitivity. *Psychology and Aging, 14,* 264–272.

Westerhof, G. J., Bohlmeijer, E., & Valenkamp, M. W. (2004). In search of meaning: A reminiscence program for older persons. *Educational Gerontology, 30,* 751–766.

Westermann, G., Mareschal, D., Johnson, M. H., Sirois, S., Spratling, M. W., & Thomas, M. S. C. (2007). Neuroconstructivism. *Developmental Science, 10,* 75–83.

Westermeyer, J. F. (1998). Predictors and characteristics of mental health among men at midlife: A 32-year longitudinal study. *American Journal of Orthopsychiatry, 68,* 265–273.

Westermeyer, J. F. (2004). Predictors and characteristics of Erikson's life cycle model among men: A 32-year longitudinal study. *International Journal of Aging and Human Development, 58,* 29–48.

Wethington, E. (2000). Expecting stress: Americans and the "midlife crisis." *Motivation and Emotion, 24,* 85–103.

Wethington, E., Kessler, R. C., & Pixley, J.E. (2005). Turning points in adulthood. In O. G. Brim, C. D. Ryff, & R. C. Kessler (Eds.), *How healthy are we? A national study of well-being at midlife* (pp. 586–613). Chicago: University of Chicago Press.

Wexler, I. D., Branski, D., & Kerem, E. (2006). War and children. *Journal of the American Medical Association, 296,* 579–581.

Weyermann, M., Rothenbacher, D., & Brenner, H. (2006). Duration of breast-feeding and risk of overweight in childhood: A prospective birth cohort study from Germany. *International Journal of Obesity, 30,* 1281–1287.

Whalley, L. (2001). *The aging brain.* London: Weidenfeld & Nicolson.

Wheeler, I. (2001). Parental bereavement: The crisis of meaning. *Death Studies, 25,* 51–66.

Wheeler, W. (2002). Youth leadership for development: Civic activism as a component of youth development programming and a strategy for strengthening civil society. In R. M. Lerner, F. Jacobs, & D. Wertlieb (Eds.), *Handbook of applied developmental science* (Vol. 2, pp. 491–506). Thousand Oaks, CA: Sage.

Whipple, E. E. (2006). Child abuse and neglect: Consequences of physical, sexual, and emotional abuse of children. In H. E. Fitzgerald, B. M. Lester, & B. Zuckerman (Eds.), *The crisis in youth mental health: Critical issues and effective programs: Vol. 1. Childhood disorders* (pp. 205–229). Westport, CT: Praeger.

Whisman, M. A., Uebelacker, L. A., Tolejko, N., Chatav, Y., & McKelvie, M. (2006). Marital discord and well-being in older adults: Is the association confounded by personality? *Psychology and Aging, 21,* 626–631.

Whitaker, D. J., Baker, C. K., & Arias, I. (2007). Interventions to prevent intimate partner violence. In L. S. Doll, S. E., Bonzo, D. A. Sleet, & J. A. Mercy (Eds.), *Handbook of injury and violence prevention* (pp. 203–221). New York: Springer Science + Business Media.

Whitbeck, L., Hoyt, D. R., & Huck, S. M. (1994). Early family relationships, intergenerational solidarity, and support provided to parents by their adult children. *Journal of Gerontology, 49,* 585–594.

Whitbourne, S. K. (1996). *The aging individual: Physical and psychological perspectives.* New York: Springer.

Whitbourne, S. K. (2001). The physical aging process in midlife: Interactions with psychological and sociocultural factors. In M. E. Lachman (Ed.), *Handbook of midlife development* (pp. 109–155). New York: Wiley.

Whitbourne, S. K. (2002). *The aging individual: Physical and psychological perspectives.* New York: Springer.

Whitbourne, S. K., & Willis, S. L. (2006). Preface. In S. K. Whitbourne & S. L. Willis (Eds.), *The baby boomers grow up* (pp. vii–ix). Mahwah, NJ: Erlbaum.

Whitbourne, S. K., Zuschlag, M. K., Elliot, L. B., & Waterman, A. S. (1992). Psychosocial development in adulthood: A 22-year sequential study. *Journal of Personality and Social Psychology, 63,* 260–271.

White, L. (2001). Sibling relationships over the life course: A panel analysis. *Journal of Marriage and Family, 63,* 555–568.

White, L. K. (1994). Coresidence and leaving home: Young adults and their parents. *Annual Review of Sociology, 20,* 81–102.

Whiteman, S. D., & Loken, E. (2006). Comparing analytic techniques to classify dyadic relationships: An example using siblings. *Journal of Marriage and Family, 68,* 1370–1382.

Whitesell, N. R., Mitchell, C. M., Spicer, P., and the Voices of Indian Teens Project Team. (2009). A longitudinal study of self-esteem, cultural identity, and academic success among American Indian adolescents. *Cultural Diversity and Ethnic Minority Psychology, 15,* 38–50.

Whiteside, M. F. (2006). Remarried systems. In L. Combrinck-Graham (Ed.), *Children in family contexts: Perspectives on treatment* (pp. 163–189). New York: Guilford.

Whiteside-Mansell, L., Bradley, R. H., Owen, M. T., Randolph, S. M., & Cauce, A. M. (2003). Parenting and children's behavior at 36 months: Equivalence between African-American and European-American mother–child dyads. *Parenting: Science and Practice, 3,* 197–234.

Whiting, B., & Edwards, C. P. (1988). A cross-cultural analysis of sex differences in the behavior of children aged 3 through 11. In G. Handel (Ed.), *Childhood socialization* (pp. 281–297). New York: Aldine de Gruyter.

Whitlock, J. L., Powers, J. L., & Eckenrode, J. (2006). The virtual cutting edge: The Internet and adolescent self-injury. *Developmental Psychology, 42,* 407–417.

Whitmer, R. A., Gunderson, E. P., Quesenberry, C. P., Jr., Zhou, J., & Yaffe, K. (2007). Body mass index in midlife and risk of Alzheimer disease and vascular dementia. *Current Alzheimer Research, 4,* 103–109.

Wichmann, C., Coplan, R. J., & Daniels, T. (2004). The social cognitions of socially withdrawn children. *Social Development, 13,* 377–392.

Wichstrøm, L. (2006). Sexual orientation as a risk factor for bulimic symptoms. *International Journal of Eating Disorders, 39,* 448–453.

Wickens, A. P. (2001). Aging and the free radical theory. *Respiration Physiology, 128,* 379–391.

Wideen, M. F., O'Shea, T., Pye, I., & Ivany, G. (1997). High-stakes testing and the teaching of science. *Canadian Journal of Education, 22,* 428–444.

Wiebe, D. J., & Williams, P. G. (1992). Hardiness and health: A social psychophysiological perspective on stress and adaptation. *Journal of Social and Clinical Psychology, 11,* 238–262.

Wigfield, A., Battle, A., Keller, L. B., & Eccles, J. S. (2002). Sex differences in motivation, self-concept, career aspiration, and career choice: Implications for cognitive development. In A. McGillicudy-De Lisi & R. De Lisi (Eds.), *Biology, society, and behavior: The development of sex differences in cognition* (pp. 93–124). Westport, CT: Ablex.

Wigfield, A., & Eccles, J. S. (1994). Children's competence beliefs, achievement values, and general self-esteem change across elementary and middle school. *Journal of Early Adolescence, 14,* 107–138.

Wigfield, A., Eccles, J. S., Schiefele, U., Roeser, R. W., & Davis-Kean, P. (2006). Development of achievement motivation. In N. Eisenberg (Ed.), *Handbook of child psychology: Vol. 3. Social, emotional, and personality development* (6th ed., pp. 933–1002). Hoboken, NJ: Wiley.

Wigfield, A., Eccles, J. S., Yoon, K. S., Harold, R. D., Arbreton, A. J., Freedman-Doan, C., & Blumenfeld, P. C. (1997). Changes in children's competence beliefs and subjective task values across the elementary school years: A three-year study. *Journal of Educational Psychology, 89,* 451–469.

Wikby, A., Maxson, P., Olsson, J., Johansson, B., & Ferguson, F. G. (1998). Changes in CD8 and CD4 lymphocyte subsets, T cell proliferation responses and non-survival in the very old: The Swedish longitudinal OCTO-immune study. *Mechanisms of Ageing and Development, 102,* 187–198.

Wilber, K. H., & McNeilly, D. P. (2001). Elder abuse and victimization. In J. E. Birren (Ed.), *Handbook of the psychology of aging* (pp. 569–591). San Diego: Academic Press.

Wilbur, J., Chandler, P. J., Dancy, B., & Lee, H. (2003). Correlates of physical activity in urban Midwestern African-American women. *American Journal of Preventive Medicine, 25,* 45–52.

Wilbur, J., Vassalo, A., Chandler, P., McDevitt, J., & Miller, A. M. (2005). Midlife women's adherence to home-based walking during maintenance. *Nursing Research, 54,* 33–40.

Wilcox, A. J., Weinberg, C. R., & Baird, D. D. (1995). Timing of sexual intercourse in relation to ovulation: Effects on the probability of conception, survival of the pregnancy, and sex of the baby. *New England Journal of Medicine, 333,* 1517–1519.

Wilke, C. J., & Thompson, C. A. (1993). First-year reentry women's perceptions of their classroom experiences. *Journal of the Freshman Year Experience, 5,* 69–90.

Wilkinson, K., Ross, E., & Diamond, A. (2003). Fast mapping of multiple words: Insights into when "the information provided" does and does not equal "the information perceived." *Applied Developmental Psychology, 24,* 739–762.

Wilkinson, R. B. (2004). The role of parental and peer attachment in the psychological health and self-esteem of adolescents. *Journal of Youth and Adolescence, 33,* 479–493.

Willatts, P. (1999). Development of means–end behavior in young infants: Pulling a support to retrieve a distant object. *Developmental Psychology, 35,* 651–667.

Wille, M. C., Weitz, B., Kerper, P., & Frazier, S. (2004). Advances in preconception genetic counseling. *Journal of Perinatal and Neonatal Nursing, 18,* 28–40.

Williams, C. (2006). Dilemmas in fetal medicine: Premature application of technology or responding to women's choice? *Sociology of Health and Illness, 28,* 1–20.

Williams, F. M. K., & Spector, T. D. (2006). Recent advances in the genetics of osteoporosis. *Musculoskeletal and Neuronal Interactions, 6,* 27–35.

Williams, J. E., Nieto, F. J., Sanford, C. P., Couper, D. J., & Tyroler, H. A. (2002). The association between trait anger and incident stroke risk: The Atherosclerosis Risk in Communities (ARIC) Study. *Stroke, 33,* 13–20.

Williams, J. M., & Currie, C. (2000). Self-esteem and physical development in early adolescence: Pubertal timing and body image. *Journal of Early Adolescence, 20,* 129–149.

Williams, K. (2003). Has the future of marriage arrived? A contemporary examination of gender, marriage, and psychological well-being. *Journal of Health and Social Relationships, 44,* 470–487.

Williams, K., & Dunne-Bryant, A. (2006). Divorce and adult psychological well-being: Clarifying the role of gender and age. *Journal of Marriage and Family, 68,* 1178–1196.

Williams, N., & Torrez, D. J. (1998). Grandparenthood among Hispanics. In M. E. Szinovacz (Ed.), *Handbook on grandparenthood* (pp. 87–96). Westport, CT: Greenwood Press.

Williams, P. E., Weis, L. G., & Rolfhus, E. (2003). *WISC-IV: Theoretical model and test blueprint.* San Antonio, TX: Psychological Corporation.

Williams, S., & Dale, J. (2006). The effectiveness of treatment for depression/depressive symptoms in adults with cancer: A systematic review. *British Journal of Cancer, 94,* 372–390.

Williamson, J., Softas-Nall, B., & Miller, J. (2003). Grandmothers raising grandchildren: An exploration of their experiences and emotions. *Counseling and Therapy for Couples with Families, 11,* 23–32.

Willinger, M., Ko, C.-W., Hoffman, H. J., Kessler, R. C., & Corwin, M. J. (2003). Trends in infant bed sharing in the United States. *Archives of Pediatrics and Adolescent Medicine, 157,* 43–49.

Willis, S. L., & Schaie, K. W. (1999). Intellectual functioning in midlife. In S. L. Willis & J. D. Reid (Eds.), *Life in the middle* (pp. 105–146). San Diego: Academic Press.

Willis, S. L., Tennstedt, S. L., Marsiske, M., Ball, K., Elias, J., & Koepke, K. M. (2006). Long-term effects of cognitive training on everyday functional outcomes in older adults. *Journal of the American Medical Association, 296,* 2805–2814.

Willoughby, J., Kupersmidt, J. B., & Bryant, D. (2001). Overt and covert dimensions of antisocial behavior. *Journal of Abnormal Child Psychology, 29,* 177–187.

Willson, A. E., Shuey, K. M., Elder, G. H., Jr., & Wickrama, K. A. S. (2006). Ambivalence in mother–adult child relations: A dyadic analysis. *Social Psychology Quarterly, 69,* 235–252.

Wilmoth, J. M. (2001). Living arrangements among older immigrants in the United States. *Gerontologist, 41,* 228–238.

Wilson, D. K., Kirtland, K. A., Ainsworth, B. E., & Addy, C. L. (2004). Socioeconomic status and perceptions of access and safety for physical activity. *Annals of Behavioral Medicine, 28,* 20–28.

Wilson, R. S., Arnold, S. E., Schneider, J. A., Kelley, J. F., Tang, Y., & Bennett, D. A. (2006). Chronic psychological distress and risk of Alzheimer's disease in old age. *Neuroepidemiology, 27,* 143–153.

Wilson, R. S., Beckett, L. A., Evans, D. A., & Bennett, D. A. (2003). Terminal decline in cognitive function. *Neurology, 60,* 1782–1787.

Windsor, T. D., Anstey, K. J., & Rodgers, B. (2008). Volunteering and psychological well-being among young–old adults: How much is too much? *Gerontologist, 48,* 59–70.

Wingfield, A., & Stine-Morrow, E. A. L. (2000). Language and speech. In F. I. M. Craik & T. A. Salthouse (Eds.), *Handbook of aging and cognition* (2nd ed., pp. 359–416). Mahwah, NJ: Erlbaum.

Wink, P. (2006). Who is afraid of death? Religiousness, spirituality, and death anxiety in late adulthood. *Journal of Religion, Spirituality and Aging, 18,* 93–110.

Wink, P. (2007). Everyday life in the Third Age. In J. B. James & P. Wink (Eds.), *Annual review of gerontology and geriatrics* (Vol. 26, pp. 243–261). New York: Springer.

Wink, P., & Dillon, M. (2002). Spiritual development across the adult life course: Findings from a longitudinal study. *Journal of Adult Development, 9,* 79–94.

Wink, P., & Dillon, M. (2003). Religiousness, spirituality, and psychosocial functioning in late adulthood: Findings from a longitudinal study. *Psychology and Aging, 18,* 916–924.

Wink, P., & Helson, R. (1993). Personality change in women and their partners. *Journal of Personality and Social Psychology, 65,* 597–605.

Wink, P., & James, J. B. (2007). Is the Third Age the crown of life? In J. B. James & P. Wink (Eds.), *Annual review of gerontology and geriatrics* (Vol. 26, pp. 305–325). New York: Springer.

Wink, P., & Schiff, B. (2002). To review or not to review? The role of personality and life events in life review and adaptation to older age. In J. D. Webster & B. K. Haight (Eds.), *Critical advances in reminiscence work* (pp. 44–75). New York: Springer.

Wink, P., & Scott, J. (2005). Does religiousness buffer against the fear of death and dying in late adulthood? Findings from a longitudinal study. *Journal of Gerontology, 60B,* P207–P214.

Winn, R., & Newton, N. (1982). Sexual activity in aging: A study of 106 cultures. *Archives of Sexual Behavior, 11,* 283–298.

Winner, E. (1986, August). Where pelicans kiss seals. *Psychology Today, 20*(8), 25–35.

Winner, E. (1988). *The point of words: Children's understanding of metaphor and irony.* Cambridge, MA: Harvard University Press.

Winner, E. (1996). *Gifted children: Myths and realities.* New York: Basic Books.

Winner, E. (2000). The origins and ends of giftedness. *American Psychologist, 55,* 159–169.

Winner, E. (2003). Creativity and talent. In M. H. Bornstein, L. Davidson, C. L. M. Keyes, K. A. Moore, & the Center for Child Well-Being (Eds.), *Well-being: Positive development across the life course* (pp. 371–380). Mahwah, NJ: Erlbaum.

Winsler, A. (2009). Still talking to ourselves after all these years: A review of current research on private speech. In A. Winsler, C. Fernyhough, & I. Montero (Eds.), *Private speech executive functioning, and the development of self-regulation.* New York: Cambridge University Press.

Winsler, A., Fernyhough, C., & Montero, I. (2009). *Private speech, executive functioning, and the development of verbal self-regulation.* New York: Cambridge University Press.

Winsler, A., Naglieri, J., & Manfra, L. (2006). Children's search strategies and accompanying verbal and motor strategic behavior: Developmental trends and relations with task performance among children age 5 to 17. *Cognitive Development, 21,* 232–248.

Winslow, R. D., Mehta, D., & Fuster, V. (2005). Sudden cardiac death: Mechanisms, therapies and challenges. *Cardiovascular Medicine, 2,* 352–360.

Winter, D. G., Torges, C. M., Stewart, A. J., Henderson-King, D., & Henderson-King, E. (2007). Pathways toward the Third Age: Studying a cohort from the "golden age." In J. B. James & P. Wink (Eds.), *The crown of life: Dynamics of the early postretirement period* (pp. 103–130). New York: Springer.

Wintergest, E. S., Maggini, S., & Hornig, D. H. (2007). Contribution of selected vitamins and trace elements to immune function. *Annals of Nutrition and Metabolism, 51,* 301–323.

Wiscott, R., & Kopera-Frye, K. (2000). Sharing of culture: Adult grandchildrens' perceptions of intergenerational relations. *International Journal of Aging and Human Development, 5,* 199–215.

Wissink, I. B., Deković, M., & Meijer, A. M. (2006). Parenting behavior, quality of the parent–adolescent relationship, and adolescent functioning in four ethnic groups. *Journal of Early Adolescence, 26,* 133–159.

Witherington, D. C. (2005). The development of prospective grasping control between 5 and 7 months: A longitudinal study. *Infancy, 7,* 143–161.

Witherington, D. C., Campos, J. J., Anderson, D. I., Lejeune, L., & Seah, E. (2005). Avoidance of heights on the visual cliff in newly walking infants. *Infancy, 7,* 285–298.

Witherington, D. C., Campos, J. J., & Hertenstein, M. J. (2001). Principles of emotion and its development in infancy. In G. Bremner & A. Fogel (Eds.), *Blackwell handbook of infant development* (pp. 427–464). Malden, MA: Blackwell.

Wojciechowski, W. C. (1998). Issues in caring for older lesbians. *Journal of Gerontological Nursing, 24,* 28–33.

Wolak, J., Finkelhor, D., Mitchell, K. J., & Ybarra, M. L. (2008). Online "predators" and their victims: Myths, realities, and implications for prevention and treatment. *American Psychologist, 63,* 111–128.

Wolak, J., Mitchell, K. J., & Finkelhor, D. (2003). Escaping or connecting? Characteristics of youth who form close online relationships. *Journal of Adolescence, 26,* 105–119.

Wolak, J., Mitchell, K., & Finkelhor, D. (2007). Unwanted and wanted exposure to online pornography in a national sample of youth Internet users. *Pediatrics, 119,* 247–257.

Wolchik, S. A., Wilcox, K. L., Tein, J.-Y. & Sandler, I. N. (2000). Maternal acceptance and consistency of discipline as buffers of divorce stressors on children's psychological adjustment problems. *Journal of Abnormal Child Psychology, 28,* 87–102.

Wolf, A. W., Jimenez, E., & Lozoff, B. (2003). Effects of iron therapy on infant blood lead levels. *Journal of Pediatrics, 143,* 789–795.

Wolfe, D. A. (2005). *Child abuse* (2nd ed.). Thousand Oaks: Sage.

Wolfe, D. A., Scott, K., Wekerle, C., & Pittman, A. (2001). Child maltreatment: Risk of adjustment problems and dating violence in adolescence. *Journal of the American Academy of Child and Adolescent Psychiatry, 40,* 282–289.

Wolfe, V. V. (2006). Child sexual abuse. In E. J. Mash & R. A. Barkley (Eds.), *Treatment of childhood disorders* (3rd ed., pp. 647–727). New York: Guilford.

Wolfelt, A. D. (1997). Death and grief in the school setting. In T. N. Fairchild (Ed.), *Crisis intervention strategies for school-based helpers* (pp. 199–244). Springfield, IL: Charles C. Thomas.

Wolff, P. H. (1966). The causes, controls and organization of behavior in the neonate. *Psychological Issues, 5*(1, Serial No. 17).

Wolff, P. H., & Fesseha, G. (1999). The orphans of Eritrea: A five-year follow-up study. *Journal of Child Psychology and Psychiatry and Allied Disciplines, 40,* 1231–1237.

Wolfinger, N. H. (2000). Beyond the intergenerational transmission of divorce: Do people replicate the patterns of marital instability they grew up with? *Journal of Family Issues, 21,* 1061–1086.

Wolfinger, N. H. (2005). *Understanding the divorce cycle.* New York: Cambridge University Press.

Wolinsky, F. D., Unverzagt, F. W., Smith, D. M., Jones R., Stoddard, A., & Tennstedt, S. L. (2006). The ACTIVE cognitive training trail and health-related quality of life: Protection that lasts for 5 years. *Journal of Gerontology, 61A,* 1324–1329.

Wolkove, N., Elkholy, O., Baltzan, M., & Palayew, M. (2007). Sleep and aging: 1. Sleep disorders commonly found in older people. *Canadian Medical Association Journal, 17,* 1299–1304.

Women's Health Initiative. (2002). Risks and benefits of estrogen plus progestin in healthy postmenopausal women: Principal results from the Women's Health Initiative randomized control trial. *Journal of the American Medical Association, 288,* 321–333.

Women's Health Initiative. (2004). Effects of conjugated equine estrogen in postmenopausal women with hysterectomy: The Women's Health Initiative Randomized Controlled Trial. *Journal of the American Medical Association, 291,* 1701–1712.

Wong, C. A., Eccles, J. S., & Sameroff, A. (2003). The influence of ethnic discrimination and ethnic identification on African American adolescents' school and socioemotional adjustment. *Journal of Personality, 71,* 1197–1232.

Wong, M. M., Nigg, J. T., Zucker, R. A., Puttler, L. I., Fitzgerald, H. E., Jester, J. M., Glass, J. M., & Adams, K. (2006). Behavioral control and resiliency in the onset of alcohol and illicit drug use: A prospective study from preschool to adolescence. *Child Development, 77,* 1016–1033.

Wood, E., Desmarais, S., & Gugula, S. (2002). The impact of parenting experience on gender stereotyped toy play of children. *Sex Roles, 47,* 39–49.

Wood, J. J., Emmerson, N. A., & Cowan, P. A. (2004). Is early attachment security carried forward into relationships with preschool peers? *British Journal of Developmental Psychology, 22,* 245–253.

Wood, J. M. (2002). Aging, driving and vision. *Clinical and Experimental Optometry, 85,* 214–220.

Wood, W., & Eagly, A. H. (2000). Once again, the origins of sex differences. *American Psychologist, 55,* 1062–1063.

Woods, B. (2008). Suicide and attempted suicide in later life. In B. Woods & L. Clare (Eds.), *Handbook of the clinical psychology of ageing* (2nd ed., pp. 111–119). Chichester, UK: Wiley.

Woodward, A. L., & Markman, E. M. (1998). Early word learning. In D. Kuhn & R. S. Siegler (Eds.), *Handbook of child psychology: Vol. 2. Cognition, perception, and language* (5th ed., pp. 371–420). New York: Wiley.

Woodward, J., & Ono, Y. (2004). Mathematics and academic diversity in Japan. *Journal of Learning Disabilities, 37,* 74–82.

Woolf, L. M. (2001). Gay and lesbian aging. *SIECUS Report, 30,* 16–21.

Woolley, J. D. (1997). Thinking about fantasy: Are children fundamentally different thinkers and believers from adults? *Child Development, 68,* 991–1011.

Woolley, J. D. (2000). The development of beliefs about direct mental–physical causality in imagination, magic, and religion. In K. S. Rosengren, C. N. Johnson, & P. L. Harris (Eds.), *Imagining the impossible* (pp. 99–156). Cambridge, UK: Cambridge University Press.

Word, S. (1996). Mortality awareness and risk-taking in late adolescence. *Death Studies, 20,* 133–148.

Worden, J. W. (2000). Toward an appropriate death. In T. A. Rando (Ed.), *Clinical dimensions of anticipatory mourning* (pp. 267–277). Champaign, IL: Research Press.

Worden, J. W. (2002). *Grief counseling and grief therapy* (3rd ed.). New York: Springer.

Worden, J. W. (2009). *Grief counseling and grief therapy* (4th ed.). New York: Springer.

World Cancer Research Fund/American Institute for Cancer Research. (2007). *Food, nutrition, physical activity, and the prevention of cancer: A global perspective.* Washington, DC: American Institute for Cancer Research.

World Education Services. (2007). *World education database.* Retrieved from www.wes.org

World Federation of Right to Die Societies. (2006). Public opinion. Retrieved from www.worldrtd.net

World Health Organization. (2000). Violence against women information pack. Retrieved from http://www.who.int/frh-whd/VAW/infopack/English

World Health Organization. (2002). *World report on violence and health.* Geneva: Author.

World Health Organization. (2005). *WHO Multi-Country Study on Women's Health and Domestic Violence Against Women.* Geneva: Author.

World Health Organization. (2008a). *The global burden of disease: 2004.* Geneva, Switzerland: Author.

World Health Organization. (2008b). The World Health Organization's Infant Feeding Recommendation. Retrieved from www.who.int/nutrition/topics/infantfeeding_recommendation/en/index.html

World Health Organization. (2008c). *World report on child injury prevention.* Geneva, Switzerland: Author.

World Health Organization. (2009a). *Estimated healthy life expectancy (HALE) at birth and age 60, by sex, WHO member states, 2002.* Retrieved from www.who.int/whosis/indicators/2007HALE0/en

World Health Organization. (2009b). Obesity and overweight. Retrieved from www.who.int/dietphysicalactivity/publications/facts/obesity/en/

World Press Review. (2004). Obesity: A worldwide issue. Retrieved from www.worldpress.org/Africa/1961.cfm

Worrell, F. C., & Gardner-Kitt, D. L. (2006). The relationship between racial and ethnic identity in black adolescents: The cross-racial identity scale and the multigroup ethnic identity measure. *Identity, 6,* 293–315.

Wray, L. A., Alwin, D. F., & McCammon, R. J. (2005). Social status and risky health behaviors: Results from the health and retirement study. *Journal of Gerontology, 60B,* S85–S92.

Wray, S. (2007). Health, exercise, and well-being: The experiences of midlife women from diverse ethnic backgrounds. *Social Theory and Health, 5,* 126–144.

Wright, B. C. (2006). On the emergence of the discriminative mode for transitive inference. *European Journal of Cognitive Psychology, 18,* 776–800.

Wright, J. C., Huston, A. C., Murphy, K. C., St. Peters, M., Pinon, M., Scantlin, R., & Kotler, J. (2001). The relations of early television viewing to school readiness and vocabulary of children from low-income families: The Early Window Project. *Child Development, 72,* 1347–1366.

Wright, K. (2003). Relationships with death: The terminally ill talk about dying. *Journal of Marital and Family Therapy, 29,* 439–454.

Wright, M., Wood, J., Lynch, T., & Clark, D. (2008). Mapping levels of palliative care development: A global view. *Journal of Pain and Symptom Management, 35,* 469–485.

Wright, M. O., & Masten, A. S. (2005). Resilience processes in development. In S. Goldstein & R. B. Brooks (Eds.), *Handbook of resilience in children* (pp. 17–37). New York: Springer.

Wright, R. O., Tsaih, S. W., Schwartz, J., Wright, R. J., & Hu, H. (2003). Associations between iron deficiency and blood lead level in a longitudinal analysis of children followed in an urban primary care clinic. *Journal of Pediatrics, 142,* 9–14.

Wright, T. A., & Bonett, D. G. (1997). The contribution of burnout to work performance. *Journal of Organizational Behavior, 18,* 491–499.

Wright, V. C., Chang, J., Jeng, G., & Macaluso, M. (2008). Assisted reproductive technology surveillance—United States, 2005. *Morbidity and Mortality Weekly Report, 57*(5), 1–23.

Wright, W. E., & Shay, J. W. (2005). Telomere biology in aging and cancer. *Journal of the American Geriatric Society, 53,* S292–S294.

Wrotniak, B. H., Epstein, L. H., Raluch, R. A., & Roemmich, J. N. (2004). Parent weight change as a predictor of child weight change in family-based behavioral obesity treatment. *Archives of Pediatric and Adolescent Medicine, 158,* 342–347.

Wu, A. M. S., Tang, C. S. K., & Kwok, T. C. Y. (2002). Death anxiety among Chinese elderly people in Hong Kong. *Journal of Aging and Health, 14,* 42–56.

Wu, G., Bazer, F. W., Cudd, T. A., Meininger, C. J., & Spencer, T. E. (2004). Maternal nutrition and fetal development. *Journal of Nutrition, 134,* 2169–2172.

Wu, L. L., Bumpass, L. L., & Musick, K. (2001). Historical and life course trajectories of nonmarital childbearing. In L. L. Wu & B. Wolfe (Eds.), *Out of wedlock: Causes and consequences of nonmarital fertility* (pp. 3–48). New York: Russell Sage Foundation.

Wu, P., Robinson, C. C., Yang, C., Hart, C. H., Olsen, S. F., Porter, C. L., Jin, S., Wo, J., & Wu, X. (2002). Similarities and differences in mothers' parenting of preschoolers in China and the United States. *International Journal of Behavioral Development, 26,* 481–491.

Wu, T., Mendola, P., & Buck, G. M. (2002). Ethnic differences in the presence of secondary sex characteristics and menarche among U.S. girls: The Third National Health and Nutrition Examination Survey, 1988–1994. *Pediatrics, 110,* 752–757.

Wu, W., Brickman, A. M., Luchsinger, J., Ferrazzano, P., Pichiule, P., Yoshita, M., & Brown, T. (2008). The brain in the age of old: The hippocampal formation is targeted differentially by diseases of late life. *Annals of Neurology, 64,* 698–706.

Wu, Y. (2006). Overweight and obesity in China. *British Medical Journal, 333,* 362–363.

Wu, Z., & Penning, M. J. (1997). Marital instability after midlife. *Journal of Family Issues, 18,* 459–478.

Wu, Z., & Pollard, M. S. (1998). Social support among unmarried childless elderly persons. *Journal of Gerontology, 53B,* S324–S335.

Wust, S., Entringer, S., Federenko, I. S., Schlotz, W., Helhammer, D. H. (2005). Birth weight is associated with salivary cortisol responses to psychosocial stress in adult life. *Psychoneuroendocrinology, 30,* 591–598.

Wyatt, J. M., & Carlo, G. (2002). What will my parents think? Relations among adolescents' expected parental reactions, prosocial moral reasoning, and prosocial and antisocial behaviors. *Journal of Adolescent Research, 16,* 646–666.

Wynn, K. (1992). Addition and subtraction by human infants. *Nature, 358,* 749–750.

Wynn, K., Bloom, P., & Chiang, W.-C. (2002). Enumeration of collective entities by 5-month-old infants. *Cognition, 83,* B55–B62.

Wynne-Edwards, K. E. (2001). Hormonal changes in mammalian fathers. *Hormones and Behavior, 40,* 139–145.

Wysong, A., Lee, P. P., & Sloan, F. A. (2009). Longitudinal incidence of adverse outcomes of age-related macular degeneration. *Archives of Ophthalmology, 127,* 320–327.

X

Xu, X., & Lai, S.-C. (2004). Gender ideologies, marital roles, and marital quality in Taiwan. *Journal of Family Issues, 25,* 318–355.

Xue, Y., & Meisels, S. J. (2004). Early literacy instruction and learning in kindergarten: Evidence from the early childhood longitudinal study—kindergarten classes of 1998–1999. *American Educational Research Journal, 41,* 191–229.

Y

Yaari, R., & Corey-Bloom, J. (2007). Alzheimer's disease. *Seminars in Neurology, 27,* 32–41.

Yaffe, K., Blackwell, T., Kanaya, A. M., Davidowitz, N., Barrett-Connor, E., & Krueger, K. (2004). Diabetes, impaired fasting glucose, and development of cognitive impairment in older women. *Neurology, 63,* 658–663.

Yaffe, K., Fox, P., Newcomer, R., Sands, L., Lindquist, K., Dane, K., & Covinsky, K. E. (2002). Patient and caregiver characteristics and nursing home placement in patients with dementia. *Journal of the American Medical Association, 287,* 2090–2097.

Yale, M. E., Messinger, D. S., Cobo-Lewis, A. B., Oller, D. K., & Eilers, R. E. (1999). An event-based analysis of the coordination of early infant vocalizations and facial actions. *Developmental Psychology, 35,* 505–513.

Yamamoto, K. (2004). The care of the dying and the grieving in Japan. In J. D. Morgan & P. Laungani (Eds.), *Death and bereavement around the world: Vol. 4. Death and bereavement in Asia, Australia, and New Zealand* (pp. 101–107). Amityville, NY: Baywood Publishing Company.

Yan, L. L., Liu, K., Matthews, K. A., Daviglus, M. L., Ferguson, T. F., & Kiefe, C. I. (2003). Psychosocial factors and risk of hypertension: The Coronary Artery Risk Development in Young Adults (CARDIA) Study. *Journal of the American Medical Association, 290,* 2138–2148.

Yang, B., Ollendick, T. H., Dong, Q., Xia, Y., & Lin, L. (1995). Only children and children with siblings in the People's Republic of China: Levels of fear, anxiety, and depression. *Child Development, 66,* 1301–1311.

Yang, C. (2008, April). *The influence of one-child policy on child rearing, family, and society in post-Mao China.* Invited address, Illinois State University.

Yang, C., Hart, C. H., Nelson, D. A., Porter, C. L., Olsen, S. F., Robinson, C. C., & Jin, S. (2004). Fathering in a Beijing Chinese sample: Associations with boys' and girls' negative emotionality and aggression. In R. D. Day & M. E. Lamb (Eds.), *Conceptualizing and measuring father involvement* (pp. 185–215). Mahwah, NJ: Erlbaum.

Yang, C.-K., & Hahn, H.-M. (2002). Cosleeping in young Korean children. *Developmental and Behavioral Pediatrics, 23,* 151–157.

Yang, S. C., & Chen, S.-F. (2002). A phenomenographic approach to the meaning of death: A Chinese perspective. *Death Studies, 26,* 143–175.

Yao, L., & Robert, S. A. (2008). The contributions of race, individual socioeconomic status, and neighborhood socioeconomic context to the self-rated health trajectories and mortality of older adults. *Research on Aging, 30,* 251–273.

Yap, M. B. H., Allen, N. B., & Ladouceur, C. D. (2008). Maternal socialization of positive affect: The impact of invalidation on adolescent emotion regulation and depressive symptomatology. *Child Development, 79,* 1415–1431.

Yarrow, M. R., Scott, P. M., & Waxler, C. Z. (1973). Learning concern for others. *Developmental Psychology, 8,* 240–260.

Yates, L. B., Djouseé, L., Kurth, T., Buring, J. E., & Gaziano, J. M. (2008). Exceptional longevity in men: Modifiable factors associated with survival and function to age 90 years. *Archives of Internal Medicine, 168,* 284–290.

Yates, T. M., Egeland, B., & Sroufe, L. A. (2003). Rethinking resilience: A developmental process perspective. In S. S. Luthar (Ed.), *Resilience and vulnerability: Adaptation in the context of childhood adversities* (pp. 243–266). New York: Cambridge University Press.

Yeh, C. J., Kim, A. B., Pituc, S. T., & Atkins, M. (2008). Poverty, loss, and resilience: The story of Chinese immigrant youth. *Journal of Counseling Psychology, 55,* 34–48.

Yehuda, R., Engel, S. M., Brand, S. R., Seckl, J., Marcus, S. M., & Berkowitz, G. S. (2005). Transgenerational effects of posttraumatic stress disorder in babies of mothers exposed to the World Trade Center attacks during pregnancy. *Journal of Clinical Endocrinology and Metabolism, 90,* 4115–4118.

Yeung, D. Y., Fung, H. H., & Lang, F. R. (2008). Self-construal moderates age differences in social network characteristics. *Psychology and Aging, 23,* 222–226.

Yeung, W. (1996). Buddhism, death, and dying. In J. K. Parry & A. S. Ryan (Eds.), *A cross-cultural look at death, dying, and religion* (pp. 74–83). Chicago: Nelson-Hall.

Yip, R., Scanlon, K., & Trowbridge, F. (1993). Trends and patterns in height and weight status of low-income U.S. children. *Critical Reviews in Food Science and Nutrition, 33,* 409–421.

Yip, T., Seaton, E. K., & Sellers, R. M. (2006). African-American racial identity across the lifespan: Identity status, identity content, and depressive symptoms. *Child Development, 77,* 1504–1517.

Yirmiya, N., Erel, O., Shaked, M., & Solomonica-Levi, D. (1998). Meta-analyses comparing theory of mind abilities of individuals with autism, individuals with mental retardation, and normally developing individuals. *Psychological Bulletin, 124,* 283–307.

Yonas, A., Elieff, C., & Arterberry, M. E. (2002). Emergence of sensitivity to pictorial depth cues: Charting development in individual infants. *Infant Behavior and Development, 25,* 295–314.

Yonas, A., & Granrud, C. E. (2006). Infants' perception of depth from cast shadows. *Perception and Psychophysics, 68,* 154–160.

Yoshida, H., & Smith, L. B. (2003). Known and novel noun extensions: Attention at two levels of abstraction. *Child Development, 74,* 564–577.

Yoshinaga-Itano, C. (2003). Early intervention after universal neonatal hearing screening: Impact on outcomes. *Mental Retardation and Developmental Disabilities Research and Reviews, 9,* 252–266.

Youn, G., Knight, B. G., Jeon, H., & Benton, D. (1999). Differences in familism values and caregiving outcomes among Korean, Korean American, and White American dementia caregivers. *Psychology and Aging, 14,* 355–364.

Young, H. M. (1998). Moving to congregate housing: The last chosen home. *Journal of Aging Studies, 12,* 149–165.

Young, J. B., & Rodgers, R. F. (1997). A model of radical career change in the context of psychosocial development. *Journal of Career Assessment, 5,* 167–172.

Young, J. F., & Mroczek, D. K. (2003). Predicting intraindividual self-concept trajectories during adolescence. *Journal of Adolescence, 26,* 589–603.

Young, T., Rabago, D., Zgierska, A., Austin, D., & Finn, L. (2002). Objective and subjective sleep quality in premenopausal, perimenopausal, and postmenopausal women in the Wisconsin Sleep Cohort Study. *Epidemiology, 26,* 667–672.

Youngblade, L. M., & Dunn, J. (1995). Individual differences in young children's pretend play with mother and sibling: Links to relationships and understanding of other people's feelings and beliefs. *Child Development, 66,* 1472–1492.

Young-Hyman, D., Tanofsky-Kraff, M., Yanovski, S. Z., Keil, M., Cohen, M. L., & Peyrot, M. (2006). Psychological status and weight-related distress in overweight or at-risk-for-overweight children. *Obesity, 14,* 2249–2258.

Youniss, J., McLellan, J. A., & Yates, M. (1997). What we know about engendering civic identity. *American Behavioral Scientist, 40,* 620–631.

Yu, B. P. (2006). Why calorie restriction would work for human longevity. *Biogerontology, 7,* 179–182.

Yu, R. (2002). On the reform of elementary school education in China. *Educational Exploration, 129,* 56–57.

Yu, S., Yarnell, J. W. G., Sweetnam, P. M., & Murray, L. (2003). What level of physical activity protects against premature cardiovascular death? The Caerphilly Study. *Heart, 89,* 502–506.

Yuan, A. S. V., & Hamilton, H. A. (2006). Stepfather involvement and adolescent well-being: Do mothers and nonresidential fathers matter? *Journal of Family Issues, 27,* 1191–1213.

Yumoto, C., Jacobson, S. W., & Jacobson, J. L. (2008). Fetal substance exposure and cumulative environmental risk in an African American cohort. *Child Development, 79,* 1761–1776.

Yunger, J. L., Carver, P. R., & Perry, D. G. (2004). Does gender identity influence children's psychological well-being? *Developmental Psychology, 40,* 572–582.

Z

Zacks, R. T., & Hasher, L. (2006) Aging and long-term memory: Deficits are not inevitable. In E. Bialystok & F. I. M. Craik (Eds.), *Lifespan cognition: Mechanisms of change* (pp. 162–177). New York: Oxford University Press.

Zafeiriou, D. I. (2000). Plantar grasp reflex in high-risk infants during the first year of life. *Pediatric Neurology, 22,* 75–76.

Zaff, J. F., Malanchuk, O., & Eccles, J. S. (2008). Predicting positive citizenship from adolescence to young adulthood: The effects of a civic context. *Applied Developmental Science, 12,* 38–53.

Zahn-Waxler, C., Kochanska, G., Krupnick, J., & McKnew, D. (1990). Patterns of guilt in children of depressed and well mothers. *Developmental Psychology, 26,* 51–59.

Zahn-Waxler, C., Radke-Yarrow, M., & King, R. M. (1979). Child-rearing and children's prosocial initiations toward victims of distress. *Child Development, 50,* 319–330.

Zahn-Waxler, C., & Robinson, J. (1995). Empathy and guilt: Early origins of feelings of responsibility. In J. P. Tangney & K. W. Fischer (Eds.), *Self-conscious emotions* (pp. 143–173). New York: Guilford.

Zahn-Waxler, C., Schiro, K., Robinson, J. L., Emde, R. N., & Schmitz, S. (2001). Empathy and prosocial patterns in young MZ and DZ twins: Development and genetic and environmental influences. In R. N. Emde & J. K. Hewitt (Eds.), *Infancy to early childhood: Genetic and environmental influences on developmental change* (pp. 141–162). New York: Oxford University Press.

Zakowski, S. G., Hall, M. H., Klein, L. C., & Baum, A. (2001). Appraised control, coping, and stress in a community sample: A test of the goodness-of-fit hypothesis. *Annals of Behavioral Medicine, 23,* 158–165.

Zane, N., & Yeh, M. (2002). The use of culturally based variables in assessment: Studies on loss of face. In K. Kurasaki, S. Okazaki, & S. Sue (Eds.), *Asian American mental health: Assessment theories and methods* (pp. 123–138). Dordrecht, Netherlands: Kluwer Academic.

Zapf, D., Seifert, C., Schmutte, B., Mertini, H., & Hotz, M. (2001). Emotion work and job stressors and their effects on burnout. *Psychology and Health, 16,* 527–545.

Zaretsky, M. D. (2003). Communication between identical twins: Health behavior and social factors are associated with longevity that is greater among identical than fraternal U.S. World War II veteran twins. *Journal of Gerontology, 58,* 566–572.

Zarit, S. H., & Eggebeen, D. J. (2002). Parent–child relationships in adulthood and later years. In M. H. Bornstein (Ed.), *Handbook of parenting, Vol. 1* (2nd ed., pp. 135–161). Mahwah, NJ: Erlbaum.

Zaslow, M. J., Weinfield, N. S., Gallagher, M., Hair, E. C., Ogawa, J. R., Egeland, B., Tabors, P. O., & De Temple, J. M. (2006). Longitudinal prediction of child outcomes from differing measures of parenting in a low-income sample. *Developmental Psychology, 42,* 27–37.

Zea, M. C., Reisen, C. A., Beil, C., & Caplan, R. D. (1997). Predicting intention to remain in college among ethnic minority and nonminority students. *Journal of Social Psychology, 137,* 149–160.

Zelazo, N. A., Zelazo, P. R., Cohen, K. M., & Zelazo, P. D. (1993). Specificity of practice effects on elementary neuromotor patterns. *Developmental Psychology, 29,* 686–691.

Zelazo, P. D., Frye, D., & Rapus, T. (1996). An age-related dissociation between knowing rules and using them. *Cognitive Development, 11,* 37–63.

Zelazo, P. D., Muller, U., Frye, D., & Marcovitch, S. (2003). The development of executive function: Cognitive complexity and control—revised. *Monographs of the Society for Research in Child Development, 68*(3), 93–119.

Zeldin, A. L., & Pajares, F. (2000). Against the odds: Self-efficacy beliefs of women in mathematical, scientific, and technological careers. *American Educational Research Journal, 37,* 215–246.

Zelinski, E., & Kennison, R. F. (2007). Not your parents' test scores: Cohort reduces psychometric aging effects. *Psychology and Aging, 22,* 546–557.

Zeman, J., Shipman, K., & Suveg, C. (2002). Anger and sadness regulation: Predictions to internalizing and externalizing symptoms in children. *Journal of Clinical Child and Adolescent Psychology, 31,* 393–398.

Zenger, T., & Lawrence, B. (1989). Organizational demography: The differential effects of age and tenure distributions on technical communication. *Academy of Management Journal, 32,* 353–376.

Zeskind, P. S., & Barr, R. G. (1997). Acoustic characteristics of naturally occurring cries of infants with "colic." *Child Development, 68,* 394–403.

Zeskind, P. S., & Lester, B. M. (2001). Analysis of infant crying. In L. T. Singer & P. S. Zeskind (Eds.), *Biobehavioral assessment of the infant* (pp. 149–166). New York: Guilford.

Zhan, H. J., & Montgomery, R. J. V. (2003). Gender and elder care in China: The influence of filial piety and structural constraints. *Gender and Society, 17,* 209–229.

Zhang, Q. F. (2004). Economic transition and new patterns of parent–adult child coresidence in urban China. *Journal of Marriage and Family, 66,* 1231–1245.

Zhou, M., & Bankston, C. L. (1998). *Growing up American: How Vietnamese children adapt to life in the United States.* New York: Russell Sage Foundation.

Zhou, M., & Xiong, S. (2005). The multifaceted American experiences of the children of Asian immigrants: Lessons for segmented assimilation. *Ethnic and Racial Studies, 28,* 1119–1152.

Zhou, X., Huang, J., Wang, Z., Wang, B., Zhao, Z., Yang, L., & Zheng-zheng, Y. (2006). Parent–child interaction and children's number learning. *Early Child Development and Care, 176,* 763–775.

Zielinski, D. S., & Bradshaw, C. P. (2006). Ecological influences on the sequelae of child maltreatment: A review of the literature. *Child Maltreatment, 11,* 49–62.

Zimmer-Gembeck, M. J., Siebenbruner, J., & Collins, W. A. (2001). Diverse aspects of dating: Associations with psychosocial functioning from early to middle adolescence. *Journal of Adolescence, 24,* 313–336.

Zimmerman, B. J., & Risemberg, R. (1997). Self-regulatory dimensions of academic learning and motivation. In G. D. Phye (Ed.), *Handbook of academic learning: Construction of knowledge* (pp. 105–125). San Diego: Academic Press.

Zimmerman, C. (2005). *The development of scientific reasoning skills: What psychologists contribute to an understanding of elementary science learning.* Report to the National Research Council, Committee on Science Learning Kindergarten through Eighth Grade. Normal, IL: Illinois State University.

Zimmerman, C. (2007). The development of scientific thinking skills in elementary and middle school. *Developmental Review, 27,* 172–223.

Zimmerman, F. J., Christakis, D. A., & Meltzoff, A. N. (2007). Television and DVD/video viewing in children younger than 2 years. *Archives of Pediatrics and Adolescent Medicine, 161,* 473–479.

Zimmerman, L. K., & Stansbury, K. (2004). The influence of emotion regulation, level of shyness, and habituation on the neuroendocrine response of three-year-old children. *Psychoneuroendocrinology, 29,* 973–982.

Zimmerman, P., & Becker-Stoll, F. (2002). Stability of attachment representations during adolescence: The influence of ego-identity status. *Journal of Adolescence, 25,* 107–124.

Zins, J. E., Garcia, V. F., Tuchfarber, B. S., Clark, K. M., & Laurence, S. C. (1994). Preventing injury in children and adolescents. In R. J. Simeonsson (Ed.), *Risk, resilience, and prevention: Promoting the well-being of all children* (pp. 183–202). Baltimore: Paul H. Brookes.

Zubenko, G. S., Zubenko, W. N., McPherson, S., Spoor, E., Marin, D. B., & Farlow, M. R. (2003). A collaborative study of the emergence and clinical features of the major depressive syndrome of Alzheimer's disease. *American Journal of Psychiatry, 160,* 857–866.

Zucker, A. N., Ostrove, J. M., & Stewart, A. J. (2002). College-educated women's personality development in adulthood: Perceptions and age differences. *Psychology and Aging, 17,* 236–244.

Zucker, K. J. (2006). "I'm half-boy, half-girl": Play psychotherapy and parent counseling for gender identity disorder. In R. L. Spitzer, M. B. First, J. B. W. Williams, & M. Gibbon (Eds.), *DSM-IV-TR Casebook: Vol. 2. Experts tell how they treated their own patients* (pp. 322–334). Washington, DC: American Psychiatric Publishing.

Zukow-Goldring, P. (2002). Sibling caregiving. In M. H. Bornstein (Ed.), *Handbook of parenting: Vol. 3* (2nd ed., pp. 253–286). Hillsdale, NJ: Erlbaum.

Zwart, M. (2007). The Dutch system of perinatal care. *Midwifery Today with International Midwife, 81*(Spring), 46.

Name Index

Italic n following page number indicates source for an illustration or figure.

I

J

O

P

U

V

W

X

Y

Subject Index

Alphabetization is letter-by-letter (e.g., "Genes" precedes "Gene therapy").

E

T